Merry Christmas 05!
and
Happy New Year!
Love,
Amelia

The blue planet: The Earth was created billions of years ago from cosmic dust and gas – water, vital to all life on Earth, covers more than two-thirds of the planet's surface

The delta of the Mississippi River on the Gulf of Mexico – the mixing of water from the gulf and the river is vividly apparent in the satellite photograph below

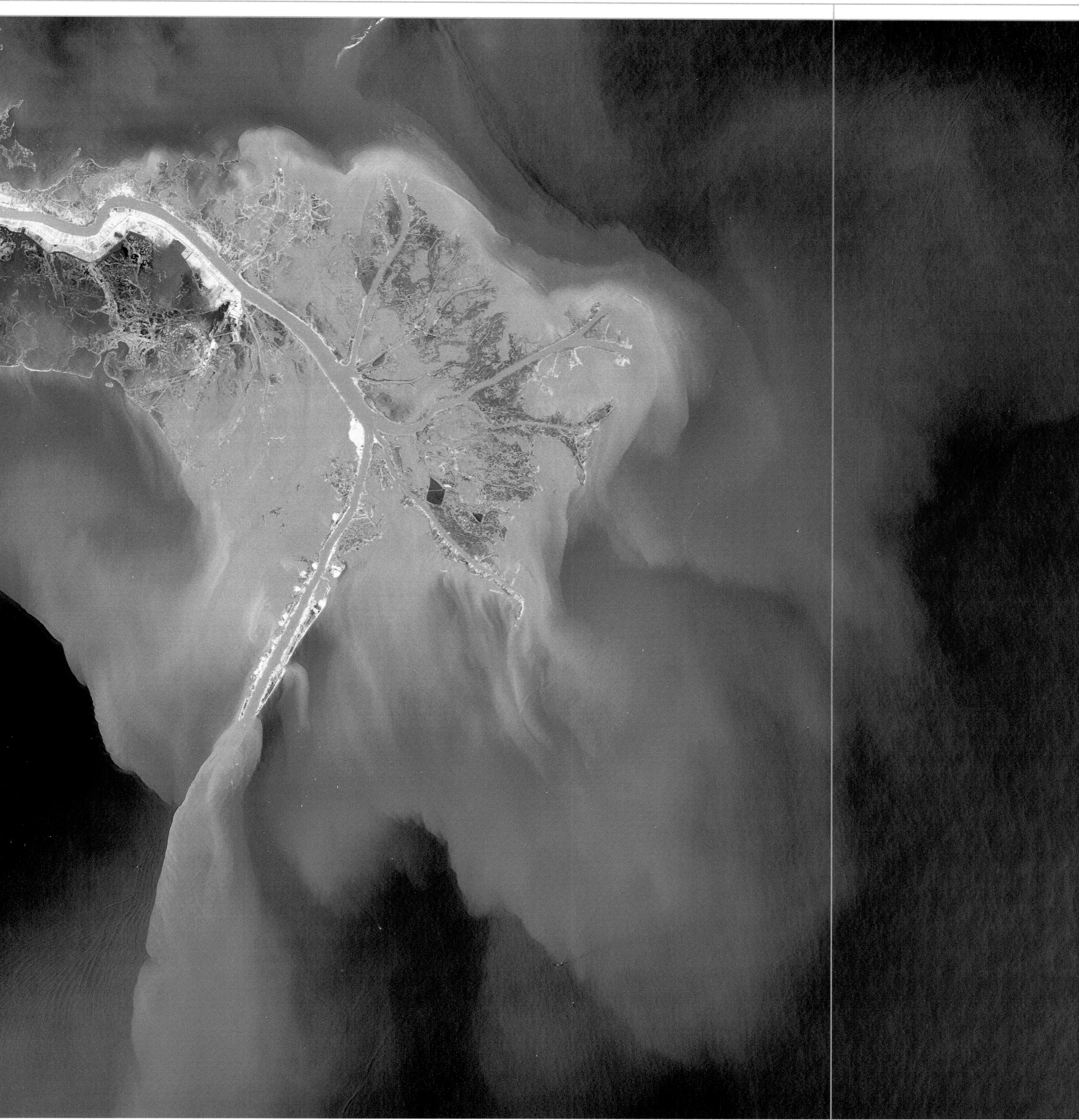

The power of wind and water erosion shaped the beautiful landscapes of the Colorado Plateau – including the sandstone arches in Arches National Park

WORLD TRAVEL ATLAS

Florence, the historic capital of Tuscany (Italy), with its Renaissance buildings and countless artistic masterpieces, is a jewel of European culture.

"The world is a book, and those who do not travel read only a page." – St. Augustine of Hippo (354-430 AD)

Preface

St. Augustine's quote is as true now as it was during his lifetime. The world has experienced many dramatic changes since then – empires have fallen, new nations have been born, and technology and global communications have made our world a smaller place – but travel remains as fascinating as ever.

In recent centuries, scientists and explorers have discovered every "terra incognita" and now use satellites to survey and photograph the Earth with incredible accuracy. Our planet, however, still offers countless surprises, adventures, and exotic wonders: the vastness of Asia, the isolated islands of the Pacific, the dense rainforests of Africa, Alaska's wilderness, ancient villages in Europe, and the summits of the Andes. Presenting all of these, and the many other fascinating places on our planet, is a difficult but rewarding task.

"A journey of a thousand miles begins with the very first step" – Lao-tzu (Chinese philosopher, 4th century BC)

And now we can begin our journey with the new World Travel Atlas. The groundbreaking concept of the atlas serves several functions: the first is to offer basic geographic knowledge of our planet with detailed and clear cartography. Further, it functions as a comprehensive travel guide in which more than 16,000 fascinating attractions are highlighted – including landscapes, national parks, cities, cultural attractions, monuments, holiday destinations, and travel routes. These sites are presented through a new system of pictograms, developed specifically for this book. With more than 2,000 texts covering the geographic and cultural aspects of the world's regions, the atlas also serves as a travel encyclopedia. Finally, it is a visually stimulating illustrated book with numerous beautiful photographs from around the world.

It is our hope that the World Travel Atlas will inspire in our readers the feeling that they are "citizens of the world" and serve as a "first step" on a fascinating journey of discovery to the countless wonders of the planet we call home. This atlas should deepen our understanding of our Earth and its multifaceted splendor, and awaken our curiosity, tolerance, and feelings of responsibility towards one another as inhabitants of this planet.

In the words of the famed Indian poet Rabindranath Tagore: "We live in this world as long as we love it"

The Publisher

Table of Contents

Islamic heritage in southern Spain: La Mezquita cathedral – once the Great Mosque of Cordoba – is a beautiful example of Moorish architecture with large chambers and splendid facades.

Beautiful landscapes on the Li River: The green, craggy mountains around the city of Guilin are situated in one of China's most scenic regions.

Map locater		X – XI
Legend – natural geographical features		XII
Legend – manmade geographical features		XIII
Explanation of symbols		XIV – XVII

The world		XVIII – 1
The world – physical map	1 : 85 Mio.	2 – 3
The world – political map	1 : 85 Mio.	4 – 5

North and Central America 6 – 47

North and Central America – physical map	1 : 45 Mio.	8
North and Central America – political map	1 : 45 Mio.	9
Alaska, Canada, Greenland	1 : 18 Mio.	10 – 11
USA, Central America	1 : 18 Mio.	12 – 13
Western Alaska		14 – 15
Southern Alaska, Northwestern Canada, Hawaiian Islands		16 – 17
Southwestern Canada, Northwestern USA		18 – 19
Western USA		20 – 21
Southwestern USA		22 – 23
Southern Canada		24 – 25
Northern Great Plains		26 – 27
Southern Great Plains, Gulf Coast		28 – 29
Newfoundland, Southeastern Canada		30 – 31
Great Lakes Region, Mid-Atlantic States		32 – 33
Southern States		34 – 35
Florida, Bahamas		36 – 37
Northern Mexico		38 – 39
Southern Mexico, Guatemala		40 – 41
Honduras, El Salvador, Nicaragua, Costa Rica, Panama		42 – 43
Cuba, Jamaica		44 – 45
Hispaniola and Lesser Antilles		46 – 47

South America 48 – 83

South America – physical map	1 : 45 Mio.	50
South America – political map	1 : 45 Mio.	51
Northern South America	1 : 18 Mio.	52 – 53
Southern South America	1 : 18 Mio.	54 – 55
Western Venezuela, Northern Colombia		56 – 57
Eastern Venezuela, Guyana, Suriname		58 – 59
Ecuador, Southern Colombia, Northern Peru		60 – 61
Amazonian Lowlands		62 – 63
Northeastern Brazil		64 – 65
Southern Peru, Northwestern Bolivia		66 – 67
Mato Grosso, Northeastern Bolivia		68 – 69
Eastern Brazil		70 – 71
Northern Chile, Southern Bolivia, Pantanal, Gran Chaco		72 – 73
Southeastern Brazil		74 – 75
North Central Chile, Central Argentina, Uruguay		76 – 77
Southern Brazil		78 – 79
South Central Chile, Pampas		80 – 81
Southern Chile, Patagonia, Falkland Islands		82 – 83

Europe 84 – 135

Europe – physical map	1 : 27 Mio.	86
Europe – political map	1 : 27 Mio.	87
Europe	1 : 18 Mio.	88 – 89
Northern Scandinavia, Iceland, Spitsbergen		90 – 91
Southern Norway, Central Sweden		92 – 93
Denmark, Southern Sweden		94 – 95
Southern Finland, Northern Baltic States		96
Southern Baltic States		97
British Isles, North		98 – 99
British Isles, South		100 – 101
Belgium, Northern France		102 – 103
Southern France		104 – 105
Northern Portugal, Northern Spain		106 – 107
Southern Portugal, Southern Spain		108 – 109
Catalonia, Balearic Islands, Corsica, Sardinia		110 – 111
Netherlands, Northern Germany		112 – 113
Southern Germany, Switzerland, Austria		114 – 115
Poland		116 – 117
Eastern Austria, Czech Republic, Slovakia, Hungary		118 – 119
Northern Italy, Slovenia, Croatia, Bosnia-Herzegovina		120 – 121
Southern Italy, Malta, Albania		122 – 123
Northern Serbia, Romania, Moldova		124 – 125
Southern Serbia and Montenegro, Bulgaria, Macedonia, Northern Greece		126 – 127
Southern Greece, Southwestern Turkey		128 – 129
Southern Turkey, Cyprus		130 – 131
Belarus, Western Russia		132 – 133
Ukraine, Southern Russia, Black Sea		134 – 135

Asia 136 – 215

Asia – physical map	1 : 54 Mio.	138
Asia – political map	1 : 54 Mio.	139
Northern Asia	1 : 18 Mio.	140 – 141
Near and Middle East	1 : 18 Mio.	142 – 143
Turkey, Caucasus Region		144 – 145
Lebanon, Syria, Israel, Jordan, Iraq		146 – 147
Northern Arabian Peninsula		148 – 149
Southern Arabian Peninsula		150 – 151
Caspian Sea Region		152 – 153
Northern Iran		154 – 155

Table of Contents

Marrakech (Morocco): Jemaa l-Fna square, located near the Koutoubia mosque, is a lively meeting place for vendors, street artists, traditional storytellers, and tourists.

Wet Tropics National Park in north-eastern Australia features fascinating flora and fauna as well as beautiful landscapes such as Milla Falls.

Southern Iran, Persian Gulf		156 – 157
Central Asia		158 – 159
Afghanistan, Northern and Central Pakistan		160 – 161
Central and Southern Pakistan		162 – 163
East Asia	1 : 18 Mio.	164 – 165
Eastern Kazakhstan, Altai Region, Western Mongolia		166 – 167
Tarim Basin, Western China		168 – 169
Tibet, Nepal, Bhutan		170 – 171
Southern Baykal Region, Northern Mongolia		172 – 173
Northern China		174 – 175
Central China		176 – 177
Southern China, Taiwan, Northern Vietnam		178 – 179
Northeastern China, Southeastern Russia, Hokkaido (Northern Japan)		180 – 181
Korea, Honshu (Central Japan)		182 – 183
Eastern China, Kyushu, Ryukyu Islands (Southern Japan)		184 – 185
Southern Asia	1 : 18 Mio.	186 – 187
Pakistan, Northern India		188 – 189
Central India		190 – 191
Southern India, Maldives, Sri Lanka		192 – 193
Eastern India, Bangladesh, Northern Myanmar		194 – 195
Northern Thailand, Laos, Cambodia, Central Vietnam		162 – 163
Southern Thailand, Malaysian Peninsula		198 – 199
Southeast Asia	1 : 18 Mio.	200 – 201
Northern Philippines, Palau		202 – 203
Southern Philippines, Northern Borneo		204 – 205
Sumatra		206 – 207
Borneo, Sulawesi		208 – 209
Java, Lesser Sunda Islands		210 – 211
Molucca Islands, New Guinea		212 – 213
Timor, Arafura Sea		214 – 215

Australia/Oceania 216 – 249

Australia/Oceania – physical map	1 : 45 Mio.	218
Australia/Oceania – political map	1 : 45 Mio.	219
Australia, New Zealand	1 : 18 Mio.	220 – 221
Northwestern Australia		222 – 223
Western Australia		224 – 225
Central Australia		226 – 227
Southwestern Australia		228 – 229
Northern Australia		230 – 231
Northeastern Australia, Great Barrier Reef		232 – 233
Eastern Australia		234 – 235
Southern Australia, Tasmania		236 – 237
New Zealand		238 – 239
Islands of the South Pacific	1 : 18 Mio.	240 – 241
Papua New Guinea		242 – 243
Bismarck Archipelago, Solomon Islands		244 – 245
New Caledonia, Vanuatu, Fiji Islands		246 – 247
Tonga, Samoa, French Polynesia		248 – 249

Africa 250 – 307

Africa – physical map	1 : 45 Mio.	252
Africa – political map	1 : 45 Mio.	253
Northern Africa	1 : 18 Mio.	254 – 255
Southern Africa	1 : 18 Mio.	256 – 257
Morocco, Northwestern Algeria		258 – 259
Northeastern Algeria, Tunisia, Northern Libya		260 – 261
Egypt		262 – 263
Western Sahara, Northern Mauritania, Northern Mali, Southwestern Algeria		264 – 265
Central Sahara		266 – 267
Cape Verde Islands, Senegal, Gambia		268 – 269
Mali		270 – 271
Southern Niger, Northern Nigeria		272 – 273
Northern Chad		274 – 275
Northern Sudan, Eritrea		276 – 277
West Africa		278 – 279
Southern Nigeria, Cameroon		280 – 281
Central African Republic, Southern Sudan		282 – 283
Highlands of Ethiopia, Horn of Africa		284 – 285
Northern Congo, Northern Democratic Republic of Congo		286 – 287
Southern Congo, Southern Democratic Republic of Congo, Northern Angola		288 – 289
Uganda, Kenya, Northern Tanzania		290 – 291
Rwanda, Burundi, Tanzania		292 – 293
Southern Angola, Western Zambia		294 – 295
Eastern Zambia, Malawi, Northern Mozambique		296 – 297
Namibia, Botswana, Western Zimbabwe		298 – 299
Eastern Zimbabwe, Southern Mozambique		300 – 301
South Africa, Lesotho, Swaziland		302 – 303
Comoros, Seychelles, Northern Madagascar		304 – 305
Madagascar, Réunion, Mauritius		306 – 307

Arctic Region, Antarctica, Oceans 308 – 317

Arctic Region	1 : 18 Mio.	310 – 311
Antarctica	1 : 18 Mio.	312 – 313
Atlantic Ocean	1 : 63 Mio.	314
Indian Ocean	1 : 45 Mio.	315
Pacific Ocean	1 : 54 Mio.	316 – 317

Index

The index explained, Abbreviations	318
International license plate codes, Symbols	319
Index to places and features	320 – 412
Photo index	413
Credits/Contributors	414

Map locator

The Loire River valley in France with its many historic towns and palaces – including Chateau Chamborg (photo) – is a UNESCO world heritage site.

Japan's former imperial capital Kyoto has been an important cultural center for more than 1,000 years. Kyoto's historic attractions include numerous shrines and temples

North and Central America

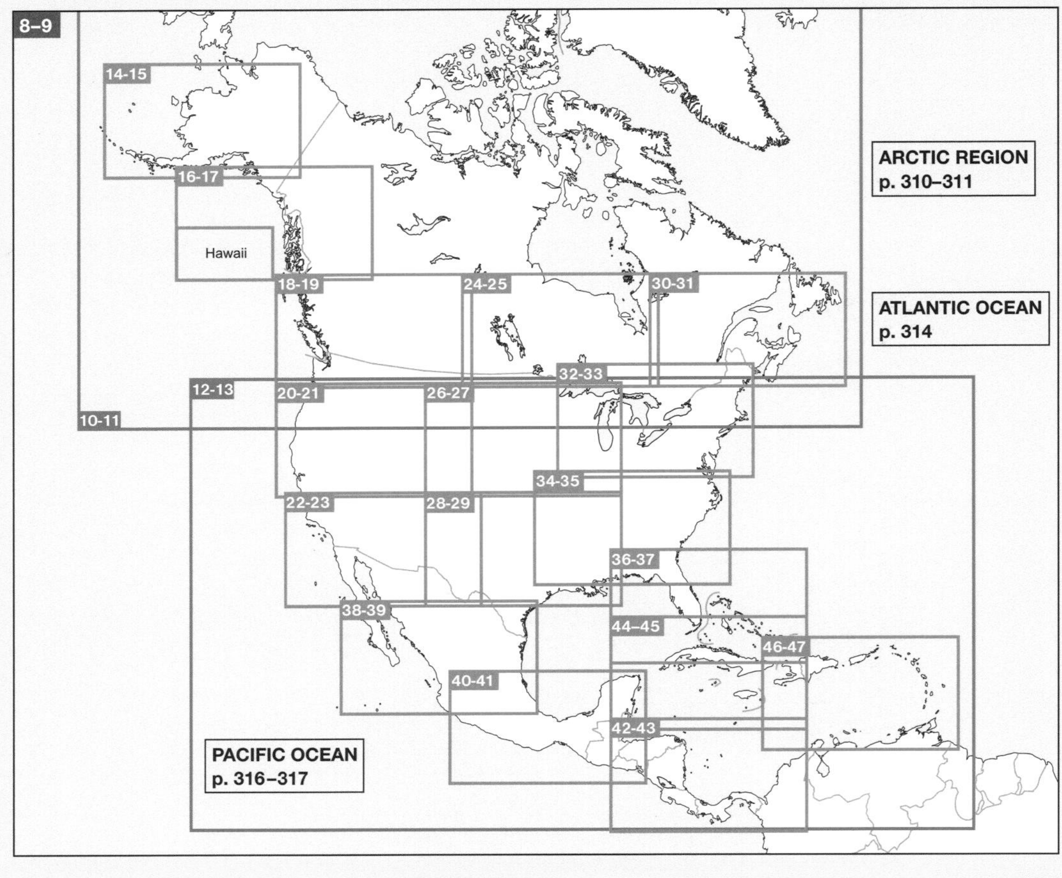

Europe

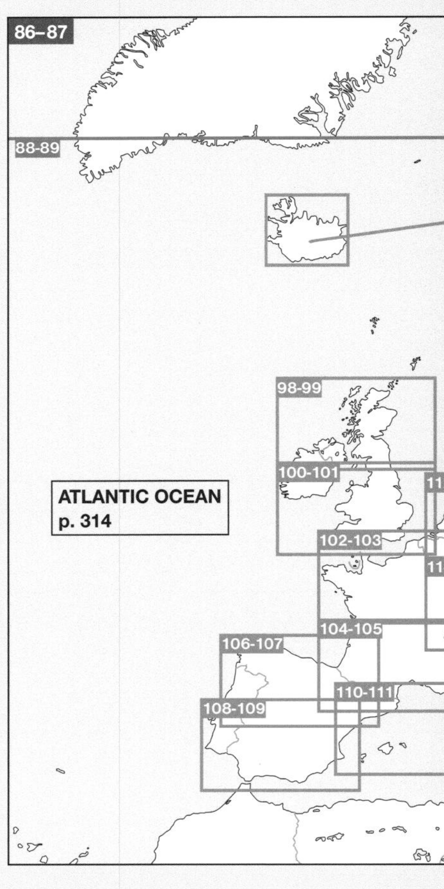

Southamerica

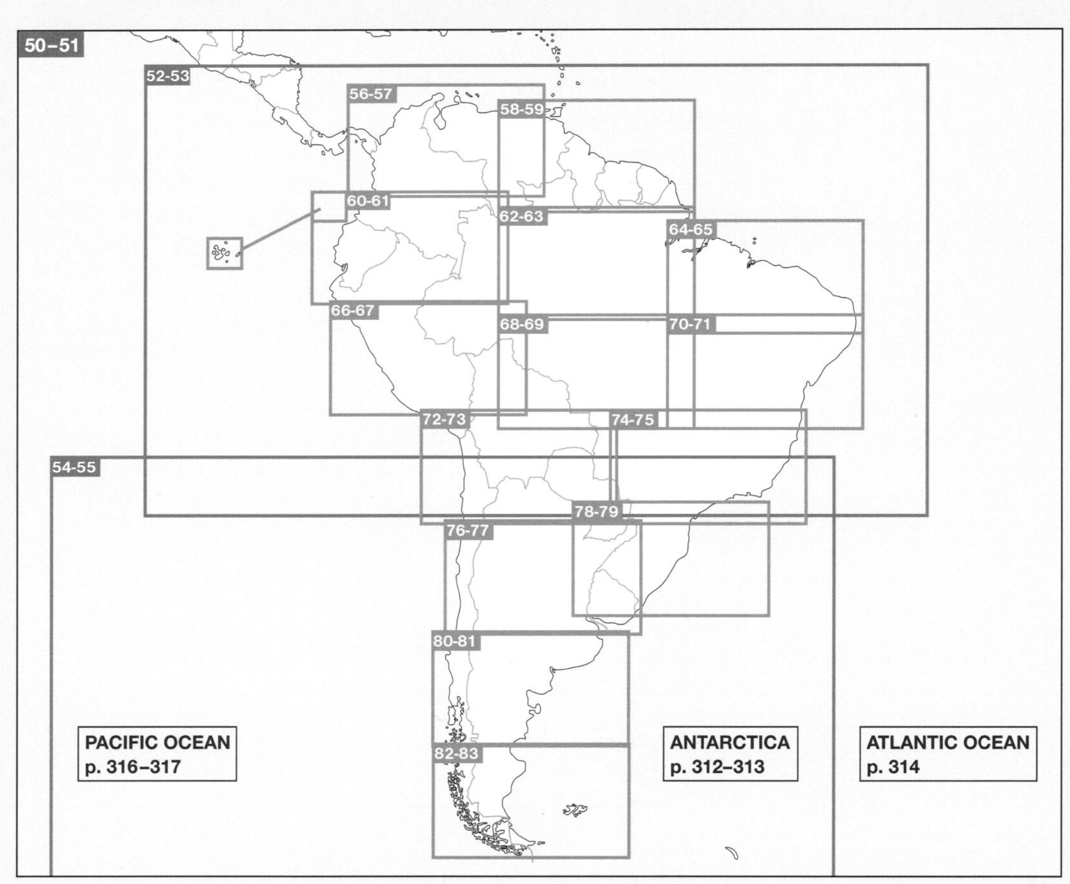

Near and Middle East, Northern

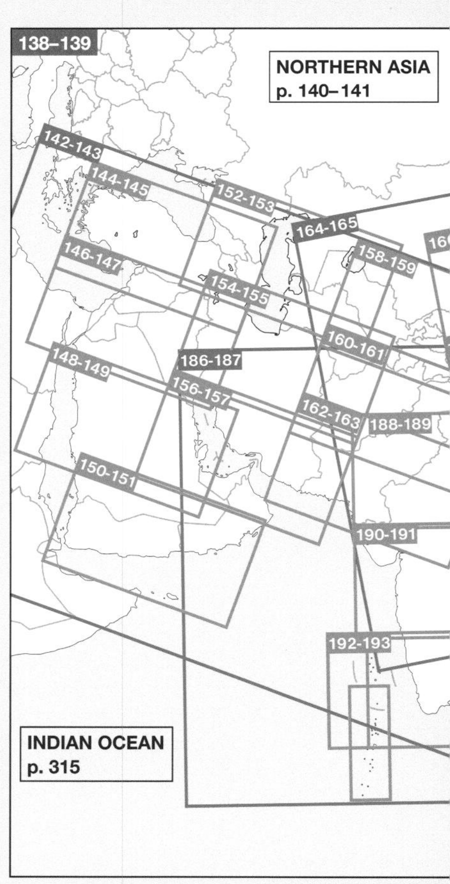

Map locator

The impressive modern skyline of Chicago along the shores of Lake Michigan. The city is a leading commercial and financial center.

Easter Island was once home to an advanced civilization. The more than 300 stone sculptures (moai) scattered around Easter Island are the most important remnants of this culture.

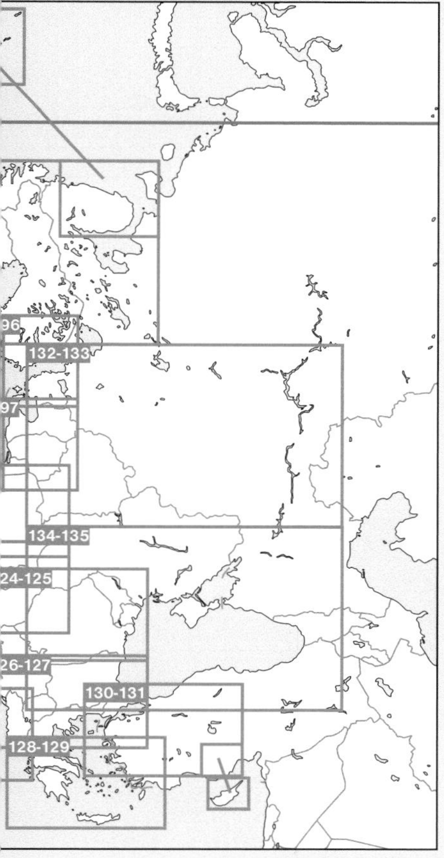

Southeastern Asia, Australia/Oceania

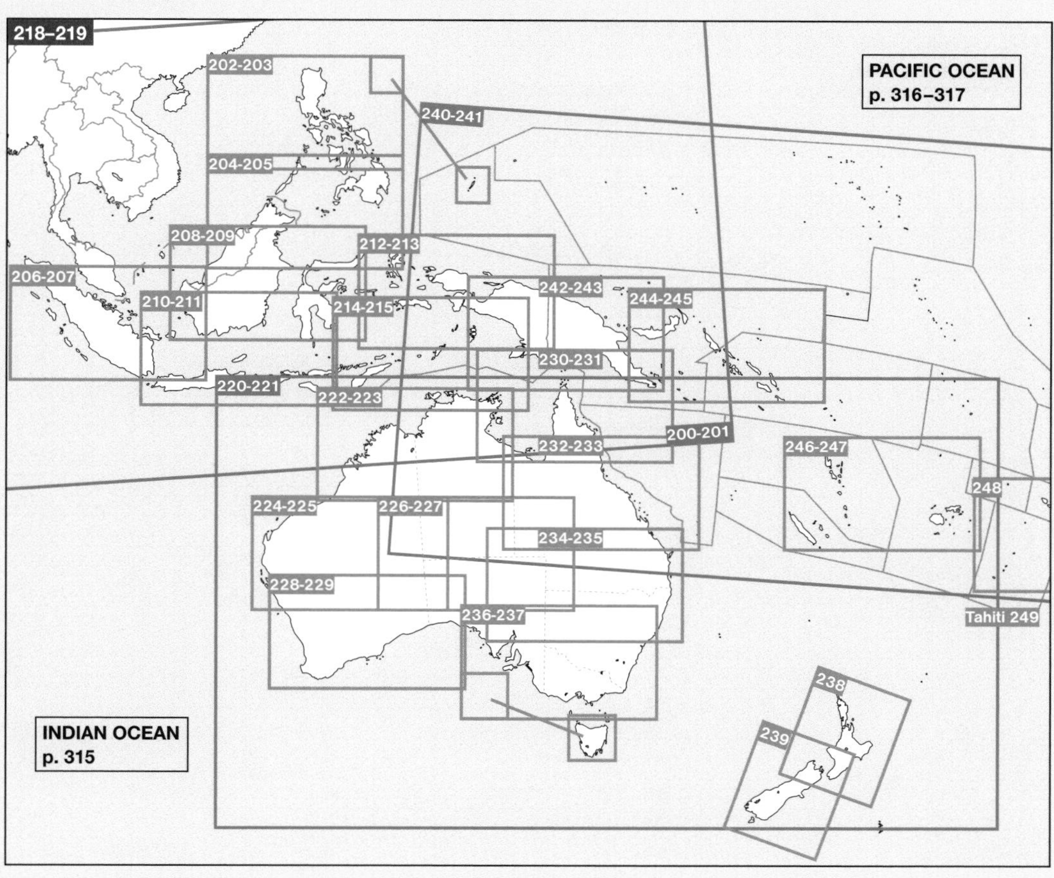

...al Asia, Southern Asia

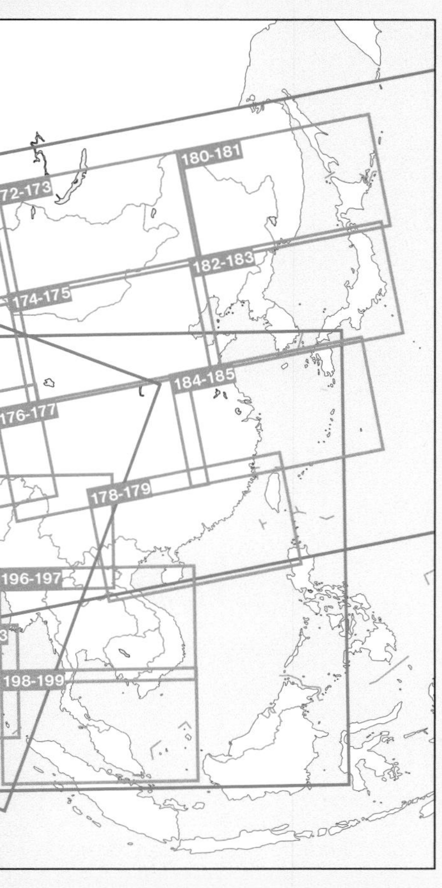

Africa

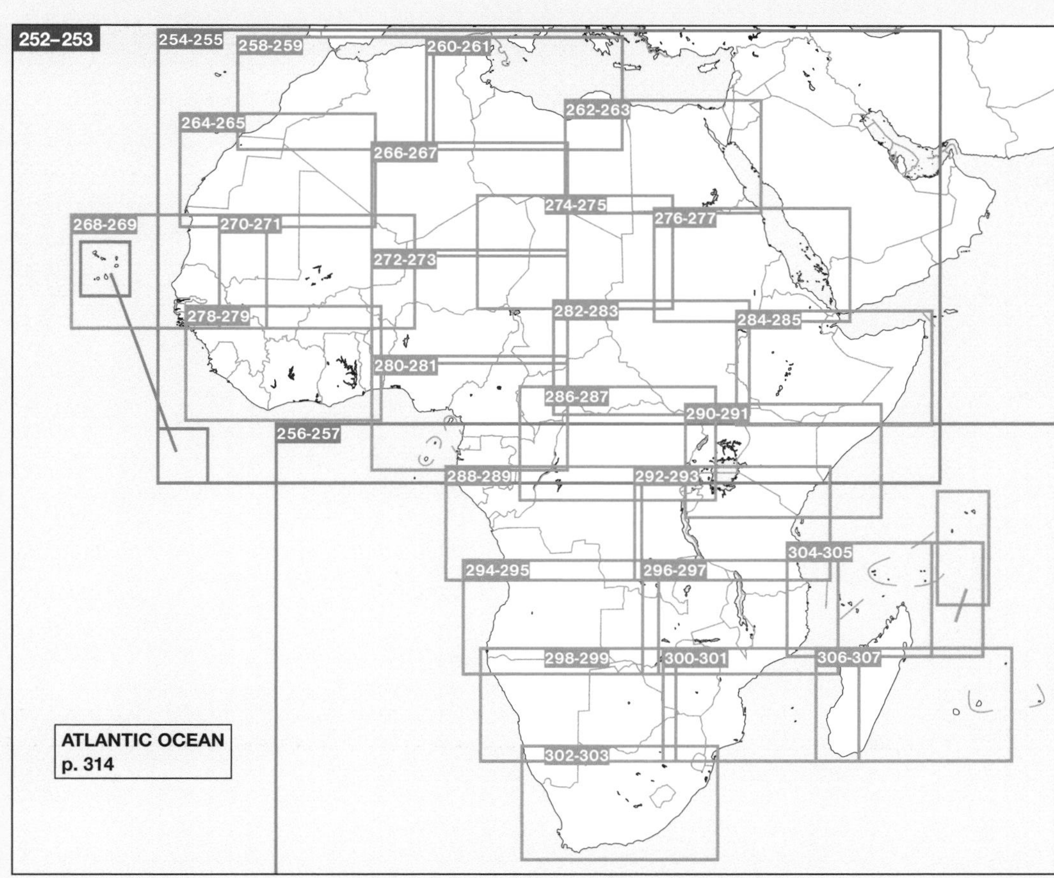

Legend • Natural geographical features

The Polynesian island of Moorea is the remnant of a massive volcano. The island, like so many in the Pacific Ocean, is surrounded by coral reefs.

The Scottish Highlands in the United Kingdom feature a variety of romantic and beautiful landscapes, including craggy mountains, pristine lakes, and rugged valleys.

Bodies of Water

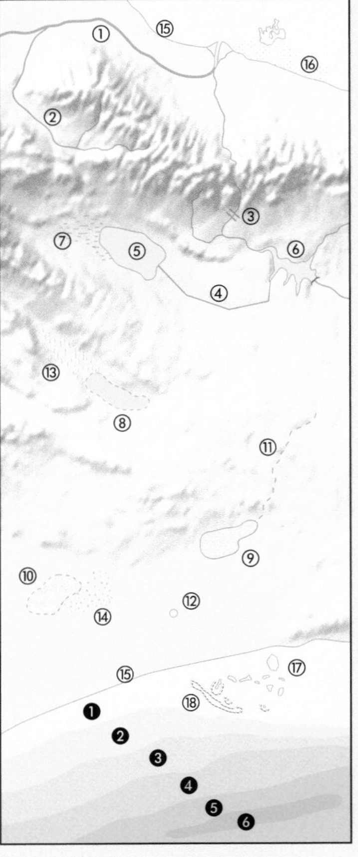

① Stream, river
② Tributary with headstreams
③ Waterfall, rapids
④ Canal
⑤ Lake
⑥ Reservoir with dam
⑦ Marsh, moor
⑧ Intermittent lake
⑨ Salt lake
⑩ Intermittent salt lake
⑪ Intermittent river (wadi)
⑫ Well, spring
⑬ Salt swamp
⑭ Salt pan
⑮ Shoreline
⑯ Mud flats
⑰ Island, archipelago
⑱ Coral reef

Depth tints

❶ 0 – 200 meters
❷ 200 – 2000 meters
❸ 2000 – 4000 meters
❹ 4000 – 6000 meters
❺ 6000 – 8000 meters
❻ below 8000 meters

Topography

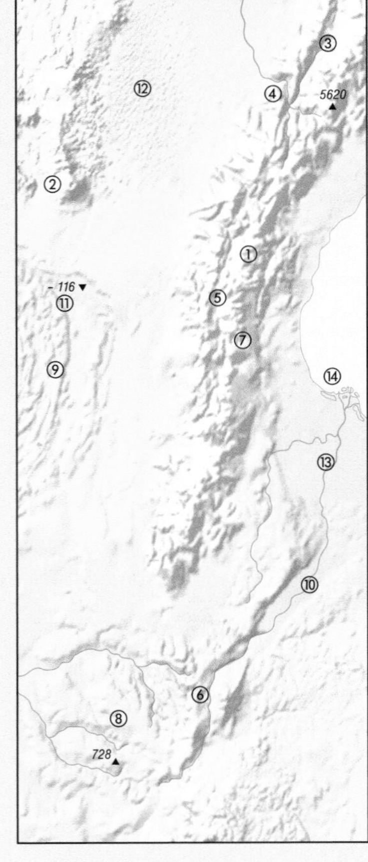

① High mountain region
② Volcano
③ V-shaped valley
④ Gorge
⑤ U-shaped valley
⑥ Canyon
⑦ Glacier in high mountain regions
⑧ Highland with valleys
⑨ Escarpment
⑩ Rift Valley
⑪ Depression
⑫ High dunes in arid areas
⑬ Lowland
⑭ Delta

Color tints of climate and vegetation zones

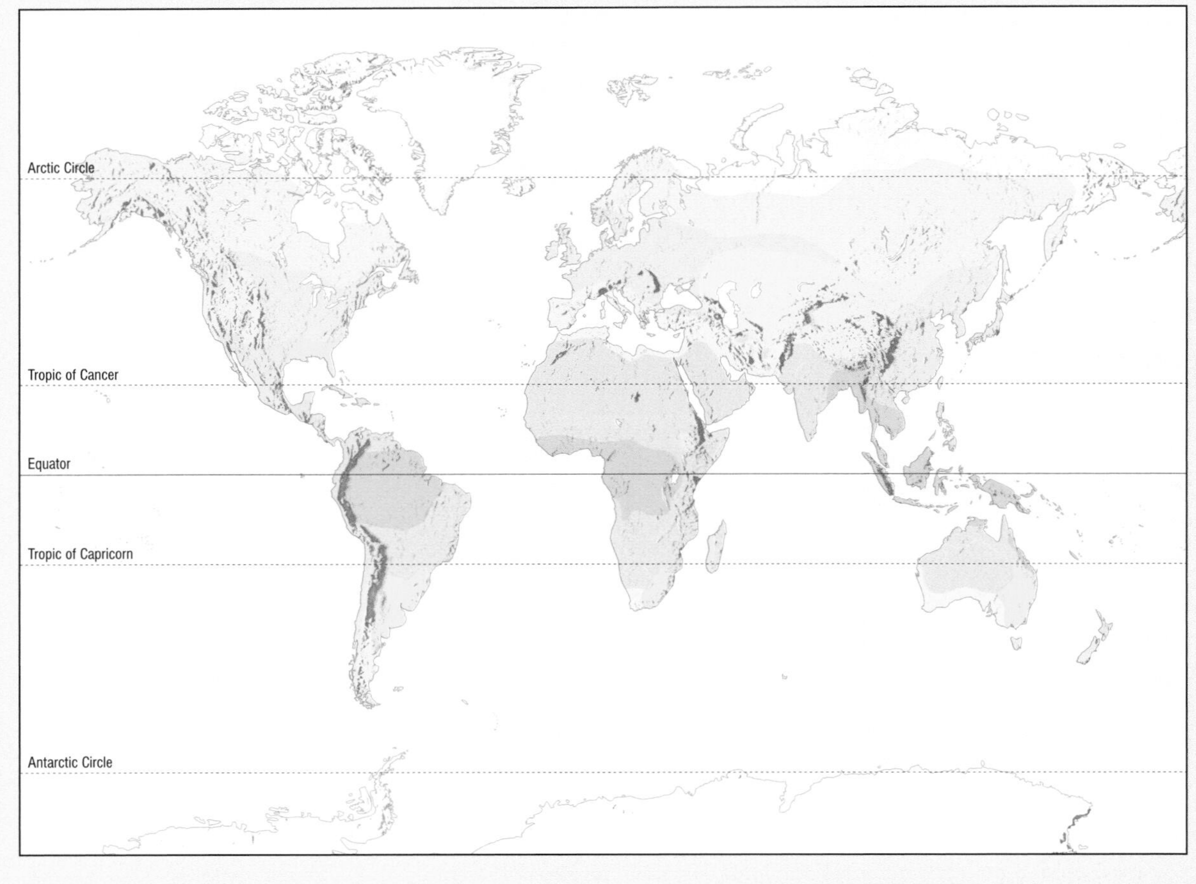

Polar and subpolar zone

Perpetual frost, all months below 0° C (32°F)

Arctic flora and Tundra (lichens, mosses, grasses, dwarf shrubs)

Boreal zone

Taiga, northern coniferous trees; pines, firs, larches, spruces

Temperate zones

Rainy climates with mild winters; deciduous broadleaf forests, mixed forests

Wintercold desert and semidesert climates; steppe, prairie, grasslands, semideserts

Subtropics

Mediterranean climate with dry summers and moist winters; broadleaved evergreen forests

Warm, summerhumid moist climate; subtropical forests

Desert and semidesert climates; open shrub lands

Tropics

Humid and dry savannas with dry seasons; woody savannas

Tropical rainforest, rainy climate with no winter; high temperatures

Beijing's historic Forbidden City was the main residence of China's monarchs and the great imperial court for many centuries.

A full moon above the skyline of San Francisco in northern California. The city's beautiful Golden Gate Bridge is one of the world's longest suspension bridges.

Settlements and transportation routes

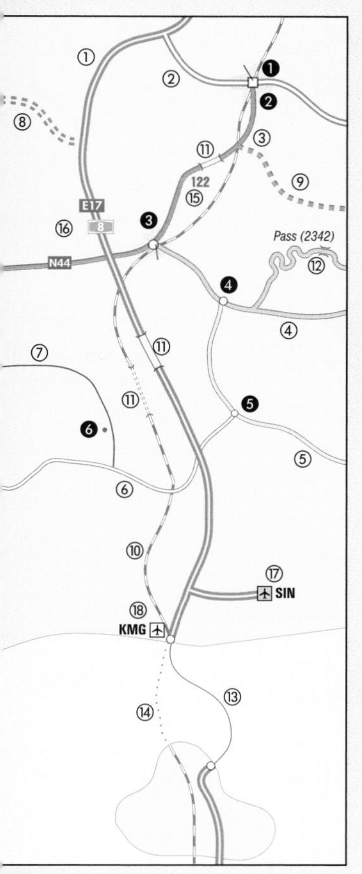

Transportation routes

① Interstate highway/motorway
② Multilane divided highway
③ Primary highway
④ Secondary highway
⑤ Main road
⑥ Secondary road
⑦ Unimproved road
⑧ Interstate highway/motorway under construction
⑨ Primary highway under construction
⑩ Railway
⑪ Tunnel
⑫ Pass with elevation in meters
⑬ Ferry, shipping route
⑭ Railway ferry
⑮ Distances in kilometers (within USA and UK in miles)
⑯ Road numbers
⑰ International Airport with IATA-code
⑱ Airport with IATA-code

Settlements

❶ Urban area
❷ Town over 1 million inhabitants
❸ Town 100,000 - 1 million inhabitants
❹ Town 10,000 - 100,000 inhabitants
❺ Town under 10,000 inhabitants
❻ Hamlet, research station

Type faces of cities and towns

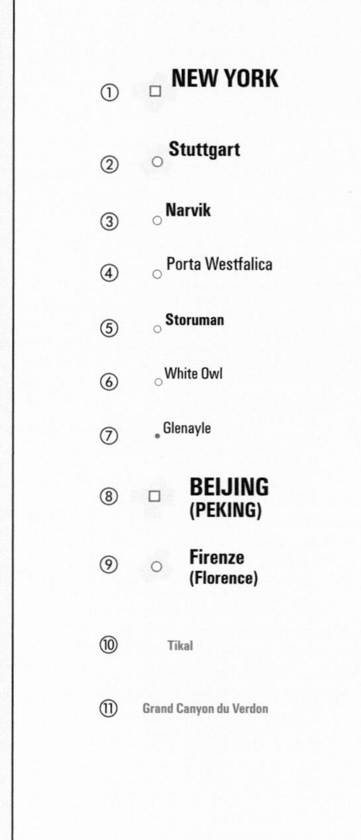

① Town over 1 million inhabitants
② Town 100,000 - 1 million inhabitants
③ Significant town 10,000 - 100,000 inhabitants
④ Town 10,000 - 100,000 inhabitants
⑤ Significant town under 10,000 inhabitants
⑥ Town under 10,000 inhabitants
⑦ Hamlet, research station
⑧ Town over 1 million inhabitants with translation
⑨ Town 100,000 - 1 million inhabitants with translation
⑩ Point of cultural interest
⑪ Point of natural interest

Political and other boundaries

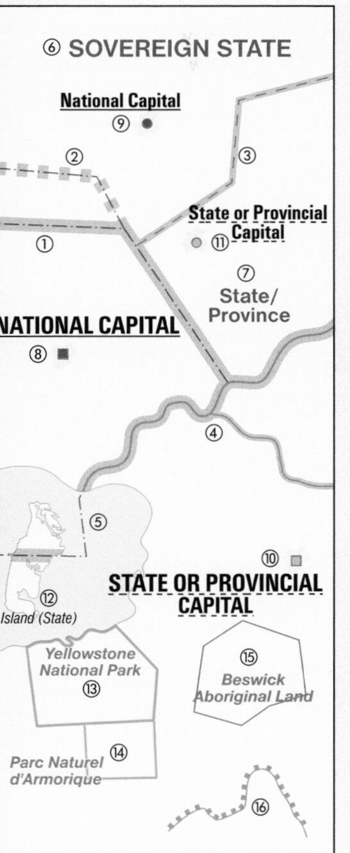

① International boundary
② Disputed international boundary
③ Administrative boundary
④ Boundary on rivers
⑤ Boundary in lake or sea
⑥ Country name
⑦ Administrative name
⑧ Capital with more than 1 million inhabitants
⑨ Capital below 1 million inhabitants
⑩ Administrative capital with more than 1 million inhabitants
⑪ Administrative capital with less than 1 million inhabitants
⑫ Dependent territory with administering country
⑬ National parks and biosphere reserves
⑭ Nature parks and other protected areas
⑮ Reservation
⑯ Walls (Great Wall of China, Hadrian's wall)

Type faces of topographic features

① *PACIFIC OCEAN*
② *GULF OF MEXICO*
Gulf of Thailand
③ *Antalya Körfezi*
④ *Elbe Rio Grande Murray*
⑤ *White Nile Suez Canal*
⑥ *HIMALAYA*
⑦ *Great Plains*
⑧ *Mt. Olympus* ▲ *2424*
⑨ - 116 ▼ *Danakil Depression*
⑩ *Tahiti*
⑪ *Cape of Good Hope*
⑫ *325*
⑬ *5425*
⑭ *Mexican Basin*
⑮ *Mariana Trench*

① Ocean
② Gulf, bay
③ Small bay, strait
④ River, lake, canal
⑤ River, lake, canal (translated)
⑥ Mountain name
⑦ Area name, landscape name
⑧ Mountain name with elevation above sea level in meters
⑨ Depression with depth below sea level in meters
⑩ Island name
⑪ Cape name
⑫ Elevation of lake above sea level
⑬ Depth in oceans and lakes
⑭ Undersea landscapes, mountains and trenches
⑮ Deepsea trench

Explanation of symbols

The passenger train services that pass through South Africa's Garden Route offer spectacular views of the Indian Ocean and the Karoo Mountains.

The landscapes of Los Glaciares National Park, including large glaciers and mountains, are among the most spectacular in the region of Patagonia. Photo: Fitz Roy Massif (3,128 meters)

Beautiful natural landscapes, fascinating wildlife, historic architecture, and vibrant cities – our world is rich in wonders. The modern cartography and layout of the World Travel Atlas highlights many of the world's attractions – unspoiled wilderness areas, the most famous and significant historic sites, culturally diverse urban areas, holiday resorts, as well as sporting venues. The system of pictograms developed specifically for this atlas gives the reader a clear impression of the diverse attractions in the world's regions. All of the pictograms featured on each map are listed and labeled in a legend at the bottom of the respective page.

The following pages offer brief characterizations of the various pictograms used in the atlas. The pictograms are divided by color into two groups: green and blue pictograms represent natural attractions, while yellow pictograms represent cultural attractions and other man-made sites. The names of significant towns and cities are highlighted in yellow throughout the atlas. Blue pictograms represent sporting and recreational facilities. Important and well-known transportation routes, including highways and shipping routes, are also highlighted in the atlas. These routes are not only highlighted by pictograms but also by distinctly-colored lines that identify each type of route.

Principal travel routes

Auto route
The maps display many of the world's most famous and historically significant roads and routes, such as the ancient Silk Road in Asia and historic Route 66 in the United States, The maps also feature important modern highways including the Pan-American Highway – which stretches from Alaska to Tierra del Fuego.

Rail road
The age of the railways started in 1804 when the world's first steam locomotive began operation in Wales. By the end of the 19th century it was possible to travel through most of Europe and North America on trains. The Orient Express, Europe's first long-distance luxury passenger line began operation in 1883 and traveled between Paris and Bucharest. The Trans-Siberian line was constructed between 1891 and 1916 with the goal of connecting Siberia to European Russia. The Trans-Siberian still runs between Moscow and Vladivostok on the Pacific Ocean almost 100 years after construction ended.

Highspeed train
The Eurostar trains travel at speeds up to 300 kilometers an hour and transport passengers between London and Brussels or Paris in less than three hours. Japan's Shinkansen line connects several of the country's major cities. In Europe, France and Germany maintain the most extensive networks of high speed trains.

Shipping route
Millions of passengers travel on cruise ships every year and experience one of the most leisurely and comfortable forms of long-distance travel. Thousands of cruise ships of vastly different sizes traverse the oceans, seas, and rivers of the world. The Caribbean Sea, Mediterranean Sea, Scandinavia, and Alaska are among the most popular locations for cruises on the open seas. Modern cruise ships offer an astounding variety of attractions including casinos, fine restaurants, shops, as well as side trips to attractive destinations on land. Most of the ships on our planet, however, are used for transporting valuable goods and natural resources between different nations and continents. Shipping plays a vital role in the global economy.

Remarkable landscapes and natural monuments

UNESCO World Natural Heritage
Since 1972, UNESCO has compiled a growing list of specially designated natural sites that are deemed to be of outstanding importance and "universal" significance.

Mountain landscape
Mountain ranges are among the most scenic areas in the world. Many of the world's ancient low-mountain ranges including the Appalachians and the Central Massif feature heavily eroded and rounded peaks. Other younger mountain ranges feature jagged and high peaks that are often covered by snow and glaciers.

Rock landscape
Many of the world's most interesting stone formations were shaped by wind and water erosion, including the natural attractions of Monument Valley National Park in the western United States.

Ravine/canyon
Canyons and Gorges are narrow and often deep valleys created by rivers and wind erosion. The Grand Canyon in the American state of Arizona is the most famous and one of the most spectacular canyons on the planet.

Extinct volcano
Volcanoes are formed when solid, liquid, or gas-like materials from the Earth's interior rise to the planet's surface. Magma passes through the structure of a volcano and leaves its crater as lava, often accompanied by plumes of hot ash. Extinct volcanoes are volcanoes that have not erupted in the last 10,000 years.

Active volcano
Geologists consider any volcano that has erupted in the last 10,000 years to be an active volcano. Most of the world's active volcanoes are concentrated in geologically active region such as areas near the boundaries of the world's tectonic plates or mid-ocean ridges. The Pacific Ring of Fire is an area of relatively frequent volcanic activity.

Geyser
Active geysers are hot springs that occasionally release plumes of water into the air. Geysers are located in volcanically active regions and many are popular tourist attractions.

Cave
Caves are formed during the crea tion of stone formations (mountains underground layers of stone, etc. or emerge later due to the erodinc effects of water that seeps into stone and often carves out entire networks of large caves containing lakes anc rivers.

Glacier
Glaciers are large fields or rivers o ice that often migrate through moun tain valleys. Glaciers are formec above the snow line in mountainous areas or in arctic regions.

River landscape
The eroding power of flowing wate formed many of the world's valleys gorges, and canyons. Most of the world's earliest civilizations were formed in fertile river valleys such as Mesopotamia or the Indus Valley Many rivers in lowland areas have large branching deltas containing delicate ecosystems.

Waterfall/rapids
Waterfalls are formed when rivers flow over an area with a sudden drop in elevation. Waterfalls are among the most stunning and popular natu ral attractions on the planet.

Lake country
Most of the world's major lakes were created by glaciers during the ice ages. Several regions including southern Finland feature a large number o lakes, often interconnected and located near one another. In additior to glacial lakes, there are many lakes formed as a result of tectonic activity, such as the many lakes in Africa's Great Rift Valley.

Desert
Vast landscapes covered by sanc dunes, sand fields, or stone with sparse rainfall. Deserts are the mos arid regions on the earth and only a few types of plants and animals car survive in these harsh environments Most deserts have major differences between night and daytime tem peratures.

Oasis
Oases are fertile islands surroundec by barren, arid deserts or steppes They are supplied with water by rivers, springs or underground groundwater repositories. Most oases feature dense vegetation.

Explanation of symbols

Thick clouds above Mount Taranaki (2,158 meters) on New Zealand's North Island, one of many active volcanoes in the Pacific Ring of Fire.

Dresden, the capital of the German state of Saxony, became a major cultural center in the 18th century. The city's waterfront along the Elbe River features many historic landmarks.

Depression
Depressions are small basins located on land but at significant depths below sea level. Many depressions - including the Dead Sea – were created through tectonic activity.

Fossil site
Fossils are the ancient remnants and traces of animals and plants that have inhabited our planet during its long history.

Nature park
Conservation areas created to protect local flora and fauna.

National park (landscape)
Large conservation areas created to protect areas of natural beauty and significant national or international importance. Development and industry are forbidden or heavily restricted in national parks. Yellowstone National Park in the United States is the world's oldest national park.

National park (flora)
This symbol designates national parks with interesting local flora.

National park (fauna)
This symbol designates national parks with a large or unique collection of local wildlife.

National park (culture)
National park with important cultural attractions such as the Native American historic sites in Mesa Verde National Park.

Biosphere reserve
Undeveloped conservation areas with pristine examples of distinct climate or vegetation zones.

Wildlife reserve
Conservation areas created for the protection of endangered animals. Selous Game Reserve in Tanzania is home to large herds of protected African elephants.

Whale watching
Boat tours providing the chance to observe whales or dolphins in their natural habitats can be found in many of the world's coastal areas.

Turtle conservation area
Specially designated coastal areas where endangered sea turtles live or lay their eggs.

Protected area for sea-lions/seals
Areas created especially for the protection of endangered seal and sea lion species.

Protected area for penguins
These protected areas were created to preserve threatened penguin colonies and offer visitors a chance to see the creatures in their habitats.

Zoo/safari park
Zoos are park-like areas that feature collections of mostly exotic animals. Safari parks are large properties open to tourists that feature wildlife.

Crocodile farm
Most alligator farms are commercial operations where animals are bred. Many are open to the public.

Coastal landscape
Coastal areas often feature diverse landscapes including beaches, cliffs, tidal flats, and large river deltas surrounded by marshlands. Some coastal areas are flat with sand dunes and land spits, while others are lined by rock formations, stony beaches, and high cliffs. The fjords of Scandinavia, Alaska, and a few other regions are among the most stunning coastal areas in the world.

Beach
Beaches are major tourist attractions and often feature numerous recreational activities. Sand beaches are common in flat coastal areas. Many of the world's most famous beaches are now lined by large tourist and residential developments.

Coral reef
Coral Reefs are formed by small animals called coral in warm, saline water. Many of the world's large coral reefs exhibit astonishing biodiversity and are accessible to divers.

Island
Islands are land masses surrounded by water. Most islands are part of island groups. The islands on our planet have a combined land area of 10.5 million km². Many of the world's islands and island groups have become popular tourist destinations.

Underwater reserve
Underwater conservation areas created to protect local marine flora and fauna.

Remarkable Cities and cultural monuments

UNESCO World Cultural Heritage
Since 1972, UNESCO has compiled a list of specially designated cultural/man-made sites that are deemed to be of outstanding importance.

Remarkable city
Cities of global importance or with an abundance of tourist attractions are marked yellow on our maps. These cities are highlighted because of their significance as tourist destinations or leading cultural centers.

Pre- and early history
Sites related to ancient human cultures and their ways of life during times before the emergence of written records. The most grandiose prehistoric sites include large megaliths created by different cultures, including the circle of stone pillars at Stonehenge in the United Kingdom.

Prehistoric rockscape
Prehistoric paintings, carvings and reliefs created by nomadic peoples during ancient times.

The Ancient Orient
Sites related to the ancient cultures that developed in the region comprising modern Anatolia (Asia Minor), Syria, Iraq, Israel, Lebanon, Iran, and in some cases Egypt during the period between 7000 BC and the time of Alexander the Great (400 BC). The Sumerians developed one of the first urban civilizations on the planet. They also developed one of the first number systems. After 2000 BC, the first large empires emerged in the region including the kingdoms of the Babylonians, Assyrians, and Hittites. The region features temples, ziggurats, and palaces from ancient times.

Ancient Egypt
One of the greatest ancient civilizations developed on the banks of the Nile River in Egypt. Around 3000 BC, Egypt was unified under the reign of one ruler for the first time. Between this time and the period of Alexander the Great's conquests, Egypt was ruled by more than 31 dynasties. The all-powerful pharaohs were considered living gods in Ancient Egypt. The ancient Egyptians developed a writing system, a calendar, and eventually advanced building techniques. In ancient Egypt, the arts were devoted primarily to religion and mythology.

Ancient Egyptian pyramids
The monumental pyramid tombs of Egyptian pharaohs were constructed during the Old Kingdom. The largest and most spectacular pyramid is the 137-meter-high Great (Cheops) Pyramid at Giza, one of the seven wonders of the ancient world.

Minoan culture
The advanced bronze-age culture of the Minoans flourished on the Greek island of Crete during ancient times. Minoan civilization first emerged during the 3rd millennium BC, after which the Minoans rapidly became the dominant power in the eastern Mediterranean. Modern Crete features the remnants of luxurious Minoan villas with impressive frescoes and interior design.

Phoenecian culture
During ancient times the area encompassing modern Israel, Lebanon, and Palestine was once the center of Phoenician culture. The Phoenicians were the dominant trading power in the Mediterranean for several centuries and founded distant colonies (Carthage).

Early African culture
Ancient African civilizations include the cultures of the Kingdom of Ghana, Axum (Ethiopia), and Kush – a complex and advanced society that developed south of Egypt.

Etruscan culture
The Etruscans probably originated in central Italy. During the 10th century BC, they conquered large sections of the Italian Peninsula before they were conquered by the Romans. Italy has numerous archeological and historic sites related to the culture of the ancient Etruscans.

Greek antiquity
No other civilization has had a greater influence of European culture than that of Ancient Greece. The city-state of Athens was one of the first basic democracies in history. The art, philosophy and architecture of Ancient Greece continue to inspire and shape our modern world. Ancient Greece was divided into city-states, many of which founded distant colonies in Southern Europe, the Middle East, and North Africa. Ancient Greek art dealt mostly with subject related to Greek mythology. The Greek city-states constructed many great struc-

Explanation of symbols

Sunset above the Pyramids of Giza: the enormous pyramids were constructed as monumental tombs during the reign of ancient Egypt's pharaohs.

Borobudur: the Buddhist complex in Indonesia features numerous sculptures and reliefs. The site was buried beneath volcanic ash for centuries until it was rediscovered in the 19th century.

Remarkable Cities and cultural monuments

tures including impressive temples and amphitheaters. During the Hellenistic period – after the death of Alexander the Great – Greek-speaking cities outside of the mainland, including Alexandria in Egypt, replaced the city-states as the centers of Greek civilization.

Roman antiquity
Over a period of centuries the once small city of Rome on the Tiber River emerged as the center of a vast and powerful empire. The Roman Empire was at its largest under the reign of the Emperor Trajan (98-117 BC) – during this period its borders extended from North Africa to Scotland and from Iberia to Mesopotamia. The Roman state that existed between 509 and 27 BC is referred to as the Roman Republic. The Roman state that was created after the reforms of Caesar Augustus is known as the Roman Empire. Roman art and culture was greatly influenced by Ancient Greek and other Mediterranean cultures. The Romans constructed impressive architectural monuments including amphitheaters, temples, and aqueducts. Roman historic sites can be found throughout Europe, the Middle East, and North Africa.

Nabatean culture
The ancient city of Petra (in modern Jordan) was first settled by the Nabataeans in the fifth century BC. By the 1st century BC, the Nabateans ruled a powerful trading empire with Petra as its capital. The monumental ruins of Petra are the grandest remnants of this ancient culture and one of many historic sites in the Middle East.

Vikings
Between the 9th and 11th centuries, Scandinavian Vikings conquered territories throughout Europe. During their centuries of conquest, the Vikings founded numerous settlements and trading posts in Russia, Western Europe, as well as in the British Isles.

Ancient India
India has a wealth of cultural and historic attractions. The Indus Valley civilization (2600-1400 BC), was one of the first advanced civilizations to emerge on the planet. Indian culture reached a highpoint during the period between the 7th and 13th centuries. Many of India's greatest Buddhist and Hindu architectural masterpieces as well as art were created during these centuries. During the Mogul era (16th and 17th century), many impressive works of Islamic architecture were created throughout the country.

Ancient China
The oldest remnants of early Chinese culture date from the era between 5000-2000 BC. The Shang dynasty (1600-1000 BC) was the most influential and advanced bronze-age culture in China. Daoism and Confucian philosophy were both developed in 5th century BC China. The first great unified Chinese empire was forged around 220 BC by Ying Zheng, the king of Qin. After the emergence of the first Chinese empire, China was ruled by various dynasties and experienced many periods of cultural and technological advancement. The country's most impressive historic sites include the Great Wall, the tomb of Emperor Qin with its army of terracotta warriors, and the Forbidden City in Beijing.

Ancient Japan
The Yamato period of Japanese history began around 400 AD. During this period, the country was ruled by an imperial court based in the city of Nara. During the 5th century the Japanese adopted the Chinese writing system and in the 6th century Buddhism arrived in the country. The Fujiwara clan dominated the country for more than 500 years starting in the 7th century. During this period the country's imperial capital was moved from Nara to Kyoto. Between 1192 and 1868, Japan was ruled by a series of shoguns (military rulers). The Meiji Era (1868-1912) saw the restoration of imperial power and the emergence of modern Japan.

Mayan culture
The Maya are an Amerindian people in southern Mexico and Central America. During pre-Columbian times, the Maya developed an advanced and powerful civilization that ruled over a vast territory. Mayan Civilization reached its cultural and technological peak around 300 AD and was eventually devastated by the arrival of Spanish conquistadors in the 16th century. Maya civilization was dominated by a series of city-states. Central America and Mexico are the sites of many grand Mayan ruins including numerous pyramids.

Inca culture
During the 15th and 16th centuries, the Incas ruled a vast empire that encompassed parts of modern-day Peru, Bolivia, Ecuador, Chile, and Argentina. The Incas built monumental stone architecture throughout their realm.

Aztec culture
During the Second Millennium BC, the Aztec people migrated into Mexico where they quickly established a powerful empire. The Aztec capital city of Tenochtitlan (modern-day Mexico City) was founded in 1325. The Aztecs constructed many grand temples and pyramids throughout their empire and made important cultural advances including the creation of a writing system and calendar.

Other ancient American cultures
Advanced Amerindian cultures appeared in both North America and the Andean regions of South America. Countless Amerindian historic sites can be found throughout the Americas.

Places of Jewish cultural interest
Judaism is the oldest of the world's major monotheist religions. The temple in Jerusalem was one of the greatest achievements of early Jewish culture – today only a section of its surrounding walls remain (the Western or Wailing Wall). Historic synagogues can be found throughout the world, a legacy of the Jewish Diaspora.

Places of Christian cultural interest
Christianity is the world's most practiced and widespread religion. Christianity is based on the teachings in the old and new testaments of the Bible. Christian religious sites, including grand churches, cathedrals, and monasteries, can be found in most regions of the world.

Places of Islamic cultural interest
Islam, one of the world's major religions, was founded by Mohammed (570-632 AD). The teachings of the Koran are the basis for Islam. Muslims around the world pray in the direction of Mecca, the religion's holiest cities. Many Muslim countries feature beautiful, historic mosques.

Places of Buddhist cultural interest
Buddhism is based on the teachings of Siddhartha Gautama (around 560-480 BC), also known as the Buddh
Most of the world's Buddhists live
East Asia. Important Buddhist site
include temples, pagodas, stupa
and monasteries.

Places of Hindu cultural interest
Most of the at least one billion fo
lowers of Hinduism, one of world'
most practiced religions, live on th
Indian subcontinent. Hinduism e
compasses a variety of beliefs an
practices, many of which are tho
sands of years old.

Places of Jainist cultural interest
Most followers of Jainism live in Indi
Jainism is based on the teachings
Mahavira, who lived in the 5th centu
BC. India features many Jainist site
including temples and monasterie

Places of Sikh cultural interest
The Sikh religious philosophy emerge
in 16th century northern India, as a
attempt to merge the teachings
Islam and Hinduism. The "Golde
Temple" in Amritsar is the mo
important Sikh religious center.

Places of Shinto cultural interest
Shinto, the native religion of Japa
is based on the reverence of ka
(nature spirits) and ancestral spirit

Places of cultural interest to othe religions
Sites related to other religious an
spiritual communities.

Places of cultural interest to indi genous peoples (native peoples)
Sites related to the culture or histo
of a region's indigenous inhabit-ant

Aborigine reservation
The almost 500,000 Aborigines
Australia form only a small portion
the continent's population. Ma
Aborigine communities administe
large land reserves.

Places of Aboriginal cultural intere
The scattered cultural sites of th
Aborigines, including countless roc
paintings, are amongst the interestin
cultural attractions in Australia.

Indian reservation
Most of the Native American rese
vations in the United States an
Canada were founded during th
19th century. Despite the history
low living standards on reservation
many Native American communitie

Explanation of symbols

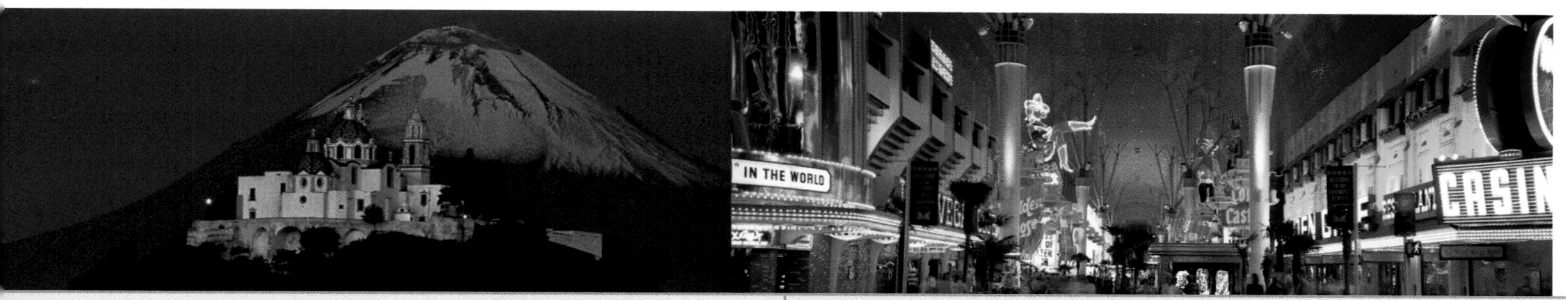

Spanish settlers built Nuestra Senora church in Cholula, Mexico atop a series of ancient Amerindian pyramids. The historic church lies close to the snow-capped volcano Popocatepetl.

Las Vegas, the largest city in the American state of Nevada, is a popular tourist destination with numerous casinos, theme hotels, and amusement parks.

Sport and leisure destinations

have successfully protected their culture and languages.

Indian Pueblo culture
The Pueblo Indians are a group of Native American communities who have lived in southwestern United States for centuries. Their traditional settlements – known as pueblos – consist of adobe buildings.

Places of Indian cultural interest
The different regions of North America feature hundreds of sites related to the history and cultures of Native Americans.

Amazonian Indians/protected area
The tropical rainforests of South America are home to dozens of Amerindian communities. During the 20th century, several land reserves were created to protect Amerindian communities in the Amazon basin.

Cultural landscape
This designation refers to rural areas with fascinating and distinctive landscapes that have been created or shaped by human settlement or land cultivation.

Historical city scape
Historic cities and towns with well-preserved architectural attractions.

Impressive skyline
Cities featuring modern skylines, such as New York City and Hong Kong.

Castle/fortress/fort
Europe features the greatest concentration of these structures.

Caravanserai
Historic inns along the ancient caravan routes of the Middle East and North Africa, especially Asia Minor and Iran.

Palace
Grand castles and palaces that once housed nobility and royalty can be found in many different regions.

Technical/industrial monument
Man-made attractions related to the achievements of industrialization and modern times.

Dam
The largest and most important dams and retaining walls on the planet.

Remarkable lighthouse
Many coastal areas feature beautiful or historic lighthouses.

Remarkable bridge
Many of the world's ancient and modern great bridges are considered engineering marvels.

Tomb/grave
Mausoleums, monuments, burial mounds, and other gravesites.

Theater of war/battlefield
Site where important battles occurred, including Waterloo in Belgium.

Monument
Sites dedicated to historic figures and important historical events.

Memorial
Site dedicated to the victims of wars and genocides.

Space mission launch site
Landing and launch sites of manned and unmanned space missions, including Cape Canaveral in Florida.

Space telescope
Radio, X-ray, and gamma-ray telescopes are important tools of modern astronomy.

Market
Important markets where local people gather to trade and purchase goods.

Festivals
Large celebrations of music and culture including the Salzburg Festival, Rio de Janeiro's Carnaval, and Mardi Gras in New Orleans.

Museum
Important collections of man-made works (art, technology, anthropology) and natural relics.

Theater
Famous theaters – presenting opera, musicals, dramas, and avant-garde productions.

World exhibition
Cities that have hosted world expositions including London and Seville, Spain.

Olympics
Cities and towns that have hosted the modern summer or winter Olympic Games.

Arena/stadium
The largest sporting venues in the world – including venues for soccer, football, baseball, rugby, hockey, and other leading sports.

Race track
Auto and motorbike racing are popular sports in many of the world's regions. The atlas highlights many of the most famous auto-racing venues including Formula 1 and NASCAR race tracks in Daytona, Indianapolis, Melbourne, and numerous other cities around the world.

Golf
Golf has become an increasingly popular sport around the world in recent decades. This atlas highlights many of the world most famous and beautiful golf courses as well as the areas that host important golf tournaments.

Horse racing
Several well-known racing courses and events are highlighted in the book, including the Ascot racecourse in England, a haunt of British high society. The Kentucky Derby is one of the most popular annual sporting events in the United States, while Hong Kong's Happy Valley draws thousands of visitors every week.

Skiing
The maps in the atlas point out the most important ski areas in the world including Chamonix in France, St. Moritz in Switzerland, and Aspen in Colorado. Many of these areas also offer facilities for other winter sports including snowboarding.

Sailing
Once a sport reserved for the very wealthy, recreational sailing is now enjoyed by millions of people. Some of the world's most beautiful sailing areas and popular marinas for recreational sailors are mentioned in the atlas.

Diving
Beautiful, colorful coral reefs and close encounters with marine life – the atlas presents popular diving from around the world.

Wind surfing
A mix of surfing and sailing, windsurfing is popular aquatic sport. The atlas points out coastal areas well suited to the sport.

Surfing
Popular coastal areas with adequate waves for surfing are highlighted – including well-known beaches in Australia, California, and Hawaii.

Canoeing/rafting
Adventurous and relaxing journeys along the world's rivers and lakes in canoes or rafts.

Seaport
Shipping remains vital for the global economy.The largest and busiest harbors in the world including the port cities of Rotterdam, Houston, and Singapore.

Deep-sea fishing
The atlas highlights many of best spots on the world's seas and oceans for recreational fishing.

Waterskiing
Beaches and lakes with ideal conditions for waterskiing.

Beach resort
Many of the world's beachside communities feature laid-back atmospheres and excellent tourist facilities. The atlas highlights popular beaches and beach towns such as Acapulco in Mexico, Waikiki in Hawaii, Hua Hin in Thailand.

Mineral/thermal spa
The atlas presents several historic and beautiful towns with spas that have attracted visitors for centuries.

Amusement/theme park
Many large and popular amusement parks are highlighted in the atlas including Walt Disney World, Sea World in California, Euro Disneyland in Paris, and Tivoli in Copenhagen.

Casino
Well known casinos including the historic casino of Monte Carlo in Monaco and the enormous resort-hotels of Las Vegas.

Hill resort
Exclusive resorts located in temperate highland areas. Mostly in Asia, hill resorts were once popular destinations for European colonial officials.

Lodge
Comfortable and in many cases luxurious camps or inns in pristine wilderness areas, mostly in Africa and North America.

A view over the crater of Mount St. Helens, an active volcano which last erupted in 1980. Mount St. Helens is proof of the awesome natural forces which continue to shape our planet.

The world

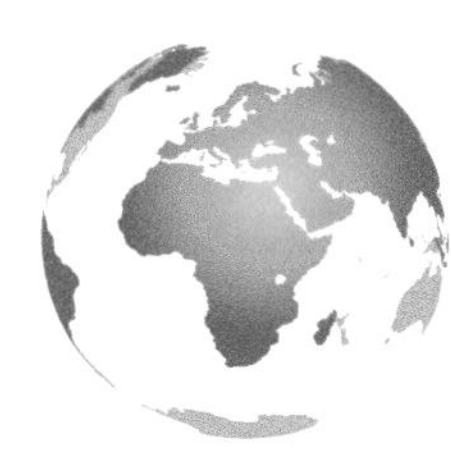

Fascinating Planet Earth: The blue jewel of the solar system. Created 4.6 billion years ago from a cloud of dust and gas, the Earth today has a fascinating mix of landscapes, flora, and fauna. Our planet is also home to countless manmade wonders, all created in the last few thousand years.

The world – physical map

The total surface area of the Earth covers 510 million km², 71% of which is covered by water and 29% by land. Most of the **world's water** is contained in the four vast oceans on our planet: Pacific, Atlantic, Indian, and the relatively small Arctic Ocean. The world's **land area** is divided between the seven continents: North America, South America, Europe, Asia, Africa, Australia, and Antarctica. While the surface of the planet's Southern Hemisphere is dominated by the oceans the Northern Hemisphere is almos equally covered by land and water. Th shape of the Earth's surface and th creation of the continents are the resul of tectonic plate movements, a proces that began billions of years ago. Catastrophic volcanic eruptions an

Light and water are the sources of all life on Earth

Heavy snowfall, extremely cold temperatures, permafrost, bright summers and dark winters are common in the world's **polar regions**. Antarctica and the Arctic (top photo) contain at least 90% of the planet's ice masses. The polar regions border on large tundras. Tundras (bottom photo) are cool regions with little precipitation and sparse, rugged vegetation.

The **taiga** is the world's largest belt of continuous forests and the world's northermost forested biome. This immense climate zone is 1,000 kilometers wide at its widest. The taiga belt stretches though Alaska and Canada in North America as well as Scandinavia in Europe and Siberia (top photo). The vast boreal forests of the taiga (bottom photo) cover around 13% of the world's land surface.

The **temperate regions** are home to vast forests with tall and green broad-leafed trees (top photo: Mixed forests in the Rocky Mountains of North America). Another side of the temperate zones are its vast grasslands and steppes, located primarily in Central Asia (Kazak Steppe), North America (Great Plains), and South America (Pampas). These mostly treeless regions receive relatively little precipitation and were once home to large numbers of gregarious animals (middle photo). The temperate zones also feature many of the world's most productive farming areas.

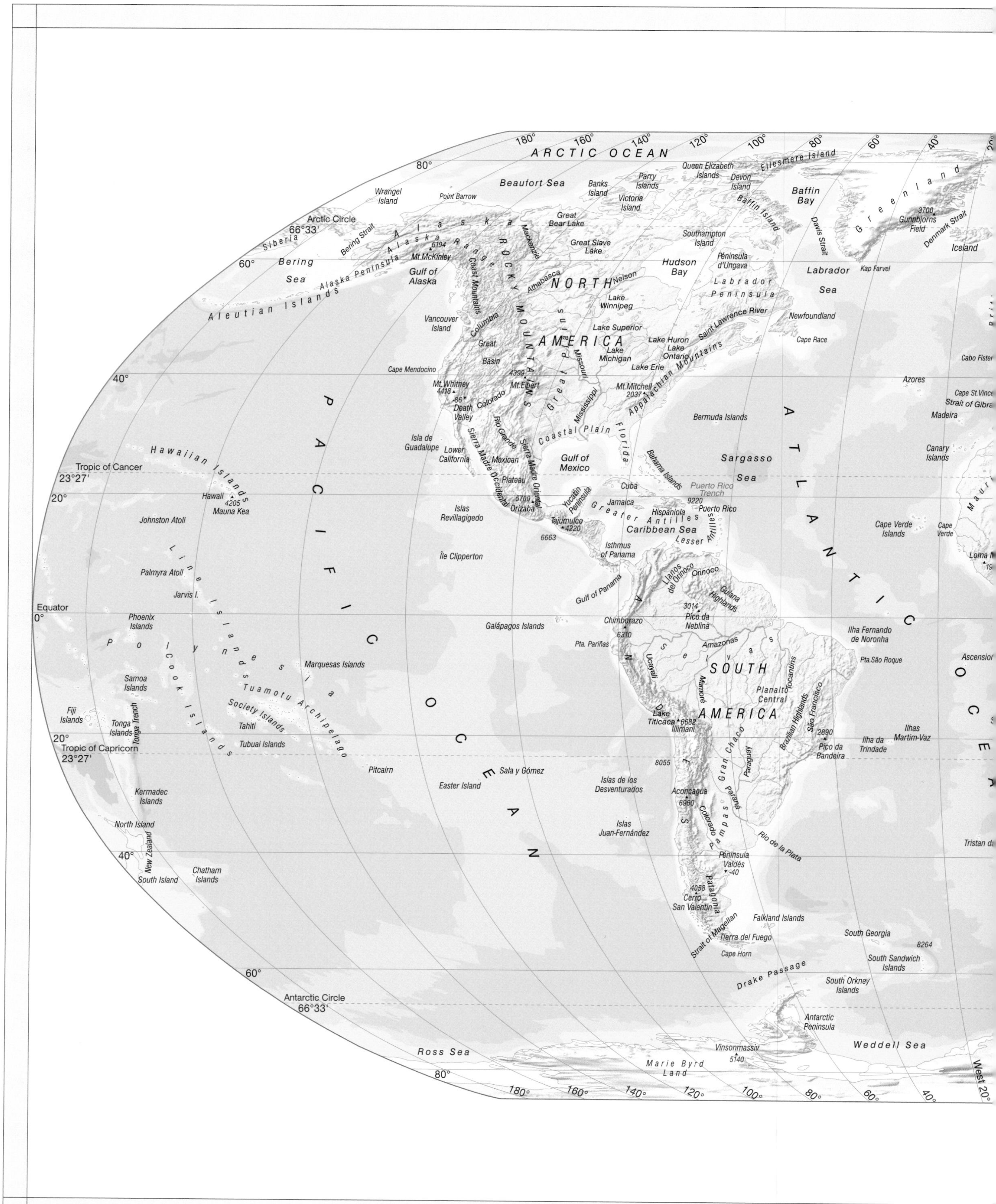

ARCTIC OCEAN
NORTH AMERICA
SOUTH AMERICA
PACIFIC OCEAN
ATLANTIC OCEAN

Scale 1:85,000,000

0 400 800 Kilometers

owerful earthquakes are not uncom- ion along the edges of the various tec- onic plates.

Compared to the total diameter of the Earth (12,700 km) the height variations on our planet's surface are small. Mount Everest, the world's tallest mountain, ises 8,850 meters, while the deepest point in the ocean, the Mariana Trench in he Pacific, extends 11,034 meters beneath the planet's surface. Including Mount Everest there are 14 mountains rising above 8,000 meters; all of them are located in Asia.

Most of the world's highest mountains are located in massive mountain chains, several of which cover large sections of the continents. The Pyrenees in Europe are the westernmost chain in an almost continuous belt of mountain systems stretching to Southeast Asia. The world's largest body of water, the Pacific Ocean, is surrounded by the circumglobal mountain belt and East Africa has a long mountain belt. Mountain chains are the source of many rivers. The longest rivers on Earth are the Nile (6,671 km) in Africa, the Amazon (6,400 km) in South America, and the Yangtze (Chang Jiang) in East Asia (6,300 km).

The location of the world's various climate and vegetation zones is dependent on many factors, including the Earth's rotation, the tilt of the Earth's axis, and ocean currents, among others. In equatorial regions constant heavy rainfall leads to the growth of thick vegetation coverage. Many tropical and subtropical regions border large arid regions; the Sahara in Africa is the world's largest desert (9 million km²). The world's temperate regions are home to green deciduous and mixed forests, and often border taiga and tundra regions.

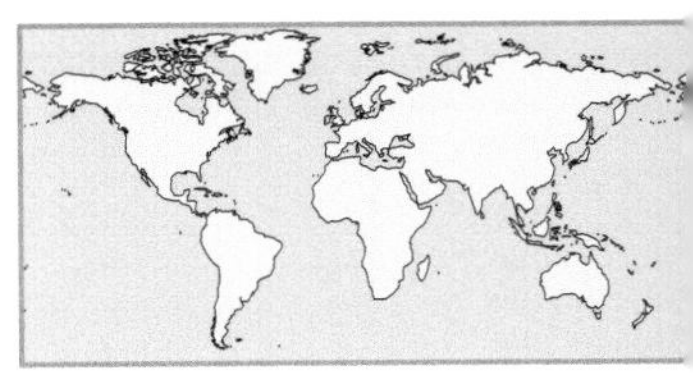

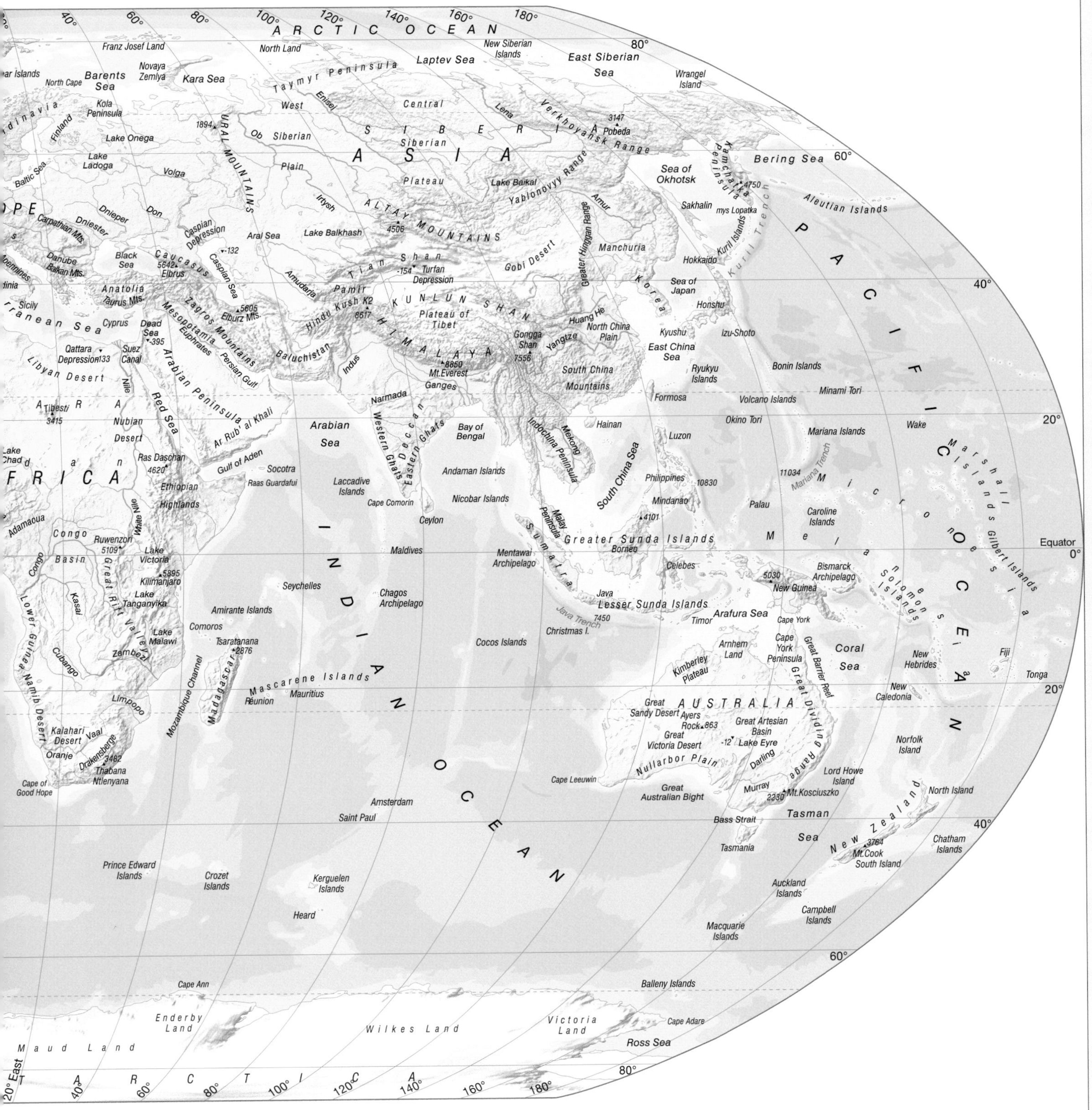

The world's **subtropical regions** are located between areas with temperate and tropical climates. Regions with Mediterranean climates (top photo) have warm summers as well as rainy winters and often border **semi-arid regions** or **deserts** (middle photo). **Humid Subtropical forests** (ferns, palms, and mangroves) often grow along the edges of the tropical regions around the equator (bottom photo).

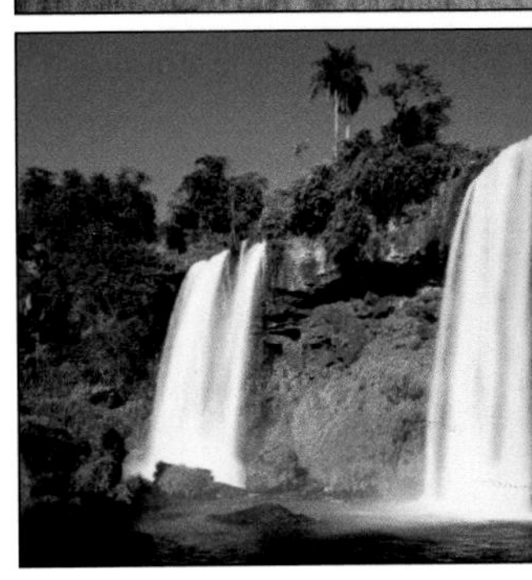

Most of the regions situated between the Tropics of Cancer and Capricorn have **tropical** or **subtropical climates**. To the north and south of most tropical rainforests are large **humid subtropical forests** or **savannahs** (top photo: Africa). The world's tropical rainforests are home to countless species of plants and animals and thick foliage (bottom photo: Brazil).

Mountain Systems (photo: Cerro Paine in Patagonia) often form distinct "climatic islands" inside of larger climate zones. Many mountain ranges feature a variety of vegetation types at different elevations. The Himalayas in Asia are the world's highest mountain system.

The world – political map

At the beginning of the 21st century there were 194 sovereign nations on our planet. During the last centuries the shape of borders around the world were changed many times. Two world wars, the decline of European colonialism, and the collapse of Communism in Europe and the Soviet Union were especially important factors in the rise of many new nations and the fall of others. At the beginning of the 20th century most of Africa was controlled by colonial powers, today the continent has 54 independent states, more than any other continent. After Africa comes Asia with 47 states, then Europe with 44, North America with 23, Australia/Oceania with 14, and South America with 13. Antarctica is the only "stateless" continent; the southernmost landmass is

United Nations headquarters along the East River in New York City

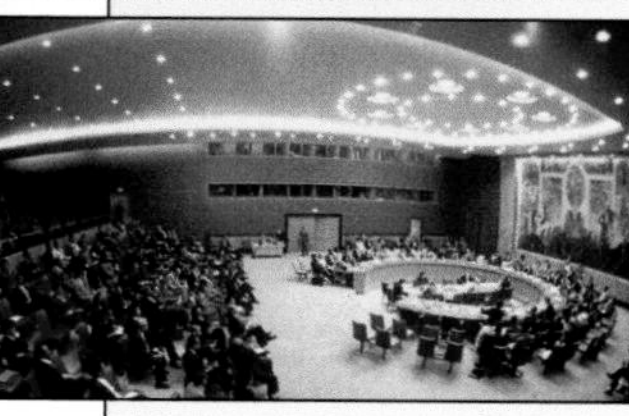

The **United Nations (UN)** is the most famous and one of the more controversial international organizations on our planet. The United Nations was founded in 1945 and declares supporting world peace, increased international cooperation, and the development of underdeveloped nations as its main goals. New York City is the site of UN headquarters but the organization has bases and offices around the world. The UN has 191 member nations; only Taiwan, the Vatican, and West Sahara (occupied by Morocco) have not joined. The major divisions of the UN are the General Assembly, the Security Council, the Economic and Social Council, the International Court of Justice, and the Secretariat. In addition, the UN also operates several organizations and special programs, including the World Health Organization (WHO), UNICEF, and UNESCO. Photos from top to bottom: United Nations flag, the Palace of Nations in Geneva, The General Assembly, The Security Council

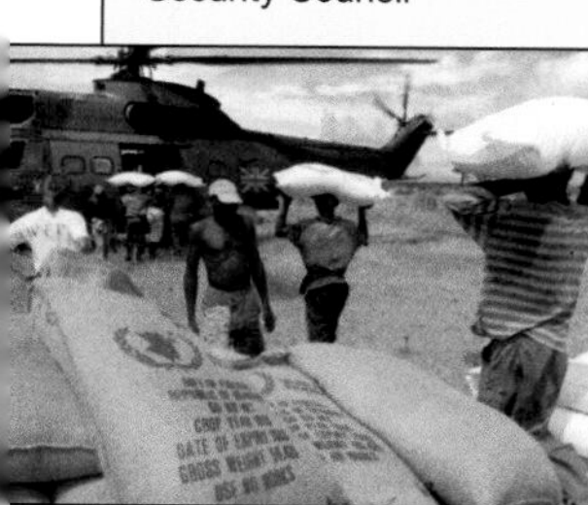

One of the UN's major concerns is the fight against hunger around the world. The **UN World Food Program (WTF)** was set up in 1963 to provide assistance in areas where food is in short supply. In 2001, the WTF fed 77 million people in 81 countries, including many of the world's refugees.

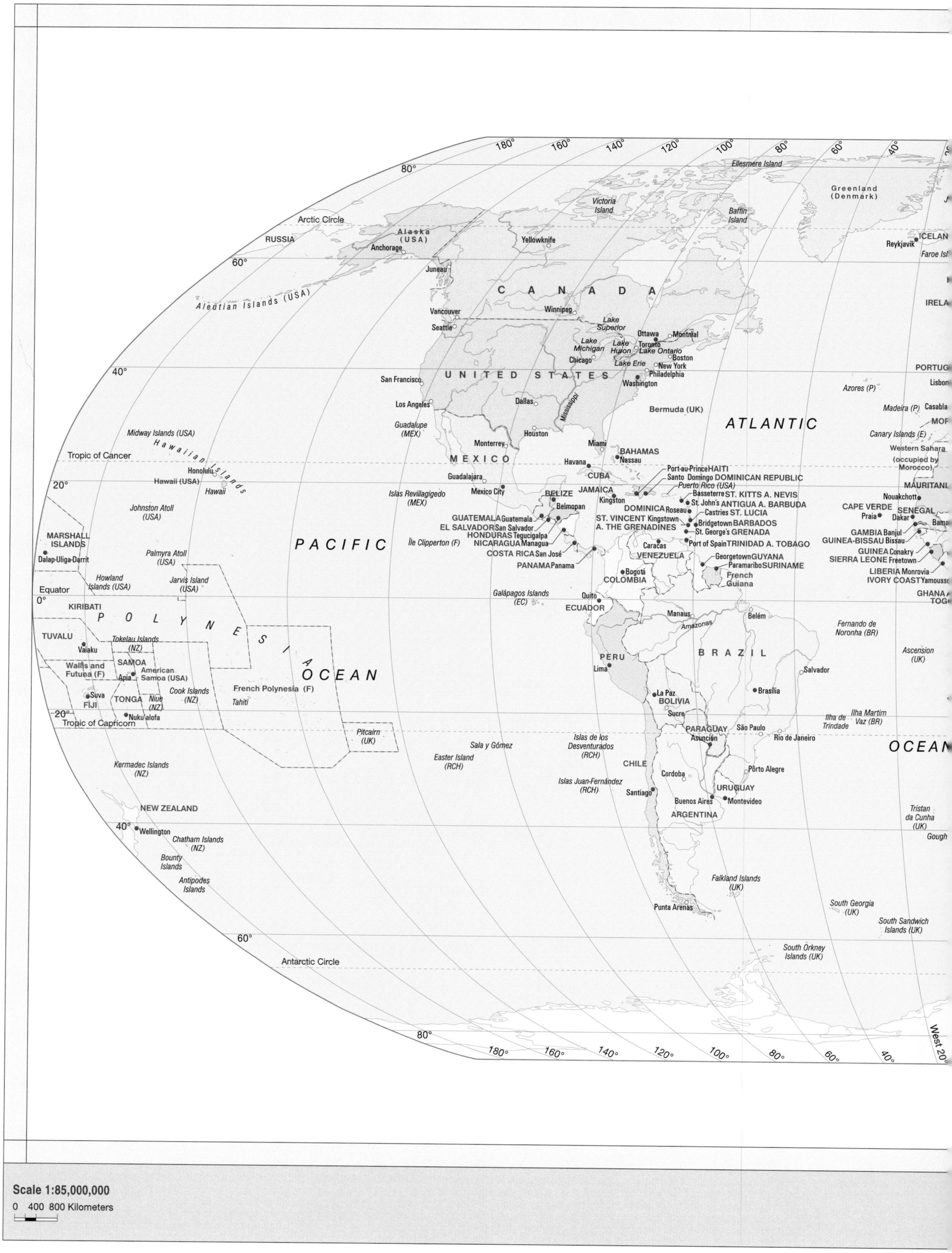

RUSSIA
Arctic Circle
Alaska (USA)
Anchorage
Aleutian Islands (USA)
Victoria Island
Baffin Island
Ellesmere Island
Greenland (Denmark)
Reykjavik
ICELAN
Faroe Isl
Yellowknife
Juneau
C A N A D A
Winnipeg
Vancouver
Seattle
Lake Superior
Lake Michigan
Lake Huron
Lake Ontario
Lake Erie
Ottawa
Montréal
Toronto
Boston
New York
Philadelphia
Washington
Chicago
San Francisco
U N I T E D S T A T E S
Los Angeles
Dallas
Mississippi
Houston
Guadalupe (MEX)
Bermuda (UK)
ATLANTIC
Azores (P)
Madeira (P)
Canary Islands (E)
Western Sahara (occupied by Morocco)
MAURITANI
IRELA
PORTUG
Lisbon
Casabla
MOR
Midway Islands (USA)
Hawaiian Islands
Honolulu
Hawaii (USA)
Hawaii
Tropic of Cancer
Monterrey
M E X I C O
Guadalajara
Mexico City
Islas Revillagigedo (MEX)
Miami
BAHAMAS
Nassau
Havana
CUBA
Port-au-Prince HAITI
Santo Domingo DOMINICAN REPUBLIC
Puerto Rico (USA)
Basseterre ST. KITTS A. NEVIS
St. John's ANTIGUA A. BARBUDA
BELIZE
Belmopan
JAMAICA
Kingston
DOMINICA Roseau
Castries ST. LUCIA
ST. VINCENT Kingstown
A. THE GRENADINES
Bridgetown BARBADOS
St. George's GRENADA
Port of Spain TRINIDAD A. TOBAGO
GUATEMALA Guatemala
EL SALVADOR San Salvador
HONDURAS Tegucigalpa
NICARAGUA Managua
COSTA RICA San José
PANAMA Panama
Île Clipperton (F)
PACIFIC
Johnston Atoll (USA)
MARSHALL ISLANDS
Dalap-Uliga-Darrit
Palmyra Atoll (USA)
Howland Islands (USA)
Jarvis Island (USA)
Equator
KIRIBATI
P O L Y N E S I A
TUVALU
Vaiaku
Tokelau Islands (NZ)
Wallis and Futuna (F)
SAMOA
Apia
American Samoa (USA)
Suva
FIJI
TONGA
Niue (NZ)
Nuku'alofa
Cook Islands (NZ)
French Polynesia (F)
Tahiti
OCEAN
Tropic of Capricorn
Pitcairn (UK)
Kermadec Islands (NZ)
Sala y Gómez
Easter Island (RCH)
Islas de los Desventurados (RCH)
Islas Juan-Fernández (RCH)
NEW ZEALAND
Wellington
Chatham Islands (NZ)
Bounty Islands
Antipodes Islands
Caracas
VENEZUELA
Georgetown GUYANA
Paramaribo SURINAME
French Guiana
Bogotá
COLOMBIA
Galápagos Islands (EC)
Quito
ECUADOR
Manaus
Amazonas
Belém
B R A Z I L
PERU
Lima
Salvador
Brasília
La Paz
BOLIVIA
Sucre
PARAGUAY
Asunción
São Paulo
Rio de Janeiro
CHILE
Córdoba
Pôrto Alegre
URUGUAY
Santiago
Buenos Aires
Montevideo
ARGENTINA
Falkland Islands (UK)
Punta Arenas
Fernando de Noronha (BR)
Ascension (UK)
Ilha de Trindade
Ilha Martim Vaz (BR)
OCEAN
Tristan da Cunha (UK)
Gough
South Georgia (UK)
South Sandwich Islands (UK)
South Orkney Islands (UK)
Antarctic Circle
Nouakchott
CAPE VERDE
Praia
SENEGAL
Dakar
GAMBIA Banjul
GUINEA-BISSAU Bissau
GUINEA Conakry
SIERRA LEONE Freetown
LIBERIA Monrovia
IVORY COAST Yamousso
GHANA
TOG
West 20°

Scale 1:85,000,000
0 400 800 Kilometers

nternational territory according to the ntarctic Treaty of 1961.
ussia is the world's largest nation in erms of area. The country covers around 7.1 million km^2 on two continents and ccupies one ninth of the world's land surace. The **smallest sovereign nation** on arth is the Vatican, the spiritual center of he Roman Catholic Church.The small ity-state covers 0.44 km^2 and is entirely urrounded by the city of Rome.

Many of the world's political **borders** developed along natural barriers such as rivers and mountains. The straight linear borders found in some countries are the result of political developments; the border between the United States and Canada is an example of such a border.
The many different nations of the world are connected to one another in many ways. **Globalization** is a popular term used to describe the increasing integration of cultures and economic markets around the world. Globalization involves not only the **trade of natural resources** and manufactured goods, but also increasingly the exchange of information, skills, and services.
In October 1999, the **world's population** exceeded six billion for the first time in history. The population density of our planet is unevenly distributed between different regions. Western Europe and India are the world's most densely populated regions. China is the most populous country with 1.3 billion inhabitants. In the year 2000, India became the second nation with a population exceeding one billion. Since 1960 the world population has doubled in size. At least 90% of current population growth occurs in the so-called developing nations; this imbalance contributes to the problems of mass hunger and poverty in many of the world's poorer regions.

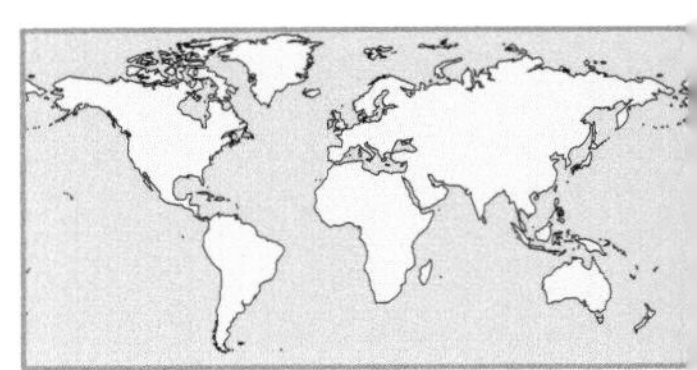

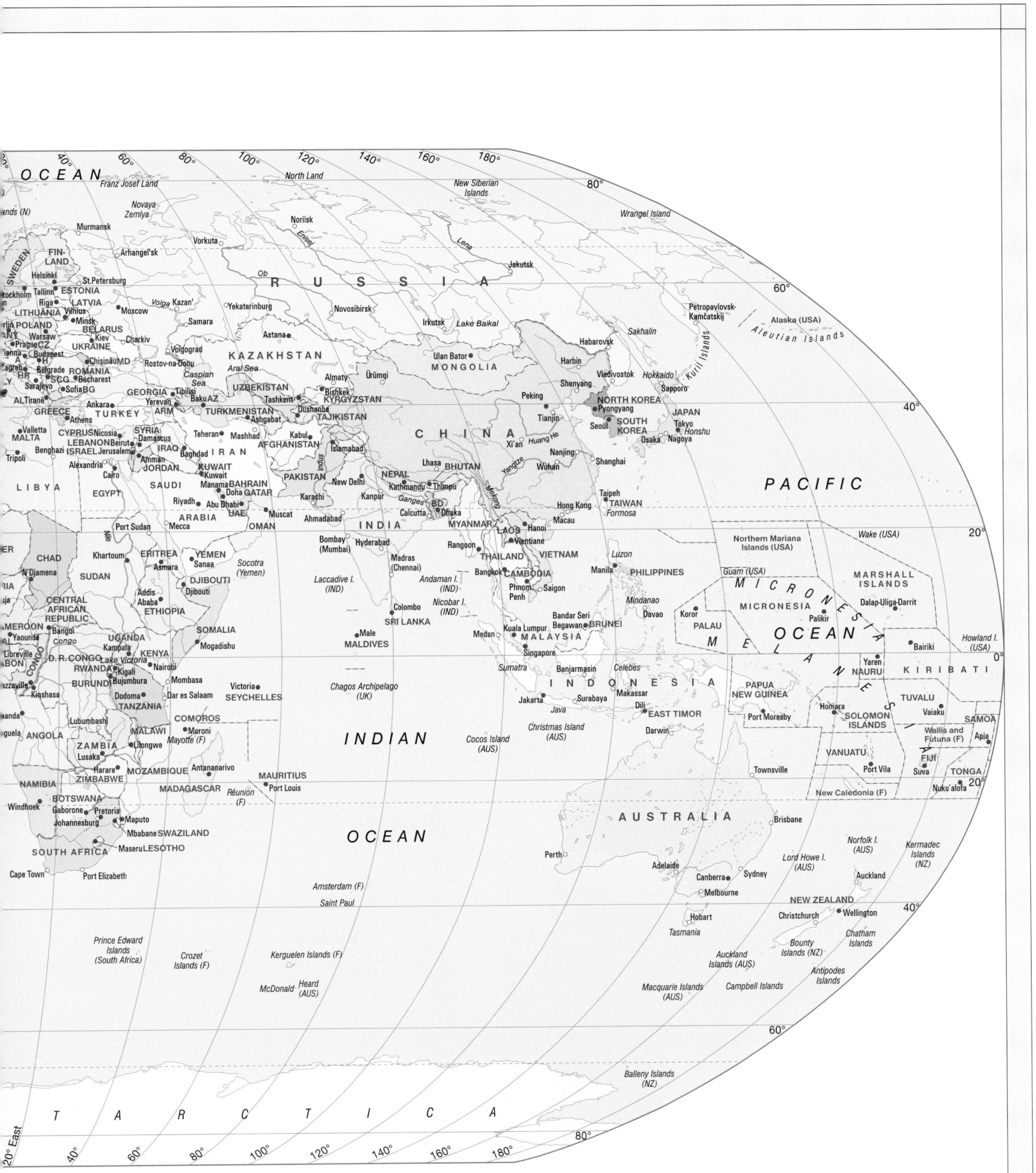

The **UN Security Council** is the only UN body authorized to make binding decisions for all of its members. The Council has 15 members, including five permanent members:

The **United States of America** is the last remaining superpower. The White House (top photo) in Washington D.C is the residence of American presidents. The United States' Senate meets in the Capitol (bottom photo).

The Kremlin has been a center of political power in **Russia** since the 13th century and is today the seat of the Russian parliament.

In 1949, Mao Zedong proclaimed the establishment of the **People's Republic of China** in fronz of Beijing's Gate of Heavenly Peace (top photo) on Tiananmen Square (bottom photo).

Paris is the cultural, economic, and political center of **France**. Photo: Place de la Concorde and the National Assembly.

Great Britain: Once the leader of a vast empire, Britain is now an important member of the European Union. Photo: The Houses of Parliament in London.

Chicago (top): The modern skyline of the city glitters next to Lake Michigan
Joshua Tree National Park (bottom): Sunset above California's Joshua Trees

Yucátan Peninsula (left): Ancient remnants of the Maya civilization on the Caribbean coast
Cascade Mountains (right): Snow and glaciers cover Mt. Rainier (4,392 m) in Washington State

North and Central America

The Golden Gate and vibrant San Francisco, the red rock formations of Monument Valley, the Grand Canyon, endless prairies, the legacy of the Maya, Aztecs, and immigrants from all corners of the globe, the colonial towns of Mexico, Caribbean Islands, historic Route 66 and Highway No. 1, and New York City... Welcome to North America.

The northern continent of the Western Hemisphere stretches from the Arctic Ocean to the Caribbean Sea. North America can be divided into three large geographic regions running from north to south. The western portion of the continent is dominated by the **Cordilleras**, a series of mountain ranges which contains Alaska's Mount McKinley (6,194 meters), the continent's tallest mountain. The Appalachian Mountains stretch through much of eastern North America. In between these two regions lie the vast Central Plains of North America. One of the continent's most interesting geographic attractions is Death Valley, the lowest point on the planet's surface.

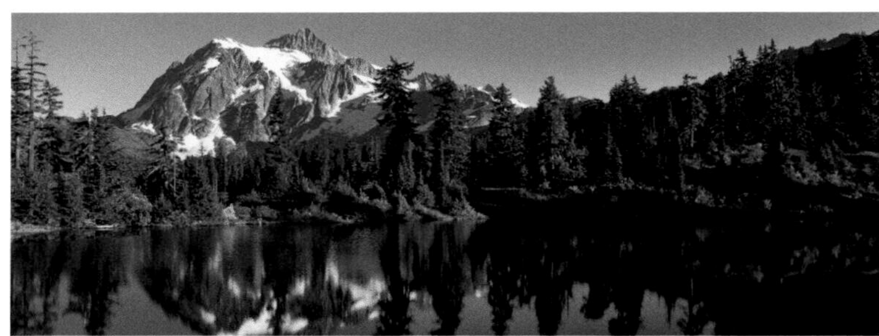

The Rocky Mountains are 4,300 kilometers long

The **Rocky Mountains**, the largest mountain chain in North America, extend through the United States and Canada. In the American Southwest, the Rocky Mountains border the Sierra Madre mountain range which extends through most of Mexico and into Central America. The Isthmus of Panama is only 50 kilometers wide. The islands of the **Caribbean** form a large chain running from Cuba to South America and are separated into two groups: the Lesser Antilles and the Greater Antilles.

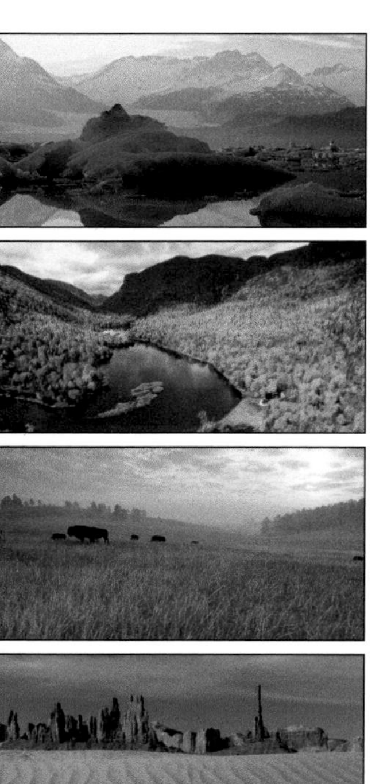

The United States is home to many diverse landscapes including (photos from top to bottom) the glaciers of Alaska's Glacier Bay, the peaks of the Rocky Mountains, the Great Plains, and Monument Valley in the deserts of the Southwest.

The Alaska Range (photo: Mount McKinley), the Rocky Mountains (Mount Elbert 4,396 meters), and the Coast Mountains (Mount Waddington 4,016 meters) all belong to the North American Cordilleras, a series of mountain ranges.

The 6,020 kilometers long Mississippi-Missouri river system is the largest river system in North America. The drainage basin of the Mississippi covers an area of 3,208,000 km^2. The Canadian Mackenzie and Yukon rivers are the second and third longest rivers on the continent respectively.

The world's largest island, Greenland (2,175,600 km^2), and the world's fifth largest island, Baffin Island (517,890 km^2), are among the many arctic islands surrounding the North American mainland. The largest islands in the Caribbean Sea are Cuba (111,000 km^2), Hispaniola (76,000 km^2), and Jamaica (10,990 km^2). St. Lucia (photo) is one of the smaller Caribbean nations with an area of 616 km^2.

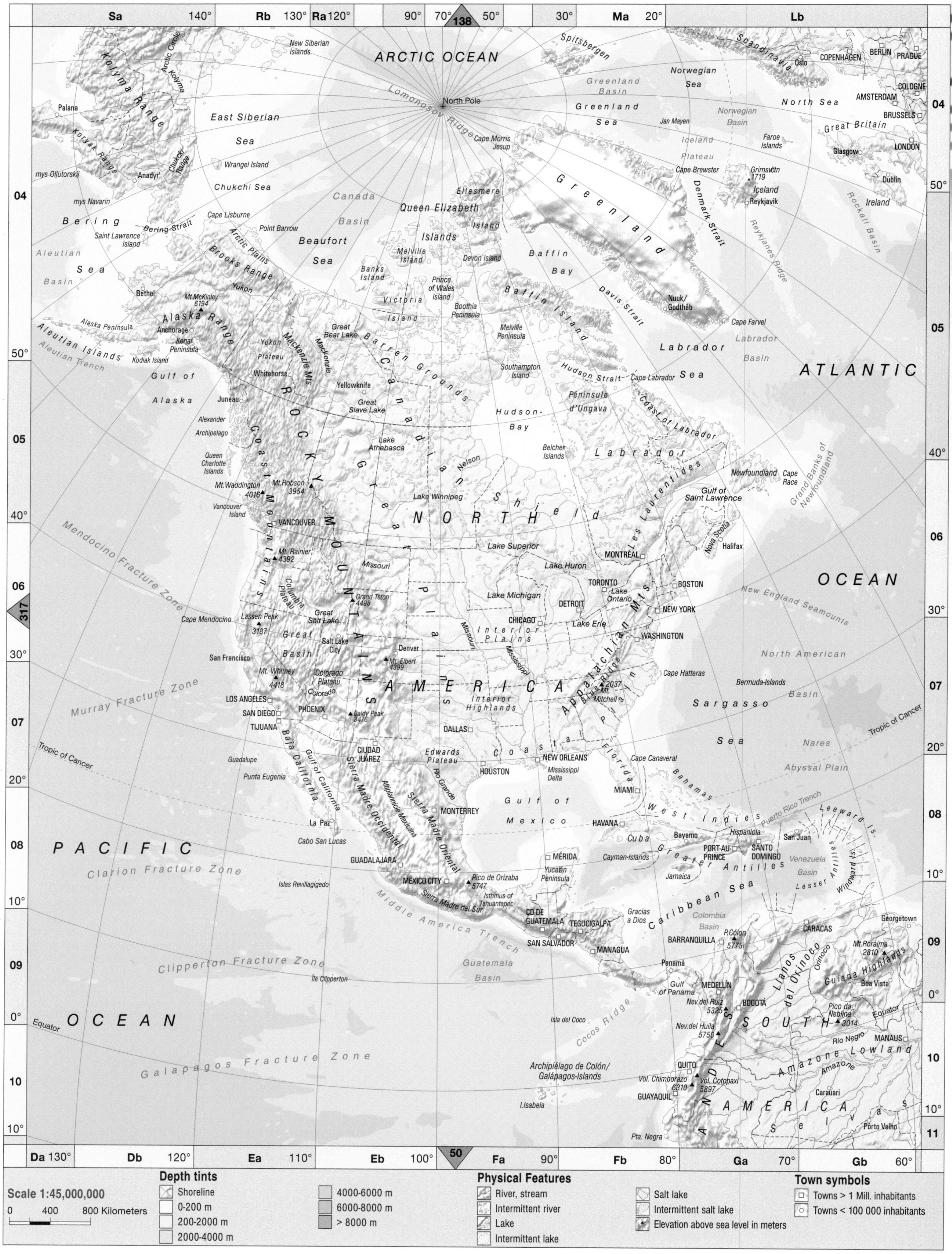

Scale 1:45,000,000
0 400 800 Kilometers

Depth tints
- Shoreline
- 0-200 m
- 200-2000 m
- 2000-4000 m
- 4000-6000 m
- 6000-8000 m
- > 8000 m

Physical Features
- River, stream
- Intermittent river
- Lake
- Intermittent lake
- Salt lake
- Intermittent salt lake
- Elevation above sea level in meters

Town symbols
- Towns > 1 Mill. inhabitants
- Towns < 100 000 inhabitants

n addition to the three larger nations on the continent (Canada, Mexico, and the United States) there are numerous smal-er North American nations. North Amer-ca's **indigenous people** (Native Amer-cans and Inuit) form only a small portion of the population in Canada and the Unit-ed States, while most Mexicans and Cen-tral Americans are at least of partial indi-genous descent.

Over the centuries millions of European immigrants settled in North America and most of the continent's population is of European descent. Millions of North Amer-icans, mostly in the United States and the Caribbean, are of African descent. Cana-da and the USA attract a large number of immigrants every year, including many migrants from neighboring Mexico.

North America is a continent with many faces

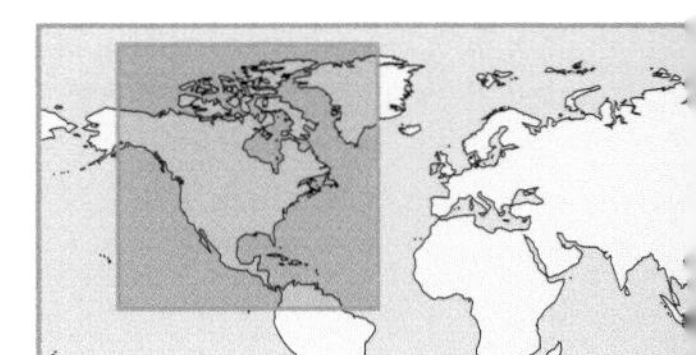

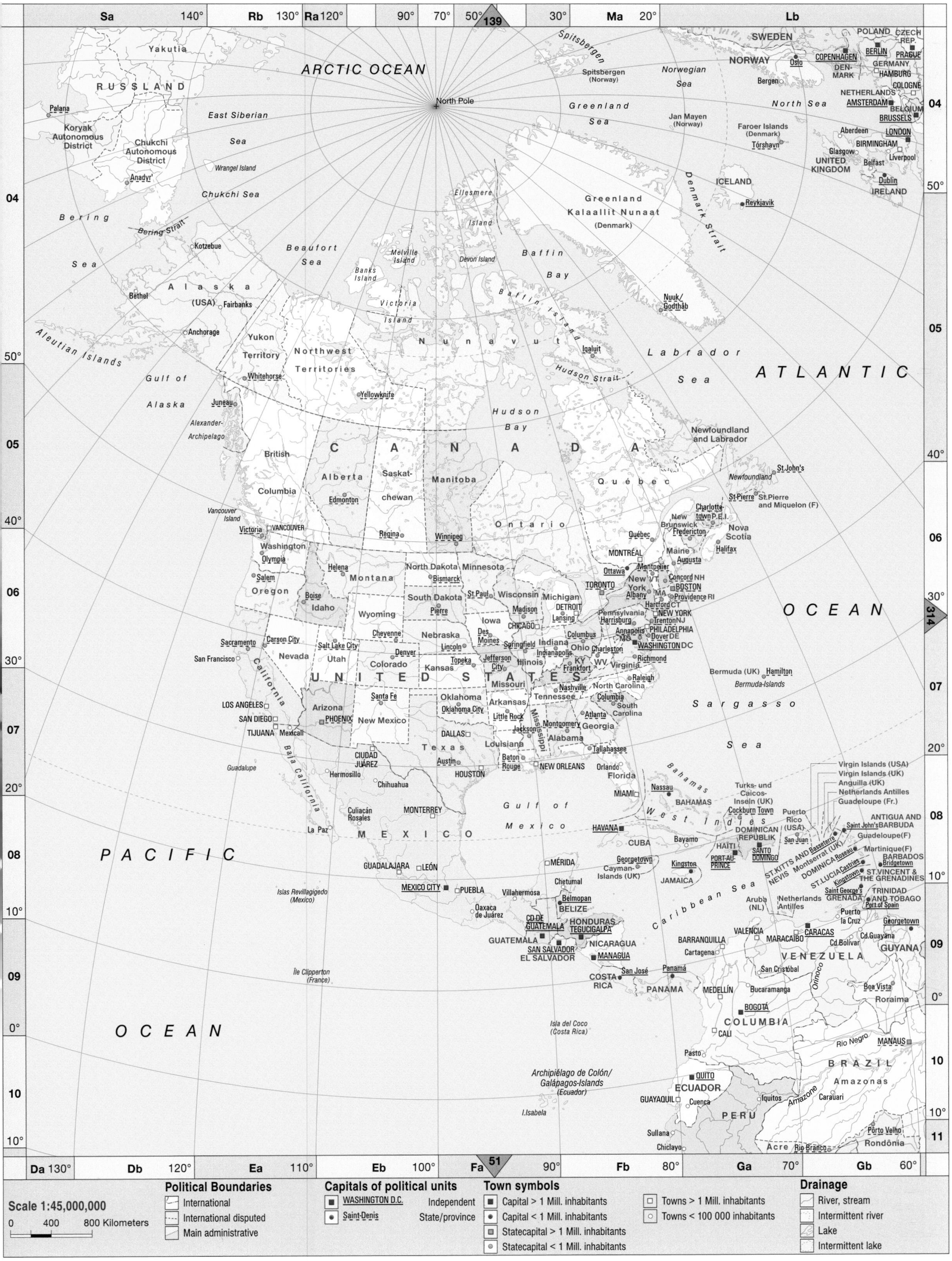

ARCTIC OCEAN — PACIFIC OCEAN — ATLANTIC OCEAN — CANADA — UNITED STATES — MEXICO

Scale 1:45,000,000

0 400 800 Kilometers

Political Boundaries
- International
- International disputed
- Main administrative

Capitals of political units
- WASHINGTON D.C. Independent
- Saint-Denis State/province

Town symbols
- Capital > 1 Mill. inhabitants
- Capital < 1 Mill. inhabitants
- Statecapital > 1 Mill. inhabitants
- Statecapital < 1 Mill. inhabitants
- Towns > 1 Mill. inhabitants
- Towns < 100 000 inhabitants

Drainage
- River, stream
- Intermittent river
- Lake
- Intermittent lake

The **indigenous people of North America** continue to struggle for recognition and equal rights, including ownership of land. In Canada, the Inuit (top photo: Inuit couple) have won control of their own self-governing region called Nunavut. Many of the Amerindians in the United States live in so-called reservations. Among the most well known Native American tribes in the United States are the Seminole in the Southeast, the Iroquois in the North-east, the Cheyenne and Lakota Sioux in the Great Plains states, and the Navajo in the Southwest. Today, Native Americans (middle photo) form only a small percentage of the American population. Central America's indigenous people form a large part of the region's population but have limited political influence (bottom photo: Cuba woman in Panama).

Canada and Alaska cover the northern half of the North American continent. Ten percent of the region is covered by bodies of water. Alaska and Canada are home to one third of the world's freshwater supply. The region borders three oceans: the Pacific, Atlantic, and Arctic Oceans. The vast majority of Canada's population lives within 300 kilometers of the American-Canadian border. Large sections of the region are sparsely populated or totally uninhabited. The Hudson Bay plain is the lowest region of Canada. The Canadian (Precambrian) Shield forms a horseshoe around the **Hudson Bay region** and is one of the world's oldest geologic features. During the ice age the entire region was covered by gigantic glaciers. To the east of the **Canadian**

An arctic sunset in Alaska's beautiful Glacier Bay **Da07**

The Bering Strait Between Alaska and Siberia – 85 kilometer wide at its narrowest point – (photo: Saint Lawrence Island)

Alaska Range The northernmost range in the North American Cordilleras – (photo: Wonder Lake in Denali National Park)

Kluane National Park Wilderness area – St. Elias Mountains (Yukon Territory) – glaciers and snowfields – Taiga wildlife and vegetation

Gulf of Alaska Glacier Bay National Park is home to 16 flowing glaciers – the Alexander Archipelago contains over 11,000 islands

The Canadian Rockies are home to glaciers and snow-covered mountains. The region also contains diverse wildlife including a large bear population. Several major rivers including the Columbia and Athabasca Rivers rise in the Rockies.

Scale 1:18,000,000

0 160 320 Kilometers

Depth tints
- Shoreline
- 0-200 m
- 200-2000 m
- 2000-4000 m
- 4000-6000 m
- 6000-8000 m
- > 8000 m

Physical Features
- River, stream
- Intermittent river
- Lake
- Intermittent lake
- Salt lake
- Intermittent salt lake
- Elevation above sea level in meters

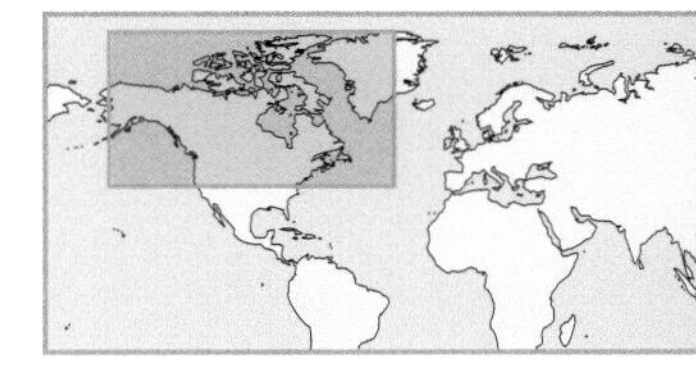

Shield lie the mountainous regions of Labrador and Baffin Island – both areas with subarctic climates. Between the Canadian Shield and the mountainous regions of eastern Canada lies the narrow valley of the **St. Lawrence River**. The lower river valley is one of Canada's most populated and economically important regions. To the west of the Canadian Shield lies the Great Plains region. These vast plains were formed during the ice ages as gigantic migrating glaciers flattened the land they passed over. The Canadian Rockies are a section of the **Cordilleras**, a long system of mountain ranges extending through South and North America. The Coast Mountains to the west of the Rockies also belong to the Cordilleras. The mountains of the Cordilleras extend into the American state of Alaska. **Alaska** is home to some of the continent's highest mountains including Mount McKinley (6,194 meters), the highest peak in North America. The **Bering Strait** borders Alaska to the west. During the last ice age, the strait formed a land bridge that connected the Asian and North American continents. It was here that the ancestors of today's Native Americans crossed into the Americas. This land bridge was also crossed by migrating animals, many of which evolved into new species found only in the Americas. Between the Canadian mainland and Greenland lies the **Arctic Archipelago**. The mountainous islands in this group have peaks rising 2,000 meters above sea level. To the northeast of Canada lies the world's largest island, Greenland. The island has a jagged coast and most of its land is covered by a layer of ice. Greenland, a Danish territory, is sparsely populated and the majority of its inhabitants are Inuits.

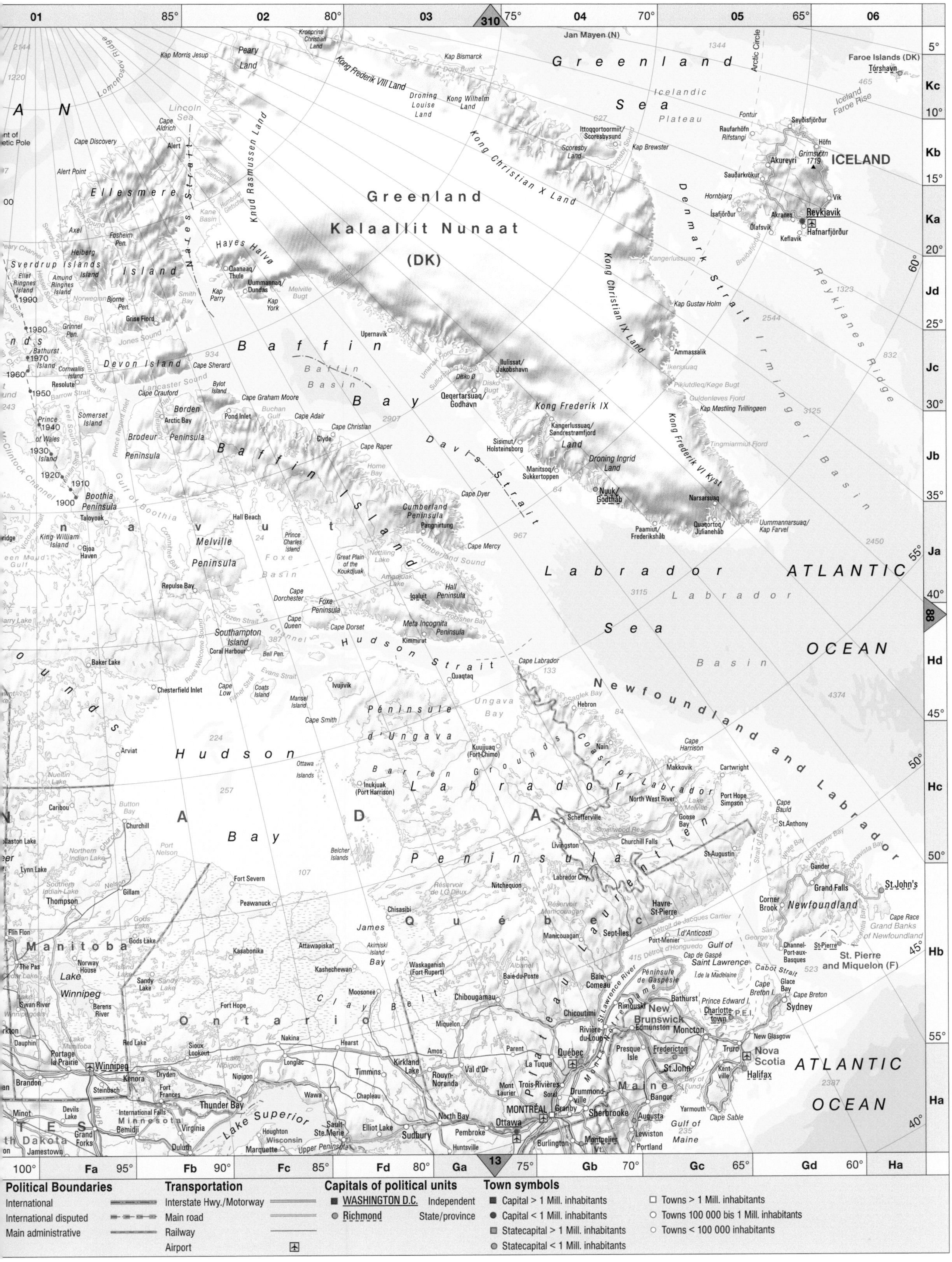

The Barren Grounds Tundra landscape covered by permafrost and sparse vegetation – subarctic flora and fauna

Manitoba One of Canada's three Prairie Provinces. Most of Manitoba lies on the Canadian Shield – Conservation areas include Riding Mountain National Park (photo)

Nunavut Canada's youngest and largest province. The region's population is 85% Inuit. Nunavut covers 20% of Canada's land area. There are few paved roads in the region and most of the territory consists of treeless tundra.

Hudson Bay Large inland sea in northeastern Canada – ice-free during four months of the year – rarely more than 200 meters deep – connected to the Atlantic at the Hudson Strait

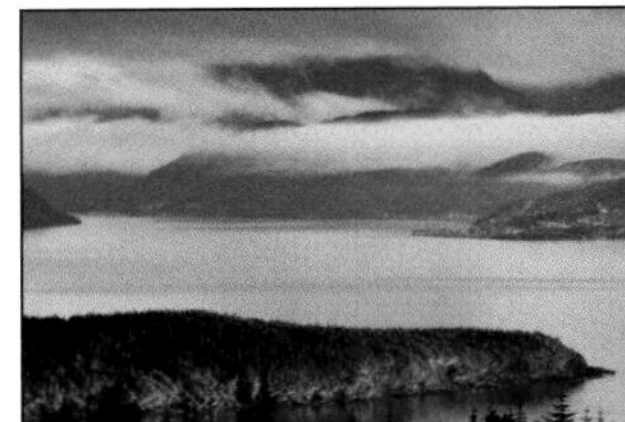

Newfoundland Easternmost province of Canada – the provincial capital is St. John's – Gros Mourne National Park (photo)

New England Region in the northeastern United States – wooded mountains – bays – pleasant islands – historic cities and towns

Political Boundaries
International
International disputed
Main administrative

Transportation
Interstate Hwy./Motorway
Main road
Railway
Airport

Capitals of political units
WASHINGTON D.C. Independent
Richmond State/province

Town symbols
Capital > 1 Mill. inhabitants
Capital < 1 Mill. inhabitants
Statecapital > 1 Mill. inhabitants
Statecapital < 1 Mill. inhabitants
Towns > 1 Mill. inhabitants
Towns 100 000 bis 1 Mill. inhabitants
Towns < 100 000 inhabitants

USA, Central America

The Pacific coast is the most geologically active region in North America. Along this coast the Pacific and American tectonic plates meet and collide with one another. Tectonic activity is also responsible for the emergence of large mountain ranges (Sierra Nevada, Rocky Mountains) in western North America. Earthquakes and tremors are common throughout the region. The Nazca and Cocos tectonic plates, which collide with the smaller Caribbean plate, are located beneath Central America. Most of the Caribbean islands and the deep **Cayman Trench** lie along the edges of the Caribbean plate. The Caymen Trench one of the world's deepest trenches, lies in the waters between Central America and Cuba. This geologically active re-

Arizona's Grand Canyon is one of the world's most visited natural attractions

Sierra Nevada Mountain range in California and Nevada – Highest Peak: Mount Whitney, 4,418 meters

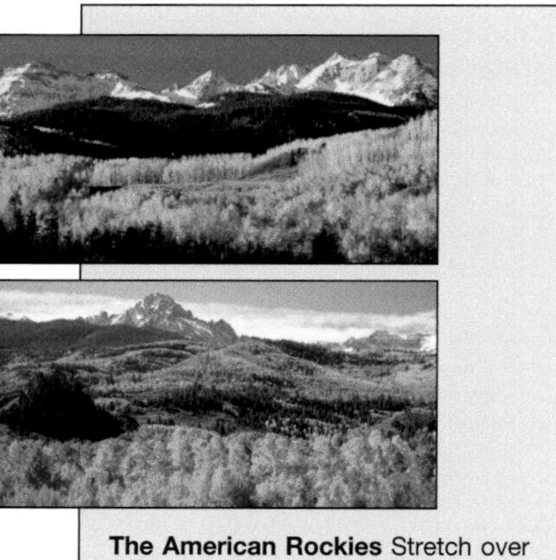

The American Rockies Stretch over 2,500 kilometers from the Canadian border to the Mexican border. Grand Teton (bottom photo) rises 4,198 meters.

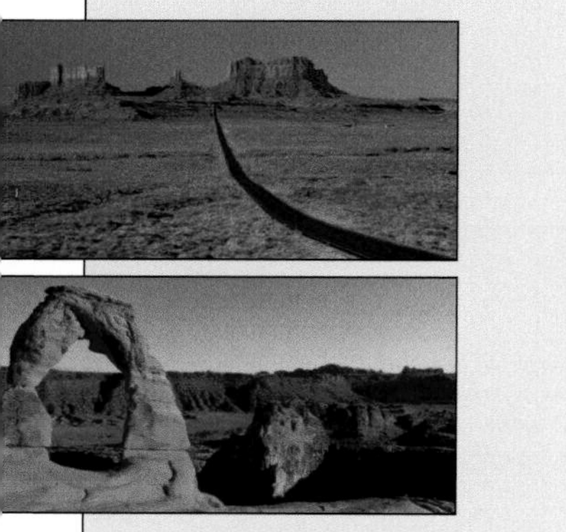

Colorado Plateau The Colorado Plateau contains many beautiful sandstone formations including Monument Valley (top photo) and Arches NP (bottom photo).

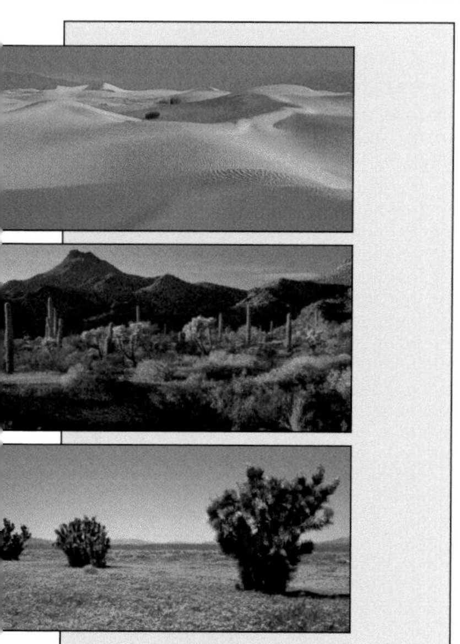

The Deserts of the Southwest North of Mexico's Sierra Madre Mountains lie the vast deserts of America's Southwest. Photos from top to bottom: Death Valley, Organ Pipe Cactus National Park, Mojave Desert.

Scale 1:18,000,000

0 160 320 Kilometers

Depth tints

- Shoreline
- 0-200 m
- 200-2000 m
- 2000-4000 m
- 4000-6000 m
- 6000-8000 m
- > 8000 m

Physical Features

- River, stream
- Intermittent river
- Lake
- Intermittent lake
- Salt lake
- Intermittent salt lake
- Elevation above sea level in meters

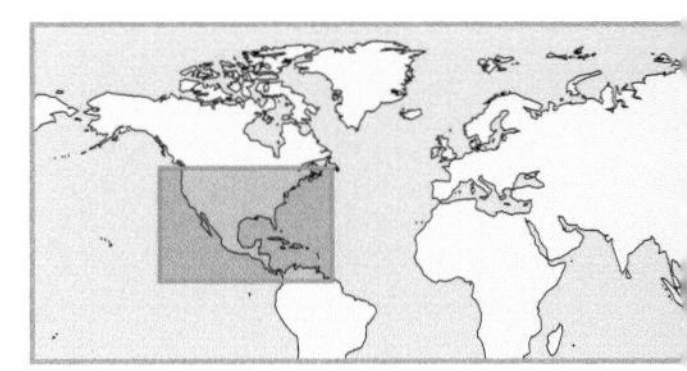

gion is home to a high number of active volcanoes. Eastern North America's present topography was created during the ice ages. Enormous migrating glaciers shaped the **Appalachian Mountains**. The glaciers also created large basins, where large lakes, such as the Great Lakes, were eventually formed.

The contiguous United States and Central America are home to many different climate zones. The northern regions of the United States have temperate climates and four distinct seasons. These temperate regions are bordered in the south by subtropical and arid regions which extend to the tropics of Central America. In the tropical regions of the Caribbean and Central America there are two distinct seasons: a rainy season and a dry season. The Caribbean islands and the coastal areas bordering the Gulf of Mexico and Caribbean Sea are often threatened by hurricanes. **Hurricanes** are powerful tropical cyclones that can cause major destruction when they hit land. Central America also suffers from powerful winds usually called **"nortes."** These winds bring bitterly cold air and rain from the United States and Canada to the Caribbean and Central America. The Atlantic coast of the United States is the most heavily populated region on the continent. The coast is home to an almost continuous area of urban and suburban development stretching north from Washington DC to Boston in New England. The United State's incredible wealth of arable land and natural resources (coal, iron ore, gold) were vital to its emergence as the world's largest economic power. The beautiful and historic colonial towns of Mexico's highlands were built with wealth generated from the region's gold and silver mines.

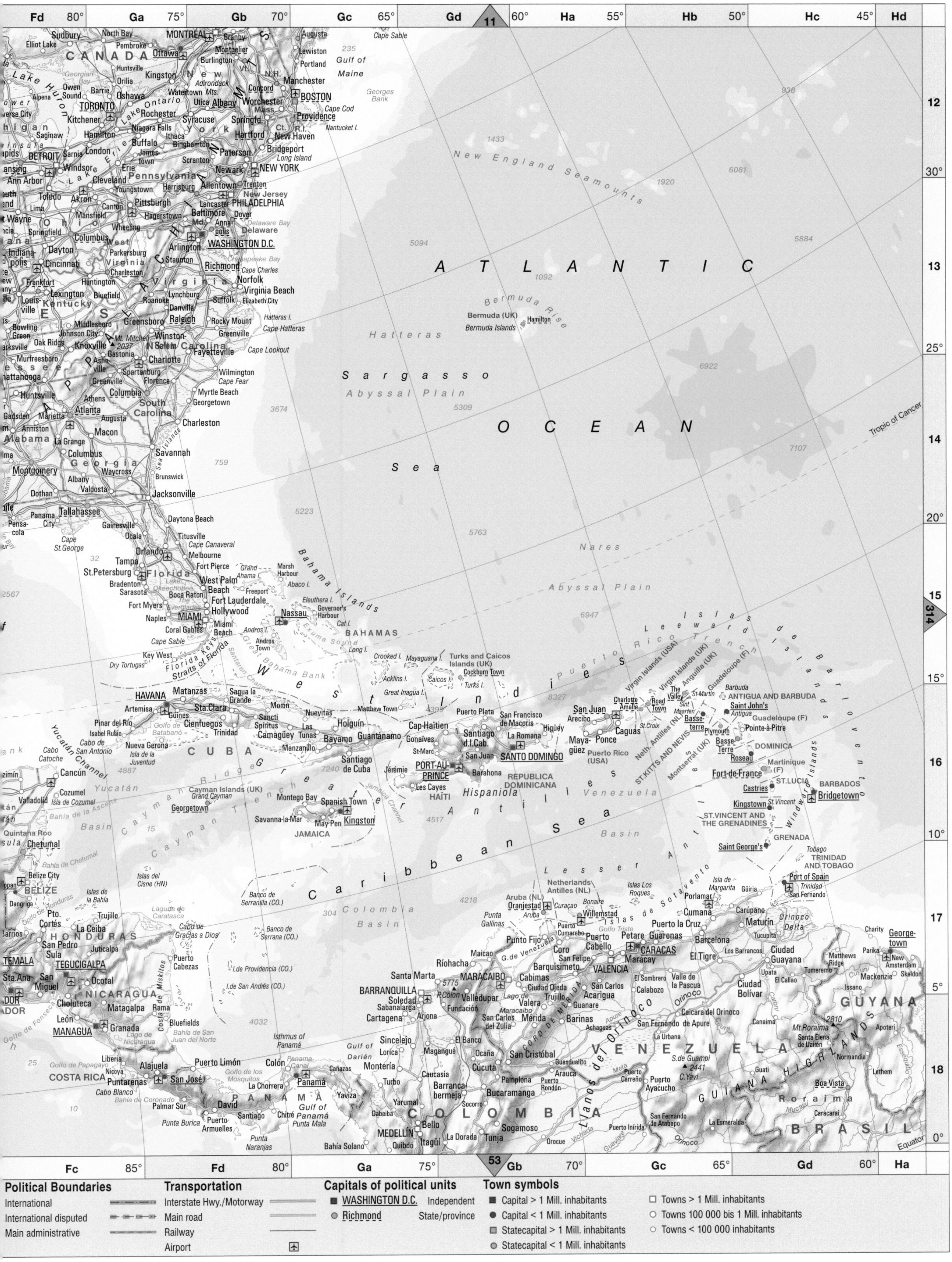

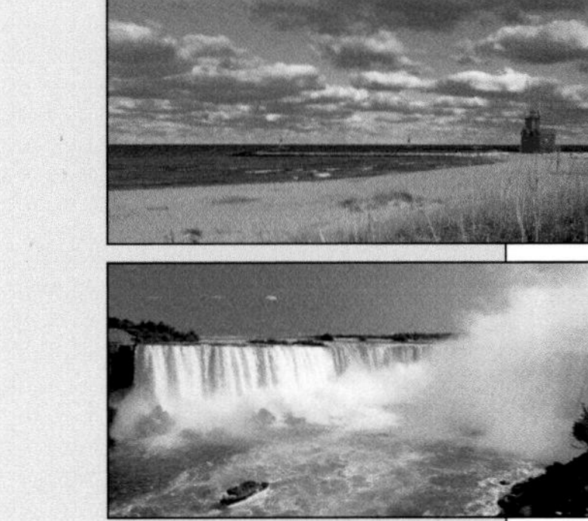

The Great Lakes The largest group of freshwater lakes in the world. Lake Michigan (top photo) is the only lake entirely in the US. Niagara Falls (bottom photo) drops into Lake Ontario.

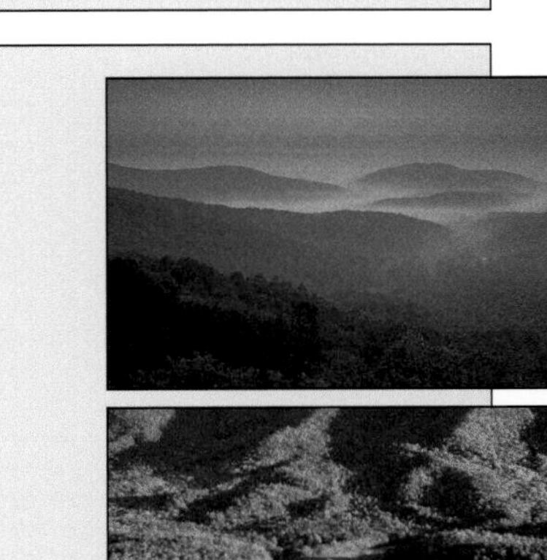

The Appalachians The Appalachians divide the eastern seaboard from the Midwest. The Smokey Mountains (top photo) are a UNESCO world heritage site. The Ridge Mountains (bottom photo) are covered by woodlands.

Sierra Madre Mountains Divided into two ranges: the Sierra Madre Oriental and Occidental – the ranges feature many volcanoes including Popocatepetl (5,452 meters)

The Caribbean Islands Consisting of the Bahamas, the Greater Antilles, and the Lesser Antilles – the Caribbean contains coral and volcanic islands (photo: St. Lucia)

Central American Cordilleras Mountain ranges between the Gulf of Tehuantepec and Columbia – more than 300 active volcanoes in the region

Political Boundaries
International
International disputed
Main administrative

Transportation
Interstate Hwy./Motorway
Main road
Railway
Airport

Capitals of political units
WASHINGTON D.C. Independent
Richmond State/province

Town symbols
Capital > 1 Mill. inhabitants
Capital < 1 Mill. inhabitants
Statecapital > 1 Mill. inhabitants
Statecapital < 1 Mill. inhabitants
Towns > 1 Mill. inhabitants
Towns 100 000 bis 1 Mill. inhabitants
Towns < 100 000 inhabitants

Alaska with an area of 1.5 million km² is the largest of the fifty American states. Alaska is a large peninsula on the northwestern edge of North America. The state shares a long border with Canada. The distance between this border and the westernmost of Alaska's Aleutian Islands is over 3,900 kilometers. The **Aleutian Islands** are a chain of small islands stretching into the North Pacific. These stormy islands lie near the edge of a continental tectonic plate and are home to several active volcanoes. Earthquakes are also common in this geologically active region.

A colorful mountain lake in Alaska

Southern Alaska is home to several mountain ranges including the Alaska and the Aleutian Ranges. **Mount McKinley** in Denali National Park is the tallest mountain in North America. The mountain was named after President William McKinley in 1897, but the state of Alaska also recognizes its indigenous name, Denali. With its base at sea level and its peak at 6,194 meters, Mount McKinley has one of the steepest vertical rises in the world.

The Alaska Range shelters **Anchorage**, Alaska's largest city, and its suburbs from the bitter cold winds of northern Alaska. The average temperature in the region i

Kotzebue Inuit settlement – large zinc deposits in the area – Nana Museum of the Arctic – (photo: Kotzebue Sound) **Bj12**

Unalakleet Traditional fishing harbor on the Norton Sound – wonderful locations for fishing **Bk14**

Inuit The name Inuit means people and since the 1970s the term has gained in popularity over the name Eskimo (raw meat eaters). The Inuit once lived from fishing and hunting but many now work in Alaska's oil industry.

National Parks and Nature Reserves Alaska has 16 nature reserves including the Alaska Maritime National Wildlife Refuge **(Bd16)**. The reserves provide protected living space for Alaska's flora and fauna. The Yukon Flats National Wildlife Refuge **(Cg12)** is home to moose, grizzlies, and wolves.

Shishaldin On Unimank Island, one of the most active volcanoes in the Aleutians, 2862 meters – last eruption in 1999 **Bj18**

Aniakchak National Monument National park in the Aleutian Range – beautiful volcanoes (photo) **Cb17**

Bering Sea

Bristol Bay

Kuskokwim Bay

Alaska Peninsula

Aleutian Islands

Scale 1:4,500,000

0 40 80 Kilometers

Principal travel routes

- Auto route
- Rail road
- Shipping route

Remarkable landscapes and natural monuments

- UNESCO World Natural Heritage
- Mountain landscape
- Ravine/canyon
- Extinct volcano
- Active volcano
- Glacier
- River landscape
- Waterfall/rapids
- Nature park
- National park (landscape)
- Wildlife reserve
- Coastal landscape

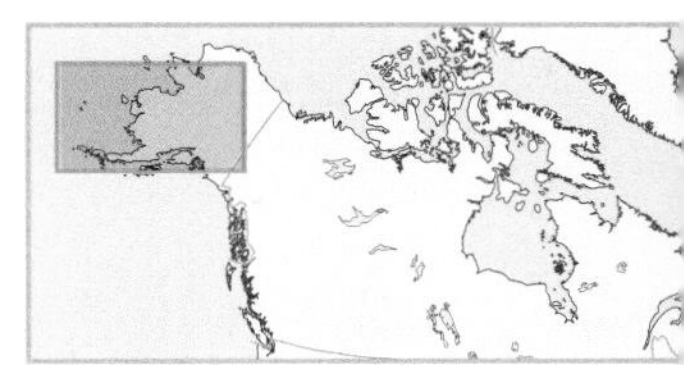

around -11° Celsius in winter and 15° Celsius during the mild summer months. The **Kenai Peninsula**, south of Anchorage, is one of many regions in Alaska with a large number of spectacular glaciers. The **Columbia Glacier** in Prince William Sound is the fastest moving glacier in the world and one of the most beautiful in Alaska. Wrangell-St. Elias National Park where the Wrangell-St. Elias, Chugach, and Alaska Ranges meet, is a UNESCO world heritage site containing numerous glaciers, mountains and ice-fields.

Western Alaska's terrain is mostly hilly with jagged coastlines, numerous bays, and natural harbors. The region is also home to the **Yukon Delta** with its abundance of wildlife. Central Alaska extends from the Brooks Range to the Arctic Circle. The **Yukon River** flows through most of central Alaska. The region consists primarily of marshy treeless land covered by permafrost, rock or soil that remains frozen throughout most of the year. **Fairbanks**, the largest city in the region and the second largest in Alaska, is only frost-free during the months of June and July. The region north of the **Brooks Range** consists of tundra with average temperatures far below freezing for most of the year. This is the so-called land of the midnight sun, a region where the sun continuously shines from May to August only to disappear during winters. The discovery of natural resources in Alaska has also been the driving force behind the state's settlement and development for over 100 years. During the 19th century, a gold rush brought a flood of migrants to the state. Despite population growth and the exploitation of natural resources, most of Alaska remains a pristine, sparsely settled wilderness.

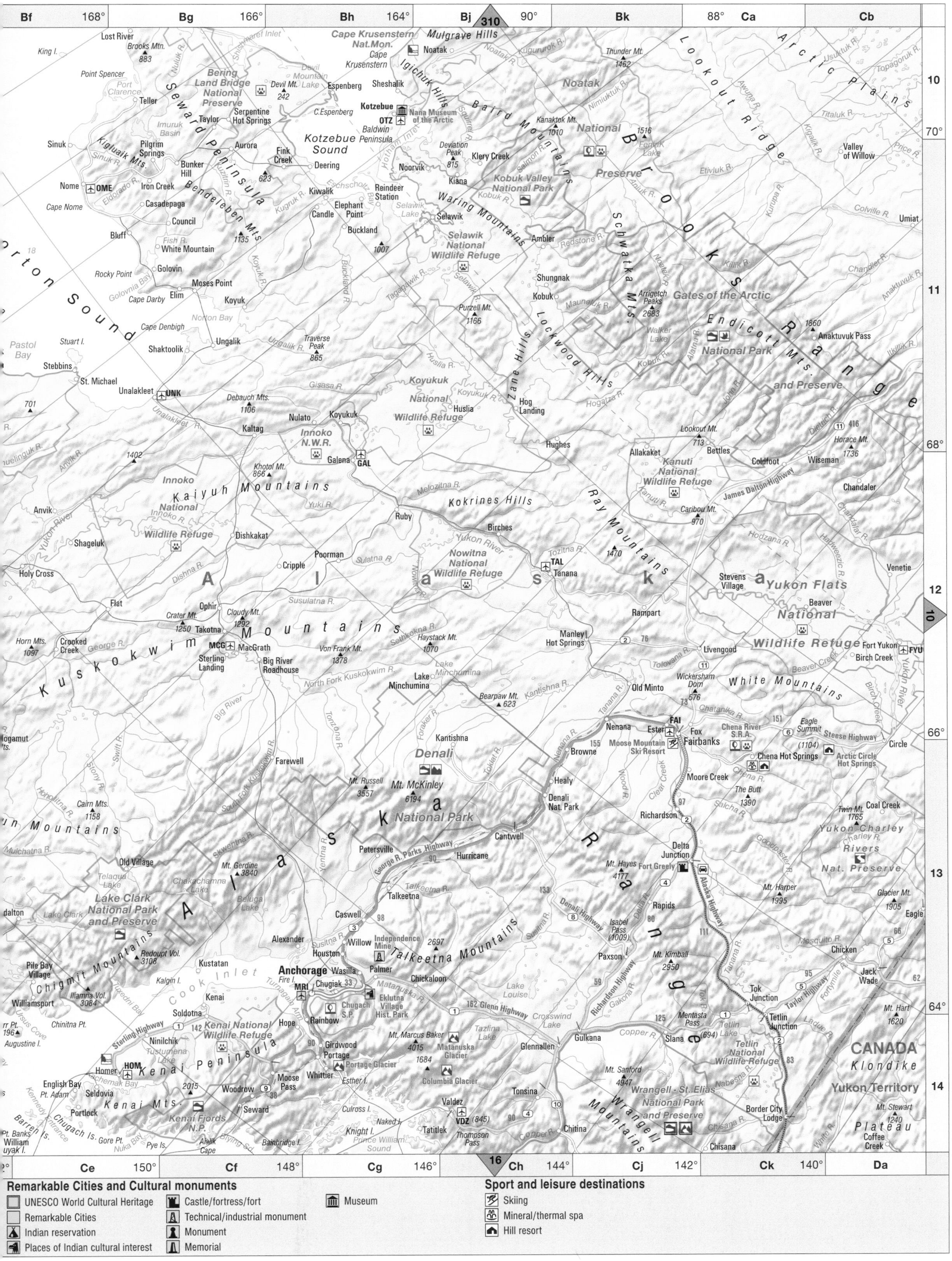

The Alaska Highway This roadway stretches through the North American wilderness. The highway starts in Dawson Creek, British Columbia and ends in Delta Junction, Alaska **Ch14**

Fairbanks Alaska's second largest city – amusement park Alaskaland – University of Alaska Museum (local history and art museum) **Cg13**

Mount McKinley The highest mountain in North America (6194 meters) – beautiful white mountain face – Wonder Lake at the foot of the mountain **Ce14**

Denali National Park Mount McKinley is the major attraction in this national park – home to herds of caribous, moose, bears and wolves **Ce14**

Anchorage Largest city in Alaska – founded in 1914 – population of 250,000 and the economic center of the state – Anchorage Museum of History and Art **CfBc**

Homer Port city on the mountainous Kenai Peninsula – gravel bar, Homer Spit – Pratt Museum (indigenous culture) **CeBb**

Portage Glacier and Lake This area lies east of Anchorage – large icebergs fall from the glaciers into the lake **CfBc**

Remarkable Cities and Cultural monuments

- UNESCO World Cultural Heritage
- Remarkable Cities
- Indian reservation
- Places of Indian cultural interest
- Castle/fortress/fort
- Technical/industrial monument
- Monument
- Memorial
- Museum

Sport and leisure destinations

- Skiing
- Mineral/thermal spa
- Hill resort

The **Alaskan Panhandle** stretches from Wrangell-St. Elias National Park south to the Canadian border at the Portland Inlet. It is home to numerous fjords and large sections of the Panhandle including the **Alexander Archipelago** are covered by temperate rainforest. The climate in this part of Alaska is influenced by warm ocean currents. The average temperature in the region is -6° Celsius in January and 13° Celsius in June. Rain or snow is common throughout the year. Fall and winter are the seasons with the most precipitation. The region's dense rainforests thrive in this wet climate. Many of the region's most beautiful rainforests are located in spectacular fjords – several of which, including the **Misty Fjord National Monument**, are protected by conservation laws. Every year betwee[n] July and September, Pacific salmo[n] migrate into the rivers of Alaska to spaw[n]. Without the salmon, the bear populatio[n] in the region would not be able to survi[ve]. Tours along the Alaskan coast giv[e] cruise ship passengers the opportunity t[o] observe Orcas, humpback whales, an[d] other types of whales. The **Inside Pas[sage]** in southeast Alaska is one of th[e] best areas for whale-watching in th[e]

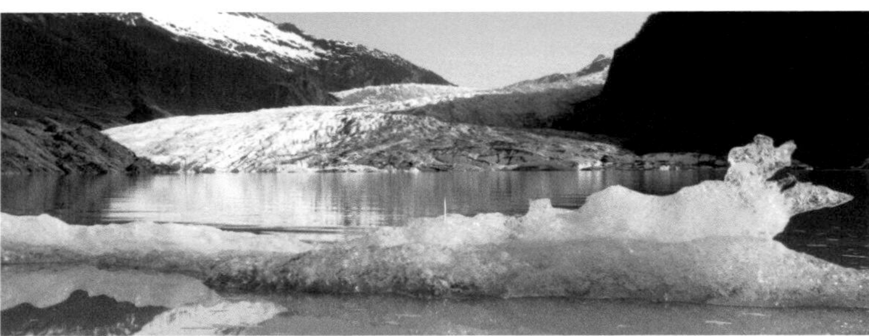

The Mendenhall Glacier near Alaska's capital city Juneau **Dc16**

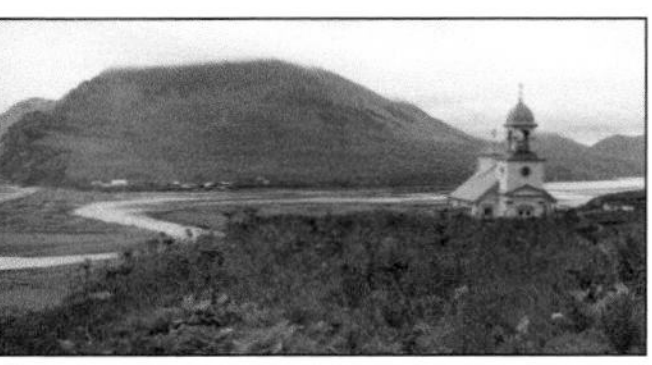

Kodiak Island Green coastline and snow covered mountains – home to the world's largest bears – the brown bears in Kodiak National Wildlife Refuge live on a diet consisting mostly of salmon **CcCd17**

Chugach Mountains Mountain range with a large number of glaciers – home to large grizzly and wolf populations **ChCj15**

Mount Huxley Tall mountain with a height of 3,828 meters in Wrangell-St. Elias National Park **Ck15**

Alexander Archipelago Islands in southeastern Alaska – fjords – the Inside Passage – humpback whale pods **DcDd17/18**

The Hawaiian Islands The archipelago is 2,400 kilometers long and has a great variety of landscapes including beaches, mountains, canyons, waterfalls, and forests. **BkCc34/36**

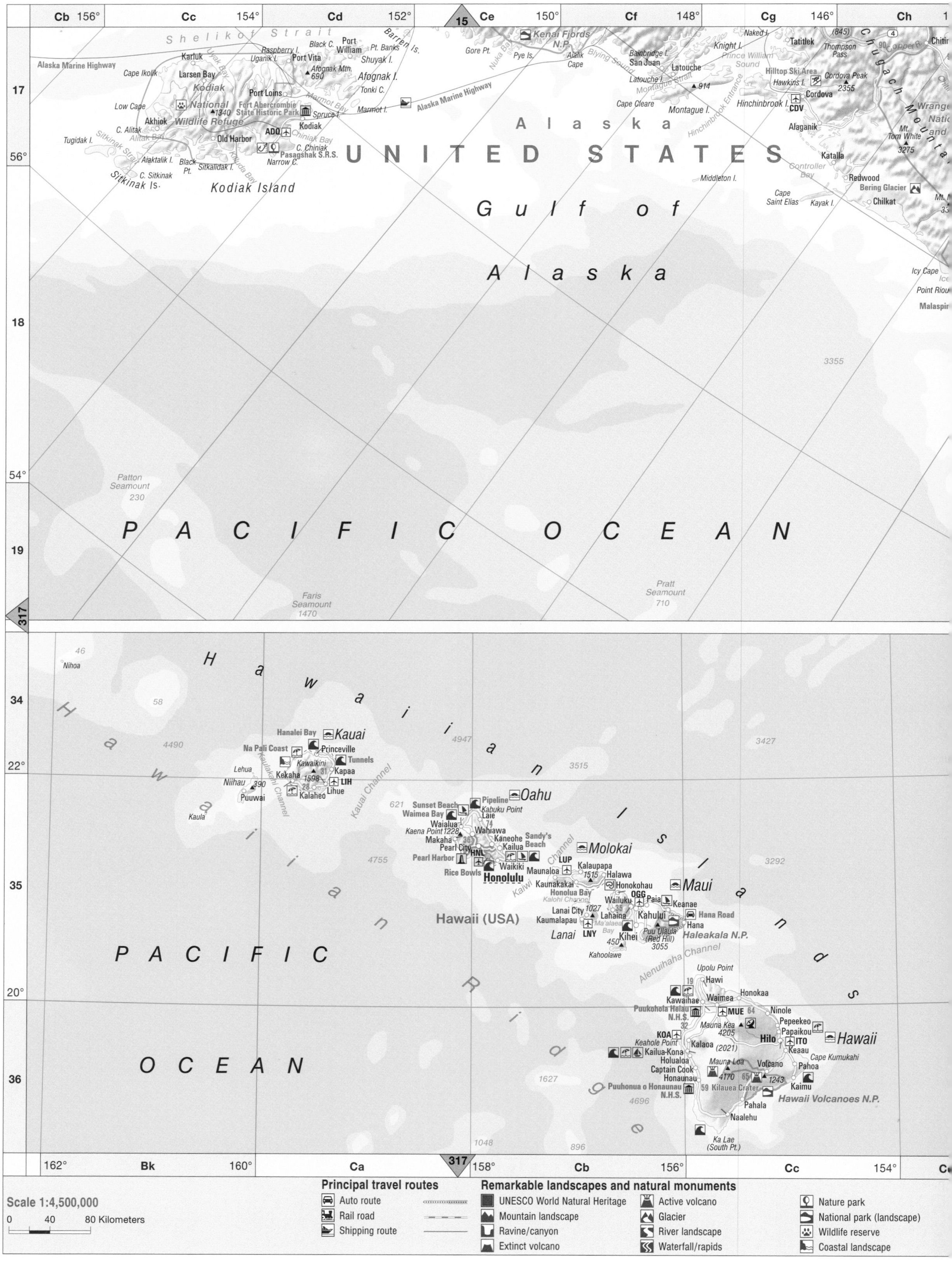

Scale 1:4,500,000
0 40 80 Kilometers

Principal travel routes
- Auto route
- Rail road
- Shipping route

Remarkable landscapes and natural monuments
- UNESCO World Natural Heritage
- Mountain landscape
- Ravine/canyon
- Extinct volcano
- Active volcano
- Glacier
- River landscape
- Waterfall/rapids
- Nature park
- National park (landscape)
- Wildlife reserve
- Coastal landscape

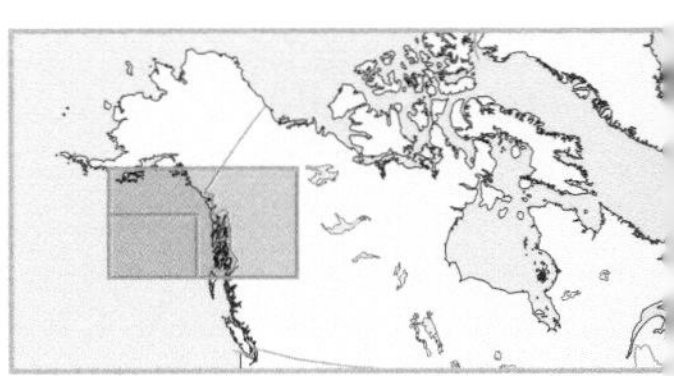

state. While the Panhandle has a mari-ime climate and heavy rainfall, the re-gions to its north as well as those farther nland are drier and have colder winters. The region around **Mount Logan** (5,959 neters) to the north of the Panhandle and the interior regions away from the coast have continental climates with less ainfall and large variations in tempera-ure during the year. In Canada's Yukon Territory and along the eastern edges of the Rockies temperatures near -50° Celsius are not uncommon during winter. In the late 19th century, the **Yukon Territory** made news around the world when large gold deposits were discovered in the area around the Klondike River. Fortune seekers from many nations came to the territory in search of wealth. Today the territory is one of the most sparsely populated regions in Canada.

Hawaii, the southernmost American state, lies in the Pacific Ocean nearly 4,000 kilometers away from the west coast of the American mainland. The state consists of six main islands: Oahu, Kauai, Maui, Lanai, Molokai, and Hawaii and at least 130 smaller islands and islets. This archipelago of volcanic islands owes its existence to a hot spot in the earth's crust. Molten lava from the hot spot hardened and accumulated over time forming underwater mountains and eventually the islands. The Hawaiian Islands are home to a variety of landscapes; tropical rainforests, white sandy beaches, black volcanic sand beaches, cliffs and canyons can all be found on the islands. Travelers on the islands can also visit the lava pools and lava flows in Hawaii Volcanoes National Park near the crater of Kilauea. Daytime temperatures on the islands range between 25° and 30° Celsius during most of the year.

Kluane National Park This national park is a world heritage site. Located in the Yukon Territory, the park contains large inaccessible glaciers and Canada's tallest mountain, Mount Logan (top photo). The park is home to wolves and grizzly bears. There are several hiking paths along Kathleen Lake (bottom photo). **CkDb15**

Nahanni National Park In the Northwest Territories – world heritage site – mountain ranges, canyons, and rivers **Dh15**

Haines Town at the northern edge of the Inside Passage – local culture in the Chilkat Center for the Performing Arts **Dc16**

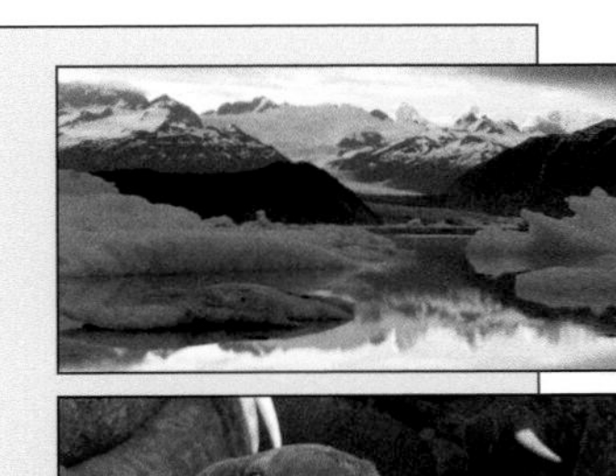

Glacier Bay National Park Glacier Bay harbors 16 glaciers, 12 of which calve into the bay. The area is a UNESCO world heritage site. Seals, walruses, and whales live in the bay. The John Hopkins Glacier is the most active in the bay calving large amounts of ice into the water. **Db16**

Hazleton Historic architecture from the colonial era – 'Ksan Indian Village Museum: recreation of a traditional Native American village **Dg18**

Remarkable Cities and Cultural monuments

- UNESCO World Cultural Heritage
- Remarkable Cities
- Places of Christian cultural interest
- Places of Indian cultural interest
- Technical/industrial monument
- Monument
- Memorial
- Space telescope
- Museum

Sport and leisure destinations

- Sailing
- Diving
- Wind surfing
- Surfing
- Canoeing/rafting
- Deep-sea fishing
- Beach resort

Southwestern Canada is a region of mountain ranges (Rocky Mountains, Coast Mountains) and vast plains that encompass parts of three Canadian provinces: British Columbia, Alberta, and Saskatchewan. Southwestern Canada is bordered by three northwestern American states: Washington, Idaho, and Montana. The tall mountains in this region, including the **Rockies**, have a major effect on the climate. Along the Pacific coast, mountains block the path of air into the interi or; the rising air cools, condenses anc falls to the ground as snow or rain. The coast is not only wetter than the interior it also has milder temperatures durinc winter. The Pacific coast is also home tc **Vancouver** and **Seattle**, the two larges urban areas in the region.

Longmire Valley in Mount Rainier National Park **Dk22**

Vancouver The city has a beautiful natural setting between mountains and the ocean – Gastown – large Chinatown – Stanley Park and its aquarium – Museum of Anthropology **Dj21**

Olympic National Park Temperate rainforest – Hoh Rainforest – Rialto Beach – Makah Indian Reservation (museum and cultural center) **DhDj21/22**

Seattle Largest city in the American Northwest – Space Needle (158 meters) – Pike Place Market – Seattle Aquarium – Seattle Art Museum **Dj22**

Mount Rainier National Park Popular area for hiking – 26 glaciers – Grove of the Patriarch – volcano – Wonderland Trail around Mount Rainier **Dk22**

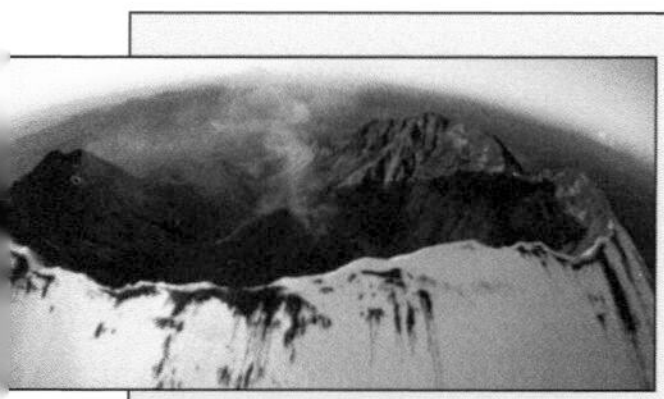

Mount St. Helens In 1980 this volcano erupted. The powerful eruption blew away the summit and north face of the mountain leaving a large crater. Coldwater Ridge Visitors Center provides information about the eruption and impressive views of the mountain and surrounding region. **Dj22**

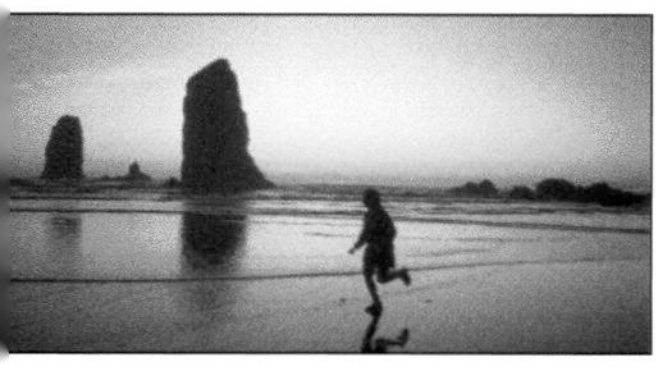

Cannon Beach Attractive coastal town – long sandy beaches – Haystack Rock (72 meters tall free-standing rock) **Dj23**

Scale 1:4,500,000
0 40 80 Kilometers

Principal travel routes
- Auto route
- Rail road
- Shipping route

Remarkable landscapes and natural monuments
- UNESCO World Natural Heritage
- Mountain landscape
- Rock landscape
- Active volcano
- Glacier
- River landscape
- Waterfall/rapids
- Nature park
- National park (landscape)
- National park (flora)
- National park (fauna)
- National park (culture)
- Wildlife reserve
- Coastal landscape
- Beach
- Underwater reserve

ne region's interior has a continental cli-ate. Summers in the interior are consi-erably warmer than on the coast and the inters are far colder. Latitude also deter-ines climate in the region – the farther orth a location in the interior is, the rawer s climate. In Edmonton, the capital of lberta, temperatures can reach -25° Cel-us in winter.

Vancouver Island was once covered y virgin rainforests, but logging has reduced the forests to a few areas including Clayoquot Sound and **Pacific Rim National Park**.

The **Queen Charlotte Islands** lie 80 kilometers away from mainland British Columbia and are home to an abundance of wildlife. The eastern **Rocky Mountains** contain interesting landscapes and some of the most beautiful **national parks** in North America, including Banff and Jasper National Parks. The Icefields Parkway, running through these two parks, is one of the world's most spectacular mountain highways. The mountains in the eastern Rockies are covered by snow and surrounded by ice and snowfields. The eastern Rockies are heavily forested and there are countless mountain lakes scattered throughout the region. To the east of the Rockies lies a region of vast prairies and grasslands. **Calgary**, the largest city in Alberta, lies at the foot of the Rockies while Edmonton, the northernmost large city in Canada, is surrounded by plains. The province Saskatchewan has an economy dominated by agriculture. The province produces around 60% of Canada's wheat. Mining (uranium and potash) also plays an important role in the province's economy. While southern Saskatchewan is covered by fields, the north is mostly forests and marshland.

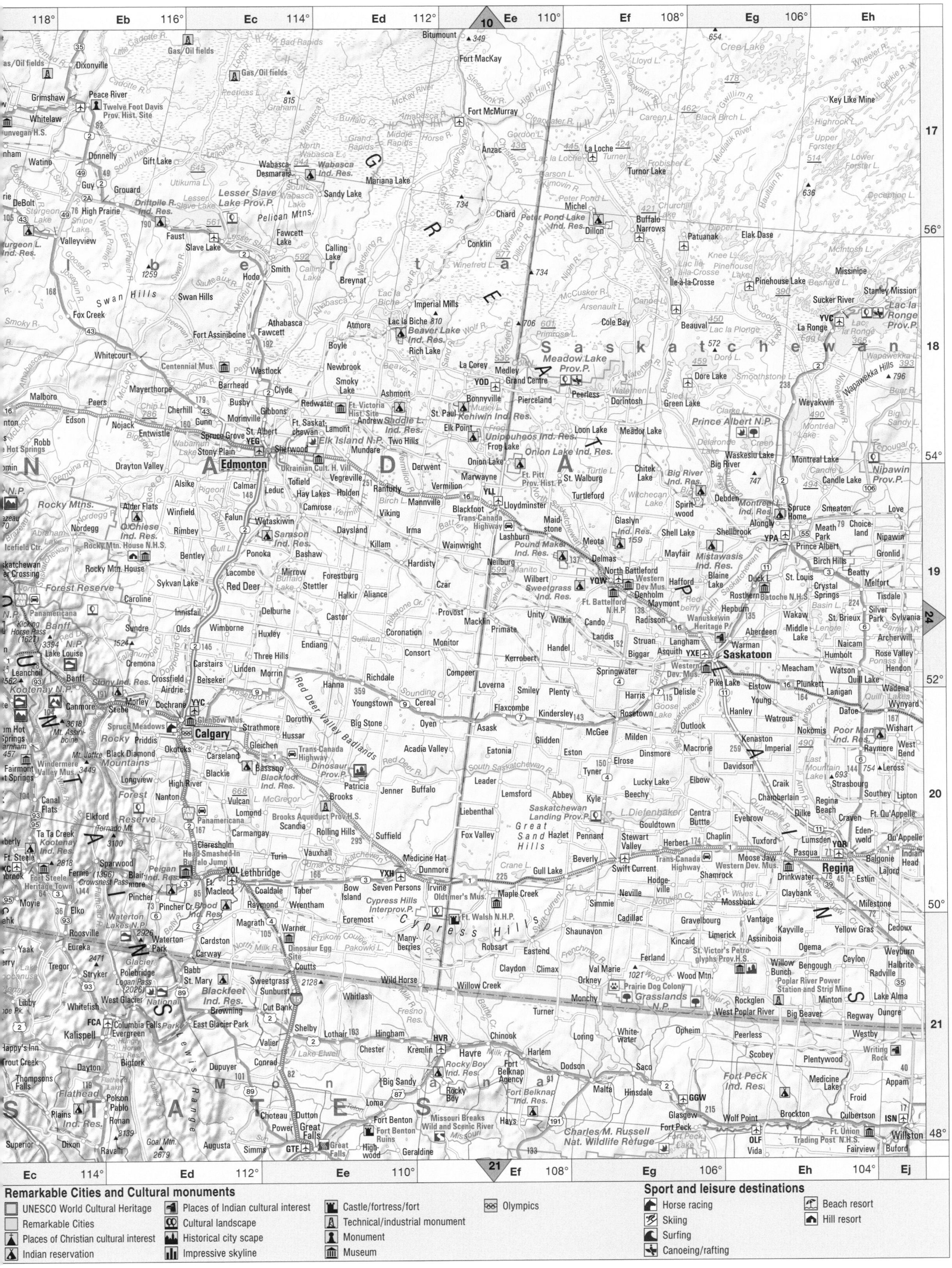

Clearwater River Beautiful river in Canada's Wells Gray Provincial Park – Dawson Falls (18 meters high) – Helmcken-Falls (137 meters high) **DkEa19**

Jasper National Park Largest national park in the Rocky Mountains (10,878 km²) – Athabasca Glacier and Athabasca Falls – Spirit Island in Maligne Lake **Ea19**

Glacier National Park (Montana, US) 400 glaciers – more than 140 kilometers of hiking trails – extreme weather conditions – Connaught train tunnel **Eb20**

Banff National Park Canada's oldest national park, founded in 1885 – resort town of Banff – rafting on the Bow River – glacial lakes including Lake Louise and Moraine Lake **Ec20**

Mount Assiniboine Mountain in Kootenay National Park – mountain wilderness in the western Rockies – Marble Canyon – the town Radium Hot Springs **Ec20**

Dinosaur Provincial Park Prehistoric dinosaur gravesite in Alberta: UNESCO world heritage site – Dinosaur Trail – bus tours to excavation sites **Ee20**

Waterton Lakes National Park National park in southern Alberta – Upper Waterton Lake – Red Rock Canyon – the historic Prince of Wales Hotel **Ec21**

Remarkable Cities and Cultural monuments

- UNESCO World Cultural Heritage
- Remarkable Cities
- Places of Christian cultural interest
- Indian reservation
- Places of Indian cultural interest
- Cultural landscape
- Historical city scape
- Impressive skyline
- Castle/fortress/fort
- Technical/industrial monument
- Monument
- Museum
- Olympics

Sport and leisure destinations

- Horse racing
- Skiing
- Surfing
- Canoeing/rafting
- Beach resort
- Hill resort

Western USA

This section of the American West stretches from the Pacific coast to the eastern edges of the **Rocky Mountains**. The Pacific coast between Oregon and Southern California is heavily developed but still contains many pristine beaches. The San Andreas Fault runs from Southern California to the northern part of the state and passes through the heavily populated metropolitan area of **San Francisco**. Mountain ranges like the Cascade and **Coast Ranges** in the north and the **Sie ra Nevada** mountains in the south hav a major effect on the climate of the Pac fic coast. These mountains form a nat ral barrier that traps moisture in the coas al areas, forming a rain shadow in th interior. California contains nine nation parks, more than any other state in th

Yosemite National Park: fascinating landscapes and wildlife **Ea26/2**

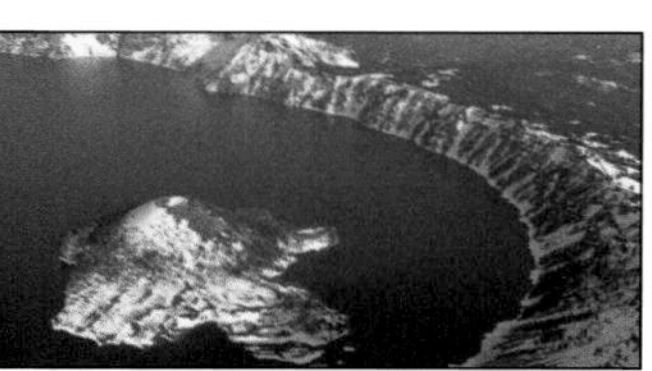

Crater Lake National Park The intense blue-colored Crater Lake is surrounded by a high crater wall – hiking trails **Dj24**

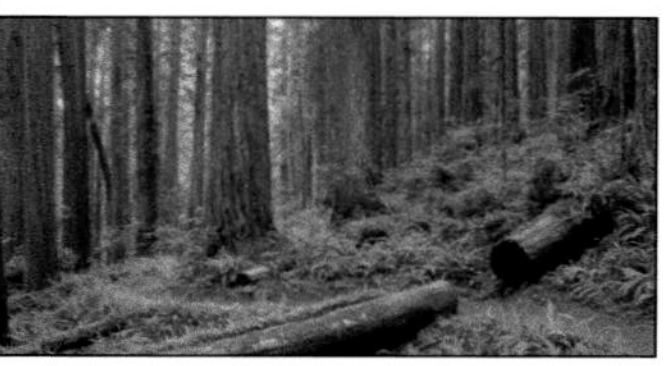

Redwood National Park The park is home to some of the world's tallest trees, the coastal Redwoods – the tallest tree in the park, Tall Tree, once measured 120 meters in height **DhDj25**

Lassen National Park This nature reserve covers 440 km² – Bumpass Hell has geothermal springs and boiling mud pools – Burney Falls (40 meters) **Dk25**

San Francisco Northern California's largest city – city population 725,000 – attractions: Fisherman's Wharf, Lombard Street, cable cars, Coit Tower, Chinatown, and Market Street shopping area **Dj27**

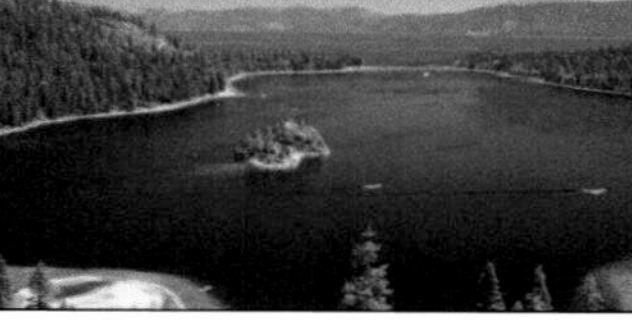

Lake Tahoe Azure blue mountain lake on the Nevada/California border – popular summer holiday destination **DkEa26**

Yosemite National Park Mountainous landscapes in western California – deep canyons, diverse wildlife, Yosemite Falls (740 meters) – panoramic views from Glacier Point **Ea26/27**

Mono Lake Remnant of an ancient inland sea – mating area for California's seagull population – unusual chalk formations called tufus **Ea26/27**

PACIFIC OCEAN

Scale 1:4,500,000
0 40 80 Kilometers

Principal travel routes
- Auto route
- Rail road
- Shipping route

Remarkable landscapes and natural monuments
- UNESCO World Natural Heritage
- Rock landscape
- Ravine/canyon
- Extinct volcano
- Active volcano
- Geyser
- Cave
- Waterfall/rapids
- Desert
- Fossil site
- Nature park
- National park (landscape)
- National park (flora)
- National park (fauna)
- Wildlife reserve
- Coastal landscape

ountry. Yellowstone National Park
western California is the most visited
ational park in the state.
he Cascade Range is part of the Paci-
c Ring of Fire and the range is home to
umerous active volcanoes. Many vol-
anoes in the range, including Mount
ood (Oregon) and Mount Shasta (Cali-
ornia), have picturesque snow-covered
eaks. To the east of the Cascade lies the
olcanic **Columbia Plateau**. Farther south, the Sierra Nevada Mountains are bordered in the east by the **Great Basin**. The Great Basin is the largest arid region in North America. The Great Basin is home to Death Valley – the lowest point in the United States – and the Great Salt Lake Desert in Utah.

The Great Basin is bordered to the east and northeast by the Rocky Mountains. Yellowstone National Park became the world's first national park when it was established in 1872. The national park is divided between three states – Idaho, Wyoming, and Montana – and lies in a volcanically active region. In addition to its geologic attractions including its famous geysers, the park also has an abundance of wildlife, including bears and buffalos. The mountains of Colorado make the state one of the most popular destinations in the western United States. The Colorado town of Vail is the site of the largest ski area in the country. Utah boasts five national parks. **Bryce Canyon** in Utah has an impressive collection of interesting stone formations. Utah's **Zion National Park** is most famous for its beautiful cliffs and canyons, while **Arches National Park's** major attractions are its many natural sandstone arches. East of the Rocky Mountains are the vast and fertile prairies of the Great Plains.

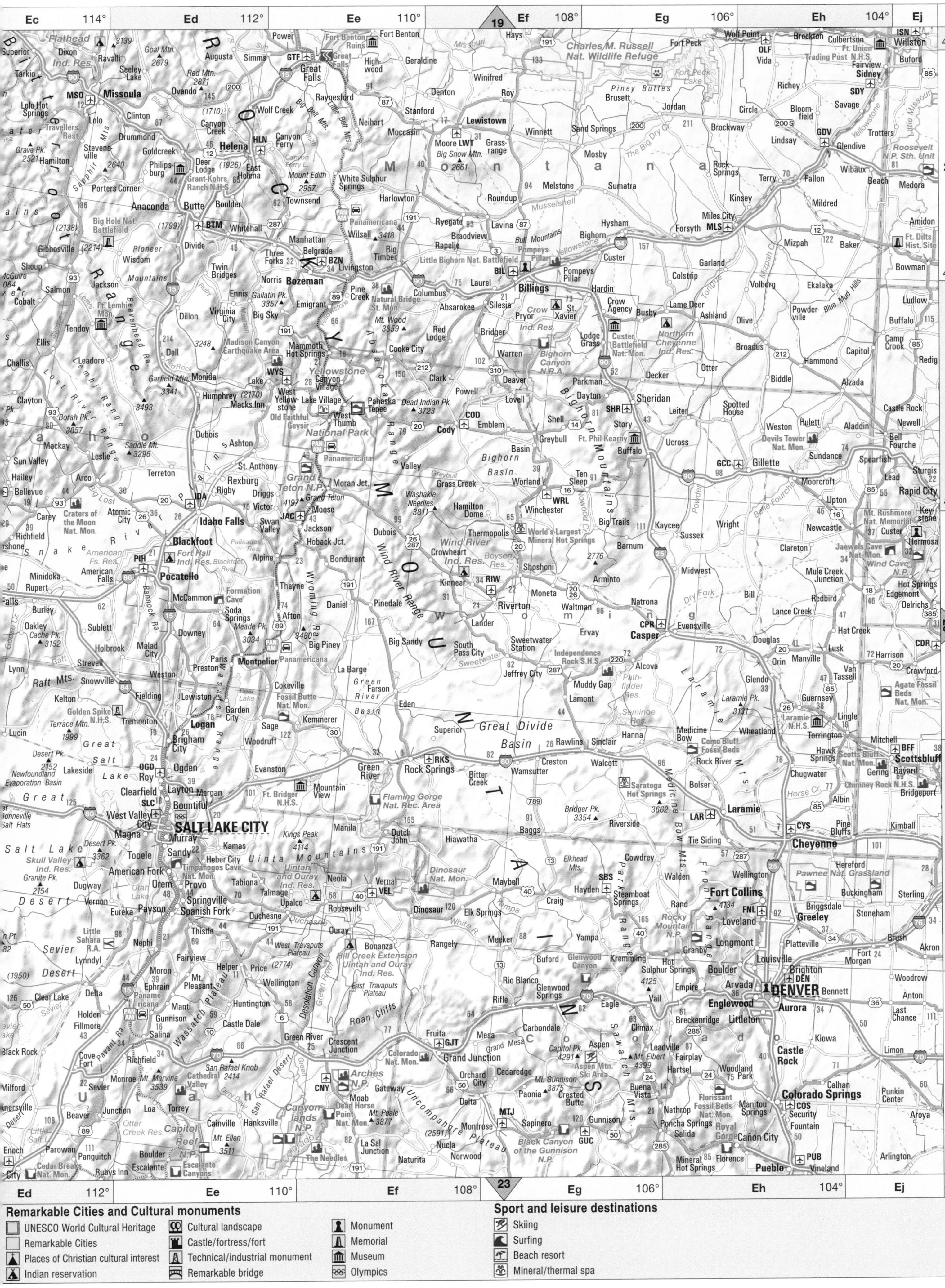

Yellowstone National Park The world's oldest national park, Yellowstone, was established in 1872. The park has an area of 9,000 km² and lies at an elevation of 2,400 meters in the Rocky Mountains. Yellowstone National Park is home to bears, buffalo, and elk. The geologically active park contains numerous hot springs and around 200 geysers. **Ee23**

Grand Teton National Park National Park in the Rocky Mountains – The Grand Teton (mountain) rises 4,197 meters – numerous mountain lakes **Ee24**

Salt Lake City Capital of Utah – population 175,000 – founded by Mormon settlers – site of the 2002 Olympic games **Ee25**

Arches National Park Erosion created the more than 200 natural stone arches in the national park **Ef26**

Canyonlands National Park National park at the meeting point of the Colorado and Green Rivers – panoramic views from the Grand View Point Overlook **EeEf26**

Kings Canyon National Park River valley surrounded by high canyon walls – home to the General Grant Tree (America's Christmas tree) **Ea27**

Remarkable Cities and Cultural monuments

- UNESCO World Cultural Heritage
- Remarkable Cities
- Places of Christian cultural interest
- Indian reservation
- Cultural landscape
- Castle/fortress/fort
- Technical/industrial monument
- Remarkable bridge
- Monument
- Memorial
- Museum
- Olympics

Sport and leisure destinations

- Skiing
- Surfing
- Beach resort
- Mineral/thermal spa

Southwestern USA

There are few regions in the world that can offer visitors the chance to visit more fascinating natural attractions than the American Southwest. The **Grand Canyon** surveyor John Wesley Powell was enthralled by what he described as a "wilderness of rocks; deep gorges, where the rivers are lost below cliffs and towers and pinnacles; and beyond them, mountains blending with the clouds." The Southwest encompasses five states:

Nevada, Colorado, Utah, Arizona, and New Mexico. The region's terrain is dominated by large basins and plateaus which are broken by tall mountains ranges such as the **Rocky Mountains** and deep river valleys. Covering 110,000 km², the Colorado Plateau encompasses some of the most beautiful national parks in th

The Mitten Buttes in Monument Valley (Arizona) **Ee27**

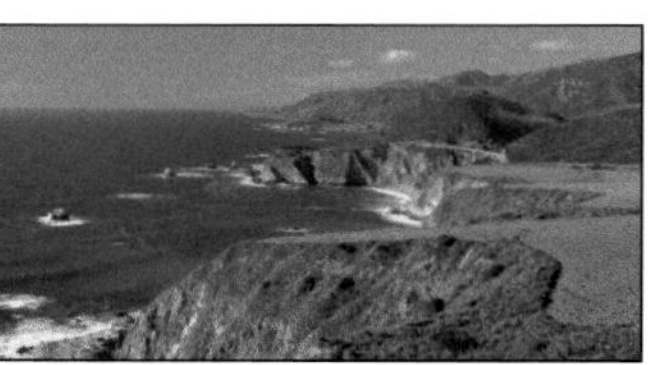

Big Sur Coastal area along California's Highway 1 – beautiful cliffs – Julia Pfeiffer State Park (beaches), Pfeiffer Big Sur State Park (redwood forests) **Dk27**

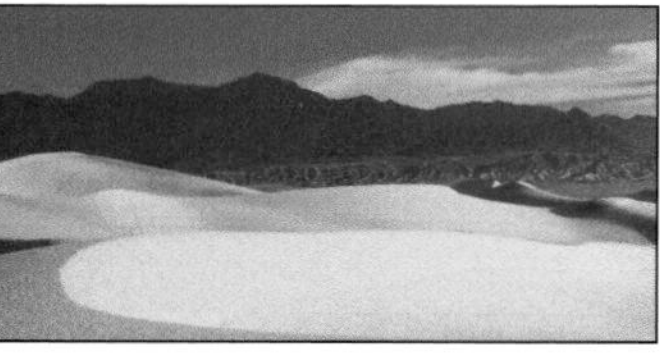

Death Valley National Park Spectacular desert landscapes – salt lakes canyons – large sand dunes **Eb27/28**

Las Vegas The city is a popular tourist destination – neon-lit Glitter Gulch has numer-ous casinos – large theme hotels and casinos – amusement parks **Ec27**

Los Angeles Second largest city in the United States – population: city 3.6 million, county 9.4 million – downtown has impressive skyscrapers – Disneyland – beach communities including Venice Beach and Santa Monica – interesting museums: Getty Center and Paul Getty Museum in Malibu **Ea29**

Joshua Tree National Park Uninhabited nature reserve in the Mojave Desert – ten meters tall Yucca trees (Joshua Trees) and unique cacti **EbEc28/29**

El Vizcaíno Reserve The world's first marine reserve for the protection of whales – whale-watching boat tours **Ec31**

Organ Pipe Cactus National Monument wilderness in the Sonora Desert – interesting desert plants **Ed29/30**

Scale 1:4,500,000
0 40 80 Kilometers

Principal travel routes
- Auto route
- Rail road
- Shipping route

Remarkable landscapes and natural monuments
- UNESCO World Natural Heritage
- Rock landscape
- Ravine/canyon
- Extinct volcano
- Cave
- Desert
- Nature park
- National park (landscape)
- National park (flora)
- National park (fauna)
- National park (culture)
- Biosphere reserve
- Wildlife reserve
- Whale watching
- Coastal landscape
- Beach

Southwest including Grand Canyon, Bryce, Zion, and Arches National Park. The **Colorado River** is the longest and most important river in the region The construction of dams in the last century has created several large artificial lakes in the region including Lake Mead and Lake Powell. The construction of the Hoover Dam is considered one of the greatest engineering achievements of the 20th century. Without the energy supplied by dams, **Las Vegas** would never have become a bright and vibrant metropolis in the middle of a desert. Large sections of Nevada, Southern California and most of the border region are covered by rocky or sandy deserts.

In addition to its natural sights, the region also offers cultural attractions, many connected to the history and culture of local Native Americans. The ancient history of the local Native Americans is displayed in the region's pueblos. The most visited pueblos are **Taos Pueblo** with its adobe buildings, **Acoma Pueblo** the "Sky City," **Mesa Verde National Park's** 700-year-old cliff buildings, and sites in Arizona's reservations.

To the west of the **Sierra Nevada** mountains lies Southern California with its beautiful beaches and the exciting urban areas of Los Angeles and San Diego. While the coastal area of Southern California is densely populated and highly developed, the interior contains many pristine wilderness areas.

The Mexican coasts along the **Gulf of California** (Sea of Cortez) are surrounded by extremely dry deserts. Many of the islands in the gulf are conservation areas. Along the coast of **Baja California** several marine reserves have been created for the protection of local whales and dolphins.

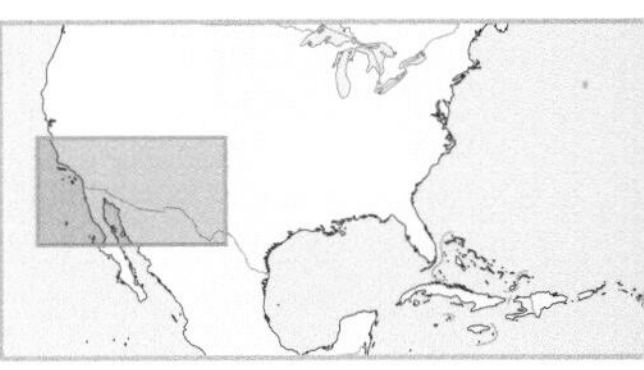

Bryce Canyon National Park Red stone formations called Hoodoos – large horseshoe shaped natural amphitheaters **Ed27**

Grand Canyon National Park The largest canyon in the world. The Grand Canyon lies in northwest Arizona and stretches 350 kilometers, created by the Colorado River over millions of years – national park – panoramic views **EdEe27/28**

Meteor Crater Meteor impact crater in Arizona – 170 meters deep and 1,250 meters wide – 40,000 years old **Ee28**

Mesa Verde National Park Canyons in southwestern Colorado – well preserved cliff settlements constructed by the Anasazi Native Americans **Ef27**

Chaco Culture N.H.P. Well preserved remnants of ancient Native American Pueblo culture – the remains of Pueblo Bonito, a structure that was once five stories tall and had 600 rooms **EfEg27/28**

Acoma Pueblo Native American village – one of the oldest permanently inhabited settlements in the Americas (founded in 1075) – often called "Sky City" **Eg28**

Carlsbad Caverns National Park Extensive network of more than 100 caves in southern New Mexico – The Big Room, a 545 meters long chamber **Eh29**

Remarkable Cities and Cultural monuments

- UNESCO World Cultural Heritage
- Remarkable Cities
- Places of Christian cultural interest
- Indian reservation
- Indian Pueblo culture
- Historical city scape
- Castle/fortress/fort
- Technical/industrial monument
- Dam
- Remarkable bridge
- Memorial
- Space mission launch site
- Space telescope
- Museum
- Theater
- Olympics

Sport and leisure destinations

- Race track
- Horse racing
- Skiing
- Wind surfing
- Surfing
- Beach resort
- Mineral/thermal spa
- Amusement/theme park

Southern Canada

The northern regions of the provinces Manitoba, Saskatchewan, Quebec, and Ontario are covered by the Canadian Shield, one of the oldest geological features on the Earth's surface. The **Canadian Shield** extends out from both sides of the Hudson Bay and covers almost half of Canada's total land area. The area's topography was shaped to a great extent by glaciers during the ice age. In terms of mineral wealth, the Canadian Shield is one of the richest regions in the world. The vast **Hudson Bay Lowlands** are a region of lakes and flat swampy land on the southern and western coasts of the bay. The province of Ontario alone encompasses several hundred thousand lakes. Central Canada has a typical continental climate with dry hot summers.

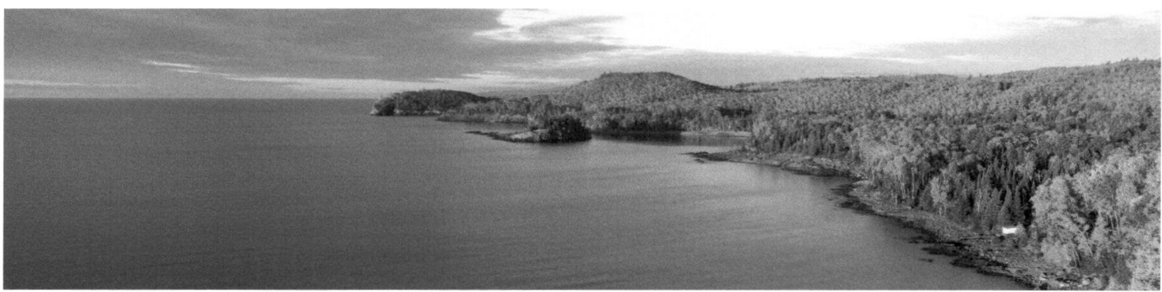

Pukaskwa National Park on the shore of Lake Superior **FgFh21**

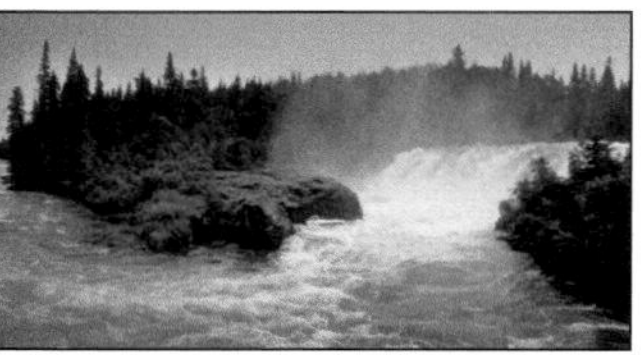

Pisew Falls Waterfall on the Grass River – located in Manitoba's Paint Lake Provincial Park **Fa18**

Grass River Provincial Park Undeveloped wilderness with countless lakes – most of the park's land is covered by permafrost – scattered forests **Ek18**

Lake Winnipeg The largest lake in Manitoba – dunes and beaches – surfing and recreational sailing areas **FaFb19/20**

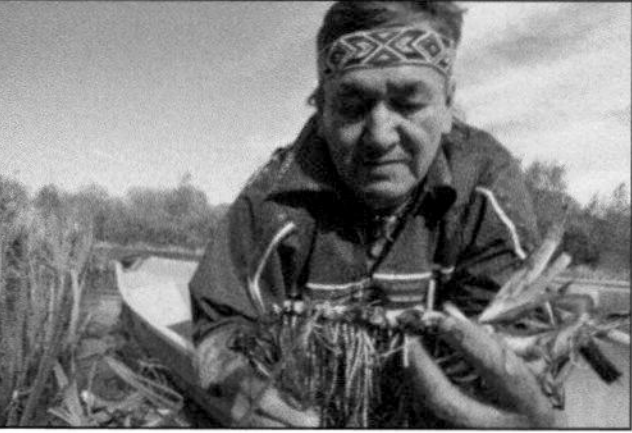

Hollow Water First Nation Land Native reservation in Manitoba – on the southern shore of Lake Winnipeg **Fb20**

Woodland Caribou Provincial Park Conservation area containing numerous lakes – caribou and bear populations **Fc20**

Lake Manitoba The smallest of Manitoba's three largest lakes (4,624 km²) – name comes from the Ojibwa language and means "Straits of the Great Spirit" **Fa20**

Winnipeg Capital city of Manitoba – population 690,000 – Winnipeg Art Gallery – French district, St. Boniface – Centennial Centre with the Manitoba Museum of Man and Nature **Fb21**

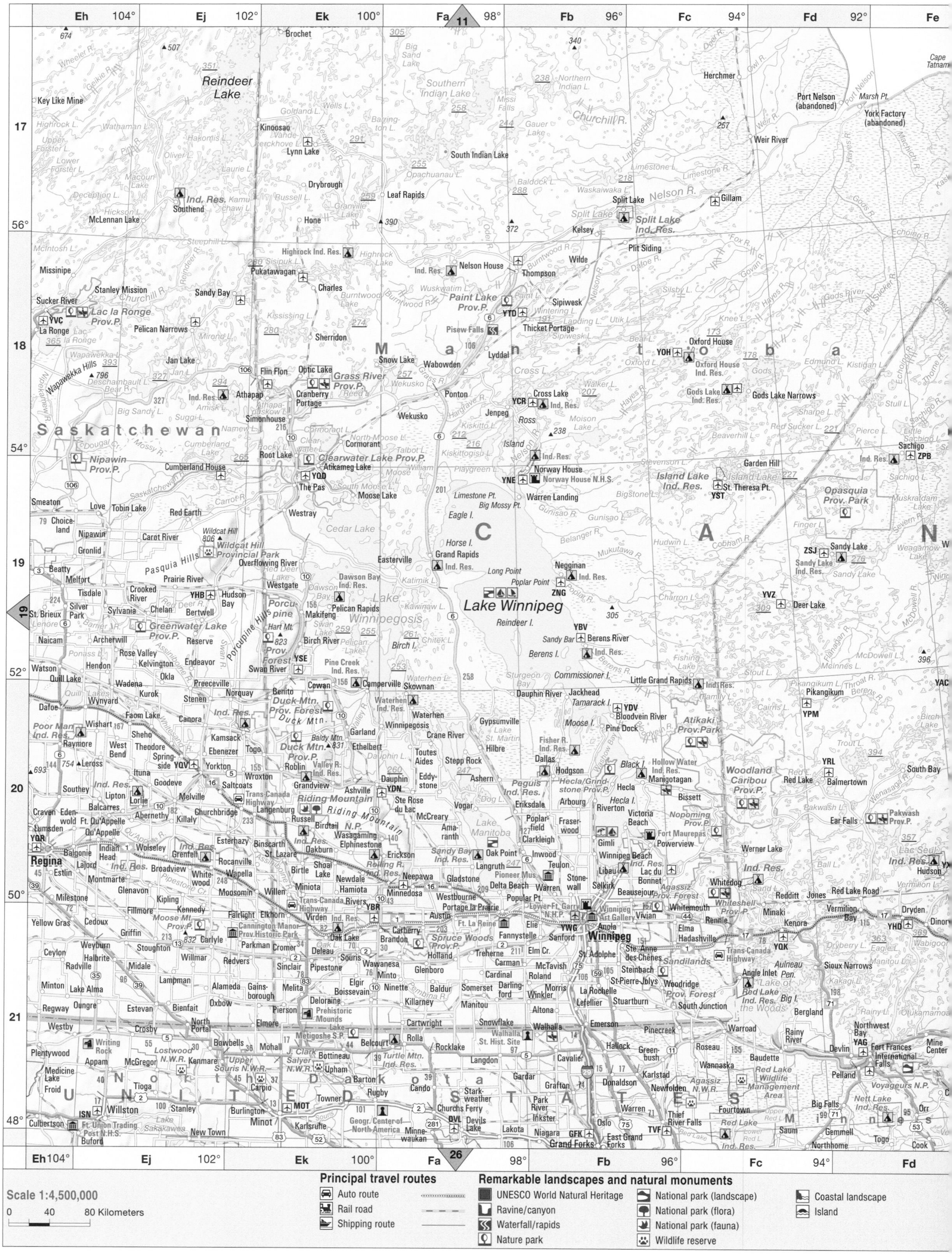

Scale 1:4,500,000
0 40 80 Kilometers

Principal travel routes
- Auto route
- Rail road
- Shipping route

Remarkable landscapes and natural monuments
- UNESCO World Natural Heritage
- Ravine/canyon
- Waterfall/rapids
- Nature park
- National park (landscape)
- National park (flora)
- National park (fauna)
- Wildlife reserve
- Coastal landscape
- Island

and bitter cold winters that are five months long in the south and even longer in northern areas. Winter temperatures around -25° Celsius and summer temperatures exceeding 25° Celsius are typical for the region. Because of the raw climate and terrain in the northern sections of southern Canada most of the region's population is concentrated in the far south near the American border. The pristine forests and lakes are best explored from the many hunting and fishing lodges scattered throughout southern Canada. Fishing and hunting in the great outdoors are favorite pastimes for much of the region's population. Southern Canada has many accessible waterways for canoeing and kayaking.

The **Trans Canada Highway** stretches from the Atlantic coast to the Pacific coast and driving along the highway provides travelers a good impression of the country's landscapes. The highway passes through forests and along lakes in **Ontario**, into the wheat fields and grasslands of the Prairie Provinces. The **Great Plains** begin west of Winnipeg in Manitoba and rise in elevation from east to west. Lake Winnipeg, one of the largest lakes in Canada, has many sandy white beaches along its edges. In addition to Lake Winnipeg, Manitoba is also home to two other large lakes, Lake Manitoba and Lake Winnipegosis, and countless smaller lakes scattered throughout the province. The central and southern sections of **Saskatchewan** are covered by vast fields used for agriculture and the province is widely known as the "breadbasket of Canada." While most of Saskatchewan is covered by flat plains, the northern section of the province, like much of neighboring Manitoba, is covered by countless lakes.

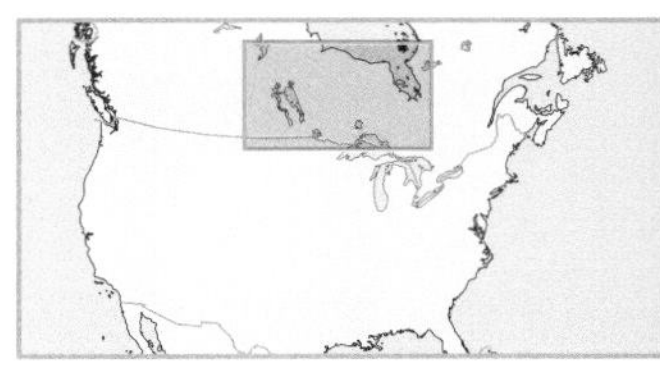

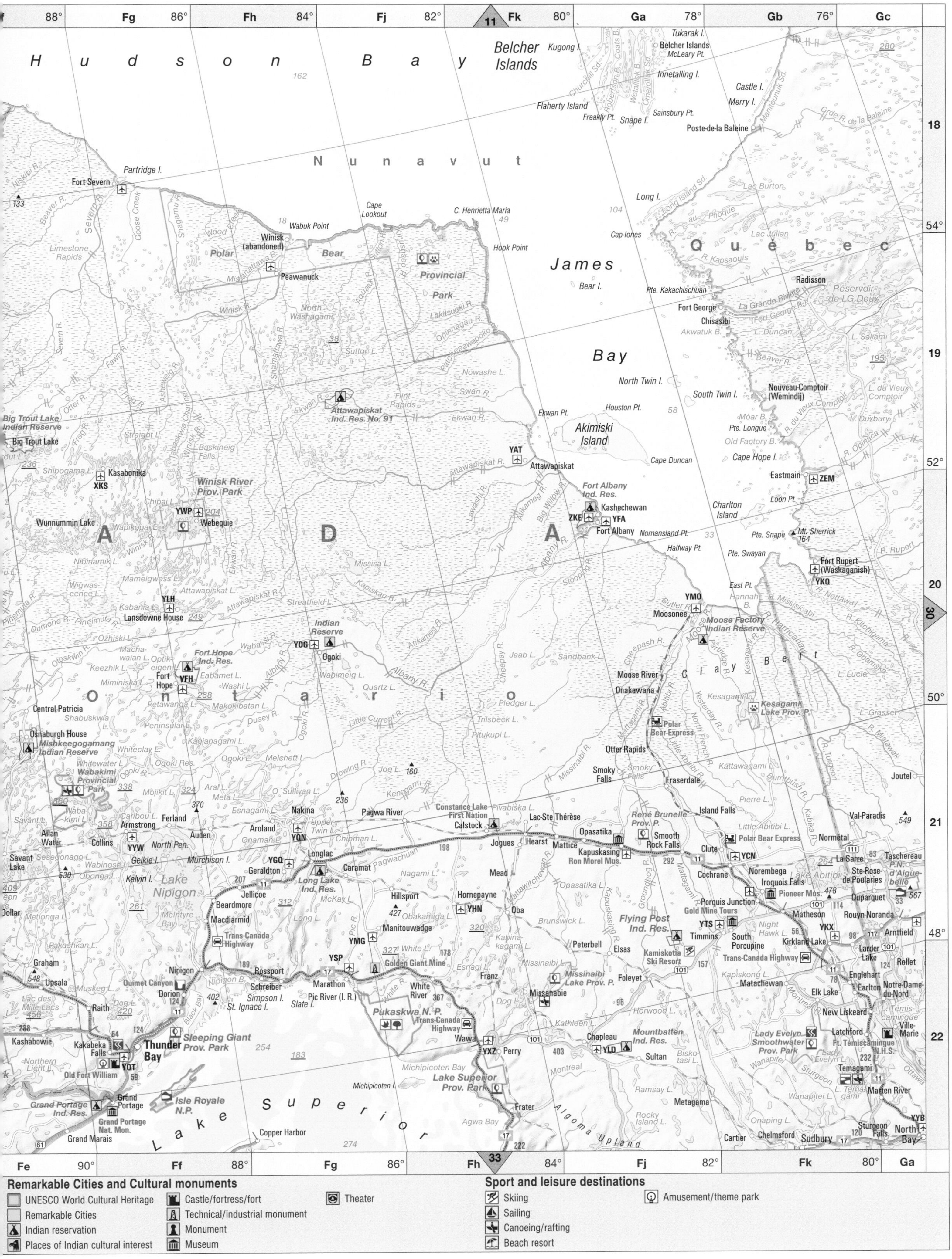

James Bay Home to Cree Indian communities – seal, whales, and walrus populations – hydroelectric projects on the Quebec coast **FjGa18-20**

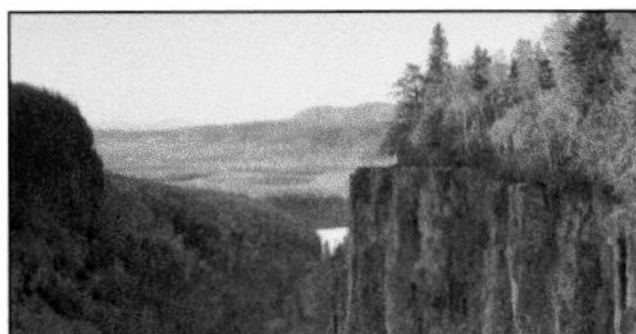

Ouimet Canyon Five kilometers long canyon in Ontario – contains rare alpine-arctic vegetation – panoramic views from platforms **Ff21**

Kakabeka Falls The name means the "waterfall over tall rocks" – the falls are 39 meters high **Ff21**

Thunder Bay Town on the northwestern coast of Lake Superior – major port for the export of Canadian grain – historic Old Fort William **Ff21**

Sleeping Giant Large land formation at the mouth of Thunder Bay – according to legend the Giant "protects" the entrance to the bay. **Ff21**

Isle Royale National Park Island in the north of Lake Superior – part of the U.S state of Michigan – only accessible with a boat or seaplane – hiking areas **Ff21/22**

Lake Temagami Beautiful lake surrounded by forests – in Ontario near the Quebec border – popular with fishers and kayakers **FkGa22**

Remarkable Cities and Cultural monuments

- UNESCO World Cultural Heritage
- Remarkable Cities
- Indian reservation
- Places of Indian cultural interest
- Castle/fortress/fort
- Technical/industrial monument
- Monument
- Museum
- Theater

Sport and leisure destinations

- Skiing
- Sailing
- Canoeing/rafting
- Beach resort
- Amusement/theme park

Northern Great Plains

Most of the American Midwest is covered by the vast flat prairies of the **Great Plains**. The western sections of the Great Plains border the **Rocky Mountains**. The area within 200 kilometers of the Rockies is dotted by several isolated hilly areas such as Badlands National Park, the Smoky Hills, and the Sandy Hills. North of the Smoky Hills lies the geographic center of the mainland United States; a monument marks the exact

location. The Great Plains tend to decline in elevation from west to east. The **Missouri Plateau** is a large plateau in the center of the United States. It borders the **Coteau des Prairies** and the **Coteau du Missouri**, two smaller significant plateaus in the region. The Midwest is home to several large river basins including the

Ft. Pierre Grassland National Park in South Dakota **Ek23**

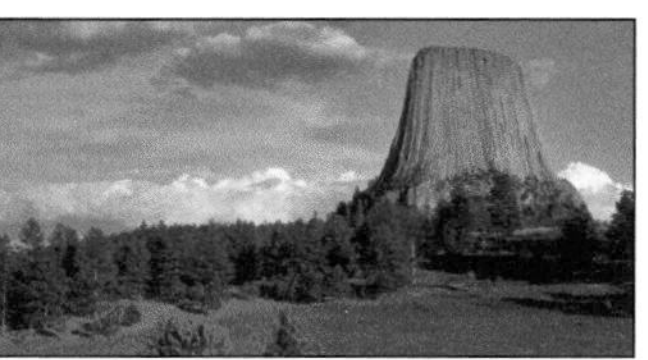

Devil's Tower tall rim of an inactive volcano (264 meters) – national monument in Wyoming **Eh23**

Mount Rushmore The faces of four American presidents carved in stone: Washington, Jefferson, Lincoln, and Roosevelt – all around 18 meters tall **Ej24**

Wind Cave National Park Extensive network of caves – Custer State Park – buffalo herds **Ej24**

Badlands National Park Large region of heavily eroded arid land – eagle, hawk and falcon populations **Ej24**

Chimney Rock 46 meters tall rock formation near the North Platte River in Nebraska **Ej25**

Denver Capital city of Colorado – metropolitan population, 2.4 million – Cherry Cheek shopping area – Country Club District – LoDo: downtown neighborhood with bars, art galleries, and boutiques – Colorado History Museum **Eh26**

Aspen Ski resort: popular with the wealthy and celebrities – dozens of ski areas – tree-lined streets **Eg26**

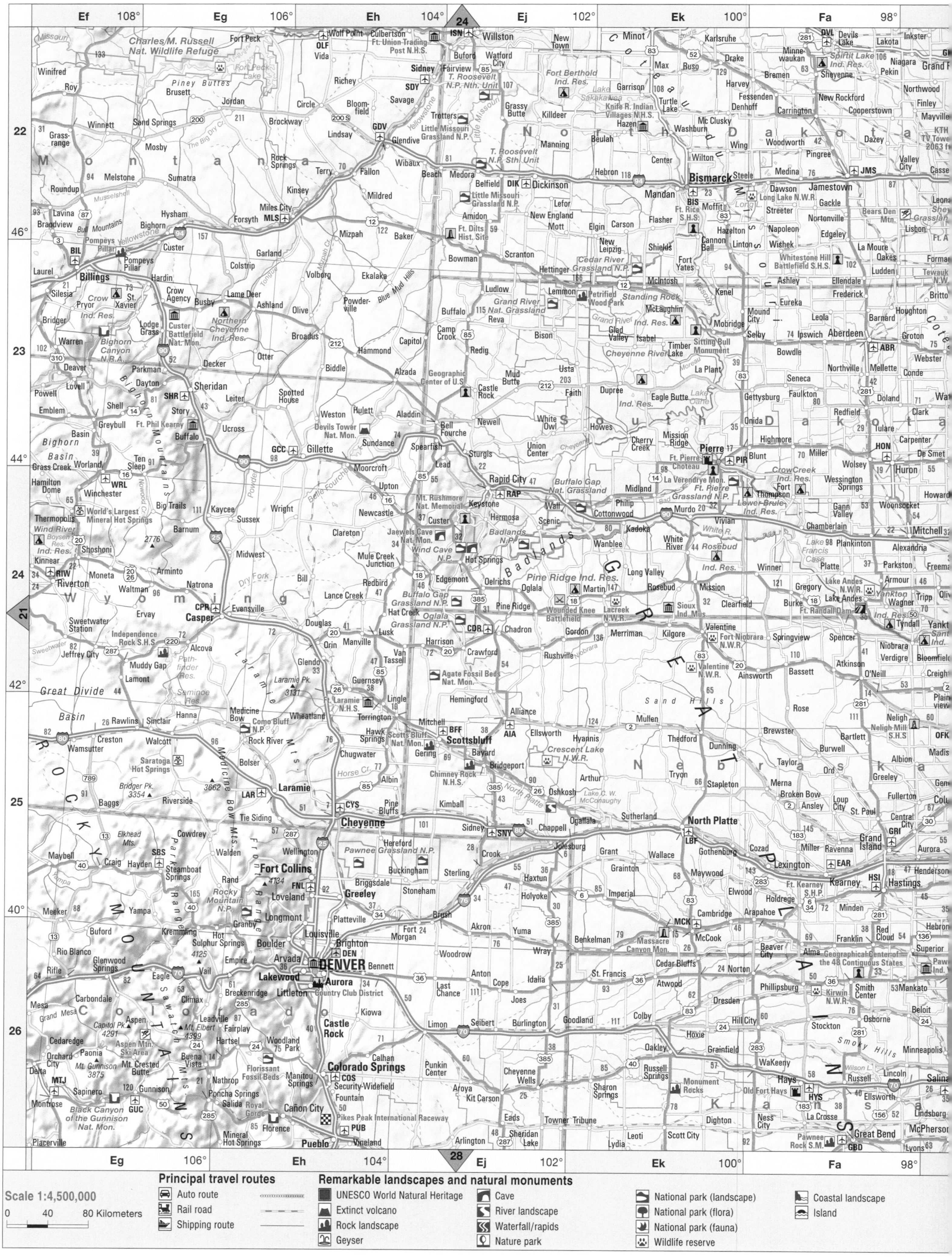

Scale 1:4,500,000
0 40 80 Kilometers

Principal travel routes
- Auto route
- Rail road
- Shipping route

Remarkable landscapes and natural monuments
- UNESCO World Natural Heritage
- Extinct volcano
- Rock landscape
- Geyser
- Cave
- River landscape
- Waterfall/rapids
- Nature park
- National park (landscape)
- National park (flora)
- National park (fauna)
- Wildlife reserve
- Coastal landscape
- Island

asin of the 3,725 meters long **Mis-ouri River**. The Missouri River begins in ontana and there are several large ams along the river's path.
he **Great Lakes**, divided between the nited States and Canada, are the largest roup of freshwater lakes in the world. he five Great Lakes cover a combined tal of 245,000 square kilometers. **Chi-ago** on Lake Michigan is the largest city the Midwest and one of the most important economic centers on the continent. America's Midwest has large deposits of mineral resources including iron ore, oil, and coal. The most important river in the region is the **Mississippi**, the continent's longest river. The basin of the Mississippi River is a fertile region that is home to countless farms. Near **St. Louis**, the Mississippi River joins with the Illinois and Missouri Rivers. The Midwest has experienced several major floods in the recent decades. Many dams and levees have been built throughout the region to protect against floods which can cause major damage to homes and agricultural areas.
Some of the most important historic sites in the United States are in the Midwest, including sites connected to the history of the region's Native Americans. **Wounded Knee** in South Dakota was the site of one of the most controversial events in the region's history. On December 29,1890, at least 150 Lakota (Sioux) men, women, and children lost their lives in a clash with the United States army.
The Midwest has four distinct seasons characterized by hot summers and very cold winters. Rainfall is heaviest in the eastern sections of the Midwest and significantly less in the western parts of the region. Major droughts hit the region at least once every 25 years.

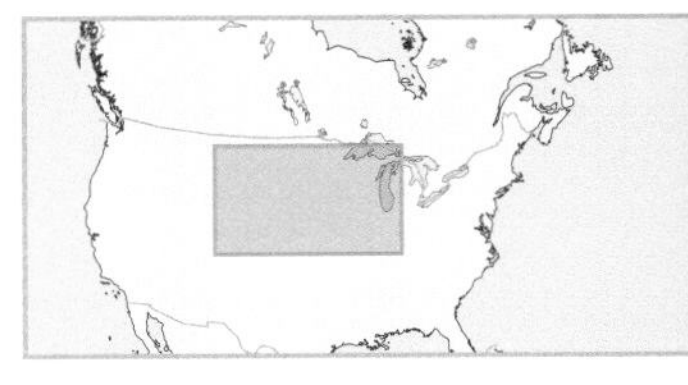

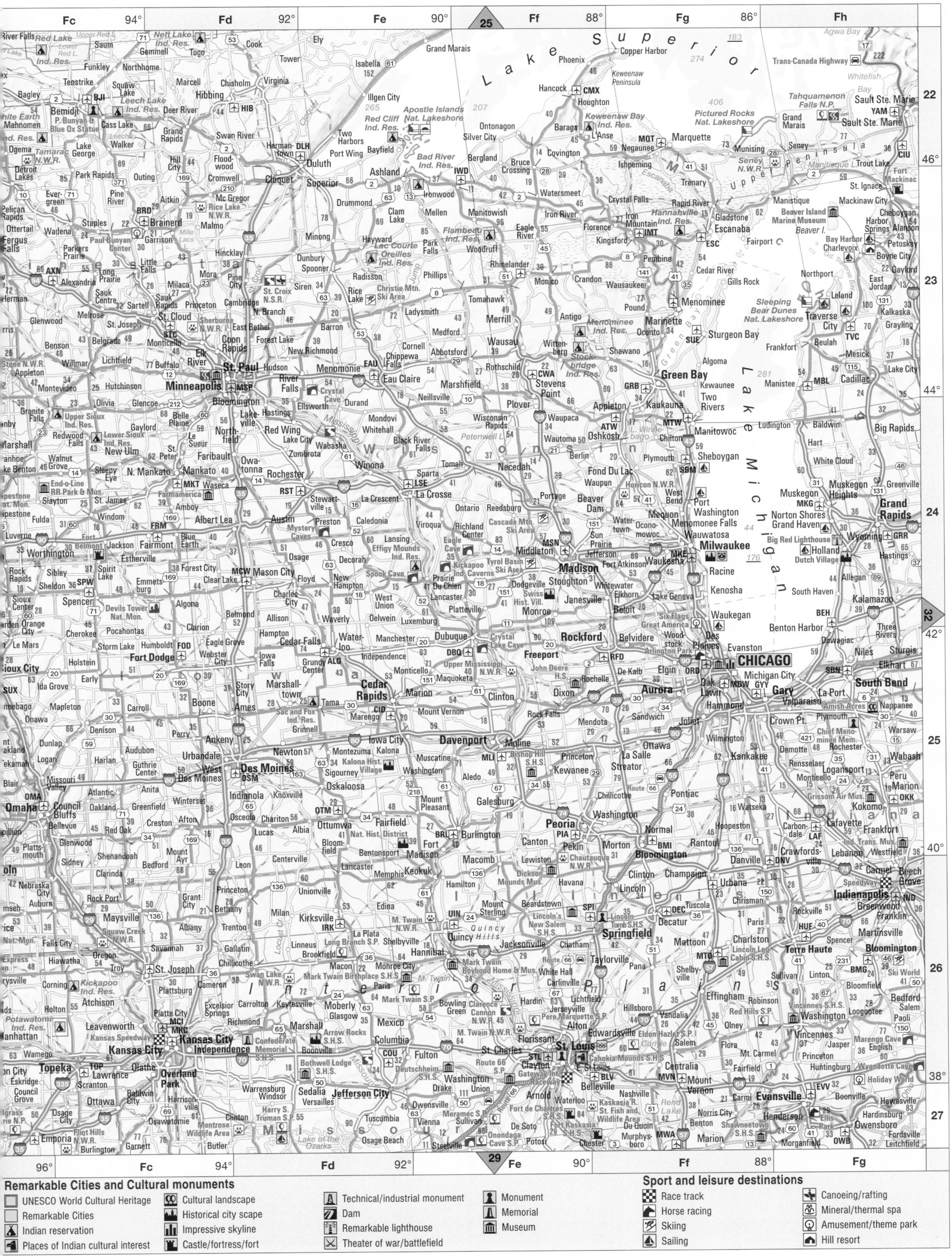

Minneapolis-St. Paul "Twin Cities" on the Mississipi River – Minnesota Capitol building (photo) in St. Paul – skyscrapers in Minneapolis – St. Anthony Falls **Fd23**

Milwaukee Largest city in Wisconsin – Performing Arts Center – historic district with 19th century architecture **Fg24**

Holland, Michigan Founded by Dutch settlers – Dutch Village theme park – Big Red Lighthouse (photo) **Fg24**

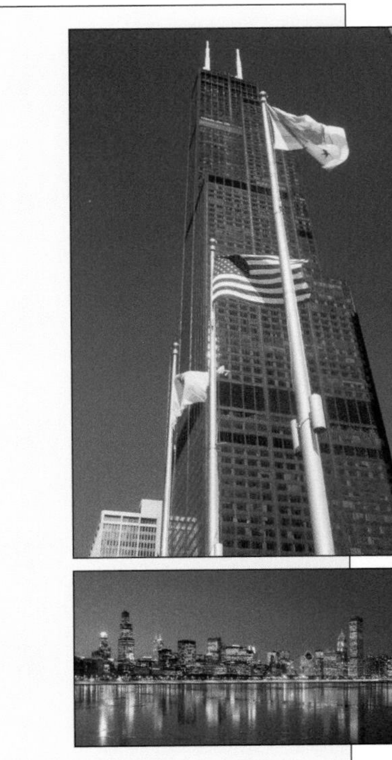

Chicago The third largest city in the United States. Chicago's metro population exceeds eight million. The city has an impressive skyline including the Sears Tower (top photo). The Art Institute of Chicago has a famous collection of art. Other attractions: beaches on the shore of Lake Michigan and an active jazz scene. **Fg25**

St. Louis Largest city in Missouri – The Jefferson National Expansion Memorial with the Gateway Arch (photo) **Fe26**

Remarkable Cities and Cultural monuments

- UNESCO World Cultural Heritage
- Remarkable Cities
- Indian reservation
- Places of Indian cultural interest
- Cultural landscape
- Historical city scape
- Impressive skyline
- Castle/fortress/fort
- Technical/industrial monument
- Dam
- Remarkable lighthouse
- Theater of war/battlefield
- Monument
- Memorial
- Museum

Sport and leisure destinations

- Race track
- Horse racing
- Skiing
- Sailing
- Canoeing/rafting
- Mineral/thermal spa
- Amusement/theme park
- Hill resort

The basin of the Mississippi-Missouri River covers a large section of the mainland United States. The basin stretches over the territory of eleven states: New Mexico and Colorado in the west; Tennessee, Alabama and Mississippi in the east; Louisiana and Texas in the south; Oklahoma and Arkansas in the basin's center; and Kansas and Missouri in the north. To the west of the basin rise the **Rocky Mountains** with peaks over 4,000 meters high. To the east of the basin a the heavily forested **Appalachi Mountains**.

The flat plains extending from the ea and west banks of the Mississippi Riv are called the **Interior Plains**.

Farther west is a region called the Inte ior Highlands encompassing the Oza

White Sands National Monument in New Mexico Eg2

Durango Silverton Narrow Gauge Railroad Historic steam engine train – travels between Durango and Silverton in southern Colorado Eg27

Rio Grande Gorge Scenic deep canyon (200 meters) – west of Taos, New Mexico – canoe and paddle boat tours Eh27

Taos Pueblo This Native American settlement in the Rio Grande Valley has been inhabited for almost 1,000 years – UNESCO world heritage site – historic Spanish mission Eh27

Bandelier National Museum West of Santa Fe – ruins of Anasazi Native American cave settlements Eg28

Santa Fe Capital city of New Mexico – located at 2,100 meters above sea level – artist colonies – historic adobe buildings – numerous art galleries and craft shops along Canyon Road Eh28

White Sands Space Harbor NASA training area for space shuttle pilots – White Sands Missile Range Museum has a collection of rockets Eg29

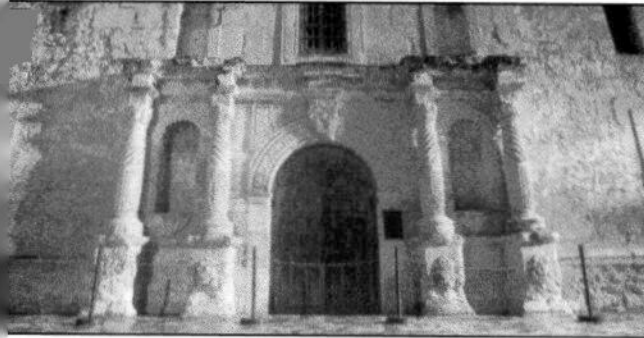

San Antonio Large city in Texas with strong Hispanic-Mexican heritage – the Alamo: originally a Spanish mission built in 1755 and the site of a historic battle, "craddle of Texan independence" Fa31

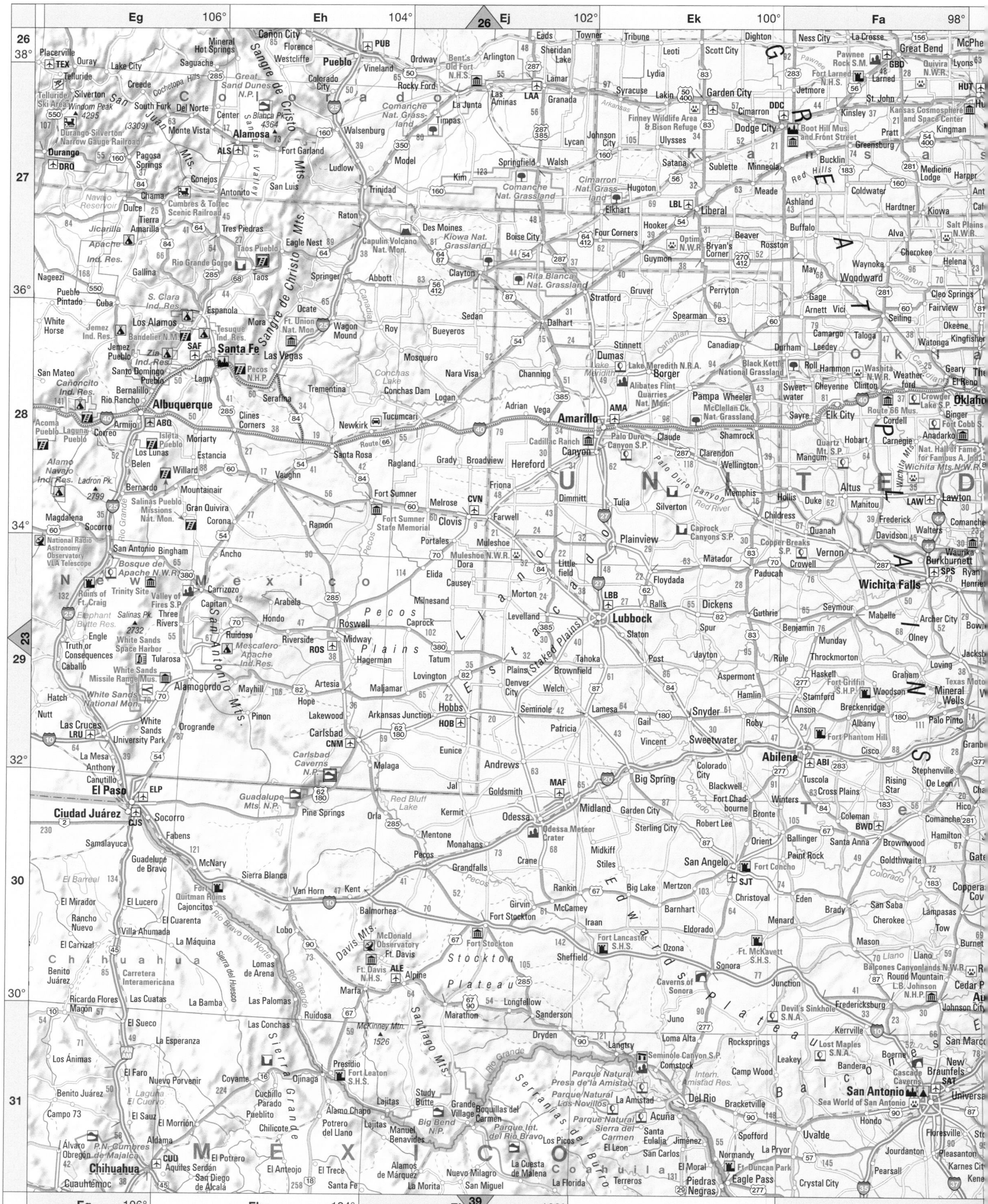

Scale 1:4,500,000

0 40 80 Kilometers

Principal travel routes

- Auto route
- Rail road
- Shipping route

Remarkable landscapes and natural monuments

- UNESCO World Natural Heritage
- Rock landscape
- Ravine/canyon
- Extinct volcano
- Cave
- River landscape
- Waterfall/rapids
- Desert
- Nature park
- National park (landscape)
- National park (flora)
- National park (fauna)
- Wildlife reserve
- Coastal landscape

ateau and the **Ouachita Mountains.** his region is heavily forested and has eep river valleys. It is crossed by many aterways including the Arkansas, anadian, and Pecos Rivers. The **Rio rande River** flows over 2,480 kilome-rs from its source in Colorado to the ulf of Mexico. East of El Paso the Rio rande forms a natural border between exas and Mexico. outh of the Mississippi-Missouri Basin lie the extremely flat and low-lying **Gulf Coast plains** which extend to the coast. This region is very humid and covered by extensive swamplands. The numerous Pueblos of **New Mexico** give visitors the chance to discover the history and culture of local Native Americans. Many of the region's Native Americans also welcome visitors to their traditional ceremonies and festivals. **Oklahoma** was once called "Indian Territory" and it was in this territory that most of the southeastern Native Americans who were expelled during the Trail of Tears were forcibly settled. There are several memorials in the state dedicated to this sad chapter in American history. For many people around the world **Texas** is still a land of cowboys and vast empty plains. Nowadays, many Texans live in large modern cities such as Dallas, San Antonio, and Houston. The state is also a major center for several high tech industries and the home of NASA's Lyndon B. Johnson Space Center in Houston. The Gulf Coast states – Mississippi, Alabama, and Louisiana – contain many historic sites including restored antebellum plantations and relics from the Spanish and French colonial eras. New Orleans, at the mouth of the Mississippi, is a vibrant city with well-preserved Spanish colonial architecture and a distinct local culture.

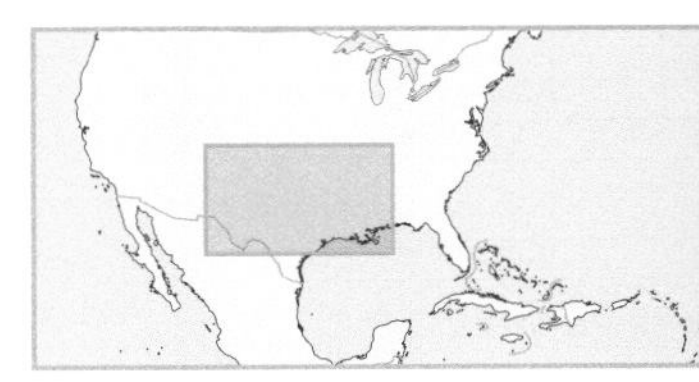

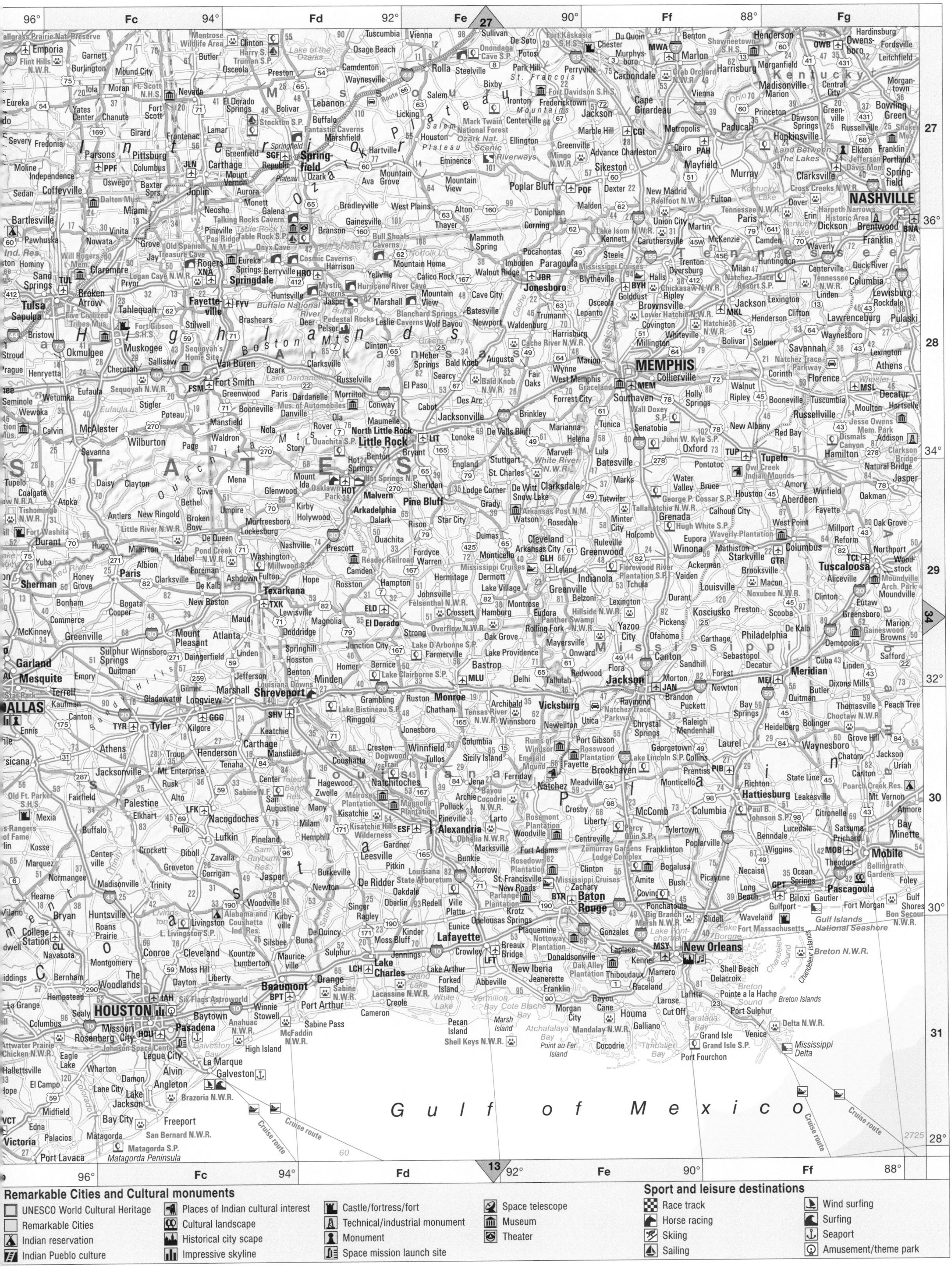

Dallas Second largest city in Texas – beautiful modern skyline – John F. Kennedy Memorial **Fb29**

Houston Important center for the oil and petrochemical industries – modern skyscrapers – Six Flags Astroworld – Lyndon B. Johnson Space Center (NASA) **Fc31**

Natchez Port city on the Mississippi – antebellum houses – Natchez African American History Museum **Fe30**

Oak Alley Plantation Restored sugar plantation on the Mississippi River – features a bed and breakfast – several movies were filmed in the area **Fe31**

New Orleans Port city in the Mississippi Delta region – lively jazz scene – birthplace of Louis Armstrong – French Quarter – Mardi Gras **Fe31**

The Mississippi River The longest river in North America. The Mississippi flows south from its source in Minnesota into the Gulf of Mexico. Tourists can take steamboat tours up the river and enjoy its landscapes. **FfFe27/31**

Remarkable Cities and Cultural monuments

- UNESCO World Cultural Heritage
- Remarkable Cities
- Indian reservation
- Indian Pueblo culture
- Places of Indian cultural interest
- Cultural landscape
- Historical city scape
- Impressive skyline
- Castle/fortress/fort
- Technical/industrial monument
- Monument
- Space mission launch site
- Space telescope
- Museum
- Theater

Sport and leisure destinations

- Race track
- Horse racing
- Skiing
- Sailing
- Wind surfing
- Surfing
- Seaport
- Amusement/theme park

Newfoundland, Canada's easternmost province, consists of two distinct regions – the large island of Newfoundland and the mainland region of **Labrador**. Newfoundland is home to the majority of the province's inhabitants. Most of the island has a maritime climate, while sparsely populated Labrador has a subarctic climate. Both areas are home to large forests and crystal clear lakes. The province of **New Brunswick** encompasses

the northernmost sections of the App
lachian Mountains. To the west of Ne
Brunswick lies the **Saint Lawren**
River which flows north into the Gulf
Saint Lawrence. The Saint Lawrence
3,000 kilometers long and is border
by fertile plains on both sides. The riv
is connected to the Great Lakes by

Lighthouse on Cape Enrage in New Brunswick **Gg**

Labrador Heavily forested, sparsely populated peninsula – long cold winters – mostly tundra **Gc19**

Les Laurentides Popular weekend destination – winter sports – abundant wildlife – beautiful autumn foliage **Ge22**

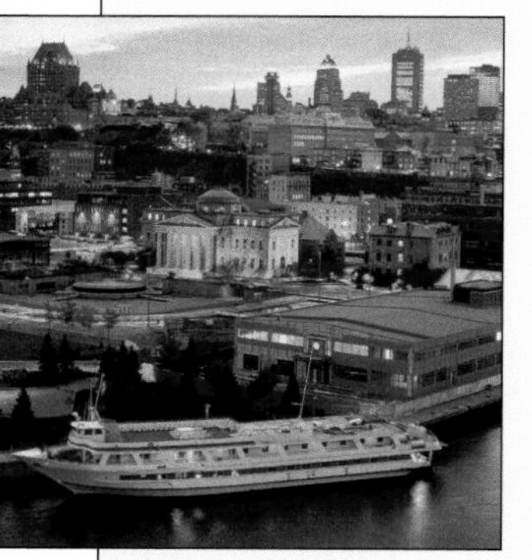

Québec City French is the dominant language in Québec's capital and second largest city. Québec City is divided into two sections. The lower town contains the military museum Musee du Fort and the Basilique-cathedrale Notre Dame built in 1647. The Upper Town contains the picturesque Petit-Champlain district. The two sections of the city are connected by stairways and a funicular. **Ge22**

Montréal Canada's second largest city – population 3.5 million – interesting mix of architectural styles, including modern skyscrapers and Victorian homes **Gd23**

Acadia National Park National park in Maine – oldest national park in the eastern United States – Cadillac Mountain (466 meters) **Gf23**

La Verendrye Nature Reserve Nature reserve covering 13,615 km² – numerous lakes and rivers – bears and elk herds **Gb22**

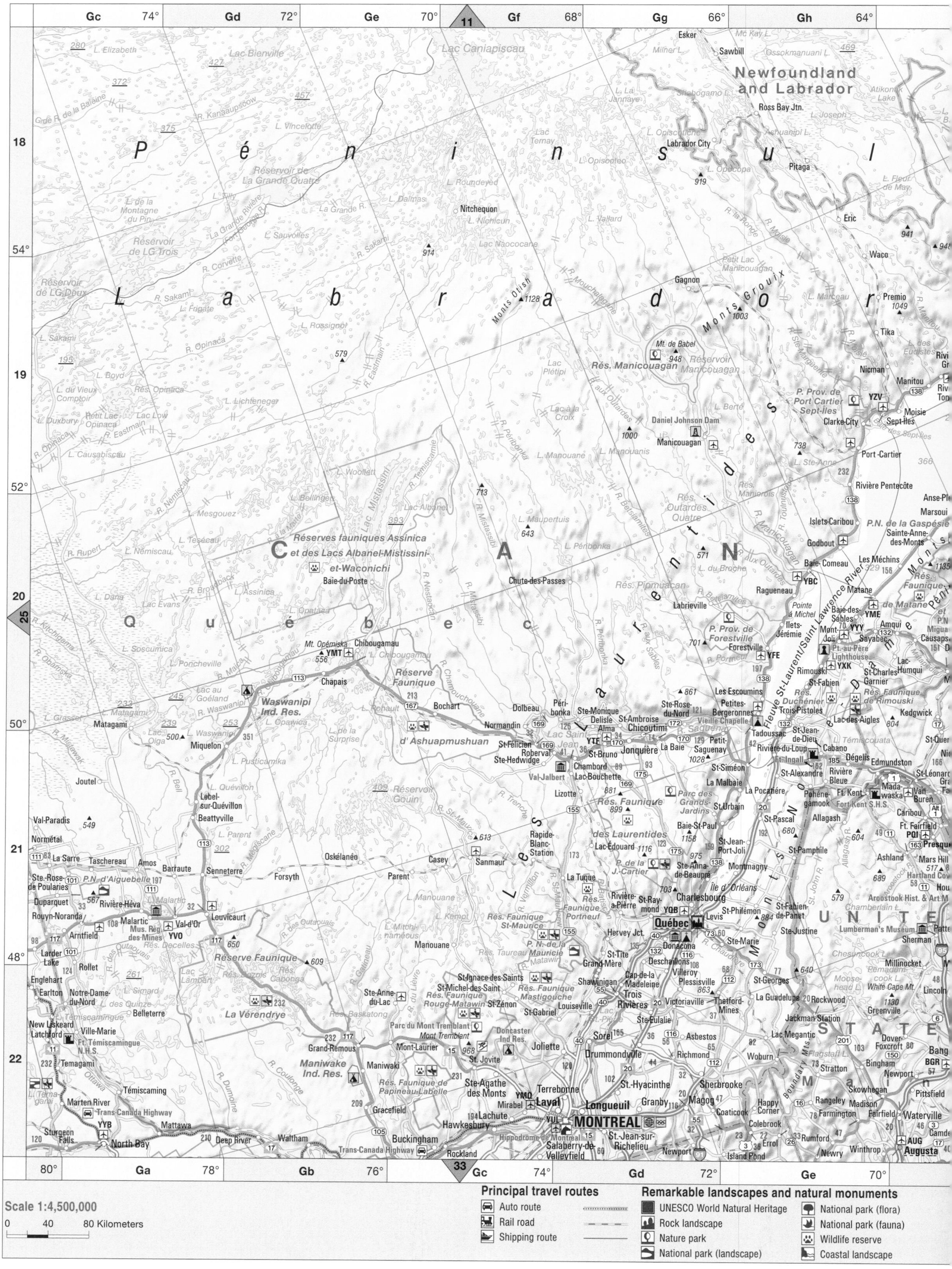

Scale 1:4,500,000
0 40 80 Kilometers

Principal travel routes
- Auto route
- Rail road
- Shipping route

Remarkable landscapes and natural monuments
- UNESCO World Natural Heritage
- Rock landscape
- Nature park
- National park (landscape)
- National park (flora)
- National park (fauna)
- Wildlife reserve
- Coastal landscape

eries of canals. **Québec** has a land area f 1.5 million km² and is the largest of anada's ten provinces. The province orders Ontario in the west, Newfound-nd and Labrador in the east, and New runswick in the southeast. Québec also hares borders with the U.S states of laine, New Hampshire, Vermont, and ew York.
anada's Atlantic provinces have long old winters and the region gets heavy precipitation during the entire year. The region's climate is greatly influenced by ocean currents and winds from the continent's interior regions. Most of central and southern Québec has a continental climate with hot summers, cold winters, and abundant rainfall. September and October are the best months to visit the region. During these months visitors can enjoy the beautiful autumn colors of the region's forests.
Eastern Canada comprises large undeveloped regions with abundant wildlife including large caribou and bear populations. Many aquatic birds inhabit the region's coasts and whales can be seen in the Saint Lawrence River.
Because of the climate, more than half of the Canadian population lives in the southeastern regions of the country. Like the rest of the population, most of Canada's 970,000 indigenous people live in the country's eastern provinces.
The state of **Maine** shares a border with the Canadian provinces of New Brunswick and Québec. There are countless small bays and islands along the jagged coast of Maine. Maine is the most sparsely populated and least developed of the New England states. The state has an abundance of wildlife including caribous and beavers. Maine's capital city, Augusta, is one of the smallest state capitals

Signal Hill 170-meter-high cliff in the harbor of Newfoundland's provincial capital, St. John's – Cabot Tower (photo) lies atop the coastal cliff – interesting radio and Morse code museum **Hd22**

Gros-Morne National Park Mountainous national park with fjords – fascinating wildlife **Hb21**

Avalon Peninsula Peninsula in western Newfoundland – location of the provincial capital, St. John's – numerous fishing villages and large bays **Hd22**

Prince Edward Island Hilly island in the Gulf of Saint Lawrence – the smallest Canadian province – lakes and attractive villages – pink sandy beaches in the south **Gj22**

Cape Breton Island Narrow peninsula in New Brunswick – mild climate – beautiful rugged landscape – distinctive local culture – Cabot Trail **Gk22/23**

Fortress of Louisbourg On Cape Breton Island – founded by the French during the colonial era – reconstructed fort with museum **Gk23**

Lunenburg Picturesque port city south of Halifax in Nova Scotia – Victorian architecture and brightly painted houses – UNESCO world heritage site – fisheries museum **Gh23**

Remarkable Cities and Cultural monuments

- UNESCO World Cultural Heritage
- Remarkable Cities
- Places of Christian cultural interest
- Indian reservation
- Historical city scape
- Castle/fortress/fort
- Technical/industrial monument
- Remarkable lighthouse
- Remarkable bridge
- Monument
- Museum
- World exhibition
- Olympics

Sport and leisure destinations

- Horse racing
- Skiing
- Sailing
- Canoeing/rafting

The five **Great Lakes** were formed at the end of the last ice age when massive glaciers carved out huge basins in the Earth's surface. When the glaciers melted these basins filled with water and formed the Great Lakes. Lake Superior is the largest and deepest of the Great Lakes with a surface area of 82,350 km^2 and a maximum depth of 200 meters. Lake Erie, with an average depth of 62 meters, is the shallowest of the Great

Lakes and drains into Lake Ontario at t spectacular Niagara Falls (60 mete high). Niagara Falls consists of thr seperate falls and together the falls a one of the most visited natural attra tions on the continent. With a combin surface area of 245,000 km^2, the Gre Lakes are the largest group of fres

A beautiful sunset above Lake Superior **FeFh21/2**

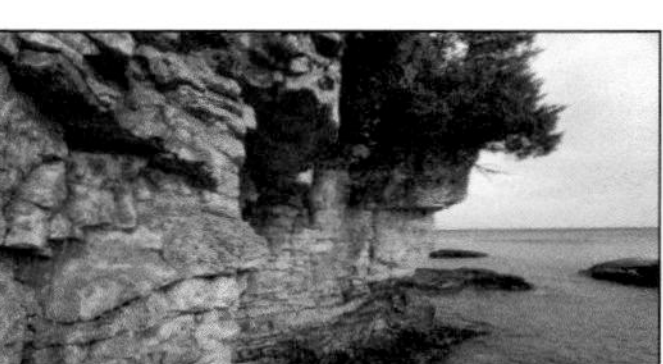

Bruce Peninsula National Park 100-kilometer-long peninsula northwest of Toronto – beaches – Bruce Trail **Fk23**

Detroit Largest city in Michigan – center of the American automobile industry – Henry and Edsel Ford Auditorium – downtown with the civic center and philharmonic – Renaissance Center **Fj24**

Cleveland Rock and Roll Hall of Fame (music history museum) – art deco shopping center, Tower City – Playhouse Square comprises four theaters **Fk25**

Toronto Canada's largest city, located on Lake Ontario – population 4.9 million – CN Tower – the financial district has art galleries and skyscrapers **Ga24**

Niagara Falls Falls descend from the Niagara River – in Ontario and New York – three separate falls: American Falls, Horseshoe Falls, and Bridal Veil Falls **Ga24**

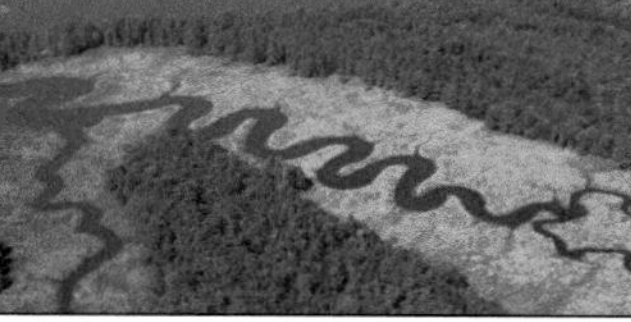

Allegany State Park Conservation area, east of Lake Erie – heavily forested area – beautiful meandering rivers **Ga24**

Philadelphia Largest city in Pennsylvania – population 1.7 million – historic sites including the Independence Hall in Independence Historical Park – excellent art collections in the Philadelphia Museum of Art and Franklin Institute **Gc26**

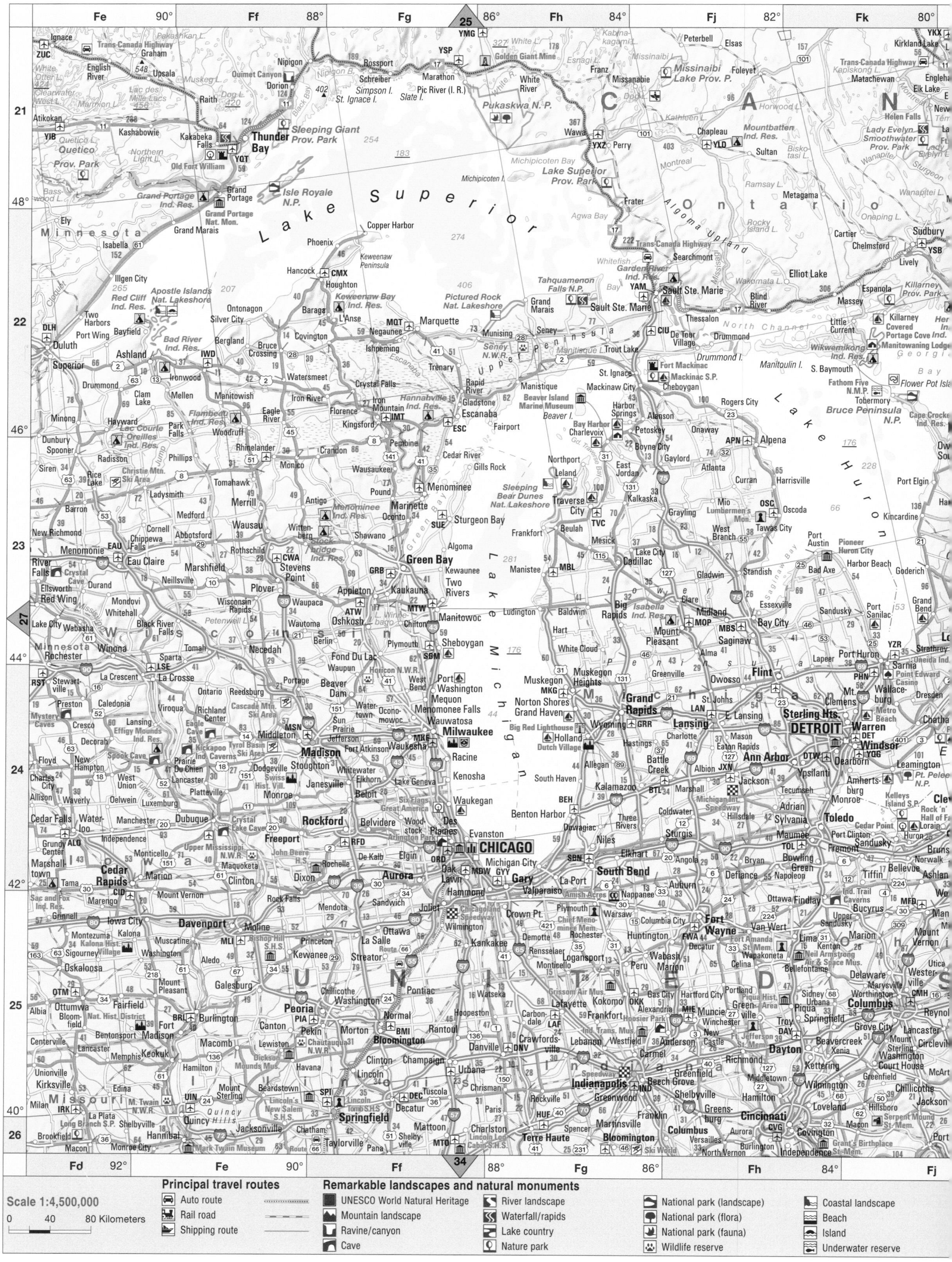

Scale 1:4,500,000

0 40 80 Kilometers

Principal travel routes
- Auto route
- Rail road
- Shipping route

Remarkable landscapes and natural monuments
- UNESCO World Natural Heritage
- Mountain landscape
- Ravine/canyon
- Cave
- River landscape
- Waterfall/rapids
- Lake country
- Nature park
- National park (landscape)
- National park (flora)
- National park (fauna)
- Wildlife reserve
- Coastal landscape
- Beach
- Island
- Underwater reserve

vater lakes in the world. The Great Lakes, which lie along the American-Canadian order, also represent the world's larest supply of potable water.
he **Appalachian Mountains** stretch om the southeastern United States to ne Canadian province of Québec. The nountains form a natural barrier between ne Eastern Seaboard of the United States and the Midwest. During the ice ges, the Appalachians were reshaped by glaciers which left the mountains shorter and rounder.
The climate of New York and **New England** is greatly influenced by ocean currents and winds. This region has hot summers with temperatures regularly exceeding 30° Celsius and cold winters with temperatures below -10° Celsius. More than 70% of New England's land is covered by deciduous forests and during autumn, the region's foliage displays bright fiery colors that attract visitors from around the world. The coniferous forests to the north of the Great Lakes are darker and less accessible than their New England counterparts. These forests are home to abundant wildlife including large elk herds and bear populations. The western Appalachians have rich coal deposits and the area around the Great Lakes is fertile and well suited for large-scale agriculture.The Great Lakes Region and the surrounding Midwestern states are responsible for most of America's grain production. The Saint Lawrence seaway is a series of canals that connect the Great Lakes to the Atlantic. The seaway was completed in 1959 and is administered by the United States and Canada. The Northeastern United States and the Great Lakes region comprise one of the world's wealthiest and most economically productive regions.

Boston New England's largest city – historic architecture – Freedom Trail – Quincy Market – panoramic views from the J. Hancock Tower **Ge24**

Martha's Vineyard Island south of Cape Cod – beaches – Victorian architecture – popular weekend destination **Ge25**

Nantucket Popular tourist destination – major whaling port in the 18th century – beaches and historic architecture **Ge25**

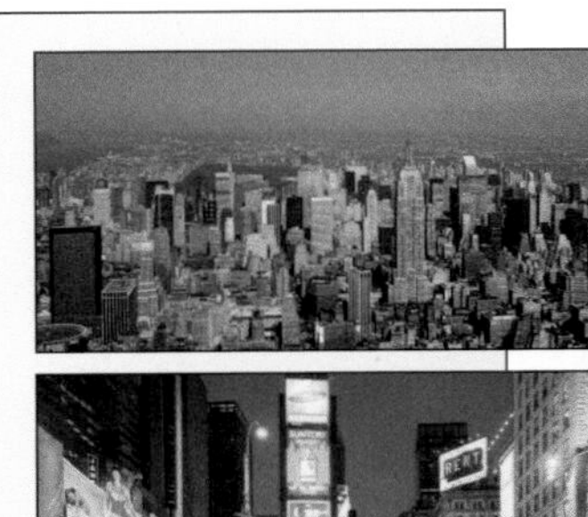

New York City Largest city in the United States with a population over eight million. Visitors can enjoy views of the city's skyline from the top of the Empire State Building. The Metropolitan Museum, Museum of Modern Art and the Guggenheim contain world class art collections. **GcGd25**

Atlantic City Gaming center in New Jersey – large casino-hotel resorts – the famous Boardwalk **Gc26**

Washington D.C. Capital of the United States – home to important government buildings including the White House and the Capitol building (photo) – The Smithsonian Institute is one of the world's most impressive collections of museums – National Gallery of Art **Gb26**

Remarkable Cities and Cultural monuments

- UNESCO World Cultural Heritage
- Remarkable Cities
- Indian reservation
- Places of Indian cultural interest
- Cultural landscape
- Historical city scape
- Impressive skyline
- Castle/fortress/fort
- Technical/industrial monument
- Monument
- Museum
- Olympics

Sport and leisure destinations

- Race track
- Horse racing
- Skiing
- Sailing
- Wind surfing
- Surfing
- Canoeing/rafting
- Deep-sea fishing
- Beach resort
- Amusement/theme park
- Casino
- Hill resort

Southern States

In the United State, the southeastern region of the country is commonly referred to as **"the South."** Next to New England the South is the American region with the clearest identity. Around the world people associate the South with images of old cotton plantations, southern gentry and the region's history of racial divisions. The South usually refers to the southeastern states between Texas and the District of Columbia. To the south of

the region lies the Gulf of Mexico and t the east, the Atlantic Ocean. The coas lines in the region are uneven and cor tain numerous bays, river deltas, barrie islands, and large natural harbors such a **Chesapeake Bay** in Virginia. The Gu Coast is a humid area with many swamps bayous, and river deltas. The flat water

A colorful "Indian summer" in the mountains of North Carolina **Fk2**

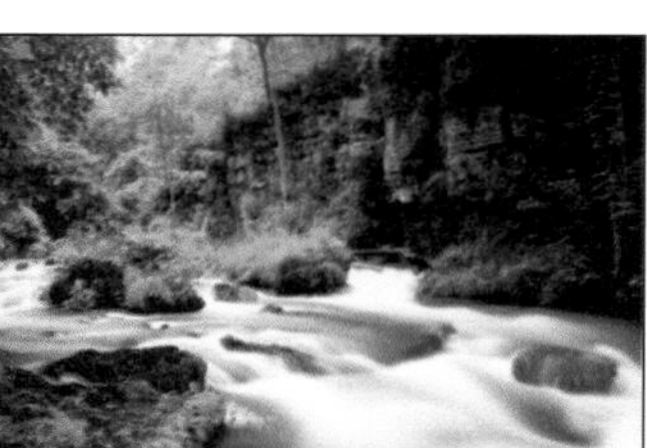

Mark Twain National Forest Protected forest in southern Missouri – hiking and bike trails, horse riding, and canoeing **Fe27**

Table Rock State Park On the northern shore of Table Rock Lake, a reservoir on the White River – camping areas **Fd27**

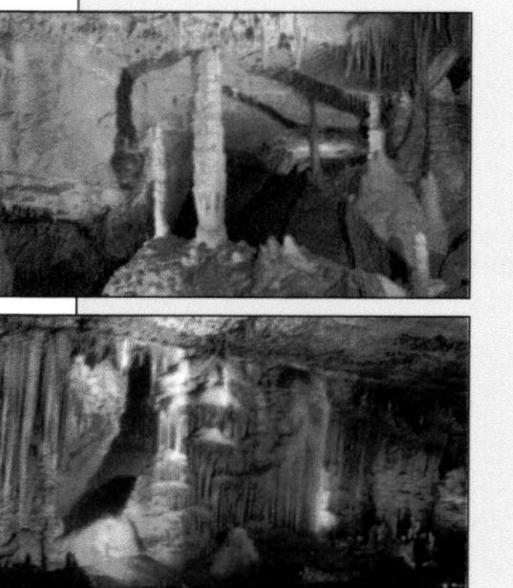

Ozark Plateau An upland region mostly in Arkansas and Missouri; partially in Kansas and Oklahoma. There are around 1,500 limestone caves in the region. **FdFe27**

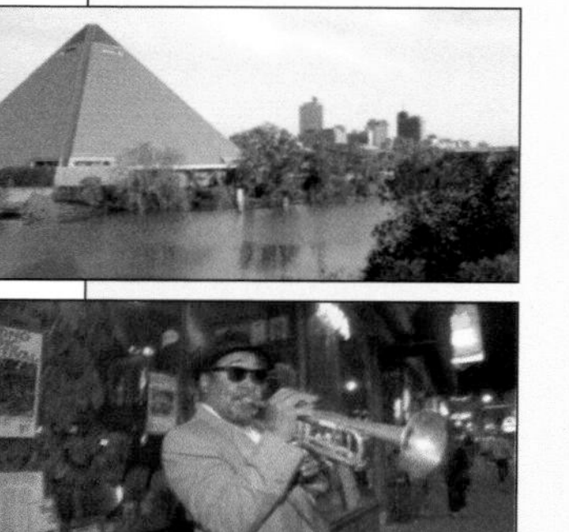

Memphis The Memphis Pyramid (top photo) is the most famous landmark of the city's skyline. The city has strong musical traditions. In addition to its famous connection to Blues, the city is also home to Graceland and Beagle Street (bottom photo) contains numerous live music venues. **Ff28**

Nashville Capital of Tennessee – population 500,000 – center of the country music industry – Country Music Hall of Fame and the Grand Ole Opry **Fg27**

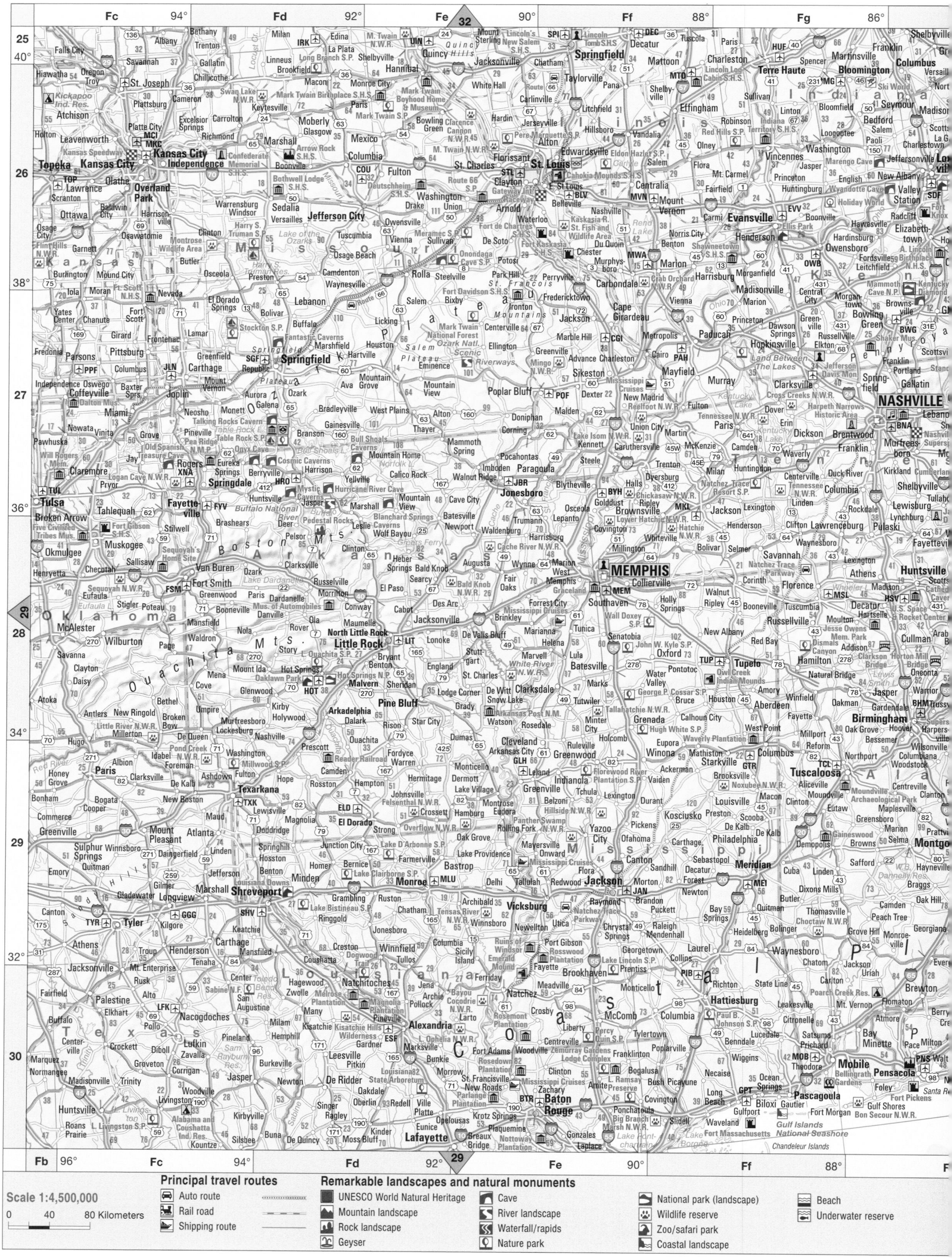

Scale 1:4,500,000

0 40 80 Kilometers

Principal travel routes

- Auto route
- Rail road
- Shipping route

Remarkable landscapes and natural monuments

- UNESCO World Natural Heritage
- Mountain landscape
- Rock landscape
- Geyser
- Cave
- River landscape
- Waterfall/rapids
- Nature park
- National park (landscape)
- Wildlife reserve
- Zoo/safari park
- Coastal landscape
- Beach
- Underwater reserve

ains along the Gulf Coast extend up to
)0 kilometers into the region's interior.
he **Mississippi River** is the longest river
North America. Near St. Louis, the Illi-
ois and Missouri Rivers merge into the
lississippi and the river flows into the
ulf of Mexico at New Orleans.
he **Appalachian Mountains** extend
rough the interior of the South. The high-
st peak in these relatively low mountains
Mount Mitchell in North Carolina which rises 2,037 meters. The southern Appalachians are home to two beautiful national parks: **Shenandoah National Park** and **Great Smoky Mountains National Park**. The 760 kilometer long **Blue Ridge Parkway** winds through the Appalachian Mountains and passes through or near many of the most beautiful areas in the region.

Many remnants of the antebellum South can still be found in the region, including historic plantations and small towns with historic districts. Some cities in the South – such as Savannah, Georgia and Charleston, South Carolina – have large collections of interesting historic architecture from the 18th and 19th centuries. Louisiana is home to the unique French influenced culture of the Cajuns who are famous for their distinct dialect and cuisine. The South boasts many sites connected to the history, culture, and arts of African-Americans, including the Martin Luther King Jr. National Historic Site in Atlanta.

Large southern cities, including Atlanta, New Orleans, and Memphis, give visitors an impression of the region's economic revival in recent decades and the rich musical heritage of the South. Jazz, Blues, Country Music, and Rock and Roll all have their roots in the Southern United States.

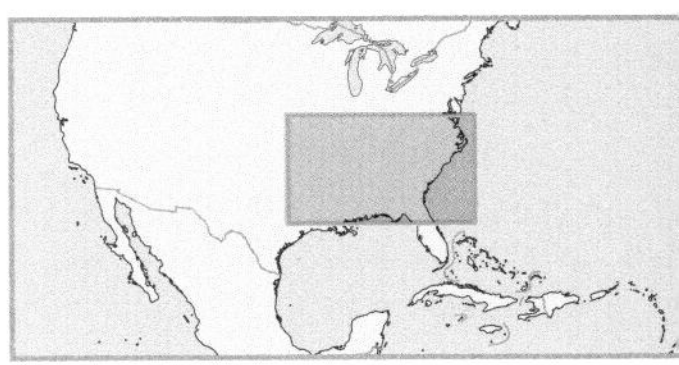

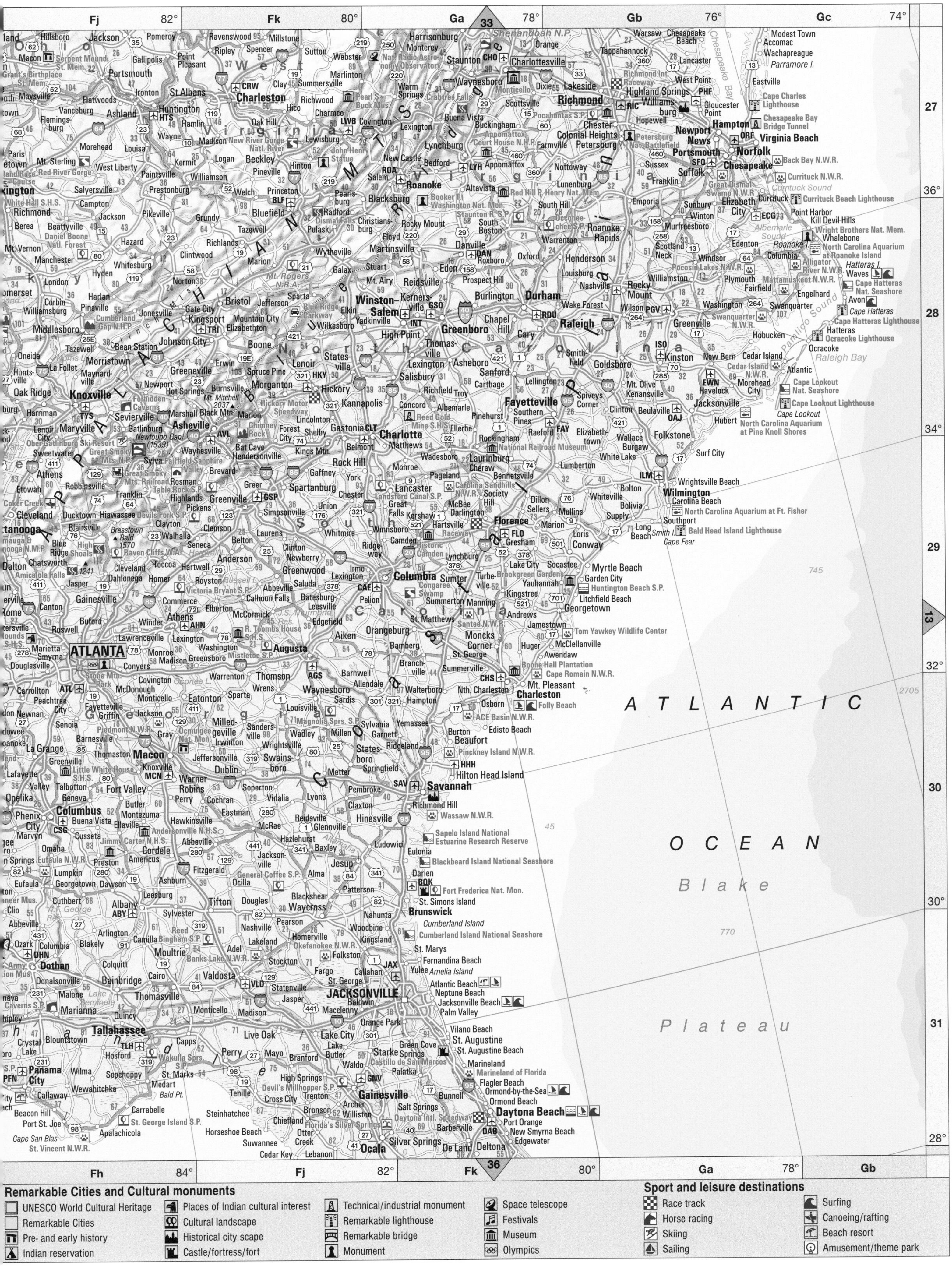

Monticello Private estate of Thomas Jefferson – designed by Jefferson in a combination of styles – world heritage site **Ga27**

Richmond Capital of Virginia and capital of the Confederacy during most of the civil war – Museum of the Confederacy **Gb27**

Great Smoky Mountains National Park In the Appalachians – world heritage site – Cherokee Native American land **Fj28**

Atlanta Georgia's state capital – site of the 1996 Olympics – CNN and Coca Cola are headquartered in the city – Martin Luther King Jr. National Historic Site **Fh29**

Charleston Historic architecture in the city center – luxury homes on East Battery (photo) – Boone Hall Plantation **Ga29**

Savannah Historic district with antebellum and Victorian architecture – tree-lined avenues – beautiful squares **Fk29**

Okefenokee National Wildlife Refuge Large swampland in Georgia – peat deposits up to 5 meters thick – alligators **Fj30**

ATLANTIC OCEAN

Blake Plateau

Remarkable Cities and Cultural monuments

- UNESCO World Cultural Heritage
- Remarkable Cities
- Pre- and early history
- Indian reservation
- Places of Indian cultural interest
- Cultural landscape
- Historical city scape
- Castle/fortress/fort
- Technical/industrial monument
- Remarkable lighthouse
- Remarkable bridge
- Monument
- Space telescope
- Festivals
- Museum
- Olympics

Sport and leisure destinations

- Race track
- Horse racing
- Skiing
- Sailing
- Surfing
- Canoeing/rafting
- Beach resort
- Amusement/theme park

Florida, Bahamas

The state of Florida consists of an 800-kilometer-long peninsula and a narrow "panhandle" in the north of the state. No part of the state is more than 100 kilometers away from the coast. To the east of Florida lies the Atlantic; to the west and south of the panhandle lies the Gulf of Mexico. The **Florida Keys** are a chain of small islands that extend along the Straits of Florida and into the **Gulf of Mexico**. The Florida Keys are connected

to the mainland by the Overseas Hig way, a series of bridges and streets. **Ke West** is the southernmost point of th mainland United States. Florida is a fl state with no major elevations; the high est areas in the state are the **Northwes Plateau** around Tallahassee and th **Central Highlands**. The state of Floric

Sandy white beach in Delnor Wiggins State Park near Naples **Fk3**

Ringling Museum of Art (Sarasota) Important collection of Flemish art including works from Peter Paul Rubens – Circus Museum **Fj32**

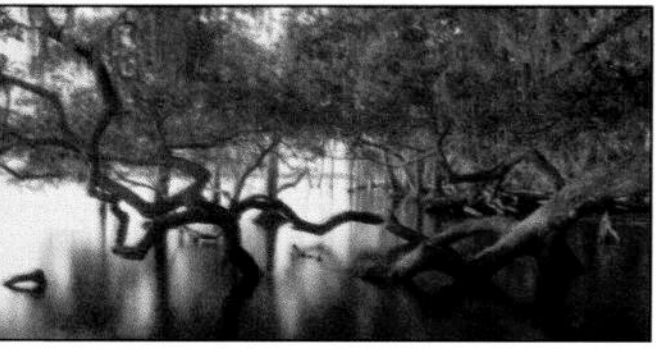

Big Cypress Seminole Indian Reservation Nature reserve with swamps and cypress forests – home to the last Florida panthers **Fk32**

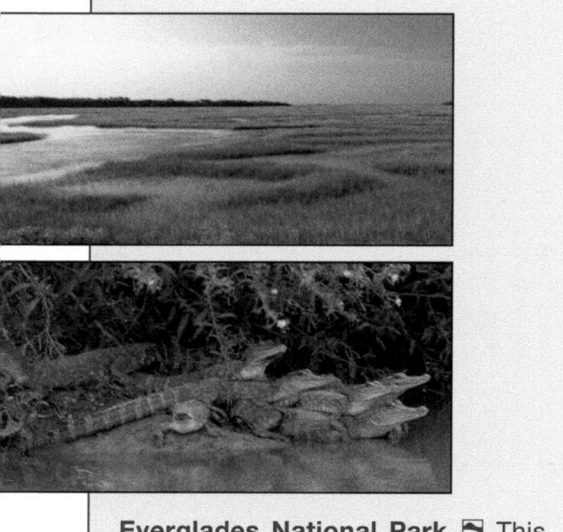

Everglades National Park This unique and delicate ecosystem covers 1.5 million acres. The Everglades are a vast flat tropical marshland covered by sawgrass and cypress trees. The national park covers only 20% of the Everglades' area. The Everglades are home to alligators, Florida panthers, and at least 300 bird species. **Fk33**

Overseas Highway This famous 180-kilometer-long highway connects the Florida Keys to the mainland **Fk33**

Key West Westernmost island of the Florida Keys – Hemingway House (museum) – Key West Aquarium on Mallory Square – Conch House in Old Town (photo) **Fk33**

St. Augustine Oldest city in the United States – historic center with Spanish colonial architecture – Castillo de San Marcos (photo) **Fk31**

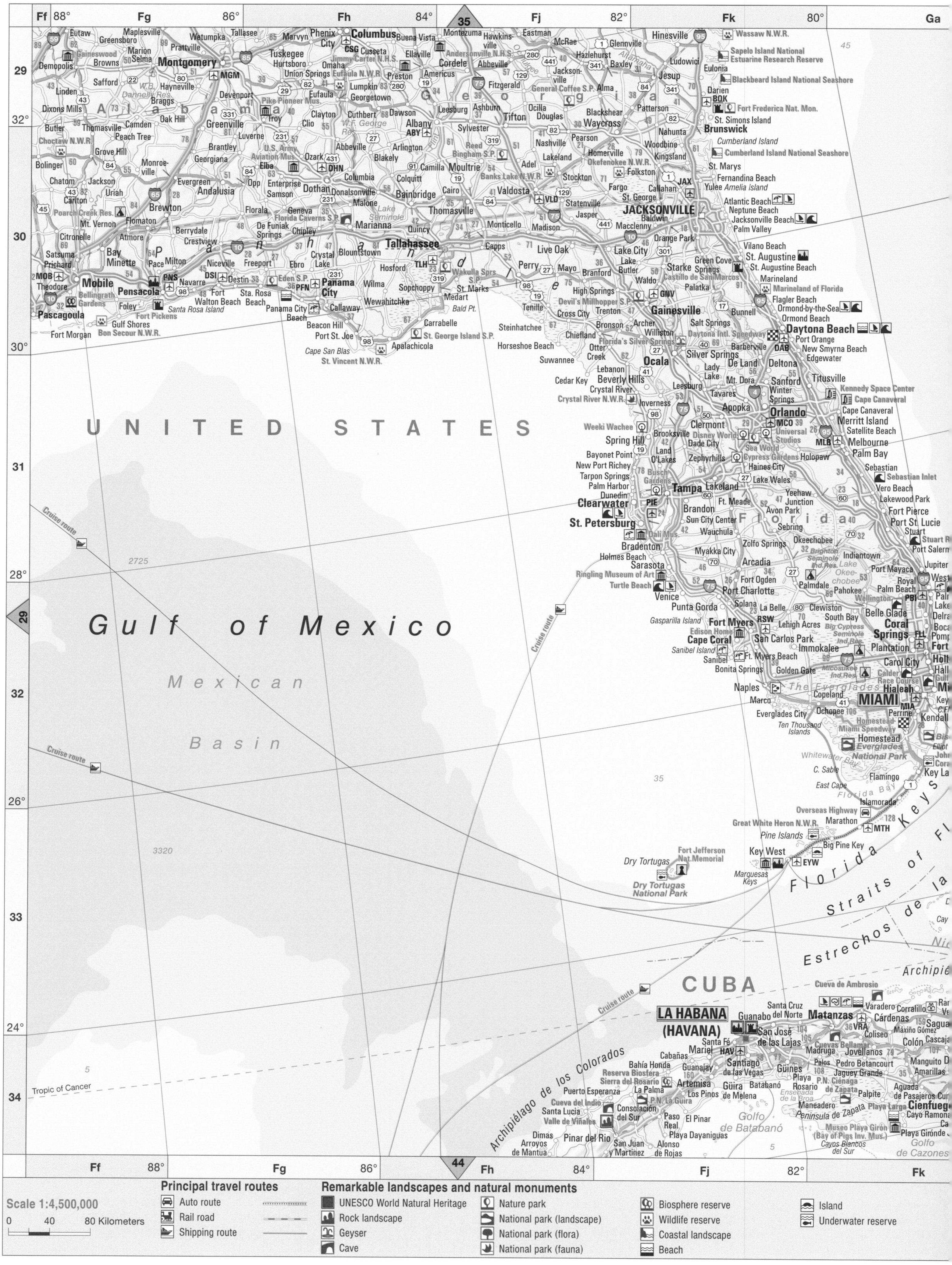

Scale 1:4,500,000

0 40 80 Kilometers

Principal travel routes

- Auto route
- Rail road
- Shipping route

Remarkable landscapes and natural monuments

- UNESCO World Natural Heritage
- Rock landscape
- Geyser
- Cave
- Nature park
- National park (landscape)
- National park (flora)
- National park (fauna)
- Biosphere reserve
- Wildlife reserve
- Coastal landscape
- Beach
- Island
- Underwater reserve

as a total area of 151,714 km² of which 1,500 km² are covered by water. Florida is home to countless lakes including Lake Okeechobee, the second rgest freshwater lake entirely in the United States. The **Everglades**, a large opical marshland with unique flora and auna, begins just south of Lake Okeechobee. Florida's coastlines total 13,000 ilometers including at least 1,800 kilometers of white sandy beaches. The **Barrier Islands** along the state's Atlantic coast are a series of islets and sandbanks that protect the coast from strong ocean waves. Many of Florida's ecosystems including the lagoons around Cape Canaveral are threatened by development. The sea turtles that gave the **Dry Tortugas** Islands their name are an endangered species like many of the state's indigenous animals.

The **Bahamas** are an island group of more than 700 islands and 2,000 islets off the southeastern coast of Florida. Because of their location, the Bahamas have a tropical climate cooled by ocean breezes. Temperatures between 28 and 33° Celsius are normal during the humid summer days. The islands get an abundance of sunshine during the entire year and most rainfall occurs between May and October.

The Bahamas have very few sources of drinkable water and there are no rivers on the islands. Because of this shortage of freshwater, the Bahamas have very few indigenous land animals. There is however an impressive variety of marine life in the surrounding waters, including large coral reefs and countless species of fish. Because of the abundant marine life and numerous shipwrecks, the Bahamas are a popular destination for recreational divers.

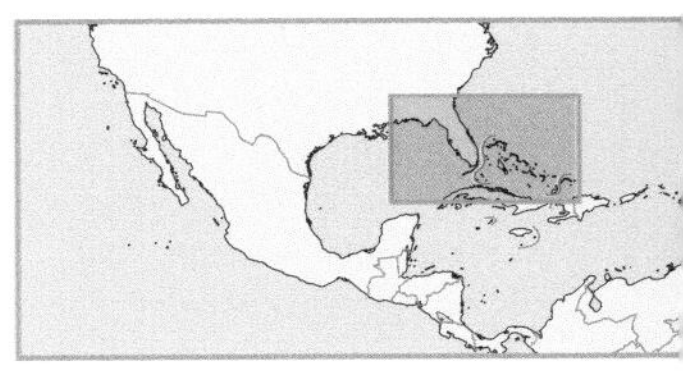

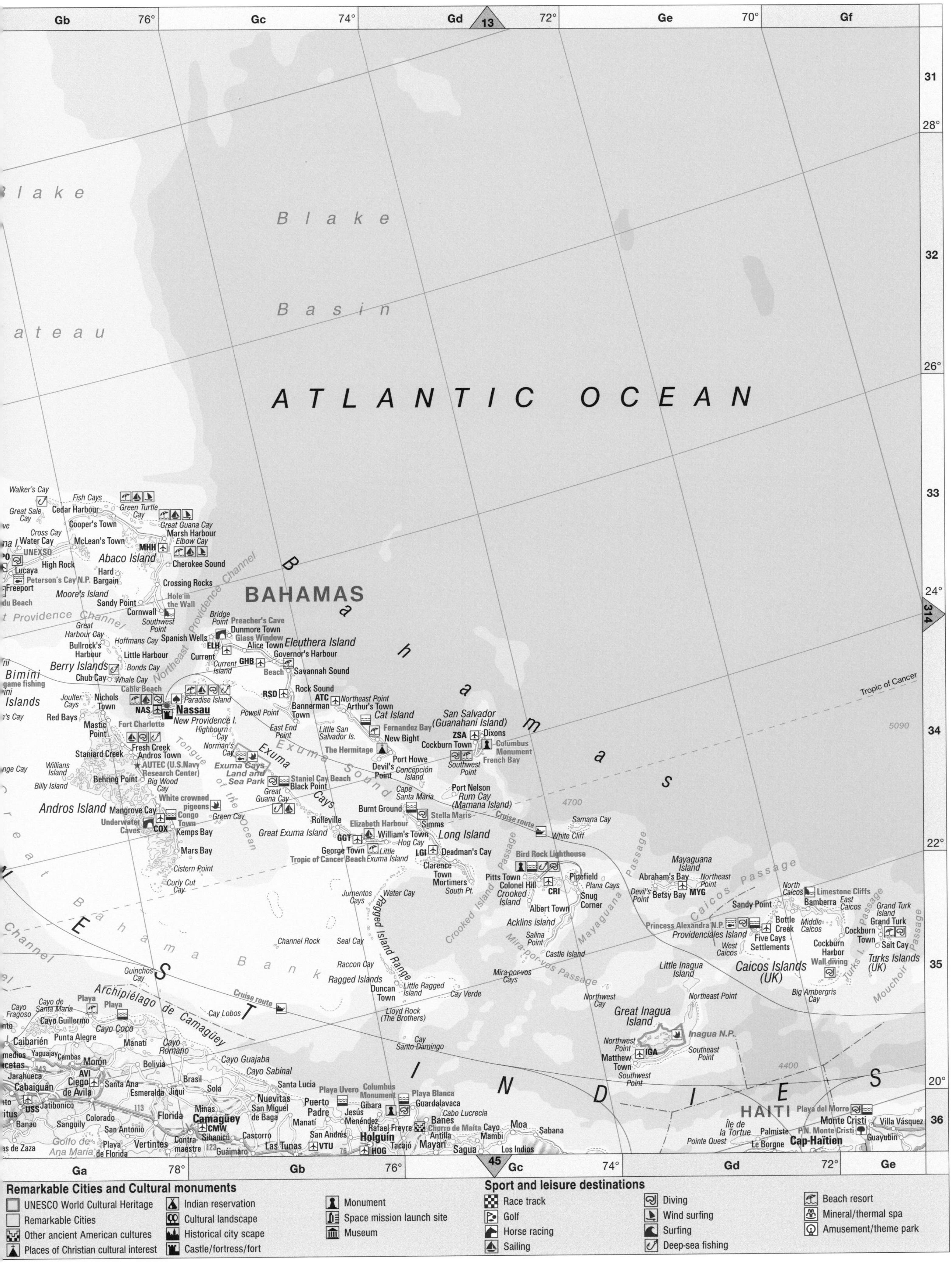

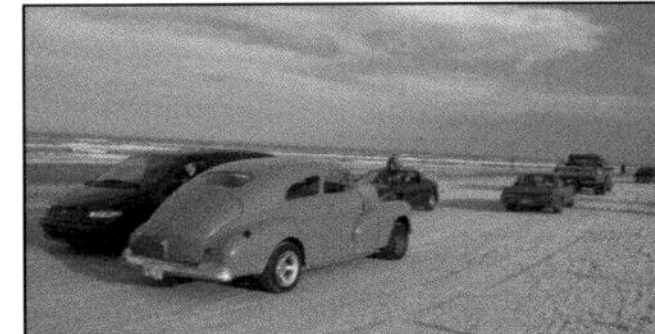

Daytona Beach Popular beach town – major car racing center – annual NASCAR event, Daytona 500 – annual Harley Davidson Bike Week **Fk31**

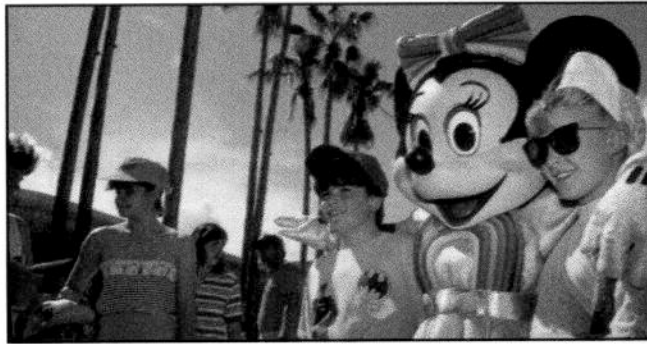

Walt Disney World Located near Orlando – four theme parks: Magic Kingdom, Epcot Center, Animal Kingdom, and Disney-MGM Studios **Fk31**

Cape Canaveral Site of Kennedy Space Center where most American space missions start – NASA Visitors Center – Astronaut Hall of Fame **Fk31**

Miami The largest urban area in Florida – population of two million in the metro area – Port of Miami – Little Havana, center of the Cuban-American cummunity – Miami Seaquarium **Fk33**

Miami Beach Part of Greater Miami – Art Deco architecture along Ocean Drive – numerous night clubs and restaurants **Fk33**

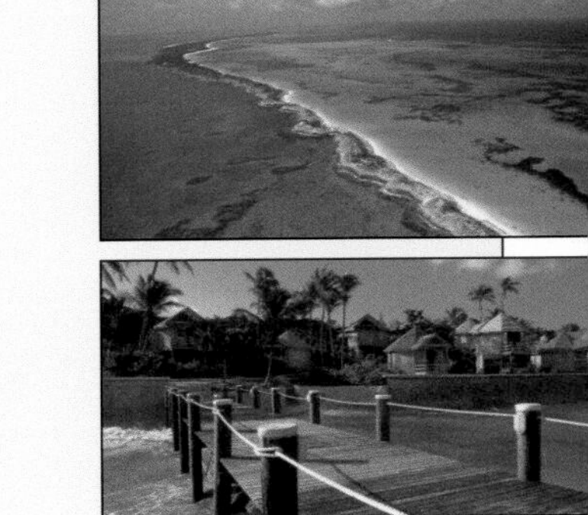

Bahamas Millions of tourists enjoy the beautiful beaches, shopping centers, and casinos in the Bahamas. The Out Islands are more peaceful and less visited than Nassau and Freeport and are home to the pristine Exuma Cays Land and Sea Park (400 km²). **Gb33**

Remarkable Cities and Cultural monuments

- UNESCO World Cultural Heritage
- Remarkable Cities
- Other ancient American cultures
- Places of Christian cultural interest
- Indian reservation
- Cultural landscape
- Historical city scape
- Castle/fortress/fort
- Monument
- Space mission launch site
- Museum

Sport and leisure destinations

- Race track
- Golf
- Horse racing
- Sailing
- Diving
- Wind surfing
- Surfing
- Deep-sea fishing
- Beach resort
- Mineral/thermal spa
- Amusement/theme park

Northern Mexico

Mexico is located in a very geologically active region. The country's territory lies in an area where three tectonic plates meet. Along the southern coast, the Cocos plate collides with and slides beneath the larger North American plate. The Cocos plate also collides with the Pacific plate along its western edges. The three plates are moving through the Earth's interior at a rate of around five centimeters per year. The tectonic activity in the region makes Mexico a country that is frequently shaken by earthquakes and tremors.

Northern Mexico is home to numerous mountain ranges including the different Sierras in **Baja California** and the large mountain ranges that extend from north to south through the country's interior.

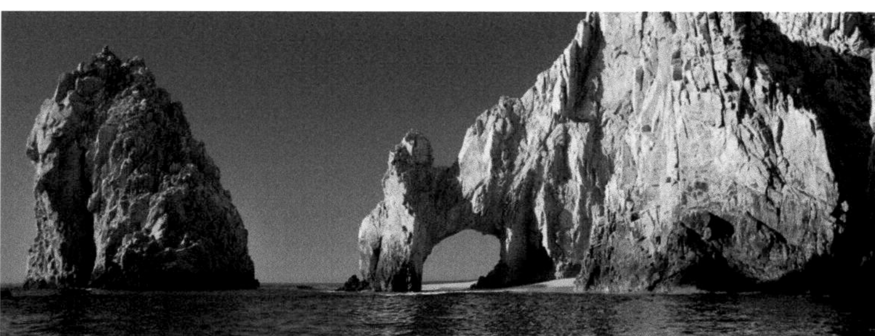

El Arco stone formations near Cabo San Lucas in Baja California **Ef34**

The two largest mountain ranges in th country are the parallel **Sierra Mad Oriental** (eastern) and **Sierra Mad Occidental** (western). The Sierra Mad Occidental declines steeply to the Pac fic coast on its western side and in th east the range declines gradually stages through the **Mexican Highland** The highest mountains in the Sier Madre Oriental range rise over 3,00 meters above sea level.

La Pintada 100-meter-long cave – contains ancient cave paintings from between 1100 BC and 1480 AD **Ed32**

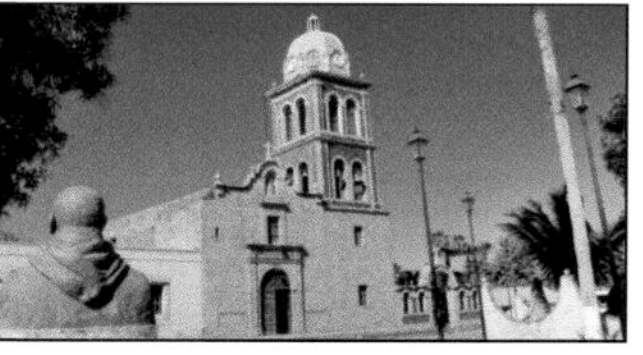

San Javier Jesuit mission in Baja California – built in 1699 – most beautiful Jesuit mission in Baja California **Ee33**

La Paz Port city in southern Baja California – palm-tree-lined promenade with cafes and seafood restaurants **Ee33**

Cascadas de Basaseachic The highest waterfall in Mexico – 246 meters high – surrounded by tropical forests **Ef31**

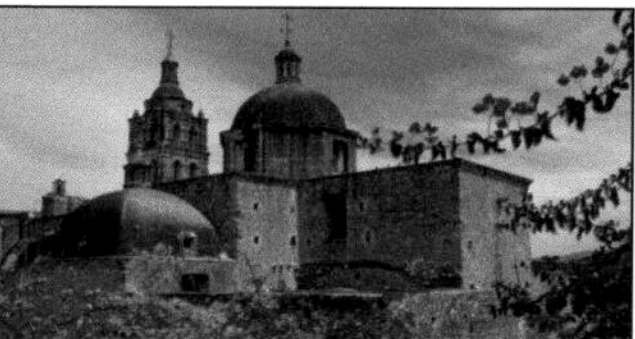

Álamos Colonial city – once a center of silver mining – Nuestra Señora de la Concepción (photo) **Ef32**

Barranca del Cobre (Copper Canyon) A series of canyons – six rivers flow through the area – lush vegetation **Eg32**

Sierra Madre Oriental Mountain range, parallel to the Sierra Madre Occidental – peaks rising over 3,000 meters **EjEk31-33**

Scale 1:4,500,000
0 40 80 Kilometers

Principal travel routes
- Auto route
- Rail road
- Shipping route

Remarkable landscapes and natural monuments
- UNESCO World Natural Heritage
- Mountain landscape
- Rock landscape
- Ravine/canyon
- Extinct volcano
- Active volcano
- Cave
- Waterfall/rapids
- Nature park
- National park (landscape)
- National park (fauna)
- Biosphere reserve
- Whale watching
- Coastal landscape
- Beach
- Underwater reserve

The Sierra Volcanica Transversal is a chain of active volcanoes that crosses Mexico between the 19th and 21st parallels of latitude. This range is home to the beautiful volcano **Popocatépetl** as well as Mexico's highest peak, the snow covered volcano **Pico de Orizaba** (5,747 meters).
The coastal regions in northern Mexico have humid tropical or subtropical climates. The Gulf of Mexico coastal region gets heavy rainfall during the entire year. Bitter cold north winds called Nortes (northers) often bring sudden cold temperatures and violent storms south into Mexico. These winds frequently cause extensive crop damage in the country's agricultural region. During summer and fall the Pacific coast is often threatened by typhoons while the eastern coasts are at risk from hurricanes.
Baja California is an arid area and indigenous plants include several species of giant cacti. The body of water between Baja California and mainland Mexico is usually called the Sea of Cortez but is also known as the Gulf of California. The Sea of Cortez is home to at least 800 different animal species.
The indigenous people of northern Mexico traditionally lived through hunting, and the cultivation of crops (especially corn and beans), and by gathering local plants including agave and yucca plants. Wine has been produced in the areas around **Parras de Fuente** since the early colonial period. The far north is home to numerous large cattle ranches and wheat farms. Irrigation is used throughout northern Mexico to support agriculture in the region.
The major source of Mexico's wealth during the colonial era was silver from the mines in the Sierra Madres.

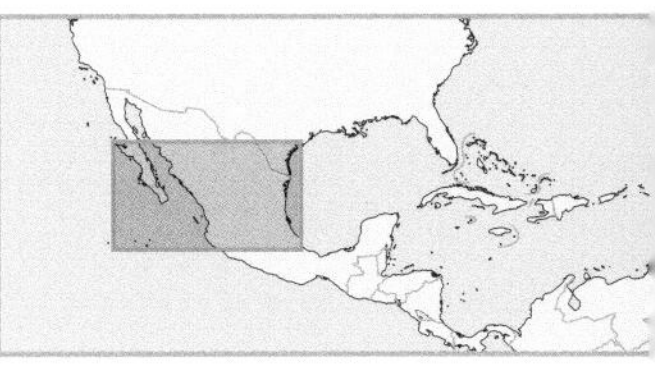

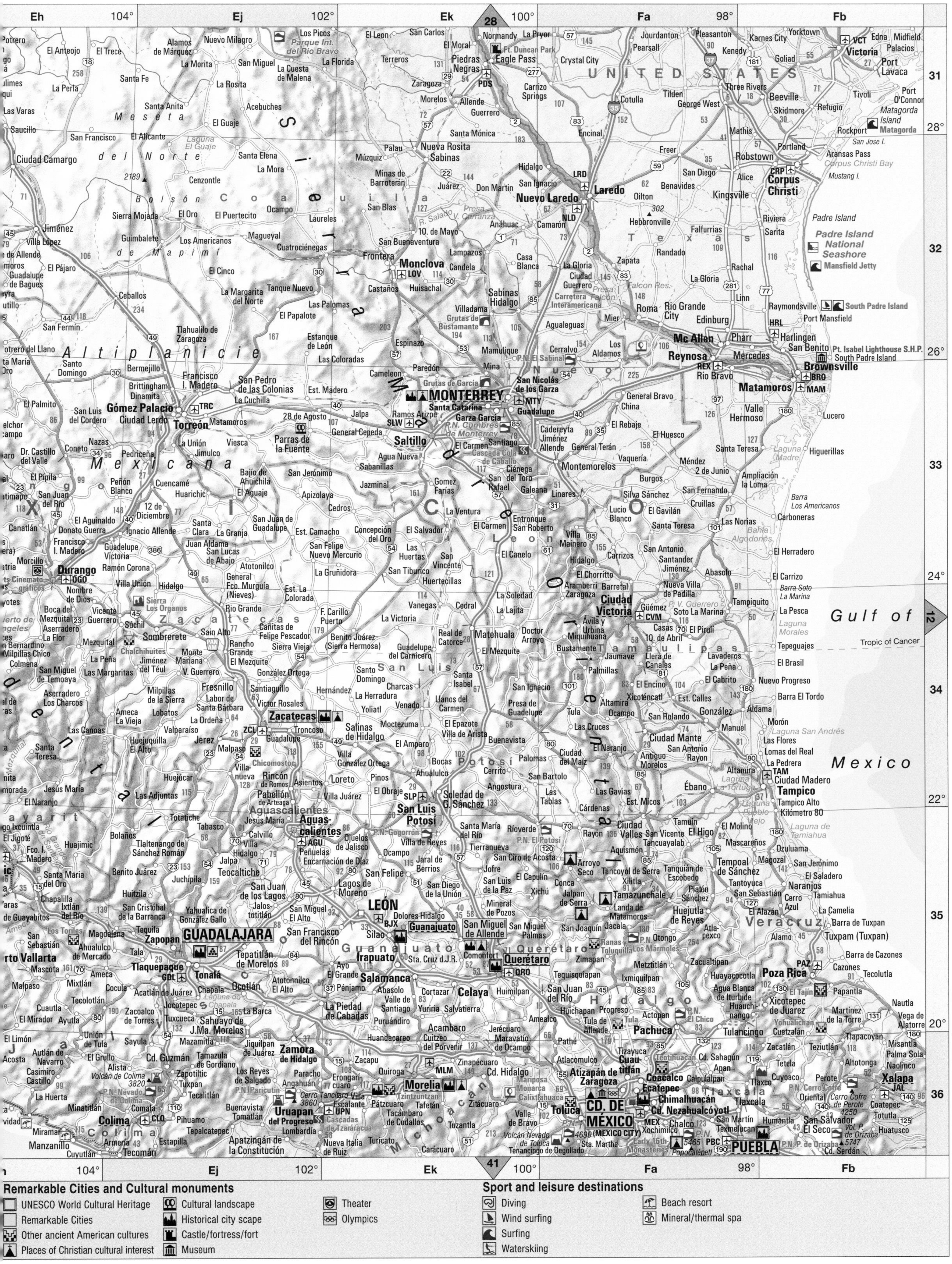

Remarkable Cities and Cultural monuments
- UNESCO World Cultural Heritage
- Remarkable Cities
- Other ancient American cultures
- Places of Christian cultural interest
- Cultural landscape
- Historical city scape
- Castle/fortress/fort
- Museum
- Theater
- Olympics

Sport and leisure destinations
- Diving
- Wind surfing
- Surfing
- Waterskiing
- Beach resort
- Mineral/thermal spa

Monterrey Third largest city in Mexico – Faro del Comercio (photo) on the Gran Plaza – Cathedral **Ek33**

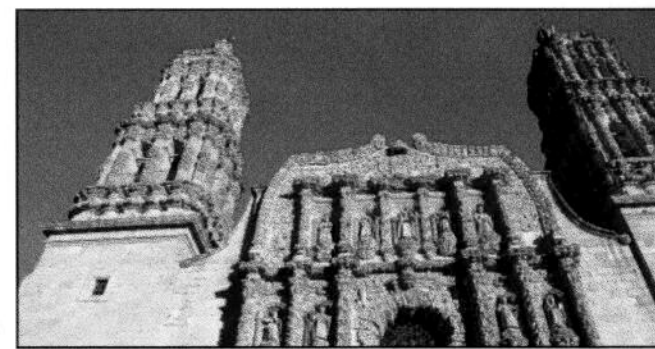

Zacatecas Colonial city founded in 1546 – the old town is a UNESCO world heritage site – baroque cathedral (photo) **Ej34**

Puerto Vallarta Popular tourist resort – population 350,000 – sandy white beaches – old town on the Rio Cuale **Eh35**

Guadalajara Second largest city in Mexico – population 6 million – colonial architecture – large market place **Ej35**

Guanajuato Once an important mining town – one of Mexico's most charming city centers – world heritage site **Ek35**

San Miguel de Allende Small city with colonial architecture – cobblestone streets – Templo de San Francisco (photo) **Ek35**

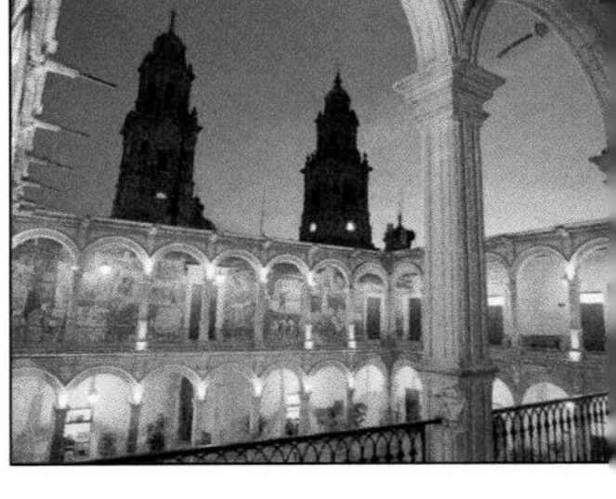

Morelia Founded in 1541 this city in Central Mexico has restored colonial architecture in its center – beautiful cathedral – palatial colonial homes **Ek36**

In geography, the region known as Central America begins to the east of the Mexican Isthmus of Tehuantepec. Most of **Mexico** (Latin America's third largest nation) belongs to the North American continent. Mexico's capital, Mexico City, lies at a elevation of 2,242 meters in the **central highlands** which are surrounded by the **Sierra Madre Oriental** and **Sierra Madre Occidental** mountains. The southern boundary of this region is defined by the **Sierra Volcánica Transversal**, a volcanic mountain chain. Well known volcanoes in this chain include Popocatépetl (5,465 m), Iztaccihuatl (5,286 m) and the highest peak, Pico de Orizaba (5,747 m).

In the heart of the **Yucatán Peninsula** lies the expansive tropical rain forest Bió

The Mayan ruins of Tulum on Mexico's Caribbean coast **Fg3**

Mexico City Templo Mayor (top photo) on Plaza de la Constitucion is a reminder of this city's Aztec heritage. Much of the city was once covered by a lake. The Cathedral Metropolitana and the famous National Anthropology Museum are important attractions. **Fa36**

Popocatépetl Active volcano – the surrounding area has interesting churches (UNESCO world heritage sites) – Nuestra Señora de los Remedios **Fa36**

Puebla Plaza de Armas – cathedral – views of Popocatépetl and Iztaccíhuatl – Iglesia Santo Domingo – the old town is a UNESCO world heritage site **Fa36**

El Tajín historic ruins – 17 ancient ball sports areas – several pyramids and viewing platforms – museum **Fb35**

Oaxaca Plaza de Armas is the city's main square – Alameda de Léon has an interesting arts and crafts market – colonial architecture in Centro Cultural de Santo Domingo (world heritage site) **Fb37**

Monte Alban Pre-Columbian ruins above Oaxaca Valley – los Danzantes, carved stone figures – the burial grounds are UNESCO world heritage sites **Fb37**

PACIFIC OCEAN

Scale 1:4,500,000

0 40 80 Kilometers

Principal travel routes

- Auto route
- Rail road
- Shipping route

Remarkable landscapes and natural monuments

- UNESCO World Natural Heritage
- Mountain landscape
- Extinct volcano
- Active volcano
- Geyser
- Cave
- Waterfall/rapids
- Nature park
- National park (landscape)
- National park (flora)
- Biosphere reserve
- Coastal landscape
- Beach
- Coral reef
- Island
- Underwater reserve

fera Calakmul/Biósfera Maya. This region which is home to countless species f flora and fauna is divided between Mexico and Guatemala.
hroughout Mexico there are numerous istoric sites from the civilizations of pre-columbian Mayans and Aztecs. Today the Mayans constitute 60% of Guatemala's opulation; a further 800,000 ethnic Mayans live in Mexico.
he southern regions of **Guatemala** are defined by a series of mountain chains. The southern and eastern highlands encompass numerous volcanoes (some active) and several lakes including **Lago de Atitlán**. The areas north of Guatemala City, Alta, and Baja Veracruz are covered by an expansive grassland with diverse vegetation.
Belize, the smallest Central American nation, has practically no noteworthy elevations. Belize is most famous for its Cayes, a collection of small islands in the Caribbean Sea. Belize is also home to the world's second largest coral reef, the Gran Recife Maya also known as the Belize Barrier Reef.
Mayan ruins and mountain chains can be found throughout **El Salvador**. Along El Salvador's southern coast, a thin plain gives way to a mountain chain comprising more than 20 active volcanoes. Near the border to **Honduras**, the Lempa river valley seperates the **Matepan** and **Chalatenango** mountains. There are many remnants of Mayan civilization in the region. The ruins at **Copán** are a designated UNESCO world heritage site.
Several river valleys extend from southwestern Honduras to the Caribbean coast in the North. In eastern regions of the country, the coast becomes increasingly wide. South of the Honduran highlands the Pacific coast is bordered by a plain.

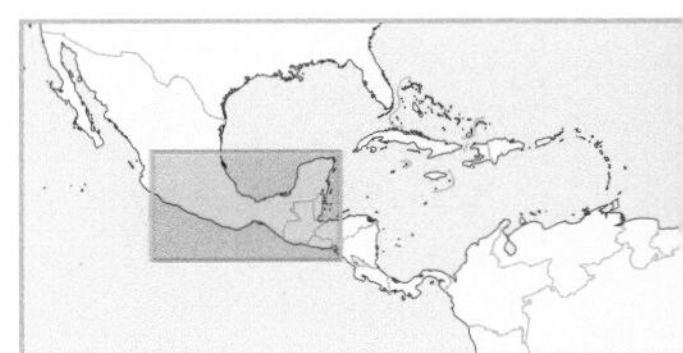

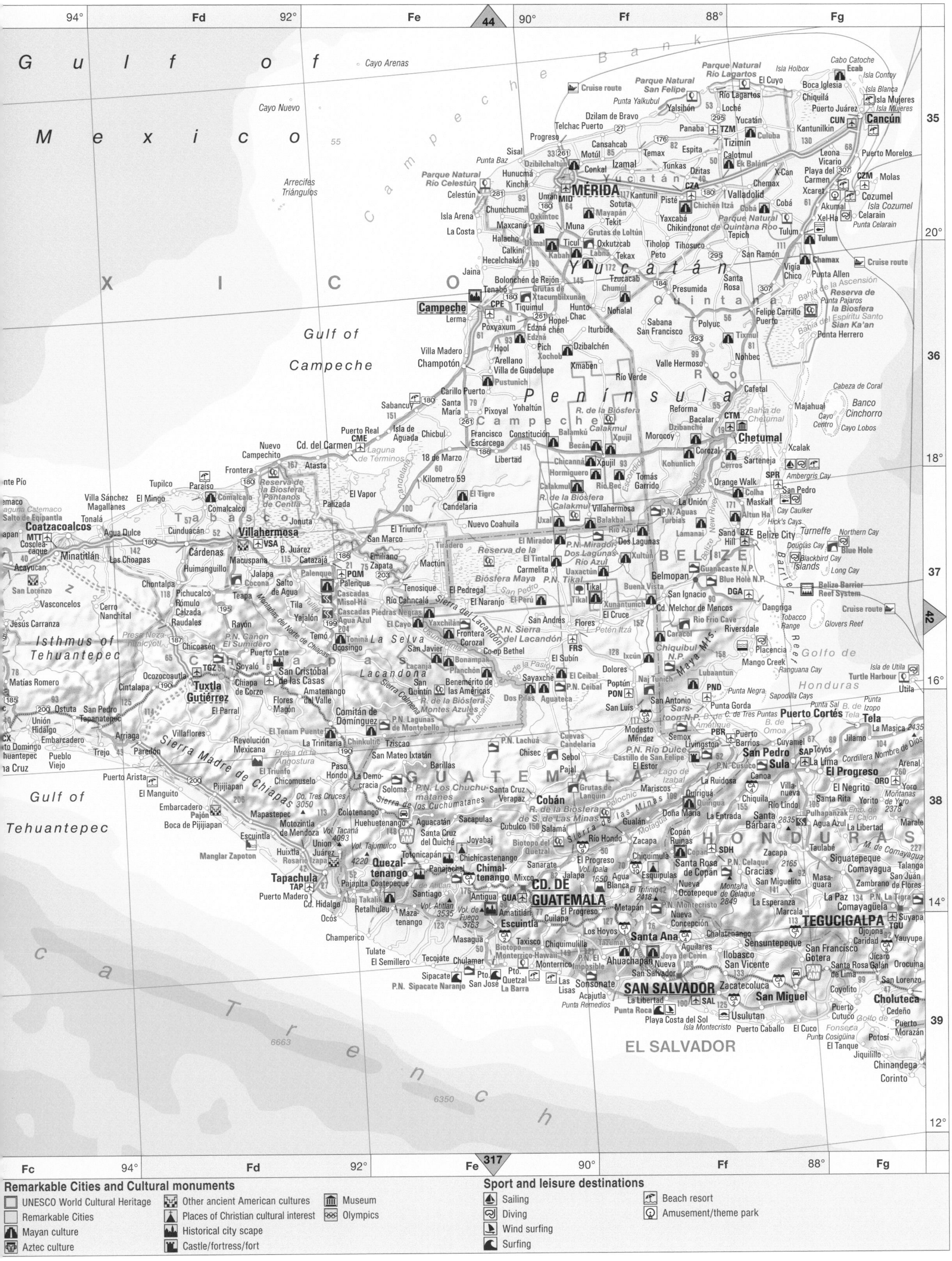

Gulf of Mexico

Gulf of Campeche

Yucatán Peninsula

Gulf of Tehuantepec

GUATEMALA

BELIZE

HONDURAS

EL SALVADOR

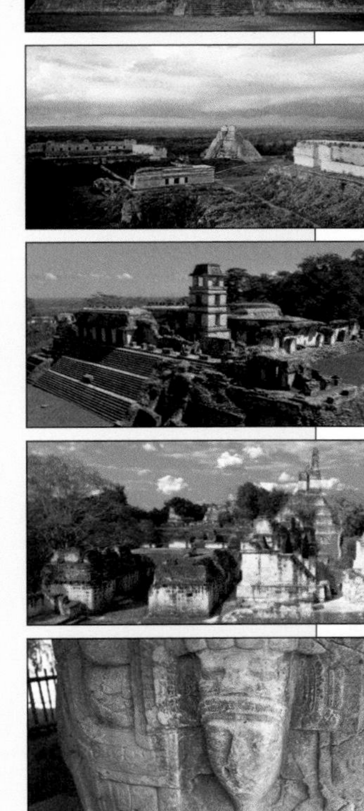

The Realm of the Maya
Even today there are mysteries surrounding the pre-Columbian Mayan culture. Several ruins of this civilization belong to UNESCO's list of World Heritage Sites including Chichén Itzá with its Pyramid of Kukulcán. The site also includes a field for ball sports and a warrior temple. Uxmal in Mexico contains an impressive pyramid; another attraction here is the so-called Governor's Palace, once an important residence for the local Maya elite. The ruins at Palenque cover an area of 16 km², but only a small portion of the site has been excavated including the Palacio with its distinctive towers. Tikal, in Guatemala, is surrounded by dense jungle but remains one of the most important Mayan archaeological sites. Photos from top to bottom: Chichén Itzá **(Ff35)**, Uxmal **(Ff35)**, Palenque **(Fd37)**, Tikal **(Ff37)**, Quiringuá **(Ff38)**

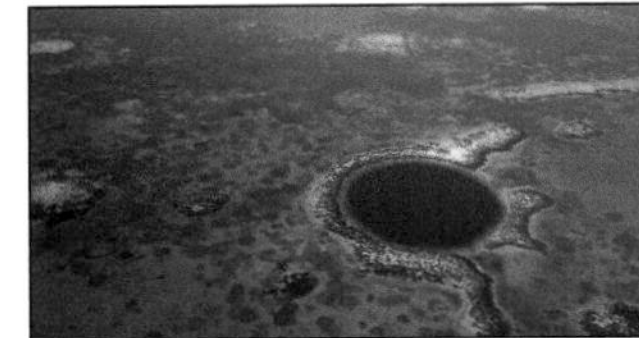

Belize Barrier Reef/Gran Recife Maya
300-kilometer-long coral reef – hundreds of small coral islands (Cayes) – UNESCO world heritage site **Fg37**

Antigua Former capital city of Guatemala with colonial achitecture – cathedral (1545) – La Merced church (1749) – Las Capuchinas monastery, 18th century **Fe38**

Remarkable Cities and Cultural monuments
- UNESCO World Cultural Heritage
- Remarkable Cities
- Mayan culture
- Aztec culture
- Other ancient American cultures
- Places of Christian cultural interest
- Historical city scape
- Castle/fortress/fort
- Museum
- Olympics

Sport and leisure destinations
- Sailing
- Diving
- Wind surfing
- Surfing
- Beach resort
- Amusement/theme park

Many geographers consider Mexico's Isthmus of Tehauntepec the starting point of Central America but the region is usually defined as consisting of the six countries between Mexico and Columbia.
The mountainous border region separating Guatemala from El Salvador and Honduras runs through an area where the North American tectonic plate collides with the Caribbean plate. The climate in Central America is overwhelmingly tropical with the exception of a few regions. Central America is home to a diverse collection of plants and animals. Many of the region's animals are unique hybrids created from the mixing of North and South American species. The thin strip of land forming the Isthmus of Panama connects North America and South America. At its narrowest, the isthmus has a width of 46 kilometers.
Expansive rainforests cover the easter[n] plains of Nicaragua and Honduras. Th[e] region is dissected by numerous rivers most of which flow into the Caribbea[n] Sea. Much of western Nicaragua is cov[-]ered by a large basin containing th[e] region's largest lake **Lago de Nicara[-]gua** (8,150 km²). South of Lago de Nica[-]ragua rise the volcanoes of the Cordi[llera]

Arenal in Costa Rica, one of many active volcanoes in this region **Fh40**

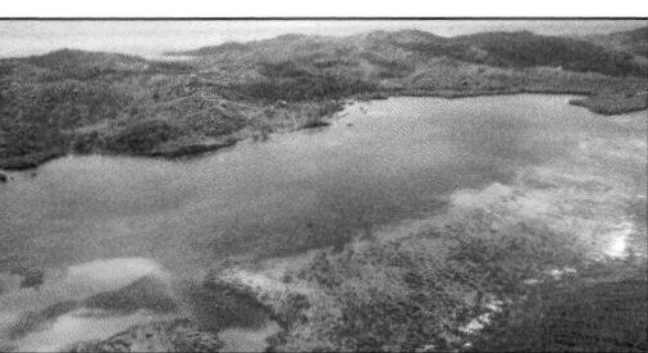

Islas de la Bahía Archipelago of coral islands off the northern coast of Honduras – Roatán is the largest island – conservation areas on the coasts **Fg37**

Copán Large Mayan temple complex in Honduras – contains many statues, all dated to between 400 and 700 AD – UNESCO world heritage site **Ff38**

Río Platano Biosphere Reserve This nature reserve is inhabited by many endangered and rare species including tapirs, jaguars (photo), red macaws, and fish species. The biosphere is also home to unique plants. Around 5,000 Paya and Miskito Amerindians live in the area. **Fh38**

Guanacaste National park in Costa Rica – savannahs and dry forests – rainforests along the slopes of inactive volcanoes – UNESCO world heritage site **Fh40**

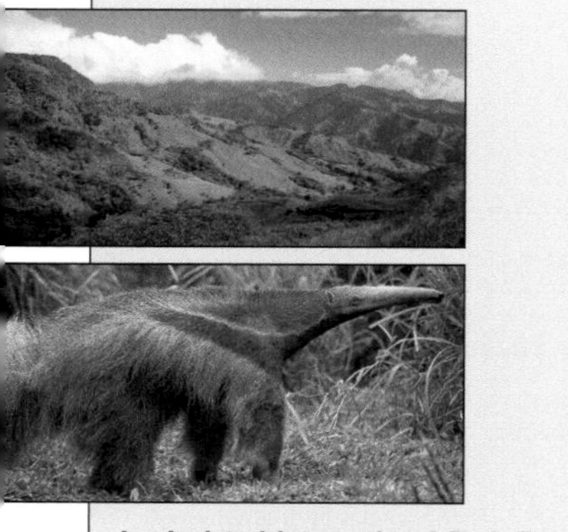

La Amistad International Park The core of a large biosphere reserve in Panama and Costa Rica. The park stretches from the swampy coast into the highlands of the Cordillera Talamanca. The area has been designated a UNESCO world heritage site. **Fj41**

HONDURAS
NICARAGUA
EL SALVADOR
COSTA RICA
GUATEMALA
BELIZE
PACIFIC OCEAN

Scale 1:4,500,000
0 40 80 Kilometers

Principal travel routes
- Auto route
- Rail road
- Shipping route

Remarkable landscapes and natural monuments
- UNESCO World Natural Heritage
- Mountain landscape
- Extinct volcano
- Active volcano
- Cave
- River landscape
- Waterfall/rapids
- Nature park
- National park (landscape)
- National park (flora)
- National park (fauna)
- Biosphere reserve
- Coastal landscape
- Beach
- Coral reef
- Underwater reserve

ra Central and Cordillera de Talaanca mountain ranges. The highest mmits in these ranges rise over 3,000 eters and several of the volcanoes are ill active including **Arenal** (1,633 eters). As with the active volcanoes, e frequent earthquakes and tremors in is region are the result of plate tecnics. In 1972, Nicaragua's capital city, anagua, was devastated by a powerful arthquake. Despite its small size, **Costa Rica** has a diverse collection of flora and fauna and several distinct climate zones. Many of the country's rainforests have been designated national parks. Many of the western areas of the country have dry savannah-like landscapes, while the eastern coast is covered by humid swampland. Most of the country's rainforests lie in the central highlands, while the northwest contains expansive dry forests. Both coasts are home to rare and endangered sea turtles. Tortuguero National Park was established solely for the protection of sea turtles and is only accessible by boat. The waters off the Caribbean coast of Central America contain several large coral reefs. The best diving areas in the region include Panama's **San Blas Islands**, the **Bocas del Toro Archipelago** in Costa Rica, and many small islands off the coast of Nicaragua and Honduras. The legacy of Spanish colonialism can be seen in the region's culture and historic architecture.

Costa Rica's Central Valley attracted more European settlers that any other area in the region because of its mild climate and good conditions for coffee cultivation and dairy farming. Many of the coastal areas and plains in Central America contain large fruit plantations which produce fruit primarily for foreign markets.

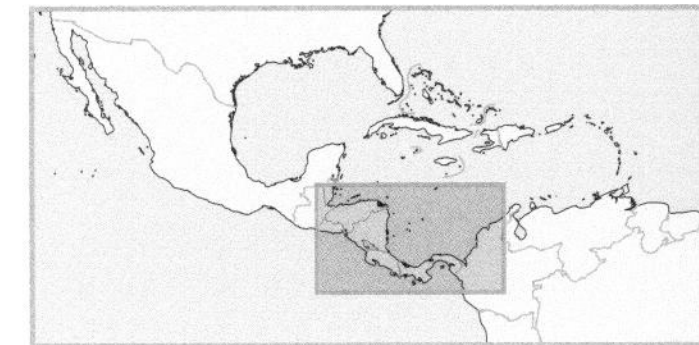

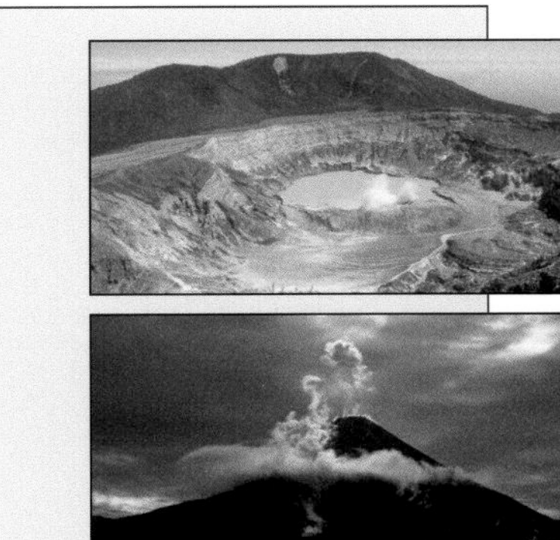

Costa Rica's Volcanoes The spectacular volcanoes along the edges of Costa Rica's Central Valley can be easily visited from the capital, San José. Many of the volcanic craters are filled with water, and natural fountains often spring from their centers. The crater of Arenal has been crowned by a plume of smoke every since the volcano's last eruption in 1968, after a century of being dormant. **Fh40**

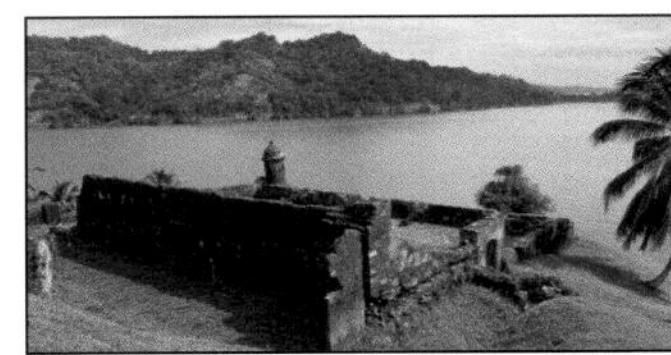

Portobelo Historic port city on Panama's Caribbean coast – Spanish style colonial architecture in the historic city center – Caribbean atmosphere – UNESCO world heritage site **Ga41**

Panama City Capital of Panama – historic old town (world heritage site) – modern skyscrapers along the bay **Ga41**

The Panama Canal Construction of the canal began in 1881 and it was opened in 1914 – 67.5 kilometers long – under American jurisdiction until 1999 – panoramic views of the canal from the Miraflores locks **Ga41**

Darién National Park National park in one of most undeveloped regions of Panama – has an abundance of unique flora and fauna – UNESCO world heritage site – Tapir (photo) **Gb42**

Remarkable Cities and Cultural monuments

- UNESCO World Cultural Heritage
- Remarkable Cities
- Mayan culture
- Other ancient American cultures
- Places of Christian cultural interest
- Historical city scape
- Castle/fortress/fort
- Technical/industrial monument
- Monument

Sport and leisure destinations

- Sailing
- Diving
- Wind surfing
- Surfing
- Canoeing/rafting
- Deep-sea fishing
- Beach resort

The 120-kilometer-wide **Yucatan Channel** separates the Yucatan Peninsula from Cuba, the largest and westernmost of the four Greater Antilles. In addition to Cuba, the **Greater Antilles** includes the islands of Jamaica, Puerto Rico, and Hispaniola. Cuba, together with the Cayman Islands and the Bahamas, lies along the southern edges of the North American tectonic plate. Jamaica and Hispaniola lie along the northern edges of the relatively small Caribbean plate. South of these two islands, the Caribbean Sea has an average depth of 5,000 meters below sea level.

The 1500-meters-deep Nicholas Channel is located off the northern coast of **Cuba**, between the island and Florida. Between the Bahamas and Cuba lies the Great Bahama Bank, a large area of relative shallow waters. There are countless co reefs near the coast of Cuba and t island is surrounded by numerous grou of small islands and sandbanks includi the **Archipiélago de Sabana** and t **Archipiélago de los Jardines de Reina**. These tropical coral island along with the **Isla de la Juventud** the southwest coast, are excellent are for diving. The abundance of coral ree

Montego Bay in Jamaica lures many tourists to its fine beaches **Gb36**

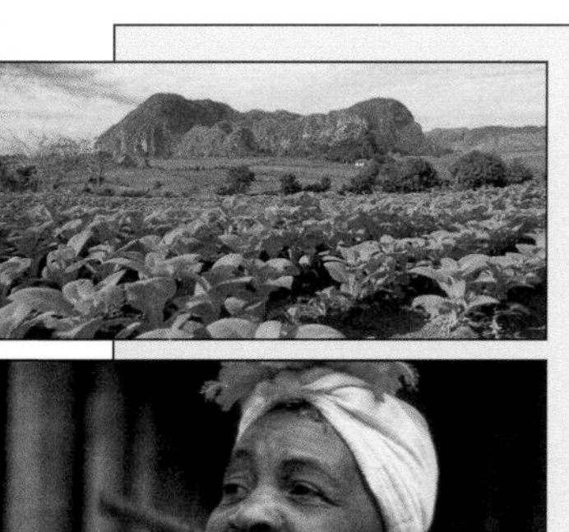

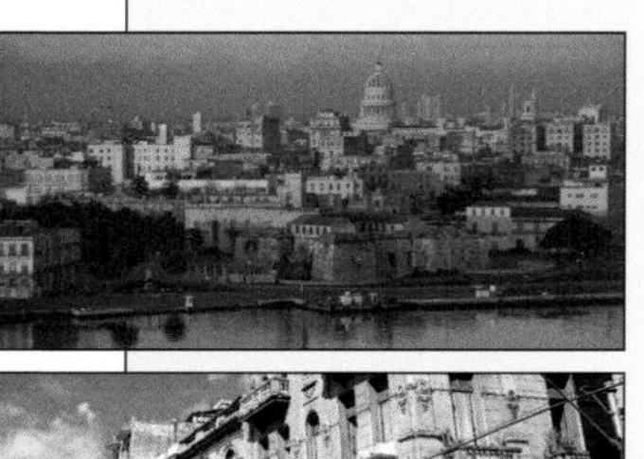

Valle de Viñales Tobacco farming is the main industry in the region around Pinar del Rio. The region contains numerous round stone formations (top photo). **Fj34**

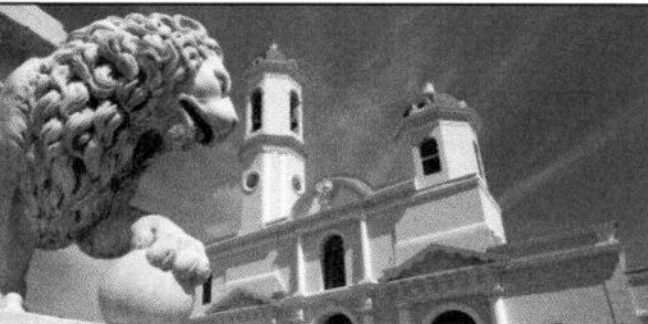

Havana Cuba's capital has impressive colonial architecture, much of which is decaying and in need of restoration. The most important landmark in the old town is the Cathedral. The historic fortress and old town are UNESCO world heritage sites. **Fj34**

Cienfuegos Important port city for the sugar industry – Piaza Marti has beautiful historic architecture – Palacio del Valle, built in Moorish style **Fk34**

The Cayman Islands The islands are the peaks of underwater mountains. The Caymans, a British territory, are one of the best areas for diving in the Caribbean. **Fk36**

Scale 1:4,500,000
0 40 80 Kilometers

Principal travel routes
- Auto route
- Rail road
- Shipping route

Remarkable landscapes and natural monuments
- UNESCO World Natural Heritage
- Rock landscape
- Cave
- Waterfall/rapids
- Nature park
- National park (landscape)
- National park (flora)
- National park (fauna)
- Biosphere reserve
- Coastal landscape
- Beach
- Coral reef
- Island
- Underwater reserve

the region can be attributed to the arm temperature, moderate salinity, and earness of the water in the region. ne island of Cuba is over 1,250 kilo- eters long and 190 kilometers at its idest. Huge round stone formations an be found in the **Valle de Viñales** nd **Sierra de los Órganos** regions of astern Cuba. The tallest stone forma- ons (Mogotes) in these areas rise 700 eters above sea level. Pico Turquino, Cuba's tallest mountain, lies in the **Sierra Maestra** Range and rises 1,972 meters. The small Cayman Islands are the summits of an underwater mountain chain. The **Cayman Islands** are a British territory consisting of three main islands: Grand Cayman, Little Cayman, and Cayman Brac. The **Cayman Trench** extends underwater north and west of the Cayman Island and descends 7,240 meters at its deepest point. The center of **Jamaica** is a mountainous region, while the coastal regions consist of plains with many beautiful beaches. The beaches and the warm climate are the two main reasons Jamaica has become one of the most famous Caribbean destinations. The island rises in elevation from east to west. The **Blue Mountains** are a series of tall hills and mountains in eastern Jamaica. They are heavily forested and feature many of the island's most beautiful landscapes. The mountains also support an important coffee growing industry. Blue Mountain Peak, the tallest mountain on the island, rises 2,292 meters. **Hurricanes** pose a major threat to almost all of the islands in the Caribbean region, including Jamaica and Cuba. During hurricane season (July to October) the region is at high risk of being struck by devastating hurricanes and tropical storms.

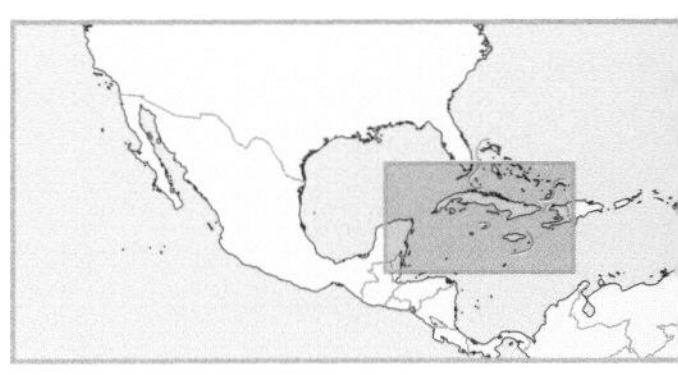

Trinidad Restored colonial city at the foot of the Sierra de Escrambray range in southwestern Cuba – UNESCO world heritage site – traditional Cuban architecture – beaches at Playa Ancon **FkGa35**

Santiago de Cuba Second largest city in Cuba – strong influence on Cuban music and dance – grave of Cuban national hero José Marti in the Cathedral at Parque Céspedes – colonial history museum in the Casa de Diego Velázquez **Gc35**

El Cobre Important pilgrimage site for Cuban Catholics since the 17th century – Basilica, built in the 20th century **Gc35**

Jamaica The island has a population of 2.7 million. Tourism is very important for the Jamaican economy. The major attractions in Negril are Eight Mile Beach and the local bars and nightclubs. Montego Bay and Ocho Rios are home to numerous beautiful small bays and Dunn's River Falls. The Blue Mountains in eastern Jamaica encompass some of the most breathtaking landscapes on the island and the last remnants of Jamaica's virgin tropical forests. Photos from top to bottom: A bay on the north coast, Ocho Rios, Dunn's River Falls, Cockpit County **Gb36**

Remarkable Cities and Cultural monuments

- UNESCO World Cultural Heritage
- Remarkable Cities
- Mayan culture
- Other ancient American cultures
- Places of Christian cultural interest
- Cultural landscape
- Historical city scape
- Castle/fortress/fort
- Palace
- Tomb/grave
- Monument
- Museum

Sport and leisure destinations

- Sailing
- Diving
- Wind surfing
- Seaport
- Deep-sea fishing
- Beach resort
- Mineral/thermal spa
- Amusement/theme park

Hispaniola and Lesser Antilles

Hispaniola, Puerto Rico, and the Lesser Antilles form a bow of islands along the eastern edges of the Caribbean tectonic plate. In this area the North American tectonic plate pushes underneath the smaller Caribbean plate. Like other regions near the collision zone of two tectonic plates, this region is home to many mountain ranges, including the highlands in the **Dominican Republic** which rise to a height of 3,200 meters above sea

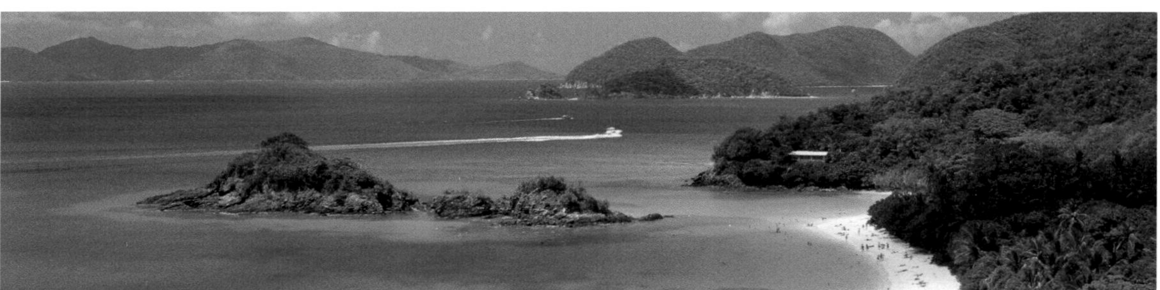

level. The tectonic activity is also re sponsible for the volcanism on many the smaller islands in the region. **Barb dos** is the region's only large island cre ted entirely from coral formations. T last major volcanic eruption in regi occurred in 1995/96 when the volca Soufrière devastated the small isla

The Virgin Islands are surrounded by beautiful tropical coasts **Gh**

Citadelle La Ferrière and Sans Souci Palace 40-meter-tall historic fortress in northern Haiti – Sans Souci Palace was built in 1807 and modeled after Versailles in France; today it is partly in ruins **Gd36**

Samaná Peninsula Peninsula with beautiful beaches in the Dominican Republic – small villages – whale-watching in Bahía de Samaná **Gf36**

Parque Nacional Los Haïtises National park in the Dominican Republic – home to unique fish and bird species – accessible caves – exotic vegetation **Gf36**

Santo Domingo Capital of the Dominican Republic – founded in 1496 – colonial old town has historic palatial homes and monasteries – Cathedral (photo) – Faro a Colon/ Columbus Lighthouse **Gf36**

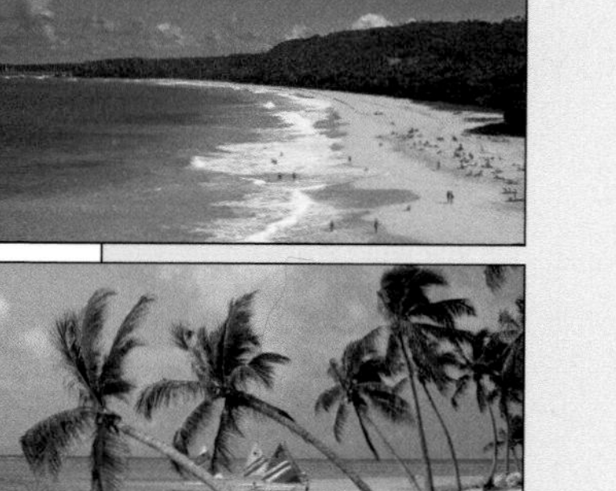

Dominican Republic The country's economy is heavily dependent on tourism. There are countless beaches in the country and windsurfing is popular. The country also has many diving areas and large resort hotels.

San Juan Capital of Puerto Rico – cruise ship port – restored colonial architecture – historic sites including UNESCO world heritage sites **Gg36**

Scale 1:4,500,000

0 40 80 Kilometers

Principal travel routes

- Auto route
- Rail road
- Shipping route

Remarkable landscapes and natural monuments

- UNESCO World Natural Heritage
- Rock landscape
- Active volcano
- Cave
- River landscape
- Waterfall/rapids
- Lake country
- Desert
- Nature park
- National park (landscape)
- National park (flora)
- National park (fauna)
- Biosphere reserve
- Coastal landscape
- Beach
- Underwater reserve

ontserrat. **Hispaniola**, the second rgest island in the Caribbean, is home several mountain ranges. The tallest ountains on the island are in the Cor-llera Central. Hispaniola's tallest moun-in, Pico Duarte, rises 3,175 meters. The ountains in the central highlands of **uerto Rico** rise to heights around 1,300 eters above sea level.

e **Lesser Antilles** are divided into two oups of islands: the Leeward Islands in the north and the Windward Islands in the south. In addition to their famous white beaches, many of the islands, including **St. Lucia** and **Dominica**, also have black beaches with dark volcanic sand. The tropical climate and fertile soil in the region make the islands ideal for the farming of tropical plants. Several islands still contain remnants of virgin tropical rainforests with unique flora and fauna. While most islands in the Lesser Antilles are covered by lush tropical forests, a few islands (most notably Aruba) have dry desert-like interiors with sparse vegetation. Because of their warm sunny climates, countless beaches, and beautiful landscapes, the Lesser Antilles attract many tourists from beyond the region. In recent decades, tourism has become the dominant industry in the region. Between July and October, the Lesser Antilles are threatened by hurricanes and many of the islands have been devastated by these powerful storms in the past. The southern islands of the Lesser Antilles are less threatened by hurricanes and have far drier climates than their northern counterparts.

The **Netherlands Antilles** – consisting of Curaçao, Bonaire, and Aruba – is the southernmost island group in the Lesser Antilles and has some of the best diving sites in the Caribbean.

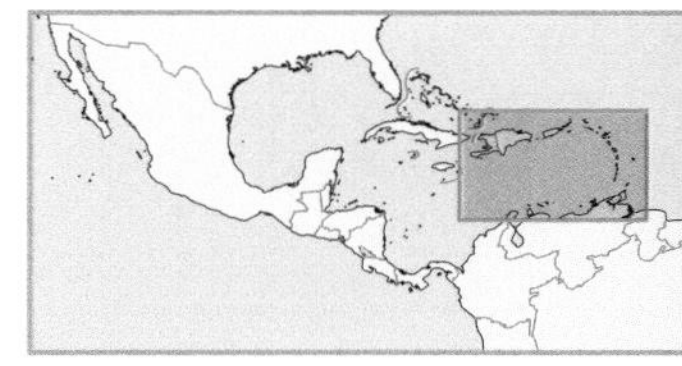

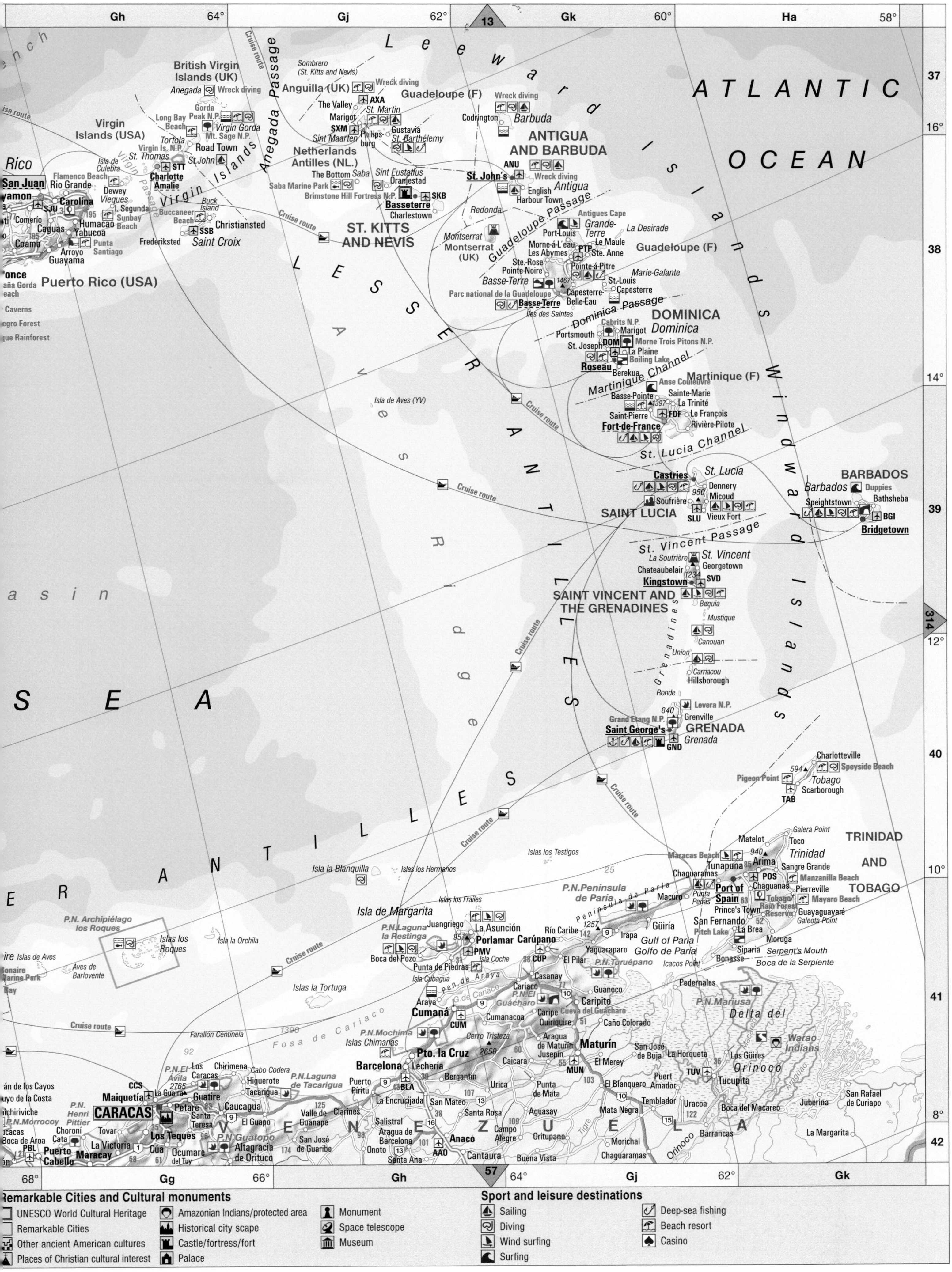

English Harbour Bay on the southern coast of Antigua – popular sailing area – site of the Antigua Sailing Week **Gk37**

Guadeloupe Overseas department of France – two distinct regions: mountainous west and flat east – coffee fields rise along the slopes of the island's volcanoes **Gk37**

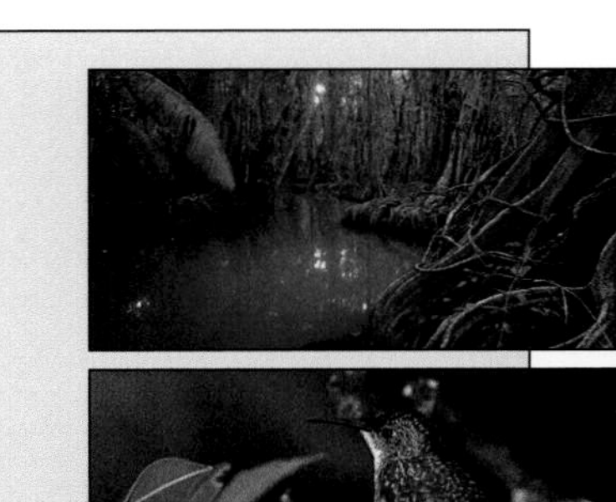

Dominica This small island has some of the most pristine rainforests in the Caribbean. The eastern coast has black beaches. The island's northwest is covered by banana fields. Trois Pitons National Park encompasses the island's virgin rainforests and is a UNESCO world heritage site. **Gk38**

Soufrière Small town on St. Lucia – sulfur springs – Pitons: round stone mountains: the highest rising 800 meters **Gk39**

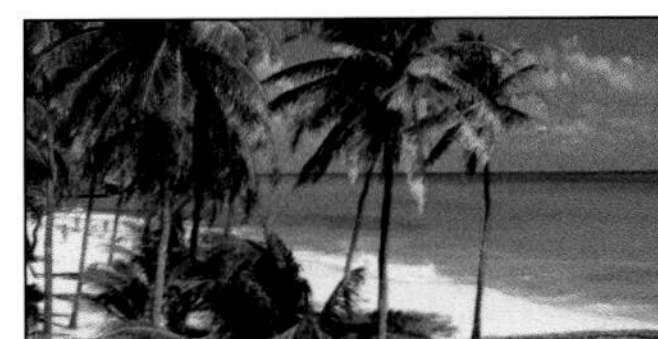

Barbados The easternmost of the Lesser Antilles islands – old sugar plantations and historic colonial estates – Harrion's Cave has stalactite-covered chambers – beautiful white beaches on the southern and western coasts **Ha39**

St. George's Grenada's capital has a beautiful harbor – the island's culture and architecture display both British and French influences – Fort George **Gk39**

Remarkable Cities and Cultural monuments

UNESCO World Cultural Heritage
Remarkable Cities
Other ancient American cultures
Places of Christian cultural interest
Amazonian Indians/protected area
Historical city scape
Castle/fortress/fort
Palace
Monument
Space telescope
Museum

Sport and leisure destinations

Sailing
Diving
Wind surfing
Surfing
Deep-sea fishing
Beach resort
Casino

Atacama (top): A snow covered beauty on the edge of Chile's most fascinating desert
Iguaçu Falls (bottom): The roaring waters of South America's widest falls

Machu Picchu (left): The remnants of an Incan "lost city" in the Peruvian highlands
Rio de Janeiro (right): Beaches and sunshine; South America's most hedonistic city

South America

From the green rainforests of the Amazon basin to the icecaps of the world's tallest volcanoes and the glaciers of Patagonia, South America has a wealth of fascinating and unique landscapes. The cultural highlights of the continent include ancient sites of Incan civilization and the legacy of European colonialism.

Compared to the other continents South America is a relatively compact landmass. The continent has smooth coastlines and a consistently flat relief – outside of the Andes. The southern continent of the western hemisphere is 7,500 kilometers long from north to south and the greatest distance from east to west measures 4,800 kilometers. The continent borders Central (and North) America at the Isthmus of Panama.

Parinacota (6,400 m), a volcano in Chile's Lauca National Park

The Andes Mountains, the world's second highest mountain range after the Himalayas, rise to the east of the continent's Pacific coast. Aconcagua in Argentina is the highest mountain in the Western Hemisphere. Other significant mountain ranges in South America include the Pakaraima Mountains in the north and the Serra do Mar in Brazil. Between these two mou tainous regions lies the vast basin of th Amazon River. With a length of 6,400 kil meters, the Amazon is the second longe river in the world after the Nile. Th marshy land of the Gran Chaco is locate north of the fertile Pampas and th sparsely populated Patagonia region. Th flat basin of the Orinoco River (2,14 kilometers) occupies a large area in north ern South America.

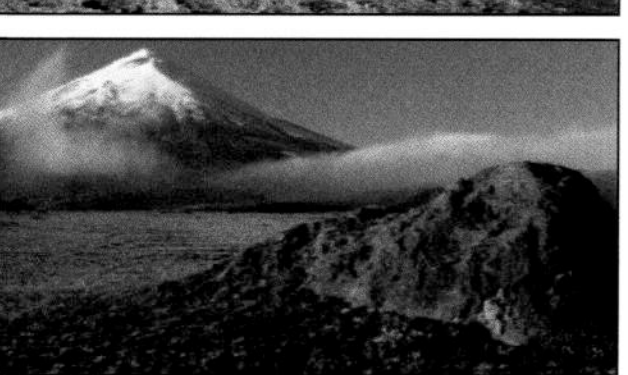

The **Andes mountain system** extends north to south along the entire length of South America. The width of the Andes ranges between 200 and 400 kilometers. The Andes are also the longest mountain chain on the planet. Aconcagua (top photo) located in the border region between Argentina and Chile is the highest mountain in the Andes and the western hemisphere. The highest active volcano in the Andes is Cotopaxi (bottom photo), located in Ecuador. Cotopaxi rises 5,897 meters high and has a beautiful snow-capped summit.

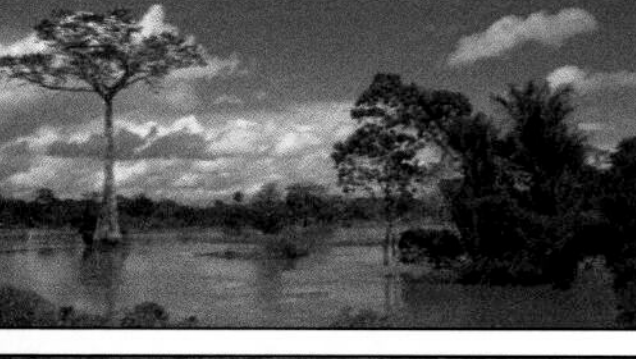

The drainage basin of the **Amazon River** is home to the world's largest tropical rain forest (middle photo). The Amazon River basin covers 3,500 km from east to west, and more than 2,000 kilometers from north to south. The Rio Negro is the largest tributary of the Amazon River and has a drainage basin with an area of 600,000 km^2. Many sections of the river are covered by dense vegetation (bottom photo). Trees in the Amazon Forest can grow over 90 meters high (top photo).

The **Iguaçu (Iguazu) Falls** are located on the border between Brazil and Argentina. The falls are between 65 and 70 meters high and three kilometers wide (top photo). **Lake Titicaca** (8,559 km^2) is the highest lake in the Andes with an elevation of 3,182 meters. Lake Maracaibo is the largest lake in South America (13,512 km^2).

Scale 1:45,000,000
0 400 800 Kilometers

Depth tints
- Shoreline
- 0-200 m
- 200-2000 m
- 2000-4000 m
- 4000-6000 m
- 6000-8000 m
- > 8000 m

Physical Features
- River, stream
- Intermittent river
- Lake
- Intermittent lake
- Salt lake
- Intermittent salt lake
- Elevation above sea level in meters

Town symbols
- Towns > 1 Mill. inhabitants
- Towns < 100 000 inhabitants

here are twelve independent nations South America as well as French Guiana, a territory of France. South America is home to 304 million people, more an half of this population lives in Brail. Centuries of contact between Euroeans, Amerindians and Africans has ade the population of South America e most ethnically and racially mixed in e world.
o other continent is as religiously homoeneous as South America. Almost 90% of the continent's people are Roman Catholics.
Migration from rural areas to cities continues to expand the population of cities in the region. In recent decades, the continent's cities have grown explosively. Most of South America's large cities are surrounded by large slums, home to the poorest members of society.

Left: Quetchua woman (Peru)
Right: Yanomami in the Amazon basin

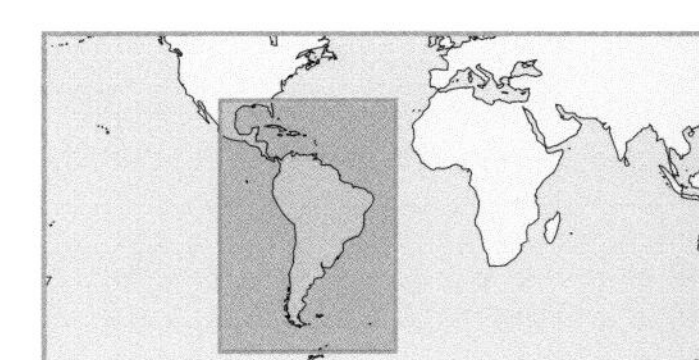

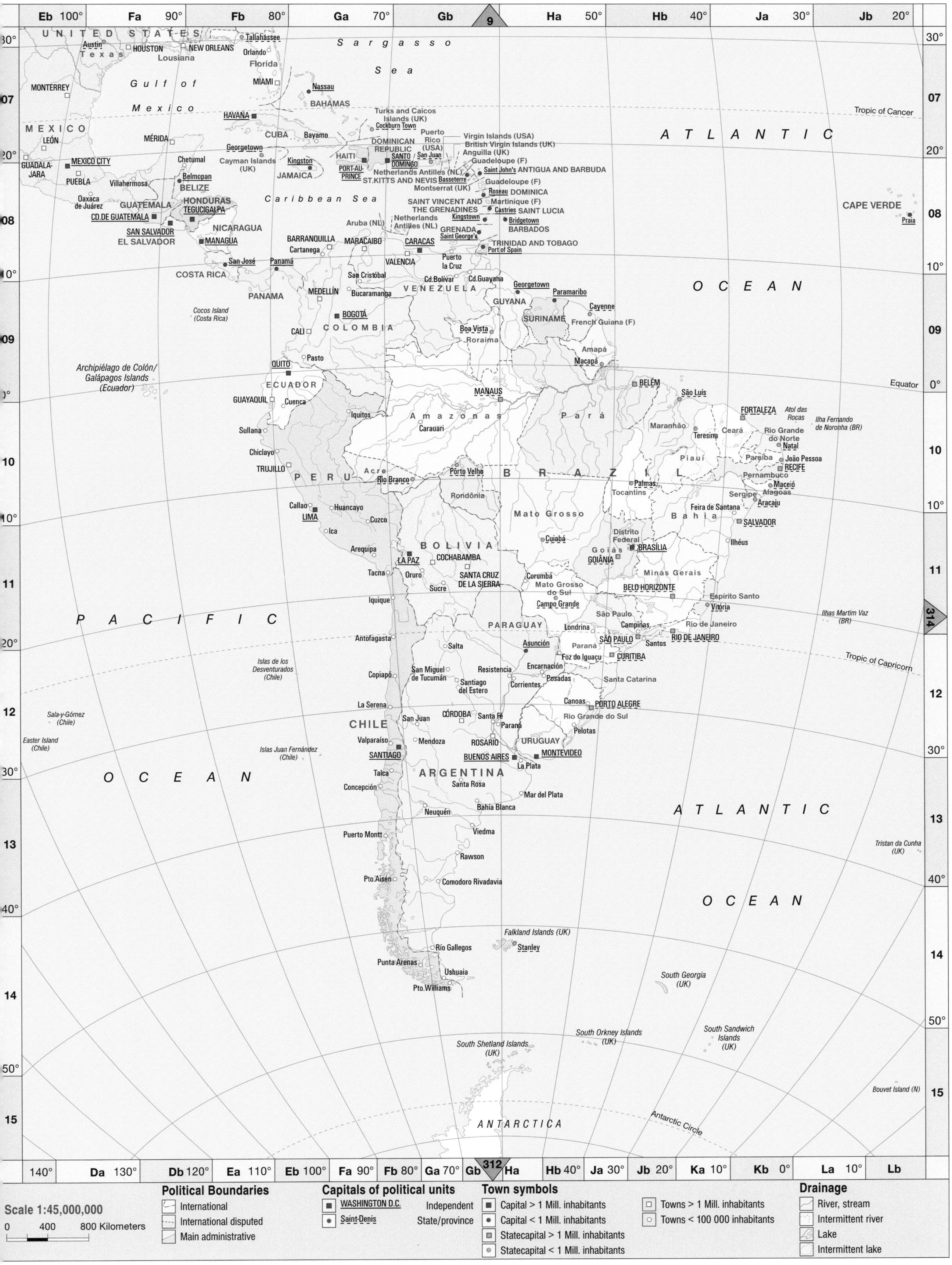

Countries and Flags
Argentina
Bolivia
Brasil
Chile
Colombia
Ecuador
Guyana
Paraguay
Peru
Suriname
Uruguay
Venezuela

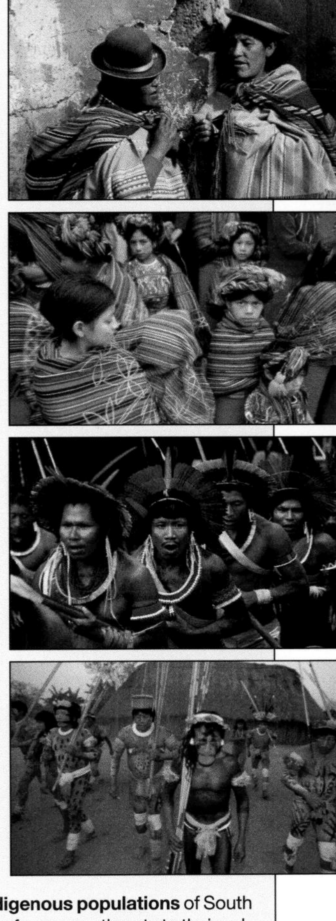

The **indigenous populations** of South America face many threats to their cultures and traditional lifestyles. One significant issue is the increasing exploitation of natural resources in the Amazon region and Andean highlands. In the next few decades, only the most isolated tribes in sparsely populated inhospitable regions will be able to preserve their traditional lifestyles in the face of pressure from the outside world. The Quechua in the Andes were traditionally llama and alpaca herders. The Yanomami are one of the largest tribes in the Amazon region, numbering at least 20,000 in Brazil and Venezuela. The Suya of Brazil are a people of farmers and hunters and gatherers. The Suya are well known for the large plates they wear in their ears and lips. Photos from top to bottom: Quechua women in Peru, Quechua girl in traditional clothing, Yanomami in the Amazon region, Suya in the Brazilian state Mato Grosso.

Scale 1:45,000,000
0 400 800 Kilometers

Political Boundaries
- International
- International disputed
- Main administrative

Capitals of political units
- WASHINGTON D.C. Independent
- Saint-Denis State/province

Town symbols
- Capital > 1 Mill. inhabitants
- Capital < 1 Mill. inhabitants
- Statecapital > 1 Mill. inhabitants
- Statecapital < 1 Mill. inhabitants
- Towns > 1 Mill. inhabitants
- Towns < 100 000 inhabitants

Drainage
- River, stream
- Intermittent river
- Lake
- Intermittent lake

Northern South America

Western South America is home to the **Andes Mountains**, one of the longest mountain ranges in the world. The Andes are an ancient mountain range created through the collision of tectonic plates. The mountain range rises 6,000 meters above sea level. Active volcanoes and frequent earthquakes are evidence that the Andes remain a geologically active region. There are several long ocean trenches off the coast of South America including the

8,000-meters-deep **Atacama Trenc**
The northern Andes in Columbia are con
prised of three parallel mountain range
the Occidental, Central, and Oriental Co
dilleras.
In Ecuador, south of Colombia, the Ande
are divided into two separate ranges.
Peru, long mountain valleys divide th

The Amazon rainforests are home to a
incredible abundance of flora and faun

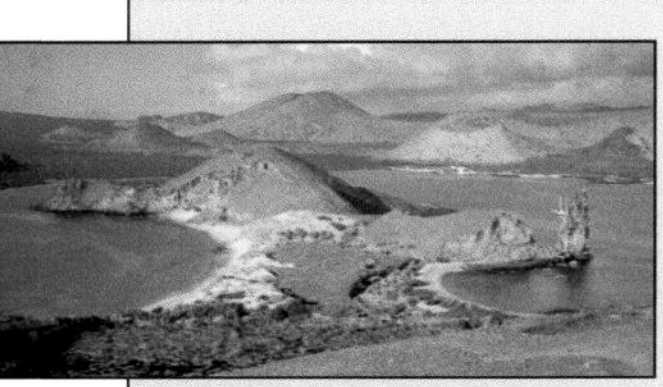

The Galapagos Islands This archipelago of volcanic islands is famous for its unique flora and fauna. Charles Darwin did much of his important research on these islands. The islands are a UNESCO world heritage site.

The Northern Andes Numerous active volcanoes – Chimborazo (photo) is the highest mountain in Ecuador (6,310 meters)

The Peruvian Andes In Peru, the Andes are divided into several ranges. In the north, the Andes are divided by the Maranon River. In the south, the mountains border the Altiplano plateau. Photos from top to bottom: Cordillera Blanca, the Cordillera Villacabamba range near Cuzco, Lake Titicaca

La Montaña (Peru) Region of lush rainforests in the eastern foothills of the Andes Mountains – abundance of wildlife and tropical plants

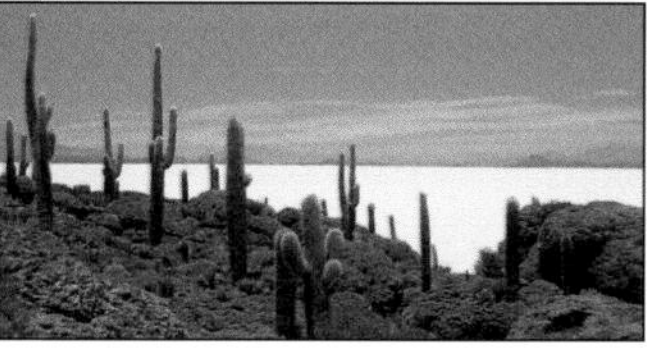

Salt Lakes in the Bolivian Andes Fascinating lakes at heights between 3,000 and 4,500 meters above sea level – unique ecosystems

Scale 1:18,000,000
0 160 320 Kilometers

Depth tints
Shoreline
0-200 m
200-2000 m
2000-4000 m
4000-6000 m
6000-8000 m
> 8000 m

Physical Features
River, stream
Intermittent river
Lake
Intermittent lake
Salt lake
Intermittent salt lake
Elevation above sea level in mete

ndes into several distinct ranges. Altilano, in southern Peru, is a large plateau urrounded by the tall mountains of the **ordillera Oriental** and **Cordillera Occiental**. The **Altiplano** contains numerus salt pans and lakes including **Lake iticaca**, the highest navigable lake in the orld. The Andes reach their maximum idth in Bolivia extending more than 700 ilometers east from the Pacific coast. he **Guiana and Brazilian Highlands**, the massive Amazon River basin, the **Llanos del Orinoco** marshland, and the plains of the **Gran Chaco** are all situated in the north of South America, to the east of the Andes. The **Amazon Basin,** the world's largest river basin, has a maximum width of 6500 km². The Amazon has more than 300 tributaries, many of which are interconnected by natural canals (iguarapes). Many of the rivers in the region split into two or more rivers – a process called bifurcation. The **Casiquiare** River, one of the longer branches of the Orinoco River, flows into the Amazon. Most of the Amazon basin is covered by thick tropical rainforests. In many of the region's rainforests, the ground is permanently covered by a shallow layer of water.

The climate in the Amazon rainforest is humid and hot with an average annual temperature around 26° Celsius. Despite human impact on the rainforest, the region is still home to an incredible abundance of unique animal and plant species. In recent decades, environmental activism and international interest in the rainforests has led to increased government protection of the region. But the biodiversity of the Amazon remains threatened. The Amazon basin contains more than half of the world's remaining rainforest areas and has a significant impact on the planet's climate.

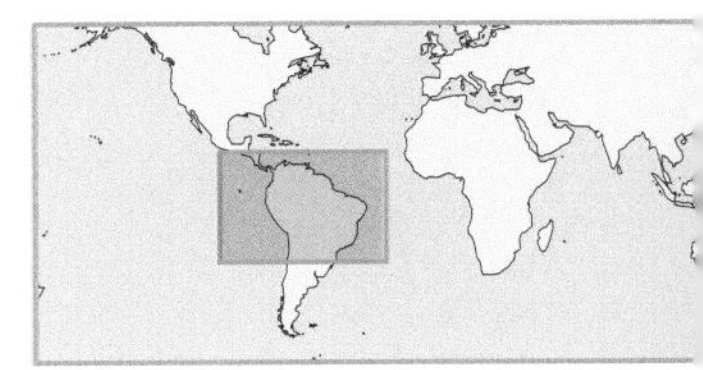

The Windward Islands The southern islands in the Lesser Antilles – Trinidad and Tobago (photo) lie near the South American coast

Guiana Highlands This highland region is one of the world's oldest geological formations. Angel Falls (top photo) in Venezuela's Canaima National Park descend from a height of more than 1,000 meters. The park is also home to Hacha Falls (bottom photo).

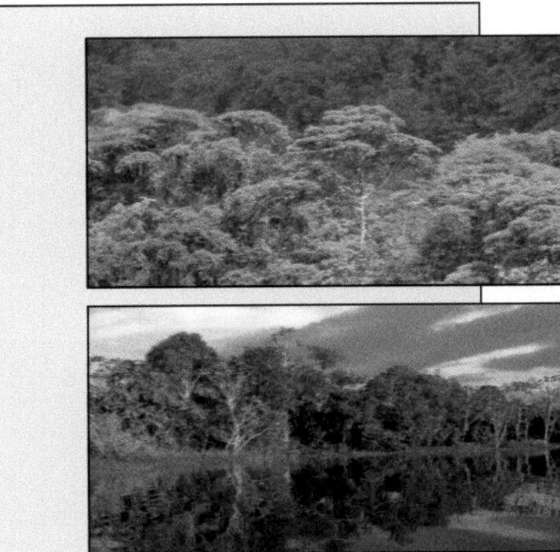

The Amazon Basin The world's largest river basin is nourished by the Amazon and its hundreds of tributaries.

Brazilian Highlands The region borders the Amazon River basin and is covered by savannahs and forests

Pantanal One of the world's largest series of wetlands. The Pantanal covers more than 230,000 km² – UNESCO world heritage site

Political Boundaries	Transportation	Capitals of political units		Town symbols	
International	Interstate Hwy./Motorway	■ WASHINGTON D.C.	Independent	■ Capital > 1 Mill. inhabitants	□ Towns > 1 Mill. inhabitants
International disputed	Main road	○ Richmond	State/province	● Capital < 1 Mill. inhabitants	○ Towns 100 000 bis 1 Mill. inhabitants
Main administrative	Railway			▣ Statecapital > 1 Mill. inhabitants	○ Towns < 100 000 inhabitants
	Airport			◉ Statecapital < 1 Mill. inhabitants	

The cone shaped southern portion of South America extends to within a few hundred kilometers of Antarctica. Mount Aconcagua, the highest mountain in South America, lies in western Argentina and rises 6959 meters. In the far south of the continent, the **Andes Mountain Range** tends to decrease in height and width. The island **Tierra del Fuego** is the southernmost region of South America. The highest mountains on the island, the last segment of the Andes, reach to height of no more than 2500 meters. Mas sive glaciers can be found in the Pata gonia region of Argentina as well as o the barren **South Georgia** and **Sout Sandwich Islands**. The landscape south of **Puerto Montt** in Chile loo remarkably similar to the fjords of Norwa

Barren mountain landscape in the southern Andes

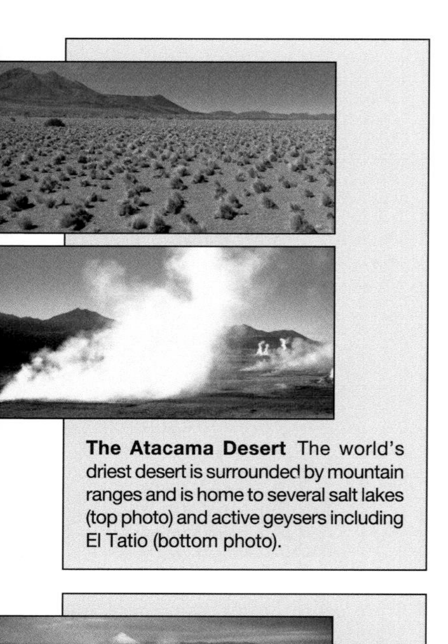

The Atacama Desert The world's driest desert is surrounded by mountain ranges and is home to several salt lakes (top photo) and active geysers including El Tatio (bottom photo).

Argentinean Lake District Argentina's Lake District encompasses snow-capped mountains and many beautiful lakes. The region is a popular tourist destination.

Patagonia Patagonia is the most sparsely settled region in Argentina. The area contains many glaciers and tall stone formations created by erosion. Photos from top to bottom: Torres del Paine NP, Los Glaciares NP, Mount Fitz Roy

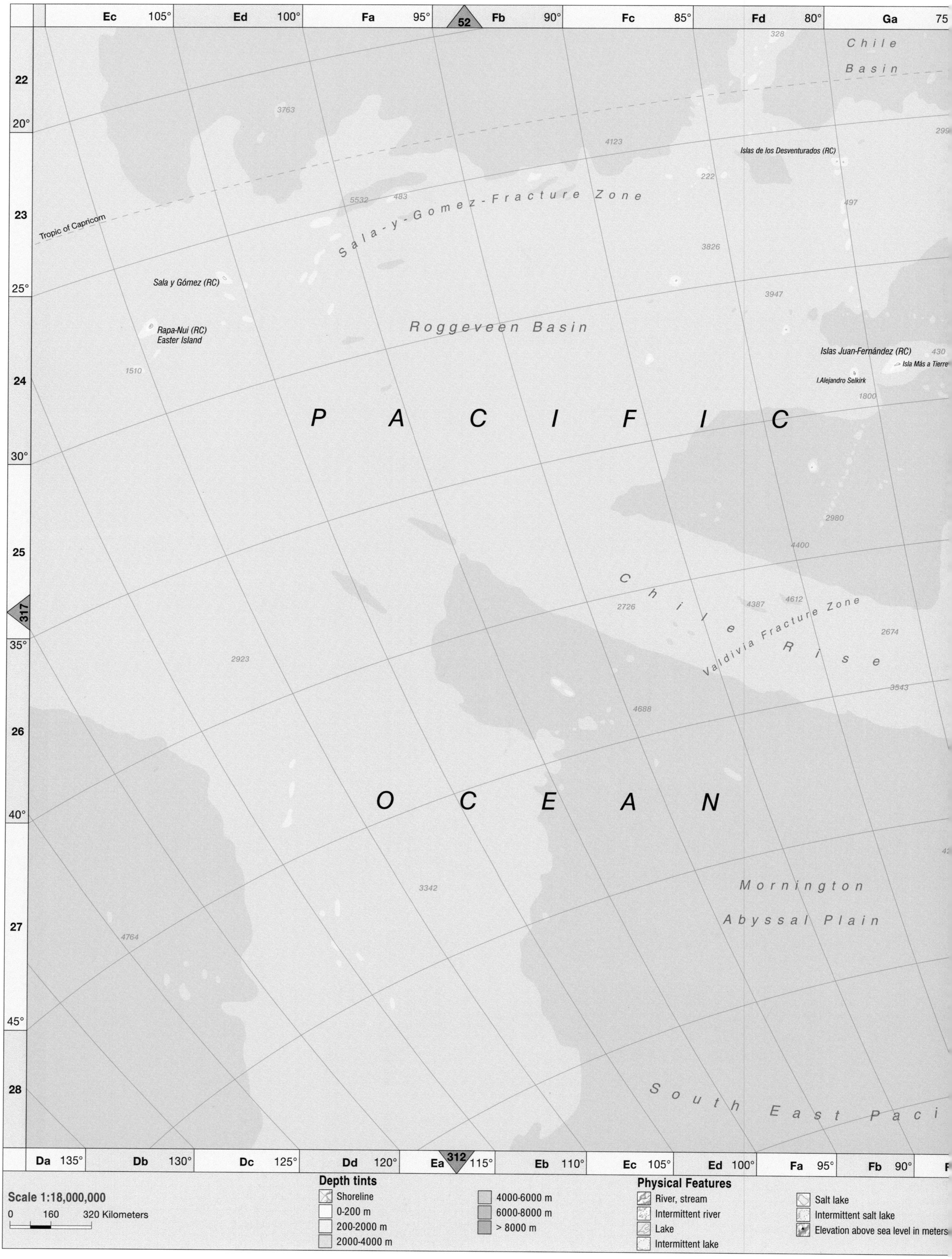

Ec 105° Ed 100° Fa 95° 52 Fb 90° Fc 85° Fd 80° Ga 75

22 20° 23 25° 24 30° 25 317 35° 26 40° 27 45° 28

Chile Basin

Islas de los Desventurados (RC)

Tropic of Capricorn

Sala-y-Gomez-Fracture Zone

Sala y Gómez (RC)

Rapa-Nui (RC)
Easter Island

Roggeveen Basin

Islas Juan-Fernández (RC)

Isla Más a Tierra

I.Alejandro Selkirk

P A C I F I C

Chile Rise

Valdivia Fracture Zone

O C E A N

Mornington Abyssal Plain

South East Paci

3763 4123 222 5532 483 497 3826 3947 1510 430 1800 2980 4400 2726 4387 4612 2674 2923 3543 4688 3342 4764

Da 135° Db 130° Dc 125° Dd 120° Ea 312 115° Eb 110° Ec 105° Ed 100° Fa 95° Fb 90°

Scale 1:18,000,000

0 160 320 Kilometers

Depth tints

Shoreline
0-200 m
200-2000 m
2000-4000 m
4000-6000 m
6000-8000 m
> 8000 m

Physical Features

River, stream
Intermittent river
Lake
Intermittent lake
Salt lake
Intermittent salt lake
Elevation above sea level in meters

nd Alaska. **Argentina's Lake District**, round San Carlos de Bariloche, is a re- on of mountains, forests and crystal- ear lakes that reminds many visitors of witzerland. The lakes were created uring the ice ages by large moving gla- ers. North of the Puerto Natales in Chile, s the **Torres del Paine** National Park ith breathtaking natural sights and nique wildlife.
ne subtropical regions of northern Chile are home to numerous volcanoes, salt lakes, and deserts including the Atacama Desert. The **Atacama Desert** is the driest area in the world. High mountain ranges surround the desert on both sides, preventing moist air from entering the region. Northern Chile's many salt lakes support delicate ecosystems with unique flora and fauna including colonies of flamingos and llamas. Two large regions cover the vast plains between the Andes in the west and the **highlands** of southern Brazil in the east – the **Gran Chaco** and the **Pampas**. Spanish settlers were the first people to bring cattle to South America, and today the Pampas and Gran Chaco are major centers for cattle ranching. The sections of the Pampas to the south and west of Buenos Aires are used mainly for crop cultivation (especially corn and wheat); Argentina is a major exporter of foodstuffs.

Patagonia is a cool, windswept, and sparsely populated region. Sheep farming is a major industry in this Argentinean frontier. The regions at the extreme south of the continent and the **Falkland Islands (Islas Malvinas)** have cool climates with abundant precipitation. Much of southern South America's population is concentrated in a few large coastal cities such as Buenos Aires, Valparaiso, and Montevideo.

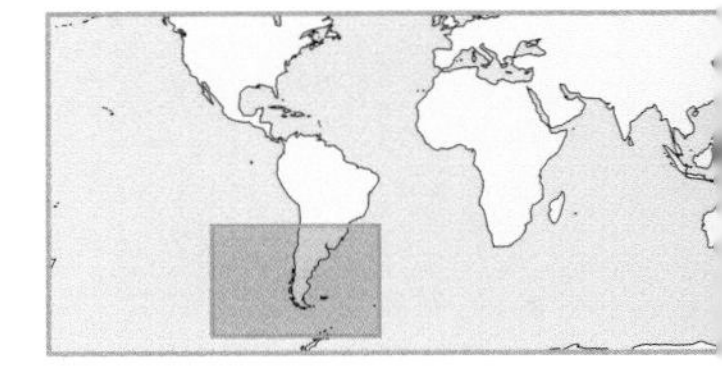

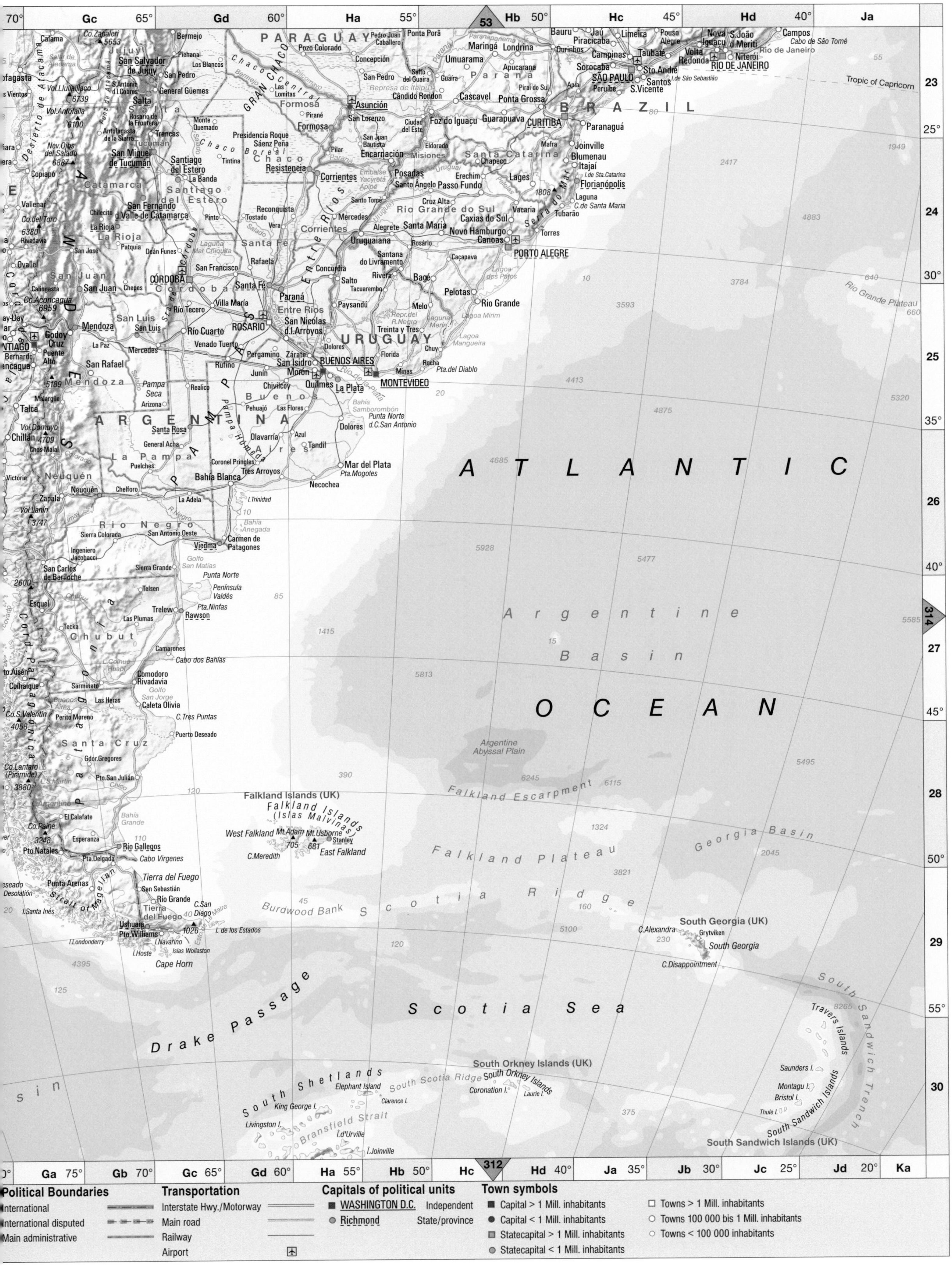

Gran Chaco Expansive grassland region in Argentina and Paraguay – subject to floods and frequent drought – pawpaw trees (photo) are common to the Gran Chaco

La Pampa Seca This dry section of the Pampas lies in the rain shadow of the Andes – major center of the Argentinean cattle ranching industry

The Pampas A region of vast fertile plains extending north and west of the Rio de la Plata – crop farming and sheep herding

The Falkland Island (Islas Malvinas) Island group in the South Atlantic – British territory – site of the 1982 Falklands War

South Georgia Discovered in 1675 – more than 160 glaciers descend from the island into the ocean – abandoned whaling station

South Shetland Islands First explored in 1819 – four island groups with a total land area of 3,687 km² – highest peak, Mount Foster (2,105 meter) – large penguin colonies

South Sandwich Islands Group of islands west of a large ocean trench – active volcanoes – the islands are covered by glaciers

Political Boundaries
International
International disputed
Main administrative

Transportation
Interstate Hwy./Motorway
Main road
Railway
Airport

Capitals of political units
WASHINGTON D.C. Independent
Richmond State/province

Town symbols
Capital > 1 Mill. inhabitants
Capital < 1 Mill. inhabitants
Statecapital > 1 Mill. inhabitants
Statecapital < 1 Mill. inhabitants
Towns > 1 Mill. inhabitants
Towns 100 000 bis 1 Mill. inhabitants
Towns < 100 000 inhabitants

Western Venezuela, Northern Colombia

The geological history of this South American region goes back to the early periods of the Earth's development. The mountains of the **Guiana Highlands**, east and south of the Orinoco River, were first formed during the Precambrian period. The oldest sections of this range were created around 2.5 billion years ago on the prehistoric super-continent Gondwanaland. The western portions of the Guiana Highlands are covered by the upland plains of the Gran Sabana. The Pemon Amerindians who inhabit the region refer to the mountains, which they consider sacred, as tepuis.

To the east of the **Gran Sabana** lies an area of plateaus and mesas. Because of their height and steep rises many of the plateaus and mountains in the highlands are isolated from surrounding region This isolation has led to the developme of unique vegetation in many areas.

Since the 1950s, the Orinoco basin Venezuela has become increasing important for the country's econon because of its vast deposits of miner resources. An even larger segment of th Venezuelan economy relies on the deposits in the region around **Lak Maracaibo**. Thanks to its large reserve

A colorful island in the Los Roques Archipelago National Park **Gg40**

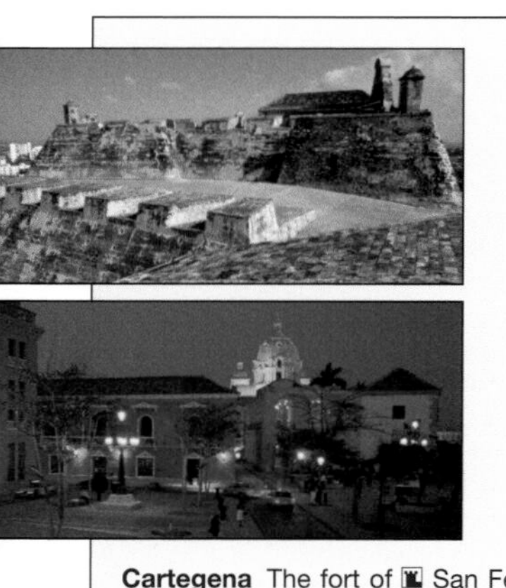

Cartegena The fort of San Felipe (top photo) protected the Spanish port Cartagena during the colonial era. The beautiful old town (bottom photo) is still surrounded by a city wall. **Gc40**

Santa Cruz de Mompox Colonial city founded in 1537 – historic Santa Barbara church was built in Moorish style **Gc41**

Río Magdalena This river was the most important transport route in the region during pre-Colombian times – several floating markets (photo) **Gd41/44**

Los Katios National Park Columbian national park adjoined to Panama's Darien National Park – mostly humid tropical swampland **Gb42**

Villa de Leyva Picturesque village in the Boyaca Highlands of Colombia – historic architecture from the colonial era **Gd43**

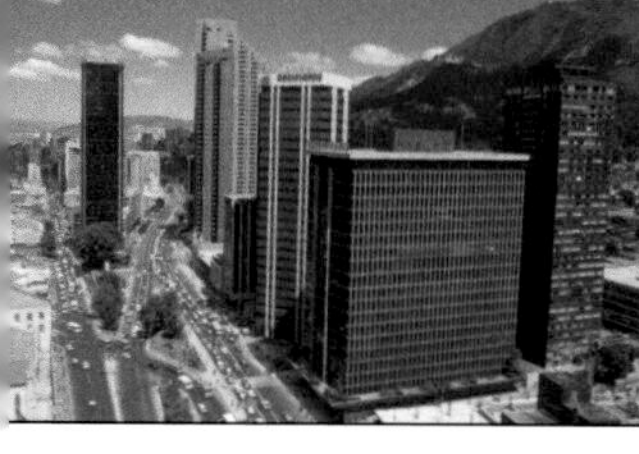

Bogotá Capital city of Colombia – population 6.8 million – historic old town: La Candelaria – modern high rises – historic architecture around Plaza Bolivar – gold museum **Gc43**

Scale 1:4,500,000

0 40 80 Kilometers

Principal travel routes

- Auto route
- Rail road
- Shipping route

Remarkable landscapes and natural monuments

- UNESCO World Natural Heritage
- Mountain landscape
- Extinct volcano
- Active volcano
- Cave
- River landscape
- Waterfall/rapids
- Lake country
- Desert
- Nature park
- National park (landscape)
- National park (flora)
- National park (fauna)
- National park (culture)
- Coastal landscape
- Beach

enezuela is one of the world's leading l producers and exporters. The coun-y's oil deposits were formed billions of ears ago in an undersea basin along the dge of the South American tectonic ate.

ollisions between the Nazca and South merican tectonic plates led to the for-ation of the **Andes Mountains** (divi-ed into three separate ranges in this egion). There are several mountains rising more than 5,000 meters in the region including snow covered **Pico Bolivar** in the Sierra de Merida, **Nevado de Tolima** (5,215 meters), and the active volcano **Nevado der Ruiz** (5,352 meters). Many of the numerous valleys in the Colombian Andes were formed by powerful rivers such as the **Rio Atrato** and **Rio Magdelena**.

The **Llanos** are a hot region of expansive prairies in the **Orinico River** basin region of Colombia and Venezuela. Because of powerful trade winds, the coastal areas in this part of northern South America are relatively dry – especially during winter. Colombia and Venezuela get most of their rainfall during the humid summer months.

During the early19th century, the German explorer and naturalist Alexander von Humboldt became the first person to identify the incredible diversity of flora and fauna in the region. Ecotourism has become an important industry in Venezuela recently with an increasing number of tourists visiting the country's wilderness areas. The rainforest and savannahs in the region often border mountainous regions with cool climates and rugged vegetation. In addition to its abundant vegetation, northwestern South America is also home to many fascinating and unique animal species.

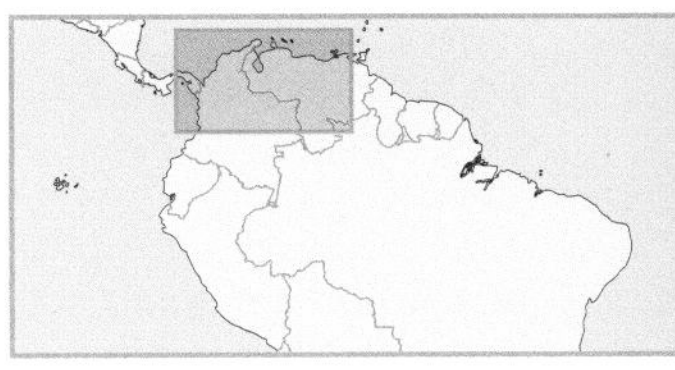

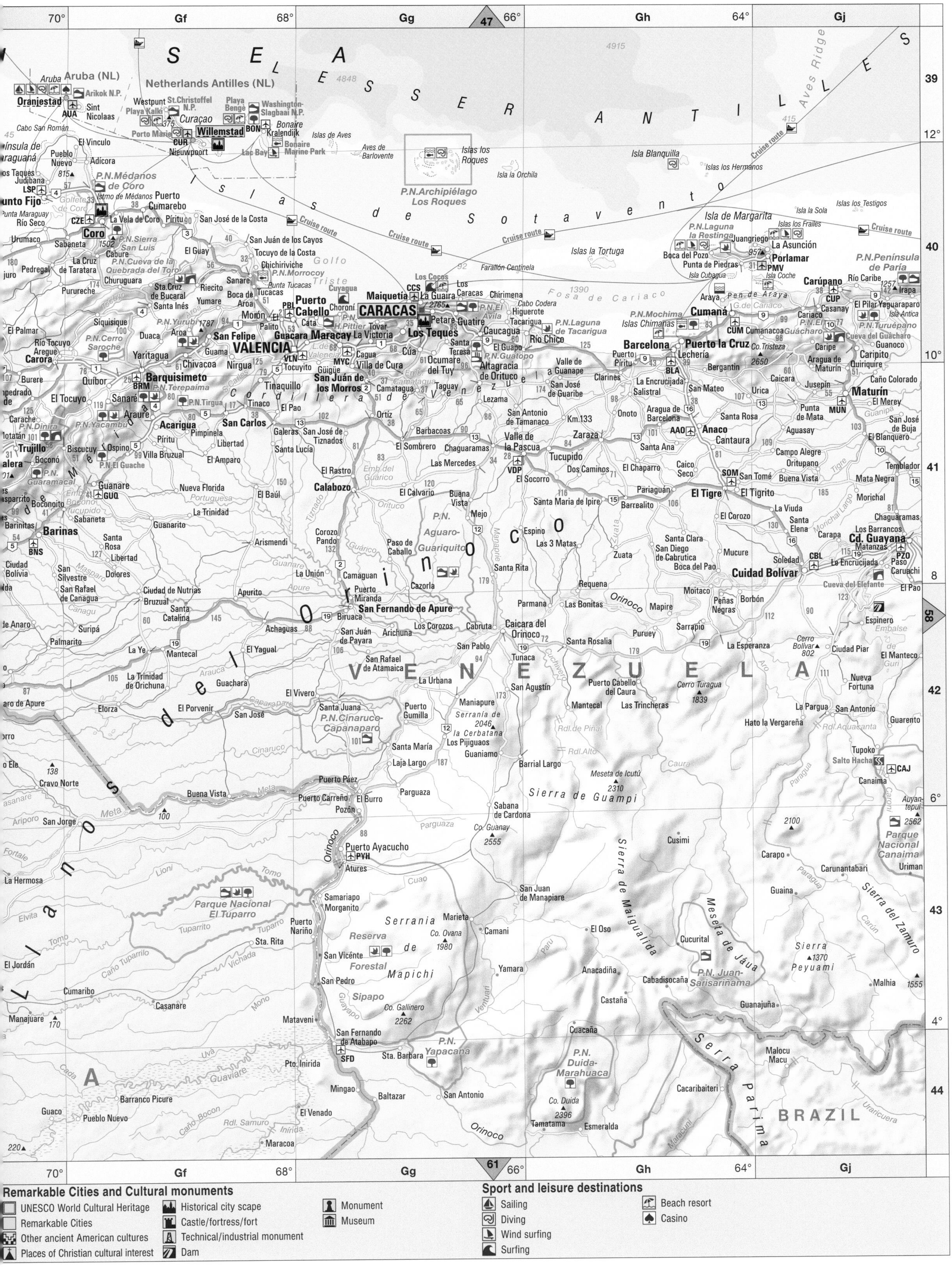

Willemstad Capital of the Netherland Antilles – on Curacao – historic quarter with Dutch architecture – oil refinery **Gf39**

Coro Historic city founded in 1527 (population 175,000) – Cathedral (1583) – UNESCO world heritage site **Gf40**

Caracas Capital of Venezuela – population of five million – historic cathedral and San Francisco Church – Casa Natal del Libertador: birthplace of Simon Bolivar **Gg40**

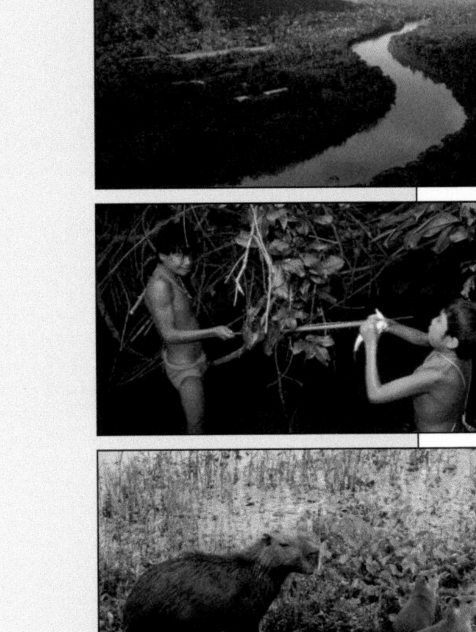

The Orinoco River The longest river (2140 kilometers) in Venezuela, passes through rainforests (top photo) including the homelands of the Yanomami (middle photo). **GgGj41/44**

Salto Hacha Terraced waterfalls along the dark Rio Carrao in the Laguna de Canaima (Venezuela) **Gj42**

Remarkable Cities and Cultural monuments

- UNESCO World Cultural Heritage
- Remarkable Cities
- Other ancient American cultures
- Places of Christian cultural interest
- Historical city scape
- Castle/fortress/fort
- Technical/industrial monument
- Dam
- Monument
- Museum

Sport and leisure destinations

- Sailing
- Diving
- Wind surfing
- Surfing
- Beach resort
- Casino

Eastern Venezuela, Guyana, Suriname

Northeastern South America comprises eastern Venezuela, the French territory French Guiana and two of the smallest nations in South America – Suriname and Guyana. The region is home to many diverse landscapes and natural attractions including tropical rainforests, high plateaus, the world's tallest waterfall, prairies, and sandy white beaches. The majority of the region's population is concentrated in eastern **Venezuela's** coastal

areas. This coastal region was one of th first areas to be settled during the Sp nish colonization of South America. Ma of the cities along the Venezuelan coas including Puerto la Cruz, experienced major hotel construction boom in th 1980s. There are still, however, undev loped beaches in places such as

Auyán-tepuí is the largest mesa in the Guiana Highlands **Gj**

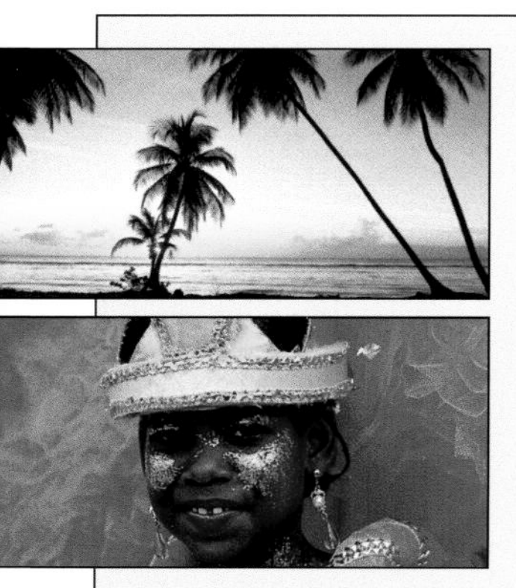

Trinidad und Tobago Pigeon Point is a beautiful series of beaches in western Tobago (top photo). Trinidad has one of the largest carnivals in the Caribbean. This small nation has a diverse population and is the birthplace of calypso music. **Gk40**

Mochima National Park National Park in northern Venezuela – includes uninhabited islands, creeks, and beaches **Gh40**

Warao Amerindians The Warao Amerindians live in the Orinoco Delta – stilt houses are common in Warao villages **Gk41**

Angel Falls The tallest waterfalls in the world – 978 meters tall – discovered in 1936 by the American pilot Jimmy Angel **Gj42/43**

Quebrada de Jaspe Terraced riverbed in a tropical rainforest – unusual, dark red-dish-orange colored stone **Gk43**

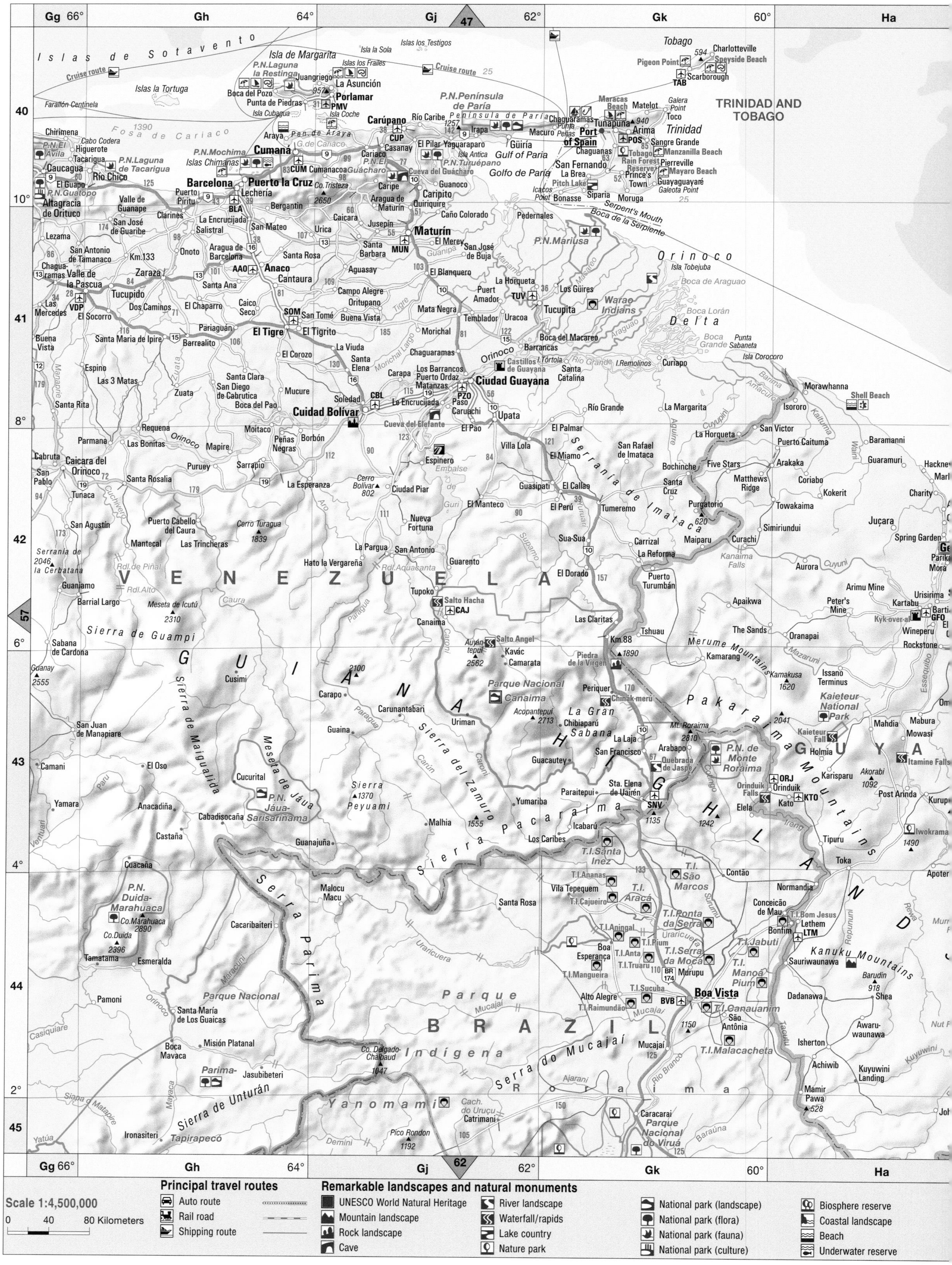

Scale 1:4,500,000
0 40 80 Kilometers

Principal travel routes
- Auto route
- Rail road
- Shipping route

Remarkable landscapes and natural monuments
- UNESCO World Natural Heritage
- Mountain landscape
- Rock landscape
- Cave
- River landscape
- Waterfall/rapids
- Lake country
- Nature park
- National park (landscape)
- National park (flora)
- National park (fauna)
- National park (culture)
- Biosphere reserve
- Coastal landscape
- Beach
- Underwater reserve

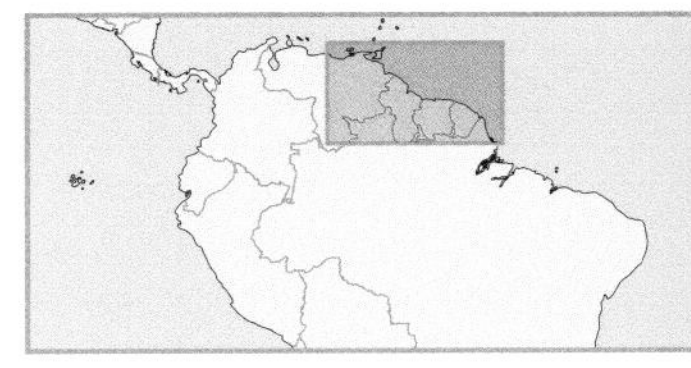

ochima National Park. Isla Marga-
a, an island off the Venezuelan coast one of the most popular tourist destiations in the region. **The Orinoco River** the most important river in the reon. Two major cities are located along e Orinoco: Ciudad Bolivar, a major port ty and Ciudad Guyana, a leading inıstrial center. The Casiquiare River onnects the Orinoco to the Rio Negro, tributary of the Amazon River.

High water levels in the Rio Negro often cause the Casiquiare to change its direction and flow backwards into the Orinoco. The **Guiana Highlands** block the path of the Orinoco and force the river to make a 1,000 kilometer detour on its way to the ocean. These highlands are one of the oldest mountain regions in the world and were once a part of the prehistoric Guiana Shield. The **Gran Sabana** in the southeastern Guiana Highlands offers fascinating landscapes. The region is home to isolated **mesas** (called tepuis locally) that rise above lush rainforests. Roraima Tepui lies along the border between Venezuela, Guyana, and Brazil. To the east of the Orinoco Delta in Venezuela are the three countries sometimes collectively known as the Guianas. **Guyana** is the westernmost of these three countries and is home to the beautiful Kaieteur Falls. East of Guyana lies **Suriname**, a former Dutch colony with an attractive capital city. **French Guiana**, the easternmost of the Guianas, is an overseas territory of France. This small territory is the location of the European Space Agency's launch center and infamous Devil's Island, a former French penal colony. Because the interior of the Guianas is covered by thick hot rainforests, the populations of all three countries are concentrated along the coast.

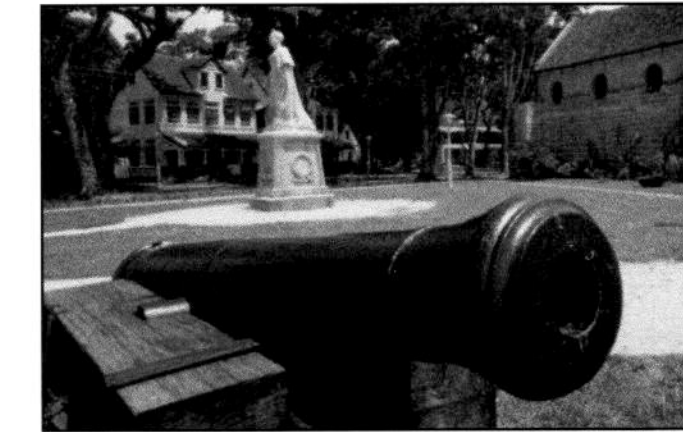

Paramaribo Capital of Suriname – Fort Zeelandia (photo) – Suriname National Museum – colonial wooden houses – UNESCO world heritage site **Hc43**

Kaieteur Falls Spectacular waterfall in Guyana – 226-meter-drop – the surrounding region is home to unique wildlife including tapirs, armadillos, and anteaters **Ha43**

Central Suriname Nature Reserve Protected ecosystem – home to rare poisonous frogs – covered by thick rainforests – UNESCO world heritage site **HbHc43/44**

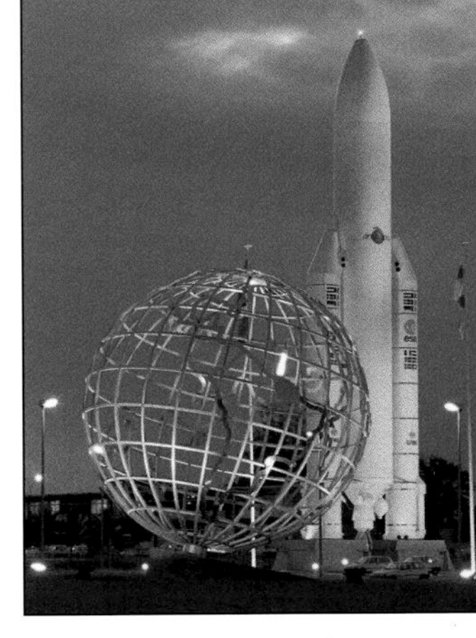

Kourou Site of the European Space Agency's launch center – space exploration museum – in French Guiana **Hd43**

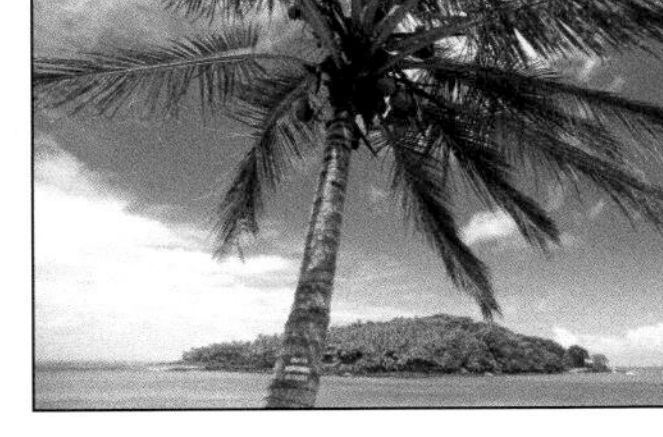

Îles du Salut Island group includes Ile du Diable (Devil's Island), once the site of an infamous French penal colony **Hd43**

Remarkable Cities and Cultural monuments
- UNESCO World Cultural Heritage
- Remarkable Cities
- Amazonian Indians/protected area
- Historical city scape
- Castle/fortress/fort
- Dam
- Space mission launch site

Sport and leisure destinations
- Sailing
- Diving
- Wind surfing
- Deep-sea fishing
- Beach resort

The equatorial region in western South America stretches into three countries: Ecuador, Peru, and Colombia. This compact region encompasses coastlines, mountainous highlands, and tropical forests. The Andes in this region are divided into three separate ranges: the **Cordillera Real** in the west, the **Cordillera Oriental** in the east, and the Cordillera Central which runs between the previous two. The three ranges, which contain several peaks above 5,000 meters, a separated by hilly highlands. The highe mountain in the region, Chimbora (6,310 meters), is an inactive volcano. Cotopaxi, the world's highest active vo cano, lies in central Ecuador. Many of t region's rivers have their sources in t western Cordilleras and flow through

Cotopaxi: one of the most beautiful peaks in the Andes **Ga**

Galápagos Islands Swallow-tailed Gulls, Galapagos Land Iguanas, and Galapagos Giant Tortoises, are a few of the many unique species on this group of islands. The islands are a UNESCO world heritage site. The Galapagos also feature unique volcanic landscapes and plant species. **FeFf45/46**

San Agustín Archeological Park Site containing more than 500 sculptures created between the 6th and 12th centuries – UNESCO world heritage site **Gb45**

El Angel Ecological Reserve Nature reserve containing rugged alpine vegetation – at heights between 3400 and 4150 meters – in northern Ecuador **GaGb45**

Quito Ecuador's capital lies 2850 meters above sea level – founded in 1534 – the old town is a UNESCO world heritage site – 16th century cathedral – La Compania and San Francisco (photo) **Ga46**

Cotopaxi The world's highest active volcano – crater diameter of 5897 meters – rugged alpine vegetation lies below the snow-covered rim **Ga46**

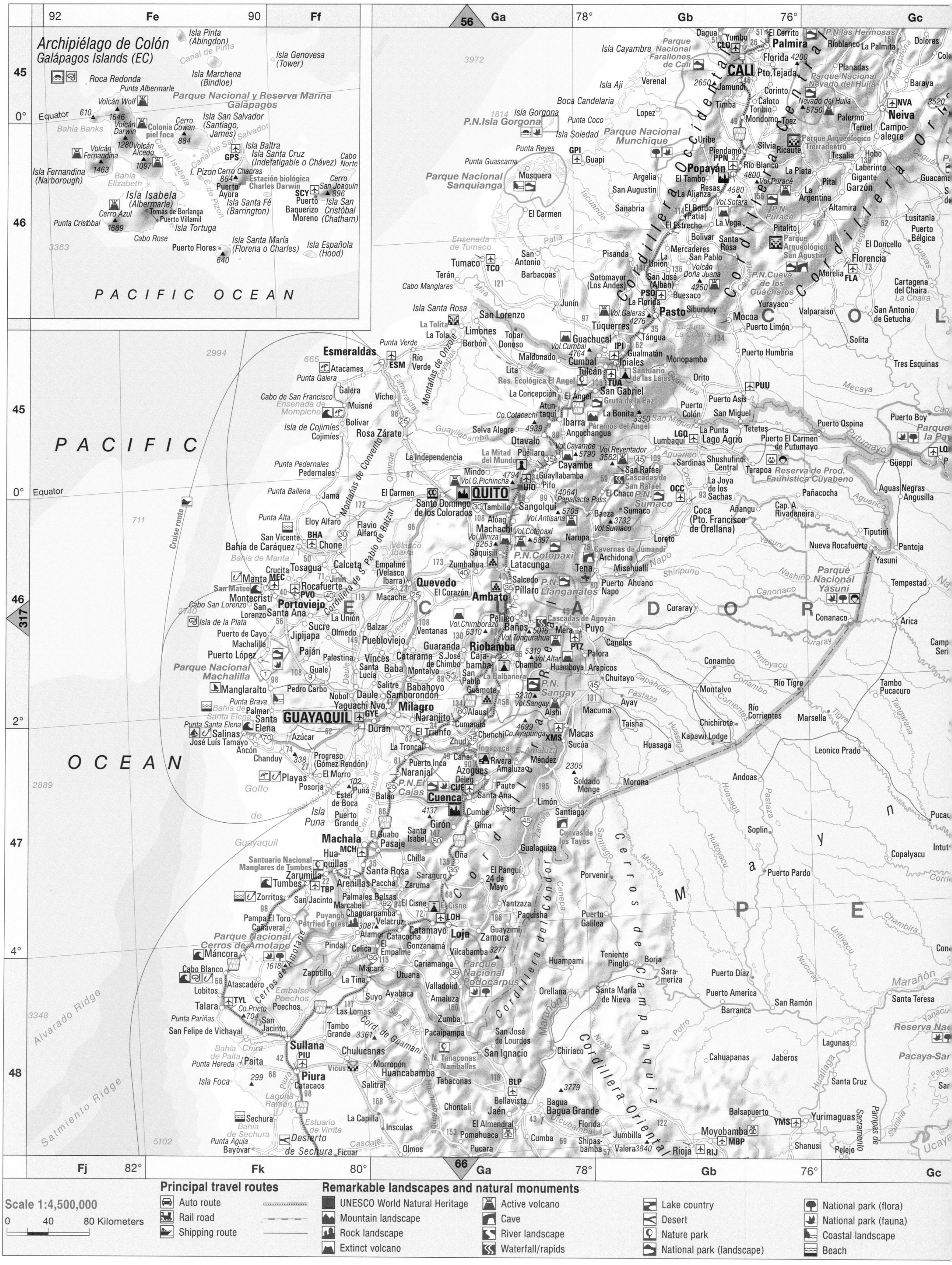

Scale 1:4,500,000

0 40 80 Kilometers

Principal travel routes

- Auto route
- Rail road
- Shipping route

Remarkable landscapes and natural monuments

- UNESCO World Natural Heritage
- Mountain landscape
- Rock landscape
- Extinct volcano
- Active volcano
- Cave
- River landscape
- Waterfall/rapids
- Lake country
- Desert
- Nature park
- National park (landscape)
- National park (flora)
- National park (fauna)
- Coastal landscape
- Beach

astal areas where they deposit fertile il important to local agriculture. Sever- important tributaries of the **Amazon ver** such as the Rio Napo and Rio San-go rise in the eastern Cordilleras. The avily forested eastern Cordilleras are rdered to the east by the plains of the **nazon River basin**. This region of nse rainforest is largely inaccessible th the exception of areas where natu- resources (natural gas and oil) are exploited. The Brazilian section of the Amazon basin contains several large land reserves created to protect the traditional lifestyles of local Amerindians. The **Galápagos Islands** are a group of volcanic islands formed on top of a so-called mantle plume. Mantle plumes are columns of molten rock that rise from deep within the earth's surface. These columns of rock force the earth's crust to rise forming volcanoes and in some cases volcanic islands. The tallest volcano on the Galápagos Islands is **Cerro Azul** rising more than 5,000 meters from the ocean floor and 1,689 meters above sea level. **Cerro Wolf** the second tallest peak on the islands rises 1,646 meters. The islands are slowly drifting eastwards toward the South American mainland. The western islands are the youngest in the group. The Galápagos Islands are most famous for their unique wildlife and the work of Charles Darwin, who conducted some of his most important research on the islands. Alcedo Crater is home to the largest colony of **Galápagos Giant Tortoises**. These famous tortoises are the largest in the world and can live as long as 150 years. The island's unique wildlife is a result of the Galápagos' geographic isolation from other land areas and the lack of large predators on the islands.

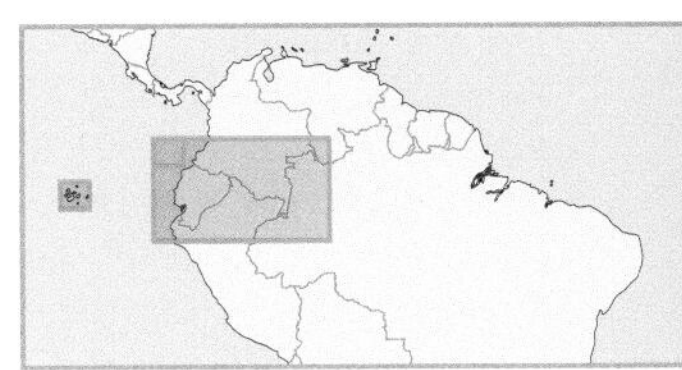

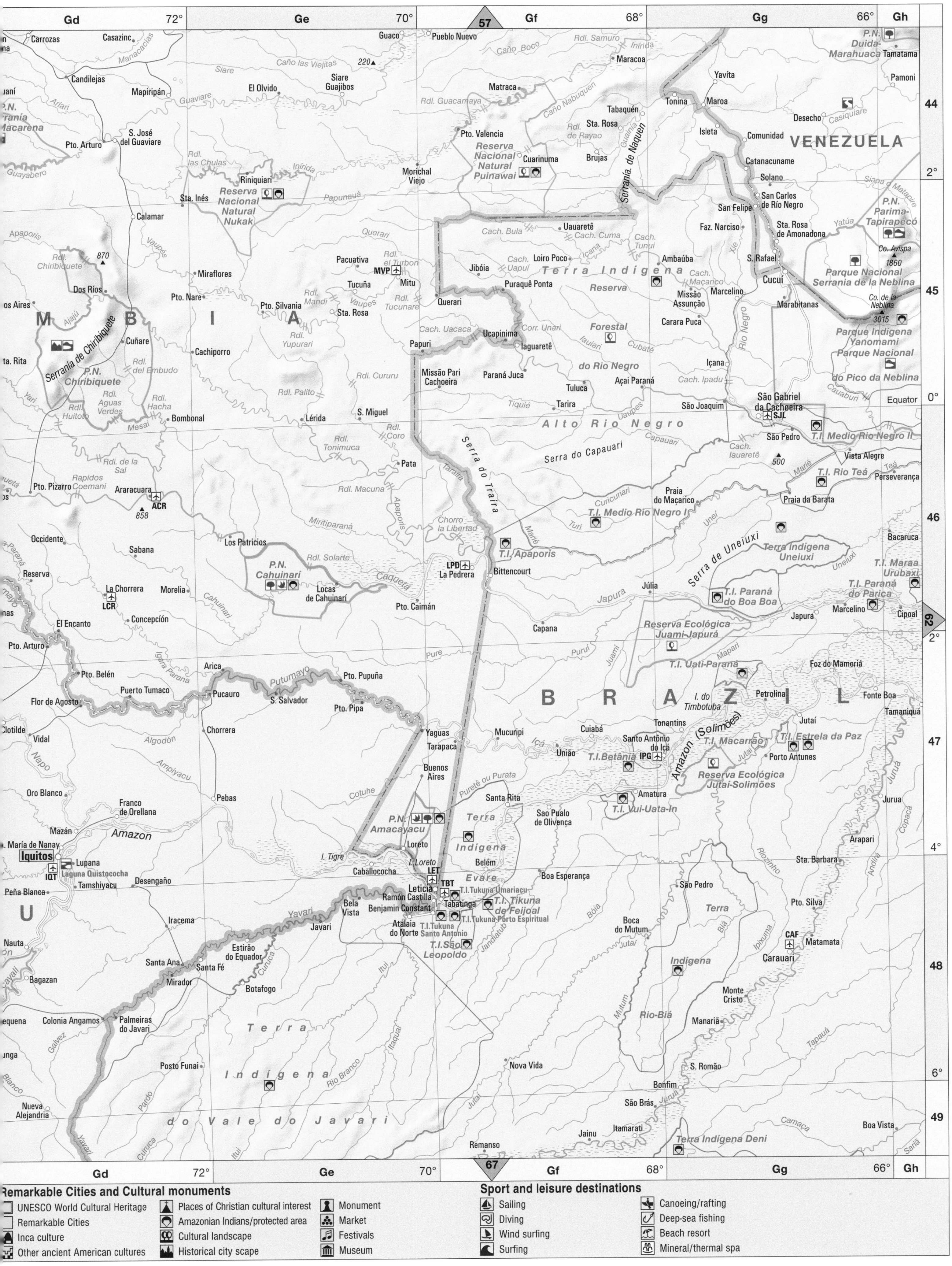

Chimborazo The highest mountain in Ecuador (6,310 meters) – inactive volcano – 16 glaciers – ice covered craters **Ga46**

Machalilla National Park National park on the Pacific coast – extensive forests – good areas for bird watching **Fk46**

Sangay National Park National park in Ecuador – Sangay volcano (5,230 meters) – home to endangered tapirs **Ga46/47**

Ingapirca Built around 1500 – complex of Incan inns and troop lodgings – once a major stop on the Incan road system **Ga47**

Cuenca Founded by the Spanish in 1557 – Catedral Nueva (photo) – historic old town with 17th and 18th century architecture – UNESCO world heritage site **Ga47**

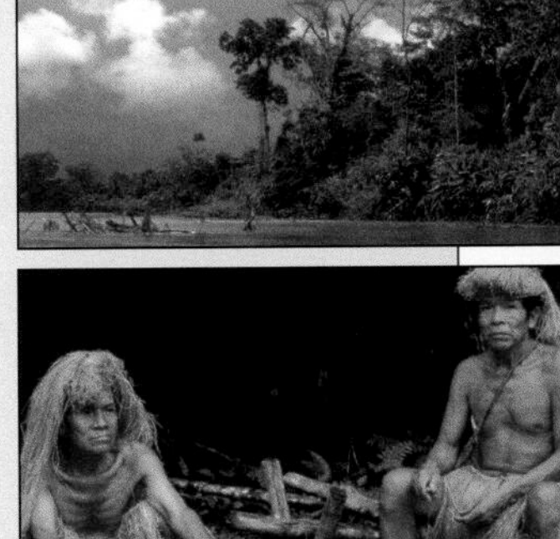

The Amerindians of the western Amazon region The Amazon basin has been inhabited by humans for at least 12,000 years. The Huaorani are one of the last nomadic tribes in Ecuador. Many of the region's Amerindians live on protected land reservations.

Remarkable Cities and Cultural monuments

- UNESCO World Cultural Heritage
- Remarkable Cities
- Inca culture
- Other ancient American cultures
- Places of Christian cultural interest
- Amazonian Indians/protected area
- Cultural landscape
- Historical city scape
- Monument
- Market
- Festivals
- Museum

Sport and leisure destinations

- Sailing
- Diving
- Wind surfing
- Surfing
- Canoeing/rafting
- Deep-sea fishing
- Beach resort
- Mineral/thermal spa

Amazonian Lowlands

The Amazon River basin is the largest river basin in the world. The drainage area of the Amazon River is larger in size than the continent of Australia. Technically the Amazon River only begins where it merges with the **Rio Negro**, 18 kilometers southeast of Manaus. The section of the river upstream from Manaus is known to Brazilians as the **Rio Solimões**. Further upstream in Peru, the name of the river reverts back to Amazon. In Peru,

several rivers that originate in the Ande including the Maranon and Huallaga, flo into the Amazon. The Amazon has seve al large tributaries such as the power Rio Negro which flow south into the Am zon. Other major tributaries such as t **Rio Madeira**, **Rio Tapajos**, and **R Xingu** flow north into the river. The wat

Sunrise above the steamy Amazon rainforest

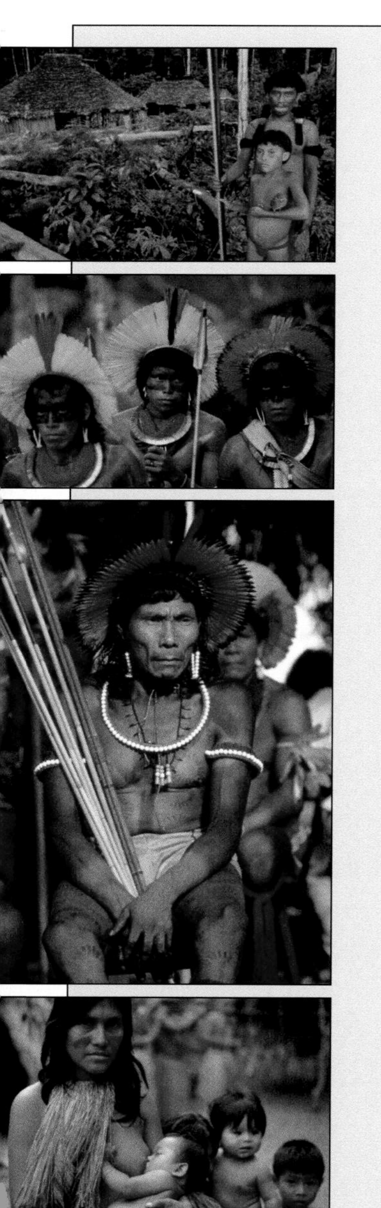

Amazon Amerindians The Yanomami are the largest Amerindian tribe in the Amazon region (top and bottom photo). Most Yanomami live in small villages of malokas (round huts) in the rainforest. They live in both Brazil and Venezuela. The Kayapo (middle photos) live in areas along the Rio Xingu. **GhGj45**

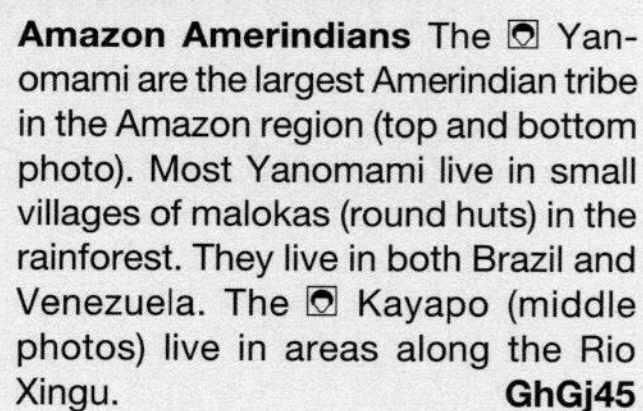

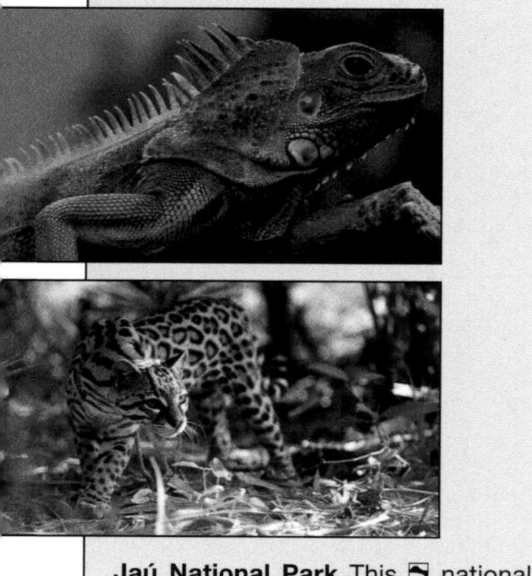

Jaú National Park This national park in the Amazon rainforest has an abundance of unique flora and fauna. The park is home to green iguanas (top photo), which can grow to be two meters long, and endangered spotted ocelots. **GjGk46/47**

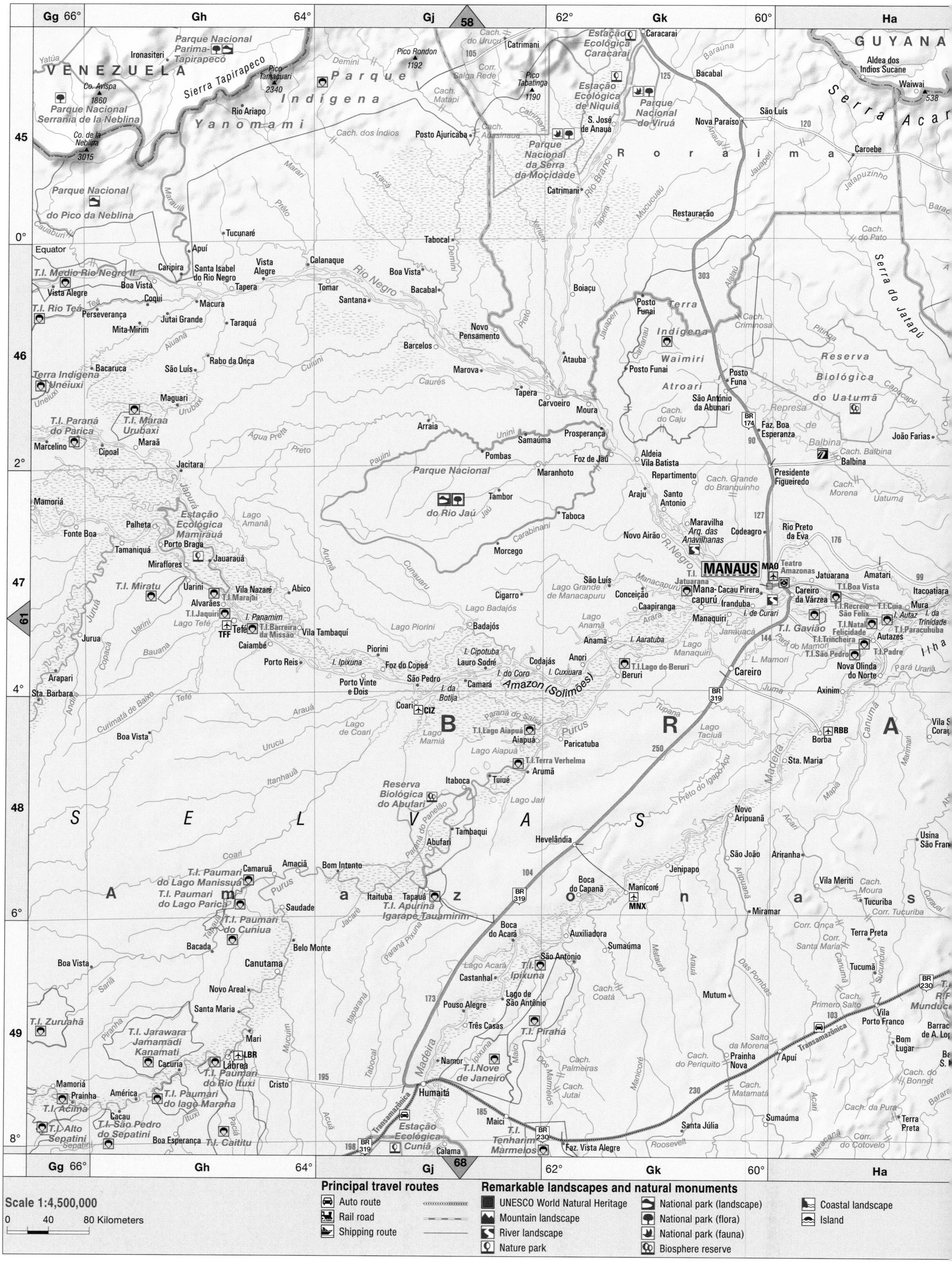

Scale 1:4,500,000

0 40 80 Kilometers

Principal travel routes

- Auto route
- Rail road
- Shipping route

Remarkable landscapes and natural monuments

- UNESCO World Natural Heritage
- Mountain landscape
- River landscape
- Nature park
- National park (landscape)
- National park (flora)
- National park (fauna)
- Biosphere reserve
- Coastal landscape
- Island

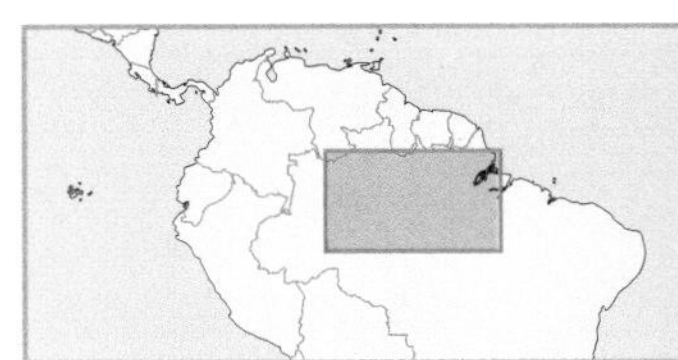

vel fluctuation of the Amazon River can be as great as 15 meters. Downstream om Manaus the river widens and is rely less than five kilometers wide. One ception to this pattern is the narrow ea of the river around **Óbidos** where the mazon is 100 meters deep and only two ometers wide. Modern geologists beve that the Amazon was created in the ection of Africa where the Sahara Desert now located. It is also known that the Amazon once flowed towards the Pacific – the opposite direction of its present course. Millions of years ago, Africa and South America formed one continent. When this continent began to break apart, and South America drifted westwards, the Andes Mountains began to form. The rising mountains forced the Amazon to finally change direction around six million years ago.

The Amazon rainforest is the largest continuous forested area in the world. Because of its dense vegetation and poor soil the Amazon rainforest remains a sparsely populated region. Logging and land clearing have done considerable damage to the rainforest. But in recent decades increased environmental awareness has led to activism and government action for the defense of the Amazon rainforest. Large sections of the rainforest are now protected in national parks such as **Jau National Park**, **Yanomami Indigenous Park**, and **Tumucumaque Park**. In the 15th century, before the arrival of Europeans, there were at least one million Amerindians living in the rainforest – today there are less than 100,000. Many tribes were enslaved, kidnapped, or wiped out by diseases during the colonial period. There are now at least 100 fewer tribes in the region than at the start of the 20th century.

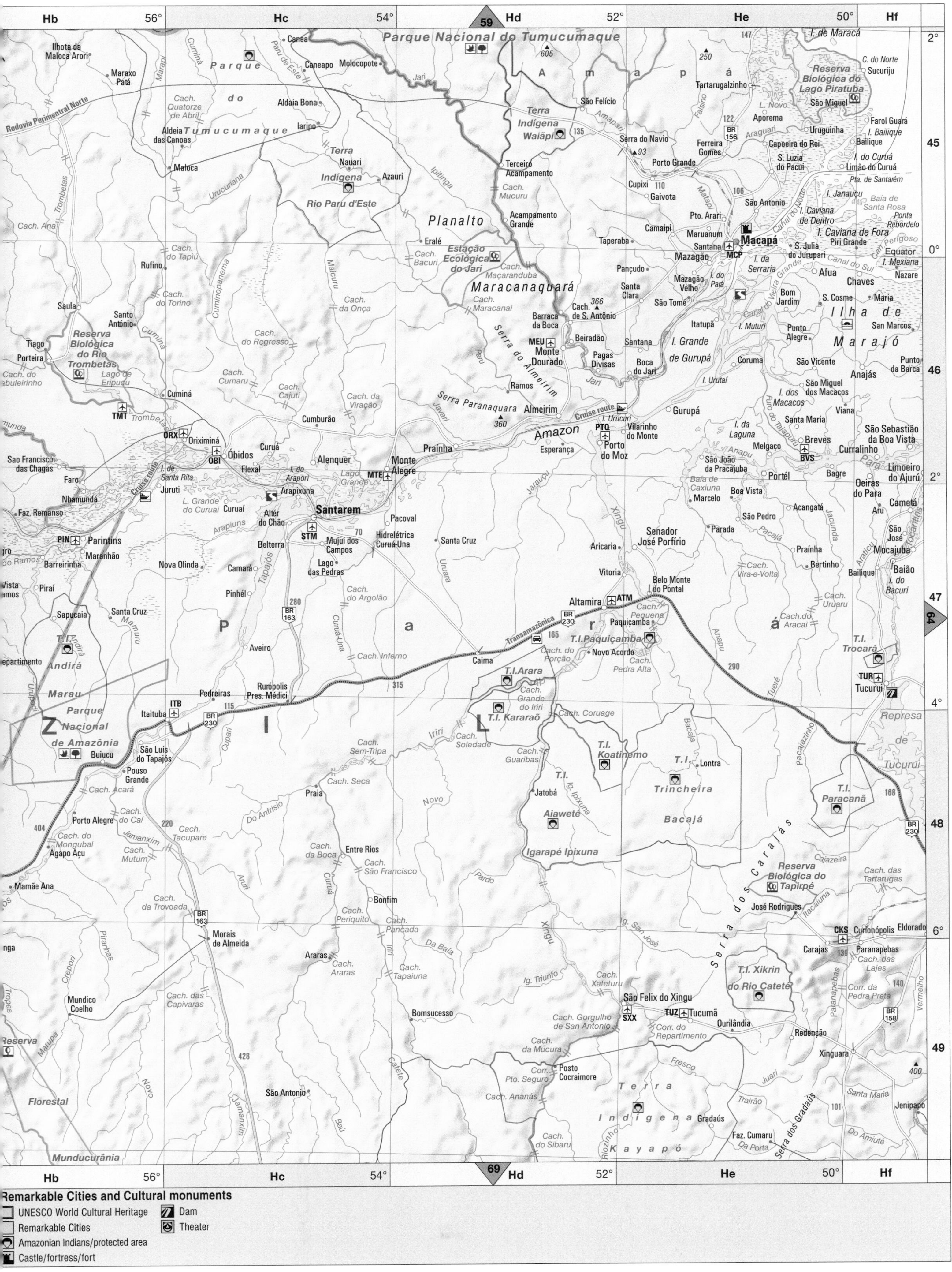

Macapá Capital of the Brazilian state Amapá – historic Fort São José was built in 1763 – Zoobotanico Park: a nature reserve inhabited by local wildlife **He45**

Along the Amazon The Amazon River is the most important transport route into the Amazon region. Because of the thick almost inaccessible rainforests many towns in the Amazon region are only connected to the outside world by ships traveling up and down the river.

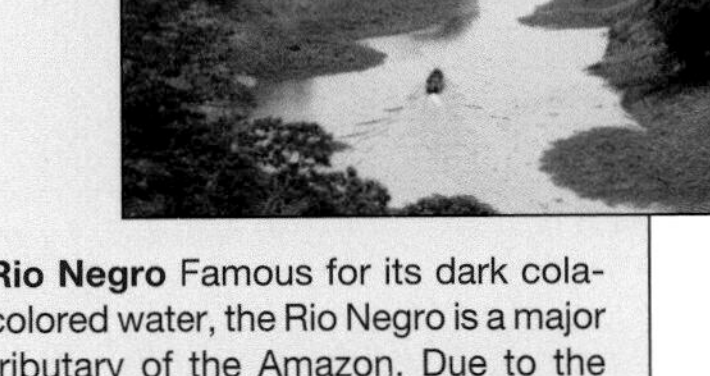

Rio Negro Famous for its dark cola-colored water, the Rio Negro is a major tributary of the Amazon. Due to the high acidity and low mineral content of its water, the Rio Negro is inhabited by few animals and insects. The river is over 1,700 kilometers long and begins as the Rio Guainia in Columbia and reaches a maximum width of 2 kilometers near Manaus. The luxury hotel Ariaú Tower in Manaus has a viewing platform which offers good views over the river and surrounding rainforests.

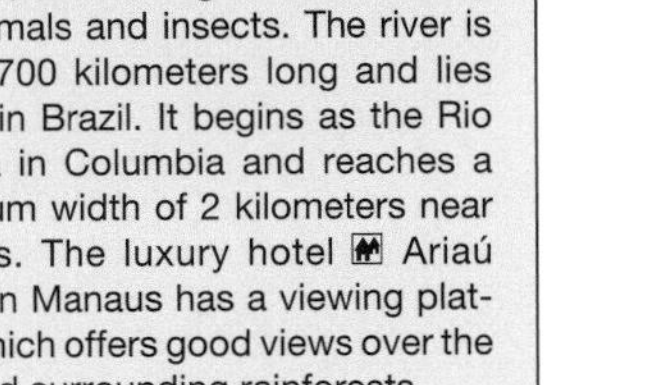

Manaus Large city in the Amazon region – center of Brazil's 19th century rubber boom – Teatro Amazonas opera house **Gk47**

Remarkable Cities and Cultural monuments

- UNESCO World Cultural Heritage
- Remarkable Cities
- Amazonian Indians/protected area
- Castle/fortress/fort
- Dam
- Theater

Northeastern Brazil

Northeastern Brazil is one of the most distinct regions in the country. The Northeast, a tropical region, is located just south of the equator which passes through the **Ilha de Marajó** in the Amazon Delta. The Ilha de Marajo has a land area roughly the size of Switzerland and is one of the largest river islands in the world. During much of the year, half of the island's land is submerged beneath the **Amazon**, **Pará**, and **Tocantins Rivers**.

In recent decades, water buffalos fro India have been introduced to the are The water buffalos are used primarily cargo transportation – there are no thousands of them in the region. One the most interesting natural phenome in the Amazon delta is a large tidal wa called **Pororoca**. The wave appears fro

The area around Canoa Quebrada has numerous beautiful, colorful cliffs **Jb**

Ilha de Marajó One of the largest river islands in the world – covers 48,000 km^2 – surrounded by rivers including the Amazon and the Tocantins **HeHf46**

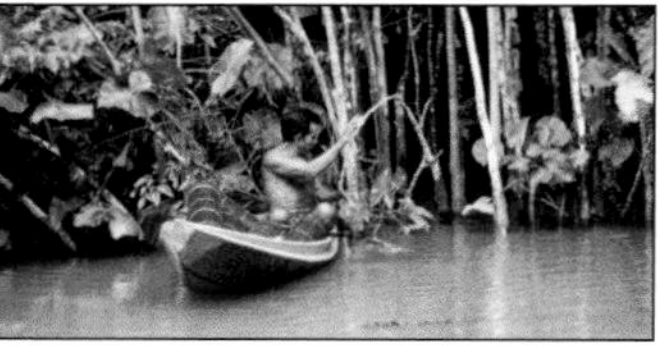

Baía de Marajó Large channel in the Amazon river delta – rich fishing grounds – dense mangrove rainforests line both banks of the channel **Hf46**

Belem Largest port in the Amazon region – Ver-o-Peso market hall (photo) – Museo Goeldi: natural history museum – Forte de Castelo (1616) **Hf46**

Alcântara Historic city with colonial architecture – Plaza Gomez de Castro – 17th century houses and churches **Hh47**

São Luís State capital of Maranhão – vibrant reggae music scene – historic city center – Catedral de Se (photo) **Hh47**

Lençóis Maranhenses National Park Coastal national park with countless large sand dunes – shallow lakes are formed during the rainy season **Hj47**

Kayapó Indigenous Land Amerindian land reserve in the Central Brazilian Highlands – most Amerindians live traditional lifestyles – large forests **He49**

Scale 1:4,500,000

0 40 80 Kilometers

Principal travel routes

- Auto route
- Rail road
- Shipping route

Remarkable landscapes and natural monuments

- UNESCO World Natural Heritage
- Cave
- River landscape
- Nature park
- National park (landscape)
- National park (flora)
- National park (fauna)
- National park (culture)
- Biosphere reserve
- Turtle conservation area
- Coastal landscape
- Beach
- Island

ebruary to May when water in the **Peri-oso Channel** (between the islands Cavi-na de Fora and Mexiana) is pushed out sea by powerful currents from the mazon. This frightening wave is often ve meters tall and more than a kilo-eter in length.
he areas south and east of the Amazon elta, including portions of the **Central razilian Highlands**, are significantly rier than the delta. The vegetation in these areas also differs from that in the delta. The humid **tropical rainforests** with their heavy rainfall extend south to the area near the city of Sao Luis. Vast grasslands called **Campos Cerrados**, with only scattered clusters of trees, border the rainforests. Between Natal and Fortaleza in the easternmost region of Brazil, the climate is shaped by strong coastal winds.
The interior regions of northeastern Brazil are covered by dry forests known as **Caatinga** in Brazilian Portuguese. These dry regions receive less than 50 millimeters of rainfall annually and are subject to frequent droughts. This is also one of the poorest regions in Brazil with many of its inhabitants living in severe poverty.
The Atlantic coast in the Northeast has many large sand dunes and long sandy beaches. The coastal areas south of Natal have humid rainy climates. During much of the colonial era, the Northeast's sugar crops were Brazil's greatest source of wealth.
Fernando de Noronha is a tropical archipelago comprising 21 volcanic islands, 350 kilometers off the coast of mainland Brazil. In an effort to preserve the archipelago's pristine beaches and unique marine life, most of the islands and the waters around them have been designated a national marine park.

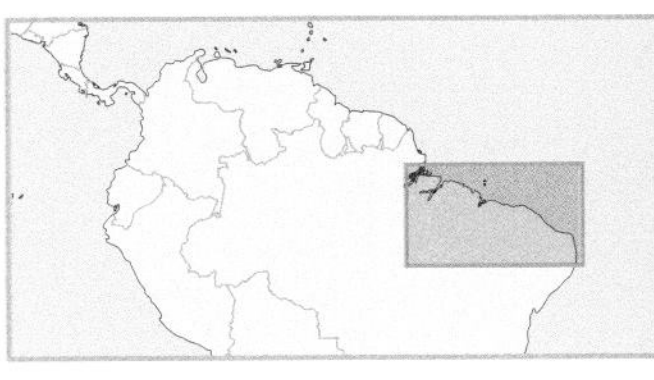

Fernando de Noronha Archipelago of volcanic islands 350 kilometers off the Brazilian coast – underwater national park around the islands – diving areas **Jd47**

Jericoacoara National Park Beautiful beaches along the Atlantic coast – sand dunes – abandoned fishing villages **Hk47**

Fortaleza Capital of the state of Ceará – population of two million – José de Alencar theatre – popular beaches – vibrant nightlife in Iracema district **Ja47**

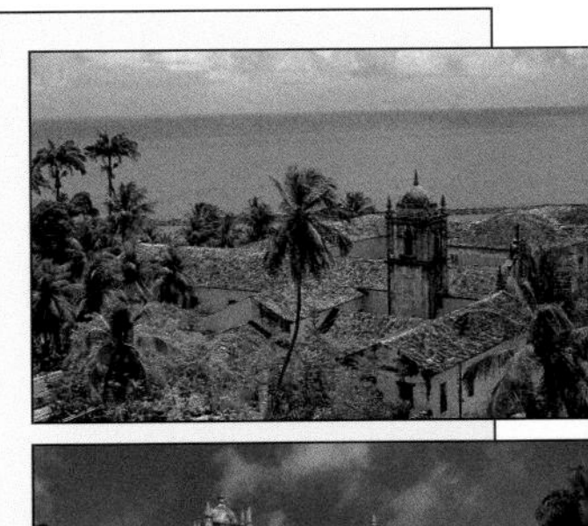

Olinda Historic city on Brazil's east coast. Olinda's old town is a designated UNESCO world heritage site. São Francisco convent (top photo) and Nossa Senhora do Carmo church (bottom photo) are two of the most beautiful buildings in the city. **Jc49**

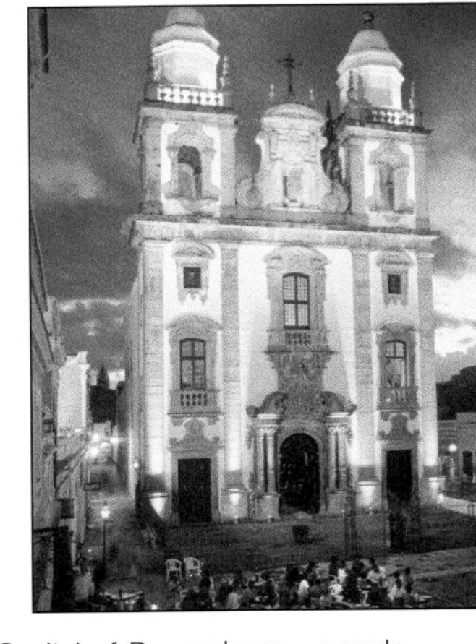

Recife Capital of Pernambuco – population 1.35 million – historic city center around the São Pedro cathedral (photo) – Recife Antigo, lively portside district **Jc50**

Remarkable Cities and Cultural monuments

- UNESCO World Cultural Heritage
- Remarkable Cities
- Prehistoric rockscape
- Places of Christian cultural interest
- Amazonian Indians/protected area
- Cultural landscape
- Historical city scape
- Castle/fortress/fort
- Dam
- Remarkable lighthouse
- Monument
- Space mission launch site
- Market
- Festivals
- Museum
- Theater

Sport and leisure destinations

- Diving
- Wind surfing
- Surfing
- Beach resort
- Amusement/theme park

Southern Peru, Northwestern Bolivia

Despite its location between the ocean and mountains the Peruvian coast is a relatively infertile and dry area. The cool **Humboldt Current**, a shallow current carrying Antarctic water, runs along the coast of **Peru**. Large fog clouds extend from the coast into the interior; however, the region gets very little rainfall. Lush green vegetation grows along the bottom edges of mountains with frequent fog coverage. A few scattered river oases are the only areas in the region capab of supporting agriculture. While the coas itself is relatively barren, the waters off th coast contain an incredible abundance o marine life. Nutrient rich water from th deep **Peru-Chile Trench** (-6,600 meters supports a complex food chain wit plankton at the bottom and ocean pre

Lake Titicaca in Peru and Bolivia is the largest lake in South America **Gf53/5**

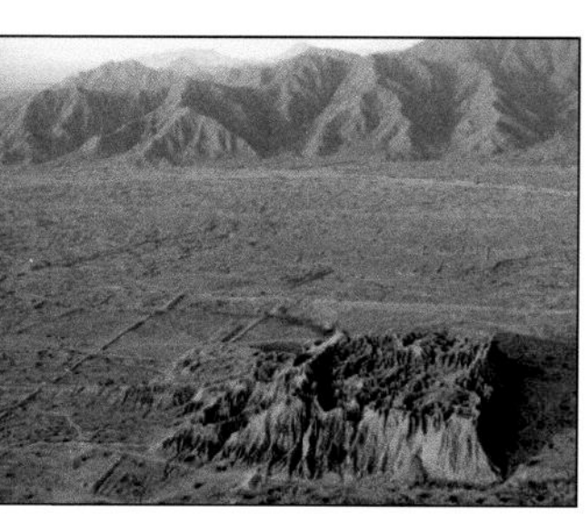

Moche Pyramids near Lambayeque Terraced ▣ adobe pyramids – ancient burial complex **Ga49**

Chan-Chan Ancient capital of the ▣ Chimú kingdom – founded in the 12th century – UNESCO world heritage site **Ga49**

Huascarán National Park Mount Huascaran rises 6,768 meters (photo) – deep ravines and glacial lakes **Gb50**

Chavín de Huántar Large settlement built by the ▣ Chavin culture around 800 BC – UNESCO world heritage site **Gb50**

Lima Capital of Peru – population 8.5 million – colonial ▣ old town – historic 17th and 18th century ▣ churches – Plaza San Martin (photo) **Gb52**

Nazca Lines ▣ A series of geometric lines and forms in the Peruvian desert – made by the Nazca between 200 and 600 BC **Gc53**

Scale 1:4,500,000
0 40 80 Kilometers

Principal travel routes
- Auto route
- Rail road
- Shipping route

Remarkable landscapes and natural monuments
- UNESCO World Natural Heritage
- Mountain landscape
- Ravine/canyon
- Active volcano
- River landscape
- Lake country
- Desert
- Oasis
- Nature park
- National park (landscape)
- National park (flora)
- National park (fauna)
- Biosphere reserve
- Protected area for sea-lions/seals
- Protected area for penguins
- Beach

tors and aquatic birds at the top. **El ño** is an natural phenomenon that cau-s the waters in the eastern Pacific to rm resulting in significant changes to e region's weather pattern. The ana-bly occurs at irregular intervals every o to seven years. El Niño has a nega-e impact on fishing and agriculture in stern South America and often results the appearence of destructive floods ong the Peruvian coast. The heavy rainfall during El Niño is a serious threat to the ancient adobe settlements built by pre-Incan coastal Amerindian cultures. These historic buildings are amongst the oldest remaining Amerindian sites in the Americas.

East of Trujillo on Peru's southern coast, the **Callejón de Huaylas Valley** separates the **Cordillera Negra** and **Cordillera Blanca Mountains**. The Ucayali River flows through the Cordillera Oriental and Cordillera Central mountain ranges. The river is one of many that feed the Amazon.

The Incas were once the most powerful nation in South American. From their capital city **Cuzco**, the Incas administered a vast empire. During the colonial era, Peru's highlands were the major center of gold mining in South America.

Lake Titicaca, situated 3,821 meters above sea level, is the largest lake in South America with an area of 8,300 km². In addition to the coast (La Costa) and the highlands (La Sierra), Peru has a third distinct region. The third region, **La Selva** is a region of rainforest-covered plains. The Selva covers more than two thirds of Peru and contains several land reserves created to protect Amerindians. The Selva has a stable climate throughout the year with warm temperatures, high humidity, and heavy rainfall.

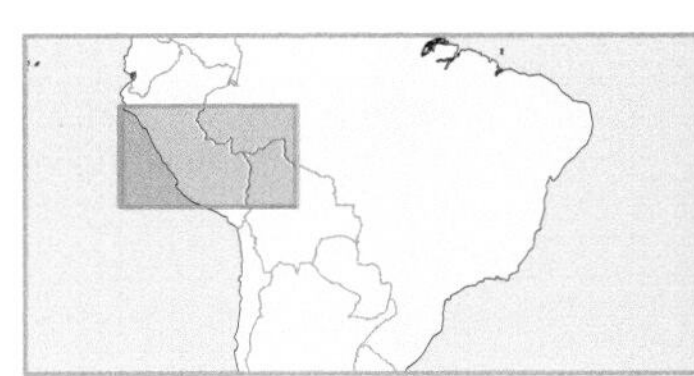

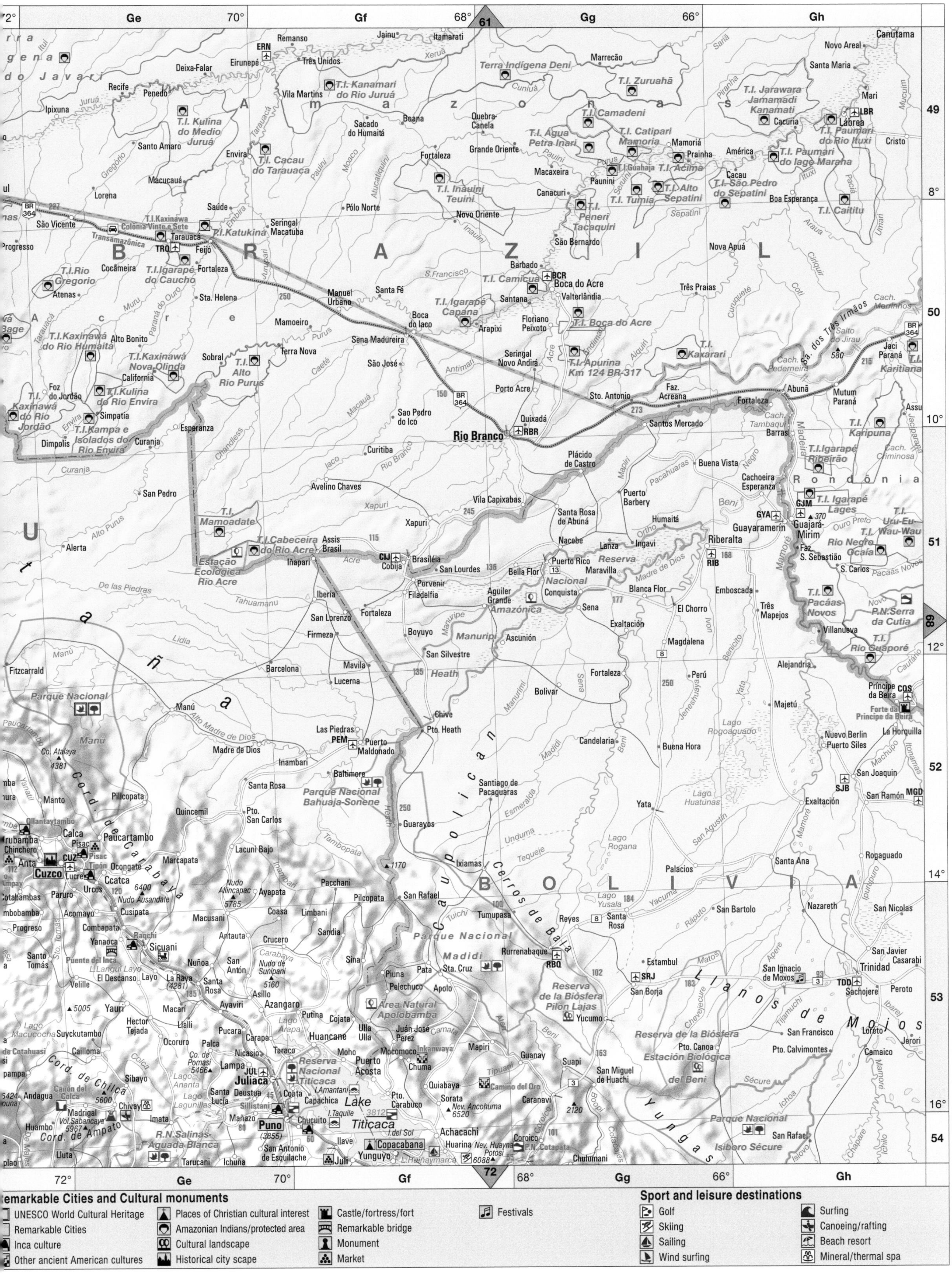

Manú National Park National Park covering 15,000 km² – over 1,000 bird species including Aras (photo) **GdGe51/52**

Bahuaja-Sonene National Park 10,914 km² – consisting of rainforests and grasslands – unique mixture of rainforest and savannah flora and fauna **Gf52**

Machu Picchu Ancient Incan fortress city located 2,400 meters above sea level. It was rediscovered in 1911. The city consists of a temple complex surrounded by dwellings. **Gd52**

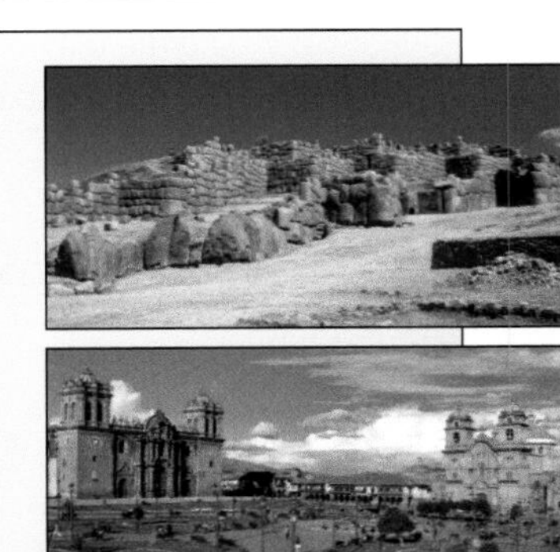

Cuzco The city was once the center of the Incan Empire. Plaza de Armas (bottom photo) was built on top of an Incan ritual site. The remnants of the Incan fortress Sacsayhuaman (top photo) are near the city. **Gd52**

Sillistani Tall towers containing burial tombs built in the pre-Incan and Incan periods – located near a small lake **Ge53**

Puno The largest city on Lake Titicaca – 3,855 meters above sea level – founded in 1668 – historic cathedral **Ge53**

Remarkable Cities and Cultural monuments

- UNESCO World Cultural Heritage
- Remarkable Cities
- Inca culture
- Other ancient American cultures
- Places of Christian cultural interest
- Amazonian Indians/protected area
- Cultural landscape
- Historical city scape
- Castle/fortress/fort
- Remarkable bridge
- Monument
- Market
- Festivals

Sport and leisure destinations

- Golf
- Skiing
- Sailing
- Wind surfing
- Surfing
- Canoeing/rafting
- Beach resort
- Mineral/thermal spa

Mato Grosso, Northeastern Bolivia

It was only after paved roads were built between the cities of Porto Velho and Cuiaba that large scale agriculture and settlement came to Mato Grosso, a Brazilian state in the country's Planalto Central region. Across the border, northeastern Bolivia remains a sparsely populated and in some areas uninhabited region. The border between Brazil and northeastern Bolivia is marked by the Marmore and Guapore Rivers.

In Portuguese, the name **Mato Grosso** means "thick grass." The region comprises two Brazilian states – Mato Grosso and Mato Grosso do Sol. Both of these states contain vast grasslands. The dry season in Mato Grosso begins in July and lasts until October. Many of the local tree species have adapted to the environ-

A flooded area of the Pantanal during the rainy season **HbHc54**

ment – hard rubbery leaves and thi bark protect them against water loss a fire. In addition, many trees store wa in complex underground root system The **Campos Cerrados** with its ma rivers and forests lies in the southe Mato Grosso and is home to several Amerindian land reserves. Despite t land reserves, many of the local Ame indian peoples are finding it increasin hard to maintain traditional lifestyle

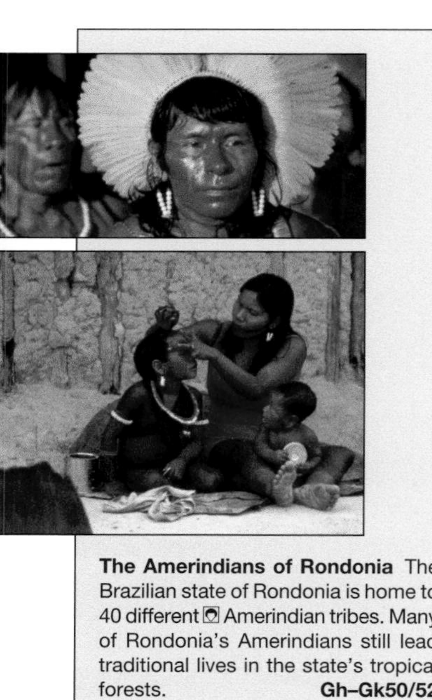

The Amerindians of Rondonia The Brazilian state of Rondonia is home to 40 different Amerindian tribes. Many of Rondonia's Amerindians still lead traditional lives in the state's tropical forests. **Gh–Gk50/52**

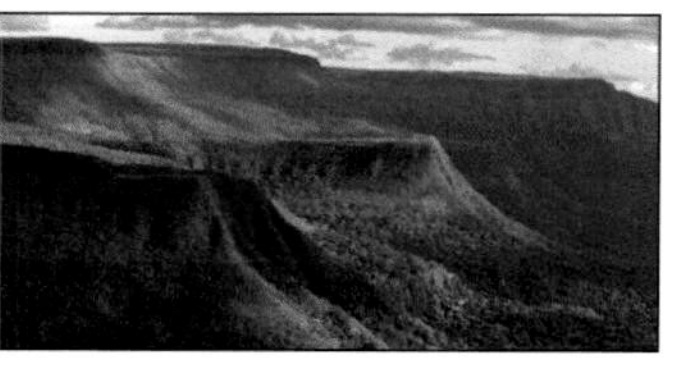

Noel Kempff National Park National park covering 15,230 km² – tropical plains and wooded plateaus – UNESCO world natural heritage site **Gk52/53**

The Mission Churches of Chiquitos The Bolivian region is the location of six historic mission churches. The churches were built between 1696 and 1760 by Jesuit missionaries and local Amerindians. **GjGk54**

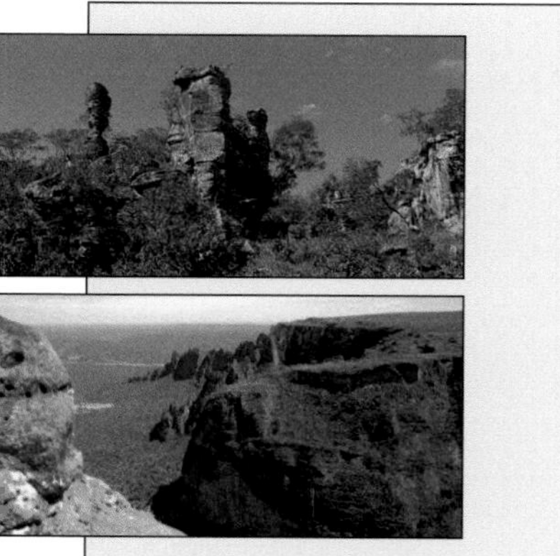

Chapada dos Guimarães National Park Brazilian national park with a total land area of 330 km². The park features many interesting stone formations including the "city of stone" (top photo). **Hc53**

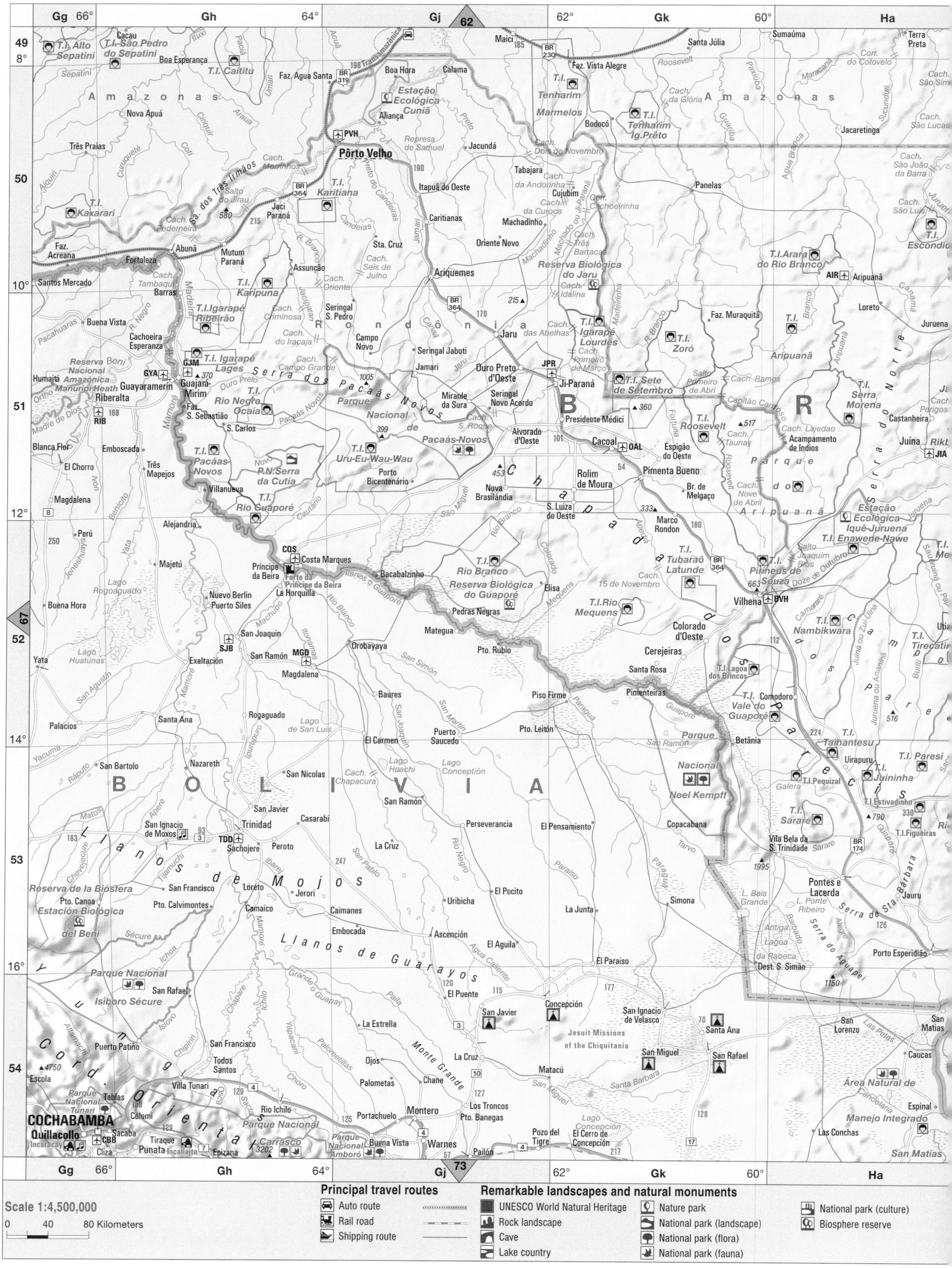

Scale 1:4,500,000
0 40 80 Kilometers

Principal travel routes
- Auto route
- Rail road
- Shipping route

Remarkable landscapes and natural monuments
- UNESCO World Natural Heritage
- Rock landscape
- Cave
- Lake country
- Nature park
- National park (landscape)
- National park (flora)
- National park (fauna)
- National park (culture)
- Biosphere reserve

uch of the land in the Campos Cerra-ɔs is used for livestock ranching. The nching industry has devastated local ildlife which the Amerindians have tra-itionally hunted. Another environmental reat to the region's ecosystems and digenous people comes from mining. ercury and other waste substances ɔm mines are polluting the region's vers and their basins.

ɔ the east of the Campos Cerrados lies the Pantanal, one of the world's largest wetlands. Because of its incredible abundance of plant and animal species, the **Pantanal** is sometimes called the "Noah's Ark" of South America. The area has a total land area of 230,000 km² of which a mere 1,350 km² is protected in conservation areas.

Between the months of December and March, the region gets extremely heavy rainfall. During these months many of the Pantanal's rivers flood their banks covering large sections of the region with water. Many of the area's animals seek shelter from the floods in the treetops or on hills. The Pantanal is inhabited by many fascinating animals and is one of the best areas in South America to view wildlife. The region is home to rare birds, large cats, and at least 230 species of fish. Capybaras, the largest rodents in the world, are common throughout the region. Anteaters, giant otters, and jaguars are just a few of the many fascinating animals visitors can see in this area.

The **Cuiabá**, the state capital of Mato Grosso, is known as the northern gateway to the Pantanal. The city is the best base for any expedition into the Pantanal. It lies near the geographic center of South America. With about half a million inhabitants, Cuiaba is also the largest city in the region.

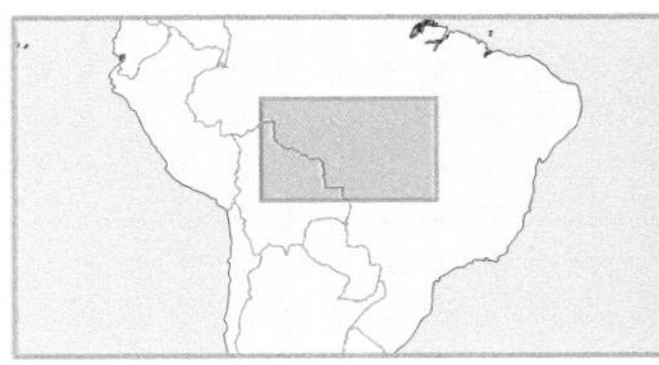

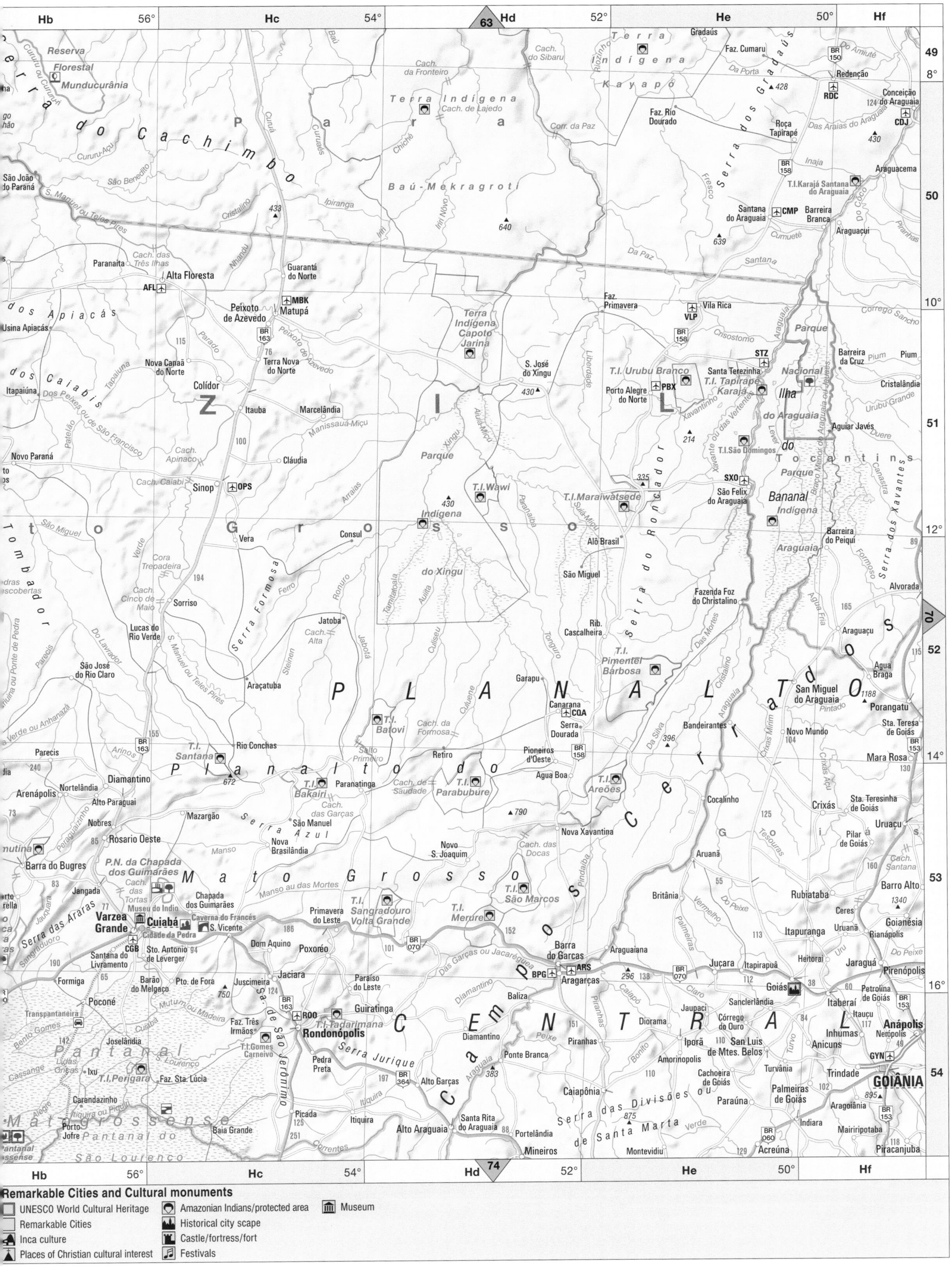

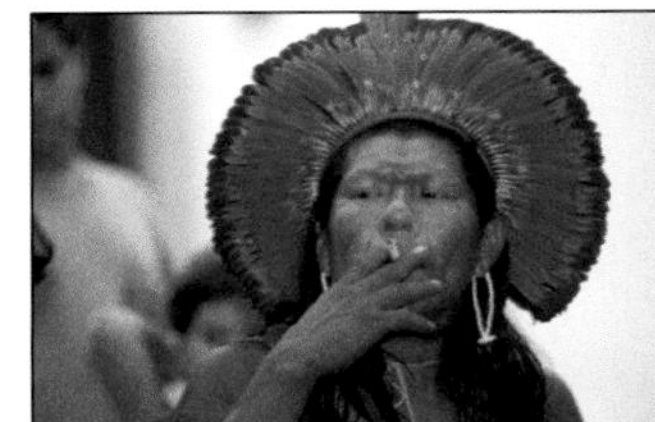

Xingu Indigenous Park Large Amerindian land reserve along the Xingu River – primarily marshland **Hd51/52**

Cuiabá State capital of Mato Grosso – the "gateway" to the Pantanal – Museo do Indio: Amerindian culture museum **Hb53**

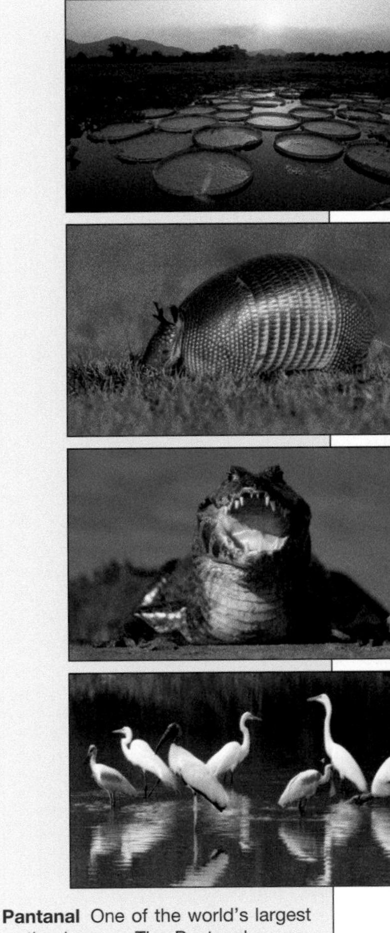

Pantanal One of the world's largest wetland areas. The Pantanal covers 230,000 km² and is home to many different species of birds, fish, amphibians and land animals. The dry season between May and September is the best time to visit the area. **HbHc54**

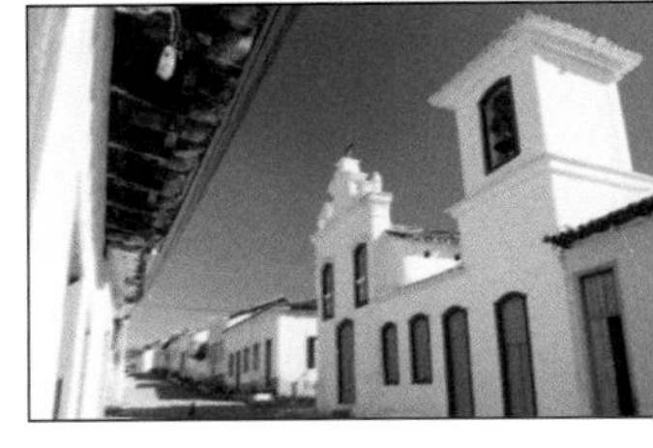

Goiás Attractive mining town with historic architecture – the town is a UNESCO world heritage site **He53**

Remarkable Cities and Cultural monuments

- UNESCO World Cultural Heritage
- Remarkable Cities
- Inca culture
- Places of Christian cultural interest
- Amazonian Indians/protected area
- Historical city scape
- Castle/fortress/fort
- Festivals
- Museum

Eastern Brazil

The highlands of the **Planalto Central** lie south of the Amazon River basin. Several tributaries of the Amazon River, including the Araguaia and Tocantins Rivers drain the western highlands of eastern Brazil. These rivers nourish huge tropical marshlands including the 300-kilometer-long **Ilha do Bananal**. These large lush tropical areas are still home to numerous Amerindian tribes. The construction of the planned capital city –

Brasilia – brought domestic and inte national attention to the sparsely pop lated Brazilian interior. The city was cor pleted in the 1960s and features unique collection of 20th century arch tecture. Soybeans are the most importa crop grown on the relatively dry sava nahs in the interior. The **Serra Geral** c

Chapada Diamantina National Park boasts spectacular gorges **Hk**

Ilha do Bananal This large "island" is a 320-kilometer-long tropical marshland surrounded by rivers including the Rio Araguaia. The area is home to the Javae and Karaja Amerindians (middle photo). The northern section of the "island" contains a national park, home to wood storks (bottom photo) and river dolphins. **He51**

Chapada dos Veadeiros National Park National park on a large plateau – numerous lakes, waterfalls and ponds **Hg52/53**

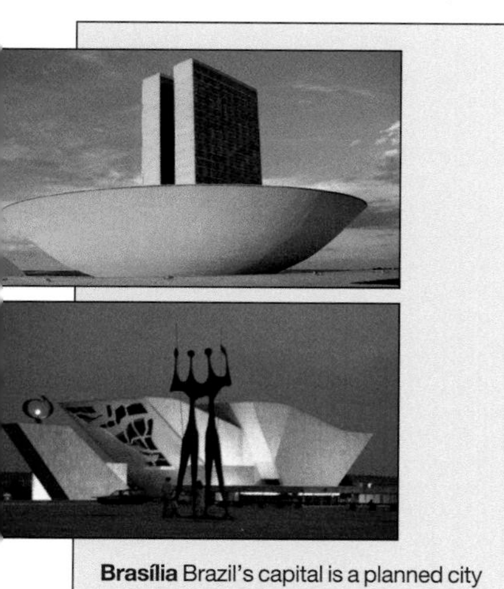

Brasília Brazil's capital is a planned city built in the 1960s. Most of the city's architecture was designed by Oscar Niemeyer, including the congress building (top photo) and Plaza of the Three Powers (bottom photo). **Hg53**

Scale 1:4,500,000

0 40 80 Kilometers

Principal travel routes

- Auto route
- Rail road
- Shipping route

Remarkable landscapes and natural monuments

- UNESCO World Natural Heritage
- Rock landscape
- River landscape
- Waterfall/rapids
- Nature park
- National park (landscape)
- National park (flora)
- National park (fauna)
- National park (culture)
- Beach

aranã and the **Serra Geral do Goiás** ountain ranges are the sources of many vers which flow into and feed the 3000- lometer-long **São Francisco River**. he São Francisco River is the third largst river in Brazil and one of the most nportant in the northeastern region. The ver was once a major transport route efore dams and reservoirs made ship avel along the river impractical.
he **Barragem de Sobradinho** is a large reservoir along the São Francisco River in the Brazilian state of Bahia. The reservoir, with a total area of 4,220 km², was created after the construction of a dam built to generate electricity. **Sertão**, known as the poorhouse of Brazil, is an extremely dry region in the interior of eastern and northeastern Brazil. The Sertao gets less than 50 millimeters of rainfall annually and long droughts are common in the region. Many of the rivers in this area dry up and disappear into the briar covered savannahs.
The coastal areas of eastern Brazil get abundant rainfall and the region is one of the world's major centers of **sugarcane production**. It was sugar production that once made the northeastern coast the richest region in colonial Brazil. Millions of African slaves were brought here to work in the sugar fields and the region's culture (including the local cuisine and religious practices) were strongly influenced by African traditions. **Cocoa farming**, concentrated near the coast, is also an important industry in the region. The Brazilian highlands contain many fascinating geological attractions – most of them formed through erosion caused by the area's many rivers. The canyons in **Chapada Diamantina** National Park feature some of the most fascinating landscapes in the region.

ATLANTIC OCEAN

Serra da Capivara National Park Nature reserve in Brazil's interior– 2,000 prehistoric rock paintings **Hj50**

Chapada Diamantina National Park Vast savannahs broken by tall, flat-topped mountains – beautiful canyons – numerous waterfalls including the 340-meter-high Cachoeira da Fumaça **Hk52**

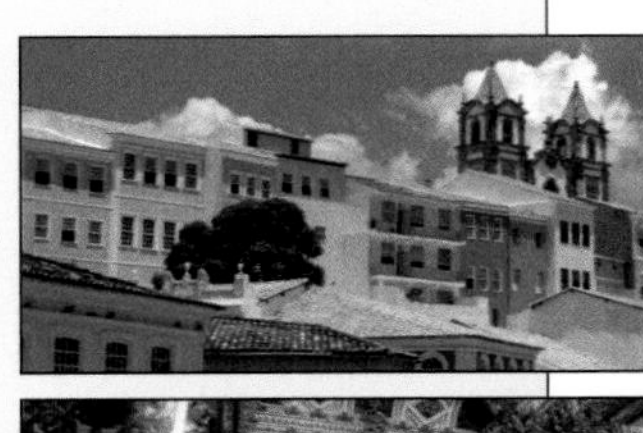

Salvador da Bahia Historic port city founded in 1549. The city has fascinating architecture. São Francisco (bottom photo) and the other historic churches in Salvador were built during the city's golden age in the 17th and 18th centuries. The Pelourinho district (top photo) contains many baroque buildings and is a UNESCO world heritage site. Salvador is a major center of Afro-Brasilian culture. **Ja52**

Ilha de Itaparica Island in the Baía de Todos os Santos (239 km²) – long sandy beaches – picturesque village of Itaparica **Ja52**

Ilha do Boipeba Island south of Salvador – undeveloped white beaches – tropical forests **Ja52**

Porto Seguro Atmospheric small town on the coast with a historic town center – Passarela do Álcool promenade **Ja54**

Remarkable Cities and Cultural monuments

- UNESCO World Cultural Heritage
- Remarkable Cities
- Prehistoric rockscape
- Places of Christian cultural interest
- Amazonian Indians/protected area
- Cultural landscape
- Historical city scape
- Dam
- Monument
- Market
- Festivals
- Theater

Sport and leisure destinations

- Golf
- Wind surfing
- Surfing
- Beach resort

The Andes Mountains, between the 17th and 24th parallels of latitude, lie in an area with a subtropical climate. The mountain range is at its widest here, stretching several hundred kilometers into the continent's interior. To the east of this section of the Andes is the **Gran Chaco**, a vast subtropical savannah. The Gran Chaco stretches through parts of Argentina, Bolivia, Paraguay and Brazil. In this part of South America the level of

precipitation tends to decrease from ea to west. The wetlands of the Pantanal ar Paraguay Chaco Boreal are nourished b the waters of the large Paraguay-Parar river system. The **Pantanal** is the larg est area of wetlands in South Americ During the rainy season between Decem ber and March much of the region lie

A row of snow-capped volcanoes near the Atacama Desert **GfGg57/5**

Iquique Port founded in 1730 – once a major export harbor for nitrates – part of Chile since 1883 – Naval History Museum – interesting coastline **Ge56**

Salar de Uyuni The largest and highest salt flat in the world – situated at a height of 5000 meters above sea level – much of the flat's surface is red due to algae – groups of flamingos **GfGg56**

Chuquicamata The world's largest copper mine – produces five percent of global copper output – 800 meters deep **Gf57**

The Atacama Desert The Atacama is the world's driest desert. Salar de Atacama, a large salt flat to the west of Cordillera Domeyko, covers 3000 km². Near the salt flat, the Valle de la Luna has strange landscapes resembling the moon's surface. Just outside of the Atacama Desert, the El Tatio Geyser Field contains a large number of active geysers in a small area. The azure blue Lake Verde in Bolivia, located at the foot of the active volcano Licancabur (5916 meters), can be reached from the Atacama through the Jama mountain pass. Photos from top to bottom: El Tatio Geyser Field, Valle de la Luna, Salar de Atacama, Lake Verde **Gf57/58**

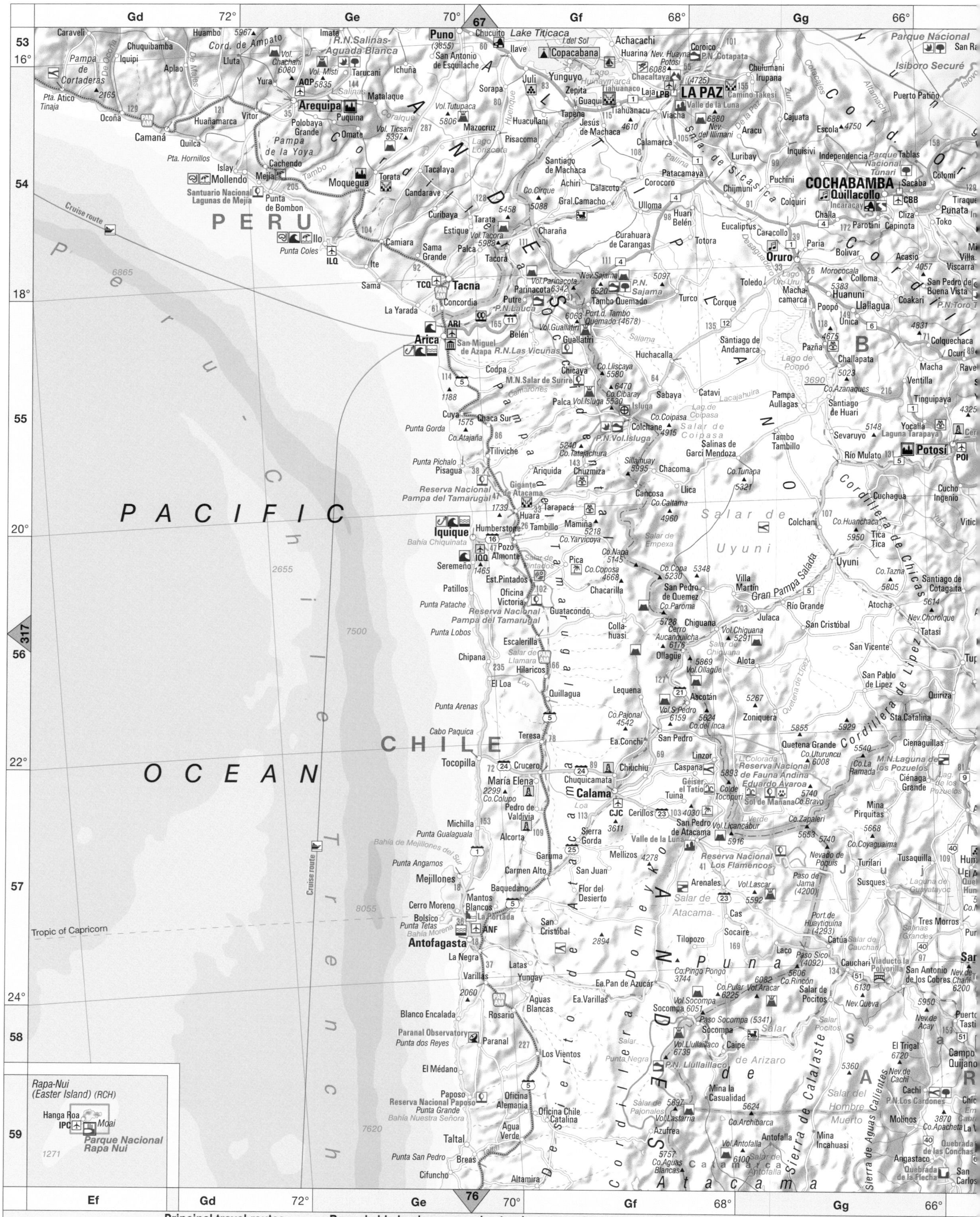

Scale 1:4,500,000

0 40 80 Kilometers

Principal travel routes

- Auto route
- Rail road
- Shipping route

Remarkable landscapes and natural monuments

- UNESCO World Natural Heritage
- Ravine/canyon
- Extinct volcano
- Active volcano
- Geyser
- Cave
- Glacier
- Lake country
- Desert
- Oasis
- Fossil site
- Nature park
- National park (landscape)
- National park (flora)
- National park (fauna)
- National park (culture)

nder a shallow layer of water. The unique ant and animal life in the Pantanal is reatened by increased tourism and griculture.

he Andes Mountains increase signifi- antly in width south of Lake Titicaca. A hain of narrow mountains covered by ense mountain rain forest rises along e eastern edges of the Gran Chaco. The Yungas in southern Bolivia is a re- on of highland rainforests between the Andes and the Amazon Basin. This transition zone is home to dense rainforests and mountainous vegetation. The watershed or divide between the Amazon and Paraguay river basins runs along the 18th parallel of latitude.

In the center of the Andes mountain range in southern Bolivia lies the **Altiplano**, a large plateau high above sea level. The Puna – the section of the Altiplano in Argentina and Chile – has unique flora and fauna. This part of South America contains many large **salt flats** (salares) scattered throughout the drier section of the Andes. Llamas, vicunas, and alpacas are among the many unique endemic animal species found in the Andes.

The largest plateau in the Andes begins near the 27th parallel of latitude in the Cordillera Domeyko range and stretches to an area of the Cordillera Oriental range just south of La Paz. Salar de Atacama and Salar de Uyuni are the most fascinating of the many salt lakes in this region. The Salar de Uyuni is the remnant of a prehistoric lake that once covered most of southern Bolivia. Salar de Uyuni, which is dry during most of the year, is also the world's largest and highest salt flat. Numerous active volcanoes and geysers are among the many other natural attractions in this fascinating region of South America.

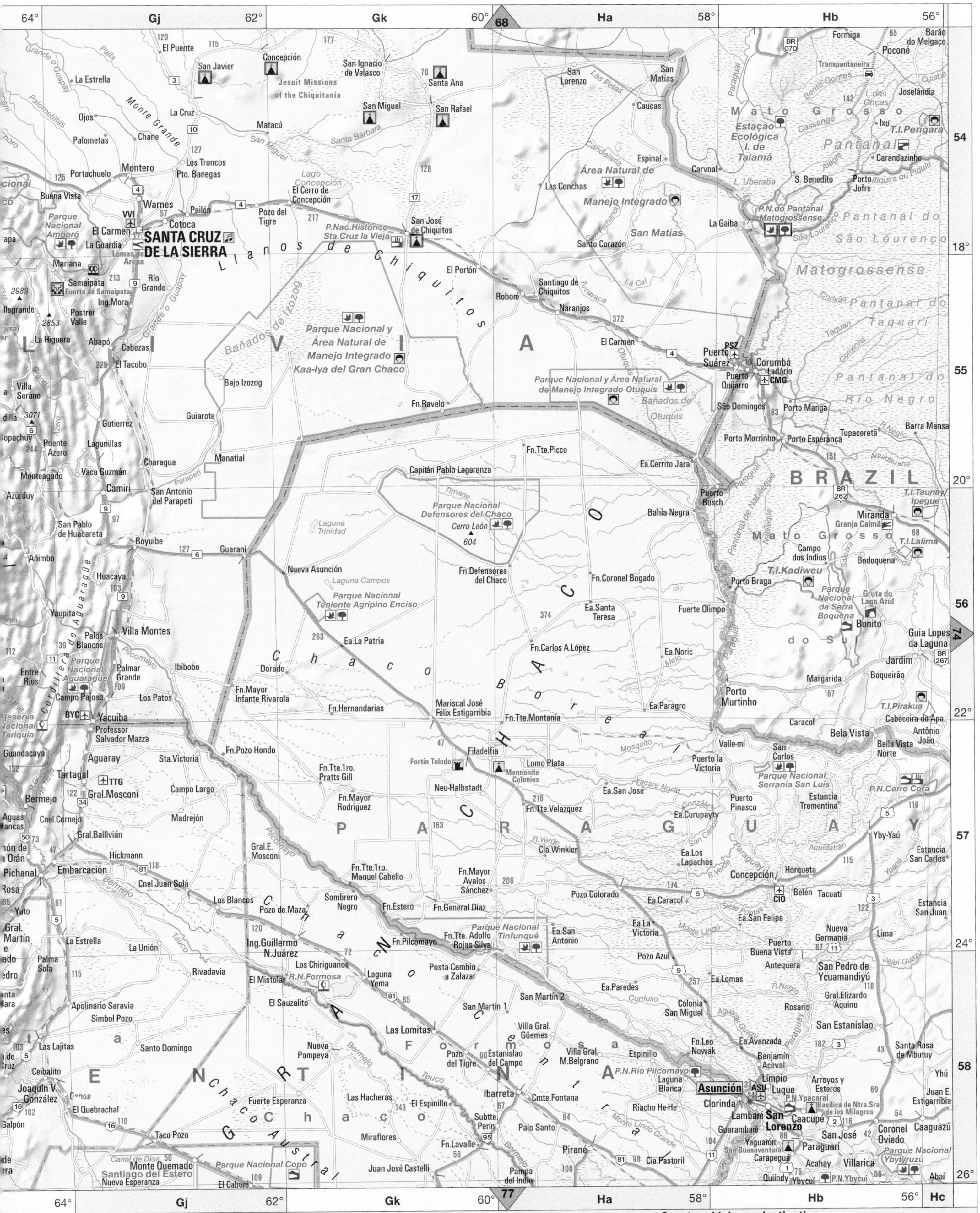

Tiahuanaco Once the center of a pre-Columbian Amerindian empire – contains the remnants of four ancient temples and pyramids – Puerto del Sol (photo) **Gf54**

La Paz The highest major city in the world located between 3,300 and 4,000 meters above sea level – founded in 1548 by the Spanish – historic city center with lively marketplace **Gf54**

Altiplano Large plateau region in the Andes – the local Amerindians have retained many of their traditions – interesting villages and markets **GfGg54-56**

Sucre Capital of Bolivia – historic old town with colonial architecture – cathedral built in the 17th century – UNESCO world heritage site **Gh55**

Potosí Historic mining town – Casa Nacional de la Moneda: coin minting museum – UNESCO world heritage site **Gh55**

Cordillera de Sama Conservation area in Altiplano (109 km²) – fascinating valley – contains four large lakes **Gh56**

Quebrada de Humahuaca 130-kilometer-long gorge in Argentina – the Rio Grande flows through the gorge – the gorge is surrounded by high stone walls **Gh57**

Remarkable Cities and Cultural monuments

- UNESCO World Cultural Heritage
- Remarkable Cities
- Prehistoric rockscape
- Inca culture
- Other ancient American cultures
- Places of Christian cultural interest
- Pl. of cult. interest to other religions
- Amazonian Indians/protected area
- Cultural landscape
- Historical city scape
- Castle/fortress/fort
- Technical/industrial monument
- Space telescope
- Market
- Festivals
- Museum

Sport and leisure destinations

- Skiing
- Sailing
- Diving
- Surfing
- Canoeing/rafting
- Deep-sea fishing
- Beach resort
- Mineral/thermal spa

Southeastern Brazil

Southeastern Brazil is the wealthiest and most heavily populated region in the country. The Southeast is home to almost half of the country's population as well as Brazil's two largest cities – **São Paulo** and **Rio de Janeiro**. A series of coastal mountain ranges, including the **Serra da Mantiqueira**, stretch along the southeastern coast. The region also features many tall and striking stone formations such as Rio's famous **Sugarloaf**. These stone formations are the remnants c ancient volcanoes.

Away from the coast, the land in the South east declines in elevation. Only a fe rivers flow through the valleys in the coas tal mountains. The region's interior cor tains several powerful rivers many c which flow through the **Brazilian High**

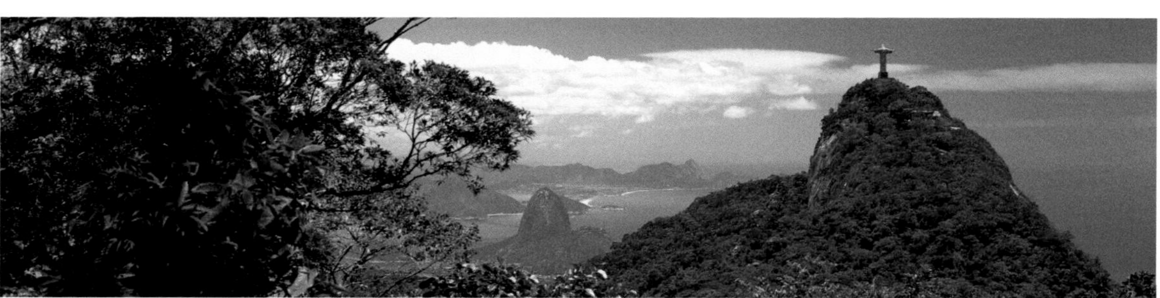

The Sugarloaf and Corcovado: the most famous of Rio's many hills. **Hj5**

Tingua Nature Reserve Nature reserve in Rio de Janeiro state – extensive virgin tropical forests **Hj57**

Serra do Mar Coastal mountain range near Rio – popular weekend destination for city residents – tropical forests **Hh57**

Parati City with historic architecture – Santa Rita de Cássia – Museum de Arte Sacra (religious artwork) **Hh57**

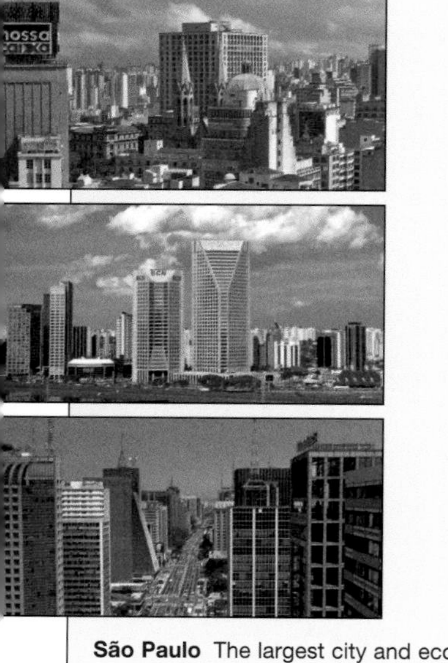

São Paulo The largest city and economic center in Brazil – metro population of at least 20 million – São Paulo Museum of Art – Teatro Municipal: historic opera house. **Hg57**

Atlantic Forest Southeast Reserves A group of 25 separate nature reserves protecting virgin tropical forests **Hg58**

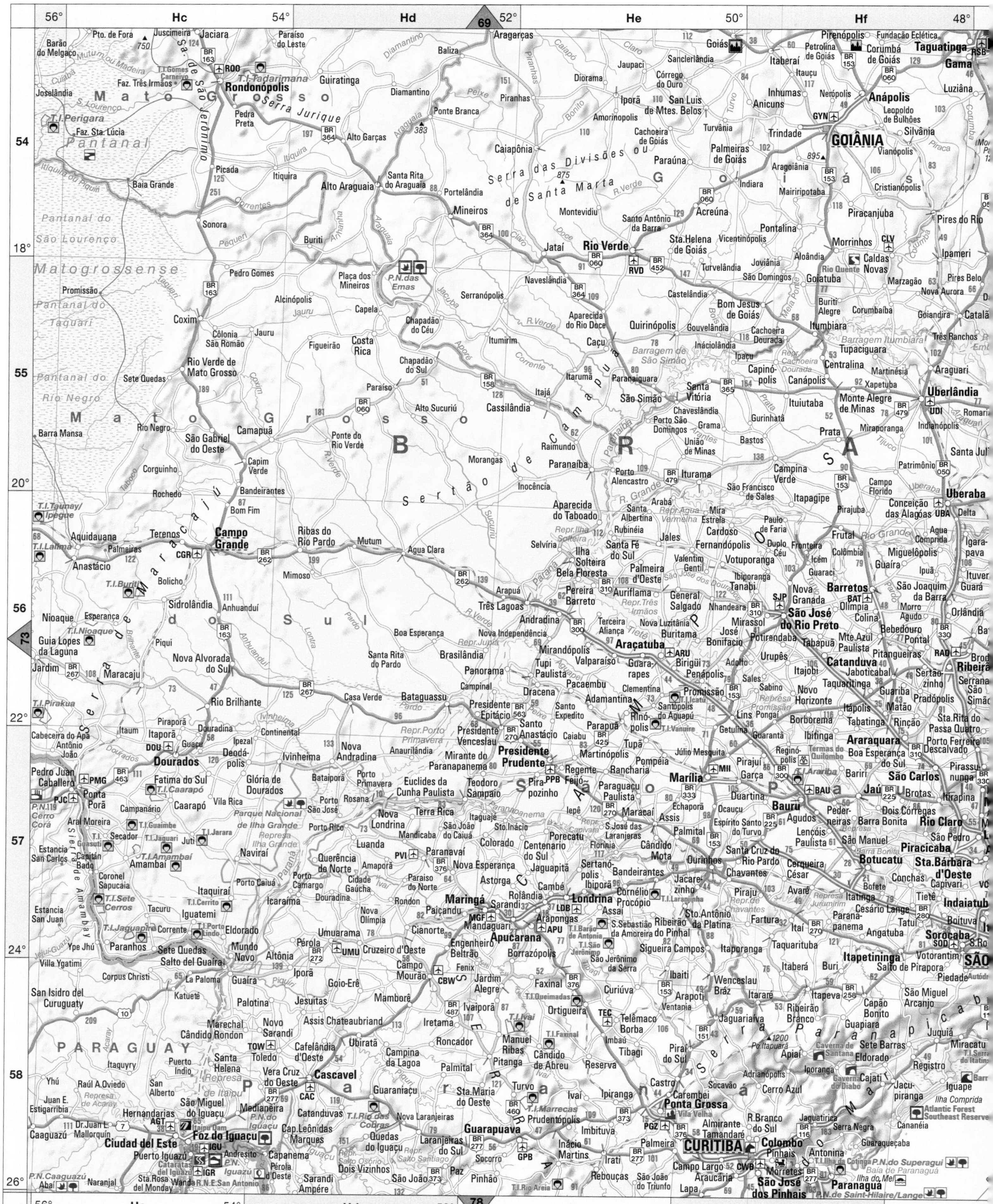

Scale 1:4,500,000

0 40 80 Kilometers

Principal travel routes
- Auto route
- Rail road
- Shipping route

Remarkable landscapes and natural monuments
- UNESCO World Natural Heritage
- Mountain landscape
- Rock landscape
- Cave
- River landscape
- Waterfall/rapids
- Lake country
- Nature park
- National park (landscape)
- National park (flora)
- National park (fauna)
- National park (culture)
- Turtle conservation area
- Beach
- Island
- Underwater reserve

ıds into the Parana and Paranaiba ɾers. The Rio Iguaçú begins in the ountains of southern Brazil. Along its urse the river flows over an eighty-ɛter-high escapement creating the most autiful waterfalls in the country. **Igu-ú Falls** – along the border between gentina and Brazil – are a crescent aped series of 275 separate falls over o kilometers in length.

e Pantanal, a large marshland covering 230,000 km², is located to the west of the **Mato Grosso** region with it vast grasslands. The **Pantanal**, one of the world's largest wetlands, is home to unique flora and fauna. The region's delicate ecosystems are increasingly threatened by agriculture and tourism.

The vast grasslands of the Mato Grosso are used mostly for livestock grazing. The highlands of southeastern Brazil are major centers for **coffee production**. Coffee farming is concentrated primarily in the area's moist river valleys. In recent decades, sheep farming and other agricultural activities have reduced the highlands' once total dependence on coffee crops. The state of **Minas Gerais**, with an area the size of France, boasts many of Brazil's most impressive historic buildings. This beautiful architecture is a legacy of the region's history as an important and wealthy mining center during the colonial era. Diamonds, gold, and iron are just a few of the mineral resources that have been mined in the state. Even today, the state produces over 90% of the precious stones mined in Brazil. The name Minas Gerais means "general mines" in Portuguese and reflects the state's historic connections to natural resources. The state's highest mountain, Pico da Bandeira, rises 2,890 meters above sea level.

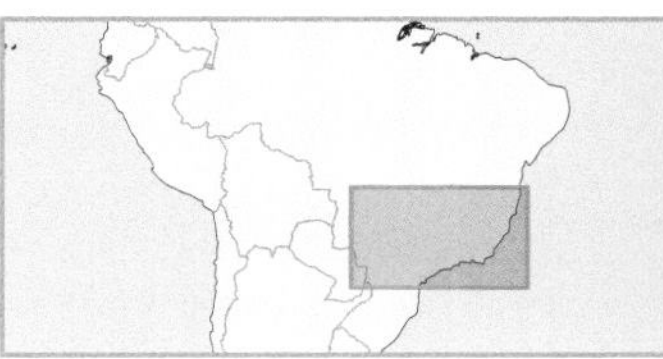

Bom Jesus de Matosinhos Sanctuary Baroque pilgrimage church – UNESCO world heritage site **Hj56**

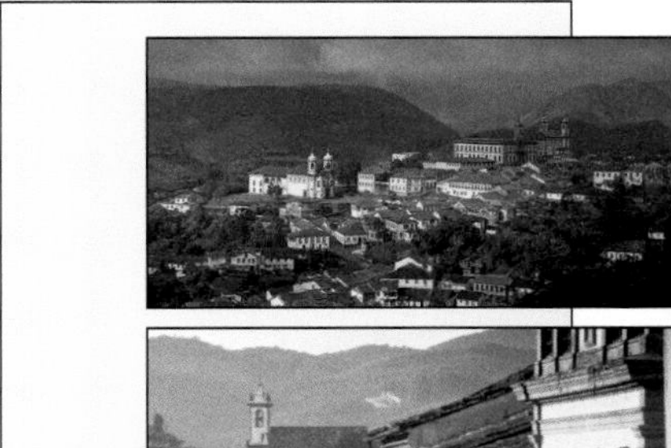

Ouro Preto City with numerous baroque buildings including São Francisco de Assis church. Ouro Preto was once a mining center. **Hj56**

Serra dos Orgãos National Park The second oldest national park in Brazil – lush tropical vegetation **Hj57**

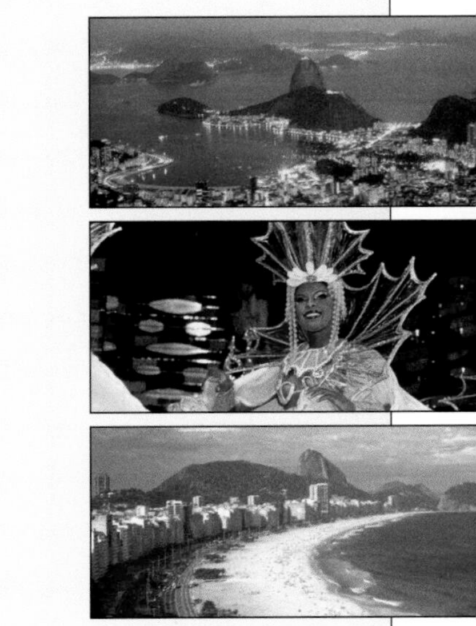

Rio de Janeiro The city, with a population of twelve million, is famous for its beaches, breathtaking natural setting and Carnaval. There are several mountains in the city. **Hj57**

emarkable Cities and Cultural monuments

- UNESCO World Cultural Heritage
- Remarkable Cities
- Places of Christian cultural interest
- Amazonian Indians/protected area
- Historical city scape
- Dam
- Festivals
- Museum

Sport and leisure destinations

- Arena/stadium
- Race track
- Horse racing
- Diving
- Wind surfing
- Surfing
- Beach resort
- Mineral/thermal spa

North Central Chile, Central Argentina, Uruguay

The section of South America between the 26th and 35th parallels of latitude exhibits a remarkable variety of landscapes and climates. The western part of the region is dominated by the **Andes Mountains**. The **South American continental shield**, which encompasses the Brazilian and Guiana highlands, is located to the north and northeast of this area. Between the Brazilian highlands and Chile lies a series of vast flat plains comprising two distinct regions: t **Pampas** in Argentina and the **Gr Chaco** in both Paraguay and Argentir **Uruguay** consists mostly of rollings h and low-lying coastal plains. Urugua principal rivers are the **Rio Urugua** along the border to Argentina – and t **Río Negro**.

Fascinating sandstone formations in Talampaya National Park **GfGg60/**

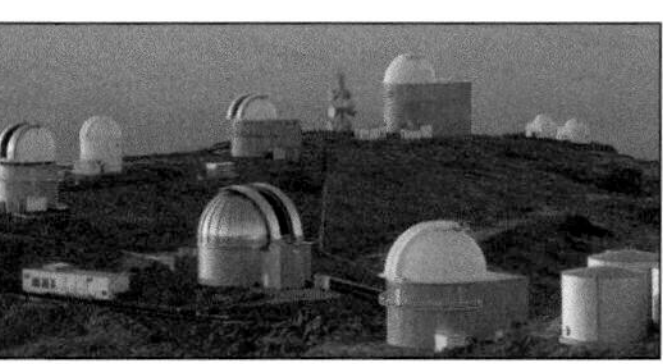

La Silla One of three large observatories in the Andes south of La Serena – twelve large telescopes **Ge60**

La Serena The second oldest city in Chile, founded in 1544 – seaside town with beaches – historic and modern architecture – the lighthouse is a city landmark **Ge60**

Valparaíso Chile's largest coastal city – the lower city features the harbor and a historic marketplace – funiculars connect the lower and upper city – Museo a Cielo Abierto, modern art museum **Ge62**

Aconcagua South America's tallest mountain (6959 meters) – Jesus statue on the Argentinean side of the mountain **Ge62**

Puente del Inca Natural bridge in western Argentina – 28 meters wide and 20 meters above the Rio Mendoza – created by mineral deposits from a natural spring **Gf62**

Santiago de Chile Capital of Chile – population of five million – historic buildings including San Francisco around Cerro Santa Lucia and Cerro San Cristobal – Museo de Arte Precolombino (pre-Columbian art) – artist district Bellavista **Ge62**

Mendoza Modern city in Argentina – the city is in a major winemaking region – Wine Museum – several wine cellars open to the public – historic Casa Giol (photo) **Gf62**

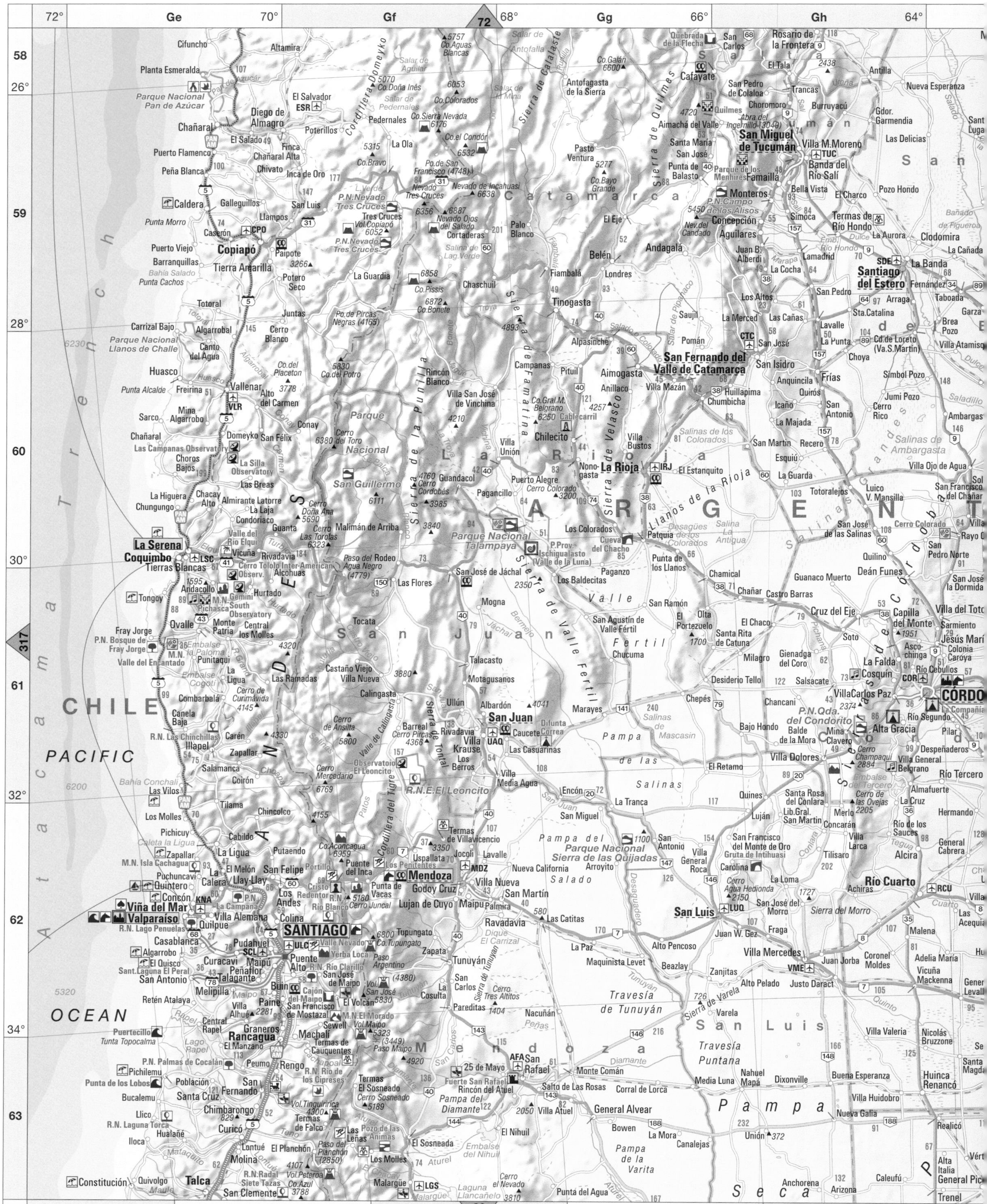

Scale 1:4,500,000
0 40 80 Kilometers

Principal travel routes
- Auto route
- Rail road
- Shipping route

Remarkable landscapes and natural monuments
- UNESCO World Natural Heritage
- Mountain landscape
- Rock landscape
- Ravine/canyon
- Extinct volcano
- Active volcano
- Cave
- Glacier
- River landscape
- Waterfall/rapids
- Lake country
- Oasis
- National park (landscape)
- National park (flora)
- National park (fauna)
- National park (culture)

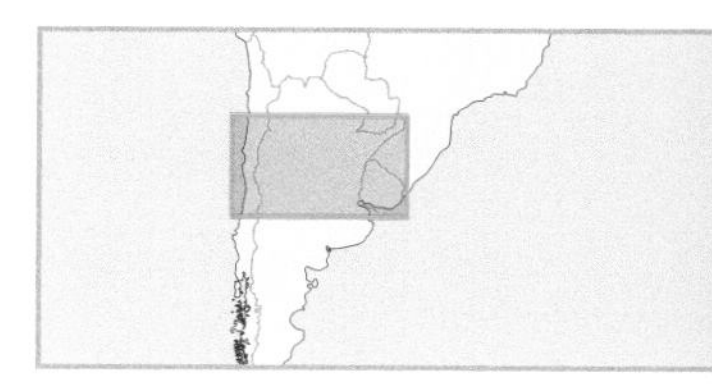

›e Río de la Plata is an estuary ›tween southern Uruguay and northern ›gentina. The estuary ranges between › and 200 kilometers in width before › flows into the Atlantic Ocean. West › Montevideo, the Rio de la Plata is a ›eshwater body – the section of the ›tuary east of the city contains salt- ›ater.

›e Pampas in Argentina is one of the ›orld's most important centers for grain production. Livestock ranching is the most important industry in the semi-arid Gran Chaco region. Argentina's Mendoza Province and Chile's **Central Valley (Valle Central)** both have subtropical climates. The two regions are also the leading centers for wine production in South America.

The **Andes Mountains** stretch the entire length of Chile. South of Chile's capital city Santiago, the Andes are divided into a coastal and interior range separated from one another by the fertile Central Valley. The interior range in this section of the Andes features **Aconcagua**, South America's highest mountain. Aconcagua rises 6959 meters above sea level and is surrounded by a large national park containing numerous glaciers and pristine mountain lakes.

The northern edges of central Chile consist of arid and semi-arid areas. Most of central Chile however has a pleasant Mediterranean climate and fertile soil. The warmer sections of central Chile are the most densely populated areas of the country and contain its two largest cities: Valparaiso and Santaigo de Chile. Santiago de Chile, the capital city of Chile, is a modern urban area with scattered historic buildings, tall skyscrapers, and a population around five million.

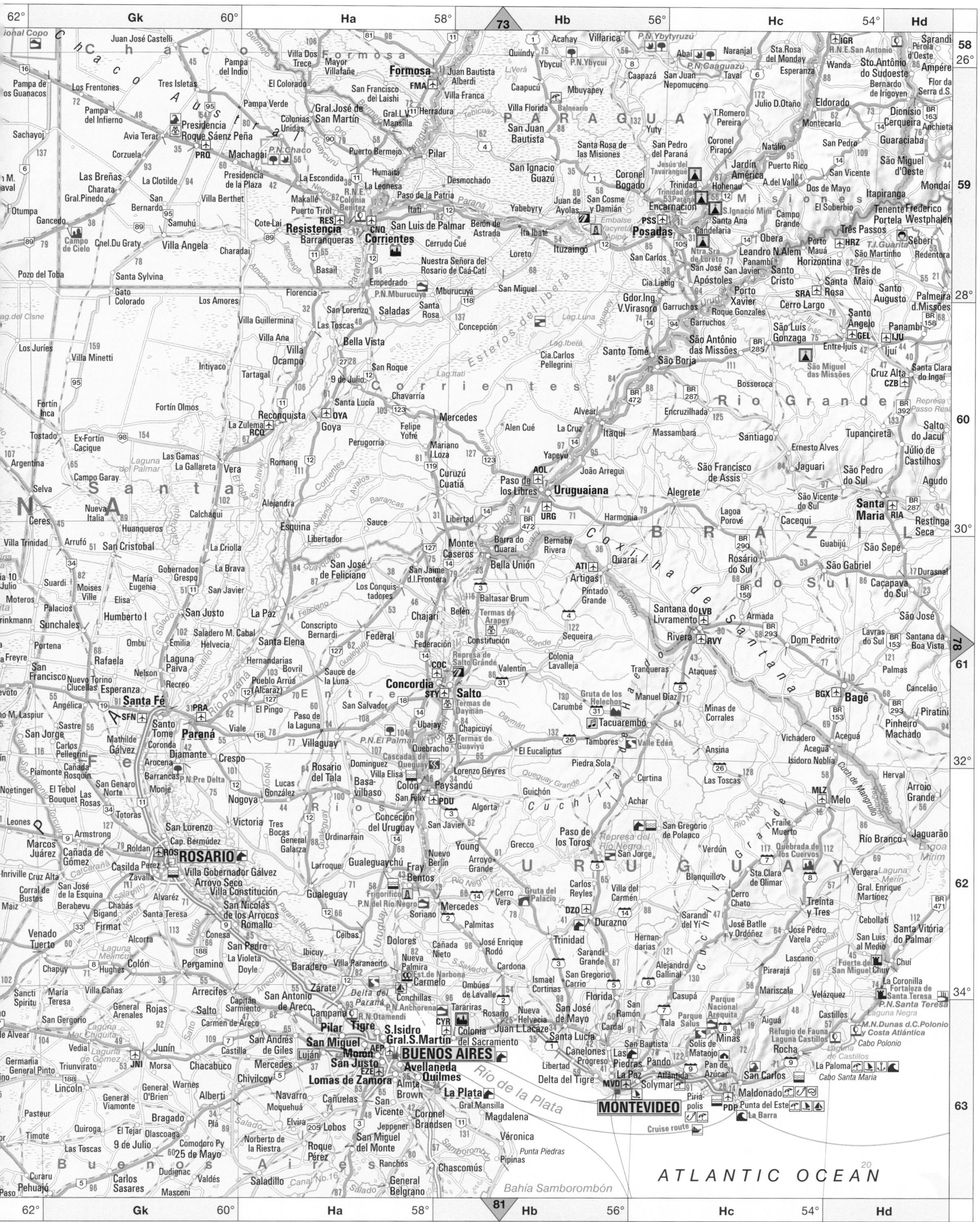

Los Menhires Park Open air museum containing 129 ancient stone monoliths (4th - 9th centuries) – located in Argentina's Tafí del Valle **Gh59**

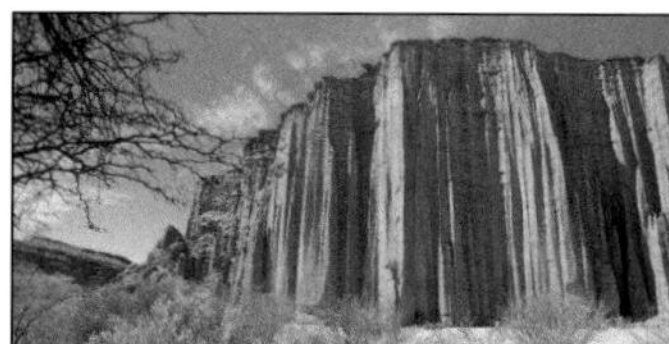

Talampaya National Park National park containing large sandstone formations – UNESCO world natural heritage site – pre-Columbian rock paintings **GfGg60/61**

Córdoba Second largest city in Argentina – population 1.2 million – location of a major university – historic baroque Iglesia Compañía de Jesús church – cathedral and city hall on the Plaza San Martin **Gh61**

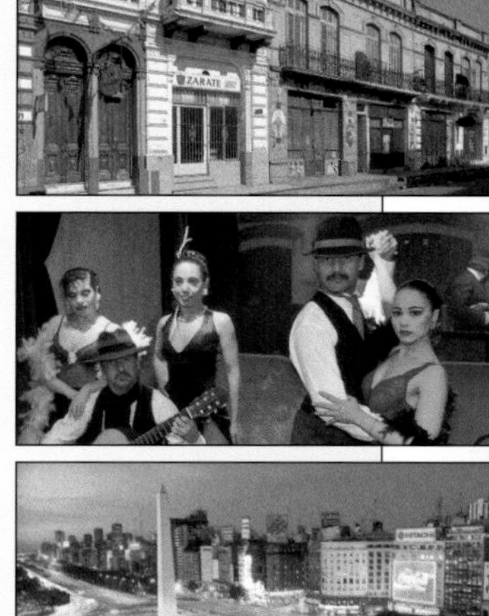

Buenos Aires The largest city and capital of Argentina was founded in 1536. Buenos Aires and its suburbs are home to 12 million people, one third of Argentina's population. The sophisticated and cosmopolitan city is famous as the birthplace of tango. La Boca is a colorful and lively neighborhood near the city's harbor. Photos from top to bottom: La Boca district, tango dancers, Plaza de la Republica **Ha63**

Montevideo Capital of Uruguay – important port city – population 1.3 million – popular sandy beaches – Parliament building (photo) **Hb63**

›emarkable Cities and Cultural monuments

- UNESCO World Cultural Heritage
- Remarkable Cities
- Prehistoric rockscape
- Other ancient American cultures
- Places of Christian cultural interest
- Amazonian Indians/protected area
- Cultural landscape
- Historical city scape
- Castle/fortress/fort
- Technical/industrial monument
- Space telescope
- Festivals

Sport and leisure destinations

- Horse racing
- Skiing
- Sailing
- Diving
- Wind surfing
- Surfing
- Canoeing/rafting
- Deep-sea fishing
- Beach resort
- Mineral/thermal spa
- Casino
- Hill resort

Southern Brazil

From Salvador in the north to Porto Allegre, a continuous series of plateaus and uplands run parallel to the **Brazilian** coast. These elevations were created millions of years ago when South America separated from the prehistoric supercontinent Gondwanaland. This region features numerous fertile valleys, unusual stone formations, and beautiful green mountains.
Large remnants of the virgin tropical

forest that once covered most of coas Brazil can be found in the **Atlan Forest Southeast Reserves**. This gro of 25 nature reserves covers an ar around 4,700 km² large.
The few rivers in the region that flow ea ward are relatively short. Most of t rivers in the region flow westward into t

Iguaçu Falls: a conglomerate of 275 separate waterfalls **Hc**

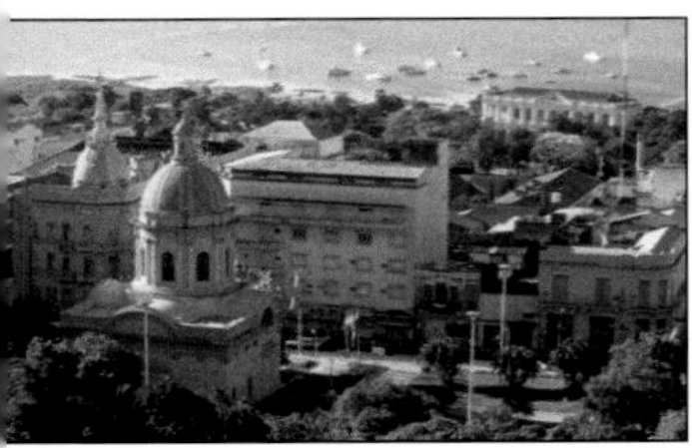

Asunción Capital city of Paraguay – population 1.2 million – Panteón Nacional de los Héroes (photo) **Hb58**

Itaipu Dam 7,700-meter-long dam – part of the world's largest hydroelectric power facility – twenty generators **Hc58**

Iguaçu (Iguaçú) National Park The national park around the spectacular Iguaçu Falls is a UNESCO world heritage site. **Hc58**

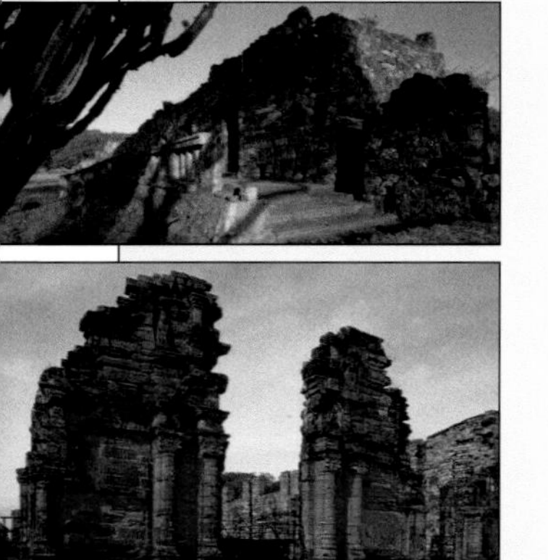

Jesuit-Guarani Missions More than 30 historic missions along the Paraná River. The 18th-century buildings once housed Jesuit missionaries and converted Amerindians. **Hc59**

Esteros del Iberá Large marshland and savannah region – unique plants – more than 300 bird species **Hb59/60**

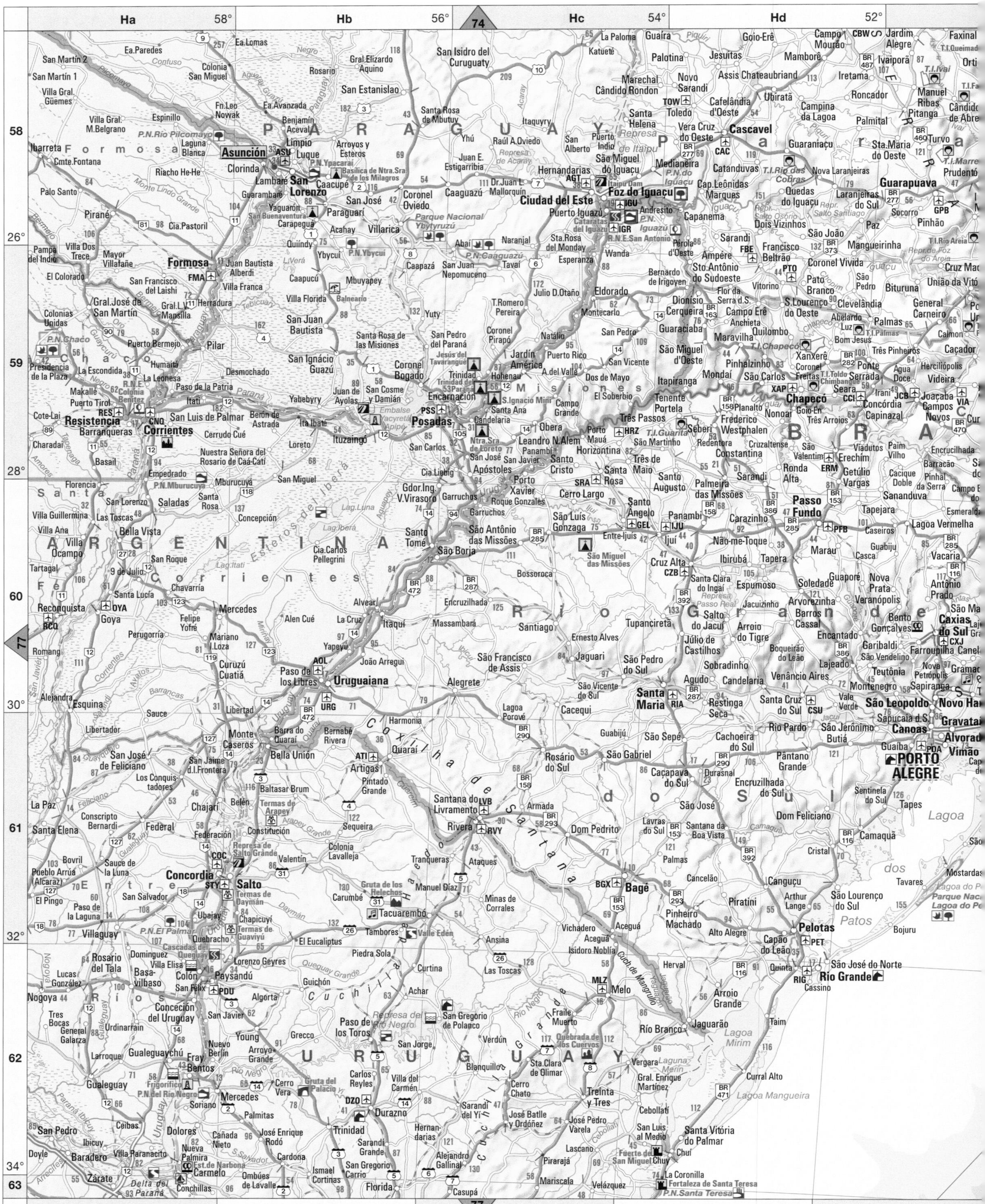

Scale 1:4,500,000
0 40 80 Kilometers

Principal travel routes
- Auto route
- Rail road
- Shipping route

Remarkable landscapes and natural monuments
- UNESCO World Natural Heritage
- Mountain landscape
- Rock landscape
- Cave
- River landscape
- Waterfall/rapids
- Lake country
- Nature park
- National park (landscape)
- National park (flora)
- National park (fauna)
- National park (culture)
- Biosphere reserve
- Coastal landscape
- Beach
- Island

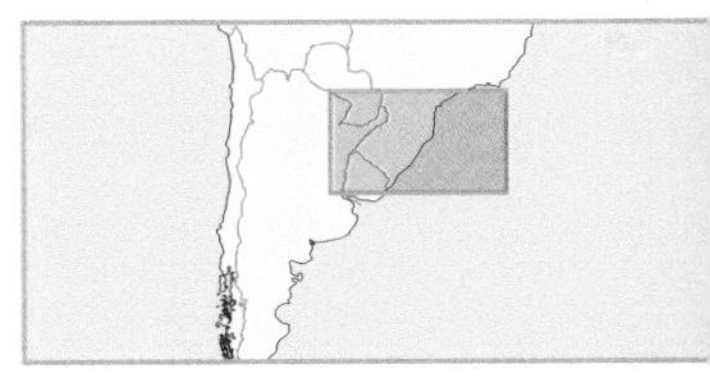

Jruguay, Paraná, or São Francisco er. The **Iguaçu River** flows over an 80 ter high drop on its way to merge with Parana River. Over centuries the er's eroding forces formed one of the eatest natural attractions in South erica. The **Iguaçu Falls** are a group 275 separate waterfalls stretched out er two kilometers. The subtropical ests of southern Brazil are home to ny interesting animals including tapirs and rare bird species. The **Esteros del Iberá** is a large marshland with abundant wildlife, located between the Uruguay and Paraná Rivers. There are several large lagoons along the coast of southern Brazil including the **Lagoa dos Patos**.

The mild subtropical climate and fertile soil of southern **Brazil** and southern **Paraguay** attracted millions of European immigrants to the region. The influence of German, Italian, and other European settlers is still evident in the region's culture and tradtions. Every year, the residents of Blumenau in Brazil celebrate the largest German style Oktoberfest in Latin America. Due to careful urban planning, Curitiba (the state capital of Parana), is generally considered the most livable urban area in Brazil. The **Planalto Meridional** is an area of hills and evergreen forests stretching from southern Brazil into Uruguay. Many of the rainforests in southern Brazil, including those around the Iguaçu Falls and east of Curitiba, are protected by conservation laws.

The **Serra Geral** and **Serra Gaúcha** ranges around Porto Alegre contain temperate vegetation. The area features many vineyards and is an important center for wine production. This is also one of the few places in Brazil where snow falls during winter.

Atlantic Forest Southeast Reserves A group of 25 nature reserves containing virgin tropical forests **Hg58**

Curitiba One of Brazil's most "livable" cities – excellent public transport system – several parks – Ópera de Arame **Hf58**

Train Route Curitiba-Paranagua Train route passing through the Serra do Mar – built between 1880 and 1885 – 110-kilometer-long route with beautiful views **Hf58**

Blumenau Brazilian city founded by German immigrants – numerous half timbered buildings – Oktoberfest **Hf59**

Florianópolis The state capital of Santa Catarina – part of the city is on an island – Ponte Hercílio Luz suspension bridge, built in the 1920s **Hf59**

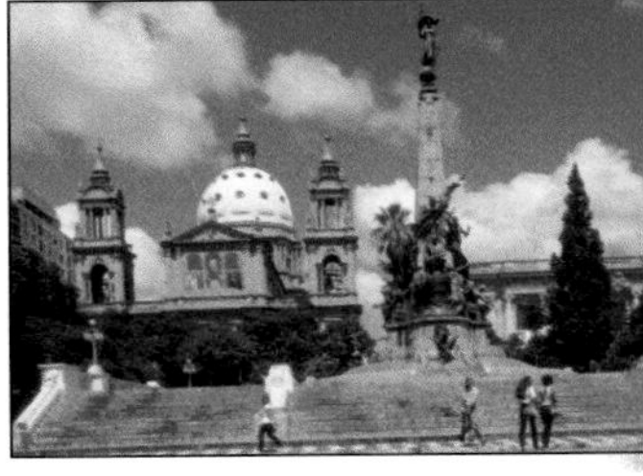

Porto Alegre Large city in Southern Brazil – German and Italian cultural influences – São Pedro Theatre – Mercado Público market – historic cathedral **He61**

Aparados da Serra National Park Contains the seven-kilometer-long Itaimbezinho gorge – two waterfalls **He60**

ATLANTIC OCEAN

Remarkable Cities and Cultural monuments

- UNESCO World Cultural Heritage
- Remarkable Cities
- Places of Christian cultural interest
- Amazonian Indians/protected area
- Cultural landscape
- Historical city scape
- Castle/fortress/fort
- Technical/industrial monument
- Dam
- Festivals

Sport and leisure destinations

- Race track
- Horse racing
- Sailing
- Diving
- Surfing
- Beach resort
- Mineral/thermal spa

The section of South America below the 36th parallel of latitude tends to rise in elevation from east to west. The Andes Mountains in the west include numerous volcanoes and are separated from the Pacific Ocean by a narrow coastal strip of land. The border between Chile and Argentina runs through the Andes in this region. South America features many of the world's tallest active volcanoes. The volcanism in the Andes is the result of collisions between three tectonic plates the Earth's crust; the Nazca, Antarc and South American plates. Tecto activity was also responsible for the cr tion of the 7,500 meter deep **Peru-C Trench** situated off the western coas South America in the Pacific Ocean. 38th parallel of latitude marks the g

Villarrica (2,847 meters): one of many beautiful active volcanos in Chile **G**

Villarrica National Park The national park is located on the southern edge of a large lake. It includes the volcanoes Villarrica (2,847 meters) and Quetrupillán. **Ge65**

Lanín National Park The volcano Lanin (3,747 meters) is situated in the center of this Argentinean national park – popular destination for mountain climbers **Ge65**

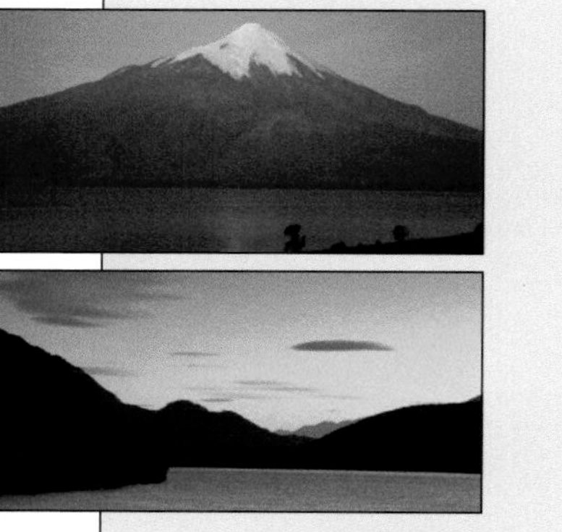

Chile's Lake District Scenic region in the Chilean Andes. The volcano Osomo (top photo) and Lago Llanquihue (bottom photo) are two of the many stunning natural attractions in this area north of Puerto Montt. **Gd66**

Isla Grande de Chiloé Large island off the coast of Patagonia – around 160 churches (gothic and baroque wooden buildings) – Castro Cathedral (photo) – UNESCO world heritage site **Gd67**

Corcovado Active volcano (2,300 meters) next to the Gulf of Corcovado in Chile – several lakes in the surrounding area **Gd67**

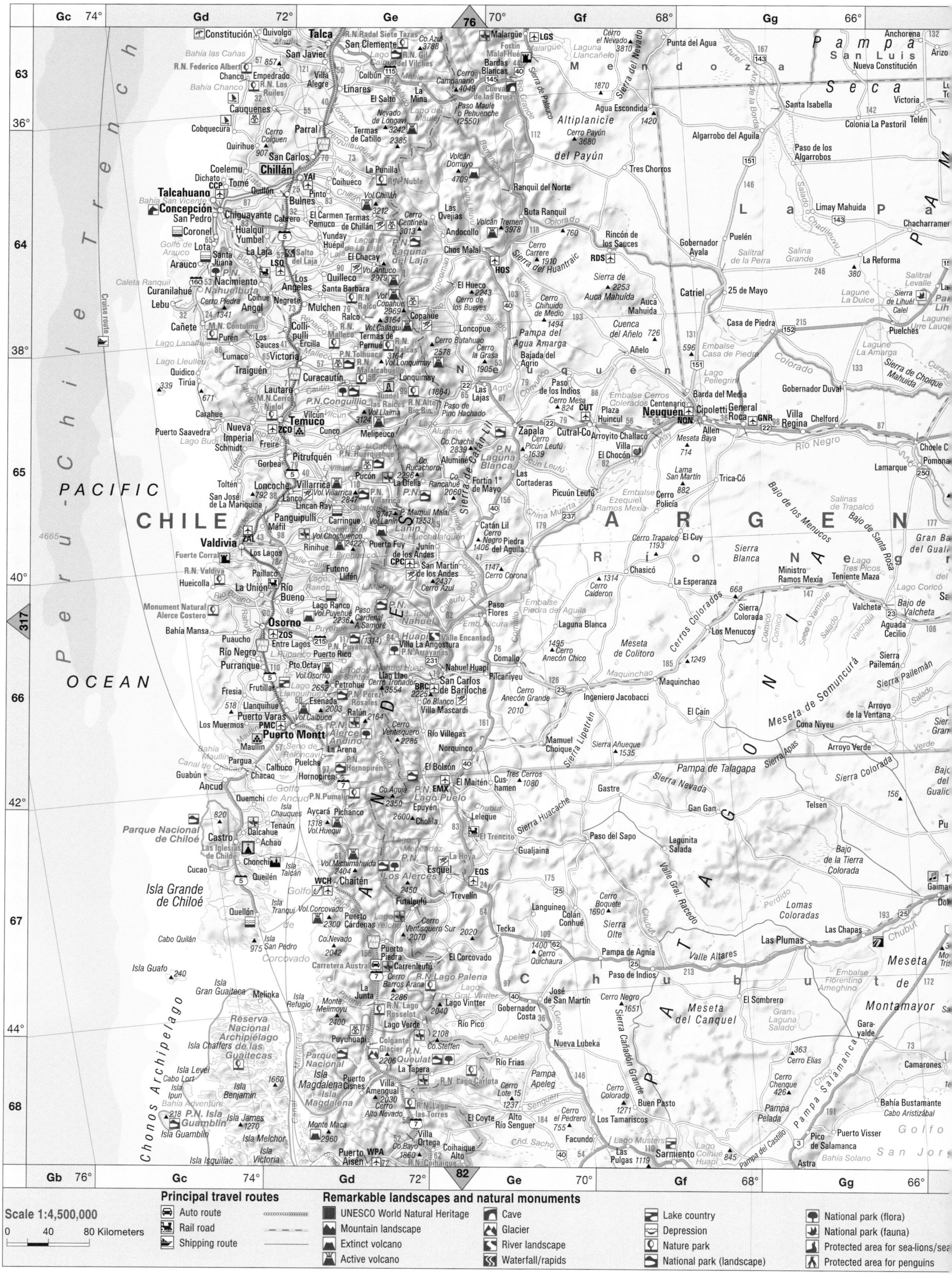

Scale 1:4,500,000

0 40 80 Kilometers

Principal travel routes

- Auto route
- Rail road
- Shipping route

Remarkable landscapes and natural monuments

- UNESCO World Natural Heritage
- Mountain landscape
- Extinct volcano
- Active volcano
- Cave
- Glacier
- River landscape
- Waterfall/rapids
- Lake country
- Depression
- Nature park
- National park (landscape)
- National park (flora)
- National park (fauna)
- Protected area for sea-lions/se
- Protected area for penguins

phic border between two distinct sec- s of the Andes: the Central and uthern Cordilleras. The Southern rdilleras extend through Patagonia and o the island Tierra del Fuego. The ge decreases in elevation from north south.
arge number of mountain lakes and ge glaciers are scattered throughout Southern Cordilleras. During the ice es, gigantic glaciers created large valleys and unique stone formations throughout the Andes Mountains. At the end of the last ice age, water released from melting glaciers caused the sea level around the region to rise. The many **fjords** along the southwestern coast of South America were created when mountainous inland areas were partially submerged by the rising ocean. Ice age glaciers also formed many new bodies of water in the Andes. Several areas in the region, including the **Chilean Lake District**, have an incredible concentration of beautiful lakes.
Ancient layers of stone are located beneath the surface of Patagonia and the Pampas in Argentina. The vast prairies of the Pampas are used primarily for grain cultivation and to a lesser extent for livestock ranching. Patagonia, the most sparsely populated section of Argetina, has a cool and dry climate. Sheep herding and mining are the most important sectors of Patagonia's economy. The Andes and the Chilean coast in this region are covered by thick evergreen forests. Many fascinating animals inhabit the eastern coast of Argentina. Punta Tombo is home to large penguin colonies and the **Valdés Peninsula** has the largest sea elephant population in Argentina. Whale watching season in the region is between July and December.

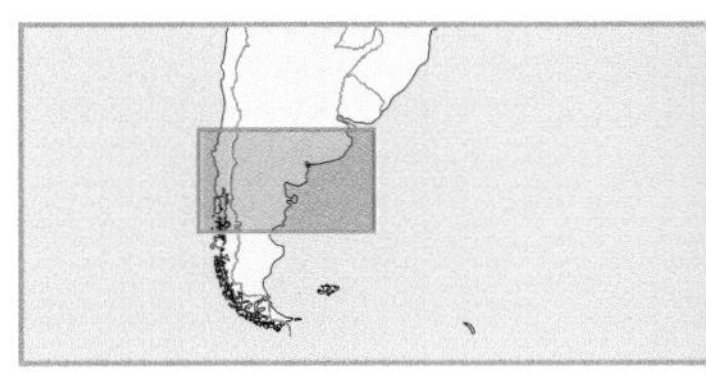

ATLANTIC OCEAN

Cerro Payún High inactive volcano (3,680 meters) – large elliptical main crater and several smaller craters **Gf64**

Laguna Blanca National Park This national park in the eastern Andes has several mountain lakes – created for the protection of rare black-necked swans **Ge65**

Nahuel Huapi National Park National park in mountainous western Argentina – tallest mountain Cerro Tronador (3,554 meters) – 100-kilometers-long glacial lake **Ge66**

Mar del Plata Popular holiday destination on Argentina's Atlantic coast – more than two million visitors in summer – large casino **Hb65**

Valdés Península The peninsula on Argentina's Atlantic coast is home to an abundance of wildlife. The cliffs at Punta Delgada and Punta Norte are inhabited by large sea elephant populations. Caleta Valdés has the area's largest population of sea lions (bottom photo). Whale watching season in the area is between July and December. **Gj67**

Cabo dos Bahías This remote coastal area is home to a large colony of Magellan penguins (photo) **Gh68**

emarkable Cities and Cultural monuments

- UNESCO World Cultural Heritage
- Remarkable Cities
- Places of Christian cultural interest
- Historical city scape
- Castle/fortress/fort
- Technical/industrial monument
- Market
- Festivals
- Dam

Sport and leisure destinations

- Race track
- Golf
- Horse racing
- Skiing
- Diving
- Wind surfing
- Surfing
- Canoeing/rafting
- Deep-sea fishing
- Beach resort
- Mineral/thermal spa
- Casino

Southern Chile, Patagonia, Falkland Islands

South America stretches south to just below the 55th parallel of latitude. While the areas along the 55th parallel of latitude in the northern hemisphere are covered by ice sheets and tundras, the southern tip of South America has a cool but temperate climate with abundant precipitation. The southernmost regions of the continent are frequently swept by powerful storms in the Pacific Ocean. Constant storms and strong winds make the area off of the coast one of the wor most dangerous ship passages. In the mountains of the Peruvian An snow begins to fall at elevations betw 4,900 and 5,300 meters above sea le In central Chile, the so-called snow begins at elevations around 2,000 met In Chile's far south, the snow line is lo

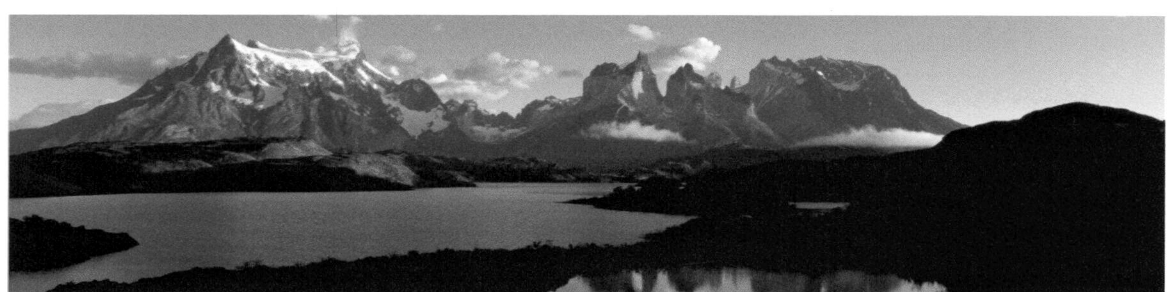

Torres del Paine: spectacular landscapes in the southern Andes **G**

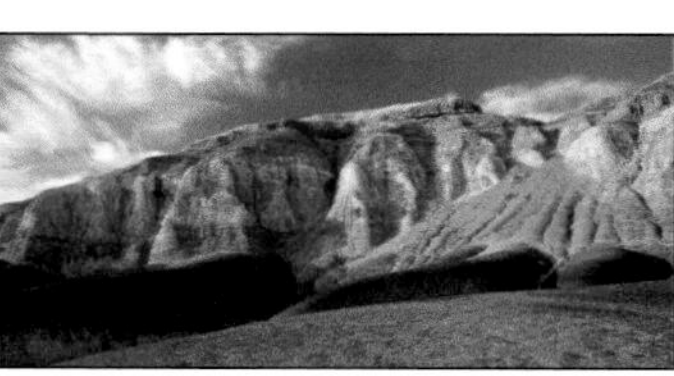

J. Ormachea Petrified Forest Argentinean petrified forest with 70-million-year old remnants of tall trees – more than 20 meter high **Gf68**

Laguna San Rafael National Park Large nature reserve (Chile) with the 45-kilometer-long San Rafael Glacier – icebergs and fjords **GcGd69**

Río Baker Valley Partially forested canyons between two large ice fields (Chile) – turquoise blue river – good fishing area **Gd69**

Cueva de las Manos The isolated canyons along the Rio Pinturas (top photo) featuring caves with 10,000-year-old paintings. These caves are a UNESCO world heritage site. The cave paintings show handprints in different colors (bottom photo). **Ge69**

Los Glaciares National Park Beautiful national park and UNESCO world heritage site between Lago Viedma and Lago Argentino. The park has many peaks including Mount Fitz Roy (top photo). The Perito Moreno Glacier (bottom photo) flows into Lago Argentino. **Gd70/71**

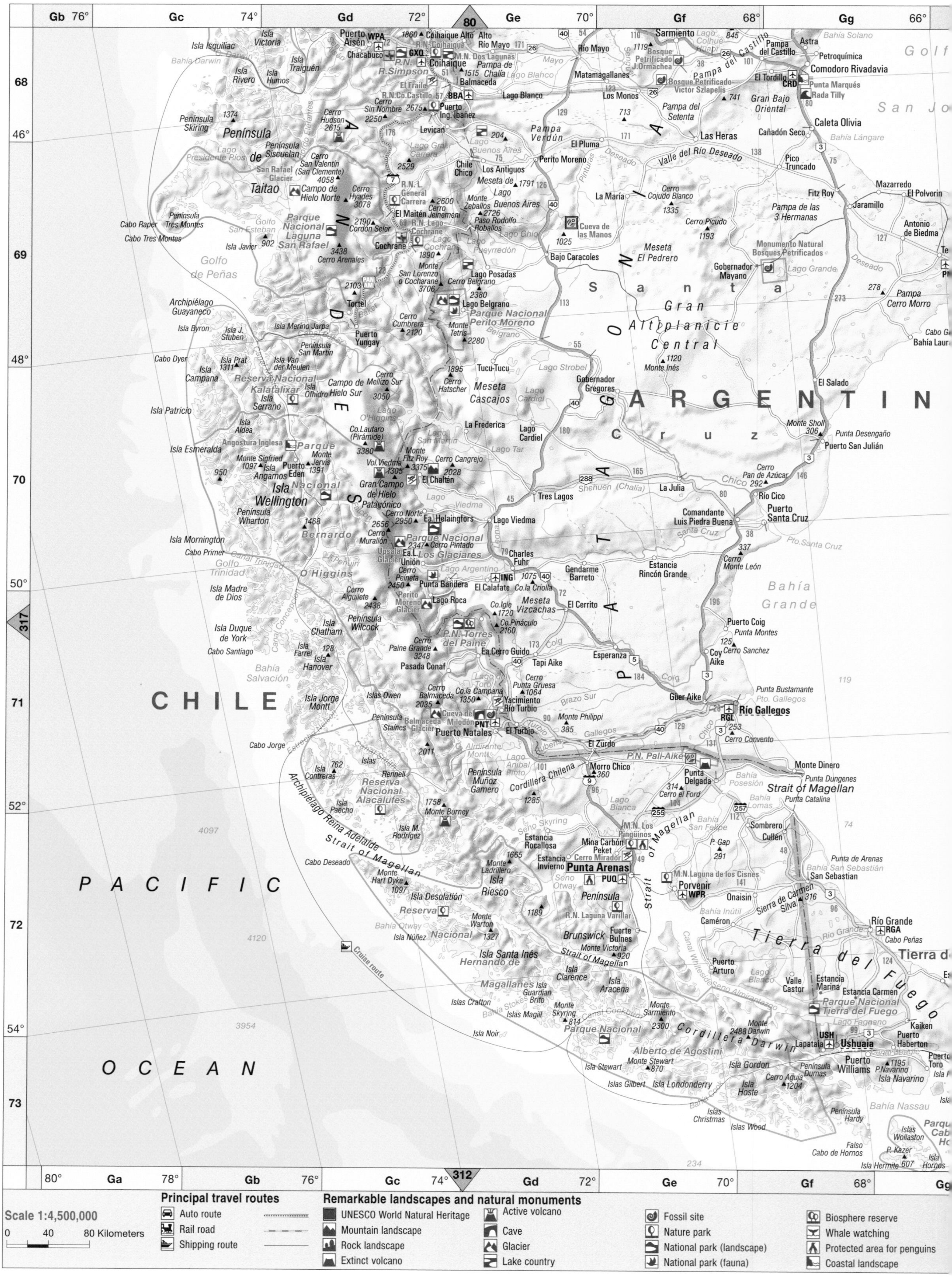

Scale 1:4,500,000

0 40 80 Kilometers

Principal travel routes

- Auto route
- Rail road
- Shipping route

Remarkable landscapes and natural monuments

- UNESCO World Natural Heritage
- Mountain landscape
- Rock landscape
- Extinct volcano
- Active volcano
- Cave
- Glacier
- Lake country
- Fossil site
- Nature park
- National park (landscape)
- National park (fauna)
- Biosphere reserve
- Whale watching
- Protected area for penguins
- Coastal landscape

›d a mere 700 meters above sea level. ›arge evergreen trees flourish along Chi- ›'s southwestern coast, an area with ›oundant rainfall. The western sections › the southern Andes exhibit sparse ›oorland vegetation. The easternmost ›ections of the southern Andes – in ›rgentina – feature vast temperate forests ›nd alpine vegetation. This area is often ›alled **Argentina's Switzerland** and ›so has many large mountain lakes including **Lago Argentino** at the foot of the Andes. The southern tip of South America comprises numerous bays, peninsulas, and lakes. The archipelago **Tierra del Fuego** is the southernmost region of South America. The archipelago consists of countless tiny islets, five smaller islands, and one large island also called Tierra del Fuego. In 1520, Ferdinand Magellan became the first European to visit the archipelago. During the 19th century, the discovery of gold attracted a large number of migrants to the region. Tierra del Fuego is now a sparsely populated region divided between Argentina and Chile.

Ushuaia in Argentina is the southernmost city in the world. The city lies on the **Beagle Channel**, which was named after the famous ship that Charles Darwin sailed with to South America. West of Ushuaia lies a mountain range named after Darwin himself, the Cordillera Darwin. Southern Patagonia is a land of fire and ice. Patatgonia features both active volcanoes, including Mount Viedma (1,305 meters), as well as numerous large glaciers. The **Falkland Islands**, known as **Islas Malvinas** in Spanish, are a British overseas territory off the southeastern coast of South America. The Falklands are home to large penguin colonies and at least 60 bird species.

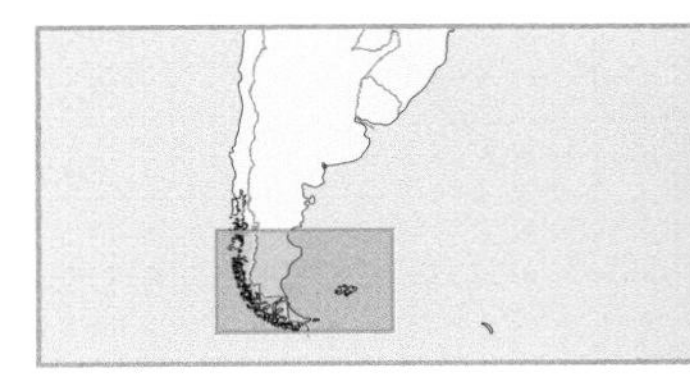

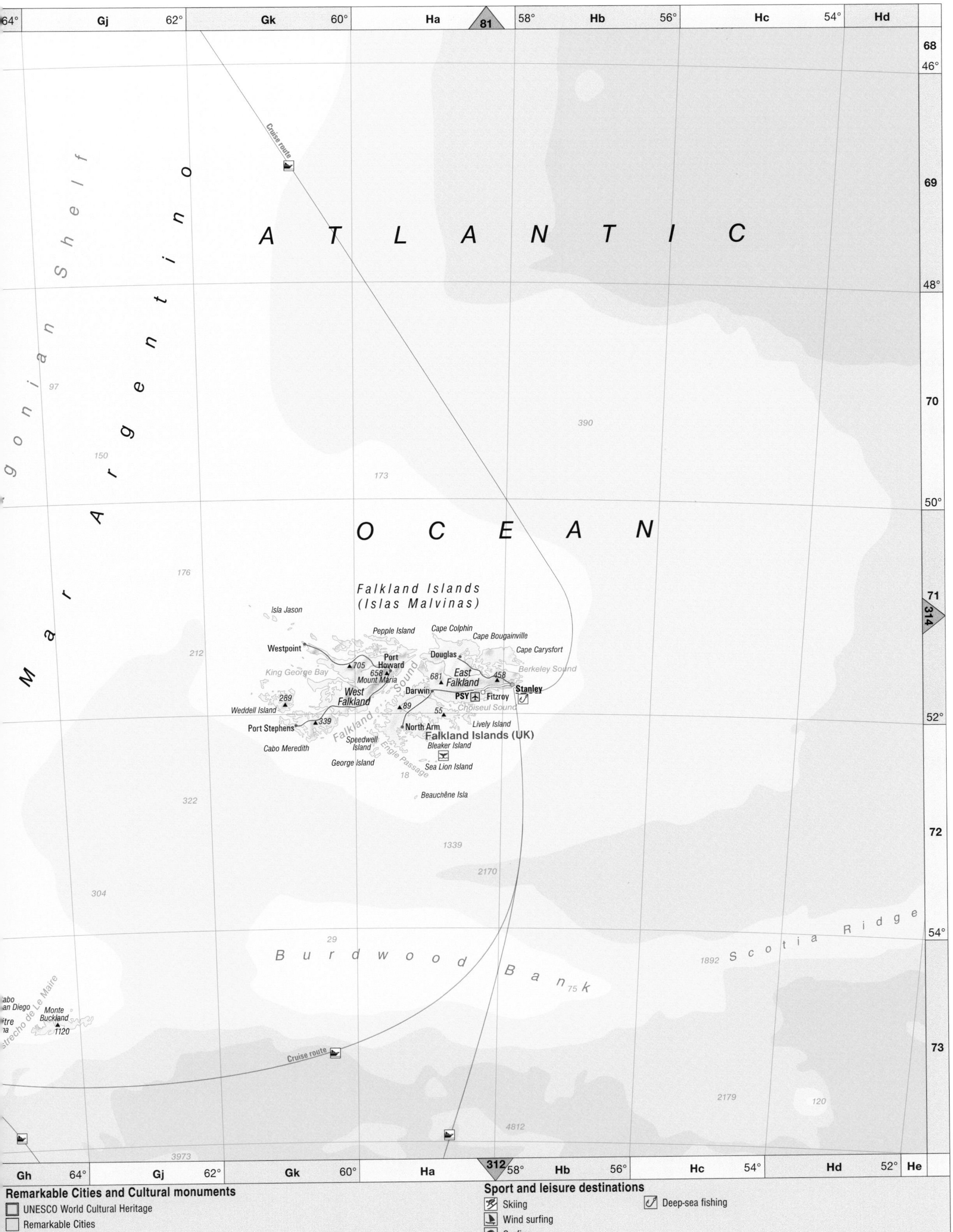

ATLANTIC OCEAN

Mar Argentino

Falkland Islands (Islas Malvinas)

Isla Jason, Pepple Island, Cape Colphin, Cape Bougainville, Cape Carysfort, Westpoint, Port Howard, Douglas, King George Bay, Mount Maria, East Falkland, Berkeley Sound, West Falkland, Darwin, PSY, Fitzroy, Stanley, Weddell Island, Choiseul Sound, Port Stephens, Lively Island, North Arm, Falkland Islands (UK), Speedwell Island, Bleaker Island, Cabo Meredith, George Island, Sea Lion Island, Beauchêne Isla, Falkland Sound, Eagle Passage

Burdwood Bank

Scotia Ridge

Cruise route

Monte Buckland 1120

Estrecho de Le Maire

Remarkable Cities and Cultural monuments

- UNESCO World Cultural Heritage
- Remarkable Cities
- Prehistoric rockscape

Sport and leisure destinations

- Skiing
- Wind surfing
- Surfing
- Canoeing/rafting
- Deep-sea fishing

Torres del Paine National Park National park on the edge of an ice field – several hiking trails – Rio Paine waterfalls **Gd71**

Punta Arenas Port city on the Straits of Magellan – beautiful cemetery – regional history museum **Ge72**

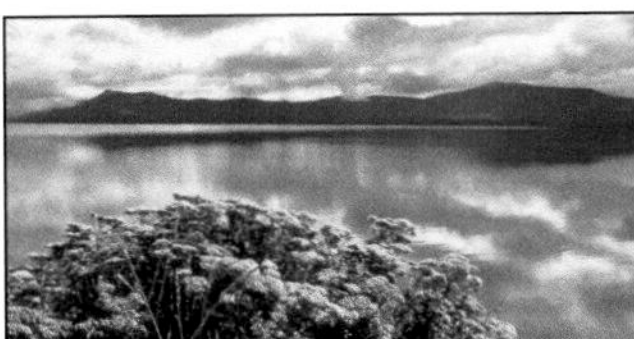

Tierra del Fuego National Park Protected mountainous region in Tierre del Fuego – only the southern portions of the park are accessible **Gf73**

Ushuaia The southernmost city in the world – 50,000 residents – Museo del Fin del Mundo, regional history and natural history museum **Gg73**

Cape Horn The southern tip of South America on the island Isla de Hornos – surrounded by stormy waters **Gg73**

The Falkland Islands (Isla Malvinas) British territory in the Atlantic Ocean. The islands are covered by grasslands. Sheep herding and fishing are the major industries. The areas outside of Port Stanley boast large bird colonies and good fishing areas. **GkHb71/72**

Salzburg (top): The Hohensalzburg fortress towers above the picturesque old town.
Andalusian countryside (bottom): storm clouds above a village in the Sierra Nevada.

Bilbao (left): The futuristic architecture of Bilbao's Guggenheim museum.
Stonehenge (right): An early Stone Age monument built to observe the stars.

Europe

The fjords and cliffs of the north, the vast green forests of Central Europe, the snow covered peaks of the Alps and Pyrenees, the sun drenched coasts of the Mediterranean, the legacy of ancient Greeks and Romans, medieval cathedrals, baroque castles, modern cities, and colorful traditions... All this and more is Europe.

With an area of 10.5 million km², Europe is the second smallest continent in size. Separated in the east from Asia by the Ural Mountains, Europe extends over 5,000 kilometers to the western coast of Ireland. From the North Cape to Crete in the Mediterranean, Europe stretches over 4,000 kilometers north to south. The **Atlantic Ocean** marks the western borders of Europe, the Mediterranean and Black Sea border the continent in the south and the Arctic Ocean lies north of the continent.

The topography Southern and Central Europe's is dominated by a bow shaped series of **mountain chains**. The mountain system extends from the Sierra Nevada, to the Pyrenees, the Alps, and the Carpathian Mountains. North of this mountain belt lies a series of **medium elevatio ranges** – including the French Massif Central, the Harz Mountains, and the Tatras – that gives way to the plains of northern and Central Europe. One of the most striking features of Europe's geography is the large number of **peninsulas** (Scandinavia, Iberia, Greece, etc.) of the continent. The European mainland is also surrounded by many **islands**, including Great Britain and Sardinia.

The beatiful rolling hills of Tuscany (Italy).

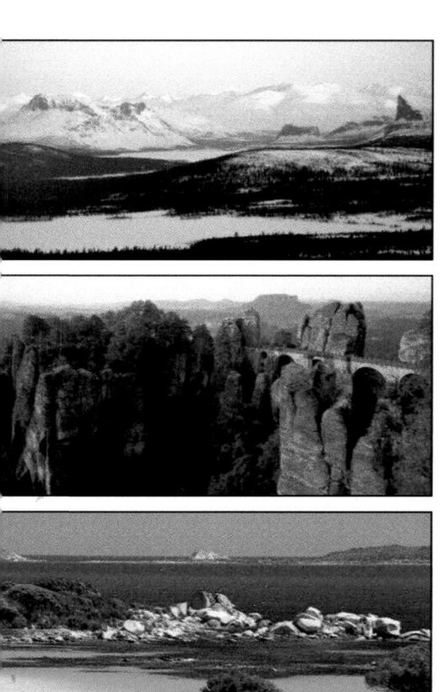

Europe's diverse landscapes developed over many millions of years and were largely shaped by the last ice ages. The ice-and snow-covered **mountainous tundra** of northern Scandinavia – including Lapland (top photo) – is a rugged and sparsely populated region. North of the tall Alps, a series of **medium-height ranges** stretches through much of Central Europe (middle photo: Sächsische Schweiz in Germany). There are also many rocky landscapes and high hills along Europe's Mediterranean coastlines (bottom photo).

The **Alps** stretch in a long band from west to east. The highest peaks are in the western areas of the Alps, including the highest alpine mountain Mont Blanc (4,807 meters). The 4,478 meter high Matterhorn (top photo) is the third highest mountain in the Alps. The second highest mountain chain in Europe is the Sierra Nevada in Spain, which encompasses many high peaks including Mulhacen (3,478 meters).

Many of the world's most famous **rivers** are located in Europe. The longest rivers in Europe are the Volga (3,530 km), the Danube (2,850 km), and the Ural (2,428 km); all three flow into the Caspian or Black Sea (top photo: the Danube in Budapest). The Rhine (1,320 km), Loire (1,020 km), and Oder (868 km) are all among the longest rivers in Europe (bottom photo: The Rhine in Switzerland).

Scale 1:27,000,000
0 160 320 Kilometers

Depth tints
Shoreline
0-200 m
200-2000 m
2000-4000 m
4000-6000 m
6000-8000 m
> 8000 m

Physical Features
River, stream
Intermittent river
Lake
Intermittent lake
Salt lake
Intermittent salt lake
Elevation above sea level in meters

Town symbols
Towns > 1 Mill. inhabitants
Towns < 100 000 inhabitants

th a **population** of 740 million, Eu-
pe is the third most populous con-
ent. Several European states have
pulations exceeding 50 million – in-
uding Italy, France, the United King-
m, Russia, and Germany. Immigrants
m outside of Europe have changed
faces of many once homogenous
ropean nations since the second half
the 20th century. With the relatively
cent **political development** in Eastern Europe – the collapse of the Soviet Union for example – many new states have emerged on the continent. The **migration** of people from eastern to western Europe and between southern and northern Europe continues to bring the continent's diverse cultures and nations closer together.

Left: Swedish child
Right: A young Russian woman

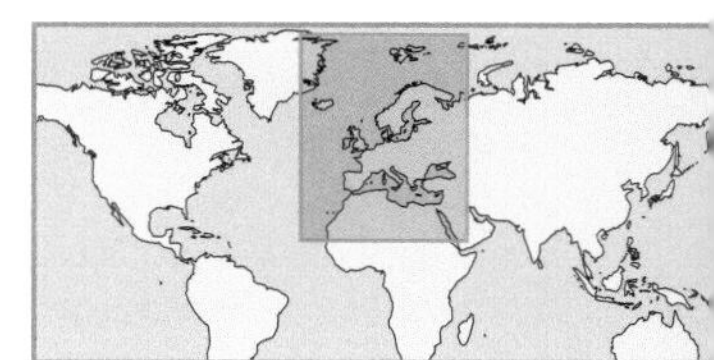

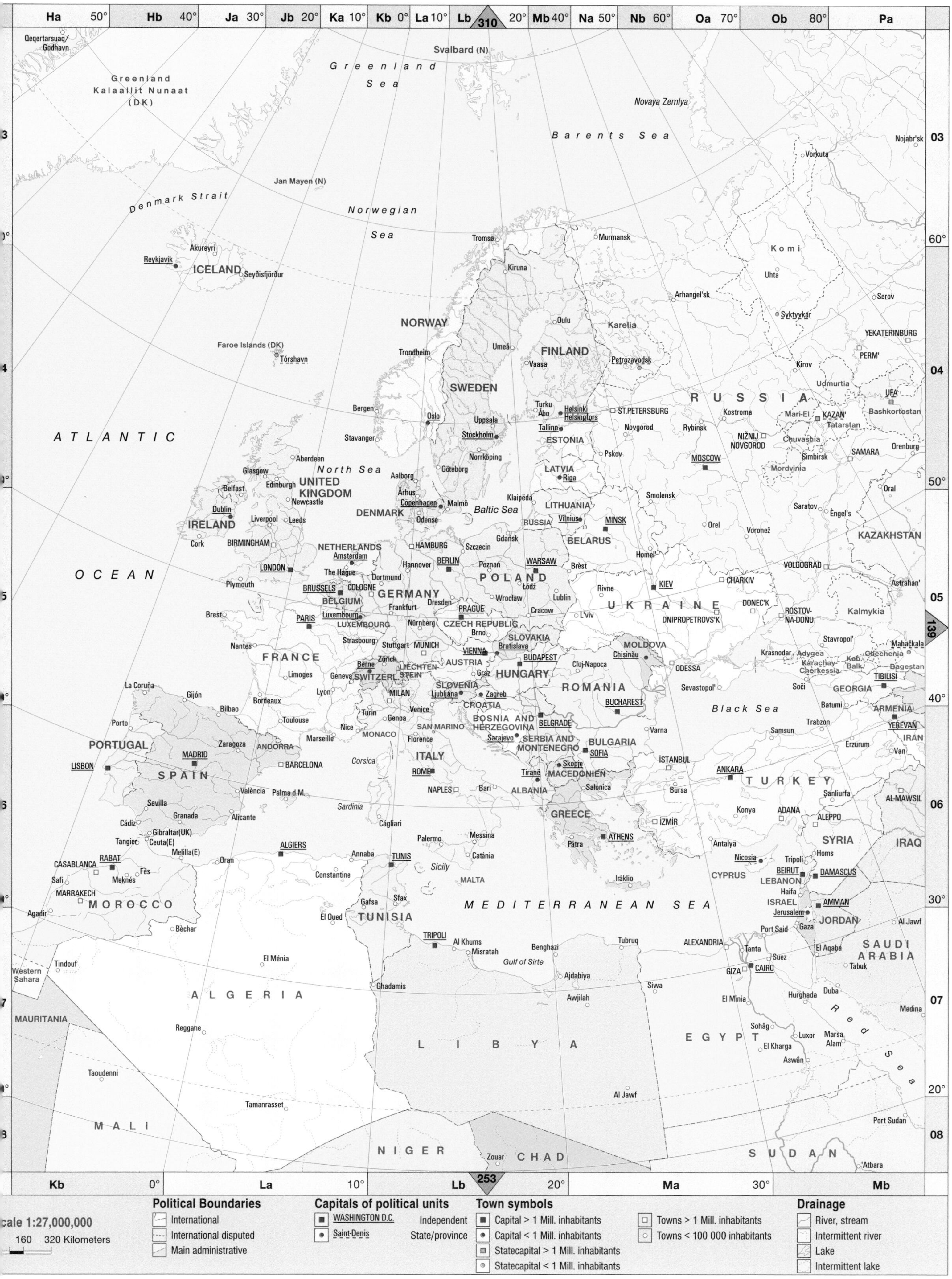

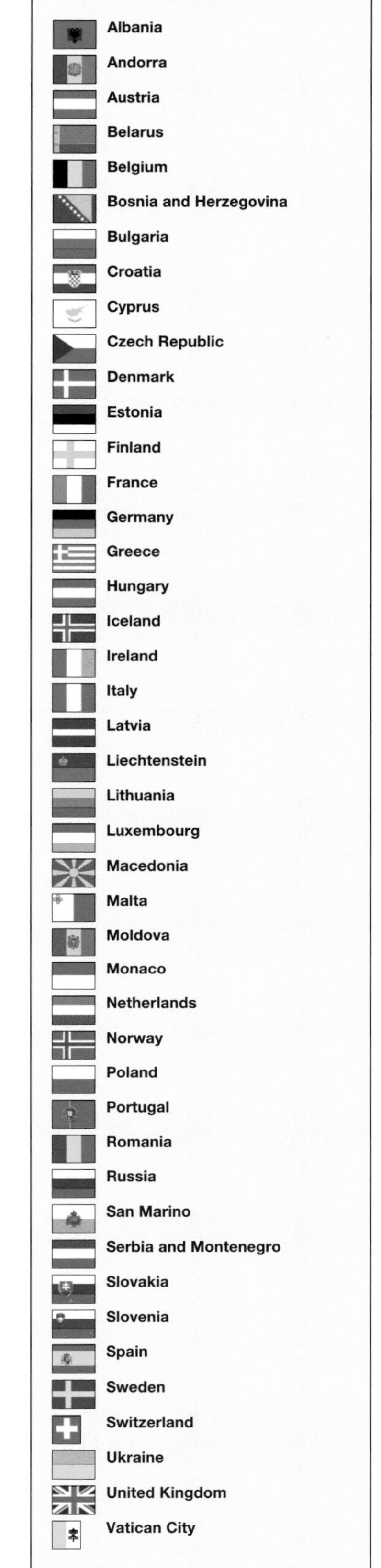

cale 1:27,000,000
160 320 Kilometers

Political Boundaries
International
International disputed
Main administrative

Capitals of political units
WASHINGTON D.C. Independent
Saint-Denis State/province

Town symbols
Capital > 1 Mill. inhabitants
Capital < 1 Mill. inhabitants
Statecapital > 1 Mill. inhabitants
Statecapital < 1 Mill. inhabitants
Towns > 1 Mill. inhabitants
Towns < 100 000 inhabitants

Drainage
River, stream
Intermittent river
Lake
Intermittent lake

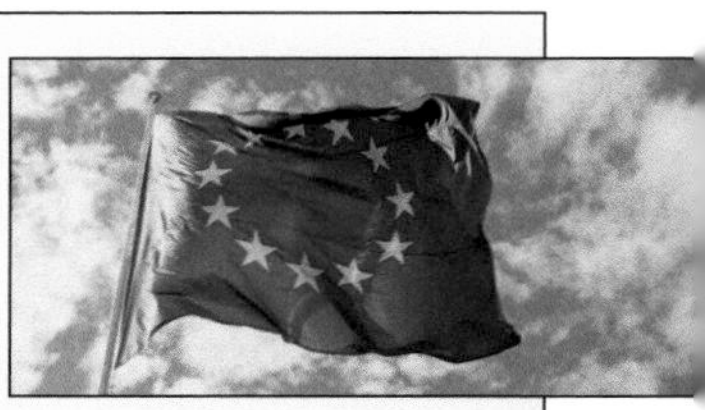

A blue flag with twelve golden stars is the official emblem of the **European Union**. Founded in the 1950s, the European Union was originally a trade alliance of six nations.

Europe

The continent of Europe is surrounded by the Atlantic Ocean, Arctic Ocean, and several marginal seas – including the Mediterranean Sea – on three sides: north, south, and west. The Ural Mountains and the Ural River are generally considered the natural boundaries that separate Europe from Asia. Geographically, Europe and Asia can be seen as two parts of a larger continent called Eurasia. Because Europe lacks a definitive border to Asia, certain regions such as Anatolia (Asia Minor) may or may not be considered European in different situations. Iceland lies on the boundary between the Eurasian and North American continental plates but is considered a European nation. Islands and peninsulas form around 34% of Europe's total area.

The Dolomites, a craggy section of the Alp's in South Tyrol-Alto Adige (Italy)

Despite the presence of several hi mountain ranges including the Alps, E rope has an average height of just 3 meters above sea, the lowest avera elevation of any continent.

Europe is a relatively small land mass b the continent features an incredible div sity of **landscapes** and geographica distinct regions including numero islands and peninsulas. The mounta ranges in western Scandinavia and nor

Iceland Volcanic island located just south of the Arctic Circle – 103,125 km² – highest mountain, Hvannadalshnukur (2,119 meters)

The British Isles Great Britain and Ireland are the main islands in this group – smaller island groups include the Shetlands, Orkneys, and Hebrides – highest mountain, Ben Nevis (1,344 meters) – photo: Dorset

The North Sea Flat marginal sea of the Atlantic Ocean – surface covering 0,575 million km² – maximum depth, 294 meters – extreme tidal range (0,5 to 7 meters)

The European Plain Series of plains encompassing lowlands in France, northern Germany (photo), and eastern Europe – stretches from the Atlantic Coast to the Urals

Massif Central Unique mountainous region in France – consists of craggy mountains (photo) and plateaus – the Rhone Valley seperates the area from the Alps

Iberian Peninsula Encompasses Spain and Portugal – circa 585,560 km² – Atlantic and Mediterranean coasts – the Pyrenees form a natural boundary between Iberia and France

Apennine Peninsula The "boot" of Italy – named after the 1,500 kilometers long Apennine Mountain Range – Sicily lies to the southwest – photo: Mount Etna

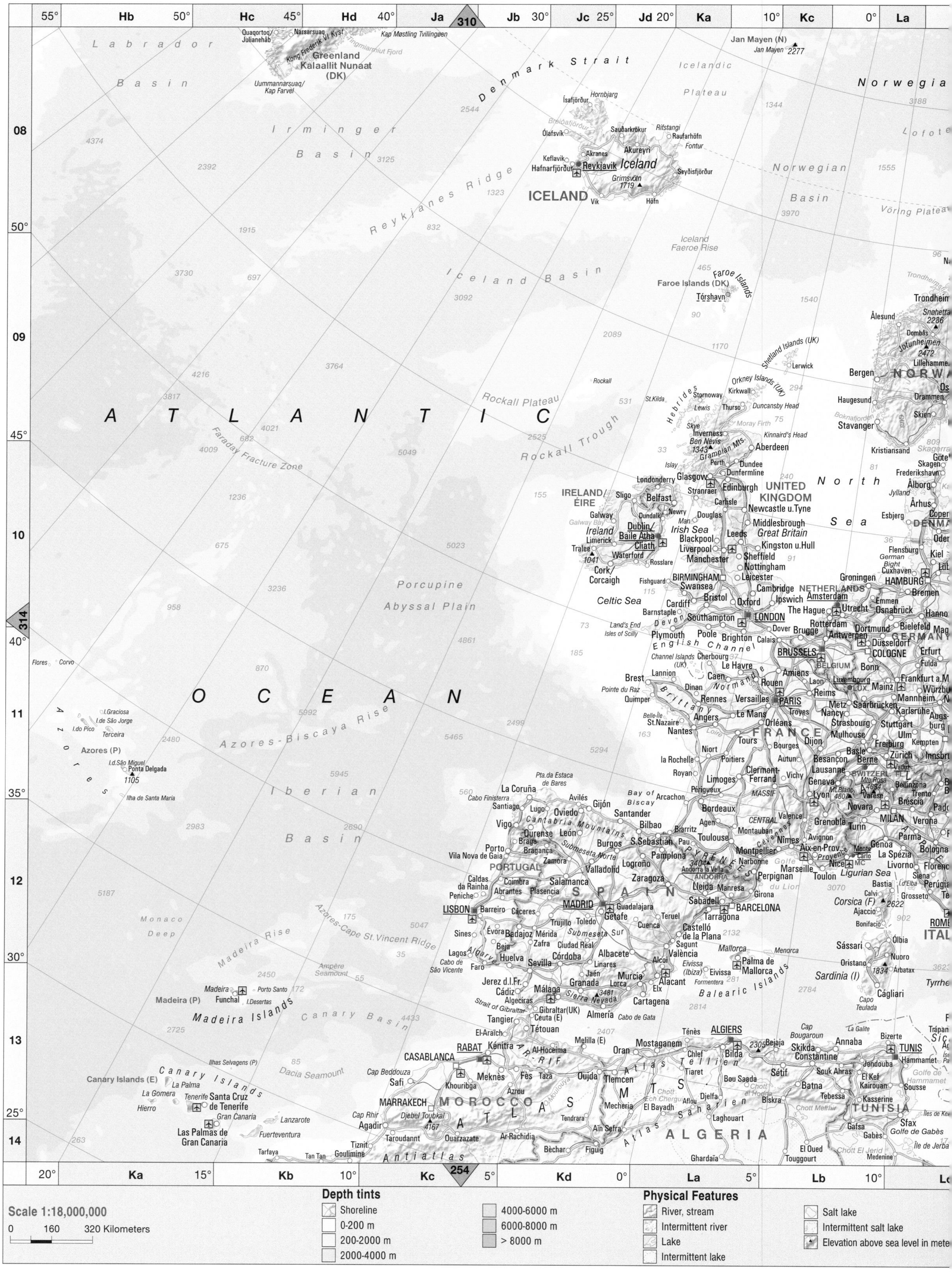

310

314

254

Scale 1:18,000,000

0 160 320 Kilometers

Depth tints

- Shoreline
- 0-200 m
- 200-2000 m
- 2000-4000 m
- 4000-6000 m
- 6000-8000 m
- > 8000 m

Physical Features

- River, stream
- Intermittent river
- Lake
- Intermittent lake
- Salt lake
- Intermittent salt lake
- Elevation above sea level in mete

ı Great Britain border lowlands and ling hills around the North Sea, the ıltic Sea, and the English Channel. Low-ıds also dominate the northwestern ges of mainland Europe in France and e Benelux countries. Most of Eastern d Central Europe is covered by a series vast plains stretching to the Ural Moun-ns. A long belt of mountain ranges tends from the western coast of main-ıd Europe to the eastern edges of the continent. This mountain belt encompasses the Pyrenees, the Alps, the Carpathian Mountains, and several smaller ranges. Most of the mountain ranges in southern and southeastern Europe – including the highlands on the Balkan Peninsula – are lateral branches of the main continental mountain belt.

Most of Europe's regions have temperate continental **climates**. Mild ocean currents (including the Gulf Stream) and winds have a significant impact on the continent's climates. During winter, Eastern Europe is often significantly colder than the western sections of the continent where the effect of ocean currents on the weather is greater. During summer, major differences in temperature between northern and southern Europe are common.

With the exception of a few areas in northern Europe with arctic and sub-arctic climates, most of Europe lies within the temperate zone. Much of the continent is covered by forests and heavily cultivated farmland. Southern Europe's coastal areas, around the Atlantic Ocean, Mediterranean, and Black Sea, have warm "Mediterranean" climates with mild winters and dry hot summers.

The many islands of the Mediterranean Sea include some of the driest and warmest areas in Europe.

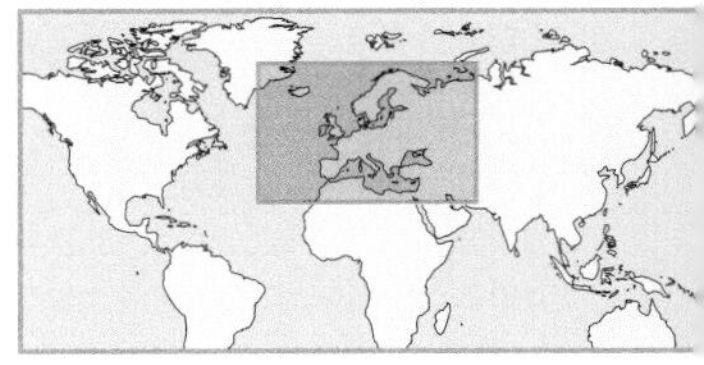

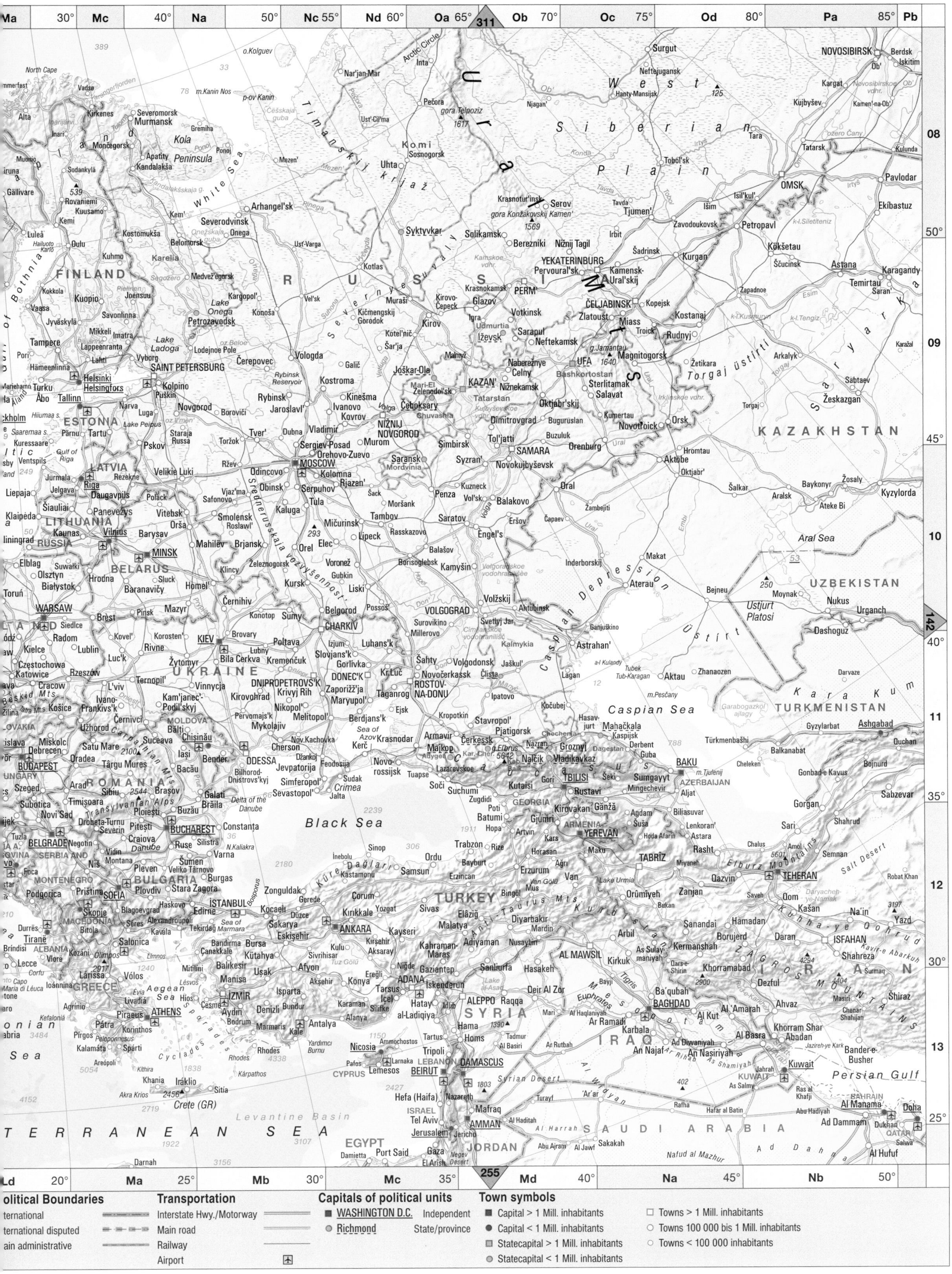

Scandinavian Peninsula Encompasses Norway, Sweden, and northern Finland – 750,000 km² – jagged western coast – numerous fjords

Baltic Sea Sea in northern Europe – maximum depth, 459 meters – largest island, Gotland (Sweden) – photo, Rügen (Germany)

The Alps High mountain range in Central Europe – length: 1,300 kilometers – highest peak, Mont Blanc in France (4,807 meters) – photo, alpine glacier in Switzerland

Balkan Peninsula Located between the Adriatic and Black Seas – circa 476,000 km² – Balkan, Pindus, and Rhodope Mountains – photo, the Dalmatian coast

Aegean Islands Island group belonging mostly to Greece – includes the Cyclades, the Sporades, Rhodes and Crete – photo: Santorini

Carpathian Mountains Mountain system stretching 1,300 kilometers – between 50 and 150 kilometers wide – consists of several distinct ranges – tallest mountain, Gerlachovsky in Slovakia (2,655 meters)

The Caucasus Mountain range stretching around 1,100 kilometers between the Black and Caspian Seas – heavily glaciered – Mount Elbrus (5,642 meters), the highest mountain in Europe

olitical Boundaries
ternational
ternational disputed
ain administrative

Transportation
Interstate Hwy./Motorway
Main road
Railway
Airport

Capitals of political units
WASHINGTON D.C. Independent
Richmond State/province

Town symbols
Capital > 1 Mill. inhabitants
Capital < 1 Mill. inhabitants
Statecapital > 1 Mill. inhabitants
Statecapital < 1 Mill. inhabitants
Towns > 1 Mill. inhabitants
Towns 100 000 bis 1 Mill. inhabitants
Towns < 100 000 inhabitants

Most of Northern Scandinavia's fascinating landscapes were formed during the last three ice ages, the most recent ending 13,000 years ago. The region boasts numerous **treeless plateaus (fjell)**, **mountain valleys**, and **fjords**. Norway's Vestfjorden is the longest fjord in the region and one of the most stunning. The Scandinavian Mountains cover most of northern Norway and stretch across the border into Sweden. Many

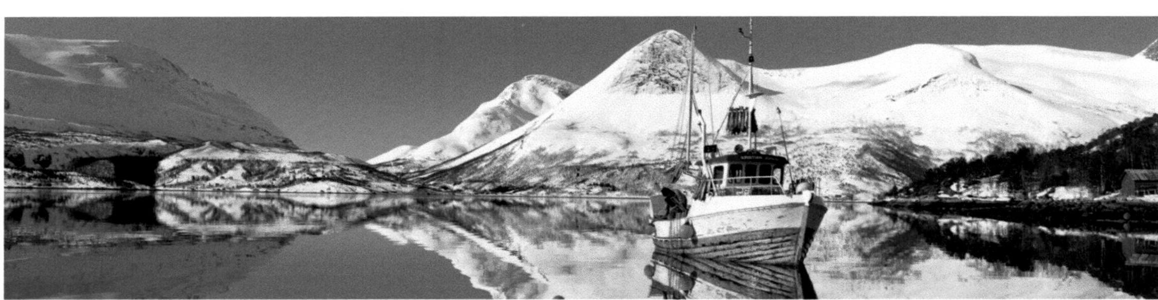

small islets and islands are located off t jagged northern coast of Norway. Nor ern Norway also features numerous pr tine rivers that flow from the interior i the sea. Lapland, a fascinating region moors and tundra lies north of the Arc Circle. The region is divided betwe Norway, Sweden, Finland, and Russ

The Mørsvikfjorden in Northern Norway **Lh**

Iceland Despite its name, ice and glaciers, cover only ten percent of this large volcanic island in the North Atlantic. Iceland's largest glacier Vatnajoekull is also the largest in Europe. The country has more than 200 volcanoes including Hekla, the most active in the country. Photos from top to bottom: Dettifoss **(Kb13)**, Hekla **(Ka14)**, Jökulsarlon Glacier **(Kb14)**.

North Cape/Nordkapp Rocky coast on the edge of an icefield – the northernmost point in Norway **Mc10**

Lofoten Norwegian island group north of the Arctic Circle – jagged mountains and fascinating rugged landscapes **Lg11/12**

Hurtigruta Famous ferries that travel regularly along the Norwegian coast from Bergen to Kirkenes.

Trondheim Capital of Norway during the Middle Ages – Nidarosdom, Norway's royal cathedral – historic warehouses (photo) on the Nidelv River **Le14**

Scale 1:4,500,000

0 40 80 Kilometers

Principal travel routes

- Auto route
- Rail road
- Shipping route

Remarkable landscapes and natural monuments

- UNESCO World Natural Heritage
- Mountain landscape
- Rock landscape
- Ravine/canyon
- Active volcano
- Geyser
- Cave
- Glacier
- River landscape
- Waterfall/rapids
- Nature park
- National park (landscape)
- National park (fauna)
- National park (culture)
- Whale watching
- Protected area for sea-lions/sea

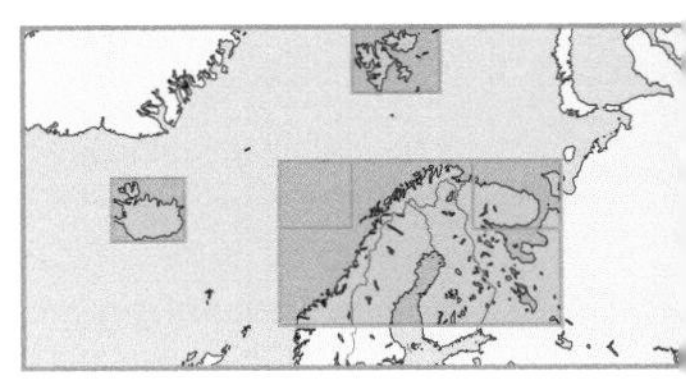

Most of Finland's more than 180,000 lakes were formed during the ice ages. Russia's Lake Ladoga, near the Finnish border, is the largest lake in Europe. Another lake in the region, Lake Onega, is the second largest in Europe.

The two most famous natural phenomena in this part of Europe are the **Aurora Borealis (northern lights)** and the **midnight sun**. In areas north of the Arctic Circle, the sun is visible during all 24 hours of the day around the 21st of June. In winter, this process is reversed and the region experiences long periods without sunlight. The spectacular light shows of the Aurora Borealis are created when energized particles from the sun plunge through the Earth's atmosphere. Like many of the world's large volcanic islands, Iceland was formed along what geologists refer to as a hotspot. On this hotspot a stream of magma rising from the earth's core breached the surface and cooled.

Iceland features active volcanoes, geysers, and gigantic glaciers. At least two thirds of the island's territory is uninhabited. The majority of the country's population is concentrated in coastal cities and towns – including the capital Reykjavik. The more than 700 hot springs on the island provide a reliable source of heat for most of the country's households.

Svalbard is an isolated Norwegian island group in the Arctic Ocean. The islands lie just 1,000 kilometers away from the North Pole. More than two thirds of the islands' land area is covered by large glaciers. The highest mountain in the island group Newtontoppen rises 1,717 meters. Svalbard is home to around 2,500 people living in a few scattered settlements. Most of the islands' inhabitants work in the fishing or coal mining industries.

Svalbard This Norwegian island group boasts fascinating mountain landscapes and large glaciers (top photo). The national parks on the islands are home to reindeer, walruses (bottom photo), and many unique bird species.

The Sámi Once known as the Lapps, around 50,000 Sámi live in Lapland. Their nomadic ancestors lived primarily from reindeer herding in the northernmost regions of Scandinavia.

Lake Inari The second largest lake north of the Arctic Circle – 1,085 km² – maximum depth, 96 meters **MdMe11**

Savonlinna Historic city surrounded by numerous lakes – Burg Olavinlinna, built in 1475 **Me15**

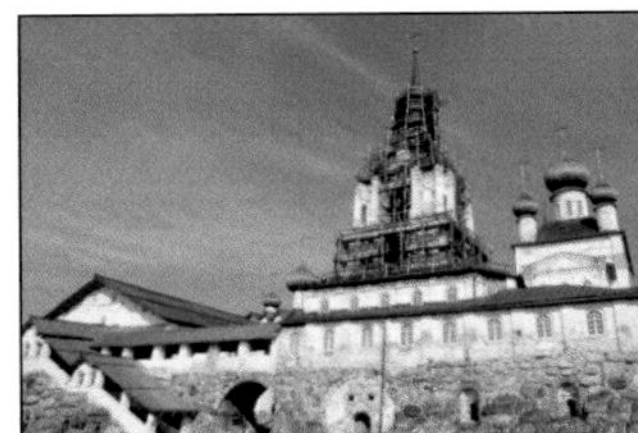

Solovetsky Monastery Historic fortified Orthodox monastery on an island – UNESCO world heritage site **Mh13**

Kiži Pogost Two beautiful historic wooden churches – on an island in Lake Onega – UNESCO world heritage site **Mh14**

Remarkable Cities and Cultural monuments

- UNESCO World Cultural Heritage
- Remarkable Cities
- Prehistoric rockscape
- Vikings
- Places of Christian cultural interest
- Historical city scape
- Castle/fortress/fort
- Technical/industrial monument
- Market
- Festivals
- Museum

Sport and leisure destinations

- Skiing
- Diving
- Wind surfing
- Canoeing/rafting
- Deep-sea fishing
- Beach resort
- Mineral/thermal spa
- Amusement/theme park
- Hill resort

Southern Norway, Central Sweden

Norway covers the western half of the Scandinavian Peninsula. The country is a land of mountains, fjords, and valleys. The 400-million-year old **Scandinavian Mountains** extend through most of Norway. The mountain range stretches over 1,500 kilometers from Southern Norway to the Arctic Ocean.

The **Jotunheimen Range**, a section of the Scandinavian Mountains, includes the two highest mountains in Scandinavia: Galdhøpiggen (2,469 meters) ar Glittertind (2,472 meters). Most of th population in southern Norway and ce tral Sweden live near or along the coas In Norway, 80% of the population live within fifteen kilometers of the sea. No way's capital city, Oslo, is also the large city in the country – with a populatic

Ålesund, the center of Norway's fishin industry is an attractive city **Lf2**

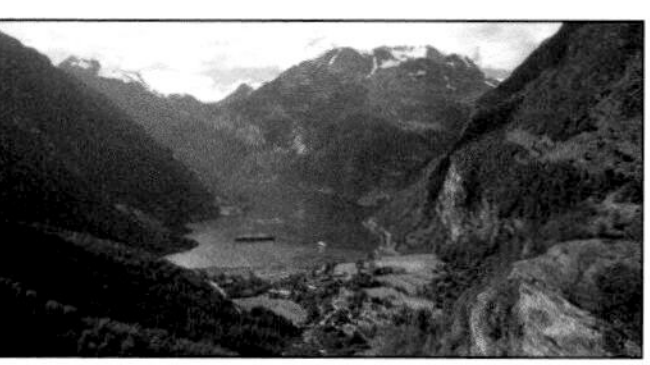

Geirangerfjorden One of the most spectacular fjords in Norway – connected to the larger Storfjord **Lg28**

Røros Former mining center – historic town center is a UNESCO world heritage site – 350-year-old wooden houses **Lm28**

Urnes Stave Church The oldest stave church – made entirely of wood in the 12th century – UNESCO world heritage site **Lg29**

Jostedalsbreen National Park Mountainous national park containing the largest glacier in Norway – glacier museum in Fjaerland **Lg29**

Lustrafjorden Fjord in southwestern Norway – deep blue water surrounded by the Sognefjell plateau **Lg29**

Bergen The second largest city in Norway and the leading port on the country's western coast – Bryggen, the medieval quarter with historic warehouses is a UNESCO world heritage site – 12th century church – interesting museums **Le30**

Oslo Norway's capital and largest city – Akerhus fortress and the interesting modern city hall (photo) – Karl Johans Gate, major city center boulevard – Royal Palace – Bygdøy museum island – the ski jump of the 1952 Olympic winter games is a local landmark **Ll31**

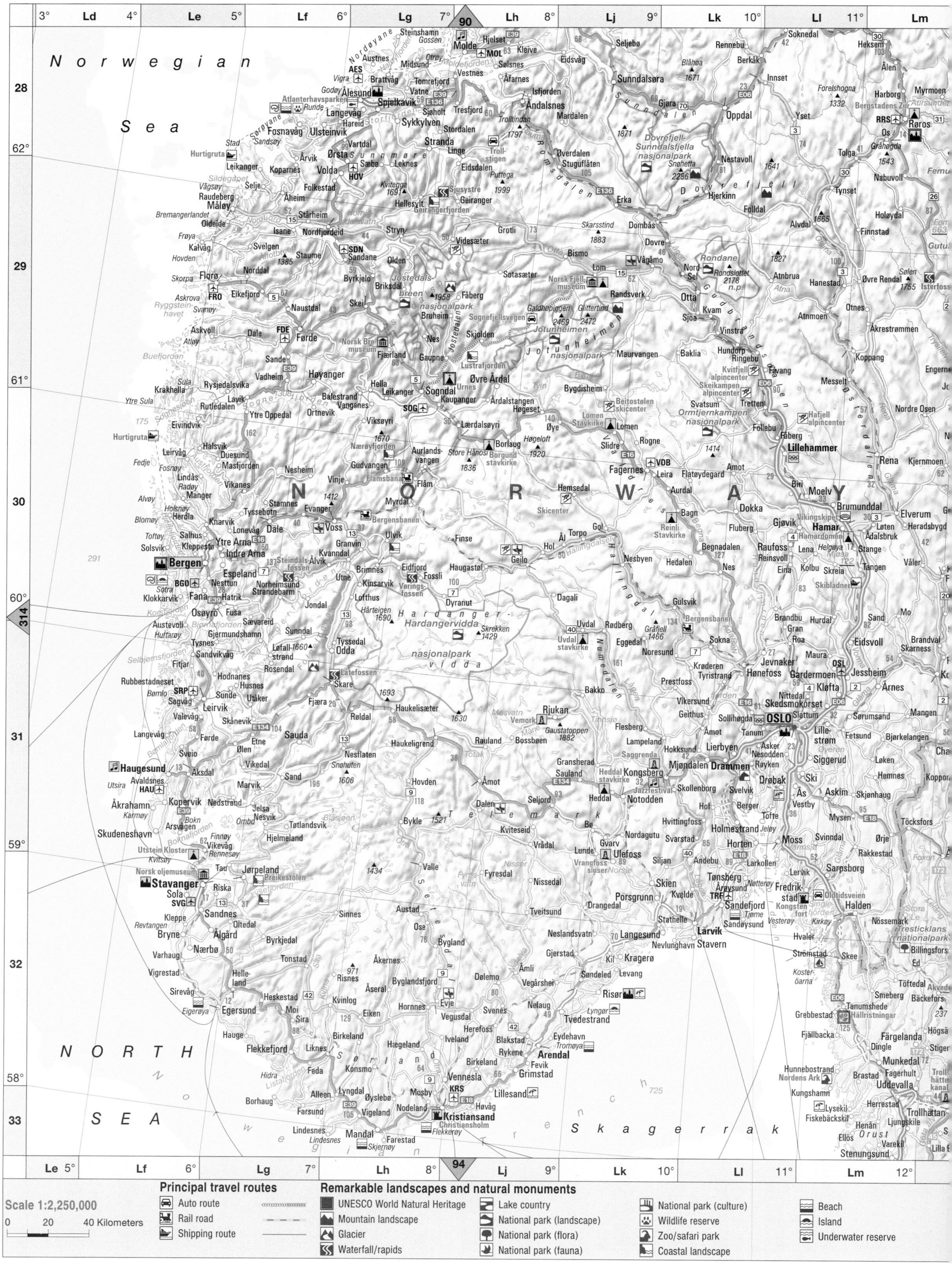

Scale 1:2,250,000

0 20 40 Kilometers

Principal travel routes

- Auto route
- Rail road
- Shipping route

Remarkable landscapes and natural monuments

- UNESCO World Natural Heritage
- Mountain landscape
- Glacier
- Waterfall/rapids
- Lake country
- National park (landscape)
- National park (flora)
- National park (fauna)
- National park (culture)
- Wildlife reserve
- Zoo/safari park
- Coastal landscape
- Beach
- Island
- Underwater reserve

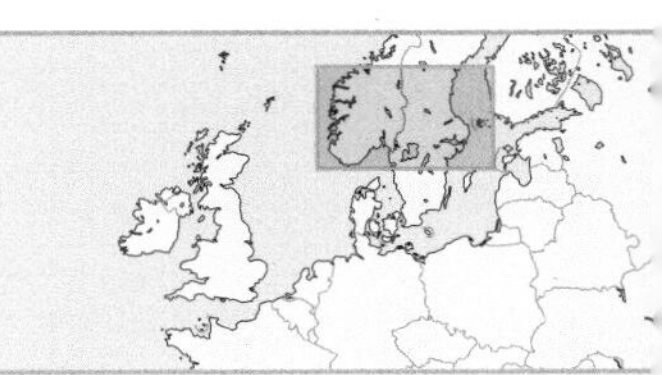

ɔproaching 800,000. The city is situa-ɘd on the Oslofjord in southeastern Nor-ay and is surrounded by forested hills nd mountains.

he numerous fjords on Norway's estern coast were formed during the last e age around 10,000 years ago. Today ese deep flooded valleys are among the ost popular tourist attractions in the ɔuntry. The longest fjords stretch over 00 kilometers inland and the deepest, Sognefjord, has a maximum depth of 1,244 meters. Eastern Norway contains many plateaus and barren treeless patches of rocky land. The area is popular with Norwegian hikers during summers. Dovrefjell and **Hardangervidda**, between Oslo and Bergen, are two of the larger plateaus in the countries. Hardangervidd is one of the largest elevated plateaus in Europe with a total area of 10,000 km^2.

Central Sweden is an expansive region of countless rivers, large pristine forests, and fertile valleys. The thousands of lakes in the region are ideal for swimmers and recreational sailors.

The area between Oslo and Stockholm features several of Europe's largest lakes – including Lake Vanern (5,600 km^2), the continent's third largest lake. Sweden's Baltic coast is lined by countless small islands and islets. Many of the islands near Stockholm are popular weekend destinations for city dwellers. Stockholm, the capital of Sweden, is the largest and most cosmopolitan city on the Scandinavian Peninsula.

Despite their northern locations, both southern Norway and central Sweden have temperate climates with cold winters and warm summers. The Gulf Stream, an ocean current, has a major effect on the climates of both regions.

Gulf of Bothnia

FINLAND

SWEDEN

BALTIC SEA

Remarkable Cities and Cultural monuments

- UNESCO World Cultural Heritage
- Remarkable Cities
- Places of Christian cultural interest
- Vikings
- Historical city scape
- Castle/fortress/fort
- Palace
- Technical/industrial monument
- Remarkable lighthouse
- Festivals
- Museum
- Olympics

Sport and leisure destinations

- Arena/stadium
- Horse racing
- Skiing
- Sailing
- Diving
- Wind surfing
- Canoeing/rafting
- Beach resort
- Mineral/thermal spa
- Amusement/theme park

Falun The oldest copper mine in the world – in use for over 1,000 years – UNESCO world heritage site – museum and visitors center **Lq30**

Darlana Province in central Sweden – beautiful Lake Siljan – expansive pristine forests cover most of the province's southeast – popular ski areas **Lp29/Lp30**

The Åland Islands Group of over 6,500 islands and islets – province of Finland – most of the population are Swedish speakers – Kastelholm, medieval castle **Lu30**

Gripsholm Castle Historic castle – built in the 16th century – on the shore of Lake Malaren **Lr31**

Drottningholm Palace Baroque palace with an extensive park – UNESCO world heritage site – residence of the Swedish Royal Family **Ls31**

Stockholm The capital of Sweden since 1634 – built on fourteen islands between the Baltic Sea and a lake – Gamla Stan, medieval old town – museum church on the island Riddarholmen – the national parliament – the Vasa Museum, Scandinavia's most visited museum **Ls31**

Skargard Islands near Stockholm Archipelago of more than 30,000 islands between Stockholm and the Baltic Sea **Lt31**

Denmark, Southern Sweden

Denmark is a small nation of rolling hills, forests, and fertile plains. The country has around 1,000 lakes and 7,300 kilometers of coastline – at least 5,000 kilometers of which feature sandy beaches. No area in Denmark is more than 55 kilometers distance from the sea. Of the 400 Danish islands, around 380 are located in the Baltic Sea.
Denmark's capital city, **Copenhagen**, is located on the country's largest and most densely populated island, **Seeland**. Much of the land on Seeland is used for agriculture but the island also has large forests, dunes, and long sand beaches. Denmark's second largest island, **Funen**, is surrounded by many smaller islands and islets. Funen is heavily forested but it is also one of most important fruit and vegetable farming areas in the coun try. **Jutland** – a peninsula between th Baltic and North Seas – is largest Danis region and is the only part of the count connected to mainland Europe. **Limfjor** a body of water that cuts through north ern Jutland, is a popular recreation destination. Most of Jutland's wester coast consists of large dunes, broa sandy beaches, and scattered bluff Southern Jutland features large coast

A Viking burial site near Aalborg (Denmark) **Lk33**

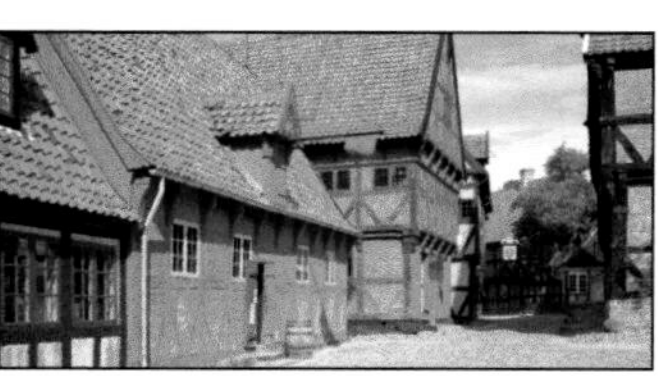

Århus Denmark's second largest city – Modern city hall – Frue Kirke – open air museum Den Gamle By (photo) **Ll34**

Egeskov Castle Beautiful Renaissance-era castle on Funen – beautiful gardens – classic car museum **Ll35**

Roskilde Former residence of the Danish monarchs – gothic cathedral built in the 12th century, burial site of Danish royalty and UNESCO world heritage site (photo) – hall with preserved Viking ships **Ln35**

Kronborg Castle Shakespeare's Hamlet Castle (Elsinore) – on the Öresund strait – UNESCO world heritage site **Ln34**

Frederiksborg Castle Renaissance era castle built in the 17th century – on a lake near Hillerod in Seeland **Ln35**

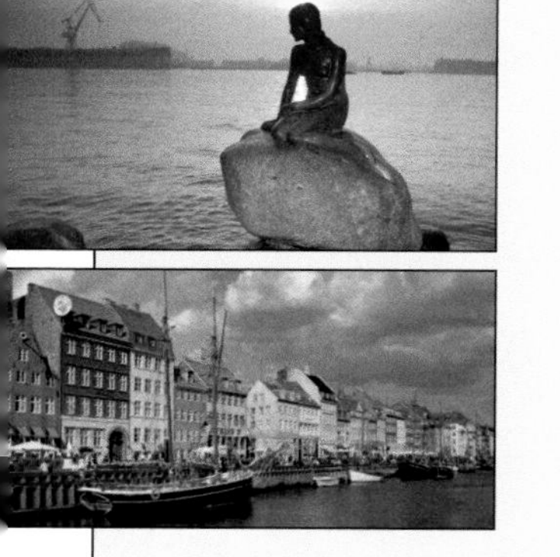

Copenhagen Capital city of Denmark since 1417. More than a million people live in the city and its surrounding area. The city is also the country's leading port and cultural center. The city's most famous landmark is the (top photo) Little Mermaid statue. South of the Nyhavn district (bottom photo), with its bars and historic architecture, lies Slottsholmen Island and Christiansborg Castle. **Ln35**

Scale 1:2,250,000
0 20 40 Kilometers

Principal travel routes
Auto route
Rail road
Shipping route

Remarkable landscapes and natural monuments
UNESCO World Natural Heritage
Rock landscape
Lake country
Nature park
National park (landscape)
National park (flora)
National park (fauna)
Protected area for sea-lions/seals
Zoo/safari park
Coastal landscape
Beach
Island

arshlands and pastures. **Rebild Bak-r National Park** south of Aalborg compasses moorlands and the largest est in Denmark. The eastern half of Jut-ld is an important agricultural region. e coastal areas of eastern Jutland are rrower than those on the peninsula's stern coast. Several long and narrow ys are located on the eastern coast of tland. **Bornholm**, the easternmost nish island, has the country's finest beaches and a variety of interesting landscapes. The **Öresund** strait separates Denmark from **Southern Sweden**. **Scania**, the southernmost region of Sweden, is covered by plains and scattered hills. Scania is densely populated and agriculture is an important sector in the region's economy. The coasts of Scania are lined with fine sand beaches. To the north of Scania lies **Blekinge**, a region of rolling hills, forests, and meadows. The **Småland** region has the most diverse collection of landscapes in Southern Sweden. Småland's natural attractions include a hilly upland, vast forests, countless moors, around 5,000 lakes, and a coast lined by many small islands. The highest elevation in Småland is **Tomtabacken** (378 meters), a hill southwest of Nässjö. **Vättern**, Sweden's second largest lake, is located to the northwest of Tomtabacken. **Öland** and **Gotland**, off the southwestern coast of Sweden, are the country's two largest island. Both islands have steep, rocky western coasts and smooth sandy eastern coasts. The historic landscapes of Öland's countryside comprise a designated world heritage site.

Southern Sweden is the location of five national parks. **Store Mosse National Park** encompasses the largest Swedish moorland outside of Lapland.

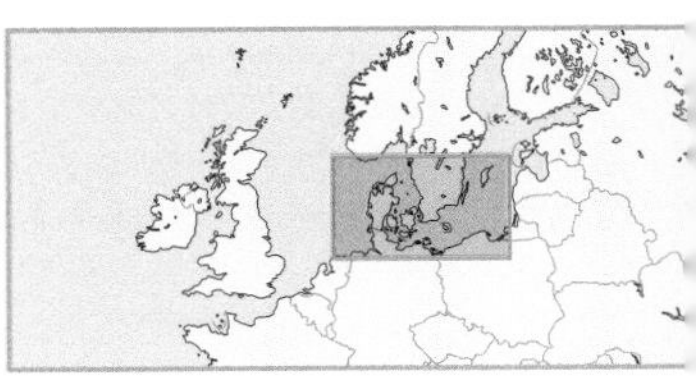

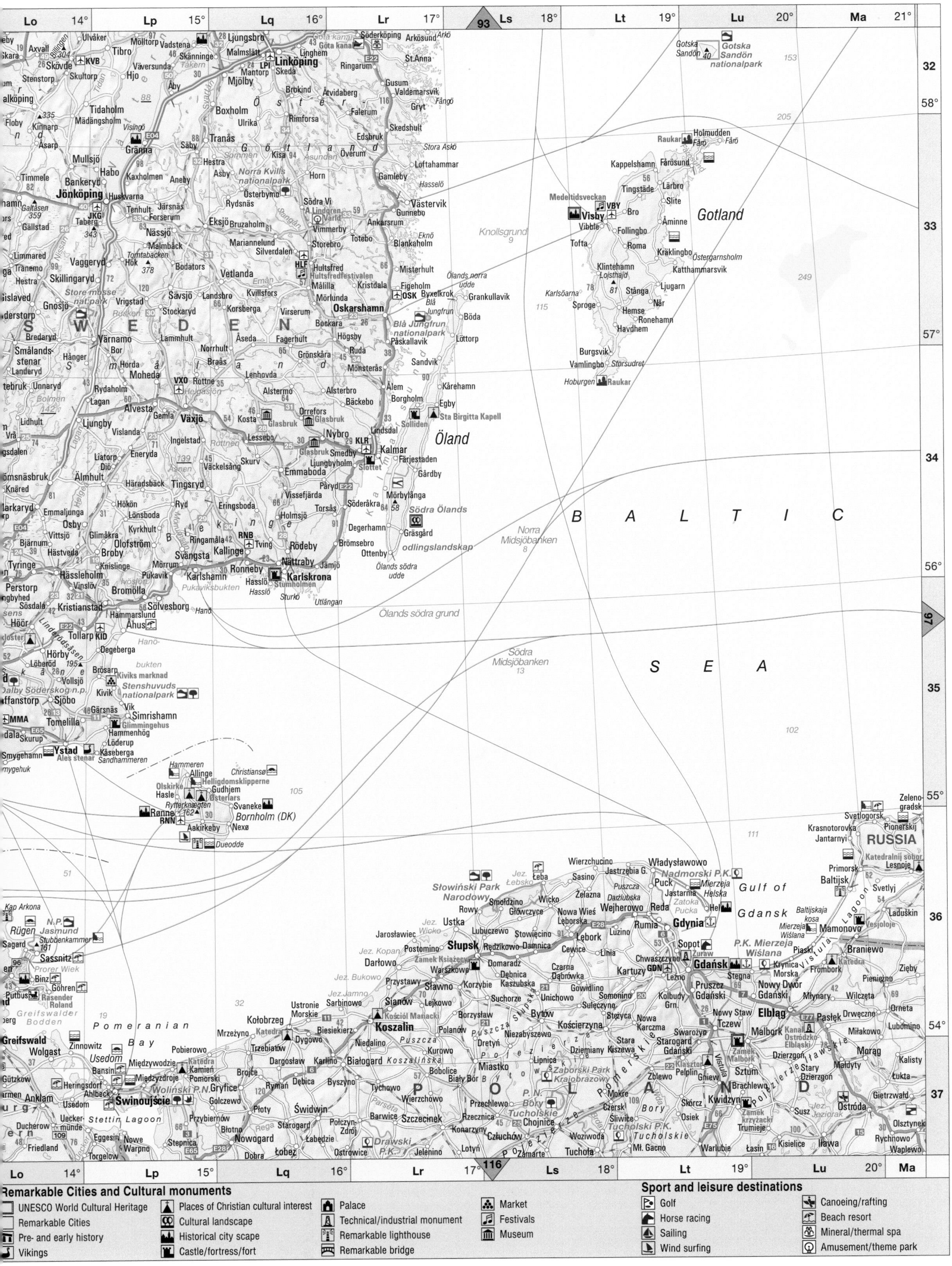

Gothenburg Important port and Sweden's second largest city – beautiful historic old town – important art museum **Lm33**

Öland Island off the southwestern coast of Sweden – UNESCO world heritage site – Sta Birgitta Chapel (photo) **Lr34**

Kalmar Castle Renaissance era fortified castle – splendid interior design – beautiful fountains **Lr34**

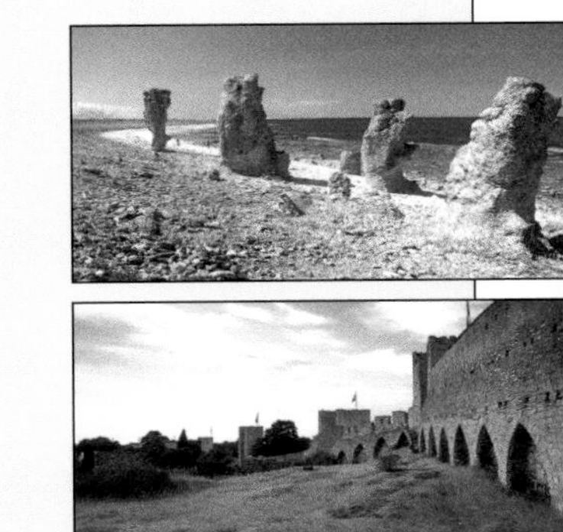

Gotland Because of its mild climate and sandy beaches, Sweden's largest island is a popular holiday destination. Gotland's many attractions include large unique rock formations called Raukar (top photo) and Visby (bottom photo), a historic city and UNESCO world heritage site on the island's coast. **Lt33**

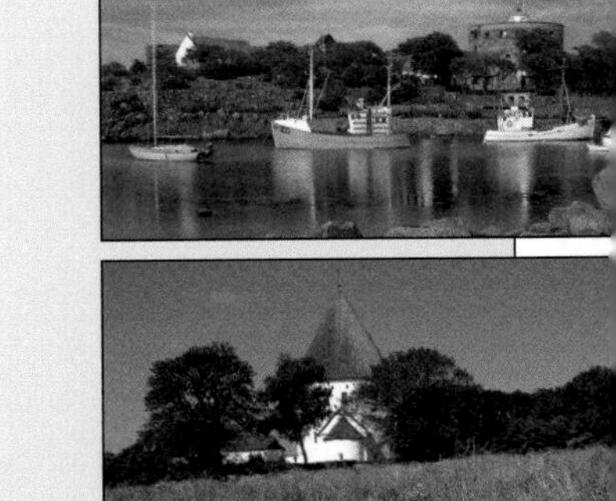

Bornholm The easternmost and fourth largest Danish island has a rocky northern coast, while its southern coast has sandy beaches, idyllic fishing villages, and historic sites. The island's landmarks are its round churches, all of which were built in the 12th and 13th centuries – including the Olskirke (bottom photo). **LpLq35**

Remarkable Cities and Cultural monuments

- UNESCO World Cultural Heritage
- Remarkable Cities
- Pre- and early history
- Vikings
- Places of Christian cultural interest
- Cultural landscape
- Historical city scape
- Castle/fortress/fort
- Palace
- Technical/industrial monument
- Remarkable lighthouse
- Remarkable bridge
- Market
- Festivals
- Museum

Sport and leisure destinations

- Golf
- Horse racing
- Sailing
- Wind surfing
- Canoeing/rafting
- Beach resort
- Mineral/thermal spa
- Amusement/theme park

The Finns call their country **Suomi**, a name meaning marshland and one that accurately describes much of southern Finland. There are at least 55,000 thousand **lakes** in southern Finland, many of which are interconnected by streams and rivers. During the ice ages, Finland was covered by large glaciers. When these glaciers melted, they created most of the country's lakes. Finland is a heavily forested country – at least 70% of the country is covered by woodlands. Finland's coa is lined with thousands of **sm islands**, only 80 of which are perm nently inhabited. The islands south of Finnish city Turku Åbo are parts of t **Skargardshavet National Park.** The **Baltic Sea** lies southeast of the **B of Finland. Saremaa** (2,710 km²) a

The Curonian Spit off the coasts of Lithuania and Kaliningrad **Ma**

Southern Finland's Lakes Lake Saimaa is the largest lake in Finland, with a total area of 1,460 km². The lake is one of at least 55,000 lakes in southern Finland alone. **Md–Na28/29**

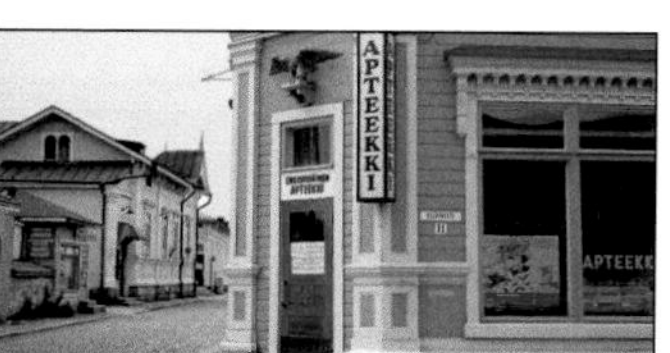

Rauma Port city on the Baltic Sea – Historic district with wooden houses – UNESCO world heritage site **Mb29**

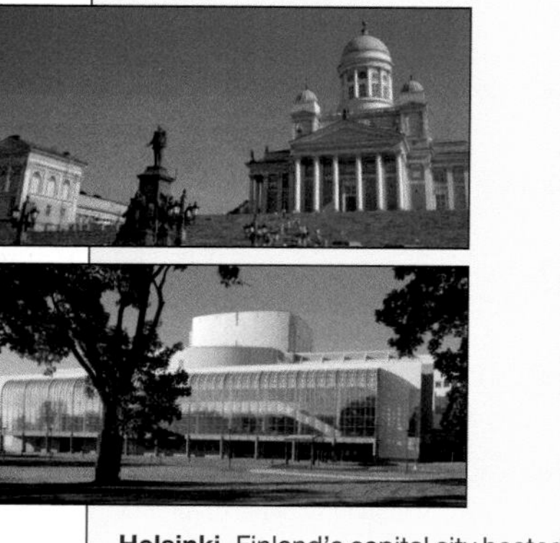

Helsinki Finland's capital city hosted the 1952 Olympics. Senate Square is the site of an impressive cathedral (top photo). The historic Suomenlinna fort and the modern National Opera House (bottom photo) are also interesting attractions. **Me30**

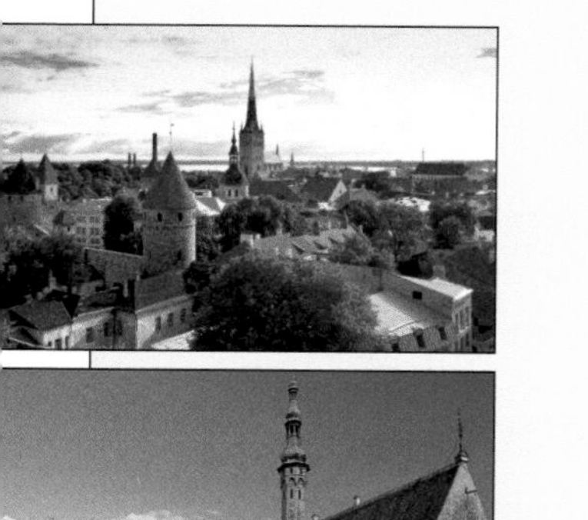

Tallinn (Reval) The capital of Estonia has a beautiful medieval old town (top photo). Town Hall Square (bottom photo) has stunning historic architecture. **Me31**

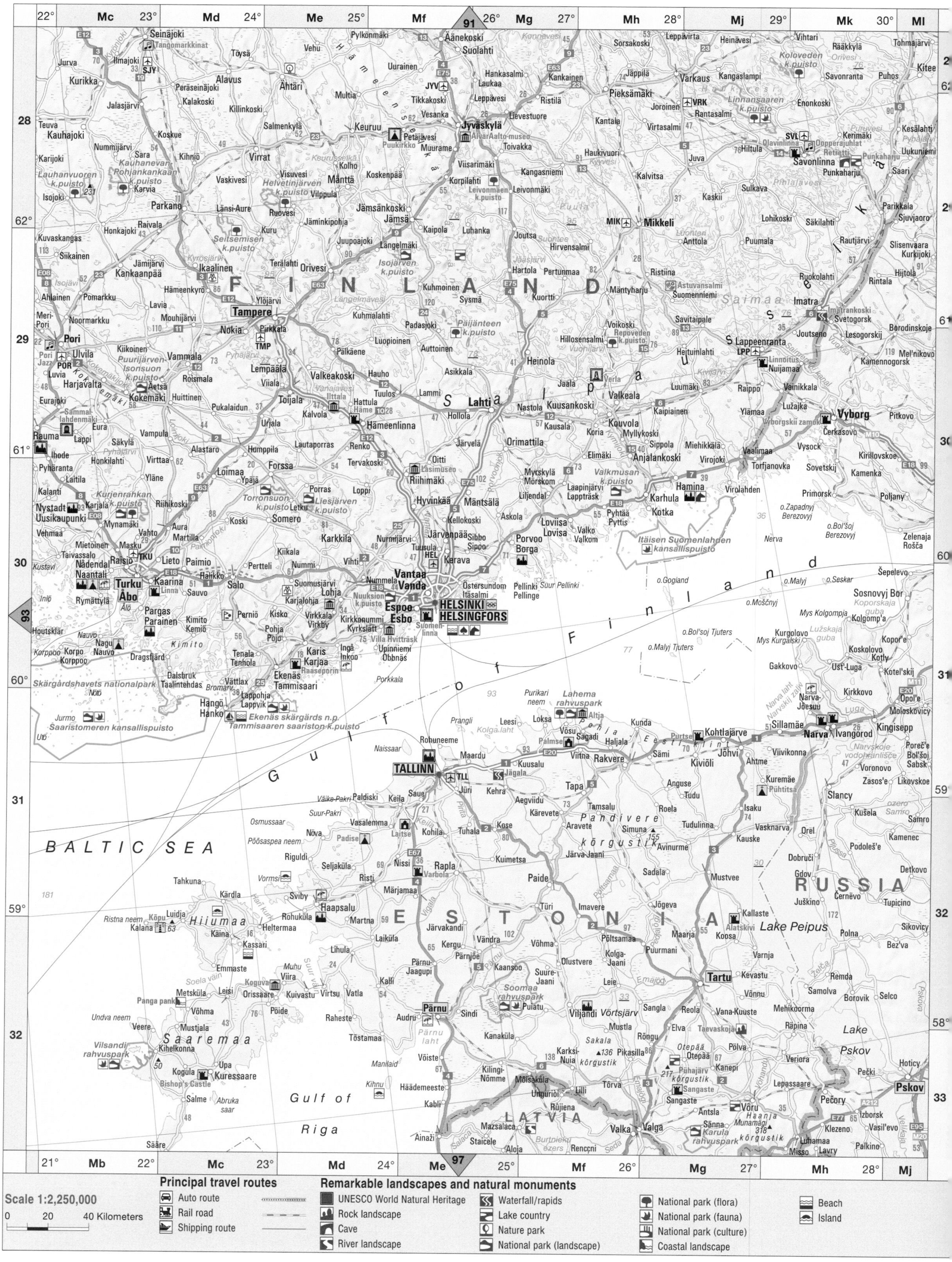

Scale 1:2,250,000
0 20 40 Kilometers

Principal travel routes
- Auto route
- Rail road
- Shipping route

Remarkable landscapes and natural monuments
- UNESCO World Natural Heritage
- Rock landscape
- Cave
- River landscape
- Waterfall/rapids
- Lake country
- Nature park
- National park (landscape)
- National park (flora)
- National park (fauna)
- National park (culture)
- Coastal landscape
- Beach
- Island

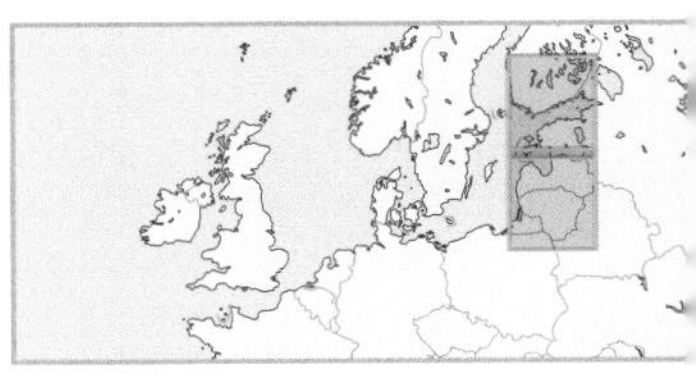

iumaa (960 km²) are the largest of the 500 islands off the coast of Estonia. ost of Estonia's land is covered by low ls and plains. Marshland and lakes ver at least a fifth of the country. The untry has extensive forests and wood oducts are among its leading exports. tonia is a very flat country with no major evations. Munnamagi, a hill rising 318 eters, is the highest point in the coun-. **Lake Peipsi** (2,673 km²) is the largest of Estonia's 1,400 lakes. Finland's capital city, Helsinki, is situated on the Gulf of Finland's northern edge across from Tallinn, the capital of Estonia. The two cities are separated by around 90 kilometers of water and linked by frequent ferry services.

The former Soviet republics **Estonia**, **Lithuania**, and **Latvia** are collectively referred to as the Baltic States. Large sections of Latvia are situated below sea level. Only the eastern and western areas of the country rise significantly above sea level. Latvia's coastline consists primarily of long sandy beaches. The western coast borders the Baltic Sea and farther east the large Gulf of Riga extends deep into the country's interior. Most of eastern Latvia consists of low lying plains, while the western section of the country is covered by numerous lakes and rolling hills. Western Latvia also features extensive, pristine forests of pine, spruce, and birch trees.

Northern and southeastern Lithuania have many high sand dunes, small lakes, and hills. The **Curonian Spit** is a narrow 98-kilometer-long strip of land between the Baltic and the Curonian Lagoon. The Neman (Nemunas) River flows from Belarus to the Baltic Sea and forms the border between Lithuania and the Russian exclave Kaliningrad.

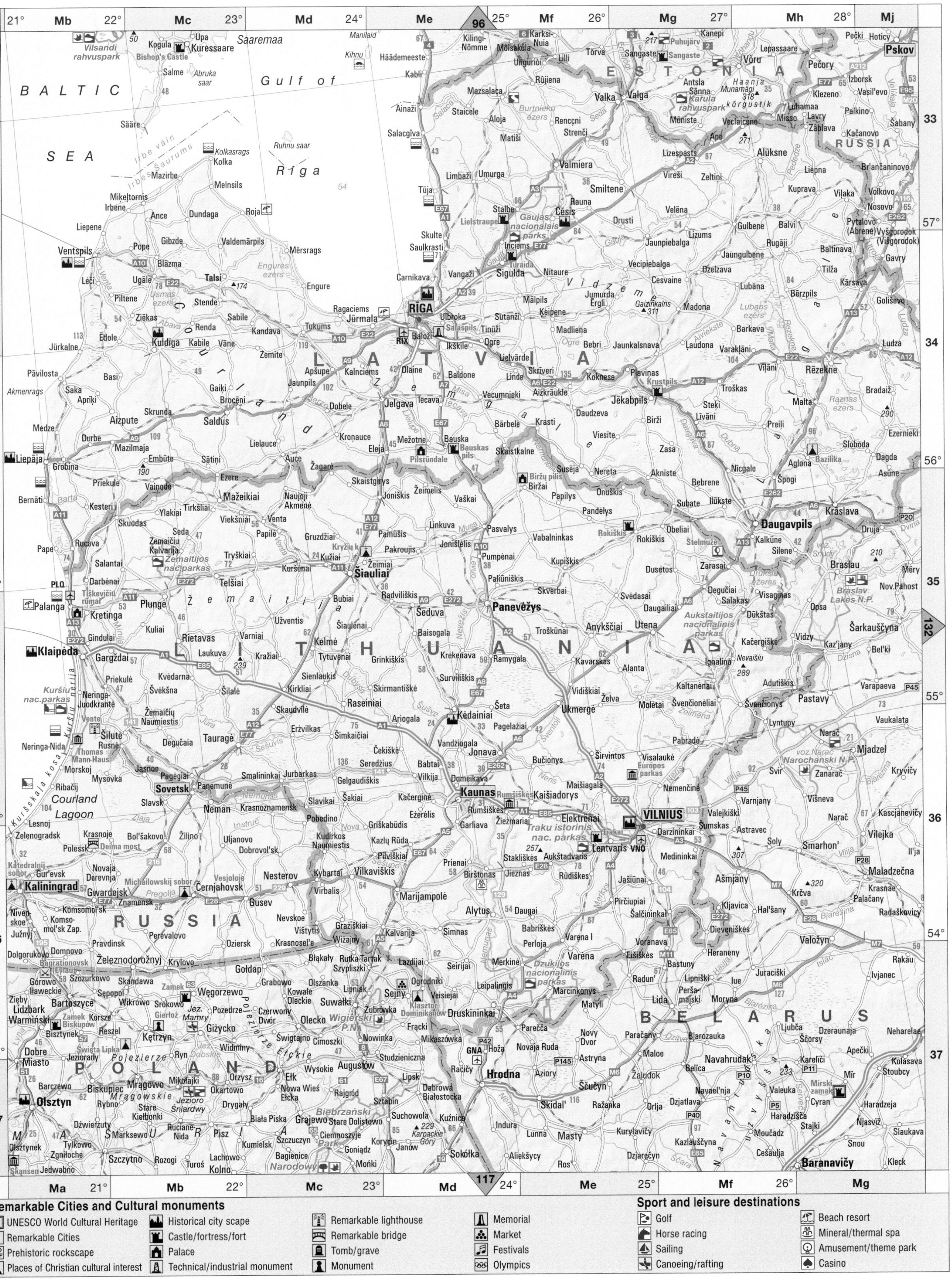

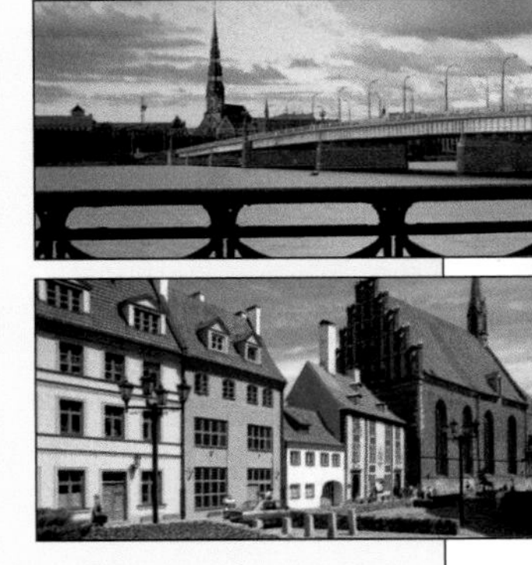

Riga St. Peter's Church (top photo) in Latvia's capital city was built in 1209. The city's historic old town (bottom photo) boasts well preserved medieval buildings and is a UNESCO world heritage site. **Me34**

Kaunas The second largest city in Lithuania – historic Jesuit church (photo) – beautiful riverside district **Md36**

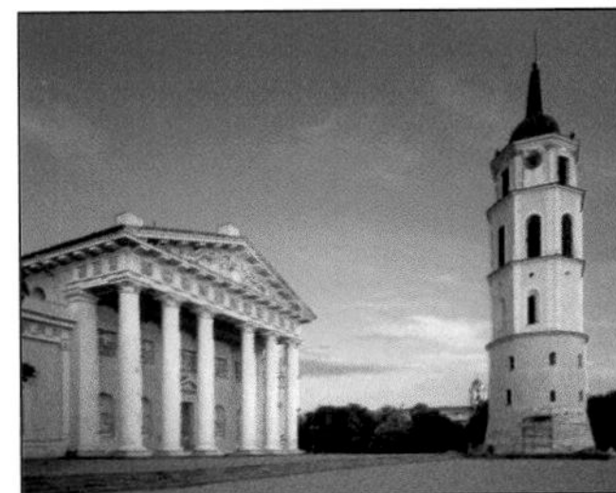

Vilnius Lithuania's capital city has a beautiful old town – UNESCO world heritage site – cathedral (photo) built in 1783 **Mf36**

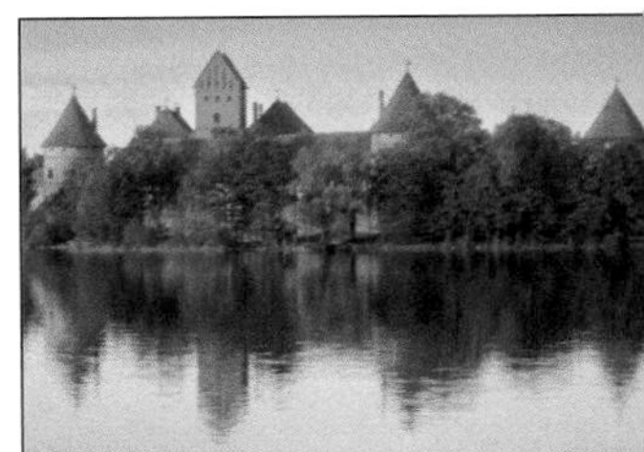

Trakai Capital of the Lithuanian kingdom during the Middle Ages – island castle (photo) in an area with many lakes **Me36**

Kaliningrad Russian exclave surrounded by Poland and Lithuania – the city was once predominantly German speaking and was called Koenigsberg – cathedral (photo) with a memorial to Immanuel Kant **Ma36**

Remarkable Cities and Cultural monuments

- UNESCO World Cultural Heritage
- Remarkable Cities
- Prehistoric rockscape
- Places of Christian cultural interest
- Historical city scape
- Castle/fortress/fort
- Palace
- Technical/industrial monument
- Remarkable lighthouse
- Remarkable bridge
- Tomb/grave
- Monument
- Memorial
- Market
- Festivals
- Olympics

Sport and leisure destinations

- Golf
- Horse racing
- Sailing
- Canoeing/rafting
- Beach resort
- Mineral/thermal spa
- Amusement/theme park
- Casino

Northern Great Britain encompasses several regions and political divisions: Northern England, Scotland, the Shetland Islands as well as the Orkney and Hebrides Islands off the coast of Scotland. Northern Ireland is a political division of the United Kingdom and shares a border with the Republic of Ireland. **Northern England** is distinctly hilly and the **Pennines**, a low mountain range, stretches through most of the region.

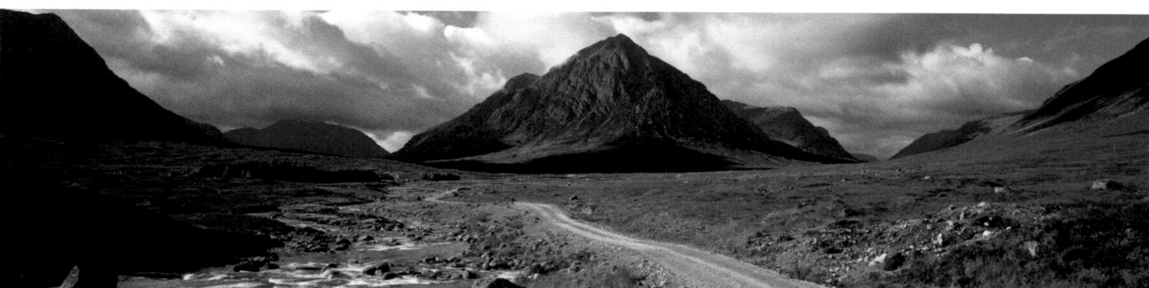

Spectacular Glen Coe in the Scottish Highlands **Kp**

Lake District National Park boas some of the most beautiful landscapes England. The national park also featu Scafell Pike (978 meters), the highe point in England. The coast of **Nort umberland** has many fine sandy be ches and is a popular area for bird a seal watching. **Scotland** can be divid

Isle of Skye Island in the Inner Hebrides – interesting attractions; Loch Coriusk and the Cullin Hills **Ko33**

Giant's Causeway Natural attraction on the coast of Northern Ireland – consists of over 40,000 black basalt columns leading to the sea – created by lava 60 million years ago – UNESCO world heritage site **Ko35**

Dunluce Castle Picturesque ruins of a castle atop a small stone hill – built in the 16th century **Ko35**

Achill Island The largest island off the coast of Ireland – hills, moors, and meadows in the island's interior – beautiful views – good beaches **Kk37**

Connemara National Park in the Republic of Ireland with fascinating coastal landscapes (top photo). The large national park features many pristine landscapes, includind moors and heaths. Doo Lough (bottom photo) often called the "black lake" is situated in a beautiful valley near Clew Bay. The park contains several nature trails and hiking paths. **KkKl37**

Clifden Castle Once the home of John d'Arcy, founder of the city of Clifden – now a beautiful ruin **Kl37**

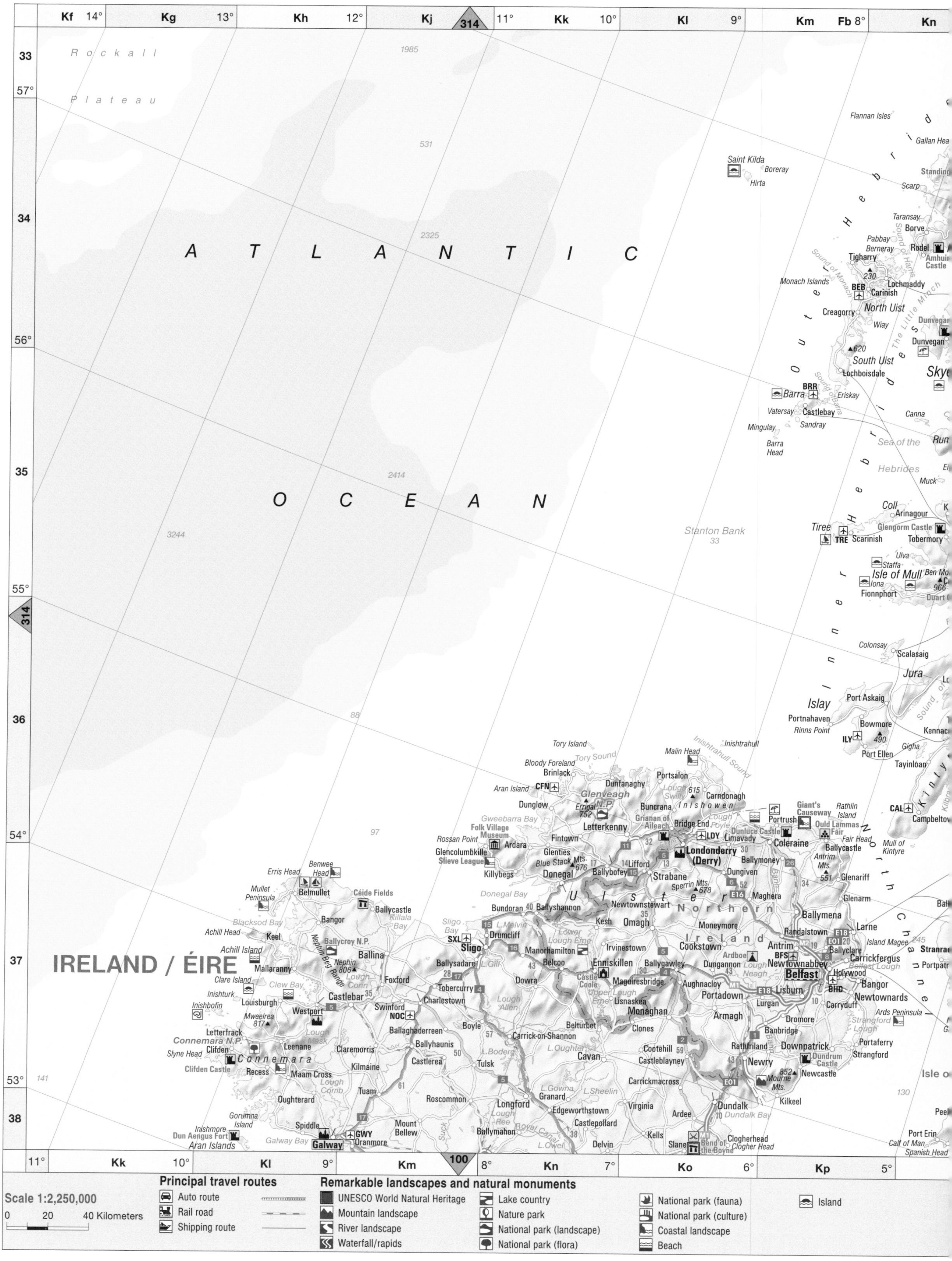

ATLANTIC OCEAN

IRELAND / ÉIRE

Scale 1:2,250,000
0 20 40 Kilometers

Principal travel routes
- Auto route
- Rail road
- Shipping route

Remarkable landscapes and natural monuments
- UNESCO World Natural Heritage
- Mountain landscape
- River landscape
- Waterfall/rapids
- Lake country
- Nature park
- National park (landscape)
- National park (flora)
- National park (fauna)
- National park (culture)
- Coastal landscape
- Beach
- Island

o three distinct geographic regions: e Southern Uplands are a region of low s and undeveloped coasts, the Cen- l Lowlands – the most densely popu- ed and fertile region, and the moun- nous Scottish Highlands with its stun- ng landscapes. The most sparsely pulated regions in Great Britain are the autiful northern and western Highlands Scotland.
n Nevis (1,344 meters), the highest mountain in Great Britain, and Loch Ness are two of the most popular tourist attractions in the Highlands. **Loch Lomond and the Trossachs National Park** in central Scotland encompass beautiful mountains and valleys. Firth and loch are Scottish words used to designate the many bays, inlets, and estuaries along the country's coast. The **Orkney Islands** and the **Hebrides** are island groups off the coast of Scotland. Like the more distant **Shetland Islands**, the Hebrides and Orkneys feature many prehistoric sites and fascinating landscapes. Much of the land on the Scottish islands is cultivated. Small scale farming together with fishing dominates the local economies of the Shetlands, Orkneys, and Hebrides.

The interior of Ireland is covered by lakes and fertile plains, while the coastal areas are rocky and hilly. The north and northwest of **Ireland** feature tree covered hills, jagged coasts, and low mountains. The summit of Slieve Donard (825 meters) in the Mourne Mountains is the highest point in Northern Ireland. Glenveagh, Connemara, and Ballycroy **National Parks** are three fascinating and beautiful nature reserves in the Republic of Ireland. The Giant's Causeway is one of many beautiful stone formations on the coast of Northern Ireland.

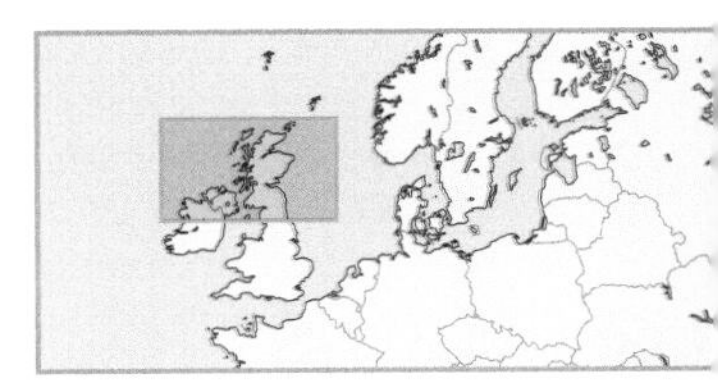

The Orkney Islands A group of seventy islands off the northern coast of Scotland – several of the islands' prehistoric sites including the Ring of Brodgar (photo) are UNESCO world heritage sites. **KrKs31/32**

Scotland's Castles Scotland has many historic castles and forts. Many of these building are well preserved and have extensive gardens. Some are open to visitors. Photos from top to bottom: Dunnottar Castle, Stalker Castle, Eilean Donan Castle

Scottish Clans The Scottish clan system was first established in 13th century. Many modern clans have their own unique tartans or woven patterns.

Edinburgh Scotland's capital and one of the most beautiful cities in the United Kingdom – annual festival – Edinburgh Castle towers above the city – medieval old town and Georgian new town – important museums **Kr35**

Hadrian's Wall Historic wall built by the Romans in the 2nd century. There are several forts and watchtowers along the wall. UNESCO world heritage site and Britain's most important Roman ruin **Ks35/36**

UNITED KINGDOM

NORTH SEA

Remarkable Cities and Cultural monuments

- UNESCO World Cultural Heritage
- Remarkable Cities
- Pre- and early history
- Roman antiquity
- Places of Christian cultural interest
- Historical city scape
- Castle/fortress/fort
- Palace
- Remarkable bridge
- Tomb/grave
- Theater of war/battlefield
- Market
- Festivals
- Museum

Sport and leisure destinations

- Golf
- Horse racing
- Skiing
- Sailing
- Diving
- Wind surfing
- Seaport
- Beach resort

Southern **Great Britain** consists of Wales as well as central and southern England. This small region encompasses diverse landscapes, including some of the most beautiful areas in the British Isles. Most of southern Britain is covered by rolling low hills and fertile plains. The south west of England is the location of Dartmoor and Exmoor National Parks, both of which contain pristine moorlands. Millions of visitors travel to England's southern coast to enjoy the many sandy beaches and majestic cliffs in the regic Devon, the Isles of Scilly, and the Is of Wight have the mildest climates Great Britain as well as attractive coa lines. The Isle of Wight is also home an abundance of wildlife including ma unique bird species. The Jurass

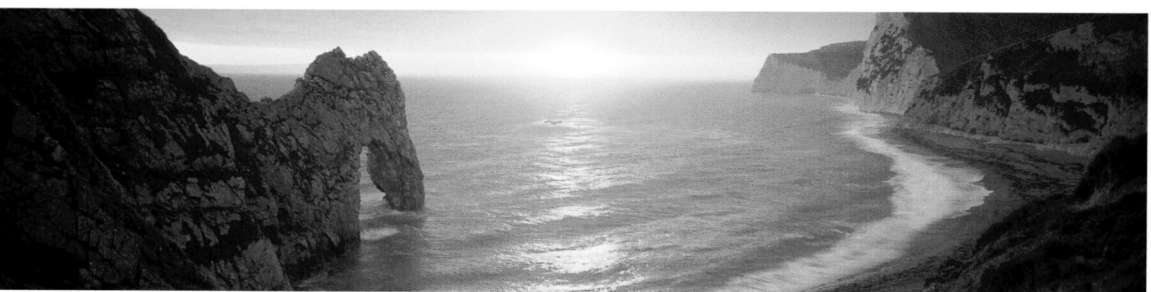

Durdle Door, an ancient natural arch c the Dorset coast **Ks**

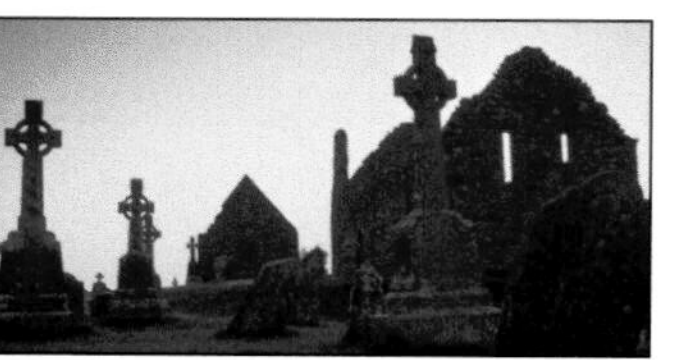

Clonmacnoise Ruins of an early Christian monastic settlement on the banks of the Shannon River – first settled by Celtic monks in the 7th century **Kn37**

Cliffs of Moher One of the Europe's most beautiful coastal cliffs – 203 meters above the ocean **Kl37/38**

Dublin Capital and cultural center of the Irish Republic – modern and cosmopolitan city – two historic cathedrals – Temple Bar, neighborhood with vibrant nightlife – museums – O'Connell Bridge (photo) – Trinity College **Ko37**

Snowdonia National Park Popular national park with tall mountains and deep valleys – Mount Snowdon is the highest mountain in Wales **KqKr37/38**

Conwy Castle Impressive example of medieval fortified architecture in the former Welsh county of Gwynedd – built in the 13th century during the reign of Edward I – UNESCO world heritage site **Kr37**

Tintern Abbey This Cistercian abbey in the Wye Valley is one of Wales' most impressive ruins – built in Gothic style during the 13th century **Ks39**

Land's End The westernmost point in Great Britain – located in Cornwall – high stone cliffs – popular tourist destination **Kp40**

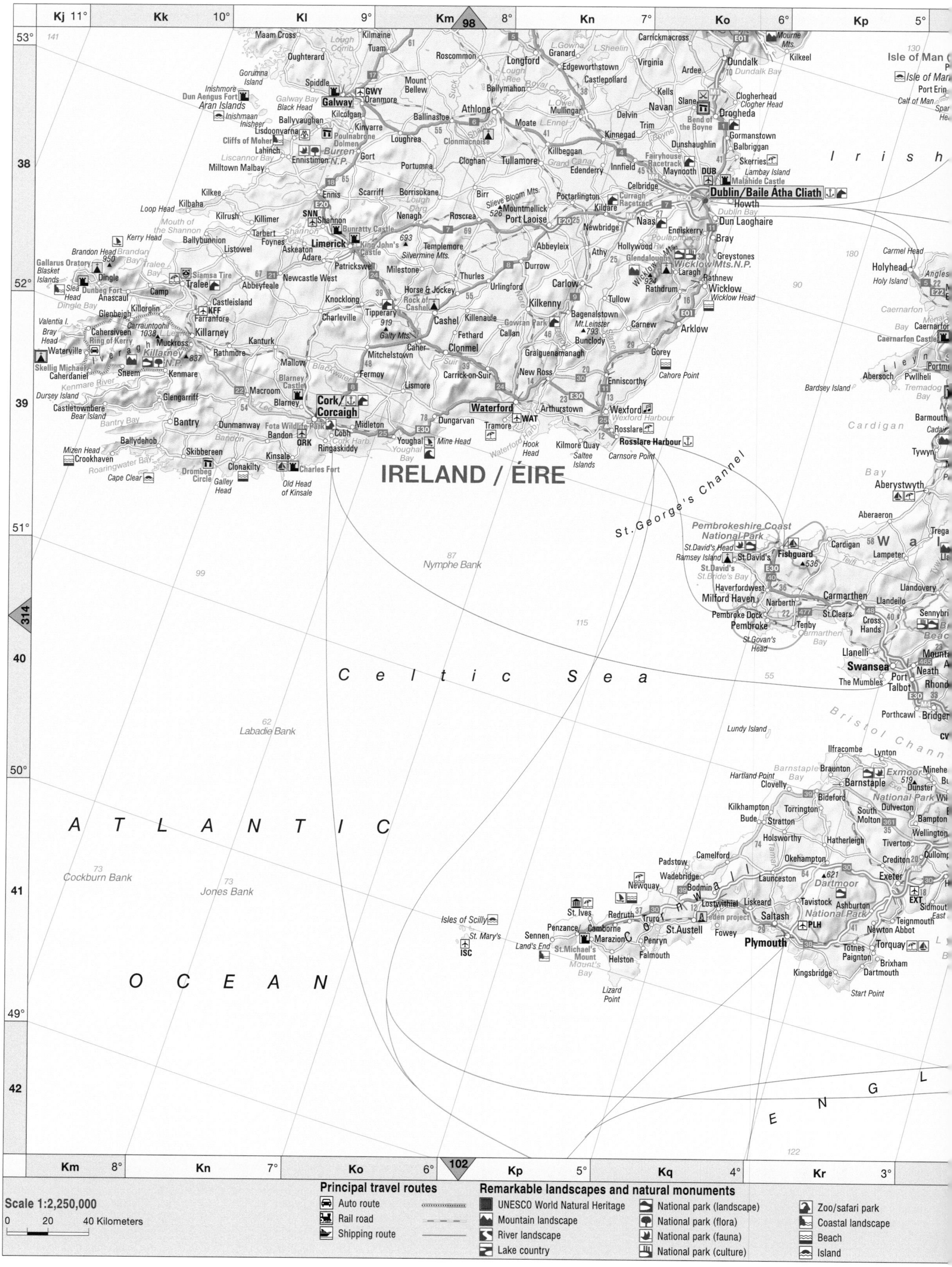

IRELAND / ÉIRE

Celtic Sea

ATLANTIC OCEAN

Scale 1:2,250,000
0 20 40 Kilometers

Principal travel routes
- Auto route
- Rail road
- Shipping route

Remarkable landscapes and natural monuments
- UNESCO World Natural Heritage
- Mountain landscape
- River landscape
- Lake country
- National park (landscape)
- National park (flora)
- National park (fauna)
- National park (culture)
- Zoo/safari park
- Coastal landscape
- Beach
- Island

-ast between East Devon and Dorset -atures prehistoric rock formations and -any important fossil sites. Outside of -ndon and its suburbs, South East Eng- -d has a largely rural character. The -uth East with its mild climate is one of -gland's most fertile regions and com- -ses deep valleys, idyllic pastures, and -nous white chalk cliffs.
-st Anglia is a low-lying region with -tensive fenlands, historic towns and small seaside resorts – located northeast of London. Much of East Anglia consists of land reclaimed from the sea through the use of canals and dikes. The **Midlands** in central England is a diverse region with both idyllic rural settings (including Cotswold) and large industrial urban areas such as Birmingham, Britain's second largest city. North of the Midland lies the historic county of Yorkshire, which features the Yorkshire Dales and the North York Moors. Lake District National Park in Cumbria has fascinating landscapes and is considered by many to be the most beautiful area in England.
Wales is largely mountainous, with the Cambrian Mountains and their foothills stretching through most of the country. Snowdonia National Park in North Wales is the location of Mount Snowdon, the highest British mountain outside of Scotland. Pembrokeshire National Park on the Welsh coast encompasses fascinating seaside landscapes and small islands. The interior of **Ireland** has numerous rivers and lakes. Most of the Republic of Ireland's land is covered by hills, moors, and fertile pastures. Carrauntoohil (1,038 meters), near the south-western coast, is the highest mountain in Ireland. The southwestern coast of Ireland also features the Ring of Kerry, a fascinating region of beautiful landscapes.

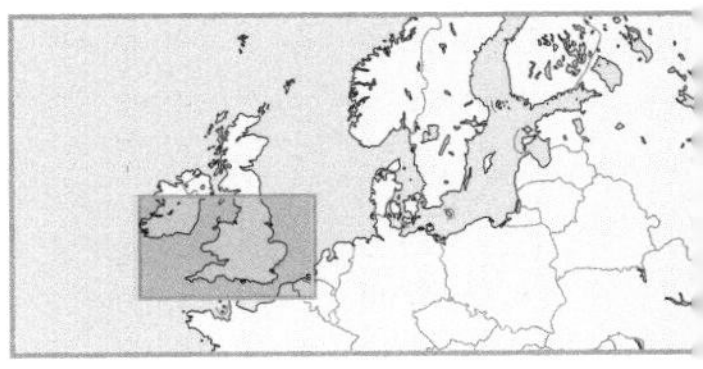

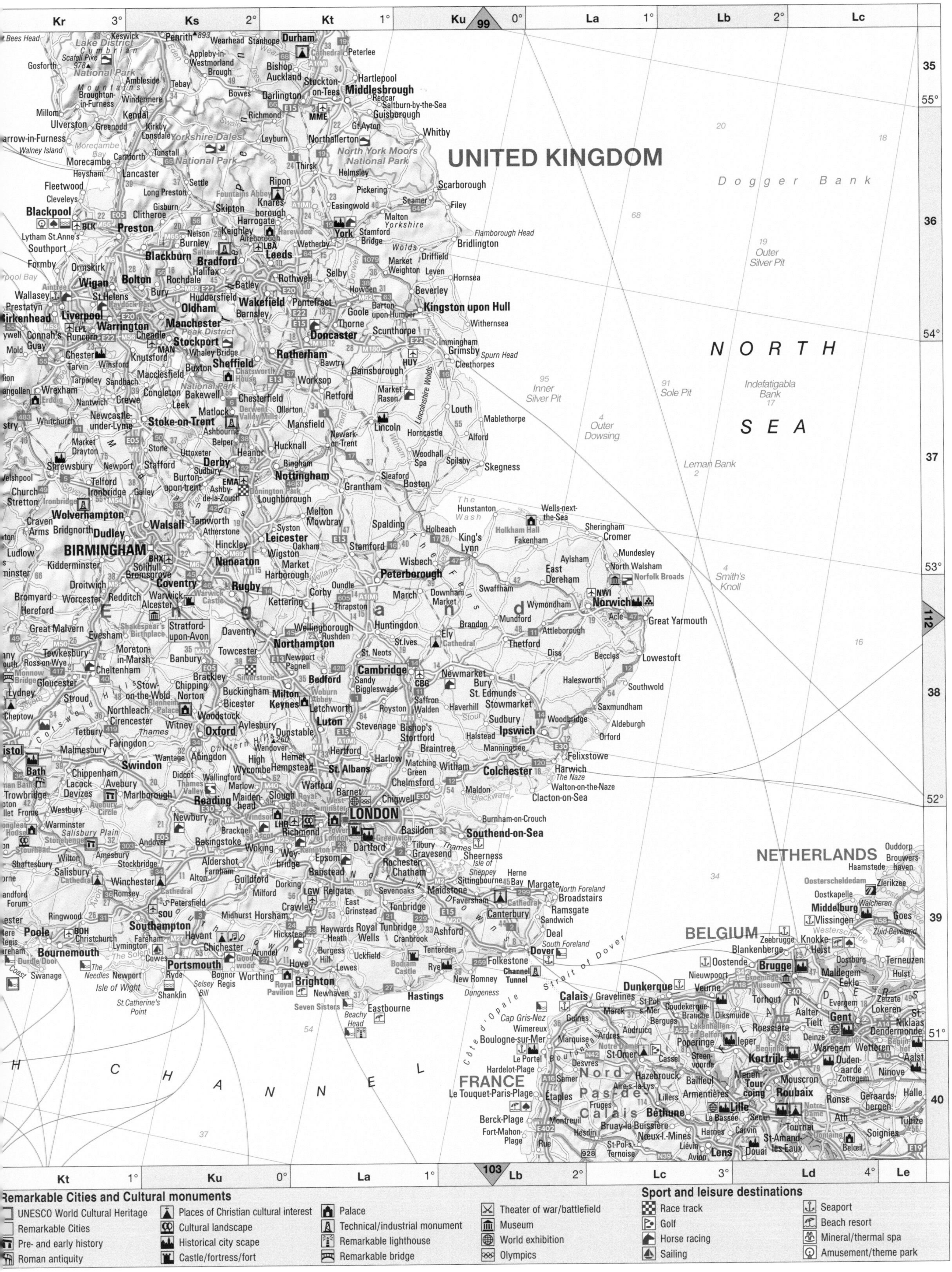

Remarkable Cities and Cultural monuments

- UNESCO World Cultural Heritage
- Remarkable Cities
- Pre- and early history
- Roman antiquity
- Places of Christian cultural interest
- Cultural landscape
- Historical city scape
- Castle/fortress/fort
- Palace
- Technical/industrial monument
- Remarkable lighthouse
- Remarkable bridge
- Theater of war/battlefield
- Museum
- World exhibition
- Olympics

Sport and leisure destinations

- Race track
- Golf
- Horse racing
- Sailing
- Seaport
- Beach resort
- Mineral/thermal spa
- Amusement/theme park

Lake District National park with spectacular landscapes and lakes – waterfalls, mountains, and gorges **KrKs36**

Blenheim Palace Largest private residence in Britain – impressive architecture and gardens – UNESCO world heritage site **Kt39**

London The capital city of the United Kingdom and a leading financial center. The cosmopolitan city has numerous attractions including; the Tower Bridge (top photo), Buckingham Palace, the British Museum. Several London attractions including the Tower of London, the Houses of Parliament (bottom photo), and Westminster Abbey are UNESCO world heritage sites. **Ku39**

Stonehenge Famous prehistoric site consisting of several large stones in a circle – built between 3000-1500 BC – mysterious origins – UNESCO world heritage site **Kt39**

Canterbury One of the oldest cities in southern England – home to a magnificent historic cathedral begun in the 12th century AD, a UNESCO world heritage site **Lb39**

The Chalk Cliffs of East Sussex This area boasts many beautiful high chalk cliffs, including the Seven Sisters **La40**

Belgium, Northern France

Belgium is one of the smallest and most densely populated states in Europe. The country is divided into two distinct geographic regions seperated by the Maas/Meuse river. The south and east of Belgium is a highland region, in contrast to the country's low lying north and west. Beyond Belgium's 70 km of coastline, with its dunes and beaches, lies a flat region of fertile polders – land claimed from the sea – and the hills of the Kempenland. **Central Belgium** is a region rolling green hills, that rise to 200 mete in height. To the south and east of Maas/Meuse lies the **Ardennes**, a de sely forested region and the location countless caves, gorges, and the Hoh Venns plateau (694 meters).

Northern France is dominated by

The famous medieval abbey Mont Sa Michael **Kt**

Brittany's Coast Beautiful cliffs – beaches – charming port cities including St. Guénolé (Photo) **Kq43**

Carnac Center of a prehistoric culture – Sites with ancient man-made stone formations and 3,000 stone monoliths **Kr43**

La Rochelle Port city (pop. 71,000) – interesting old town center – attractive Vieux Port **Kt44**

Loire Valley From Sully-sur-Loire to Chalonnes this fertile river valley forms part of a UNESCO world heritage site. Highlights of the region include the palaces at Chambord (photo,top) Chennonceaux, Amboise, and Azay-le-Rideau. Historic Blois (photo,bottom) also has a palace and the town of Saumur is dominated by an impressive castle. **Lb43**

Amiens Traditional capital of Picardy, located on the Somme river – the large Gothic cathedral Notre Dame built in the 13th century – UNESCO world heritage site **Lc41**

Versailles Louis XIV's grandiose palace, today a national museum – symbol of absolutism – the historic hall of mirrors – beautiful surrounding parks (UNESCO world heritage site) **Lc42**

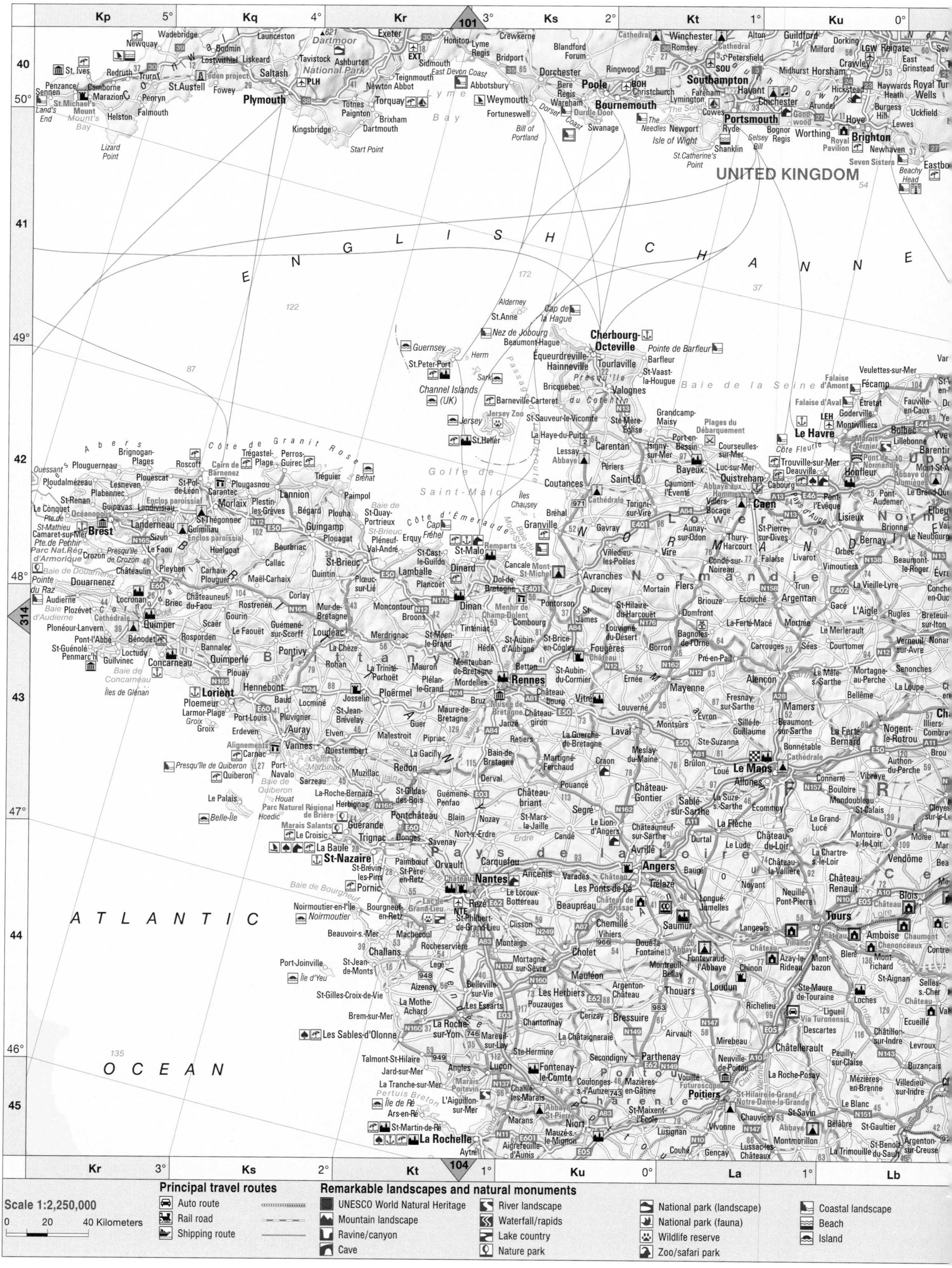

Scale 1:2,250,000
0 20 40 Kilometers

Principal travel routes
- Auto route
- Rail road
- Shipping route

Remarkable landscapes and natural monuments
- UNESCO World Natural Heritage
- Mountain landscape
- Ravine/canyon
- Cave
- River landscape
- Waterfall/rapids
- Lake country
- Nature park
- National park (landscape)
- National park (fauna)
- Wildlife reserve
- Zoo/safari park
- Coastal landscape
- Beach
- Island

ains of **Normandy** and **Picardy** and ne hills of **Brittany**. The Atlantic and nglish Channel coasts of France are rich contrasts: the white chalk cliffs of ne northern channel coast, the endless beaches in Picardy and Normandy, ne jagged coastline, bays, and islets Brittany. The **Channel Islands**, ependencies of the United Kingdom, resent some of most interesting landcapes in the region and a wealth of unique flora and fauna. The unusual chalk formations of the Côte de Granit Rose in Northern Brittany and the marsh landscape Marais Poitevin are among the many other interesting landscapes in the region.

The Loire River delta is situated to the south of Brittany. The **Loire** stretches over 1,000 km through France and is the country's longest river. Between Orleans and Angers the Loire passes through a region with an abundance of interesting cultural attractions including numerous ancient towns, palaces, and cathedrals. The **Paris basin** is located in the center of northern France. Paris, the capital of France, is one of the world's most diverse cities and the largest urban area in France by far. The city's numerous cultural, historic, and architectural highlights attract millions of visitors to the region every year. The river Seine flows 770 km though the region's farmland and beyond into the region **Champagne**, a major center of wine production. In the eastern basin, the forests of the **French Ardennes** run along the border between France and Belgium. The **Vosges** mountain range extends through the area to the southeast of the Paris basin. The range has a maximum height of 1,426 meters and descends abruptly into the Rhine Valley to its east.

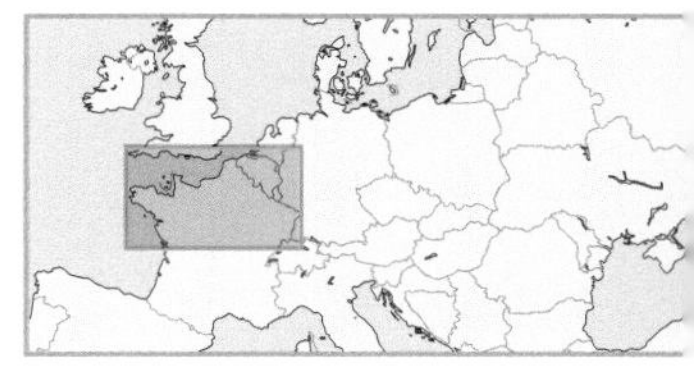

Bruges Capital of western Flanders – intact gothic city center – UNESCO world heritage site – photo: Roezenhod wharf and the Belfried tower. **Ld39**

Brussels Capital of Belgium and administrative center of the EU (pop. 950,000) – UNESCO world heritage site: La Grand Place (photo) with its guild houses and the city hall – important museums – Atomium **Le40**

Paris The capital of France (metro area pop. 12 million) has countless attractions. The banks of the Seine from the Eifel Tower to the gigantic Louvre and including the cathedrals Notre Dame and Saint Chappelle make up a UNESCO world heritage site. Photos from top to bottom: The Louvre, Arc de Triomphe, the Eifel Tower. **Lc42**

Nancy Charming city center rich in impressive 18th century architecture – three city plazas are UNESCO world heritage sites – Art Noveau museum **Lg42**

Strasbourgh Capital of Alsace (pop. 256,000) and home of the European Parliament and the Council of Europe – medieval city center and cathedral (UNESCO world heritage site) **Lh42**

Remarkable Cities and Cultural monuments

- UNESCO World Cultural Heritage
- Remarkable Cities
- Pre- and early history
- Roman antiquity
- Places of Christian cultural interest
- Cultural landscape
- Historical city scape
- Castle/fortress/fort
- Palace
- Theater of war/battlefield
- Memorial
- Market
- Festivals
- Museum
- World exhibition
- Olympics

Sport and leisure destinations

- Race track
- Golf
- Horse racing
- Wind surfing
- Beach resort
- Mineral/thermal spa
- Amusement/theme park
- Casino

Southern France comprises several distinct geographic regions. In the southwest, the Bay of Biscay, an arm of the Atlantic Ocean, borders the Aquitaine Basin. West of the Aquitaine Basin are the highlands of the Massif Central, which are separated from the French Alps by the Rhone River Valley. The Pyrenees Mountains separate France from the Iberian Peninsula.

The Aquitaine Basin, located south of the

Paris basin, is a scenic region of rollin hills crossed by many rivers such as th **Garonne**. The flat southeastern coas between the Spanish border and th Gironde Delta consists of long san beaches with many sand dunes. Th area has several seaside freshwater lake including Lac de Lacanau and Etang d

The village of Roussilon in Provence lies atop an ancient stone hill **Lf4**

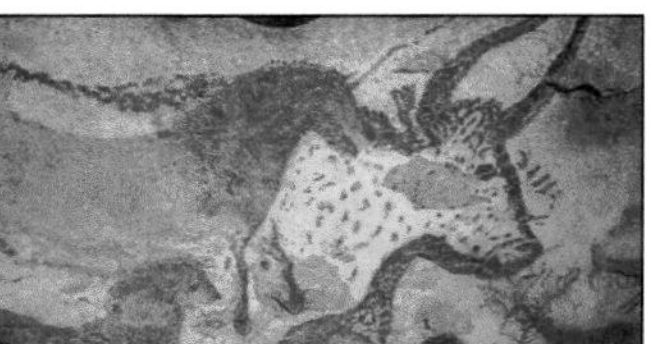

Lascaux Caves Cave in the Vezere Valley features ancient cave paintings – UNESCO world heritage site – tourists can visit an exact replica of the paintings **Lb45**

Saint-Émilion Historic city built around two hills in a winemaking region – well preserved architecture – UNESCO world heritage site **Ku46**

The Pyrenees High mountain range stretching from the Atlantic Ocean to the Mediterranean Sea – lush green valleys – unique wildlife and vegetation **Kt-Lc47/48**

Carcassonne Historic city with a largely intact medieval old town surrounded by a city wall – UNESCO world heritage site – the wall is over three kilometers long and includes 52 towers – medieval castle **Lc47**

Languedoc Region west of Provence – Cevenne Mountains and a sunny coastline – interesting gorges **Ld46**

Roman relicts in France Southern France boasts many remnants from the Roman era (200 BC - 400 AD) including temples (Nimes), triumphal arches, amphitheaters (Orange), aqueducts (Pont du Gard, top photo), and arenas (Arles, bottom photo). Many are UNESCO world heritage sites. **Le47**

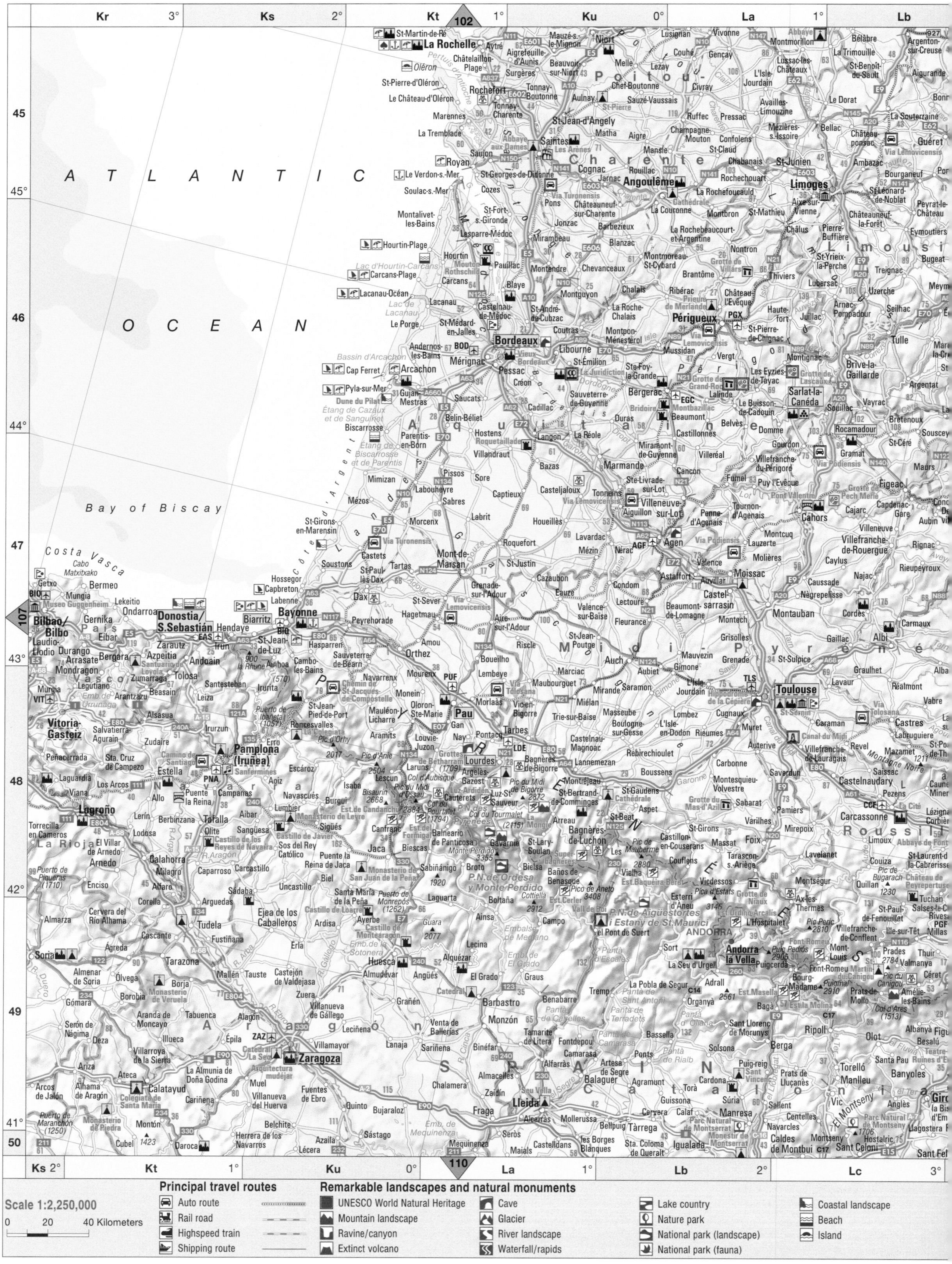

ATLANTIC OCEAN

Bay of Biscay

Scale 1:2,250,000

0 20 40 Kilometers

Principal travel routes

- Auto route
- Rail road
- Highspeed train
- Shipping route

Remarkable landscapes and natural monuments

- UNESCO World Natural Heritage
- Mountain landscape
- Ravine/canyon
- Extinct volcano
- Cave
- Glacier
- River landscape
- Waterfall/rapids
- Lake country
- Nature park
- National park (landscape)
- National park (fauna)
- Coastal landscape
- Beach
- Island

102
107
110

azaux. The 105-meter-high and 2,700-eter-long **Dune du Pilat** is the longest and dune in Europe. **Côte d'Argent** near e Spanish border encompasses Europe's largest pine forest.

ance's Bordeaux region is one of the ost productive and famous wine-aking regions in the world. Dordogne to e west of Bordeaux is a hilly region of rests, pastures, and vineyards.

ance's **Pyrenees** are green and steep. The area around the French Pyrenees is one of most pristine in Western Europe. Cirque du Gavarnie, a gigantic natural stone half-circle in Pyrenees Occidentales National Park is the most famous attraction in this region. The Massif Central which covers most of Southeastern France is a large mountainous highlands region. The **Auvergne Mountains**, a range of extinct volcanoes, form the core of the Massif Central. Between the Massif Central and the French Alps stretches the **Rhone River Valley**. The **Camargue** in the Rhone Valley is a unique wetlands area with interesting local wildlife and nature reserves.

France's **Mediterranean coast** has a warm climate with most rainfall concentrated in the winter months. The most visited section of the coast is the French Riviera or **Côte d'Azur**, as it is known in French. This world famous coastal area has beautiful cliffs and vibrant seaside resort towns. **Provence**, a charming region in southeastern France, contains many natural attractions including Gorges du Verdon, Europe's deepest canyon and the **Luberon Mountains**. The magnificent French Alps stretch from Lake Geneva to just north of the Mediterranean Coast. Mont Blanc rises 4,807 meters above sea level and is the highest mountain in Europe outside of Russia.

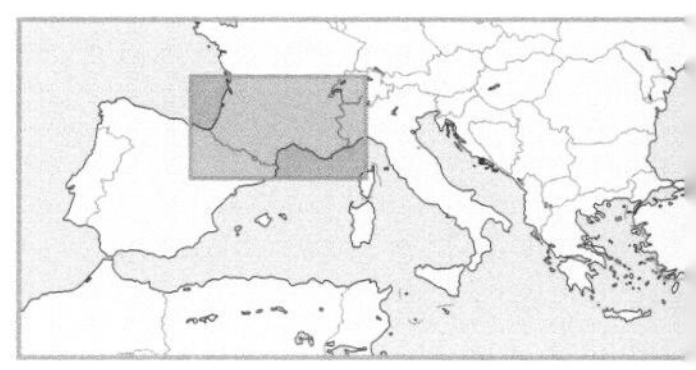

Lyon The second largest urban area in France has a historic city center with Roman ruins, medieval buildings, and Renaissance-style patrician houses – UNESCO world heritage site **Le45**

Mont Blanc The highest mountain in Europe outside of Russia – rising 4,807 meters – covered by several glaciers **Lg45**

Avignon Once a papal residence during the middle ages – historic city architecture – large Palace of the Pope – annual theater festival **Le47**

Abbaye de Sénanque Cistercian abbey in Provence – simple harmonious architecture – beautiful cloister **Lf47**

The French Riviera (Côte d'Azur) The Côte d'Azur is the section of the Meditereanean coast between Cassis and Menton. The Massif de l'Estérel (top photo) is a series of beautiful hills directly on the coast. Famous towns on the Riviera include Nice, St. Tropez, and Cannes, site of an annual film festival. **LgLh47**

Monaco Small principality on the Mediterranean coast – famous for its historic casino in Monte Carlo – annual Grand Prix auto race **Lh47**

emarkable Cities and Cultural monuments

- UNESCO World Cultural Heritage
- Remarkable Cities
- Pre- and early history
- Prehistoric rockscape
- Greek antiquity
- Roman antiquity
- Places of Christian cultural interest
- Cultural landscape
- Historical city scape
- Castle/fortress/fort
- Palace
- Technical/industrial monument
- Remarkable bridge
- Festivals
- Museum
- Olympics

Sport and leisure destinations

- Race track
- Golf
- Horse racing
- Skiing
- Wind surfing
- Beach resort
- Mineral/thermal spa
- Casino

The Bay of Biscay, an arm of the Atlantic Ocean, and the Pyrenees Mountains border the Iberian Peninsula to the north. Spain covers around four-fifths of the Iberian Peninsula's area, while Portugal and the small nation of Andorra comprise the remaining area.

The **Pyrenees** separate Iberia from France. **Monte Perdido**, the highest mountain in the Pyrenees, rises 3,350 meters above sea level. West of the Pyrenees rises the **Cordillera Cantábr ca Range**. The highest mountain the range, **Picos de Europa**, ris 2,600 meters. The Cordillera Cantabri is also the source of the 928-kilom ter-long **Ebro River** – Spain's secor longest river. The Ebro River delta the Spanish Medditerranean coast is

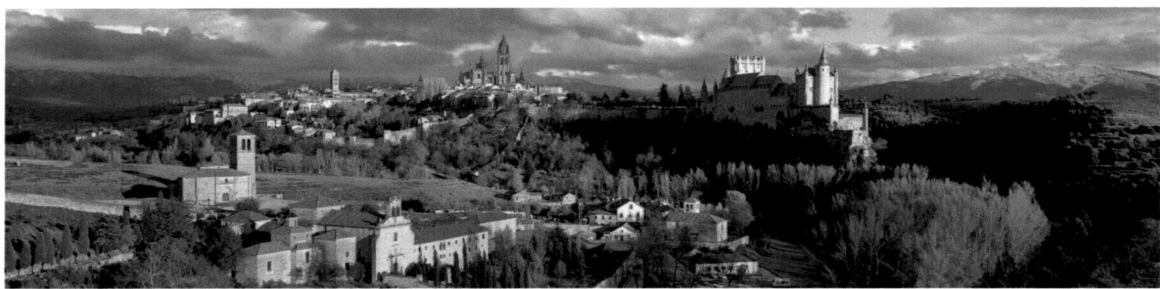

The historic skyline of Segovia (Spain) **Kq5**

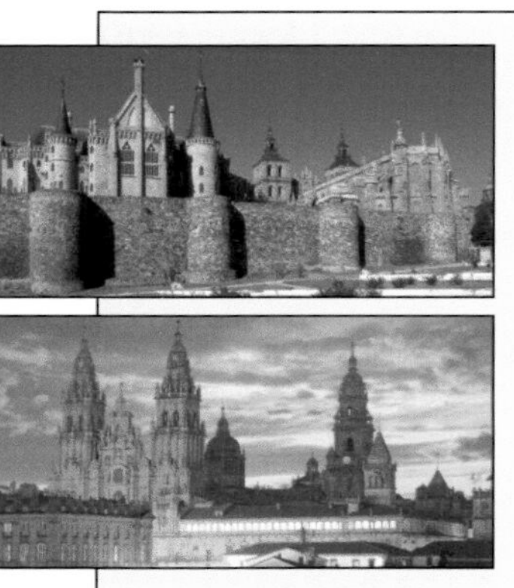

Camino de Santiago Also known as the Way of St. James, this pilgrimage route has attracted Christian pilgrims for thousands of years. The route leads to the cathedral in Santiago de Compostela (bottom photo; **Km52**), with the tomb of Saint James. The 800-kilometer-long route passes through historic Astorga (top photo; **Ko52**)

Picos de Europa National Park Mountainous nature reserve around the city of Covadonga – chamois, wolf, and bear populations – 30 kilometers from the coast – hiking trails **KpKq53**

Porto The largest city in northern Portugal – the old town is a UNESCO world heritage site – port wine cellars **Km51**

Bragança Portuguese town with a largely intact castle built in the 12th century – the old town is surrounded by an ancient city wall **Ko51**

Salamanca Historic university town – UNESCO world heritage site – beautiful Plaza Mayor – famous twin cathedrals **Kp50**

Ávila The highest city in Spain – medieval town center – 2,500-meter-long city wall with 86 towers – UNESCO world heritage site **Kq50**

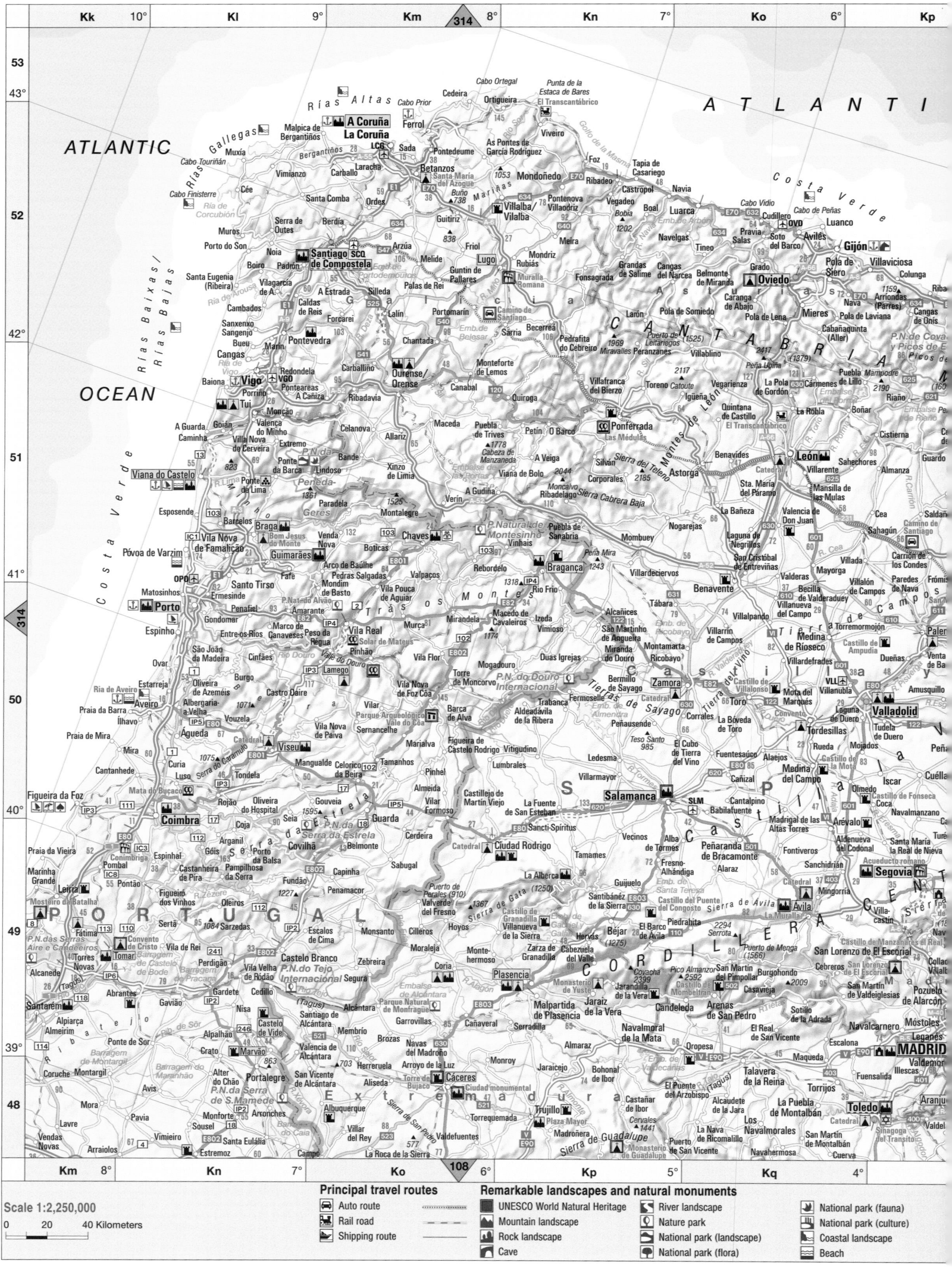

Scale 1:2,250,000

0 20 40 Kilometers

Principal travel routes

- Auto route
- Rail road
- Shipping route

Remarkable landscapes and natural monuments

- UNESCO World Natural Heritage
- Mountain landscape
- Rock landscape
- Cave
- River landscape
- Nature park
- National park (landscape)
- National park (flora)
- National park (fauna)
- National park (culture)
- Coastal landscape
- Beach

nservation area, home to many rare d fascinating birds. ...ain's **Meseta** is a large elevated pla- ...au covering much of the country. The ...rthern Meseta is separated from the ...her sections of the plateau by the **Cor- ...llera Central** Range. Several major ...ers flow through the Cordillera Central ...cluding the Tajo (Tejo: Portuguese) ...ver in the south and the Deuro/Douro ...ver in the north. The northwestern coast of the Iberian Peninsula has a rainy maritime climate. Northwestern Iberia encompasses many inland valleys with mild climates – including the **Douro Valley** in Portugal and the **Rioja** region, both major winemaking regions. The Meseta region and the Ebro River Basin get scorching temperatures in summer months, while the climate of the warm Mediterranean coast is moderated by sea breezes. During winter, strong winds can cause temperatures below freezing and even snowfall in Madrid and the Meseta. The mountains of northern Iberia receive abundant snowfall during the winter months. The Pyrenees are a popular destination for the enjoyment of winter sports such as skiing and snowboarding. The northernmost regions of Spain are often referred to as "green Spain" because of their lush vegetation and abundant rainfall. Galicia is the wettest region in Spain and the region's coast is indented by several bays. Spain's Basque Country is home to a people with a unique culture. The origins of the Basque people are unknown and their language is unrelated to any other. The Basque city of San Sebastian/Donostia is one of the most beautiful seaside towns in Europe. Portugal's **Costa Verde**, a major tourist destination, features sandy and rocky beaches.

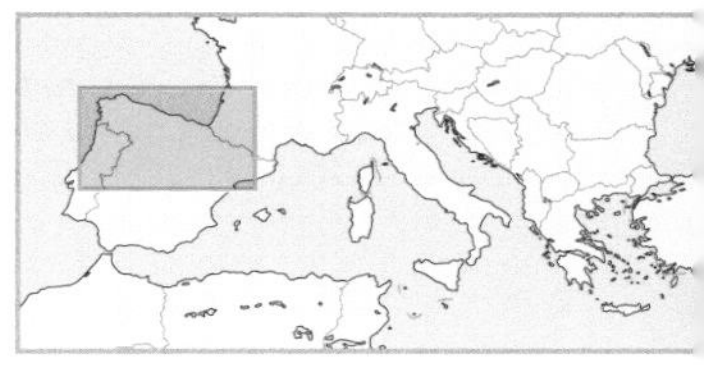

Altamira Cave with Stone Age paintings – world heritage site – cave painting replica in the neighboring museum **Kq53**

San Sebastián/Donostia Elegant seaside town on the Bay of Biscay – La Concha beach (photo) is between Monte Urgull and Monte Igueldo **Kt53**

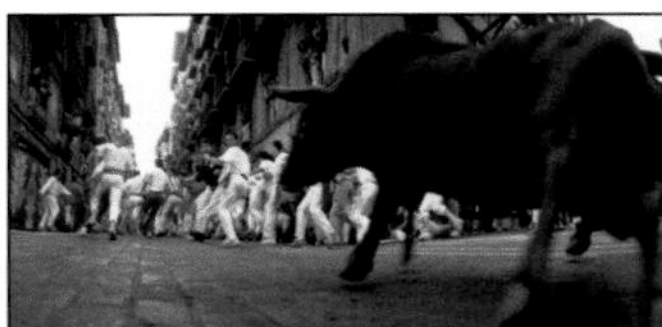

Pamplona Capital of Navarre – the city has medieval ruins and a historic center – location of the famous Fiesta de San Fernin, where young men run through narrow alleys chased by a herd of bulls **Kt52**

Ordesa y Monte Perdido National Park Located in the central Pyrenees – the national park was founded in 1918 and has several high mountain hiking trails **La52**

Zaragoza Once the residence of the kings of Aragon, today a large modern city – Basilica del Pilar (photo) **Ku51**

San Lorenzo de El Escorial Enormous monastic castle northwest of Madrid – built by Phillip II in the 16th century – burial site of Spanish monarchs since Charles V. **Kq50**

Madrid Capital of Spain and the largest city on the Iberian Peninsula – Royal Palace – Prado art museum – Plaza de la Cibeles (photo) is the intersection of several major boulevards – historic buildings on Plaza de la Villa and Plaza Mayor **Kr50**

...emarkable Cities and Cultural monuments

- UNESCO World Cultural Heritage
- Remarkable Cities
- Pre- and early history
- Prehistoric rockscape
- Roman antiquity
- Places of Jewish cultural interest
- Places of Christian cultural interest
- Cultural landscape
- Historical city scape
- Castle/fortress/fort
- Palace
- Remarkable bridge
- Market
- Festivals
- Museum

Sport and leisure destinations

- Golf
- Horse racing
- Skiing
- Wind surfing
- Seaport
- Beach resort
- Mineral/thermal spa
- Amusement/theme park

The southern half of the Iberian Peninsula encompasses many mountain ranges, called Sierras or Cordilleras in Spanish and Serra in Portuguese. Spain's highest **mountain Mulhacén** (3,481 meters) is situated twenty kilometers from the Mediterranean coast in the **Sierra Nevada Mountains**. The name Sierra Nevada means "snowy mountains" and the range gets abundant snowfall during winter. Spain's **Meseta** is a large elevated pla-

teau that extends over much of the cou try. The sections of the Meseta south a southeast of Madrid produce most of t country's grain and are known as t "breadbasket of Spain." Saffron, the mo expensive spice in the world, is also ha vested in this region. Southern Portug comprises two vast plain-covered

Windmills in La Mancha, a Spanish region south of Madrid **Ks**

Sintra Once the residence of Portuguese monarchs – UNESCO world heritage site – Paço Real palace – Palácio da Pena (photo) **Kl48**

Lisbon Capital of Portugal on the delta of the Tejo River – the old town district Alfama features historic plazas and palaces – UNESCO world heritage site: Mosteiro dos Jerónimos, Torre de Belém **Kl48**

Algarve This region in southern Portugal is a popular destination for tourists – beaches and golf courses – sandbanks and lagoons in the eastern Algarve **KmKn47**

Seville Capital of Andalucia – the cathedral is a UNESCO world heritage site – Alcázar Castle **Kp47**

Córdoba Mezquita Cathedral (photo) is a world heritage site; the cathedral is a converted mosque containing more than 850 columns **Kq47**

Ronda Picturesque and historic town in Andalucia – the two sections of the town are connected by the 98 meters high Puente Nuevo bridge – Spain's oldest bullfighting arena **Kp46**

Gibraltar British overseas territory – located on a rocky peninsula – Europe and Africa are between 14 and 44 kilometers apart in the Strait of Gibraltar **Kp46**

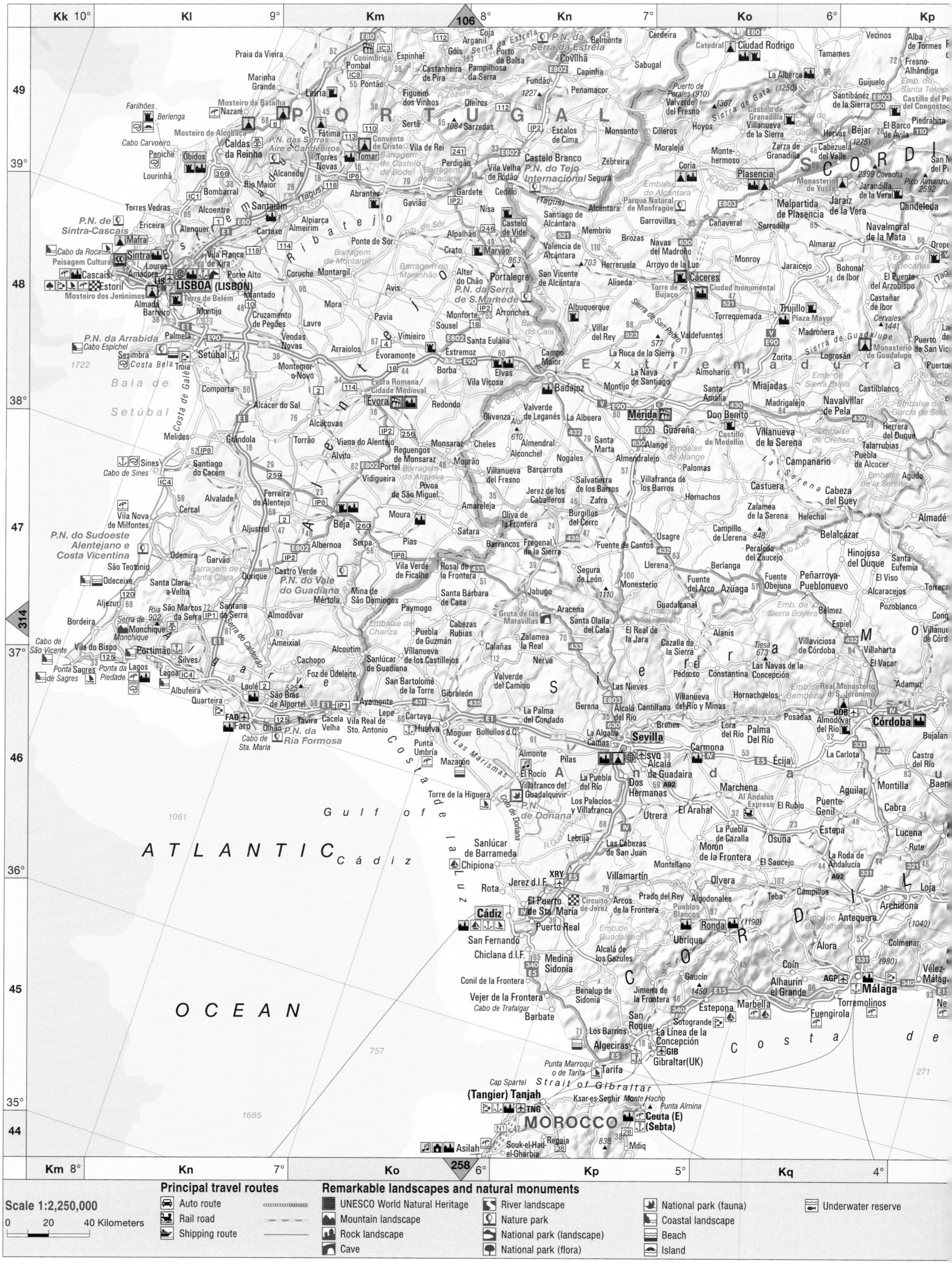

Scale 1:2,250,000

0 20 40 Kilometers

Principal travel routes

- Auto route
- Rail road
- Shipping route

Remarkable landscapes and natural monuments

- UNESCO World Natural Heritage
- Mountain landscape
- Rock landscape
- Cave
- River landscape
- Nature park
- National park (landscape)
- National park (flora)
- National park (fauna)
- Coastal landscape
- Beach
- Island
- Underwater reserve

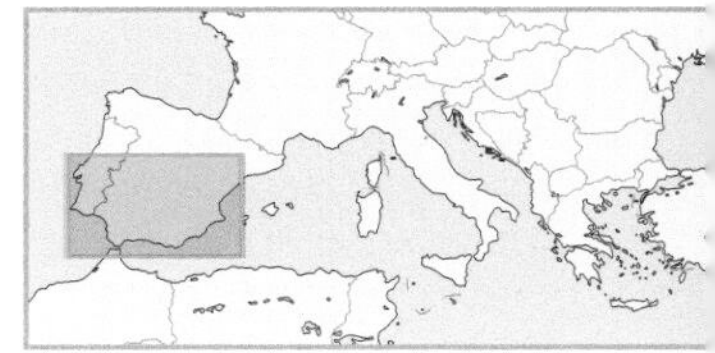

ons: the **Alentejo** and the **Ribatejo**. e Ribatejo is a major cattle ranching nter, while the Alentejo produces much Portugal's grain and most of the orld's cork supply.
ost of Portugal's Atlantic coast con- ts of sandy strips of land but the **Algar-** region has many picturesque rocky ys. The southernmost regions of Por- gal, including **Ponta de Sagres**, have editerranean climates with hot sunny summers and mild wet winters. Portugal's central coast (around Lisbon) is cooler and wetter than the southern coast because of strong Atlantic winds.

Gibraltar, a British territory, comprises a five kilometer long and 1.4 kilometer wide peninsula bordering Spain's **Costa del Sol**. The Costa del Sol with its Mediterranean beaches is one of Spain's most popular tourist destinations.

The interior of the Iberian Peninsula has a continental climate with abundant sunshine and significant differences between the seasons. In addition to grain production, citrus farming is widespread in the warmer regions of Iberia. Olive trees are common in most Mediterranean regions including Spain and Portugal.

Due to deforestation that began in the Bronze Age, southern Iberia has suffered from water shortages since the Roman era. Numerous dams have been built throughout the Iberian Peninsula to provide water for irrigation and household consumption. The few remaining wetlands in the region, including the **Tablas de Daimiel** and **Río Guadalquivir** Delta are part of **national parks** established in recent decades. During winter, these areas are home to large colonies of migrating birds. Both of these wetlands are home to endangered animals such as the Spanish lynx.

Toledo Historic city surrounded by the Rio Tajo – medieval architecture – museum in the former home of 17th century master painter El Greco **Kq49**

Aranjuez Castle and retreat of the Spanish Royal Family – gardens surrounding the castle – world heritage site **Kr50**

Monasterio de Guadalupe Monastery, west of Toledo – UNESCO world heritage site – major pilgrimage site because of its Black Madonna statue **Kp49**

Granada The town features the Alhambra Palace, a UNESCO world heriage site built during the Moorish era – Renaissance-era cathedral **Kr47**

Sierra Nevada Mountain range with a large national park – ski areas – 16 peaks rising above 3,000 meters **KrKs47**

Spanish Bullfighting The "corrida de toros" is a national passion in Spain. Bullfighting season runs from Easter until October. Picaderos and banderilleros encite the bull before a matador begins the main spectacle.

Benidorm Resort city on the Costa Blanca. The town was a sleepy fishing village until the tourism boom of the 1960s **Ku48**

emarkable Cities and Cultural monuments

- UNESCO World Cultural Heritage
- Remarkable Cities
- Phoenecian culture
- Roman antiquity
- Places of Jewish cultural interest
- Places of Christian cultural interest
- Cultural landscape
- Historical city scape
- Castle/fortress/fort
- Palace
- Space telescope
- World exhibition

Sport and leisure destinations

- Race track
- Golf
- Horse racing
- Skiing
- Sailing
- Diving
- Wind surfing
- Seaport
- Beach resort
- Mineral/thermal spa
- Amusement/theme park
- Casino

The **Pyrenees** stretch through much of **northern Spain** and separate the Iberian Peninsula from France. In addition to mountains, northern Spain also comprises fertile plains, river valleys, and beautiful coastal areas. The **Costa Brava** and **Costa Daurada** are both popular tourist destinations. Catalonia's capital, **Barcelona** is the second largest urban area in Spain and a major economic center.

The **Balearic Islands** consists of **Maj ca (Mallorca)**, **Minorca**, **Formente** **Ibiza**, as well as numerous minor islan **Cabrera**, one of the minor islan includes the Cabrera National Park. In northwestern **Majorca** rise the mou tains of the Serra de Tramuntana rang while the southeast is covered by

Les Calanche, beautiful granite stone formations on Corsica **Lj**

The Costa Brava Rocky coast north of Barcelona – popular beach towns including Cadaques **LcLd48/49**

Monserrat Monastery The most revered religious site in Catalonia – basilica containing a Black Madonna statue **Lb49**

Barcelona Catalonia's leading city is one of the most vibrant coastal cities on the Mediterranean. In addition to its many museums the city also has an abundance of interesting architecture including Casa Mila (top photo) and Palau de la Música Catalana (bottom photo), both UNESCO world heritage sites. **Lc49**

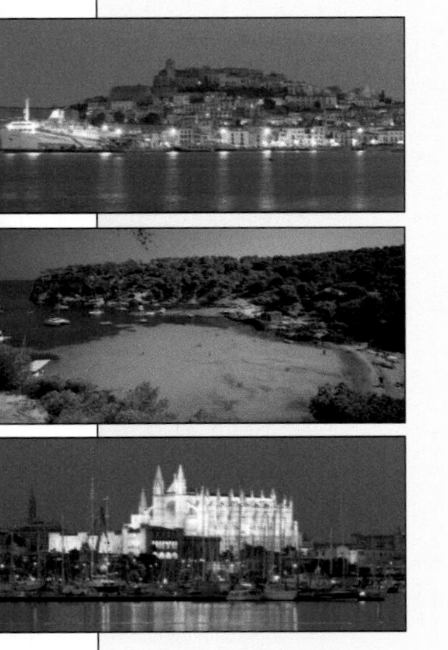

The Balearic Islands The islands are popular tourist destinations with many diverse landscapes, picturesque villages, beautiful bays, and beaches. Photos from top to bottom: Ibiza **(Lb51/52)**, beach on Majorca, Palma de Mallorca **(LcLd51)**

Scale 1:2,250,000

0 20 40 Kilometers

Principal travel routes

- Auto route
- Rail road
- Shipping route

Remarkable landscapes and natural monuments

- UNESCO World Natural Heritage
- Mountain landscape
- Rock landscape
- Ravine/canyon
- Cave
- River landscape
- Nature park
- National park (landscape)
- National park (flora)
- National park (fauna)
- Coastal landscape
- Beach
- Island
- Underwater reserve

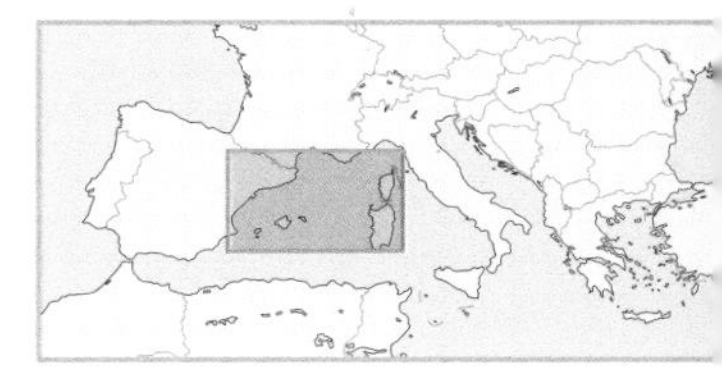

…rra de Llevant. Between the two …lands lies a large fertile plain. Majorca's …coastal areas comprise beautiful bea…es, cliffs, and bays.
…norca's 200 kilometers of coastline …clude some of the most spectacular …ys in the Mediterranean. The island's …erior consists of fertile hills in the north …d barren grassy areas in the south.
…ly **Ibiza** has beautiful coasts and is …e of Spain's most popular tourist destinations. Neighboring **Formentera** lies only a few kilometers south of Ibiza and has numerous undeveloped white sand beaches. Both Ibiza and Formentera feature coastal nature reserves.

Politically, **Corsica** is a region of France but the island has a distinctive local culture and is situated closer to Italy than France. A mountain range running from the northwest to the southeast divides Corsica into two regions. The western half of the island is a region of bays and hills, while the eastern half of the island is a region of plains with numerous sandy beaches. The large Regional Nature Park of Corsica was created in the 1970s. It covers a third of Corsica's total area and encompasses protected areas on the island's coast and in the mountainous interior.

The Italian island, **Sardinia**, boasts many beautiful caves and grottos. A mountainous highland covers most of Sardinia's interior. Around 14% of the island's territory is covered by plains, including the fertile Campidano region between the cities of Cagliari and Oristano. Sardinia also features many important archeological and historical sites including remnants of the Roman and Neolithic eras. Costa del Sud in southern Sardinia is the location of the finest beaches on the island.

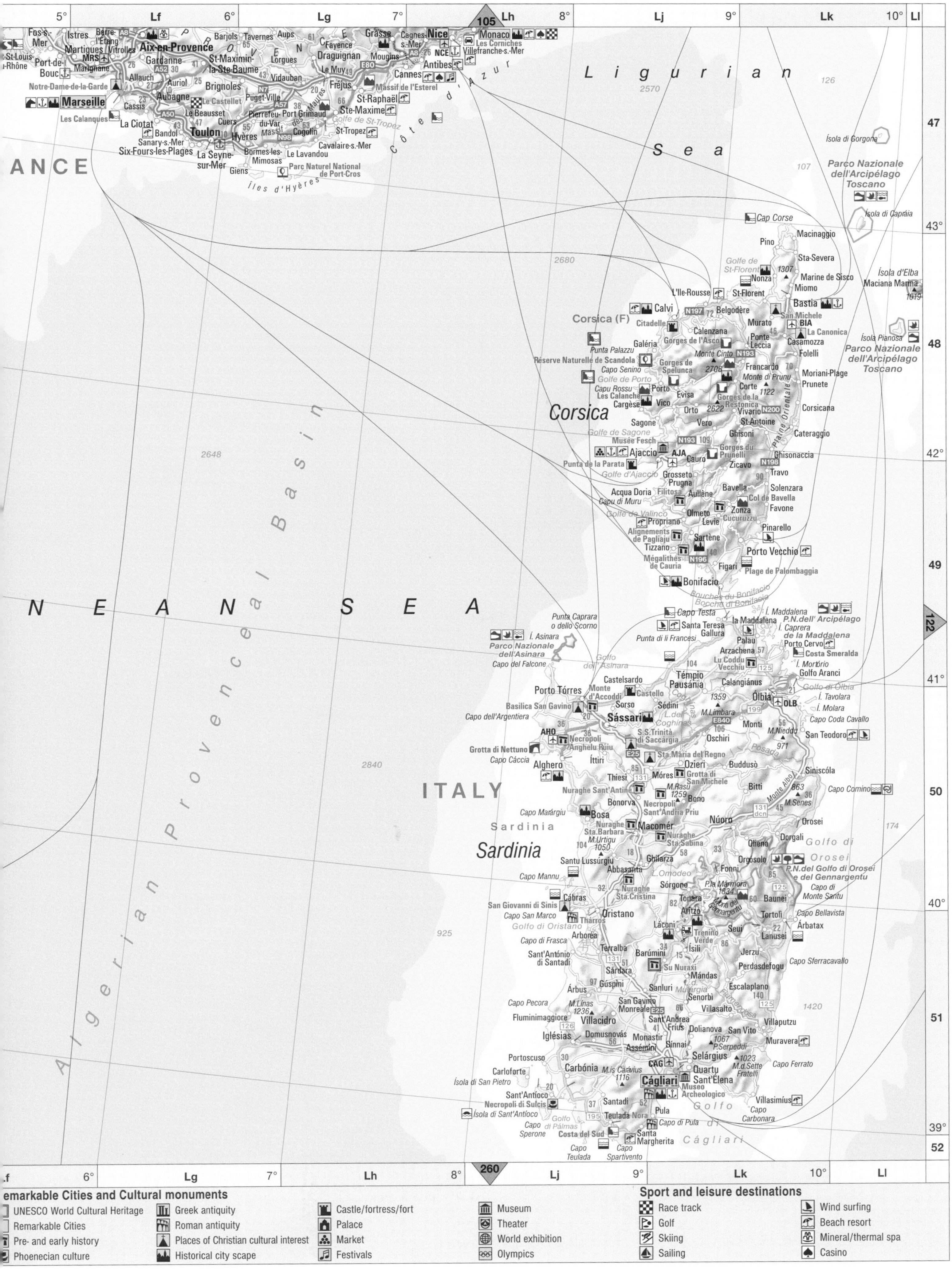

Calvi Picturesque Corsican town with beautiful beaches – La Marine, harbor district – medieval citadel **Lj48**

Gulf of Porto One of the most beautiful coastal areas on Corsica – rocky Cape Porto is a designated UNESCO world natural heritage site **Lj48**

Corte Historic Corsican city with a vibrant student population – citadel – Musee de la Corse, Corsican culture museum **Lk48**

Bonifacio Ancient city in southernmost Corsica – lively lower town – historic sailor's cemetery **Lk49**

Costa Smeralda Popular tourist destination on Sardinia – picturesque bays – turquoise blue sea **LK49**

Su Nuraxi Large prehistoric structure built by an ancient culture around 2,500 years ago – round structures – bastion with four towers and defensive walls **Lk51**

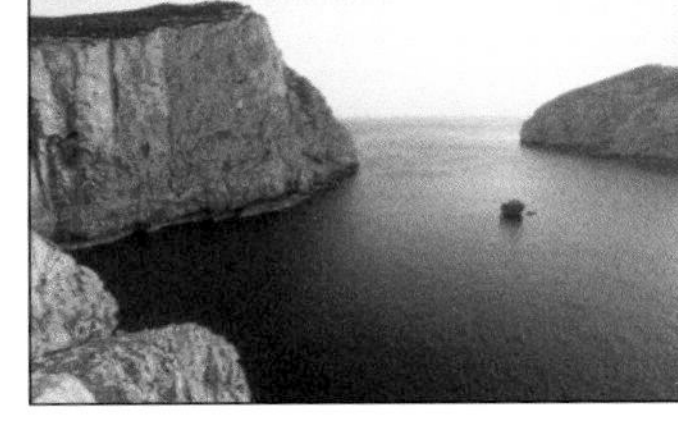

Capo Càccia Steep cliffs on the Sardinian coast – Escala di Cabiro (656 steps) lead to the Grotta di Nettuno **Lj50**

…emarkable Cities and Cultural monuments

- UNESCO World Cultural Heritage
- Remarkable Cities
- Pre- and early history
- Phoenecian culture
- Greek antiquity
- Roman antiquity
- Places of Christian cultural interest
- Historical city scape
- Castle/fortress/fort
- Palace
- Market
- Festivals
- Museum
- Theater
- World exhibition
- Olympics

Sport and leisure destinations

- Race track
- Golf
- Skiing
- Sailing
- Wind surfing
- Beach resort
- Mineral/thermal spa
- Casino

Germany is divided into several distinct geographic regions. The northern half of the country is dominated by plains and in certain areas by low mountains. The **flat, low-lying areas** in the most northern regions of Germany are relatively unfertile and are dotted with moors, small lakes, and heaths. **The North and East Frisian Islands** in the **North Sea** encompass many fascinating landscapes, including the three **national parks** in the **Wattenmeer**, a mud tideland. The German **Baltic Sea coa** is an area of bays, sandy beaches, a hanging cliffs. The largest German islan in the Baltic Sea are Fehmarn, Rüg Hiddensee, and Usedom. Behind the B tic coast is the region called Holstei Switzerland and Mecklenburg's la

Kinderdijk-Elshout: historic windmills the Dutch countryside Le

Hanseatic Towns The Hanseatic League was founded in the 13th centuries as a union of trading towns with Lübeck (top photo), now a world heritage site, as its center. Other Hanseatic towns in northern Germany include Hamburg, Wismar (bottom photo) and Greifswald.

Hamburg Germany's largest port and second largest city (pop. 1,7 million) is a major cultural center encompassing several urban lakes – most important tourist attraction: the harbor (photo) **Ll37**

Amsterdam Capital of the Netherlands (pop. 730,000) – a multicultural and tolerant city – historic villas – picturesque canals – photo: Canal with houseboats **Le38**

De Keukenhof A large park near Lisse – flowers, trees, waterways, a sea of tulips and other colorful flowers **Le38**

Rotterdam Second largest city of the Netherlands – busiest harbor in the world – photo: Erasmus bridge **Le39**

Cologne Important cultural and convention center (pop. 960,000) – most famous landmark: Cologne Cathedral (photo): UNESCO world heritage site – numerous historic churches **Lg40**

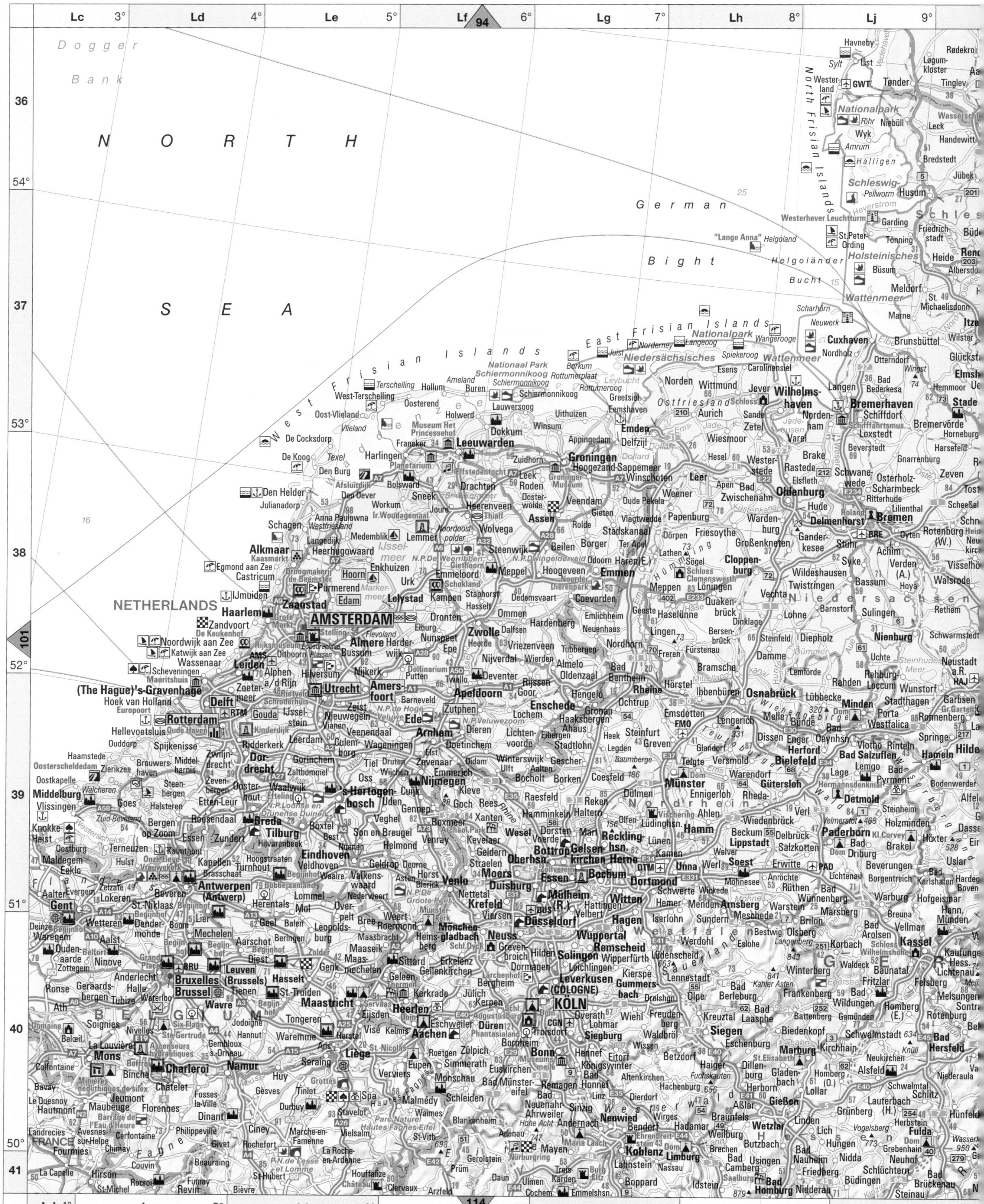

Scale 1:2,250,000

0 20 40 Kilometers

Principal travel routes

- Auto route
- Rail road
- Shipping route

Remarkable landscapes and natural monuments

- UNESCO World Natural Heritage
- Mountain landscape
- Rock landscape
- Cave
- River landscape
- Lake country
- Fossil site
- Nature park
- National park (landscape)
- National park (flora)
- National park (fauna)
- Protected area for sea-lions/seals
- Zoo/safari park
- Coastal landscape
- Beach
- Island

strict. The land surrounding the coastal ys are fertile plains that give way to the othills of central Germany's mountains. e low mountain ranges of central ermany stretch through a heavily forest- region. The region ranges between 0 and 1,200 meters in elevation. Cen- l Germany's uplands feature scenic er valleys,unique eroded stone forma- ns, and beautiful lakes. The highest ountains in the region are the Fichtel-berg (1,214 meters) in the Erz Mountains and the Brocken (1,142 meters) in the Harz Mountains.

The most important rivers in the northern half of Germany are the **Rhine**, the **Elbe**, and the **Weser**. The largest urban area in the region is the Rhine-Ruhr area – which encompasses the major cities of Cologne and Düsseldorf as well as the industrial centers along the Ruhr River.

Most of the **Netherlands** is located on the same vast plain that covers most of northern Germany. More than half of the country's land area is situated below sea level and much of the country's territory consists of land reclaimed from the sea through the use of dikes and canals. Despite having a high population density, most of the land in the country is used for agriculture. The Netherlands also has extensive forests and meadow landscapes. The country is criss-crossed by numerous canals and protected from the sea by a series of dunes and dikes. There are many good beaches along the northern and northwestern coasts. The highest point of the Netherlands is in the country's hilly southeast – (Vaalser 322 meters).

The most densely populated region in the country is the Randstad, which comprises several major cities, including Amsterdam and Rotterdam.

Rügen Baltic Sea island with diverse landscapes – white chalk cliffs (photo) in the Jasmund National Park **Lo36**

Usedom Historic seaside resort with interesting architecture – long white beaches – wealth of flora and fauna **Lp36**

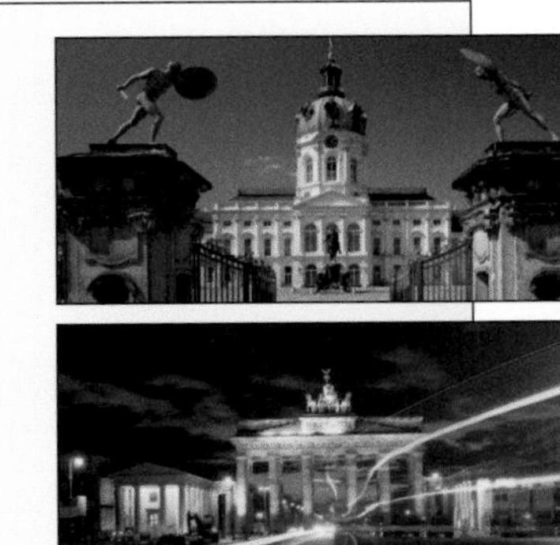

Berlin The German capital (pop. 3.39 million) has been one of Europe's leading cities since its reunification. The city has numerous cultural offerings, important museums, and the best nightlife in Germany. The city's most famous landmark is the **Brandenburg Gate** (photo, bottom). One of the city's most impressive buildings is **Charlottenburg palace** built in the 17th and 18th centuries (photo, top). **Lo38**

Potsdam-Sanssouci Summer residence of Frederick the Great – park and palace are UNESCO world heritage sites – lakeside manor on Heiligen See (photo) **Lo38**

Wartburg Impressive castle in central Germany – UNESCO world heritage site – Martin Luther's study – museum **Ll40**

Dresden "Florence on the Elbe" (pop. 480,000) – important art collection and impressive historic buildings: Zwinger, Semperoper opera house, palace **Lo39**

Remarkable Cities and Cultural monuments

- UNESCO World Cultural Heritage
- Remarkable Cities
- Pre- and early history
- Roman antiquity
- Places of Christian cultural interest
- Cultural landscape
- Historical city scape
- Impressive skyline
- Castle/fortress/fort
- Palace
- Technical/industrial monument
- Remarkable lighthouse
- Remarkable bridge
- Museum
- World exhibition
- Olympics

Sport and leisure destinations

- Arena/stadium
- Race track
- Golf
- Horse racing
- Sailing
- Wind surfing
- Beach resort
- Amusement/theme park

Southern Germany, Switzerland, Austria

The terrain of **southern Germany** is distinctly more mountainous and hilly than that of northern Germany. The region encompasses several **mountain ranges** and **highlands**. The highlands in the region include the **Upper Rhine Uplands**, an area comprising the Black Forest and the Palatinate region. The Upper Rhine Uplands are a major center for wine and fruit production because of their mild climate. The **South German "Stufenland"** is a hilly area with many natural caves in the regions of Swabia and Franconia. Between the "Stufenland" and the Rhine Basin lie numerous fertile valleys with terraced vineyards.

The **Upper Palatinate** and Bavarian Forests are heavily forested areas with sparsely populated river valleys. The Feldberg (1,493 meters) in the Bla Forest and Grosser Arber in the Bavari Forest are the highest mountains in sou ern Germany outside of the Alps.

The region south of the Danube River Bavaria forms a transition zone betwe the hilly uplands and the Alpine footh with their lakes and moors. In Germar the **Alps** rise abruptly in the southernmo sections of the country. The German Al are a 30 to 40 kilometer wide strip

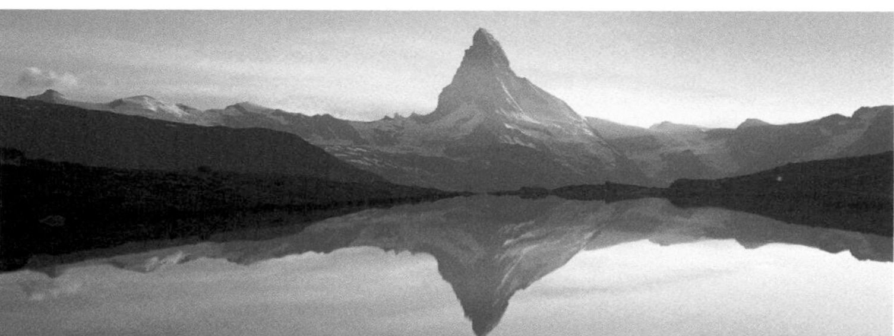

The Matterhorn is one of the most beautiful peaks in the Alps **Lh45**

The Moselle Valley German river valley and a major winemaking area – Burg Eltz (photo), a beautiful historic castle **Lh41**

The Rhine Valley The central section of the German Rhine Valley is a UNESCO world heritage site – numerous castles and fortresses – restored Burg Stahleck castle (photo) – the Lorelei Rock **Lh41**

Heidelberg Historic city on the Neckar River (photo) – picturesque old town – ruins of a medieval castle **Lj41**

Lake Constance Lake divided between Germany, Austria, and Switzerland – Reichenau Island is a world heritage site – historic castle in Meersburg (photo) **LjLk43**

Zurich Largest city and economic center of Switzerland – the Grossmuenster church (photo) is a city landmark – important museums: Rietberg Museum, Art Museum, and Swiss National Museum **Lj43**

Lake Thun The prettiest lake in the Berner Oberland region – several historic castles including Oberhofen (photo), Thun, and Spiez castles **Lh44**

Berner Oberland One of Switzerland's most beautiful regions with many lakes and mountains including Moench (photo) and Jungfrau (4,158 meters) – popular destination for mountain climbers **LgLh44**

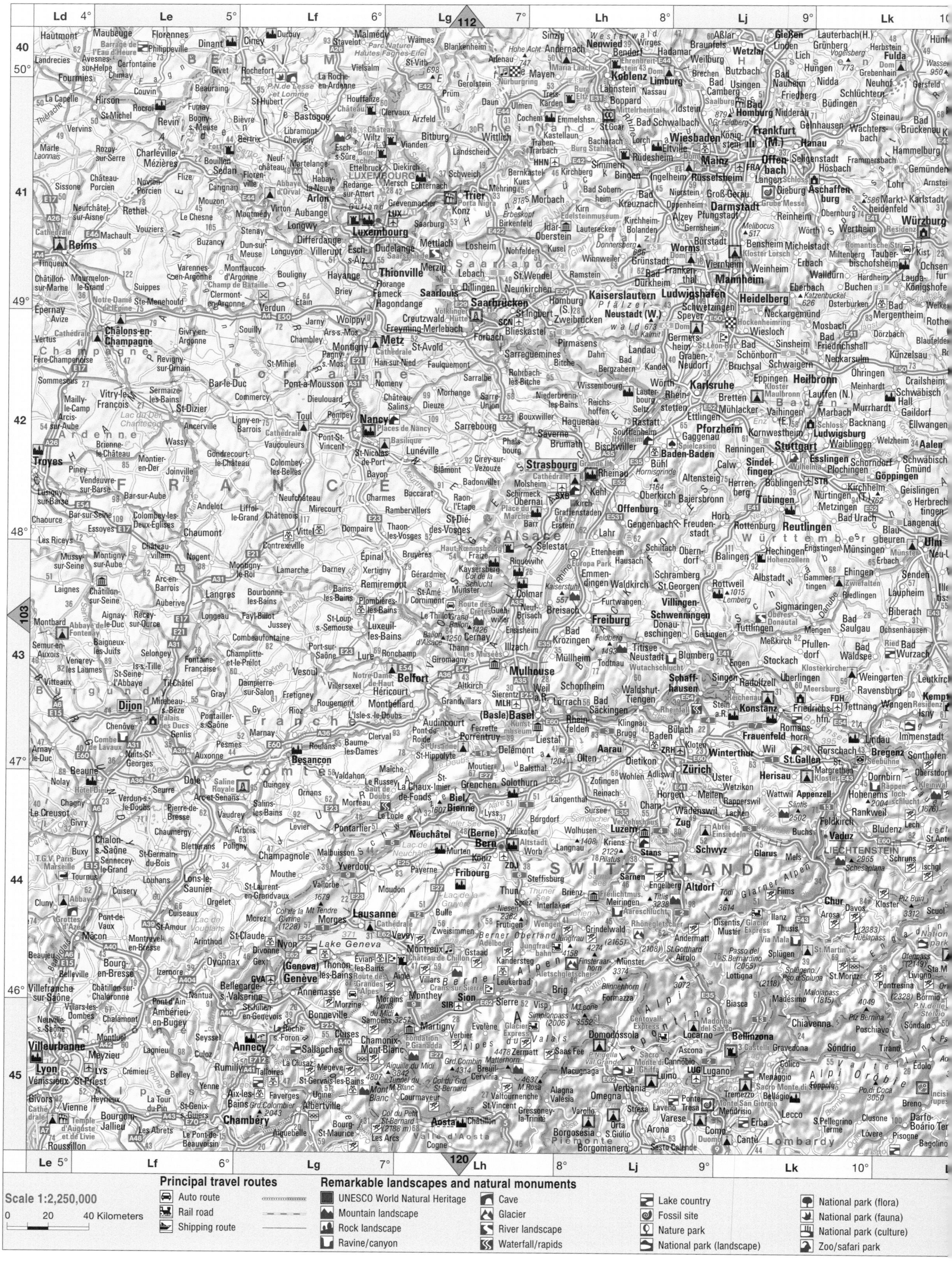

112
103
120

Scale 1:2,250,000
0 20 40 Kilometers

Principal travel routes
- Auto route
- Rail road
- Shipping route

Remarkable landscapes and natural monuments
- UNESCO World Natural Heritage
- Mountain landscape
- Rock landscape
- Ravine/canyon
- Cave
- Glacier
- River landscape
- Waterfall/rapids
- Lake country
- Fossil site
- Nature park
- National park (landscape)
- National park (flora)
- National park (fauna)
- National park (culture)
- Zoo/safari park

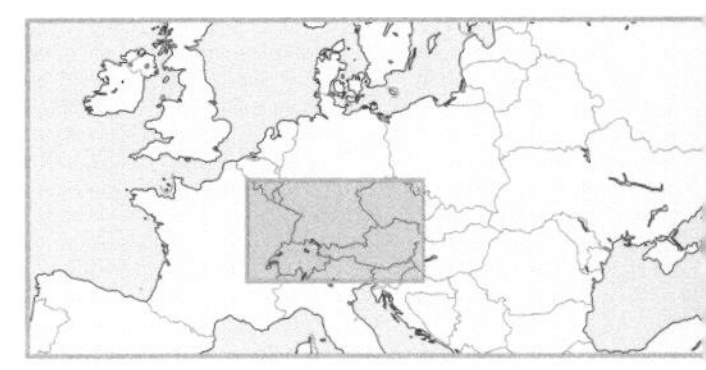

gh mountains with many picturesque ces. The **Zugspitze** (2,962 meters), near e Austrian border in Bavaria is the high- t mountain in Germany.

e Swiss Alps are divided into two main nges – northern and southern – by the **one** and **Rhine** rivers. More than two- rds of **Switzerland's** territory is cover- by the Alps. Switzerland's tallest ountains including the Matterhorn 478 meters) and Monte Rosa (4,637 meters) are located in the southern range. The **Jura Mountains**, a range in the Alps, covers most of northwestern Switzerland. Between the Jura Mountains and the southern range lies the densely populated central region of Switzerland which stretches from Lake Geneva in the west to Lake Constance in the northeast. In addition to its mountain peaks, Switzerland also features many rivers and lakes.

Austria is a small nation with a great variety of landscapes and an abundance of natural attractions. Like Switzerland much of Austria is covered by the mountains of the Alps. Austria's tallest mountains – all in the Salzburg, Tyrol, and Carinthia regions – are collectively referred to as **"Hohe Tauern."** The Grossglockner in East Tyrol rises 3,798 meters and is the highest mountain in the country. Northern Austria is dominated by the foothills of the Alps. The mountains north of the Danube are covered by large forests. The **Pannonian plain**, a fertile lowland, encompasses large sections of eastern Austria. Austria's capital, Vienna, is situated in a basin between mountain ranges and the Pannonian plain.

The **Inn** and the **Danube River** are the most important waterways in the country. Floods and avalanches in mountainous regions are the only significant natural threats to the country.

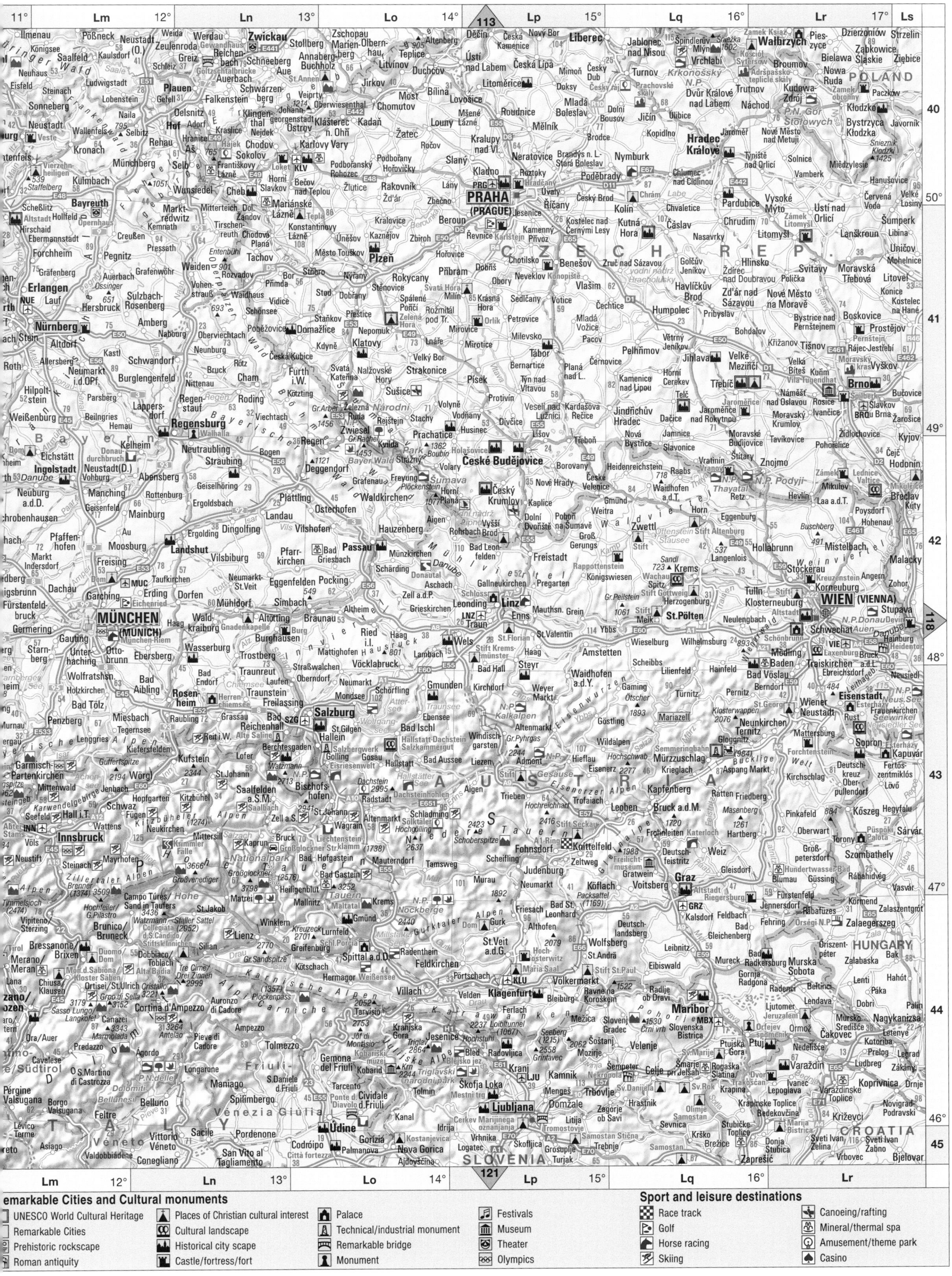

Germany's Romantic Road This popular tourist route between Würzburg and Füssen passes many popular tourist attractions. Highlights include Würzburg's royal residence (top photo) and the idyllic medieval town of Rothenburg (bottom photo). **Lk41**

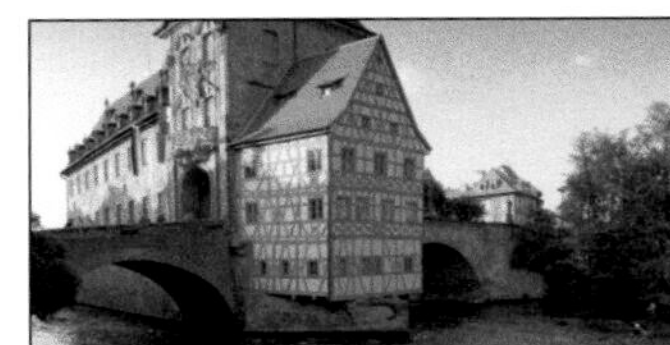

Bamberg City in Franconia – the historic old town is a UNESCO world heritage site – the old town hall (photo) is built atop a 15th century bridge **Ll41**

Augsburg Bavarian city with a history stretching over 2,000 years – Renaissance-era city hall (photo) **Ll42**

Munich The beautiful capital city of Bavaria has a vibrant cultural scene and countless historic buildings – Marienplatz – The English Garden, Europe's largest city park – medieval Church of our Lady/Frauenkirche (photo) **Lm42**

Neuschwanstein Castle World famous "fairy tale" castle built by Bavaria's Ludwig II – beautiful towers and pinnacles **Ll43**

Salzburg City in western Austria – the birthplace of Wolfgang Amadeus Mozart – annual music festival – baroque old town – historic palaces, churches, and squares – Hohensalzburg fortress **Lo43**

emarkable Cities and Cultural monuments

- UNESCO World Cultural Heritage
- Remarkable Cities
- Prehistoric rockscape
- Roman antiquity
- Places of Christian cultural interest
- Cultural landscape
- Historical city scape
- Castle/fortress/fort
- Palace
- Technical/industrial monument
- Remarkable bridge
- Monument
- Festivals
- Museum
- Theater
- Olympics

Sport and leisure destinations

- Race track
- Golf
- Horse racing
- Skiing
- Canoeing/rafting
- Mineral/thermal spa
- Amusement/theme park
- Casino

Poland

Poland can be seen as either the westernmost nation in Eastern Europe or the easternmost in Central Europe. The country can be divided into three distinct geographic regions stretching parallel to one another from north to south: the plains of western Poland, hilly areas in central Poland, and the mountainous east. Poland borders the Baltic Sea to the north. The country's 500-kilometer-long **Baltic coast** consist mostly of broad

white sandy beaches. Several lar bays and seaside lakes are located on t Baltic coast separated from the sea narrow spits of land. South of the coa in **Pomerania** lies a hilly region with hu dreds of lakes and moors. The **Vistu** Poland's longest river, flows through t center of Pomerania.

Pristine birch forests are common in t Polish region of Masuria **MaMc**

Szczecin Historic port city on the Baltic coast – Gothic town hall in the old town – national museum **Lp37**

Gdańsk (Danzig) Major port city that was once a leading member of the Hanseatic League – restored historic old town – the historic crane built in the 15th century is the city's landmark **Lt36**

Malbork Historic city in northern Poland – famous brick castle built in the 14th century by the Knights of the Teutonic Order – UNESCO world heritage site – the castle consists of three separate structures **Lu36**

Frombork Town with a Gothic town hall built on a fortified hill in the 14th century – famed astronomer Copernicus lived here in the 16th century **Lu36**

Masuria Region in northeastern Poland with many lakes and forests – holiday destination with many recreational opportunities **MaMc37**

Święta Lipka Baroque pilgrimage church – built in the 17th century – located in a heavily forested area **Mb36**

Białowieski National Park National Park on the Belorussian border – the park encompasses sections of Europe's largest remaining virgin forest – bison herds inhabit the park **MdMe38**

Scale 1:2,250,000
0 20 40 Kilometers

Principal travel routes
- Auto route
- Rail road
- Shipping route

Remarkable landscapes and natural monuments
- UNESCO World Natural Heritage
- Mountain landscape
- Rock landscape
- River landscape
- Lake country
- Nature park
- National park (landscape)
- National park (flora)
- National park (fauna)
- National park (culture)
- Coastal landscape
- Beach
- Island

e Oder and Neisse Rivers form most the border between Poland and Germany. German's capital city Berlin lies just kilometers away from the Polish border. Most of Poland is covered by vast **ains** and much of the country's land is ed for agriculture. Warsaw, Poland's pital lies on the banks of the Vistula ver in a lowlands region. The Vistula is 066 kilometers long and its basin covers er 200,000 square kilometers.

South of central Poland's plains lie the hills and uplands of Silesia and southeastern Poland. Krakow, Poland's second largest city, is located in the country's southeast. The city contains an impressive collection of well preserved historic architecture. The southernmost region of Poland is the most mountainous region in the country. The **Sudeten Mountains** form a natural border between Poland and the Czech Republic. The western **Carpathian Mountains** separate the country from the Slovak Republic. Since the collapse of the Soviet Union two new nations now border Poland to the east: Ukraine with its vast plains and heavily forested Belarus. Northeast of Poland lies Lithuania, a country that, together with Poland, ruled a vast empire during the middle ages. The Russian enclave of Kaliningrad was part of the historic German kingdom of Prussia until the end of the Second World War. Kaliningrad is now seperated from mainland Russia by the territory of Lithuania and Belarus.

Poland has a temperate continental climate with cold winters and warm summers. The climate of the country's coastal areas is significantly different from that of the interior. The Baltic coast tends to be cooler than the interior in summer and warmer than the interior in winter.

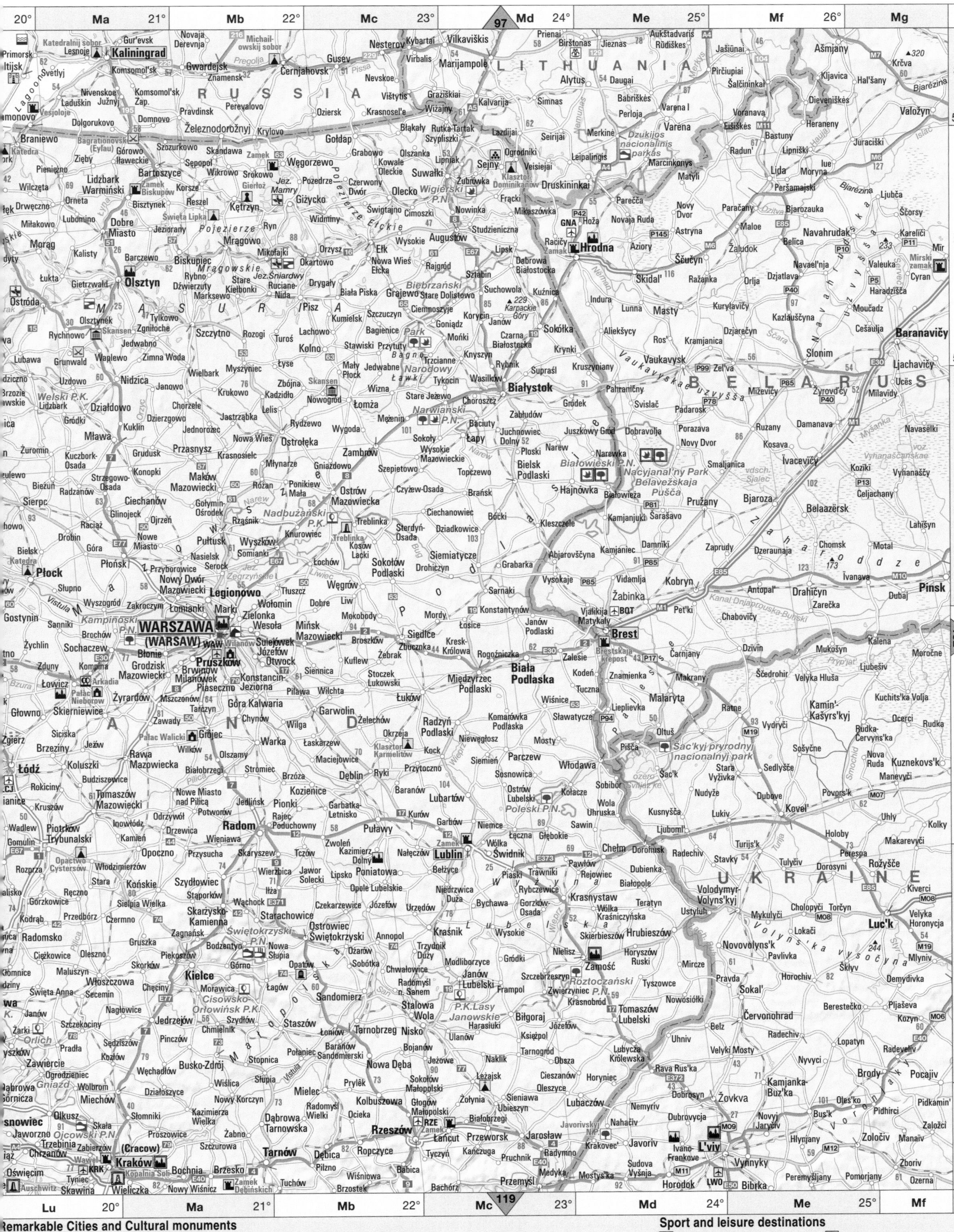

Warsaw The city's old town, a world heritage site, was largely destroyed in the Second World War and later restored. The city features the former Royal Palace and St. John's Cathedral (top photo). Market Square is surrounded by historic patrician houses (bottom photo). **Ma38**

Wrocław (Breslau) Capital of Silesia – Gothic town hall in the old town district of Rynek – historic church and cathedral on Tum Island **Ls39**

Jawór The town has a "Church of Peace" built in the 17th century (photo) – the church was designated a UNESCO world heritage site in 2001 **Lr39**

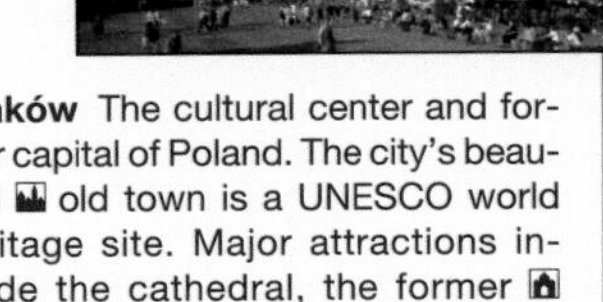

Kraków The cultural center and former capital of Poland. The city's beautiful old town is a UNESCO world heritage site. Major attractions include the cathedral, the former Royal Palace (top photo), and the large market square (bottom photo). **Lu40**

Zamość In 1508, the town was built in a wilderness on the orders of Poland's ruler Jan Zamoyski – the historic old town is a UNESCO world heritage site **Md40**

Remarkable Cities and Cultural monuments

- UNESCO World Cultural Heritage
- Remarkable Cities
- Pre- and early history
- Places of Christian cultural interest
- Cultural landscape
- Historical city scape
- Castle/fortress/fort
- Palace
- Remarkable lighthouse
- Remarkable bridge
- Theater of war/battlefield
- Monument
- Memorial
- Museum
- Theater
- Olympics

Sport and leisure destinations

- Race track
- Horse racing
- Skiing
- Canoeing/rafting
- Seaport
- Beach resort
- Mineral/thermal spa
- Amusement/theme park

Before the First World War the countries in this Central European region were all parts of the Austro-Hungarian Empire ruled by the Habsburg dynasty. The region has diverse landscapes and many cultural attractions. Most of the region is covered by mountains and rolling hills. **Bohemia** in the Czech Republic is surrounded by several mountain ranges including sections of the Erz and Sudeten Mountains which form a natural

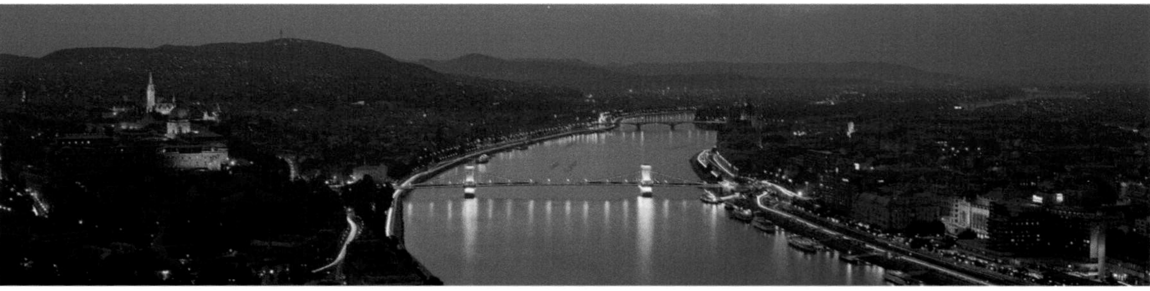

boundary between the Czech Repub and Germany, Poland, and Austria. T **Bohemian Basin** contains the Labe a Vltava, the longest rivers in the Cze Republic.

Slovakia, officially known as the Slov Republic, is a small mountainous natic Slovakia's highest mountains are locat

Budapest, Hungary's historic and bea tiful capital on the Danube River **Lu**

Mariánské Lázně Famous spa town in Bohemia – grand colonnades – historic architecture including hotels **Ln41**

Prague The capital city of the Czech Republic was founded in the 10th century. The city's extensive old town is a UNESCO world heritage site. Prague old city hall (top photo) was constructed in the 13th century from a row of seperate houses. Historic Charles Bridge and Prague Castle are two of the city's most visited attractions (bottom photo). **Lp40**

Karlštejn Castle Castle 28 kilometers southwest of Prague – built by Charles IV in the 14th century **Lp41**

Český Krumlov The old town features a hilltop castle – UNESCO world heritage site – historic Latran district – Egon Schiele Art Center **Lp42**

Bratislava Slovakia's capital and largest city – in the foothills of the Carpathian Mountains – university city – national museum – historic old town – Gothic St. Martin's Cathedral **Ls42**

Spišský hrad Largest castle in Slovakia – founded in the 12th century – UNESCO world heritage site **Ma42**

Scale 1:2,250,000

0 20 40 Kilometers

Principal travel routes

- Auto route
- Rail road
- Shipping route

Remarkable landscapes and natural monuments

- UNESCO World Natural Heritage
- Mountain landscape
- Rock landscape
- Ravine/canyon
- Cave
- River landscape
- Waterfall/rapids
- Lake country
- Nature park
- National park (landscape)
- National park (flora)
- National park (fauna)
- National park (culture)

the High Tatra Mountains, along the ›lish-Slovakian border. Gerlachovsky ›t, the highest Slovak mountain, rises ›655 meters. Slovakia's capital city, ›atislava, lies in the Danube River ›asin. The Slovakian section of the basin ›etches to the Ukrainian border and is ›e flattest region in the country. The ›arpathian Mountains begin near Bra›slava and stretch through Slovakia, ›omania, Poland, and the Ukraine.

In contrast to neighboring Slovakia, **Hungary** is mostly flat country. The vast **Pannonian plain** is the remnant of an ancient lake and covers most of southern and eastern Hungary. A major agricultural area, the Hungarian sections of the plain are called the Great Alföld or Great Hungarian Plain. Northwestern Hungary is covered by the Little Alföld, a smaller plain separated from the Great Alföld by a low mountain range. The **Danube River** flows through the middle of the Great Alföld and passes through Budapest. Hungary's capital and largest city, Budapest, is built on a series of hills. **Lake Balaton** (592 km²) in western Hungary is the largest freshwater lake in Central Europe. The shallow lake has an average depth of just 3.5 meters.

Hungary and neighboring **Austria** were once the dominant nations in the vast Astro-Hungarian Empire that once ruled most of Central Europe. Vienna, the capital of modern Austria, was once the administrative center of the empire. The region around Vienna is a transition zone between the Pannonian plain and the **Alps**. More than two-thirds of Austria's land is covered by the Alps. The **Hohen Tauern** in western and central Austria include some of the country's highest mountains including the Großglockner (3,798 meters), Austria's highest peak.

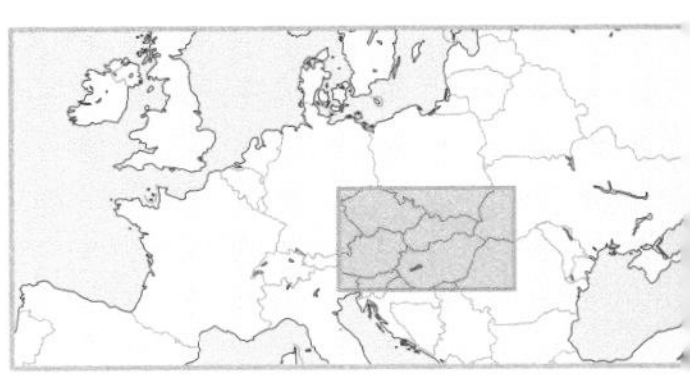

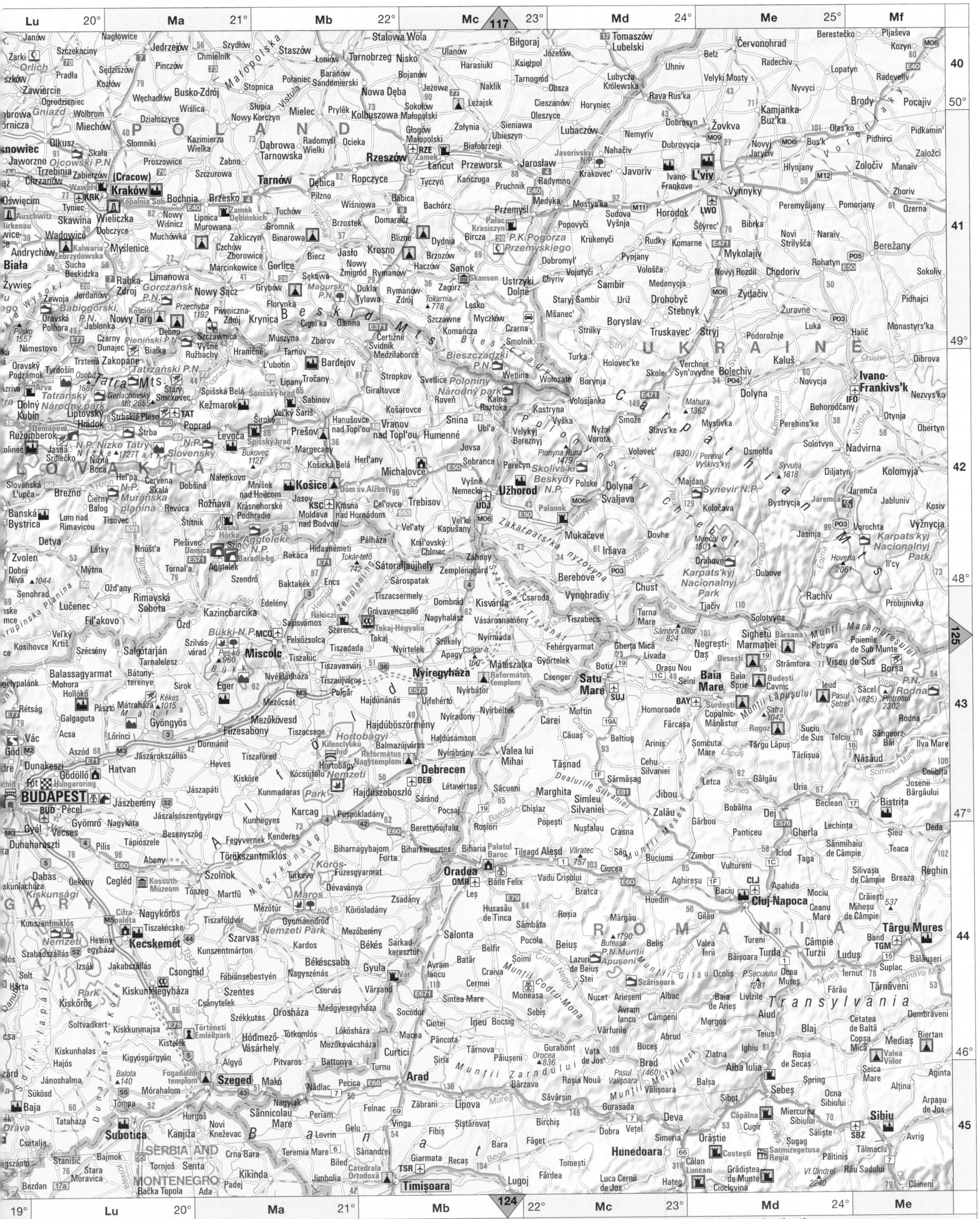

Hallstatt Picturesque village in Austrian Alps along Lake Hallstatt – historic salt mines – UNESCO world heritage site **Lo43**

Wachau Austrian winemaking region along the Danube – idyllic village – photo: Dürnstein **Lq42**

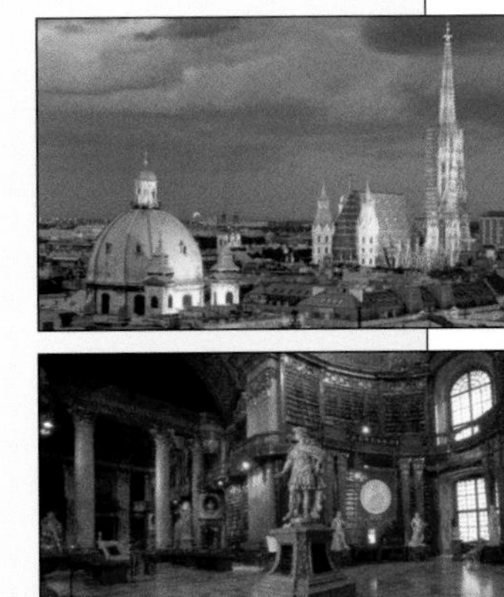

Vienna Once the center of a vast empire, Vienna is now the capital of the Austrian Republic. The charming city on the Danube is a popular tourist destination. Vienna's medieval center is surrounded by baroque and 19th century buildings. The St. Charles' and St. Stephan's cathedrals (top photo) are Vienna's most famous landmarks. The ceremonial room (bottom photo) in Vienna's old national library is the largest baroque library chamber in the world. **Lr42**

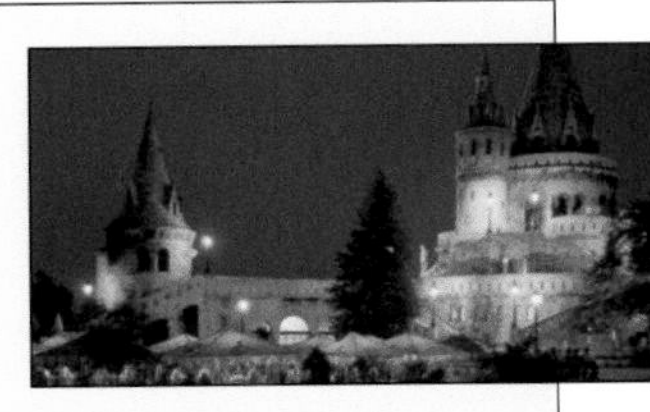

Budapest Hungary's capital city boasts countless art and architectural treasures. Castle Hill is a UNESCO world heritage site. The famous chain bridge, near the Hungarian parliament building, was completed in 1849. The area around beautiful Fisherman's Bastion (photo) offers good views of the city. **Lu43**

Hortobágyi National Park Hungarian national park – grazing areas in the Puszta – photo: cattle herd **Mb43**

Remarkable Cities and Cultural monuments

- UNESCO World Cultural Heritage
- Remarkable Cities
- Roman antiquity
- Places of Christian cultural interest
- Cultural landscape
- Historical city scape
- Castle/fortress/fort
- Palace
- Technical/industrial monument
- Remarkable bridge
- Monument
- Memorial
- Museum
- Theater
- World exhibition

Sport and leisure destinations

- Race track
- Golf
- Horse racing
- Skiing
- Wind surfing
- Canoeing/rafting
- Beach resort
- Mineral/thermal spa

Northern **Italy** consists of the northern half of the Italian mainland on the Apennine peninsula, which takes its name from the Apennine Mountains. The northernmost regions of Italy are covered by the **Alps**, the alpine foothills and many mountain lakes. Northeast of **Lake Garda**, Italy's largest lake, rise the **Dolomites**, a fascinating section of the Alps with high, craggy mountains. Mont Blanc (4,807 meters), the highest moun-

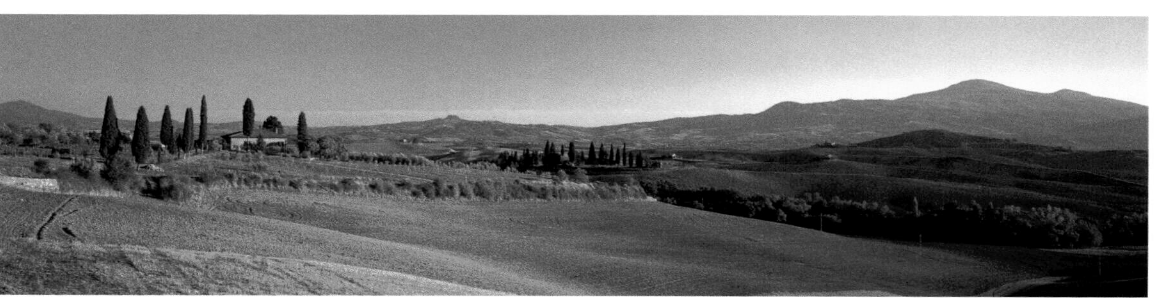

tain in Western Europe, is situated on t border between France and northe Italy. The region to the south of the al ine foothills consists of fertile plains inc ding the **Po Valley**. The **Apenni Mountains** form a natural barrier b tween the western and eastern sectio of the Italian peninsula. The western

Rolling hills cover much of Tuscany (Italy) **LlLm**

The Dolomites Alpine mountains east of Bolzano in northernmost Italy – famous peak: Marmolada (3,343 meters) – wine-making village St. Magdalena (photo) in the Villnos Valley **Lm44**

Milan The economic center of Italy and a major center of the international fashion industry – population, 2.3 million – landmark: Duomo cathedral (photo) – historic shopping center Galleria Vittorio Emanuele II – La Scala opera house **Lk45**

Lake Garda The largest lake in Italy covering 370 km² – name taken from the town Garda – amusement parks – Rocca Scalgera in Sirmione (photo) **Ll45**

Cinque Terre Beautiful rocky coast in northern Italy – interesting coastal islands – national park – picturesque villages – Vernazza has a charming harbor **Lk46**

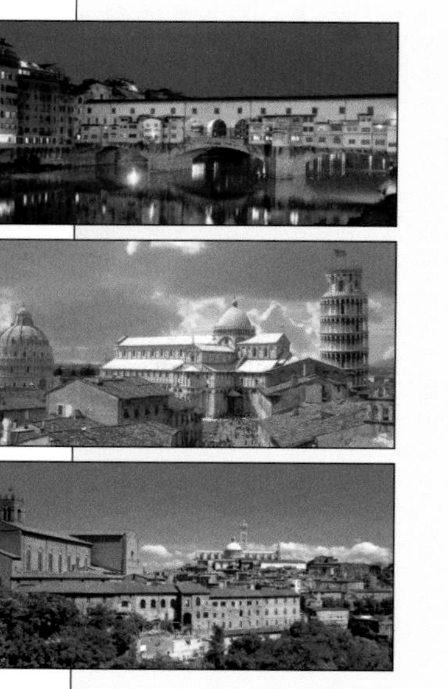

Tuscany's Historic Cities and Towns The beautiful cities and towns of Tuscany draw millions of tourists to the region. The cities feature spectacular collections of priceless art and architectural masterpieces. Photos from top to bottom: Florence **(Lm47)**, Pisa **(Ll47)**, and Sienna **(Lm47)**. All three cities are designated UNESCO world heritage sites.

Scale 1:2,250,000

0 20 40 Kilometers

Principal travel routes

- Auto route
- Rail road
- Shipping route

Remarkable landscapes and natural monuments

- UNESCO World Natural Heritage
- Mountain landscape
- Ravine/canyon
- Extinct volcano
- Cave
- Glacier
- River landscape
- Waterfall/rapids
- Lake country
- Nature park
- National park (landscape)
- National park (flora)
- National park (fauna)
- National park (culture)
- Coastal landscape
- Underwater reserve

ons of the northern peninsula are covered by rolling hills and basins, while the stern regions consist of mountain ridges and river valleys extending up to the rrow coastal areas. Northern Italy's **coasts** comprise sandy beaches, eep cliffs, lagoons, and rocky bays. e Julian Alps stretch through most mountainous Northwestern **Slovenia** region with many lakes and **Triglav** 864 meters), the country's highest mountain. Between Triglav National Park and Slovenia's coastal region lies an area with interesting natural sights including plateaus, rivers, and numerous caves. The areas south of the basin, around Ljubljana, have rolling hills covered by vineyards and fruit farms. Beyond the Mur River, in the easternmost regions of Slovenia, lie sections of the vast **Pannonian plain**.

Croatia can be divided into three distinctive geographic regions: the coastal region along the **Adriatic**, the areas on the **Pannonian plain**, and the **mountainous regions**. Croatia's jagged Adriatic coast, a popular tourist attraction, features sandy beaches, cliffs, and numerous coastal islands. The mountainous regions of Croatia include the mountains near the northern coast and between the Istria peninsula as well as the hills of northern Croatia. In eastern Croatia, the Pannonian plain stretches between the Drava and Sava rivers.

Bosnia-Herzegovina is a mountainous nation with fertile lowlands in the northern sections of the country. Central Bosnia is a heavily forested area encompassing several large valleys. The country's short **Adriatic coast** is only twenty kilometers long. Devastated by an ethnic civil war in the 1990s, the country is now in the process of rebuilding.

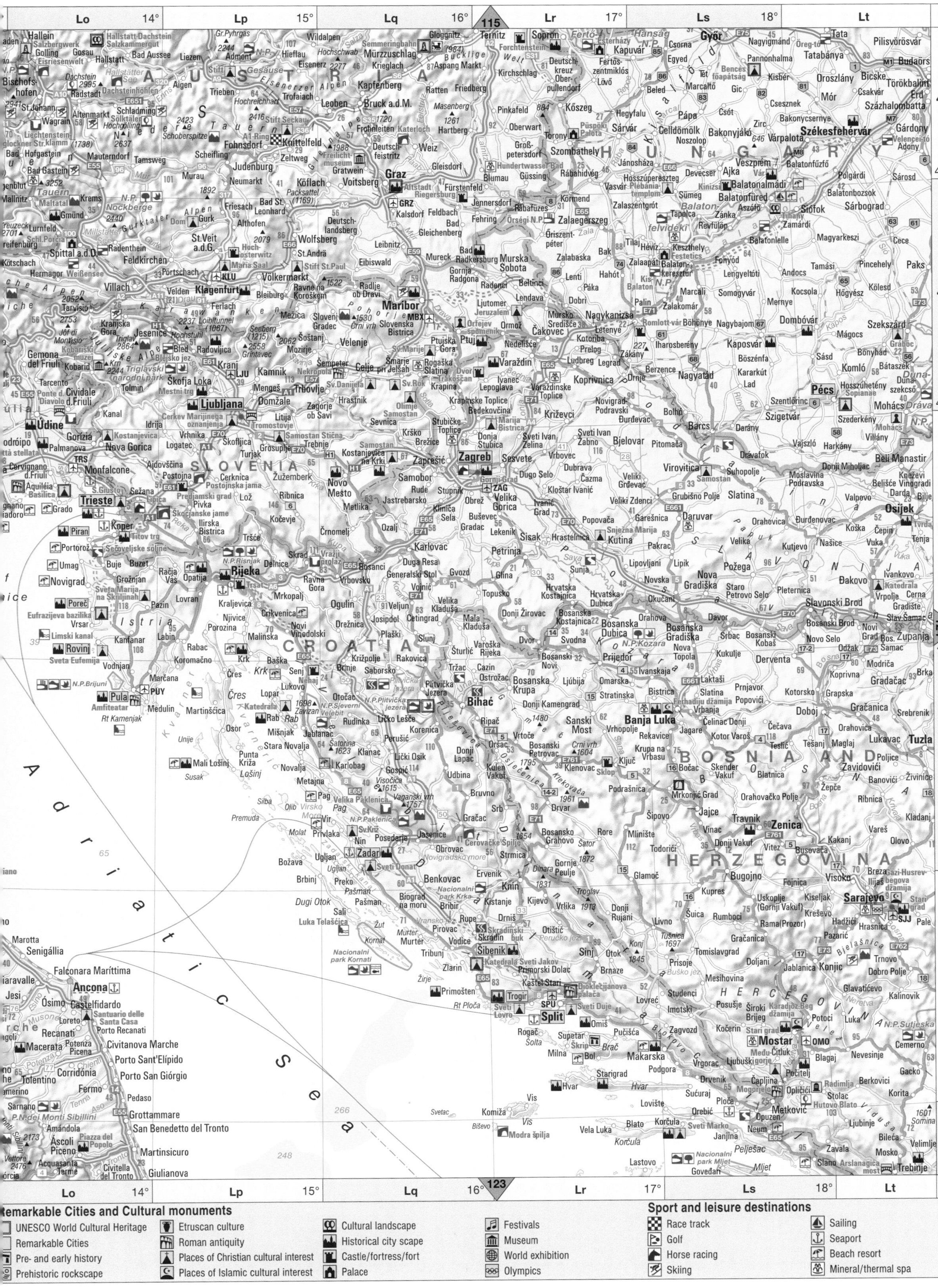

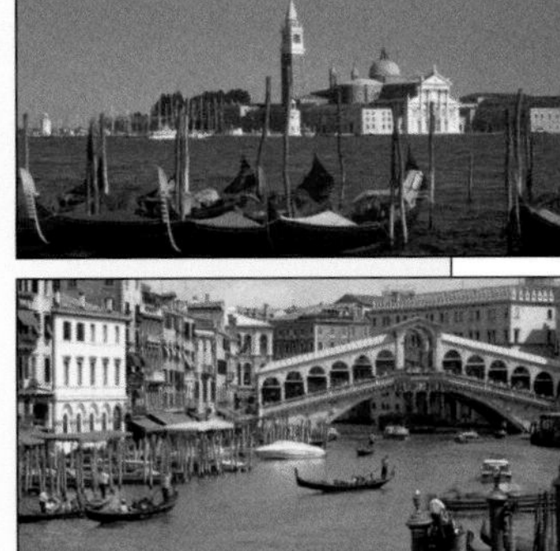

Venice Historic old town (UNESCO world heritage site) containing San Marco Piazza, St. Mark's Basilica, and the lagoon. Gondolas (top photo) are floating symbols of the city. The Canal Grande is the longest canal in Venice. The Rialto Bridge (bottom photo) is one of Venice's 400 bridges. **Ln45**

Ravenna City on Italy's Adriatic coast – San Vitale Basilica contains interesting mosaics (photo) – grave of the poet and author Dante Alighieri **Ln46**

Ljubljana Capital and largest city in Slovenia – baroque and art deco architecture in the city center – castles, palaces, and palatial houses **Lp44**

Istria Peninsula in northwestern Croatia – towns with historic Venetian architecture – Roman amphitheater in Pula – Rovinj cathedral (photo) **Lo45**

Plitvicka Jezera This Croatian national park is a UNESCO world heritage site – diverse fauna and flora – beautiful lakes – waterfalls and river rapids **Lq46**

Trogir Historic old town – UNESCO world heritage site – numerous historic churches including the St. Lawrence cathedral – palaces from the Venetian era **Lr47**

Remarkable Cities and Cultural monuments

- UNESCO World Cultural Heritage
- Remarkable Cities
- Pre- and early history
- Prehistoric rockscape
- Etruscan culture
- Roman antiquity
- Places of Christian cultural interest
- Places of Islamic cultural interest
- Cultural landscape
- Historical city scape
- Castle/fortress/fort
- Palace
- Festivals
- Museum
- World exhibition
- Olympics

Sport and leisure destinations

- Race track
- Golf
- Horse racing
- Skiing
- Sailing
- Seaport
- Beach resort
- Mineral/thermal spa

The Apennine Mountains stretch through the entire boot shaped southern half of the Italian Peninsula. The region of Abruzzo contains the highest peaks in the Apennines, including the mountains of the Gran Sasso d'Italia Range, several of which rise higher than 2,500 meters. The area north of Italy's capital city **Rome** consists of rolling hills and lakes that were formed in ancient volcanic craters. Vatican City, the spiritual center of millions of Roman Catholics, is a small sovereign state in the middle of Rome. The flat plains of Italy's southwestern coast – especially **Calabria** and the area around **Naples** – are the most volcanically active regions in Italy. In addition to the active volcanoes Mount Etna and Mount Vesuvius, the region also features dormant volcanoes and large fields of v canic stone. Numerous rivers flow par lel to the coast through the mountainc regions of southwestern Italy. The sm peninsula in southeastern Italy is cove ed by heavily cultivated, flat plains. T coastal areas in Italy's far south featu kilometers of long white sand beach and beautiful cliffs. Italy's **Amalfi Coa** region is a popular tourist destinati with lush vegetation and rocky coastline

Mount Etna on Sicily is the highest active volcano in Europe **LpLq53**

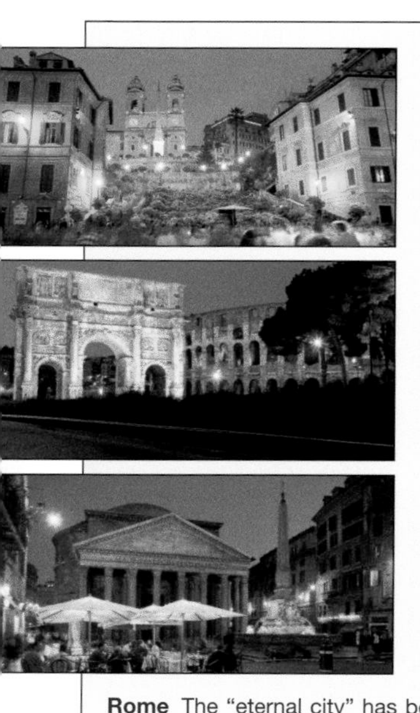

Rome The "eternal city" has been a center of western civilization for more than 2,000 years. The city, built on seven hills, has important historic buildings including the Forum Romanum and countless art treasures. The city also boasts many historic churches. Photos from top to bottom: the Spanish Steps, Arch of Constantine, and the Pantheon **Ln49**

Vatican City (The Holy See) Small sovereign enclave in Rome – residence of the Pope – Palace of the Vatican – The Sistine Chapel – St. Peter's Basilica **Ln49**

Pompeii When Mount Vesuvius erupted in 79 AD, the city of Pompeii was buried under a layer of ash and lava. More than three-quarters of the city (top photo) has been excavated. One of the most impressive sights is the Villa del Misteri (bottom photo) with its frescoes. The neighboring Roman town of Herculaneum was also buried after the eruption. **Lp50**

Capri The most beautiful island in the Gulf of Naples – grand villas – beautiful gardens – historic town center – Grotta Azzura, the world famous Blue Grotto **Lp50**

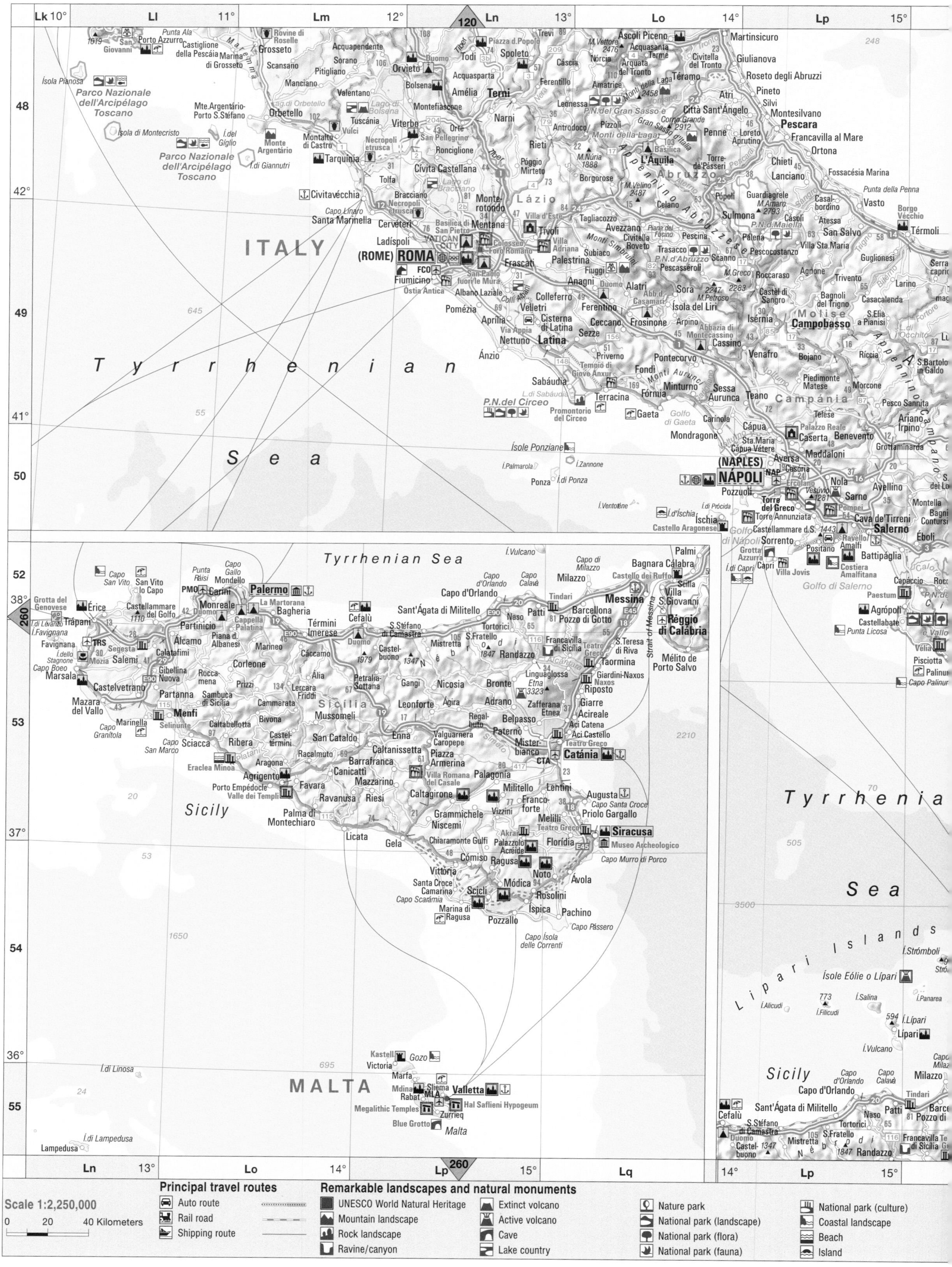

Scale 1:2,250,000

0 20 40 Kilometers

Principal travel routes

- Auto route
- Rail road
- Shipping route

Remarkable landscapes and natural monuments

- UNESCO World Natural Heritage
- Mountain landscape
- Rock landscape
- Ravine/canyon
- Extinct volcano
- Active volcano
- Cave
- Lake country
- Nature park
- National park (landscape)
- National park (flora)
- National park (fauna)
- National park (culture)
- Coastal landscape
- Beach
- Island

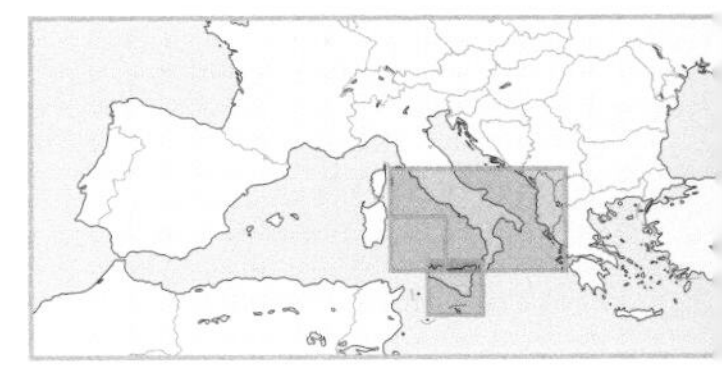

e 405-kilometer-long **Tiber River** is e longest river in southern Italy. **Sicily**, the largest Italian island, is sepa-ed from the mainland by the **Strait of essina**. The densely populated island geologically active and earthquakes e not uncommon on Sicily. Northern cily is dominated by craggy mountains, ile the island's south is a hilly yet fer- region. **Mount Etna**, Sicily's highest ountain is an active volcano which has erupted several times in recent decades. The **Aeolian Islands** off the northern coast of Sicily contain two more active volcanoes: Strómboli and Vulcano.

Malta is a nation consisting of a group of dry islands with no rivers and few sources of freshwater. The largest island in the group, also called **Malta**, is covered by hills in the southeast and valleys and fruit fields in the northwest. **Gozo**, the second largest Maltese island, is more fertile than neighboring Malta and covered by a large plateau. **Comino**, the smallest of the three inhabited islands, has many attractive beaches. The country has a pleasant Mediterranean climate and tourism is an important sector of Malta's economy.

More than three-quarters of **Albania's** territory is covered by mountains. The highest mountains are located in the northern and northeastern sections of the country. Korab, the country's highest mountain, rises 2,764 meters. Western Albania, including the coastal areas, is the least mountainous and most densely populated region in the country. Most of Albania's coast consists of marshy areas with numerous lagoons, while the south has a rocky coastline. Albania's three largest lakes are all situated along the country's borders with neighboring countries.

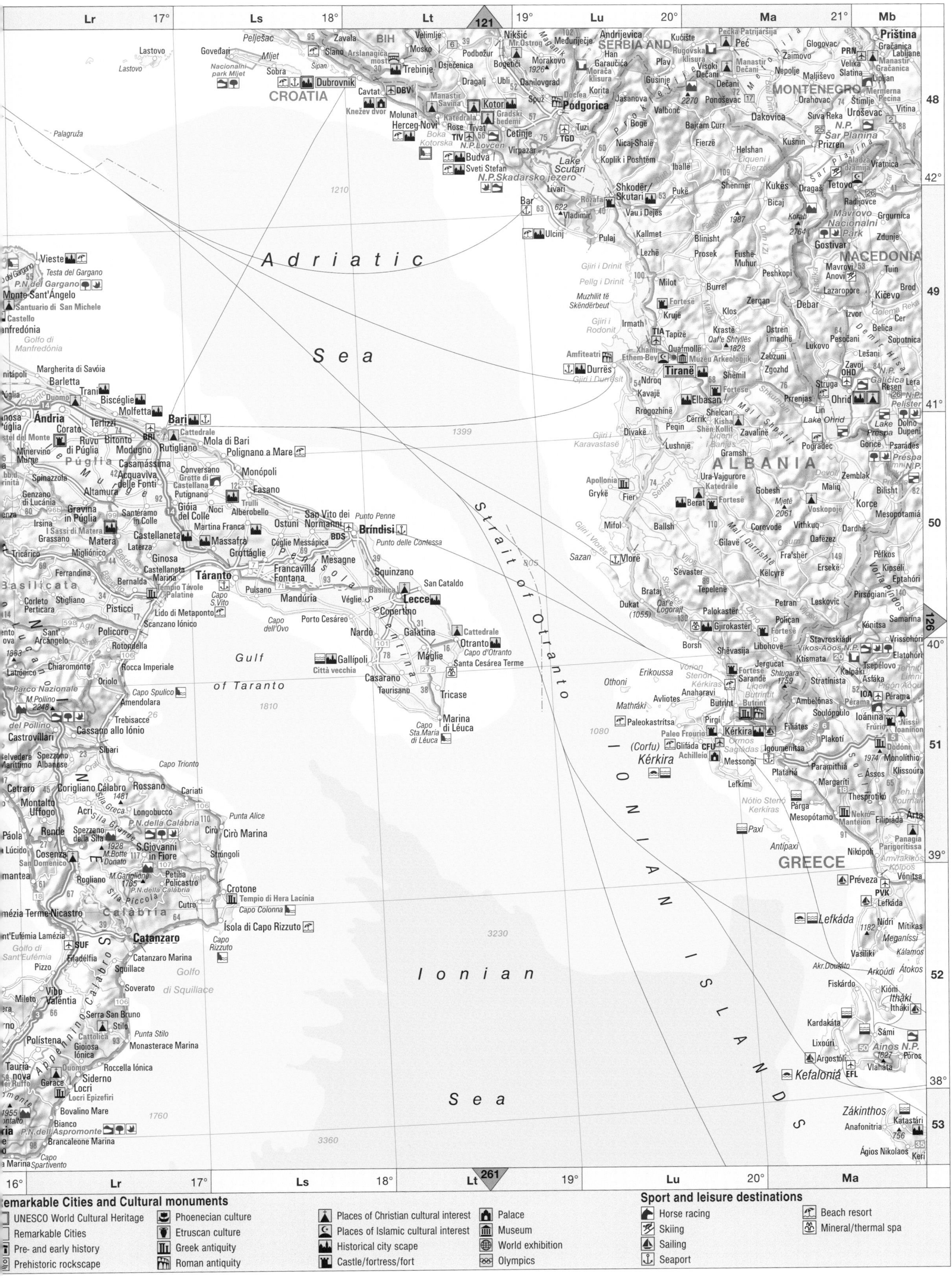

The Amalfi Coast One of Europe's most beautiful coastal areas – UNESCO world natural heritage site – Positano has charming pastel colored cottages and palaces – Santa Maria Assunta church **Lp50**

Castel del Monte Unique octagonal castle built by Frederick II in the 13th century – ornamental windows – UNESCO world heritage site **Lr49**

Aeolian Islands Seven volcanic islands north of Sicily – Strómboli and Vulcano are active volcanos – ancient ruins **LpLq52**

Agrigento Founded as a Greek colony between 600-500 BC – Greek temples in the Valley of Temples – well preserved Temple of Concord (photo) **Lo53**

Temple of Segesta Impressive and well-preserved building erected by the Dorian Greeks and never completed **Ln53**

Malta Malta's capital city Valletta (top photo) has one of the most attractive harbors in Europe and is a UNESCO world heritage site. Valletta has baroque and renaissance architecture. The Grand Master's Palace is one of the most impressive sights. Maesaxlockk (bottom photo) is a beautiful fishing village. **Lp54/55**

emarkable Cities and Cultural monuments

- UNESCO World Cultural Heritage
- Remarkable Cities
- Pre- and early history
- Prehistoric rockscape
- Phoenecian culture
- Etruscan culture
- Greek antiquity
- Roman antiquity
- Places of Christian cultural interest
- Places of Islamic cultural interest
- Historical city scape
- Castle/fortress/fort
- Palace
- Museum
- World exhibition
- Olympics

Sport and leisure destinations

- Horse racing
- Skiing
- Sailing
- Seaport
- Beach resort
- Mineral/thermal spa

West of Romania, the vast plains of the Carpathian Basin stretch south from the city of Budapest in Hungary to Belgrade in Serbia. North of Budapest rise the mountains of the **Mátra Range**, which stretches north to the Tatra Mountains in Slovakia.

The **Danube River** is the most important waterway in this region of Europe. Before it reaches its delta on the Black Sea, the Danube passes through many large cities, including Belgrade and B dapest. Large cargo ships transp goods along the Danube and the rive one of the busiest transport routes b tween Western Europe and the Balk nations. River cruises offer tourists chance to enjoy the Danube's beau Since the collapse of Yugoslavia, **Ro**

One of the wider sections of the Danube; near Orsova in Romania **Mc**

Bistrița Monastery Orthodox monastery built in the 16th century – located in the eastern Carpathian Mountains **Me43**

Cluj-Napoca Historic university town – the city has a very long and rich history – St. Michael's church (photo) **Md44**

Sighişoara Town with a well preserved medieval center – UNESCO world heritage site – birthplace of Vlad Tepes, the inspiration for Count Dracula myths **Me44**

Biertan Large church complex in Transylvania – defensive towers and high defensive walls **Me44**

Alba Iulia The largest fortress complex in Romania – ten-kilometer-long defensive walls – orthodox cathedral **Md44**

Timişoara Largest city in Romania's Banat region – historic architecture from the era of the Habsburg Empire **Mb45**

Belgrade Capital city of Serbia and Montenegro on the Danube River – population 1.2 million – Kalemegdan Fortress **Ma46**

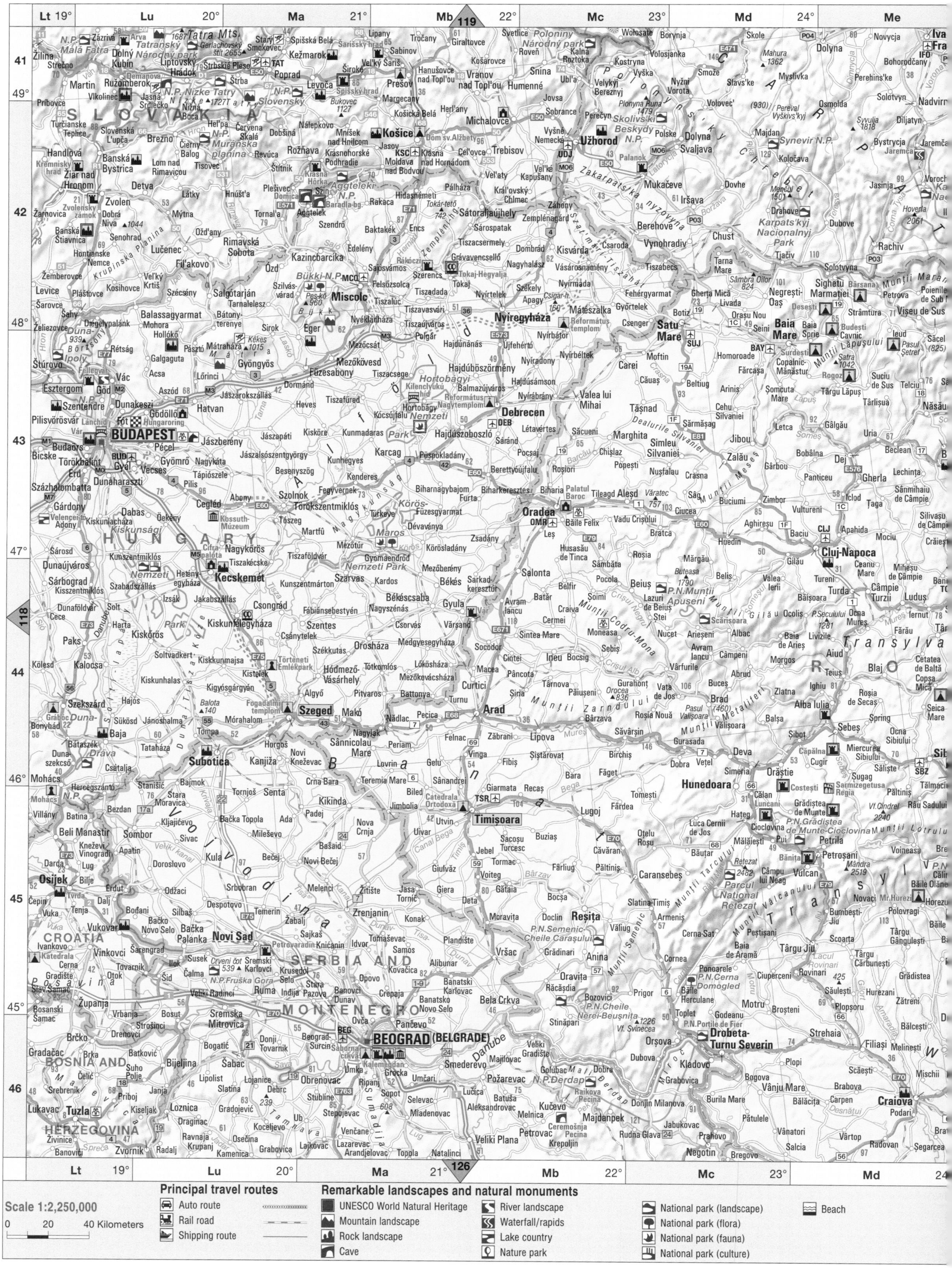

Scale 1:2,250,000

0 20 40 Kilometers

Principal travel routes

- Auto route
- Rail road
- Shipping route

Remarkable landscapes and natural monuments

- UNESCO World Natural Heritage
- Mountain landscape
- Rock landscape
- Cave
- River landscape
- Waterfall/rapids
- Lake country
- Nature park
- National park (landscape)
- National park (flora)
- National park (fauna)
- National park (culture)
- Beach

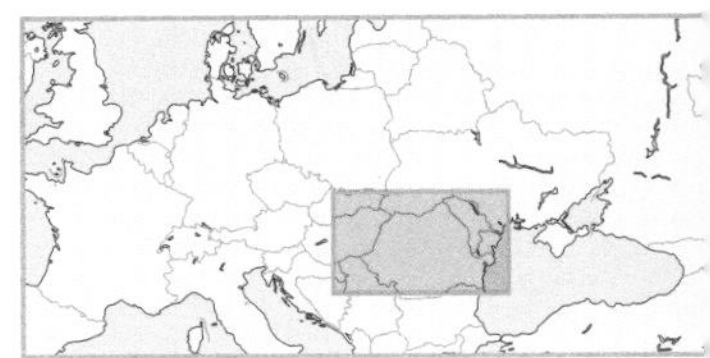

ia is the largest nation in southeastern rope. The country consists mostly of ee historic regions separated by mountain ranges and rivers: Walachia, manian Moldavia, and Transylvania. e Banat region in southeastern Roma, was Hungarian territory from the e 18th century until the end of the First rld War.

e **Carpathian Mountains** stretch ough Romania from the southeast to the northern areas along the Ukrainian border. Transylvania is a hilly region surrounded by mountains – including **Moldoveanu**, the highest mountain in Romania, rising 2,544 meters. The Romanian region of Moldavia encompasses many river valleys, inactive volcanic mountains, and the largest forest in Romania. Southern Romania is a mostly flat region containing the most productive grain growing areas in the country.

The interior area around the Black Sea coast is a fertile flat plain stretching to the Bulgarian border – a border that has been the subject of dispute more than once. The many streams and tributaries in the Danube river delta form a natural boundary between Romania and Ukraine.

Moldova is a small landlocked country between the Danube and Prut Rivers. Before its independence in 1991, Moldova was a republic in the Soviet Union. Moldova consists mainly of rolling hills and plains as well as numerous rivers. Mount Balanesti, the highest point in the country, rises just 430 meters. The country has an abundance of fertile land, a good climate, and a large winemaking industry. Modern Moldova encompasses most of the historic Romanian-speaking region of Bessarabia and still has strong cultural and historic connections to Romania.

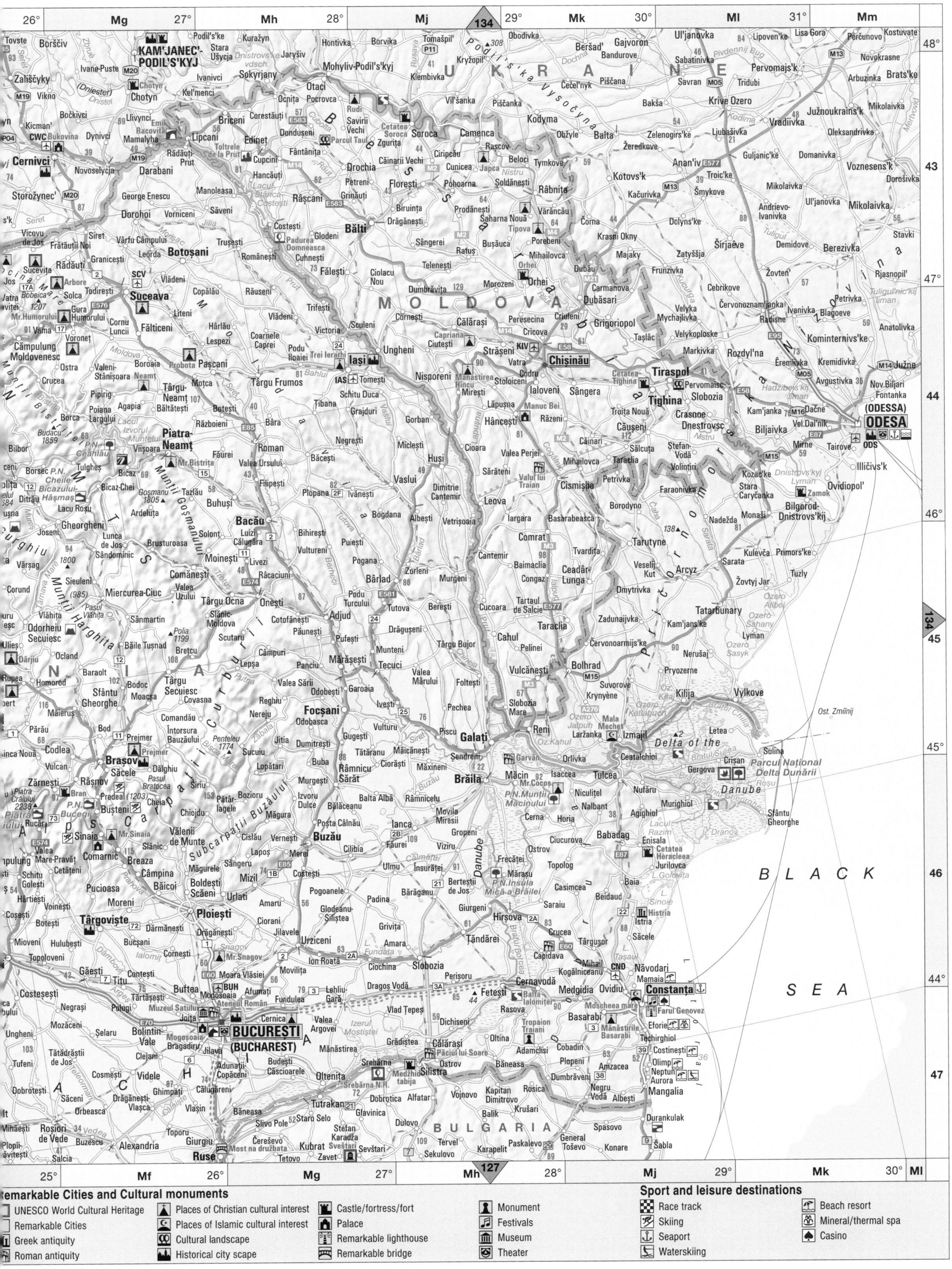

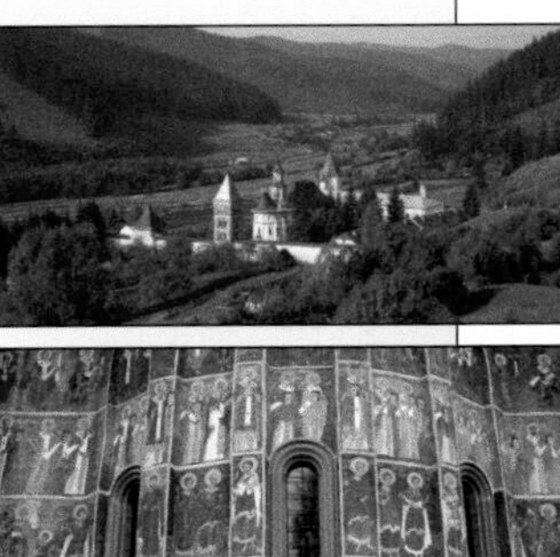

Romania's Monasteries Many of the beautifully painted churches and monasteries of northeastern Romania are UNESCO world heritage sites – including Putna (top photo), Sucevita (middle photo) with its well preserved wall paintings, and Humor Monastery (bottom photo). **MfMg43**

Chişinău Capital of Moldova – largely Stalinist era architecture – historic orthodox churches **Mj43**

Bran Castle Also known as Dracula's castle – once a citadel against the Ottoman armies – center of "Dracula" tourism **Mf45**

Bucureşti (Bucharest) Capital of Romania – population, 2.1 million – the former palace (photo) of the dictator Ceausescu now houses Romania's parliament **Mg46**

Danube River Delta UNESCO world natural heritage site – around 150 fish species – habitat for migrating birds **Mk45/46**

Remarkable Cities and Cultural monuments

- UNESCO World Cultural Heritage
- Remarkable Cities
- Greek antiquity
- Roman antiquity
- Places of Christian cultural interest
- Places of Islamic cultural interest
- Cultural landscape
- Historical city scape
- Castle/fortress/fort
- Palace
- Remarkable lighthouse
- Remarkable bridge
- Monument
- Festivals
- Museum
- Theater

Sport and leisure destinations

- Race track
- Skiing
- Seaport
- Waterskiing
- Beach resort
- Mineral/thermal spa
- Casino

Southern Serbia and Montenegro, Bulgaria, Macedonia, Northern Greece

The borders in the southern Balkans have been changed many times throughout history. Most recently, during the conflicts following the collapse of Yugoslavia in the early 1990s. Geographically, the southern Balkans is a region of mountain ranges, pristine forests, and coastal areas along the Adriatic, Aegean, and Black Seas. The high mountain range west of the steppe between Belgrade and Nis in Serbia has several peaks rising over 2,500 meters. **Durmitor National Park** is a UNESCO world heritage site with unique wildlife and the 61-kilometer-long Tara Canyon. Brown bears, chamois, and wild cats are just a few of many interesting animals inhabiting the park. While **Kosovo** comprises two large basins surrounded by mountains, neighboring Albania is a mountainous cour with a marshy coast. On the border tween **Albania** and the Former Yugos Republic of **Macedonia** lies La Ohrid. The large lake is surrounded mountains and is the deepest lake in Balkans, with a maximum depth of 2 meters. Macedonia's interior is cove by expansive mountain forests. **Bulgaria** is a relatively small nation w a great variety of landscapes. South of

Sveti Stefan: resort island on the Montenegro's Adriatic coast **Lt48**

Bay of Kotor Historic Montenegrin port city – UNESCO world heritage site – medieval wall – cathedral **Lt48**

Budva 2,500-year-old city on Montenegro's Adriatic coast – surrounded by 17 beautiful beaches, considered by many to be among the best in the region **Lt48**

Gjirokastër Albanian city – the birthplace of Albania's former Stalinist dictator Enver Hoxha – distinctive architecture – Gjirokaster Castle **Lu50**

Lake Ohrid Mountain lake between Albania and Macedonia – UNESCO world heritage site **Ma49/50**

Corfu One of the most visited Greek Islands – diverse landscapes and lush vegetation – historic palaces and monasteries – sandy beaches **Lu51**

Metéora Spectacular monasteries in northern Greece built on large rock formations – UNESCO world heritage site **Mb51**

Mount Athos The monastic community on Greece's Athos Peninsula is an important religious center encompassing 20 monasteries. Around 3,000 monks live on Mount Athos. The area is accesible by ferry only. **Me50**

Scale 1:2,250,000
0 20 40 Kilometers

Principal travel routes
- Auto route
- Rail road
- Shipping route

Remarkable landscapes and natural monuments
- UNESCO World Natural Heritage
- Mountain landscape
- Rock landscape
- Ravine/canyon
- Extinct volcano
- Cave
- River landscape
- Waterfall/rapids
- Lake country
- National park (landscape)
- National park (flora)
- National park (fauna)
- National park (culture)
- Coastal landscape
- Beach

ɔital city Sofia, rise the forested moun-ɪns of the **Vitoša Range** which ɪtend up to the **Rila Mountains**. ɪstala in the Rila Mountains rises 2,925 ɪters and is the tallest mountain in the ɪuntry. According to legend, the **Rho-ɔpe Mountains** along the Greek-Bul-ɪrian border were the home of the ɪthological figure Orpheus. The Bal-ɪns region is named after the **Balkan ɔuntains**, a long mountain range which stretches through central Bulgaria and eastern Serbia.

The **Danube River** forms a natural border between Bulgaria and Romania. The areas along the river's banks are the most fertile in the region. Bulgaria's 378-kilometer-long Black Sea coast is rocky in the north and covered by sandy beaches in the south. The coast is a major tourist attraction and has become increasingly popular in recent years. A four-hundred-kilometer-long roadway connects the Bulgarian port city of Burgas to Istanbul, the largest city in Turkey. **Istanbul** is situated on the Bosporus, a strait between the Black Sea and the Sea of Marmora. The **Dardanelles**, another important strait, connects the Sea of Marmora with the Aegean Sea.

Northern Greece like most of the country consists largely of mountainous highlands and hills. The region has a Mediterranean climate with mild winters and hot summers. **Chalkidiki Peninsula** on the coast of northern **Greece** features many beautiful beaches. The peninsula is also the location of Mount Athos, an important spiritual center of the Greek Orthodox religion. Thessaloniki, the largest city in northern Greece, is located just north of **Mount Olympus**, the home of the Greek gods in ancient mythology.

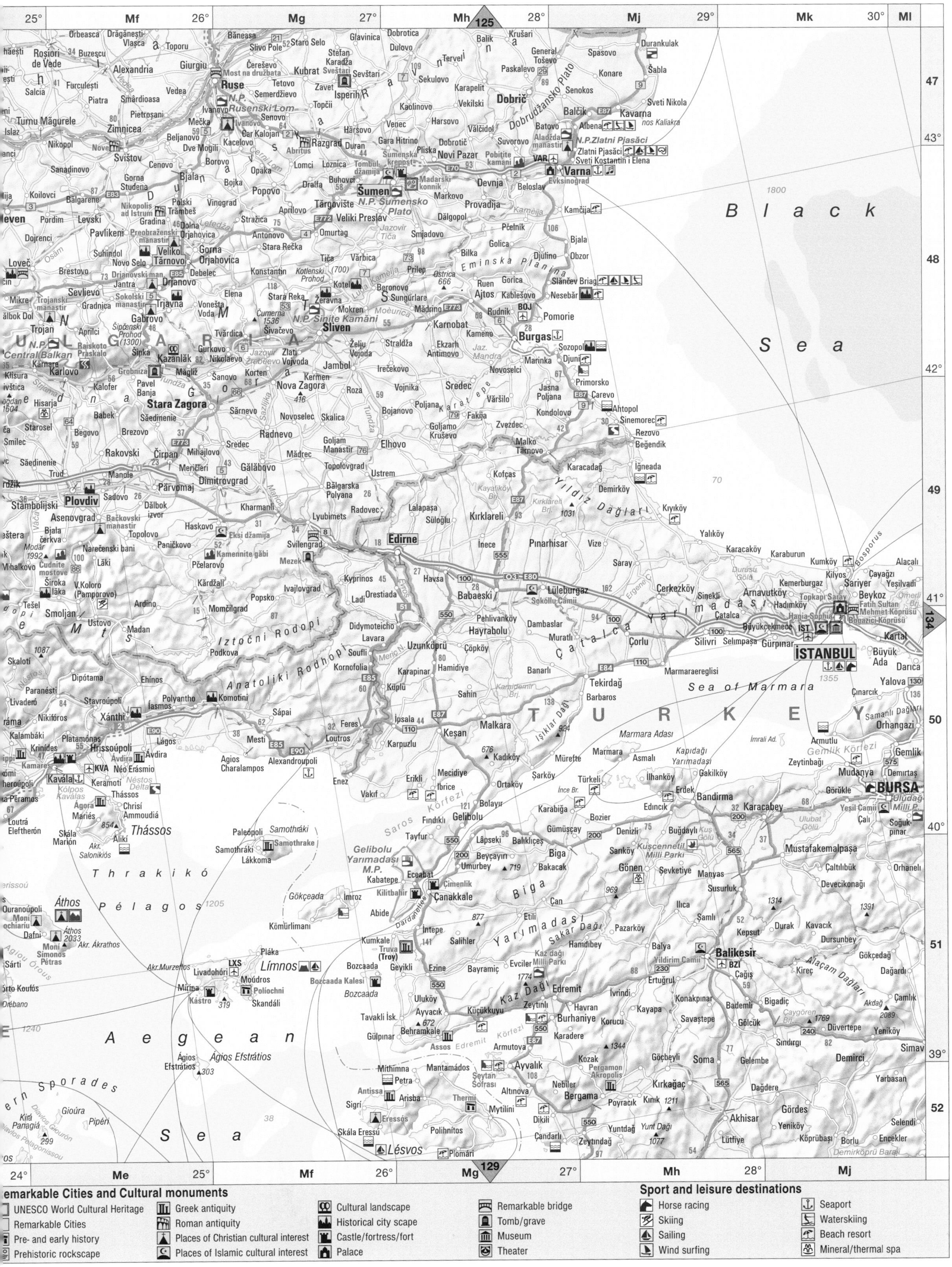

Sofia Capital city of Bulgaria – Alexander Nevsky Cathedral (photo) – St. George's Church, built in the 4th century – Archeology Museum **Md48**

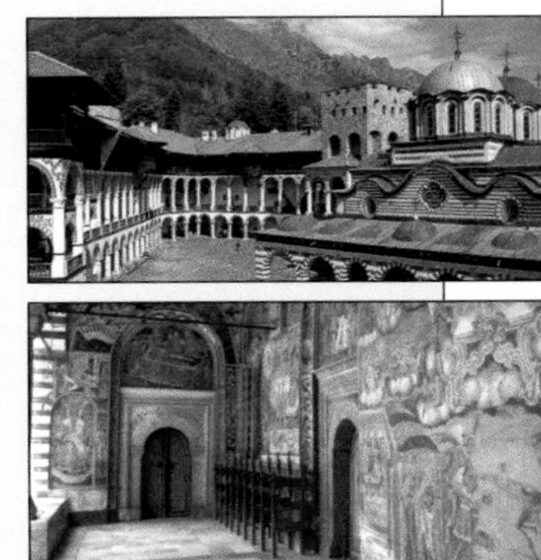

Rila Monastery Bulgarian monastery founded by Ivan Rilski in the 10th century. The unique complex has been destroyed and rebuilt several times and is an important national symbol. Photos: (top) historic church in the monastery's interior, (bottom) interior wall paintings. **Md48**

Plovdiv The second largest city in Bulgaria – Roman amphitheater – around 300 protected buildings **Me48**

Veliko Tărnovo Former capital of Bulgaria (1185-1393) – picturesque riverside architecture – ruins of Tsaravets Citadel – large student population **Mf47**

Pobitite Kamani Fields of interesting stone pillars – created by erosion millions of years ago **Mh47**

Nesebăr Ancient city first settled in the second century BC – historic city on a peninsula – the city is a designated UNESCO world heritage site – 19th century Black Sea region architecture (photo) including buildings made of stone and wood **Mh48**

emarkable Cities and Cultural monuments

UNESCO World Cultural Heritage · Remarkable Cities · Pre- and early history · Prehistoric rockscape · Greek antiquity · Roman antiquity · Places of Christian cultural interest · Places of Islamic cultural interest · Cultural landscape · Historical city scape · Castle/fortress/fort · Palace · Remarkable bridge · Tomb/grave · Museum · Theater

Sport and leisure destinations

Horse racing · Skiing · Sailing · Wind surfing · Seaport · Waterskiing · Beach resort · Mineral/thermal spa

Southern Greece consists of the southern half of mainland Greece including the Peloponnesus peninsula and most of the Greek islands, which combined comprise around one fifth of the country's land area. The region is mostly mountainous with craggy coasts, while the western Peloponnesus has a smooth coast with many sand beaches.

The **Pindos Mountains** run through the western section of mainland Greece parallel to the coast. This mountain ran looks distinctly alpine and snow cov much of the area between Decemb and April.

Athens and its surrounding areas located in the **Attica Basin**. The basin the most densely populated region Greece and is home to almost half of

The Colossus of Rhodes stood near Rhodes harbor in ancient times **MhM**

Zakynthos Byzantine Museum – historic town Zakynthos – beaches including the shipwreck beach (photo) **Ma53**

Delphí Site of the ancient Delphic Oracle, dedicated to the Greek god Apollo – the area is a UNESCO world heritage site – Temple of Apollo – remains of an ancient arena – Tholos temple **Mc52**

Corinth, Temple of Apollo Ruin of an ancient Hellenic city – Temple of Apollo remnants (photo) **Mc53**

Athens Greece's capital and largest urban area is not usually considered beautiful, but it is a fascinating city with several ancient sites. The **Acrópolis** (top photo) – with the ancient Parthenon, Erechtheum, and Propylaea – towers over the center of the city. The **Odeon** (bottom photo) is the site of an annual theatre festival in summer. **Md53**

Aegina Interesting island – the Temple of Aphaia (photo), built around 500 BC and one of Greece's most famous temples **Md53**

Epídauros Birthplace of Asclepius in Greek mythology – the well preserved ampitheater is considered a masterpiece of classic Hellenistic architecture **Md53**

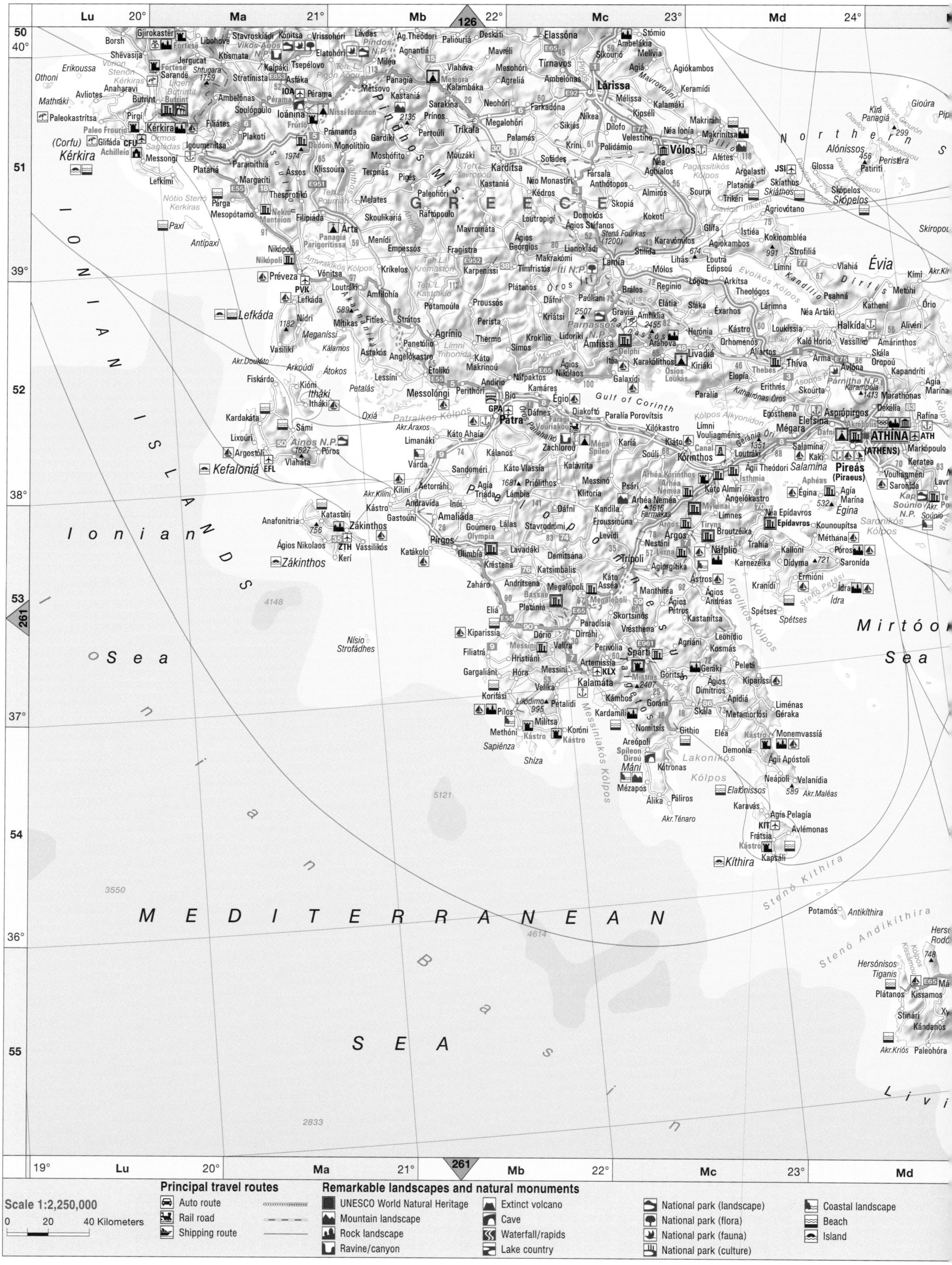

Scale 1:2,250,000
0 20 40 Kilometers

Principal travel routes
- Auto route
- Rail road
- Shipping route

Remarkable landscapes and natural monuments
- UNESCO World Natural Heritage
- Mountain landscape
- Rock landscape
- Ravine/canyon
- Extinct volcano
- Cave
- Waterfall/rapids
- Lake country
- National park (landscape)
- National park (flora)
- National park (fauna)
- National park (culture)
- Coastal landscape
- Beach
- Island

untry's population. The **Thessaly Plain** d the **Peloponnesus** are two of the ore fertile regions in Greece. There are veral large bays and gulfs between e Peloponnesus and the Isthmus of orinth.

eece's **Aegean Islands** are cover- by rolling hills and mountains. The ands are divided into several groups: e Cyclades, including Mykonos and elos, the Dodecanese, near the coast of Asia Minor, and the Sporades. Euboea is the largest of the Aegean Island, with a total land area of 3,580 km². The eastern Aegean Islands including the Dodecanese are generally wetter than their western counterparts. Rhodes has an area of 1,398 km² and is the largest island in the Dodecanese. The island was once the site of the Colossus of Rhodes, one of the "seven wonders" of the ancient world. The **Ionian Islands** are situated off the western coast of southern Greece. The Ionians consist of seven main islands and many smaller ones with lush green vegetation. **Crete**, the largest of the Greek islands, has a long history and beautiful landscapes including mountains and sandy beaches. Crete also features many important archeological sites, including many linked to the ancient Minoan civilization (3000-1400 BC).

Southwestern Turkey is a region with rolling hills, lakes, ancient towns and important archeological sites. **Pamukkale** – a spectacular site consisting of terraced white chalk formations and thermal pools – is the most interesting natural attraction in the region. The western **Aegean coast** features several bays. Southwest of Marmaris lies the so-called **Turkish Riviera**. **Ölü Deniz Bay** has fine sandy beaches and is one of the most attractive areas in the region.

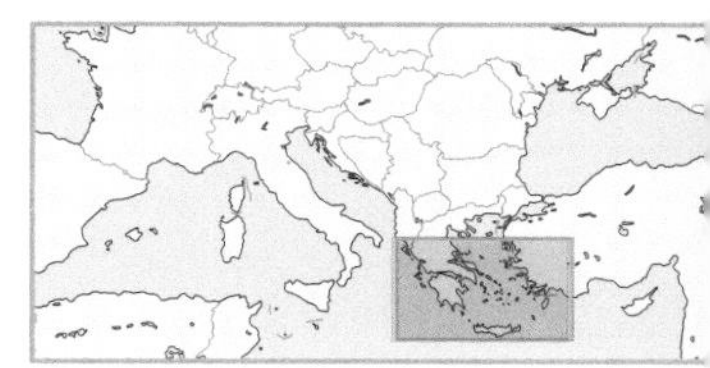

Mykonos This Aegean island is a popular tourist destination – traditional white cubic houses – windmills – beaches **Mf53**

Páros One of the Cyclades islands – Katapoliani church in Parikia (photo) – highest mountain, Profitis Ilias (775 meters) **Mf53**

Delos This was a sacred island for the ancient Greeks – "birthplace" of Apollo – the largest site of ancient Greek ruins – Terrace of the Lions with large lion statues – Temple of Apollo **Mf53**

Náxos Charming island – historic towns with Venetian architecture – reconstructed Temple of Demeter **Mf53**

Santorini Fascinating crater landscapes – typical Aegean Island architecture – Oia is the prettiest village on the island **Mf54**

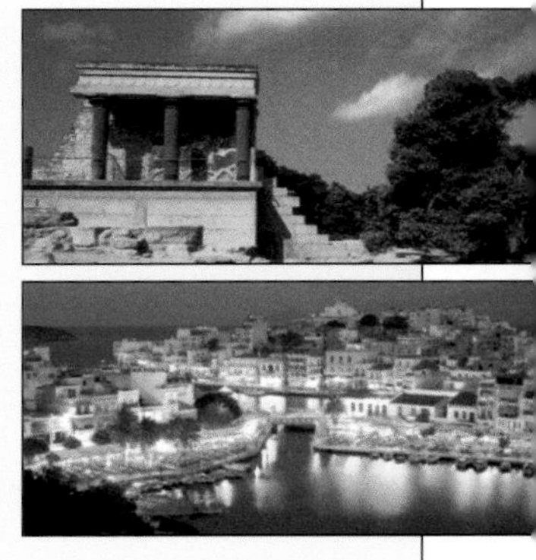

Crete The largest of the Greek islands has many diverse landscapes. Crete was home to the Minoan culture, one of the first civilizations in Europe. Around 2000 BC the Minoans built impressive palaces on the island – including the **Palace of Knossós** (top photo). **Réthimno** (bottom photo) is one of the prettiest towns on Crete with a historic old town and an idyllic harbor. **MdMg55**

emarkable Cities and Cultural monuments

- UNESCO World Cultural Heritage
- Remarkable Cities
- Pre- and early history
- The Ancient Orient
- Minoan culture
- Greek antiquity
- Roman antiquity
- Places of Christian cultural interest
- Places of Islamic cultural interest
- Historical city scape
- Castle/fortress/fort
- Palace
- Technical/industrial monument
- Tomb/grave
- Museum
- Olympics

Sport and leisure destinations

- Horse racing
- Skiing
- Sailing
- Diving
- Wind surfing
- Seaport
- Beach resort
- Mineral/thermal spa

Southern Turkey, Cyprus

"Like the head of a mare galloping from Asia into the Medditeranean", is how the famed Turkish poet Nazim Hikmet described the shape of his native country. Istanbul,the largest city in Turkey, was once the capital of the mighty Ottoman Empire. Most of **Istanbul** lies in the small European portion of Turkey (3%) on the Bosporus, a strait separating Europe from Anatolia (Asia Minor). This region between two continents has been a melting pot of different cultures since ancient times.

Sunset near Lamarka on Cyprus **MnMp55/56**

Turkey is a country surrounded by seas on three sides. The **Black Sea** and the **Sea of Marmara** are north of mainland Turkey. To the west is the **Aegean Sea** and to the south lies the Mediterranean Sea. Many of the numerous islands off the western coast of Turkey belong Greece. Ionia was the name of the coas al areas of western Turkey in ancie times. The ancient Ionians were ethnica Greek and the region features the **rui** of several ancient Hellenic cities – inclu ing Pergamon, Ephesus, Bodrum (Ha carnassus), and a site believed by ma to be the "legendary" city of Troy.

Turkey's **southern coast** is a tran tion zone between mountains and t

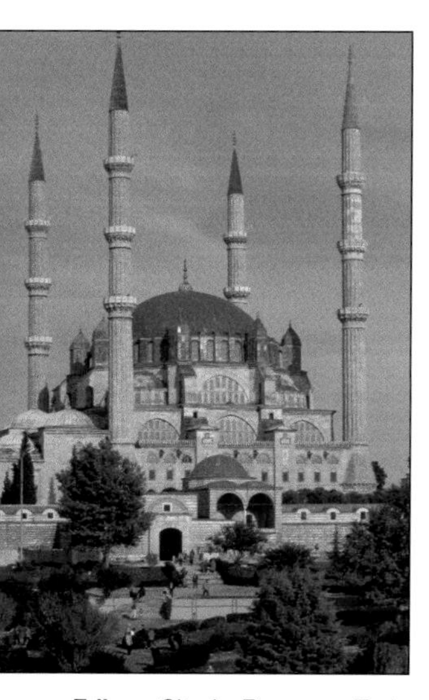

Edirne City in European Turkey – the Selimiye Mosque (photo), a masterpiece of Ottoman religious architecture – Ottoman bridges **Mg49**

İstanbul Turkey's largest city (population, 13 million) has attractions from the Roman to the modern era – including the Hagia Sofia (top photo), the Blue Mosque (middle photo), and a historic old town (bottom photo). The city is located in both Europe and Asia. **MjMk49/50**

Bursa City in northwestern Turkey – once the residence of Ottoman sultans – historic old town – The Green Mosque – Islamic cemetery (photo) **Mk50**

Pergamon This ancient coastal city was the center of an important Hellenic kingdom – large altar to Zeus and Athena – ruins of the Dionysus Temple **Mh51**

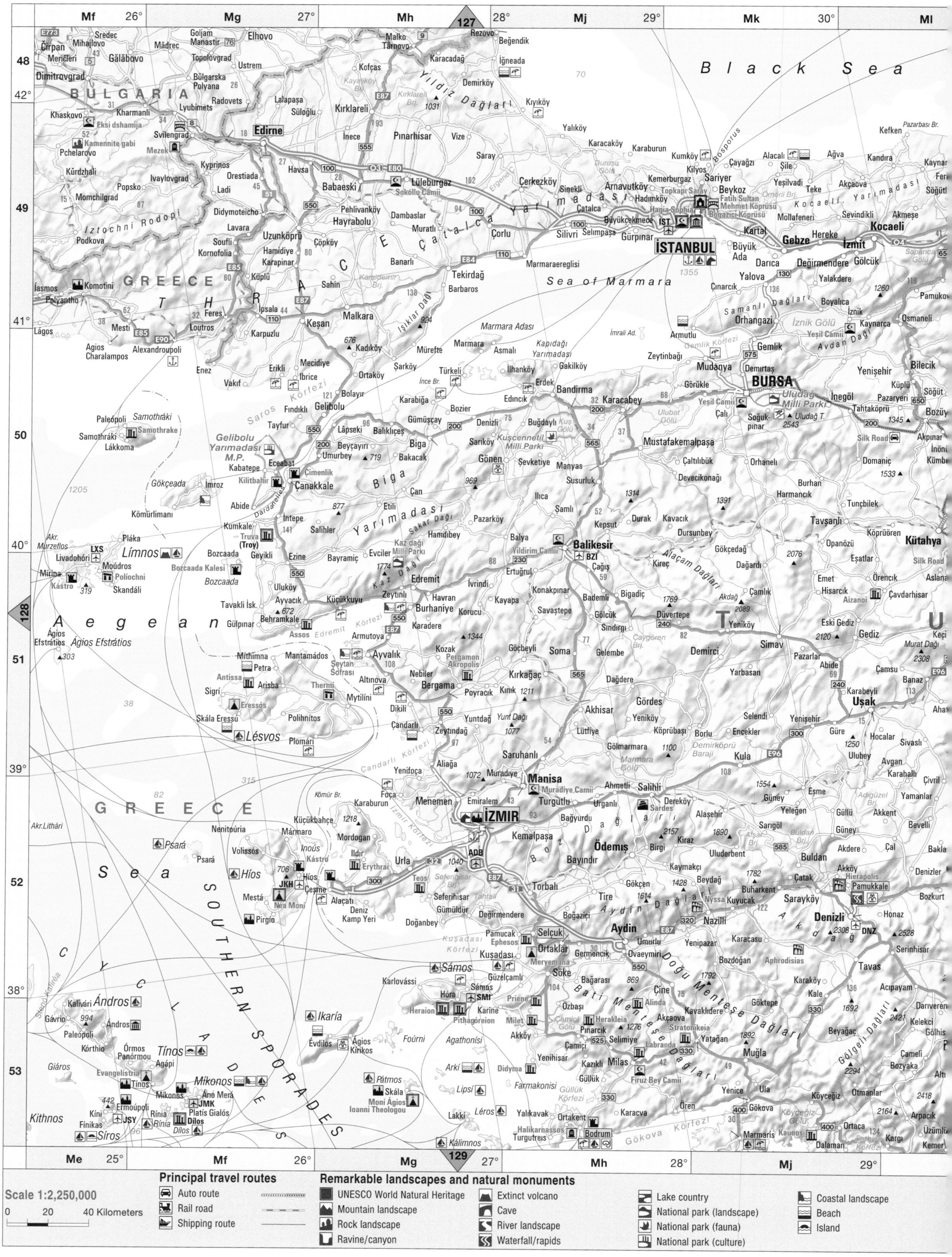

Scale 1:2,250,000
0 20 40 Kilometers

Principal travel routes
- Auto route
- Rail road
- Shipping route

Remarkable landscapes and natural monuments
- UNESCO World Natural Heritage
- Mountain landscape
- Rock landscape
- Ravine/canyon
- Extinct volcano
- Cave
- River landscape
- Waterfall/rapids
- Lake country
- National park (landscape)
- National park (fauna)
- National park (culture)
- Coastal landscape
- Beach
- Island

diterranean Sea. The southern coast s many beautiful bays and the **Lycian ast** between Marmaris and Antalya is opular tourist destination with long, ite beaches.
o large mountain ranges cover most Western Turkey: the **Pontus Moun-ns** in the north and the **Taurus Moun-ns** in the south. Between these two untain ranges lies a large, flat plateau und the large and shallow salt lake **Tuz Gölü**, the second largest lake in Turkey. Many of the settlements on the edges of the highlands in western Turkey have ancient histories and were founded by different ancient cultures, including the Romans, Hittites, and the Phrygians. **Central Anatolia** features many historic sites connected to the different cultures that once lived in the region. The ruins of Huttusa, the ancient capital of the Hittites, and Ankara, the capital of modern Turkey since 1923, are both located on Anatolia's central plateau. The city Konya has a rich collection of early Islamic art and is the birthplace of the Whirling Dervishes sect. Near Konya, lies the prehistoric ruin of Çatal Hüyük, an ancient town first settled around 7000 BC.
The region around the city of Göreme has been known by the name **Cappodocia** for many centuries and contains many unusual "lunar" landscapes as well as several active volcanoes – including Erciyes Dağı (3,916 meters) and Hasan Dağı (3,253 meters). Cappodocia's most fascinating attractions are the many homes, churches, and monasteries built into caves and stone formations during ancient times.
Cyprus is an island in the eastern Mediterranean located south of Turkey. The country's population consists mostly of ethnic Greeks and Turks.

Ephesus An important city during the ancient Greek era. Ephesus contains the ruins of temples and ceremonial sites. The Celsus Library (photo) is the most intact ancient site. **Mh53**

Pamukkale Fascinating natural attraction – UNESCO world heritage site – museum – ancient amphitheater **Mk53**

Hierapolis Ruins of a Greek/Roman settlement (photo) – UNESCO world heritage site – largest necropolis in Asia **Mk53**

Bodrum Popular seaside resort – St. Peter's Castle (photo); the historic building contains a museum **Mh53**

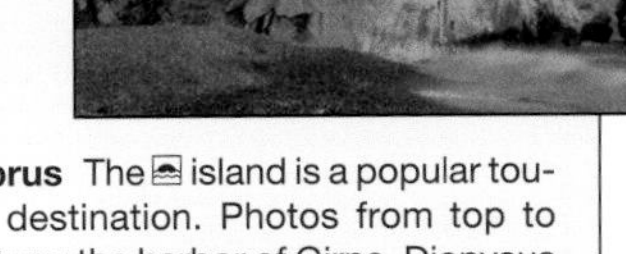

Cyprus The island is a popular tourist destination. Photos from top to bottom: the harbor of Girne, Dionysus mosaic in Paphos, Aphrodite's Rock. **MnMp55/56**

emarkable Cities and Cultural monuments

UNESCO World Cultural Heritage
Remarkable Cities
Pre- and early history
The Ancient Orient
Greek antiquity
Roman antiquity
Places of Christian cultural interest
Places of Islamic cultural interest
Historical city scape
Castle/fortress/fort
Caravanserai
Palace
Remarkable bridge
Tomb/grave
Museum

Sport and leisure destinations

Horse racing
Skiing
Sailing
Wind surfing
Canoeing/rafting
Seaport
Beach resort
Mineral/thermal spa

Belarus, Western Russia

Russia is the largest nation in the world in terms of area. The enormous size of the country has always had an influence on Russia's economy and culture. Russia stretches through two continents, numerous climate zones, and twelve time zones.

The country has a total land area of 17,075,400 km² and a population around 150 million. Most of European Russia comprises a series of vast **plains** stret-

ching up to the Ural Mountains. South Russia's capital city, Moscow, lies a lo land region encompassing sections the **Don and Oka river basins.** This lo land borders the **Central Russi Upland**, a large region of rolling hills. T **Volga Upland**, which has a maxim height of 358 meters above sea level

Russia's Valdaisky National Park contains many lakes **Mg**

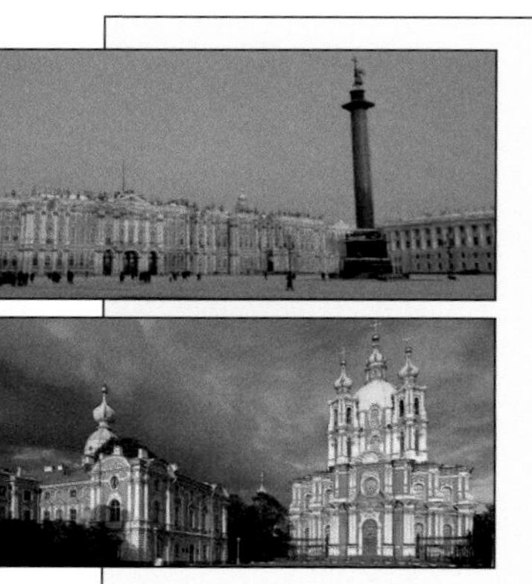

St. Petersburg The former capital of the tsars was founded in 1703 and has an abundance of beautiful architecture. Alexander Column (top photo) was erected in front of the Winter Palace. Smolny Cathedral (bottom photo) was the Soviet headquarters during the Russian Revolution. The old town is a world heritage site. **Mf16**

Palaces of the Tsars St. Petersburg is home to several grand palaces from the time of the tsars including Catherine the Great's summer palace in Pushkin (top photo) and Peterhof (bottom photo). **Mf16**

Novgorod City in northwestern Russia – during the Middle Ages Novgorod was a leading trading center – St. Sophia's – Museum of Wooden Architecture **Mf16**

Minsk Capital city of Belarus – population, 1.8 million – Belarusian National Museum – national circus – heavily damaged during the Second World War – 20th century socialist architecture **Md19**

Mir Castle Complex Historic 16th century castle in Belarus – gothic architecture – UNESCO world heritage site **Md19**

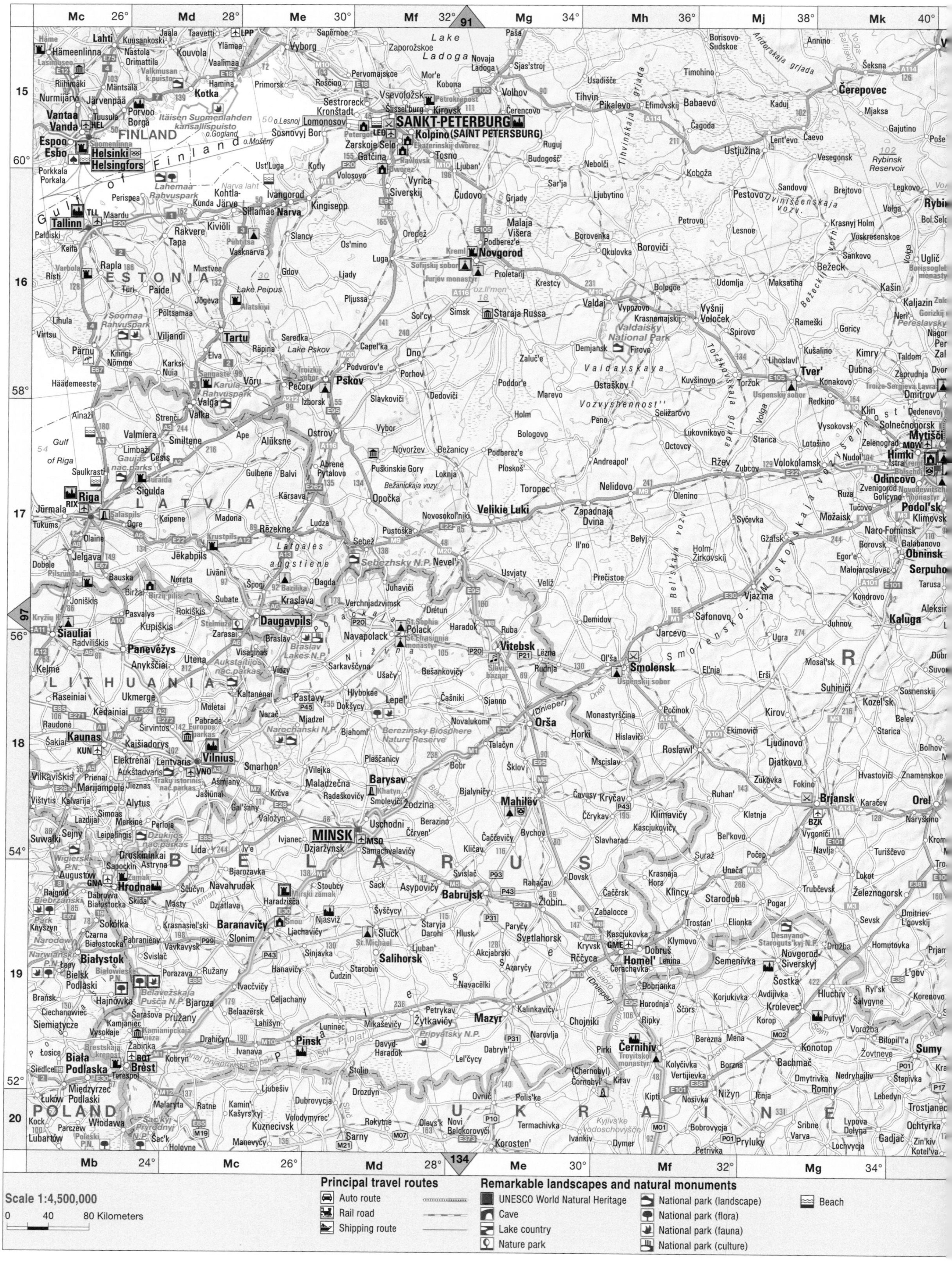

Scale 1:4,500,000
0 40 80 Kilometers

Principal travel routes
- Auto route
- Rail road
- Shipping route

Remarkable landscapes and natural monuments
- UNESCO World Natural Heritage
- Cave
- Lake country
- Nature park
- National park (landscape)
- National park (flora)
- National park (fauna)
- National park (culture)
- Beach

cated to the west of the Volga River. The ropean section of Russia is home to ost of the Russian population and is the untry's cultural heartland. European ussia is crisscrossed by many power- rivers running from north to south ncluding the 1,870-kilometer-long **Don ver** and the 3,350-kilometer-long **Volga ver**.

hen Peter the Great founded the city of **. Petersburg** in the 18th century he wanted to give his nation a major port on the Baltic Sea and a "window to the West". The largest city in Russia is the nation's capital city **Moscow**. From 1922 to 1991 the city was also the capital of the powerful Soviet Union. Northwestern Russia features many large lakes. **Lake Ladoga**, north of St. Petersburg, is the largest lake in Europe with a total area of 18,000 km². Most of European Russia has a continental climate with long, cold winters and short, dry summers. The area between the **Baltic States** and the plains of Russia and Belarus consists of large marshlands with many lakes and forests. The area is also a transition zone between the maritime climate zone of the Baltic region and the continental climate zone in most of Eastern Europe.

Belarus is located just west of European Russia and has a total land area of 207,595 km². Most of the country's territory is covered by flat plains. Agriculture and lumbering are both important sectors of the country's economy. The hills around Belarus' capital, **Minsk**, rise no more than 346 meters in height. The basins of the Desna and the Dnieper rivers encompass large marshlands including the **Pripyat marshes** along the Ukrainian border. The country has a temperate continental climate with mild winters and cool summers.

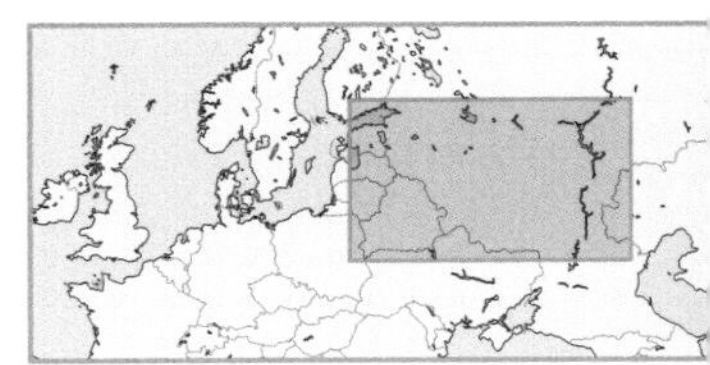

Kostroma Historic city trade center on the banks of the Volga river – Ipatievsky Monastery – resurrection church (photo) **Na17**

Pereslavl Zalessky City on the shore of Lake Pleshcheyevo – Goritsky Monastery, 14th century structure (photo) **Mk17**

Suzdal' Largest city on the Golden Ring, a historic route northeast of Moscow – impressive citadel (kremlin) – Museum of wooden architecture **Na17**

Sergiyev Posad Town near Moscow – Trinity Monastery, spectacular fortress monastery – art history museum – tsarist palace **Mk17**

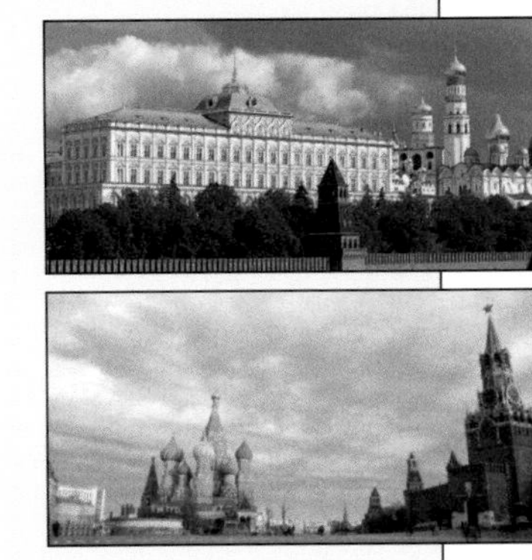

Moscow The capital city of the Russian Federation is the nation's leading cultural and economic center. Moscow has an interesting mix of medieval Russian, tsarist, and Stalinist architecture. The historic Kremlin (top photo) is Russia's most famous national landmark. Red Square (bottom photo) was once a market square and lies near St. Basil's Cathedral. **Mj18**

Volgograd Industrial city on the lower Volga – known as Stalingrad before 1961 – reconstructed in Stalinist style after the Second World War – war memorial (photo) **Nc21**

Remarkable Cities and Cultural monuments

- UNESCO World Cultural Heritage
- Remarkable Cities
- Prehistoric rockscape
- Places of Christian cultural interest
- Places of Islamic cultural interest
- Historical city scape
- Castle/fortress/fort
- Palace
- Technical/industrial monument
- Dam
- Theater of war/battlefield
- Monument
- Market
- Festivals
- Museum
- Theater
- Olympics

Sport and leisure dest.

- Beach resort
- Mineral/thermal spa
- Casino

Before it became an independent nation in 1991, **Ukraine** was politically aligned to neighboring Russia, first in the Russian Empire and later in the Soviet Union. The country is the second largest nation in Europe with a total area of 604,000 km². At least 100 distinct ethnic groups live in Ukraine. Ethnic Russians, who form one fifth of the country's population, are the largest minority group. The Crimean Peninsula was once home to a large distinct

Tatar community before they were exp led from the region by Stalin in 1944. Most of Ukraine is covered by vast plai and few areas of the country are situ ted more than 500 meters above s level. The plains of Ukraine are cover by fertile, black soil and agriculture is important sector in the nation's econon

Mount Elbrus in the central Caucasus **Na**

L'viv The former capital of the historic region Galicia. L'viv, a UNESCO world heritage site, has an abundance of beautiful architecture. The city's opera house (top photo) was built in the Viennese neo-Renaissance style. The medieval market square (bottom photo) is well preserved. **Mc21**

Kiev The capital city of Ukraine was founded in the 5th century. St. Sophia's Cathedral (top photo) was completed in 1037. Lavra Monastery (bottom photo) is a pilgrimage site for Orthodox Christians. **Mf20**

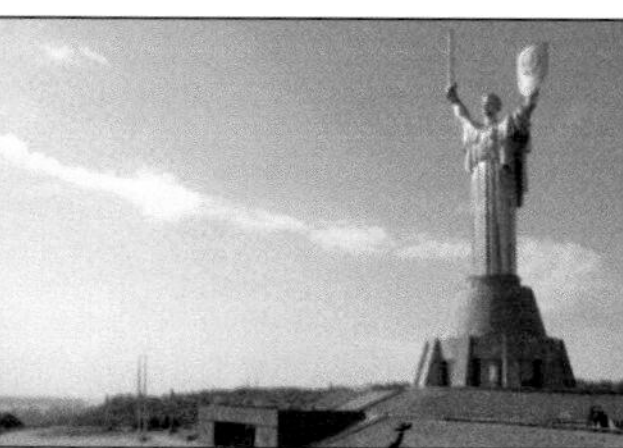

Monument to the Motherland Massive Soviet-era monument to the victory in the Second World War **Mf20**

Odessa Ukrainian port city on the Black Sea – beautiful baroque and neo-classical architecture **Mf22**

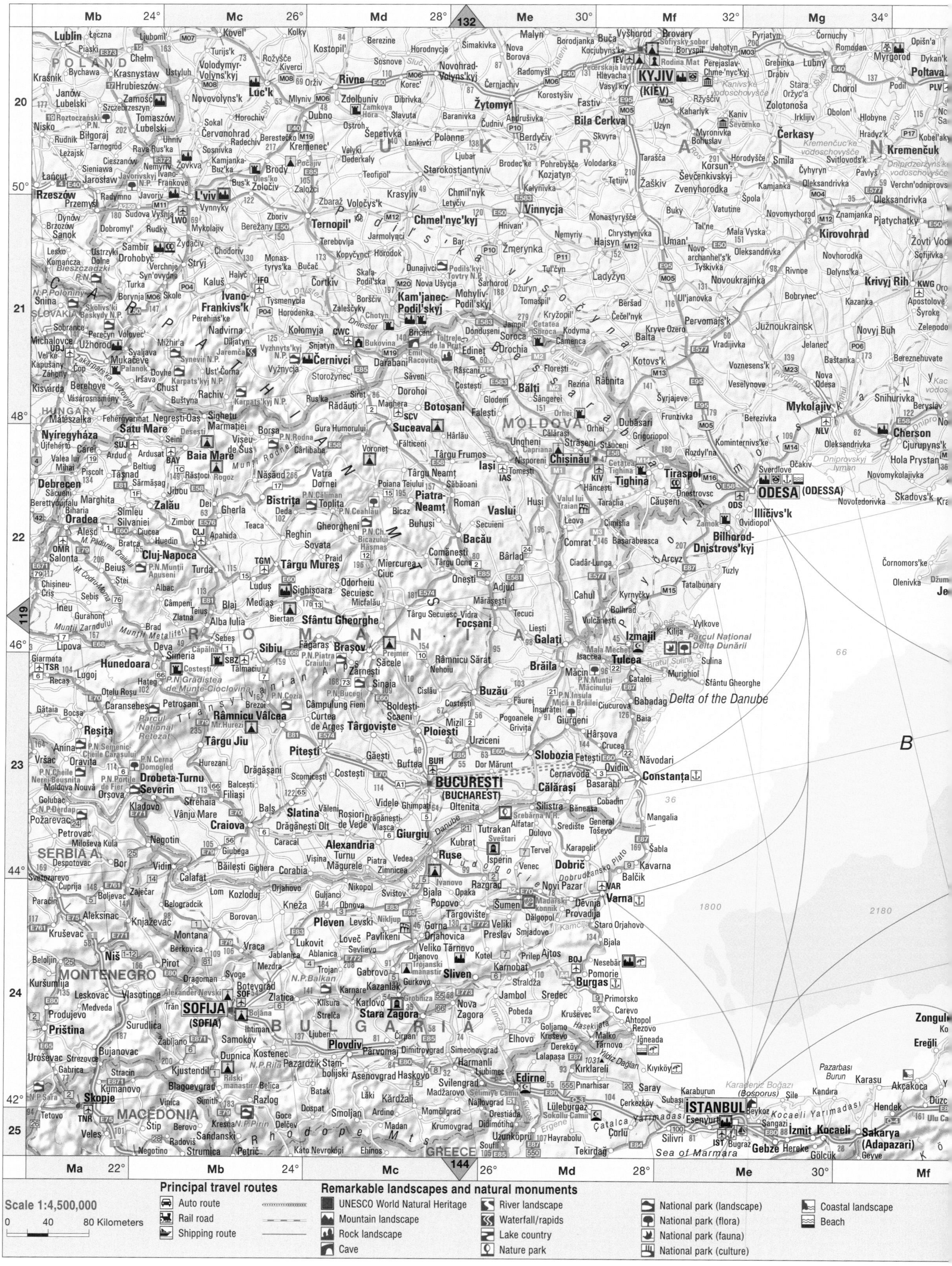

Scale 1:4,500,000

0 40 80 Kilometers

Principal travel routes

- Auto route
- Rail road
- Shipping route

Remarkable landscapes and natural monuments

- UNESCO World Natural Heritage
- Mountain landscape
- Rock landscape
- Cave
- River landscape
- Waterfall/rapids
- Lake country
- Nature park
- National park (landscape)
- National park (flora)
- National park (fauna)
- National park (culture)
- Coastal landscape
- Beach

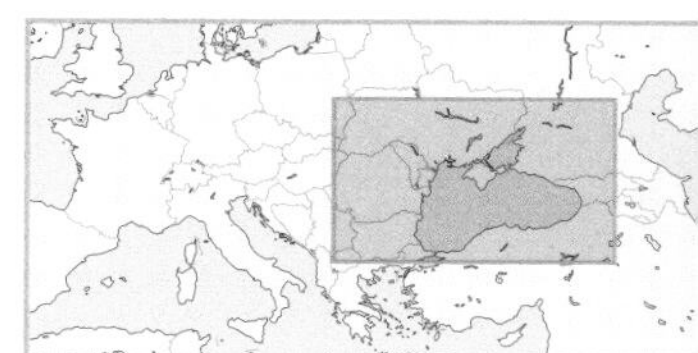

e Ukrainian Carpathians in western kraine are a 280-kilometer-long moun- n range covered by large forests of eech and fir trees. The mountain Hora overla rises 2,061 meters above sea vel and is the highest mountain in kraine. Most of southern Ukraine is vered by steppes, while the northern d eastern sections of the country fea- re expansive forests.

e **Black Sea** (maximum depth, 2,243 meters) is connected to the Mediterranean Sea by the Bosporus, the Dardanelles, and the Sea of Marmara. The **Sea of Azov** is a section of the Black Sea connected to the main body of water by the Kerch Strait. The **Crimea** consists mostly of mountain ranges, prairies, and coastal areas with numerous natural harbors and bays. The Black Sea coasts are divided between Ukraine, Russia, Bulgaria, Romania, Turkey, and Georgia. The coastal areas around the Black Sea have a climate similar to that of the Mediterranean with dry, warm summers and wet, mild winters. Western Ukraine has a temperate continental climate with wet, warm summers and cool winters. Most of eastern Ukraine, however, has a continental climate with long, cold winters and short summers. Three major rivers flow through Ukraine: the **Dniester**, the **Bug**, and the 2,200-kilometer-long **Dnieper River**. All three of these rivers flow from north to south into the Black Sea. Kiev, Ukraine's capital city, lies on the Dnieper River and stretches over seven hills.

The Greater Caucasus Mountains are located between the Black and the Caspian Seas. The mountain range is more than 1,000 kilometers long and up to 180 kilometers wide. It is also the site of several high, extinct volcanoes including Mount Elbrus, the highest mountain in Europe.

Crimea In 1783 Empress Catherine II annexed the Crimean Peninsula for the Russian Empire. Before the Russia Revolution, the Russian elite and wealthy foreign visitors built grand villas in Crimea. Photos from top to bottom: Livadia Palace, Alupka Palace, the Swallow's Nest **Mh23**

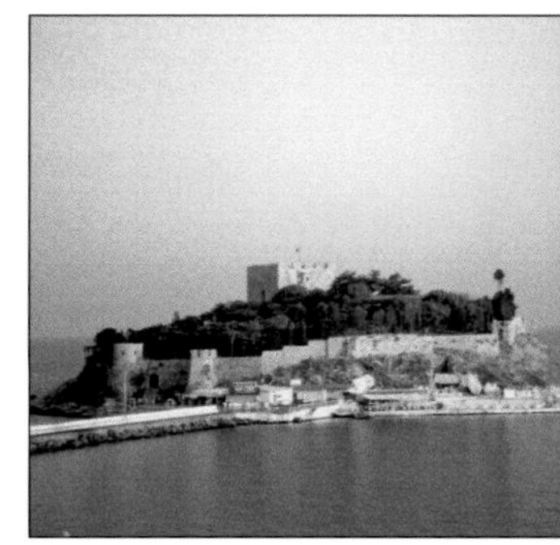

Sudak Fortified complex on a small peak rising out of the sea – built by Genovese traders in the 14th century **Mh23**

Mount Elbrus The highest mountain in Europe – in the western Caucasus – twin peaks, western peak rises 5,642 meters **Nb24**

Mestia Capital of the mountainous Georgian region Svaneti – located in the Greater Caucasus – traditional art museum **Nb24**

Kutaisi Center of the Imereti region in western Georgia – cathedral, completed in 1,033 – distinct local stone architecture **Nb24**

markable Cities and Cultural monuments

- UNESCO World Cultural Heritage
- Remarkable Cities
- Pre- and early history
- Prehistoric rockscape
- The Ancient Orient
- Greek antiquity
- Roman antiquity
- Places of Christian cultural interest
- Places of Islamic cultural interest
- Cultural landscape
- Historical city scape
- Castle/fortress/fort
- Palace
- Dam
- Tomb/grave
- Monument

Sport and leisure destinations

- Horse racing
- Skiing
- Sailing
- Wind surfing
- Canoeing/rafting
- Seaport
- Beach resort
- Mineral/thermal spa

Itsukushima (top): Shinto shrine in one of Japan's most beautiful coastal regions.
Hongkong (bottom): The glittering skyline of China's leading financial center.

Taj Mahal (left): A monument to eternal love and Islamic architecture at its finest.
Borobudur (right): The largest Buddhist temple complex in the world.

Asia

Sweeping deserts, foggy rainforests, and the tallest mountains on Earth can all be found in Asia. The ancient cultures of Mesopotamia were among the earliest civilizations. The ancient philosophies of China, Islam, Hinduism, Buddhism, as well as many other religions and cultures make Asia a continent with an incredibly rich cultural legacy.

Asia has a total area of 44.4 million km^2 and encompasses around one-third of the world's land. The continent has a maximum length of 11,000 kilometers from east to west and a maximum length of 8,500 kilometers from north to south. The vast majority of Asia's land area is situated above the equator in the northern hemisphere. Only a few areas in Southeast Asia and the Indian subcontinent are located south of the equator. The continent borders the Arctic Ocean in the north, the Pacific Ocean in the east, and the Indian Ocean in the south. In the west, Asia borders Europe, the Mediterranean Sea, North Africa and the Red Sea. The Bering Sea, a section of the Pacific, separates Siberia in northern Asia from North America. The Arabian Penin-sula, India, the Malay Peninsula, Kore and Kamchatka are the largest and mo significant of the many peninsulas on t continent. The Japanese Islands are loc ted off the northeastern coast of mainla Asia. A large belt of mountain system extends from the Caucasus (maximu height, 5,642 meters) and Pontic Mou tains (3,937 meters) in western Asia to t **Himalayas** and farther east into Sout east Asia.

Mount Everest (8,850 meters), the world's tallest mountain

Asia stretches from the frozen tundra above the Arctic Circle to the hot and humid tropics along the equator. Northern Asia is home to vast treeless plains (top photo) and central Asia encompasses many large deserts (middle photo). The climates of South and Southeast Asia (bottom photo: the Philippines) are greatly influenced by monsoon winds.

All of the world's 14 mountains rising above 8,000 meters are located in Asia, most in the Himalayas. Mount Everest in the Himalayas is the world's tallest mountain. K2 (photo), with a height of 8,611 meters is the world's second tallest mountain.

The Chang Jiang (Yangtze) River in China is the longest river in Asia with a total length of 6,300 kilometers (top photo). The Huang He/Yellow (5,460 km), Mekong (4,500 km), Amur (4,415 km), and Ob (5,400 km) Rivers are all among the longest rivers in the world. The Aral Sea, a large inland body of water, (bottom photo) has an area around 33,640 square kilometers. In recent decades the sea has shrunk dramatically in size.

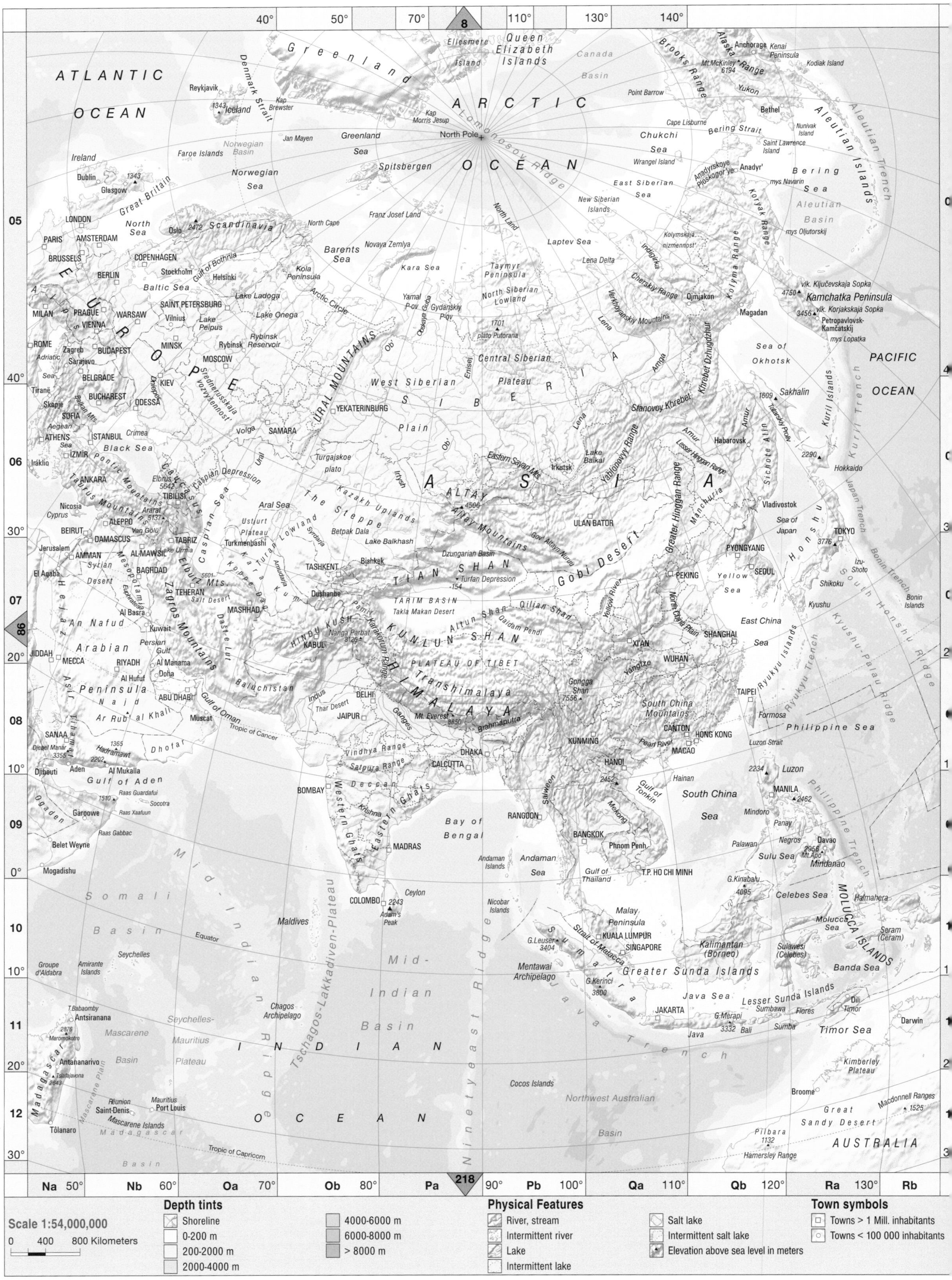

Scale 1:54,000,000
0 400 800 Kilometers

Depth tints
Shoreline
0-200 m
200-2000 m
2000-4000 m
4000-6000 m
6000-8000 m
> 8000 m

Physical Features
River, stream
Intermittent river
Lake
Intermittent lake
Salt lake
Intermittent salt lake
Elevation above sea level in meters

Town symbols
Towns > 1 Mill. inhabitants
Towns < 100 000 inhabitants

a is by far the most populated of the rld's seven continents. The continent's **pulation** of more than 3.4 billion is equally distributed. Sparsely populated ngolia has a population density of t two inhabitants per square kilometer. ngladesh, one of the world's most wded nations, has a population den- y in excess of 900 inhabitants per uare kilometer. China and India, the rld's most populous nations, are both home to more than one billion people. Most of the **world's major religions** were founded in Asia many centuries ago. Judaism, Islam and Christianity all originated in western Asia. India was the birthplace of Hinduism and Buddhism, while Taoism and Confucianism both originated in China.

Left: Veiled woman in Oman
Right: Balinese dancer

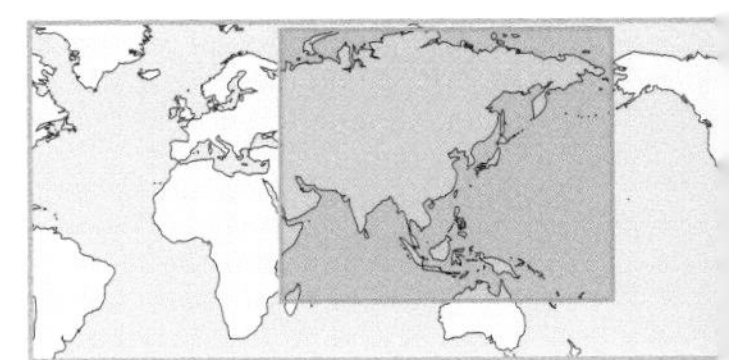

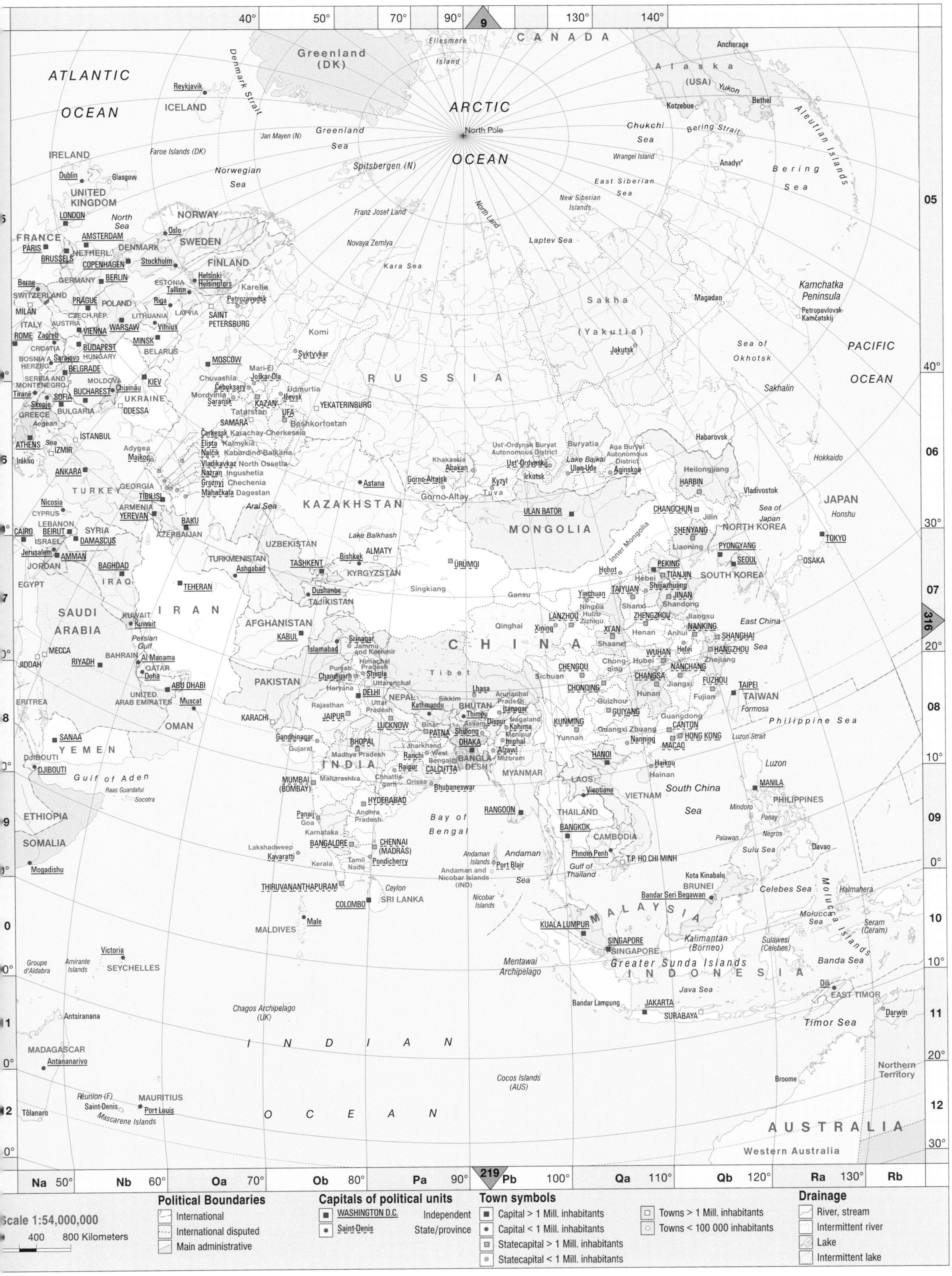

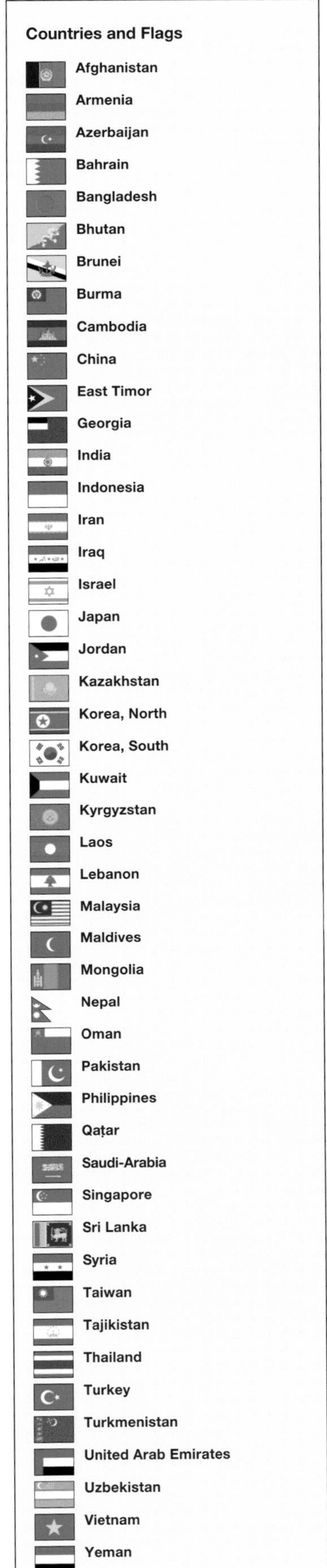

Scale 1:54,000,000
400 800 Kilometers

Political Boundaries
International
International disputed
Main administrative

Capitals of political units
WASHINGTON D.C. Independent
Saint-Denis State/province

Town symbols
Capital > 1 Mill. inhabitants
Capital < 1 Mill. inhabitants
Statecapital > 1 Mill. inhabitants
Statecapital < 1 Mill. inhabitants
Towns > 1 Mill. inhabitants
Towns < 100 000 inhabitants

Drainage
River, stream
Intermittent river
Lake
Intermittent lake

In 1967, ten Southeast Asian nations joined together to form ASEAN, a community founded to increase economic and cultural cooperation in the region. The ten members of ASEAN are Brunei, Indonesia, Cambodia, Laos, Malaysia, Myanmar (Burma), Singapore, Thailand, the Philippines, and Vietnam. ASEAN is now home to more than 500 million people and comprises several rapidly developing economies.

Northern Asia

The 2,000-kilometer-long **Ural Mountains** form a natural boundary between Asia and Europe. Naroda, the tallest peak in the mountain range, rises 1,894 meters above sea level. The Urals stretch from the steppes of southern Russia near the border of Kazakhstan to the Russian Arctic Ocean coast. East of the Urals lies **Siberia**, a region encompassing most of Russia's territory. Siberia stretches over 7,000 kilometers from the Urals to the

Pacific Ocean and the greatest distar from north to south in Siberia is arou 3,500 kilometers. The **West Siberi Plain**, the world's largest plain, covers million km² and is drained by the Ob Ri and its many tributaries. The plain is r in valuable mineral resources includ natural gas and oil.

Coastal wetlands on the Kamchatka Peninsula

Ural Mountains The "border" between Europe and Asia – Komi virgin forests, UNESCO world heritage site – southern foothills near the Russia-Kazakhstan border

West Siberian Plain Covers 2.6 million km² – large marshlands – more than 2,000 rivers – frequent flooding in summer

Yenisei River Major river in Siberia – 4,130 kilometers long – the river's basin spans 2.6 million km²

Central Siberian Plateau Series of plateaus – Putoran Mountains, tallest peak 1,701 meters – taiga and permafrost ground

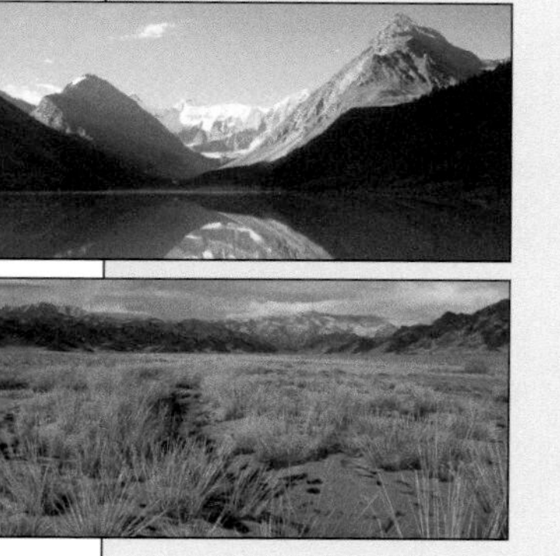

Altai The name of a region and mountain range containing Siberia's tallest mountains. Beluha, the tallest mountain rises 4,506 meters. The region encompasses diverse landscapes including steppes, forests, sub-alpine and alpine regions. Altai is also home to several rare animal species such as snow leopards.

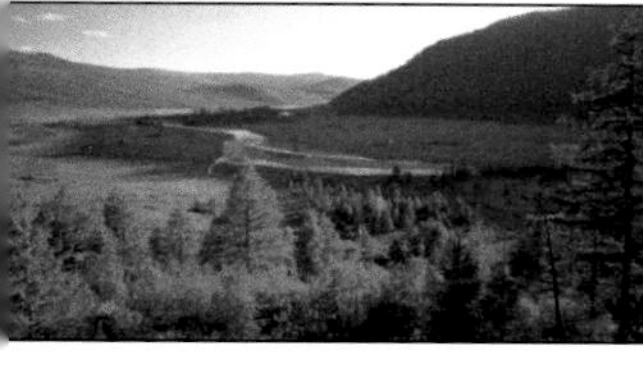

Sayan Mountains Mountain range between central and northern Asia – highest mountain, Munku Sardyk (3,491 meters) in the Eastern Sayan Mountains

Scale 1:18,000,000

0 160 320 Kilometers

Depth tints

- Shoreline
- 0-200 m
- 200-2000 m
- 2000-4000 m
- 4000-6000 m
- 6000-8000 m
- > 8000 m

Physical Features

- River, stream
- Intermittent river
- Lake
- Intermittent lake
- Salt lake
- Intermittent salt lake
- Elevation above sea level in mete

ectly to the east of the West Siberian in lies the **Central Siberian Plateau**. e plateau, located between the **Yeni- y and Lena Rivers**, covers around 3.5 lion km². The tallest peak in the pla- u region lies in the Putoran Mountains d rises 1,701 meters. The **North Sibe- n Lowlands**, a region of vast plains, etch between the plateau and the **ymyr Peninsula**. The archipelago vernaya Zemlya is situated north of this region and off the Arctic Ocean coast of Russia. **Lake Baikal** in southern Siberia is the largest freshwater lake in Asia and the world's deepest with a maximum depth of 1,620 meters. East of Lake Baikal in southern Siberia lies a region of high mountain ranges that stretch to Russia's southeastern borders. The various ranges in this region include the Altai Mountains, the Stanovoy Range, and the Eastern and Western Sayan Range.

Northeastern Siberia is also a mountainous region with numerous mountain ranges and tall peaks. The **Verkhoyansk** and **Kolyma Mountain Ranges** stretch through much of the region. The Yana, Indigirka, and Kolyma plains consist of vast infertile moorlands. The Chukchi Peninsula is mainland Siberia's easternmost region. East of the peninsula is the Bering Strait, which connects the Bering Sea and the Arctic Ocean. **Kamchatka**, a 1,250-kilometer-long peninsula in Siberia's far east, separates the Sea of Okhotsk from the Pacific Ocean. Around seven million square kilometers of Siberia's land is covered by permafrost, a layer of frozen rock and soil. There are three distinct climate and vegetation zones in Siberia: the barren arctic northern islands, a broad strip of tundra along the Arctic coast, and a large taiga region with sub-arctic forests.

OCEAN
Chukchi Sea
East Siberian Sea
New Siberian Islands
Wrangel Island
Bering Strait
Alaska (USA)
Chukotskiy Poluostrov
Chukchi Autonomous District
Bering Sea
Aleutian Basin
Koryak Autonomous District
Sakha
Yakutia
Kamchatka Peninsula
Sea of Okhotsk
PACIFIC OCEAN
Sakhalin
Kuril Islands
Kuril Trench
Stanovoy Khrebet
Lesser Hinggan Range
Greater Hinggan Range
CHINA
HOKKAIDO
JAPAN
Magadan
Petropavlovsk-Kamčatskij
Jakutsk
Habarovsk
Harbin
Sapporo
Political Boundaries
International
International disputed
Main administrative
Transportation
Interstate Hwy./Motorway
Main road
Railway
Airport
Capitals of political units
WASHINGTON D.C. Independent
Richmond State/province
Town symbols
Capital > 1 Mill. inhabitants
Capital < 1 Mill. inhabitants
Statecapital > 1 Mill. inhabitants
Statecapital < 1 Mill. inhabitants
Towns > 1 Mill. inhabitants
Towns 100 000 bis 1 Mill. inhabitants
Towns < 100 000 inhabitants

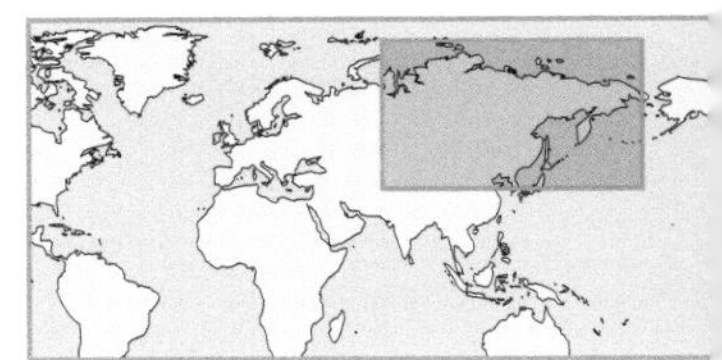

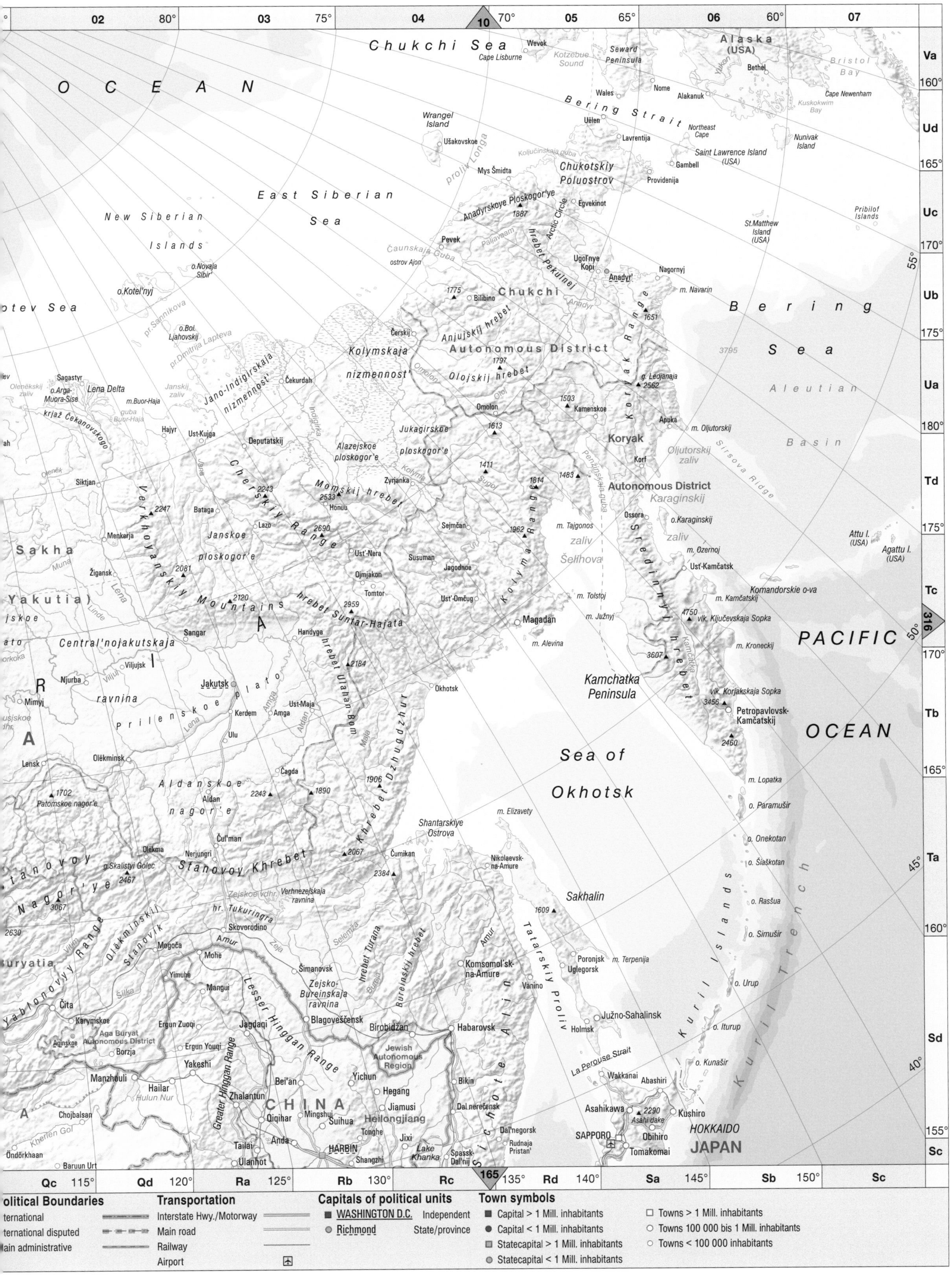

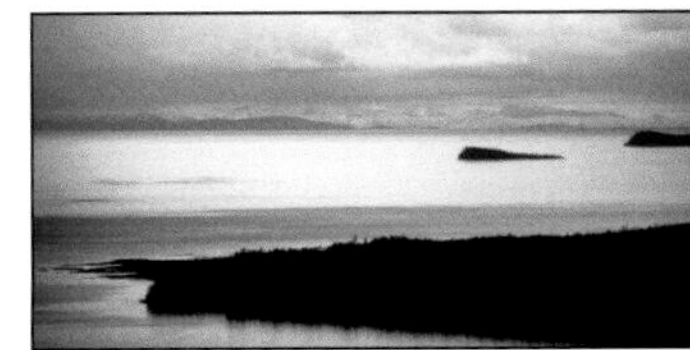

Lake Baikal 31,500 km², 636 kilometers long, and 40 to 80 kilometers wide – deepest freshwater lake on Earth, maximum depth 1,620 meters

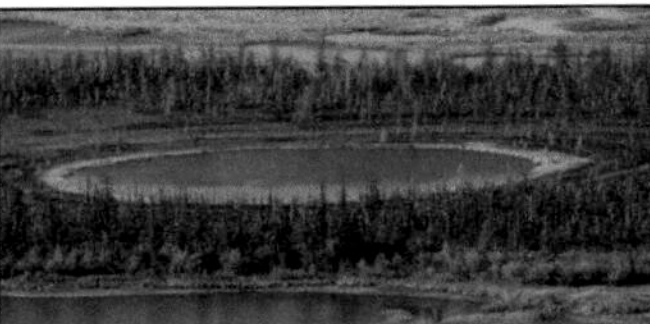

Yakutian Taiga Sub-arctic mixed forests consisting mostly of larches – permafrost ground

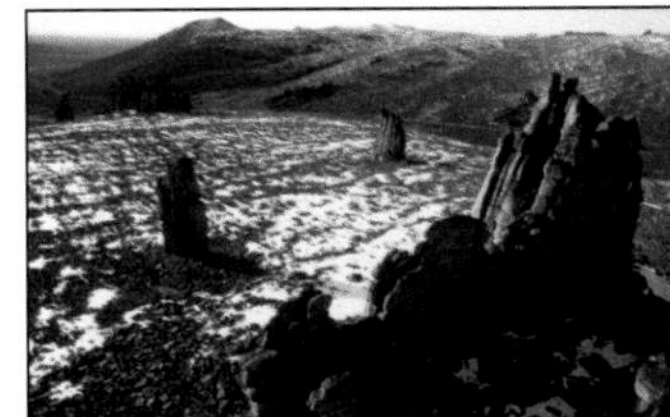

Arctic Coast Long coast consisting of infertile moorlands, river deltas, and steep rocky areas – photo: coastal area near Anadyr

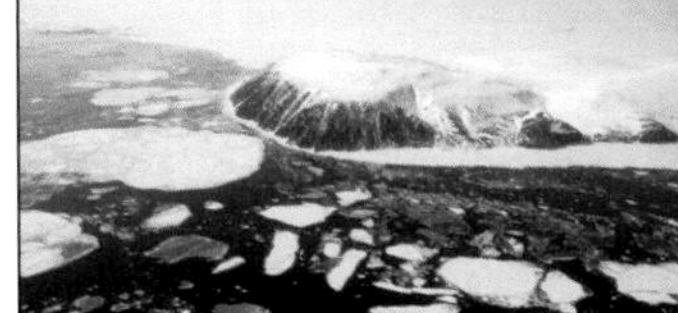

The Bering Strait Named for the Russian explorer Vitus Bering – connects the Bering Sea and the Arctic Ocean – photo: Cape Dezhnev

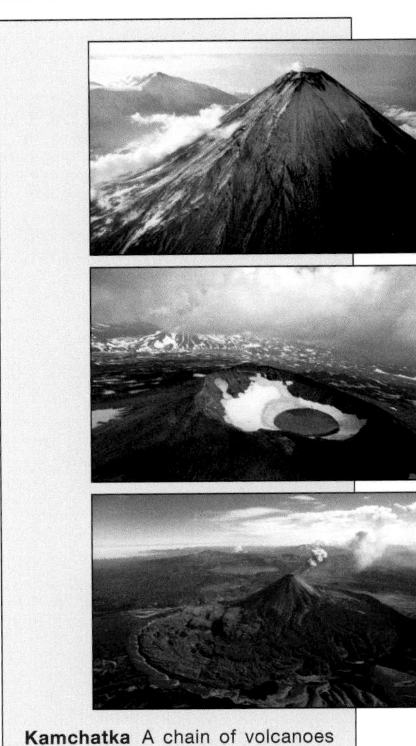

Kamchatka A chain of volcanoes runs through this 1,200-kilometer-long peninsula. The peninsula covers 350,000 km². Southeastern Kamchatka is home to many geysers. Photos from top to bottom: Kliuchevskoi (4,750 meters), Mutnovsky, Karymsky

Near and Middle East

The Middle East is a term encompassing a variety of different nations. The term usually refers to the countries along the eastern coast of the Mediterranean, on the Arabian Peninsula, and along the Persian Gulf.
Anatolia (Asia Minor) contains most of Turkey's territory. Anatolia consists of a large central plateau flanked by two tall mountain ranges; the **Taurus Mountains** in the south and the **Pontus Mountains**

in the north. The two mountain rang stretch from western Turkey to the ea ern edges of the country. **Lake Van**, T key's largest lake, is located in east Anatolia near the Iranian border.
The **Arabian Peninsula** is located b tween the Persian Gulf and the Red S and is the westernmost of Asia's su

The Indus River has a total length of 3,200 kilometers

Anatolia (Asia Minor) Large central plateau flanked by tall mountain ranges – salt lakes – photo: mountains in western Anatolia

Jordan Rift Valley The Dead Sea is the lowest point on the Earth's surface (-829 meters) – Sea of Galilee (photo) – Jordan River

Negev Desert covering most of southern Israel – the southern sections are the driest – photo: hills near the Red Sea

Sinai Peninsula Arid peninsula in Egypt – between the Gulf of Suez and the Gulf of Aqaba – photo: Mount Sinai

Euphrates River 2,500-kilometer-long river – forms the boundaries of Mesopotamia together with the Tigris River – the two rivers merge to form the Shatt al-Arab River

Rub al'Khali/ The Empty Quarter Large sand desert covering almost a third of the Arabian Peninsula – sparsely populated region

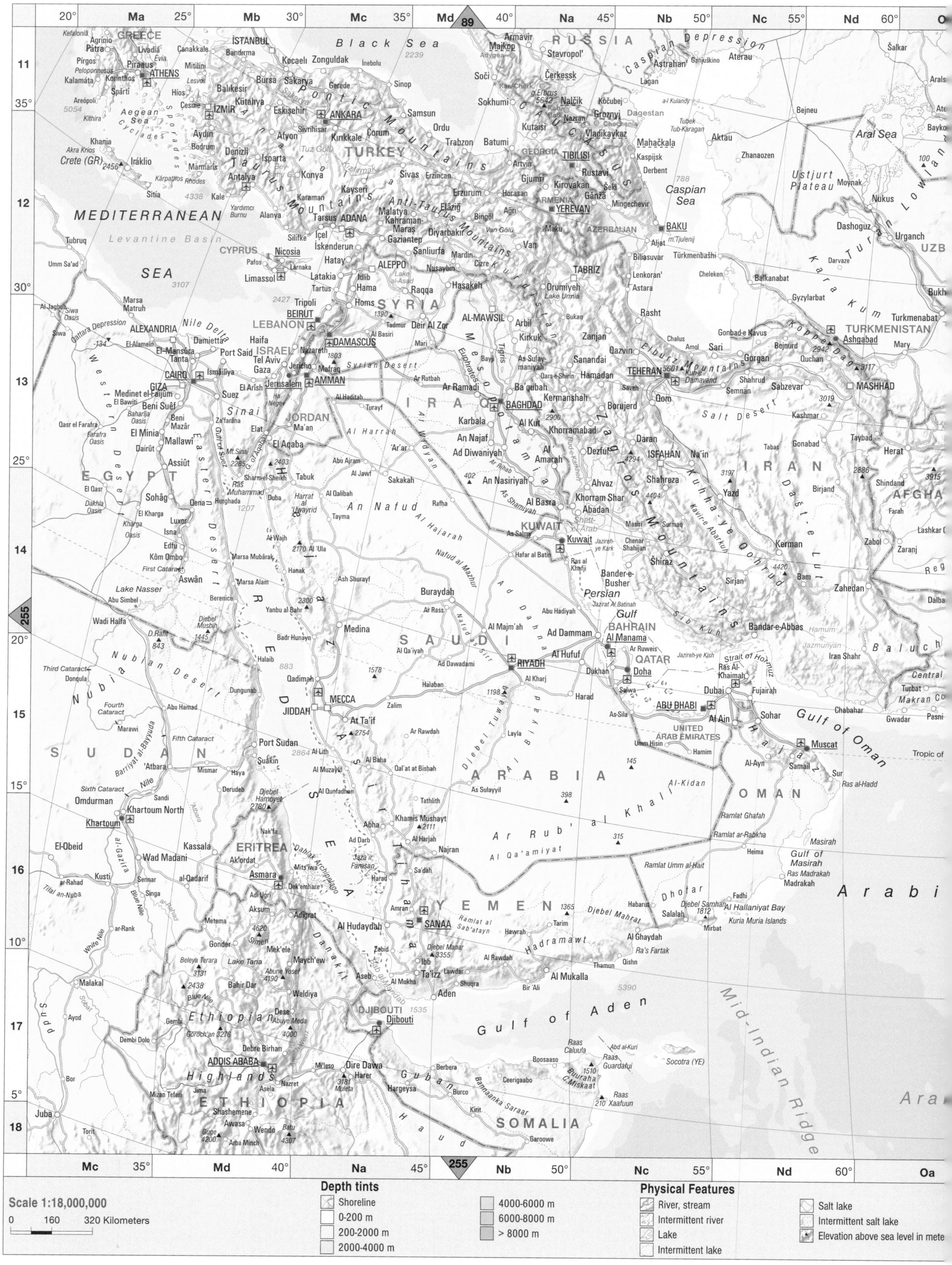

Scale 1:18,000,000
0 160 320 Kilometers

Depth tints
Shoreline
0-200 m
200-2000 m
2000-4000 m
4000-6000 m
6000-8000 m
> 8000 m

Physical Features
River, stream
Intermittent river
Lake
Intermittent lake
Salt lake
Intermittent salt lake
Elevation above sea level in mete

ntinents. The peninsula consists overelmingly of vast barren deserts and the a is an extension of Africa's Sahara sert. The coastal mountains in northstern Arabia border a region of interhighlands. The peninsula's interior is so the location of its most barren serts including the **Nafud Desert** with red sands and the Rub'al Khali. The b'al Khali covers 780,000 km² and is en referred to as the Empty Quarter because most of the area is uninhabited. Historic **Mesopotamia**, the mountainous highlands of Iran, Armenia, and the Caucasus nations are located north of the Persian Gulf. Iran is one of most mountainous nations in the Middle East. The large **Alborz** and **Zagros Mountain ranges** cover most of western and northern Iran. Damavand (5,601 meters), Iran's highest peak, is located in the Alborz Mountains. Eastern and Central Iran contain large basins with numerous salt lakes and vast deserts. **Dasht-e-Lut**, a large sand desert in central and eastern Iran, is one of the hottest places on the Earth. The **Caspian Sea**, the world's largest inland body of water, is around 1,200 kilometers long from north to south. The Caspian Sea basin is bounded in the west by the **Caucasus Mountains**. A region of vast semi-arid lowlands is located to the east of the Caspian Sea. This region encompasses the almost uninhabited **Ustjurt plateau** and the **Kara Kum** desert, a section of the **Turan lowlands**. A large endhoric body of water, the **Aral Sea**, borders this arid region.
The **Hindu Kush** mountain range in Afghanistan contains several peaks rising more than 7,000 meters including Tirich Mir (7,707 meters). The range is a branch of the **Pamir Mountains**, a mountain system extending to the Himalayas.

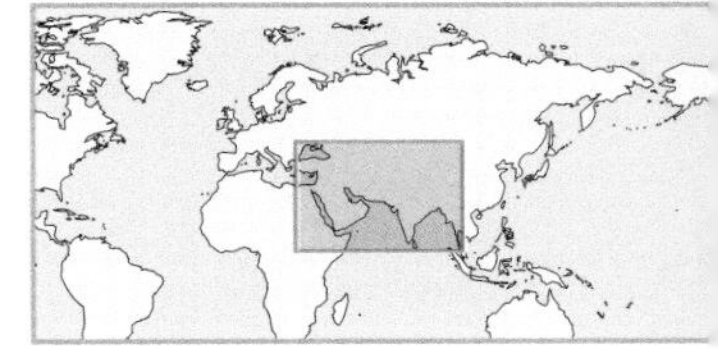

Hajar Mountains Mountain range in Oman in southeastern Arabia – tallest mountain, Jabal Shams (3,108 meters)

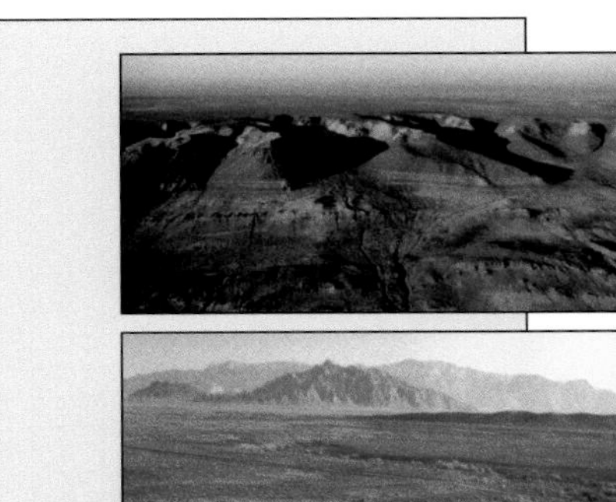

The Steppes and Deserts of Central Asia Includes the vast arid and semi arid region east of the Aral Sea; the Turan lowlands, Kazahks steppes, and Kara Kum deserts.

Alborz Mountains Range in northern Iran, extending to the Caspian Sea coast – photo: Damavand (5,601 meters)

Hindu Kush Mountain range in northeastern Afghanistan – more than 20 mountains above 7,000 meters – Tirich Mir (7,707 meters)

Toba Kakar Range Mountain range in Pakistan and Afghanistan – southeast of Kandahar – Sakir (3,092 m)

Pamir Mountains A combination of several tall mountain ranges located near the Himalayas – highest peak, Kungur (7,719 meters)

olitical Boundaries
ternational
ternational disputed
ain administrative

Transportation
Interstate Hwy./Motorway
Main road
Railway
Airport

Capitals of political units
WASHINGTON D.C. Independent
Richmond State/province

Town symbols
Capital > 1 Mill. inhabitants
Capital < 1 Mill. inhabitants
Statecapital > 1 Mill. inhabitants
Statecapital < 1 Mill. inhabitants
Towns > 1 Mill. inhabitants
Towns 100 000 bis 1 Mill. inhabitants
Towns < 100 000 inhabitants

Turkey, Caucasus Region

With a total area of 780,576 km² and a population around 68 million the Republic of Turkey has a relatively low population density. The country's territory lies on two continents: Europe and Asia. The province of Thrace which encompasses three percent of Turkey's territory is geographically European, while the rest of Turkey lies in Asia.

The historic Turkish city of **Istanbul** is situated on the Bosporus strait, the

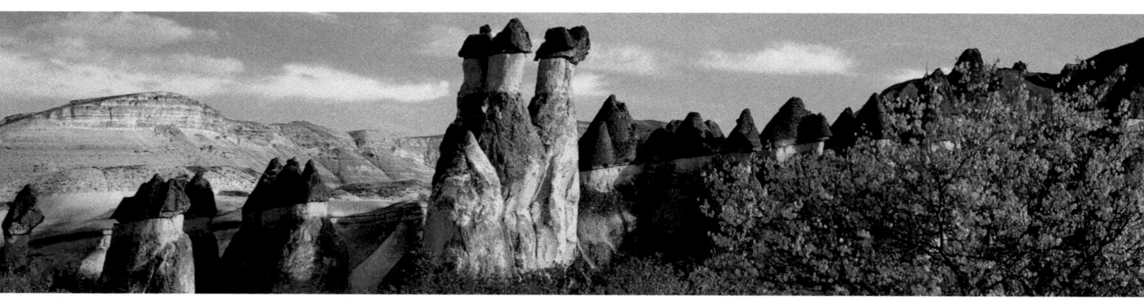

boundary between Europe and Asia. W more than ten million inhabitants Ista bul is the most populous city in Turk Turkey is divided into 80 provinces ru from the national capital **Ankara** in t mountains of Anatolia.

Turkey is home to a variety of uniq landscapes and regions. The countr

Natural stone formations near Göreme (Turkey) **Mh**

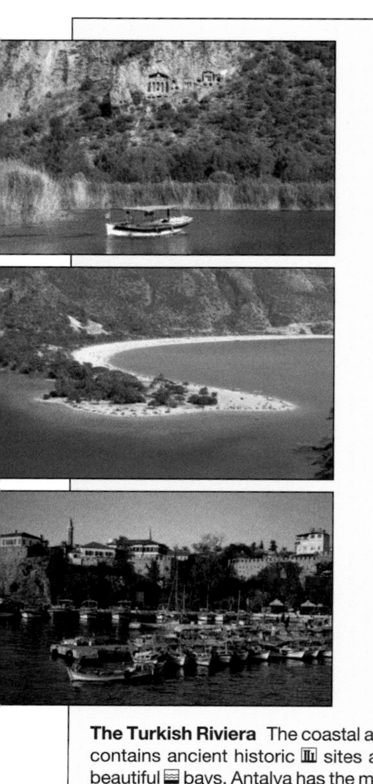

The Turkish Riviera The coastal area contains ancient historic sites and beautiful bays. Antalya has the most beautiful harbor in the region. Photos from top to bottom: ancient burial site near Daylan, the beach of Ölu Deniz, Antalya harbor **MeMf27**

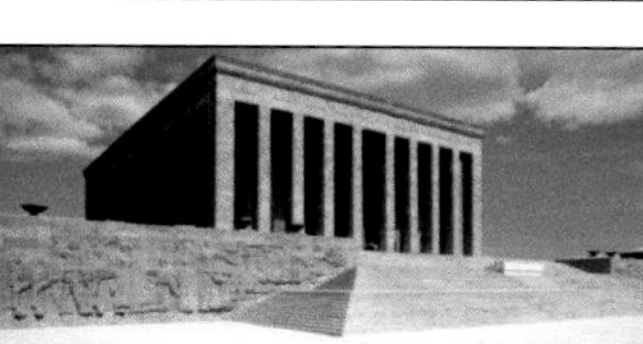

Ankara Turkey's capital – Roman ruins – Museum of Anatolian Civilization – photo: Atatürk mausoleum **Mg26**

Konya Former capital of the Seljuk Empire – Mevlevi Convent – photo: Whirling Dervishes **Mg27**

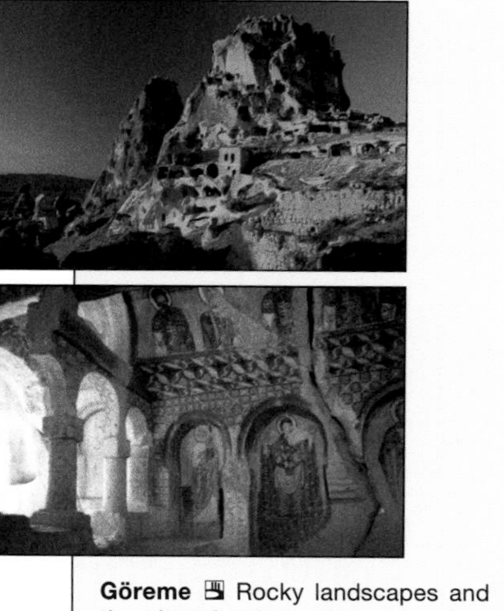

Göreme Rocky landscapes and the site of unique stone churches (top photo) in the heart of Anatolia. Göreme Museum Park (bottom photo) is a world heritage site. **Mh26**

Mc 26° Md 28° Me 134 30° Mf 32° Mg 34°

BLACK

GREECE · BULGARIA · İSTANBUL · ANKARA · TURKEY · CYPRUS · LEBANON

AEGEAN SEA

MEDITERRANEAN SEA

Levantine Basin

Me 30° Mf 32° 146 Mg 34° Mh 36° Mj 38°

Scale 1:4,500,000
0 40 80 Kilometers

Principal travel routes
- Auto route
- Rail road
- Shipping route

Remarkable landscapes and natural monuments
- UNESCO World Natural Heritage
- Mountain landscape
- Rock landscape
- Ravine/canyon
- Cave
- Waterfall/rapids
- Nature park
- National park (landscape)
- National park (flora)
- National park (fauna)
- National park (culture)
- Coastal landscape
- Beach
- Island

uthern and western coasts contain merous ancient archeological sites cluding the ruins of **Pergamon**, **Troy**, d **Ephesus**.

rthern Turkey is covered by the tall ountains and foothills of the **Pontic ountain Range** which extend to the rkish Black Sea coast. Like the north, uthern Turkey is also a mountainous gion. The **Taurus Mountain Range** d its foothills extend through most of southern Turkey. The highlands of eastern Turkey contain the nation's highest mountain **Mount Ararat**, an extinct volcano which rises 5,165 meters. Anatolia's large central plateau features many of Turkey's unique natural and cultural attractions. Several large **salt lakes** including Tuz Gölu are located in the region. **Cappodocia**, a historic region on the central plateau, is home to hundreds of unique ancient churches carved into rock formations. The ruins at Hattusa are ancient remnants of the Hittite civilization and **Konya** is the spiritual center of the Whirling Dervishes, a religious sect famous for its unique spiritual dances.

The Firat (Euphrates) and Dicle (Tigris) Rivers are the principal rivers in eastern Turkey. Several large dams constructed on the rivers have helped to transform eastern Turkey into a fertile region with productive agriculture. Eastern Turkey is the traditional homeland of Turkey's large Kurdish minority. The region is also home to **Lake Van**, Turkey's largest lake. Mountainous northeastern Turkey is covered by the foothills of the Caucasus which stretch into neighboring countries. Turkey's **Black Sea coast** is a fertile region with heavy rainfall throughout the year. The coast is the site of numerous ancient settlements and historic ruins.

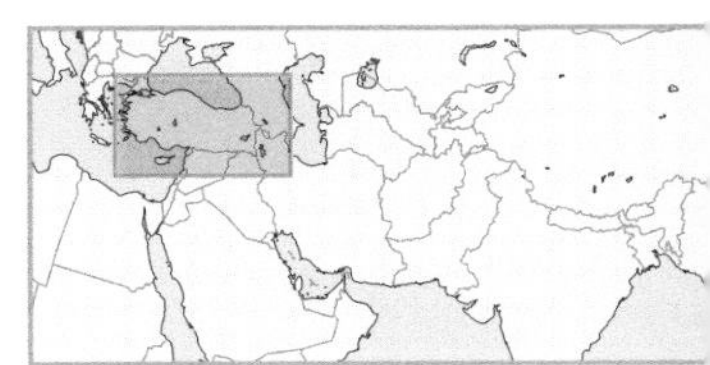

Hattuşa Ancient ruins in the Anatolian highlands – once the center of Hittite civilization – preserved city gates (photo) – UNESCO world heritage site **Mh26**

Nemrut Dağı Extensive burial site of Antiochus I (69-38 BC) – large statues of kings and gods (photo) **Mk26**

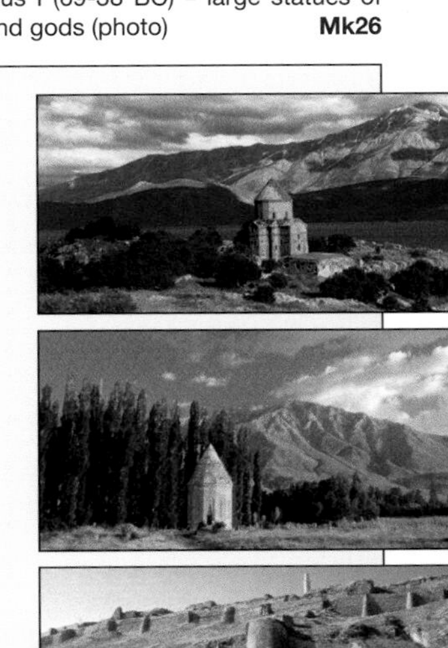

Lake Van The largest lake in Turkey was first settled around 840 BC. Photos from top to bottom: the ruins of Ahtamar church, Hasan Paşa Kümbret, castle ruins, waterfalls near Muradiye **Nb26**

Aleppo Ancient trading and cultural center in Syria – citadel containing a mosque and a Mamluk palace (photo) **Mj27**

Hatra Historic remnants of an ancient fortified city in Mesopotamia (Iraq) – Parthian architecture – large temple to Greek and Parthian gods (photo) – UNESCO world heritage site **Nb28**

Remarkable Cities and Cultural monuments

- UNESCO World Cultural Heritage
- Remarkable Cities
- Pre- and early history
- The Ancient Orient
- Greek antiquity
- Roman antiquity
- Places of Christian cultural interest
- Places of Islamic cultural interest
- Pl. of cult. interest to other religions
- Historical city scape
- Castle/fortress/fort
- Caravanserai
- Palace
- Dam
- Remarkable bridge
- Tomb/grave

Sport and leisure destinations

- Horse racing
- Skiing
- Sailing
- Wind surfing
- Canoeing/rafting
- Seaport
- Beach resort
- Mineral/thermal spa

Lebanon, Syria, Israel, Jordan, Iraq

North of the **Arabian Peninsula** is a large triangle shaped region covered mostly by deserts and semi-arid plains. Situated along the Mediterranean coast, the western section of the region is home to several mountain ranges and rift valleys. The **Lebanon** and **Anti-Lebanon Mountains** are the region's principal coastal mountain ranges. Both ranges merge with a series of smaller mountain ranges in Syria and Jordan. The **Gulf of Aqaba** and the **Jordan Rift Valley** are sectic of an enormous fracture zone that al encompasses the Great Rift Valley in A ca. The surface of the salty **Dead Sea** l around 829 meters below sea level a is the lowest point on the Earth's surfac The coasts, coastal mountains, and in rior mountains of Israel, Lebanon, Sy

Camels were once vital for travel through the Syrian desert **MjMk**

Baalbek Spiritual center for the Phoenicians and Romans – Temple of Jupiter (photo) – UNESCO world heritage site **Mj28**

Damascus Capital city of Syria – the old town is a UNESCO world heritage site – Omayyad Mosque – Saladin's mausoleum – "burial site" of St. John **Mj29**

Acre (Acco) Port city in Israel – medieval town center – historic "crusaders" buildings – Ahmed-al-Jazzar mosque **Mh29**

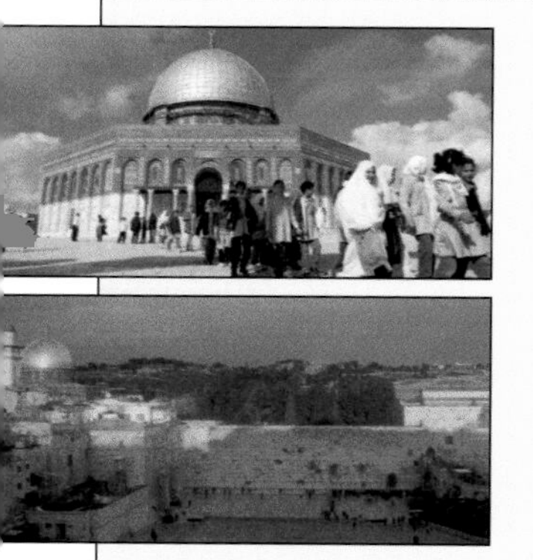

Jerusalem The capital of Israel is a holy city for three major religions; Judaism, Christianity, and Islam. The Dome of the Rock (top photo) is at the center of the Temple mount in the old city. The al-Aqsa mosque also lies in the old town. At the foot of the Temple mount is the Western Wall (bottom photo), a Jewish holy site. The Via Dolorosa stretches from the Sacred Tomb to Golgotha, where Jesus Christ was crucified. **Mh30**

The Dead Sea Saline lake – the surface, 395 meters below sea level, is the lowest point on the Earth's surface **Mh30**

Petra Capital of the Nabataean civilization – palaces and temples carved into stone walls – UNESCO world heritage site **Mh30**

Scale 1:4,500,000

0 40 80 Kilometers

Principal travel routes

- Auto route
- Rail road
- Shipping route

Remarkable landscapes and natural monuments

- UNESCO World Natural Heritage
- Mountain landscape
- Rock landscape
- Ravine/canyon
- Cave
- Waterfall/rapids
- Lake country
- Desert
- National park (landscape)
- National park (fauna)
- Wildlife reserve
- Coastal landscape
- Beach
- Coral reef
- Island
- Underwater reserve

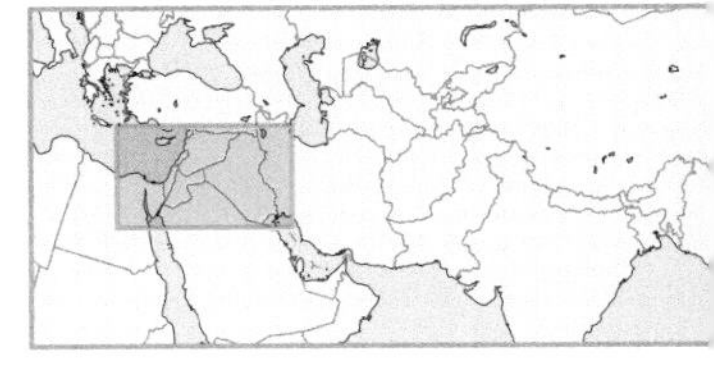

d Jordan are fertile areas that have en densely populated since ancient nes. In stark contrast to these areas, any places farther in the interior are vered by sparsely populated deserts th extremely hot daytime temperatures d freezing winters. eyond the barren deserts of Syria d the Nafud Desert in Saudi Arabia the Euphrates and Tigris Rivers. e Tigris and Euphrates both have their sources in the mountains of eastern Turkey. Together the two rivers nourish and define the historic region of Mesopotamia. **Mesopotamia** covers a large section of modern Iraq and the region is often referred to as the "cradle of civilization" because of the relatively advanced cultures that inhabited the region during ancient times.

With the use of modern technology and irrigation techniques Israel has made major agricultural advances in the extremely dry **Negev Desert** and sections of eastern **Sinai**. The Negev is dotted by numerous dried river beds called wadis which can suddenly fill with water during winter floods. The well preserved remnants of **Petra**, the ancient capital of the Nabataean culture, are located in a gorge near the Wadi Araba valley. The city was once a major trading center along the ancient trade route between Mesopotamia and the Mediterranean coast. The grand historic architecture in Syrian cities such as Damascus and Tadmor (Palmyra) are evidence that these cities were once major centers of commerce and trade.

Israel's capital city, Jerusalem, has been a melting pot of different religions and cultures since the Roman era. The city continues to attract many pilgrims of various faiths from around the world.

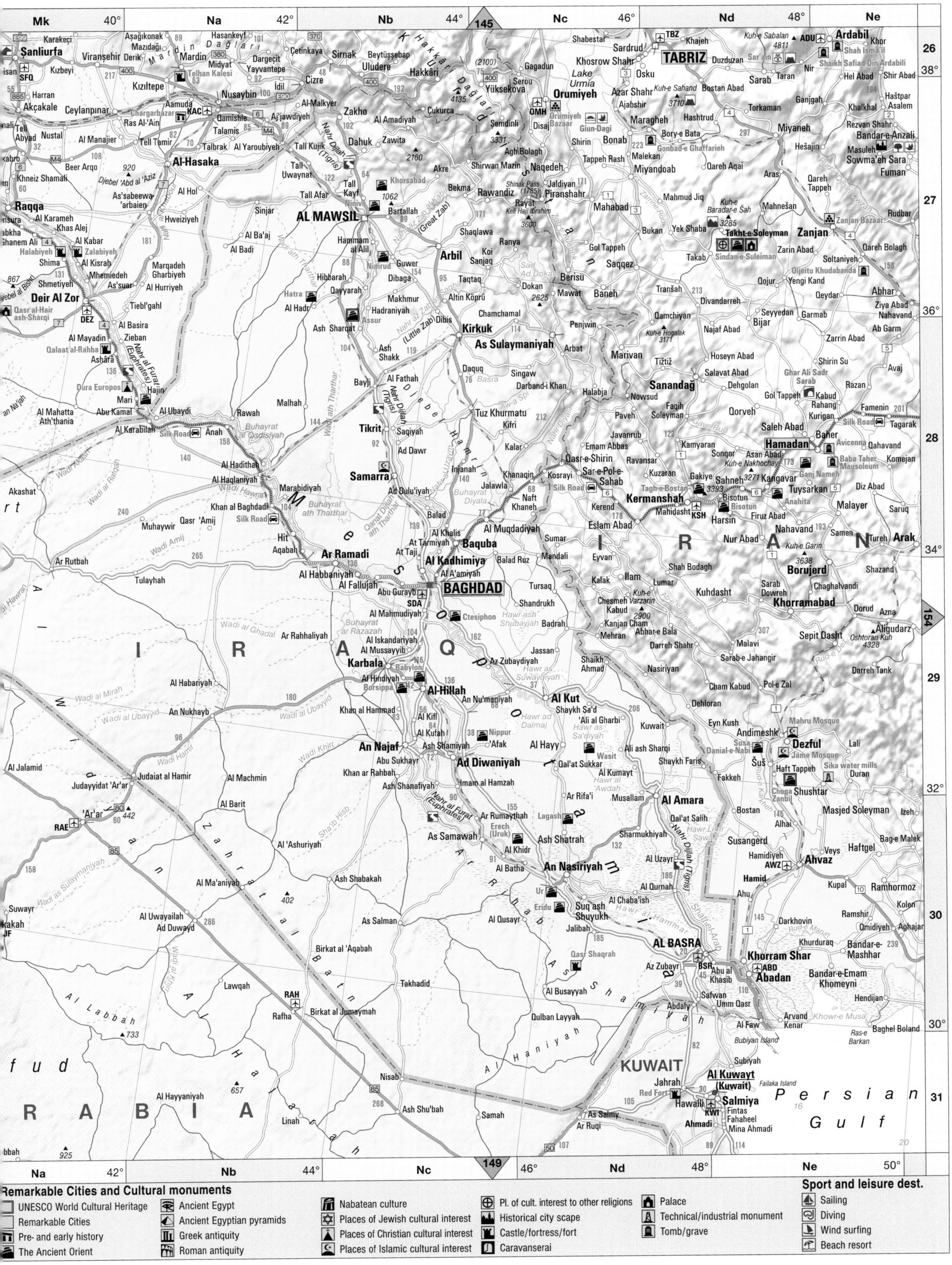

Palmyra/Tadmor ruins of an ancient city in Syria – 4,000 years old – UNESCO world heritage site – museum **Mk28**

Samarra Shiite pilgrimage site in Iraq – ruins of caliphal palaces – spiral minarets of the Great Mosque **Nb28**

Bagdad Capital of Iraq – population, 4.5 million – Tahrir Square (photo) – palaces from the Abbasids era – historic Umm el-Mahare mosques **Nc29**

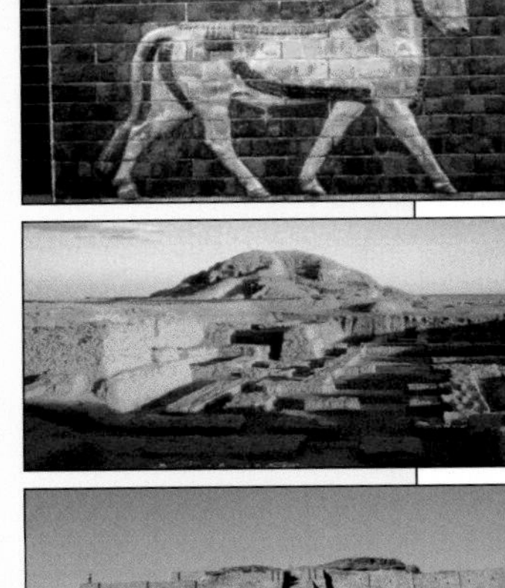

Sumerian and Babylonian Culture
The Sumerians wandered into southern Mesopotamia around 4000 BC and founded the city states of Ur and Babylon. In addition to colorful mosaics, remnants of Sumerian sculpture have also been found throughout southern Mesopotamia. Arabian nomads mixed with the Sumerians around 3500 BC. The new culture founded Ur and the world's first dynasty around 2500 BC. Photos from to bottom: section of the Babylon's Ishtar Gate, temple in Uruk, ziggurat in Ur

Euphrates The longest river in western Asia, 2,375 kilometers – source in Turkey, flows through Syria and Iraq – delta on the Persian Gulf – several large dams have been constructed along the river **MjNd27/30**

Remarkable Cities and Cultural monuments
- UNESCO World Cultural Heritage
- Remarkable Cities
- Pre- and early history
- The Ancient Orient
- Ancient Egypt
- Ancient Egyptian pyramids
- Greek antiquity
- Roman antiquity
- Nabatean culture
- Places of Jewish cultural interest
- Places of Christian cultural interest
- Places of Islamic cultural interest
- Pl. of cult. interest to other religions
- Historical city scape
- Castle/fortress/fort
- Caravanserai
- Palace
- Technical/industrial monument
- Tomb/grave

Sport and leisure dest.
- Sailing
- Diving
- Wind surfing
- Beach resort

The kingdom of **Saudi Arabia** comprises the vast majority of the Arabian Peninsula – including the central section of the peninsula with the Islamic holy cities of Mecca and Medina. Most of western Saudi Arabia is covered by a large plateau containing **vast barren stone and sand deserts**. The plateau descends in "steps" in the east and in the west it merges with the Hijaz Mountains which contain peaks rising more than 3,000 meters above sea level. Along the R Sea coast, the Hijaz Mountains dr abruptly to the sea. Saudi Arabia is hor to some of the most expansive dese in the world including the Nafud des in the country's north and the Rub'al Kh (Empty Quarter) in the south. The int ior of Saudi Arabia contains numerous

A desert highway on the Persian Gulf coast **Ne**

Madain Salah Spectacular Nebetaean rock tombs with well preserved facades – 300 kilometers north of Medina **Mj32**

Medina Historic city in western Saudi Arabia – Masjid Al Nabawi (photo), mosque and the burial site of the Islamic prophet Muhammad **Mk33**

Harrat Rahat Arid volcanic lava field south of Medina – one of twelve lava field deserts in Saudi Arabia **Na34**

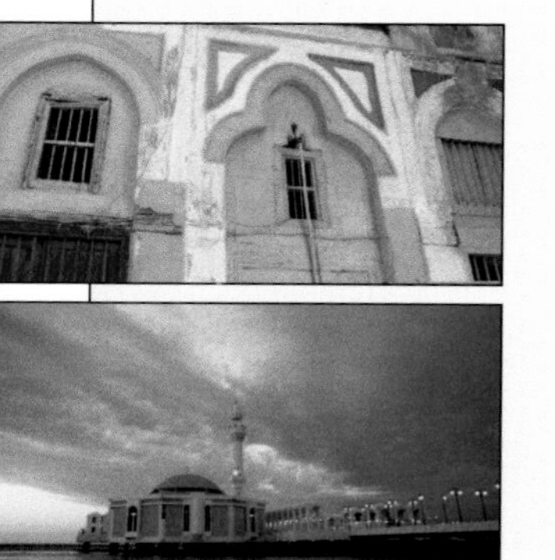

Jeddah Modern port city on the Red Sea. The city has a restored old town (top photo) with historic architecture and an old marketplace. Sixty-kilometer-long coastal road Corniche with beautiful mosques (bottom photo), palaces, and villas. **Mk35**

Mecca The most holy spiritual center of Islam – pilgrimage site visited by millions annually during the Hajj – the Prophet's Mosque containing the Kaaba (photo), which pilgrims circle seven times – Mount Arafat is 15 kilometers from the city **Mk35**

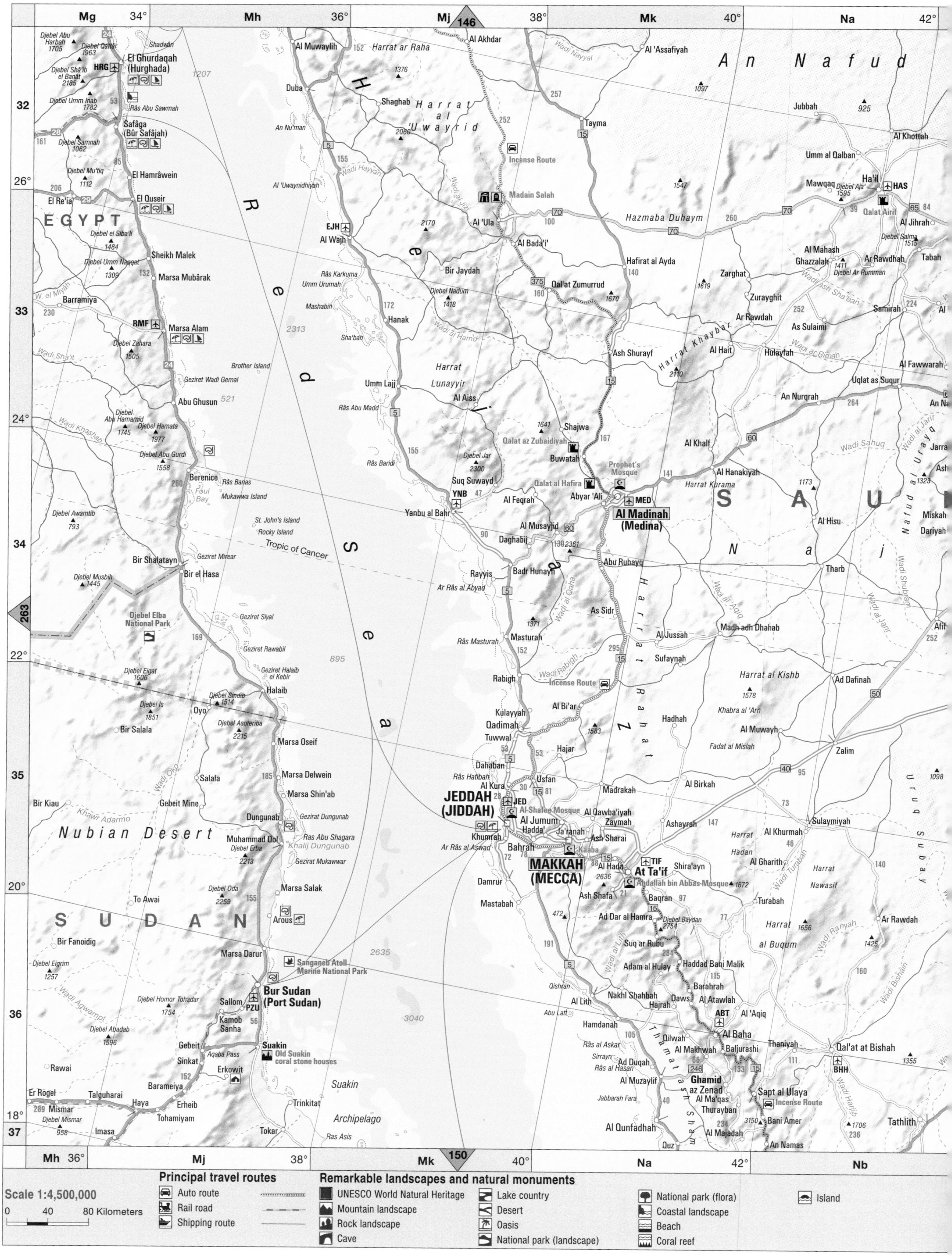

146
263
150

Scale 1:4,500,000
0 40 80 Kilometers

Principal travel routes
- Auto route
- Rail road
- Shipping route

Remarkable landscapes and natural monuments
- UNESCO World Natural Heritage
- Mountain landscape
- Rock landscape
- Cave
- Lake country
- Desert
- Oasis
- National park (landscape)
- National park (flora)
- Coastal landscape
- Beach
- Coral reef
- Island

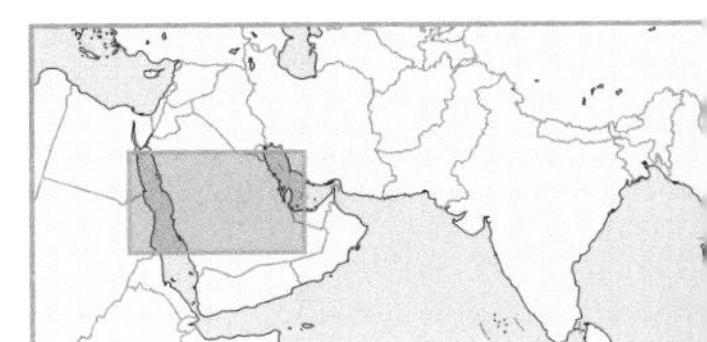

adis, dry river beds that can flood sud-
nly after rainfall.
uwait is situated on the northwestern
lge of the Arabian Peninsula. The coun-
 consists of a mostly flat **desert**
terior and a short coastline along the
ersian Gulf. Kuwait's deserts rise in
evation towards the Iraqi border and
entually rise to a maximum height of
0 meters above sea level.
ne Kingdom of **Bahrain** encompasses 33 islands in the Gulf of Bahrain. The kingdom's main island, Bahrain, consists mostly of sand dunes and marshes.

Qatar is an arid peninsula, located fifty kilometers south of Bahrain, along the western edge of the Persian Gulf. The country's interior is mostly flat, expansive deserts and semi-arid areas.

The **United Arab Emirates** is a federation of small emirates on the eastern edge of the Arabian Peninsula. More than two-thirds of the country's territory is covered by deserts. The deserts of the country extend to just before the Persian Gulf coast. A narrow three-kilometer-wide strip of fertile land stretches along the coast. Dates, mangos, bananas, and vegetables are widely cultivated in this area.

The economies of the countries in northern Arabia are dominated by the region's large oil and natural gas deposits.

Saudi Arabia's interior contains some of the hottest areas on the planet. Many of these desert areas remain almost totally uninhabited. Most of the settlements in the Saudi interior are built near oases or near the edges of the desert. Despite the high temperatures common throughout the region, low humidity makes the climates tolerable in many places. During summer, temperatures in northern Arabia often exceed 40° Celsius and in the some areas even 50° Celsius.

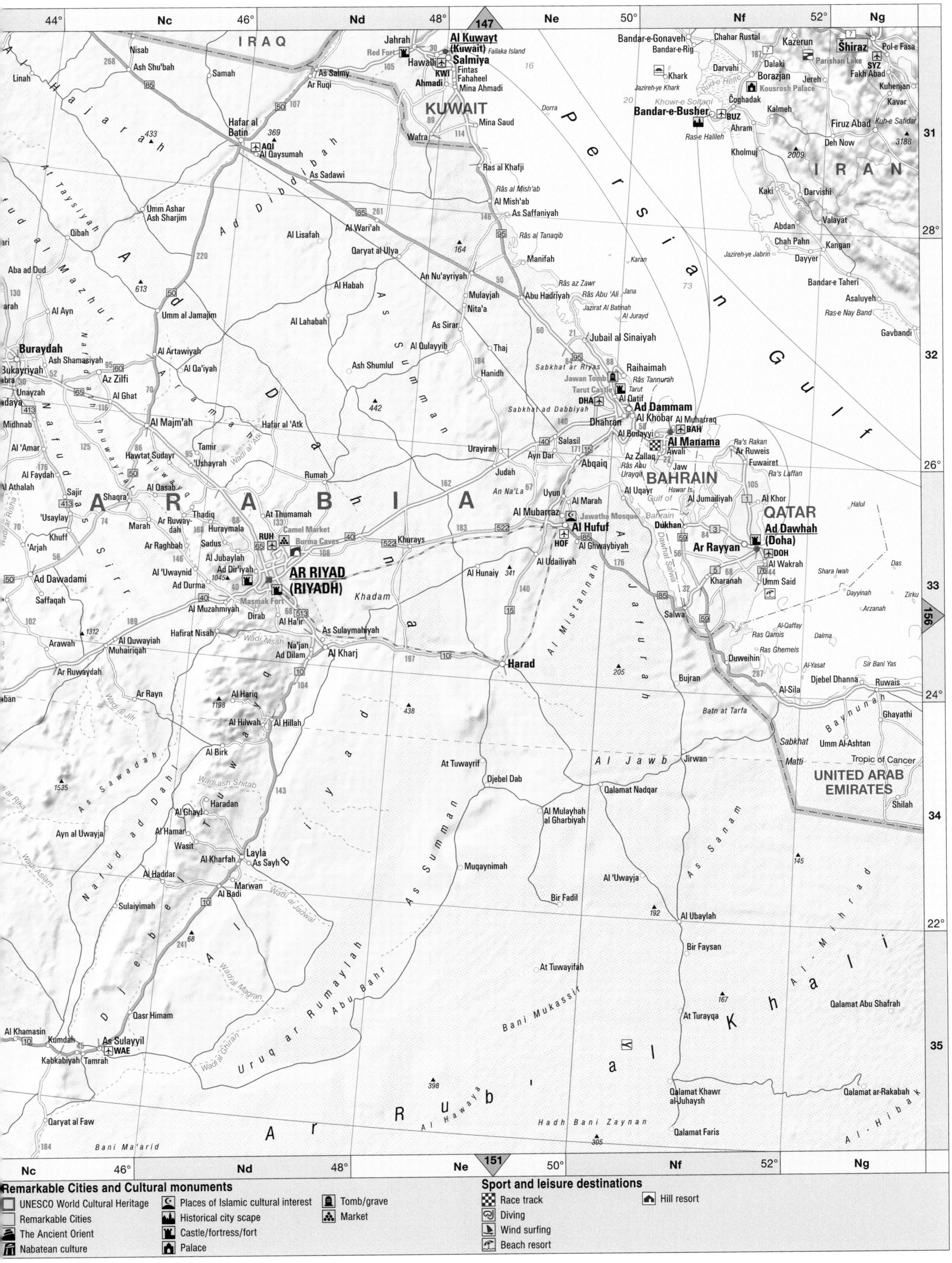

Kuwait City Capital city of the desert nation Kuwait. The three Kuwait Towers (photo) are the city's principal landmark. Major attractions include the old town, fishing harbor, and the Sief palace. **NdNe31**

Al Manama Bahrain's capital city – skyscrapers and traditional architecture – Al Fateh mosque (photo) **Nf32**

Doha Capital city of Qatar on the Persian Gulf – traditional dhows (boats) in the harbor (photo) **Nf33**

Riyadh Saudi Arabia's capital city – Dira Square with the Friday Mosque – markets – National Museum – futuristic Ministry of the Interior building (photo) **Nd33**

Ad Dir'iyah The traditional home of the Al-Saud royal dynasty – ruins of the house of Al-Saud – north of Riyadh **Nd33**

Remarkable Cities and Cultural monuments

- UNESCO World Cultural Heritage
- Remarkable Cities
- The Ancient Orient
- Nabatean culture
- Places of Islamic cultural interest
- Historical city scape
- Castle/fortress/fort
- Palace
- Tomb/grave
- Market

Sport and leisure destinations

- Race track
- Diving
- Wind surfing
- Beach resort
- Hill resort

Southern Arabian Peninsula

The south of the Arabian Peninsula encompasses Oman, Yemen, and the southernmost regions of Saudi Arabia. **Yemen** is situated on the southwestern edge of the Arabian Peninsula. The country has an area of 527,968 km². **Tihamah**, a narrow arid plain, stretches along the Red Sea coast in Western Yemen. The region is bounded in the west by a series of **mountain ranges**. The country's tallest mountain, Jabal an Nabi

Traditional architecture in Wadi Doan (Yemen) **Ne38**

Shu'ayb, is located in the mountain ranges of western Yemen. Across the border in Saudi Arabia, the **Asir Mountain range** features several mountains taller than 3,000 meters. Monsoon winds from the Indian Ocean bring sporadic rainfall to the highlands of western Yemen during summer. In ancient times, most of west-

ern Yemen was ruled by the power **Kingdom of Saba (Sheba)**, which cc trolled Arabia's valuable **frankincen trade**. North of Yemen's southern co stretches a chain of plateaus and v canoes. The **Jol mountain plate** covers a large area in the center of t country. Around 160 kilometers inlan the Yemeni highlands drop abruptly to t flat desert that covers much of the cou try's interior. Yemen's interior is home

Clay Buildings Common in Saudi Arabia's Asir Mountains region, a popular summer destination with a temperate climate **Na36**

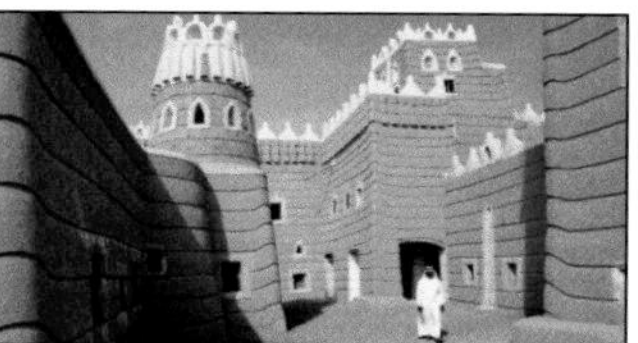

Najran Saudi province containing a large oasis – along the ancient frankincense route – Ibn Madi palace (photo) **Nc37**

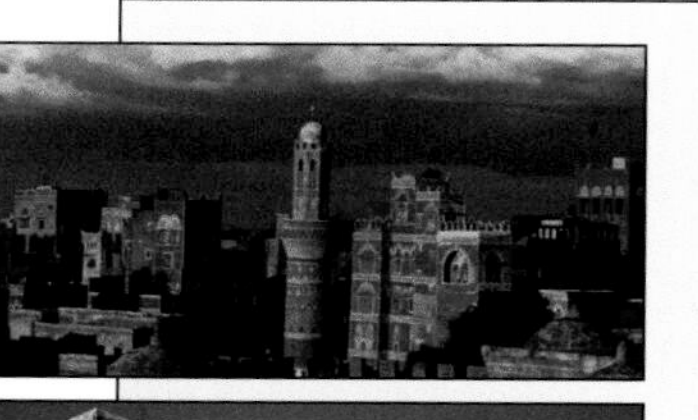

Sanaa The city's unique architecture includes traditional tower buildings (photo). The old town is a UNESCO world heritage site. The city's Great Mosque contains important old handwritten versions of the Koran. Sanaa has a vibrant marketplace (bottom photo). **Nc38**

Wadi Dahr Contains the Dar al-Hajar rock palace (photo) – summer residence of local imams **Nc38**

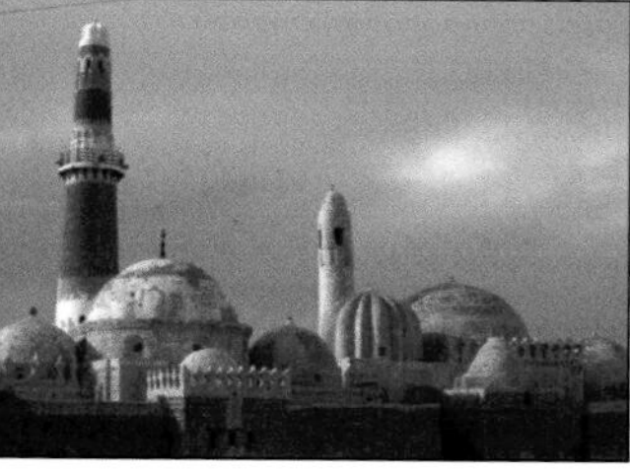

Sa'dah Location of the Al Hadi mosque (photo) – center of the Zaydi Shiites – historic old town **Nb37**

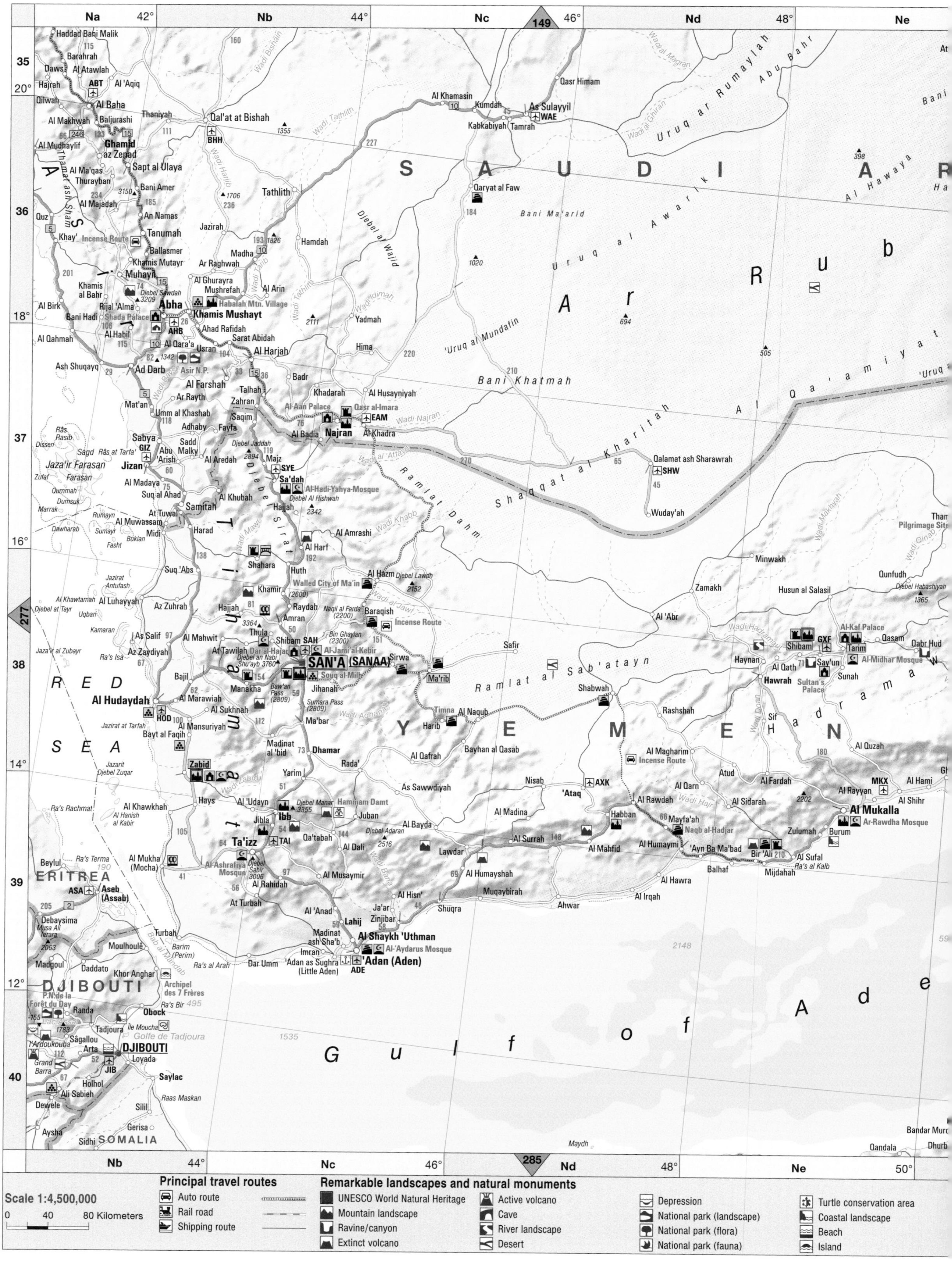

149

277

285

Scale 1:4,500,000

0 40 80 Kilometers

Principal travel routes

Auto route
Rail road
Shipping route

Remarkable landscapes and natural monuments

UNESCO World Natural Heritage
Mountain landscape
Ravine/canyon
Extinct volcano
Active volcano
Cave
River landscape
Desert
Depression
National park (landscape)
National park (flora)
National park (fauna)
Turtle conservation area
Coastal landscape
Beach
Island

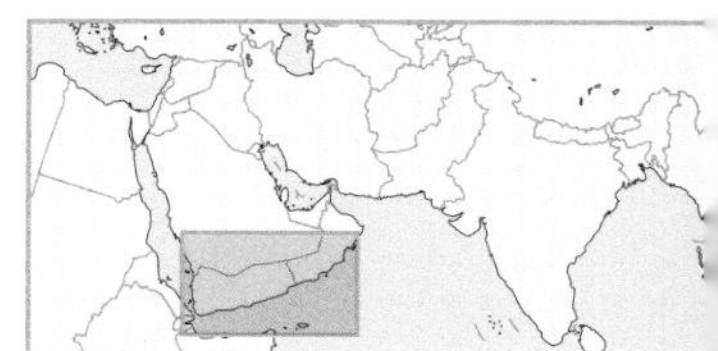

veral large dried watercourses called ıdis including the **Wadi Hadhra-awt**, the largest wadi in Arabia. **Soco- Archipelago**, a Yemeni island group the Indian Ocean is home to unique ·a. Major dams and irrigation projects vital to agriculture in arid Yemen. men coastal regions – including the ıamah – have hot humid climates, while ost of the country's highlands have nperate climates. In Yemen's vast desert regions, including the Wadi Hadhramawt and the **Ramlat Al-Sab'atayn**, temperatures regularly exceed 50° Celsius during summer. Yemen has around 20 million inhabitants and is the second most populous country on the Arabian Peninsula. Yemen's capital **Sanaa** is located in a mountainous interior region. Most of the country's population is concentrated in the temperate mountainous regions. **Najran** province in **Saudi Arabia** has strong cultural and historic connections to Yemen. Most of southern Saudi Arabia is covered by the vast and almost totally uninhabited **Ar Rub' al Khali** desert – also widely known as the Empty Quarter.

The **Sultanate of Oman** is situated on the southern edge of the Arabian Peninsula, to the east of Yemen. Oman varies between 200 and 700 kilometers in width from north to south. The Umm as Samim is a unique desert landscape with salt marshes and quicksand fields located in central Oman, along the edges of Saudi Arabia's Rub'al Khali desert. Oman's largest island territory, Masirah Island, is an important habitat for migratory birds and a breeding ground for sea turtles. **Jiddat al-Harasis** is an expansive rocky desert in central Oman that contains sanctuaries for the Arabian oryx (antelope) population.

Remarkable Cities and Cultural monuments

- UNESCO World Cultural Heritage
- Remarkable Cities
- The Ancient Orient
- Places of Islamic cultural interest
- Cultural landscape
- Historical city scape
- Castle/fortress/fort
- Palace
- Remarkable bridge
- Tomb/grave
- Market

Sport and leisure destinations

- Diving
- Seaport
- Beach resort
- Mineral/thermal spa
- Hill resort

The villages and cities of the Yemeni highlands The highlands of western Yemen are the wettest and most heavily populated region in the country. Terraced agriculture (grain, coffee, etc.) has been practiced in the area since ancient times. Tall tower buildings are common in the region's cities. Photos from top to bottom: terrace farms near Al Mahwit, Thula, Tiwala **Nb38**

Habban Village between Aden and Mukalla at the foot of a large plateau – once home to a large community of Jewish silversmiths – palaces **Nd38**

Socotra Archipelago of volcanic islands in the Indian Ocean – nature reserves – frankincense trees – dragon blood trees – sea turtles **Nh39**

Wadi Hadhramawt Situated in a valley surrounded by high plateaus, this area is the economic center of eastern Yemen. Dates, grains, and fruits are all grown here. The towering buildings of Shibam, a UNESCO world heritage site (top photo) are surrounded by an old city wall. The city of Say'un is home to a large sultan's palace (bottom photo). **Ne37/38**

Caspian Sea Region

The **Caspian Sea** covers 371,000 km² and is the largest inland body of water in the world. The sea has a maximum depth of 1,000 meters and its surface lies around 28 meters below sea level. Five nations have borders along the Caspian Sea; Russia, Kazakhstan, Turkmenistan, Azerbaijan, Armenia, and Georgia. The Caucasus is a mountainous region – between the Caspian and Black Seas – comprised of Armenia, Azerbaijan, and Georgia. The Caucasus nation of **Georgia** has an area of 69,700 km². Georgia's capital city **Tbilisi** is located along the banks of the Mtkvari River in the southwest. The Mtkvari flows from Georgia to its delta near Baku, Azerbaijan on the Caspian Sea coast. Most of northern Georgia is covered by the snowy mountains and foothills of the **Greater Ca casus** mountain range. Georgia's Bla Sea coast consists of fertile plains wit subtropical climate and abundant rainf The country's eastern coast along t Caspian Sea is an arid region with a c climate. The **Lesser Caucasus** mou tain range covers most of southwest Georgia and stretches over the bord into Armenia.

Armenia is a mountainous nation wit

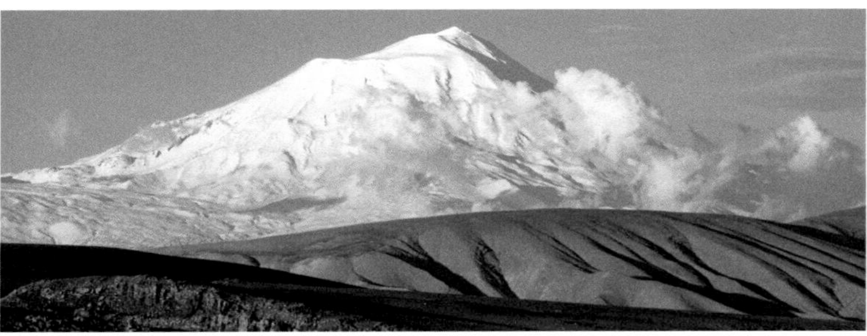

Mount Ararat rises 5,165 meters in northeastern Turkey **Nc26**

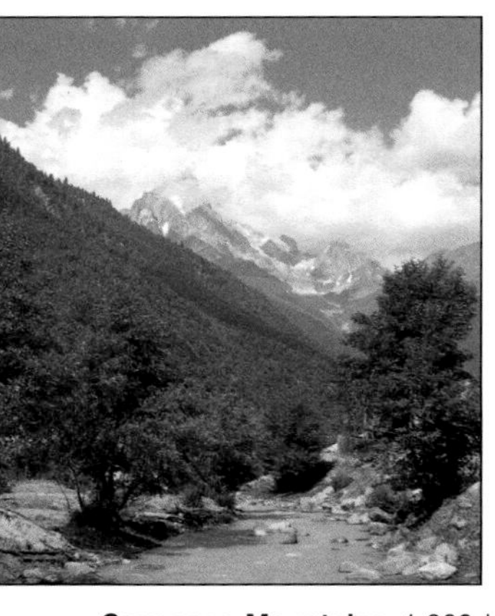

Caucasus Mountains 1,200-kilometer-long range – Greater and Lesser Caucasus – world heritage site **MkNe23/25**

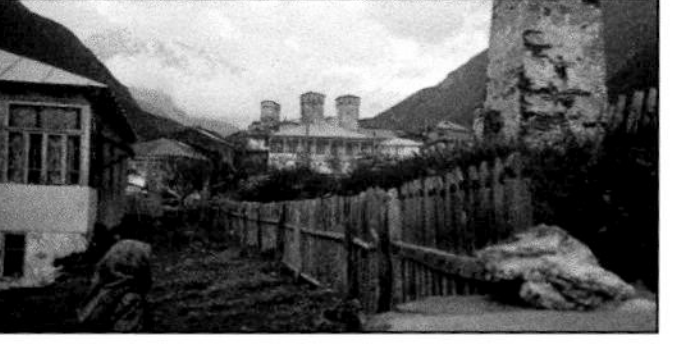

Svaneti Region in Georgia's Greater Caucasus mountains – historic homes with defensive towers (photo) – hot springs – numerous scenic hiking trails **Nb24**

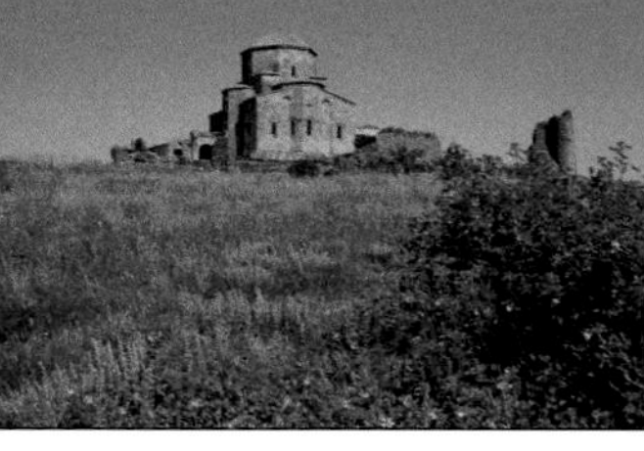

Mtskheta First settled around 3000 BC – Capital of the Georgian Kingdom of Iberia in ancient times – Svetitskhoveli cathedral, a world heritage site (photo) **Nc25**

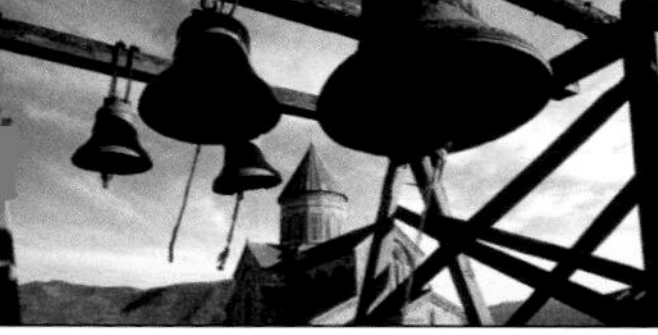

Tbilisi Georgia's capital and largest city – spas with sulfur springs – historic old town – Narikala fortress – Metekhi church (photo) **Nc25**

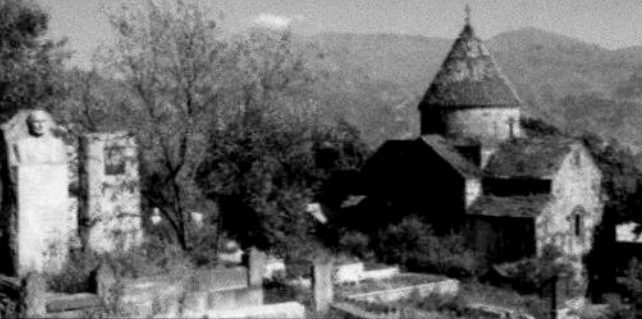

Haghpat Monastery In the mountains of northern Armenia – fortified monastery – UNESCO world heritage site **Nc25**

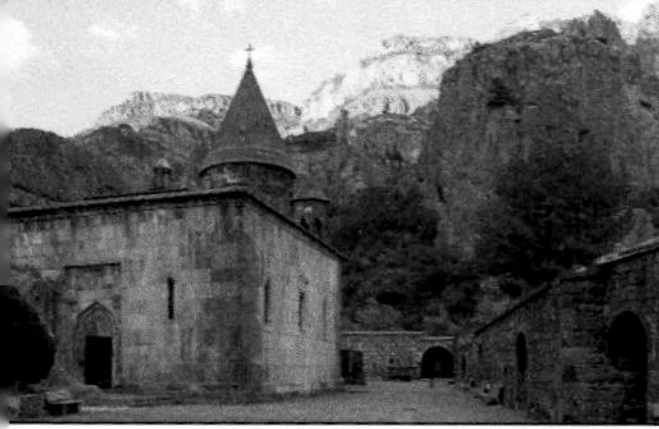

Geghard Monastery Located in Armenia's Azat Valley – stone monasteries built in the 4th century – the main building was completed in 1215 – UNESCO world heritage site **Nc25**

R U S S I A
G E O R G I A
ARMENIA
A Z E R B A I J A N
T U R K E Y
I R A N
C A S P I A N S E A
Kalmykia
Caspian Depression
ASTRAKHAN
Krasnodar
Stavropol'
Elista
Soči
Sokhumi (Sochumi)
Batumi
Kutaisi
TBILISI (TIBILISI)
YEREVAN
Gyumri
Vanadzor
Gänzä
BAKI (BAKU)
Sumqayit
Groznyj
Mahačkala
Vladikavkaz
Nal'čik
Derbent
Aktau
Erzurum
Van
TABRIZ
Ardabil
Orumiyeh
Scale 1:4,500,000
0 40 80 Kilometers
Principal travel routes
Auto route
Rail road
Shipping route
Remarkable landscapes and natural monuments
UNESCO World Natural Heritage
Mountain landscape
Rock landscape
Cave
River landscape
Waterfall/rapids
Lake country
Desert
Oasis
Depression
Nature park
National park (landscape)
National park (flora)
National park (fauna)
Biosphere reserve
Beach

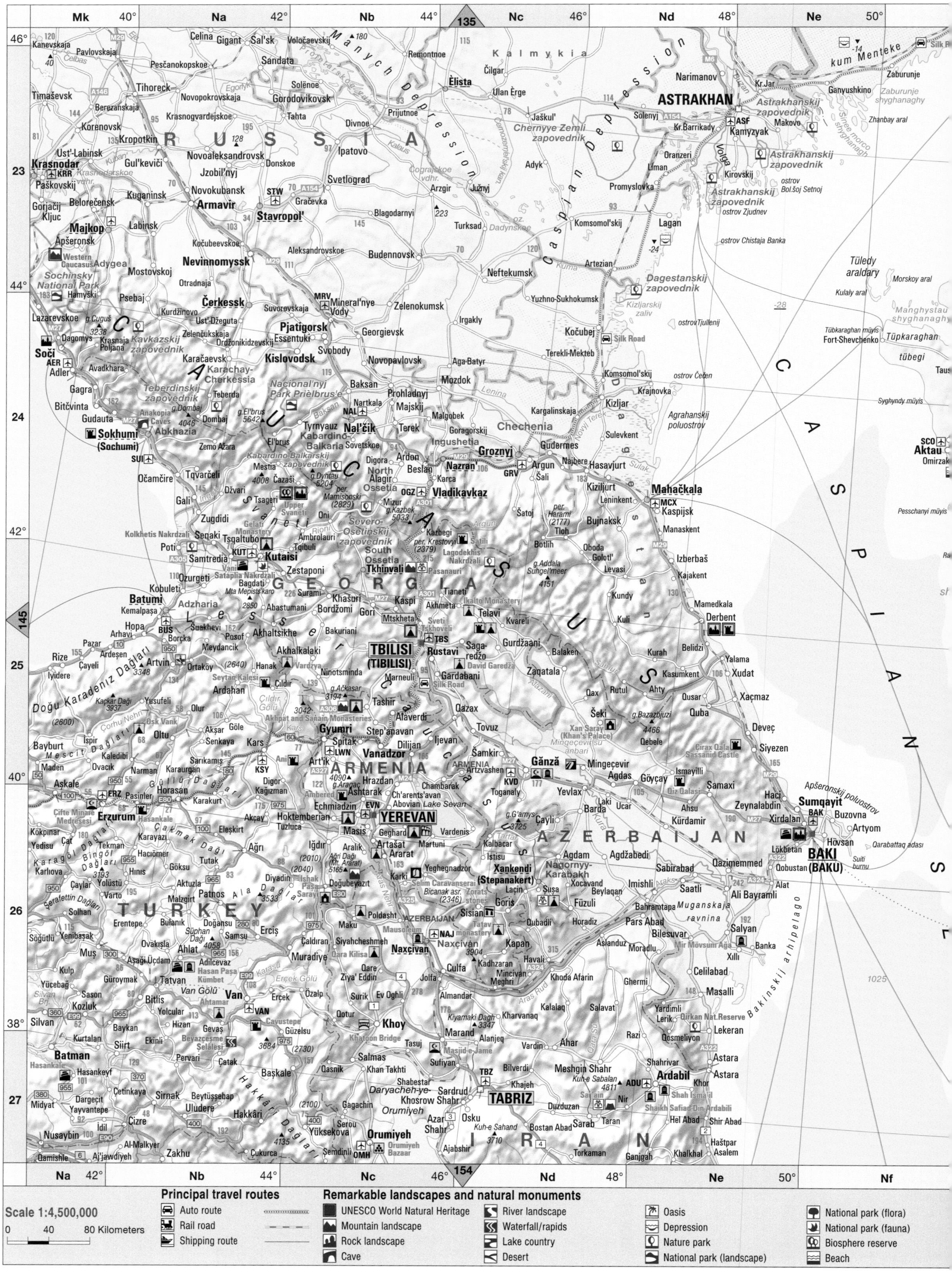

al area of 29,800 km² and a population ·und 3.8 million. Armenia is situated in ·eologically active region and the coun- is home to several dormant volca- ·es. The country's tallest mountain is ·gats Lerrnagagat (4,090 meters) near · Turkish border. Armenia's capital city **·revan** is surrounded by highlands with ·l continental climates. **Lake Sevan** is ·uated in eastern Armenia at a height of ·97 meters above sea level. In addition to Turkey and Georgia Armenia borders several other nations; in the southwest the country borders the Azeri exclave **Naxçivan**, in the far south Iran, and in the east mainland Azerbaijan.

The Azeri region of **Nagorno-Karabakh** has a mostly Armenian speaking population. The region has been at the center of a dispute between **Azerbaijan** and Armenia since the collapse of the Soviet Union. Azerbaijan is the largest of the Caucasus nations with a total area of 86,600 km². Most of northern Azerbaijan is covered by the foothills of the Greater Caucasus range. Azerbaijan's tallest mountain, Bazarduzu Dagi, rises 4,466 meters. The Kura River basin is a fertile area bordered by vast steppes. Azerbajan's capital **Baku** is situated on the **Apsheron Peninsula**. The **Üstyurt plateau** in Kazakhstan lies northeast of the Caspian Sea and west of the **Turan lowlands**. The **Aral Sea** is situated between these two regions. In recent decades, the Aral Sea has shrunk dramatically as a result of evaporation and irrigation projects. Turkmenistan's Caspian Sea coast is broken by several large bays. Garabogazkol was once the largest bay next to the Caspian Sea but the two bodies are now separated by a narrow strip of land created after a drop in the Caspian Sea's water level.

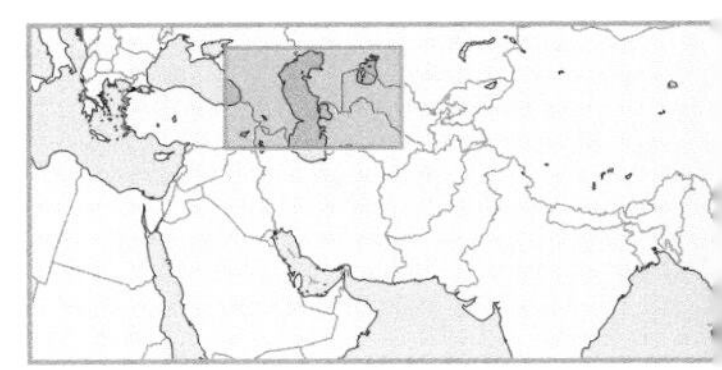

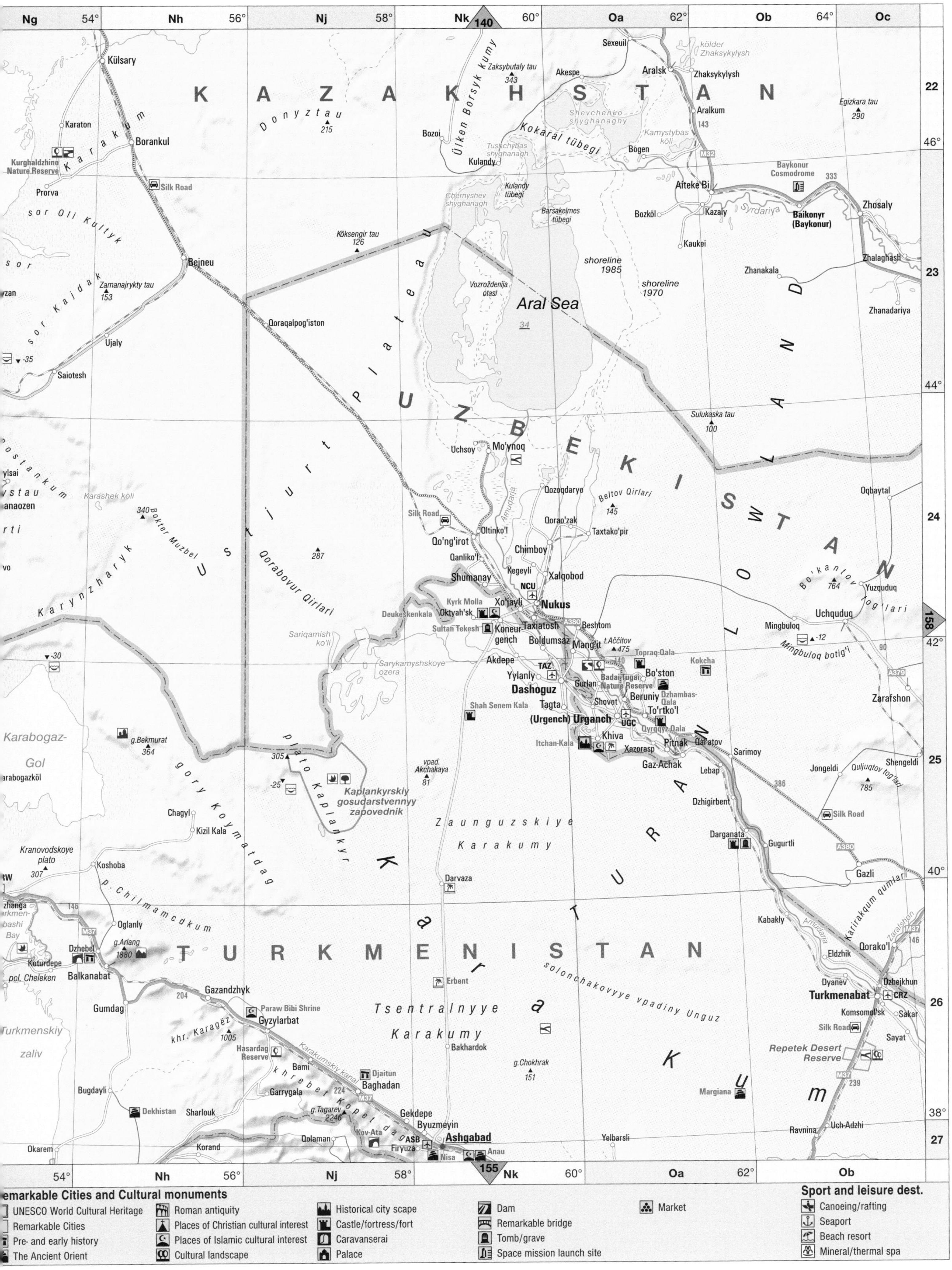

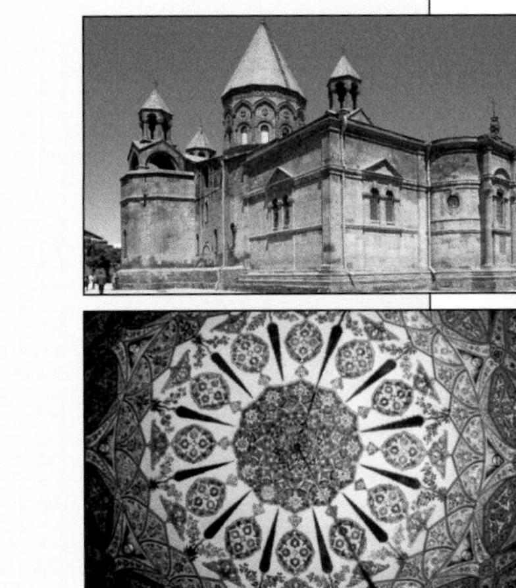

Echmiatsin A holy city for Armenian Christians. The city is the site of a historic basilica, a UNESCO world heritage site with colorful frescoes and clock towers. **Nc25**

Baku Azerbaijan's capital city on the Caspian Sea – old town with historic city wall – UNESCO world heritage site – medieval mosques and palaces **Ne25**

Baikonur Kazahkstan – launch site for the Russian space program – the first manned space flight in history with Yuri Gagarin started here in 1961 **Ob23**

Khiva Fascinating city in Uzbekistan – the old town Ichan Kala is surrounded by a city wall – mosque and palaces **Oa25**

emarkable Cities and Cultural monuments

- UNESCO World Cultural Heritage
- Remarkable Cities
- Pre- and early history
- The Ancient Orient
- Roman antiquity
- Places of Christian cultural interest
- Places of Islamic cultural interest
- Cultural landscape
- Historical city scape
- Castle/fortress/fort
- Caravanserai
- Palace
- Dam
- Remarkable bridge
- Tomb/grave
- Space mission launch site
- Market

Sport and leisure dest.

- Canoeing/rafting
- Seaport
- Beach resort
- Mineral/thermal spa

Northern Iran

The narrow **Alborz mountain range** covers much of northern **Iran** and contains the country's tallest mountain, Damavand, which rises 5,601 meters above sea level. **Teheran**, the capital of the Islamic Republic of Iran is situated on the southern edges of the Alborz Mountains. Teheran is also the largest Iranian city with around seven million residents. Northwestern Iran is a mountainous region along the country's borders to Turkey, Azerbaijan, and Armenia. This gion features narrow and shallow **La Urmia**. Along the Caspian Sea coast the northwest lies a strip of fertile a heavily cultivated plains. Most of nor western Iran has cold winters with hea snowfall and temperate dry summers w only sporadic rainfall.

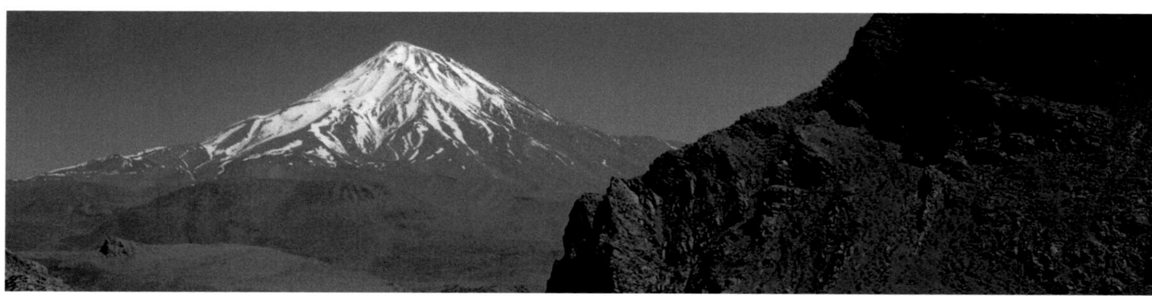

Damavand (5,601 meters), Iran's talles mountain **Ng**

Maku Town near Mount Ararat – pilgrimage site for Armenian Christians – Qara Kilisa, ancient "black church" (photo) **Nc26**

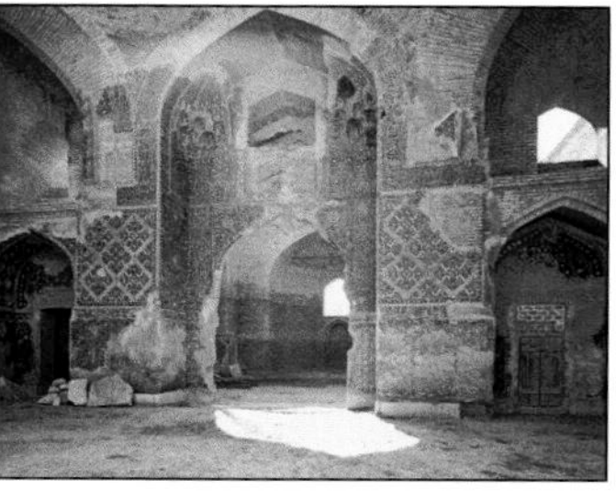

Tabriz Near the volcano Sahand – traditional bazaar – capital of Persia in the 14th century – Blue Mosque (photo) **Nd26**

Teheran The capital of Iran is situated at the foot of the Alborz Mountains. Teheran's sites includes the Golestan Palace, the mausoleum of Ayatollah Khomeini and Shahyad's Tower (photos). **Nf28**

Kermanshah Historic city in northeastern Iran – sculptures and reliefs – tomb of the Sassanian king Ardashir (photo) **Nd28**

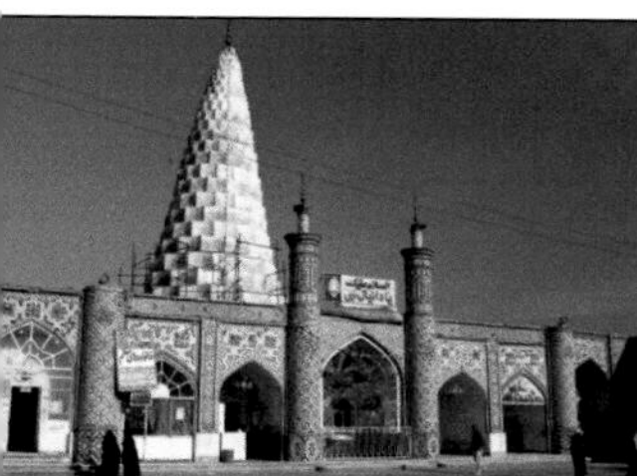

Shush (Susa) First settled around 4000 BC – capital of ancient Elam – tomb of the biblical prophet Daniel (photo) **Ne29**

Tchogha Zanbil Ruins of the ancient holy city of the Elamites – world heritage site – site of Iran's only terraced palace **Ne29**

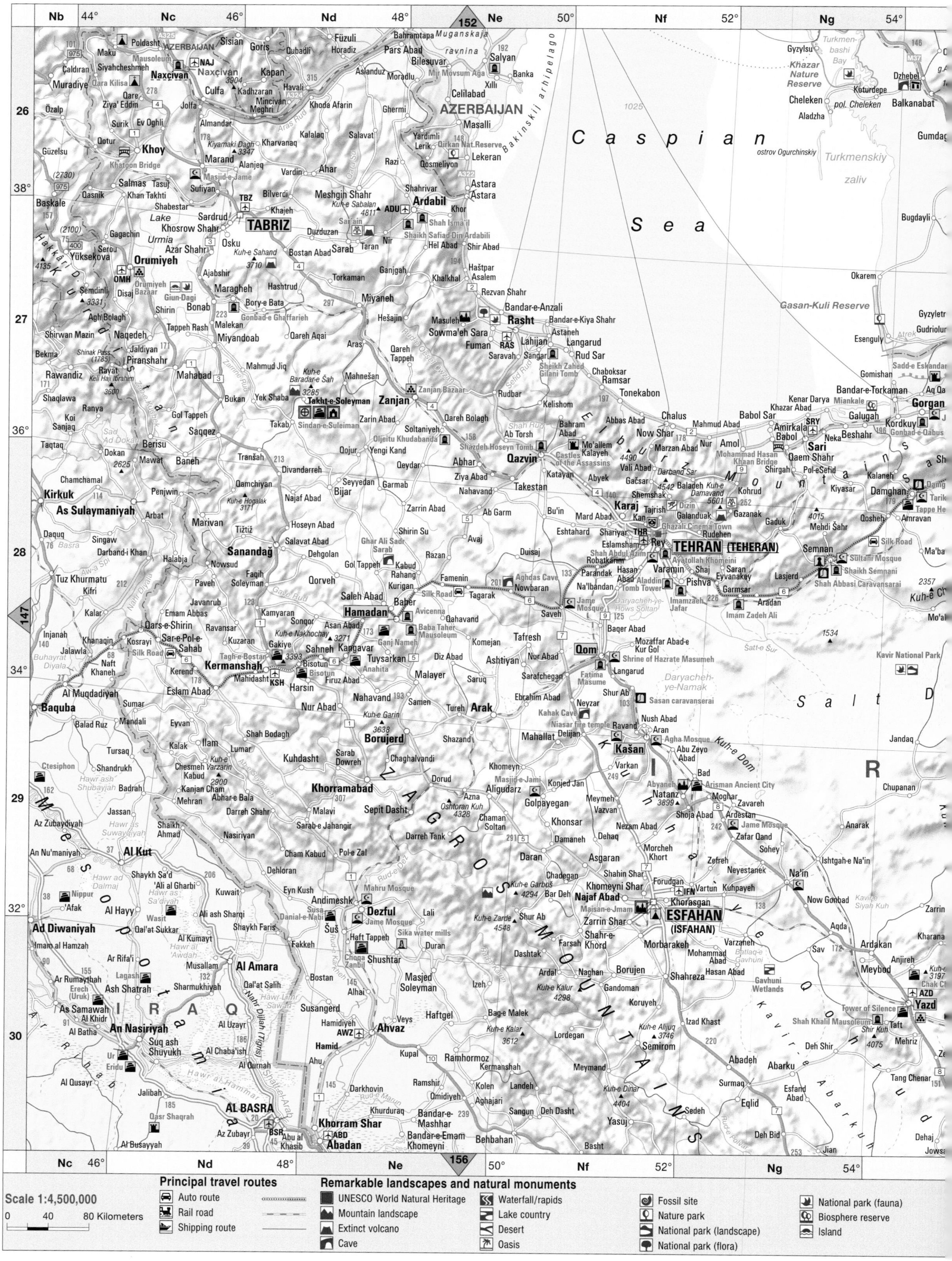

152 147 156

Scale 1:4,500,000

0 40 80 Kilometers

Principal travel routes

- Auto route
- Rail road
- Shipping route

Remarkable landscapes and natural monuments

- UNESCO World Natural Heritage
- Mountain landscape
- Extinct volcano
- Cave
- Waterfall/rapids
- Lake country
- Desert
- Oasis
- Fossil site
- Nature park
- National park (landscape)
- National park (flora)
- National park (fauna)
- Biosphere reserve
- Island

rthquakes are the common in northern n. The geologically active region is uated near the boundaries of the Arabian and Eurasian tectonic plates. The a between the cities Tabriz and Ardabil encompasses many hot natural springs d a chain of extinct volcanoes.

e **Zagros Mountains**, a series of rallel ranges, stretch from the northwest to the southeast near the borders Iraq and Turkey. Iran's Zagros Mountains contain the source of the **Karun River**, the country's only major navigable river. The river flows from Khorramshahr to the Shatt al-Arab river along the Iran-Iraq border. Iran's Central Plateau is situated west of the Zagros Mountains and has an average height of 1,220 meters. The plateau borders two large deserts: **Dasht-e Kavir** and **Dasht-e Lut**. Dasht-e Kavir covers 200,000 km^2 and is the largest salt desert in the world. It stretches between the cities Teheran, Mashhad, and Yadz. The Dasht-e Lut desert covers 166,000 km^2 and stretches to the Iran's borders with Pakistan and Afghanistan. The Iranian province of Khuzestan consists of marshlands along the Shatt al-Arab river southwest of the Zagros Mountains. Located along the border to Iraq, **Khuzestan** has major oil deposits.

Iran's southwest, southeast, and coastal areas along the Persian Gulf have humid and hot climates. Most of the country's interior regions however have hot and arid climates with little rainfall. Iran has a diverse **population** with many distinct ethnic groups. Ethnic Persians form around one half of Iran's population. Azeris, Kurds, and smaller ethnic groups comprise the remaining half of the population. The smaller ethnic groups are concentrated near Iran's borders.

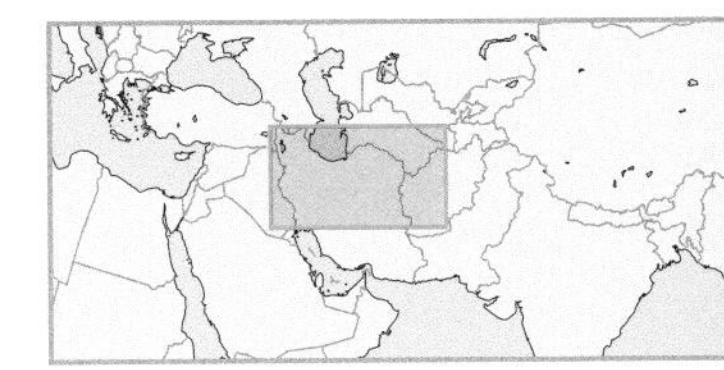

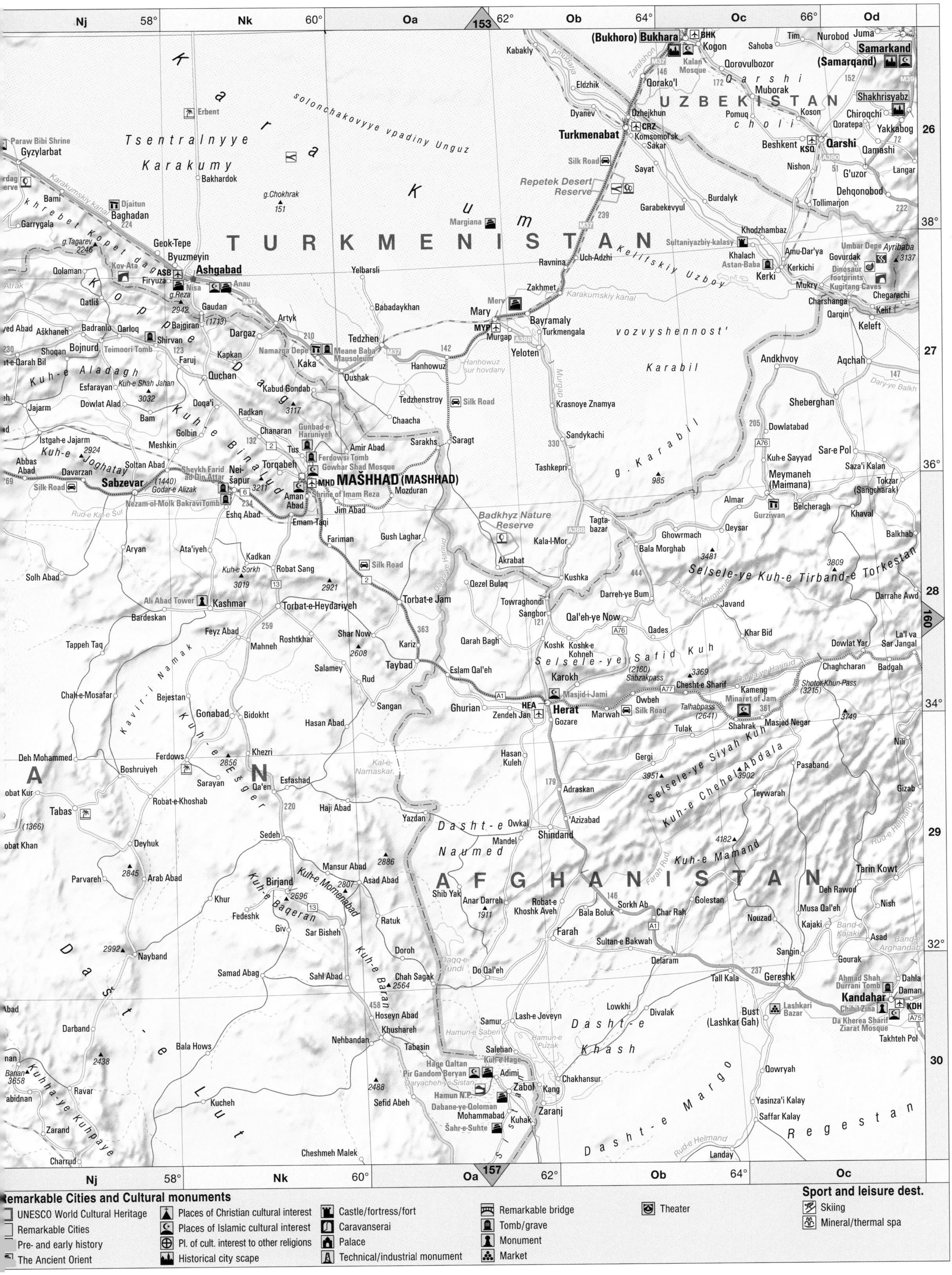

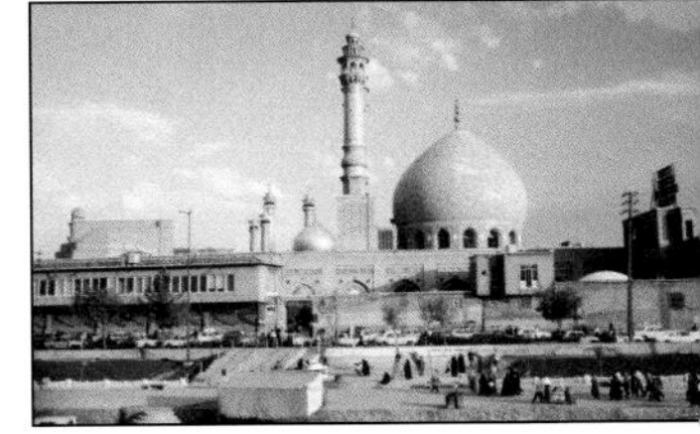

Qom Pilgrimage site and important Iranian religious center – training schools for Shiite clerics – the tomb of Fatima, sister of Imam Reza, (photo) is the town's principal attraction **Nf28**

Kashan Oasis town on the edge of a large salt desert – unique local architecture – Tabatabai House (photo) **Nf28/29**

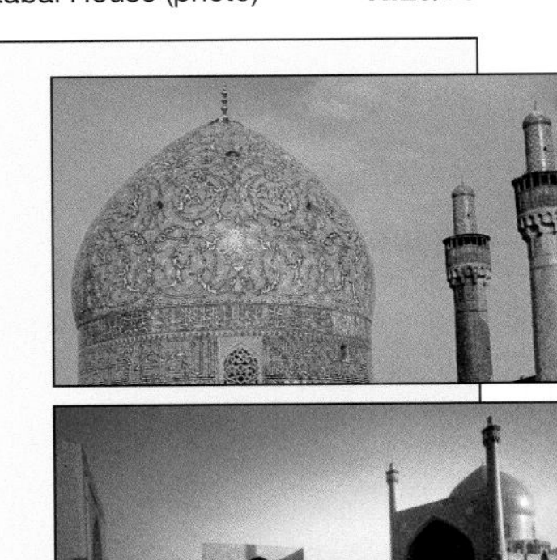

Isfahan The city is often considered the most beautiful urban area in Iran. Isfahan lies on the Zayandeh River between the mountain ranges. The Meidan Emam mosque (both photos) is a UNESCO world heritage site. **Nf29**

Yazd Beautiful old town – traditional homes topped by wind towers for cooling – center of silk production **Nh30**

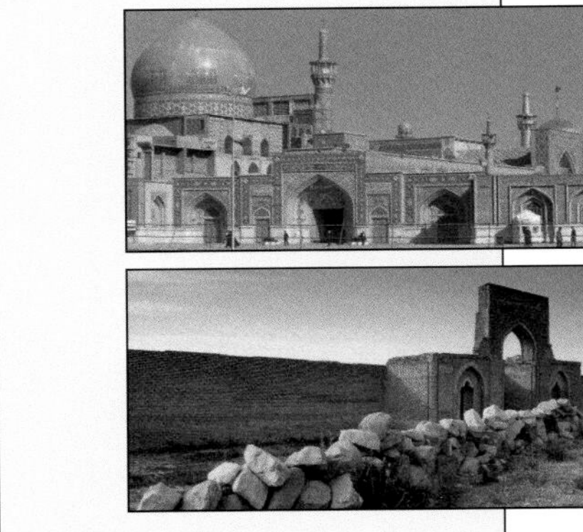

Masshad The shrine of Imam Reza (top photo) is the most revered Shiite holy site in Iran. The shrine's golden towers were built in the 17th century. Masshad contains many historic caravansaries (bottom photo). **Nk27**

153
160
157

Remarkable Cities and Cultural monuments

- UNESCO World Cultural Heritage
- Remarkable Cities
- Pre- and early history
- The Ancient Orient
- Places of Christian cultural interest
- Places of Islamic cultural interest
- Pl. of cult. interest to other religions
- Historical city scape
- Castle/fortress/fort
- Caravanserai
- Palace
- Technical/industrial monument
- Remarkable bridge
- Tomb/grave
- Monument
- Market
- Theater

Sport and leisure dest.

- Skiing
- Mineral/thermal spa

Southern Iran, Persian Gulf

The regions along the coasts of the **Persian Gulf** contain a fascinating variety of unique landscapes. With the exception of the **Al Hajar Mountains** in Oman most of the Arabian Peninsula's Persian Gulf coast consists of flat desert regions. Because of its hot and dry climate along the Persian Gulf most of the region's large towns and cities lie directly on the coast. The Persian Gulf is the site of major oil deposits and oil exports

dominate the economies of several co tries in the region including **Om** (309,500 km²) and the **United Arab E rates**. The United Arab Emirates (77,7 km²) is a federation consisting of sev emirates; Abu Dhabi, Ajman, Dubai, Fu rah, Ras al-Khaimah, Sharjah, and Ur al-Qaiwain. The **Al Batinah** coastal p

Jebel Akhdar (3,018 meters) in Oman Al Hajar Mountains **Nj**

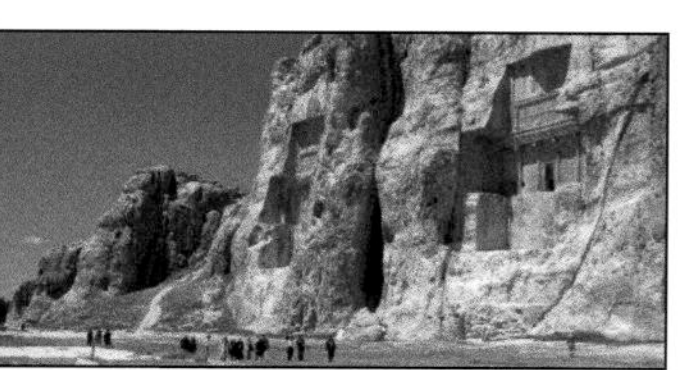

Naghshe-Rostam The tombs of four ancient Persian Kings including Darius the Great and Xerxes II – built into the side of stone cliffs – large reliefs **Ng30**

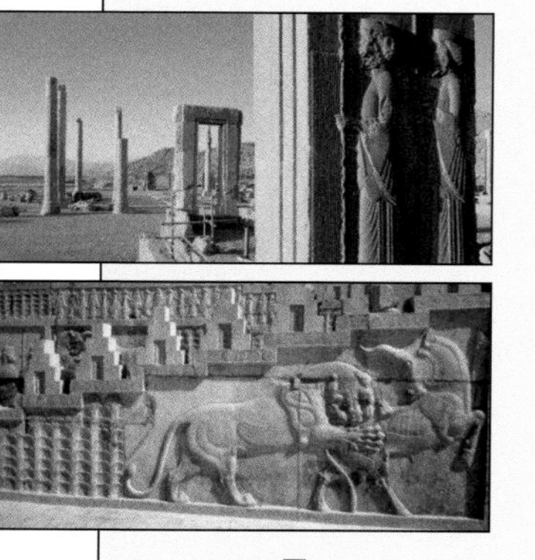

Persepolis The center of the Persian-Achaemenid Empire was founded by Darius I and destroyed by Alexander the Great around 330 BC. The **Apadana** (top photo) or reception hall was decorated with large reliefs, some depicting battles between animals (bottom photo). **Ng31**

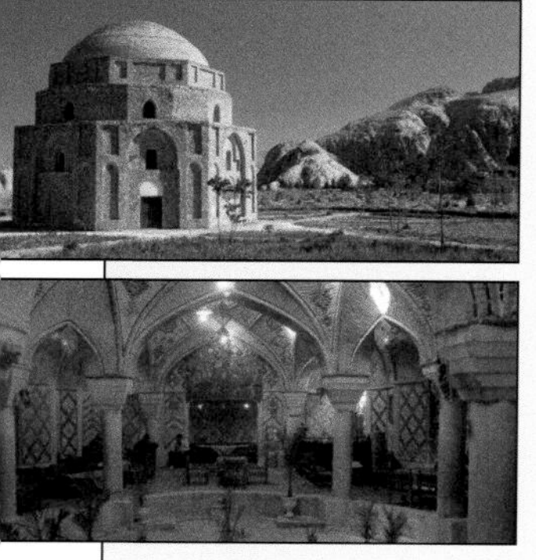

Kerman Provincial capital on the edge of the Dasht-e Lut desert. The city is known for its carpets, the Ganj-Ali-Khan Museum, 13th century mosque, and bazaar. Gonbad-e Jabalieh (top photo) and the Vakil tea house (bottom photo) are also popular attractions. **Nj30**

Bam, Arg-e-Bam Historic Iranian city with unique architecture – citadel (photo) – historic mosque and palaces – damaged by major earthquake in 2003 **Nk31**

Ras al-Khaimah Shiekdom in the United Arab Emirates – mountainous regions with wadis and scattered oases **Nj33**

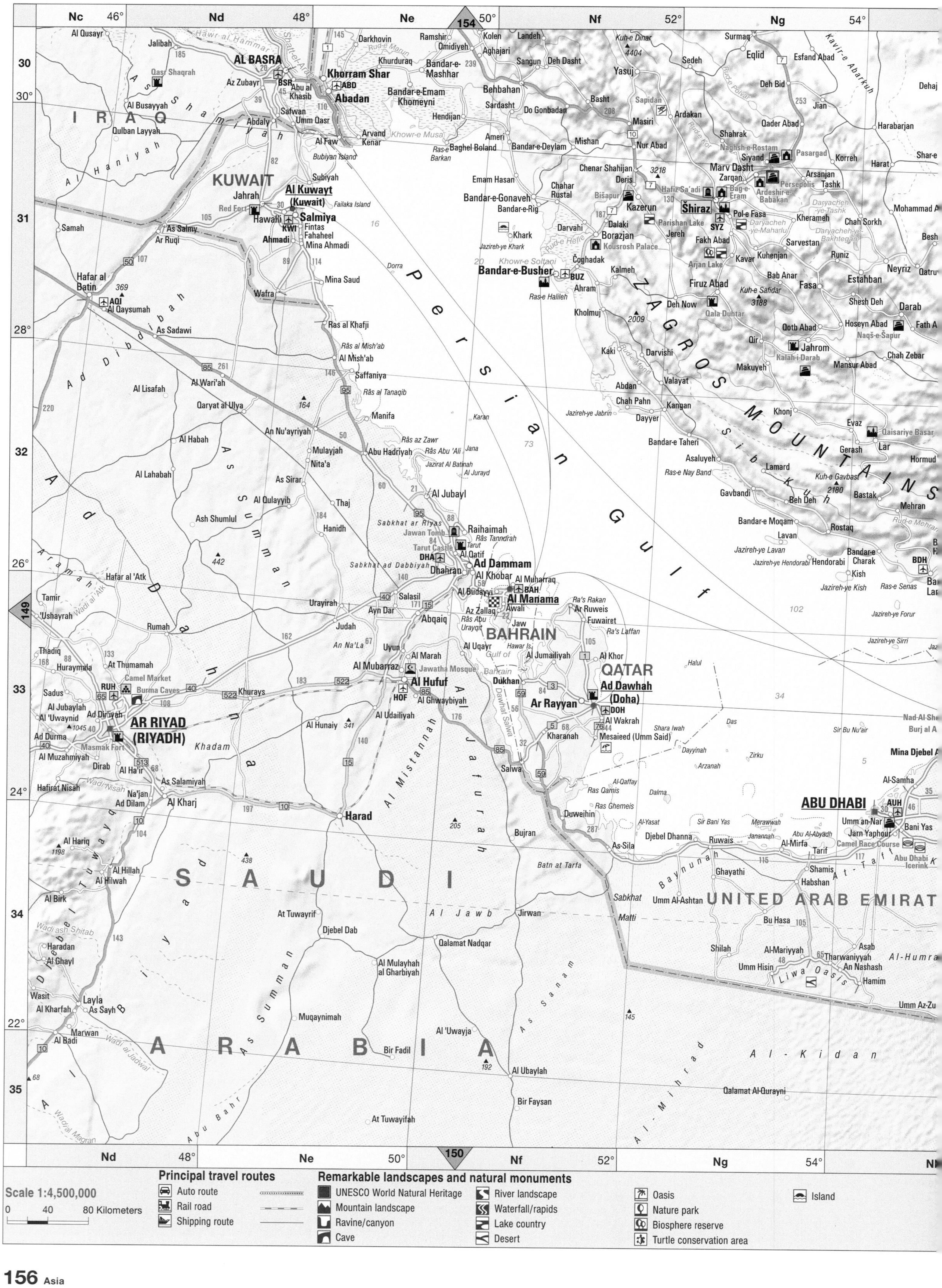

Scale 1:4,500,000
0 40 80 Kilometers

Principal travel routes
- Auto route
- Rail road
- Shipping route

Remarkable landscapes and natural monuments
- UNESCO World Natural Heritage
- Mountain landscape
- Ravine/canyon
- Cave
- River landscape
- Waterfall/rapids
- Lake country
- Desert
- Oasis
- Nature park
- Biosphere reserve
- Turtle conservation area
- Island

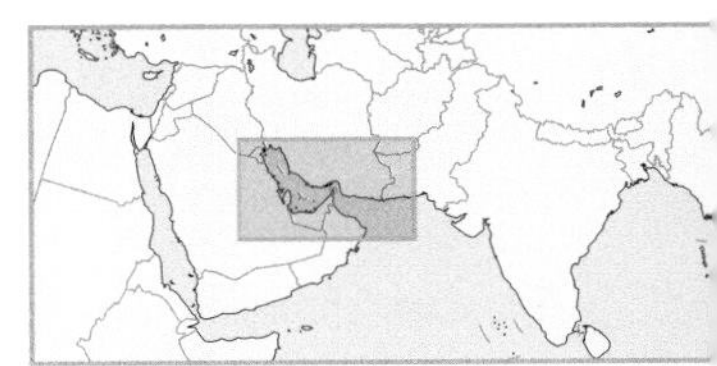

)man is a hot region with temperatu- often exceeding 50° Celsius and reme humidity in summer. Despite the sh climate, the majority of Oman's 2.5 lion inhabitants live on the coastal in. Oman's mountainous regions have arm but moderate climate with abun- nt rainfall in winter.

e **Zagros Mountains**, a series of tall ges, extend from northwestern Iran to e country's southeast. The Zagros Mountains rise abruptly to around 3,000 meters above sea level just beyond Iran's Persian Gulf coast.

Oman and Iran are separated by just 80 km of water along the narrow **Strait of Hormuz**. The strait is situated between the Persian Gulf and the Gulf of Oman. The tall craggy mountain ranges of Southern Iran and Pakistan are far younger than the heavily eroded plateaus of Southern Arabia. Several large basins are situated between the mountains of southern Iran. These basins are covered by large deserts, including the Dasht-e Lut, which contain numerous salt lakes. Because of high temperatures and evaporation many of these lakes have extremely salty water and are dry during most of the year. Southern Iran's scattered oasis towns including **Bam** and **Kerman** are dependant on groundwater supplies. Bam, one of the most ancient cities in Iran, was heavily damaged by a powerful earthquake in 2003. The Zagros Mountains of Iran and Balochistan in Pakistan have been inhabited for thousands of years. **Persepolis**, the center of an ancient Achaemenid Empire was founded around 600 BC. The city of **Shiraz** is situated on a large oasis and became an important settlement in the 7th century when it fell under the control of a powerful Arab dynasty.

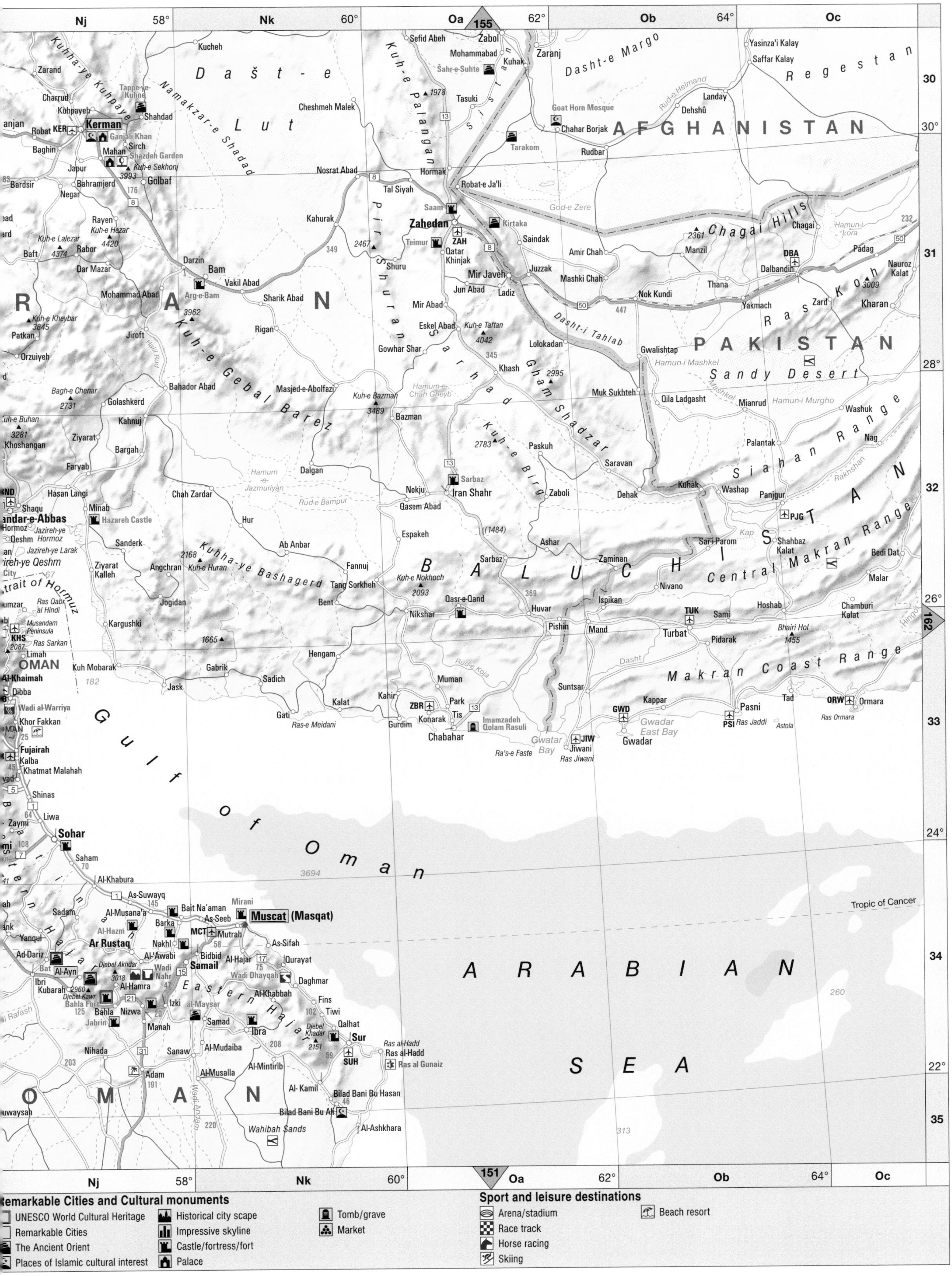

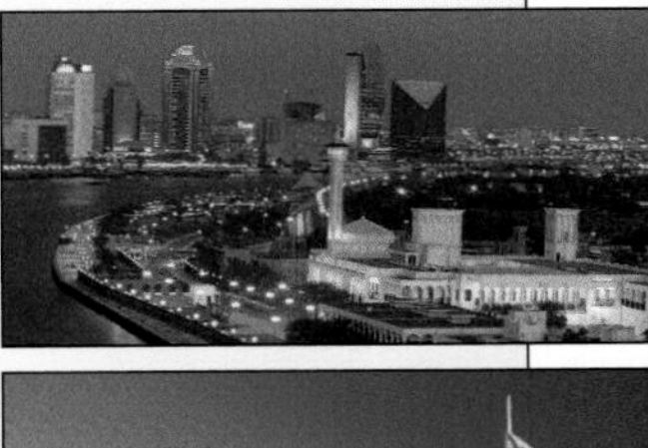

Dubai Economic center of the United Arab Emirates. The city has a modern skyline including the World Trade Center and Burj al-Arab hotel (bottom photo). The city's traditional sites include the Jumeirah mosque and the Deira district. **Nh33**

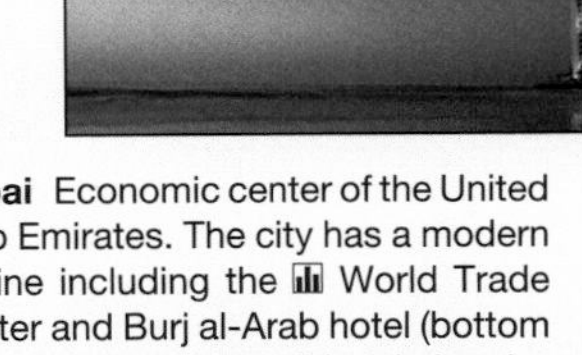

Abu Dhabi Capital of the United Arab Emirates – more than 20 parks – Al-Husn, historic fort – long seaside road (photo) – the island of Umm an-Nar features ancient graves from the 3rd century BC **Nh33**

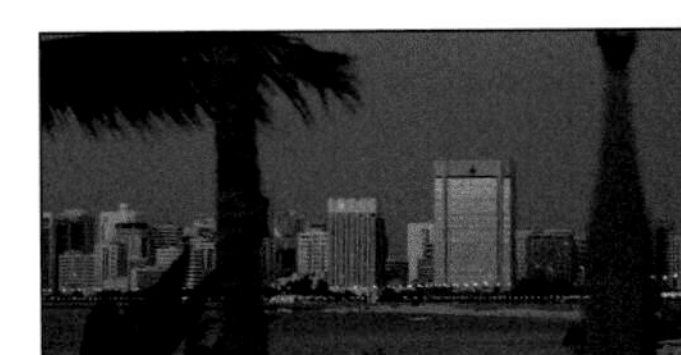

Fort Nakhl Historic fort located southwest of Muscat in Oman – defensive towers on the Nakhl oasis – hot springs **Nj34**

Muscat The capital city of Oman – major port city with a natural harbor – the forts Al Jalali (photo) and Al Mirani were built in the 16th century – Al Alam, sultan's palace – dhow harbor **Nk34**

Bahla Fort Clay fort built during the pre-Islam era – UNESCO world heritage site – expanded between the 12th and 15th centuries – long ring wall **Nj34**

Archeological sites Bat/Al Ayn/Al Khutm Bronze Age settlements including the necropolis Al Ayn – built during the 3rd millennium BC – world heritage site **Nj34**

Remarkable Cities and Cultural monuments

- UNESCO World Cultural Heritage
- Remarkable Cities
- The Ancient Orient
- Places of Islamic cultural interest
- Historical city scape
- Impressive skyline
- Castle/fortress/fort
- Palace
- Tomb/grave
- Market

Sport and leisure destinations

- Arena/stadium
- Race track
- Horse racing
- Skiing
- Beach resort

The shrinking Aral Sea lies on the **Turan Plain**, a vast arid lowland that rises no more than 34 meters above sea level. A long chain of mountain ranges stretches between the Aral Sea and the arid **Tarim Basin** in China. These ranges contain several of the world's highest mountains including **K2** (8,611 meters), the world's second highest mountain, in the Karakoram Range and Cummunism Peak (7,494 meters) in the **Pamir Range**.

The section of the **Tian Shan Mo tains** around Lake Issyk-Kul in Kyrg stan contains dozens of mountains ta than 4,000 meters. Kyrgyzstan has a t area of 2,717,300 km² and is the wor ninth largest nation in terms of size. M of the country consists of large dese and arid steppes. Along the Kazakhst

The mountains of the Pamir Range cover most of Tajikistan **OfOg26**

Kazakhs Kazakhs, the second largest Turkic ethnicity in Central Asia, are famous for their horse riding skills

Kzyl-Orda Former capital of Kazakhstan (1925-1929) – vast underground water reserves – fortress ruins (photo) **Oc23**

Tashkent Capital of Uzbekistan – major transportation center – old town with historic mosques, mausoleums, and bazaars **Oe25**

Buhkara Located on an oasis in the Kyzylkum Desert – old town, a UNESCO world heritage site – Kalan Mosque (photo) – Ark citadel **Oc26**

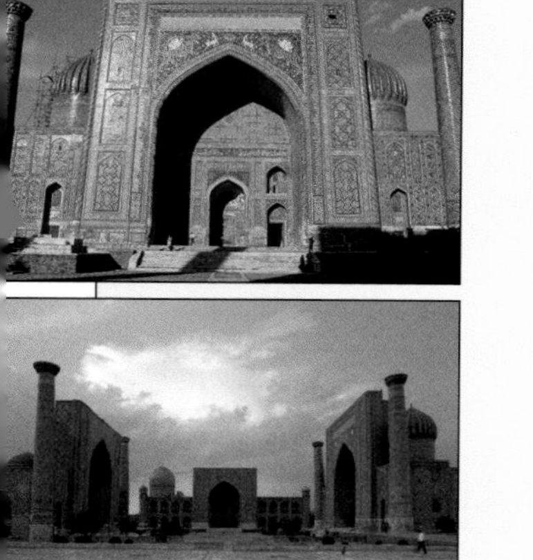

Samarkand One of the world's grandest cities during the 14th century, Samarkand is now a world heritage site. There are three historic Islamic schools on the central square Registan (bottom photo) including the Shirdar (top photo). **Od26**

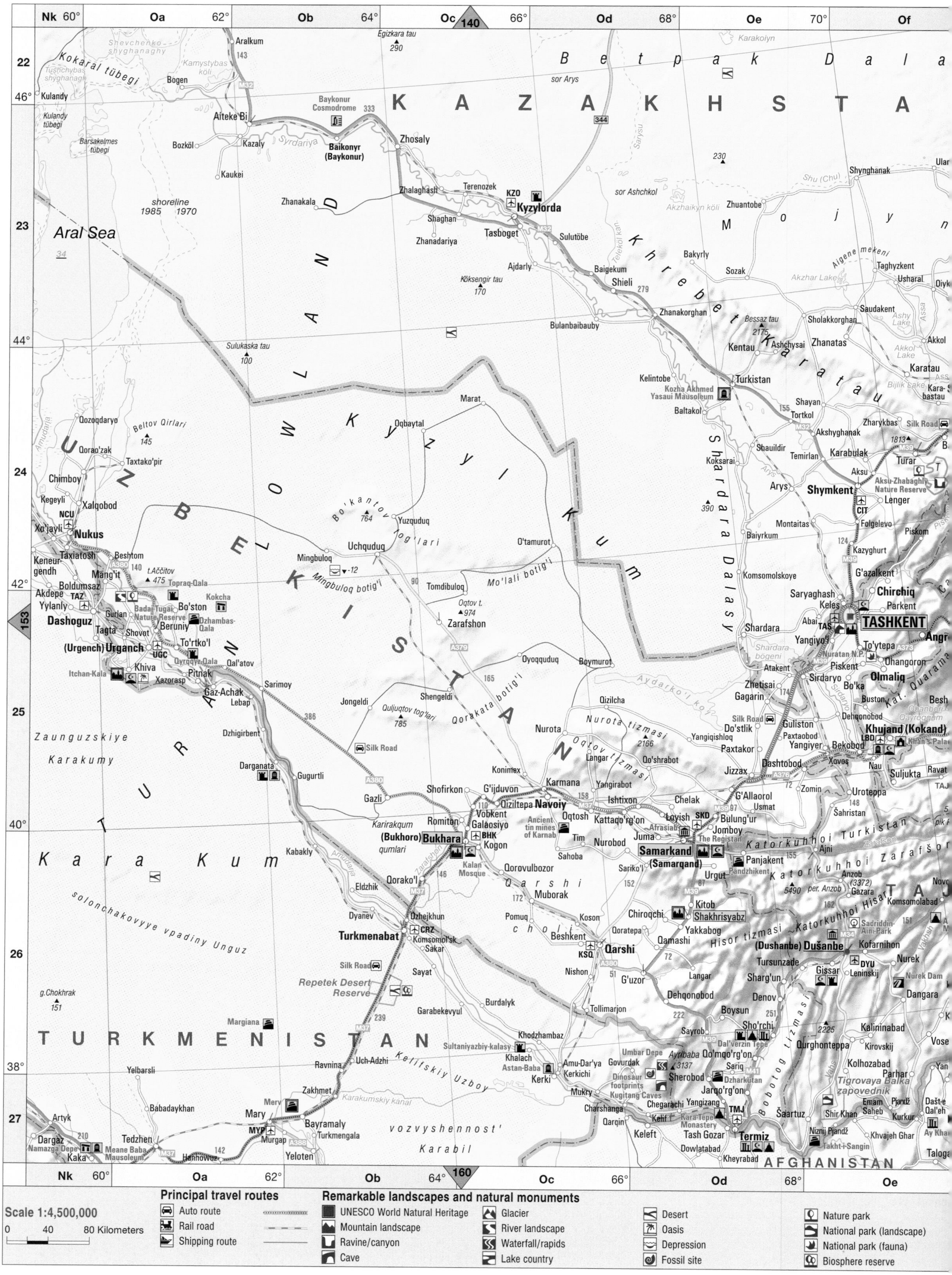

Scale 1:4,500,000
0 40 80 Kilometers

Principal travel routes
- Auto route
- Rail road
- Shipping route

Remarkable landscapes and natural monuments
- UNESCO World Natural Heritage
- Mountain landscape
- Ravine/canyon
- Cave
- Glacier
- River landscape
- Waterfall/rapids
- Lake country
- Desert
- Oasis
- Depression
- Fossil site
- Nature park
- National park (landscape)
- National park (fauna)
- Biosphere reserve

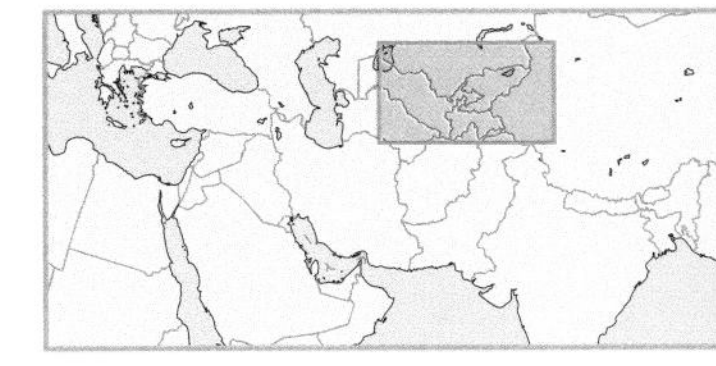

ʻgyzstan border the Tian Shan Range ms a natural boundary between the countries. **Kyrgyzstan** is a mountain-s nation and more than half of the untry's territory (198,500 km²) lies at ghts above 3,000 meters. A large per-ntage of Kyrgyzstan's population lives m traditional sheep herding in rural as. Most of the country's major towns concentrated in river valleys and in the as around Lake Issyk-Kul. Kyrgyz-stan's capital **Bishkek** is the nation's largest city with a population around 650,000. The most isolated mountainous regions are home to abundant wildlife including bears, wolves, eagles, and rare snow leopards. The area around Jalal Abad features large pristine forests. Around four percent of Kyrgyzstan's area consists of designated nature reserves and national parks.

Like neighboring Kyrgyzstan, **Tajikistan** is a mountainous nation and the Pamir Range stretches over much of its territory. The majority of Tajikistan's population is concentrated in the country's fertile river valleys. The country's capital, Dushanbe, is located near the border to Uzbekistan. Livestock ranching, cotton farming, and silk production are important sectors in the country's economy. Centuries ago many of Uzbekistan's towns including **Samarkand**, **Khiva**, and the capital **Tashkent** were important trade centers along the **Silk Road** trade route. More than three quarters of Uzbekistan is covered by arid steppes and deserts including the vast **Kara Kum** desert. The country has a mostly continental climate with hot summers and cold winters.

The mountainous areas of Uzbekistan and Tajikistan are home to large glaciers including the Inylchek Glaciers and snow capped mountains.

Almaty The largest city in Kazakhstan – former national capital and leading economic center – Zenkov cathedral – university – Pushkin Library – Palace of Culture – National Museum **Oj24**

Lake Issyk-Kul Mountain lake – hot springs along the shore – national park and UNESCO biosphere reserve **Oj24**

Tian Shan Mountains Mountain range encompassing Jengish Chokusu (7,439 meters), Khan Tengri (6,995 meters) – Inylchek Glacier **Of-Pc24/25**

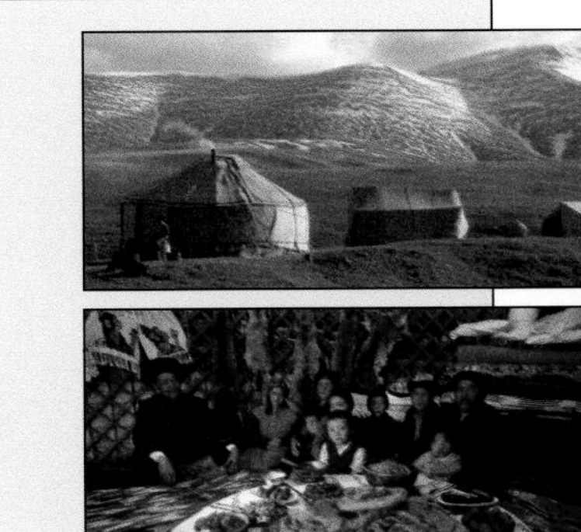

Kyrgyzstan The Kyrgyz are a Turkic people and form the majority of Kyrgyzstan's population. Most Kyrgyz are Sunni Muslims and many raise livestock in rural areas. Yurts (photos) made of wood and animal hide are the tradition homes of the Kyrgyz.

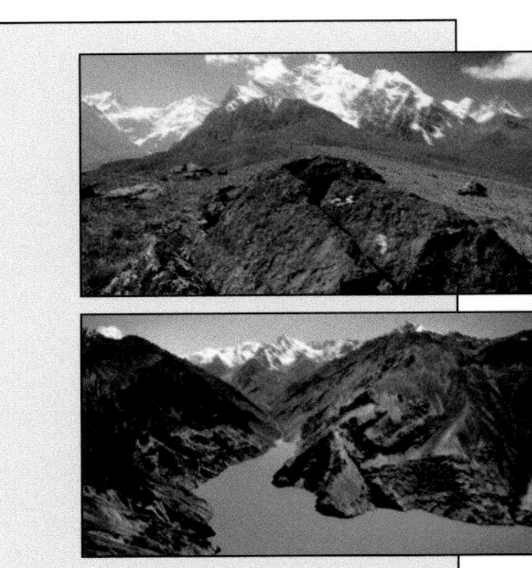

Pamir Mountains This mountain range (photos) stretches through much of Central Asia and has a total area of 60,000 km². Many of the mountains are covered by glaciers and several peaks rise above 7,000 meters. **OfOg26/27**

emarkable Cities and Cultural monuments

UNESCO World Cultural Heritage · Remarkable Cities · Pre- and early history · The Ancient Orient · Greek antiquity · Places of Islamic cultural interest · Places of Buddhist cultural interest · Historical city scape · Castle/fortress/fort · Palace · Remarkable bridge · Tomb/grave · Space mission launch site · Market · Museum · Theater

Sport and leisure destinations

Arena/stadium · Horse racing · Skiing · Sailing · Diving · Canoeing/rafting · Mineral/thermal spa · Amusement/theme park

Afghanistan, Northern and Central Pakistan

The landlocked country of **Afghanistan** has a total land area of 652,090 km². Most of Afghanistan's territory is covered by mountain ranges and valleys. Around half of the country lies at heights between 600 and 1,800 meters above sea level. The vast **Kara Kum desert** stretches over many of the regions near the border to Turkmenistan in northwestern Afghanistan. The country's south and southwest consist primarily of large basins and deserts including the Da e-Margo or "desert of death."

The tall **Hindu Kush mountain ra** begins in southwestern Afghanistan a extends through most of the cour including the central highlands. In nor eastern Afghanistan the peaks of Hindu Kush rise above 7,000 meter

Rakaposhi massif (7,788 meters) in Pakistan's Hunza Valley **Ol**

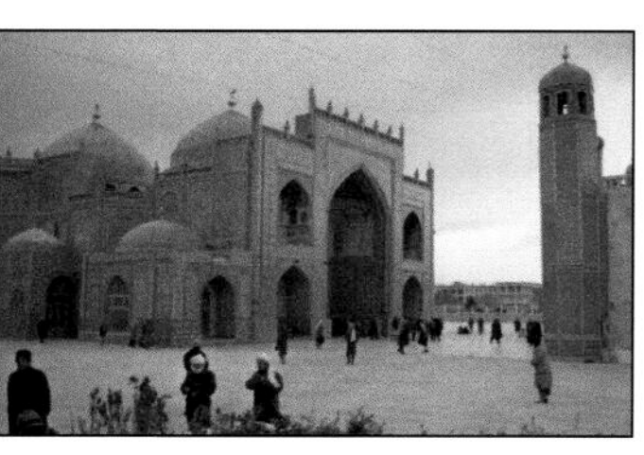

Mazar-e Sharif City in Afghanistan – Blue Mosque is reputed to be the tomb of Ali, son in law of Islamic prophet Mohammed **Od27**

Bamiyan Valley Region containing unique Buddhist art – several large historic Buddha statues were destroyed by the Taliban – UNESCO world heritage site. **Od28**

Panjshir Valley Difficult to access region north of Kabul with narrow canyons and valleys **Oe28**

Kabul Afghanistan's capital and largest city – Babur gardens – Timur Shah mausoleum – citadel and historic city wall **Oe28**

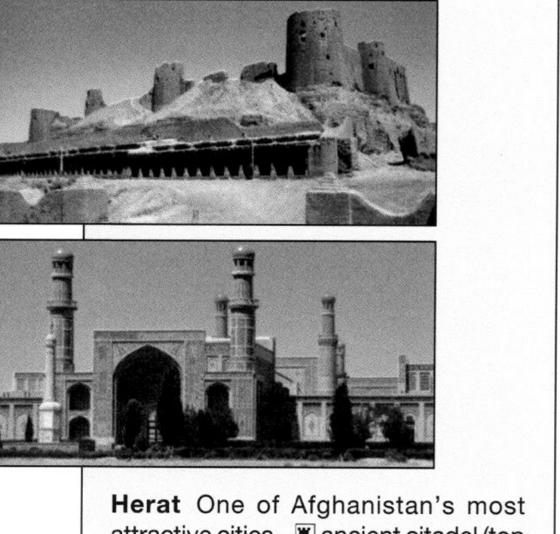

Herat One of Afghanistan's most attractive cities – ancient citadel (top photo) – old town and Masjid I Jami mosque (bottom photo). **Ob28**

Khyber Pass 53-kilometer-long path through the Hindu Kush between Pakistan and Afghanistan **Of28**

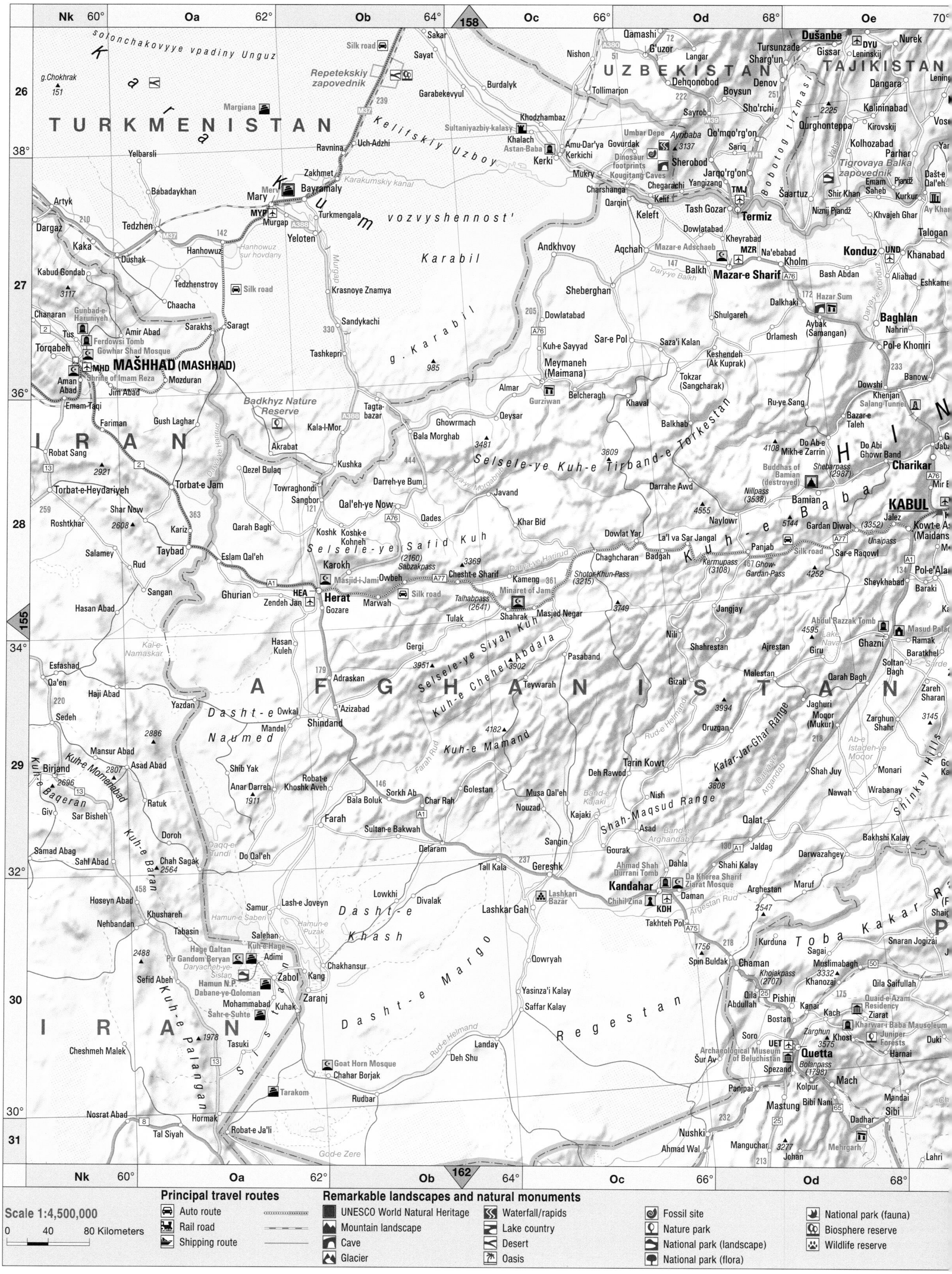

158
155
162

Scale 1:4,500,000

0 40 80 Kilometers

Principal travel routes

- Auto route
- Rail road
- Shipping route

Remarkable landscapes and natural monuments

- UNESCO World Natural Heritage
- Mountain landscape
- Cave
- Glacier
- Waterfall/rapids
- Lake country
- Desert
- Oasis
- Fossil site
- Nature park
- National park (landscape)
- National park (flora)
- National park (fauna)
- Biosphere reserve
- Wildlife reserve

ight, while the tallest peak in southstern Afghanistan barely tops 4,000 eters. **Kabul** the capital of Afghanistan situated in a mountainous region at a ght of 1,800 meters above sea level d has a population around 1.5 million. ghanistan's central highlands have a ntinental climate with hot summers d bitter cold winters. Southeastern and stern Afghanistan have arid subpical climates.

Northern **Pakistan** is covered by expansive mountain ranges that stretch into neighboring China to the east. In this region, two of the world's tallest mountain ranges border one another: the Karakoram, a section of the Hindu Kush and the Himalayas.

The Gilgit mountain range in Baltistan is home to numerous fertile river valleys with green meadows and farms. Many of the mountains in the region are covered by snow and long glaciers. The Siachen Glacier, is around 72 kilometers long.

The **Indus River** begins in Tibet and flows south through many mountain ranges in a long narrow valley. South of Peshawar, the Indus River flows through a large plain which is dissected by many of the river's tributaries including the Chenab, Ravi, Jelum, and Sutlej Rivers. The Indus River plain covers almost half of Pakistan's territory and stretches over the border into neighboring India.

Most areas in northern and central Pakistan have temperate continental climates with warm summers and cold winters. In the Punjabi city of Lahore, temperatures usually exceed 30° Celsius in summer, while frost covers many of the region's mountains during the same time.

The wet monsoon season occurs between July and October in Pakistan.

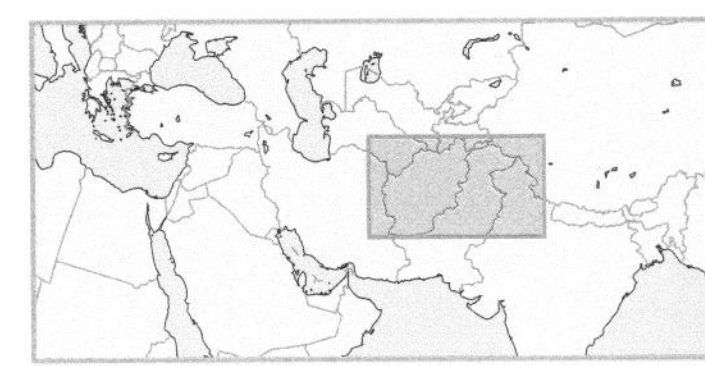

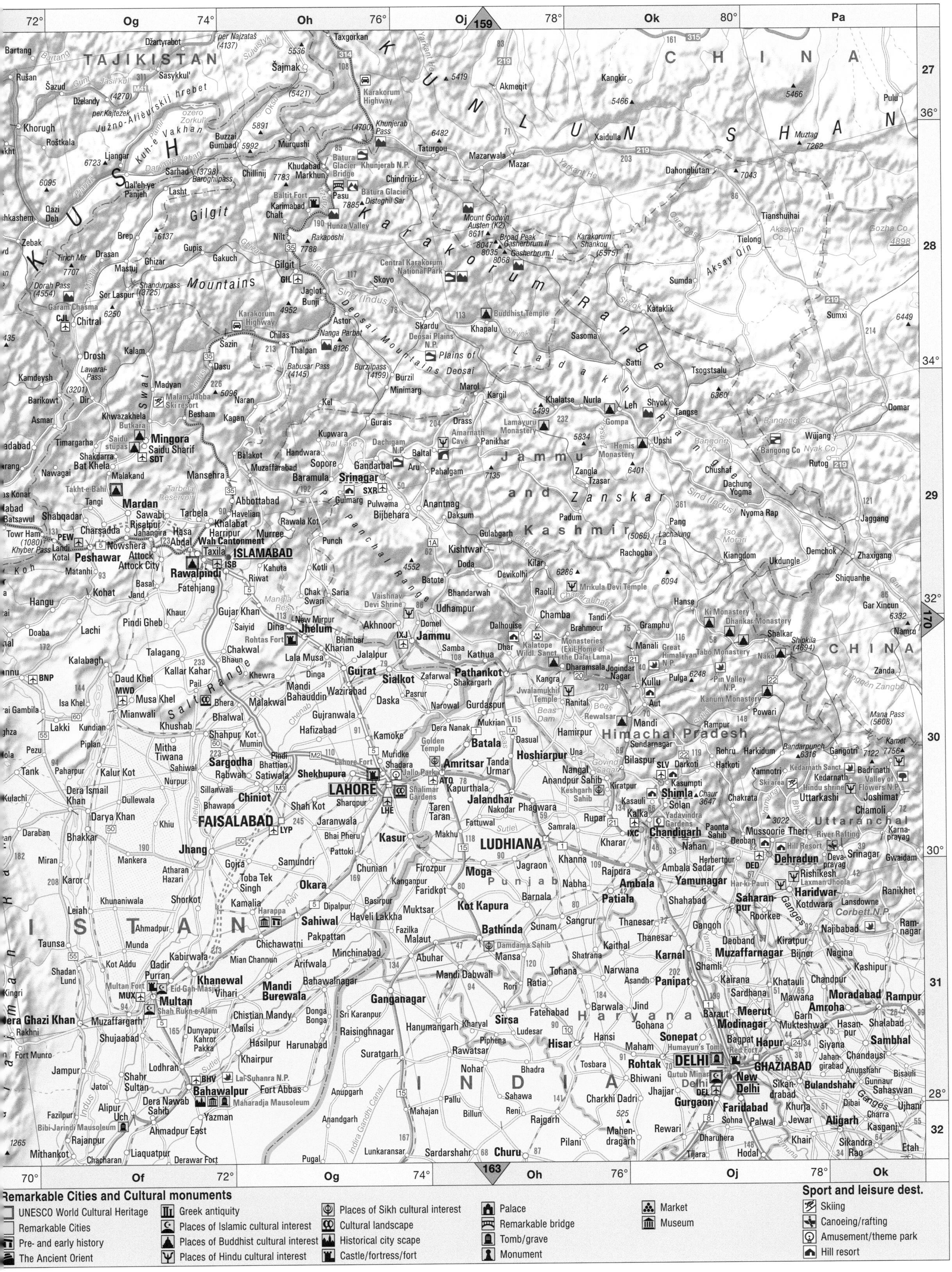

Karakoram Mountain range divided between India, China, and Pakistan: Broad Peak (8,047 meters), Gasherbrum I (8,068 meters, top photo), K2 (8,611 meters, bottom photo). **OhOk27/28**

Nanga Parbat Mountain (8,126 meters) on the western edge of the Himalayas – first climbed in 1953 **Oh28**

Baltit Fort 600-year-old fort in the Hunza Valley (Pakistan) – Tibetan-influenced architecture **Oh27**

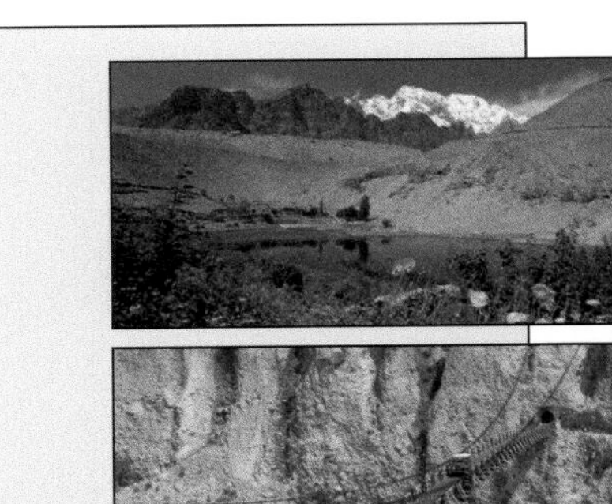

Karakoram Highway Road stretching from Islamabad in Pakistan to China. Passes the Batura glacier (top photo) and suspension bridges (bottom photo) over the Gilgit River. **Oh27**

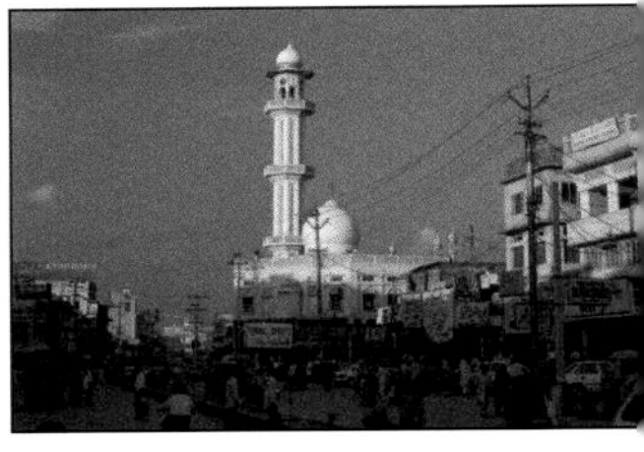

Rawalpindi City near Islamabad – southeast of Taxila archeological site – once the center of the ancient Gandhara kingdom **Og29**

159 170 163

Remarkable Cities and Cultural monuments

- UNESCO World Cultural Heritage
- Remarkable Cities
- Pre- and early history
- The Ancient Orient
- Greek antiquity
- Places of Islamic cultural interest
- Places of Buddhist cultural interest
- Places of Hindu cultural interest
- Places of Sikh cultural interest
- Cultural landscape
- Historical city scape
- Castle/fortress/fort
- Palace
- Remarkable bridge
- Tomb/grave
- Monument
- Market
- Museum

Sport and leisure dest.

- Skiing
- Canoeing/rafting
- Amusement/theme park
- Hill resort

Central and Southern Pakistan

The southern and central regions of **Pakistan** are situated east of Iran and Afghanistan, between the Arabian Sea and the Toba Kakar mountains. These regions contain a diverse group of landscapes including the deserts of Makran, the flood threatened Indus River Valley, and the arid steppes of Balochistan.

The delta of the **Indus River** is situated on the Arabian Sea, just east of Karachi. The Pakistani section of the Indus alone is around 2,200 kilometers lo… Tibet in China is the location of the In… River's source. Many smaller rivers fl… into the Indus along its path south to … Arabian Sea. The river's delta enco… passes more than 60,000 km² of w… lands.

The name of the **Punjab** region mea…

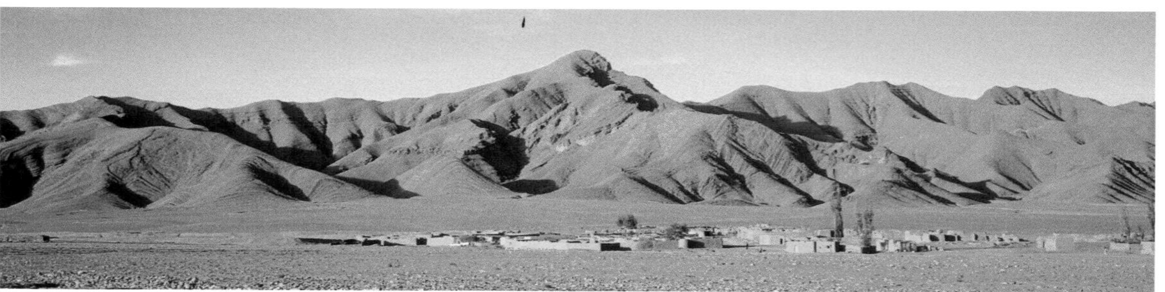

The Toba Kakar Mountains in wester… Pakistan **OdOe**

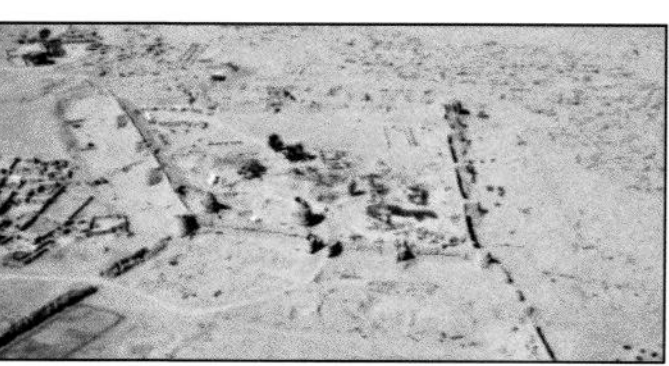

Mehrgarh Southeast of Quetta in Balochistan – first settled around 7000 BC – excavation sites (photo) – early center of agriculture – ancient pottery **Od31**

Mohenjo Daro Ruins of an ancient city and trade center built in the 3rd millenium BC – UNESCO world heritage site – citadel – Buddhist temples **Oe32**

Hyderabad Economic center of Sindh province – historic 18th century fort built by Ghulam Shah Kalhora – towers of Char Minar (photo) – Mausoleum of Sheikh Makki **Oe33**

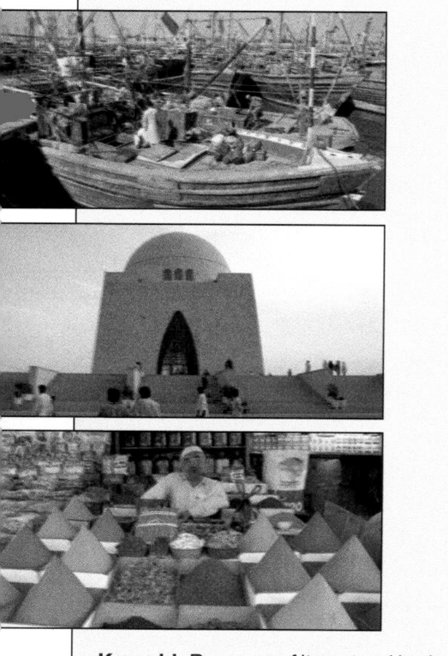

Karachi Because of its natural harbor (top photo), Pakistan's largest city has long been a major center of trade. Muhammed Ali Jinnah, the founder of Pakistan was born in the city. The Qiad-e-Azam mausoleum (middle photo) was built in his honor. The city is home to several markets including the Empress Market (bottom photo) where local goods such as jewelry and spices are sold. **Od33**

Chaukundi Located 30 kilometers east of Karachi – historic burial site – graves decorated with floral and geometric reliefs **Od33**

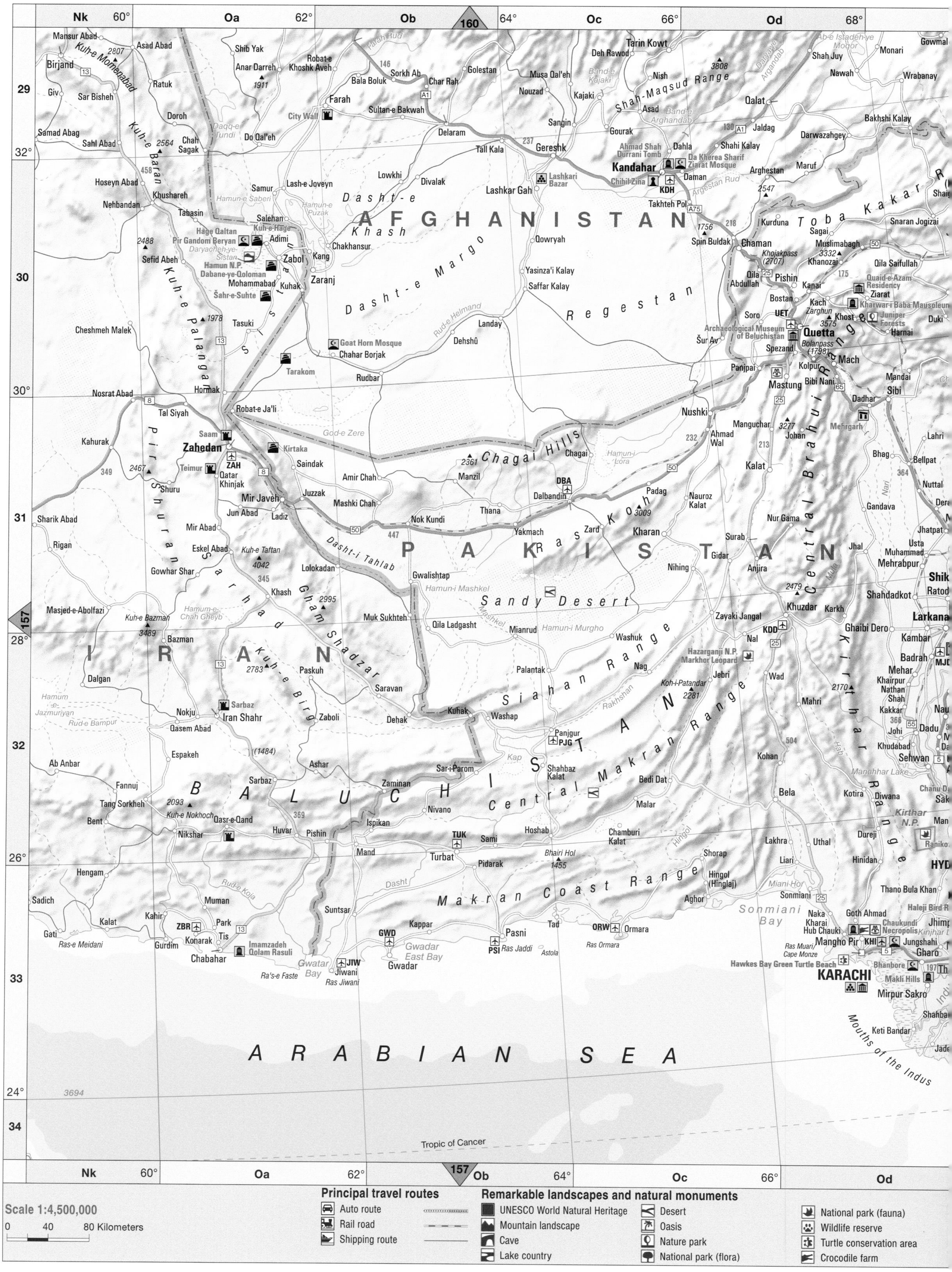

Scale 1:4,500,000

0 40 80 Kilometers

Principal travel routes

- Auto route
- Rail road
- Shipping route

Remarkable landscapes and natural monuments

- UNESCO World Natural Heritage
- Mountain landscape
- Cave
- Lake country
- Desert
- Oasis
- Nature park
- National park (flora)
- National park (fauna)
- Wildlife reserve
- Turtle conservation area
- Crocodile farm

and of five rivers." Punjab is home to veral major rivers, most of which flow o the Indus. This fertile region – which divided between India and Pakistan – as once a center of the **Sindu-Indus ver civilization**, an ancient culture unded during the 3rd millennium BC. At ast one-third of Pakistan's territory is vered by the basin of the Indus and its butaries. These regions are home to the ajority of Pakistan's 145 million inhabitants. The port city of Karachi, on Pakistan's southern coast, is the country's largest city and most important economic center. **Balochistan** is an arid region consisting of vast steppes and numerous salt pans. The region covers southwestern Pakistan and several areas across the border in Iran and Afghanistan. Balochistan is bounded by three mountain ranges: the Siahan Range, the Central Makran Range, and the Coastal Makran Range. The Sulaiman Mountains are situated in central Pakistan, on the northeastern edges of Balochistan. Most of northern Balochistan is covered by large sand deserts. The **Thar Desert** is located east of the Indus River and encompasses a large area divided between Pakistan and India. Lahore, the second largest city in Pakistan, lies near the Indian border and has a population of around 4.5 million.

Pakistan has two significant climate types: subtropical and temperate continental climate. During the rainy season, monsoon winds bring heavy rainfall to most of the country. The Indus River Valley gets little precipitation outside of winter and Balochistan is dry during the entire year. Pakistan's southern coast is a hot and humid area, while the mountains in the far north are covered by frost and snow during most of the year.

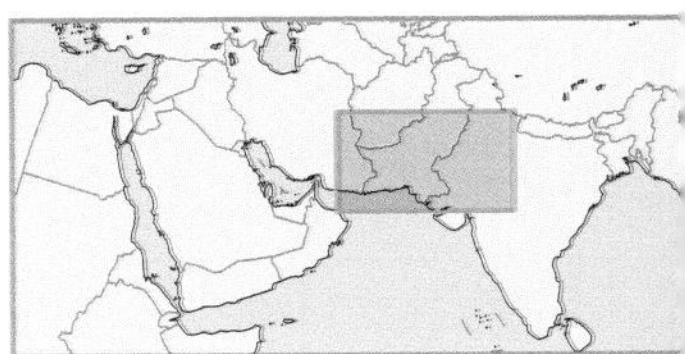

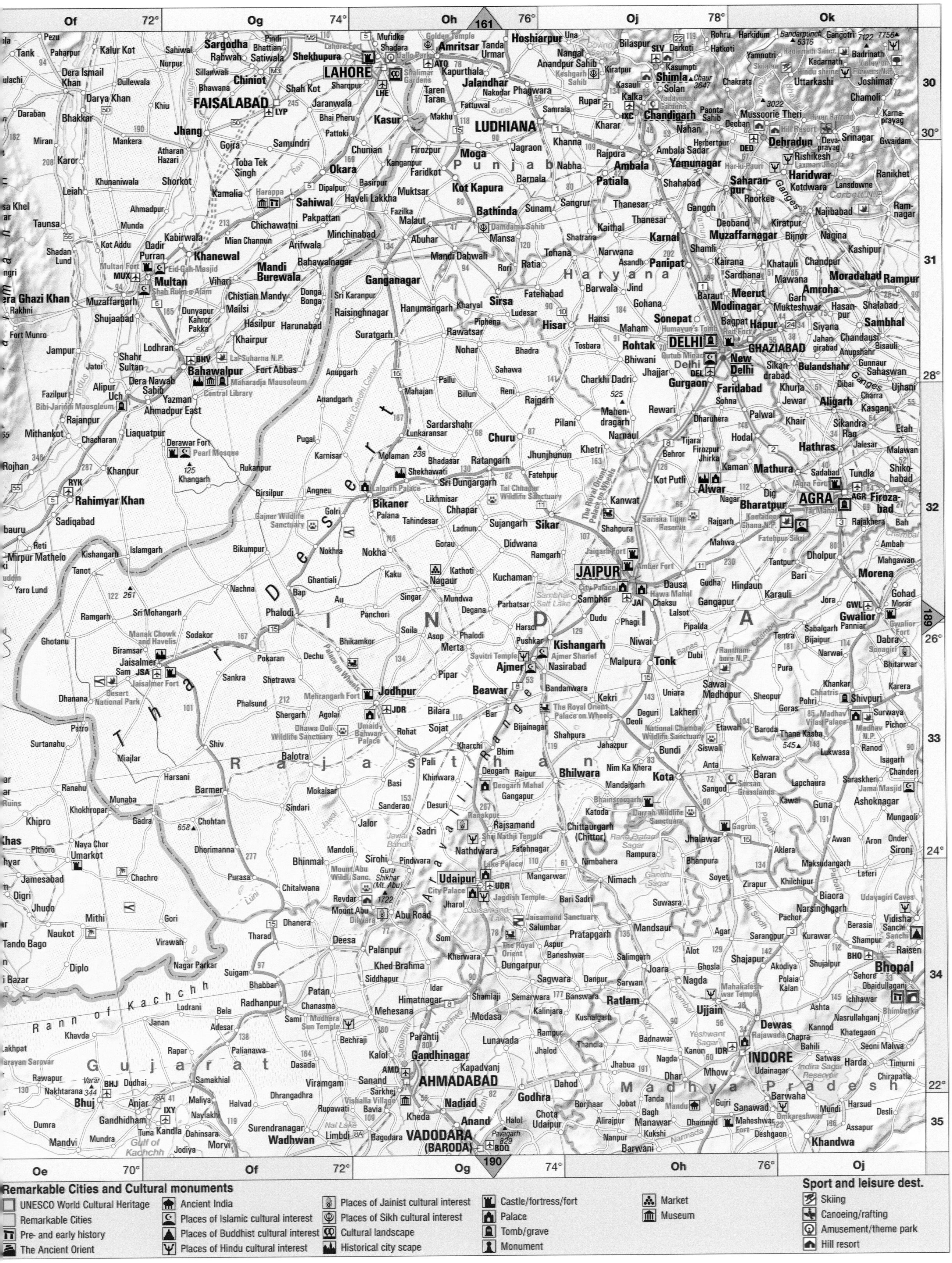

161
189
190

Remarkable Cities and Cultural monuments

- UNESCO World Cultural Heritage
- Remarkable Cities
- Pre- and early history
- The Ancient Orient
- Ancient India
- Places of Islamic cultural interest
- Places of Buddhist cultural interest
- Places of Hindu cultural interest
- Places of Jainist cultural interest
- Places of Sikh cultural interest
- Cultural landscape
- Historical city scape
- Castle/fortress/fort
- Palace
- Tomb/grave
- Monument
- Market
- Museum

Sport and leisure dest.

- Skiing
- Canoeing/rafting
- Amusement/theme park
- Hill resort

Lahore The capital of Punjab province, Lahore, flourished under the rule of the Mogul Empire during the 16th and 17th century. Lahore's fort (top photo), world heritage site, was expanded during this era. Badshahi mosque (middle photo) accommodates 60,000 worshippers. The Wazir Khan mosque (bottom photo) was built with Persian architectural influences. **Oh30**

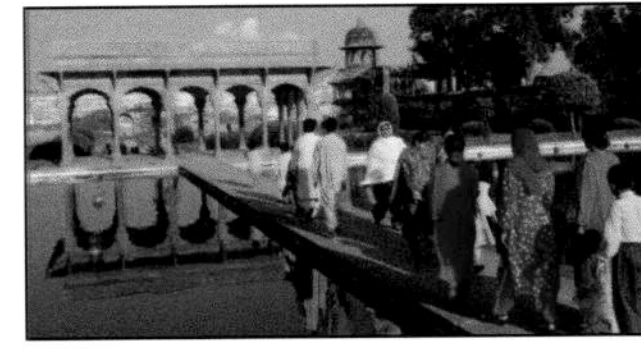

Shalimar Gardens Large gardens with terraces, canals, pavilions in Lahore – UNESCO world heritage site **Oh30**

Multan Fortified city in the Indus Valley – mausoleum of Rukn-i-Alam (photo) – silk production **Of30**

Uch Center for Islamic scholars in the 12th and 13th centuries – Persian architecture – the tomb of Bibi Jawindi (photo) was completed in 1494 **Of31**

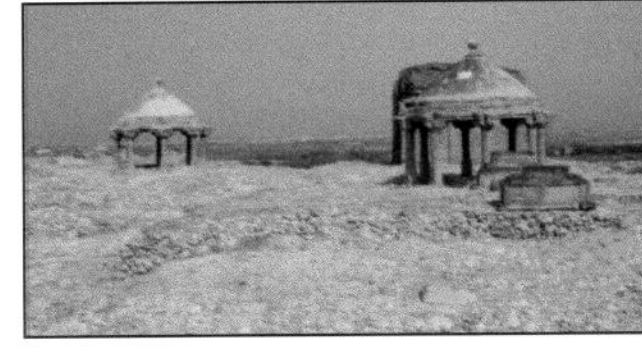

Makli Hills Necropolis Large field of tombs near Thatta, a UNESCO world heritage – mausoleum of Tarkhan **Od33**

The **People's Republic of China** is the third largest nation on earth with a total area of 9.6 million km². With around 1.3 billion inhabitants, China is also the world's most populous nation. The vast **Plateau of Tibet** in western China is the world's largest continuous upland region. Much of the plateau is covered by the **Himalayan Range** which features **Mount Everest** (8,850 meters), the world's tallest mountain. The Himalayas

separate the highlands of Central As from tropical South Asia. The **Karakora Range**, an extension of the Hindu Kus is situated northwest of the Himalaya The Karakoram features many large gl ciers and high mountains – includir **Nanga Parbat** (8,126 meters) and K (8,611 meters), the world's second hig

The Karakoram Mountains, a section c the Himalayas

Tian Shan Mountain range in central China, rising 5,000 meters – borders large deserts, steppes, and oases

Takla Makan Sand desert in the Tarim basin – Northwestern China – around 400,000 km²

Karakoram Mountain range in Afghanistan and Pakistan – contains four mountains rising over 8,000 meters

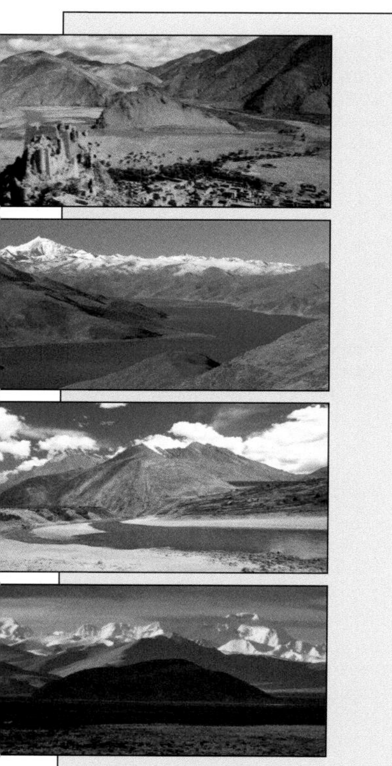

Tibet Tibet consists mostly of a two million km² large mountainous plateau. The region is widely known as the "roof of the world." Tibet's capital Lhasa was once the home of the Dalai Lama, the spiritual leader of Tibetan Buddhism. Photos from top to bottom: barren landscape in central Tibet, Yamdrok Tso lake, Brahmaputra river, Cho Oyu

North Tibetan Mountains Peaks rising above 7,000 meters – source of the Huang He and Chang Jiang Rivers – salt lakes

140
143
186

Scale 1:18,000,000
0 160 320 Kilometers

Depth tints
Shoreline
0-200 m
200-2000 m
2000-4000 m
4000-6000 m
6000-8000 m
> 8000 m

Physical Features
River, stream
Intermittent river
Lake
Intermittent lake
Salt lake
Intermittent salt lake
Elevation above sea level in meters

…t mountain. The **Quidam Basin** in cen-…l China is an arid basin between the …tun Shan and branches of the Kunlun …nge.
…vo large basins, the **Tarim basin** and …e **Dzungaria basin** stretch through …orthwestern China. Most of the arid …rim basin is covered by the vast and …ndy Takla Makan desert. The two …asins are separated by the mountains … the **Tian Shan Range**.The vast **Gobi Desert** starts to the east of the Tian Shan Range. The Gobi has an extreme climate with hot summers and bitter cold winters. It covers around 1.2 million km^2 in China and Mongolia. The Gobi is bordered in the northwest by the **Mongolian Altai**, a section of the large Altai mountain system.

Manchuria in northeastern China is bounded by three mountain ranges: the Greater and Lesser Khingan in the north and the Changbai range in the east. The Greater and Lesser Khingan ranges are relatively low mountain ranges which rise no higher than 2,000 meters.

Much of the Great Manchurian Plain in southern Manchuria is crossed by the **Huang He River**. The 4,845-kilometer-long Huang He is China's second longest river. China's longest river, the **Chang Jiang (Yangtze) River**, is around 6,300 kilometers long.

Japan is an archipelago of volcanic islands situated off the eastern coast of mainland Asia. Japan consists of four main islands: Hokkaido, Honshu, Shikoku, and Kyushu; and at least 3,300 smaller islands. All of the Japanese islands are summits of an undersea mountain range. A long mountain range stretches through the middle of the main Japanese islands and most of the country's territory is mountainous.

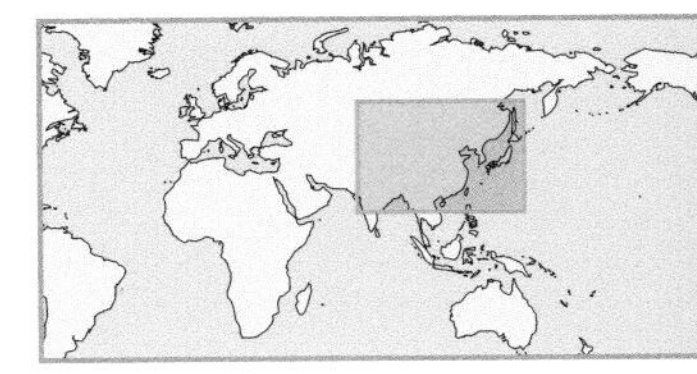

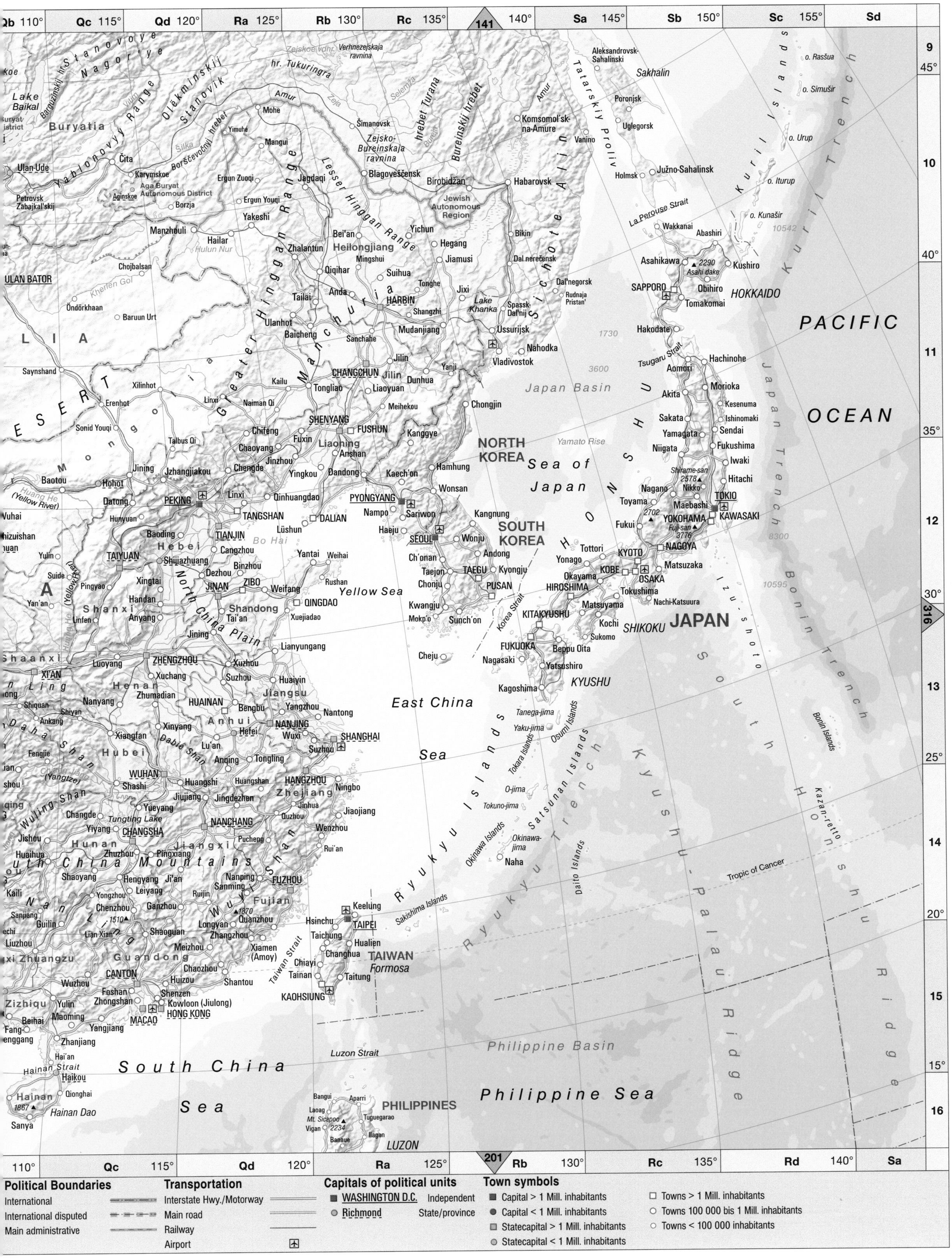

Gobi Desert East Asia's largest desert is surrounded by mountain ranges – located in northern China and southern Mongolia – dramatic climate with hot summer and bitter cold winters

Mongolian Altai Section of the Altai mountain range, divided between Russia and Mongolia – arid eastern sections – stretches into the Gobi Desert

Highlands of Central China Several mountain ranges stretch through the region – beautiful landscapes – tallest mountain, Magên Gangri (6,282 meters)

Huangshan Picturesque mountains west of Hangzhou – popular Chinese tourist destination – UNESCO world heritage site

Guilin Beautiful landscapes containing unique stone formations – along the Li River – numerous lake and rivers

Japanese Islands The volcano Mount Fuji (top photo) rises 3,776 meters on Japan's largest island Honshu. The Ryukyu Islands (bottom photo) are situated between Kyushu and Taiwan.

Political Boundaries
International
International disputed
Main administrative

Transportation
Interstate Hwy./Motorway
Main road
Railway
Airport

Capitals of political units
WASHINGTON D.C. Independent
Richmond State/province

Town symbols
Capital > 1 Mill. inhabitants
Capital < 1 Mill. inhabitants
Statecapital > 1 Mill. inhabitants
Statecapital < 1 Mill. inhabitants
Towns > 1 Mill. inhabitants
Towns 100 000 bis 1 Mill. inhabitants
Towns < 100 000 inhabitants

141
316
201

This section of Central Asia is a region of vast sparsely populated steppes and uninhabited deserts. The region encompasses sections of five nations; Kazakhstan, Tajikistan, Kyrgyzstan, and China. Many historic trade routes including the Silk Road passed through the heart of Central Asia during ancient times. Most of the larger cities in the region were, however, only founded in recent centuries. Bishek, the capital of **Kyrgyzstan** is situated in the Chu River vall The foothills of the Trans Alay Range - section of **Tian Shan** mountain syste – are located just outside of the city. T glacier-covered Tian Shan mounta range covers most of northeastern Ky gyzstan where it rises to a maximu height of 4,000 meters. Most of nor

A lush valley in China's Xinjiang province **Pb**

Trans-Ili Alatau Mountain range south of Lake Issyk-Kul – (photo) Kazakh shepherds near Almaty **OjOk24**

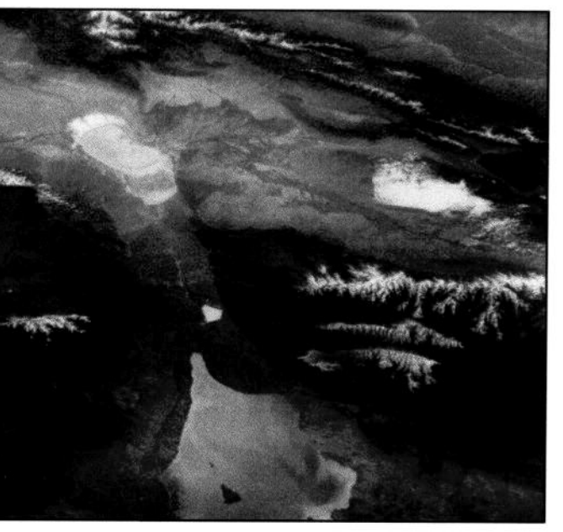

Dzungarian Gate Mountain pass between China and Kazakhstan – 3,000 meters above sea level – (photo) a satellite view of the Dzungarian Gate **Pb23**

Sayram Hu Lake in China at a height of 2,019 meters above sea level – 457 km² – maximum depth of 86 meters – colorful mountain vegetation in summer **Pa23**

Tian Shan Mountain System The system encompasses several ranges. The tallest peaks Khan Tengri (top photo; **Pa24**) and Pik Pobedy are in Kazakhstan. Inylchek Glacier (photo) is around 60 kilometers long. The turquoise lake Tian Chi is located west of Ürümqi at an elevation of 2,000 meters (bottom photo; **Pe24**).

Scale 1:4,500,000

0 40 80 Kilometers

Principal travel routes

- Auto route
- Rail road
- Shipping route

Remarkable landscapes and natural monuments

- UNESCO World Natural Heritage
- Mountain landscape
- Ravine/canyon
- Glacier
- River landscape
- Waterfall/rapids
- Lake country
- Desert
- Fossil site
- Nature park
- National park (landscape)
- Biosphere reserve
- Wildlife reserve

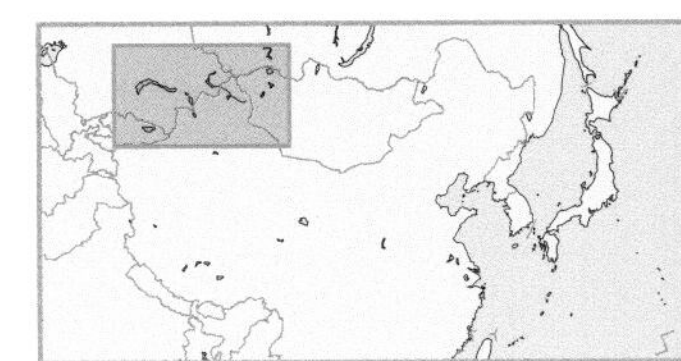

stern Kyrgyzstan's population is concentrated in two densely populated val-
s; the Talas River valley and the valley
ound **Lake Issyk-Kul**. The lake
000 km²) has a maximum depth of 700
eters and is one of the deepest fresh-
ater lakes in the world. Pik Pobedy
439 meters) and Khan Tengri (6,995
eters), the tallest mountains in Kyrgyz-
an, are both located near the border to
ina.

Most of southeastern **Kazakhstan** is covered by vast flat steppes and grasslands. The region is also the location of several mountainous areas including sections of the Tian Shan and Altai mountain systems. **Lake Balkhash** is a long and narrow body of water stretching over 600 kilometers from west to east though the steppes of southern Kazakhstan. The shallow western sections of the lake contain freshwater, while the deeper eastern sections of the lake contain salty water.

The Tian Shan Mountains separate the low lying northern sections of China's **Xinjiang Autonomous Region** from the Tarim Basin in the southern sections of the region. Most of northern Xinjiang is covered by the **Dzungarian (Junggar) Basin**. The basin itself consists of steppes and a large desert. The basin is bounded to the north by the **Altai Mountains** in Mongolia. The Altai Mountain Range rises to a maximum height above 4,000 meters. Mongolia's mountains are the source of the Irtysh River, which flows through **Lake Zaysan** in southeastern Kazakhstan. The northeastern section of the Altai stretches into the mountainous Russian republics of **Altai** and **Tuva**. The Altai is bordered to the east by a series of arid basins dotted with lakes and oases.

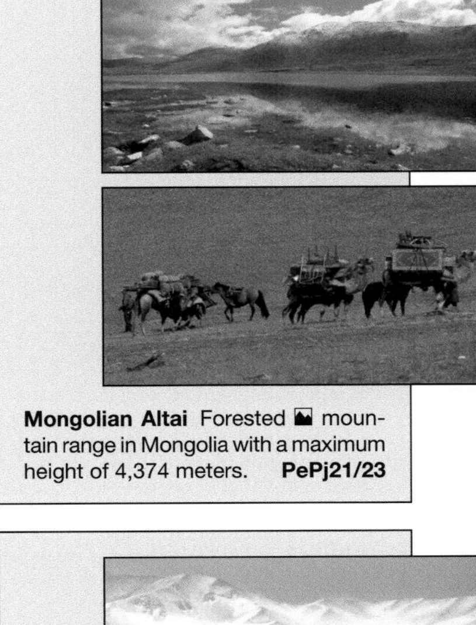

Mongolian Altai Forested mountain range in Mongolia with a maximum height of 4,374 meters. **PePj21/23**

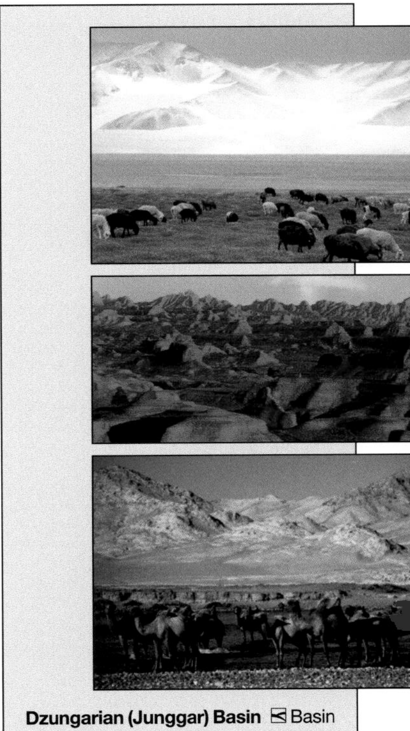

Dzungarian (Junggar) Basin Basin with grasslands and deserts. Photos from top to bottom: Grazing sheep, desert, wild camels in Dzungaria Nature Reserve **PdPe22/23**

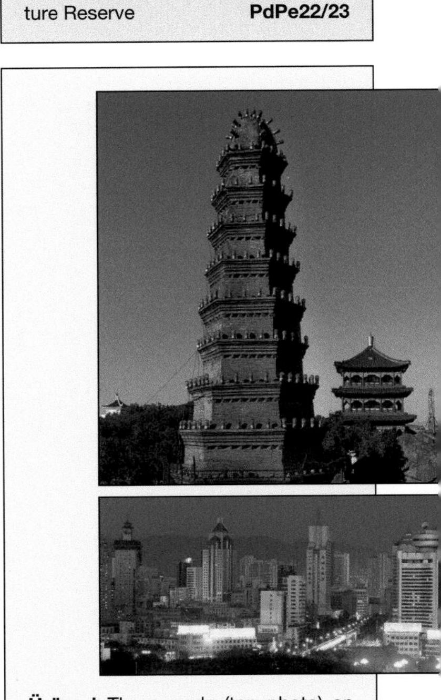

Ürümqi The pagoda (top photo) on the Red Hill is the major landmark of Ürümqi (bottom photo), capital of Xinjiang Autonomous Region. **Pd24**

Remarkable Cities and Cultural monuments

- UNESCO World Cultural Heritage
- Remarkable Cities
- Places of Islamic cultural interest
- Historical city scape
- Impressive skyline
- Castle/fortress/fort
- Tomb/grave
- Monument
- Museum
- Theater

Sport and leisure destinations

- Arena/stadium
- Horse racing
- Skiing
- Sailing
- Diving
- Canoeing/rafting
- Mineral/thermal spa

Tarim Basin, Western China

Northwestern China is home to several large basins surrounded by large mountain ranges. The largest of these basins is the massive Tarim basin which covers an area of 975,000 km². The Tarim Basin is bounded in the north, west, and south by three mountain ranges. The **Tian Shan range** which rises to a maximum height of around 7,000 meters is situated north of the Tarim basin. The **Altun Mountains** and **Kunlun Mountains**

stretch to the south and west of the bas The climates in the basin range fr semi-arid to very arid and most of basin is covered by the large **Tak Makan** desert. Because of its extre climate, the Takla Makan is totally ur habited. The only settlements in the ba lie along its edges outside of the des

Bezeklik Valley: tall stone walls and numerous caves **Pe**

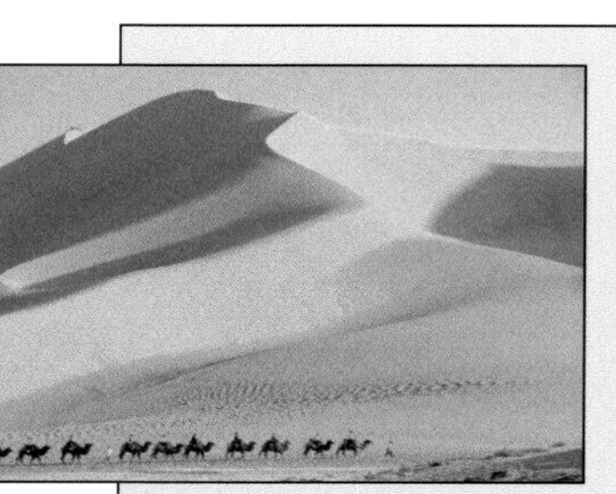

Takla Makan Large sandy desert covering the Tarim basin – scattered oasis settlements along the edges of the desert. **PaPb26**

Karakoram Highway 1,300-kilometer-long mountain roadway between Pakistan and China. Photos from top to bottom: Taxkorgan, Muztagata, Lake Karakul **Oh26/27**

The Tomb of Abahk Hoja Beautiful tomb in the city of Kashi – mosques and historic fountains on the premises **Oj26**

Id Kah Mosque The largest mosque in China – yellow brick facade – oldest sections constructed in 1445 **Oj26**

Kuqa The Thousand Buddha caves (photo) contain important Buddhist art made between the 3rd and 8th centuries **Pb25**

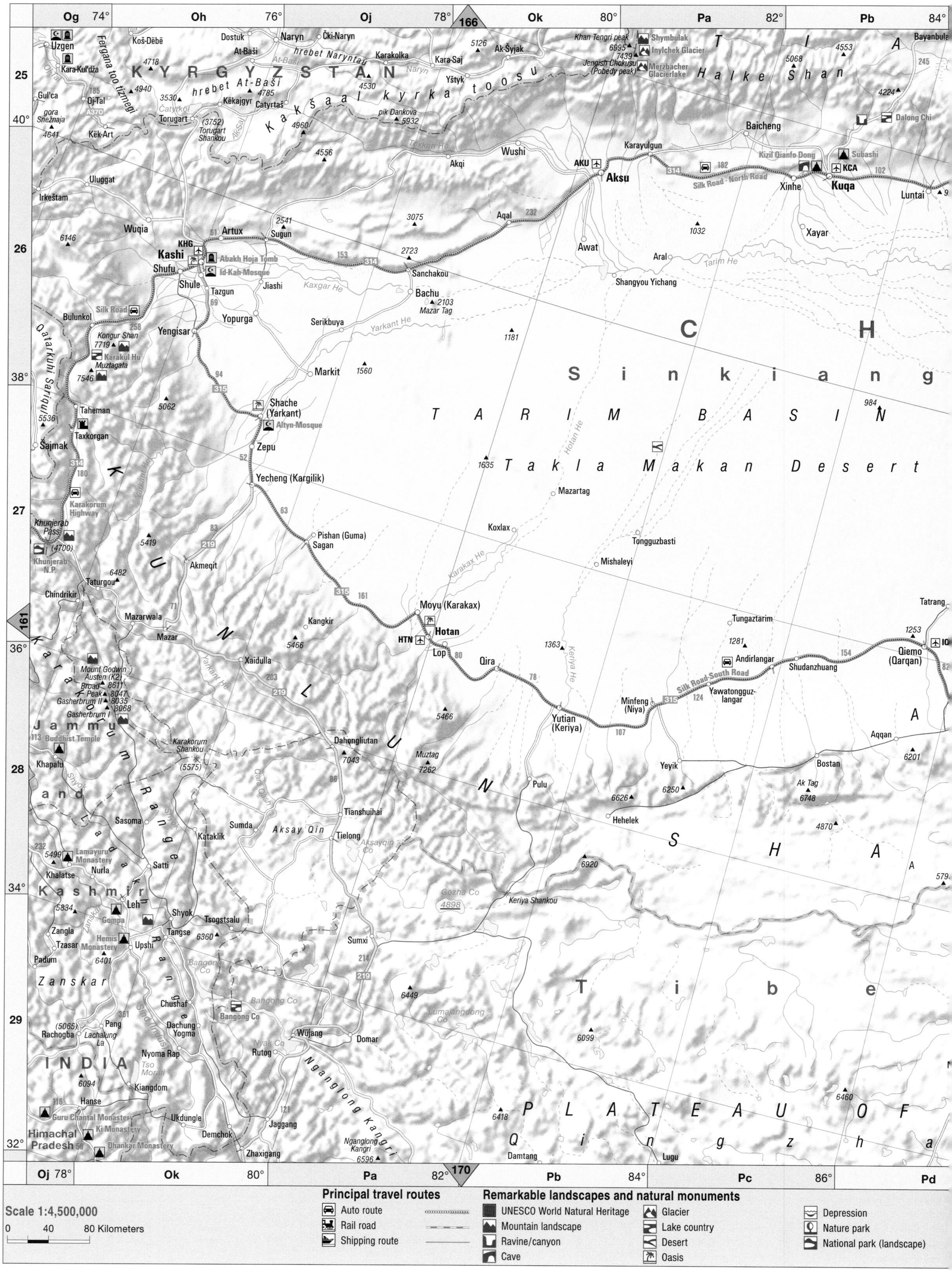

Scale 1:4,500,000

0 40 80 Kilometers

Principal travel routes

- Auto route
- Rail road
- Shipping route

Remarkable landscapes and natural monuments

- UNESCO World Natural Heritage
- Mountain landscape
- Ravine/canyon
- Cave
- Glacier
- Lake country
- Desert
- Oasis
- Depression
- Nature park
- National park (landscape)

d depend on water from snow covered untains. Turpan, on the north-tern edge of the basin, is one of the gest towns in the region. It lies in the pan Depression, which has a maxi-m depth of 505 meters below sea level. e depression is the second lowest nt on the Earth's surface, after the ad Sea. Turpan and its surroundings well known throughout China for their pe farms and Central Asian atmosphere. The town of Dunhuang is located in the western foothills of the Qilian Mountains along the historic Silk Road. The **Silk Road** was a historic trade route along which traders carried valuable Chinese silk to Europe and the Middle East.

The **Mogoa Grottoes** contain impressive Buddhist cave paintings and historic statues made between the 4th and 7th centuries. The grottoes are the major cultural attraction in the region around Dunhuang. **Kaski**, a city in the northwestern Tarim basin, is home to many different Central Asian ethnicities including Kazakhs, Uzbeks, Kyrgyz, and Uighurs. The city lies near China's borders to Kyrgyzstan, Tajikistan, and Afghanistan.

The **Karakoram Range** – an extension of the Hindu Kush – starts to the west of Kunlun Mountains. The Karakoram forms part of the border between China and Pakistan. K2, the world's second tallest mountain (8,611 meters) is situated on the Chinese-Pakistani border.

Most of the east-west extension of the Kunlun Mountains lies just north of the vast **Tibetan Plateau**. The southeastern sections of the Kunlun Mountains extend into the 200,000 km² large Qaidam basin. The arid basin consists of sand hills, salt lakes, and marshlands. There are only a few scattered settlements in this inhospitable region.

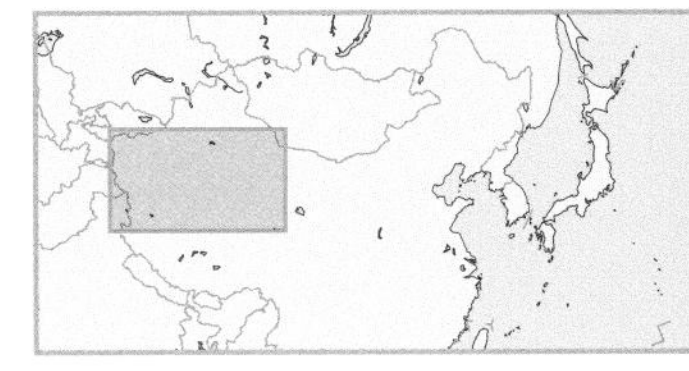

Jiaohe Ruins of a city abandoned in the 13th century – well preserved remnants of the city gates and Buddhist monasteries **Pe24**

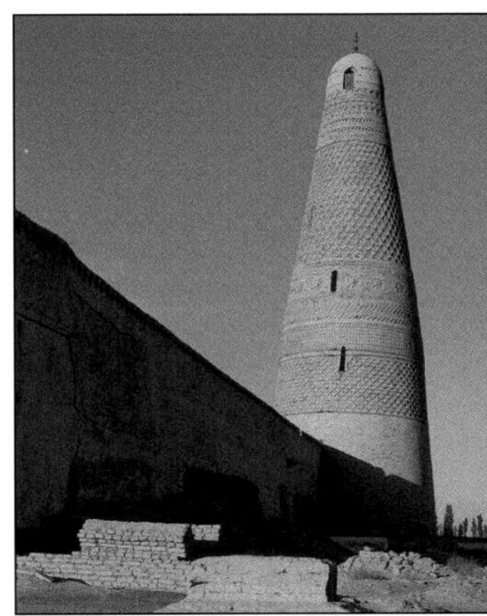

Turpan Oasis in a deep depression – Emin mosque and the Sugong Ta (photo) minaret, built in the 18th century **Pe24**

Bezeklik The Thousand Buddha Caves – 70 grottoes containing wall paintings made between the 5th and 9th century **Pe24**

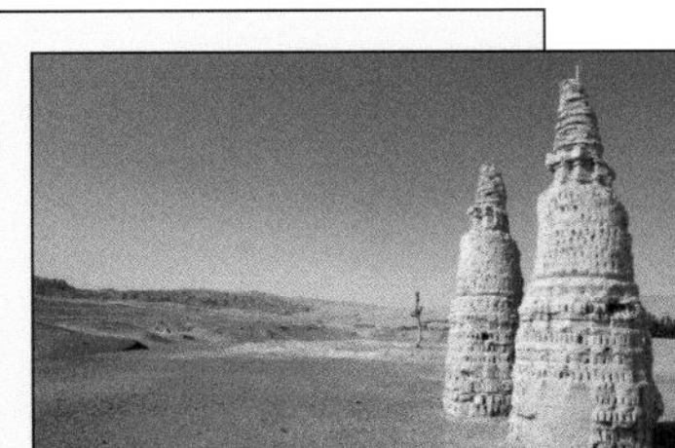

The Silk Road The historic route was first used by traders carrying silk from China to Persia around 200 BC. In addition to silk, weapons, horses, and art were traded along the road. Photo: near Dunhuang **Ph25**

Mogao Grottoes 5th century temple constructed into the side of a stone cliff – Buddhist art from different centuries **Ph25**

Crescent Moon Lake Lake surrounded by large sand dunes – beautiful views from the top of Mingsha Shan dune **Ph25/26**

emarkable Cities and Cultural monuments

- UNESCO World Cultural Heritage
- Remarkable Cities
- Ancient China
- Places of Islamic cultural interest
- Places of Buddhist cultural interest
- Castle/fortress/fort
- Tomb/grave

Because of its high elevation, the expansive Plateau of Tibet is often referred to as the "Roof of the World." The mountainous plateau encompasses most of Tibet and sections of China's Qinghai province. With an average elevation of 4,500 meters above sea level, the Plateau of Tibet is the highest plateau in the world. It consists of a large basin that declines in elevation to the north, numerous mountain ranges, and wide

valleys. Thousands of lakes and salt la are scattered throughout the area of plateau. The largest lake, **Nam** covers 1,920 km² and is considere sacred site by Tibetan Buddhists. highlands of Tibet and especially **Tanggula Shan mountain range** cont the sources of many important rivers t

Sunset above the Tibetan Himalayas **Pa**

Annapurna 40-kilometer-long mountain mass in the Himalayas – Annapurna I (8,091 meters) **PbPc31**

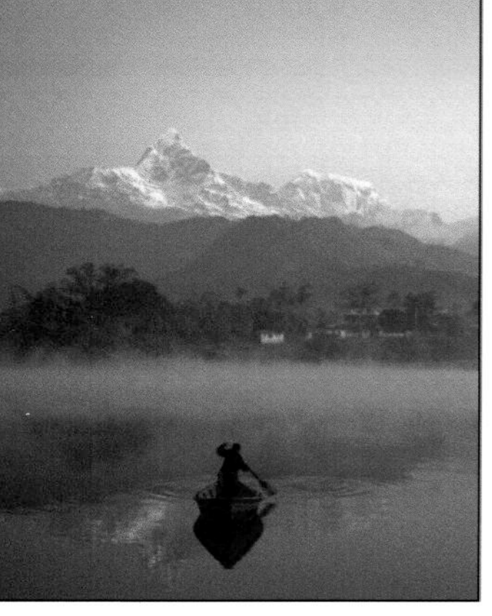

Pokhara City at the foot of the mountain Machhapuchare (6,997 meters) – lakes and forests in the surrounding area **Pc31**

Royal Chitwan National Park Situated in a pristine section of Nepal's Terai region – UNESCO world heritage site **Pc32**

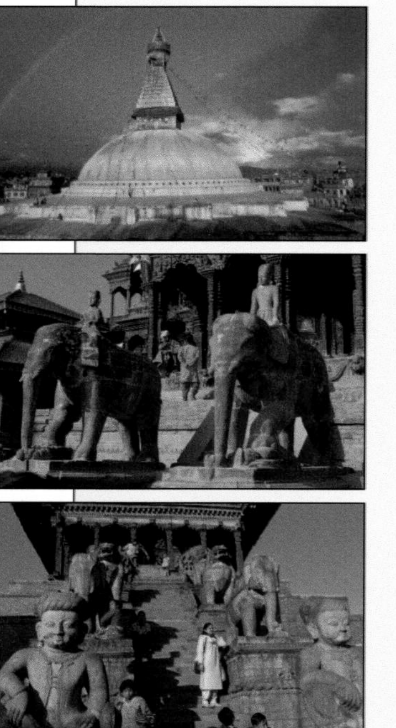

Kathmandu Valley The region of Nepal has been designated a UNESCO world heritage sites. The royal cities Kathmandu and Patan (middle photo) are home to several medieval palaces and other historic buildings. Stupas (top photo) are the holiest temples for Nepal's Buddhist community. The royal city Bhaktapur is the location of the Nyatapola (bottom photo) and Pashupatinath temples. **Pc32**

Scale 1:4,500,000

0 40 80 Kilometers

Principal travel routes

- Auto route
- Rail road
- Shipping route

Remarkable landscapes and natural monuments

- UNESCO World Natural Heritage
- Mountain landscape
- Ravine/canyon
- Glacier
- Lake country
- National park (landscape)
- National park (flora)
- National park (fauna)
- Wildlife reserve

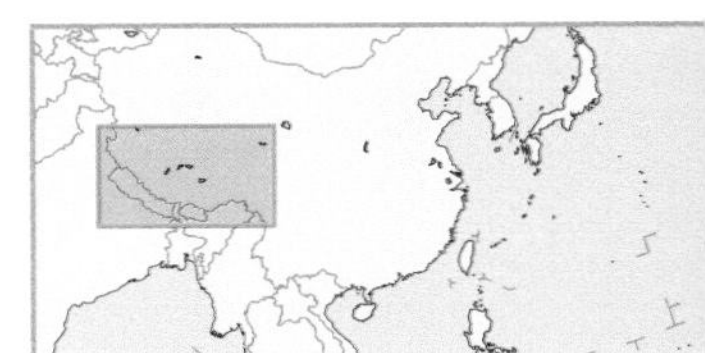

ẉ through East and Southeast Asia, cluding the Chang Jiang (Yangtze), ang He, and Mekong Rivers. Because the extreme climate, the highest eleted sections of the plateau are gene'y uninhabited. Much of the plateau's pulation lives in the numerous canyons d rivers valleys in the region's southstern section. Southeastern Tibet is the cation of several glacier covered mounns ranges and at lower elevations expansive **subtropical forests** with abundant flora and fauna including rare Tibetan white pines and (white-lipped) Thorold's deer.

The most populous area of Tibet is the valley of the **Yarlung-Zangbo (Brahmaputra) River** which flows from west to east at an elevation around 4,000 meters. According to traditional Tibetan beliefs the valley was the original "birthplace" of the Tibetan people. The valley is bordered to the north by the **Kailas Mountains** and to the south by the main range of the **Himalayas**. The Himalayas are divided between Tibet and several neighboring countries: India, Nepal and Bhutan. **Mount Everest** (8,850 meters), the world's highest mountain, is located in the Himalayas along the border between Nepal and Tibet. The Yarlung-Zango river valley features the majority of Tibet's cultural and religious attractions including the ancient cities of Lhasa and Xigaze.

Despite its small size, the **Kingdom of Nepal** has a wealth of breathtaking landscapes and cultural treasures. The country's culture has been heavily influenced by neighboring Tibet and India. Nepal is 800 kilometers long from east to west but its territory encompasses several climate zones including polar mountainous regions and subtropical marshlands.

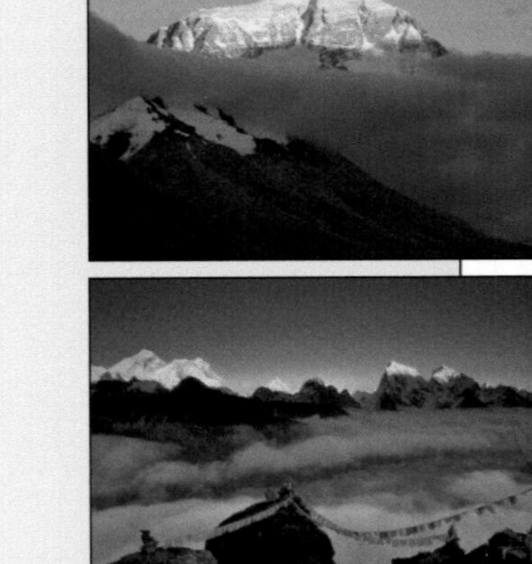

The Roof of the World The Himalayas and their foothills encompass many of the world's great mountains including Mount Everest (photo, 8,850 meters), which was first climbed in 1953. **Pd31/32**

Sagarmatha National Park The area contains glaciers, valleys, and tall peaks including Mount Everest – world heritage site – Tengpoche monastery (photo) **Pd32**

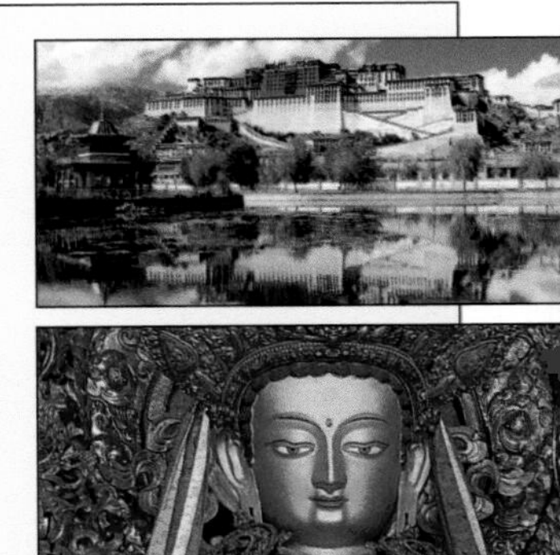

Lhasa The Potala Palace towers above Lhasa and was once the summer residence of the Dalai Lamas. The Johkang Temple contains the beautiful Meitreya chapel (bottom photo). **Pf31**

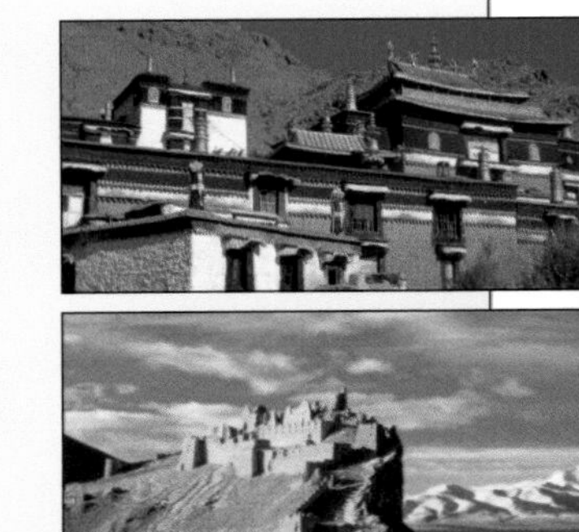

The Monasteries of Tibet Tashilhungpo (top photo; **Pe31**) monastery, founded in 1447. Samye monastery, Tibet's oldest, (bottom photo; **Pf31**) was founded around 767 AD.

Remarkable Cities and Cultural monuments

- UNESCO World Cultural Heritage
- Remarkable Cities
- Ancient China
- Places of Christian cultural interest
- Places of Islamic cultural interest
- Places of Buddhist cultural interest
- Places of Hindu cultural interest
- Places of Sikh cultural interest
- Historical city scape
- Castle/fortress/fort
- Palace
- Space telescope
- Museum

Sport and leisure destinations

- Skiing
- Canoeing/rafting
- Hill resort

Mongolia in eastern Central Asia is a nation of large plateaus, arid **steppes** and vast **deserts**. Around 80% of the country's territory is covered by mountain plateaus and lies at elevations above 1,000 meters. The western and southern sections contain several tall mountain ranges including the Mongolian-Gobi Altai which rises to a maximum height of 4,000 meters. Numerous large basins are situated between the mountains of the south

and west and many of the region's mou tains are covered by glaciers. In nor western Mongolia the mountains of t Eastern and Western Sayan mount ranges rise to maximum heights arou 3,000 meters.

The **Hangayn Mountains** are a range low and heavily eroded mountains. Th

Lake Baikal in Siberia, the world's deepest freshwater lake **Qb–Qe19/**

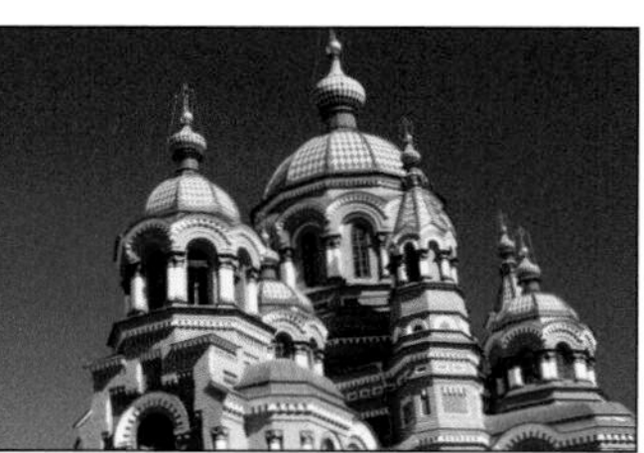

Irkutsk Russian city in eastern Siberia – Kazanskaya Church, built in the 17th century (photo) **Qc19**

Lake Khovsgol National Park Located in northeastern Mongolia, Lake Khovsgol (top photo) is the second largest lake in Mongolia. Yaks (bottom photo) are the most valuable animals for the region's inhabitants. **Qa20**

Khorgo Terkhiin Tsagaan Nuur National Park The crater of Khorgo volcano was created around 8,000 years ago – 2,240 meters high – mountain scenery **Pk21**

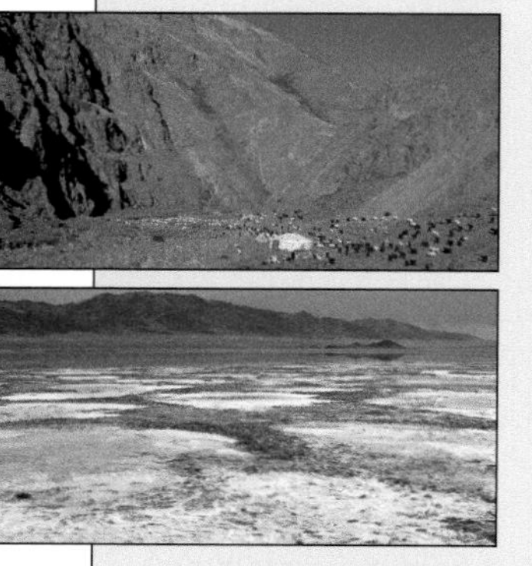

Mongolian/Gobi Altai This expansive mountain system surrounded by karst landscapes is inhabited by Mongolian nomads (top photo). The region's wildlife includes snow leopards and argali sheep. Böön Tsagaan (bottom photo) is the largest salt lake in the area. **Pk–Qb23**

Orkhon Valley Contains the meandering Orkhon River – Orkhon waterfalls – archeological sites **QaQb22**

Scale 1:4,500,000

0 40 80 Kilometers

Principal travel routes

- Auto route
- Rail road
- Shipping route

Remarkable landscapes and natural monuments

- UNESCO World Natural Heritage
- Mountain landscape
- Rock landscape
- Ravine/canyon
- Geyser
- Cave
- River landscape
- Waterfall/rapids
- Lake country
- Desert
- Nature park
- National park (landscape)
- National park (flora)
- National park (fauna)
- Wildlife reserve

ver much of central Mongolia and are oken by numerous large plains. Around e percent of Mongolia's territory is vered by forests, many of which are ncentrated in the center of the coun- . The northern foothills of the Hangayn ountains comprise an area of forested eppes which are mostly used for live- ock grazing. In contrast to the northern othills, the southern edges of the Han- yn Mountains are a mostly treeless area covered by large grasslands. Central Mongolia features numerous lakes and smaller bodies of water, many of which contain saline water.

The Mongolian section of the **Gobi desert** consists primarily of arid steppes. The desert covers much of southern Mongolia and is bordered to the north by mountain ranges and dense taiga. The Gobi is around 2,000 kilometers long. Its sandy deserts, marshes, and grassy steppes where livestock is grazed. Eastern Mongolia consists of a large plateau that is situated at heights between 800 and 1,000 meters above sea level. This plateau contains large basins with numerous salt lakes and vast steppes covered by grass.

Mongolia's rivers flow in three directions: south into China, north into Russia, and east to the Pacific Ocean.

Lake Baikal is the largest freshwater lake in Asia and the deepest lake on the planet with a maximum depth of 1,620 meters. At least 1,000 unique species inhabit the lake but its biodiversity is threatened by manmade pollution.

Mongolia has an arid and cool continental climate. Winters are dry and cold, while summers are temperate with plentiful rainfall. In Mongolia's capital **Ulaanbaatar (Ulan Bator)** temperatures often fall below -47° Celsius during winter.

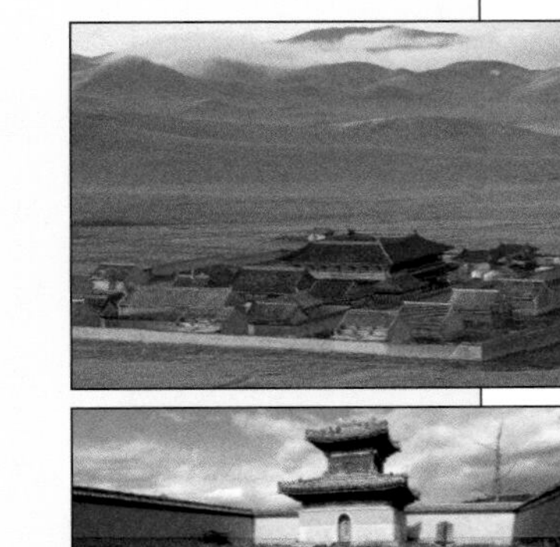

Amarbayasgalant Buddhist monastery built in the 17th century. The monastery is situated in a picturesque Mongolian valley. **Qc21**

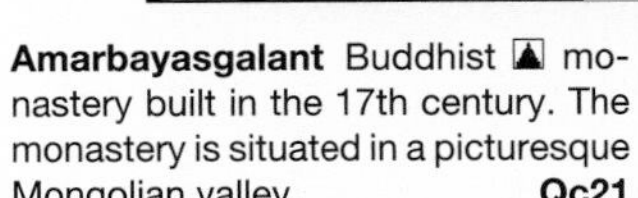

Ulaanbaatar (Ulan Bator) Mongolia's capital and largest city – the former Winter Palace now contains a museum – Mongolian temples (photo) **Qd22**

Erdene Zuu Monastery Oldest Mongolian temple, founded in 1586 – damaged in the 1930s and recently renovated **Qb22**

Shankh Monastery Heavily damaged during the early Communist era – now in the process of reconstruction **Qb22**

Ikh Gazriin Chuluu Stone formation near Mandalgovi – many interesting granite formations in the surrounding area **Qd23**

Khan Khentii Nature Reserve The birthplace and burial site of Genghis Khan, according to traditional beliefs **Qe21**

Remarkable Cities and Cultural monuments

- UNESCO World Cultural Heritage
- Remarkable Cities
- Places of Buddhist cultural interest
- Historical city scape
- Castle/fortress/fort
- Tomb/grave
- Monument
- Festivals
- Museum

Northern China

Northern China is a region of high plateaus, deserts, and craggy mountains. Northern China's topography resembles the shape of a stairway. The region's elevation rises from east to west like a series of steps or ridges. The **Alxa Plateau** in the far west of Northern China is the first in a chain of sparsely populated high plateaus covered by deserts and arid grasslands. The plateau stretches between the Mongolian border in the north and the

Qilian Shan Mountains in the south. T **Gansu (Hexi) Corridor** is over 1,000 k meters long and stretches through Gansu province. The corridor has be a major transport route to western Ch since ancient times. The Gansu Corri was once part of the ancient **Silk Ro** and the Great Wall of China runs para

The Great Wall of China is 6,700 kilometers long **Qg**

Bayanzag The valley contains excavation sites with dinosaur fossils – around 100 intact skeletons have been found here – well preserved dinosaur eggs **Qb23**

Dafo Si Large Buddhist temple built in the 11th century – largest reclining Buddha statue in China; 35 meters long **Qa26**

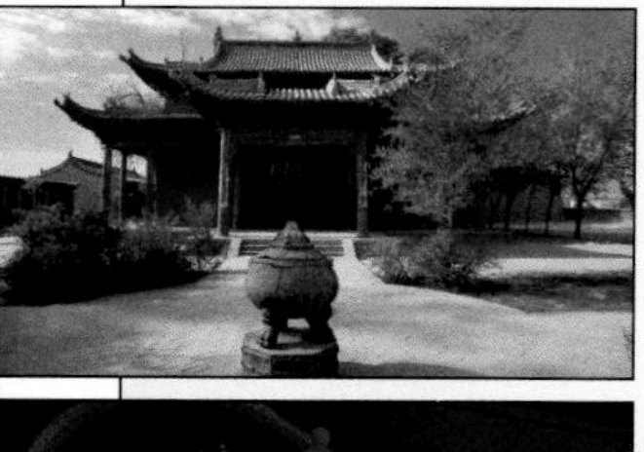

Wuwei The city is home to three major tourist attractions; the Han tomb of Leitai, the tomb of the princesses, and the Haizang temple. **Qb27**

Ta'er Si Large monastery complex built by Tibetan Buddhist lamas in the 16th century – beautiful landscapes – historic sculptures **Qa27**

Xixia Wangling Burial site containing the tombs of 72 kings and nobles from the Xixia Kingdom (1038-1227) – often called the "Pyramids of China" **Qc26**

Jiayuguan Large historic fortress built in the 14th century – the surrounding walls are 10 meters high **Pk26**

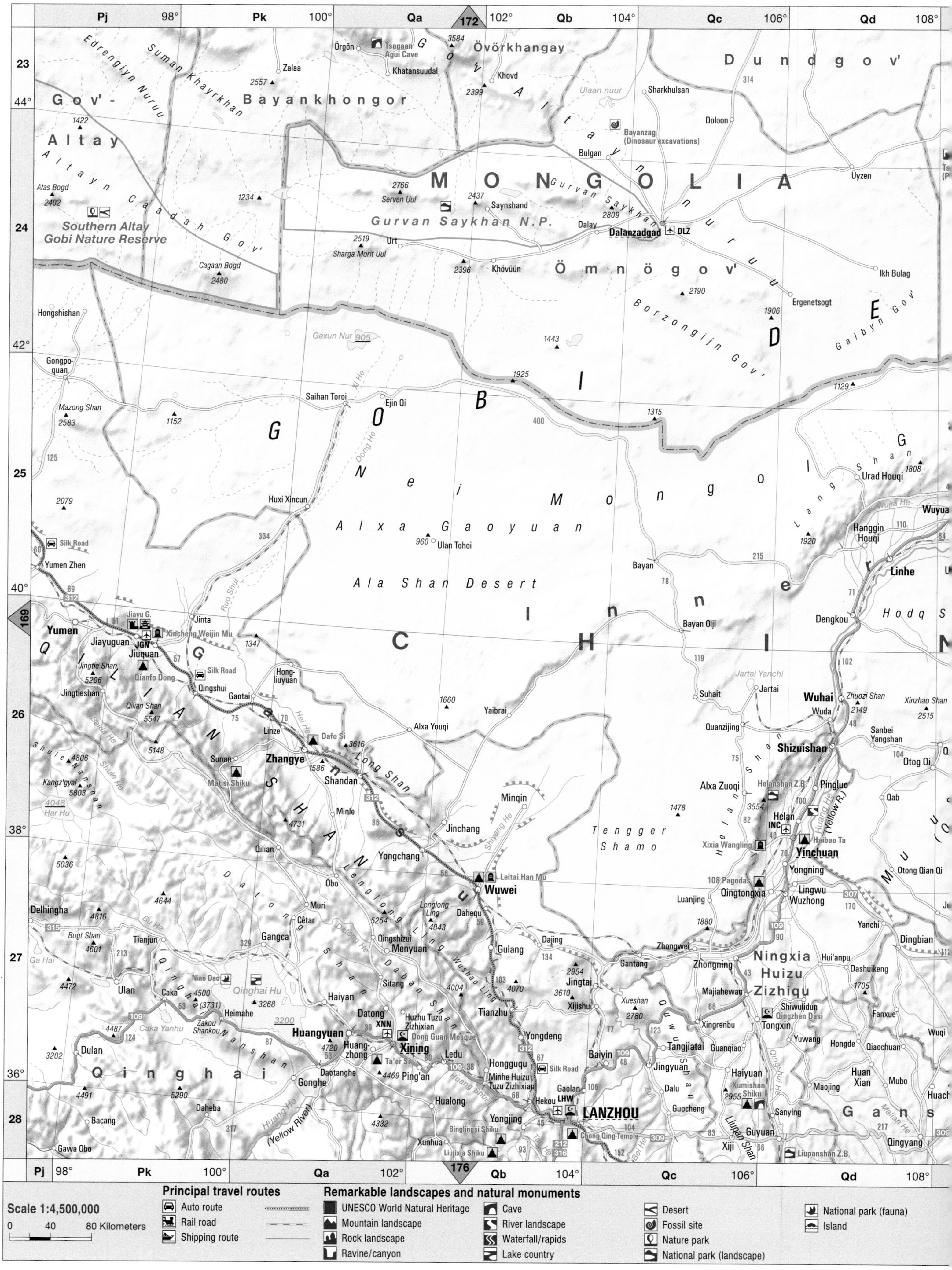

Scale 1:4,500,000
0 40 80 Kilometers

Principal travel routes
- Auto route
- Rail road
- Shipping route

Remarkable landscapes and natural monuments
- UNESCO World Natural Heritage
- Mountain landscape
- Rock landscape
- Ravine/canyon
- Cave
- River landscape
- Waterfall/rapids
- Lake country
- Desert
- Fossil site
- Nature park
- National park (landscape)
- National park (fauna)
- Island

he corridor for much of its length. The Road was not only a trade route but a meeting point for many different tures and religions. The numerous autiful mosques and Buddhist nples scattered throughout north- stern China are reminders of the cul- al interactions that took place in the ion during ancient times.

e center of Northern China is covered the **basin of the Huang He (Yellow) River**. The basin area is often considered the craddle of Chinese civilization. The Chinese name Huang-He literally means the "Yellow River" and comes from the yellow color of the silt in the river. Every year the river transports around 1.6 billion tons of silt, much of which gets deposited along its banks. The river flows north in the shape of a bow, around the Ordos Plateau. This large plateau is covered by deserts and extends east to the highlands of Shaanxi province. Wutaishan, the tallest mountain in Shaanxi province rises 3,058 meters above sea level.

The eastern sections of Northern China consist mostly of densely populated plains dissected by many rivers and canals. The **Great Wall of China**, a UNESCO world heritage site, begins in this region. It is, however, just one of many historic monuments and attractions in the region. **Beijing**, the capital of China is home to many important Chinese historic sites including Tiananmen Square and the **Forbidden City**, once the residence of China's emperors. **Qufu**, the birthplace of Confucius and the mountain **Taishan** are also located in the region and both are highly revered by the Chinese. Northern China extends east to the delta of the Huang He River on the coast of **Bo Hai**, an arm of the Pacific.

Yungang 53 grottoes with Buddhist sculptures and bas-reliefs, a UNESCO world heritage site – created in the 5th century **Qg25**

Chengde Summer palace of the Qing dynasty – Buddhist temple complex – UNESCO world heritage site **Qj25**

The Great Wall The section near Badaling has been restored – built under the Ming dynasty – museum **Qh25**

The Imperial Ming Tombs Burial site of the Ming dynasty (1368-1644) – UNESCO world heritage site – sculptures **Qj25**

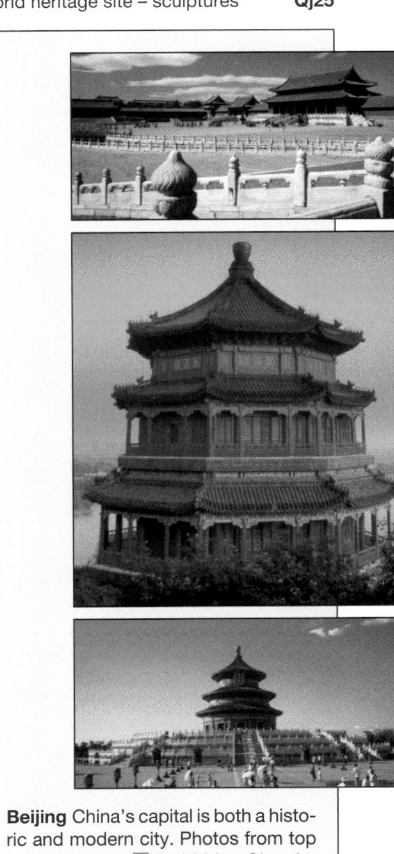

Beijing China's capital is both a historic and modern city. Photos from top to bottom: the Forbidden City, the Imperial Summer Palace, the Temple of Heaven, a UNESCO world heritage site **Qj26**

Remarkable Cities and Cultural monuments

- UNESCO World Cultural Heritage
- Remarkable Cities
- Pre- and early history
- Ancient China
- Places of Islamic cultural interest
- Places of Buddhist cultural interest
- Historical city scape
- Castle/fortress/fort
- Palace
- Technical/industrial monument
- Tomb/grave
- Monument
- Festivals
- Museum
- Theater
- Olympics
- Great Wall

Sport and leisure dest.

- Beach resort
- Mineral/thermal spa

Central China

Central China contains an incredible wealth of important cultural and natural attractions. The region also features a fascinating mix of distinct climate zones and topographies.

The western edges of Central China are covered by the **highlands of Qinghai** province and sections of the **Tibetan Plateau**. This area is home to major rivers flowing from to north to south and expansive mountain systems including the ▲

Hengduan Shan along the border be tween China and Myanmar (Burma). A in the region, the craggy and tall ▲ Dax Shan range rises above 7,000 meter Sichuan province. The source of the **Jinsha Jiang River** lies in Tibet. The ri forms the western borders of Sichu Near Yibin, the Jinsha Jiang becon

Arid plains and rugged mountains ne Labrang **Qb**

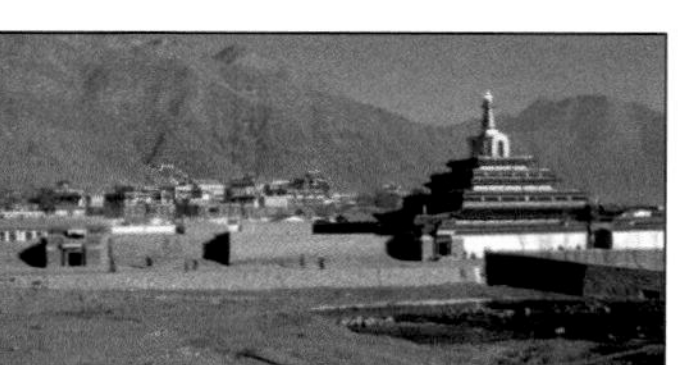

Labrang Si Monastery The largest Tibetan Buddhist (Lamaism) monastery outside of Tibet – golden stupas **Qb28**

Jiuzhaigou National park – waterfalls, steppes, and grasslands – rare plants and animals **Qb29**

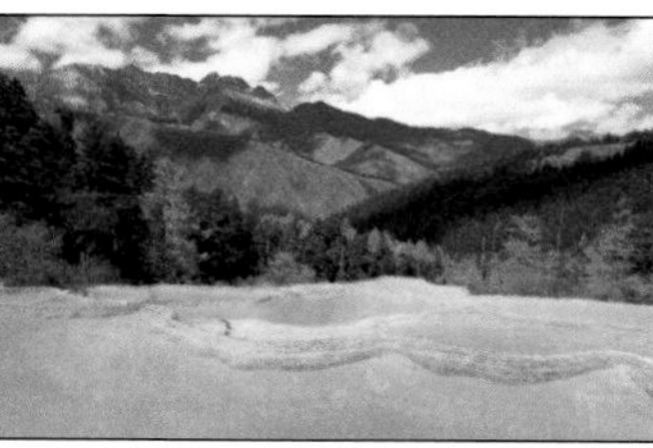

Huanglong Mountain valley – hot thermal springs and tall stone formations – large glaciers **Qb29**

Wolong Giant Panda Reserve Protected habitat of giant pandas and other endangered animals – research area for panda preservation **Qb30**

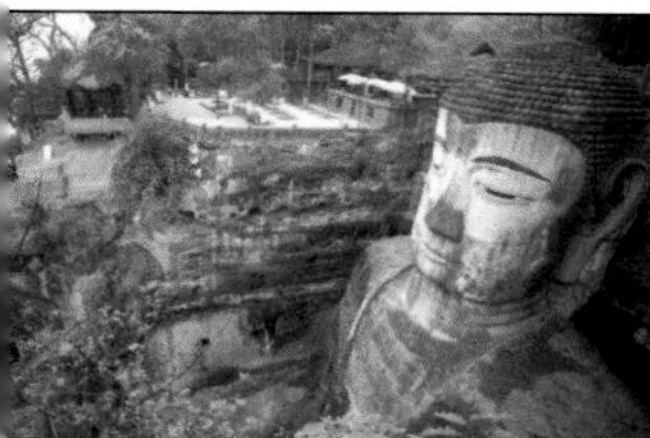

Leshan Giant Buddha Large ▲ Buddha statue built into the side of a stone wall – temple and pagoda built during the Tang era **Qb31**

Lijiang Historic town with wooden houses and cobblestone streets – UNESCO world heritage site – traditional Naxi culture **Qa32**

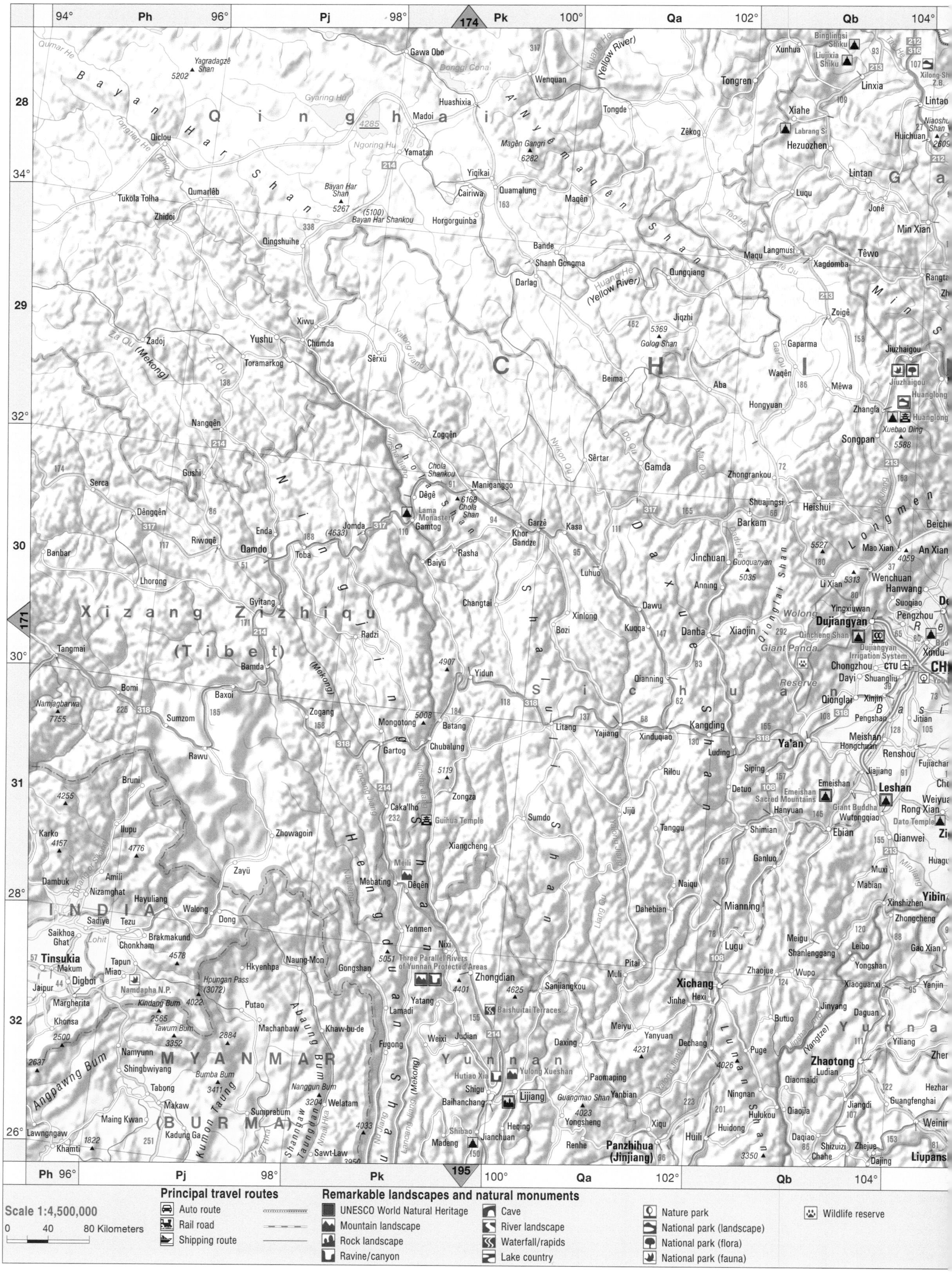

Scale 1:4,500,000
0 40 80 Kilometers

Principal travel routes
- Auto route
- Rail road
- Shipping route

Remarkable landscapes and natural monuments
- UNESCO World Natural Heritage
- Mountain landscape
- Rock landscape
- Ravine/canyon
- Cave
- River landscape
- Waterfall/rapids
- Lake country
- Nature park
- National park (landscape)
- National park (flora)
- National park (fauna)
- Wildlife reserve

e Chang Jiang (Yangtze) River, Asia's gest river. e Chang Jiang flows through the large chuan Basin, which covers most of stern Sichuan. The basin is also wide-known as the **Red Basin**, a reference its rich red soil. The mountainous stern edge of the basin is home to any important natural and cultural ractions. The sacred mountain **Emei**, e **Giant Panda Reserve** near the city of Chengdu, **Huanglong National Park** and **Juizhaigou National Park** are among the more popular attractions in the region.

Near Fengjie, the river passes through the first of the famous **Three Gorges**, a group of scenic gorge landscapes. After passing Yichang, the river flows through a large plain containing many lakes and rivers. The plain comprises sections of both the Chang Jiang River basin and the delta of the Han River. **Dongting Hu**, situated on the plain, is China's second largest freshwater lake.

The **Qin Ling Mountains** are located just north of the Sichuan Basin. The mountain range separates the subtropical regions to its south from the more temperate areas to the north. Many Chinese consider the Qin Ling Mountains a boundary between Northern and Southern China. The Wei River flows along the edges of the Qin Ling Mountains and the Wei river valley contains the city **Xi'an**. The city was once the starting point of the ancient Silk Road and is home to several important historic sites. The Wei empties into the **Huang He (Yellow) River** near the city of Tong'guan. East of the city **Luoyang**, the Huang He flows into the **North China Plain**. The large plain covers 400,000 km² and is one of China's most densely populated regions.

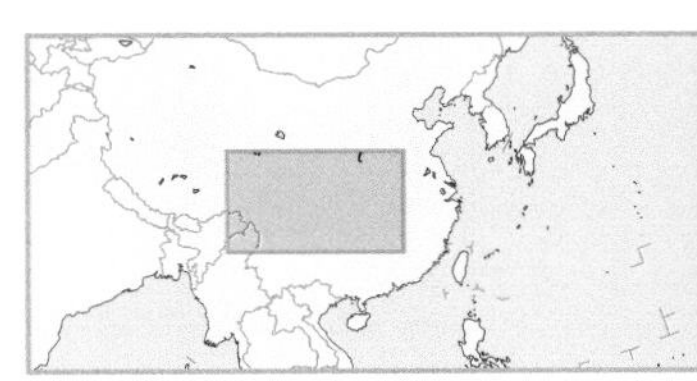

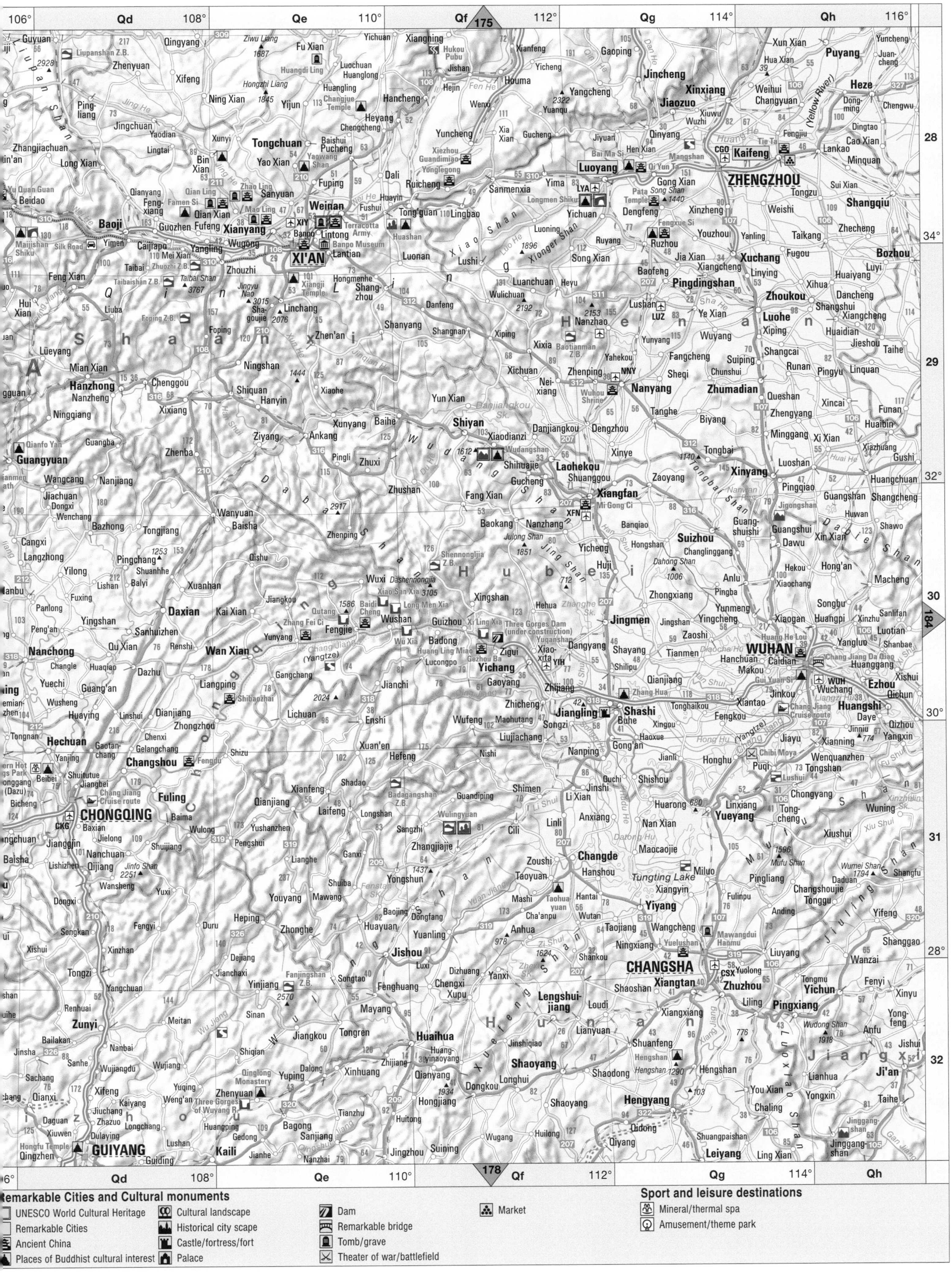

Remarkable Cities and Cultural monuments

- UNESCO World Cultural Heritage
- Remarkable Cities
- Ancient China
- Places of Buddhist cultural interest
- Cultural landscape
- Historical city scape
- Castle/fortress/fort
- Palace
- Dam
- Remarkable bridge
- Tomb/grave
- Theater of war/battlefield
- Market

Sport and leisure destinations

- Mineral/thermal spa
- Amusement/theme park

Xi'an Once a capital of China and site of the Wild Goose Pagoda (top photo) and the terracotta army in Qin Shi Huangdi's tomb (bottom photo). **Qe28**

Longmen Shiku Grottoes containing historic Buddhist art – over 2,000 statues and bas-reliefs **Qg28**

Wudang Sacred mountain for Taoists – highest peak rises 1,612 meters – Ming era temple and 36 monasteries **Qf29**

Chang Jiang (Yangtze) Some of the landscapes in the beautiful Three Gorges (top photo) will be submerged after the completion of the gigantic Three Gorges Dam (bottom photo). **Qf30**

Dazu Buddhist caves – around 50,000 colorful sculptures and bas-reliefs from the Tang and Song eras **Qc31**

Southern China is a region of low mountains and rolling hills dissected by a network of rivers and canals. Most of the region has a subtropical climate and experiences heavy rainfall.

The **Highlands of Southern China** are bordered on their western edges by the large Yunnan Plateau which contains the source of many rivers including the Wu River, a major tributary of the Chang Jiang (Yellow) River. A long chain of mountains and hills stretch northwest of highlands and into the provinces Gua[ng]dong, Jiangxi, and Fujian. **Heng Sh[an]** one of the five holy mountains in Tao[ism] and the incredibly tall "Dragon's Ba[ck]bone Terrace" near Longsheng are t[wo] of the most fascinating natural attra[c]tions in the region. The tall stone form[ations]

Stunning landscapes along the Lijian[g] River near Yangshuo Q[f33]

Guilin Beautiful landscapes along the Li River. Photos from top to bottom: Hills along the Li River, Moon Hill near Yangshuo, traditional fishers **Qf33**

Longsheng Village in northeastern Guangxi province – Dragon's Backbone Terrace – terraced rice fields on steep hills **Qf33**

Sanya City on the southern edge of Hainan, an island off the southeastern coast of China – beautiful sand beaches **Qe36**

Hoa Binh Province in northern Vietnam – ancient Vietnamese historic sites along the Black River – Perfume Pagoda **Qc35**

Halong Bay Bay of the descending Dragon – 1,600 islands – stone formations – UNESCO world heritage site **Qd35**

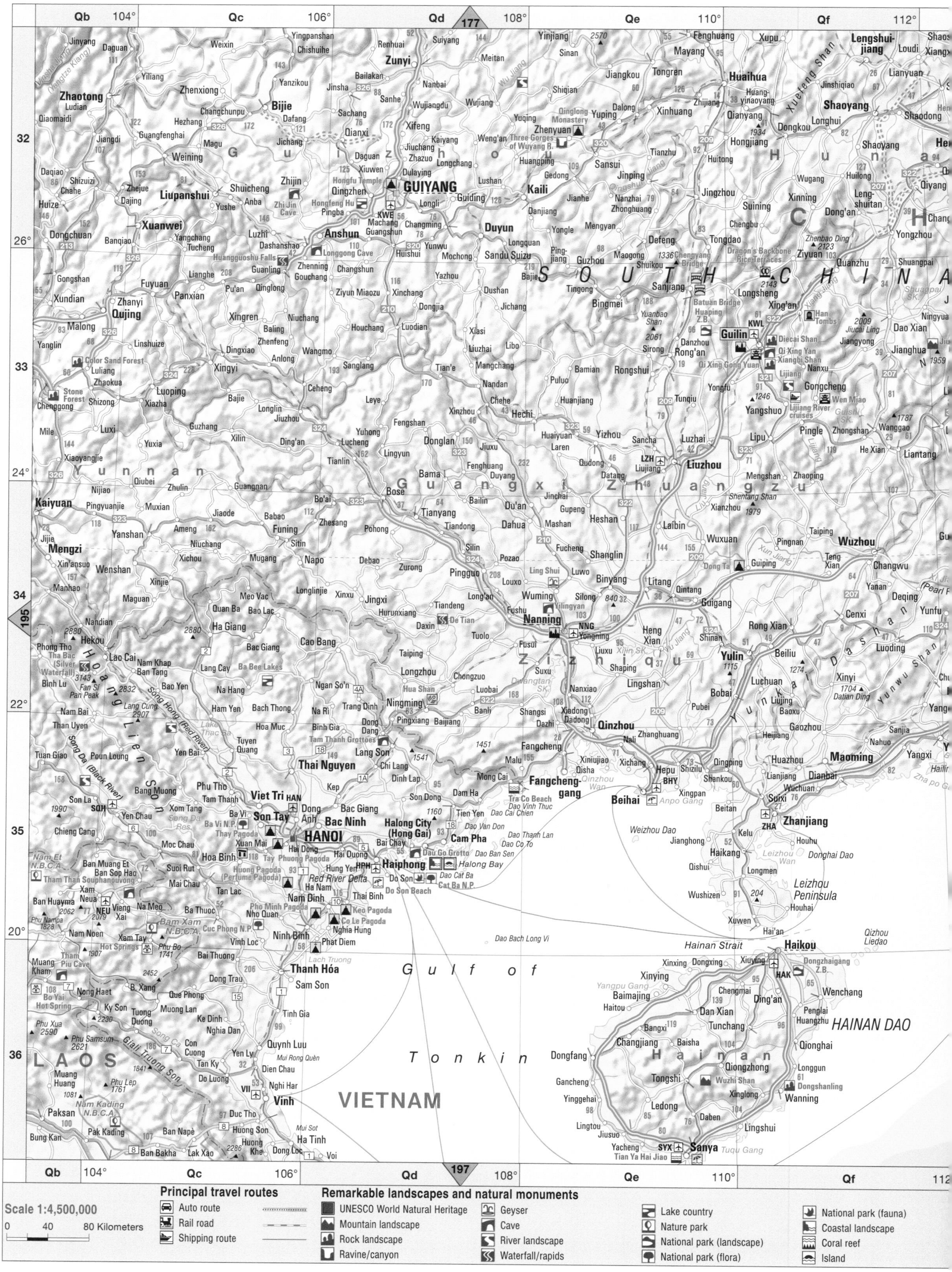

Scale 1:4,500,000

0 40 80 Kilometers

Principal travel routes

- Auto route
- Rail road
- Shipping route

Remarkable landscapes and natural monuments

- UNESCO World Natural Heritage
- Mountain landscape
- Rock landscape
- Ravine/canyon
- Geyser
- Cave
- River landscape
- Waterfall/rapids
- Lake country
- Nature park
- National park (landscape)
- National park (flora)
- National park (fauna)
- Coastal landscape
- Coral reef
- Island

ns along the **Lijiang River** near ngshuo and Guilin are known through- China for their unique beauty. The **nhua Shan range** is a small mountain ge stretching through the coastal areas southeastern China. Much of Guang- ng province's population is concen- ted in or near the **delta of the Pearl ver**. In addition to the Pearl River, veral other rivers also flow into the large lta. The historic port city of Guangzhou (Canton) is situated on the northern edge of the delta.

The northeastern section of Southern China consists of hills and low mountains extending to a coast which is broken by many bays and peninsulas. **Taiwan**, the largest island in the region is separated from mainland China by the Taiwan Strait, which has a maximum width of 200 kilometers. The majority of Taiwan's 21 million inhabitants live on the plains of western Taiwan. Most of the eastern and central sections of the island are dominated by mountain ranges. Although the island has historic ties to mainland China, Taiwan has been governed seperately from the mainland since the end of the Chinese Civil War in 1949. **Macau** and **Hong Kong** are both situated on peninsulas along the southern coast of China. Hong Kong was a British colony for more than a century and remained politically seperated from China until the city and it surroundings were integrated into the People's Republic of China in 1997. **Hainan**, a large tropical island in southernmost China, is bordered to the west by the Gulf of Tonkin. Along the western edge of the Gulf of Tonkin lies northern **Vietnam** with the country's capital Hanoi and the densely populated region in and around the **Red River delta**.

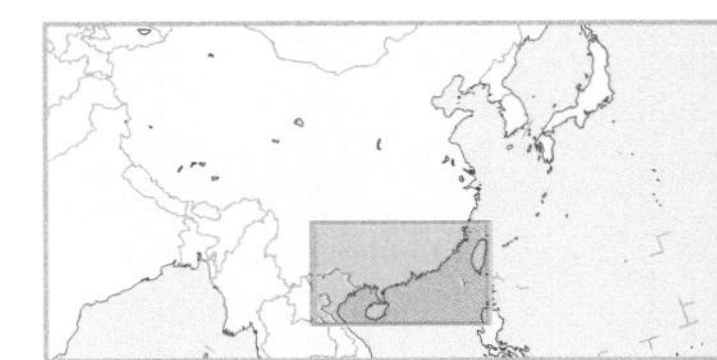

184

316

202

Hong Kong Modern skyline with beautiful towers along the waterfront (top photo). Victoria Peak offers the best views of the city (bottom photo). **Qh34**

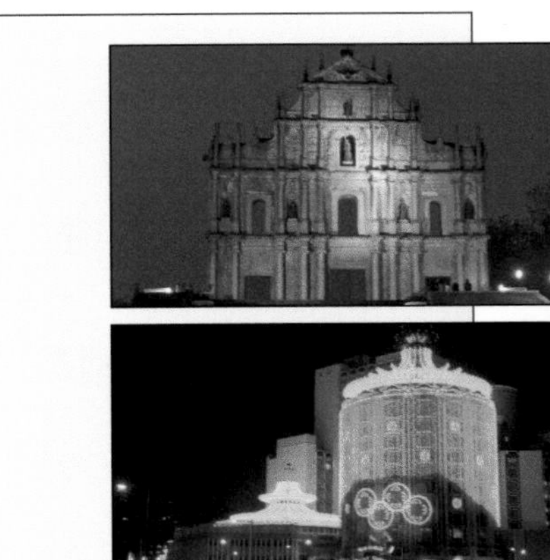

Macau St. Paul's Cathedral (top photo) and the casino (bottom photo) draw many visitors to this former Portuguese colony. **Qg34**

Taipei Taiwan's capital – population, three million – Chiang Kai-shek Memorial (photo) – national opera and concert halls **Ra33**

Taroko National Park Deep gorges – waterfalls, caves, and historic temples – hot thermal springs **Ra33**

Kaohsiung Taiwanese city – Three Phoenix Palace – Dragon and Tiger Pagodas (photo) are connected by a bridge **Ra34**

emarkable Cities and Cultural monuments

- UNESCO World Cultural Heritage
- Remarkable Cities
- Prehistoric rockscape
- Ancient China
- Places of Christian cultural interest
- Places of Islamic cultural interest
- Places of Buddhist cultural interest
- Cultural landscape
- Historical city scape
- Impressive skyline
- Castle/fortress/fort
- Remarkable bridge
- Tomb/grave
- Monument
- Festivals
- Museum

Sport and leisure destinations

- Horse racing
- Sailing
- Diving
- Wind surfing
- Seaport
- Beach resort
- Mineral/thermal spa
- Hill resort

Northeastern China, Southeastern Russia, Hokkaido (Northern Japan)

Large sections of China's three northeastern provinces are covered by expansive forests. In the past, this region of China was widely known as **Manchuria**. One of the largest forests in China stretches along the edges of the **Lesser Khingan Range**. Southwest of the range lies the densely populated Manchurian Plain, the economic center of the region. The major industrial cities **Qiqihar** and **Daqing** are both situated on the plain.

The jagged coastline of the Shakotan Peninsula (Japan) **Sa24**

Harbin in Heilongjiang province is the region's cultural center. The northeastern section of China's Northeast (Manchuria) is covered by large marshlands and bogs. This area is dissected by many rivers including the numerous tributaries of the **Amur River** (Heilong Jiang) such as the Songhua Jiang and Naoli He. With a total length of 4,416 kilometers, the Amur Ri is the fifth longest river in Asia. The Ar River – together with its tributary the **Ussuri River** (Wusuli Jiang) – forms long section of the northern border tween northeastern China and Russ **Lake Khanka** (Xingkai Hui) is a shall lake near the border with a total area 4,380 km² and a maximum depth of meters. The Laoye Ling Mountains a the eastern foothills of the Wanda Sh

Trans-Siberian Railway The famous rail link was completed in 1916 and stretches over 9,290 kilometers in both Europe and Asia. The journey between Moscow and Vladivostok takes ten days on the Trans-Siberian.

Vladivostok Russian port city on the Pacific coast – important industrial and trade center **Rf24**

Lake Wudalianchi Nature reserve – five interconnected lakes – caves containing hot thermal springs **Rd21**

Harbin Ice and Snow Festival held every January – illuminated sculptures and buildings made of ice (photo) **Rd23**

Lake Jingpo The lake is 45 kilometers long, surrounded by forests, and dotted with small islands. The beautiful 20-meter-tall Diaoshuilou waterfall is located near the lake's shore. **Re24**

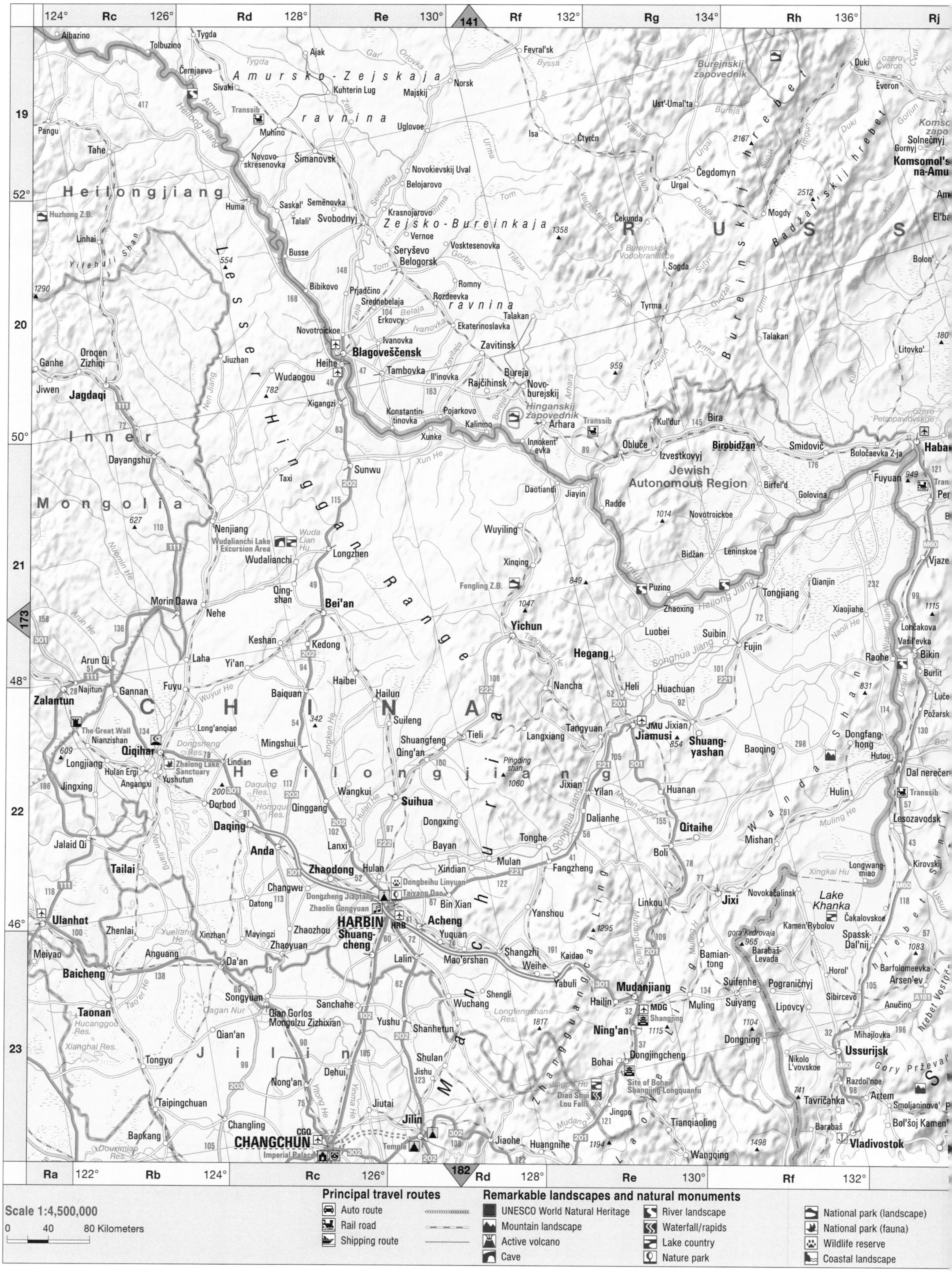

Scale 1:4,500,000

0 40 80 Kilometers

Principal travel routes

- Auto route
- Rail road
- Shipping route

Remarkable landscapes and natural monuments

- UNESCO World Natural Heritage
- Mountain landscape
- Active volcano
- Cave
- River landscape
- Waterfall/rapids
- Lake country
- Nature park
- National park (landscape)
- National park (fauna)
- Wildlife reserve
- Coastal landscape

nge stretch along the eastern border northeastern China. A wide strip of ssian territory lies between the north-most sections of China's Northeast d the Pacific Ocean. The **Sikhote n** mountain system stretches more n 1,200 kilometers along the Pacific ast of southeastern Russia between adivostok to the Amur River delta. **khalin**, the largest Russian island, is parated from the mainland by the Tartar Strait. In recent years, the island has become an important center of the Russian oil industry.

Hokkaido is the northernmost of the four main Japanese islands. The sparsely populated island encompasses twenty percent of Japan's total land area but is home to less than five percent of the national population. The island is home to three significant mountain ranges: the Kitami Range in the north, the Hidaka Range in the south, and the Ishikari Mountains in central Hokkaido. Hokkaido's tallest mountain, Asahidake, rises 2,290 meters above sea level. **Daisetsuzan National Park** in central Japan is the largest national park in Japan and contains beautiful landscapes with many high volcanoes, lakes, and forests. Shiretoko National Park is situated on an isolated peninsula in northernmost Hokkaido. **Akan National Park** in eastern Hokkaido contains the largest crater lake in Japan. **Lake Mashu**, one of the cleanest lakes in the world, has stunningly clear water. The largest body of water on Hokkaido, **Lake Kutcharo**, has an area of 80 km². Hokkaido's climate is significantly cooler from those of the other Japanese main islands. The average temperature in summer is around 20° Celsius and the island experiences heavy snowfall in winter.

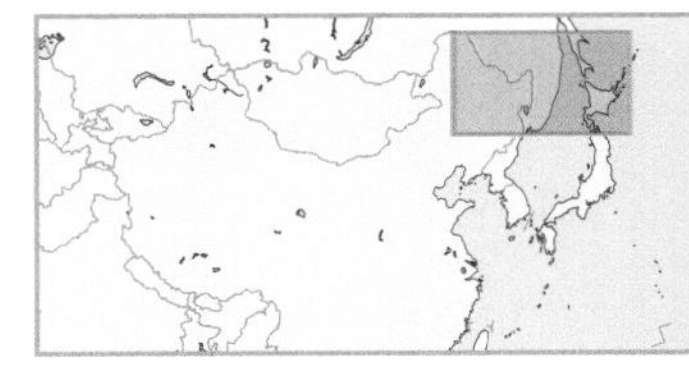

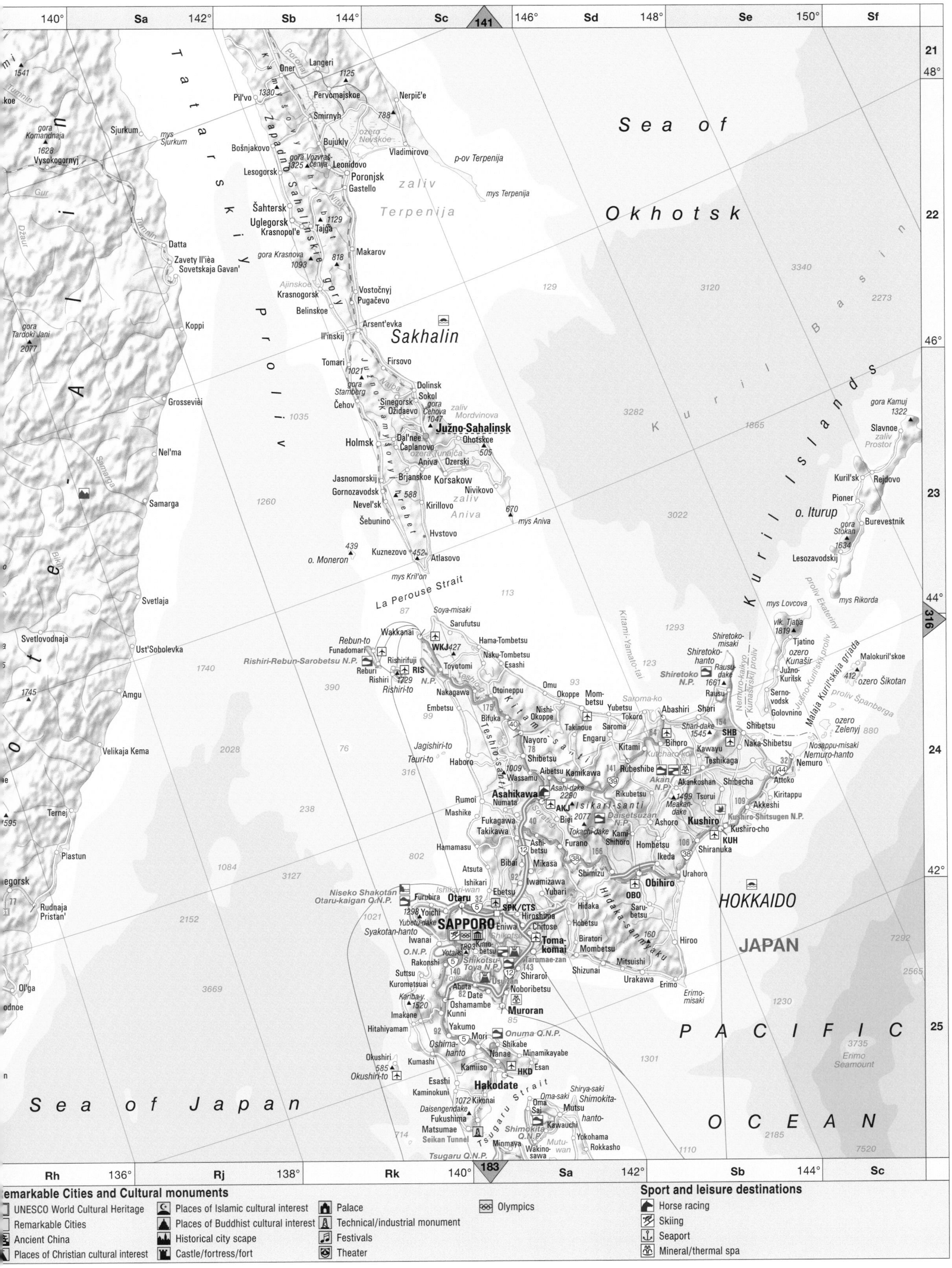

Shiretoko National Park Peninsula in northern Hokkaido – rugged landscapes encompassing several volcanos **Sc23**

Akan National Park Mountains, forests, and lakes – crater lakes: Lake Mashu and Lake Kutcharo – hot springs **Sc24**

Daisetsuzan National Park Japan's largest national park – mountains, plains, and gorges – mountain vegetation **Sb24**

Sapporo The capital city of Hokkaido prefecture – tree-lined central boulevard, Odori (photo) – Ainu Museum – botanical gardens **Sa24**

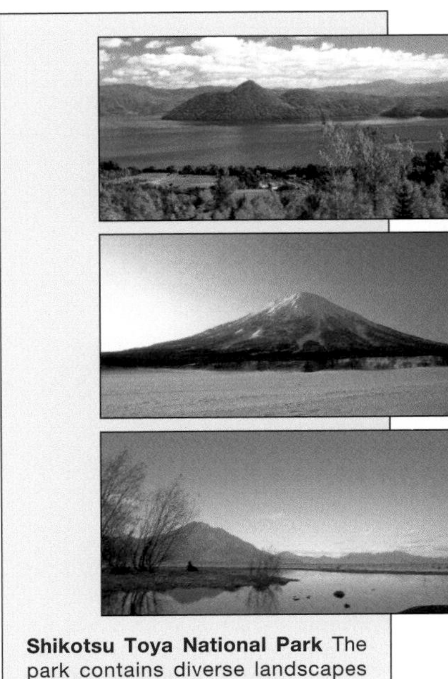

Shikotsu Toya National Park The park contains diverse landscapes including volcanoes, crater lakes, and many hot springs. Photos from top to bottom: Lake Toya, Mount Yotei, Lake Shikotsu **Sa24**

emarkable Cities and Cultural monuments

- UNESCO World Cultural Heritage
- Remarkable Cities
- Ancient China
- Places of Christian cultural interest
- Places of Islamic cultural interest
- Places of Buddhist cultural interest
- Historical city scape
- Castle/fortress/fort
- Palace
- Technical/industrial monument
- Festivals
- Theater
- Olympics

Sport and leisure destinations

- Horse racing
- Skiing
- Seaport
- Mineral/thermal spa

Korea, Honshu (Central Japan)

Korea, the "land of the morning calm" and Japan are home to many of the wealthiest and most economically developed regions in Asia. At their closest, South Korea and the Japanese island Honshu are separated by just 160 kilometers of water. North Korea shares a long border with China and a small 17 kilometer long border with Russia. Most of the **Korean Peninsula** consists of mountainous land, with the tallest mountains concentrated in the north. The **T'aebaek Mounta** stretch along the peninsula's east coast and the highest peak in the ran Sorak, rises 1,708 meters. Korea is sit ted between regions with subtropical a cold continental climates but the pen sula itself has a mostly temperate cli ate with abundant rainfall.

Mount Fuji is Japan's most revered mountain **Rk**

Pyongyang Capital of North Korea – numerous monuments, including the Tower of the Juche Idea (photo) **Rc26**

Kaesong Burial site of ancient kings – once the capital of the Koryo kingdom – one of Korea's oldest cities **Rd27**

Changdeokgung Palace Built during the Joseon Kindgom, the palace has been destroyed and rebuilt several times- **Rd27**

Seoul Capital of South Korea and the largest city on the peninsula – historic Old Seoul district – ancient royal palaces – population ten million **Rd27**

Haeinsa Temple Buddhist holy site in South Korea's Kayasan National Park – location of the Tripitaka Koreana, a Korean cultural treasure **Re28**

Kyongju The former capital of the ancient Silla Kingdom. The Pugulska temple (top photo) is considered a holy site and masterpiece of Silla architecture. The Seokguram Grotto houses a historic Buddha statue (bottom photo). **Re28**

Scale 1:4,500,000
0 40 80 Kilometers

Principal travel routes
- Auto route
- Rail road
- Highspeed train
- Shipping route

Remarkable landscapes and natural monuments
- UNESCO World Natural Heritage
- Mountain landscape
- Extinct volcano
- Active volcano
- Cave
- River landscape
- Waterfall/rapids
- Lake country
- Nature park
- National park (landscape)
- National park (flora)
- National park (fauna)
- Coastal landscape
- Beach
- Island

espite the strong cultural influence of ıpan and China, the Koreans have been ɔle to preserve their own unique culre. Since the Korean War ended ırough a ceasefire in 1953, the Korean eninsula has been divided between ıpitalist South Korea and communist ɔrth Korea. Since the 1970s, South Korea ıs undergone an incredible transformaɔn from a poor country to a major exporr with a relatively high standard of living.

In addition to its populated islands, **Japan** also consists of at least 3,000 small uninhabited islands. The country has four main islands: Hokkaido, Shikoku, Kyushu, and Honshu. Honshu is the largest and most populous Japanese island. From north to south, the main islands extend over a distance of 4,000 kilometers. The vast majority of the mountainous nation's land is unsuitable for agriculture. All of the Japanese islands are part of a large underwater mountain system and the country is situated in a geologically active region where earthquakes occur frequently. In addition to earthquakes, Japan is also threatened by other natural hazards including cyclones, tsunamis, and volcanic eruptions. There are approximately 265 volcanoes in Japan, around 60 of which are active. The tallest and most famous Japanese mountain is Mount Fuji which rises 3,776 meters.

There are many lakes scattered throughout the countryside and Japan's national parks. The country's largest lake, **Lake Biwa**, covers 674 km^2 on the island of Honshu. There are three distinct climate zones in Japan but most of the country has a temperate humid climate with plentiful rainfall. The country's largest cities, including the capital Tokyo, are among the most modern and wealthy urban areas in the world.

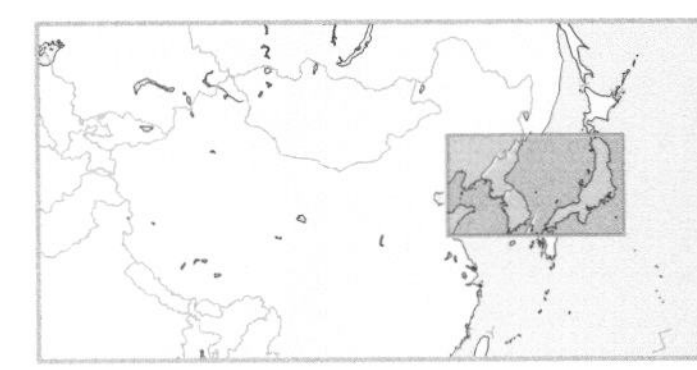

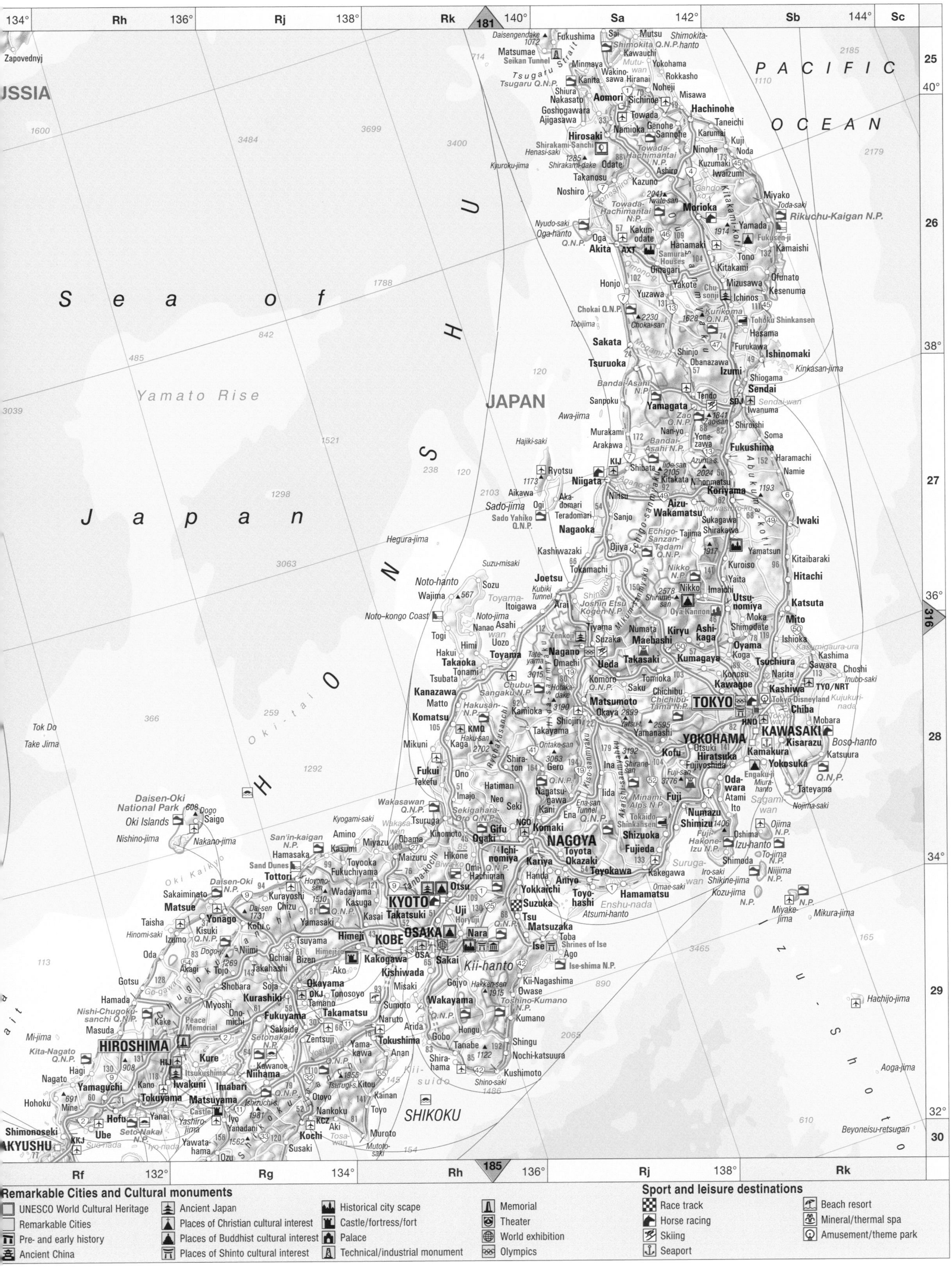

Nikko National Park Conservation area north of Tokyo – Toshugu shrine (photo) – Shinto and Buddhist architecture – rivers and waterfalls **Rk27**

Tokyo Japan's capital and largest city – Imperial Palace – Tokyo Tower (333 meters) in Shiba Park – Ginza shopping district – Shinto shrines – modern skyscrapers **Rk28**

Yokohama Japan's second largest city – leading port city in East Asia – large Chinatown **Rk28**

Kyoto Japan's historic cultural center – population 1.5 million – traditional wooden architecture – Golden Pavilion (photo) – Imperial Palace – Nanzen-ji Temple – Kyoto National Museum **Rh28**

Nara Capital of Japan until 784 AD – Todai-ji Temple, the world's largest wooden temple – Yakushiji Temple – Nara National Museum **Rh28**

Himeji the "White Heron Castle" – Japan's best preserved medieval castle – 31 buildings and 21 towers – built in the 14th century and expanded in 1581 **Rh28**

Itsukushima Shinto Shrine Important Shinto holy site on a small island near Hiroshima – built in the 13th century – world heritage site – the Red Torii gates stand on the water before the shrine (photo) **Rg28**

Remarkable Cities and Cultural monuments

- UNESCO World Cultural Heritage
- Remarkable Cities
- Pre- and early history
- Ancient China
- Ancient Japan
- Places of Christian cultural interest
- Places of Buddhist cultural interest
- Places of Shinto cultural interest
- Historical city scape
- Castle/fortress/fort
- Palace
- Technical/industrial monument
- Memorial
- Theater
- World exhibition
- Olympics

Sport and leisure destinations

- Race track
- Horse racing
- Skiing
- Seaport
- Beach resort
- Mineral/thermal spa
- Amusement/theme park

Eastern China, Kyushu, Ryukyu Islands (Southern Japan)

Eastern China is one of the world's most populous regions. The region can be divided into three distinct geographic areas. The southern sections of the region consist of rolling hills and mountains that stretch from the interior to the coast along the East China Sea. Eastern China's highlands tend to decline in height from south to north. The **Chang Jiang (Yangtze) River** basin covers the central section of eastern

China. This area consists of dense populated and low lying plains betwe the cities **Wuhan**, **Nanjing**, a **Shanghai**. The northern section eastern China includes parts of the ter perate North China Plain. The plains this region are dissected by many rive and canals. Several large lakes includi

Thousand Islands Lake near Hangzhou (China) Qk

Qufu Impressive Qing-era temple at the birthplace of Confucius – UNESCO world heritage site **Qj28**

Kaifeng City on the Huang River – Dragon Pavilion (photo) – Xiang Guo monastery – the Iron Pagoda **Qh28**

Nanjing Ancient imperial city on the Yangtze River – well preserved Ming era city walls – Ming era tombs with human and animal statues **Qk29**

Huang Shan The "Yellow Mountain" has inspired many poets and painters throughout Chinese history. Lotus Flower Peak rises 1,841 meters and is the tallest peak in the Huang Shan range. **Qk30**

Lushan National Park around Lake Poyang – UNESCO world heritage site – caves, ponds, waterfalls, steep cliffs, and jagged peaks **Qj31**

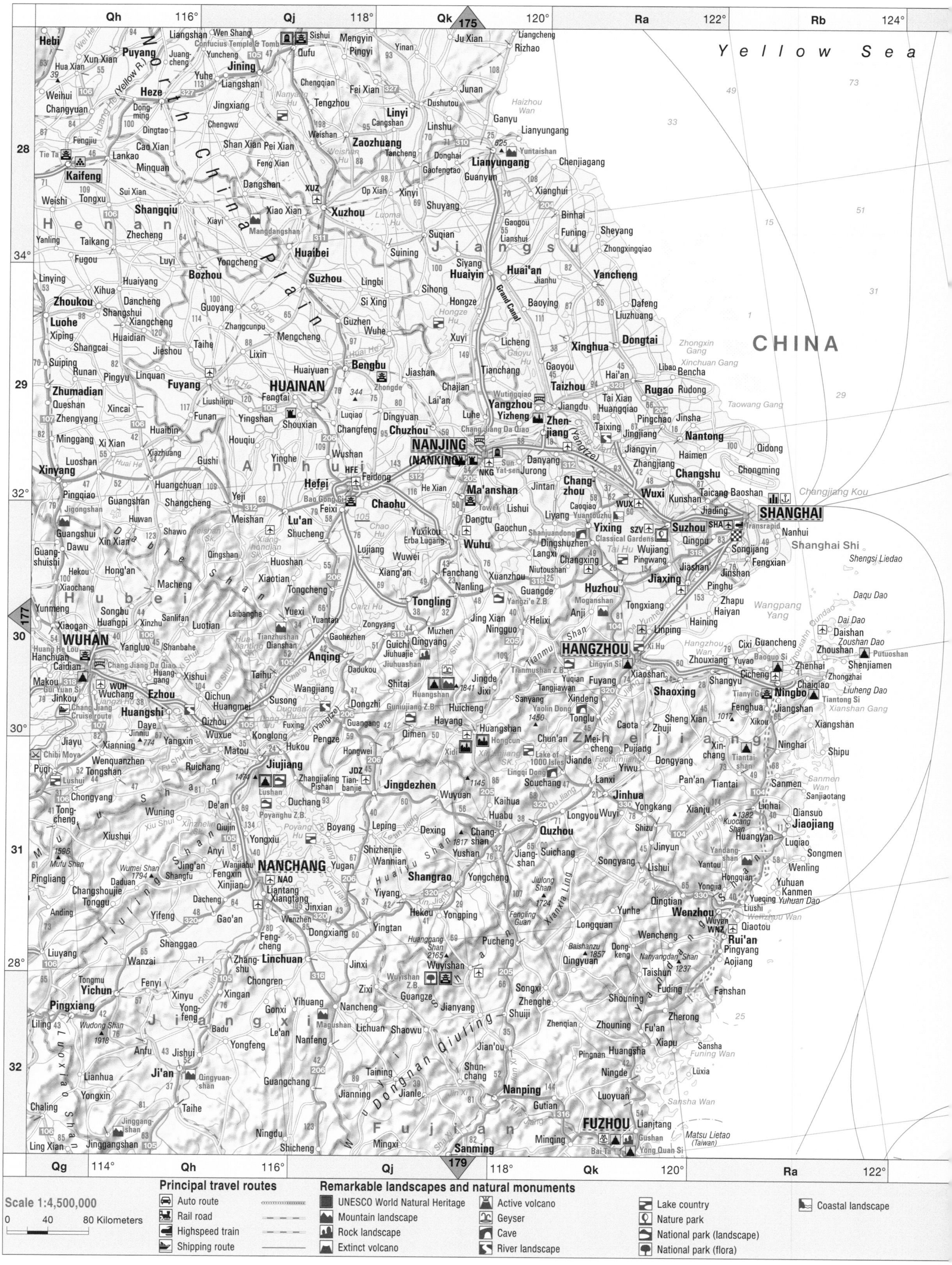

Scale 1:4,500,000
0 40 80 Kilometers

Principal travel routes
Auto route
Rail road
Highspeed train
Shipping route

Remarkable landscapes and natural monuments
UNESCO World Natural Heritage
Mountain landscape
Rock landscape
Extinct volcano
Active volcano
Geyser
Cave
River landscape
Lake country
Nature park
National park (landscape)
National park (flora)
Coastal landscape

Hongze Hu and Nanyang Hu are attered throughout the region.
e vast basin of the Chang Jiang (Yang-e) River encompasses not only the river t its many tributaries and numerous kes. The largest lake in the basin, Po-ng Hu, covers 3,500 km^2 and is also e largest freshwater lake in China.
here are many beautiful landscapes attered throughout the highlands of astern China including beautiful **Mount Wuyi** which rises 1,500 meters above sea level and the peaks of the **Huang Shan** and **Jiuhua Shan** mountain ranges. **"Thousand Island Lake"** in Zhejiang province is surrounded by lush green hills. The city **Hangzhou** is one of the starting points of the 2,000-kilometer-long **Grand Canal**, the world's longest man-made waterway.

The southern islands of **Japan** are separated from eastern China by the East China Sea. **Kyushu** is the southernmost of Japan's four main islands. Most of Kyushu is covered by rolling hills and mountains. In addition to its many historic sites, there are also many natural attractions on Kyushu including hot springs, geysers, and active **volcanoes**. **Aso National Park** features pristine landscapes around the volcano Aso and is one of several national parks on Kyushu. The subtropical Ryukyu Islands stretch over a distance of 1,200 kilometers between Kyushu and Taiwan. The islands are the southernmost Japanese island group. Despite the strong cultural influence of the Japanese main islands, the people of the **Ryukyu Islands** have maintained a distinct indigenous culture. **Okinawa**, situated halfway between Taiwan and Kyushu, is the largest and most populous island in the Ryukyu archipelago.

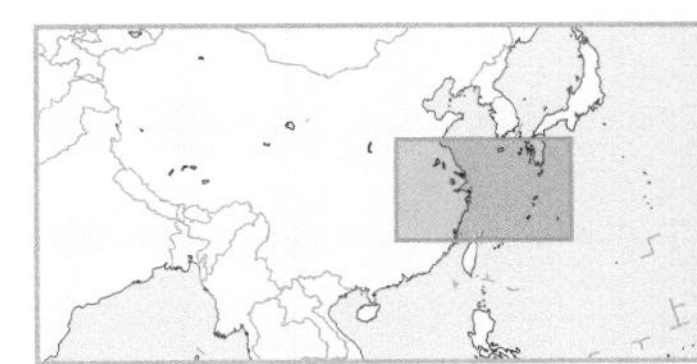

Shanghai China's largest city is a booming economic center. The Bund, a central boulevard, and Frenchtown contain historic western style architecture. In recent years, modern skyscrapers have been built in the Pudong district (top photo). The Oriental Pearl Tower (bottom photo) has become a city landmark. **Ra30**

Suzhou City on the shore of Lake Tai – major center of silk production – traditional Chinese gardens **Ra30**

Hangzhou The West Lake is famous for its beautiful pavilions and bridges. Lingyin Temple contains ancient stone sculptures and the laughing Maitreya Buddha (photo). **Ra30**

Aso National Park Located on Kyushu – Aso San (1,592 meters), large caldera containing five volcanic cones – hot springs **Rf29**

Yakushima Island National Park UNESCO world heritage site – 40 peaks above 1,000 meters – Japanese cedars **Rf30**

Ryukyu Islands Okinawa is the largest island – Gusuku, UNESCO world heritage site – historic palaces (photo) **RdRe31/32**

Remarkable Cities and Cultural monuments

- UNESCO World Cultural Heritage
- Remarkable Cities
- Ancient China
- Ancient Japan
- Places of Buddhist cultural interest
- Places of Shinto cultural interest
- Historical city scape
- Impressive skyline
- Castle/fortress/fort
- Palace
- Remarkable bridge
- Tomb/grave
- Theater of war/battlefield
- Market
- Museum

Sport and leisure destinations

- Race track
- Seaport
- Beach resort
- Mineral/thermal spa
- Amusement/theme park

Southern Asia

The section of Asia south of the Himalayan Mountain Range and China is generally divided into two distinct regions: South Asia and Southeast Asia. South Asia stretches south to the island Sri Lanka off the coast of India. The region encompasses almost the entire Indian subcontinent. A series of mountain ranges running from north to south through Pakistan and Afghanistan define the western boundaries of South Asia. The mountain ranges in the far west of South Asia include sections of the **Hindu Kush**, the **Toba Kakar Range**, the **Central Brahui Range**, and the **Makran Coast Range**. The Indian and Bangladeshi borders to Myanmar (Burma) are generally considered the borders between South Asia and Southeast Asia.

The **Thar Desert** covers a vast area b tween the Indus River Valley and Cent India. Only a small percentage of t desert's 200,000 km² is covered by sar the majority of desert consists of roc arid land broken by hills.

The Indian subcontinent cove 3,287,782 km² and encompasses t majority of South Asia, with the notat exception of Sri Lanka. The northern se tions of the subcontinent are covered

The Mekong River in the highlands of Laos

Jammu and Kashmir Beautiful mountainous region – numerous lakes and lush mountain valleys

The Ganges India's holiest river is 2,500 kilometers long and has a large delta (top photo). Important religious ceremonies occur in many places along the river.

Vindhya Range 1,000-kilometer-long mountain range – sandstone plateaus – mountain valleys – waterfalls

Tamil Nadu Mountainous region in southern India – beautiful coastlines – Dravidian culture – Nilgiri Mountains

Kerela Backwaters 1,500-kilometer-long network of canals and lagoons in Kerela (Southern India)

Sri Lanka Island republic off the coast of India – large coastal plains – mountainous interior – Adam's Peak (2,243 meters)

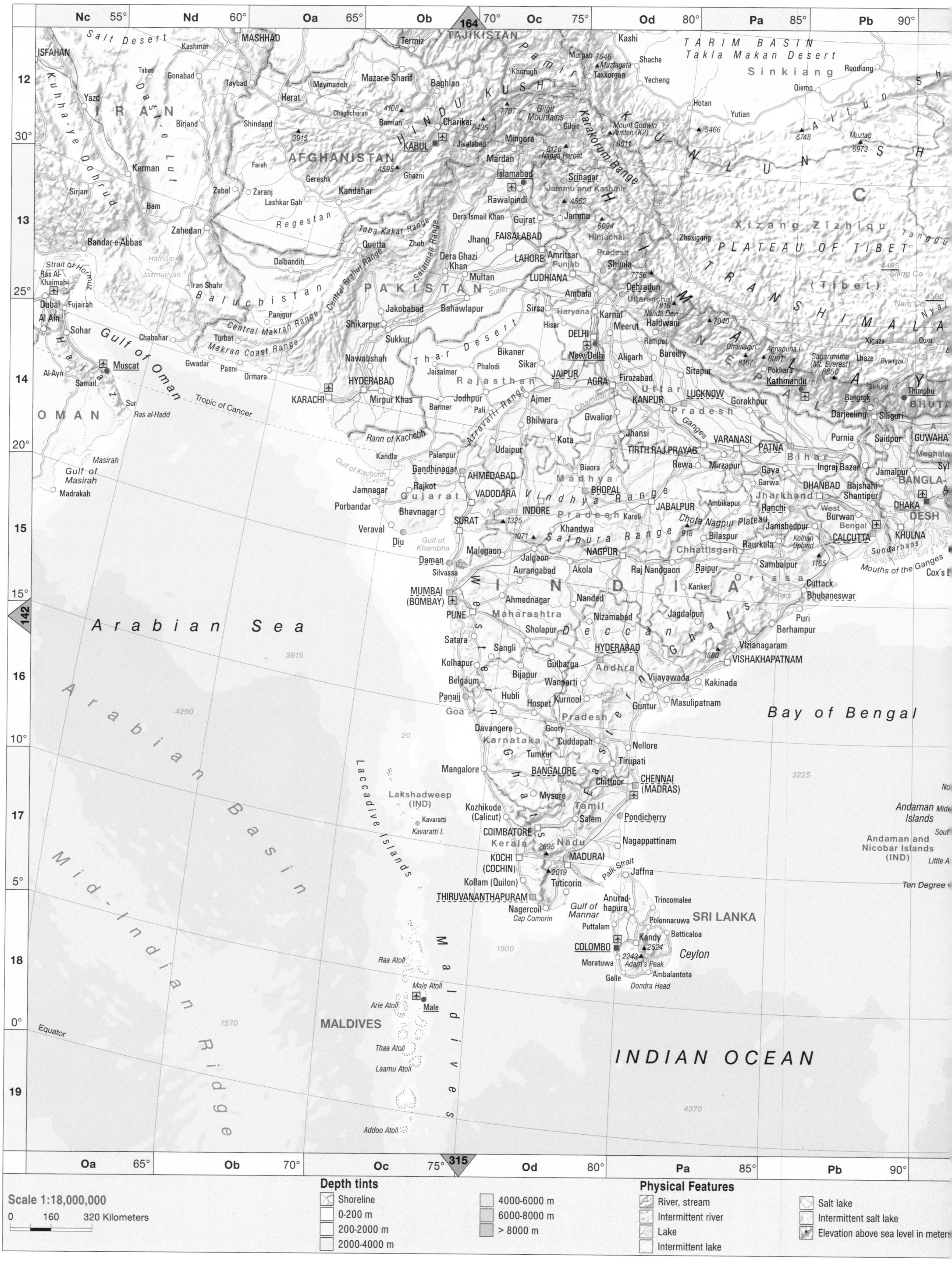

Scale 1:18,000,000

0 160 320 Kilometers

Depth tints

- Shoreline
- 0-200 m
- 200-2000 m
- 2000-4000 m
- 4000-6000 m
- 6000-8000 m
- > 8000 m

Physical Features

- River, stream
- Intermittent river
- Lake
- Intermittent lake
- Salt lake
- Intermittent salt lake
- Elevation above sea level in meters

e plains stretching out from the Ganges d Brahmaputra Rivers. South of the ains lies a series of mountain ranges d hills including the Vindhya Range d the Aravalli Hills. The **Deccan Pla-au** is a massive plateau covering most Central and Southern India. The pla-au is bounded by two mountain ranges its eastern and western edges: the stern and Western Ghats.
e island nation of **Sri Lanka** is situated off the southeastern coast of India. Sri Lanka's north is covered by savannahs which give way to the tall mountain ranges in the island's central and southern sections. The **Maldives** are a group of small coral island and atolls in the Indian Ocean. An independent country, the Maldives have a land area of 300 km².
In northeast India, the **Ganges** and **Brahmaputra** Rivers flow into a vast delta which covers 44,000 km². The fertile region in and around the delta is densely populated. The outer edges of the delta are covered by large mangrove forests called **Sundarbans**. The Patkai and Arakan mountain ranges stretch along the border between India and Myanmar, the westernmost country in Southeast Asia. The Irrawaddy River is Myanmar's longest river and principal commercial waterway. The 2,000-kilometer-long river flows south to its delta on the Indian Ocean. East of the Irraway River basin, mountainous highlands cover most of eastern Myanmar.
Southern Thailand, Cambodia, and southern Vietnam consist primarily of vast low-lying plains. This region contains the deltas of several major rivers – including the **Mekong River delta**. Southern Asia is home to many distinct regions including tropical rain forests, grassy plains, and semi-arid savannahs.

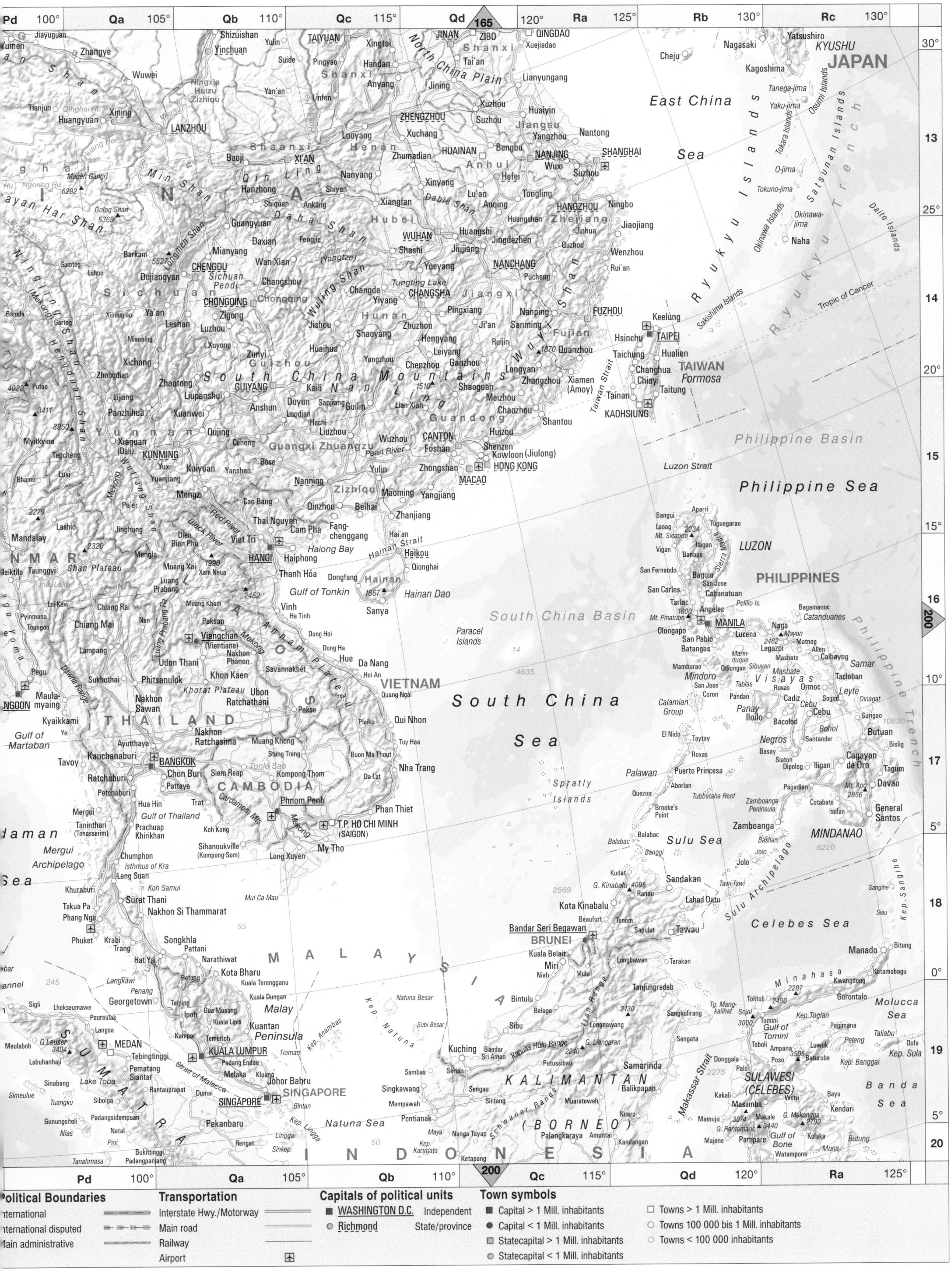

Himalayas The world's tallest mountain range boasts 14 mountains higher than 8,000 meters. Photos from top to bottom: Annapurna, Sagarmatha National Park, Runbuk Glacier

East Indian Highlands The Eastern Ghats, a mountain range on the edge of the Deccan Plateau – Simlipal National Park (photo)

The Mekong 4,500-kilometer-long river – source in the Tibetan mountains – several waterfalls – the Mekong Delta (70,000 km²)

Thai Highlands The highest mountains are concentrated in the far north – Doi Inthanon (2,590 meters)

Halong Bay Unique coastal landscape near Hanoi – around 3,000 limestone formations dot the bay

Political Boundaries
International
International disputed
Main administrative

Transportation
Interstate Hwy./Motorway
Main road
Railway
Airport

Capitals of political units
WASHINGTON D.C. Independent
Richmond State/province

Town symbols
Capital > 1 Mill. inhabitants
Capital < 1 Mill. inhabitants
Statecapital > 1 Mill. inhabitants
Statecapital < 1 Mill. inhabitants
Towns > 1 Mill. inhabitants
Towns 100 000 bis 1 Mill. inhabitants
Towns < 100 000 inhabitants

Few regions on the planet encompass as many contrasting landscapes as the northern section of the Indian subcontinent. The mountainous highlands of Pakistan (Central Grahui Range, Sulaiman Range,etc.) border the vast plains of the Indus River basin. The 3,200-kilometer-long **Indus River** nourishes the fertile plains of Punjab, a region whose name means the land of five rivers. Further south, the Indus flows through a 130-kilometer-wide river oasis in south Pakistan, a mostly arid region. This oa is the most important economic cente Pakistan. The **Thar Desert** stretch over a vast area to the west of the Inc River basin and has a total area 250,000 km². Most of the desert is situ ted in the Indian state of **Rajastan**. A

Mehrangahr Fort towers above the ancient city of Jodhpur Og

Jaisalmer Traditional home of Rajasthan's royalty – large historic fortress – grand villas **Of32**

Nagaur The site of India's largest cattle and camel market, held January and February – camel races **Og32**

Alwar Trade center with many historic buildings – impressive palace complex built in 1793 **Oj32**

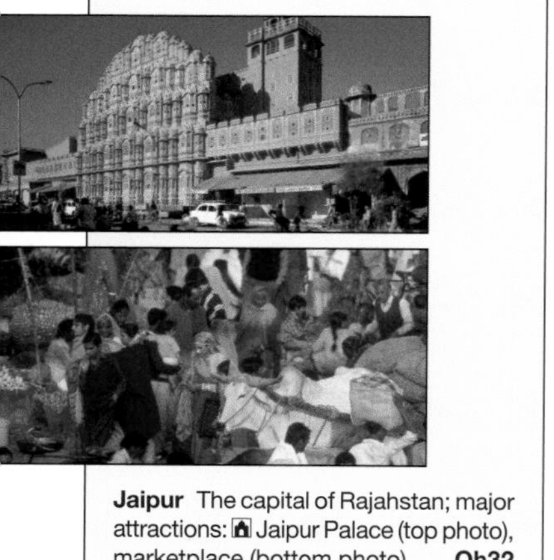

Jaipur The capital of Rajasthan; major attractions: Jaipur Palace (top photo), marketplace (bottom photo). **Oh32**

Ajmer Marble pavilions – the grave of the Sufi saint Muin-ud-din, a pilgrimage site for Muslims **Oh32**

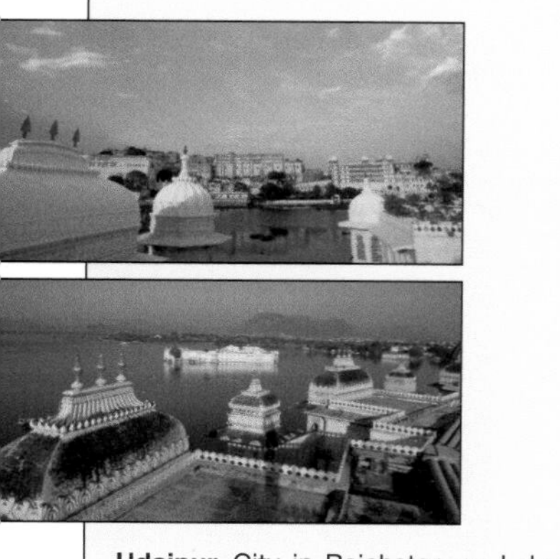

Udaipur City in Rajahstan on Lake Pichola with palaces and a beautiful natural setting. **Og33**

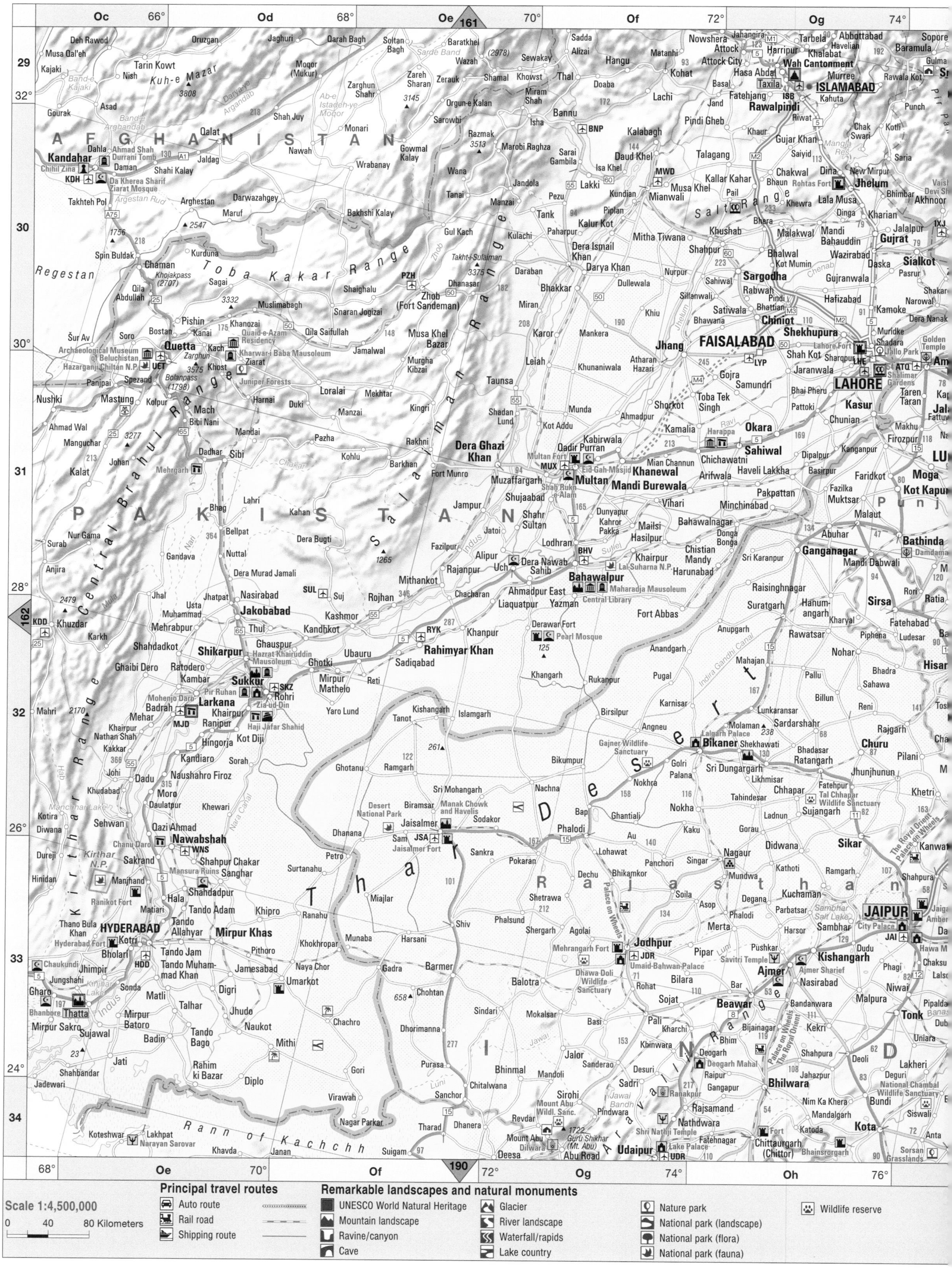

161
162
190

Scale 1:4,500,000

0 40 80 Kilometers

Principal travel routes

- Auto route
- Rail road
- Shipping route

Remarkable landscapes and natural monuments

- UNESCO World Natural Heritage
- Mountain landscape
- Ravine/canyon
- Cave
- Glacier
- River landscape
- Waterfall/rapids
- Lake country
- Nature park
- National park (landscape)
- National park (flora)
- National park (fauna)
- Wildlife reserve

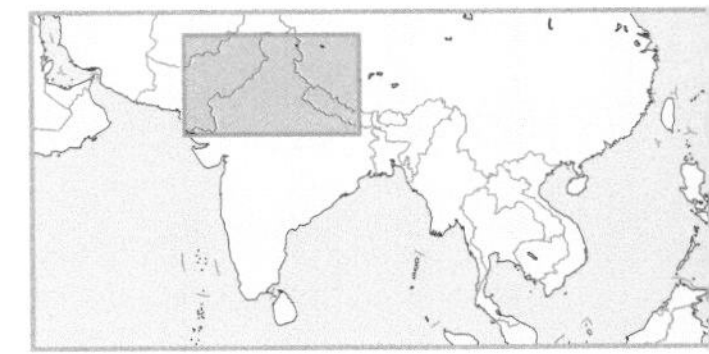

…ppes and large sand dunes cover most …the desert. The arid desert is the driest …gion in India. The fertile plains of the …nges and Brahmaputra river basins … bordered to the north by the Hima… …as and to the west by the Thar Desert. …e 2,700-kilometer-long **Ganges** …ver and its most important tributary, the …muna, flow south from their sources …the Himalayas. The two rivers merge …ar the Indian city of Allahabad. A large alluvial plain subject to frequent floods lies at the foot of the Himalayas. The plains of northern India include some of the most fertile areas in the country. An elevated plain around **Delhi** separates the Indus basin from the plains in the Ganges basin. To the north, the plains of the Ganges basin are bounded by sections of the Himalayan Range.

The **Himalayas** are the highest mountain range in the world. The range was formed millions of years ago by collisions between the Indo-Australian and Eurasian tectonic plates. The Himalayas stretch in the shape of a bow through Afghanistan, Pakistan, northern India, Nepal and Tibet (China). There are several mountains in the range that exceed 8,000 meters in height. Mount Everest (8,850 meters), the world's highest mountain, is situated along the border between Tibet and Nepal. The Himalayas separate Central Asia with its cool climates from the tropical and subtropical regions of South Asia. The Indus-Yarlung suture, an ancient trench separates the Trans-Himalayas (Tibetan Himalayas) from the main sections of the range.

The **Tibetan Plateau**, one of the world's largest plateaus, covers around two million km² and is situated mostly at elevations between 4,000 and 5,000 meters above sea level.

Remarkable Cities and Cultural monuments

- UNESCO World Cultural Heritage
- Remarkable Cities
- Pre- and early history
- Ancient India
- Places of Christian cultural interest
- Places of Islamic cultural interest
- Places of Buddhist cultural interest
- Places of Hindu cultural interest
- Places of Jainist cultural interest
- Places of Sikh cultural interest
- Cultural landscape
- Historical city scape
- Castle/fortress/fort
- Tomb/grave
- Space telescope
- Market
- Museum

Sport and leisure dest.

- Skiing
- Canoeing/rafting
- Amusement/theme park
- Hill resort

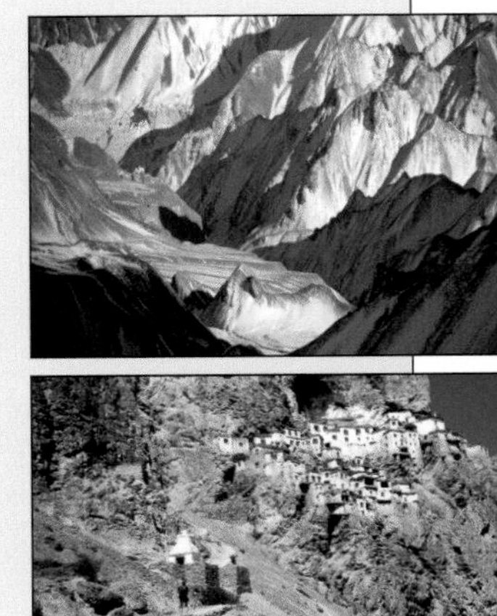

Ladakh Craggy mountainous landscapes (top photo) and the site of important Tibetan Buddhist monasteries (bottom photo). **OjOk28/29**

Amritsar The spiritual center of India's Sikh community – Golden Temple – Granth Sahib, a Sikh holy book **Oh30**

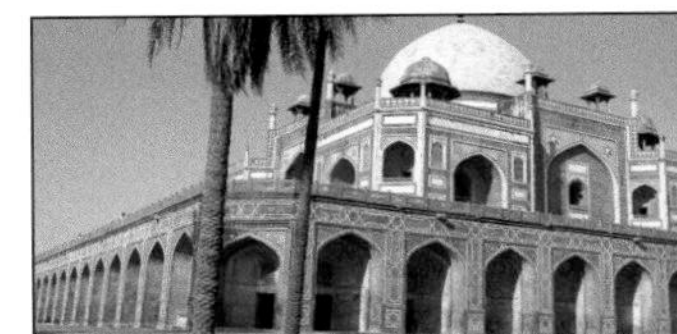

Delhi The capital city of India – population, 7.3 million – Humayan's Tomb (photo), a world heritage site – The Red Fort **Oj31**

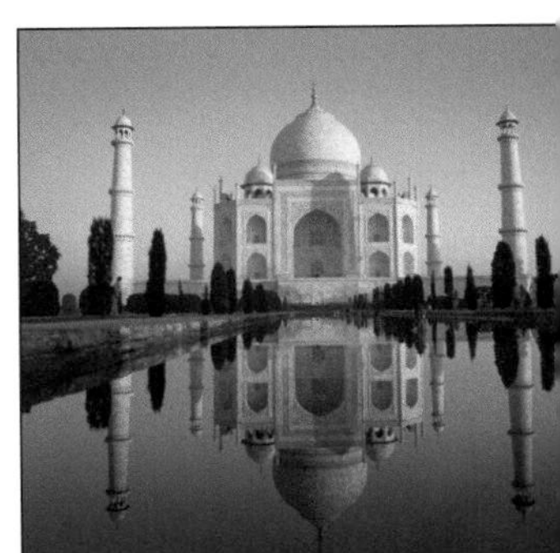

Taj Mahal Mausoleum built by Emperor Shah Jahan in memory of his wife Mumtaz Muhal – UNESCO world heritage site **Oj32**

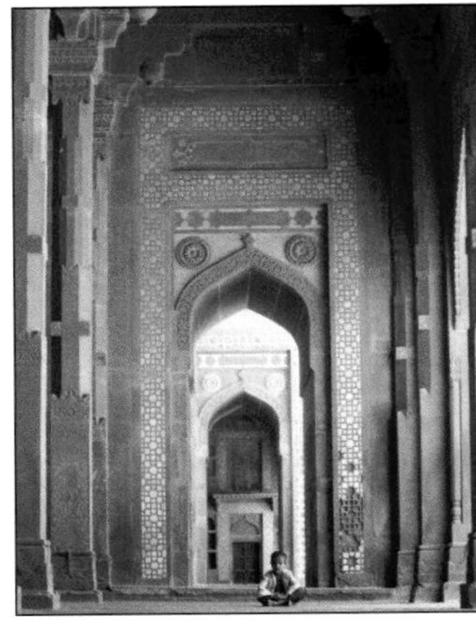

Fatehpur Sikri Residence of Emperor Akbar – built in the 16th century – UNESCO world heritage site **Oj32**

Central India

The **Rann of Kachchh** is a vast area of salty mudflats in central India that stretches along the country's Arabian Sea coast. The Gulf of Kachchh separates this area from the **Kathiawar Peninsula**. The peninsula is mostly flat and agriculture is an important part of the local economy. The vast **Deccan Plateau** covers a large section of the Indian subcontinent. To the north, the plateau borders the fertile plains of northern India and several upland areas including the **Vindhya Range** and **Saptura Ran** The Deccan Plateau is situated at heig between 800 and 1,000 meters. Toget with the coastal plains on its edges, plateau covers around half of India's t ritory. Several major rivers including Godavari (1,450 kilometers) and Krish

Ancient Fort Golconda near Hyderabad **Ok**

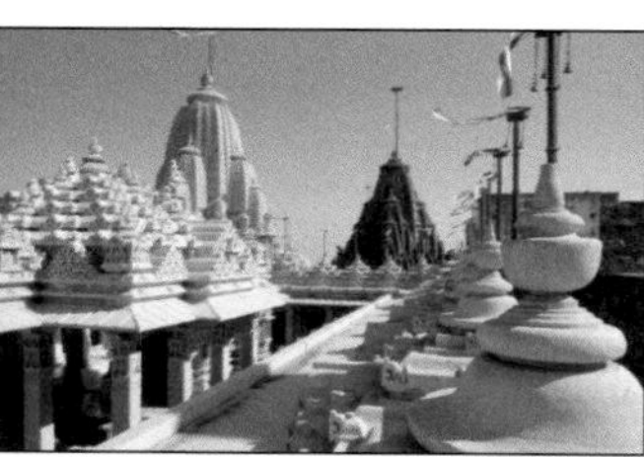

Palitana Important spiritual center of Jainism – temple district on Shetrunjaya Hill encompasses 863 buildings (photo) **Of35**

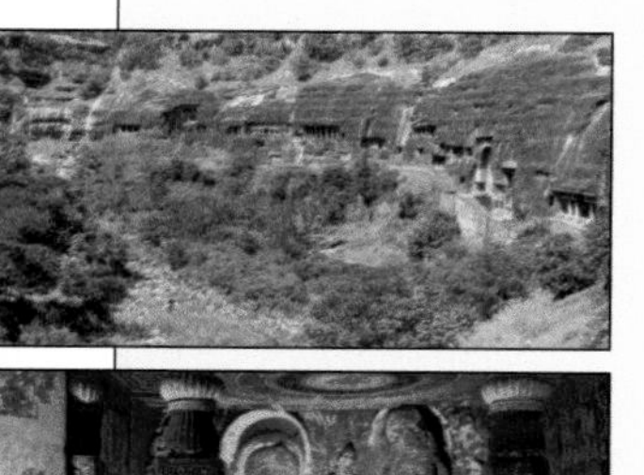

Ajanta Caves Crescent shaped caves in the side of a stone wall containing Buddhist art. The caves are a UNESCO world heritage site. **Oh35**

Ellora Caves The caves contain Buddhist, Jain, and Hindu temples and monasteries – world heritage site **Oh35**

Mumbai (Bombay) India's largest city is home to more than ten million people – large film industry (Bollywood) **Og36**

Elephanta Island Stone temples carved into caves – 7th and 8th century sculptures – UNESCO world heritage site **Og36**

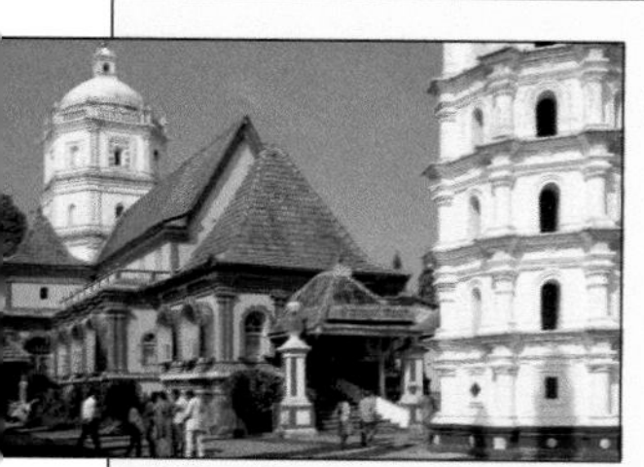

Goa The former Portuguese colony, with its beautiful beaches, is a popular tourist attraction. Goa's historic churches are world heritage sites. **Og38**

Scale 1:4,500,000

0 40 80 Kilometers

Principal travel routes

- Auto route
- Rail road
- Shipping route

Remarkable landscapes and natural monuments

- UNESCO World Natural Heritage
- Mountain landscape
- Rock landscape
- Cave
- Lake country
- Nature park
- National park (landscape)
- National park (flora)
- National park (fauna)
- Wildlife reserve
- Beach

50 kilometers) Rivers flow through the ·eau. The majority of the rivers on the ·eau empty into the Bay of Bengal. The ·er levels in these rivers are greatly ·ected by monsoon winds. Most of the ·ccan Plateau's terrain is dominated ·hills, river basins, and mountain ran·s. The northern section of the Deccan ·teau is covered by rich volcanic soils ·d many of the fields in the area are used ·grow cotton. During the monsoon season, the northern sections of the plateau get abundant rainfall. In contrast to the north, the center of the Deccan Plateau is a semi-arid region with sparse rainfall. Sorghum, grain, and peanuts are common crops in the region.

The Deccan Plateau is bounded on its western and eastern edges by two mountain ranges. The **Western Ghats** bound the plateau to the west and separate it from the **Malabar plains**, a narrow strip of lowlands along the Arabian Sea coast. The **Eastern Ghats** bound the Deccan Plateau in the east and descend gradually to the **Coromandel Coast**. The plains on the Coromandel Coast are significantly wider than those on India's western coast. Situated on the Coromandel Coast, the deltas of the Krishna and Mahanadi Rivers extends out into the Bay of Bengal. Devodi, the tallest mountain in the Eastern Ghats range rises 1,680 meters above sea level. Both the Eastern and Western Ghats get abundant rainfall and both ranges are major centers of agriculture. Rice, tea, coffee, and palm trees are the most important crops grown in the highlands.

Most of central India has a tropical climate. Central India's climate is greatly influenced by **monsoon** winds and the region has dry summers, a warm rainy season, and mild winters.

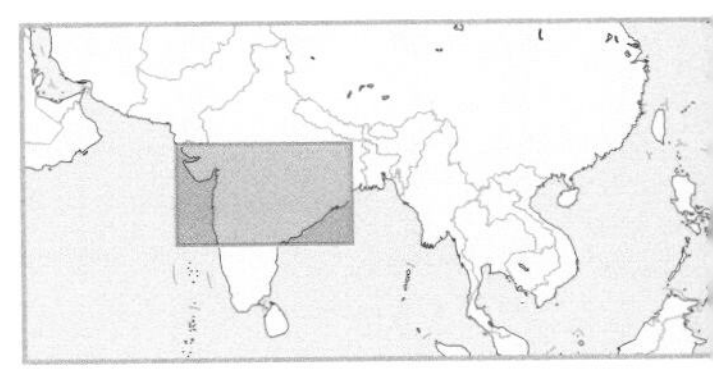

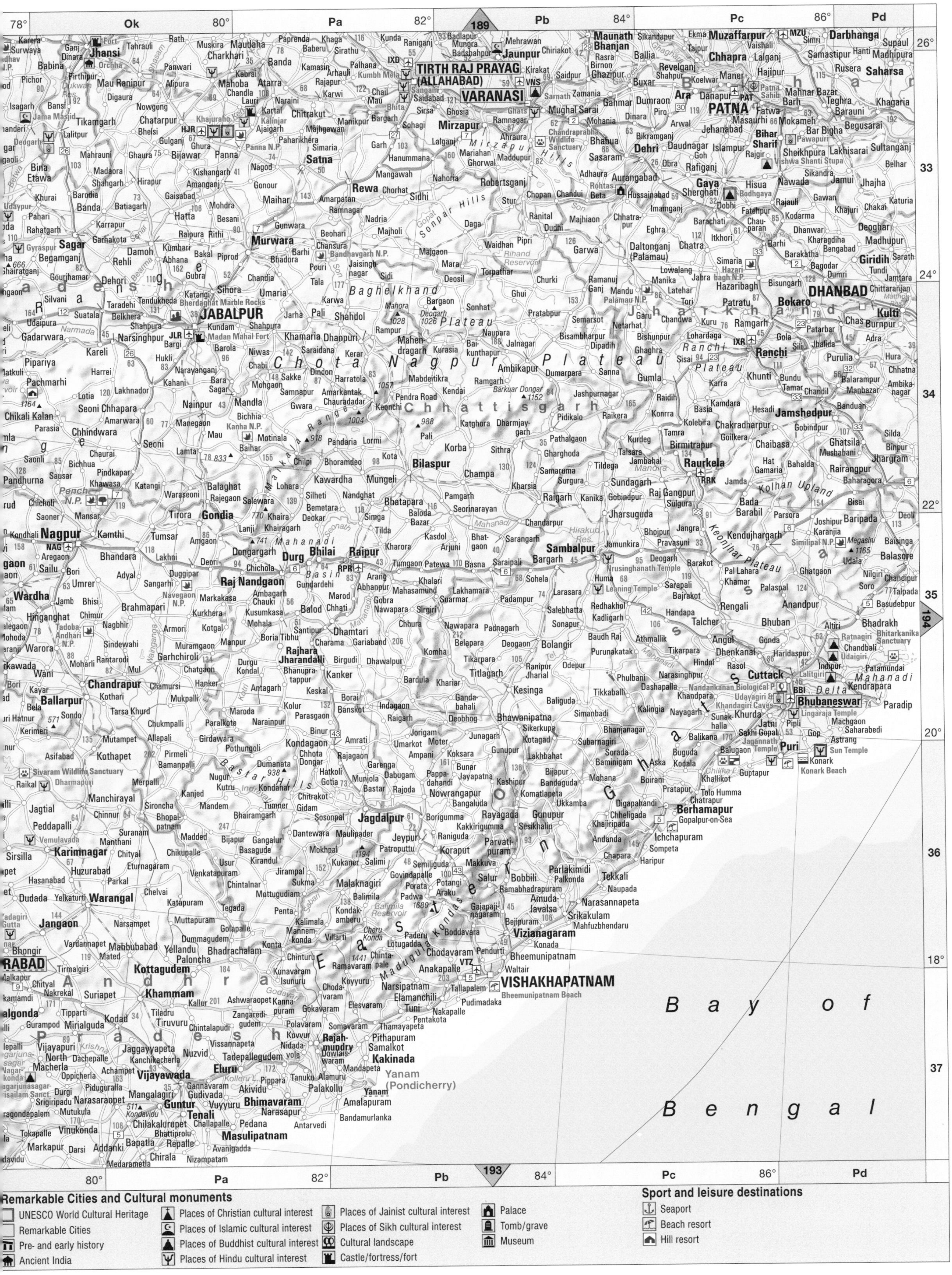

Bay of Bengal

Remarkable Cities and Cultural monuments

- UNESCO World Cultural Heritage
- Remarkable Cities
- Pre- and early history
- Ancient India
- Places of Christian cultural interest
- Places of Islamic cultural interest
- Places of Buddhist cultural interest
- Places of Hindu cultural interest
- Places of Jainist cultural interest
- Places of Sikh cultural interest
- Cultural landscape
- Castle/fortress/fort
- Palace
- Tomb/grave
- Museum

Sport and leisure destinations

- Seaport
- Beach resort
- Hill resort

Khajuraho The temple is a masterpiece of Hindu architecture – UNESCO world heritage site – famous for its sculptures **Ok33**

Varanasi (Benares) For around 2,500 years, Hindu pilgrims have traveled to this holy city for ceremonial baths in the Ganges River. The pilgrims descend steps (ghats) into the holy river. The most important religious building in the city is the Vishvanatha temple dedicated to Shiva. **Pb33**

Bodhgaya Buddhist spiritual center – Mahabodi temple, built in the 2nd century – Vajrasana – museum **Pc33**

Sanchi The oldest stupa (Buddhist shrine) in India is a UNESCO world heritage site – The Great Stupa was built over the burial site of Buddha **Oj34**

Bhubaneswar Site of historic Indian temples – Muktesvara temple (photo) was built in the 10th century **Pc35**

Puri Jagannath temple (photo), built in the 12th century, has several 65-meter-tall white pagodas – pilgrimage sites – ceremonies in honor of Jagannath (God of the Universe) – Rath Yatra Festival **Pc36**

The Maldives are a group of coral atolls located 700 kilometers off the coast of India in the Indian Ocean. The coral islands of the Maldives are situated atop a long underwater ridge with a total length of around 1,000 kilometers. Because none of the islands lie more than three meters above sea level, the small nation's existence is threatened by a possible rise in sea level that could occur as a result of global warming. The

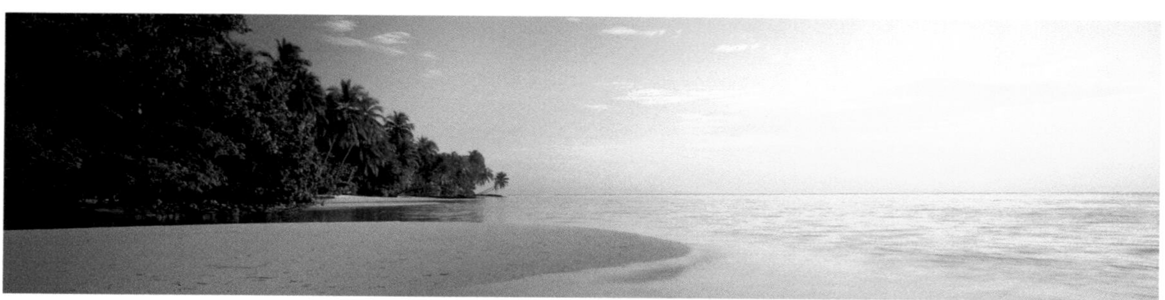

Huvadhoo Atoll has a diameter of kilometers and is the country's larg atoll.

The Eastern and **Western Ghats** situated on the edges of the **Deccan P teau** in southern India. The two moun ranges merge and form the Palani H in the far south of India. The mounta

The Maldives are home to many beautiful sandy beaches **Og41**

The Maledives This small nation encompasses 19 groups of coral islands and atolls in the Indian Ocean. The islands are home to many good diving sites. **Og42-46**

Hampi Once the capital of the Vijayanagar Empire, today it consists of large ruins – UNESCO world heritage site **Oj39**

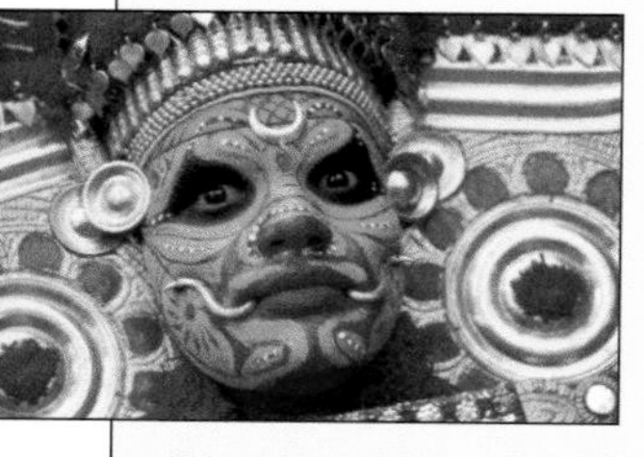

Kochi (Cochin) The port city's attractions include a historic Jewish Quarter with India's oldest synagogue and the famous Theyyam temple dancers (photo). **Oj42**

Kollam (Quilon) Holiday resort on the Malabar Coast – access to the Backwaters region – lakes and lagoons (photo) **Oj42**

Thiruvananthapuram (Trivandrum) Capital of Kerala – museum – palm tree lined Kovalam Beach **Oj42**

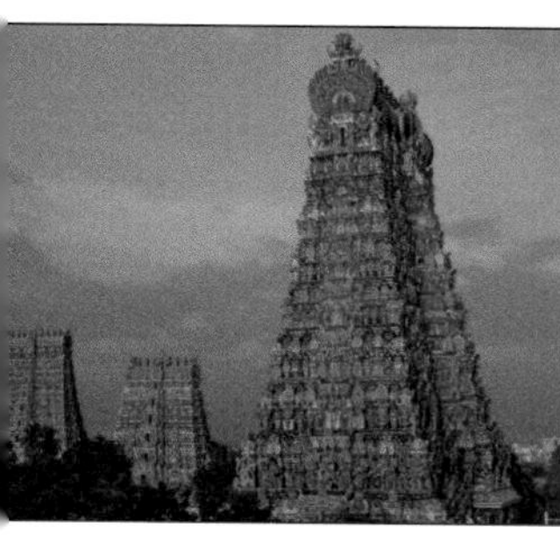

Madurai 2,000-year-old city in Tamil Nadu state – site of the large 17th century Meenakshi temple (photo) – Hall of 1,000 Pillars **Ok42**

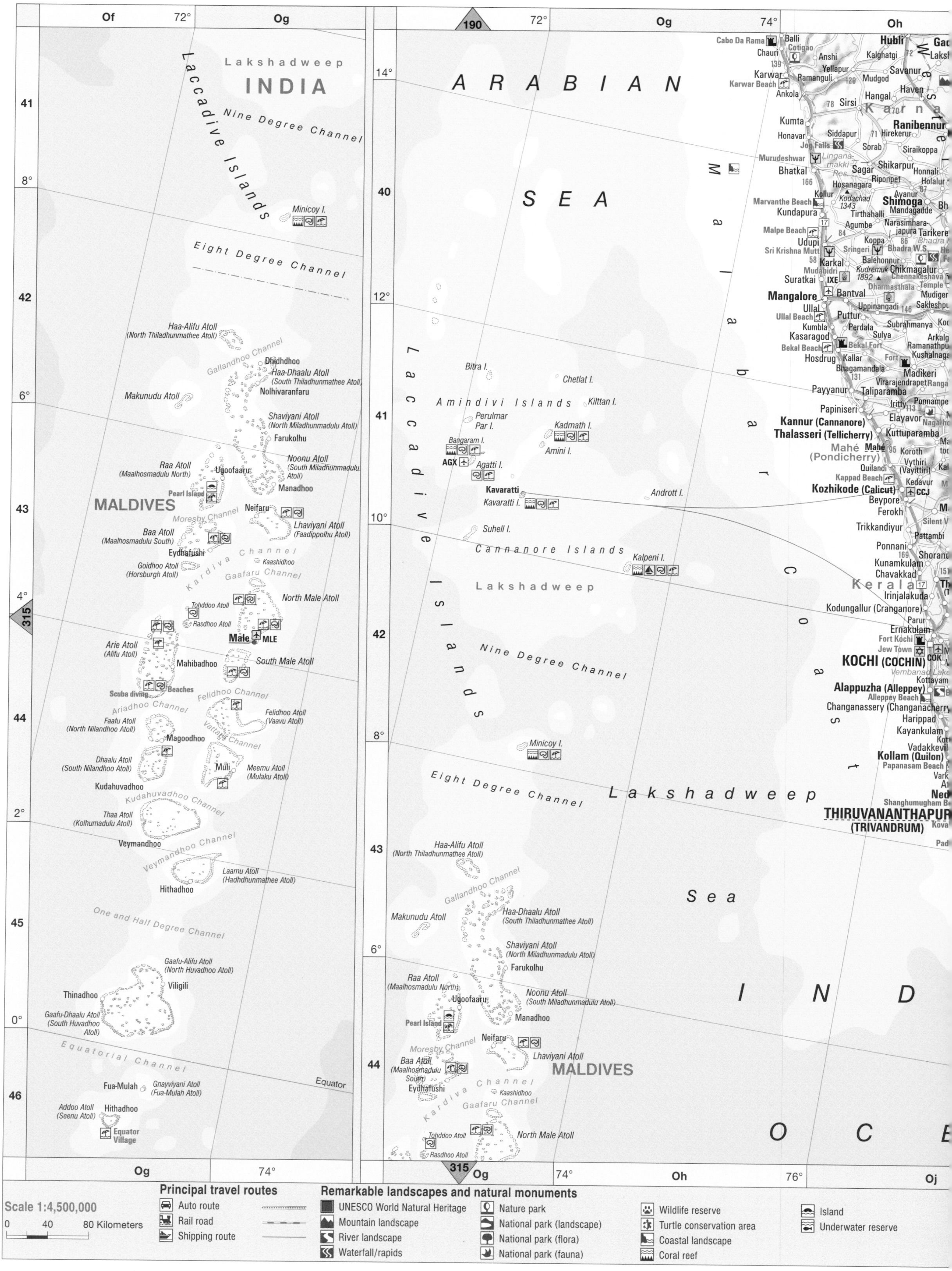

Scale 1:4,500,000

0 40 80 Kilometers

Principal travel routes

- Auto route
- Rail road
- Shipping route

Remarkable landscapes and natural monuments

- UNESCO World Natural Heritage
- Mountain landscape
- River landscape
- Waterfall/rapids
- Nature park
- National park (landscape)
- National park (flora)
- National park (fauna)
- Wildlife reserve
- Turtle conservation area
- Coastal landscape
- Coral reef
- Island
- Underwater reserve

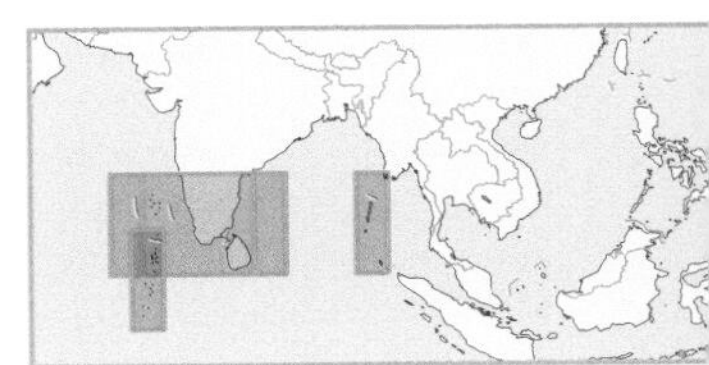

the Western Ghat fall abruptly to the 00-kilometer-long Malabar Coast. The lian state Kerala is the location of veral mountain ranges – including the **Nilgiri Hills,** which rise to a maximum ght of 2,600 meters The **Malabar ast** is a narrow strip of coastal plains ich increases in width from north to uth. Cape Comorin is the southern-st point on the Indian subcontinent. e **Kaveri River** flows 475 kilometers from its source in the Western Ghats to its delta on the Bay of Bengal.

The Gulf of Mannar and shallow Palk Bay separate the island nation **Sri Lanka** from the Indian subcontinent. **Adam's Bridge**, a chain of sand bars and coral islands between the Gulf of Mannar and Palk Bay are visible reminders of an ancient land bridge that once connected the island to India. Most of northern Sri Lanka is covered by lowlands and coastal plains. Adam's Peak is the tallest mountain in the country's central highlands with a height of 2,243 meters above sea level. Adam's Peak is highly revered by all four major religious communities on the island. Two sudden drops in elevation mark the transition between the central highlands and the plains of northern Sri Lanka. The transition zone between the two regions is home to many beautiful landscapes including a large number of waterfalls. There are noticeable differences between the topography of Sri Lanka's coastal areas. The western coast is lined by several long spits, while the eastern coast consists primarily of broad sandy beaches. The **Andaman** and **Nicobar Islands** are situated in the eastern Bay of Bengal. Both island groups belong to India. Most of the 223 islands are mountainous and most of their populations live in river deltas or on coastal plains.

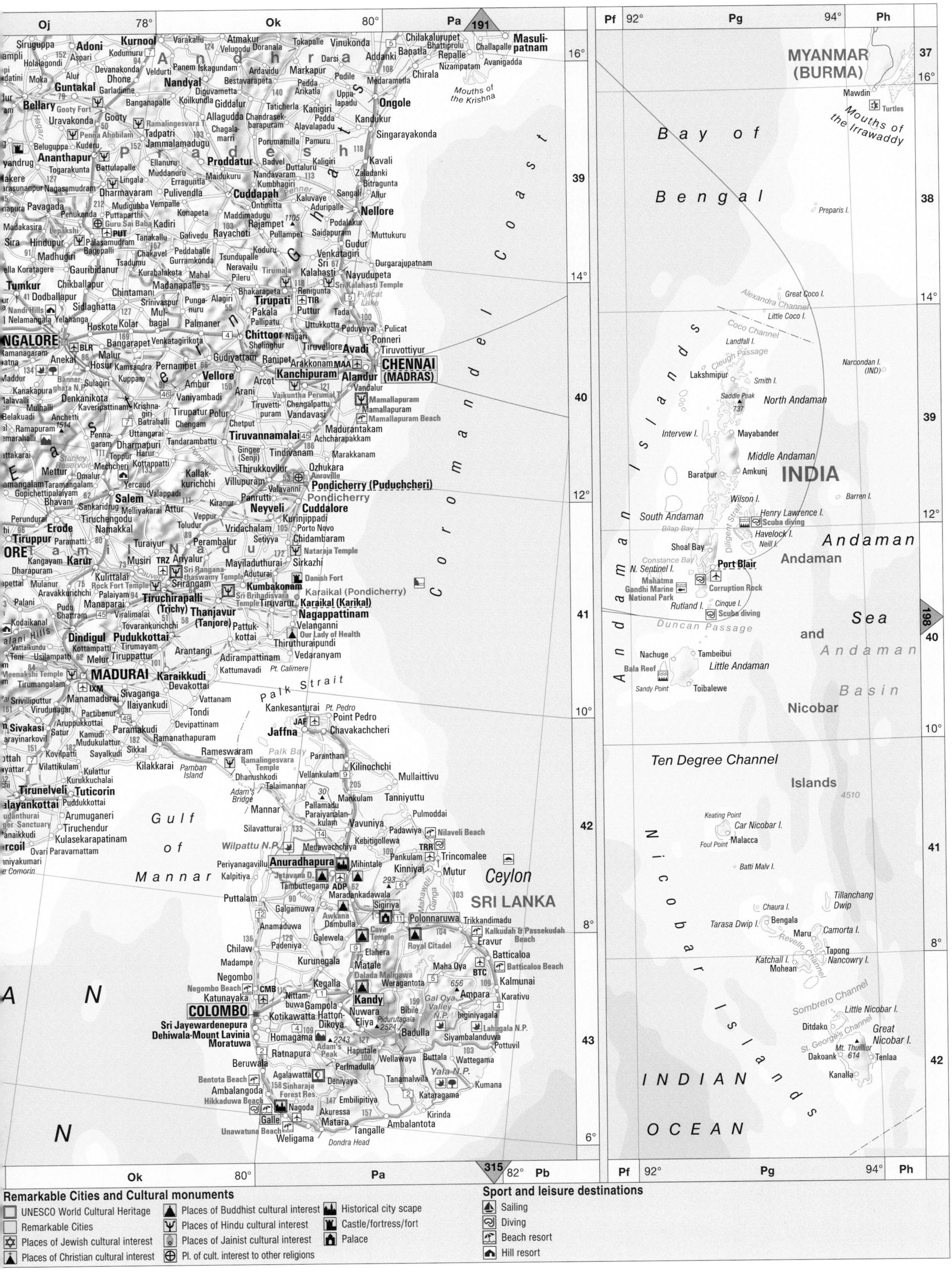

Mahabalipuram The Shore Temple was built in the eighth century and is now a world heritage site – large bas-reliefs **Pa40**

Anuradhapura The city became the first royal capital of Sri Lanka in the fourth century – ruins area covering 20 km², a world heritage site – Buddhist shrines **Pa42**

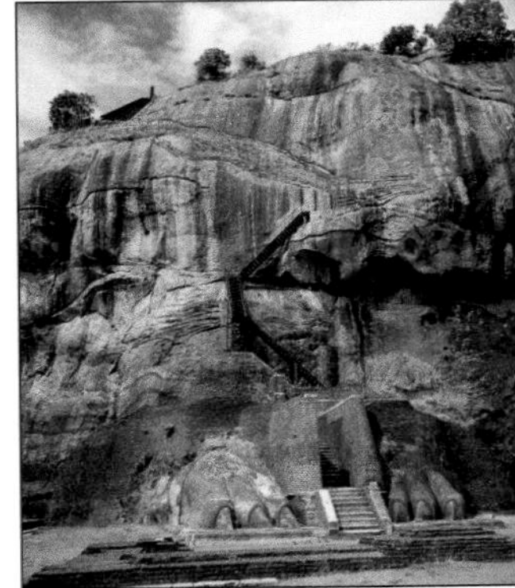

Sigiriya The ruins of King Kasyapa's palace built into the "Lion Rock" – beautiful frescoes – UNESCO world heritage site **Pa42/43**

Dambulla Five cave temples, a UNESCO world heritage site – 14 meter long reclining Buddha statue **Pa43**

Kandy Historic city in the Sri Lankan highlands – Dalada Maligawa, the temple of the sacred tooth – Esala Perahera, Hindu pageant – UNESCO world heritage site **Pa43**

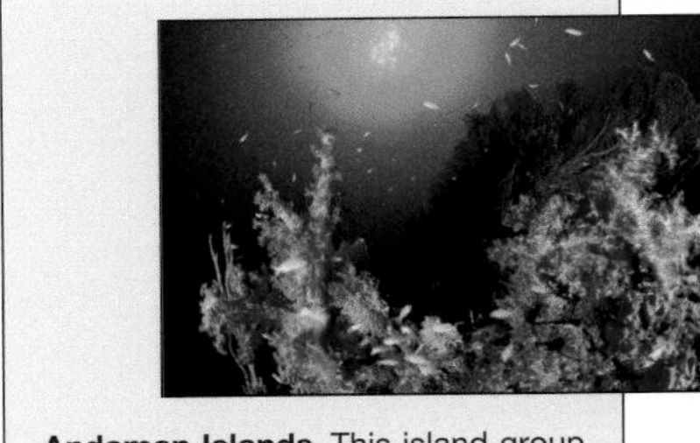

Andaman Islands This island group in the Bay of Bengal is surrounded by waters with beautiful coral reefs. The islands are a popular destination for diving. **Pg39/40**

Remarkable Cities and Cultural monuments

- UNESCO World Cultural Heritage
- Remarkable Cities
- Places of Jewish cultural interest
- Places of Christian cultural interest
- Places of Buddhist cultural interest
- Places of Hindu cultural interest
- Places of Jainist cultural interest
- Pl. of cult. interest to other religions
- Historical city scape
- Castle/fortress/fort
- Palace

Sport and leisure destinations

- Sailing
- Diving
- Beach resort
- Hill resort

Eastern India, Bangladesh, Northern Myanmar

The eastern section of the Indian subcontinent encompasses several distinct landscapes. The **Himalayas** are the world's tallest mountain range. The highest mountains in the range including Mount Everest (8,850 meters) and Lhotse (8,516 meters) are situated near the border between Nepal and Tibet (China). The lower eastern section of the Himalayas located in Bhutan, the Indian state of Arunachal Pradesh, and Yunnan

(China) is situated between 4,000 a 5,000 meters above sea level. The Ki dom of **Nepal** consists of several dist regions with major differences in ele tion. Around one fourth of the kingdo territory lies more than 4,000 met above sea level. The Kathmandu Ba has an average elevation of 1,300 r

Shwesandaw temple in Bagan; built i the 11th century **Ph**

Simtokha Dzong Historic fortified monastery in Bhutan – located on a steep hillside – founded in 1644 and rebuilt after a fire in 1907 **Pe32**

Darjeeling Indian town situated in a scenic highlands area – the historic Darjeeling Himalayan Railway (photo) is a UNESCO world heritage site **Pe32**

Kaziranga National Park This conservation area contains the world's largest population of one-horned rhinoceroses – elephant herds – world heritage site **Pg32**

Dhaka Bangladesh's capital and largest urban area – Historic mosque (photo) in the area of Lalbagh Fort **Pf34**

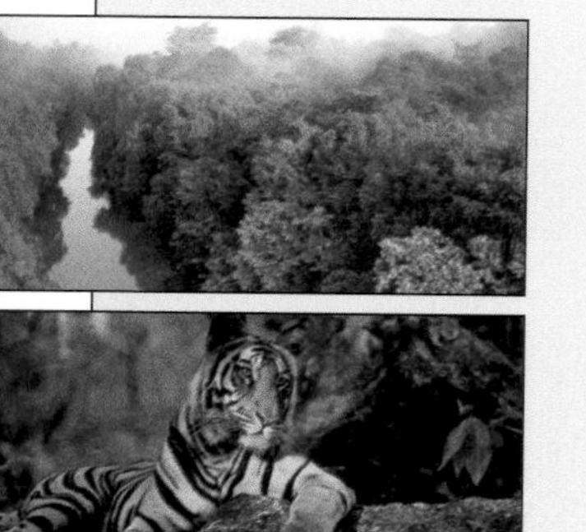

Sundarbans National Park This park, located in the Ganges delta (top photo), contains the world's largest mangrove forest. It was designated a UNESCO world heritage site in 1987. Around 250 rare Royal Bengali Tigers (bottom photo) inhabit the park. **Pe35**

Kolkata (Calcutta) India's second largest city – Victoria Memorial Hall (photo) contains an art museum **Pe34**

Scale 1:4,500,000

0 40 80 Kilometers

Principal travel routes

- Auto route
- Rail road
- Shipping route

Remarkable landscapes and natural monuments

- UNESCO World Natural Heritage
- Mountain landscape
- Rock landscape
- Ravine/canyon
- Extinct volcano
- Cave
- River landscape
- Waterfall/rapids
- Lake country
- Fossil site
- Nature park
- National park (landscape)
- National park (flora)
- National park (fauna)
- Wildlife reserve

s. In contrast to these regions, how-er, the subtropical plains of southern pal rise no higher than a few hundred ters above sea level. The 2,700-kilo-eter-long **Ganges River** flows into ngladesh from the west, while the 00-kilometer-long **Brahmaputra** ters the country from the northeast. e two rivers merge near Dhaka, the pital city of Bangladesh. The shared ta of the two rivers covers an area of 56,000 km² and extends out into the Bay of Bengal. Because of frequent tropical storms and Bangladesh's low elevation, the risk of devastating floods is the major natural threat to the country. In recent decades, several major floods have caused severe economic damage and many fatalities in densely populated Bangladesh.

The eastern edge of the Indian subcontinent and western Myanmar (Burma) are dominated by a series of mountain ranges. The Irrawaddy River basin covers much of central Myanmar. The Shan Plateau is located to the east of the basin. The expansive plateau encompasses numerous high mountains. The powerful **Salween River** flows from north to south through the plateau. Myanmar's far north is dominated by the **eastern Himalayas**.

The highlands of southeastern China feature many high mountains and several major rivers. The **Mekong (Lancang Jiang) River** flows east from its source in Tibet into Southeast Asia. After it leaves China, the river forms sections of the borders separating Laos from Myanmar and Thailand. The **Chang Jiang (Yangtze) River** is the longest waterway in Asia. The upper course of the river flows through a series of beautiful gorges in the highlands of southern China.

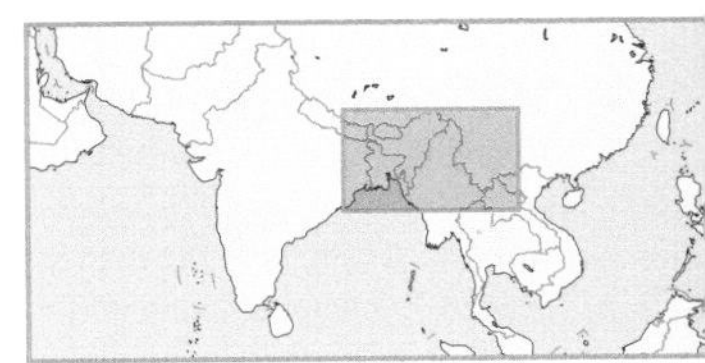

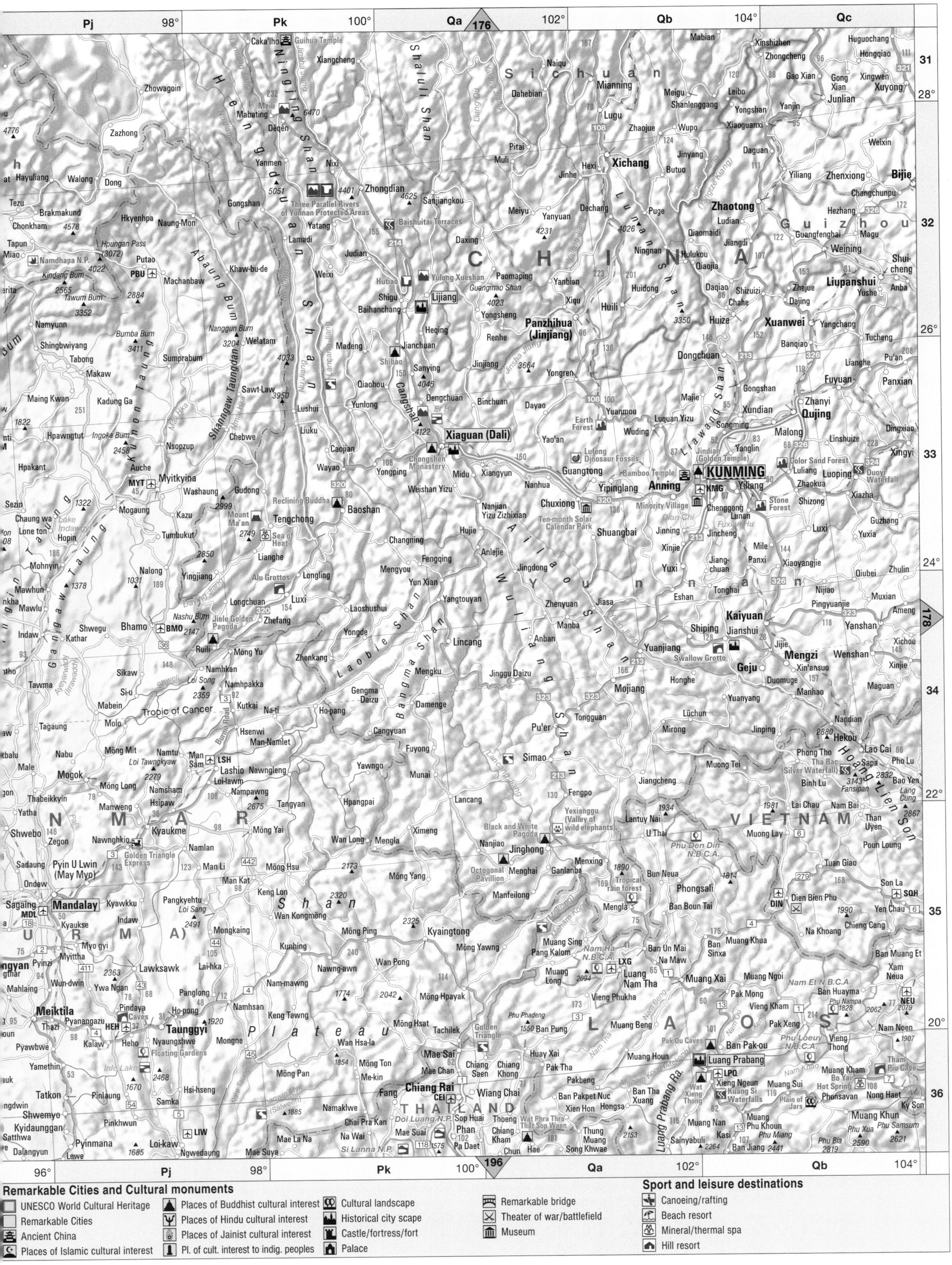

Kunming The stone forest of Shilin, a group of unusual stone formations formed over 200 million years ago **Qb33**

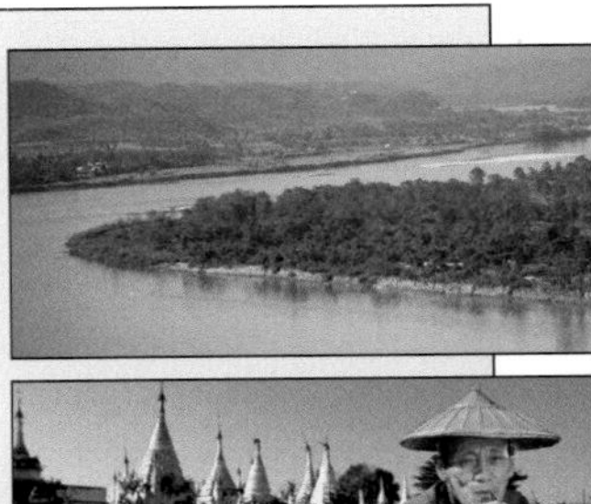

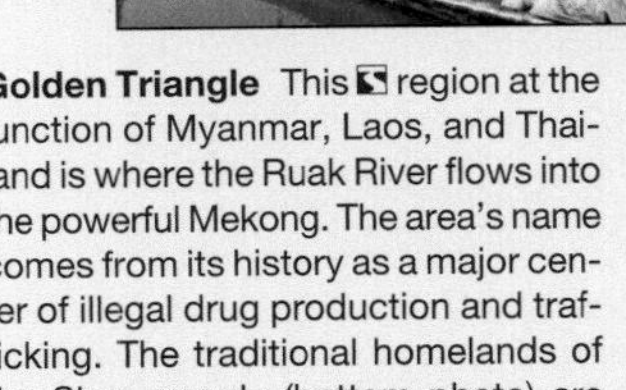

Golden Triangle This region at the junction of Myanmar, Laos, and Thailand is where the Ruak River flows into the powerful Mekong. The area's name comes from its history as a major center of illegal drug production and trafficking. The traditional homelands of the Shan people (bottom photo) are located along the northwest edges of the triangle. **Qa35**

Monywa Thanboddhay temple – the temple contains 845 small stupas – constructed between 1939 and 1952 **Ph34**

Inle Lake Unique "floating gardens" – Phaung Daw Oo monastery with the royal barge (photo) – Nga Phe monastery **Pj35**

Bagan Religious center of the Bamar people – around 2,000 well preserved and beautiful historic buildings **Ph35**

Louangphrabang (Luang Prabang) Town in Laos – Wat Xieng Thong temple, built in 1850 – traditional architecture **Qb36**

Remarkable Cities and Cultural monuments

- UNESCO World Cultural Heritage
- Remarkable Cities
- Ancient China
- Places of Islamic cultural interest
- Places of Buddhist cultural interest
- Places of Hindu cultural interest
- Places of Jainist cultural interest
- Pl. of cult. interest to indig. peoples
- Cultural landscape
- Historical city scape
- Castle/fortress/fort
- Palace
- Remarkable bridge
- Theater of war/battlefield
- Museum

Sport and leisure destinations

- Canoeing/rafting
- Beach resort
- Mineral/thermal spa
- Hill resort

Much of mainland Southeast Asia is covered by heavily forested highlands and fertile plains in the basins of the region's many powerful rivers. The Irrawaddy, Salween, Chao Phraya, and Mekong Rivers are the most important waterways in the region.

The **Irrawaddy River** flows south from its source in the Himalayas through the center of Myanmar. It's delta in southern Myanmar covers 47,800 km² and encom-

Elephant riders near Siem Reap in Cambodia **Qc**

passes one of the largest rice farm areas in the world. A narrow mount range separates the Irrawaddy from t **Thanwin River** which flows from north south near the border to Thailand. T Bilauktaung Range stretches south fr the Dawna Mountains in eastern Mya mar into the **Malay Peninsula**. Thailan

Kyaik Hti Yo Pagoda Myanmar's most important pilgrimage site – located atop the "golden rock" **Pj37**

Yangon (Rangoon) Myanmar's capital – Shwedagon Pagoda (photo), a historic holy site with a 98-meter-tall golden stupa **Pj37**

Chiang Mai The largest city in northern Thailand – Wat Chedi Luang – Wat Phra Singh (photo) – night market **Pk36**

Sukhothai Capital of the Thai Empire in the 13th century – historic park containing ancient ruins, a UNESCO world heritage site – remnants of Wat Mahathat (photo) **Pk37**

Bangkok The Chao Phraya River (bottom photo) flows through Thailand's capital and largest city. Bangkok is home to modern skyscrapers and historic architecture including the Wat Phra Kaeo. The Wat Phra Kaeo complex contains the Royal Pantheon (top photo). **Qa39**

Ayutthaya Thailand's capital and leading city until the 17th century – UNESCO world heritage site – Wat Yat Chai Mongkol **Qa38**

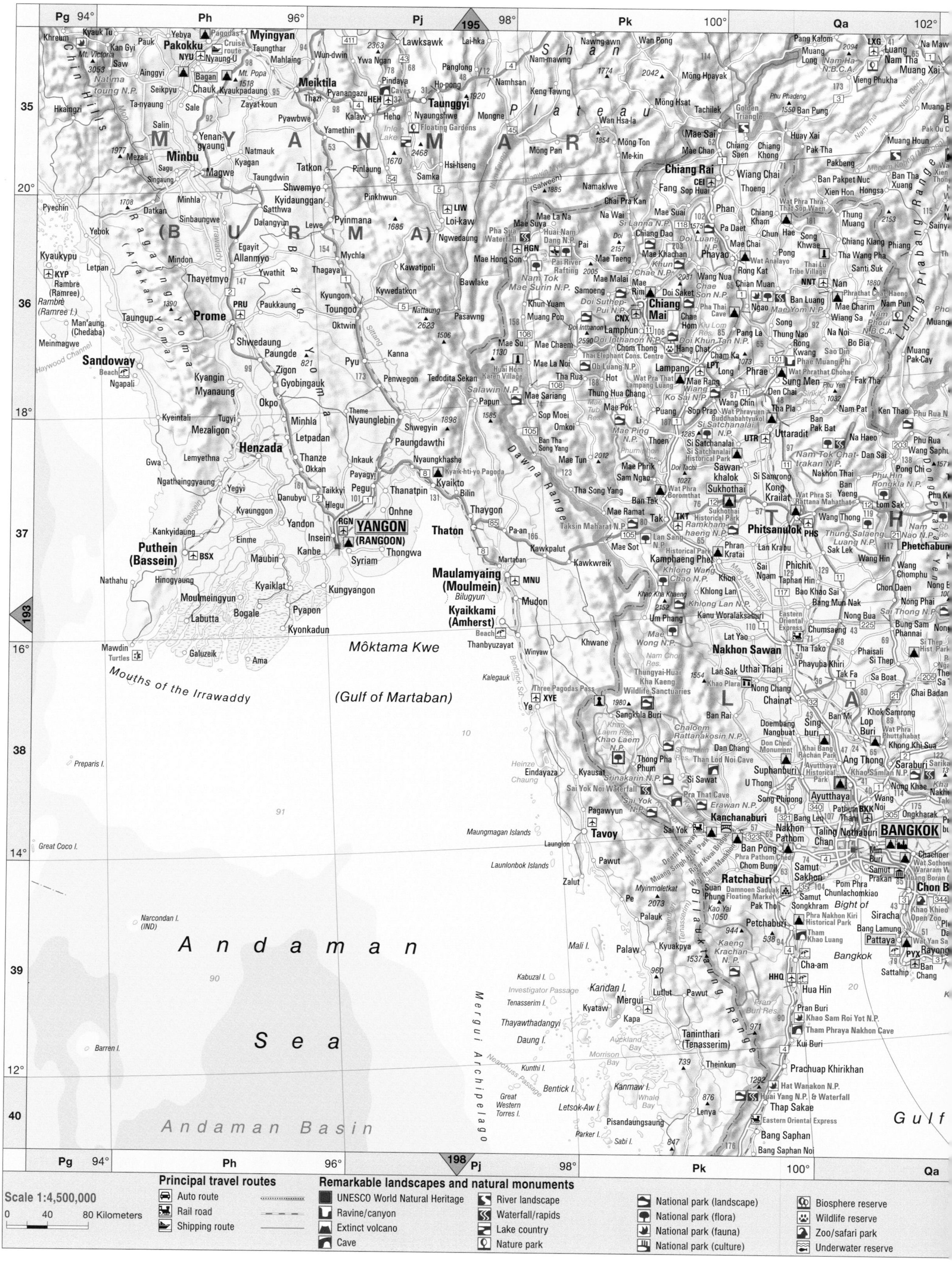

Scale 1:4,500,000

0 40 80 Kilometers

Principal travel routes

- Auto route
- Rail road
- Shipping route

Remarkable landscapes and natural monuments

- UNESCO World Natural Heritage
- Ravine/canyon
- Extinct volcano
- Cave
- River landscape
- Waterfall/rapids
- Lake country
- Nature park
- National park (landscape)
- National park (flora)
- National park (fauna)
- National park (culture)
- Biosphere reserve
- Wildlife reserve
- Zoo/safari park
- Underwater reserve

ıcipal river, the Chao Phraya, flows ough the country's central plain, one of most productive rice and fruit far- ng regions in Asia. The central plain is o considered the cradle of Thai civi- ation. After leaving the plain, the Chao raya flows south to its large delta near ngkok.
e highlands of northern and western ailand are home to many steep narrow ountain valleys. Thailand's highest mountain, **Doi Inthanon** (2,590 meters), is located in the northern highlands near Chang Mai. The **Golden Triangle** region is divided between Thailand, Laos, and Myanmar. In addition to its interesting indigenous cultures, the Golden Triangle also encompasses some of the most spectacular landscapes in Southeast Asia. Northeastern Thailand is dominated by mountain ranges and the hills of the **Khorat Plateau**.

The 4,500 meter long **Mekong River** is the fourth longest river in Asia. It flows from its source in Tibet to its delta in southern Vietnam. The river forms a long section of the border between Laos and Thailand. Further south it enters the plains of Cambodia before crossing the border into Vietnam where it reaches its 70,000 -km²-large delta on the South China Sea. Most of eastern Laos is covered by the mountains of **Annamite Chain**, which rises to a maximum height of 2,500 meters. The mountain chains form a natural barrier between Vietnam and Laos. Vietnam is a long nation from north to south but relatively narrow from east to west. The smallest distance from the western border to the eastern coast in central Vietnam is 60 kilometers. Central Vietnam consists of mountainous highlands in the interior and a narrow strip of coastal plains.

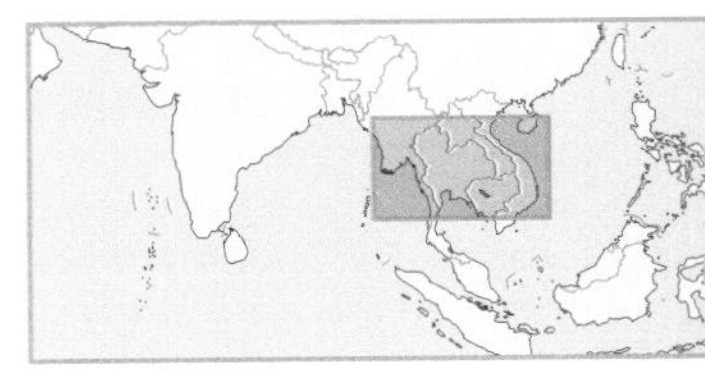

Hue Former imperial capital of Vietnam – the city contain many historic buildings – UNESCO world heritage site **Qd37**

My Son Ruins of an ancient Cham ▲ religious center – damaged during the Vietnam War – UNESCO world heritage site **Qd38**

Hoi An The old town is a UNESCO world heritage site – Hoi An's central street Duong Tran Phu is a center of the Chinese community (photo) – Japanese Bridge **Qe38**

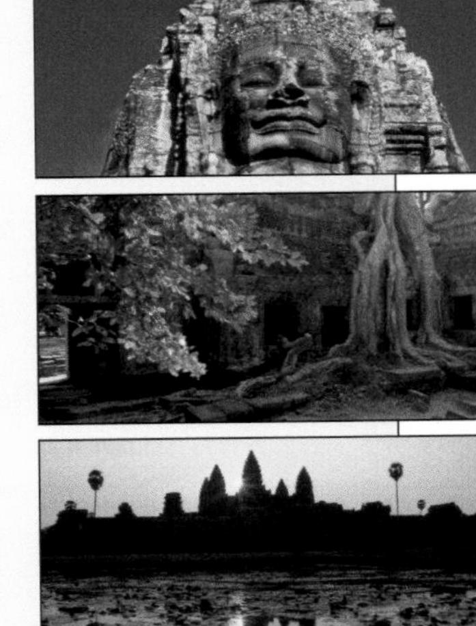

Angkor ▲ The city was the center of the Khmer Empire (802-1432 AD). Bayon temple complex features many towers with depictions of human faces (top photo). Wat Ta Prohm (middle photo) was completed in 1186. The temple Angkor Wat (bottom photo) is one of the the most impressive historic buildings in Asia. **Qb39**

Wat Phu Large ▲ temple complex at the foot of Phu Pasak (1,200 meters) – the oldest sections were completed in the 5th and 6th centuries – beautiful bas-reliefs **Qc38**

Remarkable Cities and Cultural monuments

- UNESCO World Cultural Heritage
- Remarkable Cities
- Places of Buddhist cultural interest
- Pl. of cult. interest to indig. peoples
- Cultural landscape
- Historical city scape
- Castle/fortress/fort
- Remarkable bridge
- Theater of war/battlefield
- Monument
- Memorial
- Market
- Museum

Sport and leisure destinations

- Diving
- Canoeing/rafting
- Beach resort
- Mineral/thermal spa

The **Malay Peninsula** was created around 150 million years ago. The peninsula is around 40 kilometers wide at its narrowest. Several long mountain ranges stretch from north to south through the 1,500-kilometer-long peninsula. Until recently, the mountains were a major obstacle to overland travel between the two coasts of the peninsula. Southern Thailand's pleasant climate and its many beautiful beaches attract tourists from around the world to the region. Situated off the west coast of the southern Thailand, **Phuket** is the country's largest island and a major center of the Thai tourism industry. The **Similan Islands**, a small island group north of Phuket, offer some of finest diving sites in Thailand.

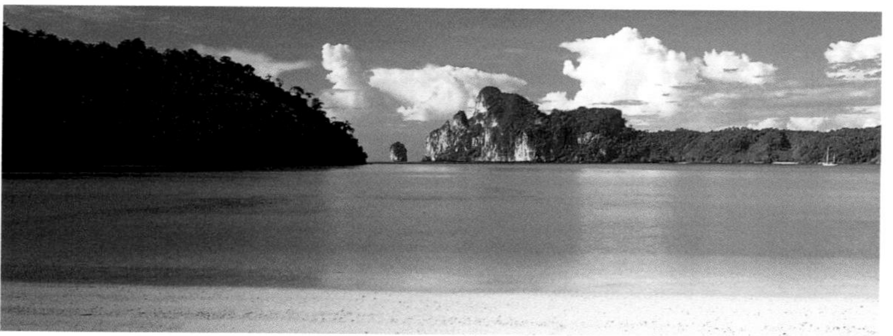

Phuket, Thailand's largest island, is a popular tourist destination **Pk41/42**

Khao Luang (1,793 meters) is the tall mountain in a long mountain chain t stretches through much of southern Th land. The mountain is surrounded b national park with fascinating flora a fauna. The mountains in this area a home to many ancient and heavily ero ed stone formations as well as cou less caves.

The alluvial plains in the western parts the Malay Peninsula contain extens

Koh Samui Island in the Gulf of Thailand (247 km²) – beautiful Chaweng beach – waterfalls: Na Muang and Hin Lat – large Buddha statue (photo) **Qa41**

Phuket Thailand's largest island (800 km²) – Phuket (town) contains historic Sino-Portuguese architecture – rainforests in Khao Phra Taeo National Park – long beaches on the island's western coast **Pk41/42**

Georgetown Capital of the Malaysian state Penang – the majority of the city's population is of Chinese descent – Chinatown (photo) – Khoo Kongsi Temple **Qa43**

Kek Lok Si Temple Located on the island Penang – Buddhist pilgrimage site – "the pagoda of 10,000 Buddhas" **Qa43**

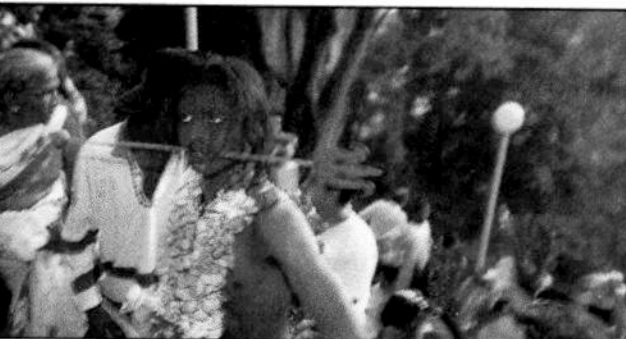

Batu Caves Site of the Thaipusam festival, a large Hindu religious gathering in Malaysia **Qa44**

Kuala Lumpur Malaysia's capital city was founded in the middle of the 19th century. The city is now the economic and cultural center of the country. Kuala Lumpur's Petronas Towers (photo, 452 meters) are among the tallest buildings in the world. **Qa44**

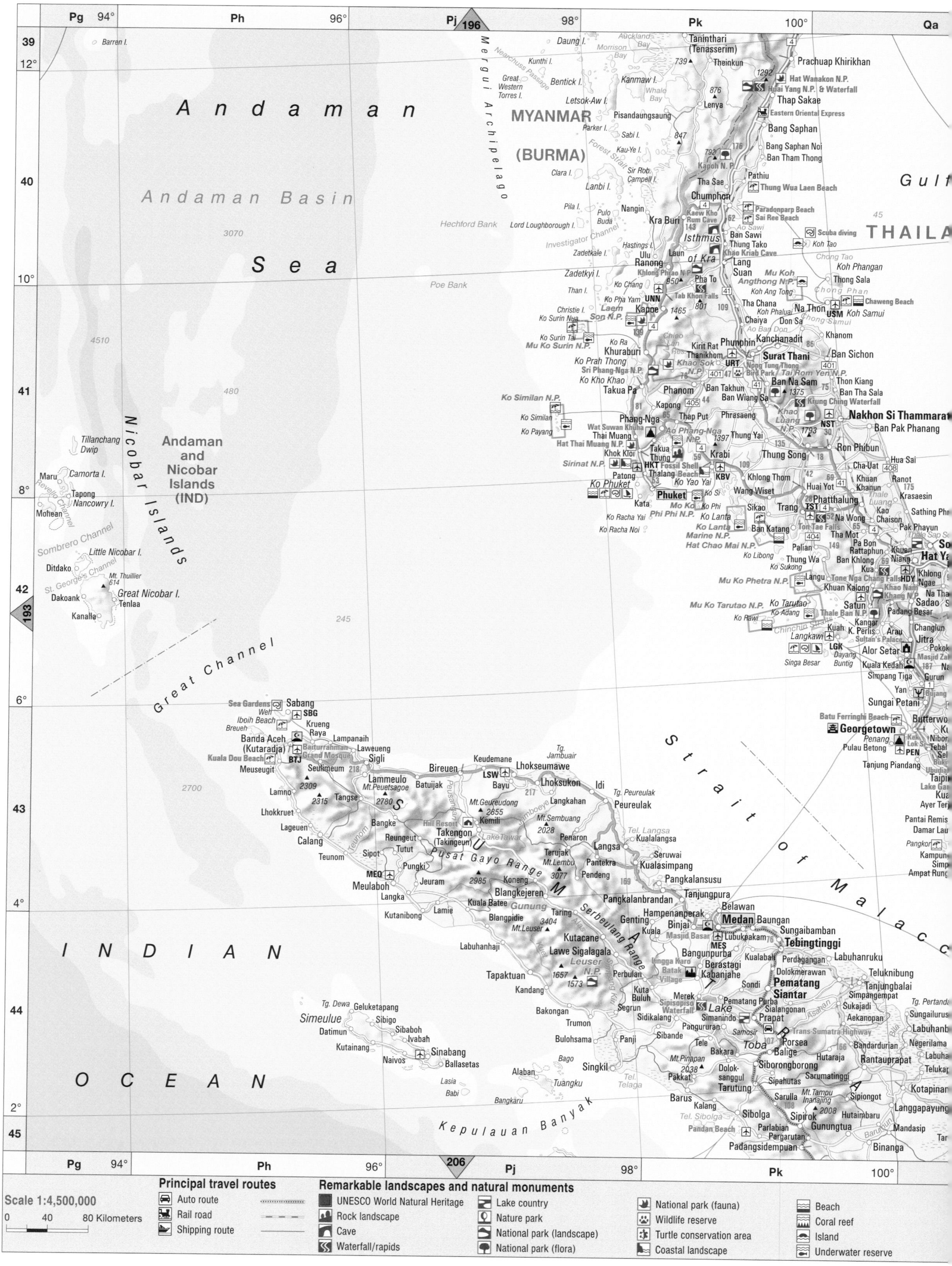

Scale 1:4,500,000

0 40 80 Kilometers

Principal travel routes

- Auto route
- Rail road
- Shipping route

Remarkable landscapes and natural monuments

- UNESCO World Natural Heritage
- Rock landscape
- Cave
- Waterfall/rapids
- Lake country
- Nature park
- National park (landscape)
- National park (flora)
- National park (fauna)
- Wildlife reserve
- Turtle conservation area
- Coastal landscape
- Beach
- Coral reef
- Island
- Underwater reserve

ce growing areas. The peninsula was nce totally covered by dense tropical inforests: today the **tropical rain-rests** cover only a portion of the re-on but they contain an incredible level bio-diversity. Many of the larger mam-als in the forests including local tigers nd rhinoceroses are considered endan-ered. Smaller animals such as apes, sects, and butterflies continue to flou-sh in the forests. The forests of the Malay Peninsula are also home to many birds, including several species of hornbills. **Taman Negara National Park** is the largest national park in Malaysia and contains large virgin rainforests. Because of logging and agriculture, only around 12 percent of the Malay Peninsula is covered by tropical rainforests. Expansive palm, rubber, and coconut plantations now occupy large sections of the countryside where rainforests once were.

Southern Thailand and Peninsular Malaysia both have tropical **climates** with high humidity and heavy rainfall during much of the year.

The Indonesian island of Sumatra is separated from Malaysia and southern Thailand by the Strait of Malacca. The western section of the island is dominated by a long mountain range. These mountains border a large plain that covers much of northeastern Sumarta. The forests in **Mount Leuser National Park** are the only remaining habitats of the endangered Sumatran orangutans. Western Sumatra's most popular attraction is **Lake Toba**, a large lake in an ancient volcanic crater.

Southern Thailand is home to most of the country's large Muslim minority. Most Malaysians are practicing Muslims but the country also has large Buddhist and Hindu communities.

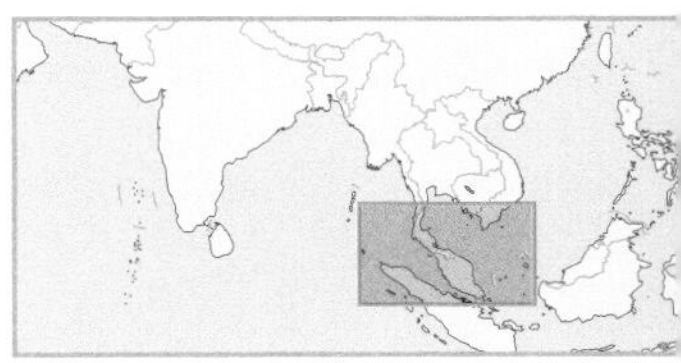

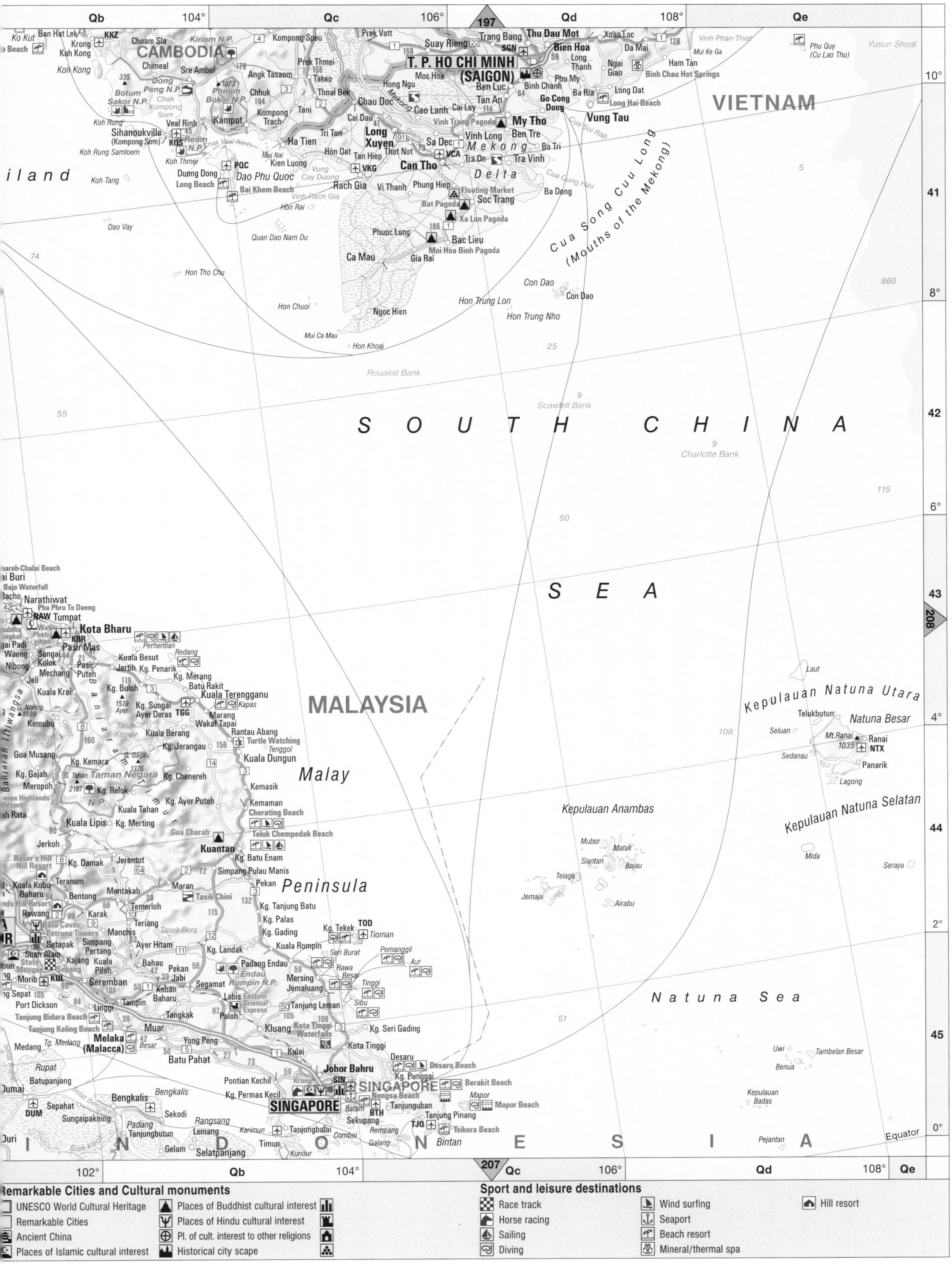

Ho Chi Minh City (Saigon) Vietnam's largest city – Temple of the Jade Emperor with a Taoist pantheon – Mariamman temple – Chinatown Cho Lon **Qd40**

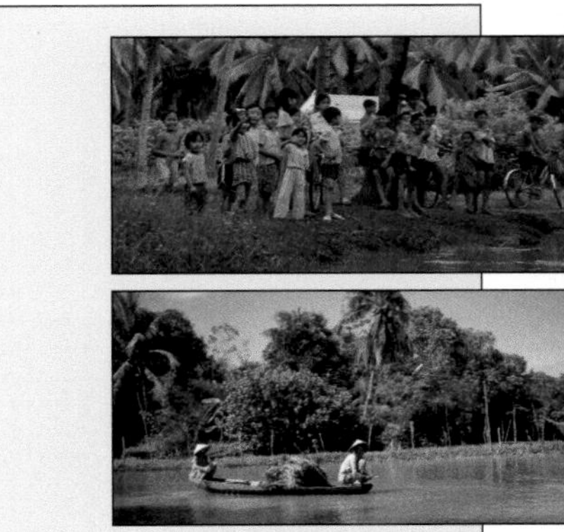

Mekong-Delta The 4,500-kilometer-long Mekong River is the longest river in Southeast Asia. The river's basin covers much of southern Vietnam. The Mekong delta features an extensive network of canals, rivers, and streams. **Qd40**

Cameron Highlands Mountain region in Malaysia – between 600 and 2,000 meters above sea level – major tea growing area since 1926 **Qa43**

Taman Negara 4,350-km²-large natio-nal park containing pristine rainforests – river rapids at Lata Berkoh **Qb43**

Singapore The island nation is connected to Peninsular Malaysia by a causeway. The ethnically diverse city is home to many notable attractions including the colonial era Raffles Hotel, markets in Orchard Road, Mariamann temple, and Jamae Mosque. Singapore is the busiest port in Southeast Asia. **Qb45**

Remarkable Cities and Cultural monuments

- UNESCO World Cultural Heritage
- Remarkable Cities
- Ancient China
- Places of Islamic cultural interest
- Places of Buddhist cultural interest
- Places of Hindu cultural interest
- Pl. of cult. interest to other religions
- Historical city scape

Sport and leisure destinations

- Race track
- Horse racing
- Sailing
- Diving
- Wind surfing
- Seaport
- Beach resort
- Mineral/thermal spa
- Hill resort

Southeast Asia

Southeast Asia is composed of six nations on mainland Asia: Vietnam, Cambodia, Laos, Thailand, and sections of Malaysia. The region also includes the countless islands that form Indonesia and the Philippines. The island of Borneo is divided between the small sultanate Brunei, Indonesia, and two Malaysian states. Myanmar (Burma), the westernmost nation in Southeast Asia features a variety of landscapes and topographies. The

eastern, northern, and western sectio of Myanmar are dominated by mountai and plateaus. Myanmar is also home numerous river valleys, rolling hills, a large lowland areas. The **Malay Peni sula** is divided between Thailand a Malaysia. A long chain of mountains stre ches from north to south through t

Rainforest in the highlands of Borneo

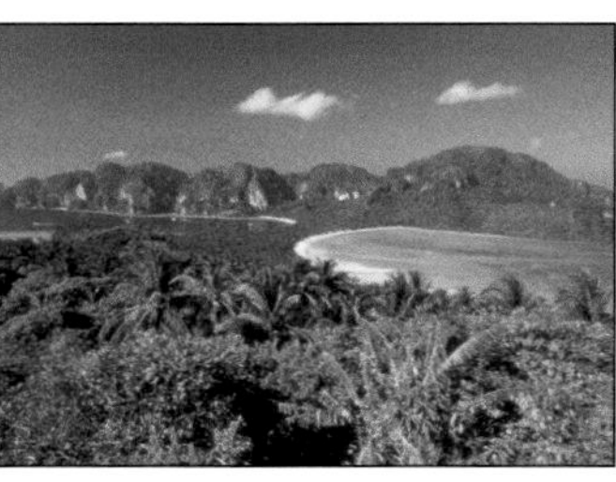

Malay Peninsula South of southern Thailand – Peninsular Malaysia and the capital Kuala Lumpur – Singapore off the southern coast

Sumatra Large Indonesian island – plains in the east – the Barisan Mountains dominate the west – Lake Toba, the largest crater lake in Southeast Asia

Borneo The world's third largest island is one of the Greater Sunda Islands. The island's craggy highlands rise to 4,100 meters at Mount Kinabalu, Borneo's tallest peak. Several national parks protect some of the island's rare flora and fauna. Photos from top to bottom: Mount Kinabalu, Gunung Mulu National Park (middle photos), Tanjung Putting National Park

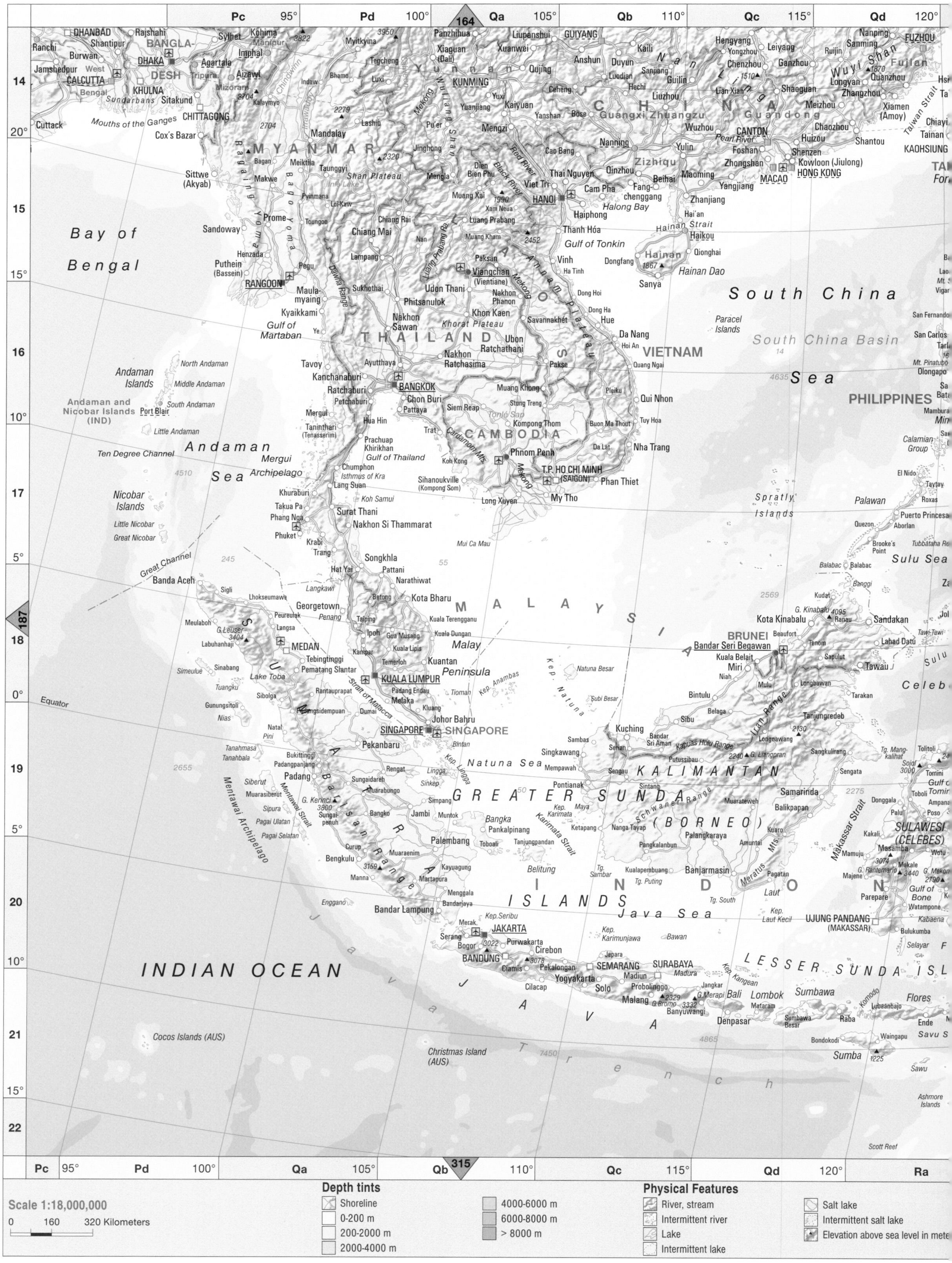

Scale 1:18,000,000
0 160 320 Kilometers

Depth tints
- Shoreline
- 0-200 m
- 200-2000 m
- 2000-4000 m
- 4000-6000 m
- 6000-8000 m
- > 8000 m

Physical Features
- River, stream
- Intermittent river
- Lake
- Intermittent lake
- Salt lake
- Intermittent salt lake
- Elevation above sea level in mete

nter of the peninsula. Singapore, a ıall island nation, is situated off the uthern coast of the peninsula. The alay Peninsula is home to many sand- one mountain ranges with unique stone rmations and extensive networks of bterranean caves.

donesia is a large mosaic of islands at were once part of an ancient sub- ntinent that connected Australia and ia. The nation is the largest archipelago in the world and encompasses more than 15,000 islands. Indonesia is located near the edges of the Eurasian, Pacific, and Indo-Australian tectonic plates. The geologically active archipelago is home to a long chain of volcanoes, several of which are still active. Borneo, Java, Sumatra, Sulawesi, and the Lesser Sunda Islands are the most important islands in Indonesia. The northern section of Borneo, the world's third largest island, is occupied by Brunei and the Malaysian states, Sabah and Sarawak. Much of Borneo's interior is covered by dense tropical rainforest, while the island's coastal areas contain large swampy plains.

New Guinea is the world's second largest island. The western half of the island forms the Indonesian province of Papua – officially known as Irian Jaya before 2002. The eastern half of the island belongs to Papua New Guinea, an independent nation since 1975. More than half of New Guinea is covered by tropical rainforest.

The **Philippines** is an archipelago of more than 7,100 islands off the southeastern coast of mainland Asia. The archipelago is located inside the so-called Pacific Ring of Fire and there are several active volcanos in the area. Luzon, the Visayas, Mindanao, Mindoro, and Palawan are the most important islands and island groups of the Philippines.

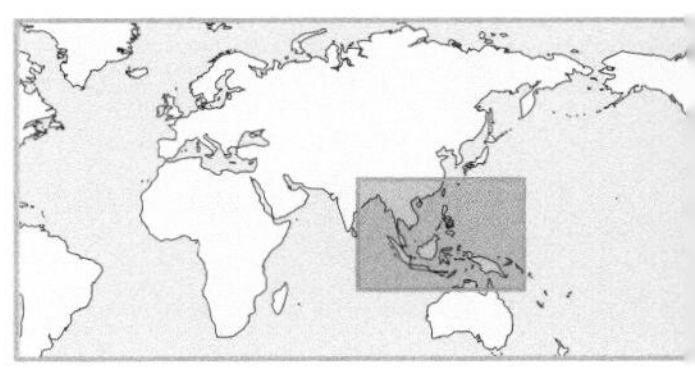

The Philippines More than 5,000 islands – active volcanoes including Mount Pinatubo (photo) – Luzon, largest island and location of the capital Manila

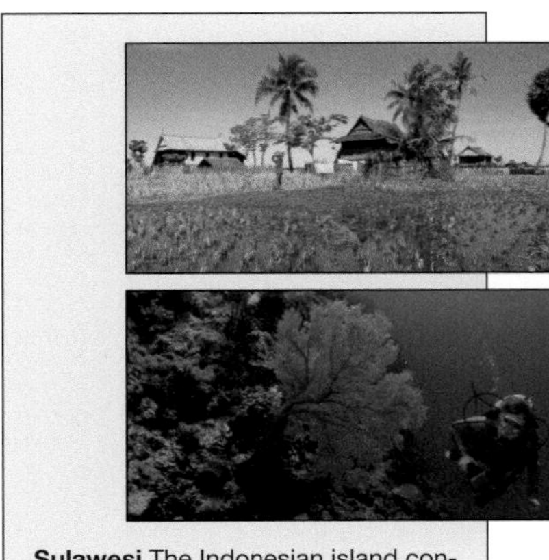

Sulawesi The Indonesian island consist of several long peninsulas with tall mountains, savannahs, traditional villages and coral reefs off the coast.

Lesser Sunda Islands The island group includes Bali (photos), Lombok, Sumba, Flores, and Komodo, home of the fascinating Komodo Dragons.

New Guinea The world's second largest island (771,900 km²) – rainforests – tallest mountain, Puncak Yaya (5,030 meters)

165

240

220

olitical Boundaries
ternational
ternational disputed
ain administrative

Transportation
Interstate Hwy./Motorway
Main road
Railway
Airport

Capitals of political units
WASHINGTON D.C. Independent
Richmond State/province

Town symbols
Capital > 1 Mill. inhabitants
Capital < 1 Mill. inhabitants
Statecapital > 1 Mill. inhabitants
Statecapital < 1 Mill. inhabitants
Towns > 1 Mill. inhabitants
Towns 100 000 bis 1 Mill. inhabitants
Towns < 100 000 inhabitants

The **Philippines** is a large archipelago encompassing more than 7,100 islands off the southeastern coast of mainland Asia. The island nation has a total land area of 300,000 km². Only around 900 of the islands that form the Philippines are permanently inhabited. The Philippines have a maximum length of 1,850 kilometers from north to south and from east to west a maximum length of 1,060 kilometers. The archipelago borders the

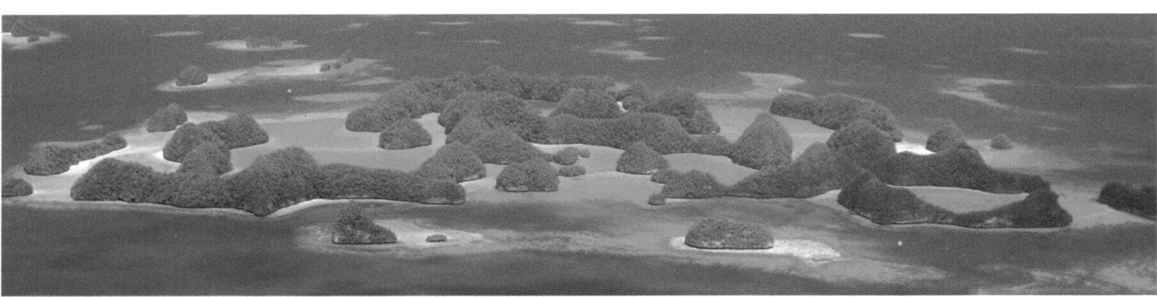

South China Sea in the west and t Pacific Ocean in the east. To the nor the archipelago is separated from Taiw by the **Luzon Strait**.
Like Indonesia, the vast number of islar in the Philippines means the country h one of the longest coastlines of any n tion in the world. The Philippines a

The islands of Palau are covered by lush tropical forests **Rh**

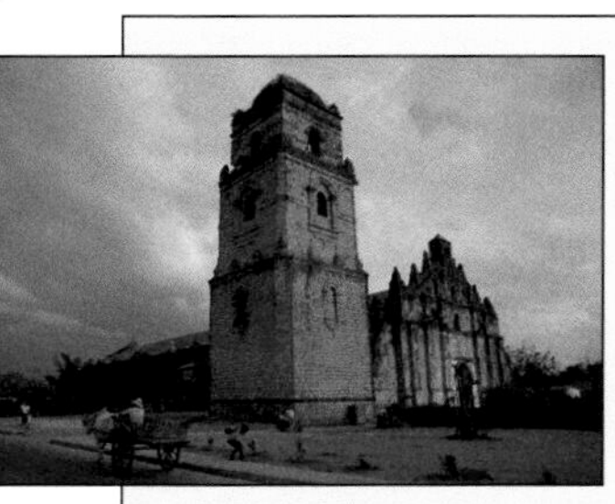

Paoay Church The historic church was built in the Baroque style and completed in 1894. Paoay church is a designated UNESCO world heritage site. **Ra37**

Vigan Spanish colonial houses in the Kamestizoan district, a world heritage site – cathedral – Ayala Museum **Ra37**

Lake Taal Beautiful 270-km²-large crater lake – the volcano Taal is located in the middle of the lake **Ra38/39**

Manila The capital of the Philippines has one of the best natural harbors in Asia. The city (top photo) is home to around ten million people. Colorful jeepneys (bottom photo) are an important means of transport in Manila. **Ra38**

Puerto Galera On the island Mindoro – beautiful natural harbor – beaches – popular tourist destination **Ra39**

Mount Pinatubo Volcano on the island Luzon – the eruption in 1991 created a 25-kilometer-high plume of smoke **Ra38**

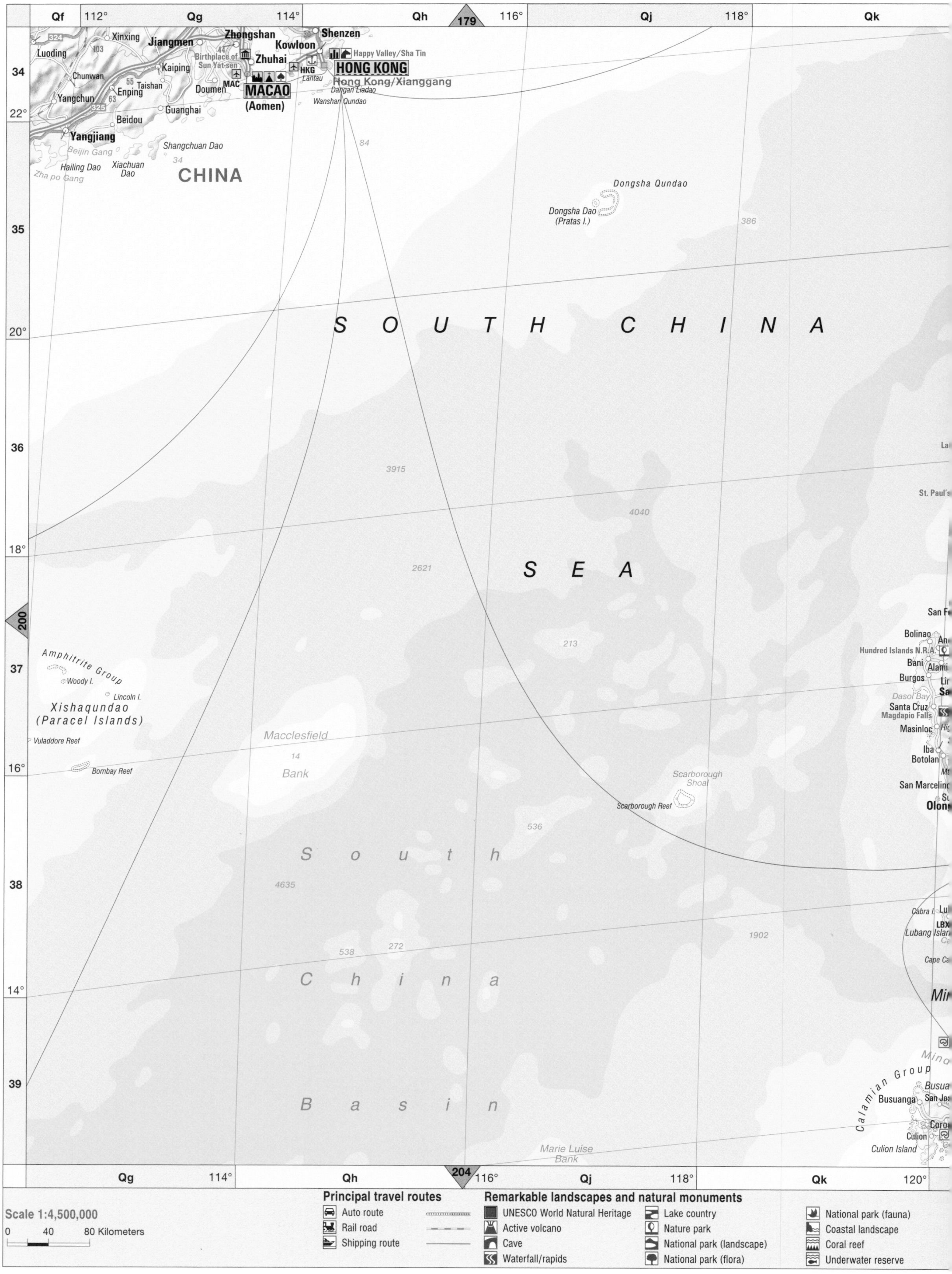

Qf 112° Qg 114° Qh 179 116° Qj 118° Qk

CHINA
Shenzen
Kowloon
Zhongshan
Jiangmen
Zhuhai
HONG KONG
Hong Kong/Xianggang
MACAO
(Aomen)
Yangjiang
Dongsha Qundao
Dongsha Dao (Pratas I.)

S O U T H C H I N A

S E A

Amphitrite Group
Xishaqundao (Paracel Islands)
Macclesfield Bank
Scarborough Shoal

S o u t h C h i n a B a s i n

Calamian Group

Qg 114° Qh 204 116° Qj 118° Qk 120°

Scale 1:4,500,000
0 40 80 Kilometers

Principal travel routes
Auto route
Rail road
Shipping route

Remarkable landscapes and natural monuments
UNESCO World Natural Heritage
Active volcano
Cave
Waterfall/rapids
Lake country
Nature park
National park (landscape)
National park (flora)
National park (fauna)
Coastal landscape
Coral reef
Underwater reserve

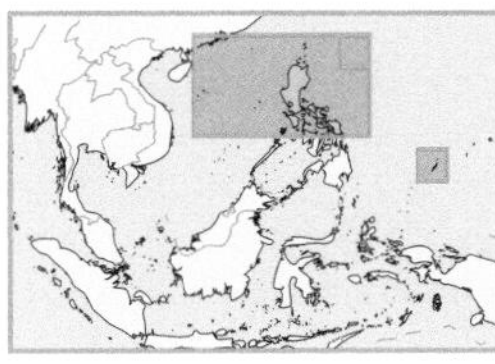

uated along the edges of several tec-
nic plates. Many of the Philippine
ands are mountainous and the coun-
is home to several active volcanoes.
e **Philippines Trench**, located off the
chipelago's eastern coasts, has a maxi-
um depth of 10,830 meters. Both the
cific Trench and the Philippine islands
ere created through the collision of tec-
nic plates in the Earth's crust.
llions of years ago the largest Philippine islands – including Luzon – were connected to mainland Asia by land bridges. After the last ice age, massive glaciers that covered much of the planet's surface began to melt causing the oceans to rise. The land bridges disappeared beneath the sea and the Philippines became a mosaic of several thousand small scattered islands.

Of the 37 volcanoes on the Philippines, 18 are still active including **Mount Pinatubo** (1,600 meters) on the island of Luzon. In 1991, a major eruption of Mount Pinatubo devastated the areas surrounding the volcano.

Luzon is the largest island in the Philippines and encompasses more than a third of the country's total area. The island is home to several powerful rivers that deposit large amounts of rich sediments in their deltas and river valleys. The **Cagayan River**, the longest river on Luzon, has a total length of 354 kilometers. **Laguna de Bay**, the largest lake in the Philippines, is located south of Manila and covers an area of 932 km².

Palau is a small island group on the western edge of Micronesia, a section of the Pacific Ocean. Most of Palau's larger islands are located near a 110-kilometer -long barrier reef. Palau has a tropical climate with warm temperatures throughout the year.

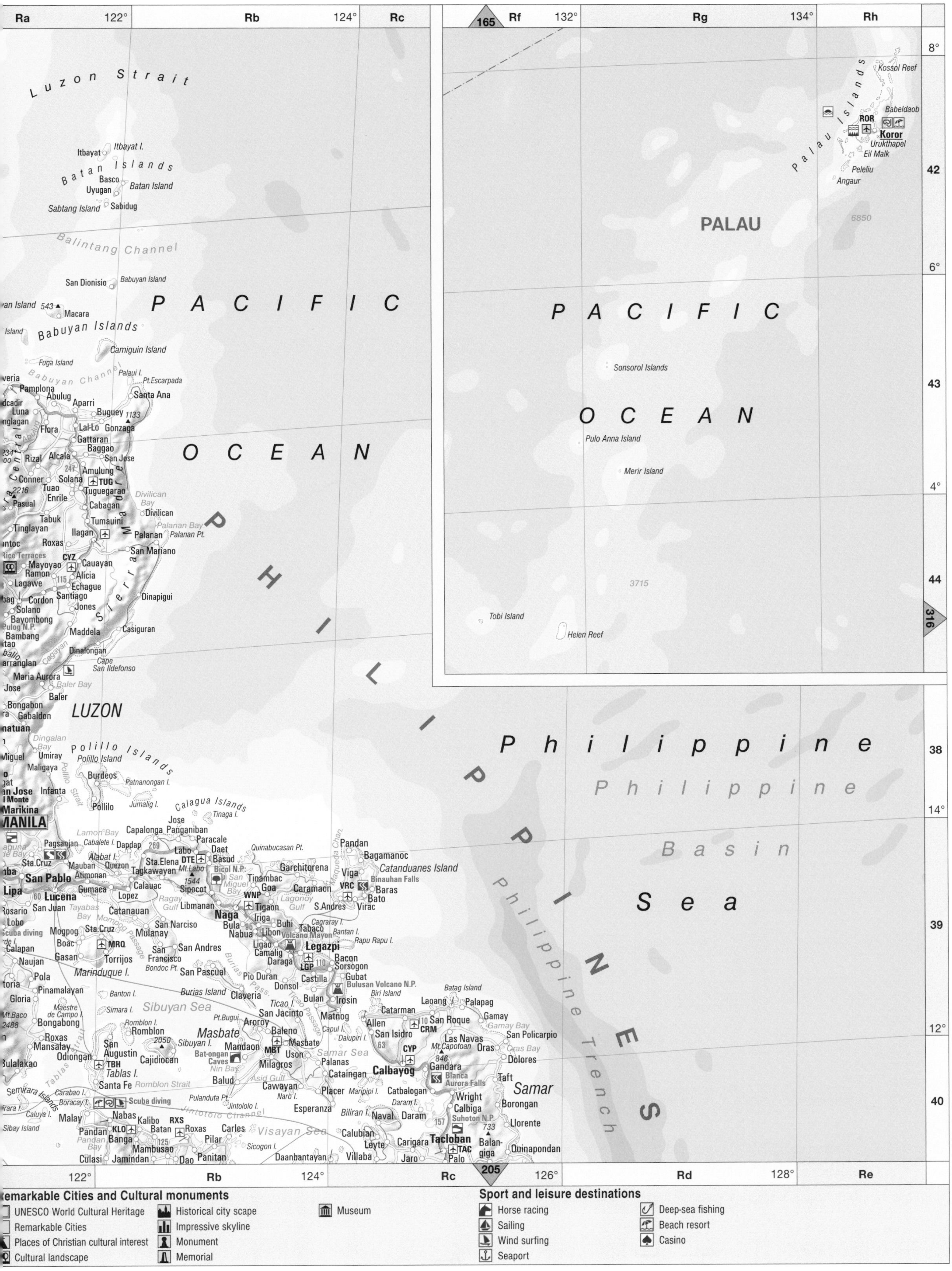

Remarkable Cities and Cultural monuments

- UNESCO World Cultural Heritage
- Remarkable Cities
- Places of Christian cultural interest
- Cultural landscape
- Historical city scape
- Impressive skyline
- Monument
- Memorial
- Museum

Sport and leisure destinations

- Horse racing
- Sailing
- Wind surfing
- Seaport
- Deep-sea fishing
- Beach resort
- Casino

Palau The island group Palau consists of 343 islands around 1,000 kilometers east of the Philippines. Coral atolls (top photo) surrounded by reefs and the Rock Islands (bottom photo) are among Palau's attractions. **Rh42**

Rice Terraces of Ifugao The high terraces in Luzon's highlands are a UNESCO world heritage site. The highest of the narrow terraces, held up by stone and clay walls, rises 1,500 meters. **Ra37**

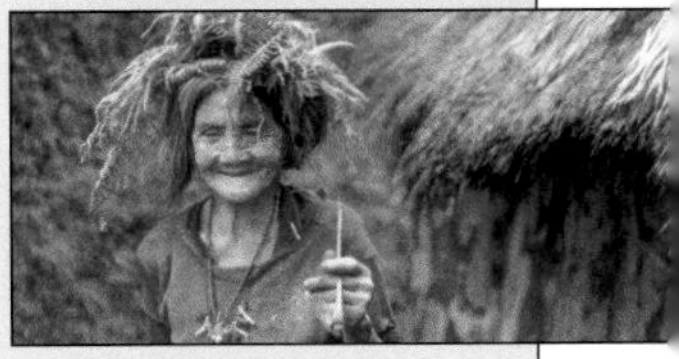

Indigenous People Most Filipinos are ethnic Malays but around twelve percent of the population consist of indigenous people whose ancestors lived on the islands before the Malays arrived. There are around 60 indigenous ethnic groups in the Philippines.

Pagsanjan River near Santa Cruz – deep gorges around Pagsanjan (Magdapio) Falls (photo) **Qk38**

Mount Mayon 2,462 meter tall volcano with a beautiful cone shaped peak – several eruptions in recent centuries **Rb39**

The many islands of the Philippines can be divided into four distinct large island groups. The northernmost group consist of the largest Filipino island Luzon and the islands surrounding it. The **Visayas** group containing the major islands of Cebu and Bohol, is located south of Luzon.

Palawan is located to the west of the other main islands in the Philippines archipelago and is separated from Borneo by a narrow strait. **Mindanao** and the **islands of Sulu** Province are located in the southeastern section of the Philippines.

The **Chocolate Hills**, a major tourist attraction on Bohol, are a series of brown cone shaped hills with average heights of 30 meters. **Negros**, the fourth largest island in the Philippines is situated b tween the islands Cebu and Pana Negros is home to fertile mountainc areas with extensive forests, subter nean caves, and large sugar plantatio The coasts of the island **Panay** cont many of the finest beaches in the Phi pines. Panay also has several importa rice farming areas, including the pla around the city of Iliolio. **Mindanao**, largest island in the southern Philippir

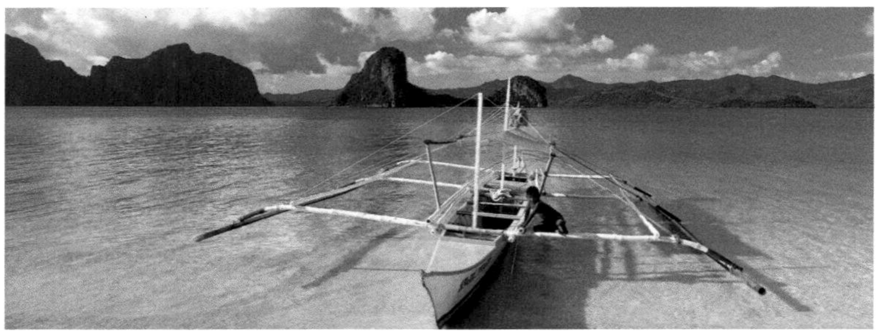

Beautiful El Nido Bay in northern Palawan **Qk40**

Paglugaban Island In the Bacuit archipelago, an island group west of El Nindo – beautiful beaches **Qk40**

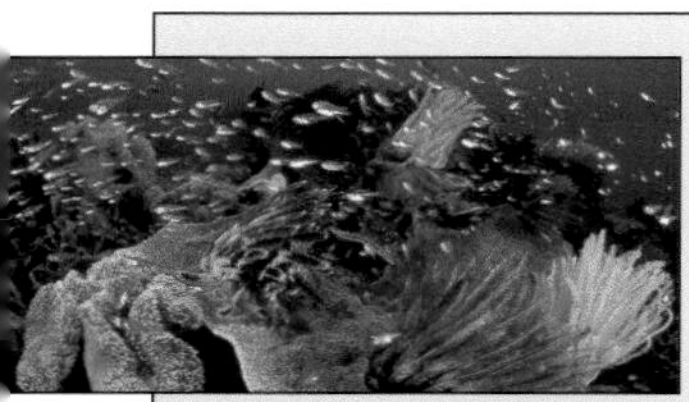

Underwater Biodiversity The waters surrounding the Philipines are home to many unique plants and animals. The Tubbataha reef (top photo) **(Qk41)** contains more than 300 types of coral. Honda Bay, north of Puerto Princesa **(Qk41)** is also home to interesting marine life. Turtle Island Marine Park **(Qj42)** contains sea turtle (bottom photo) breeding sites.

Kinabalu National Park Large rainforests – the world's largest flower – Mount Kinabalu (4,101 meters) **Qj42**

Brunei The small sultanate of Brunei is a wealthy nation with large oil reserves. The capital city Bandar Seri Begawan is home to the Sultan Omar Mosque (top photo) and the large Istana Nurul Imam palace (bottom photo: palace interior). **Qh43**

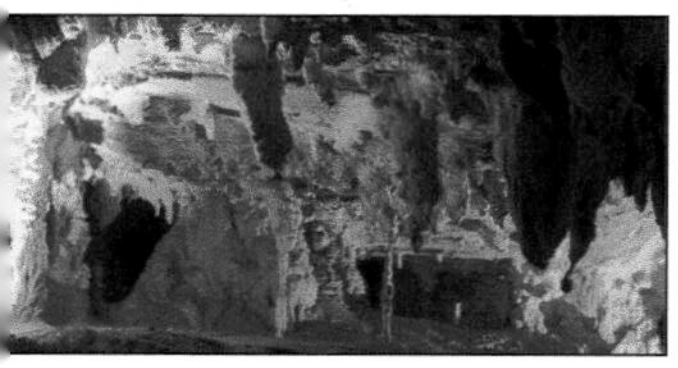

Gunung Mulu National Park Large underground cave systems – Sarawak Chamber is the largest cave chamber – UNESCO world heritage site **Qh43**

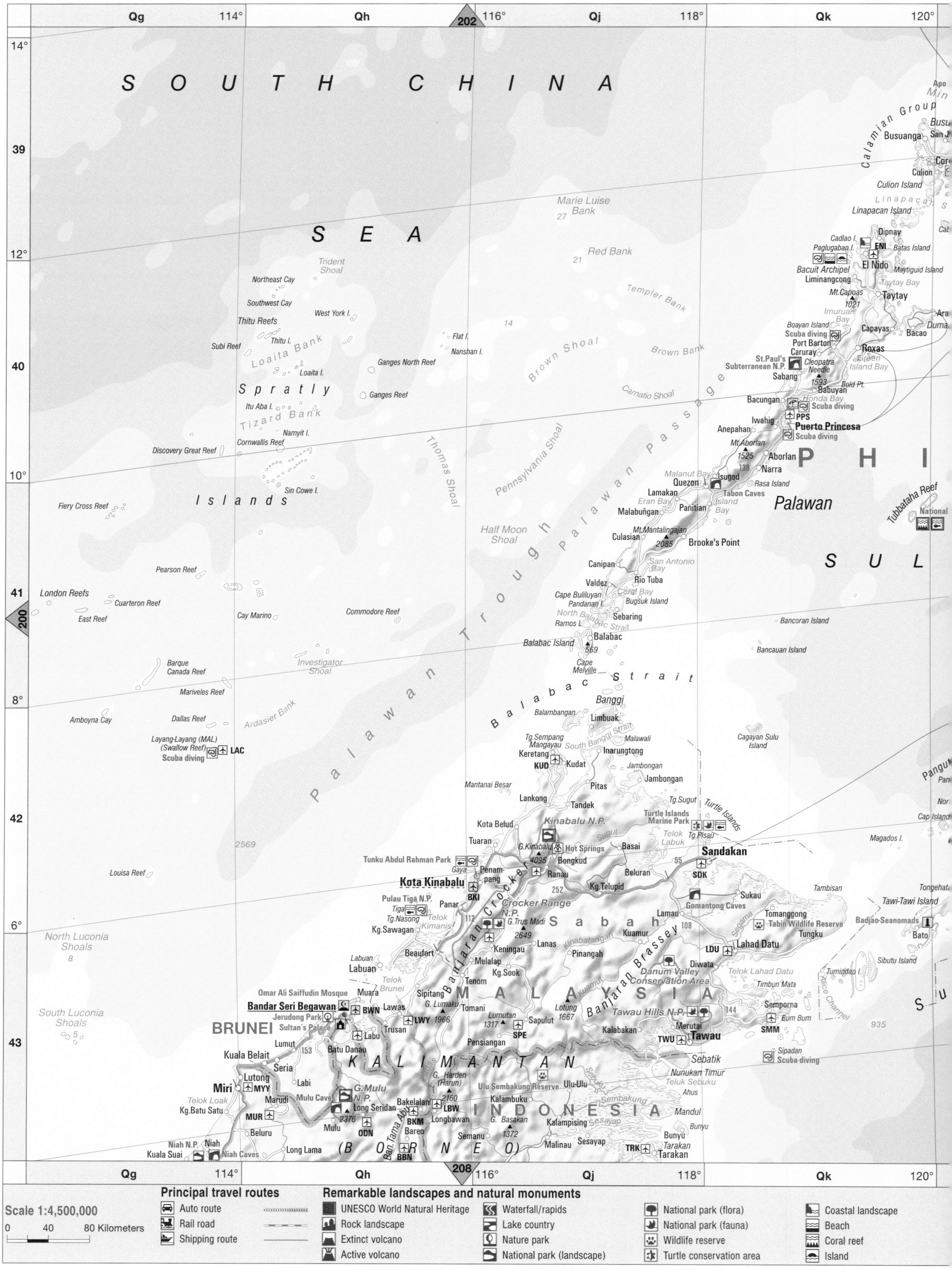

Scale 1:4,500,000
0 40 80 Kilometers

Principal travel routes
- Auto route
- Rail road
- Shipping route

Remarkable landscapes and natural monuments
- UNESCO World Natural Heritage
- Rock landscape
- Extinct volcano
- Active volcano
- Waterfall/rapids
- Lake country
- Nature park
- National park (landscape)
- National park (flora)
- National park (fauna)
- Wildlife reserve
- Turtle conservation area
- Coastal landscape
- Beach
- Coral reef
- Island

separated from the more northern and by the Mindanao Sea. Several ge mountain ranges stretch from north south through the island's interior. e mountains of Mindanao contain the urces of many major rivers that flow rough the island. Because of the large mber of rivers and abundant rainfall Mindanao, severe floods are common the island.

Mount Apo (2,956 meters) is an inactive volcano that has been dormant for several million years. The volcano is the highest point on Mindanao and in the Philippines. Mount Apo is also home to the few remaining Philippine eagles (haribon), one of the largest species of eagles in the world. Palawan is a long island that stretches from north to south between the Sulu Sea and the South China Sea. Before the end of the last ice age, the island was connected to Borneo. Of the more than 1,000 animal species that inhabit the Philippines, 232 are unique to Palawan – including the Philippine mouse deer, the world's smallest hoofed mammals. Palawan is also home to many distinct cultures and indigenous ethnicities including the Batak people, a group of semi-nomadic hunters and gatherers.

The Philippines have a hot tropical climate that is greatly influenced by **monsoon winds**. The dry season occurs between December and May and the rainy season is between June and November. The Malaysian state of Sabah occupies the northern section of the island of **Kalimantan (Borneo)**. Mount Kinabalu rises 4,101 meters and is the tallest mountain in Malaysia. The interior of **Sabah** is dominated by a large plateau and the region's northern coast is broken by many bays and inlets.

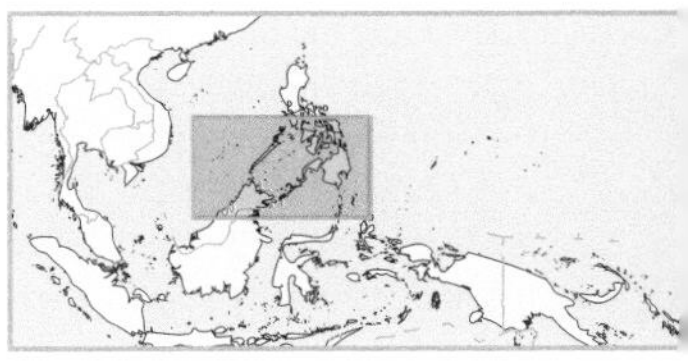

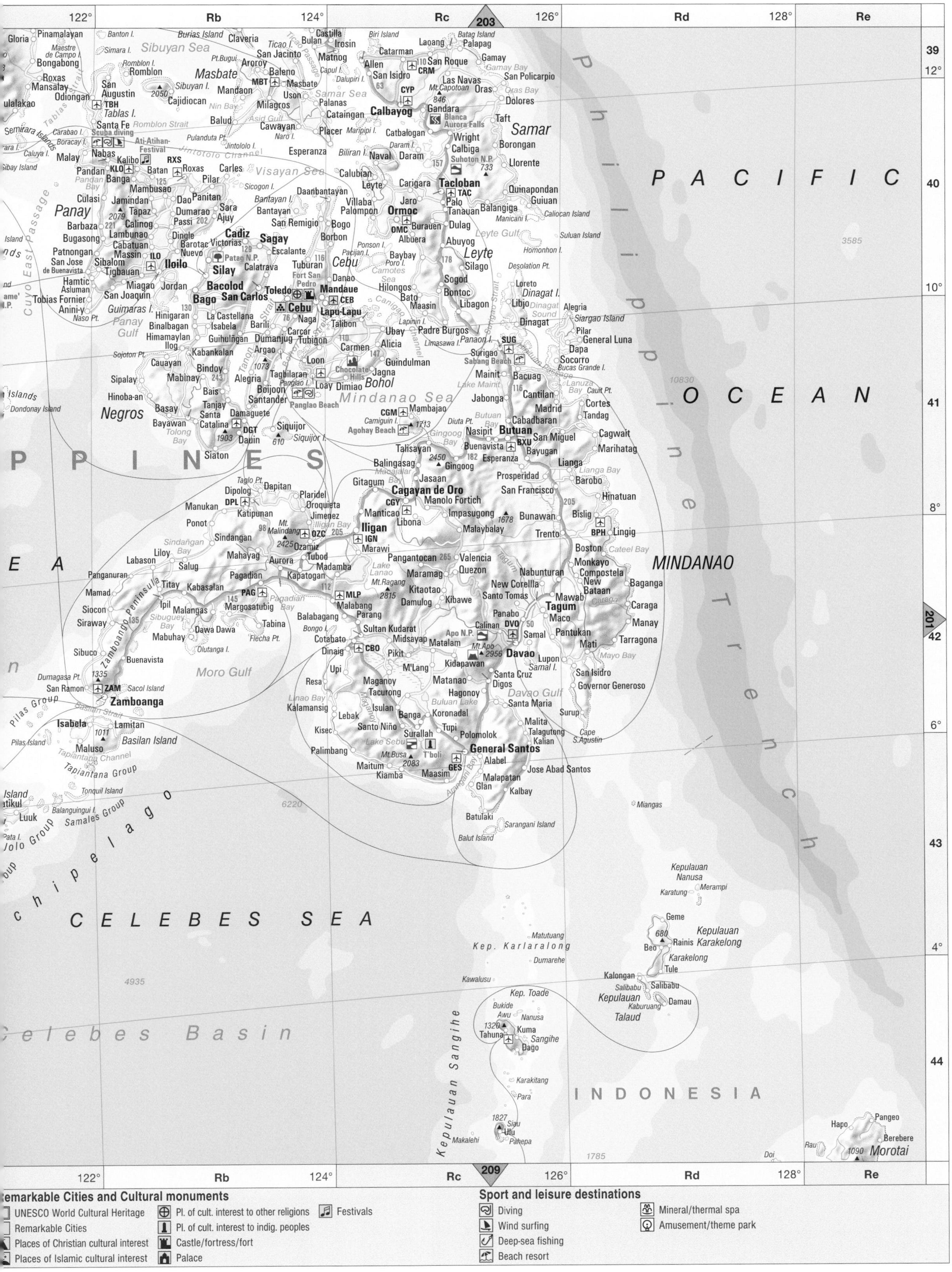

Remarkable Cities and Cultural monuments
- UNESCO World Cultural Heritage
- Remarkable Cities
- Places of Christian cultural interest
- Places of Islamic cultural interest
- Pl. of cult. interest to other religions
- Pl. of cult. interest to indig. peoples
- Castle/fortress/fort
- Palace
- Festivals

Sport and leisure destinations
- Diving
- Wind surfing
- Deep-sea fishing
- Beach resort
- Mineral/thermal spa
- Amusement/theme park

Cebu The Philippine island's attractions include Fort San Pedro, Carbon market (bottom photo), and the beautiful Taoist temple (top photo) near Cebu City. **Rb40**

Chocolate Hills Unique hills on the island of Bohol (Philippines) – 1,268 grass covered cone-shaped mounds surrounded by lush forests **Rc41**

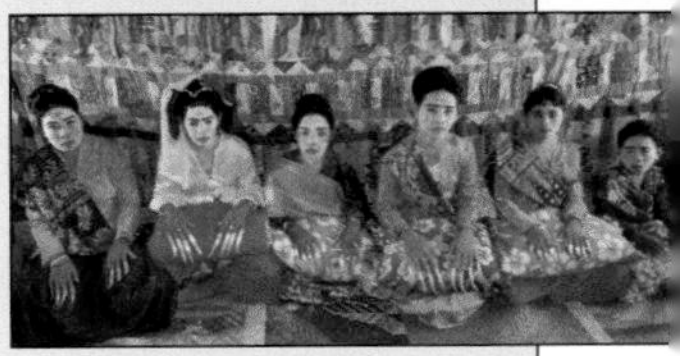

Coastal Nomads The Badjao (bottom photo) are one of several ethnic groups that inhabit the bays and coastal areas of the Philipines. Often called "sea gypsies," the Badjao live on the sea in long floating structures called lipa. Some of the nomadic coastal people have settled in permanent communities consisting of stilt houses (top photo) built atop sand banks or in shallow water. **Qk43**

Ati Atihan Festival Large festival in Kalibo – last three days in January – most famous festival in the Philipines **Rb40**

Mindanao Second largest Philippine island – capital city Davao – Lake Sebu (photo) – home to many distinct indigenous cultures **Rb-Rd41/42**

The Republic of Indonesia consists of more than 15,000 islands and islets of varying size. The vast archipelago stretches a distance of more than 5,100 kilometers from Sumatra in the west to Irian Jaya in Indonesia's far east. **Sumatra** is one of the larger Indonesian islands with a total area of 473,000 km². The eastern section of Sumatra is covered by heavily forested swampy plains, while the center and west of the island are domi-

nated by the **Barisan Mountair** Sumatra is home to ten active volc noes including Kerinci (3,800 meters) a numerous lakes including Toba La (1,700 km²), the largest lake in Southea Asia. Almost the entire southweste coast of Sumatra is covered by the Ba san Mountains and their foothills.

Rice fields and rainforests in Sumatra interior

Lake Toba The island Samosir in the middle of the lake is home to the Toba Batak people (bottom photo). The Toba have their own unique architecture (top photo). **Pk44**

Lake Maninjau One of Sumatra's most beautiful crater lakes – surrounded by thick forests **Qa46**

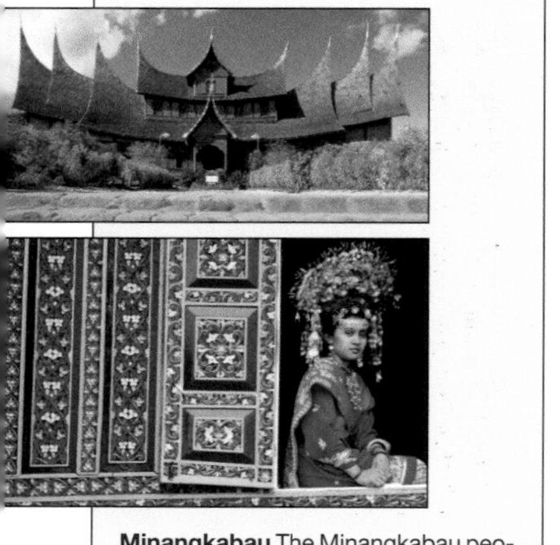

Minangkabau The Minangkabau people live around Bukittinggi and are famous for their distinctive and beautiful architecture (top photo). Their traditional culture is matriarchal. Land and property are owned and inherited by women. **Qa46**

Nias Island The indigenous people (top photo) of Nias arrived on the island before the Malays settled in Indonesia. Before 1900, the inhabitants created many large stone altars and statues (bottom photo). **Pj45**

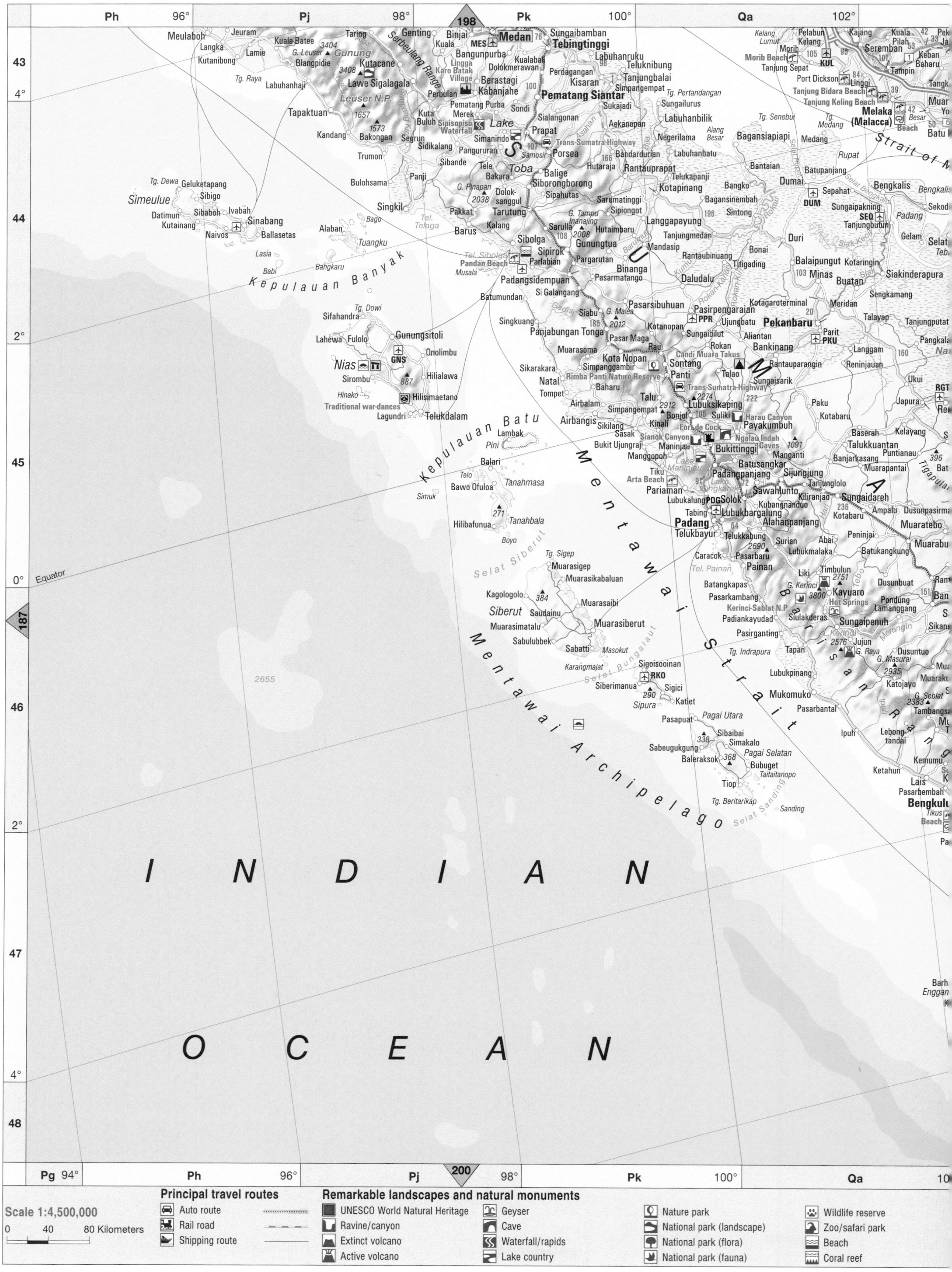

INDIAN OCEAN

Scale 1:4,500,000

0 40 80 Kilometers

Principal travel routes
- Auto route
- Rail road
- Shipping route

Remarkable landscapes and natural monuments
- UNESCO World Natural Heritage
- Ravine/canyon
- Extinct volcano
- Active volcano
- Geyser
- Cave
- Waterfall/rapids
- Lake country
- Nature park
- National park (landscape)
- National park (flora)
- National park (fauna)
- Wildlife reserve
- Zoo/safari park
- Beach
- Coral reef

ıny of Sumatra's mountainous regions home to dense tropical rainforests ıt grow at elevations below 1,000 ıters. Moss covered cloud forests are ımmon in mountainous areas above)00 meters. The rainforests of Sumatra ɔw in areas with hot humid climates and ıtain an incredible abundance of flora d fauna.
chain of small and medium sized ands is located just off the western coast of Sumatra. **Nias**, the largest island in the chain, is home to historic stone altars, traditional architecture, and a distinctive local culture.
With a population of more than two million, **Medan** is the largest city on Sumatra and the island's main economic center. Medan's city hall and main train station were built during the colonial period when the Dutch ruled Indonesia.
The section of Sumatra's eastern coast between Medan and Palembang is covered by mangrove forests. The **Trans Sumatra Highway**, completed in the 1980s, runs between Medan and the southern tip of Sumatra. Eastern Sumatra's plains are crossed by numerous rivers and small streams.
Sumatra produces many of Indonesia's most important exports – including oil, natural gas, rubber, cinnamon, coffee, tea, and tobacco.
The Strait of Malacca is a body of water with a width of just 67 kilometers at its narrowest section. It separates Sumatra from Peninsular **Malaysia** and **Singapore**, an island nation with the busiest port in Asia.
The densely populated island **Java** is located southeast of Sumatra on the opposite side of the Sundra Strait. **Borneo** is separated from Sumatra by the Karimata Strait.

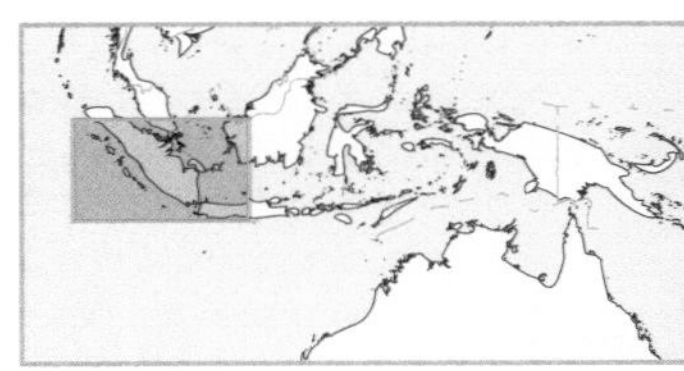

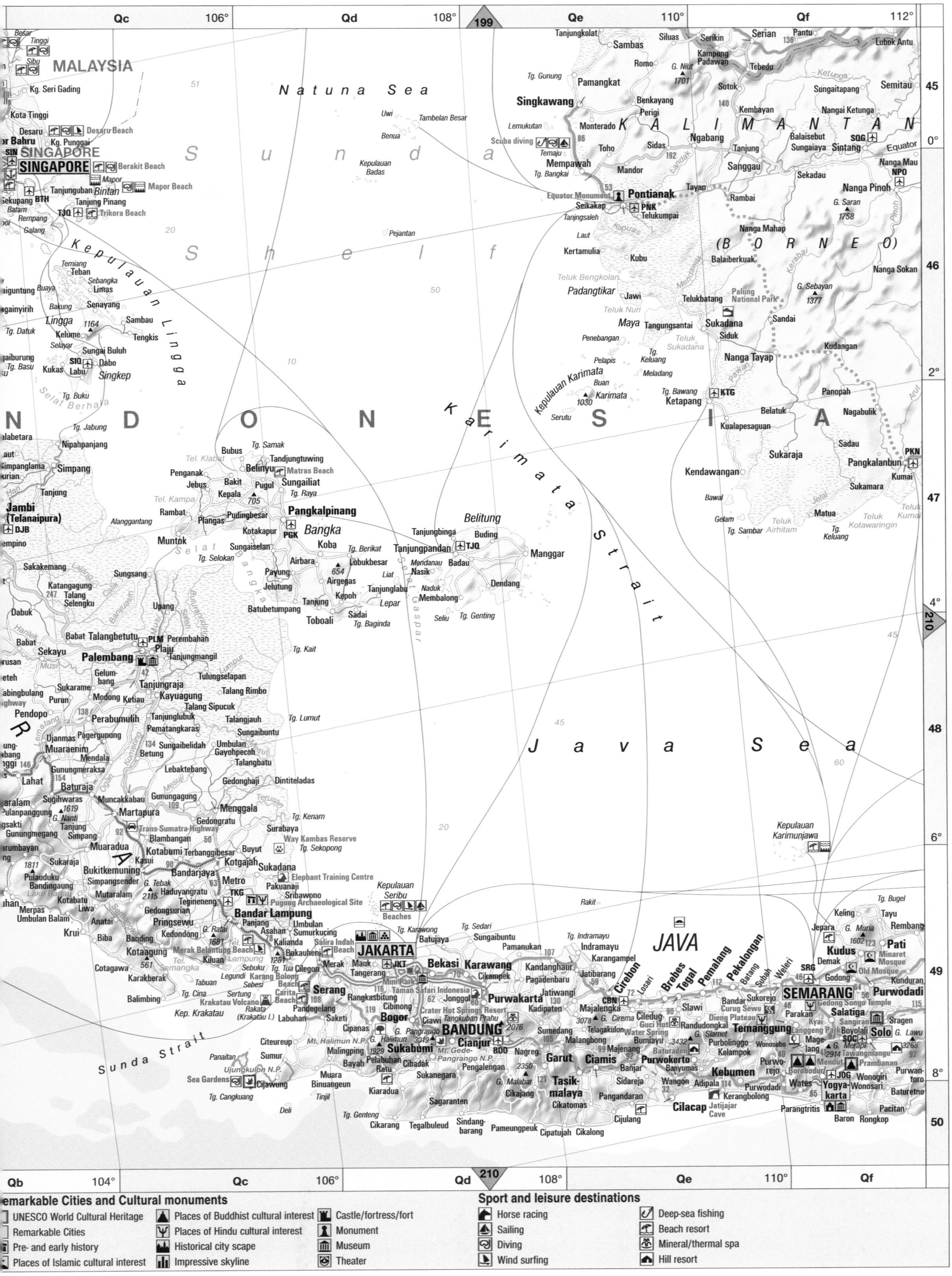

Sianok Canyon The walls of this steep canyon are 100 meters high – lush vegetation – suspension bridge **Qa46**

Gunung Kerinci 3,800-meter-high volcano in the Barisan range – eruption in 1982 – Kerinci Seblat National Park **Qa46**

Kerinci Seblat National Park The park features tropical plains, large mountain rainforests, and cloud forests. The park is home to many interesting animals including large numbers of macaques (top photo). Sumatran tigers (bottom photo) inhabit the coastal forests and highlands of the park. **Qa46**

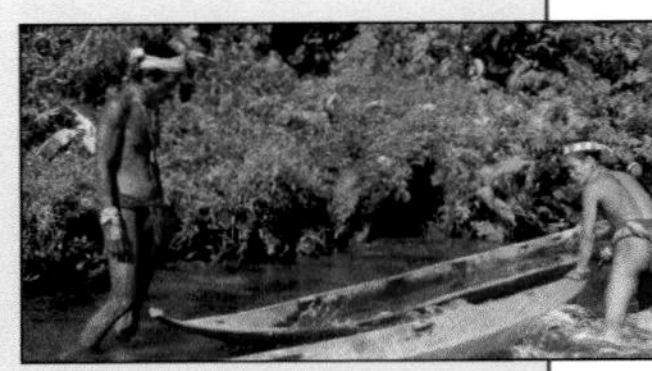

Mentawai Island Siberut is the largest island in this group off the western coast of Sumatra. The islands are home to many endemic plant and animal species. The origin of the indigenous Mentawai people (photo) is unknown. Their culture, language, and appearance differ from those of the peoples on neighboring islands. **PkQa46/47**

Palembang The largest city in southern Sumatra – oil refineries – traditional houseboats – Balaputra Museum – historic Dutch colonial fortress **Qc47**

emarkable Cities and Cultural monuments

- UNESCO World Cultural Heritage
- Remarkable Cities
- Pre- and early history
- Places of Islamic cultural interest
- Places of Buddhist cultural interest
- Places of Hindu cultural interest
- Historical city scape
- Impressive skyline
- Castle/fortress/fort
- Monument
- Museum
- Theater

Sport and leisure destinations

- Horse racing
- Sailing
- Diving
- Wind surfing
- Deep-sea fishing
- Beach resort
- Mineral/thermal spa
- Hill resort

Kalimantan (Borneo) and Sulawesi together with Java and Sumatra form the **Greater Sunda Islands**, an island group in the large Indonesian archipelago. Because of their locations near the equator all of these islands have hot tropical climates with high humidity and warm temperatures throughout the year.

Indonesia shares Borneo, the world's third largest island, with two other nations. Most of northern Borneo is occupied by two Malaysian states and t small nation Brunei. The two Malays states, **Sarawak** and **Sabah** are c vered by tropical rain forests with lu vegetation and interesting wildlife.

Brunei was once the center of a large a powerful empire that ruled over large se tions of Borneo and the Philippin

Kuching, the capital of Sarawak, is situated on the Sarawak River **Qf**

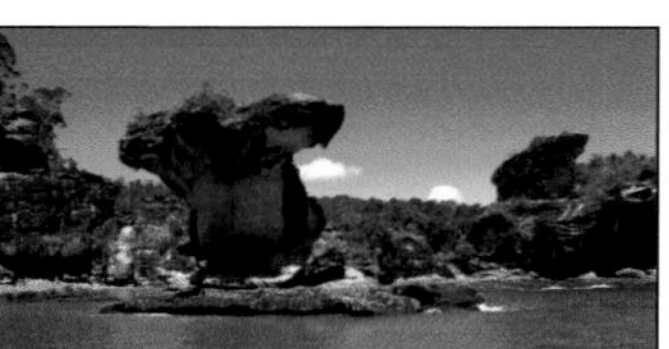

Bako National Park Lush tropical vegetation – hornbills and gibbons – interesting stone formations (photo) **Qf45**

Uma Daro The village consists of buildings constructed on stilts along the Rajang River, the longest river (560 kilometers) in Sarawak – only accessible by boat **Qf44**

National Parks of Kalimantan The tropical rainforests in Tanjung Putting National Park **(Qg47)** are home to rare birds (top photo) and orangutans (middle photo). Palung National Park encompasses mangrove forests, swamps, plains, mountain forests, and the habitats of colorful hornbills (bottom photo; **Qf46**).

Banjarmasin Important port city on the Barito River in southern Kalimantan – canals and streams – floating market – large main mosque **Qh47**

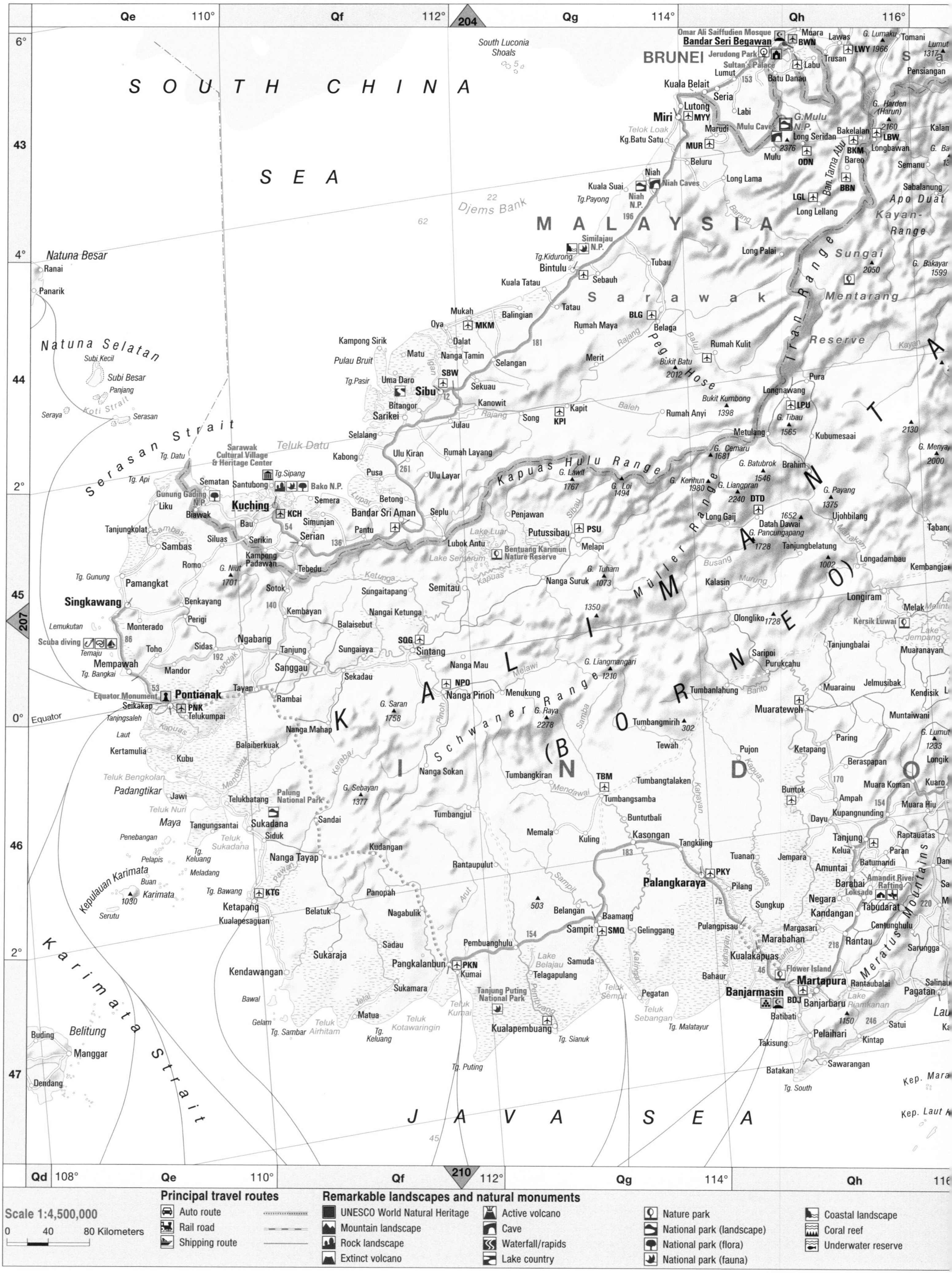

Scale 1:4,500,000

0 40 80 Kilometers

Principal travel routes

- Auto route
- Rail road
- Shipping route

Remarkable landscapes and natural monuments

- UNESCO World Natural Heritage
- Mountain landscape
- Rock landscape
- Extinct volcano
- Active volcano
- Cave
- Waterfall/rapids
- Lake country
- Nature park
- National park (landscape)
- National park (flora)
- National park (fauna)
- Coastal landscape
- Coral reef
- Underwater reserve

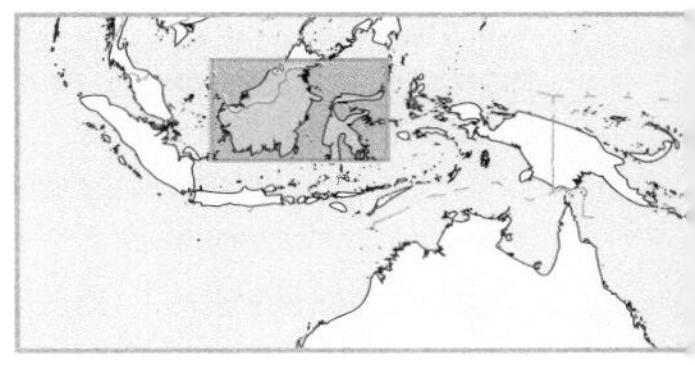

›day the country is a small sultanate ›th an impressive wealth of oil and natur- gas reserves.
›e Indonesia section of Borneo is ›lled **Kalimantan** and covers most of ›e island. Borneo's interior is dominat- › by highlands which border large ›ampy plains that cover the south and ›astal areas of the island. These plains ›e crossed by many streams and large rivers. The large oil deposits on Borneo and the logging industry dominate the economy of Kalimantan. Indonesian and foreign concerns operate oil drilling sites and oil refineries along the eastern coast of the island around the cities Tarakan, Bontang, and Balkpapan.
Kalimantan is a sparsely populated region. The majority of its 12.3 million inhabitants are concentrated in cities and towns along the coast. In the western section of Kalimantan, the population consists mostly of Malays and ethnic Chinese. The majority of the population in Kalimantan's interior consists of **Dayaks** – a term encompassing hundreds of distinct indigenous tribes. The ancestors of the Dayaks first settled Borneo more than 2,000 years ago.
The island of **Sulawesi** has a distinctive shape, consisting of four long arms of land extending out from the center of the island. The "arms" of the island consist of mountainous areas and volcanic massifs. The coastal areas of Sulawesi are the traditional homelands of the several indigenous ethnic groups with distinct cultures, including the **Makassar people**. The **Toraja people** are well known for their elaborate funerals and burial practices. The ancestors of many indigenous coastal people on Sulawesi came to the island from the Asian mainland thousands of years ago.

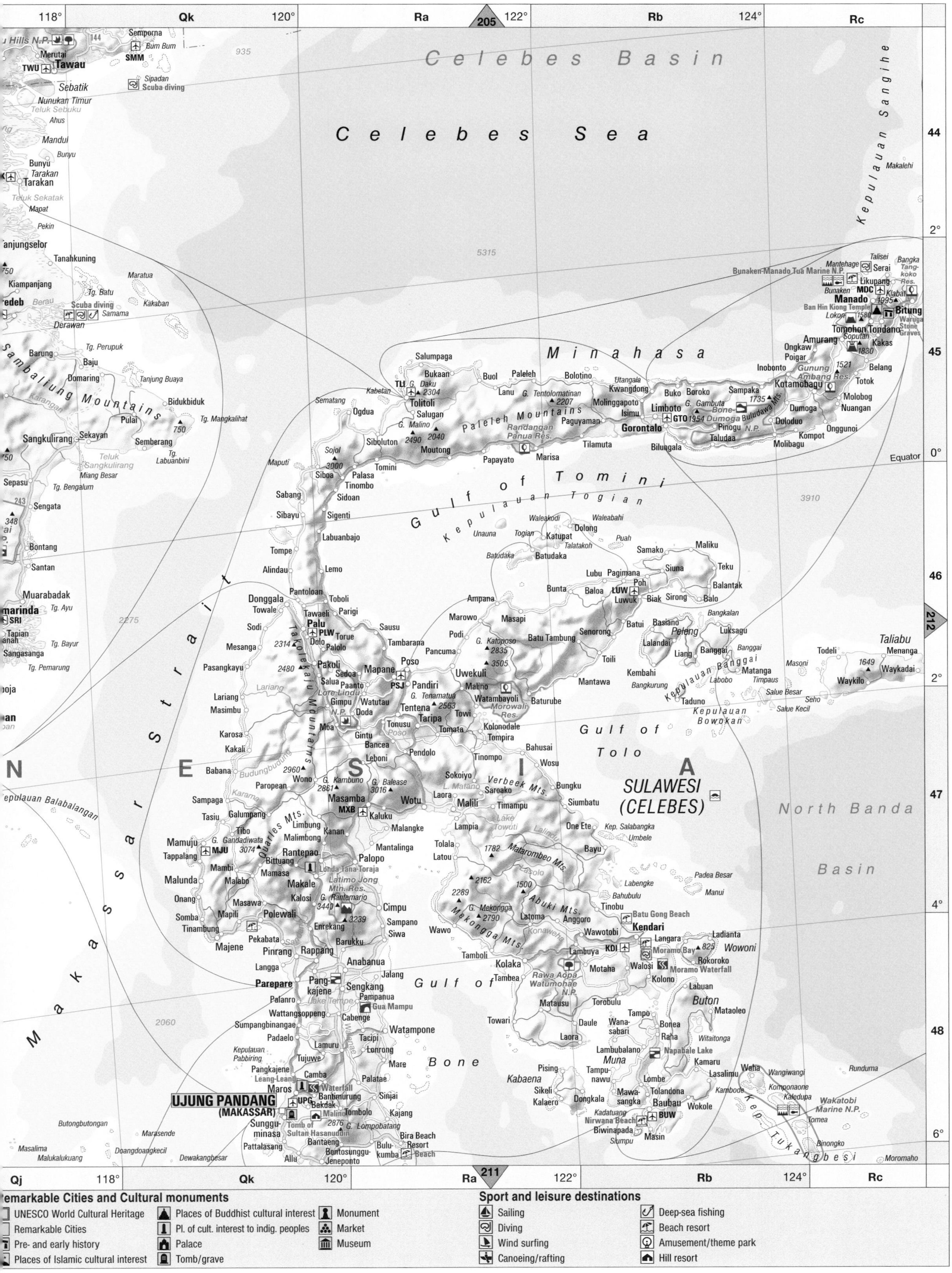

Celebes Sea · Celebes Basin · Gulf of Tomini · Gulf of Tolo · Gulf of Bone · Makassar Strait · North Banda Basin · SULAWESI (CELEBES) · UJUNG PANDANG (MAKASSAR)

Bunaken Marine National Park Extensive coral reefs (photo) – abundant marine life – good diving sites **Rc45**

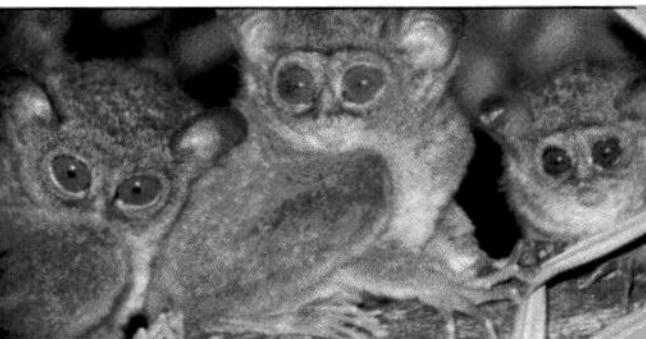

Dumoga Bone National Park Home to abundant flora and fauna including Borneo tarsiers – pristine jungle wilderness in Minahasa **Rb45**

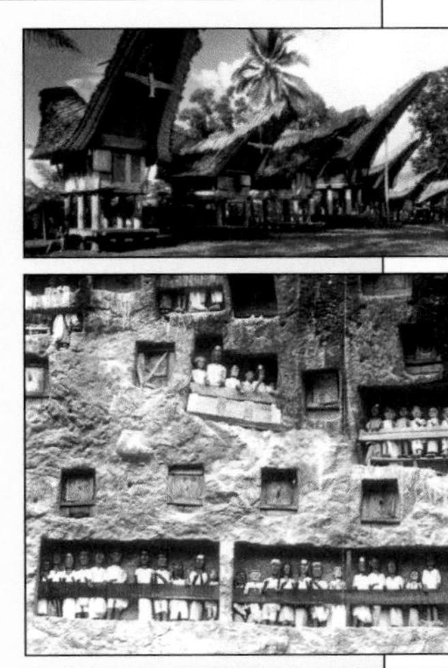

The Toraja This ethnic group lives in central Sulawesi and around the Gulf of Tomini. Death is very important in Toraja culture. The Toraja devote much of their time to organizing elaborate burial ceremonies and "death festivals." Photos from top to bottom: traditional homes, burial site with figures, sacred stones **Qk47**

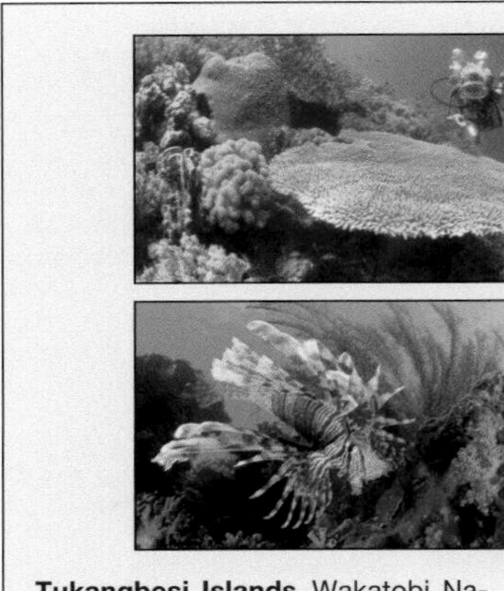

Tukangbesi Islands Wakatobi National Park, southeast of Sulawesi, contains delicate underwater ecosystems with large coral reefs and abundant marine life. **RbRc48**

Remarkable Cities and Cultural monuments

UNESCO World Cultural Heritage · Remarkable Cities · Pre- and early history · Places of Islamic cultural interest · Places of Buddhist cultural interest · Pl. of cult. interest to indig. peoples · Palace · Tomb/grave · Monument · Market · Museum

Sport and leisure destinations

Sailing · Diving · Wind surfing · Canoeing/rafting · Deep-sea fishing · Beach resort · Amusement/theme park · Hill resort

Like neighboring Sumatra, Java and the Lesser Sunda Islands are located on the southwestern edge of the Eurasian tectonic plate. The southern coasts of Java of the Lesser Sunda Islands border deep underwater trenches in the Indian Ocean while the northern coasts of these islands border the relatively shallow Java Sea. After the end of the last ice age around 10,000 years ago, the **Sunda continental shelf** was flooded by the rising seas

and Indonesia, the world's largest arc pelago was formed. The archipela encompasses more than 15,000 islan and islets.

The large number of **volcanoes** loc ted on the islands of **Indonesia** is e dence of the archipelago's location in t collision zone of two tectonic plates.

Bromo Semeru mountain massif in eastern Java **Qg**

Jakarta Capital and largest city of Indonesia – National Museum – fish market – historic Batavia district – Sunda Kelapa harbor – Ancol amusement park **Qd49**

Mount Gede Active volcano (2,958 meters) in Mount Gede Pangrango National Park – rare flora **Qd49**

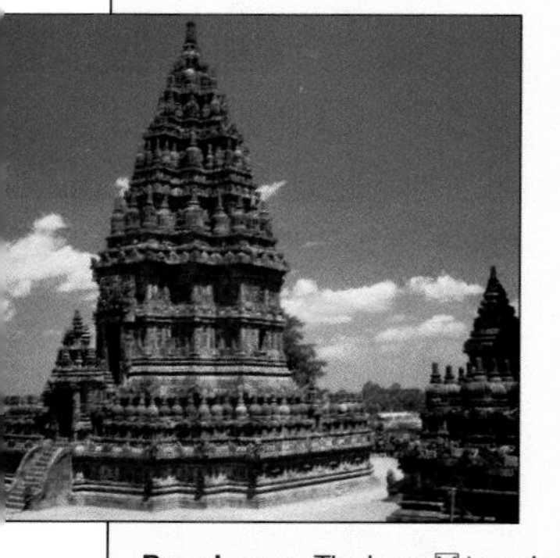

Prambanan The large temple complex, built towards the end of the 9th century, is the largest Hindu holy site in Indonesia. The complex encompasses 190 buildings including eight large temples. The 47 meter tall main temple is dedicated to Shiva and the complex is a UNESCO world heritage site. **Qf49**

Borobodur One of the largest Buddhist temples in Southeast Asia – built in the 9th century by the Sailendra dynasty – UNESCO world heritage site **Qf49**

Yogyakarta Sultanate in Indonesia, founded in the 17th century – Sultan's Palace with the central mosque – bird market – Sono Budoyo Museum **Qf49**

Krakatau Site of several major eruptions in recent centuries – new volcanic island formed in 1928 **Qc49**

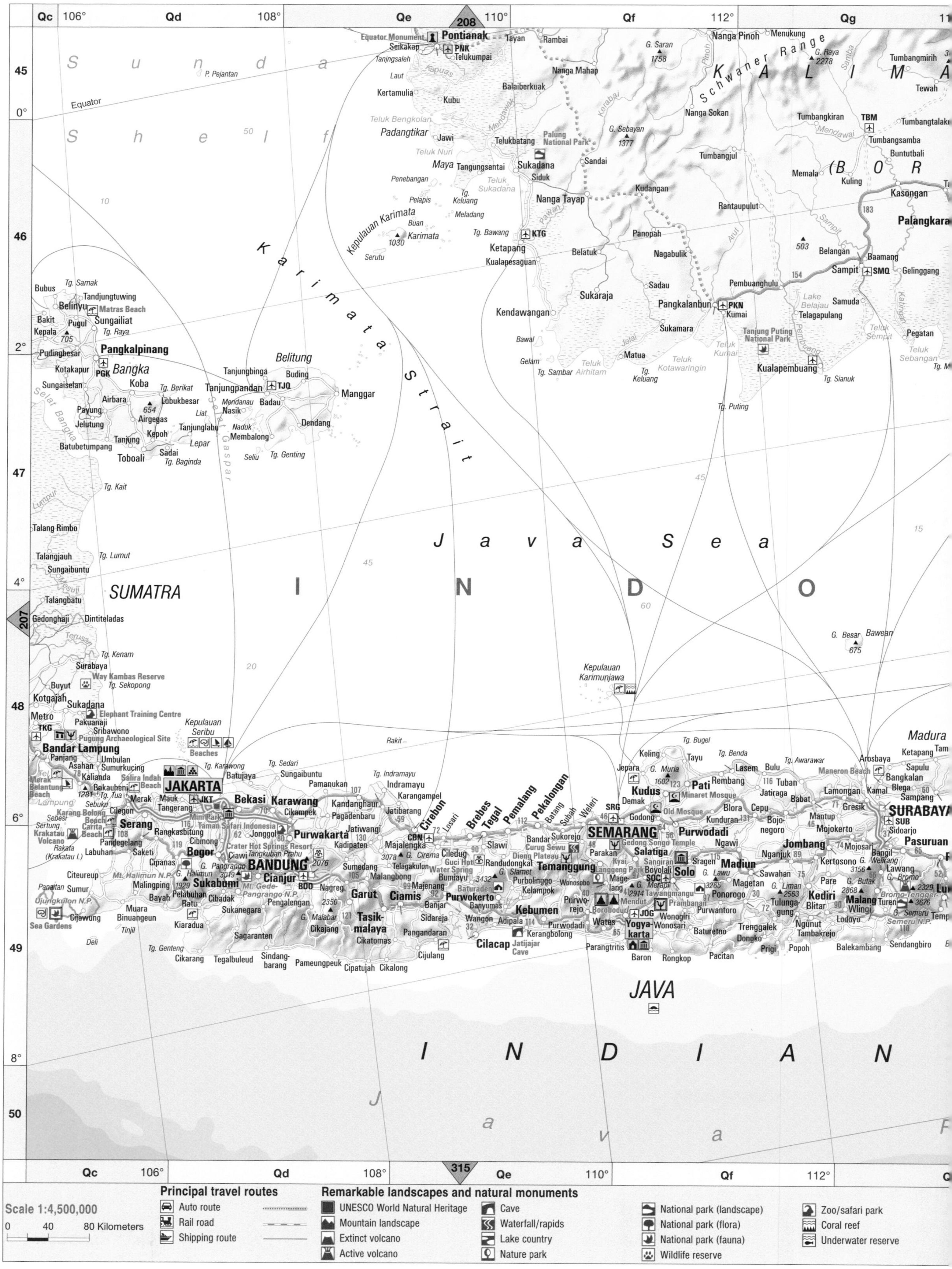

Scale 1:4,500,000

0 40 80 Kilometers

Principal travel routes

- Auto route
- Rail road
- Shipping route

Remarkable landscapes and natural monuments

- UNESCO World Natural Heritage
- Mountain landscape
- Extinct volcano
- Active volcano
- Cave
- Waterfall/rapids
- Lake country
- Nature park
- National park (landscape)
- National park (flora)
- National park (fauna)
- Wildlife reserve
- Zoo/safari park
- Coral reef
- Underwater reserve

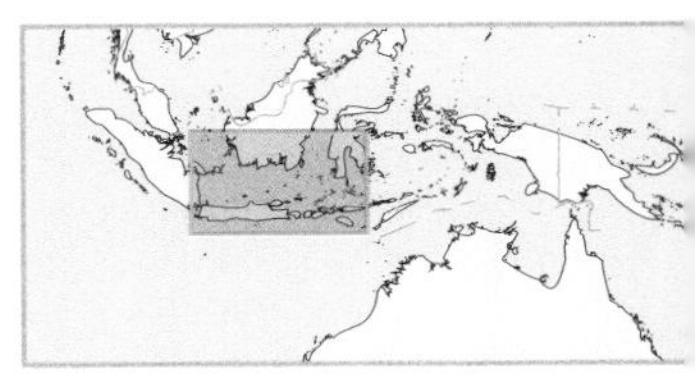

ng belt of volcanoes stretches through eninsular Malaysia, Sumatra, Java and ali. This volcanic belt also stretches east o the Lesser Sunda Islands and the and of Sulawesi. Around 76 of the vol-anoes in Indonesia have been active in cent centuries and Java alone contains 5 active volcanoes including Mount emuru (3,676 meters). The volcano rakatoa, off the west coast of Java, as the site of a major eruption in 1883.

The fertile plains and foothills on the island of **Java** are used primarily for rice farming. Rice has been the staple food throughout most of Indonesia for many centuries and the rice trade financed the construction of several historic temples including the Buddhist **Borobudur** temple and the Hindu temple complex **Prambanan**. Both of these temples have been designated world heritage sites by UNESCO because of their historic architecture. Java is one of the most densely populated regions in the world. At least two-thirds of Indonesia's 200 million inhabitants live on the island. Archeological sites suggest that Java was also one of the earliest sites of human settlement in Asia.

The island of **Bali**, like neighboring Java, is dominated by volcanic mountain chains. Bali is the only majority Hindu region in Indonesia, the world's most populous majority Muslim nation. The island's culture, architecture, and beautiful landscapes attract many tourists from around the world. The indigenous Sassaks form the majority of the island of **Lombok's** population. Most Sassaks practice a religion indigenous to Lombok called Wetu Tulu. Komodo, one of the smaller Lesser Sunda islands is home to the fascinating Komodo Dragons, the largest lizards in the world.

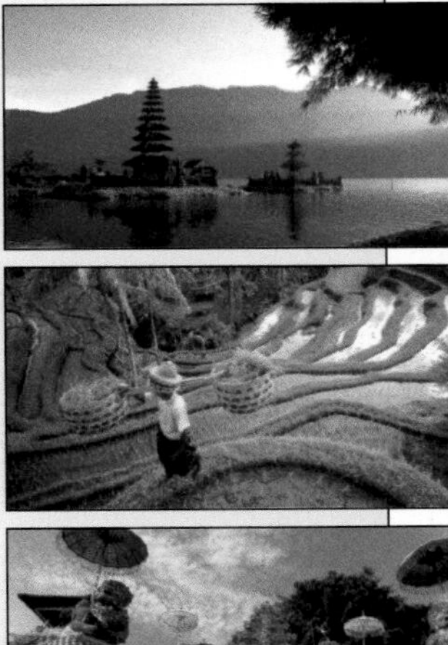

Bali The Hindu enclave in predominantly Muslim Indonesia is home to unique local cultures and religious practices. Pura Ulun Danu (top photo), in the middle of Lake Bratan, is dedicated to Shiva and Vishnu. Pura Kehen (bottom photo) is one of the six holiest temples on Bali. The island's rural areas are home to many beautiful rice terraces (middle photo). **Qh50**

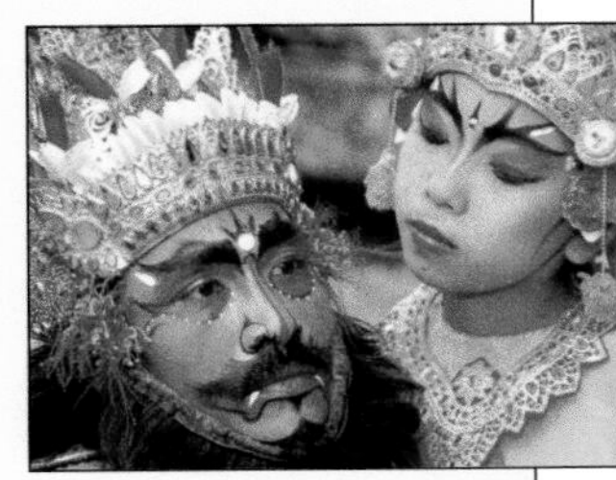

Kecak Dance The "monkey dance" is one of the most fascinating traditional Balinese dances. It is performed with more than 100 actors. The actors sit around a stage where stories of the Ramayana myth are performed. Most of the actor's potray soldiers in the moneky army of the general Hanuman.

Sumba Island (11,080 km²) in the Lesser Sunda group – traditional grass covered buildings – ancient stone megaliths scattered around the island – burial sites with large stone animal and human figures (photo) **QkRa49/50**

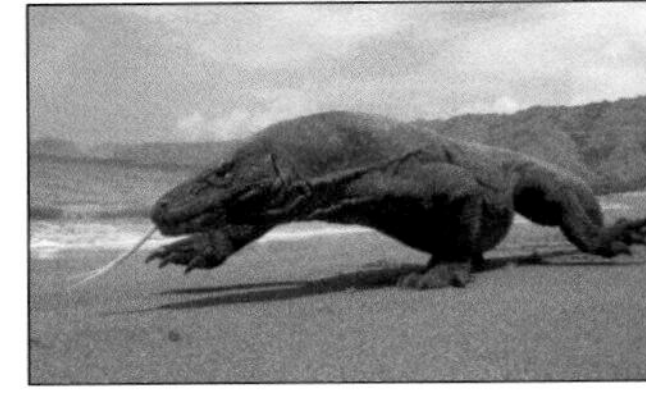

Komodo Lesser Sunda Islands – national park, a UNESCO world heritage site – home of the Komodo Dragons (photo), the largest lizards in the world **Qk49**

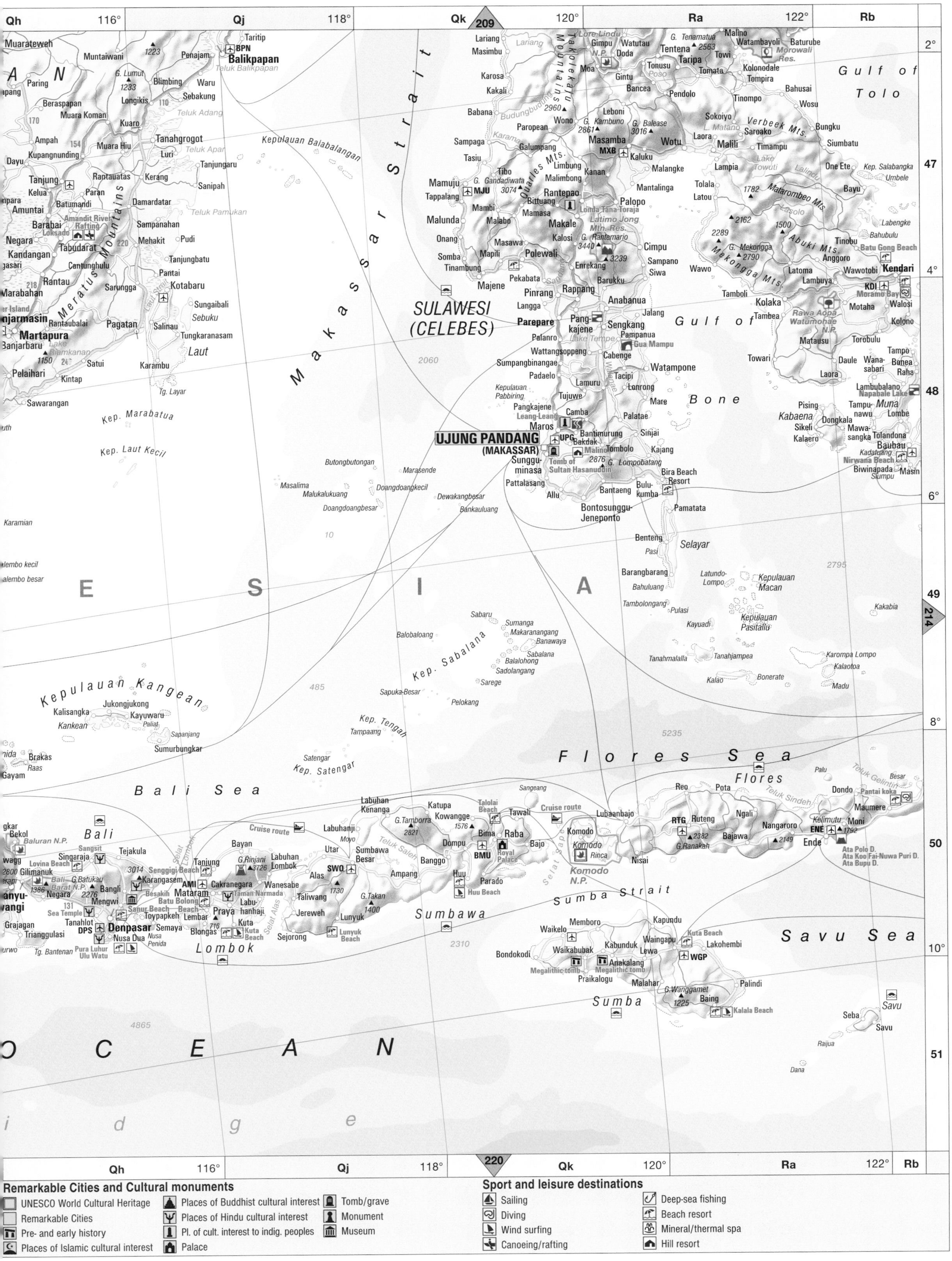

Remarkable Cities and Cultural monuments

- UNESCO World Cultural Heritage
- Remarkable Cities
- Pre- and early history
- Places of Islamic cultural interest
- Places of Buddhist cultural interest
- Places of Hindu cultural interest
- Pl. of cult. interest to indig. peoples
- Palace
- Tomb/grave
- Monument
- Museum

Sport and leisure destinations

- Sailing
- Diving
- Wind surfing
- Canoeing/rafting
- Deep-sea fishing
- Beach resort
- Mineral/thermal spa
- Hill resort

Molucca Islands, New Guinea

The Moluccas island group was once known throughout the world as the **Spice Islands**. The island group, called Maluku in Indoniesian, is situated on both sides of the equator – between Sulawesi to the northwest and Irian Jaya (Papua) to the southeast – in one of the most geologically active regions on the planet. Like the rest of Indonesia, the Moluccas were once part of vast subcontinent that connected Australia and Southeast Asia.

Millions of years ago, rising seas su merged the low lying areas of this su continent.

The **Moluccas** comprise more than 1,0 islands and form two Indonesian provi ces: Maluku and Maluku Utara. The pr duction of spices such as saffron, ging and coriander dominated the island

Palm trees and beautiful beaches are abundant in the Moluccas **Rd**

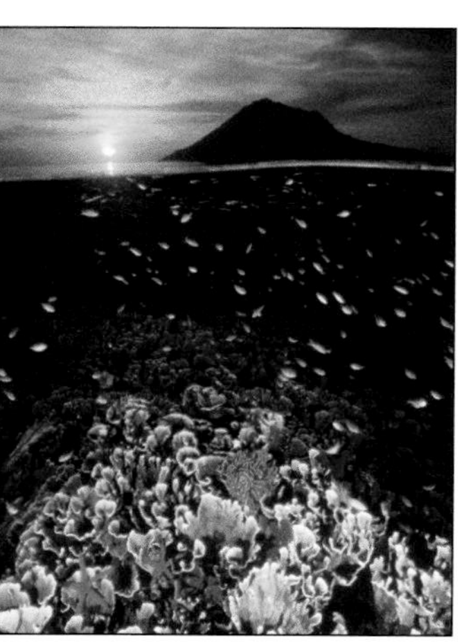

Manado Important port city and capital of North Sulawesi – fascinating coral reefs in Tua Marine National Park on the island Bunaken (photo) **Rc45**

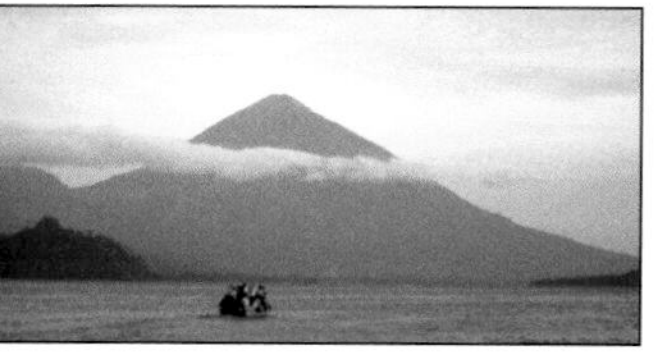

Ternate Circle shaped island – historic Dutch fort, built in 1511 – administrative center of Maluka Utara (Northern Moluccas) – Gamalama (photo) **Rd45**

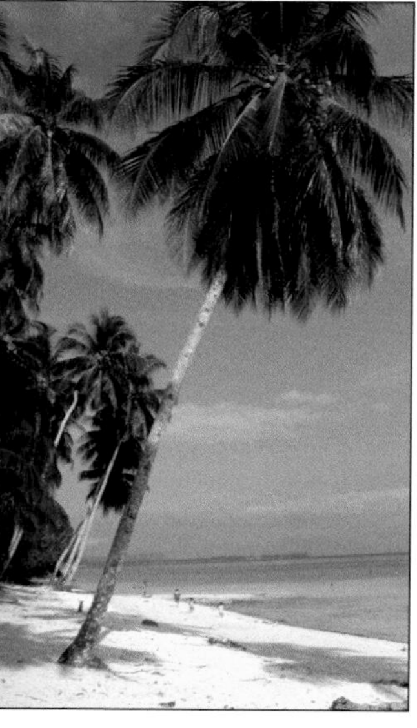

Biak population 70,000 – nature reserves – numerous white sand beaches including Adoki Beach (photo) **RhRj46**

Pandaidori Islands Small island group east of Biak – large coral reefs – beaches and diving sites on the islands' coasts **Rj46**

Yapen Island south of Biak – main settlement Serui – rainforests – numerous bird species including hornbills and cockatoos – beautiful bays **RhRj46**

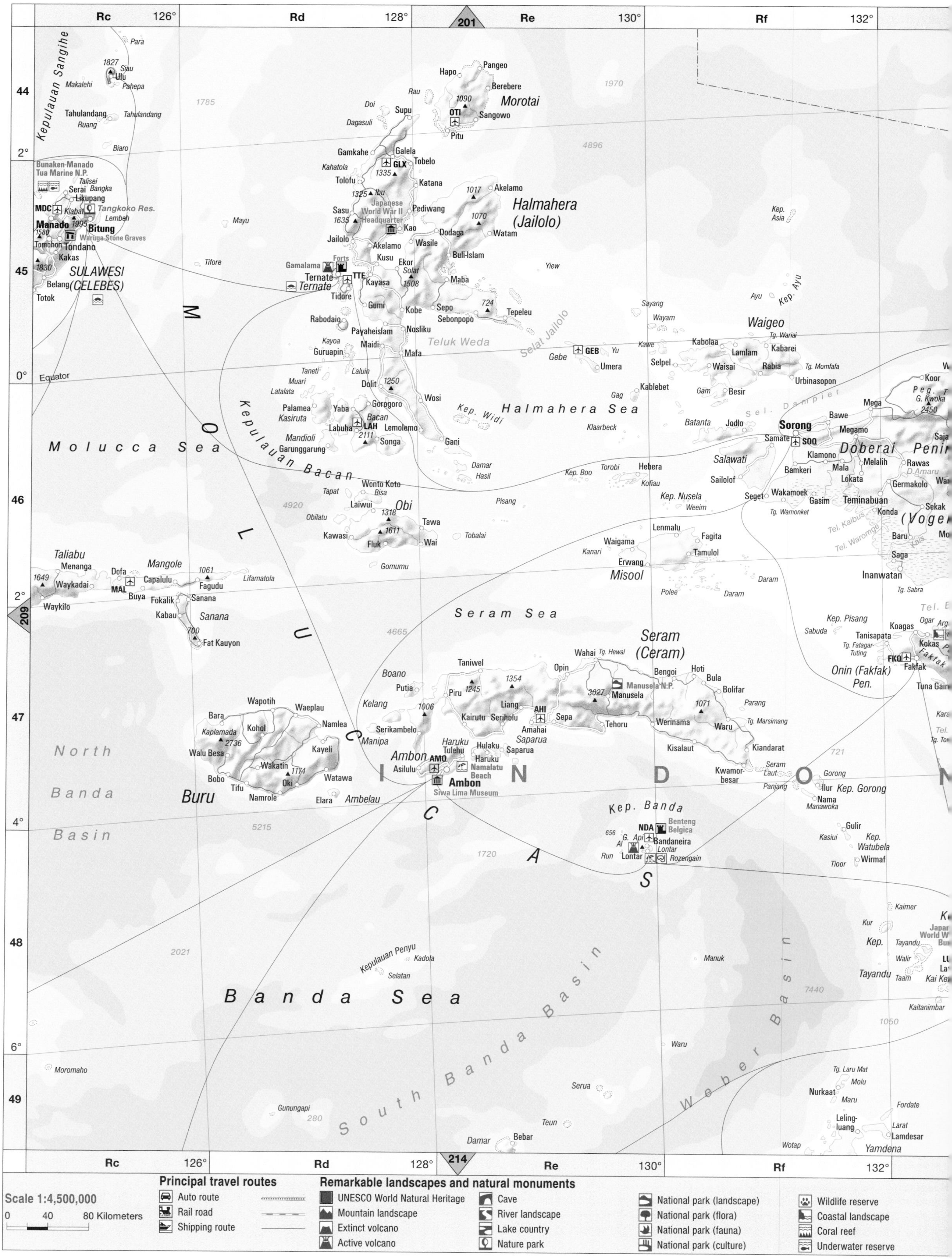

Scale 1:4,500,000

0 40 80 Kilometers

Principal travel routes

- Auto route
- Rail road
- Shipping route

Remarkable landscapes and natural monuments

- UNESCO World Natural Heritage
- Mountain landscape
- Extinct volcano
- Active volcano
- Cave
- River landscape
- Lake country
- Nature park
- National park (landscape)
- National park (flora)
- National park (fauna)
- National park (culture)
- Wildlife reserve
- Coastal landscape
- Coral reef
- Underwater reserve

onomies for many centuries. Before e 16th century, the spice trade on the oluccas was dominated by Arab and dian traders. In 1511, the Portuguese ilt their first base in the region on the and of Ternate. Shortly afterwards, e first Portguese trade ships arrived at **mbon** and the Banda Islands, the most portant centers of spice production. nbon City is the provincial capital of aluka and the most important economic center in the region. Fish, nickel, oil, and timber are now the leading exports of the Moluccas.

The Moluccas are home to countless beautiful beaches and there are extensive coral reefs near the coasts of many islands. The interiors of many islands in area are covered by dense **tropical rainforests** with an incredible abundance of unique plants. In addition to its fascinating plant life, the islands are also home to an interesting collection of land and marine animals.

With a total area of 733,000 km², **New Guinea** is the second largest island in the world. The eastern half of the island comprises most of Papua New Guinea, an independent nation since 1975. The western half of the island has been a province of Indonesia since 1969. In 2001, the name of the Indonesian province **Irian Jaya** was officially changed to Papua.

More than half of Papua's land is covered by dense tropical rainforests and the mountainous central highlands are home to expansive cloud forests. The tallest mountain in the province, **Puncak Jaya**, rises 5,030 meters above sea level and its peak is covered by snow during the entire year. Many of the areas in the province's interior are difficult to access. The coastal areas of the province are dominated by vast swampy plains.

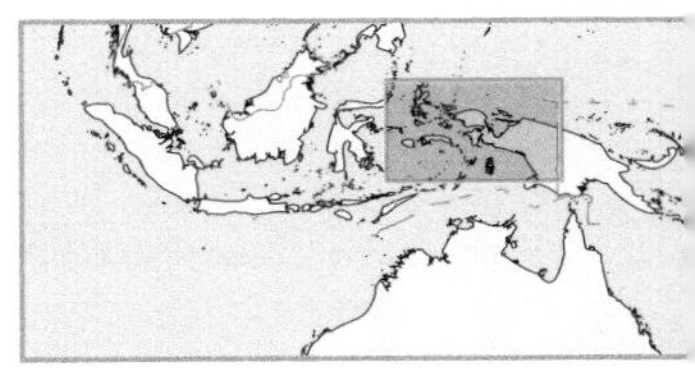

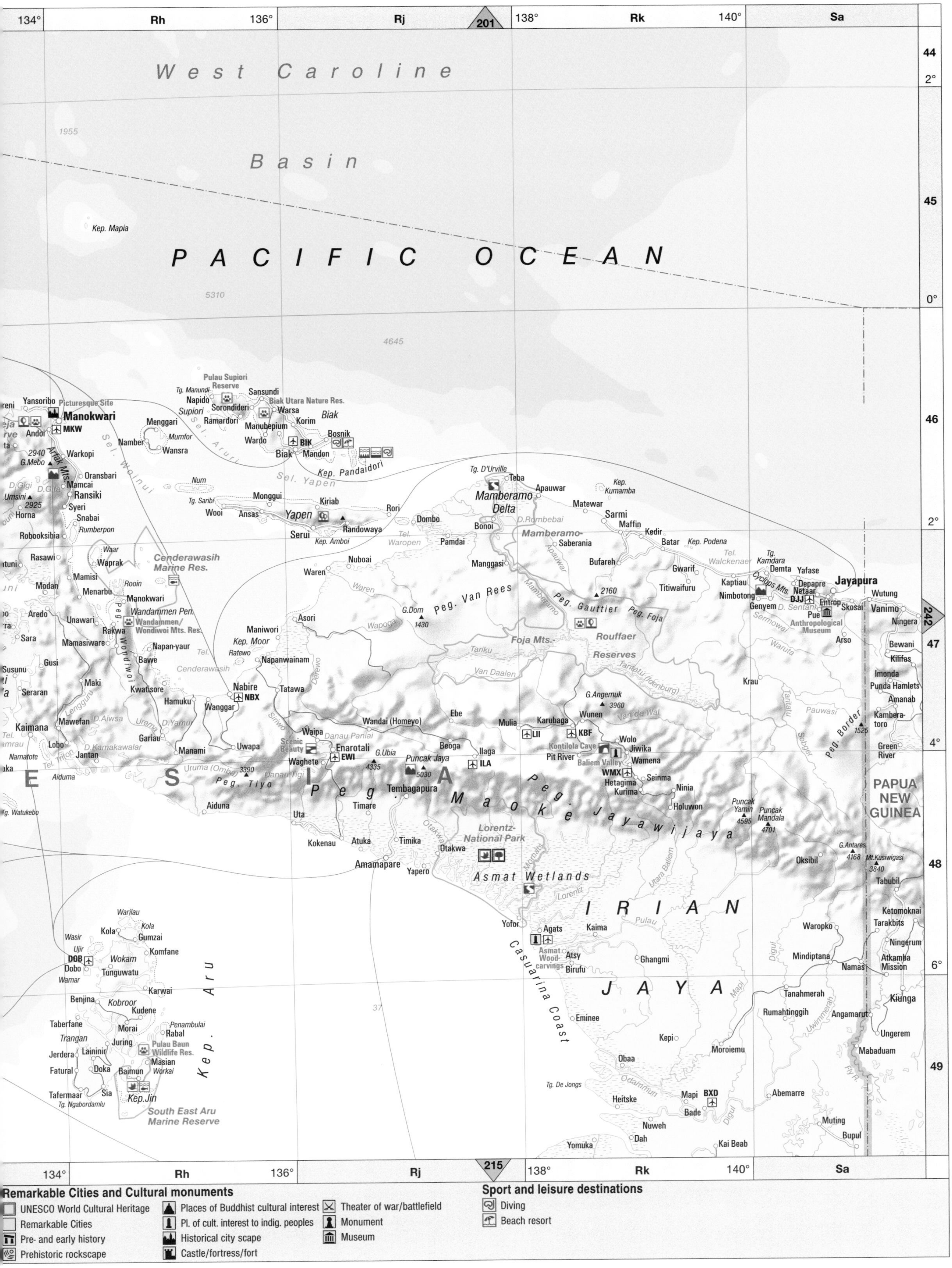

Jayapura Capital city of Papua (Irian Jaya) – located near the Cyclops Mountains, a range of rainforest covered mountains – unique birds and orchids **Sa47**

Baliem Valley The valley in Papua (Irian Jaya) is situated 1,700 meters above sea level. The indigenous Dani people form the majority of the area's population. Many small Dani villages consisting of grass covered huts are scattered throughout the valley. Like the other inhabitants of New Guinea's isolated highlands, the Dani have their own unique social systems and traditions. Photos from top to bottom: lush mountain vegetation, suspension bridge over the Baliem River, Dani people in traditional costumes **Rk48**

Jayawijaya Mountains Long mountain range in central Papua (Irian Jaya). The Jayawijaya highlands contain villages inhabited by the Dani, Lani, Jali, and Eipomek peoples. **Rk48**

Remarkable Cities and Cultural monuments

- UNESCO World Cultural Heritage
- Remarkable Cities
- Pre- and early history
- Prehistoric rockscape
- Places of Buddhist cultural interest
- Pl. of cult. interest to indig. peoples
- Historical city scape
- Castle/fortress/fort
- Theater of war/battlefield
- Monument
- Museum

Sport and leisure destinations

- Diving
- Beach resort

Southeastern Indonesia is a region containing several thousand islands scattered thorough three different seas. The region is home to a unique diversity of cultures, ethnicities, and landscapes. Southeastern Indonesia consists of the southern tip of Sulawesi, Timor, the Southern Moluccas, and the southwestern coast of Papua (Irian Jaya), an Indonesian province on New Guinea. The islands of southeastern Indonesia are located near the northernmost tip of Australia. Millions of years ago, the regions were connect by a land bridge and animals migrated both directions between Asia and Austr lia. The Arafura Sea stretches over a lar section of the area once occupied by t prehistoric land bridge. It is a shallow s with a maximum depth of just 130 mete

Isolated beach in Wakatobi Marine National Park **RbRc**

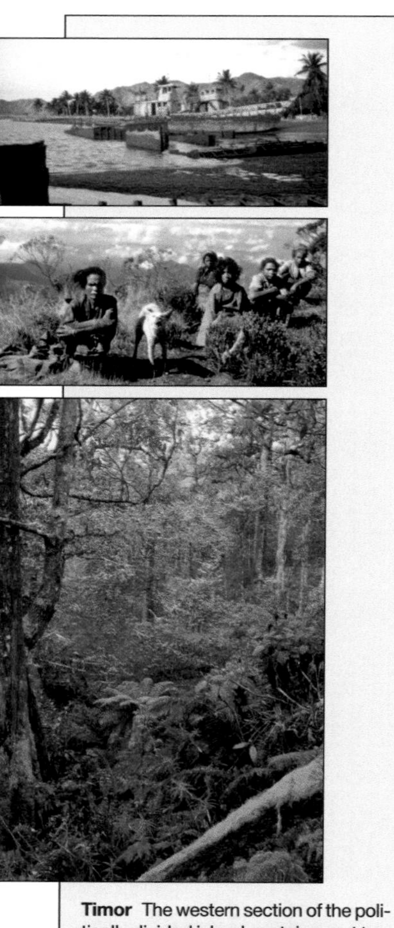

Timor The western section of the politically divided island contains vast tropical rainforests. Photos from top to bottom: the harbor of Dili, Mount Ramelau in East Timor, rainforest on Mount Mutis **Rc50**

Seram Central Moluccas – high mountains – dense rainforests – Manusela National Park – unique birds – photo: the harbor of Seram **ReRf47**

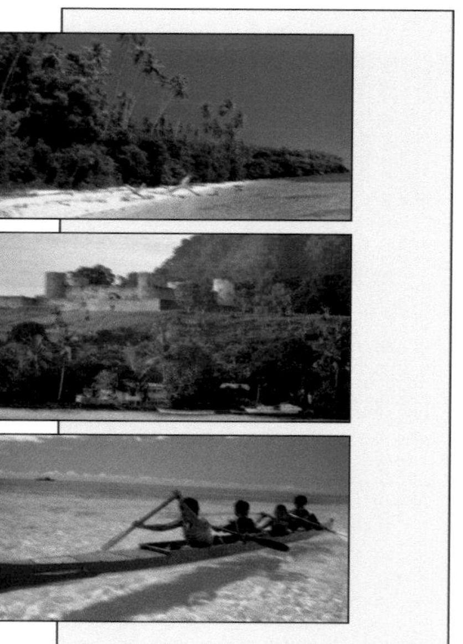

Banda Islands The islands are widely scattered and were once a center of nutmeg production. Photos from top to bottom: beach, historic Fort Benteng Belgica, traditional boat **ReRf48**

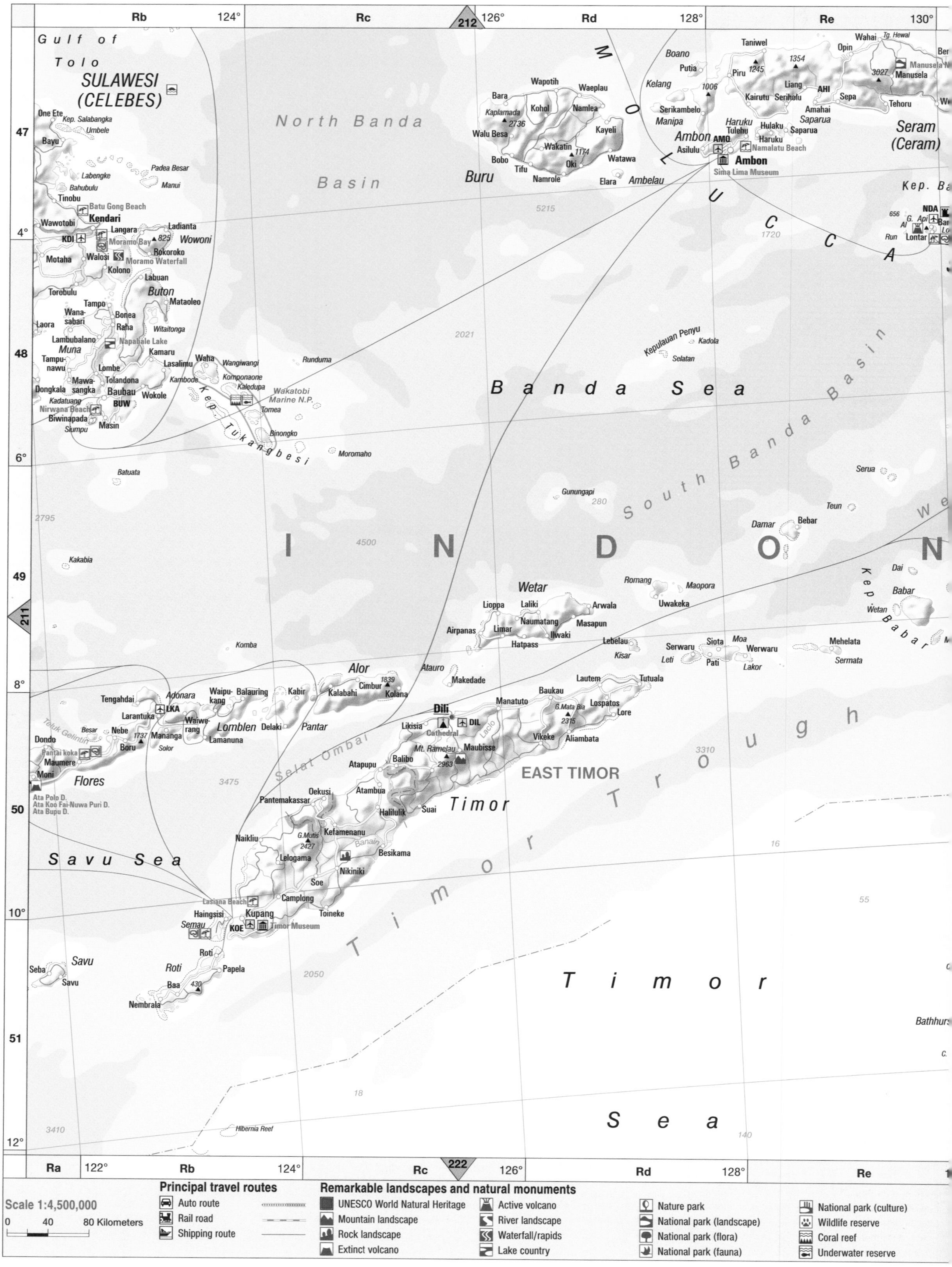

Scale 1:4,500,000
0 40 80 Kilometers

Principal travel routes
- Auto route
- Rail road
- Shipping route

Remarkable landscapes and natural monuments
- UNESCO World Natural Heritage
- Mountain landscape
- Rock landscape
- Extinct volcano
- Active volcano
- River landscape
- Waterfall/rapids
- Lake country
- Nature park
- National park (landscape)
- National park (flora)
- National park (fauna)
- National park (culture)
- Wildlife reserve
- Coral reef
- Underwater reserve

nor is the largest island in the Lesser nda group and is divided between two tions. East Timor was a Portuguese ritory for several centuries before it s occupied by Indonesia in 1975. After ong period of violent unrest, East Timor s granted its independence from Indosia in 2002. The country is home to ound 800,000 people and the port city i is the national capital. West Timor a province of Indonesia. Like neighboring Sumba, Timor is located in the western section of the Lesser Sunda island group. Timor is separated from Australia by the Timor Sea which contains the Temor Trough, an underwater trench with a maximum depth of 3,300 meters. Central Timor is dominated by a 500-kilometer-long mountain range that is interrupted by several grassy plateaus. The tallest mountain on the island, **Mount Ramelau**, rises 2,963 meters. The remaining sections of Timor's virgin rainforests are home to many fascinating birds.

With the exception of some areas dominated by swampy mangrove forest, most of the coastal areas are covered by grassy plains with scattered acacias and eucalyptus trees. The coasts are home to unique plants and animals. The flora and fauna of coastal Timor is similar to that found on other islands in the region.

The Aru Islands in the Southern Moluccas are covered by dense rainforests, home to a variety of plants and animals. The islands are located 200 kilometers off the southwestern coast of **New Guinea**. The Indonesian province Papua, formerly known as **Irian Jaya**, covers the western half of New Guinea. **Lorentz National Park** stretches from the swampy coast of Papua to the foothills of the province's central highlands.

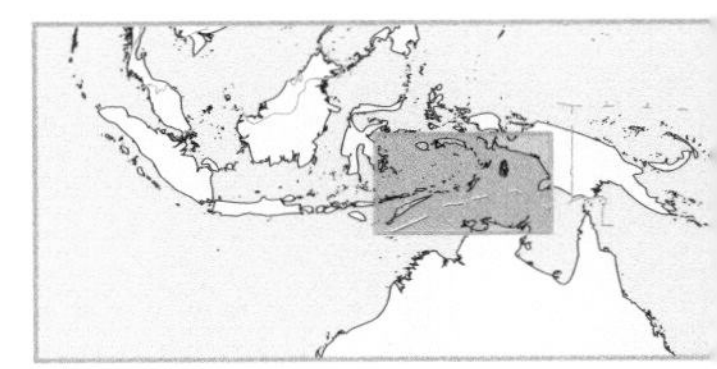

Kai Islands Three islands with around 100,000 inhabitants – main settlement Tual (photo) – beautiful beaches **Rg48**

Aru Islands South East Aru Marine Reserve – Pulau Baun Wildlife Reserve – many lagoons and coral reefs – dolphins and sea cows **Rh48/49**

Lorentz National Park The national park in Indonesia's Papua province is a UNESCO world heritage site. The park features rainforests (top photo). Many animals including birds of paradise (photo) inhabit the park. **Rj48**

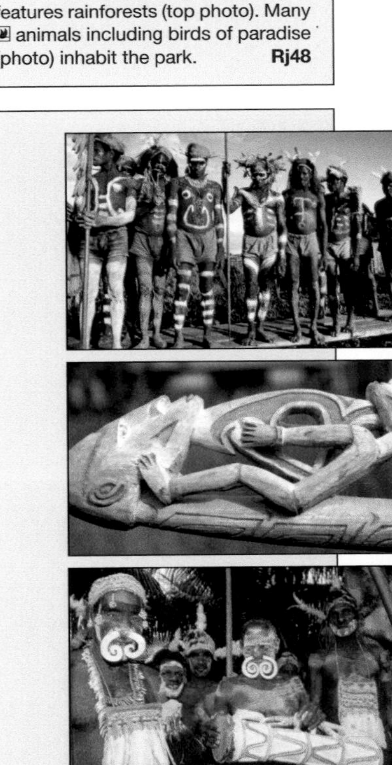

Asmat The name refers to a swampy area in western New Guinea and an indigenous ethnic group that lives in the area. The Asmat are well known for their traditional wood carvings. Photos from top to bottom: Asmat men and traditional body paintings. Wood carving, Asmat community gathering **Rk48**

Remarkable Cities and Cultural monuments

- UNESCO World Cultural Heritage
- Remarkable Cities
- Places of Christian cultural interest
- Pl. of cult. interest to indig. peoples
- Aborigine reservation
- Places of Abor. cultural interest
- Castle/fortress/fort
- Technical/industrial monument
- Theater of war/battlefield
- Museum

Sport and leisure destinations

- Diving
- Wind surfing
- Beach resort

The Olgas (top): Spectacular rock formations in the "red heart" of Australia
Sydney (bottom): Australia's largest city with its famous Opera House and the Harbour Bridge

Milford Sound (left): A stunning fjord landscape on New Zealand's South Island
Moorea (right): One of Polynesia's most beautiful islands; Moorea is covered by lush forests

Australia/Oceania

Australia is the land of the "dreamtime." The blue waters of the Great Barrier Reef, the green rainforests in the wet tropics, the red rock formations of Central Australia, and the golden sand dunes of Nambung National Park make Australia a fascinating continent rich in color and diversity.

This region of the world is comprised of two unequal parts: the massive landmass of **Australia** and the countless scattered islands of the South Pacific. The region's islands range from the very smallest of islets to large islands such as New Guinea and New Zealand.
Australia is a continent of vast distances. Most of Central and Western Australia consist of deserts. Australia's largest desert, The Great Sandy Desert, covers 520,000 km². Ayers Rock, also known by its aboriginal name Uluru, is located near the geographic center of Australia.
Australia's highest mountains are in the Australian Alps, a section of the Great Dividing Range which stretches along the eastern coast. Mount Kosciuszko (2,228 meters) is the highest mountain on the continent.

Sunset at Ayers Rock (Uluru)

The Great Barrier Reef off the no eastern coast of Australia is the wor largest coral reef. It has a total lengt more than 2,000 kilometers from nort south.
The **islands of Oceania** are usually di ed into three regions: Micronesia, Me nesia, and Polynesia. The thousands islands in Oceania, scattered over 70 lion km² in the Pacific Ocean, have a t land area around 1.3 million km².

The regions near the equator are lush and thick with vegetation (top photo: rainforest in New Guinea). **Subtropical vegetation** in the Northern Territory (middle photo, top). Mungo National Park (middle photo, bottom). **The Great Barrier Reef** (bottom photo).

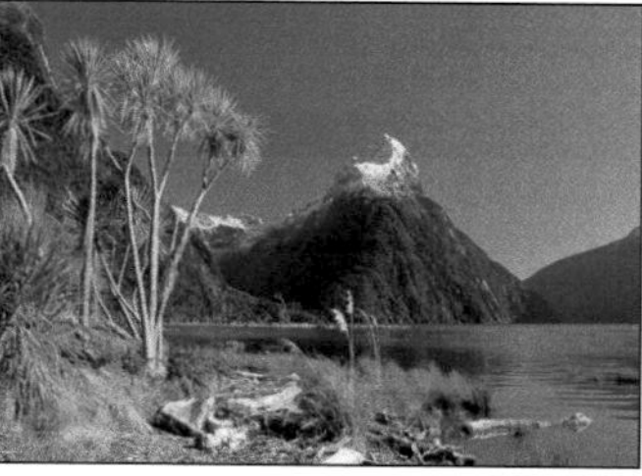

Snow covered Mount Cook in the New Zealand Alps is the tallest mountain in **New Zealand** (3,764 meters) (top photo). Fjordland National Park features some of the most beautiful landscapes in New Zealand (bottom photo: Milford Sound).

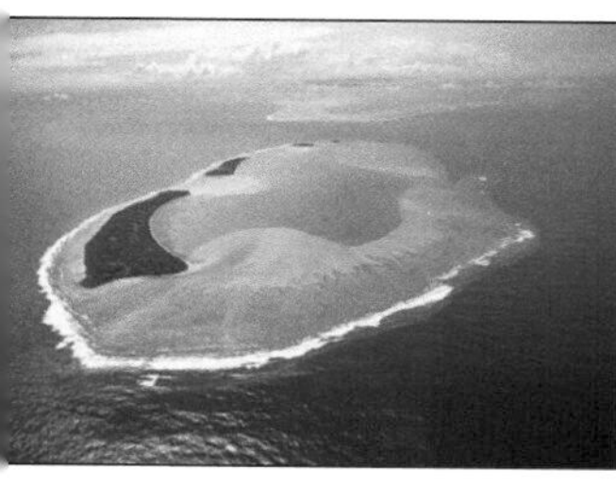

Many of the **Pacific islands** were created from coral reefs. Countless small islands in the region remain uninhabited. (photo: a small island in the Palau archipelago)

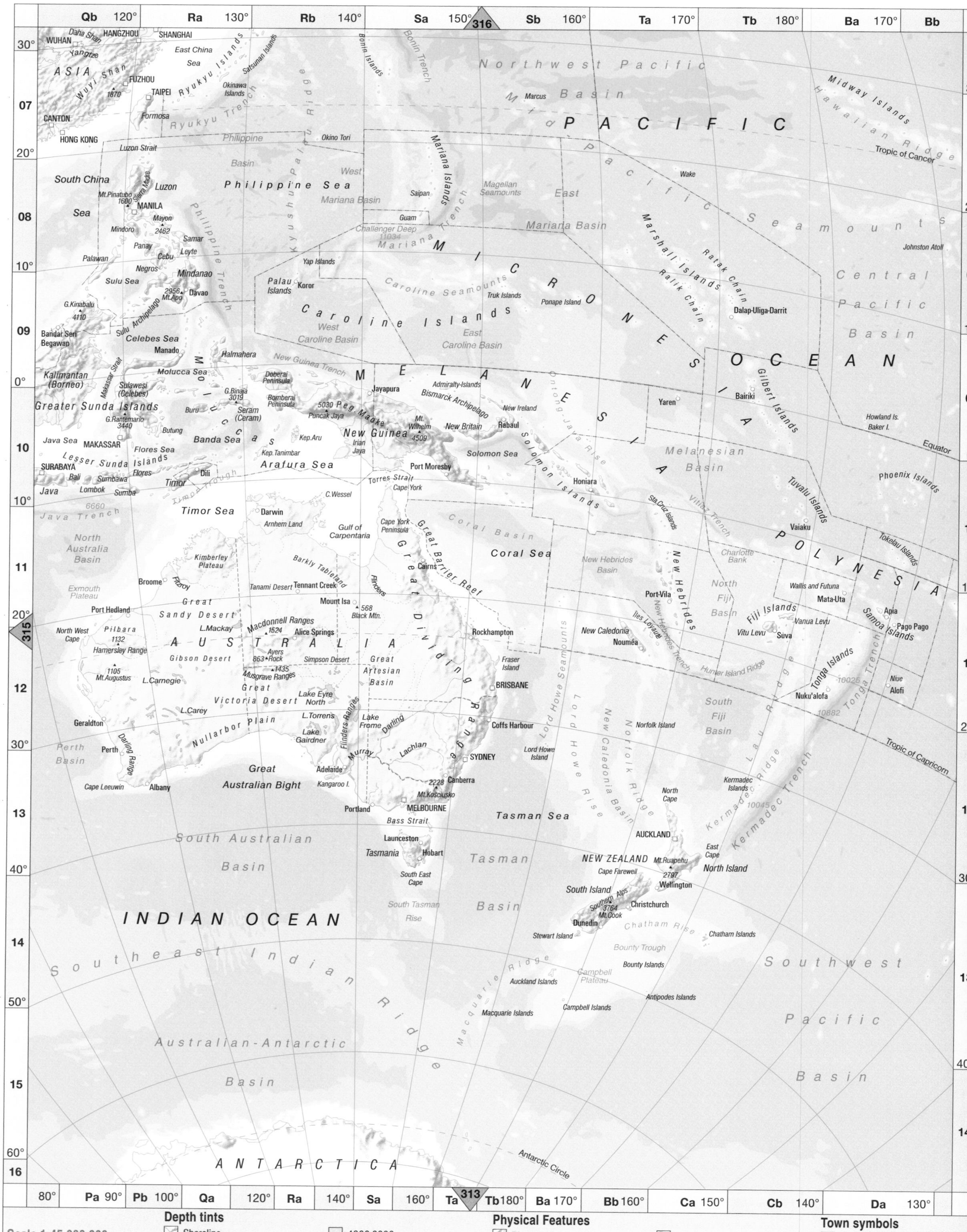

Scale 1:45,000,000
0 400 800 Kilometers

Depth tints
- Shoreline
- 0-200 m
- 200-2000 m
- 2000-4000 m
- 4000-6000 m
- 6000-8000 m
- > 8000 m

Physical Features
- River, stream
- Intermittent river
- Lake
- Intermittent lake
- Salt lake
- Intermittent salt lake
- Elevation above sea level in meters

Town symbols
- Towns > 1 Mill. inhabitants
- Towns < 100 000 inhabitants

und 90% of Australia's 19.7 million abitants occupy just 3% of the conti- it's land. The continent's population is centrated in the Southeast with the jority of people living in a few large astal cities. **Aborigines**, the continent's igenous people, represent just 2.2% he population. Most Australians are the scendants of European immigrants. er the arrival of the first Europeans at end of the 18th century, the Aborigi- nal population began to decline. Like the Aborigines, the **Maori** of New Zealand and the **Papua** of New Guinea were dramatically affected by the European colonization of their countries. These ethnic groups still struggle to preserve the most important aspects of their cultures including their languages and traditional arts.

Left: Aboriginal man of Australia
Right: Warrior of Papua New Guinea

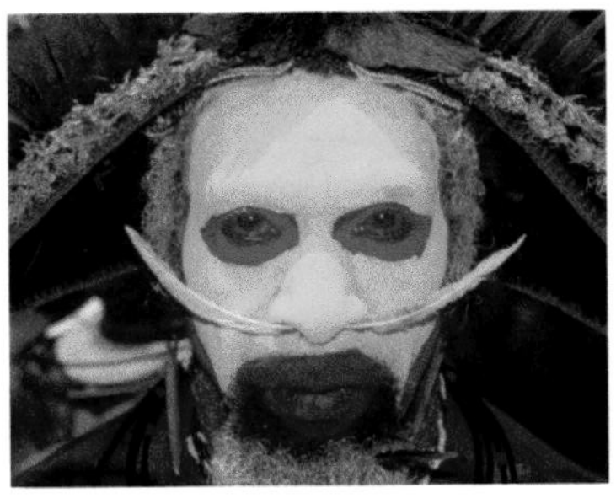

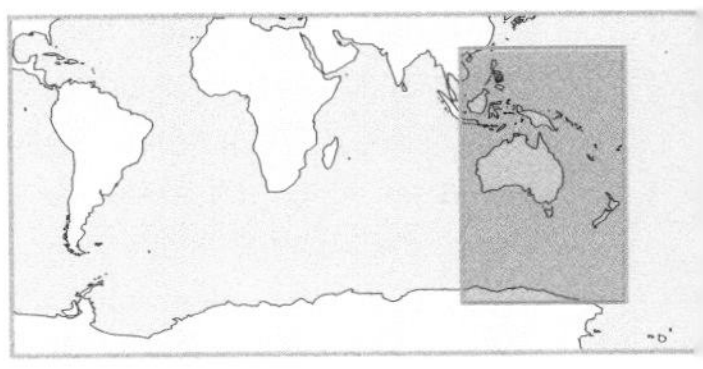

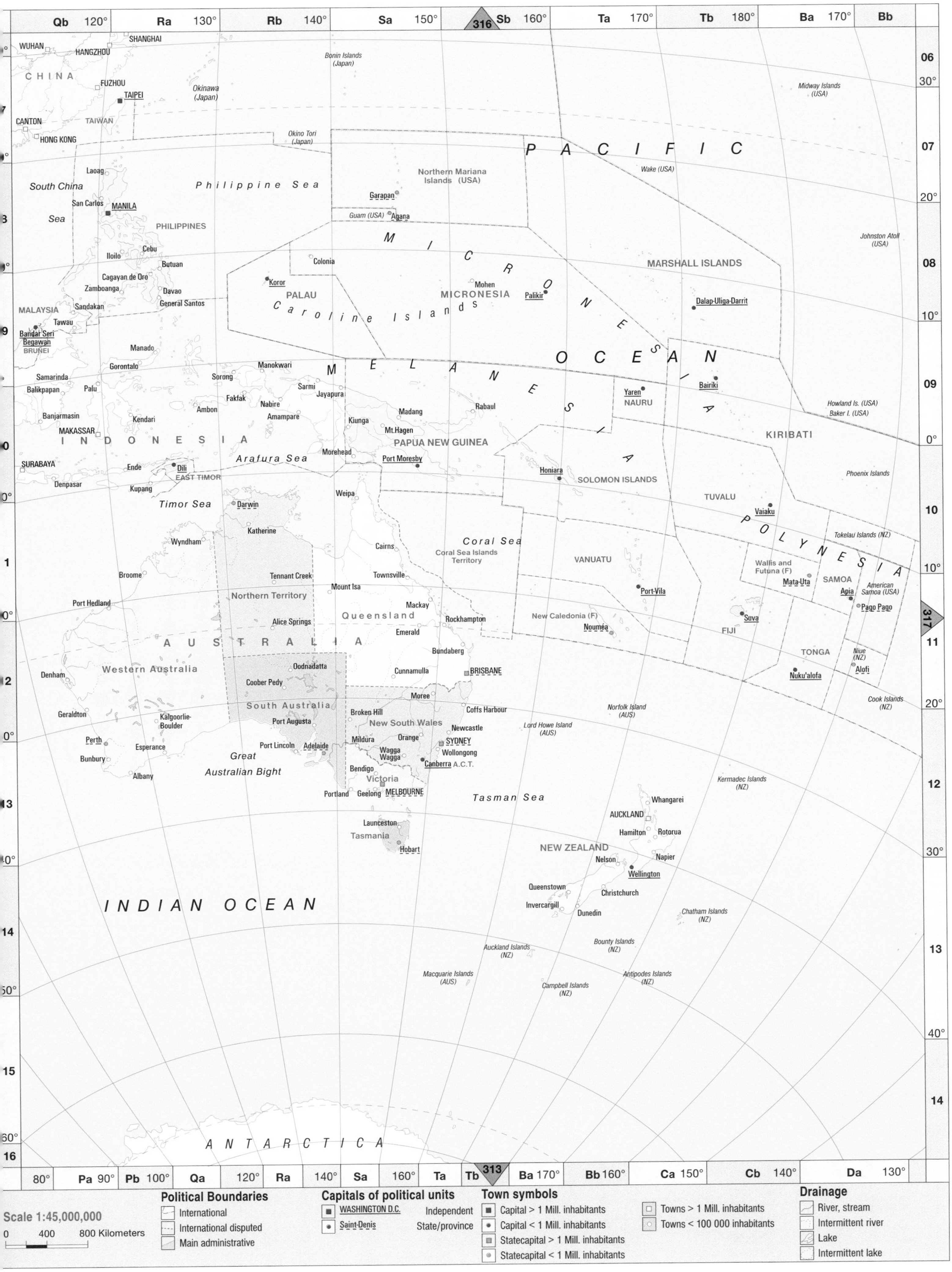

Scale 1:45,000,000
0 400 800 Kilometers

Political Boundaries
- International
- International disputed
- Main administrative

Capitals of political units
- WASHINGTON D.C. Independent
- Saint-Denis State/province

Town symbols
- Capital > 1 Mill. inhabitants
- Capital < 1 Mill. inhabitants
- Statecapital > 1 Mill. inhabitants
- Statecapital < 1 Mill. inhabitants
- Towns > 1 Mill. inhabitants
- Towns < 100 000 inhabitants

Drainage
- River, stream
- Intermittent river
- Lake
- Intermittent lake

Countries and Flags

- Australia
- Fiji
- Kiribati
- Marshall Islands
- Micronesia
- Nauru
- New Zealand
- Palau
- Papua New Guinea
- Samoa
- Solomon Islands
- Tonga
- Tuvalu
- Vanuatu

Since the 19th century the islands of the Pacific have been divided into three distinct regions: **Melanesia** in the western Pacific, **Micronesia** in the northern Pacific, and **Polynesia** in the central Pacific. Melanesian ethnic groups include the Chimbu, Enga, Motu, and Foi. Among the more famous Micronesian ethnic groups are the Chamorro, Marshall Islanders, and Palauans. The Polynesians include the indigenous Hawaiians, the Maori of New Zealand, and the Samoans. In all traditional Pacific island societies, dance, song, and traditional storytelling play important roles in the preservation of culture. Photos from top to bottom: Huli man of New Guinea, Samoan, Micronesian man, Polynesian women (all in traditional headdresses)

Australia is the smallest of the world's seven continents with a total area of 7.7 million km². The continent can be divided into three large geographic regions. The **Great Western Plateau** covers much of western and central Australia. It is situated at elevations between 200 and 800 meters above sea level. The plateau features vast deserts, including the **Great Sandy Desert**, as well as unique stone formations. The **Great Dividing Range** stretches the entire length of Austral eastern coast. A narrow strip of low-ly coastal plains is located to the eas the range. Southeastern Australia is most densely populated region on continent. Australia's two largest citie Melbourne and Sydney – are locate this region.

Pristine Lake Burbury on the Australi island of Tasmania

Arnhem Land Aboriginal land reserve in Australia's Northern Territory – aboriginal art – Gove Peninsula – Mary River (photo)

The Kimberley Region (not easily accessed) in Western Australia – 350-million-years old stone formation, Bungle Bungle (photo); a UNESCO world heritage site

Macdonnell Ranges Range of hills and mountains in central Australia – mountains rise above 1,500 meters – fascinating gorges – national park

Central Australia's Stone Formations Uluru (Ayers Rock) is 348 meters high with a diameter of nine kilometers (photo) – 600 million years old – a sacred mountain for Aborigines – Olgas (Kata Tjuta): a group of red sandstone formations

Australia's Western Coasts Shark Bay World Heritage Area is home to rare animals including humpback whales and manatees – Ningaloo Reef Marine Park

Australia's Southern Coasts Walpole-Nornalup National Park features the Valley of the Giants with its tall Karri Trees – Whale watching in Albany – Limestone Coast

South Australia The state's interior comprises large deserts and semi-arid grasslands – Stuart Highway – Eyre Highway – capital city of Adelaide – Eucla Desert (photo)

Scale 1:18,000,000
0 160 320 Kilometers

Depth tints
- Shoreline
- 0-200 m
- 200-2000 m
- 2000-4000 m
- 4000-6000 m
- 6000-8000 m
- > 8000 m

Physical Features
- River, stream
- Intermittent river
- Lake
- Intermittent lake
- Salt lake
- Intermittent salt lake
- Elevation above sea level in meters

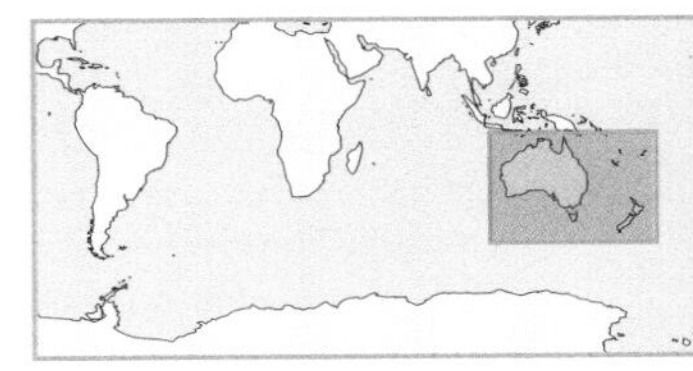

uated between the Western Plateau d the mountains of eastern Australia, ast basin covers most of central Ausia. This arid region is covered by large ndy deserts, such as the **Great Victo- Desert**, as well as large salt lakes. The ion is extremely sparsely populated d has no large cities. There are sever- vast livestock ranches scattered oughout central Australia. The major rist attractions in central Australia are the region's unique red sandstone formations including **Uluru (Ayers Rock)** and the **Olgas**.

The **Great Barrier Reef**, located off the northeastern coast of Australia, is the world's longest coral reef. The reef is more than 2,000 kilometers long and houses 400 types of coral and 1,500 fish species. **Tasmania**, Australia's largest island, features pristine forests and unique wildlife.

The ancestors of Australia's Aborigines arrived on the continent more than 50,000 years ago. There are now around 400,000 Australians of aboriginal descent. The Aborigines have been granted Australian citizenship and control of large land reserves in recent decades.

Fiji and **Vanuatu (New Hebrides)** are island groups situated east of Australia in the Pacific Ocean. **New Zealand** consists of two main islands as well as numerous smaller ones. New Zealand's North Island (115,000 km^2) has many geysers and several active volcanoes. The South Island (151,000 km^2) features tall mountain ranges, fjords, and large glaciers. The country's capital, Wellington, and the largest city, Auckland, are both situated on the North Island. In recent decades, the government of New Zealand has taken steps to preserve the culture of the indigenous Maori people.

Northern Queensland Daintree National Park (photo): rain forests, bird watching, tours along the Daintree River – Cape Tribulation with coastal rainforests

Whitsunday Islands Island group close to the Great Barrier Reef – around 70 islands – the islands are the peaks of an underwater mountain system

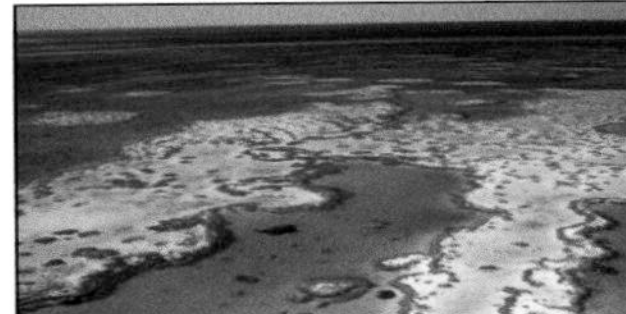

Great Barrier Reef The largest coral reef in the world – off the coast of Queensland – UNESCO world natural heritage site

Great Dividing Range Mountain range along the eastern coast of Australia – Blue Mountain National Park (photo)

Tasmania Island (68,000 km^2) around 300 kilometers south of mainland Australia – hilly terrain – temperate rain forests – 14 national parks – historic architecture in Hobart

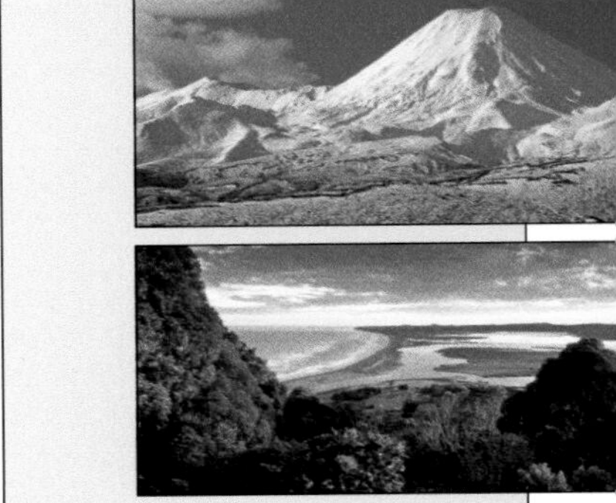

New Zealand The two main islands of this Pacific nation are home to a diverse group of beautiful landscapes. The North Island has active volcanoes including Mount Ngauruhoe (top photo). The South Island is home to the Southern Alps and Westland National Park (bottom photo).

Political Boundaries
- International
- International disputed
- Main administrative

Transportation
- Interstate Hwy./Motorway
- Main road
- Railway
- Airport

Capitals of political units
- WASHINGTON D.C. Independent
- Richmond State/province

Town symbols
- Capital > 1 Mill. inhabitants
- Capital < 1 Mill. inhabitants
- Statecapital > 1 Mill. inhabitants
- Statecapital < 1 Mill. inhabitants
- Towns > 1 Mill. inhabitants
- Towns 100 000 bis 1 Mill. inhabitants
- Towns < 100 000 inhabitants

Northwestern Australia comprises areas in the state of Western Australia and the Northern Territory. The climate in this part of the continent is mostly tropical except for a few arid areas, including the **Tanami Desert**, in the southern section of the region. The **Kimberley** (in the western part of the region) is a series of rugged plateaus and spectacular gorges near the Timor Sea coast.

The region, which has been inhabited by

Aborigines for centuries, was bar explored up until the last few decad Many areas are still difficult to travel ir a fact which has helped preserve the f cinating nature of the region. Altho northwestern Australia is three times size of England it has just 25,000 inha tants. One of the region's most interest

The Bungle Bungle: bizarre rock form tions in Western Australia **Re**

Bonaparte Archipelago A lone tropical island 850 kilometers north from Broome, off the jagged Kimberley coast **Rc53**

Prince Regent Nature Reserve nature reserve in the Kimberley region – heavy annual rainfall – the area is difficult to access – the reserve contains more than 500 unique plant species **Rc53/54**

Lake Argyle Largest man-made lake in Australia – 45 km south of the Kununurra – the damming of the Ord River made agriculture possible in the Kimberley **Re54**

Argyle Diamond Mine World's most productive diamond mine – produces one third of the world's natural diamonds – source of rare pink diamonds **Re54**

Wolfe Creek Crater Second largest meteor impact crater on Earth – on the edge of the Great Sandy Desert – only visible from the air – around 300,000 years old **Rd55**

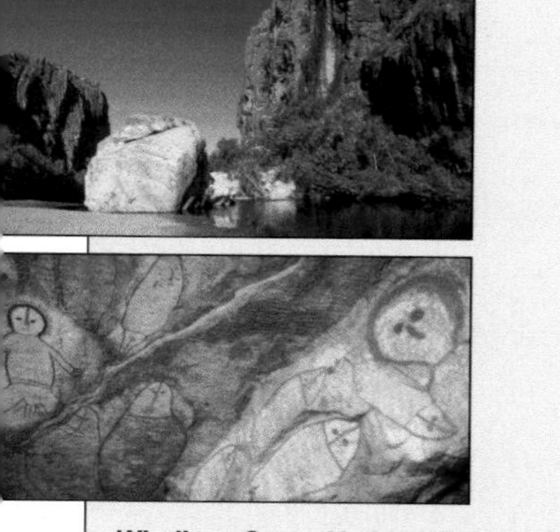

Windjana Gorge National Park (Kimberleys) Large gorge on the Lennard River (top photo). The sandstone walls of the gorge are as high as 90 meters. The area is renowned for old Aboriginal rock paintings. The most impressive paintings portray the cloud gods (bottom photo). **Rc54**

Scale 1:4,500,000

0 40 80 Kilometers

Principal travel routes

- Auto route
- Rail road
- Shipping route

Remarkable landscapes and natural monuments

- UNESCO World Natural Heritage
- Mountain landscape
- Rock landscape
- Ravine/canyon
- Geyser
- Cave
- River landscape
- Waterfall/rapids
- National park (landscape)
- National park (flora)
- National park (fauna)
- National park (culture)
- Wildlife reserve
- Crocodile farm
- Coastal landscape
- Underwater reserve

actions is the Bungle Bungle (Pur- ulu) – a group of colorful stone for- tions first discovered during the fil- ng of a television program in 1982. The vn of Kinunurra is the gateway to the nberley. The town was built in the 60s as part of a plan to dam the near- Ord River and irrigate the surrounding a. South of the Kimberley lies the city Broome, famous for its beaches and al pearl industry.

The northern part of the region including **Darwin**, the capital of the Northern Territory, is called the "Top End" by Australians. Darwin and its surroundings have a humid subtropical climate. The city with 100,000 inhabitants is the only large city in the region. For the Australian economy Darwin is the "gateway to Asia" and for many tourists the city is also important as the gateway to **Litchfield** and **Kakadu** National Parks.

In both the Top End and the Kimberley there are only two distinct seasons during the year. The Dry Season lasts from May until September, while the Wet Season lasts from November until the end of March. April and October are the transitional months between the two seasons. During the Wet Season, many areas in northwestern Australia, including Arnhem Land and Kakadu National Park, are flooded over and can only be reached by airplane. Temperatures in the region regularly exceed 35° Celsius, and humidity is high during the entire year. Coastal storms often move inland bringing heavy rainfall and floods to the interior. The coast itself is regularly threatened by powerful cyclones. July and August offer the most appealing weather for tourists wanting to explore the region, despite many areas being parched because of the low rainfall during these months.

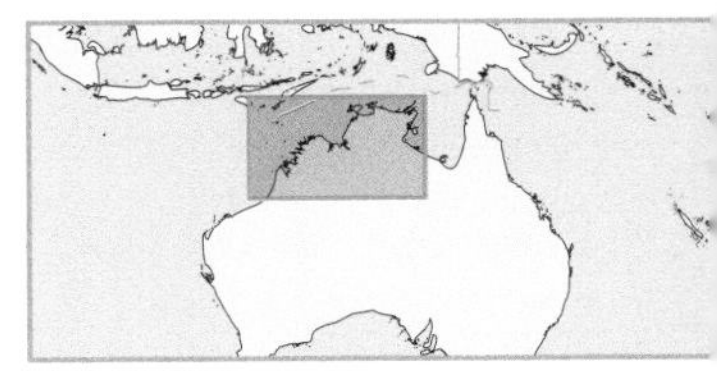

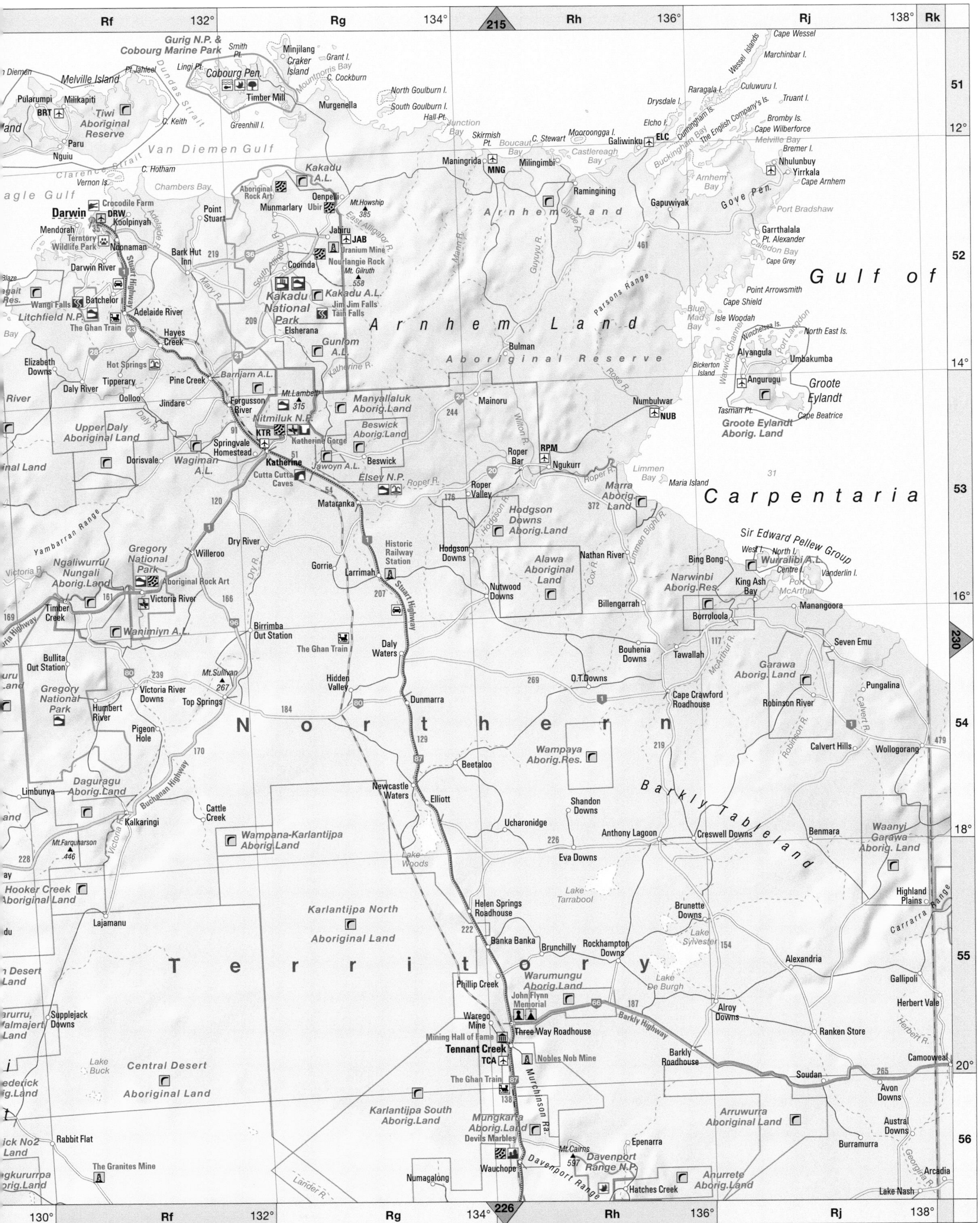

Arnhem Land Region on the edge of northwestern Australia – floods during the wet season – towns: Nhulunbuy and Yirrkala – under Aboriginal administration **Rh52/53**

Litchfield National Park Spectacular national park with Florence Falls and "The Lost City": a rock formation **Rf52**

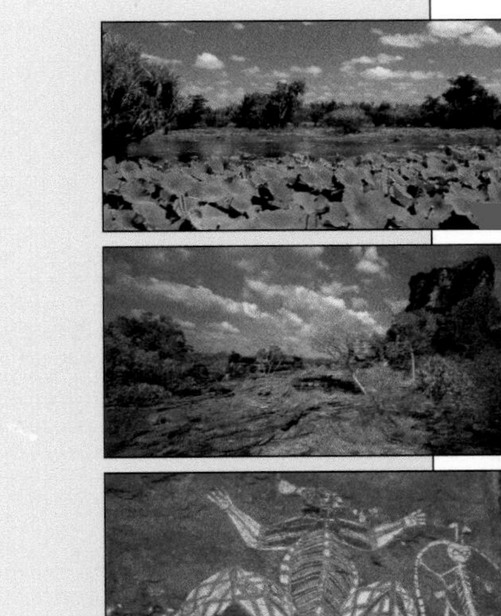

Kakadu National Park Covering 20,000 km² the national park is inhabited and governed by Aborigines. The national park, a UNESCO world heritage site, lies in the drainage area of the Alligator River. Kakadu is home to over 1,000 different plant, 300 bird, and 75 reptile species. Ubirr and Nourlangie Rock are sites of important aboriginal rock paintings. **Rg52**

Nitmiluk National Park The major attraction in this national park is Katherine Gorge, a 30-kilometer-long series of 13 gorges – cliffs with rock paintings **Rg52/53**

Devil's Marbles According to aboriginal myths these rock formations are eggs laid by the Rainbow Serpent – large round stones along the Stuart Highway **Rh56**

Remarkable Cities and Cultural monuments

- UNESCO World Cultural Heritage
- Remarkable Cities
- Pre- and early history
- Places of Christian cultural interest
- Aborigine reservation
- Places of Abor. cultural interest
- Technical/industrial monument
- Monument
- Museum

Sport and leisure destinations

- Diving
- Wind surfing
- Canoeing/rafting
- Beach resort

Western Australia

If the Australian state of Western Australia were an independent country it would be the ninth biggest nation on Earth. The state covers the western third of the continent and has a land area of 2.5 million km². Western Australia is incredibly rich in natural resources. **Pilbara**, a rocky region in Western Australia, has vast iron ore deposits. Most of the communities in the area, including Newman and Tom Price, depend on mining for their economic well being. The rock formations in bara's **Hamersley Range** are estima to be at least three million years old recent decades, significant reserves natural gas and oil have been found Western Australia's coast. Western A tralia coasts feature many delicate a unique ecosystems. The marine a

Storm clouds above the Great Sandy Desert **Rb**

Dampier Archipelago Island group near the port city of Dampier – rare plant and animal species **Qj56**

Hamersley Range Pilbara Region – vast iron ore deposits – Karijini National Park – gorges, rivers, and waterfalls **QjQk57**

Australia's West Coast Cape Range National Park has many fine beaches and coral reefs; the park is part of the Ningaloo Marine Park (UNESCO natural heritage site) **(Qg 56/57)**. The Ningaloo reef comprises at least 250 different types of coral. Shark Bay Marine Park was named for the tiger sharks in the area **(QgQh 58/59)**. Stromatolites (colonies of primitive microbes) are one of the major reasons Shark Bay was designated a world natural heritage site by UNESCO. The underwater reserves around Shark Bay and Ningaloo Reef were created to protect the animals and plants in the area. Francois Perron National Park in Shark Bay is home to rare bird species **(Qg58)**.

Kalbarri National Park River basin along the Murchison River – canyons and beautiful coastline **Qh59**

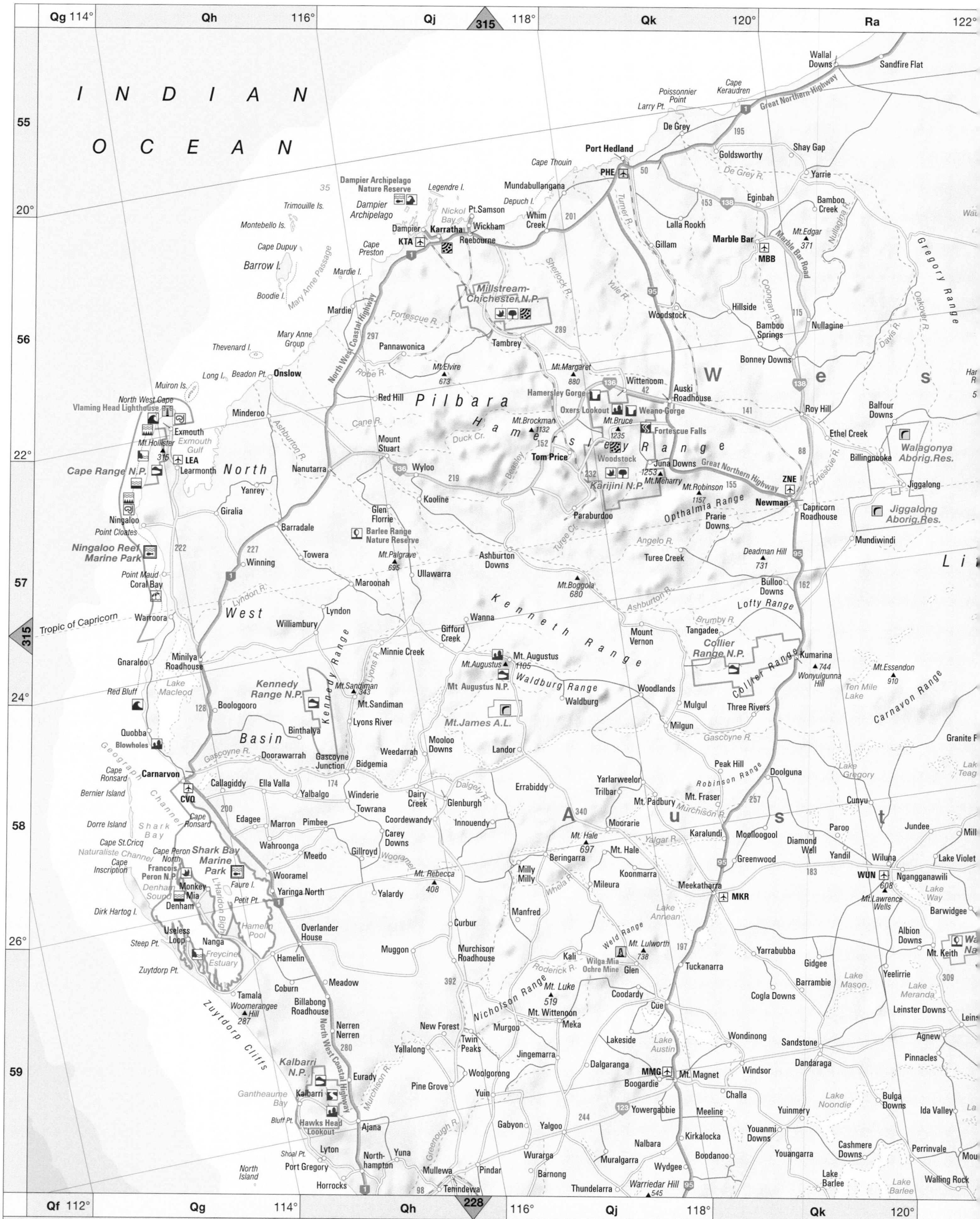

Scale 1:4,500,000
0 40 80 Kilometers

Principal travel routes
- Auto route
- Rail road
- Shipping route

Remarkable landscapes and natural monuments
- UNESCO World Natural Heritage
- Rock landscape
- Ravine/canyon
- River landscape
- Waterfall/rapids
- Nature park
- National park (landscape)
- National park (flora)
- National park (fauna)
- National park (culture)
- Biosphere reserve
- Zoo/safari park
- Coastal landscape
- Beach
- Coral reef
- Underwater reserve

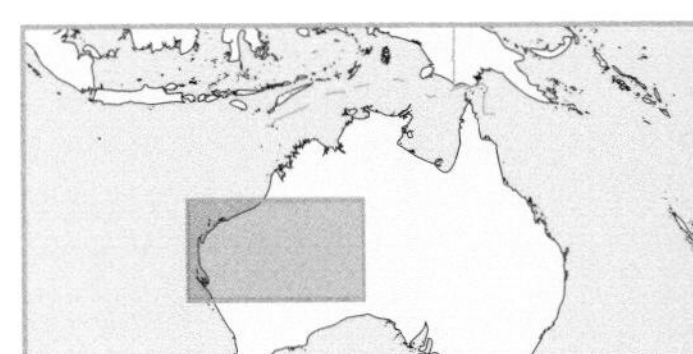

tional parks around Shark Bay and Ningaloo Reef have been desig-ted UNESCO world natural heritage es. Rare plants and animals are found both areas. Whales, dolphins, and anatees are among the many animals itors can discover in these areas. Shark y is also home to what may be the dest life forms still living on earth – the omatolites. Stromatolites are struc-es consisting of bacteria layers that grow in warm saline water. The oldest stromatolite fossils in Shark Bay are more than three billion years old.

The interior of Western Australia consists mostly of deserts and semi-arid land. Visitors to the interior will encounter a land of red sand dunes, spinifex grass, beautiful rock formations, sleepy isolated towns, and the largest livestock ranches in the world. Western Australia also encompasses the hottest areas on the continent. During the 1920s temperatures exceeding 38 degrees Celsius were recorded for 160 consecutive days in the town of **Marble Bar**. Despite the high temperatures, heavy rainfall often leads to severe flooding in the interior of Western Australia. These floods can cause major damage to roads and buildings. The northern sections of Western Australia above the Tropic of Capricorn are situated in a hurricane risk zone. Many Australian towns in this area have been heavily damaged by these powerful storms in recent decades.

The **Aborigines** of Western Australia have gained control of large areas of land in the region after a series of court rulings in recent years. Many Aboriginal leaders hope that land ownership and limited self-government will increase the confidence, influence and economic well being of their communities.

Western Australia's deserts Rudall River national park is the largest in Western Australia. Mostly desert, the park contains a system of salt lakes (Lake Dora and Lake Blanche) **(Rb57)**. The Gibson Desert Nature Reserve is home to large herds of wild horses and camels **(Rc58)**. Large sections of Western Australia's interior are under Aboriginal control.

Warburton Range Typical desert mountain range – in the center of a large Aboriginal land reserve **Rd59**

The Outback The Outback is the name Australians give to their most sparsely populated regions. Most of the Outback is desert but some of the largest farms and ranches in the country can be found here. Many dirt roads and paths in the Outback are only accessible with all terrain vehicles and some only with permission from local authorities. Several paved highways stretch through the Outback including the Stuart and Matilda Highways.

Remarkable Cities and Cultural monuments

- UNESCO World Cultural Heritage
- Remarkable Cities
- Aborigine reservation
- Places of Abor. cultural interest
- Historical city scape
- Technical/industrial monument
- Remarkable lighthouse
- Monument
- Museum

Sport and leisure destinations

- Diving
- Wind surfing
- Surfing
- Deep-sea fishing
- Beach resort

The sparsely populated interior of the world's smallest continent encompasses sections of Western Australia, South Australia, Queensland, and the Northern Territory. The region consists mostly of deserts and semi-arid regions including the **Great Victoria Desert**, **Gibson Desert** and the **Simpson Desert** with its gigantic red sand dunes. The mesa landscape is dotted with several mountain chains, including the Macdonnell Ranges, rising

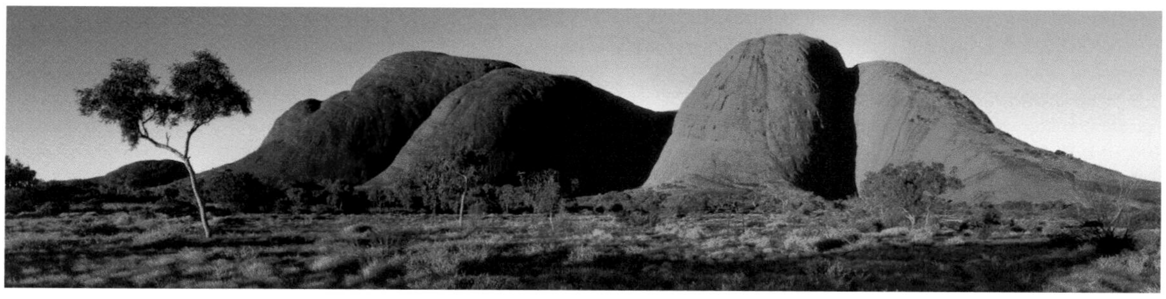

between 1,000 and 1,500 meters height. The famous stone monolith **Ul** **(Ayers Rock)** towers over the s rounding countryside and is – after We ern Australia's Mt. Augustus – the secc largest monolith on the planet. The **Olgas** (a group of red stone formatio are one of the most fascinating natu

The Olgas: sandstone formations in th "red heart" of Australia **Rf**

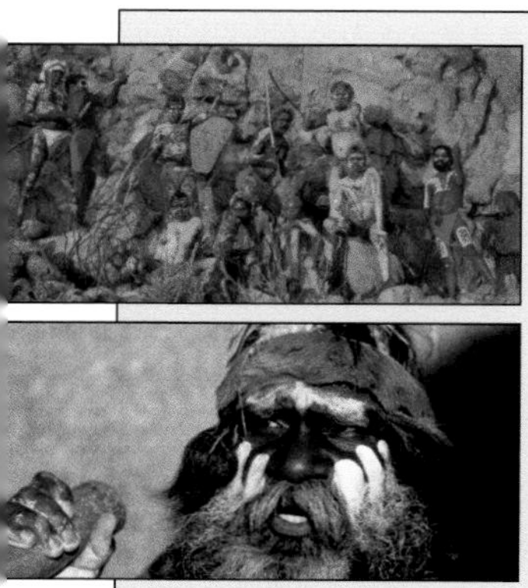

The **Aborigines** arrived on the Australian continent about 50,000 years ago. As hunters and gatherers they migrated throughout the continent with the help of songlines – oral maps passed on through the generations. The myths of the "dreamtime" are an important element of aboriginal culture. In recent decades, the Aborigines have won many legal rights.

Kings Canyon In Watarrka National Park – steep canyon walls – the Lost City: a cluster of rock formations – swimming holes – "The Garden of Eden" (photo) **Rf58**

Uluru (Ayers Rock) and **the Olgas (Kata Tjuta)** are the highlights of Central Australia's national parks. Uluru (863 meters) is 600 million years old and is considered sacred ground by many Aborigines (top/middle photo). The Olgas (bottom photo) comprise 36 round rock formations surrounded by gorges and valleys. **Rf 58**

Scale 1:4,500,000

0 40 80 Kilometers

Principal travel routes

- Auto route
- Rail road
- Shipping route

Remarkable landscapes and natural monuments

- UNESCO World Natural Heritage
- Rock landscape
- Ravine/canyon
- Geyser
- Cave
- Desert
- Nature park
- National park (landscape)
- National park (flora)
- National park (fauna)
- National park (culture)
- Biosphere reserve
- Zoo/safari park

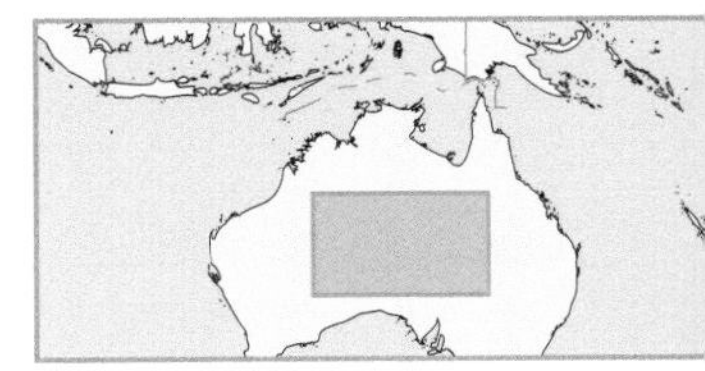

ractions in the region. The red color of e Olgas and much of central Australia caused by the high level of oxidized iron the region's soil and rocks. The **Lake re Basin** is the world's largest salt pan, ntaining a lake of the same name that both Australia's largest lake as well as e largest salt lake in the world. The sin's watershed covers one sixth of e continent and the area is usually par- ed and lifeless. Only after periods of extremely strong rainfall does the area become fertile, but this happens no more than three or four times in a century. The Lake Eyre Basin is part of the **Great Artesian Basin**, the world's largest reservoir of groundwater (1.8 million km²). During summer temperatures in Central Australia often exceed 40° Celsius. Winters in the region are more pleasant, with temperatures consistently around 20° Celsius. The outback town of **Alice Springs** is situated near the geographical center of the Australian continent. The countryside around Alice Springs is well known as the red heart of Australia and tourists flock to the region to enjoy its natural beauty. In 1987 the first paved highway through Central Australia was completed. The Stuart Highway runs between Darwin, in the Northern Territory, and Port Augusta, in South Australia. Large sections of Central Australia are tribal lands under the control of Australia's indigenous people – the Aborigines. Most of these lands are only open to visitors who have been granted permission before their arrival. The famous artwork of the Aborigines can be found throughout Central Australia. The aboriginal paintings depict myths from the "dreamtime" and are an important element in the ceremonies and spirituality of Australia's indigenous people.

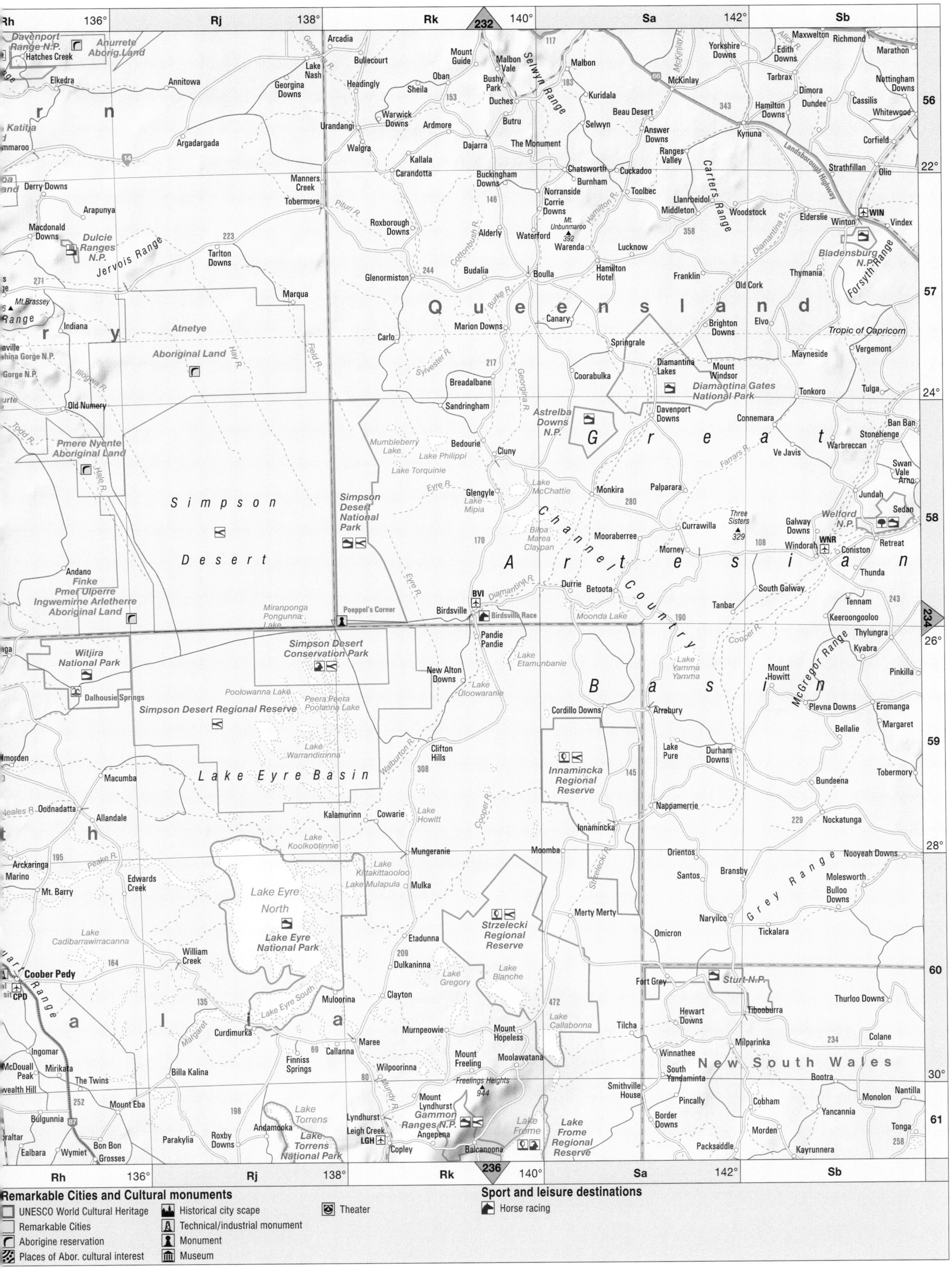

Macdonnell Ranges Mountain chain near Alice Springs – tallest peak: Mount Liebig (1,524 meters) – numerous valleys and gorges in the area – traditional Aboriginal rock paintings **Rg57**

Finke Gorge National Park canyon along the Finke river – Palm Valley with rare red cabbage palms **Rg58**

Henbury Meteorite Craters Thirteen meteorite craters – the largest crater is 15 meters deep and has a diameter of 180 meters – created 5,000 years ago **Rg58**

Chambers Pillar Tall red sandstone formation on the edge of the Simpson Desert – used by early outback explorers for orientation through the desert **Rg58**

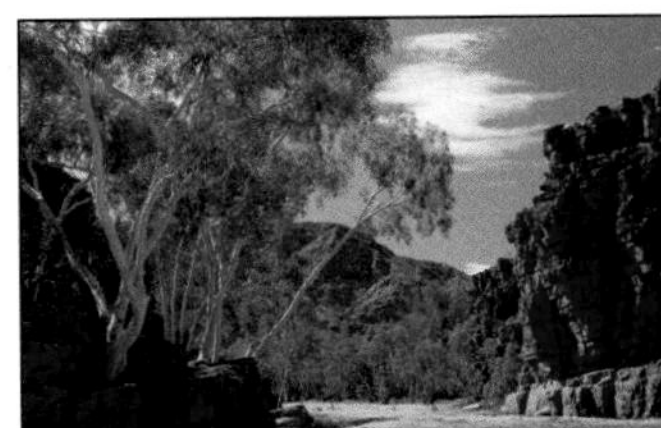

Trephina Gorge National Park Conservation area with streams and lush riverside vegetation – John Hayes Rockhole: a long narrow gorge **Rh57**

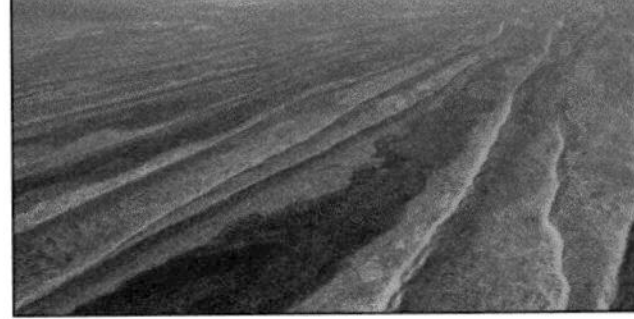

Simpson Desert National Park Large national park with beautiful desert landscapes – large sand dunes up to 20 meters tall and 100 kilometers long **Rk58**

Coober Pedy Opal mining center in the Australian outback – subterranean homes – opal mines – Mine Museum **Rh60**

Remarkable Cities and Cultural monuments

- UNESCO World Cultural Heritage
- Remarkable Cities
- Aborigine reservation
- Places of Abor. cultural interest
- Historical city scape
- Technical/industrial monument
- Monument
- Museum
- Theater

Sport and leisure destinations

- Horse racing

Southwestern Australia

Southwestern Australia covers one third of the state of Western Australia. The region's attractions include the marine life of Shark Bay, giant trees in the south, beautiful beaches on the Indian Ocean in the west, and the red sand dunes of the Great Victoria Desert in the east. The distance from Perth in the far west to Eucla (on the border to the neighboring state South Australia) is around 1,450 kilometers. The greater part of southwestern Australia is sparsely po ulated rural outback land. The terrain co sists mostly of semi-arid grasslands a parched deserts including the Gre Sandy Desert. The Nullarbor Plain is vast flat grassland with a total area 250,000 km². It is situated atop a seri of underground rivers and caves. Mu

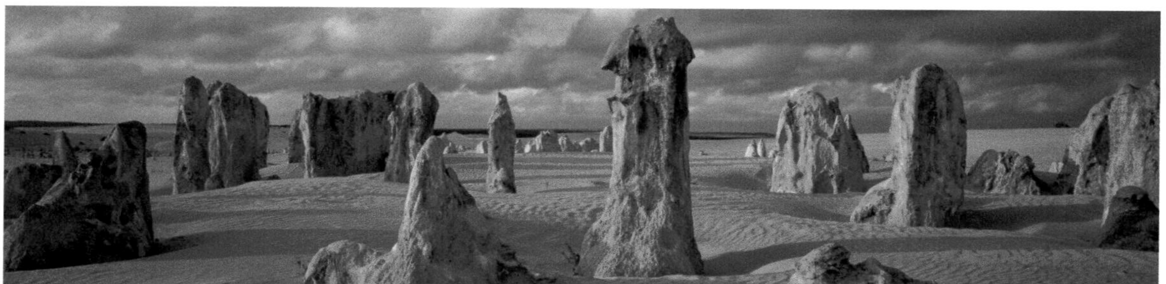

The Pinnacles: a group of limestone formations in the desert Qh

Rottnest Island Island near Perth with nice beaches – automobiles are banned on the island – diverse flora and fauna – home of Rottnest Quokka, a small mammal – Surfing area **Qh61**

Perth Capital and economic center of Western Australia (population 1.3 million) – vibrant cultural scene – beaches on the Indian Ocean **Qh61**

Leeuwin National Park National park along the coast – large accessible caves – vineyards and holiday camps **Qh62/63**

Walpole Nornalup National Park Famous for the giant Karri trees in the Valley of the Giants – Tree Top Walk: steel walkways where visitors roam through the trees 40 meters above ground **Qj63**

Albany Oldest European settlement in Western Australia (1823) – former whaling port – 18th century buildings (photo: Two People's Bay) **Qj63**

Wave Rock 350 kilometers east of Perth – a massive stone formation resembling a wave – the formation is 15 meters high and 100 meters long **Qk62**

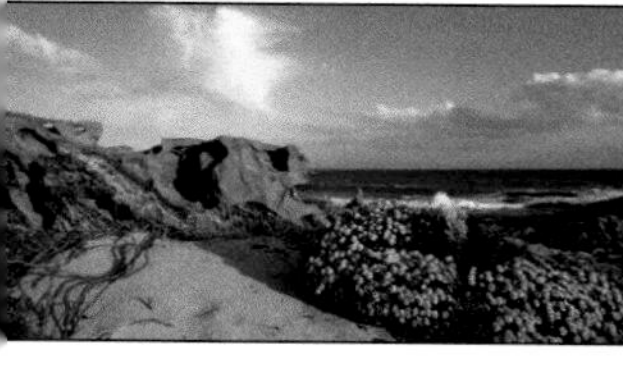

Fitzgerald National Park Park on the southern coast – rare plants and animals – deep gorges, tall cliffs, and secluded beaches **Qk62/63**

Scale 1:4,500,000
0 40 80 Kilometers

Principal travel routes
- Auto route
- Rail road
- Shipping route

Remarkable landscapes and natural monuments
- UNESCO World Natural Heritage
- Rock landscape
- Cave
- River landscape
- Nature park
- National park (landscape)
- National park (flora)
- National park (fauna)
- Biosphere reserve
- Whale watching
- Zoo/safari park
- Coastal landscape
- Beach
- Island
- Underwater reserve

the plain's surface is covered by extensive agricultural fields.
rth is the state capital and largest city Western Australia. The area surrounding the city is known as the "Heartland." **rth** – the "city of lights" – is situated tween the Indian Ocean and the Swan ver and is considered one of the most ractive cities in Australia. The sprawling city is the political, economic, and cultural capital of Western Australia. It is also the most isolated major city on the continent. Perth has a pleasant Mediterranean climate with mild winters and long hot summers.

Southwestern Australia has a milder climate than most of the continent and plentiful rainfall. The region's coastal areas feature numerous vineyards, olive tree groves, fruit gardens, and lush forests with tall karri trees. The coast is also the location of several attractive and historic seaside towns including Margaret River and Yallingup.

The so-called Heartland stretches from the edge of Perth to the eastern goldfields near Kalgoorie. It is a largely rural area with an economy heavily dependent on agriculture. Most of the area is covered by vast golden fields of grain. In recent years, an increasing number of farmers near the coast have started growing olive trees instead of more traditional crops.

The coast is also the location of many of the region's most important natural attractions. The so-called Pinnacles (in **Nambung National Park**) are a series of pointy limestone formations. **Wave Rock**, another fascinating natural attraction in the region, is a 15-meters-tall rock formation that resembles the crest of a wave. It is located near the town of Hyden in a reserve that features several other unique rock formations.

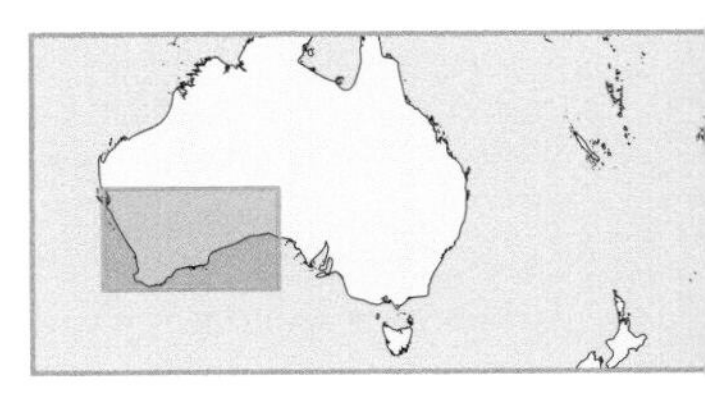

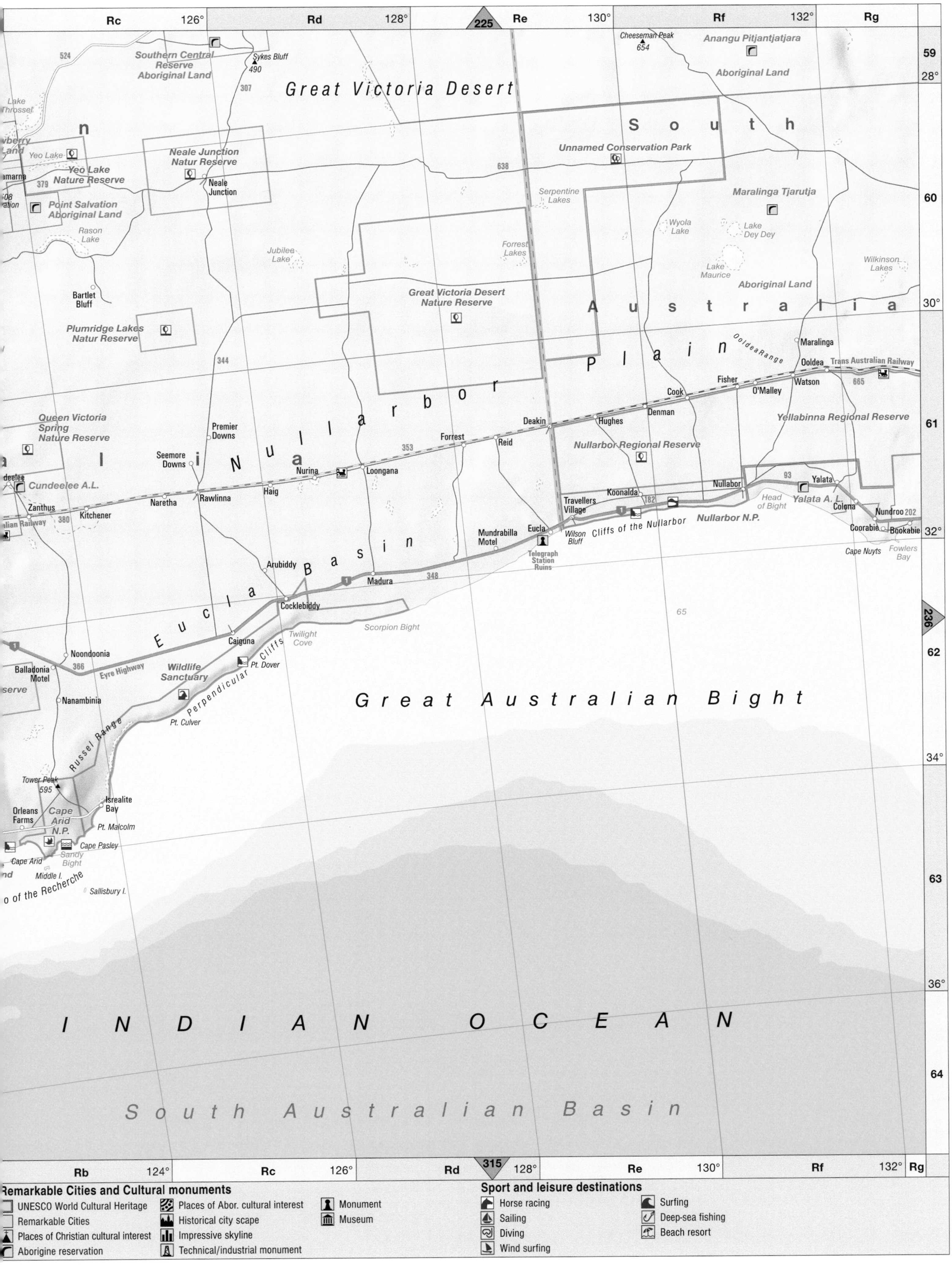

Great Victoria Desert
South Australia
Nullarbor Plain
Eucla Basin
Great Australian Bight
INDIAN OCEAN
South Australian Basin
Southern Central Reserve Aboriginal Land
Neale Junction Natur Reserve
Yeo Lake Nature Reserve
Point Salvation Aboriginal Land
Plumridge Lakes Natur Reserve
Queen Victoria Spring Nature Reserve
Unnamed Conservation Park
Great Victoria Desert Nature Reserve
Maralinga Tjarutja
Anangu Pitjantjatjara
Aboriginal Land
Yellabinna Regional Reserve
Nullarbor Regional Reserve
Nullarbor N.P.
Trans Australian Railway
Eyre Highway
Cundeelee A.L.
Yalata A.L.
Cape Arid N.P.
Wildlife Sanctuary
Kalgoorie, Zanthus, Kitchener, Naretha, Rawlinna, Haig, Nurina, Loongana, Forrest, Reid, Deakin, Hughes, Cook, Denman, Fisher, O'Malley, Watson, Ooldea, Maralinga, Nullarbor, Yalata, Colona, Nundroo, Coorabie, Bookabie, Koonalda, Travellers Village, Eucla, Wilson Bluff, Mundrabilla Motel, Madura, Arubiddy, Cocklebiddy, Caiguna, Noondoonia, Balladonia Motel, Nanambinia, Israelite Bay, Orleans Farms, Premier Downs, Seemore Downs, Bartlet Bluff, Neale Junction, Sykes Bluff, Cheeseman Peak, Tower Peak, Pt. Malcolm, Cape Pasley, Cape Arid, Sandy Bight, Middle I., Sallisbury I., Pt. Culver, Pt. Dover, Twilight Cove, Scorpion Bight, Head of Bight, Cape Nuyts, Fowlers Bay, Cliffs of the Nullarbor, Perpendicular Cliffs, Russel Range, Ooldea Range, Telegraph Station Ruins
Rb, Rc, Rd, Re, Rf, Rg; 124°, 126°, 128°, 130°, 132°; 28°, 30°, 32°, 34°, 36°; 59, 60, 61, 62, 63, 64

225
236
315

Remarkable Cities and Cultural monuments
- UNESCO World Cultural Heritage
- Remarkable Cities
- Places of Christian cultural interest
- Aborigine reservation
- Places of Abor. cultural interest
- Historical city scape
- Impressive skyline
- Technical/industrial monument
- Monument
- Museum

Sport and leisure destinations
- Horse racing
- Sailing
- Diving
- Wind surfing
- Surfing
- Deep-sea fishing
- Beach resort

Kalgoorie-Boulder Twin gold rush towns in the outback – historic mines and architecture **Ra61**

Esperance Bay Small port city – popular holiday destination – beaches – sailing and deep-sea fishing **Ra62**

Cape Le Grand National Park Hilly coastline – impressive bays with long white beaches **Rb62**

Cape Arid National Park Unique hill and coastal landscapes – beaches – natural pools with rare plants and animals **Rb62**

Nullarbor Plain The area is almost totally waterless – Australia's largest karst – little vegetation **Rc–Rf60/61**

Nullarbor Cliffs In a national park – incredible jagged and steep coastline – cliffs up to 80 meters above the Great Australian Bight **ReRf61**

Trans-Australian Railway (Perth-Sydney) Route of the legendary Indian Pacific line – runs 4,000 kilometers in just under three days – 480 km straight through the Nullarbor Plain without curves or turns

The northernmost region of Australia consists of ▨ **Arnhem Land** in the Northern Territory and **Cape York Peninsula** in the state of Queensland. The entire region has a tropical climate with high temperatures throughout the year and heavy rainfall during the so-called wet season. Much of region is inaccessible by road during the the wet season because of frequent flooding. A large portion of Northern Australia is under the administration

of local ◻ aboriginal communities. B
tween Arnhem Land and Cape York Pe
insula lies the **Gulf of Carpentaria**,
large body of water that indents Austr
lia's generally smooth coastline.
Both parts of northern Australia are ri
in **mineral resources**. Arnhem Land
major source of bauxite (aluminum or

Daintree National Park encompasses Australia's most ancient rainforests **Sc**

Aboriginal Dance A gathering of the Corroboree tribe on ◻ Groote Eylandt off the coast of Arnhem Land – traditional legends and history are told through dance **Rj52/53**

Mornington Island Main island in the Wellesley Island group (Queensland) – under the administration of local ◻ Aborigines – the main settlement is Gununa **Rk54**

Nicholson River Delta Typical central Australian basin landscapes – usually flooded or parched **Rk54**

Lizard Island Coral island in the northern section of the ▤ Great Barrier Reef National Park – fascinating marine life **Sc53**

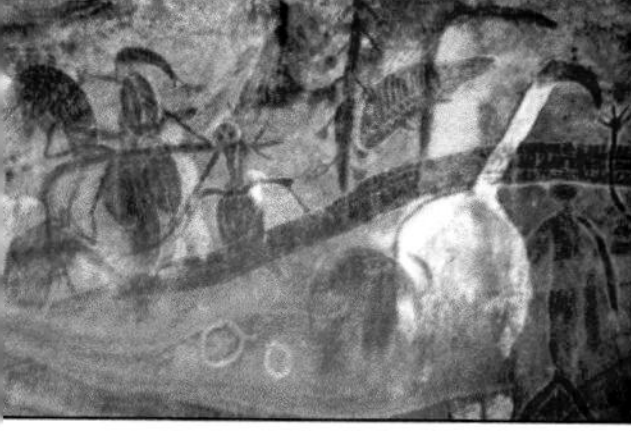

Rock Paintings near Laura Hundreds of ▨ rock paintings – some are open to the public – Split Rock and Guguyalangi are well-known and easy to reach **Sc53**

Cooktown Captain Cook stopped here in 1770 to repair his ship Endeavour – gold rush on the Palm River in 1872 – ▥ James Cook Museum **Sc53**

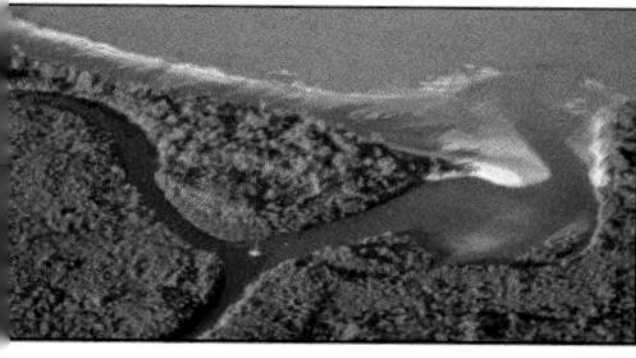

Cedar Bay National Park ◪ Tropical river delta on the Coral Sea – ◻ Wujal Wujal Aboriginal village located in the park **Sc53**

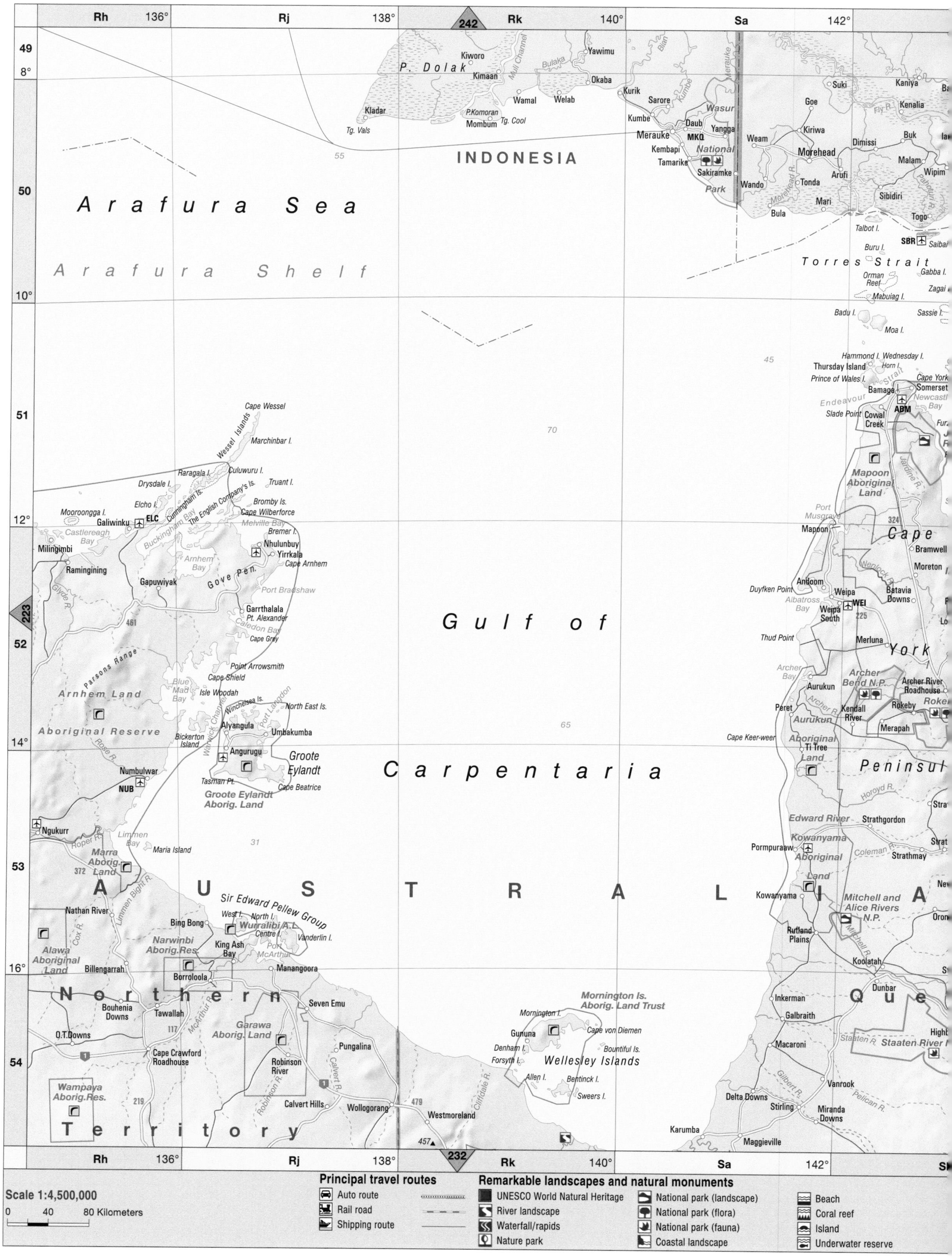

Rh 136° Rj 138° Rk 140° Sa 142°

Arafura Sea

Arafura Shelf

INDONESIA

Torres Strait

Gulf of Carpentaria

Arnhem Land Aboriginal Reserve

Groote Eylandt

Wellesley Islands

AUSTRALIA

Northern Territory

Cape York Peninsula

Scale 1:4,500,000
0 40 80 Kilometers

Principal travel routes
Auto route
Rail road
Shipping route

Remarkable landscapes and natural monuments
UNESCO World Natural Heritage
River landscape
Waterfall/rapids
Nature park
National park (landscape)
National park (flora)
National park (fauna)
Coastal landscape
Beach
Coral reef
Island
Underwater reserve

●oktown on the Cape York Peninsula s been a gold mining center since the d of the 19th century and Weipa on the ninsula's west coast is home to the gest bauxite mine in the world.

e tip of the **Cape York Peninsula** is the rthernmost area in Australia. It is a re- on of thick rainforests, flooded plains, ocodile infested rivers, large cattle ran- es, mines. The area also features veral isolated Aboriginal communities with interesting cultural attractions. North of the peninsula lie the **Torres Strait Islands**: the most northern of these islands are separated from Papua New Guinea by only a few kilometers of water.

The **Great Barrier Reef** is located off the coast of northeastern Australia. With its coral islands and diverse marine life, the Great Barrier Reef is one of the world's natural wonders. The reef's existence and its incredible biodiversity is threatened by rising ocean temperatures that may be caused by global warming. The best starting point for any expedition to the Great Barrier Reef is the city of **Cairns**. The stretch of coastline to the north and south of Cairns is one of the most popular holiday destinations in the country for both Australians and foreign tourists. Between October and April the waters off the northeastern coast are inhabited by the highly poisonous Box Jellyfish, a potential danger to swimmers in the area.

The **Atherton Tableland**, a section of the Great Dividing Range is just 10 to 15 kilometers away from the coastal area around Cairns. The 900 meter tall plateau was created 10,000 years ago as a result of volcanic activity. The breathtaking landscapes in the tableland include several crater lakes, high waterfalls and vibrant green rainforests.

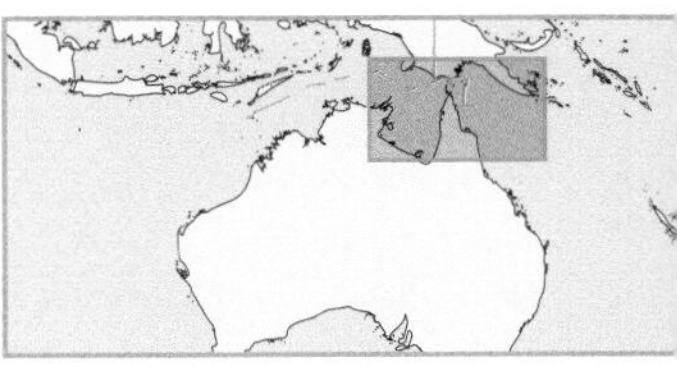

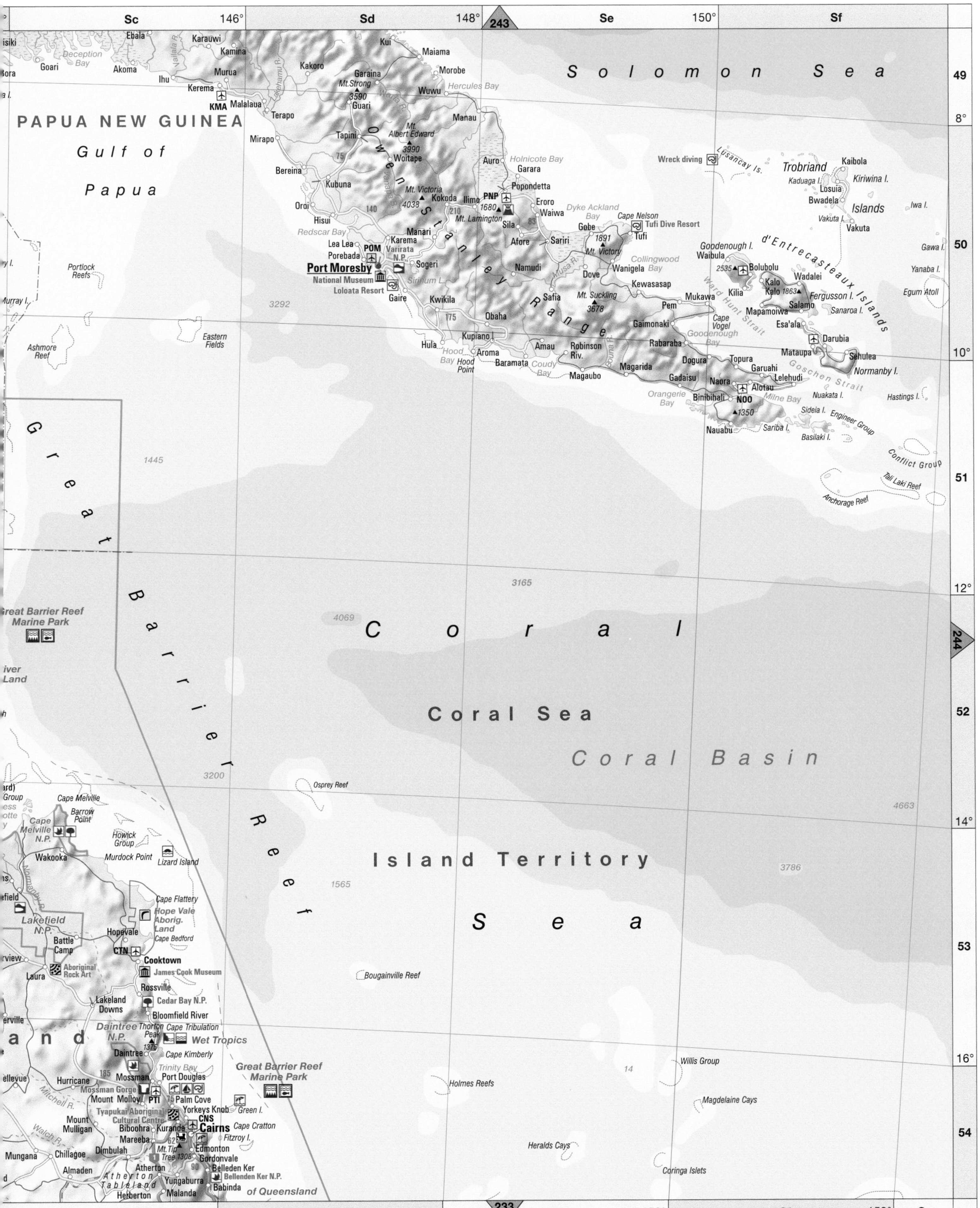

Cape Tribulation Rainforest and ocean reefs – long beaches – several ecotourism resorts **Sc54**

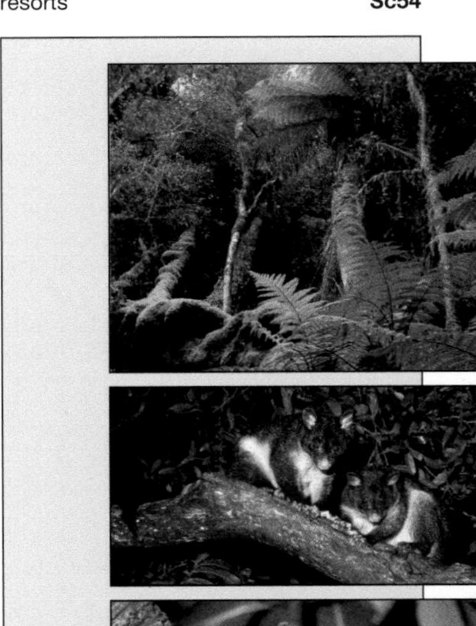

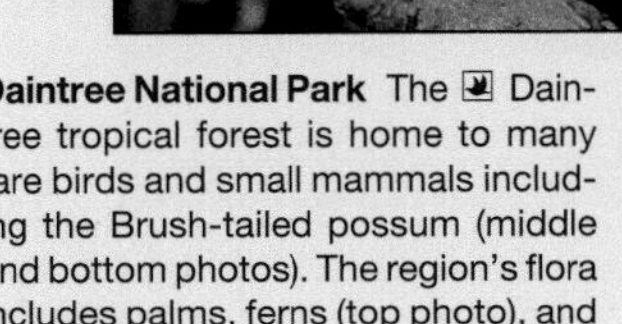

Daintree National Park The Daintree tropical forest is home to many rare birds and small mammals including the Brush-tailed possum (middle and bottom photos). The region's flora includes palms, ferns (top photo), and vines. **Sc54**

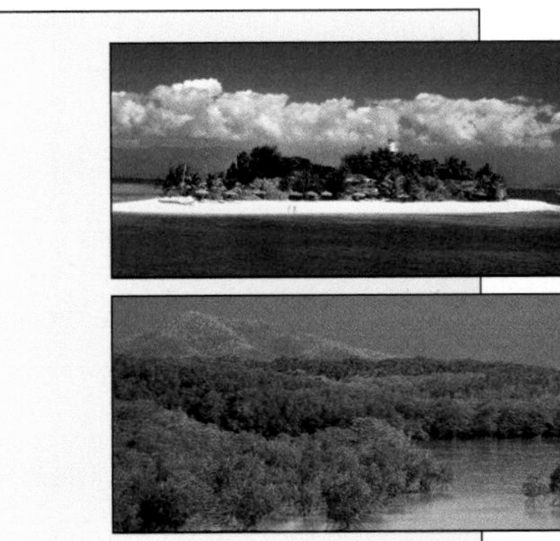

Port Douglas This popular tourist destination is a good area for sailing and diving. The barrier reef is in close proximity to the coast. The Rainforest Habitat provides information on local forests. **Sc54**

Cairnes-Kuranda train route An hour and a half ride around curves and through tunnels – passes rainforests and waterfalls – the Skyrail: the world's longest cable car **Sc54**

243

244

233

Remarkable Cities and Cultural monuments
- UNESCO World Cultural Heritage
- Remarkable Cities
- Aborigine reservation
- Places of Abor. cultural interest
- Museum

Sport and leisure destinations
- Sailing
- Diving
- Beach resort

Northeastern Australia can be roughly divided from east to west into four areas. The world's largest coral reef, the Great Barrier Reef, with its many islands, are located in the west. The reef, a UNESCO world heritage site, is over 2,300 kilometers long. It borders a narrow fertile coastal strip that extends inland up to the Great Dividing Range. The Great Dividing Range is bordered in the west by the large flat Carpentaria Basin.

The Great Barrier Reef is a chain over 2,500 separate coral reefs that sta south of the Tropic of Capricorn and stre ches almost to New Guinea. The ent reef was designated a world heritage s in 1981. Countless species of marine l inhabit the reef, including at least 4 colorful types of coral, 4,000 species

Underwater bounty: the Great Barrier Reef **Sd–Sg53/**

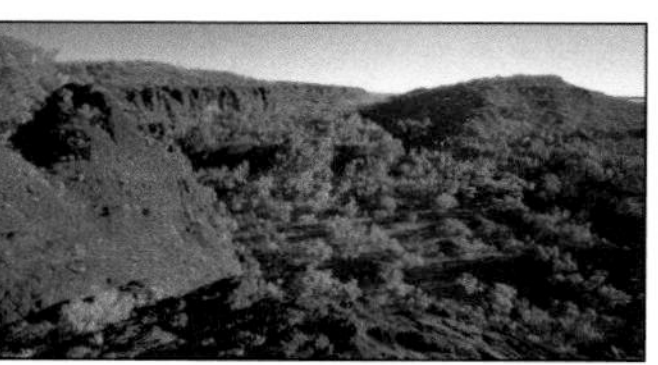

Lawn Hill National Park Green oasis in the outback – abundant wildlife – gorges and sandstone ranges **Rk55**

Fossil Mammal Site Part of Lawn Hill NP – paleontologists have found fossils of extinct mammals on the site – UNESCO world heritage site **Rk55**

Porcupine Gorge National Park The park is home to a canyon of the same name with 150-meter-high walls **Sc56**

Milla Milla Falls In the Atherton Tableland – 65-meter-wide waterfalls – most impressive during the rainy season **Sc54**

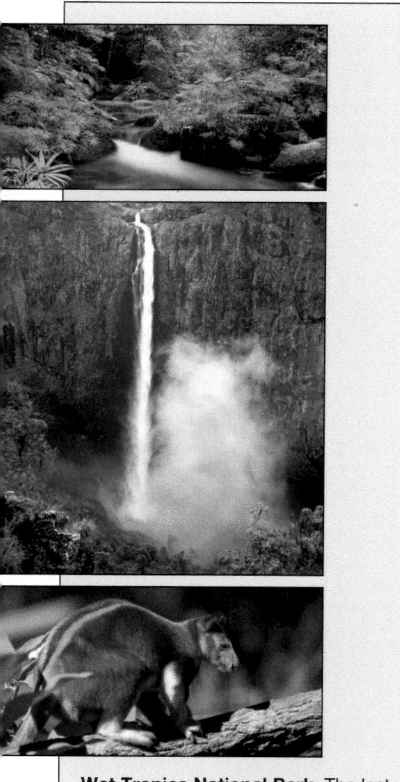

Wet Tropics National Park The last remnants of the northern Australian rainforest are in this national park (UNESCO world heritage site). Photos from top to bottom: Mossman Gorge **(Sc54)**, Wallaman Falls **(Sc55)**, tree kangaroo **ScSd54/55**

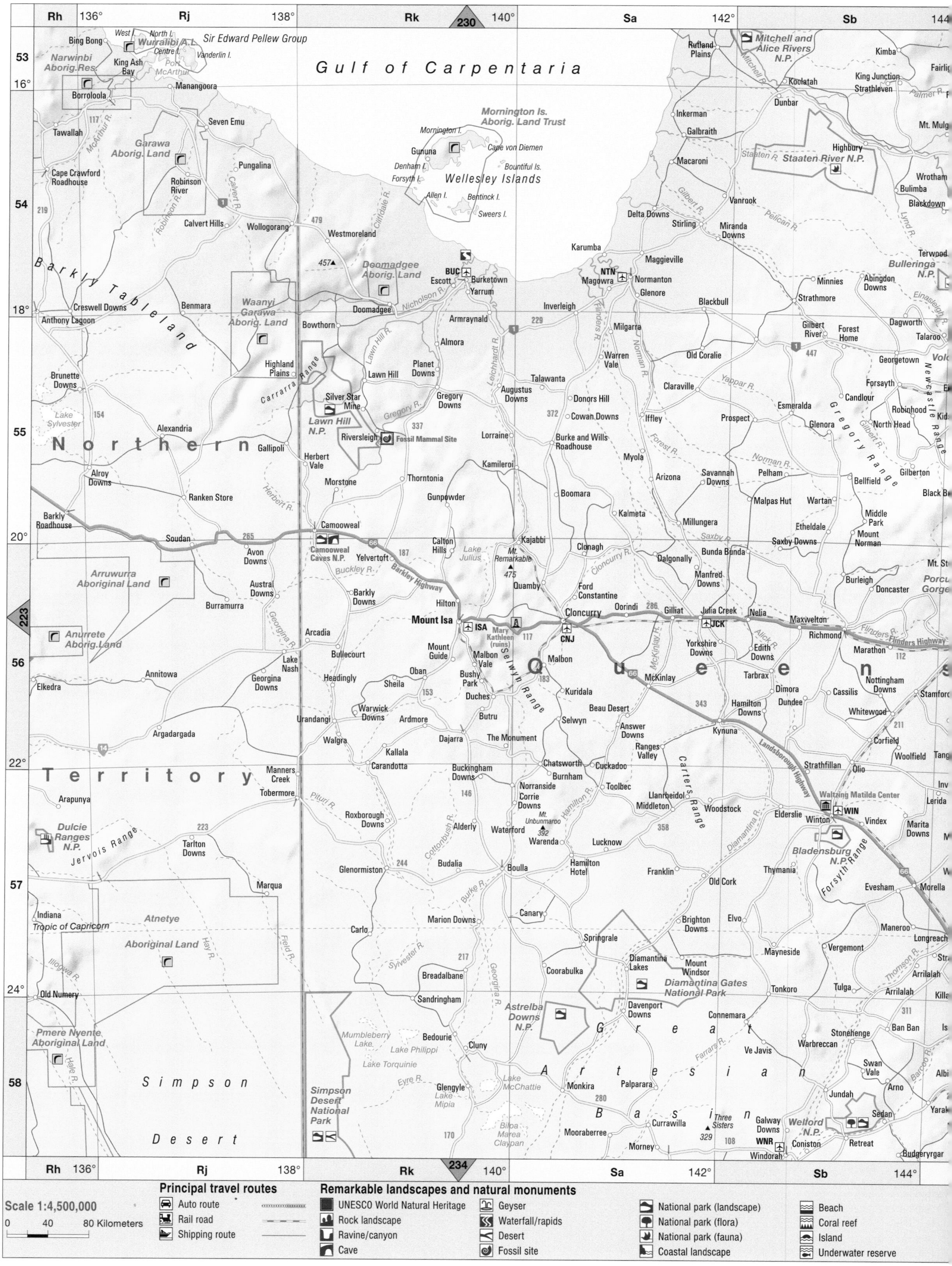

Scale 1:4,500,000
0 40 80 Kilometers

Principal travel routes
- Auto route
- Rail road
- Shipping route

Remarkable landscapes and natural monuments
- UNESCO World Natural Heritage
- Rock landscape
- Ravine/canyon
- Cave
- Geyser
- Waterfall/rapids
- Desert
- Fossil site
- National park (landscape)
- National park (flora)
- National park (fauna)
- Coastal landscape
- Beach
- Coral reef
- Island
- Underwater reserve

ollusks, 2,000 fish species, as well as e sea turtles and manatees. Global arming and coastal pollution are major eats to the health and long term sural of the reef.
rge sections of the reef are protected ture reserves, whiles others are open tourists – most traveling from coastal wns such as MacKay or Townsville. In dition to tourism, agriculture also plays important role in the regional economy of Northeastern Australia. Sugar cane is one of the most important crops grown in the region.
The mountains of the **Great Dividing Range** stretch along the entire eastern coast of Australia. In northeastern Australia, the range reaches a maximum height of 1,300 meters. The **Wet Tropics World Heritage Site** encompasses several large national parks. It contains the remaining sections of a vast rain forest that covered most of Australia 50 million years ago.
Between the Great Dividing Range and the Gulf of Carpentaria lies the Carpentaria Basin. The basin is a hot, dry region covering most of the state of **Queensland**. Despite the dry climate, floods are a major problem in the region during the rainy season. Bushfires are also a serious threat to the region.
The main industries in Northeastern Australia's sparsely populated outback are sheep and cattle ranching as well as mining. The town of Mt. Isa has an area as large as Switzerland within its city limits, with a population of less than 25,000. Because of the vast distances, airplanes play a vital role in the lives of many Outback residents. Many people rely on the Flying Doctor Service for medical care and many of the region's children are educated by the School of the Air.

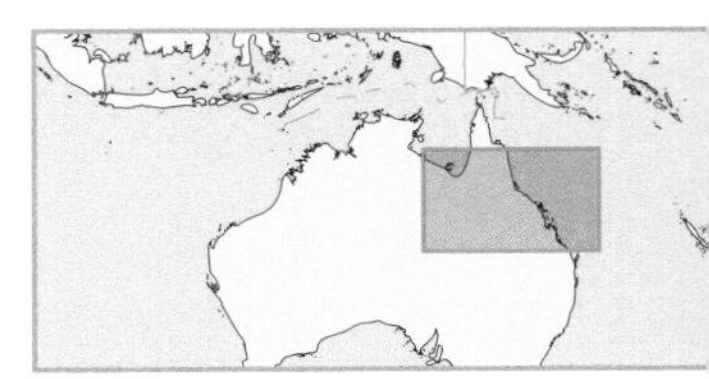

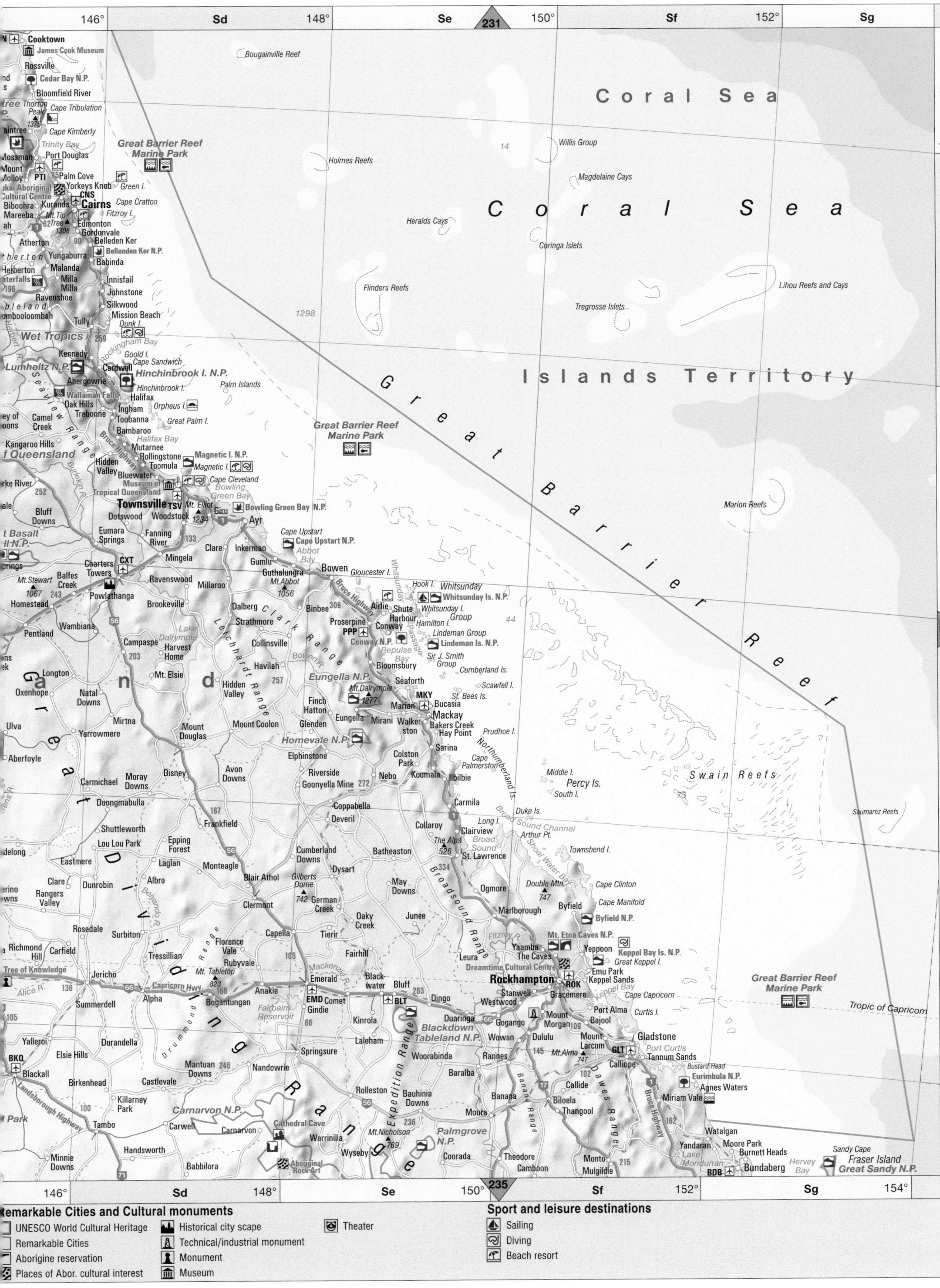

Hinchinbrook-Island National Park
Nature reserve – Mangroves and tropical forests – Mount Bowen (1,142 meters) **Sd55**

Whitsunday Island National Park
National park with azure blue water, sandy white beaches and tropical vegetation. **Se56**

Great Barrier Reef Not all of the islands in this world heritage site are coral islands; some are the remnants of mountains chains that were submerged and surrounded by coral. Reefs are formed when tiny animals called coral secrete small shells made of limestone. The accumulation of limestone eventually results in the formation of reefs. The Great Barrier Reef is home to over 2,000 fish species. Photos from top to bottom: Coral island, Reef shark, Coral formation, Clown Anemone Fish **Sd–Sg53/58**

Coral Sea

Islands Territory

Great Barrier Reef

emarkable Cities and Cultural monuments
- UNESCO World Cultural Heritage
- Remarkable Cities
- Aborigine reservation
- Places of Abor. cultural interest
- Historical city scape
- Technical/industrial monument
- Monument
- Museum
- Theater

Sport and leisure destinations
- Sailing
- Diving
- Beach resort

Eastern Australia

Eastern Australia covers portions of two Australian states: (northern) New South Wales and (southern) Queensland. The region itself is divided into three distinct sections: a narrow **coastal region**, the **Great Dividing Range**, and the open spaces of the **Outback**. The majority of the population is concentrated near the coast. **Brisbane**, the third largest city in Australia, is the economic center of the region and the capital of Queensland.

The region's economy is supported p marily by agriculture and tourism. T region's most visited tourist destinat is Surfer's Paradise on the Gold Coa The area around Coffs Harbour is a ma center for banana farming. Pineapp and sugar cane are important crops the Sunshine Coast.

Wilpena Pound in Flinders-Ranges-National Park **Rk**

Salt Lakes The largest salt lakes in the region are Lake Eyre, Lake Torren, Lake Frome and Lake Gairdner. They are all remnants of a large inland sea. All of the lakes are located in the Great Artesian Basin. **RhRk60/61**

Flinders Ranges National Park One of the oldest landscapes on earth – landscape with unusual stones – the park's major attraction is Wilpena Pound, a large natural amphitheater – Arkaroo Rock: site of Aboriginal rock paintings **Rk61**

Giant Red Kangaroo This type of Kangaroo grows up to two meters tall and is the largest marsupial in Australia. They can jump over 10 meters and can run at speeps of 80 km per hour. They can dig one meter deep to search for water in the dry outback deserts.

Mutawintji National Park Beautiful sandstone landscape – green canyons – over 300 sites with Aboriginal art – camp sites **Sb61**

Kinchega National Park On the west bank of the Darling River – streams and lakes – home to numerous species of aquatic birds (photo: Giant Eucalyptus Tree on Menindee Lake) **Sb62**

Scale 1:4,500,000
0 40 80 Kilometers

Principal travel routes
- Auto route
- Rail road
- Shipping route

Remarkable landscapes and natural monuments
- UNESCO World Natural Heritage
- Rock landscape
- Extinct volcano
- Geyser
- Cave
- Waterfall/rapids
- Lake country
- Desert
- National park (landscape)
- National park (flora)
- National park (fauna)
- Biosphere reserve
- Zoo/safari park
- Coastal landscape
- Beach
- Coral reef

f the coast of eastern Australia lies a ·ies of sand islands, including Fra- r Island – the largest sand island in the ·rld and a UNESCO world heritage site. e southern portion of the Great Bar- r Reef begins just north of Fraser and. The climate on the coast is en- ·ly subtropical and becomes warmer m south to north.

e mountains and hills of the Great viding Range are located between the Outback and the coast. The Great Dividing Range, with mountains rising above 1,600 meters, stretches along the east coast of Australia. The Great Dividing Range area has a mild climate and heavy rainfall. The area's thick rainforests include many unique ecosystems. A network of national parks and nature reserves protect the flora and fauna of the area including the unique Antarctic Beech. Many of these national parks have the interesting feature of encompassing both subtropical rainforests and temperate rainforests at higher elevations.

The western Great Dividing Range borders the flat expanses of the Australian Outback. The thinly populated **Outback** is dotted by many small settlements. Towns in the Outback are usually no more than one paved road and a few small buildings. The region also possesses some of the world's largest farms and cattle ranches. Kangaroos, Australia's "national" animals, are common in the continent's interior. Farther inland, the region's climate becomes increasingly drier and farms and ranches are replaced by parched deserts and semi-arid regions. Despite the raw climate there are a few scattered settlements deep in the interior. Most of these cities are mining towns such Broken Hill, a center for silver mining.

Remarkable Cities and Cultural monuments

- UNESCO World Cultural Heritage
- Remarkable Cities
- Aborigine reservation
- Places of Abor. cultural interest
- Historical city scape
- Technical/industrial monument
- Remarkable lighthouse
- Monument
- Space telescope
- Museum

Sport and leisure destinations

- Horse racing
- Sailing
- Diving
- Wind surfing
- Surfing
- Canoeing/rafting
- Beach resort
- Amusement/theme park

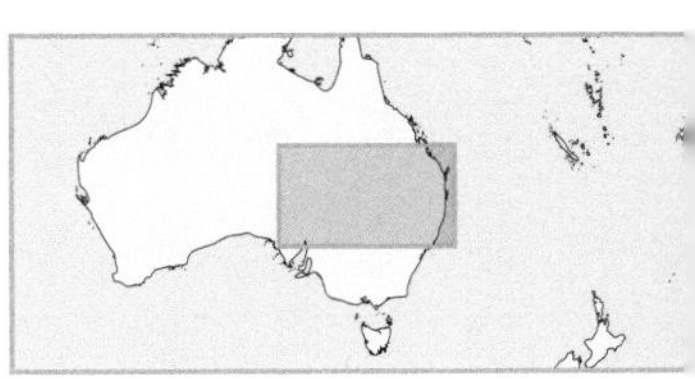

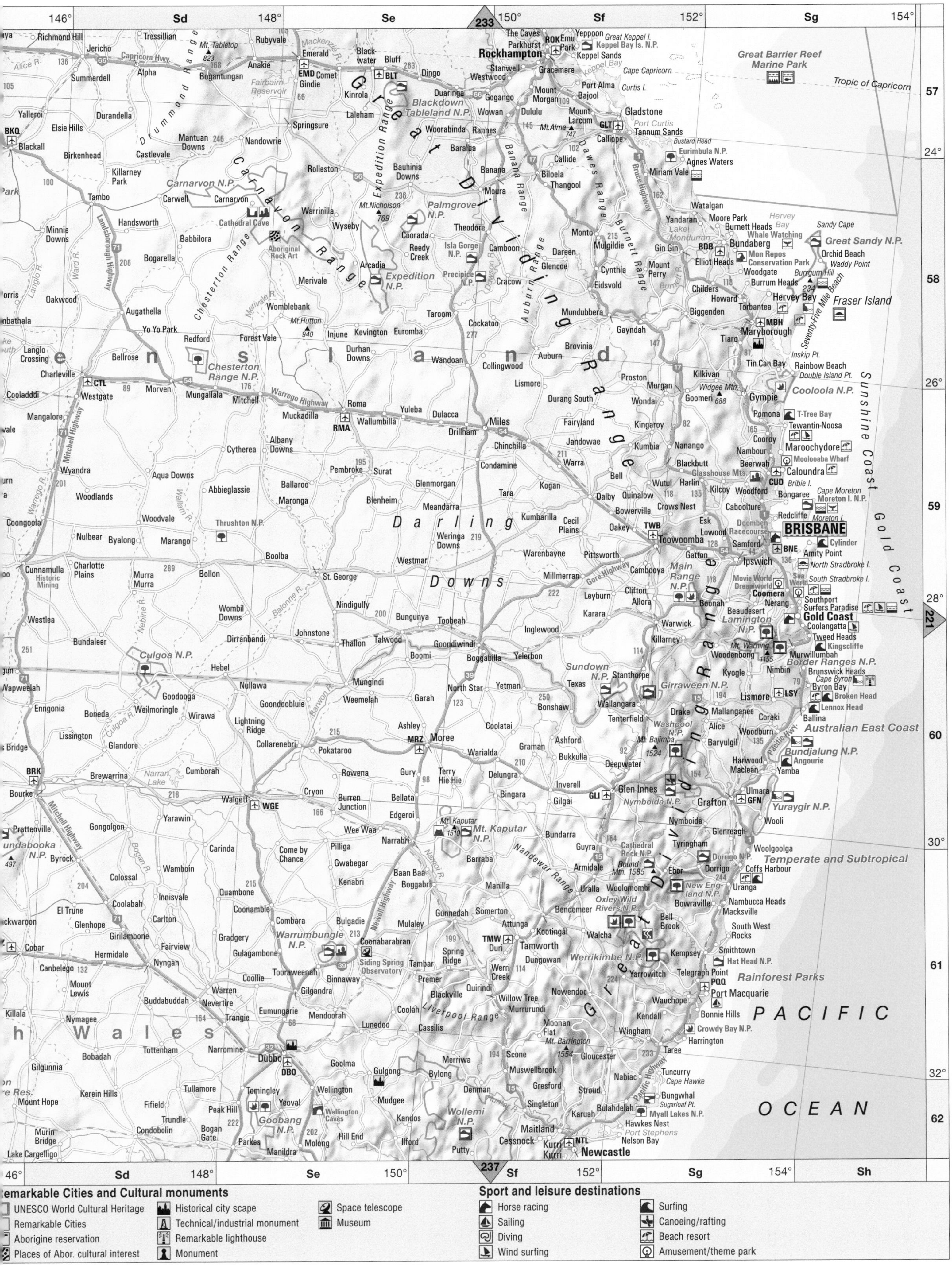

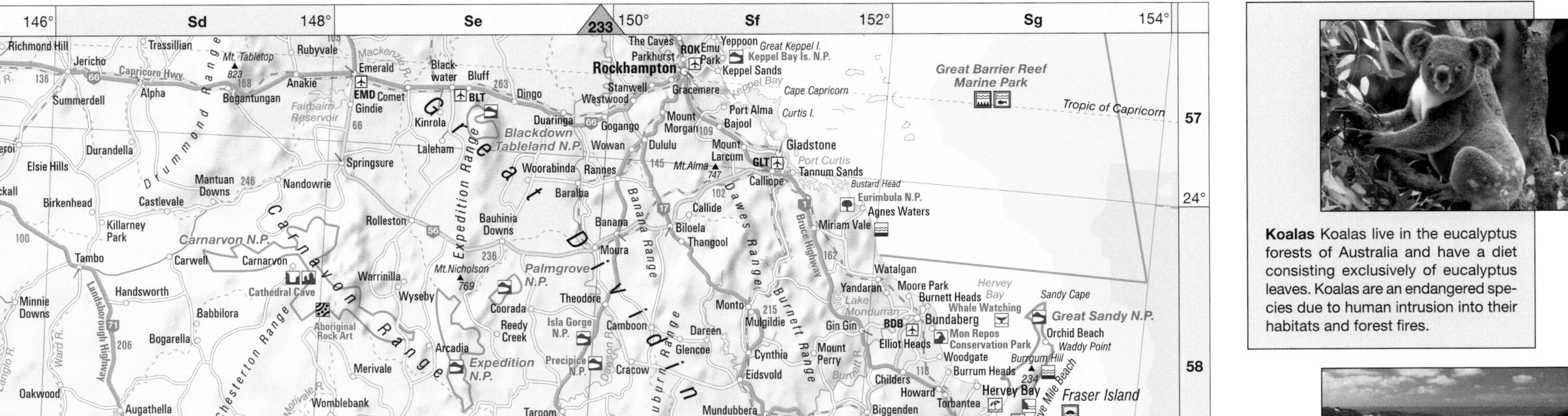

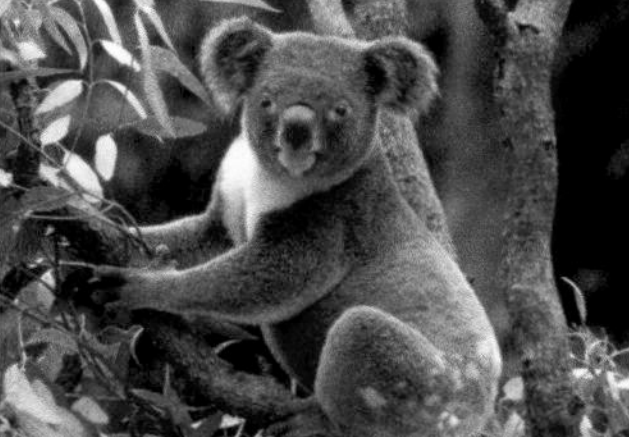

Koalas Koalas live in the eucalyptus forests of Australia and have a diet consisting exclusively of eucalyptus leaves. Koalas are an endangered species due to human intrusion into their habitats and forest fires.

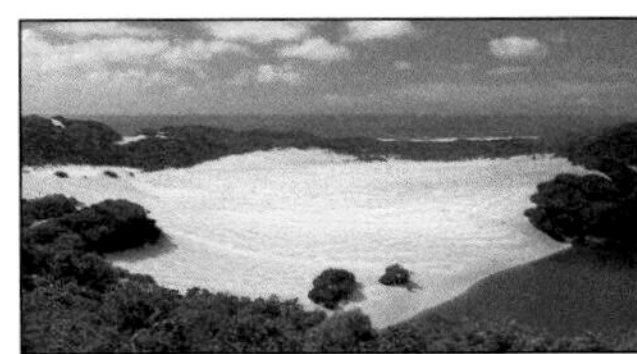

Fraser Island UNESCO world heritage site – the world's largest sand island – tall sand dunes – rainforest in the interior **Sg58**

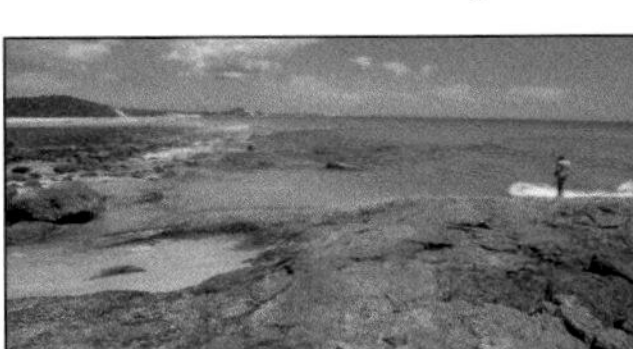

Moreton Island National Park Mount Tempest (world's tallest sand dune) – beautiful beaches – whale-watching **Sg59**

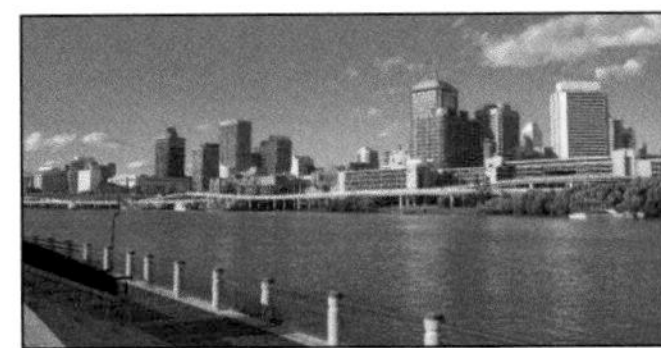

Brisbane Population 1.5 million – botanical gardens – Southbank Parklands – Cultural Center (theater, concerts, museum) **Sg59**

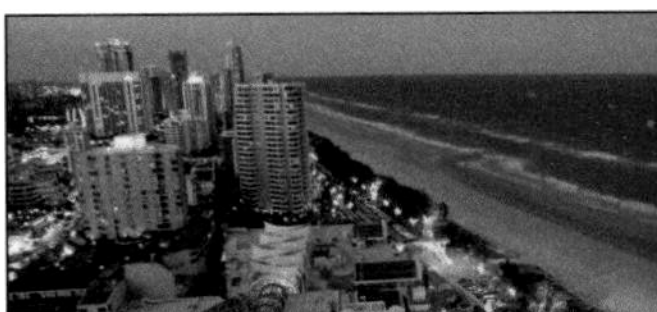

Surfers Paradise Forty kilometers of beaches – 300 days of sunshine annually – large amusement parks **Sg59**

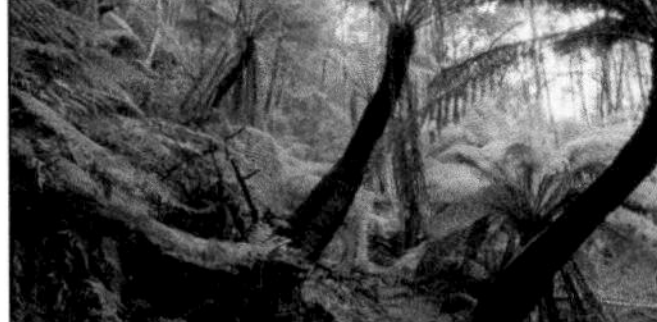

Subtropical Rain Forest Parks National Parks in the interior – humid rainforests – diverse flora and fauna **Sg60/61**

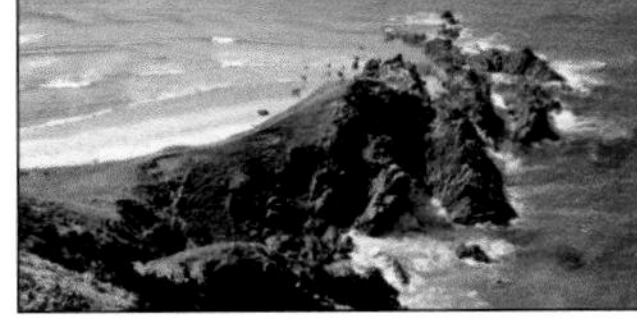

Cape Byron The easternmost point of Australia – lighthouse with an impressive view – tourist resorts in Byron Bay **Sg60**

The climate of southern Australia fits the pattern of most of the continent. The farther inland an area is, the less rainfall it gets. The region covers portions of three states: New South Wales, Victoria, and South Australia. A large percentage of the region has a subtropical climate with plentiful rainfall. Southeastern Australia is the most densely populated region on the continent and encompasses several large cities including **Sydney** and **Melbourne**. Australia's national capi Canberra, is also situated in the regi The **Great Dividing Range** – a lo mountain range that runs along the e ire east coast of Australia – begins j north of Melbourne. Mount Koscius the highest mountain in Australia, ris 2,228 meters above sea level. The mou

The Twelve Apostles near Melbourne the state of Victoria **Sb**

Mungo National Park 40,000-year-old relicts of early aboriginal culture – "Walls of China," a line of white sand dunes (UNESCO world heritage site) **Sb62**

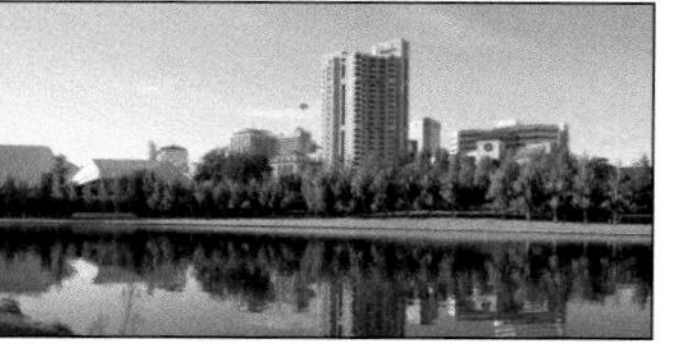

Adelaide Capital of the state of South Australia – population 1.2 million – vibrant cultural scene – one of the world's largest arts and culture festivals **Rk63**

Flinders Chase National Park Located on Kangaroo Island – cliffs and interesting rock formations – seals and sea lions **Rj63**

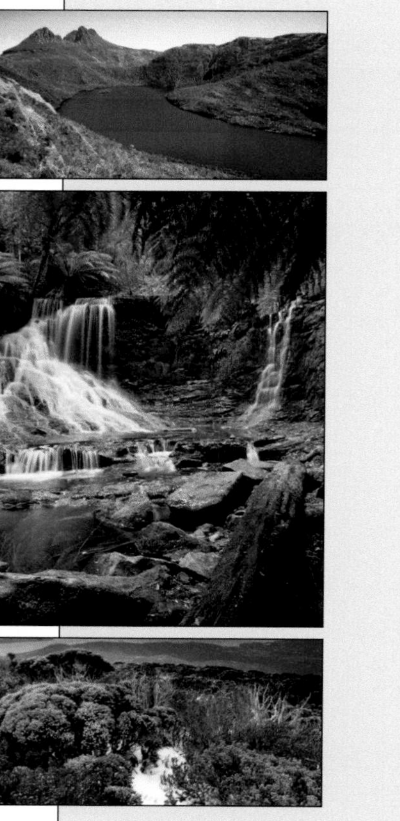

Tasmania About the size of Ireland, this hilly island was "discovered" by Abel Tasman in 1642. The island is Australia's southernmost state. Tasmania has some of the world's few remaining pristine temperate rain forest ecosystems as well as an abundance of rare animals, historic sites and 14 national parks. The rare Tasmanian Devil and the Wombat are two fascinating animals native to Tasmania. Photos from top to bottom: Cradle Mountain (Lake St. Clair National Park), Mount Field National Park, South West National Park **Sc–Se66/67**

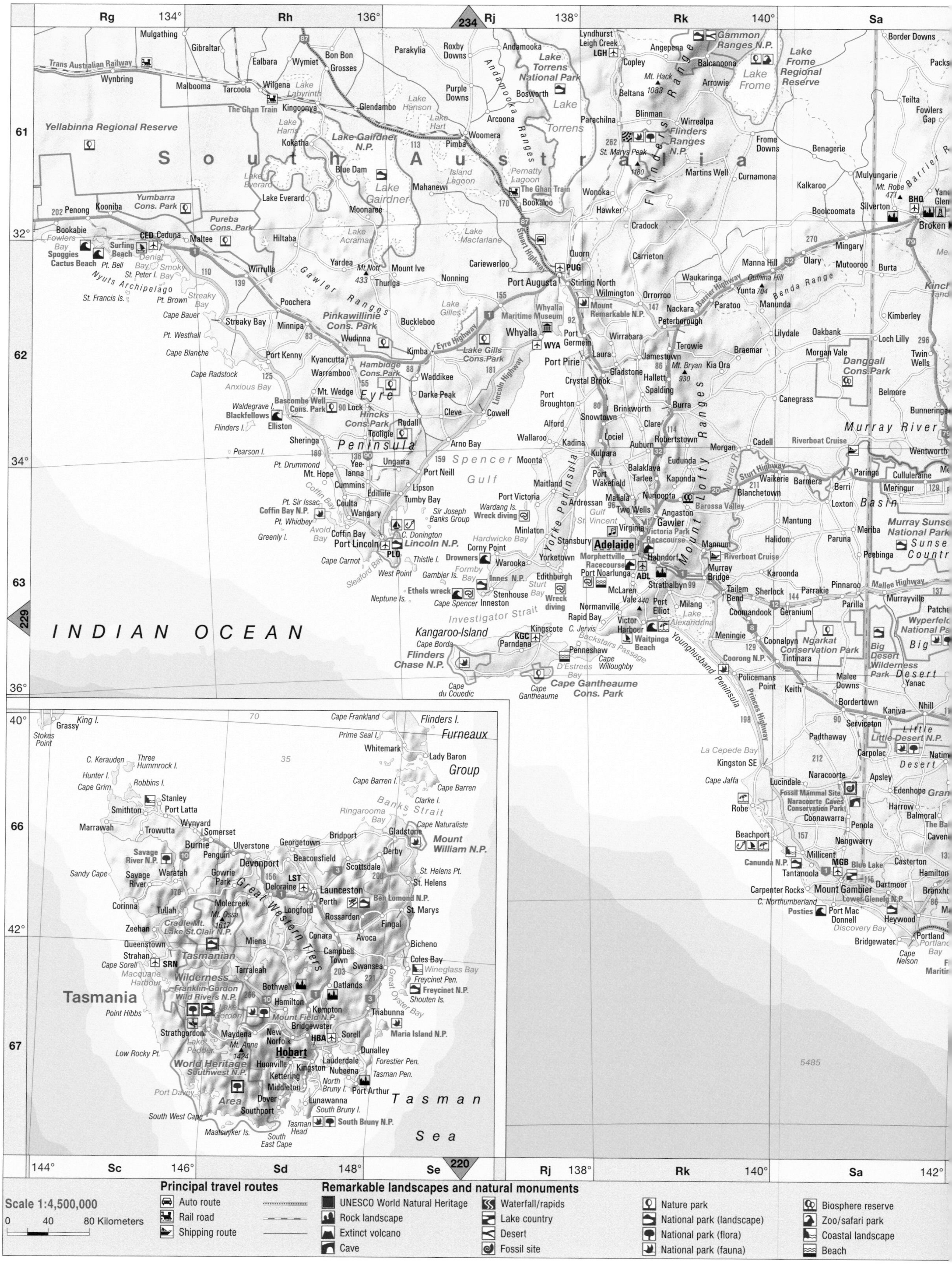

Scale 1:4,500,000
0 40 80 Kilometers

Principal travel routes
- Auto route
- Rail road
- Shipping route

Remarkable landscapes and natural monuments
- UNESCO World Natural Heritage
- Rock landscape
- Extinct volcano
- Cave
- Waterfall/rapids
- Lake country
- Desert
- Fossil site
- Nature park
- National park (landscape)
- National park (flora)
- National park (fauna)
- Biosphere reserve
- Zoo/safari park
- Coastal landscape
- Beach

n is located in the Snowy Mountains, ection of the Great Dividing Range. In e higher elevations of the mountain ge snowfall, rare in Australia, is common in winter, while in summer mountain wers cover the sides of the peaks. e source of the country's longest river, e **Murray River**, is located in the eat Dividing Range. The Murray River ws over 2,500 kilometers from east to st before reaching its delta near the city of Adelaide in South Australia. Most of Southern Australia, like the rest of the continent, consists of dry and sparsely populated countryside. Only a limited percentage of the land in the region is arable but irrigation projects have opened large areas to farming in recent decades. Countless fascinating rock formations are scattered throughout the southern outback including the sandstone mountains in the **Grampians** and the rock formations in **Mungo National Park**, the **Mount Lofty Ranges**, and the **Flinders Range**.

The bluffs west of Melbourne with their views of the **Twelve Apostles** stone formations are one of the most visited natural attractions in the region.

Kangaroo Island off the coast of South Australia is the third largest Australian island. The island is home to interesting wildlife including, koalas, wallabies, and kangaroos. The island also includes pristine coastal areas and unique flora.

Tasmania (64,880 km²) is separated from the Australian mainland by the 200-kilometer-wide Bass Strait. Tasmania's terrain is mostly hilly. Mount Ossa (1,617 meters) is the highest point on the island. Tasmania's national parks with their temperate rainforests and unique fauna encompass some of the world's most pristine natural settings.

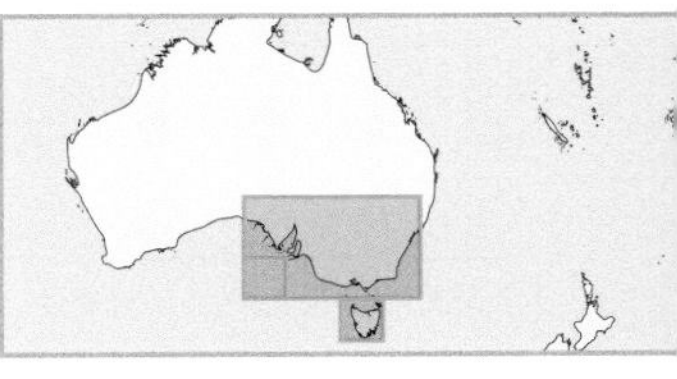

Blue Mountains Mountains rising up to 1,000 meters – named for the blue hue of the local eucalyptus trees – Three Sisters (tall rock formations) **SeSf62**

Sydney The economic center of Australia has a population of four million. Sydney is an attractive city renowned for its Harbour Bridge and the Opera House (bottom photo). The well-known Bondi and Manly beaches are popular with surfers and swimmers. **Sf62**

Canberra Capital of Australia – population 310,000 – planned city – important museums and parks **Se63**

Sovereign Hill Historic gold mining town in the Ballarat region – famous for the Eureka Stockade, a revolt by local gold miners against license fees in 1854 **Sb64**

Melbourne Capital of Victoria – population 3.5 million – second largest city in Australia – important museums include the National Gallery of Victoria (art) and the Melbourne Museum (local history) **Sc64**

Great Ocean Road Fascinating coastal route with cliffs, beaches, and forests – The "Twelve Apostles" – (photo: cliffs near the Great Ocean Road) **Sa-Sc67**

Remarkable Cities and Cultural monuments

- UNESCO World Cultural Heritage
- Remarkable Cities
- Aborigine reservation
- Places of Abor. cultural interest
- Cultural landscape
- Historical city scape
- Impressive skyline
- Castle/fortress/fort
- Space telescope
- Museum
- Theater
- Olympics

Sport and leisure destinations

- Race track
- Horse racing
- Skiing
- Sailing
- Diving
- Wind surfing
- Surfing
- Canoeing/rafting
- Deep-sea fishing
- Beach resort

New Zealand

The islands of New Zealand were created after the collision of two tectonic plates around 100 million years ago and are relatively young by geologic standards. New Zealand is one country but it consists of two mains islands and countless smaller ones. The South Island is a land of hills, mountains, lakes, and fjords. Most of the **South Island's** are the result of centuries of glacial activity. Snow-covered Mount Cook (Aoraki) in the South-

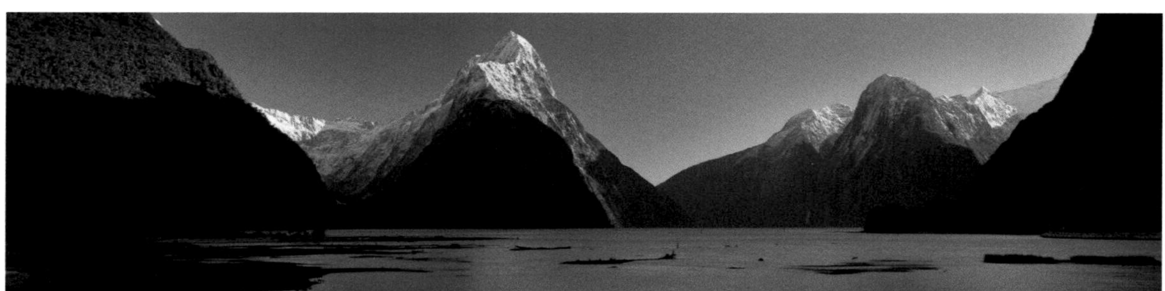

ern Alps is the highest mountain in N Zealand rising 3,764 meters above s level. Volcanic eruptions, earthquak and the forces of erosion continue shape the land of South Island.

The North Island is home to a chain volcanoes stretching from Ruape (2,797 meters) in Tongario National P

Milford Sound in Fiordland National Park on the South Island **Td**

Cape Reinga Meeting point of the Pacific Ocean and Tasman Sea – lighthouse (photo) **Tg63**

Maori The indigenous inhabitants of New Zealand are of Polynesian descent. Traditionally, the Maori lived in clans and had no concept of private property. Traditional face tattoos (moko) are becoming less common.

Auckland Cultural and economic center of New Zealand – largest city in the country – population 1.1 million – panoramic views of the city from the Sky Tower **Th64**

White Island Volcanic island 59 kilometers from the mainland – last eruption in1966 – steaming crater **Tj64**

Tongariro National Park A UNESCO world heritage site – Mount Ruapehu (2,797 meters) **Th65**

Taranaki National Park In the vicinity of the volcano Mount Taranaki (2,518 meters) – open to mountain climbers **Th65**

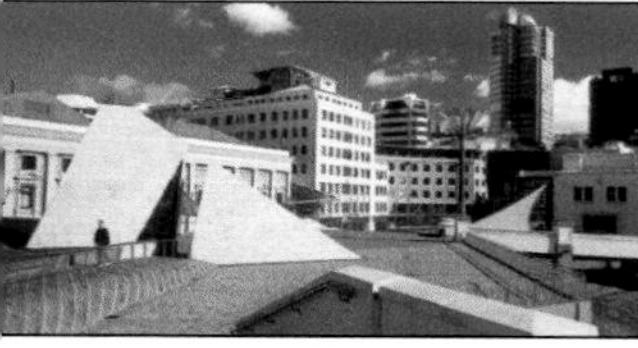

Wellington National capital – population 350,000 – Lambton Quay shopping area – Botanic Gardens – Katherine Mansfield's childhood home – waterfront – National Museum Te Papa **Th66**

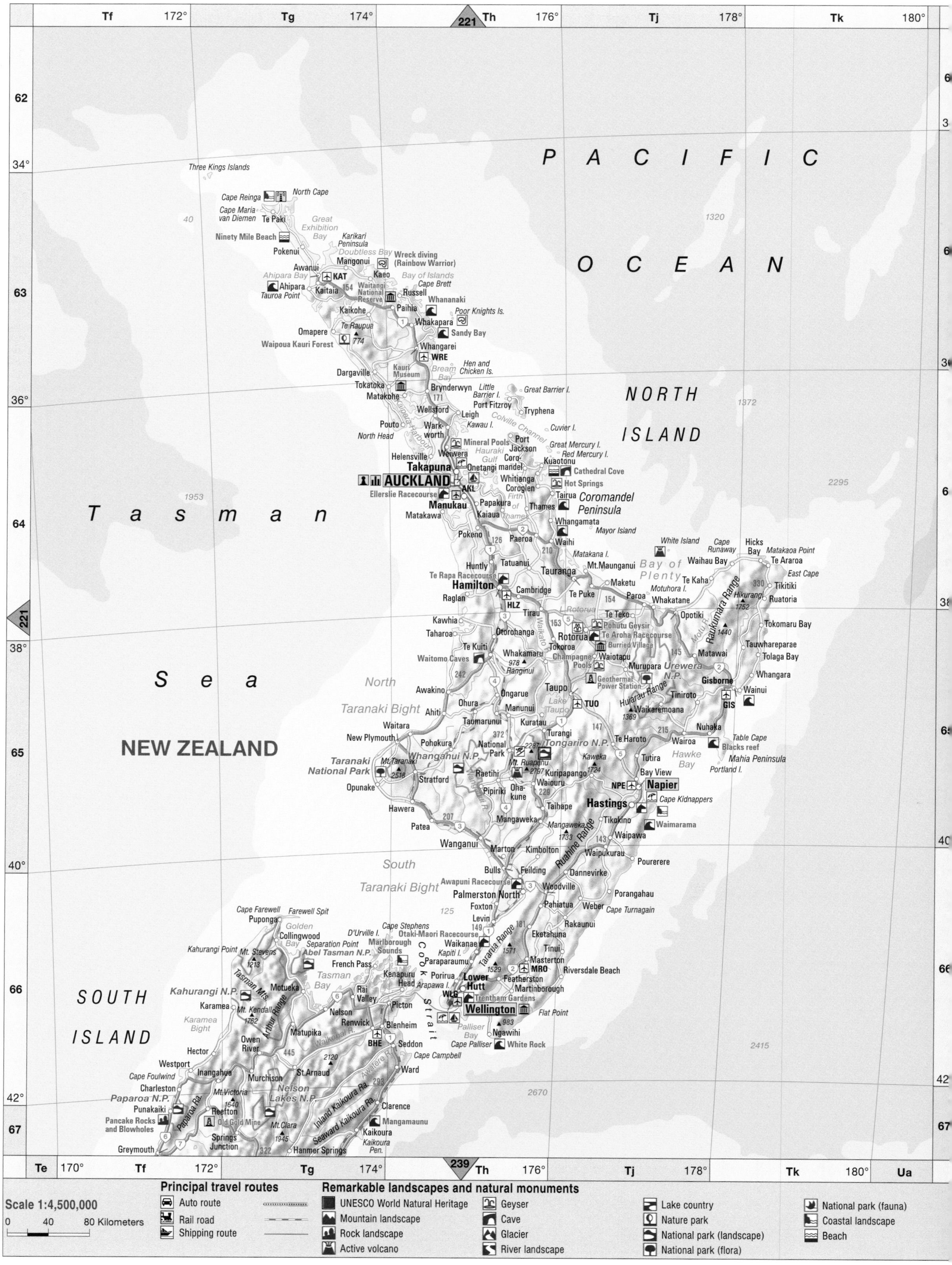

PACIFIC OCEAN

Tasman Sea

NEW ZEALAND

NORTH ISLAND

SOUTH ISLAND

Scale 1:4,500,000
0 40 80 Kilometers

Principal travel routes
- Auto route
- Rail road
- Shipping route

Remarkable landscapes and natural monuments
- UNESCO World Natural Heritage
- Mountain landscape
- Rock landscape
- Active volcano
- Geyser
- Cave
- Glacier
- River landscape
- Lake country
- Nature park
- National park (landscape)
- National park (flora)
- National park (fauna)
- Coastal landscape
- Beach

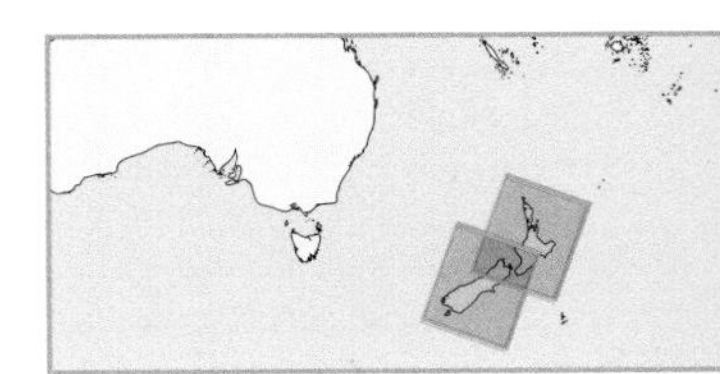

wn to **White Island** in the Bay of Plen- At the center of the North Island lies olcanic plateau containing a large mber of geysers, hot springs, boiling d pools, and steam vents.
e flora and fauna of New Zealand were e to develop isolated and undis- bed for over 80 million years until the t humans arrived on the islands. The t people to settle New Zealand were ynesians – the ancestors of the Maori who took their name from large (now extinct) birds called Moa. The early European colonists introduced new animals , including deer and possums that thrived in the New Zealand countryside. The most famous bird species in the country are the Keas (mountain parrots) as well as the bizarre **Kiwis**, the national symbol of New Zealand. The Tuatara is a small reptile indigenous to New Zealand. It is often called a living fossil because it is the last surviving member of ancient class of animals that appeared on earth even before the dinosaurs. Depending on the season, coastal New Zealand is an excellent location for watching whales, dolphins, or penguins.
Ferns are common in all of New Zealand's warmer regions. There are around 180 fern species in the country. Kauris are giant spruce trees that grow up to 50 meters in height. Most of the Kauri forests were chopped down in the 19th century, but in recent decades nature reserves and national parks have been created to save the remaining trees. The two main islands have several climates zones. The North Island with a subtropical climate is warmer than the South Island. The South Island has the more interesting landscapes of the two islands. The weather on both islands is greatly affected by ocean currents and winds.

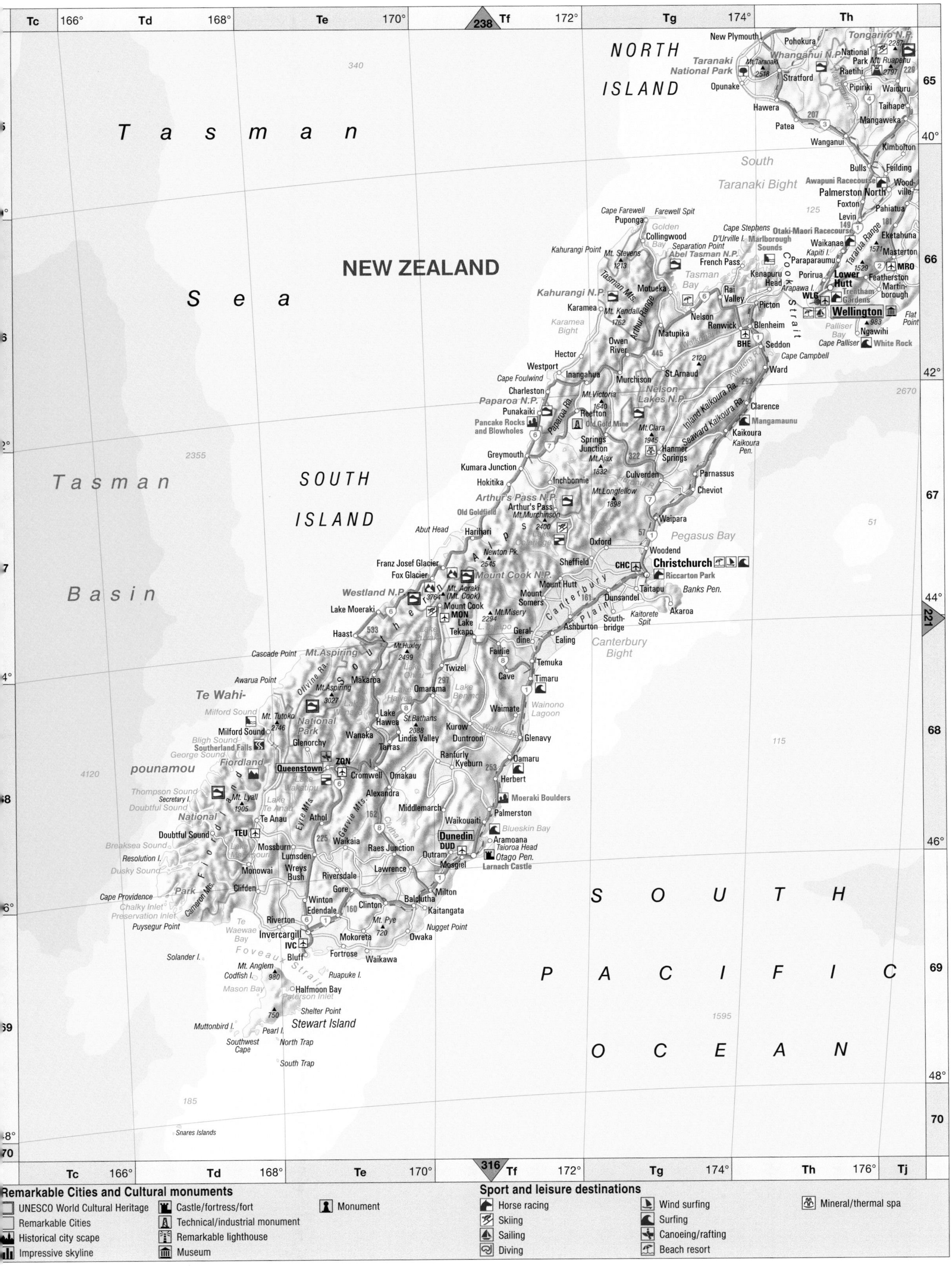

NEW ZEALAND

Tasman Sea

NORTH ISLAND

SOUTH ISLAND

SOUTH PACIFIC OCEAN

Remarkable Cities and Cultural monuments

- UNESCO World Cultural Heritage
- Remarkable Cities
- Historical city scape
- Impressive skyline
- Castle/fortress/fort
- Technical/industrial monument
- Remarkable lighthouse
- Museum
- Monument

Sport and leisure destinations

- Horse racing
- Skiing
- Sailing
- Diving
- Wind surfing
- Surfing
- Canoeing/rafting
- Beach resort
- Mineral/thermal spa

Pancake Rocks Pancake shaped limestone formations – Paparoa National Park – natural fountains **Tf67**

Lake Coleridge Mountain lake at the foot of Craigieburn Range – an hour from Christchurch – nearby Washpen Falls – Rakaia Gorge **Tf67**

Queenstown Popular tourist destination on Lake Wakatipu (Hayes) – the town lies at the foot of the Remarkables mountain range **Te68**

Mount Aspiring National Park Wilderness area in the Southern Alps – mountain climbing and ski areas – beautiful mountainous landscape in the river valleys **Te68**

Westland National Park UNESCO world heritage site on the South Island – 60 glaciers including the Franz Josef Glacier and Fox Glacier – Lake Matheson (photo) with reflections of Mount Cook (Aoraki) and Mount Tasmen **Te67**

Mount Cook National Park National park and world heritage site encompassing New Zealand's highest mountain – Mount Cook is also known by its Maori name Aoraki **Tf67**

Fiordland National Park New Zealand's largest national park (12,095 km²) – Milford Track – Sutherland Falls (580 meters high) **Td68**

Islands of the South Pacific

The South Pacific is home to thousands of islands, most of them small and uninhabitable. The Pacific Ocean has an average depth of 4,188 meters below sea level, with the western Pacific containing the deepest ocean trenches on Earth. The **Tonga Trench** drops 10,025 meters below the surface of the ocean. The **Mariana Trench** is the world's deepest ocean trench with a maximum depth of 11,034 meters. The largest trenches in the

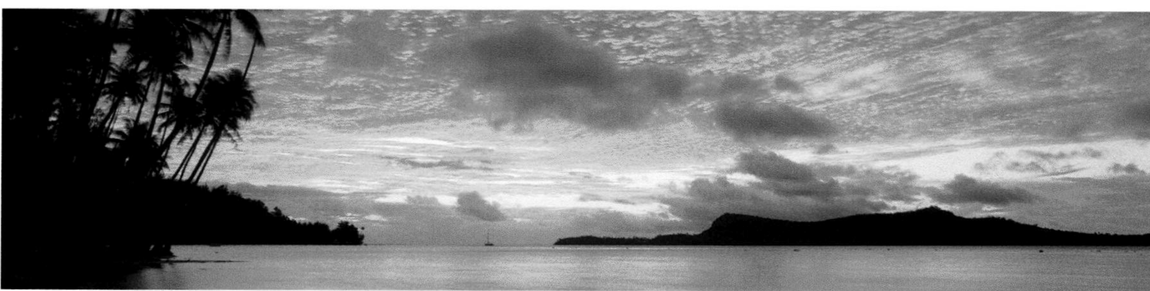

South Pacific and the “bow” shap series of island groups stretching fr New Guinea to the New Hebrides are situated along the edges of the Indi Australian tectonic plate.
Collisions between the Indian-Austral and Pacific plates resulted in the forn tion of the western Pacific's volca islands and certain mountain cha

Sunset on Fiji

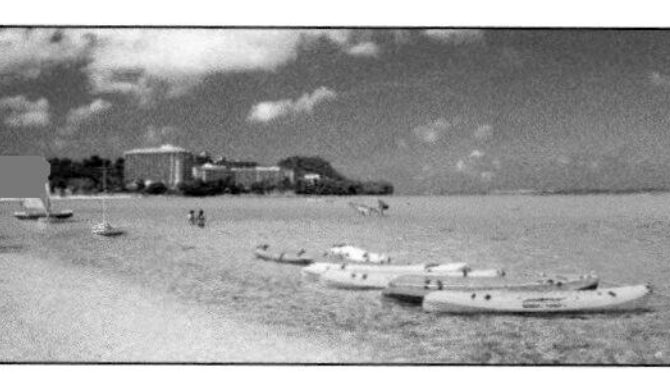

Guam United States territory – military base – War of the Pacific National Historic Park – ancient stone pillars in Latte Stone Park

Palau The Republic of Palau consists of 343 islands, only nine of which are inhabited. The republic is surrounded by a large coral reef. It has the richest collection of plants and animals of any island nation in the region.

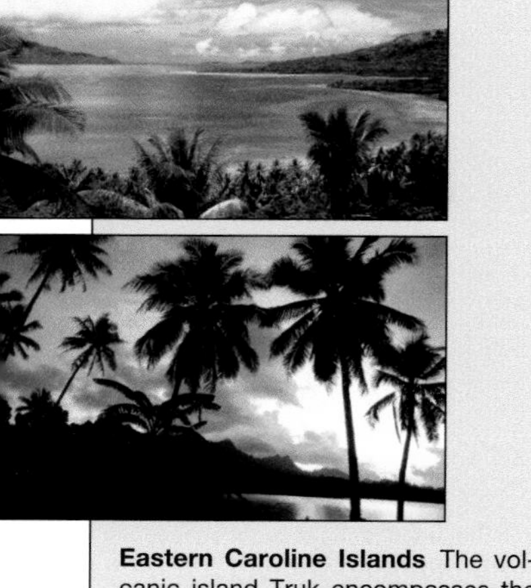

Eastern Caroline Islands The volcanic island Truk encompasses the world's largest lagoon (top photo). Kosrae (bottom photo) has an interior covered by thick rainforests.

New Guinea The world's second largest island – western portion is the Indonesian province of Papua – eastern portion is the independent state of Papua New Guinea

Bismarck Archipelago Many colorful and often rare fish inhabit the archipelago's coral reefs – (photo) a swarm of snappers

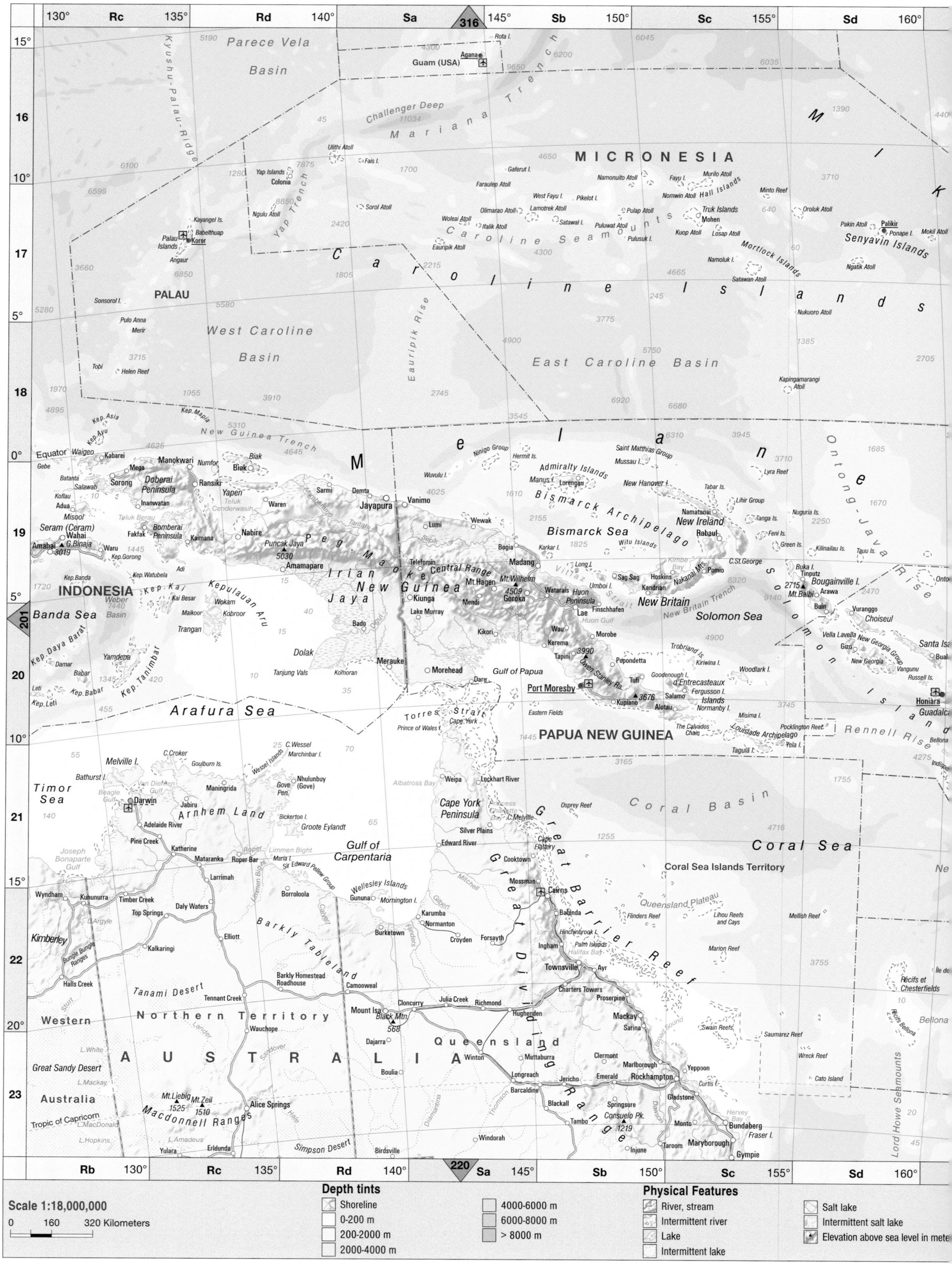

Scale 1:18,000,000
0 160 320 Kilometers

Depth tints
- Shoreline
- 0-200 m
- 200-2000 m
- 2000-4000 m
- 4000-6000 m
- 6000-8000 m
- > 8000 m

Physical Features
- River, stream
- Intermittent river
- Lake
- Intermittent lake
- Salt lake
- Intermittent salt lake
- Elevation above sea level in mete

luding the central highlands of New inea. New Guinea's highest mountain ncak Jaya rises 5,030 meters above a level. The many volcanic islands in the gion including Fiji, Bougainville Island, d Tonga are the peaks of massive derwater mountain chains. Extreme riations in the elevation of islands and ir surrounding waters are not uncom- on in the region. The Bougainville ench has a maximum depth of over 9,000 meters, while the highest peak on Bougainville Island rises 2,175 meters above sea level.

The **Pacific "Ring of Fire"** runs along the entire edge of the Pacific Ocean. The Ring of Fire encompasses 80% of the active volcanoes on the Earth's surface. Volcanic eruptions and earthquakes are common occurences in the geologically active region. Underwater earthquakes often result in the creation of destructive waves called Tsunamis that can reach 300 kilometers in length and 35 meters in height. The numbers of islands dotting the Pacific tends to decreases from west to east. Micronesia which means "small islands" consists entirely of coral islands and atolls. The islands of Micronesia are located parallel to the Melanesian islands. The large islands of Melanesia, including New Guinea and New Caledonia, are all of volcanic orgin.

The flora and fauna of the small Pacific Islands are relatively unimpressive compared to the abundance of species found on New Guinea and Australia. Animals and plants introduced by humans in recent centuries (pigs, dogs, chickens, etc.) have caused significant damage to indigenous ecosystems. Even the coconut palm, the most cliché symbol of the South Pacific, was introduced to the region by human settlers.

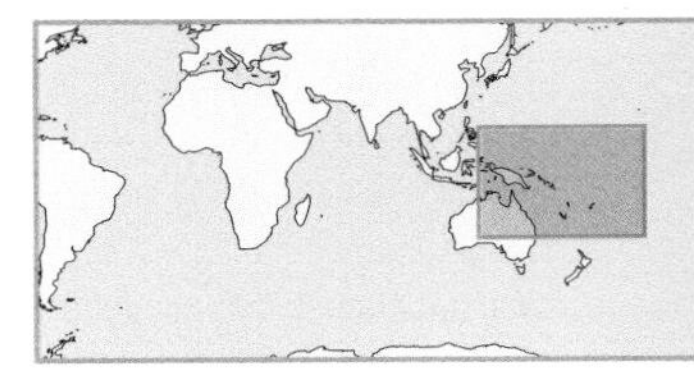

Marshall Islands Island nation consisting of two chains of atolls with over 1,200 coral islands – (photo) Reef sharks in Bikini Atoll

Tarawa Atoll One of the 17 Gilbert Islands – part of the Republic of Kiribati – the main settlement is Bairiki

Nendo Island Part of the Santa Cruz Group in the Solomon Islands – good diving areas – traditional villages

Tanna Island The island belongs to the Republic of Vanuatu. There are five active volcanoes in the archipelago encompassing Tanna. Tanna's attractions include mountain climbing on Jasur (bottom photo) and Hot Springs Lake (top photo).

Fiji Island group in Melanesia – the largest islands are Vanua Levu and Viti Levu – sunset in Naidi on Vanua Levu (photo)

Tonga Polynesian kingdom – located on the international dateline – the capital is Nuku'alofa – beautiful harbour on Vava'u (photo)

316 317 221

Political Boundaries
International
International disputed
Main administrative

Transportation
Interstate Hwy./Motorway
Main road
Railway
Airport

Capitals of political units
WASHINGTON D.C. Independent
Richmond State/province

Town symbols
Capital > 1 Mill. inhabitants
Capital < 1 Mill. inhabitants
Statecapital > 1 Mill. inhabitants
Statecapital < 1 Mill. inhabitants
Towns > 1 Mill. inhabitants
Towns 100 000 bis 1 Mill. inhabitants
Towns < 100 000 inhabitants

New Guinea, the world's second largest island, is located in the southwestern Pacific Ocean. The island is separated from Australia to the south by the narrow Torres Strait.

New Guinea owes its existence to its location near the meeting points of the Indian-Australian and Pacific tectonic plates. The collision of these plates led to the formation of the island and the mountain chain that runs through its cen-

ter. The island can be divided into th
distinct geographic regions. In the c
ter of New Guinea extends a 2,500 k
meter long chain of mountain ran
(Maoke Mountains and Central Ran
The central highlands are covered
thick tropical rainforests. The high
peaks in the region are more than 4,0

New Guinea's Central Highlands are covered by dense vegetation **Sb**

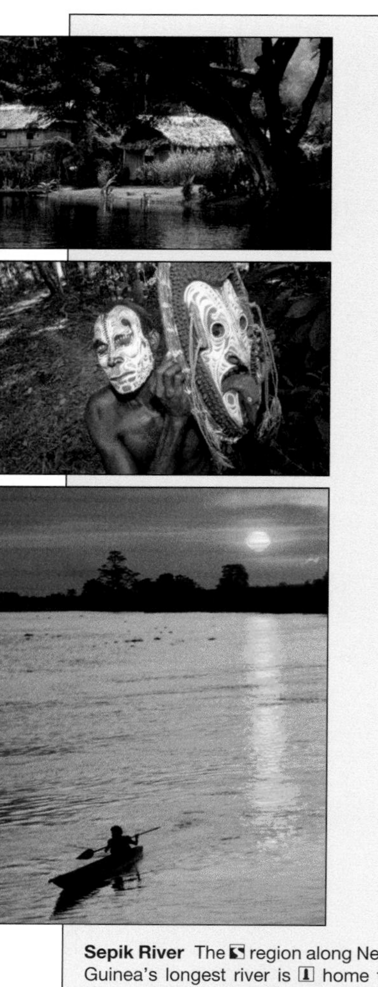

Sepik River The region along New Guinea's longest river is home to many different tribes including the Yamis and the Yawangs. Traditional masks (middle photo) are an important element of local culture. **SaSc47/48**

Lake Kutubu National Park Fascinating body of water with 14 unique species of fish – rare birds and butterflies **Sb49**

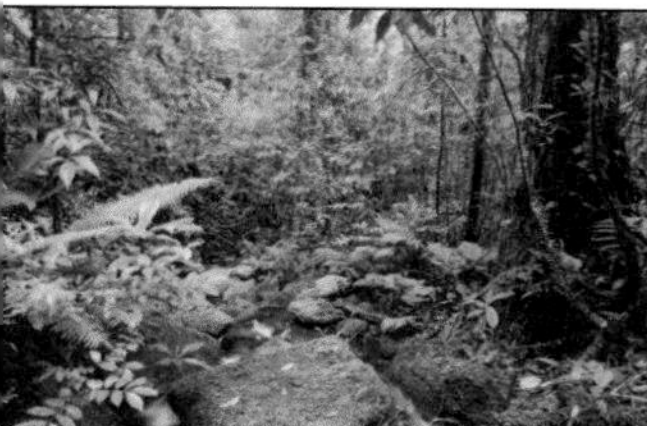

Mount Bosavi The mountain is the source of several major rivers – mountain rainforests **Sb49**

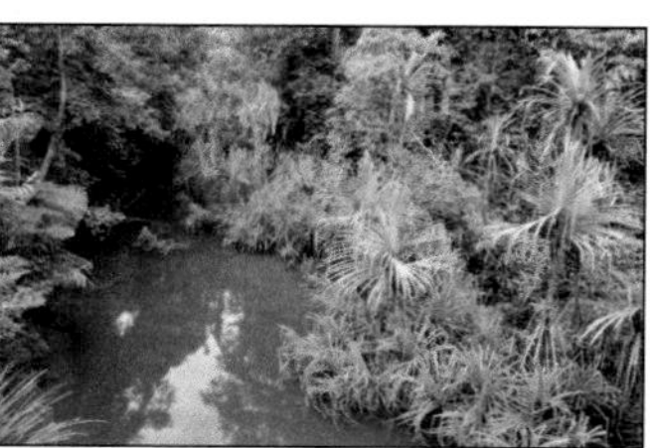

Kikori River Region Pristine rainforests – stretching from the dense mountain forests of the Central Range to the coastal areas along the Gulf of Papua **SbSc49**

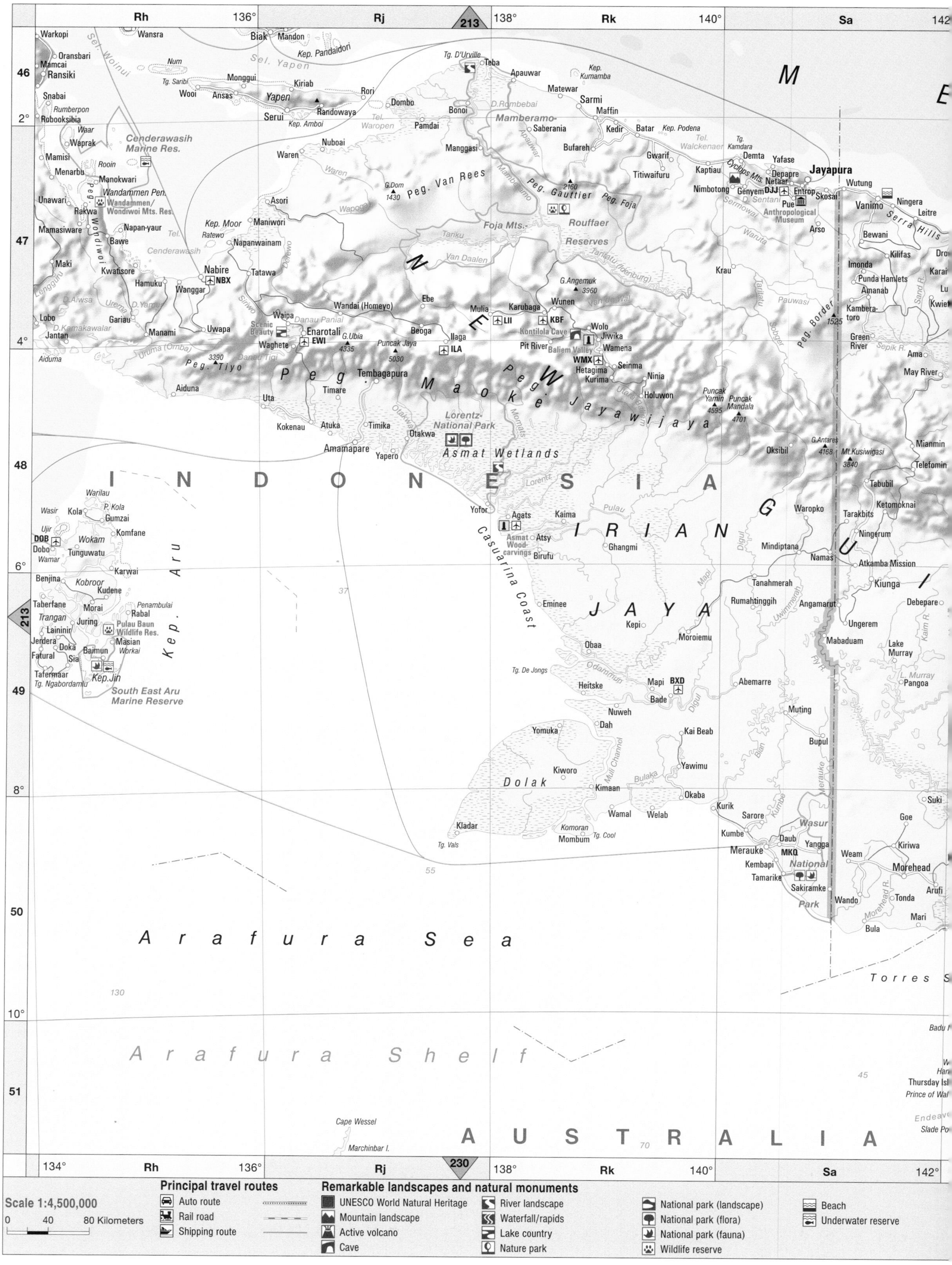

Scale 1:4,500,000
0 40 80 Kilometers

Principal travel routes
- Auto route
- Rail road
- Shipping route

Remarkable landscapes and natural monuments
- UNESCO World Natural Heritage
- Mountain landscape
- Active volcano
- Cave
- River landscape
- Waterfall/rapids
- Lake country
- Nature park
- National park (landscape)
- National park (flora)
- National park (fauna)
- Wildlife reserve
- Beach
- Underwater reserve

eters high. The highest mountain on e island, **Puncak Jaya** (5,030 meters), s in Papua (Irian Jaya), the western half New Guinea and a province of Indo- sia. The central portions of the high- ıds are home to several active **vol- noes** and earthquakes are common in e area. The isolated and difficult to cess mountain valleys in the highlands e inhabited by tribes of subsistence mers. The swampy plains south of the highlands form another distinct region of New Guinea. This region is criss-crossed by numerous rivers that flow from the mountains into the **Arafuru Sea** and **Gulf of Papua**. Because of heavy rainfall and erosion in the mountains the rivers contail large amounts much of silt, which gets deposited on the southern plains. The **Fly River,** on the southwest coast, nourishes one of the world's largest wetland areas. These wetlands were once one of the most inaccessible regions in Papua New Guinea. But mining operations have expanded in recent years, threatening the delicate ecosystem in the area. To the north of the central highlands lies a region of hills and plains. The **Sepik** and **Tariku** rivers are two of the most important rivers in the north. The waters off the northern coast contain large coral reefs. Around 60% of New Guinea is covered by dense rainforests.

New Guinea's climate is tropical but frost is not uncommon at higher elevations in the highlands. The entire island gets heavy rainfall throughout the year, especially during the rainy season from December to March.

Most of the islands to the east and northeast of New Guinea are of volcanic origins including the Bismarck Archipelago and the Trobriand Islands. This area features numerous large coral reefs.

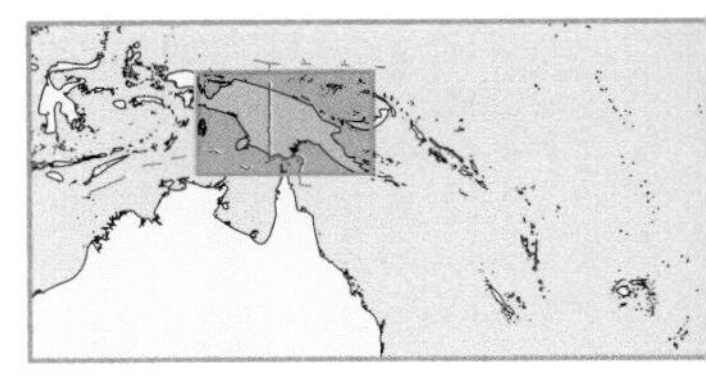

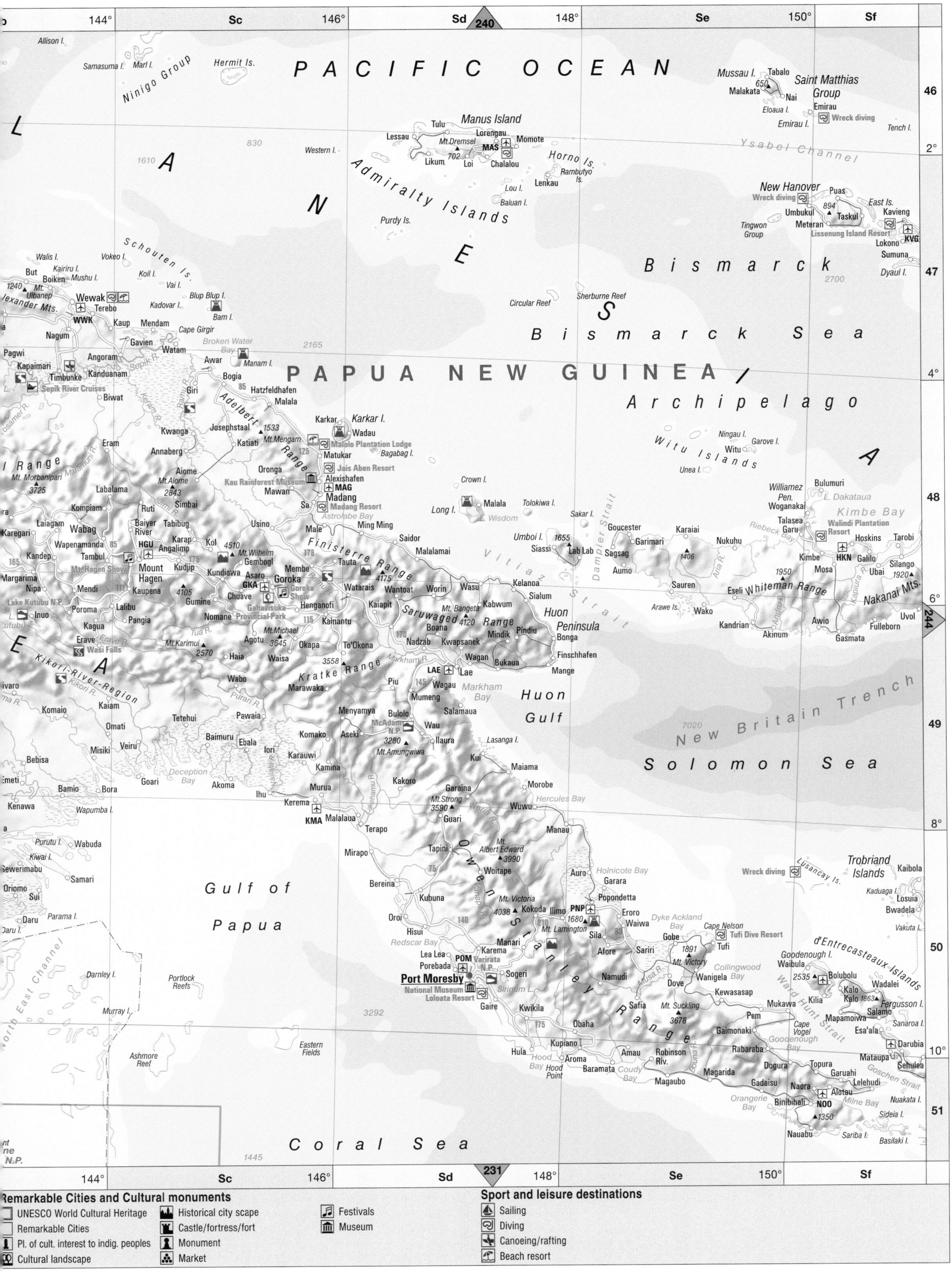

Finisterre Range Peaks over 4,000 meters – home to some of the most isolated communities in New Guinea **Sc48**

Ramu River Source is in the eastern highlands – flows parallel to the coast – forms a single flood plain with the Sepik River during the rainy season **ScSd48/49**

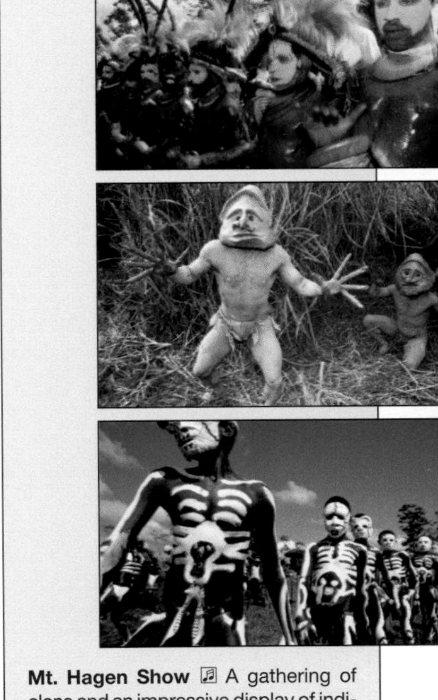

Mt. Hagen Show A gathering of clans and an impressive display of indigenous cultures. The clans compete in a "sing sing" contest. **Sc48**

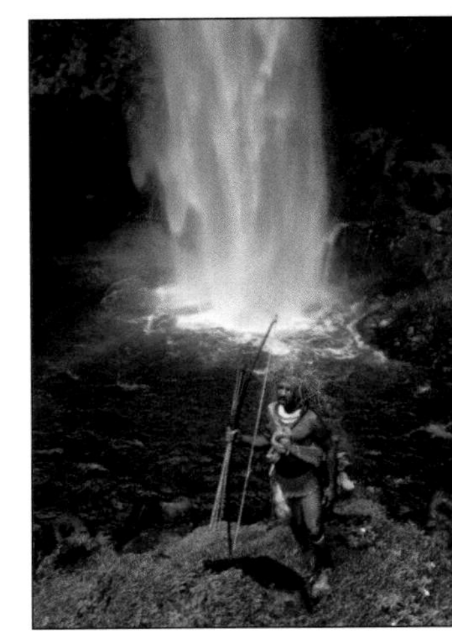

Owen Stanley Range Mountain range north of Port Moresby – waterfalls – home to isolated mountain tribes **SdSe50**

Remarkable Cities and Cultural monuments

- UNESCO World Cultural Heritage
- Remarkable Cities
- Pl. of cult. interest to indig. peoples
- Cultural landscape
- Historical city scape
- Castle/fortress/fort
- Monument
- Market
- Festivals
- Museum

Sport and leisure destinations

- Sailing
- Diving
- Canoeing/rafting
- Beach resort

The Bismarck Archipelago has two main islands: New Britain and New Ireland. Both the Bismarck Archipelago and the nearby Solomon Islands lie in the collision zone of two tectonic plates: the Indian-Australian and Pacific plates. The New Britain Trench is situated in the Solomon Sea between New Britain and the Solomon Islands. The trench reaches a depth of 9,140 meters at its deepest point. In the area around the trench, tectonic forces continue to suck pieces the ocean's floor into the Earth's mar causing the trench to expand.

The Solomon Islands and the **Bisma Archipelago** are located inside the Pa fic "Ring of Fire," which extends along edges of the Pacific Ocean. Volca islands and active volcanoes are co

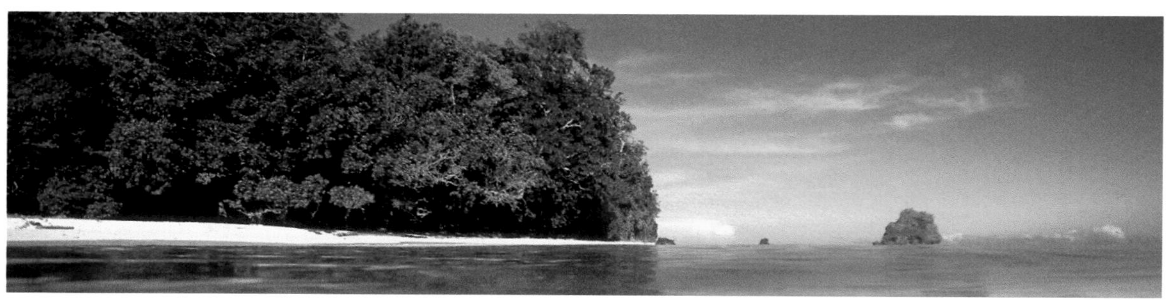

Coral islands in the New Georgia archipelago **Sj49/**

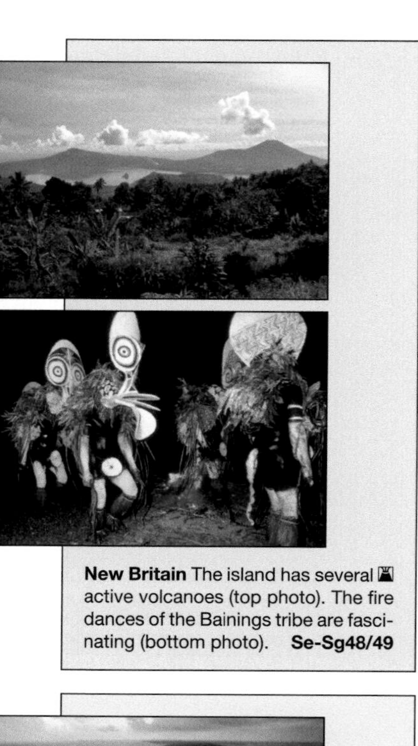

New Britain The island has several active volcanoes (top photo). The fire dances of the Bainings tribe are fascinating (bottom photo). **Se-Sg48/49**

Trobriand Islands These flat coral islands are home to a proud people with rich traditions. Photos from top to bottom: Aerial view of Kiriwina Islands, Kula dancers, spear fisher, harvest festival in a Yam village **Sf50**

New Georgia The people of New Georgia were once known as headhunters – today their traditional culture attracts visitors **Sj50**

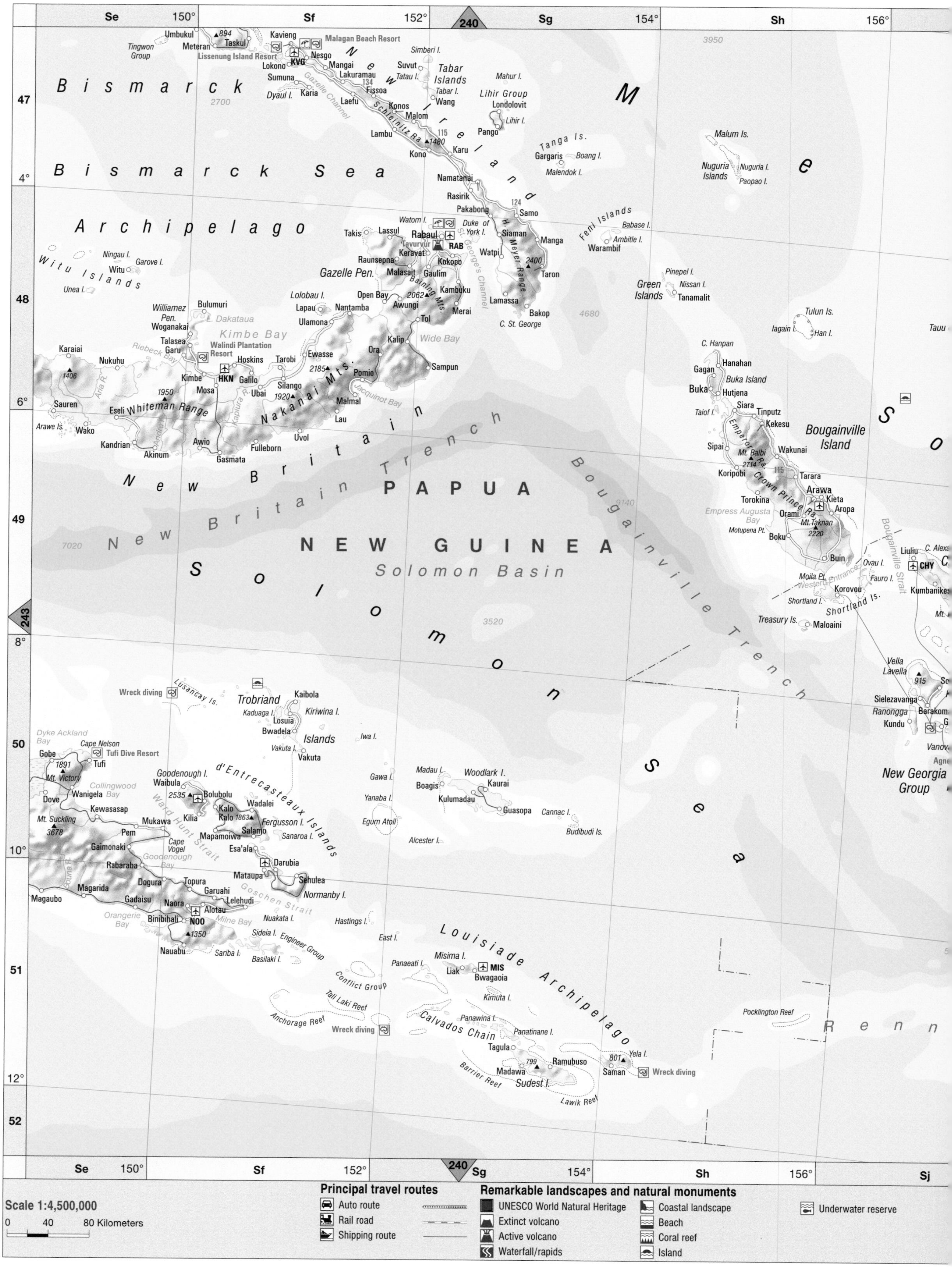

Bismarck Archipelago — Bismarck Sea — New Ireland — New Britain — PAPUA NEW GUINEA — Solomon Sea — Solomon Basin — New Britain Trench — Bougainville Trench — Bougainville Island — Trobriand Islands — d'Entrecasteaux Islands — Louisiade Archipelago — New Georgia Group

Scale 1:4,500,000

0 40 80 Kilometers

Principal travel routes

- Auto route
- Rail road
- Shipping route

Remarkable landscapes and natural monuments

- UNESCO World Natural Heritage
- Extinct volcano
- Active volcano
- Waterfall/rapids
- Coastal landscape
- Beach
- Coral reef
- Island
- Underwater reserve

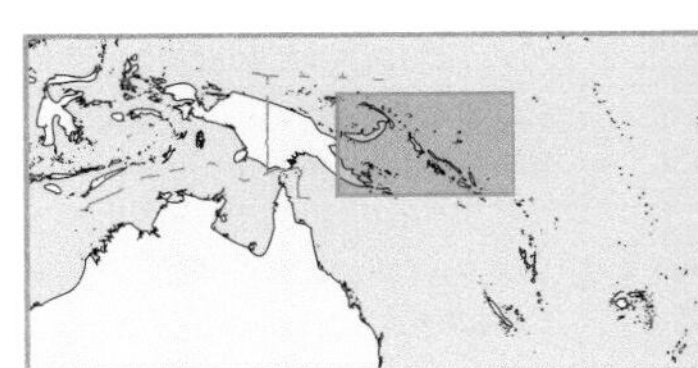

on in this region. Earthquakes and vol-
nic eruptions are constant threats to
e islands. The Bismarck Archipelago
longs to Papua New Guinea and con-
st of more than 200 islands – most
vered by dense rainforests. There are
veral **active volcanoes** in the archi-
lago including Vulcan and Tavurvur.
ew Britain and New Ireland are the two
gest islands in the archipelago.
e territory of the Solomon Islands is divided between two parallel island groups. The Solomons are located southeast of **Bougainville Island**, an island territory of Papua New Guinea. With more than 1,000 islands and a total land area of 28,000 km², the Solomon Islands form one of the largest archipelagoes in the Pacific Ocean. The island nation lies around 1,860 kilometers from Australia and stretches over a distance of approximetely 1,400 kilometers from north to south. The main islands in the archipelago (Choiseul, New Georgia, Santa Isabel, Makira, and Guadalcanal) are all of volcanic origin and are covered by thick forests.The economy of the Solomon Islands is heavily dependent on the export of crops and timber, but the abundant mineral wealth of the islands is being increasingly exploited.

Coral reefs are common along the coastline of many islands in this region of the Pacific, some extending above the water. The Louisiade Archipelago is an island group off the southeastern coast of New Guinea. The archipelago icludes several large islands of volcanic origin as well as many small coral islands. Both the Bismarck Archipelago and the Solomon Islands get abundant rainfall, especially during the rainy season. This is also the time when the risk of cyclones is greatest in the region.

The Reefs of the Solomon Islands The coral reefs off the coast of the Solomon Islands are one of the country's most popular attractions. The country's reefs are home to a diverse collection of marine plants and animals. Coral reefs are formed over many years, in warm (minimum 20° Celsius) saltwater, by colonies of coral – tiny marine animals. Photos from top to bottom: Reefs off the coast of the Solomon island, Moray eel, Clown fish, Toadstool coral, Boxfish.

Solomon Islands Melanesian island group – independent nation since 1978 – undeveloped infrastructure (photo: A wedding on the Solomons) **Sh/Tb48/51**

Rennell Island Located south of Guadalcanal – total area of 650 km² – traditonal dance troupes (photo) – the coral island is a UNESCO world heritage site – national park **SkTa51**

Remarkable Cities and Cultural monuments

- UNESCO World Cultural Heritage
- Remarkable Cities
- Pl. of cult. interest to indig. peoples
- Market

Sport and leisure destinations

- Sailing
- Diving
- Wind surfing
- Deep-sea fishing
- Beach resort

New Caledonia, Vanuatu, Fiji Islands

New Caledonia, Vanuatu and Fiji are all located in the South Pacific to the east of Australia. Many of the islands in this region are part of an expansive ancient underwater **mountain chain**. **New Caledonia** is 400 kilometers long and has a maximum width of 50 kilometers. The island has an extraordinary wealth of mineral resources including deposits of nickel, gold, copper, iron and silver. Just north of New Caledonia's main island lie

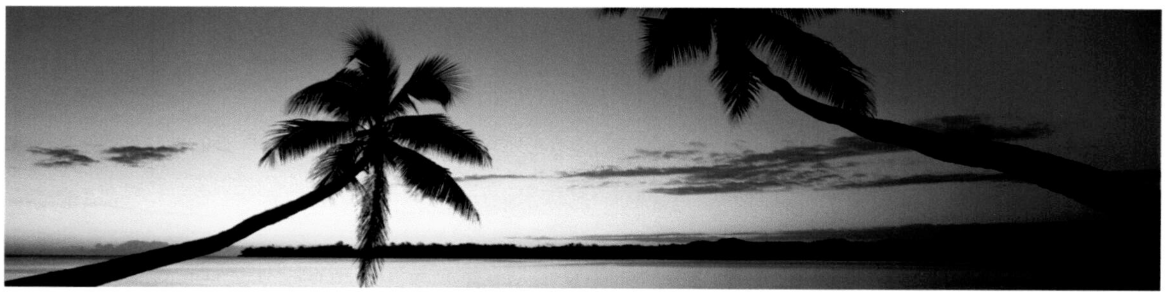

two large parallel coral reefs, the **Gra Récif de Cook** and the **Récif de Fra çais**. With the exception of the ma island, most of New Caledonia's islan are flat coral islands. The tallest mou tain in the archipelago is the Massif Humboldt (1,635 meters).
The culture of New Caledonia has be greatly influenced by the cultures

Dusk on a Fijian island **TjUa54/**

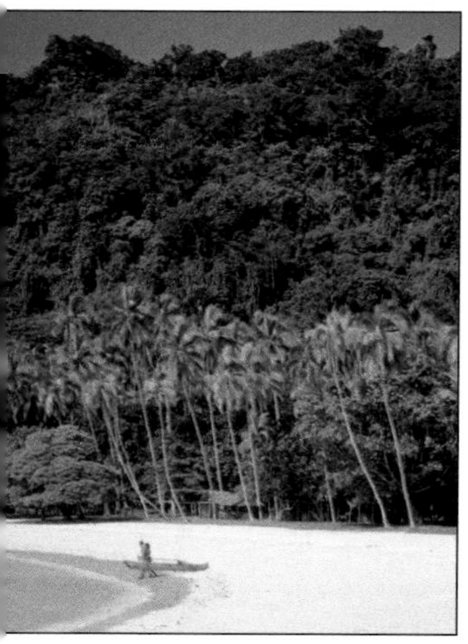

Espíritu Santo Largest island in Vanuatu – inaccessible interior – sunken warships at Million Dollar Point **Td53**

Ambrim Two active volcanoes in the island's interior – striking statues – (photos) traditional dances **Te54**

Tana The volcano Mount Yasur is the island's major attraction – manatees near Port Resolution **Te55**

New Caledonia The main island is surrounded by reefs and small coral islands (top photo). The highlands contain several beautiful waterfalls including Chute de la Madeleine (bottom photo). **TcTd56/57**

Lifou The largest and most populated of the Loyalty Islands – major town We – the local language is Drehu **Td56**

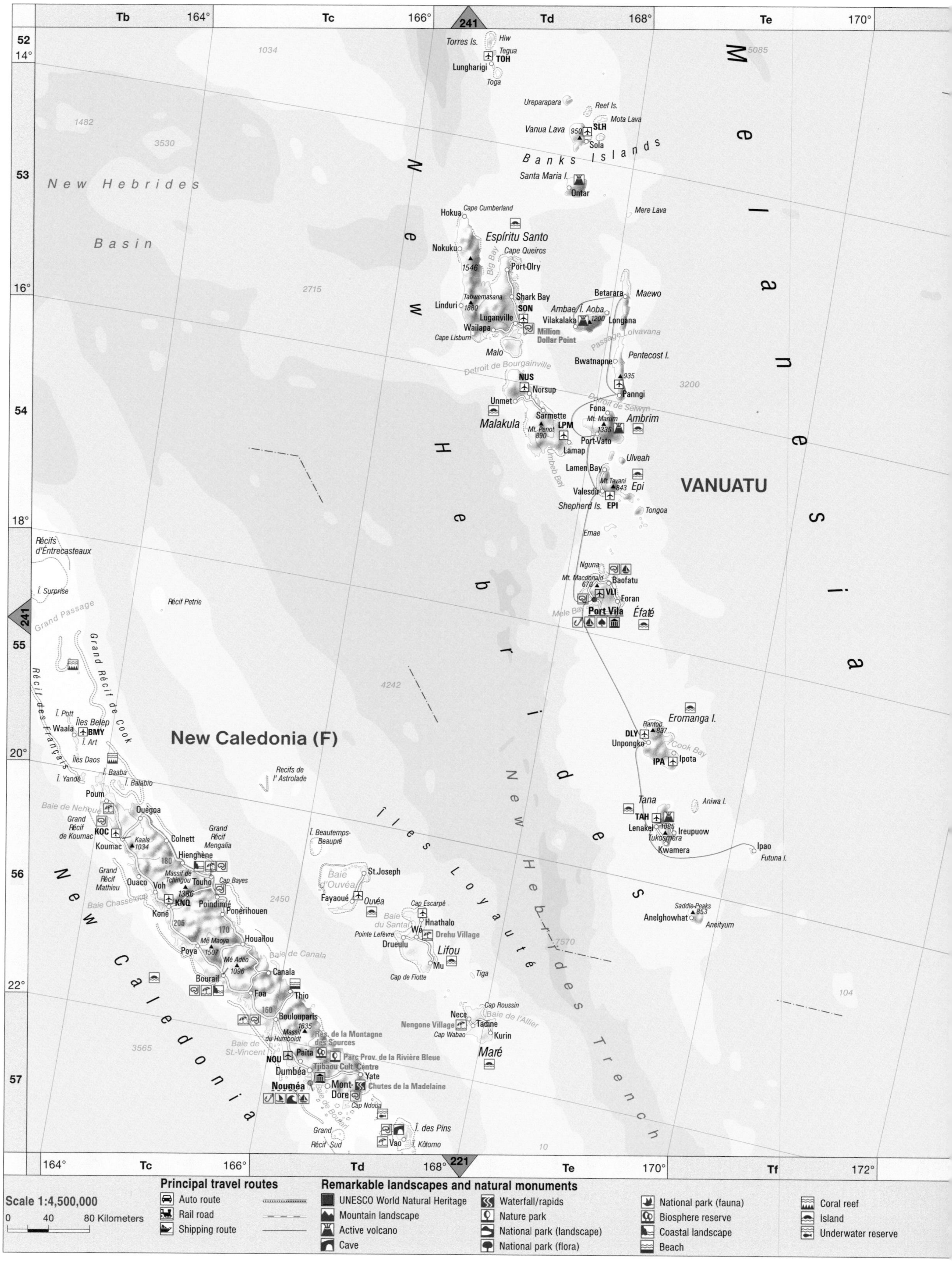

Tb
164°
Tc
166°
241
Td
168°
Te
170°
52
14°
53
16°
54
18°
55
20°
56
22°
57
Torres Is.
Hiw
Tegua
TOH
Lungharigi
Toga
Ureparapara
Reef Is.
Mota Lava
Vanua Lava
SLH
Sola
Banks Islands
Santa Maria I.
Ontar
New Hebrides Basin
Hokua
Cape Cumberland
Espíritu Santo
Cape Queiros
Nokuku
Port-Olry
Big Bay
Mere Lava
Tabwemasana
Shark Bay
SON
Linduri
Luganville
Wailapa
Cape Lisburn
Million Dollar Point
Ambae/I. Aoba
Vilakalaka
Longana
Betarara
Maewo
Passage Lolvavana
Malo
Detroit de Bourgainville
Bwatnapne
Pentecost I.
NUS
Norsup
Unmet
Panngi
Malakula
Sarmette
Mt. Penot
LPM
Fona
Mt. Marum
Ambrim
Lamap
Port-Vato
Ulveah
Lamen Bay
Mt. Tavani
Epi
Valesdir
Shepherd Is.
EPI
Tongoa
VANUATU
Emae
Nguna
Mt. Macdonald
Baofatu
VLI
Foran
Mele Bay
Port Vila
Éfaté
Melanesia
New Hebrides
Récifs d'Entrecasteaux
Î. Surprise
Grand Passage
Récif Petrie
Grand Récif de Cook
Récif des Français
Î. Pott
Waala
Îles Belep
BMY
Î. Art
Îles Daos
Î. Yandé
Î. Baaba
Î. Balabio
Poum
Baie de Nehoue
Ouégoa
Grand Récif de Koumac
KOC
Koumac
Kaala
Colnett
Grand Récif Mengalia
Hienghène
Massif de Tchingou
Grand Récif Mathieu
Ouaco
Voh
Touho
Cap Bayes
KNQ
Poindimié
Koné
Ponérihouen
Baie Chasseloup
Houaïlou
Poya
Mé Maoya
Mé Adeo
Baie de Canala
Bourail
Canala
Foa
Thio
Boulouparis
Massif du Humboldt
Rés. de la Montagne des Sources
Baie de St.-Vincent
NOU
Paita
Parc Prov. de la Rivière Bleue
Dumbéa
Tjibaou Cult. Centre
Nouméa
Mont-Dore
Yate
Chutes de la Madelaine
Cap Ndoua
Grand Récif Sud
Vao
Î. des Pins
Î. Kôtomo
New Caledonia
New Caledonia (F)
Recifs de l'Astrolabe
Î. Beautemps-Beaupré
Baie d'Ouvéa
St.Joseph
Fayaoué
Ouvéa
Îles Loyauté
Cap Escarpé
Baie du Santal
Hnathalo
Pointe Lefèvre
Wé
Drehu Village
Drueulu
Lifou
Cap de Flotte
Mu
Tiga
Nece
Cap Roussin
Baie de l'Allier
Nengone Village
Tadine
Cap Wabao
Kurin
Maré
New Hebrides Trench
Eromanga I.
Rantop
DLY
Unpongkor
Cook Bay
IPA
Ipota
Tana
Aniwa I.
TAH
Lenakel
Tukosmera
Ireupuow
Kwamera
Ipao
Futuna I.
Saddle-Peaks
Anelghowhat
Aneityum
164°
Tc
166°
Td
168°
221
Te
170°
Tf
172°
Scale 1:4,500,000
0 40 80 Kilometers
Principal travel routes
Auto route
Rail road
Shipping route
Remarkable landscapes and natural monuments
UNESCO World Natural Heritage
Mountain landscape
Active volcano
Cave
Waterfall/rapids
Nature park
National park (landscape)
National park (flora)
National park (fauna)
Biosphere reserve
Coastal landscape
Beach
Coral reef
Island
Underwater reserve

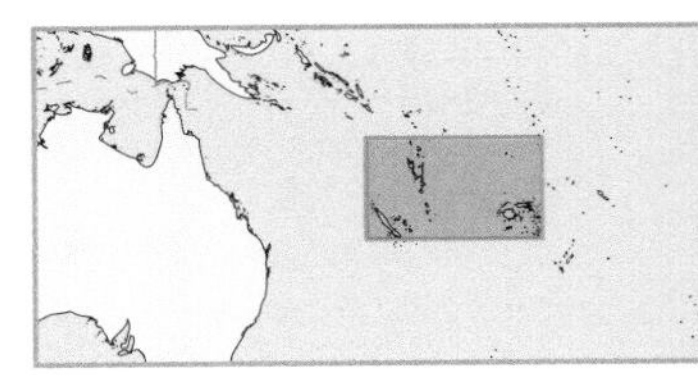

ance and the surrounding Melanesian ands. The island has been politically ked to France since the middle of the th century, and French is the dominant nguage on New Caledonia and the naller islands around it. The indigenous eople of New Caledonian – the Melasian Kanaks – now make up less than lf of the current population.

elanesia, along with Polynesia and icronesia, is one of the three regions into which the islands of the South Pacific are divided. Melanesia was given its name by 19th century Europeans because of the dark skin tones of its indigenous people. Vanuatu, also known as the **New Hebrides**, consists of over 70 islands located in the southern part of Melanesia. Most of the Melanesian islands are surrounded by large coral reefs with diverse and unique marine life. **Éfaté**, the most populated island in Vanuatu, is the location of the country's capital city, Port Vila. The islands north of Efate have a distinct climate with high temperatures and humidity. The large northern island Espiritu Santo has several good diving areas where divers can view several shipwrecks from the Second World War.

Vanua Levu (5,534 km²) and **Viti Levu** (10,388 km²) are by far the largest of the 330 **Fiji Islands**. Most of the smaller Fiji islands are separated from the two larger islands by the Nanuku Passage. There are many large reefs off the coast of the Fiji islands including the **Great Sea Reef** near Vanua Levu. The population of Fiji is almost equally divided between the indigenous (Melanesian) Fijians and Fijians of Indian descent. In recent years, ethnic tension between the two communities has led to government instability and violent clashes.

Yasawa Islands Part of the Fiji Islands – beautiful beaches – good diving areas – local cruise ship lines **Tj54**

Viti Levu Largest of the Fiji Islands – tropical highlands – Sigatoka Sand Dunes National Parks **TjTk54/55**

Coral Reefs The 100-kilometers-long Great Astrolabe Reef near Kadavu one of the world's most fascinating reefs. The Great White Wall, a white coral reef, lies in the diving areas off the coast of Taveuni. **Tk55**

Vanua Levu Second largest island in Fiji – major cities: Labasa and Savusavu – cruise lines and diving areas **Tk54**

Taveuni Volcanic "garden island" – Buma National Park with the crater lake, Lake Tagimaucia **TkUa54**

PACIFIC OCEAN

North Fiji Basin

Polynesia

TUVALU

Wallis and Futuna (F)

FIJI

Fiji Islands

Koro Sea

241

248

221

Remarkable Cities and Cultural monuments

- UNESCO World Cultural Heritage
- Remarkable Cities
- Places of Hindu cultural interest
- Pl. of cult. interest to indig. peoples
- Historical city scape
- Monument
- Museum

Sport and leisure destinations

- Sailing
- Diving
- Wind surfing
- Surfing
- Deep-sea fishing
- Beach resort
- Casino

The island kingdom of Tonga and its northern neighbor Samoa are both **Polynesian islands**. These island nations are located in the South Pacific to the northeast of New Zealand. The island groups in this section of the Pacific Ocean are separated from one another by relatively large distances. The Kingdom of **Tonga** consist of 169 islands in two parallel island chains. Tonga encompasses both coral islands and islands of volcanic

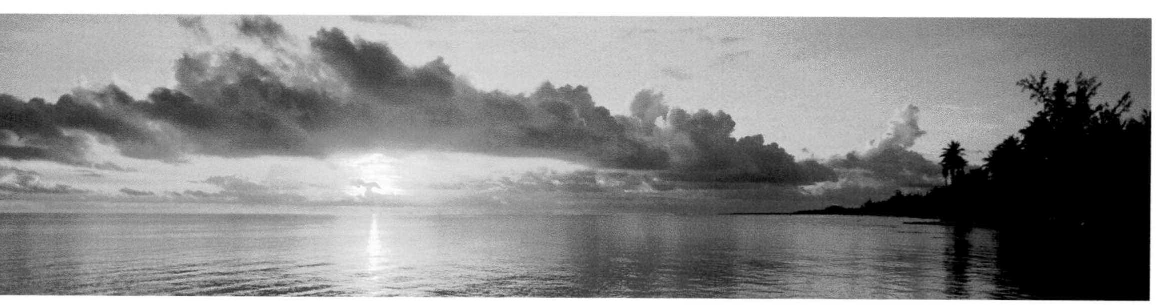

origin. The island kingdom is home several active volcanoes. The freque volcanism in Tonga is the result of t country's location near the collision zo of the Pacific and Indian-Australian te tonic plates.

The **Tonga Trench** has a maximu depth of 10,882 meters. Most of Tonga

Sunset above Rangiroa atoll in French Polynesia **Cg**

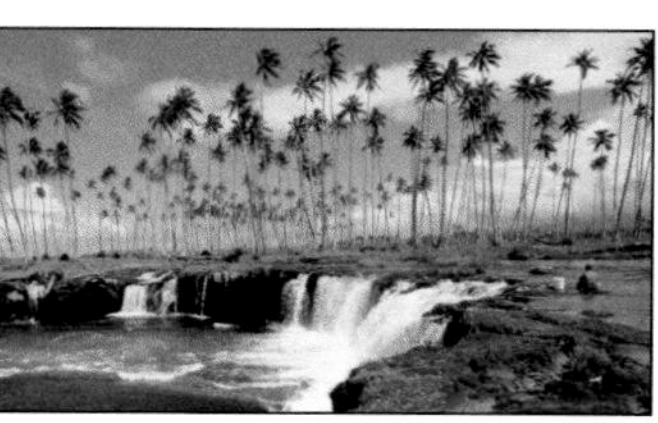

Savai'i Largest Samoan island – several volcanoes and lava fields – mountainous interior – beaches and waterfalls **Bd52**

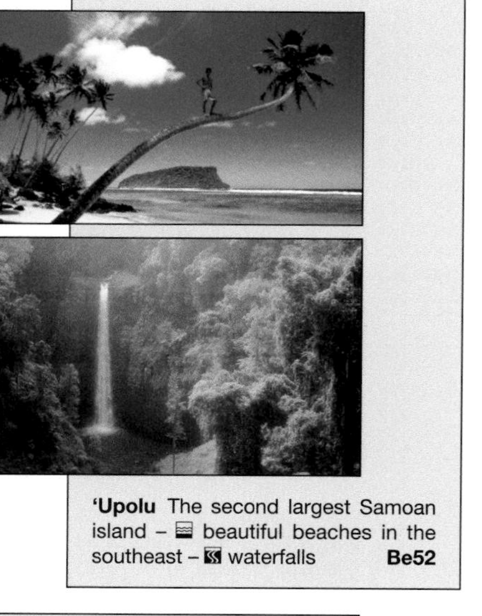

'Upolu The second largest Samoan island – beautiful beaches in the southeast – waterfalls **Be52**

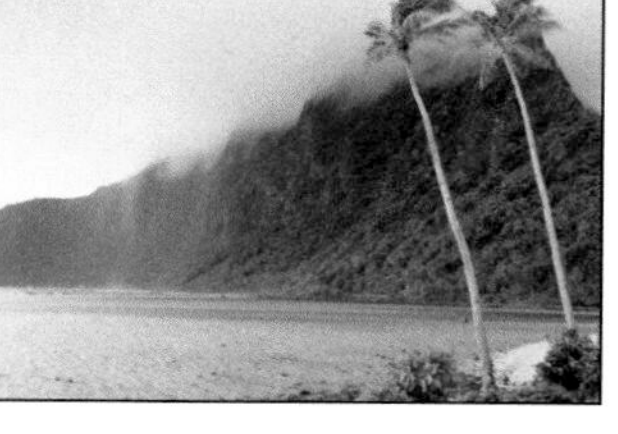

Manua Islands Three islands; Olosega, Ofu, and Ta'u – sandy beaches – mountains reaching 1,000 meters in height **Bf53**

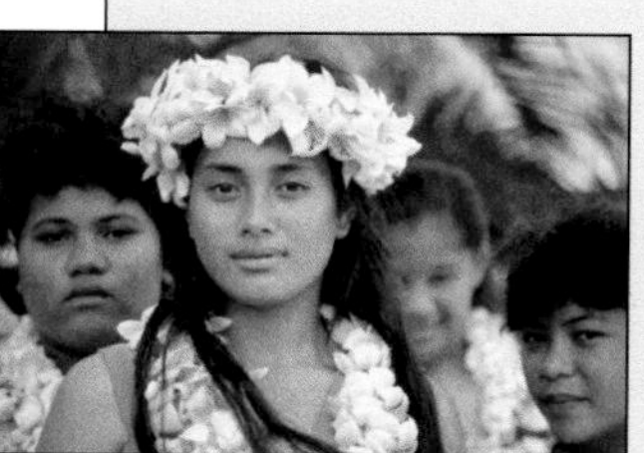

The Samoans Family and community play an important role in the lives of Samoa's 200,000 inhabitants.

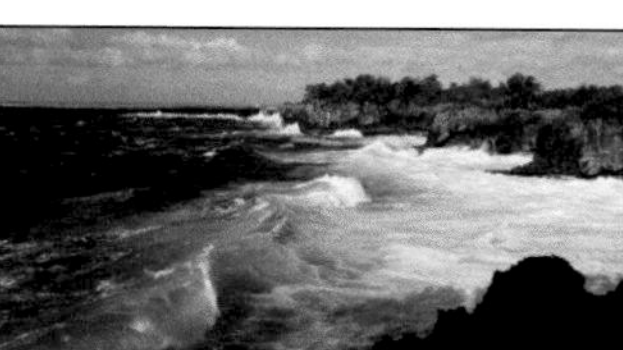

Vava'u The most beautiful of Tonga's island groups – boat expeditions through the islands – accessible caves **BcBd55**

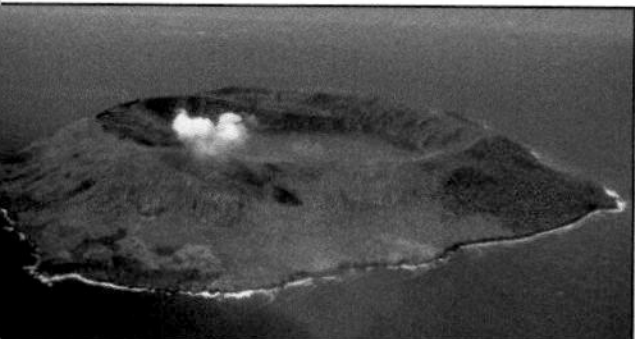

Tofua Islands Home to Tonga's most active volcanoes – the site of the famous mutiny on the ship Bounty in 1789 **Bc55**

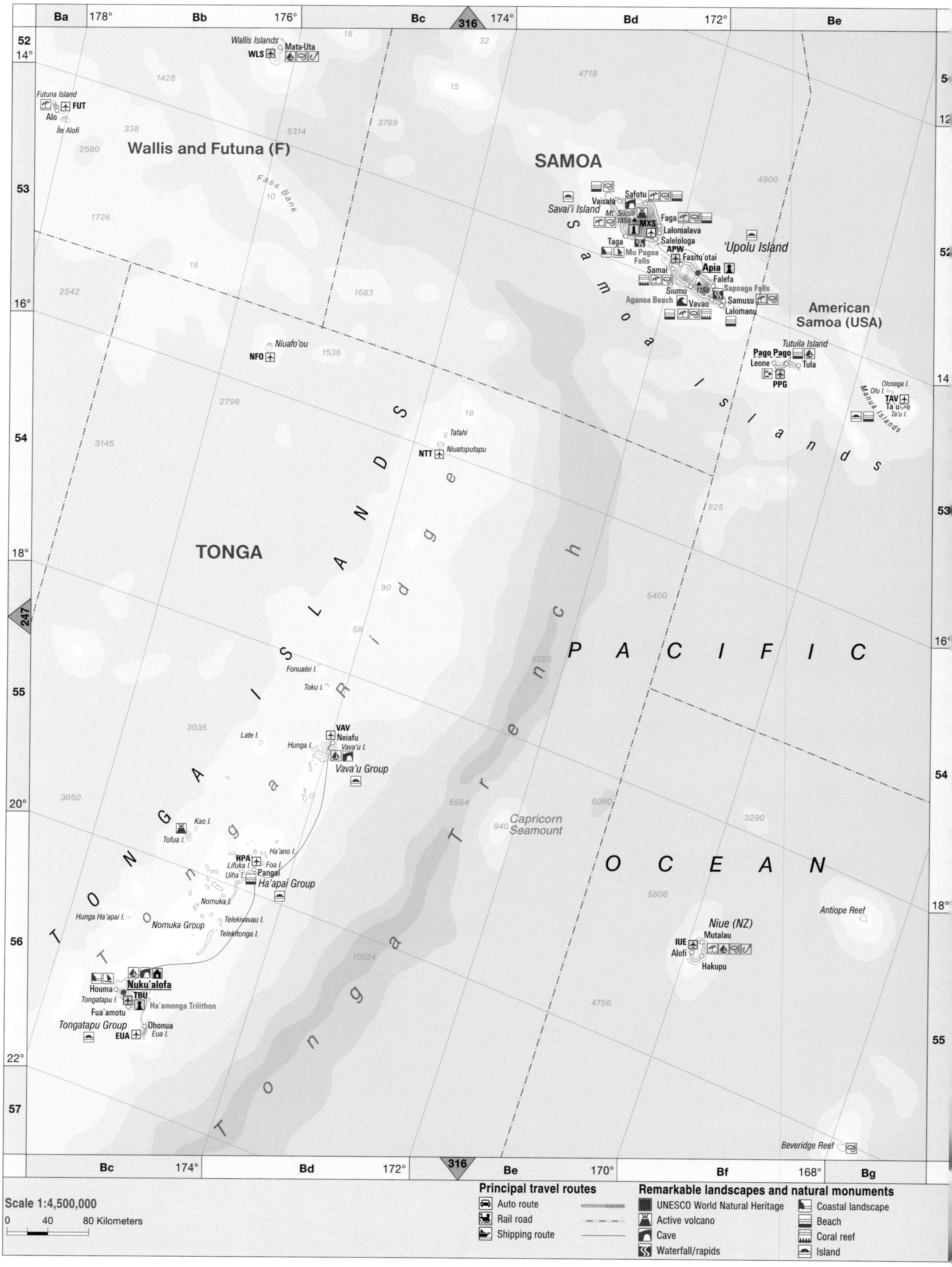

Ba
178°
Bb
176°
Bc
316
174°
Bd
172°
Be
Wallis Islands
Mata-Uta
WLS
Futuna Island
FUT
Alo
Île Alofi
Wallis and Futuna (F)
Fass Bank
SAMOA
Savai'i Island
Safotu
Vaisala
Mt. Silisili 1858
MXS
Faga
Lalomalava
Salelologa
Taga
Mu Pagoa Falls
APW
Fasito'otai
Samai
Apia
Falefa
Siumu
Sapoaga Falls
Aganoa Beach
Vavau
Samusu
Lalomanu
'Upolu Island
American Samoa (USA)
Tutuila Island
Pago Pago
Leone
Tula
PPG
Olosega I.
Ofu I.
TAV
Ta'u
Ta'u I.
Manua Islands
Samoa Islands
Niuafo'ou
NFO
Tafahi
Niuatoputapu
NTT
TONGA
Tonga Islands
Tonga Ridge
Tonga Trench
Fonualei I.
Toku I.
VAV
Neiafu
Late I.
Hunga I.
Vava'u I.
Vava'u Group
Kao I.
Tofua I.
Ha'ano I.
HPA
Lifuka I.
Foa I.
Uiha I.
Pangai
Ha'apai Group
Nomuka I.
Hunga Ha'apai I.
Nomuka Group
Telekivavau I.
Telekitonga I.
Houma
Nuku'alofa
Tongatapu I.
TBU
Ha'amonga Trilithon
Fua'amotu
Tongatapu Group
Ohonua
EUA
Eua I.
Capricorn Seamount
PACIFIC OCEAN
Antiope Reef
Niue (NZ)
Mutalau
IUE
Alofi
Hakupu
Beveridge Reef
247
Bc
174°
Bd
172°
316
Be
170°
Bf
168°
Bg

Scale 1:4,500,000

0 40 80 Kilometers

Principal travel routes

- Auto route
- Rail road
- Shipping route

Remarkable landscapes and natural monuments

- UNESCO World Natural Heritage
- Active volcano
- Cave
- Waterfall/rapids
- Coastal landscape
- Beach
- Coral reef
- Island

…stern islands – including the largest …and Tongatapu – are coral islands, …hile most of the western islands are of …lcanic origin.
…e largest islands in **Samoa** are the …eaks of large underwater volcanic …ountain chains. **Mount Matavanu** is …cated at the center of Savai'i, the larg…st Samoan island. The volcano's last …ajor eruption in 1905 forced much of the …cal population to permenantly leave the island. Because of the lovely beaches, waterfalls, and fascinating culture the Samoan Islands are considered one of most attractive destinations in the South Pacific. Despite the influence of American and European culture, the Samoans have preserved many aspects of their traditional culture.

French Polynesia consists of five archipelagos comprising more than 120 islands. The French territory is scattered over 4.5 million km² near the eastern edges of Polynesia. The volcanic **Marquesas Islands** are one of the largest island groups in French Polynesia. Poitanui (1,232 meters) is the highest volcano in the Marquesas. Over 1,000 kilometers southwest of the Marquesas Islands lie the **Tuamotu Islands** – an island group consisting entirely of atolls. The **Society Islands** are the most famous island group in French Polynesia.

Tahiti, the economic and cultural center of French Polynesia, lies at the geographic center of the territory. The capital and largest city in French Polynesia is Papeete on Tahiti. The Society Islands are divided into two groups: the Leeward and Windward Islands. All of the Society Islands are volcanic islands with rich tropical vegetation. Mount Orohena on Tahiti is the highest mountain in the territory, rising 2,241 meters above sea level.

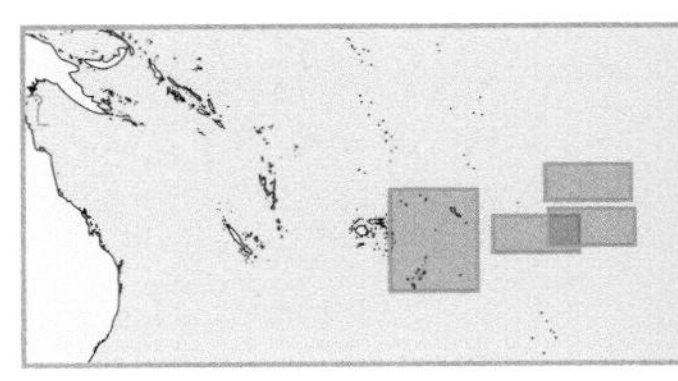

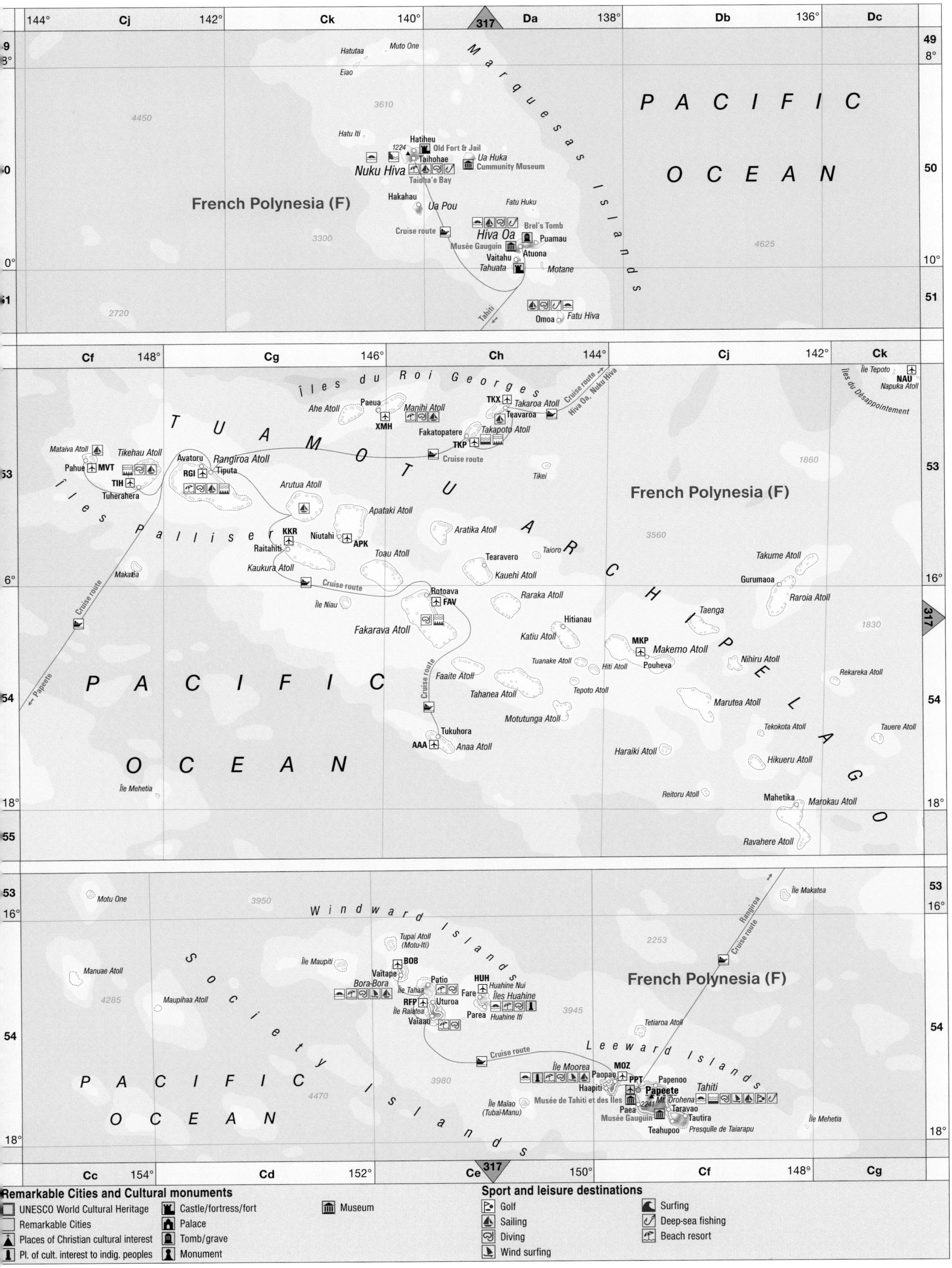

Nuku Hiva Largest of the Marquesas Islands – several deep bays – fascinating stone formations – historic fort **Ck50**

Fatu Hiva Considered the most beautiful of the Marquesas Islands – formed from two volcanic craters – sailings areas **Da51**

Bora Bora Often called the "pearl of the Pacific", the island covers 38 km². Bora Bora boasts several beautiful blue lagoons surrounded by sandy white beaches. Ferries link the island to Tahiti. **Ce54**

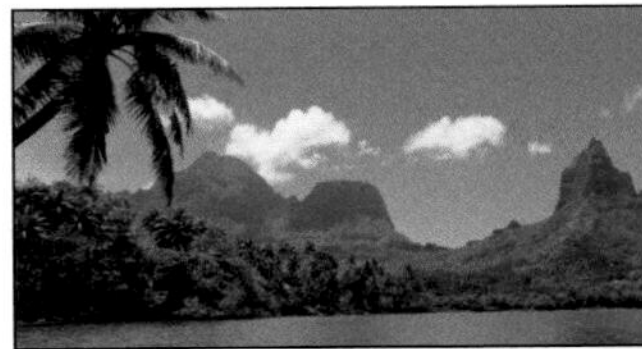

Moorea Island with peaks and lush vegetation – panoramic views from Belvedere lookout – ruins of ancient temples **Cf54**

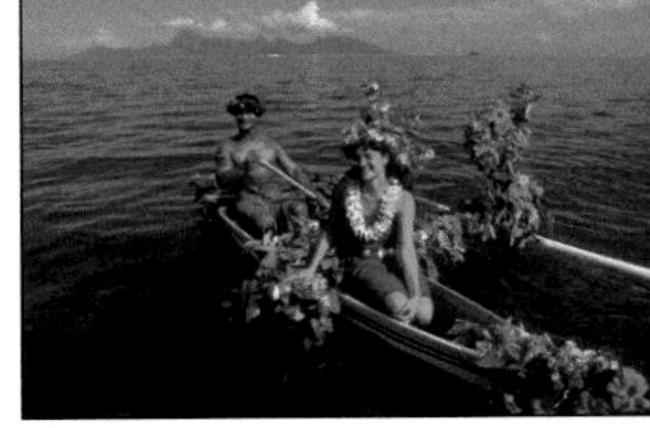

Tahiti Gauguin Museum – Musée de Tahiti et des Îles (local history and culture museum) – tall cliffs and peaks – capital city Papeete **Cf54**

Remarkable Cities and Cultural monuments

- UNESCO World Cultural Heritage
- Remarkable Cities
- Places of Christian cultural interest
- Pl. of cult. interest to indig. peoples
- Castle/fortress/fort
- Palace
- Tomb/grave
- Monument
- Museum

Sport and leisure destinations

- Golf
- Sailing
- Diving
- Wind surfing
- Surfing
- Deep-sea fishing
- Beach resort

Namaland (top): Quiver trees, a type of Aloe, are common in the deserts of southern Namibia
Abu Simbel (bottom): Colossal statues of Ramses II before the temple at Abu Simbel

Kruger National Park (left): A leopard relaxes in South Africa's most famous national park
The Seychelles (right): A tourist paradise in the Indian Ocean

Africa

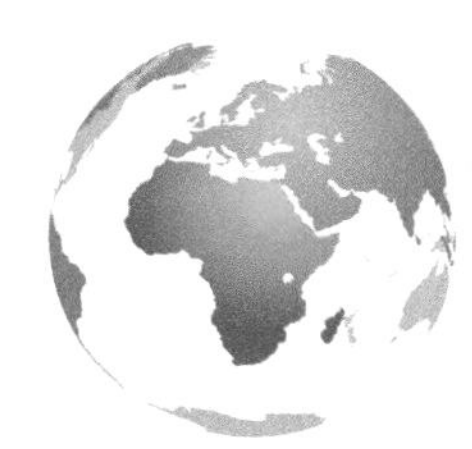

Africa was and is the continent of explorers and adventurers. The continent's wonders include vast wildernesses, the world's largest desert, the Virunga Volcanoes, steamy rainforests, the Victoria Falls, the majesty of Kilimanjaro, Egypt's pyramids, Morocco's palaces, the ruins of Great Zimbabwe, as well as its fascinating indigenous cultures.

Africa has an area of approximately 30.4 million km². The world's second largest continent encompasses around 20% of the Earth's total land area. From north to south, Africa stretches over 8,000 kilometers. Africa is separated from Europe by the Mediterranean Sea, but at the **Strait of Gibraltar** the two continents are less than 14 kilometers apart. The Red Sea is situated between northeastern Africa and the Arabian Peninsula. In the west, Africa is bordered by the Atlantic Ocean, while the Indian Ocean borders the continent to the east and southeast. The coasts of Africa are remarkably smooth with few peninsulas and large natural harbors. **Madagascar** is situated near a series of smaller island groups including the Comoros and the Seychelles. Several small island groups – including the Cape Verde Islan – are located near Africa's western coa The terrain of Africa is dominated by series of basins, including the immer Sahara basin, the Niger-Chad-White N basin, and the Congo basin. The **Gre Rift Valley**, an ancient fracture on t Earth's surface, stretches through E Africa. Many of Africa's tallest mounta – including Kilimanjaro and Mt. Kenya – a located in or near the Great Rift Valley.

Beautiful Mount Kilimanjaro is comprised of three volcanoes

With the exception of a few areas near the Mediterranean and southeastern coast on the Indian Ocean most of Africa has three types of climate/vegetation zones. The North and Southwest of the continent have **arid** and **semi-arid climates** (top photo: Dunes in the Libyan Desert). Central Africa and West Africa have humid **tropical climates** (middle photo: Rain forest in the Congo basin). The landscape in East Africa and most of Southern Africa is primarily **savannah** (bottom photo: Serengeti National Park in Tanzania).

The highest mountains in Africa (in descending order) are **Kilimanjaro** (5,895 meters), **Mt. Kenya** (photo: 5,199 meters), Mt. Ruwenzori (5,109 meters), and Ras Dashen Terara (4,620 meters). The **Atlas Mountains** is the highest range in North Africa. In southern Africa, the **Drakensberg Mountains** rise to a maximum height of 3,482 meters. Lake Assal (-155 meters) in Djibouti is the lowest point on the continent's surface.

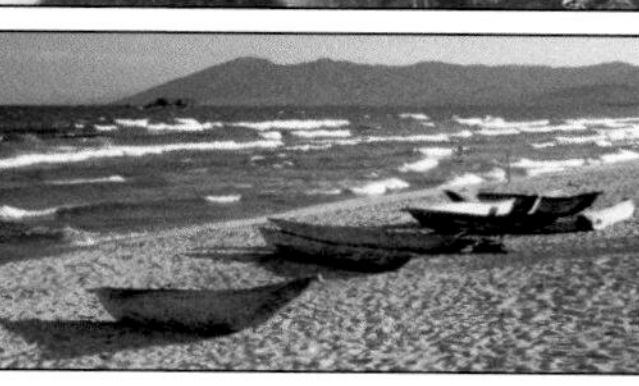

The longest river in Africa is the 6,671-kilometer-long **Nile River** (top photo). Other major rivers include the **Congo** (4,374 km), the **Niger** (4,184 km), and the **Zambezi** (2,376 km). The **Victoria Falls** (middle photo) on the Zambezi River are the continent's largest waterfalls. The largest lakes in Africa are **Lake Victoria** (68,000 km²), **Lake Tanganyika** (34,000 km²), and Lake Malawi (30,800 km²: bottom photo).

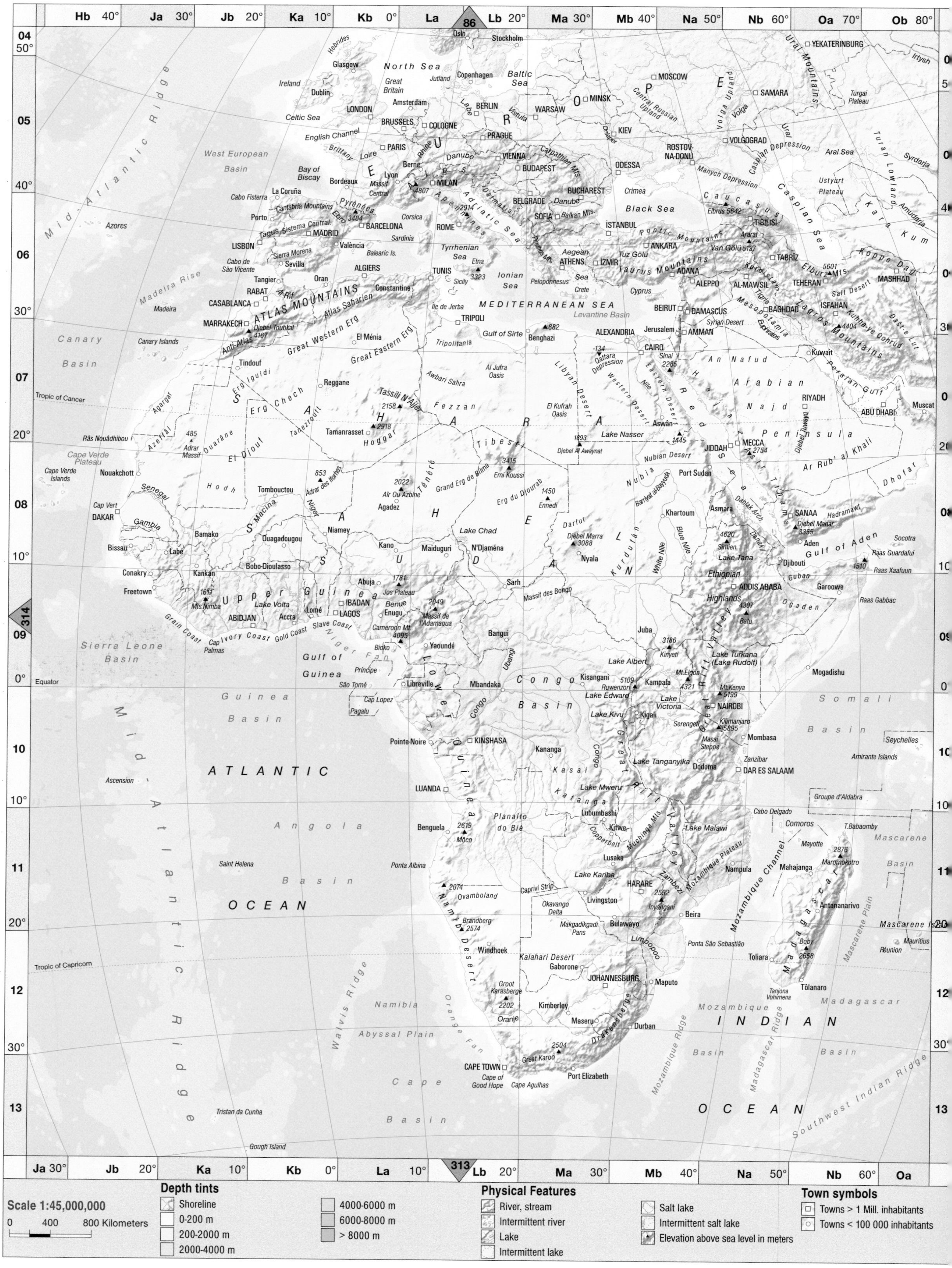

Scale 1:45,000,000

0 400 800 Kilometers

Depth tints
- Shoreline
- 0-200 m
- 200-2000 m
- 2000-4000 m
- 4000-6000 m
- 6000-8000 m
- > 8000 m

Physical Features
- River, stream
- Intermittent river
- Lake
- Intermittent lake
- Salt lake
- Intermittent salt lake
- Elevation above sea level in meters

Town symbols
- Towns > 1 Mill. inhabitants
- Towns < 100 000 inhabitants

‑ica is home to more than 700 million ople. North Africa is inhabited by a riety of ethnicities, including **Arabs**, **Ber‑ rs**, and the **Tuareg**. The areas south of e Sahara are populated mostly by dark nned black African ethnicities. Most ack Africans ethnicities are categorized o one of distinct two groups: **Bantu eaking** and **Sudanic** ethnicities. Other ajor ethnic groups in Africa include the **malis**, **Ethiopians**, and the **San**.

Africa has the highest birthrates of any continent. The rapid population growth is seen by many as a major obstacle to the continent's economic and social development. Despite widespread social problems, several African states have experienced positive economic and political developments in recent years.

Left: A Tuareg man
Right: Maasai girl in Kenya

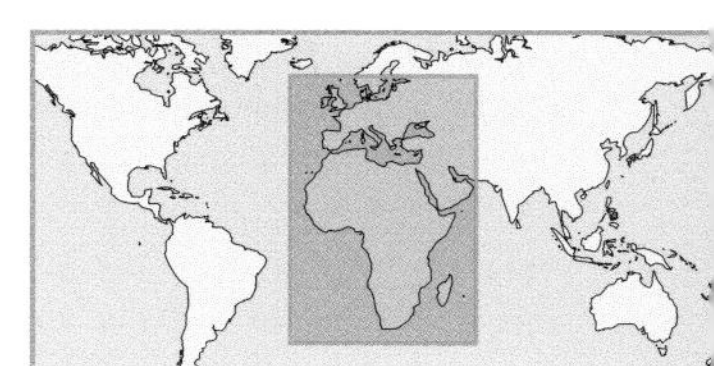

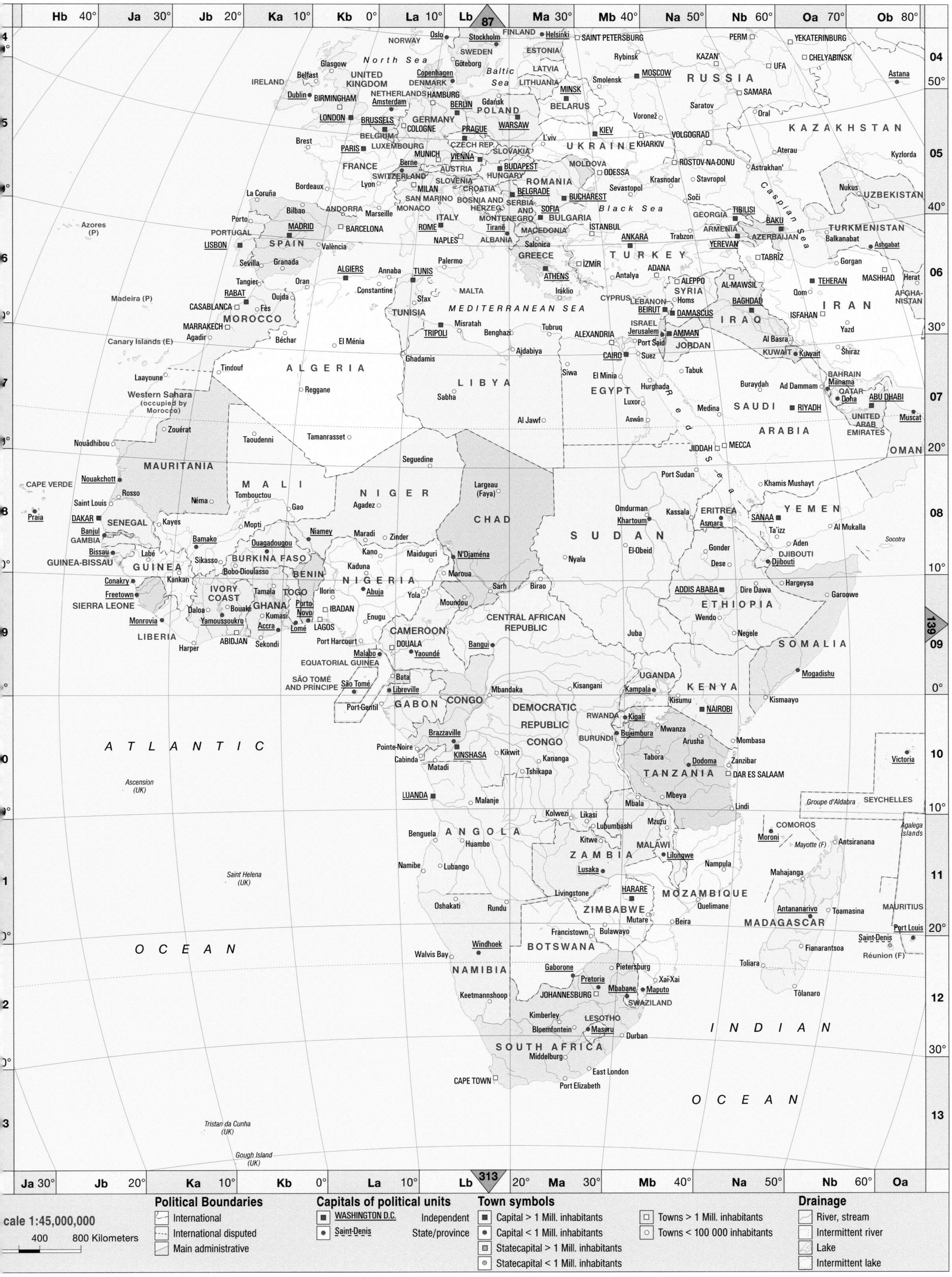

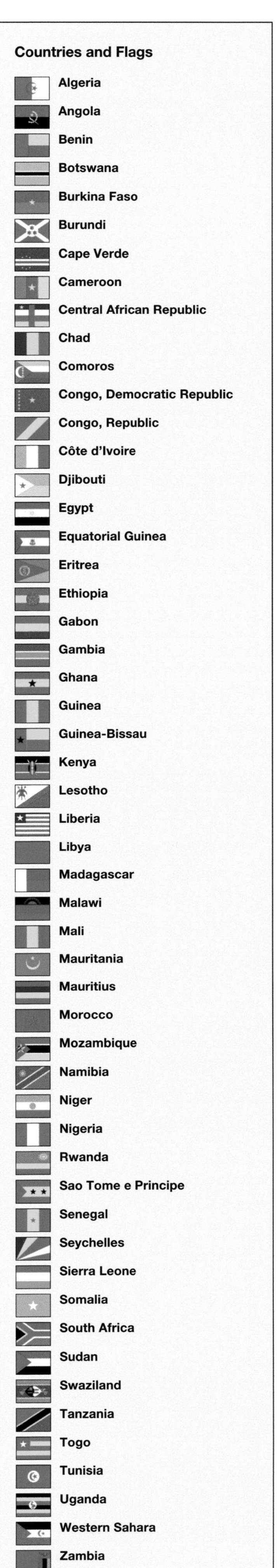

cale 1:45,000,000
400 800 Kilometers

Political Boundaries
International
International disputed
Main administrative

Capitals of political units
WASHINGTON D.C. Independent
Saint-Denis State/province

Town symbols
Capital > 1 Mill. inhabitants
Capital < 1 Mill. inhabitants
Statecapital > 1 Mill. inhabitants
Statecapital < 1 Mill. inhabitants
Towns > 1 Mill. inhabitants
Towns < 100 000 inhabitants

Drainage
River, stream
Intermittent river
Lake
Intermittent lake

Northern Africa

The northern half of Africa features many contrasting climate and vegetation zones. The Sahara Desert stretches between Africa's Mediterranean coast and the tropical regions of central and western Africa. The **Sahara**, the world's largest desert, covers more than nine million km^2. Between the Atlas Mountain range on the northwestern edge of the Sahara and the Mediterranean lies a coastal area with a hospitable subtropical climate. The

Sahel along the southern edges of t
Sahara is a transition zone between t
desert and the tropical regions of Afri
This region consists mostly of semi-a
savannahs and stretches from Senega
West Africa to Kenya in East Africa. Ce
turies ago, Arab traders and geographe
gave the Sahel its name, an Arabic wo

The vast Sahara Desert covers most o
North Africa

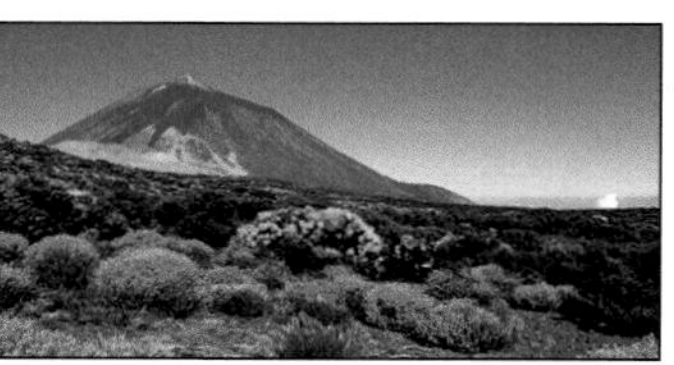

Canary Islands Spanish island group off the western coast of Africa – the highest point on the Canary Islands is Pico del Teide (photo) with a height of 3,717 meters

Atlas Mountains The Atlas mountain chain stretches through Morocco, Algeria, and Tunisia. The High Atlas (top photo, Morocco), the highest section of the chain, rises above 4,000 meters. The Sahara Atlas range (bottom photo) borders the Sahara Desert.

The **Sahara Desert** encompasses a variety of contrasting landscapes including high sand dunes, heavily eroded highlands with unusual stone formations, and flat monotonous fields of sand. Numerous fertile oases are scattered throughout the desert. Photos from top to bottom: Erg Chebbi in Morocco, The Hoggar Mountains in Algeria, Saharan village

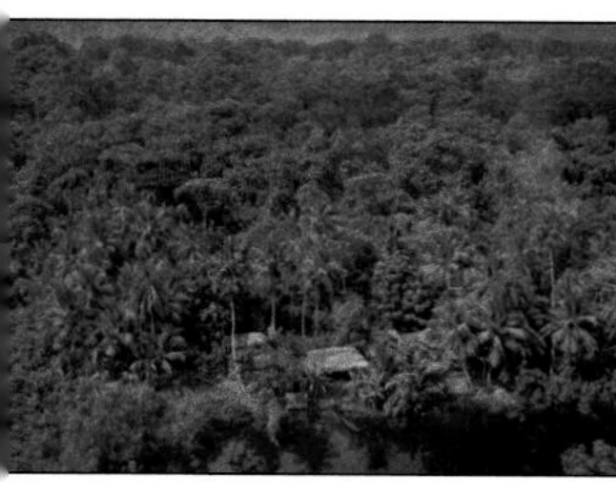

Niger River 4,184 kilometers long – the river flows from the highlands of Guinea through the Sahel and into the deserts of Mali and Niger – rainforests around the Niger's delta on the Atlantic coast

Scale 1:18,000,000
0 160 320 Kilometers

Depth tints
- Shoreline
- 0-200 m
- 200-2000 m
- 2000-4000 m
- 4000-6000 m
- 6000-8000 m
- > 8000 m

Physical Features
- River, stream
- Intermittent river
- Lake
- Intermittent lake
- Salt lake
- Intermittent salt lake
- Elevation above sea level in mete

eaning shore or border. Because of tural desertification and human land e, the Sahel is gradually expanding uth. The majority of the Sahel's inhabi-ıts are subsistence farmers or nomads. uth of the Sahel lies a belt of **forested vannahs** and **tropical rainforests** etching from the Atlantic coast to the eat Rift Valley in East Africa. The re-on is home to many ecosystems with ique flora and fauna. Rapid popula-tion growth in the region is a significant threat to this biodiversity.

The **Congo basin** encompasses the world's second largest area of tropical rainforests. Many of these forests have been designated conservation areas in recent years but illegal logging remains a problem in the region. The Congo basin is also home to many valuable mineral resources including diamonds, oil, gold, and iron ore. Unfortunately this mineral wealth has also contributed to environmental damage and the outbreak of armed conflicts in the region.

Centuries ago, European traders established bases and forts in West Africa and on islands near the region's coast. Many settlements on the West African coast would eventually become centers of the international slave trade. For many centuries, Arabian traders had a major presence on the continent's eastern coast.

Many traders and armies once traversed the deserts of North Africa in large caravans. Northern Africa's rivers – including the Nile and Niger – have been an important means of transport through the continent's interior for many centuries. The **Niger** is the longest river in West Africa with a length of 4,184 kilometers. Africa's longest river, the **Nile**, flows north from its source in Uganda to the continent's Mediterranean coast.

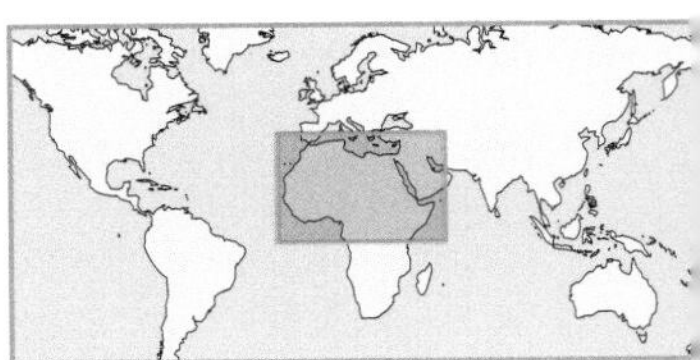

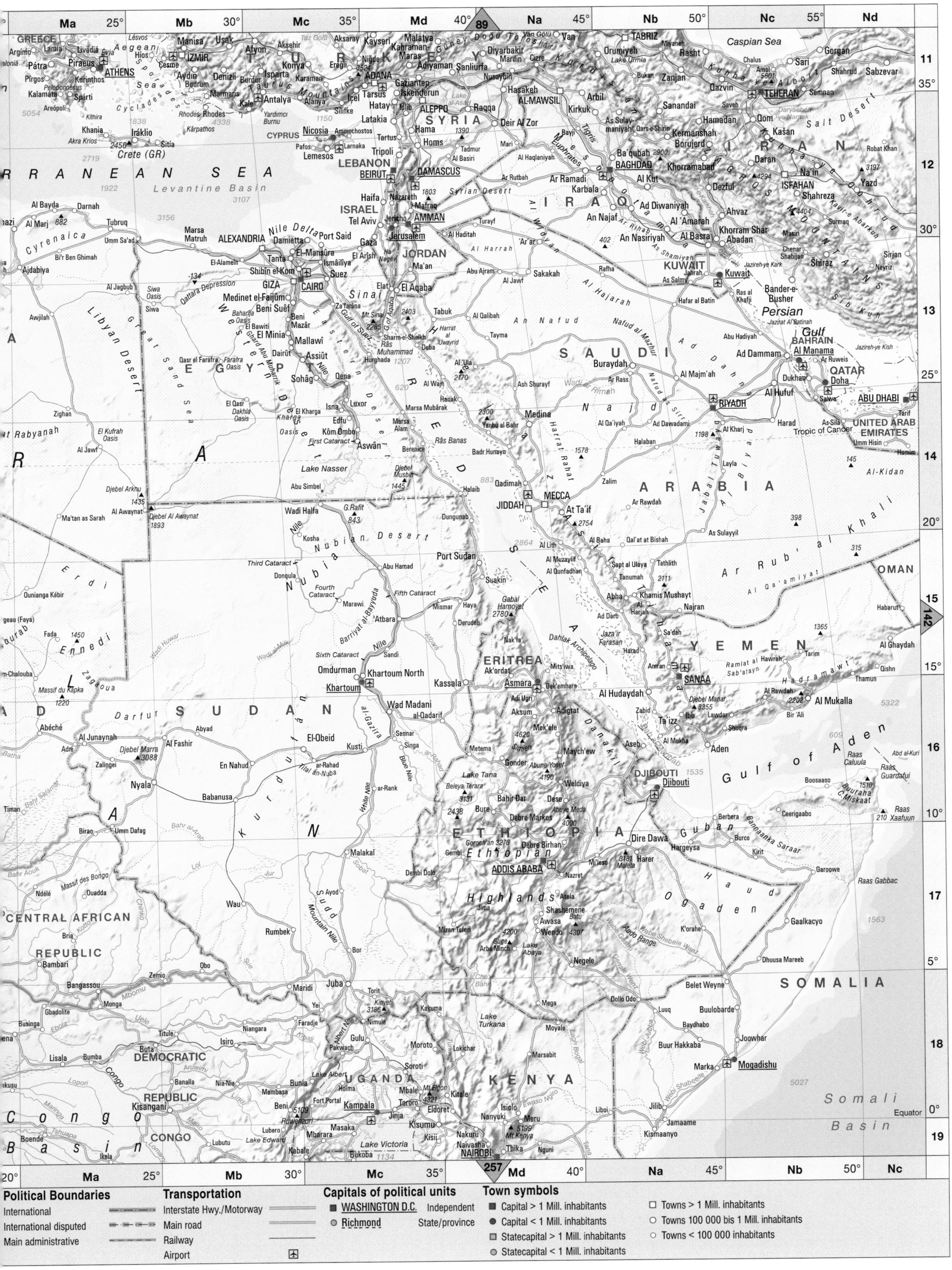

89

142

257

The Nile The Blue Nile and the White Nile Rivers begin in Ethiopia and Uganda and merge near Khartoum in Sudan. The Nile, Africa's longest river, flows north to its delta on the Mediterranean coast. Photos from top to bottom: Cairo, near Aswan, Blue Nile Falls in Ethiopia, the source of the White Nile in Uganda

Eritrea Mountainous arid nation – capital city, Asmara – fertile coastal strip along the Red Sea

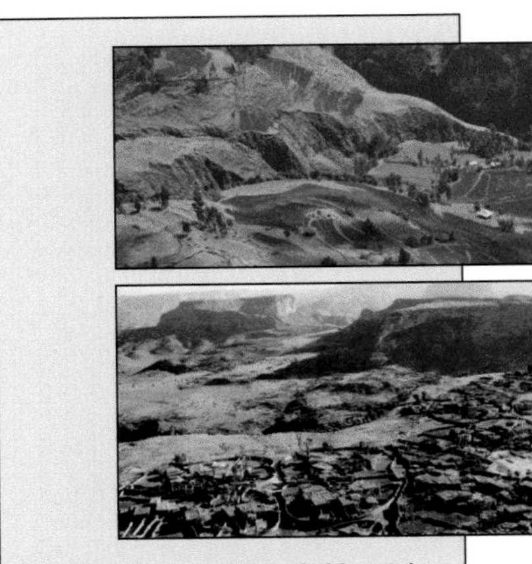

The Highlands of Ethiopia Mountainous areas cover much of Ethiopia. The country's highlands contain several massifs taller than 4,000 meters.

Somalia Desert country on the Horn of Africa – home to many desert nomads – dry river beds (photo)

Political Boundaries
- International
- International disputed
- Main administrative

Transportation
- Interstate Hwy./Motorway
- Main road
- Railway
- Airport

Capitals of political units
- WASHINGTON D.C. Independent
- Richmond State/province

Town symbols
- Capital > 1 Mill. inhabitants
- Capital < 1 Mill. inhabitants
- Statecapital > 1 Mill. inhabitants
- Statecapital < 1 Mill. inhabitants
- Towns > 1 Mill. inhabitants
- Towns 100 000 bis 1 Mill. inhabitants
- Towns < 100 000 inhabitants

The section of Africa between the equator and the continent's southern tip offers a variety of distinct climate zones, including areas with tropical and Mediterranean climates. The terrain of southern Africa is dominated by a series of large basins including the **Kalahari Basin** with its arid deserts. The **Okavango Basin** encompasses the world's largest wetland – a conservation area with abundant wildlife. The Afro-Arabian Rift Valley, an ancient geographic feature, stretc from southern Africa to western Asia East Africa, the Rift Valley diverges i two branches: the **Western** and **East (Great) Rift Valleys**. Lake Victoria, A ca's largest lake, is located in a basin tween the two branches of the Rift V ley. The Great Rift Valley contains ma

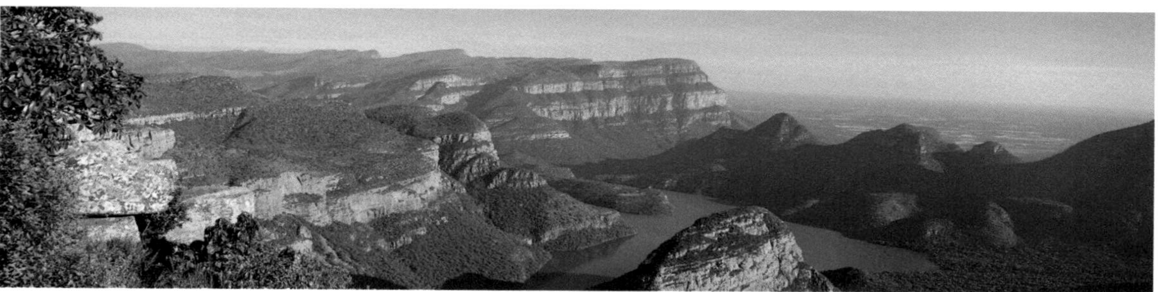

The Blyde River flows through the Dr kensberg Mountains of South Africa

Congo Basin The basin of the Congo River contains vast tropical rainforests, home to countless plants and animals

Great Escarpment The transition zone between southern Africa's highlands and coasts has beautiful, craggy landscapes

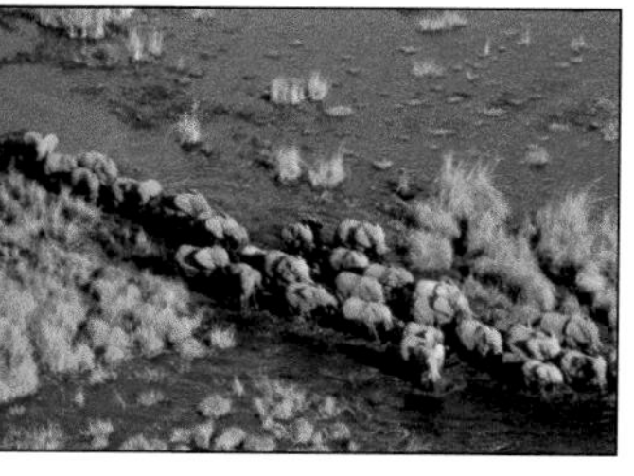

Okavango Delta Inland river delta in Botswana (15,000 km²) – numerous small streams – home to large animal herds

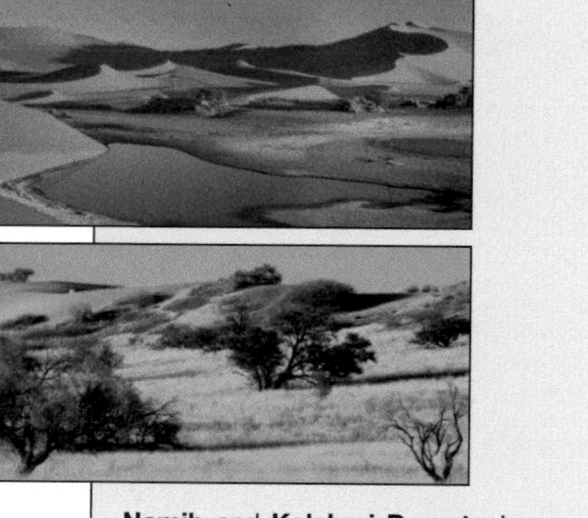

Namib and **Kalahari Deserts** Large arid areas in Botswana and Namibia. The Namib Desert (top photo) located near the Atlantic Ocean gets almost no rainfall. The arid and semi-arid steppes of the Kalahari Desert contain several seasonal rivers.

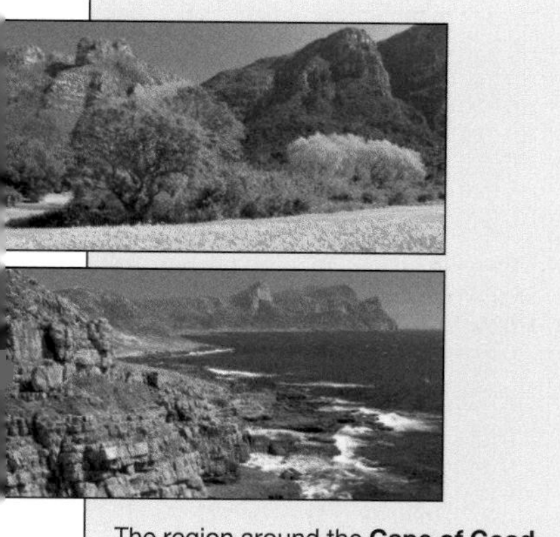

The region around the **Cape of Good Hope** (bottom photo) in South Africa has some of the country's most beautiful landscapes, unique flora, attractive beaches, and a pleasant Mediterranean climate.

Scale 1:18,000,000
0 160 320 Kilometers

Depth tints
- Shoreline
- 0-200 m
- 200-2000 m
- 2000-4000 m
- 4000-6000 m
- 6000-8000 m
- > 8000 m

Physical Features
- River, stream
- Intermittent river
- Lake
- Intermittent lake
- Salt lake
- Intermittent salt lake
- Elevation above sea level in meter

›cinating landscapes including numer-s high volcanoes and large lakes. ›unt **Kilimanjaro** (5,895 meters), Afri-'s highest mountain, lies in the Great 't Valley near the border between Tan-nia and Kenya. East Africa features ›veral large national parks and conser-›tion areas with fascinating wildlife – ›luding **Ruwenzori Mountains Natio-l Park** (Uganda), **Serengeti National ›rk** (Tanzania), and the **Masai Mara Reserve** in Kenya. Southern Africa features a long series of highlands. These highlands rise gradually to the south of the enormous Congo River basin and extend to the southern edges of the continent in South Africa. The highlands of Zimbabwe, known as the **High Veld**, consist of heavily cultivated areas where tobacco and grains are farmed. Namibia's arid and semi-arid highlands are inhabited mostly by ranchers and cattle herders. The **Okavango** and **Zambezi Rivers** are the two most significant rivers in Southern Africa. During the wetter months of the year, the Okavango Delta is transformed into a fertile wetland. The Zambezi flows east from its source in northeastern Zambia and forms the spectacular **Victoria Falls** when it crashes over a narrow gorge in Zimbabwe. Two large man-made lakes have been created along the course of the Zambezi in recent decades: Lake Kariba and Cabora Bassa Reservoir. The dams constructed on the Zambezi are vital sources of electricity for Mozambique and Zimbabwe. **Madagascar** is the largest island off the African coast and the world's fourth largest island. The island's interior is dominated by humid tropical highlands. Because of its geographic isolation, Madagascar has a unique collection of endemic flora and fauna.

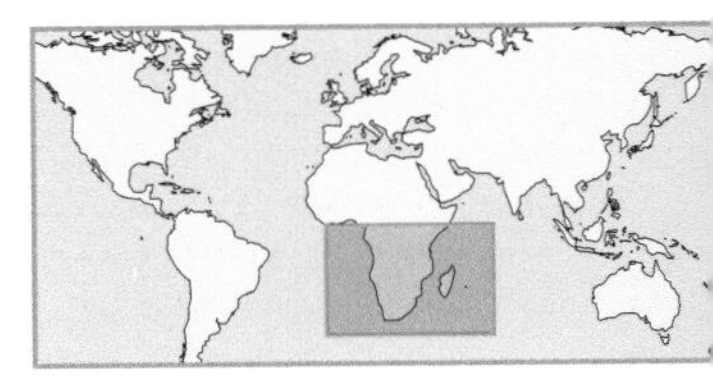

Mount Kilimanjaro Africa's highest mountain rises 5,895 meters – located in northern Tanzania – UNESCO world heritage site

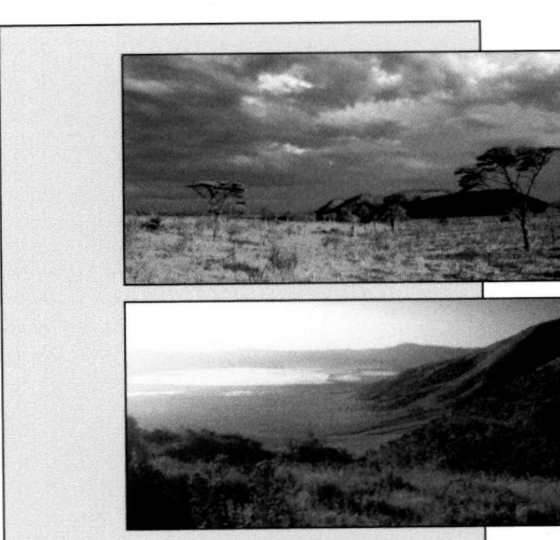

Vast **steppes** and **savannahs** cover much of East Africa, especially Kenya and Tanzania. This region features some of the continent's most famous national parks – including Serengeti National Park and the Masai Mara National Game Reserve.

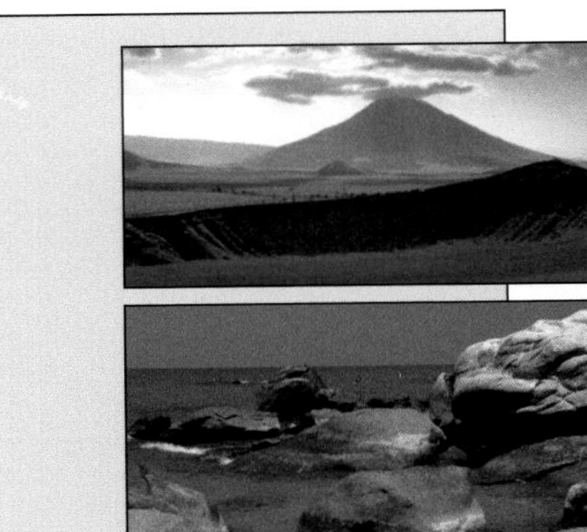

The **Great Rift Valley** and **Western Rift Valley** are ancient fault systems in Africa. Both encompass numerous volcanoes and a series of large lakes. Photos: the volcano Ol Doinyo Lengai, Lake Malawi

Drakensberg Mountains UNESCO world heritage site – mountain range in South Africa and Lesotho – thousands of ancient rock paintings created by the San people

The Highlands of Madagascar Highlands cover much of the island's interior – humid tropical and subtropical climates – national parks with diverse flora and fauna

Political Boundaries
International
International disputed
Main administrative

Transportation
Interstate Hwy./Motorway
Main road
Railway
Airport

Capitals of political units
WASHINGTON D.C. Independent
Richmond State/province

Town symbols
Capital > 1 Mill. inhabitants
Capital < 1 Mill. inhabitants
Statecapital > 1 Mill. inhabitants
Statecapital < 1 Mill. inhabitants
Towns > 1 Mill. inhabitants
Towns 100 000 bis 1 Mill. inhabitants
Towns < 100 000 inhabitants

Morocco and **Algeria** occupy the northwestern edges of Africa. There are however major geographic and political differences between the two neighboring nations. Morocco's territory is dominated by the four sections of the Atlas mountain system. The **Anti Atlas range** in southern Morocco borders the Sahara Desert. The **High Atlas range**, the tallest section of the Atlas system, contains several mountains taller than 4,000 meters. The central range of the Atlas Mo tains borders a large fertile plate called the Meseta. Northeastern Moroc is dominated by the **Rif Mountains**, northernmost section of the Atlas Mo tains in the country. Morocco conta only a small section of the Sahara the Moroccan territory Western Sah

The high mountains of the Atlas Rang in Morocco Kg

Casablanca Morocco's largest city – industrial center – major port city – the Grand Mosque Hassan II (photo) can accommodate 100,000 worshippers **Kg29**

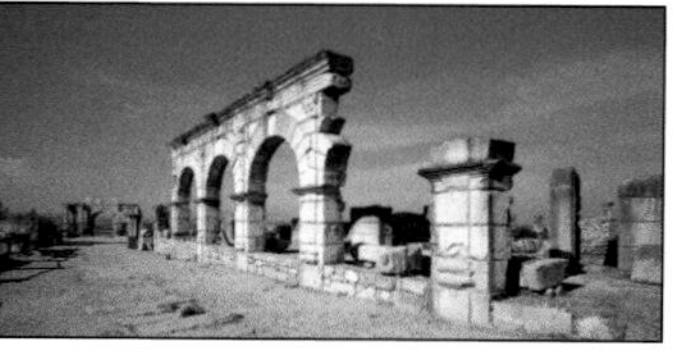

Volubilis Capital of the Roman province Mauritania Tingitania between 42-285 AD – historic ruins and mosaics – basilicas – UNESCO world heritage site **Kh28**

Fès (Fez) Royal city – Fès al Bali (photo), a UNESCO world heritage site, with historic mosques, Islamic schools – the tomb of the city's founder Moulay Idriss II is a pilgrimage site **Kh29**

Meknès Royal City – UNESCO world heritage site – city gate Bab el-Mansour (photo) – royal palaces **Kh29**

Marrakech Royal city – historic city wall, souks (Arab markets), and the Koutoubia Mosque – Jemaa el Fna square (photo) with vendors and street performers – UNESCO world heritage site **Kf30**

Tizi-n-Tichka Pass Mountain pass situated 2,260 meters above sea level in the Atlas Mountains **Kg30**

Aït Ben Haddou UNESCO world heritage site in Morocco – features ancient, ornamental adobe casbahs built by the Ben Haddou Berbers on the edge of the High Atlas mountain range **Kg30**

Scale 1:4,500,000
0 40 80 Kilometers

Principal travel routes
- Auto route
- Rail road
- Shipping route

Remarkable landscapes and natural monuments
- UNESCO World Natural Heritage
- Mountain landscape
- Rock landscape
- Ravine/canyon
- Cave
- Waterfall/rapids
- Desert
- Oasis
- National park (landscape)
- National park (flora)
- National park (fauna)
- National park (culture)
- Biosphere reserve
- Coastal landscape
- Beach

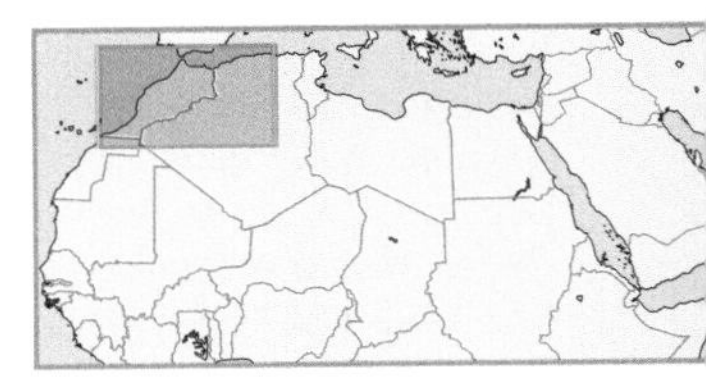

50,000 km²) consists almost entirely of esert. Western Sahara, a former panish colony, was annexed by Morocco in the 1970s. The region has a population of around 250,000 and is believed to ave valuable mineral resources.
orocco is a popular tourist destination nd the country's attractions include the ur so-called **royal cities**, historic North frican architecture, and long sand eaches on the Mediterranean coast. The Moroccans have preserved many aspects of their traditional culture despite centuries of foreign influence. The Alaouite Dynasty has been the ruling family of Morocco continuously since the 17th century.

In contrast to Morocco's history of political stability, **Algeria** has experienced political unrest and armed conflicts since its independence from France in 1962. Northern Algeria is the most fertile and densely populated region in the country. The majority of Algeria's more than 30 million inhabitants live in this region. Algeria's capital and largest city, **Algiers**, is situated on the country's Mediterranean coast. The **Tell mountain range** separates the fertile area on Algeria's Mediterranean coast from the country's interior. Further south, the **Sahara Atlas mountain range** rises to a maximum height of 2,328 meters above sea level.

Most of Algeria's territory (2,381,741 km²) is occupied by sections of the Sahara Desert. The sand dunes of the **Grand Erg Occidental** – near Timimoun – are among the most fascinating natural attractions in the interior. The **oasis towns of the M'zab region** contain distinct local architecture. This region is inhabited by the M'zabites, a Berber ethnic group with a unique culture developed during centuries of isolation.

Drâa Valley Fertile oasis on the Drâa River – numerous small farms, palm groves, traditional gardens, adobe villages, and historic casbahs **KgKh30**

Todra Gorge Beautiful gorge near the southern edge of the High Atlas mountain range – near Tinerhir **Kh30**

Merzouga Large erg – stretch of sand dunes – in southeastern Morocco near Tafilalt Oasis **Kh30**

Tipaza Algerian town – former Roman port founded by the Phoenicians – Kbor er Roumia tomb (photo) – UNESCO world heritage site **Lb27**

Great Kabylie Mountainous region in eastern Algeria – large Berber population – principal city, Tizi Ouzou – cedar forests – Djebel Djurdjura National Park **LbLc27**

Ghardaïa Largest town in the M'zab Valley – UNESCO world heritage site – distinct culture of the M'zabite Berbers – the town's unique Saharan architecture inspired prominent modernist architects **Lb29**

Taghit Oasis village surrounding by large sand dunes – located in the Grand Erg Occidental – historic rock carvings **Kj30**

Remarkable Cities and Cultural monuments

- UNESCO World Cultural Heritage
- Remarkable Cities
- Prehistoric rockscape
- Phoenecian culture
- Roman antiquity
- Places of Islamic cultural interest
- Cultural landscape
- Historical city scape
- Castle/fortress/fort
- Palace
- Tomb/grave
- Space telescope
- Market
- Festivals
- Museum

Sport and leisure destinations

- Golf
- Skiing
- Sailing
- Diving
- Surfing
- Seaport
- Beach resort
- Mineral/thermal spa

Northeastern Algeria, Tunisia, Northern Libya

The Mediterranean coasts of Libya, Algeria, and Tunisia are home to more remnants of ancient 🏛 Roman civilization than any other region in Africa. Numerous temples, amphitheaters, villas, and aqueducts from the Roman era are scattered throughout this part of the continent. Like the other countries of North Africa, the culture of Libya, Tunisia, and Algeria was shaped mostly by **Arabs** who migrated to the region from the Middle

East during the 7th and 8th centurie
After their arrival in North Africa, the Ara
rapidly replaced the indigenous **Berbe**
as the dominant ethnic group in the r
gion. The Berber populations of Lib
and Tunisia have largely adapted Ar
culture and there are few significant d
ferences between the two ethnicities

A herd of camels near the Douz oasis in Tunisia **Le:**

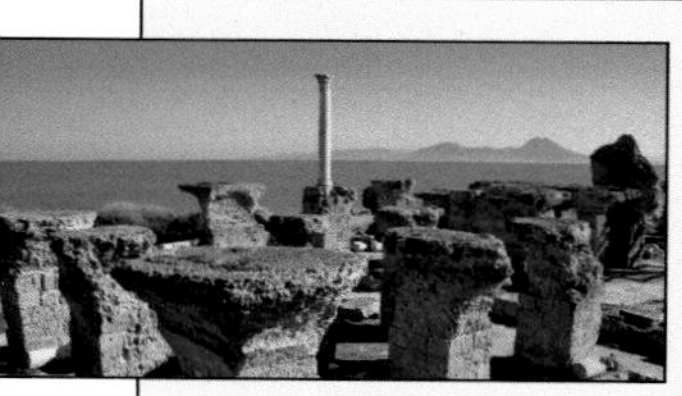

The Phoenicians In the 9th century BC, the Phoenicians founded the city of Carthage where Tunis now stands. The city became Rome's greatest challenger for control of the Mediterranean. The two powers fought three wars before Carthage was conquered.

The Romans in North Africa Around 44 BC, the Romans under the leadership of Caesar Augustus gained control over much of North Africa. The province of Africa Proconsularis encompassed most of modern Tunisia. Photos from top to bottom: Djemilla **(Lc27)**, Sufetula **(Le28)**, Djem **(Lf28)**

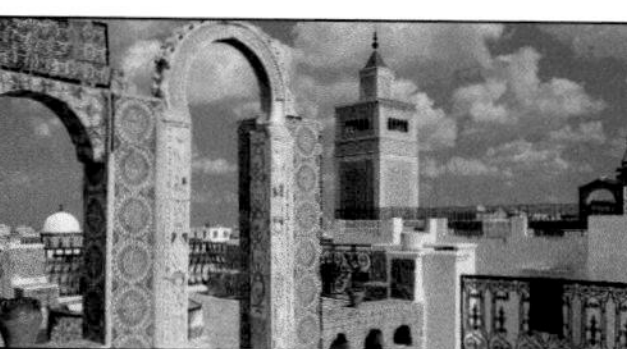

Tunis Tunisia's capital and principal city – historic 🏙 medina, a world heritage site with historic markets and mosques – 🏛 Bardo Museum – Roman and Phoenician ruins in 🏛 Carthage **Lf27**

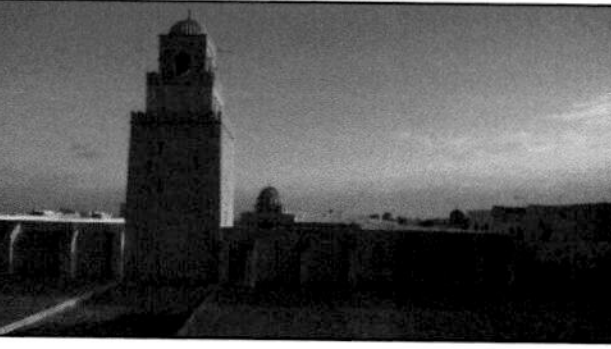

Kairouan 🏙 Religious center founded in 670 AD – historic medina: a world heritage site – 🕌 Sidi Oqba mosque (photo) **Lf28**

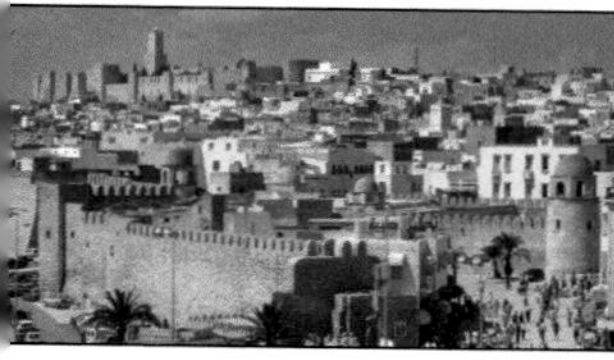

Sousse Port city with a vibrant 🏙 medina (photo), a UNESCO world heritage site – 🏰 Ribat, fortified complex and mosque built in the 9th century – casbah **Lf28**

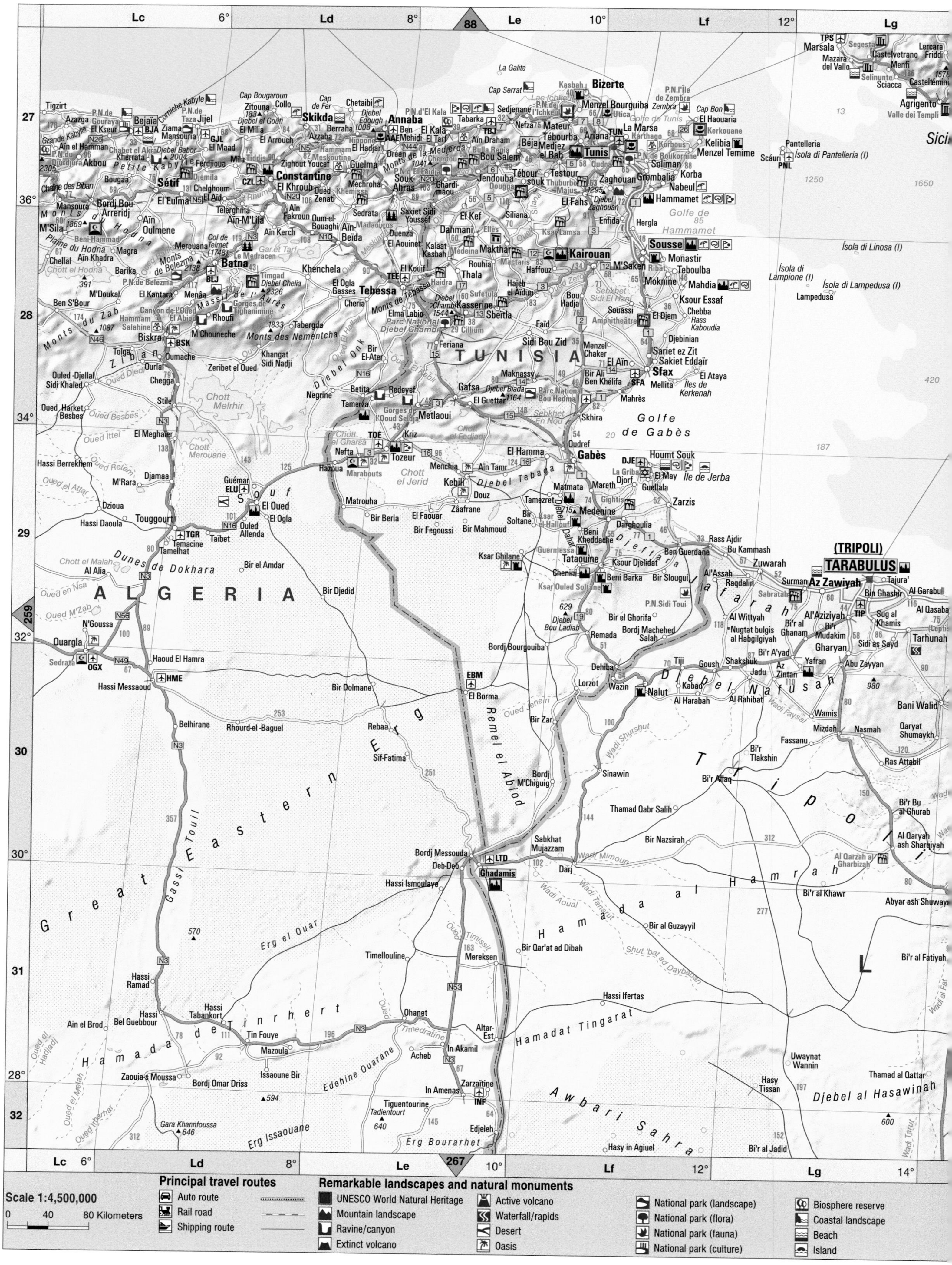

Scale 1:4,500,000
0 40 80 Kilometers

Principal travel routes
- Auto route
- Rail road
- Shipping route

Remarkable landscapes and natural monuments
- UNESCO World Natural Heritage
- Mountain landscape
- Ravine/canyon
- Extinct volcano
- Active volcano
- Waterfall/rapids
- Desert
- Oasis
- National park (landscape)
- National park (flora)
- National park (fauna)
- National park (culture)
- Biosphere reserve
- Coastal landscape
- Beach
- Island

›ya and Tunisia. In Algeria, a large seg›ent of the Berber population retreated the highlands of the Atlas Mountains ›er the Arabs arrived in the region. ›cause of their isolation, the Algerian ›rbers were better able to preserve their ›guages and traditions.

›rtheastern Algeria and most of Tuni›a are dominated by the foothills and ›ountains of the **Atlas mountain sys›m**. In contrast to these regions, **Libya** is dominated by the vast Sahara Desert. The desert extends through the country's interior and along the Mediterranean coast. Most of the Libya's **desert** consists of flat monotonous fields of sand, unlike the deserts of Tunisia and Algeria, which contain many fascinating landscapes – including the sand dunes of the **Grand Erg Oriental** and numerous shining salt flats.

Tunisia, the smallest nation in North Africa, borders the Mediterranean Sea to the north and east. The country is one of the most popular tourist destinations in Northern Africa. Tunisia's attractions include its long Mediterranean **beaches**, the beautiful **mountain villages** of the Berbers, **desert oases**, and traditional markets. The coastline between the cities Djerba and Nabeul contains many modern hotels built with local North African architectural influences. **Libya's** main tourist attractions include its ancient **archeological sites** and desert interior. Islam is the dominant religion in all of the North African countries. In Algeria, tensions between Islamic fundamentalists and the country's government have led to political instability. In Tunisia, a moderate interpretation of Islam dominates society. Polygamy is forbidden and women have the same legal rights as men in the country.

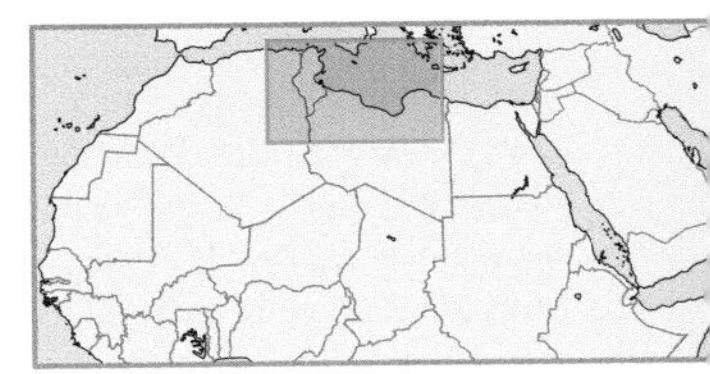

Djerba Island in the Gulf of Gàbes – Houmt Souk, a historic marketplace – La Ghirba synagogue – Jewish community since the 1st century AD – Berber architecture – sandy beaches **Lf29**

Cave Dwellings in Matmata Unusual village in the highlands of southeastern Tunisia – underground dwellings – several scenes from the Star Wars films were filmed in the town **Le29**

Tataouine Southernmost major town in Tunisia – historic mosque in Guermessa (photo), 20 kilometers from Tataouine **Lf29**

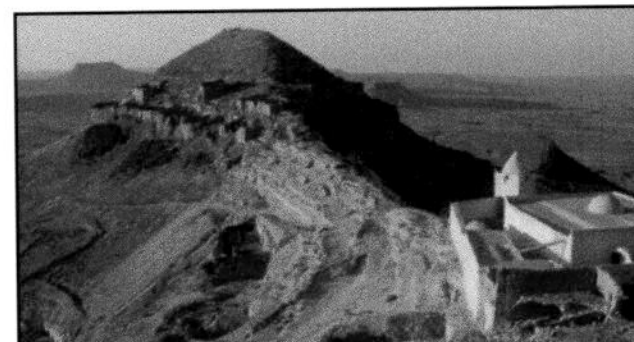

Chenini Picturesque Berber village built on a hillside – cave dwellings – Mosque of the Seven Sleepers **Lf29**

Sabratah Well preserved remnants of a Roman town on the Mediterranean coast – amphitheater, temple of Isis, and main plaza (forum) – world heritage site **Lg29**

Leptis Magna Ancient city in Libya – birthplace of the "African" emperor Septimus Severus – site of the most beautiful ruins in North Africa – world heritage site **Lh29**

Ghadamis UNESCO world heritage site – once a major trade center along a caravan route – walled old town – traditional Saharan architecture; white colored buildings and arched alleyways **Le30**

Remarkable Cities and Cultural monuments

- UNESCO World Cultural Heritage
- Remarkable Cities
- Pre- and early history
- Prehistoric rockscape
- Early african culture
- Phoenecian culture
- Greek antiquity
- Roman antiquity
- Places of Jewish cultural interest
- Places of Islamic cultural interest
- Historical city scape
- Castle/fortress/fort
- Monument
- Market

Sport and leisure destinations

- Golf
- Diving
- Seaport
- Beach resort
- Mineral/thermal spa

Egypt

The Arab Republic of Egypt is situated between the **Red Sea** to the east, the **Mediterranean Sea** to the north, and the **Sahara desert** to the west and south. The vast majority of Egypt's more than 70 million inhabitants are concentrated in around five percent of the country's territory along the banks of the Nile. Most of Egypt's territory is covered by large sand or stony deserts. Egypt has an arid climate with high temperatures during

most of the year. During winter, nighttime temperatures in the deserts often fall below 0° Celsius and the country's Mediterranean coast gets heavy rainfall.

The **Nile**, Africa's longest river, is the lifeline of Egypt. The Nile Valley, a fertile oasis on both sides of the river, has a maximum width of 25 kilometers and is

A tranquil section of the Nile Valley near Aswan **Mg33**

surrounded by deserts. The Nile ent Egypt as Lake Nasser, a large reserv created after the construction of the **Aswan High Dam** in the 1960s. The N Valley extends north from the lake to area around **Cairo**. The Nile Delta is a f tile plain crossed by branches of the riv and the most important center of ag culture in Egypt.

The **Suez Canal** connects the Red S to the Mediterranean Sea. The canal w

Marsa Matruh The westernmost major city in Egypt – Cleopatra's Bath – bay on the Mediterranean Sea – Siwa Oasis **Md30**

White Desert Between the Baharija and Farafra oases – stunning white limestone formations created by erosion **Me32**

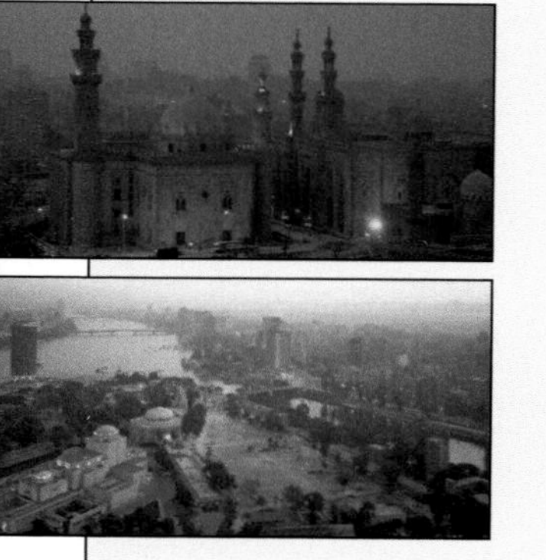

Cairo Egypt's capital has an impressive collection of Islamic art and architecture. The Mosque of Amr is the oldest mosque in Africa. During the 10th century, the Fatamid dynasty founded the Al-Azhar University, the oldest university in the Muslim world. The Sultan Hasa Mosque (top photo) was founded in the 14th century. Cairo's museums contain ancient Roman, Christian, and Islamic art. **Mf30**

Mount Catherine Monastery Located in southern Sinai on Mount Catherine (2,637 meters) – Greek-Orthodox monastery with an important collection of religious icons – historic basilica **Mg31**

Red Sea Large coral reefs between Marsa Alam and Hurghada – good diving venues – abundant marine life **Mh32**

St Simeon's Monastery Site of a monastic settlement between the 7th and 13th centuries – archeological site **Mg33**

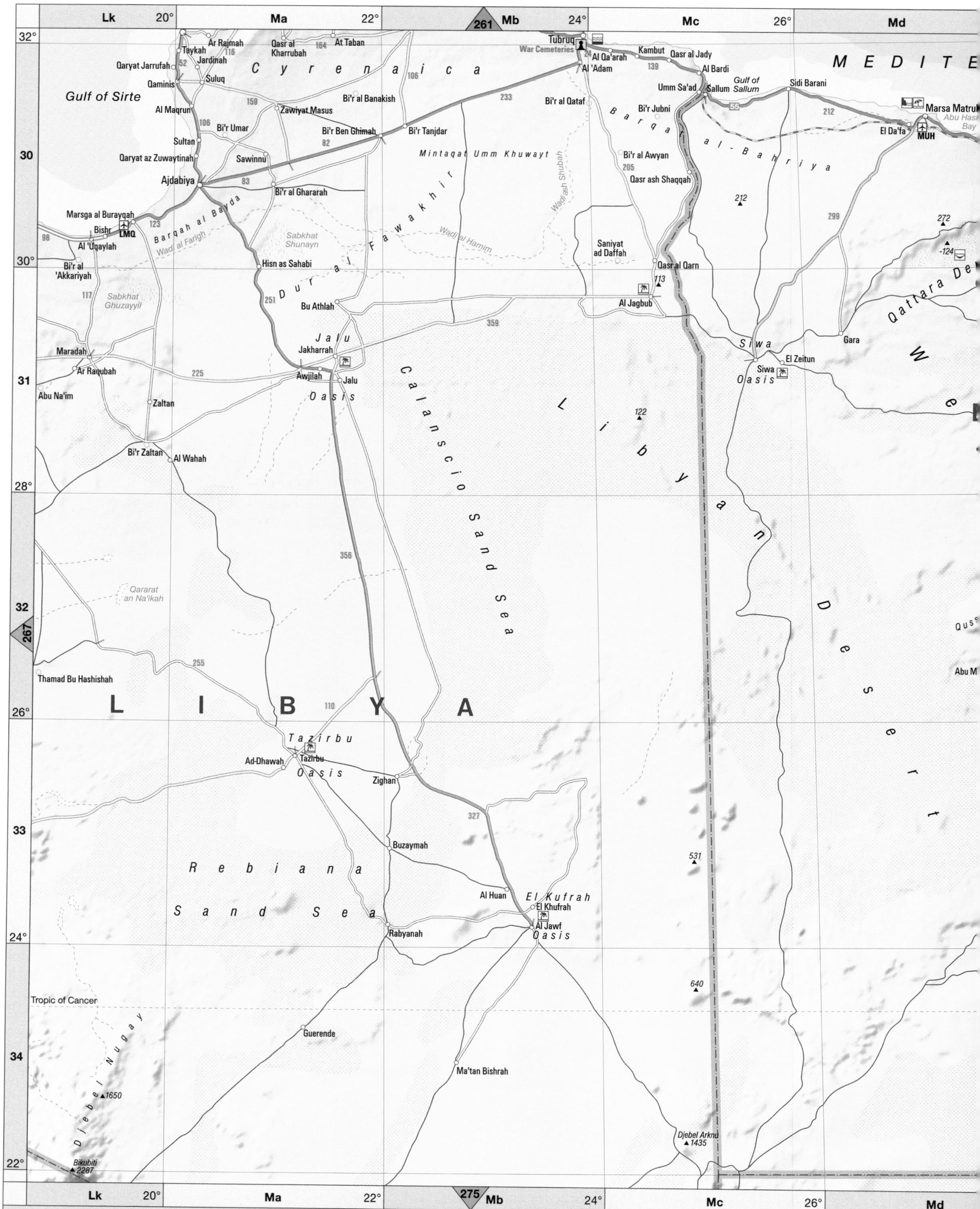

Scale 1:4,500,000
0 40 80 Kilometers

Principal travel routes
Auto route
Rail road
Shipping route

Remarkable landscapes and natural monuments
UNESCO World Natural Heritage
Mountain landscape
Rock landscape
Ravine/canyon
River landscape
Lake country
Desert
Oasis
Depression
National park (landscape)
Wildlife reserve
Coastal landscape
Beach
Coral reef
Island
Underwater reserve

ompleted in 1869 and remains one of the ost economically important waterways in e world. East of the canal, the mountain-us **Sinai Peninsula** is home to Egypt's llest mountain, Mount Catherine ,637 meters). The Sinai is also home to eautiful canyons and unique stone for-ations formed by erosion. The waters f the eastern coast of Egypt and around e Sinai Peninsula contain many color-l **coral reefs**. The reefs with their bio-diversity and natural beauty are popular tourist attractions. Tourism is an important sector of the Egyptian economy. In addition to seaside resorts and beaches, Egypt's biggest attractions are its many historic and archeological sites. The country's cultural attractions include remnants from the civilization of the ancient Egyptians, ancient Christian monuments, and Islamic architecture.

During ancient times, important overland trade routes passed along a series of oases through the deserts of Egypt and Libya into the continent's interior. The **Qattara Depression** in Egypt's interior is situated 134 meters below sea level and is one of the lowest points in Africa. **Libya** has a total land area of approximately 1.76 million km². Most of the country consists of sandy deserts located in a large basin. In the far south of Libya the **Tibesti Mountains** rise along the border to Chad. While the southern and central sections of Libya have extremely arid climates, the country's coastal region has a pleasant Mediterranean climate. The coastal regions are home to more than 95% of Libya's five million inhabitants. Of this population, a large minority are concentrated in two cities: **Benghazi** and the capital city **Tripoli**. Both cities and their surroundings are home to many well preserved ruins from the Roman era.

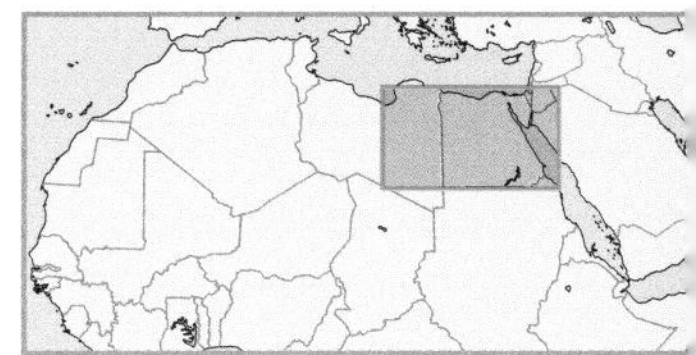

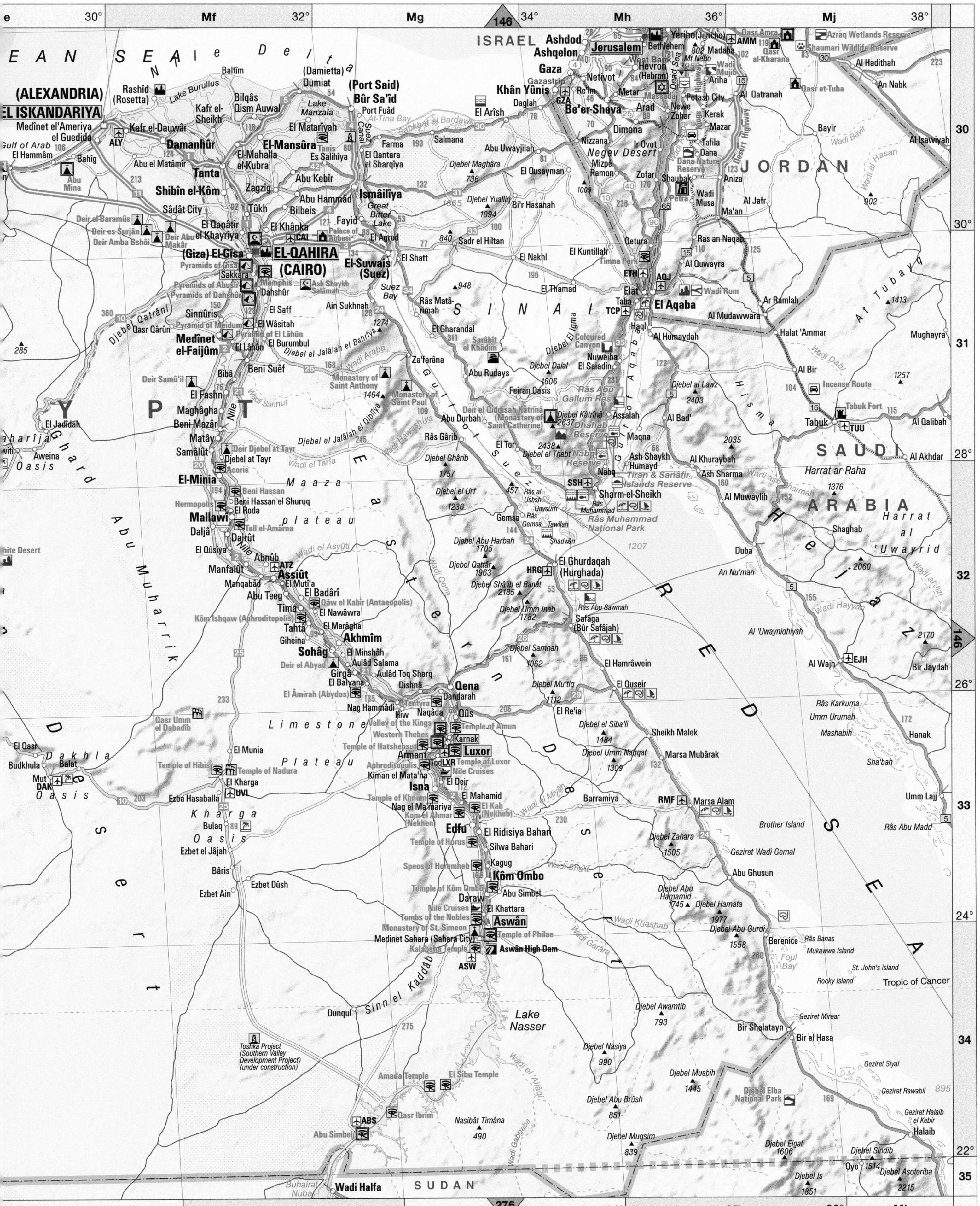

Remarkable Cities and Cultural monuments

- UNESCO World Cultural Heritage
- Remarkable Cities
- The Ancient Orient
- Ancient Egypt
- Ancient Egyptian pyramids
- Greek antiquity
- Roman antiquity
- Nabatean culture
- Places of Jewish cultural interest
- Places of Christian cultural interest
- Places of Islamic cultural interest
- Historical city scape
- Castle/fortress/fort
- Palace
- Technical/industrial monument
- Dam
- Theater of war/battlefield
- Monument

Sport and leisure dest.

- Diving
- Wind surfing
- Beach resort

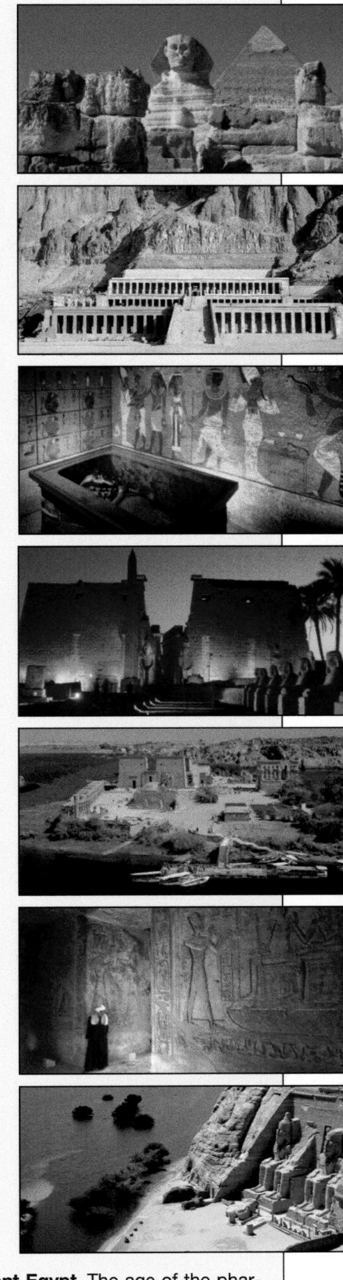

Ancient Egypt The age of the pharaohs encompasses thirty dynasties. The history of ancient Egypt is divided into three periods: the Old Kingdom (2660-2160 BC) – when most Egyptian pyramids were built, the Middle Kingdom (2040- 1785 BC), and the New Kingdom (1552-1070 BC). The years between these three periods were times of conflict and instability. Egypt contains many remnants from the civilization of the pharaohs. Photos from top to bottom: Sphinx (Giza) **(Mf31)**, Hatshepsut Temple, Tomb of Tutankhamen, Karnak **(Mg33)**, Temple of Isis, Aswan **(Mg33)**, El Seboua Temple, Lake Nasser **(Mg34)**, Temple of Ramses II (Abu Simbel) **(Mf34)**

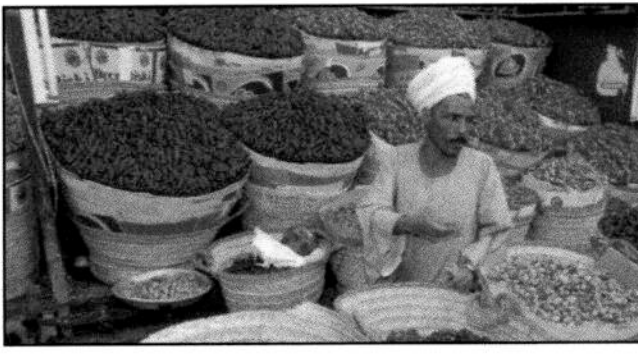

Aswan City in southern Egypt – Elephantine Island and the Temple of Satet (Satis) – two large dams in the surrounding area – Aswan has the largest Nubian population of any Egyptian city – traditional marketplaces **Mg33**

The Canary Islands and the Moroccan territory of Western Sahara are separated by a narrow stretch of the Atlantic Ocean. The Canary Islands are situated off the northwestern coast of Africa. The island group belongs to Spain and consists of seven islands; **Gran Canaria**, **Tenerife**, **Lanzarote**, **La Palma**, **La Gomera**, **El Hierro**, and **Fuerteventura**. All of the islands are of volcanic origins but most of the volcanoes on the Canaries are dormant. Popular tourist destina tions for many decades, the Cana Islands are home to many beach resor and fascinating diverse landscapes. Th western and central islands are domina ted by craggy volcanic peaks. In contra to this, the landscapes on the geological older eastern islands have been smoot

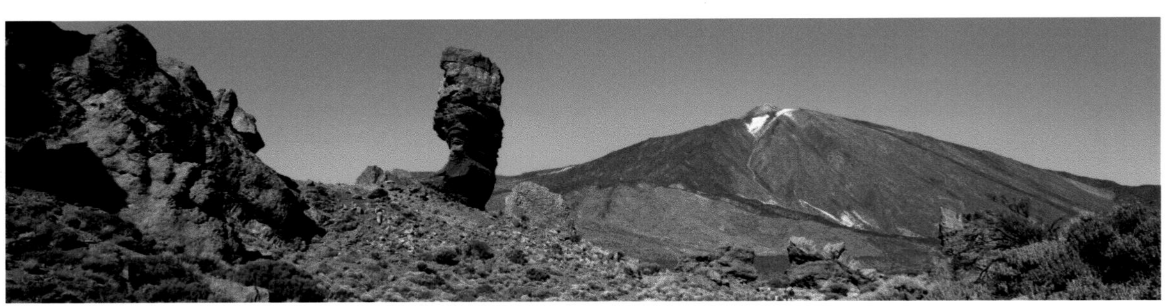

Pico del Teide: the highest mountain c the Canary Islands **Kb3**

The Canary Islands The seven Canary Islands are home to many contrasting landscapes. Ocean currents bring abundant rainfall to the smaller western islands. These islands **El Hierro**, **La Palma**, and **La Gomera** are home to lush green vegetation. Farther east, the island **Tenerife** contains stunning landscapes in its interior and beautiful beaches on its coast. **Gran Canaria** encompasses diverse landscapes including the beautiful stretch of sand dunes at Playa de Maspalomas. **Fuerteventura** and **Lanzarote** are the oldest islands in the group and contain mostly craggy volcanic landscapes. Photos from top to bottom: the observatory at Roque de Los Muchachos (La Palma) **(Kb31)**, Agulo in northern La Gomera **(Kb31)**, Garajonay National Park **(Kb31)**, Pico del Teide (Tenerife) **(Kb31)**, Playa de Maspalomas (Gran Canaria) **(Kc32)**, Fuerteventura **(KcKd31)**, Montañas del Fuego (Lanzarote) **(Kd31)**

Scale 1:4,500,000
0 40 80 Kilometers

Principal travel routes
- Auto route
- Rail road
- Shipping route

Remarkable landscapes and natural monuments
- UNESCO World Natural Heritage
- Mountain landscape
- Rock landscape
- Ravine/canyon
- Extinct volcano
- Cave
- Desert
- Oasis
- Nature park
- National park (landscape)
- National park (flora)
- National park (fauna)
- Biosphere reserve
- Coastal landscape
- Beach

314
269

by many centuries of erosion. The rival of the Spanish colonists after the th century wiped out most traces of the digenous African peoples who once inabited the Canary Islands. The indigeous people, the Gaunches, are generally elieved to have been related to the Berr ethnicities of mainland North Africa. efore the 1970s, the desert region beteen Morocco and Mauritania was Spash Sahara, a territory of Spain. After the sparsely populated region was granted its independence from Spain in 1976, the area was occupied by Morocco and Mauritania. Today the region is the Moroccan territory of **Western Sahara**. The local independence movement Polisario Front has campaigned, with the support of Algeria and often with violence, for the region's independence from Morocco. The majority of Western Sahara's around 250,000 inhabitants are native **Sahrawis**. Western Sahara landscapes are dominated by gravel and sand deserts. There are numerous salt flats scattered throughout the region, and the **Grand Erg Oriental** – near the border to Algeria – contains large wandering sand dunes.

Many of the trade routes that once connected North Africa and Sub-Saharan Africa passed through the western sections of the Sahara. Many of the scattered oasis towns in the region were once important trade centers. **Ouadâne** and **Chinguetti**, two oasis towns in Mauritania, are now both important pilgrimage sites for local Muslims. The two towns contain fascinating historic architecture including homes, libraries, and mosques made of adobe. Together with several other Mauritanian desert towns, Ouadane and Chinguetti, have been designated a UNESCO world heritage site.

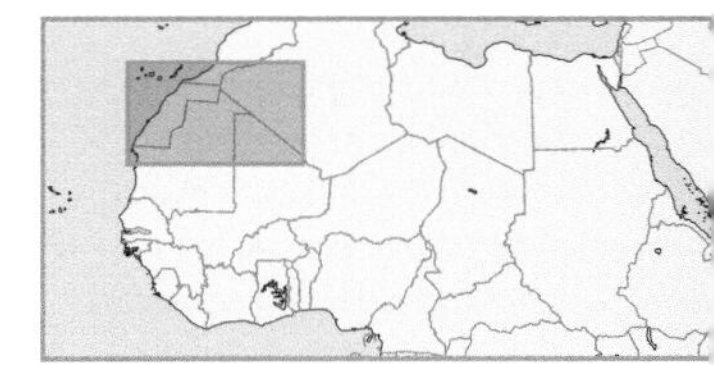

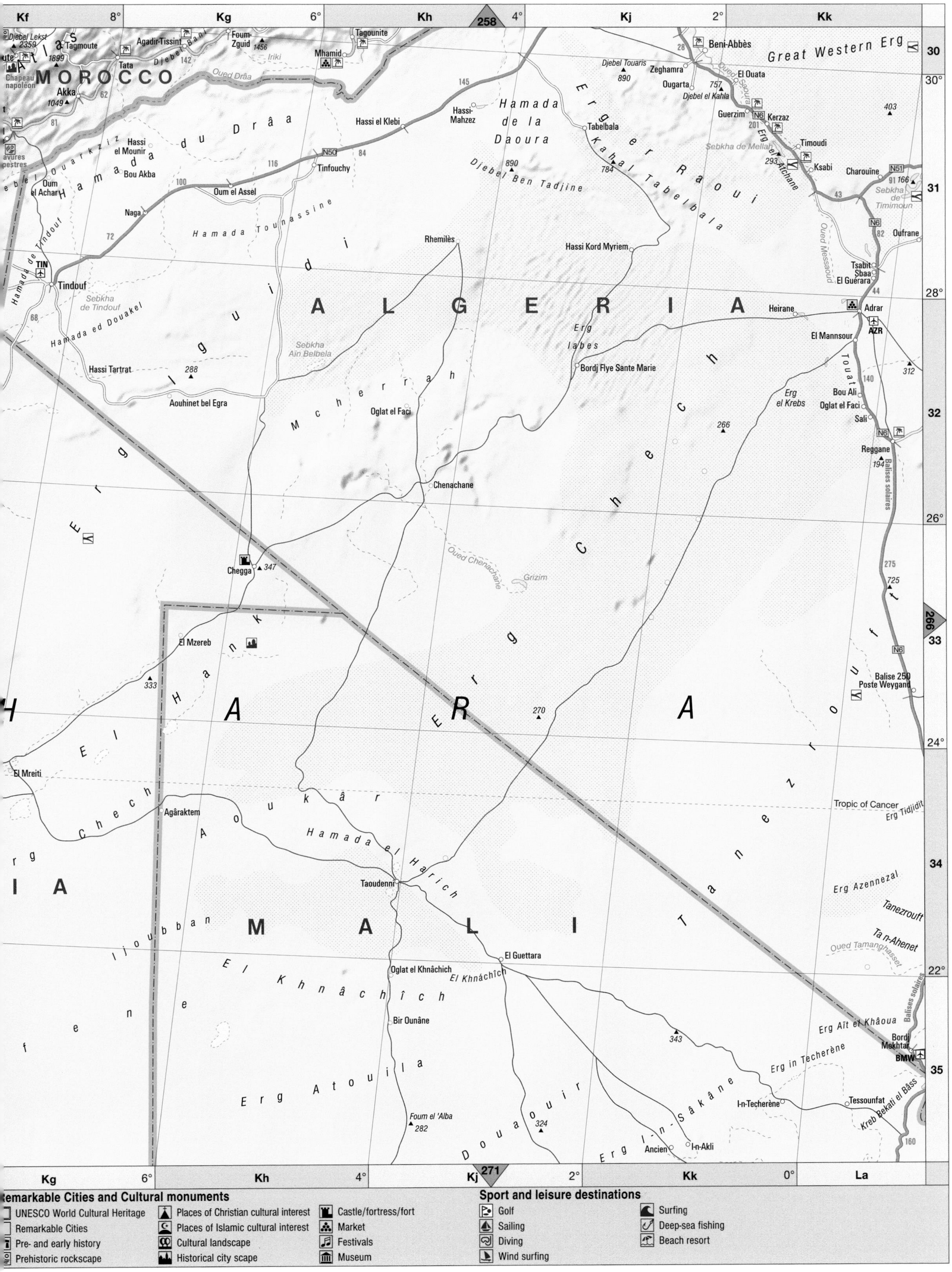

Anti-Atlas Mountain range in Morocco featuring many unusual granite formations. The region is the traditional homeland of several large Berber ethnic groups. The Chapeau Napoleon (top photo), a high stone hill, was named for its resemblance to Napoleon's hat. The red-colored villages around Tafraoute (middle photo) blend into their mountainous desert surroundings. February – when the almond trees bloom – is generally considered the best month to visit the region (bottom photo). **Kf31**

Tan-Tan The city is the administrive and economic center of Morocco's far south – camels are traded at the local livestock market (photo) once a week **Ke31**

Adrar Principal town in the Touat oasis – dwellings made from red clay in traditional Saharan style – lively market **Kk32**

Atâr Market in the Mauritanian desert – surrounded by gravel deserts, steep hills, and fields of sand dunes **Kd35**

Adrar Massif Northeastern Mauritania – tall plateau shaped by erosion – a caravan route connecting Western Sahara and Morocco passes through the sparsely populated area **Ke35**

Remarkable Cities and Cultural monuments

- UNESCO World Cultural Heritage
- Remarkable Cities
- Pre- and early history
- Prehistoric rockscape
- Places of Christian cultural interest
- Places of Islamic cultural interest
- Cultural landscape
- Historical city scape
- Castle/fortress/fort
- Market
- Festivals
- Museum

Sport and leisure destinations

- Golf
- Sailing
- Diving
- Wind surfing
- Surfing
- Deep-sea fishing
- Beach resort

The Sahara Desert occupies almost the entire northern half of the African continent. The center of the desert features interesting landscapes and cultural attractions. Five nations have borders in the central Sahara; Algeria, Libya, Chad, Niger, and Mali. Several mountain ranges form the highlands of the central Sahara including the **Hoggar** and **Tassili n'Ajjer** in Algeria, the **Aïr Mountains** in Niger, and the **Tibesti range** in Chad. All of the mountain ranges in the cent[ral] Sahara were formed during the Preca[m]brian era and originally consisted [of] smooth granite, quartz, and crystalliz[ed] stone. Erosion and volcanic activity al[te]red the shape of the region's mountai[ns] and formed the many unique stone f[or]mations throughout the central Saha[ra].

Heavily eroded mountains in the Hoggar Range **Lc/Lg**

In Salah Oasis in central Algeria – mosque and old town buildings made of red clay – surrounded by large sand dunes **Lb32**

Tassili n'Ajjer National Park UNESCO world heritage site – mountainous desert region – ancient rock paintings **Le33**

Ancient Rock Paintings in the Desert Remnants of ancient cultures that once inhabited the Sahara are scattered through Tassili n'Ajjer National Park. Scientists believe the Sahara once experienced periods of heavy rainfall in the distant past. **Le32/33**

Hoggar Mountains Mountain range in the deserts of southern Algeria – eroded volcanoes – inhabited by Tuareg communities – main settlement, Tamanrasset **LcLd34**

Tuareg merchants once dominated trade in the Sahara. The Tuareg are now scattered throughout the Sahara and the northern Sahel. Though related to the Berbers, the Tuareg have a unique culture and social structure.

Iferouâne Oasis in the Aïr Mountains of Niger – large Tuareg community – Aïr-Ténéré National Park **Le36**

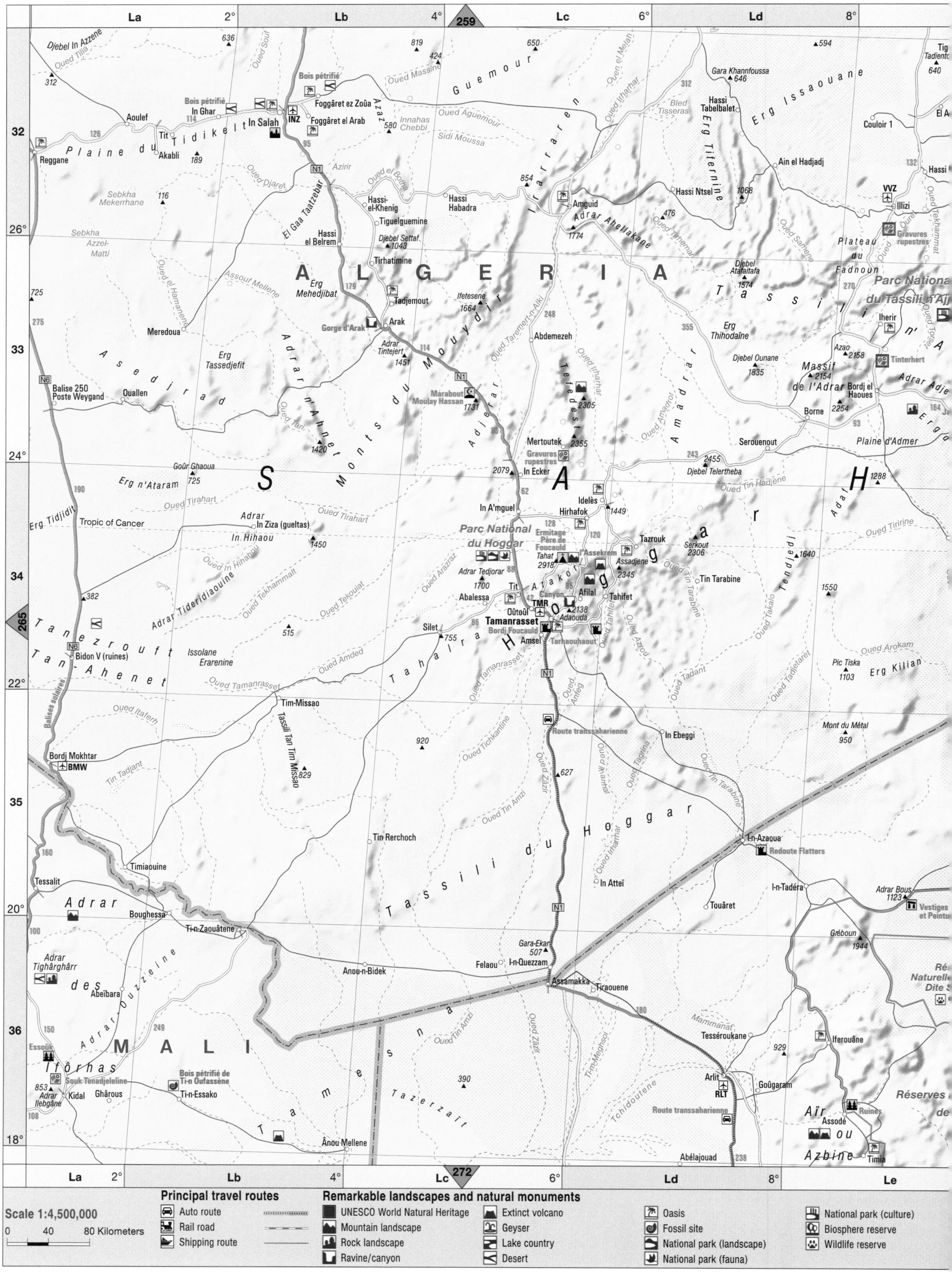

259 265 272

Scale 1:4,500,000
0 40 80 Kilometers

Principal travel routes
- Auto route
- Rail road
- Shipping route

Remarkable landscapes and natural monuments
- UNESCO World Natural Heritage
- Mountain landscape
- Rock landscape
- Ravine/canyon
- Extinct volcano
- Geyser
- Lake country
- Desert
- Oasis
- Fossil site
- National park (landscape)
- National park (fauna)
- National park (culture)
- Biosphere reserve
- Wildlife reserve

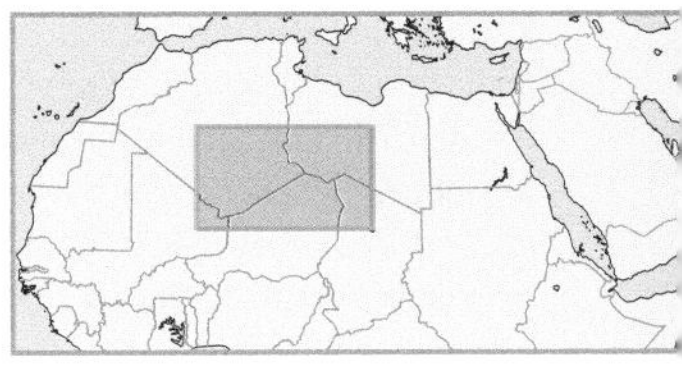

ne Hoggar Mountains are home to many ark chimney-shaped formations created volcanic activity. The highlands of bya and the Tibesti Mountains encompass many small lakes that glitter under e desert sun.

ne tallest mountain ranges in the cenal Sahara rise more than 3,000 meters bove seal level. Emi Koussi (3,415 eters) in the Tibesti Mountains is the ghest mountain in the region.

During prehistoric times, the highlands of the central Sahara were inhabited by hunter and gatherer populations which later turned to raising livestock for survival. Many ancient stone carvings and **rock paintings** depicting wild animals, livestock, gods, and dances have been found throughout the region. Many of the ancient paintings indicate that many sections of the Sahara were fertile and hospitable areas 10,000 years ago. The southern sections of the central Sahara contain many ergs – large fields of sand dunes. Most of the remaining salt caravans of the Tuareg people pass through the **Ténéré Desert** – a barren wilderness located east of the Aïr Mountains. During winter, powerful sand storms are common in the desert. The Tuareg caravans carry sorghum to oasis communities which they exchange for salt with local people. This trading relationship between the Tuareg and the isolated oasis villages of the Central Sahara has existed for centuries.

The **Tuareg** were once called the "knights of the Sahara" by Europeans because of their traditional weapons and the hierarchical structure of their society. Centuries ago, Tuareg merchants controlled trade throughout the Sahara and Tuareg warriors were feared by most communities in the Central Sahara.

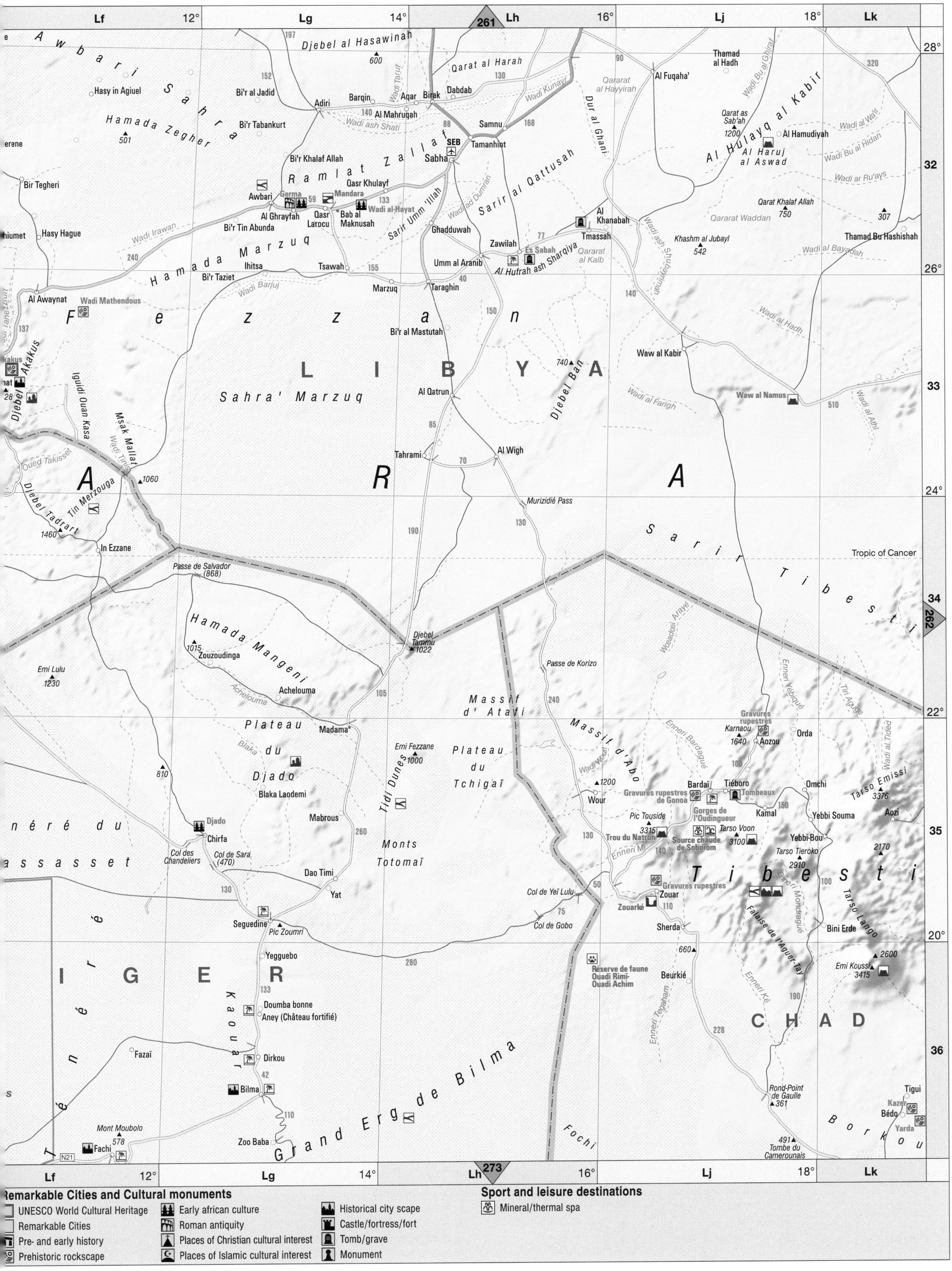

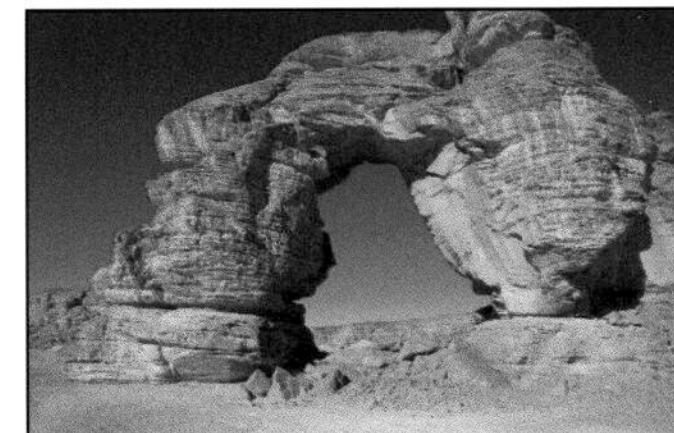

Acacus Mountains Mountain range in Libya with interesting stone formations – sand dunes and canyons – the Fozzigiaren stone arch (photo) **Lf33**

Prehistoric Art in the Acacus Mountains UNESCO world heritage site – ancient depictions of animals, dances, and peoples – between 2,000 and 20,000 years old **Lf33**

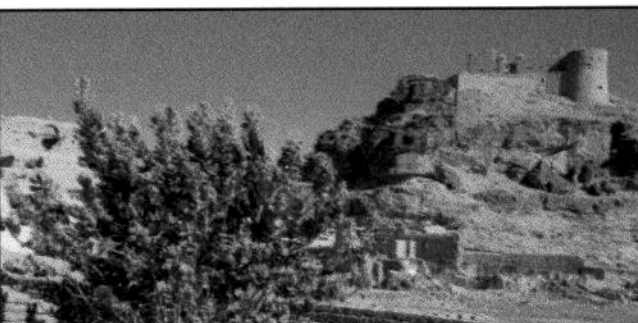

Ghat Oasis in the Acacus Mountains – beautiful abandoned old town with narrow alleys – abandoned French fort **Lf33**

Tin Merzouga Tassili n'Ajjer – desert landscapes – red sand dunes and tall column-shaped stone formations **Lf33/34**

Ancient Burial Sites of Fezzan Burial site of ancient sultans in the Libya's Fezzan region – Sahel style architecture with significant Hausa influences **Lh32**

Waw al Namus Volcano crater with a diameter of ten kilometers – a colorful saline lake is located inside the crater **Lj33**

Stone Arches of the Djado Plateau Mountainous plateau in the Tenere Desert (Niger) – ruins of Djado – major center of overland trade until the 19th century **Lg35**

Remarkable Cities and Cultural monuments

- UNESCO World Cultural Heritage
- Remarkable Cities
- Pre- and early history
- Prehistoric rockscape
- Early african culture
- Roman antiquity
- Places of Christian cultural interest
- Places of Islamic cultural interest
- Historical city scape
- Castle/fortress/fort
- Tomb/grave
- Monument

Sport and leisure destinations

- Mineral/thermal spa

Cape Verde Islands, Senegal, Gambia

Historians remain divided on the question of whether or not Greek sailing vessels traveled to the coast of Senegal during ancient times. In 1445, the Venetian sailor Alvise de Mosto reached the uninhabited **Cape Verde Islands** aboard a Portuguese trade ship. The Portuguese had already established their first base on mainland Africa near the Senegal River delta a decade before Mosto explored the Cape Verde Islands. Eventually the Cape Verde Islands became a major center the slave trade as a station between t mainland coast, where most slaves ori nated, and the European colonies in t Americas. This dark chapter of the r gion's history continued for several ce turies before the slave trade was fina ended in the 19th century.

The beautiful old town of Mindelo on the island São Vicentes **Jh**

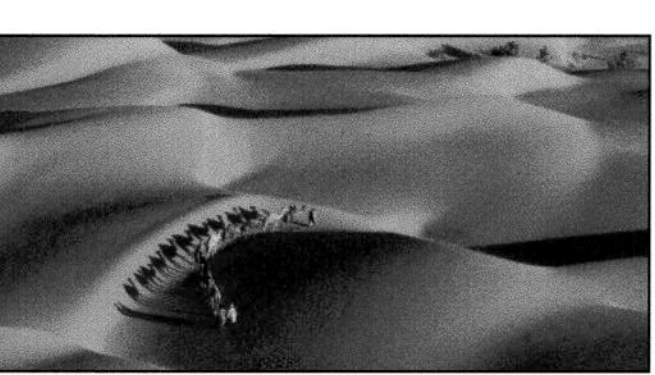

Trarza Desert region south of Nouakchott in Mauritania – inhabited by nomadic camel herders (photo) **Kc37**

Nouakchott Capital of Mauritania – attractive mosques built in typical North African style – important market – the city was a small fishing village before it became the nation's capital in 1958 **Kc36**

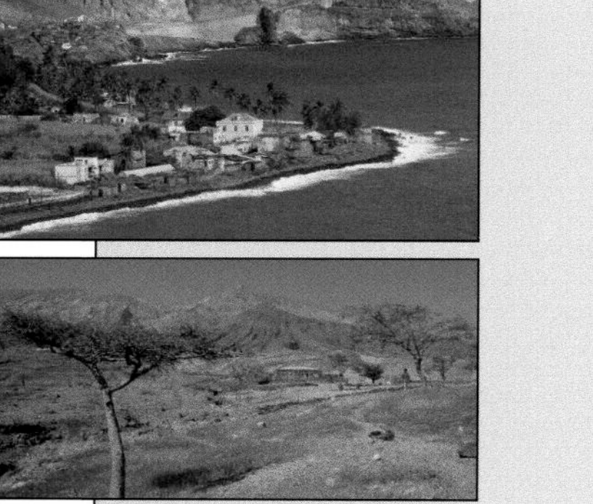

Cape Verde Islands The island group near the coast of mainland Africa is home to Iberian style colonial architecture on São Vicente, sandy beaches on the islands Sal and Maio, beautiful cliffs on Santo Antão (top photo, **Jh37**), and the volcano Pico on Fogo (bottom photo, **Jh38**).

Saint Louis Former capital of the French colony Senegal – Mauritania – colonial architecture – beaches **Kb37**

Dakar Senegal's capital city – modern business and port district, Ville Nouvelle (photo) – old town with markets and colonial buildings **Kb38**

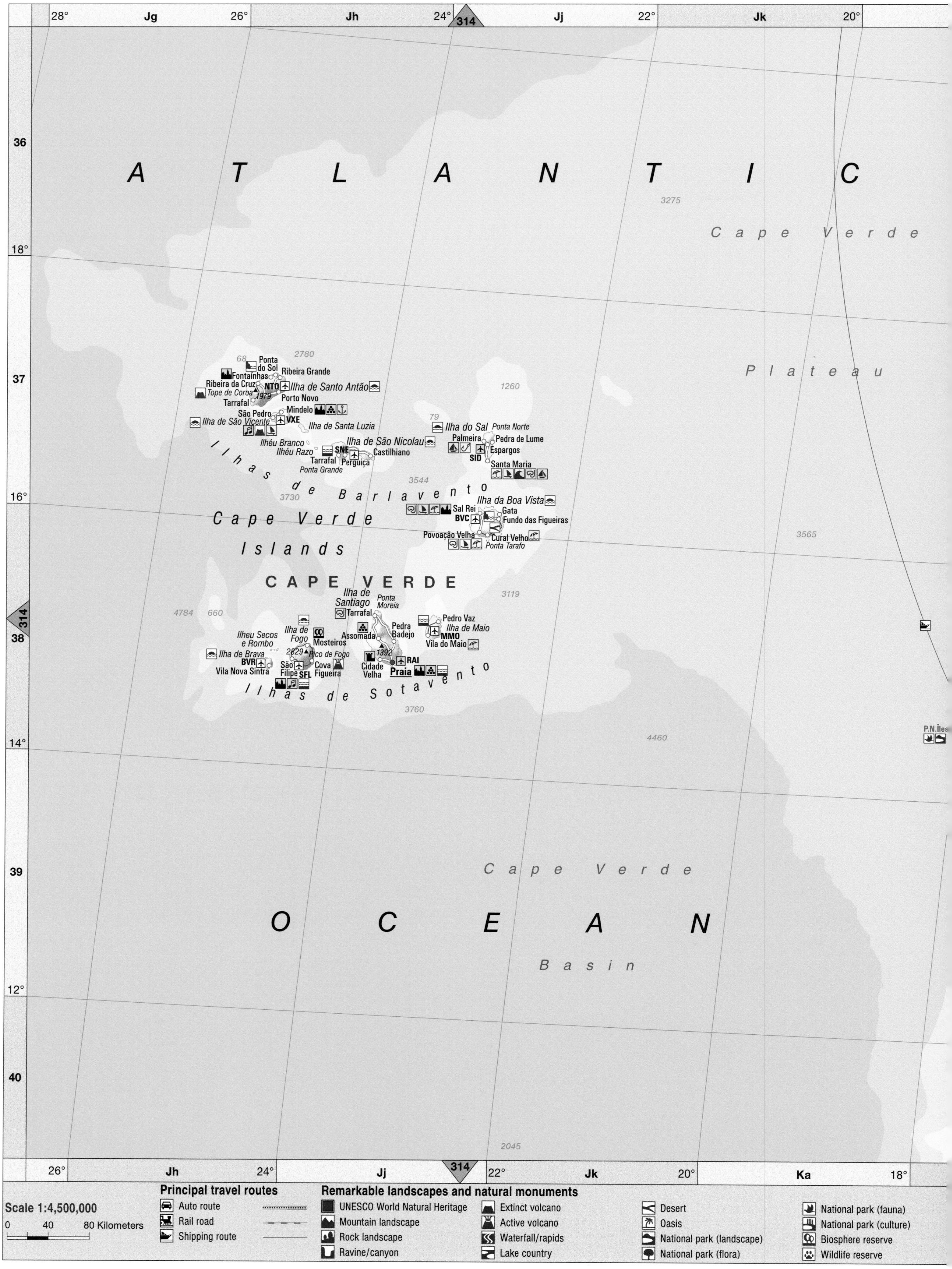

ATLANTIC OCEAN

Cape Verde Plateau

Cape Verde Basin

CAPE VERDE

Cape Verde Islands

Ilhas de Barlavento

Ilhas de Sotavento

Ilha de Santo Antão, Ponta do Sol, Ribeira Grande, Fontainhas, Ribeira da Cruz, Tope de Coroa, 1979, Porto Novo, Tarrafal, Mindelo, São Pedro, VXE, Ilha de São Vicente, Ilha de Santa Luzia, Ilhéu Branco, Ilhéu Razo, Ilha de São Nicolau, SNE, Tarrafal, Preguiça, Castilhiano, Ponta Grande, Ilha do Sal, Ponta Norte, Palmeira, Pedra de Lume, Espargos, SID, Santa Maria, Ilha da Boa Vista, Sal Rei, BVC, Gata, Fundo das Figueiras, Povoação Velha, Curral Velho, Ponta Tarafo, Ilha de Santiago, Ponta Moreia, Tarrafal, Assomada, Pedra Badejo, 1392, Cidade Velha, Praia, RAI, Pedro Vaz, Ilha de Maio, MMO, Vila do Maio, Ilheu Secos e Rombo, Ilha de Fogo, Mosteiros, 2829, Pico de Fogo, Ilha de Brava, BVR, Vila Nova Sintra, São Filipe, SFL, Cova Figueira, P.N.Îles

Scale 1:4,500,000

0 40 80 Kilometers

Principal travel routes

- Auto route
- Rail road
- Shipping route

Remarkable landscapes and natural monuments

- UNESCO World Natural Heritage
- Mountain landscape
- Rock landscape
- Ravine/canyon
- Extinct volcano
- Active volcano
- Waterfall/rapids
- Lake country
- Desert
- Oasis
- National park (landscape)
- National park (flora)
- National park (fauna)
- National park (culture)
- Biosphere reserve
- Wildlife reserve

Cape Verde is an archipelago of ten ajor islands and numerous smaller ands with a total land area of 4,033 km². inhabited until the arrival of the Portuiese, the Cape Verde Islands now have diverse population. Around 71 percent the Cape Verde Island's population is mixed white European and black rican descent. Most of the remaining opulation is of black African (28%) or ortuguese (1%) descent. The majority of the country's population is concentrated on two islands: **Santiago** and **São Vicente**.

The Cape Verde Islands are all of volcanic origin and there are several active volcanoes in the archipelago. In 1995, the volcano **Pico** (2,829 meters) on the island of Fogo was the site of a major eruption. The large western islands have mountainous interiors with many gorges and coastal cliffs.

On the African mainland between the deserts of Mauritania and the tropical forests of Guinea lies a strip of savannahs that stretches through most of Senegal and sections of Mali. The northern regions of Senegal and Mali are both occupied by sections of the Sahel, an arid transition zone south of the Sahara Desert. Severe droughts are common in both countries. The basin of the **Casamance River** in Senegal is a fertile region with abundant rainfall and lush vegetation. **Niokolo-Koba National Park** in southern Senegal is home to expansive tropical rainforests.

Senegal was a French colony for centuries and French remains the dominant language of commerce, government and education in the country. The country's capital Dakar is generally considered one of the most beautiful and culturally vibrant cities in West Africa.

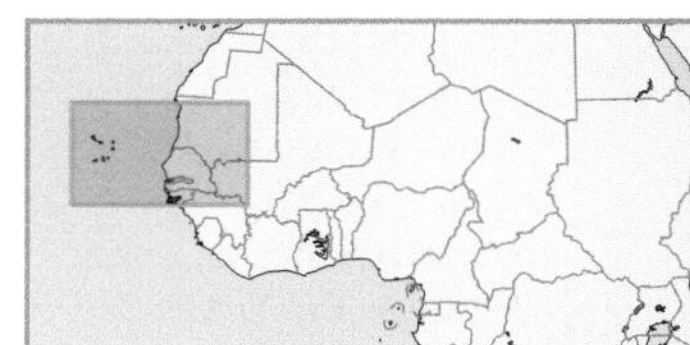

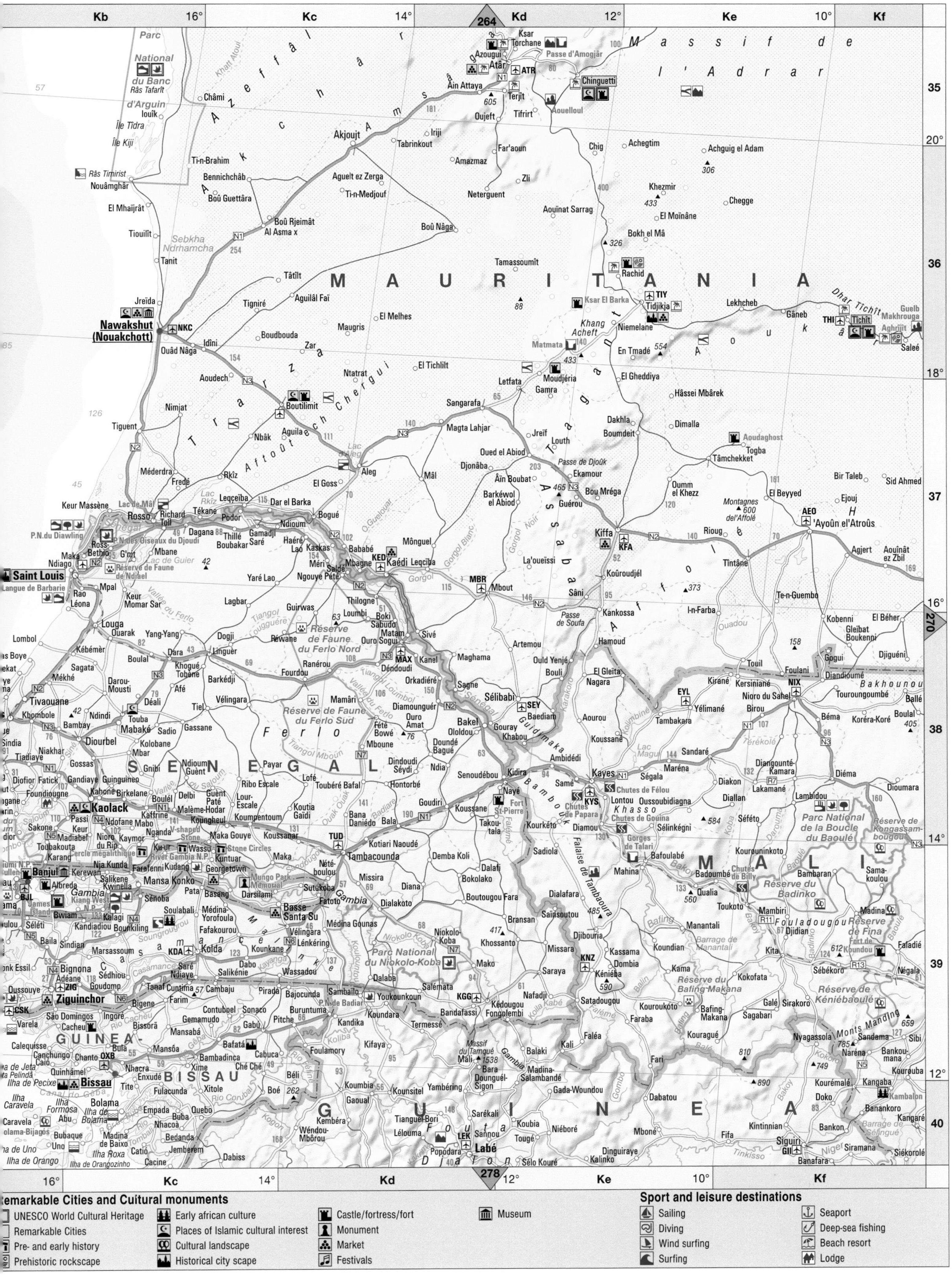

Gorée Island was a major station for European slave ships. At least two million Africans were transported from the island to slavery in the Americas. The island is now a UNESCO world heritage site with several historic sites linked to the brutal slave trade. **Kb38**

Mbour Coastal town located south of Dakar – traditional fishing industry – large resort hotels – beaches (photo) **Kb38**

Touba Important spiritual center of the Murid Muslims, Senegal's largest religious community – Great Mosque (photo) **Kc38**

Brikama Fishing village in Gambia – center of traditional wood carving and drum production **Kb39**

Gambia River 1,120 kilometers – important transport route – fertile basin – photo: village near Banjul **KbKc39**

Wassu Stone Circles Prehistoric stone monument in eastern Senegal – consists of several stone pillars up to 2.5 meters tall – may have once been used as burial site or for religious ceremonies **Kc39**

emarkable Cities and Cultural monuments

- UNESCO World Cultural Heritage
- Remarkable Cities
- Pre- and early history
- Prehistoric rockscape
- Early african culture
- Places of Islamic cultural interest
- Cultural landscape
- Historical city scape
- Castle/fortress/fort
- Monument
- Market
- Festivals
- Museum

Sport and leisure destinations

- Sailing
- Diving
- Wind surfing
- Surfing
- Seaport
- Deep-sea fishing
- Beach resort
- Lodge

The Niger, Africa's third longest river, flows from its source in the highlands of Guinea to the arid and semi-arid regions of Mali and Niger. The crescent-shaped river has one of the most unusual forms of any major waterway in the world. The river's course was a mystery to the western world for many centuries and several explorers lost their lives while attempting to study the Niger. The Niger flows northeast from Guinea into Mali,

where it continues to flow northea through the country's desert. In easte Mali, the Niger suddenly changes dire tion and the river flows south into t neighboring country Niger. Farther sou the river enters Nigeria and flows to delta on the Gulf of Guinea coast.
The Niger has been an important tran

Wetlands along the banks of the Nige River **Kk**

Chinguetti Mauritanian trade center – historic mosque, a pilgrimage site – old town with abandoned homes buried beneath sand dunes **Kd35**

Tichît On the caravan route between Chinguetti and Timbuktu – desert region with large sand dunes **Kf36**

Falaise de Tambaoura Stone hills near Kayes in western Mali – tallest point, 485 meters **Ke39**

Bamako Capital city of Mali – lively Marché Rose market (photo) – National Museum with traditional masks and relics **Kf39**

Mopti Port city on the Niger River – adobe mosque (photo) – large marketplace near the harbor where local produce is sold – center for the production of traditional Fulbe clothing **Kh38**

Djenné Ancient trade center on the Bani River – Islamic schools and mosques – large adobe mosques – weekly market – UNESCO world heritage site **Kh39**

Korientzé Port city on the Niger River – beautiful traditional architecture – historic mosque – livestock market **Kj38**

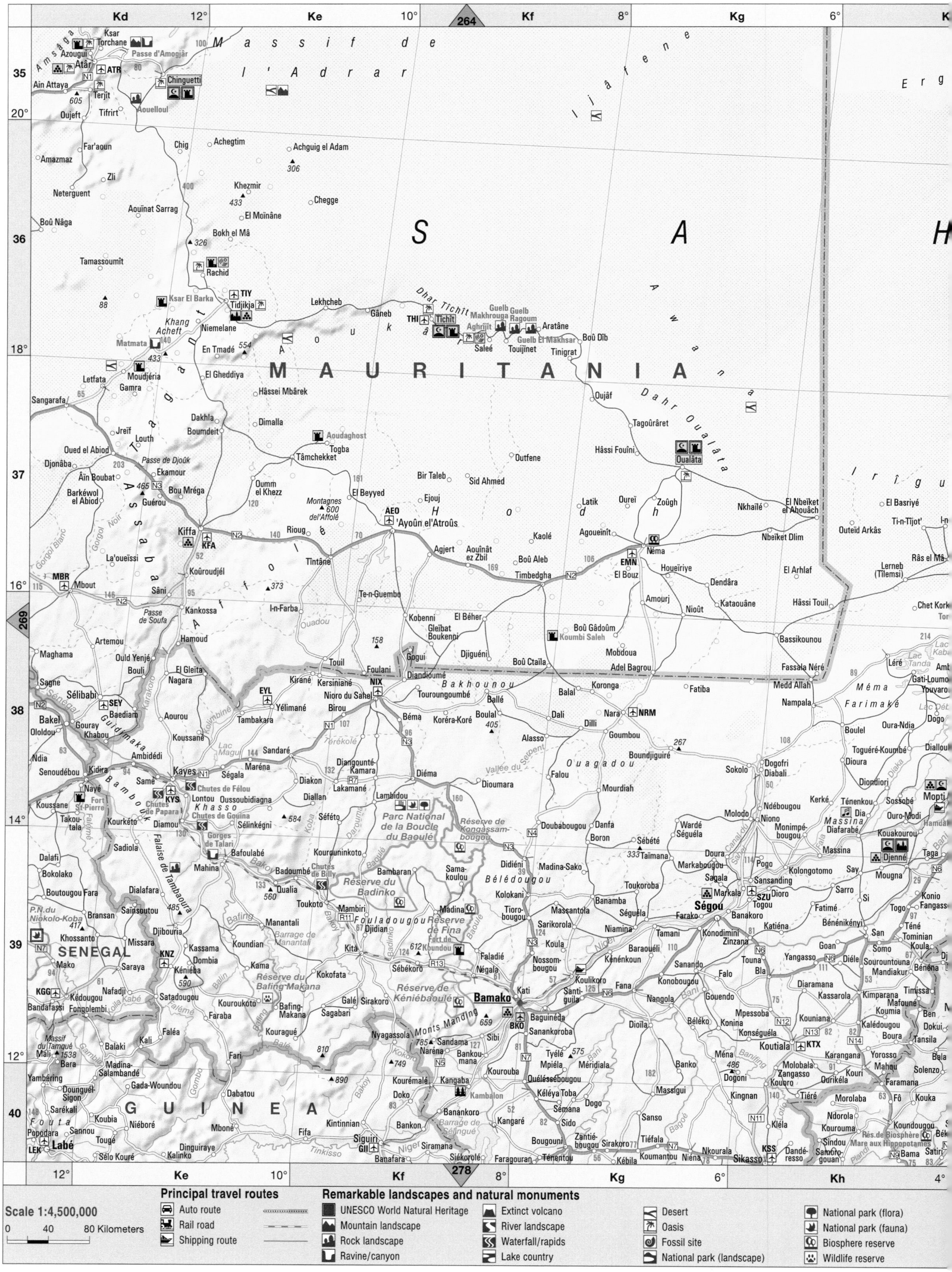

Scale 1:4,500,000
0 40 80 Kilometers

Principal travel routes
- Auto route
- Rail road
- Shipping route

Remarkable landscapes and natural monuments
- UNESCO World Natural Heritage
- Mountain landscape
- Rock landscape
- Ravine/canyon
- Extinct volcano
- River landscape
- Waterfall/rapids
- Lake country
- Desert
- Oasis
- Fossil site
- National park (landscape)
- National park (flora)
- National park (fauna)
- Biosphere reserve
- Wildlife reserve

rtation route over the centuries and
any important cities and trade bases
veloped along the river's banks. Cen-
ies ago, **Timbuktu** was a wealthy
nter of trade and education. In many
ltures, the name Timbuktu has be-
me a synonym for distant and exotic
aces. Timbuktu's golden age has long
ded and a small settlement between
Sahara and the Niger River is all that
mains of the once glorious African city.

Other ancient cities near the Niger River including Mali's capital **Bamako** have continued to grow in population and economic importance.

Only ruins remain of **Kumbi (Koumbi Saleh)**, the last capital of the powerful Ghana Empire and once the largest city in West Africa. Today few caravans travel through the southern Sahara. Most modern caravans are led by Berber or Tuareg salt traders who carry their products from northern Mali to river ports on the Niger.

Mali and **Niger** are two of the most sparsely populated countries in Africa. Both countries have land areas of around 1.3 million km² and around ten million inhabitants. The arid northern sections of Mali and Niger are the most sparsely populated regions in both countries.

Burkina Faso, known as Upper Volta before 1984, is located south of Mali and Niger. The country has a total area of 274,000 km² and its territory consists mostly of savannahs. The countryside is home to vast plains and numerous small villages consisting of adobe structures. More than 160 distinct ethnic groups inhabit the country. The Mossi people are the largest ethnic group in the country. Between the 11th and 19th centuries the Mossi ruled a large and powerful empire.

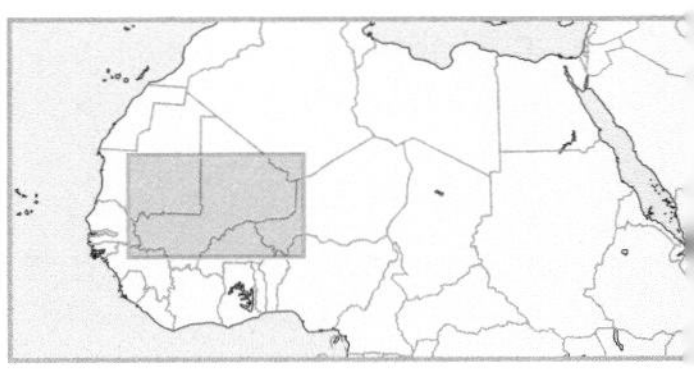

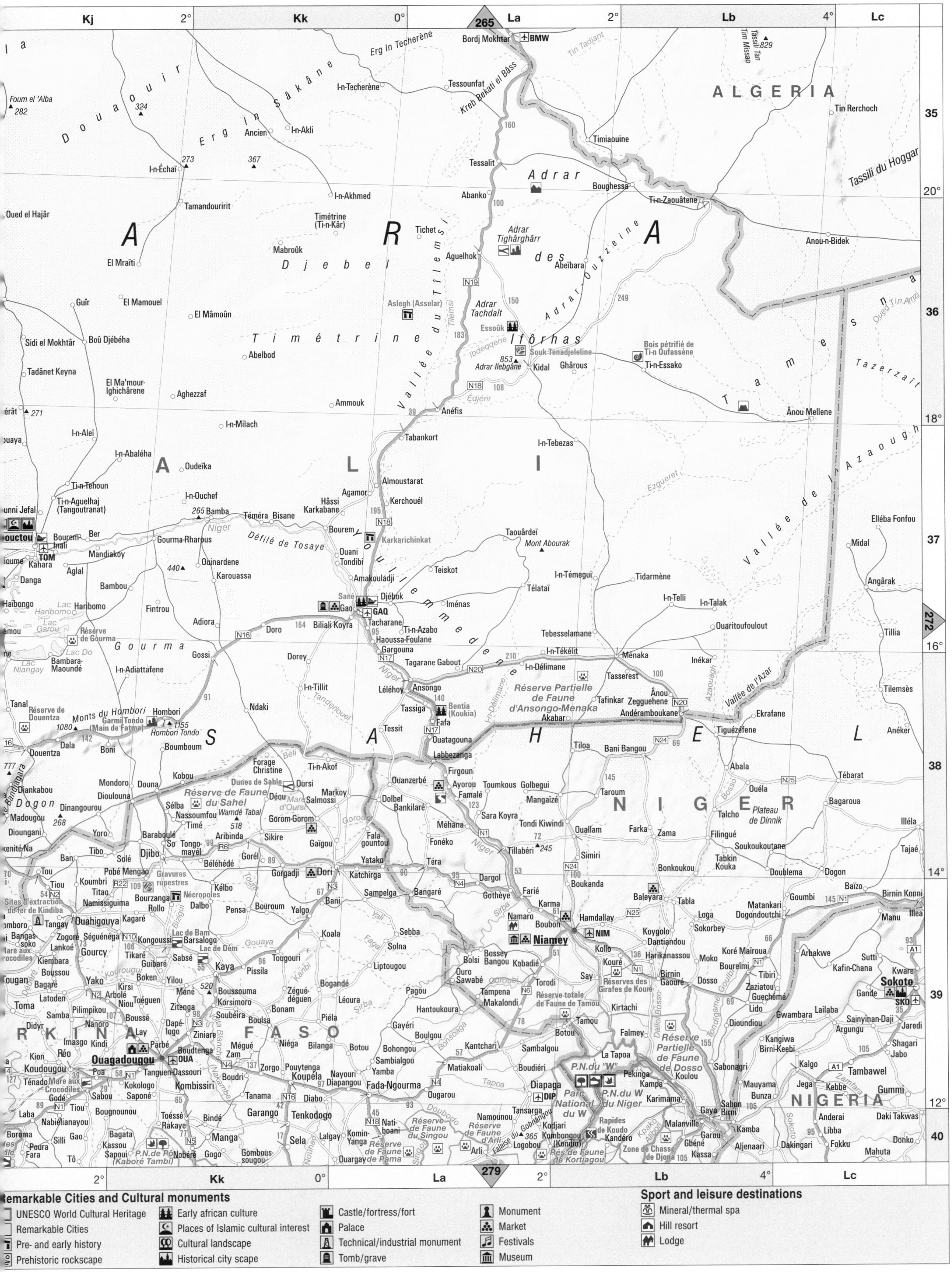

Timbuktu (Tombouctou) Historic city in Mali – Sankore and Djinguere-Ber mosques – Tuareg markets – UNESCO world heritage site **Kj37**

Goundam River port on a tributary of the Niger River – mosque in traditional local style (photo) **Kj37**

Niger River Important transport route (4,160 kilometers) – the river flows through West Africa, from Guinea to Nigeria **Kk37**

Hombori Highlands Heavily eroded plateau in Mali – highest point, Hombori Tondo (1,155 meters) **Kj38**

The central plateau of Mali is home to the **Dogon**, a people who have preserved many aspects of their culture. Photos from top to bottom: Bandiagara cliffs, Dogon village, Dogon in traditional masks **Kj38**

emarkable Cities and Cultural monuments

UNESCO World Cultural Heritage
Remarkable Cities
Pre- and early history
Prehistoric rockscape
Early african culture
Places of Islamic cultural interest
Cultural landscape
Historical city scape
Castle/fortress/fort
Palace
Technical/industrial monument
Tomb/grave
Monument
Market
Festivals
Museum

Sport and leisure destinations

Mineral/thermal spa
Hill resort
Lodge

Southern Niger, Northern Nigeria

Arab traders and cartographers named the transition zone between Sahara and the savannahs of Africa the **Sahel**, an Arabic word for shore or boundary. Drought and land erosion are common problems throughout the Sahel. For centuries, the Sahel has been expanding into once fertile regions to its south. Desertification has also expanded the Sahara into areas that were once part of the Sahel. **Lake Chad** is one of the most

interesting geographic features in t Sahel. The lake is the remnant of an a cient inland sea that once covered a lar section of western Africa. After the c mate in the region changed and the Sah ra began to expand, the inland sea w greatly reduced in size. Although sev al rivers flow into Lake Chad, the la

The barren Ténéré Desert in north-eastern Niger **Le36/**

Teguidda-n-Tessoumt Important center of salt production in Niger – salt is produced using ancient techniques – the salt mines are open to visitors **Ld37**

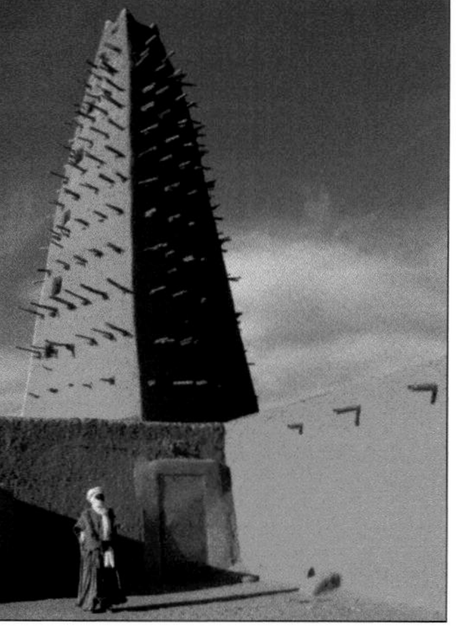

Agadez Historic trade and political center on the edge of the Aïr Mountains – adobe mosque built in the 15th century (photo) – important regional market – home to the Aïr-Tuareg sultans **Ld37**

Niamey Capital city of Niger – population of 400,000 – markets – Anthropology Museum **Lb39**

W National Park National Park in Niger between forests and savannahs – UNESCO world heritage site – elephant, buffalo, and hippopotamus populations **Lb39**

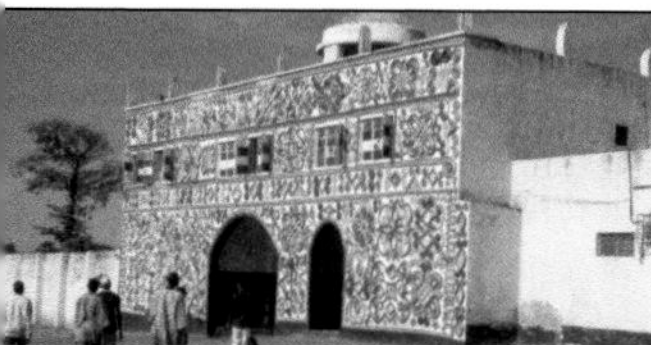

Zaria One of several historic Hausa city states in northern Nigeria – historic palace (photo) – the city is surrounded by a well preserved defensive wall – large traditional marketplace **Ld40**

Kainji Lake National Park Nigeria's oldest national park – 5,340 km² of savannahs and forests – buffalo, warthog, baboon, and waterbuck populations **Lc41**

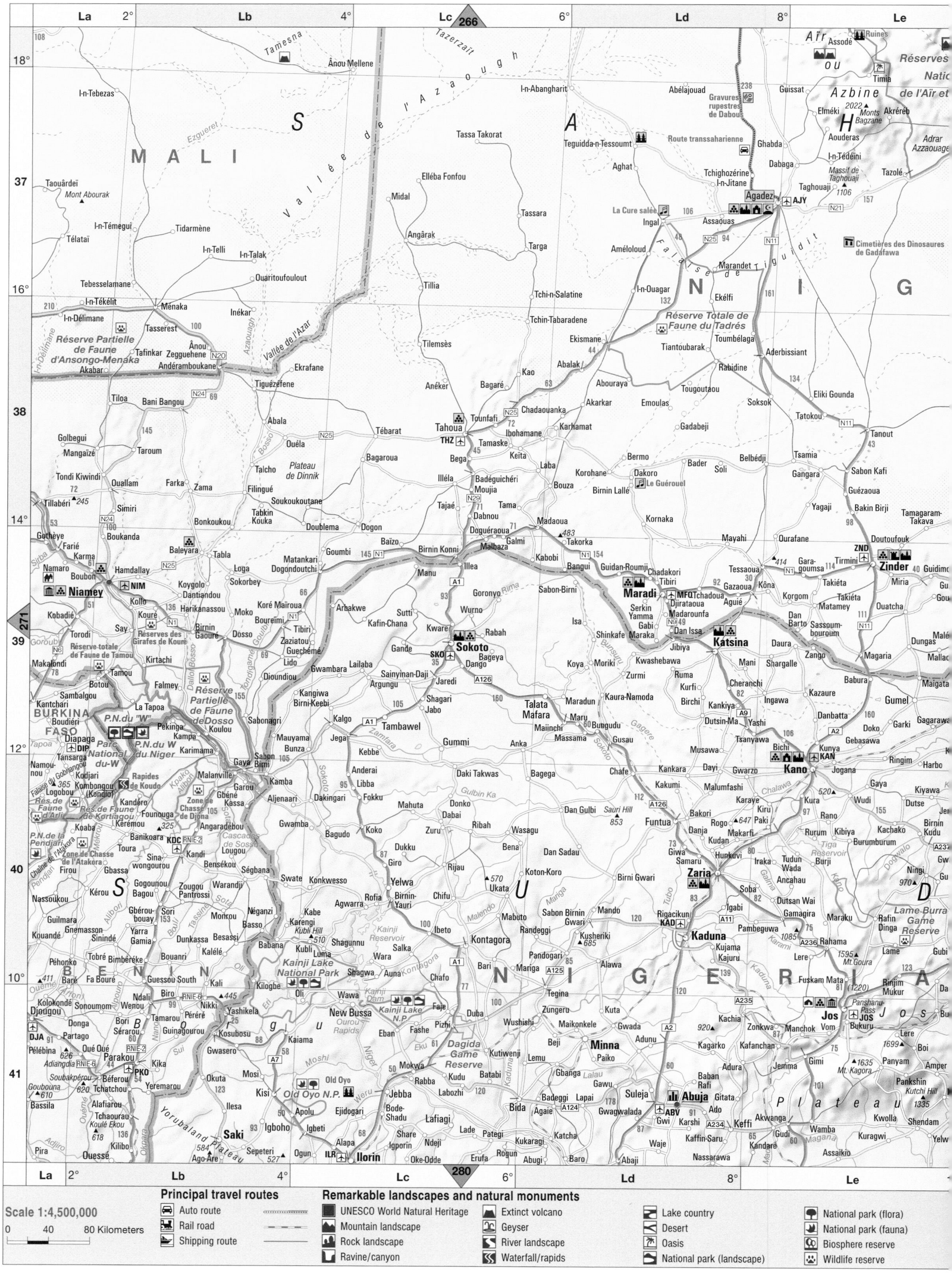

La 2° Lb 4° Lc 6° Ld 8° Le

266
271
280

Scale 1:4,500,000

0 40 80 Kilometers

Principal travel routes

- Auto route
- Rail road
- Shipping route

Remarkable landscapes and natural monuments

- UNESCO World Natural Heritage
- Mountain landscape
- Rock landscape
- Ravine/canyon
- Extinct volcano
- Geyser
- River landscape
- Waterfall/rapids
- Lake country
- Desert
- Oasis
- National park (landscape)
- National park (flora)
- National park (fauna)
- Biosphere reserve
- Wildlife reserve

ntinues to decrease in size every year. ke Chad now covers a maximum area 17,000 km² but its area varies signifi- ntly depending on the level of rainfall the region. obab trees, acacias, bushes and hard ass are the most common types of vege- ion found throughout the Sahel. The mi-nomadic **Tuareg** and **Fulbe** peoples th graze livestock in the Sahel regions southern Niger and northern Nigeria.

In contrast to the western sections of the Sahara, the desert regions of **northern Niger** offer many interesting and unique landscapes. The region contains the beautiful natural terraces in the Aïr Mountain range and the vast sand dune fields of the Ténéré Desert – located in the **Aïr et du Ténéré National Nature Reserve**. Unique stone formations, **Aïr-Tuareg** villages, and the historic town of **Agadez** are just a few of the numerous noteworthy tourists attractions in northern Niger.

Between the 16th and 19th centuries, the city states of the Hausa people flourished throughout **southern Niger** and **northern Nigeria**. **Sokoto**, **Kano**, and **Zaria** in Nigeria as well as **Maradi** and **Zinder** in Niger were all powerful city states which often formed alliances and fought wars against one another. The power of the city states came to an abrupt end after European colonizers gained control of the region. Some of the cities and towns in the region feature historic palaces and mosques built when the city states were at their most powerful. Despite influence from other cultures, the Hausa still value their culture and traditional social structures. Symbolic visits from members of the nobility are common during ceremonies in Hausa communities.

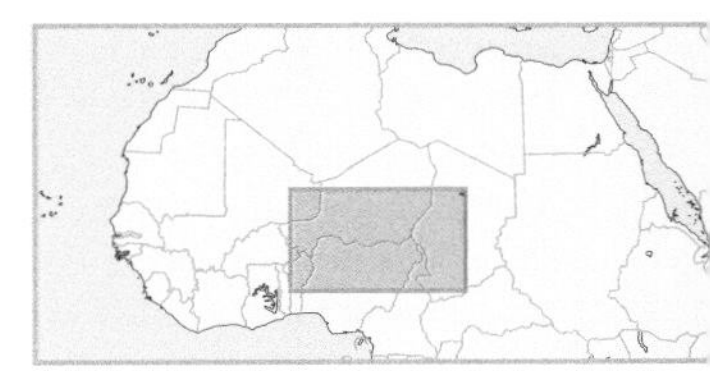

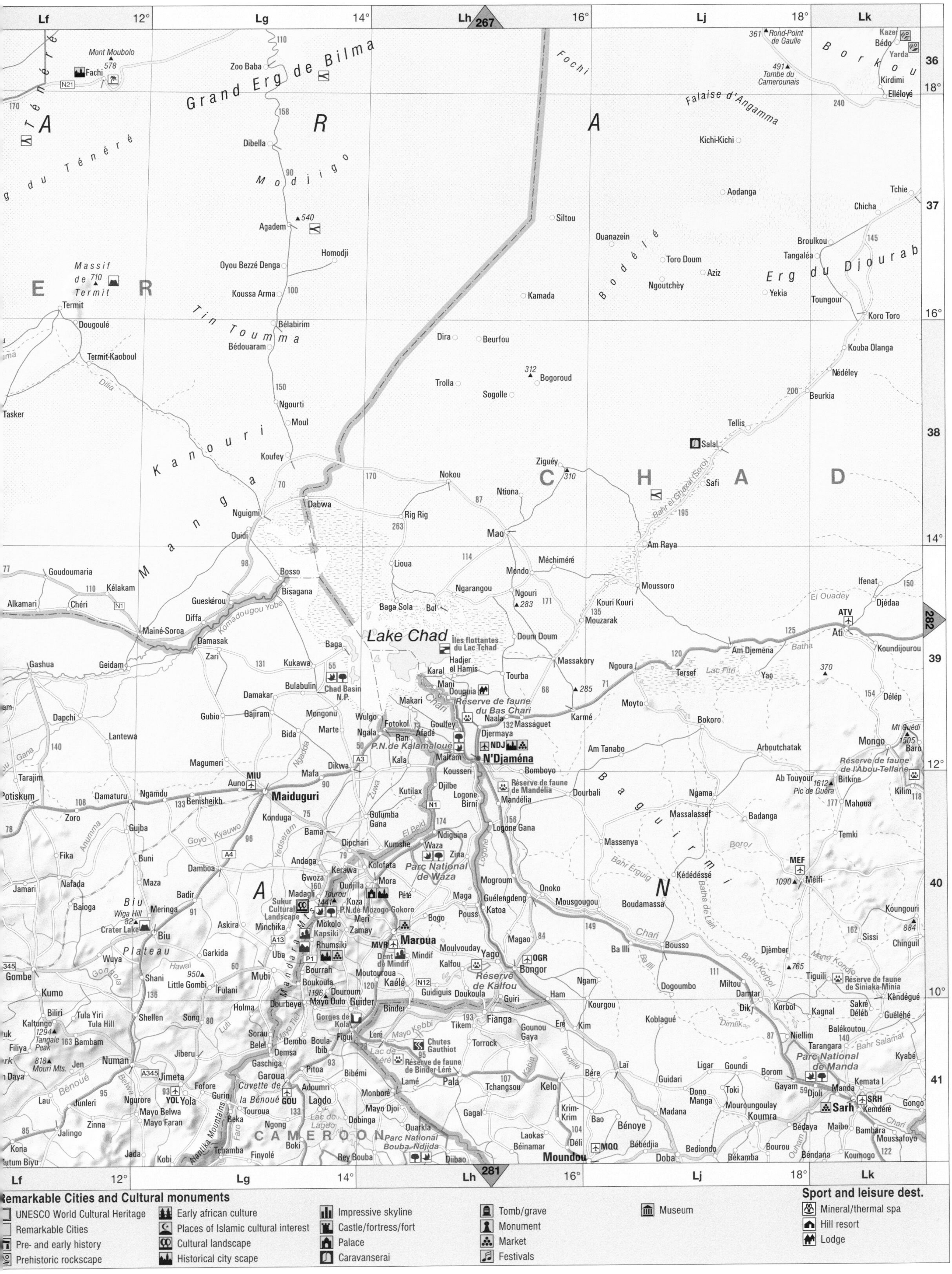

Aïr et du Ténéré National Nature Reserve The sand dunes and the granite mountains of the Aïr range are inhabited by a variety of rare desert animals including antelopes and ostriches. The reserve is a UNESCO world heritage site. **Le36/37**

Fachi Oasis on the caravan route between Agadez and Blima – rest stop with subterranean wells (photo) – traditional adobe architecture **Lf36**

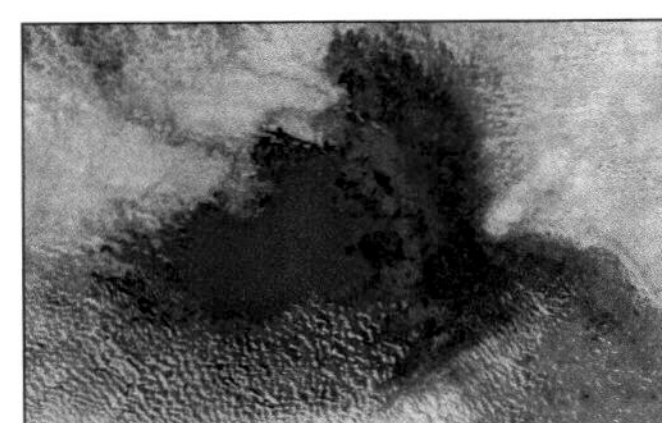

Lake Chad Shallow lake with a maximum depth of 1.5 meters – maximum area of around 20,000 km² – large hippopotamus populations **LgLh38/39**

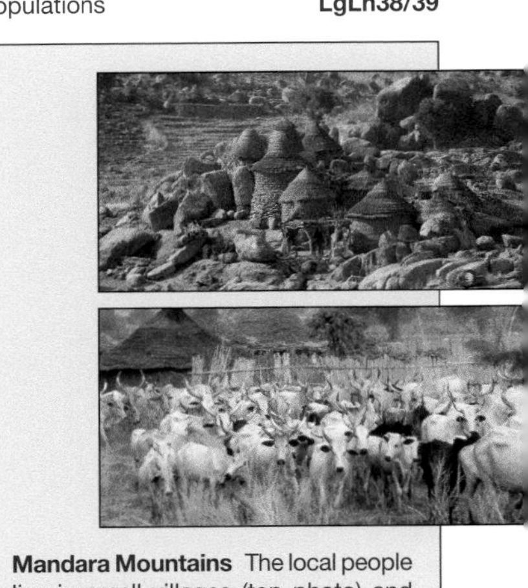

Mandara Mountains The local people live in small villages (top photo) and cultivate their land in northern Cameroon and Nigeria according to ancient methods of terrace farming and livestock (bottom photo) grazing. **Lg40**

Remarkable Cities and Cultural monuments

- UNESCO World Cultural Heritage
- Remarkable Cities
- Pre- and early history
- Prehistoric rockscape
- Early african culture
- Places of Islamic cultural interest
- Cultural landscape
- Historical city scape
- Impressive skyline
- Castle/fortress/fort
- Palace
- Caravanserai
- Tomb/grave
- Monument
- Market
- Festivals
- Museum

Sport and leisure dest.

- Mineral/thermal spa
- Hill resort
- Lodge

Northern Chad

Northern **Chad** is situated on the eastern edges of the central Sahara Desert. The sparsely populated region is relatively unexplored and remains difficult to access. The **Tibesti Mountain** range is an ancient group of volcanoes in northern Chad and southernmost Libya. Many of the ancient volcanoes' peaks collapsed after the mountains became inactive leaving behind gigantic craters, which often contain small lakes.

Many deep and narrow gorges c through the older sections of the Tibe Mountain range. Water from rainfall a underground springs often accumula inside the gorges, transforming them ir fertile oases with lush vegetation. E cause of the labyrinth-like shape of t gorges in the Tibesti Mountains, many a

Trou du Natron: an ancient caldera in the Tibesti Mountains **Lj**

Bardai Fertile oasis at the foot of the Tibesti Mountains – ancient rock paintings and pre-Islamic burial sites **Lj35**

Rock Paintings of Gonoa Prehistoric art including depictions of people, elephants, cattle, and giraffes **Lj35**

Tibesti Mountains The mountain range is located mostly in northern Chad but also extends into the neighboring countries of Libya and Niger. The ancient highlands extend over an area of more than 100,000 km² and feature a variety of interesting natural attractions including volcanic craters up to ten kilometers in diameter and the mountain Emi Koussi. **LjLk35**

Zouar Oasis Located on the edge of the Tibesti Mountains – Zoarke Valley has water holes (gueltas) and dense vegetation – ancient rock paintings **Lj35**

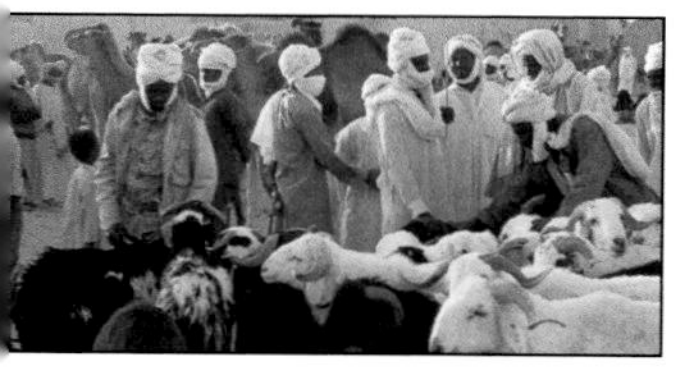

Faya Oasis city and important trade center for Tubu and Daza merchants in central Chad – along the caravan route between Lake Chad and Sudan **Lk37**

Salai Caravansary One of several trade centers along the caravan route between Lake Chad and Tripoli via Faya – livestock market **Lj38**

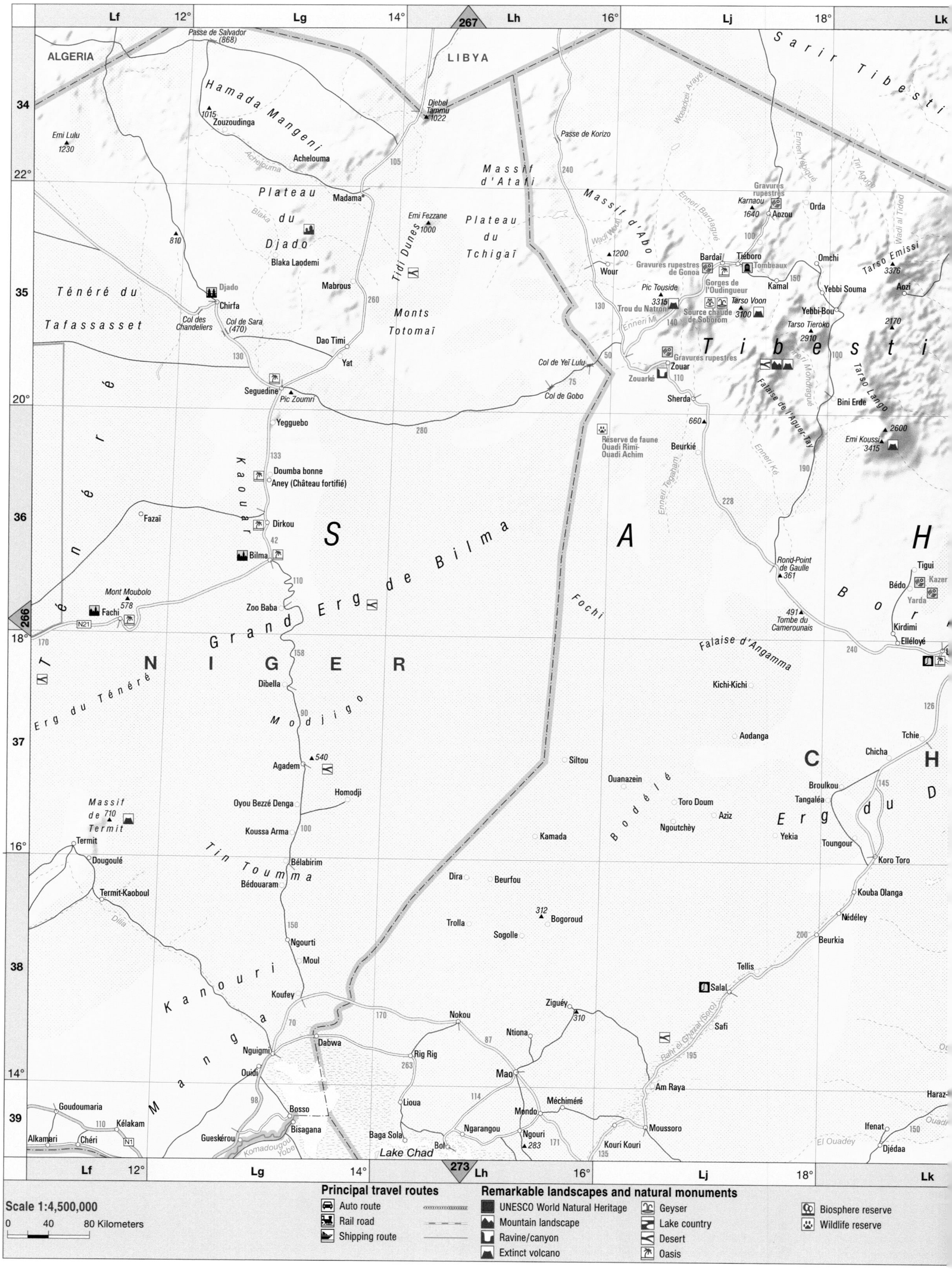

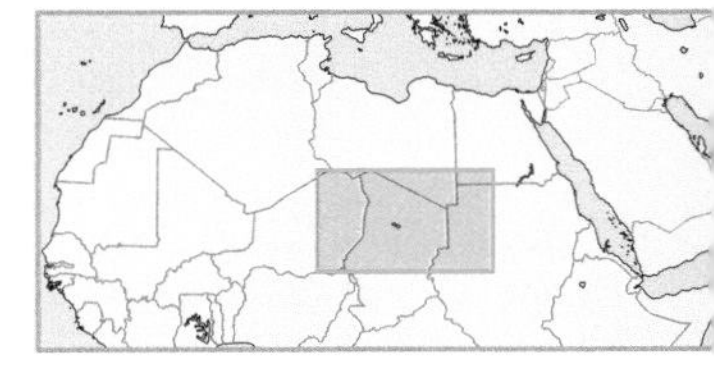

ficult to access and are rarely visited people from outside the region. e Tubu, a semi-nomadic group of live- ock breeders, are one of the larger eth- groups in the isolated highlands. They ve a reputation as an independent peo- e that avoids contact with other com- unities. For centuries, the Tubu resisted e domination of Islamic sultans and ntinue to resist the influence of modern ad's central government.

To the south, Chad borders the junction of Nigeria, Niger, and Cameroon around **Lake Chad**.

As in other areas of the Sahara, several caravan routes once passed through northern Chad. These routes were, however, far more dangerous and less widely traveled than most other caravan routes through the Sahara. In the 19th century, western explorers traveled to northern Chad to study the region. Some of these explorers lost their lives there and northern Chad has remained a dangerous area for outsiders, even in modern times. The region's underdeveloped infrastructure, the xenophobia of the Tubu people, and the countless land mines planted by the Libyan army are some of the factors and dangers that complicate travel in northern Chad.

West of the Tibesti Mountains lies the **Djado Plateau**, a large elevated tableland. The plateau features several sites with ancient rock paintings created by prehistoric cultures that once inhabited the region. The **Enneri Blaka Valley** stretches through the Djado Plateau. During prehistoric times, the valley was a fertile region with lush vegetation. The area was home to a large population of livestock breeders and hunters. These ancient peoples left behind fascinating relics that depict the area as it once was.

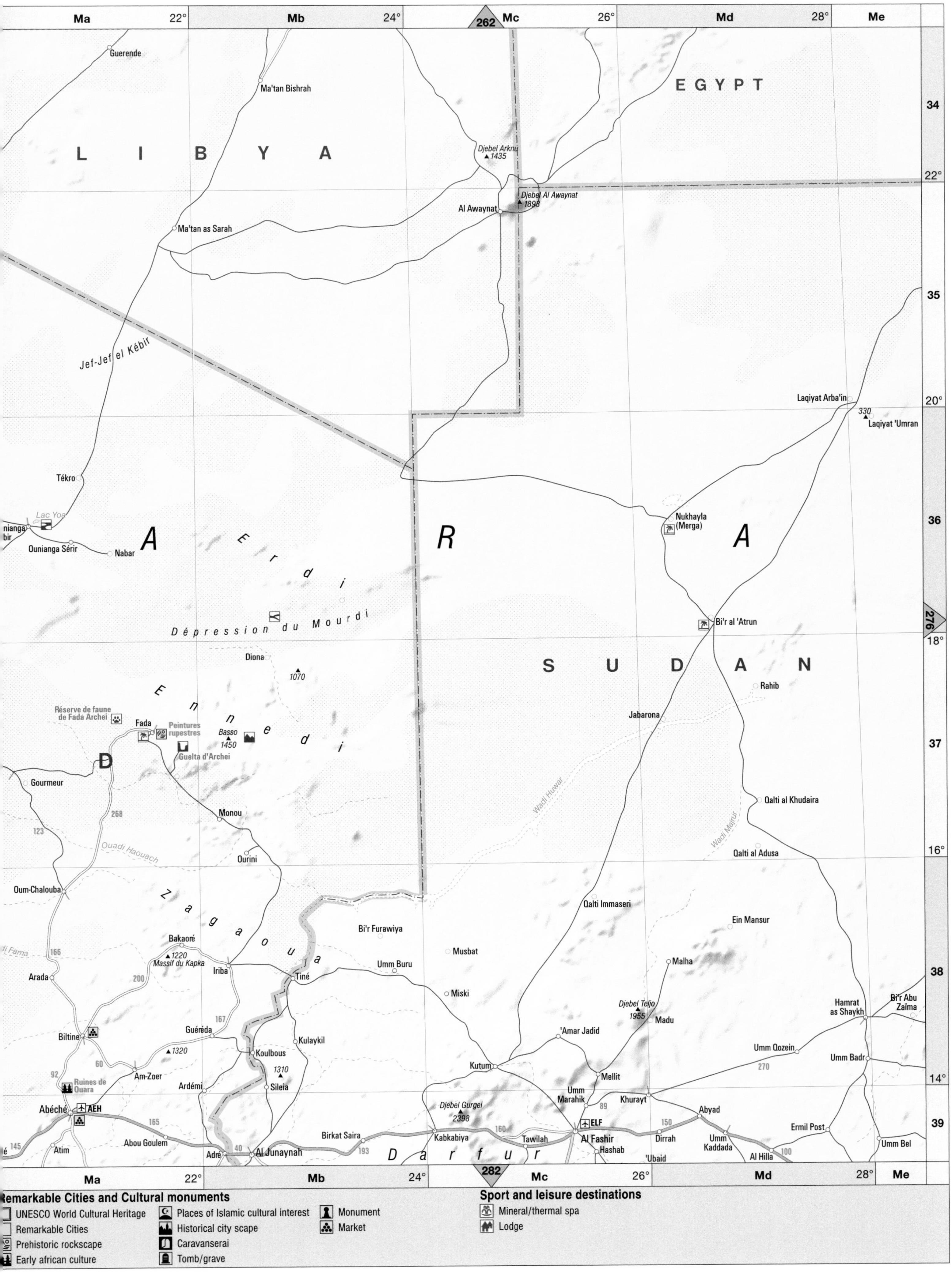

Ma 22° Mb 24° 262 Mc 26° Md 28° Me

LIBYA EGYPT SUDAN

Guerende, Ma'tan Bishrah, Djebel Arknu 1435, Djebel Al Awaynat 1893, Al Awaynat, Ma'tan as Sarah, Jef-Jef el Kébir, Laqiyat Arba'in, 330, Laqiyat 'Umran, Tékro, Lac Yoa, Ounianga Sérir, Nabar, Nukhayla (Merga), Erdi, Dépression du Mourdi, Bi'r al 'Atrun, Diona, 1070, Ennedi, Réserve de faune de Fada Archei, Fada, Peintures rupestres, Basso 1450, Guelta d'Archei, Rahib, Jabarona, Gourmeur, 268, Monou, Wadi Huwar, Qalti al Khudaira, Wadi Magrur, 123, Ouadi Haouach, Ourini, Qalti al Adusa, Oum-Chalouba, Zagaoua, Qalti Immaseri, Ein Mansur, Bakaoré, Bi'r Furawiya, Musbat, 1220 Massif du Kapka, Iriba, Tiné, Umm Buru, Malha, Arada, 166, 200, Miski, Hamrat as Shaykh, Bi'r Abu Zaima, Djebel Teljo 1955, Madu, Biltine, 167, Guéréda, 'Amar Jadid, Kulaykil, 1320, Koulbous, Umm Qozein, Umm Badr, 60, 1310, Kutum, 270, 92, Ruines de Ouara, Am-Zoer, Ardémi, Sileia, Mellit, Umm Marahik, Khurayt, Abéché, AEH, Djebel Gurgei 2398, 89, Abyad, 165, 160, ELF, 150, Ermil Post, Kabkabiya, Tawilah, Al Fashir, Dirrah, Umm Kaddada, Umm Bel, 145, Atim, Abou Goulem, Birkat Saira, Hashab, 'Ubaid, Al Hilla, 100, Adré, 40, Al Junaynah, 193, Darfur

34, 22°, 35, 20°, 36, 276, 18°, 37, 16°, 38, 14°, 39

Ma 22° Mb 24° 282 Mc 26° Md 28° Me

Remarkable Cities and Cultural monuments

UNESCO World Cultural Heritage, Remarkable Cities, Prehistoric rockscape, Early african culture, Places of Islamic cultural interest, Historical city scape, Caravanserai, Tomb/grave, Monument, Market

Sport and leisure destinations

Mineral/thermal spa, Lodge

Lac Yoa Saline lake situated below sea level between the Tibesti and Ennedi Plateau – fascinating landscapes with dunes and stone formations **Ma36**

Historic Caravan Routes Until the 19th century caravans transported goods between Tripoli on the Mediterranean coast and the kingdoms around Lake Chad. Today the caravans are limited to local trade between communities in northern Chad. Most modern caravans in the region are led by Tuareg or Tubu merchants. Camels remain the principal means of overland travel through the regions. **Lj38/Lk37**

Ennedi Plateau The region is a transition zone between the Tibesti Mountains and the Sahara. Ancient rock paintings depict the once fertile region before the expansion of the Sahara Desert. **Ma/Mb37**

Guelta d'Archei Canyon in the Ennedi Plateau region – natural springs – habitat of Saharan crocodiles **Ma37**

Biltine Important market for the Tubu, Shoa, and Wadai peoples – ruins of the ancient city Ouara **Ma38**

Northern Sudan, Eritrea

Around 38 million people live in **Sudan**, Africa's largest country with a total area of 2.5 million km². Sudan borders Egypt to the north and Kenya, Uganda, and Congo to the south. The country also borders the Red Sea, Eritrea, and Ethiopia to the east. North of Sudan's capital **Khartoum**, the Nile River valley separates the **Libyan** and **Nubian Deserts**. The sections of the Nile Valley near the Nubian Desert are home to many histo-

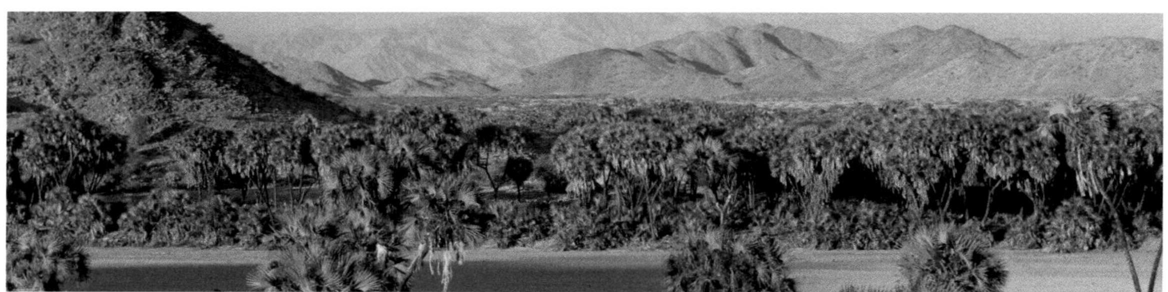

ric cultural sites built by ancient Egyp ians and Nubians. Lake Nasser, a lar reservoir created after Egypt damm the Nile in the 1970s, extends across t Egyptian border into the northernmo region of Sudan around Wadi Halfa. In Khartoum, the Blue Nile and White N merge to form the Nile River proper. T

The oasis of Wadi Baraka (Eritrea) is surrounded by barren deserts **Mj38/**

Wadi Halfa Town in northern Sudan – the older sections of the town were submerged after the creation of Lake Nasser **Mf36**

Dongola Sudanese city founded in the 19th century – date palm groves – ruins of Kawa including an ancient temple **Mf37**

Karima Ruins of an ancient imperial city – pyramids (photo) containing the graves of Kushite monarchs – UNESCO world heritage site **Mf37**

Meroe Capital of the Kush Kingdom after the 7th century BC – royal burial site after the 3rd century BC – tall pyramids – subterranean burial chambers **Mg38**

Musawwarat es Sufra Ancient temple dedicated to the lion god Apademak – built around 220 BC – reliefs depicting gods – restored between 1960 and 1970 **Mg38**

Naqa Temple of Apademak built during the 1st century BC – Temple of Amun built in the 1st century BC – Roman ruins from the 3rd century AD **Mg38**

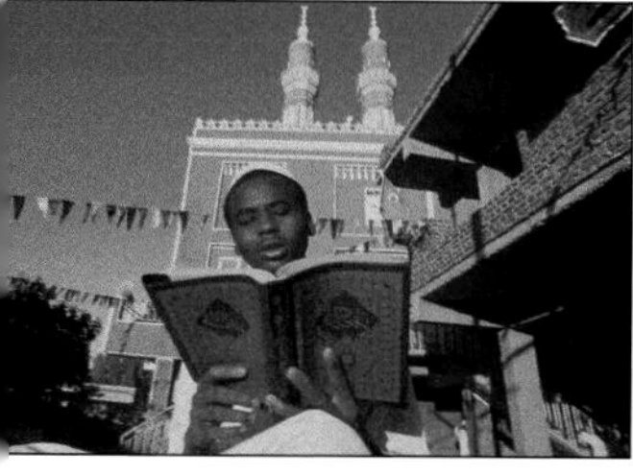

Omdurman One of Sudan's major cities – large marketplace – mausoleum of the Mahdi, a 19th century Sudanese religious leader **Mg39**

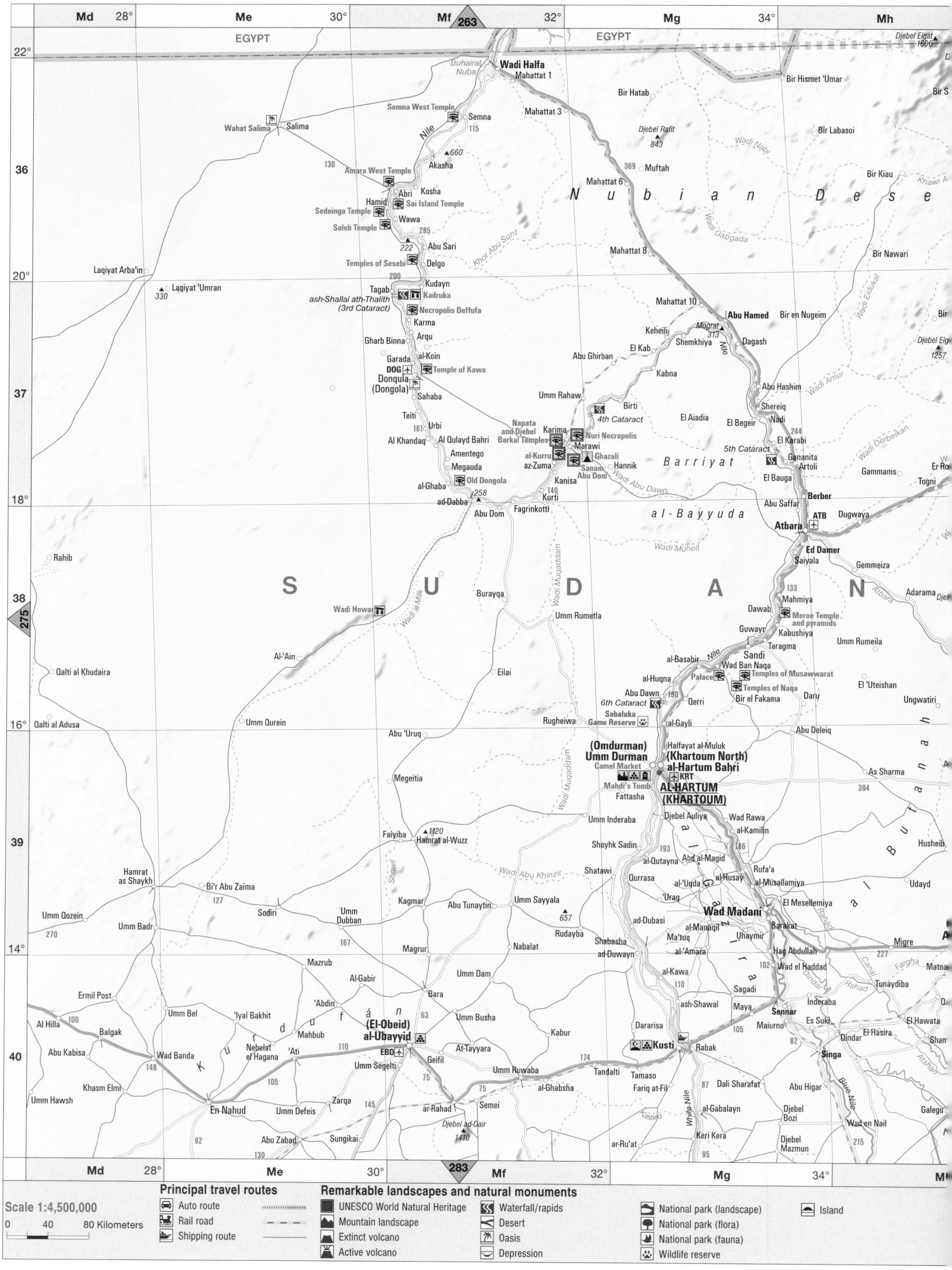

Scale 1:4,500,000
0 40 80 Kilometers

Principal travel routes
- Auto route
- Rail road
- Shipping route

Remarkable landscapes and natural monuments
- UNESCO World Natural Heritage
- Mountain landscape
- Extinct volcano
- Active volcano
- Waterfall/rapids
- Desert
- Oasis
- Depression
- National park (landscape)
- National park (flora)
- National park (fauna)
- Wildlife reserve
- Island

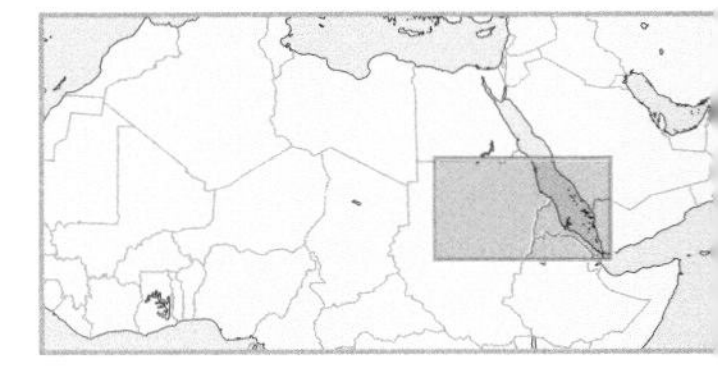

:bara River, the Nile's northernmost ajor tributary, flows from Ethiopia to the :y of Atbara in Sudan, where it enters e Nile. Al-Jazirah (Gezira), a Sudanese gion between the **Blue Nile** and **White le** is a leading center of agriculture. A ng mountain range with a maximum ight of 2,259 meters stretches along e **Red Sea** coast of Sudan. **Dindar ational Park** near the Sudanese-Ethio- an border is home to interesting wildlife including lion, leopard, elephant, and giraffe populations. Northern Sudan has an arid hot climate with sparse rainfall.

Eritrea is a small nation located on East Africa's Red Sea coast. The country has a total area of 121,444 km^2 and a population of 3.5 million. An ancient mountain range stretches from north to south over much of Eritrea's territory. A narrow and arid strip of coastal plains separates the Eritrean highlands from the Red Sea. The stony deserts of the northern highlands are inhabited mostly by nomadic peoples, while the population of the southwestern highlands consists largely of subsistence farmers. Southeastern Eritrea is dominated by mountains and sections of the arid Danakil Plain. The northern highlands of Ethiopia extend to the country's borders with Eritrea and Sudan. These highlands are the source of several rivers – including the Blue Nile and Atbara Rivers. The highlands of Ethiopia have a mostly subtropical climate with heavy rainfall during summer. In Simien National Park and around Ethiopia's highest mountain, **Ras Dashen** (4,620 meters), snow occasionally falls during winter. The arid **Danakil** plain, an extension of the Great Rift Valley, is situated at an average elevation of 116 meters below sea level in northeastern Ethiopia and southern Eritrea.

Sanganeb Atoll Large coral reefs in the Red Sea – interesting diving sites – the atoll was designated a national park in 1990, because of its fascinating marine life **Mj37**

Wadi Baraka Stony desert in the northern highlands of Ethiopia – inhabited by nomadic livestock breeders during the rainy season **Mj38/39**

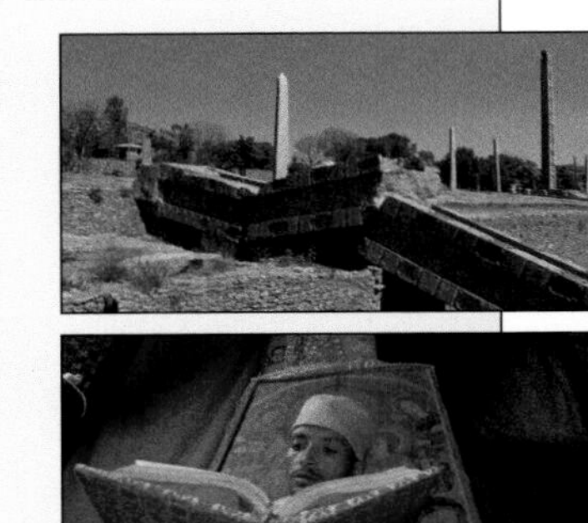

Axum The ancient city in northern Ethiopia was the capital of the Kingdom of Axum. The city features many historic sites (top photo). The Ethiopian Orthodox Church believes the Ark of the Covenant is housed in Axum. **Mk39**

Simien Mountains National Park Temperate highlands (1,900 - 4,430 meters) in northern Ethiopia – habitat of the walia ibex and Simien fox **Mk40**

Gondar The city was the capital of Ethiopia between the 17th and 19th centuries AD. During the reign of Emperor Fasilidas many grand buildings, including palaces (top photo), churches (bottom photo), and monasteries, were built in the city. The local architecture features Arabian and Portuguese influences. **Mj40**

Remarkable Cities and Cultural monuments

- UNESCO World Cultural Heritage
- Remarkable Cities
- Pre- and early history
- Ancient Egypt
- Early african culture
- Places of Christian cultural interest
- Places of Islamic cultural interest
- Cultural landscape
- Historical city scape
- Castle/fortress/fort
- Caravanserai
- Palace
- Tomb/grave
- Monument
- Market

Sport and leisure destinations

- Diving
- Beach resort
- Hill resort

148
150
284

West Africa

The landscapes of West Africa range from semi-desert areas along the southern edges of the Sahel to dense tropical forests. Several long rivers – including the **White Volta** (Ghana) – flow through the region to the Atlantic Ocean. The **Niger River**, one of Africa's longest waterways, rises in the highlands of Guinea. West Africa has a largely smooth coast with only a few major lagoons and bays. The region's coastal areas consist

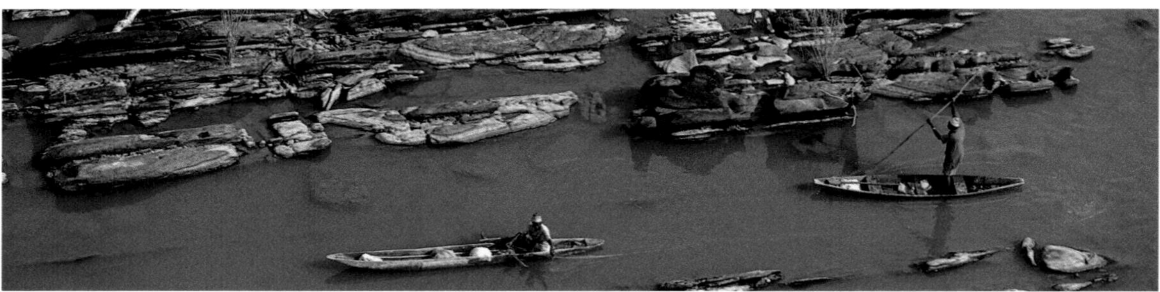

mostly of large mangrove forests a swamps. In contrast to the low-lyi coast, West Africa's interior consis mostly of expansive flat plateaus brok by scattered mountain ranges. Most West Africa was once covered by den tropical rainforests. Most of the regior forests have been cleared in recent ce

Traditional fishers on the Comoé Rive in Côte d'Ivoire **Kj**

Freetown Sierra Leone's capital – King James market – heavily damaged during a recent civil war **Kd41**

Yawri Bay Deep bay on Sierra Leone's Atlantic coast – home to many marine animals including turtles, crabs, and a variety of fish species – fishing villages **Kd41**

Tiwai Island Wildlife Sanctuary Nature reserves (13 km²) on a small island in the Moa River – large primate population (colobus monkeys) – home to crocodiles and more than 120 bird species **Ke42**

Man Major city in western Cote d'Ivoire – located at the foot of the heavily forested Toura Mountains – traditional mask festivals, mostly in February **Kg42**

Lac du Buyo Manmade lake on the Sassandra River in Cote d'Ivoire – important power plant – beautiful shoreline – abundant animal life **Kg42**

Parc National de Taï Conservation area (33,000 km²) in Cote d'Ivoire – UNESCO world heritage site – tropical rainforests – abundant wildlife **Kg43**

Yamoussoukro Administrative capital of Cote d'Ivoire – presidential palace – Notre Dame de la Paix (photo) **Kh42**

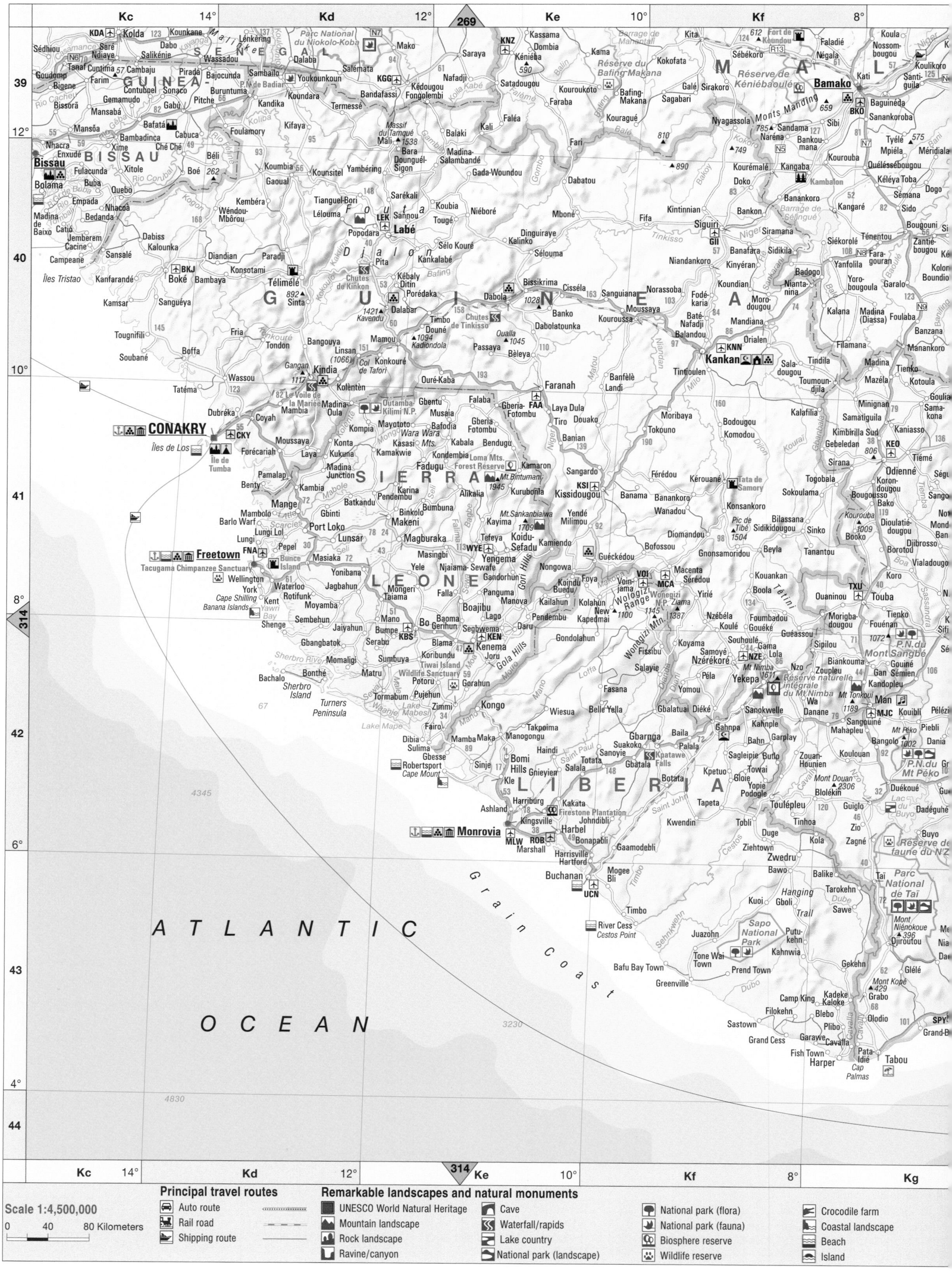

ATLANTIC OCEAN

Scale 1:4,500,000

0 40 80 Kilometers

Principal travel routes

- Auto route
- Rail road
- Shipping route

Remarkable landscapes and natural monuments

- UNESCO World Natural Heritage
- Mountain landscape
- Rock landscape
- Ravine/canyon
- Cave
- Waterfall/rapids
- Lake country
- National park (landscape)
- National park (flora)
- National park (fauna)
- Biosphere reserve
- Wildlife reserve
- Crocodile farm
- Coastal landscape
- Beach
- Island

…ries for cultivation or to create space for …ettlements. The region is rich in **mineral …esources,** including diamonds and gold. …nese natural resources drew European …aders to the region after the 17th cen…ry. The Portuguese constructed several …rts and trading bases along the West …frican coast before the start of colonial…m. The region was not only a center for …e trade of minerals but also ivory and, …agically, millions of human slaves.

Several powerful kingdoms flourished in West Africa before the start of the colonial era, including the kingdoms of Dahomey and Ashanti. Many West African kingdoms offered serious resistance to the European powers. Modern West Africa is home to an incredible variety of ethnic groups. Many ethnic groups in the region are now separated by borders created during the colonial era without regard to local demographics and history.

Despite foreign influences, most West African peoples were able to maintain many of their traditions. Indigenous animist beliefs are widely practiced throughout the region as is Christianity. Vodun, a naturist religion centered on ancestor worship, originated on the coast of West Africa and was carried to the Americas by slaves from the region. During the 1990s, West Africa was the scene of several bloody civil wars. **Liberia** and **Sierra Leone** have been devastated by long armed conflicts. Several West African countries, however, have recently experienced significant economic and political developments – most notably Ghana, which is now a democracy after decades of dictatorship. Unlike most other African regions, West Africa has plentiful potential energy sources. The region's rivers are a convenient source of electricity for several countries.

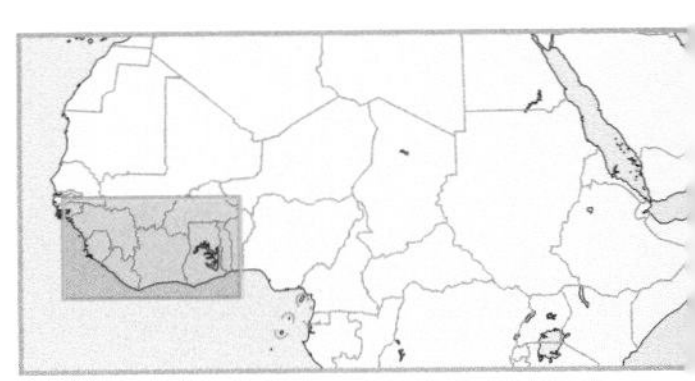

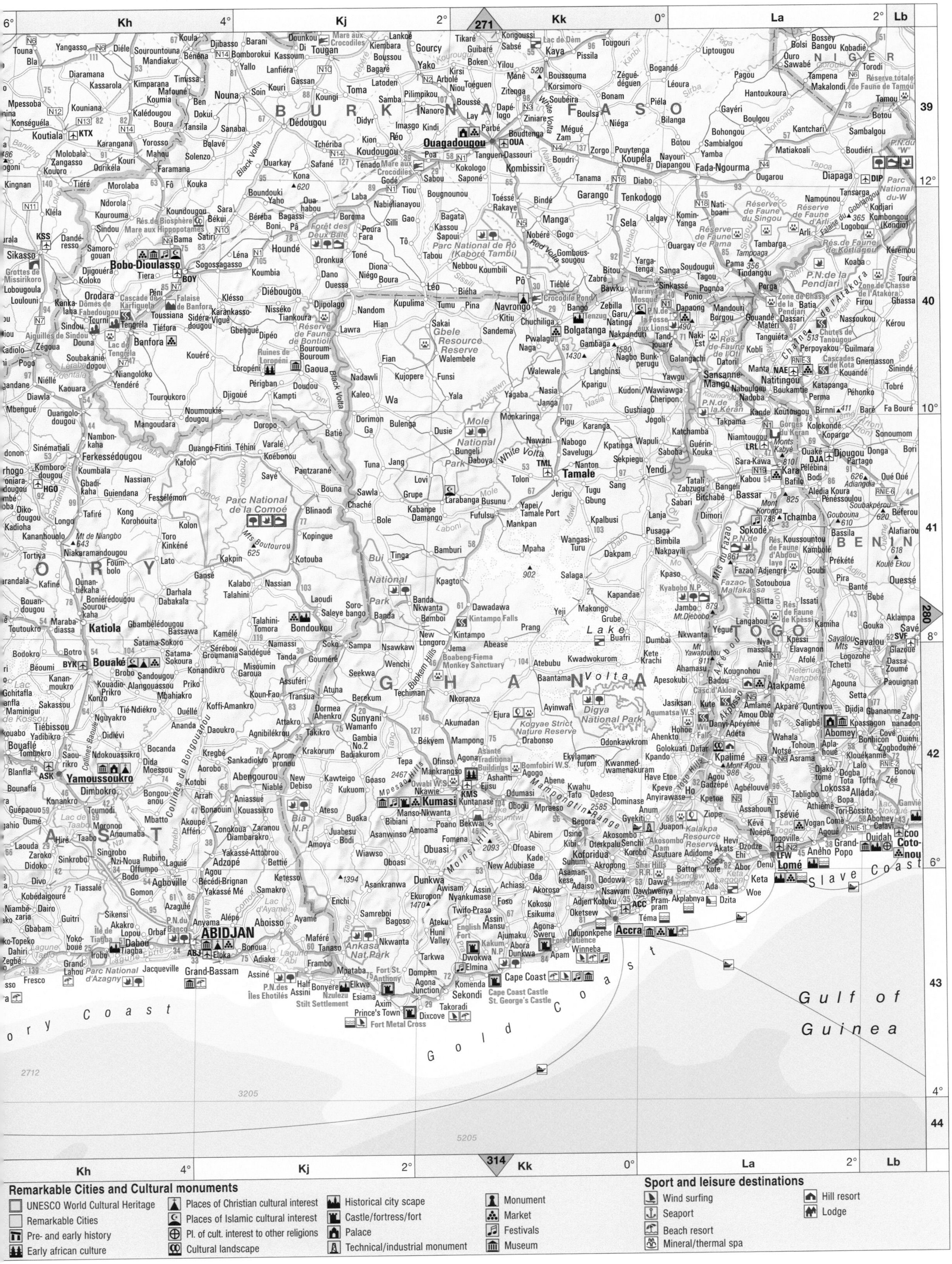

Bobo-Dioulasso The second largest city in Burkina-Faso – adobe mosques and dwellings (photo) – large marketplace – annual music festival **Kh40**

Parc National de la Comoé Conservation area (11,500 km²) in Cote d'Ivoire – UNESCO world heritage site – sacred sites of the Lobi and Dyula peoples **Kj41**

Abidjan Economic and cultural center of Cote d'Ivoire – population 2 million – large markets – St. Paul's cathedral – national museum **Kh43**

Lake Volta Man-made lake created in 1965 on the White Volta River in Ghana – power plant in Akosombo Dam – ferry and freighter traffic – fishing boats (photo) – Digya National Park **KkLa41/42**

Ashanti Largest ethnic group in Ghana – the city of Kumasi, a UNESCO world heritage site, is the traditional center of Ashanti culture – traditional wooden art **Kk42**

St. George's Castle One of several forts founded by the Portuguese on West Africa's coast – UNESCO world heritage site – once a center for slave trading **Kk43**

Abomey Once the capital of the powerful Dahomey Kingdom – royal palace built in the 17th century, a UNESCO world heritage site – museum **La42**

Remarkable Cities and Cultural monuments

- UNESCO World Cultural Heritage
- Remarkable Cities
- Pre- and early history
- Early african culture
- Places of Christian cultural interest
- Places of Islamic cultural interest
- Pl. of cult. interest to other religions
- Cultural landscape
- Historical city scape
- Castle/fortress/fort
- Palace
- Technical/industrial monument
- Monument
- Market
- Festivals
- Museum

Sport and leisure destinations

- Wind surfing
- Seaport
- Beach resort
- Mineral/thermal spa
- Hill resort
- Lodge

The vast delta of the Niger stretches through an area 200 kilometers wide in southern Nigeria on the country's coast along the Gulf of Guinea and Bight of Benin. North of Nigeria's swampy and low lying coastal areas is a region of rolling hills. The hills of southern Nigeria stretch east to the **Adamaoua Mountains** in Cameroon, which rise to a maximum height of 2,460 meters. The mountain range is covered mostly by tropical

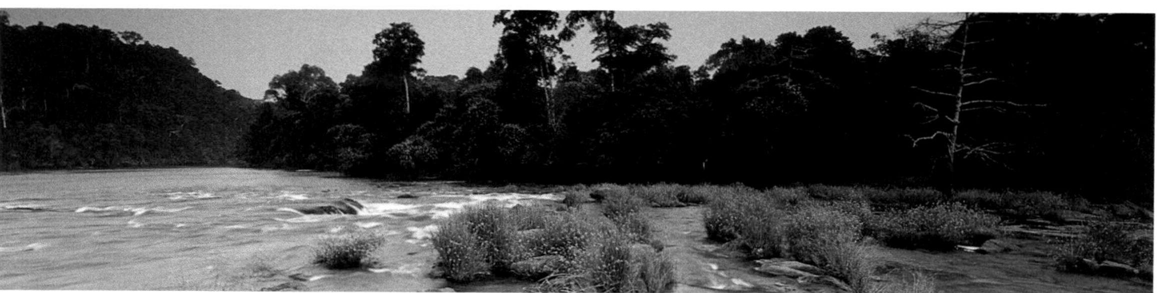

forests, and several national parks she ter the area's abundant flora and faun Western Cameroon is home to sever tall active and inactive volcanoes. Th summit of the highest volcano in th region, **Mount Cameroon** (4,09 meters), is the highest point in West Afr ca. **Isla de Bioko**, a volcanic island c

Tropical rainforests in Dja Nature Reserve (Cameroon) **Lg4**

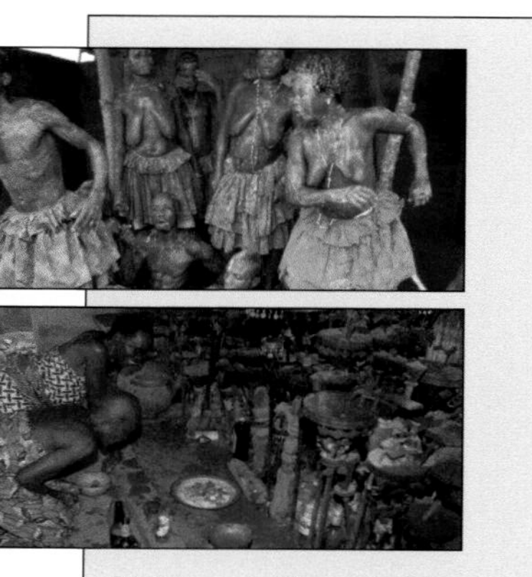

Vodun and other **animist religions** are widely practiced in West and Central Africa. Respect for ancestors and nature spirits are among the central beliefs of most indigenous religions in the regions. **Lb42**

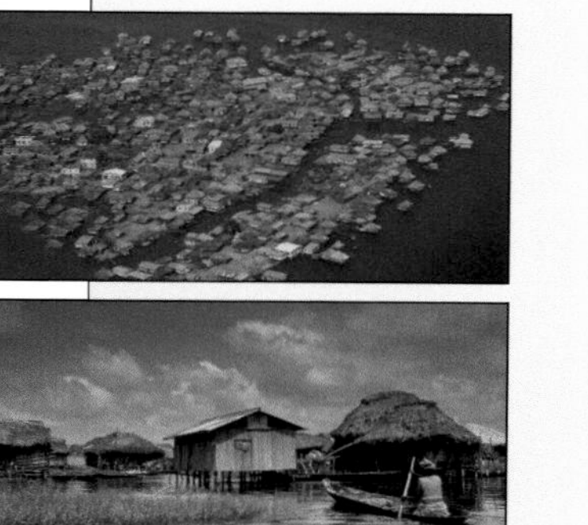

Lac Nokoué The village **Ganvié** with its floating market and homes is located inside a small lagoon on the edge of Lake Nokoue in Benin. **Lb42**

Lagos Most of Nigeria's largest city is built on several islands near the country's southern coast – National Museum and Balogun Market on Lagos Island **Lb42**

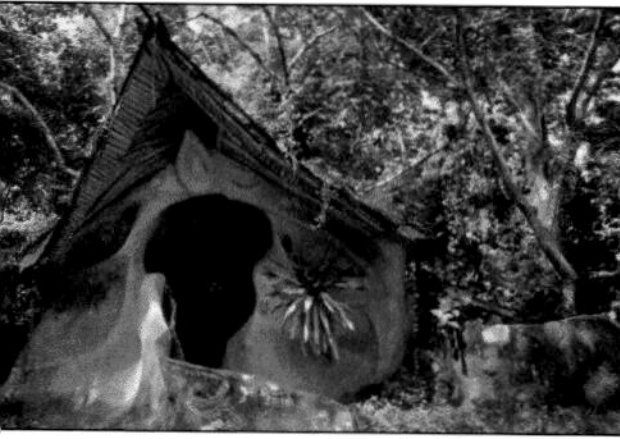

Osogbo Spiritual center of several indigenous religious groups, located in Nigeria – shrine to the deity Osun (photo) **Lc42**

Lake Nyos Lake in a volcanic crater – in 1986 the lake erupted releasing a cloud of poisonous gas that killed many inhabitants in the surrounding area **Lf42**

Scale 1:4,500,000
0 40 80 Kilometers

Principal travel routes
- Auto route
- Rail road
- Shipping route

Remarkable landscapes and natural monuments
- UNESCO World Natural Heritage
- Mountain landscape
- Rock landscape
- Active volcano
- Cave
- River landscape
- Waterfall/rapids
- Lake country
- Nature park
- National park (landscape)
- National park (flora)
- National park (fauna)
- National park (culture)
- Biosphere reserve
- Coastal landscape
- Beach

Cameroon's coast, is an extension of e large volcanic mountain range on e mainland. The 918-kilometer-long anaga River flows into the Atlantic cean at its delta in southernmost ameroon.

ne Adamaoua highlands are a transi- on zone between the semi-arid regions northern Cameroon and the country's umid tropical south, which encompas- es some of the wettest areas on the planet. Northern Cameroon consists mostly of semi-arid savannahs, while the south and the coastal regions are home to large tropical rainforests.

To the south, Cameroon is bordered by the Republic of Congo, a country in the Congo River basin, which shares its name with the larger Democratic Republic of Congo, once known as Zaire. The Ubangi River, the largest tributary of the Congo, is fed by several smaller rivers that rise in the highlands of Cameroons. The Ubangi forms sections of the border between the Republic of Congo (capital: Brazzaville) and the Democratic Republic of Congo (capital: Kinshasa). The sections of the **Congo basin** west of the Ubangi are covered by large swampy wetlands. These wetlands are mostly nourished by the many tributaries of the Ubangi and the area contains expansive rainforests. In densely populated southern Nigeria, large rainforest areas have been cleared in recent decades for use as agricultural land. Southern Cameroon, Gabon, and the two Congo states, however, still contain vast and intact tropical rainforests. The rainforests in the Congo Basin constitute the second largest area of tropical rainforests on the planet. These vast forests are inhabited by many animals including several endangered ape species.

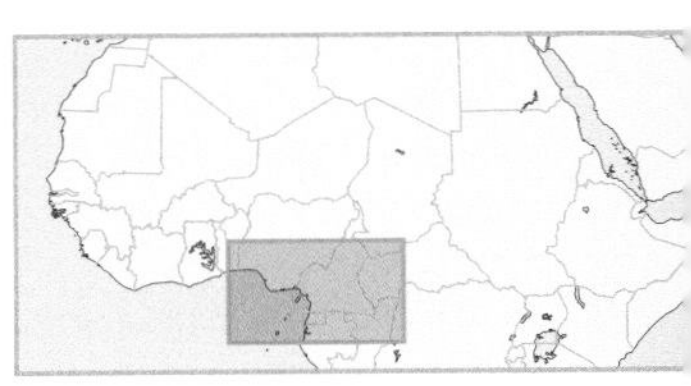

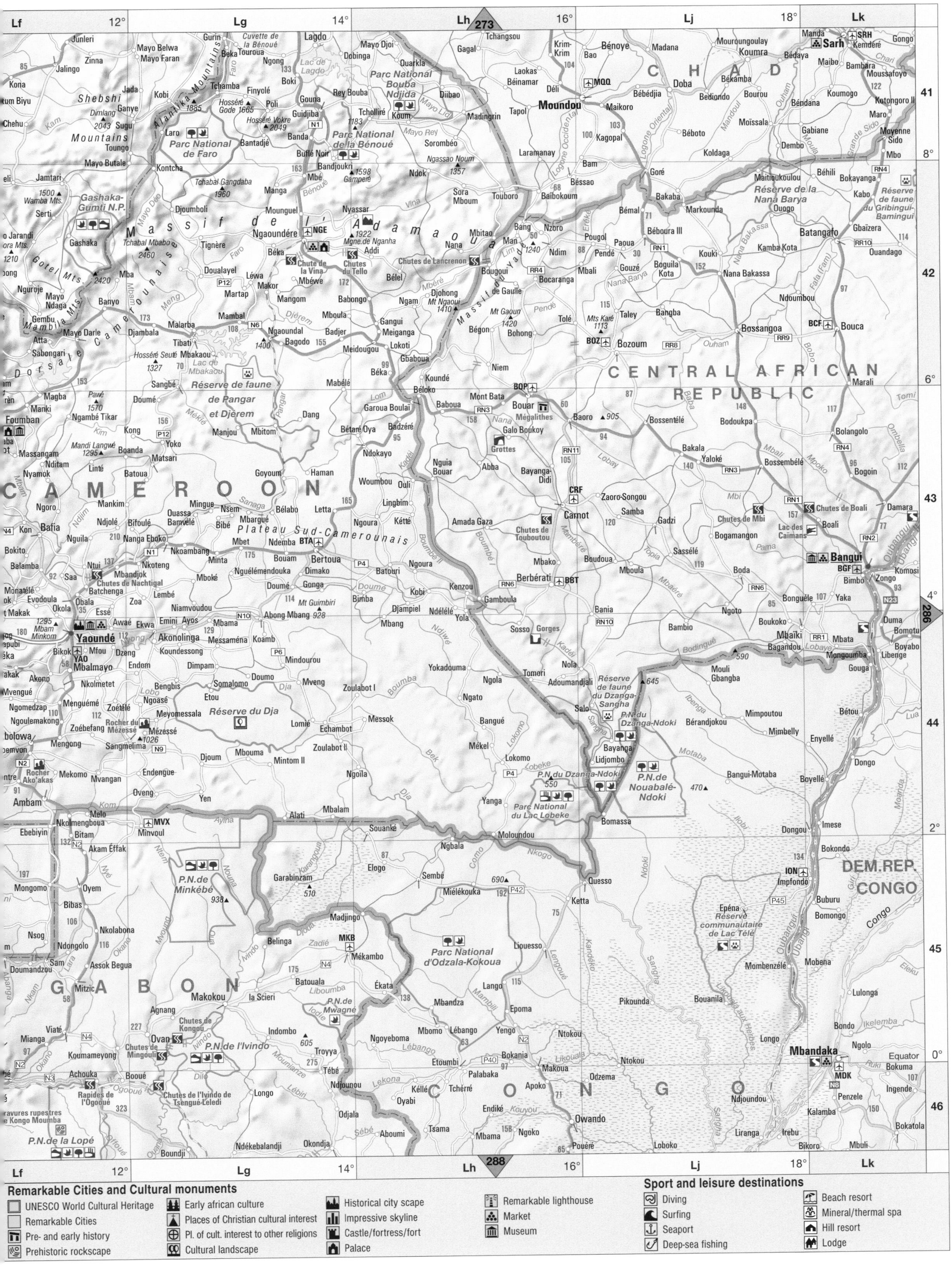

Korup National Park Large national park in western Cameroon (1,255 km²) – tropical rainforests – ape colonies **Le43**

Rey Bouba Fulani sultanate in northern Cameroon – traditional festivals in honor of the local sultan **Lh41**

Foumban Capital of a sultanate in Cameroon – sultan's palace – anthropology museum – Tam Tam house with 10-meter-long drums (photo) **Lf43**

Yaoundé Cameroon's capital city – modern skyline – presidential palace (photo) – Museum of African Art – central marketplace **Lf44**

Dja Faunal Reserve Nature reserve in southeastern Cameroon – UNESCO world heritage site – tropical rainforests – gorilla colonies **Lg44**

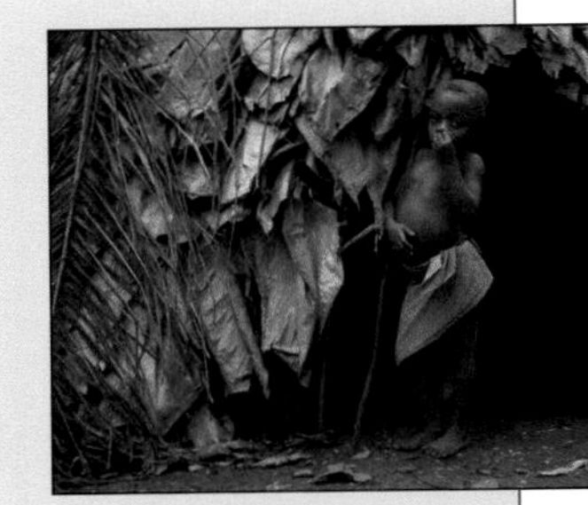

Pygmies of Central Africa Several hunter and gatherer pygmy groups live in the rainforests of Central Africa. The pygmies live in small close-knit clans.

Remarkable Cities and Cultural monuments

- UNESCO World Cultural Heritage
- Remarkable Cities
- Pre- and early history
- Prehistoric rockscape
- Early african culture
- Places of Christian cultural interest
- Pl. of cult. interest to other religions
- Cultural landscape
- Historical city scape
- Impressive skyline
- Castle/fortress/fort
- Palace
- Remarkable lighthouse
- Market
- Museum

Sport and leisure destinations

- Diving
- Surfing
- Seaport
- Deep-sea fishing
- Beach resort
- Mineral/thermal spa
- Hill resort
- Lodge

The region between the Sahel's southern edges in Sudan and the **tropical rainforests** of Central Africa offers a variety of landscapes and climates. The northern sections of the region – in southern Sudan and the Central African Republic – consist of arid land with eroded soil and sparse vegetation. Nomadic livestock herders including the Tubu people form a large proportion of the inhospitable area's population. The **Marrah Moun-**

tain range (Jabal Marra), a chain of extinct volcanoes stretching through se tions of Sudan and Chad, is one of t most fascinating geographic features this region. In stark contrast to the ba ren surrounding plains, the sides of t mountains are covered by dense veg tation. Southern Chad is a transiti

A small Nuba village in the highlands o southern Sudan **Mf39/4**

Marrah Mountains The chain of extinct volcanoes is a relatively fertile mountain range with a maximum height of 3,088 meters. **Mc39**

Saint Floris National Park The large nature reserve in the Central African Republic is a habitat for cheetahs and rhinoceroses (middle photo). The park's wetlands are home to flocks of pelicans (bottom photo). **Ma41**

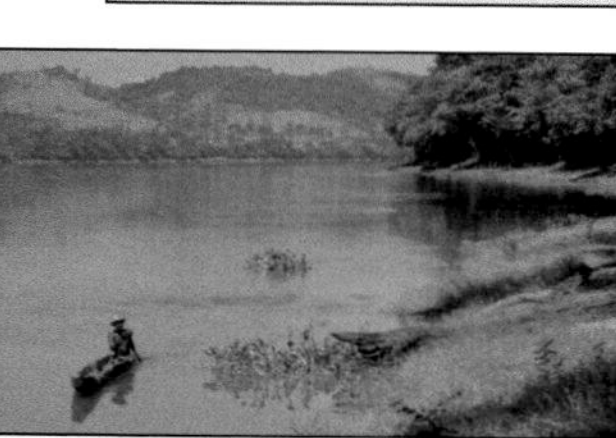

Ubangi River along the border between the Central African Republic and the Republic of Congo – rapids near Gele **Lk43**

Chutes de Boali 50 meters high and 250 meters wide waterfall near Bangui in the Central African Republic **Lk43**

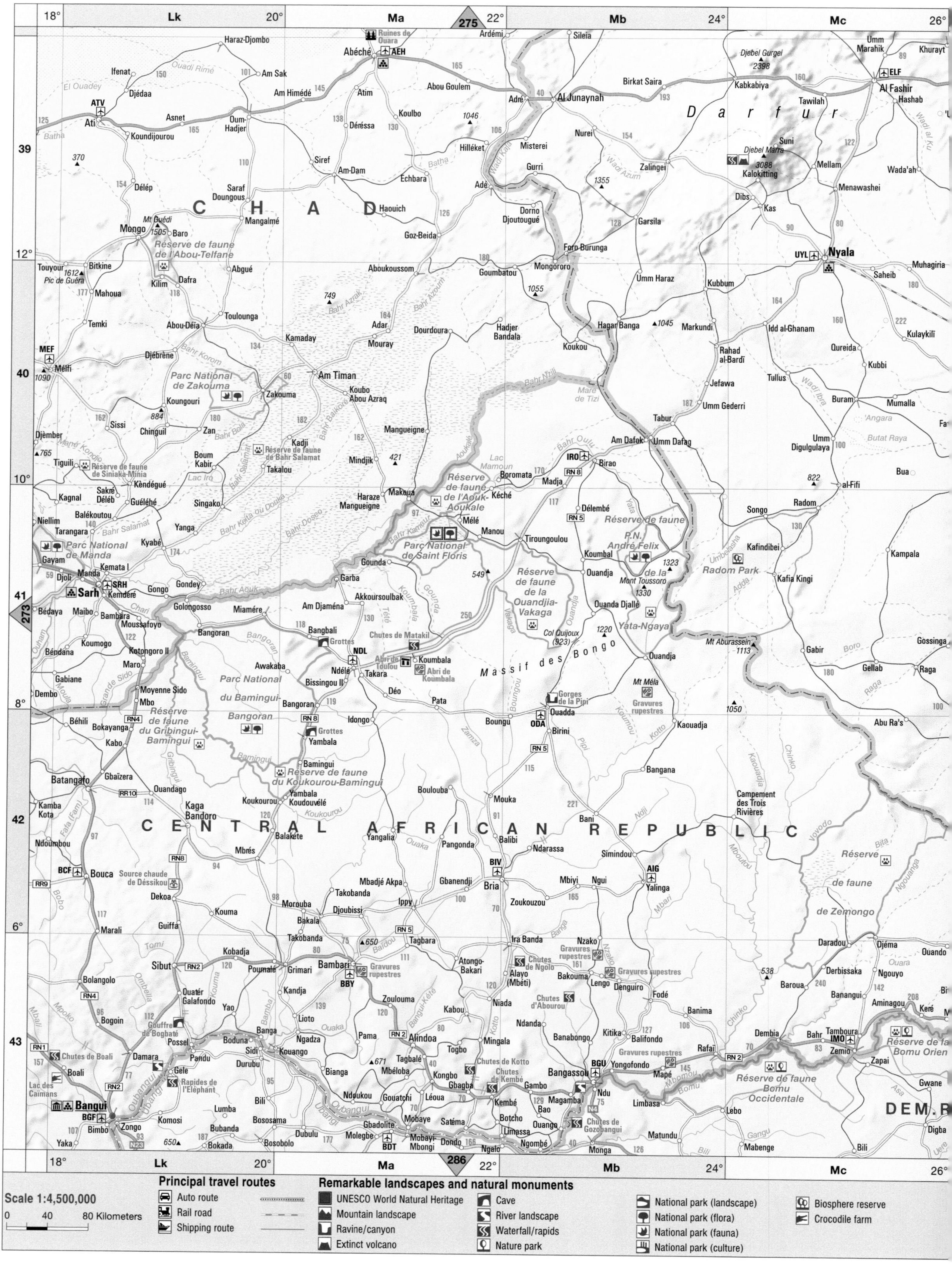

Scale 1:4,500,000

0 40 80 Kilometers

Principal travel routes

- Auto route
- Rail road
- Shipping route

Remarkable landscapes and natural monuments

- UNESCO World Natural Heritage
- Mountain landscape
- Ravine/canyon
- Extinct volcano
- Cave
- River landscape
- Waterfall/rapids
- Nature park
- National park (landscape)
- National park (flora)
- National park (fauna)
- National park (culture)
- Biosphere reserve
- Crocodile farm

ne between the arid Sahel and the st tropical rainforests of Central Africa. e region consists of a flat basin dis- cted by countless streams and rivers. e **Chari (Shari)**, one of southern Chad's incipal rivers, contributes most of the ater that flows into Lake Chad. Most of uthern Chad's population consists of bsistence farmers and Sudanic lan- uage-speaking ethnicities. The culture the **Sara people**, a collection of closely related ethnicities, includes a complex and ancient mythology well studied by Western anthropologists, before and after the colonial era.

The **White Nile River (Al-bahr Al-abyad)** flows north from the city of Malakal through southern and central Sudan before it merges with the Blue Nile in Khartoum. The Sudd is a swampy plain in southern Sudan that is watered by several rivers including the White Nile. The area's terrain is greatly affected by the water levels of these rivers. In addition to large papyrus swamps, the **Sudd** also encompasses large grasslands that frequently are flooded in summer.

In Chad and Sudan the border between the arid Sahel and the fertile forests and savannahs to its south are also borders between different religious communities. In both countries, tensions between Muslim, Christians and Animists have led to violent conflicts. Both Chad and Sudan have experienced drawn out civil wars between the Muslims in their northern regions and the mostly Christian and Animist communities in their southern regions. In Chad, the civil war lasted for almost three decades before a ceasefire was agreed upon in the mid 1990s. Southern Sudan remains the site of violent conflicts and widespread human rights abuses.

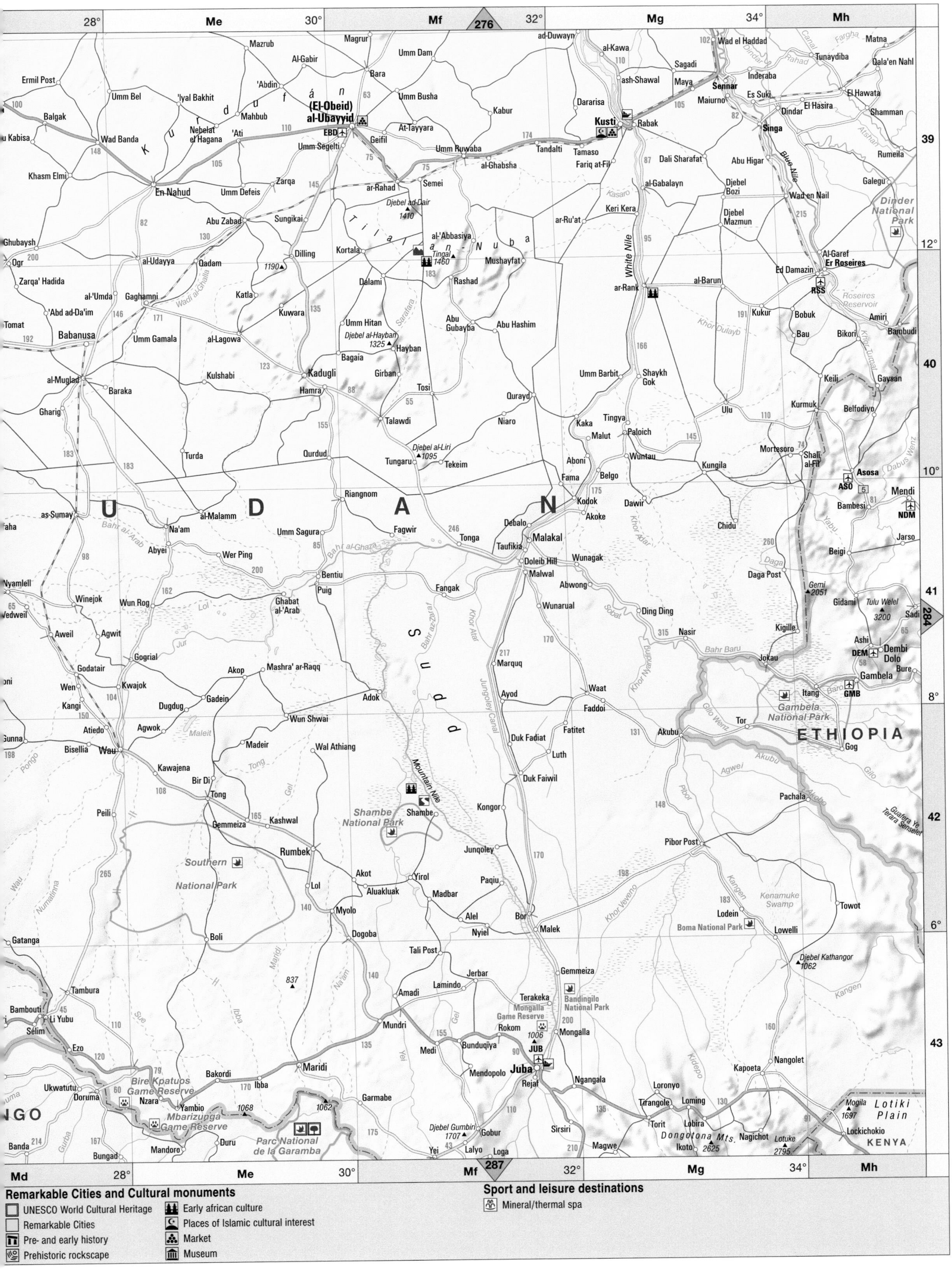

Nuba Mountains Fertile mountainous region in eastern Sudan – inhabited by Nuba ethnicities and Arabic-speaking nomads **Mf39/40**

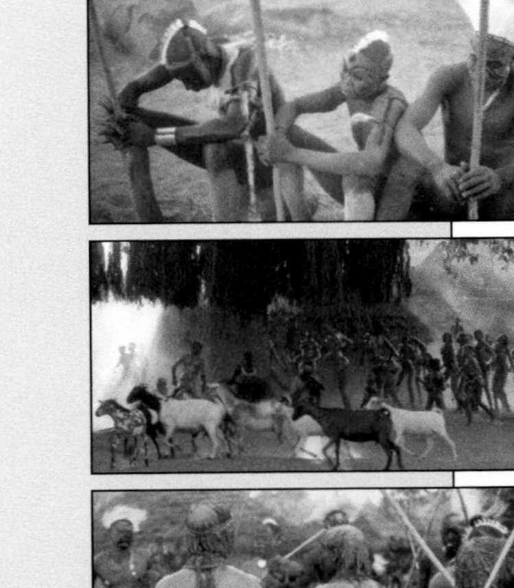

The Nuba This group of ethnicities inhabits the mountainous regions of Sudan and has preserved many of its ancient traditions. The Nuba, who are considered backward by their Arabic-speaking neighbors, have suffered from government-supported expulsions and discrimination.

Sudd Marshland along the edges of the White Nile in central Sudan – inhabited by livestock breeders **Mf41/42**

Shambe National Park Swamp south of the Sudd region – habitat of the Nile lechwe and fascinating birds (photo) **Mf42**

Boma National Park Savannah in southern Sudan – wild dogs – large antelope herds **Mg42**

Remarkable Cities and Cultural monuments

- UNESCO World Cultural Heritage
- Remarkable Cities
- Pre- and early history
- Prehistoric rockscape
- Early african culture
- Places of Islamic cultural interest
- Market
- Museum

Sport and leisure destinations

- Mineral/thermal spa

Highlands of Ethiopia, Horn of Africa

Ethiopia in East Africa is a mountainous country with a total area of 1.13 million km^2. The country's capital, **Addis Ababa**, has a population of nearly three million and is situated at a height of 2,400 meters above sea level. Ras Dashen Terara (4,260 meters) in the Simien Mountains is the country's highest mountain. Ethiopia's highlands have a mostly temperate climate with temperatures below 20° Celsius during most of the year.

The highlands decline in steps to t eastern section of the country, a regi dominated by savannahs and desert Eastern Ethiopia is an arid region w sparse rainfall. The Danakil Plain, in nort eastern Ethiopia and southeastern Eritr is one of the hottest and driest areas the world.

Traditional two-story dwellings with thatched roofs in Ethiopia **Mk**

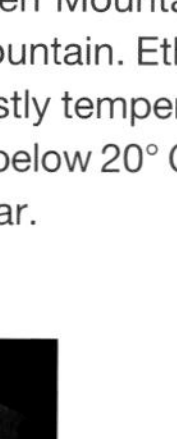

Daga Estifanos Ancient mausoleum containing the tombs of several Ethiopian emperors – on an island in Lake Tana – monasteries and churches in the area **Mj40**

Abuna Josef Massif Heavily eroded mountain (4,190 meters) – one of the highest peaks in the Ethiopian highlands **Mk39**

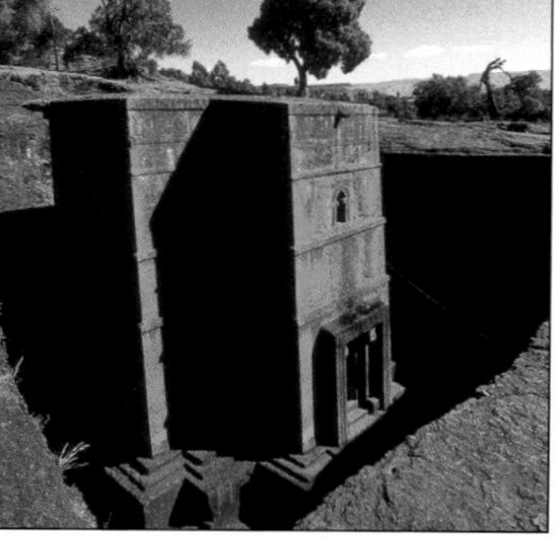

Lalibela Important spiritual center of Ethiopian Christianity, often called the Ethiopian Jerusalem – monolithic cave churches, UNESCO world heritage sites – Beta Georgis church (photo) **Mk39**

Lower Valley of the Awash River Excavation sites containing ancient hominid remains, the oldest are more than 3.2 million years old – world heritage site **Na40**

Lake Assal Body of water situated 155 meters below sea level – one of the deepest points on the Earth's surface – salt caravan routes between the lake and Bati **Nb40**

Harer Principal city of Ethiopia's Muslim minority – founded in 1520 – walled old town – more than 90 mosques **Nb41**

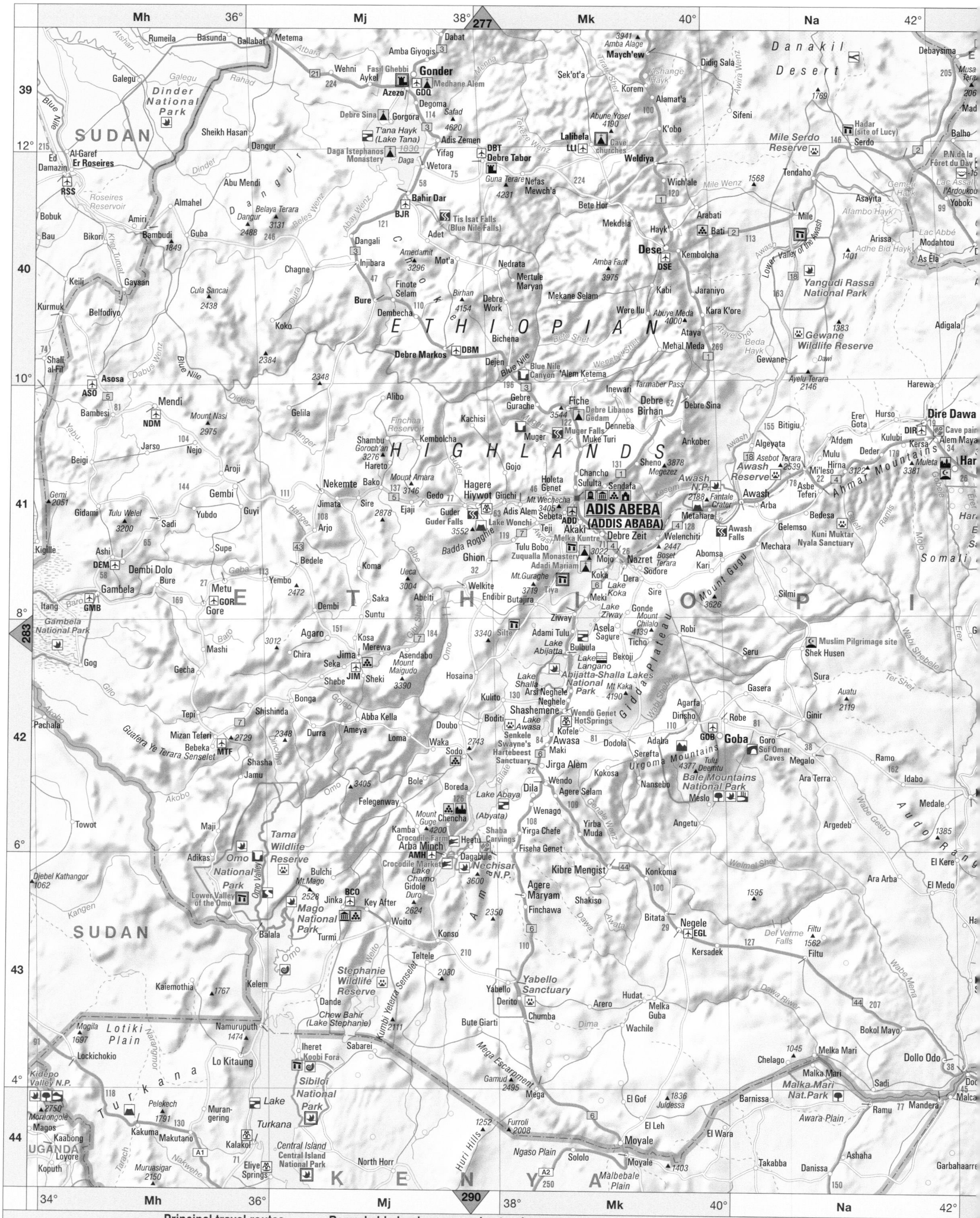

Scale 1:4,500,000
0 40 80 Kilometers

Principal travel routes
- Auto route
- Rail road
- Shipping route

Remarkable landscapes and natural monuments
- UNESCO World Natural Heritage
- Mountain landscape
- Rock landscape
- Ravine/canyon
- Extinct volcano
- Cave
- River landscape
- Waterfall/rapids
- Lake country
- Desert
- Depression
- National park (landscape)
- National park (flora)
- National park (fauna)
- Wildlife reserve
- Crocodile farm

e western edges of the Ethiopian high-nds are more fertile and receive signi-cantly more rainfall than the eastern dges. **Lake Tana**, in the northwestern ghlands, is the largest body of water in hiopia with an area of around 3,000 n². The lake is also the source of the **ue Nile River**. The **Omo River**, one of hiopia's principal rivers, rises in the uthern highlands and flows to **Lake urkana** (Rudolf) in Kenya. Gambela National Park near the Sudanese border consists of marshy savannahs crossed by many rivers and streams. The **Great Rift Valley** runs through the middle of the Ethiopian highlands. In Ethiopia, the Great Rift Valley encompasses a chain of large lakes. **Lake Assal**, on the Danakil Plain in Djibouti, is one of the deepest points on the Earth's surface with an average elevation of 155 meters below sea level. **Djibouti**, a small nation with an area of 23,200 km², is situated on East Africa's coast next to the Gulf of Aden and the Red Sea. Like the countries it borders, Djibouti consists primarily of deserts and volcanic highlands. **Somalia** has a 3,025-kilometer-long coastline along the Gulf of Aden and the Indian Ocean. Somalia's terrain consists of hilly **deserts** and mountainous highlands along the country's northern coast. Humidity levels on the northern coast regularly exceed 80 percent during the rainy season. Somalia's capital **Mogadishu** is also the largest city in the country.

Ethiopia and the Horn of Africa region are home to more than 70 ethnic groups who speak dozens of different languages. Most Ethiopians are Christians. The Ethiopian Orthodox Church was founded in the 4th century AD. Somalia has been a predominantly Muslim nation since the 12th century.

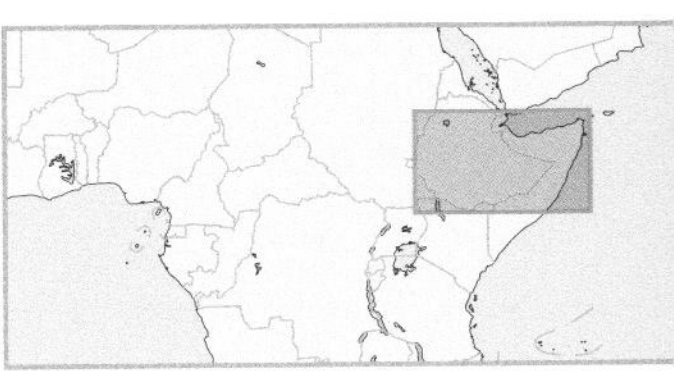

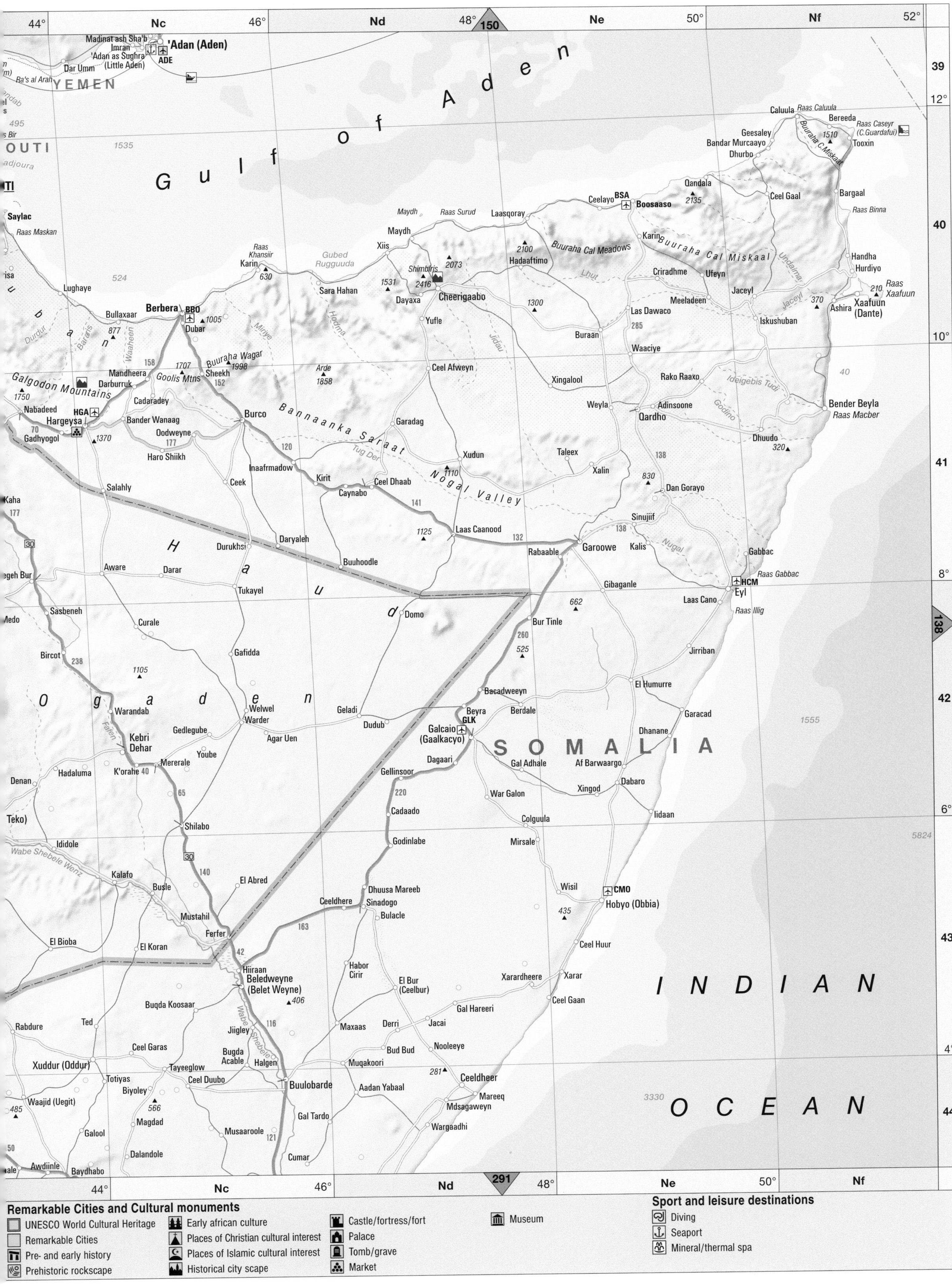

Awash National Park Fantale crater – habitat for Oryx-antelopes, leopards, and Kudus **MkNa41**

Addis Ababa Ethiopia's capital – St. George's cathedral (photo) – Menelik Mausoleum – Gebbi Palace – Anthropology Museum – marketplace **Mk41**

Nechisar National Park Ethiopian national park in the Great Rift Valley – home to rare animal species **Mj42/43**

Mursi The nomadic Mursi people have lived in the Omo River Valley in southwestern Ethiopia for hundreds of years. Adult Mursi women wear large plates (photo) in their ears and lower lips. **Mj43**

Hargeysa Commercial center in northwestern Somalia – located in an agricultural region – marketplace (photo) **Nc41**

Somali Desert The arid regions of Somalia are inhabited mostly by nomadic herders – frequent sand storms **Nc-Ne40/41**

Webe Shebel River The river rises in Ethiopia's highlands – numerous agrarian villages along the river's banks **Nc43**

Remarkable Cities and Cultural monuments

- UNESCO World Cultural Heritage
- Remarkable Cities
- Pre- and early history
- Prehistoric rockscape
- Early african culture
- Places of Christian cultural interest
- Places of Islamic cultural interest
- Historical city scape
- Castle/fortress/fort
- Palace
- Tomb/grave
- Market
- Museum

Sport and leisure destinations

- Diving
- Seaport
- Mineral/thermal spa

The gigantic basin of the Congo River consists of vast tropical rainforests and swamps. It stretches through most of Central Africa. Situated near the equator, the region has a tropical climate with high temperatures and heavy rainfall throughout the year. Countless unique tropical plant and animal species inhabit the largely inaccessible rainforests in the region. The construction of roads stretching from east to west though the rainforests and ship traffic on the river h greatly expanded the limits of hum settlement in the region. Large sectio of Central Africa's rainforests have be cleared in recent decades by miners, lo gers, and a growing population in ne of farming land. Habitat loss, poachir and civil wars have brought several sp

The Ruwenzori Mountains are coverec by thick tropical vegetation **Me**

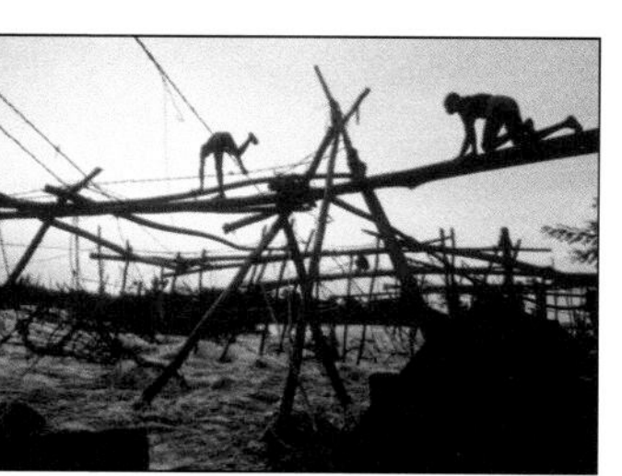

Wagenia Fishing Grounds Fishing area on the Congo River near Boyoma Falls – the local fishermen still rely on centuries-old traditional methods (photo) – near the city of Kisangani **Mc45**

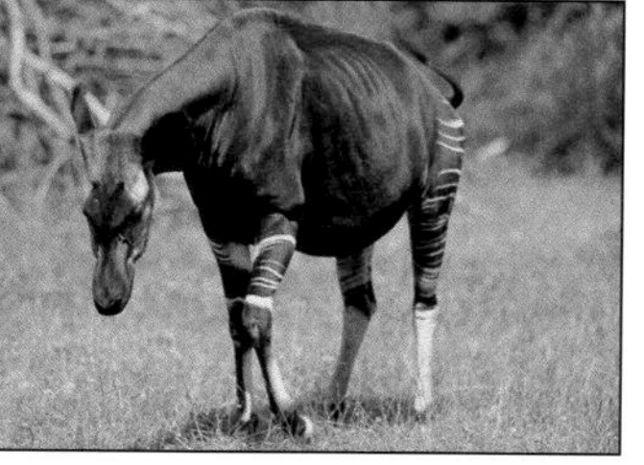

Okapi Wildlife Reserve Conservation area and habitat for endangered Okapis in eastern Congo – UNESCO world heritage site – several waterfalls **Me45**

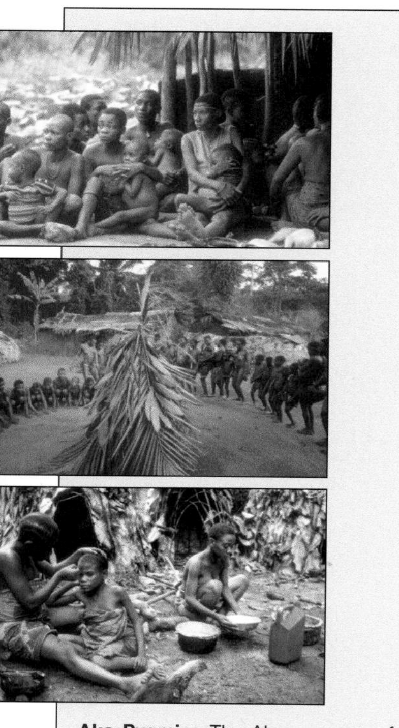

Aka Pygmies The Aka, a group of Pygmy communities, live in the upper valley of the Congo River. Like most other Pygmies, the Aka are hunter-gatherers and live in small clans. They reside in heavily forested areas. Their traditional lifestyles are increasingly threatened by outside influences. Traditional knowledge and beliefs are passed down the generations though songs and storytelling.

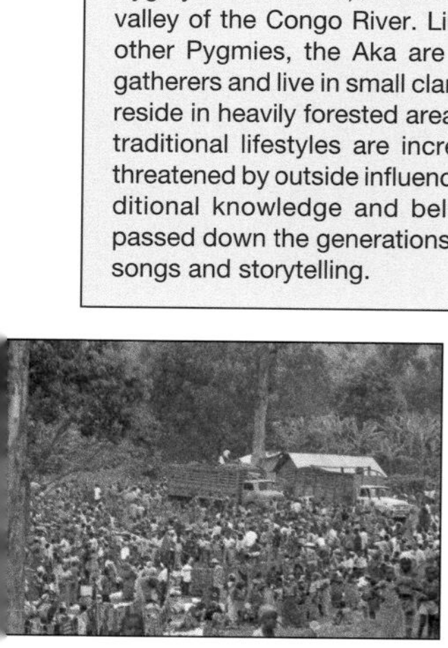

Rutshuru Small city on the southern edge of Virunga National Park – large produce market (photo) – Rutshuru waterfalls: three kilometers outside of the city **Me46**

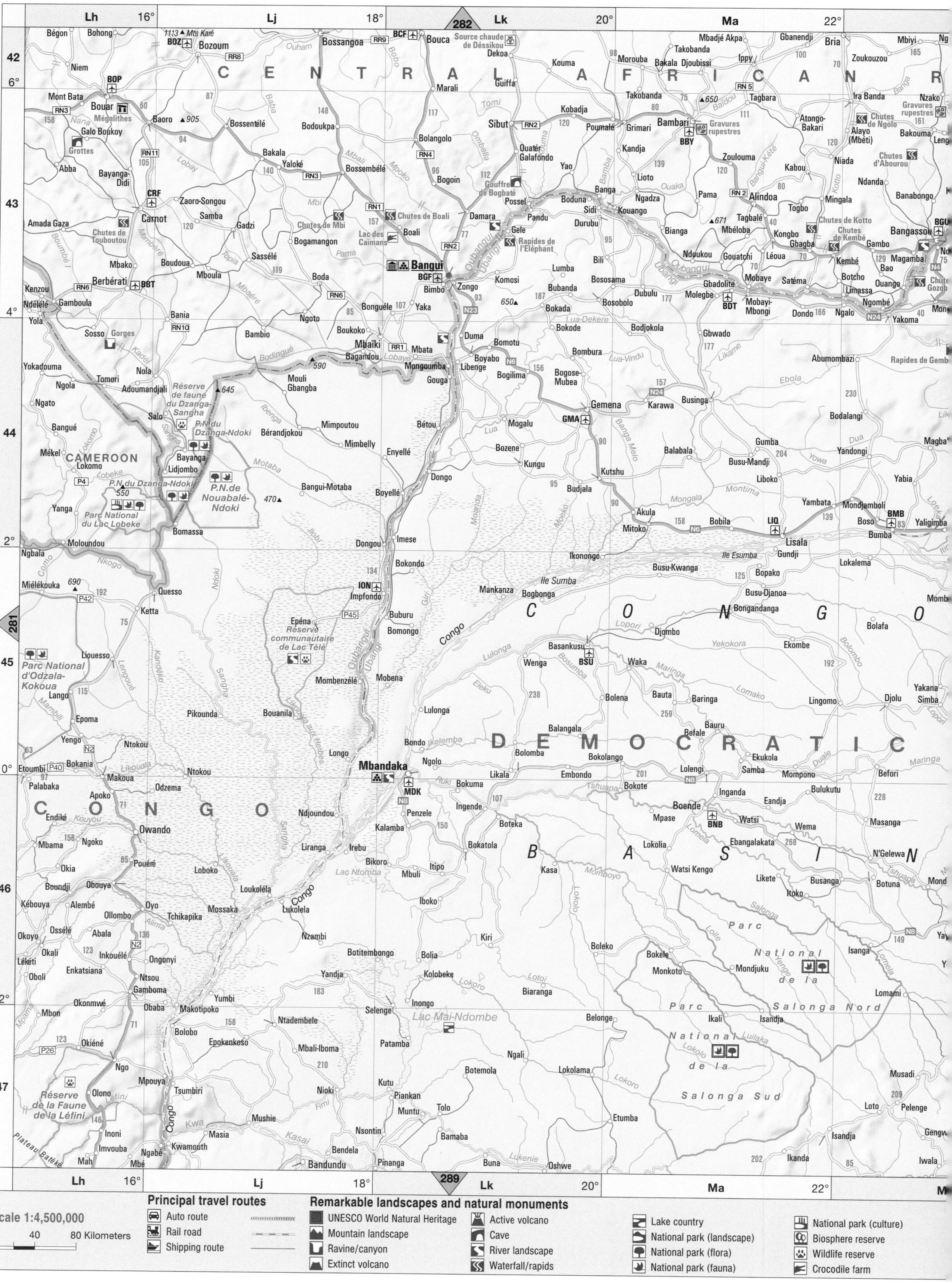

Scale 1:4,500,000
0 40 80 Kilometers

Principal travel routes
- Auto route
- Rail road
- Shipping route

Remarkable landscapes and natural monuments
- UNESCO World Natural Heritage
- Mountain landscape
- Ravine/canyon
- Extinct volcano
- Active volcano
- Cave
- River landscape
- Waterfall/rapids
- Lake country
- National park (landscape)
- National park (flora)
- National park (fauna)
- National park (culture)
- Biosphere reserve
- Wildlife reserve
- Crocodile farm

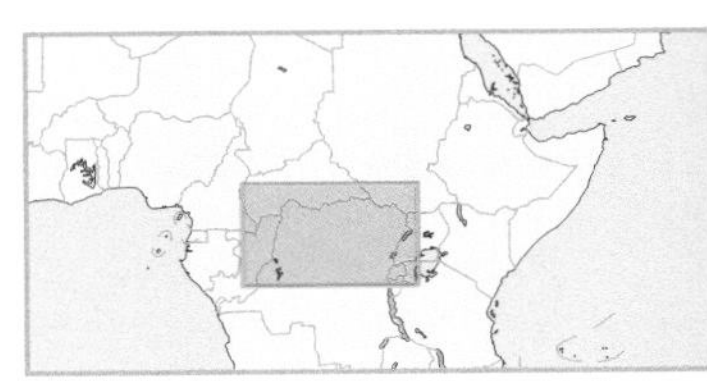

›s in the Congo basin including the ›gion's mountain gorillas and forest ele›ants to the verge of extinction. The ›ngo basin is the traditional homeland several hunter-gatherer ethnic groups ›llectively referred to as Pygmies be›use of their small statures. Most Pyg›es live in small clans and music plays important role in the culture of almost of their communities. The majority of › basin's population is formed by members of Bantu-language-speaking ethnicities. The ancestors of the Bantu-speaking ethnicities arrived in the Congo basin after they migrated from their original homelands in the borders of modern-day Nigeria at least 2,000 years ago.

Most of the Congo basin consists of flat low-lying areas. However, the eastern edge of the basin near Lake Victoria is a mountainous region encompassing countless large and small lakes. The **Ruwenzori** and **Vurangi** mountain ranges are situated on the eastern edge of the Albertine (Western) Rift Valley, an extension of the Great Rift Valley. The jagged Ruwenzori Mountain range rises to a maximum height of 5,109 meters and encompasses several large glaciers. These rainy and humid highlands are home to unique endemic vegetation including unusually large flowers and weeds. Among the animals in the Ruwenzori Mountains, the region's birds and primates are the most fascinating and studied. Many historians believe the Ruwenzori Mountains are the "Mountains of the Moon" described by the Greco-Egyptian geographer Ptolemy during the 2nd century AD. Ptolemy and many other geographers believed the mountain range contained the source of the Nile River. In the 19th century, explorers proved that the White Nile rises from Lake Victoria.

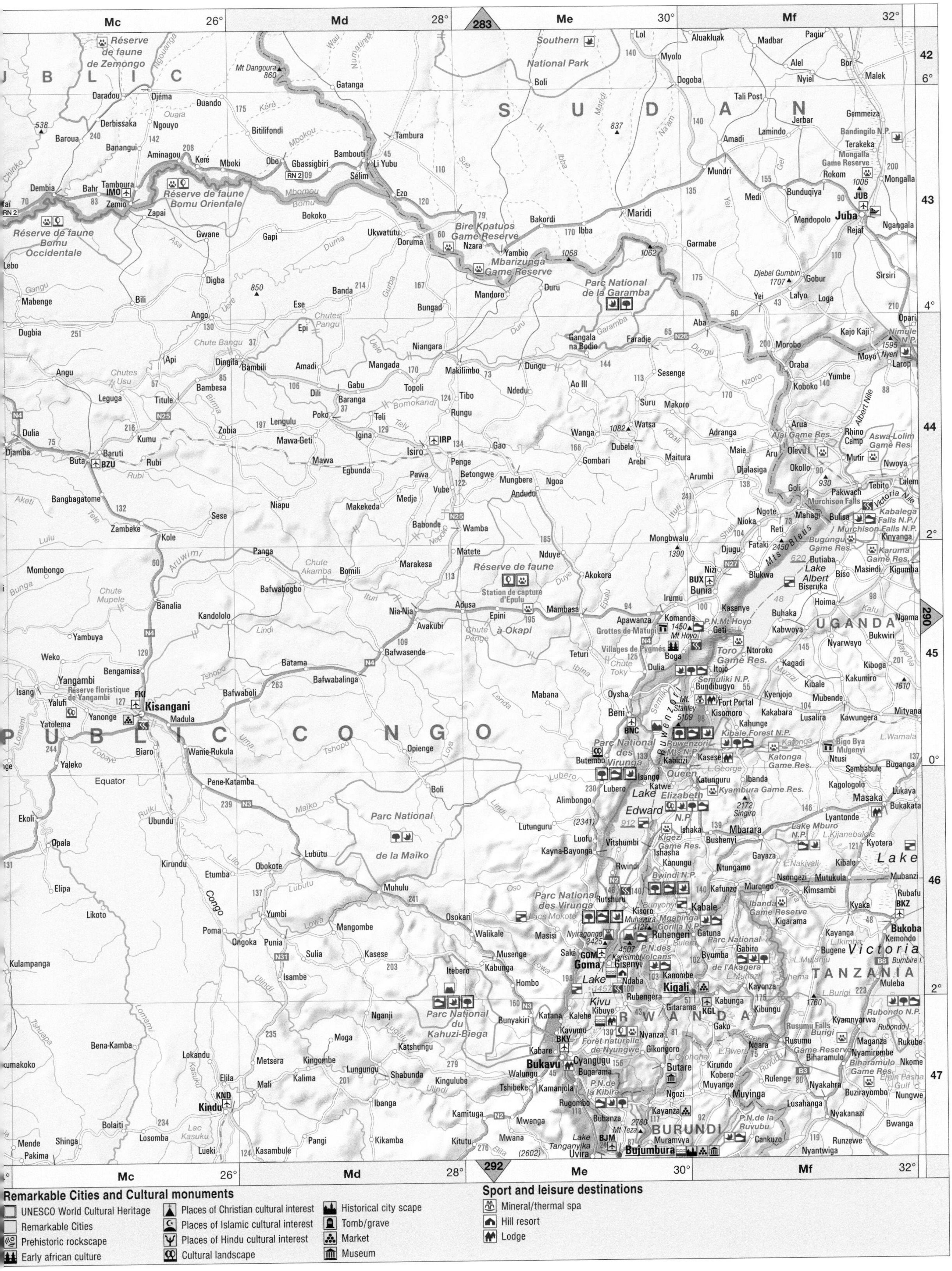

Ruwenzori National Park/ Virunga National Park The two neighboring national parks are located along the border between Uganda and the Democratic Republic of Congo. Both parks encompass volcanic mountain chains and contain many unique plants species. Photos from top to bottom: mountain valley, giant lobelias, Jackson's chameleon **Me45**

Mountain Gorillas Virunga and Ruwenzori National Parks are home to around 250 mountain gorillas. Their survival is threatened by poaching and wars **Me46**

Volcanoes of Central Africa Virunga National Park is home to several active volcanoes. The 3,425 meter tall volcano Nyiragongo is the most active in the region. **Me46**

Remarkable Cities and Cultural monuments

- UNESCO World Cultural Heritage
- Remarkable Cities
- Prehistoric rockscape
- Early african culture
- Places of Christian cultural interest
- Places of Islamic cultural interest
- Places of Hindu cultural interest
- Cultural landscape
- Historical city scape
- Tomb/grave
- Market
- Museum

Sport and leisure destinations

- Mineral/thermal spa
- Hill resort
- Lodge

The powerful **Congo River** gives its name to two nations in central Africa: the **Republic of Congo** also known as Congo-Brazzaville and the **Democratic Republic of Congo** or Congo-Kinshasa, formerly Zaire. Both Congo nations contain vast areas of dense tropical rainforests and the Congo River is the most important transportation route in the region. **Kinshasa** (population: 4.5 million) and **Brazzaville** (population: 950,000), the two capital cities of the Congo nations, are both located on the banks on the river.

Gabon (267,667 km²), a nation to the north of the Republic of Congo has a terrain and tropical climate similar to that of the two Congo Nations. Gabon's coastal areas consist of flat plains, while the interior consists mostly of low hills. Alm all of Gabon's territory is located in basin of the **Ogooue River**. The 8 kilometer-long river rises in the Repub of Congo and flows to its delta Gabon's Atlantic coast.

Gabon and the two Congo nations ha **equatorial tropical climates** with h levels of humidity and heavy rain throughout the entire year. All three cou tries are home to vast tropical rainfore

The Congo River: Africa's socond longest river

Lambaréné Hospital in the rainforests of Gabon – founded in 1913 by Dr. Albert Schweitzer, who was buried nearby **Lf46**

Moukalaba-Doudou National Park Large conservation area in southwestern Gabon – Nyanga savannah, rainforests, and swamps – elephants and gorillas **Lf47**

Conkouati-Douli National Park Sea turtle habitats – elephants, gorillas, chimpanzees (photo) **Lf47/48**

Kinshasa The capital of the Democratic Republic of Congo – cathedrals and mosques – large marketplaces **Lh48**

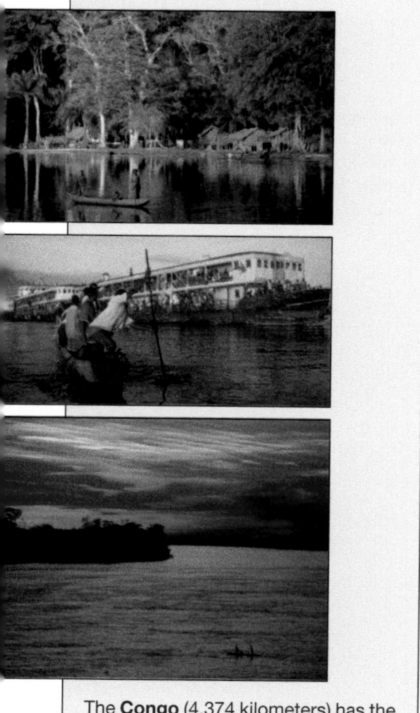

The **Congo** (4,374 kilometers) has the largest river basin in Africa. The river is a vital transport route for Central Africa and several large cities are located on its banks.

Scale 1:4,500,000
0 40 80 Kilometers

Principal travel routes
- Auto route
- Rail road
- Shipping route

Remarkable landscapes and natural monuments
- UNESCO World Natural Heritage
- Mountain landscape
- Rock landscape
- Ravine/canyon
- Cave
- River landscape
- Waterfall/rapids
- Lake country
- National park (landscape)
- National park (flora)
- National park (fauna)
- National park (culture)
- Biosphere reserve
- Wildlife reserve
- Whale watching
- Turtle conservation area

Southern Congo, Southern Democratic Republic of Congo, Northern Angola

th amazing levels of biodiversity. Sev- al **national parks** have been created the region's rainforests to protect in- genous flora and fauna from the ef- cts of deforestation and habitat loss. e region's primates, including gorillas d chimpanzees, are especially endan- red and several reserves have been eated solely for the protection of these imals.
antu-language-speaking ethnic groups form the vast majority of Central Africa's population. Before the beginning of European colonization in the 19th century, the region was dominated by several powerful African kingdoms. The Luba-Lunda kingdoms were famous for their wealth of gold reserves and controlled large areas in the Congo Basin before the colonial era. By the beginning of the 20th century most of the Congo Basin had fallen under the control of European colonial powers. In recent decades, the vast mineral wealth of the Congo Basin has been a driving force behind the region's frequent armed conflicts and civil wars. Tension between the many ethnic groups in Central Africa has also been a major factor behind the region's conflicts and political instability.

Northern **Angola**, unlike the rest of the country, has a wet tropical climate similar to other regions near the equator. The climate along Angola's long **Atlantic coast** is strongly influenced by ocean currents, such as the Benguela Current. The **central plateau** in Angola's interior rises to heights above 2,000 meters. The plateau declines gradually in the north and more abruptly in the south. Most of Angola's territory is covered by savannahs and semi-arid regions. Angola has large deposits of natural resources, including oil, copper, and diamonds.

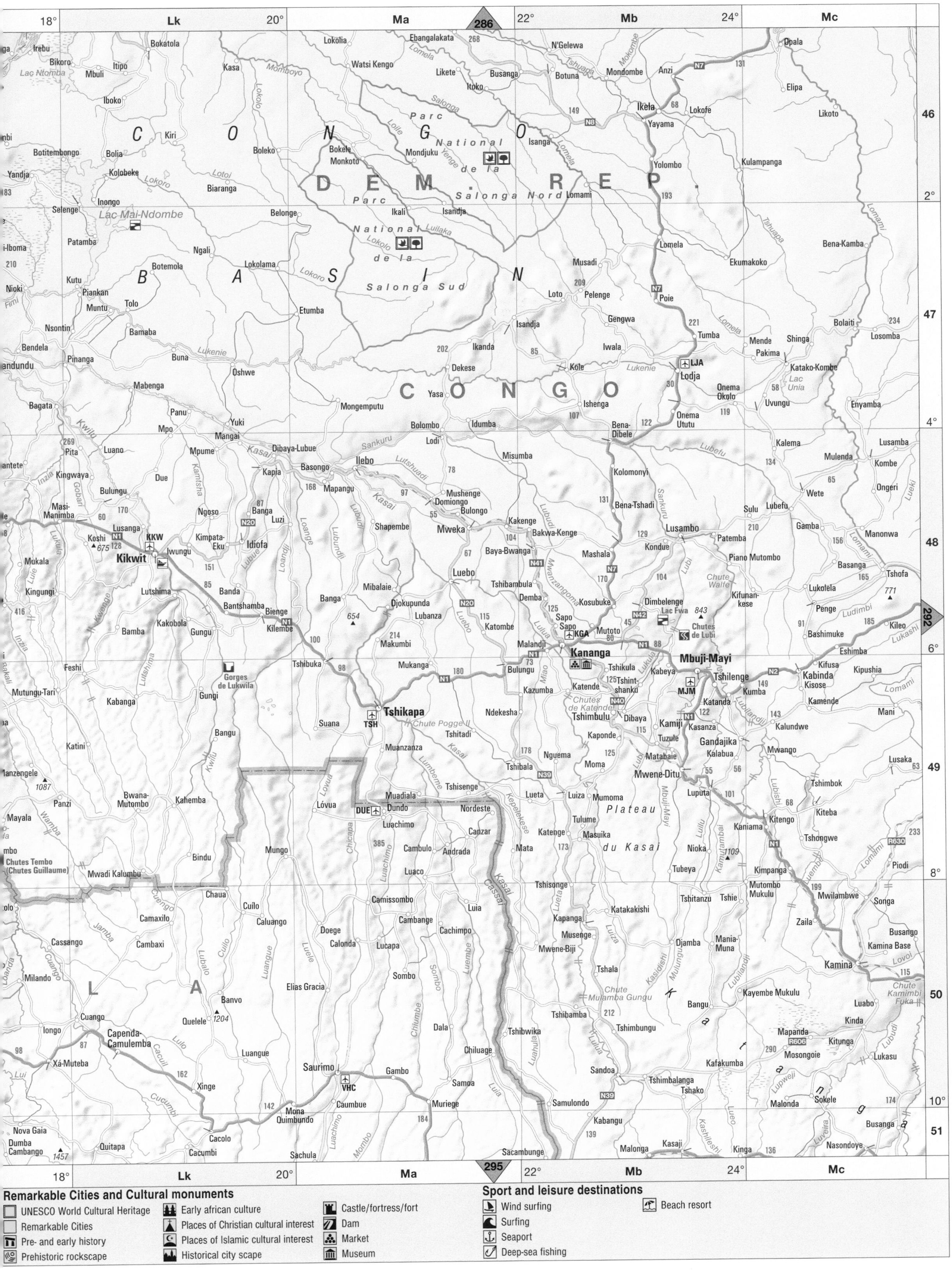

Salonga National Park The world's largest tropical rainforest reserve (36,000 km²) is a UNESOC world heritage site and is home to fascinating animals including elephants and chimpanzees. The park is accessible only by river boat. Photos from top to bottom: rainforest, mandrill baboon, mustached monkey, a group of bonobos **Ma46/47**

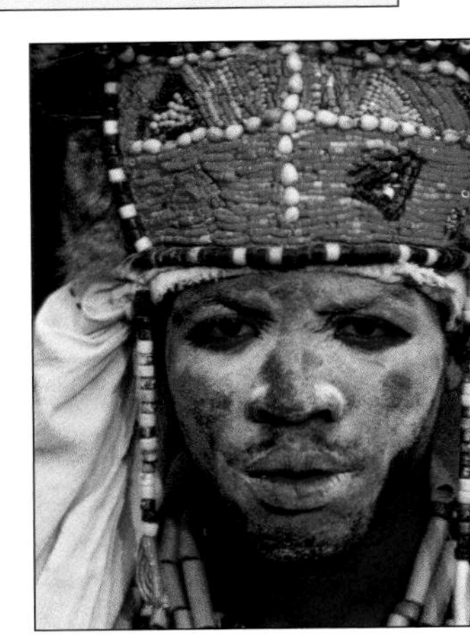

Katanga Ethnically diverse region in the Democratic Republic of Congo (Kinshasa) – photo: medicine man

Remarkable Cities and Cultural monuments

- UNESCO World Cultural Heritage
- Remarkable Cities
- Pre- and early history
- Prehistoric rockscape
- Early african culture
- Places of Christian cultural interest
- Places of Islamic cultural interest
- Historical city scape
- Castle/fortress/fort
- Dam
- Market
- Museum

Sport and leisure destinations

- Wind surfing
- Surfing
- Seaport
- Deep-sea fishing
- Beach resort

The **East African Rift System** is the most spectacular geographic feature in East Africa. The East African Rift System is part of a larger rift system called the Afro-Arabian Rift Valley. The Afro-Arabian Rift Valley was formed more than 30 million years ago after the African and Asian continental plates separated from one another. The 7,000-kilometer-long rift valley extends from the Jordan Valley in Israel through the Red Sea and down to

the southern edges of East Africa. T width of the East African Rift Syste ranges between 50 and 300 kilomete In East Africa, the Rift Valley diverg into two sections: the Eastern (Great) F Valley and the Western Rift Valley. Both sections of the East African R System contain volcanic mountain rang

Masai-Mara Reserve in Kenya features fascinating flora and fauna **Mh**

Lake Turkana (Rudolf) Lake (6,000 km²) in northwestern Kenya – traditional homeland of the Turkana people **MhMj43/44**

The Afro-Arabian Rift Valley 7,000 kilometers long – extends from Israel to East Africa – volcanic mountain ranges **Mj44/45**

Lake Bogoria Located in the Great Rift Valley – high salt and mineral content – geysers – flamingo flocks (photo) **Mj45**

The Masai This famed group of seminomadic livestock herders lives in several East African countries. The Masai have maintained many of their traditions despite increasing contact with other ethnic groups.

Masai Mara National Reserve The northernmost section of the Serengeti is divided into two zones by Tanzania's government. The northern zone is inhabited by Masai herders and the southern zone is a conservation area for wildlife. The reserve is home to large herds of gnus (top photo), lions (middle photo), and water buffalo (bottom photo). **Mh46**

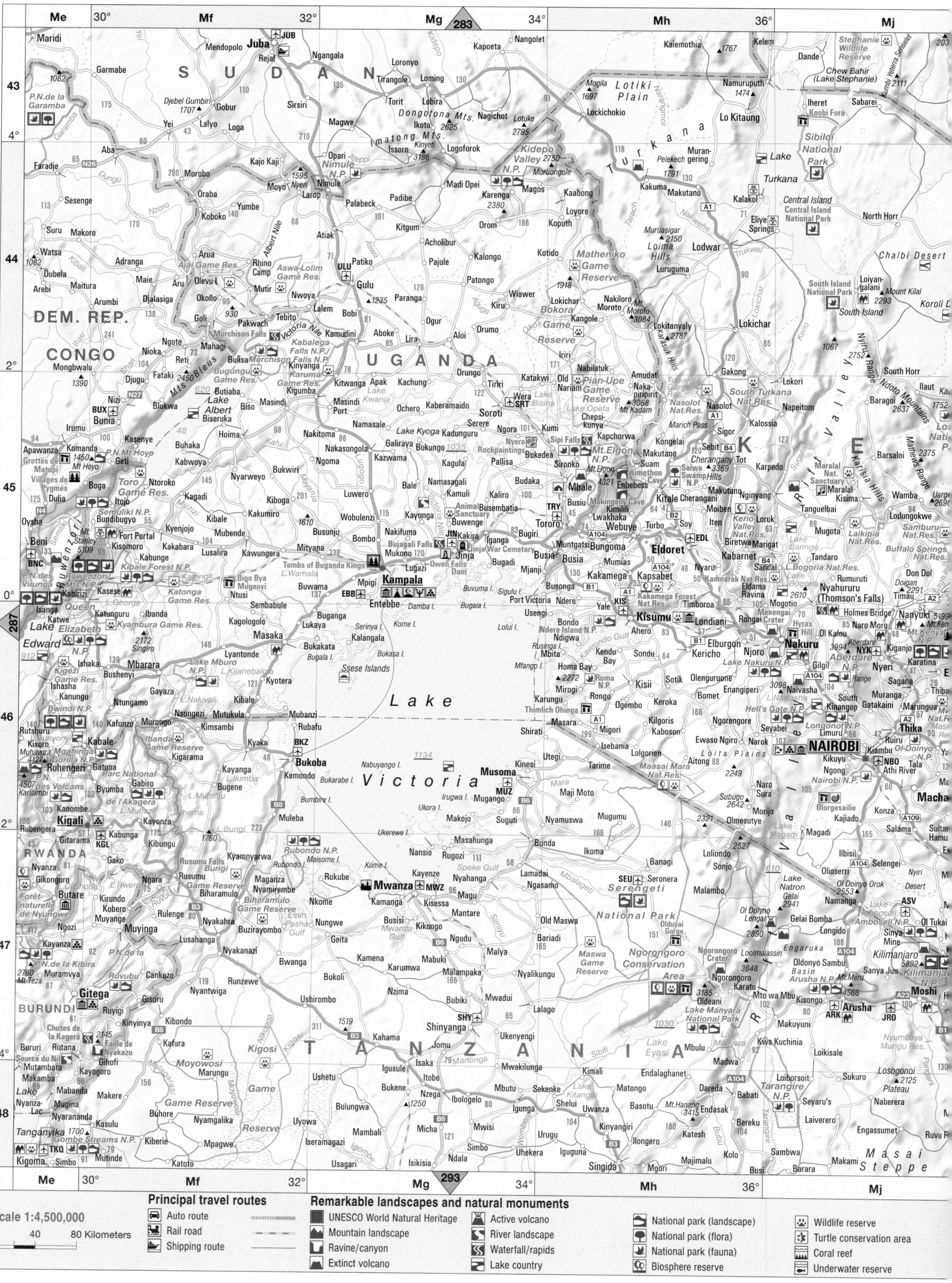

Scale 1:4,500,000

0 40 80 Kilometers

Principal travel routes

- Auto route
- Rail road
- Shipping route

Remarkable landscapes and natural monuments

- UNESCO World Natural Heritage
- Mountain landscape
- Ravine/canyon
- Extinct volcano
- Active volcano
- River landscape
- Waterfall/rapids
- Lake country
- National park (landscape)
- National park (flora)
- National park (fauna)
- Biosphere reserve
- Wildlife reserve
- Turtle conservation area
- Coral reef
- Underwater reserve

cluding the **Virunga Mountains** along e Ugandan-Rwandan border and the **wenzori Range**. The Great Rift Valley East Africa also contains a series of ge lakes. **Lake Victoria**, the world's cond largest freshwater lake, is locad in a large basin between the eastern d western sections of the rift system. any important archeological disco-ries have been made in the Great Rift lley during modern times. The Great Rift Valley's climate and terrain are ideal for the preservation of organic remains and the bones of prehistoric humans, and extinct hominid species have been discovered at many sites throughout East Africa.

Both Kenya and Tanzania contain a series of highlands that stretch from the countries' coasts into their interiors. These **highlands** rise to 2,000 meters in elevation and the savannahs they encompass are home to many large wild animals, including elephants and lions. The Serengeti, a wilderness in northern Tanzania, contains several nature reserves with abundant wildlife and beautiful landscapes. The highlands of Tanzania and Kenya feature several of Africa's highest mountains, including **Mount Kenya** (5,199 meters) and **Mount Kilimanjaro** (5,892 meters) – the second highest and highest mountain on the continent. The 400-kilometer-long **Tana River**, which flows from Kenya's interior to the Indian Ocean, is the most important river in the highlands.

Somalia is situated on a plateau with an average elevation of 500 meters. Most of the country's terrain consists of semi-arid savannahs and deserts. A narrow strip of humid plains stretches along the country's coast, and northern Somalia features a region of arid highlands.

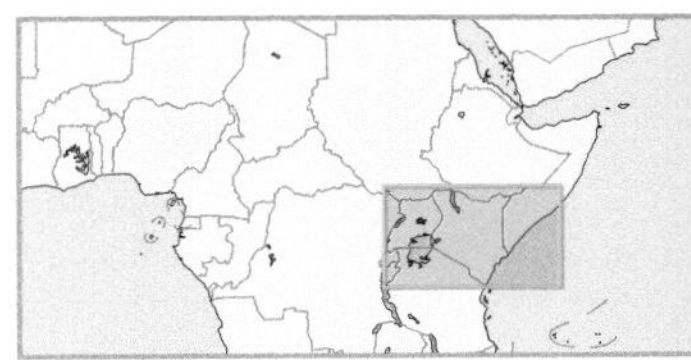

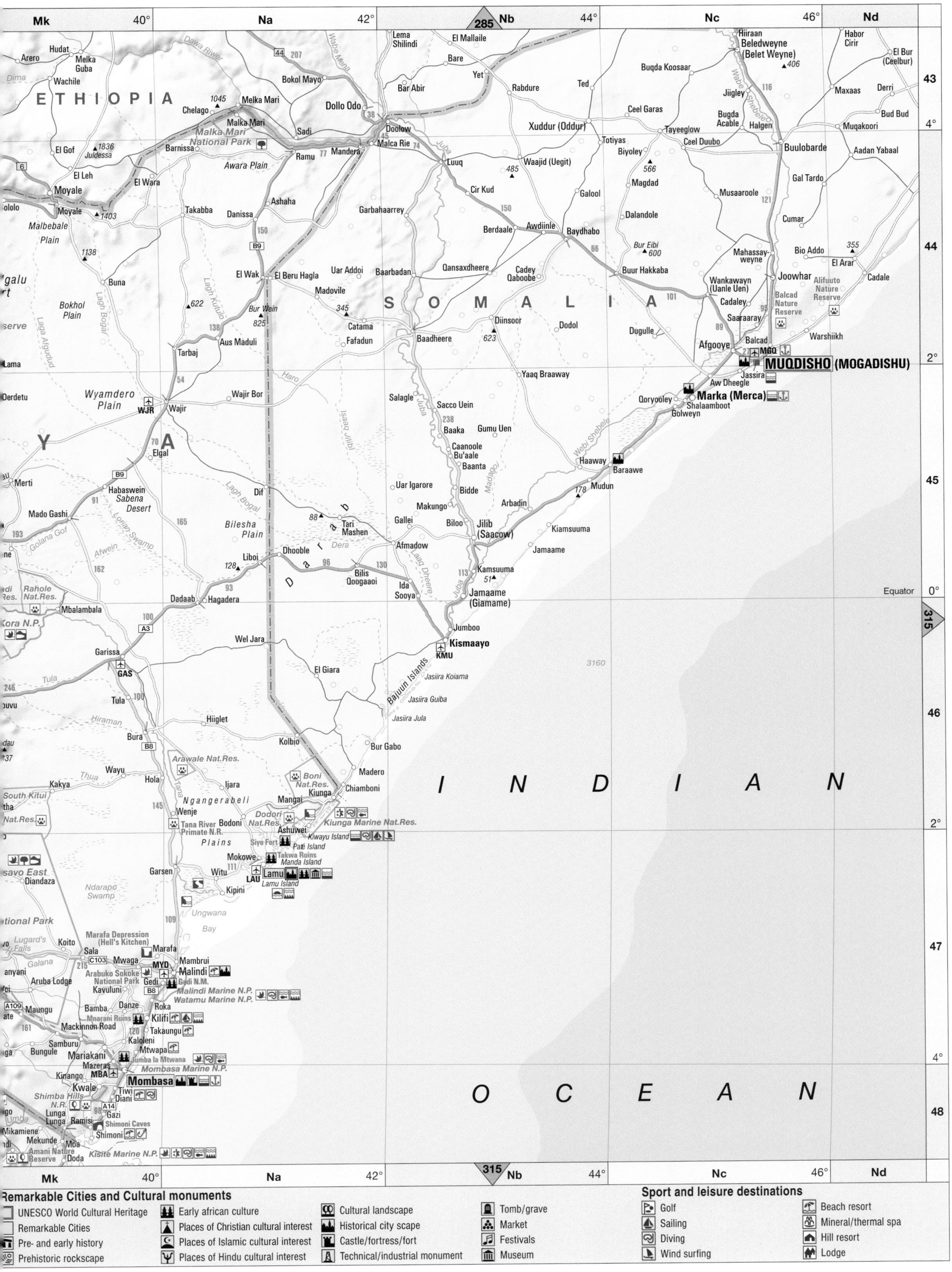

Samburu The Samburu people are closely related to the Masai. Like the Masia, the Samburu are traditionally semi-nomadic cattle herders.

Samburu National Reserve Conservation area in a semi-arid region with large antelope herds (photo) and gerenuks **Mj45**

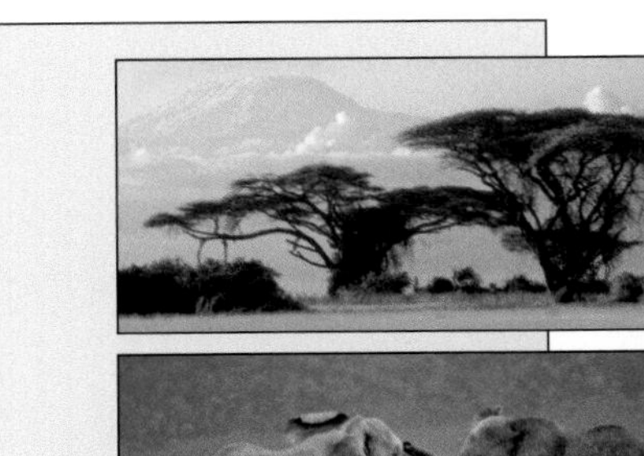

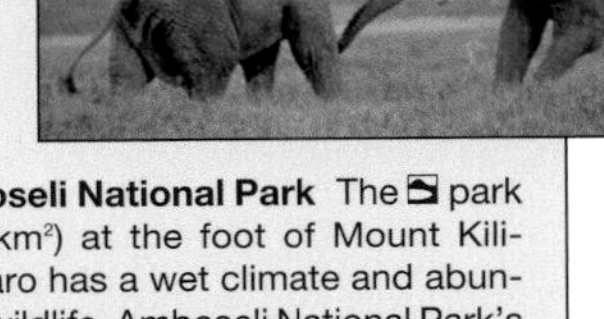

Amboseli National Park The park (400 km²) at the foot of Mount Kilimanjaro has a wet climate and abundant wildlife. Amboseli National Park's unique vegetation (top photo) and large elephant herds (bottom photo) are major attractions. **Mj47**

Lamu UNESCO world heritage site – port city located on an island in the Indian Ocean – Swahili architecture in the well preserved old town – beaches **Na47**

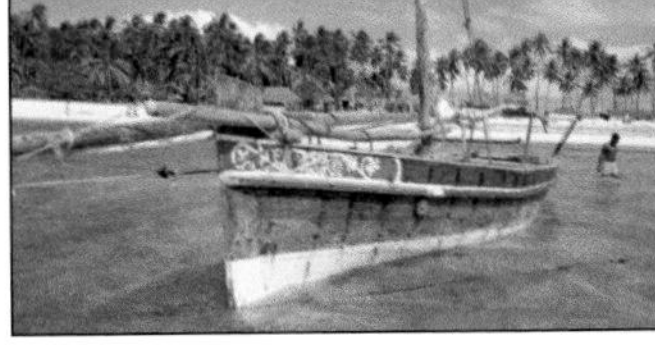

Watamu Bay Beautiful beaches on the Kenyan coast – Marine National Park with coral reefs – diving sites **Na47**

Mombasa Kenya's leading port city – historic Fort Jesus, built in the 17th century – Swahili old town **Mk48**

Remarkable Cities and Cultural monuments

- UNESCO World Cultural Heritage
- Remarkable Cities
- Pre- and early history
- Prehistoric rockscape
- Early african culture
- Places of Christian cultural interest
- Places of Islamic cultural interest
- Places of Hindu cultural interest
- Cultural landscape
- Historical city scape
- Castle/fortress/fort
- Technical/industrial monument
- Tomb/grave
- Market
- Festivals
- Museum

Sport and leisure destinations

- Golf
- Sailing
- Diving
- Wind surfing
- Beach resort
- Mineral/thermal spa
- Hill resort
- Lodge

East Africa and the eastern sections of Central Africa comprise many landscapes and geographic regions. The **Mitumba Mountain range** in western East Africa stretches over a distance of 1,200 kilometers parallel to Lake Tanganyika. In the west, the range borders the basin of the Congo River. The section of the Mitumba range south of **Lake Kivu** rises to a height of 2,600 meters and descends in elevation abruptly near the Great Rift Valley. The most remarkable geographic fe ture in this region is the East African R System, which is divided into two se tions: the Western (Albertine) and Easte (Great) Rift Valley. The Western Rift V ley contains numerous lakes includi Lake Kivu and **Lake Tanganyika**, t longest lake in Africa.

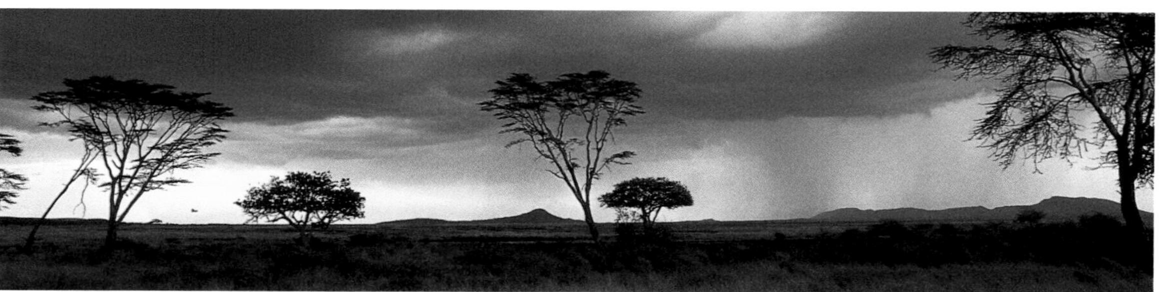

Storm clouds above the savannahs of the Serengeti in Tanzania **Mh**

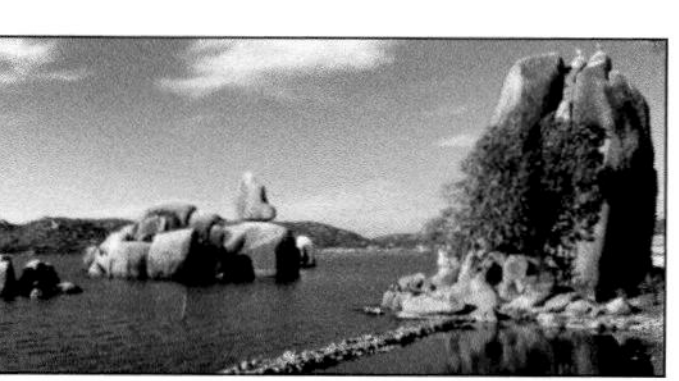

Lake Victoria The world's second largest freshwater lake (68,800 km²) – source of the White Nile River – the lake's endemic fauna is threatened by the Nile perch **Mg46/47**

Akagera National Park 2,800 km² – located in the Kagera (Akagera) River basin – buffalo and antelope populations **Mf46**

Nyungwe National Park The 970 km² large nature reserve encompasses tropical rainforests inhabited by many rare birds and endangered primates including chacma baboons (bottom photo). **Me47**

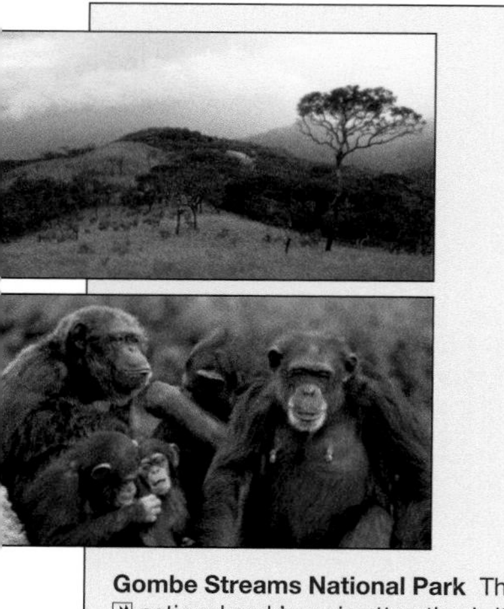

Gombe Streams National Park The national park's main attraction is its chimpanzee population, made famous by the work of Jane Goodall. Despite the creation of the nation park, the primates remain endangered. **Me48**

Rusha National Park The third largest national park in Tanzania with an area of 12,800 km² – hotels and camp sites in the park – views of Mount Kilamanjaro **Mh49**

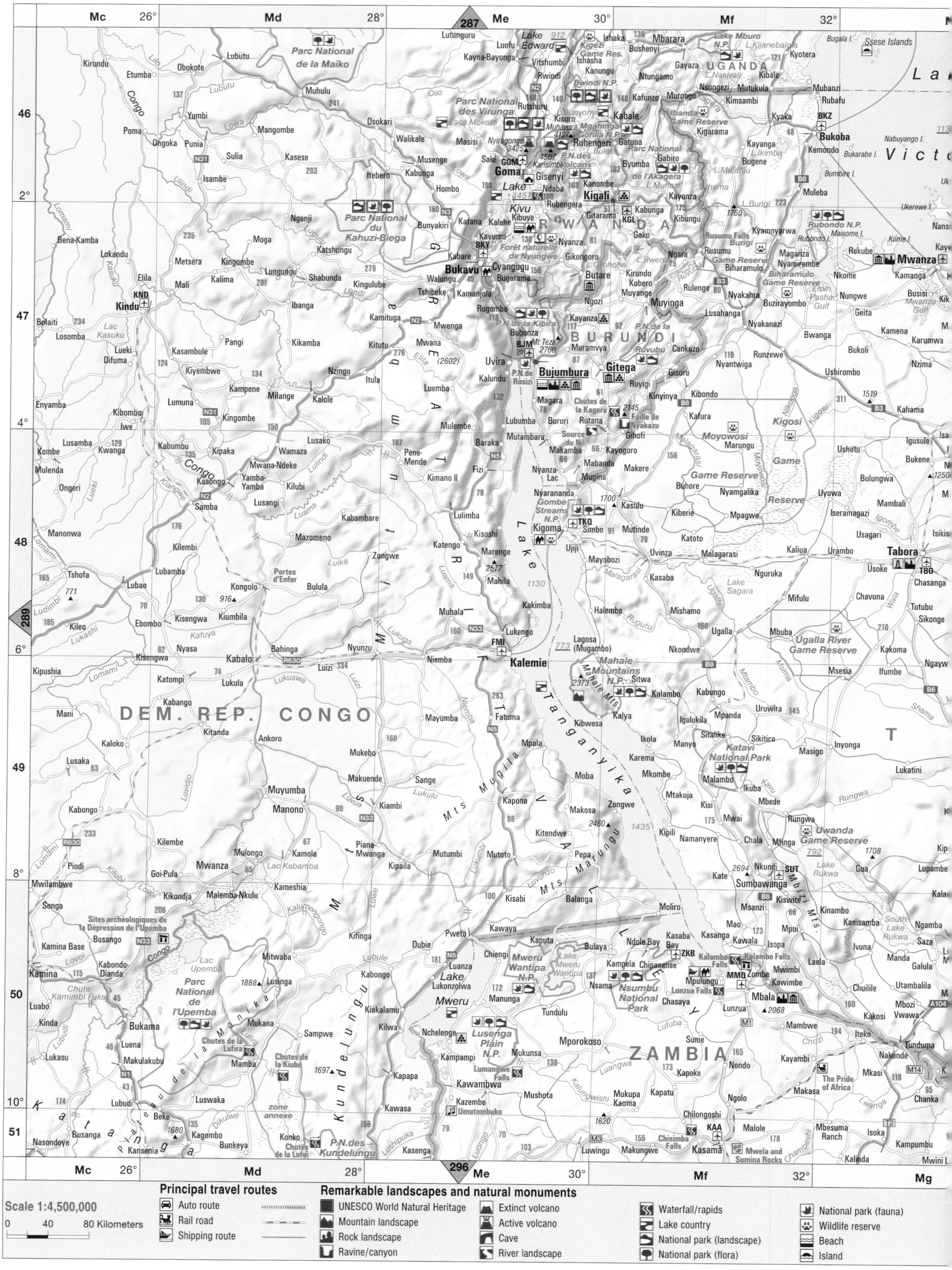

Scale 1:4,500,000
0 40 80 Kilometers

Principal travel routes
- Auto route
- Rail road
- Shipping route

Remarkable landscapes and natural monuments
- UNESCO World Natural Heritage
- Mountain landscape
- Rock landscape
- Ravine/canyon
- Extinct volcano
- Active volcano
- Cave
- River landscape
- Waterfall/rapids
- Lake country
- National park (landscape)
- National park (flora)
- National park (fauna)
- Wildlife reserve
- Beach
- Island

e mountains of the Ruwenzori and unga ranges are located to the east Lake Kinu. The mountains in both nges are covered by dense tropical nforests inhabited by endangered ountain gorillas. The foothills of the wenzori Mountains are the source of Kagera (Akagera) River, the most isoed source of the Nile River. The area tween the western and eastern secns of the East African Rift System contains a large, flat basin. Much of this basin is occupied by **Lake Victoria**, Africa's largest lake. The savannahs of Tanzania's **Serengeti National Park** are located directly south of Lake Victoria. Many large animals inhabit the park including groups of lions, elephants, buffalos, zebras, and leopards. The most interesting geographic feature in the national park is the Ngorongoro crater, which has an area of 260 km². The Great (Eastern) Rift Valley stretches through Kenya and Tanzania. Like the Western Rift, it contains a series of large lakes including Lake Natron, Lake Eyasi, and Lake Manyara. **Lake Natron**, located in northern Tanzania, contains numerous active geysers and water with high mineral content. The large volcanic mountains on the edge of the Eastern Rift have been dormant for centuries or thousands of years. One of these mountains, **Mount Kilimanjaro**, is the highest mountain in Africa with a height of 5,892 meters. Although generally considered inactive, many geologists believe molten lava continues to accumulate within Mount Kilimanjaro and that the volcano could erupt in the future.

East Africa's coastal regions consist of a narrow strip of low-lying plains. The coast has been a meeting point for African and Asian cultures for many centuries.

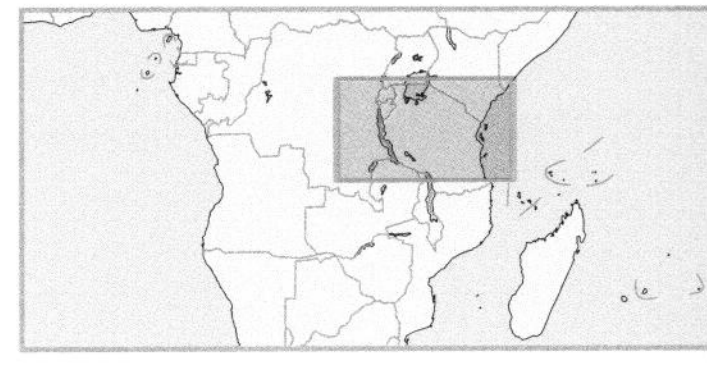

291

INDIAN OCEAN

315

297

Remarkable Cities and Cultural monuments

- UNESCO World Cultural Heritage
- Remarkable Cities
- Pre- and early history
- Prehistoric rockscape
- Early african culture
- Places of Christian cultural interest
- Historical city scape
- Castle/fortress/fort
- Technical/industrial monument
- Market
- Festivals
- Museum

Sport and leisure destinations

- Golf
- Sailing
- Diving
- Wind surfing
- Seaport
- Deep-sea fishing
- Beach resort
- Hill resort
- Lodge

Serengeti National Park 14,500 km² – incredible abundance of wildlife – UNESCO world heritage site **Mh47**

Olduvai Gorge Ngorongoro Conservation Area – archeological site containing tools created by Homo erectus hominids, the ancestors of modern humans **Mh47**

Ngorongoro Conservation Area The area around the 260 km² large Ngorongoro volcanic crater is a UNESCO world heritage site and is inhabited by large herds of gnus and zebras. The Masai people graze their cattle in the area during certain times of the year. **Mh47**

Mount Kilimanjaro Africa's tallest mountain (5,892 meters) – national park, a UNESCO world heritage site **Mj47**

Lake Manyara Mineral rich lake in the Great Rift Valley – national park inhabited by lions and a large flamingo population (photo) **Mh47**

Zanzibar UNESCO world heritage site – historic Stone Town contains traditional Swahili architecture – vibrant harbor – beaches – diving sites **Mk49**

The western and southern sections of Angola encompass two distinct geographic regions: the coastal lowlands near the Atlantic Ocean and the highlands of the Bié Plateau. The climate of the coastal lowlands is heavily influenced by ocean currents and the vast **Namib Desert** stretches along Angola's coast. The width of the Namib Desert ranges between 80 and 130 kilometers in Angola. Dense fog frequently blankets the areas directly on Angola's Atlar coast. Rainfall is extremely sparse in coastal lowlands farther away from ocean.

The fertile **Bié Plateau** is a flat elevat plateau with an average elevation 1,500 meters. The highest point on plateau is the summit of the mountair

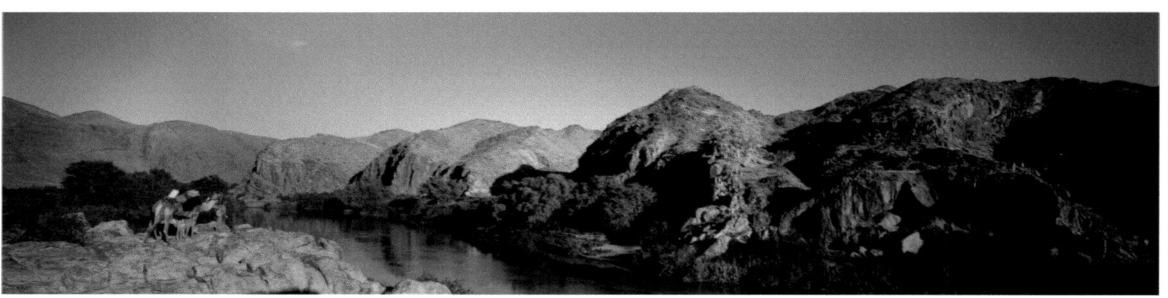

The Cunene River flows through Namibia and Angola Lg

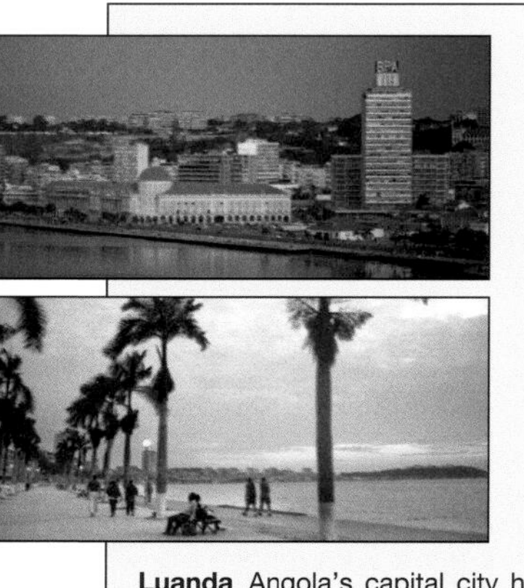

Luanda Angola's capital city has Portuguese colonial architecture, lively markets, and long sandy beaches on the Ilha de Luanda. **Lg50**

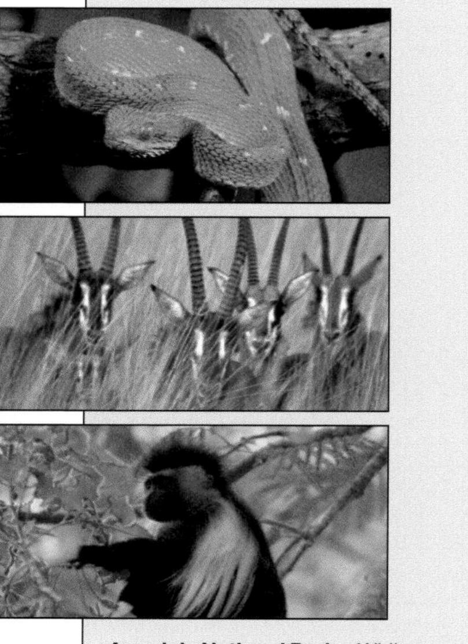

Angola's National Parks While some animals including the African bush viper (top photo) and the Angolan colobus monkey (bottom photo) continue to flourish in the country's national park, others such as the sable antelope (middle photo) remain endangered.

Epupa Falls River rapids and a 35 meter tall waterfall on the Cunene River – inhabited by the nomadic Himba people – baobabs – large crocodile population **Lg54**

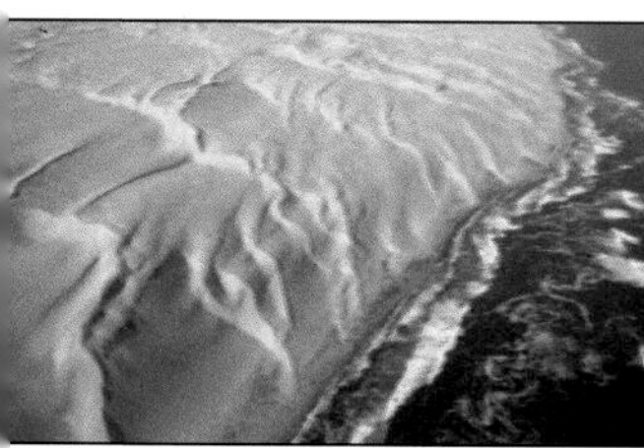

Skeleton Coast Dangerous coast stretching through Namibia and Angola – frequent fog and a large number of sandbars – numerous shipwrecks – national park **Lf54/55**

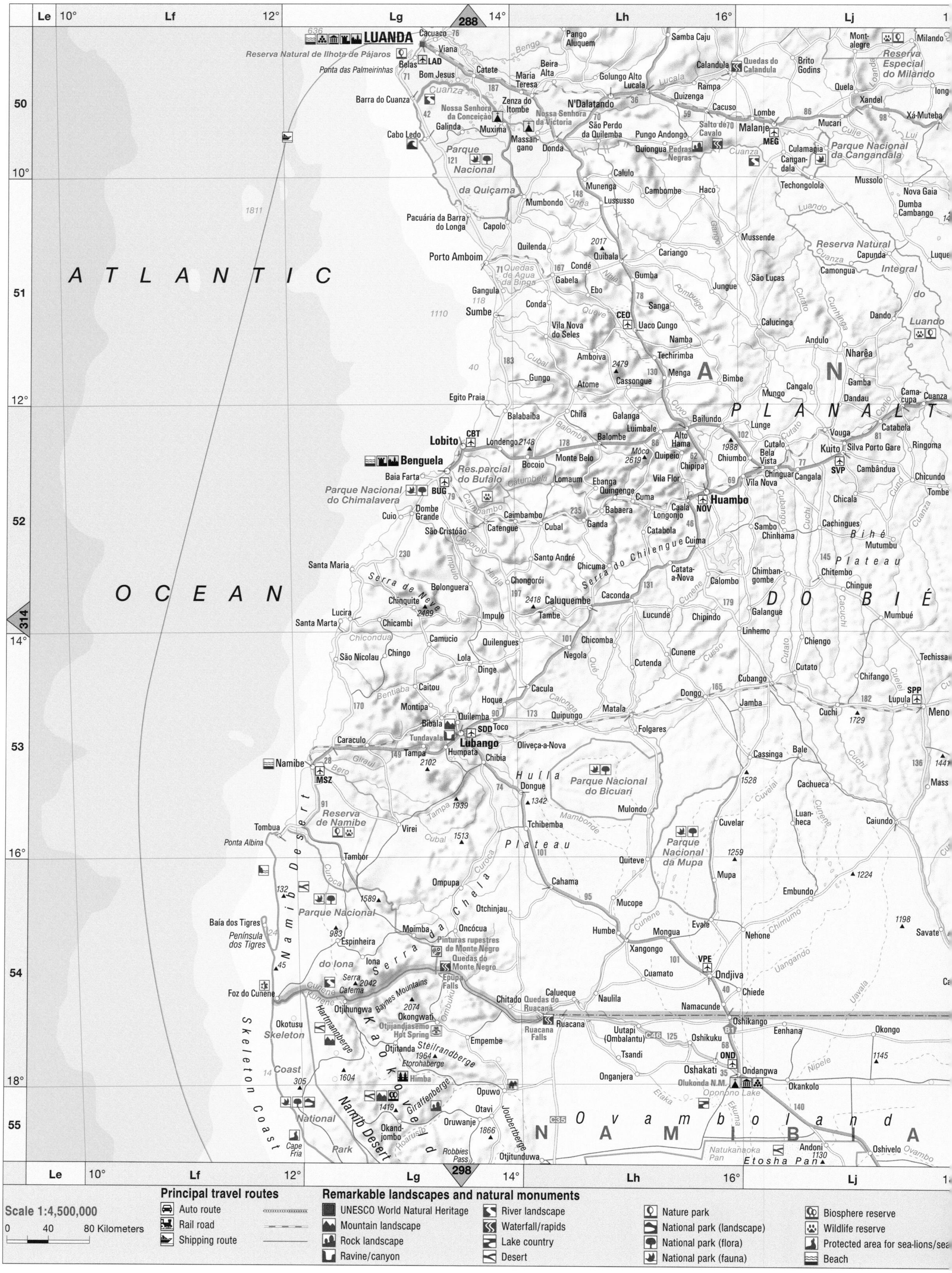

Scale 1:4,500,000

0 40 80 Kilometers

Principal travel routes

- Auto route
- Rail road
- Shipping route

Remarkable landscapes and natural monuments

- UNESCO World Natural Heritage
- Mountain landscape
- Rock landscape
- Ravine/canyon
- River landscape
- Waterfall/rapids
- Lake country
- Desert
- Nature park
- National park (landscape)
- National park (flora)
- National park (fauna)
- Biosphere reserve
- Wildlife reserve
- Protected area for sea-lions/sea
- Beach

Moco (2,619 meters). Many rivers and small streams flow through the plateau. Most of the larger rivers in the region flow south towards the Okavango River basin or north to the Cuanza (Kwanza) River and its many tributaries. The lower course of the **Cunene River** forms a long section of the border between Namibia and Angola. The Bié Plateau comprises several distinct vegetation zones including temperate savannahs in the south and tropical rainforests in the plateau's northwestern sections. Angola is rich in mineral resources – including oil, diamonds, iron ore, copper, and gold. These resources (especially oil) are the country's most valuable exports and dominate its trade with other nations. Despite the growing importance of mining, most of Angola's people work as farmers or agricultural laborers.

The **highlands of Zambia** consist primarily of dry forests and large marshlands (near the country's rivers). The country is home to abundant fauna; large herds of elephants, buffalos, and zebras inhabit Zambia's savannahs. The border region around the junction of Angola, Namibia, Zambia, and Botswana is dominated by two large rivers: the Okavango River (1,800 kilometers) rises on the Bié Plateau in Angola and the **Zambezi** (2,736 kilometers), which rises in northwestern Zambia. The Zambezi River forms the **Victoria Falls** (128 meters) when it flows over a narrow gorge near the border between Zimbabwe and Zambia.

The **Caprivi Strip** was created by colonial officials who wanted to control the route between Namibia (then a German colony) and the Zambezi River. Consisting of marshlands, the area is home to many hippopotamuses and crocodiles.

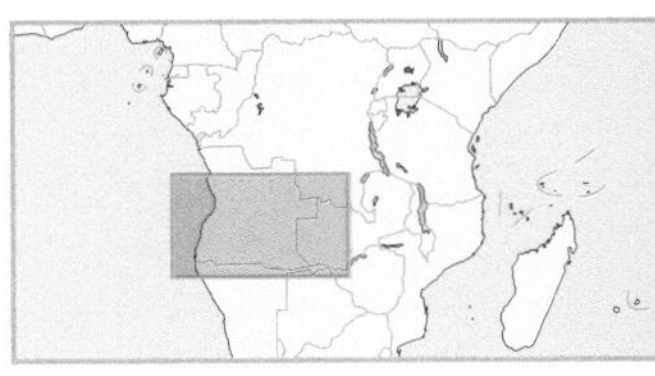

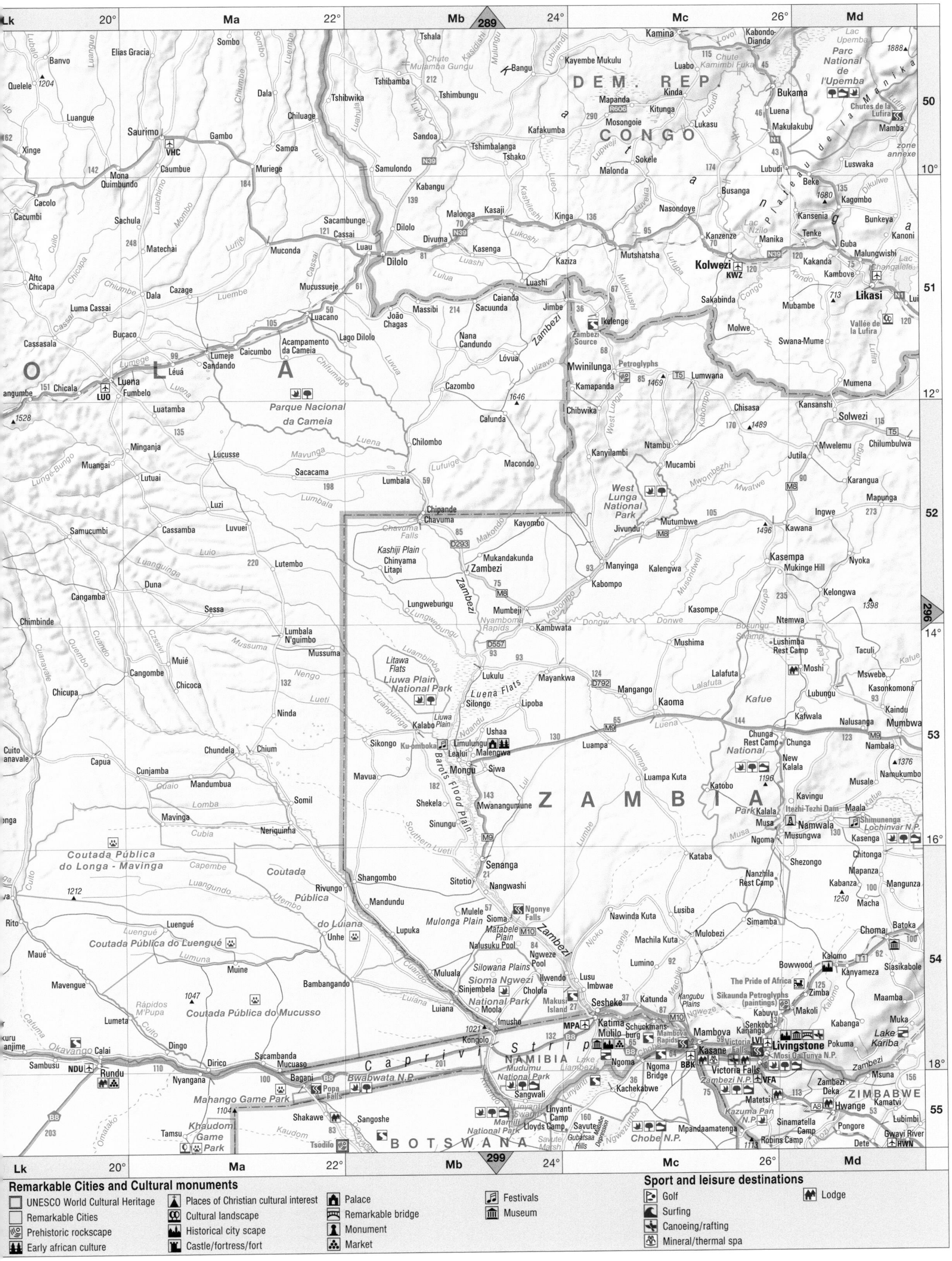

West Lunga National Park Swamps and swampy forests between the West Lunga and Kabompo Rivers – elephants, buffalos, and hippopotamuses **Mc52**

Zambezi Major river in southern Africa (2,750 kilometers) – rises in northern Zambia – several national parks in the river basin – river boat tours **MbMc54**

Victoria Falls The waterfalls, a UNESCO world heritage site, are situated on the border between Zimbabwe and Zambia. Victoria Falls drop more than 100 meters off the side of a long narrow gorge. **Mc54**

Kwando River The river rises on the Bié Plateau in Angola and flows through the Caprivi Strip – Mudumu National Park – crocodiles and hippopotamuses **Mb55**

Okavango River The Okavango rises in Angola and flows over a distance of 1,800 kilometers to a large inland delta in the Kalahari Desert – ancient San rock paintings in the Tsodilo Hills **LkMa54/55**

Remarkable Cities and Cultural monuments

- UNESCO World Cultural Heritage
- Remarkable Cities
- Prehistoric rockscape
- Early african culture
- Places of Christian cultural interest
- Cultural landscape
- Historical city scape
- Castle/fortress/fort
- Palace
- Remarkable bridge
- Monument
- Market
- Festivals
- Museum

Sport and leisure destinations

- Golf
- Surfing
- Canoeing/rafting
- Mineral/thermal spa
- Lodge

Eastern Zambia, Malawi, Northern Mozambique

The majority of Zambia's territory is covered by dense tropical forests. Two major rivers rise in the country: the **Zambezi River** rises in northern Zambia and the **Luapula River**, which rises in the **Bangweulu Swamps**. The Zambezi (2,736 kilometers) forms a long section of the border between Zambia and Zimbabwe. Zambia contains around 45 percent of southern Africa's freshwater reserves. The banks of the Zambezi and

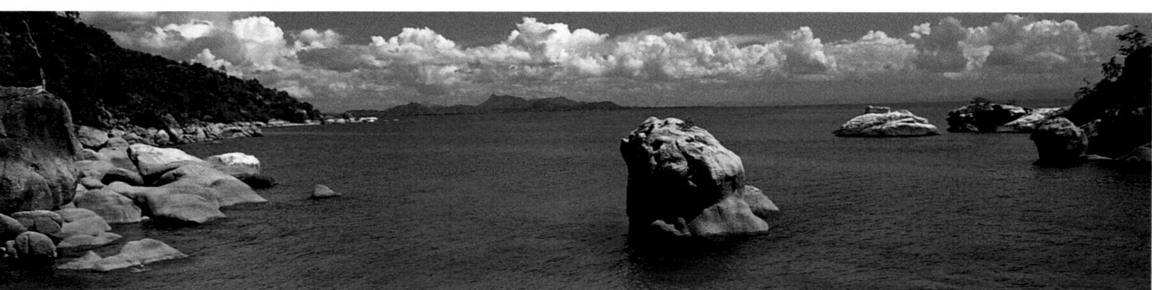

its major tributaries contain large swam py areas. Zambia's vast tropical forest are home to many endangered animal including elephants and chimpanzees The country's government has create several national parks in the recen decades in an effort to protect loca wildlife. Along Zambia's northern borde

Lake Malawi has a wealth of unique flora and fauna **MgMh50/5**

Chimfunshi Chimpanzee Sanctuary Africa's largest wildlife orphanage rescues injured and orphaned chimpanzees **Md52**

South Luangwa National Park (Zambia, 9,050 km²) – lions, elephants, giraffes, and leopards **Mf52**

Kafue National Park (Zambia, 22,400 km²) – large forests – endangered elephant population – antelopes (photo) **McMd53**

Cabora Bassa Dam Major dam on the Zambezi River – 200-kilometer-long reservoir – important source of electricity for Mozambique **MfMg53**

Mana Pools National Park The park, a UNESCO world heritage site, is located in the Zambezi River basin. During the dry season, the area teems with wildlife including Nile crocodiles (bottom photo) and rare white rhinoceroses (top photo). **Me53/54**

Lake Kariba Large reservoir created by the Kariba Dam on the Zambezi River – recreation facilities **MdMe54**

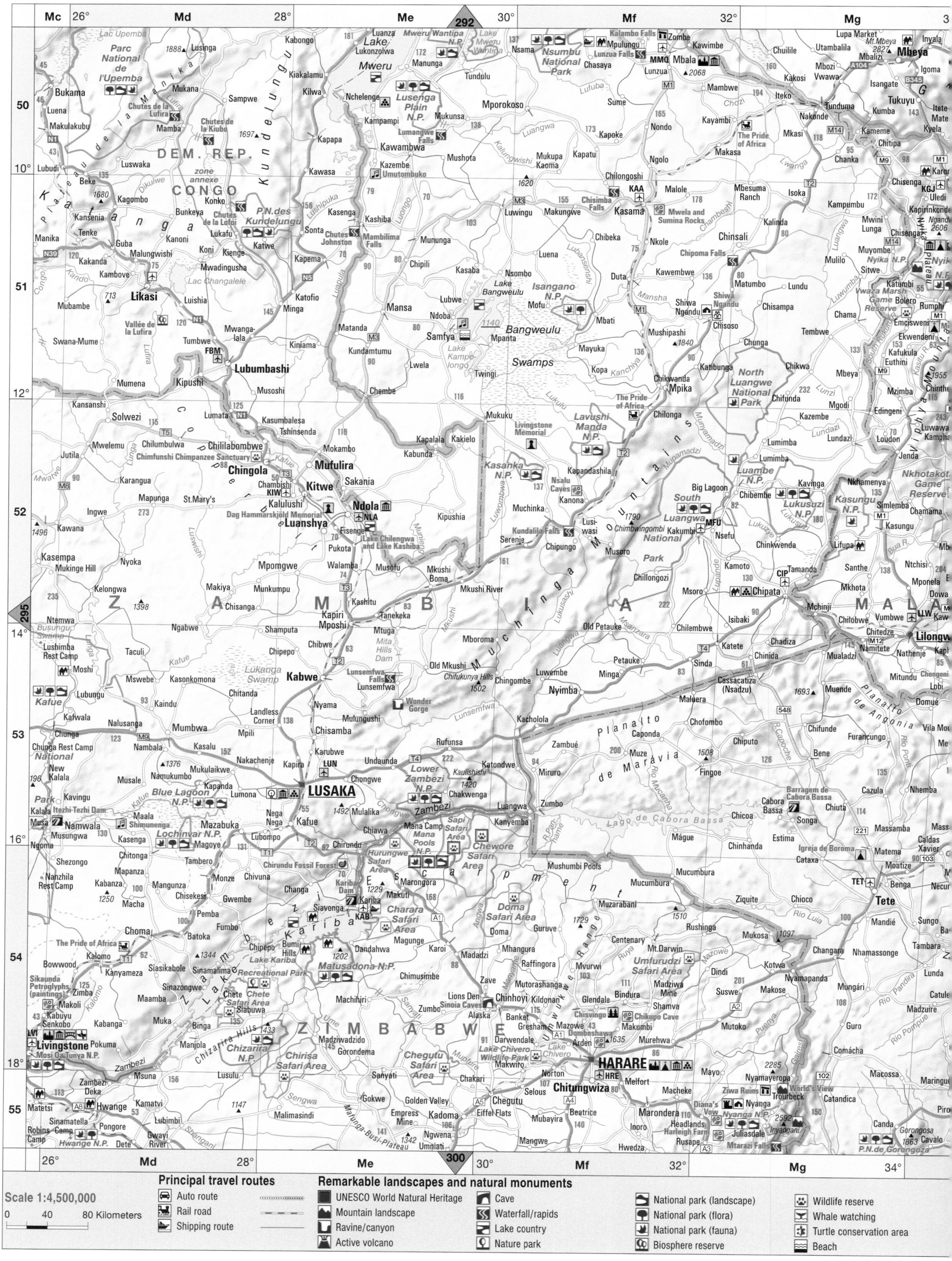

Scale 1:4,500,000
0 40 80 Kilometers

Principal travel routes
- Auto route
- Rail road
- Shipping route

Remarkable landscapes and natural monuments
- UNESCO World Natural Heritage
- Mountain landscape
- Ravine/canyon
- Active volcano
- Cave
- Waterfall/rapids
- Lake country
- Nature park
- National park (landscape)
- National park (flora)
- National park (fauna)
- Biosphere reserve
- Wildlife reserve
- Whale watching
- Turtle conservation area
- Beach

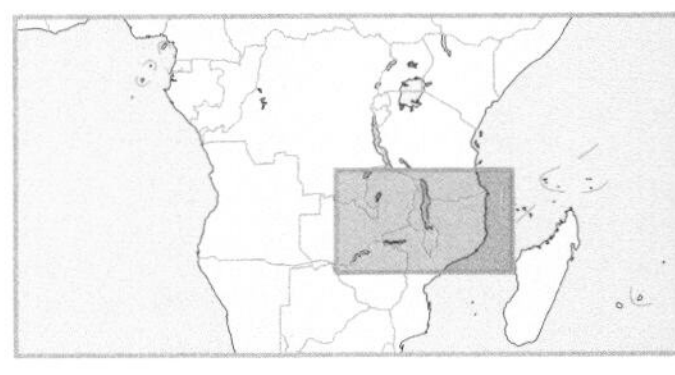

ith the Democratic Republic of Congo es the so-called **"copper belt"** – a region with abundant mineral resources. he **Muchinga Mountains** (1,840 eters), in northeastern Zambia, form e largest mountain range in the country. **Lake Malawi**, also widely known as ake Nyasa, is located in the southern ection of the **Great Rift Valley**, which tretches from north to south through ost of Malawi. Africa's third largest lake has a total length of 600 kilometers from north to south and 90 km from east to west. More than 1,000 endemic fish species inhabit the lake, including around 500 species of perch. The lake is surrounded by a series of highlands: Viphya Highlands, Livingstone Mountains, and Nyika Plateau.

Mozambique borders Malawi, Zambia, Zimbabwe, and South Africa in the west; and the Indian Ocean in the east. The northern half of Mozambique is a flat region with an average elevation of 1,000 meters above sea level and abundant rainfall. Several isolated highland areas are scattered throughout northern Mozambique. In general, the region's elevation rises gradually from east to west. Mount Namuli, the tallest mountain in Northern Mozambique, rises 2,420 meters. Vast tropical forests once covered large sections of northern Mozambique. Most of the remaining tropical rainforests in the country are located in the far north around Lake Malawi.

Northern Mozambique has a **rocky coastline** with many steep cliffs. Numerous small islands and long coral reefs are situated directly off the coast. Many of the islands near the coast are home to abundant animal life and beautiful, isolated beaches.

Lake Malawi National Park UNESCO world heritage site – abundant marine life – cormorants and egrets – (photo) Monkey Bay **Mh53**

Liwonde National Park Located in the Shire River basin – the local wildlife is threatened by poaching – large lion and elephant populations **Mh53**

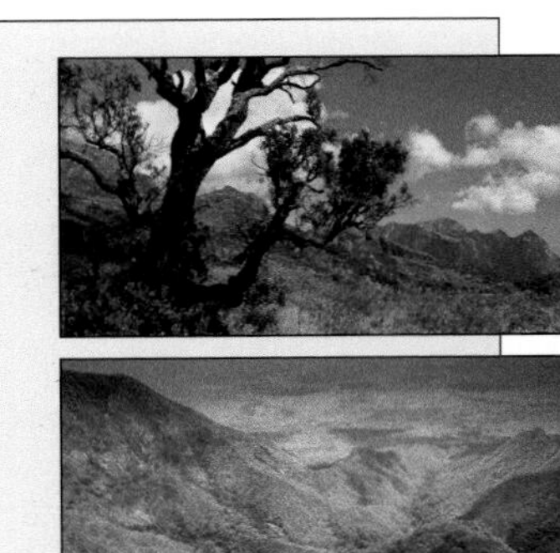

Mulanje Mountains The mountain Sapitwa (3,001 meters) in southeastern Malawi is the highest mountain in the range (top photo) and the country. Tropical rainforests cover large sections of the mountains and their foothills, while other sections are covered by shrubs and grass. The area features extensive hiking trails. **Mh53**

Ilha do Ibo Island in the Quirimbas Archipelago – Portuguese fort – sandy beaches – large coral reefs off the coast – sea turtles **Na52**

Ilha de Moçambique UNESCO world heritage site – former capital of Portuguese East Africa – Fort Sao Sebastiao – mosques – churches **Na53**

Gurué Highland region in Mozambique – Monte Namuli (2,240 meters) – tea plantations (photo) **Mj53**

Remarkable Cities and Cultural monuments

UNESCO World Cultural Heritage
Remarkable Cities
Pre- and early history
Prehistoric rockscape
Early african culture
Places of Christian cultural interest
Places of Islamic cultural interest
Cultural landscape
Historical city scape
Castle/fortress/fort
Dam
Remarkable bridge
Monument
Market
Festivals
Museum

Sport and leisure destinations

Diving
Wind surfing
Canoeing/rafting
Seaport
Beach resort
Mineral/thermal spa
Amusement/theme park
Lodge

Botswana and **Namibia** consist mostly of semi-arid and arid regions such as the **Kalahari Desert**. The **Namib Desert** stretches over 1,500 kilometers along the southwestern coast of Africa. It is generally considered one of the most barren and inhospitable deserts in the world. The Namib contains no large oases or significant bodies of water. The desert does however contain several **dry watercourses** that occasionally carry water through the desert after periods of heav rainfall in Namibia's highlands.

The **Sossusvlei** area in the Nam Desert contains the tallest sand dunes the world. Some of the sand dunes in th area are more than 300 meters tall. Nam bia's Atlantic coast features many lor sand dunes and the waters directly off th

The Caprivi Strip: a sparsely populated wilderness in Namibia **Mb5**

Kaokoveld Mountainous region in northwestern Namibia – homelands of the Himba people (photo) – deep mountain valleys – elephants **Lg54/55**

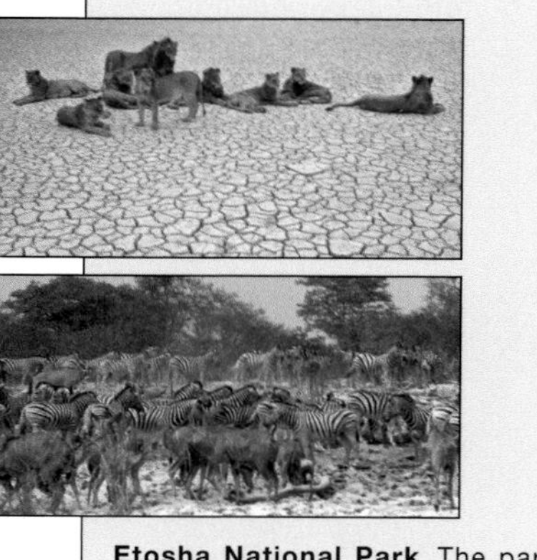

Etosha National Park The park (22,000 km²) encompasses the large Etosha saltpan and is home to many large wild animals. Guided tours provide visitors the chance to see lions (top photo), antelopes, zebras, gnus (bottom photos) and other animals up close. **LhLj55**

Spitzkoppe The "Matterhorn" of Namibia – granite formation in southern Damaraland – ancient San rock paintings – popular destination for rock-climbers **Lh56**

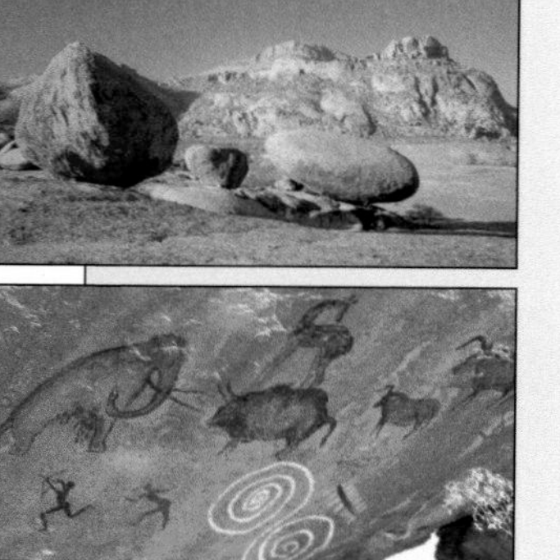

Erongo Mountains The mountain range between the Namib Desert and Namibia's Central Highlands features many unusual eroded stone formations (top photo). Ancient rock paintings found in the area suggest the region was once considerably more fertile than it currently is. **Lh56**

Namib-Naukluft Park Protected desert wilderness – Naukluft Mountains – sand dunes in Sossusvlei (photo) **Lh57/59**

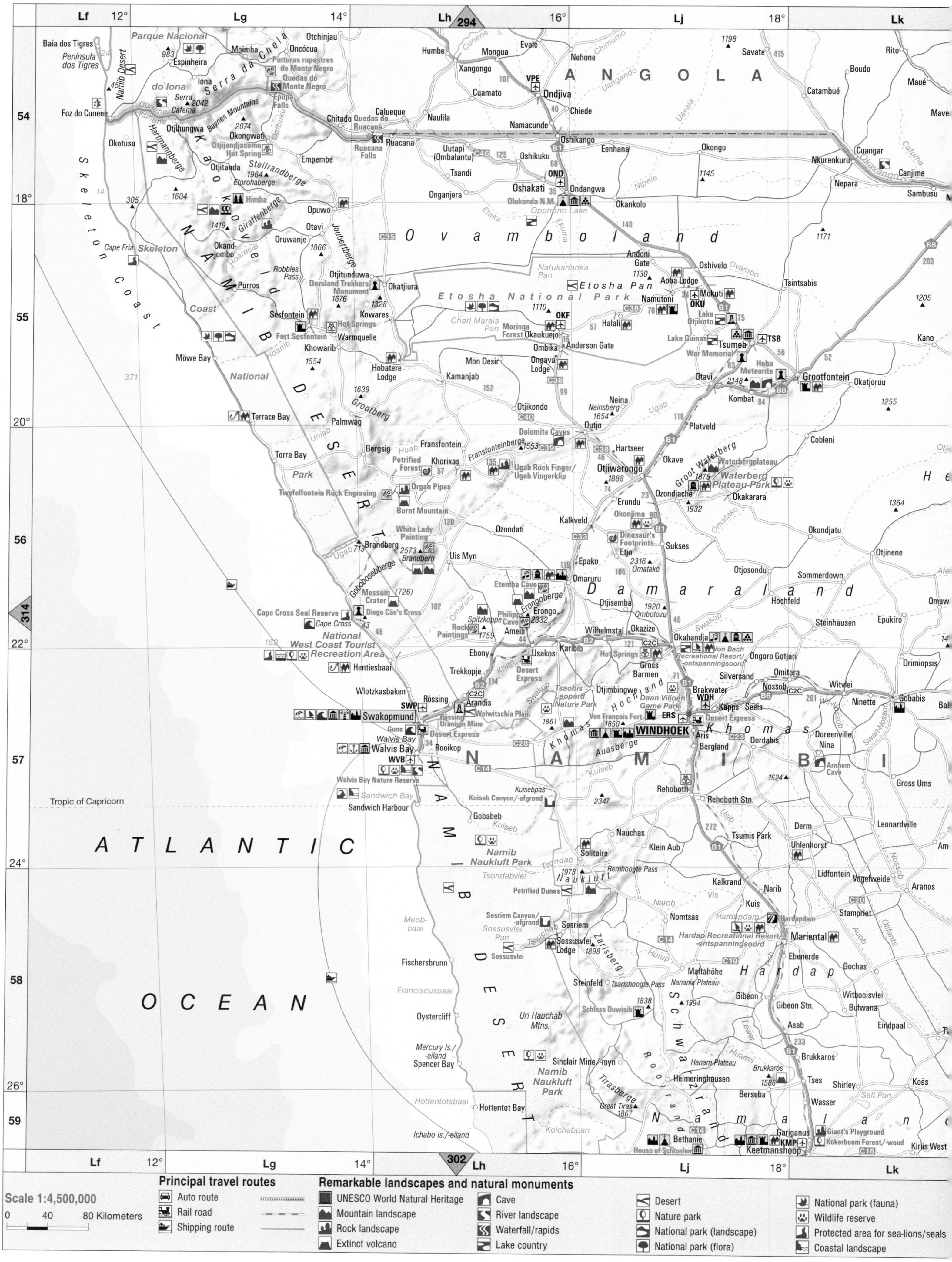

Scale 1:4,500,000
0 40 80 Kilometers

Principal travel routes
- Auto route
- Rail road
- Shipping route

Remarkable landscapes and natural monuments
- UNESCO World Natural Heritage
- Mountain landscape
- Rock landscape
- Extinct volcano
- Cave
- River landscape
- Waterfall/rapids
- Lake country
- Desert
- Nature park
- National park (landscape)
- National park (flora)
- National park (fauna)
- Wildlife reserve
- Protected area for sea-lions/seals
- Coastal landscape

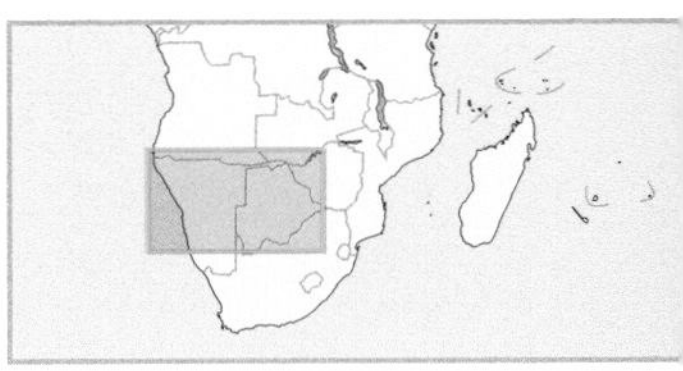

›ast contain countless small sand bars. ›amibia's northern coast is known as ›e "Skeleton Coast" because the large ›umber of sandbars and dense fog once ›d to frequent shipwrecks in the area. ›e Kalahari Desert is significantly more ›rtile and hospitable than the Namib. ›e region's desert plants survive in the ›id climate by storing water collected ›ring the rainy season. ›ocated in Botswana, the **Okavango River** delta is the largest inland river delta in the world. During much of the year, water from the Okavango turns this section of the Kalahari Desert into a fertile wetland with small islands and swamps. Both the Okavango delta and the areas surrounding it are home to abundant flora and fauna. Large sections of the Okavango delta have been declared conservation areas by the governments of Namibia and Botswana.

Namibia's Central Highlands stretch through much of the country's interior between the Namib Desert and the arid plains of eastern Namibia. The region consists of ancient, craggy mountains. The southern section of the highlands is particularly arid and rainfall is extremely sparse in the area. The northern sections of the highlands get moderate rainfall and the area is heavily cultivated.

Namibia is one of the most sparsely populated countries in the world with a population of less than two million. The country's economy is dominated by the export of natural resources, such as diamonds and uranium. Namibia's neighbor, **Botswana**, is also a sparsely populated nation with valuable natural resources. Botswana also has a long history of impressive economic growth and political stability.

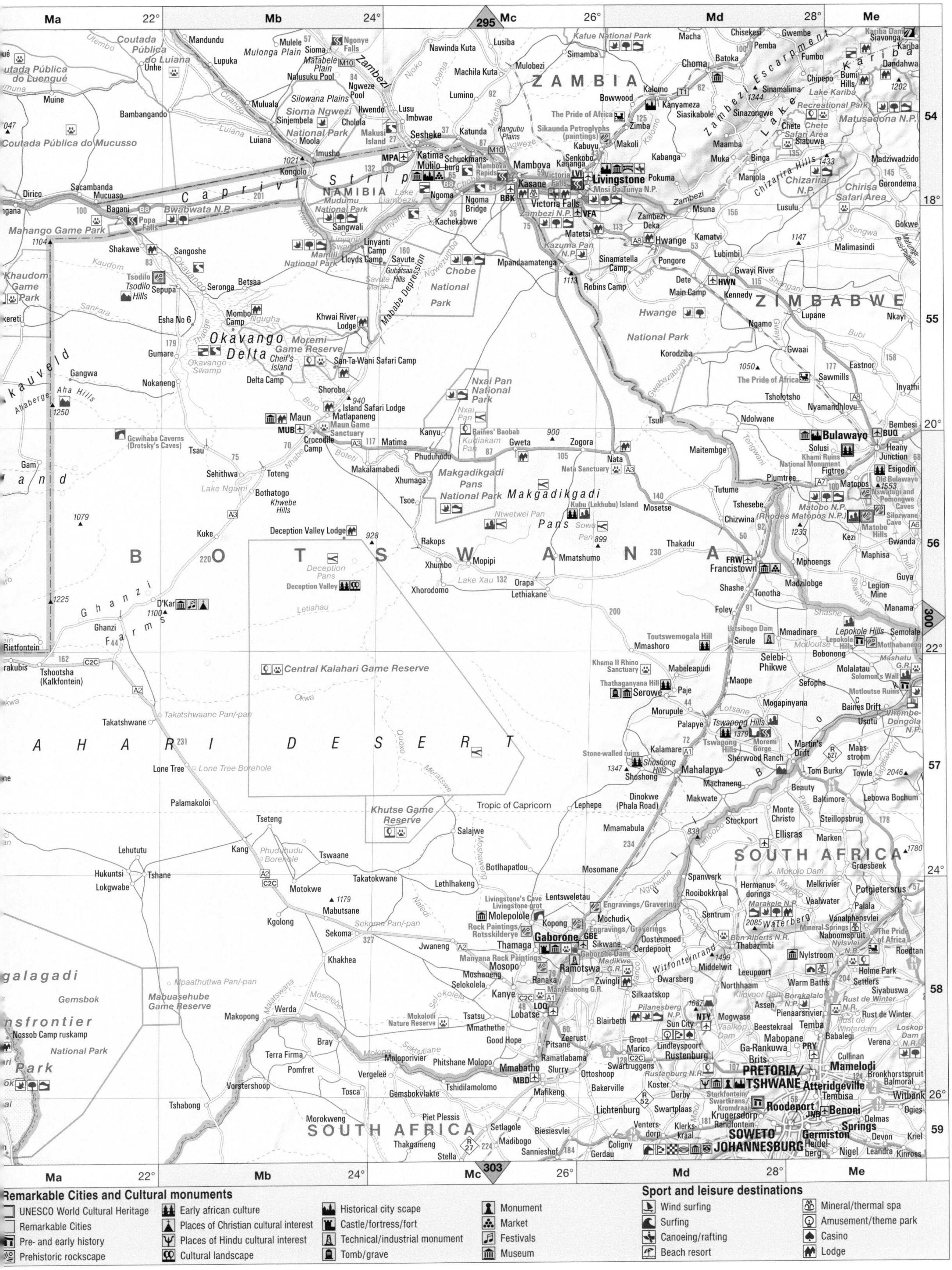

Chobe National Park National Park along the Chobe River in Botswana – home to large elephant herds **Mc55**

Okavango Delta The UNESCO world heritage site comprises the world's largest inland delta. During the rainy season, the Okavango River floods large sections of the Kalahari Desert (top photo). The delicate ecosystem in the delta supports a diverse collection of plants (middle photo) and wild animals (bottom photo). **Mb55**

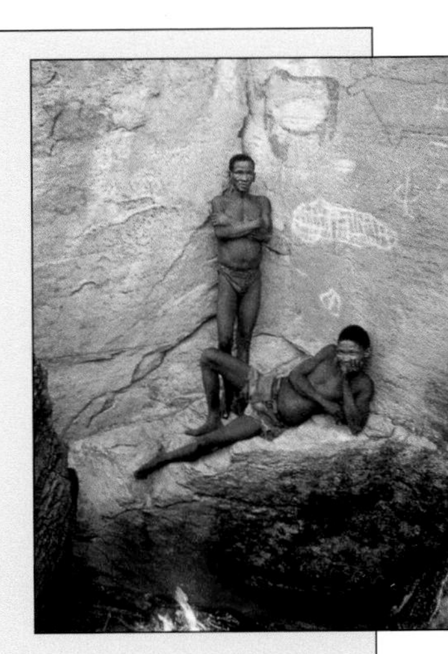

The San, also known as Bushmen, have inhabited southern Africa longer than any other group. Over time, the San have been pushed into the less fertile areas of the region. Most of the San in Nambia and Botswana have abandoned their traditional nomadic hunter-gatherer lifestyles.

Remarkable Cities and Cultural monuments

- UNESCO World Cultural Heritage
- Remarkable Cities
- Pre- and early history
- Prehistoric rockscape
- Early african culture
- Places of Christian cultural interest
- Places of Hindu cultural interest
- Cultural landscape
- Historical city scape
- Castle/fortress/fort
- Technical/industrial monument
- Tomb/grave
- Monument
- Market
- Festivals
- Museum

Sport and leisure destinations

- Wind surfing
- Surfing
- Canoeing/rafting
- Beach resort
- Mineral/thermal spa
- Amusement/theme park
- Casino
- Lodge

Eastern Zimbabwe, Southern Mozambique

The beautiful mountainous landscapes of eastern Zimbabwe and northern South Africa with their abundant wildlife are a major contrast to the coastal lowlands of Mozambique. The variety of **Zimbabwe's** landscapes range from the barren arid sections of the Kalahari Basin in the west to the mountainous regions covered by dense tropical vegetation in the country's east. The highlands of central and eastern Zimbabwe, like the highlands on the other side of the **Limpo[po] River** in South Africa, consist of ancie[nt] mountain ranges. Zimbabwe's talle[st] mountain, **Inyangani**, rises 2,5[..] meters above sea level in the border r[e]gion near Mozambique. The area of fo[r]ested savannahs along the Limpo[po] River between South Africa and Zi[mbabwe]

A pristine forest in the Umfurudzi Safa[ri] Area (Zimbabwe) **Mf[54]**

Domboshawa Area in Zimbabwe with ancient cave paintings – holy site for several local communities **Mf54**

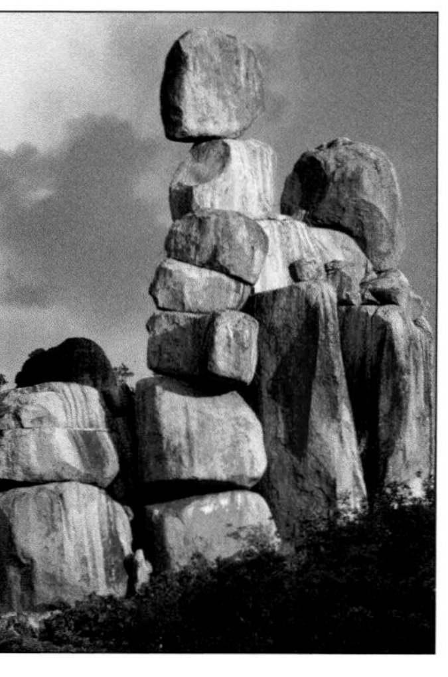

Matobo National Park Nature reserve in Zimbabwe with many ancient stone formations and rock paintings – UNESCO world heritage site **Me56**

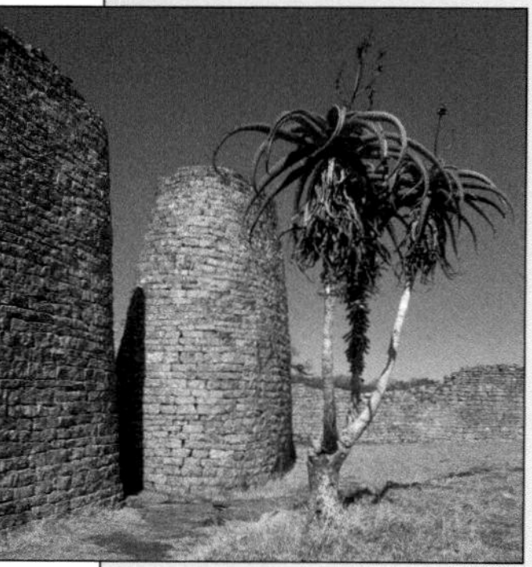

Great Zimbabwe (UNESCO world heritage site) Historic ruins of a powerful African kingdom that flourished between the 12th and 15th centuries. Great Zimbabwe was once home to 20,000 people. The ruins constitute one of sub-Saharan Africa's greatest archeological sites. **Mf56**

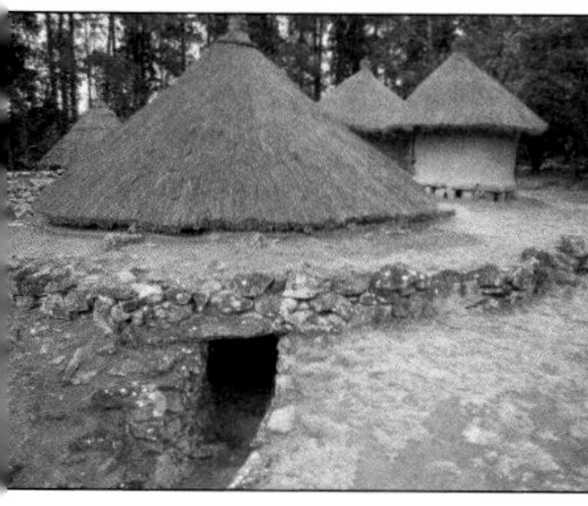

Nyanga National Park Mountainous region in Zimbabwe with tropical forests and several waterfalls – Remains of abandoned settlements built in the 17th and 18th centuries – Rhodes Museum **Mg55**

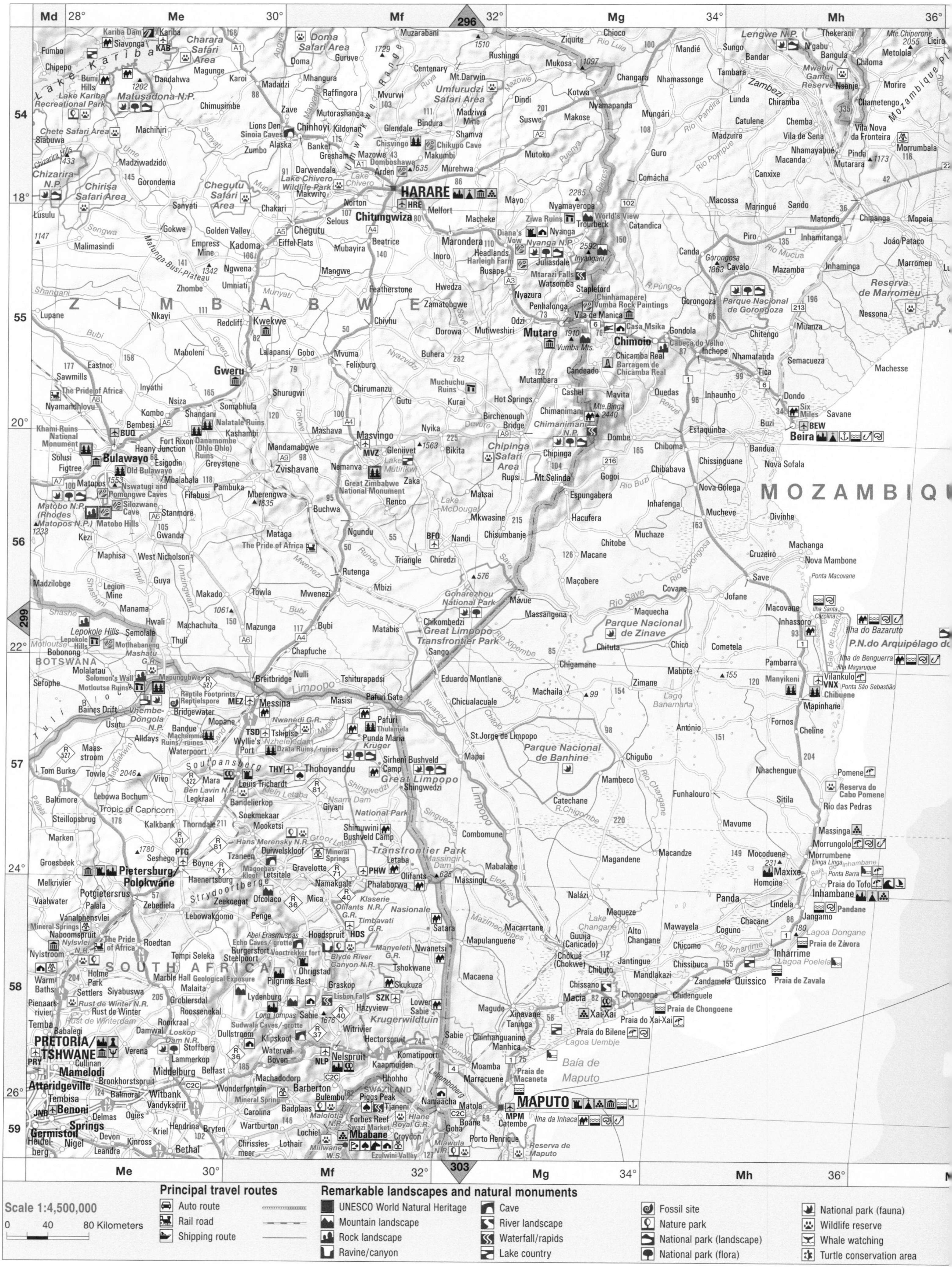

Scale 1:4,500,000
0 40 80 Kilometers

Principal travel routes
- Auto route
- Rail road
- Shipping route

Remarkable landscapes and natural monuments
- UNESCO World Natural Heritage
- Mountain landscape
- Rock landscape
- Ravine/canyon
- Cave
- River landscape
- Waterfall/rapids
- Lake country
- Fossil site
- Nature park
- National park (landscape)
- National park (flora)
- National park (fauna)
- Wildlife reserve
- Whale watching
- Turtle conservation area

abwe is known as the **lowveld**. The re-
on is home to many wild animals and
ncompasses several nature reserves
cluding Matusadona National Park in
mbabwe. The **Great Dyke**, a long series
hills and ridges, stretches through
orthwest Zimbabwe around 60 kilo-
eters west of the capital Harare. The
ncient geological formation consists of
recambrian-era stone containing an
oundance of natural resources.

Mozambique has a total area of 812,379 km² and around 17 million inhabitants. In contrast to neighboring Zimbabwe, only the northern and western sections of Mozambique are mountainous. Most of the country consists of low-lying plains crossed by several major rivers, including the **Zambezi** and **Limpopo Rivers**. Most of Mozambique's regions have tropical or subtropical climates with abundant rainfall. The only significant exceptions are the country's northern highlands which have more temperate climates because of their relatively high elevations. The **Great Limpopo Transfrontier Park** (30,000 km²) is a multi-national nature reserve created to protect the threatened flora and fauna in the border region between Zimbabwe, Mozambique, and South Africa. The western section of the park, created in 2002, encompasses South Africa's famous **Kruger National Park**. Mozambique's Indian Ocean coast is also home to several nature reserves, created in recent decades to protect the area's biodiversity on land and in the waters off the coast. Across the **Mozambique Channel**, the coast areas of **Madagascar** are inhabited by many rare and endangered animals. The waters around Madagascar contain large coral reefs with fascinating marine life.

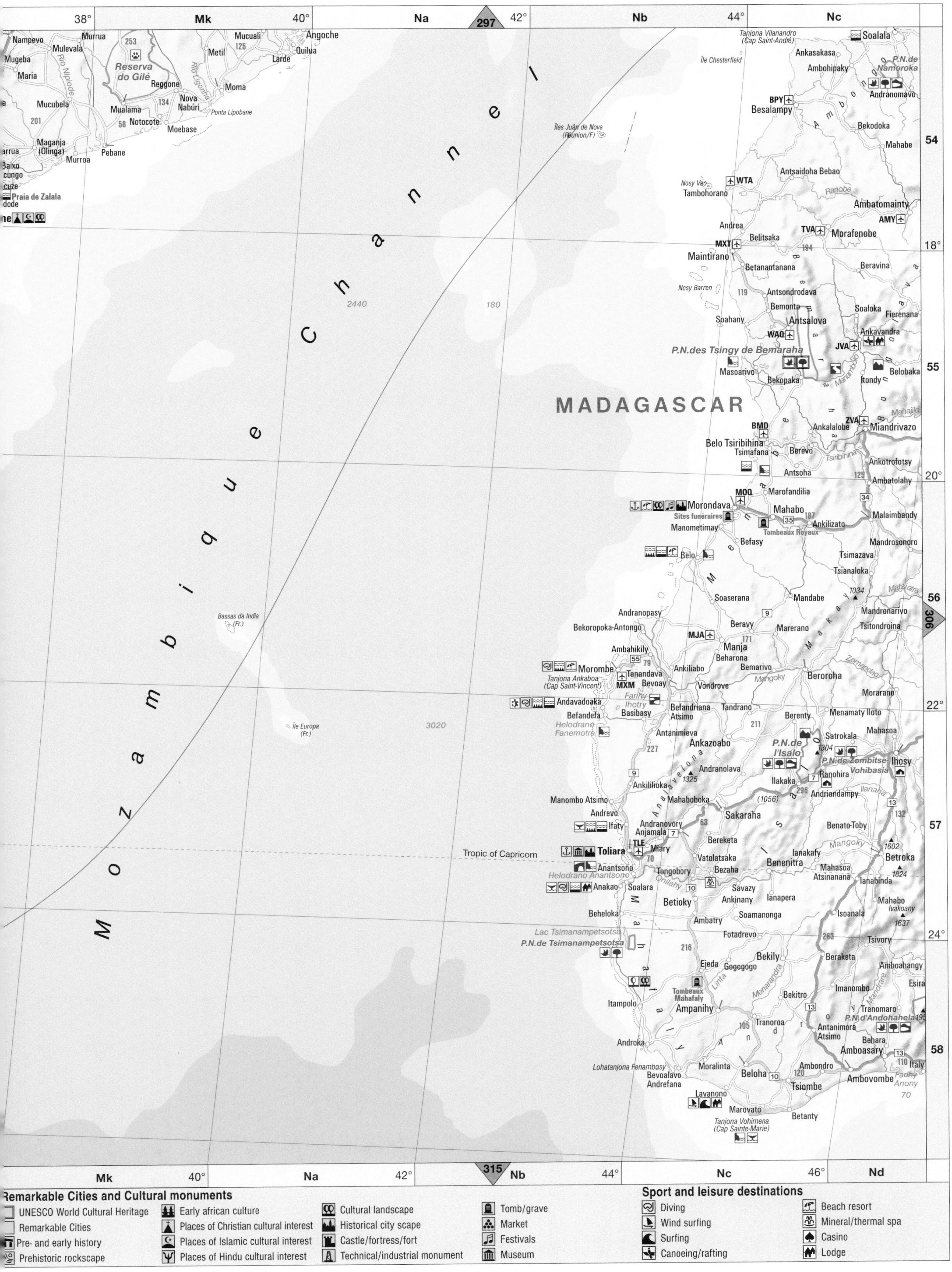

Kruger National Park The South African park (20,000 km²) was founded in 1898. More than 150 mammals inhabit the park including leopards (top photo), giraffes (middle photo), and buffalo (bottom photo). The Great Limpopo Transfrontier Park (36,000 km²), founded in 2002, encompasses Kruger National Park and areas in Zimbabwe and Mozambique. **Mf57/58**

Blyde River Canyon South African canyon – 26 kilometers long and 800 meters deep – the three rondavels **Mf58**

Swaziland The kingdom of Swaziland is a mountainous country with a total area of 17,363 km². Swaziland maintained at least nominal independence through centuries of European colonization in southern Africa. Ethnic Swazis form the overwhelming majority of the population and the king holds supreme power over the country's government. **Mf58/59**

Maputo Mozambique's capital city – Portuguese colonial architecture and art nouveau train station designed by Gustave Eiffel – lively markets – modern art museum – vibrant cultural scene **Mg58**

MADAGASCAR

Mozambique Channel

Remarkable Cities and Cultural monuments
- UNESCO World Cultural Heritage
- Remarkable Cities
- Pre- and early history
- Prehistoric rockscape
- Early african culture
- Places of Christian cultural interest
- Places of Islamic cultural interest
- Places of Hindu cultural interest
- Cultural landscape
- Historical city scape
- Castle/fortress/fort
- Technical/industrial monument
- Tomb/grave
- Market
- Festivals
- Museum

Sport and leisure destinations
- Diving
- Wind surfing
- Surfing
- Canoeing/rafting
- Beach resort
- Mineral/thermal spa
- Casino
- Lodge

South Africa, Lesotho, Swaziland

With a population exceeding 40 million and a total area of 1.2 million km², the Republic of South Africa is one of the largest and most populous countries in sub-Saharan Africa. Together with Namibia and the kingdoms Lesotho and Swaziland, South Africa comprises a region with an amazing diversity of landscapes and topographies. The region encompasses semi-arid areas in the Karoo and the Namib Desert, subtropical forests near the Indian Ocean coast, and t craggy mountains of the Drakensbe Range, a section of southern Africa Great Escarpment. The many natior parks and nature reserves in sout ern Africa are refuges for many of t region's animals, some of which a threatened by extinction. Kruger Natior

Southern Africa's arid regions feature beautiful and unique vegetation

Fish River Canyon National Park 161-kilometer-long and 550 meter deep canyon – largest canyon system in Africa **Lj59**

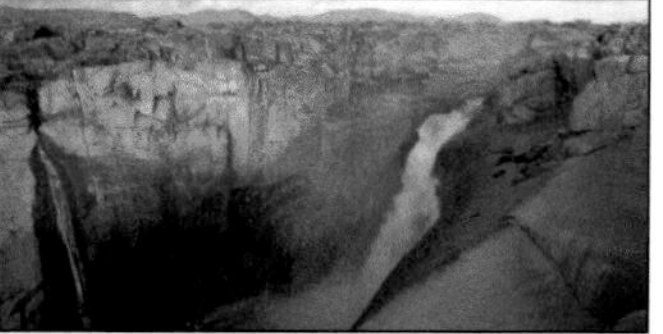

Augrabies National Park Stunning waterfalls and stone formations – Oranje River – antelope, leopard, and rhinoceros populations **Ma60**

West-Coast-Nationalpark Beautiful conservation area around a lagoon near the village of Langebaan – a diverse collection of birds inhabit the area **Lk62**

Cape Town South Africa's most beautiful city is located on a peninsula between the Indian and Atlantic Oceans. The city has become one of Africa's most visited destinations since the end of apartheid. Cape Town's historic district and modern business center (top photo) are situated at the foot of Table Mountain. The surrounding areas feature spectacular landscapes (bottom photo). **Lk62/63**

Little Karoo Semi-arid region near the Swart Mountains – ostrich farms – numerous vineyards **Ma62**

Garden Route Beautiful landscapes along South Africa's southern coast – sandy beaches (photo) **Mb63**

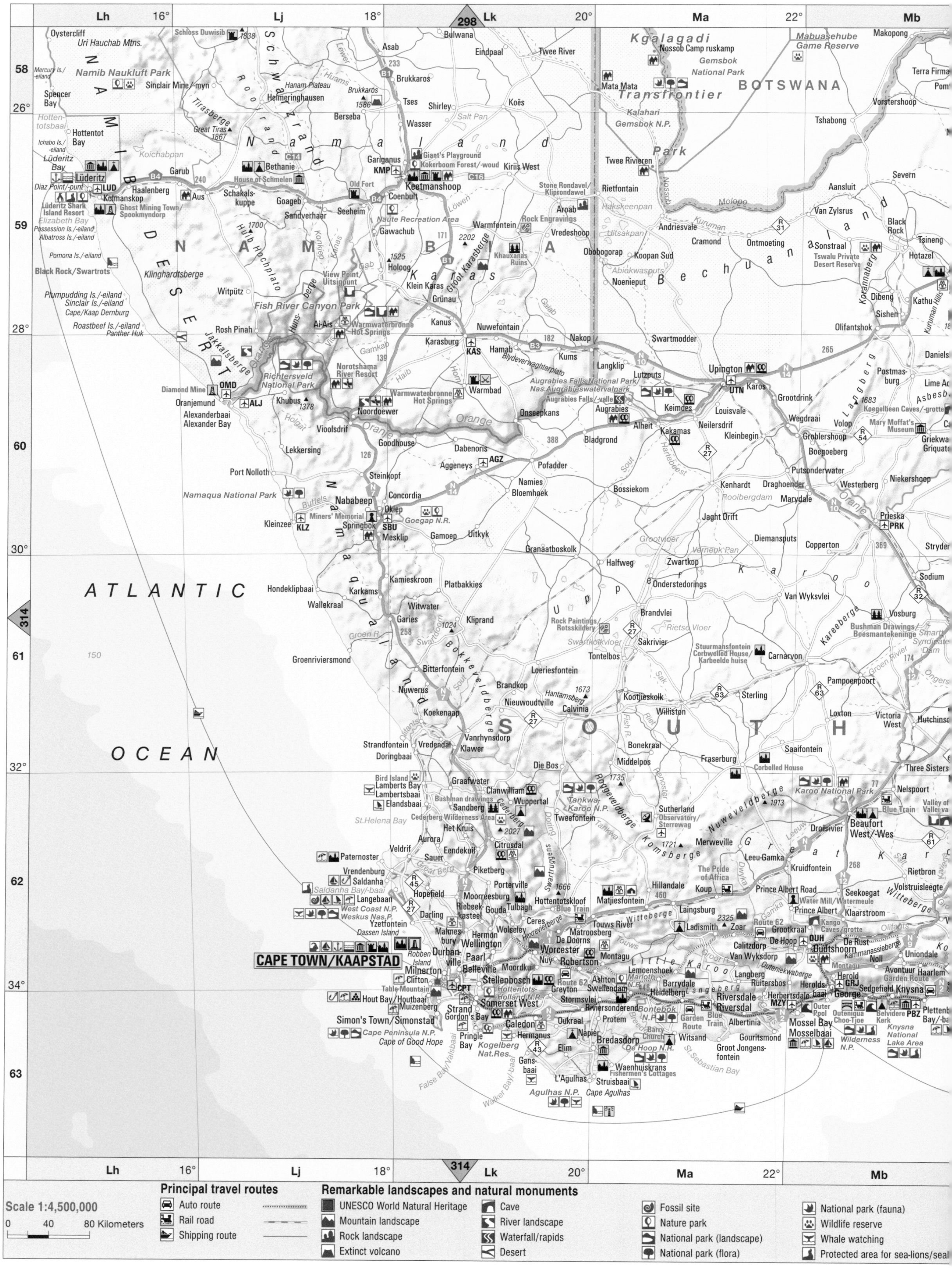

Scale 1:4,500,000
0 40 80 Kilometers

Principal travel routes
- Auto route
- Rail road
- Shipping route

Remarkable landscapes and natural monuments
- UNESCO World Natural Heritage
- Mountain landscape
- Rock landscape
- Extinct volcano
- Cave
- River landscape
- Waterfall/rapids
- Desert
- Fossil site
- Nature park
- National park (landscape)
- National park (flora)
- National park (fauna)
- Wildlife reserve
- Whale watching
- Protected area for sea-lions/seal

ark in South Africa is the most famous ature reserve in the region. The park is ome to many of the animals typically ssociated with the region, including ephants, lions, and rhinoceroses. The dian and Atlantic Ocean coasts of outh Africa are popular areas for whale, olphin, and seal watching.

he region around the Cape of Good ope has a Mediterranean climate. The ape Region is also home to a unique type of vegetation called Fynbos, the smallest of the world's floral kingdoms. The Fynbos classification comprises more than 8,500 different plant species, all of which are found within a 70,000 km²-large-area in southwestern South Africa.

South Africa has a wealth of natural resources. Johannesburg, the largest city in southern Africa, developed into a major city after a gold rush in nearby mines during the late 19th century. Uranium, nickel, and platinum are also important resources produced in South Africa. South Africa has the largest and most developed economy in Africa.

Although black Africans form a majority of the country's population, South Africa is also home to millions of Asians, whites, and people of mixed ethnicity. For several decades South Africa was ruled by a government that enforced strict racial segregation and denied most of the country's people the right to vote. Although apartheid was ended in the 1990s, there are still major economic differences between the ethnic groups of South Africa. Most urban black and mixed-race South Africans live in townships, areas with mostly substandard housing. The largest ethnic groups in the country are the Xhosa and Zulu peoples. The San people (Bushmen) have lived in southern Africa for thousands of years.

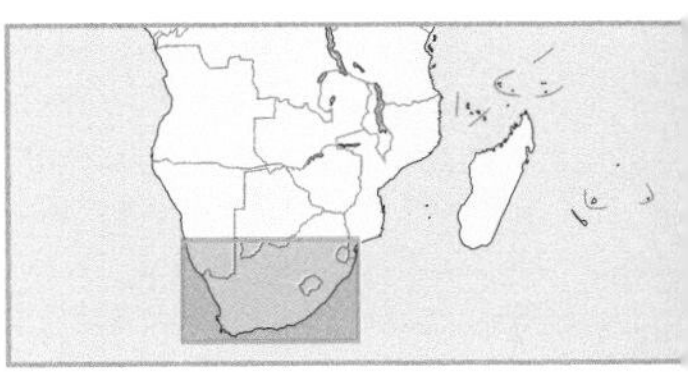

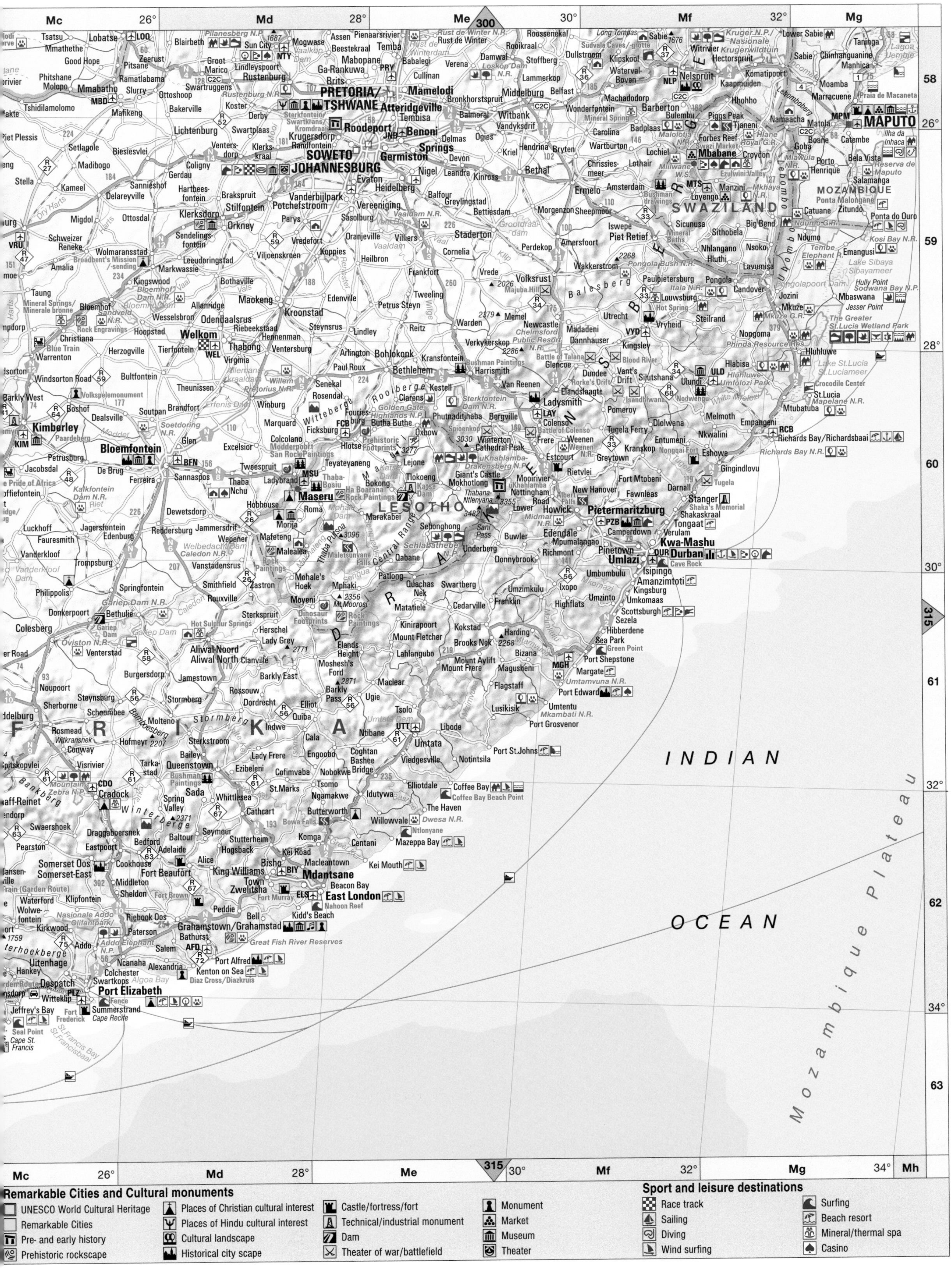

Johannesburg Major industrial and financial center in South Africa – the township of Soweto borders the city – important museums **MdMe59**

Lesotho The mountainous kingdom features the highest mountain in southern Africa – Thabana Ntlenyana (3,482 meters), beautiful highland regions, and distinct local cultures. The indigenous Sotho people form the overwhelming majority of the country's population. **MdMe60/61**

Drakensberg 250-kilometer-long mountain range with a maximum height of 3,842 meters – San rock painting **Me60**

Greater St. Lucia Wetland Park Coastal marshlands – UNESCO world heritage site – crocodiles, rhinoceros, and hippopotamuses – whale watching **Mg59**

Zulu The more than five million Zulus form the largest ethnic group in southern Africa. Most of the region's Zulu population is concentrated in the Kwa-Zulu-Natal region. During the 19th century, the Zulus fiercely resisted European colonization under the reign of Shaka Zulu.

Durban South African port city on the Indian Ocean coast – large Indian community – Juma Mosque – Victoria Street Market – Sea World aquarium – beaches and beachside hotels **Mf60**

Remarkable Cities and Cultural monuments

- UNESCO World Cultural Heritage
- Remarkable Cities
- Pre- and early history
- Prehistoric rockscape
- Places of Christian cultural interest
- Places of Hindu cultural interest
- Cultural landscape
- Historical city scape
- Castle/fortress/fort
- Technical/industrial monument
- Dam
- Theater of war/battlefield
- Monument
- Market
- Museum
- Theater

Sport and leisure destinations

- Race track
- Sailing
- Diving
- Wind surfing
- Surfing
- Beach resort
- Mineral/thermal spa
- Casino

Most of the large islands scattered in the **Indian Ocean** were created millions of years ago when the landmass **Gondwanaland** drifted apart, forming the different continents of our planet. Sri Lanka and Madagascar are the largest of the many islands scattered throughout the sections of the Indian Ocean between Asia and Africa. Other large islands that once dotted the ocean were submerged after a rise in global sea level. The Seychelles are the peaks of a mountain cha that once stretched across one of the landmasses that disappeared benea the ocean.

The Comoros were created through vo canic activity, millions of years later tha the Seychelles or Madagascar. **Ka thala** (2,361 meters) on the island Gra

Palm trees and sandy beaches on the island of La Digue (Seychelles) **Nh**

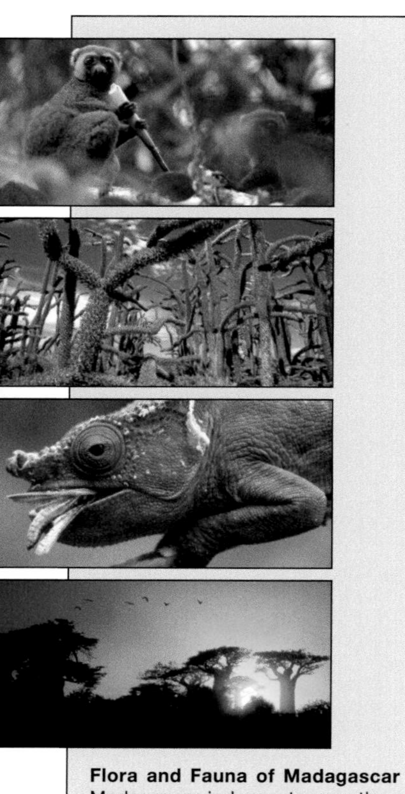

Flora and Fauna of Madagascar
Madagascar is home to countless endemic plants and animals, many of which remain undiscovered. Madagascar's unique animals developed in isolation from other regions, and new species are still being discovered on the island. The government of Madagascar has created several nature reserves to protect the island's biodiversity. Photos from top to bottom: golden bamboo lemur, octopus trees, Parson's chameleon, baobab trees

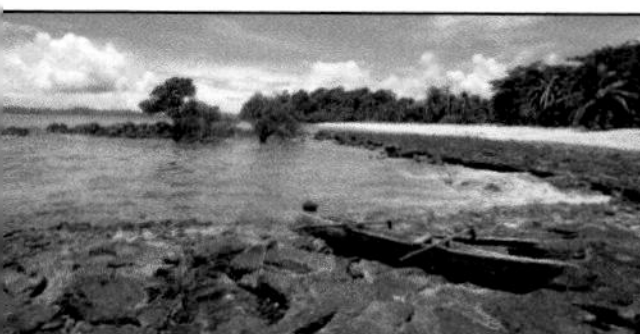

Nosy Be Island with long white sandy beaches – thick tropical vegetation and volcanoes – Nosy Faly – the island's main town Hell-Ville features attractive colonial architecture **Ne52**

Réserve Spéciale d'Ankarana Karst landscapes with numerous subterranean caves – subterranean rivers – crocodile population – baobab groves containing the graves of local kings **Ne52**

Cirque Rouge Beautiful stone formation near the city of Mahajanga – popular tourist destination **Nd53**

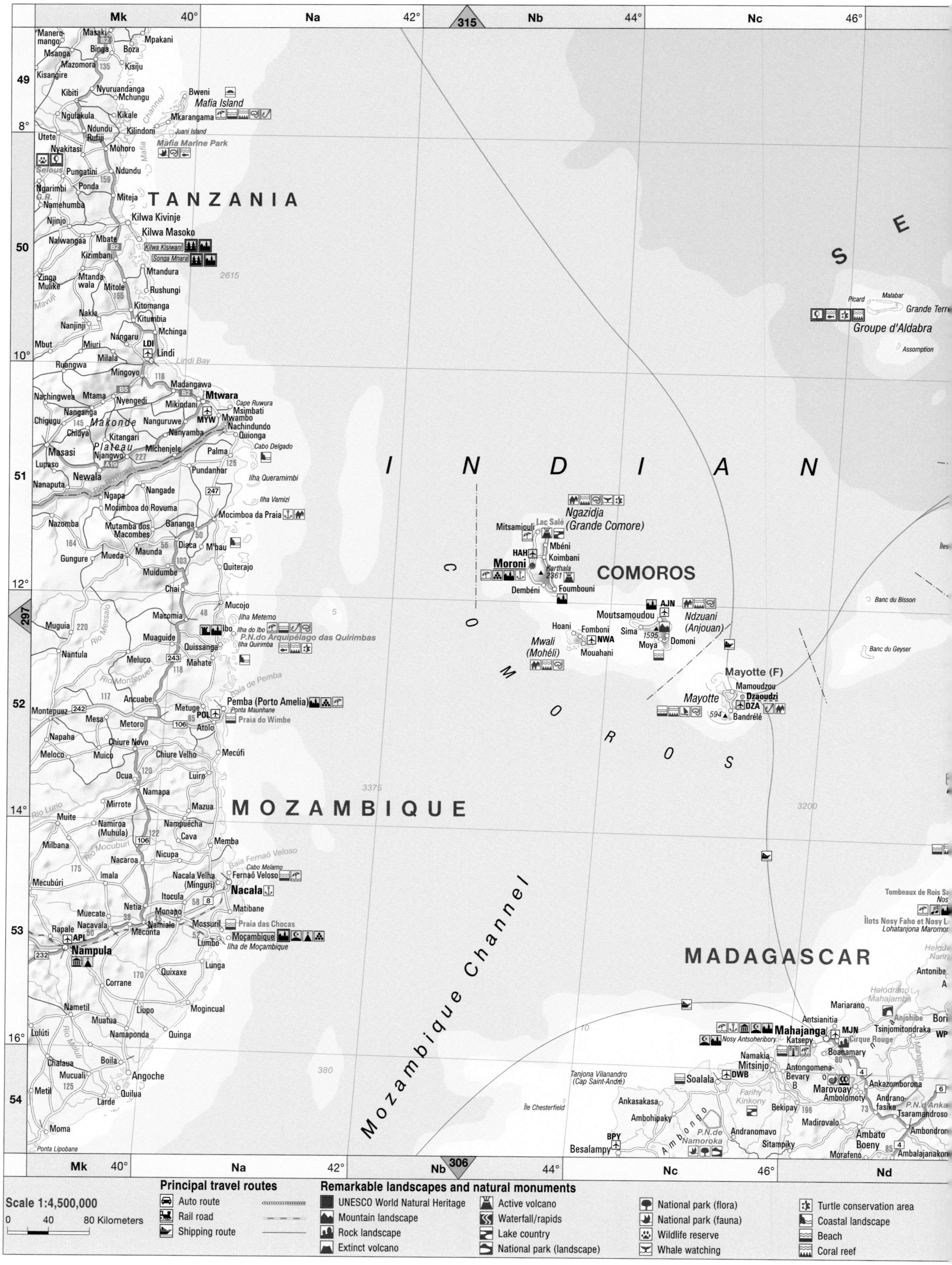

TANZANIA
MOZAMBIQUE
COMOROS
MADAGASCAR
INDIAN OCEAN
Mozambique Channel

Scale 1:4,500,000
0 40 80 Kilometers

Principal travel routes
- Auto route
- Rail road
- Shipping route

Remarkable landscapes and natural monuments
- UNESCO World Natural Heritage
- Mountain landscape
- Rock landscape
- Extinct volcano
- Active volcano
- Waterfall/rapids
- Lake country
- National park (landscape)
- National park (flora)
- National park (fauna)
- Wildlife reserve
- Whale watching
- Turtle conservation area
- Coastal landscape
- Beach
- Coral reef

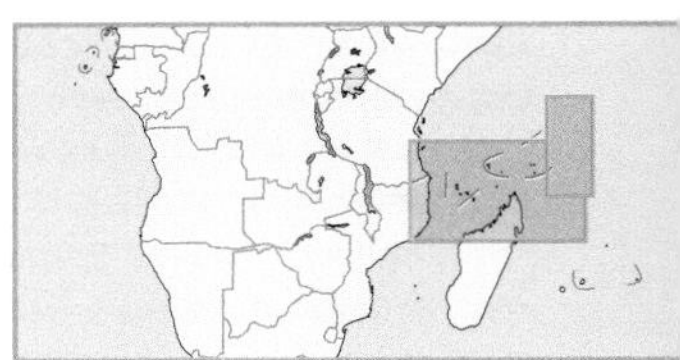

omore (Ngazidja) is the youngest and ne of more active volcanoes in the island roup. The volcanoes on Mayotte and Moheli, the oldest of the Comoro Islands, ave been dormant for centuries. All of he major Comoro Islands have mountainous interiors surrounded by narrow trips of flat coastal land. The flora and auna of the islands is similar to that of Madagascar. Many of the islands' indigenous species have become extinct in recent centuries because of human activities including logging and farming. The discovery of a live coelacanth in the waters around the Comoros in 1938 shocked the scientific world. Before this discovery, the unusual fish-like creatures were believed to have become extinct millions of years ago.

Madagascar (590,000 km²), the world's fourth largest island, is situated 400 kilometers off the coast of mainland Africa. The island encompasses several topographies and distinct climate zones ranging from humid subtropical to semi-arid. Madagascar's isolation from other landmasses led to the development of many unique plants and animals. The island's lemur population is widely studied by scientists from around the world. Like Madagascar, the **Seychelles** (454 km²) are home to an abundance of unique endemic flora and fauna. Thousands of Seychelles green turtles and several rare bird species inhabit the **Aldabra Atoll**. The Seychelles are an archipelago of more than 100 islands, only a third of which are inhabited. The central islands, including Mahe and Praslin, have mountainous interiors. These islands have heavy levels of rainfall during most of the year and are covered by dense green vegetation. The outer islands of the Seychelles are mostly flat coral islands with arid climates.

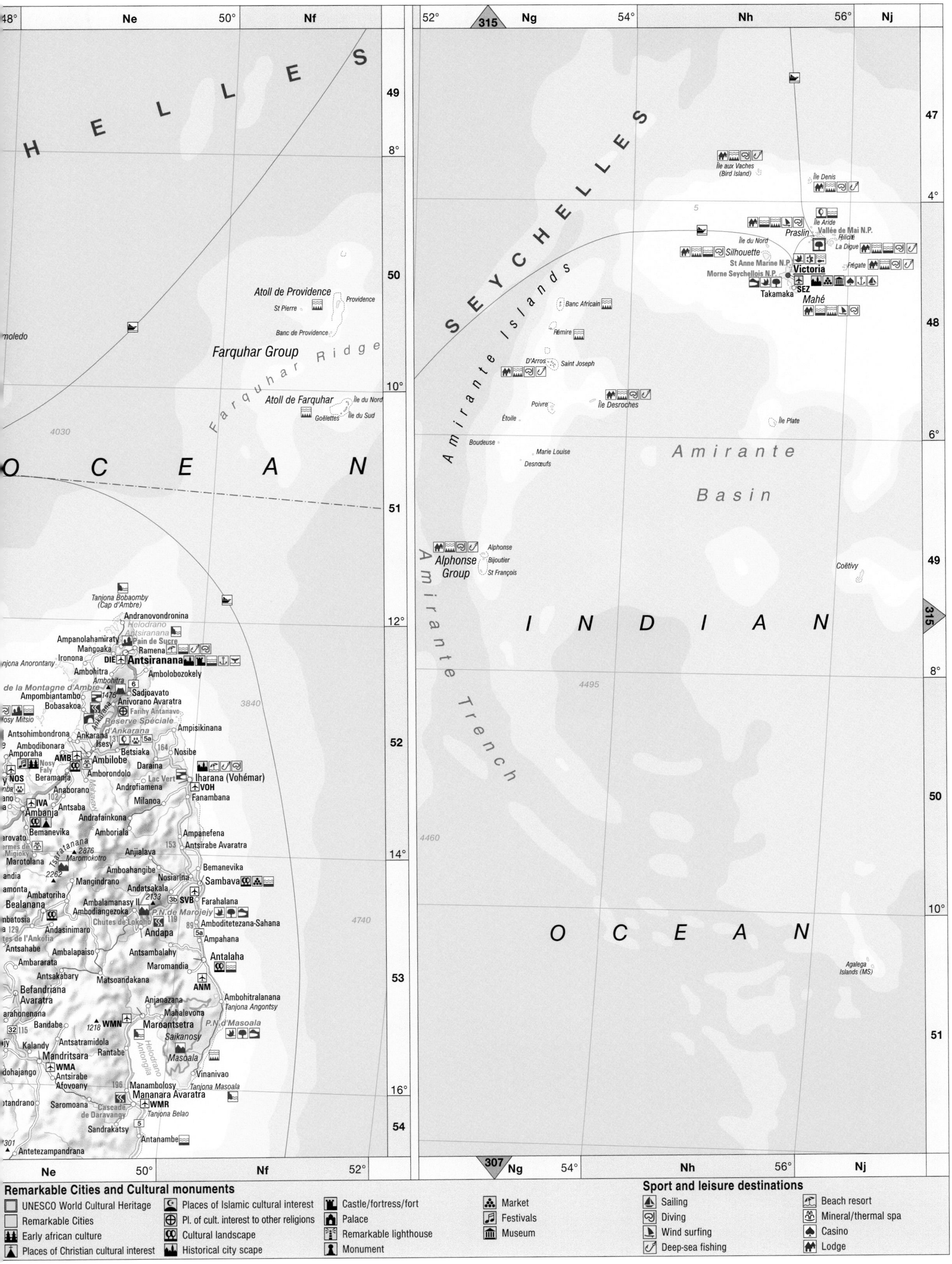

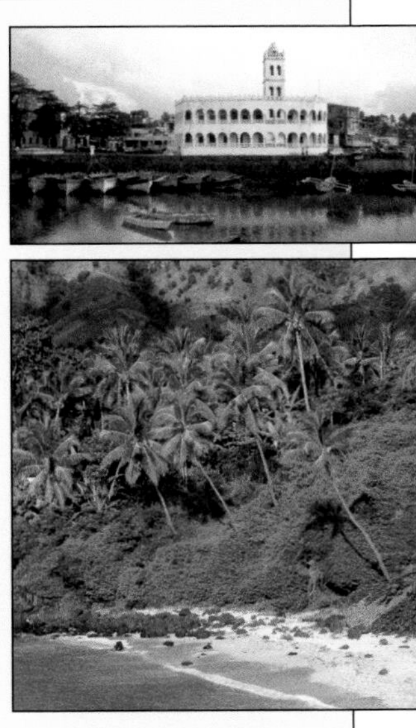

Comoros Moroni (top photo) on the island Grande Comore is the capital of the Comoros. The island of Anjouan (bottom photo) has beautiful undeveloped beaches. **NbNc51/52**

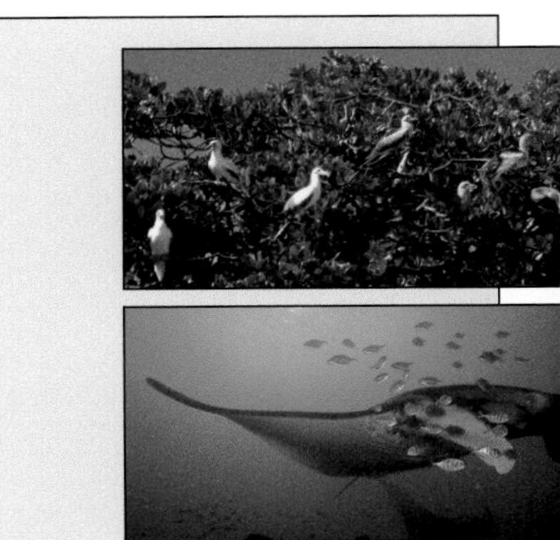

Aldabra Atoll The atoll, a UNESCO world heritage site, is home to many animals including red-footed boobies (top photo) and large manta rays (bottom photo). **Nd50**

Praslin Vallée de Mal, a UNESCO world heritage site, contains coco-de-mer palm forests – diving sites **Nh48**

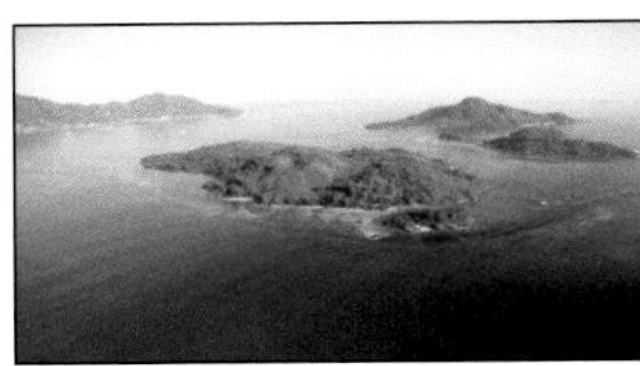

St. Anne National Marine Park Five islands (photo) – spawning ground for turtles – diving sites **Nh48**

Frégate Island Privately owned island in the Seychelles – beaches and diving sites – exclusive holiday resort **Nh48**

Remarkable Cities and Cultural monuments

- UNESCO World Cultural Heritage
- Remarkable Cities
- Early african culture
- Places of Christian cultural interest
- Places of Islamic cultural interest
- Pl. of cult. interest to other religions
- Cultural landscape
- Historical city scape
- Castle/fortress/fort
- Palace
- Remarkable lighthouse
- Monument
- Market
- Festivals
- Museum

Sport and leisure destinations

- Sailing
- Diving
- Wind surfing
- Deep-sea fishing
- Beach resort
- Mineral/thermal spa
- Casino
- Lodge

Madagascar, Réunion, Mauritius

The islands of **Madagascar**, **Mauritius**, and **Réunion** are situated on the western edge of the Indian Ocean. This region features a unique mixture of African and Asian cultural influences. The majority of Mauritius' population consists of people whose ancestors came from the Indian subcontinent to work as field laborers on the island. The French territory Réunion has large ethnic European (especially French), African, and Asian

communities. Madagascar is home t dozens of distinct indigenous ethn groups and religious communities. Th majority of Madagascar's people, how ever, are the descendants of both (Mala Southeast Asians and black Africa ancestors. Eastern Madagascar's terra is dominated by ancient mountains (up t

Lac d'Itasy (Madagascar): a lake surrounded by volcanic highlands **Nd5**

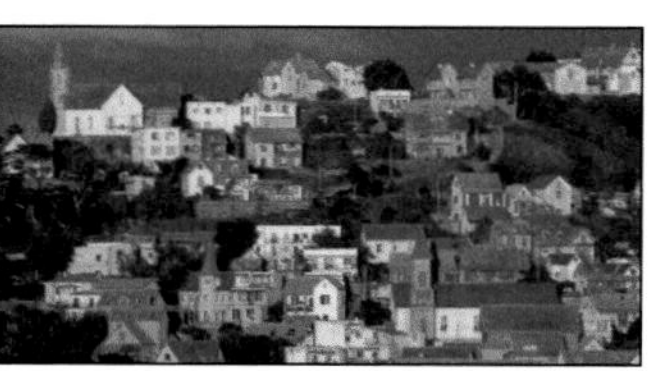

Antananarivo Madagascar's capital and largest city – vibrant weekly market on Fridays: Zoma – wooden royal palace: Rova – colonial-era architecture **Nd55**

Lac d'Itasy Beautiful lake situated 2,300 meters above sea level, west of Antananarivo – volcanic landscapes – home to large bird populations **Nd55**

The **Tsingy de Bemaraha Strict Nature Reserve** features fascinating heavily eroded landscapes (bottom photo) and is a designated UNESCO world heritage site. Tall baobab trees (top photo) are common throughout the area. The dense tropical rainforests in the reserves are home to many lemurs and birds. **Nc55**

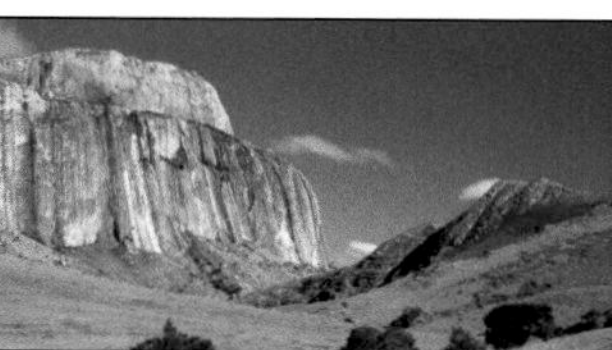

Rocher d'Ifandana Granite hills in Madagascar's southern highlands – located near Andringitra National Park, which also feature numerous granite formations **Nd56**

Isalo National Park Mountainous conservation area featuring unique stone formations – deep gorges with beautiful tropical vegetation **Nc57**

Befandefa Town on Madagascar's southwestern coast – coral reefs and isolated beaches – sheltered lagoons **Nb57**

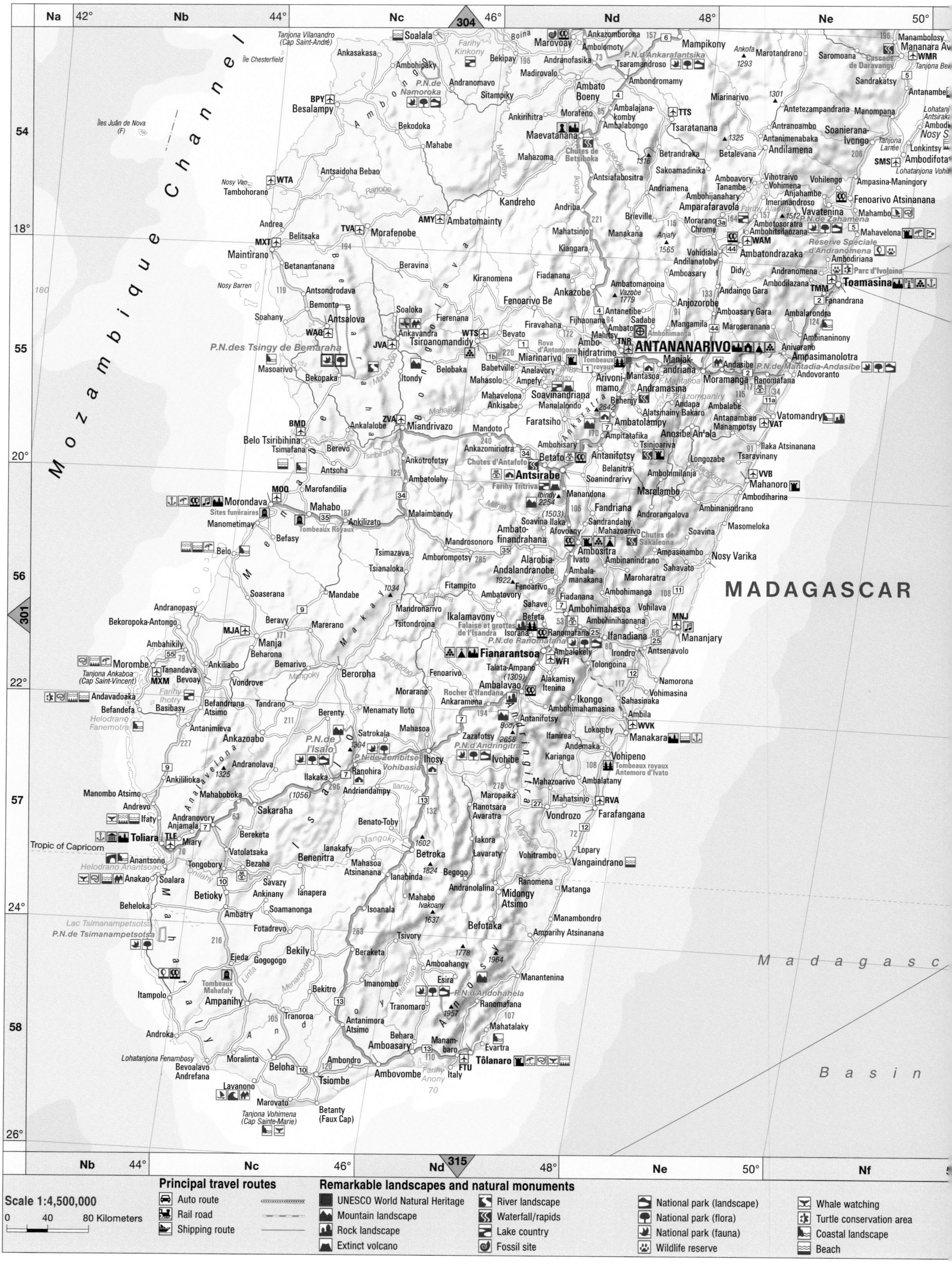

MADAGASCAR

Mozambique Channel

Madagascar Basin

ANTANANARIVO

Scale 1:4,500,000
0 40 80 Kilometers

Principal travel routes
- Auto route
- Rail road
- Shipping route

Remarkable landscapes and natural monuments
- UNESCO World Natural Heritage
- Mountain landscape
- Rock landscape
- Extinct volcano
- River landscape
- Waterfall/rapids
- Lake country
- Fossil site
- National park (landscape)
- National park (flora)
- National park (fauna)
- Wildlife reserve
- Whale watching
- Turtle conservation area
- Coastal landscape
- Beach

,500 meters high) including the **Ankaatra Mountains**. The eastern edges of hese mountain ranges are covered by ense tropical rainforests. Due to ocean urrents and moist winds, Madagascar's astern coast is a region of heavy rainfall nd high humidity. Southwestern Madaascar is bounded to the north and east y two high mountain massifs. The reion is largely arid with sparse rainfall hroughout the year and scattered dry forests. Much of Madagascar's land is cultivated including the country's large highlands. Rice, the staple food of most Madagascans, is widely cultivated for domestic consumption, while coffee is the leading export crop.

Madagascar's amazing abundance of unique endemic flora and fauna is largely the result of the island's geographic isolation. The island's fifteen endemic lemur species are perhaps the most fascinating and studied native creatures found there. Of the more than 230 reptiles on Madagascar around 95% are native to the island, including 38 types of chameleons.

The small islands of Réunion and Mauritius are both part of the Mascarene Archipelago in the Indian Ocean. The archipelago developed above a so-called hot spot, an area on the ocean's floor where magma rises from the Earth's mantle. Mauritius, the oldest island in the group, is around eight million years old, while Réunion was formed three million years ago. The volcano **Piton de la Fournaise** (2,632 meters) on Réunion is one of the world's most active in terms of lava production. The highlands around the dormant volcano **Piton de Neiges** are covered by dense tropical vegetation. Mauritius is surrounded by a long ring of **coral reefs**.

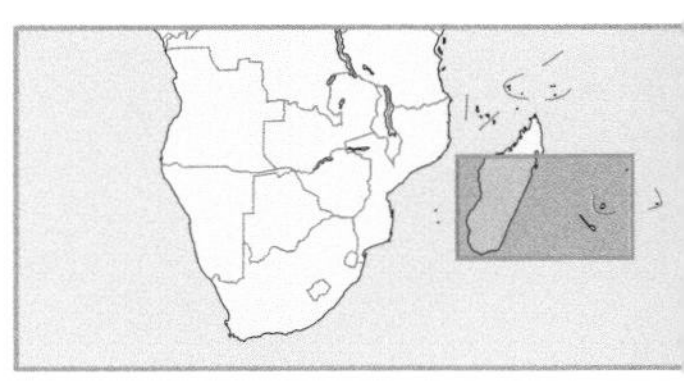

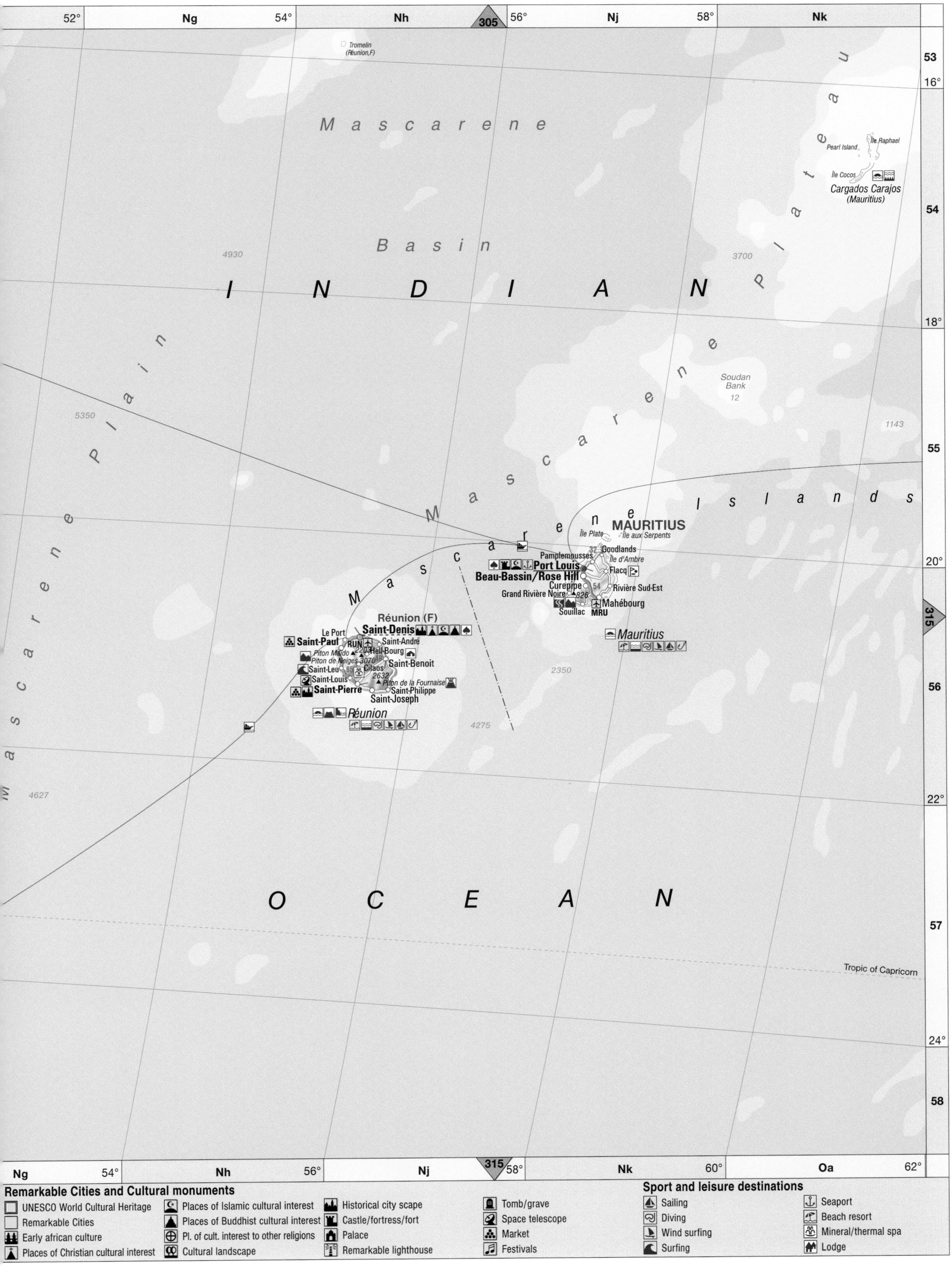

INDIAN OCEAN

Mascarene Basin

MAURITIUS

Réunion (F)

Remarkable Cities and Cultural monuments

- UNESCO World Cultural Heritage
- Remarkable Cities
- Early african culture
- Places of Christian cultural interest
- Places of Islamic cultural interest
- Places of Buddhist cultural interest
- Pl. of cult. interest to other religions
- Cultural landscape
- Historical city scape
- Castle/fortress/fort
- Palace
- Remarkable lighthouse
- Tomb/grave
- Space telescope
- Market
- Festivals

Sport and leisure destinations

- Sailing
- Diving
- Wind surfing
- Surfing
- Seaport
- Beach resort
- Mineral/thermal spa
- Lodge

Andringitra National Park Mountainous national park in southeastern Madagascar – fascinating endemic flora including numerous rare orchids – also home to several lemur species and rare butterflies **Nd57**

Mahafaly Tribal Tombs Sacred site for the Mahafaly people – wooden statues and animal horns adorn the tombs **Nc58**

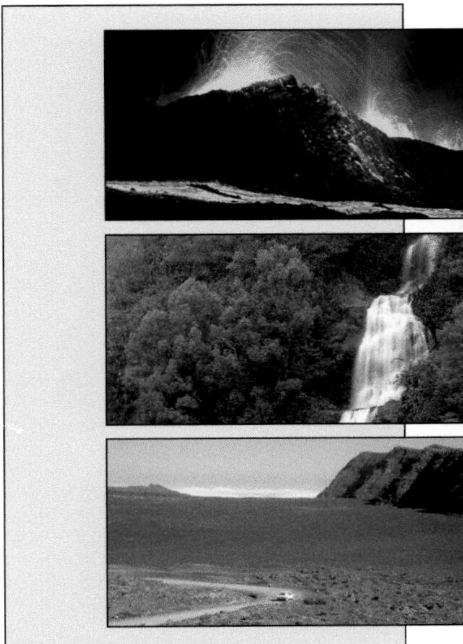

Réunion The island (2,500 km²) features beautiful volcanic highlands. **Piton de la Fournaise** (top and bottom photos) frequently releases large amounts of lava from its summit (middle photo: Cirque de Salazie). **Nh56**

Mauritius has several interesting stone formations including **Trois Mamelles** (top photo) and **Morne Brabant** (middle photo). Ethnic Indians (bottom photo) form the majority of Mauritius' population. **Nj56**

North Frisia (top): Historic lighthouse near Westerhever, Germany
Okayama (bottom): A stunning sunset above islands in Japan's Inland Sea

The Atlantic (left): Colorful marine inhabitants of the deep blue sea
The Pacific (right): Huge waves demonstrate the incredible power of the oceans

Arctic Region, Antarctica, Oceans

The immense oceans shape the face of our "blue planet." The Pacific, Atlantic, Indian, and Arctic oceans cover more than two thirds of the planet's surface. Even today most of the oceans' landscapes remain unexplored. Around the polar regions the world's oceans give way to the barren ice masses of the Arctic and Antarctica. These inhospitable regions were a magnet to famous explorers including Admiral Richard E. Byrd and Robert F. Scott.

Arctic Region

Unlike most of the world's regions, the Arctic has no clear geographic definition. The Arctic usually refers to the cold treeless regions around the North Pole. The Arctic encompasses the Arctic Ocean and its adjacent bodies of water – including Baffin Bay, the Beaufort Sea, the Greenland Sea, the Laptev Sea, and the Bering Sea. The Arctic also consists of the countless islands in the region and some sections of mainland

North America (Canada and Alaska Europe, and Asia. 
The **Arctic** has a total area of 28 millic km². Of the 10 million km² of land the Arctic, 5 million km² lie in **Canad** around 4 million km² is equally divide between **Greenland** and **Russia**, an the remaining arctic land lies in **Alask**

The Arctic is home to several large mammal species including Polar Bears

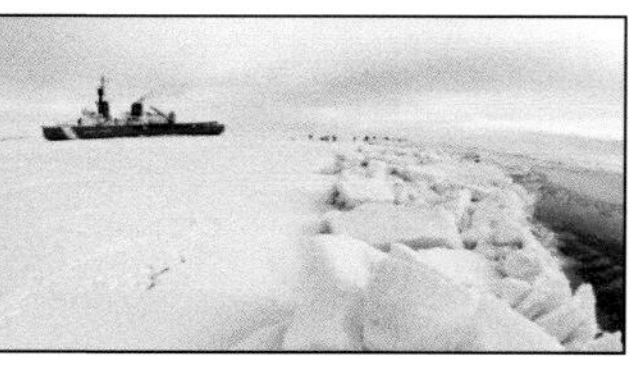

Many of the ice-covered areas along **Alaska's Arctic coast** (photo) are only navigable by icebreakers.

Ellesmere Island Canadian island near northeastern Greenland – mountainous island with peaks rising to 3,000 meters – covered by glaciers.

Baffin Island Canada's largest arctic island – the north is mountainous and covered by glaciers – the west is marshy and flat

Icebergs can travel the oceans for up to ten years – most of an iceberg's mass lies underwater – photo: icebergs in the Labrador Sea

Greenland covers 2.17 million km² and is the largest island in the world. The island is self-governing but politically associated with Denmark. Geographically the island is a section of the North American continent. The island has around 56,000 inhabitants, mostly Inuit. In the Inuit language, Greenland is called Kalaallit Nunaat (land of people). Over 80 percent of the island's surface is covered by ice. The thickest layer of ice on the island is around 3,400 meters thick. The Humboldt Glacier is over 100 kilometers wide. It is the largest glacier in the Northern Hemisphere.

Scale 1:18,000,000
0 160 320 Kilometers

Depth tints
- Shoreline
- 0-200 m
- 200-2000 m
- 2000-4000 m
- 4000-6000 m
- 6000-8000 m
- > 8000 m

Physical Features
- River, stream
- Intermittent river
- Lake
- Intermittent lake
- Salt lake
- Intermittent salt lake
- Elevation above sea level in meters

nd **Norway**. The center of the Arctic is overed by water and ice masses.
ne **Arctic Ocean** is the smallest of the orld's four oceans. The Arctic Ocean is eparated from the Pacific Ocean by the arrow Bering Strait. It also shares a uch longer border with the Atlantic cean. The Arctic Ocean has a total area around 14 million km². In winter, most the ocean's surface is covered by a yer of **ice** between three to four meters thick. During summer the extent of this ice layer decreases and the coastal areas around the ocean become navigable for ships. The Arctic is the shallowest of the oceans with an average depth around 1,200 meters. Fram Basin is the deepest point with a maximum depth of 4,665 meters. A large percentage of the Arctic's land area, especially in Greenland and Canada, is covered by ice during the entire year. Most of the remaining land is covered by **permafrost**, layers of frozen soil or rock that temporarily thaw in summer covering the land with water. Most of the Arctic's landscapes, including the many beautiful fjords in the region, were formed during or near the end of the last ice ages.
Life in the Arctic is strongly influenced by the extreme days and nights in the region. Long dark winter months with little sunshine are followed by short summers with almost continuous daylight. Despite the extreme climate, the Arctic is home to many fascinating animal species including polar bears, reindeer and walruses. The North Pole is warmed by ocean currents and is therefore not the coldest place in the Arctic. Ojmjakon, in northeastern Siberia, has the coldest average temperatures in the region. Temperatures around -78° Celsius have been recorded in the area.

Laptev Sea
Kara Sea
Barents Sea
East Siberian Sea
Taymyr Peninsula
Novaya Zemlya
Franz Josef Land (RUS)
Svalbard (N)
Central Siberian Plateau
West Siberian Plain
URAL MOUNTAINS
RUSSIA
NORWAY
FINLAND
KAZAKSTAN
CHINA
Political Boundaries
International
International disputed
Main administrative
Transportation
Interstate Hwy./Motorway
Main road
Railway
Airport
Capitals of political units
WASHINGTON D.C. Independent
Richmond State/province
Town symbols
Capital > 1 Mill. inhabitants
Capital < 1 Mill. inhabitants
Statecapital > 1 Mill. inhabitants
Statecapital < 1 Mill. inhabitants
Towns > 1 Mill. inhabitants
Towns 100 000 bis 1 Mill. inhabitants
Towns < 100 000 inhabitants

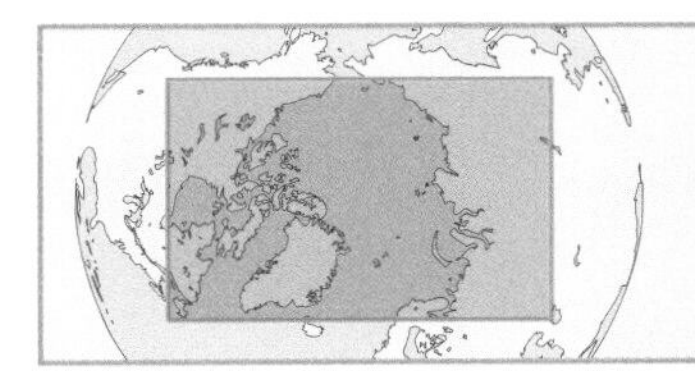

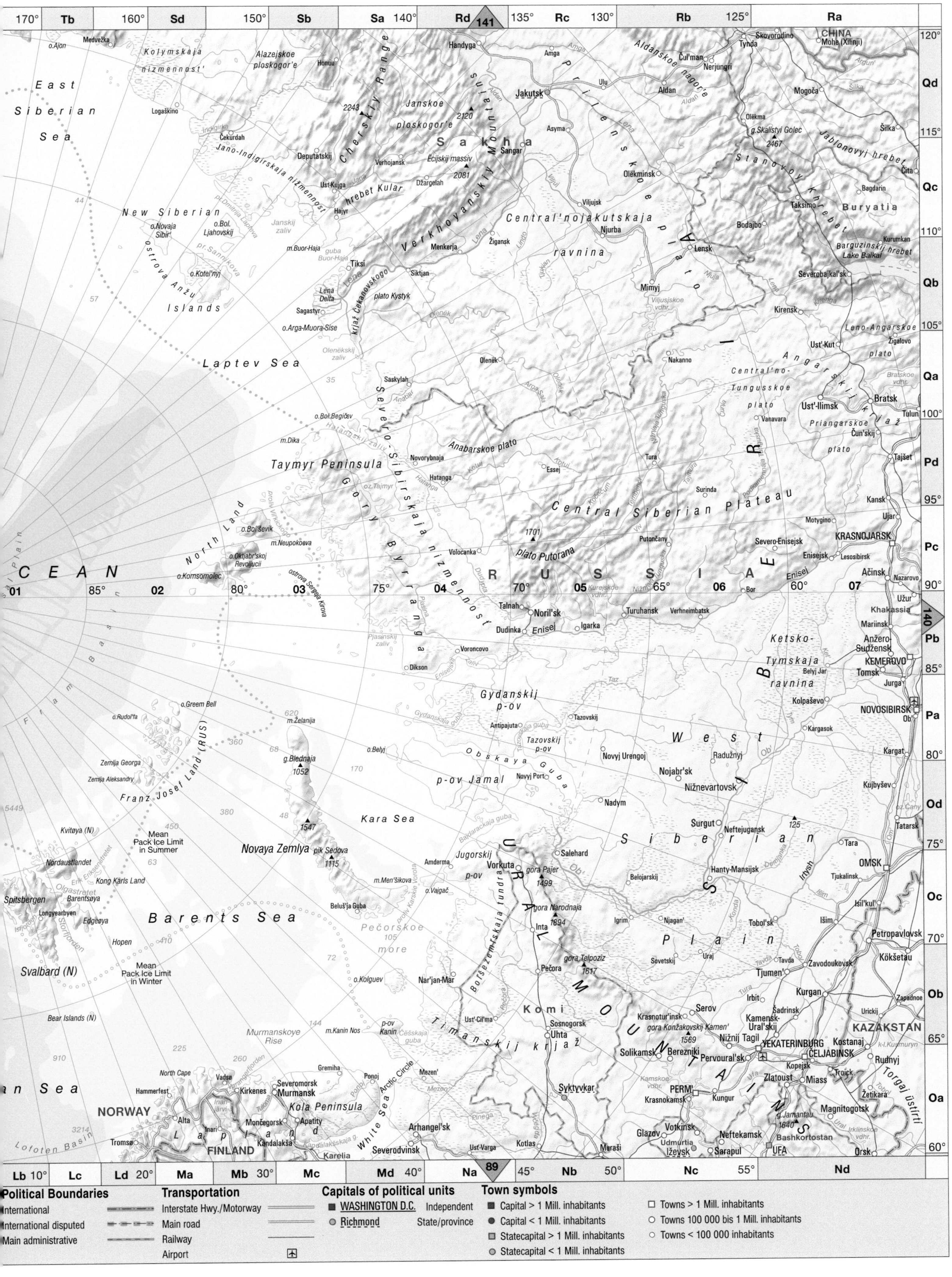

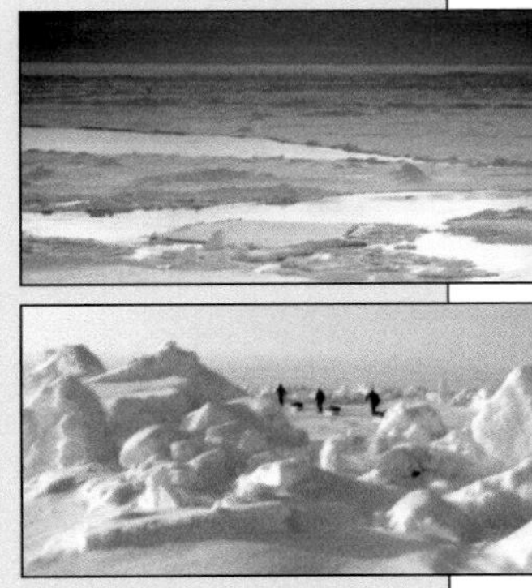

The Geographic **North Pole** is also known as True North. Unlike the Magnetic North Pole, the Geographic North Pole has a fixed position. The North Pole lies in the Arctic Ocean and is occasionally free of ice, despite the cold temperatures in the area.

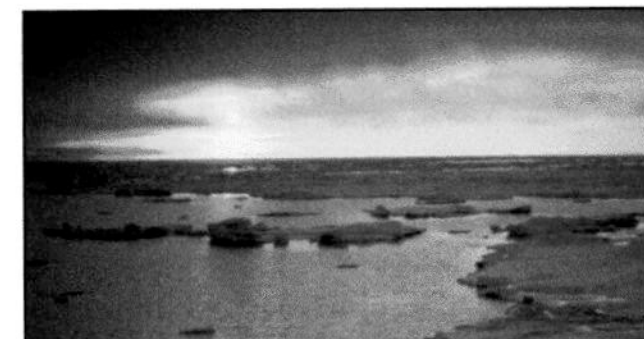

The ice sheet on the Arctic Ocean often reaches the **Siberian coast**. At least 10 million km² of Arctic Ocean is covered by ice.

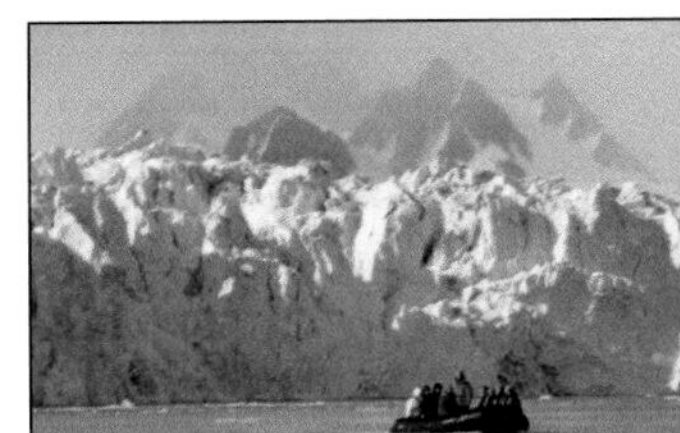

The **Monaco Glacier** (photo) in the Liefdefjord is one of the most spectacular glaciers on the Norwegian island Spitsbergen.

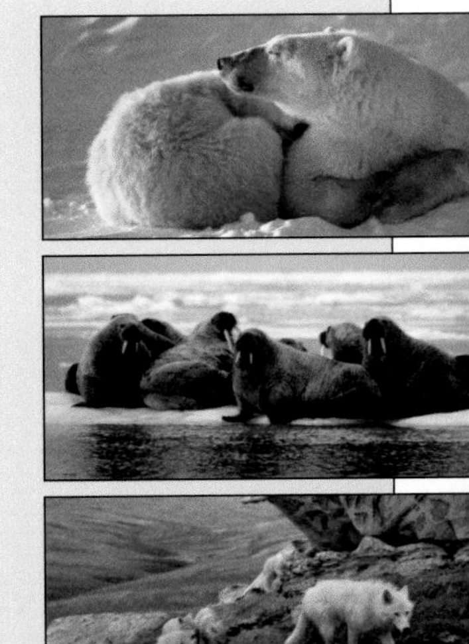

Despite its raw climate the Arctic is home to many species of animal life. Some **animals** like the arctic foxes are active throughout the year while others including polar bears hibernate during the coldest months. Adult polar bears can weigh over 1,000 kilograms and are the largest predators in the Arctic. Whales, walruses, caribous, and reindeer continue to play an important part in the diet of indigenous people in the Arctic. Photos from top to bottom: Polar bears, Walruses, Arctic foxes

Antarctica occupies most of the area in the Antarctic Circle. The **Antarctic Peninsula** extends over 1,900 kilometers towards South America. Most of the continent is covered by a layer of ice that is, in some places, up to 4,000 meters thick. Less than five percent of the continent is free of ice; primarily coastal areas including Victoria Land and Wilkes Land. Antarctica has an average land area of around 14 million km² but it increases or decreases in size depending on the se son. The **ice layer** is thickest at the ce ter of the continent and declines in thic ness towards Antarctica's edges. Mou Vernon is the highest mountain on t continent. The mountain is 4,897 mete high and it was first climbed in 196 The area around the **South Pole** is situ ted 2,804 meters above sea level. T

The Transantarctic Mountains

Because of its cold temperatures and storms Antarctica is almost uninhabitable. Penguins (photo) live in large colonies in order to survive in this harsh environment.

The **Antarctic Peninsula** (photo) lies between the Weddell Sea and the Bellingshausen Sea. The Peninsula is over 1,200 kilometers long. Mount Jackson is the highest point in the region, rising almost 4,190 meters.

Every year huge ice masses break away from Antarctica and flow into the oceans as new **icebergs**. In May 2002, a massive iceberg measuring 6,336 km² (larger than the US state of Delaware) broke away from the Ross Shelf. Photo: Icebergs in the Amundsen Sea

The **Transantarctic Mountains** (photo) are located near the South Pole and rise above 4,000 meters. The highest peak in the mountain chain is Mount Kirckpatrick with a total height of 4,528 meters above sea level.

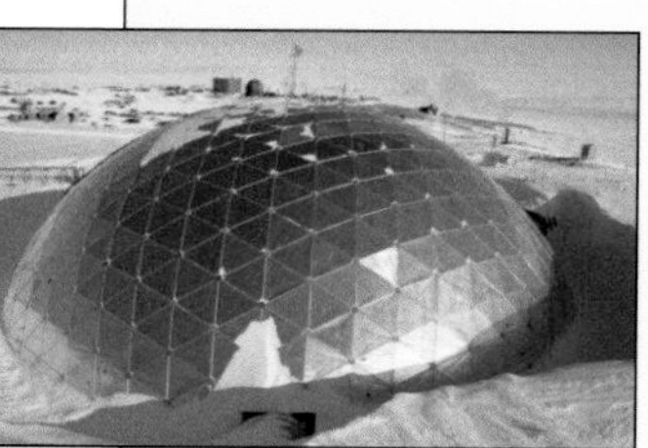

The American research base **Amundsen-Scott Base** (photo) lies near the Geographic South Pole. Other American bases lie on the Ross Sea (McMurdo) and on Anvers Island (Palmer Station). The station was built in 1956 and has been in use since then. A geodesic dome forms part of the station.

Mount Minto (4,165 meters) is the highest mountain in Victoria Land. Many volcanoes rise high above the ice covered surface of Antarctica.

Scale 1:18,000,000

0 160 320 Kilometers

Depth tints
- Shoreline
- 0-200 m
- 200-2000 m
- 2000-4000 m
- 4000-6000 m
- 6000-8000 m
- > 8000 m

Physical Features
- River, stream
- Intermittent river
- Lake
- Intermittent lake
- Salt lake
- Intermittent salt lake
- Elevation above sea level in meters

erage elevation of the continent is 340 meters. The large bays in the Ross a and Weddell Sea divide western Ant- ctica from the rest of the continent. etween these two regions lies the **Tran- ntarctic Moutain Range**. Mount patrick, the highest peak in this range, es 4,528 meters.

e ice mass covering the continent is ozen but active. Large glaciers fre- ently break away from the continent's edges and become icebergs. Rivers of ice in the continent's interior continously create new glaciers. There are several large ice shelves on the continent including the Ross Shelf (490,000 km²) and Filchner Ronne Shelf (450,000 km²). The continent is surrounded by the world's stormiest waters.

Antarctica is the coldest place on Earth. Temperatures reaching -89.2° Celsius have been recorded at Vostok Climate Station in western Antarctica. Even in summer most of Antarctica has temperatures below the freezing point. The Antarctic Peninsula, which extends to South America, is Anarctica's warmest region. Geologists believe Antarctica has large reserves of natural resources including oil, gold and natural gas. **The Antarctic Treaty**, signed in 1959, declares that the continent will be used peacefully for the mutual benefit of all mankind. The Antarctic Treaty Sytem has stopped any potential mining efforts or permanent land claims on the continent. Antarctica is the only continent with no permanent human inhabitants and there are also no large land animals on the continent. In 1985 scientists discovered a hole in the **ozone layer** above Antarctica. At the beginning of the 21st century the hole – believed to be a result of industrial pollution – was four times the size of Australia.

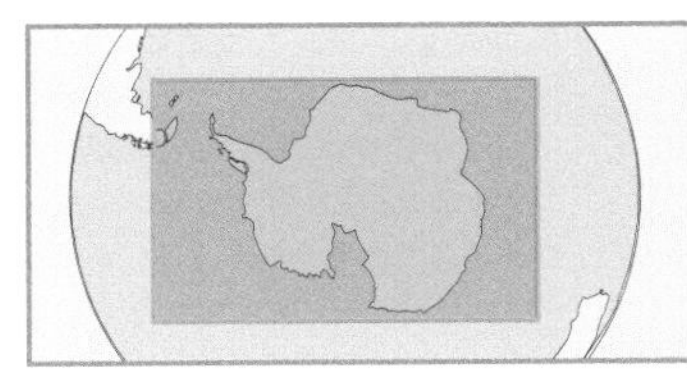

As many as 2,500 scientists work in the over **50 international research stations** in Antarctica. In addition, almost 12,000 tourists visited the continent in 2001/2002.

On January 17, 1912 the Briton Robert F. Scott reached the **South Pole** after Roald Amundsen. Scott died on the way back from the pole. A memorial (photo) to Scott has been erected in Antarctica.

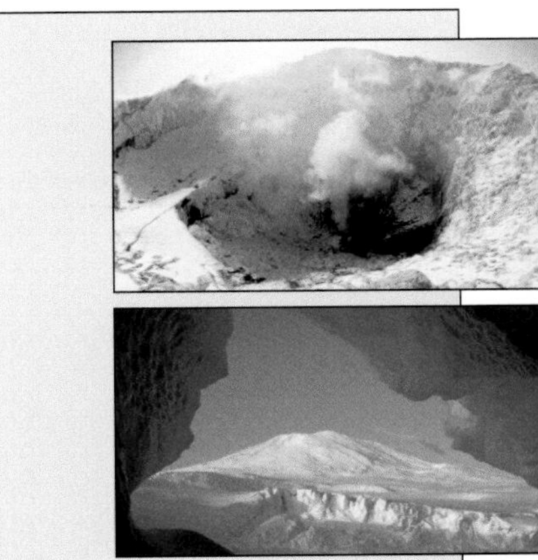

Mount Erebus (3,795 meters) on Ross Island is the highest active volcano in Antarctica

Lützow-Holm-Bay lies between Enderby Land and Queen Maud Land – impressive glaciers

The Mawson Coast (photo) is the location of the Australian research station (Mawson Station).

Cape Darnley borders MacKenzie Bay. This area is home to a large colony of Emperor Penguins.

Political Boundaries
- nternational
- nternational disputed
- Main administrative

Transportation
- Interstate Hwy./Motorway
- Main road
- Railway
- Airport

Capitals of political units
- WASHINGTON D.C. Independent
- Richmond State/province

Town symbols
- Capital > 1 Mill. inhabitants
- Capital < 1 Mill. inhabitants
- Statecapital > 1 Mill. inhabitants
- Statecapital < 1 Mill. inhabitants
- Towns > 1 Mill. inhabitants
- Towns 100 000 bis 1 Mill. inhabitants
- Towns < 100 000 inhabitants

Atlantic Ocean

With its adjacent seas, the Atlantic covers 106.6 million km² of the Earth's surface and is (after the Pacific) the second largest ocean. The Atlantic is bounded by four continents. The largest of these seas are the Mediterranean (3 million km²) and the North Sea (575,000 km²) to the east of the Atlantic and the Caribbean Sea (2.6 million km²) and Gulf of Mexico (1.8 million km²) to the ocean's west. The Mid-Atlantic Ridge, an under-

water mountain system, runs through t middle of the ocean. The deepest pc in the Atlantic is Milwaukee Deep (-9,2 meters) in the Puerto Rico Trench. Ma of the islands in the Atlantic – such as t Azores and Cape Verde Islands – a the peaks of vast underwater mount systems.

A lighthouse on the rocky Atlantic coa of Maine

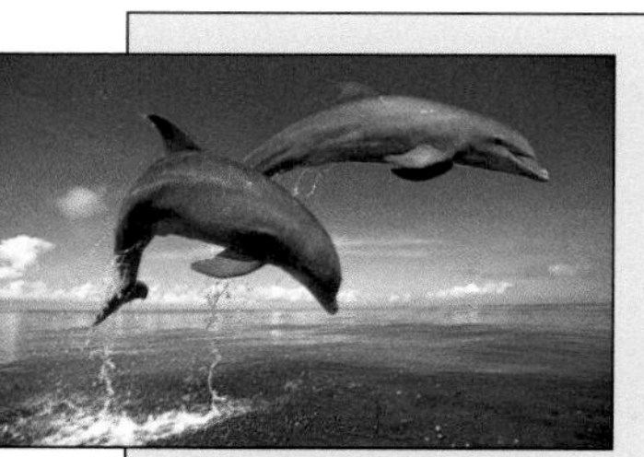

Many of the **marine animals** in the Atlantic Ocean travel great distances during the year. Some animals including dolphins (photo) and whales migrate in groups called pods or schools.

The **Mediterranean Sea** The largest sea adjacent to the Atlantic. It connects with the Atlantic at the Strait of Gibraltar. Major islands in the sea include Sicily, Cyprus, Crete, Corsica, and Malta. Photo: The Greek island Mykonos

The largest **island** in the Atlantic is Greenland (2,175,600 km²), which lies north of mainland North America. The largest island in the Carribean is Cuba (111,000 km²). Great Britain (219,801 km²) and Iceland (103,000 km²) are the largest European islands in the Atlantic. Photos from top to bottom: Iceland, Ireland, an island in the Caribbean Sea, the Falkland Islands

Scale 1:63,000,000

0 400 800 Kilometers

Depth tints

- Shoreline
- 0-200 m
- 200-2000 m
- 2000-4000 m
- 4000-6000 m
- 6000-8000 m
- > 8000 m

Physical Features

- River, stream
- Intermittent river
- Lake
- Intermittent lake
- Salt lake
- Intermittent salt lake
- Elevation above sea level in meters

e Indian Ocean covers arround 74.1 llion km² and is the world's third larg- ocean. The Indian Ocean is surroun- d by four continents; Africa, Asia, stralia, and Antarctica. It borders the antic Ocean on the meridian at 20 grees east and the Pacific Ocean on e meridian at 147 degrees east. There e numerous bodies of water adjacent the Indian Ocean, including the Red a, Persian Gulf, Arabian Sea, the Great Australian Bight, and the Bay of Bengal. The deepest point in the Indian Ocean is the **Java Trench** which extends 7,450 meters below the surface. The average depth of the ocean is around 3,850 meters. Java, Sumatra, Sri Lanka and Madagascar are the largest islands in the ocean.

Sunset over the Arabian Sea near the coast of southern India

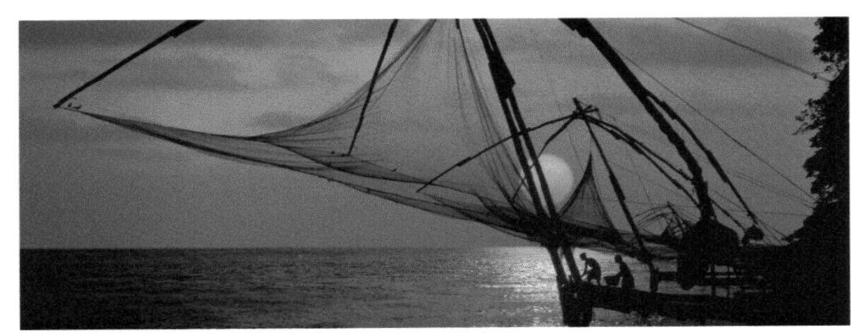

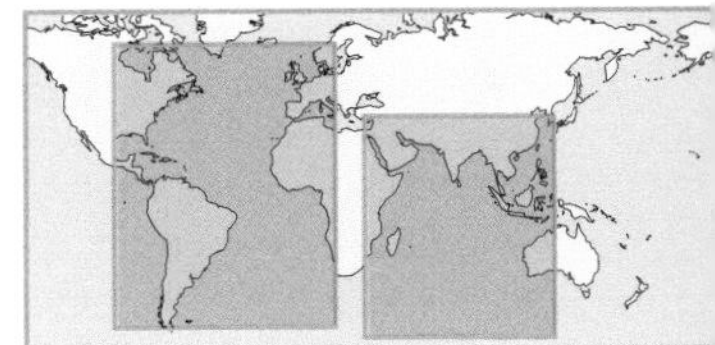

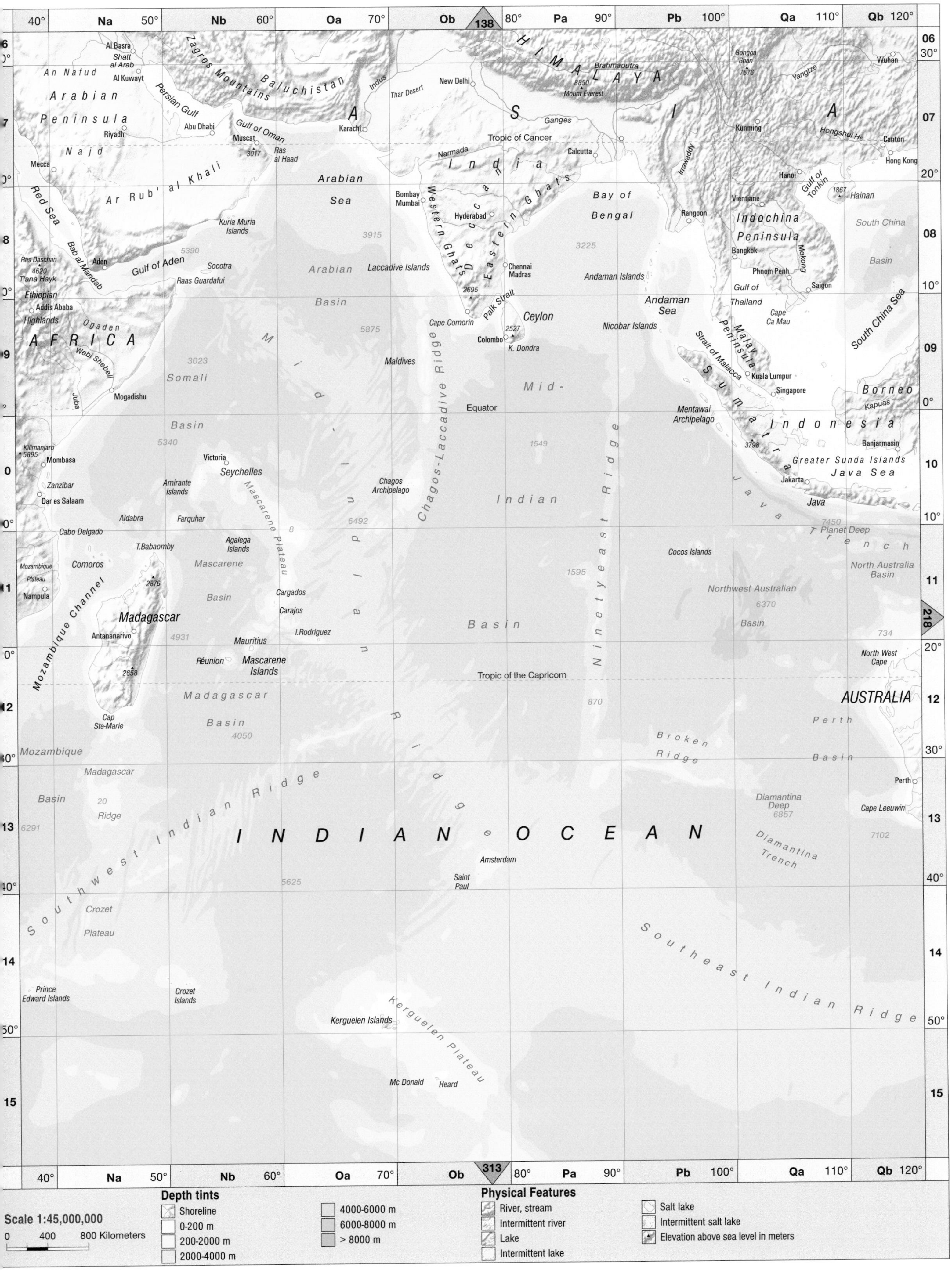

The Indian Ocean is home to diverse **marine life** and many areas are open to divers. Whale sharks (top photo) are often 15 meters long. Manta Rays (bottom photo) live near the ocean floor and belong to a family of fish related to sharks.

Because of high temperatures and evaporation many of the Indian Ocean's **adjacent seas**, including the Red Sea (top photo), have a high salt content. In many of the large gulfs around the ocean, water temperatures can reach 32 degrees. (bottom photo: Gulf of Thailand).

Five tectonic plates are situated beneath the Indian Ocean. Many of the ocean's volcanic islands lie near the edges of these plates. Mauritius (top photo) is of volcanic origin. The Seychelles (bottom photo) are coral islands. Madagascar (587,040 km²) is the largest island in the Indian Ocean.

138
218
313

Scale 1:45,000,000

0 400 800 Kilometers

Depth tints

- Shoreline
- 0-200 m
- 200-2000 m
- 2000-4000 m
- 4000-6000 m
- 6000-8000 m
- > 8000 m

Physical Features

- River, stream
- Intermittent river
- Lake
- Intermittent lake
- Salt lake
- Intermittent salt lake
- Elevation above sea level in meters

The **Pacific** is the superlative of the world's four oceans. The ocean was first named the "Pacific" (peaceful) by 16th century European explorers who mistook it for a calm body of water. It is the largest ocean in the world with an area of 181.6 million km² and it covers more than a third of the planet's surface. Even without its adjacent seas the Pacific covers 166.2 million km², a larger area than all the land on the planet combined.

The Pacific is also the deepest of [the] oceans with an average depth of 4,2[…] meters. The deepest point in the Pac[ific] is the Challenger Deep in the **Marian[a] Trench** with a depth of 11,034 mete[rs]. More than half of the unfrozen water [on] the planet is contained in the Pacific. T[he] **International Date Line** runs through [the] middle of the ocean.

Beautiful Bora Bora in French Polyne[sia]

Most of **the Pacific's animals** live between the ocean's surface and a depth of 200 meters and eat plankton and algae. Photos from top to bottom: Giant Pacific Octopus, Blue Whales, Giant Jellyfish, Tiger Shark

The **Great Barrier Reef** off the northeastern coast of Australia covers an area of 205,000 km². The reef is home to more than 400 species of coral, 2,000 species of fish, and many other forms of marine life.

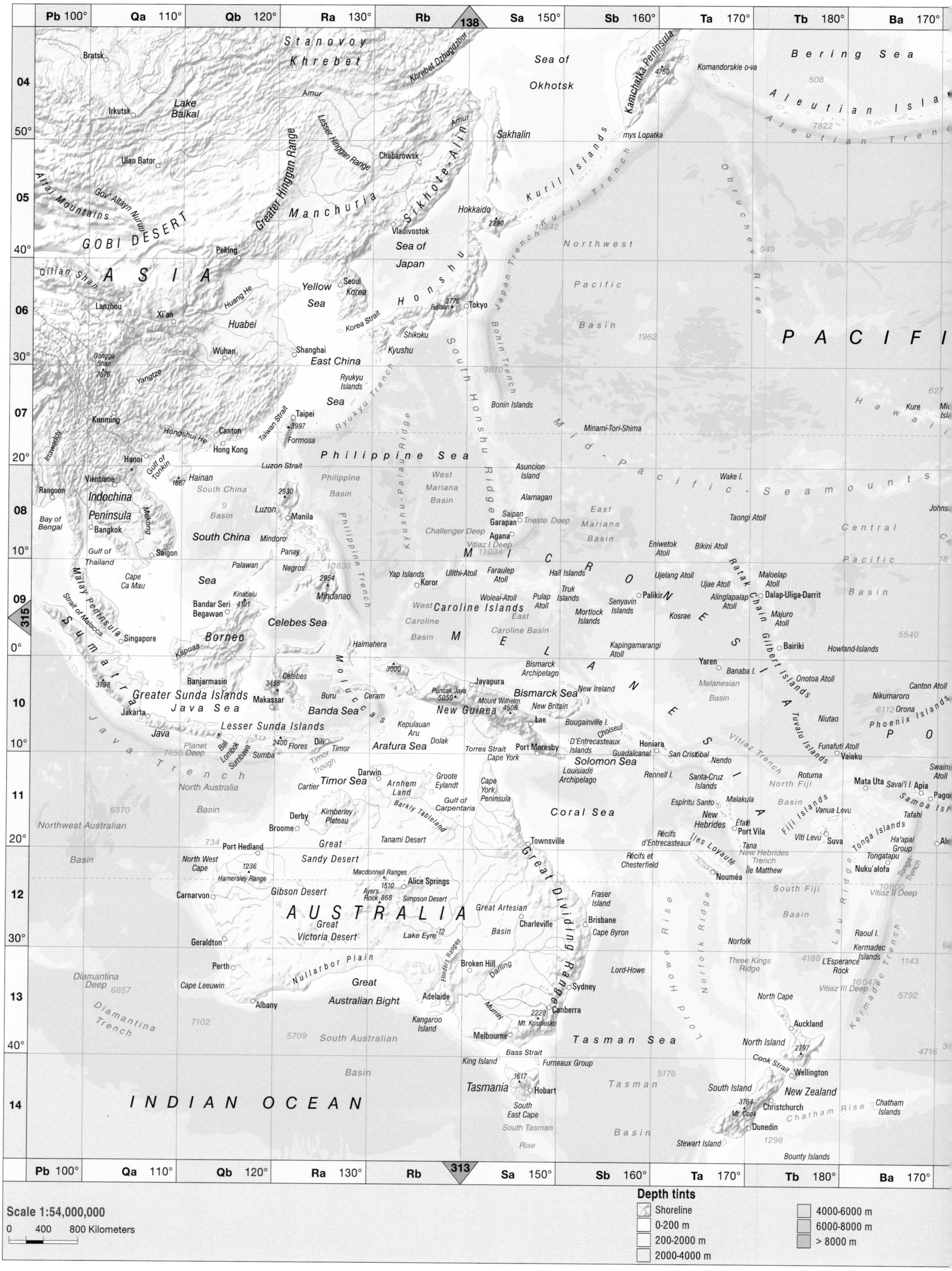

Pb 100° | Qa 110° | Qb 120° | Ra 130° | Rb 138 | Sa 150° | Sb 160° | Ta 170° | Tb 180° | Ba 170°

04 | 50° | 05 | 40° | 06 | 30° | 07 | 20° | 08 | 10° | 09 | 315 | 0° | 10 | 10° | 11 | 20° | 12 | 30° | 13 | 40° | 14

Stanovoy Khrebet · Sea of Okhotsk · Bering Sea · Aleutian Isla[nds] · Kamchatka Peninsula · Komandorskie o-va · Lake Baikal · Irkutsk · Bratsk · Sakhalin · mys Lopatka · Kuril Islands · Kuril Trench · Ulan Bator · Chabarowsk · Greater Hinggan Range · Lesser Hinggan Range · Sikhote-Alin · Altai Mountains · Gobi Altayn Nuruu · GOBI DESERT · Manchuria · Hokkaido · Vladivostok · Sea of Japan · Northwest Pacific Basin · Peking · ASIA · Qilian Shan · Yellow Sea · Seoul · Korea · Honshu · Tokyo · Lanzhou · Xi'an · Huang He · Huabei · Korea Strait · Shikoku · Kyushu · Wuhan · Shanghai · East China Sea · Yangtze · Ryukyu Islands · Ryukyu Trench · Bonin Trench · Bonin Islands · South Honshu Ridge · PACIFI[C] · Kunming · Hongshui He · Canton · Hong Kong · Taipei · Taiwan Strait · Formosa · Minami-Tori-Shima · Mid-Pacific Seamounts · Hanoi · Gulf of Tonkin · Philippine Sea · Hainan · Luzon Strait · Philippine Basin · West Mariana Basin · Kyushu-Palau Ridge · Asuncion Island · Wake I. · Rangoon · Vientiane · Indochina Peninsula · Mekong · South China Basin · Luzon · Manila · Alamagan · Saipan · Garapan · Trieste Deep · East Mariana Basin · Taongi Atoll · Bay of Bengal · Bangkok · South China Sea · Mindoro · Challenger Deep · Agana · Vitiaz I Deep · Gulf of Thailand · Saigon · Panay · Philippine Trench · MICRONESIA · Eniwetok Atoll · Bikini Atoll · Central Pacific Basin · Palawan · Negros · Cape Ca Mau · Yap Islands · Koror · Ulithi-Atoll · Faraulep Atoll · Hall Islands · Truk Islands · Ujelang Atoll · Ujae Atoll · Maloelap Atoll · Ratak Chain · Malay Peninsula · Strait of Malacca · Kinabalu · Mindanao · Woleai-Atoll · Pulap Atoll · Senyavin Islands · Palikir · Ailinglapalap Atoll · Dalap-Uliga-Darrit · Bandar Seri Begawan · West Caroline Basin · Caroline Islands · East Caroline Basin · Mortlock Islands · Kosrae · Majuro Atoll · Singapore · Borneo · Celebes Sea · Halmahera · Kapingamarangi Atoll · Gilbert Islands · Bairiki · Howland-Islands · Sumatra · Kapuas · Moluccas · Bismarck Archipelago · Yaren · Banaba I. · Onotoa Atoll · Canton Atoll · Banjarmasin · Celebes · Jayapura · Melanesian Basin · Nikumaroro · Greater Sunda Islands · Makassar · Buru · Ceram · Puncak Jaya · Mount Wilhelm · Bismarck Sea · New Ireland · New Britain · Phoenix Islands · Jakarta · Java Sea · Banda Sea · New Guinea · Lae · Bougainville I. · Niutao · Lesser Sunda Islands · Kepulauan Aru · Choiseul · Tuvalu Islands · POLYNESIA · Java · Java Trench · Bali · Lombok · Sumbawa · Sumba · Flores · Dili · Timor · Dolak · Arafura Sea · Torres Strait · Port Moresby · D'Entrecasteaux Islands · Honiara · Guadalcanal · San Cristobal · Solomon Sea · Nendo · Vitiaz Trench · Funafuti Atoll · Vaiaku · Planet Deep · Timor Trough · Darwin · Cape York · Louisiade Archipelago · Rennell I. · Rotuma · Mata Uta · Savai'i I. · Apia · North Australia Basin · Cartier · Timor Sea · Arnhem Land · Groote Eylandt · Gulf of Carpentaria · Cape York Peninsula · Santa-Cruz Islands · North Fiji Basin · Samoa Islands · Barkly Tableland · Espiritu Santo · Malakula · Fiji Islands · Vanua Levu · Tafahi · Northwest Australian Basin · Derby · Kimberley Plateau · Coral Sea · New Hebrides · Efate · Port Vila · Viti Levu · Suva · Broome · Great Sandy Desert · Tanami Desert · Townsville · Récifs d'Entrecasteaux · Iles Loyauté · Tana · New Hebrides Trench · Tonga Islands · Ha'apai Group · Port Hedland · North West Cape · Hamersley Range · Macdonnell Ranges · Récifs et Chesterfield · Ile Matthew · Tongatapu · Nuku'alofa · Tonga Trench · Nouméa · Alice Springs · Simpson Desert · Carnarvon · Gibson Desert · Ayers Rock · Great Dividing Range · Fraser Island · South Fiji Basin · Vitiaz II Deep · AUSTRALIA · Great Artesian Basin · Charleville · Brisbane · Cape Byron · Great Victoria Desert · Lake Eyre · Lau Ridge · Raoul I. · Kermadec Islands · Geraldton · Norfolk · Norfolk Ridge · Lord Howe Rise · Nullarbor Plain · Flinders Ranges · Broken Hill · Darling · Lord-Howe · Three Kings Ridge · L'Esperance Rock · Perth · Cape Leeuwin · Great Australian Bight · Sydney · Vitiaz III Deep · Kermadec Trench · Diamantina Deep · Adelaide · Murray · Canberra · North Cape · Albany · Diamantina Trench · Kangaroo Island · Mt. Kosciusko · Auckland · South Australian Basin · Melbourne · Tasman Sea · North Island · Bass Strait · Cook Strait · Wellington · King Island · Furneaux Group · Tasman Basin · South Island · New Zealand · Chatham Rise · Chatham Islands · Tasmania · Hobart · Mt. Cook · Christchurch · INDIAN OCEAN · South East Cape · South Tasman Rise · Dunedin · Stewart Island · Bounty Islands

Pb 100° | Qa 110° | Qb 120° | Ra 130° | Rb 313 | Sa 150° | Sb 160° | Ta 170° | Tb 180° | Ba 170°

Scale 1:54,000,000

0 400 800 Kilometers

Depth tints

- Shoreline
- 0-200 m
- 200-2000 m
- 2000-4000 m
- 4000-6000 m
- 6000-8000 m
- > 8000 m

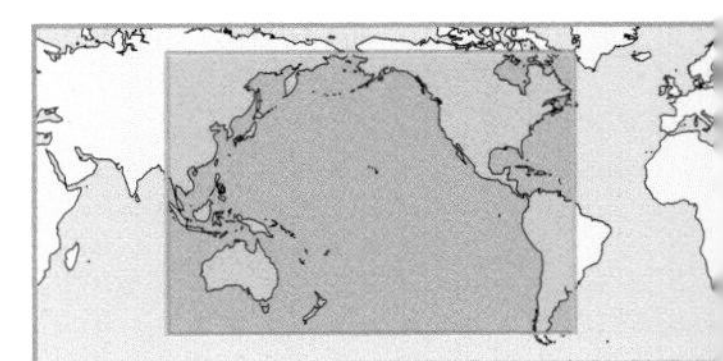

ıe largest bodies of water bordering the ıcific include the East China Sea and ellow Sea in the west, the Gulf of Alas- ı and Bering Sea in the north, the Sea Cortez in the east, and the Ross Sea the south. The farthest distance from ırth to south in the Pacific – from the ering Strait to Antarctica – covers ound 15,500 kilometers. The Straits Malacca are often considered the esternmost section of the Pacific. From east to west the greatest distance in the Pacific Ocean measures around 17,500 kilometers.

There are an estimated 25,000 islands in the Pacific, more than in all the other oceans combined. Most of the Pacific's islands lie south of the equator.

Several large underwater mountain chains rise in the Pacific Ocean. The East Pacific Rise is an **underwater mountain chain** stretching 8,700 kilometers through the Pacific, parallel to the South American coast. It is one section of the Pacific's massive mid-oceanic ridge. Magma from the earth's core runs out of these mountains, hardens, and becomes part of the ocean's floor.

The Pacific "Ring of Fire" encircles the entire ocean and is a zone of frequent volcanic eruptions and earthquakes. The zone contains numerous mountain ranges and trenches including the Mariana Trench, the Japan Trench and Cascade Mountains. In addition to earthquakes and eruptions, the coastal areas in the Pacific are also threatened by powerful cyclones and tsunamis. Many of the islands near the Asian mainland, including New Guinea, the Philippines and Taiwan, are of volcanic origin. In the southern and central Pacific the countless islands are divided into three regions: Polynesia, Micronesia, and Melanesia.

The Pacific region features many **active volcanoes**. The **Kamtchaka Peninsula** (top photo) and the **Andes Mountains** encompass (bottom photo) some of the world's most active volcanoes.

Mauna Kea on **Hawaii's Big Island** is a spectacular sight. The mountain stretches 5,500 meters from the ocean's floor to its surface. Its total height, above and below water, is around 9,700 meters.

The islands of Melanesia and Micronesia are situated in the western Pacific, northeast of Australia. Palau archipelago (photo) belongs to Micronesia.

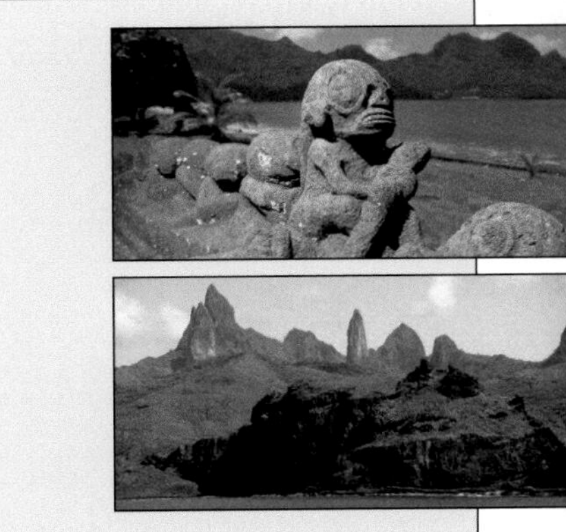

The **islands of Polynesia** lie in the central Pacific. The Samoan Islands (top photo) lie near the western edges of Polynesia. The Marquesas Islands (bottom photo) are a part of French Polynesia.

The **Easter Islands** lie 3,500 kilometers off the coast of South America. Its famous statues (photo) are called Moai.

hysical Features

- River, stream
- Intermittent river
- Lake
- Intermittent lake
- Salt lake
- Intermittent salt lake
- Elevation above sea level in meters

The index explained

All of the places named on the maps in the atlas are listed in the atlas index. The place names are listed alphabetically. Special symbols and letters including accents and umlauts are ignored in the order of the index. For example, the letters Á, Ä, Â are all categorized under A, and Ź, Ż, Ž are all treated as the standard Latin letter Z. Written characters consisting of two letters joined together (ligatures) are treated as two separate characters in the index: for example, words beginning with the character Æ would be indexed under AE.
The most commonly used abbreviations in the atlas – including N.P. for national park or N.W.R. for national wildlife refuge – are also used in the index. These abbreviations are listed and explained on this page (below). Generic geographic terms (sea, bay, etc.) and word articles (the, le, el, etc.) were used in the order of the index: for example, the Gulf of Mexico is listed under G and Le Havre, France is listed under L.
A special aspect of the atlas is the detailed and specially developed system of pictograms it features. These pictograms highlight famous travel routes, scenic landscapes, natural attractions, man-made attractions, cultural sites, as well as sporting, vacation, and recreation facilities. These pictograms also appear in the index (up to three per place nam
The pictograms provide a basic overvi of the attractions featured in a particu area. The meanings of all of the pic grams featured in the atlas are explain on the following page. In addition these pictograms, the index also fe tures special symbols to provide inform tion about the political status of cert places including states, provinces, a capital cities. Virtually all of the plac

Abbreviations

Abb. – Abbey, abbaye (French), abbadia (Span.), abbazia (Ital.)
Abor. – Aboriginal (indigenous inhabitants of Australia)
Aborig. – Aboriginal (indigenous inhabitants of Australia)
Ad. – Adas (Turkish) = Island
Ág. – Ági -os, -a, -i (Greek) = Saint
A.L. – Aboriginal Land = Aboriginal land reserve in Australia
Ban. – Banjaran (Malaysian) = mountain range
Bol'. – Bol'-šoj, -šaja, -šoe (Russian) = large-
C. – Cape, cap (French), cabo (Span./Port.), capo (Ital.)
Can. – Canal
Cast. – Castle, castel (French.), castillo (Span.), castelo (Port.), castello (Ital.)
Cd. – Ciudad (Span.), cidade (Port.) = city
Co. – Cerro (Span.) = mountain, hill
Conv. – Convento (Span.) = monastery
Cord. – Cordillera (Span.) = mountain range
Corr. – Corrente (Port.), corriente (Ital./Span.) = river
Cr. – Creek
D. – Dake (Jap.) = mountain
D. – Danau (Indonesian) = lake
Dağ. – Dağlar, dağları (Turkish) = mountain range
Ea. – Estancia (Span.) = estate
Emb. – Embalse (Span.), embassament (catalonian) = reservoir
Ens. – Ensenada (Span./Port.) = small bay
Erm. – Ermita (Span.) = hermitage
Est. – Estación (Span.) = rail station
Faz. – Fazenda (Port.) = estate
Fl. – Fleuve (French) = river
Fs. – waterfalls
g. – gawa (Jap.) = river
G. – Gora (Russian), góra (Polish), gunung (Indonesian) = mountain
Gde. – Grande (Span./French) = large
Geb. – Gebirge (German), gebergte (Dutch) = mountain range
Grd. – Grand (French) = large
Gt. – Great-
Hist. – Historic, historical
Hr. – Hrebet (Russian) = high
Ht. – Haut (French) = high-
Hte. – Haute (French) = high-
Hts. – Haut -s, -es (French) = high-
Hwy. – Highway
I. – Isla (Span.), ilha (Port.) = island
Î. – Île (French) = island
Ind. – Indian/ Native Americans
Ind.Res. – Indian Reservation = Native American land reserves in North America
Is. – Islands
Îs. – Îles (French) = islands
Jaz. – Jazovir (Bulg.) = reservoir
Jct. – Junction
Jez. – Jezioro (Pol.), jezero (Czech/Slovak./Serb./Croat./Slov.) = lake
Kan. – Kanal (Turk./Rus.), kanaal (Dutch), kanał (Pol.) = canal
Kep. – Kepulauan (Malaysian) = archipelago
Kg. – Kampong (Malaysian), kampung (Khmer) = village
Kör. – Körfezi (Turk.) = gulf, bay
L. – Lake, lac (French), lago (Ital./Span./Port.), loch, lough (Gaelic)
M. – Mys (Rus./Ukr.) = cape
Mal. – Malo, -yj, -aja, -oe (Rus.) = small
Mem. – Memorial
Mon. – Monastery, monastère (French.), monasterio (Span.), monastero (Ital.)
M.P. – Milli Parkı (Turk.) = national park
Mt. – Mount, mont (French)
Mta. – Montagna (Ital.), montaña (Span.) = mountain range
Mte. – Monte (Ital./Span./Port.), montagne (French) = mountain
Mtes. – Montes (Span./Port.), montagnes (French) = mountains
Mţi. – Munţii (Romanian) = mountain range
Mti. – Monti (Ital.) = mountain range
Mtn. – Mountain
Mtns. – Mountains
Mts. – Mountains, Monts (French)
Mus. – Musée (French), museo (Span.), museu (Port.) = museum
N. – North, Northern, Norte (Ital./Span./Port.), Norra (Swedish), Nørdre (Norwegian), Nørre (Danish), Nord (German)
Nac. – Nacional (Span.), Nacional'-nyj, -aja, -oe (Russian) = national
Naz. – Nazionale (Ital.) = national
N.B.C.A. – National Biodiversity and Conservation Area = protected natural area
Nev. – Nevado (Span.) = snow-covered mountain peaks
N.H.P. – National Historic Park
N.H.S. – National Historic Site
Niž. – Niž-e, -nij, -naja, -neje (Russian) = lower-
Nižm. – Nižmennost' (Rus.) = plain
N.M.P. – National Military Park
N.P. – National Park, Nationalpark (Swedish), nasjonal park (Norwegian), Nemzeti Park (Hungarian)
N.R. – Nature Reserve, Natuurreservaat (Dutch)
N.R.A. – National Recreation Area
N.S. – National Seashore
N.Sra. – Nossa Senhora (Port.) = our lady (Mary, the mother of Jesus)
Nva. – Nueva (Span.) = new-
Nvo. – Nuevo (Span.) = new-
N.W.R. – National Wildlife Refuge
o. – Ostrov (Rus.) = island
P. – Port (English and French), puerto (Span./Port.), porto (Ital.) = harbor
Peg. – Pegunungan (Indonesian) = mountain
Pen. – Peninsula, péninsule (franz.), península (Span.), penisola (Ital.)
Pk. – Peak
P.N. – Parc National (French), parque nacional (Span./Port.), parco nazionale (Ital.) = national park
p-ov. – Poluostrov (Rus.) = peninsula
Pres. – Presidente (Span./Port.) = president
Prov. – Provincial, Province
Pse. – Passe (French) = Pass
Pso. – Paso (Span.), passo (Ital.) = Pass
Pt. – Point
Pta. – Punta (Span./Port.) = point
Pte. – Pointe (French) = point
Pto. – Punto (Ital.) = point
Q.N.P. – Quasi National Park (Jap.) = national park
R. – River, rivière (French), río (Span.), ribeiro, rio (Port.), rîu (Romanian), reka (Bulgarian)
Ra. – Range
Rep. – Republic, république (French), república (Span./Port.), republicca (Ital.)
Repr. – Represa (Port.) = dam
Res. – Reserva (Span.), réserve (French) = nature reserve
Res. – Reservoir, réservoir (French)
Resp. – Respublika (Russian) = Republik
s. – San (Jap.) = mountain
S. – San (Span./Ital.), são (Port.) = saint
Sanc./Sanct. – Sanctuary
Sd. – Sound, sund (German, Danish, Norwegian, Swedish)
Sel. – Selat (Indonesian) = strait
Sg. – Song (Vietnamese) = river
S.H.P. – State Historic Park
S.H.S. – State Historic Site
Sk. – Shuiku (Chinese) = reservoir
S.M. – State Monument
S.P. – State Park
Sr. – Sredn -e, -ij, -jaja (Russian) = central, middle
Sra. – Sierra (Span.), serra (Port./Ital.) = mountain range
St./St – Saint (English and French), sankt (German, Dutch)
Sta. – Santa (Span./Port./Ital.) = saint
Star. – Star -o, -yj, -aja, -oe (Russian) old-
Ste – Sainte (French) = saint
Sth. – South, southern
St.Mem. – State Memorial
Sto. – Santo (Span./Port.) = Saint
Str. – Street, Strait, stretto (Italian), stræde (Danish), stret (Norwegian)
t. – tau (Kaz.) = mountain
T. – Take (Jap.) = peak, summit
T. – Temple
Tel. – Teluk (Indonesian) = bay
Tg. – Tanjung (Indonesian) = cape
T.I. – Terra Indígena (Port.), territorio indigena (Span.) = indigenous land reservation in Latin America
Vdhr. – Vodohranilišče (Russian) = reservoir
Vel. – Velik -o, -ij, -yki, -oe (Rus.) = large-
Verh. – Verhn -ee, -ie, -ij, -jaja (Rus.) mountain
Vill. – Village
vlk. – Vulkan (Rus.) = volcano
Vol. – Volcano, volcan (French), volcán (Span.)
Vul. – Vulkan (German.), Vulcano (Ital./Romanian) = volcano
W.A. – Wilderness Area
Wildl. – Wildlife
W.S. – Wildlife Sanctuary
Y. – Yama (Jap.) = mountain, mountain range
Zal. – Zaliv (Russian), zalew (Polish) bay
Zap. – Zapovednik (Russian) = nature reserve
Z.B. – Nature reserve in the People's Republic of China
Zp. – Zapadn -e, -ji, -aja, -noe (Russian) = west, western

ted in the atlas have a country reference; these nations are identified by eir international license (registration) ate codes. The various international ense codes are identified on this page. the case of communities and areas at are located on or between the borrs of two nations, the license plate des of both nations are listed and parated by a backslash. e names of areas and geographic features that cannot be assigned to specific states, such as the Atlantic Ocean, are followed by the page number of a map featuring the area and the number of the map grid box in which the area is depicted on the map.

Niue		**NZ**	164	Bf55
Place name	Pictograms	Nation	Page	Map grid

nternational license (registration) plate code

	Austria
FG	Afghanistan
G	Antigua and Barbuda
	Albania
ND	Andorra
NG	Angola
RM	Armenia
JS	Australia
Z	Azerbaijan
	Belgium
D	Bangladesh
DS	Barbados
	Burkina Faso
G	Bulgaria
	Belize
IT	Bhutan
H	Bosnia and Herzegovina
OL	Bolivia
R	Brazil
RN	Bahrain
RU	Brunei
S	Bahamas
J	Burundi
Y	Belarus
	Cuba
AM	Cameroon
DN	Canada
H	Switzerland
	Cote d'Ivoire
	Sri Lanka
O	Colombia
OM	Comoros
R	Costa Rica
CV	Cape Verde
CY	Cyprus
CZ	Czech Republic
D	Germany
DARS	Western Sahara
DJI	Djibouti
DK	Denmark
DOM	Dominican Republic
DVRK	Korea, North
DY	Benin
DZ	Algeria
E	Spain
EAK	Kenya
EAT	Tanzania
EAU	Uganda
EC	Ecuador
ER	Eritrea
ES	El Salvador
EST	Estonia
ET	Egypt
ETH	Ethiopia
F	France
FIN	Finland
FJI	Fiji
FL	Liechtenstein
FSM	Micronesia
G	Gabon
GB	Great Britain
GCA	Guatemala
GE	Georgia
GH	Ghana
GNB	Guinea-Bissau
GQ	Equatorial Guinea
GR	Greece
GUY	Guyana
H	Hungary
HN	Honduras
HR	Croatia
I	Italy
IL	Israel
IND	India
IR	Iran
IRL	Ireland
IRQ	Iraq
IS	Iceland
J	Japan
JA	Jamaica
JOR	Jordan
K	Cambodia
KIR	Kiribati
KN	Saint Kitts and Nevis
KS	Kyrgyzstan
KSA	Saudi Arabia
KWT	Kuwait
KZ	Kazakhstan
L	Luxembourg
LAO	Laos
LAR	Libya
LB	Liberia
LS	Lesotho
LT	Lithuania
LV	Latvia
M	Malta
MA	Morocco
MAL	Malaysia
MC	Monaco
MD	Moldova
MEX	Mexico
MH	Marshall Islands
MK	Macedonia
MNG	Mongolia
MOC	Mozambique
MS	Mauritius
MV	Maldives
MW	Malawi
MYA	Burma
N	Norway
NAM	Namibia
NAU	Nauru
NEP	Nepal
NIC	Nicaragua
NL	Netherlands
NZ	New Zealand
OM	Oman
P	Portugal
PA	Panama
PAL	Palau
PE	Peru
PK	Pakistan
PL	Poland
PNG	Papua New Guinea
PY	Paraguay
Q	Qatar
RA	Argentina
RB	Botswana
RC	Taiwan
RCA	Central African Republic
RCB	Republic of the Congo
RCH	Chile
RDC	Democratic Republic of the Congo
RG	Guinea
RH	Haiti
RI	Indonesia
RIM	Mauritania
RL	Lebanon
RM	Madagascar
RMM	Mali
RN	Niger
RO	Romania
ROK	Korea, South
ROU	Uruguay
RP	Philippines
RSM	San Marino
RT	Togo
RUS	Russia
RWA	Rwanda
S	Sweden
SA	South Africa
SD	Swaziland
SGP	Singapore
SCG	Serbia and Montenegro
SK	Slovakia
SLO	Slovenia
SME	Suriname
SN	Senegal
SOL	Solomon Islands
SP	Somalia
STP	São Tomé und Príncipe
SUD	Sudan
SY	Seychelles
SYR	Syria
TCH	Chad
THA	Thailand
TIM	East Timor
TJ	Tajikistan
TM	Turkmenistan
TN	Tunisia
TO	Tonga
TR	Turkey
TT	Trinidad and Tobago
TUV	Tuvalu
UA	Ukraine
UAE	United Arab Emirates
USA	United States of America
UZB	Uzbekistan
V	Vatican City
VN	Vietnam
VRC	China
VU	Vanuatu
WAG	Gambia
WAL	Sierra Leone
WAN	Nigeria
WD	Dominica
WG	Grenada
WL	Saint Lucia
WS	Samoa
WV	Saint Vincent and the Grenadines
YE	Yemen
YV	Venezuela
Z	Zambia
ZW	Zimbabwe

ymbols used in the index

City
State
Capital
Province
Provincial Capital

rincipal travel routes

Auto route
Rail road
Highspeed train
Shipping route

emarkable landscapes and atural monuments

UNESCO World Natural Heritage
Mountain landscape
Rock landscape
Ravine/canyon
Extinct volcano
Active volcano
Geyser
Cave
Glacier
River landscape
Waterfall/rapids
Lake country
Desert
Oasis
Fossil site
Depression
Nature park
National park (landscape)
National park (flora)
National park (fauna)
National park (culture)
Biosphere reserve
Wildlife reserve
Whale watching
Turtle conservation area
Protected area for sea-lions/seals
Protected area for penguins
Zoo/safari park
Crocodile farm
Coastal landscape
Beach
Coral reef
Island
Underwater reserve

Remarkable Cities and cultural monuments

UNESCO World Cultural Heritage
Pre- and early history
Prehistoric rockscape
The Ancient Orient
Ancient Egypt
Ancient Egyptian pyramids
Minoan culture
Phoenecian culture
Early African culture
Etruscan culture
Greek antiquity
Roman antiquity
Nabatean culture
Vikings
Ancient India
Ancient China
Ancient Japan
Mayan culture
Inca culture
Aztec culture
Other ancient American cultures
Places of Jewish cultural interest
Places of Christian cultural interest
Places of Islamic cultural interest
Places of Buddhist cultural interest
Places of Hindu cultural interest
Places of Jainist cultural interest
Places of Sikh cultural interest
Places of Shinto cultural interest
Places of cultural interest to other religions
Places of cultural interest to indigenous peoples (native peoples)
Aborigine reservation
Places of Aboriginal cultural interest
Indian reservation
Indian Pueblo culture
Places of Indian cultural interest
Amazonian Indians/protected area
Cultural landscape
Historical city scape
Impressive skyline
Castle/fortress/fort
Caravanserai
Palace
Technical/industrial monument
Dam
Remarkable lighthouse
Remarkable bridge
Tomb/grave
Theater of war/battlefield
Monument
Memorial
Space mission launch site
Space telescope
Market
Festivals
Museum
Theater
World exhibition
Olympics

Sport and leisure destinations

Arena/stadium
Race track
Golf
Horse racing
Skiing
Sailing
Diving
Windsurfing
Surfing
Canoeing/rafting
Seaport
Deep-sea fishing
Waterskiing
Beach resort
Mineral/thermal spa
Amusement/theme park
Casino
Hill resort
Lodge

Special index pictograms

Bodies of Water
Canal
Other physical names
Pass
Underwater topography

wa IND (GUJ) 190 Og35
war YE 150 Nd39
Ais NAM 302 Lj59
Ais Hot Springs NAM 302 Lj59
Ais Warmwaterbrönne NAM 302 Lj59
aktalik Island USA 16 Cd17
alik Cape USA 15 Cf16
apuá BR (AM) 62 Gj48
awetë Igarapé Ipixuna, T.I. BR 63 Hd48
ban UAE 156 Nh33
ere E 107 Kt52
etsu J 181 Sb24
hach D 115 Lm42
luna RI 213 Rh48
luna RI 213 Rh48
ma River PNG 242 Sb49
ere WAN 280 Ld42
gen A 115 Lo42
gen A 115 Lp43
gene mekeni KZ 158 Oe23
giali GR 129 Mf54
gialousa CY 131 Mp55
gle CH 114 Lg44
gnay-le-Duc F 103 Le43
gre F 104 La45
grefeuille-d'Aunis F 104 Ku44
guá ROU 77 Hc63
guebelle F 105 Lg45
guebelle, P.N. d' CDN 30 Ga21
gues F 105 Le46
gues-Mortes F 105 Le47
güestortes i Estany de Sant Maurici, P.N. de E 110 La48
guilete, Cerro RCH 82 Gd71
guille du Midi F 105 Lg45
guilles F 105 Lg46
guilles de Sindou BF 279 Kh40
guillon F 104 La46
gurande F 104 Lb44
hole IND 190 Oh38
i PE 66 Gb50
awa J 183 Rk26
ken USA (SC) 35 Fk29
lao Shan VRC 195 Qa33
efroide F 105 Lg46
eron AUS (NT) 226 Rg57
gandi PA 43 Ga41
nginae Atoll MH 241 Tb16
nglapalag Atoll MH 241 Tb17
ly-sur-Noye F 103 Lc41
uk Atoll MH 241 Tb16
nachá del Valle RA (TU) 76 Gh59
nogasta RA (LR) 76 Gg60
norés BR (MG) 75 Hk55
nabulak KZ 166 Of21
n al Arab SYR 147 Mk27
n Attaya RIM 264 Kd35
nazi LV 97 Me33
n-Beïda DZ 260 Ld28
n Benian DZ 259 Lb27
n Benimathar MA 259 Kj28
n Ben Tili RIM 264 Kf33
n Bessem DZ 259 Lb27
n Boubat RIM 269 Kd37
n Dara SYR 146 Mj27
n Defla DZ 259 La27
n Deheb DZ 259 La28
n Draham TN 260 Le27
n-Ech-Chair MA 259 Kj29
n el Bell DZ 259 Lb28
n el Brod DZ 260 Lc31
n el Hadja DZ 259 La28
n-el-Hadjadj DZ 259 Lb31
n el Hadjar DZ 266 Lc32
n el Hadjel DZ 259 Lb28
n el Hamara DZ 259 Lb28
n el Hamman DZ 259 Lc27
n el Melh DZ 259 Lc28
n-el-Türck DZ 259 Kk28
n Fakroun DZ 260 Ld28
n Fekan DZ 259 La28
nggyi MYA 194 Ph35
nhoa F 104 Kt47
n Kerch DZ 260 Ld28
n Kermes DZ 259 La28
n Khadra DZ 259 Lc28
n-Leuh MA 258 Kh29
n Madhi DZ 259 Lb29
n Mahdi DZ 260 Ld27
nos N.P. GR 128 Ma52
n Oulmene DZ 260 Lc28
n Oussera DZ 259 Lb28
nsa E 110 La48
n Sefra DZ 259 Kk29
n Skhouna DZ 259 La28
n Sukhnah ET 263 Mg31
nsworth USA (NE) 26 Fa24
n Tamr TN 260 Le29
n Taya DZ 259 Lb27
n Tédelès DZ 259 La28
n Témouchent DZ 259 Kk28
ntree GB 101 Ks37
ome PNG 243 Sc48
ome, Mount PNG 243 Sc48
quile BOL 72 Gh55
quiri BR 67 Gg50
abu RI 199 Qd44
aines F 103 Lb41
asca I 120 Lh46
balam RI 206 Pk45
bangis RI 206 Pk45
bara RI 207 Qd47
drie CDN (AB) 19 Ec20
eborough GB 101 Kt37
e-sur-l'Ador F 104 Ku47
e-sur-la-Lys F 103 Lc40
gegas RI 207 Qd47
i BR (PE) 71 Ja50
lie AUS (QLD) 233 Se56
olo CH 114 Lj44
ou Azbine RN 266 Le36
panas RI 214 Rc49
vault F 102 Ku44
wa IND (UPH) 189 Ok32
yk KZ 166 Oj20
sch D 115 Ll41
shihik CDN (YT) 17 Db15
shihik Lake CDN 17 Db15
sne F 103 Ld41
ana E 109 Ku48
ape PNG 242 Sb47
-Baha MA 258 Kf30
Ben Haddou MA 258 Kg30
eke Bi KZ 158 Ob23
-Hamane MA 258 Kg30
kin USA (MN) 27 Fd22
-Melloul MA 258 Kf30
Morrhad MA 258 Kh30
ong EAK 290 Mh46
-Ourir MA 258 Kg30
Sadane MA 258 Kh30
ambe BR 62 Gh46
ad RO 124 Md44
Aiuiá-Miçu BR 69 Hd51
Aiviekste LV 97 Mg34
Aix-en-Othe F 103 Ld42
Aix-en-Provence F 105 Lf47
Aixe-sur-Vienne F 104 Lb45
Aix-les-Bains F 105 Lf45
Aiy Adi ETH 277 Mk40
Aiyar Reservoir IND 191 Pc34
Aiyetoro WAN 280 Lb42
Aiyetoro WAN 280 Lc42
Aiyrtas KZ 166 Oj21
Aizanoi TR 130 Mk51
Aizawl IND (MZR) 194 Pg34
Aizenay F 102 Kt44
Aizkraukle LV 97 Mf34
Aizpute LV 97 Mb34
Aizu-Wakamatsu J 183 Rk27
Ajabshir IR 154 Nc27
Ajaccio F 111 Lj49
Ajai Game Reserve EAU 290 Mf44
Ajaigarh IND (MPH) 191 Pa33
Ajajú CO 61 Gd45
Ajak RUS 180 Rd19
Ajana AUS (WA) 224 Qh59
Ajanta IND (MHT) 190 Oh35
Ajanta Caves IND 190 Oh35
Ajaokuta WAN 280 Ld42
Ajarani BR 58 Gk44
Ajasse WAN 280 Lc41
Ajasso WAN 280 La42
Ajax, Mount NZ 239 Tg67
Aj Bogd Uul MNG 167 Ph23
Ajdabiya LAR 261 Ma30
Ajdar UA 133 Mk21
Ajdarly KZ 158 Oc23
Ajdir MA 259 Kj28
Ajdovščina SLO 121 Lo45
Ajigasawa J 183 Sa25
Ajinskoe RUS 181 Sb21
Aj'jawdiyeh SYR 147 Na27
Ajjibal Attadmur Iych SYR 146 Mj28
Ajka H 118 Ls43
Ajman UAE 156 Nh33
Ajmer IND (RJT) 188 Oh32
Ajmer Sharief IND 188 Oh32
Ajni TJ 158 Oe26
Ajo USA (AZ) 22 Ed29
Ajoda WAN 280 Lc42
Ajoya MEX (SL) 38 Eg33
Ajra IND (MHT) 190 Oh37
Ajrestan AFG 160 Od29
Ajtos BG 127 Mh48
Ajtte S 90 Lk12
Ajumaku GH 279 Kk43
Ajuruteua BR (PA) 64 Hg46
Ajuy RP 205 Rb40
Akabar RMM 271 La38
Akabli DZ 266 La32
Akadomari J 183 Rk27
Akadyr KZ 166 Og21
Aka-Eze WAN 280 Ld43
Akagera, P.N. de l' RWA 292 Mf46
Akagi J 183 Rg28
Akaishi-sanmyakhu J 183 Rk28
Akakbe CAM 280 Le43
Akaki ETH 284 Mk41
Akakro CI 279 Kh43
Akakus LAR 267 Lf33
Akala SUD 277 Mj39
Akalkot IND (MHT) 190 Oj37
Akam Éffak G 281 Lf45
Akamkpa WAN 280 Le43
Akanda, P.N. d' G 280 Le45
Akankoshan J 181 Sc24
Akan N.P. J 181 Sc24
Akarkar RN 272 Ld38
Akarnaniká GR 128 Mb52
Akaroa NZ 239 Tg67
Akasame PNG 243 Sb49
Akasha SUD 276 Mf36
Akashat IRQ 147 Mk29
Akassa WAN 280 Ld43
Akat Amnuai THA 197 Qb37
Akats GH 279 La42
Akbado DY 279 Lb42
Akbarpur IND (UPH) 189 Pb32
Akbelenli TR 131 Mf53
Akbou DZ 259 Lc27
Akçaabat TR 145 Mk25
Akçadağ TR 145 Mk26
Akçakale TR 145 Mk27
Akçakent TR 131 Mp51
Akçakısla TR 131 Mq51
Akçakoca TR 131 Mm49
Akçakoca Dağları TR 131 Mm50
Akçalar TR 144 Mj27
Akçalı Dağları TR 144 Mg27
Akçaova TR 130 Mj53
Akçaova TR 130 Mk49
Akçay TR 131 Mk54
Akçay TR 145 Nb25
Akchâr RIM 264 Kc35
Akcjabrski BY 132 Me19
Akdağ TR 130 Mj51
Akdağ TR 130 Mj53
Akdağ TR 131 Mq51
Ak Dağlar TR 131 Mk54
Akdağmadeni TR 131 Mq51
Akdepe TM 153 Nk24
Akdere TR 130 Mk52
Ak-Dovurak RUS (TUV) 167 Pf20
Akébou RT 279 La42
Akelamo RI 212 Rd45
Akelamo RI 212 Re45
Aken D 113 Ln39
Åkernes N 92 Lh32
Åkersberga S 93 Lt31
Åkers styckebruk S 93 Ls31
Akespe KZ 153 Oa22
Aketi RDC 287 Mb44
Aketi RDC 287 Mc44
Akhalkalaki GE 152 Nb25
Akhaltsikhe GE 152 Nb25
Akhiok USA (AK) 16 Cc17
Akhisar TR 129 Mh52
Akhmeta GE 152 Nc25
Akhmim ET 263 Mf32
Akhnoor IND 161 Oh29
Akhpat and Sanain Monasteries ARM 152 Nc25
Aki J 183 Rg29
Akiachak USA (AK) 14 Bk15
Akiéni G 288 Lg46
Akimiski Island CDN 25 Fk19
Akın TR 131 Mo51
Akıncı Burnu TR 144 Mh27
Akinum PNG 243 Se49
Akita J 183 Sa26
Akividu IND (APH) 191 Pa37
Akjoujt RIM 269 Kc36
Akka MA 258 Kf31
Akkajaure S 90 Lj12
Akkent TR 130 Mk52
Akkeshi J 181 Sc24
'Akko IS 146 Mh29
Akkol KZ 158 Of24
Akkol Lake KZ 158 Of24
Akkoursoulbak RCA 282 Ma41
Akköy TR 129 Mh53
Akköy TR 130 Mk53
Akköy TR 144 Mg26
Akkum KZ 158 Of24
Ak Kuprak = Keshendeh AFG 160 Od27
Akkuş TR 145 Mj25
Aklampa DY 280 Lb41
Aklera IND (RJT) 190 Oj33
Akmektep KZ 167 Pb22
Akmenrags LV 97 Mb34
Akmeqit VRC (XUZ) 168 Oj27
Akmeşe TR 130 Ml50
Akniste LV 97 Mf34
Aknoul MA 259 Kj28
Ako J 183 Rh28
Akobo ETH 283 Mg42
Akodiya IND (MPH) 190 Oj34
Akok G 280 Le45
Akoke SUD 283 Mg41
Akokora RDC 287 Me45
Akola IND (MHT) 190 Oj35
Akoma PNG 243 Sc49
Akom II CAM 281 Lf44
Akono CAM 281 Lf44
Akonolinga CAM 281 Lg44
Akop SUD 283 Me41
Akorabi GUY 58 Ha43
Akordat ER 277 Mj39
Akören TR 131 Mn53
Akören TR 144 Mg27
Akoroso GH 279 Kk43
Akosombo GH 279 La42
Akosombo Dam GH 279 La42
Akot IND (MHT) 190 Oj35
Akot SUD 283 Mf42
Akoupé CI 279 Kj42
Akparé RT 279 La42
Akpınar TR 130 Ml51
Akpınar TR 131 Ml51
Akpınar TR 131 Mo51
Akpınar TR 131 Mp51
Akplabnya GH 279 La43
Akposso RT 279 La42
Akqi VRC (XUZ) 168 Ok25
Akrabat TM 155 Oa28
Åkrahamn N 92 Lf31
Akrai I 122 Lp53
Akranes IS 90 Jj13
Akre IRQ 147 Nb27
Akréréb RN 272 Le37
Åkrestrømmen N 92 Lm29
Akron USA (CO) 26 Ej25
Akron USA (IA) 27 Fb24
Akron USA (OH) 33 Fk25
Akrópolis GR 128 Md53
Akrópolis GR 129 Mj54
Akropong GH 279 Kk42
Akrotiri CY 131 Mn56
Akrotiri GR 129 Mf54
Akrotíri Ágios Ioánnis GR 129 Mf55
Akrotíri Ákrathos GR 127 Me50
Akrotíri Áraxos GR 128 Mb52
Akrotíri Doukáto GR 128 Ma52
Akrotíri Drépano GR 127 Md51
Akrotíri Kassándra GR 126 Md51
Akrotíri Kilíni GR 128 Mb53
Akrotíri Kímis GR 128 Me52
Akrotíri Kriós GR 128 Md55
Akrotíri Lithári GR 129 Me52
Akrotíri Lithino GR 129 Me56
Akrotíri Maléas GR 128 Md54
Akrotíri Murzeflos GR 127 Mf51
Akrotíri Palioúri GR 127 Md51
Akrotíri Salonikiós GR 127 Me50
Akrotíri Soúnio GR 128 Me53
Akrotíri Ténaro GR 128 Mc54
Akša RUS 173 Qg20
Ak-Saj KS 159 Oh25
Aksaj RUS 135 Mk22
Akşar TR 145 Nb25
Aksaray TR 131 Mp52
Aksay VRC (GSU) 169 Ph26
Aksay Qin 161 Ok28
Aksayqin Co 161 Ok28
Aksdal N 92 Lf31
Akşehir TR 131 Mm52
Akşehir Gölü TR 131 Mm52
Akseki TR 131 Mm53
Akshatau KZ 166 Og22
Akshyghanak KZ 158 Oe24
Aksoran tau KZ 166 Oh21
Aksu KZ 158 Oe24
Aksu KZ 166 Oe23
Aksu KZ 166 Ok23
Aksu TR 131 Ml54
Aksu TR 131 Mm53
Aksu VRC (XUZ) 168 Pa25
Aksuat KZ 166 Pb22
Aksuat KZ 167 Pb21
Aksu-Ayuly KZ 166 Og21
Aksubaevo RUS (TAR) 133 Nf18
Aksu Canyon KZ 158 Of24
Aksu Çay TR 131 Ml53
Aksum ETH 277 Mk39
Aksumite royal city of Kohaito ER 277 Mk39
Aksu-Zhabaghly Nature Reserve KZ 158 Of24
Ak-Şyjak KS 159 Ok25
Ak Tag VRC 168 Pc27
Ak-Tal KS 159 Oh25
Aktanys RUS (TAR) 133 Nh18
Aktarsk RUS 133 Nc20
Aktas KZ 166 Og21
Aktaš RUS (ALT) 167 Pd20
Aktau KZ 152 Nf24
Aktaz VRC (XUZ) 169 Pd26
Aktoghai KZ 166 Oh21
Aktoghai KZ 166 Ok22
Aktuzla TR 145 Nb26
Akubu SUD 283 Mg42
Akubu SUD 283 Mg42
Akula RDC 286 Ma44
Akulurak USA (AK) 14 Bh14
Akumadan GH 279 Kk42
Akumal MEX (QTR) 41 Fg35
Akune J 185 Rf29
Akun Island USA 14 Bh18
Akuraj RUS 173 Qj20
Akure WAN 280 Lc42
Akuressa CL 193 Pa43
Akureyri IS 90 Ka13
Akuseki-jima J 185 Re31
Akutan USA (AK) 14 Bh18
Akutan Island USA 14 Bg18
Akutukpa WAN 280 Ld41
Håverud Akvedukt S 92 Ln32
Akvinu River CDN 19 Ec18
Akwanga WAN 272 Le41
Akwatuk Bay CDN 25 Ga19
Akwaya CAM 280 Le42
Akyab = Sittwe MYA 194 Pg35
Akyaka TR 131 Mo54
Akyazı TR 130 Ml50
Akyma GUY 58 Ha43
Akyurt TR 131 Mo50
Akzhaikyn köli KZ 158 Od23
Akzhal KZ 166 Oh22
Akzhar KZ 166 Oh23
Akzhar KZ 166 Oj23
Akzhar KZ 167 Pb22
Akzhar Lake KZ 158 Oe23
Ål N 92 Lj30
Al RI 212 Re48
Ala S 93 Ls29
Al A'amiyah IRQ 147 Nc29
Al-Aan Palace KSA 150 Nc37
Ala-Archa Canyon KS 159 Oh24
Ala-Archa N.P. KS 159 Oh24
Alabama USA 13 Fc12
Alabama and Coushatta Ind. Res. USA 29 Fc30
Alaban RI 198 Pj44
Alabat Island RP 203 Rb38
al-'Abbasiya SUD 283 Mf39
Ala-Bel KS 159 Og24
Alabel RP 205 Rc42
Al 'Abr YE 150 Nd37
Ala-Buka KS 159 Of25
Ala-Buka KS 159 Oh25
Alaca TR 131 Mp50
Alacahan TR 145 Mj26
Alacalı TR 130 Mk49
Alaçam TR 144 Mh25
Alaçam Dağları TR 130 Mj51
Alacami TR 131 Mn54
Alacant E 109 Ku48
Alaçatı TR 129 Mg52
Ala Dağlar TR 131 Mq53
Ala Dağlar TR 145 Nb26
Ala DağlarTasarı Milli Parkı TR 131 Mq53
Al 'Adam LAR 261 Mb30
Aladdin USA (WY) 21 Eh23
Aladdin Tomb Tower IR 154 Nf28
Aladža džamija MK 126 Ma48
Aladža manastir BG 127 Mh47
Aladzha TM 153 Ng26
Alaejos E 106 Kp51
Alafiarou DY 272 Lb41
Alaganik USA (AK) 16 Ch15
Alaganik Lake USA 14 Ca16
Alagir RUS (SOA) 152 Nc24
Alagiri IND (APH) 193 Ok40
Alag Khayrkhan Uul MNG 167 Ph23
Alagna Valésia I 120 Lh45
Alag nuur MNG 167 Ph23
Alagoa Grande BR (PB) 65 Jc49
Alagoas BR 53 Ja20
Alagoinhas BR (CE) 65 Ja47
Alagoinhas BR (BA) 71 Ja52
Alagón E 107 Kt51
Alagoninha do Piauí BR (PI) 65 Hk49
Alahan TR 144 Mg27
Alahanpanjang RI 206 Qa46
Al-'Ain SUD 276 Me38
Al Ain UAE 157 Nh33
Al Aiss KSA 148 Mk33
Al-Ajaiz OM 151 Nj36
Alajskij hrebet KS 159 Of26
Alajuela CR 42 Fh40
Alakamisy Itenina RM 306 Nd56
Alakanuk USA (AK) 14 Bh14
Al Akhdar KSA 146 Mj31
Alaköl KZ 166 Oh22
Alakol KZ 166 Pa22
Alakuko WAN 280 Lc42
Alakurtti RUS 91 Mf12
Alalaú BR 62 Gk46
Al Alia DZ 260 Lc29
Al A'lyaneh SYR 146 Mk28
Al Amadiyah IRQ 147 Nb27
Al 'Amar KSA 149 Nc33
Al Amara IRQ 147 Nd30
al-'Amara SUD 276 Mg39
Alamat'a ETH 277 Mk40
Alambie AUS (NSW) 234 Sb61
Alamdo VRC (TIB) 171 Ph30
Alameda CDN (SK) 24 Ej21
Alamikamba NIC 42 Fh39
Alaminos RP 202 Qk37
Alamo MEX (VC) 40 Fb35
Álamo Chapo MEX (CHH) 23 Eh31
Alamogordo USA (NM) 23 Eh29
Alamo Lake USA 22 Ed28
Alamo Navajo Ind. Res. USA 23 Eg28
Alamor EC 60 Fk47
Álamos MEX (SO) 38 Ef32
Alamosa USA (CO) 23 Eh27
Alamos de Márquez MEX (COH) 23 Ej31
Al Amrashi YE 150 Nc37
Alamuru IND (APH) 191 Pa37
Al ,Anad YE 150 Nc39
Åland = Ahvenanmaa FIN 93 Lu30
Aland IND (KTK) 190 Oj37
Al Andalus Expreso E 109 Kr47
Älandsbro S 93 Ls28
Ålands hav S 93 Lu30
Alandur IND (TNU) 193 Pa40
Alanga G 288 Lg46
Alang Besar RI 198 Qa44
Alange E 108 Ko48
Alanggantang RI 207 Qc46
Alangouassou CI 279 Kh42
Alanis E 108 Kp48
Alanjeq IR 154 Nd26
Alanson USA (MI) 32 Fh23
Alanta LT 97 Mf35
Alantika Mountains WAN 281 Lg41
Alanya TR 131 Mm54
Alapa WAN 272 Lc41
Alaplı TR 131 Mm49
Alappuzha IND (KER) 192 Oj41
Al ,Aqiq KSA 148 Na35
Alarahan Caravanserai TR 131 Mm54
Alaraz E 106 Kp50
Alarcón E 109 Ks49
Al Aredah KSA 150 Nb37
Al Arin KSA 150 Nb36
Alarobia-Andalandranobe RM 306 Nd56
Al Artawiyah KSA 149 Nc32
Alas RI 198 Pj44
Alas RI 211 Qj50
Alaşehir TR 130 Mj52
Al-Ashkhara OM 157 Nk35
Al-Ashrafiya Mosque YE 150 Nb39
Al 'Ashuriyah IRQ 147 Nb30
Alaska USA 10 Ca06
Alaska ZW 296 Mf54
Alaska Highway USA 15 Ch14
Alaska Marine Highway USA (AK) 14 Cb17
Alaska Maritime Wildlife Refuge USA (AK) 14 Bg18
Alaska Peninsula USA 10 Bd07
Alaska Peninsula Wildlife Refuge USA 14 Ca17
Alaska Range USA 15 Ce14
Al Asma x RIM 269 Kc36
Alassa CY 131 Mn56
Al 'Assafiyah KSA 146 Mk31
Al'Assah LAR 260 Lf29
Alássio I 120 Lj47
Alasso RMM 270 Kf38
Alastaro FIN 96 Mc30
Alat AZ 152 Ne26
Al Atawlah KSA 148 Na35
Alataw Shankou KZ/VRC 166 Pb23
Al Athalah KSA 149 Nb33
Alati CAM 281 Lg44
Alatna River USA 15 Cd12
Alatri I 122 Lo49
Alatsinainy Bakaro RM 306 Nd55
Alatskivi EST 96 Mh32
Alatyr' RUS 133 Nc18
Alatyr' RUS (CHU) 133 Nd18
Alausí EC 60 Ga47
Alaverdi ARM 152 Nc25
Alavus FIN 96 Md28
Alawa WAN 272 Ld40
Alawa A.L. AUS 223 Rh53
Al-'Awabi OM 157 Nj34
Al Awaynat LAR 267 Lf33
Al Awaynat LAR 275 Mc35
Al-'Awir UAE 156 Nh33
Al-'Aydarus Mosque YE 150 Nc39
Al Ayn KSA 149 Nc32
Al-Ayn OM 157 Nj34
Alayo RCA 286 Mb43
Al-'Ayun MA/DARS 264 Kd32
Alazani AZ/GE 152 Nd25
Alazejskoe ploskogor'e RUS 141 Sb05
Al'Aziziyah LAR 260 Lg29
Al Azraq JOR 146 Mj30
Alb CH 114 Lj43
Alba I 120 Lj46
Al Ba'aj IRQ 147 Na27
Al Bab SYR 146 Mj27
Albac RO 124 Mc44
Albacete E 109 Kt48
Al Bad' KSA 146 Mh31
Al Bada'i' KSA 148 Mk32
Al Badaya KSA 149 Nb33
Alba de Tormes E 106 Kp50
Al Badi IRQ 147 Na28
Al Badi KSA 149 Nb35
Al Badia KSA 150 Nc37
Ålbæk DK 94 Ll33
Ålbæk Bugt DK 94 Ll33
Al Baha KSA 148 Na36
Albaida E 109 Ku48
Alba Iulia RO 124 Md44
Albalate del Arzobispo E 107 Ku51
Albalate de Zorita E 109 Ks50
Al Baleed OM 151 Nh37
Alban CO 56 Gc43
Alban = San José CO 60 Gb45
Alban F 104 Lc47
Albania AL 126 Lu50
Albano Laziale I 122 Ln49
Albany AUS (WA) 228 Qj63
Albany USA (OR) 20 Dj23
Albany USA (MO) 27 Fc25
Albany USA (TX) 28 Fa29
Albany USA (NY) 33 Gd24
Albany USA (KY) 35 Fh27
Albany USA (GA) 35 Fh30
Albanyà E 110 Lc48
Albany Downs AUS (QLD) 235 Se59
Albany River CDN 25 Fh20
Al Bardi LAR 262 Mc30
Albardón RA (SJ) 76 Gf61
Al Barit IRQ 147 Nb30
Albarracín E 109 Kt50
al-Barun SUD 283 Mg40
al-Basabir SUD 276 Mg38
Al Basira SYR 147 Na28
Al Basiri SYR 146 Mj28
Al Basra IRQ 147 Nd30
Al Basra IRQ 147 Nd30
Al Batha IRQ 147 Nc30
Albatross Bay AUS 230 Sa52
Albatross-eiland NAM 302 Lh59
Albatross Island NAM 302 Lh59
Al Bayda LAR 261 Ma29
Al Bayda YE 150 Nc38
Albazino RUS 180 Rc19
Albemarle USA (NC) 35 Fk28
Albemarle Sound USA 35 Gb27
Albena BG 127 Mj47
Albenga I 120 Lj46
Albentosa E 109 Ku50
Albergaria-a-Velha P 106 Km50
Alberga River AUS 227 Rh59
Albermarle = Isla Isabela EC 60 Fe46
Albernoa P 108 Kn47
Alberobello I 123 Ls50
Albersdorf D 112 Lk36
Albert F 103 Lc40
Alberta CDN 10 Ea08
Albert Edward, Mount PNG 243 Sd50
Albert Falls SA 303 Mf60
Alberti RA (BA) 77 Gk63
Albert I Land N 84 Lf06
Albertinia SA 302 Ma63
Albert Lea USA (MN) 27 Fd24
Albert Nile EAU 255 Mc18
Alberto de Agostini, P.N. RCH 82 Ge73
Alberton CDN (PE) 31 Gh22
Albert Town BS 37 Gc34
Albertville F 105 Lg45
Albertville USA (AL) 34 Fg28
Albeşti RO 125 Mh44
Albeşti RO 125 Mj47
Albi F 104 Lc47
Albia USA (IA) 27 Fd25
Al Bi'ar KSA 148 Mk34
Albilbah AUS (QLD) 234 Sc58
Albin USA (WY) 21 Eh25
Albina SME 59 Hc43
Albion USA (CA) 20 Dj26
Albion USA (TX) 29 Fa29
Albion USA (MI) 32 Fh24
Albion USA (NY) 33 Ga24
Albion Downs AUS (WA) 224 Ra59
Al Bir KSA 146 Mj31
Al Birk KSA 149 Nd34
Al Birk KSA 150 Na36
Al Birkah KSA 148 Na35
Al Bir Lahlou DARS 264 Kf32
Al Biyad KSA 149 Nd35
Albocàsser E 110 La50
Alborea E 109 Kt49
Ålborg DK 94 Lm36
Ålborg Bugt DK 94 Ll34
Albox E 109 Ks47
Albreda WAG 269 Kb39
Albro AUS (QLD) 233 Sd57
Albstadt D 114 Lk42
Al Budayyi BRN 156 Nf32
Albuera RP 205 Rc40
Albufeira P 108 Km47
Al Bukayriyah KSA 149 Nb32
Albuñol E 109 Kr46
Albuquerque E 108 Kn49
Albuquerque USA (NM) 23 Eg28
Al Buraimi OM 157 Nh33
Albury AUS (NSW) 237 Sd64
Al Busayta KSA 146 Mk30
Al Busayyah IRQ 147 Nd30
al Butanah SUD 276 Mh39
Alcácer do Sal P 108 Km48
Alcáçovas P 108 Km48
Alcala RP 203 Ra37
Alcalá de Guadaira E 108 Kp47
Alcalá de Henares E 109 Kr50
Alcalá del Júcar E 109 Kt49
Alcalá de los Gazules E 108 Kp46
Alcalá del Río E 108 Kp47
Alcalá de Xivert E 110 La50
Alcalá la Real E 108 Kr47
Alcamo I 122 Ln53
Alcanar E 110 La50
Alcanede P 108 Km49
Alcañices E 106 Ko51
Alcañiz E 107 Ku51
Alcântara BR (MA) 64 Hh47
Alcántara E 108 Ko49
Alcántara I 122 Lq53
Alcantarilla E 109 Kt47
Alcaracejos E 108 Kq48
Alcaraz = Pueblo Arrúa RA (ER) 77 Ha61
Alcarràs E 110 La49
Alcaudete E 108 Kq47
Alcaudete de la Jara E 108 Kq49
Alcazaba de Almería E 109 Ks46
Alcázar de San Juan E 109 Kr49
Alcedo, Volcán EC 60 Fe46
Alcester GB 101 Kt38
Alcester Island PNG 244 Sg50
Alčevs'k UA 135 Mk21
Al Chaba'ish IRQ 147 Nd30
Alcinópolis BR (MS) 74 Hd55
Alcira RA (CD) 76 Gh62
Alcobaça BR (BA) 75 Ja54
Alcoba de los Montes E 108 Kq49
Alcoentre P 108 Km49
Alcohuas RCH 76 Ge61
Alcoi E 109 Ku48
Alcolea del Pinar E 109 Ks51
Alconchel E 108 Kn48
Alcoota AUS (NT) 227 Rh57
Alcorisa E 109 Ku50
Alcorta RA (SF) 77 Gk62
Alcorta RCH 72 Gf57
Alcoutim P 108 Kn47
Alcova USA (WY) 21 Eg24
Alcoy = Alcoi E 109 Ku48
Alcublas E 109 Ku49
Alcúdia E 110 Ld51
Aldaia Bona BR (PA) 63 Hc45
Al Dali YE 150 Nc39
Aldama MEX (CHH) 23 Eh31
Aldama MEX (TM) 39 Fa34
Aldan RUS 141 Rb07
Aldan RUS 141 Rc07
Aldanskoe nagor'e RUS 141 Ra07
Aldar MNG 172 Pj22
Aldeadávila de la Ribera E 106 Ko51
Aldea del Rey E 109 Kr48
Aldea dos Indios Sucane GUY 62 Ha45
Aldeburgh GB 101 Lb38
Aldeia das Canoas BR (PA) 63 Hc45
Aldeia Viçosa ANG 288 Lh50
Aldeia Vila Batista BR (AM) 62 Gk46
Aldenueva del Codonal E 106 Kq51
Alder Creek USA (NY) 33 Gc24
Alder Flats CDN (AB) 19 Ec19
Alderly AUS (QLD) 232 Rk57
Alderney GB 102 Ks41
Aldershot GB 101 Ku39
Aldersyde AUS (WA) 228 Qj62
Aldeyjarfoss IS 90 Kb13
Al Dibin YE 151 Nf37
Al Djebel al Akhdar LAR 261 Ma29
Al Eatrah KSA 148 Nb33
Åled S 95 Ln34
Aledia Koura DY 279 La41
Aledo USA (IL) 27 Fe25
Aleg RIM 269 Kd37
Alegre BR 68 Ha53
Alegre BR 69 Hb54
Alegre BR (MG) 75 Hg55
Alegre BR (ES) 75 Hk56
Alegrete BR (RS) 78 Hc60
Alegria RP 205 Rb41
Alegria RP 205 Rd40
Alëhovščina RUS 91 Mg15
Alej RUS 167 Pa20
Alejandra RA (SF) 77 Ha60
Alejandro Gallinal ROU 77 Hc62
Alejandro Humboldt, P.N. C 45 Gc35
Aleknagik USA (AK) 14 Ca16
Aleksandro Gaj RUS 133 Ne20
Aleksandrov RUS 132 Mk17
Aleksandrovac SCG 124 Mb46
Aleksandrovac SCG 126 Mb47
Aleksandrovskoe RUS 152 Nb23
Aleksandrów Kujawski PL 116 Lt38
Aleksandrów Łódzki PL 117 Lu39
Alekseevka RUS 133 Mk20
Alekseevka RUS 133 Nb20
Alekseevka RUS 133 Nf19
Alekseevskaja RUS 133 Nb20
Alekseevskoe RUS (TAR) 133 Nf18
Aleksin RUS 132 Mj18
Aleksinac SCG 126 Mb47
Alel SUD 283 Mf42
Älem S 95 Lr34
Alèmbé G 281 Lf46
Alembé RCB 288 Lh46
Alembeyli TR 131 Mp50
'Alem Ketema ETH 284 Mk40
Alem Maya ETH 284 Na41
Alem Paraíba BR (MG) 75 Hj56
Ålen N 92 Lm28
Alençon F 102 La42
Alen Cué RA (CR) 77 Hb60
Alenquer BR (PA) 63 Hc46
Alenquer P 108 Km48
Alentejo P 108 Kn48
Alenuihaha Channel USA 16 Cb35
Alépé CI 279 Kj43
Aleppo SYR 146 Mj28
Alerce Andino, P.N. RCH 80 Gd66
Alert DK 11 Gd02
Alerta PE 67 Ge51
Alert Bay CDN (BC) 18 Dg20
Alert Point CDN 11 Fb02
Alès F 105 Le46
Aleşd RO 124 Mc43
Alessándria I 120 Lj46
Ales stenar S 95 Lp35
Ålesund N 92 Lg28
Aletschgletscher CH 114 Lh44
Aleutian Basin USA 10 Ba07
Aleutian Islands USA 10 Bc08
Aleutian Range USA 14 Cb17
Aleutian Trench USA 10 Bc08
Alexander USA (AK) 15 Ce15
Alexander Archipelago USA 10 Da07
Alexanderbaai SA 302 Lj60
Alexander Bay SA 302 Lj60
Alexander City USA (AL) 35 Fh29
Alexander Graham Bell N.H.S. CDN 31 Gk22
Alexander Island 312 Ga32
Alexander Morrison N.P. AUS 228 Qh60
Alexander-Nevski BG 126 Md48
Alexandra NZ 239 Te68
Alexandra Channel MYA 193 Pg38
Alexandria AUS (NT) 223 Rj55
Alexandria BR (RN) 65 Ja49
Alexandria ET 263 Me30
Alexándria GR 126 Mc50
Alexandria RO 127 Mf47
Alexandria SA 303 Md62
Alexandria USA (SD) 26 Fa24
Alexandria USA (MN) 27 Fc23
Alexandria USA (LA) 29 Fd30
Alexandria USA (IN) 32 Fh25
Alexandria USA (VA) 33 Gb26
Alexandroupoli GR 127 Mf50
Alexandrovskij Zavod RUS 173 Qj20
Alexeck NAM 298 Lk56
Alexis Creek CDN (BC) 18 Dj19
Alexishafen PNG 243 Sc48
Al Faid Majir LAR 260 Lh29
Alfalfa USA (OR) 20 Dk23
Al Fallujah IRQ 147 Nb29
Al Fardah YE 150 Ne38
Alfaro E 107 Kt52
Alfarràs E 110 La49
Al Farshah KSA 150 Nb37
Al Fashir SUD 282 Mc39
Al-Fatah OM 157 Nj34
Alfatar BG 125 Mh47
Al Fathah IRQ 147 Nb28
Al Fatk YE 151 Ng37
Al Faw IRQ 147 Ne31
Al Fawwarah KSA 148 Nb32
Al Faydah KSA 149 Nc33
Al Faydami YE 151 Ng37
Alfeld D 112 Lk39
Alfenas BR (MG) 75 Hh56
Al Feqrah KSA 148 Mk33
al-Fifi SUD 282 Mc40
Alfioó GR 128 Mb53
Alföld H 119 Ma43
Alfonsina MEX (BC) 22 Ec31
Alfonsine I 120 Ln46
Alford AUS (SA) 236 Rj62
Alford GB 99 Ks33
Alford GB 101 La37
Ålfotbreen N 92 Lf29
Alfredo Wagner BR (SC) 79 Hf59
Alfta S 93 Lr29
Al Fuqaha' LAR 267 Lj32
al-Gabalayn SUD 276 Mg40
Al-Gabir SUD 283 Me39
Al Garabull LAR 260 Lg29
Ålgård N 92 Lf32
Al-Garef SUD 283 Mh40
Algarroba RA (BA) 81 Gj65
Algarrobal RCH 76 Ge60
Algarrobal RCH 76 Ge60
Algarrobo CO 56 Gc40
Algarrobo RCH 76 Ge62
Algarrobo del Aguila RA (LP) 80 Gg64
Algarve P 108 Km47
al-Gayli SUD 276 Mg38
al-Gazira SUD 276 Mg39
Algeciras E 108 Kp46
Algena ER 277 Mk38
Algeria DZ 253 Kb07
Algerian Provenceal Basin 111 Lf51
Algeyata ETH 284 Na41
al-Ghaba SUD 276 Mf37
al-Ghabsha SUD 283 Mf39
Al Ghandura SYR 146 Mj27
Al Gharith KSA 148 Na35
Al Ghat KSA 149 Nc32
Al Ghaydah YE 151 Ng37
Al Ghayl KSA 149 Nd34
Alghero I 111 Lj50
Al Ghrayfah LAR 267 Lg32
Al Ghurayra KSA 150 Nb36
Al Ghwaybiyah KSA 149 Ne33
Algiers DZ 259 Lb27
Algoa Bay SA 303 Md62
Algodões BR (PE) 71 Jb50
Algodón PE 61 Gd47
Algodonales E 108 Kp46
Algoma USA (WI) 32 Fg23
Algoma Upland CDN 25 Fj22
Algona USA (IA) 27 Fc24
Algonguin Prov. Park CDN 33 Ga23
Algonquin Upland CDN 33 Ga23
Algorta ROU 77 Hb62
Algyő H 119 Ma44
Al Habah KSA 149 Nd32
Al Habariyah IRQ 147 Nb29
Al Habbaniyah IRQ 147 Nb29
Al Habil KSA 150 Nb36
Al Hada KSA 148 Na35
Al Haddar KSA 149 Nc34
Al Haditah KSA 146 Mj30
Al Hadithah IRQ 147 Nb28
Al-Hadi-Yahya-Mosque YE 150 Nb37
Al Hadr IRQ 147 Nb28
Alhai IR 154 Ne30
Al Ha'ir KSA 149 Nd33
Al Hait KSA 148 Na33
Al-Hajar OM 157 Nk34
Al Hajarah KSA 147 Nb31
Al Halbeh SYR 146 Mk28
Al Hallaniyah OM 151 Nh37
Al Hallaniyat Bay OM 151 Nh37
Al Hamad KSA 147 Mk30
Alhama de Aragón E 107 Kt51
Alhama de Granada E 108 Kr46
Alhama de Murcia E 109 Kt47
Al Hamar KSA 149 Nd34
Alhambra E 109 Kr47
Alhambra E 109 Kr48
Alhambra USA (CA) 22 Ea28
Al Hami YE 150 Ne38
Al-Hamra OM 157 Nj34
Al Hamudiyah LAR 267 Lj32
Al Hanakiyah KSA 148 Na33
Al Hanish al Kabir YE 150 Nb39
Al Haniyah KSA 147 Nc31
Al Haqlaniyah IRQ 147 Nb28
Al Harabah LAR 260 Lf30
Al Harf YE 150 Nc37
Al Hariq KSA 149 Nd34
Al Harjah KSA 150 Nb36
Al Harrah KSA 146 Mk30
Al-Hartum SUD 276 Mg39
al-Hartum Bahri SUD 276 Mg39
Al Haruj al Aswad LAR 267 Lj32
Al-Hasaka SYR 147 Na27
Al Hassiane DARS 264 Kc32
Alhaurín el Grande E 108 Kq46
Al Hawaya KSA 149 Ne35
Al Hawra YE 150 Nd39
Al Hayy IRQ 147 Nc29
Al Hayyaniyah KSA 147 Nb31
Al-Hazm OM 157 Nj34
Al Hazm YE 150 Nc37
Alheit SA 302 Ma60
Al-Hibak KSA 151 Ng35
Al Hilla SUD 283 Md39
Al-Hillah IRQ 147 Nc29
Al Hillah KSA 149 Nd34
Al Hilwah KSA 149 Nd34
Al Hindiyah IRQ 147 Nc29
Al Hisn' YE 150 Nc39
Al Hisu KSA 148 Na33
Al Hoceima MA 259 Kj28
Al Hol SYR 147 Na27
Al Huan LAR 262 Mb33
Al Hudaydah YE 150 Nb38
Al Hufrah KSA 146 Mk31
Al-Hufrah al-Janubiyah OM 151 Nh36
Al Hufrah ash Sharqiya LAR 267 Lh32
Al Hufuf KSA 149 Ne33
Al Hulayq al Kabir LAR 267 Lj32
Al Humaydah KSA 146 Mh31
Al Humaymi YE 150 Nd38
Al Humayshah YE 150 Nc39
Al-Humrah UAE 156 Nh34
Al Hunaiy KSA 149 Ne33
al-Huqna SUD 276 Mg38
Al Hurriyeh SYR 147 Na28
al-Husay SUD 276 Mg39
Al Husayniyah KSA 150 Nc37
Al-Huwaysah OM 157 Nj35
Ália I 122 Lo53
Aliabad AFG 160 Oe27
Ali Abad IR 154 Nh27
Ali Abad IR 157 Nh31
Ali Abad Tower IR 155 Nk28
Aliaga E 109 Ku50
Aliağa TR 129 Mg52
Aliákmonas GR 126 Mb50
'Ali al Gharbi IRQ 147 Nd29
Aliambata TIM 214 Rd50
Aliança BR (RO) 68 Gj50
Aliança BR (PE) 71 Jc49
Aliance CDN (AB) 19 Ee19
Aliantan RI 206 Qa45
Alíartos GR 128 Md52
Ali ash Sharqi IRQ 147 Nd29
Alibag IND (MHT) 190 Og36
Alibates Flint Quarries Nat. Mon. USA 28 Ek28
Ali Bayramli AZ 152 Ne26
Alibo ETH 284 Mj41
Alibori DY 271 Lb40
Alibunar SCG 124 Ma45
Alicante = Alacant E 109 Ku48
Alice AUS (NSW) 235 Sg60
Alice SA 303 Md62
Alice USA (TX) 39 Fa32
Alice Arm CDN (BC) 17 Df18
Alice Channel MAL/RP 204 Qk43
Alice River AUS 233 Sc57
Alice Springs AUS (NT) 226 Rg57
Alice Town BS 37 Ga33
Alice Town BS 37 Gb33
Aliceville USA (AL) 29 Ff29
Ali Chuk USA (AZ) 22 Ed30
Alicia RP 203 Ra37
Alicia RP 205 Rc41
Alick River AUS 232 Sb56
Aliekšycy BY 97 Md37
Alifu Atoll = Arie Atoll MV 192 Og44
Alifuuto Nature Reserve SP 291 Nc44
Aliganj IND (UPH) 189 Ok32
Aligarh IND (UPH) 189 Ok32
Alignements de Pagliaju F 111 Lj49
Aligudarz IR 154 Ne29
Álika GR 128 Mc54
Alikalia WAL 278 Ke41
'Ali Kheyl AFG 160 Oe29
Al Ikhwan YE 151 Ng39
Alikí GR 127 Me50
Alíko GR 129 Mf54
Alima RCB 286 Lj46
Alimbongo RDC 287 Me46
Alimiá GR 129 Mh54
Alinda TR 129 Mh53
Alindau RI 209 Qk46
Alindoa RCA 286 Ma43
Alingsås S 94 Ln33
Alipur IND (WBG) 194 Pe34
Alipur PK 163 Of31
Alipura IND (MPH) 191 Ok33
Alipur Duar IND (WBG) 194 Pe32
Alirajpur IND (MPH) 190 Oh34
Al Irqah YE 150 Nd39
Ali Sabieh DJI 284 Nb40
Al Isawiyah KSA 146 Mk30
Aliseda E 108 Ko49
Alishan RC 179 Ra34
Alishan RC 179 Ra34
Al Iskandariyah IRQ 147 Nc29
Alista MEX (JLC) 40 Ej36
Alitak Bay USA 16 Cc17
Alivéri GR 128 Me52
Aliwal-Noord SA 303 Md61
Aliwal North SA 303 Md61
Alizai PK 161 Of29
Al Jafr JOR 146 Mj30
Al Jafurah KSA 149 Nf33

nba VRC (GZH) 178 Qc32
nban VRC (YUN) 195 Qa34
nbyon DVRK 182 Rd26
ncahau WAN 272 Le40
nce LV 97 Mc33
ncenis F 102 Kt43
ncerville F 103 Lf42
nchetti IND (TNU) 193 Oj40
nchieta BR (ES) 75 Hk56
nchieta BR (SC) 78 Hd59
ncho USA (NM) 23 Eh29
nchorage USA (AK) 15 Cf15
nchorage Reef PNG 244 Sf51
nchor Bay USA (CA) 20 Dj26
nchorena RA (SL) 76 Gh63
nchorena, P.N. ROU 77 Hb63
ncien RMM 265 Kk35
ncient tin mines of Karnab UZB 158 Oc26
ncohuma, Nevado BOL 67 Gf53
ncón EC 60 Fk47
ncón PE 66 Gb51
ncona I 121 Lo47
ncuabe MOC 297 Mk52
ncud RCH 80 Gd66
ncy-le-Franc F 103 Le43
nda RP 202 Qk37
nda VRC (HLG) 180 Rc22
ndacollo RCH 76 Ge61
ndaga WAN 273 Lg40
ndagalá RA (CA) 76 Gg59
ndagua PE 67 Gd53
ndahuaylas PE 66 Gd52
ndaiá BR 75 Hh55
ndaingo Gara RM 306 Ne55
ndal IND (WBG) 194 Pd34
ndalsnes N 92 Lh28
ndalucía E 108 Ko47
ndalusia USA (AL) 34 Fg30
ndaman and Nicobar Islands IND 186 Pb16
ndaman Basin 198 Ph40
ndaman Islands IND 186 Pc16
ndaman Sea IND 187 Pd16
ndamarca PE 66 Gc53
ndamooka AUS (SA) 236 Rj61
ndamooka Ranges AUS 236 Rj61
ndanda IND (ORS) 191 Pc36
ndanoo AUS (NT) 227 Rh58
ndapa RM 305 Ne53
ndapa RM 306 Nd55
ndarai BR (BA) 71 Hk52
ndasibe RM 306 Ne55
ndasinimaro RM 305 Ne53
ndatsakala RM 305 Ne53
ndavadoaka RM 306 Nb57
ndeba Ye Midir Zerf Chaf ER 277 Na39
ndebu N 92 Ll31
ndelot F 103 Lf42
ndemaka RM 306 Nd57
ndenes N 90 Lj11
nderai WAN 272 Lc40
ndéramboukane RMM 271 Lb38
nderdalen n.p. N 90 Lj11
nderlecht B 103 Le40
ndermatt CH 114 Lj44
ndernach D 112 Lh40
ndernos-les-Bains F 104 Kt46
nderson USA (CA) 20 Dj25
nderson USA (IN) 32 Fh25
nderson USA (SC) 35 Fj28
nderson Gate NAM 298 Lh55
ndersonville N.H.S. USA 35 Fh29
nderstorp S 95 Lo33
ndes CO 56 Gc43
ndes 50 Ga10
ndfjorden N 90 Lj11
ndhra Lake IND 190 Og36
ndhra Pradesh IND 186 Od15
ndijan UZB 159 Og25
ndijon UZB 159 Og25
ndilamena RM 306 Ne54
ndilana RM 305 Ne52
ndilanatoby RM 306 Ne54
ndimeshk IR 154 Ne29
nding VRC (HUN) 177 Qg31
ndirá BR 61 Gg48
ndirá BR 63 Hb47
ndirá Marau, T.I. BR 63 Hb47
ndırın TR 144 Mj27
ndírio GR 128 Mb52
ndirlangar VRC (XUZ) 168 Pb27
ndirobal BR (MA) 64 Hh47
ndižanskoe vodohranilišče KS 159 Og25
ndjogo G 288 Lg46
ndkhvoy AFG 160 Oc27
ndoain E 107 Ks53
ndoany RM 305 Ne52
ndoas PE 66 Gb47
ndocollo RA (NE) 80 Ge64
ndocs H 118 Ls44
ndohahela, P.N. d' RM 306 Nd58
ndohajango RM 305 Ne53
ndoi RI 213 Rg46
ndong ROK 182 Re27
ndoni Gate NAM 298 Lj55
ndoom AUS (QLD) 230 Sa52
ndorra AND 104 Lb48
ndorra la Vella AND 110 Lb48
ndorskaja grjada RUS 132 Mj16
ndover GB 101 Kt39
ndovoranto RM 306 Ne55
ndøya N 90 Lh11
ndrada ANG 289 Ma49
ndradas BR (MG) 75 Hg57
ndradina BR (SP) 74 He56
ndrafiakinena RM 305 Ne52
ndramasina RM 306 Nd55
ndranofasika RM 306 Nd54
ndranolalina RM 306 Nd57
ndranolava RM 306 Nc57
ndranomavo RM 306 Nc54
ndranomena RM 306 Ne55
ndranopasy RM 306 Nb56
ndranosamonta RM 305 Ne53
ndranovondronina RM 305 Ne52
ndranovory RM 306 Nc57
ndratx E 110 Lc51
ndravida GR 128 Mb53
ndrea RM 306 Nc54
ndreafsky River USA 15 Bj14
ndreapol' RUS 132 Mg17
ndre-Lahl N 91 Lh06
ndré Felix, P.N. RCA 282 Mb41
ndrelândia BR (MG) 75 Hh56
ndrequice BR (MG) 75 Hh55
ndresito RA (MI) 74 Hc58
ndrevo RM 306 Nb57
Andrew CDN (AB) 19 Ed19
Andrews USA (TX) 23 Ej29
Andrews USA (SC) 35 Ga29
Ándria I 123 Lr49
Andriamena RM 306 Nd54
Andriandampy RM 306 Nc57
Andriba RM 306 Nd54
Andriesvale SA 302 Ma59
Andrievo-Ivanivka UA 125 Ml43
Andrijevica SCG 126 Lu48
Andringitra RM 306 Nd57
Andringitra, P.N. d' RM 306 Nd57
Andritsena GR 128 Mb53
Androfiamena RM 305 Ne52
Androka RM 306 Nc58
Androrangalova RM 306 Nd56
Ándros GR 129 Me53
Ándros GR 129 Me53
Andros Island BS 37 Ga33
Andros Town BS 37 Gb33
Andrott Island IND 192 Og41
Androy RM 306 Nc58
Andru River PNG 243 Se49
Andruškva UA 134 Me20
Andrychów PL 119 Lu41
Andselv N 90 Lk11
Andújar E 108 Kq48
Andulo ANG 294 Lj51
Anduze F 105 Ld46
Andy Warhol Museum USA 33 Ga25
Aneby S 95 Lp33
Anecón Chico, Cerro RA 80 Gf66
Anecón Grande, Cerro RA 80 Ge66
Anéfis RMM 271 La36
Anegada GB 47 Gh36
Anegada Passage 47 Gj36
Aného RT 279 La42
Aneityum VU 246 Te56
Anekal IND (KTK) 193 Oj40
Anéker RN 272 Lc38
Anelghowhat VU 246 Te56
Añelo RA (NE) 80 Gf65
Anepahan RP 204 Qk41
Aney RN 274 Lg36
Anfile Bay ER 277 Na39
Anfu VRC (JGX) 184 Qh32
Angahuán MEX (MHC) 40 Ej36
Angalimp PNG 243 Sc48
Angamali IND (KER) 192 Oj41
Angamuthu PNG 242 Sa49
Angangxi VRC (HLG) 180 Rb22
Angara RUS 140 Qa08
'Angara SUD 282 Mc40
Angaradébou DY 272 Lb40
Angarak RN 272 Lc37
Angarapa A.L. AUS 227 Rh57
Angarsk RUS 172 Qb19
Angarskij krjaž RUS 140 Qa07
Angas Downs AUS (NT) 226 Rg58
Angastaco RA (SA) 72 Gg58
Angaston AUS (SA) 236 Rk63
Angatuba BR (SP) 74 Hf57
Angaur PAL 203 Rh42
Angba WAN 280 Ld42
Angchran IR 157 Nj32
Ånge S 93 Lq28
Angeles RP 202 Ra38
Ängelholm S 94 Ln34
Angélica RA (SF) 77 Gk61
Angelókastro GR 128 Mb52
Angelókastro GR 128 Md53
Angelo River AUS 224 Qk57
Ängelsberg S 93 Lq31
Angels Camp USA (CA) 20 Dk26
Angemuk, Gunung RI 213 Rk47
Angepena AUS (SA) 227 Rk61
Angereb ETH 277 Mj40
Angereb Wenz ETH 277 Mj40
Angermanland S 90 Lj14
Angermünde D 113 Lo37
Angern A 115 Lr42
Angers F 102 Ku43
Angerville F 103 Lb42
Ängesön S 90 Ma14
Angetu ETH 284 Mk42
Anggoro RI 209 Ra47
Angical BR (BA) 70 Hh51
Angico BR (TO) 64 Hg49
Angicos BR (RN) 65 Jb48
Angicos BR (BA) 70 Hj51
Angkor Wat K 197 Qb39
Angk Tasaom K 197 Qc40
Angle Inlet USA (MN) 24 Fc21
Anglem, Mount NZ 239 Td69
Anglès E 110 Lc49
Anglès F 102 Kt44
Anglesea AUS (VIC) 237 Sc65
Anglesey GB 100 Kq37
Angleton USA (TX) 29 Fc31
Anglure F 103 Ld42
Angnu IND (RJT) 188 Og31
Ango RDC 287 Mc43
Angochangua EC 60 Ga45
Angoche MOC 297 Mk54
Angol RCH 80 Gd64
Angola AND 253 Lb11
Angola USA (IN) 32 Fh25
Angola Basin 256 La21
Angoon USA (AK) 17 Dc17
Angoram PNG 243 Sc48
Angostura MEX (SL) 38 Ef33
Angostura MEX (SLP) 39 Ek34
Angostura Inglesa RCH 82 Gc70
Angoulême F 104 La45
Angourie AUS 235 Sg60
Angpawing Bum MYA 195 Ph32
Angra dos Reis BR (RJ) 75 Hh57
Angren KS 158 Of25
Ängsö n.p. S 93 Lr31
Ang Thong THA 196 Qa38
Ang Tra Peang Thmor W.S. K 197 Qb39
Anguang VRC (JLN) 180 Rb23
Angueretá BR (MG) 75 Hh55
Angüés E 107 Ku52
Anguilla GB 47 Gj36
Anguilla GB 47 Gj36
Anguilla Cays BS 37 Ga34
Anguille Mts. CDN 31 Ha21
Angul IND (ORS) 191 Pc35
Anguo VRC (HBI) 175 Qh26
Anguran IR 157 Nh32
Angurugu AUS (NT) 223 Rj53
Anguse EST 96 Mg31
Angusilla PE 60 Gc46
Angwa ZW 296 Me54
Anhai VRC (FJN) 179 Qk33
Anholt DK 94 Lm34
Anhua VRC (HUN) 177 Qf31
Anhuandui BR (MS) 74 Hc56
Anhuandui BR 74 Hc56
Anhui VRC 165 Qd12
Ani TR 145 Nb25
Aniak USA (AK) 15 Ca15
Aniakchak Nat.Mon. and Preserve USA 14 Ca17
Aniassué CI 279 Kj42
Anicuns BR (GO) 74 Hf54
Anié RT 279 La41
Anié RT 279 La42
Anikino RUS 173 Ra19
Anil BR (MA) 64 Hh47
Anillaco RA (LR) 76 Gg60
Animas USA (NM) 23 Ef30
Anímbo BOL 73 Gh56
Anina RO 124 Mb45
Aningal, T.I. BR 58 Gk44
Anini-y RP 205 Ra40
Anísio de Abreu BR (PI) 70 Hj50
Anita USA (IA) 27 Fc25
Anıtkaya TR 131 Ml52
Anıtlı TR 131 Mn54
Aniuk River USA 15 Cb11
Aniva RUS 181 Sb22
Anivorano RM 306 Ne55
Anivorano Avaratra RM 305 Ne52
Aniwa Island VU 246 Te55
Aniyo J 183 Rj28
Aniza JOR 146 Mh30
Anjafy RM 306 Nd54
Anjahambe RM 306 Ne54
Anjalankoski FIN 96 Mg30
Anjamala RM 306 Nb57
Anjanazana RM 305 Ne53
Anjangaon IND (MHT) 190 Oj35
Anjar IND (GUJ) 190 Of34
Anjar RL 146 Mh29
Anji VRC (ZJG) 184 Qk30
Anjialava RM 305 Ne53
Anjialava RM 305 Ne53
Anjimangirana RM 304 Nd53
Anjira PK 152 Od31
Anjireh IR 154 Nh29
Anjohibe RM 304 Nd53
Anjoman AFG 161 Of28
Anjou F 102 Ku42
Anjouan = Ndzuani COM 304 Nc52
Anjozorobe RM 306 Nd55
Anju DVRK 182 Rc26
Anjuba VRC (SCH) 177 Qc30
Anjuj RUS 181 Rj21
Anjujskij hrebet RUS 141 Ta05
Anka WAN 272 Lc39
Ankalabe RM 306 Nc55
Ankang VRC (SAA) 177 Qe29
Ankara TR 131 Mn51
Ankarafantsika, P.N. d' RM 304 Nd54
Ankaramena RM 306 Nd56
Ankaramy RM 305 Ne52
Ankarana RM 305 Ne52
Ankarana RM 305 Ne52
Ankaratra RM 306 Nd55
Ankarsrum S 95 Lr33
Ankasakasa RM 306 Nc54
Ankasa Nature Park GH 279 Kj43
Ankatafa RM 305 Ne52
Ankavandra RM 306 Nc55
Ankazoabo RM 306 Nc57
Ankazobe RM 306 Nd55
Ankazomborona RM 306 Nd54
Ankazomiriotra RM 306 Nd55
Ankeny USA (IA) 27 Fd25
Ankerika RM 304 Nd53
An Khe VN 197 Qe39
Ankiliabo RM 306 Nb56
Ankililoaka RM 306 Nb57
Ankilizato RM 306 Nc56
Ankinany RM 306 Nc57
Ankirihitra RM 306 Nd54
Ankisabe RM 306 Nd55
Anklam D 113 Lo37
Ankleshwar IND (GUJ) 190 Og35
Ankober ETH 284 Mk41
Ankofa RM 305 Ne54
Ankola IND (KTK) 192 Oh39
Ankoro RDC 292 Md49
Ankotrofotsy RM 306 Nc55
Ankpa WAN 280 Ld42
Anlejie VRC (YUN) 195 Qa33
Anliu VRC (GDG) 179 Qh34
An Loc VN 197 Qd40
Anlong VRC (GZH) 178 Qc33
Anlong Veng K 197 Qc38
Anlu VRC (HUB) 177 Qg30
Anmyon Do ROK 182 Rd27
Anna RUS 133 Na20
Annaba DZ 260 Ld27
Annaberg PNG 243 Sc48
Annaberg-Buchholz D 113 Ln40
An Nabhaniyah KSA 148 Nb33
An Nabk KSA 146 Mj30
An'nabk SYR 146 Mj28
An Nafud KSA 147 Mk31
An Najaf IRQ 147 Nc29
An Na'la KSA 149 Ne33
An Namas KSA 150 Nb36
Annam Plateau LAO/VN 197 Qc36
Annan GB 99 Kr36
Anna Paulowna NL 112 Le38
Annapolis USA (MD) 33 Gb26
Annapolis Royal CDN (NS) 31 Gh23
Annapurna I NEP 170 Pb31
Annapurna II NEP 170 Pc31
An-Naqdah OM 151 Nk35
Ann Arbor USA (MI) 32 Fj24
Anna Regina GUY 58 Ha42
An Nashash UAE 156 Nh34
An Nasiriyah IRQ 147 Nd30
An'nasra SYR 146 Mj28
Annecy F 105 Lg45
Annemasse F 105 Lg44
Anne, Mount AUS 236 Sd67
Annette Island USA 17 De18
Annette Island Ind. Res. USA 17 De18
Anning VRC (SCH) 176 Qa30
Anning VRC (YUN) 195 Qb33
Annino RUS 132 Mj16
Anniston USA (AL) 35 Fh29
Annitowa AUS (NT) 227 Rj56
Annivka UA 135 Mj22
Annofliyah LAR 261 Lj30
Annonay F 105 Le45
Annopol PL 117 Mb40
Annot F 105 Lg47
Annotto Bay JA 45 Gb36
Annoual MA 259 Kj28
An Nu'ayriyah KSA 149 Ne32
An Nukhayb IRQ 147 Nb29
An Nu'man KSA 148 Mh32
An Nu'maniyah IRQ 147 Nc29
An Nuqrah KSA 148 Na33
Anola CDN (MB) 24 Fb21
Áno Merá GR 129 Mf53
Año Nuevo USA (CA) 20 Dj27
Áno Poróia GR 126 Md49
Anori BR (AM) 62 Gk47
Anosibe An'ala RM 306 Ne55
Anosy RM 306 Nd58
Anoual MA 259 Kj29
Anoumaba CI 279 Kh42
Ânou Mellene RMM 266 Lc36
Anou-n-Bidek DZ 266 Lc36
Ânou Zegguehene RMM 271 Lb38
Áno Vrondoú GR 126 Md49
An Ping Qiao VRC 179 Qk33
Anpo Gang VRC 178 Qe35
Anqing VRC (AHU) 184 Qj30
Anqiu VRC (SDG) 175 Qk27
Anquincila RA (CA) 76 Gh60
Anröchte D 112 Lj39
Anroville IND 193 Ok41
Ans B 103 Lf40
Ansai VRC (SAA) 175 Qe27
Ansas RI 213 Rh46
Ansbach D 115 Ll41
Anse-à-Galets RH 46 Gd36
Anse-àVeau RH 46 Gd36
Anseba Shet ER 277 Mk38
Anse Couleuvre F 47 Gk38
Anse-Pleureuse CDN (QC) 30 Gh21
Anserma CO 56 Gc43
Anshan VRC (LNG) 182 Rb25
Anshi IND (KTK) 192 Oh39
Anshun VRC (GZH) 178 Qc32
Ansilta, Cerro de RA 76 Gf61
Ansina ROU 77 Hc61
Ansley USA (NE) 26 Fa25
Anson USA (TX) 28 Fa29
Anson Bay AUS 223 Rf52
Ansongo RMM 271 La38
Ansuiek KZ 166 Oh23
Answer Downs AUS (QLD) 232 Sa56
Anta IND (RJT) 190 Oj33
Anta PE 67 Gd52
Antabamba PE 67 Gd53
Antaeopolis = Qâw el Kabir ET 263 Mf32
Antagarh IND (CGH) 191 Pa35
Antakya TR 144 Mj27
Antalaha RM 305 Nf53
Antalya TR 131 Ml54
Antalya Körfezi TR 131 Ml54
Antanambao Manampotsy RM 306 Ne55
Antanambe RM 306 Ne54
Antananarivo RM 306 Nd55
Antanetibe RM 306 Nd55
Antanifotsy RM 306 Nd55
Antanifotsy RM 306 Nd57
Antanimenabaka RM 306 Ne54
Antanimieva RM 306 Nb57
Antanimora Atsimo RM 306 Nc58
Antarctica ANT 312 Ga35
Antarctic Peninsula ANT 312 Gd32
Antares, Gunung RI 213 Sa48
Antarvedi IND (APH) 191 Pa37
Antas BR (BA) 71 Ja51
Antas BR 78 He60
Antas, T.I. BR 58 Gk44
Antauta PE 67 Ge53
Antelao I 120 Ln44
Antelope Canyon USA 23 Ee27
Antelope Summit USA 20 Ec26
Antelope Wells USA (NM) 23 Ef30
Antequera E 108 Kq46
Antequera PY 73 Hb58
Antetezampandrana RM 306 Ne54
Anthony USA (NM) 23 Eg29
Anthony USA (KS) 28 Fb27
Anthony Island CDN 18 De19
Anthony Lagoon AUS (NT) 223 Rh54
Anthótopos GR 128 Mc51
Anti-Atlas MA 258 Kf31
Antibes F 105 Lh47
Antiga Lagoa da Rabeca BR 68 Ha53
Antigo USA (WI) 32 Ff23
Antigonish CDN (NS) 31 Gj23
Antigua AG 47 Gk37
Antigua GCA 41 Fe38
Antigua and Barbuda 47 Gk37
Antigues Cape F 47 Gk37
Antiguo Morelos MEX (TM) 39 Fa34
Antikithira GR 128 Md55
Anti Lebanon RL 146 Mj29
Antilla C 45 Gc35
Antilla RA (SA) 76 Gh59
Antimari BR 67 Gf50
Antimilos GR 128 Me54
Antiochia ad Pisidiam TR 131 Mm52
Antipajuta RUS 140 Od05
Antiparos GR 129 Mf53
Antiparos GR 129 Mf54
Antipaxi GR 128 Ma51
Antipodes Islands 218 Ba14
Antisana, Volcán EC 60 Ga46
Antissa GR 129 Mg51
Anti-Taurus Mountains TR 142 Md11
Antlers USA (OK) 29 Fc28
Antnäs S 90 Ma13
Antofagasta RCH 72 Ge57
Antofagasta de la Sierra RA (CA) 76 Gg59
Antofalla RA (CA) 72 Gg58
Antofalla, Volcán RA 72 Gg58
Anton USA (CO) 26 Ej26
Antongomena-Bevary RM 304 Nc53
Antonibe RM 304 Nd53
Antonin PL 116 Ls39
Antonina BR (PR) 74 Hf58
Antonina do Norte BR (CE) 65 Ja49
Antônio BR 71 Hj53
Antônio BR 75 Hj55
Antônio MOC 300 Mh57
Antônio Carlos BR (MG) 75 Hj56
Antonio de Biedma RA (SC) 82 Gg69
Antônio Dias BR (MG) 75 Hj55
Antônio João BR (MS) 74 Hc57
Antônio Prado BR (RS) 78 He60
Antonito USA (CO) 23 Eg27
Antonovo BG 127 Mg47
Antopal' BY 117 Me38
Antracyt UA 135 Mk21
Antranoambo RM 306 Ne54
Antrim GB 98 Ko36
Antrim Mountains GB 98 Ko35
Antrodoco I 122 Lo48
Antsaba RM 305 Ne52
Antsahabe RM 305 Ne53
Antsahampano RM 305 Ne52
Antsaidoha Bebao RM 306 Nc54
Antsakabary RM 305 Ne53
Antsalova RM 306 Nc55
Antsambalahy RM 305 Ne53
Antsatramidola RM 305 Ne53
Antsenavolo RM 306 Ne56
Antsiafabositra RM 306 Nd54
Antsianitia RM 304 Nd53
Antsirabe RM 306 Nd55
Antsirabe Afovoany RM 305 Ne53
Antsirabe Avaratra RM 305 Ne52
Antsiranana RM 305 Ne52
Antsla EST 96 Mg33
Antsoha RM 306 Nc55
Antsohihy RM 305 Nd53
Antsohimbondrona RM 305 Ne52
Antsondrodava RM 306 Nc55
Anttola FIN 96 Mh29
Antu VRC (JLN) 182 Re24
Antuco, Volcán RCH 80 Ge64
Antwerp B 103 Le39
Antwerpen B 103 Le39
Anučino RUS 180 Rg24
Anuj RUS 167 Pc20
Anum GH 279 Kh42
Anum GH 279 La42
Anumma WAN 273 Lf40
Anupgarh IND (RJT) 188 Og31
Anupshahr IND (UPH) 189 Ok31
Anuradhapura CL 193 Pa42
Anurrete A.L. AUS 227 Rh56
Anvak Island USA 14 Bj18
Anvik USA (AK) 15 Bk14
Anvik River USA 15 Bk14
Anxi VRC (GSU) 169 Ph25
An Xian VRC (SCH) 176 Qc30
Anxiang VRC (HUN) 177 Qg31
Anxious Bay AUS 236 Rh62
Anyama CI 279 Kh43
Anyang ROK 182 Rd27
Anyang VRC (HNN) 175 Qh27
A'Nyêmaqên Shan VRC 176 Pk28
Anyi VRC (JGX) 184 Qh31
Anyirawase GH 279 La42
Anykščiai LT 97 Mf35
Anyuan VRC (JGX) 179 Qh33
Anza USA (CA) 22 Eb29
Anza-Borrego Desert S.P. USA 22 Eb29
Anzac CDN (AB) 19 Ee17
Anze VRC (SAX) 175 Qg27
Anzi RDC 286 Mb46
Anzin F 103 Ld40
Ánzio I 122 Ln49
Anzob TJ 158 Oe26
Aoba Lodge NAM 298 Lj55
Ao Ban Don THA 198 Pk41
Aodanga TCH 273 Lj37
Aoga-jima J 183 Rk29
Aohan Qi VRC (NMZ) 175 Qk24
Aoiz E 107 Kt52
Aoji DVRK 182 Rf24
Aojiang VRC (ZJG) 184 Ra32
Ao Kongkang THA 197 Qb39
Aola SOL 245 Ta50
Aomen = Macao VRC (MAC) 179 Qg34
Aomori J 183 Sa25
Aonla IND (UPH) 189 Ok31
Ao Phang-Nga N.P. THA 198 Pk41
Aorobo CI 279 Kj42
Ao Sawi THA 198 Pk40
Aosta I 120 Lh45
Ao Trat THA 197 Qb39
Aoudaghost RIM 269 Ke37
Aoudech RIM 269 Kc37
Aouderas RN 272 Le37
Aoueloul RIM 264 Kd35
Aoufouss MA 259 Kh30
Aouhinet bel Egra DZ 265 Kg32
Aouinât ez Zbil RIM 270 Kf37
Aouinet Sarrag RIM 269 Kd36
Aoukalé RCA/TCH 282 Ma40
Aoukâr RIM 269 Ke36
Aoukâr RMM 265 Kh34
Aoulef DZ 266 La32
Aoulouz MA 258 Kf30
Aourir-n'-Ouassel MA 258 Kg30
Aourou RMM 269 Ke38
Aoussard DARS 264 Kc34
Aozi TCH 274 Lk35
Aozou TCH 267 Lj35
Apache Creek USA (NM) 23 Ef29
Apache Junction USA (AZ) 23 Ee29
Apache Lake USA 23 Ee29
Apacheta, Cerro RA 72 Gg58
Apagy H 119 Mb43
Apahida RO 124 Md44
Apaikwa GUY 58 Gk42
Apak EAU 290 Mg45
Apalachicola USA (FL) 35 Fh31
Apam GH 279 Kk43
Apamea SYR 146 Mj28
Apan MEX (HDG) 40 Fa36
Apaporis CO 61 Ge46
Apaporis, T.I. BR 61 Gf46
Aparados da Serra, P.N. BR 78 He60
Aparawatatja AUS (SA) 226 Rh59
Aparecida, Nossa Senhora BR 75 Hh57
Aparecida do Rio Doce BR (GO) 74 He55
Aparecida do Taboado BR (MS) 74 He56
Aparri RP 203 Ra36
Apastovo RUS (TAR) 133 Ne18
Apataki Atoll F 249 Cg53
Apatin SCG 124 Lt45
Apatity RUS 140 Mc05
Apatou F 59 Hc43
Apatzingán de la Constitución MEX (MHC) 40 Ej36
Apauwar RI 213 Rk46
Apauwar RI 213 Rk47
Apawanza RDC 287 Me45
Ape LV 97 Mg33
Apečki BY 97 Mg37
Apedia BR 68 Gk52
Apeldoorn NL 112 Lg38
Apen D 112 Lh37
Apennines I 86 Lb05
Apere BOL 67 Gh53
Apesokubi GH 279 La42
Aphéas GR 128 Md53
Aphrodisias TR 130 Mj53
Aphrodites Rock CY 131 Mn56
Aphroditopolis = Kôm Ishqaw ET 263 Mf32
Aphroditopolis ET 263 Mg33
Api NEP 170 Pa30
Apia CO 56 Gc43
Apia WS 248 Be52
Apiacás BR (MT) 69 Hb50
Apiaí BR (SP) 74 Hf58
Apiaka Kayabi, T.I. BR 69 Hb51
Apidiá GR 128 Mc54
Api, Gunung RI 212 Re48
Apinajes BR (PA) 64 Hf48
Apinayé, T.I. BR 64 Hg49
Apinópolis BR (MG) 75 Hg56
Apio SOL 245 Ta50
Apizolaya MEX (ZCT) 39 Ej33
Aplahoué DY 279 La42
Aplao PE 72 Gd54
Apodi BR (RN) 65 Jb48
Apodi BR 65 Jb48
Apo Duat Range RI 208 Qh44
Apo East Passage RP 202 Ra39
Apoera SME 59 Hb43
Apoko RCB 281 Lh46
Apolda D 113 Lm39
Apolinario Saravia RA (SA) 73 Gj58
Apollo Bay AUS (VIC) 237 Sb65
Apollonia AL 126 Lu50
Apollonia LAR 261 Mb29
Apolo BOL 67 Gf53
Apólonas GR 129 Mf53
Apolu WAN 272 Lc41
Apo, Mount RP 205 Rc42
Apo N.P. RP 205 Rc42
Apopka USA (FL) 36 Fk31
Aporé BR 74 Hd55
Apo Reef RP 202 Ra39
Apo Reef N.P. RP 202 Ra39
Aporema BR (AP) 63 He45
Apostle Islands Nat. Lakeshore USA 32 Fe22
Apóstoles RA (MI) 77 Hc59
Apostolove UA 134 Mg22
Apoteri GUY 58 Ha43
Appalachian Mountains USA 13 Fd12
Appam USA (ND) 24 Ej21
Äppelbo S 93 Lo30
Appennino Lucano I 123 Lq50
Appennino Abruzzese I 122 Lo48
Appennino Calabro I 123 Lr52
Appennino Campano I 122 Lp49
Appennino Ligure I 120 Lj46
Appennino Tosco-Emiliano I 120 Ll46
Appennino Umbro-Marchegiano I 121 Ln47
Appenzell CH 114 Lk43
Appingedam NL 112 Lg37
Appleby-in-Westmorland GB 99 Ks36
Appleton USA (MN) 27 Fc23
Appleton USA (WI) 32 Ff23
Appomattox USA (VA) 35 Ga27
Appomattox Court House N.H.P. USA 35 Ga27
Approuague F 59 Hd44
Apricena I 122 Lq49
Apriķi LV 97 Mb34
Aprilci BG 127 Me48
Aprilia I 122 Ln49
Aprilovo BG 127 Mg47
April River PNG 243 Sb48
Apromponou CI 279 Kj42
Apropuk Lake USA 14 Bh15
Apšeronsk RUS 135 Mk23
Apšeronskij poluostrov AZ 152 Ne25
Apsley AUS (VIC) 236 Sa64
Apsley CDN (ON) 33 Ga23
Apšupe LV 97 Md34
Apt F 105 Lf47
Apti IND (MHT) 190 Og36
Apucarana BR (PR) 74 He57
Apuí BR (AM) 62 Gh46
Apuí BR (AM) 62 Ha49
Apuka RUS 141 Tb06
Apure YV 57 Gg41
Apurimac PE 66 Gd52
Apurinã Igarapé Tauamirim, T.I. BR 62 Gj48
Apurina Km 124 BR-317, T.I. BR 67 Gg50
Apurito YV 57 Gf41
Aqabah IRQ 147 Nb29
Aqaba Pass SUD 277 Mj37
Aqal VRC (XUZ) 168 Ok25
Aqar LAR 267 Lh32
Aqchah AFG 160 Od27
Aqda IR 154 Ng29
A'qeirbat SYR 146 Mj28
Aqiq SUD 277 Mk37
Aqitag VRC 169 Pf25
Aq Qaleh IR 154 Nh27
Aqqan VRC (XUZ) 168 Pc27
Aqqikkol Hu VRC 169 Pe27
Aqua Downs AUS (QLD) 235 Sd59
Aquarium and Marine Center (Shippagan) CDN 31 Gh22
Aquatuk River CDN 25 Fh18
Aqueduct USA (NY) 33 Gd25
Aquidabán PY 73 Hb57
Aquidauana BR 73 Hb55
Aquidauana BR (MS) 74 Hc56
Aquila MEX (MHC) 40 Ej36
Aquiléia I 121 Lo45
Aquiles Serdán MEX (CHH) 23 Eh31
Aquin RH 46 Gd36
Aquiraz BR (CE) 65 Ja47
Aquismón MEX (SLP) 40 Fa35
Aquitaine F 104 Ku46
Ara IND (BIH) 191 Pc33
Ara Arba ETH 284 Na43
Arab USA (AL) 34 Fg28
Arabá BR (SP) 74 He55
Arab Abad IR 155 Nj29
Araban TR 144 Mj27
Arabapo YV 58 Gk43
Arabati ETH 284 Mk40
Arabela USA (NM) 23 Eh29
Arabian Basin 315 Oa08
Arabian Oryx Sanctuary OM 151 Nj35
Arabian Peninsula 142 Na07
Arabian Sea 142 Oa15
Arabiyeh Sagireh SYR 146 Mk27
Arabuko Sokoke N.P. EAK 291 Mk47
Araç TR 144 Mg25
Aracá BR 62 Gj45
Aracaju BR (SE) 71 Jb51
Aracar, Volcán RA 72 Gg58
Araçás BR (BA) 71 Ja52
Aracataca CO 56 Gc40
Aracá, T.I. BR 58 Gk44
Aracati BR (CE) 65 Jb48
Aracatiaçu BR 65 Ja47
Araçatuba BR (MT) 69 Hc52
Araçatuba BR (SP) 74 He56
Araceli RP 204 Ra40
Aracena E 108 Ko47
Araci BR (BA) 71 Ja51
Aracruz BR (ES) 75 Hk55
Aracu BOL 72 Gg54
Araçuaí BR (MG) 75 Hj54
Araçuaí BR 75 Hj54
Aracuta BR (BA) 71 Hk53
Arad IL 146 Mh30
Arad RO 124 Mb44
Arada TCH 275 Ma38
Aradan IR 154 Ng28
Aradan RUS 167 Pg19
Aradippou CY 131 Mo56
Arafali ER 277 Mk39
Arafura Sea AUS/RI 215 Rf50
Arafura Shelf 215 Rg51
Aragarças BR (GO) 69 Hd53
Arage WAN 280 Le41
Aragoiânia BR (GO) 74 Hf54
Aragón E 107 Kt51
Aragona I 122 Lo53
Araguacema BR (TO) 70 Hf50
Araguaçu BR (TO) 70 Hf52
Araguaçui BR (TO) 70 Hf50
Aragua de Barcelona YV 57 Gh41
Aragua de Maturín YV 58 Gj41
Araguaia BR 69 He51
Araguaiana BR (MT) 69 He53
Araguaína BR (TO) 64 Hf49
Araguanã BR (TO) 64 Hf49
Araguao YV 58 Gk41
Araguari BR 63 He45
Araguari BR (MG) 74 Hf55
Araguari BR 74 Hg55
Araguatins BR (TO) 64 Hf48
Aráhova GR 128 Mc52
Arahthos GR 128 Mb51
Araí BR (GO) 70 Hg52
Arai J 183 Rk27
Araioses BR (MA) 65 Hj47
Araju BR (AM) 62 Gk47
Arak DZ 266 Lb33
Arak IR 154 Ne28
Arakaka GUY 58 Ha42
Arakan Yoma MYA 196 Pj36
Arakawa J 183 Rk26
Arakht AFG 161 Of27
Arakkonam IND (TNU) 193 Ok40
Araks AZ 152 Ne26
Araku IND (APH) 191 Pb36
Aral KS 159 Oh25
Aral VRC (XUZ) 168 Pa25
Aralık TR 145 Nc26
Aralık TR 145 Na25
Aralkum KZ 153 Ob22
Aral Lake CDN 25 Fg20
Aral Moreira BR (MS) 74 Hc57
Aral Sea KZ/UZB 153 Nk23
Aralsk KZ 140 Oa09
Aralsk KZ 153 Oa22
Aramac River AUS 233 Sc57
Aramah KSA 149 Nc32
Arambagh IND (WBG) 194 Pd34
Aramberri MEX (NL) 39 Fa33
Arame BR (MA) 64 Hh48
Aramia River PNG 242 Sb49
Aramits F 104 Ku47
Aramoana NZ 239 Tf68
Aran IR 154 Nf28
Arancay PE 66 Gb50
Aranda de Duero E 107 Kr51
Aranda de Moncayo E 107 Kt51
Arandis NAM 298 Lh57
Arandjelovac SCG 124 Ma46
Arang IND (CGH) 191 Pa35
Arangani Bay RP 205 Rc43
Arani IND (TNU) 193 Ok40
Aran Island IRL 98 Km36
Aran Islands IRL 100 Kl37
Aranjuez E 109 Kr50
Aranos NAM 298 Lk58
Aransas Pass USA (TX) 39 Fb32
Arantangi IND (TNU) 193 Ok41
Arantes BR 74 He55
Arantzazu E 107 Ks52
Aranuka Atoll KIR 241 Tc19
Araouane RMM 271 Kj36
Arapahoe USA (NE) 26 Fa25
Arapari BR (AM) 61 Gg47
Arapari BR (PA) 64 Hf48
Arapawa Island NZ 239 Th66
Arapey Grande ROU 77 Hb61
Arapicos EC 60 Gb46
Arapiraca BR (AL) 71 Jb50
Arapiuns BR 63 Hc47
Arapixi BR (AM) 67 Gf50
Arapixuna BR (PA) 63 Hc47
Arapkir TR 145 Mk26
Araponga BR (PR) 74 He57
Arapoti BR (PR) 74 Hf58
Arapuá BR (MS) 74 He56
Arapunya AUS (NT) 227 Rh57
Araputanga BR (MT) 68 Ha53
'Ar'ar KSA 147 Na30
Arara BR 62 Gk47
Araracuara CO 61 Gd46
Arara do Rio Branco, T.I. BR 68 Ha50
Araranguá BR (SC) 79 Hf60
Araraquara BR (SP) 74 Hf56
Araras BR (PA) 63 Hc49
Araras BR (SP) 74 Hg57
Ararat ARM 152 Nc26
Ararat AUS (VIC) 237 Sb64
Ararat = Ağrı Dağı TR 145 Nc26
Arara, T.I. BR 63 Hd47
Araruama BR (RJ) 75 Hj57
Ararendá BR (CE) 65 Hk48
Arari BR (MA) 64 Hh47
Araria IND (BIH) 194 Pd32
Arariba, T.I. BR 74 Hf57
Araribóia, T.I. BR 64 Hg48
Araripe BR (CE) 65 Hk49
Araripina BR (PE) 71 Hk49
Aras IR 154 Nd27
Aras de Alpuente E 109 Kt49
Aras Rud 154 Nd26
Arataca BR (BA) 71 Ja53
Aratâne RIM 270 Kf36
Ara Terra ETH 284 Na42
Araticu BR 63 Hf47
Aratika Atoll F 249 Ch53
Arau MAL 198 Qa42
Arauá BR 62 Gh48
Arauá BR 62 Gh49
Arauá BR 67 Gh50
Arauá BR (SE) 71 Jb51
Arauca CO 57 Ge42
Arauca CO/YV 57 Ge42
Araucária BR (PR) 79 Hf58
Arauco RCH 80 Gd64
Araure YV 57 Gf41
Aravakkurichchi IND (TNU) 193 Oj41
Aravalli Range IND 188 Og33
Aravan KS 159 Og25
Aravete EST 96 Mf31
Arawa PNG 244 Sh49
Arawah KSA 149 Nc34
Arawale Nature Reserve EAK 291 Na46
Arawe Islands PNG 243 Se49
Araxá BR (MG) 75 Hg55
Araya YV 57 Gh40
Arayat RP 203 Ra38
Arba ETH 284 Na41
Arbadin SP 291 Nb45
Arbakwe WAN 272 Lc39
Arba Minch ETH 284 Mj43
Arba Minch Crocodile Market ETH 284 Mj43
Arbaoua MA 258 Kh28
Arbat IRQ 147 Nc28
Árbatax I 111 Lk51
Arbil IRQ 147 Nc27
Arboga S 93 Lq31
Arbois F 105 Lf44
Arbolé BF 271 Kj39
Arboledas RA (BA) 81 Gk64
Arboletes CO 56 Gb41
Arbore RO 125 Mf43
Arborea I 111 Lj51
Arbourg CDN (MB) 24 Fb20
Arboutchatak TCH 273 Lj39
Arbrå S 93 Lr29
Arbre du Ténéré RN 272 Le37
Arbroath GB 99 Ks34
Årbus I 111 Lj51
Arbuzinka UA 125 Mm43
Arcabuco CO 56 Gd43
Arcachon F 104 Kt46
Arcadia AUS (QLD) 232 Rk56
Arcadia AUS (QLD) 235 Se58
Arcadia USA (FL) 36 Fk32
Arcahaie RH 46 Gd36
Arcata USA (CA) 20 Dh25
Arc de Triomphe d'Orange F 105 Le46
Arčedinskaja RUS 133 Nb21
Arcelia MEX (GUR) 40 Ek36
Arc-en-Barrois F 103 Lf43
Arc-et-Senans F 103 Lf43
Archaeological Museum of Beluchistan PK 160 Od30
Archangelskij sobor RUS 133 Nb17
Archäologischer Park Xanten D 112 Lg39
Archena E 109 Kt48
Archer USA (FL) 36 Fj31
Archer Bay AUS 230 Sa52
Archer Bend N.P. AUS 230 Sb52
Archer City USA (TX) 28 Fa29
Archer River AUS 230 Sa52
Archer River Roadhouse AUS (QLD) 230 Sb52
Archers Post EAK 290 Mj45
Archerwill CDN (SK) 19 Eh19
Arches N.P. USA 21 Ef26
Archibald USA (LA) 29 Fe29
Archibarca, Cerro RA 72 Gg58
Archidona E 108 Kq47
Archidona EC 60 Gb46
Archie USA (LA) 29 Fe30
Archipelago of the Recherche AUS 229 Rb63
Archipel des 7 Frères DJI 285 Nb39
Archipiélago de Bocas del Toro PA 42 Fj41
Archipiélago de Camagüey C 45 Gb34
Archipiélago de Colón EC 60 Fe45
Archipiélago de las Perlas PA 43 Ga41
Archipiélago de los Canarreos C 44 Fj35
Archipiélago de los Colorados C 44 Fh34
Archipiélago de los Jardines de la Reina C 45 Ga35
Archipiélago de Sabana C 44 Fk34
Archipiélago de San Blás PA 43 Ga41
Archipiélago de Solentiname NIC 42 Fh40
Archipiélago Guayaneco RCH 82 Gc69
Archipiélago Los Roques, P.N. YV 57 Gg40
Archipiélago Reina Adelaide RCH 82 Gc72
Arcidosso I 120 Lm48
Arcipélago de la Maddalena, P.N. dell' I 111 Lk49
Arcipélago Toscano, P.N. dell' I 120 Lk47
Arcis-sur-Aube F 103 Le42
Arckaringa AUS (SA) 227 Rj59
Arco I 120 Ll45
Arco USA (ID) 21 Ed24
Arco de Baúlhe P 106 Kn51
Arcoona AUS (SA) 236 Rj61
Arcos BR (MG) 75 Hh56
Arcos de Jalón E 107 Ks51
Arcos de la Frontera E 108 Kp46
Arcot IND (TNU) 193 Ok40
Arcoverde BR (PE) 71 Jb50
Arctic Bay CDN 11 Fd04
Arctic Circle Hot Springs USA 15 Ch13
Arctic Ocean 310 Dd02
Arctic Plains USA 15 Cb11
Arctowski ANT (PL) 312 Ha31
Arcyz UA 125 Mk45
Ardabil IR 154 Ne26
Ardahan TR 145 Nb25
Ardakan IR 154 Nh29
Ardakan IR 156 Nf30
Ardal IR 154 Nf30
Årdalstangen N 92 Lh29
Ardara IRL 98 Km36
Ardasier Bank 204 Qh42
Ardatov RUS 133 Nb18
Ardavidu IND (APH) 193 Ok39
Ardboe GB 98 Ko36
Arde SP 285 Nd41
Ardèche F 105 Le46
Ardee IRL 100 Ko37
Ardeluța RO 125 Mg44
Ardémi TCH 275 Mb38
Arden DK 94 Lk34
Arden ZW 296 Mf54
Ardennes B/F 103 Le41
Ardentes F 102 Lb44
Ardes F 105 Ld45
Ardeșen TR 145 Na25
Ardeshir-e-Babakan IR 156 Ng31
Ardestan IR 154 Ng29
Ardgartan GB 99 Kq34

olo SOL 245 Sk49
o Loc VN 197 Qd40
olun VRC (SCH) 177 Qc29
oma WAL 278 Ke41
oqing VRC (HLG) 180 Rg22
oro RCA 281 Lh43
oshan VRC (SHG) 184 Ra30
oshan VRC (YUN) 195 Pk33
o Ta Shan VRC 175 Qe27
otianman Z.B. VRC 177 Qf29
oulé RMM 269 Kf39
oxu VRC (GDG) 178 Qf34
o Yen VN 178 Qc34
oying VRC (JGS) 184 Qk29
p IND (RJT) 188 Og32
patla IND (APH) 193 Pa39
paume F 103 Lc40
q'a KSA 148 Nb32
qer Abad IR 154 Nf28
qran KSA 148 Na35
quba IRQ 147 Nc29
quedano RCH 72 Gf57
r IND (RJT) 188 Oh32
r SCG 126 Lu48
r UA 134 Md21
ra RG 269 Kd39
ra RI 212 Rd47
ra RO 124 Mb45
ra RO 125 Mh43
ra SUD 283 Mf39
ra WAN 273 Lf40
raawe SP 291 Nc45
rabai RI 208 Qh47
ra Banki IND (UPH) 189 Pa32
rabaš RUS 182 Rf24
rabaš-Levada RUS 180 Rf23
r Abir ETH 284 Nb43
rachati IND (BIH) 191 Pc33
rachois CDN (QC) 31 Gh21
rachois Pond Prov. Park CDN 31 Ha21
racoa C 45 Gc35
racuxi BR 62 Ha45
raderes RH 46 Gd36
radero RA (BA) 77 Ha62
radla-barlang H 119 Ma42
raga USA (MI) 32 Ff22
răganu RO 125 Mh46
ragoi EAK 290 Mj45
rah IND (UPH) 189 Pa32
rahanuddin BD 194 Pf34
rahona DOM 46 Ge36
rahrah KSA 148 Na35
ra Imambara IND 189 Pa32
ra-Issa RMM 270 Kh38
rajas de Melo E 109 Ks50
raka ER 277 Mj39
raka RDC 292 Me48
raka SUD 277 Mj38
raka SUD 283 Md40
rakaldo E 107 Ks53
rakat SUD 276 Mg39
rakatha IND (JKD) 191 Pc33
raki AFG 160 Oe29
rakoma SOL 244 Sj49
rakot IND (ORS) 191 Pc35
ralba AUS (QLD) 235 Se58
ramanni GUY 58 Ha42
ramata PNG 243 Se51
ramati IND (MHT) 190 Oh36
rameiya SUD 277 Mj37
ramula 161 Oh28
ran IND (RJT) 190 Oj33
ranavičy BY 97 Mg37
ranga MAL 208 Qh44
ranga RDC 287 Md44
ranga RDC 287 Me44
rangbarang RI 211 Ra49
rani BF 270 Kj39
ranivka UA 134 Md20
ranoa CO 56 Gc40
ranof USA (AK) 17 Dc17
ranof Island USA 17 Dc17
ranów PL 117 Mc39
ranów Sandomierski PL 117 Mb40
rão de Antonia, T.I. BR 74 He57
rão de Grajaú BR (MA) 64 Hj49
rão de Melgaço BR (RO) 58 Gk51
rão do Melgaço BR (MT) 74 Hc54
raolt RO 125 Mf44
raouéli RMM 270 Kg39
raqish YE 150 Nc38
raqueville F 104 Lc46
rara EAT 293 Mj48
rarati BR 62 Ha49
raris SP 285 Nc40
ras RP 203 Rc39
ra Sagar IND (MPH) 191 Pa34
rataria Bay USA 29 Ff31
rate CI 279 Kh42
ratkhel AFG 160 Oe29
ratpur IND (AAN) 193 Pg39
rauli IND (BIH) 189 Pc32
raúna BR 62 Gk45
rauni IND (BIH) 194 Pd33
raut IND (UPH) 189 Oj31
ravinskaja niznenost RUS 140 Oc07
ray K 197 Qc39
raya CO 60 Gc44
rbacena BR (MG) 75 Hj56
rbacoas CO 56 Gd40
rbacoas CO 60 Ga45
rbacoas YV 57 Gg41
rbado BR (AM) 67 Gg50
rbado BR 68 Ha53
rbados BDS 47 Ha39
rbados 47 Ha39
rbalha BR (CE) 65 Ja49
rbaros TR 130 Mh50
rbastro E 110 La48
rbate E 108 Kp46
rbaza RP 205 Rb40
rbazum OM 151 Nh37
rbele LV 97 Me34
rberton SA 300 Mf58
rberville USA (FL) 36 Fk31
rbezieux F 104 Ku45
r Bigha IND (BIH) 191 Pc33
rbosa CO 56 Gc42
rbosa CO 56 Gd42
rbuda AG 47 Gk37
rca RO 126 Md47
rca de Alva P 106 Ko51
rcaldin AUS (QLD) 233 Sc57
rcarena BR (PA) 64 Hf46
rcarrota E 108 Ko48
rcău RO 124 Mc43
rcellona Pozzo di Gotto I 122 Lq52
rcelona E 110 Lc49
rcelona PE 67 Gf51
Barcelona YV 57 Gh40
Barcelonnette F 105 Lg46
Barcelos BR (AM) 62 Gj46
Barcelos P 106 Km51
Bárcena de Pie de Concha E 107 Kq53
Barcin PL 116 Ls38
Barcoo River AUS 234 Sb58
Barcs H 121 Ls45
Barczewo PL 117 Ma37
Barda AZ 152 Nd25
Barda del Medio RA (RN) 80 Gf65
Bardaï TCH 267 Lj35
Bardakçı TR 131 Ml51
Bardas Blancas RA (MD) 80 Gf63
Barddhaman = Burwan IND (WBG) 194 Pd34
Bar Deh IR 154 Nf29
Bardejov SK 119 Mb41
Bardeskan IR 155 Nj28
Bardi I 120 Lk46
Bardoc AUS (WA) 228 Ra61
Bardoli IND (GUJ) 190 Og35
Bardonécchia I 120 Lg45
Bardsey Island GB 100 Kq38
Bardsir IR 157 Nj30
Bardstown USA (KY) 34 Fh27
Bardula IND (CGH) 191 Pb35
Baré DY 279 La41
Bare ETH 284 Nb43
Bareilly IND (UPH) 189 Ok31
Bareli IND (MPH) 191 Ok34
Bareilan AUS (NSW) 237 Sd63
Barentin F 102 La41
Barentsburg N 91 Lh06
Barentsøya N 91 Mb06
Barents Sea 86 Mb02
Barentu ER 277 Mj39
Barenya AUS (QLD) 232 Sc56
Bareo MAL 208 Qh44
Barfleur F 102 Kt41
Barfolomeevka RUS 180 Rg23
Barga I 120 Ll46
Barga VRC (TIB) 170 Pa30
Bargaal SP 285 Nf40
Bargah IR 157 Nj32
Bargaon IND (CGH) 191 Pb34
Bargarh IND (UPH) 191 Pa33
Bargarh IND (ORS) 191 Pb35
Bargi IND (MPH) 191 Ok34
Bargteheide D 113 Ll37
Barguzin RUS (BUR) 173 Qe19
Barguzin RUS 173 Qf19
Barguzinskij Hrebet RUS 141 Qb08
Barguzinskij hrebet RUS 173 Qe19
Barh IND (BIH) 191 Pc33
Barhaj IND (UPH) 189 Pb32
Bar Harbor USA (MA) 33 Gf23
Barhau RI 206 Qb48
Barhi IND (MPH) 191 Pa34
Barhi IND (JKD) 191 Pc33
Bari I 123 Lr49
Bari IND (RJT) 189 Oj32
Bari WAN 272 Lc40
Ba Ria VN 197 Qd40
Bariadi EAT 293 Mg47
Barichara CO 56 Gd42
Barik OM 151 Nj35
Barika DZ 260 Lc28
Barikowt AFG 161 Of28
Barili RP 205 Rb40
Barillas GCA 41 Fe38
Barim YE 150 Nb39
Barima GY 58 Gk41
Barinas YV 57 Ge41
Baringa RDC 286 Ma45
Barinitas YV 57 Ge41
Baripada IND (ORS) 194 Pd35
Bariri BR (SP) 74 Hf57
Bâris ET 263 Mf33
Bari Sadri IND (RJT) 190 Oh33
Barisal BD 194 Pf34
Barisan Range RI 206 Qa46
Barisan Range RI 206 Qa46
Barito RI 208 Qh46
Barito RA (SA) 73 Gh57
Barito, P.N. RA 73 Gh57
Barjols F 105 Lg47
Barka OM 157 Nj34
Barkam VRC (SCH) 176 Qb30
Barkava LV 97 Mg34
Barkédji SN 269 Kc38
Barkerville CDN (BC) 18 Dk19
Barkerville Hist. Town CDN 18 Dk19
Barkéwo el Abiod RIM 269 Kd37
Barkhan PK 163 Oe31
Bark Hut Inn AUS (NT) 223 Rf52
Barkley Highway AUS 232 Rk56
Barkley Sound CDN 18 Dh21
Barkly Downs AUS (QLD) 232 Rk56
Barkly East SA 303 Md61
Barkly Highway AUS 223 Rh55
Barkly Pass SA 303 Md61
Barkly Roadhouse AUS (NT) 223 Rh55
Barkly Tableland AUS 223 Rh54
Barkly West SA 303 Mc60
Barkol VRC (XUZ) 169 Pg24
Barkol Hu VRC 169 Pg24
Barkuar Dongar IND 191 Pb34
Bârlad RO 125 Mh44
Bârlad RO 125 Mh44
Bar-le-Duc F 103 Lf42
Barlee Range Nature Reserve AUS (WA) 224 Qh57
Barletta I 123 Lr49
Barlik RUS 167 Pf20
Barlinek PL 116 Lq37
Barlo Warf WAL 278 Kd41
Barma RI 212 Rg46
Barmedman AUS (NSW) 237 Sd63
Barmer IND (RJT) 188 Of33
Barmera AUS (SA) 236 Sa63
Barmouth GB 100 Kq38
Barnala IND (PJB) 188 Oh30
Barnard USA (SD) 26 Fa23
Barnato AUS (NSW) 234 Sc61
Barnaul RUS 140 Pa08
Barnesville USA (MN) 27 Fb22
Barnesville USA (GA) 35 Fh29
Barnet GB 101 Ku39
Barnett River Gorge AUS 222 Rd54
Barneveld NL 112 Lf38
Barneville-Carteret F 102 Kt41
Barnhart USA (TX) 28 Ek30
Barnim D 113 Lo38
Barnissa EAK 291 Na44
Barnjarn A.L. AUS 223 Rg52
Barnong AUS (WA) 228 Qj60
Barnsley GB 101 Kt37
Barnstaple GB 100 Kq39
Barnstaple Bay GB 100 Kq39
Barnstorf D 112 Lj38
Barnum USA (WY) 21 Eg24
Barnwell USA (SC) 35 Fk29
Baro ETH 283 Mh41
Baro TCH 282 Lk39
Baro WAN 272 Ld41
Barobo RP 205 Rd41
Baroda IND (MPH) 188 Oj33
Baroda = Vadodara IND (GUJ) 190 Og34
Barodia IND (MPH) 191 Ok33
Baroe SA 303 Mc62
Baroghilpass AFG/PK 161 Og27
Barola IND (MPH) 191 Pa34
Barolo I 120 Lh46
Baron RI 210 Qf50
Barora Island SOL 245 Sk49
Barora Ite Island SOL 245 Sk49
Barossa Valley AUS 236 Rk63
Barotac Nuevo RP 205 Rb40
Barots Flood Plain Z 295 Mb53
Baroua RCA 287 Mc43
Barovo MK 126 Mc49
Barpeta IND (ASM) 194 Pf32
Barqah al Bayda LAR 261 Ma30
Barqat al-Bahriya ET/RN 262 Mc30
Barqin LAR 267 Lg32
Barque Canada Reef 204 Qg41
Barquisimeto YV 57 Gf40
Barra BR (BA) 70 Hj51
Barra BR 74 Hg58
Barra BR 74 Hg58
Barra GB 98 Kn34
Barra Alegre BR (MG) 75 Hj55
Barraba AUS (NSW) 235 Sf61
Barra Bonita BR (SP) 74 Hf57
Barraca da Boca BR (AP) 63 Hd46
Barraca de A.Lopes BR (PA) 62 Ha49
Barracão BR (RS) 78 He59
Barracão do Barreto BR (MT) 68 Ha50
Barracas E 109 Ku50
Barra da Estiva BR (BA) 71 Hk52
Barradale AUS (WA) 224 Qh57
Barra de Cazones MEX (VC) 40 Fb35
Barra de Itabapoana BR (RJ) 75 Hk56
Barra de Navidad MEX (JLC) 39 Eh36
Barra de São Francisco BR (ES) 75 Hk55
Barra de São Manuel BR (AM) 62 Ha49
Barra de Tuxpan MEX (VC) 40 Fb35
Barra do Bugres BR (MT) 69 Hb53
Barra do Cai BR (BA) 75 Ja54
Barra do Choça BR (BA) 71 Hk53
Barra do Corda BR (MA) 64 Hh48
Barra do Cuanza ANG 288 Lg50
Barra do Dande ANG 288 Lg50
Barra do Garcas BR (MT) 69 Hd53
Barra do Guaicuí BR (MG) 75 Hh54
Barra do Mendes BR (BA) 71 Hj51
Barra do Quarai BR (RS) 78 Hb61
Barra do Tarrachi BR (BA) 71 Ja50
Barra El Tordo MEX (TM) 39 Fb34
Barrafranca I 122 Lp53
Barrage Al-Massira MA 258 Kg29
Barrage de l'Eau d'Heure B 103 Le40
Barrage de Manantali RMM 269 Ke39
Barrage de Matadi RDC 288 Lg48
Barrage de Sélingué RMM 269 Kf40
Barrage Djorf-Torba DZ 259 Kj30
Barrage El-Mansour-Eddahbi MA 258 Kg30
Barrage Hassan-Addakhil MA 259 Kh29
Barragem de Cabora Bassa MOC 296 Mg53
Barragem de Castelo de Bode P 108 Km49
Barragem de Chicamba Real MOC 300 Mg55
Barragem de Itaparica BR 71 Ja50
Barragem de Montargil P 108 Km49
Barragem de Moxotó BR 71 Ja50
Barragem de Pedra BR 71 Hk52
Barragem de Pracana P 108 Kn49
Barragem de Santa Clara P 108 Km47
Barragem de São Simão BR 74 He55
Barragem de Serra da Mesa BR 70 Hf53
Barragem de Sobradinho BR 71 Hj50
Barragem do Alqueva P 108 Kn48
Barragem do Caia P 108 Kn49
Barragem do Maranhão P 108 Kn49
Barragem Itumbiara BR 74 Hf55
Barrage Mohamed V MA 259 Kj28
Barragem Pedro do Cavalo BR 71 Ja52
Barrage S.M. Ben Abdellah MA 258 Kg29
Barra Grande BR (BA) 71 Ja52
Barra Head GB 98 Kn34
Barra Los Americanos MEX 39 Fb33
Barra Mansa BR (MS) 73 Hb55
Barramansa BR (RJ) 75 Hh57
Barrambie AUS (WA) 224 Qj59
Barramiya ET 263 Mg33
Barranca PE 60 Gb48
Barranca PE 66 Gb51
Barrancabermeja CO 56 Gd42
Barranca del Cobre MEX 38 Eg32
Barranca del Cobre, P.N. MEX 38 Eg32
Barranca de Upia CO 56 Gd43
Barrancas RA (SF) 77 Gk62
Barrancas RA 77 Ha60
Barrancas RA 80 Ge64
Barrancas YV 58 Gj41
Barranca Sinforosa MEX 38 Eg32
Barranc d'Algendar E 110 Ld51
Barranco de Loba CO 56 Gc41
Barranco Picure CO 57 Gf44
Barrancos P 108 Ko48
Barranda E 109 Kt48
Barranqueras RA (CH) 77 Ha59
Barranquilla CO 56 Gc40
Barranquillas RCH 76 Ge59
Barranquitas YV 56 Gd40
Barras BR (PI) 65 Hj48
Barras BR (RO) 68 Gh51
Barra Seca BR (RJ) 75 Hk56
Barra Soto La Marina MEX 39 Fb34
Barraute CDN (QC) 30 Gb21
Barra Velha BR (SC) 79 Hf59
Barra Velha, T.I. BR 75 Ja54
Barrax E 109 Ks49
Barr'd Harbour CDN (NF) 31 Hb20
Barre USA (VT) 33 Gd23
Barreal RA (SJ) 76 Gf61
Barrealito YV 57 Gh41
Barreira Branca BR (PA) 69 He50
Barreira da Cruz BR (TO) 70 Hf51
Barreira da Missão, T.I. BR 62 Gh47
Barreira do Peiqui BR (TO) 70 Hf52
Barreiras BR (BA) 70 Hh52
Barreirinha BR (AM) 63 Hb47
Barreirinhas BR (MA) 65 Hj47
Barreiro P 108 Kl48
Barreiros BR (PE) 71 Jc50
Barreiros BR (SC) 79 Hf59
Barrême F 105 Lg47
Barren Grounds CDN 10 Dd05
Barren Grounds CDN 11 Gb07
Barren Is. USA 15 Cd16
Barren Island IND 193 Pg39
Barretal MEX (TM) 39 Fa33
Barretos BR (SP) 74 Hf56
Barrett Lake CDN (BC) 18 Dg18
Barrhead CDN (AB) 19 Ec18
Barrial Largo YV 57 Gg42
Barrie CDN (ON) 33 Ga23
Barriere CDN (BC) 18 Dk20
Barrier Highway AUS 234 Sc61
Barrier Range AUS 234 Sa61
Barrier Reef BH 41 Fg37
Barrier Reef PNG 244 Sg51
Barrier River CDN 19 Eh19
Barrière = Isla Santa Fé EC 60 Fe46
Barrington Lake CDN 24 Ek17
Barrington, Mount AUS 237 Sf62
Barringun AUS (NSW) 235 Sc60
Barriyat al-Bayyuda SUD 276 Mg37
Barro Alto BR (GO) 70 Hf53
Barroção BR (MG) 75 Hj54
Barro Duro BR (MA) 65 Hj47
Barro Duro BR (PI) 65 Hj48
Barron USA (WI) 27 Fe23
Barros Arana, Cerro RCH 80 Gd67
Barros Cassal BR (RS) 78 Hd60
Barrow IRL 100 Ko38
Barrow USA 10 Cb04
Barrow Creek AUS (NT) 226 Rg56
Barrow-in-Furness GB 101 Kr36
Barrow Island AUS 224 Qh56
Barrow Point AUS 231 Sc53
Barrow Strait CDN 11 Fa04
Barruelo de Santullán E 107 Kq52
Barry GB 100 Kr39
Barry Church SA 302 Ma63
Barrydale SA 302 Ma62
Barry's Bay CDN (ON) 33 Gb23
Barsakelmes tübegi KZ 153 Nk23
Barsalogo BF 271 Kk39
Barsaloi EAK 290 Mj45
Barsana IND (RJT) 189 Ok32
Barsatas KZ 166 Ok21
Barsi IND (MHT) 190 Oh36
Barskoon KS 159 Oj24
Barstow USA (CA) 22 Eb28
Bar-sur-Aube F 103 Le42
Bar-sur-Seine F 103 Le42
Barta LV 97 Mb34
Bartallah IRQ 147 Nb27
Bartang TJ 159 Of26
Bartang TJ 159 Of26
Bartel USA (CA) 20 Dk25
Barth D 113 Ln36
Bartica GUY 58 Ha42
Bartın TR 144 Mg25
Bartlesville USA (OK) 29 Fb27
Bartlett Bluff AUS (WA) 229 Rc60
Bartlett USA (NE) 26 Fa25
Bartolomé Masó C 45 Gb35
Barton USA (ND) 24 Ek21
Barton-upon-Humber GB 101 Ku37
Bartoszyce PL 117 Ma36
Barú CO 56 Gc40
Baru RI 206 Qb48
Baru RI 212 Rg46
Barudin GUY 58 Ha44
Barueri BR (SP) 74 Hg57
Baruipur IND (WBG) 194 Pe34
Barukku RI 209 Ra47
Barúmini I 111 Lk51
Barumun RI 206 Pk45
Barun RUS (KAL) 133 Nc22
Barung RI 209 Qj46
Barung RI 210 Qg50
Baruth D 113 Lo38
Baruunkharaa MNG 172 Qd21
Baruunturuun MNG 167 Ph21
Baruun Urt MNG 173 Qg22
Barvala IND (GUJ) 190 Of34
Barvas GB 99 Kn32
Barvinkove UA 135 Mj21
Barwaha IND (MPH) 190 Oj34
Barwala IND (HYA) 188 Oh31
Barwani IND (MPH) 190 Oh35
Barwice PL 116 Lr37
Barwidgee AUS (WA) 224 Ra59
Barwidgi AUS (QLD) 232 Sc54
Barwon River AUS 235 Se60
Barycz PL 116 Lr39
Baryš RUS 133 Nd19
Barysav BY 132 Me18
Barylgil AUS (NSW) 235 Sg60
Bârzava RO 124 Mb44
Bârzava RO 124 Mb45
Basacato del Este GQ 280 Le44
Basagude IND (CGH) 191 Pa36
Basaguke VRC (TIB) 170 Pc31
Basai MAL 204 Qj42
Bašaid SCG 124 Ma45
Basaidu IR 156 Nh32
Basail RA (CH) 77 Ha59
Basak K 197 Qc40
Basakan, Gunung RI 208 Qj44
Basal PK 161 Og29
Basali RDC 287 Mb45
Basang WAG 269 Kc39
Basanga RDC 289 Mc48
Basankusu RDC 286 Lk45
Basantpur IND (BIH) 189 Pc32
Basar IND (APH) 190 Oj36
Basarabeasca MD 125 Mj44
Basarabi RO 125 Mj46
Basaseachic MEX (CHH) 38 Ef31
Basavana Bagevadi IND (KTK) 190 Oh37
Basavilbaso RA (ER) 77 Ha62
Basay RP 205 Rb41
Baščelakskij hrebet RUS 167 Pb20
Basco RP 203 Ra35
Bascombe Well Conservation Park AUS 236 Rh62
Bascov RO 125 Me46
Baseer SYR 146 Mj29
Basel CH 114 Lh43
Base Naval Azopardo RA (BA) 81 Ha64
Basento I 123 Lr50
Baserah RI 206 Qa46
Bash Abdan AFG 160 Oe27
Bashaw CDN (AB) 19 Ed19
Bashee SA 303 Me62
Bashee Bridge SA 303 Me61
Bashimuke RDC 289 Mc48
Bashkortostan 89 Nd08
Basht IR 156 Nf30
Basi IND (RJT) 188 Og33
Basi LV 97 Mb34
Basia IND (JKD) 191 Pc34
Basiano RI 209 Rb46
Basibasy RM 306 Nb57
Basilaki Island PNG 244 Sf51
Basilan Island RP 205 Rb42
Basilan Strait RP 205 Ra42
Basildon GB 101 La39
Basilica d'Aquila I 122 Lo48
Basilica d'Aquiléia I 121 Lo45
Basilica di Lecce I 123 Lt50
Basilica di San Francesco d'Assisi I 120 Ln47
Basilica di San Pietro I 122 Ln49
Basilica of Bom Jesus IND 190 Og38
Basilica San Gavino I 111 Lj50
Basilicata I 123 Lr50
Basilique de Saint-Nicolas-de-Port F 103 Lg42
Basilique Notre-Dame de Paray-le-Monial F 105 Le44
Basilique Notre Dame de Port de Clermont-Ferrand F 105 Ld45
Başın TR 131 Mo53
Basin USA (WY) 21 Ef23
Basingstoke GB 101 Kt39
Basin Head Fisheries Mus. CDN 31 Gj22
Basin Lake CDN 19 Eh19
Basirka WAN 273 Lf40
Basirpur PK 161 Og30
Baška HR 121 Lp46
Başkale TR 145 Nb26
Baskan KZ 166 Ok23
Baskatong CDN 33 Gc22
Baskineig Falls CDN 25 Fg19
Başkomutan Milli Parkı TR 131 Ml52
Başkomutan Tarihi Milli Parkı TR 130 Mk52
Başkuyu TR 131 Mn52
Baslar TR 131 Mm53
Basle CH 114 Lh43
Başmakçı TR 131 Ml53
Basmath IND (MHT) 190 Oj36
Basna IND (CGH) 191 Pb35
Basoda IND (MPH) 191 Oj34
Basoko RDC 287 Mb45
Basongo RDC 289 Ma48
Basotu EAT 293 Mh48
Basra IRQ 147 Nc28
Bassa CI 278 Kg43
Bassac GR 128 Mb53
Bassano CDN (AB) 19 Ed20
Bassano del Grappa I 120 Lm45
Bassar RT 279 La41
Bassaula WAN 281 Lg43
Bassawa CI 279 Kh41
Basse Casamance, P.N. du SN 269 Kb39
Bassein MYA 196 Ph37
Bassein = Puthein MYA 196 Ph37
Bassein Beach IND 190 Og36
Basselata E 110 Lb48
Basse-Pointe F 47 Gk38
Basse Santa Su WAG 269 Kc39
Basse Terre F 47 Gk37
Basse-Terre F 47 Gk37
Basseterre KN 47 Gj37
Bassett USA (NE) 26 Fa24
Bassikounou RIM 270 Kh38
Bassila DY 279 La41
Bassin Bleu RH 46 Gd36
Bassin d'Arcachon F 104 Kt46
Bassin de Thau F 105 Ld47
Basso DY 272 Lb40
Basso TCH 275 Mb37
Bass Strait AUS 220 Sa26
Bassum D 112 Lj38
Basswood Lake USA 24 Fd21
Båstad S 94 Ln34
Bastak IR 156 Nh32
Bastam Jame Mosque IR 154 Nh27
Baštanka UA 134 Mg22
Bastar IND (CGH) 191 Pa36
Bastar Hills IND 191 Pa36
Basti IND (UPH) 189 Pb32
Bastia F 111 Lk48
Bastia Umbra I 120 Ln47
Bastogne B 103 Lf41
Bastos BR (MG) 74 Hf55
Bastrop USA (TX) 29 Fb30
Bastrop USA (LA) 29 Fe29
Bastuny BY 97 Mf36
Basu RI 207 Qb46
Basua WAN 280 Le42
Basud RP 203 Rb38
Basudebpur IND (ORS) 194 Pd35
Basunda SUD 277 Mh40
Bat OM 157 Nj34
Bāta BG 127 Me48
Bata GQ 280 Le45
Batabanó C 44 Fj34
Batabi WAN 272 Lc41
Batac RP 203 Ra37
Batacosa MEX (SO) 38 Ef32
Bataga RUS 141 Rc05
Batag Island RP 203 Rc39
Bataguassu BR (MS) 74 Hd56
Bataiporã BR (MS) 74 Hd57
Batajsk RUS 135 Mk22
Batak BG 127 Me49
Batakan RI 208 Qh48
Batala IND (PJB) 188 Oh30
Batalha BR (PI) 65 Hj48
Batam RI 207 Qb45
Batama RDC 287 Md45
Batan RP 205 Rb40
Batang RI 210 Qe49
Batang VRC (SCH) 176 Pk31
Batanga G 280 Le46
Batangafo RCA 282 Lk42
Batangas RP 203 Ra39
Batangkapas RI 206 Qa46
Batan Island RP 203 Rb35
Batan Islands RP 203 Ra35
Batanovci BG 126 Mc48
Batanta RI 212 Rf46
Batar RI 213 Rk47
Batár RO 124 Mb44
Batas Island RP 204 Qk40
Bátaszék H 119 Lt44
Batatais BR (SP) 74 Hg56
Batavia USA (NY) 33 Ga24
Batavia Downs AUS (QLD) 230 Sb52
Bat Cave USA (NC) 35 Fj28
Batcham CAM 280 Lf43
Batchelor AUS (NT) 223 Rf52
Batchenga CAM 281 Lf43
Batea E 110 La49
Batemans Bay AUS (NSW) 237 Sf63
Batemans Bay AUS 237 Sf63
Baté-Nafadji RG 278 Kf40
Bates USA (OR) 20 Ea23
Batesburg Leesville USA (SC) 35 Fk29
Batesville USA (AR) 29 Fe28
Batesville USA (MS) 29 Ff28
Bath GB 101 Ks39
Bath USA (NY) 33 Gb24
Bath USA (MA) 33 Gf24
Batha TCH 273 Lj39
Batha de Lairi TCH 273 Lj40
Batheaston AUS (QLD) 233 Se57
Bathhurst Island AUS 223 Rf51
Bathinda IND (PJB) 188 Oh30
Bathsheba BDS 47 Ha39
Ba Thuoc VN 178 Qc35
Bathurst AUS (NSW) 237 Se62
Bathurst CDN (NB) 31 Gh22
Bathurst SA 303 Md62
Bathurst Inlet CDN 10 Ec05
Bathurst Island CDN 11 Fa03
Bati ETH 284 Na40
Batia DY 279 La40
Batiagarh IND (MPH) 191 Ok33
Batibati RI 208 Qh47
Batié BF 279 Kj41
Bati Menteşe Dağları TR 129 Mh53
Batina HR 124 Lt45
Batinah OM 157 Nj33
Bati Toroslar TR 144 Mf27
Batkandu WAL 278 Kd41
Batken UZB 158 Of25
Batkhaan Uul Nature Reserve MNG 172 Qb22
Bat Khela PK 161 Of28
Batković BIH 124 Lu46
Batlaq-e Gavhuni IR 154 Nf29
Batley GB 101 Kt37
Batman TR 145 Na27
Batna DZ 260 Ld28
Batn at Tarfa KSA 149 Nf34
Bato RP 203 Rc39
Bato RP 204 Qk43
Bato RP 205 Rc40
Ba To VN 197 Qe38
Batoche N.H.S. CDN 19 Eg19
Batoka Z 296 Md54
Bat Ölziyt MNG 172 Qc21
Baton Rouge USA (LA) 29 Fe30
Batonyterenye H 119 Lu43
Batopilas MEX (CHH) 38 Eg32
Batote 161 Oh29
Batoua CAM 281 Lg43
Batouala G 281 Lg45
Batouri CAM 281 Lh44
Batovi, T.I. BR 69 Hd52
Batovo BG 127 Mh47
Bat Pagoda VN 199 Qc41
Batrahalli IND (TNU) 193 Ok40
Batroun RL 146 Mh28
Batsawul AFG 161 Of28
Båtsfjord N 91 Me10
Battambang K 197 Qb39
Batticaloa CL 193 Pa43
Battenberg D 112 Lj39
Batticaloa Beach CL 193 Pa43
Batti Malv Island IND 193 Pg41
Battipáglia I 122 Lp50
Battistero di Firenze I 120 Lm47
Battistero di Parma I 120 Ll46
Battle Camp AUS (QLD) 231 Sc53
Battle Creek USA 19 Ef21
Battle Creek USA (MI) 32 Fh24
Battle Mountain USA (NV) 20 Eb25
Battle of Colenso SA 303 Me60
Battle of Talana SA 303 Mf60
Battle River CDN 19 Ed19
Battonya H 119 Mb44
Batu GH 279 La42
Batuapalle IND (APH) 193 Oj39
Batuampar RI 206 Qb46
Batuan Bridge VRC 178 Qe33
Batuata RI 214 Rb49
Batubetumpang RI 207 Qd47
Batu Bolong Beach RI 211 Qj50
Batubrok, Gunung RI 208 Qh45
Batu Caves MAL 199 Qa44
Batudaka RI 209 Ra46
Batudaka RI 209 Ra46
Batu Danau MAL 204 Qh43
Batu Ferringhi Beach MAL 198 Qa43
Batu Gong Beach RI 209 Rb47
Batuijak RI 198 Pj43
Batujaya RI 210 Qd49
Batukangkung RI 206 Qb47
Batukau, Gunung RI 211 Qh50
Batulaki RP 205 Rc43
Batulintang RI 207 Qb47
Batumandi RI 208 Qh47
Batumi GE 145 Na25
Batumi GE 152 Na25
Batumundan RI 206 Pk45
Batu Pahat MAL 199 Qb45
Batupanjang RI 206 Qa45
Baturaden RI 210 Qe49
Batura Glacier PK 161 Oh27
Batura Glacier Bridge PK 161 Oh27
Baturaja RI 207 Qc48
Batu Rakit MAL 199 Qb43
Baturetno RI 210 Qf50
Baturité BR (CE) 65 Ja48
Baturube RI 209 Ra46
Batuša SCG 124 Mb46
Batusangkar RI 206 Qa46
Batu Tambung RI 209 Rb46
Batyrevo RUS (CHU) 133 Nd18
Baú BR 63 Hc49
Bau MAL 208 Qf45
Bau SUD 283 Mh40
Bauana BR 62 Gh47
Bauang RP 202 Ra37
Baubau RI 209 Rb48
Bauchi WAN 272 Le40
Baud F 102 Kr43
Baudette USA (MN) 24 Fc21
Baudh Raj IND (ORS) 191 Pc35
Baudo CO 56 Gb43
Baugé F 102 Ku43
Bauhaus D 113 Ln39
Bauhausbauten und klassisches Weimar D 113 Lm40
Bauhinia Downs AUS (QLD) 235 Se58
Bauhinia TM 214 Rd50
Baumberge D 112 Lh39
Baú-Mekragroti, T.I. BR 69 Hd50
Baume-les-Dames F 103 Lg43
Bauna BD 194 Pe33
Baunatal D 112 Lk39
Baunei I 111 Lk50
Baungan RI 198 Pk44
Baures BOL 68 Gj52
Bauru BR (SP) 74 Hf57
Bauru RDC 286 Ma45
Bauska LV 97 Me34
Bauskas pils LV 97 Me34
Bauta RDC 286 Ma45
Bāutar RO 124 Mc45
Bautzen D 113 Lp39
Bauyrzhan KZ 158 Of24
Bavaria = Bayern D 115 Lm42
Bavay F 103 Ld40
Bavella F 111 Lk49
Båven S 93 Lr31
Ba Vì VN 178 Qc35
Bavla IND (GUJ) 190 Og34
Baviácora MEX (SO) 23 Ee31
Baxoi VRC (TIB) 171 Pj30
Ba Vì N.P. VN 178 Qd35
Bawal RI 208 Qf47
Bawangaja IND 190 Oh35
Baw'an Pass YE 150 Nb38
Bawe RI 212 Rf46
Bawe RI 213 Rh47
Bawean RI 210 Qg48
Bawku GH 279 Kh40
Bawlake MYA 196 Pj36
Bawley Point AUS 237 Sf63
Bawli Bazar MYA 194 Pg35
Bawo LB 278 Kf43
Bawo Ofuloa RI 206 Pk46
Bawtry GB 101 Kt37
Baxian VRC (CGQ) 177 Qd31
Baxkorgan VRC (XUZ) 169 Pf26
Baxley USA (GA) 35 Fj30
Baxoi VRC (TIB) 171 Pj30
Baxter Springs USA (KS) 29 Fc27
Bay RMM 271 Kj39
Baya-Bwanga RDC 289 Mb48
Bayaguana DOM 46 Gf36
Bayah RI 210 Qd49
Bayaha IND (BIH) 189 Pc32
Bayamo C 45 Gb35
Bayamon USA (PR) 47 Gg36
Bayan MNG 167 Ph22
Bayan MNG 172 Qb22
Bayan MNG 173 Qf22
Bayan RI 211 Qj50
Bayan VRC (NMZ) 174 Qc25
Bayan VRC (HLG) 180 Rd22
Bayanbulag MNG 172 Pk22
Bayanbulag MNG 172 Pk23
Bayanbulag MNG 173 Qe22
Bayanbulak VRC (XUZ) 166 Pc24
Bayanga RCA 281 Lj44
Bayanga-Didi RCA 281 Lh43
Bayangol MNG 167 Ph23
Bayan Har Shan VRC 171 Ph28
Bayan Har Shan VRC 171 Pj28
Bayan Har Shankou VRC 171 Pj28
Bayankhongor MNG 172 Pk23
Bayankhongor MNG 172 Qa22
Bayankhoshuu MNG 167 Pg21
Bayan Obo VRC (NMZ) 175 Qe25
Bayan Ölgiy MNG 167 Pe21
Bayan Olji VRC (NMZ) 174 Qc25
Bayan-Ovoo MNG 167 Ph23
Bayan Ovoo MNG 173 Qf21
Bayansayr MNG 172 Pk23
Bayan Shan VRC 169 Pj27
Bayanteeg MNG 172 Qa23
Bayantökhöm MNG 172 Qc22
Bayantsagaan MNG 172 Qa21
Bayan Uul MNG 167 Pe21
Bayanzag (Dinosaur excavations) MNG 174 Qb23
Bayard USA (NM) 23 Ef29
Bayard USA (NE) 26 Ej25
Bayasgalant MNG 173 Qg22
Bayat TR 207 Qb47
Bayat TR 130 Mk52
Bayat TR 131 Ml52
Bayat TR 131 Ml53
Bayat TR 131 Mp50
Bayata C 45 Gc35
Bayawan RP 205 Rb41
Bayaz IR 156 Nh30
Bayaziyeh IR 154 Nh29
Baybay RP 205 Rc40
Bay Bulls CDN (NF) 31 Hd22
Bayburt TR 145 Na25
Bay City USA (TX) 29 Fc31
Bay City USA (MI) 32 Fj24
Baydhabo SP 291 Nb44
Bay du Nord Wilderness Res. CDN 31 Hc21
Bayerische Alpen D 115 Lm43
Bayerischer Wald D 115 Ln41
Bayerischer Wald, N.P. D 115 Lo42
Bayern D 115 Lm42
Bayeux F 102 Ku41
Bayfield USA (WI) 27 Fe22
Bayhan al Qasab YE 150 Nc38
Bay Harbor USA 32 Fh23
Bayındır TR 129 Mh52
Bayındır Barajı TR 131 Mn50
Bayir JOR 146 Mj30
Bayizhen VRC (TIB) 171 Ph31
Bayji IRQ 147 Nb28
Baykan TR 145 Na26
Baykonur KZ 158 Ob23
Baykonur Cosmodrome KZ 158 Ob23
Baylamören TR 131 Mo50
Bay Minette USA (AL) 34 Fg30
Baynes Mountains NAM 294 Lg54
Baynunah UAE 156 Ng34
Bayo, Cerro RCH 80 Gd68
Bay of Bengal 186 Pb15
Bay of Biscay F/E 104 Ks46
Bay of Campeche MEX 41 Fd36
Bay of Fundy CDN 31 Gg23
Bay of Islands AUS 238 Th63
Bay of Islands CDN 31 Ha21
Bay of Plenty AUS 238 Tj64
Bay of Whales 312 Bd34
Bayo Grande, Cerro RA 76 Gg59
Bayombong RP 203 Ra37
Bayon F 103 Lg42
Bayonet Point USA (FL) 36 Fj31
Bayonne F 104 Kt47
Bayou Cane USA (LA) 29 Fe31
Bayou Cocodrie N.W.R. USA 29 Fe30
Bayóvar PE 66 Fk48
Bayramaly TM 155 Ob27
Bayramiç TR 130 Mg51
Bayreuth D 115 Lm41
Bayshint MNG 167 Pf21
Bayshint MNG 172 Qc22
Bay Shore USA (NY) 33 Gd25
Bay Springs USA (MS) 29 Ff30
Bayt al Faqih YE 150 Nb38
Baytik Shan VRC/MNG 167 Pf23
Baytown USA (TX) 29 Fc31
Bay Tree CDN (AB) 18 Ea18
Bayu RI 198 Pj43
Bayu RI 209 Rb47
Bayugan RP 205 Rc41
Bayum Gol He VRC 169 Pj27
Bay View NZ 238 Tj65
Baza E 109 Ks47
Bazar-e Taleh AFG 160 Oe28
Bazarnye Mataki RUS (TAR) 133 Nf18
Bazarnyi Karabulak RUS 133 Nd19
Bazas F 104 Ku46
Bazhong VRC (SCH) 177 Qd30
Bazhou VRC (HBI) 175 Qj26
Bazman IR 157 Oa32
Beach USA (ND) 26 Ej22
Beach Haven USA (NJ) 33 Gc26
Beach Park BR 65 Ja47
Beachport AUS (SA) 236 Sa64
Beachy Head GB 101 La40
Beacon AUS (WA) 228 Qj61
Beacon USA (NY) 33 Gd25
Beacon Bay SA 303 Md62
Beacon Hill USA (FL) 35 Fh31
Beaconsfield AUS (TAS) 236 Sd66
Beadon Point AUS 224 Qh56
Beagle Bay AUS (WA) 222 Rb54
Beagle Bay A.L. AUS 222 Rb54
Beagle Gulf AUS 223 Rf52
Bealanana RM 305 Ne53
Bean Station USA (TN) 35 Fj27
Bear Cove CDN (BC) 18 Dg20
Beardmore CDN (ON) 25 Fg21
Beardmore Glacier 313 Tc35
Beardmore South Camp USA 313 Ta35
Beardstown USA (IL) 27 Fe25
Bearhead River CDN 19 Eb17
Bear Island CDN 25 Fk18
Bear Island IRL 100 Kl39
Bear Islands N 86 Ma02
Bear Lake CDN 24 Fb18
Bear Lake USA 21 Ee25
Bearma IND 191 Ok34
Bearpaw Mountain USA 15 Ce13
Bear River CDN 19 Eh18
Bears Den Mtn. USA 26 Fa22
Beas IND 188 Oh30
Beasain E 107 Ks53
Beas Dam IND 189 Oj30
Beas de Segura E 109 Ks48
Beasley AUS 224 Qj57
Beata Ridge 46 Gd38
Beatrice USA (NE) 27 Fb25
Beatrice ZW 300 Mf55
Beatton River CDN (BC) 17 Dk17
Beatton River CDN 17 Dk17
Beatty CDN (SK) 19 Eh19
Beatty USA 22 Eb27
Beattyville CDN (QC) 30 Gb21
Beattyville USA (KY) 35 Fj27
Beau-Bassin MS 307 Nj56
Beaucaire F 105 Le47
Beauce F 102 Lb42
Beauchêne Isla GB 83 Ha72
Beau Desert AUS (QLD) 232 Sa56
Beaudesert AUS (QLD) 235 Sg60
Beaufort AUS (VIC) 237 Sb64
Beaufort MAL 204 Qh43
Beaufort USA (SC) 35 Fk29
Beaufort Castle RL 146 Mh29
Beaufort Sea 10 Cd04
Beaufort Wes SA 302 Mb62
Beaufort-West SA 302 Mb62
Beaugency F 102 Lb43
Beaujeu F 105 Le44
Beaujolais F 105 Le44
Beaumaris Castle GB 100 Kq37
Beaumont F 104 La46
Beaumont USA (TX) 29 Fc30
Beaumont-de-Lomagne F 104 La47
Beaumont-Hague F 102 Kt41
Beaumont-le-Roger F 102 La41
Beaumont-sur-Sarthe F 102 La42
Beaune F 103 Le43
Beaupréau F 102 Ku43
Beauraing B 103 Le40
Beaurepaire F 105 Lf45
Beausejour CDN (MB) 24 Fb20
Beauty SA 299 Md57
Beauvais F 103 Lc41
Beauval CDN (SK) 19 Eg18
Beauvoir-sur-Mer F 102 Ks44
Beauvoir-sur-Niort F 104 Ku44

ka IND 191 Oj34
IND (MPH) 190 Oj35
IND (MPH) 189 Ok32
IND (RJT) 188 Og33
IND (MHT) 191 Ok35
IND 191 Pa33
nika Sanctuary IND
135
ar IND (MPH) 189 Ok33
i IND (MHT) 190 Og36
IND (HYA) 188 Oj31
ur IND (UPH) 189 Ok32
IND 191 Oj34
IND (ORS) 191 Pc35
IND (MHT) 190 Oj36
BD 194 Pf34
PK 162 Oe33
on IND (UPH) 189 Ok32
IND (APH) 191 Ok37
IND (MPH) 190 Oj34
atnam IND (CGH)
36
deo IND (CGH) 191
IND (BIH) 189 Pc32
IND (MHT) 190 Oh36
IND (ORS) 191 Pc35
eswar IND (ORS) 191
IND (GUJ) 190 Oe34
al IND (MHT) 190 Oh35
BHT 186 Pb13
R 61 Gg48
279 Kj43
PE 66 Gb49
IND (WBG) 194 Pe33
WAN 280 Le43
al 209 Rb46
RI 213 Rj46
RI 213 Rj46
ra Nature Reserve RI
46
ka PL 117 Mc37
dlaska PL 117 Md38
PL 119 Ma41
egi PL 117 Ma39
egi PL 117 Mc40
d PL 116 Lq36
e PL 117 Md40
ski P.N. PL 117 Md37
ża PL 117 Md38
r PL 116 Lr37
k PL 117 Md37
RI 242 Sa49
I 123 Lr52
RCA 286 Ma43
na CI 278 Kg42
GH 279 Kj42
IND (MPH) 190 Oj34
RDC 286 Lk46
RDC 287 Mc45
RI 212 Rc44
F 104 Kt47
CH 114 Lj44
MAL 208 Qe45
T 263 Mf31
RI 207 Qc48
I 181 Sa24
ANG 294 Lg53
G 281 Lf45
I 120 Lm47
AM 281 Lg43
CAM 273 Lg41
D 114 Lk42
GH 279 Kj42
ndi Mausoleum PK
31
RUS 180 Rd20
CL 193 Pa43
PK 162 Od31
AUS (QLD) 233 Sc54
G 288 Lf47
UA 119 Me41
F 59 Hd44
AL 126 Ma49
asr. ARM/AZ 152 Nc26
BR (MG) 75 Hj56
RO 125 Mg44
ei RO 125 Mf44
TR 131 Mm51
GB 101 Kt39
RUS 180 Rh22
ETH 284 Mk40
VRC (CGQ) 177 Qd31
AUS (TAS) 236 Se66
IND (MPH) 191 Pa34
IND (MPH) 191 Ok35
WAN 272 Le39
Island AUS 223 Rj52
RP 203 Rb39
H 118 Lt43
P.N. do ANG 294
RUS (BUR) 172 Qd20
D (MHT) 190 Oh36
WAN 272 Ld41
WAN 273 Lg39
IND (KTK) 190 Oj37
OM 157 Nk34
SP 291 Nb45
d USA (ME) 33 Ge24
USA (MT) 21 Eh23
GB 100 Kq39
AUS (WA) 224 Qh58
IR 155 Nk28
DZ 266 La34
MAL 199 Qa43
uk RI 209 Qk45
NEP 170 Pc32
RUS (YAO) 180 Rf22
93 Lr31
ski Park Narodowy
Mc37
PL 119 Mb41
opf D 112 Lj40
BF 279 Kk40
181 Sb24
nne CH 114 Lh43
107 Ku52
PL 116 Lr40
e D 112 Lj38
e CH 114 Lh43
PL 117 Lu37
120 Lj45
CI 279 Kg41
E 110 La48
PL 117 Lu38
Biała PL 119 Lu41
odlaski PL 117 Md38
ittel D 113 Ll37
CDN (SK) 24 Ej21
RDC 289 Lk48
VN 197 Qd40
PL 116 Lq39
Biel CH 114 Lh43
AUS (QLD) 235 Sc59
y PL 116 Lt40
RO 124 Me44
PL 116 Ls39
E 107 Ku52
Biese D 113 Lm38
Biesiekierz PL 116 Lr36
Biesiesvlei SA 303 Mc59
Bieszczady PL 119 Mc41
Bieszczadzki P.N. PL 119 Mc41
Bièvre B 103 Lf41
Bieżuń PL 117 Lu38
Biferno I 122 Lp49
Bifoulé CAM 281 Lg43
Bifoun G 280 Lf46
Bifuka J 181 Sb23
Biga TR 130 Mh50
Bigadiç TR 130 Mj51
Big Ambergris Cay GB 37 Ge35
Bigand RA (SF) 77 Gk62
Biga Yarımadası TR 130 Mg50
Big Baldy USA 21 Ec23
Big Bay VU 246 Td53
Big Bear Creek CDN (BC) 18 Dj20
Big Beaver CDN (SK) 19 Eh21
Big Belt Mts. USA 21 Ee22
Big Bend SD 303 Mf59
Big Bend N.P. USA 23 Ej31
Big Branch Marsh N.W.R. USA 29 Fe30
Big Creek CDN (BC) 18 Dj20
Big Creek USA (ID) 21 Ec23
Big Cypress Seminole Ind.Res. USA 36 Fk32
Big Desert AUS 236 Sa63
Big Desert Wilderness Park AUS 236 Sa63
Bigene GNB 269 Kc39
Big Falls USA (MN) 24 Fd21
Bigfork USA (MT) 19 Ec21
Biggar CDN (SK) 19 Eg19
Biggar GB 99 Kr35
Bigge Island AUS 222 Rc53
Biggenden AUS (QLD) 235 Sg58
Biggleswade GB 101 Ku38
Big Hole SA 303 Mc60
Big Hole Nat. Battlefield USA 21 Ed23
Bighorn USA (MT) 21 Eg22
Bighorn Basin USA 21 Ef23
Bighorn Canyon N.R.A. USA 21 Ef23
Bighorn Mountains USA 21 Eg23
Bight of Bangkok T 196 Qa39
Bight of Benin 280 Lb43
Bight of Biafra 280 Ld43
Bigi Polka SME 59 Hc43
Big Island CDN 24 Fc21
Big Kalzas Lake CDN 17 Dc14
Big Koniuji Island USA 14 Ca18
Big Lagoon Z 296 Mg52
Big Lake USA (TX) 28 Ek30
Big Lake Ranch CDN (BC) 18 Dk19
Big Lost USA 21 Ed24
Big Mossy Pt. CDN 24 Fa19
Bignona SN 269 Kb39
Bigo Bya Mugenyi EAU 290 Mf45
Bigoray River CDN 19 Ec19
Big Pine USA (CA) 20 Ea27
Big Pine USA (FL) 36 Fk33
Big Piney USA (WY) 21 Ee24
Big Pond CDN (NS) 31 Gk23
Big Rapids USA (MI) 32 Fh24
Big Red Lighthouse USA 32 Fg24
Big River CDN (SK) 19 Eg19
Big River USA 21 Ec24
Big River USA 15 Cc14
Big River Ind. Res. CDN 19 Eg19
Big River Roadhouse USA (AK) 15 Cc14
Big Rock USA (CA) 22 Eb29
Big Salmon Range CDN 17 Dd15
Big Salmon River CDN 17 Dc15
Big Sand Lake CDN 24 Fa17
Big Sandy USA (MT) 19 Ee21
Big Sandy USA (WY) 21 Ef24
Big Sandy Lake CDN 19 Eh18
Big Sky USA (MT) 21 Ee23
Big Smokey Valley USA 20 Eb26
Big Snow Mtn. USA 21 Ef22
Big South Fork Nat. River and Rec. Area USA 35 Fh27
Big Spring USA (TX) 28 Ek29
Big Stone CDN (AB) 19 Ee20
Bigstone Lake CDN 24 Fb19
Big Stone N.W.R. USA 27 Fb23
Big Sur USA (CA) 22 Dk27
Big Timber USA (MT) 21 Ef23
Big Trails USA (WY) 21 Eg24
Big Trout Lake CDN 25 Fe19
Big Trout Lake CDN (ON) 25 Ff19
Big Trout Lake Indian Reserve CDN 25 Ff19
Biguaçu BR (SC) 79 Hf59
Big Water USA (UT) 23 Ee27
Big Willow River CDN 25 Fj19
Big Wood Cay BS 37 Gb33
Bihać BIH 121 Lq46
Bihar IND 186 Pb13
Biharamulo EAT 292 Mf47
Biharamulo Game Reserve EAT 292 Mf47
Biharia RO 124 Mb43
Bihariganj IND (BIH) 194 Pd33
Biharkeresztes H 119 Mb43
Biharnagybajom H 119 Mb43
Bihar Sharif IND (BIH) 191 Pc33
Bihé Plateau ANG 294 Lj52
Bihireşti RO 125 Mh44
Bihoro J 181 Sc24
Bihoua RCB 288 Lg47
Bihpur IND (BIH) 194 Pd33
Bija RUS 167 Pd20
Bijainagar IND (RJT) 188 Oh33
Bijaipur IND (MPH) 189 Oj32
Bijapur IND (KTK) 190 Oh37
Bijapur IND (CGH) 191 Pa36
Bijapur IND (ORS) 191 Pb36
Bijar IR 154 Nd28
Bijawar IND (MPH) 191 Ok33
Bijbehara IND 161 Oh29
Bijeljina BIH 124 Lu46
Bijelo Polje SCG 126 Lu47
Bij-Hem = Bol'šoj Enisej RUS 167 Ph19
Bijie VRC (GZH) 178 Qc32
Bijlik Lake KZ 158 Of24
Bijnapalli IND (APH) 190 Ok37
Bijnor IND (UPH) 189 Ok31
Bijoutier SY 305 Ng49
Bijsk RUS 140 Pb08
Bikaner IND (RJT) 188 Og31
Bikapur IND (UPH) 189 Pb32
Bikar Atoll MH 241 Tc16
Bikin RUS 180 Rh22
Bikin RUS 180 Rh22
Bikini Atoll MH 241 Tb16
Bikita ZW 300 Mf56
Bikok CAM 281 Lf44
Bikori SUD 283 Mh40
Bikoro RDC 286 Lk46
Bikou VRC (GSU) 177 Qc29
Bikramganj IND (BIH) 191 Pc33
Bikubiti LAR/TCH 262 Lk34
Bikumpur IND (RJT) 188 Og32
Bila RI 198 Qa44
Bila Cerkva UA 134 Mf21
Bilad Bani Bu Ali OM 157 Nk34
Bilad Bani Bu Hasan OM 157 Nk34
Bilala RCB 288 Lg48
Bilanga BF 271 Kk39
Bilanga G 288 Lf47
Bilap Bay IND 193 Pg40
Bilara IND (RJT) 188 Og32
Bilaspur IND (HPH) 189 Oj30
Bilaspur IND (UPH) 189 Pa32
Bilaspur IND (CGH) 191 Pb34
Bilassana RG 278 Kf41
Bilate ETH 284 Mk42
Bilauktaung Range MYA/THA 196 Pk39
Bilbao = Bilbo E 107 Ks53
Bilbeis ET 263 Mf30
Bilbo = Bilbao E 107 Ks53
Bilbor RO 125 Mf43
Bílčice CZ 118 Ls41
Bildudalur IS 90 Jj13
Bileća BIH 126 Lt48
Bilecik TR 130 Mk50
Biled RO 124 Ma45
Bilehra IND (UPH) 189 Pa32
Bilesha Plain EAK 291 Na45
Bilesuvar AZ 152 Ne26
Bilgoraj PL 117 Mc40
Bilgorod-Dnistrovs'kij UA 125 Ml44
Bilgram IND (UPH) 189 Pa32
Bilhaur IND (UPH) 189 Pa32
Bili RDC 286 Lk43
Bili RDC 287 Mb43
Bili RDC 287 Mc43
Biliali Koyra RMM 271 La37
Bilibino RUS 141 Tb05
Bilin MYA 196 Pj37
Bilina CZ 118 Lo40
Biling La VRC/NEP 170 Pa30
Biliran Island RP 205 Rc40
Biliri WAN 273 Lf41
Bilisht AL 126 Ma50
Bilis Qooqaaoi SP 291 Na45
Biljaivka UA 125 Ml44
Biljari, Nov. UA 125 Ml44
Bilje HR 124 Lt45
Bilka BG 127 Mh48
Bill USA (WY) 21 Eh24
Billabong Roadhouse AUS (WA) 224 Qh59
Billa Kalina AUS (SA) 227 Rj60
Billdal S 94 Lm33
Billengarrah AUS (NT) 223 Rh53
Billiluna AUS (WA) 222 Rd55
Billiluna A.L. AUS 222 Rd55
Billingen S 93 Lo32
Billingnooka AUS (WA) 224 Ra57
Billings USA (MT) 21 Ef23
Billingsfors S 92 Ln32
Bill of Portland GB 101 Ks40
Billom F 105 Ld45
Billun IND (RJT) 188 Oh31
Billy Island BS 37 Ga33
Bilma RN 274 Lg36
Biloela AUS (QLD) 235 Sf58
Bilohirs'k UA 135 Mh23
Bilokurakyne UA 133 Mk21
Biloo SP 291 Nb45
Bilopill'a UA 132 Mh20
Bilovec CZ 118 Ls41
Bilovods'k UA 133 Mk21
Biloxi USA (MS) 29 Ff30
Bilpa Marea Claypan AUS 234 Rk58
Bilqâs Qism Auwal ET 263 Mf30
Biltine TCH 275 Ma38
Bilto N 90 Ma11
Bilugyun MYA 196 Pj37
Bilungala RI 209 Rb45
Bilverdi IR 154 Nd26
Bima RI 211 Qk50
Bimba CAM 281 Lh43
Bimbe ANG 294 Lh51
Bimbéréke DY 272 Lb40
Bimbijy AUS (WA) 228 Qk60
Bimbila GH 279 La41
Bimbo RCA 286 Lk43
Bimini Islands BS 37 Ga33
Bina Etawa IND (MPH) 191 Ok33
Binalbagan RP 205 Rb40
Binanga RI 206 Pk45
Binarowa PL 119 Mb41
Binauhan Falls RP 203 Rc39
Binbee AUS (QLD) 233 Sd56
Binche B 103 Le40
Binchuan VRC (YUN) 195 Qa33
Bindé BF 279 Kk40
Binder TCH 273 Lh41
Bindi Bindi AUS (WA) 228 Qj61
Bindki IND (UPH) 189 Pa32
Bindloe = Isla Marchena EC 60 Fe45
Bindoy RP 205 Rb41
Bindu RDC 289 Lk49
Bindura ZW 296 Mf54
Binéfar E 110 La49
Bin-el-Ouidane MA 258 Kg29
Binga EAT 293 Mk49
Binga ZW 296 Md54
Bingara AUS (NSW) 235 Sf60
Bing Bong AUS (NT) 223 Rj53
Bingen D 114 Lh41
Binger USA (OK) 28 Fa28
Bingham GB 101 Ku38
Bingham USA (NM) 23 Eg29
Bingham USA (MA) 33 Gf23
Binghamton USA (NY) 33 Gc24
Bin Ghashir LAR 260 Lg29
Bin Ghaylan YE 150 Nc38
Bingintelok RI 207 Qb47
Binglingsi Shiku VRC 174 Qb28
Bingmei VRC (GZH) 178 Qe33
Bingöl TR 145 Na26
Bingöl Dağları TR 145 Na26
Bingsjö S 93 Lq29
Binhai VRC (JGS) 184 Qk28
Binh Chanh VN 197 Qd40
Binh Chau Hot Springs VN 197 Qd40
Binh Dinh VN 197 Qe39
Binh Gia VN 178 Qd35
Binh Lu VN 195 Qb34
Binh Son VN 197 Qe38
Binibihali PNG 244 Sf51
Bini Erde TCH 274 Lk35
Binjai RI 198 Pk44
Bin Jawwad LAR 261 Lk30
Binkolo WAL 278 Ke41
Bin Lam VN 197 Qe38
Binnaway AUS (NSW) 235 Se61
Binneringie AUS (WA) 228 Rb61
Binongko RI 209 Rc48
Binpur IND (WBG) 194 Pd34
Binscarth CDN (MB) 24 Ek20
Bintagoungou RMM 271 Kj37
Bintan RI 207 Qc45
Binthalya AUS (WA) 224 Qh58
Bintuhan RI 207 Qb48
Bintulu MAL 208 Qg44
Bintumani, Mount WAL 278 Ke41
Bintuni RI 213 Rg47
Binur IND (CGH) 191 Pa36
Bin Xian VRC (SAA) 177 Qe28
Bin Xian VRC (HLG) 180 Rd23
Binyang VRC (GZG) 178 Qe34
Binz D 113 Lo36
Binzhou VRC (SDG) 175 Qk27
Bio Addo SP 291 Nc44
Biobio RCH 80 Gd64
Bioča SCG 126 Lu48
Biograd na moru HR 121 Lq47
Biogradska Gora, N.P. SCG 126 Lu48
Biokovo HR 121 Ls47
Biosphere II USA 23 Ee29
Biotopo del Quetzal GCA 41 Fe38
Biotopo Monterrico-Hawaii GCA 41 Fe39
Biougra MA 258 Kf30
Bipindi CAM 280 Lf44
Bipok CAM 281 Lf43
Biquinhas BR (MG) 75 Hh55
Bira RUS (YAO) 180 Rg21
Bira RUS 180 Rg21
Bira Beach Resort RI 211 Ra48
Bi'r Abu Zaïma SUD 276 Me39
Birak LAR 267 Lh32
Bi'r al 'Akkariyah LAR 261 Lk30
Bi'r al 'Alaqah LAR 260 Lh31
Bi'r al 'Atrun SUD 275 Md36
Bi'r al Awyan LAR 262 Mc30
Bi'r al Banakish LAR 261 Ma30
Bi'r al Fatiyah LAR 260 Lh31
Bi'r al Ghanam LAR 260 Lg29
Bi'r al Gharaqah LAR 261 Ma30
Bir al Guzayyil LAR 260 Lf31
Bir 'Ali YE 150 Ne38
Bir Ali Ben Khélifa TN 260 Lf28
Bi'r al Jadid LAR 267 Lg32
Bi'r al Kammuniyan LAR 261 Lj31
Bi'r al Khawr LAR 260 Lg30
Bi'r Allaq LAR 260 Lf30
Bi'r al Mastutah LAR 267 Lh33
Bi'r al Muwaylih LAR 261 Lk31
Bi'r al Qaf LAR 261 Lh31
Bi'r al Qataf LAR 261 Mb30
Bi'r al 'Utaylah LAR 261 Lj31
Bi'r al Washkah LAR 261 Lh31
Birampur IND (WBG) 194 Pd35
Bir 'Amrâne RIM 264 Kf34
Biramsar IND (RJT) 188 Of32
Bir Anzarane DARS 264 Kc34
Birao RCA 282 Mb40
Bi'r ar Rijl LAR 261 Lh31
Bi'r ash Shahwi LAR 260 Lh30
Biratnagar NEP 170 Pd32
Biratori J 181 Sb24
Bi'r A'yad LAR 260 Lg29
Bir Bel Guerdâne RIM 264 Ke33
Bi'r Ben Ghimah LAR 261 Ma30
Bir Beria TN 260 Le29
Bi'r Bin 'Isa LAR 261 Lh30
Bi'r Bu al Ghurab LAR 260 Lg30
Birch Creek USA (AK) 15 Ch12
Birch Creek USA 15 Ch12
Birchenough Bridge ZW 300 Mg55
Birches USA (AK) 15 Cd13
Birch Hills CDN (SK) 19 Eh19
Birchi WAN 272 Ld39
Birchip AUS (VIC) 237 Sb63
Birchiş RO 124 Mc45
Birch Island CDN 24 Fa19
Birch Lake CDN 19 Ee19
Birch Lake CDN 24 Fd20
Birch River CDN (MB) 24 Ek19
Bircot ETH 285 Nb42
Bircza PL 119 Mc41
Bi'r Dhu'fan LAR 260 Lh30
Bir Di SUD 283 Me42
Bird Island SA 302 Lk62
Bird Island = Île aux Vaches SY 305 Nh47
Bir Djedid DZ 260 Ld29
Bir Dolmane DZ 260 Le30
Bird Rock Lighthouse BS 37 Gc34
Birdsville AUS (QLD) 234 Rk58
Birdsville Race AUS 234 Rk58
Birdtail CDN (MB) 24 Ek20
Birecik TR 145 Mk27
Bire Kpatuos Game Reserve SUD 283 Me43
Bir el Amdar DZ 260 Ld29
Bir El-Ater DZ 260 Le28
Bir el Fakama SUD 276 Mg38
Bir el Gâreb RIM 264 Kb35
Bir el Ghorifa TN 260 Lf29
Bir el Hasa SUD 263 Mh34
Birendranagar NEP 170 Pa31
Bir en Nugeim SUD 276 Mh37
Biretwa EAK 290 Mh45
Bireuen RI 198 Pj43
Bir Fadil KSA 149 Ne34
Bir Fanoidig SUD 276 Mh37
Bir Fegoussi TN 260 Le29
Birfel'd RUS (YAO) 180 Rg21
Bi'r Furawiya SUD 275 Mb38
Bir Gandouz DARS 264 Kb35
Birganj NEP 170 Pc32
Birgi TR 130 Mj52
Birgudi IND (CGH) 191 Pa35
Bir Hadi KSA 151 Nf36
Birhan ETH 284 Mj40
Bi'r Hasanah ET 263 Mg30
Bir Hatab SUD 276 Mg36
Bir Hismet ,Umar SUD 276 Mh36
Biri N 92 Ll30
Biri SUD 282 Md42
Biri SUD 282 Md42
Biria EAT 293 Mg50
Birigüi BR (SP) 74 He56
Biri Island RP 203 Rc39
Biritingas BR (BA) 71 Ja51
Birjand IR 155 Nk29
Bir Jaydah KSA 148 Mj32
Bir-Jdid MA 258 Kg29
Bi'r Jimi LAR 261 Lh29
Bi'r Jubni LAR 262 Mc30
Birka S 93 Ls31
Birkat al 'Aqabah IRQ 147 Nb30
Birkat al Jumaymah KSA 147 Nb31
Birkat Saira SUD 282 Mb39
Birkeland N 92 Lh32
Birkeland N 92 Lj32
Birkelane SN 269 Kc38
Birkenau PL 119 Lu41
Birkenfeld D 114 Lh41
Birkenhead AUS (QLD) 235 Sd58
Birkenhead GB 101 Kr37
Birkerød DK 94 Ln35
Bi'r Khalaf Allah LAR 267 Lg32
Bir Kiau SUD 276 Mh36
Bir Labasoi SUD 276 Mh36
Birlik KZ 159 Og24
Birlik KZ 166 Og23
Birma RDC 287 Mc44
Birma RUS 180 Re20
Bir Mahmoud TN 260 Le29
Birmingham GB 101 Ks38
Birmingham USA (AL) 34 Fg29
Birmitrapur IND (ORS) 191 Pc34
Bir Mogreïn RIM 264 Ke33
Bi'r Mudakim LAR 260 Lg29
Bir Nawari SUD 276 Mh36
Bir Nazirah LAR 260 Lf30
Birnie Atoll KIR 241 Ub19
Birni Gwari WAN 272 Ld40
Birni-Keebi WAN 272 Lc39
Birnin RN 272 Le38
Birnin Gaouré RN 271 Lb39
Birnin Konni RN 272 Lc39
Birnin Kudu WAN 272 Le40
Birnin Lallé RN 272 Ld38
Birnin-Yauri WAN 272 Lc40
Birniwa WAN 272 Lf39
Birnni DY 279 La41
Birnon IND (UPH) 191 Pb33
Biro DY 272 Lb41
Birobidžan RUS (YAO) 180 Rg21
Birou RMM 270 Kf38
Bir Ounâne RMM 265 Kj35
Birpara IND (WBG) 194 Pe32
Bir Qar'at ad Dibah LAR 260 Le31
Bi'r Qaryas LAR 261 Lj31
Birr IRL 100 Kn37
Birricannia AUS (QLD) 233 Sc57
Birrimba Out Station AUS (NT) 223 Rg53
Birrindudu AUS (NT) 223 Re55
Bir Salala SUD 276 Mh36
Birsay GB 99 Kr31
Bir Senia DZ 259 Kk29
Bir Shalatayn ET 263 Mh34
Bir Shari KSA 149 Nb32
Birsilpur IND (RJT) 188 Og31
Bir Slougui TN 260 Le29
Bir Soltane TN 260 Le29
Birštonas LT 97 Me36
Bi'r Tabankurt LAR 267 Lg32
Bir Taleb RIM 270 Kf37
Bir-Tam-Tam MA 259 Kh29
Bi'r Tanjdar LAR 261 Mb30
Bi'r Taziet LAR 267 Lg33
Bir Tegheri LAR 267 Lf32
Birthplace of Mahatma Gandhi IND 190 Oe35
Birthplace of Sun Yat-sen VRC 179 Qg34
Birti SUD 276 Mg37
Bi'r Tin Abunda LAR 267 Lg32
Bi'r Tlakshin LAR 260 Lg30
Birtle CDN (MB) 24 Ek20
Bi'r Turbah LAR 261 Ma29
Biruaca YV 57 Gg42
Birufu RI 213 Rk48
Biruința MD 125 Mj43
Bir Umar LAR 261 Ma30
Biržai LT 97 Me34
Bi'r Zaltan LAR 261 Lk31
Bir Zar TN 260 Lf30
Birži LV 97 Mf34
Biržų pilis LT 97 Me34
Bisa RI 212 Rd46
Bisáccia I 122 Lq49
Bisagana WAN 273 Lg39
Bisai IND (ORS) 194 Pd34
Bisalpur IND (UPH) 189 Ok31
Bisambharpur IND (CGH) 191 Pb34
Bisanadi Nature Reserve EAK 291 Mk45
Bisane RMM 271 La37
Bišapur IR 156 Nf31
Bisauli IND (UPH) 189 Ok31
Bisaurin E 107 Ku52
Bisbee USA (AZ) 23 Ef30
Bisca Mare RO 125 Mg45
Biscarrosse F 104 Kt46
Biscayne N.P. USA 36 Fk33
Biscéglie I 123 Lr49
Bischofshofen A 115 Lo43
Bischofswerda D 113 Lp39
Bischwiller F 103 Lh42
Biscoe Islands 312 Gc32
Biscucuy YV 57 Gf41
Bisellia SUD 283 Md42
Biseruka EAU 287 Mf45
Biševo HR 121 Lq48
Bisha ER 277 Mj39
Bishkek KS 158 Oh24
Bisho SA 303 Md62
Bishop USA (CA) 20 Ea27
Bishop Auckland GB 99 Kt36
Bishop Hill S.H.S. USA 32 Fe25
Bishop's Falls CDN (NF) 31 Hc21
Bishop's Stortford GB 101 La39
Bishr LAR 261 Lk30
Bishunpur IND (JKD) 191 Pc34
Bishu Shanzhuang VRC 175 Qj25
Biskotasi Lake CDN 25 Fj22
Biskra DZ 260 Lc28
Biskupiec PL 117 Ma37
Bislig RP 205 Rd41
Bismarck USA (ND) 26 Ek22
Bismarck Archipelago PNG 240 Sb19
Bismarck Sea PNG 240 Sb19
Bismark D 113 Lm38
Bismil TR 145 Na27
Bismo N 92 Lj29
Biso EAU 287 Mf45
Bison USA (SD) 26 Ej23
Bisonó DOM 46 Ge36
Bisotun IR 154 Nd28
Bisotun IR 154 Nd28
Bispgården S 93 Lr28
Bissau GNB 269 Kc40
Bissett CDN (MB) 24 Fc20
Bissikrima RG 278 Ke40
Bissingou II RCA 282 Ma41
Bissorã GNB 269 Kc39
Bistreț RO 126 Md47
Bistrica BIH 121 Ls46
Bistrica SCG 126 Lu47
Bistrica SCG 126 Lu48
Bistrița RO 124 Me43
Bistrița RO 125 Mf43
Bisungarh IND (JKD) 191 Pc33
Biswan IND (UPH) 189 Pa32
Bisztynek PL 117 Ma36
Bita RCA 282 Mc42
Bitam G 281 Lf44
Bitangor MAL 208 Qf44
Bitata ETH 284 Mk43
Bitburg D 114 Lg41
Bitchabé RT 279 La41
Bitche F 103 Lh41
Bitčvinta GE 152 Na24
Bithoor IND 189 Pa32
Bitigiu ETH 284 Na41
Bitilifondi RCA 287 Md43
Bitjug RUS 133 Na20
Bitkine TCH 282 Lk40
Bitlis TR 145 Nb26
Bitola MK 126 Mb49
Bitonto I 123 Lr49
Bitou BF 279 Kk40
Bitoutouk CAM 280 Lf44
Bitragunta IND (APH) 193 Ok39
Bitra Island IND 192 Og41
Bittencourt BR (AM) 61 Gf46
Bitter Creek USA (WY) 21 Ef25
Bitterfeld D 113 Ln39
Bitterfontein SA 302 Lk61
Bitterroot Range USA 21 Ec22
Bitti I 111 Lk50
Bittuang RI 209 Qk47
Bitumount CDN (AB) 19 Ee17
Bitung RI 209 Rc45
Bituruna BR (PR) 78 He59
Biu WAN 273 Lg40
Biu Plateau WAN 273 Lg40
Bivona I 122 Lo53
Biwa-ko J 183 Rh28
Biwat PNG 243 Sb48
Biwinapada RI 209 Rb48
Bixby USA (MO) 29 Fe27
Biyang VRC (HNN) 177 Qg29
Biye K'obe ETH 284 Nb40
Biyoley SP 291 Nc44
Bizana SA 303 Me61
Bizen J 183 Rh28
Bizerte TN 260 Le27
Bizhe KZ 166 Oj23
Bizigui BF 271 Kk39
Bjahoml' BY 132 Me18
Bjala BG 127 Mf47
Bjala BG 127 Mh48
Bjala čerkva BG 127 Me49
Bjala Slatina BG 126 Md47
Bjalyničy BY 132 Me19
Bjarčzina BY 132 Me18
Bjarèzina BY 97 Mg36
Bjarèzina BY 132 Me19
Bjargtangar IS 90 Jh13
Bjärnum S 95 Lo34
Bjaroza BY 117 Me38
Bjarozauka BY 97 Mf37
Bjärred S 95 Lo35
Bjästa S 90 Lk14
Bjelašnica BIH 121 Lt47
Bjelovar HR 121 Lr45
Bjerkvik N 90 Lj11
Bjerringbro DK 94 Lk34
Björbo S 93 Lp30
Bjørkelangen N 92 Lm31
Björklinge S 93 Ls30
Björkö S 93 Lt31
Björksele S 90 Lk13
Bjørnafjorden N 92 Lf30
Björnberg S 93 Lp31
Bjorne Peninsula CDN 11 Fc03
Björnlandets n.p. S 90 Lk14
Björnrike S 93 Lo28
B. Juárez, P.N. MEX 40 Fb37
Bjurholm S 90 Lk14
Bjursås S 93 Lq30
Bjuv S 95 Ln34
Bla RMM 270 Kh39
Blace SCG 126 Mb47
Blackall AUS (QLD) 235 Sc58
Black and White Pagoda VRC 195 Qa34
Black Bay CDN 25 Ff21
Blackbeard Island National Seashore USA 35 Fk30
Black Bear River CDN 25 Fe18
Black Birch Lake CDN 19 Eg17
Blackbird Cay BH 41 Fg37
Black Braes AUS (QLD) 232 Sc55
Blackbull AUS (QLD) 232 Sa54
Blackburn GB 101 Ks37
Blackbutt AUS (QLD) 235 Sg59
Black C. USA 15 Cd16
Black Canyon of the Gunnison N.P. USA 21 Eg26
Black Diamond CDN (AB) 19 Ec20
Blackdown AUS (QLD) 232 Sb54
Blackdown Tableland N.P. AUS 233 Se57
Black Duck River CDN 25 Ff17
Blackfeet Ind. Res. USA 19 Ed21
Blackfellows AUS 236 Rh62
Blackfoot CDN (AB) 19 Ee19
Blackfoot USA 21 Ed22
Blackfoot USA (ID) 21 Ed24
Blackfoot Ind. Res. CDN 19 Ed20
Blackfoot Res. USA 21 Ee24
Black Forest D 114 Lh43
Blackgate AUS (NSW) 237 Sb62
Black Head IRL 100 Kl37
Blackie CDN (AB) 19 Ed20
Black Irtysh KZ 167 Pc22
Black Island CDN 24 Fb20
Black Kettle National Grassland USA 28 Fa28
Black Lake USA 14 Ca17
Black Mountain IND 194 Pf32
Black Mountain USA (NC) 35 Fj28
Black Mountain N.P. BHT 194 Pf32
Black Mountains GB 101 Kr39
Black Point BS 37 Gb33
Blackpool GB 101 Kr37
Black Pt. USA 16 Cd17
Black Range USA 23 Eg29
Black River JA 45 Gb36
Black River USA 23 Ee29
Black River VN 178 Qb35
Black River Falls USA (WI) 27 Fe23
Black Rock NAM 302 Lh59
Black Rock SA 302 Mb59
Black Rock USA (UT) 21 Ed26
Black Rock Desert USA 20 Ea25
Blacksburg USA (VA) 35 Fk27
Black Sea 86 Mb05
Blackshear USA (GA) 35 Fj30
Blacksod Bay IRL 98 Kk36
Blacks reef NZ 238 Tj65
Blackville AUS (NSW) 235 Sf61
Black Volta GH/BF 279 Kk40
Blackwater AUS (QLD) 233 Se57
Blackwater IRL 100 Km38
Blackwell USA (TX) 28 Ek29
Blackwell USA (OK) 28 Fb27
Bladensburg N.P. AUS 232 Sb57
Bladgrond SA 302 Lk60
Blaenavon GB 101 Kr39
Bláfell IS 90 Ka13
Blagaj BIH 121 Ls47
Blagodarnyj RUS 152 Nb23
Blagoeve UA 125 Ml44
Blagoevgrad BG 126 Md48
Blagoveščenka RUS 140 Pa08
Blagoveščensk RUS 180 Rd20
Blåhøa N 92 Lk28
Blahoveščensky sobor UA 133 Mj20
Blain F 102 Kt43
Blaine Lake CDN (SK) 19 Eg19
Blair USA (NE) 27 Fb25
Blair Athol AUS (QLD) 233 Sd57
Blairbeth SA 299 Md58
Blairgowrie GB 99 Kr34
Blair Castle GB 99 Kr34
Blairmore CDN (AB) 19 Ec21
Blairquhan Castle GB 99 Kq33
Blairsden USA (CA) 20 Dk26
Blairsville USA (GA) 35 Fj28
Blaj RO 124 Md44
Blå Jungfrun S 95 Lr33
Blå Jungfrun n.p. S 95 Lr33
Blaka RN 267 Lg35
Blaka Laodemi RN 267 Lg35
Błąkały PL 117 Mc36
Blake Basin 37 Gc31
Blakely USA (GA) 35 Fh30
Blake Plateau 37 Ga30
Blakstad N 92 Lj32
Blama WAL 278 Ke42
Blambangan RI 207 Qc48
Blâmont F 103 Lg42
Blanca Aurora Falls RP 205 Rc40
Blanca Flor BOL 67 Gg51
Blancagrande RA (BA) 81 Gk64
Blanca Peak USA 23 Eh27
Blanchard Springs Caverns USA 29 Fd28
Blanche Channel SOL 245 Sj50
Blanche Marievallen SME 59 Hb43
Blanchetown AUS (SA) 236 Rk63
Blanco Encalada PE 72 Ge58
Blanco, P.N. RCH 42 Fh40
Blandford Forum GB 101 Ks40
Blanding USA (UT) 23 Ef27
Blanes E 110 Lc49
Blanfla CI 279 Kh42
Blangkejeren RI 198 Pj43
Blangpidie RI 198 Pj44
Blangy-sur-Bresle F 103 Lb41
Blankaholm S 95 Lr33
Blankenberge B 103 Ld39
Blankenburg D 113 Ll39
Blankenheim D 112 Lg40
Blanquillo ROU 77 Hc62
Blantyre MW 297 Mh53
Blanzac F 104 La45
Blarney IRL 100 Km39
Blarney Castle IRL 100 Km39
Blåsjøen N 92 Lg31
Blasket Islands IRL 100 Kk38
Błaszki PL 116 Lt39
Blatnica BIH 121 Ls46
Blato HR 121 Lr48
Blaubeuren D 114 Lk42
Blaufelden D 114 Lk41
Blåvand DK 94 Lj35
Blåvands Huk DK 94 Lj35
Blavet F 102 Kr43
Blawagg RI 211 Qh50
Blaye F 104 Ku45
Blayney AUS (NSW) 237 Se62
Blaževo SCG 126 Ma47
Blāzma LV 97 Mc33
Bleaker Island GB 83 Ha72
Blebo LB 278 Kg43
Bleckede D 113 Ll37
Bled SLO 121 Lp44
Bled Tisseras DZ 266 Ld32
Blega RI 210 Qg49
Bleiburg A 115 Lp44
Bleikvassli N 90 Lg13
Blejsko jezero SLO 121 Lp44
Blekinge S 95 Lp34
Bléneau F 103 Lc43
Blenheim AUS (QLD) 235 Se59
Blenheim NZ 239 Tg66
Blenheim Palace GB 101 Kt39
Bleré F 102 La43
Blesmanspos SA 303 Mc59
Bletterans F 105 Lf44
Blida DZ 259 Lb27
Blieskastel D 114 Lh41
Bligh Sound AUS 239 Td68
Bligh Water FJI 247 Tj54
Blimbing RI 208 Qj46
Blina AUS (WA) 222 Rc54
Blinaodi CI 279 Kj41
Blind Channel CDN (BC) 18 Dh20
Blind River CDN (ON) 32 Fj22
Blinisht AL 126 Lu49
Blinman AUS (SA) 236 Rk61
Blinnenhorn CH 114 Lj44
Bliss Landing CDN (BC) 18 Dh20
Blitar RI 210 Qg50
Blitta RT 279 La41
Blizne PL 119 Mb41
Block Island USA 33 Ge25
Bloemfontein SA 303 Md60
Bloemhoek SA 302 Lk60
Bloemhof SA 303 Mc59
Bloemhofdam SA 303 Mc59
Bloemhof Dam Nature Reserve SA 303 Md59
Blois F 102 Lb43
Blokhus DK 94 Lk33
Blolékin CI 278 Kg42
Blombacka S 93 Lo31
Blomøy N 92 Le30
Blönduós IS 90 Jk13
Blongas RI 211 Qj50
Blonie PL 117 Ma38
Blood Ind. Res. CDN 19 Ed21
Blood River SA 303 Mf60
Bloods Range AUS 226 Re58
Bloodvein River CDN (MB) 24 Fb20
Bloodvein River CDN 24 Fb20
Bloody Foreland IRL 98 Km35
Bloomfield USA (MT) 21 Eh22
Bloomfield USA (NM) 23 Eg27
Bloomfield USA (NE) 26 Fb24
Bloomfield USA (IA) 27 Fd25
Bloomfield USA (IN) 34 Fg26
Bloomfield River AUS (QLD) 231 Sc53
Bloomington USA (MN) 27 Fd23
Bloomington USA (IL) 32 Ff25
Bloomington USA (IN) 34 Fg26
Bloomsburg USA (PA) 33 Gb25
Bloomsbury AUS (QLD) 233 Se56
Blora RI 210 Qf49
Blossom Village GB 45 Fk36
Błotno PL 116 Lq37
Blountstown USA (FL) 35 Fh30
Blowholes AUS 224 Qg58
Blowholes OM 151 Ng37
Blubber Bay CDN (BC) 18 Dh21
Bludenz A 114 Lk43
Blue BH 41 Ff36
Blueberry River CDN 17 Dk17
Blue Dam AUS (SA) 236 Rh61
Blue Earth USA (MN) 27 Fc24
Bluefield USA (WV) 35 Fk27
Bluefields NIC 42 Fj39
Blue Grotto M 122 Lp55
Blue Hills of Couteau CDN 31 Hb22
Blue Hole BH 41 Fg37
Blue Hole N.P. BH 41 Ff37
Blue Lagoon N.P. Z 296 Md53
Blue Lake AUS 236 Sa64
Blue Lake USA (CA) 20 Dj25
Blue Mud Bay AUS 223 Rj52
Blue MountainLake USA (NY) 33 Gc24
Blue Mountains USA 20 Ea23
Blue Mountains USA 33 Gb25
Blue Mountains N.P. AUS 237 Sf62
Blue Mts. N.P. JA 45 Gb36
Blue Mud Hills USA 21 Ef22
Blue Nile ETH 284 Mh40
Blue Nile SUD 255 Mc16
Blue Nile Canyon ETH 284 Mk40
Blue Nile Falls = Tis Isat Falls ETH 284 Mj40
Blue Rapids USA (KS) 27 Fb26
Blue Ridge USA (GA) 35 Fh28
Blue Ridge USA 35 Fk27
Blue Ridge Parkway USA 35 Fk27
Blue River CDN (BC) 18 Ea19
Blueskin Bay AUS 239 Tf68
Blue Stack Mountains IRL 98 Km36
Blue Train SA 302 Lk62
Blue Train (Garden Route) SA 303 Mc62
Bluewater AUS (QLD) 233 Sd55
Bluff AUS (QLD) 233 Se57
Bluff NZ 239 Te69
Bluff PA 42 Fj41
Bluff USA (AK) 15 Bj13
Bluff USA (UT) 23 Ef27
Bluff Downs AUS (QLD) 233 Sc55
Bluffers Park CDN 33 Ga24
BluffFace Range AUS 222 Rd54
Bluff Point AUS 224 Qh59
Blukwa RDC 287 Mf45
Blumau A 115 Lr43
Blumberg D 114 Lj43
Blumenau BR (SC) 79 Hf59
Blunt USA (SD) 26 Fa23
Blup Blup Island PNG 243 Sc47
Bly USA (OR) 20 Dk24
Blyde River Canyon Nature Reserve SA 300 Mf58
Blydeverwaghterplato SA 302 Lk60
Blying Sound USA 15 Cf16
Blyth GB 99 Kt35
Blythe USA (CA) 22 Ec29
Blytheville USA (AR) 29 Ff28
Bni-Boufrah MA 259 Kh28
Bø N 92 Lk31
Bo WAL 278 Ke42
Boa CI 278 Kg41
Boabeng-Fiema Monkey Sanctuary GH 279 Kk42
Boac RP 203 Ra39
Boaco NIC 42 Fh39
Boa Esperança BR (RR) 58 Gk44
Boa Esperança BR (AM) 61 Gf48
Boa Esperança BR (AM) 62 Gh49
Boa Esperança BR (MS) 74 Hd56
Boa Esperança BR (MG) 75 Hh56
Boa Esperança do Sul BR (SP) 74 Hf56
Boagis PNG 244 Sg50
Boa Hora BR (RO) 68 Gj50
Bo'ai VRC (YUN) 178 Qd34
Boajibu WAL 278 Ke41
Boal E 106 Ko53
Boali RCA 286 Lk43
Boana BR (AM) 67 Gf49
Boana PNG 243 Sd49
Boanamary RM 304 Nd53
Boanda CAM 281 Lf43
Boane MOC 303 Mg59
Boang Island PNG 244 Sg47
Boano RI 212 Rd47
Boa Nova BR (BA) 71 Hk53
Boardman USA (OR) 20 Ea23
Boardman USA (OH) 33 Fk25
Boat Basin CDN (BC) 18 Dg21
Boat of Garten GB 99 Kr33
Boa Viagem BR (CE) 65 Ja48
Boa Vista BR (RR) 58 Gk44
Boa Vista BR (AM) 62 Gh46
Boa Vista BR (AM) 62 Gh48
Boa Vista BR (AM) 62 Gh49
Boa Vista BR (AM) 62 Gj46
Boa Vista BR (PA) 63 He47
Boa Vista da Ramos BR (AM) 63 Hb47
Boa Vista do Tupim BR (BA) 71 Hk52
Boa Vista, T.I. BR 62 Ha47
Boayan Island RP 204 Qk40
Boaz USA (AL) 34 Fg28
Bobadah AUS (NSW) 237 Sd62
Bobai VRC (GZG) 178 Qf34
Bobâlna RO 124 Md43
Bobasakoa RM 305 Ne52
Bobbejaanland B 103 Le39
Bobbili IND (APH) 191 Pb36
Böbbio I 120 Lk46
Bobé DY 279 La41
Bobeica RO 125 Mf43

ou Salem TN 260 Le27
ouse USA (AZ) 22 Ed29
ou Sfer DZ 259 Kk28
oussac F 104 Lc44
oussé BF 271 Kk39
oussens F 104 La47
oussès TCH 273 Lj40
oussou BF 271 Kj39
oussouma BF 271 Kk39
outilimit RIM 269 Kc37
outiller RH 46 Gd36
outougou Fara SN 269 Kd39
ouvet Island 50 La15
ouxwiller F 103 Lh42
ouza RN 272 Ld38
ouzghaïa DZ 259 La27
ovalino Mare I 123 Lr52
ova Marina I 123 Lq53
ovbjerg Fyr DK 94 Lj34
ovenden D 112 Lk39
oves F 103 Lc41
ovino I 122 Lq49
ovril RA (ER) 77 Ha61
owa Falls SA 303 Md62
owbells USA (ND) 24 Ej21
owdle USA (SD) 26 Fa23
owdon USA (GA) 35 Fh29
owen AUS (QLD) 233 Se56
owen RA (MD) 76 Gg63
owen River AUS 233 Sd56
owerville AUS (QLD) 235 Sf59
owes GB 101 Kt36
owie USA (TX) 29 Fb29
ow Island CDN (AB) 19 Ee21
owling Green USA (MO) 27 Fe26
owling Green USA (OH) 32 Fj25
owling Green USA (KY) 34 Fg27
owling Green Bay AUS 233 Sd55
owling Green Bay N.P. AUS 233 Sd55
owman USA (ND) 26 Ej22
owmore GB 98 Ko35
owning AUS (NSW) 237 Se63
owraville AUS (NSW) 235 Sg61
ow River CDN 19 Ed20
owron Lake Prov. Park CDN 18 Dk19
owser CDN (BC) 18 Dh21
owthorn AUS (QLD) 232 Rk55
oxberg D 113 Lp39
oxholm S 95 Lq32
oxmeer NL 112 Lg39
oxtel NL 112 Lf39
oxwood Hill AUS (WA) 228 Qk63
oyabat TR 144 Mh25
oyabo RDC 286 Lk44
oyaca CO 56 Gd43
Yai Hot Spring LAO 197 Qb36
oyakro CI 279 Kh42
oyalı TR 131 Mo49
oyalı TR 131 Mo52
oyalıca TR 130 Mk50
oyang VRC (JGX) 184 Qj31
oyele RCB 286 Lk44
oyle CDN (AB) 19 Ed18
oyle IRL 98 Km37
oylston CDN (NS) 31 Gk23
oymurot UZB 158 Od25
oyne SA 300 Me57
oyne City USA (MI) 32 Fh23
oyo RI 206 Pk46
oyolali RI 210 Qf49
oysen Res. USA 21 Ef24
oysun UZB 158 Od26
oyuibe BOL 73 Gj56
oyup Brook AUS (WA) 228 Qj62
oyuyo BOL 67 Gf51
oza EAT 293 Mk48
oza EAT 293 Mk49
ozan TR 130 Mk53
ozanbai KZ 167 Pb21
ozashchy tübegi KZ 152 Nf23
ožava HR 121 Lp46
ozburun TR 129 Mj54
ozburun Yarımadası TR 129 Mj54
ozcaada TR 130 Mg51
ozcaada Adası TR 130 Mg51
oz Dağları TR 129 Mh52
ozdoğan TR 130 Mj53
ozen = Bolzano I 120 Lm44
ozene RDC 286 Lk44
ozhou VRC (AHU) 184 Qh29
ozi VRC (SCH) 176 Qa30
ozier TR 130 Mh50
ozioru RO 125 Mg45
ozkir TR 131 Mn53
ozkir TR 131 Mo50
ozköl KZ 153 Oa23
ozkurt TR 130 Mk53
ozok Yaylası TR 131 Mq51
ozouls F 105 Lc46
ozoum RCA 281 Lj42
ozova TR 131 Ml53
ozova TR 145 Mk27
ozovici RO 124 Md46
oztepe TR 131 Mp51
oztepe TR 131 Mq50
ozüyük TR 130 Ml51
ozyaka TR 130 Mk53
ozyazı TR 131 Mn54
ozyazı TR 144 Mg27
ozzolo I 120 Ll45
a I 120 Lh46
aås S 95 Lq33
abova RO 124 Md46
ač HR 121 Lr47
acciano I 122 Ln48
acebridge CDN (ON) 33 Ga23
achlewo PL 116 Lt37
äcke S 93 Lq28
acketville USA (TX) 28 Ek31
ackley GB 101 Kt38
acknell GB 101 Ku39
aço do Norte BR (SC) 79 Hf60
aço Menor do Araguaia ou Jauaés BR 69 He51
ad RO 124 Mc44
adaiž LV 97 Mh34
ádano I 123 Lr50
ádeni RO 125 Me44
adenton USA (FL) 36 Fj32
adford GB 101 Kt37
adford USA (PA) 33 Ga25
adley USA (CA) 22 Dk28
adley Reef SOL 245 Ta49
adleyville USA (MO) 29 Fd27
ady USA (TX) 28 Fa30
ae GB 99 Kt30
ædstrup DK 94 Lk35
Braemar AUS (SA) 236 Rk62
Braemar GB 99 Kr33
Braga P 106 Km51
Bragadiru RO 125 Mf46
Bragado RA (BA) 77 Gk63
Bragança BR (PA) 64 Hg46
Bragança P 106 Ko51
Bragança Paulista BR (SP) 75 Hg57
Braggs USA (AL) 34 Fg29
Brahestadt FIN 91 Mc13
Brahim RI 208 Qh45
Brahmanbaria BD 194 Pf34
Brahmapari IND (MHT) 191 Ok35
Brahmaputra IND 194 Pg32
Brahmour IND (HPH) 189 Oj29
Braidwood AUS (NSW) 237 Se63
Brăila RO 125 Mh45
Braine F 103 Ld41
Brainerd USA (MN) 27 Fc22
Braintree GB 101 La39
Brak SA 300 Me57
Brakas RI 211 Qh49
Brake D 112 Lj37
Brakel D 112 Lk39
Brakmakund IND (ARP) 195 Pj32
Brakspruit SA 303 Md59
Brakwater NAM 298 Lj57
Brålanda S 92 Ln32
Brálos GR 128 Mc52
Bramming DK 94 Lj35
Brämön S 93 Ls28
Brampton CDN (ON) 33 Ga24
Brampton GB 99 Ks36
Bramsche D 112 Lj38
Bramsöfjärden S 93 Ls30
Bramwell AUS (QLD) 230 Sb52
Bran RO 125 Mf45
Branäs S 93 Ln30
Brancaleone Marina I 123 Lr53
Branch CDN (NF) 31 Hd22
Branchville USA (SC) 35 Fk29
Brandberg NAM 298 Lh56
Brandberg NAM 298 Lh56
Brandbu N 92 Ll30
Brande DK 94 Lk35
Brandenburg D 113 Lo38
Brandenburg D 113 Ln38
Brand-Erbisdorf D 113 Lo40
Brandfort SA 303 Md60
Brandkop SA 302 Lk61
Brandö FIN 93 Mb30
Brandö FIN 93 Mb30
Brandon CDN (MB) 24 Fa21
Brandon GB 101 La38
Brandon USA (SD) 27 Fb24
Brandon USA (MS) 29 Ff29
Brandon USA (FL) 36 Fj32
Brandon Bay IRL 100 Kk38
Brandon Head IRL 100 Kk38
Brandval N 92 Lm30
Brandvlei SA 302 Ma61
Brandýs nad Labem-Stará Boleslav CZ 118 Lp40
Branford USA (FL) 36 Fj31
Braniewo PL 117 Ma36
Branitzer Park D 113 Lp39
Br'anka UA 135 Mk21
Bränna S 92 Ln32
Bransan SN 269 Kd39
Bransby AUS (QLD) 234 Sa60
Bransfield Strait 312 Ha31
Brańsk PL 117 Mc38
Branson USA (MO) 29 Fd27
Brantford CDN (ON) 33 Fk24
Brantôme F 104 La45
Branxholme AUS (VIC) 236 Sa64
Braodview USA (MT) 21 Ef22
Brás BR (AM) 62 Ha46
Bras d'Or Lake CDN 31 Gk23
Brashears USA (AR) 29 Fd28
Brasil C 45 Gb35
Brasilândia BR (MS) 74 Hd56
Brasilândia de Minas BR (MG) 75 Hh54
Brasiléia BR (AC) 67 Gf51
Brasília BR (DF) 70 Hg53
Brasília de Minas BR (MG) 75 Hh54
Brasília, P.N. de BR 70 Hg53
Braslândia BR (DF) 70 Hf53
Braslau BY 97 Mh35
Braslav Lakes N.P. BY 97 Mh35
Brasnorte BR (MT) 68 Ha51
Brasópolis BR (MG) 75 Hh57
Brașov RO 125 Mf45
Brass WAN 280 Ld43
Brasschaat B 103 Le39
Brassey, Mount AUS 227 Rh57
Brasstown Bald USA 35 Fj28
Brastad S 92 Lm32
Brąszewice PL 116 Lt39
Brataj AL 126 Lu50
Bratca RO 124 Mc44
Bratislava SK 118 Ls42
Bratislavský hrad SK 118 Ls42
Bratovoești RO 124 Md46
Bratsk RUS 140 Qa07
Brats'ke UA 125 Mm43
Bratskoe-vodohranilišce RUS 140 Qa07
Brattfjället S 93 Ln29
Brattleboro USA (VT) 33 Gd24
Brattmon S 93 Ln30
Brattvåg N 92 Lg28
Brațul Borcea RO 125 Mh46
Brațul Chilia RO 125 Mk45
Brațul Sfântu Gheorghe RO 125 Mk45
Brațul Sulina RO 125 Mk45
Bratunac BIH 126 Lu46
Braulio Carrillo, P.N. CR 42 Fj40
Braunau A 115 Lo42
Braunfels D 112 Lj40
Braunlage D 113 Ll39
Braunschweig D 113 Ll38
Braunton GB 100 Kq39
Bråviken S 93 Lr32
Brawley USA (CA) 22 Ec29
Bray IRL 100 Ko37
Bray SA 299 Mb58
Bray Head IRL 100 Kk39
Bray-sur-Seine F 103 Ld42
Bray-sur-Somme F 103 Lc41
Brazatortas E 108 Kq48
Brazeau, Mount CDN 18 Eb19
Brazeau River CDN 19 Eb19
Brazil 51 Ha10
Brazil Basin 53 Jb21
Brazilian Highlands BR 53 Hd22
Brazoria N.W.R. USA 29 Fc31
Brazos USA 29 Fb30
Brazo Sur del Río RA 82 Ge71
Brazzaville RCB 288 Lh48
Brbinj HR 121 Lp46
Brčko BIH 124 Lt46
Brda PL 116 Ls37
Breadalbane AUS (QLD) 232 Rk57
Breaksea Sound AUS 239 Td68
Bream Bay NZ 238 Th63
Brea Pozo RA (SE) 76 Gj60
Breas PE 72 Ge58
Breaux Bridge USA (LA) 29 Fe30
Breaza RO 124 Me44
Breaza RO 125 Mf45
Brebes RI 210 Qe49
Brechen D 112 Lj40
Brechin GB 99 Ks34
Breckenridge USA (CO) 21 Eh26
Breckenridge USA (MN) 27 Fb22
Breckenridge USA (TX) 28 Fa29
Břeclav CZ 118 Lr42
Brecon GB 100 Kr39
Brecon Beacons N.P. GB 100 Kr39
Breda NL 112 Le39
Bredaryd S 95 Lo33
Bredasdorp SA 302 Ma63
Bredbo AUS (NSW) 237 Se63
Bredstedt D 112 Lj36
Bree B 103 Lf39
Breede SA 302 Ma63
Breeza Plains AUS (QLD) 231 Sc53
Bregalnica MK 126 Mb49
Bregenz A 114 Lk43
Bregovo BG 126 Mc46
Bréhal F 102 Kt42
Bréhat F 102 Ks42
Breiðafjörður IS 90 Jj13
Breiðdalsvik IS 90 Kd13
Breil-sur-Roya F 105 Lh47
Breisach D 114 Lh42
Breitbridge ZW 300 Mf57
Breivikbotn N 90 Mb10
Brejão da Caatinga BR (BA) 71 Hk51
Brejo BR (MA) 65 Hj47
Brejo da Madre de Deus BR (PE) 71 Jb50
Brejo da Onça BR (PI) 65 Hk48
Brejo de São Félix BR (MA) 64 Hj48
Brejo do Cruz BR (PB) 65 Jb49
Brejo Grande BR (SE) 71 Jb51
Brejolândia BR (BA) 70 Hj52
Brejo Santo BR (CE) 65 Ja49
Brejtovo RUS 132 Mj16
Brekken N 92 Lm28
Brekstad N 90 Le14
Brel's Tomb F 249 Da50
Bremangerlandet N 92 Le29
Brembo I 120 Lk45
Bremen D 112 Lj37
Bremen USA (ND) 26 Fa22
Bremer Bay AUS (WA) 228 Qk63
Bremerhaven D 112 Lj37
Bremer Island AUS 223 Rj52
Bremer Range AUS 228 Ra62
Bremerton USA (WA) 18 Dj22
Bremervörde D 112 Lk37
Brem-sur-Mer F 102 Kt44
Breń PL 116 Lq37
Brenes E 108 Kp47
Brenner A/I 115 Lm43
Breno I 120 Ll45
Brenta I 120 Ll44
Brenta I 120 Lm45
Brentley USA (AL) 34 Fg30
Brentwood USA (TN) 34 Fg27
Brep PK 161 Og27
Bréscia I 120 Ll45
Bressanone = Brixen I 120 Lm44
Bressay GB 99 Kt30
Bressuire F 102 Ku44
Brest BY 117 Md38
Brest F 102 Kq42
Brestovac SCG 126 Mc46
Brestovo BG 127 Me47
Bretaña PE 61 Gc48
Brețcu RO 125 Mg44
Bretenoux F 104 Lb46
Breteuil F 103 Lc41
Breteuil-sur-Iton F 102 La42
Breton, P.N.W.R. USA 29 Ff31
Breton Sound USA 29 Ff31
Bretten D 114 Lj41
Breueh RI 198 Ph43
Breuil-Cervinia I 120 Lh45
Breuna D 112 Lk39
Brevard USA (NC) 35 Fj28
Breves BR (PA) 63 He46
Brewarrina AUS (NSW) 235 Sd60
Brewer USA (MA) 33 Gf23
Brewster USA (NE) 26 Fa25
Brewton USA (AL) 34 Fg30
Breynat CDN (AB) 19 Ed18
Breza BIH 121 Lt46
Brežice SLO 121 Lq45
Brezina DZ 259 La29
Breznik BG 126 Mc48
Brezno SK 119 Lu42
Brezoi RO 124 Me45
Brezovo BG 127 Mf48
Bria RCA 282 Ma42
Briançon F 105 Lg46
Briare F 103 Lc43
Bribbaree AUS (NSW) 237 Sd63
Bribie Island AUS 235 Sg59
Bribir HR 121 Lq47
Bribri CR 42 Fj41
Briceni MD 125 Mh42
Bricquebec F 102 Kt41
Bridge End IRL 98 Kn35
Bridge Lake CDN (BC) 18 Dk20
Bridgend GB 100 Kr39
Bridge Point BS 37 Gb33
Bridgeport USA (CA) 20 Ea26
Bridgeport USA (NE) 26 Ej25
Bridgeport USA (CT) 33 Gd25
Bridger USA (MT) 21 Ef23
Bridger Peak USA 21 Eg25
Bridgeton USA (NJ) 33 Gc26
Bridgetown BDS 47 Ha39
Bridgetown CDN (NS) 31 Gh23
Bridgeville USA (CA) 20 Dj25
Bridgewater AUS (VIC) 236 Sa65
Bridgewater AUS (TAS) 236 Sd67
Bridgewater AUS (VIC) 237 Sb64
Bridgewater CDN (NS) 31 Gh23
Bridgewater SA 300 Me57
Bridgnorth GB 101 Ks38
Bridgwater GB 100 Ks39
Bridlington GB 101 Ku36
Bridoire F 104 Lf45
Bridport AUS (TAS) 236 Sd66
Bridport GB 100 Ks40
Brie F 103 Ld42
Briec F 102 Kr42
Brie-Comte-Robert F 103 Lc42
Brienne-le-Château F 103 Le42
Brienz CH 114 Lj44
Brienzer See CH 114 Lj44
Brieville RM 306 Nd54
Briey F 103 Lf41
Brig CH 114 Lh44
Brigde River CDN 18 Dj20
Briggsdale USA (CO) 21 Eh25
Brigham City USA (UT) 21 Ee25
Bright AUS (VIC) 237 Sd64
Brighton GB 101 Ku40
Brighton USA (CO) 21 Eh26
Brighton Downs AUS (QLD) 232 Sa57
Brighton Seminole Ind.Res. USA 36 Fk32
Brignogan-Plages F 102 Kq42
Brignoles F 105 Lg47
Brihuega E 109 Ks50
Brijuni, N.P. HR 121 Lo46
Brikama WAG 269 Kb39
Briksdal N 92 Lg29
Brilhante BR 74 Hc56
Brilon D 112 Lj39
Brimnes N 92 Lg30
Brimstone Hill Fortress N.P. KN 47 Gj37
Brindisi I 123 Ls50
Brinje HR 121 Lq46
Brinkley USA (AR) 29 Fe28
Brinkmann RA (CD) 77 Gj61
Brinkworth AUS (SA) 236 Rk62
Brinlack IRL 98 Km35
Brin-Navolok RUS 91 Na14
Brinnon USA (WA) 18 Dj22
Brintbodarna S 93 Lp30
Brionne F 102 La41
Brioude F 105 Ld45
Briouze F 102 Ku42
Brisbane AUS (QLD) 235 Sg59
Brisighella I 120 Lm46
Bristol CDN (NB) 30 Gg22
Bristol GB 101 Ks39
Bristol USA (CT) 33 Gd25
Bristol USA (VA) 35 Fj27
Bristol Bay USA 14 Ca17
Bristol Channel GB 100 Kr39
Bristow USA (OK) 29 Fb28
Britânia BR (GO) 69 He53
Britannia CDN (NF) 31 Hd21
British Columbia CDN 10 Dc07
British Virgin Islands USA 47 Gh36
Brito Godins ANG 288 Lj50
Brits SA 299 Md58
Britstown SA 302 Mb61
Brittany F 102 Kr43
Brittany F 102 Kr42
Brittingham MEX (DGO) 39 Ej33
Britton USA (SD) 26 Fb23
Brive-la-Gaillarde F 104 Lb45
Briviesca E 107 Kr52
Brixen = Bressanone I 120 Lm44
Brixham GB 100 Kr40
Brjansk RUS 132 Mh19
Brjanskoe RUS 181 Sb22
Brjánslækur IS 90 Jj13
Brka BIH 124 Lt46
Brnaze HR 121 Lr47
Brno CZ 118 Lr41
Bro S 95 Lt33
Broach = Bharuch IND (GUJ) 190 Og35
Broad Arrow AUS (WA) 228 Ra61
Broad Bay GB 99 Ko32
Broadbent's Mission SA 303 Mc59
Broadbent's Sending SA 303 Mc59
Broadford GB 98 Kp33
Broad Law GB 99 Kr35
Broad Peak 161 Oj28
Broad Sound AUS 233 Se57
Broad Sound Channel AUS 233 Sf57
Broadsound Range AUS 233 Se57
Broadstairs GB 101 Lb39
Broadus USA (MT) 21 Eh23
Broadview CDN (SK) 24 Ej20
Broadview USA (NM) 23 Ej28
Brobo CI 279 Kh42
Broby S 95 Lp34
Broćeni LV 97 Mc34
Brochet CDN (MB) 24 Ek17
Brochów PL 117 Ma38
Brocken D 113 Ll39
Brockman, Mount AUS 224 Qj57
Brockton USA (MT) 19 Eh21
Brockton USA (MA) 33 Ge24
Brockville CDN (ON) 33 Gc23
Brockway USA (MT) 21 Eh22
Brockway USA (PA) 33 Ga25
Brod BIH 126 Lt47
Brod MK 126 Mb49
Brod MK 126 Mb50
Brodarevo SCG 126 Lu47
Brodce CZ 118 Lp40
Brodec'ke UA 134 Me21
Brodeur Peninsula CDN 11 Fc04
Brodick GB 98 Kp35
Brodie Castle GB 99 Kr33
Brodina de Jos RO 125 Mf43
Brodnica PL 117 Lu37
Brodowski BR (SP) 74 Hg56
Brody UA 117 Mf40
Brogan USA (OR) 20 Eb23
Brojce PL 116 Lq37
Broke Inlet AUS 228 Qj63
Broken Arrow USA (OK) 29 Fc27
Broken Bay AUS 237 Sf62
Broken Bow USA (NE) 26 Fa25
Broken Bow USA (OK) 29 Fc28
Broken Head AUS 235 Sg60
Broken Hill AUS (NSW) 234 Sa61
Broken Ridge 315 Pb13
Broken Skull River CDN 17 Df14
Broken Water Bay PNG 243 Sc47
Brokind S 95 Lq32
Brokopondo SME 59 Hc43
Brokopondo-stuwmeer SME 59 Hc43
Brokoyo CI 278 Kg43
Bromaderry AUS (NSW) 237 Sf63
Bromarv FIN 96 Mc31
Bromby Islands AUS 223 Rj51
Brome D 113 Ll38
Brommö S 93 Lo32
Bromo, Gunung RI 210 Qg49
Bromölla S 95 Lp34
Bromo-Tengger-Semeru N.P. RI 210 Qg50
Brömsebro S 95 Lr34
Bromsgrove GB 101 Ks38
Bromyard GB 101 Ks38
Brønderslev DK 94 Lk33
Broni I 120 Lk45
Bronkhorstspruit SA 299 Me58
Brønnøysund N 90 Lg13
Bronson USA (FL) 36 Fj31
Bronte I 122 Lp53
Bronte USA (TX) 28 Ek30
Brooke's Point RP 204 Qj41
Brookeville AUS (QLD) 233 Sd56
Brookfield USA (MO) 27 Fd26
Brookgreen Gardens USA 35 Ga29
Brookhaven USA (LA) 29 Fe30
Brookings USA (OR) 20 Dh24
Brookings USA (SD) 26 Fb23
Brooks CDN (AB) 19 Ee20
Brooks Aqueduct Prov. H.S. CDN 19 Ee20
Brooks Mtn. USA 15 Bg13
Brooks Nek SA 303 Me61
Brooks Range USA 15 Cc11
Brooksville USA (MS) 29 Ff29
Brooksville USA (FL) 36 Fj31
Brookton AUS (WA) 228 Qj62
Broome AUS (WA) 222 Rb54
Broome Crocodile Park AUS 222 Rb54
Broomehill AUS (WA) 228 Qj62
Broons F 102 Ks42
Brora GB 99 Kr32
Brørup DK 94 Lk35
Brösarp S 95 Lp35
Broșteni RO 124 Mc46
Broszków PL 117 Mc38
Brotas BR (SP) 74 Hf57
Brotas de Macaúbas BR (BA) 71 Hj52
Brother Island ET 263 Mh33
Brothers USA (OR) 20 Dk24
Broto E 107 Ku52
Brottby S 93 Lt31
Brou F 102 Lb42
Brough GB 99 Ks36
Broughton-in-Furness GB 101 Kr36
Broughton Island CDN 18 Dg20
Broulee AUS (NSW) 237 Sf63
Broulkou TCH 274 Lk37
Broumov CZ 118 Lr40
Brouwershaven NL 112 Ld39
Brovary UA 134 Mf20
Brovinia AUS (QLD) 235 Sf58
Brovst DK 94 Lk33
Brown Bank 204 Qj40
Browne USA (AK) 15 Cf13
Brownfield USA (TX) 23 Ej29
Browning USA (MT) 19 Ed21
Browns USA (AL) 34 Fg29
Brown's Cay BS 37 Ga33
Brown Shoal 204 Qj40
Brown's Town JA 45 Gb36
Brownsville USA (TN) 29 Ff28
Brownsville USA (KY) 34 Fg27
Brownsville USA (TX) 39 Fb33
Brownsweg SME 59 Hc43
Brownwood USA (TX) 28 Fa30
Browse Island AUS 222 Rb53
Brozas E 108 Ko49
Bruay-la-Buissière F 103 Lc40
Bruce USA (MS) 29 Ff29
Bruce Crossing USA (MI) 32 Ff22
Bruce Highway AUS 233 Sd55
Bruce, Mount AUS 224 Qk57
Bruce Peninsula N.P. CDN 32 Fk23
Bruce Rock AUS (WA) 228 Qk61
Bruchsal D 114 Lj41
Bruck A 115 Ln43
Bruck D 115 Ln41
Bruck an der Leitha A 115 Lr42
Bruck an der Mur A 115 Lq43
Brüel D 113 Lm37
Brugg CH 114 Lj43
Brugge B 103 Ld39
Bruheim N 92 Lh29
Bruja Beach MEX 38 Eg34
Brujas CO 61 Gf44
Brukkaros NAM 298 Lj58
Brukkaros NAM 298 Lk58
Bruksmiljö S 93 Lq31
Brûlon F 102 Ku43
Brumado BR (BA) 71 Hk53
Brumath F 103 Lh42
Brumby River AUS 224 Qk58
Brumov-Bylnice CZ 118 Lt41
Brumunddal N 92 Ll30
Brunchilly AUS (NT) 223 Rh55
Brundby DK 94 Ll35
Bruneau USA (ID) 20 Ec24
Bruneau USA 20 Ec24
Bruneck = Brunico I 120 Lm44
Brunei BRU 200 Qc17
Brunette Downs AUS (NT) 223 Rh55
Brunette Island CDN 31 Hb22
Brunflo S 90 Lh14
Bruni IND (ARP) 195 Pj31
Brunico = Bruneck I 120 Lm44
Brunsbüttel D 112 Lk37
Brunswick AUS (WA) 228 Qh62
Brunswick USA (OH) 32 Fk25
Brunswick USA (ME) 33 Ge24
Brunswick USA (GA) 35 Fk30
Brunswick Heads AUS (NSW) 235 Sg60
Brunswick Lake CDN 25 Fj21
Bruntál CZ 118 Ls41
Brunt Ice Shelf 312 Jd34
Brus SCG 126 Mb47
Brusarci BG 126 Mc47
Brusett USA (MT) 21 Eg22
Brush USA (CO) 26 Ej25
Brus Laguna HN 42 Fh38
Brusque BR (SC) 79 Hf59
Brussel B 103 Le40
Brussels B 103 Le40
Brüssow D 113 Lp37
Brusturoasa RO 125 Mg44
Bruvno HR 121 Lq46
Bruxelles B 103 Le40
Bruyères F 103 Lg42
Bruz F 102 Kt42
Bruzaholm S 95 Lq33
Bruzual YV 57 Gf41
Brvenik SCG 126 Ma47
Brwinow PL 117 Ma38
Bryan USA (TX) 29 Fb30
Bryan USA (OH) 32 Fh25
Bryan Coast 312 Fd33
Bryan, Mount AUS 236 Rk62
Bryan's Corner USA (OK) 28 Ek27
Bryant USA (AR) 29 Fd28
Bryce Canyon N.P. USA 23 Ed27
Brynderwyn NZ 238 Th64
Bryne N 92 Lf32
Bryten SA 303 Mf59
Brzeg PL 116 Ls40
Brzeg Dolny PL 116 Lr39
Brześć Kujawski PL 116 Lt38
Brzesko PL 119 Ma41
Brzeszcze PL 117 Lu40
Brzeszcze PL 119 Lu41
Brzeziny PL 117 Lu39
Brzostek PL 119 Mb41
Brzóza PL 117 Mb39
Brzozie Lubawskie PL 117 Lu37
Brzozów PL 119 Mc41
Bua FJI 247 Tk54
Bua SUD 282 Mc40
Bu'aale SP 291 Nb45
Bua Bay FJI 247 Tk54
Buafri GH 279 Kk41
Buaka GH 279 Kj42
Buala SOL 245 Sk50
Bualpui IND (MZR) 194 Pg33
Buan RI 208 Qe46
Bua River Z 296 Mg52
Buatan RI 206 Qa45
Bu Athlah LAR 261 Ma31
Buaya RI 207 Qc45
Bu'ayrat al Hasun LAR 261 Lh30
Buba GNB 269 Kc40
Buba RO 125 Mg45
Bubanda RDC 286 Lk43
Bubanza BU 292 Me47
Bubaque GNB 269 Kc40
Bubi ZW 299 Me55
Bubi ZW 300 Mf56
Bubiai LT 97 Md35
Bubiki EAT 292 Mg47
Bubiyan Island KWT 156 Ne31
Bubu EAT 290 Mh48
Bubuget RI 206 Qa47
Bubus RI 207 Qc46
Buca FJI 247 Tk54
Buča UA 134 Mf20
Bučač UA 134 Mc21
Buçaco ANG 295 Ma51
Bucak TR 131 Ml53
Bucalemu RCH 76 Gd63
Bucaramanga CO 56 Gd42
Bucareli Bay USA 17 Dd18
Bucas Grande Island RP 205 Rd41
Bucasia AUS (QLD) 233 Se56
Buccaneer Archipelago AUS 222 Rb53
Buccaneer Beach USA 47 Gh36
Buccino I 122 Lq50
Bucegi, P.N. RO 125 Mf45
Bucerias MEX (NYT) 39 Eh35
Buces RO 124 Mc44
Buchan AUS (VIC) 237 Se64
Buchanan LB 278 Ke43
Buchanan Highway AUS 223 Rf54
Buchan Gulf CDN 11 Gb04
Buchans CDN (NF) 31 Hb21
Bucharest RO 125 Mg46
Buchen D 114 Lk41
Buchholz D 112 Lk37
Buchloe D 115 Ll42
Buchs CH 114 Lk43
Buchwa ZW 300 Mf56
Buchy F 102 Lb41
Bučionys LT 97 Me35
Buciumi RO 124 Md43
Buckeye USA (AZ) 22 Ed29
Buckhannon USA (WV) 33 Fk26
Buckhaven GB 99 Kr34
Buckingham CDN (QC) 33 Gc23
Buckingham GB 101 Ku39
Buckingham USA (CO) 26 Ej25
Buckingham USA (VA) 35 Ga27
Buckingham Bay AUS 223 Rh52
Buckingham Downs AUS (QLD) 232 Rk57
Buck Island USA 47 Gh37
Buckland USA (AK) 15 Bk13
Buckland River USA 15 Bk13
Buckleboo AUS (SA) 236 Rj62
Buckley River AUS 232 Rk56
Bucklige Welt A 115 Lq43
Bucklin USA (KS) 28 Fa27
Bucksport USA (MA) 33 Gf23
Buckwaroon AUS (NSW) 235 Sc61
Bučovice CZ 118 Lr41
Buco Zau ANG 288 Lg48
Bucșani RO 125 Mf46
București RO 125 Mg46
Bucyrus USA (OH) 32 Fj25
Buczek PL 117 Lu39
Bud N 90 Ld14
Budacu RO 125 Mf43
Budaka EAU 290 Mg45
Budalia AUS (QLD) 232 Rk57
Budalin MYA 195 Ph34
Bu Dang VN 197 Qd40
Budaörs H 119 Lt43
Budapest H 119 Lu43
Búðardalur IS 90 Jk13
Budaun IND (UPH) 189 Ok31
Budawang N.P. AUS 237 Sf63
Bud Bud SP 285 Nd43
Buddabuddah AUS (NSW) 235 Sd61
Budd Coast 313 Qc32
Buddha Mountain RC 179 Ra34
Buddha Park THA 197 Qc38
Buddhas of Bamian AFG 160 Oe28
Buddhist Monastery IND 194 Pf32
Buddhist Temple PK 161 Oj28
Buddon Ness GB 99 Ks34
Buddusò I 111 Lk50
Bude GB 100 Kq40
Büdelsdorf D 112 Lk36
Budennovsk RUS 152 Nc23
Budești RO 124 Md43
Budești RO 124 Me45
Budești RO 125 Mg46
Buđevo SCG 126 Ma47
Budgerygar AUS (QLD) 234 Sb58
Budgewoi AUS (NSW) 237 Sf62
Budibudi Islands PNG 244 Sg50
Buding RI 207 Qd47
Büdingen D 114 Lk40
Budjala RDC 286 Lk44
Budkhula ET 263 Me33
Budogošč' RUS 132 Mg16
Budongquan VRC (QHI) 171 Pg28
Budrio I 120 Lm46
Budungbudung RI 209 Qk47
Budva SCG 126 Lt48
Budziszewice PL 117 Lu39
Budzyń PL 116 Lr38
Buéa CAM 280 Le43
Buëch F 105 Lf46
Buedu WAL 278 Ke41
Buefjorden N 92 Le29
Buela ANG 288 Lh48
Buena USA (WA) 18 Dk22
Buena Esperanza RA (SL) 76 Gh63
Buena Hora BOL 67 Gg52
Buenaventura C 45 Gb35
Buenaventura CO 56 Gb44
Buenaventura MEX (CHH) 23 Eg31
Buena Vista BOL 67 Gg51
Buena Vista BOL 73 Gj54
Buena Vista GCA 41 Ff37
Buenavista MEX (CHH) 38 Eg32
Buenavista MEX (SLP) 39 Ek34
Buenavista RP 205 Rb42
Buenavista RP 205 Rc41
Buena Vista USA (CO) 21 Eg26
Buena Vista USA (GA) 35 Fh29
Buena Vista USA (VA) 35 Ga27
Buena Vista YV 57 Gf42
Buena Vista YV 57 Gg41
Buena Vista YV 58 Gj41
Buenavista Alta PE 66 Ga50
Buenavista de Valdavia E 106 Kq52
Buena Vista Island SOL 245 Sk50
Buena Vista Lake USA 22 Ea28
Buenavista Tomatlán MEX (MHC) 40 Ej36
Buendia E 109 Ks50
Buenga ANG 288 Lj49
Bueno Brandão BR (MG) 75 Hg57
Buenópolis BR (MG) 75 Hh54
Buenos Aires CO 56 Gc43
Buenos Aires CO 56 Gd44
Buenos Aires CO 61 Gd45
Buenos Aires CO 61 Ge47
Buenos Aires CR 42 Fj41
Buenos Aires MEX (CHH) 23 Ef30
Buenos Aires PE 66 Gb49
Buenos Aires RA 55 Gd26
Buenos Aires RA (BA) 77 Ha63
Buen Pasto RA (CB) 80 Gf68
Buerarema BR (BA) 71 Ja53
Buesaco CO 60 Gb45
Bueu E 106 Km52
Bueyeros USA (NM) 23 Ej28
Bueyes, Cerro de los RA 80 Ge64
Bufareh RI 213 Rk47
Buffalo CDN (AB) 19 Ee20
Buffalo USA (WY) 21 Eg23
Buffalo USA (SD) 26 Ej23
Buffalo USA (MN) 27 Fd23
Buffalo USA (OK) 28 Fa27
Buffalo USA (TX) 29 Fb30
Buffalo USA (MO) 29 Fd27
Buffalo USA (NY) 33 Ga24
Buffalo Gap Grassland N.P. USA 26 Ej24
Buffalo Gap Nat. Grassland USA 26 Ek23
Buffalo Lake CDN 19 Ed19
Buffalo Narrows CDN (SK) 19 Ef18
Buffalo National River USA 29 Fd28
Buffalo River CDN 19 Ed17
Buffalo Springs Nature Reserve EAK 290 Mj45
Buffels SA 302 Lj60
Buflé Noir CAM 281 Lg41
Buford USA (CO) 21 Eg26
Buford USA (ND) 26 Ej22
Buford USA (GA) 35 Fh28
Buftea RO 125 Mf46
Bug PL 117 Mc38
Buga CO 56 Gb44
Buga MNG 167 Ph22
Buga WAN 280 Ld41
Bugadi EAU 290 Mg45
Bugaia Island EAU 290 Mg46
Bugala Island EAU 290 Mg46
Bugana WAN 280 Ld42
Bugango EAT 287 Mf46
Bugant MNG 172 Qd21
Bugarama RWA 292 Me47
Bugasong RP 205 Rb40
Bugda Acable SP 285 Nc43
Bugdayli TM 153 Nh26
Buğdaylı TR 130 Mh50
Bugeat F 104 Lb45
Bugene EAT 287 Mf46
Bugojno BIH 121 Ls46
Bugsuk Island RP 204 Qj41
Bugt VRC (NMZ) 173 Ra21
Bugt Shan VRC 174 Pk27
Buguda IND (ORS) 191 Pc36
Buguey RP 203 Ra36
Bugul'ma RUS (TAR) 133 Ng18
Bugul'minsko-Belebeevskaja vozvyšennost' RUS 133 Nf18
Bugunda RUS (BUR) 173 Qh19
Bugungu Game Reserve EAU 290 Mf44
Buguruslan RUS 133 Ng19
Buhairat Nuba SUD 276 Mf36
Buhaka EAU 287 Mf45
Buharkent TR 130 Mj53
Bu Hasa UAE 156 Ng34
Buhayrat al Qadisiyah IRQ 147 Nb28
Buhayrat ar Razazah IRQ 147 Nb29
Buhayrat ath Tharthar IRQ 147 Nb29
Bu He VRC 174 Pk27
Buhe VRC (HUB) 177 Qg30
Buhera ZW 300 Mf55
Buhi RP 203 Rb39
Bühl D 114 Lj42
Buhore EAT 292 Mf48
Buhovci BG 127 Mg47
Buhovo BG 126 Md48
Buhtarminskoe sukojmasy KZ 167 Pc21
Buhuși RO 125 Mg44
Buick CDN (BC) 17 Dk17
Buigiri EAT 293 Mh49
Builth Wells GB 100 Kr38
Bu'in IR 154 Nf28
Buin PNG 244 Sh49
Buin RCH 76 Ge62
Bui N.P. GH 279 Kj41
Buinsk RUS (TAR) 133 Ne18
Buique BR (PE) 71 Jb50
Buir Nur MNG/VRC 173 Qj22
Buitepos NAM 298 Lk57
Buiucu BR (PA) 63 Hb48
Buj RUS 133 Na16
Bujagali Falls EAU 290 Mg45
Bujalance E 108 Kq47
Bujang Valley MAL 198 Qa43
Bujanovac SCG 126 Mb48
Bujaraloz E 107 Ku51
Bujaru BR (PA) 65 Hf46
Buje HR 121 Lo45
Buji BR (PI) 65 Hk48
Bujnaksk RUS (DAG) 152 Nd24
Bujran KSA 149 Nf33
Bujukly RUS 181 Sb21
Bujumbura BU 292 Me47
Buk PNG 242 Sb50
Buka PNG 244 Sh48
Bukaan RI 209 Ra45
Bukačače RUS 173 Qj19
Bukadaban Feng VRC 169 Pf27
Buka Island PNG 244 Sh48
Bukakata EAU 287 Mf46
Bukama RDC 292 Mc50
Bu Kammash LAR 260 Lf29
Bukan IR 154 Nd27
Bukanovskaja RUS 133 Nb21
Bukarabe Island EAT 290 Mg46
Bukasa Island EAU 290 Mg46
Bukatatonoa Reefs FJI 247 Ua55
Bukaua PNG 243 Sd49
Bukavu RDC 292 Me47
Bukedea EAU 290 Mh45
Bukene EAT 292 Mg48
Bukhara UZB 158 Oc26
Bukhit SUD 283 Md40
Bukhoro UZB 158 Oc26
Bukide RI 205 Rc44
Bukit Batu MAL 208 Qg44
Bukit Kaba RI 206 Qb47
Bukitkemuning RI 207 Qc48
Bukit Kumbong MAL 208 Qh45
Bukit Larut MAL 198 Qa43
Bukittinggi RI 206 Qa46
Bukit Ujungraj RI 206 Pk46
Bükk H 119 Ma42
Bukkapatna IND (KTK) 193 Oj40
Bükki N.P. H 119 Ma42
Bukkulla AUS (NSW) 235 Sf60
Buklan YE 150 Nb37
Buko RI 209 Rb45
Bukoba EAT 287 Mf46
Bukoli EAT 292 Mg47
Bukovec SK 119 Ma42
Bukovik SCG 126 Mb47
Bukovina UA 125 Mf42
Bukrane RI 215 Rf49
Buktyrma KZ 167 Pc21
Bukungo EAU 290 Mg45
Bukuru WAN 277 Le41
Bukwiri EAU 287 Mf45
Buky UA 134 Mf21
Bula GNB 269 Kc39
Bula PNG 242 Sa50
Bula RI 212 Rf47
Bula RP 203 Rb39
Bula Atuma ANG 288 Lh50
Bulabulin WAN 273 Lg39
Bülach CH 114 Lj43
Bulacle SP 285 Nd43
Bulag MNG 172 Qe21
Bulagansk RUS (BUR) 173 Qf19
Bulahdelah AUS (NSW) 237 Sg62
Bulaka RI 242 Rk49
Bulak Gölü TR 131 Mn52
Bulalacao Island RP 204 Ra40
Bulalakao RP 203 Ra39
Bulan RP 203 Rb39
Bulanbaibauby KZ 158 Od24
Bulandshahr IND (UPH) 189 Oj31
Bulanghee VRC (SAA) 175 Qe26
Bulangu WAN 272 Lf39
Bulanık TR 145 Nb26
Bulanlak TR 145 Mk25
Bulaq ET 263 Mf33
Bulawayo ZW 300 Me56
Bulaya Z 292 Mf50
Bulbula ETH 284 Mk42
Bulchi ETH 284 Mj43
Buldan TR 130 Mj52
Buldana IND (MHT) 190 Oj35
Buldan Baraj TR 130 Mj52
Buldibuyo PE 66 Gb50
Bulembu SD 300 Mf58
Bulenga GH 279 Kj41
Bulgadie AUS (NSW) 235 Se61
Bulga Downs AUS (WA) 228 Qk60
Bulgan MNG 167 Pg22
Bulgan MNG 172 Qb21
Bulgan MNG 172 Pk23
Bulgan MNG 172 Qa20
Bulgan MNG 172 Qb21
Bulgan MNG 174 Qb23
Bulgan gol MNG 167 Pf22
Bulgan Gol Nature Reserve MNG 167 Pf23
Bulgar RUS (TAR) 133 Ne18
Bulgaria BG 127 Me48
Bulguksa Temple ROK 182 Re28
Bulgunnia AUS (SA) 227 Rh61
Buli-Islam RI 212 Re45
Bulimba AUS (QLD) 232 Sb54
Bulisa EAU 287 Mf44
Bulkley River CDN 17 Dg18
Bullaballing AUS (WA) 228 Ra61
Bulla Regia TN 260 Le27
Bullaring AUS (WA) 228 Qj62
Bullas E 109 Kt48
Bullaxaar SP 285 Nc40
Bulle CH 114 Lh44
Bullecourt AUS (QLD) 232 Rk56
Bulleringa N.P. AUS 232 Sb54
Bullfinch AUS (WA) 228 Qk61
Bullhead City USA (AZ) 22 Ec28
Bulli AUS (NSW) 237 Sf63
Bullita Out Station AUS (NT) 223 Rf54
Bull Mountains USA 21 Ef22
Bulloo Downs AUS (WA) 224 Qk58
Bulloo Downs AUS (QLD) 234 Sb60
Bulloo River AUS 234 Sc59
Bullo River AUS (NT) 223 Re53
Bull River CDN 19 Ec20
Bullrock's Harbour BS 37 Gb33
Bulls NZ 238 Th66
Bull Shoals Caverns USA 29 Fd27
Bull Shoals Lake USA 29 Fd27
Bulman AUS (NT) 223 Rh52
Bulnayn Nuruu MNG 172 Pj21
Bulnay Uul MNG 172 Pk21
Bulnes RCH 80 Gd64
Bulolo PNG 243 Sd49
Bulohsama RI 198 Pj44
Bulongo RDC 289 Ma48
Bultfontein SA 303 Md60
Bulu RI 210 Qf49
Buluan Lake RP 205 Rc42

C

risí Ammoudiá GR 127 Me50
risman USA (IL) 32 Fg26
rissiesmeer SA 303 Mf59
ristchurch GB 101 Kt40
ristchurch NZ 239 Tg67
ristiana SA 303 Mc59
ristianburg GUY 58 Ha42
ristiansburg USA (VA) 35
Fk27
ristiansfeld DK 94 Lk35
ristianshölm N 92 Lh32
ristiansø DK 95 Lq35
ristian Sound USA 17 Dc17
ristiansted USA (VI) 47 Gh37
ristie Island MYA 198 Pj41
ristie Mtn. Ski Area USA
32 Fe23
ristina Lake CDN (BC) 18
Eb21
ristina River CDN 19 Ee17
ristina Creek AUS (WA)
222 Rc55
ristmas Creek AUS 222 Rd55
ristmas Island AUS 200 Qb21
ristmas Ridge 316 Bb08
ristmas Valley USA (OR)
20 Dk24
ristoval USA (TX) 28 Ek30
rudim CZ 118 Lq41
rystal Springs USA (LA)
29 Fe30
rystynivka UA 134 Me21
rzanów PL 117 Lu40
u KS 159 Oh24
u = Shu KZ 158 Oe23
uadanga BD 194 Pe34
uave PNG 243 Sc49
ubalung VRC (SCH) 176 Pk31
ub Cay BS 37 Gb33
ubu-Sangaku N.P. J 183 Rj27
ubut RA 55 Gc27
ubut RA 80 Gg67
uchi Lake CDN 18 Dh18
uchiliga GH 279 Kk40
ucuito PE 67 Gf53
ucuma RA (SJ) 76 Gg61
ucuri CO 56 Gc42
u Dang Sin VN 197 Qe39
ufut-Kale UA 135 Mg23
ugach Is. USA 15 Ce16
ugach Mountains USA 16
Ch15
ugach S.P. USA 15 Cf15
ugay PE 66 Gb49
ugiak USA (AK) 15 Cf15
ugoku-sanchi J 183 Rg28
ugwater USA (WY) 21 Eh25
uhuichupa MEX (CHH) 23
Ef31
ui BR (RS) 78 Hd62
uille EAT 292 Mg50
uitayo EC 60 Gb46
uka EAK 290 Mj46
ukchi Autonomous District
RUS 141 Tb05
ukchi Plateau 310 Bd03
ukchi Sea RUS 141 Uc04
ukmpalli IND (MHT) 191 Pa36
uknagar BD 194 Pe34
ukotskiy Poluostrov RUS
141 Ua05
ulamar GCA 41 Fe39
ulaphon Reservoir THA
196 Qa37
ula Vista USA (CA) 22 Eb29
ulluncani, Cerro BOL 73
Gh55
ulucanas PE 60 Fk48
ulumani BOL 72 Gg54
uluut gol MNG 172 Qa21
uma BOL 67 Gf53
umba ETH 284 Mk43
umbicha RA (CA) 76 Gg60
umbo BR (MG) 75 Hg55
umda VRC (QHI) 171 Pj29
umphae THA 196 Qb37
umphon THA 198 Pk40
umphon Buri THA 197 Qb38
um Phuang THA 197 Qb38
umpi PE 66 Gd53
umsaeng THA 196 Qa38
umuch PE 66 Ga49
umul MEX 41 Ff36
un THA 196 Qa36
un'an VRC (ZJG) 184 Qk31
unchi EC 60 Ga47
'unch'on ROK 182 Rd27
unchucmil MEX (YT) 41 Fe35
undela ANG 295 Ma53
unga Z 295 Mc53
unga Z 296 Mg51
ungang DVRK 182 Rd25
unga Rest Camp Z 295 Mc53
'ungju ROK 182 Rd27
'ungmu ROK 182 Re28
ungui PE 66 Gd52
ungungo RCH 76 Ge60
ungyang Shanmo RC 179
Ra34
unian PK 161 Og30
unshui VRC (HNN) 177 Qg29
unwan VRC (GDG) 178 Qf34
unya EAT 292 Mg50
uor Phnom Kravanh K 197
Qb39
uor Phnum Dangrek K 197
Qb38
upaca PE 66 Gc52
upanan IR 154 Nh29
uPha VN 197 Qd39
u Prong VN 197 Qd39
uquibamba PE 67 Gd53
uquibambilla PE 67 Gd53
uquicamata RCH 72 Gf57
uquis PE 66 Gb50
ur CH 114 Lk44
urachandpur IND (MNP)
194 Pg33
urcampa PE 66 Gc52
urchbridge CDN (SK) 24 Ek20
urchill CDN 11 Fa07
urchill CDN 11 Fb07
urchill Falls CDN 11 Gd08
urchill Lake CDN 19 Ef17
urchill Mountains 313 Sc35
urchill River CDN 19 Ef18
urchill Sound CDN 25 Ga17
urchs Ferry USA (ND) 24
Fa21
urch Stretton GB 101 Ks38
uria Range NEP 170 Pa31
uria Range NEP 170 Pb32
urín PE 66 Gb51
urki IND (CGH) 191 Pb34
uru IND (RJT) 188 Oh31
urubamba PE 66 Gb50
uruguara YV 57 Gf40
u Se VN 197 Qe39
ushaf 161 Ok29
uska Mts. USA 23 Ef27

Chu-sonji J 183 Sa26
Chust KS 158 Of25
Chust UA 119 Md42
Chute Akamba RDC 287 Md45
Chute Bangu RDC 287 Mc44
Chute de la Vina CAM 281 Lg42
Chute-des-Passes CDN (QC)
30 Ge21
Chute Kamimbi Fuka RDC
289 Mc50
Chute Mulamba Gungu RDC
289 Mb50
Chute Mupele RDC 287 Mc45
Chute Penge RDC 287 Me45
Chute Pogge II RDC 289 Ma49
Chutes d'Abourou RCA 282
Mb43
Chutes d'Antafofo RM 306 Nd55
Chutes de Béla RCB/RDC
288 Lh48
Chutes de Betsiboka RM 306
Nd54
Chutes de Billy RMM 270 Kf39
Chutes de Boali RCA 282 Lk43
Chutes de Bouenza RCB 288
Lg47
Chutes de Dibouangui G 288
Lf46
Chutes de Félou RMM 269 Ke38
Chutes de Gouina RMM 269
Ke38
Chutes de Gozobangui RDC
286 Mb43
Chutes de Katende RDC 289
Mb49
Chutes de Kembé RCA 282
Ma43
Chutes de Kinkon RG 278 Kd40
Chutes d'Ekom CAM 280 Lf43
Chutes de Kongou G 281 Lg45
Chutes de Kotto RCA 282 Ma43
Chutes de la Kagera BU 292
Me47
Chutes de la Kiubo RDC 292
Md50
Chutes de la Lobé CAM 280
Le44
Chutes de la Lofoi RDC 296
Md51
Chutes de la Lufira RDC 292
Md50
Chutes de la Madelaine F 246
Td57
Chutes de Lancrenon CAM
281 Lh42
Chutes de l'Ankofia RM 305
Ne53
Chutes de l'Ivindo de Tsengué
Leledi G 281 Lg46
Chutes de Livingstone RDC
288 Lg48
Chutes de Lokoho RM 305 Ne53
Chutes de Loufoulakari RCB/
RDC 288 Lh48
Chutes de Lubi RDC 289 Mb49
Chutes de Matakil RCA 282
Ma41
Chutes de Mbi RCA 281 Lj43
Chutes de Mingouli G 281 Lg45
Chutes de Nachtigal CAM
281 Lf43
Chutes de Ngolo RCA 282 Mb43
Chutes de Papara RMM 269
Ke38
Chutes de Poubara G 288 Lg46
Chutes de Sakaleona RM 306
Nd56
Chutes de Tanougou DY 279
La40
Chutes de Tinkisso RG 278
Ke40
Chutes de Touboutou RCA
281 Lh43
Chutes de Zongo RCB 288 Lh48
Chutes d'Inga RDC 288 Lg48
Chutes du Tello CAM 281 Lg42
Chutes Gauthiot TCH 273 Lh41
Chutes Guillaume = Chutes Tembo
RDC 289 Lj49
Chutes Johnston RDC 296 Me51
Chutes Kasongo-Lunda RDC
289 Lj49
Chutes Pangu RDC 287 Md44
Chutes Tembo RDC 289 Lj49
Chutes Usu RDC 287 Mc44
Chute Toky RDC 287 Me45
Chute Wafie RDC 289 Mb48
Chutine Landing CDN (BC)
17 De17
Chuvashia RUS 133 Nd18
Chuwangsan N.P. ROK 182
Re27
Chuxiong VRC (YUN) 195 Qa33
Chuy ROU 77 Hd62
Chuzhou VRC (AHU) 184 Qk29
Chuzmiza RCH 72 Gf55
Chvaletice CZ 118 Lq40
Chwaka EAT 293 Mk49
Chwałowice PL 117 Mb40
Chwaszczyno PL 116 Lt36
Chynów PL 117 Mb39
Chynthiana USA (KY) 35 Fh26
Chyriv UA 119 Mc41
Chyulu Hills N.P. EAK 290 Mj47
Ciamis RI 210 Qe49
Cianjur RI 210 Qd49
Cianorte BR (PR) 74 Hd57
Ciawi RI 210 Qd49
Cibadak RI 210 Qd49
Cibaray, Cerro BOL 72 Gf55
Cibinong RI 210 Qd49
Cibit RUS (ALT) 167 Pd20
Cibuta MEX (SO) 23 Ee30
Çiçekdağı TR 131 Mp51
Cícero Dantas BR (BA) 71 Ja51
Cićevac SCG 126 Mb47
Cicheng VRC (ZJG) 184 Ra31
Cicia FJI 247 Ua54
Cidade da Pedra BR 69 Hc53
Cidade Gaúcha BR (PR) 74
Hd57
Cidade Medieval de Évora
P 108 Kn48
Cidade Velha CV 268 Jj38
Cide TR 144 Mg25
Ciechanów PL 117 Ma38
Ciechanowiec PL 117 Mc38
Ciechocinek PL 116 Lt38
Ciego de Ávila C 45 Ga35
Ciemnik PL 116 Lq37
Ciemnoszyje PL 117 Mc37
Ciénaga de Ayapel CO 56 Gc43
Ciénaga de Oro CO 56 Gc41
Ciénaga de Pedeguita CO
56 Gb42
Ciénaga de Zapata, P.N. C
44 Fk34
Ciénaga de Zapatosa CO 56
Gd41
Ciénaga Grande CO 56 Gc41

Ciénaga Grande RA (PJ) 72
Gg57
Ciénaga Grande de Santa Marta
CO 56 Gc40
Ciénaga Guájaro CO 56 Gc40
Ciénaga Iguana CO 56 Gc41
Ciénagas de Catatumbo, P.N.
YV 56 Ge41
Ciénagas RA (PJ) 72 Gh57
Ciénega CO 56 Gc40
Ciénega del Toro MEX (NL)
39 Ek33
Ciénega Prieta MEX (CHH)
38 Eg32
Cienfuegos C 44 Fk34
Čierny Balog SK 119 Lu42
Cieszanów PL 117 Md40
Cieszyn PL 118 Lt41
Cieza E 109 Kt48
Ciężkowice PL 117 Lu40
Cifrapalota H 119 Lu44
Çiftehan TR 131 Mp53
Çifteler TR 131 Mm51
Çifte Minare Medresesi TR
145 Na26
Çiftlik TR 131 Mp52
Cifuentes C 44 Fk34
Cifuentes E 109 Ks50
Cifuncho PE 72 Ge58
Cigarette Springs Cave USA
23 Ee27
Cigarro BR (AM) 62 Gj47
Cigel'ka SK 119 Mb41
Cigliano I 120 Lj45
Cihanbeyli TR 131 Mn52
Cihanbeyli Yaylası TR 131 Mn52
Cijawung RI 210 Qc49
Cijulang RI 210 Qe49
Cikajang RI 210 Qd49
Cikalong RI 210 Qe49
Cikampek RI 210 Qd49
Cikarang RI 210 Qd49
Cikatomas RI 210 Qe49
Cikobia FJI 247 Ua53
Čikoj MNG 173 Qf21
Čikoj RUS (BUR) 172 Qd20
Čikoj RUS 172 Qd20
Čikokon RUS 173 Qf20
Cilacap RI 210 Qe49
Cilaos F 307 Nh56
Çıldır TR 145 Nb25
Çıldır Gölü TR 145 Nb25
Ciledug RI 210 Qe49
Cilegon RI 210 Qd49
Cilento I 122 Lq50
Cilento e Vallo di Diano, P.N. del
I 122 Lq50
Čilgar RUS (KAL) 135 Nc22
Cili VRC (HUN) 177 Qf31
Cilibia RO 125 Mh45
Çilimli TR 131 Mm50
Cillas E 109 Kt50
Cilleros E 108 Ko50
Cillium TN 260 Le28
Čil'na RUS 133 Ne18
Cima USA (CA) 22 Ec28
Cimarron USA (KS) 28 Ek27
Cimarron USA 28 Ek27
Cimarron Nat. Grassland USA
28 Ek27
Cimbur RI 214 Rc50
Çimenlik TR 130 Mg50
Çimenliyeniköy TR 144 Mg26
Cimetières des Dinosaures de
Gadafawa RN 272 Le37
Cimitarra CO 56 Gd42
Cimljansk RUS 135 Nb22
Cimljanskoe Vodohranilišče
RUS 133 Nb21
Cimoszki PL 117 Mc37
Cimpu RI 209 Ra47
Çimşit TR 131 Mn51
Çınar TR 145 Na27
Çınarcık TR 130 Mk50
Cinaruco YV 57 Gf42
Cinaruco-Capanaparo, P.N. YV
57 Gg42
Cincinnati USA (OH) 32 Fh26
Çine TR 130 Mj53
Ciney B 103 Lf40
Cinfães P 106 Km51
Cingoli I 121 Lo47
Cinque Island IND 193 Pg40
Cinque Terre I 120 Lk46
Cinque Terre, P.N. delle I
120 Lk46
Cintalapa MEX (CHP) 41 Fd37
Cintei RO 124 Mb44
Cintra RA (CD) 77 Gj62
Cioara MD 125 Mj44
Ciocănești RO 125 Mf43
Ciochina RO 125 Mh46
Cioclovina RO 124 Md45
Ciolacu Nou MD 125 Mh43
Ciorani RO 125 Mg46
Ciorăști RO 125 Mh45
Cipanas RI 210 Qd49
Cipatujah RI 210 Qe49
Cipó BR (BA) 71 Ja51
Cipoal BR (AM) 62 Gh46
Cipolletti RA (RN) 80 Gg65
Čiprovski manastir BG 126
Mc47
Cir RUS 133 Nb21
Çırax Qala Sassanid Castle AZ
152 Ne25
Circeo, P.N. del I 122 Ln49
Circle USA (AK) 15 Ch13
Circle USA (MT) 21 Eh22
Circleville USA (OH) 32 Fj26
Circuit de Catalunya E 110 Lc49
Circuit Nelson Piquet BR 75
Hj57
Circuito de Jerez E 108 Kp46
Circuit Ricardo Tormo E 109
Ku49
Circular Reef PNG 243 Sd47
Cirebon RI 210 Qe49
Cirema, Gunung RI 210 Qe49
Cirencester GB 101 Kt39
Cirey-sur-Vezouze F 103 Lg42
Ciriè I 120 Lh45
Ciripcău MD 125 Mj43
Ciriquiri BR 67 Gh50
Cir Kud SP 291 Nb44
Cirò I 123 Ls51
Ciro Marina I 123 Ls51
Ciemiśla MD 125 Mj44
Cisneros CO 56 Gc42
Cisowsko-Orłowiński Park
Krajobrazowy PL 117 Ma40
Cisséla RG 278 Ke40

Cisterna di Latina I 122 Ln49
Cistern Point BS 37 Gb34
Cistierna E 106 Kp52
Čita RUS 173 Qg19
Čita RUS 173 Qh19
Citadelle/Sans Souci RH
45 Gd36
Citadelle de Calvi F 111 Lj48
Citeureup RI 210 Qd49
Čitluk BIH 121 Ls47
Citronelle USA (AL) 29 Ff30
Citrusdal SA 302 Lk62
Citrus Heights USA (CA) 20
Dk26
Città Alta di Bergamo I 120 Lk45
Cittadella I 120 Lm45
Città della Pieve I 120 Lm48
Città del Palladio I 120 Lm45
Città di Castello I 120 Lm47
Città Sant'Angelo I 122 Lp48
City Palace IND 188 Oh32
City Palace IND 190 Og33
Ciucea RO 124 Mc44
Ciucurova RO 125 Mj46
Ciudad Altamirano MEX (GUR)
40 Ek36
Ciudad Bolívia YV 57 Ge41
Ciudad Camargo MEX (CHH)
39 Eh32
Ciudad Constitución MEX (BCS)
38 Ee33
Ciudad Cortes CR 42 Fj41
Ciudad de Guatemala GCA
41 Fe38
Ciudad del Carmen MEX (CAM)
41 Fe36
Ciudad del Este PY 74 Hc58
Ciudad del Maíz MEX (SLP)
39 Fa34
Ciudad de México MEX
(MEX) 40 Fa36
Ciudad de México MEX
(MEX) 40 Fa36
Ciudad de Nutrias YV 57 Gf41
Ciudad Encantada E 109 Ks50
Ciudad Guayana YV 58 Gj41
Ciudad Guerrero MEX (TM)
39 Fa32
Ciudad Guzmán MEX (JLC)
40 Ej36
Ciudad Hidalgo MEX (MHC)
40 Ek36
Ciudad Hidalgo MEX (CHP)
41 Fd38
Ciudad Huitzuco MEX (GUR)
40 Fa36
Ciudad Insurgentes MEX (BCS)
38 Ee33
Ciudad Ixtepec MEX (OAX)
41 Fc37
Ciudad Juárez MEX (CHH)
23 Eg30
Ciudad Lerdo MEX (DGO)
39 Ej33
Ciudad Lerdo de Tejada MEX
(VC) 41 Fc36
Ciudad Madero MEX (TM) 39
Fb34
Ciudad Mante MEX (TM) 39
Fa34
Ciudad Melchor de Mencos
GCA 41 Ff37
Ciudad monumental de Cáceres
E 108 Ko49
Ciudad Mutis = Bahía Solano
CO 56 Gb42
Ciudad Neily CR 42 Fj41
Ciudad Nezahualcóyotl MEX
(MEX) 40 Fa36
Ciudad Obregon MEX (SO)
38 Ef32
Ciudad Ojeda YV 56 Ge40
Ciudad Perdida CO 56 Gd40
Ciudad Piar YV 58 Gj42
Ciudad Real E 109 Kr48
Ciudad Rodrigo E 106
Ko50
Ciudad Sahagún MEX (HDG)
40 Fa36
Ciudad Serdán MEX (PUE)
40 Fb36
Ciudad Valles MEX (SLP) 40
Fa35
Ciudad Victoria MEX (TM)
39 Fa34
Ciuperceni RO 124 Md46
Ciutadella E 110 Ld50
Ciutești MD 125 Mj43
Cividale del Friuli I 121 Lo44
Civil'sk RUS (CHU) 133 Nd18
Civita Castellana I 122 Ln48
Civitanova Marche I 121 Lo47
Civitavecchia I 122 Lm48
Civitella del Tronto I 122 Lo48
Civitella Roveto I 122 Lo49
Civray F 104 La44
Çivril TR 130 Mk52
Cixi VRC (ZJG) 184 Ra30
Cizre TR 145 Nb27
Cjurupyns'k UA 134 Mg22
Čkalovsk RUS 133 Nb17
Čki-Naryn KS 159 Oj25
Clacton-on-Sea GB 101 Lb39
Clair Engle Lake USA 20 Dj25
Clairview AUS (QLD) 233 Se57
Clamecy F 103 Ld43
Clam Lake USA (WI) 27 Fe22
Clan Donald Centre GB 98 Kp33
Clanton USA (AL) 34 Fg29
Clanville SA 303 Md61
Clanwilliam SA 302 Lk62
Claonaig GB 98 Kp35
Claquato Church USA 18 Dj22
Clara Island MYA 198 Pj40
Clara, Mount NZ 239 Tg67
Claraville AUS (NT) 227 Rh57
Claraville AUS (QLD) 232 Sa55
Clare AUS (QLD) 233 Sc57
Clare AUS (QLD) 233 Sd55
Clare AUS (SA) 236 Rk62
Clare USA (MI) 32 Fh24
Clare Island IRL 98 Kk37
Claremont USA (NH) 33 Gd24
Claremont Point AUS 231 Sb52
Claremore USA (OK) 29 Fc27
Claremorris IRL 98 Kl37
Clarence NZ 239 Tg67
Clarence Cannon N.W.R. USA
27 Fe26
Clarence Island 312 Hb31
Clarence Strait AUS 223 Rf52
Clarence Strait USA 17 Dd18
Clarence Town BS 37 Gc34
Clarendon USA (TX) 28 Ek28
Clarens SA 303 Me60
Clarenville CDN (NF) 31 Hc21
Claresholm CDN (AB) 19 Ed20
Clareton USA (WY) 21 Eh24
Clarinda USA (IA) 27 Fc25

Clarines YV 57 Gh41
Clarion USA (IA) 27 Fd24
Clarion USA (PA) 33 Ga25
Clarion Fracture Zone 317 Cb08
Clark USA (WY) 21 Ef23
Clark USA (SD) 26 Fb23
Clarke-City CDN (QC) 30 Gg20
Clarke Island AUS 236 Se66
Clarke Lake CDN 19 Eg18
Clarke River AUS (QLD) 233
Sc55
Clarkia USA (ID) 18 Eb22
Clarkleigh CDN (MB) 24 Fa20
Clark Range AUS 233 Sd56
Clarksburg USA (WV) 33 Fk26
Clarksdale USA (MS) 29 Fe28
Clark's Harbour CDN (NS)
31 Gh24
Clarkson SA 303 Mc63
Clarkson Bridge USA 34 Fg28
Clarks Point USA (AK) 14 Ca16
Clarkston USA (WA) 20 Eb22
Clarksville USA (TX) 29 Fc29
Clarksville USA (AR) 29 Fd28
Clarksville USA (TN) 34 Fg27
Claro BR 69 He54
Claro BR 74 He54
Claro dos Poções BR (MG)
75 Hh54
Claromecó RA (BA) 81 Gk65
Classical Gardens VRC
184 Ra30
Claude USA (TX) 28 Ek28
Cláudia BR (MT) 69 Hc51
Claudio BR (MG) 75 Hh56
Clausthal-Zellerfeld D 113 Ll39
Claveria RP 203 Ra36
Claveria RP 203 Rb39
Claxton USA (GA) 35 Fk29
Clay USA (WV) 35 Fk26
Claybank CDN (SK) 19 Eh20
Clay Belt CDN 25 Fk20
Clay Center USA (KS) 26 Fb26
Claydon CDN (SK) 19 Ef21
Clayoquot Sound CDN 18 Dg21
Clayton AUS (SA) 227 Rk60
Clayton USA (ID) 21 Ec23
Clayton USA (NM) 23 Ej27
Clayton USA (MO) 27 Fe26
Clayton USA (OK) 29 Fc28
Clayton USA (AL) 35 Fh30
Clayton USA (NY) 33 Gb23
Clayton USA (GA) 35 Fj28
Clear Creek USA 15 Cg13
Cleardale CDN (AB) 19 Ea17
Clearfield USA (UT) 21 Ed25
Clearfield USA (PA) 33 Ga25
Clearfield USA (SD) 26 Ek24
Clearlake USA (CA) 20 Dj26
Clear Lake USA 20 Dj26
Clear Lake USA (UT) 21 Ed26
Clear Lake USA (SD) 27 Fb23
Clear Lake USA (IA) 27 Fd24
Clear Lake Reservoir USA
20 Dk25
Clear Prairie CDN (AB) 19 Ea17
Clearwater CDN (BC) 18 Dk20
Clearwater USA 20 Eb22
Clearwater USA (FL)
36 Fj32
Clearwater Creek CDN 17 Dg14
Clearwater Lake CDN 24 Ek18
Clearwater Lake Prov. Park
CDN 24 Ek18
Clearwater Mountains USA
21 Ec22
Clearwater River CDN 19 Ee17
Clearwater West Lake CDN
24 Fd21
Cleburne USA (TX) 28 Fb29
Cle Elum USA (WA) 18 Dk22
Clejani RO 125 Mf46
Clelles F 105 Lf46
Clementina BR (SP) 74 He56
Clemson USA (SC) 35 Fj28
Cleopatra Needle RP 204 Qk40
Cleo Springs USA (OK) 28 Fa27
Clermont AUS (QLD) 233 Sd57
Clermont F 103 Lc41
Clermont USA (FL) 36 Fk31
Clermont-en-Argonne F 103
Lf41
Clermont-Ferrand F 105
Ld45
Clermont-l'Hérault F 105 Ld47
Clerval F 103 Lg43
Cles I 120 Lm44
Cleugh Passage IND 193 Pg39
Cleve AUS (SA) 236 Rj62
Clevedon GB 101 Ks39
Cleveland USA (TX) 29 Fc30
Cleveland USA (MS) 29 Fe29
Cleveland USA (OH) 32 Fk25
Cleveland USA (TN) 35 Fh28
Cleveland USA (GA) 35 Fj28
Clevelândia BR (PR) 78 Hd59
Clevelan Pen. USA 17 Dd18
Cleveleys GB 101 Kr37
Clew Bay IRL 98 Kl37
Clewiston USA (FL) 36 Fk32
Clifden IRL 98 Kk36
Clifden NZ 239 Td69
Clifden Castle IRL 98 Kk36
Cliffdale River AUS 232 Rk54
Cliffs of Moher IRL 100 Kl38
Cliffs of the Nullarbor AUS
229 Re61
Clifton AUS (QLD) 235 Sf59
Clifton SA 302 Lk62
Clifton USA (AZ) 23 Ef29
Clifton USA (TN) 34 Fg28
Clifton Bridge GB 101 Ks39
Clifton Hills AUS (SA) 227 Rk59
Cli Lake CDN 17 Dj15
Climax CDN (SK) 19 Ef21
Climax USA (CO) 21 Eg26
Climax USA (MN) 26 Fb22
Clinch Mts. USA 35 Fj27
Clines Corners USA (NM) 23
Eh28
Clinton CDN (BC) 18 Dk20
Clinton NZ 239 Te69
Clinton USA (WA) 18 Dj21
Clinton USA (MT) 21 Ed22
Clinton USA (MO) 27 Fd26
Clinton USA (IA) 27 Fe25
Clinton USA (OK) 28 Fa28
Clinton USA (AR) 29 Fd28
Clinton USA (LA) 29 Fe30
Clinton USA (IL) 32 Ff25
Clinton USA (AL) 34 Fg29
Clinton USA (SC) 35 Fk28
Clinton USA (NC) 35 Ga28
Clinton-Colden Lake CDN 10
Ec06
Clintwood USA (VA) 35 Fj27
Clio USA (AL) 35 Fh30
Clipperton Fracture Zone 317
Cb09

Clisson F 102 Kt43
Čilsta RUS (KAL) 135 Nc22
Clitheroe GB 101 Ks37
Cliza BOL 72 Gg54
Clodomira RA (SE) 76 Gh59
Cloghan IRL 100 Kn37
Clogher Head IRL 100 Ko37
Clogherhead IRL 100 Ko37
Clonagh AUS (QLD) 232 Sa56
Clonakilty IRL 100 Km39
Clonbrook GUY 59 Hb42
Cloncurry AUS (QLD) 232 Sa56
Cloncurry River AUS 232 Sa56
Clones IRL 98 Kn36
Clonmacnoise IRL 100 Kn37
Clonmel IRL 100 Kn38
Cloppenburg D 112 Lj38
Cloquet USA (MN) 27 Fd22
Cloquet USA 27 Fd22
Clorinda RA (FO) 73 Hb58
Cloridorme CDN (QC) 31 Gh21
Cloudy Mount USA 15 Cb14
Clovelly GB 100 Kq40
Cloverdale USA (CA) 20 Dj26
Clovis USA (CA) 20 Ea27
Clovis USA (NM) 23 Ej28
Cloyes-sur-le-Loir F 102 Lb43
Čl'ton RUS 133 Nd21
Cucellas RA (SF) 77 Gk61
Cluj-Napoca RO 124 Md44
Cluny AUS (QLD) 234 Rk58
Cluny F 105 Le44
Cluses F 105 Lg44
Clusone I 120 Lk45
Clute CDN (ON) 25 Fk21
Clutha River AUS 239 Te68
Clyde CDN 11 Gc04
Clyde CDN (AB) 19 Ed18
Clyde GB 99 Kr35
Clydebank GB 99 Kq35
Clyde River CDN (NS) 31 Gh24
Cna RUS 133 Na19
Coacalco MEX (MEX) 40 Fa36
Coaceral BR (BA) 70 Hh51
Coachella USA (CA) 22 Eb29
Coahuila MEX 12 Ed13
Coakari BOL 72 Gg55
Coalcomán de Vázquez Pallares
MEX (MHC) 40 Ej36
Coal Creek USA (AK) 15 Cj13
Coaldale CDN (AB) 19 Ed21
Coaldale USA (NV) 20 Eb26
Coalgate USA (OK) 29 Fb28
Coalinga USA (CA) 22 Dk27
Coal River CDN 17 Dg15
Coal River CDN (BC) 17 Dg16
Coamo USA (PR) 47 Gg36
Coaraci BR (BA) 71 Ja53
Coari BR 62 Gh48
Coari BR (AM) 62 Gj48
Comănele Caprei RO 125 Mh43
Coasa PE 67 Ge53
Coastal Plain USA 8 Fa06
Coast Mountains CDN/USA
8 Db04
Coast of Labrador CDN 11 Gd07
Coast Ranges USA 12 Dd11
Coata PE 67 Gf53
Coatepec MEX (VC) 40 Fb36
Coatepeque GCA 41 Fe38
Coaticook CDN (QC) 33 Ge23
Coats Bay CDN 25 Ga17
Coats Island CDN 11 Fd06
Coats Land ANT 312 Jb34
Coatzacoalcos MEX (VC) 41
Fc36
Cobá MEX 41 Fg35
Cobá MEX (QTR) 41 Fg35
Cobadin RO 125 Mj46
Cobalt USA (ID) 21 Ec23
Cobán GCA 41 Fe38
Cobanlar TR 131 Ml52
Cóbano CR 42 Fh41
Cobar AUS (NSW) 235 Sc61
Cobblestones AUS 228 Oh62
Cobden AUS (VIC) 237 Sb65
Cobh IRL 100 Km39
Cobham AUS (NSW) 234 Sb61
Cobham River CDN 24 Fc19
Cobija BOL 67 Gf51
Cobleni NAM 298 Lk56
Cobleskill USA (NY) 33 Gc24
Cobos RA (SA) 73 Gh58
Cobourg CDN (ON) 33 Ga24
Cobourg Peninsula AUS 223
Rg51
Cobquecura RCH 80 Gd64
Cobúe MOC 297 Mh52
Coburg D 115 Ll40
Coburn AUS (WA) 224 Qh59
Coca E 106 Kq51
Coca EC 60 Gb46
Coca EC 60 Gb46
Cocachacra PE 66 Gb51
Cocal BR (PI) 65 Hk47
Cocalinho BR (MA) 64 Hh47
Cocalinho BR (MT) 69 He53
Cocameira BR (AC) 67 Ge50
Cochabamba BOL 72 Gg54
Cochabamba PE 66 Ga49
Cochem D 114 Lh40
Cochetopa Hills USA 23 Eg27
Cochin = Kochi IND (KER)
192 Oj42
Cochran USA (GA) 35 Fj29
Cochrane CDN (AB) 19 Ec20
Cochrane CDN (ON) 25 Fk21
Cochrane RCH 82 Gd69
Cochkäöl KZ 166 Of21
Cockatoo AUS (QLD) 235 Sf58
Cockatoo Island AUS 222 Rb54
Cockburn Bank 100 Km41
Cockburn Harbor GB 37 Ge35
Cockburn Town BS 37
Gc33
Cockburn Town GB 37 Ge35
Cockermouth GB 99 Kr36
Cocklebiddy AUS (WA) 229
Rd62
Coclecito PA 43 Fk41
Coco CR 42 Fh40
Coco HN/NIC 42 Fj38
Cocobeach G 280 Le45
Cocoal BR (CE) 65 Hk49
Cocos Channel IND 193 Pg39
Cococi BR (CE) 65 Hk49
Cocodrie USA (LA) 29 Fe31
Cocoland NIC 42 Fj38
Cocona MEX 41 Fd37
Coconparra N.P. AUS 237 Sd63
Cocorna CO 56 Gc42
Cocos BR (BA) 70 Hh53
Cocos Island CR 52 Fc17
Cocos Islands AUS 200 Pd21
Cocos Ridge 52 Fc18
Cocula MEX (VC) 40 Fb36
Cocula MEX (JLC) 40 Ej35
Codajás BR (AM) 62 Gj47
Codeagro BR (AM) 62 Gk47
Codemin BR (GO) 70 Hf53

Codfish Island NZ 239 Td69
Codigoro I 120 Ln46
Codlea RO 125 Mf45
Codó BR (MA) 64 Hj48
Codo del Pozuzo PE 66 Gc50
Codogno I 120 Lk45
Codozinho BR (MA) 64 Hh48
Codpa RCH 72 Gf55
Codrington AG 47 Gk37
Codróipo I 121 Ln45
Codru MD 125 Mj44
Cody USA (WY) 21 Ef23
Coelemu RCH 80 Gd64
Coelho Neto BR (MA) 65 Hj48
Coenbult NAM 302 Lk59
Coengua PE 66 Gd51
Coeur d'Alene Ind. Res. USA
18 Eb22
Coeur d'Alene Lake USA 18
Eb22
Coesfeld D 112 Lh39
Coëtivy SY 305 Nj49
Coeur d'Alene USA (ID) 18 Eb22
Coevorden NL 112 Lg38
Coffee Bay SA 303 Me62
Coffee Bay Beach Point SA
303 Me62
Coffee Bay Beach Point SA
303 Me62
Coffee Creek CDN (YT) 17 Da14
Coffeyville USA (KS) 29 Fc27
Coffin Bay AUS (SA) 236 Rh63
Coffin Bay AUS 236 Rh63
Coffin Bay N.P. AUS 236 Rh63
Coffs Harbour AUS (NSW)
235 Sg61
Cofimvaba SA 303 Md61
Cofre de Perote, Cerro MEX
39 Fb36
Cogâlnic MD 125 Mj44
Čoghadak IR 156 Nf31
Coghinas I 111 Lk50
Coghtan SA 303 Me61
Cogla Downs AUS (WA) 224
Qj59
Cognac F 104 Ku45
Cogne I 120 Lh45
Cogolin F 105 Lg47
Čograjskoe vodohranilišče RUS
152 Nc23
Çoğun TR 131 Mp51
Coguno MOC 300 Mh58
Cohoes USA (NY) 33 Gd24
Cohuna AUS (VIC) 237 Sc63
Coig RA 82 Gf71
Coihaique RCH 82 Gd68
Coihaique Alto RCH 80 Ge68
Coihue RCH 80 Gd64
Coihueco RCH 80 Ge64
Coimbatore IND (TNU) 193 Oj41
Coimbra P 106 Km50
Coin E 108 Kq46
Coipasa, Cerro BOL 72 Gf55
Coirón RCH 76 Ge61
Coja P 106 Kn50
Cojata PE 67 Gf53
Cojimies EC 60 Fk45
Cojúa YV 56 Ge40
Cojudo Blanco, Cerro RA 82
Gf69
Çokak TR 144 Mj27
Coker Creek USA 35 Fh28
Cokeville USA (WY) 21 Ee24
Çokören TR 131 Mn51
Colac AUS (VIC) 237 Sb65
Colán Conhué RA (CB) 80 Gf67
Colane AUS (NSW) 234 Sb60
Colares BR (PA) 64 Hf46
Colatina BR (ES) 75 Hk55
Colazolo RA (CD) 76 Gj61
Colbún RCH 80 Ge63
Colby USA (KS) 26 Ek26
Colca PE 67 Ge53
Colcabamba PE 66 Gd52
Colchane RCH 72 Gf55
Colchani BOL 72 Gg56
Colchester GB 101 La39
Colchester SA 303 Mc62
Colcolano SA 303 Md60
Col d'Allos F 105 Lg46
Col d'Ares E 104 Lc48
Col d'Aubisque F 104 Ku48
Cold Bay USA (AK) 14 Bj18
Col de Bavella F 111 Lk49
Col de Gobo RN 267 Lh35
Col de la Croix Haute F 105 Lf46
Col de la Schlucht F 103 Lh42
Col de l'Iseran F 105 Lh45
Col de l'Izoard F 105 Lg46
Col de Montgenèvre F 105 Lg46
Col de Sara RN 267 Lg35
Col des Chandeliers RN 267
Lg35
Col de Tafori RG 278 Kd40
Col de Telmet DZ 260 Ld28
Col de Yeï Lulu RN 267 Lh35
Colditz D 113 Ln39
Cold Lake CDN 19 Ef18
Coldspring Mtn. CDN 17 Db14
Cold Springs USA (NV) 20 Eb26
Coldstream GB 99 Ks35
Col du Galibier F 105 Lg45
Col du Grand Saint-Bernard
I/CH 114 Lh45
Col du Lautaret F 105 Lg45
Col du Petit St-Bernard F/I
105 Lg45
Col du Pourtalet F 104 Ku48
Col du Tourmalet F 104 La48
Col du Zad MA 258 Kh29
Coldwater USA (KS) 28 Fa27
Coldwater USA (MI) 32 Fh25
Coleambally AUS (NSW) 237
Sc63
Cole Bay CDN (SK) 19 Ef18
Colebrook USA (NH) 33 Ge23
Colegiata de Santa María de
Calatayud E 107 Kt51
Colekeplaas SA 303 Mc62
Coleman USA (TX) 28 Fa30
Coleman River AUS 230 Sb53
Colenso SA 303 Me60
Co Le Pagoda VN 178 Qd35
Colera E 110 Ld48
Coleraine GB 98 Ko35
Coles Bay AUS (TAS) 236 Se67
Colesberg SA 303 Mc61
Colfax USA (WA) 20 Eb22
Colfax USA (ND) 26 Fb22
Colfontaine B 103 Ld40
Colgante Glacier RCH 80 Gd68
Colgong IND (BIH) 194 Pd33
Colguiola SP 285 Nd42
Colha BH 41 Ff37
Colibita RO 124 Me43
Cólico I 120 Lk44
Colidor BR (MT) 69 Hc51
Coligny SA 303 Md59
Colima MEX 40 Ej36

Colima MEX (COL) 40 Ej36
Colima, Volcán de MEX 40 Ej36
Colina BR (SP) 74 Hf56
Colina RCH 76 Ge62
Colinas BR (MA) 64 Hh49
Colinas do Tocantins BR (TO)
70 Hf50
Colinet CDN (NF) 31 Hd22
Colintraive GB 99 Kp35
Coliseo C 44 Fk34
Coll GB 98 Ko34
Collado Bajo E 109 Kt50
Collado-Villalba E 109 Kr50
Collahuasi RCH 72 Gf56
Collarenebri AUS (NSW) 235
Se60
Collaroy AUS (QLD) 233 Se57
Coll de Rates E 109 Ku48
Collécchio I 120 Ll46
Collector AUS (NSW) 237 Se63
Colle della Maddalena F/I
120 Lg46
Colle di Val d'Elsa I 120 Lm47
Colleferro I 122 Lo49
College Place USA (WA) 20
Ea22
College Station USA (TX) 29
Fb30
Collegiata di San Cándido I
120 Ln44
Colli Albani I 122 Ln49
Collie AUS (WA) 228 Qj62
Collie Bay AUS 222 Rc54
Collier Range AUS 224 Qk58
Collier Range N.P. AUS 224
Qk58
Collierville USA (TN) 29 Ff28
Collines Baoulé CI 279 Kh42
Collines de Bongouanou CI
279 Kh42
Collingullie AUS (NSW) 237
Sd63
Collingwood AUS (QLD) 235
Sf59
Collingwood CDN (ON) 33 Fk23
Collingwood NZ 239 Tg66
Collingwood Bay PNG 243 Se50
Collins CDN (ON) 25 Ff20
Collins USA (MS) 29 Ff30
Collinsville AUS (QLD) 233 Sd56
Collipulli RCH 80 Gd64
Collmberg D 113 Lo39
Collo DZ 260 Ld27
Colloma BOL 72 Gg55
Collón Cura RA 80 Ge66
Colmar F 103 Lh42
Colmars F 105 Lg46
Colméia BR (TO) 70 Hf50
Colmena MEX (DGO) 39 Eh34
Colmenar E 108 Kq46
Colmenar Viejo E 109 Kr50
Colnett F 246 Tc56
Cologne D 112 Lg40
Colo-i-Suva Forest Reserve FJI
247 Tk54
Colombey-les-Belles F 103 Lf42
Colombey-les-Deux-Églises F
103 Le42
Colômbia BR (SP) 74 Hf56
Colombia C 45 Gb35
Colombia CO 56 Gc44
Colombia 51 Ga09
Colombia Basin 46 Gc38
Colombo BR (PR) 74 Hf58
Colombo CL 193 Ok43
Colomí BOL 72 Gh54
Colón C 44 Fk34
Colón PA 43 Ga41
Colón RA (BA) 77 Gk62
Colón RA (ER) 77 Ha62
Colona AUS (SA) 229 Rg61
Colonelganj IND (UPH) 189
Pa32
Colonel Hill BS 37 Gc34
Colônia BR 71 Ja53
Colonia FSM 240 Rh17
Colonia 10 de Julio RA (CD)
77 Gj61
Colonia Angamos PE 61 Gd48
Colonia Carlos Pellegrini RA
(CR) 77 Hb60
Colonia Caroya RA (CD) 76 Gj61
Colonia del Sacramento
ROU 77 Hb63
Colònia de Sant Jordi E 110
Lc51
Colônia do Piauí BR (PI) 65 Hj49
Colonia Dora RA (SE) 76 Gj60
Colonia La Pastoril RA (LP)
80 Gg64
Colonia Lavalleja ROU 77 Hb61
Colonial Beach USA (VA) 33
Gb26
Colonial Heights USA (VA)
35 Gb27
Colonia Liebig RA (CR) 77 Hc59
Colonia Marina RA (CD) 77 Gj61
Colonia Pastoril RA (FO) 73
Ha58
Colonia San Miguel PY 73 Ha58
Colônia São Romão BR (MS)
74 Hc55
Colonias Unidas RA (CH) 77
Ha59
Colonia Winkler PY 73 Ha57
Colonsay GB 98 Ko34
Colorado BR 68 Gj52
Colorado BR (PR) 74 He57
Colorado C 45 Ga35
Colorado, Cerro RA 76 Gg60
Colorado, Cerro RA 80 Gf68
Colorado RA 80 Gg65
Colorado USA 12 Ec11
Colorado USA 23 Ee27
Colorado USA 28 Fa30
Colorado City USA (AZ) 22 Ed27
Colorado City USA (CO) 23
Eh27
Colorado City USA (TX) 28 Ek29
Colorado Desert USA 22 Ec29
Colorado d'Oeste BR (RO)
68 Gk52
Colorado Nat. Mon. USA 21
Ef26
Colorado Plateau USA 23 Ee27
Colorados, Cerro RA/RCH
76 Gf59
Colorado Springs USA (CO)
21 Eh26
Color Sand Forest VRC 195
Qb33
Colossal AUS (NSW) 235 Sd61
Colosseo I 122 Ln49
Colotenango GCA 41 Fe38
Colotlipa MEX (GUR) 40 Fa37
Coloured Canyon ET 263 Mh31
Colquechaca BOL 72 Gh55
Colquen, Cerro RCH 80 Gd64
Col Quijoux RCA 282 Mb41
Colquiri BOL 72 Gg54

rixas Açu BR 69 Hf53
rixas Mirim BR 69 He52
rna Bara SCG 124 Ma45
rna Reka MK 126 Mb50
rni vrh BIH 121 Lr46
rni vrh SLO 121 Lq44
rnomelj SLO 121 Lq45
roajingolong N.P. AUS 237 Se64
roatia HR 121 Lp45
rocker Range N.P. MAL 204 Qj43
rockett USA (TX) 29 Fc30
rocodile SA 299 Md58
rocodile Camp RB 299 Mb56
rocodile Farm AUS 223 Rf52
rocodile Farm (Abaya Hayk') ETH 284 Mj42
rocodile Pond GH 279 Kk40
rocq F 105 Lc45
roissilles F 103 Lc40
romarty GB 99 Kq33
romer CDN (MB) 24 Ek21
romer GB 101 Lb38
romwell NZ 239 Te68
romwell USA (MN) 27 Fd22
ronulla Point AUS 237 Sf63
rook USA (CO) 26 Ej25
rooked USA 20 Dk23
rooked Creek USA (AK) 15 Ca15
rooked Island BS 37 Gc34
rooked Island USA 14 Bk16
rooked Island Passage BS 37 Gc34
rooked River CDN 18 Dj18
rooked River CDN (SK) 24 Ej19
rookhaven IRL 100 Kl39
rookston USA (MN) 27 Fb22
rookwell AUS (NSW) 237 Se63
rosby USA (ND) 24 Ej21
rosby USA (LA) 29 Fe30
ross WAN 280 Le43
ross Cay BS 37 Ga32
ross City USA (FL) 36 Fj31
ross Creeks N.W.R. USA 34 Fg27
rossett USA (AR) 29 Fe29
ross Fell GB 99 Ks36
rossfield CDN (AB) 19 Ec20
ross Hands GB 100 Kq39
rossing Rocks BS 37 Gb32
ross Lake CDN (MB) 24 Fb18
ross Lake CDN 24 Fb18
rossmore AUS (QLD) 232 Sc57
rosson Ice Shelf 312 Ec33
ross Plains USA (TX) 28 Fa29
ross River N.P. WAN 280 Le42
ross Sound USA 17 Db16
rossville USA (TN) 35 Fh28
rosswind Lake USA 15 Ch14
rotone I 123 Ls51
row Agency USA (MT) 21 Eg23
rowCreek Ind. Res. USA 26 Fa23
rowder Lake S.P. USA 28 Fa28
rowdy Bay N.P. AUS 235 Sg61
rowell USA (TX) 28 Fa29
rowheart USA (WY) 21 Ef24
row Ind. Res. USA 21 Ef23
rowley USA (LA) 29 Fd30
rown Island PNG 243 Sd48
rownpoint USA (NM) 23 Ef28
rown Point USA (IN) 32 Fg25
rown Prince Range PNG 244 Sh49
rowpara BD 194 Pg34
row River CDN 17 Dh16
rows Nest AUS (QLD) 235 Sg59
rowsnest Pass CDN 19 Ec21
roydon SD 303 Mf59
rozet Islands 315 Nb14
rozet Plateau 315 Na14
rozon F 102 Kq42
rucea RO 125 Mf43
rucea RO 125 Mj46
rucero PE 67 Gf53
rucero RCH 72 Gf57
ruces C 44 Fk34
rucita EC 60 Fk46
ruden Bay GB 99 Kt33
ruillas MEX (TM) 39 Fa33
ruz Alta BR (RS) 78 Hd60
ruz Alta RA (CD) 77 Gk62
ruzaltense BR (RS) 78 Hd59
ruzamento de Pegões P 108 Km48
ruz das Almas BR (BA) 71 Ja52
ruz del Eje RA (CD) 76 Gh61
ruzeiro BR (SP) 75 Hh57
ruzeiro MOC 300 Mh56
ruzeiro d'Oeste BR (PR) 74 Hd57
ruzeiro do Sul BR (AC) 67 Gd49
ruz Grande MEX (GUR) 40 Fa37
ruzília BR (MG) 75 Hh56
ruz Machado BR (PR) 78 He59
rveni čot SCG 124 Lu45
ryon AUS (NSW) 235 Se60
rysdale, Mount CDN 17 Dj17
rystal Brook AUS (SA) 236 Rk62
rystal Cave USA 27 Fd23
rystal City USA (TX) 39 Fa31
rystal Falls USA (MI) 32 Ff22
rystal Lake USA (FL) 35 Fh30
rystal Lake Cave USA 32 Fe24
rystal River USA (FL) 36 Fj31
rystal River N.W.R. USA 36 Fj31
rystal Springs CDN (SK) 19 Eh19
sakvár H 118 Lt43
sánytelek H 119 Ma44
saroda H 119 Mc42
sátalja H 119 Lu44
senger H 119 Mc43
sesznek H 118 Ls43
sigar-heg H 119 Mc43
songrád H 119 Ma44
sorna H 118 Ls43
sorvás H 119 Ma44
sót H 118 Ls43
tesiphon IRQ 147 Nc29
tyrčn RUS 180 Rf20
úa YV 57 Gg40
uacaña YV 57 Gh43
ua Cung Hau VN 199 Qd41
uaio ANG 295 Ma53
uajinicuilapa MEX (GUR) 40 Fa37
uale ANG 288 Lj50
uamato ANG 294 Lh54
uamba MOC 297 Mj53
uanavale ANG 295 Lk53
Cuando RB 295 Mb54
Cuangar ANG 295 Lk54
Cuango ANG 288 Lj49
Cuango ANG 289 Lj50
Cuango ANG 289 Lk50
Cuanza ANG 288 Lg50
Cuanza ANG 294 Lj51
Cuanza ANG 294 Lj52
Cuao YV 57 Gg43
Cuareím BR/ROU 77 Hb61
Cuárenta Casas MEX 23 Ef31
Cuarinuma CO 61 Gf44
Cuarteron Reef 204 Qg41
Cuarto RA 76 Gh62
Cua Soi Rap VN 197 Qd40
Cua Song Cuu Long 199 Qd41
Cuatir ANG 294 Lk54
Cuatrociénegas MEX (COH) 39 Ej32
Cuauhtémoc MEX (CHH) 38 Eg31
Cuautitlán MEX (MEX) 40 Fa36
Cuautla MEX (JLC) 39 Eh35
Cuautla MEX (MOR) 40 Fa36
Cuba C 44 Fk35
Cuba USA (NM) 23 Eg27
Cuba USA (AL) 29 Ff29
Cu Bai VN 197 Qd37
Cubal ANG 294 Lg53
Cubal ANG 294 Lh51
Cubal ANG 294 Lh52
Cubango ANG 294 Lj53
Cubango ANG 294 Lk54
Cubara CO 56 Gd42
Cubatão BR (SP) 75 Hg57
Cubaté BR 61 Gf45
Cubel E 107 Kt51
Cubia ANG 295 Ma53
Cubolta MD 125 Mh42
Çubuk TR 131 Mo50
Çubuk Baraj TR 131 Mo50
Cubulco GCA 41 Fe38
Cucao RCH 80 Gc67
Cuchagua BOL 72 Gg55
Cuchi ANG 294 Lj53
Cuchi ANG 294 Lj53
Cuchilla de Haedo ROU 77 Hb61
Cuchilla de Mangrullo ROU 77 Hd62
Cuchilla Grande ROU 77 Hc62
Cuchillo-Co RA (LP) 80 Gh65
Cuchillo Parado MEX (CHH) 23 Eh31
Cuchivero YV 57 Gh42
Cucho Ingenio BOL 72 Gh55
Cuchuverachi MEX (SO) 23 Ef30
Cuckadoo AUS (QLD) 232 Sa57
Čučkovo RUS 133 Na18
Cucoara MD 125 Mj44
Cuc Phong N.P. VN 178 Qd35
Cucuí BR (AM) 61 Gg45
Cucumbi ANG 289 Lk50
Cucurital YV 57 Gh43
Cucurpé MEX (SO) 23 Ee30
Cucuruzzu F 111 Lk49
Cúcuta CO 56 Gd42
Cuddalore IND (TNU) 193 Ok41
Cuddapah IND (APH) 193 Ok39
Cudillero E 106 Ko53
Čudnite mostove BG 127 Me49
Čudniv UA 134 Me20
Čudovo RUS 132 Mf16
Čudzin BY 132 Md19
Cue AUS (WA) 224 Qj59
Cuebe ANG 294 Lj53
Cueio ANG 294 Lj53
Cuelei ANG 294 Lj53
Cuéllar E 106 Kq51
Cuemba ANG 294 Lk52
Cuenca E 109 Ks50
Cuenca EC 60 Ga47
Cuenca del Añelo RA 80 Gf65
Cuencamé MEX (DGO) 39 Ej33
Cuengo ANG 289 Lk50
Cuernavaca MEX (MOR) 40 Fa36
Cuero USA (TX) 29 Fb31
Cuers F 105 Lg47
Cuerva E 109 Kq49
Cuestecitas CO 56 Gd40
Cueto C 45 Gc35
Cuetzalán MEX (PUE) 40 Fb35
Cueva de Altamira E 107 Kq53
Cueva de Ambrosio C 44 Fk34
Cueva de la Quebrada del Toro, P.N. YV 57 Gf40
Cueva de las Brujas RA 80 Gf63
Cueva de las Manos RA 82 Ge69
Cueva del Chacho RA 76 Gg61
Cueva del Elefante YV 57 Gj42
Cueva del Guácharo YV 57 Gj40
Cueva del Indio C 44 Fj34
Cueva del Milodón RCH 82 Gd71
Cueva de los Guácharos, P.N. CO 60 Gb45
Cueva de Nerja E 108 Kr46
Cuevas Bellamar C 44 Fk34
Cuevas Candelaria GCA 41 Fe38
Cuevas del Almanzora E 109 Kt47
Cuevas de los Tayos EC 60 Ga47
Cugir RO 124 Md45
Cugnaux F 104 Lb47
Čuhloma RUS 133 Nb16
Cuhnești MD 125 Mh43
Čuhujv UA 133 Mj21
Cuiabá BR (AM) 61 Gf47
Cuiabá BR (MT) 69 Hb53
Cuiabá BR 69 Hb54
Cuia, T.I. BR 62 Ha47
Cuicatlán MEX (OAX) 40 Fb37
Cuidad Bolívar YV 58 Gj41
Cuidad de Loreto RA (SE) 76 Gh60
Cuije ANG 289 Lj50
Cuijk NL 112 Lf39
Cuilapa GCA 41 Fe38
Cuillin Hills GB 98 Ko33
Cuillin Sound GB 98 Ko33
Cuilo ANG 288 Lh49
Cuilo ANG 289 Lk50
Cuílo ANG 289 Lk50
Cuilo-Futa ANG 288 Lh49
Cuilo Pombo ANG 288 Lh49
Cuima ANG 294 Lh52
Cuimba ANG 288 Lh49
Cuio ANG 294 Lg52
Cuipo PA 43 Fk41
Cuira o Monos CO 61 Gd46
Cuiriri ANG 295 Lk53
Cuiseaux F 105 Lf44
Cuisery F 105 Lf44
Cuité BR (PB) 65 Jb49
Cuito ANG 295 Lk54
Cuito Cuanavale ANG 295 Lk53
Cuitzeo del Porvenir MEX (MHC) 40 Ek36
Cuiuni BR 62 Gh46
Cuiyun Lang VRC 177 Qc29
Cuja RUS 167 Pd20
Cujubim BR (RO) 68 Gk50
Çukurca TR 145 Nb27
Çukurköpru TR 144 Mh27
Çukurkuyu TR 131 Mp53
Çukurova TR 144 Mh27
Culamagia ANG 288 Lj50
Culan F 105 Lc44
Cu Lao Cham VN 197 Qe38
Cu Lao Re VN 197 Qe38
Cu Lao Thu = Phu Quy VN 197 Qe40
Cula Sancai ETH 284 Mh40
Culasi RP 205 Rb40
Culasian RP 204 Qj41
Culbertson USA (MT) 19 Eh21
Culburra AUS (NSW) 237 Sf63
Culcairn AUS (NSW) 237 Sd63
Culebras PE 66 Ga50
Culemborg NL 112 Lf39
Culfa AZ 152 Nc26
Culgoa N.P. AUS 235 Sd60
Culgoa River AUS 235 Sd60
Culiacán MEX (SL) 38 Eg33
Culion RP 204 Ra40
Culion Island RP 204 Qk40
Culiseu BR 69 Hd52
Cúllar-Baza E 109 Ks47
Cullen GB 99 Ks33
Cullén RCH 82 Gf72
Cullera E 109 Ku49
Cullinan SA 299 Me58
Cullman USA (AL) 34 Fg28
Cullompton GB 100 Kr40
Culluleraine AUS (VIC) 236 Sa63
Čul'man RUS 141 Rb07
Culoz F 105 Lf45
Culpaulin AUS (NSW) 234 Sb61
Culpeper USA (VA) 33 Ga26
Culpina BOL 73 Gh56
Culross Island USA 15 Cg15
Culuba MEX 41 Fg35
Culuene BR 69 Hd52
Culuwuru Island AUS 223 Rj51
Culverden NZ 239 Tg67
Čulym RUS 140 Pa07
Culyšman RUS 167 Pe20
Culyšmanskoe nagor'e RUS 167 Pe20
Culzean Castle GB 99 Kq35
Cuma ANG 294 Lh52
Cumaná YV 57 Gh40
Cumanacoa YV 58 Gj40
Cumanayagua C 44 Fk34
Cumandá EC 60 Ga47
Cumar SP 291 Nc44
Cumaral CO 56 Gd43
Cumari BR (GO) 70 Hg53
Cumaribo CO 57 Gf43
Cumba PE 60 Ga48
Cumbal CO 60 Gb45
Cumbal, Volcán CO 60 Gb45
Cumbe EC 60 Ga47
Cumberland USA (MD) 33 Ga26
Cumberland Caverns USA 34 Fg28
Cumberland Downs AUS (QLD) 233 Sd57
Cumberland Gap N.H.P. USA 35 Fj27
Cumberland House CDN (SK) 24 Ej19
Cumberland Island USA 35 Fk30
Cumberland Island National Seashore USA 35 Fk30
Cumberland Islands AUS 233 Se56
Cumberland Lake CDN 24 Ek18
Cumberland Peninsula CDN 10 Gd05
Cumberland Sound CDN 10 Gc05
Cumbernauld GB 99 Kr35
Cumbi ANG 288 Lg49
Cumborah AUS (NSW) 235 Sd60
Cumbrera, Cerro RCH 82 Gd69
Cumbres de Majalca, P.N. MEX 23 Eg31
Cumbres de Monterrey, P.N. MEX 39 Ek33
Cumbres & Toltec Scenic Railroad USA 23 Eg27
Cumbrian Mountains GB 99 Kr36
Cumburão BR (PA) 63 Hc46
Čumerna BG 127 Mf48
Čumić SCG 126 Ma46
Čumikan RUS 141 Rd08
Cuminá BR (PA) 63 Hb46
Cuminá BR 63 Hb46
Cuminopanema BR 63 Hc46
Cummins AUS (SA) 236 Rh63
Cummins Range AUS 222 Rd55
Community Museum F 249 Da50
Cumnock GB 99 Kq35
Cumpas MEX (SO) 23 Ef31
Çumra TR 144 Mg27
Cumueté BR 69 He50
Čuna RUS 140 Pd07
Cunani BR (AP) 59 He44
Cuñare CO 61 Gd45
Cunauaru BR 62 Gj47
Cunco RCH 80 Gd65
Cund ANG 294 Lj52
Cunday CO 56 Gc43
Cundeelee AUS (WA) 229 Rb61
Cundeelee A.L. AUS 229 Rb61
Cunderdin AUS (WA) 228 Qj61
Cunduacán MEX (TB) 41 Fd36
Cunene ANG 294 Lg54
Cunene ANG 294 Lh53
Cunene ANG 294 Lj53
Cúneo I 120 Lh46
Cunhambebe BR (RJ) 75 Hh57
Cunhaú BR (RN) 65 Jc49
Cunhinga ANG 294 Lj51
Cunicea MD 125 Mj43
Cuniuá BR 67 Gg49
Cunjamba ANG 295 Ma53
Cunlhat F 105 Ld45
Cunnamulla AUS (QLD) 235 Sc60
Cunningham Islands AUS 223 Rj51
Cuntima GNB 269 Kc39
Cunyu AUS (WA) 224 Ra59
Cuorgnè I 120 Lh45
Cupar GB 99 Kr34
Cupari BR 63 Hc48
Cupcini MD 125 Mh42
Cupica CO 43 Gb42
Cupica CO 56 Gb42
Cupisnique, Cerro PE 66 Ga49
Cupixi BR (AP) 63 He45
Ćuprija SCG 126 Mb47
Curaça BR 71 Ja50
Curaçá BR (BA) 71 Ja50
Curaçao NL 57 Gf39
Curacautín RCH 80 Ge65
Curacavi RCH 76 Ge62
Curachi GUY 58 Gk42
Curacó RA 80 Gh65
Curahuara de Carangas BOL 72 Gf54
Curale ETH 285 Nc42
Cural Velho CV 268 Jj37
Curanilahué RCH 80 Gd64
Curanja PE 67 Ge50
Curanja PE 67 Ge51
Curaray EC 60 Gb46
Curaray PE 61 Gc47
Curaru RA (BA) 77 Gj63
Curauaí BR 62 Ha48
Curbur AUS (WA) 224 Qh59
Curdimurka AUS (SA) 227 Rj60
Curepipe MS 307 Nj56
Curia P 106 Km50
Curiapo YV 58 Gk41
Curibaya PE 72 Ge54
Curicó RCH 76 Ge63
Curicuriari BR 61 Gf46
Curi Leuvú RA 80 Ge64
Curimatá BR (PI) 70 Hh51
Curimatá de Baixo BR 62 Gh48
Curimávida, Cerro de RCH 76 Ge61
Curionópolis BR (PA) 64 Hf48
Curitiba BR (AC) 67 Gf51
Curitiba BR (PR) 74 Hf58
Curitibanos BR (SC) 78 He59
Curiúva BR (PR) 74 He58
Curly Cut Cay BS 37 Gb34
Curnamona AUS (SA) 236 Rk61
Curoca ANG 294 Lg54
Curragh Racetrack IRL 100 Ko37
Currais BR (PI) 70 Hj50
Currais Novos BR (RN) 65 Jb49
Curral Alto BR (RS) 78 Hd62
Curral de Pedra BR (PI) 65 Hk49
Curralinho BR (PA) 64 Hf46
Curral Novo do Piauí BR (PI) 71 Hk50
Curran USA (MI) 32 Fj23
Currant USA (NV) 20 Ec26
Curranyalpa AUS (NSW) 234 Sc61
Currawilla AUS (QLD) 234 Sa58
Currawinya AUS (QLD) 234 Sc60
Currawinya N.P. AUS 235 Sc60
Current BS 37 Gb33
Current Island BS 37 Gb33
Currie AUS (TAS) 237 Sb65
Currie USA (NV) 20 Ec25
Currituck USA (NC) 35 Gb27
Currituck Beach Lighthouse USA 35 Gc27
Currituck N.W.R. USA 35 Gc27
Currituck Sound USA 35 Gc27
Curtain Springs AUS (NT) 226 Rf58
Curtea de Argeș RO 125 Me45
Curtici RO 124 Mb44
Curtina ROU 77 Hb62
Curtis Island AUS 233 Sf57
Curtis Island AUS 237 Sd65
Curtis Island NZ 221 Ua25
Curu BR 65 Ja47
Curuá BR (PA) 63 Hc46
Curuá BR 63 Hc48
Curuaés BR 69 Hc50
Curuaí BR (PA) 63 Hc47
Curuá-Una BR 63 Hc47
Curuca BR 61 Ge48
Curuçã BR (PA) 64 Hg46
Curucay PE 60 Gc47
Curug Sewu RI 210 Qe49
Curup RI 206 Qb47
Curuqueté BR 67 Gh50
Cururu-Açu BR 69 Hb50
Cururu ou Cururu-ri BR 69 Hb50
Cururupu BR (MA) 64 Hh46
Curuzú Cuatiá RA (CR) 77 Ha60
Curvelo BR (MG) 75 Hh55
Cushabatay PE 66 Gc49
Cushamen RA (CB) 80 Ge67
Cushing USA (OK) 29 Fb28
Cusimi YV 57 Gh43
Cusipata PE 67 Ge52
Cusset F 105 Ld44
Cusseta USA (GA) 35 Fh29
Cusso ANG 294 Lh53
Custer USA (MT) 21 Eg22
Custer USA (SD) 26 Ej24
Custer Battlefield Nat. Mon. USA 21 Eg23
Custódia BR (PE) 71 Jb50
Cusuco, P.N. HN 41 Ff38
Cutalo ANG 294 Lj52
Cutato ANG 294 Lj53
Cutato ANG 294 Lj53
Cut Bank USA (MT) 19 Ed21
Cutbank River CDN 18 Ea18
Čuteevo RUS (TAR) 133 Nd18
Cutenda ANG 294 Lh53
Cutervo PE 66 Ga49
Cuthbert USA (GA) 35 Fh30
Cut Off USA (LA) 29 Fe31
Čutove UA 134 Mh21
Cutral-Co RA (NE) 80 Gf65
Cutro I 123 Lr51
Cuttack IND (ORS) 191 Pc35
Cutta Cutta Caves AUS 223 Rg53
Cutzamala de Pinzón MEX (GUR) 40 Ek36
Cuvelai ANG 294 Lj53
Cuvelar ANG 294 Lh53
Cuvette de Doany RM 305 Nd53
Cuvette de la Bénoué CAM 273 Lg41
Cuvier Island NZ 238 Th64
Cuvo ANG 294 Lh51
Cuxhaven D 112 Lj37
Cuya RCH 72 Ge55
Cuyagua YV 57 Gg40
Cuyagua YV 57 Gg40
Cuyahoga Valley N.P. USA 33 Fk25
Cuyama USA (CA) 22 Ea28
Cuyamel HN 41 Ff38
Cuyo RP 205 Ra40
Cuyoaco MEX (PUE) 40 Fb36
Cuyo East Passage RP 205 Ra40
Cuyo ‚English Game' Subterranean N.P. RP 205 Ra40
Cuyo Island RP 205 Ra40
Cuyo Islands RP 205 Ra40
Cuyo West Passage RP 204 Ra40
Cuyuni GUY 58 Ha42
Cuyupini YV 58 Gk41
Cuyutlán MEX (COL) 39 Eh36
Cuzco PE 67 Ge52
Čvur RUS 180 Rj20
Cwmcarn GB 100 Kr39
Cyangugu RWA 292 Me47
Cybinka PL 116 Lp38
Cyclades GR 128 Md53
Cyclops Mountains RI 213 Sa47
Čyhyryn UA 134 Mg21
Cylinder AUS 235 Sg59
Cynthia AUS (QLD) 235 Sf58
Cypress Gardens USA 36 Fk31
Cypress Hills CDN 19 Ef21
Cypress Hills Interprov. Park CDN 19 Ee21
Cyprus CY 131 Mo55
Cyran BY 97 Mg37
Cyrenaica LAR 261 Ma31
Cyrene = Shahhât LAR 261 Ma29
Cyrrhus SYR 146 Mj27
Cytherea AUS (QLD) 235 Sd59
Czaplinek PL 116 Lr37
Czar CDN (AB) 19 Ee19
Czarna PL 119 Mc41
Czarna Białostocka PL 117 Md37
Czarna Dąbrówka PL 116 Ls36
Czarnków PL 116 Lr38
Czarny Dunajec PL 119 Lu41
Czchów PL 119 Ma41
Czechowice-Dziedzice PL 119 Lu41
Czech Republic CZ 118 Lp41
Czekarzewice PL 117 Mb39
Czermno PL 117 Ma39
Czersk PL 116 Ls37
Czerwieńsk PL 116 Lq38
Czerwionka-Leszczyny PL 116 Lt40
Czerwony Dwór PL 117 Mc36
Częstochowa PL 117 Lu40
Człopa PL 116 Lr37
Człuchów PL 116 Ls37
Czssivi ANG 295 Ma53
Czyżew-Osada PL 117 Mc38

D

Da'an VRC (JLN) 180 Rc23
Daanbantayan RP 205 Rc40
Daan Viljoen Game Park NAM 298 Lj57
Dabaga EAT 293 Mh50
Dabaga RN 272 Le37
Dabagram IND (WBG) 194 Pe34
Dabai WAN 272 Lc40
Da Baía BR 63 Hd49
Dabajuro YV 57 Ge40
Dabaka IND (ASM) 194 Pg32
Dabakala CI 279 Kh41
Dabancheng VRC (XUZ) 167 Pe24
Dabane-ye-Qoloman IR 155 Oa30
Daban Shan VRC 174 Qa27
Dabaro SP 285 Ne42
Dabas H 119 Lu43
Daba Shan VRC 177 Qe29
Dabat ETH 277 Mj40
Dabatou RG 278 Ke40
Dabdab LAR 267 Lh32
Dabeiba CO 56 Gb42
Dabeiyuan Monastery VRC 175 Qj26
Daben VRC (HAN) 178 Qe36
Dabenoris SA 302 Lk60
Dabhoi IND (GUJ) 190 Og34
Dąbie PL 116 Lq38
Dąbie PL 116 Lt38
Dabie Shan VRC 184 Qh30
Dabilja MK 126 Mc49
Dabiss RG 269 Kc40
Dabnou RN 272 Lc38
Dabo RI 207 Qc46
Dabo SN 269 Kc39
Daboh IND (MPH) 189 Ok33
Dabola RG 278 Ke40
Dabolatounka RG 278 Ke40
Dabou CI 279 Kh43
Daboya GH 279 Kk41
Dabra IND (MPH) 189 Ok33
Dabrowa Białostocka PL 117 Md37
Dąbrowa Górnicza PL 117 Lu40
Dąbrowa Tarnowska PL 117 Ma40
Dabryn' BY 132 Me20
Dabsan Hu VRC 169 Ph27
Dabugam IND (ORS) 191 Pb36
Dabuk RI 207 Qb47
Dăbuleni RO 126 Me47
Dabus Wenz ETH 283 Mh40
Dabwa TCH 273 Lg38
Dac Glei VN 197 Qd38
Dachau D 115 Lm42
Dacheng VRC (JGX) 184 Qh31
Dachengzhuang VRC (HBI) 175 Qj26
Dachepalle IND (APH) 191 Ok37
Dachigam N.P. PK 161 Oh28
Dachstein A 115 Lo43
Dachsteinhöhlen A 115 Lo43
Dachung Yogma 161 Ok29
Dacia Seamount 254 Kb12
Dačice CZ 118 Lq41
Dačne UA 125 Ml44
Dac Song VN 197 Qd39
Dac To VN 197 Qd38
Dadaab EAK 291 Na45
Dadanawa GUY 58 Ha44
Daddato DJI 277 Nb40
Dade City USA (FL) 36 Fj31
Dadéguhé CI 278 Kg42
Dadeville USA (AL) 35 Fh29
Dadhar PK 162 Od31
Dadong VRC (GZG) 178 Qe34
Dadra and Nagar Haveli IND 190 Og35
Dadu PK 162 Od32
Daduan VRC (JGX) 184 Qh31
Dadu He VRC 176 Qb30
Dadukou VRC (AHU) 184 Qj30
Daet RP 203 Rb38
Dafang VRC (GZH) 178 Qc32
Dafanpu VRC (NMZ) 175 Qf26
Dafar GH 279 La42
Dafeng VRC (JGS) 184 Ra29
Dáfnes GR 128 Mb52
Dafni GR 127 Me50
Dáfni GR 128 Mc52
Dáfni GR 128 Mc53
Dafní GR 128 Md53
Dafoe CDN (SK) 19 Eh20
Dafoe River CDN 24 Fc18
Dafo Si VRC 174 Qa26
Dafra TCH 282 Lk40
Daga IND (MPH) 191 Pb33
Daga SUD 283 Mg41
Dagaari SP 285 Nd42
Dagabule ETH 284 Mj43
Daga Istephanos Monastery ETH 284 Mj40
Dagali N 92 Lj30
Dagana SN 269 Kc37
Daga Post SUD 283 Mg41
Dağardı TR 130 Mj51
Dagash SUD 276 Mg37
Dagasuli RI 212 Rd44
Dagda LV 97 Mh34
Dağdere TR 130 Mj52
Dagestan RUS 145 Nd24
Dagestanskij zapovednik RUS 152 Nd23
Daghabij KSA 148 Mk34
Dag Hammarskjöld Memorial Z 296 Me52
Daghandeli KZ 166 Oj21
Daghmar OM 157 Nk34
Dagida Game Reserve WAN 272 Lc41
Daginggou VRC 182 Ra24
Daglah ET 263 Mh30
Daglung VRC (TIB) 171 Pf31
Dago RI 205 Rc44
Dagomys RUS 135 Mk24
Dagua CO 56 Gb44
Daguan VRC (SCH) 176 Qc31
Daguan VRC (GZH) 178 Qd32
Daguan VRC (YUN) 195 Qb32
Dagu Fort VRC 175 Qj26
Dagupan RP 202 Ra37
Daguragu A.L. AUS 223 Rf54
Dagworth AUS (QLD) 232 Sb54
Dagzê Co VRC 170 Pd30
Dah RI 242 Rk49
Dahaban KSA 148 Mk35
Dahadinni River CDN 17 Dh14
Dahanu IND (MHT) 190 Og36
Dahanu Beach IND 190 Og35
Daheba VRC (QHI) 174 Pk28
Dahebian VRC (SCH) 176 Qa31
Dahequ VRC (GSU) 174 Qb27
Dahinsara IND (GUJ) 190 Of34
Dahiri CI 279 Kh43
Dahla AFG 160 Oc30
Dahlak Archipelago ER 277 Na39
Dahlak Marine N.P. ER 277 Na39
Dahlonega USA (GA) 35 Fj28
Dahmani TN 260 Le28
Dahme D 113 Lo39
Dahn D 114 Lh41
Dahongliutan 161 Ok27
Dahong Shan VRC 177 Qg30
Dahra Oil Field LAR 261 Lj31
Dahr Oualâta RIM 270 Kg37
Dahshûr ET 263 Mf31
Dahua VRC (GZG) 178 Qe34
Dahuk IRQ 147 Nb27
Da Huoai VN 197 Qd40
Dai RI 214 Re49
Dai Dao VRC 184 Rb30
Daïet Akhicha DZ 259 La31
Dai Hai VRC 175 Qg25
Dai Island SOL 245 Ta49
Dai Lanh Beach VN 197 Qe39
Dailekh NEP 170 Pa31
Daimiel E 109 Kr49
Daingerfield USA (TX) 29 Fc29
Daintree AUS (QLD) 233 Sc54
Daintree N.P. AUS 233 Sc54
Dainzú MEX 40 Fb37
Daireaux RA (BA) 81 Gk64
Dairo CI 279 Kh43
Dairût ET 263 Mf32
Dairy Creek AUS (WA) 224 Qh58
Dai-sen J 183 Rg28
Daisengendake J 181 Sa25
Daisen-Oki N.P. J 183 Rg27
Daisen-Oki N.P. J 183 Rg28
Daisetsuzan N.P. J 181 Sb24
Daishan VRC (ZJG) 184 Rb30
Daisy USA (OK) 29 Fc28
Daito Islands J 185 Rf33
Dai Xian VRC (SAX) 175 Qg26
Daiyun Shan VRC 179 Qk33
Dajabón DOM 46 Ge36
Dajarra AUS (QLD) 232 Rk56
Dajing VRC (GSU) 174 Qb27
Dajing VRC (YUN) 195 Qb32
Da Juh VRC (QHI) 169 Pg27
Dakar SN 269 Kb38
Dakawa EAT 293 Mj49
Dakawa EAT 293 Mj49
Daketa ETH 284 Nb42
Da Kherea Sharif Ziarat Mosque AFG 160 Oc30
Dakhla DARS 264 Kc34
Dakhla RIM 269 Ke37
Dakhla Oasis ET 263 Me33
Dakhlet Nouâd- hibou RIM 264 Kd35
Dakingari WAN 272 Lc40
Daki Takwas WAN 272 Lc40
Dak Mil VN 197 Qd39
Dak Nong VN 197 Qd40
Dako GH 279 Kk41
Dakoank IND (AAN) 193 Pg42
Dakoro RN 272 Ld38
Dakovica SCG 126 Ma48
Đakovo HR 121 Lt45
Katedrala u Đakovu HR 121 Lt45
Dakpam GH 279 Kk41
Dakshin Gangotri ANT (IND) 313 Lc32
Daksum 161 Oh29
Daku, Gunung RI 209 Ra45
Dala ANG 289 Ma50
Dala ANG 295 Ma51
Dala RMM 271 Kj38
Dala SOL 245 Ta50
Dalaba SN 269 Kd39
Dalabar RG 278 Kd40
Dalada Maligawa CL 193 Pa43
Dalad Qi VRC (NMZ) 175 Qf25
Dalafi SN 269 Kd39
Dalahaj RUS (BUR) 172 Qb20
Dalai Nur VRC 175 Qj24
Dalai Shan VRC 169 Pj26
Dalaki IR 156 Nf31
Dalälven S 93 Lq30
Dalaman TR 129 Mj54
Dalami SUD 283 Mf40
Dalandole SP 291 Nc44
Dalangyun MYA 196 Ph36
Dalanzadgad MNG 174 Qc24
Dalap-Uliga-Darrit MH 241 Tc17
Dalark USA (AR) 29 Fd29
Dalarna S 93 Lo29
Dalarö S 93 Lt31
Dalat MAL 208 Qf44
Da Lat VN 197 Qe40
Dalay MNG 174 Qb24
Dalbandin PK 162 Oc31
Dalbeattie GB 99 Kr36
Dalberg AUS (QLD) 233 Sd56
Dalbo BF 271 Kk39
Dălbok Dol BG 127 Me48
Dălbok izvor BG 127 Mf48
Dalbosjön S 93 Ln32
Dalby AUS (QLD) 235 Sf59
Dalby Söderskog n.p. S 95 Lo35
Dalcahue RCH 80 Gd67
Dale N 92 Lf29
Dale N 92 Lf30
Dalen N 92 Lj31
Dalfors S 93 Lq29
Dalfsen NL 112 Lg38
Dalgan IR 157 Nk32
Dalgaranga AUS (WA) 224 Qj59
Dalgety River AUS 224 Qj58
Dălghiu RO 125 Mf45
Dălgi Del BG 126 Mc47
Dalgonally AUS (QLD) 232 Sa56
Dălgopol BG 127 Mh47
Dalhalla S 93 Lq30
Dalhart USA (TX) 23 Ej27
Dalhouise IND (HPH) 189 Oj29
Dalhousie CDN (NB) 30 Gg21
Dalhousie Springs AUS 227 Rj59
Dali RMM 270 Kg38
Dali VRC (SAA) 177 Qe28
Dali = Xiaguan VRC (YUN) 195 Qa33
Dalian VRC (LNG) 182 Ra26
Dalianhe VRC (HLG) 180 Re22
Dalías E 109 Ks46
Dalimb IND (MHT) 190 Oj37
Dalí Museum (Saint Petersburg) USA 36 Fj32
Daling He VRC 175 Qk25
Dali Sharafat SUD 276 Mg40
Dalj HR 124 Lt45
Daljâ ET 263 Mf32
Dalkeith GB 99 Kr35
Dalkhaki AFG 160 Od27
Dalkola IND (WBG) 194 Pd33
Dal Lake 161 Oh28
Dallas CDN (MB) 24 Fb20
Dallas USA (OR) 20 Dj23
Dallas USA (TX) 29 Fb29
Dallas Reef 204 Qg42
Dalli WAN 281 Lf41
Dall Island USA 17 Dd18
Dallol Bosso RN 271 Lb39
Dalma UAE 156 Ng33
Dalmacija HR 121 Lq46
Dalmally GB 99 Kq34
Dalmatia 86 Lb05
Dalmeny AUS (NSW) 237 Sf64
Dalmose DK 94 Lm35
Dal'nee RUS 181 Sb22
Dal'negorsk RUS 181 Rh23
Dal nerečensk RUS 180 Rg23
Daloa CI 278 Kg42
Dalol ETH 277 Na39
Dalol Crater ER 277 Na39
Dalol Saltlake and Hot Springs ETH 277 Na39
Dalong VRC (HUN) 178 Qe32
Dalong Chi VRC 168 Pb24
Dalrymple, Mount AUS 233 Se56
Dalsbruk = Taalintehdas FIN 96 Mc30
Dalsjöfors S 95 Lo33
Dals Långed S 92 Ln32
Dalsmynni IS 90 Jk13
Dalton USA (GA) 35 Fh28
Daltonganj IND (JKD) 191 Pc33
Dalton Mus. USA 29 Fc27
Dalu IND (MGA) 194 Pf33
Dalu VRC (GSU) 174 Qc27
Daludalu RI 206 Qa45
Dalupiri Island RP 203 Ra36
Dalupiri Island RP 203 Rc39
Dal'verzin Tepe UZB 158 Od27
Dalvík IS 90 Ka13
Dalwallinu AUS (WA) 228 Qj61
Dalwhinnie GB 99 Kq34
Daly City USA (CA) 20 Dj27
Daly River AUS (NT) 223 Rf52
Daly River AUS 223 Rf53
Daly River A.L. AUS 223 Rf53
Dalyup AUS (WA) 228 Ra62
Daly Waters AUS (NT) 223 Rg54
Damaguete RP 205 Rb41
Da Mai VN 197 Qd40
Damakar WAN 273 Lg39
Daman AFG 160 Oc30
Daman IND 190 Og35
Daman IND (DAD) 190 Og35
Damanava BY 117 Mf38
Damaneh IR 154 Nf29
Damango GH 279 Kk41
Damanhûr ET 263 Mf30
Damaqun Shan VRC 175 Qh25
Damar RI 212 Re46
Damar RI 214 Re49
Damara RCA 286 Lk43
Damaraland NAM 298 Lj56
Damardatar RI 208 Qh47
Damar Laut MAL 198 Qa43
Damasak WAN 273 Lg39
Damas Cays BS 36 Fk34
Damascus SYR 146 Mj29
Damaskinía GR 126 Mb50
Damaturu WAN 273 Lf40
Damau RI 205 Rd44
Damauli NEP 170 Pc32
Damba ANG 288 Lh49
Damba KZ 153 Nf22
Damba Island EAU 290 Mg46
Dambam WAN 273 Lf40
Dambaslar TR 130 Mh49
Damboa WAN 273 Lg40
Dâmbovița RO 125 Mf46
Dambri Waterfall VN 197 Qd40
Dambuk IND (ARP) 195 Ph31
Dambulla CL 193 Pa43
Damdama Sahib IND 188 Oh31
Da Meio BR 70 Hh52
Dame Marie RH 46 Gc36
Damenge VRC (YUN) 195 Pk34
Damghan IR 154 Nh27
Damghan Caravansarai IR 154 Nh27
Dam Ha VN 178 Qd35
Damianópolis BR (GO) 70 Hg53
Damietta ET 263 Mf30
Damji BHT 194 Pe32
Damlacık TR 145 Mk27
Dammartin-en-Goële F 103 Lc41
Damme D 112 Lj38
Damnica PL 116 Ls36
Damnïkï BY 117 Me38
Damnoen Saduak Floating Market THA 196 Pk39
Damodar IND 194 Pd34
Damoh IND (MPH) 191 Ok34
Damon USA (TX) 29 Fc31
Damon Point USA (WA) 18 Dh22
Dampar WAN 272 Lf41
Dampier AUS (WA) 224 Qj56
Dampier Archipelago AUS 224 Qj56
Dampier Archipelago Nature Reserve AUS 224 Qj56
Dampier Downs AUS (WA) 222 Rb55
Dampierre-sur-Salon F 103 Lf43
Dampier Strait PNG 243 Se48
Damqawt YE 151 Ng37
Dam Qu VRC 171 Pg29
Damra IND (MGA) 194 Pf33
Damrur KSA 148 Mk35
Damtang VRC (TIB) 170 Pb29
Damtar TCH 273 Lj40
Damulog RP 205 Rc42
Damwal SA 300 Me58
Damxung VRC (TIB) 171 Pf30
Dana JOR 146 Mh30
Dana RI 211 Ra51
Danakil ETH 277 Na40
Danakil Depression ETH 277 Na40
Danakil Desert ETH 277 Na40
Danamombe (Dhlo Dhlo) Ruins ZW 300 Me56
Dana, Mount USA 14 Bk18
Dana Nature Reserve JOR 146 Mh30
Danane CI 278 Kf42
Da Nang VN 197 Qe37
Danao RP 205 Rc40
Danapur IND (BIH) 191 Pc33
Danau Aiwsa RI 213 Rh47
Danau Amaru RI 212 Rg46
Danau Gigi RI 213 Rg46
Danau Gita RI 213 Rg46
Danau Kamakawalar RI 213 Rh47
Danau Paniai RI 213 Rj47
Danau Rombebai RI 213 Rj46
Danau Sentani RI 213 Sa47
Danau Tigi RI 213 Rj48
Danau Yamur RI 213 Rh47
Danba VRC (SCH) 176 Qa30
Dan Barto RN 272 Le39
Danbatta WAN 272 Le39
Danbury USA (CT) 33 Gd25
Danby Lake USA 22 Ec28
Dan Chang THA 196 Pk38
Dancheng VRC (HNN) 184 Qh29
Dandahwa ZW 296 Me54
Dandaraga AUS (WA) 228 Qk60
Dandaragan AUS (WA) 228 Qh61
Dandarah ET 263 Mg32
Dande ANG 294 Lj51
Dande ETH 284 Mj43
Dandeli IND (KTK) 190 Oh38
Dandenong AUS (VIC) 237 Sc64
Dandérosso RMM 279 Kh40
Dando ANG 294 Lj51
Dandong VRC (LNG) 182 Rc25
Danfa RMM 270 Kg38
Danfeng VRC (SAA) 177 Qf29
Danforth USA (ME) 30 Gg23
Dang CAM 281 Lg43
Danga RMM 271 Kj37
Dangali ETH 284 Mj40
Dangan Liadao VRC 179 Qh34
Dangara TJ 158 Oe26
Dangchang VRC (GSU) 176 Qc28
Dange ANG 288 Lh50
Danggali Conservation Park AUS 236 Sa62
Danggou VRC (LNG) 182 Rc26
Dang He VRC 169 Ph26
Dangjin Shankou VRC 169 Ph26
Dango WAN 272 Lc39
Dan Gorayo SP 285 Ne41
Dangriga BH 41 Ff37
Dangriga BH 41 Ff37
Dangshan VRC (AHU) 184 Qj28
Dangtu VRC (AHU) 184 Qk30
Dan Gulbi WAN 272 Ld40
Dangur ETH 283 Mh39
Dangur ETH 284 Mj40
Dangur ETH 284 Mj40
Dangyang VRC (HUB) 177 Qf30
Dan He VRC 177 Qg28
Da Nhim Lake VN 197 Qe40
Dania CI 278 Kg42
Daniel USA (WY) 21 Ee24
Daniel Boone Natl. Forest USA 35 Fj27
Daniel Johnson Dam CDN 30 Gf20
Danielskuil SA 302 Mb60
Danilov RUS 132 Na16
Danilovgrad SCG 126 Lu48
Danilovka RUS 133 Nc20
Daning VRC (SAX) 175 Qf27
Danish Fort IND 193 Ok41
Danissa EAK 291 Na44
Dan Issa RN 272 Ld39
Danja WAN 272 Ld40
Danjiang VRC (GZH) 178 Qe32
Danjiangkou VRC (HUB) 177 Qf29
Danjiangkou Shuiku VRC 177 Qf29
Danjo-gunto J 185 Re29
Dank OM 157 Nj34
Dan Khun Thot THA 196 Qa38
Dankov RUS 133 Mk19
Danlí HN 42 Fg38
Dannelly Res. USA 34 Fg29
Dannenberg D 113 Lm37
Dannevirke NZ 238 Tj66
Dannhauser SA 303 Mf60
Dano BF 279 Kj40
Danpur IND (RJT) 190 Oh34
Dan Sadau WAN 272 Ld40
Dan Sai THA 196 Qa37
Danskøya N 91 Lf06
Dansville USA (NY) 33 Gb24
Dantan IND (WBG) 194 Pd35
Dante = Xaafuun SP 285 Nf40
Dantewara IND (CGH) 191 Pa36
Dantiandou RN 271 Lb39
Danube 86 Ma05
Danubyu MYA 196 Ph37
Danum Valley Conservation Area MAL 204 Qj43
Danville USA (AR) 29 Fd28
Danville USA (IL) 32 Fg25
Danville USA (PA) 33 Gb25
Danville USA (KY) 35 Fh27
Danville USA (VA) 35 Ga27
Dan Xian VRC (HAN) 178 Qe36
Danxiashan VRC 179 Qg33
Danyang VRC (JGS) 184 Qk29
Danyi-Apéyémé RT 279 La42
Danze EAK 293 Mk47

E

Elx E 109 Ku48
Ely GB 101 La38
Ely USA (NV) 20 Ec26
Ely USA (MN) 27 Fe22
El Yagual YV 57 Gf42
El Yunque C 45 Gc35
El Yunque Rainforest USA 47 Gh36
Elze D 112 Lk38
El Zeitun ET 262 Mc31
El Zúlia CO 56 Gd42
El Zurdo RA (SC) 82 Ge71
Emae VU 246 Te54
Emajõgi EST 96 Mg32
Emali EAK 293 Mj47
Emam Abbas IR 154 Nc28
Emam Hasan IR 156 Nf31
Emam Saheb AFG 160 Oe27
Emam Taqi IR 155 Nk27
Emån S 95 Lq33
Emangusi SA 303 Mg59
Emas, P.N. das BR 74 Hd55
Embalse Alicura RA 80 Ge66
Embalse Amaluza EC 60 Ga47
Embalse Bocono Tucupido YV 57 Gf41
Embalse Cabra Corral RA 72 Gh58
Embalse Camatagua YV 57 Gg41
Embalse Casa de Piedra RA 80 Gg65
Embalse Cerros Colorados RA 80 Gf65
Embalse Cogotí RCH 76 Ge61
Embalse de Aguilar de Campóo E 106 Kq52
Embalse de Alange E 108 Ko48
Embalse de Alarcón E 109 Ks49
Embalse de Alcántara E 108 Ko49
Embalse de Almendra E 106 Ko51
Embalse de Arbón E 106 Ko53
Embalse de Belesar E 106 Kn52
Embalse de Bembézar E 108 Kp47
Embalse de Buendía E 109 Ks50
Embalse de Cíjara E 108 Kq49
Embalse de Contreras E 109 Kt49
Embalse de El Cajon HN 41 Fg38
Embalse de El Grado E 110 La48
Embalse de Entrepeñas E 109 Ks50
Embalse de Gabriel y Galán E 108 Ko50
Embalse de García de Sola E 108 Kp49
Embalse de Giribaile E 109 Kr48
Embalse de Guadalcacín E 108 Kp46
Embalse de Guadalhorce E 108 Kq46
Embalse de Guri YV 57 Gj42
Embalse de Jándula E 109 Kr48
Embalse de la Serena E 108 Kp48
Embalse de la Sotonera E 107 Ku52
Embalse de las Portas E 106 Kn52
Embalse del Cenajo E 109 Kt48
Embalse del Chanza E 108 Kn47
Embalse del Ebro E 107 Kr53
Embalse del Guárico YV 57 Gg41
Embalse del Nihuil RA 76 Gf63
Embalse del Pintado E 108 Kp47
Embalse del Porma E 106 Kp52
Embalse del Rumblar E 109 Kr48
Embalse del Tercero RA 76 Gh62
Embalse de Mediano E 110 La48
Embalse de Mequinenza E 110 La49
Embalse de Negratín E 109 Ks47
Embalse de Orellana E 108 Kp48
Embalse de Portodemouros E 106 Km52
Embalse de Riaño E 106 Kp52
Embalse de Ricobayo E 106 Kp51
Embalse de Santa Teresa E 106 Kp50
Embalse de Sierra Boyera E 108 Kp48
Embalse de Sierra Brava E 108 Kp49
Embalse de Urrunaga E 107 Ks52
Embalse de Valdecañas E 108 Kp49
Embalse de Valdemojón E 108 Kq47
Embalse Ezequiel Ramos Mexia RA 80 Gf65
Embalse Florentino Ameghino RA 80 Gg67
Embalse la Paloma RCH 76 Ge61
Embalse Paso de las Piedras RA 81 Gk65
Embalse Peñol CO 56 Gc42
Embalse Piedra del Aguila RA 80 Ge66
Embalse Poechos PE 60 Fk48
Embalse Río Hondo RA 76 Gh59
Embalse Yacyretá Apipé PY/RA 77 Hb59
Embarcación RA (SA) 73 Gh57
Embarcadero MEX (OAX) 41 Fc37
Embarcadero MEX (CHP) 41 Fd38
Emb del Guadalmena E 109 Ks48
Embetsu J 181 Sa23
Embi KZ 140 Nd09
Embilipitiya CL 193 Pa43
Embira BR 67 Ge49
Emblem USA (WY) 21 Ef23
Embocada BOL 68 Gj53
Embondo RDC 286 Lk45
Emboscada BOL 67 Gh51
Embrun F 105 Lg46
Embu EAK 290 Mj46
Embundo ANG 294 Lj54
Embyn LV 97 Mb34
Emca RUS 91 Na14
Emcisweni MW 296 Mg51
Emden D 112 Lh37
Emecik TR 129 Mh54
Emeishan VRC (SCH) 176 Qb31
Emeishan Sacred Mountains VRC 176 Qb31
Emel KZ 166 Pb22
Emel'janovskaja RUS 91 Na13
Emerald AUS (QLD) 233 Se57
Emerald Mound USA 29 Fe30
Emeriau Point AUS 222 Rb54
Emerson CDN (MB) 24 Fb21
Emesa SYR 146 Mj28
Emet TR 130 Mk51
Emeti PNG 243 Sb49
Emi Fezzane RN 267 Lh35
Emigrant USA (MT) 21 Ee23
Emi Koussi TCH 274 Lk36
Emilia RA (SF) 77 Gk61
Emiliano Zapata MEX (CHP) 41 Fe37
Emilia-Romagna I 120 Ll46
Emil Racovita MD 125 Mg42
Emi Lulu RN 267 Lf34
Emin VRC (XUZ) 167 Pb22
Eminee RI 242 Rk49
Eminence USA (MO) 29 Fe27
Emin He VRC 166 Pb22
Emini CAM 281 Lg44
Emin Pasha Gulf EAT 287 Mf47
Eminska Planina BG 127 Mh48
Emiralem TR 129 Mh52
Emirau PNG 243 Se46
Emirau Island PNG 243 Se46
Emirdağ TR 131 Mf26
Emir Dağları TR 144 Mm51
Emirgazi TR 131 Mo53
Emirler TR 131 Mn51
Emlichheim D 112 Lg38
Emmaboda S 95 Lq34
Emmaljunga S 95 Lo34
Emmaste EST 96 Mc32
Emmel AUS (QLD) 234 Sc58
Emmeloord NL 112 Lf38
Emmelshausen D 114 Lh40
Emmen NL 112 Lg38
Emmendingen D 114 Lh42
Emmerich D 112 Lg39
Emmetsburg USA (IA) 27 Fc24
Emmett USA (ID) 20 Eb24
Emmiganuru IND (APH) 190 Oj38
Emmonak USA (AK) 15 Bh14
Emory USA (TX) 29 Fc29
Emoulas RN 272 Lg38
Empada GNB 269 Kc40
Empalmé EC 60 Ga46
Empalme MEX (SO) 38 Ee32
Empangeni SA 303 Mf60
Empedrado RA (CR) 77 Ha59
Empedrado RCH 80 Gd63
Empembe NAM 294 Lg54
Emperor Range PNG 244 Sh48
Empessós GR 128 Mb51
Empire USA (CO) 21 Eh26
Empoli I 120 Ll47
Emporia USA (KS) 27 Fb26
Emporia USA (VA) 35 Gb27
Emporium USA (PA) 33 Ga25
Empress Augusta Bay PNG 244 Sh49
Empress Mine ZW 300 Me55
Ems D 112 Lh38
Emsdetten D 112 Lh38
Ems-Jade-Kanal D 112 Lh37
Emu Hill AUS (WA) 228 Qk62
Emu Park AUS (QLD) 233 Sf57
Ena J 183 Rj28
Enånger S 93 Lr29
Enangiperi EAK 290 Mh46
Enarotali RI 213 Rj47
Ena-san Tunnel J 183 Rj28
Enawene-Nawe, T.I. BR 68 Ha52
Enbebess EAK 290 Mh45
Encantado BR (RS) 78 He60
Encarnación PY 77 Hc59
Encarnación de Díaz MEX (JLC) 40 Ej35
Encekler TR 130 Mj52
Enchi GH 279 Kj43
Encinal USA (TX) 39 Fa31
Encinitas USA (CA) 22 Eb29
Enciso E 107 Ks52
Encoje ANG 288 Lh49
Encón RA (SJ) 76 Gg62
Encontrados YV 56 Gd41
Encruzilhada BR (SC) 78 He59
Encruzilhada BR (BA) 71 Hk53
Encruzilhada BR (RS) 78 Hc60
Encruzilhada do Sul BR (RS) 78 Hd61
Encs H 119 Mb42
Enda VRC (TIB) 171 Pj30
Endagikot EAT 293 Mh50
Endako CDN (BC) 18 Dh18
Endalaghanet EAT 293 Mh48
Endasak EAT 293 Mh48
Endau EAK 291 Mk46
Endau EAK 291 Mk46
Endau Rompin N.P. MAL 199 Qb44
Ende RI 211 Ra50
Endeavor CDN (SK) 24 Ej19
Endeavour Strait AUS 230 Sb51
Endelave DK 94 Ll35
Endengue CAM 281 Lg44
Enderbury Atoll KIR 241 Ub19
Enderby CDN (BC) 18 Ea20
Enderbyland ANT 313 Na32
Endiang CDN (AB) 19 Ed20
Endibir ETH 284 Mj41
Endicott USA (NY) 33 Gb24
Endicott Mts. USA 15 Cd12
Endiké RCB 281 Lh46
Endimari BR 67 Gg50
End-o-Line RR Park & Mus. USA 27 Fc23
Endom CAM 281 Lg44
Eneabba AUS (WA) 228 Qh60
Energía RA (BA) 81 Ha65
Eneryda S 95 Lp34
Enez TR 130 Mg50
Enfida TN 260 Lf27
Enfield CDN (NS) 31 Gj23
Engadin CH 114 Ll44
Engaku-ji J 183 Rk28
Engaru J 181 Sb23
Engaruka Basin EAT 290 Mj47
Engassumet EAT 293 Mj48
Enge N 90 Le14
Engelberg CH 114 Lj44
Engelhard USA (NC) 35 Gc28
Engen D 114 Lj43
Engenheiro Beltrão BR (PR) 74 Hd57
Engenheiro Dolabela BR (MG) 75 Hh54
Engenheiro Navarro BR (MG) 75 Hj54
Enger D 112 Lj38
Engerneset N 92 Ln29
Enggano RI 206 Qb48
Engh VRC (NMZ) 173 Qk20
Engineer CDN (BC) 17 Dc16
Engineer Group PNG 244 Sf51
England GB 101 Ks38
England USA (AR) 29 Fe28
Engle USA (NM) 23 Eg29
Englehart CDN (ON) 33 Ga22
Engle Passage GB 83 Ha72
English USA (IN) 34 Fg26
English Bay USA (AK) 15 Ce16
English Channel 102 Kr41
English Coast 312 Gb33
English Fort GH 279 Kk43
English Harbour East CDN (NF) 31 Hc22
English Harbour Town AG 47 Gk37
English Harbour West CDN (NF) 31 Hc22
English River CDN (ON) 25 Fe21
Engoobo SA 303 Md61
Engravings RB 299 Md58
Engre Rios = Malema MOC 297 Mj53
Engstingen D 114 Lk42
Enguera E 109 Ku48
Enguidanos E 109 Kt49
Engure LV 97 Md33
Engures ezers LV 97 Mc33
Enid USA (OK) 28 Fb27
Enisala RO 125 Mj46
Enisej RUS 140 Pb05
Enisej RUS 140 Pb05
Enisejsk RUS 140 Pc07
Enisejskij zaliv RUS 140 Od04
Eniwa J 181 Sa24
Eniwetok Atoll MH 240 Ta16
Enjil MA 259 Kh29
Enkatsiana RCB 288 Lh46
Enkhuizen NL 112 Lf38
Enklinge FIN 93 Ma30
Enkodak FIN 91 Mb11
Enköping S 93 Ls31
Enna I 122 Lp53
En Nahud SUD 283 Me39
Ennedi TCH 275 Mb37
Enneri Bardagué TCH 267 Lj35
Enneri Ké TCH 267 Lj36
Enneri Mi TCH 267 Lj35
Enneri Mondragué TCH 267 Lj35
Enneri Tegaham TCH 267 Lj36
Enneri Yébiqué TCH 267 Lj34
Enngonia AUS (NSW) 235 Sc60
Ennigerloh D 112 Lj39
Ennis IRL 100 Km38
Ennis USA (MT) 21 Ee23
Ennis USA (TX) 29 Fb29
Enniscorthy IRL 100 Ko38
Enniskerry IRL 100 Ko37
Enniskillen GB 98 Kn36
Ennistimon IRL 100 Kl38
Enns A 115 Lp42
Enns A 115 Lp43
Enoch USA (UT) 21 Ed27
Enonkoski FIN 96 Mj28
Enontekiö FIN 91 Mb11
Enping VRC (GDG) 178 Qg34
Enrekang RI 209 Qk47
Enrile RP 203 Ra37
Enriquillo DOM 46 Ge37
Enschede NL 112 Lg38
Ensenada MEX (BC) 22 Eb30
Ensenada de Calabozo YV 56 Ge40
Ensenada de Garachiné PA 43 Ga41
Ensenada de la Broa C 44 Fj34
Ensenada de Mompiche EC 60 Fk45
Ensenada de Tumaco CO 60 Ga45
Ensenada Los Muertos MEX (BCS) 38 Ef34
Ensenada Pabellones MEX 38 Eg33
Enshi VRC (HUB) 177 Qe30
Enshu-nada J 183 Rj28
Ensisheim F 103 Lh43
Entebbe EAU 290 Mg45
Entenbühl D 115 Ln41
Enterprise USA (OR) 20 Eb23
Enterprise USA (UT) 20 Ed27
Enterprise USA (AL) 35 Fh30
Entiako River CDN 18 Dh19
En Tmadé RIM 269 Ke36
Entrance CDN (AB) 19 Eb19
Entraygues-sur-Truyère F 104 Lc46
Entre-Ijuís BR (RS) 78 Hc60
Entre Lagos RCH 80 Gd66
Entre-os-Rios P 106 Km51
Entre Rios BOL 73 Gh56
Entre Rios BR (PA) 63 Hc48
Entre Rios BR (BA) 71 Ja51
Entre Rios RA 55 Ha25
Entre Rios de Minas BR (MG) 75 Hh56
Entrevaux F 105 Lg47
Entrocamento BR (MA) 64 Hg48
Entrocamento BR (MA) 64 Hh49
Entroncamento BR (MA) 64 Hh47
Entronque San Roberto MEX (NL) 39 Ek33
Entrop RI 213 Sa47
Entumeni SA 303 Mf60
Entwistle CDN (AB) 19 Ec19
Enugu WAN 280 Ld42
Enugu Ezike WAN 280 Ld42
Enumclaw USA (WA) 18 Dj22
Envermeu F 103 Lb41
Envigado CO 56 Gc42
Enviken S 93 Lq30
Envira BR (AM) 67 Ge49
Enxudé GNB 269 Kc40
Enyamba RDC 289 Mc47
Enyellé RCB 286 Lk44
Enz D 114 Lj42
Enza I 120 Ll46
Čornobyl' UA 132 Mf20
Epako NAM 298 Lj56
Epe NL 112 Lg38
Epe WAN 280 Lb42
Epéna RCB 281 Lj45
Epenarra AUS (NT) 223 Rh56
Épernay F 103 Ld41
Ephesos TR 129 Mh53
Ephrain USA (UT) 21 Ee26
Ephrata USA (WA) 18 Ea22
Epi RDC 287 Md44
Epi RDC 287 Me44
Epi VU 246 Te54
Epidavros GR 128 Md53
Épila E 107 Kt51
Épinal F 103 Lg42
Epini RDC 287 Me45
Epiphania SYR 146 Mj28
Episkopí GR 129 Me55
Epizana BOL 72 Gh54
Epokenkoso RDC 288 Lj47
Epoma RCB 281 Lh45
Eppingen D 114 Lj41
Epping Forest AUS (QLD) 233 Sd57
Epsom GB 101 Ku39
Eptahóri GR 126 Mb50
Epukiro NAM 298 Lk56
Epukiro NAM 299 Ma56
Epulu RDC 287 Me45
Epupa Falls NAM 298 Lg54
Epuyén RA (CB) 80 Ge67
Equatorial Channel MV 192 Og46
Equatorial Guinea 253 La09
Equator Monument RI 208 Qe45
Equator Village MV 192 Og46
Équeurdreville-Hainneville F 102 Kt41
Eraballi IND (KTK) 193 Oj39
Eraclea Minoa I 122 Lo53
Erahtur RUS 133 Na18
Eralé BR (PA) 63 Hd45
Eram PNG 243 Sb48
Eran Bay RP 204 Qj41
Erátira GR 126 Mb50
Erave PNG 243 Sb49
Erave River PNG 243 Sb49
Eravikulam N.P. IND 193 Oj41
Eravur CL 193 Pa43
Erawan Cave THA 196 Qb37
Erawan N.P. THA 196 Pk38
Erba I 120 Lk45
Erbaa TR 144 Mj25
Erbach D 114 Lj41
Erbach D 114 Lk42
Erba Lugang VRC (AHU) 184 Qk30
Erbent TM 153 Nk26
Erbeskopf D 114 Lh41
Erçek TR 145 Nb26
Erçek Gölü TR 145 Nb26
Ercilla RCH 80 Gd65
Erciş TR 145 Nb26
Erciyes Dağı TR 131 Mq52
Ercolano I 122 Lp50
Erd H 119 Lt43
Erdaobaihe VRC (JLN) 182 Re24
Erddig GB 101 Ks37
Erdeentsav MNG 173 Qh21
Erdek TR 130 Mh50
Erdemli TR 144 Mh27
Erdenet MNG 172 Pk21
Erdenet MNG 172 Qc21
Erdenetsogt MNG 172 Qa22
Erdene Zuu Monastery MNG 172 Qb22
Erdeven F 102 Kr43
Erdi TCH 275 Mb36
Erding D 115 Lm42
Erdre F 102 Kt43
Erdut HR 124 Lu45
Eré TCH 273 Lh41
Erebus, Mount 313 Tc34
Erech IRQ 147 Nc30
Erechim BR (RS) 78 Hd59
Ereğli TR 131 Mm49
Ereğli TR 131 Mp53
Ereğli Ovası TR 131 Mo53
Eréké RCA 281 Lj42
Eremiivka UA 125 Ml44
Eremitu RO 125 Me44
Eréndira MEX (BC) 22 Eb30
Eréndira MEX (MHC) 40 Ek36
Erenhot VRC (NMZ) 175 Qg24
Ereñler Dağlari TR 131 Mn53
Erentepe TR 145 Na26
Erer ETH 284 Nb42
Ereré BR (CE) 65 Ja48
Erer Gota ETH 284 Na41
Eressós GR 129 Mf51
Erfenis Dam SA 303 Md60
Erfoud MA 259 Kh30
Erft D 112 Lg40
Erfurt D 113 Lm40
Erg Aït el Khâoua DZ/RMM 265 La35
Ergani TR 145 Mk26
Erg Atouila RMM 265 Kh35
Erg Azenezal DZ 265 La34
Erg Bourarhet DZ 260 Le32
Erg Chech DZ 265 Kj33
Erg Chech RIM 265 Kg34
Erg d'Admer DZ 266 Le33
Erg du Djourab TCH 273 Lk37
Erg du Ténéré RN 273 Lf37
Ergel MNG 175 Qe24
Erg el Atchane DZ 259 Kk31
Erg el Ouar DZ 260 Ld31
Ergene Çay TR 130 Mh49
Ergenetsogt MNG 174 Qd24
Ergeni RUS 135 Nc22
Erg er Raoui DZ 259 Kj31
Erg labes DZ 259 Kj32
Erg Iguidi DZ 258 Kg32
Erg In-Sâkâne RMM 265 Kk35
Erg in Techerène RMM 265 Kk35
Erg Issaouane DZ 260 Ld32
Erg Kilian DZ 266 Le34
Ergli LV 97 Mf34
Erg Mehedjibat DZ 266 Lb33
Erg n'Ataram DZ 266 La34
Ergolding D 115 Ln42
Ergoldsbach D 115 Ln42
Erg Tassedjefit DZ 266 Lb33
Erg Tihodaïne DZ 266 Ld33
Erg Tidjidit DZ 265 La34
Erg Tifernine DZ 266 Ld32
Ergun He VRC/RUS 173 Ra20
Ergun Youqi VRC (NMZ) 173 Ra20
Ergun Zuoqi VRC (NMZ) 173 Ra20
Er Hai VRC 195 Qa33
Erheib SUD 277 Mj37
Eri WAN 272 Lb41
Eriba SUD 277 Mj38
Eric CDN (QC) 30 Gh20
Érice I 122 Ln52
Ericeira P 108 Kl48
Erickson CDN (MB) 24 Fa20
Eridu IRQ 147 Nd30
Erie USA (PA) 33 Fk24
Erigât RMM 270 Kh36
Erik Eriksenstretet N 91 Mc06
Erikli TR 130 Mg50
Erikoussa GR 128 Lu51
Eriksdale CDN (MB) 24 Fa20
Erikub Atoll MH 241 Tb17
Ermitage Père de Foucauld DZ 266 Lc34
Erimo J 181 Sb24
Erimo-misaki J 181 Sb25
Erimo Seamount J 181 Sc25
Erin USA (TN) 34 Fg27
Eringsboda S 95 Lq34
Eriskay GB 98 Kn33
Erithrés GR 128 Md52
Eritrea ER 253 Mb08
Erka N 92 Lj28
Erkelenz D 112 Lg39
Erkhet MNG 172 Qb21
Erkhet Uul MNG 172 Qa22
Erkilet TR 131 Mq52
Erkner D 113 Lo38
Erkovcy RUS 180 Re20
Erkowit SUD 277 Mj37
Erla E 107 Ku52
Erlangen D 115 Lm41
Erldunda AUS (NT) 226 Rg58
Erlistoun AUS (WA) 228 Rb60
Ermelo SA 303 Mf59
Ermenek TR 144 Mg27
Ermesinde P 106 Km51
Ermil Post SUD 283 Md39
Ermióni GR 128 Md53
Ermis RUS 133 Nb18
Ermoúpoli GR 129 Me53
Ernakulam IND (KER) 192 Oj42
Ernée F 102 Ku42
Ernesto Alves BR (RS) 78 Hc60
Ernest Sound USA 17 Dd18
Erode IND (TNU) 193 Oj41
Eromanga AUS (QLD) 234 Sb59
Eromanga Island VU 246 Te55
Erongari cuaro MEX (MHC) 40 Ek36
Erongo NAM 298 Lh56
Erongoberge NAM 298 Lh56
Eroro PNG 243 Se50
Erpengdianzi VRC (LNG) 182 Rc25
Erquy F 102 Ks42
Errabiddy AUS (WA) 224 Qj58
Erragondapalem IND (APH) 191 Ok37
Erraguntla IND (APH) 193 Ok39
Errego MOC 297 Mj54
Errigal IRL 98 Km35
Erris Head IRL 98 Kk36
Erro E 107 Kt52
Er Rogel SUD 276 Mh37
Errol USA (NH) 33 Ge23
Er Roseires SUD 283 Mh40
Ersaf MA 259 Kj28
Ersekë AL 126 Ma50
Erši RUS 132 Mh18
Erskine USA (MN) 27 Fb22
Erstein F 103 Lh42
Erta Ale ETH 277 Na40
Ertai VRC (XUZ) 167 Pf22
Ertil' RUS 133 Na20
Ertis 140 Pa08
Ertix He VRC 167 Pd22
Ertuğrul TR 130 Mh51
Ertuğrulköy TR 131 Mm51
Erufa WAN 272 Lc41
Erundu NAM 298 Lj56
Eruwa WAN 280 Lb42
Ervália BR (MG) 75 Hj56
Ervay USA (WY) 21 Eg24
Ervenik HR 121 Lq46
Ervy-le-Châtel F 103 Ld42
Erwang RI 212 Re46
Erwin USA (TN) 35 Fj27
Erwitte D 112 Lj39
Erythrai TR 129 Mg52
Erzen AL 126 Lu49
Erzgebirge D/CZ 115 Ln40
Érzin RUS (TUV) 167 Ph20
Erzincan TR 145 Mk26
Erzurum TR 145 Na26
Erzvilkas LT 97 Mc35
Esa'ala PNG 244 Sf50
Esan J 181 Sa25
Esashi J 181 Sa25
Esashi J 181 Sb23
Eşatlar TR 130 Mk51
Esbjerg DK 94 Lj35
Esbo = Espoo FIN 96 Me30
Escada BR (PE) 71 Jc50
Escalada E 107 Kr52
Escalante RP 205 Rb40
Escalante USA (UT) 23 Ee27
Escalante USA 23 Ee27
Escalante Canyons USA 23 Ee27
Escalante Desert USA 21 Ed27
Escalaplano I 111 Lk51
Escalerilla RCH 72 Gf56
Escalona E 109 Kq50
Escalos de Cima P 108 Kn49
Escanaba USA 27 Fg22
Escároz E 107 Kt52
Eschede D 113 Ll38
Eschenburg D 112 Lj40
Esch-s-Alzette L 103 Lf41
Eschscholtz Bay USA 15 Bk12
Esch-s-Sûre L 103 Lf41
Eschwege D 112 Ll39
Eschweiler D 112 Lg40
Escola BOL 72 Gg54
Escondido MEX 41 F36
Escondido NIC 42 Fh39
Escondido USA (CA) 22 Eb29
Escondido, T.I. BR 68 Ha50
Escott AUS (QLD) 232 Rk54
Escoumins CDN (QC) 30 Gf21
Escravos WAN 280 Lc43
Escudero ANT (RCH) 312 Ha30
Escuinapa MEX (SL) 38 Eh34
Escuintla GCA 41 Fe38
Escuintla MEX (CHP) 41 Fd38
Escuminac CDN (NB) 31 Gh22
Escus BG 127 Me47
Ese RDC 287 Md43
Eséka CAM 281 Lf44
Eseli PNG 243 Se49
Eşen TR 129 Mk54
Esenada RCH 80 Gd66
Esens D 112 Lh37
Esenyurt TR 144 Me25
Esfahan IR 154 Nf29
Esfand Abad IR 154 Ng30
Esfand Abad IR 154 Ng30
Esfarayan IR 155 Nj27
Esfashad IR 155 Nk29
Esfolado BR 64 Hh49
Eshan VRC (YUN) 195 Qb33
Esha Ness GB 99 Kt30
Esha No 6 RB 299 Mb55
Eshimba RDC 289 Mc48
Eshkamesh AFG 160 Oe27
Eshkashem AFG 161 Of27
Eshowe SA 303 Mf60
Eshq Abad IR 155 Nk27
Eshtahard IR 154 Nf28
Esigodini ZW 300 Me56
Esik KZ 159 Oj24
Esikuma GH 279 Kk43
Esino I 121 Lo47
Esira RM 306 Nd58
Esk AUS 235 Sg59
Eskdale AUS (VIC) 237 Sd64
Eskel Abad IR 157 Oa31
Esker CDN (NF) 30 Gg19
Eskifjörður IS 90 Kd13
Eski Gediz TR 130 Mk51
Eski Gümüş TR 131 Mp53
Eskil TR 131 Mo52
Eskilstuna S 93 Lr31
Eski-Nookat KS 159 Og25
Eskipazar TR 131 Mn50
Eskişehir TR 131 Ml51
Eskridge USA (KS) 27 Fb26
Eslam Abad IR 154 Nd28
Eslam Qal'eh AFG 160 Oa28
Eslamsham IR 154 Nf28
Eslohe D 112 Lj39
Eslöv S 95 Lo35
Eşme TR 130 Mj52
Eşmekaya TR 131 Mo52
Esmeralda AUS (QLD) 232 Sb55
Esmeralda BOL 67 Gg52
Esmeralda BR (RS) 78 He60
Esmeralda C 45 Ga35
Esmeralda YV 58 Gh44
Esmeraldas EC 60 Ga45
Esmeraldas EC 60 Ga45
Es Mercadal E 110 Le50
Esnagami Lake CDN 25 Fg20
Esnagi Lake CDN 25 Fh21
Espakeh IR 157 Oa32
Espalion F 105 Lc46
Espanola CDN (ON) 32 Fk22
Espanola USA (NM) 23 Eg28
Espargos CV 268 Jj37
Espartillar RA (BA) 81 Gk64
Espeland N 92 Lf30
Espenberg USA (AK) 15 Bj12
Esperança BR (PA) 63 Hd46
Esperança BR (PB) 65 Jc49
Esperança BR (MS) 74 Hc56
Esperance AUS (WA) 228 Ra62
Esperance Bay AUS 228 Ra62
Esperance Highway AUS 228 Ra62
Esperantina BR (PI) 65 Hj47
Esperantinópolis BR (MA) 64 Hh48
Esperanza MEX (SO) 38 Ef32
Esperanza PE 67 Ge50
Esperanza RA (SF) 77 Gk61
Esperanza RA (MI) 77 Hc59
Esperanza RA (SC) 82 Ge71
Esperanza RP 205 Rc40
Esperanza RP 205 Rc41
Esperanza ANT (RA) 312 Ha31
Espiel E 108 Kp48
Espigão do Oeste BR (RO) 68 Gk51
Espigão Mestre BR 70 Hh52
Espina, I. E 110 La50
Espinal BOL 73 Ha54
Espinal CO 56 Gc43
Espinama E 106 Kq53
Espinazo MEX (NL) 39 Ek32
Espinero YV 58 Gj42
Espinhal P 106 Km50
Espinheira ANG 294 Lg54
Espinho P 106 Km51
Espinillo RA (FO) 73 Ha58
Espino YV 57 Gh41
Espinosa BR (MG) 70 Hj53
Espinosa de los Monteros E 107 Kr53
Espírito Santo BR 53 Hd22
Espírito Santo do Turvo BR (SP) 74 Hf57
Espírito São do Pinhal BR (SP) 75 Hg57
Espiritu RP 203 Ra37
Espiritu Santo VU 246 Td53
Espita MEX (YT) 41 Ff35
Es Pla E 110 Ld51
Esplanada BR (BA) 71 Jb51
Espoo = Esbo FIN 96 Me30
Esposende P 106 Km51
Espumoso BR (RS) 78 Hd60
Espungabera MOC 300 Mg56
Esqueda MEX (SO) 21 Ef30
Esquel RA (CB) 80 Ge67
Esquina RA (CR) 77 Ha60
Esquipulas GCA 41 Ff38
Esquipulas NIC 42 Fh39
Esquiú RA (CA) 76 Gh60
Esrefoğlu Camii TR 131 Mm53
Es Sabah LAR 267 Lh32
Es Salihiya ET 263 Mg30
Essaouira MA 258 Kf30
Essé CAM 281 Lf43
Essej RUS 140 Qa05
Essen B 103 Le39
Essen D 112 Lh39
Essendon, Mount AUS 224 Ra58
Essentuki RUS 152 Nb23
Essequibo GUY 58 Ha43
Essex USA (CA) 22 Ec28
Essexville USA (MI) 32 Fj24
Esslingen D 114 Lk42
Essoûk RMM 271 La36
Essoyes F 103 Le42
Es Suki SUD 276 Mg40
Estaçao Catur MOC 297 Mh52
Estação de Narbona ROU 77 Ha62
Estação Ecológica Caracaraí BR 62 Gk45
Estação Ecológica Cuniã BR 68 Gj50
Estação Ecológica da Serra das Araras BR 69 Hb53
Estação Ecológica de Niquiá BR 62 Gk45
Estação Ecológica do Jari BR 63 Hd46
Estação Ecológica Ilha de Taiamã BR 69 Hb54
Estação Ecológica Ilhas Maracá e Jipióca BR 59 He44
Estação Ecológica Iquê-Juruena BR 68 Ha52
Estação Ecológica Mamirauá BR 62 Gh47
Estação Ecológica Maracá BR 58 Ha44
Estação Ecológica Rio Acre BR 67 Ge51
Estaca Zero BR (PI) 65 Hj48
Estación Baquéira-Beret E 110 La48
Estación biológica Charles Darwin EC 60 Fe45
Estación Calles MEX (TM) 39 Fa34
Estación Camacho MEX (ZCT) 39 Ej33
Estación Cerler E 110 La48
Estación Coyotes MEX (DGO) 39 Eh34
Estación de Candanchú E 107 Ku52
Estación del Formigal E 107 Ku52
Estación Dimas MEX (SL) 38 Eg34
Estación La Colorada MEX (ZCT) 39 Ej34
Estación la Molina E 110 Lb48
Estación Madero MEX (COH) 39 Ej33
Estación Masella E 110 Lb48
Estación Micos MEX (SLP) 39 Fa34
Estación Ordino-Arcalís AND 110 Lb48
Estación Pintados RCH 72 Gf56
Estación Sierra Nevada E 109 Kr47
Estado de Guerrero, P.N. MEX 40 Fa37
Estahban IR 156 Nh31
Estaing F 105 Lc46
Estambul BOL 67 Gg53
Estância BR (SE) 71 Jb51
Estancia USA (NM) 23 Eg28
Estancia Avanzada PY 73 Hb58
Estancia Caracol PY 73 Ha57
Estancia Carmen RA (TF) 82 Gf73
Estancia Cerrito Jara PY 73 Ha55
EstanciaCerro Guido RCH 82 Gd71
Estancia Conchi RCH 72 Gf57
Estancia Curupayty PY 73 Ha57
Estancia Helaingfors RA (SC) 82 Gd70
Estancia Invierno RCH 82 Ge72
Estancia La Patria PY 73 Gk56
Estancia La Victoria PY 73 Ha57
Estancia Lomas PY 73 Ha58
Estancia Los Lapachos PY 73 Ha57
Estancia L.Unión RA (SC) 82 Gd71
Estancia María Luisa RA (TF) 82 Gg73
Estancia Marina RA (TF) 82 Gf73
Estancia Noric PY 73 Ha56
Estancia Pan de Azucár PE 72 Gf58
Estancia Paragro PY 73 Ha56
Estancia Paredes PY 73 Ha58
Estancia Policarpo RA (TF) 83 Gh73
Estancia Rincón Grande RA (SC) 82 Gf71
Estancia Rocallosa RCH 82 Ge72
Estancia San Antonio PY 73 Ha57
Estancia San Carlos PY 74 Hc57
Estancia San Felipe PY 73 Hb57
Estancia San José PY 73 Ha57
Estancia San Juan PY 74 Hc57
Estancia San Pablo RA (TF) 82 Gg73
Estancia Santa Teresa PY 73 Ha56
Estancia Trementina PY 73 Hb57
Estancia Varillas PE 72 Gf58
Estandarte BR (MA) 64 Hh46
Estanislao del Campo RA (FO) 73 Gk58
Estanque de León MEX (COH) 39 Ej32
Estapilla MEX (COL) 40 Ej36
Estaquinba MOC 300 Mh55
Estarreja P 106 Km50
Estcourt SA 303 Me60
Esteli NIC 42 Fg39
Estella E 107 Ks52
Estepa E 108 Kq47
Este, P.N. del DOM 46 Gf36
Estepona E 108 Kp46
Ester USA (AK) 15 Cg13
Estercuel E 109 Ku50
Ester de Boca EC 60 Fk47
Schloss Esterházy A 115 Lr43
Esterhazy CDN (SK) 24 Ej20
Esterházy H 118 Lr43
Esternay F 103 Ld42
Estero Agiabampo MEX 38 Ef32
Esteros del Iberá RA 77 Hb60
Esterri d'Àneu E 110 Lb48
Estevan CDN (SK) 24 Ej21
Estevan Group CDN 18 Df19
Esther Island USA 15 Cf15
Estherville USA (IA) 27 Fc24
Estima MOC 296 Mg53
Estique PE 72 Ge54
Estirão do Equador BR (AM) 61 Ge48
Estirão do Robojo BR (AM) 67 Gd49
Estissac F 103 Ld42
Estiva BR 64 Hh49
Estivadinho, T.I. BR 68 Ha53
Estiva do Campo BR (MA) 64 Hh49
Estlin CDN (SK) 19 Eh20
Eston CDN (SK) 19 Ef20
Estonia EST 96 Me32
Estoril P 108 Kl48
Estrecho de Le Maire RA 83 Gh73
Estrecho de Yucatán 44 Fh35
Estrecho Nelson RCH 82 Gc71
Estrechos de la Florida 37 Fk34
Estreito BR (MA) 64 Hg49
Estrela da Paz, T.I. BR 61 Gg47
Estremadura P 108 Kl48
Estremoz P 108 Kn48
Estuario de Virrita PE 60 Fk48
Esztergom H 118 Lt43
Etadunna AUS (SA) 227 Rk60
Etah IND (UPH) 189 Ok32
Étain F 103 Lf41
Etaka NAM 294 Lh55
Étampes F 103 Lc42
Étang de Bages et de Sigean F 105 Ld47
Étang de Berre F 105 Lf47
Étang de Biscarrosse et de Parentis F 104 Kt46
Étang de Cazaux et de Sanguinet F 104 Kt46
Étang de Vaccarès F 105 Le47
Étaples F 103 Lb40
Etawah IND (RJT) 188 Oj33
Etawah IND (UPH) 189 Ok32
Etchojoa MEX (SO) 38 Ef32
Etemba Cave NAM 298 Lh56
Etembue GQ 280 Le45
Ethelbert CDN (MB) 24 Ek20
Ethel Creek AUS (WA) 224 Ra57
Etheldale AUS (QLD) 232 Sb55
Ethel Lake CDN 17 Db14
Ethels wreck AUS 236 Rj63
Ethiopia ETH 253 Mb09
Ethiopian Highlands ETH 284 Mj40
Etili TR 130 Mg51
Etivluk River USA 15 Cb11
Etjo NAM 298 Lj56
Etna I 122 Lp53
Etne N 92 Lf31
Étoile SY 305 Ng48
Etolikó GR 128 Mb52
Etolin Island USA 17 Dd17
Etolin Point USA 14 Ca16
Etolin Strait USA 14 Bh15
Etoraheberge NAM 294 Lg54
Etosha N.P. NAM 298 Lh55
Etosha Pan NAM 298 Lj55
Etou CAM 281 Lg44
Etoumbi RCB 281 Lh45
Etowah USA (TN) 35 Fh28
Etrépagny F 103 Lb41
Étretat F 102 La41
Etropole BG 126 Md48
Etropolski manastir BG 127 Me48
Etsch = Ådige I 120 Ll44
Ettelbruck L 103 Lg41
Ettenheim D 114 Lh42
Etten-Leur NL 112 Le39
Et-Tleta-de-Oued-Laou MA 259 Kh28
Ettlingen D 114 Lj42
Et-Tnine MA 258 Kf30
Ettumanur IND (KER) 192 Oj42
Etumba RDC 287 Mc46
Etumba RDC 289 Ma47
Eturnagaram IND (APH) 191 Pa36
Etzikom Coulée CDN 19 Ee21
Eu F 103 Lb40
Eua Island TO 248 Bc56
Euca BR (AP) 59 He44
Eucaliptus BOL 72 Gg54
Eucla AUS (WA) 229 Re61
Eucla Basin AUS 229 Rc62
Euclid USA (OH) 32 Fk25
Euclides da Cunha BR (BA) 71 Ja51
Euclides da Cunha Paulista BR (SP) 74 Hd57
Eudora USA (AR) 29 Fe29
Eudunda AUS (SA) 236 Rk63
Eufaula USA (OK) 29 Fc28
Eufaula USA (AL) 35 Fh30
Eufaula Lake USA 29 Fc28
Eufaula N.W.R. USA 35 Fh29
Eufrasio Loza RA (CD) 76 Gj60
Eufrazijeva bazilika HR 121 Lo45
Eugene USA (OR) 20 Dj23
Eugowra AUS (NSW) 237 Se62
Eulo AUS (QLD) 235 Sc60
Eulonia USA (GA) 35 Fk30
Eumara Springs AUS (QLD) 233 Sd55
Eumungarie AUS (NSW) 235 Se61
Eunápolis BR (BA) 75 Ja54
Eungella AUS (QLD) 233 Se56
Eungella N.P. AUS 233 Se56
Eunice USA (NM) 23 Ej29
Eunice USA (LA) 29 Fd30
Eupen B 103 Lg40
Euphrates IRQ 142 Na12
Eupora USA (MS) 29 Ff29
Eura FIN 96 Mc29
Eurady AUS (WA) 224 Qh59
Eurajoki FIN 96 Mb29
Eureka USA (MT) 19 Ec21
Eureka USA (CA) 20 Dh25
Eureka USA (NV) 20 Ec26
Eureka USA (UT) 21 Ed26
Eureka USA (SD) 26 Fa23
Eureka USA (KS) 29 Fb27
Eureka Springs USA (AR) 29 Fd27
Euribulla N.P. AUS 235 Sf58
Euromba AUS (QLD) 235 Se58
Europa Park D 114 Lh42
Europoort NL 112 Ld39
Europos parkas LT 97 Mf36
Eurora AUS (VIC) 237 Sc64
Euro Speedway D 113 Lo39
Euskirchen D 112 Lg40
Euston AUS (NSW) 237 Sb63
Eutaw USA (AL) 34 Fg29
Euthini MW 296 Mg51
Eutin D 113 Ll36
Eutsuk Lake CDN 18 Dg19
Eva Downs AUS (NT) 223 Rh55
Evakkokeskus FIN 91 Md14
Evale ANG 294 Lh54
Evandale CDN (NB) 31 Gg23
Evangelistria GR 129 Mf53
Evanger N 92 Lg30
Evans Ice Stream 312 Ga34
Evans Strait CDN 11 Fd06
Evanston USA (WY) 21 Ee25
Evanston USA (IL) 32 Fg24
Evansville USA (IN) 34 Fg27
Evare, T.I. BR 61 Gf47
Evartra RM 306 Nd58
Evaton SA 303 Md59
Evaux-les-Bains F 105 Lc44
Evaz IR 156 Ng32
Evciler TR 130 Mg51
Évdilos GR 129 Mg53
Evenki Autonomous District RUS 140 Pc05
Evensville USA (WY) 21 Eg24
Everard Junction AUS (WA) 225 Rc58
Everard Park AUS (SA) 226 Rh59
Everard Ranges AUS 226 Rg59
Everest, Mount NEP/VRC 170 Pd31
Everett USA (WA) 18 Dj22
Evergem B 103 Ld39
Everglades City USA (FL) 36 Fk33
Everglades National Park USA 36 Fk33
Evergreen USA (MT) 19 Ec21
Evergreen USA (MN) 27 Fc22
Evergreen USA (AL) 34 Fg30
Evertsberg S 93 Lo29
Evesham AUS (QLD) 232 Sb57
Evesham GB 101 Kt38
Évia GR 128 Me52
Évia GR 128 Md52
Évian-les-Bains F 105 Lg44
Evijärvi FIN 91 Mb14
Evinayong GQ 281 Lf45
Evisa F 111 Lj48
Evje N 92 Lh32
Evksinograd BG 127 Mh47
Evlanovo RUS 133 Mj19
Evodoula CAM 281 Lf43
Ev Oghli IR 154 Nc26
Evoikós Kólpos GR 128 Md52
Evolène CH 114 Lh44

F

G

adein SUD 283 Me41
adyhogol SP 285 Nb41
ading N.P., Gunung MAL 208 Qe45
adis RI 206 Pk45
adjač UA 132 Mh20
ádor E 109 Ks46
adra PK 163 Of33
adsden USA (AL) 34 Fh29
aduk IR 154 Ng28
adwal IND (APH) 190 Oj37
adzi RCA 281 Lj43
ærum DK 94 Ll33
ăești RO 125 Mf46
aeta I 122 Lo49
aferut Island FSM 240 Sb17
affney USA (SC) 35 Fk28
afidda ETH 285 Nc42
afsa TN 260 Le28
ag RI 212 Re46
agachin IR 154 Nc27
agal TCH 273 Lh41
agan PNG 244 Sh48
agarawa WAN 272 Le39
agargarh IND (UPH) 189 Pb32
agarin UZB 158 Oe25
agau, Gunung MAL 199 Qb42
age USA (OK) 28 Fa27
agere WAN 272 Ld39
aggenau D 114 Lj42
aghamni SUD 283 Me40
agince SCG 126 Mb48
agino RUS 133 Nc18
agnef S 93 Lq30
agnoa CI 279 Kh42
agra GE 152 Na24
agron IND 190 Oj33
a Hai VRC 169 Pj27
ahavisuka Provincial Park PNG 243 Sc49
ahkom IR 157 Nh31
ahmar IND (UPH) 191 Pb33
ahnpa LB 278 Kf42
ai EAK 291 Mk46
aiab NAM 302 Lk59
aibanda BD 194 Pe33
aighat NEP 170 Pd32
aigou BF 271 Kk38
aiki LV 97 Mc34
ail A 115 Ln44
ail USA (TX) 28 Ek29
aildorf D 114 Lk42
ailey GB 101 Ks38
aillac F 104 Lb47
aillon F 102 Lb41
aiman RA (CB) 80 Gh67
aimonaki PNG 243 Se50
ainesville USA (TX) 29 Fb29
ainesville USA (MO) 29 Fd27
ainesville USA (GA) 35 Fj28
ainesville USA (FL) 36 Fj31
ainesvood USA 34 Fg29
ainsborough CDN (SK) 24 Ek21
ainsborough GB 101 Ku37
airdner AUS (WA) 228 Qk63
aire PNG 243 Sd50
airesi ZW 296 Mg54
airloch GB 99 Kp33
aisabad IND (MPH) 191 Ok33
aithersburg USA (MD) 33 Gb26
aivota BR (AP) 63 He45
ai Xian VRC (LNG) 182 Rb25
aizinkalns LV 97 Mf34
ajapajinagaram IND (APH) 191 Pb36
ajendragarh IND (KTK) 190 Oh38
ajiram WAN 273 Lf40
ajiram WAN 273 Lg39
ajner W.S. IND 188 Og32
ajol IND (WBG) 194 Pe33
ajutino RUS 132 Mk16
ajvoron UA 125 Mk42
akem WAN 280 Le42
akem WAN 280 Le42
akilköy TR 130 Mj50
akiye IR 154 Nd28
akkovo RUS 96 Mj31
ako RWA 292 Mf47
akona USA (AK) 15 Ch14
akona River USA 15 Ch14
akong EAK 290 Mh44
akuch 161 Og27
ala VRC (TIB) 170 Pe31
alăbovo BG 127 Mf48
al Adhale SP 285 Nd42
alán CO 56 Gd42
alán, Cerro RA 76 Gg59
alana EAK 291 Mk47
alanduak IR 154 Nf28
alang RI 207 Qc45
alanga ANG 294 Lh52
alangachi RT 279 La40
alangue ANG 294 Lj52
alanta SK 118 Ls42
alaosiyo UZB 158 Oc26
alápagos Fracture Zone 317 Cb10
alápagos Islands EC 60 Fe45
alas MAL 199 Qb43
alashiels GB 99 Ks35
alați RO 125 Mj45
alatina I 123 Lt50
alátista GR 126 Md50
alax USA (VA) 35 Fk27
alaxidi GR 128 Mc52
albraith AUS (QLD) 232 Sa54
albraith CDN (BC) 17 Dd16
albyn Gov' MNG 174 Qd24
alcia SP 285 Nd42
aldar E 264 Kc31
aldhøpiggen N 92 Lj29
alé RMM 270 Kf39
aleana MEX (CHH) 23 Eg30
aleana MEX (NL) 39 Ek33
alegu SUD 276 Mh40
alegu SUD 276 Mh40
alela RI 212 Rd45
alena USA (AK) 15 Cb13
alena USA (MO) 29 Fd27
alena Bay CDN (BC) 18 Eb20
alenbecker See D 113 Lo37
alecta Point TT 58 Gk40
alera BR 68 Ha53
alera E 109 Ks47
alera EC 60 Fk45
alera Point TT 58 Gk40
aleras VY 57 Gf41
aleras, Volcán CO 60 Gb45
aleria F 111 Lj48
aleria degli Uffizi I 120 Lm47
alesburg USA (IL) 27 Fe25
aleti ETH 284 Na41
aleton USA (PA) 33 Gb25
alewela CL 193 Pa43
algaguta H 119 Lu43
algamuwa CL 193 Pa43
Gălgău RO 124 Md43
Galgodon Mountains SP 285 Nb41
Gal Hareeri SP 285 Nd43
Galheirã BR 70 Hh52
Gali GE 152 Na24
Galibi SME 59 Hc43
Galič RUS 133 Nb16
Galicia E 106 Km52
Galičica, N.P. MK 126 Ma49
Galičskaja vozvyšennost' RUS 133 Nb16
Galiléia BR (MG) 75 Hk55
Galilo PNG 244 Sf48
Galim CAM 280 Lf43
Galinda ANG 288 Lg50
Galiraya EAU 290 Mg45
Galivedu IND (APH) 193 Ok40
Galiwinku AUS (NT) 223 Rh52
Gallabat SUD 277 Mj40
Galladhoo Channel MV 192 Og42
Gallan Head GB 98 Kn32
G'Allaorol UZB 158 Od26
Gallarate I 120 Lj45
Gallarus Oratory IRL 100 Kk38
Gallatin USA (MO) 27 Fd26
Gallatin USA (TN) 34 Fg27
Gallatin Peak USA 21 Ee23
Galle CL 193 Pa43
Gallegos RA 82 Ge71
Galleguillos RCH 76 Ge59
Gallei SP 291 Nb45
Galley Head IRL 100 Km39
Galliano USA (LA) 29 Fe31
Gallina USA (NM) 23 Eg27
Gallinazo YV 56 Gd41
Gallinero, Cerro YV 57 Gg43
Gallipoli AUS (NT) 223 Rj55
Gallipoli I 123 Ls50
Gallipolis USA (OH) 35 Fj26
Gällivare S 90 Ma12
Gallneukirchen A 115 Lp42
Gällö S 93 Lq28
Gallo Mts. USA 23 Ef28
Gällstad S 95 Lo33
Gallup USA (NM) 23 Ef28
Galma WAN 272 Le40
Galmi RN 272 Lc39
Galo Boukoy RCA 281 Lh43
Galool SP 291 Nb44
Gal Oya Valley N.P. CL 193 Pa43
Galsi IND (WBG) 194 Pd34
Galt USA (CA) 20 Dk26
Gal Tardo SP 291 Nc44
Galtåsen S 95 Lo33
Galtat Zemmour DARS 264 Kd33
Galtström S 93 Ls28
Galty Mountains IRL 100 Km38
Galugah IR 154 Ng27
Galula EAT 292 Mg50
Galumpang RI 209 Qk47
Galuutyn Canyon MNG 172 Pk22
Galuzeik MYA 196 Pj38
Galveston USA (TX) 29 Fc31
Galveston Bay USA 29 Fc31
Galvez PE 61 Gd48
Gálvez RA (SF) 77 Gk62
Galway IRL 100 Kl37
Galway Bay IRL 100 Kl37
Galway Downs AUS (QLD) 234 Sb58
Gam NAM 299 Ma56
Gam RI 212 Rf46
Gama BR (DF) 70 Hf54
Gama RG 278 Kf42
Gamadji Saré SN 269 Kc37
Gamagira WAN 272 Le40
Gamalama RI 212 Rd45
Gamana WAN 280 Le42
Gamarra CO 56 Gd41
Gamawa WAN 273 Lf39
Gamay RP 203 Rc39
Gamay Bay RP 203 Rc39
Gamba ANG 294 Lj51
Gamba G 288 Le47
Gamba RDC 289 Mc48
Gamba VRC (TIB) 170 Pe31
Gambaga GH 279 Kk40
Gambela ETH 283 Mh41
Gambela N.P. ETH 283 Mg42
Gambell USA 10 Bb06
Gambia WAG 269 Kb39
Gambia 253 Ka08
Gambia No.2 GH 279 Kj42
Gambier Islands AUS 236 Rj63
Gambo ANG 289 Lh53
Gambo CDN (NF) 31 Hc21
Gambo RCA 286 Mb43
Gamboa PA 43 Ga41
Gamboma RCB 288 Lh46
Gamboula RCA 281 Lh43
Gambuta, Gunung RI 209 Rb45
Gamda VRC (SCH) 176 Qa29
Gamdou RN 272 Le39
Gameh IR 155 Nj27
Gameleira BR (PB) 65 Jc49
Gamia DY 272 Lb40
Gaming A 115 Lq43
Gamka SA 302 Ma62
Gamkab NAM 302 Lj60
Gamkahe RI 212 Rd45
Gamle By DK 94 Ll34
Gamleby S 95 Lr33
Gammams SUD 276 Mh37
Gammelbo S 93 Lq31
Gammelstaden S 90 Mb13
Gammertingen D 114 Lk42
Gammon Ranges N.P. AUS 227 Rk61
Gamoep SA 302 Lk60
Gamperé CAM 281 Lh42
Gampola CL 193 Pa43
Gamra RIM 269 Kd37
Gamtog VRC (SCH) 176 Pk30
Gamud ETH 284 Mk43
Gan CI 278 Kg42
Gan F 104 Ku47
Ganado USA (AZ) 23 Ef28
Gananga MOC 297 Na51
Gananita SUD 276 Mg37
Gananoque CDN (ON) 33 Gb23
Ganapatipule Beach IND 190 Og37
Gancedo RA (CH) 77 Gk59
Gancheng VRC (HAN) 178 Qe36
Ganda ANG 294 Lh52
Gandaba ETH 284 Nb42
Gandabahali IND (ORS) 191 Pb35
Gandadiwata, Gunung RI 209 Qk47
Gandajika RDC 289 Mb49
Gandak IND 189 Pc32
Gandara RP 203 Rc39
Gandara RP 205 Rc40
Gandarbal 161 Oh28
Gandava PK 162 Od31
Gande WAN 272 Lc39
Ganden VRC 171 Pf31
Gander CDN (NF) 31 Hc21
Gander Bay CDN (NF) 31 Hc21
Ganderkesee D 112 Lj37
Gander Lake CDN 31 Hc21
Gander River CDN 31 Hc21
Gandesa E 110 La49
Gandhidham IND (GUJ) 190 Of34
Gandhinagar IND (GUJ) 190 Og34
Gandhi Sagar IND 190 Oh33
Gandia E 109 Ku48
Gandiaye SN 269 Kb38
Gando-ko J 183 Sa26
Gandoman IR 154 Nf30
Gandorhun WAL 278 Ke41
Gandu BR (BA) 71 Ja52
Gâneb RIM 269 Ke36
Ganesh NEP/VRC 170 Pc31
Gangakher IND (MHT) 190 Oj36
Gangalur IND (CGH) 191 Pa36
Gan Gan RA (CB) 80 Gf67
Gangan RG 278 Kd40
Ganganagar IND (RJT) 188 Og31
Ganga Nuur Nature Reserve MNG 173 Qg23
Gangapur IND (RJT) 188 Oh33
Gangapur IND (RJT) 188 Oj32
Gangara RN 272 Le38
Gangaw MYA 194 Ph34
Gangawati IND (KTK) 193 Oj39
Gangca VRC (QHI) 174 Qa27
Gangchang VRC (CGQ) 177 Qe30
Gangdisê Shan VRC 170 Pa29
Ganges F 105 Ld47
Ganges IND 189 Ok31
Ganges North Reef 204 Qh40
Ganges Reef 204 Qh40
Ganghwa Dolmen Site ROK 182 Rd28
Gangi I 122 Lp53
Gango ANG 294 Lh51
Gangoh IND (UPH) 189 Oj31
Gangola BHT 194 Pf32
Gangotri IND (UTT) 189 Ok30
Gangrampur IND (WBG) 194 Pe33
Gangte Goemba BHT 194 Pf32
Gangtok IND (SIK) 194 Pe32
Gangu RDC 282 Mc43
Gangu VRC (GSU) 177 Qc28
Gangui CAM 281 Lh42
Gangula ANG 294 Lg51
Gangwa RB 299 Ma55
Ganhe VRC (NMZ) 173 Rb20
Gani RI 212 Re46
Ganjali Khan IR 157 Nj30
Ganj Dinara IND (MPH) 189 Ok33
Ganjgah IR 154 Ne27
Gan Jiang VRC 179 Qh32
Ganj Nameh IR 154 Ne28
Ganlanba VRC (YUN) 195 Qa35
Ganluo VRC (SCH) 176 Qb31
Ganmain AUS (NSW) 237 Sd63
Gannan VRC (HLG) 180 Rb22
Gannat F 105 Ld44
Gannavaram IND (APH) 191 Pa37
Gann Valley USA (SD) 26 Fa23
Gano RA (SA) 73 Gh58
Ganquan VRC (SAA) 175 Qe27
Gansbaai SA 302 Lk63
Gansé CI 279 Kj41
Gansen VRC (QHI) 169 Pg27
Gansu VRC 164 Pd10
Gantang VRC (NHZ) 174 Qc27
Gantheaume Bay AUS 224 Qg59
Gantheaume Point AUS 222 Rb55
Ganvié DY 280 Lb42
Ganxi VRC (HUN) 177 Qe31
Ganye WAN 281 Lg41
Ganyesa SA 303 Mc59
Ganyu VRC (JGS) 184 Qk28
Ganyushkino KZ 152 Ne22
Gänzä AZ 152 Nd25
Ganzhou VRC (JGX) 179 Qh33
Gao BF 279 Kj40
Gao RMM 271 Kk37
Gao'an VRC (JGX) 184 Qh31
Gaochang Gucheng VRC 169 Pe24
Gaochun VRC (JGS) 184 Qk30
Gaofengtao VRC (SDG) 184 Qk28
Gaogou VRC (JGS) 184 Qk28
Gaohezhen VRC (AHU) 184 Qj30
Gaojiabu VRC (SAA) 175 Qf26
Gaolan VRC (GSU) 174 Qb27
Gaomi VRC (SDG) 175 Qk27
Gaoping VRC (SAX) 177 Qg28
Gaoshan VRC (FJN) 179 Qk33
Gaotai VRC (GSU) 174 Pk26
Gaotanchang VRC (SCH) 177 Qd30
Gaotang VRC (SDG) 175 Qj27
Gaoua BF 279 Kj40
Gaoual RG 278 Kd40
Gao Xian VRC (SCH) 176 Qc31
Gaoyang VRC (HUB) 177 Qf30
Gaoyi VRC (HBI) 175 Qh27
Gaoyou VRC (JGS) 184 Qk29
Gaoyou Hu VRC 184 Qk29
Gaozhou VRC (GDG) 178 Qf35
Gap F 105 Lg46
Gapan RP 203 Ra38
Gapi RDC 287 Md43
Gapuwiyak AUS (NT) 223 Rh52
Gar' RUS 180 Re19
Gar VRC 170 Pa29
Gara ET 262 Md31
Garabekevyul TM 155 Oc26
Garabinzam RCB 281 Lg45
Garacad SP 285 Ne42
Garachico E 264 Kb31
Garachiné PA 43 Ga41
Garada SUD 276 Mf37
Garadag SP 285 Nd41
Gara-Ekar DZ 266 Lc36
Garagoa CO 56 Gd43
Garagoumsa RN 272 Le39
Garah AUS (NSW) 235 Se60
Gara Hitrino BG 127 Mg47
Garaina PNG 243 Sd49
Garajonay, P.N. de E 264 Kb31
Gara Khannfoussa DZ 260 Ld32
Gara Lăkatnik BG 126 Md47
Garalo RMM 278 Kg40
Garamba RDC 287 Me44
Garamba, P.N. de la RDC 287 Me43
Garam Chasma PK 161 Of27
Garampani IND (ASM) 194 Pg33
Garango BF 279 Kk40
Garanhuns BR (PE) 71 Jb50
Ga-Rankuwa SA 299 Md58
Garapan USA 201 Sb15
Garapu BR (MT) 69 Hd52
Garara PNG 243 Se50
Garawa A.L. AUS 223 Rj54
Garayalde RA (CB) 80 Gg68
Garba RCA 282 Ma41
Garbahaarrey SP 291 Nb44
Garbatka-Letnisko PL 117 Mb39
Garba Tula EAK 291 Mk45
Garberville USA (CA) 20 Dj25
Gârbou RO 124 Md43
Garbów PL 117 Mc39
Garbsen D 112 Lk38
Garça BR (SP) 74 Hf57
Garching D 115 Lm42
Garchitorena RP 203 Rb39
Garda I 120 Ll45
Gardabani GE 152 Nc25
Gardan Diwal AFG 160 Oe28
Gardanne F 105 Lf47
Gardar USA (ND) 24 Fb21
Gårdby S 95 Lr34
Gardelegen D 113 Lm38
Garden City USA (UT) 21 Ee25
Garden City USA (KS) 28 Ek27
Garden City USA (TX) 28 Ek30
Garden City USA (SC) 35 Ga29
Gardendale USA (AL) 34 Fg29
Garden Hill CDN (MB) 24 Fc19
Garden of the Sleeping Giant FJI 247 Tj54
Garden Route SA 302 Ma63
Gardermoen N 92 Lm30
Gardete P 108 Kn49
Gardez AFG 160 Oe29
Gardiki GR 128 Mb51
Garding D 112 Lj36
Gardner = Nikumaroro KIR 241 Ub19
Gardner USA (LA) 29 Fd30
Gardnerville USA (NV) 20 Ea26
Gardone Riviera I 120 Ll45
Gardone Val Trompia I 120 Ll45
Gárdony H 119 Lt43
Garenga IND (CGH) 191 Pb36
Garešnica HR 121 Lr45
Garéssio I 120 Lj46
Gare Tigre F 59 Hd43
Gar et Tarf DZ 260 Ld28
Garfield Mtn. USA 21 Ed23
Garford AUS (SA) 226 Rg60
Gargaliáni GR 128 Mb53
Gargango RMM 270 Kh37
Gargano, P.N. del I 123 Lr49
Gargaris PNG 244 Sg47
Gargouna RMM 271 La38
Gargždai LT 97 Mb35
Garh IND (MPH) 191 Pa33
Garhakota IND (MPH) 191 Ok34
Garhbeta IND (WBG) 194 Pd34
Garhchiroli IND (MHT) 191 Ok35
Garhmuktesar IND (UPH) 189 Ok31
Gariaband IND (CGH) 191 Pb35
Gariau RI 213 Rh47
Garibaldi BR (RS) 78 He60
Garibaldi CDN (BC) 18 Dj20
Garibaldi USA (OR) 20 Dj23
Garibaldi Prov. Park CDN 18 Dj21
Gariep Dam SA 303 Mc61
Gariep Dam Nature Reserve SA 303 Mc61
Garies SA 302 Lk61
Gariganus NAM 302 Lk59
Garigliano I 122 Lo49
Garimari PNG 243 Se48
Garimpinho BR (TO) 64 Hf49
Garin Shehu WAN 272 Lf41
Garissa EAK 291 Mk46
Garkem WAN 280 Le42
Garki WAN 272 Le39
Garkida WAN 273 Lg40
Garladinne IND (APH) 193 Oj39
Garland CDN (MB) 24 Ek20
Garland USA (MT) 21 Eh22
Garland USA (TX) 29 Fb29
Garlasco I 120 Lj45
Garliava LT 97 Md36
Gărljano BG 126 Mc48
Garmab IR 154 Ne28
Garmabe SUD 287 Mf43
Garmisch-Partenkirchen D 115 Lm43
Garmi Tondo (Main de Fatma) RMM 271 Kk38
Garmsar IR 154 Ng28
Garnett USA (KS) 29 Fc26
Garnett USA (SC) 35 Fk29
Garoaia RO 125 Mh45
Garonne F 104 Ku46
Garoowe SP 285 Ne41
Garopaba BR (SC) 79 Hf60
Garou DY 272 Lb40
Garoua CAM 273 Lg41
Garoua CI 279 Kj42
Garoua Boulaï CAM 281 Lh43
Garove Island PNG 243 Se48
Garphyttan S 93 Lp31
Garphyttans n.p. S 93 Lp31
Garplay LB 278 Kf42
Gar Qu VRC 176 Qb29
Garrafão do Norte BR (PA) 64 Hg46
Garré RA (BA) 81 Gj64
Garrison USA (UT) 21 Ed26
Garrison USA (ND) 26 Ek22
Garrison USA (MN) 27 Fd22
Garrovillas E 108 Ko49
Garrthalala AUS (NT) 223 Rj52
Garrucha E 109 Kt47
Garruchos BR (RS) 78 Hc60
Garruchos RA (CR) 77 Hc60
Garrygala TM 153 Nj26
Garry Lake CDN 10 Ed05
Garsen EAK 293 Na47
Garsila SUD 282 Mb39
Gärsnäs S 95 Lp35
Garson Lake CDN 19 Ef17
Gartempe F 104 La44
Gartog VRC (TIB) 176 Pk31
Gartz D 113 Lp37
Garu GH 279 Kk40
Garu IND (JKD) 191 Pc34
Garu PNG 243 Se48
Garuahi PNG 244 Sf51
Garub NAM 302 Lj59
Garubhasa IND (ASM) 194 Pf32
Garuma RCH 72 Gf57
Garunggarung RI 212 Rd46
Garut RI 210 Qd49
Garuva BR (SC) 79 Hf59
Garvăn RO 125 Mj45
Garvão P 108 Km47
Garve GB 99 Kq33
Garvie Mountains NZ 239 Te68
Garwa IND (JKD) 191 Pb33
Garwolin PL 117 Mb39
Gar Xincun VRC (TIB) 170 Pa29
Gary USA (IN) 32 Fg25
Garza RA (SE) 76 Gj60
Garza Garcia MEX (NL) 39 Ek33
Garzê VRC (SCH) 176 Pk30
Garzón CO 60 Gc44
Gasan RP 203 Ra39
Gas Bay AUS 228 Qh63
Gas Chambers USA (OR) 20 Dh23
Gaschiga CAM 273 Lg41
Gas City USA (IN) 32 Fh25
Gascogne F 104 Ku47
Gascogne F 104 Ku47
Gascoyne Junction AUS (WA) 224 Qh58
Gascoyne River AUS 224 Qg58
Gash ER 277 Mj39
Gashaka WAN 281 Lf42
Gashaka-Gumti N.P. WAN 281 Lf42
Gasherbrum I PK 161 Oj28
Gasherbrum II 161 Oj28
Gash Setit Wildlife Reserve ER 277 Mj39
Gas Hu VRC 169 Pf27
Gashua WAN 273 Lf39
Gashunchaka VRC (QHI) 169 Ph27
Gashun Gobi VRC 169 Pg25
Gasim RI 212 Rf46
Gasmata PNG 244 Sf49
Gaspar BR (SC) 79 Hf59
Gasparilla Island USA 36 Fj32
Gaspé CDN (QC) 31 Gh21
Gaspésie, P.N. de la CDN 30 Gg21
Gasquet USA (CA) 20 Dj25
Gassan BF 271 Kj39
Gassane SN 269 Kc38
Gassi Touil DZ 260 Ld30
Gassol WAN 273 Lf41
Gastello RUS 181 Sb21
Gastonia USA (NC) 35 Fk28
Gastoúni GR 128 Mb53
Gastre RA (CB) 80 Gf67
Gästrikland S 93 Lr30
Gata CV 268 Jj37
Gataga River CDN 17 Dg16
Gătaia RO 124 Mb45
Gatakaini EAK 290 Mj46
Gatanga SUD 283 Md42
Gatčina RUS 132 Mf16
Gatčina Dworez RUS 132 Mf16
Gate City USA (VA) 35 Fj27
Gatehouse of Fleet GB 99 Kq36
Gateshead GB 99 Kt36
Gates of the Arctic National Park and Preserve USA 15 Cc12
Gatesville USA (TX) 28 Fb30
Gateway USA (CO) 21 Ef26
Gateway International Raceway USA (IL) 34 Fe26
Gathto Creek CDN 17 Dh16
Gati IR 157 Nk33
Gati-Loumo RMM 270 Kh38
Gatineau CDN (QC) 33 Gc23
Gatlinburg USA (TN) 35 Fj28
Gatma Dağı TR 144 Me26
Gato Colorado RA (SF) 77 Gk60
Gattaran RP 203 Ra36
Gattinara I 120 Lj45
Gatton AUS (QLD) 235 Sg59
Gatú PA 43 Fk41
Gatuna RWA 287 Mf46
Gaturiano BR (PI) 65 Hk49
Gau FJI 247 Tk55
Gaucín E 108 Kp46
Gaudan TM 155 Nk27
Gauer Lake CDN 24 Fb17
Gauja LV 97 Me33
Gaujas n.p. LV 97 Mf33
Gaulim PNG 244 Sg48
Gaultois CDN (NF) 31 Hc22
Gaupne N 92 Lh29
Gauribidanur IND (KTK) 193 Oj40
Gauripur IND (ASM) 194 Pe32
Gaurnadi BD 194 Pf34
Gaussberg 313 Pb32
Gaustatoppen N 92 Lj31
Gautier USA (MS) 29 Ff30
Gauting D 115 Lm42
Gavarnie F 104 Ku48
Gavbandi IR 156 Ng32
Gávdopoúla GR 128 Md56
Gávdos GR 129 Me56
Gave Rud IR 154 Nd28
Gavhuni Wetlands IR 154 Ng29
Gavião BR 71 Hk53
Gavião P 108 Kn49
Gavião, T.I. BR 62 Ha47
Gavien PNG 243 Sc49
Gaviota Beach USA 22 Dk28
Gävle S 93 Ls30
Gävlebukten S 93 Ls30
Gavorrano I 120 Ll48
Gavray F 102 Kt42
Gavrilov-Jam RUS 133 Mk17
Gávrio GR 129 Me53
Gávros GR 126 Mb50
Gavry RUS 97 Mh34
Gawachub NAM 302 Lj59
Gawa Island PNG 244 Sf50
Gawan IND (JKD) 191 Pc33
Gawa Obo VRC (QHI) 176 Pk28
Gawler AUS (SA) 236 Rk63
Gawler Ranges AUS 236 Rh62
Gaworzyce PL 116 Lq39
Gawu WAN 272 Ld41
Gaxun Nur VRC 174 Qa24
Gaya IND (BIH) 191 Pc33
Gaya MAL 204 Qj42
Gaya RN 272 Lb40
Gaya WAN 272 Le40
Gayam RI 211 Qh49
Gayam TCH 273 Lj41
Gayaza EAU 287 Mf46
Gayéri BF 271 La39
Gaylord USA (MN) 27 Fc23
Gaylord USA (MI) 32 Fh23
Gaya River CDN 17 Df13
Gayndah AUS (QLD) 235 Sf58
Gaysan SUD 283 Mh40
Gaza IS 146 Mh30
Gaz-Achak TM 153 Oa25
G'azalkent UZB 158 Oe25
Gazanak IR 154 Ng28
Gazandzhyk TM 153 Nh26
Gazaoua RN 272 Ld39
Gazara TJ 158 Oe26
Gaza Strip IS 146 Mh30
Gazelle Channel PNG 244 Sf47
Gazelle Peninsula PNG 244 Sf48
Gazi EAK 293 Mk48
Gaziantep TR 144 Mj27
Gazi-Husrev-begova džamija BIH 121 Lt47
Gazimağusa CY 131 Mo55
Gazimağusa = Ammochostos CY 131 Mo55
Gazimur RUS 173 Qk19
Gazimurskij Zavod RUS 173 Qk20
Gazipaşa TR 144 Mg27
Gazli UZB 158 Ob25
Gazligölakören TR 131 Ml52
Gbabam CI 279 Kh43
Gbaboua CAM 281 Lh42
Gbadikaha CI 279 Kh41
Gbadolite RDC 286 Ma43
Gbagba RCA 286 Ma43
Gbaïzera RCA 282 Lk42
Gbalatuai LB 278 Kf42
Gbambélédougou CI 279 Kh41
Gbananme DY 280 Lb42
Gbanbala CI/RG 278 Kf41
Gbanendji RCA 282 Ma42
Gbanga WAN 272 Ld41
Gbangbatok WAL 278 Kd42
Gbarnga LB 278 Kf42
Gbassa DY 272 Lb40
Gbassigbiri RCA 287 Md43
Gbatala LB 278 Kf42
Gbele Resource Reserve GH 279 Kj40
Gbéné DY 272 Lb40
Gbengué BF 279 Kj40
Gbentu WAL 278 Ke41
Gberia-Fotombu RG 278 Ke41
Gberia Fotombu WAL 278 Ke41
Gbéroubouay DY 272 Lb40
Gbesse LB 278 Ke42
Gbétitapéa CI 278 Kg42
Gbinti WAL 278 Kd41
Gbodonon CI 279 Kh41
Gboko WAN 280 Le42
Gboli LB 278 Kf43
Gbon CI 278 Kg41
Gbongan WAN 280 Lc42
Gbung GH 279 Kk41
Gbwado RDC 286 Ma44
Gcwihaba Caverns RB 299 Ma56
Gdańsk PL 116 Lt36
Gdov RUS 96 Mh32
Gdyel DZ 259 Kk28
Gdynia PL 116 Lt36
Geary USA (OK) 28 Fa28
Geba ETH 284 Mk41
Gebasawa WAN 272 Le39
Gebe RI 212 Re46
Gebeit SUD 277 Mj37
Gebeit Mine SUD 277 Mj36
Gebeledan CI 278 Kf41
Gebitudatuo VRC (QHI) 169 Pg26
Gebiz TR 131 Ml53
Gebre Guracha ETH 284 Mk41
Gebze TR 130 Mk50
Gecha ETH 283 Mh42
Gedaref SUD 276 Mh39
Gedi EAK 293 Mk47
Gediksaray TR 131 Mq50
Gedi National Monument EAK 293 Na47
Gediz TR 130 Mk51
Gedlegube ETH 285 Nc42
Gedo ETH 284 Mj41
Gedong VRC (GZH) 178 Qe32
Gedonghaji RI 207 Qc48
Gedongratu RI 207 Qc48
Gedong Songo Temple RI 210 Qf49
Gedongsurian RI 207 Qc48
Gedser DK 94 Lm36
Geel B 103 Lf39
Geelong AUS (VIC) 237 Sc65
Geelvink Channel AUS 228 Qg60
Geesaley SP 285 Nf40
Geeste D 112 Lh38
Geesthacht D 113 Ll37
Gefell D 113 Lm40
Gegentala Caoyuan VRC 175 Qf25
Geghard ARM 152 Nc25
Gê'gyai VRC (TIB) 170 Pa29
Geidam WAN 273 Lf39
Geifi SUD 283 Mf39
Geikie Gorge N.P. AUS 222 Rc55
Geikie Island CDN 25 Ff20
Geikie River CDN 19 Eh17
Geilenkirchen D 112 Lg40
Geilo N 92 Lj30
Geiranger N 92 Lh28
Geirangerfjorden N 92 Lg28
Geiro EAT 293 Mj49
Geiselhöring D 115 Ln42
Geisenfeld D 115 Lm42
Géiser el Tatio RCH 72 Gf57
Geisingen D 114 Lj43
Geislingen D 114 Lk42
Geita EAT 292 Mg47
Geithus N 92 Lk31
Geju VRC (YUN) 195 Qb34
Gekdepe TM 153 Nj26
Gekehn LB 278 Kg43
Gel SUD 283 Me42
Gel SUD 283 Mf43
Gela I 122 Lp53
Geladaindong VRC 171 Pf29
Geladi ETH 285 Nd42
Gelai EAT 290 Mj47
Gelai Bomba EAT 293 Mj47
Gelam RI 206 Qb45
Gelam RI 208 Qf47
Gelangchang VRC (CGQ) 177 Qd30
Gelati Monastery GE 152 Nb24
Geldern D 112 Lg39
Geldrop NL 112 Lf39
Gele RDC 286 Lk43
Geleen NL 112 Lf40
Gelembe TR 130 Mj51
Gelemso ETH 284 Na41
Gelendost TR 131 Mm52
Gelendžik RUS 135 Mk23
Gelgaudiškis LT 97 Mc35
Gelibolu TR 130 Mg50
Gelibolu Yarımadası Milli Parkı TR 130 Mg50
Gelila ETH 284 Mj41
Gelinggang RI 208 Qg47
Gelingüllü Barajı TR 131 Mq51
Gellab SUD 282 Mc41
Gellinsoor SP 285 Nd42
Gelnhausen D 114 Lk40
Gelsenkirchen D 112 Lh39
Gelting D 113 Lk36
Gelu RO 124 Mb44
Geluketapang RI 198 Ph44
Gelumbang RI 207 Qc47
Gemamudo GNB 269 Kc39
Gembi ETH 283 Mh41
Gembloux-sur-Orneau B 103 Le40
Gembogl PNG 243 Sc48
Gembu WAN 281 Lf42
Geme RI 205 Rd43
Gemena RDC 286 Lk44
Gemeri Hayk ETH 284 Na40
Gemi ETH 283 Mh41
Gemini South Observatory RCH 76 Ge61
Gemla S 95 Lp34
Gemlik TR 130 Mk50
Gemlik Körfezi TR 130 Mj50
Gemmeiza SUD 276 Mh38
Gemmeiza SUD 283 Me42
Gemmeiza SUD 287 Mf43
Gemmell USA (MN) 27 Fc22
Gemona del Friuli I 121 Lo44
Gemsa ET 263 Mg32
Gemsbok N.P. RB 299 Ma58
Gemsbokvlakte SA 299 Mc58
Gemünden D 112 Lj40
Gemünden D 114 Lk40
Genale Wenz ETH 284 Mk42
Gençay F 104 La44
Gencek TR 131 Mm53
Gendarme Barreto RA (SC) 82 Ge71
General Acha RA (LP) 80 Gh64
General Alvear RA (MD) 76 Gg63
General Alvear RA (BA) 81 Gk64
General Arenales RA (BA) 77 Gk63
General Ballivián RA (SA) 73 Gj57
General Belgrano RA (BA) 77 Ha63
General Bravo MEX (NL) 39 Fa33
General Cabrera RA (CD) 76 Gj62
General Camacho BOL 72 Gf54
General Carneiro BR (PR) 78 He59
General Cepeda MEX (COH) 39 Ek33
General Coffee S.P. USA 35 Fj30
General Conesa RA (RN) 81 Gh66
General Conesa RA (BA) 81 Hb64
General Daniel Cerri RA (BA) 81 Gj65
General Elizardo Aquino PY 73 Hb58
General Enrique Martínez ROU 77 Hd62
General Enrique Mosconi RA (FO) 73 Gj57
General Francisco Murguía (Nieves) MEX (ZCT) 39 Ej33
General Galarza RA (ER) 77 Ha62
General Güemes RA (SA) 73 Gh58
General Guido RA (BA) 81 Hb64
General José de San Martín RA (CH) 77 Ha59
General Juan Madariaga RA (BA) 81 Hb64
General Juan N. Álvarez, P.N. MEX 40 Fa37
General La Madrid RA (BA) 81 Gk64
General Lavalle RA (BA) 81 Hb64
General Levalle RA (CD) 76 Gj63
General Lucio Victorio Mansilla RA (FO) 77 Ha59
General Luna RP 205 Rd41
General Mansilla RA (BA) 77 Hb63
General M. Belgrano, Cerro RA 76 Gg60
General Mosconi RA (SA) 73 Gj57
General O'Brien RA (BA) 77 Gk63
General Pico RA (LP) 76 Gj63
General Pinedo RA (CH) 77 Gk59
General Pinto RA (BA) 77 Gk63
General Roca RA (RN) 80 Gg65
General Salgado BR (SP) 74 He56
General Sampaio BR (CE) 65 Ja48
General San Martín RA (BA) 77 Ha63
General San Martín RA (LP) 81 Gj64
General Santos RP 205 Rc42
Generalski Stol HR 121 Lq45
General Terán MEX (NL) 39 Fa33
General Toševo BG 127 Mj47
General Viamonte RA (BA) 77 Gk63
General Villegas RA (BA) 77 Gj63
Geneseo USA (NY) 33 Gb24
Geneva CH 114 Lg44
Geneva USA (NE) 26 Fb25
Geneva USA (NY) 33 Gb24
Geneva USA (GA) 35 Fh29
Geneva USA (AL) 35 Fh30
Genève CH 114 Lg44
Gengenbach D 114 Lj42
Gengis Khan Mausoleum VRC 175 Qe26
Gengis Khan Monument MNG 173 Qf21
Gengma Daizu VRC (YUN) 195 Pk34
Gengwa RDC 289 Mb47
Gen He VRC 173 Qk20
Genk B 103 Lf40
Genkainada J 185 Rf29
Genlis F 103 Lf43
Gennep NL 112 Lg39
Genoa AUS (VIC) 237 Se64
Genoa I 120 Lj46
Genoa USA (NE) 27 Fb25
Genohe J 183 Sa25
Génolhac F 105 Ld46
Génova I 120 Lj46
Gent B 103 Ld39
Genteng RI 211 Qh50
Genthin D 113 Ln38
Genting RI 198 Pk44
Genting Highlands Hill Resort MAL 199 Qa44
Gentio do Ouro BR (BA) 71 Hj51
Genyem RI 213 Sa47
Genzano di Lucánia I 123 Lr50
Geograph Channel AUS 224 Qg58
Geographe Bay AUS 228 Qh62
Geographical Center of the 48 Contiguous States USA 26 Fa26
Geographic Center of North America USA (ND) 24 Fa21
Geographic Center of U.S. USA 26 Ej23
Geological Exposure SA 300 Mf58
George SA 302 Mb63
George USA (WA) 18 Ea22
George VI Ice Shelf 312 Gc33
George Enescu RO 125 Mg42
George Gill Range AUS 226 Rf58
George Island GB 83 Ha72
George P. Cossar S.P. USA 34 Ff28
George Reservoir USA 35 Fh30
George River USA 15 Cb14
George R. Parks Highway USA 15 Ce14
Georges Bank 13 Gc10
George Sound AUS 239 Td68
Georgetown AUS (QLD) 232 Sb55
Georgetown AUS (TAS) 236 Sd66
George Town BS 37 Gc34
Georgetown GB 44 Fk36
Georgetown GUY 58 Ha42
Georgetown MAL 198 Qa43
Georgetown USA (TX) 28 Fb30
Georgetown USA (LA) 29 Fe30
Georgetown USA (DE) 33 Gc26
Georgetown USA (KY) 35 Fh26
Georgetown USA (GA) 35 Fh30
Georgetown USA (SC) 35 Ga29
Georgetown WAG 269 Kc39
Georgetown WV 47 Gk39
George V Land 313 Sb33
George Washington Birthplace Nat. Mon. USA 33 Gb26
George West USA (TX) 39 Fa31
Georgia GE 145 Nb24
Georgia USA 13 Fd12
Georgia Basin 55 Ja29
Georgiana USA (AL) 34 Fg30
Georgian Bay CDN 32 Fk23
Georgian Bay Islands N.P. CDN 33 Ga23
Georgievsk RUS 152 Nb23
Georgina Downs AUS (NT) 227 Rj56
Georgina River AUS 232 Rk57
Georg von Neumayer ANT (D) 312 Kc33
Gera D 113 Ll40
Gera D 113 Ln40
Geraardsbergen B 103 Ld40
Gerace I 123 Lr52
Gerakarou GR 126 Md50
Geráki GR 128 Mc53
Gerakini GR 126 Md50
Geraldine NZ 239 Tf68
Geraldine USA (MT) 21 Ee22
Geraldo Toco Preto, T.I. BR 64 Hh48
Geraldton AUS (WA) 228 Qh60
Geraldton CDN (ON) 25 Fg21
Gerania Óri GR 128 Md52
Geranium AUS (SA) 236 Sa63
Gérardmer F 103 Lg42
Gerash IR 156 Nh32
Gerdau SA 303 Md59
Gerdine, Mount USA 15 Cd15
Gerede TR 131 Mn50
Gerena E 108 Ko47
Gereshk AFG 160 Oc30
Gérgal E 109 Ks47
Gergi AFG 160 Ob29
Gergova RO 125 Mk45
Gerickes SA 302 Mb63
Gerihun WAL 278 Ke42
Gering USA (NE) 26 Ej25
Geriş TR 131 Mm54
Gerisa SP 285 Nb40
Gerlach USA (NV) 20 Ea25
Gerlachovský štít SK 119 Ma41
Germa LAR 267 Lg32
Germakolo RI 212 Rg46
German Bight D 112 Lh36
German Creek AUS (QLD) 233 Se57
Germania RA (BA) 77 Gj63
Germansen Landing CDN (BC) 17 Dh18
Germany 87 La04
Germencik TR 129 Mh53
Germering D 115 Lm42
Germersheim D 114 Lj41
Germiston SA 303 Me59
Gernika E 107 Ks53
Gernsheim D 114 Lj41
Gero J 183 Rj28
Gerogievka KZ 166 Pa21
Gerolstein D 112 Lg40
Gerolzhofen D 114 Ll41
Gerona RP 202 Ra38
Gers F 104 La46
Gersfeld D 114 Lk40
Gersthofen D 115 Ll42
Gêrzê VRC (TIB) 170 Pc29
Gesäuse, N.P. A 115 Lp43
Gescher D 112 Lh39
Gesunda S 93 Lp30
Gèsves B 103 Lf40
Geta FIN 93 Lu30
Getafe E 109 Kr50
Geti RDC 287 Mf45
Getinge S 94 Ln34
Gettorf D 113 Lk36
Getty Center USA (CA) 22 Ea28
Gettysburg USA (SD) 26 Fa23
Gettysburg USA (PA) 33 Gb26
Gettysburg N.M.P. USA 33 Gb26
Getúlio Vargas BR (RS) 78 Hd59
Getxo E 107 Kr53
Getz Ice Shelf 312 Dd33
Geureudong, Mount RI 198 Pj43
Gevaş TR 145 Nb26
Gevgelija MK 126 Mc49
Gevrai IND (MHT) 190 Oh36
Gewandhaus in Zwickau D 113 Ln40
Gewane ETH 284 Na40
Gewane Wildlife Reserve ETH 284 Na40
Gex F 105 Lg44
Geyik Dağları TR 144 Mf27
Geyikli TR 130 Mg51
Geyve TR 130 Mf50
Gezhou Ba VRC 177 Qf30

osséré Vokre CAM 281 Lg41
osston USA (LA) 29 Fd29
osszúhetény H 118 Lt44
osszúpereszteg H 118 Ls43
ostalric E 110 Lc49
ostens F 104 Ku46
osur IND (TNU) 193 Oj40
ot THA 196 Pk36
otaka-dake J 183 Rj27
ot... VRC (XUZ) 168 Ok27
otan He VRC 168 Pa26
otazel SA 302 Mb59
ôtel-Dieu F 103 Le43
otham Inlet USA 15 Bk12
oti RI 212 Rf47
oticy RUS 96 Mj33
oting S 90 Lj13
o Tri An VN 197 Qd40
ot Springs USA 22 Ed29
ot Springs USA (SD) 26 Ej24
ot Springs USA (AR) 29 Fd28
ot Springs USA (NC) 35 Fj28
ot Springs ZW 300 Mg55
ot Springs N.P. USA 29 Fd28
ot Sulphur Springs SA
303 Md61
ot Sulphur Springs USA (CO)
21 Eg25
ottentot Bay NAM 302 Lh59
ottentotsbaai NAM 298 Lh59
ottentots-Holland Nature
Reserve SA 302 Lk63
ottentotskloof SA 302 Lk62
ouaïlou F 246 Tc56
ouat F 102 Ks43
ouchang VRC (GZH) 178 Qd33
oudan F 103 Lb42
oueillès F 104 La46
oueïriye RIM 270 Kg37
ouffalize B 103 Lf40
oughton USA (SD) 26 Fa23
oughton USA (MI) 32 Ff22
ouhai VRC (GDG) 178 Qf35
ouhu VRC (GDG) 178 Qf35
oulton USA (ME) 30 Gg22
ouma TO 248 Bc56
ouma USA (LA) 29 Fe31
ouma VRC (SAX) 177 Qf28
oumt Souk TN 260 Lf29
oundé BF 279 Kj40
ouqiu VRC (AHU) 184 Qj29
ourtin F 104 Kt45
ourtin-Plage F 104 Kt45
ouse of Schmelen NAM
302 Lj59
ouston CDN (BC) 18 Dg18
ouston USA (AK) 15 Cf15
ouston USA (TX) 29 Fc31
ouston USA (MO) 29 Fe27
ouston USA (MS) 29 Ff29
ouston Pt. CDN 25 Fk19
outbaai SA 302 Lk63
out Bay SA 302 Lk63
outman Abrolhos AUS 228
Qg60
outon GB 99 Kr32
outskari FIN 93 Mb30
outskär FIN 96 Mb30
ouxia VRC (XUZ) 167 Pd24
ov DK 94 Ll35
ova S 93 Lp32
ovåg N 92 Lj32
ovärken S 93 Lo28
ovden N 92 Le29
ovden N 92 Lh31
ove GB 101 Ku40
overla UA 119 Me42
ovoro SOL 245 Sj50
ovsan AZ 152 Nf25
ovsta S 93 Lq31
ovu-Aksy RUS (TUV) 167 Pg20
owakil ER 277 Na39
owakil Bay ER 277 Na39
oward AUS (QLD) 235 Sg58
oward USA (SD) 26 Fb23
owden GB 101 Ku37
owe, Mount 312 Ca36
owes USA (SD) 26 Ej23
owick SA 303 Mf60
owick Group AUS 231 Sc53
owland Islands USA 241 Ub18
owli IND (ASM) 194 Pf32
owship, Mount AUS 223 Rg52
owth IRL 100 Ko37
oxie USA (KS) 26 Ek26
öxter D 112 Lk39
oxtolgay VRC (XUZ) 167 Pd22
oxud VRC (XUZ) 169 Pd24
oya D 112 Lk38
oyanger N 92 Lg29
oyerswerda D 113 Lp39
oylandet N 90 Lg13
oyono-sen J 183 Rh28
oyos E 108 Ko50
oza BY 97 Md37
ozoviótissa GR 129 Mf54
pakant MYA 195 Pk34
pangpai MYA 195 Pk34
pawngtut MYA 195 Pj33
pungan Pass IND/MYA 195
Pj32
radčany CZ 118 Lp40
radec Králové CZ 118 Lq40
radec nad Moravicí CZ 118
Ls41
rádek nad Nisou CZ 118 Lp40
radyz'k UA 134 Mg21
ranice CZ 118 Ln40
ranice CZ 118 Ls41
ranične SK 119 Ma41
rasnica BIH 121 Lt47
rastelnica HR 121 Lr45
rastnik SLO 121 Lq44
razdan ARM 152 Nc25
rebet Akademika Obruceva
RUS 172 Pj20
rebet At-Baši KS 159 Oh25
rebet Bijskaja Griva RUS
167 Pd19
rebet Cagan-Hurtej RUS
173 Qf20
rebet Čerskogo RUS 173 Qg20
rebet Črmana MNG 173 Qg21
rebet Hamar-Daban RUS 172
Qb20
rebet Homi RUS 181 Rk20
rebet Horumnug Tajga RUS
172 Pj20
rebet Iolgo RUS 167 Pd20
rebet Kukulbej RUS 173 Qj20
rebet Malyj Hamar-Daban RUS
172 Qc20
rebet Muzkol TJ 159 Og26
rebet Naryntau KS 159 Oj25
rebet Pekulnej RUS 141 Td05
rebet Sajljuge MNG/RUS
167 Pe21
rebet Sengilan RUS 172 Pj20
rebet Sinij RUS 180 Rg23
rebet Stanovik MNG 173 Qg21
hrebet Suntar-Hajata RUS
141 Rd06
Hrebet Tukuringra RUS 141
Ra08
hrebet Turana RUS 141 Rc08
hrebet Ujukskij RUS 167 Pg20
hrebet Ulahan-Bom RUS 141
Rd06
hrebet Ulan-Burgasy RUS 172
Qe19
hrebet Vostočnnyj Sinij RUS
180 Rg24
Hrissoúpoli GR 127 Me50
Hristiáni GR 128 Mb53
Hrodna BY 97 Md37
Hron SK 119 Lu42
Hronský Beňadik SK 118 Lt42
Hrubieszów PL 117 Md40
Hrušovský Hrad SK 118 Lt42
Hrušuvacha UA 135 Mj21
Hrvatska Dubica HR 121 Lr45
Hrvatska Kostajnica HR 121
Lr45
Hsenwi MYA 195 Pk34
Hsi-hseng MYA 195 Pj35
Hsinchu RC 179 Ra33
Hsinying RC 179 Ra34
Hsipaw MYA 195 Pj34
Hsuen Shan RC 179 Ra33
Hti lin MYA 194 Ph35
Hua'an VRC (FJN) 179 Qj33
Huab NAM 298 Lh56
Huabu VRC (ZJG) 184 Qk31
Huacachina PE 66 Gc53
Huacaña PE 66 Gc53
Huacaya BOL 73 Gj56
Huacaybamba PE 66 Gb50
Huachi VRC (GSU) 174 Qd27
Huacho PE 66 Gb51
Huachón PE 66 Gc51
Huachuan VRC (HLG) 180 Rf22
Huacrachuco PE 66 Gb50
Huacullani PE 72 Gf54
Huade VRC (NMZ) 175 Qg25
Huadian VRC (JLN) 182 Rd24
Huagu VRC (SCH) 176 Qc31
Huahaizi VRC (QHI) 169 Ph26
Hua Hin THA 196 Pk39
Huahine Iti F 249 Ce54
Huahine Nui F 249 Ce54
Huahua = Wawa NIC 42 Fh38
Huai'an VRC (HBI) 175 Qh25
Huai'an VRC (JGS) 184 Qk29
Huaibei VRC (AHU) 184 Qj29
Huaibin VRC (HNN) 184 Qh29
Huaidian VRC (HNN) 184 Qh29
Huai Hat N.P. THA 197 Qc37
Huai He VRC 184 Qj29
Huai Hom Karen Village THA
196 Pj36
Huaihua VRC (HUN) 178 Qf32
Huaiji VRC (GDG) 178 Qg34
Huailai VRC (HBI) 175 Qh25
Huai Nam Dang N.P. THA 196
Pk36
Huainan VRC (AHU) 184 Qj29
Huairen VRC (SAX) 175 Qg26
Huairou VRC (BJG) 175 Qj25
Huaiyang VRC (HNN) 184 Qh29
Huaiyin VRC (JGS) 184 Qk29
Huai Yot THA 198 Pk42
Huaiyuan VRC (GZG) 178 Qe33
Huaiyuan VRC (AHU) 184 Qj29
Huaiyu Shan VRC 184 Qj31
Huajapan de León MEX (OAX)
40 Fb37
Huajialing VRC (GSU) 177 Qc28
Hualanzi VRC (LNG) 182 Rc25
Huajimic MEX (NYT) 39 Eh35
Hualañé RCH 76 Ge63
Hualapai Ind. Res. USA 22 Ed28
Hualapai Mt. Park USA 22 Ed28
Hualianting Shuiku VRC 184
Qj30
Hualien RC 179 Ra33
Huallaga PE 60 Gc48
Huallanca PE 66 Gb50
Hualong VRC (QHI) 174 Qb27
Hualqui RCH 80 Gd64
Huamachuco PE 66 Ga49
Huamali PE 66 Gc51
Huambo ANG 294 Lh52
Huambo PE 67 Gd53
Huamboya EC 60 Ga46
Huampami PE 60 Ga48
Huams NAM 298 Lj58
Huamuxtitlán MEX (GUR) 40
Fa37
Huañamarca PE 72 Gd54
Huanan VRC (HLG) 180 Rf22
Huancabamba PE 60 Ga48
Huancabamba PE 60 Ga48
Huancan PE 66 Gc52
Huancane PE 67 Gf53
Huancano PE 66 Gc52
Huancapallac PE 66 Gb50
Huanca Sancos PE 66 Gc52
Huancavelica PE 66 Gc52
Huancayo PE 66 Gc52
Huanchaca, Cerro BOL 72 Gg56
Huancilla RA (CD) 76 Gj62
Huandacareo MEX (MHC) 40
Ek36
Huangchuan VRC (HNN) 184
Qh29
Huangdi Ling VRC 177 Qe28
Huanggang VRC (HUB) 184
Qh30
Huanggangliang VRC 175 Qj24
Huanggang Shan VRC 184 Qj32
Huangguoshu Falls VRC 178
Qc33
Huang He VRC 165 Qc11
Huanghe Kou VRC 175 Qk27
Huang He Lou VRC 184 Qh30
Huanghua VRC (HBI) 175 Qj26
Huangjianyu VRC 179 Qj33
Huangling VRC (SAA) 177 Qe28
Huang Ling Miao VRC 177 Qf30
Huanglong VRC (SAA) 177
Qe28
Huanglong Si VRC 176 Qb29
Huanglong Z.B. VRC 176
Qb29
Huangmei VRC (HUB) 184 Qh30
Huangnihe VRC (JLN) 182 Rd24
Huangpi VRC (HUB) 184 Qh30
Huangping VRC (GZH) 178
Qd32
Huangqiao VRC (JGS) 184 Ra29
Huangqi Hai VRC 175 Qg25
Huangsha VRC (FJN) 184 Qk32
Huangshan VRC 184 Qj30
Huangshan VRC (AHU) 184
Qk31
Huangshi VRC (HUB) 184 Qh30
Huang Shui VRC 174 Qb27
Huangyaguan VRC 175 Qj25
Huangyan VRC (ZJG) 184 Ra31
Huangyinaoyang VRC (HUN)
178 Qf32
Huangyuan VRC (QHI) 174 Qa27
Huangzhong VRC (QHI) 174
Qa27
Huangzhu VRC (HAN) 178 Qf36
Huanjiang VRC (GZG) 178 Qe33
Huanquelén RA (BA) 81 Gk64
Huanqueros RA (SF) 77 Gk61
Huanren VRC (LNG) 182 Rc25
Huanta PE 66 Gc52
Huant Hatun Külliyesi TR 131
Mq52
Huánuco PE 66 Gb50
Huánuco Viejo PE 66 Gb50
Huanuni BOL 72 Gg55
Huan Xian VRC (GSU) 174 Qd27
Huanza PE 66 Gb51
Huaping Yü RC 179 Ra33
Huaping Z.B. VRC 178 Qe33
Huaqiao VRC (SCH) 177 Qd30
Huaquillas EC 60 Fk47
Huara RCH 72 Gf56
Huaral PE 66 Gb51
Huarás PE 66 Gb50
Huari PE 66 Gb50
Huari PE 66 Gb52
Huari Belén BOL 72 Gf54
Huarichic MEX (DGO) 39 Ej33
Huarina BOL 72 Gf54
Huarmey PE 66 Ga51
Huarong VRC (HUN) 177 Qg31
Huásabas MEX (SO) 23 Ef31
Huasaga EC 60 Gb47
Huasaga PE 60 Gb47
Hua Sai THA 198 Qa42
Huascarán, P.N. PE 66 Gb50
Huasco RCH 76 Ge60
Huasco RCH 76 Ge60
Huashan VRC 177 Qf28
Huashaoying VRC 178 Qd34
Huashaoying VRC (HBI) 175
Qh25
Huashilou VRC 182 Ra27
Huashixia VRC (QHI) 176 Pk28
Huatabampo MEX (SO) 38 Ef32
Huatugou VRC (QHI) 169 Pf26
Huatusco MEX (VC) 40 Fb36
Huauchi nango MEX (HDG)
40 Fa35
Huaura PE 66 Gb51
Huautla MEX (OAX) 40 Fb36
Hua Xian VRC (GDG) 179 Qg34
Hua Xian VRC (HNN) 184 Qh28
Huayacocotla MEX (VC) 40 Fa35
Huayin VRC (SAA) 177 Qf28
Huaying VRC (SCH) 177 Qd30
Huayllay PE 66 Gb51
Huayna Potosi, Nevado BOL
67 Gf54
Huaytará PE 66 Gc52
Huaytiquina, Port.de RA/RCH
72 Gg57
Huayuan VRC (HUN) 177 Qe31
Huay Xai LAO 195 Qa35
Huazhou VRC (GDG) 178 Qf35
Huazi VRC (LNG) 182 Rb25
Hubbard USA (TX) 29 Fb30
Hubbard, Mount CDN 17 Da15
Hubbards CDN (NS) 31 Gh23
Hubbell Trading Post N.H.S.
USA 23 Ef28
Hub Chauki PK 162 Od33
Hubei VRC 165 Qc12
Hubert USA (NC) 35 Gb28
Hubli IND (KTK) 190 Oh38
Hubynycha UA 135 Mh21
Hucanggou Reservoir VRC
180 Rb23
Huchacalla BOL 72 Gf55
Huchang DVRK 182 Rd25
Hucknall GB 101 Kt37
Hudan RUS 173 Qe20
Hudat ETH 284 Mk43
Huddersfield GB 101 Kt37
Hude D 112 Lj37
Huder VRC (NMZ) 173 Ra20
Hudiksvall S 93 Ls29
Hudiksvallfjärden S 93 Ls29
Hudson CDN (ON) 24 Fd20
Hudson, Cerro RCH 82 Gd69
Hudson USA (WI) 27 Fd23
Hudson USA (NY) 33 Gd24
Hudson Bay CDN 11 Gb06
Hudson Bay CDN (SK) 24 Ej19
Hudson Canyon 33 Gd26
Hudson Falls USA (NY) 33 Gd24
Hudson Mountains 312 Fa33
Hudson's Hope CDN (BC) 17
Dk17
Hudson Strait CDN 11 Fc06
Hudu He VRC 177 Qg31
Hudwin Lake CDN 24 Fc19
Hue VN 197 Qd37
Huedin RO 124 Md44
Huehuetenango GCA 41 Fe38
Hueicolla RCH 80 Gd66
Huejúcar MEX (JLC) 39 Ej34
Huejuquilla El Alto MEX (JLC)
39 Ej34
Huejutla de Reyes MEX (HDG)
40 Fa35
Huelgoat F 102 Kr42
Huelma E 109 Kr47
Huelva E 108 Ko47
Huéneja E 109 Ks47
Huenque PE 72 Gf54
Huepac MEX (SO) 23 Ee31
Huépil RCH 80 Ge64
Huequi, Volcán RCH 80 Gd67
Huércal-Overa E 109 Kt47
Huerquehue, P.N. RCH 80 Ge65
Huertecillas MEX (SLP) 39 Ek33
Huesca E 107 Ku52
Huéscar E 109 Ks47
Huetamo de Nuñez MEX (MHC)
40 Ek36
Huete E 109 Ks50
Huftarøy N 92 Lf30
Huger USA (SC) 35 Ga29
Hughenden AUS (QLD) 232
Sc56
Hughes AUS (SA) 229 Re61
Hughes RA (SF) 77 Gk62
Hughes USA (AK) 15 Cc12
Hugh River AUS 226 Rg58
Hugh White S.P. USA 34 Ff29
Hugo USA (OK) 29 Fc29
Hugoton USA (KS) 28 Ek27
Huguochang VRC (SCH) 177
Qc31
Hui'an VRC (FJN) 179 Qk33
Hui'anpu VRC (NHZ) 174 Qd27
Huiarau Range NZ 238 Tj65
Huib Hochplato NAM 302 Lj59
Huichang VRC (JGX) 179 Qh33
Huichapan MEX (HDG) 40 Fa35
Huicheng VRC (AHU) 184 Qk31
Huichon DVRK 182 Rd25
Huichuan VRC (GSU) 176 Qb28
Huidong VRC (GDG) 179 Qh34
Huidong VRC (SCH) 195 Qb32
Hui He VRC 173 Qk21
Huila, Nevado del CO 60 Gc44
Huilai VRC (GDG) 179 Qj34
Huila Plateau ANG 294 Lh53
Huili VRC (SCH) 195 Qb32
Huillapima RA (CA) 76 Gh60
Huilong VRC (HUN) 178 Qf32
Huimanguillo MEX (TB) 41 Fd37
Huimbayoc PE 66 Gb49
Huimilpan MEX (QRT) 40 Ek35
Huimin VRC (SDG) 175 Qj27
Huinan VRC (JLN) 182 Rd24
Huinca Renancó RA (CD) 76
Gh63
Huining VRC (GSU) 177 Qc28
Huisachal MEX (COH) 39 Ek32
Huishui VRC (GZH) 178 Qd32
Huiten Nur VRC 171 Pg28
Huitong VRC (HUN) 178 Qe32
Huitoyacu PE 60 Gb47
Huittinen FIN 96 Mc29
Huitzila MEX (ZCT) 40 Ej35
Hui Wangmu VRC 169 Pg24
Hui Xian VRC (GSU) 177 Qd29
Huixtla MEX (CHP) 41 Fd38
Huiyang VRC (GDG) 179 Qh34
Huize VRC (YUN) 195 Qb32
Huizhou VRC (GDG) 179 Qh34
Huji VRC (HUB) 177 Qg30
Hujie VRC (YUN) 195 Qa33
Hukeri IND (KTK) 190 Oh37
Hukli IND (MPH) 191 Ok34
Hukou VRC (JGX) 184 Qj31
Hukou Pubu VRC 177 Qf28
Hukuntsi RB 289 Ma57
Hula PNG 243 Sd51
Hul'ajpole UA 135 Mj22
Hulaku RI 212 Re47
Hulan VRC (HLG) 180 Rd23
Hulan Ergi VRC (HLG) 180 Rb22
Hulan He VRC 180 Rd22
Hulayfah KSA 148 Na32
Hulett USA (WY) 21 Eh23
Hulin VRC (HLG) 180 Rg23
Huliyar IND (KTK) 193 Oj40
Hull CDN (QC) 33 Gc23
Hull = Orona KIR 241 Ub19
Hully Point SA 303 Mg59
Hulst NL 112 Ld39
Hultsfred S 95 Lq33
Hultsfredfestivalen S 95 Lq33
Hulubești RO 125 Mf46
Hulu He VRC 177 Qe28
Hulukou VRC (SCH) 195 Qb32
Hulun Buir Shadi VRC 173 Qk21
Hulun Nur VRC 173 Qj21
Huma IND (ORS) 191 Pb35
Huma VRC (HLG) 180 Rd20
Humacao USA (PR) 47 Gh36
Humahuaca RA (PJ) 72 Gh57
Humaitá BOL 67 Gg51
Humaitá BR (AM) 62 Gj49
Humaitá PY 77 Ha59
Humanes E 109 Kr50
Humansdorp SA 303 Mc63
Humantla MEX (TXL) 40 Fb36
Humariza MEX (CHH) 38 Eg32
Humay PE 66 Gc52
Humaya MEX 38 Eg33
Humayun's Tomb IND 189
Oj31
Humbe ANG 294 Lh54
Humber GB 101 Ku37
Humberstone RCH 72 Gf56
Humberto de Campos BR (MA)
64 Hj47
Humberto I RA (SF) 77 Gk61
Humbert River AUS (NT) 223
Rf54
Humboldt USA (NV) 20 Ea25
Humboldt USA (IA) 27 Fc24
Humboldt Gletscher DK 11
Gd03
Humboldt Redwoods State Park
USA 20 Dj25
Humbolt CDN (SK) 19 Eh19
Humeburn AUS (QLD) 235 Sc59
Humenné SK 119 Mb42
Humgarh IND (WBG) 194 Pd34
Humla NEP 170 Pa30
Humlum D 112 Lh38
Humpata ANG 294 Lg53
Humphrey USA (ID) 21 Ed23
Humpolec CZ 118 Lq41
Humppila FIN 96 Mb30
Humptulips USA (WA) 18 Dj22
Hün LAR 261 Lh31
Húnaflói IS 90 Js13
Hunan VRC 165 Qc13
Hunasagi IND (KTK) 190 Oj37
Hunchun VRC (JLN) 182 Rf24
Hundertwasser-Bad A 115 Lr43
Hundested DK 94 Lm35
Hundorp N 92 Lk29
Hundred Islands N.R.A. RP
202 Qk37
Hunedoara RO 124 Mc45
Hünfeld D 112 Lk40
Hunga Ha'apai Island TO 248
Bc56
Hunga Island TO 248 Bc55
Hungaroring H 119 Lu43
Hungary H 119 Lt43
Hungen D 112 Lj40
Hungerford AUS (QLD) 234
Sc60
Hungnam DVRK 182 Rd26
Hungry Horse Reservoir USA
19 Ed21
Hungund IND (KTK) 190 Oj37
Hung Yen VN 178 Qd35
Huni Valley GH 279 Kk43
Hunjiang VRC (JLN) 182 Rd25
Hunkuvi WAN 272 Ld40
Hunnebostrand S 92 Lm32
Hunsberge NAM 302 Lj59
Hunsrück D 114 Lh41
Hunstanton GB 101 La38
Hunstein Range PNG 243 Sb48
Hunsur IND (KTK) 192 Oj40
Hunte D 112 Lj38
Hunter Island AUS 236 Sc66
Hunter Island CDN 18 Df20
Hunter Island Ridge 218 Tb11
Hunter River AUS 237 Sf62
Hunters USA (WA) 18 Ea21
Hunter Valley AUS 237 Sf62
Huntingburg USA (IN) 34 Fg26
Huntingdon GB 101 Ku38
Huntingdon USA (TN) 29 Ff28
Huntingdon USA (PA) 33 Ga25
Huntington USA (OR) 20 Eb23
Huntington USA (UT) 21 Ee26
Huntington USA (IN) 32 Fh25
Huntington USA (WV) 35 Fj26
Huntington Beach USA (CA)
22 Eb29
Huntington Beach S.P. USA
35 Ga29
Huntly GB 99 Ks33
Huntly NZ 238 Th64
Hunto-Chac MEX (YT) 41 Ff36
Huntsville CDN (ON) 33 Ga23
Huntsville USA (TX) 29 Fc30
Huntsville USA (AR) 29 Fd27
Huntsville USA (AL) 34 Fg28
Huntsville USA (TN) 35 Fh27
Hunucmá MEX (YT) 41 Ff35
Hunyuan VRC (SAX) 175 Qg26
Hunza PK 161 Oh27
Hunza Valley PK 161 Oh27
Huocheng VRC (XUZ) 166 Pa23
Huolingol VRC (NMZ) 173 Qk23
Huolin He MNG 173 Ra23
Huong Hoa VN 197 Qd37
Huong Khe VN 197 Qc36
Huong Pagoda VN 178 Qd35
Huong Son VN 197 Qc36
Huon Gulf PNG 243 Sd49
Huon Peninsula PNG 243 Sd49
Huonville AUS (TAS) 236 Sd67
Huoshan VRC (AHU) 184 Qj30
Huoshaoshan VRC 167 Pe23
Huoyan Shan VRC 169 Pe24
Huozhou VRC (SAX) 175 Qf27
Hur IR 157 Nk32
Hura IND (WBG) 194 Pd34
Huraymala KSA 149 Nd33
Hurbanovo SK 118 Lt43
Hurdal N 92 Lm30
Hurdiyo SP 285 Nf40
Hureidhen OM 151 Nh36
Hure Qi VRC (NMZ) 182 Ra24
Hurezani RO 124 Md46
Hurghada ET 263 Mg32
Huri Hills EAK 284 Mj44
Hurley USA (NM) 23 Ef29
Huron USA (SD) 26 Fa23
Huron USA (OH) 32 Fj25
Huronia Museum CDN 33 Ga23
Hurricane USA (AK) 15 Cf14
Hurricane USA (UT) 22 Ed27
Hurricane River Cave USA
29 Fd27
Hurshi IND (WBG) 194 Pe33
Hurso ETH 284 Na41
Hurstbridge AUS (VIC) 237
Sc64
Hurtado RCH 76 Ge61
Hurtado RCH 76 Ge61
Hurtigruta N 90 Lf13
Hurtigruta N 92 Le30
Hurtsboro USA (AL) 35 Fh29
Hurungwe Safari Area ZW 296
Me54
Hurunui River NZ 239 Tg67
Hurunxiang VRC (GZG) 178
Qd34
Hurup DK 94 Lj34
Hurzuf UA 135 Mh23
Husasău de Tinca RO 124 Mb44
Húsavík IS 90 Kb12
Husheib SUD 276 Mh39
Huși RO 125 Mj44
Husinec CZ 118 Lp41
Huskisson AUS (NSW) 237 Sf63
Huskvarna S 95 Lp33
Huslia USA (AK) 15 Cb13
Huslia River USA 15 Cb13
Husnes N 92 Lf31
Hussainabad IND (JKD) 191
Pc33
Hussar CDN (AB) 19 Ed20
Husum D 112 Lk36
Husum S 90 Lk14
Husun al Salasil YE 150 Ne37
Hutaimbaru RI 206 Pk45
Hutaraja RI 198 Pk44
Hutchinson SA 302 Mb61
Hutchinson USA (MN) 27 Fc23
Hutchinson USA (KS) 28 Fb27
Huth YE 150 Nb37
Hutiao VRC 195 Qa32
Hutjena PNG 244 Sh48
Hutou VRC (HLG) 180 Rg23
Hutovo Blato BIH 121 Ls47
Hutton, Mount AUS 235 Se58
Huttonsville USA (WV) 33 Fk26
Hutubi VRC (XUZ) 167 Pd23
Hutup NAM 298 Lj58
Huu RI 211 Qk50
Huu Beach RI 211 Qk50
Huvar IR 157 Oa32
Huvin Hippargi IND (KTK)
190 Oj37
Huwan VRC (HNN) 184 Qh30
Huxi Xincun VRC (NMZ) 174
Qa25
Huxley CDN (AB) 19 Ed20
Huxley, Mount NZ 239 Te68
Huxley, Mount USA 16 Ck15
Huy B 103 Lf40
Hüyük TR 131 Mm53
Huzhong Z.B. VRC 173 Rb20
Huzhu VRC (ZJG) 184 Ra30
Huzhu Tuzu Zizhixian VRC (QHI)
174 Qa27
Hužir RUS 172 Qd19
Huzurabad IND (APH) 191 Ok36
Hvaler N 92 Lm31
Hvalynsk RUS 133 Ne19
Hvammstangi IS 90 Jk13
Hvannadalshnúkur IS 90 Kb13
Hvar HR 121 Lr47
Hvar HR 121 Lr47
Hvastoviči RUS 132 Mh19
Hveragerði IS 90 Jk13
Hveravellir IS 90 Ka13
Hvide Sande DK 94 Lj35
Hvittingfoss N 92 Lk31
Hvolsvöllur IS 90 Jk14
Hvorostjanka RUS 133 Ne19
Hvstovo RUS 181 Sb22
Hwali ZW 300 Me56
Hwange ZW 297 Md55
Hwange N.P. ZW 299 Md55
Hwaseong Fortress ROK
182 Rd27
Hwasun Dolmen Site ROK
182 Rd28
Hwedza ZW 300 Mf55
Hweiziyeh SYR 147 Na27
Hyades, Cerro RCH 82 Gd69
Hyannis USA (NE) 26 Ek25
Hyannis USA (MA) 33 Ge25
Hydaburg USA (AK) 17 Dd18
Hyden AUS (WA) 228 Qk62
Hyden USA (KY) 35 Fj27
Hyde Park USA (VT) 33 Gd23
Hyder USA (AK) 17 De18
Hyderabad IND (APH) 191 Ok37
Hyderabad PK 162 Oe33
Hyères F 105 Lg47
Hyesan DVRK 182 Re25
Hyland Bay AUS 223 Re52
Hyland Plateau CDN 17 Df15
Hyland River CDN 17 Df15
Hyltebruk S 95 Lo34
Hyperittfossen N 91 Lj06
Hyrax Hill EAK 290 Mj46
Hysham USA (MT) 21 Eg22
Hyuga J 185 Rf29
Hyuga-nada J 185 Rf29
Hyvinkää FIN 96 Me30

I

Ía GR 129 Mf54
Iaciara BR (GO) 70 Hg53
Iaco PE 67 Gf51
Iaçu BR (BA) 71 Hk52
Iagain Island PNG 244 Sh48
Iaguaretê BR (AM) 61 Gf45
Iakora RM 306 Nd57
Ia Krang PoCo VN 197 Qd38
Ialomița RO 125 Mf46
Ialoveni MD 125 Mj44
Ialpug MD 125 Mj44
Iamara PNG 243 Sb50
Ianabinda RM 306 Nc57
Ianakafy RM 306 Nc57
Ianapera RM 306 Nc57
Ianca RO 125 Mh45
Iapim BR (AC) 66 Gd49
Iargara MD 125 Mj44
Iaripo BR (PA) 63 Hc45
Iași RO 125 Mh43
Iasmos GR 127 Mf49
Iauiari BR 61 Gf45
Iba RP 202 Qk38
Ibacari BR (BA) 71 Ja53
Ibadan WAN 280 Lb42
Ibague CO 56 Gc43
Ibaiti BR (PR) 74 He57
Ibalé AL 126 Lu48
Ibanda EAU 287 Mf46
Ibanda Game Reserve EAT
292 Mf46
Ibanga RDC 292 Md47
Ibar SCG 126 Ma48
Ibarantim BR (BA) 71 Ja53
Ibarej BOL 67 Gh53
Ibaretama BR (CE) 65 Ja48
Ibarra EC 60 Ga45
Ibarreta RA (FO) 73 Ha58
Ibatiba BR (ES) 75 Hk56
Ibb YE 150 Nc39
Ibba SUD 283 Me43
Ibba SUD 287 Me43
Ibbenbüren D 112 Lh38
Ibdeqqene RMM 271 La36
Ibeas de Juarros E 107 Kr52
Ibek TR 131 Mq50
Ibembo RDC 287 Mb44
Ibembo RDC 287 Mc44
Ibenga RCB 281 Lj44
Iberia PE 61 Gc48
Iberia PE 67 Gf51
Iberian Basin 88 Ka10
Ibertioga BR (MG) 75 Hj56
Ibeto WAN 272 Lc40
Ibi E 109 Ku48
Ibi WAN 280 Le41
Ibiá BR (MG) 75 Hg55
Ibiaí BR (MG) 75 Hh54
Ibiassucê BR (BA) 71 Hj53
Ibibobo BOL 73 Gj56
Ibicuí BR (BA) 71 Ja53
Ibicuí BR 77 Hc60
Ibicuy RA (ER) 77 Ha62
Ibimirim BR (PE) 71 Jb50
Ibina RDC 287 Me45
Ibindy RM 306 Nd56
Ibipeba BR (BA) 71 Hj51
Ibipetum BR (BA) 70 Hj51
Ibipira BR (MA) 64 Hh47
Ibipitanga BR (BA) 71 Hj52
Ibiporã BR (PR) 74 He57
Ibiporanga BR (SP) 74 Hf56
Ibiquera BR (BA) 71 Hk52
Ibiraba BR (BA) 70 Hj51
Ibiraci BR (MG) 74 Hg56
Ibirama BR (SC) 79 Hf59
Ibirama, T.I. BR 79 Hf59
Ibiranhém BR (BA) 75 Hk54
Ibirataia BR (BA) 71 Ja53
Ibirité BR (MG) 75 Hh56
Ibirubá BR (RS) 78 Hd60
Ibitiara BR (BA) 71 Hj52
Ibitinga BR (SP) 74 Hf56
Ibiza = Eivissa E 110 Lb51
Ibiza = Eivissa E 110 Lb52
Ibó BR (PE) 71 Ja50
Ibo MOC 297 Na52
Ibohamane RN 272 Lc38
Iboih Beach RI 198 Ph43
Iboko RDC 286 Lk46
Ibologelo EAT 292 Mg48
Ibonma RI 213 Rg47
Iboro WAN 280 Lb42
Ibotirama BR (BA) 70 Hj52
Ibra OM 157 Nk34
Ibra RI 212 Rg48
Ibrahimpatan IND (APH) 191
Ok37
Ibrahim Rauza IND 190 Oh37
Ibri OM 157 Nj34
Ibrice TR 130 Mg50
Ibrjaevo RUS 133 Ng18
Ibu RI 212 Rd45
Ibusuki J 185 Rf30
Içá BR 61 Gf47
Ica PE 66 Gc53
Ica PE 66 Gc53
Icabarú YV 58 Gk43
Icacos Point YV 58 Gj40
Içana BR 61 Gf45
Içana BR (AM) 61 Gg45
Icaño RA (CA) 76 Gh60
Icapuí BR (CE) 65 Jb48
Icaraí de Amontada BR
(CE) 65 Ja47
Icaraima BR (PR) 74 Hd57
Icatu BR (MA) 64 Hh47
Icatú, T.I. BR 74 He56
Ice Bay USA 16 Ck16
Ice Cape USA 10 Ca04
Ice Caves USA 20 Dk24
Icefield Ctr. CDN 19 Eb19
Içel TR 144 Mh27
Iceland IS 90 Ka12
Iceland IS 90 Jk13
Iceland Basin 88 Jd07
Iceland Faeroe Rise 88 Kb06
Icelandic Plateau 88 Ka05
Icém BR (SP) 74 Hf56
İçerçumra TR 144 Mg27
Ice Stream A 312 Cc35
Ice Stream B 312 Cc35
Ice Stream C 312 Cd35
Ice Stream D 312 Cd35
Ice Stream E 312 Cd35
Ichabo-eiland NAM 298 Lh59
Ichabo Island NAM 298 Lh59
Ichalkaranji IND (MHT) 190
Oh37
Ichchapuram IND (APH)
191 Pc36
Iche MA 259 Kk29
Ichenhausen D 114 Ll42
Icheu WAN 280 Ld42
Ichhawar IND (MPH) 190 Oj34
Ichilo BOL 67 Gh54
Ichinomiya J 183 Rj28
Ichinoseki J 183 Sa26
Ichkeul, P.N. de l' TN 260
Le27
Ichoa BOL 67 Gh53
Ich'on DVRK 182 Rd26
Ich'on ROK 182 Rd27
Ichuña PE 72 Ge54
Iclod RO 124 Md44
İçmeler TR 129 Mj54
Ičnja UA 132 Mg20
Icó BR (CE) 65 Ja49
Icoca ANG 288 Lj49
Icy Cape USA 16 Ck16
Icy Strait USA 17 Dc16
Ida RUS 172 Qb19
Ida SP 291 Nb45
Idabato CAM 280 Le43
Idabel USA (OK) 29 Fc29
Idabo ETH 284 Na42
Idaga Hamus ETH 277 Mk39
Ida Grove USA (IA) 27 Fc24
Idah WAN 280 Ld42
Idaho USA 12 Ea10
Idaho Falls USA (ID) 21 Ee24
Idalia USA (CO) 26 Ej26
Idalia N.P. AUS 235 Sc58
Idanre WAN 280 Lc42
Ida-Oumarkt MA 258 Kf31
Idar IND (GUJ) 190 Og34
Idar-Oberstein D 114 Lh41
Ida Valley AUS (WA) 228 Ra60
Idd al-Ghanam SUD 282 Mc40
Idelgebis Tudi SP 285 Nf41
Ideles DZ 266 Lc34
Idenao CAM 280 Le43
Idenburg = Taritatu RI 213 Rk47
Ider gol MNG 172 Pk21
Idgaon BD 194 Pg35
Idgaon BD 194 Pg35
Idi RI 198 Pj43
Ididole ETH 285 Nb43
İdil TR 145 Na27
Idini RIM 269 Kc37
Idiofa RDC 289 Lk48
Id-Kah-Mosque VRC 168 Oj26
Idlib SYR 146 Mj28
Idoani WAN 280 Lc42
Idodi EAT 293 Mh49
Idodoma EAT 293 Mj49
Idogo WAN 280 Lb42
Idongo RCA 282 Ma42
Ídra GR 128 Md53
Ídra GR 128 Md53
Idracowra AUS (NT) 226 Rg58
Idre S 93 Ln29
Idrefjäll S 93 Ln29
Idrija SLO 121 Lp45
Idstein D 114 Lj40
Idumba RDC 289 Ma47
Idutywa SA 303 Me62
Idvor SCG 124 Ma45
Iecava LV 97 Me34
Iecava LV 97 Me34
Ie-jima J 185 Rd32
Iepê BR (SP) 74 He57
Ieper B 103 Lc40
Ierápetra GR 129 Mf55
Ierissós GR 127 Md50
Iernut RO 124 Me44
Iernut RO 124 Me43
Ifakara EAT 293 Mj50
Ifaki WAN 280 Lc42
Ifalik Atoll FSM 240 Sa17
Ifanadiana RM 306 Nd56
Ifanirea RM 306 Nd57
Ifaty RM 306 Nb57
Ife WAN 280 Lc42
Ifenat TCH 282 Lk39
Iferouâne RN 266 Le36
Ifetedo WAN 280 Lc42
Ifetesene DZ 266 Lc33
Iffezheim D 114 Lj42
Iffley AUS (QLD) 232 Sa55
Ifjord N 91 Md10
Ifon WAN 280 Lc42
Ifrane MA 258 Kh29
Ifumbe EAT 292 Mg49
Igabi WAN 272 Ld40
Igalukila EAT 292 Mf49
Igalula EAT 292 Mg48
Igam MAL 208 Qf44
Iganga EAU 290 Mg45
Igangan WAN 280 Lb42
Igapo BR (RN) 65 Jc48
Igaporã BR (BA) 70 Hj52
Igara Parana CO 61 Gd47
Igarapava BR (SP) 74 Hg56
Igarapé BR (MG) 75 Hh56
Igarapé-Açu BR (PA) 64 Hg46
Igarapé Capana, T.I. BR 67
Gf50
Igarapé do Caucho, T.I. BR
67 Ge50
Igarapé Grande BR (MA) 64
Hh48
Igarapé Ipixuna BR 63 Hd48
Igarapé Lages, T.I. BR 67 Gh51
Igarapé Lourdes, T.I. BR 68
Gk51
Igarapé Mirim BR (PA) 64 Hf46
Igarapé Ribeirão, T.I. BR 67
Gh51
Igarapé São José BR 63 He48
Igarapé Triunfo BR 63 Hd49
Igarité BR (BA) 70 Hj51
Igarka RUS 140 Pb05
Igarra WAN 280 Ld42
Igatpuri IND (MHT) 190 Og36
Igawa EAT 293 Mh50
Igbeti WAN 272 Lc41
Igbogor WAN 280 Lc42
Igboho WAN 272 Lb41
Igbo-Oro WAN 280 Lb42
Igbor WAN 280 Le42
Iğdecik TR 131 Mm51
Iğdir TR 131 Mq50
Iğdır TR 145 Nc26
Ige RUS 180 Rf19
Iggesund S 93 Ls29
Igherm MA 258 Kf30
Ighiu RO 124 Md44
Igichuk Hills USA 15 Bj12
Igina RDC 287 Md44
Igina RDC 287 Me44
Igiugig USA (AK) 14 Cc16
Igle, Cerro RA 82 Gd71
Iglésias I 111 Lj51
Igli DZ 259 Kj30
Ignace CDN (ON) 24 Fe21
Ignacio Allende MEX (DGO)
39 Ej33
Ignalina LT 97 Mg35
Ignarassú BR (PE) 71 Jc49
Ignatovo RUS 91 Mj15
İğneada TR 130 Mh49
Igoma EAT 292 Mg50
Igombe EAT 290 Mg48
Igornachoix Bay CDN 31 Hb20
Igoumenitsa GR 128 Ma51
Igporin WAN 272 Lc41
Igreja de Boroma MOC 296
Mg53
Igreja de Nossa Senhora do
Rosário dos Pretos BR 71
Ja52
Igreja de São Francisco BR
71 Ja52
Igrita WAN 280 Ld43
Iguaçu BR 74 Hd58
Iguaçu, P.N. do BR 74 Hd58
Iguai BR (BA) 71 Hk53
Iguala MEX (GUR) 40 Fa36
Igualada E 110 Lb49
Iguape BR (SP) 74 Hg58
Iguará BR 64 Hj47
Iguatemi BR (MS) 74 Hc57
Iguatu BR (CE) 65 Ja49
Iguazú, P.N. BR/RA 74 Hc58
Iguéla G 288 Le46
Igüeña E 106 Ko52
Iguetti RIM 264 Kf33
Iguguna EAT 293 Mh48
Iguidi Ouan Kasa LAR 267 Lf33
Igunga EAT 293 Mg48
Igusule EAT 292 Mg47
Iharana RM 305 Ne52
Iharosberény H 118 Ls44
Iheret EAK 284 Mj43
Iherir DZ 266 Le33
Iheya J 185 Rd32
Iheya-jima J 185 Rd32
Ihiala WAN 280 Ld43
Ihitsa LAR 267 Lg33
Ihlara TR 131 Mp52
Ihode FIN 96 Mb30
Ihosy RM 306 Nd57
Ihsaniye TR 131 Ml51
Ihsaniye TR 131 Ml51
Ihu PNG 243 Sc49
Ihugh WAN 280 Le42
Ihumbu EAT 293 Mh49
Ihuo WAN 280 Ld43
Iida J 183 Rj28
Iidaan SP 285 Ne42
Iide-san J 183 Rk27
Iiesia LT 97 Md36
Iil He VRC 166 Pa24
Iisalmi FIN 91 Md14
Iittala FIN 96 Me29
Ij IND (APH) 190 Oj37
Ija RUS 172 Pk19
Ijafene RIM 264 Kf35
Ijara EAK 291 Na46
Ijebu-Igbo WAN 280 Lb42
Ijebu-Ode WAN 280 Lb42
Ijen-Merapi Maelang Reserves
RI 211 Qh50
Ijevan ARM 152 Nc25
IJmuiden NL 112 Le38
Ijoubban RMM 265 Kg33
Ijoukak MA 258 Kf30
IJssel NL 112 Lg38
IJsselmeer NL 112 Lf38
IJsselstein NL 112 Lf38
Ijuí BR 77 Hc60
Ijuí BR (RS) 78 Hd60
Ikaalinen FIN 96 Md29
Ikalamavony RM 306 Nd56
Ikali RDC 289 Ma47
Ikalto Monastery GE 152 Nc25
Ikanbujimal VRC (XUZ) 169
Pe26
Ikanda RDC 289 Ma47
Ikang WAN 280 Le43
Ikanga EAK 291 Mk46
Ikare WAN 280 Lc42
Ikaria GR 129 Mg53
Ikast DK 94 Lk34
Ikatskij hrebet RUS 173 Qf19
Ikauna IND (UPH) 189 Pa32
Ikebe WAN 280 Lb42
Ikeda J 181 Sb24
Ikeja WAN 280 Lb42
Ikela RDC 286 Mb46
Ikelemba RDC 281 Lk45
Ikelenge Z 295 Mc51
Ikem WAN 280 Ld42
Ikengué G 288 Le46
Ikere WAN 280 Lc42
Ikerssuaq DK 11 Jb05
Ikh Bogd Uul MNG 172 Pk21
Ikh Bogd Uul MNG 172 Qa23
Ikh Bulag MNG 174 Qd24
Ikh Gazaryn Chuluu MNG 172
Qd23
Ikh Khayrkhan MNG 172 Qc22
Ikh Khenteyn Nuruu MNG 173
Qe21
Ikh Nuuruudyn Khotgor MNG
167 Ph21
Ikhšüüj MNG 172 Qd21
Iki J 185 Re29
Ikire WAN 280 Lc42
Ikirun WAN 280 Lc42
Iki-Tsushima Q.N.P. J 182 Re28
İkizce TR 131 Mn51
İkizören TR 131 Mo50
İkiztepe TR 144 Mj25
Ikola EAT 292 Mf49
Ikole WAN 280 Lc42
Ikom WAN 280 Le42
Ikonda EAT 293 Mh47
Ikomu WAN 280 Lb41
Ikongo RM 306 Nd56
Ikongo EAT 293 Mh49
Ikonongo RDC 286 Lk45
Ikoo EAK 291 Mk46
Ikopa RM 306 Nd54
Ikorodu WAN 280 Lb42
Ikot Ekpene WAN 280 Ld43
Ikoto SUD 283 Mg43
Ikoy G 288 Lf46
Ikškile LV 97 Me34
Ikuba EAT 292 Mf49
Ikungi EAT 293 Mh48
Ikutha EAK 293 Mk47
Ilaga RI 213 Rj47
Ilagan RP 203 Ra37
Ilaiyankudi IND (TNU) 193 Ok42
Ilaji WAN 280 Lb42
Ilaka Afovoany RM 306 Nd56
Ilaka Atsinanana RM 306 Ne55
Ilakaka RM 306 Nc57
Ilam IR 154 Nd29
Ilam NEP 170 Pd32
Ilan RC 179 Ra33
Ilanana RM 306 Nc57
Ilangali EAT 293 Mh49
Ilanz CH 114 Lk44

užnyj RUS (KAL) 152 Nc23
uzua Morava SCG 126 Mc48
uzzak PK 162 Oa31
walamukhi Temple IND 189 Oj29
waneng RB 299 Mc58
wderup DK 94 Lm35
ylland Bank 94 Lh34
yväskylä FIN 96 Mf28
zobil'nyj RUS 135 Na23

K

2 = Mount Godwin Austen PK 161 Oj28
aaba KSA 148 Mk35
aabong EAU 290 Mh44
aaimanston SME 59 Hb43
aala F 246 Tc56
aamanen FIN 91 Md11
aansoo EST 96 Mf32
aap Dernburg NAM 302 Lh59
aapmuiden SA 300 Mf58
aapstad SA 302 Lk62
aaresuvanto FIN 90 Mb11
aarina FIN 96 Mc30
aashidhoo MV 192 Og43
abaca TR 131 Mm50
abaena RI 211 Ra48
abaga G 288 Lg46
abah MEX 41 Ff35
abakly TM 153 Ob26
abala WAL 278 Ke41
abale EAU 287 Me46
abalebo-stuwmeer(projected) SME 59 Hb43
abalega Falls N.P. = Murchison Falls N.P. EAU 290 Mf44
abalı TR 144 Mh25
abalo RDC 292 Md49
abambare RDC 292 Md48
abanbai KZ 166 Pa23
abanbai KZ 166 Pb22
abanga RDC 289 Lk49
abango Z 296 Md54
abango RDC 292 Md49
abangu RDC 295 Mb51
abania Lake CDN 25 Ff19
abanjahe RI 198 Pk44
abankalan RP 205 Rb41
abanpe GH 279 Kj41
abanza Z 296 Md54
abao LAR 260 Lf30
abara FJI 247 Ua55
abardino-Balkaria RUS 145 Nb24
abardino-Balkarskij zapovednik RUS 152 Nb24
abare RDC 292 Me47
abarei RI 212 Rf46
abarnet EAK 290 Mh45
abasalan RP 205 Rb42
abatepe TR 130 Mg50
abau RI 212 Rc47
abba WAN 280 Ld42
abdalis S 90 Ma12
abe WAN 272 Lc40
abelvåg N 90 Lh11
aberamaido EAU 290 Mg45
abetan RI 209 Ra45
abeya RDC 289 Mb49
abi ETH 284 Mk40
abia TCH 273 Lh41
abika River CDN 25 Ga21
abile LV 97 Mc34
abinakagami Lake CDN 25 Fh21
abinburi THA 196 Qa38
abinda RDC 289 Mc49
abir RI 214 Rc50
abirizi EAU 287 Me45
abirwala PK 161 Of30
abkabiya SUD 282 Mc39
abkabiyah KSA 149 Nc35
ablebet RI 212 Re46
ableŝovo BG 127 Mh48
abli EST 96 Me32
abna SUD 276 Mg37
abo RCA 282 Lk42
abobi RN 272 Lc39
abola RI 212 Rf46
abompo Z 295 Mb52
abompo Z 295 Mc52
abondo-Dianda RDC 292 Mc50
abong MAL 208 Qf45
abongo RDC 292 Mc49
abongo RDC 292 Me50
aboson EAK 290 Mh46
abou RCA 286 Ma43
abou RT 279 La41
abrai IND (UPH) 191 Pa33
abrousse SN 269 Kb39
abud Gondab IR 155 Nk27
abud Rahang IR 154 Ne28
abul AFG 160 Oe28
abumbu RDC 292 Md48
abunda RDC 296 Me52
abunduk RI 211 Qk50
abunga RDC 287 Me46
abunga RWA 287 Mf46
abungo EAT 292 Mf49
abur SUD 283 Mf39
aburuang RI 205 Rd44
abushiya SUD 276 Mg38
abuwe RI 206 Qb48
abuyu Z 295 Mc54
abuzal Island MYA 196 Pj39
abwe Z 296 Me53
abwoya EAU 287 Mf45
abwum PNG 243 Sd49
açarlı TR 131 Mo51
acelovo BG 127 Mg47
acerginé LT 97 Md36
acergiškė LT 97 Mg35
ach PK 160 Od30
achako WAN 272 Le40
achekabwe RB 299 Mc55
achemak Bay USA 15 Ce16
achia WAN 272 Ld41
achisi ETH 284 Mj41
acholola Z 296 Mf53
achovka UA 134 Mg22
achovs'ke vodoschovyšče UA 135 Mh22
achovs'kyj kanal UA 135 Mh22
achulu MW 297 Mh53
achung EAU 290 Mg45
açkar Dağı TR 145 Na25
açkar Dağlari Milli Parkı TR 131 Mm53
acug RUS 172 Qc19
aćurivka UA 125 Mk43
aczorów PL 116 Lq40
adaiyanallur IND (TNU) 193 Oj42
adakkal IND (TNU) 192 Oj42
adam, Mount EAU 290 Mh45
adań CZ 118 Lo40
Kadatuang RI 209 Rb48
Kadavu FJI 247 Tk55
Kadavu Passage FJI 247 Tk55
Kade GH 279 Kk42
Kadéï CAM/RCA 281 Lh44
Kadeke LB 278 Kg43
Kadhzaran ARM 152 Nd26
Kadijivka UA 135 Mk21
Kadıköy TR 130 Mg50
Kadina AUS (SA) 236 Rj62
Kadınhanı TR 131 Mn52
Kadin most BG 126 Mc48
Kadioha CI 279 Kh41
Kadiolo RMM 279 Kh40
Kadiondola RG 278 Ke40
Kadipaten RI 210 Qe49
Kadiri IND (APH) 193 Ok39
Kadirli TR 144 Mj27
Kadısehri TR 131 Mq50
Kadiweu, T.I. BR 73 Hb56
Kadji TCH 282 Ma40
Kadkan IR 155 Nk28
Kadligarh IND (ORS) 191 Pc35
Kadmath Island IND 192 Og41
Kado WAN 280 Le42
Kadoka USA (SD) 26 Ek24
Kadola RI 212 Rd48
Kadoma ZW 300 Me55
Kadovar Island PNG 243 Sc47
Kadrifakovo MK 126 Mc49
Kadruka SUD 276 Mf37
Kaduaga Island PNG 244 Sf50
Kadugli SUD 283 Me40
Kaduj RUS 132 Mj16
Kaduma MYA 195 Ph34
Kaduna WAN 272 Lc41
Kaduna WAN 272 Ld40
Kadung Ga MYA 195 Pj32
Kadunguru EAU 290 Mg45
Kadur IND (KTK) 192 Oj40
Kadyj RUS 133 Nb17
Kadzidło PL 117 Mb37
Kaech'on DVRK 182 Rc26
Kaélé CAM 273 Lh40
Kaena Point USA 16 Ca35
Kaeng Khlo THA 197 Qb37
Kaeng Krachan N.P. THA 196 Pk39
Kaeng Tana N.P. THA 197 Qc38
Kaeo NZ 238 Tg63
Kaesong DVRK 182 Rd27
Kaevanga SOL 245 Sk50
Kaew Kho Rum Cave THA 198 Pk40
Kaf KSA 146 Mj30
Kafakumba RDC 289 Mb50
Kafanchan WAN 272 Le41
Kafar-Jar-Ghar Range AFG 160 Od29
Kaffin-Saru WAN 272 Ld41
Kaffrine SN 269 Kc38
Kafia Kingi SUD 282 Mc41
Kafin-Chana WAN 272 Lc39
Kafindibei SUD 282 Mc41
Kafiné CI 279 Kh41
Kafin Hausa WAN 272 Le39
Kåfjord N 91 Mc10
Kafolo CI 279 Kh41
Kafountine SN 269 Kb39
Kafr el-Dauwâr ET 263 Mf30
Kafr el-Sheikh ET 263 Mf30
Kafu EAU 287 Mf45
Kafue Z 296 Me52
Kafue Z 296 Me53
Kafue N.P. Z 295 Mc53
Kafukula MW 296 Mg51
Kafunzo EAU 287 Mf46
Kafura EAT 292 Mf47
Kafuya RDC 292 Md48
Kafwala Z 296 Md53
Kaga J 183 Rj27
Kaga Bandoro RCA 282 Lk42
Kagadi EAU 287 Mf45
Kagan PK 161 Og28
Kagaré BF 271 Kk39
Kagarko WAN 272 Ld41
Kagera EAT/EAU 287 Mf46
Kagianagami Lake CDN 25 Fg20
Kağızman TR 145 Nb25
Kagmar SUD 276 Mf39
Kagnal TCH 282 Lk41
Kagologolo RI 206 Pk46
Kagomba RDC 296 Md51
Kagopal TCH 281 Lj41
Kagora, Mount WAN 272 Le41
Kagoshima J 185 Rf30
Kagoshima wan J 185 Rf30
Kagua PNG 243 Sb49
Kagug ET 263 Mg33
Kagula EAU 290 Mg45
Kaha ETH 285 Nb41
Kahak Cave IR 154 Nf28
Kahal Tabelbala DZ 259 Kj31
Kahama EAT 292 Mg47
Kahan PK 162 Oe31
Kahani IND (MPH) 191 Ok34
Kahara RMM 271 Kj37
Kaharlyk UA 134 Mf21
Kahatola RI 212 Rd45
Kahayan RI 208 Qh47
Ka-Hem = Malyj Enisej RUS 172 Pj20
Kahemba RDC 289 Lk49
Kahir IR 157 Oa33
Kahla D 113 Lm40
Kahler Asten D 112 Lj39
Kahmoo AUS (QLD) 235 Sc60
Kahnple LB 278 Kf42
Kahnuj IR 157 Nj32
Kahnwie LB 278 Kf43
Kahone SN 269 Kc38
Kahoolawe USA 16 Cb35
Kahramanmaras TR 144 Mj27
Kahror Pakka PK 163 Of31
Kahuku Point USA 16 Cb35
Kahului USA 16 Cb35
Kahunge EAU 287 Mf45
Kahurak IR 157 Nk31
Kahurangi N.P. NZ 239 Tg66
Kahurangi Point NZ 239 Tg66
Kahurestan IR 156 Nh32
Kahuta PK 161 Og29
Kahuzi-Biega, P.N. du RDC 292 Md47
Kai RI 213 Rg48
Kaiam PNG 243 Sb49
Kaiapit PNG 243 Sd49
Kaiaua NZ 238 Th64
Kaibab Ind. Res. USA 23 Ed27
Kai Besar RI 212 Rg48
Kaibola PNG 244 Sf50
Kaichui, Mount SOL 245 Ta50
Kaidao VRC (HLG) 180 Re23
Kaidu He VRC 169 Pc24
KaiDulan RI 212 Rg48
Kaiemothia SUD 283 Mh43
Kaieteur Fall GUY 58 Ha43
Kaieteur National Park GUY 58 Ha43
Kaifeng VRC (HNN) 184 Qh28
Kaigani USA (AK) 17 Dd18
Kaihua VRC (ZJG) 184 Qk31
Kaiken RA (TF) 82 Gg73
KaiKetjil RI 212 Rg48
Kaikohe NZ 238 Tg63
Kaikoura NZ 239 Tg67
Kaikoura Peninsula NZ 239 Tg67
Kailahun WAL 278 Ke41
Kailash = Kangrinboqê Feng VRC 170 Pa30
Kaili VRC (GZH) 178 Qd32
Kailu VRC (NMZ) 182 Ra24
Kailua USA (HI) 16 Cb35
Kailua-Kona USA (HI) 16 Cc36
Kaima RI 213 Rk48
Kaimana RI 213 Rg47
Kaimer RI 212 Rg48
Kaimganj IND (UPH) 189 Ok32
Kaim River PNG 242 Sa49
Kaimu USA (HI) 16 Cc36
Käina EST 96 Mc32
Kainan J 183 Rh29
Kainantu PNG 243 Sc49
Kainar KZ 159 Of24
Kainar KZ 166 Oj21
Kaindu Z 296 Md53
Kaindy KS 159 Og24
Kainji Dam WAN 272 Lc41
Kainji Lake N.P. WAN 272 Lc40
Kainji Reservoir WAN 272 Lc40
Kaipara-Harbour NZ 238 Th64
Kaipiainen FIN 96 Mh30
Kaiping VRC (GDG) 179 Qg34
Kaipola FIN 96 Mf29
Kairakty KZ 166 Og21
Kairana IND (UPH) 189 Oj31
Kaireni RI 213 Rg46
Kairiru Island PNG 243 Sb47
Kairouan TN 260 Lf28
Kairuku EAT 292 Mf49
Kairutu RI 212 Re47
Kais RI 212 Rg46
Kaiserslautern D 114 Lh41
Kaiserstuhl D 114 Lh42
Kaisi IND (MZR) 194 Pg34
Kaišiadorys LT 97 Me36
Kaisut Desert EAK 290 Mj45
Kaitaia NZ 238 Tg63
Kaitangata NZ 239 Te69
Kaitanimbar RI 212 Rg49
Kaithal IND (HYA) 189 Oj31
Kaitorete Spit NZ 239 Tg67
Kaituma GUY 58 Ha41
Kaiwi Channel USA 16 Cb35
Kai Xian VRC (CGQ) 177 Qe30
Kaiyang VRC (GZH) 178 Qd32
Kaiyuan VRC (LNG) 182 Rc24
Kaiyuan VRC (YUN) 195 Qb34
Kaiyuan Temple VRC 179 Qk33
Kaiyuh Mountains USA 15 Ca14
Kajaani FIN 91 Md13
Kajabbi AUS (QLD) 232 Sa56
Kajakent RUS (DAG) 152 Nd24
Kajaki AFG 160 Oc29
Kajang MAL 199 Qa44
Kajang RI 211 Ra48
Kajeray AFG 160 Oe29
Kajgaon IND (MHT) 190 Oh35
Kajiado EAK 290 Mj46
Kajlagarh IND (WBG) 194 Pd34
Kajlastuj RUS 173 Qk21
Kajo Kaji SUD 287 Mf44
Kajola WAN 280 Lc42
Kajrat KZ 133 Ne20
Kajsackoe RUS 133 Nd21
Kajuru WAN 272 Ld40
Kaka SUD 283 Mg40
Kaka TM 155 Nk27
Kaka USA (AZ) 22 Ed29
Kakaban RI 209 Qk44
Kakabara EAU 287 Mf45
Kakabeka Falls CDN (ON) 25 Ff21
Kakabia RI 211 Rb49
Kakadu A.L. AUS 223 Rg52
Kakadu A.L. AUS 223 Rg52
Kakadu N.P. AUS 223 Rg52
Kakagi Lake CDN 24 Fd21
Kakali RI 209 Qk46
Kakamas SA 302 Ma60
Kakamega EAK 290 Mh45
Kakamega Forest Nature Reserve EAK 290 Mh45
Kakamoéka RCB 288 Lg48
Kaka, Mount ETH 284 Mk42
Kakanda RDC 296 Md51
Kakanj BIH 121 Lt46
Kakas RI 209 Rc45
Kakata LB 278 Ke42
Kakching IND (MNP) 194 Ph33
Kakdwip IND (WBG) 194 Pe35
Kake J 183 Rg28
Kake USA (AK) 17 Dd17
Kakegawa J 183 Rk28
Kakenge RDC 289 Ma48
Kakeroma-jima J 185 Re31
Kaki IR 155 Nf31
Kakielo RDC 296 Me52
Kakimba RDC 292 Me48
Kakinada IND (APH) 191 Pb37
Kakira EAU 290 Mg45
Kakkar PK 162 Od32
Kakki IND 192 Oj42
Kakkirigumma IND (ORS) 191 Pb36
Kakobola RDC 289 Lk48
Kakogawa J 183 Rh28
Kakol PL 116 Lt38
Kakoma EAT 292 Mg48
Kakopetria CY 131 Mn55
Kakoro PNG 243 Sd49
Kakosi EAT 292 Mg50
Kakpin CI 279 Kj41
Kakrala IND (UPH) 189 Ok32
Kakrima RG 269 Kd40
Kaksa IND (WBG) 194 Pd34
Kakšaal kyrka toosu KS/VRC 159 Oj25
Kaku IND (RJT) 188 Og32
Kakuma EAK 290 Mh44
Kakumbi Z 296 Mf52
Kakumi WAN 272 Ld40
Kakumiro EAU 287 Mf45
Kakum N.P. GH 279 Kk43
Kakunodate J 183 Sa26
Kakwa Prov. Rec. Area CDN 18 Dk18
Kakwa River CDN 18 Ea18
Kakya EAK 291 Mk46
Kala WAN 273 Lh39
Kalaallit Nunaat DK 11 Hd03
Kalaat Kasbah TN 260 Le28
Kalabagh PK 161 Of29
Kalabahi RI 214 Rc50
Kalabakan MAL 204 Qj43
Kalabo CI 279 Kj41
Kalabo Z 295 Mb53
Kalabsha Temple ET 263 Mg34
Kalabua RDC 289 Mb49
Kalač RUS 133 Na20
Kalač-na-Donu RUS 133 Nb21
Kaladar CDN (ON) 33 Gb23
Ka Lae USA 16 Cc36
Kalaero RI 211 Ra48
Kalafilia RG 278 Kf41
Kalafo ETH 285 Nc43
Kalagi SN 269 Kc39
Kalahari Desert RB 299 Ma57
Kalahari Gemsbok N.P. SA 302 Ma59
Kalaheo USA (HI) 16 Ca35
Kalah-i-Darab IR 156 Ng31
Kalaia BD 194 Pf34
Kalaichumb TJ 159 Of26
Kalaigaon IND (ASM) 194 Pf32
Kala-I-Mor TM 155 Ob28
Kalajoki FIN 91 Mb13
Kalak IR 154 Nd29
Kalakol EAK 290 Mh44
Kalakoski FIN 96 Md28
Kalakpa Resource Reserve GH 279 La42
Kalala Z 295 Mc53
Kalala Beach RI 211 Ra51
Kalalaq IR 154 Nd26
Kalam IND (MHT) 191 Ok35
Kalam PK 161 Og28
Kalamáki GR 126 Mc51
Kalamaloué, P.N. de CAM 273 Lh39
Kalamansig RP 205 Rc42
Kalamare RB 299 Md57
Kalamáta GR 128 Mc53
Kalamazoo USA (MI) 32 Fh24
Kalamba RDC 286 Lk46
Kalambáka GR 126 Mb51
Kalambáki GR 127 Me49
Kalambo Falls Z 292 Mf50
Kalambuku RI 208 Qj44
Kalamnuri IND (MHT) 190 Oj36
Kálamos GR 128 Ma52
Kalampising RI 208 Qj44
Kalamurinn AUS (SA) 227 Rk59
Kalana EST 96 Mc32
Kalana RMM 278 Kf40
Kalančak UA 134 Mg22
Kalándra GR 126 Md51
Kalandy RM 305 Ne53
Kalaneh IR 154 Nf27
Kalan Eylgah AFG 161 Of27
Kalang RI 206 Pk45
Kalangala EAU 290 Mg46
Kalangali EAT 292 Mg50
Kalangali EAT 293 Mh49
Kalanguj RUS 173 Qj20
Kalannie AUS (WA) 228 Qj61
Kalan Mosque UZB 158 Oc26
Kalanti FIN 96 Mb30
Kalao RI 211 Ra49
Kalaoa USA (HI) 16 Cc36
Kalaotoa RI 211 Ra49
Kala Oya CL 193 Pa42
Kalapahar IND (MNP) 194 Pg33
Kalapur BD 194 Pf34
Kalar IRQ 147 Nc28
Kalarada BD 194 Pe34
Kälarne S 93 Lr28
Kalarua MYA 194 Pg35
Kalasin RI 208 Qh45
Kalasin THA 197 Qb37
Kalat IR 157 Nk33
Kalat PK 162 Od31
Kalatope W.S. IND 189 Oj29
Kalaupapa USA (HI) 16 Cb35
Kalaus RUS 152 Nb23
Kalavad IND (GUJ) 190 Of34
Kalavárda GR 129 Mh54
Kalávrita GR 128 Mc52
Kalaw MYA 195 Pj35
Kalaymyo MYA 194 Ph34
Kalba UAE 157 Nj33
Kalbacar AZ 152 Nc25
Kalban OM 151 Nk35
Kalbarri AUS (WA) 228 Qh59
Kalbarri N.P. AUS 224 Qh59
Kalbay RP 205 Rc43
Kalbe D 113 Lm38
Kalbinskij toglari KZ 166 Pa21
Kaldera GR 129 Mf54
Kale IND (MHT) 190 Og37
Kale TR 130 Mj53
Kale TR 144 Me27
Kalecık TR 131 Mo50
Kaledibi TR 145 Na25
Kalédougou RMM 270 Kh39
Kaledupa RI 209 Rb48
Kalegauk MYA 196 Pj38
Kalehe RDC 292 Me47
Kaléle DY 272 Lb40
Kalema EAT 293 Mh48
Kalema RDC 289 Mc48
Kalemegdan SCG 124 Ma46
Kalemie RDC 292 Me48
Kalémié? UA 117 Mf39
Kal-e-Namaskar IR 155 Oa29
Kalenga RUS 172 Qc19
Kalengwa Z 295 Mc52
Kaleo GH 279 Kj40
Kalérgo GR 128 Me52
Kalevala RUS (KAR) 91 Mf13
Kalewa MYA 194 Ph34
Kalfou CAM 273 Lh40
Kalga RUS 173 Qk20
Kalghatgi IND (KTK) 192 Oh39
Kalgin Island USA 15 Cd15
Kalgo WAN 272 Lc39
Kalgoorlie AUS (WA) 228 Ra61
Kalguddering AUS (WA) 228 Qj61
Kali AUS (WA) 224 Qj59
Kali DY 272 Lb40
Kali NEP 170 Pa31
Kali RMM 269 Ke39
Kaliakain BD 194 Pf33
Kalian RP 205 Rc42
Kalianda RI 207 Qc48
Kalianget RI 211 Qg49
Kalibo RP 205 Rb40
Kalichandbari BD 194 Pf34
Kali Gandaki NEP 170 Pb32
Kali Gandaki River Rafting NEP 170 Pb31
Kali Gandaki (World's deepest gorge) NEP 170 Pb31
Kaligiri IND (APH) 193 Ok39
Kalima RDC 292 Md47
Kalimantan RI 200 Qc18
Kálimnos GR 129 Mg53
Kálimnos GR 129 Mg54
Kalimpong IND (WBG) 194 Pe32
Kalinda Z 296 Mg51
Kalinga AUS (QLD) 231 Sb53
Kalingia IND (ORS) 191 Pc35
Kalinina RUS 133 Nc17
Kalininabad TJ 158 Oe27
Kaliningrad RUS 97 Ma36
Kalinino RUS 180 Re21
Kalininsk RUS 133 Nc20
Kalinjar IND 191 Pa33
Kalinjara IND (RJT) 190 Oh34
Kalinkavičy BY 132 Me19
Kalinko RG 278 Ke40
Kalinovik BIH 121 Lt47
Kalip PNG 244 Sf48
Kalipéfki GR 126 Mc51
Kalipur BD 194 Pf35
Kaliro EAU 290 Mg45
Kalis SP 285 Ne41
Kalisah SYR 146 Mj27
Kalisangka RI 211 Qh49
Kali Sindh IND 190 Oj34
Kalisko PL 117 Lu39
Kalispel Ind. Res. USA 18 Eb21
Kalispell USA (MT) 19 Ec21
Kalisty PL 117 Ma37
Kalisz PL 116 Lt39
Kalisz Pomorski PL 116 Lq37
Kalithéa GR 126 Md50
Kalitva RUS 135 Na21
Kaliua EAT 292 Mf48
Kalivári GR 129 Me53
Kalix S 90 Mb13
Kalixälven S 91 Mb12
Kaliyaganj IND (WBG) 194 Pe33
Kaljazin RUS 132 Mj17
Kalka IND (HYA) 189 Oj30
Kalkalpen, N.P. A 115 Lp43
Kalkan TR 129 Mk54
Kalkaringi AUS (NT) 223 Rf54
Kalkaroo AUS (SA) 236 Sa61
Kalkaska USA (MI) 32 Fh23
Kalkbank SA 300 Me57
Kalkfontein = Tshootsha RB 299 Ma57
Kalkfontein Dam Nature Reserve SA 303 Mc60
Kalkrand NAM 298 Lj58
Kalkudah Beach CL 193 Pa43
Kalkūne LV 97 Mg35
Kalkveld NAM 298 Lj56
Kallakkurichchi IND (TNU) 193 Ok41
Kallala AUS (QLD) 232 Rk56
Kallam IND (MHT) 190 Oh36
Kallambella IND (KTK) 193 Oj40
Kållands halvö S 93 Ln32
Kållandsö S 93 Lo32
Kallar IND (KER) 192 Oh40
Kallar Kahar PK 161 Og29
Kallaste EST 96 Mh32
Kållered S 94 Ln33
Kalli EST 96 Me32
Kallidaikurichi IND (TNU) 193 Oj42
Kallinge S 95 Lq34
Kallithéa GR 126 Mc51
Kallmet AL 126 Lu49
Kalloní GR 128 Md53
Kallsjön S 90 Lg14
Kallur IND (APH) 191 Pa37
Kalma IND (KTK) 190 Oj37
Kalmar S 95 Lr34
Kalmarsund S 95 Lr34
Kalmeh IR 156 Nf31
Kalmeta AUS (QLD) 232 Sa55
Kalmit D 114 Lj41
Kal'mius UA 135 Mj22
Kalmthout B 103 Le39
Kalmunai CL 193 Pa43
Kalmykia RUS 135 Nc22
Kalmykovskij RUS 133 Nb21
Kalna SCG 126 Mc47
Kálna nad Hronom SK 118 Lt42
Kalná Roztoka SK 119 Mc42
Kalnciems LV 97 Md34
Kalocsa H 119 Lt44
Kalofer BG 127 Me48
Kalohi Channel USA 16 Cb35
Kaló Horío GR 128 Md52
Kalo Kalo PNG 244 Sf50
Kaloke LB 278 Kg43
Kalokitting SUD 282 Mc39
Kaloko RDC 292 Mc49
Kalol IND (GUJ) 190 Og34
Kalole RDC 292 Md47
Kaloleni EAK 293 Mk47
Kalomo Z 295 Md54
Kalomo Z 296 Md54
Kalona USA (MO) 27 Fe25
Kalona Hist. Village USA 32 Fe25
Kalongan RI 205 Rd44
Kalongo EAU 290 Mg44
Kalosi RI 209 Qk47
Kalossia EAK 290 Mh45
Kalouamoutou G 288 Lg46
Kalounka RG 278 Kc40
Kalourat, Mount SOL 245 Ta50
Kalpáki GR 128 Ma51
Kalpeni Island IND 192 Og41
Kalpetta IND (KER) 192 Oj41
Kalpi IND (UPH) 189 Ok32
Kalpitiya CL 193 Ok42
Kalsdorf A 115 Lq44
Kalskag USA (AK) 15 Bk15
Kalso CDN (BC) 19 Eb21
Kaltag USA (AK) 15 Ca13
Kaltanėnai LT 97 Mf35
Kaltenkirchen D 113 Ll37
Kaltern = Caldaro I 120 Lm44
Kaltungo WAN 273 Lf41
Kaluga RUS 132 Mj18
Kalugerovc BG 127 Me48
Kaluku RI 209 Ra47
Kalulushi Z 296 Me52
Kalumburu AUS (WA) 222 Rd53
Kalumburu A.L. AUS 222 Rd53
Kalumengongo RDC 292 Md50
Kalundborg DK 94 Lm35
Kalundu RDC 292 Me47
Kalundwe RDC 289 Mc49
Kalungwishi Z 292 Me50
Kalur Kot PK 161 Of29
Kaluš UA 119 Me41
Kaluvaye IND (APH) 193 Ok39
Kalvåg N 92 Le29
Kalvarija LT 97 Md36
Kalvitsa FIN 96 Mh29
Kalvola FIN 96 Me29
Kalwakurti IND (APH) 191 Ok37
Kalwaria Zebrzydowska PL 119 Lu41
Kalya EAT 292 Mf49
Kalyan IND (MHT) 190 Og36
Kalyandrug IND (APH) 193 Oj39
Kalynivka UA 134 Me21
Kalzhat KZ 159 Pa24
Kam WAN 281 Lf41
Kama RMM 269 Ke39
Kamada TCH 273 Lh37
Kamaday TCH 282 Ma40
Kamaishi J 183 Sa26
Kamakura J 183 Rk28
Kamakusa GUY 58 Ha43
Kamakwie WAL 278 Kd41
Kamal RI 210 Qg49
Kamal TCH 267 Lj35
Kamalia PK 161 Og30
Kamalpur IND (TRP) 194 Pf33
Kaman IND (RJT) 189 Oj32
Kaman TR 131 Mo51
Kamanga EAT 292 Mg47
Kamanjab NAM 298 Lh55
Kamanjola RDC 292 Me47
Kamapanda Z 295 Mc51
Kamaran YE 150 Nb38
Kamarang GUY 58 Gk43
Kamareddi IND (APH) 191 Ok36
Kamares GR 127 Me50
Kamáres GR 128 Mb52
Kamáres GR 129 Me53
Kamári GR 129 Mf54
Kamaron WAL 278 Ke41
Kamaru RI 209 Rb48
Kamas USA (UT) 21 Ee25
Kamasin IND (UPH) 191 Pa33
Kamatvi ZW 299 Md55
Kamba ETH 284 Mj42
Kamba WAN 272 Lb40
Kamba Kota RCA 281 Lj42
Kambalda AUS (WA) 228 Ra61
Kambalon RMM 278 Kf40
Kambam IND (TNU) 193 Oj42
Kambambe ANG 288 Lh50
Kambánis GR 126 Mc50
Kambar PK 162 Od32
Kambeng IND (ARP) 194 Ph31
Kamberatoro PNG 242 Sa47
Kambia WAL 278 Kd41
Kambikatoto EAT 292 Mg49
Kambode RI 209 Rb48
Kambolé RT 279 La41
Kámbos GR 128 Mc54
Kambove RDC 296 Md51
Kambuku PNG 244 Sg48
Kambuno, Gunung RI 209 Ra47
Kamburu EAK 290 Mj46
Kambut LAR 262 Mc30
Kambwata Z 295 Mb53
Kamcha-i THA 197 Qc37
Kamchatka Peninsula RUS 141 Sc07
Kamčija BG 127 Mh47
Kamčija BG 127 Mh47
Kamdara IND (JKD) 191 Pc34
Kamdeysh AFG 161 Of28
Kameel SA 303 Mc59
Kamélé CI 279 Kj41
Kameme MW 292 Mg50
Kamen D 112 Lh39
Kamena EAT 292 Mg47
Kamende RDC 289 Mc49
Kamenec RUS 96 Mj32
Kameng AFG 160 Oc28
Kameng IND 194 Pg32
Kamenica BG 126 Md49
Kamenica SCG 124 Lu46
Kamenice nad Lipou CZ 118 Lq41
Kamenka KZ 133 Nf20
Kamenka RUS 96 Mk30
Kamenka RUS 133 Mk20
Kamenka RUS 133 Nb19
Kamenka RUS 167 Pc20
Kamen'-na-Ob' RUS 140 Pa08
Kamennite găbi BG 127 Mf49
Kamennogorsk RUS 96 Mk30
Kamenný Přívoz CZ 118 Lp41
Kameno BG 127 Mh48
Kamen'Rybolov RUS 180 Rg23
Kamenskij RUS 133 Nc20
Kamenskoe RUS 141 Tb06
Kamensk-Sahtinskij RUS 135 Na21
Kamensk-Ural'skij RUS 140 Oa07
Kamenz D 113 Lp39
Kameshia RDC 292 Md50
Kameškovo RUS 133 Na17
Kamet IND 189 Ok30
Kamianieckaja vieza BY 117 Md38
Kamień PL 117 Ma39
Kamiendo WAL 278 Ke41
Kamień Pomorski PL 116 Lp37
Kamieskroon SA 302 Lj61
Kamiha RT 279 La41
Kamiiso J 181 Sa25
Kamiji RDC 289 Mb49
Kamikawa J 181 Sb24
Kamikaze Peace Museum J 185 Rf30
Kami-koshiki-jima J 185 Re30
Kamileroi AUS (QLD) 232 Rk55
Kamina PNG 243 Sc49
Kamina RDC 289 Mc50
Kamina Base RDC 289 Mc50
Kamin'-Kašyrs'kyj UA 117 Me39
Kamino-jima J 182 Re28
Kaminokuni J 181 Sa25
Kamioka J 183 Rj27
Kámiros GR 129 Mh54
Kamishak Bay USA 15 Cd16
Kami-Shihoro J 181 Sb24
Kamiskotia Ski Resort CDN 25 Fk21
Kamişlı TR 131 Mp53
Kamışlıkuyu TR 131 Mp53
Kamitsushima J 182 Re28
Kamituga RDC 292 Me47
Kami-Yaku J 185 Rf30
Kam'janec'-Podil's'kyj UA 125 Mg42
Kamjaniec BY 117 Md38
Kamjanjuki BY 117 Md38
Kam'janka UA 125 Ml44
Kamjanka UA 134 Mg21
Kamjanka-Buz'ka UA 117 Me40
Kam'jans'ke UA 125 Mk45
Kamloops CDN (BC) 18 Dk20
Kamloops Ind. Res. CDN 18 Dk20
Kamloops Plateau CDN 18 Dk20
Kammanassieberge SA 302 Mb62
Kamnarok Nature Reserve EAK 290 Mh45
Kamnik SLO 121 Lp44
Kamob Sanha SUD 277 Mj37
Kamoke PK 161 Oh30
Kamola RDC 292 Md49
Kamoto Z 296 Mg52
Kamp A 115 Lq42
Kamp 52 SME 59 Hb43
Kampa DY 271 Lb39
Kampa do Rio Amõnea, T.I. BR 67 Gd50
Kampa e Isolados do Rio Envira, T.I. BR 67 Ge50
Kampala EAU 290 Mg45
Kampala SUD 282 Mc41
Kampampi Z 292 Me50
Kampar MAL 199 Qa43
Kampar RI 206 Qb45
Kampe WAN 280 Lc41
Kampela Z 292 Mf50
Kampen NL 112 Lf38
Kampene RDC 292 Md47
Kamphaeng Phet THA 196 Pk37
Kamphambale MW 296 Mg52
Kampinoski P.N. PL 117 Ma38
Kampli IND (KTK) 193 Oj39
Kampong Padawan MAL 208 Qf45
Kampong Sirik MAL 208 Qf44
Kampong Sralao K 197 Qc38
Kampong Taben K 197 Qc39
Kampot K 197 Qc40
Kampti BF 279 Kj40
Kampumbu Z 296 Mg51
Kampung Ayer Puteh MAL 199 Qb43
Kampung Batu Enam MAL 199 Qb44
Kampung Batu Satu MAL 204 Qg43
Kampung Buloh MAL 199 Qb43
Kampung Chenereh MAL 199 Qb43
Kampung Damak MAL 199 Qb44
Kampung Gading MAL 199 Qb44
Kampung Gajah MAL 198 Qa43
Kampung Gajah MAL 199 Qa43
Kampung Jerangau MAL 199 Qb43
Kampung Kemara MAL 199 Qb43
Kampung Koh MAL 198 Qa43
Kampung Landak MAL 199 Qb44
Kampung Laut RI 207 Qb46
Kampung Merang MAL 199 Qb43
Kampung Merting MAL 199 Qb43
Kampung Nibong MAL 199 Qa43
Kampung Palas MAL 199 Qb44
Kampung Penarik MAL 199 Qb43
Kampung Permas Kecil MAL 199 Qb45
Kampung Punggai MAL 199 Qc45
Kampung Relok MAL 199 Qb43
Kampung Sawagan MAL 204 Qh43
Kampung Seri Gading MAL 199 Qc45
Kampung Sook MAL 204 Qj43
Kampung Sungai Ayer Deras MAL 199 Qb43
Kampung Tanjung Batu MAL 199 Qb44
Kampung Tekek MAL 199 Qc44
Kampung Telupid MAL 204 Qj43
Kamsack CDN (SK) 24 Ek20
Kamsamba EAT 292 Mg50
Kamsandra IND (KTK) 193 Ok40
Kamsar RG 278 Kc40
Kamskoe Ust'e RUS (TAR) 133 Ne18
Kamskoe vdhr. RUS 140 Nd07
Kamsuuma SP 291 Nb45
Kamthi IND (MHT) 191 Ok35
Kamtsha RDC 289 Lk48
Kamuchawi Lake CDN 24 Ej17
Kamudi IND (TNU) 193 Ok42
Kamudini EAU 290 Mg44
Kamuli EAU 290 Mg45
Kamutambai RDC 289 Mb49
Kamuwongo EAK 291 Mk46
Kamyaran IR 154 Nd28
Kamysanovka KS 159 Oh24
Kamyšin RUS 133 Nc20
Kamyšovyj hrebet RUS 181 Sb21
Kamystybas köli KZ 153 Oa22
Kamyzyak RUS 152 Ne22
Kan IR 154 Nf28
Kanab USA (UT) 23 Ed27
Kanab Creek USA 22 Ed27
Kanacea FJI 247 Ua54
Ka Nae THA 197 Qc37
Kanai PK 160 Od30
Kanaima Falls GUY 58 Gk42
Kanaka RI 213 Rg47
Kanakapura IND (KTK) 193 Oj40
Kanakatte IND (KTK) 192 Oj40
Kanakono CI 279 Kg40
Kanaktok Mount USA 15 Bk12
Kanaküla EST 96 Mf32
Kanal SLO 121 Lo44
Kanal Dnjaprouska-Buhski BY 117 Me38
Kanal Dunav-Tisa-Dunav SCG 124 Ma45
Kanalla IND (AAN) 193 Pg42
Kanal Ostródzko-Elbląski PL 117 Lu36
Kanamari do Rio Juruá, T.I. BR 67 Gf49
Kanan RI 209 Ra47
Kananaskis River CDN 19 Ec20
Kananga RDC 289 Mb48
Kananga Z 295 Mc54
Kanangra-Boyd N.P. AUS 237 Sf62
Kananhouolo CI 279 Kh41
Kananmoukro CI 279 Kh42
Kanari RI 212 Re46
Kanas NAM 302 Lj59
Kanaš RUS (CHU) 133 Nd18
Kanatak USA (AK) 14 Cb17
Kanazawa J 183 Rj27
Kanbe MYA 196 Ph37
Kanbi BF 271 Kk39
Kanchanaburi THA 196 Pk38
Kanchanadit THA 198 Pk41
Kanchanpur NEP 170 Pd32
Kanchenjunga IND/NEP 194 Pe32
Kanchenjunga Conservation Area NEP 170 Pd32
Kanchikacherla IND (APH) 191 Pa37
Kanchipuram IND (TNU) 193 Ok40
Kanchiya Z 296 Mf51
Kańczuga PL 119 Mc41
Kandahar AFG 160 Oc30
Kandalakša RUS 140 Mc05
Kandalakšskaja guba RUS 140 Mc05
Kandang RI 198 Pj44
Kandangan RI 208 Qh47
Kandanghaur RI 210 Qe49
Kandan Island MYA 196 Pk39
Kándanos GR 128 Md55
Kandar RI 215 Rf50
Kandare WAN 272 Le41
Kandava LV 97 Mc33
Kande RT 279 La41
Kandéko RCB 281 Lj45
Kandel D 114 Lj41
Kandenmarai IND 190 Oj37
Kandep PNG 243 Sb48
Kandéro DY 272 Lb40
Kandersteg CH 114 Lh44
Kandhkot PK 163 Oe31
Kandi DY 272 Lb40
Kandi IND (WBG) 194 Pe34
Kandiadiou SN 269 Kb39
Kandiana RMM 278 Kg40
Kandiaro PK 162 Oe32
Kandi Bagh AFG 161 Of28
Kandika RG 269 Kd39
Kandila GR 128 Mc53
Kandil Bouzou RN 273 Lf38
Kandílio GR 128 Md52
Kandıra TR 130 Ml49
Kandja RCA 286 Ma43
Kandla IND (GUJ) 190 Of34
Kando RDC 295 Md51
Kandololo RDC 287 Mc45
Kandopleu CI 278 Kg42
Kandos AUS (NSW) 237 Se62
Kandreho RM 306 Nd54
Kandrian PNG 243 Se49
Kandry RUS 133 Nh18
Kanduanam PNG 243 Sb48
Kandukur IND (APH) 193 Ok39
Kandy CL 193 Pa43
Kane Basin DK 11 Gc03
Kanektok River USA 14 Bk16
Kanel SN 269 Kd38
Kanela Buriti Velho, T.I. BR 64 Hh49
Kaneohe USA (HI) 16 Cb35
Kanepi EST 96 Mg33
Kanevskaja RUS 135 Mk22
Kanfanar HR 121 Lo45
Kanfarandé RG 278 Kc40
Kang AFG 160 Oa30
Kang RB 299 Mb57
Kanga EAT 292 Mg49
Kanga EAT 293 Mj49
Kangaba RMM 278 Kf40
Kangal TR 145 Mj26
Kangan IR 156 Ng32
Kanganpur PK 161 Oh30
Kangar MAL 198 Qa42
Kangaré RMM 278 Kf40
Kangaroo Hills AUS (QLD) 233 Sc55
Kangaroo-Island AUS 236 Rj63
Kangaslampi FIN 96 Mj28
Kangasniemi FIN 96 Mg29
Kangavar IR 154 Nd28
Kangayam IND (TNU) 193 Oj41
Kangding VRC (SCH) 176 Qa30
Kangdong DVRK 182 Rd26
Kangen SUD 283 Mg42
Kangerlussuaq = Søndrestrømfjord DK 11 Hb05
Kangerlussuaq DK 11 Hb05
Kangeta EAK 290 Mj45
Kanggye DVRK 182 Rd25
Kanghwa ROK 182 Rd27
Kanghwa Do ROK 182 Rd27
Kangi SUD 283 Md41
Kangiwa WAN 271 Lb39
Kangkir VRC (XUZ) 168 Ok27
Kangmar VRC (TIB) 171 Pe31
Kangnung ROK 182 Re27
Kango G 280 Lf45
Kango Caves SA 302 Mb62
Kangogrotte SA 302 Mb62
Kangole EAU 290 Mh44
Kangonde EAK 290 Mj46
Kangping VRC (LNG) 182 Rb24
Kangra IND (HPH) 189 Oj29
Kangrinboqê Feng VRC 170 Pa30
Kangto VRC/IND 171 Pg32
Kangubu Plains Z 295 Mc54
Kangxian VRC (GSU) 177 Qc29
Kan Gyi MYA 194 Ph35
Kangz'gyai VRC 169 Pj26
Kanha N.P. IND 191 Pa34
Kani CI 278 Kg41
Kani J 183 Rj28
Kani MYA 194 Ph34
Kaniama RDC 289 Mc49
Kaniasso CI 278 Kg41
Kanigiri IND (APH) 193 Ok39
Kani-Gogouna RMM 271 Kj38
Kanika IND (ORS) 191 Pb35
Kanioume RMM 271 Kj38
Kanisa SUD 276 Mf37
Kanita J 183 Sa25
Kaniv UA 134 Mf21
Kaniva AUS (VIC) 236 Sa64
Kanivs'ke vodoschovyšče UA 134 Mf21
Kaniya PNG 243 Sb49
Kanjan Cham IR 154 Nd29
Kanjanka EAT 292 Mg48
Kanjed IND (CGH) 191 Pa36
Kanji-dong DVRK 182 Re25
Kanjiroba NEP 170 Pb31
Kanjiža SCG 124 Ma44
Kanka EAT 293 Mh49
Kankaanpää FIN 96 Mc29
Kankainen FIN 96 Mg28
Kankakee USA (IL) 32 Fg25
Kankalabé RG 278 Ke40
Kankalaha BF 279 Kh40
Kankan RG 278 Kf40
Kankara WAN 272 Ld40
Kankean RI 211 Qh49
Kankelaba RMM 278 Kg40
Kanker IND (CGH) 191 Pa35
Kankesanturai CL 193 Pa42
Kankiya WAN 272 Ld39
Kankossa RIM 269 Ke38
Kankyidaung MYA 196 Ph37
Kanmaw Island MYA 198 Pk40
Kanmen VRC (ZJG) 184 Ra31
Kanna MYA 196 Pj36
Kan Nack VN 197 Qe38
Kannad IND (MHT) 190 Oh35
Kannapolis USA (NC) 35 Fk28
Kannapuram IND (APH) 191 Pa37
Kannauj IND (UPH) 189 Ok32
Kanniyakumari IND (TNU) 193 Oj42
Kannod IND (MPH) 190 Oj34
Kannur IND (KER) 192 Oh41
Kano J 183 Rf28

Lamadi VRC (YUN) 195 Pk32
Lamadrid RA (TU) 76 Gh59
La Majada RA (CA) 76 Gh60
Lamakan RP 204 Qj41
Lamalaga DARS 264 Kb34
La Malbaie CDN (QC) 30 Ge22
La Malène F 105 Ld46
Lama Monastery VRC 176 Pk30
Lamanai BH 41 Ff37
La Mancha E 109 Ks49
La Manche Prov. Park CDN 31 Hd22
Lamandongahao VRC (NMZ) 175 Qf26
La Manta CO 56 Gc41
Lamanuna RI 214 Rb50
Lamap VU 246 Td54
La Máquina MEX (CHH) 23 Eh30
Lamar USA (CO) 28 Ej26
Lamar USA (MO) 29 Fc27
Lamarche F 103 Lf42
Lamard IR 156 Ng32
La Margarita YV 58 Gk41
La Margarita del Norte MEX (COH) 39 Ej32
La María RA (SC) 82 Gf69
Lamarque RA (RN) 80 Gh65
La Marque USA (TX) 29 Fc31
La Marsa TN 260 Lf27
La Martorana I 122 Lo52
Lamas PE 61 Gc47
Lamas PE 66 Gb49
Lama San Martin RA 80 Gf65
La Masica HN 42 Fg38
Lamassa PNG 244 Sg48
Lamastre F 105 Le46
La Mata CO 56 Gd41
Lamau MAL 204 Qj43
La Maya C 45 Gc35
Lamayuru Monastery PK 161 Oj28
Lambach A 115 Lo43
Lambak RI 206 Pk45
Lamballe F 102 Ks42
Lambaré PY 73 Hb58
Lambaréné G 280 Lf46
Lambari BR (MG) 75 Hh56
Lambayeque PE 66 Ga49
Lambay Island IRL 100 Ko37
Lambell, Mount AUS 223 Rg53
Lambert Glacier 313 Ob33
Lambertsbaai SA 302 Lk62
Lamberts Bay SA 302 Lk62
Lambesc F 105 Lf47
Lambi SOL 245 Sk50
Lâmbia GR 128 Mb53
Lambidou RMM 270 Kf38
Lambina AUS (SA) 226 Rj59
Lambrama PE 67 Gd52
Lambu PNG 244 Sf47
Lambubalano RI 209 Rb48
Lambunao RP 205 Rb40
Lambuya RI 209 Rb47
Lambuyen RI 215 Rf49
la Mé CI 279 Kj43
Lamé TCH 273 Lh41
Lame WAN 272 Le40
Lame Burra Game Reserve WAN 272 Le40
Lame Deer USA (MT) 21 Eg23
Lamego P 106 Kn51
Lamen Bay VU 246 Te54
Lamèque CDN (NB) 31 Gh22
La Merced PE 66 Gc51
La Merced RA (CA) 76 Gh60
La Mesa CO 56 Gc43
La Mesa USA (NM) 23 Eg29
Lamesa USA (TX) 28 Ek29
l'Ametlla de Mar E 110 La50
Lamézia Terme-Nicastro I 123 Lr52
Lami FJI 247 Tk55
Lamía GR 128 Mc52
Lamie RI 198 Pj44
La Mina RCH 80 Ge63
Lamindo SUD 287 Mf43
Lamington N.P. AUS 235 Sg60
La Misa MEX (SO) 23 Ee31
La Misión MEX (BC) 22 Eb29
La Mitad del Mundo EC 60 Ga45
Lamitan RP 205 Rb42
Lamlam RI 212 Rf46
Lammerkop SA 300 Me58
Lammermuir Hills GB 99 Ks35
Lammeulo RI 198 Ph43
Lammhult S 95 Lp33
Lammi FIN 96 Mf29
Lamno RI 198 Ph43
Lamon Bay RP 203 Ra38
Lamongan RI 210 Qg49
La Mongie F 104 La48
Lamont CDN (AB) 19 Ed19
Lamont USA (WY) 21 Eg24
Lamont USA (CA) 22 Ea28
La Montaña PE 52 Gb20
La Mora MEX (COH) 39 Ej32
La Mora RA (MD) 76 Gg63
La Morita MEX (COH) 39 Ej31
La Mothe-Achard F 102 Kt44
Lamotrek Atoll FSM 240 Sb17
La Motte F 105 Lg46
Lamotte-Beuvron F 103 Lc43
La Moure USA (ND) 26 Fa22
Lampa PE 66 Gd53
Lampa PE 67 Ge53
Lampanaih RI 198 Ph43
Lampang THA 196 Pk36
Lam Pao Reservoir THA 197 Qb37
Lampasas USA (TX) 28 Fa30
Lampazos MEX (NL) 39 Ek32
Lampedusa I 122 Ln55
Lampedusa I 260 Lg28
Lampeland N 92 Lk31
Lampeter GB 100 Kq38
Lam Phai THA 198 Qa42
Lamphun THA 196 Pk36
Lampia RI 209 Ra47
Lam Plaimat THA 197 Qb38
Lampman CDN (SK) 24 Ej21
Lamta IND (MPH) 191 Pa34
Lamti BHT 194 Pf32
Lam tok MYA 194 Pg34
Lamu EAK 293 Na47
Lamud PE 66 Gb49
Lamu Island EAK 291 Na47
La Muralla de Ávila E 106 Kq50
La Muralla, P.N. HN 42 Fg38
La Mure F 105 Lf46
Lamuru RI 211 Ra48
Lamy USA (NM) 23 Eh28
Lana I 120 Lm44
Lanai USA 16 Cb35
Lanai City USA (HI) 16 Cb35
Lanaja E 107 Ku51
Lanark GB 99 Kr35
Lanas MAL 204 Qj43
La Nava de Ricomalillo E 108 Kq49
La Nava de Santiago E 108 Ko49
Lanbi Island MYA 198 Pk40
Lancang VRC (YUN) 195 Qa34
Lancang Jiang VRC 195 Qa34
Lancaster GB 101 Ks36
Lancaster USA (CA) 22 Ea28
Lancaster USA (MO) 27 Fd25
Lancaster USA (WI) 27 Fe24
Lancaster USA (OH) 32 Fj26
Lancaster USA (NH) 33 Ge23
Lancaster USA (SC) 35 Fk28
Lancaster USA (PA) 33 Gb25
Lancaster USA (VA) 35 Gb27
Lancaster Sound CDN 11 Fd04
Lance Creek USA (WY) 21 Eh24
Lancefield AUS (VIC) 237 Sc64
Lancelin AUS (WA) 228 Qh61
Lancester USA (PA) 33 Gb25
Lánchid H 119 Lu43
Lanciano I 122 Lp48
Lanco RCH 80 Gd65
Łańcut PL 117 Mc40
Landa de Matamoros MEX 39 Fa35
Landak RI 208 Qe45
Landana ANG 288 Lg48
Landau D 114 Lj41
Landau D 115 Ln42
Landay AFG 160 Ob30
Land Between The Lakes USA 34 Ff27
Landeck A 114 Ll43
Landeh IR 154 Nf30
Lander USA (WY) 21 Ef24
Landerneau F 102 Kq42
Lander River AUS 226 Rg56
Landeryd S 95 Lo33
Landes F 104 Kt47
Landete E 109 Kt49
Landfall Island IND 193 Pg39
Land Glacier 312 Cc33
Landi RG 278 Ke40
Landi Kotal PK 161 Of28
Landing Lake CDN 24 Fb18
Landis CDN (SK) 19 Ef19
Landivisiau F 102 Kq42
Landless Corner Z 296 Me53
Landmannalaugar IS 90 Ka14
Land O'Lakes USA (FL) 36 Fj31
Landor AUS (WA) 224 Qj58
Landrecies F 103 Ld40
Landri Sales BR (PI) 64 Hj49
Landsberg D 113 Ln39
Landsberg D 115 Ll42
Landsbro S 95 Lp33
Landscheid D 114 Lg41
Land's End GB 100 Kp40
Landsford Canal S.P. USA 35 Fk28
Landshut D 115 Ln42
Landskrona S 95 Ln35
Landsortsdjupet 93 Lt32
Landvetter S 94 Ln33
Lane City USA (TX) 29 Fb31
La Negra RA (BA) 81 Ha64
La Negra RCH 72 Ge57
Lane Poole Conservation Res. AUS (WA) 228 Qj62
Lanfiéra BF 271 Kj39
Langå DK 94 Lk34
Langa PE 66 Gb52
Långå S 93 Lo28
Langabou RT 279 La41
La'nga Co VRC 170 Pa30
Langadas GR 126 Md50
Langa de Duero E 107 Kr51
Langa-Langa RDC 288 Lj47
Langanes IS 90 Kc12
Langar UZB 158 Oc25
Langar UZB 158 Od26
Langara RI 209 Rb48
Langara Island USA 17 Dd18
Langarud IR 154 Nf27
Langarud IR 154 Nf28
Långås S 94 Ln34
Langatabbetja SME 59 Hc43
Langberg SA 302 Ma62
Langberg SA 302 Mb60
Langbinsi GH 279 Kk40
Lang Cay VN 178 Qc34
Lang Cung VN 178 Qc35
Langdon USA (ND) 24 Fa21
Langeac F 105 Ld45
Langeais F 102 La43
Lange Anna D 112 Lh36
Langebaan SA 302 Lj62
Langeberg SA 302 Ma62
Langedijk NL 112 Le38
Langeland DK 94 Ll35
Langelandsbælt DK 94 Ll36
Längelmäki FIN 96 Me29
Längelmävesi FIN 96 Me29
Langen D 112 Lj37
Langen D 114 Lj41
Langenau D 114 Ll42
Langenberg D 112 Lj39
Langenburg CDN (SK) 24 Ek20
Langenhagen D 112 Lk38
Langenlois A 115 Lq42
Langenthal CH 114 Lh43
Langenzenn D 115 Ll41
Langeoog D 112 Lh37
Langerak DK 94 Ll34
Langeri RUS 181 Sb20
Langesund N 92 Lk32
Langevåg N 92 Lf31
Langevåg N 92 Lg28
Langfeng VRC (HBI) 175 Qj26
Langford CDN (BC) 18 Dj21
Langga RI 209 Qk47
Langgam RI 206 Qa45
Langgapayung RI 206 Pk45
Langgur RI 212 Rg48
Langham CDN (SK) 19 Eg19
Langholm GB 99 Ks35
Langjökull IS 90 Jk13
Langka RI 198 Pj43
Langkahan RI 198 Pj43
Langkawi MAL 198 Pk42
Langklip SA 302 Ma60
Langkofel = Sasso Lungo I 120 Lm44
Langlo Crossing AUS (QLD) 235 Sc59
Langlo River AUS 235 Sc58
Langmusi VRC (GSU) 176 Qb28
Langnau CH 114 Lh44
Lango RCB 281 Lh45
Langogne F 105 Ld46
Langon F 104 Ku46
Langøya N 90 Lh11
Langqên Zangbo VRC 170 Pa30
Langres F 103 Lf43
Langruth CDN (MB) 24 Fa20
Langsa RI 198 Pj43
Lang Shan VRC 174 Qd25
Långshyttan S 93 Lr30
Långsjöby S 90 Lj13
Lang Son VN 178 Qd35
Lang Suan THA 198 Pk41
Langtang NEP 170 Pc31
Langtang WAN 272 Le41
Langtang N.P. NEP 170 Pc31
Långträsk S 90 Ma13
Langtry USA (TX) 28 Ek31
Langu THA 198 Pk42
Langue de Barbarie, P.N. de la SN 269 Kb38
Languedoc F 104 Lc47
Languedoc-Roussillon F 105 Ld46
Langueyú RA 81 Ha64
Languineo RA (CB) 80 Ge67
Langxi VRC (AHU) 184 Qk30
Langxiang VRC (HLG) 180 Re22
Langzhong VRC (SCH) 177 Qc30
Lanigan CDN (SK) 19 Eh20
Lanigan Creek CDN 19 Eh20
Lanín, P.N. RA 80 Ge65
Lanín, Volcán RCH 80 Ge65
Läppe S 93 Lq31
Lappeenranta FIN 96 Mj29
Lappersdorf D 115 Ln41
Lappfjärd = Lapväärtti FIN 93 Mb28
Lappi FIN 96 Mb29
Lappohja = Lappvik FIN 96 Md31
Lappoluobbal N 91 Mb11
Lappträsk = Laapinjärvi FIN 96 Mg30
Lappvik = Lappohja FIN 96 Md31
Laprida RA (BA) 81 Gk64
La Pryor USA (TX) 28 Fa31
Lapseki TR 130 Mg50
Laptev Sea RUS 141 Qd03
Lapua FIN 91 Mb14
La Puebla de Cazalla E 108 Kp47
La Puebla del Río E 108 Ko47
La Puebla de Montalbán E 109 Kq49
La Puebla de Valverde E 109 Ku50
La Puerta MEX (BC) 22 Ec29
La Puerta RA (CD) 76 Gj61
La Puerta YV 57 Ge41
Lapu-Lapu RP 205 Rc40
La Punilla RCH 80 Ge64
La Punta EC 60 Gb45
La Punta RA (SE) 76 Gh60
La Purísima MEX (BCS) 38 Ed32
Lăpuș RO 124 Me43
La Push USA (WA) 18 Dh22
Lăpușna MD 125 Mj44
Lăpușna MD 125 Mj44
Lăpușna RO 125 Mf44
Lapväärtti = Lappfjärd FIN 93 Mb28
Lapwai USA (ID) 18 Eb22
Łapy PL 117 Mc38
Laqiyat Arba'in SUD 276 Me36
Laqiyat 'Umran SUD 276 Me37
La Quiaca RA (PJ) 72 Gh57
L'Aquila I 122 Lo48
Lar IND (UPH) 189 Pb32
Lar IR 156 Nh32
Lara AUS (VIC) 237 Sc64
Lara G 281 Lf45
Larabanga GH 279 Kk41
Laracha E 106 Km53
Larache MA 258 Kg28
Lara de los Infantes E 107 Kr52
Laragh IRL 100 Ko37
Laragne-Montéglin F 105 Lf46
La Ramada, Cerro BOL/RA 72 Gg57
Laramanay TCH 281 Lh41
Laramarca PE 66 Gc52
Laramate PE 66 Gc53
Laramie USA (WY) 21 Eh25
Laramie Mts. USA 21 Eh24
Laramie Peak USA 21 Eh24
Laranja BR (PI) 71 Hk50
Laranjeiras do Sul BR (PR) 74 Hd58
Laranjinha, T.I. BR 74 He57
Larantuka RI 214 Rb50
Larasara IND (ORS) 191 Pb35
La Rastra MEX (SL) 39 Eh34
Larat RI 215 Rg49
La Raya PE 67 Ge53
Larba DZ 259 Lb27
L'Arbresle F 105 Le45
Lärbro S 95 Lt33
Lärchenhof D 112 Lg39
Larde MOC 297 Mk54
Larderello I 120 Ll47
Larder Lake CDN (ON) 25 Ga21
l'Ardoukouba DJI 284 Nb40
Laredo E 107 Kr53
Laredo USA (TX) 39 Fa32
La Reforma C 44 Fj35
La Reforma MEX (SO) 22 Ee31
La Reforma MEX (SL) 38 Ef33
La Reforma RA (LP) 80 Gg64
La Reforma YV 58 Gk42
Laren VRC (GZG) 178 Qe33
La Réole F 104 Ku46
Largeau TCH 274 Lk37
Largentière F 105 Le46
L'Argentière-la Bessée F 105 Lg46
Largs GB 99 Kq35
la Rhune F 104 Kt47
Lariang RI 209 Qk46
Lariang RI 209 Qk46
La Ribera MEX (BCS) 38 Ef34
La Rica CO 56 Gc42
Lárimna GR 128 Md52
Larino I 122 Lp49
La Rioja E 107 Ks52
La Rioja RA 55 Gc26
La Rioja RA (LR) 76 Gg60
Lárissa GR 126 Mc51
Larkana PK 162 Oe32
Lark Harbour CDN (NF) 31 Ha21
Larkollen N 92 Ll31
Larmor-Plage F 102 Kr43
Larnach Castle NZ 239 Tf68
Larnaka CY 131 Mo56
Larnaka Gulf CY 131 Mo55
Lárnax CY 131 Mo56
Larned USA (KS) 28 Fa26
Laro CAM 281 Lg41
La Robla E 106 Kp52
La Roca de la Sierra E 108 Ko49
La Rochebeaucourt-et-Argentine F 104 La45
La-Roche-Bernard F 102 Ks43
La Roche-Chalais F 104 La45
La Roche-en-Ardenne B 103 Lf40
La Rochefoucauld F 104 La45
La Rochelle CDN (MB) 24 Fb21
La Rochelle F 102 Kt44
La Roche-Posay F 102 La44
La Roche-sur-Foron F 105 Lg44
La Roche-sur-Yon F 102 Kt44
La Roda E 109 Ks49
La Roda de Andalucía E 108 Kq47
La Romana DOM 46 Gf36
Larón E 106 Ko52
La Ronge CDN (SK) 19 Eh18
Larop EAU 287 Mf44
Laroquebrou F 104 Lc46
Larose USA (LA) 29 Fe31
La Rosita CO 57 Ge43
La Rosita MEX (COH) 39 Ej31
La Rosita NIC 42 Fh39
Larrimah AUS (NT) 223 Rg53
Larrimah Historic Railway Station AUS (NT) 223 Rg53
Larroque RA (ER) 77 Ha62
Larry Point AUS 224 Qk55
Larry's River CDN (NS) 31 Gk23
Lars Christensen Coast 313 Ob32
Larsen Bay USA (AK) 16 Cc17
Larsen Ice Shelf 312 Gd32
Larto USA (LA) 29 Fe30
La Ruidosa GCA 41 Ff38
Laruns F 104 Ku48
Larvik N 92 Lk31
Laržanka UA 125 Mj45
Las 3 Matas YV 57 Gh41
Las Acequias RA (CD) 76 Gj62
Las Adjuntas MEX (JLC) 39 Ej34
Lasalimu RI 209 Rb48
La Salitrera MEX (GUR) 40 Ek37
La Sal Junction USA (UT) 21 Ef26
La Salle USA (IL) 32 Ff25
La Salvetat-sur-Agout F 104 Lc47
Las Aminas USA (CO) 28 Ej26
Lasanga Island PNG 243 Sd49
La Sanne CH 114 Lh44
Las Armas RA (BA) 81 Hb64
La Sarre CDN (QC) 25 Ga21
Las Arrias RA (CD) 76 Gj61
Las Bocas MEX (SO) 38 Ef32
Las Bonitas YV 57 Gh42
Las Breas RCH 76 Ge60
Las Breñas RA (CH) 77 Gk59
Las Cabezas de San Juan E 108 Kp46
Las Cabras MEX (SL) 38 Eh34
La Scala I 120 Lk45
Las Calenturas MEX (SO) 22 Ed30
Las Campanas Observatory RCH 76 Ge60
Las Cañas RA (CA) 76 Gh60
Lascano ROU 77 Hc62
Las Canoas MEX (DGO) 39 Eh34
Lascar, Volcán RCH 72 Gg57
Las Casuarinas RA (SJ) 76 Gf61
Las Catitas RA (MD) 76 Gf62
Lascelles AUS (VIC) 237 Sb63
Las Chapas RA (CB) 80 Gg67
Las Choapas MEX (VC) 41 Fc37
La Scie CDN (NF) 31 Hc21
la Scieri G 281 Lg45
Las Claritas YV 58 Gk42
Las Coloradas MEX (COH) 39 Ek32
Las Conchas BOL 73 Ha54
Las Conchas MEX (CHH) 23 Eh31
Las Cortaderas RA (NE) 80 Ge65
Las Cruces MEX (DGO) 39 Eh34
Las Cruces MEX (TM) 39 Fa34
Las Cruces USA (NM) 23 Eg29
Las Cuatas MEX (CHH) 23 Eh30
Las Dawaco SP 285 Ne40
Las Delicias CO 56 Ge43
Las Delicias RA (SE) 76 Gh59
La SelvaLacandona MEX 41 Fe37
Lasem RI 210 Qf49
la Sénia E 110 La50
La Serena E 108 Kp48
La Serena RCH 76 Ge60
Las Estrellas MEX (SO) 22 Ed31
La Seu de Palma de Mallorca E 110 Lc51
La Seu d'Urgell E 110 Lb48
La Seyne-sur-Mer F 105 Lf47
Las Flores MEX (TM) 39 Fb34
Las Flores RA (SJ) 76 Gf61
Las Flores RA (BA) 81 Ha64
Las Galeras DOM 46 Gf36
Las Garzas RA (SF) 77 Gk60
Las Gaviotas MEX (SLP) 39 Fa34
Las Glorias MEX (SL) 38 Ef33
Las Guacamayas MEX (MHC) 40 Ej36
Las Hacheras RA (CH) 73 Gk58
Lashburn CDN (SK) 19 Ef19
Lash-e Joveyn AFG 160 Oa30
Las Heras RA (SC) 82 Gf69
las Hermosas, P.N. CO 56 Gc44
Lashio MYA 195 Pj34
Lashkar Gah AFG 160 Oc30
Lashkari Bazar AFG 160 Oc30
Lasht PK 161 Og27
Las Huertas MEX (ZCT) 39 Ek33
Lasia RI 198 Pj44
Lasiana Beach RI 214 Rb51
Las Iglesias de Chiloé RCH 80 Gd67
L'Asile RH 46 Gd36
La Silla Observatory RCH 76 Ge60
Lasimuseo FIN 96 Me30
Łasin PL 116 Lu37
Lasjerd IR 154 Ng28
Łask PL 117 Lu39
Łaskarzew PL 117 Mb39
Laskó H 119 Ma43
Laskowice PL 116 Lt37
Las Lajas RA (NE) 80 Ge65
Las Lajitas MEX (SL) 38 Ef32
Las Lajitas RA (SA) 73 Gh58
Las Leñas RA (MD) 76 Ge63
Las Lisas GCA 41 Fe39
Las Lomas PE 60 Fk48
Las Lomitas RA (FO) 73 Gk58
Las Margaritas MEX (DGO) 39 Eh34
Las Marismas E 108 Ko47
Las Martinas C 44 Fh35
Las Médulas E 106 Ko52
Las Mercedes YV 57 Gg41
Las Minas PA 43 Fk42
Las Navas RP 203 Rc39
Las Navas de la Concepción E 108 Kp47
Las Negras E 109 Ks46
Las Nieves E 108 Ko47
Las Norias MEX (TM) 39 Fa33
Las Nutrias RA (BA) 81 Ha65
La Solana E 109 Kr48
La Soledad CO 56 Ge43
La Soledad MEX (DGO) 38 Eg33
La Soledad MEX (NL) 39 Ek33
La Soledad PA 43 Fk42
Lasolo RI 209 Ra47
Las Orquídeas, P.N. CO 56 Gb42
La Sortija RA (BA) 81 Gk65
La Soufrière WV 47 Gk39
La Souterraine F 104 Lb44
Las Ovejas RA (NE) 80 Ge64
Lasovo SCG 126 Mc47
Las Palmas PE 66 Gc50
Las Palmas de Gran Canaria E 264 Kc31
Las Palomas MEX (CHH) 23 Eh30
Las Palomas MEX (COH) 39 Ek32
Las Pedroñeras E 109 Ks49
Las Perdices RA (CD) 76 Gj62
Las Petas BOL 68 Ha54
La Spézia I 120 Lk46
Las Piedras PE 67 Gf52
Las Piedras ROU 77 Hb63
Las Plumas RA (CB) 80 Gg67
Las Pulgas RA (CB) 80 Gf68
Las Ramadas RCH 76 Ge61
Las Rosas RA (SF) 77 Gk62
Lassance BR (MG) 75 Hh54
l'Assekrem DZ 266 Lc34
Lassen Volcanic N.P. USA (CA) 20 Dk25
Lassul PNG 244 Sf48
Las Tablas MEX (SLP) 39 Fa34
Las Tablas PA 43 Fk42
Låstad S 93 Lo32
Lastarria, Volcán RCH/RA 72 Gf58
Last Chance USA (CO) 26 Ej26
Las Tinajas RA (SE) 76 Gj59
Last Mountain Lake CDN 19 Eh20
Las Torolas, Cerro RA/RCH 76 Gf60
Las Toscas RA (BA) 77 Gk63
Las Toscas RA (SF) 77 Ha60
Las Toscas ROU 77 Hc62
Lastoursville G 288 Lg46
Lastovo HR 123 Lr48
Lastovo HR 123 Lr48
Las Trincheras YV 57 Gh42
Las Trojes HN 42 Fh38
Las Tunas C 45 Gb35
Las Tunitas MEX (BCS) 38 Ee33
La Suze-sur-Sarthe F 102 La43
Las Varas MEX (CHH) 23 Ef31
Las Varas MEX (CHH) 39 Eh31
Las Varas MEX (NYT) 39 Eh35
Las Varillas RA (CD) 77 Gj61
Las Vegas USA (NV) 22 Ec27
Las Vegas USA (NM) 23 Eh28
Las Vegas (La Tasajera) MEX (DGO) 39 Eh33
Las Ventas con Peña Aguilera E 109 Kq49
Las Vilos RCH 76 Ge61
Las Viñas E 109 Kr47
Las Virgenes, Volcán MEX 38 Ed32
La Tabatière CDN (QC) 31 Ha20
Latacunga EC 60 Ga46
Latady Island 312 Ga33
Latakia SYR 144 Mh28
Latalata RI 212 Rd46
la Tapera RCH 80 Ge68
La Tapoa RN 271 Lb39
Latas RCH 72 Gf57
La Tasajera MEX (SO) 23 Ef31
Latchford CDN (ON) 33 Ga22
Låtefossen N 92 Lg31
Latehar IND (JKD) 191 Pc34
Late Island TO 248 Bc55
Laterza I 123 Lr50
Latgale LV 97 Mg34
Latham AUS (WA) 228 Qj60
Lathen D 112 Lh38
Latheron GB 99 Kr32
La Ticla MEX 40 Ej36
La Tigra, P.N. HN 42 Fg38
Latik RIM 270 Kg37
Latimo Jong Mountain Reserve RI 209 Ra47
Latina I 122 Ln49
La Tina PE 60 Ga48
La Tinaja MEX (VC) 40 Fb36
La Tinaja de Bartolo MEX (DGO) 39 Eh33
La Tinidad RP 203 Ra37
Latisana I 121 Lo45
Látky SK 119 Lu42
Lato CI 279 Kh41
La Toba E 109 Kt50
Latoden BF 271 Kj39
La Tola EC 60 Ga45
La Toma RA (SL) 76 Gh62
Latorycja UA 119 Mc42
Latou RI 209 Ra47
Latouche USA (AK) 15 Cg15
Latouche Island USA 16 Cf16
La Tour du-Pin F 105 Lf45
Látrabjarg IS 90 Jj13
La Trampa PE 66 Fk49
La Tranca RA (SL) 76 Gg62
La Tranche-sur-Mer F 102 Kt44
La Tremblade F 104 Kt45
La Trimouille F 104 Lb44
La Trinidad YV 57 Gf41
La Trinidad de Orichuna YV 57 Gf42
La Trinitaria MEX (CHP) 41 Fd37
La Trinité F 47 Gk38
La Trinité-Porhoët F 102 Ks42
Latrobe USA (PA) 33 Ga25
La Troncal EC 60 Ga47
Latrónico I 123 Lq50
La Troya RA 76 Gf60
Latundo-Lompo RI 211 Ra49
La Tunia CO 61 Gd45
La Tuque CDN (QC) 30 Gd22
Latur IND (MHT) 190 Oj36
Latvia LV 97 Mc34
Lat Yao THA 196 Pk38
Lau PNG 244 Sf48
Lau WAN 273 Lf41
Lau Basin 221 Ua22
Lauca, P.N. RCH 72 Gf55
Lauchhammer D 113 Lo39
Lauda-Königshofen D 114 Lk41
Lauder GB 99 Ks35
Lauderdale AUS (TAS) 236 Sd67
Laudio-Llodio E 107 Ks53
Laudona LV 97 Mg34
Lauenburg D 113 Ll37
Lauf D 115 Lm41
Laufen D 115 Ln43
Lauffen (Neckar) D 114 Lk41
Laugarbakki IS 90 Jk13
Laughlin USA (NV) 22 Ec28
Lauhanvuoren kansallispuisto FIN 96 Mc28
Laujar de Andarax E 109 Ks46
Laukaa FIN 96 Mf28
Laukuva LT 97 Mc35
Laun THA 198 Pk40
Launceston AUS (TAS) 236 Sd66
Launceston GB 100 Kq40
Launglon MYA 196 Pk38
La Unión CO 56 Gb43
La Unión CO 60 Gb45
La Unión E 109 Ku47
La Unión EC 60 Fk46
La Unión HN 42 Fg38
La Unión MEX (DGO) 39 Ej33
La Unión MEX (GUR) 40 Ek37
La Unión MEX (QTR) 41 Ff37
La Unión PE 66 Gb50
La Unión RA (SA) 73 Gj57
La Unión RCH 80 Gd66
La Unión RCH 80 Gd66
La Unión YV 57 Gg41
Laulounbok Islands MYA 196 Pj39
Laupheim D 114 Lk42
Laura AUS (QLD) 231 Sc53
Laura AUS (SA) 236 Rk62
La Urbana YV 57 Gg42
Laurel USA (MT) 21 Ef23
Laurel USA (MS) 29 Ff30
Laureles MEX (COH) 39 Ej32
Laurel Park USA (MD) 33 Gb26
Laurencekirk GB 99 Ks34
Laurens USA (SC) 35 Fj28
Laurentians = Les Laurentides CDN 30 Gb22
Lauri IND (MPH) 191 Pa33
Lauria I 123 Lq50
La Uribe CO 56 Gb43
La Uribe CO 60 Gc44
Lau Ridge 218 Tb12
Laurie Lake CDN 24 Ej17
Laurinburg USA (NC) 35 Ga28
Lauriya Mandangarh IND (BIH) 189 Pc32
Lauro de Freitas BR (BA) 71 Ja52
Lauro Muller BR (SC) 79 Hf60
Lauro Sodré BR (AM) 62 Gj47
Lausanne CH 114 Lg44
Lausche D 113 Lp40
Lausitzer Neiße D 113 Lp39
Laussat F 59 Hd43
Laut RI 199 Qe43
Laut RI 208 Qe46
Laut RI 208 Qh47
Lautaporras FIN 96 Md30
Lautaro RCH 80 Gd65
Lautaro, Cerro RCH 82 Gd70
Lautem TIM 214 Rd50
Lauterbach (Hessen) D 112 Lk40
Lauterecken D 114 Lh41
Lautoka FJI 247 Tj54
Laut Strait RI 208 Qj47
Lauwersoog NL 112 Lg37
Lauzerte F 104 Lb46
Lava Beds Nat. Mon. USA (CA) 20 Dk25
Lavadáki GR 128 Mb53
Lavaderos MEX (TM) 39 Fa34
Laval CDN (QC) 33 Gd23
Laval F 102 Ku42
la Vall d'Uixó E 109 Ku49
Lavalle RA (MD) 76 Gf62
Lavalle RA (SE) 76 Gh60
Lavan IR 156 Ng32
Lavanono RM 306 Nc58
Lavara GR 127 Mg49
Lavaraty RM 306 Nd57
Lavardac F 104 La46
Lava Tubes AUS 233 Sc55
Lavaur F 104 Lb47
Lávdas GR 126 Mb50
La Vega CO 60 Gb44
La Vega DOM 46 Ge36
La Vela de Coro YV 57 Gf40
Lavelanet F 104 Lb48
Lavello I 123 Lq49
Laveno I 120 Lj45
La Ventura MEX (COH) 39 Ek33
La Verendrye Mon. USA 26 Ek23
Laverton AUS (WA) 228 Rb60
Laverton Downs AUS (WA) 228 Rb60
Lavia FIN 96 Mc29
La Victoria MEX (SLP) 39 Ek34
La Victoria YV 56 Ge42
La Victoria YV 57 Gg40
La Vieille-Lyre F 102 La42
Lavik N 92 Lf29
La Vila Joiosa E 109 Ku48
La Viña RA (SA) 72 Gh58
Lavina USA (MT) 21 Ef22
Lavitola RA (BA) 77 Gk62
La Visite, P.N. RH 46 Gd36
La Viuda YV 58 Gj41
La Voulte-sur-Rhône F 105 Le46
Lavras BR (MG) 75 Hh56
Lavras de Mangabeira BR (CE) 65 Ja49
Lavras do Sul BR (RS) 78 Hd61
Lavre P 108 Km48
Lavrentija RUS 141 Ub05
Lavrio GR 128 Me53
Lavrovo RUS 91 Mj16
Lavry RUS 96 Mh33
Lavumisa SD 303 Mf59
Lavushi Manda N.P. Z 296 Mf52
Lawaki FJI 247 Tk54
Lawang RI 210 Qg49
Lawarai Pass PK 161 Of28
Lawas MAL 204 Qh43
Lawashi River CDN 25 Fj19
Lawdar YE 150 Nc39
Law Dome 313 Qc32
Lawe Sigalagala RI 198 Pj44
Laweueng RI 198 Ph43
Lawha IND (MHT) 190 Oj36
Lawik Reef PNG 244 Sg51
Lawit, Gunung RI 208 Qg45
Lawksawk MYA 195 Pj35
Lawley River N.P. AUS 222 Rc53
Lawn CDN (NF) 31 Hc22
Lawn Bay CDN 31 Hc22
Lawngmasu IND (MZR) 194 Pg34
Lawngngaw MYA 195 Ph32
Lawn Hill AUS (QLD) 232 Rk55
Lawn Hill N.P. AUS 232 Rk55
Lawn Hill River AUS 232 Rk55
Lawqah KSA 147 Nb31
Lawra GH 279 Kj40
Lawrence NZ 239 Te68
Lawrence USA (KS) 27 Fc26
Lawrence USA (MA) 33 Ge24
Lawrenceburg USA (TN) 34 Fg28
Lawrence House CDN 31 Gj23
Lawrenceville USA (GA) 35 Fj29
Lawrence Wells, Mount AUS 224 Ra59
Lawson AUS (NSW) 237 Sf62
Lawton USA (OK) 28 Fa28
Lawton USA (PA) 33 Gb25
Lawu, Gunung RI 210 Qf49
Laxå S 93 Lp32
Laxenburg A 115 Lr42
Laxford Bridge GB 99 Kq32
Laxi VRC (SDG) 182 Ra27
Laxman Jhoola IND 189 Ok30
Lay BF 271 Kk39
Lay F 102 Kt44
Laya RG 278 Kd41
Laya Dula RG 278 Ke41
Layang-Layang MAL 204 Qg42
La Yarada PE 72 Ge55
La Ye YV 57 Gf42
Layla KSA 149 Nd34
Layo PE 67 Ge53
Layshi MYA 194 Ph33
Layton USA (UT) 21 Ee25
Laytonville USA (CA) 20 Dj26
Laž RUS 133 Ne17
Lazarevac SCG 124 Ma46
Lazarevskoe RUS 135 Mk24
Lázaro Cárdenas MEX (BC) 22 Ec30
Lázaro Cárdenas MEX (MHC) 40 Ej37
Lazaropore MK 126 Ma49
Lazdijai LT 97 Md36
Lázio I 122 Ln48
Lazo RUS 141 Rd05
Lazo RUS 180 Rg24
La Zulema RA (SF) 77 Gk60
Lazuri de Beiuș RO 124 Mc44
Lead USA (SD) 26 Ej23
Leader CDN (SK) 19 Ef20
Leading Tickles CDN (NF) 31 Hc21
Leadore USA (ID) 21 Ed23
Leadville USA (CO) 21 Eg26
Leaf Rapids CDN (MB) 24 Fa17
Leahy USA (WA) 18 Ea22
Leakesville USA (MS) 29 Ff30
Leakey USA (TX) 28 Fa31
Lea Leau PNG 243 Sd50
Lealui Z 295 Mb53
Leamington CDN (ON) 32 Fj24
Le'an VRC (JGX) 184 Qh32
Leanchoil CDN (BC) 19 Eb20
Leander Point AUS 228 Qh60
Leandro RA (BA) 81 Ha65
Leandro N.Alem RA (MI) 77 Hc59
Leang-Leang RI 211 Qk48
Leaning Temple IND 191 Pc35
Leanja RM 304 Nd53
Le'an Jiang VRC 184 Qj31
Learmonth AUS (WA) 224 Qh57
Leavenworth USA (WA) 18 Dk22
Leavenworth USA (KS) 27 Fc26
Łeba PL 116 Ls36
Lebach D 114 Lg41
Lebak RP 205 Rc42
Lebaktebang RI 207 Qc48
Lébamba G 288 Lf47
Lebane SCG 126 Mb48
Lébango RCB 281 Lh45
Lébango RCB 281 Lh45
Lebanon RL 146 Mh29
Lebanon USA (OR) 20 Dj23
Lebanon USA (MO) 29 Fd27
Lebanon USA (IN) 32 Fg25
Lebanon USA (PA) 33 Gb25
Lebanon USA (NH) 33 Gd24
Lebanon USA (TN) 34 Fg27
Lebanon USA (KY) 34 Fh27
Lebanon USA (FL) 36 Fj31
Lebanon, Mount RL 146 Mh29
Lebap TM 153 Oa25
Le Barón MEX (CHH) 23 Eg30
Le Beausset F 105 Lf47
Lebed' RUS 167 Pd19
Lebedjan RUS 133 Mk19
Lebedyn UA 132 Mh20
Lebel-sur-Quévillon CDN (QC) 25 Gb21
Lebel-sur-Quévillon CDN (QC) 30 Gb21
Lébiri G 281 Lg46
Le Blanc F 102 Lb44
Lebo RDC 286 Mb43
Lebombo SD 303 Mf59
Lebongtandai RI 206 Qa47
Leboni RI 209 Ra47
Lebon Régis BR (SC) 78 He59
Le Borgne RH 46 Gd36
Lębork PL 116 Ls36
Le Bourg-d'Oisans F 105 Lg45
Lebowa Bochum SA 300 Me57
Lebowakgomo SA 300 Me58
Lebrija CO 56 Gd42
Lebrija E 108 Ko46
Lebu RCH 80 Gd64
Le Buisson-de-Cadouin F 104 La46
Le Castellet F 105 Lf47
Le Cateau-Cambrésis F 103 Ld40
Le Catelet F 103 Ld41
Le Caylar F 105 Ld47
Lecce I 123 Lt50
Lecco I 120 Lk45
Lécera E 107 Ku51
Lech A 114 Ll43
Lech D 115 Ll42
L'Echalp F 105 Lg46
Lechang VRC (GDG) 179 Qg33
Le Château-d'Oléron F 104 Kt45
Le Châtelet F 105 Lc44
Lecheria YV 57 Gh40
Le Chesne F 103 Le41
Le Cheylard F 105 Le46
Lechinta RO 124 Me43
Lechtaler Alpen A 114 Ll43
Léči LV 97 Mb33
Lecina E 110 La48
Leciñena E 107 Ku51
Leck D 112 Lj36
Le Conquet F 102 Kq42
Le Creusot F 105 Le44
Le Croisic F 102 Ks43
Le Crotoy F 103 Lb40
Lectoure F 104 La47
Łęczna PL 117 Mc39
Łęczyca PL 116 Lq37
Łęczyca PL 117 Lu38
Ledesma E 106 Kp51
Ledmore GB 99 Kq32
Lednice-Valtice CZ 118 Lr42
Ledong VRC (HAN) 178 Qe36
Le Donjon F 105 Ld44
Le Dorat F 104 Lb44
Le Doubs CH 114 Lh43

orough GB 101 Kt38
Conn IRL 98 Kl36
Corrib IRL 98 Kl37
erg IRL 100 Km38
Ennel IRL 100 Kn37
Foyle IRL/GB 98 Kn35
Gill IRL 98 Km36
Gowna IRL 98 Kn37
eane IRL 100 Kl38
Mask IRL 98 Kl37
Melvin IRL 98 Km36
Neagh GB 98 Ko35
Oughter IRL 98 Kn37
Owel IRL 100 Kn37
ea IRL 100 Km37
Ree IRL 100 Kn37
Sheelin IRL 98 Kn37
Swilly IRL 98 Kn35
DY 272 Lb40
s F 105 Lf44
RUS (KAR) 91 Mg12
i RCB 288 Lh48
USA (KY) 35 Fj26
Downs AUS (WA) 222
Reef 204 Qg42
urg CDN (NS) 31 Gk23
rg USA (NC) 35 Ga27
rgh IRL 98 Kl37
le CDN (NS) 31 Gk23
sland CDN 18 De19
ille CDN (QC) 30 Gd22
de Archipelago PNG
g51
na DK 94 Ln35
na USA 12 Fb12
na Downs USA (LA)
29
na State Arboretum USA
30
nd PNG 243 Sd47
ichardt SA 300
le SA 302 Ma60
le USA (CO) 21 Eh26
le USA (MS) 29 Ff29
le USA (KY) 34 Fh26
le USA (GA) 35 Fj29
le Ridge 221 Ub24
ia GR 128 Md52
la RCB 286 Lj46
o RCB 288 Lh47
Gucheng VRC 169
P 108 Kn47
i RMM 279 Kh40
Park AUS (QLD) 233
CAM 280 Le43
SN 269 Kd38
RCB 288 Lh48
CZ 118 Lo40
ty USA (NE) 26 Fa25
s F 104 Ku47
o BR (AP) 59 He44
P 108 Kl48
cale SN 269 Kc38
ã P 108 Kl49
BF 271 Kj39
AUS (NSW) 235 Sc61
GB 101 La37
RIM 269 Kd37
GR 129 Me53
Edipsoú GR 128 Md52
Eleftherón GR 127 Me50
GR 128 Mb52
GR 128 Md53
igí GR 128 Mc51
GR 127 Mg50
ou RCB 288 Lg47
é F 102 Ku42
urt CDN (QC) 30 Gb21
Luzon F 104 Ku47
s F 102 Lb41
é-du-Désert F 102 Kt42
F 103 Lc42
urg SA 303 Mf59
VRC (GZG) 178 Qe34
er S 90 Ma13
N.P. SCG 126 Lt48
CDN (SK) 19 Eh19
BG 127 Me47
d USA (CO) 21 Eh25
d USA (OH) 32 Fh26
USA (WY) 21 Ef23
k USA (NV) 20 Ea25
I 120 Ll45
CDN (SK) 19 Ef20
Leap JA 45 Gb37
GH 279 Kk41
= Lovisa FIN 96 Mg30
Beach RI 211 Qh50
USA (TX) 28 Fa29
on USA (NM) 23 Ej29
= Loviisa FIN 96 Mg30
HR 121 Ls47
S 93 Lo29
vallen S 93 Lo29
H 118 Lr43
RDC 289 Mc50
e CZ 118 Lp40
HR 121 Lp45
HR 121 Lr47
RO 124 Ma45
ruk S 93 Ls30
ANG 289 Ma49
ANG 289 Ma49
ANG 295 Mb51
RDC 287 Md46
ng IND (JKD) 191 Pc33
pe USA 16 Cc17
USA (ID) 21 Ec22
USA (MA) 33 Ge24
SUD 283 Mg43
NAM 302 Lk59
erg D 113 Lo38
SA 303 Me60
Arrow Lake CDN 18 Ea21
Brule Ind. Res. USA
23
Forster Lake CDN 19
Ft. Garry N.H.P. CDN
20
Glenelg N.P. AUS 236
Guinea 252 Lb09
Hatchie N.W.R. USA
28
Hutt NZ 238 Th66
Lough Erne GB 98 Kn36
Normandie F 102 Ku42
Peninsula USA 32 Fh24
Post CDN (BC) 17 Df16
Red Lake USA 24 Fc21
Sabie SA 300 Mf58
Sackville CDN (NS)
23
Sioux Ind. Res. USA
23

Lower Valley of the Awash ETH 284 Na40
Lower Valley of the Omo ETH 284 Mh43
Lower Zambezi N.P. Z 296 Me53
Lowestoft GB 101 Lb38
Lowest Point in U.S. USA 22 Eb27
Łowicz PL 117 Lu38
Lowkhi AFG 160 Ob30
Lowman USA (ID) 20 Ec23
Lowood AUS (QLD) 235 Sg59
Low Rocky Point AUS 236 Sc67
Lowry Ind. Ruins USA 23 Ef27
Lowville USA (NY) 33 Gc24
Loxstedt D 112 Lj37
Loxton AUS (SA) 236 Sa63
Loxton SA 302 Mb61
Loya RDC 287 Md45
Loyada DJI 285 Nb40
Loyds River CDN 31 Hb21
Loyengo SD 303 Mf59
Loyish UZB 158 Od26
Loyore EAU 290 Mh44
Lož SLO 121 Lp45
Loznica BG 127 Mg47
Loznica SCG 124 Lu46
Ložnikovo RUS 173 Qj20
Lozova UA 135 Mj21
Lozoyuela E 109 Kr50
Ltyentye Apurte A.L. AUS 227 Rh58
Lua RDC 281 Lk44
Luabo MOC 300 Mj55
Luabo RDC 289 Mc50
Luacano ANG 295 Ma51
Luachimo ANG 289 Ma49
Luachimo ANG 289 Ma49
Luachimo ANG 289 Ma51
Luaco ANG 289 Ma49
Lua-Dekere RDC 286 Lk44
Luahula RDC 289 Mb50
Luali RDC 288 Lg48
Luama RDC 292 Me48
Luambe N.P. Z 296 Mg52
Luambimba Z 295 Mb53
Luampa Z 295 Mc53
Luampa Z 295 Mc53
Luampa Kuta Z 295 Mc53
Lu'an VRC (AHU) 184 Qj30
Luanchuan VRC (HNN) 177 Qf29
Luanco E 106 Kp53
Luanda ANG 288 Lg50
Luanda BR (PR) 74 Hd57
Luando ANG 288 Lj51
Luando ANG 294 Lk51
Luang Nam Tha LAO 195 Qa35
Luango ANG 288 Lg48
Luang Pho Phra Chai THA 197 Qb37
Luang Prabang LAO 196 Qb36
Luang Prabang Range LAO 196 Qa36
Luangue ANG 289 Lk50
Luangue ANG 289 Lk50
Luanguinga Z 295 Mb53
Luangundo ANG 295 Ma54
Luangwa Z 292 Mf50
Luangwa Z 296 Mf53
Luangwa Z 296 Mg51
Luan He VRC 175 Qk26
Luanheca ANG 294 Lj53
Luanjing VRC (NMZ) 174 Qc27
Luano RDC 289 Lk48
Luanping VRC (HBI) 175 Qj25
Luanshya Z 296 Me52
Luan Toro RA (LP) 80 Gh64
Luan Xian VRC (HBI) 175 Qk26
Luanza RDC 292 Me50
Luapula RDC/Z 296 Me51
Luarca E 106 Ko53
Luashi RDC 295 Mb51
Luashi RDC 295 Mb51
Luassingua ANG 294 Lk53
Luatamba ANG 295 Ma52
Luau ANG 295 Mb51
Lua-Vindu RDC 286 Ma44
Luba GQ 280 Le44
Lubaanbajo RI 211 Qk50
Lubaantun BH 41 Ff37
Lubaczów PL 117 Md40
Lubalo ANG 289 Lk50
Lubamba RDC 292 Mc48
Lubań PL 116 Lq39
Lubāna LV 97 Mg34
Lubang RP 202 Ra39
Lubang Island RP 202 Ra39
Lubango ANG 294 Lg53
Lubansenshi Z 296 Mf51
Lubans ezers LV 97 Mg34
Lubanza RDC 289 Ma48
Lubao RDC 292 Mc48
Lubartów PL 117 Mc39
Lubawa PL 117 Lu37
Lübbecke D 112 Lj38
Lübbenau (Spreewald) D 113 Lo39
Lübben (Spreewald) D 113 Lo39
Lubbock USA (TX) 28 Ek29
Lubec USA (ME) 31 Gg23
Lübeck D 113 Ll37
Lübecker Bucht D 113 Lm36
Lubefu RDC 289 Mb48
Lubefu RDC 289 Mc48
Lubero RDC 287 Me46
Lubero RDC 287 Me46
Lubersac F 104 Lb45
Lubi RDC 289 Mb48
Lubiąż PL 116 Lr39
Lubień Kujawski PL 117 Lu38
Lubilandji RDC 289 Mb50
Lubimbi ZW 299 Md55
Lubin PL 116 Lr39
Lubishi RDC 289 Mc49
Lubjaniki RUS 133 Na18
Lublin PL 117 Mc39
Lubliniec PL 116 Lt40
Lubniewice PL 116 Lq38
Lubny UA 134 Mg21
Lubok Antu MAL 208 Qf45
Lubomino PL 117 Ma36
Lubompo Z 296 Md53
Luboń PL 116 Lr38
L'ubotin SK 119 Ma41
Lubsko PL 116 Lp39
Lubu RI 209 Rb46
Lubuczewo PL 116 Ls36
Lubudi RDC 289 Ma48
Lubudi RDC 289 Mb48
Lubudi RDC 289 Mc50
Lubudi RDC 292 Mc50
Lubue RDC 289 Lk48
Lubukalung RI 206 Qa46
Lubukbargalung RI 206 Qa46
Lubukbesar RI 206 Qb46
Lubukbesar RI 207 Qd47
Lubuklinggau RI 207 Qb47
Lubukmalaka RI 206 Qa46

Lubukpakam RI 198 Pk44
Lubukpinang RI 206 Qa47
Lubuksikaping RI 206 Qa45
Lubuktapi RI 207 Qb48
Lubule RDC 292 Md50
Lubumba RDC 292 Me47
Lubumbashi RDC 296 Md51
Lubundji RDC 289 Ma48
Lubungu Z 296 Md53
Lubutu RDC 287 Md46
Lubutu RDC 287 Md46
Lubwe Z 296 Me51
Lubycza Królewska PL 117 Md40
Lübz D 113 Ln37
Luca Cernii de Jos RO 124 Mc45
Lucala ANG 288 Lh50
Lucala ANG 288 Lh50
Lucanas PE 66 Gc53
Lucapa ANG 289 Ma50
Lucas USA (IA) 27 Fd25
Lucas do Rio Verde BR (MT) 69 Hc52
Lucas González RA (ER) 77 Ha62
Lucaya BS 37 Ga32
Lucca I 120 Ll47
Lucea JA 45 Ga36
Luce Bay GB 98 Kq36
Lucedale USA (MS) 29 Ff30
Lučegorsk RUS 180 Rh22
Lucena E 108 Kq47
Lucena RP 203 Ra39
Luc-en-Diois F 105 Lf46
Lučenec SK 119 Lu42
Lucera I 122 Lq49
Lucerna PE 67 Gf52
Lucero MEX (TM) 39 Fb33
Lucheng VRC (SAX) 175 Qg27
Lucheng VRC (GZG) 178 Qd33
Luchenza MW 297 Mh53
Luchima MOC 297 Mh53
Lüchow D 113 Lm38
Luchuan VRC (GZG) 178 Qf34
Lüchun VRC (YUN) 195 Qb34
Lucia USA (CA) 22 Dk28
Lučica SCG 124 Mb46
Lucin USA (UT) 21 Ed25
Lucindale AUS (SA) 236 Sa64
Lucio Blanco MEX (TM) 39 Fa33
Lucira ANG 294 Lg52
Luc'k UA 117 Mf40
Luckau D 113 Lo39
Luckenwalde D 113 Lo38
Luckhoff SA 303 Mc60
Lucknow AUS (QLD) 232 Sa57
Lucknow IND (UPH) 189 Pa32
Lucky Lake CDN (SK) 19 Eg20
Lucma PE 66 Ga49
Lucma PE 67 Gd52
Lu Coddu Vecchiu I 111 Lk49
Luçon F 102 Kt44
Lucongpo VRC (HUB) 177 Qf30
Lucossa ANG 288 Lh48
Lucre PE 67 Ge52
Luc-sur-Mer F 102 Ku41
Lucunde ANG 294 Lh52
Lucunga ANG 288 Lh49
Lucunga ANG 288 Lh49
Lucusse ANG 295 Ma52
Lüda VRC (LNG) 182 Ra26
Luda Kamčija BG 127 Mg48
Ludbreg HR 121 Lr44
Ludden USA (ND) 26 Fa22
Lüdenscheid D 112 Lh39
Lüderitz NAM 302 Lh59
Lüderitz Bay NAM 302 Lh59
Lüderitz Shark Island Resort NAM 302 Lh59
Ludesar IND (HYA) 188 Oh31
Ludhiana IND (PJB) 188 Oh30
Ludian VRC (YUN) 195 Qb32
Ludimbi RDC 289 Mc48
Luding VRC (SCH) 176 Qb31
Lüdinghausen D 112 Lh39
Ludington USA (MI) 32 Fg24
Ludlow GB 101 Ks38
Ludlow USA (CA) 22 Eb28
Ludlow USA (CO) 23 Eh27
Ludlow USA (SD) 26 Ej23
Ludomy PL 116 Lr38
Ludowici USA (GA) 35 Fk30
Luduș RO 124 Me44
Ludvika S 93 Lq30
Ludwigsburg D 114 Lk42
Ludwigsfelde D 113 Lo38
Ludwigshafen D 114 Lj41
Ludwigslust D 113 Lm37
Ludza LV 97 Mh34
Ludza LV 97 Mh34
Luebo RDC 289 Ma48
Luebo RDC 289 Ma48
Lueki RDC 289 Mc48
Lueki RDC 292 Mc47
Luele ANG 289 Ma50
Luemba RDC 292 Me47
Luembe ANG 289 Ma50
Luembe RDC 289 Mc49
Luena ANG 295 Lk51
Luena ANG 295 Mb52
Luena RDC 292 Mc50
Luena Z 295 Mc53
Luena Z 296 Mf51
Luena Flats Z 295 Mb53
Luengué ANG 295 Ma54
Luengué ANG 295 Ma54
Lueo RDC 289 Mb51
Lueta RDC 289 Mb49
Lueta RDC 289 Mb50
Lueti ANG 295 Ma53
Lüeyang VRC (SAA) 177 Qd29
Lufeng VRC (GDG) 179 Qh34
Lufeng Dinosaur Fossils VRC 195 Qa33
Lufico ANG 288 Lg49
Lufije ANG 295 Ma51
Lufimi RDC 288 Lj48
Lufira RDC 292 Md50
Lufkin USA (TX) 29 Fc30
Lufu RDC 288 Lg48
Lufuba Z 292 Mf50
Lufuige ANG 295 Mb52
Lufupa RDC 295 Mc51
Lufupa Z 295 Mc52
Lug HR 124 Lt45
Lug SCG 124 Ma46
Luga RUS 96 Mj31
Luga RUS 132 Me16
Lugano CH 114 Lj45
Luganville VU 246 Td53
Lugard's Falls EAK 291 Mk47
Lugazi EAU 290 Mg45
Lugela MOC 297 Mj54
Lughaye SP 285 Nb40
Lugo E 106 Kn52
Lugo I 120 Lm46
Lugogo EAU 290 Mg45
Lugoj RO 124 Mb45
Lugovoi KZ 159 Og24

Lugu VRC (TIB) 170 Pc29
Lugu VRC (SCH) 176 Qb31
Lugulu RDC 287 Md47
Lugus Island RP 205 Ra43
Luh RUS 133 Nb17
Luh RUS 133 Nb17
Luhamaa EST 96 Mh33
Luhanka FIN 96 Mf29
Luhans'k UA 135 Mk21
Luhe VRC (GDG) 179 Qh34
Luhe VRC (JGS) 184 Qk29
Luhovicy RUS 133 Mk18
Luhuo VRC (SCH) 176 Qa30
Lui ANG 289 Lj50
Lui Z 295 Mb53
Luia ANG 289 Ma50
Luia ANG 289 Ma50
Luiana ANG 295 Mb54
Luiana RB 295 Mb54
Luico V.Mansilla RA (CD) 76 Gh60
Luidja EST 96 Mc32
Luie RDC 289 Lj48
Luika RDC 292 Md48
Luilaka RDC 286 Ma47
Luilu RDC 289 Mb49
Luimbale ANG 294 Lh52
Luinga ANG 288 Lh50
Luino I 120 Lj45
Luio ANG 295 Ma52
Luiro MOC 297 Na52
Luís Correia BR (PI) 65 Hk47
Luis Domingues BR (MA) 64 Hh46
Luishia RDC 296 Md51
Luislândia BR (MG) 75 Hh54
Luislândia do Oeste BR (MG) 75 Hh54
Luiza RDC 289 Mb49
Luiza RDC 289 Mb50
Luizavo ANG 295 Mb51
Luizi RDC 292 Md49
Luizi RDC 292 Md49
Luizi Călugăra RO 125 Mg44
Luiz Viana BR (BA) 71 Hk50
Luján RA (SL) 76 Gh62
Luján RA (BA) 77 Ha63
Lujan de Cuyo RA (MD) 76 Gf62
Lujiang VRC (AHU) 184 Qj30
Luka BIH 121 Lt47
Luka SCG 126 Mc46
Luka UA 119 Me41
Lukafu RDC 296 Md51
Lukajanov RUS 133 Nc18
Lukanga Swamp Z 296 Md53
Lukang Folk Arts Festival RC 179 Ra34
Lukashi RDC 289 Mc48
Lukasu RDC 289 Mc50
Luka Telašćica HR 121 Lq47
Lukatini EAT 292 Mg49
Lukavac BIH 124 Lt46
Lukaya EAU 287 Mf46
Luke, Mount AUS 224 Qj59
Lukengo RDC 292 Me48
Lukenie RDC 286 Lk47
Lukeville USA (AZ) 22 Ed30
Lukimwa EAT 297 Mh51
Lukiv UA 117 Me39
Lukole EAT 293 Mk49
Lukolela RDC 286 Lj46
Lukolela RDC 289 Mc48
Lukonzolwa RDC 292 Me50
Lukose EAT 293 Mj49
Lukoshi RDC 295 Mb51
Lukovit BG 127 Me47
Lukovnikovo RUS 132 Mh17
Lukovo HR 121 Lp46
Lukovo MK 126 Ma49
Łuków PL 117 Mc39
Lukozi ZW 295 Md55
Luksagu RI 209 Rb46
Łukta PL 117 Ma37
Lukuga RDC 292 Me48
Lukula RDC 288 Lg48
Lukula RDC 288 Lg48
Lukula RDC 289 Lj48
Lukula RDC 289 Mb48
Lukula RDC 292 Md49
Lukuliro EAT 293 Mk50
Lukuliro EAT 293 Mk50
Lukulu RDC 292 Me49
Lukulu Z 295 Mb53
Lukulu Z 296 Mf51
Lukumbi RDC 292 Me49
Lukumburu EAT 293 Mh50
Lukuni RDC 289 Lj48
Lukusashi Z 296 Mf52
Lukusuzi Z 296 Mg52
Lukusuzi N.P. Z 296 Mg52
Lukuswa RDC 292 Md49
Lukuzye Z 296 Mg52
Lukwasa IND (MPH) 191 Oj33
Lukwika EAT 297 Mk51
Lula USA (MS) 29 Fe28
Luleå S 90 Mb13
Luleälven S 90 Ma13
Lüleburgaz TR 130 Mh49
Luliang VRC (YUN) 195 Qb33
Lüliang Shan VRC 175 Qf27
Lulimba RDC 292 Me48
Lulindi RDC 292 Md48
Luling USA (TX) 28 Fb31
Lulo ANG 289 Lk50
Lulong VRC (HBI) 175 Qk26
Lulonga RDC 286 Lk45
Lulonga RDC 286 Lk45
Lulu RDC 287 Mc44
Lulua RDC 289 Mb48
Lulúti MOC 297 Mk53
Lulworth, Mount AUS 224 Qj59
Luma WAN 272 Lc40
Luma Cassai ANG 295 Lk51
Lumaco RCH 80 Gd65
Lumajang RI 210 Qg50
Lumajangdong Co VRC 168 Pa28
Lumaku, Gunung MAL 204 Qh43
Lumangwe Falls Z 292 Me50
Lumar IR 154 Nd29
Lumata RDC 296 Md52
Lumba RDC 286 Lk43
Lumbala ANG 295 Ma52
Lumbala ANG 295 Mb52
Lumbala N'guimbo ANG 295 Ma53
Lumbaquí EC 60 Gb45
Lumbe Z 295 Mc53
Lumbeme RDC 289 Ma49
Lumberman's Museum USA 30 Gf22
Lumbermen's Mon. USA 32 Fj23
Lumberton USA (TX) 29 Fc30
Lumberton USA (NC) 35 Ga28
Lumbier E 107 Kt52
Lumbini NEP 170 Pb32
Lumbo MOC 297 Na53
Lumbrales E 106 Ko50
Lumbreras RA (SA) 73 Gh58

Lumby CDN (BC) 18 Ea20
Lumding IND (ASM) 194 Pg33
Lumege ANG 295 Ma51
Lumeje ANG 295 Ma51
Lumene RDC 288 Lj48
Lumeta ANG 295 Ma54
Lumezzane I 120 Ll45
Lumholtz N.P. AUS 233 Sc55
Lumi PNG 242 Sb47
Lumimba Z 296 Mg52
Lumimba Z 296 Mg52
Lumino Z 295 Mc54
Lumona Z 296 Md53
Lumparland FIN 93 Ma30
Lumpkin USA (GA) 35 Fh30
Lumpur RI 207 Qc47
Lumsden CDN (SK) 19 Eh20
Lumsden NZ 239 Te68
Lumuna ANG 295 Ma54
Lumuna RDC 292 Md47
Lumut BRU 204 Qh43
Lumut MAL 199 Qa44
Lumutan MAL 204 Qj43
Lumut, Gunung RI 208 Qh46
Lumwana Z 295 Mc51
Lün MNG 172 Qc22
Luna RP 202 Ra37
Luna RP 203 Ra36
Luna USA (NM) 23 Ef29
Lunahuana PE 66 Gb52
Lunan VRC (YUN) 195 Qb33
Lunan Shan VRC 195 Qb32
Lunar Crater USA 20 Ec26
Lunavada IND (GUJ) 190 Og34
Lunawanna AUS (TAS) 236 Sd67
Lunca Corbului RO 125 Me46
Lunca de Jos RO 125 Mf44
Luncani RO 124 Md45
Lund CDN (BC) 18 Dh21
Lund S 95 Lo35
Lund USA (UT) 21 Ed27
Lunda MOC 296 Mh54
Lundazi Z 296 Mg52
Lundazi Z 296 Mg52
Lunde N 92 Lk31
Lunde S 93 Ls28
Lunder DK 94 Lk35
Lundu EAT 297 Mh51
Lundu Z 296 Mg51
Lundy Island GB 100 Kq39
Lüneburg D 113 Ll37
Lüneburger Heide D 112 Lk37
Lunel F 105 Le47
Lünen D 112 Lh39
Lunenburg CDN (NS) 31 Gh23
Lunenburg USA (VA) 35 Ga27
Lunéville F 103 Lg42
Lunga MOC 297 Na53
Lunga Z 295 Md53
Lunga Lunga EAK 293 Mk48
Lunge ANG 294 Lj52
Lungé-Bungo ANG 295 Lk52
Lunggar VRC (TIB) 170 Pb30
Lungharigi VU 246 Td52
Lungi WAL 278 Kd41
Lungi Lol WAL 278 Kd41
Lunglei IND (MZR) 194 Pg34
Lungshan Temple RC 179 Ra33
Lungthung IND (TRP) 194 Pf34
Lungungu RDC 292 Md47
Lungwebungu Z 295 Mb52
Lungwebungu Z 295 Mb52
Luni IND 188 Of33
Luninec BY 132 Md19
Luning USA (NV) 20 Ea26
Lunino RUS 133 Nc19
Lunkaransar IND (RJT) 188 Og31
Lunna BY 97 Me37
Lunsar WAL 278 Kd41
Lunsemfwa Z 296 Me53
Lunsemfwa Z 296 Me53
Lunsemfwa Falls Z 296 Me53
Luntai VRC (XUZ) 168 Pc25
Lunyere EAT 297 Mh51
Lunyuk RI 211 Qj50
Lunyuk Beach RI 211 Qj50
Lunzi Z 296 Mg51
Lunzu MW 297 Mh53
Lunzua Z 292 Mf50
Lunzua Falls Z 292 Mf50
Luobai VRC (GZG) 178 Qd34
Luobei VRC (HLG) 180 Rf22
Luobuzhuang VRC (XUZ) 169 Pe26
Luochuan VRC (SAA) 177 Qe28
Luodian VRC (GZH) 178 Qd33
Luoding VRC (GDG) 178 Qf34
Luofu RDC 287 Me46
Luofushan VRC 179 Qh34
Luo He VRC 177 Qf28
Luohe VRC (HNN) 184 Qh29
Luoma Hu VRC 184 Qk28
Luonan VRC (SAA) 177 Qf28
Luongo Z 292 Me51
Luoning VRC (HNN) 177 Qf28
Luonteri FIN 96 Mh29
Luoping VRC (YUN) 178 Qc33
Luopioinen FIN 96 Me29
Luoshan VRC (HNN) 184 Qh29
Luotian VRC (HUB) 184 Qh30
Luotuoquanzi VRC (XUZ) 169 Ph24
Luoxiao Shan VRC 179 Qg32
Luoyang VRC (HNN) 177 Qg28
Luoyuan VRC (FJN) 184 Qk32
Luozi RDC 288 Lh48
Lupa EAT 292 Mg50
Lupahira EAT 293 Mh50
Lupa Market EAT 292 Mg50
Lupambela EAT 292 Mg49
Lupana PE 61 Gd47
Lupande Z 296 Mf52
Lupane ZW 299 Md55
Lupar MAL 208 Qf45
Lupaso EAT 297 Mk51
Lupembe EAT 293 Mh50
Lupéron DOM 46 Ge36
Lupiro EAT 293 Mj50
Lupon RP 205 Rd42
Lupuka Z 295 Mb54
Lupula ANG 294 Lj53
Luputa RDC 289 Mb49
Lupweji RDC 289 Mc50
Luqiao VRC (AHU) 184 Qj29
Luqiao VRC (ZJG) 184 Ra31
Luqu VRC (GSU) 176 Qb28
Luquan Yizu VRC (YUN) 195 Qb33
Luque PY 73 Hb58
Luquembo ANG 294 Lj51
Lurcy-Lévis F 105 Lc44
Lure F 103 Lg43
Lurgan GB 98 Ko36
Luri RI 208 Qj47
Luribay BOL 72 Gg54
Lurín PE 66 Gb52
Lúrio MOC 297 Mj53
Lurnfeld A 115 Lo44

Luruguma EAK 290 Mh44
Lusahanga EAT 292 Mf47
Lusaka RDC 289 Mc49
Lusaka Z 296 Me53
Lusako RDC 292 Md48
Lusalira EAU 287 Mf45
Lusamba RDC 289 Mc48
Lusambo RDC 289 Mb48
Lusancay Islands PNG 244 Sf50
Lusanga RDC 289 Lk48
Lusangi RDC 292 Md48
Lusenga Plain N.P. Z 292 Me50
Lushan VRC 175 Qk27
Lushan VRC (HNN) 177 Qg29
Lushan VRC (GZH) 178 Qd32
Lushan VRC 184 Qj31
Lushi VRC (HNN) 177 Qf28
Lushimba Rest Camp Z 295 Mc53
Lushipuka Z 292 Me51
Lushnjë AL 126 Lu50
Lushoto EAT 293 Mk48
Lushui VRC 177 Qg31
Lushui VRC (YUN) 195 Pk33
Lushuihe VRC (JLN) 182 Rd24
Lüshun VRC (LNG) 182 Ra26
Lusiba Z 295 Mc54
Lusignan F 102 La44
Lusignan GUY 58 Ha42
Lusigny-sur-Barse F 103 Le42
Lusikisik SA 303 Me61
Lusinga RDC 292 Md50
Lusitania CO 60 Gc44
Lusiwasi Z 296 Mf52
Lusk USA (WY) 21 Eh24
Luso P 106 Km50
Luss GB 99 Kq34
Lussac-les-Châteaux F 104 La44
Lussan F 105 Le46
Lussenga ANG 288 Lg49
Lussusso ANG 294 Lh51
Lustrafjorden N 92 Lh29
Lusu Z 295 Mc54
Lusulu ZW 299 Md55
Luswaka RDC 292 Md50
Luswishi Z 296 Me52
Lutao RC 179 Ra34
Lutembo ANG 295 Ma52
Lütfiye TR 129 Mh52
Luth SUD 283 Mf42
Luthergedenkstätte Eisleben D 113 Lm39
Luthergedenkstätte Wittenberg D 113 Ln39
Lutherstadt Eisleben D 113 Lm39
Lutherstadt Wittenberg D 113 Ln39
Luti SOL 244 Sj49
Luti WAN 273 Lg41
Lütjenburg D 113 Ll36
Lutlut MYA 196 Pk39
Luton GB 101 Ku39
Lutong MAL 204 Qh43
Łutselk'e CDN 10 Eb06
Lutshima RDC 289 Lk48
Lutshuadi RDC 289 Ma48
Lutuai ANG 295 Ma52
Lutuhyne UA 135 Mk21
Lutunguru RDC 287 Me46
Lututów PL 116 Lt39
Lützow-Holm bukta 313 Md32
Lutzputs SA 302 Ma60
Luuk RP 205 Ra43
Luumäki FIN 96 Mh30
Luuq SP 291 Nb44
Luveira RDC 289 Mc51
Luverne USA (MN) 27 Fb24
Luverne USA (AL) 34 Fg30
Luvia FIN 96 Mb29
Luvidjo RDC 292 Md49
Luvo ANG 288 Lh48
Luvu RDC 288 Lg48
Luvua ANG 295 Mb51
Luvua RDC 292 Md49
Luvuei ANG 295 Ma52
Luvunzo RDC 292 Me49
Luwawa MW 296 Mg52
Luwe RDC 292 Me50
Luwegu EAT 293 Mj50
Luwembe Z 296 Mf53
Luwero EAU 290 Mg45
Luwingu Z 296 Me51
Luwo VRC (GZG) 178 Qe34
Luwombwa Z 296 Me52
Luwuk RI 209 Rb46
Luwumba Z 296 Mg51
Luxembourg L 103 Lg41
Luxembourg L 103 Lg41
Luxemburg USA (IA) 27 Fe24
Luxeuil-les-Bains F 103 Lg43
Luxi VRC (HUN) 177 Qf31
Luxi VRC (YUN) 195 Pk33
Luxi VRC (YUN) 195 Qb33
Lüxia VRC (FJN) 184 Ra32
Luxikegongba VRC (TIB) 170 Pd30
Luxor ET 263 Mg33
Luxor ET 263 Mg33
Luyando PE 66 Gc50
Luyi VRC (HNN) 184 Qh29
Luz BR (MG) 75 Hh55
Lužajka RUS 96 Mj30
Luz-Ardiden F 104 Ku48
Luzern CH 114 Lj43
Luzhai VRC (GZG) 178 Qe33
Luzhi VRC (GZH) 178 Qc32
Luzhou VRC (SCH) 177 Qc31
Luzi ANG 295 Ma52
Luzi RDC 289 Lk48
Luziâna BR (GO) 74 Hg54
Luzilândia BR (PI) 65 Hj47
Luzino PL 116 Lt36
Luzon RP 203 Ra38
Luzon Strait 200 Ra14
Luz-Saint-Sauveur F 104 Ku48
Lužskaja guba RUS 96 Mj31
Luzy F 105 Ld44
L'viv UA 119 Md41
Lwakhaka EAK 290 Mh45
Lwanga Z 292 Mg50
Lwela Z 296 Me51
Lwówek Śląski PL 116 Lq39
Lyall, Mount NZ 239 Td68
Lyantonde EAU 287 Mf46
Lycan USA (CO) 23 Ej27
Lychen D 113 Lo37
Lycksele S 90 Lk13
Lyddal CDN (MB) 24 Fa18
Lydenburg SA 300 Mf58
Lydia USA (KS) 28 Ek26
Lydiannasundet N 91 Me06
Lydney GB 101 Ks39
Lyell Island CDN 18 De19
Lygnern S 94 Ln33
Lykso SA 303 Mc59
Lyle USA (WA) 20 Dk23
Lyman UA 125 Mk45

Lyme Bay GB 100 Kr40
Lyme Regis GB 100 Ks40
Lymington GB 101 Kt40
Łyna PL 117 Ma36
Lynchburg USA (TN) 34 Fg28
Lynchburg USA (SC) 35 Fk28
Lynchburg USA (VA) 35 Ga27
Lynden USA (WA) 18 Dj21
Lyndhurst AUS (SA) 227 Rk61
Lyndhurst AUS (QLD) 232 Sc55
Lyndon AUS (WA) 224 Qh57
Lyndon River AUS 224 Qh57
Lyndonville USA (VT) 33 Gd23
Lynd River AUS 232 Sb54
Lyngdal N 92 Lh32
Lyngen N 90 Ma11
Lyngør N 92 Lk32
Lyngseidet N 90 Ma11
Lynn USA (UT) 21 Ed25
Lynn USA (MA) 33 Ge24
Lynn Canal USA 17 Dc16
Lynndyl USA (UT) 21 Ed26
Lynn Haven USA (FL) 35 Fh30
Lynn Lake CDN (MB) 24 Ek17
Lynton GB 100 Kr39
Lyntupy BY 97 Mg35
Lyon F 105 Le45
Lyon Mountain USA (NY) 33 Gd23
Lyons USA (KS) 28 Fa26
Lyons USA (NY) 33 Gb24
Lyons USA (GA) 35 Fj29
Lyons Falls USA (NY) 33 Gc24
Lyons-la-Forêt F 103 Lb41
Lyons River AUS 224 Qh58
Lypci UA 133 Mj20
Lypova Dolyna UA 132 Mg20
Łyse PL 117 Mb37
Lysefjorden N 92 Lg32
Lysekil S 92 Lm32
Lysi CY 131 Mo55
Lyskovo RUS 133 Nc17
Lysøysundet N 90 Le14
Lyss CH 114 Lh43
Lystrup DK 94 Ll34
Lysvik S 93 Lo31
Lysyčans'k UA 135 Mk21
Lysye Gory RUS 133 Nc20
Lytham Saint Anne's GB 101 Ks37
Lyton AUS (WA) 228 Qh60
Lytton CDN (BC) 18 Dk20
Lyubimets BG 127 Mg49

M

Ma CAM 281 Lf42
Maala Z 296 Md53
Ma'alaea Bay USA 16 Cb35
Maalhosmadulu North = Raa Atoll MV 192 Og43
Maalhosmadulu South = Baa Atoll MV 192 Og43
Maamba Z 296 Md54
Maam Cross IRL 98 Kl37
Ma'an CAM 281 Lf44
Ma'an JOR 146 Mh30
Maanit MNG 172 Qb21
Maanit MNG 172 Qd22
Ma'an, Mount VRC 195 Pk33
Maanselkä FIN 91 Me12
Maanselkä FIN 91 Me14
Ma'anshan VRC (AHU) 184 Qk30
Maardu EST 96 Mf31
Ma'aret Mokhouz SYR 146 Mj28
Maarianhamina = Mariehamn FIN 93 Lu30
Maarja EST 96 Mg32
Ma'arrat an-Nu'man SYR 146 Mj28
Maas NL 112 Lg39
Maasai Mara Nature Reserve EAK 290 Mh46
Maasbracht NL 112 Lf39
Maaseik B 103 Lf39
Maasim RP 205 Rc43
Maasin RP 205 Rc40
Maasmechelen B 103 Lf40
Maasstroom SA 300 Me57
Maastricht NL 112 Lf40
Maatsuyker Islands AUS 236 Sd67
Maazaplateau ET 263 Mf32
Mâaziz MA 258 Kg29
Maba RI 212 Re45
Mababe Depression RB 299 Mc55
Ma'bad IR 154 Nh28
Mabaduam PNG 242 Sa49
Mabaia ANG 288 Lh49
Mabaké SN 269 Kc38
Mabalacat RP 202 Ra38
Mabalane MOC 300 Mg57
Mabana RDC 287 Me45
Mabanda BU 292 Me48
Ma'bar YE 150 Nc38
Mabarangandu EAT 293 Mj50
Mabating VRC (YUN) 176 Pk31
Mabdeitikra IND (CGH) 191 Pb34
Mabein MYA 195 Pj34
Mabel Creek AUS (SA) 227 Rh60
Mabélé CAM 281 Lg42
Mabeleapudi RB 299 Md57
Mabelle USA (TX) 28 Fa29
Mabenga RDC 289 Lk47
Mabenge RDC 287 Mc43
Mabian VRC (SCH) 176 Qb31
Mabinay RP 205 Rb41
Mablethorpe GB 101 La37
Mabo SN 269 Kc39
Mabokweni EAT 293 Mk48
Mabole WAL 278 Kd41
Maboleni ZW 300 Me55
Mabopane SA 299 Me58
Mabote MOC 300 Mh57
Mabou CDN (NS) 31 Gk22
Mabroûk RMM 271 Kk36
Mabrous RN 267 Lg35
Mabruk LAR 261 Lj30
Mabton USA (WA) 20 Dk22
Mabuasehube Game Reserve RB 299 Mb58
Mabuhay RP 205 Rb42
Mabuiag Island AUS 230 Sb50
Mabuki EAT 292 Mg47
Mabura GUY 58 Ha43
Mabuto WAN 272 Lc40
Mabutsane RB 299 Mb58
Macache EC 60 Ga46
Macachin RA (LP) 81 Gj64
Macaé BR (RJ) 75 Hk57
Macaena MOC 300 Mg58
Macaíba BR (RN) 65 Jc48
Macajalar Bay RP 205 Rc41
Macajuba BR (BA) 71 Hk52

Macanda MOC 297 Mh54
Macandze MOC 300 Mg57
Macane MOC 300 Mg56
Macao VRC 179 Qg35
Macao VRC (MAC) 179 Qg34
Macapá BR (AP) 63 He45
Macará EC 60 Ga48
Macara RP 203 Ra36
Macaracas PA 43 Fk42
Macarani BR (BA) 71 Hk53
Macareo YV 58 Gk41
Macarí PE 67 Ge53
Maçaroca BR (BA) 71 Hk50
Macaroni AUS (QLD) 232 Sa54
Macarrão, T.I. BR 61 Gg47
Macarrtane MOC 300 Mg58
Macarthur AUS (VIC) 236 Sb65
Macas EC 60 Ga47
Macatanja MOC 297 Mj54
Macaú BR (RN) 65 Jb48
Macauá BR 67 Gf50
Macauari BR (AM) 62 Ha46
Macaúba BR (TO) 64 Hg48
Macaúbas BR (BA) 70 Hj52
Macauley Island NZ 221 Ua25
Macaxeira BR (AM) 67 Gg49
Macclenny USA (FL) 35 Fj30
Macclesfield GB 101 Ks37
Macclesfield Bank 202 Qh37
Macdiarmid CDN (ON) 25 Ff21
Macdonald Downs AUS (NT) 227 Rh57
Macdonald, Mount VU 246 Te54
Macdonnell Ranges AUS 226 Rg57
Macea RO 124 Mb44
Maceda E 106 Kn52
Macedo de Cavaleiros P 106 Ko51
Macedonia MK 126 Mb49
Maceió BR (AL) 71 Jc50
Macenta RG 278 Kf41
Macerata I 121 Lo47
MacGrath USA (AK) 15 Cc14
Mach PK 162 Od31
Macha BOL 72 Gg55
Macha Z 296 Md54
Machacalis BR (MG) 75 Hk54
Machacamarca BOL 72 Gg55
Machachi EC 60 Ga46
Machachuta ZW 300 Me56
Machadinho BR (RO) 68 Gj50
Machadinho BR 68 Gj50
Machado BR (MG) 75 Hh56
Machadodorp SA 300 Mf58
Machado ou Ji-Paraná BR 68 Gk50
Machagai RA (CH) 77 Gk59
Machaila MOC 300 Mg57
Machakos EAK 290 Mj46
Machala EC 60 Ga47
Machalí RCH 76 Ge63
Machalilla EC 60 Fk46
Machalilla, P.N. EC 60 Fk46
Machanbaw MYA 195 Pj32
Machaneng RB 299 Md57
Machang VRC (GZH) 178 Qd32
Machanga MOC 300 Mh56
Machault F 103 Le41
Machawaian Lake CDN 25 Ff20
Machecoul F 102 Kt44
Macheke ZW 300 Mf55
Machemmaruines SA 300 Me57
Machemma Ruins SA 300 Me57
Macheng VRC (HUB) 184 Qh30
Macherla IND (APH) 191 Ok37
Machesse MOC 300 Mh55
Machgaon IND (ORS) 194 Pd35
Machhapuchare NEP 170 Pb31
Machias USA (ME) 31 Gg23
Machichi River CDN 24 Fe17
Machihiri ZW 296 Me54
Machila Kuta Z 295 Mc54
Machile Z 295 Mc54
Machina WAN 272 Lf39
Machinga MW 297 Mh53
Machiques YV 56 Gd40
Machu Picchu PE 67 Gd52
Machupo BOL 67 Gh52
Machynlleth GB 100 Kr38
Macia MOC 300 Mg58
Maciana Marina I 120 Ll48
Maciejowice PL 117 Mb39
Măcin RO 125 Mj45
Macinaggio F 111 Lk48
Mackay AUS (QLD) 233 Se56
Mackay USA (ID) 21 Ed24
Mac Kean Island KIR 241 Ub19
Mackenzie CDN 10 Dd06
Mackenzie CDN (BC) 18 Dj18
Mackenzie Bay CDN 10 Da05
Mackenzie Bay 313 Oc32
Mackenzie King Island CDN 11 Ec03
Mackenzie Mountains CDN 17 Df14
Mackinac S.P. USA 32 Fh23
Mackinaw City USA (MI) 32 Fh23
Mackinnon Road EAK 293 Mk47
Macklin CDN (SK) 19 Ef19
Macks Inn USA (ID) 21 Ee23
Macksville AUS (NSW) 235 Sg61
Maclean AUS (NSW) 235 Sg60
Maclean Strait CDN 10 Ed03
Macleantown SA 303 Md62
Maclear SA 303 Me61
Macmillan Pass CDN 17 Df14
Macmillan Plateau CDN 17 Dd14
Macmillan River CDN 17 Dc14
Maco RP 205 Rc42
Maçobere MOC 300 Mg56
Macocola ANG 288 Lj49
Macomb USA (IL) 27 Fe25
Macomér I 111 Lj50
Macomia MOC 297 Na52
Mâcon F 105 Le44
Macon USA (MO) 27 Fd26
Macon USA (MS) 29 Ff29
Macon USA (OH) 32 Fj26
Macon USA (GA) 35 Fj29
Macondo ANG 295 Mb52
Macossa MOC 296 Mg54
Macoun Lake CDN 24 Ej17
Macovane MOC 300 Mh56
Macquarie Harbour AUS 236 Sc67
Macquarie Islands 218 Sb15
Macquarie Ridge 218 Sb15
Mac Robertson Land 313 Nd33
Macroom IRL 100 Km39
Macrorie CDN (SK) 19 Eg20
Mactaris TN 260 Le28
Mactún MEX (TB) 41 Fe37
Macucauá BR (AM) 67 Ge49
Macugnaga I 120 Lh45
Macuira, P.N. CO 56 Ge39
Macuma EC 60 Gb47
Macumba AUS (SA) 227 Rj59

i RI 213 Rh46
IND (APH) 191 Ok36
'kala RUS (DAG) 152
gwess Lake CDN 25
odi SA 299 Me58
s F 102 La42
CAM 280 Le43
N.P. RB 299 Mb55
n RCH 72 Gf56
gui CI 279 Kh42
Pawa GUY 58 Ha44
RI 213 Rh47
IND (MZR) 194 Pg34
anat RN 266 Ld36
oth Cave AUS 228 Qh63
oth Cave N.P. USA
j27
oth Hot Springs USA
21 Ee23
oth Lakes USA (CA)
a27
oth Springs USA (AR)
a27
date, T.I. BR 67 Ge51
iro BR (AC) 67 Gf50
as BR (MG) 70 Hj53
ovo RUS 117 Lu36
né BOL/BR 67 Gh51
iá BR (AM) 67 Gg49
RG 278 Kd40
dzou F 304 Nc52
kony RM 306 Nd54
dre E 106 Kp53
ng GH 279 Kk42
ngtin Range GH 279
WAN 280 Lb42
'o MOC 297 Mj52
Choique RA (RN) 80
Malal, P. RA/RCH 80
RI 209 Qk47
que MEX (NL) 39 Ek32
o RB 299 Ma57
e Kalesi TR 144 Mg27
u BR 63 Hb47
ovo RUS (TAR) 133 Nf18
CI 278 Kg42
RCA 281 Lh42
F 59 Hd43
F 59 Hd43
acias CO 56 Gd44
amp ZW 296 Me53
apurú BR (AM) 62 Gk47
apurú BR 62 Gk47
or E 110 Ld51
hoo MV 192 Og43
RI 209 Rc45
UA 119 Mf41
ua NIC 42 Fg39
OM 157 Nj34
a BR (PB) 65 Ja49
are CO 57 Ge43
amana NEP 170 Pc31
ana RM 306 Nd54
ara RM 306 Nd57
Chowk and Havelis IND
f32
ha YE 150 Nb38
londo RM 306 Nd55
IND (HPH) 189 Oj29
a UAE 157 Nh33
a ZW 300 Me56
adurai IND (TNU) 193
baro RM 306 Nd58
bolo RM 306 Nc55
bolosy RM 306 Ne54
bondro RM 306 Nd57
ensalo FIN 91 Md13
RI 213 Rh47
Island PNG 243 Sc48
oc Island RP 205 Ra40
ara RM 306 Nd57
ara Avaratra RM 306
dona RM 306 Nd56
ga RI 214 Rb50
gatang AUS (VIC) 237
goora AUS (NT) 223 Rj53
ary RM 306 Ne56
koro RMM 278 Kg40
ali RMM 269 Ke39
enina RM 306 Nd58
oddy IND (KER) 192 Oj41
ur IND (APH) 191 Ok37
arai IND (TNU) 193 Ok41
Pass VRC/IND 170 Ok30
Pools N.P. ZW 296
rie YV 57 Gg41
uiri BR (AM) 62 Gk47
BR (PE) 71 Jb50
PNG 243 Sd50
a BR (AM) 61 Gg48
PE 66 Gb51
VRC (XUZ) 167 Pd23
arowar = Mapam Yumco
170 Pa30
He VRC 167 Pc23
Hu VRC 167 Pd23
kent RUS (DAG) 152
u NEP 170 Pc31
sas USA (VA) 33 Gb26
Tiger Reserve IND
f32
tir Dečani SCG 126 Ma48
tir Đurđevi Stupovi SCG
Lu48
itirea RO 125 Mg46
itirea Bistriţa RO 125
itirea Cocoş RO 125 Mj45
itirea Cozia RO 124 Me45
itirea Hincu MD 125 Mj43
itirea Humorului RO
Mf43
itirea Hurezi RO 124
itirea Sinaia RO 125 Mf45
itirea Snagov RO 125
tir Gračanica SCG 126
tirile Basarabi RO 125
tir Kalenić SCG 126 Ma47
tir Ljubostinja SCG 126
tir Manasija SCG 126
tir Mileševa SCG 126
tir Ostrog SCG 126 Lu48

Manastir Ravanica SCG 126 Mb47
Manastir Savina SCG 126 Lt48
Manastir Sopoćani SCG 126 Ma47
Manastir Studenica SCG 126 Ma47
Manastir Žiča SCG 126 Ma47
Manat KZ 167 Pb21
Manati C 45 Ga34
Manati C 45 Gb35
Manati USA (PR) 47 Gg36
Manatial BOL 73 Gj55
Manatuto TIM 214 Rc50
Manau PNG 243 Sd50
Man'aung MYA 196 Pg36
Manaure CO 56 Gd40
Manaus BR (AM) 62 Gk47
Manavgat TR 131 Mm54
Manavgat Baraj TR 131 Mm54
Manavgat Şelâlesi TR 131 Mm54
Manawar IND (MPH) 190 Oh34
Manawoka RI 212 Rf48
Manay RP 205 Rd42
Mañazo PE 67 Ge53
Manba VRC (YUN) 195 Qa34
Manbazar IND (WBG) 194 Pd34
Manbej SYR 146 Mj27
Mancha Khiri THA 197 Qb37
Mancha Real E 109 Kr47
Mancheng Hanmu Tombs VRC 175 Qh26
Manchester GB 101 Ks37
Manchester USA (IA) 27 Fe24
Manchester USA (CT) 33 Gd25
Manchester USA (NH) 33 Ge24
Manchester USA (TN) 35 Fh28
Manchester USA (KY) 35 Fj27
Manchester Center USA (VT) 33 Gd24
Manchhar Lake PK 162 Od32
Manching D 115 Lm42
Manchirayal IND (APH) 191 Ok36
Manchis MAL 199 Qb44
Manchok WAN 272 Le41
Manchuria VRC 165 Ra10
Manciano I 122 Lm48
Mancora PE 60 Fk48
Mancos USA (CO) 23 Ef27
Mand PK 162 Ob32
Manda BD 194 Pe33
Manda EAT 292 Mg50
Manda EAT 297 Mh51
Manda TCH 282 Lk41
Mandabe RM 306 Nc56
Mandagadde IND (KTK) 192 Oh40
Mandaguari BR (PR) 74 He57
Mandah RI 207 Qb46
Mandai PK 162 Oe31
Manda Island EAK 291 Na47
Mandal MNG 172 Pk21
Mandal MNG 172 Qd21
Mandal N 92 Lh32
Mandalay MYA 195 Pj35
Mandalay N.W.R. USA 29 Fe31
Mandalgarh IND (RJT) 188 Oh33
Mandalgov' MNG 172 Qd23
Mandali IRQ 147 Nc29
Mandamabgwe ZW 300 Mf56
Mandan USA (ND) 26 Ek22
Mandaon RP 203 Rb39
Mandapeta IND (APH) 191 Pb37
Manda, P.N.de TCH 273 Lk41
Mandara LAR 267 Lg32
Mandara Mountains WAN 273 Lg40
Mândas I 111 Lk51
Mandasip RI 206 Pk45
Mandaue RP 205 Rb40
Mandeb AFG 160 Oa29
Mandélia TCH 273 Lh40
Mandem IND (CGH) 191 Pa36
Mandera EAK 291 Na44
Mandera USA (CA) 20 Dk27
Mandeville JA 45 Gb36
Mandheera SP 285 Nc41
Mandi IND (HPH) 189 Oj30
Mandi IND (GUJ) 190 Og35
Mandiakoy RMM 271 Kj38
Mandiakur RMM 270 Kh39
Mandiana RG 278 Kf40
Mandi Bahauddin PK 161 Og29
Mandi Burewala PK 161 Og30
Mandicaba BR (PR) 74 Hd57
Mandi Dabwali IND (PJB) 188 Oh31
Mandié MOC 296 Mg54
Mandi Langwé CAM 281 Lf43
Mandimba MOC 297 Mh53
Mandioli RI 212 Rd46
Mandira IND 191 Pc34
Mandji = Sangala G 288 Lf46
Mandla IND (MPH) 191 Pa34
Mandlakazi MOC 300 Mg58
Mando WAN 272 Ld40
Mandoli IND (RJT) 188 Og33
Mandon RI 213 Rj46
Mandor RI 208 Qe45
Mandoro RDC 287 Me43
Mandoto RM 306 Nd55
Mandoul TCH 281 Lj41
Mandouri RT 279 La40
Mândra RO 124 Md45
Mandráki GR 129 Mh54
Mandrare RM 306 Nd58
Mandritsara RM 305 Ne53
Mandronarivo RM 306 Nc56
Mandrosonoro RM 306 Nd56
Mandsaur IND (MPH) 190 Oh34
Mandu IND 190 Oh34
Mandu IND (JKD) 191 Pc34
Mandul RI 209 Qj44
Mandumbua ANG 295 Ma53
Mandundu Z 295 Mb54
Mandurah AUS (WA) 228 Qh62
Mandúria I 123 Ls50
Mandvi IND (GUJ) 190 Oe34
Mandwa Beach IND 190 Og36
Mandya IND (KTK) 193 Oj40
Mané BF 271 Kk39
Mâne N 92 Lj31
Maneadero C 44 Fk34
Maneadero MEX (BC) 22 Eb30
Manegaon IND (MPH) 191 Oa34
Mané Kondjo TCH 273 Lk40
Maner IND (BIH) 191 Pc33
Manèrbio I 120 Ll45
Maneromango EAT 293 Mk49
Manerson Beach RI 210 Qg49
Maneroo AUS (QLD) 232 Sb57
Manevyči UA 117 Mf39
Manfalût ET 263 Mf32
Manfeilong VRC (YUN) 195 Qa35
Manfred AUS (WA) 224 Qj59
Manfred Downs AUS (QLD) 232 Sa56

Manfredónia I 123 Lq49
Manga BF 279 Kk40
Manga BR (MG) 70 Hj53
Manga CAM 281 Lg42
Manga PNG 244 Sg48
Manga RN 273 Lg38
Mangada RDC 287 Md44
Mangada RDC 287 Me44
Manga Grande ANG 288 Lg49
Mangai EAK 291 Na46
Mangai PNG 244 Sf47
Mangai RDC 289 Lk48
Mangaïzé RN 271 La38
Mangalagiri IND (APH) 191 Pa37
Mangalia RO 125 Mj47
Mangalmé TCH 282 Lk39
Mangalore AUS (QLD) 235 Sd59
Mangalore AUS (VIC) 237 Sc64
Mangalore IND (KTK) 192 Oh40
Mangalvedha IND (MHT) 190 Oh37
Mangamaunu NZ 239 Tg67
Mangamila RM 306 Nd55
Mangango Z 295 Mc53
Manganti RI 206 Qa46
Mangaon IND (MHT) 190 Og36
Mangarwar IND (RJT) 190 Oh33
Mangawah IND (MPH) 191 Pa33
Mangaweka NZ 238 Th65
Mangaweka NZ 238 Tj65
Mangchang VRC (GZG) 178 Qd33
Mangdangshan VRC 184 Qj28
Mange PNG 243 Sd49
Mange WAL 278 Kd41
Mangen N 92 Lm31
Manger N 92 Lf30
Manggar RI 207 Qe47
Manggasi RI 213 Rj47
Manggopoh RI 206 Qa46
Mangho Pir PK 162 Od33
Manghystau KZ 152 Nf24
Manghystau shyghanaghy KZ 152 Nf23
Manghystau üstirti KZ 153 Ng24
Mangial IND (MHT) 190 Oj36
Mangindrano RM 305 Ne53
Mang'it UZB 153 Oa24
Mangkururrpa A.L. AUS 226 Re56
Manglaralto EC 60 Fk46
Manglares CO 56 Gb43
Mangla Reservoir PK 161 Og29
Manglar Zapoton MEX 41 Fd38
Mangnai VRC (QHI) 169 Pf27
Mangnai Zhen VRC (QHI) 169 Pf26
Mangoaka RM 305 Ne52
Mangochi MW 297 Mh53
Mango Creek BH 41 Ff37
Mango Creek BH 41 Ff37
Mangoky RM 306 Nc56
Mangoky RM 306 Nc57
Mangole RI 212 Rc46
Mangom CAM 281 Lg42
Mangombe RDC 287 Md46
Mangonui NZ 238 Tg63
Mangoro RM 306 Ne55
Mangoudara BF 279 Kh41
Mangral IND (GUJ) 190 Of35
Mangrove Cay BS 37 Ga32
Mangrove Cay BS 37 Gb33
Mangrul Pir IND (MHT) 190 Oj35
Mangshan VRC 177 Qg28
Mangualde P 106 Kn50
Manguchar PK 162 Od31
Mangueigne TCH 282 Ma40
Mangueira, T.I. BR 58 Gk44
Mangueirinha BR (PR) 78 Hd58
Manguel Creek AUS (WA) 222 Rb54
Mangui VRC (NMZ) 173 Rb19
Manguito C 44 Fk34
Mangum USA (OK) 28 Fa28
Mangungu RDC 288 Lj48
Mangunza Z 296 Md54
Mangut RUS 173 Qg21
Mangwe ZW 300 Mf55
Manhamade MOC 297 Mj54
Manhao VRC (YUN) 195 Qb34
Manhattan USA (MT) 21 Ee23
Manhattan USA (KS) 27 Fb26
Manhica MOC 300 Mg58
Manhuaçu BR 75 Hj55
Manhuaçu BR (MG) 75 Hj56
Manhumirim BR (MG) 75 Hk56
Manhup Kale UA 135 Mg23
Mani CO 56 Gd43
Máni GR 128 Mc54
Mani RDC 289 Mc49
Mani TCH 273 Lh39
Mani WAN 272 Ld39
Mania RM 306 Nd56
Maniago I 121 Ln44
Mania-Muna RDC 289 Mb50
Maniapure YV 57 Gg42
Manicani Island RP 205 Rc40
Manicoré BR (AM) 62 Gk48
Manicoré BR 62 Gk49
Manicouagan CDN (QC) 30 Gf20
Manifah KSA 149 Ne32
Maniganggo VRC (SCH) 176 Pk30
Manigotagan CDN (MB) 24 Fb20
Manihari IND (BIH) 194 Pd33
Manihi Atoll F 249 Ch53
Manihiki Atoll NZ 241 Ud21
Manika IND (JKD) 191 Pc34
Manika RDC 295 Mc51
Manikganj BD 194 Pe34
Manikpur IND (UPH) 191 Pa33
Manila RP 203 Ra38
Manila USA (UT) 21 Ef25
Manila Bay RP 203 Ra38
Manilaid EST 96 Me32
Manildra AUS (NSW) 237 Se62
Manilla AUS (NSW) 235 Sf61
Maningrida AUS (NT) 223 Rh52
Maninjau RI 206 Qa46
Manipa RI 212 Rd47
Manipur IND 187 Pc13
Manisa TR 129 Mh52
Manises E 109 Ku49
Manissauá-Miçu BR 69 Hc51
Manistee USA (MI) 32 Fg23
Manistique USA (MI) 32 Fg23
Manitique Lake USA 27 Fh22
Manitoba CDN 11 Fa08
Manito Lake CDN 19 Ef19
Manitou CDN (MB) 24 Fa21
Manitou CDN (QC) 30 Gh20
Manitou USA (OK) 28 Fa28
Manitou Lake CDN 24 Fd21
Manitoulin Island CDN 32 Fj23
Manitounuk Sound CDN 25 Gb18
Manitou Springs USA (CO) 21 Eh26

Manitouwadge CDN (ON) 25 Fh21
Manitowaning Lodge CDN 32 Fk23
Manitowish USA (WI) 27 Fe22
Manitowoc USA (WI) 32 Fg23
Manitsoq = Sukkertoppen DK 11 Hb05
Maniwake Ind. Res. CDN 30 Gb22
Maniwaki CDN (QC) 30 Gc22
Maniwori RI 213 Rh47
Manizales CO 56 Gc43
Manja RM 306 Nc56
Manjakandriana RM 306 Nd55
Manjamba MOC 297 Mh52
Manjar Sumba IND (MHT) 190 Oh36
Manjeri IND (KER) 192 Oj41
Manjhand PK 162 Oe33
Manjira W.S. IND 190 Ok37
Manjlegaon IND (MHT) 190 Oj36
Manjo CAM 280 Le43
Manjola ZW 296 Md54
Manjou CAM 281 Lg43
Manjra IND 190 Oj36
Mankachar IND (ASM) 194 Pe33
Mankanza RDC 286 Lk45
Månkarbo S 93 Ls30
Man Kat MYA 195 Pk35
Mankato USA (KS) 26 Fa26
Mankato USA (MN) 27 Fd23
Mankera PK 161 Of30
Mankhan MNG 172 Qa20
Mankhan Nature Reserve MNG 167 Pg22
Manki CAM 281 Lf43
Mankim CAM 281 Lg43
Mankono CI 279 Kg41
Mankpan GH 279 Kk41
Mankrangso GH 279 Kk42
Mankulam CL 193 Pa42
Manley Hot Springs USA (AK) 15 Ce13
Man Li MYA 195 Pj34
Manlleu E 110 Lc49
Manmad IND (MHT) 190 Oh35
Manna RI 207 Qb48
Manna Hill AUS (SA) 236 Rk62
Man-Namlet MYA 195 Pk34
Mannar CL 193 Ok42
Mannemkonda IND (ORS) 191 Pa36
Manners Creek AUS (NT) 227 Rj57
Mannheim D 114 Lj41
Manni VRC (TIB) 170 Pd28
Manning USA (ND) 26 Ej22
Manning USA (SC) 35 Fk29
Manning Prov. Park CDN 18 Dk21
Manning Range, Mount AUS 228 Qk60
Manning Strait SOL 245 Sj49
Manningtree GB 101 Lb39
Mann Ranges AUS 226 Re58
Mann River AUS 223 Rh52
Mannum AUS (SA) 236 Rk63
Mannville CDN (AB) 19 Ee19
Mano LB/WAL 278 Ke42
Mano WAL 278 Kd41
Manoá Pium, T.I. BR 58 Gk44
Manogongu LB 278 Ke42
Manohardi BD 194 Pf33
Manokwari RI 213 Rh46
Manokwari RI 213 Rh47
Manole BG 127 Me48
Manoleasa RO 125 Mh43
Manolo Fortich RP 205 Rc41
Manoma RUS 181 Rj21
Manombo Atsimo RM 306 Nb57
Manometimay RM 306 Nc56
Manompana RM 306 Ne54
Manonga EAT 290 Mg47
Manono RDC 292 Md49
Manonwa RDC 289 Mc48
Manor IND (MHT) 190 Og36
Manorhamilton IRL 98 Km36
Manori Beach IND 190 Og36
Manosque F 105 Lf47
Manou RCA 282 Ma41
Manouane CDN (QC) 30 Gc22
Manova WAL 278 Ke41
Manp'o DVRK 182 Rd25
Manpur IND (CGH) 191 Pa35
Manqabâd ET 263 Mf32
Manra KIR 241 Ub19
Manresa E 110 Lb49
Mansa IND (PJB) 188 Oh31
Mansa Z 296 Me51
Mansabá GNB 269 Kc39
Mansa Konko WAG 269 Kc39
Mansalay RP 203 Ra39
Man Sam MYA 195 Pj34
Mansar IND (MHT) 191 Ok35
Mansehra PK 161 Og28
Mansel Island CDN 11 Fd06
Mansfeld D 113 Lm39
Mansfield AUS (VIC) 237 Sd64
Mansfield GB 101 Kt37
Mansfield USA (AR) 29 Fc28
Mansfield USA (OH) 32 Fj25
Mansfield USA (PA) 33 Gb25
Mansfield Jetty USA (TX) 39 Fb32
Mansfiled USA (LA) 29 Fd30
Mansha Z 296 Mf51
Mansi MYA 195 Ph33
Mansiari IND (UTT) 189 Pa30
Mansidão BR (BA) 70 Hh51
Mansilla E 107 Kr52
Mansilla E 107 Ks52
Mansilla de las Mulas E 106 Kp52
Mansinha BR (TO) 70 Hg50
Mansión CR 42 Fh40
Mansle F 104 La45
Manso BR 69 Hc53
Mansôa GNB 269 Kc39
Manso au das Mortes BR 69 Hc53
Manson Creek CDN (BC) 17 Dh18
Manso-Nkwanta GH 279 Kk42
Mansoura DZ 259 Lc27
Mansourah DZ 259 Kk28
Mansur Abad IR 155 Nk29
Mansur Abad IR 156 Ng31
Mansura Ruins PK 163 Oe33
Manta DY 279 La40
Manta EC 60 Fk46
Mantadia-Andasibe, P.N.de RM 306 Ne55
Mantalinga RI 209 Ra47
Mantalingajan, Mount RP 204 Qj41
Mantamádos GR 129 Mg51
Mantanai Besar MAL 204 Qj42
Mantare EAT 292 Mg47
Mantaro PE 66 Gc51

Mantasoa RM 306 Nd55
Mantawa RI 209 Rb46
Manteca USA (CA) 20 Dk27
Mantecal YV 57 Gf42
Mantecal YV 57 Gh42
Mantehage RI 209 Rc45
Mantena BR (MG) 75 Hk55
Mantes-la-Jolie F 103 Lb42
Mantes-la-Ville F 103 Lb42
Manthani IND (APH) 191 Ok36
Manthiréa GR 128 Mc53
Manti USA (UT) 21 Ee26
Manticao RP 205 Rc41
Manto HN 42 Fg38
Manto PE 67 Gd52
Mantorp S 93 Lq32
Mantos Blancos RCH 72 Ge57
Mántova I 120 Ll45
Mantralayam IND (APH) 190 Oj38
Mäntsälä FIN 96 Mf30
Mänttä FIN 96 Me28
Mantua C 44 Fh34
Mantuan Downs AUS (QLD) 235 Sd58
Mantung AUS (SA) 236 Sa63
Mantup RI 210 Qg49
Manturovo RUS 133 Nc16
Mäntyharju FIN 96 Mg29
Mäntyluoto FIN 93 Mb29
Manu IND (TRP) 194 Pg34
Manú PE 67 Ge51
Manú PE 67 Ge52
Manu WAN 272 Lc39
Manuae Atoll F 249 Cc54
Manua Islands USA 248 Bf53
Manubepium RI 213 Rh46
Manuc Bei MD 125 Mj44
Manuel MEX (TM) 39 Fa34
Manuel Alves BR 70 Hf51
Manuel Alves Grande BR 64 Hg49
Manuel Alves Pequeno BR 64 Hg50
Manuel Antonio, P.N. CR 42 Fh41
Manuel Benavides MEX (CHH) 23 Ej31
Manuel Díaz ROU 77 Hc61
Manuel Emídio BR (PI) 64 Hj49
Manuel J.Cobo RA (BA) 81 Hb63
Manuel Ribas BR (PR) 74 He58
Manuel Tames C 45 Gc35
Manuel Urbano BR (AC) 67 Gf50
Manuel Vitorino BR (BA) 71 Hk53
Manui RI 209 Rb47
Manuk RI 212 Rf48
Manukan RP 205 Rb41
Manukau NZ 238 Th64
Manunda AUS (SA) 236 Rk62
Manunga Z 292 Me50
Manunui NZ 238 Th65
Manú, P.N. PE 67 Ge52
Manur IND (MHT) 190 Oh36
Manurimí BOL 67 Gg52
Manuripe BOL 67 Gf51
Manusela RI 212 Re47
Manusela N.P. RI 212 Re47
Manus Island PNG 243 Sd46
Manvi IND (KTK) 190 Oj38
Manville USA (WY) 21 Eh24
Manweng MYA 195 Pj34
Many USA (LA) 29 Fd30
Manyallaluk A.L. AUS 223 Rg53
Manyame ZW 296 Mf54
Manyana Rock Paintings RB 299 Mc58
Manyani EAK 293 Mk47
Manyapadu IND (APH) 190 Oj38
Manyas TR 130 Mh50
Manyberries CDN (AB) 19 Ee21
Manych Depression RUS 135 Nb22
Manyelanong Game Reserve RB 299 Mc58
Manyeleti Game Reserve SA 300 Mf58
Manyémen CAM 280 Le43
Many Farms USA (AZ) 23 Ef27
Manyikeni MOC 300 Mh57
Manyinga Z 295 Mc52
Manyo EAT 292 Mf49
Manyoni EAT 293 Mh48
Manypeaks AUS (WA) 228 Qk63
Manzai PK 160 Oe30
Manzai PK 161 Of29
Manzanares CO 56 Gc43
Manzanares E 109 Kr48
Manzanilla Beach TT 58 Gk40
Manzanillo C 45 Gb35
Manzanillo MEX (COL) 39 Eh36
Manzengele RDC 289 Lj49
Manzhouli VRC (NMZ) 173 Qj21
Manzil PK 162 Ob31
Manzini SD 303 Mf59
Manzshir Monastery MNG 172 Qd22
Manzurka RUS 172 Qd19
Mao DOM 46 Ge36
Maó E 110 Le51
Mao EAT 292 Mf50
Mao TCH 273 Lh38
Maocaojie VRC (HUN) 177 Qg31
Mao'ershan VRC (HLG) 180 Rd23
Maogong VRC (GZH) 178 Qe32
Maohutang VRC (HUB) 177 Qf30
Maojing VRC (GSU) 174 Qd27
Maokeng SA 303 Md59
Mao Ling VRC 177 Qe28
Maoming VRC (GDG) 178 Qf35
Maope RB 299 Md57
Maopora RI 214 Rd49
Mao Xian VRC (SCH) 176 Qb30
Mapagoro EAT 293 Mg50
Mapai MOC 300 Mf57
Mapamoiwa PNG 244 Sf50
Mapam Yumco VRC 170 Pa30
Mapanda RDC 289 Mc50
Mapane RI 209 Ra46
Mapangu RDC 289 Ma48
Mapanza Z 296 Md54
Mapari BR 61 Gg47
Mapastepec MEX (CHP) 41 Fd38
Mapat RI 209 Qj44
Mapati RCB 288 Lg47
Mapé RCA 286 Mb43
Mapelane Nature Reserve SA 303 Mg60
Maphisa ZW 300 Me56
Mapi RI 242 Rk49
Mapi RI 242 Rk49
Mapiá BR 62 Ha48
Mapili RI 209 Qk47
Mapinhane MOC 300 Mh57
Mapire YV 57 Gh42
Mapiri BOL 67 Gf53
Mapiri BOL 67 Gg51

Mapiripán CO 61 Gd44
Maple Creek CDN (SK) 19 Ef21
Maple Ridge CDN (BC) 18 Dj21
Maplesville USA (AL) 34 Fg29
Mapleton USA (IA) 27 Fc24
Mapoon AUS (QLD) 230 Sa52
Mapoon A.L. AUS 230 Sb51
Mapor RI 207 Qc45
Mapor Beach RI 207 Qc45
Mapuera BR 63 Hb46
Mapulanguene MOC 300 Mg58
Mapunga Z 296 Md52
Mapungubwe SA 300 Me57
Mapusa IND (GOA) 190 Og38
Maputi RI 209 Qk45
Maputo MOC 300 Mg58
Maqên VRC (QHI) 176 Qa28
Maqna KSA 146 Mh31
Maqrat YE 151 Nf38
Maqteïr RIM 264 Ke35
Maqu VRC (GSU) 176 Qb29
Maquan He VRC 170 Pb31
Maquecha MOC 300 Mg56
Maqueda E 109 Kq50
Maqueda Channel RP 203 Rc39
Maquela do Zombo ANG 288 Lh49
Maqueze MOC 300 Mg58
Maquia PE 66 Gc49
Maquinchao RA (RN) 80 Gf66
Maquinchao RA 80 Gf66
Maquinista Levet RA (MD) 76 Gg62
Maquoketa USA (IA) 27 Fe24
Mara EAT 290 Mh46
Mara IND (MPH) 191 Pb34
Mara SA 300 Me57
Maraã BR (AM) 62 Gh46
Maraa Urubaxi, T.I. BR 62 Gh46
Marabá BR (PA) 64 Hf48
Marabadiassa CI 279 Kh41
Marabahan RI 208 Qh47
Marabidiyah IRQ 147 Nb29
Marabitanas BR (AM) 61 Gg45
Marabout Moulay Hassan DZ 266 Lc33
Marabouts TN 260 Ld29
Maracá BR (AP) 59 He44
Maracaçumé BR 64 Hh46
Maracaçumé BR (MA) 64 Hh47
Maracaí BR (SP) 74 He57
Maracaibo YV 56 Ge40
Maracaju BR (MS) 74 Hc56
Maracanã BR 62 Ha49
Maracanã BR (PA) 64 Hg46
Maracanã BR (MA) 64 Hj47
Maracanaú BR (CE) 65 Ja47
Maracás BR (BA) 71 Hk52
Maracas Beach TT 58 Gk40
Maracay YV 57 Gg40
Maracoa CO 57 Gf44
Maracuni YV 57 Gf44
Maradah LAR 261 Lk31
Maradankadawala CL 193 Pa42
Maradi RN 272 Ld39
Maradun WAN 272 Ld39
Marafa EAK 293 Mk47
Marafa Depression (Hell's Kitchen) EAK 291 Mk47
Maragheh IR 154 Nd27
Maragogi BR (AL) 71 Jc50
Maragogipe BR (BA) 71 Ja52
Marah KSA 149 Nc33
Marahoue, P.N.de la CI 279 Kg42
Marais Poitevin F 102 Kt44
Marais Salants F 102 Ks43
Marais Vernier F 102 La41
Maraiwatsede, T.I. BR 69 He51
Marajai, T.I. BR 62 Gh47
Maraka RN 272 Ld39
Marakabei LS 303 Me60
Marakei Atoll KIR 241 Tc18
Marakele N.P. SA 299 Md58
Marakesa RDC 287 Md45
Marakhayy YE 150 Nf38
Marakhi Reservoir IND 194 Pd33
Marakkanam IND (TNU) 193 Ok40
Maraku WAN 272 Le40
Maralal EAK 290 Mj45
Maralal Nature Sanctuary EAK 290 Mj45
Maraldy KZ 167 Pc21
Marale HN 42 Fg38
Marali RCA 282 Lk42
Maralinga AUS (SA) 229 Rf61
Maralinga Tjarutja A.L. AUS 226 Rf60
Maramag RP 205 Rc42
Maramasike SOL 245 Ta50
Marambio ANT (RA) 312 Ha31
Maramuni River PNG 243 Sb48
Maran MAL 199 Qb44
Marana USA (AZ) 23 Ee29
Maranalgo AUS (WA) 228 Qj60
Marand IR 154 Nc26
Marandala CI 279 Kh41
Marandet RN 272 Ld37
Maranello I 120 Ll46
Marang MAL 199 Qb43
Marango AUS (QLD) 235 Sd59
Maranguape BR (CE) 65 Ja47
Maranhão BR 53 Hc20
Maranhão BR (AM) 63 Hb47
Maranhão BR 70 Hf53
Maranhoto BR (AM) 62 Gj47
Marañón PE 60 Gc48
Marans F 102 Ku44
Maranura PE 67 Gd52
Marapa RA 76 Gh59
Marapanim BR (PA) 64 Hg46
Marapi BR 63 Hb45
Mar Argentino 83 Gh71
Marari BR 62 Gh45
Mara Rosa BR (GO) 70 Hf52
Marasende RI 211 Qk48
Mărăşeşti RO 125 Mh45
Mărașu RO 125 Mh46
Marat UZB 158 Oc24
Marataízes BR (ES) 75 Hk56
Maratea I 123 Lq50
Marathon AUS (QLD) 232 Sb56
Marathon CDN (ON) 25 Fg21
Marathon USA (TX) 23 Ej30
Marathon USA (FL) 36 Fk33
Marathónas GR 128 Md52
Maratua RI 209 Qk44
Maraú BR (BA) 71 Ja53
Marau BR (RS) 78 Hd60
Maraudeur F 59 Hd44
Marauiá BR 62 Gh45
Maravatío de Ocampo MEX (MHC) 40 Ek36
Maravilha BR (AM) 62 Gk47
Maravilha BR (SC) 78 Hd59
Maravilhas BR (MG) 75 Hh55
Maravilla BOL 67 Gg51
Marawah LAR 261 Ma29

Marawaka PNG 243 Sc49
Marawi RP 205 Rc41
Marawi SUD 276 Mf37
Maraxo Patá BR (PA) 63 Hb45
Marayes RA (SJ) 76 Gg61
Marayoun RL 146 Mh29
Mar'ayt YE 151 Nf37
Marazion GB 100 Kp40
Marbach D 114 Lk42
Marbella E 108 Kq46
Marble Bar AUS (WA) 224 Qk56
Marble Bar Road AUS 224 Ra56
Marble Canyon USA (AZ) 23 Ee27
Marble Hall SA 300 Me58
Marble Hill USA (MO) 29 Ff27
Marble Point ANT (USA) 313 Tb34
Marburg D 112 Lj40
Marcabelí EC 60 Ga47
Marcal H 118 Ls43
Marcala HN 42 Fg38
Marcali H 118 Ls44
Marcaltő H 118 Ls43
Marčana HR 121 Lo46
Marcapata PE 67 Ge52
Marcapomacocha PE 66 Gb51
Marcelândia BR (MT) 69 Hc51
Marcelino BR (AM) 61 Gg45
Marcelino BR (AM) 61 Gg46
Marcell USA (MN) 27 Fd22
Marcelo BR (PA) 63 He47
March A 115 Lr42
March GB 101 La38
Marchagee AUS (WA) 228 Qj61
Marche I 120 Lo47
Marche-en-Famenne B 103 Lf40
Marchena E 108 Kp47
Marchenoir F 102 Lb43
Marchinbar Island AUS 223 Rj51
Marciac F 104 La47
Marcigny F 105 Le44
Marcilla RP 202 Ra39
Marcillac-la-Croisille F 104 Lc45
Marcinkonys LT 97 Me36
Marcinkowice PL 119 Ma41
Marcionilio Sousa BR (BA) 71 Hk52
Marck F 103 Lb40
Marco USA (FL) 36 Fk33
Marco de Canaveses P 106 Km51
Marconi N.H.S. CDN 31 Ha22
Marco Rondon BR (RO) 68 Gk52
Marcos Juárez RA (CD) 77 Gj62
Marcos Parente BR (PI) 65 Hj49
Marcoux USA (MN) 27 Fb22
Marcus Baker, Mount USA (AK) 15 Cg15
Mard Abad IR 154 Nf28
Mardalen N 92 Lj28
Mardan PK 161 Og28
Mar de Ajó RA (BA) 81 Hb64
Mar de Espanha BR (MG) 75 Hj56
Mar del Plata RA (BA) 81 Hb65
Mardie AUS (WA) 224 Qh56
Mardie Island AUS 224 Qh56
Mardin TR 145 Na27
Mardin Dağları TR 145 Na27
Maré F 246 Te56
Mare RI 211 Ra48
Marea del Portillo C 45 Gb36
Mare aux Crocodiles de Dounkou BF 271 Kj39
Mare aux Crocodiles de Sabou BF 271 Kj39
Marechal Cândido Rondon BR (PR) 74 Hc58
Marechal Deodoro BR (AL) 71 Jc50
Mare de Tizi RCA/TCH 282 Mb40
Mare d'Oursi BF 271 Kk38
Maree AUS (SA) 227 Rk60
Mareeba AUS (QLD) 233 Sc54
Mareeq SP 285 Nd44
Maremma I 122 Lm48
Maréna RMM 269 Ke38
Marenge RDC 292 Me48
Marengo USA (IA) 27 Fd25
Marengo Cave USA 34 Fg26
Marennes F 104 Kt45
Marerano RM 306 Nc56
Mareth TN 260 Lf29
Mareuil-sur-Lay F 102 Kt44
Mar'evka RUS 133 Ne19
Marevo RUS 132 Mg17
Marfa M 122 Lp55
Marfa USA (TX) 23 Eh30
Margao IND (GOA) 190 Og38
Margaree Forks CDN (NS) 31 Gk22
Margaret AUS 227 Rj60
Margaret AUS (QLD) 234 Sb59
Margareteville USA (NY) 33 Gc24
Margaret, Mount AUS 224 Qj57
Margaret River AUS 222 Rd55
Margaret River AUS (WA) 228 Qh62
Margarida BR (MS) 73 Hb56
Margarima PNG 243 Sb49
Margaríti GR 128 Ma51
Margaritove RUS 135 Mk22
Margasari RI 208 Qh47
Margate GB 101 Lb39
Margate SA 303 Mf61
Mărgău RO 124 Mc44
Margecany SK 119 Mb42
Margherita IND (ASM) 195 Ph32
Margherita di Savóia I 123 Lr49
Marghita RO 124 Mc43
Margiana TM 153 Oa26
Marg'ilon UZB 159 Of25
Margone I 120 Lh45
Margonin PL 116 Ls38
Margosatubig RP 205 Rb42
Marguerite CDN (BC) 18 Dj19
Marguerite Bay 312 Gc32
Margyang VRC (TIB) 171 Pe31
Marhamat UZB 159 Og25
Marhanec' UA 135 Mh22
Marhoum DZ 259 Kk28
Mari BR (AM) 62 Gh49
Mari PNG 242 Sa50
Mari SYR 147 Na28
Maria BR (PA) 64 Hf46
Maria MOC 297 Mj54
Maria PE 66 Gb49
Maria Aurora RP 203 Ra38
María Elena RCH 72 Gf57
María Eugenia RA (SF) 77 Gk61
Mariager DK 94 Lk34
Mariager Fjord DK 94 Ll34
Mariahan IND (UPH) 191 Pb33
María Ignacia RA (BA) 81 Ha64
Maria Island AUS 223 Rh53

Maria Island N.P. AUS 236 Se67
Mariakani EAK 293 Mk47
Maria Laach D 112 Lh40
Maria Laach D 112 Lh40
Mariala N.P. AUS 235 Sc59
Marialva P 106 Kn50
Maria, Mount GB 83 Ha71
Marian AUS (QLD) 233 Se56
Mariana BOL 73 Gj55
Mariana BR (MG) 75 Hj56
Mariana Islands 218 Sa08
Mariana Trench 218 Sa08
Mariani IND (ASM) 194 Ph32
Marianna USA (AR) 29 Fe28
Marianna USA (FL) 35 Fh30
Mariannelund S 95 Lq33
Mariano I.Loza RA (CR) 77 Ha60
Marianópolis BR (MA) 64 Hh48
Mariánské Lázně CZ 118 Ln41
Mariarano RM 304 Nd53
Maria Saal A 115 Lp44
Maria Teresa ANG 288 Lh50
María Teresa RA (SF) 77 Gk63
Mariazell A 115 Lq43
Ma'rib YE 150 Nc38
Maribo DK 94 Lm36
Maribor SLO 121 Lq44
Marica BG 126 Md48
Marica BG 127 Mf48
Maricá BR (RJ) 75 Hj57
Maricaban Island RP 203 Ra39
Marical Caceres PE 66 Gc52
Maricao USA (PR) 47 Gg36
Marico SA 299 Md58
Maridi SUD 283 Me43
Maridi SUD 287 Me43
Marié BR 61 Gf46
Marie Byrd Land ANT 312 Ed34
Mariefred S 93 Ls31
Marie Galante F 47 Gk38
Mariehamn = Maarianhamina FIN 93 Lu30
Mariel C 44 Fj34
Mari-El RUS 133 Ne17
Marie Louise SY 305 Ng49
Marie Luise Bank 204 Qj40
Marielyst DK 94 Lm36
Marienberg D 113 Lo40
Mariental NAM 298 Lj58
Mariés GR 127 Me50
Mariestad S 93 Lo32
Marieta YV 57 Gg43
Marietta USA (OH) 33 Fk26
Marietta USA (GA) 35 Fh29
Mariga WAN 272 Lc40
Mariga WAN 272 Ld40
Marigat EAK 290 Mh45
Marignane F 105 Lf47
Marigot F 47 Gj36
Marigot RH 46 Gd36
Marigot WD 47 Gk38
Marihatag RP 205 Rd41
Marija Bistrica HR 121 Lr44
Marijampolė LT 97 Md36
Marikal IND (APH) 190 Oj37
Marikina RP 203 Ra38
Marília BR (SP) 74 Hf57
Marimari BR 62 Ha48
Marimba ANG 289 Lj50
Marín E 106 Km52
Marina di Belvedere I 123 Lq51
Marina di Carrara I 120 Ll46
Marina di Cetraro I 123 Lq51
Marina di Grosseto I 120 Ll48
Marina di Léuca I 123 Lt51
Marina di Pisa I 120 Ll47
Marina di Ragusa I 122 Lp54
Marina di Ravenna I 120 Ln46
Marina Plains AUS (QLD) 231 Sb53
Mariñas E 106 Kn53
Marinduque Island RP 203 Ra39
Marine de Sisco F 111 Lk48
Marineland USA (FL) 36 Fk31
Marineland of Florida USA 36 Fk31
Marinella I 122 Ln53
Marineo I 122 Lo53
Mariner Glacier 313 Tb33
Marinette USA (WI) 32 Fg23
Maringá BR (PR) 74 He57
Maringa RDC 286 Ma45
Maringué MOC 296 Mh54
Maringues F 105 Ld45
Marinha Grande P 108 Km49
Marinho de Fernando de Noronha, P.N. BR 65 Jd47
Marinho dos Abrolhos, P.N. BR 75 Ja55
Marinka BG 127 Mh48
Marino de Pta. Francés- Pta. Pdernales, P.N. C 44 Fj35
Marino de Vallarta, P.N. MEX 38 Eh35
Marino G. de Chiriquí, P.N. PA 42 Fj41
Marino Isla Bastimentos, P.N. PA 43 Fk41
Marino Las Baulas, P.N. CR 42 Fh40
Marion USA (KS) 27 Fb26
Marion USA (IA) 27 Fe24
Marion USA (AR) 29 Fe28
Marion USA (IL) 29 Ff27
Marion USA (KY) 29 Ff27
Marion USA (IN) 32 Fh25
Marion USA (OH) 32 Fj25
Marion USA (AL) 34 Fg29
Marion USA (VA) 35 Fk27
Marion USA (NC) 35 Fk28
Marion USA (SC) 35 Ga28
Marion Downs AUS (QLD) 232 Rk57
Marion Reefs AUS 233 Sf55
Maripasoula F 59 Hd44
Maripipi Island RP 205 Rc40
Mariposa USA (CA) 20 Ea27
Mariposa Monarca MEX 40 Ek36
Mariquita CO 56 Gc43
Marisa RI 209 Ra45
Mariscala ROU 77 Hc63
Mariscal José Félix Estigarribia PY 73 Gk56
Mariscos GCA 41 Ff38
Marita Downs AUS (QLD) 232 Sb57
Maritime Alps F 105 Lg46
Maritime Museum AUS 228 Qh60
Mariusa, P.N. YV 58 Gj41
Marivan IR 154 Nd28
Mariveles RP 202 Ra38
Mariveles Reef 204 Qg42
Märjamaa EST 96 Me32
Marka SP 291 Nc45
Markabougou RMM 270 Kg39
Markabygd N 90 Lf14

Miheşu de Câmpie RO 124 Me44
Mihintale CL 193 Pa42
Mihnevo RUS 132 Mj18
Mihona IND (MPH) 189 Ok32
Mijdahah YE 150 Ne38
Mijek DARS 264 Kd34
Mi-jima J 183 Rf28
Mikamiene EAT 293 Mk48
Mikasa J 181 Sa24
Mikaševičy BY 132 Md19
Mikaszówka PL 117 Md37
Mikata EAT 293 Mj49
Mikeļtornis LV 97 Mc33
Mikindani EAT 297 Na51
Mikir Hills IND 194 Pg32
Mikkeli FIN 96 Mh29
Miknas MA 258 Kh29
Mikolaivka UA 125 Ml43
Mikolaivka UA 125 Mm43
Mikolaivka UA 125 Mm43
Mikołajki PL 117 Mb37
Mikolongo MW 296 Mh54
Mikołów PL 117 Lt40
Mikonos GR 129 Mf53
Mikonos GR 129 Mf53
Mikouyi G 288 Lg46
Mikre BG 107 Me47
Mikulčice CZ 118 Ls42
Mikulov CZ 118 Lr42
Mikumi EAT 293 Mj49
Mikumi N.P. EAT 293 Mj49
Mikum-sanmyaku J 183 Rk27
Mikuni J 183 Rj27
Mikura-jima J 183 Rk29
Mila DZ 260 Ld27
Milaca USA (MN) 27 Fd23
Miladinovci MK 126 Mb49
Milagres BR (CE) 65 Ja49
Milagres BR (BA) 71 Ja52
Milagro E 107 Kt52
Milagro EC 60 Ga47
Milagro RA (LR) 76 Gh61
Milagros RP 203 Rb39
Miłakowo PL 117 Ma36
Milala EAT 293 Mk50
Milam USA (TX) 29 Fd30
Milam Glacier IND 189 Pa30
Milan I 120 Lk45
Milan USA (MO) 27 Fd25
Milan USA (TN) 29 Ff28
Milando ANG 289 Lj50
Milang AUS (SA) 236 Rk63
Milange MOC 297 Mh54
Milange RDC 292 Md47
Milano I 120 Lk45
Milano USA (TX) 29 Fb30
Milanoa RM 305 Ne52
Milanówek PL 117 Ma38
Milas TR 129 Mh53
Milavidy BY 117 Mf38
Milazzo I 122 Lq52
Milbana MOC 297 Mk53
Milbank USA (SD) 27 Fb23
Milbanke Sound CDN 18 Df19
Milden CDN (SK) 19 Eg20
Mildred USA (MT) 21 Eh22
Mildura AUS (NSW) 236 Sb63
Mile ETH 284 Na40
Mile VRC (YUN) 195 Qb33
Miléa GR 126 Mb51
Milepa MOC 297 Mj51
Miles AUS (QLD) 235 Sf59
Miles City USA (MT) 21 Eh22
Mile Serdo Reserve ETH 284 Na40
Mileševo SCG 124 Lu45
Mi'leso ETH 284 Na41
Milestone CDN (SK) 19 Eh20
Milestone IRL 100 Km38
Milet TR 129 Mh53
Mileto I 123 Lr52
Mileura AUS (WA) 224 Qj59
Milevsko CZ 118 Lp41
Mile Wenz ETH 284 Na40
Milford GB 101 Ku39
Milford USA (UT) 21 Ed26
Milford USA (DE) 33 Gc26
Milford USA (CT) 33 Gd25
Milford Haven GB 100 Kp39
Milford Sound NZ 239 Td68
Milford Sound NZ 239 Td68
Milgarra AUS (QLD) 232 Sa55
Milgun AUS (WA) 224 Qk58
Miliana DZ 259 Lb27
Mili Atoll MH 241 Tc17
Milići BIH 126 Lu46
Milicz PL 116 Ls39
Milikapiti AUS (NT) 223 Rf51
Milin CZ 118 Lp41
Miling AUS (WA) 228 Qj61
Milingimbi AUS (NT) 223 Rh52
Militello I 122 Lp53
Militsa GR 128 Mb54
Milk River USA 19 Ee21
Milla Milla AUS (QLD) 233 Sc54
Millaroo AUS (QLD) 233 Sd56
Millas F 104 Lc48
Millau F 105 Ld46
Mill City USA (OR) 20 Dj23
Milledgeville USA (GA) 35 Fj29
Mille Lacs Lake USA 27 Fd22
Millen USA (GA) 35 Fk29
Miller SA 302 Mb62
Miller USA (SD) 26 Fa23
Miller USA (NE) 26 Fa25
Miller, Mount USA 16 Cj15
Miller, Mount 313 Tb35
Millerovo RUS 133 Na21
Millersburg USA (OH) 32 Fk25
Millerton USA (OK) 29 Fc29
Millerton USA (NY) 33 Gd25
Millertown CDN (NF) 31 Hb21
Millican USA (OR) 20 Dk24
Millicent AUS (SA) 236 Sa64
Milligan Hills CDN 17 Dk17
Millijiddie A.L. AUS 222 Rc55
Millington USA (TN) 29 Ff28
Millinocket USA (MA) 30 Gf23
Million Dollar Point VU 246 Td53
Millmerran AUS (QLD) 235 Sf59
Millom GB 101 Kr36
Millport USA (AL) 29 Ff29
Millrose AUS (WA) 224 Ra59
Millstätter See A 115 Lo44
Millstone USA (WV) 33 Fk26
Millstream-Chichester N.P. AUS 224 Qj56
Milltown CDN (NF) 31 Hc22
Milltown Malbay IRL 100 Kl38
Millungera AUS (QLD) 232 Sa55
Millville USA (NJ) 33 Gc26
Millwood S.P. USA 29 Fd29
Milly Milly AUS (WA) 224 Qj59
Milmersdorf D 113 Lo37
Milna HR 121 Lr47
Milne Bay PNG 244 Sf51
Milner Lake CDN 30 Gg19
Milnerton SA 302 Lk62
Milnesand USA (NM) 23 Ej29
Milo RG 278 Kf40
Milos GR 129 Me54
Milos GR 129 Me54
Milot AL 126 Lu49
Milot RH 46 Gd36
Milówka PL 119 Lu41
Milparinka AUS (NSW) 234 Sa60
Milpillas de la Sierra MEX (ZCT) 39 Ej34
Milpitas USA (CA) 20 Dk27
Miltenberg D 114 Lk41
Milton CDN (NS) 31 Gh23
Milton NZ 239 Te69
Milton USA (FL) 34 Fg30
Milton Brandão BR (PI) 65 Hk48
Milton Freewater USA (OR) 20 Ea23
Milton Keynes GB 101 Ku38
Miltou TCH 273 Lj40
Miluo VRC (HUN) 177 Qg31
Milwaukee USA (WI) 32 Fg24
Milwaukee deep 46 Gg36
Milwaukie USA (OR) 20 Dj23
Milybulak KZ 166 Oh21
Mimbelly RCB 281 Lj44
Mimili AUS (SA) 226 Rh59
Miminiska L CDN 25 Ff20
Mimizan F 104 Kt46
Mimoň CZ 118 Lp40
Mimongo G 288 Lf46
Mimosa Rocks N.P. AUS 237 Se64
Mimoso BR (MS) 74 Hd56
Mimoso do Oeste BR (BA) 70 Hh52
Mimpoutou RCB 281 Lj44
Mimyj RUS 141 Qc06
Mina, Cerro CO 56 Gd41
Mina MEX (NL) 39 Ek33
Mina USA (NV) 20 Ea26
Mina Ahmadi KWT 156 Ne31
Mina Algarrobo RCH 76 Ge60
Minab IR 157 Nj32
Mina Carbón Peket RCH 82 Ge72
Minaçu BR (GO) 70 Hf52
Mina de São Domingos P 108 Kn47
Mina Djebel Ali UAE 156 Nh33
Minahasa RI 209 Rb45
Mina Incahuasi RA (CA) 72 Gg58
Minaki CDN (ON) 24 Fc21
Mina la Casualidad RA (SA) 72 Gf58
Minami Alps N.P. J 183 Rk28
Minami-Daito J 185 Rf33
Minami-Daito-Jima J 185 Rf33
Minamikayabe J 181 Sa25
Minami-Tane J 183 Rf30
Minamurra AUS 237 Sf63
Mina Pirquitas RA (PJ) 72 Gg57
Minaret Mosque RI 210 Qf49
Minaret of Jam AFG 160 Oc28
Minas C 45 Gb35
Minas RI 206 Qa45
Minas ROU 77 Hc63
Mina Saud KWT 156 Ne31
Minas Basin CDN 31 Gh23
Minas de Barroterán MEX (COH) 39 Ek32
Minas de Corrales ROU 77 Hc61
Minas de Matahambre C 44 Fh34
Minas Gerais BR 53 Hc22
Minas Novas BR (MG) 75 Hj54
Minatitlán MEX (COL) 39 Eh36
Minatitlán MEX (VC) 41 Fc37
Minaya E 109 Ks49
Minbu MYA 194 Ph35
Min Buri THA 196 Qa39
Minbyar MYA 194 Pg35
Minchika WAN 273 Lg40
Minchinabad PK 161 Og30
Mincivan AZ 152 Nd26
Mindanao RP 205 Rd42
Mindanao Sea RP 205 Rc41
Mindelheim D 114 Ll42
Mindelo CV 268 Jh37
Minden D 112 Lj38
Minden USA (NE) 26 Fa25
Minden USA (LA) 29 Fd29
Minderoo AUS (WA) 224 Qh56
Mindif CAM 273 Lh40
Mindik PNG 243 Sd49
Mindiptana RI 213 Sa48
Mindjik TCH 282 Ma40
Mindo EC 60 Ga46
Mindon MYA 196 Ph36
Mindoro RP 202 Ra39
Mindoro Strait RP 202 Ra39
Mindouli RCB 288 Lh48
Mindourou CAM 281 Lg44
Minduri BR (MG) 75 Hh56
Mine J 182 Re28
Mine J 183 Rf28
Mine Center CDN (ON) 24 Fd21
Minehead GB 100 Kr39
Mine Head IRL 100 Kn39
Mineiros BR (GO) 74 Hd54
Mineral USA (CA) 20 Dk25
Mineral de Cucharas MEX (NYT) 39 Eh34
Mineral del Chico MEX (HDG) 40 Fa35
Mineral de Pozos MEX (GJT) 40 Ek35
Mineral Hot Springs USA (CO) 23 Eh26
Mineral'nye Vody RUS 152 Nb23
Mineral Springs SA 300 Mf57
Mineral Water Spring MNG 172 Qc22
Mineral Water Springs MNG 172 Qe23
Mineral Wells USA (TX) 28 Fa29
Miners' Memorial SA 302 Lj60
Miners' Mus. CDN 31 Gh23
Minersville USA (UT) 21 Ed26
Minervino Murge I 123 Lr49
Minfeng VRC (XUZ) 168 Pb27
Minga RDC 296 Md51
Minga Z 296 Mf53
Mingan RCA 286 Ma43
Mingan CDN (QC) 31 Gh20
Minganja ANG 295 Ma52
Mingao CO 57 Gg44
Mingary AUS (SA) 236 Sa62
Mingbuloq UZB 158 Ob24
Mingbuloq botig'i UZB 158 Ob24
Mingeçevir AZ 152 Nd25
Mingeçevir su anbari AZ 152 Nd25
Mingela AUS (QLD) 233 Sd55
Mingenew AUS (WA) 228 Qh60
Minggang VRC (HNN) 184 Qh29
Minghoshan VRC (GSU) 169 Ph25
Mingin MYA 194 Ph34
Mingin Taung MYA 195 Ph33
Minglanilla E 109 Kt49
Ming Ming PNG 243 Sd48
Mingo N.W.R. USA 34 Fe27
Mingora PK 161 Og28
Mingorria E 106 Kq50
Mingoyo EAT 297 Mk51
Mingshashan VRC 169 Ph26
Mingshui VRC (HLG) 180 Rc22
Ming Tombs VRC 175 Qj25
Mingue CAM 281 Lg43
Mingulay GB 98 Kn34
Minguri = Nacala Velha MOC 297 Na53
Mingxi VRC (FJN) 184 Qj32
Minhe Huizu Tuzu Zizhixian VRC (GSU) 174 Qb27
Minhla MYA 196 Ph36
Minhla MYA 196 Ph37
Minho P 106 Km51
Minićevo SCG 126 Mc47
Minicoy Island IND 192 Og42
Minidoka USA (ID) 21 Ed24
Minignan CI 278 Kg41
Minija LT 97 Mb35
Minilya Roadhouse AUS (WA) 224 Qh57
Minimarg 161 Oh28
Mining Hall of Fame AUS 223 Rh55
Miniota CDN (MB) 24 Ek20
Mini Park RI 210 Qd49
Miniss Lake CDN 25 Fe20
Ministro Ramos Mexía RA (RN) 80 Gg66
Min Jiang VRC 176 Qb29
Min Jiang VRC 184 Qk32
Minjilang AUS (NT) 223 Rg51
Minkébé, P.N.de G 281 Lg45
Minlaton AUS (SA) 236 Rj63
Minle VRC (GSU) 174 Qa26
Minmaya J 183 Sa25
Minna WAN 272 Ld41
Minna Bluff 313 Tc34
Minneapolis USA (MN) 27 Fd23
Minneapolis USA (KS) 26 Fb26
Minnedosa CDN (MB) 24 Fa20
Minneola USA (KS) 28 Fa27
Minnesota USA 12 Fa09
Minnewaukan USA (ND) 24 Fa21
Minnie Downs AUS (QLD) 235 Sc58
Minnies AUS (QLD) 232 Sb54
Minnipa AUS (SA) 236 Rh62
Minnitaki Lake CDN 24 Fe21
Minong USA (WI) 27 Fe22
Minority Village VRC 195 Qb33
Minot USA (ND) 24 Ek21
Minqin VRC (GSU) 174 Qb26
Minqing VRC (FJN) 184 Qk32
Minquan VRC (HNN) 184 Qh28
Min Shan VRC 176 Qb29
Minsk BY 132 Md19
Mińsk Mazowiecki PL 117 Mb38
Minta CAM 281 Lg43
Mintable AUS (SA) 226 Rh59
Mintaqat Umm Khuwayt LAR 261 Mb30
Minter City USA (MS) 29 Fe29
Mintlaw GB 99 Ks33
Minto CDN (YT) 17 Db14
Minto CDN (MB) 24 Ek21
Minton II CAM 281 Lg44
Minto, Mount 313 Tc33
Minton CDN (SK) 19 Eh21
Minto Reef 244 Sc17
Minturno I 122 Lo49
Minu Dašt IR 154 Nh27
Minvoul G 281 Lg44
Minwakh YE 150 Ne37
Min Xian VRC (GSU) 176 Qb28
Minz gol MNG 172 Qe21
Mio USA (MI) 32 Fh23
Miomo F 111 Lk48
Mionica SCG 126 Ma46
Mioveni RO 125 Me46
Miquelon CDN (QC) 30 Gb21
Miquelon F 31 Hb22
Miquihuana MEX (TM) 39 Fa34
Mira CO 60 Ga45
Mira E 109 Kt49
Mira I 120 Ln45
Mira P 106 Km50
Mir Abad IR 157 Oa31
Mirabela BR (MG) 75 Hh54
Miracatu BR (SP) 74 Hg58
Miracema BR (RJ) 75 Hj56
Miracema do Tocantins BR (TO) 70 Hf50
Miracosta PE 66 Ga49
Mirador BR (AM) 61 Gd48
Mirador BR (MA) 64 Hh49
Mirador- Dos Lagunas- Río Azul, P.N. GCA 41 Ff37
Mirador, P.N. de BR 64 Hh49
Mira Estrela BR (SP) 74 He55
Miraflores BR (AM) 62 Gh47
Miraflores CO 56 Gd43
Miraflores CO 61 Ge45
Miraflores RA (CH) 73 Gk58
Miragoâne RH 46 Gd36
Miraí BR (MG) 75 Hj56
Miraj IND (MHT) 190 Oh37
Miramar BR (AM) 62 Gk48
Miramar MEX (COL) 39 Eh36
Miramar RA (CD) 77 Gj61
Miramar RA (BA) 81 Hb65
Miramas F 105 Le47
Mirambeau F 104 Ku45
Miramichi Bay CDN 31 Gh22
Miramont-de-Guyenne F 104 La46
Miram Shah PK 161 Oe29
Miran PK 161 Of30
Miran VRC (XUZ) 169 Pe26
Miranda BR (MS) 73 Hb56
Miranda BR 73 Hb56
Miranda MOC 297 Mh52
Miranda de Ebro E 107 Ks52
Miranda do Douro P 106 Ko51
Miranda do Norte BR (MA) 64 Hh47
Miranda Downs AUS (QLD) 232 Sa54
Mirande F 104 La47
Mirandela P 106 Kn51
Mirandiba BR (PE) 71 Ja50
Mirándola I 120 Lm46
Mirandópolis BR (MG) 71 Hk53
Mirandópolis BR (SP) 74 He56
Mirani AUS (QLD) 233 Se56
Mirani Lake OM 157 Nk34
Mirante da Sura BR (RO) 68 Gj51
Mirano I 120 Ln45
Miranorte BR (TO) 70 Hf50
Miranponga Pongunna Lake AUS 227 Rj58
Mirante BR (BA) 71 Hk53
Mirante do Paranapanema BR (SP) 74 Hd57
Mirapo PNG 243 Sd50
Miraporanga BR (MG) 74 Hf55
Mira-por-vos Cays BS 37 Gc34
Mira-por-vos Passage BS 37 Gc34
Mirassol BR (SP) 74 Hf56
Mirassol d'Oeste BR (MT) 68 Ha53
Miratu, T.I. BR 62 Gh47
Miravalles E 106 Ko52
Mir Bachech Kowt AFG 160 Oe28
Mirbat OM 151 Nh37
Mircze PL 117 Md40
Mirebalais RH 46 Gd36
Mirebeau F 102 La44
Mirebeau-sur-Bèze F 103 Lf43
Mirecourt F 103 Lg42
Mirepoix F 104 Lb47
Mireşti MD 125 Mj44
Mirgani IND (BIH) 189 Pc32
Miri MAL 204 Qg43
Miria RN 272 Le39
Mirialguda IND (APH) 191 Ok37
Miriam Vale AUS (QLD) 235 Sf58
Mirikata AUS (SA) 227 Rh60
Mirina GR 127 Mf51
Mirina Kástro GR 127 Mf51
Miriñay RA 77 Hb60
Mirinzal BR (MA) 64 Hh47
Miritiparaná CO 61 Ge46
Miriye SP 285 Nc40
Mir Javeh IR 157 Oa31
Mirleft MA 258 Ke31
Mir Mövsum Ağa AZ 152 Ne26
Mirne UA 125 Ml44
Mirnyj RUS 91 Na14
Mirnyj ANT (RUS) 313 Pc32
Miroč SCG 124 Mc46
Mirogi EAK 290 Mh46
Mirond Lake CDN 24 Ej18
Mirong VRC (YUN) 195 Qb34
Mirool AUS (NSW) 237 Sd63
Mirosławiec PL 116 Lr37
Mirotice CZ 118 Lp41
Mirovice CZ 118 Lp41
Mirow D 113 Ln37
Mirpur Batoro PK 162 Oe33
Mirpur Khas PK 163 Oe33
Mirpur Mathelo PK 163 Oe31
Mirpur Sakro PK 162 Od33
Mirrote MOC 297 Mk52
Mirrow CDN (AB) 19 Ed19
Mirsale SP 285 Nd43
Mirski zamak BY 97 Mg37
Mirtna AUS (QLD) 233 Sd56
Mirtóon Sea GR 128 Md53
Mirtos GR 129 Mf55
Miruro MOC 296 Mf53
Mirzapur IND (UPH) 191 Pb33
Mirzapur Hills IND 191 Pb33
Misa LV 97 Me34
Misahualli EC 60 Gb46
Misaki EAT 293 Mh48
Misaki J 183 Rh28
Misaki J 185 Rg29
Misantla MEX (VC) 40 Fb36
Misau WAN 273 Lf40
Misawa J 183 Sa25
Mischii RO 124 Md46
Miscolc H 119 Ma42
Miscou Centre CDN (NB) 31 Gh22
Misele RDC 289 Lj48
Misery, Mount NZ 239 Tf67
Mishagua PE 67 Gd51
Mishaleyi VRC (XUZ) 168 Pa26
Mishamo EAT 292 Mf48
Mishan IR 156 Nf30
Mishan VRC (HLG) 180 Rf23
Mishanattawa River CDN 25 Fh18
Mishkeegogamang Indian Reserve CDN 25 Fe20
Misiki PNG 243 Sb49
Misima EAT 293 Mk48
Misima Island PNG 244 Sg51
Misinchinka Ranges CDN 18 Dj18
Misiones RA 55 Hb24
Misiones franciscanas de la Sierra Gorda de Querétaro = Arroyo Seco, Jalpan de Serra, Landa de Matamoros MEX 39 Fa35
Misión Platanal YV 58 Gh44
Misión San Fernando de Velicatá MEX 22 Ec31
Misión San Francisco de Borja Adac MEX 22 Ed31
Misión Santa Gertrudis MEX (BC) 22 Ed31
Misión Santa María de los Angeles MEX 22 Ec31
Miskah KSA 148 Nb33
Miski SUD 275 Mc38
Mismar SUD 276 Mh37
Mišnjak HR 121 Lp46
Misole EAT 292 Mg48
Misool RI 212 Re47
Misoumin CI 279 Kj42
Misratah LAR 261 Lh29
Misrikh IND (UPH) 189 Pa32
Missanabie CDN (ON) 25 Fh21
Missão Assunção BR (AM) 61 Gg45
Missão Pari Cachoeira BR (AM) 61 Gf45
Missão Velha BR (CE) 65 Ja49
Missara SN 269 Ke39
Misséni RMM 279 Kg40
Missi Falls CDN 24 Fb17
Missinaibi Lake CDN 25 Fj21
Missinaibi Lake Prov. Park CDN 25 Fj21
Missinaibi River CDN 25 Fj20
Missinipe CDN (SK) 19 Eh18
Mission CDN (BC) 18 Dj21
Mission USA (SD) 26 Ek24
Mission Beach AUS (QLD) 233 Sd54
Mission Ridge USA (SD) 26 Ek23
Mission San Buenaventura USA 22 Ea28
Mission San Juan Capistrano USA 22 Eb29
Mission San Luis Obispo USA 22 Dk28
Mission Santa Barbara USA 22 Ea28
Mission San Xavier del Bac USA 23 Ee29
Missira SN 269 Kd39
Missisagi CDN 32 Fj22
Missisa Lake CDN 25 Fh19
Mississauga CDN (ON) 33 Ga24
Mississippi USA 12 Fb12
Mississippi USA (AR) 29 Fe28
Mississippi Cruises USA 34 Fe29
Mississippi Delta USA 29 Ff31
Misso EST 96 Mh33
Missoula USA (MT) 21 Ed22
Missour MA 259 Kj29
Missouri USA 12 Fb11
Missouri USA 29 Fe26
Missouri USA 26 Ek23
Missouri Breaks Wild and Scenic River USA 19 Ef22
Missouri City USA (TX) 29 Fc31
Missouri Valley USA (IA) 27 Fc25
Mistawasis Ind. Res. CDN 19 Eg19
Mistelbach A 115 Lr42
Misterbianco I 122 Lp53
Misterei SUD 282 Mb39
Misterhult S 95 Lr33
Misti, Volcán PE 72 Ge54
Mistletoe S.P. USA 35 Fj29
Mistrás GR 128 Mc53
Mistretta I 122 Lp53
Misty Fjords Nat. Mon. USA 17 De18
Misumba RDC 289 Ma48
Misumi J 185 Rf29
Mita Hills Dam Z 296 Me53
Mita-Mirim BR (AM) 62 Gh46
Mita Mita AUS (VIC) 237 Sd64
Mitan OM 151 Ng36
Mitatib SUD 277 Mj38
Mitchell AUS (QLD) 235 Sd59
Mitchell USA (OR) 20 Dk23
Mitchell USA (NE) 26 Ej25
Mitchell USA (SD) 26 Fa24
Mitchell USA (SD) 26 Fb24
Mitchell and Alice Rivers N.P. AUS 230 Sb53
Mitchell Falls AUS 222 Rc53
Mitchell Highway AUS 235 Sd59
Mitchell Highway AUS 235 Sd61
Mitchell, Mount USA 13 Fd11
Mitchell, Mount USA 35 Fj28
Mitchell River AUS (WA) 222 Rc53
Mitchell River AUS 230 Sb53
Mitchell River N.P. AUS 222 Rc53
Mitchelstown IRL 100 Km38
Miteja EAT 293 Mk50
Mitémele GQ 280 Lf45
Mithankot PK 163 Of31
Mitha Tiwana PK 161 Og29
Mithi PK 163 Oe33
Mithimna GR 129 Mg51
Mitiamo AUS (VIC) 237 Sc64
Mitikas GR 128 Ma52
Mitkof Island USA 17 Dd17
Mitla MEX 40 Fb37
Mito J 183 Sa27
Mitoko RDC 286 Ma44
Mitole EAT 293 Mk50
Mitomoni EAT 297 Mh51
Mitrašinci MK 126 Mc49
Mitrofania Island USA 14 Ca18
Mitrofanovka RUS 133 Mk21
Mitrovo SCG 126 Ma47
Mitsamiouli COM 304 Nb51
Mitsinjo RM 304 Nc53
Mitsiwa ER 277 Mk39
Mitsiwa Channel ER 277 Mk39
Mitsuishi J 181 Sb24
Mitsushima J 182 Re28
Mittådalen S 93 Ln28
Mittellandkanal D 112 Lh38
Mittelrheintal D 114 Lh40
Mittenwald D 115 Lm43
Mittersill A 115 Ln43
Mitterteich D 115 Ln41
Mittweida D 113 Ln40
Mitu CO 61 Ge45
Mitundu MW 296 Mg53
Mitunguu EAK 290 Mj46
Mitwaba RDC 292 Md50
Mityana EAU 290 Mg45
Mitzic G 281 Lf45
Miura-hanto J 183 Rk28
Miuri EAT 293 Mk50
Mixco GCA 41 Fe38
Mixtlán MEX (JLC) 39 Eh35
Miya WAN 272 Le40
Miyake-jima J 183 Rk28
Miyako J 183 Sa26
Miyakonojo J 185 Rf30
Miyandoab IR 154 Nd27
Miyaneh IR 154 Nd27
Miyanoura-dake J 185 Rf30
Miyazaki J 185 Rf30
Miyazu J 183 Rh28
Miyun VRC (BJG) 175 Qj25
Miyun He VRC 175 Qj25
Mizan Teferi ETH 283 Mh42
Mizdah LAR 260 Lg30
Mizen Head IRL 100 Kl39
Mïževïčy BY 117 Mf38
Mizhi VRC (SAA) 175 Qf27
Mizil RO 125 Mg45
Mizoram IND 186 Pc14
Mizpah USA (MT) 21 Eh22
Mizpah CRiver USA 21 Eh22
Mizpé Ramon IL 146 Mh30
Mizque BOL 72 Gh54
Mizque BOL 72 Gh54
Mizuho ANT (J) 313 Nb32
Mizur RUS (SOA) 152 Nc24
Mizusawa J 183 Sa26
Mjadzel BY 97 Mg36
Mjaksa RUS 132 Mk16
Mjanji EAU 290 Mg45
Mjetë AL 126 Ma50
Mjölby S 93 Lq32
Mjönäs S 93 Lo31
Mjøndalen N 92 Lk31
Mjörn S 94 Ln33
Mjøsa N 92 Ll30
Mkalamo EAT 293 Mk48
Mkambati Nature Reserve SA 303 Me61
Mkanga EAT 293 Mg49
Mkangira EAT 293 Mj50
Mkarangama EAT 293 Mk49
Mkasi Z 292 Mg50
Mkata EAT 293 Mk48
Mkharram Foqani SYR 146 Mj28
Mkhaya Nature Reserve SD 303 Mf59
Mkhota MW 296 Mg52
Mkoani EAT 293 Mk48
Mkokotoni EAT 293 Mk48
Mkomazi EAT 293 Mk48
Mkomazi SA 303 Mf61
Mkomazi Game Reserve EAT 293 Mj47
Mkombe EAT 292 Mf49
Mkuchika EAT 297 Mk51
Mkushi Z 296 Me52
Mkushi Boma Z 296 Me52
Mkushi River Z 296 Me52
Mkuze SA 303 Mg59
Mkuze Game Reserve SA 303 Mg59
Mkwaja EAT 293 Mk48
Mkwasine ZW 300 Mf56
Mladá Boleslav CZ 118 Lp40
Mladá Vožice CZ 118 Lp41
Mladenovac SCG 124 Ma46
Mlandizi EAT 293 Mj49
Mlandizi EAT 293 Mk49
M'Lang RP 205 Rc42
Mlava SCG 126 Mb46
Mława PL 117 Ma37
Mlawula Nature Reserve SD 303 Mf59
Mlebniko RUS (MEL) 133 Ne17
Mligaji EAT 293 Mk48
Mlilwane W.S. SD 303 Mf59
Mlinište BIH 121 Lr46
Mljet HR 123 Ls48
Mljet, N.P. HR 121 Ls48
Młodasko PL 116 Lr38
Mlogoszyn PL 117 Lu38
Mloka EAT 293 Mk49
Młynary PL 117 Lu36
Młynarze PL 117 Mb38
Mlyniv UA 117 Mf40
Mmabatho SA 299 Mc58
Mmadinare RB 299 Md56
Mmamabula RB 299 Md57
Mmashoro RB 299 Md56
Mmathethe RB 299 Mc58
Mmatshumo RB 299 Mc56
Mnarani Ruins EAK 291 Mk47
Mnero EAT 297 Mk51
Mníšek nad Hnilcom SK 119 Ma42
Mnyani EAT 293 Mh49
Mo GH 279 La41
Mo N 92 Lm30
Moa BR 66 Gd49
Moa C 45 Gc35
Moa EAT 293 Mk48
Moa RI 209 Rd46
Moa RI 214 Re50
Moa WAL 278 Ke42
Moab USA (UT) 21 Ef26
Moaco BR 67 Gf49
Moacşa RO 125 Mf45
Moai RCH 72 Ef59
Moa Island AUS 230 Sb51
Moala FJI 247 Tk55
Mo'alleman IR 154 Nh28
Mo'allem Kalayeh IR 154 Nf27
Moama AUS (NSW) 234 Sc61
Moamba MOC 300 Mg58
Moanda G 288 Lg46
Moanda RDC 281 Lk44
Moapa R. Ind. Res. USA 22 Ec27
Moara Vlăsiei RO 125 Mg46
Móar Bay CDN 25 Ga19
Moate IRL 100 Kn37
Moatize MOC 296 Mg54
Moba RDC 292 Me49
Mobara J 183 Sa28
Mobaye RCA 286 Ma43
Mobayi-Mbongi RDC 286 Ma43
Mobdoua RIM 270 Kg38
Mobeetie USA (TX) 28 Ek28
Mobena RDC 286 Lk45
Moberly USA (MO) 27 Fd26
Mobile USA (AL) 34 Fg30
Mobile AUS (QLD) 234 Sc59
Mobridge USA (SD) 26 Ek23
Moca DOM 46 Ge36
Moca GQ 280 Le44
Mocajuba BR (PA) 64 Hf47
Mocambinho BR (MG) 70 Hh53
Moçambique MOC 297 Na53
Mocambo BR (BA) 71 Hk52
Moccasin USA (CA) 20 Dk27
Moccasin USA (MT) 21 Ef22
Moc Chau VN 178 Qc35
Moce FJI 247 Ua55
Mocha YE 150 Nb39
Moche Pirámides PE 66 Ga50
Moche Pirámides (Túcume) PE 66 Ga49
Mochima, P.N. YV 57 Gh40
Moc Hoa VN 197 Qc40
Mochong VRC (GZH) 178 Qd32
Mochudi RB 299 Md58
Mochumi PE 66 Ga49
Mochy PL 116 Lr38
Mocimboa da Praia MOC 297 Na51
Mocimboa do Rovuma MOC 297 Mk51
Mociu RO 124 Me44
Möckern D 113 Lm38
Mockfjärd S 93 Lp30
Môco ANG 294 Lk52
Mocoa CO 60 Gb45
Mococa BR (SP) 74 Hg56
Mocoduene MOC 300 Mh57
Mocomoco BOL 67 Gf53
Mocorito MEX (SL) 38 Eg33
Mocorón HN 42 Fh38
Moctezuma MEX (SO) 23 Ef31
Moctezuma MEX (SLP) 39 Ek34
Mocuba MOC 297 Mj54
Mocupe PE 66 Ga49
Močurica BG 127 Mg48
Modahtou DJI 284 Na40
Modan RI 213 Rg47
Modane F 105 Lg45
Modăr BG 127 Me49
Modasa IND (GUJ) 190 Og34
Modder SA 303 Mc60
Modderpoort San Rock Paintings SA 303 Md60
Model USA (CO) 23 Eh27
Módena I 120 Ll46
Modena USA (UT) 20 Ed27
Modesto USA (CA) 20 Dk27
Modesto Méndez GCA 41 Ff38
Modest Town USA (VA) 33 Gc27
Modhera Sun Temple IND 190 Og34
Módica I 122 Lp54
Modigliana I 120 Lm46
Modinagar IND (UPH) 189 Oj31
Modjigo RN 273 Lg37
Modlborzyce PL 117 Mc40
Mödling A 115 Lr42
Modong RI 207 Qc47
Modot MNG 173 Qe22
Modra špilja HR 121 Lr48
Modriča BIH 121 Lt46
Modugno I 123 Lr49
Moe AUS (VIC) 237 Sd65
Moebase MOC 297 Mk54
Moeko RDC 286 Lk44
Moelv N 92 Ll30
Moengo SME 59 Hc43
Moeraki Boulders NZ 239 Tf68
Moerkesung VRC (TIB) 170 Pc30
Moers D 112 Lg39
Moffat GB 99 Kr35
Moffen N 91 Lh05
Moffet Pt. USA 14 Bj18
Moffit USA (ND) 26 Ek22
Moftin RO 124 Mc43
Mofu Z 296 Mf51
Moga IND (PJB) 188 Oh30
Moga RDC 292 Md47
Mogadishu SP 291 Nc44
Mogadouro P 106 Ko51
Mogalu RDC 286 Lk44
Mogami-gawa J 183 Sa26
Moganshan VRC 175 Qk30
Mogao Ku VRC 169 Ph25
Mogapinyana RB 299 Md57
Mogaung MYA 195 Pj33
Mogdy RUS 180 Rg20
Mogee Bli LB 278 Kf43
Moghar IR 154 Ng29
Moghrar DZ 259 Kk29
Mogila EAK 283 Mh43
Mogilno PL 116 Ls38
Mogincual MOC 297 Na53
Moglenitsa GR 126 Mc50
Mogliano Véneto I 120 Ln45
Mogna RA (SJ) 76 Gf61
Mogoča RUS 141 Ra08
Mogojtuj RUS (AGB) 173 Qh20
Mogok MYA 195 Pj34
Mogorjelo BIH 121 Ls47
Mogoşoaia RO 125 Mf46
Mogosoaia RO 125 Mg46
Mogotio EAK 290 Mh45
Mogpog RP 203 Ra39
Mograt SUD 276 Mg37
Mogroum TCH 273 Lh40
Moguer E 108 Ko47
Mogumber AUS (WA) 228 Qj61
Mogwase SA 299 Md58
Mogzon RUS 173 Qg20
Mohács H 119 Lt44
Mohács H 121 Lt45
Mohala IND (CGH) 191 Pa35
Mohale Dam LS 303 Md60
Mohale's Hoek LS 303 Md61
Mohall USA (ND) 24 Ek21
Mohammabad IR 155 Oa30
Mohammad Abad IR 154 Ng29
Mohammad Abad IR 156 Nj30
Mohammad Abad IR 157 Nj31
Mohammad Agha AFG 160 Oe28
Mohammad Hasan Khaan Bridge IR 154 Ng27
Mohammadia DZ 259 La28
Mohammedia MA 258 Kg29
Mohana IND (ORS) 191 Pc36
Mohanganj BD 194 Pf33
Mohania IND (BIH) 191 Pb33
Mohanlalganj IND (UPH) 189 Pa32
Mohanpur NEP 170 Pd32
Moharli IND (MHT) 191 Ok35
Mohdra IND (MPH) 191 Ok33
Mohe VRC (HLG) 173 Rb19
Mohe VRC (HLG) 173 Rb19
Mohean IND (AAN) 193 Pg42
Mohed S 93 Lr29
Moheda S 95 Lp34
Mohéli = Mwali COM 304 Nb52
Mohelnice CZ 118 Lr41
Mohen FSM 240 Sc17
Mohenjo Daro PK 162 Oe32
Mohgaon IND (MPH) 191 Pa34
Möhne D 112 Lj39
Möhnesee D 112 Lj39
Mohnyin MYA 195 Pj33
Moho PE 67 Gf53
Mohoda IND (MHT) 191 Ok35
Mohol IND (MHT) 190 Oh37
Mohora H 119 Lu43
Mohoro EAT 293 Mk50
Mohyliv-Podil's'kyj UA 125 Mh42
Moi N 92 Lg32
Moiben EAK 290 Mh45
Moi Hoa Binh Pagoda VN 199 Qc41
Moila Point PNG 244 Sh49
Moimba ANG 294 Lg54
Moincêr VRC (TIB) 170 Pa30
Moineşti RO 125 Mg44
Moinsi Hills GH 279 Kk42
Mo i Rana N 90 Lh12
Mõisaküla EST 96 Mf32
Moises Ville RA (SF) 77 Gk61
Moisie CDN (QC) 30 Gg20
Moison Lake CDN 24 Fb18
Moissac F 104 Lb46
Moïssala TCH 281 Lj41
Moitaco YV 57 Gh41
Möja S 93 Lt31
Mojácar E 109 Kt47
Mojados E 106 Kq51
Mojave USA (CA) 22 Ea28
Mojave Desert USA 22 Eb28
Mojave National Preserve USA 22 Ec28
Mojiang VRC (YUN) 195 Qa34
Moji das Cruzes BR (SP) 75 Hg57
Moji-Guaçu BR (SP) 74 Hg57
Mojikit Lake CDN 25 Ff20
Moji-Mirim BR (SP) 74 Hg57
Mojiquiçaba BR (BA) 75 Ja54
Mojo ETH 284 Mk41
Mojo ETH 284 Na41
Mojokerto RI 210 Qg49
Mojosari RI 210 Qg49
Moju BR 64 Hf47
Mojynkum KZ 158 Oe23
Mojynty KZ 166 Og22
Moka DY 280 Lb42
Moka IND (KTK) 193 Oj39
Moka J 183 Sa27
Mokalsar IND (RJT) 188 Og33
Mokambo RDC 296 Me52
Mokameh IND (BIH) 191 Pc33
Mokhotlong LS 303 Me60
Mokhpal IND (CGH) 191 Pa36
Mokil Atoll FSM 240 Sd17
Möklinta S 93 Lr30
Moknine TN 260 Lf28
Moko RN 271 Lb39
Mokobody PL 117 Mc38
Mokokchung IND (NGL) 194 Ph32
Mokolo CAM 273 Lg40
Mokolo SA 299 Md58
Mokolo Dam SA 299 Md57
Mokolodi Nature Reserve RB 299 Mc58
Mokombe RDC 286 Mb46
Mo Ko Phi Phi N.P. THA 198 Pk42
Mokoreta NZ 239 Te69
Mokowe EAK 293 Na47
Mokp'o ROK 182 Rd28
Mokre PL 116 Ls37
Mokren BG 127 Mg48
Mokrous RUS 133 Nd20
Mokša RUS 133 Nb19
Mokšan RUS 133 Nc19
Möktama Kwe T 196 Pj38
Mokuti NAM 298 Lj55
Mokwa WAN 272 Lc41
Mol B 103 Lf39
Mola di Bari I 123 Ls49
Molalatau RB 300 Mf57
Mo'lali botig'i UZB 158 Oc25
Molaly KZ 166 Ok23
Molaman IND (RJT) 188 Og31
Molas MEX (QTR) 41 Fg35
Molat HR 121 Lp46
Mold GB 101 Kr37
Moldava nad Bodvou SK 119 Mb42
Moldavia RO 125 Mg43
Molde N 92 Lh28
Moldo-Too KS 159 Oh25
Moldova MD 125 Mh43
Moldova RO 125 Mg43
Moldoveanu RO 125 Me45
Moldray KZ 166 Ok20
Mole GH 279 Kk41
Molecreek AUS (TAS) 236 Sd66
Molegbe RDC 286 Ma43
Molem N.P. IND 190 Oh38
Mole N.P. GH 279 Kk41
Molepolole RB 299 Mc58
Môle-SaintNicolas RH 46 Gd3
Molesworth AUS (QLD) 234 Sb60
Molėtai LT 97 Mf35
Molfetta I 123 Lr49
Molibagu RI 209 Rb45
Molières F 104 Lb46
Molina E 109 Kt50
Molina RCH 76 Ge63
Molina de Segura E 109 Kt48
Moline USA (IL) 27 Fe25
Moline USA (KS) 29 Fb27
Molinella I 120 Lm46
Molinggapoto RI 209 Rb45
Molinos RA (SA) 72 Gg58
Moliro RDC 292 Mf50
Molise I 122 Lp49
Molkom S 93 Lo31
Mollafeneri TR 130 Mk50
Mollendo PE 72 Gd54
Mollerin Lake AUS 228 Qj61
Mollerussa E 110 La49
Mollisfossen N 90 Ma11
Mölln D 113 Ll37
Mölltorp S 93 Lp32
Molo MYA 195 Pj34
Molobala RMM 270 Kh39
Molobog RI 209 Rc45
Molocopote BR (PA) 63 Hc45
Molodezhnaja ANT (RUS) 313 Na33
Molodo RMM 270 Kg38
Molokai USA 16 Cb35
Molong AUS (NSW) 237 Se62
Molong IND (ASM) 194 Pg33
Molopo RB/SA 299 Mc58
Moloporivier SA 299 Mc58
Molos GR 128 Mc52
Moloskovicy RUS 96 Mk31
Moloundou CAM 281 Lh44
Molsheim F 103 Lh42
Molteno SA 303 Md61
Molu RI 215 Rf49
Molucca Islands RI 201 Rb19
Molucca Sea RI 201 Ra19
Molumbo MOC 297 Mj53
Molunat HR 123 Lt48
Molwe RDC 295 Mc51
Moma MOC 297 Mk54
Moma RDC 289 Mb49
Momalgi WAL 278 Kd42
Momats RI 213 Rk48
Momba AUS (NSW) 234 Sb61
Momba EAT 292 Mg50
Mombaça BR (CE) 65 Ja48
Mombasa EAK 293 Mk4
Mombasa Marine N.P. EAK 291 Mk48
Mombenzélé RCB 281 Lj45
Mombetsu J 181 Sb23
Mombetsu J 181 Sb24
Mombo ANG 289 Ma51
Mombo Camp RB 299 Mb5
Mombongo RDC 286 Mb45
Mombongo RDC 287 Mc45
Momboyo RDC 286 Lk46
Mombuey E 106 Ko52
Mombum RI 242 Rk50
Momčilgrad BG 127 Mf49
Mommark DK 94 Ll36
Momote PNG 243 Sc49
Momotombo, Volcán NIC 42 Fg39
Mompiche EC 60 Fk45
Mompog Passage RP 203 Rb
Mompono RDC 286 Ma45
Momskij hrebet RUS 141 Sb0
Møn DK 94 Ln35
Mon IND (NGL) 194 Ph32
Mon MYA 194 Ph35
Monach Islands GB 98 Kn33
Monaco MC 105 Lh47
Monaco Deep 254 Jd12
Monadyr KZ 166 Of21
Monaghan IRL 98 Ko36
Monahans USA (TX) 23 Ej30
Mona Passage DOM/USA 46 Gf36
Monapo MOC 297 Na53
Mona Quimbundo ANG 289 Lk50
Monarch Mtn. CDN 18 Dh20
Monari AFG 160 Oe29
Monaši UA 125 Ml44
Monasterace Marina I 123 Lr5
Monasterio de Guadalupe E 108 Kp49
Monasterio de Leyre E 107 Kt52
Monasterio de Piedra E 107 Kt51
Monasterio de San Juan de la Peña E 107 Ku52
Monasterio de Veruela E 107 Kt51

onasterio de Yuste E 108 Kp50
onastero di Sabiona = Kloster Säben I 120 Lm44
onastery of Saint Anthony ET 263 Mg31
onastery of Saint Catherine ET 263 Mg31
onastery of Saint Paul ET 263 Mg31
onastery of Saint Simeon ET 263 Mg33
onastir I 111 Lk51
onastir TN 260 Lf28
onastyrščina RUS 132 Mf18
onastyrs'ka UA 119 Mf41
onastyryšče UA 134 Me21
onastyrys'ka UA 134 Mc21
onatélé CAM 281 Lf43
onboré CAM 273 Lh41
oncada E 109 Ku49
oncalieri I 120 Lh45
oncalvo E 106 Ko52
oncalvo I 120 Lj45
onção BR (MA) 64 Hh47
onção E 106 Km52
ončegorsk RUS 140 Mc05
önchengladbach D 112 Lg39
onchique P 108 Km47
onchy CDN (SK) 19 Eg21
oncks Corner USA (SC) 35 Fk29
onclova MEX (COH) 39 Ek32
oncontour F 102 Ks42
oncton CDN (NB) 31 Gh22
ondaí BR (SC) 78 Hd59
ondéjar E 109 Kr50
ondello I 122 Lo52
on Desir NAM 298 Lh55
ondim de Basto P 106 Kn51
ondjamboli RDC 286 Mb44
ondjamboli RDC 287 Mc44
ondjuku RDC 286 Ma46
ondo EAT 293 Mh48
ondo TCH 273 Lh39
ondocino USA (CA) 20 Dj26
ondolfo I 121 Lo47
ondombe RDC 286 Mb46
ondoñedo CO 60 Gb44
ondoñedo E 106 Kn53
ondoro CI 278 Kg41
ondoro RMM 271 Kk38
ondoubleau F 102 La43
ondovì I 120 Lh46
ondovi USA (WI) 27 Fe23
ondragone I 122 Lo49
ondrian Island AUS 229 Rb63
ondriz E 106 Kn53
ondsee A 115 Lo43
ondy RUS (BUR) 172 Qa20
oné CAM 280 Le42
oneague JA 45 Gb36
oneasa RO 124 Mc44
onein F 104 Ku47
onemvassiá GR 128 Md54
onemvassiá Kástro GR 128 Md54
onesterio E 108 Ko48
onestir de Montserrat E 110 Lb49
onestir de Sant Cugat E 110 Lc49
onestir Santes Creus E 110 Lb49
oneta USA (WY) 21 Eg24
onett USA (MO) 29 Fd27
oneymore GB 98 Ko36
onfalcone I 121 Lo45
onforte P 108 Kn49
onga RDC 286 Mb43
ongala RDC 286 Ma44
ongala SUD 287 Mf43
ongala Game Reserve SUD 283 Mf43
ongbwalu RDC 287 Mf45
ong Cai VN 178 Qd35
ongemputu RDC 289 Ma47
ongeri WAL 278 Ke41
ongers Lake AUS 228 Qj60
ongge RI 212 Rg46
onggui RI 213 Rh46
öng Hpayak MYA 195 Pk35
öng Hsat MYA 195 Pk35
öng Hsu MYA 195 Pk34
ongkaing MYA 195 Pj35
ongla BD 194 Pe34
öng Long MYA 195 Pj34
öng Mit MYA 195 Pj34
ongne MYA 195 Pj35
ongo TCH 282 Lk39
ongo WAL 278 Kd41
ongol Daguran Nature Reserve MNG 173 Qh21
ongol Els MNG 167 Ph22
ongolia MNG 139 Pb05
ongomo GQ 281 Lf45
ongonu WAN 273 Lg39
ongororo TCH 282 Mb39
ongotong VRC (TIB) 176 Pk31
ongoumba RCA 286 Lk44
öng Pan MYA 195 Pk35
öng Ping MYA 195 Pk35
öng Ton MYA 195 Pk35
ongu Z 295 Mb53
ongua ANG 294 Lh54
onguel RIM 269 Kd37
öng Yai MYA 195 Pk34
öng Yang MYA 195 Pk35
öng Yawng MYA 195 Qa35
öng Yu MYA 195 Pk34
onheim D 115 Ll42
önh Hajrhan MNG 167 Pf22
oni RI 211 Ra50
oni Ágios Ioanni Theologou GR 129 Mg53
oni Arkádi GR 129 Me55
oniatis CY 131 Mn56
onico USA (WI) 32 Ff23
onida USA (MT) 21 Ed23
oni Dochiariu GR 127 Me50
onimpébougou RMM 270 Kh38
oni Simonos Pétras GR 127 Me50
onistrol-d'Allier F 105 Ld46
onistrol-sur-Loire F 105 Le45
oni Timiou Prodromou GR 126 Md49
onitor CDN (AB) 19 Ee19
onitor Range USA 20 Eb26
onitos CO 56 Gb41
onje RA (SF) 77 Gk62
onkaringa GH 279 Kk40
onkayo RP 205 Rd42
onkey Bay MW 297 Mh53
onkey Mia AUS (WA) 224 Qg58
önkhbulag MNG 172 Qb22
Mońki PL 117 Mc37
Monkira AUS (QLD) 234 Sa58
Monkoto RDC 286 Ma46
Monmouth GB 101 Ks39
Monmouth Park USA (NJ) 33 Gc25
Monnow Bridge GB 101 Ks39
Mono CO 57 Gf43
Mono RT 279 La42
Monobamba PE 66 Gc51
Mono Lake USA 20 Ea26
Monolíthio GR 128 Mb51
Monólithos GR 129 Mh54
Monolon AUS (NSW) 234 Sb61
Monopamba CO 60 Gb45
Monópoli I 123 Ls50
Monou TCH 275 Mb37
Monóvar E 109 Ku48
Monowai NZ 239 Td68
Monreal del Campo E 109 Kt50
Monreale I 122 Lo52
Mon Repos Conservation Park AUS 235 Sg58
Monroe USA (WA) 18 Dk22
Monroe USA (OR) 20 Dj23
Monroe USA (UT) 21 Ed26
Monroe USA (LA) 29 Fd29
Monroe USA (WI) 32 Ff24
Monroe USA (MI) 32 Fj25
Monroe USA (NY) 33 Gc25
Monroe USA (GA) 35 Fj29
Monroe USA (NC) 35 Fk28
Monroe City USA (MO) 27 Fe26
Monroeville USA (AL) 34 Fg30
Monrou DY 272 Lb40
Monrovia LB 278 Ke42
Monroy E 108 Ko49
Monroyo E 109 Ku50
Mons B 113 Ld40
Monsanto P 106 Kn50
Monsaraz P 108 Kn48
Monschau D 112 Lg40
Monsèlice I 120 Lm45
Monsenhor Gil BR (PI) 65 Hj48
Mons Klint DK 94 Ln36
Mönsterås S 95 Lr33
Mont Abourak RMM 271 La37
Montagnac F 105 Ld47
Montagnana I 120 Lm45
Montagna Azul Paulista BR (SP) 74 Hf56
Montagne d'Ambre, P.N.de la RM 305 Ne52
Montagne de Lure F 105 Lf46
Montagne de Nganha CAM 281 Lh42
Montagne du Lubéron F 105 Lf47
Montagne Noire F 104 Lc47
Montagnes Arawa F 59 Hd44
Montagnes del'Affolé RIM 269 Ke37
Montagnes Trinité F 59 Hd43
Mont Agou RT 279 La42
Montagu SA 302 Ma62
Montague CDN (PE) 31 Gj22
Montague Island USA 16 Cg16
Montague Sound AUS 222 Rc53
Montague Strait USA 16 Cg16
Mont Aigoual F 105 Ld46
Montaigu F 102 Kt44
Montaitas KZ 158 Oe24
Montalbán E 109 Ku50
Montalcino I 120 Lm47
Montalegre ANG 289 Lj50
Montalegre P 106 Kn51
Montalivet-les-Bains F 104 Kt45
Montalto I 123 Lq52
Montalto di Castro I 122 Lm48
Montalto Uffogo I 123 Lr51
Montalvânia BR (MG) 70 Hh53
Montalvo CO 56 Gc42
Montalvo EC 60 Ga46
Montalvo EC 60 Gb47
Montamarta E 106 Kp51
Montana BG 126 Md47
Montana USA 12 Eb09
Montaña de Celaque HN 41 Ff38
Montaña de Comayagua HN 41 Fg38
Montaña Punta Piedra HN 42 Fh38
Montaña Punta Piedra HN 42 Fh38
Montañas de Colón HN 42 Fh38
Montañas de Colón HN 42 Fh38
Montañas de Comayagua HN 42 Fg38
Montañas de Convento EC 60 Ga46
Montañas del Norte de Chiapas MEX 41 Fd37
Montañas de Onzole EC 60 Ga45
Montañas de Patuca HN 42 Fh38
Montañas de Patuca HN 42 Fh38
Montañas de Yoro HN 41 Fg38
Montañas de Yoro HN 42 Fg38
Montanha BR (ES) 75 Hk55
Montargil P 108 Km49
Montargis F 103 Lc43
Montasio I 121 Lo44
Montauban F 104 Lb47
Montauban-de-Bretagne F 102 Ks42
Montauk USA (NY) 33 Gd25
Montbard F 103 Le43
Mont Bata RCA 281 Lh43
Montbazillac F 104 La46
Montbazon F 102 La43
Montbéliard F 103 Lg43
Mont Bellevue de l'Inini F 59 Hd44
Mont Bélo RCB 288 Lg48
Mont Birougou G 288 Lg46
Mont Birougou, P.N.de G 288 Lg46
Montblanc E 110 Lb49
Montbrison F 105 Le45
Montbron F 104 La45
Montceau-les-Mines F 105 Le44
Montchanin F 105 Le44
Mont Cotica F 59 Hc43
Montcuq F 104 Lb46
Mont-de-Marsan F 104 Ku47
Mont de Niangbo CI 279 Kh41
Montdidier F 103 Lc41
Mont-Dore F 246 Td57
Mont Doumo CI 278 Kg42
Mont du Métal DZ 266 Le35
Monteagle AUS (QLD) 233 Sd57
Monteagudo BOL 73 Gj55
Monte Alban MEX 40 Fb37
Monte Albo I 111 Lk50
Monte Alegre BR (PA) 63 Hc46
Monte Alegre de Goiás BR (GO) 70 Hg52
Montealegre del Castillo E 109 Kt48
Monte Alegre de Minas BR (MG) 74 Hf55
Monte Alén, P.N.de G 280
Lf45
Monte Amaro I 122 Lp48
Monte Amiata I 120 Lm48
Monte Argentário I 122 Lm48
Monte Argentário-Porto San Stéfano I 122 Lm48
Monte Azul BR (MG) 70 Hj53
Montebello Islands AUS 224 Qh56
Montebelluna I 120 Ln45
Monte Belo ANG 294 Lh52
Monte Binga MOC/ZW 300 Mg55
Monte Botte Donato I 123 Lr51
Monte Buckland RA 83 Gh73
Monte Burney RCH 82 Gd72
Monte Calvo I 123 Lq49
Monte Campana RA 83 Gh73
Montecarlo RA (MI) 77 Hc59
Monte Carmelo BR (MG) 74 Hg55
Monte Caseros RA (CR) 77 Hb61
Montecatini Terme I 120 Ll47
Montécchio Emilia I 120 Ll46
Montécchio Maggiore I 120 Lm45
Monte Cervati I 122 Lq50
Montech F 104 Lb47
Monte Chiperone MOC 297 Mh54
Monte Christo SA 299 Md57
Monte Cimone I 120 Ll46
Monte Cinto F 111 Lk48
Monte Comán RA (MD) 76 Gg63
Monte Creek CDN (BC) 18 Ea20
Monte Cristi DOM 46 Ge36
Montecristi EC 60 Fk46
Monte Cristi, P.N. RH 46 Ge36
Monte Cristo BR (AM) 61 Gg48
Montecristo, P.N. ES 41 Ff38
Monte d'Accoddi I 111 Lj50
Monte Darwin RCH 82 Gf73
Monte die Sette Fratelli I 111 Lk51
Monte Dinero RA (SC) 82 Gf72
Monte di Prunu F 111 Lk48
Monte Dourado BR (PA) 63 Hd46
Montefalco I 120 Ln48
Monte Falterona I 120 Lm47
Montefiascone I 122 Ln48
Monte Fitz Roy RA 82 Gd70
Monteforte de Lemos E 106 Kn52
Montefrío E 108 Kq47
Monte Gariglione I 123 Lr51
Montego Bay JA 45 Gb36
Monte Grande BOL 68 Gj54
Monte Greco I 122 Lp49
Monte Hart Dyke RCH 82 Gc72
Montehermoso E 108 Ko50
Monte Hermoso RA (BA) 81 Gk65
Monte Inés RA 82 Gf70
Monteiro BR (PB) 65 Jb49
Monte is Carávius I 111 Lj51
Monte Jervis RCH 82 Gc70
Monte Ladrillero RCH 82 Gc71
Monte León, Cerro RA 82 Gf71
Monte Leone I 120 Lj44
Montelibano CO 56 Gc42
Montélimar F 105 Le46
Montelimar NIC 42 Fg40
Monte Limbara I 111 Lk50
Monte Linas I 111 Lj51
Monte Lindo PY 73 Ha57
Monte Lindo Grande RA 73 Ha58
Montella I 122 Lq50
Montellano E 108 Kp46
Montello USA (NV) 21 Ec25
Monte Mabu MOC 297 Mj54
Monte Maca RCH 80 Gd68
Monte Maiz RA (CD) 77 Gj62
Monte Mariana MEX (ZCT) 39 Ej34
Monte Melimoyu RCH 80 Gd68
Montemorelos MEX (NL) 39 Fa33
Montemor-o-Novo P 108 Km48
Monte Namuli MOC 297 Mj53
Montendre F 104 Ku45
Montenegro BR (RS) 78 He60
Monte Nieddu I 111 Lk50
Monte Núria I 122 Lo48
Monte Pascoal BR 75 Ja54
Monte Pascoal, P.N.de BR 75 Ja54
Monte Patria RCH 76 Ge61
Monte Perdido E 110 La48
Monte Petroso I 122 Lo49
Monte Philippi RA 82 Ge71
Monte Pio MEX (VC) 41 Fc36
Monte Plata DOM 46 Gf36
Monte Pollino I 123 Lr51
Montepuez MOC 297 Mk52
Montepulciano I 120 Lm47
Monte Quemado RA (SE) 73 Gj58
Monteradó RI 208 Qe45
Monte Rasu I 111 Lk50
Montereau F 103 Lc42
Monte Rei BR (MG) 70 Hh53
Monterey USA (CA) 20 Dk27
Monterey USA (VA) 33 Ga26
Monterey Bay USA 20 Dj27
Montería CO 56 Gc41
Monteriggioni I 120 Lm47
Montero BOL 73 Gj54
Monteros RA (TU) 76 Gh59
Monte Rosa I/CH 114 Lh45
Monterosso al Mare I 120 Lk46
Monterotondo I 122 Ln48
Monterrey MEX (NL) 39 Ek33
Monterrico GCA 41 Fe39
Montes Altos BR (MA) 64 Hg48
Monte San Giorgio CH 114 Lj45
Monte San Lorenzo o Cocharane RCH 82 Gd69
Monte San Savino I 120 Lm47
Monte Sant'Angelo I 123 Lq49
Monte Santo BR (BA) 71 Ja51
Monte Santo de Minas BR (MG) 75 Hg56
Monte Sarmiento RCH 82 Ge73
Montes Claros BR (MG) 75 Hj54
Montes de León E 106 Ko52
Montes de Oca RA (BA) 81 Gj65
Montes de Toledo E 109 Kq49
Monte Senes I 111 Lk50
Monte Sholl RA 82 Gg70
Monte Sigfried RCH 82 Gc70
Montesilvano I 122 Lp48
Monte Sirino I 123 Lq50
Monte Skyring RCH 82 Gd73
Montesquieu-Volvestre F 104 Lb47
Monte Stewart RCH 82 Ge73
Monte Tetris RA 82 Gd70
Monte Triste RA 80 Gh67
Monte Urtigu I 111 Lj50
Montevarchi I 120 Lm47
Monte Velino I 122 Lo48
Monte Vettore I 121 Lo48
Monte Victoria RCH 82 Ge72
Montevideo ROU 77 Hb63
Montevideo USA (MN) 27 Fc23
Montevidiu BR (GO) 74 He54
Monte Viso I 120 Lh46
Monte Vista USA (CO) 23 Eg27
Monte Volturino I 123 Lq50
Monte Vúlture I 122 Lq50
Monte Warton RCH 82 Gd72
Monte Wilson PE 66 Gb53
Monte Zeballos RA 82 Ge69
Montezuma BR (MG) 70 Hj53
Montezuma USA (IA) 27 Fd25
Montezuma USA (GA) 35 Fj29
Montezuma Castle Nat. Mon. USA 23 Ee28
Montfaucon-d'Argonne F 103 Lf41
Montfaucon-en-Velay F 105 Le45
Montgomery USA (TX) 29 Fc30
Montgomery USA (AL) 34 Fg29
Montgomery Island AUS 222 Rc53
Montgomery Pass USA 20 Ea26
Mont Guimbiri CAM 281 Lg43
Montguyon F 104 Ku45
Monthey CH 114 Lg44
Mont Hoyo RDC 287 Me45
Mont Hoyo, P.N. RDC 287 Mf45
Monti I 111 Lk50
Monti Aurunci I 122 Lo49
Mont Iboundji G 288 Lf46
Monticello USA (UT) 23 Ef27
Monticello USA (MN) 27 Fd23
Monticello USA (IA) 27 Fe24
Monticello USA (AR) 29 Fe29
Monticello USA (LA) 29 Fe30
Monticello USA (IN) 32 Fg25
Monticello USA 33 Ga26
Monticello USA (NY) 33 Gc25
Monticello USA (KY) 35 Fh27
Monticello USA (GA) 35 Fj29
Monticello USA (FL) 35 Fj30
Montichiari I 120 Ll45
Monticiano I 120 Lm47
Monti del Gennargentu I 111 Lk50
Monti della Laga I 122 Lo48
Montier-en-Der F 103 Le42
Montignac F 104 Lb45
Montigny F 103 Lg41
Montigny-le-Roi F 103 Lf43
Montigny-sur-Aube F 103 Le43
Monti Jesi MOC 297 Mh52
Montijo E 108 Ko48
Montijo P 108 Km48
Montilla E 108 Kq47
Montima RDC 286 Ma44
Montipa ANG 294 Lg53
Monti Sibillini I 121 Lo48
Monti Sibillini, P.N.dei I 121 Lo47
Mont Simbruini I 122 Lo49
Montivilliers F 102 La41
MontJoli CDN (QC) 30 Gf21
Mont Kopé CI 278 Kg43
Mont Koronga RT 279 La41
Mont-Laurier CDN (QC) 30 Gc22
Mont-Louis F 104 Lc48
Montluçon F 105 Lc44
Montluel F 105 Lf45
Mont Mabanda G 288 Lf47
Montmagny CDN (QC) 30 Ge22
Montmarault F 105 Lc44
Montmartre CDN (SK) 24 Ej20
Montmédy F 103 Lf41
Mont Méla RCA 282 Mb41
Mont Mimongo G 288 Lg46
Montmirail F 103 Ld42
Montmorau-Saint-Cybard F 104 La45
Montmorency F 103 Lc42
Montmorillon F 104 La44
Mont Moubolo RN 267 Lf36
Mont Mounier F 105 Lg46
Mont Ngaoui CAM/RCA 281 Lh42
Mont Niénokoue CI 278 Kg43
Mont Nimba CI 278 Kf42
Monto AUS (QLD) 235 Sf58
Montoire-sur-le-Loir F 102 La43
Mont Oku CAM 281 Lf42
Montón E 107 Kt51
Montoro E 108 Kq48
Mont Péko CI 278 Kg42
Mont Péko, P.N.du CI 278 Kg42
Mont Pelat F 105 Lg46
Mont Pelé G 288 Lf47
Montpelier USA (ID) 21 Ee24
Montpelier USA (VT) 33 Gd23
Montpellier F 105 Ld47
Mont Pelvoux F 105 Lg46
Montpon-Ménestérol F 104 La45
Montreal CDN 25 Fj22
Montréal CDN (QC) 33 Gd23
Montreal Lake CDN (SK) 19 Eh18
Montréal Lake CDN 19 Eh18
Montreal L. Ind. Res. CDN 19 Eh19
Montreal River CDN 25 Fk22
Montréjeau F 104 La47
Montreuil F 103 Lb40
Montreuil-Bellay F 102 Ku43
Montreux CH 114 Lg44
Montreux CH 114 Lg44
Montrevel-en-Bresse F 105 Lf44
Montrichard F 102 La43
Montrond-les-Bains F 105 Le45
Montrose CDN (BC) 18 Eb21
Montrose GB 99 Ks34
Montrose USA (CO) 21 Eg26
Montrose USA (AR) 29 Fe29
Montrose Wildlife Area USA 27 Fd26
Montrouis RH 46 Gd36
Montroy E 109 Ku49
Mont-Saint-Aignan F 102 Lb41
Mont-Saint-Michel F 102 Kt42
Montsalvy F 104 Lc46
Mont Sangbé, P.N.du CI 278 Kg42
Monts Bagzane RN 272 Le37
Monts Bamboutos CAM 280 Lf43
Monts Bleus RDC 287 Mf44
Monts Boutourou CI 279 Kj41
Monts Chic-Chocs CDN 30 Gh21
Monts de Belezma DZ 260 Lc28
Monts de Beni-Snassen MA 259 Kj28
Monts de Cristal G 281 Lf45
Monts de Cristal, P.N.des G 280 Lf45
Monts de Daïa DZ 259 Kk28
Monts de la Medjerda DZ/TN 260 Le27
Monts de Ouled Naïl DZ 259 Lb28
Monts des Ksour DZ 259 Kk29
Monts des Nementcha DZ 260 Ld28
Monts des Traras DZ 259 Kk28
Monts de Tébassa DZ 260 Ld28
Monts de Tlemcen DZ 259 Kk28
Monts du Cantal F 105 Lc45
Monts du Hodna DZ 259 Lc28
Monts du Hombori RMM 271 Kj38
Monts du Mouydir DZ 266 Lb33
Monts du Zab DZ 259 Lc28
Montségur F 104 Lb48
Montseny E 110 Lc49
Montserrat E 110 Lb49
Montserrat GB 47 Gj37
Montserrat GB 47 Gj37
Monts Grouix CDN 30 Gg20
Montsinery F 59 Hd43
Monts Kabyé RT 279 La41
Monts Manding RMM 269 Kf39
Monts Marungu RDC 292 Me49
Monts Mitumba RDC 292 Me48
Monts Mugila RDC 292 Me49
Monts Notre-Dame CDN 30 Gf22
Monts Otish CDN 30 Ge19
Monts Totomaï RN 267 Lh35
Montsûrs F 102 Ku42
Mt Tendre CH 114 Lg44
Mont Ténibre F 105 Lg46
Mont Teza BU 287 Me47
Mont Tonkoui CI 278 Kg42
Mont Toussoro RCA 282 Mb41
Mont Tremblant CDN 30 Gc22
Montuïri E 110 Lc51
Mont Ventoux F 105 Lf46
Monument Hill S.H.S. USA 29 Fb31
Monument Natural Alerce Costero RCH 80 Gd66
Monumento ao Padre Cícero BR (CE) 71 Ja49
Monumento Batalla de Junín PE 66 Gc51
Monumento Natural Ballena Franca Austral RA 81 Gj67
Monumento Natural Bosques Petrificados RA 82 Gf69
Monumento Natural Cerro Ñielol RCH 80 Gd65
Monumento Natural Contulmo RCH 80 Gd64
Monumento Natural Dos Lagunas RCH 82 Ge68
Monumento Natural Dunas d.C.Polonio y Costa Atlántica ROU 77 Hd63
Monumento Natural El Morado RCH 76 Ge62
Monumento Natural Isla Cachagua RCH 76 Ge62
Monumento Natural Laguna de los Cisnes RCH 82 Ge72
Monumento Natural Laguna de los Pozuelos RA 72 Gh57
Monumento Natural Los Pingüinos RCH 82 Ge72
Monumento Natural Pichasca RCH 76 Ge61
Monumento Natural Salar de Surire RCH 72 Gf55
Monumento Natural Valle del Encantado RCH 76 Ge61
Monument Rocks USA 26 Ek26
Monuments romains et romans d'Arles F 105 Le47
Monument Valley Navajo Tribal P. USA 23 Ee27
Monywa MYA 195 Ph34
Monza I 120 Lk45
Monze VRC (TIB) 171 Pg29
Monze Z 296 Md54
Monzón E 110 La49
Monzón PE 66 Gb50
Mooi SA 299 Md59
Mooirivier SA 303 Me60
Moojeeba AUS (QLD) 231 Sb53
Mooketsi SA 300 Mf57
Moola Z 295 Mb54
Moolawatana AUS (SA) 227 Rk60
Moolloogool AUS (WA) 224 Qj59
Moolooaba Wharf AUS 235 Sg59
Mooloo Downs AUS (WA) 224 Qh58
Moomba AUS (SA) 227 Sa60
Moonan Flat AUS (NSW) 235 Sf61
Moonaree AUS (SA) 236 Rh61
Moonda Lake AUS 234 Sa58
Moonee Valley Racecourse AUS (VIC) 237 Sc64
Moonstone Beach USA (CA) 22 Dk28
Moonta AUS (SA) 236 Rj63
Moonya AUS (QLD) 233 Sc57
Moonyoonooka AUS (WA) 228 Qh60
Moora AUS (WA) 228 Qj61
Mooraberree AUS (QLD) 234 Sa58
Moorarie AUS (WA) 224 Qj58
Moorcroft USA (WY) 21 Eh23
Moordkuil SA 302 Lk62
Moore USA (MT) 21 Ef22
Moore Creek USA (AK) 15 Cg13
Moorefield USA (WV) 33 Ga26
Moore Islands, Sir G. AUS 222 Rd52
Moore Park AUS (QLD) 235 Sg58
Moore River N.P. AUS 228 Qh61
Moore's Island BS 37 Ga32
Moorhead USA (MN) 27 Fb22
Mooroongga Island AUS 223 Rh51
Moorosi, Mount LS 303 Me61
Moorreesburg SA 302 Lk62
Moosburg D 115 Lm42
Moose USA (WY) 21 Ee24
Moose Factory Indian Reserve CDN 25 Fk20
Moosehead Lake CDN 30 Gf23
Moose Island CDN 24 Fb20
Moose Jaw Creek CDN 19 Eh20
Moose Lake CDN (MB) 24 Ek19
Moose Lake CDN 24 Fa19
Moose Law CDN (SK) 19 Eh20
Moose Mountain Ski Resort USA (AK) 15 Cg13
Moose Mt. Prov. Park CDN 24 Ej21
Moose Pass USA (AK) 15 Cf15
Moose River CDN (ON) 25 Fk20
Moose River CDN 25 Fk20
Moosomin CDN (SK) 24 Ek20
Moosonee CDN (ON) 25 Fk20
Mootwingee AUS (NSW) 234 Sb61
Mop IND (MHT) 190 Oj36
Mopane SA 300 Me57
Mopeia MOC 297 Mh54
Mopipi RB 299 Mc56
Mopti RMM 270 Kh38
Moqatta SUD 277 Mh39
Moqor AFG 160 Od29
Moquegua PE 72 Ge54
Moquehuá RA (BA) 77 Ha63
Mór H 118 Lt43
Mora CAM 273 Lh40
Mora E 109 Kr49
Mora GUY 58 Ha42
Mora P 108 Km48
Mora S 93 Lp30
Mora USA (NM) 23 Eh28
Mora USA (MN) 27 Fd23
Morabgi IND (MHT) 190 Oh37
Moraća klisura SCG 126 Lu48
Moradabad IND (UPH) 189 Ok31
Morada Nova BR (CE) 65 Ja48
Morada Nova de Minas BR (MG) 75 Hh55
Mora de Rubielos E 109 Ku50
Moradlu IR 154 Ne26
Morado, Cerro RA 72 Gh57
Morafeno RM 306 Nd54
Morafenobe RM 306 Nc54
Morąg PL 117 Lu37
Mórahalom H 119 Lu44
Morai RI 213 Rh49
Moraine St. Park USA 33 Ga25
Morais de Almeida BR (PA) 63 Hc49
Morakovo SCG 126 Lu48
Morakowo PL 116 Ls38
Móra la Nova E 110 La49
Moral de Calatrava E 109 Kr48
Moraleja E 108 Ko50
Moralinta RM 306 Nc58
Moramanga RM 306 Ne55
Moramo Bay RI 209 Rb48
Moramo Waterfall RI 209 Rb48
Moran USA (KS) 29 Fc27
Morangas BR (MS) 74 Hd55
Moran Junction USA (WY) 21 Ee24
Morant Cays JA 45 Gb37
Morar IND (MPH) 189 Ok32
Morarano RM 306 Nd56
Morarano Chrome RM 306 Ne54
Morărești RO 125 Me45
Moratalla E 109 Kt48
Moratuwa CL 193 Ok43
Morava CZ 118 Ls41
Moravia CZ 118 Lr41
Moravica SCG 126 Ma47
Moravița RO 124 Mb45
Morávka CZ 118 Lt41
Moravská Třebová CZ 118 Lr41
Moravské Budějovice CZ 118 Lq41
Moravské Lieskové SK 118 Ls42
Moravský Beroun CZ 118 Ls41
Moravský kras CZ 118 Lr41
Moravský Krumlov CZ 118 Lr41
Morawa AUS (WA) 228 Qj60
Morawhanna GUY 58 Gk41
Morawica PL 117 Ma40
Moray Downs AUS (QLD) 233 Sd56
Moray Firth GB 99 Kr33
Morbach D 114 Lh41
Morbanipari, Mount PNG 243 Sb48
Morbarakeh IR 154 Nf29
Mörbylånga S 95 Lr34
Morcego BR (AM) 62 Gj47
Morcenx F 104 Ku46
Morcheh Khort IR 154 Nf29
Morcillo MEX (DGO) 39 Eh33
Morcone I 122 Lp49
Mordaga VRC (NMZ) 173 Ra20
Mordelles F 102 Kt42
Morden AUS (NSW) 234 Sb61
Mordogan TR 129 Mg52
Mordovo RUS 133 Na19
Mordvinia RUS 133 Nb18
Mordy PL 117 Mc38
Mor'e RUS 132 Mf15
Moreau USA 26 Ek23
Morecambe GB 101 Ks36
Morecambe Bay GB 101 Ks36
Moreda E 109 Kr47
Moree AUS (NSW) 235 Se60
Morée F 102 Lb43
Morehead PNG 242 Sa50
Morehead USA (KY) 35 Fj26
Morehead City USA (NC) 35 Gb28
Morehead River PNG 242 Sa50
Moreilândia BR (PE) 71 Ja49
Moreli CDN (PE) 31 Gj22
Morelia CO 60 Gc45
Morelia CO 61 Gd46
Morelia MEX (MHC) 40 Ek36
Morella AUS (QLD) 232 Sb57
Morella E 110 Ku50
Morelos MEX (SO) 38 Ee31
Morelos MEX (COH) 39 Ek31
Morelos MEX 40 Fa36
Moremi Game Reserve RB 299 Mb55
Moremi Gorge RB 299 Md57
Morena IND (MPH) 189 Oj32
Moreni RO 125 Mf46
Mores I 111 Lj50
Moresby Channel MV 192 Og43
Moresby Island CDN 18 Dd19
Moreton AUS (QLD) 230 Sb52
Moreton-in-Marsh GB 101 Kt39
Moreton Island AUS 235 Sg59
Moreton Island N.P. AUS 235 Sg59
Moret-sur-Loing F 103 Lc42
Moreuil F 103 Lc41
Morez F 105 Lg44
Morfou = Güzelyurt CY 131 Mo55
Morfou Bay CY 131 Mn55
Morgan AUS (SA) 236 Rk63
Morgan USA (UT) 21 Ee25
Morgan City USA (LA) 29 Fe31
Morganfield USA (KY) 34 Fg27
Morgan Hill USA (CA) 20 Dk27
Morganito YV 57 Gg43
Morganton USA (NC) 35 Fk28
Morgantown USA (WV) 33 Ga26
Morgantown USA (KY) 34 Fg27
Morgan Vale AUS (SA) 236 Sa62
Morgenzon SA 303 Me59
Morges CH 114 Lg44
Morgins CH 114 Lg44
Morgongåva S 93 Lr31
Morgos RO 124 Md44
Morgram IND (WBG) 194 Pe33
Morgun-Tajga RUS 167 Pf20
Morhange F 103 Lg42
Mori J 181 Sa24
Mori VRC (XUZ) 169 Pf24
Moriah, Mount USA 20 Ec26
Moriani-Plage F 111 Lk48
Moriarty USA (NM) 23 Eg28
Morib MAL 199 Qa44
Moribaya RG 278 Kf41
Morib Beach MAL 199 Qa44
Morice Lake CDN 18 Dg19
Morice River CDN 18 Dg18
Moricetown CDN (BC) 18 Dg18
Morichal YV 58 Gj41
Morichal Largo YV 57 Gj41
Morichal Viejo CO 61 Ge44
Morigbadougou RG 278 Kf41
Morija LS 303 Md60
Morijo EAK 290 Mh46
Moriki WAN 272 Ld39
Morin Dawa VRC (NMZ) 180 Rc21
Morinville CDN (AB) 19 Ed19
Morioka J 183 Sa26
Morire MOC 297 Mh54
Morișaca RO 125 Mg43
Moritzburg D 113 Lo39
Morjärv S 91 Mb12
Morki RUS (MEL) 133 Ne17
Morkoka RUS 141 Qc06
Mörkret S 93 Ln29
Morlaàs F 104 Ku47
Morlaix F 102 Kr42
Morley CDN (AB) 19 Ec20
Mörlunda S 95 Lq33
Morne-à-l'Eau F 47 Gk37
Morne Seychellois N.P. SY 305 Nh48
Morne Trois Pitons N.P. WD 47 Gk38
Morney AUS (QLD) 234 Sa58
Mornington Abyssal Plain 54 Fb29
Mornington Island AUS 232 Rk54
Mornington Islands A.L. Trust AUS 232 Rk54
Mórnos GR 128 Mc52
Moro PE 66 Ga50
Moro PK 162 Od32
Moro USA (OR) 20 Dk23
Morobe PNG 243 Sd49
Morobo SUD 287 Mf44
Morocco 253 Kb06
Moroćne UA 117 Mf39
Morococala BOL 72 Gg55
Morocoy MEX (QTR) 41 Ff36
Morodougou RG 278 Kf40
Morogoro EAT 293 Mj49
Moro Gulf RP 205 Rb42
Moroiemu RI 242 Rk49
Morokweng SA 302 Mb59
Morolaba BF 279 Kh40
Morolica HN 42 Fg39
Moromaho RI 209 Rc49
Morombe RM 306 Nb56
Morón C 45 Ga34
Mörön MEX (TM) 39 Fb34
Mörön MNG 172 Qa21
Mörön MNG 173 Qf22
Morón RA (BA) 77 Ha63
Moron USA (UT) 21 Ee26
Morón YV 57 Gf40
Morona EC 60 Gb47
Morona PE 60 Gb47
Morondava RM 306 Nc56
Morón de Almazán E 107 Ks51
Morón de la Frontera E 108 Kp47
Moroni COM 304 Nb51
Moronou CI 279 Kh42
Moron Us VRC 171 Pg28
Morotai RI 212 Re44
Moroto EAU 290 Mh44
Moroto, Mount EAU 290 Mh44
Morotuto YV 56 Gd41
Morouba RCA 282 Ma42
Morowali Reserve RI 209 Ra46
Morozeni MD 125 Mj43
Morozovsk RUS 135 Na21
Morpará BR (BA) 70 Hj51
Morpeth GB 99 Kt35
Morphettville Racecourse AUS (SA) 236 Rk63
Morretes BR (PR) 74 Hf58
Morrilton USA (AR) 29 Fd28
Morrin CDN (AB) 19 Ed20
Morrinhos BR (GO) 74 Hf54
Morris CDN (MB) 24 Fb21
Morris USA (MN) 27 Fc23
Morris, Mount AUS 226 Rf59
Morrison Bay MYA 196 Pk39
Morristown USA (TN) 35 Fj27
Morrito NIC 42 Fh40
Morro LB/WAL 278 Ke42
Morro Agudo BR (SP) 74 Hf56
Morro Bay USA (CA) 22 Dk28
Morro Branco BR (PI) 70 Hh50
Morro Branco, T.I. BR 64 Hg48
Morro Cabeça no Tempo BR (PI) 70 Hj50
Morro Chico RCH 82 Ge72
Morrocoy, P.N. YV 57 Gf40
Morro da Igreja BR 79 Hf60
Morro de São Paulo = Ilha de Tinharé BR 71 Ja52
Morro do Chapéu BR (BA) 71 Hk51
Morro do Padre BR 70 Hg54
Morro Jable E 264 Kc31
Morropón PE 60 Ga48
Morros BR (MA) 64 Hh47
Morro Uruçuí BR (PI) 70 Hh50
Morro Velho BR (MA) 64 Hg49
Morrow USA (LA) 29 Fe30
Mörrum S 95 Lp34
Morrumbala MOC 297 Mh54
Morrumbene MOC 300 Mh57
Mörrumsån S 95 Lp34
Morrungolo MOC 300 Mh57
Mors DK 94 Lj34
Morsa RA (BA) 77 Gk63
Moršank RUS 133 Na19
Morsi IND (MHT) 191 Ok35
Mörsil S 90 Lg14
Morskoj RUS 97 Ma35
Mörskom = Myrskylä FIN 96 Mf30
Morskoy aral KZ 152 Nf23
Morsovo RUS 133 Nb19
Morstone AUS (QLD) 232 Rk55
Mørsvik N 90 Lh12
Mørsvikfjorden N 90 Lh12
Mortagne-au-Perche F 102 La42
Mortagne-sur-Sèvre F 102 Ku44
Mortain F 102 Ku42
Mortara I 120 Lj45
Morteau F 105 Lg43
Mortesoro SUD 283 Mh40
Mortimers BS 37 Gc34
Mortlake AUS (VIC) 237 Sb65
Mortlock Islands FSM 240 Sc17
Mortlock Islands PNG 244 Sj48
Morton USA (WA) 18 Dj22
Morton USA (TX) 23 Ej29
Morton USA (MS) 29 Ff29
Morton USA (IL) 32 Ff25
Morton N.P. AUS 237 Sf63
Mortrée F 102 La42
Moruga TT 58 Gk40
Morundah AUS (NSW) 237 Sd63
Moruongole EAU 284 Mh44
Morupule RB 299 Md57
Moruya AUS (NSW) 237 Sf63
Morven AUS (QLD) 235 Sd59
Morvi IND (GUJ) 190 Of34
Morwell AUS (VIC) 237 Sd65
Moryna PL 97 Mf37
Morzhovoi Bay USA (AK) 14 Bj18
Morzine F 105 Lg44
Morzyczyn PL 116 Lp37
Mosa PNG 244 Sf48
Mosal'sk RUS 132 Mh18
Mosbach D 114 Lk41
Mosby N 92 Lh32
Mosby USA (MT) 21 Eg22
Moscheea mare RO 125 Mj46
Moscow RUS 132 Mj18
Moscow USA (ID) 20 Eb22
Moscow University Ice Shelf 313 Qd32
Mosel D 114 Lg41
Moselebe RB 299 Mb58
Moselle F 103 Lg42
Moser River CDN (NS) 31 Gj23
Moses Lake USA (WA) 18 Ea22
Moses, Mount USA 20 Eb25
Moses Point USA (AK) 15 Bj13
Mosetse RB 299 Md56
Mosfellsbær IS 90 Jk13
Mosgiel NZ 239 Tf68
Moshaneng RB 299 Mc58
Moshaweng RB 299 Mc57
Moshesh's Ford SA 303 Md61
Moshi EAT 293 Mj47
Moshi WAN 272 Lc41
Moshi Z 296 Md53
Moshófito GR 128 Mb51
Mosi WAN 272 Lb41
Mosina PL 116 Lr38
Mosi Oa Tunya N.P. Z 299 Mc54
Mosite RDC 287 Mb45
Mosjøen N 90 Lg13
Moskenesøya N 90 Lg12
Mosko BIH 126 Lt48
Moskva RUS 132 Mj18
Moslavina Podravska HR 121 Ls45
Mosle Creek CDN 18 Dh20
Mosnikovskaja RUS 91 Mj15
Mosomane RB 299 Md57
Mosongoie RDC 289 Mc50
Mosonmagyaróvár H 118 Ls43
Mosopo RB 299 Mc58
Mosqueiro BR (PA) 64 Hf46
Mosquera CO 60 Ga44
Mosquero USA (NM) 23 Ej28
Mosquitia HN 42 Fh38
Mosquitia HN 42 Fh38
Mosquito BR (TO) 64 Hg49
Mosquito BR 71 Hk53
Mosquito PY 73 Ha57
Mosquito River USA 15 Cj13
Moss N 92 Ll31
Mossaka RCB 286 Lj46
Mossbank CDN (SK) 19 Eh21
Moss Bluff USA (LA) 29 Fd30
Mossburn NZ 239 Te68
Mosselbaai SA 302 Mb63
Mossel Bay SA 302 Mb63
Mossendjo RCB 288 Lg47
Mossgiel AUS (NSW) 237 Sc62
Moss Hill USA (TX) 29 Fc30
Moss Landing USA (CA) 20 Dk27
Mossman AUS (QLD) 233 Sc54
Mossman Gorge AUS (QLD) 233 Sc54
Mossoró BR (RN) 65 Jb48
Mossuril MOC 297 Na53
Moss Vale AUS (NSW) 237 Sf63
Mossy River CDN 24 Ej18
Most CZ 118 Lo40
Mostaganem DZ 259 La28
Mostar BIH 121 Ls47
Mostardas BR (RS) 78 He61
Mosteiro da Batalha P 108 Km49
Mosteiro de Alcobaça P 108 Kl49
Mosteiro dos Jerónimos P 108 Kl48
Mosteiros CV 268 Jh38
Most na družbata BG 127 Mf47
Mostóles E 109 Kr50
Mostovskoj RUS 135 Na23
Mosty PL 117 Md39
Mostys'ka UA 119 Md41

Møsvatn N 92 Lj31
Mot'a ETH 284 Mj40
Motaba RCB 281 Lj44
Mota del Cuervo E 109 Ks49
Mota del Marqués E 106 Kp51
Motagua GCA 41 Ff38
Motagusanos RA (SJ) 76 Gf61
Motaha RI 209 Rb48
Motal BY 117 Mf38
Motala S 93 Lq32
Motala S 93 Lq32
Mota Lava VU 246 Td52
Motane F 249 Da50
Motatán YV 57 Ge41
Motatán YV 57 Ge41
Moțca RO 125 Mg43
Moter IND (ORS) 191 Pb36
Moteros RA (CD) 77 Gk61
Moth IND (UPH) 189 Ok33
Motherwell GB 99 Kq35
Motihari IND (BIH) 189 Pc32
Motilla del Palancar E 109 Kt49
Motinala IND (MPH) 191 Pa34
Motlhabaneng RB 300 Me56
Motloutse RB 299 Me56
Motloutse Ruins RB 300 Me57
Motobu J 185 Rd32
Motokwe RB 299 Mb58
Motozintla de Mendoza MEX (CHP) 41 Fd38
Motril E 109 Kr46
Motru RO 124 Mc46
Motru RO 124 Mc46
Mott USA (ND) 26 Ej22
Mottugudiam IND (CGH) 191 Pa36
Motueka NZ 239 Tg66
Motuhora Island NZ 238 Tj64
Motu-Iti F 249 Ce54
Motul MEX (YT) 41 Ff35
Motu One F 249 Cc53
Motupe PE 66 Ga49
Motupena Point PNG 244 Sh49
Motu River AUS 238 Tj65
Motutunga Atoll F 249 Ch54
Motygino RUS 140 Pc07
Mouahani COM 304 Nb52
Moučadz BY 97 Mf37
Mouchoirbank 46 Ge35
Mouchoir Passage BS 37 Ge35
Moudjéria RIM 269 Kd37
Moudon CH 114 Lg44
Moúdros GR 127 Mf51
Mougamou G 288 Lg46
Mougins F 105 Lg47
Mougna RMM 270 Kh39
Mouhijärvi FIN 96 Md29
Mouila G 288 Lf46
Moujia RN 272 Lc38
Mouka RCA 282 Ma42
Moukabou G 288 Lf46
Moukalaba-Doudou, P.N.de G 288 Lf47
Moukoundou G 288 Lf47
Moul RN 273 Lg38
Moula TCH 281 Lk41
Moulamein AUS (NSW) 237 Sc63
Moulay Bouâzza MA 258 Kg29
Moulay-Bousselham MA 258 Kg28
Moulay-Idriss MA 258 Kh28
Mould Bay CDN 10 Dd03
Mouléngui Binza G 288 Lf47
Moulhoulé DJI 277 Nb40
Mouli Gbangba RCB 281 Lj44
Moulins F 105 Ld44
Moulmein = Maulamyaing MYA 196 Pj37
Moulmeingyun MYA 196 Ph37
Moulton USA (AL) 34 Fg28
Moultrie USA (GA) 35 Fj30
Moulvouday CAM 273 Lh40
Moumba G 288 Lf47
Mounanko CAM 280 Le44
Mound City USA (SD) 26 Fa23
Mound City USA (KS) 29 Fc26
Moundou TCH 273 Lj41
Moundsville USA (WV) 33 Fk26
Moundville USA (AL) 34 Fg29
Moundville Archaeological Park USA 34 Fg29
Moungoundou-Sud RCB 288 Lg47
Moung Russei K 197 Qb39
Mounguel CAM 281 Lg42
Mounianze G 281 Lg45
Mount Abbot AUS 233 Sd56
Mount Aborlan RP 204 Qk41
Mount Abu IND (RJT) 188 Og33
Mount Abu = Guru Shikhar IND 188 Og33
Mount Abu W.S. IND 188 Og33
Mount Adams USA 18 Dk22
Mountainair USA (NM) 23 Eg28
Mountain Ash GB 100 Kr39
Mountain City USA (NV) 20 Ec25
Mountain City USA (TN) 35 Fk27
Mountain Grove USA (MO) 29 Fd27
Mountain Home USA (ID) 20 Ec24
Mountain Home USA (AR) 29 Fd27
Mountain Nile SUD 255 Mc17
Mountain Pass USA (CA) 22 Ec28
Mountain Railway IND 193 Oj41
Mountain River CDN 17 Df13
Mountain View USA (WY) 21 Ee25
Mountain View USA (AR) 29 Fd28
Mountain View USA (MO) 29 Fe27
Mountain Village USA (AK) 14 Bj14
Mountain Zebra N.P. SA 303 Mc62
Mount Aiome PNG 243 Sc48
Mount Airy USA (NC) 35 Fk27
Mount Ajax NZ 239 Tg67
Mount Albert Edward PNG 243 Sd50
Mount Alfred AUS (QLD) 235 Sc59
Mount Alma AUS 235 Sf58
Mount Amara ETH 284 Mj41
Mount Amhurst AUS (WA) 222 Rd55
Mount Amungwiwa PNG 243 Sd49
Mount Anglem NZ 239 Td69
Mount Anne AUS 236 Sd67
Mount Aoraki NZ 239 Tf67
Mount Apo RP 205 Rc42
Mount Ararat = Ağrı Dağı TR 145 Nc26
Mount Arkell CDN 17 Dc15
Mount Arlington Heights CDN (NF) 31 Hd22
Mount Aspiring NZ 239 Te68
Mount Aspiring N.P. NZ 239 Te68
Mount Assiniboine CDN 19 Ec20
Mount Atouat VN 197 Qd38
Mount Augustus AUS 224 Qj58
Mount Aylift SA 303 Me61
Mount Ayr USA (IA) 27 Fc25
Mount Baco RP 203 Ra39
Mount Bajimba AUS 235 Sg60
Mount Baker USA 18 Dk21
Mount Balbi PNG 244 Sh48
Mount Ball AUS 222 Rd55
Mount Bangeta PNG 243 Sd49
Mount Barker AUS (WA) 228 Qj63
Mount Barnett AUS (WA) 222 Rc54
Mount Barrington AUS 237 Sf62
Mount Barry AUS (SA) 227 Rh60
Mountbatten Ind. Res. CDN 32 Fj22
Mount Beauty AUS (VIC) 237 Sd64
Mount Bellew IRL 100 Km37
Mountbenger GB 99 Kr35
Mount Berlin 312 Da34
Mount Bintumani WAL 278 Ke41
Mount Boggola AUS 224 Qj57
Mount Bona USA 17 Ck15
Mount Bonaparte USA 18 Ea21
Mount Bosavi PNG 243 Sb49
Mount Brassey AUS 227 Rh57
Mount Brazeau CDN 19 Eb19
Mount Brockman AUS 224 Qj57
Mount Bruce AUS 224 Qk57
Mount Bryan AUS 236 Rk62
Mount Buller AUS 237 Sd64
Mount Busa RP 205 Rc42
Mount Cairns AUS 223 Rh56
Mount Calavite RP 202 Ra39
Mount Callaghan USA 20 Eb26
Mount Capoas RP 204 Qk40
Mount Capotoan RP 203 Rc39
Mount Carleton CDN 30 Gg22
Mount Carleton Prov. Park CDN 30 Gg22
Mount Carmel USA (IL) 34 Fg26
Mount Carmel Junction USA (UT) 23 Ed27
Mount Carter AUS 230 Sb52
Mount Chiginagak USA 14 Cb17
Mount Chilalo ETH 284 Mk41
Mount Clara NZ 239 Tg67
Mount Clemens USA (MI) 32 Fj24
Mount Columbia CDN 19 Eb19
Mount Connor AUS 222 Rd53
Mount Cook AUS 228 Qj62
Mount Cook CDN 17 Ck15
Mount Cook NZ 239 Tf67
Mount Cook = Mount Aoraki NZ 239 Tf67
Mount Cook N.P. NZ 239 Tf67
Mount Coolon AUS (QLD) 233 Sd56
Mount Cornish AUS 222 Rd56
Mount Crillon CDN 17 Dj17
Mount Currie Ind. Res. CDN 18 Dj20
Mount Dalrymple AUS 233 Se56
Mount Dana USA 14 Bk18
Mount Darwin ZW 296 Mf54
Mount Davis AUS 226 Re59
Mount de Babel CDN 30 Gf20
Mount Deering AUS 225 Re58
Mount Denison AUS (NT) 226 Rg57
Mount Desert Island USA 31 Gf23
Mount Djebobo GH/RT 279 La41
Mount Dockrell AUS 222 Rd55
Mount Dora USA (FL) 36 Fk31
Mount Douglas AUS (QLD) 233 Sd56
Mount Douglas USA (AK) 15 Cd16
Mount Downton CDN 18 Dh19
Mount Draper USA 17 Da16
Mount Dremsel PNG 243 Sd47
Mount Eba AUS (SA) 227 Rh61
Mount Ebenezer Roadhouse AUS (NT) 226 Rg58
Mount Edgar AUS 224 Ra56
Mount Edith USA 21 Ee22
Mount Eduni CDN 17 Df13
Mount Edward AUS 226 Rf57
Mount Edward 312 Gc34
Mount Edziza Prov. Park CDN 17 De17
Mount Elbert USA (CO) 21 Eg26
Mount Elgon EAU/EAK 290 Mh45
Mount Elgon N.P. EAU/EAK 290 Mh45
Mount Ellen USA 21 Ee26
Mount Elliot AUS 233 Sd55
Mount Elsie AUS (QLD) 233 Sd56
Mount Elvire AUS 224 Qj56
Mount Enterprise USA (TX) 29 Fc30
Mount Erebus 313 Tc34
Mount Essendon AUS 224 Ra58
Mount Etna Caves N.P. AUS 233 Sf57
Mount Everest NEP/VRC 170 Pd31
Mount Fairweather CDN 17 Db16
Mount Farnham CDN 18 Eb20
Mount Farquharson AUS 223 Rf54
Mount Field N.P. AUS 236 Sd67
Mount Fletcher SA 303 Me61
Mount Frakes 312 Ea34
Mount Frankland N.P. AUS 228 Qj63
Mount Fraser AUS (WA) 224 Qk58
Mount Frederick A.L. AUS 223 Re55
Mount Frederick No2 A.L. AUS 223 Re56
Mount Freeling AUS (SA) 227 Rk60
Mount Frere SA 303 Me61
Mount Fridtjof Nansen 312 Bd36
Mount Gambier AUS (SA) 236 Sa64
Mount Garnet AUS (QLD) 233 Sc54
Mount Gede-Pangrango N.P. RI 210 Qd49
Mount Gelia AUS (WA) 228 Rb60
Mount Gerdine USA (AK) 15 Cd15
Mount Geureudong RI 198 Pj43
Mount Gilruth AUS 223 Rg52
Mount Godwin Austen PK 161 Oj28
Mount Gordon AUS 228 Ra62
Mount Goura WAN 272 Le40
Mount Grenfell Aboriginal Cave Paintings AUS 235 Sc61
Mount Grillon USA 17 Db16
Mount Guge ETH 284 Mj42
Mount Gugu ETH 284 Mk41
Mount Guide AUS (QLD) 232 Rk56
Mount Gunnison USA 21 Eg26
Mount Guraghe ETH 284 Mk41
Mount Hack AUS 236 Rk61
Mount Hagen PNG 243 Sc48
Mount Hagen Show PNG 243 Sc48
Mount Hale AUS 224 Qj58
Mount Hale AUS (WA) 224 Qj59
Mount Halimun N.P. RI 210 Qd49
Mount Hamilton USA 20 Ec26
Mount Hanang EAT 290 Mh48
Mount Hann AUS 222 Rc53
Mount Harper USA (AK) 15 Cj13
Mount Harris AUS 226 Re58
Mount Hart CDN 15 Ck14
Mount Hay AUS 226 Rg57
Mount Hayes USA (AK) 15 Cg14
Mount Hebron USA (CA) 20 Dk25
Mount Hermon RL 146 Mh29
Mount Hickman CDN 17 De17
Mount Hinkley AUS 225 Re59
Mount Hollister AUS 224 Qg57
Mount Hood USA 20 Dk23
Mount Hope AUS (SA) 236 Rh63
Mount Hope AUS (NSW) 237 Sc62
Mount Hopeless AUS (SA) 227 Rk60
Mount House AUS (WA) 222 Rc54
Mount Howe 312 Ca36
Mount Howitt AUS (QLD) 234 Sb59
Mount Howship AUS 223 Rg52
Mount Hubbard CDN 17 Da15
Mount Hutt NZ 239 Tf67
Mount Hutton AUS 235 Se58
Mount Huxley NZ 239 Te68
Mount Huxley USA 16 Ck15
Mount Ida AUS (WA) 228 Ra60
Mount Ida USA (AR) 29 Fd28
Mount Illbillee AUS 226 Rg59
Mount Isa AUS (QLD) 232 Rk56
Mount Ive AUS (SA) 236 Rj62
Mount Jackson AUS (WA) 228 Qk61
Mount Jackson 312 Gd33
Mount Jacques Cartier CDN 30 Gh21
Mount James A.L. AUS 224 Qj58
Mount Jefferson USA 20 Dk23
Mount Jefferson USA 20 Eb26
Mount Joffre CDN 19 Ec20
Mount Joyce 313 Sd34
Mount Junction AUS 222 Re55
Mount Kadam EAU 290 Mh45
Mount Kagora WAN 272 Le41
Mount Kaichui SOL 245 Ta50
Mount Kaka ETH 284 Mk42
Mount Kalourat SOL 245 Ta50
Mount Kaputar AUS 235 Sf61
Mount Kaputar N.P. AUS 235 Sf61
Mount Karimui PNG 243 Sc49
Mount Karoma PNG 242 Sb48
Mount Katmai USA 14 Cc16
Mount Kaye AUS 237 Se64
Mount Keith AUS (WA) 224 Ra59
Mount Kendall NZ 239 Tg66
Mount Kenya EAK 290 Mj46
Mount Kenya N.P. EAK 290 Mj46
Mount Kilal EAK 290 Mj44
Mount Kimball USA (AK) 15 Ch14
Mount Kirkpatrick 313 Ta35
Mount Kosciuszko AUS 237 Se64
Mount Kusiwigasi PNG 242 Sa48
Mount Labo RP 203 Rb39
Mount Lacy AUS 222 Rc54
Mount Lambell AUS 223 Rg53
Mount Lamington PNG 243 Se50
Mount Larcum AUS (QLD) 233 Sf57
Mount Lawrence Wells AUS 224 Ra59
Mount Lebanon RL 146 Mh29
Mount Leichhardt AUS 226 Rg56
Mount Leinster IRL 100 Ko38
Mount Leisler AUS 226 Re57
Mount Lembu RI 198 Pj43
Mount Lesueur AUS 228 Qh61
Mount Leuser RI 198 Pj44
Mount Lewis AUS (NSW) 235 Sd61
Mount Liebig AUS 226 Rf57
Mount Lister 313 Ta34
Mount Lofty Ranges AUS 236 Rk63
Mount Logan CDN 17 Ck15
Mount Longfellow NZ 239 Tg67
Mount Longhurst 313 Sd34
Mount Luke AUS 224 Qj59
Mount Lulworth AUS 224 Qj59
Mount Lyall NZ 239 Td68
Mount Lyndhurst AUS (SA) 227 Rk61
Mount Ma'an VRC 195 Pk33
Mount Macdonald VU 246 Te54
Mount Madden AUS (WA) 228 Qk62
Mount Madley AUS 225 Rb58
Mount Magnet AUS (WA) 228 Qj60
Mount Mago ETH 284 Mj43
Mount Maiden AUS 225 Rb59
Mount Maigudo ETH 284 Mj42
Mount Maitabi SOL 244 Sj49
Mount Malindang RP 205 Rb41
Mount Manning Range AUS 228 Qk60
Mount Mantalingajan RP 204 Qj41
Mount Marcus Baker USA (AK) 15 Cg15
Mount Margaret AUS 224 Qj57
Mount Margaret AUS (WA) 228 Rb60
Mount Maria GB 83 Ha71
Mount Markham 313 Tb35
Mount Marum VU 246 Te54
Mount Marvine USA 21 Ee26
Mount Maunganui NZ 238 Tj64
Mount Mbeya EAT 292 Mg50
Mount McClintock 313 Sd34
Mount McGuire USA 21 Ec23
Mount McKinley USA (AK) 15 Ce14
Mount McLoughlin USA 20 Dj24
Mount Meharry AUS 224 Qk57
Mountmellick IRL 100 Kn37
Mount Mengam PNG 243 Sc48
Mount Menzies 313 Oa33
Mount Meru EAT 290 Mj47
Mount Michael PNG 243 Sc49
Mount Miller USA 16 Cj15
Mount Miller 313 Tb35
Mount Minto 313 Tc33
Mount Misery NZ 239 Tf67
Mount Mitchell USA 35 Fj28
Mount Molloy AUS (QLD) 233 Sc54
Mount Moorosi LS 303 Me61
Mount Morbanipari PNG 243 Sb48
Mount Morgan AUS (QLD) 233 Sf57
Mount Moriah USA 20 Ec26
Mount Moroto EAU 290 Mh44
Mount Morris AUS 226 Rf59
Mount Morris AUS (QLD) 235 Sc58
Mount Moses USA 20 Eb25
Mount Mulgrave AUS (QLD) 232 Sb54
Mount Mulligan AUS (QLD) 233 Sc54
Mount Mulya AUS (NSW) 234 Sc61
Mount Murchinson NZ 239 Tf67
Mount Mye CDN 17 Dd14
Mount Nansen CDN 17 Db14
Mount Nasi ETH 284 Mk41
Mount Nebo JOR 146 Mh30
Mount Nellie AUS 222 Rc54
Mount Nicholson AUS 235 Se58
Mount Norman AUS (QLD) 232 Sb55
Mountnorris Bay AUS 223 Rg51
Mount Northampton 313 Tb33
Mount Nott AUS 236 Rh62
Mount Okora WAN 280 Ld42
Mount Olga AUS 226 Rf58
Mount Olive USA (NC) 35 Ga28
Mount Olympus USA 18 Dj22
Mount Opémiska CDN 30 Gc20
Mount Oratia USA 14 Bk16
Mount Ord AUS 222 Rc54
Mount Orohena F 249 Cf54
Mount Ossa AUS 236 Sd66
Mount Padbury AUS (WA) 224 Qk58
Mount Palgrave AUS 224 Qh57
Mount Panshan VRC 175 Qj25
Mount Parker AUS 222 Re54
Mount Patterson CDN 17 Dc13
Mount Pattullo CDN 17 Df17
Mount Peale USA 21 Ef26
Mount Pearl CDN (NF) 31 Hd22
Mount Penot VU 246 Td54
Mount Perry AUS (QLD) 235 Sf58
Mount Petras 312 Dc34
Mount Peuetsagoe RI 198 Pj43
Mount Peulik USA 14 Cb17
Mount Pfizner AUS 226 Rh57
Mount Pinapan RI 198 Pk44
Mount Pinatubo RP 202 Ra38
Mount Pinos USA 22 Ea28
Mount Pleasant USA (UT) 21 Ee26
Mount Pleasant USA (MO) 29 Fd26
Mount Pleasant USA (TX) 29 Fc29
Mount Pleasant USA (MI) 32 Fh24
Mount Pleasant USA (SC) 35 Ga29
Mount Plummer USA 14 Ca15
Mount Popa MYA 195 Ph35
Mount Popomanaseu SOL 245 Ta50
Mount Pulog N.P. RP 203 Ra37
Mount Pye NZ 239 Te69
Mount Queen Bess CDN 18 Dh20
Mount Ragang RP 205 Rc42
Mount Rainier N.P. USA 18 Dk22
Mount Ramelau TIM 214 Rc50
Mount Ranai RI 199 Qe43
Mount Ratz CDN 17 Dd17
Mount Rebecca AUS 224 Qh59
Mount Remarkable AUS 222 Rd54
Mount Remarkable AUS 232 Rk56
Mount Remarkable N.P. AUS 236 Rk62
Mount Revelstoke N.P. CDN 18 Eb20
Mount Robe AUS 234 Sa61
Mount Robinson AUS 224 Qk57
Mount Robson CDN 18 Ea19
Mount Robson Prov. Park CDN 18 Ea19
Mount Rogers N.R.A. USA 35 Fk27
Mount Roosevelt CDN 17 Dd16
Mount Roraima GUY/YV 58 Gk43
Mount Ruapehu NZ 238 Th65
Mount Rungwe EAT 293 Mh50
Mount Rupert SA 303 Mc60
Mount Rushmore Nat. Memorial USA 26 Ej24
Mount Russell USA (AK) 15 Ce14
Mount Ryan AUS 237 Se62
Mount Sage N.P. GB 47 Gh36
Mount Saint Gregory CDN 31 Ha21
Mount Saint Helens Nat. Volcanic Mon. USA 18 Dj22
Mount Sandiman AUS (WA) 224 Qh58
Mount Sandiman AUS 224 Qh58
Mount Sanford USA (AK) 15 Ch14
Mount Sankanbiaiwa WAL 278 Ke41
Mount Sasari SOL 245 Sk50
Mount Saunders 313 Tb36
Mount's Bay GB 100 Kp40
Mount Seelig 312 Ed35
Mount Selinda ZW 300 Mg56
Mount Selous CDN 17 Dd14
Mount Sembuang RI 198 Pj43
Mount Shasta USA 20 Dj25
Mount Shasta USA (CA) 20 Dj25
Mount Sherrick CDN 25 Ga20
Mount Sicapoo RP 203 Ra37
Mount Sidley 312 Dc34
Mount Silisili WS 248 Bd52
Mount Siple 312 Dc33
Mount Sir James MacBrien CDN 17 Dg14
Mount Skinner AUS (NT) 226 Rh57
Mount Somers NZ 239 Tf67
Mount Spokane S.P. USA 18 Eb22
Mount Stanley EAU/RDC 287 Mf45
Mount Steele CDN 17 Ck15
Mount Sterling USA (IL) 27 Fe25
Mount Sterling USA (OH) 32 Fj26
Mount Sterling USA (KY) 35 Fj26
Mount Stevens NZ 239 Tg66
Mount Stewart AUS 233 Sc56
Mount Stewart CDN 15 Da14
Mount Stinear 313 Ob33
Mount Strong PNG 243 Sd49
Mount Stuart AUS (WA) 224 Qj57
Mount Sturgeon AUS (QLD) 232 Sc56
Mount Suckling PNG 243 Se50
Mount Sulen PNG 242 Sb47
Mount Sullivan AUS 223 Rf54
Mount Surprise AUS (QLD) 232 Sc55
Mount Tabletop AUS 233 Sd57
Mount Takahe 312 Eb34
Mount Taknan PNG 244 Sh49
Mount Taranaki NZ 238 Th65
Mount Tavani VU 246 Te54
Mount Thuillier IND 193 Pg42
Mount Tipton USA 22 Ec28
Mount Tip Tree AUS (QLD) 233 Sc54
Mount Tobin USA 20 Eb25
Mount Tom White USA 16 Cj15
Mount Tops AUS 226 Rg56
Mount Trumbull USA 22 Ed27
Mount Tutoko NZ 239 Te68
Mount Ulbanep PNG 243 Sb47
Mount Unbunmaroo AUS 232 Sa57
Mount Vangunu SOL 245 Sj50
Mount Vernon AUS (WA) 224 Qk58
Mount Vernon USA (WA) 18 Dj21
Mount Vernon USA (OR) 20 Ea23
Mount Vernon USA (MO) 27 Fe25
Mount Vernon USA (IL) 27 Ff26
Mount Vernon USA (MO) 29 Fd27
Mount Vernon USA (OH) 32 Fj25
Mount Vernon USA (AL) 34 Fg30
Mount Vernon USA (KY) 35 Fh27
Mount Victor 313 Mc33
Mount Victoria MYA 194 Pg35
Mount Victoria NZ 239 Tg67
Mount Victoria PNG 243 Sd50
Mount Victory PNG 243 Se50
Mount Waddington CDN 18 Dh20
Mount Walton AUS 228 Qk61
Mount Warning AUS 235 Sg60
Mount Washington USA (KY) 34 Fh26
Mount Wechecha ETH 284 Mk41
Mount Wedge AUS (SA) 236 Rh62
Mount Wells AUS 222 Rd54
Mount Wharton 313 Ta35
Mount Whitney USA 22 Ea27
Mount Wilhelm PNG 243 Sc48
Mount Will CDN 17 Df17
Mount William AUS 236 Sb64
Mount William N.P. AUS 236 Se66
Mount Willoughby AUS (SA) 227 Rj59
Mount Wilson CDN 17 Df14
Mount Windsor AUS (QLD) 232 Sa57
Mount Wittenoon AUS (WA) 224 Qj59
Mount Wood USA 21 Ee23
Mount Woodroffe AUS 226 Rf59
Mount Yawatoutou GH/RT 279 La42
Mount Zeil AUS 226 Rg57
Mouping VRC (SDG) 182 Ra27
Moura AUS (QLD) 235 Se58
Moura BR (AM) 62 Gk46
Moura P 108 Kn48
Mourão P 108 Kn48
Mouray TCH 282 Ma40
Mourdiah RMM 270 Kg38
Mourenx F 104 Ku47
Mouri Mountains WAN 273 Lf41
Mourmelon-le-Grand F 103 Le41
Mourne Mountains GB 98 Kp36
Mouroungoulay TCH 273 Lj41
Mousa GB 99 Kt30
Mousa Broch GB 99 Kt30
Mouscron B 103 Ld40
Mousgougou TCH 273 Lj40
Moussa Castle RL 146 Mh29
Moussafoyo TCH 282 Lk41
Moussaya RG 278 Kd41
Moussaya RG 278 Ke40
Moussoro TCH 273 Lj39
Moustiers-Sainte-Marie F 105 Lg47
Moutamba RCB 288 Lg47
Mouthe F 105 Lg44
Mouth of the Shannon IRL 100 Kl38
Mouths of the Amazon BR 64 Hf45
Mouths of the Ganges IND 194 Pe35
Mouths of the Indus PK 162 Od33
Mouths of the Irrawaddy MYA 196 Pj38
Mouths of the Krishna IND 193 Pa39
Mouths of the Mekong 199 Qd41
Moutier CH 114 Lh43
Moûtiers F 105 Lg45
Moutindi G 288 Lf47
Moutong RI 209 Ra45
Mouton Rothschild F 104 Ku45
Moutourousa CAM 273 Lh40
Moutsamoudou COM 304 Nc52
Moutsoúna GR 129 Mf53
Mouy F 103 Lc41
Mouyondzi RCB 288 Lg47
Mouzáki GR 128 Mb51
Mouzarak TCH 273 Lh39
Mouzon F 103 Lf41
Movie World AUS 235 Sg59
Movila Miresii RO 125 Mh45
Movilița RO 125 Mg46
Mowanjum AUS (WA) 222 Rb54
Mowanjum A.L. AUS 222 Rb54
Mowasi GUY 58 Ha43
Möwe Bay NAM 298 Lg55
Moxotó BR 71 Jb50
Moya COM 304 Nc52
Moyale EAK 291 Mk44
Moyale ETH 291 Mk44
Moyamba WAL 278 Kd41
Moyen Atlas MA 258 Kh29
Moyeni LS 303 Md61
Moyenne Sido RCA 282 Lk41
Moyhu AUS (VIC) 237 Sd64
Moyie CDN (BC) 19 Ec21
Moyie Springs USA (ID) 19 Eb21
Mo'ynoq UZB 153 Nk24
Moyo EAU 287 Mf44
Moyo RI 211 Qj50
Moyobamba PE 66 Gb49
Moyogalpa NIC 42 Fh40
Moyowosi EAT 292 Mf48
Moyowosi Game Reserve EAT 292 Mf48
Moyto TCH 273 Lj39
Moyu VRC (XUZ) 168 Ok27
Moyuela E 107 Ku51
Mozăceni RO 125 Mf46
Mozaffar Abad-e Kur Gol IR 154 Nf28
Možaisk RUS 132 Mj18
Mozambique 253 Mb11
Mozambique Basin 257 Md24
Mozambique Channel 257 Na22
Mozambique Plateau 257 Md22
Mozambique Ridge 257 Md25
Mozdok RUS (SOA) 152 Nc24
Mozduran IR 155 Oa27
Mozia I 122 Ln53
Mozirje SLO 121 Lp44
Mozogo-Gokoro, P.N.de WAN 273 Lg40
Mpaathutlwa Pan RB 299 Mb58
Mpaathutlwapan RB 299 Mb58
Mpagwe EAT 292 Mf48
Mpaha GH 279 Kk41
Mpahani EAT 293 Mk49
Mpal SN 269 Kb38
Mpala RDC 292 Me49
Mpama RDC 286 Lh47
Mpanda EAT 292 Mf49
Mpandaamatenga RB 299 Mc55
Mpanga EAT 293 Mj49
Mpanta Z 296 Me51
Mpase RDC 286 Ma46
Mpataba GH 279 Kj43
Mpatora EAT 293 Mk50
Mpé RCB 288 Lh47
Mpesao Hills GH 279 Kj42
Mpessoba RMM 270 Kh39
Mphaki LS 303 Me61
Mphoengs ZW 299 Md56
Mphwayungu EAT 293 Mh49
Mpiéla RMM 270 Kg39
Mpigi EAU 290 Mg45
Mpika Z 296 Mf51
Mpili Z 296 Md53
Mpo RDC 289 Lk48
Mpoko RCA 281 Lk43
Mpomgwe Z 296 Me52
Mponde EAT 293 Mh48
Mponela MW 296 Mg52
Mporokoso Z 292 Mf50
Mpouya RCB 288 Lj47
Mpraeso GH 279 Kk42
Mpui EAT 292 Mf50
Mpulungu Z 292 Mf50
Mpumalanga SA 303 Mf60
Mpunde RDC 289 Lk48
Mpurukasese EAT 297 Mj51
Mpwapwa EAT 293 Mj49
Mrągowo PL 117 Mb37
M'Rara DZ 260 Lc29
Mrauk-U MYA 194 Pg35
Mrčajevci SCG 126 Ma47
Mrežičko MK 126 Mc49
Mrikula Devi Temple IND 189 Oj29
Mrirt MA 258 Kh29
Mrkonjić Grad BIH 121 Ls46
Mrkopalj HR 121 Lp45
Mrohaung = Mrauk-U MYA 194 Pg35
Mrzežyno PL 116 Lq36
M'Saken TN 260 Lf28
Msak Mallat LAR 267 Lf33
Msalalo EAT 293 Mh48
Msanec' UA 119 Mc41
Msanga EAT 293 Mk49
Msangasi EAT 293 Mk48
Msanzara Z 296 Mf52
Msanzi EAT 292 Mf50
Msata EAT 293 Mk49
Mscislav BY 132 Mf19
Msechela EAT 297 Mj51
Mšené Lázně CZ 118 Lp40
Msesia EAT 292 Mg49
M'Sied MA 258 Ke31
M'Sila DZ 259 Lc28
Msima EAT 292 Mf49
Msimbati EAT 297 Na51
Msoro Z 296 Mf52
Msuna ZW 299 Md55
Mswebe Z 296 Md53
Mswega EAT 293 Mj50
Mszczonów PL 117 Ma39
Mt Aburassein RCA/SUD 282 Mb41
Mtakataka MW 296 Mh53
Mtakuja EAT 292 Mf49
Mtama EAT 297 Mk51
Mtamble EAT 293 Mk48
Mtambo EAT 292 Mf48
Mta Mepists'karo GE 152 Nb25
Mtamvuna SA 303 Mf61
Mtan SYR 146 Mj29
Mtandawala EAT 293 Mk50
Mtandura EAT 293 Mk50
Mtanila EAT 292 Mg49
Mtarazi Falls ZW 300 Mg55
Mt Augustus N.P. AUS 224 Qj58
Mt Dangoura RCA/SUD 283 Md42
Mtembwe EAT 293 Mj50
Mtera Reservoir EAT 293 Mh49
Mt Gaoun RCA 281 Lh42
Mt Guédi TCH 273 Lk39
Mtito Andei EAK 293 Mk47
Mtondo EAT 293 Mk50
Mtongwe EAT 293 Mk48
Mto wa Mbu EAT 293 Mh47
Mts du Fazao RT 279 La41
Mts Karé RCA 281 Lj42
Mtskheta GE 152 Nc25
Mtubatuba SA 303 Mg60
Mtuga Z 296 Me53
Mtukula EAT 297 Mj51
Mtwapa EAK 293 Mk47
Mtwara EAT 297 Na51
Mu F 246 Td56
Muabanama MOC 297 Mj53
Muadiala RDC 289 Ma49
Muaguide MOC 297 Na52
Mualadzi MOC 296 Mg53
Mualama MOC 297 Mk54
Muaná BR (PA) 64 Hf46
Muanda RDC 288 Lg48
Muangai ANG 295 Lk52
Muang Beng LAO 195 Qa35
Muang Boran THA 196 Qa39
Muang Houn LAO 195 Qa35
Muang Huang LAO 197 Qb36
Muang Kham LAO 197 Qb36
Muang Khong LAO 197 Qc38
Muang Khua LAO 195 Qb35
Muang Khun LAO 197 Qb36
Muang Long LAO 195 Qa35
Muang Nan LAO 196 Qa36
Muang Ngoi LAO 195 Qb35
Muang Pa LAO 196 Qa36
Muang Pak-Cay LAO 196 Qa36
Muang Phin LAO 197 Qd37
Muang Phu Khoun LAO 196 Qb36
Muang Pon THA 196 Pj36
Muang Samsip THA 197 Qc38
Muang Sing LAO 195 Qa35
Muang Singh Historical Park THA 196 Pk38
Muang Sui LAO 197 Qb36
Muang Xai LAO 195 Qb35
Muanza MOC 300 Mh55
Muanzanza RDC 289 Ma49
Muapula MOC 297 Mj52
Muaquia MOC 297 Mj52
Muar MAL 199 Qb44
Muara BRU 204 Qh43
Muaraaman RI 206 Qb47
Muarabadak RI 209 Qj46
Muarabeliti RI 207 Qb47
Muara Binuangeun RI 210 Qc49
Muarabungo RI 206 Qb46
Muaradua RI 207 Qc48
Muaraenim RI 207 Qb47
Muara Hiu RI 208 Qh46
Muarainu RI 208 Qh46
Muaraklingi RI 207 Qb47
Muara Koman RI 208 Qh46
Muarakuwis RI 206 Qb47
Muaranayan RI 208 Qj46
Muarapangean RI 208 Qj44
Muarapantai RI 206 Qa46
Muararupit RI 207 Qb47
Muarasaibi RI 206 Pk46
Muarasaung RI 207 Qb48
Muarasiberut RI 206 Pk46
Muarasigep RI 206 Pk46
Muarasikabaluan RI 206 Pk46
Muarasimatalu RI 206 Pk46
Muarasoma RI 206 Pk45
Muaratalang RI 206 Qb47
Muaratebo RI 206 Qb46
Muaratembesi RI 207 Qb46
Muarateweh RI 208 Qh46
Muarawahau RI 209 Qj45
Muari RI 212 Rd46
Muatua MOC 297 Mk53
Mubambe RDC 296 Md51
Mubanzi EAU 287 Mf46
Mubayira ZW 300 Mf55
Mubende EAU 287 Mf45
Mubi WAN 273 Lg40
Mubo VRC (GSU) 174 Qd27
Muborak UZB 158 Oc26
Mubrani RI 213 Rg46
Mubur RI 199 Qd44
Mucajaí BR (RR) 58 Gk44
Mucajaí BR 58 Gk44
Mucanha Z 295 Mc52
Mucari ANG 289 Lj50
Muchaze MOC 300 Mg56
Muchea AUS (WA) 228 Qh61
Mucheve MOC 300 Mh56
Muchinga Mountains Z 296 Mf52
Muchinka Z 296 Mf52
Muchówka PL 119 Ma41
Muchuchu Ruins ZW 300 Mf55
Muck GB 98 Ko34
Muckadilla AUS (QLD) 235 Se59
Mučkapskij RUS 133 Nb20
Muckross IRL 100 Kl38
Muco CO 56 Ge43
Mucojo MOC 297 Na52
Muconda ANG 295 Ma51
Mucondo ANG 288 Lh50
Mucope ANG 294 Lh54
Mucopo MOC 297 Mj54
Mucuaso ANG 295 Ma54
Mucubela MOC 297 Mj54
Mucuchies YV 57 Ge41
Mucucuaú BR 62 Gk45
Mucugê BR (BA) 71 Hk52
Mucuim BR 62 Gh49
Mucumbura MOC 296 Mf54
Mucumbura ZW 296 Mf54
Mucupia MOC 301 Mj55
Mucur TR 131 Mp51
Mucure YV 57 Gh41
Mucuri BR (BA) 75 Ja55
Mucuri BR 75 Ja55
Mucurici BR (ES) 75 Hk55
Mucuripi BR (AM) 61 Gf47
Mucussueje ANG 295 Ma51
Mudabidri IND 192 Oh40
Mudang Jiang VRC 180 Re23
Mudanjiang VRC (HLG) 180 Re23
Mudan Jiang VRC 180 Rf22
Mudanthurai Tiger Sanctuary IND 193 Oj42
Mudanya TR 130 Mj50
Mud Butte USA (SD) 26 Ej23
Muddanuru IND (APH) 193 Ok39
Muddebihal IND (KTK) 190 Oj
Muddus n.p. S 90 Ma12
Muddy Gap USA (WY) 21 Eg2
Mudgal IND (KTK) 190 Oj37
Mudgee AUS (NSW) 237 Se62
Mudgod IND (KTK) 192 Oh39
Mudhai OM 151 Ng37
Mudhol IND (KTK) 190 Oh37
Mudigere IND (KTK) 192 Oh4
Mudigubba IND (APH) 193 Oj
Mudjatik River CDN 19 Eg17
Mudon MYA 196 Pj37
Mudukulattur IND (TNU) 193 Ok42
Mudumalai Sanctuary IND 192 Oj41
Mudumu N.P. NAM 299 Mb
Mudun SP 291 Nb45
Muecate MOC 297 Mk53
Mueda MOC 297 Mk51
Muel E 107 Kt51
Mueller Range AUS 222 Rd55
Muembe MOC 297 Mh52
Muende MOC 296 Mg53
Muftah SUD 276 Mg36
Mufulira Z 296 Me52
Mufu Shan VRC 177 Qg31
Mufu Shan VRC 184 Qh31
Mugambo = Lagosa EAT 292 Me48
Mugang VRC (YUN) 178 Qc34
Mugango EAT 290 Mg46
Muganskaja ravnina AZ 152 Ne26
Mugeba MOC 297 Mj54
Mugello I 120 Lm46
Mügeln D 113 Lo39
Muger ETH 284 Mk41
Muger ETH 284 Mk41
Muger Falls ETH 284 Mk41
Muggon AUS (WA) 224 Qh59
Mughal Sarai IND (UPH) 191 Pb33
Mughayra KSA 146 Mj31
Mughsayl OM 151 Nq37
Mugina BU 292 Me48
Muğla TR 130 Mj53
Mugling NEP 170 Pc32
Müglitztal D 113 Lo40
Mugota EAK 290 Mj45
Mug Qu VRC 171 Pg29
Muguia MOC 297 Mk52
Mugumu EAT 290 Mh46
Muhagiria SUD 282 Mc40
Muhairiqah KSA 149 Nc34
Muhala RDC 292 Me48
Muhammad Qol SUD 277 Mj3
Muhavura EAU/RWA 292 Me
Muhayil KSA 150 Nb36
Muhaywir IRQ 147 Na29
Muheza EAT 293 Mj48
Muheza EAT 293 Mk48
Muhinji Chini EAT 293 Mk50
Muhino RUS 180 Rd19
Mühlacker D 114 Lj42
Mühldorf D 115 Ln42
Mühlhausen D 113 Ll39
Mühlig-Hofmann-fjella 313 Lb
Mühlviertel A 115 Lp42
Muhoi Kondui RUS 173 Qg19
Muhoršibir RUS (BUR) 172 Qd20
Muhovo BG 126 Md48
Muhu EST 96 Md32
Muhula = Namiroa MOC 297 Mk53
Muhulu RDC 287 Md46
Muhuwesi EAT 297 Mj51
Mui Ca Mau VN 199 Qc41
Mui Chan May Dong VN 197 Qe37
Muico MOC 297 Mk52
Mui Doc VN 197 Qd37
Muidumbe MOC 297 Mk51
Muié ANG 295 Ma53
Mui Ke Ga VN 197 Qe40
Mui Ke Ga VN 197 Qe40
Mui Lai VN 197 Qd37
Mui Nai VN 199 Qc40
Mui Nam Tram VN 197 Qe38
Muine ANG 295 Ma54
Mui Ne VN 197 Qe40
Mui Ne Beach VN 197 Qe40
Mui Ron VN 197 Qd36
Mui Rong Quèn VN 197 Qc36
Muiron Islands AUS 224 Qh56
Mui Sot VN 197 Qc36
Muite MOC 297 Mk53
Muizenberg SA 302 Lk63
Mujšin RUS 173 Qh19
Muju ROK 182 Rd27
Mujui dos Campos BR (PA) 63 Hc47
Muka Z 296 Md54
Mukačeve UA 119 Mc42
Mukah MAL 208 Qg44
Mukala RDC 289 Lj48
Mukana RDC 292 Md50
Mukandakunda Z 295 Mb52
Mukanga RDC 289 Ma49
Mukanya EAT 293 Mj50
Mukawa PNG 243 Se50
Mukawwa Island ET 263 Mh3
Mukdahan THA 197 Qc37
Mukdahan N.P. THA 197 Qc37
Mukebo RDC 292 Me49
Muke Turi ETH 284 Mk41
Mukilteo USA (WA) 18 Dj22
Mukinbudin AUS (WA) 228 Qk61
Mukinge Hill Z 295 Mc52
Mu Ko Chang N.P. THA 197 Qb39
Mu Koh Angthong N.P. THA 198 Pk41
Mukomuko RI 206 Qa47
Mukono EAU 290 Mg45
Mu Ko Phetra N.P. THA 198 Pk42
Mukosa ZW 296 Mg54
Mu Ko Surin N.P. THA 198 Pj4
Mukošyn UA 117 Mf39
Mu Ko Tarutao N.P. THA 198 Pk42
Mukpalli IND (MHT) 191 Pa36
Mukrian IND (PJB) 188 Oh30
Mukry TM 155 Oc27
Muk Sukhteh IR 157 Ob31
Muktsar IND (PJB) 188 Oh30
Mukuku Z 296 Me52

Mukulaikwe Z 296 Md53
Mukulushi RDC 295 Mc51
Mukunsa Z 292 Me50
Mukupa Kaoma Z 292 Mf50
Mukur = Moqor AFG 160 Od29
Mukutawa River CDN 24 Fb19
Mukutungu EAT 293 Mj50
Mul IND (MHT) 191 Ok35
Mula E 109 Kt48
Mula PK 162 Od31
Mulaku Atoll = Meemu Atoll MV 192 Og44
Mulaley AUS (NSW) 235 Se61
Mulalika Z 296 Me53
Mulan VRC (HLG) 180 Re23
Mulanay RP 203 Rb39
Mulanje MW 297 Mh54
Mulanje Mountains MW 297 Mh53
Mulanur IND (TN) 193 Oj41
Mulatos CO 56 Gb41
Mulayjah KSA 149 Ne32
Mulbagal IND (KTK) 193 Ok40
Mulchatna River USA 15 Cc15
Mulchen RCH 80 Gd64
Mulde D 113 Ln39
Muleba EAT 287 Mf46
Mule Creek Junction USA (WY) 21 Eh24
Mulegé MEX (BCS) 38 Ed32
Mulele Z 295 Mb54
Mulembe RDC 292 Me47
Mulenda RDC 289 Mc48
Muleshoe USA (TX) 23 Ej28
Muleta ETH 284 Na41
Mulevala MOC 297 Mj54
Mulga Park AUS (NT) 226 Rf58
Mulgathing AUS (SA) 236 Rg61
Mulgildie AUS (QLD) 235 Sf58
Mulgrave CDN (NS) 31 Gk23
Mulgrave Hills USA (AK) 15 Bj12
Mulgul AUS (WA) 224 Qk58
Mulhacén E 109 Kr47
Mulhalli IND (KTK) 193 Oj40
Mülheim (Ruhr) D 112 Lg39
Mulhouse F 103 Lh43
Muli MV 192 Og44
Muli VRC (SCH) 195 Qa32
Mulia RI 213 Rj47
Muli Channel RI 242 Rk49
Mulika Lodge EAK 291 Mk45
Mulilo Z 296 Mg51
Muling VRC (HLG) 180 Rf23
Muling He VRC 180 Rg23
Mulka AUS (SA) 227 Rk60
Mulaittivu CL 193 Pa42
Mullen USA (NE) 26 Ek24
Muller Range PNG 242 Sb48
Müller Range RI 208 Qg45
Mullet Peninsula IRL 98 Kk36
Mullewa AUS (WA) 228 Qh60
Müllheim D 114 Lh43
Mullingar IRL 100 Kn37
Mullins USA (SC) 35 Ga28
Mull of Galloway GB 98 Kq36
Mull of Kintyre GB 98 Kp35
Müllrose D 113 Lp38
Mullsjö S 95 Lo33
Mulobezi Z 295 Mc54
Mulock Glacier 313 Sd34
Mulondo ANG 294 Lh53
Mulonga Plain Z 295 Mb54
Mulongo RDC 292 Md49
Muloorina AUS (SA) 227 Rj60
Mulshi IND (MHT) 190 Og36
Mulshi Lake IND 190 Og36
Multai IND (MPH) 191 Ok35
Multan PK 161 Of30
Multan Fort PK 161 Of30
Multia FIN 96 Me28
Mulu ETH 284 Na41
Mulu MAL 208 Qh44
Muluala Z 295 Mb54
Mulu Caves MAL 204 Qh43
Mulungu RDC 289 Mb50
Mulungushi Z 296 Me53
Mulu N.P., Gunung MAL 204 Qh43
Mulyungarie AUS (SA) 236 Sa61
Muma RDC 286 Mb44
Muma RDC 287 Mc44
Mumalla SUD 282 Mc40
Muman IR 157 Oa33
Mumbai IND (MHT) 190 Og36
Mumbeji Z 295 Mb52
Mumbleberry Lake AUS 234 Rk58
Mumbondo ANG 294 Lh51
Mumbué ANG 294 Lj52
Mumbwa Z 296 Md53
Mumena RDC 296 Md51
Mumeng PNG 243 Sd49
Mumfor RI 213 Rh46
Mumias EAK 290 Mh45
Mummballup AUS (WA) 228 Qj62
Mumoma RDC 289 Mb49
Mun RI 213 Rg48
Muna MEX (YT) 41 Ff35
Muna RI 209 Rb48
Muna RUS 141 Qd05
Munaba IND (RJT) 188 Of33
Munai VRC (YUN) 195 Pk34
Munaishy KZ 152 Ng24
Munamägi EST 96 Mh33
Munaya CAM 280 Le43
Muncakkabau RI 207 Qc48
Münchberg D 115 Lm40
Müncheberg D 113 Lp38
München D 115 Lm42
München-Riem D 115 Lm42
Munchique, P.N. CO 60 Gb44
Muncho Lake CDN (BC) 17 Dh16
Muncho Lake Prov. Park CDN 17 Dh16
Muncie USA (IN) 32 Fh25
Munda PK 161 Of30
Munda SOL 244 Sj50
Mundabullangana AUS (WA) 224 Qk56
Mundare CDN (AB) 19 Ed19
Mundargi IND (KTK) 192 Oh39
Mundaú BR (CE) 65 Ja47
Munday USA (TX) 28 Fa29
Mundemba CAM 280 Le43
Mundesley GB 101 Lb38
Mundford GB 101 La38
Mundi IND (MPH) 190 Oj34
Mundico Coelho BR (PA) 63 Hb49
Mundiwindi AUS (WA) 224 Ra57
Mundo Marino RA 81 Hb64
Mundo Novo BR (BA) 71 Hk51
Mundo Novo BR (MS) 74 Hc57
Mundra IND (GUJ) 190 Oe34
Mundrabilla Motel AUS (WA) 229 Re61
Mundri SUD 287 Mf43
Mundubbera AUS (QLD) 235 Sf58
Mundul AFG 161 Of28
Mundwa IND (RJT) 188 Og32
Mundy River AUS 227 Rk61
Munenga ANG 294 Lh51
Munera E 109 Ks49
Mungaa EAT 293 Mh48
Mungallala AUS (QLD) 235 Sd59
Mungana AUS (QLD) 232 Sc54
Mungaoli IND (MPH) 191 Ok33
Mungári MOC 296 Mg54
Mungeli IND (CGH) 191 Pa34
Mungeranie AUS (SA) 227 Rk60
Mungia E 107 Ks53
Mungilli A.L. AUS 225 Rc58
Mungindi AUS (NSW) 235 Se60
Mungkarta A.L. AUS 223 Rh56
Munglinup AUS (WA) 228 Ra62
Mungo ANG 289 Lk49
Mungo ANG 294 Lj51
Mungo N.P. AUS 237 Sb62
Mungo Park Memorial WAG 269 Kc39
Mungra Badshahpur IND (UPH) 191 Pb33
Munhango ANG 295 Lk52
Munich D 115 Lm42
Munieng RDC 296 Me52
Muniesa E 107 Ku51
Munim BR 64 Hj47
Munising USA (MI) 32 Fg22
Muniungu RDC 288 Lj48
Muniz Freire BR (ES) 75 Hk56
Munjola IND (CGH) 191 Pa36
Munka-Ljungby S 95 Ln34
Munkebo DK 94 Ll35
Munkedal S 92 Lm32
Munkfors S 93 Lo31
Munkumpu Z 296 Md52
Munmarlary AUS (NT) 223 Rg52
Munnar IND (KER) 193 Oj41
Munsan ROK 182 Rd27
Munshiganj BD 194 Pf34
Munshir Hat BD 194 Pf34
Münsingen D 114 Lk42
Münster CH 114 Lj44
Münster D 112 Lh39
Münster D 113 Ll38
Munster F 103 Lh42
Münster zu Ulm D 114 Ll42
Muntaiwani RI 208 Qh46
Munteni RO 125 Mh45
Muntgatsi EAK 290 Mh45
Munții Apuseni, P.N. RO 124 Mc44
Munții Bistriței RO 125 Mf43
Munții Călimani RO 125 Me43
Munții Codru-Moma RO 124 Mc44
Munții Făgărașului RO 125 Me45
Munții Gilău RO 124 Md44
Munții Goșmanului RO 125 Mg44
Munții Gurghiu RO 125 Mf44
Munții Harghita RO 125 Mf44
Munții Lăpușului RO 124 Md43
Munții Lotrului RO 124 Md45
Munții Măcinului, P.N. RO 125 Mj45
Munții Maramureșului RO 124 Me43
Munții Meseș RO 124 Md43
Munții Metaliferi RO 124 Mc44
Munții Semenic RO 124 Mc45
Munții Tarcului RO 124 Mc45
Munții Vâlcanului RO 124 Md45
Munții Zarndului RO 124 Mc44
Muntok RI 207 Qc47
Muntu RDC 289 Lk47
Munukata J 185 Rf29
Munungu Z 296 Me51
Munyamadzi Z 296 Mf52
Munyati ZW 300 Mf55
Münzkirchen A 115 Lo42
Munzur Dağları TR 145 Mk26
Munzur Vadisi Milli Parkı TR 145 Mk26
Muoco MOC 297 Mj52
Muodoslompolo S 91 Mb12
Muong Lan VN 197 Qc36
Muong Lay VN 195 Qb35
Muong Man VN 197 Qe40
Muong Tei VN 195 Qb34
Muonio FIN 91 Mb12
Mupa ANG 294 Lh54
Mu Pagoa Falls WS 248 Bd52
Mupamadzi Z 296 Mf52
Mupa, P.N.da ANG 294 Lh53
Mupfure ZW 296 Me54
Muqakoori SP 285 Nd43
Muqaybirah YE 150 Nd39
Muqaynimah KSA 149 Ne34
Muqdisho SP 291 Nc44
Muqshin OM 151 Nh36
Muquém BR (GO) 70 Hf53
Muqui BR (ES) 75 Hk56
Mur A 115 Lo43
Mura BR (AM) 62 Ha47
Muradiye TR 129 Mh52
Muradiye TR 145 Nb26
Muradiye Camii TR 129 Mh52
Murakami J 183 Rk26
Muralgarra AUS (WA) 228 Qj60
Muralla Romana de Lugo E 106 Kn52
Murallón, Cerro RA/RCH 82 Gd70
Muramgaon IND (MHT) 191 Pa35
Muramvya BU 292 Me47
Muranga EAK 290 Mj46
Murangering EAK 290 Mh44
Muránska planina, N.P. SK 119 Lu42
Muraral IND (WBG) 194 Pd33
Murat F 105 Lc45
Murat Dağı TR 130 Mk52
Muratlı TR 130 Mh49
Murato F 111 Lk48
Murau A 115 Lp43
Muravera I 111 Lk51
Murberget S 93 Ls28
Murça P 106 Kn51
Murchinson Range AUS 223 Rh55
Murchison AUS (VIC) 237 Sc64
Murchison NZ 239 Tg66
Murchison Falls EAU 290 Mf44
Murchison Falls N.P. = Kabalega Falls N.P. EAU 290 Mf44
Murchison Island CDN 25 Ff21
Murchison River AUS 224 Qh59
Murchison Roadhouse AUS (WA) 224 Qh59
Murcia E 109 Kt47
Murcia E 109 Kt47
Mur-de-Barrez F 105 Lc46
Mur-de-Bretagne F 102 Ks42
Murdo USA (SD) 26 Ek24
Murdochville CDN (QC) 31 Gh21
Murdock Point AUS 231 Sc53
Murdurnu TR 131 Mm50
Mureck A 115 Lq44
Mürefte TR 130 Mh50
Murehwa ZW 296 Mf54
Mureibit SYR 146 Mk27
Mureș RO 124 Me44
Muret F 104 Lb47
Murfreesboro USA (AR) 29 Fd28
Murfreesboro USA (TN) 34 Fg28
Murfreesboro USA (NC) 35 Gb27
Murg D 114 Lj42
Murgab TJ 159 Oh26
Murgan AUS (QLD) 235 Sf59
Murgap TM 155 Ob27
Murgap TM 155 Ob27
Murgaš BG 126 Md48
Murgenella AUS (NT) 223 Rg51
Murgeni RO 125 Mj44
Murgești RO 125 Mg45
Murgha Kibzai PK 161 Oe30
Murghob TJ 159 Og26
Murgia E 107 Ks52
Murgoo AUS (WA) 224 Qj59
Muri VRC (QHI) 174 Qa27
Muriaé BR 75 Hj56
Muriaé BR (MG) 75 Hj56
Muria, Gunung RI 210 Qf49
Muribeca BR (CE) 65 Ja48
Muricilândia BR (TO) 64 Hf49
Muricizal BR 64 Hf49
Muridke PK 161 Oh30
Muriege ANG 289 Ma50
Muriel Lake CDN 19 Ee18
Murilo Atoll FSM 240 Sc17
Murin Bridge AUS (NSW) 237 Sd62
Murindó CO 56 Gb42
Muritiba BR (BA) 71 Ja52
Müritz D 113 Ln37
Müritz, N.P. D 113 Ln37
Murizidié Pass LAR 267 Lh34
Murliganj IND (BIH) 194 Pd33
Murmansk RUS 140 Mc05
Murnau D 115 Lm43
Murnpeowie AUS (SA) 227 Rk60
Muro E 110 Ld51
Muro del Alcoy E 109 Ku48
Muro Lucano I 122 Lq50
Murom RUS 133 Nb18
Murongo EAT 287 Mf46
Muroran J 181 Sa24
Muros E 106 Kl52
Muroto J 185 Rh29
Murphy USA (ID) 20 Eb24
Murphysboro USA (IL) 29 Ff27
Murqushi 161 Oh27
Murra Murra AUS (QLD) 235 Sd60
Murray USA (UT) 21 Ee25
Murray USA (KY) 29 Ff27
Murray Bridge AUS (SA) 236 Rk63
Murray Downs AUS (NT) 227 Rh56
Murray Fracture Zone 317 Ca07
Murray Harbour CDN (PE) 31 Gj22
Murray Island AUS 231 Sb50
Murray River AUS 228 Qj62
Murray River AUS 237 Sc63
Murray River Basin AUS 236 Sa62
Murraysburg SA 302 Mb61
Murray's Falls GUY 58 Ha44
Murray Sunset N.P. AUS 236 Sa63
Murrayville AUS (VIC) 236 Sa63
Murree PK 161 Og29
Murrhardt D 114 Lk42
Murri CO 56 Gb42
Murroa MOC 297 Mj54
Murrua MOC 297 Mj54
Murrumateman AUS (NSW) 237 Se63
Murrumbidgee River AUS 237 Sd63
Murrumburrah AUS (NSW) 237 Se63
Murrupula MOC 297 Mk53
Murrurundi AUS (NSW) 235 Sf61
Murska Sobota SLO 121 Lr44
Mursko Središće HR 121 Lr44
Murtajapur IND (MHT) 190 Oj35
Murten CH 114 Lh44
Murter HR 121 Lq47
Murter HR 121 Lq47
Murtle Lake CDN 18 Ea19
Muru BR 67 Ge50
Murua PNG 243 Sc49
Muruasigar EAK 284 Mh44
Murud IND (MHT) 190 Og36
Murud IND (MHT) 190 Oj36
Murud Beach IND 190 Og36
Murudeshwar IND 192 Oh39
Murunkan CL 193 Ok42
Murupara NZ 238 Tj65
Murupu BR (RR) 58 Gk44
Murura MOC 297 Mh54
Murwara IND (MPH) 191 Pa34
Murwillumbah AUS (NSW) 235 Sg60
Mürz A 115 Lq43
Mürzzuschlag A 115 Lq43
Muş TR 145 Na26
Musa LT 97 Me34
Musa Z 295 Mc53
Musa Z 295 Mc53
Musaaroole SP 291 Nc44
Musadi RDC 289 Mb47
Musafirkhana IND (UPH) 189 Pa32
Musaia WAL 278 Ke41
Musa Khel PK 161 Of29
Musa Khel Bazar PK 161 Oe30
Musala BG 126 Md48
Musala RI 206 Pk45
Musale Z 296 Mc53
Musallam IRQ 147 Nd30
Musan DVRK 182 Re24
Musandam Peninsula OM 157 Nj32
Musa Qal'eh AFG 160 Oc29
Musa River PNG 243 Se50
Musashi J 185 Rf29
Musawa WAN 272 Ld39
Musbat SUD 275 Mc38
Muscat OM 157 Nk34
Muscat OM 157 Nk34
Muscatine USA (MO) 27 Fe25
Musée de Bretagne F 102 Kt42
Musée de Tahiti et des Îles F 249 Cf54
Musée Fesch F 111 Lj49
Musée Gauguin F 249 Cf54
Musée Gauguin F 249 Da50
Musenge RDC 287 Me46
Musenge RDC 289 Mb50
Museo Archeologico I 122 Lq53
Museo del Oro CO 56 Gc43
Museo Guggenheim E 107 Ks53
Museo Playa Girón (Bay of Pigs Inv. Mus.) C 44 Fk34
Museu do Índio (Cuiabá) BR 69 Hb53
Museu Goeldi (Belém) BR (PA) 64 Hf46
Museum Het Princessehof NL 112 Lf37
Museum of Automobiles USA 29 Fd28
Museum of Cape Breton Heritage CDN 31 Gk22
Museum of Central Australia AUS 226 Rg57
Museum of Northern British Columbia CDN 17 De18
Museum of Tropical Queensland AUS 233 Sd55
Museum Rég. des Mines CDN 30 Ga21
Museumsinsel in Berlin D 113 Lo38
Museumsmeile D 112 Lh40
Musgrave Harbour CDN (NF) 31 Hd21
Musgrave Range AUS 226 Rf59
Mushabani IND (JKD) 194 Pd34
Mushayfat SUD 283 Mf40
Mushenge RDC 289 Ma48
Mushie RDC 288 Lj47
Mushima Z 295 Mc53
Mushipashi Z 296 Mf51
Mushota Z 292 Me50
Mushrefah KSA 150 Nb36
Mushu Island PNG 243 Sb47
Mushumbi Pools ZW 296 Mf54
Musi RI 207 Qc47
Musin WAN 280 Lb42
Musiné EC 60 Fk45
Musiri IND (TNU) 193 Ok41
Muskeg Lake CDN 25 Ff21
Muskegon USA (MI) 32 Fg24
Muskegon Heights USA (MI) 32 Fg24
Muskeg River CDN 17 Dj15
Muskira IND (UPH) 189 Ok33
Muskö S 93 Lt31
Muskogee USA (OK) 29 Fc28
Muskratdam Lake CDN 24 Fd19
Muskwa River CDN 17 Dh16
Muslimabagh PK 160 Od30
Muslim Pilgrimage site of Shek Husen ETH 284 Na42
Musofu Z 296 Me52
Musoma EAT 290 Mg46
Musombe EAT 293 Mh49
Musondweji Z 295 Mc52
Musone I 121 Lo47
Musorka RUS 133 Ne19
Musoro Z 296 Mf52
Musoshi RDC 296 Md51
Musquodoboit Harbour CDN (NS) 31 Gj23
Mussau Island PNG 243 Se46
Musselburgh GB 99 Kr35
Musselshell USA 21 Ef22
Mussende ANG 294 Lj51
Musserra ANG 288 Lg49
Mussidan F 104 La45
Mussolo ANG 294 Lj51
Mussomeli I 122 Lo53
Mussoorie IND (UTT) 189 Ok30
Mussuma ANG 295 Ma53
Mussuma ANG 295 Ma53
Mussy-sur-Seine F 103 Le43
Mustafabad IND (UPH) 189 Pa33
Mustafa Kara Paşa Camii TR 144 Mh25
Mustafakemalpaşa TR 130 Mj50
Mustafa-paša džamija MK 126 Mb49
Mustahil ETH 285 Nc43
Mustang NEP 170 Pb31
Mustang Island USA 39 Fb32
Mustér = Disentis CH 114 Lj44
Mustique WV 47 Gk39
Mustjala EST 96 Mc32
Mustla EST 96 Mf32
Mustvee EST 96 Mg32
Musu Dan DVRK 182 Re25
Musungwa Z 295 Mc53
Muswellbrook AUS (NSW) 237 Sf62
Muszyna PL 119 Ma41
Mut ET 263 Me33
Mut TR 144 Mg27
Mutala MOC 297 Mj53
Mutalau NZ 248 Bf55
Mutale SA 300 Mf57
Mutamba dos Macombes MOC 297 Mk51
Mutambara BU 292 Me48
Mutambara ZW 300 Mg55
Mutampet IND (APH) 191 Ok36
Mutaralam RI 207 Qc48
Mutarara MOC 297 Mh54
Mutare ZW 300 Mg55
Mutarnee AUS (QLD) 233 Sd55
Mutatá CO 56 Gb42
Mutawintji N.P. AUS 234 Sb61
Mutha EAK 291 Mk46
Mutianyu VRC 175 Qj25
Mutiene RDC 288 Lh48
Mutinde EAT 292 Mf48
Muting RI 242 Sa49
Mutinlupa RP 203 Ra38
Mutir EAU 287 Mf44
Mutis, Gunung RI 214 Rc50
Mutiweshiri ZW 300 Mf55
Mutoko ZW 296 Mg54
Mutombo Mukulu RDC 289 Mc50
Mutomo EAK 291 Mk46
Muto One F 249 Ck49
Mutooroo AUS (SA) 236 Sa62
Mutorashanga ZW 296 Mf54
Mutoto RDC 289 Mb48
Mutoto RDC 292 Me49
Mutoto-saki J 185 Rh29
Mutrah OM 157 Nk34
Mutshatsha RDC 295 Mc51
Mutsu J 181 Sa25
Mutthaburra AUS (QLD) 232 Sc57
Muttalıp TR 131 Ml51
Muttapuram IND (APH) 191 Pa37
Muttonbird Island NZ 239 Td69
Muttukuru IND (APH) 193 Pa39
Mutúali MOC 297 Mj53
Mutuati EAK 291 Mk45
Mutukula EAU 287 Mf46
Mutukula IND (APH) 191 Ok37
Mutum BR 61 Gf48
Mutum BR (AM) 62 Gk49
Mutum BR (MS) 74 Hd56
Mutum BR (MG) 75 Hk55
Mutumbi RDC 292 Me49
Mutum Biyu WAN 273 Lf41
Mutumbo ANG 294 Lj52
Mutumbwe Z 295 Mc52
Mutum Daya WAN 273 Lf41
Mutum ou Madeira BR 69 Hc54
Mutum Paraná BR (RO) 68 Gh50
Mutungu-Tari RDC 289 Lj49
Mutur CL 193 Pa42
Mutu-wan J 183 Sa25
Muurame FIN 96 Mf28
Mu us Shamo VRC 174 Qd26
Muvattupuzha IND (KER) 192 Oj42
Muxi VRC (SCH) 176 Qb31
Muxia E 106 Kl53
Muxian VRC (YUN) 178 Qc34
Muxima ANG 288 Lg50
Muyange BU 292 Mf47
Muyinga BU 292 Mf47
Muy Muy NIC 42 Fh39
Muyombe Z 296 Mg51
Muyuka CAM 280 Le43
Muyumba RDC 292 Md49
Muzaffarabad PK 161 Og28
Muzaffargarh PK 161 Of30
Muzaffarnagar IND (UPH) 189 Oj31
Muzaffarpur IND (BIH) 189 Pc32
Muzambinho BR (MG) 75 Hg56
Muzarabani ZW 296 Mf54
Muze MOC 296 Mf53
muzej-usad'ba „Tarhany" RUS 133 Nb19
Muzeul Satului RO 125 Mf46
Muzhen VRC (AHU) 184 Qj30
Muzhlit të Skënderbeut AL 126 Lu49
Muzillac F 102 Ks43
Muzizi EAU 287 Mf45
Muzo CO 56 Gc43
Muzo CO 56 Gd42
Múzquiz MEX (COH) 39 Ek32
Muztag VRC 168 Pa27
Muztag VRC 169 Pd27
Muztagata VRC 168 Oh26
Mvangan CAM 281 Lf44
Mveng CAM 281 Lg44
Mvengué CAM 281 Lf44
Mvomero EAT 293 Mj49
Mvoung G 281 Lg45
Mvouti RCB 288 Lg48
Mvuma ZW 300 Mf55
Mvurwi ZW 296 Mf54
Mwabvi Game Reserve MW 297 Mh54
Mwadi Kalumbu RDC 289 Lk49
Mwadingusha RDC 296 Md51
Mwadui EAT 292 Mg47
Mwaga EAK 293 Mk47
Mwagné, P.N.de G 281 Lg45
Mwai EAT 292 Mf49
Mwakilunga EAT 293 Mg47
Mwala EAT 293 Mh50
Mwali COM 304 Nb52
Mwamagembe EAT 293 Mg49
Mwambo EAT 297 Na51
Mwana RDC 292 Me47
Mwana-Ndeke RDC 292 Md48
Mwanangumune Z 295 Mb53
Mwangalala RDC 296 Md51
Mwango RDC 289 Mb49
Mwanza EAT 292 Mg47
Mwanza MW 296 Mh53
Mwanza RDC 292 Md49
Mwanza Gulf EAT 290 Mg47
Mwanzangoma RDC 289 Mb48
Mwatate EAK 293 Mk47
Mwatwe Z 295 Mc52
Mwea Nature Reserve EAK 290 Mj46
Mweelrea IRL 98 Kl37
Mweka RDC 289 Ma48
Mwela and Sumina Rocks Z 296 Mf51
Mwelemu Z 296 Md52
Mwendi EAT 293 Mk50
Mwene-Biji RDC 289 Mb50
Mwene-Ditu RDC 289 Mb49
Mwenezi ZW 300 Mf56
Mwenezi ZW 300 Mf56
Mwenga RDC 292 Me47
Mweru Wantipa N.P. Z 292 Me50
Mwilambwe RDC 289 Mc50
Mwimbi EAT 292 Mf50
Mwingi EAK 291 Mk46
Mwingi Nature Reserve EAK 291 Mk46
Mwinilunga Z 295 Mc51
Mwini Lunga Z 296 Mg51
Mwinilunga Petroglyphs Z 295 Mc51
Mwisi EAT 292 Mg48
Mwitika EAK 291 Mk46
Mwitikiri EAT 293 Mh49
Mwombezhi Z 295 Mc52
Myakka City USA (FL) 36 Fj32
Myall Lakes N.P. AUS 237 Sg62
Myalup AUS 228 Qh62
Myanaung MYA 196 Ph36
Myangan Ugalfat Uul MNG 172 Qa22
Myanmar MYA 139 Pb07
Mychajlivka UA 135 Mh22
Mychla MYA 196 Pj36
Myczków PL 119 Mc41
Mye, Mount CDN 17 Dd14
Myingyan MYA 195 Ph35
Myinmoletkat MYA 196 Pk39
Myinmu MYA 195 Ph35
Myitkyina MYA 195 Pj33
Myittha MYA 195 Pj35
Myjava SK 118 Ls42
Mykénai GR 128 Mc53
Mykolajiv UA 119 Md41
Mykolajiv UA 134 Mf22
Mykolajivka UA 135 Mg23
Mykulyči UA 117 Me40
My Lai VN 197 Qe38
Myllykoski FIN 96 Mg30
Mymensingh BD 194 Pf33
Mynämäki FIN 96 Mc30
Mynarai KZ 166 Og23
Mynfontein SA 302 Mb61
Myo gyi MYA 195 Pj35
Myola AUS (QLD) 232 Sa55
Myolo SUD 283 Me42
Myoshi J 183 Rg28
Myotha MYA 195 Ph35
Myoyang San DVRK 182 Rd25
Myra TR 144 Mf27
Myrdal N 92 Lh30
Mýrdalsjökull IS 90 Ka14
Myre N 90 Lh11
Myres Castle GB 99 Kr34
Myrgorod UA 134 Mg21
Myrmoen N 92 Lm28
Myronivka UA 134 Mf21
Myrskylä = Mörskom FIN 96 Mf30
Myrtle Beach USA (SC) 35 Ga29
Myrtle Creek USA (OR) 20 Dj24
Myrtle Point USA (OR) 20 Dh24
Myrtou CY 131 Mo55
Myrviken S 93 Lp28
Mys Alevina RUS 141 Sc07
Mys Aniva RUS 181 Sb22
Myšanka BY 117 Mf38
Mys Buor-Haja RUS 141 Rc04
Mys Elizavety RUS 141 Sa08
Mysen N 92 Lm31
Mys Gamova RUS 182 Rf24
Mysingen S 93 Lt32
Mys Južnyj RUS 141 Sd07
Mys Kamčatskij RUS 141 Ta07
Mys Kanin Nos RUS 140 Na05
Mys Kolgompja RUS 96 Mj31
Mys Kril'on RUS 181 Sb23
Mys Kroneckij RUS 141 Ta08
Mys Kurgalski RUS 96 Mj31
Myślenice PL 119 Lu41
Myślibórz PL 116 Lp38
Myslivka UA 119 Md42
Mys Lopatka RUS 141 Sd08
Mys Lovcova RUS 181 Sd23
Mys Navarin RUS 141 Td06
Mys Neupokoeva RUS 140 Pd03
Mys Oljutorskij RUS 141 Tc07
My Son VN 197 Qd38
Mysore IND (KTK) 193 Oj40
Mysore Palace IND 193 Oj40
Mysovka RUS 97 Mb35
Mys Ozernoj RUS 141 Ta07
Mys Rikorda RUS 181 Sd23
Mys Sjurkum RUS 181 Sa20
Mys Šmidta RUS 141 Ua05
Mys Tajgonos RUS 141 Sd06
Mys Terpenija RUS 181 Sc21
Mystery Caves USA 27 Fd24
Mystic Caverns USA 29 Fd27
Mys Tolstoj RUS 141 Sd07
Mys Želanija RUS 140 Pb03
Myszków PL 117 Lu40
Myszyniec PL 117 Mb37
My Tho VN 197 Qd40
Mytilini GR 129 Mg51
Mytišči RUS 132 Mj18
Mytna SK 119 Lu42
Mývatn IS 90 Kb13
M'Zab DZ 259 Lb29
Mže CZ 118 Ln41
Mzenga EAT 293 Mk49
Mziha EAT 293 Mj48
Mzimba MW 296 Mg51
Mzimkulu SA 303 Mf61
Mzimvuba SA 303 Me61
Mzuzu MW 296 Mh51

N

Naab D 115 Ln41
Naala TCH 273 Lh39
Naalehu USA (HI) 16 Cc36
Na'am SUD 283 Me41
Na'am SUD 283 Me43
Naama DZ 259 Kk29
Naantali = Nådendal FIN 96 Mc30
Naas IRL 100 Ko37
Nababeep SA 302 Lj60
Nabadeed SP 285 Nb41
Nabadwip IND (WBG) 194 Pe34
Nabalat SUD 276 Mf39
Nabar TCH 275 Ma36
Nabas RP 205 Rb40
Nabavatu FJI 247 Tk54
Nabburg D 115 Ln41
Naberera EAT 293 Mj48
Naberežny Čelny RUS (TAR) 133 Ng18
Nabesna River USA 15 Cj14
Nabeul TN 260 Lf27
Nabha IND (PJB) 189 Oj30
Nabiac AUS (NSW) 237 Sg62
Nabi Ayoub OM 151 Ng37
Nabiéliananyou BF 279 Kj40
Nabiganj BD 194 Pf33
Nabilatuk EAU 290 Mh44
Nabileque BR 73 Hb56
Nabire RI 213 Rh47
Nabk Anu Qasr KSA 146 Mk30
Nabogo GH 279 Kk41
Naboomspruit SA 299 Me58
Naboulgou RT 279 La40
Nabouwalu FJI 247 Tk54
Nabq ET 263 Mh31
Nabq Reserve ET 263 Mh31
Nabu MYA 195 Pj34
Nabua RP 203 Rb39
Nabulus IS 146 Mh29
Nabunturan RP 205 Rc42
Nabuvoll N 92 Lm28
Nabuyango Island EAT 290 Mg46
Nacala MOC 297 Na53
Nacala Velha MOC 297 Na53
Nacaroa MOC 297 Mk53
Nacavala MOC 297 Mk53
Nacebe BOL 67 Gg51
Nachacachi MEX (CHH) 38 Eg32
Nachindundo MOC 297 Na51
Nachingwea EAT 297 Mk51
Nachna IND (RJT) 188 Of32
Náchod CZ 118 Lr40
Na Chuak THA 197 Qb38
Nachuge IND (AAN) 193 Pg40
Nacimiento RCH 80 Gd64
Nacional'nyj Park Pričlbrus'e RUS 152 Nb24
Nackara AUS (SA) 236 Rk62
Naco MEX (SO) 23 Ef30
Naco USA (AZ) 23 Ef30
Nacogdoches USA (TX) 29 Fc30
Nacori Chico MEX (SO) 23 Ef31
Nacozari Viejo MEX (SO) 23 Ef30
Nacuñán RA (MD) 76 Gg63
Nad Al Sheba UAE 156 Nh33
Nadamu Dahui VRC 175 Qh24
Nadarzyce PL 116 Lr37
Nadawli GH 279 Kj40
Nadbużański Park Krajobrazowy PL 117 Mb38
Nådendal = Naantali FIN 96 Mc30
Nadežda UA 125 Mk44
Nadi FJI 247 Tj54
Nadi SUD 276 Mg37
Nadiad IND (GUJ) 190 Og34
Nādlac RO 124 Ma44
Nadmorski Park Krajobrazowy PL 116 Lt36
Nadoba RT 279 La40
Nador MA 259 Kj28
Nadria IND (MPH) 191 Pa33
Naduk RI 207 Qd47
Nadvirna UA 119 Me42
Nadym RUS 140 Oc05
Nadzab PNG 243 Sd49
Na'ebabad AFG 160 Od27
Naejangsan N.P. ROK 182 Rd28
Nærbø N 92 Lf32
Nærøyfjorden N 92 Lg30
Næstved DK 94 Lm35
Nafada WAN 273 Lf40
Nafadji SN 269 Ke39
Náfpaktos GR 128 Mb52
Náfplio GR 128 Mc53
Naft Khaneh IRQ 147 Nc28
Nafud ad Dahi KSA 149 Nc35
Nafud al Ghuwaytah KSA 146 Mk31
Nafud al Mazhur KSA 149 Nb32
Nafud al Urayq KSA 148 Nb33
Nafud as Sirr KSA 149 Nc33
Nafud ath Thuwayrat KSA 149 Nc32
Nag PK 162 Oc32
Naga DZ 258 Kg31
Naga GH 279 Kk40
Naga RP 203 Rb39
Naga RP 205 Rb40
Nagabulik RI 208 Qf47
Nagai Island USA 14 Bk18
Nagaj IND (MHT) 190 Oh37
Nagajbakovo RUS 133 Ng18
Naga-jima J 185 Rf29
Nagaland IND 187 Pc13
Nagamangala IND (KTK) 193 Oj40
Nagami Lake CDN 25 Fh21
Nagano J 183 Rk27
Nagaoka J 183 Rk27
Nagaon IND (ASM) 194 Pg32
Nagappattinam IND (TNU) 193 Ok41
Nagapur IND (MHT) 190 Oj36
Nagar IND (RJT) 189 Oj32
Nagara RMM 269 Ke38
Nagarhole IND (KTK) 192 Oj40
Nagarhole N.P. IND 193 Oh41
Nagari IND (TNU) 193 Ok40
Nagarjunakonda IND 191 Ok37
Nagarjunasagar IND 191 Ok37
Nagarjunasagar-Srisailam Sanctuary IND 191 Ok37
Nagar Karnul IND (APH) 190 Ok37
Nagarote NIC 42 Fg39
Nagar Parkar PK 163 Of33
Nagarze VRC (TIB) 171 Pf31
Nagasaki J 185 Re29
Nagasamudram IND (APH) 193 Oj39
Nagasari IND (GUJ) 190 Of35
Nagash Mosque ETH 277 Mk40
Nagato J 183 Rf28
Nagatsugawa J 183 Rj28
Nagaur IND (RJT) 188 Og32
Nagbhir IND (MHT) 191 Ok35
Nagbo GH 279 Kk41
Nagda IND (MPH) 191 Oh34
Nagda IND (MPH) 190 Oh34
Nageezi USA (NM) 23 Eg27
Nag el Ma'mariya ET 263 Mg33
Nagercoil IND (TNU) 193 Oj42
Naggen S 93 Lq28
Nag Hammâdi ET 263 Mg32
Nagina IND (UPH) 189 Ok31
Nagichot SUD 283 Mg43
Nagina IND (UPH) 189 Ok31
Nagłowice PL 117 Ma40
Nago J 185 Rd32
Nagod IND (MPH) 191 Pa33
Nagoda CL 193 Pa43
Nagomba EAT 297 Mk51
Nagor'e RUS 132 Mk17
Nagorno-Karabakh ARM 145 Nc26
Nagornyj RUS 141 Td06
Nagothana IND (MHT) 190 Og36
Nagoya J 183 Rj28
Nagpur IND (MHT) 191 Ok35
Nagqu VRC (TIB) 171 Pg30
Nagreg RI 210 Qd49
Nagu = Nauvo FIN 96 Mb30
Nagua DOM 46 Gf36
Nagum PNG 243 Sb49
Nagurunguru A.L. AUS 223 Re54
Nagyatád H 118 Ls44
Nagybajom H 118 Ls44
Nagyhalász H 119 Mb42
Nagyigmánd H 118 Lt43
Nagykanizsa H 118 Lr44
Nagykáta H 119 Lu43
Nagykőrös H 119 Lu43
Nagykunság H 119 Ma43
Nagylak H 119 Ma44
Nagyszénás H 119 Ma44
Naha J 185 Rd32
Nahačiv UA 117 Md40
Na Haeo THA 196 Qa37
Nahan IND (HPH) 189 Oj30
Na Hang VN 178 Qc34
Nahanni Butte CDN (NWT) 17 Dj15
Nahanni National Park CDN 17 Dh15
Nahanni Range CDN 17 Dj15
Nahariya IL 146 Mh29
Nahavand IR 154 Ne28
Nahavand IR 154 Ne28
Nahe D 114 Lh41
Naheleg ER 277 Na38
Nahlin CDN (BC) 17 Dd16
Nahlin Plateau CDN 17 Dd16
Nahodka RUS 183 Rg24
Nahoon Reef SA 303 Md62
Nahoon Reef SA 303 Md62
Nahoria IND (MPH) 191 Pb33
Nahoton EAT 297 Mj51
Nahr al Khabour SYR 147 Na27
Nahr al-Qash SUD 277 Mj39
Nahr al Uzaym IRQ 147 Nc28
Nahr az Zab al Kabir IRQ 147 Nb28
Nahr az Zab as Saghir IRQ 147 Nb27
Nahr Diyala IRQ 147 Nc28
Nahrin AFG 160 Oe27
Nahuelbuta, P.N. RCH 80 Gd64
Nahuel Huapi RA (RN) 80 Ge66
Nahuel Huapi, P.N. RA 80 Ge66
Nahuel Mapá RA (SL) 76 Gg63
Nahunta USA (GA) 35 Fk30
Nahuo VRC (GDG) 178 Qf35
Nai PNG 243 Se46
Naica MEX (CHH) 39 Eh32
Naicam CDN (SK) 19 Eh19
Naij Tal VRC (QHI) 171 Ph28
Naikliu RI 214 Rb50
Naikoon Prov. Park CDN 18 De19
Naila D 115 Lm40
Naiman Qi VRC (NMZ) 182 Ra24
Nain CDN 11 Gd07
Na'in IR 154 Ng29
Nainital IND (UTT) 189 Ok31
Nainpur IND (MPH) 191 Pa34
Naiopue MOC 297 Mj53
Naipé MOC 297 Mk53
Naiqu VRC (SCH) 176 Qa31
Nairai FJI 247 Tk54
Nairn GB 99 Kr33
Nairobi EAK 290 Mj46
Nairobi N.P. EAK 290 Mj46
Naissaar EST 96 Me31
Naitaba FJI 247 Ua54
Naivasha EAK 290 Mj46
Naivos RI 198 Pj44
Najac F 104 Lb46
Najaf Abad IR 154 Nd28
Najaf Abad IR 154 Nf29
Na'jan KSA 149 Nd33
Najba RUS 181 Sb22
Najbere RUS (CHE) 152 Nd24
Najd KSA 148 Na33
Nájera E 107 Ks52
Najibabad IND (UPH) 189 Ok31
Najitun VRC (NMZ) 180 Rb22
Najran KSA 150 Nc37
Naj Tunich GCA 41 Ff37
Nakachenje Z 296 Md53
Nakadori-jima J 185 Re29
Nakagawa J 181 Sb23
Nakagusuku Castle J 185 Rd32
Naka Kharai PK 162 Od33
Nakambe = Volta Blanche BF 271 Kk39
Nakambe GH 279 Kk39
Nakamura J 185 Rg29
Nakanai Mountains PNG 244 Sf48
Nakanno RUS 141 Qb06
Nakano-jima J 183 Rg27
Nakano-jima J 185 Re31
Nakapalle IND (APH) 191 Pb37
Nakapanya EAT 297 Mj51
Nakapiripirit EAU 290 Mh45
Nakartiaganj IND (BIH) 189 Pc32
Nakasato J 183 Sa25
Naka-Shibetsu J 181 Sc24
Nakasongola EAU 290 Mg45
Naka-Tane J 185 Rf30
Nakatsu J 185 Rf29
Nakawale EAT 297 Mh51
Nakchamik Island USA 14 Cb17
Naked Island USA 15 Cg15
Nakfa ER 277 Mk38
Nakfa Wildlife Reserve ER 277 Mk38
Nakhl OM 157 Nj34
Nakhl Shahbah KSA 148 Na35
Na Khoang VN 195 Qb35
Nakhola IND (ASM) 194 Pg32
Nakhon Nayok THA 196 Qa38
Nakhon Pathom THA 196 Qa39
Nakhon Phanom THA 197 Qc37
Nakhon Ratchasima THA 197 Qb38
Nakhon Sawan THA 196 Qa38
Nakhon Si Thammarat THA 198 Pk41
Nakhon Thai THA 196 Qa37
Nakhtarana IND (GUJ) 190 Oe34
Naki-Est RT 279 La40
Nakifuma EAU 290 Mg45
Nakiloro EAU 290 Mh44
Nakina CDN (ON) 25 Fg20
Nakitoma EAU 290 Mg45
Nakla EAT 293 Mk50
Na Klang THA 196 Qb37
Naklik PL 117 Mc40
Nakło nad Notecią PL 116 Ls37
Naknek USA (AK) 14 Cb16
Naknek Lake USA (AK) 14 Cc16
Nako IND 189 Ok30
Nakodar IND (PJB) 188 Oh30
Nakonde Z 292 Mg50
Nakop NAM 302 Lk60
Nakpanduri GH 279 Kk40
Nakpayili GH 279 La41
Nakrekal IND (APH) 191 Ok37
Nakskov DK 94 Lm36
Näkten S 93 Lp28
Nakuru EAK 290 Mj46
Nakusp CDN (BC) 18 Eb20
Naku-Tombetsu J 181 Sb23
Nakwehe EAK 284 Mh44
Nal PK 162 Od32
Nalatale Ruins ZW 300 Me55
Nalaykh MNG 172 Qd22
Nalázi MOC 300 Mg58
Na'lbandan IR 154 Nf28
Nalbant RO 125 Mj45
Nalbara AUS (WA) 228 Qj60
Nalbari IND (ASM) 194 Pf32
Nal'čik RUS (KBA) 152 Nb24
Naldurg IND (MHT) 190 Oj37
Nałęczów PL 117 Mc39
Naledi RB 299 Mc58
Nálepkovo SK 119 Ma42
Nalgonda IND (APH) 191 Ok37
Nalhati IND (WBG) 194 Pd33
Nalhiapur IND (UPH) 189 Pb32
Nali VRC (GZG) 178 Qe35
Nal Lake IND 190 Of34
Nallıhan TR 131 Mm50
Nalong MYA 195 Pj33
Nalusanga Z 296 Md53
Nalusuku Pool Z 295 Mb54
Nalut LAR 260 Lf30
Nalwangaa EAT 293 Mk50
Nalžovské Hory CZ 118 Lo41
Nama RI 212 Rf48
Namaacha MOC 300 Mg58
Namacunde ANG 294 Lh54
Namacurra MOC 297 Mj54
Namadgi N.P. AUS 237 Se63
Namakgale SA 300 Mf57
Namakia RM 304 Nc53
Namakkal IND (TNU) 193 Ok41
Namaklwe MYA 196 Pk36
Namakzar-e Shadad IR 157 Nj30

Namaland NAM 298 Lj59
Namalatu Beach RI 212 Re47
Namanga EAK 293 Mj47
Namangan UZB 159 Of25
Namanjavira MOC 297 Mj54
Namanyere EAT 292 Mf49
Namapa MOC 297 Mk52
Namaponda MOC 297 Mk53
Namaqualand SA 302 Lj61
Namaqua N.P. SA 302 Lj60
Namaro RN 271 La39
Namarrói MOC 297 Mj53
Namas RI 213 Sa48
Namasagali EAU 290 Mg45
Namasale EAU 290 Mg45
Namassi CI 279 Kj42
Namatanai PNG 244 Sg47
Namatele EAT 293 Mk50
Namatote RI 213 Rg47
Na Maw LAO 195 Qa35
Namazga Depe TM 155 Nk27
Namba ANG 294 Lh51
Nam Bai VN 195 Qb34
Nambala Z 296 Md53
Nambazo MW 297 Mh53
Nam Beng LAO 195 Qa35
Namber RI 213 Rh46
Nambi AUS (WA) 228 Ra60
Nambikwara, T.I. BR 68 Ha52
Nambinda EAT 293 Mj50
Nambol IND (MNP) 194 Pg33
Nambonkaha CI 279 Kh41
Nambour AUS (QLD) 235 Sg59
Nambuangongo ANG 288 Lh50
Nambucca Heads AUS (NSW) 235 Sg61
Nambung N.P. AUS 228 Qh61
Namche Bazar NEP 170 Pd32
Nam Chon Reservoir THA 196 Pk38
Namco VRC (TIB) 171 Pf30
Nam Co VRC 171 Pf30
Namdalen N 90 Lg13
Namdhapa N.P. IND 195 Pj32
Nam Dinh VN 178 Qd35
Nämdö S 93 Lt31
Nämdöfjärden S 93 Lt31
Namehumba EAT 293 Mk50
Na Meo LAO 178 Qc35
Nameri N.P. IND 194 Pg32
Náměšť nad Oslavou CZ 118 Lr41
Námestovo SK 119 Lu41
Nametil MOC 297 Mk53
Nam Et N.B.C.A. LAO 195 Qb35
Namew Lake CDN 24 Ej18
Namhae Do ROK 182 Rd28
Nam Ha N.B.C.A. LAO 195 Qa35
Namhan Gang DVRK 182 Rd27
Namhkan MYA 195 Pj34
Namhpakka MYA 195 Pj34
Namhsan MYA 195 Pj35
Namhta MYA 195 Ph33
Nami MAL 198 Qa42
Namialo MOC 297 Mk53
Namib Desert ANG 294 Lf54
Namib Desert NAM 298 Lg55
Namibe ANG 294 Lg53
Namibia 253 Lb12
Namibia Abyssal Plain 256 Lb24
Namib Naukluft Park NAM 298 Lh57
Namidobe MOC 297 Mj54
Namie J 183 Sa27
Namies SA 302 Lk60
Namina MOC 297 Mk53
Namioka J 183 Sa25
Namipit RP 203 Ra37
Namiquipa MEX (CHH) 23 Eg31
Namir MNG 167 Pf21
Namiroa MOC 297 Mk53
Namissiguima BF 271 Kj39
Namitete MW 296 Mg53
Namjagbarwa VRC 171 Ph31
Nam Kading N.B.C.A. LAO 197 Qc36
Nam Khao LAO 197 Qc36
Nam Khap Ban Tang VN 178 Qc34
Namlan MYA 195 Pj34
Namlea RI 212 Rd47
Namling VRC (TIB) 170 Pe31
Nam-mawng MYA 195 Pk35
Nam Nao N.P. THA 196 Qa37
Nam Ngum Reservoir LAO 197 Qc36
Nam Noen LAO 195 Qb35
Namoi River AUS 235 Se61
Namoluk Island FSM 240 Sc17
Namonuito Atoll FSM 240 Sb17
Namor BR (AM) 62 Gj49
Namorik Atoll MH 241 Tb17
Namoroka, P.N.de RM 306 Nc54
Namorona RM 306 Ne56
Nam Ou LAO 195 Qb35
Namounou BF 279 La40
Nampa USA (ID) 20 Eb24
Nampagan MYA 195 Ph33
Nampala RMM 270 Kh38
Nam Pat THA 196 Qa37
Nampawng MYA 195 Pj34
Nampevo MOC 297 Mj54
Nam Phoui N.B.C.A. LAO 196 Qa36
Nampingo EAT 293 Mj50
Nämpnäs FIN 93 Mb28
Nampo DVRK 182 Rc26
Nampuécha MOC 297 Na52
Nampula MOC 297 Mk53
Nam Pun THA 196 Qa36
Nampungu EAT 297 Mj51
Namrole RI 212 Rd47
Namru VRC (TIB) 170 Pa30
Namsê La NEP/VRC 170 Pb31
Namsham MYA 195 Pj34
Namsos N 90 Lf13
Namsskogan N 90 Lg13
Namtabung RI 215 Rf50
Nam Taung MYA 195 Pj35
Nam Tha LAO 195 Qa35
Nam Theun LAO 197 Qc37
Nam Theun N.B.C.A. LAO 197 Qc37
Nam Tok Chattrakan N.P. THA 196 Qa37
Nam Tok Mae Surin N.P. THA 196 Pk36
Namtu MYA 195 Pj34
Namu CDN (BC) 18 Dg20
Namu Atoll MH 241 Tb17
Namudi PNG 243 Se50
Namuka-i-lau FJI 247 Ua55
Namukumbo Z 296 Md53
Namuno MOC 297 Mk52
Nam Un Reservoir THA 197 Qb37
Namur B 103 Le40
Namuruputh EAK 283 Mh43
Namutoni NAM 298 Lj55
Namwala Z 296 Md53
Namwon ROK 182 Rd28
Nam Xeng LAO 195 Qb35
Namyit Island 204 Qh40
Namysłów PL 116 Ls39
Namyunn MYA 195 Pj32
Nan THA 196 Qa36
Nana CAM 281 Lh42
Nana RCA 281 Lh43
Nana Bakassa RCA 281 Lj42
Nana Bakassa RCA 281 Lj42
Nana Barya RCA 281 Lj42
Nana Candundo ANG 295 Mb51
Nanae J 181 Sa25
Nanaimo CDN (BC) 18 Dj21
Nanambinia AUS (WA) 229 Rb62
Nana Museum of the Arctic USA (AK) 15 Bj12
Nanango AUS (QLD) 235 Sg59
Nanania Plateau NAM 298 Lj58
Nanao J 183 Rj27
Nan'ao Dao VRC 179 Qj34
Nanaputa EAT 297 Mk51
Nanarup AUS (WA) 228 Qk63
Nanay PE 60 Gc47
Nanbai VRC (GZH) 178 Qd32
Nanbu VRC (SCH) 177 Qd30
Nancha VRC (HLG) 180 Re22
Nanchang VRC (JGX) 184 Qh31
Nanchan Si VRC 175 Qg26
Nancheng VRC (JGX) 184 Qj32
Nanchititla, P.N. MEX 40 Ek36
Nanchong VRC (SCH) 177 Qd30
Nanchuan VRC (CGQ) 177 Qd31
Nancowry Island IND 193 Pg42
Nancy F 103 Lg42
Nanda Devi IND 189 Pa30
Nanda Devi N.P. IND 189 Ok30
Nandaime NIC 42 Fg40
Nandaly AUS (VIC) 237 Sb63
Nandan VRC (GZG) 178 Qd33
Nandankanan Biological Park IND 191 Pc35
Nandavaram IND (APH) 193 Ok39
Nanded IND (MHT) 190 Oj36
Nandewar Range AUS 235 Sf61
Nandgaon IND (MHT) 191 Oj35
Nandgaon Kaji IND (MHT) 190 Oj35
Nandghat IND (CGH) 191 Pa35
Nandi ZW 300 Mf56
Nandian VRC (YUN) 195 Qb34
Nandi Hills IND 193 Oj40
Nandikotkur IND (APH) 190 Ok38
Nandom GH 279 Kj40
Nandowrie AUS (QLD) 235 Sd58
Nandura IND (MHT) 190 Oj35
Nandurbar IND (MHT) 190 Oh35
Nandyal IND (APH) 193 Ok39
Nanfeng VRC (JGX) 184 Qj32
Nanga AUS (WA) 224 Qg59
Nangade MOC 297 Mk51
Nanga Eboko CAM 281 Lg43
Nanga Ketunga RI 208 Qf45
Nangal IND (PJB) 189 Oj30
Nanga Mahap RI 208 Qf46
Nanga Mau RI 208 Qf46
Nangandu EAT 293 Mj49
Nanganga EAT 297 Mk51
Nanga Parbat PK 161 Oh28
Nanga Pinoh RI 208 Qf46
Nangaroro RI 211 Ra50
Nangaru EAT 293 Mk50
Nanga Sokan RI 208 Qf46
Nanga Suruk RI 208 Qg45
Nanga Tamin MAL 208 Qg44
Nanga Tayap RI 208 Qf46
Nangazê Co VRC 170 Pd30
Nanggun Bum MYA 195 Pk32
Nangin MYA 198 Pk40
Nangis F 103 Ld42
Nango J 185 Rf29
Nangola RMM 270 Kg39
Nangolet SUD 283 Mg43
Nangong VRC (HBI) 175 Qh27
Nangqên VRC (QHI) 171 Pj29
Nang Rong THA 197 Qb38
Nanguruwe EAT 297 Na51
Nangwarry AUS (SA) 236 Sa64
Nangwashi Z 295 Mb54
Nang Xian VRC (TIB) 171 Pg31
Nan Hua VRC 179 Qg33
Nanhua VRC (YUN) 195 Qa33
Nanhui VRC (SHG) 184 Ra30
Nanjangud IND (KTK) 193 Oj40
Nanjiang VRC (SCH) 177 Qd29
Nanjian Yizu Zizhixian VRC (YUN) 195 Qa33
Nanjiao VRC (YUN) 195 Qa34
Nanjing VRC (JGS) 184 Qk29
Nanjinji EAT 293 Mk50
Nankang VRC (JGX) 179 Qh33
Nanking VRC (JGS) 184 Qk29
Nankoku J 183 Rg29
Nankova ANG 295 Lk54
Nankunshan VRC 179 Qg34
Nanle VRC (HNN) 175 Qh27
Nan Ling VRC 178 Qg33
Nanling VRC (AHU) 184 Qk30
Nanlixa MOC 297 Mj52
Nanning VRC (GZG) 178 Qe34
Nannup AUS (WA) 228 Qh63
Nano DY 272 Lb41
Na Noi THA 196 Qa36
Nanoro BF 271 Kj39
Nanpara IND (UPH) 189 Pa32
Nanpeng Liedao VRC 179 Qj34
Nanping VRC (SCH) 176 Qc29
Nanping VRC (HUB) 177 Qg31
Nanping VRC (FJN) 184 Qk32
Nanpur IND (MPH) 190 Oh34
Nanri Dao VRC 179 Qk33
Nanripo MOC 297 Mk53
Nansebo ETH 284 Mk42
Nansei Islands J 185 Rc33
Nansen, Mount CDN 17 Db14
Nansen Sound CDN 11 Fc03
Nan Shan VRC 167 Pd24
Nanshan Island 204 Qh40
Nanshui Shuiku VRC 179 Qg33
Nansio EAT 292 Mg47
Nantamba PNG 244 Sf48
Nanterre F 103 Lc42
Nantes F 102 Kt43
Nanteuil-le-Haudouin F 103 Lc41
Nanti, Gunung RI 207 Qb48
Nantilla AUS (NSW) 234 Sb61
Nanton CDN (AB) 19 Ed20
Nanton GH 279 Kk41
Nantong VRC (JGS) 184 Ra29
Nantou RC 179 Ra34
Nantua F 105 Lf44
Nantucket USA (MA) 33 Ge25
Nantucket Island USA 33 Gf25
Nantucket Shoals USA 33 Ge25
Nantucket Sound USA 33 Gf25
Nantula MOC 297 Mk52
Nantuto MOC 297 Mj53
Nantwich GB 101 Ks37
Nanuku Passage FJI 247 Ua54
Nanumanga TUV 241 Td20
Nanumea Atoll TUV 241 Td20
Nanuque BR (MG) 75 Hk54
Nanusa RI 205 Rc44
Nanutarra AUS (WA) 224 Qh57
Nanvakfak Lake USA (AK) 14 Bk16
Nanwan Reservoir VRC 177 Qg29
Nanxi VRC (SCH) 176 Qc31
Nan Xian VRC (HUN) 177 Qg31
Nanxiao VRC (GZG) 178 Qe34
Nanxiong VRC (GDG) 179 Qh33
Nanxu VRC (GZG) 178 Qf33
Nanyamba EAT 297 Mk51
Nanyang VRC (HNN) 177 Qg29
Nanyangdan Shan VRC 184 Ra32
Nanyang Hu VRC 184 Qj28
Nan-yo J 183 Sa26
Nanyuki EAK 290 Mj46
Nanzamu VRC (LNG) 182 Rc25
Nanzhai VRC (GZH) 178 Qe32
Nanzhang VRC (HUB) 177 Qf30
Nanzhao VRC (HNN) 177 Qg29
Nanzheng VRC (SAA) 177 Qd29
Nanzhila Rest Camp Z 295 Mc54
Naogaon BD 194 Pe33
Naoli He VRC 180 Rg22
Naolinco MEX (VC) 40 Fb36
Não-me-Toque BR (RS) 78 Hd60
Naora PNG 244 Sf51
Náousa GR 129 Mf53
Naoussa GR 126 Mc50
Napa, Cerro BR/RCH 72 Gf56
Napa USA (CA) 20 Dj26
Napabale Lake RI 209 Rb48
Napadogan CDN (NB) 31 Gg22
Napaha MOC 297 Mk52
Napaiskak USA (AK) 14 Bk15
Na Pali Coast USA 16 Ca34
Napanwainam RI 213 Rh47
Napan-yaur RI 213 Rh47
Napata and Djebel Barkal Temples SUD 276 Mf37
Napeitom EAK 290 Mj45
Napido RI 213 Rh46
Napier NZ 238 Tj65
Napier SA 302 Lk63
Napier Downs AUS (WA) 222 Rc54
Napier Mountains 313 Nc32
Naples I 122 Lp50
Naples USA (FL) 36 Fk32
Napo PE 60 Gc46
Napo VRC (GZG) 178 Qc34
Napoleon AUS (QLD) 234 Sc59
Napoleon USA (ND) 26 Fa22
Napoleon USA (OH) 32 Fh25
Nápoli I 122 Lp50
Nappamerrie AUS (QLD) 234 Sa59
Nappanee USA (IN) 32 Fh25
Napperby AUS (NT) 226 Rg57
Napuka Atoll F 249 Ck53
Naqāda ET 263 Mg33
Naqb al-Hadjar YE 150 Nd38
Naqadeh IR 154 Nc27
Naqil al Farda YE 150 Nc38
Naqš-e-Šapur IR 156 Nh31
När S 95 Lt33
Nara J 183 Rh28
Nara RMM 270 Kg38
Narać BY 97 Mg36
Nara Canal PK 163 Oe32
Naracoorte AUS (SA) 236 Sa64
Naracoorte Caves Conservation Park AUS 236 Sa64
Naraďv UA 119 Me41
Naraha IND (BIH) 194 Pd32
Naraini IND (UPH) 191 Pa33
Narainpur IND (CGH) 191 Pa36
Naran PK 161 Og28
Narang AFG 161 Of28
Narangmor EAK 284 Mh43
Naranjal EC 60 Ga47
Naranjal PY 77 Hc58
Naranjito EC 60 Ga47
Naranjos BOL 73 Ha55
Naranjos MEX (VC) 40 Fb35
Narao J 185 Re29
Narasannapeta IND (APH) 191 Pc36
Narasapur IND (APH) 191 Pa37
Narasaraopet IND (APH) 191 Pa37
Narasimharajapura IND (KTK) 192 Oh40
Narasinghpur IND (ORS) 191 Pc35
Naratasty RUS 133 Ng18
Narathiwat THA 199 Qa42
Nara Visa USA (NM) 23 Ej28
Naravuka FJI 247 Tk54
Narayanganj BD 194 Pf34
Narayanganj IND (MPH) 191 Pa34
Narayangaon IND (MHT) 190 Og36
Narayanpet IND (APH) 190 Oj37
Narayan Sarovar IND 190 Oe34
Narberth GB 100 Kq39
Narbonne F 105 Ld47
Narborough = Isla Fernandina EC 60 Fe46
Narcondan Island IND 196 Ph39
Nardò I 123 Lt50
Nardoo AUS (NSW) 234 Sc60
Narečenski bani BG 127 Me49
Narellen AUS (NSW) 237 Sf63
Narembeen AUS (WA) 228 Qk62
Naréna RMM 270 Kf39
Nares Abyssal Plain 13 Gc14
Nares Strait 11 Gb03
Naretha AUS (WA) 229 Rc61
Narew PL 117 Mb38
Narew PL 117 Md38
Narewka PL 117 Md38
Nargund IND (KTK) 190 Oh38
Nari PK 162 Od31
Na Ri VN 178 Qd34
Narib NAM 298 Lj58
Narijn gol MNG 167 Pg20
Narimanov RUS 152 Nd22
Narin Gol VRC 169 Pf27
Narin Nur VRC (NMZ) 174 Qe26
Narita J 183 Sa28
Nar'jan-Mar RUS 140 Nc05
Narlı TR 144 Mj27
Narmada IND 186 Oc14
Narman TR 145 Na25
Narnaul IND (HYA) 188 Oj31
Narni I 122 Ln48
Narob NAM 298 Lj58
Narochanski N.P. BY 97 Mg36
Naro-Fominsk RUS 132 Mj18
Naro Island RP 205 Rb40
Narok EAK 290 Mh46
Naro Moru EAK 290 Mj46
Narooma AUS (NSW) 237 Sf64
Naro Sura EAK 290 Mh46
Narovlja BY 132 Me20
Narowal PK 161 Oh29
Närpes = Närpiö FIN 93 Mb28
Narphung BHT 194 Pf32
Närpiö = Närpes FIN 93 Mb28
Narra RP 204 Qk41
Narrabri AUS (NSW) 235 Se61
Narragansett Bay USA 33 Ge25
Narrandera AUS (NSW) 237 Sd63
Narran Lake AUS 235 Sd60
Narrawallee Beach AUS 237 Sf63
Narraway River CDN 18 Dk18
Narrogin AUS (WA) 228 Qj62
Narromine AUS (NSW) 237 Se62
Narrow C. USA 16 Cd17
Narrowsburg USA (NY) 33 Gc25
Narsampet IND (APH) 191 Ok37
Narsapur IND (APH) 190 Ok37
Narsarsuaq DK 11 Hc06
Narsi IND (MHT) 190 Oj36
Narsinghgarh IND (MPH) 190 Oj34
Narsinghpur IND (MPH) 191 Ok34
Narsipatnam IND (APH) 191 Pb37
Nart MNG 172 Qc21
Nart VRC (NMZ) 175 Qh24
Nartkala RUS (KBA) 152 Nb24
Naru-jima J 185 Re29
Naruja EC 60 Gb46
Naruto J 183 Rh28
Narva EST 96 Mj31
Narvacan RP 202 Ra37
Narva-Jõesuu EST 96 Mj31
Narva laht EST/RUS 96 Mh31
Närvijoki FIN 93 Mb28
Narvik N 90 Lj11
Narvskij zaliv EST/RUS 96 Mh31
Narvskoje vodohranilišče RUS 96 Mj31
Narwai IND (MPH) 189 Oj33
Narwana IND (HYA) 188 Oj31
Narwiańs P.N. PL 117 Mc37
Narwinbi Aboriginal Reserve AUS 223 Rj53
Naryilco AUS (QLD) 234 Sa60
Naryn KS 159 Oh25
Naryn KS 159 Oj25
Naryn KZ 166 Oh23
Naryn RUS (TUV) 167 Ph20
Narynkol KZ 159 Pa24
Naryškino RUS 132 Mh19
Nås S 93 Lp30
Năsăud RO 124 Me43
Nasavrky CZ 118 Lq41
Nasbinals F 105 Ld46
Nascentes do Rio Parnaíba, P.N.das BR 70 Hh51
Nash Harbor USA (AK) 14 Bg15
Nashiño EC 60 Gb46
Nashua USA (NH) 33 Ge24
Nashu Bum MYA 195 Pj33
Nashville USA (AR) 29 Fd29
Nashville USA (TN) 34 Fg27
Nashville USA (GA) 35 Fj30
Nashville USA (NC) 35 Ga28
Nashville Superspeedway USA (TN) 34 Fg27
Nashwaak Bridge CDN (NB) 31 Gg22
Nasia GH 279 Kk40
Nasia GH 279 Kk40
Nasibât Timâna ET 263 Mg34
Našice HR 121 Lt45
Nasielsk PL 117 Ma38
Näsijärvi FIN 96 Md29
Nasik IND (MHT) 190 Og36
Nasik RI 207 Qd47
Nasik Road IND (MHT) 190 Og36
Nasi, Mount ETH 284 Mh41
Nasionale Addo Olifantpark SA 303 Mc62
Nasionale Augrabieswatervalpark SA 302 Ma60
Nasionale Krugerwildtuin = Kruger N.P. SA 300 Mf57
Nasipit RP 205 Rc41
Nasir SUD 283 Mg41
Nasirabad IND (RJT) 188 Oh32
Nasirabad PK 162 Oe31
Nasiriyan IR 154 Nd29
Nasmah LAR 260 Lg30
Naso I 122 Lp52
Nasolot EAK 290 Mh45
Nasolot Nature Reserve EAK 290 Mh45
Nason SME 59 Hc43
Nasondoye RDC 295 Mc51
Naso Point RP 205 Ra40
Nasorolevu FJI 247 Tk54
Nasrapur IND (MHT) 190 Og36
Nasrullahganj IND (MPH) 190 Oj34
Nassarawa WAN 272 Ld41
Nassau BS 37 Gb33
Nassau D 112 Lh40
Nassau Island NZ 241 Uc21
Nass Basin CDN 17 Df17
Nassian CI 279 Kj41
Nassian CI 279 Kj41
Nässjö S 95 Lp33
Nassoukou DY 279 La40
Nassoumfou BF 271 Kk38
Nass River CDN 17 Df18
Nastola FIN 96 Mf30
Nasugbu RP 202 Ra38
Nasuragheria SOL 245 Tb51
Näsviken S 93 Lr29
Nata PA 43 Fk41
Nata RB 299 Md56
Nataja MW 297 Mh53
Natal BR (TO) 64 Hf48
Natal BR (RN) 65 Jc48
Natal RI 206 Pk45
Natal Downs AUS (QLD) 233 Sd56
Natal Felicidade, T.I. BR 62 Ha47
Natalinci SCG 126 Ma46
Natálio PY 77 Hc59
Natanz IR 154 Nf29
Nataraja Temple IND 193 Ok41
Nata Sanctuary RB 299 Md56
Natational Wool Museum AUS 237 Sc65
Natchez USA (LA) 29 Fe30
Natchez Trace Parkway USA 34 Fe29
Natchez Trace Parkway USA 34 Fg28
Natchez Trace Resort S.P. USA 34 Ff28
Natchitoches USA (LA) 29 Fd30
Natewa Bay FJI 247 Tk54
Nathahu MYA 196 Ph37
Nathan River AUS (NT) 223 Rh53
Na Thawi THA 198 Qa42
Nathdwara IND (RJT) 188 Og33
Nathenje MW 296 Mg53
Na Thon THA 198 Pk41
Nathorst Land N 91 Lh07
Nathrop USA (CO) 21 Eg26
Na-ti MYA 195 Pk34
Natiboani BF 279 La40
Natimuk AUS (VIC) 236 Sa64
Natinga = Garu GH 279 Kk40
National Chambal W.S. IND 188 Oj33
National Hall of Fame for Famous A. Ind. USA 28 Fa28
National Hist. District (Bentonsport) USA 32 Fe25
National Park NZ 238 Th65
National Radio Astronomy Observatory USA 33 Ga26
National Radio Astronomy Observatory VLA Telescope USA 23 Eg29
National Railroad Museum USA 35 Ga28
National West Coast Tourist Recreation Area NAM 298 Lg56
Nation River CDN 18 Dh18
Natitingou DY 279 La40
Natividade BR (TO) 70 Hg51
Natla River CDN 17 Df14
Nat ma toung N.P. MYA 194 Pg35
Natmauk MYA 195 Ph35
Natore BD 194 Pe33
Natrona USA (WY) 21 Eg24
Nattai N.P. AUS 237 Sf63
Nättarö S 93 Lt32
Nattaung MYA 196 Pj36
Nättraby S 95 Lq34
Natuco MOC 297 Mj52
Natukanaoka Pan NAM 294 Lh55
Natuna Besar RI 199 Qe43
Natuna Sea RI 199 Qd45
Natural Arch USA 35 Fh27
Natural Bridge USA (AL) 34 Fg28
Natural Bridge St. Mon. USA 21 Ee23
Naturaliste Channel AUS 224 Qg58
Naturaliste Plateau 221 Qc25
Naturita USA (CO) 21 Ef26
Naturno = Naturns I 120 Ll44
Naturns = Naturno I 120 Ll44
Naturpark Brownsberg SME 59 Hc43
Natuurreservaat Boven Coesewijne SME 59 Hc43
Natuurreservaat Brinckheuvel SME 59 Hc43
Natuurreservaat Centraal Suriname SME 59 Hb43
Natuurreservaat Copi SME 59 Hc43
Natuurreservaat Coppename Monding SME 59 Hc43
Natuurreservaat Galibi SME 59 Hc43
Natuurreservaat Hertenrits SME 59 Hb42
Natuurreservaat Peruvia SME 59 Hc43
Natuurreservaat Sipaliwini SME 59 Hb44
Natuurreservaat Wane Kreek SME 59 Hc43
Natuurreservaat Wia-Wia SME 59 Hc43
Nau TJ 158 Oe25
Nauabu PNG 244 Sf51
Nauari BR (PA) 63 Hc45
Naubise NEP 170 Pc32
Nauchas NAM 298 Lj57
Nauders A 114 Ll44
Nauela MOC 297 Mj53
Nauen D 113 Ln38
Naugachhia IND (BIH) 194 Pd33
Naujan RP 203 Ra39
Naujoji Akmenė LT 97 Mc34
Naukluft NAM 298 Lj58
Naukot PK 163 Oe33
Naulila ANG 294 Lh54
Naumatang RI 214 Rd49
Naumburg D 113 Lm39
Naumovskij RUS 135 Na22
Naungmo MYA 194 Ph33
Naung-Mon MYA 195 Pj32
Naupada IND (APH) 191 Pc36
Naupara IND (CGH) 191 Pb34
Nauroz Kalat PK 162 Oc31
Nauru NAU 241 Tb19
Nauru 219 Ta10
Naushahro Firoz PK 162 Oe32
Nausori FJI 247 Tk55
Naustdal N 92 Lf29
Nauta PE 61 Gd48
Nautanwa IND (UPH) 189 Pb32
Naute Recreation Area NAM 302 Lk59
Nautla MEX (VC) 40 Fb35
Nautsi RUS 91 Me11
Nauvo = Nagu FIN 96 Mb30
Nauvo FIN 96 Mb30
Nava E 106 Kp53
Navacëlki BY 132 Me19
Navacerrada E 109 Kr50
Navael'nja BY 97 Mf37
Navahermosa E 109 Kq49
Navahrudak BY 97 Mf37
Navahrudskae uzvyšša BY 97 Mf37
Navajo Ind. Res. USA 23 Ef27
Navajo Reservoir USA (NM) 23 Eg27
Naval RP 205 Rc40
Navalcarnero E 109 Kq50
Navalgund IND (KTK) 190 Oh38
Navalmanzano E 106 Kq51
Navalmoral de la Mata E 108 Kp49
Navalvillar de Pela E 108 Kp49
Navan IRL 100 Ko37
Navapolack BY 132 Me18
Navapur IND (MHT) 190 Og35
Navarcles E 110 Lb49
Navarra E 107 Kt52
Navarre USA (FL) 34 Fg30
Navarrenx F 104 Ku47
Navarrés E 109 Ku49
Navarro RA (BA) 77 Ha63
Navarro USA (CA) 20 Dj26
Navascués E 107 Kt52
Navas del Madroño E 108 Ko49
Navašëlki BY 117 Mg38
Navašino RUS 133 Nb18
Navasota USA (TX) 29 Fb30
Navassa Island C 45 Gc36
Navegantes BR (SC) 79 Hf59
Navegaon N.P. IND 191 Pa35
Nävekvarn S 93 Lr32
Navelgas E 106 Ko53
Navelândia BR (GO) 74 He55
Navia E 106 Ko53
Navio BR 71 Jb50
Navios MEX (DGO) 39 Eh34
Navirai BR (MS) 74 Hc57
Naviti FJI 247 Tj54
Navlakhi IND (GUJ) 190 Of34
Navlja RUS 132 Mh19
Năvodari RO 125 Mj46
Navoi UZB 158 Oc25
Navojoa MEX (SO) 38 Ef32
Navolato MEX (SL) 38 Eg33
Navoloki RUS 133 Na17
Navrongo GH 279 Kk40
Navsari IND (GUJ) 190 Og35
Navua FJI 247 Tk55
Nawa SYR 146 Mj29
Nawabganj BD 194 Pe33
Nawabshah PK 162 Oe32
Nawada IND (BIH) 191 Pc33
Nawagai PK 161 Of28
Nawah AFG 160 Od29
Na Wai THA 196 Pk36
Nawakshut RIM 269 Kb36
Nawani GH 279 Kk41
Nawapara BD 194 Pe34
Nawapara IND (ORS) 191 Pb35
Nawinda Kuta Z 295 Mc54
Nawng-awn MYA 195 Pk35
Nawnghkio MYA 195 Pj34
Nawngleng MYA 195 Pk34
Nawngpuawng MYA 194 Ph33
Na Wong THA 198 Pk42
Naxçivan AZ 145 Nd26
Naxçivan AZ 152 Nc26
Náxos GR 129 Mf53
Náxos GR 129 Mf53
Naxos I 122 Lq53
Nay F 104 Ku47
Naya Chor PK 163 Oe33
Nayagarh IND (ORS) 191 Pc35
Nayagram IND (WBG) 194 Pd34
Nayakanhatti IND (KTK) 193 Oj39
Nayarit MEX 39 Eh35
Nayau FJI 247 Ua54
Nayband IR 155 Nj29
Nayé SN 269 Kd38
Naylowr AFG 160 Od28
Nayoro J 181 Sb24
Nayouri BF 271 La39
Nayudupeta IND (APH) 193 Ok40
Nazaré BR (AP) 59 He44
Nazaré BR (PA) 64 Hf46
Nazaré BR (TO) 64 Hg49
Nazaré BR (BA) 71 Ja52
Nazaré P 108 Kl49
Nazareth BOL 68 Gh53
Nazareth CO 56 Gc43
Nazareth IS 146 Mh29
Nazareth Speedway USA (PA) 33 Gc25
Nazas MEX (DGO) 39 Eh33
Nazca PE 66 Gc53
Nazca Ridge 52 Fd23
Naze J 185 Re31
Nazerat IS 146 Mh29
Nazilli TR 130 Mj53
Nazko CDN (BC) 18 Dj19
Nazko River CDN 18 Dj19
Nazomba MOC 297 Mk51
Nazran' RUS (ING) 152 Nc24
Nazret ETH 284 Mk41
Nbâk RIM 269 Kc37
Nbeïket Dlim RIM 270 Kg37
Ncanaha SA 303 Mc62
Nchelenge Z 292 Me50
Ncue GQ 281 Lf44
Ndaba RWA 287 Me46
Ndaki RMM 271 Kk38
Ndala EAT 292 Mg48
N'Dalatando ANG 288 Lh50
Ndali DY 272 Lb41
Ndanda RCA 286 Mb43
Ndandu Z 295 Mb53
Ndangane SN 269 Kb38
Ndarapo Swamp EAK 291 Mk47
Ndarassa RCA 282 Mb42
Ndébougou RMM 270 Kh38
Ndeji WAN 272 Lc41
Ndékebalandji G 281 Lg46
Ndekesha RDC 289 Mb49
Ndélé RCA 282 Ma41
Ndélélé CAM 281 Lh43
Ndemba CAM 281 Lg43
Ndendé G 288 Lf47
Ndere EAK 290 Mh45
Ndere Island N.P. EAK 290 Mh46
N'dhala Gorge N.P. AUS 227 Rh57
Ndia SN 269 Kd38
Ndiago RIM 269 Kb37
Ndiguina CAM 273 Lh40
Ndigwa EAK 290 Mh46
Ndikiniméki CAM 281 Lf43
Ndikoko CAM 281 Lf43
Ndim RCA 281 Lh42
Ndindi G 288 Lf47
Ndindi SN 269 Kb38
Ndioum SN 269 Kc37
Ndioum Guènt SN 269 Kc38
Nditam CAM 281 Lf43
Ndiya WAN 280 Ld43
N'Djamena TCH 273 Lh39
Ndji RCA 282 Mb42
Ndjim CAM 281 Lf43
Ndjolé CAM 281 Lf43
Ndjolé G 281 Lf46
Ndjoundou RCB 286 Lj46
Ndjounou G 281 Lg46
Ndjwé CAM 281 Lh44
Ndoba Z 296 Me51
Ndofane SN 269 Kc39
Ndok CAM 281 Lh42
Ndokama CAM 280 Lf43
Ndokayo CAM 281 Lh43
Ndoki RCB 281 Lj45
Ndokouassikro CI 279 Kh42
Ndola Z 296 Me52
Ndole EAT 293 Mj49
Ndole Bay Z 292 Mf50
Ndolwane ZW 299 Md55
Ndom CAM 281 Lf43
Ndondo SOL 245 Ta50
Ndongolo G 281 Lf45
Ndop CAM 280 Lf43
Ndora Mountains WAN 281 Lf42
Ndorola BF 279 Kh40
Ndoto Mountains EAK 290 Mj45
Ndougou G 288 Le46
Ndoukou RCA 286 Ma43
Ndoumbou RCA 281 Lj42
Ndrog AL 126 Lu49
Ndu CAM 281 Lf42
Ndu RDC 286 Mb43
Nduli EAT 293 Mh49
Ndumo SA 303 Mg59
Ndumo Game Reserve SA 303 Mg59
Ndundu EAT 293 Mk50
Ndundu Rufiji EAT 293 Mk49
Nduye RDC 287 Me45
Nduzani COM 304 Nc52
Néa Aghíalos GR 128 Mc51
Néa Artáki GR 128 Md52
Néa Epidavros GR 128 Md53
Néa Fókea GR 126 Md50
Neah Bay USA (WA) 18 Dh21
Néa Ionía GR 128 Mc51
Néa Kalikrátia GR 126 Md50
Neale Junction AUS (WA) 229 Rc60
Neale Junction Nature Reserve AUS 229 Rc60
Neales River AUS 227 Rh59
Néa Mihanióna GR 126 Mc50
Néa Moni GR 129 Mg52
Néa Moudania GR 126 Md50
Neamț RO 125 Mg43
Néa Péramos GR 127 Me50
Neápoli GR 126 Mb50
Neápoli GR 128 Md54
Neápoli GR 129 Mf55
Nearchuss Passage MYA 196 Pj40
Neath GB 100 Kr39
Néa Triglia GR 126 Md50
Néa Zihni GR 127 Md49
Nebbou BF 279 Kk40
Nebe RI 214 Rb50
Nebelat el Hagana SUD 283 Me39
Nebelhorn D 114 Ll43
Nebiler TR 130 Mj51
Nebine River AUS 235 Sd60
Neblina, Cerro de la EC 60 Fk46
Nebo AUS (QLD) 233 Se56
Nebolči RUS 132 Mg16
Nebo, Mount JOR 146 Mh30
Nebraska USA 12 Ed10
Nebraska City USA (NE) 27 Fc25
Nébrodi I 122 Lp53
Necaise USA (MS) 29 Ff30
Nece F 246 Td56
Necedah USA (WI) 27 Fe24
Nechako River CDN 18 Dh19
Nechi CO 56 Gc41
Nechí CO 56 Gc42
Nechisar N.P. ETH 284 Mj43
Neckar D 114 Lj42
Neckargemünd D 114 Lj41
Neckarsulm D 114 Lk41
Necochea RA (BA) 81 Ha65
Necoclé CO 56 Gb41
Nécropoles de Bourzanga BF 271 Kk39
Necropoli Anghelu Rúiu I 111 Lj50
Necropoli di Sulcis I 111 Lj51
Necropoli etrusca Cervéteri I 122 Ln49
Necropoli etrusca Tarquinia I 122 Lm48
Necropoli Sant'Andria Priu I 111 Lj50
Necropolis Deffufa SUD 276 Mf37
Necungas MOC 296 Mh54
Nédéley TCH 274 Lk38
Nedelišće HR 121 Lr44
Nederweert NL 112 Lf39
Nedong VRC 171 Pf31
Nedryhajliv UA 132 Mg20
Nedstrand N 92 Lf31
Nedumangad IND (KER) 192 Oj42
Needles CDN (BC) 18 Ea21
Needles USA (CA) 22 Ec28
Neepawa CDN (MB) 24 Fa20
Nefasit ER 277 Mk39
Nefas Mewch'a ETH 284 Mk40
Nefta TN 260 Ld29
Neftejugansk RUS 140 Oc06
Neftekumsk RUS 152 Nc23
Nefza TN 260 Le27
Negage ANG 288 Lh49
Négala RMM 270 Kf39
Nega Nega Z 296 Me53
Néganzi DY 272 Lb40
Negar IR 157 Nj31
Negara RI 208 Qh47
Negara RI 211 Qh50
Negaunee USA (MI) 32 Fg22
Negele ETH 284 Mk43
Negerilama RI 198 Qa44
Negev Desert IS 146 Mh30
Negginan CDN (MB) 24 Fb19
Neghele ETH 284 Mk42
Negola ANG 294 Lh53
Negomano MOC 297 Mk51
Negombo CL 193 Ok43
Negombo Beach CL 193 Ok43
Negotin SCG 126 Mc46
Negotino MK 126 Mc49
Negrași RO 125 Mf46
Nègrepelisse F 104 Lb46
Negrești RO 125 Mh44
Negrești-Oaș RO 124 Md43
Negrete RCH 80 Gd64
Negribreen N 91 Lk06
Negril JA 45 Ga36
Negril Beach JA 45 Ga36
Negril Point JA 45 Ga36
Negrine DZ 260 Ld28
Negro, Cerro RA 80 Ge65
Negro, Cerro RA 80 Gf68
Negros RP 205 Rb41
Negru Vodă RO 125 Mj47
Neguac CDN (NB) 31 Gh22
Nehaevski RUS 133 Na20
Nehaj HR 121 Lp46
Nehalem USA 18 Dj23
Nehalem USA (OR) 20 Dj23
Neharelae BY 97 Mh37
Nehbandan IR 155 Oa30
Nehe VRC (HLG) 180 Rc21
Nehone ANG 294 Lj54
Neiafu TO 248 Bd55
Neiba DOM 46 Ge36
Neifaru MV 192 Og43
Neihart USA (MT) 21 Ee22
Neijiang VRC (SCH) 176 Qc31
Neil Armstrong Air & Space Mus. USA 32 Fh25
Neilburg CDN (SK) 19 Ef19
Neilersdrif SA 302 Ma60
Neill Island IND 193 Pg40
Neillsville USA (WI) 27 Fe23
Neilton USA (WA) 18 Dj22
Nei Mongol Gaoyuan VRC 174 Qa25
Neina NAM 298 Lj55
Neinsberg NAM 298 Lj56
Neišapur IR 155 Nk27
Neiva CO 60 Gc44
Neixiang VRC (HNN) 177 Qf29
Neja RUS 133 Nb16
Neja RUS 133 Nb16
Nejdek CZ 118 Ln40
Neji MEX (BC) 22 Eb29
Nejime J 185 Rf30
Nejo ETH 283 Mh41
Nejsvetejsi Trojice CZ 118 Ls41
Neka IR 154 Ng27
Nekemte ETH 284 Mj41
Nekla PL 116 Ls38
Nekmard BD 194 Pe33
Nekob MA 258 Kh30
Nekrasovskoe RUS 133 Na17
Nekró Manteíon GR 128 Ma51
Nelamangala IND (KTK) 193 Oj40
Nelaug N 92 Lj32
Nelia AUS (QLD) 232 Sb56
Nelidovo RUS 132 Mg17
Neligh USA (NE) 26 Fa24
Neligh Mill S.H.S USA 26 Fa24
Nellie, Mount AUS 222 Rc54
Nelligere IND (KTK) 193 Oj40
Nellore IND (APH) 193 Ok39
Nel'ma RUS 181 Rk22
Nelson CDN (BC) 18 Eb21
Nelson GB 101 Ks37
Nelson NZ 239 Tg66
Nelson RA (SF) 77 Gk61
Nelson Bay AUS (NSW) 237 Sg62
Nelson Forks CDN (BC) 17 Dh16
Nelson House CDN (MB) 24 Fa18
Nelson Island USA 14 Bh15
Nelson Lakes N.P. NZ 239 Tg67
Nelson River CDN 24 Fc17
Nelspoort SA 302 Mb62
Nelspruit SA 300 Mf58
Néma RIM 270 Kg37
Nemaiah Valley CDN (BC) 18 Dj20
Nëman BY 97 Md37
Neman RUS 97 Mc35
Nemanva ZW 300 Mf56
Nembrala RI 214 Rb51
Nemenčinė LT 97 Mf36
Nemours F 103 Lc42
Nemrut Dağı TR 145 Mk26
Nemrut Dağı Milli Parkı TR 145 Mk27
Nemšová SK 118 Lt42
Nemunas 97 Mc35
Nemunelis LV/LT 97 Me34
Nemuro J 181 Sc24
Nemuro-hanto J 181 Sc24
Nemuro-kaikyo J/RUS 181 Sc24
Nemyriv UA 117 Md40
Nemyriv UA 134 Me21
Nenagh IRL 100 Km38
Nenana USA (AK) 15 Cf13
Nenana River USA 15 Cf13
Nendo SOL 241 Tb21
Nene GB 101 La38
Nenets Autonomous District RUS 140 Nd05
Nenggiri MAL 199 Qa43
Nengo ANG 295 Ma53
Nengone Village F 246 Td56
Nenitoúria GR 129 Mf52
Nen Jiang VRC 180 Rc20
Nenjiang VRC (HLG) 180 Rc21
Neno MW 297 Mh53
Nenoksa RUS 91 Mk13
Neo J 183 Rj28
Néo Erásmio GR 127 Me50
Neohóri GR 126 Mb51
Neola USA (UT) 21 Ee25
Néo Monastíri GR 128 Mc51
Néo Petritsi GR 126 Md49
Neopolis BR (SE) 71 Jb51
Neosho USA (MO) 29 Fc27
Néos Marmarás GR 127 Md50
Néos Skopós GR 126 Md49
Nepal NEP 186 Pa13
Nepalganj NEP 170 Pa31
Nepara NAM 294 Lk54
Nepean CDN (ON) 33 Gc23
Nepeña PE 66 Ga50
Nephi USA (UT) 21 Ee26
Nephin IRL 98 Kl37
Nephin Beg Range IRL 98 Kl36
Nepisiguit Bay CDN 31 Gh22
Nepisiguit River CDN 31 Gg22
Nepoko RDC 287 Md44
Nepolje SCG 126 Ma48
Nepomuk CZ 118 Lo41
Neptun RO 125 Mj47
Neptune Beach USA (FL) 35 Fk30
Neptune Islands AUS 236 Rj63
Nera I 122 Ln48
Nera RO 124 Mb46
Nérac F 104 La46
Nerang AUS (QLD) 235 Sg59
Neratovice CZ 118 Lp40
Neravailu IND (APH) 193 Ok40
Nerča RUS 173 Qj19
Nerčinsk RUS 173 Qj20
Nerčugan RUS 173 Qj19
Nerehta RUS 133 Na17
Nereju RO 125 Mg45
Neresheim D 114 Ll42
Nereta LV 97 Mf34
Neretva BIH 121 Ls47

Neringa-Juodkrantė LT 97 Mb35
Neringa-Nida LT 97 Ma35
Neriquinha ANG 295 Ma53
Neris LT 97 Me36
Nerja E 108 Kr46
Nerjungri RUS 141 Ra07
Nerka Lake USA (AK) 14 Ca16
Nerl' RUS 132 Mj17
Nérondes F 103 Lc44
Nerópolis BR (GO) 74 Hf54
Nerpič'e RUS 181 Sc21
Nerpio E 109 Ks48
Nerren Nerren AUS (WA) 224 Qh59
Nerrima AUS (WA) 222 Rc55
Nerušaj UA 125 Mk45
Nerva E 108 Ko47
Nerva RUS 96 Mh30
Nervi I 120 Lk46
Nes N 92 Lh29
Nes N 92 Lk30
Nesbyen N 92 Lk30
Nesebăr BG 127 Mh48
Nesflaten N 92 Lg31
Nesgo PNG 244 Sf47
Nesheim N 92 Lg30
Neskaupstaður IS 90 Kd13
Neslandsvatn N 92 Lk32
Nesle F 103 Lc41
Nesna N 90 Lg12
Nesodden N 92 Ll31
Ness City USA (KS) 26 Fa26
Nessona MOC 300 Mh55
Nestáni GR 128 Mc53
Nestavoll N 92 Lk28
Nesterov RUS 97 Mc36
Nesterovo RUS (BUR) 172 Qd19
Nestiary RUS 133 Nc17
Néstos GR 127 Me49
Néstos Délta GR 127 Me50
Nesttun N 92 Lf30
Nesvik N 92 Lg31
Netaar RI 213 Sa47
Netanya IL 146 Mh29
Netarhat IND (JKD) 191 Pc34
Nétéboulou SN 269 Kd39
Neterguent RIM 269 Kd36
Nethang-Temple VRC 171 Pf31
Netherlands NL 112 Ld38
Netherlands Antilles NL 46 Gf39
Netia MOC 297 Mk53
Netivot IL 146 Mh30
Neto I 123 Lr51
Netrakona BD 194 Pf33
Nettetal D 112 Lg39
Nettilling Lake CDN 10 Gb05
Nettuno I 122 Ln49
Neubrandenburg D 113 Lo37
Neubukow D 113 Lm36
Neuburg an der Donau D 115 Lm42
Neuchâtel CH 114 Lg44
Neuenhagen D 113 Lo38
Neuenhaus D 112 Lg38
Neuenkirchen D 112 Lk37
Neuf-Brisach F 103 Lh42
Neufchâteau B 103 Lf41
Neufchâteau F 103 Lf42
Neufchâtel-en-Bray F 103 Lb41
Neufchâtel-sur-Aisne F 103 Le41
Neufundland und Labrador CDN 11 Ha07
Neuhaus (Amt Neuhaus) D 113 Ll37
Neuhaus am Rennweg D 113 Lm40
Neuhof D 114 Lk40
Neuillé-Pont-Pierre F 102 La43
Neukirchen A 115 Ln43
Neukirchen D 112 Lk40
Neulengbach A 115 Lq42
Neum BIH 121 Ls48
Neumarkt A 115 Lo43
Neumarkt A 115 Lp43
Neumarkt in der Oberpfalz D 115 Lm41
Neumarkt-Sankt Veit D 115 Ln42
Neumünster D 113 Lk36
Neunburg D 115 Ln41
Neung-sur-Beuvron F 102 Lb43
Neunkirchen A 115 Lr43
Neunkirchen D 114 Lh41
Neuquén RA 55 Gb26
Neuquén RA 80 Gf64
Neuquén RA (NE) 80 Gf65
Neuruppin D 113 Ln38
Neusiedl A 115 Lr43
Neusiedler See A 115 Lr43
Neusiedler See-Seewinkel, N.P. A 115 Lr43
Neuss D 112 Lg39
Neustadt bei Coburg D 115 Lm40
Neustadt (Aisch) D 115 Ll41
Neustadt am Rübenberge D 112 Lk38
Neustadt (Donau) D 115 Lm42
Neustadt/Dosse D 113 Ln38
Neustadt-Glewe D 113 Lm37
Neustadt (Holstein) D 113 Ll36
Neustadt (Orla) D 113 Lm40
Neustadt (Weinstraße) D 114 Lj41
Neustift A 115 Lm43
Neustrelitz D 113 Lo37
Neutral Junction AUS (NT) 226 Rg56
Neutraubling D 115 Ln42
Neu-Ulm D 114 Ll42
Neuvic F 104 Lc45
Neuville-aux-Bois F 103 Lc42
Neuville-de-Poitou F 102 La44
Neuville-sur-Saône F 105 Le45
Neuvy-sur-Barangeon F 103 Lc43
Neuwerk D 112 Lj37
Neuwied D 112 Lh40
Nevada USA 12 Ea11
Nevada USA (MO) 29 Fc27
Nevada City USA (CA) 20 Dk26
Nevado, Cerro el RA 76 Gf63
Nevado, Cerro RCH 80 Gd67
Nevado Ancohuma BOL 67 Gf53
Nevado Chorolque BOL 72 Gh56
Nevado Coropuna PE 67 Gd53
Nevado de Acay RA 72 Gg58
Nevado de Cachi RA 72 Gg58
Nevado de Chañi RA 72 Gh58
Nevado de Colima, P.N. MEX 40 Ej36
Nevado de Incahuasi RA/RCH 76 Gf59
Nevado del Candado RA 76 Gg59
Nevado del Huila CO 60 Gc44
Nevado del Huila, P.N. CO 60 Gc44
Nevado del Illimani BOL 72 Gg54
Nevado de Longaví RCH 80 Ge64
Nevado de Poquis RA/RCH 72 Gg57
Nevado de Ruiz CO 56 Gc43
Nevado de Tolima CO 56 Gc43
Nevado Huayna Potosi BOL 67 Gf54
Nevado Ojos del Salado RCH/RA 76 Gf59
Nevado Queva RA 72 Gg58
Nevado Sajama BOL 72 Gf55
Nevado Salcantay PE 67 Gd52
Nevado Tres Cruces RA/RCH 76 Gf59
Nevado Tres Cruces, P.N. RCH 76 Gf59
Nevaišiu LT 97 Mg35
Nevasa IND (MHT) 190 Oh36
Neveklov CZ 118 Lp41
Nevel' RUS 132 Me17
Nevel'sk RUS 181 Sa22
Nevers F 103 Ld44
Nevertire AUS (NSW) 235 Sd61
Neves BR 64 Hh49
Nevesinje BIH 121 Lt47
Nevestino BG 126 Mc48
Nevėžis LT 97 Me35
Neville CDN (SK) 19 Eg21
Nevinnomyssk RUS 135 Na23
Nevlunghavn N 92 Lk32
Nevşehir TR 131 Mp52
Nevskoe RUS 97 Mc36
New Adubiase GH 279 Kk42
New Aiyansh CDN (BC) 17 Df18
Newala EAT 297 Mk51
New Albany USA (MS) 29 Ff28
New Albany USA (IN) 34 Fh26
New Alton Downs AUS (SA) 227 Rk59
New Amsterdam GUY 59 Hb42
Newark USA (OH) 32 Fj25
Newark USA (NJ) 33 Gc25
Newark USA (DE) 33 Gc26
Newark-on-Trent GB 101 Ku37
New Bataan RP 205 Rd42
New Bedford USA (MA) 33 Ge25
Newberg USA (OR) 20 Dj23
New Bern USA (NC) 35 Gb28
Newberry USA (SC) 35 Fk28
Newberry Nat. Vol. Mon. USA 20 Dk24
New Bight BS 37 Gc33
New Boston USA (TX) 29 Fc29
New Braunfels USA (TX) 28 Fa31
Newbridge IRL 100 Ko37
New Britain PNG 240 Sb20
New Britain USA (CT) 33 Gd25
New Britain Trench PNG 240 Sc20
Newbrook CDN (AB) 19 Ed18
New Brunswick CDN 11 Gc09
New Brunswick USA (NJ) 33 Gc25
Newburgh USA (NY) 33 Gc25
Newbury GB 101 Kt39
Newburyport USA (MA) 33 Ge24
New Bussa WAN 272 Lc41
New Caledonia F 219 Ta12
New Caledonia 221 Ta23
New Caledonia Basin 218 Ta12
Newcastle AUS (NSW) 237 Sf62
Newcastle CDN (NB) 31 Gh22
Newcastle GB 98 Kt36
Newcastle SA 303 Me59
Newcastle USA (WY) 21 Eh24
New Castle USA (IN) 32 Fh26
New Castle USA (PA) 33 Fk25
New Castle USA (VA) 35 Fk27
Newcastle Bay AUS 230 Sb51
Newcastle Range AUS 232 Sb55
Newcastle-under-Lyme GB 101 Ks38
Newcastle upon Tyne GB 99 Kt36
Newcastle Waters AUS (NT) 223 Rg54
Newcastle West IRL 100 Kl38
New Corella RP 205 Rc42
Newdale CDN (MB) 24 Ek20
New Debiso GH 279 Kj42
Newdegate AUS (WA) 228 Qk62
New Delhi IND (DEL) 189 Oh31
New Denver CDN (BC) 18 Eb21
New Dixie AUS (QLD) 230 Sb53
Newell USA (SD) 26 Ej23
Newell Highway AUS 235 Se61
Newellton USA (LA) 29 Fe29
New England USA (ND) 26 Ej22
New England N.P. AUS 235 Sg61
New England Seamounts 13 Gd11
Newe Zohar IL 146 Mh30
Newfolden USA (MN) 24 Fb21
New Forest AUS (WA) 224 Qh59
Newfound Gap USA 35 Fj28
Newfoundland CDN 11 Ha09
Newfoundland Basin 314 Hb05
Newfoundland Evaporation Basin USA 21 Ed25
New Georgia SOL 245 Sj50
New Georgia Group SOL 244 Sj50
New Georgia Sound SOL 244 Sj49
New Germany CDN (NS) 31 Gh23
New Glasgow CDN (NS) 31 Gj23
New Guinea RI/PNG 242 Rj47
New Guinea Trench 218 Rb09
Newhalem USA (WA) 18 Dk21
Newhalen USA (AK) 15 Cc16
New Halfa SUD 276 Mh39
New Hamilton USA (AK) 15 Bj14
New Hampshire USA 33 Ge24
New Hampton USA (IA) 27 Fd24
New Hanover PNG 243 Se47
New Hanover SA 303 Mf60
Newhaven GB 101 La40
New Haven USA (CT) 33 Gd25
New Hazleton CDN (BC) 17 Dg18
New Hebrides 221 Tb22
New Hebrides Basin 221 Ta22
New Hebrides Trench 218 Ta11
New Iberia USA (LA) 29 Fe31
New Ireland PNG 240 Sc19
New Jersey USA 33 Gc25
New Kalala Z 295 Mc53
New Kapedmai LB 278 Kf41
Newkirk USA (NM) 23 Eh28
New Knockhock USA (AK) 14 Bh14
New Lanark GB 99 Kr35
New Leipzig USA (ND) 26 Ek22
New Lexington USA (OH) 32 Fj26
New Liskeard CDN (ON) 33 Ga22
New London USA (CT) 33 Gd25
New Longoro GH 279 Kj41
New Madrid USA (MO) 29 Ff27
Newman AUS (WA) 224 Qk57
Newmarket GB 101 La38
New Martinsville USA (WV) 33 Fk26
New Meadows USA (ID) 20 Eb23
New Mexico USA 12 Ec12
New Mirpur 161 Og29
Newnan USA (GA) 35 Fh29
New Norcia AUS (WA) 228 Qj61
New Norfolk AUS (TAS) 236 Sd67
New Orleans USA (LA) 29 Fe31
New Orleans USA (LA) 29 Fe31
New Paltz USA (NY) 33 Gc25
New Philadelphia USA (OH) 33 Fk25
New Pine Creek USA (OR) 20 Dk24
New Plymouth NZ 238 Th65
New Plymouth USA (ID) 20 Eb24
Newport CDN (NS) 31 Gh23
Newport GB 101 Ks38
Newport GB 101 Ks39
Newport GB 101 Kt40
Newport USA (WA) 18 Eb21
Newport USA (OR) 20 Dh23
Newport USA (AR) 29 Fe28
Newport USA (VT) 33 Gd23
Newport USA (NH) 33 Gd24
Newport USA (RI) 33 Ge25
Newport USA (MA) 33 Gf23
Newport USA (TN) 35 Fj28
Newport News USA (VA) 35 Gb27
Newport Pagnell GB 101 Ku38
New Port Richey USA (FL) 36 Fj31
New Providence Island BS 37 Gb33
Newquay GB 100 Kp40
New Richmond CDN (QC) 31 Gh21
New Richmond USA (WI) 27 Fd23
New Ringold USA (OK) 29 Fc28
New River Gorge Natl. River USA 35 Fk27
New Roads USA (LA) 29 Fe30
New Rochelle USA (NY) 33 Gd25
New Rockford USA (ND) 26 Fa22
New Romney GB 101 La40
New Ross IRL 100 Ko38
Newry AUS (NT) 222 Re54
Newry GB 98 Ko36
Newry USA (ME) 33 Ge23
New Schwabenland 313 Lb33
New Siberian Islands RUS 141 Sa03
New Smyrna Beach USA (FL) 36 Fk31
New South Wales AUS 220 Sa25
Newstead AUS (VIC) 237 Sc64
New Stuyahok USA (AK) 14 Cb16
Newton USA (IA) 27 Fd25
Newton USA (KS) 28 Fb26
Newton USA (TX) 29 Fd30
Newton USA (MS) 29 Ff29
Newton USA (NJ) 33 Gc25
Newton Abbot GB 100 Kr40
Newton Hills CDN (NS) 31 Gj23
Newtonmore GB 99 Kq33
Newton Peak NZ 239 Tf67
Newton Stewart GB 99 Kq36
Newtontoppen N 91 Lj06
Newtown GB 101 Kr38
New Town USA (ND) 26 Ej22
Newtownabbey GB 98 Kp36
Newtownards GB 98 Kp36
Newtown Saint Boswells GB 99 Ks35
Newtownstewart GB 98 Kn36
New Ulm USA (MN) 27 Fc23
New Waterford CDN (NS) 31 Gk22
New Westminster CDN (BC) 18 Dj21
New York USA 13 Ga10
New York USA (NY) 33 Gd25
New Zealand 219 Ta14
Nexø DK 95 Lq35
Neyestanek IR 154 Ng29
Neyriz IR 156 Nh31
Neyveli IND (TNU) 193 Ok41
Neyzar IR 154 Nf28
Nezam Abad IR 154 Nf29
Nezam-ol-Molk BakraviTomb IR 155 Nk27
Nez de Jobourg F 102 Kt41
Nez Perce Ind. Res. USA 20 Eb22
Ngaanyatjarra Land Council A.L. AUS 225 Rd57
Ngabang RI 208 Qe45
Ngabé RCB 288 Lj47
N'gabu MW 297 Mh54
Ngabwe Z 296 Md52
Ngadda WAN 273 Lg39
Ngadza RCA 286 Ma43
Ngai Giao VN 197 Qd40
Ngajira EAT 293 Mh49
Ngala WAN 273 Lh39
Ngalau Indah Caves RI 206 Qa46
Ngali RDC 289 Lk47
Ngali RI 211 Ra50
Ngaliwurru/Nungali A.L. AUS 223 Rf53
Ngalo RDC 286 Mb43
Ngalurrtja A.L. AUS 226 Rf57
Ngam CAM 281 Lh42
Ngam TCH 273 Lj40
Ngama TCH 273 Lj40
Ngamakwe SA 303 Md62
Ngamba EAT 292 Mg50
Ngambé CAM 281 Lf43
Ngambé Tikar CAM 281 Lf43
Ngamdu WAN 273 Lg40
Ngamo ZW 299 Md55
Ngamring VRC (TIB) 170 Pd31
Nganda MW 296 Mg51
Nganda SN 269 Kc39
Ngandane CI 279 Kh40
Ngangala SUD 287 Mf43
Ngangerabeli Plains EAK 291 Na46
Ngangganawili AUS (WA) 224 Ra59
Ngangla Rinco VRC 170 Pb30
Nganglong Kangri VRC 170 Pa29
Nganji RDC 292 Md47
Nganjuk RI 210 Qf49
Ngan So'n VN 178 Qd34
Nganzi ANG 288 Lg48
Ngao THA 196 Pk36
Ngaoundal CAM 281 Lg42
Ngaoundéré CAM 281 Lg42
Ngapa MOC 297 Mk51
Ngapali MYA 196 Ph36
Ngara EAT 292 Mf47
Ngarangou TCH 273 Lh39
Ngarimbi EAT 293 Mk50
Ngarkat Conservation Park AUS 236 Sa63
Ngasamo EAT 293 Mg47
Ngasao Plain EAK 284 Mk44
Ngassao Noum CAM 281 Lh42
Ngathainggyaung MYA 196 Ph37
Ngatik Atoll FSM 240 Sd17
Ngato CAM 281 Lh44
Ngawi RI 210 Qf49
Ngawihi NZ 238 Th66
Ngaywa EAT 292 Mg48
Ngbala RCB 281 Lh44
N'Gelewa RDC 286 Mb46
Ngerengere EAT 293 Mk49
Nggatokae SOL 245 Sk50
Nggela Pile SOL 245 Ta50
Nggela Sule SOL 245 Ta50
Nghia Dan VN 197 Qc36
Nghia Hung VN 178 Qd35
Nghi Har VN 197 Qc36
Ngiapanda EAT 293 Mk49
Ngidinga RDC 288 Lh48
Nginyang EAK 290 Mh45
Ngo RCB 288 Lh47
Ngoasé CAM 281 Lg44
Ngoc Co Rinh VN 197 Qe38
Ngoc Hien VN 199 Qc41
Ngoc Linh VN 197 Qd38
Ngog Mapubi CAM 281 Lf44
Ngoïla CAM 281 Lh44
Ngoko RCB 281 Lh46
Ngola CAM 281 Lh44
Ngol Kedju WAN 280 Le42
Ngolo RDC 286 Lk45
Ngolo Z 292 Mf50
Ngoma EAT 287 Mf45
Ngoma NAM 295 Mc54
Ngoma Z 295 Mc53
Ngoma Bridge RB 295 Mc54
Ngoma Tsé-Tsé RCB 288 Lh48
Ngombé RCA 286 Mb43
Ngomedzap CAM 281 Lf44
Ngong CAM 273 Lg41
Ngong EAK 290 Mj46
Ngonga CAM 280 Lf43
Ngongo RCB 288 Lf47
Ngonye Falls Z 295 Mb54
Ngora EAU 290 Mg45
Ngorengore EAK 290 Mh46
Ngoring Hu VRC 171 Pj28
Ngorkou RMM 271 Kj38
Ngoro CAM 281 Lf43
Ngorongoro EAT 293 Mh47
Ngorongoro Conservation Area EAT 293 Mh47
Ngorongoro Crater EAT 293 Mh47
Ngoso RDC 289 Lk48
Ngote RDC 287 Mf44
Ngoto RCA 281 Lj43
Ngotwane RB 299 Md58
Ngouanga RCA 282 Mc42
Ngoulemakong CAM 281 Lf44
Ngoulonkila RCB 288 Lh47
Ngouma RMM 271 Kj38
Ngoumgbi G 288 Le46
Ngounié G 288 Lf46
Ngoura CAM 281 Lh43
Ngoura CAM 281 Lh43
Ngoura TCH 273 Lj39
Ngouri TCH 273 Lh39
Ngourti RN 273 Lg38
N'Goussa DZ 259 Lc29
Ngoutchéy TCH 273 Lj37
Ngouye Pété SN 269 Kd37
Ngouyo RCA 287 Mc43
Ngovayang CAM 281 Lf44
Ngoyeboma RCB 281 Lh45
Ngozi BU 292 Me47
Ngudu EAT 292 Mg47
Nguélémendouka CAM 281 Lg43
Nguema RDC 289 Mb49
Ngugha RB 299 Mb55
Ngui RCA 282 Mb42
Nguia Bouar RCA 281 Lh43
Nguigmi RN 273 Lg38
Nguila CAM 281 Lf43
Nguiu AUS (NT) 223 Rf51
Ngukurr AUS (NT) 223 Rh53
Ngulakula EAT 293 Mk49
Ngulu Atoll FSM 240 Rd17
Nguna VU 246 Te54
Ngundu ZW 300 Mf56
Nguni EAK 291 Mk46
Ngunut RI 210 Qg50
Nguroje WAN 281 Lf42
Ngurore WAN 273 Lg41
Nguru WAN 273 Lf39
Nguruka EAT 292 Mf48
Ngurumanhija EAT 297 Mj51
Ngut CAM 280 Le43
Nguyakro CI 279 Kh42
Ngwale EAT 297 Mj51
Ngwedaung MYA 196 Pj36
Ngwena ZW 300 Me55
Ngweze NAM/RB 295 Mc54
Ngweze Pool Z 295 Mb54
Ngwezumba RB 295 Mc55
Ngwo CAM 280 Le42
Nhabe RB 299 Mb56
Nhachengue MOC 300 Mh57
Nhacoà GNB 269 Kc40
Nhacra GNB 269 Kc40
Nhamassonge MOC 296 Mg54
Nhamatanda MOC 300 Mh55
Nhamayabué MOC 297 Mh54
Nhamunda BR 63 Hb46
Nhamundá BR (PA) 63 Hb47
Nhamundá Mapuera, T.I. BR 62 Ha46
Nhandeara BR (SP) 74 He56
Nhandu BR 69 Hc50
Nharêa ANG 294 Lj51
Nha Trang VN 197 Qe39
Nhemba MOC 296 Mg53
Nhia ANG 294 Lh51
Nhill AUS (VIC) 236 Sa64
Nhlangano SD 303 Mf59
Nho Quan VN 178 Qc35
Nhulunbuy AUS (NT) 223 Rj52
Niablé CI 279 Kj42
Niada RCA 286 Ma43
Niafounké RMM 270 Kh38
Niagara USA (ND) 26 Fb22
Niagara Falls CDN (ON) 33 Ga24
Niagara Falls USA (NY) 33 Ga24
Niagara Falls USA/CDN 33 Ga24
Niagué CI 278 Kg43
Niah MAL 208 Qg44
Niah Caves MAL 208 Qg44
Niah N.P. MAL 208 Qg44
Niakaramandougou CI 279 Kh41
Niakhar SN 269 Kb38
Nialaha'u Point SOL 245 Ta50
Niambézaria CI 279 Kh43
Niamey RN 271 Lb39
Niamina RMM 270 Kg39
Niamtougou RT 279 La41
Niamvoudou CAM 281 Lg43
Nianda RG 278 Kf40
Niandankoro RG 278 Kf40
Nianfissa CI 278 Kg41
Nianfors S 93 Lr29
Niangara RDC 287 Md44
Niangara RDC 287 Me44
Niangoloko BF 279 Kh40
Niani CI 278 Kg43
Nia-Nia RDC 287 Md45
Nianing SN 269 Kb38
Niantanina RMM 278 Kf40
Nianyu IND (ARP) 194 Ph32
Nianzishan VRC (HLG) 180 Rb22
Niao Dao VRC 174 Pk27
Niaoshu Shan VRC 176 Qc28
Niapidou CI 278 Kg43
Niapu RDC 287 Md44
Niapu RDC 287 Me44
Niari RCB 288 Lg47
Niari RCB 288 Lh47
Niaro SUD 283 Mf40
Nias RI 206 Pj45
Niasar fire temple IR 154 Nf28
Nibe DK 94 Lk34
Nibinamik Lake CDN 25 Ff19
Nibong Tebal MAL 198 Qa43
Nicage MOC 297 Mk52
Nicaj-Shalë AL 126 Lu48
Nicaragua 42 Fg39
Nicasio PE 67 Ge53
Nice F 105 Lh47
Niceville USA (FL) 34 Fg30
Nicgale LV 97 Mg34
Nichinan J 185 Rf30
Nichlaul IND (UPH) 189 Pb32
Nicholas Channel BS 36 Ga34
Nicholasville USA (KY) 35 Fh27
Nichole BD 194 Pe33
Nicholson AUS (WA) 222 Re55
Nicholson, Mount AUS 235 Se58
Nicholson Range AUS 224 Qj59
Nicholson River AUS 232 Rk54
Nichols Town BS 37 Ga33
Nickerie SME 59 Hb43
Nickerson Ice Shelf 312 Cc34
Nickol Bay AUS 224 Qj56
Nicman CDN (QC) 30 Gg20
Nicobar Islands IND 186 Pc17
Nicola Mameet Ind. Res. CDN 18 Dk20
Nicola River CDN 18 Dk20
Nicolás Bruzzone RA (CD) 76 Gh63
Nicosia CY 131 Mo55
Nicosia I 122 Lp53
Nicótera I 123 Lq52
Nicoya CR 42 Fh40
Nictau CDN (NB) 30 Gg22
Nicuadala MOC 297 Mj54
Niculitel RO 125 Mj45
Nicupa MOC 297 Na53
Nidadavole IND (APH) 191 Pa37
Nidda D 114 Lk40
Nidelva N 92 Lj32
Nidri GR 128 Ma52
Nidzica PL 117 Ma37
Niéboré RG 278 Ke40
Niebüll D 112 Lj36
Niedalino PL 116 Lr36
Niederaula D 112 Lk40
Niederbronn-les-Bains F 103 Lh42
Niedere Tauern A 115 Lp43
Niederlausitz D 113 Lp39
Niedersachsen D 112 Lj38
Niedersächsisches Wattenmeer, N.P. D 112 Lh37
Niedrzwica Duża PL 117 Mc39
Niefang GQ 280 Lf45
Niéga BF 271 Kk39
Niégo BF 279 Kj40
Niekershoop SA 302 Mb60
Nielisz PL 117 Md40
Niéllé CI 279 Kh40
Niellim TCH 273 Lj41
Niem RCA 281 Lh42
Niemba RDC 292 Me48
Niemba RDC 292 Me49
Niemce PL 117 Mc39
Niemelane RIM 269 Ke36
Niemisel S 90 Mb13
Niéna RMM 279 Kg40
Nienburg D 112 Lk38
Nierstein D 114 Lj41
Niesen CH 114 Lh44
Niesky D 113 Lp39
Nieu-Bethesda SA 303 Mc61
Nieuw Amsterdam SME 59 Hc43
Nieuwegein NL 112 Lf38
Nieuw Nickerie SME 59 Hb43
Nieuwoudtville SA 302 Lk61
Nieuwpoort B 103 Lc39
Nieuwpoort NL (NA) 57 Gf39
Nieva PE 60 Gb48
Nieweglosz PL 117 Mc39
Niezabyszewo PL 116 Ls36
Nifi KSA 149 Nb33
Niğde TR 131 Mp53
Niğde Kalesi TR 131 Mp53
Nigel SA 303 Me59
Niger 254 La16
Niger 253 La08
Niger Delta WAN 280 Lc43
Niger Fan 254 La16
Nigeria 253 La09
Nighasan IND (UPH) 189 Pa31
Night Hawk Lake CDN 25 Fk21
Nightmote USA (AK) 14 Bh15
Nigrangombe EAT 293 Mj50
Nigrita GR 126 Md50
Nigua 46 Ge36
Niha Caves RL 146 Mh29
Nihada OM 157 Nj34
Nihessiue MOC 297 Mk53
Nihing PK 162 Oc31
Nihiru Atoll F 249 Cj54
Nihoa USA 16 Bk34
Nihonmatsu J 183 Sa27
Niigata J 183 Rk27
Niihama J 183 Rg29
Niihau USA 16 Bk35
Niijima J 183 Rk28
Niimi J 183 Rg28
Niitsu J 183 Rk27
Nijar E 109 Ks46
Nijiao VRC (YUN) 195 Qb33
Nijkerk NL 112 Lf38
Nij Laluk IND (ASM) 194 Pg32
Nijmegen NL 112 Lf39
Nijverdal NL 112 Lg38
Nikea GR 126 Mc51
Nikel' RUS 91 Mf11
Nikíforos GR 127 Me49
Nikiniki RI 214 Rc50
Nikitas GR 127 Md50
Nikitskij monastyr RUS 132 Mk17
Nikkaluokta S 90 Lk12
Nikki DY 272 Lb41
Nikko J 183 Rk27
Nikko N.P. J 183 Rk27
Nikoemvon CAM 281 Lf44
Nikolaevka RUS 133 Nd19
Nikolaevo BG 127 Mf48
Nikolaevsk RUS 133 Nc21
Nikolaevsk-na-Amure RUS 141 Sa08
Nikolo L'vovskoe RUS 180 Rf24
Nikol'sk RUS 133 Nd19
Nikonga EAT 292 Mf47
Nikopol BG 127 Me47
Nikopol' UA 134 Mh22
Nikópoli GR 128 Ma51
Nikópoli GR 128 Ma51
Nikopolis ad Istrum BG 127 Mf47
Niksar TR 144 Mj25
Nikshar IR 157 Oa32
Nikšić SCG 126 Lt48
Nikumaroro KIR 241 Ub19
Nikunau Island KIR 241 Td19
Nilanga IND (MHT) 190 Oj36
Nilaveli Beach CL 193 Pa42
Nile ET 255 Mc13
Nile SUD 276 Mg37
Nile Delta ET 263 Mf30
Niles USA (MI) 32 Fg25
Nilgiri IND (ORS) 194 Pd35
Nili AFG 160 Od29
Nilka VRC (XUZ) 166 Pb24
Nilpass AFG 160 Od28
Nilphamari BD 194 Pe33
Nilt 161 Oh27
Nimach IND (MPH) 190 Oj33
Niman RUS 180 Rg20
Nimbahera IND (RJT) 190 Oh33
Nimbin AUS (NSW) 235 Sg60
Nimbotong RI 213 Sa47
Nimes F 105 Le47
Nimiuktuk River USA 15 Ca11
Nimjat RIM 269 Kc37
Nim Ka Khera IND (RJT) 188 Oh33
Nimmitabel AUS (NSW) 237 Se64
Nimrod Glacier 313 Sd35
Nimrud IRQ 147 Nb27
Nimule SUD 290 Mg44
Nimule N.P. SUD 290 Mg44
Nin HR 121 Lq46
Nina NAM 298 Lk57
Nin Bay RP 203 Rb39
Ninda ANG 295 Ma53
Nindigully AUS (QLD) 235 Se60
Nine Degree Channel IND 192 Og42
Ninette CDN (MB) 24 Fa21
Ninette NAM 298 Lk57
Ninetyeast Ridge 315 Pa12
Ninety Mile Beach AUS 237 Sd65
Ninety Mile Beach NZ 238 Tg63
Ningaloo AUS (WA) 224 Qg57
Ningaloo Reef Marine Park AUS 224 Qg57
Ning'an VRC (HLG) 180 Re23
Ningari RMM 271 Kj38
Ningau Island PNG 243 Se48
Ningbo VRC (ZJG) 184 Ra31
Ningcheng VRC (NMZ) 175 Qk25
Ningde VRC (FJN) 184 Qk32
Ningdu VRC (JGX) 184 Qh32
Ningera PNG 242 Sa47
Ningerum PNG 242 Sa48
Ningguo VRC (AHU) 184 Qk30
Ninghai VRC (ZJG) 184 Ra31
Ninghe VRC (TJN) 175 Qj26
Ningi WAN 272 Le40
Ningjing Shan VRC 176 Pj30
Ningming VRC (GZG) 178 Qd34
Ningnan VRC (SCH) 195 Qb32
Ningqiang VRC (SAA) 177 Qd29
Ningshan VRC (SAA) 177 Qe29
Ningwu VRC (SAX) 175 Qg26
Ningxia Huizu Zizhiqu VRC 165 Qb11
Ning Xian VRC (GSU) 177 Qd28
Ningxiang VRC (HUN) 177 Qg31
Ningyuan VRC (HUN) 178 Qf33
Ninh Binh VN 178 Qc35
Ninh Hoa VN 197 Qe39
Ninh Son VN 197 Qe40
Ninoa RI 213 Rk48
Ninigo Group PNG 243 Sc46
Ninilchik USA (AK) 15 Ce15
Ninive IRQ 147 Nb27
Ninjin VRC (SDG) 175 Qj27
Ninohe J 183 Sa25
Ninole USA (HI) 16 Cc36
Niños Héroes MEX (SL) 38 Ef32
Ninotsminda GE 152 Nb25
Ninove B 103 Le40
Nioaque BR (MS) 74 Hc56
Nioaque, T.I. BR 74 Hc56
Niobrara USA 26 Ek24
Niobrara USA (NE) 26 Fa24
Niodior SN 269 Kb39
Niofoin CI 279 Kg41
Nioka RDC 287 Mf44
Nioka RDC 289 Mb49
Nioki RDC 289 Lj47
Niokolo Koba SN 269 Kd39
Niokolo-Koba SN 269 Kd39
Niokolo-Koba, P.N.du SN 269 Kd39
Niono RMM 270 Kh38
Nioro du Rip SN 269 Kc39
Nioro du Sahel RMM 270 Kf38
Niort F 102 Ku44
Niou BF 271 Kk39
Nioût RIM 270 Kg37
Nipa PNG 243 Sb49
Nipahpanjang RI 207 Qc46
Nipani IND (KTK) 190 Oh37
Nipawin CDN (SK) 19 Eh19
Nipawin Prov. Park CDN 19 Eh19
Nipekamew River CDN 19 Eh18
Nipele NAM 294 Lj55
Nipepe MOC 297 Mj52
Niphad IND (MHT) 190 Oh35
Nipigon CDN (ON) 25 Ff21
Nipigon Bay CDN 25 Ff21
Nipin River CDN 19 Ef18
Nipiodi MOC 297 Mj54
Nipomo USA (CA) 22 Dk28
Nippur IRQ 147 Nc29
Niquelândia BR (GO) 70 Hf53
Niquero C 45 Gb35
Nir IR 154 Nd26
Nira IND (MHT) 190 Oh36
Nirgua YV 57 Gf40
Nirmal IND (APH) 191 Ok36
Nirwana Beach RI 209 Rb48
Niš SCG 126 Mb47
Nisa P 108 Kn49
Nisa TM 155 Nk27
Nisab KSA 147 Nc31
Nisab YE 150 Nd38
Nisai RI 211 Qk50
Nišava SCG 126 Mc47
Niscemi I 122 Lp53
Niseko Shakotan Otaru-kaigan Q.N.P. J 181 Sa24
Nish AFG 160 Oc29
Nishi VRC (HUN) 177 Qf31
Nishi-Chugokusanchi Q.N.P. J 183 Rg28
Nishino-jima J 183 Rg27
Nishi-no-Omote J 185 Rf30
Nishi-Okoppe J 181 Sb23
Nishi-Sonogi-hanto J 185 Re29
Nishon UZB 158 Oc26
Nisiá Petalii GR 128 Me53
Nísio Strofádhes GR 128 Ma53
Niška Banja SCG 126 Mc47
Niskibi River CDN 25 Ff17
Nisko PL 117 Mc40
Nisling River CDN 17 Da14
Nisou CY 131 Mo55
Nisporeni MD 125 Mj43
Nissan S 95 Lo33
Nissan Island PNG 244 Sh48
Nissedal N 92 Lj31
Nisséko BF 279 Kj40
Nisser N 92 Lj31
Nissi EST 96 Me31
Nissi Ioannon GR 128 Ma51
Nissiros GR 129 Mh54
Nissum Bredning DK 94 Lj34
Nissum Fjord DK 94 Lj34
Nistru MD 125 Mk44
Nisutlin River CDN 17 Dd15
Nisut Plateau CDN 17 De15
Nita'a KSA 149 Ne32
Nita Downs AUS (WA) 222 Ra55
Nitaure LV 97 Mf33
Nitchequon CDN (QC) 30 Ge19
Niterói BR (RJ) 75 Hj57
Nith GB 99 Kr35
Nitinat CDN (BC) 18 Dh21
Niti Pass VRC/IND 170 Ok30
Nitmiluk N.P. AUS 223 Rg53
Nitra SK 118 Ls42
Nitra SK 118 Lt42
Nitrianske Pravno SK 118 Lt42
Nitriansky hrad SK 118 Lt42
Nittambuwa CL 193 Pa43
Nittedal N 92 Ll30
Nittenau D 115 Ln41
Nittur IND (KTK) 193 Oj40
Nituj RUS 181 Sb21
Niuafo'ou TO 248 Bc53
Niuatoputapu TO 248 Bd53
Niuchang VRC (GZH) 178 Qc33
Niuchang VRC (YUN) 178 Qc34
Niue NZ 248 Bf55
Niulakita TUV 241 Td21
Niumi N.P. WAG 269 Kb39
Niutahi F 249 Cg53
Niutao TUV 241 Td20
Niut, Gunung RI 208 Qe45
Niutoushan VRC (AHU) 184 Qk30
Niuzhuang VRC (LNG) 182 Rb25
Nivala FIN 91 Mc14
Nivano PK 162 Ob32
Nivelles B 103 Le40
Nivenskoe RUS 97 Ma36
Nivernais F 103 Ld43
Nivikovo RUS 181 Sb22
Niwai IND (RJT) 188 Oh32
Niwas IND (MPH) 191 Pa34
Nixi VRC (YUN) 195 Pk32
Nixon USA (NV) 20 Ea26
Nixon USA (TX) 28 Fb31
Niya = Minfeng VRC (XUZ) 168 Pb27
Nizamabad IND (APH) 190 Ok36
Nizamabad Temple IND 190 Ok36
Nizamghat IND (ARP) 195 Ph31
Nizampatam IND (APH) 193 Pa39
Nizam Sagar IND 190 Oj36
Nizi RDC 287 Mf45
Nizina Wielkopolska PL 116 Lq39
Nizip TR 144 Mj27
Nizke Tatry SK 119 Lu42
Nizke Tatry, N.P. SK 119 Lu42
Nižná Boca SK 119 Lu42
Nižnaja Čir RUS 133 Nb21
Nižnaja Lomov RUS 133 Nb19
Nižnekamsk RUS (TAR) 133 Nf18
Nižnekamskoe Vodohranilišče RUS 133 Ng18
Nižnetambovskoe RUS 181 Rk20
Nižnevartovsk RUS 140 Od06
Nižnij Casučej RUS 173 Qh20
Nižnij Novgorod RUS 133 Nb17
Nižnij Pjandž TJ 158 Oe27
Nižnij Tagil RUS 140 Nd07
Nižnjaja Tunguska RUS 140 Pc05
Nizwa OM 157 Nj34
Nižyn UA 132 Mf20
Nizza Monferrato I 120 Lj46
Nizzana IL 146 Mh30
Njagan' RUS 140 Ob06
Njaiama-Sewafe WAL 278 Ke41
Nja Kunda WAG 269 Kc39
Njangwe EAT 297 Mk51
Njasviž BY 97 Mg37
Njenje EAT 293 Mk50
Njinjo EAT 293 Mk50
Njivice HR 121 Lp45
Njojane RB 299 Ma57
Njoko Z 295 Mc54
Njombe EAT 293 Mh49
Njombe EAT 293 Mh50
Njoro EAK 290 Mh46
Njupeskär S 93 Ln29
Njurba RUS 141 Qd06
Njurundabommen S 93 Ls28
Nkalagu WAN 280 Ld42
Nkam G 281 Lf45
Nkambe CAM 281 Lf42
Nkan G 280 Le45
Nkawie GH 279 Kk42
Nkayi RCB 288 Lg48
Nkayi ZW 300 Me55
Nkhaile RIM 270 Kg37
Nkhamenya MW 296 Mg52
Nkhata Bay MW 296 Mh51
Nkhotakota MW 296 Mh52
Nkhotakota Game Reserve MW 296 Mg52
Nko RCB 288 Lh47
Nkoambang CAM 281 Lg43
Nkogo RCB 281 Lh45
Nkolabona G 281 Lf45
Nkole Z 296 Mf51
Nkolmengboua G 281 Lf44
Nkolmetet CAM 281 Lf44
Nkome EAT 292 Mf47
Nkomfap WAN 280 Le42
Nkomi G 288 Lf46
Nkondwe EAT 292 Mf48
Nkongjok CAM 280 Lf43
Nkongsamba CAM 280 Le43
Nkon Ngok CAM 281 Lf43
Nkoranza GH 279 Kk42
Nkoteng CAM 281 Lg43
Nkoué RCB 288 Lh47
Nkourala RMM 279 Kg40
Nkula Falls MW 297 Mh53
Nkundi EAT 292 Mf49
Nkungulu MW 297 Mh53
Nkurenkuru NAM 295 Lk54
Nkwalini SA 303 Mf60
Nkwanta GH 279 Kj43
Nkwanta GH 279 La41
Nmai Hka MYA 195 Pk33
Nnewi WAN 280 Ld42
No.24 Well AUS (WA) 225 Rb57
No.35 Well AUS (WA) 225 Rc57
Noailles F 103 Lc41
Noakhali BD 194 Pf34
Noanama CO 56 Gb43
Noatak USA (AK) 15 Bj12
Noatak National Preserve USA (AK) 15 Bk11
Noatak River USA 15 Bj12
Nobadeer (Nantucket) USA 33 Gf25
Nobeoka J 185 Rf29
Nobéré BF 279 Kk40
Nobles Nob Mine AUS 223 Rh55
Nobokwe SA 303 Md61
Nobol EC 60 Fk46
Noboribetsu J 181 Sa24
Nobres BR (MT) 69 Hb53
Nochi-katsuura J 183 Rh29
Noci I 123 Ls50
Nockatunga AUS (QLD) 234 Sb59
Nockberge, N.P. A 115 Lo44
Nocoleche AUS (NSW) 234 Sc60
Nocona USA (TX) 28 Fb29
Noda J 183 Sa25
Nodeland N 92 Lh32
Nödinge-Nol S 94 Ln33
Nodwengu SA 303 Mf60
Noel CDN (NS) 31 Gj23
Noel Kempff, P.N. BOL 68 Ha53
Noenieput SA 302 Ma59
Noépé RT 279 La42
Noetinger RA (CD) 77 Gj62
Nœux-les-Mines F 103 Lc40
Nogales E 108 Ko48
Nogales MEX (SO) 23 Ee30
Nogales MEX (VC) 40 Fb36
Nogales USA (AZ) 23 Ee30
Nogal Valley SP 285 Nd41
Nogamut USA (AK) 15 Cb15
Nogarejas E 106 Ko52
Nogata J 185 Rf29
Nogent F 103 Lf42
Nogent-le-Roi F 102 Lb42
Nogent-le-Rotrou F 102 La42
Nogent-sur-Seine F 103 Ld42
Noginsk RUS 132 Mk18
Nogoya RA (ER) 77 Ha62
Nogoyá RA 77 Ha62
Noguera E 109 Kt50
Nohalal MEX (YT) 41 Ff36
Nohar IND (RJT) 188 Oh31
Nohbec MEX (QTR) 41 Ff36
Noheji J 183 Sa25
Nohfelden D 114 Lh41
Noia E 106 Km52
Noirétable F 105 Ld45
Noirmoutier F 102 Ks44
Noirmoutier-en-l'Île F 102 Ks44
Nojack CDN (AB) 19 Ec19
Nojima-saki J 183 Rk28
Nokaneng RB 299 Mb55
Nokha IND (RJT) 188 Og32
Nokhra IND (RJT) 188 Og32
Nokia FIN 96 Md29
Nokju IR 157 Oa32
Nok Kundi PK 162 Ob31
Nokomis CDN (SK) 19 Eh20
Nokou TCH 273 Lh38
Nokuku VU 246 Td53
Nola I 122 Lp50
Nola RCA 281 Lj44
Nola USA (AR) 29 Fd28
Nolay F 103 Le44
Nolhivaranfaru MV 192 Og42
Noli EAT 297 Mk51
Noll SA 302 Mb62
Nom VRC (XUZ) 169 Ph24
Noma misaki J 185 Rf30
Nomane PNG 243 Sc49
Nomansland Pt. CDN 25 Fk19
Nombre de Dios MEX (DGO) 39 Eh34
Nome USA (AK) 15 Bh13
Nomeny F 103 Lg42
Nomgon MNG 172 Qc21
Nomhon VRC (QHI) 169 Pj27
Nomitsis GR 128 Mc54

yika Plateau MW 296 Mg51
yikine SN 269 Kb39
yikon Qu VRC 176 Qa29
yima VRC (TIB) 170 Pd30
yimba Z 296 Mf53
yiminiama RMM 271 Kj38
yingchi VRC (TIB) 171 Ph31
yírábrány H 119 Mc43
yiradony H 119 Mb43
yiragongo RDC 287 Me46
yirbátor H 119 Mc43
yirbéltek H 119 Mc43
yirgyháza H 119 Mb43
yiri Desert EAK 290 Mj47
yirmada H 119 Mc42
yirtelek H 119 Mb43
yiru Range EAK 290 Mj44
ykøbing F DK 94 Lm36
ykøbing M DK 94 Lj34
ykøbing S DK 94 Lm35
yköping S 93 Lr32
ykroppa S 93 Lp31
ykvarn S 93 Ls31
ylstroom SA 299 Me58
ylsvlei Nature Reserve SA 300 Me58
ymagee AUS (NSW) 237 Sd62
ymboida AUS (NSW) 235 Sg60
ymboida N.P. AUS 235 Sg60
ymburk CZ 118 Lq40
ymphe Bank 100 Kn39
ynäshamn S 93 Ls32
yngan AUS (NSW) 235 Sd61
yoka Z 296 Md52
yoma Rap 161 Ok29
yommalat LAO 197 Qc37
yon CH 114 Lg44
yong CAM 280 Lf44
yons F 105 Lf46
yororo EAT 293 Mh50
yřany CZ 118 Lo41
yrud N 91 Me11
ysa PL 116 Lr40
ysa PL 116 Ls40
ysäter S 93 Ln31
yssa TR 130 Mj53
ystadt = Uusikaupunki FIN 93 Mb30
ysted DK 94 Lm36
yudo-saki J 183 Rk25
yumbaya Mungu Reservoir EAT 290 Mj47
yunzu RDC 292 Md48
yuruandanga EAT 293 Mk49
yuts Archipelago AUS 236 Rg62
yvyci UA 117 Me40
yžni Sirohozy UA 135 Mh22
yžni Torhaji UA 134 Mh22
yžni Vorota UA 119 Md42
yzn'ohirs'kyj UA 135 Mh23
zako RCA 282 Mb43
zako RCA 286 Mb43
zambi RCB 288 Lf47
zambi RDC 286 Lj46
zara SUD 287 Me43
zassi RCB 288 Lg48
zébéla RG 278 Kf41
zega EAT 292 Mg48
zérékoré RG 278 Kf42
'Zeto ANG 288 Lg49
zheleledam SA 300 Mf57
zi CI 279 Kh42
zima EAT 292 Mg47
zingu RDC 292 Md47
zi-Noua CI 279 Kh42
zo CI 278 Kg42
zo RG 278 Kf42
zoia EAK 290 Mh45
zoro RCA 281 Lh42
zoro RDC 287 Mf44
zulezu Stilt Settlement GH 279 Kj43

O

ahu USA 16 Ca35
ak Alley Plantation USA 29 Fe31
akbank AUS (SA) 236 Sa62
akburn CDN (MB) 24 Ek20
akdale USA (LA) 29 Fd30
akes USA (ND) 26 Fa22
akey AUS (QLD) 235 Sf59
ak Grove USA (LA) 29 Fe29
ak Grove USA (AL) 34 Fg29
akham GB 101 Ks38
ak Harbour USA (WA) 18 Dj21
ak Hill USA (AL) 34 Fg30
ak Hill USA (WV) 35 Fk26
ak Hills AUS (QLD) 233 Sc55
akhurst USA (CA) 20 Ea27
ak Lake CDN (MB) 24 Ek21
ak Lake CDN 24 Ek21
akland USA (CA) 20 Dj27
akland USA (IA) 27 Fc25
akland USA (MD) 33 Ga26
akland USA (NE) 27 Fb25
aklands AUS (NSW) 237 Sd63
ak Lawn USA (IL) 32 Fg25
aklawn Park USA (AR) 29 Fd28
akley USA (ID) 21 Ed24
akley USA (KS) 26 Ek26
akman USA (AL) 34 Fg29
akover River AUS 224 Ra56
ak Point CDN (MB) 24 Fa20
akridge USA (OR) 20 Dj24
ak Ridge USA (TN) 35 Fh27
akville CDN (ON) 33 Ga24
akville USA (WA) 18 Dj22
akwood AUS (QLD) 235 Sd58
aky Creek AUS (QLD) 233 Se57
amaru NZ 239 Tf68
asis USA (NV) 21 Ec25
asis II ANT (RUS) 313 Qa32
ates Land 313 Sd33
atlands AUS (TAS) 236 Sd67
axaca MEX (OAX) 40 Fb37
axaca MEX 40 Fb37
b' RUS 140 Ob06
ba CDN (ON) 25 Fh21
ba WAN 280 Lc42
baa RI 242 Rk49
baa RCB 288 Lh46
baha PNG 243 Se50
baidullaganj IND (MPH) 191 Oj34
bakamiga Lake CDN 25 Fh21
bala CAM 281 Lf43
balapuram IND (APH) 193 Oj39
bama J 183 Rh28
ban AUS (QLD) 232 Rk56
ban GB 98 Kp34
ban WAN 280 Le43
Obanazawa J 183 Sa26
Obanbori Qayroqqum TJ 158 Of25
Oban Hills WAN 280 Le43
O Barco E 106 Ko52
Obbia = Hobyo SP 285 Ne43
Obbnäs = Upinniemi FIN 96 Me30
Obcina Mare RO 125 Mf43
Obehie WAN 280 Ld43
Öbektaş TR 131 Mo53
Öbek Tepe TR 131 Mp50
Obele WAN 280 Ld42
Obeliai LT 97 Mf35
Obeliscs of Cascase ER 277 Mk39
Obera RA (MI) 77 Hc59
Oberammergau D 115 Lm43
Oberes Donautal D 114 Lk42
Ober-Gatlinburg Ski Resort USA 35 Fj28
Oberhausen D 112 Lg39
Oberkirch D 114 Lj42
Oberlausitz D 113 Lp39
Oberlin USA (LA) 29 Fd30
Obernai F 103 Lh42
Obernburg D 114 Lk41
Oberndorf A 115 Lo43
Oberndorf D 114 Lj42
Oberon AUS (NSW) 237 Se62
Oberpfälzer Wald D 115 Ln41
Oberpullendorf A 115 Lr43
Oberstdorf D 114 Ll43
Oberviechtach D 115 Ln41
Oberwart A 115 Lr43
Oberwiesenthal D 115 Ln40
Obi RI 212 Rd46
Obi WAN 280 Le41
Obiaruku WAN 280 Ld43
Óbidos BR (PA) 63 Hc46
Óbidos P 108 Kl49
Obihiro J 181 Sb24
Obilatu RI 212 Rd46
Obispo Trejo RA (CD) 76 Gj61
Obitočna kosa UA 135 Mj22
Ob Luang N.P. THA 196 Pk36
Obluče RUS (YAO) 180 Rf21
Obninsk RUS 132 Mj18
Obo RCA 287 Md43
Obo VRC (QHI) 174 Qa27
Oboasi GH 279 Kk42
Obobogorap SA 302 Ma59
Obock DJI 277 Nb40
Oboda RUS (BAG) 152 Nd24
Obodivka UA 125 Mk42
Obogu GH 279 Kk42
Obojan RUS 132 Mj20
Obokote RDC 287 Md46
Oboli RCB 288 Lh46
Obolo WAN 280 Ld42
Obolon' UA 134 Mg21
Obonga Lake CDN 25 Ff21
Oborniki PL 116 Lr38
Oborniki Śląskie PL 116 Lr39
Oborowo PL 116 Lt38
Obory CZ 118 Lp41
Obouya RCB 288 Lh46
Obozerskij RUS 91 Na14
Obra IND (BIH) 191 Pc33
Obrenovac SCG 124 Ma46
Obrež HR 121 Lq45
O'Brien USA (OR) 20 Dj24
Obrovac HR 121 Lq46
Obruchev Rise 316 Ta05
Obruk TR 131 Mo52
Obruk TR 131 Mp53
Obruk Yaylâsı TR 131 Mo52
Observatoio El Leoncito RA 76 Gf61
Observatorio Calar Alto E 109 Ks47
Observatorio de S. Pedro MEX 22 Ec30
Observatory Inlet CDN 17 Df18
Obskaya Guba RUS 140 Oc05
Obuasi GH 279 Kk42
Obubra WAN 280 Le42
Obudu WAN 280 Le42
Obudu Cattle Ranch WAN 280 Le42
Obusa RUS (UOB) 172 Qb19
Obzor BG 127 Mh48
Obžyle UA 125 Mk43
Očakiv UA 134 Mf22
Očamčire GE 152 Nb24
Ocampo MEX (CHH) 38 Ef31
Ocampo MEX (DGO) 39 Eh32
Ocampo MEX (COH) 39 Ej32
Ocampo MEX (TM) 39 Fa34
Ocampo MEX (GJT) 40 Ek35
Ocaña CO 56 Gd41
Ocaña E 109 Kr49
Ocate USA (NM) 23 Eh27
Ocauçu BR (SP) 74 Hf57
Occidente CO 61 Gd46
Occoneechee S.P. USA 35 Ga27
Ocean Cape USA 16 Ck16
Ocean City USA (MD) 33 Gc26
Ocean City USA (NJ) 33 Gc26
Ocean Falls CDN (BC) 18 Dg19
Océanopolis F 102 Kq42
Ocean Shores USA (WA) 18 Dh22
Ocean Shores USA (WA) 18 Dh22
Oceanside USA (CA) 22 Eb29
Oceanside Harbor USA (CA) 22 Eb29
Ocean Springs USA (MS) 29 Ff30
Ocerci UA 117 Mf39
Očeretuvate UA 135 Mh22
Ochero EAU 290 Mg45
Ochiai J 183 Rg28
O'Chiese Ind. Res. CDN 19 Ec19
Ochil Hills GB 99 Kr34
Ochobo WAN 280 Lc42
Ochopee USA (FL) 36 Fk33
Ocho Rios JA 45 Gb36
Ochsenfurt D 114 Ll41
Ochsenhausen D 114 Lk42
Ochtrup D 112 Lh38
Ochtyrka UA 132 Mh20
Ocieka PL 117 Mb40
Ocilla USA (GA) 35 Fj30
Ockelbo S 93 Lr30
Ocland RO 125 Mf44
Ocmulgee USA 35 Fj30
Ocmulgee Nat. Mon. USA 35 Fj29
Ocna Mureș RO 124 Md44
Ocna Sibiului RO 124 Me44
Ocnele Mari RO 124 Me45
Ocnița MD 125 Mh42
Ocoliș RO 124 Md44
Ocoña PE 72 Gd54
Oconee Lake USA 35 Fj29
Ocongate PE 67 Ge52
Oconomowoc USA (WI) 32 Ff24
Oconto USA (WI) 32 Fg23
Ocoruro PE 67 Ge53
Ocós GCA 41 Fd38
Ocosingo MEX (CHP) 41 Fe37
Ocotal NIC 42 Fg39
Ocotlán MEX (JLC) 40 Ej35
Ocotlán de Morelos MEX (OAX) 40 Fb37
Ocozocoautla MEX (CHP) 41 Fd37
Ocracoke USA (NC) 35 Gc28
Ocracoke Lighthouse USA 35 Gc28
Ocros PE 66 Gb51
Ocros PE 66 Gd52
Octogonal Pavillion VRC 195 Qa35
Octovcy RUS 132 Mg17
Ocua MOC 297 Mk52
Ocucaje PE 66 Gc53
Ocumare del Tuy YV 57 Gg40
Ocurí BOL 72 Gh55
Oda GH 279 Kk43
Oda J 183 Rg28
Odáðahraun IS 90 Kb13
Odaejin DVRK 182 Re25
Odaesan N.P. ROK 182 Re27
Ödåkra S 94 Ln34
Odammun RI 242 Rk49
Odan NEP 170 Pa31
Odate J 183 Sa25
Odawara J 183 Rk28
Odda N 92 Lg30
Odden Færgehavn DK 94 Lm35
Odder DK 94 Ll35
Oddsta GB 99 Ku30
Oddur = Xuddur SP 285 Nb43
Odeceixe P 108 Km47
Odei River CDN 24 Fa17
Odemira P 108 Km47
Ödemiş TR 129 Mh52
Odendaalsrus SA 303 Md59
Odensbacken S 93 Lq31
Odense DK 94 Ll35
Odepur IND (ORS) 191 Pb35
Oder D 113 Lp38
Oderbruch D 113 Lp38
Oderzo I 120 Ln45
Odesa UA 134 Mf22
Odessa UA 134 Mf22
Odessa USA (WA) 18 Ea22
Odessa USA (TX) 23 Ej30
Odet F 102 Kr42
Odienné CI 278 Kg41
Odighi WAN 280 Lc42
Odimba G 288 Le46
Odincovo RUS 132 Mj18
Odiongan RP 203 Ra39
Odivelas P 108 Km48
Odjala G 281 Lg46
Odobasca RO 125 Mg45
Odobeşti RO 125 Mh45
Odolanów PL 116 Ls39
Odonkawkrom GH 279 Kk42
O'Donnell River AUS 222 Rd55
Odoorn NL 112 Lg38
Odorheiu Secuiesc RO 125 Mf44
Odra PL 116 Ls40
Odry CZ 118 Ls41
Odrzywół PL 117 Ma39
Ødsted DK 94 Lk35
Odumasi GH 279 Kk42
Odunboğazı TR 131 Mo51
Odupontkpehe GH 279 Kk43
Odžaci SCG 124 Lu45
Odžak BIH 121 Lt45
Odzala-Kokoua, P.N.d' RCB 281 Lh45
Odzema RCB 286 Lj46
Odzi ZW 300 Mg55
Odziba RCB 288 Lh47
Oebisfelde D 113 Lm38
Oeiras BR (PI) 65 Hj49
Oeiras do Pará BR (PA) 64 Hf46
Ökény H 119 Lu43
Oekusi TIM 214 Rc50
Oelrichs USA (SD) 26 Ej24
Oelsnitz D 115 Ln40
Oelwein USA (IA) 27 Fe24
Oeno 317 Da12
Oenpelli AUS (NT) 223 Rg52
Oettingen D 115 Ll42
Oetz A 115 Ll43
Ofa WAN 280 Lc41
Ofahoma USA (MS) 29 Ff29
Ofanto I 123 Lr49
Ofcolaco SA 300 Mf58
Ofenpass CH 114 Ll44
Ofere WAN 280 Ld41
Offenbach D 114 Lj40
Offenburg D 114 Lh42
Offoué G 281 Lf46
Offumpo CI 279 Kh43
Oficina Alemania PE 72 Gf58
Oficina Chile PE 72 Gf58
Oficina Victoria RCH 72 Gf56
Ofin GH 279 Kk42
Ofin GH 279 Kk42
Ofoase GH 279 Kk42
Ofugo WAN 280 Ld42
Ofu Island USA 248 Bf53
Ofunato J 183 Sa26
Oga J 183 Rk26
Ogaden ETH 285 Nc42
Oga-hanto J 183 Rk26
Ogaki J 183 Rj28
Ogallala USA (NE) 26 Ek25
Ogbomosho WAN 280 Lc41
Ogani WAN 280 Ld43
Ogar RI 212 Rg47
Ogba WAN 280 Lc42
Ogbesse WAN 280 Lc42
Ogbomoso WAN 280 Lc41
Ogden USA (UT) 21 Ee25
Ogdensburg USA (NY) 33 Gc23
Ogdua RI 209 Ra45
Ogea Levu FJI 247 Ua55
Ogema CDN (SK) 19 Eh21
Ogema USA (MN) 27 Fc22
Ogembo EAK 290 Mh46
Ogi J 183 Rk27
Ogies SA 303 Me59
Ogiala USA (SD) 26 Ej24
Oglala Grassland N.P. USA 26 Ej24
Oglanly TM 153 Nh26
Oglat Berabert DZ 259 Kj30
Oglat el Faci DZ 265 Kh32
Oglat el Faci DZ 265 Kk32
Oglat el Khnâchich RMM 265 Kj35
Oglat Marhboura DZ 259 Kk29
Oglio I 120 Ll45
Ogmore AUS (QLD) 233 Se57
Ognon F 103 Lg43
Ogoja WAN 280 Le42
Ogoki CDN 25 Fh20
Ogoki Lake CDN 25 Fg20
Ogoki Reservoir CDN 25 Ff20
Ogoki River CDN 25 Fg20
Ogooué G 281 Lf46
Ogorelyši RUS (KAR) 91 Mh14
Ogosta BG 126 Md47
Ogošte SCG 126 Mb48
Ogou RT 279 La41
Ogr SUD 283 Md39
Ogre LV 97 Me34
Ogre LV 97 Mf34
Ogrodniki PL 117 Md36
Ogrodzieniec PL 117 Lu40
Oğulcuk TR 131 Mq51
Ogulin HR 121 Lq45
Ogun WAN 272 Lc41
Ogun WAN 280 Lb42
Ogur EAU 290 Mg44
Ogurugu WAN 280 Ld42
Oğuzeli TR 131 Mo52
Oğuzlar TR 131 Mp50
Ogwashi-Uku WAN 280 Ld42
Ohafia WAN 280 Ld43
Ohakune NZ 238 Th65
Ohangoron UZB 158 Oe25
O'Higgins, Gral.B. ANT (RCH) 312 Ha31
Ohio USA 13 Fd10
Ohio USA 27 Fg27
Ohogamuit USA (AK) 14 Bk15
Ohonua TO 248 Bc56
Ohotsk RUS 141 Sa07
Ohotskoe RUS 181 Sb22
Ohra D 113 Ll40
Ohrid MK 126 Ma49
Ohrigstad SA 300 Mf58
Öhringen D 114 Lk41
Ohura NZ 238 Th65
Oiapoque BR 59 Hd44
Oiapoque BR (AP) 59 He44
Oiapoque, T.I. BR 59 He44
Oil City USA (PA) 33 Ga25
Oil Gathering Station LAR 261 Lj31
Oilton USA (TX) 39 Fa32
Oiseaux du Djoudi, P.N.des SN 269 Kb37
Oisemont F 103 Lb41
Oita J 183 Rf29
Oital KZ 159 Og24
Oitti FIN 96 Mf30
Oiyk KZ 158 Of24
Oja de Liebre MEX 38 Ec32
Ojai USA (CA) 22 Ea28
Ojat IND 190 Of35
Ojcowski P.N. PL 117 Lu40
Öje S 93 Lo30
Oje WAN 280 Ld42
Ojika-jima J 185 Re29
Ojima J 183 Rk28
O-jima J 183 Rk28
Ojinaga MEX (CHH) 23 Eh31
Ojito de Camellones MEX (DGO) 38 Eg33
Ojiya J 183 Rk27
Ojmjakon RUS 141 Sa06
Ojmur RUS (BUR) 172 Qd19
Ojobo WAN 280 Lc43
Ojojona HN 42 Fg39
Ojos BOL 73 Gj54
Ojos del Salado, Nevado RCH/RA 76 Gf59
Ojos Negros E 109 Kt50
Ojrzeń PL 117 Ma38
Oj-Tal KS 159 Og25
Oj-Tal KS 159 Oh25
Oju WAN 280 Le42
Ojuelos de Jalisco MEX (JLC) 40 Ek35
Öjung S 93 Lq29
Oka RUS 132 Mj18
Oka RUS 172 Qa19
Oka WAN 280 Lc42
Okaba RI 242 Rk50
Okahandja NAM 298 Lj56
Okakarara NAM 298 Lk56
Okanagan Falls CDN (BC) 18 Ea21
Okanagan Ind. Res. CDN 18 Ea20
Okanagan Lake CDN 18 Ea21
Okanagan Valley CDN 18 Ea21
Okandjombo NAM 298 Lg55
Okankolo NAM 294 Lj54
Okano G 281 Lf45
Okano G 281 Lf45
Okanogan USA (WA) 18 Ea21
Okanogan Range CDN 18 Dk21
Okanogan River USA 18 Ea21
Okapa PNG 243 Sc49
Okara PK 161 Og30
Okartowo PL 117 Mb37
Okasawara-shoto J 165 Sa13
Okata WAN 280 Lb41
Okatjiura NAM 298 Lh55
Okatjoruu NAM 298 Lh55
Okaukuejo NAM 298 Lh55
Okavango NAM/ANG 298 Lk54
Okavango RB 299 Mb55
Okavango Delta RB 299 Mb55
Okavango Swamp RB 299 Mb55
Okave NAM 298 Lj56
Okaya J 183 Rk27
Okayama J 183 Rg28
Okazaki J 183 Rj28
Okazize NAM 298 Lj56
Okeechobee USA (FL) 36 Fk32
O'Keefe Hist. Ranch CDN 18 Ea20
Okeene USA (OK) 28 Fa27
Okefenokee N.W.R. USA 35 Fj30
Okehampton GB 100 Kq40
Oke-Iho WAN 280 Lb41
Okene WAN 280 Ld42
Oke-Odde WAN 272 Lc41
Oké Owe DY 280 Lb41
Oker D 113 Ll38
Oketsew GH 279 Kk43
Okha IND (GUJ) 190 Oe34
Okha Mathi IND (GUJ) 190 Oe34
Okhotsk RUS 141 Sa07
Oki RI 212 Rd47
Okia RCB 288 Lh46
Oki-Daito-Jima J 185 Rf33
Okiéné RCB 288 Lh47
Okiep SA 302 Lj60
Okigwe WAN 280 Ld43
Oki Islands J 183 Rg27
Oki Kaikyo J 183 Rg28
Okila G 288 Lg46
Okinawa J 185 Rd32
Okinawa Islands J 185 Re33
Okinawa-jima J 185 Re32
Okinoerabu-jima J 185 Re32
Okino-jima J 185 Rg29
Oki-tai J 183 Rh27
Okitipupa WAN 280 Lc42
Okkan MYA 196 Ph37
Okla CDN (SK) 24 Ej19
Oklahoma USA 12 Fa11
Oklahoma City USA (OK) 28 Fb28
Okmulgee USA (OK) 29 Fc28
Oko WAN 280 Lc42
Okok EAU 290 Mg44
Okola CAM 281 Lf43
Okollo EAU 287 Mf44
Okondja G 281 Lg46
Okondjatu NAM 298 Lk56
Okongo NAM 294 Lj54
Okongwati NAM 294 Lg54
Okonjima NAM 298 Lj56
Okonmwé RCB 288 Lh47
Okoppe J 181 Sb23
Okora, Mount WAN 280 Ld42
Okotoks CDN (AB) 19 Ec20
Okotusu NAM 294 Lf54
Okouyo CI 278 Kg43
Okoyo RCB 288 Lh46
Okpala-Ngwa WAN 280 Ld43
Okpara DY 272 Lb41
Okpo MYA 196 Ph36
Okrika WAN 280 Ld43
Okrzeja PL 117 Mc39
Oksapmin PNG 242 Sb48
Oksbøl DK 94 Lj35
Øksfjord N 90 Mb10
Oksibil RI 213 Sa48
Oksovskij RUS 91 Mk14
Okstindane N 91 Lh06
Oksu AFG 161 Oh27
Oktjabr' KZ 140 Nd09
Oktjabr'sk RUS 133 Ne19
Oktjabr'skij RUS 133 Nb22
Oktjabr'skij RUS 133 Ng18
Oktwin MYA 196 Pj36
Oktyab'sk TM 153 Nk24
Oku CAM 281 Lf42
Oku J 185 Re32
Okubie WAN 280 Lc43
Okučani HR 121 Ls45
Okuchi J 185 Rf29
Okulovka RUS 132 Mg16
Okundi WAN 280 Le42
Okurcalar TR 131 Mm54
Okushiri J 181 Rk24
Okushiri-to J 181 Rk24
Okuta WAN 272 Lb41
Okwa RB 299 Ma57
Okwa RB 299 Mb57
Okwoga WAN 280 Ld41
Olá PA 43 Fk41
Ola USA (AR) 29 Fd28
Ólafsfjörður IS 90 Ka12
Olaf V Land N 91 Lk06
Olaine LV 97 Md34
Olancha USA (CA) 22 Eb27
Olanchito HN 42 Fg38
Öland S 95 Lr34
Ölands norra udde S 95 Ls33
Ölands södra grund 95 Lr35
Ölands södra udde S 95 Lr34
Olargues F 104 Lc47
Olaria BR (PI) 65 Hk47
Olary AUS (SA) 236 Sa62
Olascoaga RA (BA) 77 Gk63
Olathe USA (KS) 27 Fc26
Olavarría RA (BA) 81 Gk64
Olavinlinna FIN 96 Mj29
Oława PL 116 Ls40
Olbernhau D 113 Lo40
Ólbia I 111 Lk50
Old Bulawayo ZW 300 Me56
Old Coralie AUS (QLD) 232 Sa55
Old Cork AUS (QLD) 232 Sa57
Old Crow CDN 10 Da05
Old Dongola SUD 276 Mf37
Oldeani EAT 293 Mh47
Oldeide N 92 Lf29
Olden N 92 Lg29
Oldenburg D 112 Lj37
Oldenburg in Holstein D 113 Ll36
Oldenzaal NL 112 Lg38
Olderfjord N 91 Mc10
Old Factory Bay CDN 25 Ga19
Old Faithful Geysir USA 21 Ee23
Old Forge USA (NY) 33 Gc24
Old Fort NAM 302 Lj59
Old Fort Hays USA 26 Fa26
Old Fort & Jail F 249 Da50
Old Fort Niagara S.H.S. & Fort Niagara L.H. USA 33 Ga24
Old Fort William CDN 25 Ff21
Old Ft. Henry CDN 33 Gb23
Old Ft. Parker S.H.S. USA 29 Fb30
Old Gold Mine NZ 239 Tf67
Oldham GB 101 Ks37
Old Harbor USA (AK) 16 Cd17
Old Head of Kinsale IRL 100 Km39
Old Irontown Ruins USA 22 Ed27
Old Man of Hoy GB 99 Kr32
Oldman River CDN 19 Ec21
Old Maswa EAT 293 Mg47
Oldmeldrum GB 99 Ks33
Old Minto USA (AK) 15 Cf13
Old Mkushi Z 296 Me53
Old Mosque RI 210 Qf49
Old Nariam EAU 290 Mh45
Old Numery AUS (NT) 227 Rh58
Ol-Doinyo N.P. EAK 290 Mj46
Ol Doinyo Orok EAK 290 Mj47
Ol Doinyo Lengai EAT 293 Mh47
Oldonyo Sambu EAT 293 Mj47
Old Orchard Beach USA (ME) 33 Ge24
Old Oyo WAN 272 Lc41
Old Oyo N.P. WAN 272 Lc41
Old Perlican CDN (NF) 31 Hd21
Old Petauke Z 296 Mf53
Olds CDN (AB) 19 Ec20
Old Sitka USA (AK) 17 Dc17
Old Spanish Treasure Cave USA 29 Fc27
Old Suakin coral stone houses SUD 277 Mj37
Oldtidsveien N 92 Lm31
Oldtimer's Mus. (Maple Creek) CDN (SK) 19 Ef21
Old Town USA (MA) 33 Gf23
Olduvai Gorge EAT 293 Mh47
Old Village USA (AK) 15 Cc15
Old wagon bridge SA 303 Mc60
Old Wives Lake CDN 19 Eh20
Öldziyt gol MNG 172 Pk22
Olean USA (NY) 33 Ga24
Olecko PL 117 Mc36
Oléggio I 120 Lj45
Oleiros P 108 Kn49
Olëkma RUS 141 Ra07
Olëkminsk RUS 141 Ra06
Olëkminskij Stanovik RUS 141 Qd08
Oleksandrivka UA 125 Mm43
Oleksandrivka UA 134 Mf21
Oleksandrivka UA 134 Mg21
Oleksandrivka UA 134 Mh21
Oleksandrivka UA 134 Mg22
Oleksandrivka UA 135 Mj21
Ølen N 92 Lf31
Olenëk RUS 141 Qc05
Olenëk RUS 141 Qd04
Olenëkskij zaliv RUS 141 Qd04
Olengui RUS 173 Qg20
Olenguruone EAK 290 Mh46
Olenino RUS 132 Mg17
Olenivka UA 134 Mg23
Oléron F 104 Kt45
Oles'ko UA 119 Me41
Olešnica PL 116 Ls39
Olesno PL 116 Lt40
Oleszno PL 117 Ma40
Oleszyce PL 117 Md40
Olevs'k UA 132 Md20
Olevu I EAU 287 Mf44
Olex USA (OR) 20 Dk23
Olfen D 112 Lh39
Ol'ga RUS 181 Rh24
Olga, Mount AUS 226 Rf58
Olgastretet N 91 Mb06
Ölgiy MNG 167 Pf21
Ølgod DK 94 Lj35
Olhão P 108 Kn47
Ol'hi RUS 133 Na19
Olho d'Agua das Flores BR (AL) 71 Jb50
Ol'hovatka RUS 133 Mk20
Ol'hovka RUS 133 Nc21
Oli DY 272 Lb40
Oli WAN 272 Lc41
Olib HR 121 Lp46
Oliena I 111 Lk50
Olifants NAM 298 Lk58
Olifants SA 300 Mf57
Olifants SA 302 Lk61
Olifants SA 302 Mb62
Olifants Game Reserve SA 300 Mf58
Olifantshoek SA 302 Mb59
Olimarao Atoll FSM 240 Sb17
Olímbia GR 128 Mb53
Olimje Samostan SLO 121 Lq44
Olimp RO 125 Mj47
Olímpia BR (SP) 74 Hf56
Olimpiáda GR 127 Md50
Olimpos Beydağları Milli Parkı TR 131 Ml54
Olinalá MEX (GUR) 40 Fa37
Olinda BR (PI) 65 Hj48
Olinda BR (PE) 71 Jc49
Olindina BR (BA) 71 Ja51
Olinga = Maganja MOC 297 Mj54
Olio AUS (QLD) 232 Sb56
Oliserri EAK 293 Mj47
Oliete E 107 Kt52
Oliva E 109 Ku48
Oliva RA (CD) 76 Gj62
Oliva de la Frontera E 108 Ko48
Olive USA (MT) 21 Eh23
Oliveça-a-Nova ANG 294 Lg53
Oliveira BR (MG) 75 Hh56
Oliveira de Azeméis P 106 Km50
Oliveira do Hospital P 106 Kn50
Oliveira dos Brejinhos BR (BA) 70 Hj52
Olivenza E 108 Kn48
Oliver Lake CDN 24 Ej17
Olivet F 102 Lb43
Olivet USA (SD) 26 Fb24
Olivia USA (MN) 27 Fc23
Olivine Range NZ 239 Te68
Oljeitu Khudabanda IR 154 Ne27
Oljutorskij zaliv RUS 141 Tb07
Ol Kalou EAK 290 Mj46
Olkusz PL 117 Lu40
Ollagüe RCH 72 Gf56
Ollagüe, Volcán BOL/RCH 72 Gf56
Ollantaytambo PE 67 Gd52
Ollerton GB 101 Kt37
Ollombo RCB 288 Lh46
Olmaliq UZB 158 Oe25
Olmedo E 106 Kq51
Olmedo EC 60 Fk46
Olmesutye EAK 290 Mh46
Olmeto F 111 Lj49
Olmos PE 66 Ga48
Olney USA (TX) 28 Fa29
Oloči RUS 173 Qk20
Olodio CI 278 Kg43
Olofström S 95 Lp34
Ologbo Game Reserve WAN 280 Lc42
Oloibiri WAN 280 Ld43
Oloitokitok EAK 293 Mj47
Oloj RUS 141 Ta05
Ololdou SN 269 Kd38
Olomburi SOL 245 Ta50
Olomouc CZ 118 Ls41
Olonec RUS (KAR) 91 Mg15
Olongapo RP 202 Ra38
Olongliko RI 208 Qh46
Olonki RUS (UOB) 172 Qb19
Olono RCB 288 Lh47
Olorgesailie EAK 290 Mj46
Oloron-Sainte-Marie F 104 Ku47
Olosega Island USA 248 Bf53
Olot E 110 Lc48
Olovjannaja RUS 173 Qh20
Olovo BIH 121 Lt46
Olpad IND (GUJ) 190 Og35
Olpe D 112 Lh39
Ol'ša RUS 132 Mf18
Olsberg D 112 Lj39
Olshammar S 93 Lp32
Olskirke DK 95 Lp35
Olszamy PL 117 Ma39
Olszanka PL 117 Mc36
Olsztyn PL 117 Ma37
Olsztynek PL 117 Ma37
Olszyna PL 116 Lp39
Olt RO 124 Me45
Olta RA (LR) 76 Gg61
Oltedal N 92 Lg32
Olten CH 114 Lh43
Olteniţa RO 125 Mg46
Oltet RO 124 Me46
Oltina RO 125 Mh46
Oltinko'l UZB 153 Nk24
Oltu TR 145 Na25
Ol Tukai EAK 293 Mj47
Oltuš BY 117 Md39
Oluanpi RC 179 Ra34
Oluanpi RC 179 Ra35
Ölü Deniz TR 129 Mk54
Olukonda National Monument NAM 298 Lh54
Oluközü TR 131 Mp51
Oluku WAN 280 Lc42
Olu Malua = Three Sisters Islands SOL 245 Tb51
Olumo Rock WAN 280 Lb42
Olur TR 145 Nb25
Olustvere EST 96 Mf32
Olutanga Island RP 205 Rb42
Ölvega E 107 Kt51
Olvera E 108 Kp46
Ólymbos GR 129 Mh55
Olympia GR 128 Mb53
Olympia USA (WA) 18 Dj22
OlympicMountains USA 18 Dj22
Olympic N.P. USA 18 Dj22
Olympos CY 131 Mn56
Olympos GR 126 Mc50
Olympos N.P. GR 126 Mc50
Olympus, Mount USA 18 Dj22
Olynthos GR 126 Md50
Ölziyt MNG 172 Qa21
Oma J 181 Sa25
Oma VRC (TIB) 170 Pb29
Omachi J 183 Rj27
Omae-saki J 183 Rk28
Omagari J 183 Sa26
Omagh GB 98 Kn36
Omaha USA (NE) 27 Fc25
Omaha USA (GA) 35 Fh29
Omaha Ind. Res. USA 27 Fb24
Omak USA (WA) 18 Ea21
Omakau NZ 239 Te68
Omakwia GUY 58 Ha43
Omali GR 126 Mb50
O'Malley AUS (SA) 229 Rf61
Omalur IND (TNU) 193 Ok41
Oman OM 139 Nb07
Omapere NZ 238 Tg63
Omar Ali Saifudien Mosque BRU 204 Qh43
Omarama NZ 239 Te68
Omarolluk Sound CDN 25 Ga17
Omarska BIH 121 Lr46
Omaruru NAM 298 Lh56
Omaruru NAM 298 Lh56
Omas PE 66 Gb52
Oma-saki J 181 Sa25
Omatako NAM 298 Lj56
Omatako NAM 298 Lk56
Omate PE 72 Ge54
Omati PNG 243 Sb49
Omawewozonyanda NAM 298 Lk56
Omba = Uruma RI 213 Rh48
Ombalantu = Uutapi NAM 294 Lh54
Ombella RCA 281 Lk43
Ombika NAM 298 Lh55
Ombo N 92 Lf31
Ombotozu NAM 298 Lj56
Omboué G 288 Le46
Ombrone I 120 Lm48
Ombu RA (SF) 77 Gk61
Ombúes de Lavalle ROU 77 Hb62
Ombuku NAM 294 Lg54
Omchi TCH 267 Lj35
Omdurman SUD 276 Mg39
Omegna I 120 Lj45
Omeo AUS (VIC) 237 Sd64
Ömerli Baraj TR 130 Mk50
Ometepec MEX (GUR) 40 Fa37
Om Hajer ER 277 Mj39
Omicron AUS (QLD) 234 Sa60
Omidiyeh IR 154 Ne30
Omi-Hachiman J 183 Rj28
Omineca Mountains CDN 17 Dg17
Omineca River CDN 17 Dh18
Omirzak KZ 152 Nf24
Omiš HR 121 Lr47
Omitara NAM 298 Lk57
Omkareshwar IND 190 Oj34
Omkoi THA 196 Pk37
Ommen NL 112 Lg38
Ömnögovi MNG 174 Qb24
Omo ETH 284 Mj42
Omo F 249 Da51
Omoko SA 303 Md62
Omoku WAN 280 Ld43
Omolon RUS 141 Sd05
Omolon RUS 141 Ta05
Omono-gawa J 183 Sa26
Omo N.P. ETH 284 Mh43
Omo Strict Nature Reserve WAN 280 Lc42
Omo Valley ETH 284 Mh43
Ompomouéna G 288 Lf46
Ompupa ANG 294 Lg54
Omsk RUS 140 Oc08
Omu J 181 Sb23
Omu-Aran WAN 280 Lc41
Omuo WAN 280 Lc42
Omura-wan J 185 Re29
Omurtag BG 127 Mg47
Omuta J 185 Rf29
Oña EC 60 Ga47
Ona RUS 167 Pe19
Ona RUS 173 Qf19
Onaisin RCH 82 Gf72
Onakawana CDN (ON) 25 Fk20
Onaman Lake CDN 25 Fg20
Onang RI 209 Qk47
Onaping Lake CDN 25 Fk22
Onawa USA (IA) 27 Fb24
Onaway USA (MI) 32 Fh23
Onbinisan TR 145 Mk25
Oncativo RA (CD) 76 Gj61
Oncócua ANG 294 Lg54
Onda E 109 Ku49
Ondangwa NAM 294 Lh54
Ondarroa E 107 Ks53
Ondava SK 119 Mb41
Ondaw MYA 195 Ph34
Onder IND (MPH) 191 Oj33
Onderstedorings SA 302 Ma61
Ondjiva ANG 294 Lh54
Ondo WAN 280 Lc42
Ondores PE 66 Gb51
Öndörkhaan MNG 173 Qf22
One and Half Degree Channel MV 192 Og45
One Ete RI 209 Rb47
Onega RUS 91 Mk14
Onega RUS 91 Mk14
Önege KZ 133 Nd21
Oneida USA (NY) 33 Gc24
Oneida USA (TN) 35 Fh27
Oneida Ind. Res. CDN 32 Fk24
O'Neill USA (NE) 26 Fa24
Onema Okolo RDC 289 Mb47
Onema Ututu RDC 289 Mb47
Oneonta USA (NY) 33 Gc24
Oneonta USA (AL) 34 Fg29
Oner RUS 181 Sb20
Onești RO 125 Mg44
Onetangi NZ 238 Th64
One Tree AUS (NSW) 237 Sc63
Onežskaja guba RUS 91 Mh13
Onga G 288 Lh46
Onganjera NAM 294 Lh54
Ongarue NZ 238 Th65
Ongava Lodge NAM 298 Lh55
Ongeri RDC 289 Mb48
Ongers SA 302 Mb61
Ongerup AUS (WA) 228 Qk62
Onggunoi RI 209 Rc45
Ongi MNG 172 Qb23
Ongi gol MNG 172 Qb22
Ongiyn Monastery MNG 172 Qc23
Ongjin DVRK 182 Rc27
Ongkaw RI 209 Rc45
Ongkharak THA 196 Qa38
Ongniud Qi VRC (NMZ) 175 Qk24
Ongoka RDC 287 Md46
Ongole IND (APH) 193 Ok39
Ongonyi RCB 286 Lj46
Ongoro Gotjari NAM 298 Lj57
Onhne MYA 196 Pj37
Oni GE 152 Nb24
Oni WAN 280 Lc42
Onich GB 99 Kp34
Onida USA (SD) 26 Ek23
Onilahy RM 306 Nc57
Onin Peninsula RI 212 Rf47
Onion Lake CDN (SK) 19 Ef19
Onion Lake Ind. Res. CDN 19 Ef19
Onitsha WAN 280 Ld42
Ono FJI 247 Tk55
Ono J 183 Rj28
Onofio HN 42 Fg38
Ono-i-Lau FJI 221 Ua23
Onoko TCH 273 Lh40
Onolimbu RI 206 Pj45
Onomichi J 183 Rg28
Onon MNG 173 Qf21
Onon RUS 173 Qg20
Onon-Bal'džinskij hrebet MNG 173 Qf21
Onondaga Cave S.P. USA 27 Fe26
Onondaga Cave S.P. USA 34 Fe26
Onon Gol MNG 173 Qf21
Onoto YV 57 Gh41
Onotoa Atoll KIR 241 Td19
Onseepkans NAM 302 Lk60
Onslow AUS (WA) 224 Qh56
Ontake-san J 183 Rj27
Ontar VU 246 Td53
Ontario CDN 11 Fb08
Ontario USA (OR) 20 Eb23
Ontario USA (CA) 22 Eb28
Ontario USA (WI) 27 Fe24
Ontario Peninsula CDN 32 Fk24
Ontario Place CDN 33 Ga24
Ontimitta IND (APH) 193 Ok39
Ontinyent E 109 Ku48
Ontmoeting SA 302 Ma59
Ontonagon USA (MI) 32 Ff22
Ontong Java Atoll SOL 245 Sk48
Ontong-Java Rise 240 Sd19
Ontur E 109 Kt48
Onuma Q.N.P. J 181 Sa24
Onuškis LT 97 Mf34
Onverwacht SME 59 Hc43
Onward USA (MS) 29 Fe29
Onwul WAN 280 Le42
Onyx Cave USA 29 Fd27
Onzaga CO 56 Gd42
Onze-Lieve-Vrouwekerk B 103 Le39
Oobagooma AUS (WA) 222 Rc54
Oodnadatta AUS (SA) 227 Rj59
Oodweyne SP 285 Nc41
Oog van Kuruman SA 302 Mb59
Ooldea AUS (SA) 229 Rf61
Oolloo AUS (NT) 223 Rf52
Oombulgurri A.L. AUS 222 Rd53
Oona River CDN (BC) 17 De18
Oopmyn SA 303 Mc60
Oorindi AUS (QLD) 232 Sa56
Oos-Londen SA 303 Md62
Oostburg NL 112 Ld39
Oostende B 103 Lc39
Oosterend NL 112 Lf37
Oosterhout NL 112 Le39
Oostermoed SA 299 Md58
Oosterschelde NL 112 Ld39
Oosterscheldedam NL 112 Ld39
Oosterwolde NL 112 Lg38
Oostkapelle NL 112 Ld39
Oost-Vlieland NL 112 Lf37
Ootacamund IND (TNU) 192 Oj41
Ootsa Lake CDN (BC) 18 Dg19
Ootsa Lake CDN 18 Dh19
Ooty = Ootacamund IND (TNU) 192 Oj41
Opachuanau Lake CDN 24 Fa17
Opactwo Cystersów Sulejów PL 117 Lu39
Opaka BG 127 Mg47
Opala RDC 287 Mc46
Opal Deposit AUS 227 Rh60
Opanözü TR 130 Mk51
Opari SUD 290 Mg44
Oparić SCG 126 Mb47
Opasatika CDN (ON) 25 Fj21
Opasatika Lake CDN 25 Fj21
Opasquia Prov. Park CDN 24 Fd19
Opatija HR 121 Lp45
Opatów PL 116 Lt39
Opatów PL 117 Mb40
Opava CZ 118 Ls41
Opelika USA (AL) 35 Fh29
Opelousas USA (LA) 29 Fd30
Opémiska, Mount CDN 30 Gc20
Open Bay PNG 244 Sf48
Opernhaus Bayreuth D 115 Lm41
Opheim USA (MT) 19 Eg21
Ophir USA (AK) 15 Cb14
Ophir USA (OR) 20 Dh24
Opi WAN 280 Ld42
Opienge RDC 287 Md45
Opin RI 212 Re47
Opinnagau River CDN 25 Fj18
Opišn'a UA 134 Mh21
Opličići BIH 121 Ls47
Opobo WAN 280 Ld43
Opočka RUS 132 Me17
Opoczno PL 117 Ma39
Opole PL 116 Ls40
Opol'e RUS 96 Mj31
Opole Lubelskie PL 117 Mb39
Opunono Lake NAM 298 Lh55
Opotiki NZ 238 Tj65
Opovo SCG 124 Ma45
Opp USA (AL) 35 Fg30
Oppdal N 92 Lk28
Oppenheim D 114 Lj41
Oppicherla IND (APH) 191 Ok37
Opportunity USA (WA) 18 Eb22
Opsa BY 97 Mg35

P

ontenova Villaodriz E 106 Kn53
ont-en-Royans F 105 Lf45
ontes e Lacerda BR (MT) 68 Ha53
onte Serrada BR (SC) 78 He59
onte Tresa I 120 Lj45
ontevedra E 106 Km52
ontgibaud F 105 Lc45
onthieu F 103 Lb40
ontiac USA (IL) 32 Ff25
ontianak RI 208 Qe46
ontian Kechil MAL 199 Qb45
ontic Mountains TR 142 Mc10
ontivy F 102 Ks42
ont-l'Abbé F 102 Kq43
ont-l'Evêque F 102 La41
onto Alto do Tocantins BR (TO) 70 Hg51
ontoise F 103 Lc41
ontokerasiá GR 126 Md49
onton AUS 229 Rb61
onton CDN (MB) 24 Fa18
ontorson F 102 Kt42
ontotoc USA (MS) 29 Ff28
ontrémoli I 120 Lk46
ontresina CH 114 Lk44
onts E 110 Lb49
ont-Sainte-Maxence F 103 Lc41
ont-Saint-Esprit F 105 Le46
ont-Saint-Vincent F 103 Lg42
ont-sur-Yonne F 103 Ld42
ont Valentré F 104 Lb46
ontypool GB 101 Kr39
onuga PA 43 Fk42
ony Express Station USA 27 Fb26
onza I 122 Ln50
oochera AUS (SA) 236 Rh62
oole GB 101 Kt40
ool Malebo RDC 288 Lh48
oolowanna Lake AUS 227 Rj59
ool's Cove CDN (NF) 31 Hc22
ooncarie AUS (NSW) 237 Sb62
oopó BOL 72 Gg55
oor Knights Islands NZ 238 Th63
oorman USA (AK) 15 Cc13
oor Man Ind. Res. CDN 19 Eh20
õõsaspea neem EST 96 Md31
oowong AUS (VIC) 237 Sc65
op KS 158 Of25
opa G 288 Lg46
opa Falls NAM 299 Ma55
opagaon NEP 170 Pb31
opa, Mount MYA 195 Ph35
opayán CO 60 Gb44
opčevo MNE 126 Mc49
ope LV 97 Mb33
openguine SN 269 Kb38
operinge B 103 Lc40
opești RO 124 Mc43
opielów PL 116 Ls40
oplar Bluff USA (MO) 29 Fe27
oplarfield CDN (MB) 24 Fb20
oplar Point CDN 24 Fb19
oplar River CDN 19 Eg21
oplar River CDN 24 Fb19
oplar River Power Station and Strip Mine CDN 19 Eh21
oplarville USA (MS) 29 Ff30
opocatépetl MEX 40 Fa36
opodara RG 278 Kd40
opof Island USA 14 Bk18
opoh RI 210 Qf50
op-kabaka RDC 288 Lj48
opoli I 122 Lo48
opomanaseu, Mount SOL 245 Ta50
opondetta PNG 243 Se50
opovača HR 121 Lr45
opovići BIH 121 Ls46
opovo BG 127 Mg47
opovyči UA 119 Mc41
oppi PL 116 Lt39
opp I 120 Lm47
oprad SK 119 Ma41
oprad SK 119 Ma41
opšica SCG 126 Mb47
opsko BG 127 Mf49
optún GCA 41 Ff37
opular Point CDN (MB) 24 Fb20
opulónia I 120 Ll48
oquis, Nevado de RA/RCH 72 Gg57
orangahau NZ 238 Tj66
orangatu BR (GO) 70 Hf52
orata IND (ORS) 191 Pb36
orazava BY 117 Me38
orbandar IND (GUJ) 190 Oe35
orcher Island CDN 18 De19
orcuna E 108 Kq47
orcupine USA (AK) 17 Db16
orcupine Abyssal Plain 88 Ka09
orcupine Gorge N.P. AUS 232 Sc56
orcupine Hills CDN 24 Ek19
orcupine Prov. Forest CDN 24 Ek19
ordenone I 121 Ln45
ordim BG 127 Me47
ore CO 56 Ge43
orebada PNG 243 Sd50
orebeni MD 125 Mj43
oreč HR 121 Lo45
orecatu BR (PR) 74 He57
oreč'e RUS 96 Mj31
orédaka RG 278 Kd40
orga DY 279 La40
orgera PNG 243 Sb48
orhov RUS 132 Me17
ori DVRK 182 Rd25
ori FIN 96 Mb29
ori Jazz FIN 96 Mb29
orirua NZ 238 Th66
orisvatn IS 90 Ka13
orjus S 90 Lk12
orkkala FIN 96 Me31
orlákshöfn IS 90 Jk14
orlamar YV 58 Gj40
ormpuraaw AUS (QLD) 230 Sa53
ornic F 102 Ks43
oro Island RP 205 Rc40
oroma PNG 243 Sb49
oronaj RUS 181 Sb21
orongurup AUS (WA) 228 Qj63
oronjsk RUS 181 Sb21
oros GR 128 Ma52
óros GR 128 Md53
orosozero RUS (KAR) 91 Mg14
orozina E 107 Kp51
orquinhos-Aldeia Chinela, T.I. BR 64 Hh49
orquis Junction CDN (ON) 25 Fk21
Porras FIN 96 Md30
Porrentruy CH 114 Lh43
Porretta Terme I 120 Ll46
Porriño E 106 Km52
Porsangenfjorden N 91 Mc10
Porsea RI 198 Pk44
Porsgrunn N 92 Lk31
Þórshöfn IS 90 Kc12
Þórsmörk IS 90 Ka14
Portachuelo BOL 73 Gj54
Portadown GB 98 Ko36
Portaferry GB 98 Kp36
Portage USA (AK) 15 Cf15
Portage USA (WI) 32 Ff24
Portage Glacier USA 15 Cf15
Portage la Prairie CDN (MB) 24 Fa20
Portal BR 71 Hk50
Port Alberni CDN (BC) 18 Dh21
Port Albert AUS (VIC) 237 Sd65
Portalegre P 108 Kn49
Portales USA (NM) 23 Ej28
Port Alexander USA (AK) 17 Dc17
Port Alfred ZA 303 Md62
Port Alice CDN (BC) 18 Dg20
Port Alma AUS (QLD) 233 Sf57
Porta Nigra D 114 Lg41
Port Antonio JA 45 Gb36
Portara GR 129 Mf53
Portarlington IRL 100 Kn37
Port Arthur AUS (TAS) 236 Sd67
Port Arthur USA (TX) 29 Fd31
Port Arthur = Lüshun VRC (LNG) 182 Ra26
Port Askaig GB 98 Ko35
Port au Choix N.H.S. CDN 31 Hb20
Port Augusta AUS (SA) 236 Rj62
Port au Port Bay CDN 31 Ha21
Port-au-Prince RH 46 Gd36
Port Austin USA (MI) 32 Fj23
Port aux Choix CDN (NF) 31 Hb20
Portavadie GB 98 Kp35
Port Aventura E 110 Lb49
Porta Westfalica D 112 Lj38
Port Barton RP 204 Qk40
Port Bickerton CDN (NS) 31 Gk23
Port Blair IND (AAN) 193 Pg40
Port Blandford CDN (NF) 31 Hc21
Port Bradshaw AUS 223 Rj52
Port Broughton AUS (SA) 236 Rj62
Port Burwell Prov. Park CDN 33 Fk24
Port Campbell AUS (VIC) 237 Sb65
Port -Cartier CDN (QC) 30 Gg20
Port Charlotte USA (FL) 36 Fj32
Port Chilkoot USA (AK) 17 Dc16
Port Clarence USA 15 Bg13
Port Clements CDN (BC) 18 Dd19
Port Clinton USA (OH) 32 Fj25
Port Colborne CDN (ON) 33 Ga24
Port Curtis AUS 233 Sf57
Port d'Addaia E 110 Le50
Port-Daniel CDN (QC) 31 Gh21
Port Davey AUS 236 Sc67
Port-de-Bouc F 105 Le47
Port-de-Paix RH 46 Gd36
Port de Pollença E 110 Ld51
Port d'es Torrent E 110 Lb52
Port Dickson MAL 199 Qa44
Port Douglas AUS (QLD) 233 Sc54
Port Edward CDN (BC) 18 De18
Port Edward SA 303 Mf61
Porteira BR (PA) 63 Hb46
Porteirinha BR (MG) 70 Hj53
Portel BR (PA) 63 He46
Portel P 108 Kn48
Portelândia BR (GO) 74 Hd54
Port Elgin CDN (ON) 32 Fk23
Port Elizabeth SA 303 Mc62
Port Ellen GB 98 Ko35
Port Elliot AUS (SA) 236 Rk63
Portena RA (CD) 76 Gj61
Port-en-Bessin F 102 Ku41
Port Erin GB 98 Kq36
Porters Corner USA (MT) 21 Ed22
Porterville SA 302 Lk62
Porterville USA (CA) 22 Ea27
Portes d'Enfer RDC 292 Md48
Port Essington CDN (BC) 18 Df18
Port Fairy AUS (VIC) 236 Sb65
Port Fitzroy NZ 238 Th64
Port Fourchon USA (LA) 29 Fe31
Port Fuád ET 263 Mg30
Port-Gentil G 280 Le46
Port Germein AUS (SA) 236 Rk62
Port Gibson USA (LA) 29 Fe30
Port Gregory AUS (WA) 228 Qh60
Port Grimaud F 105 Lg47
Port Grosvenor SA 303 Me61
Port Hacking AUS 237 Sf63
Port Harcourt WAN 280 Ld43
Port Hardy CDN (BC) 18 Dg20
Port Harrison = Inukjuak CDN 11 Ga07
Port Hastings CDN (NS) 31 Gk23
Porthcawl GB 100 Kr39
Port Hedland AUS (WA) 224 Qk56
Port Heiden USA (AK) 14 Ca17
Port Heiden USA (AK) 14 Ca17
Porthill USA (ID) 19 Eb21
Port Hope CDN (ON) 33 Ga24
Port Hope Simpson CDN 11 Ha08
Port Howard GB 83 Ha71
Port Howe BS 37 Gc33
Port Huron CDN (ON) 32 Fj24
Portile de Fier, P.N. RO 124 Mc46
Portillo RCH 76 Ge62
Portimão P 108 Km47
Portinatx E 110 Lb51
Port Jackson AUS 237 Sf62
Port Jackson NZ 238 Th64
Port Jervis USA (NJ) 33 Gc25
Port-Joinville F 102 Ks44
Port Kembla AUS (NSW) 237 Sf63
Port Kenny AUS (SA) 236 Rh62
Portland AUS (VIC) 236 Sa65
Portland USA (OR) 20 Dj23
Portland USA (IN) 32 Fh25
Portland USA (ME) 33 Ge24
Portland USA (TN) 34 Fg27
Portland USA (TX) 39 Fb32
Portland Bay AUS 236 Sa65
Portland Bigth JA 45 Gb37
Portland Channel USA 17 De18
Portland Creek Pond CDN 31 Hb20
Portland Inlet CDN 17 De18
Portland Island NZ 238 Tj65
Portland Point JA 45 Gb37
Portland Roads AUS (QLD) 230 Sb52
Port Langdon AUS 223 Rj52
Port-la-Nouvelle F 105 Ld47
Port Laoise IRL 100 Kn37
Port Latta AUS (TAS) 236 Sc66
Port Lavaca USA (TX) 29 Fb31
Port Lincoln AUS (SA) 236 Rh63
Portlock USA (AK) 15 Ce16
Portlock Reefs PNG 243 Sc50
Port Loins USA (AK) 16 Cd17
Port Loko WAL 278 Kd41
Port Loring CDN (ON) 32 Fk23
Port-Louis F 47 Gk37
Port-Louis F 102 Kr43
Port Louis MS 307 Nj56
Port MacDonnell AUS (VIC) 236 Sa65
Port Macquarie AUS (NSW) 235 Sg61
Port Mansfield USA (TX) 39 Fb32
Port Maria JA 45 Gb36
Port Mayaca USA (FL) 36 Fk32
Port McArthur AUS 223 Rj53
Portmeirion GB 100 Kq38
Port-Menier CDN (QC) 31 Gh21
Port Moller USA (AK) 14 Bk18
Port Moller USA (AK) 14 Bk18
Portmore JA 45 Gb37
Port Moresby PNG 243 Sd50
Port Musgrave AUS 230 Sa51
Portnacroish GB 99 Kp34
Portnahaven GB 98 Ko35
Port-Navalo F 102 Ks43
Port Neill AUS (SA) 236 Rj63
Port Nelson BS 37 Gc34
Port Nelson CDN 24 Fd17
Port Nelson (abandoned) CDN 24 Fd17
Port Neville CDN (BC) 18 Dg20
Port Noarlunga AUS (SA) 236 Rk63
Port Nolloth SA 302 Lj60
Porto BR (PI) 65 Hj47
Porto F 111 Lj48
Porto P 106 Km51
Porto Acre BR (AC) 67 Gg50
Porto Alegre BR (PA) 63 Hb48
Porto Alegre BR (RS) 78 He61
Porto Alegre STP 280 Ld45
Porto Alegre do Norte BR (MT) 69 He51
Porto Alencastro BR (MG) 74 He55
Porto Alto P 108 Km48
Porto Amboim ANG 294 Lg51
Porto Amelia = Pemba MOC 297 Na52
Porto Antunes BR (AM) 61 Gg47
Porto Arari BR (AP) 63 He45
Porto Azzurro I 120 Ll48
Portobelo PA 43 Ga41
Portobelo, P.N. PA 43 Ga41
Porto Bicentenário BR (RO) 68 Gj51
Porto Braga BR (AM) 62 Gh47
Porto Braga BR (MS) 73 Hb56
Porto Caiuá BR (MS) 74 Hd57
Porto Calvo BR (AL) 71 Jc50
Porto Camargo BR (PR) 74 Hd57
Porto Cervo I 111 Lk49
Porto Cesáreo I 123 Ls50
Porto Chique BR (MG) 75 Hh54
Porto D'Oronor USA (TX) 39 Fb31
Portocristo E 110 Ld51
Porto da Balsa P 106 Kn50
Porto da Folha BR (SE) 71 Jb50
Porto de Galinhas BR (PE) 71 Jc50
Porto de Pedras BR (AL) 71 Jc50
Porto do Mangue BR (RN) 65 Jb48
Porto do Moz BR (PA) 63 Hd46
Porto dos Gaúchos BR (MT) 69 Hb51
Porto do Son E 106 Km52
Porto Empédocle I 122 Lo53
Porto Esperança BR (MS) 73 Hb55
Porto Esperidião BR (MT) 68 Ha53
Porto Estrella BR (MT) 69 Hb53
Portoferráio I 120 Ll48
Porto Ferreira BR (SP) 74 Hg56
Portofino I 120 Lk46
Port of Ness GB 99 Ko32
Porto Franco BR (MA) 64 Hg49
Port of Spain TT 58 Gk40
Porto Grande BR (AP) 63 He45
Portogruaro I 121 Ln45
Porto Henrique MOC 303 Mg59
Porto Jofre BR (MT) 73 Hb54
Porto Koufós GR 127 Md51
Porto Lindo, T.I. BR 74 Hc57
Port-Olry VU 246 Td53
Pörtom = Pirttikylä FIN 93 Mb28
Portomaggiore I 120 Lm46
Porto Manga BR (MS) 73 Hb55
Porto Marie NL 57 Gf39
Portomarín E 106 Kn52
Porto Mauá BR (RS) 78 Hc59
Porto Morrinho BR (MS) 73 Hb55
Porto Murtinho BR (MS) 73 Hb56
Porto Nacional BR (TO) 70 Hf51
Porto-Novo CV 268 Jh37
Porto-Novo DY 280 Lb42
Porto Novo IND (TNU) 193 Ok41
Porto Primavera BR (MS) 74 Hd57
Port Orange USA (FL) 36 Fk31
Porto Recanati I 121 Lo47
Porto Reis BR (AM) 62 Gh47
Port Orford USA (OR) 20 Dh24
Porto Rico BR (PR) 74 Hd57
Portorož SLO 121 Lo45
Porto San Giórgio I 121 Lo47
Porto Sant'Elpídio I 121 Lo47
Porto Santo P 88 Ka12
Porto São Domingos BR (MG) 74 He55
Porto São José BR (MS) 74 Hd57
Porto Sauipe BR (BA) 71 Jb52
Portoscuso I 111 Lj51
Porto Seguro BR (BA) 75 Ja54
Porto Silva BR (AM) 61 Gg48
Porto Tolle I 120 Ln46
Porto Tôrres I 111 Lj50
Porto União BR (SC) 78 He59
Porto Vecchio F 111 Lk49
Pôrto Velho BR (RO) 68 Gj50
Portovénere I 120 Lk46
Portoviejo EC 60 Fk46
Porto Vinte e Dois BR (AM) 62 Gj47
Porto Viro I 120 Ln45
Porto Walter BR (AC) 67 Gd50
Porto Xavier BR (RS) 78 Hc59
Portpatrick GB 98 Kp36
Port Phillip Bay AUS 237 Sc65
Port Pirie AUS (SA) 236 Rj62
Port Radium CDN 10 Ea05
Portree GB 98 Ko33
Portrush GB 98 Ko35
Port Said ET 263 Mg30
Port Said ET 263 Mg30
Port Saint Joe USA (FL) 35 Fh31
Port Saint Johns SA 303 Me61
Port-Saint-Louis-du-Rhône F 105 Le47
Port Saint Lucie USA (FL) 36 Fk32
Port Salerno USA (FL) 36 Fk32
Portsalon IRL 98 Kn35
Port Sanilac USA (MI) 32 Fj24
Pörtschach A 115 Lp44
Port Shepstone SA 303 Mf61
Port Simpson CDN (BC) 17 De18
Portsmouth GB 101 Kt40
Portsmouth USA (NH) 33 Ge24
Portsmouth USA (OH) 35 Fj26
Portsmouth USA (VA) 35 Gb27
Portsmouth WD 47 Gk38
Portsoy GB 99 Ks33
Port Stephens AUS 237 Sg62
Port Stephens GB 83 Gk72
Port Steward = Moojeeba AUS (QLD) 231 Sb53
Port Sudan SUD 277 Mj37
Port Sulphur USA (LA) 29 Ff31
Port-sur-Saône F 103 Lg43
Port Talbot GB 100 Kr39
Porttipahdan tekojärvi FIN 91 Md11
Portugal 87 Kb05
Portugalete E 107 Kr53
Portuguesa YV 57 Gf41
Portumna IRL 100 Km37
Port-Vato VU 246 Te54
Port-Vendres F 104 Ld48
Port Victoria AUS (SA) 236 Rj63
Port Victoria EAK 290 Mh45
Port Vila VU 246 Te54
Port Vita USA (AK) 16 Cd16
Port Wakefield AUS (SA) 236 Rk63
Port Warrender AUS (WA) 222 Rc53
Port Washington USA (WI) 32 Fg24
Port William USA (AK) 16 Cd16
Port Wing USA (WI) 27 Fe22
Porumamilla IND (APH) 193 Ok39
Porvenir BOL 67 Gf51
Porvenir PE 60 Gb47
Porvenir RCH 82 Ge72
Porvenir Cumuripa MEX (SO) 38 Ef31
Porvoo = Borga FIN 96 Mf30
Porvoonjoki FIN 96 Mf30
Porzellanmanufaktur Meissen D 113 Lo39
Porzuna E 109 Kq49
Posada I 111 Lk50
Posadas E 108 Kp47
Posadas RA (MI) 77 Hc59
Posavina HR 121 Lr45
Posedarje HR 121 Lq46
Pošehon'e RUS 132 Mk16
Po Sha Nu Tower VN 197 Qe40
Posio FIN 91 Me12
Positano I 122 Lp50
Poso RI 209 Ra46
Posof TR 145 Nb25
Posong ROK 182 Rd28
Posoria EC 60 Fk47
Posse BR (GO) 70 Hg53
Possel RCA 286 Lk43
Possessioneiland NAM 302 Lh59
Possession Island NAM 302 Lh59
Pößneck D 113 Lm40
Possoś' RUS 133 Mk20
Post USA (OR) 20 Dk23
Post USA (TX) 28 Ek29
Poșta Călnău RO 125 Mg45
Posta Cambio a Zalazar RA (FO) 73 Gk58
Post Arinda GUY 58 Ha43
Post Falls USA (ID) 18 Eb22
Posties AUS 236 Rj63
Postmasburg SA 302 Mb60
Posto Ajuricaba BR (AM) 62 Gj45
Posto Cocraimore BR (PA) 68 Hd49
Posto Funa BR (AM) 62 Gk46
Posto Funai BR (AP) 59 He44
Posto Funai BR (AM) 61 Gd48
Posto Funai BR (AM) 62 Gk46
Posto Funai BR (AM) 62 Gk46
Posto Funai BR (AM) 62 Ha46
Postojna SLO 121 Lp45
Postojnska jama SLO 121 Lp45
Postomino PL 116 Lr36
Posto Uaça BR (AP) 59 He44
Postrer Valle BOL 73 Gj55
Posušje BIH 121 Ls47
Pota RI 211 Ra50
Potala VRC 171 Pf31
Potam MEX (SO) 38 Ee32
Potamós GR 128 Md55
Potamoúla GR 128 Mb52
Potangi IND (ORS) 191 Pb36
Potash City JOR 146 Mh30
Potawatomi Ind. Res. USA 27 Fc26
Potchefstroom SA 303 Md59
Potcoava RO 125 Me46
Poté BR (MG) 75 Hk54
Poteau USA (OK) 29 Fc28
Potengi BR 65 Jc48
Potenza I 121 Lo47
Potenza I 123 Lq50
Potenza Picena I 121 Lo47
Poterillos RCH 76 Gf59
Potero Seco RCH 76 Ge59
Potes E 106 Kq53
Potfontein SA 303 Mc61
Potgietersrus SA 299 Me58
Potholes Reservoir USA 18 Ea22
Pothungoli IND (CGH) 191 Pa36
Poti BR 65 Hj48
Poti GE 152 Na24
Potiguara, T.I. BR 65 Jc49
Potin IND (ARP) 194 Pg32
Potiraguá BR (BA) 71 Ja53
Potirendaba BR (SP) 74 Hf56
Potiskum WAN 273 Lf40
Pot Mountain USA 21 Ec22
Potoci BIH 121 Ls47
Potomac Highlands USA 33 Fk26
Potoru WAL 278 Ke42
Potosí BOL 72 Gh55
Potosí GUY 58 Ha42
Potosí NIC 42 Fg39
Potosí USA (MO) 29 Fe27
Potrero del Llano MEX (CHH) 23 Eh31
Potrero del Llano MEX (DGO) 39 Eh32
Potro PE 60 Gb48
Potro, Cerro del RA/RCH 76 Gf60
Potsdam D 113 Lo38
Potsdam USA (NY) 33 Gc23
Pottsville USA (PA) 33 Gb25
Pottuvil CL 193 Pa43
Pötürge TR 145 Mk26
Potworów PL 117 Ma39
Pouancé F 102 Kt43
Pouch Cove CDN (NF) 31 Hd22
Pouébo RCB 281 Lh46
Poughkeepsie USA (NY) 33 Gd25
Pougol RCA 281 Lj42
Pouh K 197 Qc39
Pouheva F 249 Cj54
Poulaphouca Reservoir IRL 100 Ko37
Poulnabrone Dolmen IRL 100 Kl37
Poum F 246 Tc56
Pouma CAM 281 Lf44
Poumalé RCA 286 Lk43
Poum USA (WI) 32 Ff23
Pound Maker Ind. Res. CDN 19 Ef19
Poun VN 178 Qc35
Poura BF 279 Kj40
Pourerere NZ 238 Tj66
Pouri IND (MPH) 191 Pa34
Pouso Alegre BR (AM) 62 Gj49
Pouso Alegre BR (MG) 75 Hh57
Pouso Grande BR (PA) 63 Hb48
Pouso Redondo BR (SC) 79 Hf59
Pouss CAM 273 Lh40
Pouto NZ 238 Th64
Pouytenga BF 271 Kk39
Pouzauges F 102 Ku44
Považska Bystrica SK 118 Lt41
Poverty Beach USA 33 Gc26
Povoação BR (ES) 75 Ja55
Povoação Velha CV 268 Jj37
Póvoa de São Miguel P 108 Kn48
Póvoa de Varzim P 106 Km51
Povorot RUS (BUR) 172 Qd20
Povors'k UA 117 Mf39
Powari IND (HPH) 189 Ok30
Powder USA 21 Eg23
Powderville USA (MT) 21 Eh23
Powell USA (WY) 21 Ef23
Powell Point AUS 228 Ra62
Powell Point BS 37 Gb33
Powell River CDN (BC) 18 Dh21
Power USA (MT) 19 Ee22
Powerview CDN (MB) 24 Fb20
Powis Castle GB 101 Kr38
Powlathanga AUS (QLD) 233 Sc56
Poxoréo BR (MT) 69 Hc53
Poxyaxum MEX (CAM) 41 Fe36
Poya F 246 Tc56
Poyang Hu VRC 184 Qj31
Poyanghu Z.B. VRC 184 Qj31
Poyracık TR 130 Mh51
Poyraz TR 131 Mn51
Poysdorf A 115 Lr42
Poytug UZB 159 Og25
Pozanti TR 131 Mp53
Pozao VRC (GZG) 178 Qd34
Požarevac SCG 124 Mb46
Poza Rica MEX (VC) 40 Fb35
Požarskoe RUS 180 Rh22
Pozedrze PL 117 Mb36
Požega HR 121 Ls45
Požega SCG 126 Ma47
Pozhan PL 116 Lr38
Pozo Alcón E 109 Ks47
Pozo Almonte RCH 72 Gf56
Pozo Azul PY 73 Ha58
Pozoblanco E 108 Kq48
Pozo-Cañada E 109 Kt48
Pozo Colorado PY 73 Ha57
Pozo Coyote MEX (SO) 22 Ed31
Pozo de las Animas RA 76 Gf63
Pozo del Molle RA (CD) 77 Gj62
Pozo del Tigre BOL 73 Gj54
Pozo del Tigre RA (FO) 73 Gk58
Pozo del Toba RA (SE) 77 Gj59
Pozo de Maza RA (FO) 73 Gk57
Pozohondo E 109 Kt48
Pozo Hondo RA (SE) 76 Gh59
Pozón YV 57 Gg42
Pozuelo de Alarcón E 109 Kr50
Pozuzo PE 66 Gc50
Pozuzo PE 66 Gc51
Pozzallo I 122 Lp54
Pozzuoli I 122 Lp50
Pra GH 279 Kk43
Prača BIH 126 Lt47
Prachatice CZ 118 Lo41
Prachinburi THA 196 Qa38
Prachovské skály CZ 118 Lq40
Prachuap Khirikhan THA 198 Pk40
Pradelles F 105 Ld46
Prades E 110 La49
Prades F 104 Lc48
Pradła PL 117 Lu40
Prado BR (BA) 75 Ja54
Prado E 109 Kr50
Prado del Rey E 108 Kp46
Pradoluengo E 107 Kr52
Prádópolis BR (SP) 74 Hf56
Præstø DK 94 Ln35
Prague CZ 118 Lp40
Prague USA (OK) 29 Fb28
Praha CZ 118 Lp40
Prahova RO 125 Mf45
Prahovo SCG 126 Mc46
Praia BR (PA) 63 Hc48
Praia CV 268 Jj38
Práia a Mare I 123 Lq51
Praia da Baleia BR (CE) 65 Ja47
Praia da Barata BR (AM) 61 Gg46
Praia da Barra P 106 Km50
Praia da Conceição BR (PE) 71 Jc49
Praia das Chocas MOC 297 Na53
Praia da Vieira P 108 Km49
Praia de Chongoene MOC 300 Mh58
Praia de Macaneta MOC 300 Mg58
Praia de Mira P 106 Km50
Praia de Zalala MOC 297 Mj54
Praia de Zavala MOC 300 Mh58
Praia de Závora MOC 300 Mh58
Praia do Bilene MOC 300 Mg58
Praia do Forte BR (BA) 71 Ja52
Praia do Maçarico BR (AM) 61 Gg46
Praia do Tofo MOC 300 Mh57
Praia do Wimbe MOC 297 Na52
Praia do Xai-Xai MOC 300 Mg58
Praia Grande BR (SP) 75 Hg58
Praia Grande BR (SC) 79 Hf60
Praid RO 125 Mf44
Praikalogu RI 211 Qk50
Prainha BR (PA) 63 Hd46
Prainha BR (PA) 63 He47
Prainha BR (AM) 67 Gg49
Prainha Nova BR (AM) 62 Gk49
Prairie AUS (QLD) 232 Sc56
Prairie Dog Colony CDN 19 Eg21
Prairie Du Chien USA (WI) 27 Fe24
Prairie River CDN (SK) 24 Ej19
Prakham K 197 Qc39
Prakhon Chai THA 197 Qb38
Pralognan F 105 Lg45
Pra-Loup F 105 Lg46
Prámanda GR 128 Mb51
Prambanan RI 210 Qf49
Prampram GH 279 La43
Pran Buri THA 196 Pk39
Pran Buri Reservoir THA 196 Pk39
Prang GH 279 Kk41
Prangli EST 96 Me31
Prapat RI 198 Pk44
Prarie Downs AUS (WA) 224 Qk57
Prasat THA 197 Qb38
Prasat Sadok Kok Thom THA 197 Qb39
Prasat Sikhoraphum THA 197 Qb38
Praserganj IND (WBG) 194 Pe35
Praslin SY 305 Nh48
Prastio CY 131 Mo55
Praszka PL 116 Lt39
Prata BR (MG) 74 Hf55
Prata BR 74 Hf55
Pratabpur IND (CGH) 191 Pb34
Pratapgad Fort IND 190 Og37
Pratapgarh IND (RJT) 190 Oh33
Ratapur IND (ORS) 191 Pc36
Pratas Islands VRC 179 Qj35
Prat, C.A. ANT (RCH) 312 Ha31
Prategi BR (BA) 71 Ja52
Prathai THA 197 Qb38
Pra That Cave THA 196 Pk38
Prato I 120 Lm47
Prats de Lluçanès E 110 Lc49
Prats-de-Mollo F 104 Lc48
Pratt USA (KS) 28 Fa27
Prattenville AUS (NSW) 235 Sc61
Pratt Seamount 16 Cj17
Prattville USA (AL) 34 Fg29
Pratudão BR 70 Hh53
Pravara Sangam IND (MHT) 190 Oh36
Pravasuni IND (ORS) 191 Pc35
Pravčická brána CZ 118 Lp41
Pravda UA 117 Me40
Pravdinsk RUS 97 Mb36
Pravec BG 126 Md48
Pravia E 106 Ko53
Praya RI 211 Qj50
Preacher's Cave BS 37 Gb33
Precipice N.P. AUS 235 Sf58
Prečistoe RUS 132 Mg18
Prečistoe RUS 132 Na16
Predajane SCG 126 Mc48
Predaltajskaja ravnina RUS 167 Pb20
Predazzo I 120 Lm44
Predbajkal'skaja vpadina RUS 172 Qc19
Predeal RO 125 Mf45
Pre Delta, P.N. RA 77 Gk62
Predeşti RO 124 Md46
Predjamski grad SLO 121 Lp45
Preeceville CDN (SK) 24 Ej19
Pré-en-Pail F 102 Ku42
Preetz D 113 Ll36
Pregarten A 115 Lp42
Pregolja RUS 97 Mb36
Pregonero YV 56 Ge41
Prehistoric Footprints LS 303 Me60
Prehistoric Mounds CDN 24 Ek21
Preikestolen N 92 Lg31
Preiļi LV 97 Mg34
Prejmer RO 125 Mf45
Prejmer RO 125 Mf45
Prékété DY 279 La41
Preko HR 121 Lq46
Prek Thmei K 197 Qc40
Prek Vatt K 197 Qc40
Prelog HR 121 Lr44
Premer AUS (NSW) 235 Se61
Prémery F 103 Ld43
Premier Downs AUS (WA) 229 Rc61
Premio CDN (QC) 30 Gh20
Premnitz D 113 Ln38
Premuda HR 121 Lp46
Prend Town LB 278 Kf43
Prenn Falls VN 197 Qe40
Prenti Downs AUS (WA) 225 Rb59
Prentiss USA (MS) 29 Ff30
Prenzlau D 113 Lo37
Preobraženski manastir BG 127 Mf47
Preparis Island MYA 193 Pg38
Prequiça BR 65 Hj47
Přerov CZ 118 Ls41
Presa de Guadelupe MEX (SLP) 39 Ek34
Presa de la Angostura MEX 41 Fd37
Presa Falcón MEX 39 Fa32
Presa J. López Portillo MEX 38 Eg33
Presa M. Alemán MEX 40 Fb36
Presa Nezahualcyotl MEX 41 Fd37
Presa Nova Ponte BR 74 Hg55
Presa P. Elias Calles MEX 23 Ef31
Presa V. Carranza MEX 39 Ek32
Prescott USA (WA) 20 Ea22
Prescott USA (AZ) 22 Ed28
Prescott USA (AR) 29 Fd29
Preservation Inlet USA 239 Td69
Preševo SCG 126 Mb48
Presidencia de la Plaza RA (CH) 77 Ha59
Presidencia Roque Sáenz Peña RA (CH) 77 Gk59
Presidente Dutra BR (MA) 64 Hh48
Presidente Eduardo Frei ANT (RCH) 312 Ha30
Presidente Epitácio BR (SP) 74 He56
Presidente Figueiredo BR (AM) 62 Gk47
Presidente Getúlio BR (SC) 79 Hf59
PresidenteJânio Quadros BR (BA) 71 Hk53
Presidente Juscelino BR (MA) 64 Hh47
Presidente Juscelino BR (MG) 75 Hh55
Presidente Kennedy BR (TO) 70 Hf50
Presidente Médici BR (RO) 68 Gk51
Presidente Olegário BR (MG) 75 Hg55
Presidente Prudente BR (SP) 74 He57
Presidente Vargas BR (MA) 64 Hh47
Presidente Venceslau BR (SP) 74 He56
Presidio USA (TX) 23 Eh31
Presjaka SCG 126 Lt48
Prešov SK 119 Mb42
Préspa N.P. GR 126 Mb50
Presque Isle USA (ME) 30 Gg22
Presque Isle S.P. USA 33 Fk24
Presqu'île de Crozon F 102 Kq42
Presqu'île de Quiberon F 102 Kr43
Presquile de Taiarapu F 249 Cf54
Presqu'île du Cotentin F 102 Kt41
Presqu'ile Prov. Park CDN 33 Gb23
Pressac F 104 La44
Pressath D 115 Lm41
Pressa Lake CDN 25 Fe21
Prestatyn GB 101 Kr37
Prestfoss N 92 Lk30
Preštice CZ 118 Lo41
Preston GB 101 Ks37
Preston USA (NV) 20 Ec26
Preston USA (ID) 21 Ee24
Preston USA (MN) 27 Fd24
Preston USA (MO) 29 Fd27
Preston USA (MS) 29 Ff29
Preston USA (GA) 35 Fh30
Prestonburg USA (KY) 35 Fj27
Prestwick GB 99 Kq35
Presumida MEX (QTR) 41 Ff36
Prêto BR 62 Gh45
Prêto BR 62 Gh46
Prêto BR 62 Gj46
Prêto BR 68 Gj50
Prêto BR 70 Hg54
Prêto BR 70 Hh51
Prêto do Candeiras BR 68 Gj50
Prêto do Igapó-Açu BR 62 Gk48
Pretoria SA 299 Me58
Pretzsch D 113 Ln39
Prevelly AUS 228 Qh62
Prevelly Park AUS 228 Qh63
Préveza GR 128 Ma52
Prevost River CDN 17 De14
Prey Khmer K 197 Qc39
Prey Veng K 197 Qc40
Priangarskoe plato RUS 140 Pd07
Priargunsk RUS 173 Qk20
Pribilof Islands USA 14 Bf17
Priboj BIH 124 Lt46
Priboj SCG 126 Lu47
Priboj SCG 126 Mc48
Pribojska Goleša SCG 126 Lu47
Příbor CZ 118 Lt41
Pribovce SK 119 Lt41
Příbram CZ 118 Lp41
Pribyslav CZ 118 Lq41
Price USA (UT) 21 Ee26
Price Island CDN 18 Df19
Price River USA 15 Cd11
Prichard USA (AL) 29 Ff30
Pričornomors'ka Nizovina UA 125 Mk45
Priddis CDN (AB) 19 Ec20
Priego E 109 Ks50
Priego de Córdoba E 108 Kq47
Priekule LT 97 Mb35
Priekule LV 97 Mb34
Prienai LT 97 Md36
Priene TR 129 Mh53
Prieska SA 302 Mb60
Priest Lake USA 18 Eb21
Prieto, Cerro PE 60 Fk48
Prieuré de Merlande F 104 La45
Prievidza SK 118 Lt42
Prigi RI 210 Qf50
Prigor RO 124 Mc46
Prijedor BIH 121 Lr46
Prijepolje SCG 126 Lu47
Prijutnoe RUS (KAL) 135 Nb22
Prijutnoe RUS (KAL) 152 Nb23
Prijutovo RUS 133 Ng19
Priko CI 279 Kj42
Prilenskoe plato RUS 141 Ra06
Prilep BG 127 Mg48
Prilep MK 126 Mb49
Prilike SCG 126 Ma47
Primate CDN (SK) 19 Ef19
Primavera BR (PA) 64 Hg46
Primavera do Leste BR (MT) 69 Hc53
Přimda CZ 118 Ln41
Primeira Cruz BR (MA) 64 Hj47
Primero RA 76 Gj61
Prime Seal Island AUS 236 Sd66
Primorsk RUS 96 Mj30
Primorsk RUS 117 Lu36
Primorsk RUS 133 Nc21
Primors'ke UA 125 Ml45
Primorskij Dolac HR 121 Lr47
Primorskij hrebet RUS 172 Qc19
Primorsko BG 127 Mh48
Primorsko-Ahtarsk RUS 135 Mk22
Primošten HR 121 Lq47
Primrose Lake CDN 19 Ef18
Prince Albert CDN (SK) 19 Eh19
Prince Albert SA 302 Mb62
Prince Albert Mountains 313 Sd34
Prince Albert N.P. CDN 19 Eg18
Prince Albert Peninsula CDN 10 Ea04
Prince Albert Road SA 302 Ma62
Prince Albert Sound CDN 10 Ea04
Prince Alexander Mountains PNG 243 Sb47
Prince Charles Island CDN 10 Ga05
Prince Edward Island CDN 31 Gj22
Prince Edward Island CDN 31 Gj22
Prince Edward Island N.P. CDN 31 Gj22
Prince Edward Islands 315 Na14
Prince Frederick Harbour AUS 222 Rc53
Prince George CDN (BC) 18 Dj19
Prince of Wales Island AUS 230 Sb51
Prince of Wales Island CDN 11 Fa04
Prince of Wales Islands USA 17 Dd18
Prince of Wales Strait CDN 10 Ea04
Prince Olav Mountains 312 Ba36
Prince Patrick Island CDN 10 Dd03
Prince Regent Inlet CDN 11 Fb04
Prince Regent Nature Reserve AUS (WA) 222 Rc53
Prince Regent River AUS 222 Rc53
Prince Rupert CDN (BC) 18 De18
Princesa Isabel BR (PB) 65 Ja49
Princes Highway AUS 236 Rk64
Princess Alexandra N.P. GB 37 Ge35
Princess Charlotte Bay AUS 231 Sb53
Princess Elizabeth Land 313 Od33
Princess Island CDN 18 Df19
Prince's Town GH 279 Kj43
Prince's Town TT 58 Gk40
Princeton CDN (BC) 18 Dk21
Princeton USA (OR) 20 Ea24
Princeton USA (MN) 27 Fd23
Princeton USA (MO) 27 Fd25
Princeton USA (IL) 32 Ff25
Princeton USA (IN) 34 Fg26
Princeton USA (KY) 34 Fg27
Princeton USA (WV) 35 Fk27
Princetown AUS (VIC) 237 Sb65
Princeville USA (HI) 16 Ca34
Prince William Sound USA 15 Cg15
Principe STP 280 Ld45
Principe Cannel CDN 18 De19
Príncipe da Beira BR (RO) 68 Gh52
Prineville USA (OR) 20 Dk23
Pringamosa CO 56 Gc43
Pringle Bay SA 302 Lk63
Pringsewu RI 207 Qc48
Prinos GR 126 Mb51
Prinsesse Ragnhild kyst 313 Mb33
Prins Karls Forland N 91 Lf06
Priólithos GR 128 Mc53
Priolo Gargallo I 122 Lq53
Priozërsk RUS (KAR) 91 Mf15
Pripjat' RUS 119 Md19
Pripyatsky N.P. BY 132 Md20
Prisoje BIH 121 Ls47
Priština SCG 126 Mb48
Pritzwalk D 113 Ln37
Privas F 105 Le46
Priverno I 122 Lo49
Privlaka HR 121 Lq46
Privolžsk RUS 133 Na17
Prizren SCG 126 Ma48
Prizzi I 122 Lo53
Prjadčino RUS 180 Rd20
Prjamicino RUS 132 Mh20
Prjaža RUS (KAR) 91 Mg15
Prnjavor BIH 121 Ls46
Probijnivka UA 119 Me43
Probolinggo RI 210 Qg49
Probota RO 125 Mg43
Prodănești MD 125 Mj43
Proddatur IND (APH) 193 Ok39
Professor Salvador Mazza BOL 73 Gj57
Progreso EC 60 Fk47
Progreso MEX (HDG) 40 Fa35
Progreso MEX (YT) 41 Ff35
Progreso PE 67 Gd53
Progreso ROU 77 Hb63
Progress ANT (RUS) 313 Od32
Progresso BR (AC) 67 Gd50
Prohladnyj RUS (KBA) 152 Nc24
Proklętije SCG/AL 126 Lu48
Prokop'evsk RUS 140 Pb08
Prokuplje SCG 126 Mb47
Proletarij RUS 132 Mf16
Proletarsk RUS 135 Na22
Proletarskoe Vodohranilišče RUS 135 Na22
Proliv Dmitrija Lapteva RUS 141 Rd04
proliv Ekateriny RUS 181 Sd23
proliv Karskie Vorota RUS 140 Nd04
proliv Longa RUS 141 Td04
Proliv Sannikova RUS 141 Rd04
proliv Španberga RUS 181 Sd24
proliv Vil'kickogo RUS 140 Qa03
Prome MYA 196 Ph36
Promissão BR (MS) 74 Hc55

Q

R

Romaškino RUS 133 Nf19
Romblon RP 203 Rb39
Romblon Island RP 203 Rb39
Romblon Strait RP 203 Rb39
Rome I 122 Lr49
Rome USA (NY) 33 Gc24
Rome USA (GA) 35 Fh28
Romilly-sur-Seine F 103 Ld42
Romiton UZB 158 Oc26
Romlott-vár H 118 Ls44
Rommani MA 258 Kg29
Romney USA (WV) 33 Ga26
Romny RUS 180 Re20
Romny UA 132 Mg20
Rømø DK 94 Lj35
Romo RI 208 Qe45
Romodan UA 134 Mg21
Romorantin-Lanthenay F 102 Lb43
Rømø Sommerland DK 94 Lj35
Romsdalen N 92 Lh28
Romsey GB 101 Kt40
Rómulo Calzada MEX (TB) 41 Fd37
Ron IND (KTK) 190 Oh38
Ronan USA (MT) 19 Ec22
Roncador BR (PR) 74 Hd58
Roncador Reef SOL 245 Sk49
Roncesvalles E 107 Kt53
Ronchamp F 103 Lg43
Ronciglione I 122 Ln48
Ronda E 108 Kp46
Ronda Alta BR (RS) 78 Hd59
Rondane n.p. N 92 Lk29
Rønde DK 94 Ll34
Ronde WG 47 Gk39
Rondeador, T.I. BR 64 Hh48
Rondeau Prov. Park CDN 32 Fk24
Rondon BR (PR) 74 Hd57
Rondon do Pará BR (PA) 64 Hf48
Rondônia BR 52 Gd21
Rondonópolis BR (MT) 74 Hc54
Rond-Point de Gaulle TCH 267 Lj36
Rondslottet N 92 Lk29
Ronehamn S 95 Lt33
Rongai EAK 290 Mh46
Rong'an VRC (GZG) 178 Qe33
Rongbon Cave THA 196 Qa39
Rongbuk Monastery VRC 170 Pd31
Rongcheng VRC (SDG) 182 Rb27
Rongelap Atoll MH 241 Tb16
Rongerik Atoll MH 241 Tb16
Rongjenj IND (MGA) 194 Pf33
Rong Kat THA 196 Pk36
Rongkop RI 210 Qf50
Rong Kwang THA 196 Qa36
Rongo EAK 290 Mh46
Rongshui VRC (GZG) 178 Qe33
Rõngu EST 96 Mg32
Rong Xian VRC (SCH) 176 Qc31
Rong Xian VRC (GZG) 178 Qf34
Ronien Daun Sam K 197 Qb39
Ron Morel Mus. CDN 25 Fj21
Rønne DK 95 Lp35
Ronne Bay 312 Gb33
Ronneby S 95 Lq34
Ronne Ice Shelf ANT 312 Gd34
Rönnenberg D 112 Lk38
Rönnöfors S 90 Lg14
Ron Phibun THA 198 Pk41
Ronse B 103 Ld40
Ronuro BR 69 Hc52
Roodeport SA 303 Md59
Rooibergdam SA 302 Ma60
Rooiberge LS 303 Me60
Rooibokkraal SA 299 Md58
Rooikop NAM 298 Lh57
Rooikraal SA 300 Me58
Rooin RI 213 Rh47
Rooirand NAM 298 Lj58
Roorkee IND (UTT) 189 Oj31
Roosendaal NL 112 Le39
Roosevelt BR 68 Gk50
Roosevelt USA (UT) 21 Ef25
Roosevelt Campobello Internat. Park CDN 31 Gg23
Roosevelt Island 312 Bc34
Roosevelt, Mount CDN 17 Dh16
Roosevelt N.P. Nth. Unit USA 26 Ej22
Roosevelt N.P. Sth. Unit USA 26 Ej22
Roosevelt, T.I. BR 68 Gk51
Roossenekal SA 300 Me58
Roosville CDN (BC) 19 Ec21
Root Lake CDN (MB) 24 Ek18
Root River CDN 17 Dh14
Ropar IND (PJB) 189 Oj30
Ropczyce PL 117 Mb40
Roper Bar AUS (NT) 223 Rh53
Roper River AUS 223 Rh53
Roper Valley AUS (NT) 223 Rh53
Ropotovo MK 126 Mb49
Roquefort F 104 Ku46
Roque Gonzales BR (RS) 78 Hc60
Roque Pérez RA (BA) 77 Ha63
Roquesteron F 105 Lh47
Roquetaillade F 104 Ku46
Roquetas de Mar E 109 Ks46
Roquetes E 110 La50
Roraima BR 53 Gd18
Roraima, Mount GUY/YV 58 Gk43
Rore BIH 121 Lr46
Rori IND (PJB) 188 Oh31
Rori RI 213 Rj46
Rorke's Drift SA 303 Mf60
Røros N 92 Lm28
Rorschach CH 114 Lk43
Rørvik N 90 Lf13
Ros' BY 97 Me37
Ros' UA 134 Mf21
Rošal' RUS 133 Mk18
Rosal de la Frontera E 108 Kn47
Rosales RP 203 Ra38
Rosalia USA (WA) 18 Eb22
Rosalindbank 45 Fk37
Rosamorada MEX (NYT) 39 Eh34
Rosana BR (SP) 74 Hd57
Rosans F 105 Lf46
Rosário BR (MA) 64 Hh47
Rosario DOM 46 Ge36
Rosario MEX (SO) 38 Ef32
Rosario PE 72 Ge58
Rosario PY 73 Hb58
Rosario RA (SF) 77 Gk62
Rosario ROU 77 Hb63
Rosario RP 202 Ra37
Rosario RP 203 Ra39
Rosario YV 56 Gd40
Rosario de la Frontera RA (SA) 73 Gh58
Rosario de Lerma RA (SA) 72 Gh58
Rosario del Tala RA (ER) 77 Ha62
Rosário do Sul BR (RS) 78 Hc61
Rosario Izapa MEX 41 Fd38
Rosário Oeste BR (MT) 69 Hb53
Rosarito MEX (BC) 22 Eb29
Rosarito MEX (BCS) 38 Ee32
Rosarno I 123 Lq52
Rosa Zárate EC 60 Ga45
Rosburg USA (WA) 18 Dj22
Roscales E 106 Kq52
Roščino RUS 132 Me15
Roscoff F 102 Kr42
Roscommon IRL 98 Km37
Roscrea IRL 100 Kn38
Rose SCG 126 Lt48
Rose USA (NE) 26 Fa24
Roseau USA (MN) 24 Fc21
Roseau WD 47 Gk38
Rose BlacheHarbour Le Cou CDN (NF) 31 Ha22
Rosebud AUS (VIC) 237 Sc65
Rosebud USA (SD) 26 Ek24
Rosebud Ind. Res. USA 26 Ek24
Rosebud River CDN 19 Ed20
Roseburg USA (OR) 20 Dj24
Rose Creek CDN 19 Ec19
Rosedale AUS (QLD) 233 Sd57
Rosedale USA (MS) 29 Fe29
Rosedown Plantation USA 29 Fe30
Rose Harbour CDN (BC) 18 De19
Rose Hill = Beau-Bassin MS 307 Nj56
Rosehill Gardens AUS (NSW) 237 Sf62
Roseires Reservoir SUD 283 Mh40
Rosemont Plantation USA 29 Fe30
Rosenberg USA (TX) 29 Fc31
Rosendal N 92 Lg31
Rosendal SA 303 Md60
Rosengarten D 112 Lk37
Rosenheim D 115 Ln43
Rose Point CDN 17 De18
Rose Prairie CDN (BC) 17 Dk17
Rose River AUS 223 Rh52
Roses E 110 Ld48
Roseto degli Abruzzi I 122 Lp48
Rosetown CDN (SK) 19 Eg20
Rosetta ET 263 Mf30
Rose Valley CDN (SK) 24 Ej19
Rosewood AUS (NT) 222 Re54
Rosh Pinah NAM 302 Lj59
Roshtkhar IR 155 Nk28
Roșia RO 124 Mc44
Roșia de Secaș RO 124 Md44
Roșia Nouă RO 124 Mc44
Rosica BG 125 Mh47
Rosice CZ 118 Lr41
Rosignano Marittimo I 120 Ll47
Rosignano Solvay I 120 Ll47
Rosignol GUY 59 Hb42
Roșiori RO 124 Mb43
Roșiori de Vede RO 125 Me46
Roskilde DK 94 Ln35
Roskilde Rockfestival DK 94 Ln35
Roslagen S 93 Lt30
Roslavl' RUS 132 Mg19
Rosman USA (NC) 35 Fj28
Rosmead SA 303 Mc61
Rosolini I 122 Lp54
Rosoman MK 126 Mb49
Rosporden F 102 Kr43
Rossano I 123 Lr51
Rossan Point IRL 98 Km36
Rossarden AUS (TAS) 236 Sd66
Ross Bay Jtn. CDN (NF) 30 Gg19
Ross-Bethio SN 269 Kb37
Ross Ice Shelf ANT 312 Bd35
Rössing NAM 298 Lh57
Rössing Uranium Mine NAM 298 Lh57
Rossington CDN 24 Fb18
Ross Lake USA 18 Dk21
Rosslare IRL 100 Ko38
Rosslare Harbour IRL 100 Ko38
Roßlau D 113 Ln39
Rosso RIM 269 Kc37
Ross-on-Wye GB 101 Ks39
Rossouw SA 303 Md61
Rossport CDN (ON) 25 Fg21
Ross River CDN (YT) 17 Dd15
Ross River CDN 17 De14
Ross Sea ANT 312 Bd33
Rosston USA (OK) 28 Fa27
Rosston USA (AR) 29 Fd29
Røssvatnet N 90 Lh13
Rossville AUS (QLD) 231 Sc53
Rosswood CDN (BC) 17 Df18
Rosswood Plantation USA 29 Fe30
Røst N 90 Lg12
Rostaq AFG 160 Oe27
Rostaq IR 156 Ng32
Rosthern CDN (SK) 19 Eg19
Roštkala TJ 159 Of27
Rostock D 113 Ln36
Rostov RUS 132 Mk17
Rostov-na-Donu RUS 135 Mk22
Rostrenen F 102 Kr42
Røsvik N 90 Lh12
Roswell USA (NM) 23 Eh29
Roswell USA (GA) 35 Fh28
Rot S 93 Lp29
Rota E 108 Ko46
Rota USA 201 Sb16
Rot am See D 114 Ll41
Rotenburg D 112 Lk39
Rotenburg (Wümme) D 112 Lk37
Roth D 115 Lm41
Rothenburg (Tauber) D 114 Ll41
Rothera ANT (UK) 312 Gc32
Rotherham GB 101 Kt37
Rothesay GB 99 Kp35
Rothschild USA (WI) 32 Ff23
Rothwell GB 101 Kt37
Roti RI 214 Rb51
Roti RI 214 Rb51
Rotifunk WAL 278 Kd41
Roto AUS (NSW) 237 Sc62
Rotoava F 249 Ch54
Rotondella I 123 Lr50
Rotorua NZ 238 Tj65
Rotsskildery SA 302 Ma61
Rotsskildergy RB 299 Mc58
Rott D 115 Ln42
Rotten CH 114 Lj44
Rottenburg D 114 Lj42
Rottenburg D 115 Ln42
Rotterdam NL 112 Le39
Rottnaälven S 92 Ln30
Rottne S 95 Lp33
Rottnen S 95 Lq34
Rottneros S 93 Lo31
Rottnest Island AUS 228 Qh61
Rottumeroog NL 112 Lg37
Rottumerplaat NL 112 Lg37
Rottweil D 114 Lj42
Rotuma FJI 241 Td21
Rötz D 115 Ln41
Roualist Bank 199 Qc41
Roubaix F 103 Ld40
Roudnice CZ 118 Lp40
Rouen F 102 Lb41
Rougemont F 103 Lg43
Rough Rock USA (AZ) 23 Ef27
Rouhia TN 260 Le28
Rouillac F 104 Ku45
Roulans F 103 Lg43
Roumsiki CAM 273 Lg40
Round Mountain AUS 235 Sg61
Round Mountain USA (TX) 28 Fa30
Round Pd. CDN 31 Hb21
Round Rock USA (AZ) 23 Ef27
Round Rock USA (TX) 28 Fb30
Roundup USA (MT) 21 Ef22
Round Valley Ind. Res. USA 20 Dj26
Roura F 59 Hd43
Rousay GB 99 Kr31
Roussillon F 105 Le45
Roussillon F 105 Lf47
Route 62 SA 302 Lk62
Route 66 USA 27 Fd26
Route 66 USA 28 Eh28
Route 66 Mus. USA 28 Fa28
Route 66 S.P. USA 27 Fe26
Route des Crêtes F 103 Lg43
Route des Grandes Alpes F 105 Lg46
Route des Kasbahs MA 258 Kg30
Route Napoléon F 105 Lg47
Route transsaharienne DZ/RN 266 Lc35
Rouxville SA 303 Md61
Rouyn-Noranda CDN (QC) 25 Ga21
Rova d'Antongona RM 306 Nd55
Rovaniemi FIN 91 Mc12
Rovato I 120 Lk45
Roven' SK 119 Mb41
Roven'ki RUS 133 Mk21
Rover USA (AR) 29 Fd28
Roverto I 120 Lm45
Rövershagen D 113 Ln36
Roverud N 92 Ln30
Rovigo I 120 Lm45
Rovinari RO 124 Md46
Rovine di Roselle I 120 Lm48
Rovinj HR 121 Lo45
Rovnoe RUS 133 Nd20
Rów PL 116 Lp38
Rowena AUS (NSW) 235 Se60
Rowley Shoals AUS 220 Qd22
Rowy PL 116 Ls36
Roxas RP 203 Ra37
Roxas RP 203 Ra39
Roxas RP 204 Qk40
Roxas RP 205 Rb40
Roxboro USA (NC) 35 Ga27
Roxborough Downs AUS (QLD) 232 Rk57
Roxby Downs AUS (SA) 236 Rj61
Roxen S 93 Lq32
Roy USA (UT) 21 Ed25
Roy USA (MT) 21 Ef22
Roy USA (NM) 23 Eh28
Royal Bardia N.P. NEP 170 Pa31
Royal Botanic Gardens GB 101 Ku39
Royal Canal IRL 100 Kn37
Royal Chitwan N.P. NEP 170 Pc32
Royal Citadel CL 193 Pa43
Royal City USA (WA) 18 Ea22
Royal Gorge USA 21 Eh26
Royal Manas N.P. BHT 194 Pf32
Royal N.P. AUS 237 Sf63
Royal Palace RI 211 Qk50
Royal Palm Beach USA (FL) 36 Fk32
Royal Pavilion GB 101 Ku40
Royal Randwick AUS (NSW) 237 Sf62
Royal Sukla Phanta N.P. NEP 170 Pa31
Royal Tombs VN 197 Qd37
Royal Tunbridge Wells GB 101 La39
Royan F 104 Kt45
Roye F 103 Lc41
Roy Hill AUS (WA) 224 Qk57
Røyken N 92 Ll31
Røykfossen N 90 Ma11
Røyrvik N 90 Lg13
Royston GB 101 Ku38
Royston USA (GA) 35 Fj28
Roza BG 127 Mg48
Rozafa AL 126 Lu48
Rožaj SCG 126 Ma48
Rožan PL 117 Mb38
Rozay-en-Brie F 103 Lc42
Rozdeevka RUS 180 Re20
Rozdol'ne UA 134 Mg23
Rozdyl'na UA 125 Mi44
Roženovo RUS 133 Nd17
Rozengain RI 212 Rf48
Roženski manastir BG 126 Md49
Rozivka UA 135 Mj22
Rožmitál pod Tremšínem CZ 118 Lo41
Rožňava SK 119 Ma42
Rožnov pod Radhoštěm CZ 118 Lt41
Rozogi PL 117 Mb37
Rožok RUS 133 Nb18
Rozoy-sur-Serre F 103 Le41
Rozprza PL 117 Lu39
Roztoczański P.N. PL 117 Md40
Roztoky CZ 118 Lp40
Rozvadov CZ 118 Ln41
Rožyšče UA 117 Mf40
Rrogozhinë AL 126 Lu49
Rtiščevo RUS 133 Nb19
Rt Kamenjak HR 121 Lo46
Rt Ploča HR 121 Lq47
Ruacana NAM 294 Lh54
Ruacana Falls NAM 298 Lh54
Ruaha N.P. EAT 293 Mh49
Ruahine Range NZ 238 Tj66
Ruang RI 212 Rc44
Ruangwa EAT 297 Mk51
Ruapehu, Mount NZ 238 Th65
Ruapuke Island NZ 239 Te69
Ruatoria NZ 238 Tk64
Ruba BY 132 Mf18
Rubafu EAT 287 Mf46
Rubbestadneset N 92 Lf31
Rubeho Mountains EAT 293 Mj49
Rubengera RWA 292 Me47
Rubens RA 82 Ge71
Rubeshibe J 181 Sb24
Rubi RDC 287 Mc44
Rubiás E 106 Kn53
Rubiataba BR (GO) 70 Hf53
Rubinéia BR (SP) 74 He56
Rubio CI 279 Kh42
Rubio YV 56 Gd42
Rubondo N.P. EAT 292 Mf47
Rubuga EAT 292 Mg48
Ruby USA (AK) 15 Cc13
Ruby USA (WA) 18 Eb21
Ruby USA 21 Ed23
Ruby Lake USA 20 Ec25
Ruby Mts. USA 20 Ec25
Ruby Mts. Scenic Area USA 20 Ec25
Ruby Range CDN 17 Da15
Rubys Inn USA (UT) 22 Ed27
Rubyvale AUS (QLD) 233 Sd57
Ruby Valley USA (NV) 20 Ec25
Rucachoroi, Cerro RA 80 Ge65
Rucăr RO 125 Mf45
Rucava LV 97 Mb34
Rucheng VRC (HUN) 179 Qg33
Ruciane-Nida PL 117 Mb37
Rud IR 155 Oa28
Ruda S 95 Lr33
Rudall AUS (SA) 236 Rj62
Rudall River N.P. AUS 225 Rb57
Rudarpur IND (UPH) 189 Pb32
Ruda Śląska PL 116 Lt40
Rudauli IND (UPH) 189 Pa32
Rudayba SUD 276 Mf39
Rudbar AFG 160 Ob30
Rudbar IR 154 Ne27
Rude HR 121 Lq45
Rud-e Atrak IR 155 Nh27
Rud-e Bampur IR 157 Nk32
Rud-e Dez IR 154 Ne29
Rud-e Helle IR 156 Ng31
Rud-e Helmand AFG 160 Ob30
Rudehen IR 154 Nf28
Rud-e Kal-e Šur IR 155 Nj27
Rud-e Karun IR 154 Ne29
Rud-e Koja IR 157 Oa33
Rud-e Kor IR 156 Ng30
Rud-e Kul IR 157 Nh32
Rud-e Marun IR 156 Ne30
Rud-e Mehran IR 156 Nh32
Rud-e Mond IR 156 Ng31
Rud-e Polvar IR 156 Ng30
Rud-e Qesel Owzan IR 154 Ne27
Rüdersdorf D 113 Lo38
Rüdesheim D 114 Lh41
Rudhauli IND (UPH) 189 Pb32
Rudi MD 125 Mh42
Rudilla E 109 Kt50
Rudinka HR 121 Lq46
Rudiškės LT 97 Me36
Rudka UA 117 Mf39
Rudka-Červyns'ka UA 117 Mf39
Rudkøbing DK 94 Ll36
Rudky UA 119 Md41
Rudna Glava SCG 124 Mc46
Rudnaja Pristan' RUS 181 Rh23
Rudnichnyi KZ 166 Ok23
Rudnik BG 127 Mh48
Rudnik SCG 126 Ma46
Rudniki PL 116 Lt39
Rudnja RUS 132 Mf18
Rudnyj KZ 140 Oa08
Rudo BIH 126 Lu47
Rudolstadt D 113 Lm40
Rudong VRC (JGS) 184 Ra29
Rudrapur IND (UTT) 189 Ok31
Rud Sar IR 154 Nf27
Rue F 103 Lb40
Rueda E 106 Kq51
Ruen BG 127 Mh48
Ruente Nacional CO 56 Gd43
Ruetz A 115 Lm43
Rufa'a SUD 276 Mg39
Ruffec F 104 La44
Rufiji EAT 293 Mk49
Rufino BR (PA) 63 Hb46
Rufino RA (SF) 77 Gj63
Rufisque SN 269 Kb38
Rufrufua RI 212 Rg47
Rufunsa Z 296 Me53
Rugaga EAT 293 Mj48
Rugāji LV 97 Mh33
Ruganga EAT 293 Mh50
Rugao VRC (JGS) 184 Ra29
Rugby GB 101 Kt38
Rugby USA (ND) 24 Ek21
Rügen D 113 Lo36
Rugheiwa SUD 276 Mf38
Rugles F 102 La42
Rugombo BU 292 Me47
Rugovska klisura SCG 126 Ma48
Rugozi EAT 292 Mg47
Rugufu EAT 292 Mf48
Ruguj RUS 132 Mg16
Ruhan' RUS 132 Mg19
Ruhengeri RWA 287 Me46
Ruhland D 113 Lo39
Ruhner Berg D 113 Lm37
Ruhnu saar EST 97 Md33
Ruhr D 112 Lh39
Ruhuhu EAT 293 Mh50
Ruhuji EAT 293 Mh50
Rui'an VRC (ZJG) 184 Ra32
Rui Barbosa BR (BA) 71 Hk52
Ruichang VRC (JGX) 184 Qh31
Ruicheng VRC (SAX) 177 Qf28
Ruidera E 109 Ks48
Ruidosa USA (TX) 23 Eh30
Ruidoso USA (NM) 23 Eh29
Ruijin VRC (JGX) 179 Qj33
Ruiki RDC 287 Mc46
Ruili VRC (YUN) 195 Pj33
Ruines d'Assodé RN 266 Le36
Ruines de Loropéni BF 279 Kj40
Ruïnes d'Empúries E 110 Ld48
Ruines de Ouara TCH 275 Ma38
Ruins of Aksum ETH 277 Mk39
Ruins of Ft. Craig USA 23 Eg29
Ruins of Sambor K 197 Qc39
Ruins of Windsor USA 29 Fe30
Ruiru EAK 290 Mj46
Ruitersbos SA 302 Mb62
Ruiz, Nevado de CO 56 Gc43
Ruiz MEX (SL) 38 Ef33
Ruiz Cortines, P. A. MEX 38 Ef32
Rūjiena LV 97 Mf33
Rukanga EAK 293 Mk47
Ruki RDC 281 Lh46
Rukube EAT 292 Mg47
Rule USA (TX) 28 Fa29
Rulenge EAT 292 Mf47
Ruleville USA (MS) 29 Fe29
Rum GB 98 Ko33
Ruma SCG 124 Lu45
Ruma WAN 272 Ld39
Rumah KSA 149 Nd33
Rumah Anyi MAL 208 Qg45
Rumah Kulit MAL 208 Qh44
Rumah Layang MAL 208 Qf45
Rumah Maya MAL 208 Qg44
Rumahtinggih RI 242 Sa49
Ruma N.P. EAK 290 Mh46
Rumayn YE 150 Nb37
Rumbek SUD 283 Me42
Rumberpon RI 213 Rh46
Rumboci BIH 121 Ls47
Rumburk CZ 113 Lp40
Rum Cay BS 37 Gc34
Rumeila SUD 276 Mh40
Rumford USA (ME) 33 Ge23
Rumia PL 116 Lt36
Rumilly F 105 Lf45
Rumoi J 181 Sa24
Rumphi MW 296 Mg51
Rumpi Hills CAM 280 Le43
Rumšiškės LT 97 Me36
Rumuruti EAK 290 Mj45
Run RI 212 Re48
Runan VRC (HNN) 184 Qh29
Runcorn GB 101 Ks37
Runde N 92 Lf28
Runde ZW 300 Mf56
Rundfloen N 92 Ln29
Rundu NAM 295 Lk54
Runduma RI 209 Rc48
Runesten DK 94 Lk35
Rungsted DK 94 Ln35
Rungu RDC 287 Md44
Rungu RDC 287 Me44
Rungwa EAT 292 Mf49
Rungwa EAT 292 Mg49
Rungwa EAT 292 Mg49
Rungwa Game Reserve EAT 293 Mh49
Rungwe, Mount EAT 293 Mh50
Runiz IR 156 Ng31
Runmarö S 93 Lt31
Runn S 93 Lq30
Runni IND (BIH) 189 Pc32
Runtuna S 93 Ls32
Runzewe EAT 292 Mf47
Ruokojärvi FIN 91 Mc12
Ruokolahti FIN 96 Mj29
Ruoqiang VRC (XUZ) 169 Pe26
Ruo Shui VRC 174 Pk25
Ruovesi FIN 96 Me29
Rupanyup AUS (VIC) 237 Sb64
Rupat RI 206 Qa45
Rupawati IND (GUJ) 190 Og34
Rupe HR 121 Lq47
Rupea RO 125 Mf44
Rupert USA (ID) 21 Ed24
Rupia EAT 293 Mj50
Rupia EAT 293 Mj50
Ruppert Coast 312 Cd34
Rupsi ZW 300 Mg56
Ruptsovsk RUS 167 Pa20
Rur D 112 Lg40
Rura IND (UPH) 189 Ok32
Rurópolis Presidente Médici BR (PA) 63 Hc48
Rurrenabaque BOL 67 Gg53
Rurum WAN 272 Le40
Rušan TJ 159 Of27
Rusape ZW 300 Mg55
Rusava UA 125 Mj42
Ruse BG 127 Mf47
Rusenski Lom, N.P. BG 127 Mg47
Rusera IND (BIH) 194 Pd33
Rushan VRC (SDG) 182 Ra27
Rushden GB 101 Ku38
Rushinga ZW 296 Mg54
Rushungi EAT 293 Mk50
Rushville USA (NE) 26 Ej24
Rusizi, P.N.de la BU 292 Me47
Rusk USA (TX) 29 Fc30
Rusken S 95 Lp33
Rusné LT 97 Mb35
Ruso THA 199 Qa42
Ruso USA (ND) 26 Ek22
Russas BR (CE) 65 Jb48
Russell CDN (MB) 24 Ek20
Russell NZ 238 Th63
Russell USA (KS) 26 Fa26
Russell Fiord USA 17 Da16
Russell Islands SOL 245 Sk50
Russell Lake CDN 24 Ek17
Russell Lake USA 35 Fj28
Russell, Mount USA (AK) 15 Ce14
Russell Springs USA (KS) 26 Ek26
Russellville USA (AL) 34 Fg28
Russel Range AUS 229 Rb62
Rüsselsheim D 114 Lj41
Russellville USA (AR) 29 Fd28
Russia RUS 139 Oa03
Russkaya ANT (RUS) 312 Da33
Russkij Kameškir RUS 133 Nd19
Russkiy Sever N.P. RUS 91 Mk15
Russlleville USA (KY) 34 Fg27
Rust A 115 Lr43
Rustavi GE 152 Nc25
Rust de Winter SA 299 Me58
Rust de Winterdam SA 299 Me58
Rust de Winter Nature Reserve SA 300 Me58
Rust de Winter Nature Reserve SA 303 Me58
Rustenburg GUY 59 Hb43
Rustenburg SA 299 Md58
Rustenburg Nature Reserve SA 303 Md58
Rusterfjelbma N 91 Me10
Ruston USA (LA) 29 Fd29
Rusumu EAT 292 Mf47
Rusumu Falls EAT 292 Mf47
Ruszów PL 116 Lq39
Rutana BU 292 Me47
Rute E 108 Kq47
Ruteng RI 211 Ra50
Rutenga ZW 300 Mf56
Rutete EAT 293 Mj50
Rutford Ice Stream 312 Fd34
Rüthen D 112 Lj39
Rutherfordton USA (NC) 35 Fj28
Ruthin GB 101 Kr37
Ruti PNG 243 Sc48
Rutigliano I 123 Lr49
Rutka-Tartak PL 117 Mc36
Rutland USA (VT) 33 Gd24
Rutland Island IND 193 Pg40
Rutland Plains AUS (QLD) 230 Sa53
Rutledalen N 92 Lf29
Rutog VRC (TIB) 170 Ok29
Rutshuru RDC 287 Me46
Rutukira EAT 293 Mh51
Rutul RUS (DAG) 152 Nd25
Ruunaankosket FIN 91 Mf14
Ruvo di Púglia I 123 Lr49
Ruvu EAT 293 Mk49
Ruvu EAT 293 Mk49
Ruvubu EAT 287 Mf47
Ruvubu, P.N.de la RWA 292 Mf47
Ruvuma EAT/MOC 297 Mj51
Ruvu Remiti EAT 293 Mj48
Ruwais UAE 156 Ng33
Ruwenzori RDC/EAU 290 Me45
Ruwenzori Mountains N.P. EAU 290 Me45
Ruya ZW 296 Mf54
Ruyang VRC (HNN) 177 Qg28
Ru-ye Sang AFG 160 Od28
Ruyigi BU 292 Mf47
Ruyuan VRC (GDG) 179 Qg33
Ruza RUS 132 Mj18
Ruzaevka RUS (MOR) 133 Nc18
Ruzany BY 117 Me38
Ruzhou VRC (HNN) 177 Qg28
Ružomberok SK 119 Lu41
Rwanda 253 Ma10
Rwindi RDC 287 Me46
Ry DK 94 Lk34
Ryan USA (OK) 28 Fb29
Ryan, Mount AUS 237 Se62
Rybachye KZ 166 Pa22
Rybczewice PL 117 Mc39
Rybinsk RUS 132 Mk16
Rybinsk Reservoir RUS 132 Mk16
Rybnik PL 116 Lt40
Rybno PL 117 Md37
Rybno PL 117 Mb37
Rybnoe RUS 133 Mk18
Rybreka RUS (KAR) 91 Mh15
Rychłocice PL 116 Lt39
Rychnowo PL 117 Ma37
Rychtal PL 116 Ls39
Rychwał PL 116 Lt38
Ryd S 95 Lp34
Rydaholm S 95 Lp34
Rydberg Peninsula 312 Ga33
Ryde GB 101 Kt40
Rydet S 94 Lm33
Rydsnäs S 95 Lq33
Rydzewo PL 117 Mb37
Rye GB 101 La40
Ryegate USA (MT) 21 Ef22
Ryggsteinhavet N 92 Le29
Rykene N 92 Lj32
Ryke Yseøyane N 91 Mc07
Ryki PL 117 Mb39
Ryl'sk RUS 132 Mh20
Rymań PL 116 Lq37
Rymanów PL 119 Mb41
Rymanów-Zdrój PL 119 Mb41
Rýmařov CZ 118 Ls41
Rymättylä FIN 96 Mb30
Ryn PL 117 Mb37
Ryn-kum KZ 133 Nd21
Ryohakusanchi J 183 Rj27
Ryotsu J 183 Rk26
Rypin PL 117 Lu37
Ryšjedalsvika N 92 Lf29
Rytterknægten DK 95 Lp35
Ryukyu Islands J 165 Ra13
Ryukyu Trench J 165 Rb14
Rząśnik PL 117 Mb38
Rzecznica PL 116 Ls37
Rzepin PL 116 Lp38
Rzeszów PL 117 Mb40
Ržev RUS 132 Mh17
Ržyščiv UA 134 Mf21

S

Sa PNG 243 Sc48
Sa RMM 270 Kh38
Saa CAM 281 Lf43
Sa'a SOL 245 Ta50
Saacow = Jilib SP 291 Nb45
Saadani Game Reserve EAT 293 Mk48
Saaifontein SA 302 Ma61
Saalbach A 115 Ln43
Saalburg D 114 Lj40
Saale D 113 Lm40
Saalfeld D 113 Lm40
Saalfelden am Steinernen Meer A 115 Ln43
Saam IR 157 Oa31
Saan SYR 146 Mj28
Saanich CDN (BC) 18 Dj21
Saar D 114 Lh41
Saaranpaä SP 291 Nc44
Saarbrücken D 114 Lg41
Saarburg D 114 Lg41
Sääre EST 97 Mc33
Saaremaa EST 96 Mc32
Saari FIN 96 Mk29
Saarijärvi FIN 91 Mc14
Saaristomeren kansallispuisto = Skärgårdshavets n.p. FIN 96 Mb31
Saarland D 114 Lg41
Saarlouis D 114 Lg41
Saarschleife D 114 Lg41
Šaartuz TJ 158 Oe27
Saas Fee CH 114 Lh44
Saatli AZ 152 Ne26
Saba NL (NA) 47 Gj37
Šabac SCG 124 Lu46
Sabadell E 110 Lc49
Sabah MAL 204 Qj43
Sabaiya SUD 282 Md42
Sabak MAL 199 Qa44
Sabak Bernam RI 211 Qk49
Sabalana RI 211 Qk49
Sabalanung RI 208 Qj44
Sabalgarh IND (MPH) 189 Oj32
Sabaluka Game Reserve SUD 276 Mg38
Saba Marine Park NL (NA) 47 Gj37
Sabana C 45 Gc35
Sabana CO 61 Gd46
Sabana SME 59 Hc43
Sabana de Cardona YV 57 Gg42
Sabana de la Mar DOM 46 Gf36
Sabana Grande YV 57 Ge41
Sabanalarga CO 56 Gc40
Sabanalarga CO 56 Gc42
Sabanalarga CO 56 Gd43
Sabana San Francisco MEX (QTR) 41 Ff36
Sabancaya, Volcán PE 67 Ge53
Sabancuy MEX (CAM) 41 Fe36
Sabaneta CO 56 Gd42
Sabaneta DOM 46 Ge36
Sabaneta YV 57 Gf40
Sabaneta YV 57 Gf41
Sabang RI 198 Ph43
Sabang RI 209 Qk45
Sabang RP 204 Qk40
Sabang Beach RP 205 Rc41
Sabanillas MEX (COH) 39 Ek33
Şabanözü TR 131 Mn51
Şabanözü TR 131 Mo50
Sabarat F 104 Lb47
Sabarei EAK 284 Mj43
Sabari GH 279 La41
Sabari IND 191 Pa36
Sabarmati IND 190 Og34
Sabaru RI 211 Qk49
Sabatinivka UA 125 Ml42
Sabatti RI 206 Pk46
Sabáudia I 122 Lo49
Sabaya BOL 72 Gf55
Saba Yoi THA 198 Qa42
Sabbioneta I 120 Ll45
Sabena Desert EAK 291 Mk45
Saberania RI 213 Rk47
Sabeugukgung RI 206 Qa47
Sabha LAR 267 Lh32
Sabidug RP 203 Ra35
Sabie MOC 300 Mg58
Sabie SA 300 Mf58
Sabi Island MYA 198 Pk40
Sabile LV 97 Mc33
Sabiñánigo E 107 Ku52
Sabinas MEX (COH) 39 Ek32
Sabinas Hidalgo MEX (NL) 39 Ek32
Sabine USA 29 Fd30
Sabine Land N 91 Lk06
Sabine N.F. USA 29 Fc30
Sabine N.W.R. USA 29 Fd31
Sabine Pass USA (TX) 29 Fd31
Sabine Peninsula CDN 11 Eb03
Sabino BR (SP) 74 Hf56
Sabinópolis BR (MG) 75 Hj55
Sabinosa E 264 Ka32
Sabinov SK 119 Mb41
Sabirabad AZ 152 Ne26
Sabkhat ad Dabbiyah KSA 149 Ne32
Sabkhat al Hayshah LAR 261 Lh30
Sabkhat ar Riyas KSA 149 Ne32
Sabkhat el Bardawil ET 263 Mg30
Sabkhat Ghuzayyil LAR 261 Lk31
Sabkhat Hawaza KSA 146 Mk30
Sabkhat Matti UAE 156 Nf34
Sabkhat Mujazzam LAR 260 Lf30
Sabkhat Shunayn LAR 261 Ma30
Sabkhat Tawurgha LAR 261 Lh29
Sabkhat Umm al 'Izam LAR 261 Lh30
Šabla BG 127 Mj47
Sablayan RP 203 Ra39
Sable Island CDN 31 Gk23
Sable Island Bank 31 Gk24
Sablé-sur-Sarthe F 102 Ku43
Sa Boat THA 196 Qa38
Saboba GH 279 La41
Saboeiro BR (CE) 65 Ja49
Sabomi WAN 280 Lc42
Sabonagri RN 271 Lb39
Sabon Birni RN 272 Lb40
Sabon-Birni WAN 272 Ld39
Sabon Birnin Gwari WAN 272 Ld40
Sabongari CAM 281 Lf42
Sabongida WAN 280 Lc42
Sabon Kafi RN 272 Le38
Saborna crkva SCG 124 Ma46
Saborsko HR 121 Lq46
Sabou BF 271 Kj39
Sabratah LAR 260 Lg29
Sabres F 104 Ku46
Sabrina Coast 313 Ra32
Sabsé BF 271 Kk39
Sabtaev KZ 140 Ob09
Sabtang Island RP 203 Ra35
Sabuda RI 212 Rf47
Sabugal P 106 Kn50
Sabulubbek RI 206 Pk46
Sabuncupınar TR 130 Ml51
Säby S 95 Lp33
Sabya KSA 150 Nb37
Sabzakpass AFG 160 Ob28
Sabzevar IR 155 Nj27
Sacaba BOL 72 Gg54
Sacacama ANG 295 Ma52
Sacado do Humaitá BR (AM) 67 Gf49
Sacama CO 56 Gd42
Sacambanda ANG 295 Ma54
Sacamburge ANG 295 Mb51
Sacanche PE 66 Gb49
Sac and Fox Ind. Res. USA 27 Fd24
Sacanta RA (CD) 76 Gj61
Sacapulas GCA 41 Fe38
Sacco Uein SP 291 Nb45
Sacecorbo E 109 Ks50
Sacedón E 109 Ks50
Săcel RO 124 Me43
Săcele RO 125 Mf45
Săcele RO 125 Mj46
Săceni RO 125 Mf46
Sachang VRC (GZH) 178 Qd32
Sachayoj RA (SE) 77 Gk59
Sachida IND (ARP) 194 Pg32
Sachigo CDN 20 Fe18
Sachigo Lake CDN 24 Fd19
Sachigo River CDN 24 Fe18
Sachna BD 194 Pf33
Sachojere BOL 68 Gh53
Sachsen D 113 Lo39
Sachsen-Anhalt D 113 Lm38
Sachsenring D 113 Ln40
Sachs Harbour CDN 10 Dd04
Sächsische Schweiz, N.P. D 113 Lp40
Sachula ANG 295 Ma51
Saçıkara TR 144 Mg26
Sacile I 120 Ln45
Sack BY 132 Md19
Šack RUS 133 Na18
Šac'k UA 117 Md39
Sacks USA (AL) 34 Fh29
Šac'kyj pryrodnyj n.p. UA 117 Md39
Saco USA (MT) 19 Eg21
Saco USA (ME) 33 Ge24
Sacol Island RP 205 Rb42
Sacoșu Turcesc RO 124 Mb45
Sacramento BR (MG) 74 Hg55
Sacramento USA 20 Dj25
Sacramento USA (CA) 20 Dk26
Sacre ou Timalacia BR 68 Ha52
Sacro Monte di Ghiffa I 120 Lj45
Sacro Monte di Oropa I 120 Lh45
Sacro Monte di Serralunga di Crea I 120 Lj45
Sacro Monte di Soccorso I 120 Lk45
Sacro Monte di Valperga Canavese I 120 Lh45
Sacta BOL 68 Gh54
Săcueni RO 124 Mc43
Sacuriuina ou Ponte de Pedra BR 69 Hb52
Sacuunda ANG 295 Mb51
Sada E 106 Km53
Sada SA 303 Md62
Sádaba E 107 Kt52
Sadabad IND (UPH) 189 Ok32
Sadabe RM 306 Nd55
Sadad SYR 146 Mj28
Sad Ad Dokan IRQ 147 Nc27
Sa'dah YE 150 Nb37
Sadai RI 207 Qd47
Sadala EST 96 Mg32
Sadam OM 157 Nj34
Sada-misaki J 185 Rg29
Sadani EAT 293 Mk49
Sadao THA 198 Qa42
Sadaseopet IND (APH) 190 Oj37
Sâdât City ET 263 Mf30
Sadau RI 208 Qf47
Sadaung MYA 195 Ph34
Sadda PK 161 Of29
Sadd-e Eskandar IR 154 Nh27
Saddle L. Ind. Res. CDN 19 Ee18
Saddle Mount USA 21 Ed24
Saddle Peak IND 193 Pg39
Saddle-Peaks USA 27 Te56
Sadd Malky KSA 150 Nb37
Sa Dec VN 199 Qc40
Sadh OM 151 Nh37
Sadi ETH 283 Mh41
Sadi ETH 284 Na43
Sadich IR 157 Nk32
Sadio SN 269 Kc38
Sadiola RMM 269 Ke39
Sadiqabad PK 163 Of31
Sadiya IND (ASM) 195 Ph32
Sadjoavato RM 305 Ne52
Sado-jima J 183 Rk27
Sadolangang RI 211 Qk49
Sadova RO 126 Md47
Sadovo BG 127 Me48
Sadovoe RUS (KAL) 133 Nc22
Sado Yahiko Q.N.P. J 183 Rk27
Sadr el Hiltan ET 263 Mg30
Sadri IND (RJT) 188 Og33
Sadriddin-Aini-Park TJ 158 Oe26
Šadrinsk RUS 140 Oa07
Sadus KSA 149 Nd33
Sæbø N 92 Lg28
Sæby DK 94 Ll33
Săedinenie BG 127 Me48
Săedinenie BG 127 Mf48
Saelices E 109 Ks49
Saerra de São Domingos BR 70 Hg53
Sævareid N 92 Lf30
Safad ETH 277 Mj40
Safaha SUD 283 Md41
Safané BF 271 Kj39
Safara P 108 Kn48
Safed Koh PK 161 Of29
Saffaqah KSA 149 Nc33
Saffar Kalay AFG 160 Oc30
Säffle S 93 Ln31
Safford USA (AZ) 23 Ef29
Safford USA (AL) 34 Fg29
Saffron Walden GB 101 La38
Safi MA 258 Kf29
Safi TCH 273 Lj38
Safia PNG 243 Se50
Safipur IND (UPH) 189 Pa32
Safir YE 150 Nd38
Safita SYR 146 Mj28
Safonovo RUS 132 Mg18
Safotu WS 248 Bd52
Safranbolu TR 144 Mg25
Safwan IRQ 147 Nd30
Såg RO 124 Mc43
Saga J 185 Rf29
Saga RI 212 Rg47
Saga VRC (TIB) 170 Pc31
Sagabari RMM 270 Kf39
Sagadi EST 96 Mg31
Sagadi SUD 276 Mg40
Sagai PK 160 Od30
Sagaing MYA 195 Ph35
Sagala RMM 270 Kg39
Sagalassos TR 131 Ml53
Sagallou DJI 284 Nb40
Sagami-wan J 183 Rk28
Sagamu WAN 280 Lb42
Sagan KZ 166 Ok20
Sagan VRC (XUZ) 168 Ok27
Sagana EAK 290 Mj46
Sagar IND (MPH) 191 Ok34
Sagar IND (KTK) 192 Oh39
Sagaranten RI 210 Qd49
Sagard D 113 Lo36
Sagaredžo GE 152 Nc25
Sagaria BD 194 Pf34
Sagarmatha = Mount Everest NEP/VRC 170 Pd31
Sagarmatha N.P. NEP 170 Pd32
Sagarpara IND (WBG) 194 Pe33
Sagastyr RUS 141 Rb04
Sagata SN 269 Kb38
Sagauli IND (BIH) 189 Pc32
Sagay RP 205 Rb40
Sagd KSA 150 Na37
Sage USA (WY) 21 Ee25
Saggrenda N 92 Lk31
Saghand IR 154 Nh29
Saginaw USA (MI) 32 Fj24
Saginaw Bay USA 32 Fj24
Saglepie LB 278 Kf42
Saglek Bay CDN 11 Gd07
Sagne RIM 269 Kd38
Šagonar RUS (TUV) 167 Pg20
Sagone F 111 Lj48
Sağpazar TR 131 Mp50
Sagra E 109 Ks47
Sagrada Familia E 110 Lc49
Sagres P 108 Km46
Sagsag PNG 243 Se48
Sagu MYA 194 Ph35
Saguache USA (CO) 23 Eg26
Sagua deTánamo C 45 Gc35
Sagua la Grande C 44 Fk34
Saguaro N.P. USA 23 Ee29
Sagunt E 109 Ku49
Sagunto = Sagunt E 109 Ku49
Sagure ETH 284 Mk42
Sagvåg N 92 Lf31
Sagwara IND (RJT) 190 Oh34
Sa'gya VRC (TIB) 170 Pd31
Sahaba SUD 276 Mf37
Sahabad IND (UPH) 189 Ok31
Sahagún CO 56 Gc41
Sahagún E 106 Kp52

Saham OM 157 Nj33
Sahara 254 Kc14
Saharabedi IND (ORS) 194 Pd35
Sahara City = Medinet Sahara ET 263 Mg34
Saharanpur IND (UPH) 189 Oj31
Saharna Nouă MD 125 Mj43
Saharsa IND (BIH) 194 Pd33
Sahasinaka RM 306 Nd56
Sahaswan IND (UPH) 189 Ok31
Sahavato RM 306 Ne56
Sahave RM 306 Nd56
Sahawa IND (RJT) 188 Oh31
Sahechores E 106 Kp52
Saheib SUD 282 Mc40
Sahel 254 Lb15
Sahib PK 163 Of31
Sahibganj IND (JKD) 194 Pd33
Sahin TR 130 Mg49
Sahiwal PK 161 Og30
Sahiwal PK 161 Og30
Sah Kuh IR 154 Nh27
Sahl Abad IR 155 Nk29
Sahneh IR 154 Nd28
Sahoba UZB 158 Oc26
Sahoué G 280 Le45
Sahra' Marzuq LAR 267 Lg33
Sahra Surt LAR 261 Lj30
Šahr-e-Suhte IR 155 Oa30
Šahristan TJ 158 Oe26
Sahtaneh River CDN 17 Dk16
Šahtersk RUS 181 Sb21
Šahty RUS 135 Na22
Sahuaripa MEX (SO) 23 Ef31
Sahuaro MEX (SO) 22 Ed30
Sahuayo de J.Ma. Morelos MEX (MHC) 40 Ej35
Šahun'ja RUS 133 Nd17
Šahy SK 119 Lt42
Sai J 181 Sa25
Saibai Island AUS 230 Sb50
Sai Buri THA 199 Qa42
Sai-Cinza, T.I. BR 62 Ha49
Saïda DZ 259 La28
Saïda RL 146 Mh29
Saidabad IND (UPH) 191 Pb33
Said Abu Bakr al-Mirgani ER 277 Mk39
Saidapuram IND (APH) 193 Ok39
Saïdia MA 259 Kj28
Saidor PNG 243 Sd48
Saidpur BD 194 Pe33
Saidpur IND (UPH) 191 Pb33
Saidu Sharif PK 161 Og28
Saigo stupas PK 161 Og28
Saigō J 183 Rg27
Saigon VN 197 Qd40
Saiha IND (MZR) 194 Pg34
Saihan Toroi VRC (NMZ) 174 Qa25
Sai Island Temple SUD 276 Mf36
Saikanosy Ampasindava RM 304 Nd52
Saikanosy Masoala RM 305 Nf53
Saikhoa Ghat IND (ASM) 195 Ph32
Saiki J 185 Rf29
Saillans F 105 Lf46
Sailolof RI 212 Rf46
Sailu IND (MHT) 191 Ok35
Saimaa FIN 96 Mj29
Saimenski kanal FIN/RUS 96 Mj29
Sain Alto MEX (ZCT) 39 Ej34
Saindak PK 162 Oa31
Sai Ngam THA 196 Pk37
Sainsbury Pt. CDN 25 Ga18
Sainsoutou SN 269 Ke39
Saint Abb's Head GB 99 Ks35
Saint Adolphe CDN (MB) 24 Fb21
Saint-Affrique F 105 Lc47
Saint-Agrève F 105 Le46
Saint-Aignan F 102 Lb43
Saint Alban's CDN (NF) 31 Hc22
Saint Albans GB 101 Ku39
Saint Albans USA (VT) 33 Gd23
SaintAlbans USA (WV) 35 Fk26
Saint Albert CDN (AB) 19 Ed19
Saint Albert Dome PNG 242 Sb48
Saint-Alexandre CDN (QC) 30 Gf22
Saint-Amand-en-Puisaye F 103 Ld43
Saint-Amand-les-Eaux F 103 Ld40
Saint-Amand-Montrond F 103 Lc44
Saint-Ambroise CDN (QC) 30 Ge21
Saint-Ambroix F 105 Le46
Saint-Amé F 103 Lg42
Saint-Amour F 105 Lf44
Saint-André F 307 Nh56
Saint-André-de-Cubzac F 104 Ku45
Saint-André-de-l'Eure F 102 Lb42
Saint-André-les-Alpes F 105 Lg46
Saint Andrew CDN (NB) 31 Gg23
Saint Andrew's CDN (NF) 31 Ha22
Saint Andrews GB 99 Ks34
Saint Andrews GB 99 Ks34
Saint Anne GB 102 Ks41
Saint Anne Marine N.P. SY 305 Nh48
Saint Ann's Bay CDN 31 Gk22
Saint Anthony CDN 11 Ha08
Saint Anthony USA (ID) 21 Ee24
Saint-Antoine F 111 Lk48
Saint Arnaud AUS (VIC) 237 Sb64
Saint Arnaud NZ 239 Tg66
Saint-Aubin-d'Aubigné F 102 Kt42
Saint-Aubin-du-Cormier F 102 Kt42
Saint-Augustin CDN (QC) 31 Ha20
Saint Augustine USA (FL) 36 Fk31
Saint Augustine Beach USA (FL) 36 Fk31
Saint Austell GB 100 Kq40
Saint-Austremoine d'Issoire F 105 Ld45
Saint-Avold F 103 Lg41
Saint Barthélemy F 47 Gj37
Saint Bathans NZ 239 Te68
Saint-Beat F 104 La48
Saint Bees Head GB 99 Kr36
Saint Bees Islands AUS 233 Se56
Saint-Benoit F 307 Nh56
Saint-Benoît-du-Sault F 104 Lb44
Saint Bernard F 59 Hd43
Saint-Bertrand-de-Comminges F 104 La47
Saint-Bonnet F 105 Lg46
Saint Brendan's CDN (NF) 31 Hd21
Saint-Brévin-les-Pins F 102 Ks43
Saint-Brice-en-Cögles F 102 Kt42
Saint Bride's CDN (NF) 31 Hc22
Saint Bride's Bay GB 100 Kp39
Saint-Brieuc F 102 Ks42
Saint Brieux CDN (SK) 19 Eh19
Saint-Bruno CDN (QC) 30 Ge21
Saint-Calais F 102 La43
Saint-CaSaint-le-Guildo F 102 Ks42
Saint Catharines CDN (ON) 33 Ga24
Saint Catherine's Point GB 101 Kt40
Saint-Céré F 104 Lb46
Saint-Chamond F 105 Le45
Saint Charles USA (MO) 27 Fe26
Saint Charles USA (AR) 29 Fe28
Saint Charles USA (MD) 33 Gb26
Saint-Chély-d'Apcher F 105 Ld46
Saint-Chinian F 104 Lc47
Saint-Claud F 104 La45
Saint-Claude F 105 Lf44
Saint Clears GB 100 Kq39
Saint Cloud USA (MN) 27 Fc23
Saint Cloud USA (FL) 36 Fk31
Saint Croix CDN (NB) 31 Gg23
Saint Croix USA 27 Fd23
Saint Croix USA 47 Gh37
Saint Croix N.S.R. USA 27 Fd23
Saint David's GB 100 Kp39
Saint David's Head GB 100 Kp39
Saint-Denis F 103 Lc42
Saint-Denis F 307 Nh56
Saint-Dié-des-Vosges F 103 Lg42
Saint-Dizier F 103 Le42
Saint-Doulchard F 103 Lc43
Sainte-Agathe des Monts CDN 30 Gc22
Sainte-Annade-Beaupré CDN (QC) 30 Ge22
Sainte Anne CDN (MB) 24 Fb21
Sainte Anne F 47 Gk37
Sainte-Annedes-Monts CDN (QC) 30 Gg21
Sainte-Annedu-Lac CDN (QC) 30 Gc22
Sainte-Énimie F 105 Ld46
Sainte-Eulalie CDN (QC) 30 Gd22
Sainte-Foy-la-Grande F 104 La46
Sainte-Egrève F 105 Lf45
Sainte-Hedwidge CDN (QC) 30 Gd21
Sainte-Hermine F 102 Kt44
Sainte-Justine CDN (QC) 30 Ge22
Saint Elias Mountains CDN 17 Da15
Saint-Élie F 59 Hd43
Sainte-Livrade-sur-Lot F 104 La46
Saint-Eloy-les-Mines F 105 Lc44
Sainte-Madeleine de Vézelay F 103 Lc43
Sainte-Marie CDN (QC) 30 Ge22
Sainte-Marie F 47 Gk38
Sainte-Maure-de-Touraine F 102 La43
Sainte-Maxime F 105 Lg47
Sainte-Menehould F 103 Le41
Sainte-Mère-Église F 102 Kt41
Saint-Émilion F 104 Ku46
Sainte-Monique CDN (QC) 30 Ge21
Sainte-Rose F 47 Gk37
Sainte-Rosede Poularies CDN (QC) 25 Ga21
Sainte Rose du Lac CDN (MB) 24 Fa20
Sainte-Rosedu-Nord CDN (QC) 30 Ge21
Saintes F 104 Ku45
Sainte-Savine F 103 Le42
Sainte-Sévère-sur-Indre F 104 Lc44
Saintes-Maries-de-la-Mer F 105 Le47
Sainte-Suzanne F 102 Ku42
Saint-Étienne F 105 Le45
Saint-Étienne-de-Saint-Geoirs F 105 Lf45
Saint-Étienne-du-Rouvray F 102 Lb41
Saint-Étienne-en-Dévoluy F 105 Lf46
Saint-Étienne-les-Orgues F 105 Lf46
Saint-Fabien CDN (QC) 30 Gf21
Saint-Fabiende-Panet CDN (QC) 30 Ge22
Saint-Fargeau F 103 Ld43
Saint-Félicien CDN (QC) 30 Gd21
Saint Fergus GB 99 Kt33
Saint-Florent F 111 Lk48
Saint-Florentin F 103 Ld42
Saint-Florent-sur-Cher F 103 Lc44
Saint Floris, P.N.de RCA 282 Ma41
Saint-Flour F 105 Ld45
Saint-Fort-sur-Gironde F 104 Ku45
Saint Francis USA (KS) 26 Ek26
Saint Francis USA 29 Fe28
Saint Francis Bay SA 303 Mc63
Saint Francis Islands AUS 236 Rg62
Saint Francisville USA (LA) 29 Fe30
Saint Francois Mountains USA 29 Fe27
Saint-Gabriel CDN (QC) 30 Gd22
Saint-Gaudens F 104 La47
Saint Gaudens N.H.S. USA 33 Gd24
Saint-Gaultier F 102 Lb44
Saint-Geniez-d'Olt F 105 Lc46
Saint-Genix-sur-Guiers F 105 Lf45
Saint George AUS (QLD) 235 Se60
Saint George CDN (NB) 31 Gg23
Saint George USA (UT) 22 Ed27
Saint George USA (GA) 35 Fj30
Saint George USA (SC) 35 Fk29
Saint George, Cape PNG 244 Sg48
Saint George Island USA 14 Bf17
Saint George Island S.P. USA 36 Fh31
Saint-Georges CDN (QC) 30 Ge22
Saint George's CDN (NF) 31 Ha21
Saint Georges F 59 He44
Saint George's WG 47 Gk39
Saint George's Bay (NFL) CDN 31 Ha21
Saint George's Bay (NS) CDN 31 Gk23
Saint George's Castle GH 279 Kk43
Saint George's Channel IND 193 Pg42
Saint George's Channel PNG 244 Sg48
St.George's Channel 100 Ko39
Saint-Georges-de-Didonne F 104 Ku45
Saint-Germain-du-Bois F 105 Lf44
Saint-Germain-en-Laye F 103 Lc42
Saint-Germain-Laval F 105 Le45
Saint-Gervais-d'Auvergne F 105 Lc44
Saint-Gervais-les-Bains F 105 Lg45
Saint-Gildas-des-Bois F 102 Ks43
Saint-Gilles F 105 Le47
Saint-Gilles-Croix-de-Vie F 102 Kt44
Saint-Girons F 104 Lb48
Saint-Girons-en-Marensin F 104 Kt47
Saint Govan's Head GB 100 Kq39
Saint Gregory, Mount CDN 31 Ha21
Saint-Guénolé F 102 Kq43
Saint-Guilhem-le-Désert F 105 Ld47
Saint Helena GB 253 Kb11
Saint Helena GB 256 Kc22
Saint Helena Bay SA 302 Lk62
Saint Helens AUS (TAS) 236 Se66
Saint Helens GB 101 Ks37
Saint Helens USA (OR) 20 Dj23
Saint Helens Nat. Volcanic Mon., Mount USA 18 Dj22
Saint Helens Point AUS 236 Se66
Saint Helier GB 102 Ks41
Sainthia IND (WBG) 194 Pd34
Saint-Hilaire-du-Harcouët F 102 Kt42
Saint-Hilaire-le-Grand de Poitiers F 102 La44
Saint-Hippolyte F 103 Lg43
Saint-Hippolyte-du-Fort F 105 Ld47
Saint-Honoré-les-Bains F 103 Ld44
Saint-Hubert B 103 Lf40
Saint-Hyacinthe CDN (QC) 33 Gd23
Saint Ignace USA (MI) 32 Fh23
Saint-Ignace-des-Saints CDN (QC) 30 Gd22
Saint Ignace Island CDN 25 Fg21
Saint-Imier CH 114 Lg43
Saint Ives GB 100 Kp40
Saint Ives GB 101 Ku38
Saint-James F 102 Kt42
Saint James USA (MN) 27 Fc24
Saint-Jean-Brévelay F 102 Ks43
Saint-Jean-d'Angely F 104 Ku45
Saint-Jeande-Dieu CDN (QC) 30 Gf21
Saint-Jean-de-Luz F 104 Kt47
Saint-Jean-de-Maurienne F 105 Lg45
Saint-Jean-de-Monts F 102 Ks44
Saint-Jean-Pied-de-Port F 104 Kt47
Saint-Jean-Port-Joli CDN (QC) 30 Ge22
Saint-Jean-Poutge F 104 La47
Saint-Jean-surRichelieu CDN (QC) 33 Gd23
Saint Joe USA 19 Ec22
Saint John CDN (NB) 31 Gg23
Saint John GB 47 Gh36
Saint John LB 278 Kf42
Saint John USA (KS) 28 Fa27
Saint John Bay CDN 31 Hb20
Saint John Island CDN 31 Hb21
Saint John River CDN 31 Gg23
Saint John River USA 30 Gf22
Saint John's AG 47 Gk37
Saint John's CDN (NF) 31 Hd22
Saint Johns USA (AZ) 23 Ef28
Saint Johns USA (MI) 32 Fh24
Saint Johnsbury USA (VT) 33 Gd23
Saint John's Island ET 263 Mj34
Saint John's Town of Dalry GB 99 Kq35
Saint Jorge de Limpopo MOC 300 Mg57
Saint Joseph F 246 Td56
Saint-Joseph F 307 Nh56
Saint Joseph SY 305 Ng48
Saint Joseph USA (MI) 27 Fc23
Saint Joseph USA (MO) 27 Fc26
Saint Joseph's CDN (NF) 31 Hd22
Saint Jovite CDN (QC) 30 Gc22
Saint-Julien-en-Genevois F 105 Lg44
Saint-Junien F 104 La45
Saint-JuSaint-en-Chaussée F 103 Lc41
Saint-Just-en-Chevalet F 105 Ld45
Saint-Justin F 104 Ku47
Saint-Just-Saint-Rambert F 105 Le45
Saint Kilda GB 98 Km33
Saint Kitts and Nevis 47 Gj37
Saint-Lary-Soulan F 104 La48
Saint-Laurent-de-la-Cabrerisse F 104 Lc47
Saint-Laurent- de-la-Salanque F 104 Lc48
Saint Laurent du Maroni F 59 Hc43
Saint-Laurent-en-Grandvaux F 105 Lf44
Saint Lawrence AUS (QLD) 233 Se57
Saint Lawrence Island USA 14 Be14
Saint Lawrence River CDN 30 Gf21
Saint Lazare CDN (MB) 24 Ek20
Saint-Léonard CDN (NB) 30 Gg22
Saint-Léonard-de-Noblat F 104 Lb45
Saint Leu F 307 Nh56
Saint-Leu F 307 Nh56
Saint-Lô F 102 Kt41
Saint Louis CDN (SK) 19 Eh19
Saint-Louis F 47 Gk38
Saint-Louis F 307 Nh56
Saint Louis SN 269 Kb37
Saint Louis USA (MO) 27 Fe26
Saint-Loup-sur-Semouse F 103 Lg43
Saint Lucia SA 303 Mg60
Saint Lucia WL 47 Gk38
Saint Lucia 47 Gk39
Saint Lucia Channel 47 Gk38
Saint Magnus Bay GB 99 Kt30
Saint-Maixent-l'École F 102 Ku44
Saint-Malo F 102 Ks42
Saint-Marc RH 46 Gd36
Saint-Marcellin F 105 Lf45
Saint Maries USA (ID) 18 Eb22
Saint Marks SA 303 Md62
Saint Marks USA (FL) 35 Fh30
Saint-Mars-la-Jaille F 102 Kt43
Saint Martin F 47 Gj36
Saint-Martin-de-Ré F 102 Kt44
Saint-Martin-du-Canigou F 104 Lc48
Saint Martins CDN (NB) 31 Gh23
Saint-Martin-Vésubie F 105 Lh46
Saint Mary USA (MT) 19 Ed21
Saint Mary River CDN 19 Ed21
Saint Marys AUS (TAS) 236 Se66
Saint Mary's GB 100 Ko41
Saint Marys USA (WV) 33 Fk26
Saint Marys USA (PA) 33 Ga25
Saint Marys USA (GA) 35 Fk30
Saint Mary's Z 296 Md52
Saint Mary's Bay CDN 31 Hd22
Saint Marys Peak AUS 236 Rk61
Saint-Mathieu F 104 La45
Saint Matthew Island USA 14 Bd15
Saint Matthews USA (SC) 35 Fk29
Saint Matthias Group PNG 243 Se46
Saint-Maximin-la-Sainte-Baume F 105 Lf47
Saint-Médard-en-Jalles F 104 Ku46
Saint-Méen-le-Grand F 102 Ks42
Saint Michael USA (AK) 15 Bj14
Saint Michaels USA (AZ) 23 Ef28
Saint Michael's Mount GB 100 Kp40
Saint-Michel F 103 Le41
SaintMichel de l'Attalaye RH 46 Gd36
Saint-Michel-des-Saint CDN (QC) 30 Gd22
Saint-Mihiel F 103 Lf42
Saint Mungo GB 99 Kq35
Saint-Nazaire F 102 Ks43
Saint Neots GB 101 Ku38
Saint-Nicolas- de-Port F 103 Lg42
Saint-Omer F 103 Lc40
Saintonge F 104 Ku45
Saint-Pamphile CDN (QC) 30 Gf22
Saint-Pascal CDN (QC) 30 Gf22
Saint Paul CDN (AB) 19 Ee18
Saint-Paul F 307 Nh56
Saint Paul LB 278 Ke42
Saint Paul USA (AK) 14 Be17
Saint Paul USA (NE) 26 Fa25
Saint Paul USA (MN) 27 Fd23
Saint Paul 315 Ob13
Saint-Paul-de-Fenouillet F 104 Lc48
Saint-Paulien F 105 Ld45
Saint Paul Island CDN 31 Gk22
Saint Paul Island USA 14 Be17
Saint-Paul-lès-Dax F 104 Kt47
Saint Paul's Cathedral RP 203 Ra38
Saint Paul's Subterranean N.P. RP 204 Qk40
Saint-Péray F 105 Le46
Saint-Père-en-Retz F 102 Ks43
Saint Peter CDN (NS) 31 Gk23
Saint Peter USA (MN) 27 Fd23
Saint Peter Island AUS 236 Rg62
Saint Peter-Port GB 102 Ks41
Saint Peters CDN (PE) 31 Gj22
Saint Petersburg RUS 132 Mf16
Saint Petersburg USA (FL) 36 Fj32
Saint-Philbert-de-Grand-Lieu F 102 Kt43
Saint-Philémon CDN (QC) 30 Ge22
Saint-Philippe F 307 Nh56
Saint-Pierre F 31 Hb22
Saint-Pierre F 31 Hb22
Saint-Pierre F 47 Gk38
Saint-Pierre F 104 Lc47
Saint-Pierre F 307 Nh56
Saint Pierre SY 305 Nf50
Saint-Pierre and Miquelon F 31 Hb22
Saint-Pierre-de-Chignac F 104 La45
Saint-Pierre-d'Oléron F 104 Kt45
Saint-Pierre-Jolys CDN (MB) 24 Fb21
Saint-Pierre-le-Moûtier F 103 Ld44
Saint-Pierre-sur-Dives F 102 Ku41
Saint-Pol-de-Léon F 102 Kr42
Saint-Pol-sur-Mer F 103 Lc39
Saint-Pol-sur-Ternoise F 103 Lc40
Saint-Pons-de-Thomières F 104 Lc47
Saint-Pourçain-sur-Sioule F 105 Ld44
Saint-Priest F 105 Le45
Saint-Privat F 104 Lc45
Saint-Quay-Portrieux F 102 Ks42
Saint-Quentin CDN (NB) 30 Gg22
Saint-Quentin F 103 Ld41
Saint-Raphaël F 105 Lg47
Saint-Raymond CDN (QC) 30 Ge22
Saint-Rémy-de-Provence F 105 Le47
Saint-Renan F 102 Kq42
Saint-Saëns F 103 Lb41
Saint-Saulge F 103 Ld43
Saint-Sauveur-en-Puisaye F 103 Ld43
Saint-Sauveur-le-Vicomte F 102 Kt41
Saint-Sauveur-sur-Tinée F 105 Lh46
Saint-Savin F 102 La44
Saint Sebastian Bay SA 302 Ma63
Saint-Seine-l'Abbaye F 103 Le43
Saint-Sernin F 104 Lb47
Saint-Sever F 104 Ku47
Saint Shotts CDN (NF) 31 Hd22
Saint-Siméon CDN (QC) 30 Gf22
Saint Simons Island USA (GA) 35 Fk30
Saint Stephen CDN (NB) 31 Gg23
Saint-Sulpice F 104 Lb47
Saint François SY 305 Ng49
Saint-Thégonnec F 102 Kr42
Saint Theresa Point CDN (MB) 24 Fc19
Saint Thomas CDN (ON) 32 Fk24
Saint Thomas USA 47 Gh36
Saint-Tite CDN (QC) 30 Gd22
Saint-Tropez F 105 Lg47
Saint Urbain CDN (QC) 30 Ge22
Saint-Ursanne CH 114 Lh43
Saint-VaaSaint-la-Hougue F 102 Kt41
Saint-Valéry-en-Caux F 102 La41
Saint-Valery-sur-Somme F 103 Lb40
Saint-Vallier F 105 Le45
Saint Victor's Petroglyphs Prov. H.S. CDN 19 Eh21
Saint Vincent I 120 Lh45
Saint Vincent WV 47 Gk39
Saint Vincent and the Grenadines 47 Gk39
Saint Vincent N.W.R. USA 36 Fh31
Saint Vincent Passage 47 Gk39
Saint-Vith B 103 Lg40
Saint Walburg CDN (SK) 19 Ef19
Saint Xavier USA (MT) 21 Eg23
Saint-Yorre F 105 Ld44
Saint-Yrieix-la-Perche F 104 Lb45
Saint-Zénon CDN (QC) 30 Gd22
Sainyabuli LAO 196 Qa36
Sainyinan-Daji WAN 272 Lc39
Saiotesh KZ 153 Ng23
Saïoua CI 278 Kg42
Saipal NEP 170 Pa31
Saipan USA 201 Sb15
Saipina BOL 73 Gh55
Sai Ree Beach THA 198 Pk40
Saisombun LAO 197 Qb36
Saissac F 104 Lc47
Sai Thong N.P. THA 196 Qa38
Saito J 185 Rf29
Saiwa Swamp N.P. EAK 290 Mh45
Saiyala SUD 276 Mg38
Saiyid PK 161 Og29
Sai Yok THA 196 Pk38
Sai Yok Noi Waterfall THA 196 Pk38
Sai Yok N.P. THA 196 Pk38
Sajam RI 212 Rg46
Sajama BOL 72 Gf55
Sajama, Nevado BOL 72 Gf55
Sajama, P.N. BOL 72 Gf55
Sajano-Šušenskoevodohranilišče RUS 167 Pf19
Sajir KSA 149 Nc33
Sajkaš SCG 124 Ma45
Sajkyn KZ 133 Nd21
Sajmak TJ 159 Oh27
Sajó H 119 Ma42
Sajósvámos H 119 Ma42
Sak SA 302 Ma61
Saka ETH 284 Mj41
Saka LV 97 Mb34
Saka MA 259 Kj28
Sakabinda RDC 295 Mc51
Sakaeo THA 197 Qb39
Sakaevi TR 131 Mo50
Sakai GH 279 Kj40
Sakai J 183 Rh28
Sakaide J 183 Rg28
Sakaiminato J 183 Rg28
Sakai N.P. J 185 Re29
Sakakah KSA 147 Na30
Sakakemang RI 207 Qb47
Sakala kõrgustik EST 96 Mf32
Sakania RDC 296 Me52
Sakar TM 153 Ob26
Sakaraha RM 306 Nc57
Sakar Dağı TR 130 Mh51
Sakar Island PNG 243 Se48
Sakartvelo = Georgia GE 145 Nb25
Sakartvelo = Georgia GE 145 Nb25
Sakarya = Adapazarı TR 130 Ml50
Sakarya TR 144 Mf25
Sakassou CI 279 Kh42
Sakata J 183 Rk26
Sakbayeme CAM 281 Lf43
Saké RDC 287 Me46
Saken KZ 166 Og21
Sakété DY 280 Lb42
Saketi RI 210 Qd49
Sakha RUS 141 Qc05
Sakhalin RUS 141 Sa08
Sakhi Gopal IND (ORS) 191 Pc36
Sakhon Nakhon THA 197 Qc37
Saki WAN 272 Lb41
Šakiai LT 97 Md36
Sakiet Eddaïr TN 260 Lf28
Sakiet Sidi Youssef TN 260 Le27
Säkilahti FIN 96 Mk29
Sakiramke RI 242 Sa50
Sakishima Islands J 165 Ra14
Sakju DVRK 182 Rc25
Sakkara ET 263 Mf31
Sakke IND (MPH) 191 Pa34
Sak Lek THA 196 Qa37
Sakleshpur IND (KTK) 192 Oh40
Sakoamadinika RM 306 Ne54
Sakone SN 269 Kb39
Sakony RUS 133 Nb18
Sakrand PK 162 Oe32
Sakré Déléb TCH 282 Lk41
Sakri IND (MHT) 190 Oh35
Sakri IND (BIH) 194 Pd32
Sakrivier SA 302 Ma61
Sakskøbing DK 94 Lm36
Saku J 183 Rk27
Saky UA 135 Mg23
Sakya Monastery VRC 170 Pe31
Sakyatan TR 131 Mn53
Säkylä FIN 96 Mc29
Sal RUS 135 Na22
Sala EAK 293 Mk47
Sala S 93 Lr31
Sala SK 118 Ls42
Salaberry-deValleyfield CDN (QC) 33 Gc23
Salaca LV 97 Me33
Salacgriva LV 97 Me33
Sala Consilina I 123 Lq50
Saladas RA (CR) 77 Ha60
Saladero M.Cabal RA (SF) 77 Gk61
Saladillo RA 76 Gj60
Saladillo RA 77 Gj62
Saladillo RA 77 Gk62
Saladillo RA (BA) 77 Ha63
Salado RA 76 Gj59
Salado RA 80 Ge64
Salado RA 80 Gg66
Salado RA 80 Gh66
Salado RA 81 Gj64
Salado RA 81 Hb63
Salado o Chadileuvu RA 80 Gg64
Salado o Colorado RA 76 Gg60
Saladougou RG 278 Kf40
Salaga GH 279 Kk41
Salagle SP 291 Nb45
Salahly SP 285 Nc41
Salaiman Range PK 163 Oe31
Salajwe RB 299 Mc57
Salakas LT 97 Mg35
Šalakuša RUS 91 Na14
Salal TCH 273 Lj38
Salala LB 278 Ke42
Salala SUD 277 Mj36
Salalah OM 151 Nh37
Salama EAK 290 Mj46
Salamá GCA 41 Fe38
Salamá HN 42 Fg38
Salamajärven kansallispuisto FIN 91 Mc14
Salamanca E 106 Kp50
Salamanca MEX (GJT) 40 Ek35
Salamanca PA 43 Ga41
Salamanca RCH 76 Ge61
Salamanca USA (NY) 33 Ga24
Salamanga MOC 303 Mg59
Salamaua PNG 243 Sd49
Salamey IR 155 Nk28
Salamina CO 56 Gc40
Salamina CO 56 Gc43
Salamina GR 128 Md53
Salamiyyeh SYR 146 Mj28
Salamo PNG 244 Sf50
Salang-Tunnel AFG 160 Oe28
Salantai LT 97 Mb34
Salar de Aguilar RCH 76 Gf58
Salar de Antofalla RA 72 Gg58
Salar de Arizaro RA 72 Gg58
Salar de Atacama RCH 72 Gf57
Salar de Cauchari RA 72 Gg57
Salar de Chiguana BOL 72 Gg56
Salar de Coipasa BOL 72 Gf55
Salar de Empexa BOL 72 Gf56
Salar de la Mina RA 76 Gg59
Salar del Hombre Muerto RA 72 Gg58
Salar de Llamara RCH 72 Gf56
Salar de Pajonales RCH 72 Gf58
Salar de Pedernales RCH 76 Gf59
Salar de Pintados RCH 72 Gf56
Salar de Pipanaco RA 76 Gg60
Salar de Pocitos RA (SA) 72 Gg58
Salar de Uyuni BOL 72 Gg56
Salar Pocitos RA 72 Gg58
Salar Punta Negra RCH 72 Gf58
Salas E 106 Ko53
Salas PE 66 Ga49
Salas de los Infantes E 107 Kr52
Salasil KSA 149 Ne32
Salaspils LV 97 Me34
Salatiga RI 210 Qf49
Sălătrucu RO 125 Me45
Salavan LAO 197 Qd38
Salavat IR 154 Nd26
Salavat RUS 140 Nd08
Salavat Abad IR 154 Nd28
Sala Vichey K 197 Qc39
Salawati RI 212 Rf46
Salawin N.P. THA 196 Pj36
Sala y Gómez RCH 54 Ec24
Sala-y-Gomez-Fracture Zone 54 Fa24
Salayie LB 278 Kf42
Salazar RA (BA) 81 Gj64
Salbris F 103 Lc43
Salcabamba PE 66 Gc52
Salcantay, Nevado PE 67 Gd52
Salcedo EC 60 Ga46
Salcha River USA 15 Ch13
Salcia RO 124 Mc46
Salcia RO 126 Mc46
Salcia RO 126 Me47
Salcia RO 127 Me47
Šalčininkai LT 97 Mf36
Sălcuța MD 125 Mk44
Salda Gölü TR 130 Mk53
Saldaña CO 56 Gc44
Saldaña E 106 Kq52
Saldanha SA 302 Lj62
Saldanhabaai SA 302 Lj62
Saldanha Bay SA 302 Lj62
Saldé SN 269 Kd37
Saldungaray RA (BA) 81 Gk65
Saldus LV 97 Mc34
Sale AUS (VIC) 237 Sd65
Salé MA 258 Kg28
Sale MYA 194 Ph35
Salebhatta IND (ORS) 191 Pb35
Saleé RIM 270 Kf36
Saleh RI 207 Qc47
Saleh Abad IR 154 Ne28
Salehard AFG 160 Oa30
Salelologa WS 248 Bd52
Salem IND (TNU) 193 Ok41
Salem SA 303 Md62
Salem USA (OR) 20 Dj23
Salem USA (SD) 26 Fb24
Salem USA (MO) 29 Fe27
Salem USA (NJ) 33 Gc26
Salem USA (IN) 34 Fg26
Salem USA (VA) 35 Fk27
Salémata SN 269 Kd39
Salemi I 122 Ln53
Salem Plateau USA 29 Fe27
Sälen S 93 Lo29
Sälenfjällen S 93 Lo29
Salerno I 122 Lp50
Salers F 104 Lc45
Sales BR (SP) 74 Hf56
Salesópolis BR (SP) 74 Hg57
Salewara IND (CGH) 191 Pa35
Saleye CI 279 Kj41
Salgado BR 65 Ja49
Salgado BR (SE) 71 Jb51
S'Algar E 110 Le51
Salgótarján H 119 Lu42
Salgrund FIN 93 Mb28
Salgueiro BR (PE) 71 Ja50
Salher IND 190 Og35
Salhus N 92 Lf30
Sali DZ 265 Kk32
Sali HR 121 Lq47
Sali RA 76 Gh59
Šali RUS (CHE) 152 Nc24
Salibabu RI 205 Rd44
Salibabu RI 205 Rd44
Salida USA (CO) 21 Eh26
Saliente Alto E 109 Ks47
Salighé RT 279 La42
Salihler TR 130 Mj51
Salihler TR 131 Mm51
Salihli TR 130 Mj52
Salihorsk BY 132 Md19
Salikene WAG 269 Kc39
Salikénie SN 269 Kc39
Salima MOC 297 Mj52
Salima MW 296 Mh52
Salima SUD 276 Me36
Salimgarh IND (RJT) 190 Oh34
Salimi IND (ORS) 191 Pb36
Salin MYA 194 Ph35
Salina USA (UT) 21 Ee26
Salina USA (KS) 26 Fb26
Salina Colorado Grande RA 81 Gj65
Salina Cruz MEX (OAX) 41 Fc37
Salina de Laguna Verde RA 76 Gf59
Salina del Gualicho RA 80 Gh66
Salina Grande RA 80 Gg64
Salina La Antigua RA 76 Gg60
Salina Point BS 37 Gc34
Salinas BR (MG) 75 Hj54
Salinas EC 60 Fk47
Salinas MEX (CHH) 38 Eg32
Salinas MEX (VC) 40 Fc36
Salinas PE 66 Fk49
Salinas RA 76 Ge61
Salinas USA (CA) 20 Dk27
Salinas de Ambargasta RA 76 Gh60
Salinas de Garci Mendoza BOL 72 Gg55
Salinas de Hidalgo MEX (SLP) 39 Ek34
Salinas de los Colorados RA 76 Gg60
Salinas de Mascasin RA 76 Gg61
Salinas de Trapalcó RA 80 Gg65
Salinas Grandes RA 72 Gg57
Salinas Grandes RA 76 Gh60
Salinas Grandes RA 81 Gj64
Salinas Grandes RA 81 Gj65
Salinas Grandes RA 81 Gj67
Salinas las Barrancas RA 81 Gj65
Salinas Peak USA 23 Eg29
Salinas Pueblo Missions Nat. Mon. USA 23 Eg28
Salinau RI 208 Qj47
Saline Royale F 103 Lf43
Salinópolis BR (PA) 64 Hg46
Salins-les-Bains F 105 Lf44
Salira Indah Beach RI 210 Qd48
Salisbury CDN (NB) 31 Gh22
Salisbury GB 101 Kt39
Salisbury USA (MD) 33 Gc26
Salisbury USA (NC) 35 Fk28
Salisbury Plain GB 101 Kt39
Salispuedas MEX 22 Eb30
Sălişte RO 124 Md45
Salistral YV 57 Gh41
Salitral PE 60 Ga48
Salitral de la Perra RA 80 Gg64
Salitral Levalle RA 80 Gh64
Salitre BR (CE) 65 Hk49
Salitre BR 71 Hk51
Salitre EC 60 Ga46
Salitrillo MEX (PUE) 40 Fb36
Salka WAN 272 Lc40
Šalkar KZ 140 Nd09
Salkhad SYR 146 Mj29
Salladillo RA 77 Gk61
Sallanches F 105 Lg45
Sallent E 110 Lb49
Salling DK 94 Lj34
Salliqueló RA (BA) 81 Gj64
Sallisaw USA (OK) 29 Fc28
Sallisbury Island AUS 229 Rb63
Sallom SUD 277 Mj37
Sallum ET 262 Mc30
Salmaná ET 263 Mg30
Salmanlı TR 131 Mp51
Salmas IR 154 Nc26
Salme EST 96 Mc32
Salmenkylä FIN 96 Mg28
Salmerón E 109 Ks50
Salmiya KWT 156 Ne31
Salmo CDN (BC) 18 Eb21
Salmon USA 20 Eb23
Salmon USA (ID) 21 Ed23
Salmon Arm CDN (BC) 18 Ea20
Salmon Falls USA 20 Ec25
Salmon Gums AUS (WA) 228 Ra62
Salmon River CDN 18 Dj18
Salmon River USA 15 Ca12
Salmon River Mountains USA 21 Ec23
Salmossi BF 271 Kk38
Salo FIN 96 Md30
Salò I 120 Ll45
Salo RCA 281 Lj44
Salobra BR 73 Hb56
Salon IND (UPH) 189 Pa32
Salon-de-Provence F 105 Lf47
Salonga RDC 286 Ma46
Salonga Nord, P.N.de la RDC 289 Ma46
Salonga Sud, P.N.de la RDC 289 Ma47
Salonica GR 126 Mc50
Salonta RO 124 Mb44
Saloum SN 269 Kb39
Salpausselkä FIN 96 Mf29
Sal Rei CV 268 Jj37
Salsacate RA (CD) 76 Gh61
Salsbruket N 90 Lf13
Salses-le-Château F 104 Lc48
Sal'sk RUS 135 Na22
Salsomaggiore Terme I 120 Lk46
Salt SA 302 Mb62
Salta RA 55 Gc24
Salta RA (SA) 72 Gh58
Saltaire GB 101 Kt37
Saltash GB 100 Kq40
Saltburn-by-the-Sea GB 101 Ku36
Salt Cay GB 37 Ge35
Saltcoats CDN (SK) 24 Ej20
Salt Desert IR 154 Ng28
Saltee Islands IRL 100 Ko38
Saltery Bay CDN (BC) 18 Dh21
Saltfjellet-Svartisen n.p. N 90 Lh12
Saltholm DK 94 Ln35
Saltillo MEX (COH) 39 Ek33
Salt Lake City USA (UT) 21 Ee25
Salto BR (SP) 74 Hg57
Salto I 122 Ln48
Salto MEX (SL) 38 Eg33
Salto RA (BA) 77 Gk63
Salto RA 77 Gk63
Salto ROU 77 Hb61
Salto Angel YV 58 Gj42
Salto da Divisa BR (MG) 75 Ja54
Salto da Morena BR 62 Gk49
Salto das Sete Quedas BR 69 Hb50
Salto de Agua MEX (CHP) 41 Fd37
Salto de Cavalo ANG 288 Lh50
Salto de Eqipantla MEX 41 Fc36
Salto de Las Rosas RA (MD) 76 Gf63
Salto del Guaíra PY 74 Hc58
Salto de Pirapora BR (SP) 74 Hg57
Salto do Jacuí BR (RS) 78 Hd60
Salto do Jirau BR 67 Gh50
Salto Hacha YV 57 Gj42
Salto Joaquim Rios BR 68 Ha52
Salton Sea USA 22 Ec29
Salto Primeiro BR 69 Hc53
Salt Pan NAM 298 Lk59
Salt Plains N.W.R. USA 28 Fa27
Salt Range PK 161 Og29
Salt River USA 23 Ee29
Salt River Canyon USA 23 Ee29
Salt Springs USA (FL) 36 Fk31
Saltstraumen N 90 Lh12
Saltvik FIN 93 Ma30
Saltwater Hot Springs RC 179 Ra34
Salua RI 209 Qk46
Saluda USA (SC) 35 Fk29
SalueBesar RI 209 Rb46
Salue Kecil RI 209 Rb47
Salug RP 205 Rb41
Salugan RI 209 Ra45
Salumbar IND (RJT) 190 Oh33
Salumpaga RI 209 Ra45
Salur IND (APH) 191 Pb36
Saluzzo I 120 Lh46
Salvador BR (BA) 71 Ja52
Salvaterra BR (PA) 64 Hf46
Salvatierra MEX (GJT) 40 Ek35
Salvatierra-Agurain E 107 Ks52
Salvatierra de los Barros E 108 Ko48
Salween 196 Pk36
Salyan AZ 152 Ne26
Salyersville USA (KY) 35 Fj27
Šalygyne UA 132 Mh20
Salza A 115 Lq43
Salzach A 115 Ln43
Salzach D 115 Ln42
Salzbergwerk A 115 Lo43
Salzburg A 115 Lo43
Salzgitter D 113 Ll38
Salzkotten D 112 Lj39
Salzwedel D 113 Lm38
Sam G 281 Lf45
Sam IND (RJT) 188 Of32
Sama PE 72 Ge54
Samachique MEX (CHH) 38 Eg32
Samachvalavičy BY 132 Md19
Samad OM 157 Nk34
Samad Abag IR 155 Nk29
Samagaltaj RUS (TUV) 167 Ph20
Samana Grande PE 72 Ge54
Samah KSA 147 Nc31
Samai WS 248 Bd52
Samail OM 157 Nj34
Samaipata BOL 73 Gj55
Samakhial IND (GUJ) 190 Of34
Samako RI 209 Rb46
Samakona CI 278 Kg41
Samakoulou RMM 270 Kf39
Samakro CI 279 Kj43
Samal RP 205 Rc42
Samalayuca MEX (CHH) 23 Eg30
Samales Group RP 205 Ra43
Samal Island RP 205 Rc42
Samalkot IND (APH) 191 Pb37
Samalut ET 263 Mf31
Samana RI 209 Qk44
Saman PNG 244 Sh51
Samaná DOM 46 Gf36
Samana Cay BS 37 Gd34
Samanco PE 66 Ga50
Samanda IND (MGA) 194 Pf33
Samandağ TR 144 Mh27
Samangan = Aybak AFG 160 Oe27
Samanlı Dağları TR 130 Mk50
Samar RP 205 Rc40
Samara CR 42 Fh41
Samara RUS 133 Nf19
Samarga RUS 181 Rk22
Samarga RUS 181 Rk22
Samari PNG 243 Sb50
Samaria N.P. GR 128 Me55
Samariapo YV 57 Gg43
Samarina GR 126 Mb50
Samarinda RI 209 Qj46
Samarkand UZB 158 Od26
Samarqand UZB 158 Od26
Samarra IRQ 147 Nb28
Samar Sea RP 203 Rc39
Samarskaya Luka N.P. RUS 133 Ne19
Samarskoye KZ 167 Pb21
Samaru WAN 272 Ld40
Samaruma IND (CGH) 191 Pb34
Samastipur IND (BIH) 191 Pc33
Samasuma Island PNG 243 Sc46
Samate RI 212 Rf46
Samatiguila CI 278 Kg41
Samatwa EAT 293 Mj48
Samaúma BR (AM) 62 Gj46
Šamaxi AZ 152 Ne25

Samba BF 271 Kj39
Samba RCA 281 Lj43
Samba RDC 286 Me45
Samba RDC 292 Md48
Samba RI 208 Qg46
Samba RI 161 Oh29
Samba Caju ANG 288 Lh50
Sambaíllo RG 269 Kd39
Sambalgou BF 271 La39
Sambaliung Mountains RI 209 Qj45
Sambalpur IND (ORS) 191 Pb35
Sambas RI 208 Qe45
Sambas RI 208 Qe45
Sâmbăta RO 124 Mc44
Sambau RI 207 Qc46
Sambava RM 305 Nf53
Sambhal IND (UPH) 189 Ok31
Sambhar IND (RJT) 188 Oh32
Sambhar Salt Lake IND 188 Oh32
Sambialgou BF 271 La39
Sambir UA 119 Md41
Sambito BR 65 Hk49
Sambo ANG 294 Lj52
Samboja RI 209 Qj46
Samborombón RA 77 Hb63
Samborondón EC 60 Ga46
Sâmbra Oilor RO 124 Md43
Sambro CDN (NS) 31 Gj23
Sambuca di Sicilia I 122 Lo53
Samburu EAK 293 Mk47
Samburu Nature Reserve EAK 290 Mj45
Sambusu NAM 295 Lk54
Sambwa EAT 293 Mj48
Samch'ok ROK 182 Re27
Samch'onp'o ROK 182 Re28
Samding Monastery VRC 171 Pf31
Same EAT 293 Mj48
Samé RMM 269 Ke38
Samen IR 154 Ne28
Samer F 103 Lb40
Samford AUS (QLD) 235 Sg59
Samfya Z 296 Me51
Samhah YE 151 Ng39
Samharam OM 151 Nh37
Sämi EST 96 Mg31
Sámi GR 128 Ma52
Sami IND (GUJ) 190 Of34
Sami PK 162 Ob32
Sâmica BG 127 Me49
Samirah KSA 148 Nb32
Samiria PE 60 Gc48
Samitah KSA 150 Nb37
Samjiyon DVRK 182 Re25
Samka MYA 195 Pj35
Şamkir AZ 152 Nc25
Samlaut W.S. K 197 Qb39
Şamlı TR 130 Mh51
Sammallahdenmäki FIN 96 Mb29
Samnapur IND (MPH) 191 Pa34
Sam Ngao THA 196 Pk37
Samnu LAR 267 Lh32
Samo PNG 244 Sg47
Samoa ANG 289 Ma50
Samoa 219 Ba11
Samoa Islands WS/USA 241 Ub21
Samobor HR 121 Lq45
Samoded RUS 91 Na14
Samoeng THA 196 Pk36
Samoëns F 105 Lg44
Samofalovka RUS 133 Nc21
Samohaji = Vasco da Gama IND (GOA) 190 Og38
Samokov BG 126 Md48
Samolva RUS 96 Mh32
Samorogouan BF 279 Kh40
Sámos GR 129 Mg53
Sámos GR 129 Mg53
Samos SCG 124 Ma45
Samosir RI 198 Pk44
Samostan Stična SLO 121 Lp45
Samothrake GR 127 Mf50
Samothráki GR 127 Mf50
Samothráki GR 127 Mf50
Samoyé RG 278 Kf42
Sampa GH 279 Kj42
Sampaga RI 209 Qk47
Sampaka RI 209 Rb45
Sampanahan RI 208 Qj47
Sampang RI 210 Qg49
Sampano RI 209 Ra47
Sampelga BF 271 La39
Samphamit Falls K/LAO 197 Qc38
Sampit RI 208 Qg47
Sampit RI 208 Qg47
Sampun PNG 244 Sg48
Sampwe RDC 292 Md50
Samrala IND (PJB) 189 Oj30
Samraong K 197 Qb38
Sam Rayburn Res. USA 29 Fc30
Samreboi GH 279 Kj43
Samro RUS 96 Mj32
Samsang VRC (TIB) 170 Pb30
Samsø DK 94 Ll35
Samsø Bælt DK 94 Ll35
Samson USA (AL) 35 Fh30
Sam Son VN 197 Qc36
Samson Ind. Res. CDN 19 Ed19
Samsu TR 145 Nb26
Samsun TR 144 Mj25
Samtens D 113 Lo36
Samthar IND (UPH) 189 Ok33
Samtredia GE 152 Nb24
Samucumbi ANG 295 Lk52
Samuda RI 208 Qg47
Samuhú RA (CH) 77 Gk59
Samulondo RDC 289 Mb50
Samundri PK 161 Og30
Samur AFG 160 Oa30
Samur RUS 152 Nd25
Samurai Houses J 183 Sa26
Samusu WS 248 Be52
Samut Prakan THA 196 Qa39
Samut Sakhon THA 196 Qa39
Samut Songkhram THA 196 Qa39
Samye Monastery VRC 171 Pf31
San PL 117 Mb40
San RMM 270 Kh39
Sana BIH 121 Lr46
San'a YE 150 Nc38
Sanaa YE 150 Nc38
Sanaba BF 270 Kj39
Sanabria CO 60 Gb44
Sanadinovo BG 127 Me47
SANAE IV ANT (SA) 312 Kd33
Sanaga CAM 280 Lf44
San Agustín BOL 67 Gg52
San Agustín YV 57 Gg42
San Agustin de Valle Fértil RA (SJ) 76 Gg61
Sanak USA (AK) 14 Bj18
Sanak Island USA 14 Bj18
Sanak Islands USA 14 Bj18
San Alberto PY 74 Hc58
San Alejandro PE 66 Gc50
Sanam Abu Dom SUD 276 Mf37
Sanamxai LAO 197 Qd38
Sanana RI 212 Rd47
Sanana RI 212 Rd47
Sanand IND (GUJ) 190 Og34
Sanandağ IR 154 Nd28
Sanando RMM 270 Kg39
Sânandrei RO 124 Mb45
San Andrés C 45 Gb35
San Andrés CO 42 Fk39
San Andrés E 264 Kb31
San Andrés GCA 41 Ff37
San Andres RP 203 Rb39
San Andres RP 203 Rc39
San Andrés de Giles RA (BA) 77 Ha63
San Andrés Tuxtla MEX (VC) 41 Fc36
Sananduva BR (RS) 78 He59
San Angelo USA (TX) 28 Ek30
Sanankoroba RMM 270 Kg39
San Antón PE 67 Ge53
San Antonio BH 41 Ff37
San Antonio BH 41 Ff37
San Antonio C 45 Ga35
San Antonio CO 60 Ga45
San Antonio MEX (CHH) 23 Eg30
San Antonio MEX (BCS) 38 Ef34
San Antonio MEX (TM) 39 Fa33
San Antonio RA (SL) 76 Gg62
San Antonio RA (CA) 76 Gh60
San Antonio RCH 76 Ge62
San Antonio USA (NM) 23 Eg29
San Antonio USA (TX) 28 Fa31
San Antonio YV 57 Gg44
San Antonio YV 58 Gj42
San Antonio Bay RP 204 Qj41
San Antonio de Areco RA (BA) 77 Ha63
San Antonio de Caparo YV 56 Ge42
San Antonio de Esquilache PE 72 Ge54
San Antonio de Getucha CO 60 Gc45
San Antonio de los Cobres RA (SA) 72 Gg58
San Antonio del Parapetí BOL 73 Gj55
San Antonio del Sur C 45 Gc35
San Antonio de Táchira YV 56 Gd42
San Antonio de Tamanaco YV 57 Gg41
San Antonio Mts. USA 23 Eh29
San Antonio Oeste RA (RN) 80 Gh66
San Antonio Rayon MEX (TM) 39 Fa34
Sanarate GCA 41 Fe38
Sanare YV 57 Gf40
Sanaré YV 57 Gf41
Sanaroa Island PNG 244 Sf50
Sanary-sur-Mer F 105 Lf47
Sanasomboun LAO 197 Qc38
San Augustín CO 60 Gb44
San Augustín MEX (BC) 22 Ec31
San Augustin RP 203 Rb39
San Augustine USA (TX) 29 Fc30
Sanaw OM 157 Nj34
Sanaw YE 151 Nf37
Sanawad IND (MPH) 190 Oj34
San Bartolo BOL 67 Gg53
San Bartolo MEX (SLP) 39 Ek34
San Bartolo PA 43 Fk41
San Bartolo PE 66 Gb52
San Bartolomé de la Torre E 108 Kn47
San Bartolomé de Tirajana E 264 Kc32
San Bartolomeo in Galdo I 122 Lq49
San Bautista ROU 77 Hc63
Sanbei Yangshan VRC (NMZ) 174 Qd26
San Benedetto del Tronto I 121 Lo48
San Benedetto Po I 120 Ll45
San Benito GCA 42 Fg39
San Benito USA (TX) 39 Fb32
San Benito Abad CO 56 Gc41
San Benito Mtn. USA 22 Dk27
San Bernado RA (BA) 81 Gk64
San Bernardino USA (CA) 22 Eb28
San Bernardino de Milpillas Chico MEX (DGO) 39 Eh34
San Bernard N.W.R. USA 29 Fc31
San Bernardo MEX (SO) 38 Ef32
San Bernardo MEX (DGO) 39 Eh32
San Bernardo RA (CH) 77 Gk59
San Bernardo del Viento CO 56 Gc41
San Blas MEX (SL) 38 Ef32
San Blas MEX (NYT) 39 Eh35
San Blas MEX (COH) 39 Ek32
San Blas PA 43 Ga41
San Borja BOL 67 Gg53
San Borjitas MEX 38 Ed32
San Buenaventura MEX (COH) 39 Ek32
Sanca CDN (BC) 19 Eb21
Sancak TR 145 Na26
San Carlos CR 42 Fh40
San Carlos GQ 280 Le44
San Carlos MEX (BC) 22 Ec31
San Carlos MEX (COH) 28 Ek31
San Carlos MEX (BCS) 38 Ed33
San Carlos MEX (SO) 38 Ee32
San Carlos NIC 42 Fh40
San Carlos PA 43 Ga41
San Carlos PY 73 Ha57
San Carlos PY 73 Hb57
San Carlos RA (SA) 72 Gh58
San Carlos RA (MD) 76 Gf62
San Carlos RA 76 Gf63
San Carlos RA (CR) 77 Hc59
San Carlos RCH 80 Ge64
San Carlos ROU 77 Hc63
San Carlos RP 202 Ra38
San Carlos RP 205 Rb40
San Carlos USA (AZ) 23 Ee29
San Carlos YV 57 Gf41
San Carlos YV 57 Gf41
San Carlos de Bariloche RA (RN) 80 Ge66
San Carlos de Bolívar RA (BA) 81 Gk64
San Carlos de Guaroa CO 56 Gd44
San Carlos del Zulia YV 56 Ge41
San Carlos de Río Negro YV 61 Gg45
San Carlos Ind. Res. USA 23 Ee29
San Carlos Lake USA 23 Ee29
San Carlos Park USA (FL) 36 Fk32
San Cataldo I 122 Lo53
San Cataldo I 123 Lt50
San Cayetano CO 56 Gc43
San Cayetano RA (BA) 81 Ha65
Sancerre F 103 Lc43
Sancha VRC (SAX) 175 Qf26
Sancha VRC (GZG) 178 Qe33
Sanchahe VRC (JLN) 180 Rc23
Sanchakou VRC (XUZ) 168 Ok26
Sánchez DOM 46 Gf36
Sanchez, Cerro RA 82 Gf71
Sanchi IND (MPH) 191 Oj34
Sanchi IND 191 Oj34
Sanchidrián E 106 Kq50
Sanchor IND (RJT) 188 Of33
San Christobal DOM 46 Ge36
San Christoval Range CDN 18 De19
San Cirilo, Cerro PE 66 Ga49
San Ciro de Acosta MEX (SLP) 40 Fa35
San Clemente E 109 Ks49
San Clemente RCH 80 Ge63
San Clemente = Cerro San Valentín RCH 82 Gd69
San Clemente USA (CA) 22 Eb29
San Clemente del Tuyú RA (BA) 81 Hb64
San Clemente Island USA 22 Ea29
Sanclerlândia BR (GO) 74 He54
Sancoins F 103 Lc44
Sancos PE 66 Gd53
San Cosme y Damián PY 77 Hb59
San Cristóbal BOL 72 Gg56
San Cristóbal RA (SF) 77 Gk61
San Cristóbal RCH 72 Gf57
San Cristóbal YV 56 Gd42
San Cristóbal de Entreviñas E 106 Kp52
San Cristóbal de la Barranca MEX (JLC) 40 Ej35
San Cristóbal de las Casas MEX (CHP) 41 Fd37
San Cristobal Wash USA 22 Ed29
Sancti Spíritu RA (SF) 77 Gj63
Sancti-Spíritus C 45 Ga35
Sancti-Spíritus E 106 Ko50
Sanctuaire de Mont Iboundji G 288 Lf46
Sančursk RUS 133 Nd17
Sand N 92 Lg31
Sand N 92 Lm30
Sand SA 300 Me57
Sanda FIN 93 Ma30
Sandai RI 208 Qf46
Sandakan MAL 204 Qk43
Sandal EAK 290 Mh45
Sandama RMM 270 Kf39
Sandan K 197 Qd39
Sandando ANG 295 Ma51
Sandane N 92 Lg29
Sandang RI 209 Qk47
San Daniele di Friuli I 121 Lo44
Sandanski BG 126 Md49
Sandaré RMM 269 Ke38
Sandata RUS 135 Na22
Sanday GB 99 Ks31
Sandbach GB 101 Ks37
Sandbank Lake CDN 25 Fj20
Sandbanks Prov. Park CDN 33 Gb23
Sandberg SA 302 Lk62
Sande D 112 Lj37
Sande N 92 Lf29
Sande N 92 Ll31
Sandefjord N 92 Ll31
Sandefjord Ice Bay 313 Oc32
Sandégué CI 279 Kj42
Sandema GH 279 Kk40
Sanderao IND (RJT) 188 Og33
Sandercock Nunataks 313 Nc32
Sanderk IR 157 Nj32
Sanders USA (AZ) 23 Ef28
Sanderson USA (TX) 23 Ej30
Sandersville USA (GA) 35 Fj29
Sandfire Flat AUS (WA) 224 Ra55
Sandhammeren S 95 Lp35
Sand Hill BH 41 Ff37
Sand Hill BH 41 Ff37
Sandhill USA (MS) 29 Ff29
Sand Hills GUY 58 Ha42
Sand Hills USA 26 Ek24
Sandi SUD 276 Mg38
Sandia PE 67 Gf53
San Diego USA (CA) 22 Eb29
San Diego USA (TX) 39 Fa32
San Diego de Alcalá MEX (CHH) 39 Eh31
San Diego de Cabrutica YV 57 Gh41
San Diego de la Unión MEX (GJT) 40 Ek35
Sandıklı TR 131 Ml52
Sandila IND (UPH) 189 Pa32
Sandilands Prov. Forest CDN 24 Fb21
Sandiman, Mount AUS 224 Qh58
Sanding RI 206 Qa47
Sandino C 44 Fh34
Sand in Taufers = Campo Túres I 120 Lm44
San Dionisio RP 203 Ra36
Sandl A 115 Lq42
Sand Lake CDN 24 Fc20
Sandnes N 92 Lf32
Sandnessjøen N 90 Lg12
Sando MOC 296 Mh54
Sandoa RDC 289 Mb50
Sandoméri GR 128 Mb53
Sandomierz PL 117 Mb40
Sândominic RO 125 Mf44
Sandön FIN 90 Ma14
San Donà di Piave I 120 Ln45
Sandougou CI 279 Kh42
Sandougou SN 269 Kc39
Sandovo RUS 132 Mj16
Sandoway MYA 196 Ph36
Sandøysund N 92 Ll31
Sandpit CDN (BC) 18 De19
Sand Point USA (AK) 14 Bk18
Sandpoint USA (ID) 18 Eb21
Sandrakatsy RM 306 Ne54
Sandrandahy RM 306 Nd56
Sandray GB 98 Kn34
Sandringham AUS (QLD) 226 Rk58
Sand River CDN 19 Ee18
Sand River PNG 242 Sa47
Šandrivka UA 135 Mh21
Sandsøy N 92 Lf28
Sand Springs USA (MT) 21 Eg22
Sand Springs USA (OK) 29 Fb27
Sandstad N 90 Le14
Sandstone AUS (WA) 224 Qj59
Sandur IND (KTK) 193 Oj39
Sandusky USA (MI) 32 Fj24
Sandusky USA (OH) 32 Fj25
Sandu Suizu VRC (GZH) 178 Qd32
Sandveld Nature Reserve SA 303 Mc59
Sandverhaar NAM 302 Lj59
Sandvik S 95 Lr33
Sandvika N 90 Lg13
Sandviken S 93 Lr30
Sandvikvåg N 92 Lf31
Sandwich GB 101 Lb39
Sandwich USA (IL) 32 Ff25
Sandwich Bay NAM 298 Lh57
Sandwich Harbour NAM 298 Lh57
Sandwip Island BD 194 Pf34
Sandy GB 101 Ku38
Sandy USA (UT) 21 Ee25
Sandy Bar CDN 24 Fb19
Sandy Bay NZ 238 Th63
Sandy Bay Ind. Res. CDN 24 Fa20
Sandy Bight AUS 229 Rb62
Sandy Cape AUS 235 Sg58
Sandy Cape AUS 236 Sc66
Sandy Desert PK 162 Ob31
Sandy Hills USA 29 Fc29
Sandykachi TM 155 Ob27
Sandy Lake CDN (AB) 19 Ed18
Sandy Lake CDN (ON) 24 Fd19
Sandy Lake CDN 24 Fd19
Sandy Lake CDN 31 Hb21
Sandy Lake Ind. Res. CDN 24 Fd19
Sandy Point BS 37 Gb32
Sandy Point GB 37 Gd35
Sandy Point IND 193 Pg40
Sandy's Beach USA (HI) 16 Cb35
San Estanislao CO 56 Gc40
San Estanislao PY 73 Hb58
San Esteban HN 42 Fh38
San Esteban de Gormaz E 107 Kr51
San Evaristo MEX (BCS) 38 Ee33
San Faustino MEX (BC) 22 Eb29
San Felipe CO 56 Gc40
San Felipe CO 61 Gg45
San Felipe MEX (BC) 22 Ec30
San Felipe MEX (GJT) 40 Ek35
San Felipe RCH 76 Ge62
San Felipe YV 57 Gf40
San Felipe de Jesús MEX (CHH) 38 Eg32
San Felipe de Vichayal PE 60 Fk48
San Felipe Jalapa de Díaz MEX (OAX) 40 Fb36
San Felipe Nuevo Mercurio MEX (ZCT) 39 Ej33
San Félix RCH 76 Ge60
San Félix ROU 77 Ha62
San Félix YV 56 Ge40
San Ferdinando di Púglia I 123 Lq49
San Fermín MEX (DGO) 39 Eh32
Sanfermines E 107 Kt52
San Fernando BOL 73 Ha54
San Fernando E 108 Ko46
San Fernando MEX (TM) 39 Fa33
San Fernando RCH 76 Ge63
San Fernando RP 202 Ra37
San Fernando RP 203 Ra38
San Fernando TT 58 Gk40
San Fernando de Apure YV 57 Gg42
San Fernando de Atabapo YV 57 Gg43
San Fernando del Valle de Catamarca RA (CA) 76 Gh60
Sånfjällets n.p. S 93 Lo28
Sanford CDN (MB) 24 Fb21
Sanford USA (ME) 33 Ge24
Sanford USA (NC) 35 Ga28
Sanford USA (FL) 36 Fk31
Sanford, Mount USA (AK) 15 Ch14
San Francesco d'Arezzo I 120 Lm47
San Francisco BOL 68 Gh53
San Francisco BOL 72 Gh54
San Francisco MEX (CHH) 39 Eh32
San Francisco PA 43 Fk41
San Francisco PE 66 Gd52
San Francisco RA (CD) 76 Gj61
San Francisco RP 203 Rb39
San Francisco RP 205 Rc41
San Francisco USA (CA) 20 Dj27
San Francisco YV 58 Gk43
San Francisco de Becerra HN 42 Fg38
San Francisco de Bellocq RA (BA) 81 Gk65
San Francisco de Borja MEX (CHH) 38 Eg32
San Francisco de la Paz HN 42 Fg38
San Francisco del Chañar RA (CD) 76 Gj60
San Francisco del Laishi RA (FO) 77 Ha59
San Francisco del Monte de Oro RA (SL) 76 Gg62
San Francisco del Rincón MEX (GJT) 40 Ek35
San Francisco de Mostazal RCH 76 Ge62
San Francisco Gotera ES 41 Ff39
San Francisquito MEX (BC) 22 Ed31
San Fratello I 122 Lp52
Sang GH 279 Kk41
Sanga ANG 294 Lh51
Sanga BF 279 La40
Sanga = Makaloge MOC 297 Mh52
Sanga RMM 271 Kj38
San Gabriel EC 60 Gb45
San Gabriel Mts. USA 22 Ea28
Sangala G 288 Lf46
San Galgano I 120 Lm47
Sangali IND (APH) 193 Ok39
San Gallan PE 66 Gb52
Sangam IND 191 Pa33
Sangameshwar IND (MHT) 190 Og37
Sangamner IND (MHT) 190 Oh36
Sangan IR 155 Oa28
Sanganeb Atoll Marine N.P. SUD 277 Mj37
Sangar IR 154 Ne27
Sangar RUS 141 Rb06
Sangarafa RMM 269 Kd39
Sangardo RG 278 Ke41
Sangareddi IND (APH) 190 Oj37
Sangarhi IND (MHT) 191 Pa35
Sangasanga RI 209 Qj46
Sangaste EST 96 Mg33
Sangatanga G 280 Le46
San Gavino Monreale I 111 Lj51
Sangay, P.N. EC 60 Ga46
Sangay, Volcán EC 60 Ga47
Sangbé CAM 281 Lg42
Sangbor AFG 160 Ob28
Sangcharak = Tokzar AFG 160 Od28
Sang Chom THA 196 Qb36
Sange RDC 292 Me49
Sangeang RI 211 Qk50
San Genaro Norte RA (SF) 77 Gk62
Sangenjo = Sanxenxo E 106 Km52
Sângeorgiu de Pădure RO 125 Me44
Sângeorz-Băi RO 124 Me43
Sanger USA (CA) 22 Ea27
Sângera MD 125 Mk44
Sângerei MD 125 Mj43
Sangerfield USA (NY) 33 Gc24
San Gergorio RA (SF) 76 Gj63
Sangerhausen D 113 Lm39
San Germán USA (PR) 47 Gg36
Sângeru RO 125 Mg45
Sanggan He VRC 175 Qh25
Sanggau RI 208 Qf45
Sangha RCB 281 Lj45
Sanghar PK 163 Oe32
Sangihe RI 205 Rc44
San Gil CO 56 Gd42
San Gimignano I 120 Lm47
Sangin AFG 160 Oc29
San Giovanni I 120 Ll48
San Giovanni di Sinis I 111 Lj51
San Giovanni in Fiore I 123 Lr51
San Giovanni in Persiceto I 120 Lm46
San Giovanni Rotondo I 123 Lq49
San Giovanni Valdarno I 120 Lm47
Sangiran RI 210 Qf49
San Giuliano Terme I 120 Ll47
San Giusto di Trieste I 121 Lo45
Sangiyn Dalai nuur MNG 172 Pk21
Sangiyn Dalay MNG 172 Pj23
Sangiyn Dalay MNG 172 Qa22
Sangkhla Buri THA 196 Pk38
Sangkulirang RI 209 Qj45
Sangkum Andet K 197 Qd39
Sangla EST 96 Mg32
Sangliang VRC (GZH) 178 Qd33
Sangli IND (MHT) 190 Oh37
Sanglia Dol RI 215 Rf49
Sangmelima CAM 281 Lg44
Sango ZW 300 Mf56
Sangod IND (RJT) 190 Oj33
Sangola IND (MHT) 190 Oh37
Sangolqui EC 60 Ga46
Sangoshe RB 299 Mb55
Sangouani CI 278 Kg41
Sangouiné CI 278 Kg42
Sangowo RI 212 Re44
Sangradouro Volta Grande, T.I. BR 69 Hd53
Sangraduoro BR 69 Hb53
Sangre de Christo Mts. USA 23 Eh27
Sangre de Cristo Mts. USA 23 Eh27
San Gregorio PE 66 Gd50
San Gregorio Carrio ROU 77 Hb62
San Gregorio de Polanco ROU 77 Hc62
Sangre Grande TT 58 Gk40
Sangro I 122 Lp48
Sangrur IND (PJB) 188 Oh30
Sangsang VRC (TIB) 170 Pd31
Sangsit RI 211 Qh50
Sangüesa E 107 Kt52
Sanguéya RG 278 Kd40
Sanguiana RG 278 Ke40
San Guillermo, P.N. RA 76 Gf60
Sanguily C 45 Ga35
Sangun IR 154 Nf30
Sangwali NAM 299 Mb55
Sangzhi VRC (HUN) 177 Qf31
Sanhe VRC (NMZ) 173 Ra20
Sanhe VRC (GZH) 178 Qd32
Sanhuizhen VRC (SCH) 177 Qd30
Sâni RIM 269 Ke37
Sanibel USA (FL) 36 Fj32
Sanibel Island USA 36 Fj32
San Ignacio BH 41 Ff37
San Ignacio BH 41 Ff37
San Ignacio BH 41 Ff37
San Ignacio BH 41 Ff37
San Ignacio CR 42 Fh41
San Ignacio MEX (BCS) 38 Ed32
San Ignacio MEX (SL) 38 Ef33
San Ignacio MEX (SL) 38 Eg34
San Ignacio MEX (SLP) 39 Ek34
San Ignacio MEX (NL) 39 Fa32
San Ignacio PE 60 Ga48
San Ignacio de Moxos BOL 68 Gh53
San Ignacio de Velasco BOL 73 Gk54
San Ignacio Guazú PY 77 Hb59
San Ignacio Mini RA 77 Hc59
San Ignacio Mini RA (MI) 77 Hc59
San Ignacio Río Muerto MEX (SO) 38 Ee32
San'in-kaigan N.P. J 183 Rh28
Sanipah RI 208 Qj47
Sani Pass LS/SA 303 Me60
San Isidro NIC 42 Fg39
San Isidro RA (CA) 76 Gh60
San Isidro RA (BA) 77 Ha63
San Isidro RP 203 Rc39
San Isidro RP 205 Rd42
San Isidro de El General CR 42 Fj41
San Isidro del Curuguaty PY 74 Hc58
Sanitz D 113 Ln36
Saniyat ad Daffah LAR 262 Mc30
San Jacinto PE 60 Fk47
San Jacinto PE 60 Fk48
San Jacinto RP 203 Rb39
San Jaime de la Frontera RA (ER) 77 Ha61
San Javier BOL 68 Gh53
San Javier E 109 Ku47
San Javier MEX (BCS) 38 Ee33
San Javier MEX (CHP) 41 Fe37
San Javiér RA 77 Ha60
San Javier RA (SF) 77 Ha61
San Javier RA (MI) 77 Hc59
San Javier RCH 80 Ge63
San Javier ROU 77 Ha62
Sanjay Gandhi N.P. IND 190 Og36
San Jerónimo MEX (ZCT) 39 Ej33
San Jerónimo MEX (VC) 40 Fb35
Sanjia VRC (GDG) 178 Qf35
Sanjiang VRC (GZG) 178 Qe33
Sanjiangkou VRC (YUN) 195 Qa32
Sanjiaotang VRC (ZJG) 184 Ra31
Sanjo J 183 Rk27
San Joaquim BR (PA) 64 Hf46
San Joaquín BOL 68 Gh52
San Joaquín BOL 68 Gj52
San Joaquín, Cerro EC 60 Ff46
San Joaquín MEX (QRT) 40 Fa35
San Joaquin RP 205 Rb40
San Joaquin Valley USA 22 Ea27
San Jorge CO 56 Gc41
San Jorge CO 57 Gf42
San Jorge NIC 42 Fh40
San Jorge RA (SF) 77 Gk61
San Jorge ROU 77 Hc62
San Jorge Island SOL 245 Sk50
San José CO 60 Gb45
San José CR 42 Fh41
San José E 109 Ks46
San José HN 42 Fg38
San José MEX 22 Ec31
San Jose PY 73 Hb58
San José RA (CA) 76 Gg59
San José RA (CA) 76 Gh60
San José RA (MI) 77 Hc59
San José RCH 80 Gd65
San Jose RP 202 Ra39
San Jose RP 203 Ra37
San Jose RP 203 Ra38
San Jose RP 203 Ra39
San Jose USA (CA) 20 Dk27
San José YV 57 Gf42
San Jose de Buenavista RP 205 Ra40
San José de Buja YV 58 Gj41
San José de Chimbo EC 60 Ga46
San José de Chiquitos BOL 73 Gk54
San José de Comondú MEX (BCS) 38 Ee32
San José de Feliciano RA (ER) 77 Ha61
San José de Gracia MEX (BCS) 38 Ed32
San José de Guaribe YV 57 Gh41
San José de Jáchal RA (SJ) 76 Gf61
San José de la Costa YV 57 Gf40
San José de la Dormida RA (CD) 76 Gj61
San José de la Esquina RA (SF) 77 Gk62
San José de La Mariquina RCH 80 Gd65
San José de las Lajas C 44 Fj34
San José de las Salinas RA (CD) 76 Gh60
San José del Bocay NIC 42 Fh39
San José del Cabo MEX (BCS) 38 Ef34
San José del Guaviare CO 61 Gd44
San Jose del Monte RP 203 Ra38
San José del Morro RA (SL) 76 Gh62
San Jose de los Molinos PE 66 Gc52
San José de Lourdes PE 60 Ga48
San José del Palmar CO 56 Gb43
San José del Progreso MEX (OAX) 40 Fb37
San José de Maipo RCH 76 Ge62
San José de Mayo ROU 77 Hb63
San José de Moradillas MEX (SO) 23 Ee31
San José de Ocoa DOM 46 Ge36
San José de Pimas MEX (SO) 23 Ee31
San Jose de Quero PE 66 Gc52
San José de Tiznados YV 57 Gg41
San Jose Island USA 39 Fb32
San Jose River CDN 18 Dk20
San José, Volcán RA/RCH 76 Gf62
San Juan CO 56 Gb43
San Juán CR/NIC 42 Fh40
San Juan DOM 46 Ge36
San Juan PE 66 Gc53
San Juan RA 55 Gc25
San Juan RA 76 Gf61
San Juan RA (SJ) 76 Gf61
San Juan RA 76 Gg62
San Juan RCH 72 Gf57
San Juan RP 203 Ra39
San Juan USA (AK) 15 Cf15
San Juan USA 23 Ee27
San Juan USA (PR) 47 Gg36
San Juán YV 56 Gd40
San Juan Bautista PY 77 Hb59
San Juan de Arama CO 56 Gd44
San Juán de Flores HN 42 Fg38
San Juan de Guadalupe MEX (DGO) 39 Ej33
San Juán del César CO 56 Gd40
San Juán de Limay NIC 42 Fg39
San Juán de los Cayos YV 57 Gf40
San Juan de los Lagos MEX (BC) 22 Ec30
San Juan de los Lagos MEX (JLC) 40 Ej35
San Juán de los Morros YV 57 Gg41
San Juan del Río MEX (SO) 23 Ef30
San Juan del Río MEX (DGO) 39 Eh33
San Juan del Río MEX (QRT) 40 Fa35
San Juan del Sur NIC 42 Fh40
San Juan de Manapiare YV 57 Gg43
San Juán de Payara YV 57 Gg42
San Juán de Urabá CO 56 Gb41
San Juan de Yanac PE 66 Gc52
San Juan Evangelista MEX (VC) 41 Fc37
San Juanico MEX (BCS) 38 Ed32
San Juanito MEX (CHH) 38 Eg32
San Juan Ixcaquixtla MEX (PUE) 40 Fb36
San Juan Mts. USA 23 Eg27
San Juan Nepomuceno CO 56 Gc41
San Juan Nepomuceno PY 77 Hc59
San Juan N.H.P. USA 18 Dj21
San Juan y Martinez C 44 Fj34
San Justo RA (SF) 77 Gk61
San Justo RA (BA) 77 Ha63
Sankadiokro CI 279 Kj42
Sankanbiaiwa, Mount WAL 278 Ke41
Sankara RB 299 Mb55
Sankarani RG/RMM 278 Kf40
Sankarayinarkovil IND (TNU) 193 Oj42
Sankaridrug IND (TNU) 193 Oj41
Sankeshwar IND (KTK) 190 Oh37
Sankha THA 197 Qb38
Sankok TR 131 Mm53
Sankosh BHT 194 Pf32
Sankovo RUS 132 Mj17
Sankra IND (RJT) 188 Of32
Sankt Andrä A 115 Lp44
Sankt Anna S 93 Lr32
Sankt Annen in Annaberg-Buchholz D 113 Ln40
Sankt Anton A 114 Ll43
Sankt Brigitta FIN 91 Mb14
Sankt Efrasinnia monastyr BY 132 Me18
Sankt Elisabeth in Marburg D 112 Lj40
Sankt Florian A 115 Lp42
Sankt Gallen CH 114 Lk43
Sankt Georgen D 114 Lj42
Sankt Georg in Wiener Neustadt A 115 Lr43
Sankt Gilgen A 115 Lo43
Sankt Goar D 114 Lh40
Sankt Gotthard CH 114 Lj44
Sankt Ingbert D 114 Lh41
Sankt Jakob A 115 Ln44
Sankt Johann A 115 Ln43
Sankt Johann A 115 Lo43
Sankt Leon-Rot D 114 Lj41
Sankt Margrethen CH 114 Lk43
Sankt Martin CH 114 Lk44
Sankt Michael BY 132 Md19
Sankt Michaelisdonn D 112 Lk36
Sankt Moritz CH 114 Lk44
Sankt-Peterburg RUS 132 Mf16
Sankt Peter-Ording D 112 Lj36
Sankt Pölten A 115 Lq42
Sankt Sophia BY 132 Me18
Sankt Ulrich = Ortisei I 120 Lm44
Sankt Valentin A 115 Lp42
Sankt Veit an der Glan A 115 Lp44
Sankt Vika S 93 Ls32
Sankt Wendel D 114 Lh41
Sankuru RDC 289 Ma48
Sankuru RDC 289 Mb48
San Leo I 120 Ln47
San Leonardo de Yagüe E 107 Kr51
Sanlifan VRC (HUB) 184 Qh30
Şanlıurfa TR 145 Mk27
San Lorenzo BOL 73 Ha54
San Lorenzo EC 60 Fk46
San Lorenzo EC 60 Ga45
San Lorenzo HN 42 Fg39
San Lorenzo MEX 41 Fc37
San Lorenzo, Cerro PE 66 Gb49
San Lorenzo PE 67 Gf51
San Lorenzo PY 73 Hb58
San Lorenzo RA 77 Gk62
San Lorenzo RA (CR) 77 Ha60
San Lorenzo de Calatrava E 109 Kr48
San Lorenzo de El Escorial E 109 Kq50
San Lorenzo de El Escorial E 109 Kq50
San Lorenzo de la Parrilla E 109 Ks49
San Lourdes BOL 67 Gf51
Sanlúcar de Barrameda E 108 Ko46
Sanlúcar de Guadiana E 108 Kn47
San Lucas BOL 72 Gh56
San Lucas MEX (BCS) 38 Ef34
San Lucas USA (CA) 22 Dk27
San Lucas de Abajo MEX (ZCT) 39 Ej33
San Lúcido I 123 Lr51
San Luís C 45 Gc35
San Luis CO 56 Gc42
San Luís GCA 41 Ff37
San Luis MEX (BC) 22 Ec31
San Luis PE 66 Gb50
San Luis RA 55 Gc25
San Luis RA (SL) 76 Gg62
San Luis RCH 76 Gf59
San Luis USA (AZ) 22 Ec29
San Luis USA (CO) 23 Eh27
San Luis al Medio ROU 77 Hd62
San Luis de la Loma MEX (GUR) 40 Ek37
San Luis de la Paz MEX (GJT) 40 Ek35
San Luis del Cordero MEX (DGO) 39 Eh33
San Luis de Montagnes Belos BR (GO) 74 He54
San Luis de Palmar RA (CR) 77 Ha59
San Luis de Shuaro PE 66 Gc51
San Luis Gonzaga MEX (BCS) 38 Ee33
San Luis Obispo USA (CA) 22 Dk28
San Luis Potosí MEX (SLP) 39 Ek34
San Luis Potosí MEX 39 Ek34
San Luis Río Colorado MEX (SO) 22 Ec29
San Luis Valley USA 23 Eh27
Sanluri I 111 Lj51
San Manuel USA (AZ) 23 Ee29
San Marcelino RP 202 Ra38
San Marco I 120 Ln45
San Marco MEX (TB) 41 Fe37
San Marco in Lámis I 123 Lq49
San Marcos BR (PA) 64 Hf46
San Marcos CO 56 Gc41
San Marcos MEX (GUR) 40 Fa37
San Marcos MEX (GUR) 40 Fa37
San Marcos PE 66 Ga49
San Marcos USA (TX) 28 Fb31
San Mariano RP 203 Rb37
San Marino AUS (SA) 227 Rh60
San Marino RSM (San Marino) 120 Ln47
San Marino RSM 120 Ln47
San Martín BOL 68 Gj52
San Martín RA (MD) 76 Gf62
San Martín RA (CA) 76 Gh60
Sânmartin RO 125 Mf44
San Martín ANT (RA) 312 Gc32
San Martín 1 RA (FO) 73 Ha58
San Martín 2 RA (FO) 73 Ha58
San Martín de Frómista E 106 Kq52
San Martín de los Andes RA (NE) 80 Ge66
San Martín del Pimpollar E 106 Kp50
San Martín de Montalbán E 109 Kq49
San Martín de Valdeiglesias E 109 Kq50
San Martino di Castrozza I 120 Lm44
San Martín Texmelucan MEX (PUE) 40 Fa36
San Mateo CR 42 Fh41
San Mateo EC 60 Fk46
San Mateo EC 60 Fk46
San Mateo USA (CA) 20 Dj27
San Mateo USA (NM) 23 Eg28
San Mateo YV 57 Gh41
San Mateo Ixtatán GCA 41 Fe38
San Matías BOL 73 Ha54
Sanmaur CDN (QC) 30 Gd22
Sanmen VRC (ZJG) 184 Ra31
Sanmen Wan VRC 184 Ra31
Sanmenxia VRC (HNN) 177 Qf28
San Miguel BOL 68 Gj54
San Miguel CO 60 Gb45
San Miguel CO 61 Ge45
San Miguel CO/EC 60 Gb45
San Miguel ES 41 Ff39
San Miguel MEX (COH) 39 Ej31
San Miguel MEX (JLC) 40 Ej35
San Miguel PA 43 Ga41
San Miguel PE 66 Gb49
San Miguel PE 66 Gd52
San Miguel RA (MD) 76 Gg62
San Miguel RA (BA) 77 Ha63
San Miguel RA (CR) 77 Hb59
San Miguel RP 203 Ra38
San Miguel RP 205 Rd41
San Miguel USA 22 Dk28
San Miguel USA (AZ) 23 Ee30
San Miguel Bay RP 203 Rb39
San Miguel de Allende MEX (GJT) 40 Ek35
San Miguel de Azapa RCH 72 Ge55
San Miguel de Baga C 45 Gb35
San Miguel de Huachi BOL 67 Gg53
San Miguel del Cantil MEX (DGO) 38 Eg33
San Miguel del Monte RA (BA) 77 Ha63
San Miguel de Salinas E 109 Ku47
San Miguel de Temoaya MEX (DGO) 39 Eh34
San Miguel de Tucumán RA (TU) 76 Gh59
San Miguel do Araguaia BR (GO) 69 He52
San Miguelito HN 41 Ff38
San Miguelito MEX (SO) 23 Ef30
San Miguelito NIC 42 Fh40
San Miguelito PA 43 Ga41
San Miguel Palmas MEX (QRT) 40 Fa35
San Miguel Suchixtepec MEX (OAX) 40 Fb37
Sânmihaiu de Câmpie RO 124 Me44
Sanming VRC (FJN) 184 Qj32
San Miniato I 120 Ll47
Sânna EST 96 Mg33
Sanna IND (CGH) 191 Pb34
San Narciso RP 203 Rb39
Sannaspos SA 303 Md60
San Nicandro Gargánico I 122 Lq49
San Nicolas BOL 68 Gh53
San Nicolás MEX (SO) 38 Ef31
San Nicolás de la Joya MEX (CHH) 38 Eg32
San Nicolas de los Arrocos RA (BA) 77 Gk62
San Nicolás de los Garza MEX (NL) 39 Ek33
San Nicolas Island USA 22 Ea29
Sânnicolau Mare RO 124 Ma44
Sannieshof SA 303 Mc59
Sanniki PL 117 Lu38
Sannohe J 183 Sa25
Sannou RG 278 Kd40
Sanok PL 119 Mc41
Sanokwelle LB 278 Kf42
San Onofre CO 56 Gc41
San Onofre USA (CA) 22 Eb29
Šanovo BG 127 Mf48
Sanoyie LB 278 Kf42
San Pablo BOL 68 Gj53
San Pablo CO 56 Gd42
San Pablo CO 60 Gb45
San Pablo EC 60 Ga46
San Pablo PE 66 Ga49
San Pablo RP 203 Ra38
San Pablo YV 57 Gg42
San Pablo de Huacareta BOL 73 Gj56
San Pablo de Lípez BOL 72 Gg56
San Paolo fuori le Mura I 122 Ln49
San Pascual RP 203 Rb39
San Pedro BH 41 Ff37
San Pedro BH 41 Ff37
San Pédro CI 278 Kg43
San Pedro E 109 Ks48
San Pedro GCA 41 Ff37
San Pedro MEX (BC) 22 Ed31
San Pedro PE 60 Gb48
San Pedro PE 67 Ge51
San Pedro RA (PJ) 73 Gh58
San Pedro RA (SE) 76 Gh59
San Pedro RA (BA) 77 Ha62

San Pedro RA (MI) 77 Hc59
San Pedro RCH 72 Gf56
San Pedro RCH 80 Gd64
San Pedro YV 57 Gg43
San Pedro Amuzgos MEX (OAX) 40 Fa37
San Pedro Channel USA 22 Ea29
San Pedro de Atacama RCH 72 Gf57
San Pedro de Buena Vista BOL 72 Gh55
San Pedro de Cachi PE 66 Gc52
San Pedro de Colaloa RA (TU) 76 Gh59
San Pedro de Coris PE 66 Gc52
San Pedro de las Colonias MEX (COH) 39 Ej33
San Pedro de la Soledad MEX (BCS) 38 Ef34
San Pedro de Lloc PE 66 Ga49
San Pedro del Norte NIC 42 Fh39
San Pedro del Paraná PY 77 Hb59
San Pedro del Pinatar E 109 Ku47
San Pedro de Quemez BOL 72 Gf56
San Pedro de Ycuamandiyú PY 73 Hb58
San Pedro d.M. DOM 46 Gf36
San Pedro Juchatengo MEX (OAX) 40 Fb37
San Pedro Norte RA (CD) 76 Gh61
San Pedro Sula HN 41 Ff38
San Pedro Tapanatepec MEX (OAX) 41 Fc37
San Pedro Totolapan MEX (OAX) 40 Fb37
San Pedro, Volcán RCH 72 Gf56
San Pellegrino Terme I 120 Lk45
Sanpoil River USA 18 Ea21
Sanpoku J 183 Rk26
San Policarpio RP 203 Rc39
Sanquhar GB 99 Kr35
Sanquianga, P.N. CO 60 Ga44
San Quintín MEX (BC) 22 Ec30
San Quintín MEX (CHP) 41 Fe37
San Quirico d'Orcia I 120 Lm47
San Rafael BOL 67 Gf52
San Rafael BOL 72 Gh54
San Rafael BOL 73 Gk54
San Rafael CO 61 Gg45
San Rafael CR 42 Fh40
San Rafael EC 60 Gb46
San Rafael MEX (BCS) 38 Ec32
San Rafael MEX (NL) 39 Ek33
San Rafael PE 66 Gb51
San Rafael RA (MD) 76 Gf63
San Rafael YV 56 Ge40
San Rafael de Atamaica YV 57 Gg42
San Rafael de Canagua YV 57 Ge41
San Rafael de Imataca YV 58 Gk42
San Rafael Desert USA 21 Ee26
San Rafael Glacier RCH 82 Gd69
San Rafael Knob USA 21 Ee26
San Ramón BOL 68 Gh52
San Ramón BOL 68 Gj53
San Ramón BOL 68 Gk53
San Ramón C 45 Gb35
San Ramón CR 42 Fh40
San Ramón MEX (QTR) 41 Ff35
San Ramón PE 60 Gb48
San Ramón PE 66 Gc51
San Ramón RA (LR) 76 Gg61
San Ramón ROU 77 Hc63
San Ramón RP 205 Ra42
San Ramón de la Nueva Orán RA (SA) 73 Gh57
San Remigio RP 205 Rb40
San Remo AUS (VIC) 237 Sc65
San Remo I 120 Lh47
San Rolando MEX (TM) 39 Fa34
San Roque E 108 Kp46
San Roque RA (CR) 77 Ha60
San Roque RP 203 Rc39
Sans Souci, Citadelle/ RH 45 Gd36
San Saba USA (TX) 28 Fa30
Sansalé RG 278 Kc40
San Salvador BS 37 Gc33
San Salvador ES 41 Ff39
San Salvador PE 61 Ge47
San Salvador RA (ER) 77 Ha61
San Salvador ROU 77 Hb62
San Salvador de Jujuy RA (PJ) 72 Gh58
San Salvador El Seco MEX (PUE) 40 Fb36
San Salvo I 122 Lp48
Sansanding RMM 270 Kh39
Sansanne-Mango RT 279 La40
Sansarpur IND (UPH) 189 Pa31
San Sebastián = Donostia E 107 Ks53
San Sebastián MEX (JLC) 39 Eh35
San Sebastián MEX (VC) 40 Fa35
San Sebastian RA (TF) 82 Gf72
San Sebastian USA (PR) 47 Gg36
San Sebastián de la Gomera E 264 Kb31
San Sebastián de los Reyes E 109 Kr50
San Sebastián Zinacatepec MEX (PUE) 40 Fb36
San Sebastião do Uatumã BR (AM) 63 Hb47
Sansepolcro I 120 Ln47
San Severino Marche I 121 Ln47
San Severo I 122 Lq49
Sansha VRC (FJN) 184 Ra32
Sansha Wan VRC 184 Qk32
Sanshui VRC (GDG) 179 Qg34
San Silvestre BOL 67 Gf51
San Silvestre YV 57 Ge41
San Simón BOL 68 Gj52
Sanski Most BIH 121 Lr46
Sanso RMM 278 Kg40
San Stéfano di Camastra I 122 Lp52
Sansui VRC (GZH) 178 Qe32
Sansundi RI 213 Rh46
Sansu-ri DVRK 182 Rd25
Santa PE 66 Ga50
Santa PE 66 Ga50
Santa USA (ID) 18 Eb22
Santa Albertina BR (SP) 74 He55
Santa Amalia E 108 Ko49
Santa Ana BOL 68 Gh52
Santa Ana BOL 73 Gh56
Santa Ana C 45 Ga35
Santa Ana CO 56 Gc41
Santa Ana EC 60 Fk46
Santa Ana EC 60 Ga47
Santa Ana ES 41 Ff38
Santa Ana MEX (SO) 23 Ee30
Santa Ana PE 61 Gd48
Santa Ana PE 66 Gc53
Santa Ana RA (MI) 77 Hc59
Santa Ana RP 203 Rb36
Santa Ana USA (CA) 22 Eb29
Santa Ana YV 56 Gd41
Santa Ana YV 57 Gh41
Santa Ana Island SOL 245 Tb51
Santa Anita MEX (BCS) 38 Ef34
Santa Anita MEX (COH) 39 Ej31
Santa Anita Park USA (CA) 22 Eb28
Santa Anita Park USA (CA) 22 Eb28
Santa Anna USA (TX) 28 Fa30
Santa Barbara BOL 68 Gk54
Santa Barbara BR (AM) 61 Gg48
Santa Barbara BR (MG) 75 Hj55
Santa Barbara CO 56 Gc43
Santa Bárbara E 109 Ks47
Santa Bárbara HN 41 Ff38
Santa Bárbara MEX (CHH) 38 Ej32
Santa Barbara RCH 80 Gd64
Santa Barbara USA (CA) 22 Ea28
Santa Barbara YV 56 Ge42
Santa Barbara YV 57 Gg44
Santa Barbara YV 58 Gj41
Santa Barbara Channel USA 22 Dk28
Santa Bárbara de Casa E 108 Kn47
Santa Bárbara d'Oeste BR (SP) 74 Hg57
Santa Barbara Island USA 22 Ea29
Santa Birgitta Kapell S 95 Lr34
Santa Brigida BR (BA) 71 Ja50
Santa Catalina CO 56 Gc40
Santa Catalina PA 43 Fk42
Santa Catalina PE 66 Ga49
Santa Catalina PE 66 Gc49
Santa Catalina RA (PJ) 72 Gg56
Santa Catalina RA (SE) 76 Gh60
Santa Catalina RP 205 Rb41
Santa Catalina YV 57 Gf42
Santa Catalina YV 58 Gk41
Santa Catalina Island USA 22 Ea29
Santa Catarina BR 55 Hb24
Santa Catarina MEX (BC) 22 Ec31
Santa Catarina MEX (NL) 39 Ek33
Santa Cecilia BR (SC) 78 He59
Santa Cecilia CR 42 Fh40
Santa Cesárea Terme I 123 Lt50
Santa Clara BR (AP) 63 He46
Santa Clara C 45 Ga34
Santa Clara MEX (DGO) 39 Ej33
Santa Clara RA (PJ) 73 Gh58
Santa Clara USA (UT) 22 Ed27
Santa Clara YV 57 Gh41
Santa Clara-a-Velha P 108 Km47
Santa Clara de Olimar ROU 77 Hc62
Santa Clara do Ingaí BR (RS) 78 Hd60
Santa Clara Ind. Res. USA 23 Eg28
Santa Clotilde PE 61 Gd47
Santa Coloma de Queralt E 110 Lb49
Santa Comba E 106 Km53
Santa Croce Camerina I 122 Lp54
Santa Cruz BOL 67 Gf53
Santa Cruz BR (AM) 61 Gg46
Santa Cruz BR (PA) 63 Hd47
Santa Cruz BR (RN) 65 Jb49
Santa Cruz BR (RO) 68 Gj50
Santa Cruz BR (PE) 71 Hk50
Santa Cruz BR (ES) 75 Hk55
Santa Cruz CR 42 Fh40
Santa Cruz MEX (NYT) 38 Eh35
Santa Cruz MEX (NYT) 39 Eh35
Santa Cruz PE 60 Gc48
Santa Cruz PE 66 Gb51
Santa Cruz RA 55 Gb28
Santa Cruz RA 82 Gf71
Santa Cruz RCH 76 Ge63
Santa Cruz RP 202 Qk38
Santa Cruz RP 203 Ra38
Santa Cruz RP 203 Ra39
Santa Cruz RP 203 Rb39
Santa Cruz RP 205 Rc42
Santa Cruz USA (CA) 20 Dj27
Santa Cruz YV 58 Gk42
Santa Cruz Cabrália BR (BA) 75 Ja54
Santa Cruz das Palmeiras BR (SP) 74 Hg56
Santa Cruz de Bucaral YV 57 Gf40
Santa Cruz de Campezo E 107 Ks52
Santa Cruz de la Palma E 264 Kb31
Santa Cruz de la Sierra BOL 73 Gj54
Santa Cruz del Norte C 44 Fk34
Santa Cruz del Quiché GCA 41 Fe38
Santa Cruz del Sur C 45 Ga35
Santa Cruz de Mompox CO 56 Gc41
Santa Cruz de Mudela E 109 Kr48
Santa Cruz de Succhabamba PE 66 Ga49
Santa Cruz de Tenerife E 264 Kb31
Santa Cruz d.J.R. MEX (GJT) 40 Ek35
Santa Cruz do Arari BR (PA) 64 Hf46
Santa Cruz do Rio Pardo BR (SP) 74 Hf57
Santa Cruz dos Milagres BR (PI) 65 Hj48
Santa Cruz do Sul BR (RS) 78 Hd60
Santa Cruz Island USA 22 Ea29
Santa Cruz Islands SOL 241 Tb21
Santa Cruz Verapaz GCA 41 Fe38
Santadi I 111 Lj51
Santa Eduwiges MEX (SO) 23 Ee31
Santa Elena EC 60 Fk47
Santa Elena MEX (COH) 39 Ej32
Santa Elena RA (ER) 77 Ha61
Santa Elena, Cerro RA 80 Gh68
Santa Elena RP 203 Rb38
Santa Elena YV 58 Gj41
Santa Elena de Uairén YV 58 Gk43
Santa Eleodora RA (BA) 77 Gj63
Santa Eufemia E 108 Kq48
Santa Eugenia E 106 Km52
Santa Eulalia E 109 Kt50
Santa Eulalia MEX (COH) 28 Ek31
Santa Eulália P 108 Kn48
Santa Eulària des Riu E 110 Lb52
Santa Fé BR (AM) 61 Gd48
Santa Fé BR (AM) 67 Gf50
Santa Fé C 44 Fj34
Santa Fe CO 56 Ge42
Santa Fé E 109 Kr47
Santa Fe MEX (BCS) 38 Ee33
Santa Fe MEX (CHH) 39 Ej31
Santa Fé PA 43 Fk41
Santa Fé PA 43 Ga41
Santa Fé RA 55 Gd25
Santa Fé RA (SF) 77 Gk61
Santa Fe RP 203 Rb38
Santa Fe USA (NM) 23 Eh28
Santa Fe de Antioquia CO 56 Gc42
Santa Fé de Minas BR (MG) 75 Hh54
Santa Fé do Sul BR (SP) 74 He56
Santa Filomena BR (PI) 70 Hh50
Santa Filomena BR (PE) 71 Hk50
Sant'Ágata di Militello I 122 Lp52
Santa Helena BR (MA) 64 Hh47
Santa Helena BR (AC) 67 Ge50
Santa Helena BR (PR) 74 Hc58
Santa Helena de Cusima CO 56 Ge43
Santa Helena de Goiás BR (GO) 74 He54
Santai VRC (SCH) 176 Qc30
Santa Inês BR (MA) 64 Hh47
Santa Inês BR (BA) 71 Ja52
Santa Inés CO 61 Gd45
Santa Inés YV 57 Gf40
Santa Inez, T.I. BR 58 Gk43
Santa Isabel EC 60 Ga47
Santa Isabel MEX (SLP) 39 Ek34
Santa Isabel NIC 42 Fh40
Santa Isabel PA 43 Ga41
Santa Isabel PE 60 Gc48
Santa Isabel SOL 245 Sk49
Santa Isabel do Araguaia BR (PA) 64 Hf49
Santa Isabel do Rio Negro BR (AM) 62 Gh46
Santa Isabella RA (LP) 80 Gg64
Santa Juana RCH 80 Gd64
Santa Juana YV 57 Gg42
Santa Júlia BR (AM) 62 Gk49
Santa Juliana BR (MG) 74 Hg55
Santa Lucía C 44 Fh34
Santa Lucía C 45 Gb35
Santa Lucía EC 60 Ga46
Santa Lucía PE 67 Ge53
Santa Lucía RA (CR) 77 Ha60
Santa Lucía ROU 77 Hb63
Santa Lucía YV 57 Gf41
Santa Lucia Bank USA 22 Dk28
Santa Lucia Range USA 22 Dk28
Santa Luz BR (PI) 70 Hh50
Santaluz BR (BA) 71 Ja51
Santa Luzia BR (PA) 64 Hg46
Santa Luzia BR (MA) 64 Hh47
Santa Luzia BR (PB) 65 Jb49
Santa Luzia BR (BA) 71 Ja53
Santa Luzia BR (MG) 75 Hj55
Santa Luzia do Paruá BR (MA) 64 Hh47
Santa Magdalena RA (CD) 76 Gj63
Santa Margherita I 111 Lj52
Santa Maria ANG 294 Lg52
Santa Maria BR (AM) 62 Gh49
Santa Maria BR (AM) 62 Ha48
Santa Maria BR (PA) 63 He46
Santa Maria BR 63 Hf49
Santa Maria BR (BA) 71 Ja53
Santa Maria BR (RS) 78 Hd60
Santa Maria CH 114 Ll44
Santa Maria CO 56 Gd43
Santa Maria CV 268 Jj37
Santa Maria HN 42 Fg38
Santa Maria MEX (BC) 22 Ec30
Santa Maria MEX (SO) 22 Ee31
Santa Maria MEX (CAM) 41 Fe36
Santa Maria RA (CA) 76 Gg59
Santa Maria RP 205 Rc42
Santa Maria USA (CA) 22 Dk28
Santa Maria YV 56 Ge41
Santa Maria YV 57 Gg42
Santa María Asunción Tlaxiaco MEX (OAX) 40 Fb37
Santa María Ayoquezco MEX (OAX) 40 Fb37
Santa Maria Cápua Vétere I 122 Lp49
Santa Maria da Boa Vista BR (PE) 71 Ja50
Santa Maria da Vitória BR (BA) 70 Hh52
Santa Maria de Ipire YV 57 Gh41
Santa Maria de Jetibá BR (ES) 75 Hk56
Santa Maria de la Peña E 107 Ku52
Santa Maria del Azogue E 106 Km53
Santa Maria del Camí E 110 Lc51
Santa Maria delle Grazie I 120 Lk45
Santa Maria del Oro MEX (DGO) 39 Eh33
Santa Maria del Oro MEX (NYT) 39 Eh35
Santa Maria de las Guaicas YV 58 Gh44
Santa Maria del Páramo E 106 Kp52
Santa Maria del Regno I 111 Lj50
Santa María del Río MEX (SLP) 40 Ek35
Santa Maria de Nanay PE 61 Gd47
Santa Maria de Nieva PE 60 Gb48
Santa Maria do Oeste BR (PR) 74 He58
Santa Maria do Suaçuí BR (MG) 75 Hj55
Santa Maria do Tocantins BR (TO) 70 Hg50
Santa María Ecatepec MEX (OAX) 40 Fc37
Santa María Huatulco MEX (OAX) 40 Fb38
Santa María Huazolotitlán MEX (OAX) 40 Fb37
Santa Maria Island VU 246 Td53
Santa Maria la Real de Nieva E 106 Kq51
Santa Marinella I 122 Lm48
Santa Mario do Pará BR (PA) 64 Hg46
Santa Marta ANG 294 Lg52
Santa Marta CO 56 Gc40
Santa Marta E 108 Ko48
Santa Martha MEX (BCS) 38 Ed33
Santa Martha MEX (MEX) 40 Fa36
Santa Mónica MEX (COH) 39 Ek31
Santa Monica USA (CA) 22 Ea28
Santan RI 209 Qj46
Santana BR (AM) 62 Gj46
Santana BR (AP) 63 He45
Santana BR (AP) 63 He46
Santana BR (MA) 64 Hg48
Santana BR (AM) 67 Gg50
Santana BR 69 He50
Santana BR (BA) 70 Hh52
Santana CO 56 Gc44
Santana CO 56 Gd42
Santana da Boa Vista BR (RS) 78 Hd61
Santana da Serra P 108 Km47
Santana de Pirapama BR (MG) 75 Hh55
Santana do Acaraú BR (CE) 65 Hk47
Santana do Araguaia BR (PA) 69 He50
Santana do Cariri BR (CE) 65 Ja49
Santana do Ipanema BR (AL) 71 Jb50
Santana do Livramento BR (MT) 69 Hb53
Santana do Livramento BR (RS) 78 Hc61
Santana do Matos BR (RN) 65 Jb48
Santana, T.I. BR 69 Hc53
Santander E 107 Kr53
Santander RP 205 Rb41
Santander Jiménez MEX (TM) 39 Fa33
Sant'Andrea Frius I 111 Lk51
Sant'Ángelo dei Lombardi I 122 Lq50
Sant'Ángelo Lodigia I 120 Lk45
Sant'Antioco I 111 Lj51
Sant Antoni de Portmany E 110 Lb52
Sant'Antonio di Santadi I 111 Lj51
Santanyí E 110 Ld51
Santa Olalla del Cala E 108 Ko47
Santa Pau E 110 Lc48
Santa Paula USA (CA) 22 Ea28
Santa Pola E 109 Ku48
Sant' Apollinare Nuovo di Ravenna I 120 Ln46
Santa Quitéria BR (CE) 65 Hk48
Santa Quitéria do Maranhão BR (MA) 65 Hj47
Santarcángelo I 123 Lr50
Santarcángelo di Romagna I 120 Ln46
Santarem BR (PA) 63 Hc47
Santarém P 108 Km49
Santarém Novo BR (PA) 64 Hg46
Santaren Channel BS 37 Ga33
Santa Rita BR (AM) 61 Gf47
Santa Rita BR (MA) 64 Hh47
Santa Rita BR (PB) 65 Jc49
Santa Rita CO 57 Gf43
Santa Rita CO 61 Gd45
Santa Rita HN 42 Fg38
Santa Rita MEX (BCS) 38 Ee33
Santa Rita NIC 42 Fg39
Santa Rita YV 56 Ge40
Santa Rita YV 57 Gg41
Santa Rita de Cássia BR (BA) 70 Hh51
Santa Rita de Catuna RA (LR) 76 Gg61
Santa Rita do Araguaia BR (GO) 74 Hd54
Santa Rita do Pardo BR (MS) 74 Hd56
Santa Rita do Passa Quatro BR (SP) 74 Hg56
Santa Rita do Sapucaí BR (MG) 75 Hh57
Santa Rosa BOL 67 Gg53
Santa Rosa BR (RR) 58 Gj44
Santa Rosa BR (RO) 68 Gk52
Santa Rosa BR (TO) 70 Hf51
Santa Rosa BR (RS) 78 Hc59
Santa Rosa CO 56 Gc42
Santa Rosa CO 60 Gb45
Santa Rosa CO 61 Ge45
Santa Rosa CO 61 Gf44
Santa Rosa EC 60 Ga47
Santa Rosa MEX (SO) 38 Ef31
Santa Rosa MEX (QTR) 41 Ff36
Santa Rosa PE 66 Ga49
Santa Rosa PE 67 Ge52
Santa Rosa PE 67 Ge53
Santa Rosa RA (SA) 73 Gh57
Santa Rosa RA (CR) 77 Ha60
Santa Rosa RA (LP) 81 Gh64
Santa Rosa USA (CA) 20 Dj26
Santa Rosa USA (AZ) 22 Ed29
Santa Rosa USA (NM) 23 Eh28
Santa Rosa YV 56 Gd41
Santa Rosa YV 57 Gf41
Santa Rosa YV 57 Gh41
Santa Rosa Beach USA (FL) 35 Fg30
Santa Rosa da Vigia BR (PA) 64 Hf46
Santa Rosa de Abuná BOL 67 Gg51
Santa Rosa de Amonadona YV 61 Gg45
Santa Rosa de Copán HN 41 Ff38
Santa Rosa de las Misiones PY 77 Hb59
Santa Rosa del Conlara RA (SL) 76 Gh62
Santa Rosa de Lima BR (SC) 79 Hf60
Santa Rosa de Lima ES 42 Fg39
Santa Rosa del Monday PY 74 Hc58
Santa Rosa del Río Primera RA (CD) 76 Gj61
Santa Rosa de Mbutuy PY 73 Hb58
Santa Rosa de Ocopa PE 66 Gc51
Santa Rosa de Socco PE 66 Gb51
Santa Rosa de Viterbo BR (SP) 74 Hg56
Santa Rosa Island USA 22 Dk29
Santa Rosa Island USA 34 Fg30
Santa Rosalía MEX (BCS) 38 Ed32
Santa Rosalía YV 57 Gh42
Santa Rosa, P.N. CR 42 Fh40
Šantarskie ostrova RUS 141 Rd07
Santa Severa F 111 Lk48
Santa Sylvina RA (CH) 77 Gk59
Santa Teresa BR 70 Hf52
Santa Teresa MEX (NYT) 39 Eh34
Santa Teresa MEX (TM) 39 Fa33
Santa Teresa MEX (TM) 39 Fb33
Santa Teresa PE 60 Gc48
Santa Teresa RA (SF) 77 Gk62
Santa Teresa YV 57 Gg40
Santa Teresa de Goiás BR (GO) 70 Hf52
Santa Teresa di Riva I 122 Lq53
Santa Teresa do Tocantins BR (TO) 70 Hg51
Santa Teresa Gallura I 111 Lk49
Santa Teresa, P.N. ROU 77 Hd62
Santa Teresinha de Goiás BR (GO) 70 Hf53
Santa Teresita RA (BA) 81 Hb64
Santa Terezinha BR (MT) 69 He51
Santa Terezinha BR (SC) 79 He59
Santa Theresa AUS (NT) 227 Rh58
Santa Victoria RA (SA) 72 Gh57
Santa Victoria RA (SA) 73 Gj57
Santa Vitória BR (MG) 74 He55
Santa Vitória do Palmar BR (RS) 78 Hd62
San-Ta-Wani Safari Camp RB 299 Mb55
Santaworld S 93 Lp30
Sant Carles de la Ràpita E 110 La50
Sant Carles de Peralta E 110 Lb51
Sant Celoni E 110 Lc49
Sante Bennur IND (KTK) 192 Oh39
Santee Ind. Res. USA 26 Fb24
Santee N.W.R. USA 35 Fk29
Sant'Elia a Pianisi I 122 Lp49
Santemarahalli IND (KTK) 193 Oj41
San Teodoro I 111 Lk50
Santéramo in Colle I 123 Lr50
Santerno I 120 Lm46
Santerre F 103 Lc41
Santesteban E 107 Kt53
Sant'Eufémia Lamézia I 123 Lr52
Sant Feliu de Guíxols E 110 Ld49
Sant Francesc de Formentera E 110 Lb52
Santhe MW 296 Mg52
Santhià I 120 Lj45
Santiago BR (RS) 78 Hc60
Santiago CR 42 Fh41
Santiago EC 60 Ga47
Santiago GCA 41 Fe38
Santiago MEX (NL) 39 Ek33
Santiago PA 43 Fk41
Santiago PE 60 Gb47
Santiago RCH 76 Ge62
Santiago RP 203 Ra37
Santiago Astata MEX (OAX) 40 Fc38
Santiago Choapan MEX (OAX) 40 Fc37
Santiago de Alcántara E 108 Kn49
Santiago de Anchucaya PE 66 Gb52
Santiago de Andamarca BOL 72 Gg55
Santiago de Cao PE 66 Ga49
Santiago de Chiquitos BOL 73 Ha55
Santiago de Chocorvos PE 66 Gc52
Santiago de Chuco PE 66 Ga50
Santiago de Compostela E 106 Km52
Santiago de Cotagaita BOL 72 Gh56
Santiago de Cuba C 45 Gc35
Santiago de Huari BOL 72 Gg55
Santiago de las Vegas C 44 Fj34
Santiago del Estero RA 55 Gd24
Santiago del Estero RA (SE) 76 Gh59
Santiago de los Caballeros MEX (SL) 38 Eg33
Santiago de los Cabelloros DOM 46 Ge36
Santiago del Teide E 264 Kb31
Santiago de Machaca BOL 72 Gf54
Santiago de Pacaguaras BOL 67 Gf52
Santiago do Cacém P 108 Km48
Santiago Ixcuintla MEX (NYT) 39 Eh35
Santiago,James = Isla San Salvador EC 60 Fe46
Santiago Juxtlahuaca MEX (OAX) 40 Fb37
Santiago Mts. USA 23 Ej31
Santiago Papasquiaro MEX (DGO) 39 Eh33
Santiago Pinotepa Nacional MEX (OAX) 40 Fa37
Santiago Tuxtla MEX (VC) 41 Fc36
Santiaguillo MEX (ZCT) 39 Ej34
Santibánez de la Sierra E 106 Kp50
San Tiburico MEX (ZCT) 39 Ek33
Santiguila RMM 270 Kg39
Santillana del Mar E 107 Kq53
San Timoteo YV 56 Ge41
Santipur IND (CGH) 191 Pa35
Säntis CH 114 Lk43
Santissima Trinità di Saccàrgia I 111 Lj50
Santisteban del Puerto E 109 Kr48
Santi Suk THA 196 Qa36
Sant Joan d'Alacant E 109 Ku48
Sant Llorenç de Morunys E 110 Lb48
Sant Mateu E 110 La50
Santo Amaro BR (AM) 67 Ge49
Santo Amaro BR (BA) 71 Ja52
Santo Anastácio BR (SP) 74 He56
Santo André ANG 294 Lh52
Santo André BR (PA) 64 Hf46
Santo André BR (SP) 75 Hg57
Santo Ângelo BR (RS) 78 Hc60
Santo Antonio BR (AM) 62 Gk47
Santo António BR (PA) 63 Hb46
Santo Antônio BR (MA) 64 Hh46
Santo Antônio BR (RN) 65 Jc49
Santo Antonio BR (RO) 67 Gg50
Santo Antonio BR 70 Hf51
Santo António STP 280 Ld45
Santo Antônio da Barra BR (GO) 74 He54
Santo Antônio da Platina BR (PR) 74 He57
Santo Antonio de Leverger BR (MT) 69 Hb53
Santo Antônio do Içá BR (AM) 61 Gg47
Santo Antônio do Jacinto BR (MG) 75 Hk54
Santo Antônio do Sudoeste BR (PR) 78 Hd59
Santo Augusto BR (RS) 78 Hd59
Santo Corazón BOL 73 Ha54
Santo Cristo BR (RS) 78 Hc59
Santo Domingo C 44 Fk34
Santo Domingo DOM 46 Gf36
Santo Domingo MEX 22 Ec30
Santo Domingo MEX (BCS) 38 Ee33
Santo Domingo MEX (DGO) 39 Eh33
Santo Domingo MEX (SLP) 39 Ek34
Santo Domingo NIC 42 Fh39
Santo Domingo RA (SA) 73 Gj58
Santo Domingo YV 56 Gd42
Santo Domingo de Acobamba PE 66 Gc51
Santo Domingo de la Calzada E 107 Ks52
Santo Domingo de los Colorados EC 60 Ga46
Santo Domingo de Silos E 107 Kr51
Santo Domingo Pueblo USA (NM) 23 Eg28
Santo Domingo Tehuantepec MEX (OAX) 41 Fc37
Santo Estevão BR (BA) 71 Ja52
Santo Expedito BR (SP) 74 He56
Santo Inácio BR (BA) 70 Hj51
Santo Inácio BR (PR) 74 He57
San Tomé YV 57 Gh41
Santoña E 107 Kr53
Santonia F 59 Hc43
Santo Niño RP 205 Rc42
Santo Onofre BR 70 Hj52
Santópolis do Aguapú BR (SP) 74 He56
Santos AUS (QLD) 234 Sa60
Santos BR (SP) 75 Hg57
Santos Dumont BR (MG) 75 Hj56
Santos Lugares RA (SE) 76 Gj59
Santos Mercado BOL 67 Gg50
Santos Reyes Nopala MEX (OAX) 40 Fb37
Santo Tirso P 106 Km51
Santo Tomás MEX (BC) 22 Eb30
Santo Tomás MEX (CHH) 23 Eg31
Santo Tomás NIC 42 Fh39
Santo Tomas PE 67 Gd53
Santo Tomás PE 67 Gd53
Santo Tomas RP 205 Rc42
Santo Tome RA (SF) 77 Gk61
Santo Tomé RA (CR) 77 Hb60
Sant Pere de Rodes E 110 Ld48
Santpur IND (KTK) 190 Oj36
Santuari de Lluc E 110 Lc51
Santuari de Sant Salvador E 110 Ld51
Santuario de las Lajas CO 60 Gb45
Santuario delle Santa Casa I 121 Lo47
Santuario de Loyola E 107 Ks53
Santuario di San Michele I 123 Lq49
Santuário do Bom Jesus BR 75 Hj56
Santuario Laguna El Peral RCH 76 Ge62
Santuario Nacional Calipuy PE 66 Ga50
Santuario Nacional de Ampay PE 67 Gd52
Santuario Nacional Huayllay PE 66 Gb51
Santuario Nacional Lagunas de Mejía PE 72 Ge54
Santuario Nacional Manglares de Tumbes PE 60 Fk47
Santuario Nacional Tanaconas Namballes PE 60 Ga48
Santubong MAL 208 Qf45
Santu Lussùrgiu I 111 Lj50
Sant Vicenç E 110 Lb49
San Ubaldo NIC 42 Fh40
Sanup Plateau USA 22 Ed28
Sanur Beach RI 211 Qh50
San Valentín, Cerro RCH 82 Gd69
San Vicente BOL 72 Gg56
San Vicente CO 56 Gd42
San Vicente EC 60 Fk46
San Vicente ES 41 Ff39
San Vicente MEX (BC) 22 Eb30
San Vicente RA (BA) 77 Ha63
San Vicente RA (MI) 77 Hc59
San Vicénte YV 57 Gg43
San Vicente de Alcántara E 108 Kn49
San Vicente de Caguan CO 60 Gc44
San Vicente de Cañete PE 66 Gb52
San Vicente de la Barquera E 107 Kq53
San Vicente Tancuayalab MEX (SLP) 40 Fa35
San Victor GUY 58 Gk42
San Vincente MEX (SLP) 39 Ek33
San Vincenzo I 120 Ll47
San Vitale di Ravenna I 120 Ln46
San Vito CR 42 Fj41
San Vito I 111 Lk51
San Vito al Tagliamento I 121 Ln45
San Vito dei Normanni I 123 Ls50
San Vito lo Capo I 122 Ln52
Sanxenxo = Sangenjo E 106 Km52
Sanya VRC (HAN) 178 Qe36
Sanya Juu EAT 293 Mj47
Sanyang VRC (AHU) 184 Qk30
Sanyati ZW 296 Me54
Sanyati ZW 296 Me54
Sanying VRC (NHZ) 174 Qd27
Sanying VRC (YUN) 195 Qa32
Sanyuan VRC (SAA) 177 Qe28
Sanza I 122 Lq50
Sanza Pombo ANG 288 Lh49
São Antônia BR (RR) 58 Gk44
São Antonio BR (AM) 62 Gk49
São Antonio BR (PA) 63 Hc49
São Antonio BR (AP) 63 He45
São Antônio da Abunari BR (AM) 62 Gk46
São Antônio das Missões BR (RS) 78 Hc60
São Antonio de Jesus BR (BA) 71 Ja52
São Antônio de Padua BR (RJ) 75 Hj56
São Antônio do Amparo BR (MG) 75 Hh56
São Antônio do Monte BR (MG) 75 Hh56
São Antônio dos Lopes BR (MA) 64 Hh48
São Bartolomeu BR 70 Hg54
São Benedito BR (CE) 65 Hk48
São Benedito BR 69 Hb50
São Benedito BR (MT) 73 Hb54
São Benedito do Rio Preto BR (MA) 64 Hj47
São Bento BR (MA) 64 Hh47
São Bento BR 71 Jc49
São Bento do Norte BR (RN) 65 Jb48
São Bento do Sul BR (SC) 79 Hf59
São Bernardo BR (MA) 65 Hj47
São Bernardo BR (AM) 67 Gg50
São Bernardo do Campo BR (SP) 75 Hg57
São Borja BR (RS) 78 Hc60
São Brás BR (AM) 61 Gf49
São Brás de Alportel P 108 Kn47
São Caetano BR (PE) 71 Jb50
São Caetano de Odivelas BR (PA) 64 Hf46
São Carlos BR (RO) 68 Gh51
São Carlos BR (SP) 74 Hg57
São Carlos BR (SC) 78 Hd59
São Cosme BR (PA) 63 He46
São Cristóão ANG 294 Lg52
São Cristóvão BR (SE) 71 Jb51
São Cristóvão do Sul BR (SC) 78 He59
São Desidério BR (BA) 70 Hh52
São Desidério BR 70 Hh52
São Domingos BR (MA) 64 Hh49
São Domingos BR (GO) 70 Hg52
São Domingos BR (MS) 73 Hb55
São Domingos BR (GO) 74 Hf54
São Domingos GNB 269 Kb39
São Domingos do Capim BR (PA) 64 Hg46
São Domingos do Capim Novo BR (PA) 64 Hg47
São Domingos do Maranhão BR (MA) 64 Hh48
São Domingos do Prata BR (MG) 75 Hj55
São Domingos, T.I. BR 69 He51
São Felicio BR (AP) 63 Hd45
São Felix do Araguaia BR (MT) 69 He51
São Felix do Coribe BR (BA) 70 Hh52
São Felix do Xingu BR (PA) 63 He49
São Fidelis BR (RJ) 75 Hk56
São Filipe CV 268 Jh38
São Francisco BR 67 Gf50
São Francisco BR (MG) 70 Hh53
São Francisco BR 71 Jb50
São Francisco BR 75 Hh54
São Francisco das Chagas BR (AM) 63 Hb47
São Francisco das Chagas BR 65 Ja48
São Francisco das Chagas BR (PI) 70 Hh50
São Francisco de Assis BR (RS) 78 Hc60
São Francisco de Paula BR (RS) 78 He60
São Francisco de Sales BR (MG) 74 Hf55
São Francisco do Maranhão BR (MA) 65 Hj49
São Francisco do Sul BR (SC) 79 Hf59
São Gabriel BR (RS) 78 Hc61
São Gabriel da Cachoeira BR (AM) 61 Gg46
São Gabriel da Palha BR (ES) 75 Hk55
São Gabriel de Goiás BR (GO) 70 Hg53
São Gabriel do Oeste BR (MS) 74 Hc55
São Geraldo do Araguaia BR (PA) 64 Hf49
São Gonçalo do Abaeté BR (MG) 75 Hh55
São Gonçalo do Amarante BR (CE) 65 Ja47
São Gonçalo dos Campos BR (BA) 71 Ja52
São Gotardo BR (MG) 75 Hg55
São Hill EAT 293 Mh50
São Ifigênia de Minas BR (MG) 75 Hj55
São Jerônimo BR (RS) 78 He60
São Jerônimo da Serra BR (PR) 74 He57
São Jerônimo, T.I. BR 74 He57
São João BR (AM) 62 Gk48
São João BR (PR) 78 Hd58
São João Batista BR (MA) 64 Hh47
São João Batista BR (SC) 79 Hf59
São João da Barra BR 68 Ha50
São João da Barra BR (RJ) 75 Hk56
São João da Boa Vista BR (SP) 75 Hg56
São João d'Aliança BR (GO) 70 Hg53
São João da Madeira P 106 Km50
São João da Ponte BR (MG) 70 Hh53
São João da Pracajuba BR (PA) 63 He46
São João da Serra BR (PI) 65 Hk48
São João del Rei BR (MG) 75 Hh56
São João de Pirbas BR (PA) 64 Hg46
São João de Rio Pardo BR (SP) 75 Hg56
São João do Araguaia BR (PA) 64 Hf48
São João do Caiuá BR (PR) 74 Hd57
São João do Paraiso BR (MG) 71 Hk53
São João do Paraná BR (PA) 69 Hb50
São João do Piauí BR (PI) 71 Hj50
São João dos Patos BR (MA) 64 Hj49
São João dos Poleiros BR (MA) 64 Hj48
São João do Tigre BR (PB) 65 Jb50
São João do Triunfo BR (PR) 79 He58
São João Evangelista BR (MG) 75 Hj55
São Joaquim BR (AM) 61 Gg45
São Joaquim BR (SC) 79 Hf60
São Joaquim da Barra BR (SP) 74 Hg56
São Joaquim, P.N.de BR 79 Hf60
São José BR (PA) 64 Hf47
São José BR (AC) 67 Gf50
São José BR (RS) 78 Hd61
São José BR (SC) 79 Hf59
São José das Laranjeras BR (SP) 74 He57
São José da Tapera BR (AL) 71 Jb50
São José de Anaua BR (RR) 62 Gk45
São José de Belmonte BR (PE) 71 Ja49
São José de Mipibu BR (RN) 65 Jc49
São José de Piranhas BR (PB) 65 Ja49
São Jose de Ribamar BR (MA) 64 Hh47
São José do Caciporé BR (AP) 59 He44
São José do Cerrito BR (SC) 78 He59
São José do Egito BR (PE) 71 Jb49
São José do Norte BR (RS) 78 Hd61
São José do Peixe BR (PI) 65 Hj49
São José do Piria BR (PA) 64 Hg46
São José do Rio Claro BR (MT) 69 Hb52
São José do Rio Preto BR (SP) 74 Hf56
São José dos Ausentes BR (RS) 79 He60
São José dos Campos BR (SP) 75 Hh57
São José dos Dourados BR 74 He56
São José dos Martírios BR (TO) 64 Hf49
São José dos Pinhais BR (PR) 79 Hf58
São José do Xingu BR (MT) 69 Hd51
São Julia do Jurupari BR (PA) 63 He45
São Leopoldo BR (RS) 78 He60
São Leopoldo, T.I. BR 61 Gf48
São Lourenço BR 73 Hb54
São Lourenço BR (MG) 75 Hh57
São Lourenço do Oeste BR (SC) 78 Hd59
São Lourenço do Sul BR (RS) 78 Hd61
São Lucas ANG 294 Lj51
São Luís BR (AM) 62 Gh46
São Luís BR (RR) 62 Gk45
São Luís BR (AM) 62 Gk47
São Luís BR (MA) 64 Hh47
São Luís do Quitunde BR (AL) 71 Jc50
São Luís do Tapajós BR (PA) 63 Hb48
São Luis Gonzaga BR (MA) 64 Hh48
São Luís Gonzaga BR (RS) 78 Hc60
São Luiza do Oeste BR (RO) 68 Gk51
São Luzia do Pacui BR (AP) 63 He45
São Manuel BR (MT) 69 Hc53
São Manuel BR (SP) 74 Hf57
São Manuel ou Teles Pires BR 69 Hb50
São Marcos BR 74 Hg54
São Marcos BR (RS) 78 He60
São Marcos da Serra P 108 Km47
São Marcos, T.I. BR 58 Gk44
São Marcos, T.I. BR 69 Hd53
São Martinho BR (RS) 78 Hd59
São Martinho de Angueira P 106 Ko51
São Mateus BR 75 Hk55
São Mateus BR (ES) 75 Ja55
São Mateus do Maranhão BR (MA) 64 Hh48
São Mateus do Sul BR (PR) 79 He58
São Miguel BR (AP) 63 He45
São Miguel BR (RN) 65 Ja49
São Miguel BR 68 Gj51
São Miguel BR 69 Hb52
São Miguel BR (MT) 69 Hd52
São Miguel BR 70 Hg53

co Mendes BR (PI) 65
9
onpass CH 114 Lj44
on Desert AUS 227 Rj58
on Desert Conservation
: AUS 227 Rk59
on Desert N.P. AUS
Rk58
on Desert Regional
erve AUS 227 Rk59
on Island CDN 25 Fg21
onville USA (SC) 35 Fj28
IND (BIH) 189 Pc32
hamn S 95 Lp35
RUS 132 Mf16
ha Dzong BHT 194 Pe32
RI 206 Pj46
a EST 96 Mg31
jan MAL 208 Qf45
PE 67 Gf53
ng RI 198 Pj44
go SP 285 Nd43
ga del Transíto E 109
9
ET 263 Mg31
RO 125 Mf45
a MEX 38 Eg34
nga I 120 Lm47
aica YV 56 Ge40
alima Z 296 Md54
atella Camp ZW 299
5
VRC (GZH) 178 Qe32
DVRK 182 Rc26
aşa TR 131 Ml52
n LAR 260 Lf30
ongourou DY 272 Lb40
ngwe Z 296 Md54
ngwe MYA 196 Ph36
TR 131 Mn51
TR 145 Mj26
Nouă RO 125 Mf45
CO 56 Gc41
ejo CO 56 Gc41
on DVRK 182 Rc26
on DVRK 182 Rc26
r CDN (MB) 24 Ek21
r USA (WY) 21 Eg25
reiland NAM 302 Lh59
r Island NAM 302 Lh59
r Mills CDN (BC) 18 Dk18
r Mine NAM 298 Lj58
rmyn NAM 298 Lj58
r's Bay GB 99 Kr32
we Island 204 Qh41
IND 189 Ok33
Z 296 Mf53
DK 94 Ll33
-e-Suleiman IR
Nd27
gan RP 205 Rb41
gan Bay RP 205 Rb41
gbarang RI 210 Qd49
a G 288 Lf46
IND (RJT) 188 Of33
ingen D 114 Lj42
vahi IND (MHT) 191 Ok35
IND (KTK) 190 Oj37
ur IND (KTK) 190 Oj38
durg Fort IND 190 Oh37
EST 96 Me32
SN 269 Kb38
n SN 269 Kb39
u TR 130 Mj51
er IND (MHT) 191 Ok36
BF 279 Kh40
BF 279 Kh40
SN 269 Kb38
morco shyghanaghy KZ
Ne22
rsk RUS 181 Sb22
TR 130 Mj49
atiali CI 279 Kh41
orec BG 127 Mh48
P 108 Km47
E 110 Ld51
CI 279 Kh42
SUD 276 Mg40
Besar MAL 198 Pk42
o TCH 282 Lk41
ore SGP 200 Qa18
ore SGP 207 Qb45
IND (RJT) 188 Og32
aja RI 211 Qh50
ayakonda IND (APH)
Pa39
ng MYA 194 Ph35
v IRQ 147 Nc28
ri THA 196 Qa38
hingbyin = Maungdaw
194 Pg35
D 114 Lj43
USA (LA) 29 Fd30
a EAT 293 Mh48
j RUS 133 Ne19
EAU 287 Mf46
wang RI 208 Qe45
p RI 207 Qc46
RI 198 Pj44
ang RI 206 Pk45
fjorden N 92 Lm31
ton AUS (NSW) 237 Sf62
hat IND (MNP) 194 Pg33
S 93 Lt30
BF 271 La40
BD 194 Pe33
bo CI 279 Kh42
edeze MOC 300 Mf57
e DVRK 182 Rd26
aja Forest Reserve CL
Pa43
g DVRK 182 Rd25
.ipjagi RUS 133 Mk20
é DY 272 Lb40
ola I 111 Lk50
Kamăni, N.P. BG 127
8
HR 121 Lr47
RI 211 Ra48
vina SCG 126 Lu47
IRQ 147 Na27
SYR 146 Mj28
ka BY 132 Md19
LB 278 Ke42
abela Z 295 Mb54
sé RT 279 La40
SUD 277 Mj37
ng VRC 164 Pa11
RG 278 Kf41
bo CI 279 Kh42
do DVRK 182 Rc26
I 111 Lk51
nary F 59 Hd43
nary F 59 Hd43
IND (MHT) 190 Oh36
Kaddâb ET 263 Mg34
N 92 Lg32
I 123 Lr50
mbre, Cerro RCH 82
8

Sinnûris ET 263 Mf31
Sinodskoe RUS 133 Nd20
Sinoia Caves ZW 296 Mf54
Sinop BR (MT) 69 Hc51
Sinop TR 144 Mh25
Sinop Burun TR 144 Mh24
Sinoquipe MEX (SO) 23 Ee30
Sinsheim D 114 Lj41
Sinsicap PE 66 Ga49
Sinta RG 278 Kd41
Sintang RI 208 Qf45
Sint Christoffel N.P. NL 57 Gf39
Sintea Mare RO 124 Mb44
Sint Eustatius NL (NA) 47 Gj37
Sint Francisbaai = Saint Francis Bay SA 303 Mc63
Sint Luciameer = Lake Saint Lucia SA 303 Mg60
Sint Maarten NL (NA) 47 Gj37
Sint Nicolaas NL (AR) 57 Gf39
Sint-Niklaas B 103 Le39
Sintong RI 206 Qa45
Sintra P 108 Kl48
Sint-Truiden B 103 Lf40
Sinú CO 56 Gb41
Sinuiju DVRK 182 Rc25
Sinujiif SP 285 Ne41
Sinuk USA (AK) 15 Bg13
Sinuk River USA 15 Bh13
Sinungu Z 295 Mb53
Sinya Mine EAT 293 Mj47
Sinzig D 112 Lh40
Sió H 119 Lt44
Siocon RP 205 Rb42
Siodjuru SOL 245 Ta50
Siófok H 118 Lt44
Sioma Z 295 Mb54
Sioma Ngwezi N.P. Z 299 Mb54
Sion CH 114 Lh44
Siota RI 214 Rd50
Siota SOL 245 Ta50
Sioux Center USA (IA) 27 Fb24
Sioux City USA (IA) 27 Fb24
Sioux Falls USA (SD) 27 Fb24
Sioux Ind. Mus. USA 26 Ek24
Sioux Lookout CDN (ON) 24 Fe20
Sioux Narrows CDN (ON) 24 Fc21
Sipacate GCA 41 Fe39
Sipacate Naranjo, P.N. GCA 41 Fe39
Sipadan MAL 204 Qk43
Sipahutas RI 198 Pk44
Sipai PNG 244 Sh48
Sipalay RP 205 Rb41
Sipaliwini SME 59 Hb44
Šipan HR 123 Ls48
Sipán PE 66 Ga49
Siparia TT 58 Gk40
Šipčenski Prohod BG 127 Mf48
Sipi CO 56 Gb43
Sipi Falls EAU 290 Mh45
Sipilou CI 278 Kf42
Siping VRC (SCH) 176 Qb31
Siping VRC (JLN) 182 Rc24
Sipiongot RI 206 Pk45
Sipirok RI 206 Pk45
Sipisopiso Waterfall RI 198 Pk44
Sipitang MAL 204 Qh43
Sipiwesk CDN (MB) 24 Fb18
Sipiwesk Lake CDN 24 Fb18
Šipka BG 127 Mf48
Siple Coast 312 Cb35
Siple Dome 312 Cc35
Siple, Mount 312 Dc33
Sipocot RP 203 Rb39
Sipoo = Sibbo FIN 96 Mf30
Sipot RI 198 Pj43
Šipovo BIH 121 Ls46
Sippola FIN 96 Mh30
Sipura RI 206 Pk47
Siqu VRC (GDG) 179 Qh34
Siquia NIC 42 Fh39
Siquia NIC 42 Fh39
Siquijor RP 205 Rb41
Siquijor Island RP 205 Rb41
Siquisique YV 57 Gf40
Sir IND (UPH) 189 Pb32
Sira IND (KTK) 193 Oj40
Sira N 92 Lg32
Sira N 92 Lg32
Siracha THA 196 Qa39
Siracusa I 122 Lq53
Siraikoppa IND (KTK) 192 Oh39
Sirakoro RMM 270 Kf39
Sirakoro RMM 278 Kg40
Siramana RG 278 Kf40
Şiran TR 145 Mk25
Sirana CI 278 Kg41
Sirasso CI 279 Kg41
Sirathu IND (UPH) 191 Pa33
Sirattana THA 197 Qc38
Siraway RP 205 Rb42
Sirba RN 271 La39
Sir Bani Yas UAE 156 Ng33
Sir Bu Nu'air UAE 156 Nh33
Sirch IR 157 Nj30
Sirdaryo UZB 158 Oe25
Sirdaryo UZB 158 Oe25
Sire ETH 284 Mj41
Sire ETH 284 Mk41
Sir Edward Pellew Group AUS 223 Rj53
Siref TCH 282 Ma39
Siren USA (WI) 27 Fd23
Siret RO 125 Mg43
Siret RO 125 Mg43
Sirevåg N 92 Lf32
Sirgiri IND (CGH) 191 Pb35
Sirheni Bushveld Camp SA 300 Mf57
Şiria RO 124 Mb44
Sirigani BD 194 Pe33
Sirikit Reservoir THA 196 Qa37
Sirinat N.P. THA 198 Pk41
Sirinhaém BR (PE) 71 Jc50
Sirinumu Lake PNG 243 Sd50
Siriu RO 125 Mg45
Siriwo RI 213 Rh47
Siriworra RI 213 Rg47
Širjaeve UA 125 Ml43
Sir James MacBrien, Mount CDN 17 Dg14
Sirjan IR 157 Nh31
Sir Joseph Banks Group AUS 236 Rj63
Sirkazhi IND (TNU) 193 Ok41
Sirkeli TR 131 Mn50
Sirmione I 120 Ll45
Sírna GR 129 Mg54
Sirnak TR 145 Nb27
Sirohi IND (RJT) 188 Og33
Sirok H 119 Ma43
Široka lăka BG 127 Me49
Široké SK 119 Ma41
Široki Brijeg BIH 121 Ls47
Sirombu RI 206 Pj45
Sironcha IND (MHT) 191 Ok36

Sirong RI 209 Rb46
Sirong VRC (GZG) 178 Qe33
Sironj IND (MPH) 191 Oj33
Sironko EAU 290 Mh45
Siros GR 129 Me53
Sirrayn KSA 148 Na36
Sir Robert Campell Island MYA 198 Pk40
Sirsa IND (HYA) 188 Oh31
Sirsa IND (UPH) 191 Pb33
Sirsi IND (KTK) 192 Oh39
Sirsilla IND (APH) 191 Ok36
Sirsiri SUD 287 Mf43
Sirsirtara HN 42 Fh38
Sirsova Ridge RUS 141 Tc07
Sırtköy TR 131 Mm53
Siruguppa IND (KTK) 193 Oj39
Sirur IND (MHT) 190 Oh36
Sirur Tajband IND (MHT) 190 Oj36
Širvintos LT 97 Me35
Sirwa YE 150 Nc38
Sirwar IND (KTK) 190 Oj37
Sisa PE 66 Gb49
Sisai IND (JKD) 191 Pc34
Sisak HR 121 Lr45
Sisaket THA 197 Qc38
Sisal MEX (YT) 41 Fe35
Si Samrong THA 196 Pk37
Sisante E 109 Ks49
Si Satchanalai THA 196 Pk37
Si Satchanalai Historical Park THA 196 Pk37
Si Satchanalai N.P. THA 196 Pk37
Si Sawat THA 196 Pk38
Sishen SA 302 Mb59
Sishilang VRC (NMZ) 174 Qe26
Sishui VRC (SDG) 175 Qj28
Sisian ARM 152 Nc26
Sisimut = Holsteinsborg DK 11 Hb05
Sisipuk Lake CDN 24 Ek18
Siskiyou Mts. USA 20 Dj25
Sison RP 202 Ra37
Si Songkhram THA 197 Qc37
Sisophon K 197 Qb39
Sissano PNG 242 Sb47
Sissédougou CI 278 Kg41
Sisseton USA (SD) 26 Fb23
Sissi TCH 282 Lk40
Sissili BF 279 Kk40
Sissone F 103 Ld41
Sistan TM 155 Oa30
Şiştarovaţ RO 124 Mb44
Sistema Ibérico E 107 Ks52
Sisteron F 105 Lf46
Sisters USA (OR) 20 Dk23
Siswali IND (RJT) 188 Oj33
Sitakund BD 194 Pf34
Sitalike EAT 292 Mf49
Sitamarhi IND (BIH) 189 Pc32
Sitampiky RM 306 Nd54
Sitang VRC (QHI) 174 Qa27
Sitapur IND (UPH) 189 Pa32
Sitar IND (WBG) 194 Pe32
Sitasjaure S 90 Lj12
Sites archéologiques de la Dépression de l'Upemba RDC 292 Md50
Sites d'extraction de fer de Kindiba BF 271 Kj39
Sites funéraires de Morondava RM 306 Nc56
Sitges E 110 Lb49
Sithe THA 197 Qb37
Si Thep THA 196 Qa38
Si Thep Historical Park THA 196 Qa38
Sithobela SD 303 Mf59
Sithonia GR 127 Me50
Sithra IND (CGH) 191 Pb34
Sitia GR 129 Mg55
Sitiecito C 44 Fk34
Sitila MOC 300 Mh57
Sitin VRC (YUN) 178 Qc34
Sitio d'Abadia BR (GO) 70 Hg53
Sitio do Mato BR (BA) 70 Hj52
Sitio Novo BR (MA) 64 Hg48
Sitio Novo do Tocantins BR (TO) 64 Hg48
Sitka USA (AK) 17 Dc17
Sitkalidak Island USA 16 Cd17
Sitka Sound USA 17 Dc17
Sitkinak Is. USA 16 Cd17
Sitkinak Strait USA 16 Cc17
Sitnica SCG 126 Ma48
Sitohóri GR 126 Md50
Sitona ER 277 Mj39
Sitotio Z 295 Mb54
Sittang MYA 196 Pj36
Sittard NL 112 Lf40
Sittingbourne GB 101 La39
Sitting Bull Monument USA 26 Ek23
Sittwe MYA 194 Pg35
Situbondo RI 211 Qh49
Situwa EAT 292 Mf49
Sitwe Z 296 Mg51
Si-u MYA 195 Pj34
Siulakderas RI 206 Qa46
Siumbatu RI 209 Rb47
Siumpu RI 209 Rb48
Siumu WS 248 Be52
Siuna NIC 42 Fh39
Siuna RI 209 Rb46
Siuri IND (WBG) 194 Pd34
Sivac SCG 124 Lu45
Sivačevo BG 127 Mg48
Sivaganga IND (TNU) 193 Ok42
Sivakasi IND (TNU) 193 Oj42
Sivaki RUS 180 Rd19
Sivaram WS 248 IND 191 Ok36
Sivas TR 144 Mj26
Sivasli TR 130 Mk52
Sivé RIM 269 Kd38
Siverek TR 145 Mk27
Siverskij RUS 132 Mf16
Sivers'kyi Donec' UA 135 Mj21
Sivrihisar TR 131 Mm51
Siwa ET 262 Mc31
Siwa RI 209 Ra47
Siwa Z 295 Mb53
Siwa Lima Museum RI 212 Re47
Siwan IND (BIH) 189 Pc32
Siwa Oasis ET 262 Mc31
Sixes USA (OR) 20 Dh24
Six Flags B 103 Le40
Six Flags Astroworld USA (TX) 29 Fc31
Six Flags Great America USA 32 Ff24
Six-Fours-les-Plages F 105 Lf47
Si Xing VRC (AHU) 184 Qj29
Six Miles MOC 300 Mh55
Six Nations Ind. Res. CDN 33 Fk24
Sixth Cataract SUD 276 Mg38

Siyabuswa SA 299 Me58
Siyahcheshmeh IR 154 Nc26
Siyambalanduwa CL 193 Pa43
Siyana IND (UPH) 189 Ok31
Siyand IR 156 Ng30
Siyang VRC (JGS) 184 Qk29
Siyezen AZ 152 Ne25
Siyu Fort EAK 291 Na47
Sızır TR 131 Mq51
Siziwang Qi VRC (NMZ) 175 Qf25
Sızma TR 131 Mn52
Sizun F 102 Kq42
Sjælland DK 94 Lm35
Sjain RUS 180 Rh22
Sjanno BY 132 Me18
Sjas'stroj RUS 132 Mg15
Sjaunja naturreservat S 90 Lk12
Sjenica SCG 126 Lu47
Sjerogošte SCG 126 Lu48
Sjeverni Velebit, N.P. HR 121 Lq46
Sjoa N 92 Lk29
Sjøasen N 90 Lf13
Sjöbo S 95 Lo35
Sjøholt N 92 Lg28
Sjötofta S 95 Lo33
Sjötorp S 93 Lo32
Sjøvegan N 90 Lj11
Sjuntorp S 94 Ln32
Sjuøyane N 91 Ma05
Sjurkum RUS 181 Sa20
Sju søstre N 90 Lg13
Sjusystre N 90 Lh12
Sjuvjaoro RUS 96 Mk29
Skabro SYR 147 Mk27
Skadarsko jezero, N.P. SCG 126 Lu48
Skadovs'k UA 134 Mg22
Skælskør DK 94 Lm35
Skærbæk DK 94 Lj35
Skaftafell IS 90 Kb14
Skaftung FIN 93 Mb28
Skagastrond IS 90 Jk13
Skagen DK 94 Ll33
Skagens museum DK 94 Ll33
Skagern S 93 Lp32
Skagerrak 94 Lj33
Skagit Prov. Park CDN 18 Dk21
Skagit River USA 18 Dk21
Skaill GB 99 Ks32
Skaistgirys LT 97 Md34
Skaistkalne LV 97 Me34
Skála GR 128 Mc54
Skála GR 129 Mg53
Skala PL 117 Lu40
Skála Eressú GR 129 Mf51
Skálafellsjökull IS 90 Kb13
Skála Marión GR 127 Me50
Skála Oropoú GR 128 Md52
Skala-Podil'ska UA 134 Md21
Skälderviken S 94 Ln34
Skalica BG 127 Mg48
Skalica SK 118 Ls42
Skaloti GR 127 Me49
Skandáli GR 127 Mf51
Skandawa PL 117 Mb36
Skanderborg DK 94 Lk34
Skåne S 95 Lo35
Skånevik N 92 Lf31
Skänninge S 93 Lq32
Skara S 93 Lo32
Skara Brae GB 99 Kr31
Skarberget N 90 Lj11
Skärblacka S 93 Lq32
Skardu 161 Oh28
Skare N 92 Lg31
Skåre S 93 Lo31
Skärgårdshavets n.p. = Saaristomeren kansallispuisto FIN 96 Mb31
Skärhamn S 94 Lm33
Skarness N 92 Lm30
Skärplinge S 93 Ls30
Skärså S 93 Ls29
Skarsfjället S 92 Ln28
Skarsstind N 92 Lj29
Skaryszew PL 117 Mb39
Skarżysko-Kamienna PL 117 Ma39
Skåt BG 126 Md47
Skattkärr S 93 Lo31
Skattungbyn S 93 Lp29
Skaudvilė LT 97 Mc35
Skawina PL 119 Lu41
Skaymat DARS 264 Kc33
Skazar AFG 161 Of27
Skeby S 93 Lo32
Skeda S 93 Lq32
Skedshult S 95 Lr32
Skedsmokorset N 92 Lm30
Skee S 92 Lm32
Skeena Mountains CDN 17 Df17
Skeena River CDN 18 Df18
Skegness GB 101 La37
Skei N 90 Le14
Skei N 92 Lg29
Skeiðarársandur IS 90 Kb14
Skeikampen alpincenter N 92 Ll29
Skeldon GUY 59 Hb43
Skeleton Coast NAM 298 Lf54
Skeleton Coast N.P. NAM 298 Lg55
Skellefteå S 90 Ma13
Skellefteälven S 90 Lk13
Skelleftehamn S 90 Ma13
Skellig Michael IRL 100 Kk39
Skelton Glacier 313 Sd34
Skender Vakuf BIH 121 Ls46
Skene S 94 Ln33
Skepasti GR 129 Me55
Skerries IRL 100 Ko37
Skhira TN 260 Lf28
Skhirat MA 258 Kg29
Skhour-Rehamna MA 258 Kg29
Ski N 92 Ll31
Ski Area Cairngorm Mountains GB 99 Kr33
Ski Area Nevis Range GB 99 Kp34
Skiáthos GR 128 Md51
Skiáthos GR 128 Md51
Skibbereen IRL 100 Kl39
Skibladner N 92 Lm30
Skibotn N 90 Ma11
Skidal' BY 97 Me37
Skidegate CDN (BC) 18 Dd19
Skidegate Inlet CDN 18 De19
Skidmore USA (TX) 39 Fb31
Skien N 92 Lk31
Skierbieszów PL 117 Md40
Skierniewice PL 117 Ma39
Skikda DZ 260 Ld27
Skillingaryd S 95 Lp33
Skinnastaður IS 90 Kb12
Skinnskatteberg S 93 Lq31

Skipton AUS (VIC) 237 Sb64
Skipton GB 101 Ks37
Skirmantiškė LT 97 Md35
Skirmish Point AUS 223 Rh51
Skiropoúla GR 128 Me52
Skiros GR 128 Me52
Skive DK 94 Lk34
Ski World USA 34 Fg26
Skjern DK 94 Lj35
Skjern Å DK 94 Lj35
Skjernøy N 92 Lh33
Skjervøy N 90 Ma10
Skjolden N 92 Lh29
Skjønhaug N 92 Lm31
Sklop BIH 121 Lr46
Šklov BY 132 Mf18
Šklyv UA 117 Mf40
Škocjanske jame SLO 121 Lp45
Skoczów PL 118 Lt41
Škofja Loka SLO 121 Lp44
Škofljica SLO 121 Lp45
Skógafoss IS 90 Ka14
Skógar IS 90 Ka14
Skoghall S 93 Lo31
Skogskyrkogården S 93 Lt31
Skoki PL 116 Ls38
Skokloster S 93 Ls31
Skole UA 119 Md41
Skolivs'ki Beskydy N.P. UA 119 Mc42
Skollenborg N 92 Lk31
Skópelos GR 128 Md51
Skópelos GR 128 Md51
Skopiá GR 128 Mc51
Skopin RUS 133 Mk19
Skopje MK 126 Mb48
Skopsko Kale MK 126 Mb48
Skórcz PL 116 Lt37
Skorków PL 117 Ma40
Skorodnoe RUS 133 Mj20
Skorogoszcz PL 116 Ls40
Skoroszyce PL 116 Ls40
Skorovatn N 90 Lg13
Skorpa N 92 Le29
Skørping DK 94 Lk34
Skortsinós GR 128 Mc53
Skosai RI 213 Sa47
Skotterud N 92 Ln31
Skoulikariá GR 128 Mb51
Skoura MA 258 Kg30
Skoúrta GR 128 Md52
Skövde S 93 Lo32
Skovorodino RUS 141 Ra08
Skowhegan USA (MA) 33 Gf23
Skownan CDN (MB) 24 Fa20
Skoyo 161 Oh28
Skrá GR 126 Mc49
Skrad HR 121 Lp45
Skradin HR 121 Lq47
Skradinski buk HR 121 Lq47
Skreia N 92 Lm30
Skrekken N 92 Lh30
Škrip HR 121 Lr47
Skriveri LV 97 Mf34
Skrunda LV 97 Mc34
Skudeneshavn N 92 Lf31
Skukuza SA 300 Mf58
Skuleskogens n.p. S 90 Lk14
Skulgam N 90 Lk11
Skull Valley Ind. Res. USA 21 Ed25
Skulsk PL 116 Lt38
Skulte LV 97 Me33
Skultorp S 95 Lo32
Skultuna S 93 Lr31
Skuodas LT 97 Mb34
Skuon K 197 Qc39
Skurup S 95 Lo35
Skurv S 95 Lq34
Skutari = Shkodër AL 126 Lu48
Skutskär S 93 Ls30
Skverbai LT 97 Me35
Skvyra UA 134 Me21
Skwentna River USA 15 Cd15
Skwierzyna PL 116 Lq38
Sky Blu ANT (UK) 312 Gb33
Skye GB 98 Ko33
Skykomish USA (WA) 18 Dk22
Skyline Caverns USA 33 Ga26
Skytrain Ice Rise 312 Ga34
Skyttorp S 93 Ls30
Slade Point AUS 230 Sb51
Slagelse DK 94 Lm35
Slamet, Gunung RI 210 Qe49
Slana USA (AK) 15 Cj14
Slănčev Briag BG 127 Mh48
Slancy RUS 96 Mj31
Slane IRL 100 Ko37
Slaney IRL 100 Ko37
Slănic RO 125 Mf45
Slănic-Moldova RO 125 Mg44
Slano HR 123 Ls48
Slaný CZ 118 Lp40
Śląskie PL 116 Lq39
Slate Falls CDN (ON) 24 Fe20
Slate Island CDN 25 Fg21
Slatina BIH 121 Ls46
Slatina HR 121 Ls45
Slatina RO 124 Mc45
Slatina SCG 124 Lu46
Slatina-Timiş RO 124 Mc45
Slaton USA (TX) 28 Ek29
Slattum N 92 Ll31
Slaukava BY 97 Mg37
Slav'anka RUS 182 Rf24
Slave Coast DY/WAN 280 Lb42
Slave Lake CDN (AB) 19 Ec18
Slavharad BY 132 Mf19
Slavic bazaar BY 132 Mf18
Slavičín CZ 118 Ls41
Slavinja SCG 126 Mc47
Slavinja SCG 126 Mc47
Slavjansk na-Kubani RUS 135 Mk23
Slavkoviči RUS 132 Me17
Slavnoe RUS 181 Se23
Slavonice CZ 118 Lq42
Slavonija HR 121 Ls45
Slavonski Brod HR 121 Lt45
Slavonski Šamac HR 121 Lt45
Slavsk RUS 97 Mb35
Slavs'ke UA 119 Md42
Slavuta UA 134 Md20
Sławatycze PL 117 Md39
Slawi RI 210 Qe49
Sławno PL 116 Lr36
Slayton USA (MN) 27 Fc24
Sleaford GB 101 Ku38
Sleaford Bay AUS 236 Rh63
Slea Head IRL 100 Kk38
Sled Lake CDN 19 Eg18
Sleeping Bear Dunes Nat. Lakeshore USA 32 Fg23
Sleeping Giant Prov. Park CDN 25 Ff21
Sleepy Eye USA (MN) 27 Fc23
Ślesin PL 116 Lt38

Slidell USA (LA) 29 Ff30
Slidre N 92 Lj29
Sliema M 122 Lp55
Slieve Bloom Mountains IRL 100 Kn37
Slieve League IRL 98 Km36
Sligachan GB 98 Ko33
Sligo IRL 98 Km36
Sligo Bay IRL 98 Km36
Slim DZ 259 Lb28
Slisenvaara RUS 96 Mk29
Šlissel'burg RUS 132 Mf16
Slite S 95 Lt33
Slivata BG 126 Md47
Sliven BG 127 Mg48
Slivnica BG 126 Md48
Slivo Pole BG 127 Mg47
Śliwice PL 116 Lt37
Sljudjanka RUS 172 Qb20
Sloboda LV 97 Mh34
Slobozia MD 125 Mk44
Slobozia RO 125 Mh46
Slobozia Mare MD 125 Mj45
Slocan CDN (BC) 18 Eb21
Słomniki PL 117 Ma40
Slonim BY 117 Mf37
Slough GB 101 Ku39
Slovakia SK 119 Lu42
Slovenia SLO 121 Lp45
Slovenj Gradec SLO 121 Lq44
Slovenska Bistrica SLO 121 Lq44
Slovenská L'upča SK 119 Lu42
Slovenský, N.P. SK 119 Ma42
Slovinka RUS 133 Nb16
Slovjans'k UA 135 Mj21
Słowiński P.N. PL 116 Ls36
Stubice PL 116 Lp38
Sluck BY 132 Md19
Sluč UA 132 Md20
Slunj HR 121 Lq45
Słupca PL 116 Ls38
Słupia PL 117 Mb40
Słupno PL 117 Lu38
Słupsk PL 116 Lr36
Slurry SA 299 Mc58
Slussfors S 90 Lj13
Slyne Head IRL 98 Kk37
Småland S 95 Lp33
Smålandsfarvandet DK 94 Lm35
Smålandsstenar S 95 Lo33
Smalininkai LT 97 Mc35
Smaljaniča BY 117 Me38
Small Malaita = Maramasike SOL 245 Ta50
Smallwood Reservoir CDN 11 Gd08
Smara DARS 264 Ke32
Smârdioasa RO 127 Mf47
Smarhon' BY 97 Mg36
Šmarje pri Jelšah SLO 121 Lq44
Smartt Syndicate Dam SA 302 Mb61
Smeaton CDN (SK) 19 Eh19
Smeberg S 92 Lm32
Smedby S 95 Lr34
Smederevo SCG 124 Ma46
Smedjebacken S 93 Lq30
Smethport USA (PA) 33 Ga25
Smidovič RUS (YAO) 180 Rg21
Śmierdnica PL 116 Lp37
Smigiel PL 116 Lr38
Smila UA 134 Mf21
Smilec BG 127 Me48
Smiley CDN (SK) 19 Ef20
Smiltene LV 97 Mf33
Smirnyh RUS 181 Sb21
Smith CDN (AB) 19 Ed18
Smith USA 21 Ee22
Smith Bay CDN 11 Ga03
Smith Center USA (KS) 26 Fa26
Smithers CDN (BC) 18 Dg18
Smith Ferry USA (ID) 20 Eb23
Smithfield SA 303 Md61
Smithfield USA (NC) 35 Ga28
Smith Group, Sir J. AUS 233 Se56
Smith Island IND 193 Pg39
Smith Island USA 35 Gb29
Smith Point AUS 223 Rg51
Smith River CDN (BC) 17 Dg16
Smith's Knoll 101 Lc38
Smithton AUS (TAS) 236 Sc66
Smithtown AUS (NSW) 235 Sg61
Smithville USA (WV) 33 Fk26
Smithville USA (TN) 34 Fh28
Smithville House AUS (NSW) 234 Sa61
Smjadovo BG 127 Mh47
Smochid UA 117 Mf39
Smogulec PL 116 Ls37
Smoke Creek Desert USA 20 Ea25
Smoke Hole Caverns USA 33 Ga26
Smoky Bay AUS 236 Rg62
Smoky Falls CDN (ON) 25 Fj20
Smoky Falls CDN 25 Fk20
Smoky Hills USA 26 Fa26
Smoky Lake CDN (AB) 19 Ed18
Smoky River CDN 19 Ea18
Smøla N 90 Ld14
Smołdzino PL 116 Ls36
Smolenice SK 118 Ls42
Smolensk RUS 132 Mg18
Smolensko-Moskovskaja vozvyšennosť RUS 132 Mg18
Smolevići BY 132 Me18
Smoljan BG 127 Me49
Smoljaninovo' RUS 180 Rg24
Smol'noe UA 119 Mh42
Smolsko BG 126 Md48
Smooth Rock Falls CDN (ON) 25 Fk21
Smoothstone Lake CDN 19 Eg18
Smože UA 119 Md42
Smygehamn S 95 Lo35
Smygehuk S 95 Lo35
Šmykove UA 125 Ml43
Smyley Island 312 Ga33
Smyrna USA (DE) 33 Gc26
Smyrna USA (GA) 35 Fh29
Smyšljaevsk RUS 133 Nf19
Snabai RI 213 Rh46
Snaefell GB 98 Kq36
Snæfell IS 90 Kc13
Snake and Manjang Caverns ROK 185 Rd29
Snake Indian River CDN 18 Ea19
Snake Island AUS 237 Sd65
Snake River USA 20 Eb23
Snake River Canyon USA 20 Eb22
Snake River Plains USA 21 Ed24

Snape Island CDN 25 Ga18
Snaran Jogizai PK 160 Oe30
Snares Islands NZ 239 Td70
Snåsa N 90 Lg13
Snåsavatnet N 90 Lf13
Snedsted DK 94 Lj34
Sneek NL 112 Lf37
Sneekermeer NL 112 Lf37
Sneem IRL 100 Kl39
Sneeuberg SA 303 Mc61
Snežnaja RUS 172 Qc20
Sniebal IND (MZR) 194 Pg34
Snieżka PL 116 Lq40
Snieznik Klodzki PL 116 Lr40
Snihurivka UA 134 Mg22
Snina SK 119 Mc42
Snipe Lake CDN 19 Eb18
Snjatyn UA 125 Mf42
Snježna Marija HR 121 Lr45
Snøhetta N 92 Lk28
Snøhuten N 92 Lg31
Snoqualmie Pass USA (WA) 18 Dk22
Snøtoppen N 91 Lk05
Snou BY 97 Mg37
Snoul K 197 Qd39
Snoul W.S. K 197 Qd39
Snowdon GB 100 Kq37
Snowdonia N.P. GB 100 Kr38
Snowflake CDN (MB) 24 Fa21
Snowflake USA (AZ) 23 Ee28
Snow Hill USA (MD) 33 Gc26
Snow Lake CDN (MB) 24 Ek18
Snow Lake USA (AR) 29 Fe28
Snow Mount USA 20 Dj26
Snowshoe Peak USA 19 Ec21
Snowtown AUS (SA) 236 Rk62
Snowville USA (UT) 21 Ed25
Snowy Mountains AUS 237 Se64
Snowy River AUS 237 Se64
Snowy River N.P. AUS 237 Se64
Snug Corner BS 37 Gd34
Snyder USA (TX) 28 Ek29
So BF 271 Kk38
Soacha CO 56 Gc43
Soahany RM 306 Nc55
Soalala RM 306 Nc54
Soalara RM 306 Nb57
Soaloka RM 306 Nc55
Soamanonga RM 306 Nc57
Soanierana-Ivongo RM 306 Ne54
Soanindrarivy RM 306 Nd55
Soan River PNG 242 Sb49
Soap Lake USA (WA) 18 Ea22
Soaserana RM 306 Nc56
Soata CO 56 Gd42
Soave I 120 Lm45
Soavina RM 306 Nd56
Soavina RM 306 Ne56
Soavinandriana RM 306 Nd55
Soba WAN 272 Le40
Sobaek Sanmaek ROK 182 Rd28
Sobaeksan N.P. ROK 182 Re27
Sobat SUD 283 Mg41
Soberania, P.N. PA 43 Ga41
Sobger RI 213 Sa47
Sobibór PL 117 Md39
Sobinka RUS 133 Na18
Sobo-Katamuki Q.N.P. J 185 Rf29
Sobolevo RUS 133 Na18
Sobótka PL 117 Mb40
Sobra HR 123 Ls48
Sobradinho BR (DF) 70 Hg53
Sobradinho BR (BA) 71 Hk50
Sobradinho BR (RS) 78 Hd60
Sobrado BR 70 Hg52
Sobral BR (CE) 65 Hk47
Sobral BR (AC) 67 Ge50
Sobrance SK 119 Mc42
Søby DK 94 Ll36
Socaire RCH 72 Gg57
Socastee USA (SC) 35 Ga29
Socavão BR (PR) 74 Hf58
Sochaczew PL 117 Ma38
Sochinsky N.P. RUS 135 Mk23
Soči RUS 135 Mk24
Society Hill USA (SC) 35 Ga28
Society Islands 317 Ca11
Socodor RO 124 Mb44
Socompa PE 72 Gf58
Socompa RA (SA) 72 Gf58
Socompa, Volcán RCH/RA 72 Gf58
Socorro BR (PR) 74 He58
Socorro BR (SP) 75 Hg57
Socorro CO 56 Gd42
Socorro RP 205 Rc41
Socorro USA (NM) 23 Eg28
Socorro USA (TX) 23 Eg30
Socota CO 56 Gd42
Socota PE 66 Ga49
Socotra YE 151 Nh39
Soc Trang VN 199 Qc41
Socuéllamos E 109 Ks49
Soda Creek CDN (BC) 18 Dj19
Sodakor IND (RJT) 188 Of32
Sodankylä FIN 91 Md12
Soda Springs USA (ID) 21 Ee24
Söderåkra S 95 Lr34
Söderarm S 93 Lu31
Söderåsens n.p. S 95 Lo35
Söderbärke S 93 Lq30
Söderfors S 93 Ls30
Söderhamn S 93 Ls29
Söderköping S 93 Lq32
Södermanland S 93 Lr31
Södertälje S 93 Ls31
Söderåsen S 93 Ls31
Södervik S 93 Lt31
Sodi RI 209 Qk46
Sodiri SUD 276 Me39
Sodium SA 302 Mb61
Sodo ETH 284 Mj42
Sodore ETH 284 Mk41
Södra Kvarken S 93 Lu30
Södra Midsjöbanken 95 Ls35
Södra Ölands odlingslandskap S 95 Lr34
Södra Vi S 95 Lq33
Sodwana Bay N.P. SA 303 Mg59
Soe RI 214 Rc50
Soekmekaar SA 300 Me57
Soela väin EST 96 Mc32
Soeng San THA 197 Qb38
Soesdyke GUY 58 Ha42
Soest D 112 Lj39
Soetdoring Nature Reserve SA 303 Md60
Sofádes GR 128 Mc51
Sofara RMM 270 Kh38
Sofia BG 126 Md48
Sofia RM 305 Ne53
Sofia BG 126 Md48
Sofijivka UA 134 Mg21

Sofijskij sobor RUS 132 Mf16
Sofiysky sobor UA 134 Mf20
Sof Omar Caves ETH 284 Na42
Soforog RUS (KAR) 91 Mf13
Sofular TR 131 Mp52
Sogakofe GH 279 La42
Sogamoso CO 56 Gd43
Soğanlı Valley TR 131 Mp52
Sogda RUS 180 Rg20
Sögel D 112 Lh38
Sogeri PNG 243 Sd50
Sogndal N 92 Lh29
Sognefjellsvegen N 92 Lj29
Sognefjorden N 92 Lf29
Sognesjøen N 92 Le29
Sogod RP 205 Rc40
Sogolle TCH 273 Lh38
Sogoot MNG 172 Pk21
Sogossagasso BF 279 Kh40
Soguip'o ROK 185 Rd29
Soğukpınar TR 130 Mk50
Soğuksu TR 130 Ml50
Soğuksu Milli Parkı TR 131 Mn50
Söğüt TR 130 Ml50
Söğüt TR 131 Mk53
Söğüt Dağı TR 130 Mk53
Söğütlü TR 130 Ml50
Söğütlü TR 145 Na26
Sog Xian VRC (TIB) 171 Pg30
Sohåg ET 263 Mf32
Sohagi IND (MPH) 191 Pa33
Sohar OM 157 Nj33
Sohela IND (ORS) 191 Pb35
Sohey IR 154 Ng29
Sohna IND (HYA) 189 Oj31
Sohós GR 126 Md50
Sohuksan Do ROK 185 Rc28
Soignies B 103 Le40
Soila IND (RJT) 188 Og32
Şoimi RO 124 Mc44
Soin BF 270 Kj39
Soini FIN 91 Mc14
Sointula CDN (BC) 18 Dg20
Soissons F 103 Ld41
Soja J 183 Rg28
Sojat IND (RJT) 188 Og33
Sojol RI 209 Ra45
Sojoson Man DVRK 182 Rc26
Sojoton Point RP 205 Rb41
Sokal' UA 117 Me40
Sokch'o ROK 182 Re26
Söke TR 129 Mh53
Sokele RDC 289 Mc50
Sokhumi GE 145 Na24
Sokhumi GE 152 Na24
Sokna N 92 Lk30
Soknedal N 92 Ll28
Soko CI 279 Kj42
Soko Banja SCG 126 Mb47
Sokodé RT 279 La41
Sokoiyo RI 209 Ra47
Sokol RUS 181 Sb22
Sokolac BIH 126 Lt47
Sokoliv UA 119 Mf41
Sokółka PL 117 Md37
Sokollu Camii TR 130 Mh49
Sokolo RMM 270 Kg38
Sokolov CZ 118 Ln40
Sokołów Małopolski PL 117 Mc40
Sokołów Podlaski PL 117 Mc38
Sokolski manastir BG 127 Mf48
Sokoły PL 117 Mc38
Sokorbey RN 271 Lb39
Sokoto WAN 271 Lc40
Sokoto WAN 272 Lc39
Sokoulama RG 278 Kf41
Sokoura RMM 270 Kj39
Soksok RN 272 Ld38
Sokyrjany UA 125 Mh42
Sola C 45 Gb35
Sola N 92 Lf32
Sola VU 246 Td52
Sola de Vega MEX (OAX) 40 Fb37
Solahpet IND (KTK) 190 Oj37
Solan IND (HPH) 189 Oj30
Solana RP 203 Ra37
Solana USA (FL) 36 Fk32
Solana del Pino E 109 Kq48
Solander Island NZ 239 Td69
Solânea BR (PB) 65 Jc49
Solano RP 203 Ra37
Solano YV 61 Gg45
Solar de Mateus P 106 Kn51
Solares E 107 Kr53
Solat RI 212 Rd45
Solberg S 90 Lj14
Solca RO 125 Mf43
Sol'cy RUS 132 Mf16
Soldado Monge EC 60 Gb47
Şoldăneşti MD 125 Mj43
Sol de Julio RA (SE) 76 Gj60
Sol de Mañana BOL 72 Gg57
Sölden A 115 Lm44
Soldotna USA (AK) 15 Ce15
Solé BF 271 Kj38
Soleb Temple SUD 276 Mf36
Solec Kujawski PL 116 Lt37
Soledad CO 56 Gc40
Soledad USA (CA) 20 Dk27
Soledad YV 58 Gj41
Soledad de Doblado MEX (VC) 40 Fb36
Soledad de G. Sánchez MEX (SLP) 39 Ek34
Soledade BR (PB) 65 Jb49
Soledade BR (RS) 78 Hd60
Solemar BR (SP) 74 Hg58
Sølen N 92 Lm29
Solënoe RUS 135 Nb22
Solenyj RUS 152 Nd22
Solenzara F 111 Lk49
Solenzo BF 270 Kh39
Sole Pit 101 Lb37
Solh Abad IR 155 Nj28
Solhan TR 145 Na26
Soli RN 272 Ld38
Solihull GB 101 Kt38
Solikamsk RUS 140 Nd07
Soliman TN 260 Lf27
Solimões = Amazon BR 62 Gk47
Solingen D 112 Lh39
Solis de Mataojo ROU 77 Hc63
Solita CO 60 Gc45
Solitaire NAM 298 Lj57
Söltäler A 115 Lo43
Sollebrunn S 94 Ln32
Sollefteå S 90 Lj14
Sollentuna S 93 Ls31
Söller E 110 Lc51
Sollidén S 95 Lr34
Sollihøgda N 92 Ll31
Solna BF 271 La39
Solncevo RUS 133 Mj20
Solnečnogorsk RUS 132 Mj17
Solnečnyj RUS 180 Rj20
Solnice CZ 118 Lr40

Solo RI 210 Qf49
Šolohovskij RUS 135 Na21
Solok RI 206 Qa46
Sololo EAK 291 Mk44
Soloma GCA 41 Fe38
Solomon Islands 219 Ta10
Solomon Islands 240 Sc20
Solomon Sea PNG 240 Sc20
Solomon's Wall RB 300 Me57
Solon VRC (NMZ) 173 Ra22
solonchakovyye vpadiny Unguz TM 153 Nk26
Solone UA 134 Mh21
Solonešnoe RUS 167 Pc20
Solongtyn davaa MNG 172 Pk21
Solonópole BR (CE) 65 Ja48
Solonț RO 125 Mg44
Solor RI 214 Rb50
Solothurn CH 114 Lh43
Solotvyn UA 119 Me42
Solotvyna UA 119 Md43
Soloveckie RUS 91 Mh13
Solovetsky monastyr RUS 91 Mh13
Solovevsk RUS 173 Qh21
Sølsnes N 92 Lh28
Solsona E 110 Lb49
Solsvik N 92 Le30
Solt H 119 Lu44
Šolta HR 121 Lr47
Soltan Abad IR 155 Nj27
Soltan Bagh AFG 160 Oe29
Soltaniyeh IR 154 Ne27
Soltau D 112 Lk38
Solti-lapály H 119 Lu44
Soltvadkert H 119 Lu44
Solusi ZW 300 Me56
Solvang USA (CA) 22 Dk28
Solvarbo S 93 Lq30
Sölvesborg S 95 Lp34
Solway Firth GB 99 Kr36
Solwezi Z 296 Md52
Soly BY 97 Mg36
Solymar ROU 77 Hc63
Sol y Nieve E 109 Kr47
Som IND (RJT) 190 Og33
Soma J 183 Sa27
Soma TR 130 Mh51
Somabhula ZW 300 Me55
Somadougou RMM 270 Kh38
Somaén E 107 Ks51
Somain F 103 Ld40
Somalia 253 Na09
Somali Basin 315 Nb09
Somali Plateau ETH 284 Na41
Somalomo CAM 281 Lg44
Somavaram IND (APH) 191 Pb37
Somba RI 209 Qk47
Sombo ANG 289 Ma50
Sombo ANG 289 Ma50
Sombor SCG 124 Lu45
Sombrerete MEX (ZCT) 39 Ej34
Sombrero KN 47 Gj36
Sombrero RCH 82 Gf72
Sombrero Channel IND 193 Pg42
Sombrero Negro RA (FO) 73 Gk57
Sombrio BR (SC) 79 Hf60
Şomcuta Mare RO 124 Md43
Somdet THA 197 Qb37
Somero FIN 96 Md30
Somers AUS (VIC) 237 Sc65
Somerset AUS (QLD) 230 Sb51
Somerset AUS (TAS) 236 Sc66
Somerset CDN (MB) 24 Fa21
Somerset USA (PA) 33 Ga26
Somerset USA (KY) 35 Fh27
Somerset-East SA 303 Mc62
Somerset Island CDN 11 Fb04
Somerset Oos SA 303 Mc62
Somerset West SA 302 Lk63
Somerton AUS (NSW) 235 Sf61
Someș RO 124 Md43
Someșul RO 124 Md44
Someșul Mare RO 124 Me43
Somianki PL 117 Mb38
Somina ANG 295 Ma53
Somina BIH 121 Lt48
Somina SCG 126 Lt48
Somme F 103 Lb40
Sommen S 95 Lq33
Sömmerda D 113 Lm39
Sommerdown NAM 298 Lk56
Sommesous F 103 Le42
Sommières F 105 Le47
Somo RMM 270 Kh39
Somogyvár H 118 Ls44
Somonino PL 116 Lt36
Somosomo FJI 247 Ua54
Somotillo NIC 42 Fg39
Sompeta IND (APH) 191 Pc36
Som Poi THA 197 Qb38
Sompolno PL 116 Lt38
Somra MYA 194 Ph33
Son IND 191 Pb33
Son IND 194 Pg33
Soná PA 43 Fk41
Sonaco GNB 269 Kc39
Sonagiri IND 189 Ok33
Sonai-Rupa N.P. IND 194 Pg32
Sonamukhi BD 194 Pe33
Sonamukhi IND (WBG) 194 Pd34
Sonapur IND (ORS) 191 Pb35
Sonar IND 191 Ok34
Sonari IND (ASM) 194 Ph32
Sonarigaon IND (ASM) 194 Ph32
Sonbong DVRK 182 Rf24
Sonch'on DVRK 182 Rc26
Soncillo E 107 Kr52
Sonda PK 162 Oe33
Søndalo I 120 Ll44
Sondeled N 92 Lk32
Sønderborg DK 94 Lk36
Sønder Nissum DK 94 Lj34
Sønder Omme DK 94 Lj35
Sondershausen D 113 Ll39
Søndersø DK 94 Ll35
Søndervig DK 94 Lj34
Sondi RI 198 Pk44
Sondo IND (MHT) 191 Ok36
Son Dong VN 178 Qd35
Søndrestrømfjord = Kangerlussuaq DK 11 Hb05
Sondrio I 120 Lk44
Sondu EAK 290 Mh46
Son en Breugel NL 112 Lf39
Sonepat IND (HYA) 189 Oj31
Song MAL 208 Qg45
Song THA 196 Qa36
Song WAN 273 Lg41
Songa MOC 296 Mg53
Songa RDC 289 Mc50
Songa RI 212 Rd46
Songa Mnara EAT 293 Mk50
Songaw Lagoon GH 279 La43
Song Ba VN 197 Qe39
Songbu VRC (HUB) 184 Qh30
Song Ca VN 197 Qd36
Song Cau VN 197 Qe39
Song Da VN 178 Qb35
Song Da Reservoir VN 178 Qc35
Song Dong Nai VN 197 Qd40
Songea EAT 297 Mh51
Songgwangsa Temple ROK 182 Rd28
Song Hong VN 178 Qc34
Songhua Hu VRC 182 Rd24
Songhua Jiang VRC 180 Re22
Songjiang VRC (SHG) 184 Ra30
Songir IND (GUJ) 190 Og34
Songir IND (MHT) 190 Oh35
Songjiang VRC (JLN) 182 Re24
Songjianghe VRC (JLN) 182 Rd24
Songkan VRC (GZH) 177 Qd31
Songkhla THA 198 Qa42
Songkhon LAO 197 Qc37
Song Khwae THA 196 Qa36
Song-Köl KS 159 Oh25
Songkou VRC (FJN) 179 Qk33
Songling VRC (NMZ) 173 Ra22
Song Ling VRC 175 Qk25
Song Luy VN 197 Qe40
Songmen VRC (ZJG) 184 Ra31
Songming VRC (YUN) 195 Qb33
Songnim DVRK 182 Rc26
Songnisan N.P. ROK 182 Rd27
Songo ANG 288 Lh49
Songo SUD 282 Mc41
Songo-lolo RDC 288 Lh48
Songpan VRC (SCH) 176 Qb29
Song Phinong THA 196 Qa38
Songshu VRC (TIB) 170 Pa30
Song Shan VRC 177 Qg28
Songshan Z.B. VRC 175 Qh25
Songtao VRC (GZH) 177 Qe31
Songxi VRC (FJN) 184 Qk32
Song Xian VRC (HNN) 177 Qg28
Songyang VRC (ZJG) 184 Qk31
Songyu ROK 182 Re27
Songyuan VRC (JLN) 180 Rc23
Songzi VRC (HUB) 177 Qf30
Songzi He VRC 177 Qf30
Sonhat IND (CGH) 191 Pb34
Son Hiep VN 197 Qe39
Son Hoa VN 197 Qe39
Sonid Youqi VRC (NMZ) 175 Qg24
Sonid Zuoqi VRC (NMZ) 175 Qg24
Sonjo EAT 293 Mh47
Sonkwale Mountains WAN 280 Le42
Son La VN 195 Qb35
Son Mbong CAM 281 Lf44
Sonmiani PK 162 Od33
Sonmiani Bay PK 162 Od33
Sonneberg D 113 Lm40
Sono BR 75 Hh54
Sonoita USA (AZ) 23 Ee30
Sonoma Range USA 20 Eb25
Sonora BR (MS) 74 Hc54
Sonora MEX 12 Eb13
Sonora USA (CA) 20 Dk27
Sonora USA (TX) 28 Ek30
Sonoran Desert USA 22 Ec29
Sonora Pass USA 20 Ea26
Sonoumom DY 272 Lb41
Sonoyta MEX (SO) 22 Ed30
Sonozo CI 279 Kg41
Sonpar Hills IND 191 Pb33
Sonpuri IND (GUJ) 190 Of35
Sonqor IR 154 Nd28
Sonseca E 109 Kr49
Sonsón CO 56 Gc43
Sonsonate ES 41 Ff39
Sonsorol Islands PAL 203 Rg43
Sonstraal SA 302 Mb59
Sonta RDC 296 Me51
Sontang RI 206 Qa45
Son Tay VN 178 Qc35
Sonthofen D 114 Ll43
Sontra D 112 Lk39
Soomaa rahvuspark EST 96 Mf32
Sooya SP 291 Nb45
Sopachuy BOL 73 Gh55
Sopchoppy USA (FL) 35 Fh30
Soperton USA (GA) 35 Fj29
Sophie F 59 Hd43
Sop Huai THA 196 Pk36
Sopianae H 118 Lt44
Sopinusa RI 212 Rg47
Soplin PE 60 Gb47
Sop Moei THA 196 Pj37
Sopo SUD 282 Md41
Sopore 161 Oh28
Sopot PL 116 Lt36
Sopot SCG 124 Ma46
Sopotnica MK 126 Mb49
Sop Prap THA 196 Pk37
Sopron H 118 Lr43
Soprtrân CO 56 Gc42
Soputan RI 209 Rc45
Sora I 122 Lo49
Sorab IND (KTK) 192 Oh39
Sorada IND (ORS) 191 Pc36
Sorah PK 163 Oe32
Söråker S 93 Ls28
Soraksan ROK 182 Re26
Soraksan N.P. ROK 182 Re26
Sora Mboum CAM 281 Lh42
Soran KZ 166 Og21
Sorano I 122 Lm48
Sorapa PE 72 Gf54
sor Arys KZ 158 Od23
sor Ashchkol KZ 158 Od23
Sorata BOL 67 Gf53
Sorati-gawa J 181 Sc24
Sorau WAN 273 Lg41
Søraust-Svalbard naturreservat N 91 Ma07
Sorbas E 109 Ks47
Sörbygden S 93 Lr28
Sördellen S 93 Lr29
Sore F 104 Ku46
Sorel CDN (QC) 30 Gd22
Sorell AUS (TAS) 236 Sd67
Soresina I 120 Lk45
Sør-Flatanger N 90 Lf13
Sørfonna N 91 Mb06
Sörforsa S 93 Lr29
Sórgono I 111 Lk50
Sorgues-l'Ouvèze F 105 Le46
Sorgun TR 131 Mq51
Sør-Gutvika N 90 Lf13
Sori DY 272 Lb40
Soria E 107 Ks51
Soriano ROU 77 Ha62
sor Kajdak KZ 153 Ng23
Sørkappøya N 91 Lj07
Sorkh Ab AFG 160 Ob29
Sørland N 92 Lg32
Sor Laspur PK 161 Og27
Sørli N 90 Lg13
Sornac F 104 Lc45
Sorø DK 94 Lm35
Soro IND (ORS) 194 Pd35
Soro PK 160 Od30
Soro = Bahr el Ghazal TCH 273 Lj38
Sorobango CI 279 Kj41
Soroca MD 125 Mj42
Sorocaba BR (SP) 74 Hg57
Soroč'i Gory RUS (TAR) 133 Nf18
Sorol Atoll FSM 240 Sa17
sor Oli Kultyk KZ 153 Ng23
Sorombéo CAM 281 Lh41
Sorondideri RI 213 Rh46
Sorong RI 212 Rf46
Sororé BR 64 Hf48
Sororó, T.I. BR 64 Hf48
Soroti EAU 290 Mg45
Sørøyane N 92 Lf28
Sorrento CDN (BC) 18 Ea20
Sorrento I 122 Lp50
Sorriso BR (MT) 69 Hc52
Sorsakoski FIN 96 Mh28
Sorsan Grasslands IND 190 Oj33
Sorsele S 90 Lj13
Sorso I 111 Lj50
Sorsogon RP 203 Rc39
Sør-Spitsbergen n.p. N 91 Lj07
Sørstraumen N 90 Ma11
Sort E 110 Lb48
Sortavala RUS (KAR) 91 Mf15
Sortland N 90 Lh11
Sørumsand N 92 Lm31
Sørvågen N 90 Lg12
Sørvattnet S 93 Lr28
Sørvika N 92 Lm28
Sosan ROK 182 Rd27
Sosan Haean N.P. ROK 182 Rd27
Sösdala S 95 Lo34
Sos del Rey Católico E 107 Kt52
Sosedka RUS 133 Nb19
Sosneado, Cerro RA 76 Gf63
Sosnenskij RUS 132 Mj19
Sosnogorsk RUS 140 Nc06
Sosnove UA 134 Md20
Sosnove-Ozërskoe RUS (BUR) 173 Qf19
Sosnovka RUS 133 Na19
Sosnovka RUS 133 Nf17
Sosnovyj Bor RUS 96 Mk31
Sosnowica PL 117 Md39
Sosnowiec PL 117 Lu40
Soso Bay FJI 247 Tk55
Sosolo SOL 244 Sj49
Sosonpal IND (CGH) 191 Pa36
Sospel F 105 Lh47
Sosso RCA 281 Lh44
Sossobé RMM 270 Kh38
Sossusvlei NAM 298 Lh58
Sossusvlei Lodge NAM 298 Lh58
Sossusvlei Pan NAM 298 Lh58
Šoštanj SLO 121 Lq44
Šostka UA 132 Mg20
Sosúa DOM 46 Ge36
Sosýčne UA 117 Me39
Sota DY 272 Lb40
Sotara, Volcán CO 60 Gb44
Sotasæter N 92 Lh29
Soteapan MEX (VC) 41 Fc36
Sotian RMM 279 Kg40
Sotik EAK 290 Mh46
Sotillo de la Adrada E 106 Kq50
Sotla SLO/HR 121 Lq44
Soto RA (CD) 76 Gh61
Soto del Barco E 106 Ko53
Sotogrande E 108 Kp46
Sotok RI 208 Qf45
Soto La Marina MEX (TM) 39 Fa34
Sotomayor CO 60 Gb45
Sotouboua RT 279 La41
Sotra N 92 Lf30
Sottunga FIN 93 Ma30
Sottunga FIN 93 Ma30
Sotuta MEX (YT) 41 Ff35
Souanké RCB 281 Lh44
Souassi TN 260 Lf28
Soubakaniédogou BF 279 Kh40
Soubakpérou DY 279 La41
Soubané RG 278 Kc40
Soubéira BF 271 Kk39
Soubré CI 278 Kg43
Souchang VRC (ZJG) 184 Qk31
Soudan AUS (NT) 223 Rj56
Soudan Bank 305 Nj56
Soudougui BF 279 La40
Soué DZ 260 Ld29
Soufflenheim F 103 Lh42
Soufli GR 127 Mg49
Soufrière WL 47 Gk39
Sougueur DZ 259 La28
Souhoulé RG 278 Kf42
Souillac F 104 Lb46
Souillac MS 307 Nj56
Souilly F 103 Lf41
Souk-Ahras DZ 260 Ld27
Souk-el-Arba-des-Beni-Hassan MA 258 Kh28
Souk-el-Arba-du-Rharb MA 258 Kg28
Souk-Jemâa-de-Oulad-Abbou MA 258 Kg29
Soukoukoutane RN 271 Lb38
Souk Tenadjeleline RMM 271 La36
Soul ROK 182 Rd27
Soul ROK 182 Rd27
Soulabali SN 269 Kc39
Soulac-sur-Mer F 104 Kt45
Soúli GR 128 Mc53
Souliou GR 128 Ma51
Soulis Pond CDN 31 Hc21
Soulópoulo GR 128 Ma51
Sounding Creek CDN 19 Ee20
Sound of Barra IRL 98 Kn33
Sound of Harris GB 98 Kn33
Sound of Jura GB 98 Kp35
Sound of Monach GB 98 Kn33
Sound of Mull GB 98 Kp34
Sound of Sleat GB 99 Kp33
Sounds of Starlight Theatre AUS 226 Rg57
Soungrougrou SN 269 Kc39
Souq al-Mihk YE 150 Nc38
Source Bleu de Meski MA 259 Kh30
Source chaude de Déssikou RCA 282 Lk42
Source chaude de Soborom TCH 274 Lj35
Source du Nil BU 292 Me47
Sour-el-Ghozlane DZ 259 Lb27
Souris CDN (MB) 24 Ek21
Souris CDN (PE) 31 Gj22
Souris USA 24 Ek21
Sourou RMM 271 Kj39
Souroukaha CI 279 Kh41
Sourountouna RMM 270 Kh39
Sourpi GR 128 Mc51
Sousa BR (PB) 65 Ja49
Sousceyrac F 104 Lc46
Sousel P 108 Kn48
Sous-Massa, P.N. MA 258 Kf30
Sousse TN 260 Lf28
Soustons F 104 Kt47
Sout SA 302 Lk61
Sout SA 302 Ma60
South Africa 253 Ma13
South Alligator River AUS 223 Rg52
Southampton GB 101 Kt40
Southampton USA (NY) 33 Gd25
Southampton Island CDN 11 Fd06
South Andaman IND 193 Pg39
South Australia AUS 220 Rc24
South Australian Basin 218 Ra14
Southaven USA (MS) 29 Ff28
South Banda Basin RI 214 Rd49
South Banggi Strait MAL 204 Qj42
Southbank CDN (BC) 18 Dh18
South Bay CDN (ON) 24 Fd20
South Bay USA (FL) 36 Fk32
South Baymouth CDN (ON) 32 Fj23
South Bend USA (IN) 32 Fg25
South Bimini BS 37 Ga33
South Boston USA (VA) 35 Ga27
South Brahmaputra Hills IND 194 Pg33
South Branch CDN (NF) 31 Ha22
Southbridge NZ 239 Tg67
South Brook CDN (NF) 31 Hb21
South Brookfield CDN (NS) 31 Gh23
South Bruny Island AUS 236 Sd67
South Bruny N.P. AUS 236 Sd67
South Carolina USA 13 Fd12
South Cay CO 43 Fk38
South Channel RP 202 Ra38
South China Basin 200 Qc15
South China Mountains VRC 178 Qd33
South China Sea 200 Qc15
South Coast Highway AUS 228 Ra62
South Dakota USA 12 Ed10
South Downs GB 101 Ku40
South East Aru Marine Reserve RI 213 Rh49
South East Cape AUS 236 Sd67
Southeast Cape USA 14 Bf14
Southeast Forests N.P. AUS 237 Se64
Southeast Indian Ridge 218 Qa14
South East Pacific Basin 54 Ed30
South East Point AUS 237 Sd65
Southeast Point BS 37 Gd35
Southend CDN (SK) 24 Ej17
Southend-on-Sea GB 101 La39
Southerland Falls NZ 239 Td68
Southern Alps NZ 239 Te68
Southern Altay Gobi Nature Reserve MNG 174 Pj24
Southern Central Reserve A.L. AUS 225 Rc59
Southern Cross AUS (WA) 228 Qk61
Southern Indian Lake CDN 24 Fa17
Southern Laos Cruise LAO/K 197 Qc38
Southern Lau Group FJI 247 Ua55
Southern Lueti Z 295 Mb53
Southern N.P. SUD 283 Me42
Southern Pines USA (NC) 35 Ga28
Southern Sporades GR 129 Mf52
Southern Uplands GB 99 Kq35
Southey CDN (SK) 19 Eh20
South Fiji Basin 218 Tb12
South Foreland GB 101 Lb39
South Fork USA (CO) 23 Eg27
South Fork Kuskokwim River USA 15 Cd14
SouthFrancisco de Macoris DOM 46 Ge36
South Galway AUS (QLD) 234 Sb58
Southgate River CDN 18 Dh20
South Georgia GB 55 Ja29
South Georgia GB 55 Ja29
South Goulburn Island AUS 223 Rg51
South Gut Saint Ann's CDN (NS) 31 Gk22
South Harbour CDN (NS) 31 Gk22
South Hatia Island BD 194 Pf34
South Haven USA (MI) 32 Fg24
South Heart River CDN 19 Eb18
South Hill USA (VA) 35 Ga27
South Honshu Ridge 165 Rd12
South Horr EAK 290 Mj45
South Huvadhoo Atoll = Gaafu-Dhaalu Atoll MV 192 Og45
South Indian Lake CDN (MB) 24 Fa17
South Island AUS 233 Sf56
South Island EAK 290 Mj44
South Island NZ 239 Te67
South Island N.P. EAK 290 Mj44
South Junction CDN (MB) 24 Fc21
South Kinangop EAK 290 Mj46
South Kitui Nature Reserve EAK 291 Mk46
South Korea ROK 139 Ra06
South Lake Rukwa EAT 292 Mg50
South Lake Tahoe USA (NV) 20 Ea26
South Luangwa N.P. Z 296 Mf52
South Luconia Shoals 204 Qg43
South Male Atoll MV 192 Og44
South Miladhunmadulu Atoll = Noonu Atoll MV 192 Og43
South Molton GB 100 Kr39
South Moose Lake CDN 24 Ek19
South Mtn. USA 20 Eb24
South Nahanni River CDN 17 Dh15
South Nilandhoo Atoll = Dhaalu Atoll MV 192 Og44
Southold USA (NY) 33 Gd25
South Orkney Islands GB 55 Hc30
South Orkney Islands GB 55 Hc30
South Ossetia GE 145 Nc24
South Padre Island USA (TX) 39 Fb32
South Padre Island USA (TX) 39 Fb32
South Pass City USA (WY) 21 Ef24
South Pole ANT 312 Ga36
South Porcupine CDN (ON) 25 Fk21
Southport AUS (QLD) 235 Sg59
Southport AUS (TAS) 236 Sd67
Southport CDN (PE) 31 Hd21
Southport GB 101 Kr37
Southport USA (NC) 35 Ga29
South Prince of Wales Wilderness USA 17 Dd18
South Pt. BS 37 Gc34
South Pt. = Ka Lae USA 16 Cc36
South River of Georgia CDN 18 Dh21
South Ronaldsay GB 99 Ks32
South Rukuru River MW 296 Mg51
South Salmara IND (ASM) 194 Pf33
South Sandwich Islands GB 55 Jc31
South Sandwich Islands GB 55 Jc31
South Sandwich Trench 55 Jc29
South Saskatchewan River CDN 19 Ef20
South Scotia Ridge 55 Hb31
South Shetland Islands ANT 312 Ha31
South Shields GB 99 Kt36
South Sioux City USA (NE) 27 Fb24
South Solomon Trench 240 Ta21
South Stradbroke Island AUS 235 Sg59
South Taranaki Bight NZ 238 Th66
South Tasman Rise 218 Sa14
South Thiladhunmathee Atoll = Haa-Dhaalu Atoll MV 192 Og42
South Thompson River CDN 18 Ea20
South Trap NZ 239 Td69
South Tucson USA (AZ) 23 Ee29
South Turkana Nature Reserve EAK 290 Mh45
South Twin Island CDN 25 Ga19
South Twin Lake CDN 31 Hc21
South Tyne GB 99 Ks36
South Uist GB 98 Kn33
South Wabasca Lake CDN 19 Ed18
South West Cape AUS 236 Sc67
Southwest Cape NZ 239 Td69
Southwest Cay 204 Qh40
Southwest Gander River CDN 31 Hc21
Southwest Indian Ridge 315 Na14
Southwest Miramichi River CDN 31 Gg22
Southwest N.P. AUS 236 Sd67
Southwest Pacific Basin 317 Cb13
Southwest Point BS 37 Gb33
Southwest Point BS 37 Gc34
Southwest Point BS 37 Gd35
South West Rocks AUS (NSW) 235 Sg61
Southwold GB 101 Lb38
South Yandaminta AUS (NSW) 234 Sa60
Souto Soares BR (BA) 71 Hk52
Soutpan NAM 298 Lk57
Soutpan SA 303 Md60
Soutpansberg SA 300 Me57
Souvigny F 105 Ld44
Sovata RO 125 Mf44
Soverato I 123 Lr52
Sovereign Hill AUS 237 Sb64
Sovetsk RUS 97 Mb35
Sovetskaja RUS 133 Nb21
Sovetskaja RUS 135 Na23
Sovetskaja Gavan' RUS 181 Sa21
Sovetskaya ANT (RUS) 313 Pb34
Sovetskij RUS 96 Mj30
Sovetskij RUS (MEL) 133 Ne17
Sovetskoe RUS (KBA) 152 Nb24
Sowa Pan RB 299 Mc56
Sowczyce PL 116 Lt40
Soweto SA 303 Md59
Sowia Góra PL 116 Lq38
Sowma'eh Sara IR 154 Ne27
Soy EAK 290 Mh45
Soyaló MEX (CHP) 41 Fd37
Soya-misaki J 181 Sb23
Soyet IND (MPH) 190 Oj33
Soyo ANG 288 Lg49
Soyuz ANT (RUS) 312 Gc33
Sozak KZ 158 Oe23
Sozopol BG 127 Mh48
Sozu J 183 Rj27
Spa B 103 Lf40
Spain 87 Kb06
Spalding AUS (SA) 236 Rk62
Spalding GB 101 Ku38
Spálené Poříčí CZ 118 Lo41
Spaniard's Bay CDN (NF) 31 Hd22
Spanish Fork USA (UT) 21 Ee25
Spanish Head GB 98 Kq36
Spanish Town JA 45 Gb37
Spanwerk SA 299 Md58
Sparks USA (NV) 20 Ea26
Sparreholm S 93 Lr31
Sparta USA (WI) 27 Fe24
Sparta USA (TN) 34 Fh28
Sparta USA (GA) 35 Fj29
Sparta USA (NC) 35 Fk27
Spartanburg USA (SC) 35 Fk28
Spárti GR 128 Mc53
Sparwood CDN (BC) 19 Ec21
Spas-Klepiki RUS 133 Na18
Spaso Jakovlenskij monastyr RUS 132 Mk17
Spasovo BG 127 Mj47
Spassk-Dal'nij RUS 180 Rg23
Spassk-Rjaznaskij RUS 133 Na18
Spatsizi Plateau CDN 17 Df17
Spatsizi Plateau Wilderness Prov. Park CDN 17 Df17
S.Paulo e S.Pedro BR 53 Jc18
Spean Bridge GB 99 Kq34
Spearfish USA (SD) 26 Ej23
Spearman USA (TX) 28 Ek27
Speculator USA (NY) 33 Gc24
Speedwell Island GB 83 Ha72
Speightstown BDS 47 Ha39
Speke Gulf EAT 290 Mg47
Spello I 120 Ln47
Spencer USA (NE) 26 Fa24
Spencer USA (IA) 27 Fc24
Spencer USA (WV) 33 Fk26
Spencer USA (IN) 34 Fg26
Spencer USA (TN) 34 Fh28
Spencer Bay NAM 298 Lh58
Spencer Bridge CDN (BC) 18 Dk20
Spencer Gulf AUS 236 Rj63
Spentrup DK 94 Ll34
Speos of Horemheb ET 263 Mg33
Sperrin Mountains GB 98 Kn36
Spessart D 114 Lk41
Spétses GR 128 Md53
Spétses GR 128 Md53
Spey GB 99 Kr33
Speyer D 114 Lj41
Speyside Beach TT 58 Gk40
Spezand PK 160 Od30
Spezzano Albanese I 123 Lr51
Spezzano della Sila I 123 Lr51
Spiddle IRL 100 Kl37
Spiekeroog D 112 Lh37
Spielcasino Baden-Baden D 114 Lj42
Spiez CH 114 Lh44
Spijkenisse NL 112 Le39
Špilberk CZ 118 Lr41
Spileon Dirou GR 128 Mc54
Spileo Stalaktiton GR 129 Mf53
Spilimbergo I 121 Ln44
Spiljani SCG 126 Ma48
Spilsby GB 101 La37
Spinazzola I 123 Lr50
Spin Buldak AFG 160 Od30
Špindlerův Mlýn CZ 118 Lq40
Spioenkop SA 303 Me60
Spirit Lake USA (IA) 27 Fc24
Spirit River CDN (AB) 19 Ea18
Spiritwood CDN (SK) 19 Eg19
Spirovo RUS 132 Mh17
Spirtit Lake Ind. Res. USA 26 Fa22
Spišská Belá SK 119 Ma41
Spišský hrad SK 119 Ma42
Spiti ARM 152 Nc25
Spitsbergen N 91 Lg06
Spitskopvlei SA 303 Mc61
Spittal an der Drau A 115 Lo44
Spitz A 115 Lq42
Spitzkoppe NAM 298 Lh56
Spitzkoppe Rock Paintings NAM 298 Lh56
Spiveys Corner USA (NC) 35 Ga28
Spjelkavik N 92 Lg28
Split HR 121 Lr47
Split Lake CDN (MB) 24 Fb17
Split Lake CDN 24 Fb17
Split Lake Ind. Res. CDN 24 Fb17
Splügen CH 114 Lk44
Splügenpass = Passo dello Spluga I/CH 114 Lk44
Spodsbjerg DK 94 Ll36
Spofford USA (TX) 28 Ek31
Spoggies AUS 236 Rg62
Špogi LV 97 Mg34
Spokane USA (WA) 18 Eb22
Spokane House USA 18 Eb22
Spokane Ind. Res. USA 18 Eb22
Špola UA 134 Mf21
Spoleto I 122 Ln48
Spook Cave USA 32 Fe24
Spookmyndorp NAM 302 Lh59
Spooner USA (WI) 27 Fe23
Sporades GR 89 Mb11
Spotorno I 120 Lj46
Spotted House USA (WY) 21 Eh23
Spottrup DK 94 Lj34
Sprague USA (WA) 18 Eb22
Sprague USA 20 Dk24
Spratly Islands 204 Qh40
Spray USA (OR) 20 Ea23
Spreča BIH 124 Lt46
Spree D 113 Lp39
Spreewald D 113 Lp39
Spremberg D 113 Lp39
Sprengisandur IS 90 Ka13
Spring RO 124 Md45
Springbok SA 302 Lj60
Spring Creek AUS (QLD) 232 Sc55
Spring Creek USA (NV) 20 Ec25
Springdale CDN (NF) 31 Hb21
Springdale USA (AR) 29 Fc27
Springe D 112 Lk38
Springer USA (NM) 23 Eh27
Springerville USA (AZ) 23 Ef28
Springfield USA (OR) 20 Dj23
Springfield USA (CO) 23 Ej27
Springfield USA (IL) 27 Ff26
Springfield USA (MO) 29 Fd27
Springfield USA (OH) 32 Fj26
Springfield USA (MA) 33 Gd24
Springfield USA (VT) 33 Gd24
Springfield USA (TN) 34 Fg27
Springfield USA (KY) 34 Fh27
Springfield USA (GA) 35 Fk29
Springfield Plateau USA 29 Fd27
Springfontein SA 303 Mc61
Spring Garden GUY 58 Ha42
Springhill CDN (NS) 31 Gh23
Springhill USA (LA) 29 Fd29
Spring Hill USA (FL) 36 Fj31
Springsure AUS (QLD) 232 Sa57
Spring Ridge AUS (NSW) 235 Sf61
Springs SA 303 Me59
Springside CDN (SK) 24 Ej20
Springs Junction NZ 239 Tg67
Springsure AUS (QLD) 235 Se58
Springvale AUS (WA) 222 Rd54
Springvale USA (ME) 33 Ge24
Springvale Homestead AUS (NT) 223 Rg53
Spring Valley SA 303 Md62
Springview USA (NE) 26 Fa24
Springville USA (UT) 21 Ee25
Springville USA (NY) 33 Ga24
Springwater CDN (SK) 19 Ef19
Sproge S 95 Lt33
Spruce Grove CDN (AB) 19 Ed19
Spruce Home CDN (SK) 19 Eh19
Spruce Island USA 16 Cd17
Spruce Meadows CDN (AB) 19 Ec20
Spruce Pine USA (NC) 35 Fj28
Spruce Woods Prov. Park CDN 24 Fa21
Spur USA (TX) 28 Ek29
Spurn Head GB 101 La37
Spuž SCG 126 Lu48
Squamish CDN (BC) 18 Dj21
Squarnish River CDN 18 Dj20
Squaw Creek N.W.R. USA 27 Fc25
Squaw Lake USA (MN) 27 Fc22
Squaw Valley USA (CA) 20 Dk26
Squillace I 123 Lr52
Squinzano I 123 Lt50
Squires Mem. Prov. Park CDN 31 Hb21
Squirrel River USA 15 Bk12
Sragen RI 210 Qf49
Sravanabelgola IND 192 Oj40
Sravasti IND 189 Pb32
Srb HR 121 Lr46
Srbac BIH 121 Ls45
Srbica SCG 126 Ma48
Srbobran SCG 124 Lu45
Srbovac SCG 126 Ma48
Srdiečko SK 119 Lu42
Sre Ambel K 197 Qb40
Srebărna BG 125 Mh46
Srebărna Nature Reserve BG 125 Mg47
Srebrenica BIH 126 Lu46
Srebrenik BIH 124 Lt46
Sredec BG 127 Mf48
Sredec BG 127 Mh48
Sredinnyj hrebet RUS 141 Ta07
Sredna Gora BG 127 Me48
Srednebelaja RUS 180 Re20
Srednerusskaja vozvyšennost' RUS 133 Mj19
Sre Koki K 197 Qd39
Srem PL 116 Ls38
Sremska Mitrovica SCG 124 Lu46
Sremski Karlovci SCG 124 Lu45
Sre Noy K 197 Qc39
Sre Peang K 197 Qb39
Sretensk RUS 173 Qj19
Sribawono RI 207 Qc48
Sribne UA 132 Mg20
Sri Brihadisvara Temple IND 193 Ok41
Sri Chaitanya Temple BD 194 Pf33
Sri Dungargarh IND (RJT) 188 Oh31
Srigiripadu IND (APH) 191 Ok37
Sri Jayewardenepura CL 193 Ok43
Srikakulam IND (APH) 191 Pb36
Sri Kalahasti IND (APH) 193 Ok40
Sri Kalahasti Temple IND 193 Ok40
Sri Karanpur IND (RJT) 188 Og31
Sri Krishna Mutt IND 192 Oh40
Sri Lanka CL 186 Pa17
Srimangal BD 194 Pf33
Sri Mohangarh IND (RJT) 188 Of32
Srinagar IND (UTT) 189 Ok30
Srinagar 161 Oh28
Srinakarin N.P. THA 196 Pk38
Srinakarin Reservoir THA 196 Pk38
Sringeri IND 192 Oh40
Srinivaspur IND (KTK) 193 Ok40
Sri Phang-Nga N.P. THA 198 Pk41
Srirangam IND (TNU) 193 Ok41
Sri Ranganathaswamy Temple IND 193 Ok41
Srirangapatna IND (KTK) 193 Oj40
Srisailam IND (APH) 191 Ok37
Srivilliputtur IND (TNU) 193 Oj42
Środa Wielkopolska PL 116 Ls38
Srokowo PL 117 Mb36
Srostki RUS 167 Pc19
Sr'reenshamali SYR 147 Mk27
Ssese Islands EAU 290 Mg46
Staaten River AUS 232 Sb54
Staaten River N.P. AUS 232 Sb54
Stabbursdalen n.p. N 91 Mc10
Stachy CZ 118 Lo41
Stack Skerry GB 99 Kq31
Stad N 92 Lf28
Stade D 112 Lk37
Staderton SA 303 Me59
Stadskanaal NL 112 Lh38
Stadthagen D 112 Lk38
Stadtlohn D 112 Lg38
Staffa GB 98 Ko34
Staffanstorp S 95 Lo35
Staffelberg D 115 Lm40
Stafford GB 101 Ks38
Stagira GR 127 Md50
Stahnsdorf D 113 Lo38
Stajki BY 97 Mg37
Staked Plains = Llano Estacado USA 23 Ej29
Stakliškės LT 97 Me36
Stalbe LV 97 Mf33
Stalker Castle GB 99 Kp34
Ställdalen S 93 Lp31
Staller Sattel I/A 115 Ln44
Staloluokta S 90 Lj12
Staloluokta fjällstation S 90 Lj12
Stalowa Wola PL 117 Mc40
Stambolijski BG 127 Me48
Stamford AUS (QLD) 232 Sb56
Stamford GB 101 Ku38
Stamford USA (TX) 28 Fa29
Stamford USA (CT) 33 Gd25
Stamford Bridge GB 101 Ku37
Stamnes N 92 Lf30
Stampriet NAM 298 Lk58
Stamsund N 90 Lg11
Stânceni RO 125 Mf44
Standing Rock Ind. Res. USA 26 Ek23
Standing Stone S.P. USA 34 Fh27
Standish USA (MI) 32 Fj24
Stanford USA (MT) 21 Ee22
Stanford USA (KY) 35 Fh27
Stånga S 95 Lt33
Stangån S 95 Lq33
Stange N 92 Lm30
Stanger SA 303 Mf60
Stanhope AUS (VIC) 237 Sc64
Stanhope GB 99 Ks36
Staniard Creek BS 37 Gb33
Stanica Bagaevskaja RUS 135 Na22
Staniel Cay Beach BS 37 Gb33
Stanišić SCG 124 Lu45
Staňkov CZ 118 Lo41
Stanley AUS (TAS) 236 Sc66
Stanley GB 83 Hb71
Stanley USA (ND) 24 Ej21
Stanley Mission CDN (SK) 19 Eh18
Stanley, Mount EAU/RDC 287 Mf45
Stanley Reservoir IND 193 Oj41
Stanmore ZW 300 Me56
Stanovoe RUS 133 Mk19
Stanovoj hrebet RUS 141 Ra07
Stanovoye Nagor'ye RUS 141 Qc07
Stanovoy Khrebet RUS 141 Ra07
Stans CH 114 Lj44
Stansbury AUS (SA) 236 Rj63
Stansmore Range AUS 225 Rd56
Stanthorpe AUS (QLD) 235 Sf60
Stanton Bank GB 98 Kn34
Stanwell AUS (QLD) 233 Sf57
Stanwell Park AUS (NSW) 237 Sf63
Stanwood USA (WA) 18 Dj21
Stanyčno-Luhans'ke UA 135 Mk21
Staphorst NL 112 Lg38
Stapleford ZW 300 Mg55
Staples USA (MN) 27 Fc22
Stapleton USA (NE) 26 Ek25
Staporków PL 117 Ma39
Stara PL 117 Lu39
Stara Caryčanka UA 125 Mk44
Starachowice PL 117 Mb39
Staraja Russa RUS 132 Mf17
Stara Kiszewa PL 116 Lt36
Stara Moravica SCG 124 Lu45
Stara Novalja HR 121 Lp46
Stara Oržyc'a UA 134 Mg21
Stara Pazova SCG 124 Ma46
Stara Rečka BG 127 Mg47
Stara Reka BG 127 Mg48
Stara Sajmyrzino RUS (TAR) 133 Nd18
Stara Ušycja UA 125 Mh42
Stara Vyžívka UA 117 Me39
Stara Zagora BG 127 Mf48
Star City USA (AR) 29 Fe29
Stare Dolistowo PL 117 Mc37
Stare Jeżewo PL 117 Mc37
Stare Kiełbonki PL 117 Mb37
Stare Strącze PL 116 Lr39
Stargard Szczeciński PL 116 Lq37
Stårheim N 92 Lf29
Starica RUS 132 Mh17
Starica RUS 132 Mh19
Starigrad HR 121 Lr47
Stari grad Mostar BIH 121 Ls47
Stari grad Sarajevo BIH 121 Lt47
Stari Ras SCG 126 Ma47
Stark USA (FL) 36 Fj31
Starkville USA (MS) 29 Ff29
Starkweather USA (ND) 24 Fa21
Starnberg D 115 Lm42
Starnberger See D 115 Lm43
Starobil's'k UA 133 Mk21
Starobin BY 132 Md19
Starodub RUS 132 Mg19
Starogard PL 116 Lq37
Starogard Gdański PL 116 Lt37
Starojur'evo RUS 133 Na19
Starokostjantyniv UA 134 Md21
Starominskaja RUS 135 Mk22
Staro Nagoričane MK 126 Mb48
Staro Petrovo Selo HR 121 Ls45
Starosel BG 127 Me48
Staro Selo BG 127 Mg47
Starotitarovskaja RUS 135 Mj23
Starožilovo RUS 133 Mk18
Start Point GB 100 Kr40
Stary Dvor RUS 133 Na17
Stary Dzierzgoń PL 117 Lu37
Staryi Oskol RUS 133 Mj20
Stary Ivanovka RUS 133 Nf18
Staryja Darohi BY 132 Me19
Staryj Bajsarovo RUS (TAR) 133 Ng18
Staryj Kulatka RUS 133 Nd19
Staryj Račejka RUS 133 Ne19
Staryj Sambir UA 119 Mc41
Starý Smokovec SK 119 Ma41
Staßfurt D 113 Lm39
Staszów PL 117 Mb40
State College USA (PA) 33 Gb25
State Line USA (MS) 29 Ff30
State Mosque MAL 199 Qa44
Statenville USA (GA) 35 Fj30
Statesboro USA (GA) 35 Fk29
Statesville USA (NC) 35 Fk28
Stathelle N 92 Lk31
Station de capture d'Epulu RDC 287 Me45
Statue of Liberty USA 33 Gd25
Staume N 92 Lf29
Staunton USA (VA) 33 Ga26
Staunton R. S.P. USA 35 Ga27
Stavanger N 92 Lf32
Stave SCG 126 Lu46

Teluk Sebuku RI 209 Qj44
Teluk Sekatak RI 209 Qj44
Teluk Semangka RI 207 Qc48
Teluk Sempit RI 208 Qg47
Teluk Sibolga RI 206 Pk45
Teluk Sindeh RI 211 Ra50
Teluk Sukadana RI 208 Qe46
Teluk Telaga RI 198 Pj44
Teluk Triton RI 213 Rg47
Telukumpai RI 208 Qe46
Teluk Walckenaer RI 213 Rk47
Teluk Waromge RI 212 Rf46
Teluk Waropen RI 213 Rj47
Teluk Weda RI 212 Re45
Tely RDC 287 Md44
Téma GH 279 Kk43
Temacine DZ 260 Ld29
Temagami CDN (ON) 33 Ga22
Temaju RI 208 Qe45
Temanggung RI 210 Qf49
Temax MEX (YT) 41 Ff35
Temba SA 299 Me58
Tembagapura RI 213 Rj48
Tembe Elephant Reserve SA 303 Mg59
Tembenči RUS 140 Pd05
Tembesi RI 207 Qb47
Tembe, T.I. BR 64 Hf47
Tembhurni IND (MHT) 190 Oh37
Tembilahan RI 207 Qb46
Tembisa SA 299 Me58
Tembladera PE 66 Ga49
Temblador YV 58 Gj41
Tembleque E 109 Kr49
Tembo RDC 289 Lj49
Tembo Aluma ANG 289 Lj49
Tembwe Z 296 Mg51
Temecula USA (CA) 22 Eb29
Temelli TR 131 Mn51
Temelon GQ 281 Lf45
Téméra RMM 271 La37
Temerin SCG 124 Lu45
Temerloh MAL 199 Qb44
Temiang RI 207 Qc45
Teminabuan RI 212 Rf46
Temirlan KZ 158 Oe24
Temirovka KS 159 Oj24
Temirtau KZ 166 Og20
Témiscaming CDN (QC) 33 Ga22
Temki TCH 282 Lk40
Temman-gu J 185 Rf29
Temnik RUS 172 Qc20
Temó MEX (CHP) 41 Fd37
Te-Moak Ind. Res. USA 20 Ec25
Temora AUS (NSW) 237 Sd63
Témoris MEX (CHH) 38 Ef32
Temósachic MEX (CHH) 23 Eg31
Tempe USA (AZ) 23 Ee29
Tempeh RI 210 Qg50
Tempestad PE 60 Gc46
Tempino RI 207 Qb46
Tempio di Giove Ánxur I 122 Lo49
Tempio di Hera Lacinia I 123 Ls51
Tempio Malatestiano di Rimini I 120 Ln46
Témpio Pausània I 111 Lk50
Tempio Távole Palatine I 123 Lr50
Temple USA (TX) 29 Fb30
Temple Bay AUS 230 Sb52
Temple d'Auguste et de Livie F 105 Le45
Templemore IRL 100 Kn38
Temple of Amun ET 263 Mg33
Temple of Hatshepsut ET 263 Mg33
Temple of Haven VRC 175 Qj25
Temple of Hibis ET 263 Mf33
Temple of Horus ET 263 Mg33
Temple of Kawa SUD 276 Mf37
Temple of Khnum ET 263 Mg33
Temple of Kôm Ombo ET 263 Mg33
Temple of Luxor ET 263 Mg33
Temple of Nadura ET 263 Mf33
Temple of Philae ET 263 Mg33
Temple of Poseidón GR 128 Me53
Temple of Yeha ETH 277 Mk39
Templer Bank 204 Qj40
Temples of Musawwarat SUD 276 Mg38
Temples of Naqa SUD 276 Mg38
Temples of Sesebi SUD 276 Mf36
Templin D 113 Lo37
Tempoal de Sánchez MEX (VC) 40 Fa35
Tempué ANG 295 Lk52
Temrjuk RUS 135 Mj23
Temuco RCH 80 Gd65
Temuka NZ 239 Tf68
Tena EC 60 Gb46
Tenabo MEX (CAM) 41 Fe35
Tenacatita MEX (JLC) 39 Eh36
Ténado BF 271 Kj39
Tenaha USA (TX) 29 Fc30
Tenakee Springs USA (AK) 17 Dc17
Tenala = Tenhola FIN 96 Md30
Tenali IND (APH) 191 Pa37
Tenamatua, Gunung RI 209 Ra46
Tenancingo de Degollado MEX (MEX) 40 Fa36
Tenasserim = Tanintharì MYA 196 Pk39
Tenasserim = Tanintharì MYA 196 Pk39
Tenasserim Island MYA 196 Pj39
Tenaún RCH 80 Gd67
Tenby GB 100 Kq39
Tench Island PNG 243 Sf46
Tendaho ETH 284 Na40
Ten Degree Channel IND 186 Pc16
Tendilla E 109 Ks50
Tendjedj DZ 266 Ld34
Tendo J 183 Sa26
Tendoy USA (ID) 21 Ed23
Tendrara MA 259 Kk29
Tendukheda IND (MPH) 191 Ok34
Téné RMM 270 Kh39
Ténenkou RMM 270 Kh38
Tenente Portela BR (RS) 78 Hd59
Ténentou RMM 278 Kg40
Tenerapa MEX (DGO) 39 Eh33
Ténéré RN 267 Lf36
Ténéré du Tafassasset RN 267 Lf35
Tenerife E 264 Kb31
Ténès DZ 259 La27
Tengahdai RI 214 Rb50
Tengchong VRC (YUN) 195 Pk33
Tenggarong RI 209 Qj46
Tengger Shamo VRC 174 Qc26
Tenggol MAL 199 Qb42
Tengréla BF 279 Kh40
Tengréla CI 279 Kg40
Te-n-Guembo RIM 270 Kf37
Tengwani ZW 299 Md56
Teng Xian VRC (GZG) 178 Qf34
Tengzhou VRC (SDG) 184 Qj28
Tenharim Igarapé Prêto, T.I. BR 68 Gk50
Tenharim Marmelos, T.I. BR 68 Gk50
Tenhola = Tenala FIN 96 Md30
Tenhult S 95 Lp33
Teni IND (TNU) 193 Oj41
Teniente Agripino Enciso, P.N. PY 73 Gk56
Teniente Luis Carvajal ANT (RCH) 312 Gc32
Teniente Maza RA (RN) 80 Gg66
Teniente Pinglo PE 60 Gb48
Tenille USA (FL) 36 Fj31
Tenindewa AUS (WA) 228 Qh60
Tenja HR 121 Lt45
Tenkasi IND (TNU) 193 Oj42
Tenke RDC 296 Md51
Tenkodogo BF 279 Kk40
Tenlaa IND (AAN) 193 Pg42
Tenmalai IND (KER) 192 Oj42
Ten Mile Lake AUS 224 Ra58
Ten Mile Pond CDN 31 Hc21
Ten-month Solar Calendar Park VRC 195 Qa33
Tenna I 121 Lo47
Tennam AUS (QLD) 234 Sb58
Tennant Creek AUS (NT) 223 Rh55
Tennessee USA 13 Fc11
Tennessee N.W.R. USA 34 Ff27
Tennessee N.W.R. USA 34 Fg28
Teno RCH 76 Ge63
Tenom MAL 204 Qh43
Tenosique MEX (TB) 41 Fe37
Tenoûmer RIM 264 Ke34
Tensas River N.W.R. USA 29 Fe29
Ten Sleep USA (WY) 21 Eg23
Tenstrike USA (MN) 27 Fc22
Tentek KZ 166 Pa23
Tentena RI 209 Ra46
Tenterden GB 101 La39
Tenterfield AUS (NSW) 235 Sf60
Ten Thousand Islands USA 36 Fk33
Tentolomatinan, Gunung RI 209 Rb45
Tentra IND (MPH) 189 Oj32
Tentyra ET 263 Mg32
Tenzug GH 279 Kk40
Teocaltiche MEX (JLC) 40 Ej35
Teodoro Sampaio BR (SP) 74 Hd57
Teofilândia BR (BA) 71 Ja51
Teófilo Otoni BR (MG) 75 Hk54
Teofipol' UA 134 Md21
Teolândi BR (BA) 71 Ja52
Teomabal Island RP 205 Ra42
Teos TR 129 Mg52
Teotihuacán MEX 40 Fa36
Teotitlán de Flores Magón MEX (OAX) 40 Fb36
Teotitlán del Valle MEX (OAX) 40 Fb37
Teovo MK 126 Mb49
Tepa GH 279 Kj42
Tepache MEX (SO) 23 Ef31
Te Paki NZ 238 Tg63
Tepalcatepec MEX (MHC) 40 Ej36
Tepalcingo MEX (MOR) 40 Fa36
Tepatitlán de Morelos MEX (JLC) 40 Ej35
Tepeguajes MEX (TM) 39 Fb34
Tepehuanes MEX (DGO) 38 Eh33
Tepelenë AL 126 Lu50
Tepeleu RI 212 Re45
Tepere MOC 297 Mk52
Tepexi de Rodríguez MEX (PUE) 40 Fb36
Tepi ETH 283 Mh42
Tepic MEX (NYT) 39 Eh35
Tepich MEX (QTR) 41 Ff35
Teplá CZ 118 Ln41
Teplice CZ 118 Lo40
Teploe RUS 133 Mj19
Teplokljucenka KS 159 Ok24
Teporechi MEX (CHH) 38 Eg32
Tepoto Atoll F 249 Ch54
Tepoztlán MEX (MOR) 40 Fa36
Te Puke NZ 238 Tj64
Tequeje BOL 67 Gg52
Tequila MEX (JLC) 40 Ej35
Tequisquiapan MEX (QRT) 40 Fa35
Téra RN 271 La38
Teradomari J 183 Rk27
Terakeka SUD 287 Mf43
Terälahti FIN 96 Md29
Téramo I 122 Lo48
Terán CO 60 Ga45
Terang AUS (VIC) 237 Sb65
Teranum MAL 199 Qa44
Te Rapa Racecourse NZ 238 Th64
Ter Apel NL 112 Lh38
Terapo PNG 243 Sd50
Teratyn PL 117 Md40
Te Raupua NZ 238 Tg63
Terbanggibesar RI 207 Qc48
Terbuny RUS 133 Mk19
Tercan TR 145 Na26
Terceira P 88 Jc11
Terceira Aliança BR (SP) 74 He56
Terceiro Acampamento BR (AP) 63 Hd45
Tercero RA 76 Gj62
Terdal IND (KTK) 190 Oh37
Terebo PNG 243 Sb49
Terebovlja UA 134 Mc21
Terek RUS (KBA) 152 Nc24
Terekhol IND 190 Og38
Terekli-Mekteb RUS (DAG) 152 Nc23
Térékolé RMM 269 Kf38
Terekti KZ 166 Oe21
Terekti KZ 167 Pc21
Terelj MNG 172 Qd22
Teremia Mare RO 124 Ma45
Teren'ga RUS 133 Ne19
Terenkůdyk KZ 133 Ne21
Terenos BR (MS) 74 Hc56
Terenozek KZ 158 Oc23
Terepaima, P.N. YV 57 Gf41
Teresa RCH 72 Gf56
Teresina BR (PI) 65 Hj48
Teresópolis BR (RJ) 75 Hj57
Teresva UA 119 Md42
Terezinha de Goiás BR (GO) 70 Hg52
Tergnier F 103 Ld41
Teriang MAL 199 Qb44
Terjit RIM 264 Kd35
Terlizzi I 123 Lr49
Termachivka UA 132 Me20
Termas de Arapey ROU 77 Hb61
Termas de Catillo RCH 80 Ge64
Termas de Cauquenes RCH 76 Ge63
Termas de Chillán RCH 80 Ge64
Termas de Daymán ROU 77 Hb61
Termas de Falco RCH 76 Ge63
Termas de Gravatal BR 79 Hf60
Termas de Guaviyú ROU 77 Hb61
Termas de Pernué RCH 80 Ge65
Termas de Reyes RA 72 Gh58
Termas de Río Hondo RA (SE) 76 Gh59
Termas de Villavicencio RA (MD) 76 Gf62
Termas do Quilombo BR 74 Hf56
Termas El Sosneado RA (MD) 76 Ge63
Terme TR 145 Mj25
Terme di Lurisia I 120 Lh46
Termessé RG 269 Kd39
Termessos TR 131 Ml54
Termessos Milli Parkı TR 144 Mf27
Términi Imerese I 122 Lo53
Termit RN 273 Lf37
Termit-Kaoboul RN 273 Lf38
Térmoli I 122 Lp49
Ternate RI 212 Rd45
Terney RUS 181 Rj23
Terneuzen NL 112 Ld39
Terni I 122 Ln48
Ternitz A 115 Lr43
Ternopil' UA 134 Mc21
Territory Wildlife Park AUS 223 Rf52
Terowie AUS (SA) 236 Rk62
Terpnás GR 128 Mb51
Terra Alta BR (PA) 64 Hg46
Terrace CDN (BC) 18 Df18
Terrace Bay NAM 298 Lg55
Terrace (Long Island) USA 33 Ge25
Terrace Mtn. USA 21 Ed25
Terracina I 122 Lo49
TerracottaArmy VRC 177 Qe28
Terra de Areia BR (RS) 79 He60
Terra Firma SA 299 Mb58
Terrâk N 90 Lg13
Terralba I 111 Lj51
Terra Mitica E 109 Ku48
Terra Nova BR (AC) 67 Gf50
Terra Nova BR (PE) 71 Ja50
Terra Nova B. ANT (I) 313 Tc33
Terra Nova do Norte BR (MT) 69 Hc51
Terra Nova N. P. CDN 31 Hd21
Terra Preta BR (AM) 62 Ha49
Terra Preta BR (AM) 62 Hh49
Terra Rica BR (PR) 74 Hd57
Terrassa E 110 Lc49
Terre Adélie 313 Rd32
Terrebonne CDN (QC) 33 Gd23
Terre Clarie 313 Rc32
Terre Haute USA (IN) 32 Fg26
Terrell USA (TX) 29 Fb29
Terreros MEX (COH) 28 Ek31
Terreton USA (ID) 21 Ed24
Terry USA (MT) 21 Eh22
Terry Hie Hie AUS (NSW) 235 Sf60
Tersakan Gölü TR 131 Mo52
Terschelling NL 112 Lf37
Tersef TCH 273 Lj39
Ter Shet ETH 284 Na42
Teruel CO 60 Gc44
Teruel E 109 Kt50
Terujak RI 198 Pj43
Terusan RI 207 Qb47
Terusan RI 207 Qc48
Tervakoski FIN 96 Me30
Tervel BG 127 Mh47
Tervo FIN 91 Md14
Tervola FIN 91 Mc12
Terwood AUS (QLD) 232 Sb54
Tesalia CO 60 Gc44
Tešanj BIH 121 Ls46
Tešel BG 127 Me49
Teseny ER 277 Mj39
Tes gol MNG 167 Pg20
Tes-Hem RUS 167 Ph20
Teshikaga J 181 Sc24
Teshio-gawa J 181 Sb23
Tešica SCG 126 Mb47
Teskej Ala-Too KS 159 Oj24
Teslić BIH 121 Ls46
Teslin CDN (YT) 17 Dd15
Teslin Lake CDN 17 Dd16
Teslin River CDN 17 Dc15
Tesluï RO 124 Me46
Teso Santo E 108 Kp51
Tesouras BR 69 He53
Tessalit RMM 271 La35
Tessaoua RN 272 Ld39
Tesséroukane RN 266 Ld36
Tessit RMM 271 La38
Tessounfat RMM 271 La35
Testa del Gargano I 123 Lr49
Testour TN 260 Le27
Tesugue Ind. Res. USA 23 Eh28
Tét H 118 Ls43
Tetachuk Lake CDN 18 Dh19
Tetari, Cerro CO/YV 56 Gd40
Tetari IND (UPH) 189 Pb32
Tetbury GB 101 Ks39
Tetcela River CDN 17 Dj15
Tete MOC 296 Mg54
Tété RCA 282 Ma41
Tête-à-la Baleine CDN (QC) 31 Ha20
Tetehui PNG 243 Sc49
Tête Jaune Cache CDN (BC) 18 Ea19
Te Teko NZ 238 Tj65
Tetela MEX (PUE) 40 Fb36
Tetepare SOL 245 Sj50
Tetere SOL 245 Ta51
Teteriv UA 134 Me20
Teterow D 113 Ln37
Tetetes EC 60 Gb45
Teteven BG 127 Me48
Tetiaroa Atoll F 249 Cf54
Tetijiv UA 134 Me21
Tétini RG 278 Kf41
Tetlin Junction USA (AK) 15 Cj14
Tetlin Lake USA 15 Cj14
Tetlin National Wildlife Refuge USA 15 Cj14
Teton USA 19 Ee22
Tétouan MA 258 Kh28
Tetovo BG 127 Mg47
Tetovo MK 126 Ma48
Tettnang D 114 Lk43
Teturi RDC 287 Me45
Teuchern D 113 Ln39
Teuco LAR 261 Ma29
Teuco RA 73 Gk58
Teulada I 111 Lj52
Teulada-Moraira E 109 La48
Teulon CDN (MB) 24 Fb20
Teun RI 214 Re49
Teunom RI 198 Ph43
Teunom RI 198 Ph43
Teuri-to J 181 Sa23
Teutoburger Wald D 112 Lj38
Teutônia BR (RS) 78 He60
Teutonic AUS (WA) 228 Ra60
Teuva FIN 93 Mb28
Teverya IS 146 Mh29
Teviot GB 99 Ks35
Te Waewae Bay NZ 239 Td69
Tewah RI 208 Qg46
Te Wahi-pounamu NZ 239 Td68
Tewantin-Noosa AUS (QLD) 235 Sg59
Tewaukon N.W.R. USA 26 Fb22
Tewkesbury GB 101 Ks39
Têwo VRC (GSU) 176 Qb28
Tewure WAN 280 Lc41
Texada Island CDN 18 Dh21
Texarkana USA (TX) 29 Fc29
Texas AUS (NSW) 235 Sf60
Texas USA 12 Fa12
Texas Motor Speedway USA (TX) 28 Fb29
Texas Rangers Hall of Fame USA 29 Fb30
Texel NL 112 Le38
Teyateyaneng LS 303 Md60
Teywarah AFG 160 Oc29
Teziutlán MEX (PUE) 40 Fb36
Tezpur IND (ASM) 194 Pg32
Tezu IND (ARP) 195 Pj32
Tezzeron Lake CDN 18 Dh18
Tfaritiy DARS 264 Ke32
T.G.V. Paris-Marseille F 105 Le45
Thaa Atoll MV 192 Og44
Thaba-Bosiu LS 303 Md60
Tha Bac VN 195 Qb34
Thabana-Ntlenyana LS 303 Me60
Thaba Nchu SA 303 Md60
Thaba Putsoa LS 303 Md60
Thabazimbi SA 299 Md58
Thabeikkyin MYA 195 Pj34
Tha Bo THA 197 Qb37
Thabong SA 303 Md59
Tha Champa THA 197 Qc37
Tha Chana THA 198 Pk41
Thach Tru VN 197 Qe38
Thadiq KSA 149 Nc33
Thadlaskein IND (MGA) 194 Pg33
Thagaya MYA 196 Pj36
Thai Binh VN 178 Qd35
Thai Elephant Conservation Centre THA 196 Pk36
Thailand T 139 Qa08
Thai Lu Tribe Village THA 196 Qa36
Thai Muang THA 198 Pk41
Thaing-ngin MYA 194 Pg34
Thai Nguyen VN 178 Qc35
Thaj KSA 149 Ne32
Thakadu RB 299 Md56
Thakgameng SA 303 Mc59
Tha Khaek LAO 197 Qc37
Thal PK 161 Of29
Thala TN 260 Le28
Thalabarivat K 197 Qc39
Thalang THA 198 Pk41
Thalasseri IND (KER) 192 Oh41
Thale Ban N.P. THA 198 Qa42
Thale Luang THA 198 Qa41
Thale Sap Songkhla THA 198 Qa42
Thallon AUS (QLD) 235 Se60
Thalpan 161 Oh28
Thamad al Hadh LAR 267 Lj32
Thamad al Qattar LAR 260 Lh31
Thamad Bu Hashishah LAR 267 Lk32
Thamad Bu Maras LAR 261 Lk31
Thamad Qabr Salih LAR 260 Lf30
Thamaga RB 299 Mc58
Tha Mai THA 197 Qb39
Thamantha MYA 195 Ph34
Thamarit OM 151 Nh37
Thamat ash Sham KSA 148 Na36
Thamayapeta IND (APH) 191 Pb37
Thames GB 101 Kt39
Thames NZ 238 Th64
Thames Valley GB 101 Kt39
Tham Jang Cave LAO 196 Qb36
Tham Khao Luang THA 196 Qa39
Tha Mot THA 198 Qa42
Tham Phra THA 196 Qa37
Tham Phraya Nakhon Cave THA 196 Pk39
Tham Phu Kham Cave LAO 196 Qb36
Tham Piu Cave LAO 197 Qb36
Tham Than Souphanouvong LAO 178 Qc35
Thamud YE 150 Ne37
Thamun YE 151 Nf38
Thana PK 162 Ob31
Thana Kasba IND (RJT) 191 Oj33
Thanatpin MYA 196 Pj37
Thanbyuzayat MYA 196 Pj38
Thandla IND (MPH) 190 Oh34
Thane IND (MHT) 190 Og36
Thanesar IND (HYA) 189 Oj31
Thang Binh VN 197 Qe38
Thangool AUS (QLD) 235 Sf58
Thanh Hóa VN 197 Qc36
Than Island MYA 198 Pj41
Thaniyah KSA 148 Nb36
Thanjavur IND (TNU) 193 Ok41
Than Lod Noi Cave THA 196 Pk38
Thanlon IND (MNP) 194 Pg33
Thann F 103 Lh43
Thano Bula Khan PK 162 Od33
Than Uyen VN 195 Qb35
Thanwin Myit MYA 196 Pk35
Thanze MYA 196 Ph37
Thaoge RB 299 Mb55
Thaon-les-Vosges F 103 Lg42
Tha Pla THA 196 Qa37
Thap Lan N.P. THA 197 Qb38
Thap Put THA 198 Pk41
Thap Sakae THA 198 Pk40
Tharad IND (GUJ) 190 Of33
Tharb KSA 148 Na33
Thar Desert IND/PK 188 Of32
Thargomindah AUS (QLD) 234 Sb59
Thárros I 111 Lj51
Tha Rua THA 196 Pk36
Tharwaniyyah UAE 156 Ng34
Tha Sae THA 198 Pk40
Tha Song Yang THA 196 Pk37
Thássos GR 127 Me50
Thássos GR 127 Me50
Tha Tako THA 196 Qa38
Thatcher USA (AZ) 23 Ef29
Thathaganyana Hill RB 299 Md57
Thaton MYA 196 Pj37
That Phanom THA 197 Qc37
That Sikhotabong LAO 197 Qc37
Thatta PK 162 Od33
Tha Uthen THA 197 Qc37
Tha Wang Pha THA 196 Qa36
Thaya A 115 Lq42
Thayatal, N.P. A 115 Lq42
Thayawthadangyi MYA 196 Pj39
Thayer USA (MO) 29 Fe27
Thayetmyo MYA 196 Ph36
Thaygon MYA 196 Pj37
Thayne USA (WY) 21 Ee24
Thay Pagoda VN 178 Qd35
Thazi MYA 195 Pj35
The Alley JA 45 Gb37
The Alps AUS 233 Se57
The Ancient City = Muang Boran THA 196 Qa39
Théâtre antique d'Orange F 105 Le46
The Balconies AUS 236 Sb64
The Bayon K 197 Qb39
Thebes GR 128 Md52
The Big Dry CRiver USA 21 Eg22
The Bottom NL (NA) 47 Gj37
The Brothers = Lloyd Rock BS 37 Gc35
The Brothers = Al Ikhwan YE 151 Ng39
The Butt USA (AK) 15 Ch13
The Caves AUS (QLD) 233 Sf57
The Cheviot Hills GB 99 Ks35
The Cove Palisades S.P. USA 20 Dk23
The Dalles USA (OR) 20 Dk23
Thedford USA (NE) 26 Ek25
The English Company's Islands AUS 223 Rj51
The Entrance AUS (NSW) 237 Sf62
The Everglades USA 36 Fk32
The Fens GB 101 La38
The Grampians AUS 236 Sb64
The Greater Saint Lucia Wetland Park SA 303 Mg59
The Great Wall VRC 175 Qj25
The Hague NL 112 Le38
The Haven SA 303 Me62
The Hermitage BS 37 Gc33
The Hoek SA 302 Lk63
Theinkun MYA 198 Pk40
Thekerani MW 297 Mh54
Thekkady IND (KER) 193 Oj41
The Lakes N.P. AUS 237 Sd65
The Little Minch GB 98 Ko33
Theme MYA 196 Pj36
The Minch GB 99 Kp32
The Monument AUS (QLD) 232 Rk56
The Mumbles GB 100 Kq39
The Naze GB 101 Lb39
The Needles GB 101 Kt40
The Needles USA 21 Ef26
Thenia DZ 259 Lb27
Theniet El Had DZ 259 Lb28
Theniet El Had, P.N.de DZ 259 La28
The North Sound GB 99 Ks31
Thenzawl IND (MZR) 194 Pg34
Theodore AUS (QLD) 235 Sf58
Theodore CDN (SK) 24 Ej20
Theodore USA (AL) 29 Ff30
Theodor Roosevelt Lake USA 23 Ee29
The Olgas AUS 226 Rf58
Theológos GR 128 Md52
Thepa THA 198 Qa42
The Pas CDN (MB) 24 Ek19
The Penines GB 101 Kt36
The Pride of Africa Z 299 Md54
Thep Sa Thit THA 196 Qa38
Théra GR 129 Mf54
The Registan UZB 158 Od26
Theri IND (UTT) 189 Ok30
Thermes de Migioky RM 305 Ne52
Thermí GR 129 Mg51
Thermo GR 128 Mb52
Thermopolis USA (WY) 21 Ef24
The Rock AUS (NSW) 237 Sd63
Theron Mountains 312 Jc34
The Royal Orient IND 188 Oh32
The Sands GUY 58 Gk42
The Slot = New Georgia Sound SOL 244 Sj49
The Solent GB 101 Kt40
The Sound DK 94 Ln35
Thesprotikó GR 128 Ma51
Thessalon CDN (ON) 32 Fj22
Thessaloníki GR 126 Mc50
The Steppe KZ 140 Oa09
Thetford GB 101 La38
Thetford Mines CDN (QC) 30 Ge22
Thet ke gyin MYA 194 Ph34
The Twins AUS (SA) 227 Rh60
Theunissen SA 303 Md60
The Valley GB 47 Gj36
Thevenard Island AUS 224 Qh56
The Village USA (OK) 28 Fb28
The Wash GB 101 La38
The Wedge USA (CA) 22 Eb29
The Witties NIC 42 Fj38
The Woodlands USA (TX) 29 Fc30
Thialf NL 112 Lg38
Thíamis GR 128 Ma51
Thiba EAK 290 Mj46
Thiboudaux USA (LA) 29 Fe31
Thicket Portage CDN (MB) 24 Fb18
Thief River Falls USA (MN) 24 Fb21
Thiel Mountains 312 Fc36
Thiene I 120 Lm45
Thien Giang VN 199 Qc40
Thiérache F 103 Ld41
Thiers F 105 Ld45
Thiès SN 269 Kb38
Thiesi I 111 Lj50
Thika EAK 290 Mj46
Thillé Boubakar SN 269 Kc37
Thilogne SN 269 Kd38
Thimad al Fata'im LAR 261 Lk30
Thimlich Ohinga EAK 290 Mh46
Thimphu BHT 194 Pe32
Thinadhoo MV 192 Og45
Thingsai IND (MZR) 194 Pg34
Thio F 246 Td56
Thionville F 103 Lg41
Thira = Santorini GR 129 Mf54
Thira GR 129 Mf54
Thira GR 129 Mf54
Third Cataract SUD 276 Mf37
Third Cataract SUD 276 Mf37
Thirsk GB 101 Kt36
Thirukkovilur IND (TNU) 193 Ok41
Thiruthuraipundi IND (TNU) 193 Ok41
Thiruvananthapuram IND (KER) 192 Oj42
Thisted DK 94 Lj34
Thistle USA (UT) 21 Ee26
Thistle Island AUS 236 Rj63
Thitani EAK 290 Mj46
Thitu Island 204 Qh40
Thitu Reefs 204 Qh40
Thíva GR 128 Md52
Thiviers F 104 La45
Thizy F 105 Le44
Thkov K 197 Qb39
Thma Pok K 197 Qb39
Thnal Bek K 197 Qc40
Thoen THA 196 Pk37
Thoeng THA 196 Qa36
Thohoyandou SA 300 Mf57
Tholária GR 129 Mf54
Thomas Mann Haus LT 97 Mb35
Thomas Shoal 204 Qh41
Thomaston USA (GA) 35 Fh29
Thomaston Corner CDN (NB) 31 Gg23
Thomasville USA (AL) 34 Fg30
Thomasville USA (GA) 35 Fj30
Thomasville USA (NC) 35 Fk28
Thomonde RH 46 Ge36
Thompson CDN (MB) 24 Fb18
Thompson Pass USA 15 Ch15
Thompson River CDN 18 Dk20
Thompsons Falls USA (MT) 19 Ec22
Thompson Sound AUS 239 Td68
Thomson USA (GA) 35 Fj29
Thomson River AUS 232 Sb57
Thomson's Falls = Nyahururu EAK 290 Mj45
Thong Pha Phum THA 196 Pk38
Thong Sala THA 198 Pk41
Thongwa MYA 196 Pj37
Thon Hai VN 197 Qd37
Thon Kiang THA 198 Pk41
Thonon-les-Bains F 105 Lg44
Thoreau USA (NM) 23 Ef28
Thorndale SA 300 Me57
Thorne GB 101 Ku37
Thorne River CDN 24 Fe18
Thornton GB 99 Kr35
Thorntonia AUS (QLD) 232 Rk55
Thorshavnheiane 313 Mc33
Thorsminde DK 94 Lj34
Thorton Peak AUS (QLD) 233 Sc54
Thot Not VN 199 Qc40
Thouars F 102 Ku44
Thoubal IND (MNP) 194 Ph33
Thowada Goemba BHT 194 Pf32
Thowak SUD 277 Mh39
Thrace GR/TR 127 Mf49
Thrakikó Pélagos GR 127 Me50
Thrapston GB 101 Ku38
Thredbo Village AUS (NSW) 237 Se64
Three Forks USA (MT) 21 Ee23
Three Gorges Dam VRC 177 Qf30
Three Gorges of Wuyang R. VRC 178 Qe32
Three Hills CDN (AB) 19 Ed20
Three Hummock Island AUS 236 Sc66
Three Kings Islands NZ 238 Tg63
Three Kings Ridge 221 Tc25
Three Pagodas Pass THA 196 Pk38
Three Parallel Rivers of Yunnan Protected Areas VRC 176 Pk32
Three Rivers AUS (WA) 224 Qk58
Three Rivers USA (NM) 23 Eg29
Three Rivers USA (MI) 32 Fh25
Three Rivers USA (TX) 39 Fa31
Three Sisters AUS 234 Sa58
Three Sisters AUS 237 Sf62
Three Sisters SA 302 Mb61
Three Sisters USA 20 Dk23
Three Sisters Islands SOL 245 Tb51
Three Springs AUS (WA) 228 Qh60
Three Way Roadhouse AUS (NT) 223 Rh55
Thrissur IND (KER) 192 Oj41
Throat River CDN 24 Fd20
Throckmorton USA (TX) 28 Fa29
Throssell Range AUS 224 Ra57
Thrumching La N.P. BHT 194 Pf32
Thrushton N.P. AUS 235 Sd59
Thua EAK 291 Mk46
Thuburbo Majus TN 260 Le27
Thu Dau Mot VN 197 Qd40
Thud Point AUS 230 Sa52
Thueyts F 105 Le46
Thuillier, Mount IND 193 Pg42
Thuir F 104 Lc48
Thul PK 162 Oe31
Thula YE 150 Nb38
Thulamela SA 300 Mf57
Thule = Qaanaaq DK 11 Gc03
Thuli ZW 299 Me56
Thuli ZW 300 Me56
Thun CH 114 Lh44
Thunda AUS (QLD) 234 Sb58
Thundelarra AUS (WA) 228 Qj60
Thunder Bay CDN (ON) 25 Ff21
Thuner See CH 114 Lh44
Thung Hua Chang THA 196 Pk36
Thung Muang THA 196 Qa36
Thung Nao THA 196 Qa36
Thung Salaeng Luang N.P. THA 196 Qa37
Thung Song THA 198 Pk41
Thung Tako THA 198 Pk40
Thung Wa THA 198 Pk42
Thung Wua Laen Beach THA 198 Pk40
Thung Yai THA 198 Pk41
Thungyai-Huai Kha Kaeng Wildlife Sanctuaries THA 196 Pk38
Thur CH 114 Lk43
Thurayban KSA 148 Na36
Thüringen D 113 Ll40
Thüringer Wald D 113 Ll40
Thurles IRL 100 Kn38
Thurlga AUS (SA) 236 Rh62
Thurloo Downs AUS (NSW) 234 Sb60
Thurmond Res. USA 35 Fj29
Thursby GB 99 Kr36
Thursday Island AUS (QLD) 230 Sb51
Thurso GB 99 Kr32
Thurso GB 99 Kr32
Thury-Harcourt F 102 Ku42
Thusis CH 114 Lk44
Thutade Lake CDN 17 Dg17
Thwaites Glacier 312 Ec34
Thyborøn DK 94 Lj34
Thylungra AUS (QLD) 234 Sb59
Thymania AUS (QLD) 232 Sb57
Thyolo MW 297 Mh54
Thysville = Mbanza-Ngungu RDC 288 Lh48
Tiabge CI 279 Kh43
Tiadiaye SN 269 Kb38
Tiago BR (PA) 63 Hb46
Tiahuanaco BOL 72 Gf54
Tiahuanacu BOL 72 Gf54
Tianbanjie VRC (JGX) 184 Qj31
Tianchang VRC (AHU) 184 Qk29
Tian Chi VRC 167 Pd24
Tianchi VRC 182 Re24
Tiandeng VRC (GZG) 178 Qd34
Tiandong VRC (GZG) 178 Qd34
Tian'e VRC (GZG) 178 Qd33
Tianeti GE 152 Nc24
Tiangol Louggueré SN 269 Kc38
Tiangol Loumbol SN 269 Kd38
Tiangol Mboun SN 269 Kc38
Tianguá BR (CE) 65 Hk47
Tianguel-Bori RG 278 Kd40
Tianjin VRC (TJN) 175 Qj26
Tianjin Shi VRC 175 Qj26
Tianjun VRC (QHI) 174 Pk27
Tiankoura BF 279 Kj40
Tianlin VRC (GZG) 178 Qd33
Tianmen VRC (HUB) 177 Qg30
Tianmu Shan VRC 184 Qk30
Tianmushan Z.B. VRC 184 Qk30
Tianqiaoling VRC (JLN) 182 Re24
Tian-Shan' VRC 166 Pa24
Tianshui VRC (GSU) 177 Qc28
Tianshuihai 161 Ok28
Tiantai VRC (ZJG) 184 Ra31
Tiantaishan VRC 184 Ra32
Tiantong Si VRC 184 Ra32
Tiantoubarak RN 272 Ld38
Tian Ya Hai Jiao VRC 178 Qe36
Tianyang VRC (GZG) 178 Qd34
Tianyi Ge VRC 184 Ra32
Tianzhen VRC (SAX) 175 Qh25
Tianzhou Jiaotang VRC 182 Ra27
Tianzhu VRC (GSU) 174 Qb27
Tianzhu VRC (GZH) 178 Qe32
Tianzhushan VRC 184 Qj30
Tiaret DZ 259 La28
Tiaro AUS (QLD) 235 Sg58
Tiassalé CI 279 Kh43
Tibagi BR 74 He57
Tibagi BR (PR) 74 He58
Tibana CO 56 Gd43
Tibana RO 125 Mh43
Tibati CAM 281 Lg42
Tibau BR (RN) 65 Jb48
Tibau, Gunung RI 208 Qh45
Tibel'ti RUS 172 Qb20
Tiber I 122 Ln48
Tiberghamine DZ 259 La31
Tiberias IS 146 Mh29
Tibesti TCH 274 Lj35
Tibet VRC 165 Pb12
Tibilisi GE 145 Nc25
Tibiri RN 271 Lb39
Tibiri RN 272 Ld39
Tibo BF 271 Kj38
Tibo RDC 287 Md44
Tibo RDC 287 Me44
Tibo RI 209 Qk47
Tibooburra AUS (NSW) 234 Sb60
Tibro S 93 Lp32
Tibú CO 56 Gd41
Tiburon RH 46 Gc36
Tiča BG 127 Mg48
Tica MOC 300 Mh55
Ticao Island RP 203 Rb39
Ticao Passage RP 203 Rb39
Tica Tica BOL 72 Gg56
Tichet RMM 271 La36
Tichit RIM 270 Kf36
Tichla DARS 264 Kc35
Ticho ETH 284 Mk42
Ticino CH 114 Lj44
Tickalara AUS (QLD) 234 Sb60
Ticonderoga USA (NY) 33 Gd24
Ticsani, Volcán PE 72 Ge54
Ticul MEX (YT) 41 Ff35
Tidaholm S 95 Lo32
Tidal River AUS (VIC) 237 Sd65
Tidan S 93 Lp32
Tidan S 95 Lp32
Tidarmène RMM 271 Lb37
Tiddim MYA 194 Pg34
Tiddis DZ 260 Ld27
Tidi Dunes RN 274 Lh35
Tidjikja RIM 269 Ke36
Tidone I 120 Lk46
Tidore RI 212 Rd45
Tiébissou CI 279 Kh42
Tiéblé BF 279 Kk40
Tiebl'gahl SYR 147 Na28
Tiéboro TCH 267 Lj35
Tiefa VRC (LNG) 182 Rb24
Tiéfala RMM 278 Kg40
Tiéfora BF 279 Kh40
Tiel NL 112 Lf39
Tiel SN 269 Kc38
Tieli VRC (HLG) 180 Re22
Tieling VRC (LNG) 182 Rb24
Tielong 161 Ok28
Tielt B 103 Ld40
Tiemba CI 278 Kg41
Tiémé CI 278 Kg41
Tié-Ndiékro CI 279 Kh42
Tienen B 103 Le40
Tiéningboué CI 279 Kh41
Tienko CI 278 Kg40
Tienko CI 278 Kg41
Tien Yen VN 178 Qd35
Tiera BF 279 Kh40
Tiéré RMM 279 Kh40
Tierfontein SA 303 Md60
Tierir AUS (QLD) 233 Se57
Tierp S 93 Ls30
Tierra Amarilla RCH 76 Ge59
Tierra Amarilla USA (NM) 23 Eg27
Tierra Blanca MEX (VC) 40 Fb36
Tierra Colorada MEX (GUR) 40 Fa37
Tierra de Campos E 106 Kp51
Tierra del Fuego RA 82 Gg73
Tierra del Fuego RA 82 Gf72
Tierra del Fuego, P.N. RA 82 Gg73
Tierra del Vino E 106 Kp51
Tierralta CO 56 Gb41
Tierranueva MEX (SLP) 40 Ek3
Tierras Blancas RCH 76 Ge61
Tierras de Sayago E 106 Ko51
Tiesa E 108 Kp47
Tie Siding USA (WY) 21 Eh25
Tie Ta VRC 184 Qh28
Tieté BR 74 He56
Tieté BR (SP) 74 Hg57
Tieyon AUS (SA) 226 Rh59
Tiffin USA (OH) 32 Fj25
Tiflét MA 258 Kg29
Tifore RI 212 Rd45
Tifrit RIM 264 Kd35
Tifton USA (GA) 35 Fj30
Tifu RI 212 Rd47
Tiga F 246 Td56
Tiga MAL 204 Qh43
Tigalda Island USA 14 Bh18
Tigaon RP 203 Rb39
Tigapulan Mountains RI 206 Qb46
Tiga Reservoir WAN 272 Le40
Tigbauan RP 205 Rb40
Tiger USA (WA) 18 Eb21
Tiger Island GUY 58 Ha42
Tigharry GB 98 Kn33
Tighenif DZ 259 La28
Tighina MD 125 Mk44
Tignère CAM 281 Lg42
Tigniré RIM 269 Kc36
Tignish CDN (PE) 31 Gh22
Tigoumatene RMM 270 Kh37
Tigre PE 60 Gc47
Tigre RA (BA) 77 Ha63
Tigre YV 57 Gj41
Tigris IRQ 142 Na11
Tigrovaya Balka zapovednik TJ 158 Oe27
Tiguelguemine DZ 266 Lb32
Tiguent RIM 269 Kb37
Tiguentourine DZ 266 Le32
Tiguézéfene RN 271 Lb38
Tigui TCH 274 Lk36
Tiguili TCH 282 Lk40
Tigzirt DZ 259 Lc27
Tihamat YE 150 Nb37
Tihany H 118 Ls44
Tiholop MEX (YT) 41 Ff35
Tihoreck RUS 135 Na23
Tihosuco MEX (QTR) 41 Ff35
Tihvin RUS 132 Mg16
Tihvinskaja grjada RUS 132 Mh16
Tiilikkajärven kansallispuisto FIN 91 Me14
Tijamuchi BOL 67 Gh53
Tijara IND (RJT) 189 Oj32
Tiji LAR 260 Lf29
Tijuana MEX (BC) 22 Eb29
Tijuca, P.N.da BR 75 Hj57
Tijucas BR (SC) 79 Hf59
Tijuco BR 74 Hf55
Tika CDN (QC) 30 Gh20
Tikal GCA 41 Ff37
Tikal GCA 41 Ff37
Tikal, P.N. GCA 41 Ff37
Tikamgarh IND (MPH) 191 Ok3
Tikanlik VRC (XUZ) 169 Pd25
Tikaré BF 271 Kk39
Tikarpara IND (ORS) 191 Pb35
Tikarpara IND (ORS) 191 Pc35
Tikehau Atoll F 249 Cf53
Tikei F 249 Ch53
Tikem TCH 273 Lh41
Tikitiki NZ 238 Tk64
Tikkaballi IND (ORS) 191 Pc35
Tikkakoski FIN 96 Mf28
Tiko CAM 280 Le43
Tikokino NZ 238 Tj65
Tikopia SOL 241 Tb21
Tikota IND (KTK) 190 Oh37
Tikrit IRQ 147 Nb28
Tikša RUS (KAR) 91 Mg13
Tiku RI 206 Pk46
Tikuna de Feijoal, T.I. BR 61 Gf48
Tikus RI 206 Qb47
Tikveško ezero MK 126 Mb49
Tila MEX (CHP) 41 Fd37
Tiladru IND (APH) 191 Pa37
Tilaiya Reservoir IND 191 Pc33
Tilaj H 118 Ls44
Tilal an-Nuba SUD 283 Mf39
Tilama RCH 76 Ge62
Tilamuta RI 209 Rb45
Tilbooroo AUS (QLD) 235 Sc59
Tilburg NL 112 Lf39
Tilbury GB 101 La39
Tilcara RA (PJ) 72 Gh57
Tilcha AUS (SA) 227 Sa60

Til-Châtel F 103 Lf43
Tilda IND (CGH) 191 Pa35
Tildega IND (ORS) 191 Pb34
Tilden USA (TX) 39 Fa31
Tileagd RO 124 Mc43
Tilemsen MA 258 Ke31
Tilemsès RN 272 Lc38
Tilemsi = Lerneb RMM 270 Kh37
Tilemsi RMM 271 La36
Tilisaro RA (SL) 76 Gh62
Tiliviche RCH 72 Gf55
Tillabéri RN 271 La38
Tillamook USA (OR) 20 Dj23
Tillamook Bay USA 20 Dh23
Tillanchang Dwip IND 193 Pg41
Tillberga S 93 Lr31
Tillia RN 272 Lc37
Tillsonburg CDN (ON) 33 Fk24
Tiloa RN 271 Lb38
Tilpozo RCH 72 Gf57
Tilos GR 129 Mh54
Tilpa AUS (NSW) 234 Sc61
Tilrhempt DZ 259 Lb29
Tiltagoonah AUS (NSW) 234 Sc61
Tilža LV 97 Mh34
Tim RUS 133 Mj20
Tim UZB 158 Oc26
Tima ET 263 Mf32
Timahdite MA 258 Kh29
Timampu RI 209 Ra47
Timane PY 73 Gk56
Timanfaya, P.N.de E 264 Kd31
Timanskiy Kryazh RUS 86 Na03
Timare RI 213 Rj48
Timargarha PK 161 Of28
Timaru NZ 239 Tf68
Timaševsk RUS 135 Mk23
Timau EAK 290 Mj45
Timba CO 60 Gb44
Timbalier Bay USA 29 Fe31
Timbauba BR (PE) 71 Jc49
Timbavati Game Reserve SA 300 Mf58
Timbedgha RIM 270 Kf37
Timber Creek AUS (NT) 223 Rf53
Timber Lake USA (SD) 26 Ek23
Timberline Lodge Ski Area USA 20 Dk23
Timber Mill AUS (NT) 223 Rg51
Timber Mtn. USA 20 Ec26
Timbiras BR (MA) 64 Hj48
Timbó BR (SC) 79 Hf59
Timbo LB 278 Kf43
Timbo LB 278 Kf43
Timbo RG 278 Ke40
Timbó Grande BR (SC) 78 He59
Timboroa EAK 290 Mh45
Timbulun RI 206 Qa46
Timbuni RI 213 Rg46
Timbunke PNG 243 Sb48
Timbun Mata MAL 204 Qk43
Timé BF 271 Kk38
Timétrine RMM 271 Kk36
Timfristós GR 128 Mb52
Timgad DZ 260 Ld28
Timia RN 266 Le36
Timiaouine DZ 271 La35
Timika RI 213 Rj48
Timimoun DZ 259 La31
Timiş RO 124 Mb45
Timişoara RO 124 Mb45
Timissa RMM 270 Kh39
Timme-Meghsi RN 266 Ld36
Timmele S 95 Lo33
Timmelsjoch A/I 120 Lm44
Timmins CDN (ON) 25 Fk21
Timm-Missao DZ 266 Lb35
Timna YE 150 Nc38
Timna Park IL 146 Mh31
Timohino RUS 132 Mj16
Timok SCG 126 Mc47
Timon BR (MA) 65 Hj48
Timor TIM 214 Rc50
Timor Museum RI 214 Rb51
Timor Sea 214 Rd51
Timor Trough 214 Rc51
Timoshino RUS 133 Nc17
Timote RA (BA) 77 Gj63
Timoteo BR (MG) 75 Hj55
Timotes YV 57 Ge41
Timoudi DZ 259 Kk31
Timpanogos Cave Nat. Mon. USA 21 Ee25
Timpas USA (CO) 23 Ej27
Timpaus RI 209 Rb46
Timrå S 93 Ls28
Timun RI 207 Qb45
Timurni IND (MPH) 190 Oj34
Tina SA 303 Me61
Tinaco YV 57 Gf41
Tinaga Island RP 203 Rb38
Ti-n-Aguelhaj RMM 271 Kj37
Ti-n-Akof BF 271 Kk38
Tin Alkoum DZ 267 Lf33
Tinambac RP 203 Rb39
Tinambung RI 209 Qk47
Ti-n-Bessais RIM 264 Kf34
Ti-n-Brahim RIM 269 Kc36
Tin Can Bay AUS (QLD) 235 Sg58
Tindangou BF 279 La40
Tindari I 122 Lq52
Tindila RG 278 Kf40
Tindivanam IND (TNU) 193 Ok40
Tindouf DZ 265 Kf32
Tiné SUD 275 Mb38
Tinejdad MA 258 Kh30
Tineo E 106 Ko53
Tinerhir MA 258 Kh30
Ti-n-Essako RMM 271 Lb36
Tinfouchy DZ 258 Kh31
Tin Fouye DZ 260 Ld31
Tin Fouye DZ 260 Le31
Tinfunqué, P.N. PY 73 Ha57
Tinga GH 279 Kj41
Tingal SUD 283 Mh40
Tinggi MAL 199 Qc44
Tinglayan RP 203 Ra37
Tinglev DK 94 Lk36
Tingmiarmiut Fjord DK 11 Hd06
Tingo María PE 66 Gb50
Tingo María, P.N. PE 66 Gb50
Tingong VRC (GZH) 178 Qe33
Tingri VRC (TIB) 170 Pd31
Tingsryd S 95 Lp34
Tingstäde S 95 Lt33
Tinguipaya BOL 72 Gh55
Tinguiririca, Volcán RCH 76 Ge63
Tingvoll N 90 Le14
Tingwon Group PNG 243 Se47
Tingya SUD 283 Mg40
Tinh Gia VN 197 Qc36
Tinhoa CI 278 Kf42
Tinian USA 201 Sb15
Tinigrat RIM 270 Kf36
Tinigua, P.N. CO 61 Gc44
Tiniroto NZ 238 Tj65
Tinjil RI 210 Qc49
Ti-n-Kâr = Timétrine RMM 271 Kk36
Tinkisso RG 269 Kf40
Tinlot B 103 Lf40
Ti-n-Medjouf RIM 269 Kc36
Tin Merzouga DZ 267 Lf34
Tinnenburra AUS (QLD) 235 Sc60
Tinnsjø N 92 Lj31
Tinobu RI 209 Rb47
Tinogasta RA (CA) 76 Gg60
Tinombo RI 209 Ra45
Tinompo RI 209 Ra47
Tinos GR 129 Mf53
Tinos GR 129 Mf53
Tinputz PNG 244 Sh48
Tinqueux F 103 Ld41
Tin Rerchoch DZ 266 Lc35
Tinsukia IND (ASM) 195 Ph32
Tin Tadjant DZ 266 La35
Tintâne RIM 269 Ke37
Tintang RI 209 Qj45
Tin Tarabine DZ 266 Ld34
Ti-n-Tehoun RMM 271 Kj37
Tinténiac F 102 Kt42
Tinterhert DZ 266 Le33
Tintern Abbey GB 101 Ks39
Ti-n-Tijot' RMM 270 Kh37
Tintina RA (SE) 77 Gj59
Tintinara AUS (SA) 236 Sa63
Tintioulen RG 278 Kf40
Tin Toumma RN 273 Lg37
Tinui NZ 238 Tj66
Tinūži LV 97 Me34
Ti-n-Zaouâtene RMM 271 Lb36
Tinzouline MA 258 Kg30
Tioga USA (ND) 24 Ej21
Tioman MAL 199 Qc44
Tione di Trento I 120 Ll44
Tioneste USA (PA) 33 Ga25
Tionk Essil SN 269 Kb39
Tioor RI 212 Rf48
Tiop RI 206 Qa47
Tiorobougou RMM 270 Kf39
Tioroniaradougou CI 279 Kh41
Tiou BF 271 Kj39
Tiou BF 279 Kj40
Tiouilit RIM 269 Kb36
Tipaza DZ 259 Lb27
Tipón PE 67 Gd52
Tipova MD 125 Mj43
Tipparti IND (APH) 191 Ok37
Tipperary AUS (NT) 223 Rf52
Tipperary IRL 100 Km38
Tipton, Mount USA 22 Ec28
Tip Tree, Mount AUS (QLD) 233 Sc54
Tiptur IND (KTK) 193 Oj40
Tipuani BOL 67 Gf53
Tipuru GUY 58 Ha43
Tiputa F 249 Cg53
Tiputini EC 60 Gc46
Tiquié BR 61 Gf45
Tiquimul MEX (CAM) 41 Fe36
Tiranë AL 126 Lu49
Tirangole SUD 283 Mg43
Tirano I 120 Ll44
Tiran & Sanâfir Islands Reserve ET 263 Mh32
Tiraouene RN 266 Ld36
Tiraque BOL 72 Gh54
Tiras Shet ETH 277 Mk40
Tirasberge NAM 298 Lj58
Tiraspol MD 125 Mk44
Tirau NZ 238 Th64
Tire TR 129 Mh52
Tirebolu TR 145 Mk25
Tirecatinga, T.I. BR 68 Ha52
Tiree AUS (QLD) 233 Sc56
Tiree GB 98 Ko34
Tirgaran AFG 161 Of27
Tirgua, P.N. YV 57 Gf41
Tirhatimine DZ 266 Lb33
Tiri Aguige TCH 267 Lk34
Tirich Mir PK 161 Of27
Tiriri EAU 290 Mg45
Tirkšliai LT 97 Mc34
Tirlta AUS (NSW) 234 Sb61
Tirmalgiri IND (APH) 191 Ok37
Tirmini RN 272 Le39
Tirnavos GR 126 Mc51
Tiro RG 278 Ke41
Tirol = Tirolo I 120 Lm44
Tirolo = Tirol I 120 Lm44
Tirora IND (MHT) 191 Pa35
Tiros BR (MG) 75 Hh55
Tiroungoulou RCA 282 Mb41
Tirrénia I 120 Ll47
Tirschenreuth D 115 Ln41
Tirthahalli IND (KTK) 192 Oh40
Tirth Raj Prayag IND (UPH) 191 Pa33
Tirûa RCH 80 Gd65
Tiruchendur IND (TNU) 193 Ok42
Tiruchengodu IND (TNU) 193 Oj41
Tiruchirapalli IND (TNU) 193 Ok41
Tirumala IND 193 Ok40
Tirumangalam IND (TNU) 193 Oj42
Tirumayam IND (TNU) 193 Ok41
Tirunelveli IND (TNU) 193 Oj42
Tirupati IND (APH) 193 Ok40
Tiruppattur IND (TNU) 193 Ok40
Tiruppattur IND (TNU) 193 Ok41
Tiruppur IND (TNU) 193 Oj41
Tirután PE 66 Gc49
Tiruvannamalai IND (TNU) 193 Ok40
Tiruvarur IND (TNU) 193 Ok41
Tiruvellore IND (TNU) 193 Ok40
Tiruvettipuram IND (TNU) 193 Ok40
Tiruvottiyur IND (TNU) 193 Pa40
Tiruvuru IND (APH) 191 Pa37
Tiryns GR 128 Mc53
Tis IR 157 Oa33
Tisa SCG 124 Ma45
Tišća BIH 126 Lt46
Tisdale CDN (SK) 19 Eh19
Tisgaon IND (MHT) 190 Oh36
Tisgui-Remz MA 258 Kf31
Tishomingo USA (OK) 29 Fb28
Tishomingo N.W.R. USA 29 Fb28
Tišina RUS 180 Rf20
Tis Isat Falls ETH 284 Mj40
Tiškevičiu rūmai LT 97 Mb35
Tisnaren S 93 Lq32
Tišnov CZ 118 Lr41
Tisovec SK 119 Lu42
Tissemsilt DZ 259 La28
Tisvildeleje DK 94 Ln34
Tisza H 119 Ma44
Tiszabecs H 119 Mc42
Tiszacsege H 119 Mb43
Tiszacsermely H 119 Mb42
Tiszadada H 119 Mb42
Tiszafüldvár H 119 Ma44
Tiszafüred H 119 Ma43
Tiszakécske H 119 Ma44
Tiszalúc H 119 Mb42
Tiszaújváros H 119 Mb43
Tiszavasvári H 119 Mb43
Tit DZ 266 La32
Tit DZ 266 Lc34
Titaluk River USA 15 Cc11
Titalya IND (WBG) 194 Pe32
Titan Dome 312 Tb36
Titao BF 271 Kj39
Titay RP 205 Rb42
Tite GNB 269 Kc40
Titigading RI 206 Qa45
Titisee-Neustadt D 114 Lj43
Titiwaifuru RI 213 Rk47
Titlagarh IND (ORS) 191 Pb35
Titlis CH 114 Lj44
Tit-Mellil MA 258 Kg29
Titran N 90 Le14
Ti-Tree AUS (NT) 226 Rg57
Ti Tree AUS (QLD) 230 Sa53
Titu RO 125 Mf46
Titusville USA (PA) 33 Ga25
Titusville USA (FL) 36 Fk31
Titwan MA 258 Kh28
Tiumpan Head GB 99 Ko32
Tivaouane SN 269 Kb38
Tivat SCG 126 Lt48
Tiveden S 93 Lp32
Tivedens n.p. S 93 Lp32
Tiverton GB 100 Kr40
Tivoli DK 94 Ln35
Tivoli I 122 Ln49
Tivoli USA (TX) 39 Fb31
Tiwai Island Wildlife Sanctuary WAL 278 Ke42
Tiwi EAK 293 Mk48
Tiwi OM 157 Nk34
Tiwi Aboriginal Reserve AUS 223 Rf51
Tixmul MEX 41 Ff36
Tixtla de Guerrero MEX (GUR) 40 Fa37
Tiya ETH 284 Mk41
Tiyama J 183 Rk27
Tiyo ER 277 Na39
Tizard Bank 204 Qh40
Tizayuca MEX (MEX) 40 Fa36
Tizimín MEX (YT) 41 Ff35
Tizi-n-Bachkoum MA 258 Kh30
Tizi-n-Tairhemt MA 259 Kh29
Tizi-n-Tarhatine MA 258 Kg30
Tizi-n-Test MA 258 Kg30
Tizi-n-Tichka MA 258 Kg30
Tizi-n-Tinififft MA 258 Kg30
Tizi Ouzou DZ 259 Lc27
Tiznado YV 57 Gg41
Tiznit MA 258 Kf31
Tižtiž IR 154 Nd28
Tizzano F 111 Lj49
Tjačiv UA 119 Md42
Tjæreborg DK 94 Lj35
Tjällmo S 93 Lq32
Tjaneni SD 303 Mf59
Tjan'-šan' KS 159 Of24
Tjatino RUS 181 Sd23
Tjatja, vulkan RUS 181 Sd23
Tjentište BIH 126 Lt47
Tjibaou Cultural Centre F 246 Td57
Tjøme N 92 Ll31
Tjörn S 94 Lm33
Tjøtta N 90 Lg13
Tjumen' RUS 140 Ob07
Tjuvfjorden N 91 Ma07
Tkhinvali GE 152 Nc24
Tlacoapa MEX (GUR) 40 Fa37
Tlacolula de Matamoros MEX (OAX) 40 Fb37
Tlacotalpan MEX (VC) 40 Fc36
Tlahualilo de Zaragoza MEX (DGO) 39 Ej32
Tlaltenango de Sánchez Román MEX (ZCT) 40 Ej35
Tlapacoyan MEX (VC) 40 Fb36
Tlapa de Comonfort MEX (GUR) 40 Fa37
Tlapehuala MEX (GUR) 40 Ek36
Tlaquepaque MEX (JLC) 40 Ej35
Tlaxcala MEX (TXL) 40 Fa36
Tlaxcala MEX 40 Fa36
Tlaxco MEX (TXL) 40 Fa36
Tlell CDN (BC) 18 De19
Tlemcen DZ 259 Kk28
Tlemcen, P.N.de DZ 259 Kk28
Tleta-Akhssass MA 258 Kf31
Tleta-Henchane MA 258 Kf30
Tlevak StRiver USA 17 Dd18
Tlisan LAR 261 Lj31
Tloh RUS (DAG) 152 Nd24
Tlokoeng LS 303 Me60
Tłuchowo PL 117 Lu38
Tłuszcz PL 117 Mb38
Tmassah LAR 267 Lh32
Tmeïmichât RIM 264 Kc35
Tnaot K 197 Qc39
Tô BF 279 Kj40
Toad River CDN 17 Dh16
Toamasina RM 306 Ne55
Toau Atoll F 249 Cg53
To Awai SUD 276 Mh36
Toay RA (LP) 81 Gh64
Toba J 183 Rj28
Toba RMM 278 Kg40
Toba VRC (TIB) 171 Pj30
Tobacco Range BH 41 Fg37
Tobago TT 58 Gk40
Tobago Rain Forest Reserve TT 58 Gk40
Toba Inlet CDN 18 Dh20
Toba Kakar Range PK 160 Od30
Tobalai RI 212 Re46
Tobar Donoso EC 60 Ga45
Tobarra E 109 Kt48
Toba Tek Singh PK 161 Og30
Tobeatic Wildlife Management Area CDN 31 Gh23
Tobelo RI 212 Rd45
Tobercurry IRL 98 Km36
Tobermore AUS (NT) 227 Rj57
Tobermory AUS (QLD) 234 Sb59
Tobermory CDN (ON) 32 Fk23
Tobermory GB 98 Ko34
Tobias Barreto BR (SE) 71 Jb51
Tobias Fornier RP 205 Ra40
Tobi Island PAL 203 Rf44
Tobijima J 183 Rk26
Tobin Lake AUS 225 Rc56
Tobin Lake CDN (SK) 24 Ej19
Tobin, Mount USA 20 Eb25
Tobique River CDN 30 Gg22
Toblach = Dobbiaco I 120 Ln44
Tobli LB 278 Kf42
Toboali RI 207 Qd47
Tobol RUS 140 Ob07
Toboli RI 209 Ra46
Tobol'sk RUS 140 Ob07
Tobré DY 272 Lb40
Toca CO 56 Gd43
Tocache Nuevo PE 66 Gb50
Tocaia BR (PI) 65 Hj48
Tocaima CO 56 Gc43
Tocancipa CO 56 Gd43
Tocantinia BR (TO) 70 Hf50
Tocantinópolis BR (TO) 64 Hg49
Tocantins BR 53 Hc19
Tocantins BR 53 Hc21
Tocantinzinho BR 70 Hf53
Tocata RA (SJ) 76 Gf61
Toccoa USA (GA) 35 Fj28
Toch'o Do ROK 185 Rd28
Töcksfors S 92 Lm31
Toco ANG 294 Lg53
Toco TT 58 Gk40
Tocoa HN 42 Fh38
Tocopilla RCH 72 Ge57
Tocopuri, Cerro de BOL 72 Gg57
Tocra = Teuchira LAR 261 Ma29
Tocumwal AUS (NSW) 237 Sc63
Tócura CO 56 Gb42
Tocuyito YV 57 Gf40
Tocuyo YV 57 Gf40
Tocuyo de la Costa YV 57 Gf40
Tod ET 263 Mg33
Toda-saki J 183 Sa26
Todd River AUS 227 Rh58
Todeli RI 209 Rc46
Tödi CH 114 Lj44
Todi I 122 Ln48
Todireşti RO 125 Mg43
Todmorden AUS (SA) 227 Rj59
Todoriči BIH 121 Ls46
Todos Santos BOL 72 Gh54
Todos Santos MEX (BCS) 38 Ee34
Todtnau D 114 Lh43
Todupulai IND (KER) 192 Oj42
Todžinskaja kotlovina RUS 172 Pj19
Toéguen BF 271 Kk39
Toéni BF 271 Kj39
Toéssé BF 279 Kk40
Toez CO 60 Gb44
Toffa DY 280 Lb42
Tofield CDN (AB) 19 Ed19
Tofino CDN (BC) 18 Dh21
Tofsingdalens n.p. S 93 Ln28
Toft GB 99 Kt30
Tofta S 94 Ln33
Tofta S 95 Lt33
Tofte N 92 Ll31
Toftedal S 92 Lm32
Toftlund DK 94 Lk35
Toftøy N 92 Le30
Tofua Island TO 248 Bc55
Tog ETH 285 Nb41
Toga VU 246 Td52
Toganaly AZ 152 Nd25
Togarakunta IND (APH) 193 Oj39
Togba RIM 269 Ke37
Togbo RCA 286 Ma43
Togi J 183 Rj27
Togiak USA (AK) 14 Bk16
Togiak Bay USA (AK) 14 Bk16
Togiak National Wildlife Refuge USA (AK) 14 Bk16
Togiak River USA (AK) 14 Bk16
Togian RI 209 Ra46
tog'lari Aččitov UZB 153 Oa24
Togni SUD 276 Mh37
Togo CDN (SK) 24 Ek20
Togo PNG 243 Sb50
Togo RMM 270 Kh39
Togo USA (MN) 27 Fd22
Togo 253 La09
Togobala RG 278 Kg41
Togo Hills GH 279 La42
Togoroma CO 56 Gb43
Togou RMM 270 Kh39
Togoville RT 279 La42
Tögrög MNG 167 Pg22
Tögrög MNG 167 Ph23
Togton VRC (NMZ) 175 Qf25
Toguéré-Koumbé RMM 270 Kh38
Tohamiyam SUD 277 Mj37
Tohana IND (HYA) 188 Oh31
Tohddoo Atoll MV 192 Og43
Tohmajärvi FIN 96 Ml28
Toho RI 208 Qe45
Tohoku Shinkansen J 183 Sa26
Toholampi FIN 91 Mc14
Tohoun RT 279 La42
Toibalewe IND (AAN) 193 Pg40
Toijala FIN 96 Md29
Toili RI 209 Rb46
Toineke RI 214 Rc51
Toivakka FIN 96 Mg28
To-jima J 183 Rk28
Tojo J 183 Rg28
Toka GUY 58 Ha43
Tokachi-dake J 181 Sb24
Tokaido Shinkansen J 183 Rk28
Tokaj H 119 Mb42
Tokaj-Hegyalja H 119 Mb42
Tokamachi J 183 Rk27
Tokapalle IND (APH) 193 Ok39
Tokar SUD 277 Mj37
Tokara Islands J 185 Re31
Tokara Strait J 185 Rf30
Tokarevka RUS 133 Na19
Tokarnia PL 119 Mc41
Tokár-tető H 119 Mb42
Tokat TR 144 Mj25
Tokatoka NZ 238 Th64
Tokchokto Do ROK 182 Rd27
Tokch'on DVRK 182 Rd26
Tok Do ROK 183 Rf27
Tokelau NZ 241 Ub20
Tokelau Islands NZ 241 Ub20
Tökhöm MNG 174 Qe23
Toki TCH 273 Lj41
Tok Junction USA (AK) 15 Cj14
Toklat River USA 15 Ce14
Tokluman TR 131 Mo51
Tokmak KS 159 Oh24
Tokmak UA 135 Mh22
Toko BOL 72 Gh54
Tokomaru Bay NZ 238 Tk65
Tokoro J 181 Sc23
Tokoroa NZ 238 Th65
Tokouno RG 278 Kf41
Tok River USA 15 Cj14
Toksum VRC (XUZ) 169 Pe24
Toktoghule reservoir KS 159 Og25
Toktogul KS 159 Og25
Toku Island TO 248 Bc55
Tokuno-jima J 185 Re32
Tokunoshima J 185 Re32
Tokushima J 183 Rh28
Tokuyama J 183 Rf28
Tokwe ZW 300 Mf55
Tokyo J 183 Rk28
Tokyo-Disneyland J 183 Rk28
Tokyo-wan J 183 Rk28
Tokyrauyn KZ 166 Oh21
Tokysan N.P. ROK 182 Rd28
Tokzar AFG 160 Od28
Tol PNG 244 Sg48
Tolaga Bay NZ 238 Tk65
Tolala RI 209 Ra47
Tôlanaro RM 306 Nd58
Tolandona RI 209 Rb48
Tolbo MNG 167 Pf21
Tolbo nuur MNG 167 Pe21
Tolbuzino RUS 180 Rc19
Toldo Chimbangue, T.I. BR 78 Hd59
Tolé RCA 281 Lh42
Tole Bi KZ 159 Og24
Toledo BOL 72 Gg55
Toledo BR (PR) 74 Hd58
Toledo E 109 Kq49
Toledo RP 205 Rb40
Toledo USA (WA) 18 Dj22
Toledo USA (OR) 20 Dj23
Toledo USA (OH) 32 Fj25
Toledo Bend Reservoir USA 29 Fd30
Tolentino I 121 Lo47
Tolfa I 122 Lm48
Tolga DZ 260 Lc28
Tolga N 92 Ll28
Tolgskij monastyr RUS 133 Na17
Tolhuaca, P.N. RCH 80 Ge65
Toli VRC (XUZ) 166 Pb23
Toliara RM 306 Nb57
Tolima, Nevado de CO 56 Gc43
Tolitoli RI 209 Ra45
Tol'jatti RUS 133 Ne19
Tollarp S 95 Lo35
Tollensesee D 113 Lo37
Tollimarjon UZB 158 Oc26
Tolmezzo I 121 Lo44
Tolmin SLO 121 Lo44
Tolo RDC 289 Lk47
Tolofu RI 212 Rd45
Tolo Humma IND (ORS) 191 Pc36
Tolokiwa Island PNG 243 Sd48
Tolon GH 279 Kk41
Tolong Bay RP 205 Rb41
Tolongoina RM 306 Nd56
Tolosa E 107 Ks53
Toloyana River USA 15 Cf13
Tolsan Do ROK 182 Rd28
Toltén RCH 80 Gd65
Toltén RCH 80 Gd65
Toltrele de la Prut MD 125 Mh42
Tolú CO 56 Gc41
Toluca MEX (MEX) 40 Fa36
Toludur IND (TNU) 193 Ok41
Toluk KS 159 Og25
Toluviejo CO 56 Gc41
Tom' RUS 180 Re20
Toma BF 271 Kj39
Tomah USA (WI) 27 Fe24
Tomahawk USA (WI) 32 Ff23
Tomakivka UA 135 Mh22
Tomakomai J 181 Sa24
Tomanggong MAL 204 Qk43
Tomani MAL 204 Qh43
Tomaniivi FJI 247 Tk54
Tomar BR (AM) 62 Gj46
Tomar KZ 166 Oh22
Tomar P 108 Km49
Tomari RUS 181 Sb22
Tomarovka RUS 133 Mj20
Tomarza TR 144 Mh26
Tomás PE 66 Gc52
Tomás de Borlanga EC 60 Fe46
Tomaševac SCG 124 Ma45
Tomás Garrido MEX (QTR) 41 Ff36
Tomašpil' UA 125 Mj42
Tomas Romero Pereira PY 77 Hc59
Tomaszów Lubelski PL 117 Md40
Tomaszów Mazowiecki PL 117 Lu39
Tomat SUD 283 Md40
Tomata RI 209 Ra46
Tomatlán MEX (JLC) 39 Eh36
Tombe ANG 294 Lj52
Tombeaux de Rois Sakalava RM 304 Nd53
Tombeaux Mahafaly RM 306 Nc58
Tombeaux royaux Antemoro d'Ivato RM 306 Nd57
Tombeaux royaux d'Antananarivo RM 306 Nd55
Tombeaux Royaux de Mahabo RM 306 Nc56
Tombeaux (Tiéboro) TCH 274 Lj35
Tombe du Camerounais TCH 267 Lj36
Tombel CAM 280 Le43
Tomboco ANG 288 Lg49
Tomb of Sultan Hasanuddin RI 211 Qk48
Tombokro CI 279 Kh42
Tombolo RI 211 Ra48
Tombos BR (MG) 75 Hj56
Tombouctou RMM 271 Kj37
Tombs of Buganda Kings EAU 290 Mg45
Tombs of the Nobles ET 263 Mg33
Tombstone USA (AZ) 23 Ee30
Tombstone Courthouse S.H.P. USA 23 Ee30
Tombua ANG 294 Lf53
Tombul-džamija BG 127 Mg47
Tom Burke SA 300 Me57
Tomdibuloq UZB 158 Oc25
Tomé RCH 80 Gd64
Tomea RI 209 Rb48
Tomé-Açu BR (PA) 64 Hf47
Tomelilla S 95 Lo35
Tomelloso E 109 Kr49
Tomeşti RO 124 Mc45
Tomeşti RO 125 Mh43
Tomi RCA 281 Lk43
Tomina BOL 73 Gh55
Tomingley AUS (NSW) 237 Se62
Tomini RI 209 Ra45
Tominian RMM 270 Kh39
Tomintoul GB 99 Kr33
Tomioka J 183 Rk27
Tomislavgrad BIH 121 Ls47
Tomkinson Ranges AUS 225 Re59
Tomma N 90 Lg12
Tomo CO 57 Gf43
Tomochic MEX (CHH) 38 Eg31
Tomohon RI 209 Rc45
Tomori RCA 281 Lh44
Tomortei VRC (QHI) 169 Pf26
Tomortei VRC (NMZ) 175 Qg25
Tompa H 119 Lu44
Tompe RI 209 Qk46
Tompet RI 206 Pk45
Tompira RI 209 Ra47
Tompi Seleka SA 300 Me58
Tompkinsville USA (KY) 34 Fh27
Tom Price AUS (WA) 224 Qj57
Tomrefjord N 92 Lg28
Tomsk RUS 140 Pb07
Toms River USA (NJ) 33 Gc26
Tomtabacken S 95 Lp33
Tomtor RUS 141 Sa06
Tomu RI 212 Rg47
Tom White, Mount USA 16 Cj15
Tom Yawkey Wildlife Center USA 35 Ga29
Tónachic MEX (CHH) 38 Eg31
Tonalá MEX (JLC) 40 Ej35
Tonalá MEX (VC) 41 Fc36
Tonami J 183 Rj27
Tonantins BR (AM) 61 Gg47
Tonara I 111 Lk50
Tonate F 59 Hd43
Tonbridge GB 101 La39
Tonda PNG 242 Sa50
Tondano RI 209 Rc45
Tondela P 106 Km50
Tønder DK 94 Lj36
Tondi IND (TNU) 193 Ok42
Tondibi RMM 271 La37
Tondidarou RMM 270 Kh37
Tondigamé Goulbi RN 271 Lb39
Tondi Kiwindi RN 271 La38
Tondon RG 278 Kd40
Toné BF 279 Kj40
Tone-gawa J 183 Rk27
Tonekabon IR 154 Nf27
Tone Nga Chang Falls THA 198 Qa42
Tone Wai Town LB 278 Kf43
Tong SUD 283 Me42
Tong SUD 283 Me42
Tonga AUS (NSW) 234 Sb61
Tonga CAM 281 Lf43
Tonga SUD 283 Mf41
Tonga 219 Ba11
Tongaat SA 303 Mf60
Tongaat Beach SA 303 Mf60
Tong'an VRC (FJN) 179 Qk33
Tonga Ridge TO 248 Bc56
Tongariro N.P. NZ 238 Th65
Tongatapu Group TO 248 Bc56
Tongatapu Island TO 248 Bc56
Tonga Trench TO 248 Bd56
Tongbai VRC (HNN) 177 Qg29
Tongbai Shan VRC 177 Qg29
Tongcheng VRC (HUB) 177 Qg31
Tongcheng VRC (AHU) 184 Qj30
Tongchon DVRK 182 Rd26
Tongchuan VRC (SAA) 177 Qe28
Tongdao VRC (HUN) 178 Qe32
Tongde VRC (QHI) 176 Qa28
Tongehatan Point RP 204 Ra43
Tongeren B 103 Lf40
Tonggu VRC (JGX) 184 Qh31
Tong'guan VRC (SAA) 177 Qf28
Tongguan VRC (YUN) 195 Qa34
Tongguzbasti VRC (XUZ) 168 Pa26
Tonggu Zhang VRC 179 Qj33
Tonghae ROK 182 Re27
Tonghai VRC (YUN) 195 Qb33
Tonghaikou VRC (HUB) 177 Qg30
Tonghe VRC (HLG) 180 Re23
Tonghua VRC (JLN) 182 Rc25
Tongi BD 194 Pf34
Tongjiang VRC (SCH) 177 Qd30
Tongjiang VRC (HLG) 180 Rg22
Tongken He VRC 180 Rd22
Tongliao VRC (NMZ) 182 Rb24
Tongling VRC (AHU) 184 Qj30
Tonglu VRC (ZJG) 184 Qk31
Tongnan VRC (CGQ) 177 Qc30
Tongoa VU 246 Te54
Tongobory RM 306 Nc57
Tongomayél BF 271 Kk38
Tongoni Ruins EAT 293 Mk48
Tongoy RCH 76 Ge61
Tongren VRC (QHI) 176 Qa28
Tongren VRC (GZH) 178 Qe32
Tongshan VRC (HUB) 184 Qh31
Tongshi VRC (HAN) 178 Qe36
Tongtian He VRC 171 Ph28
Tongue GB 99 Kq32
Tongue USA 21 Eg23
Tongue of the Ocean BS 37 Gb33
Tonguro BR 69 Hd52
Tongwe EAT 293 Mk48
Tong Xian VRC (BJG) 175 Qj26
Tongxiang VRC (ZJG) 184 Ra30
Tongxin VRC (NHZ) 174 Qc27
Tongxu VRC (HNN) 184 Qh28
Tongyu VRC (SAX) 175 Qg27
Tongyu VRC (JLN) 180 Rb23
Tongzi VRC (GZH) 177 Qd31
Tonhe MYA 194 Ph33
Tonichi MEX (SO) 23 Ef31
Tonina CO 61 Gg44
Toniná MEX 41 Fe37
Tonk IND (RJT) 188 Oh32
Tonka RMM 271 Kj37
Tonki C. USA 16 Ce16
Tonkino RUS 133 Nd17
Tonkoro AUS (QLD) 232 Sb57
Tonle Kong K 197 Qd39
Tonle San K 197 Qd38
Tonlé Sap K 197 Qc39
Tonle Sap Biosphere Reserve K 197 Qc39
Tonle Srepok K 197 Qd39
Tonnay-Boutonne F 104 Ku45
Tonnay-Charente F 104 Ku45
Tonneins F 104 La46
Tonnerre F 103 Ld43
Tönning D 112 Lj36
Tono J 183 Sa26
Tonopah USA (NV) 20 Eb26
Tonosí PA 43 Fk42
Tonosoyo J 183 Rh28
Tonotha RB 299 Md56
Tonozero RUS (KAR) 91 Mf13
Tonquil Island RP 205 Ra42
Tonšaevo RUS 133 Nd17
Tonsaket USA (WA) 18 Ea21
Tønsberg N 92 Ll31
Tonsina USA (AK) 15 Ch15
Tonstad N 92 Lh32
Ton Tae Falls THA 198 Pk42
Tontelbos SA 302 Ma61
Tonto Nat. Mon. USA 23 Ee29
Tonusu RI 209 Ra46
Tonya TR 145 Mk25
Tonzona River USA 15 Cd14
Toobanna AUS (QLD) 233 Sd55
Toobeah AUS (QLD) 235 Se60
Toodyay AUS (WA) 228 Qj61
Tooele USA (UT) 21 Ed25
To'Okona PNG 243 Sd49
Toolbec AUS (QLD) 232 Sa57
Tooligie AUS (SA) 236 Rh62
Toolondo AUS (VIC) 236 Sa64
Toombs House S.H.S. USA 35 Fj29
Toompine AUS (QLD) 234 Sc59
Toomula AUS (QLD) 233 Sd55
Toora AUS (VIC) 237 Sd65
Toora-Hem RUS (TUV) 172 Pj19
Tooraie AUS (NSW) 235 Sc61
Tooraweenah AUS (NSW) 235 Se61
Toorcomt MNG 167 Pg20
Toowoomba AUS (QLD) 235 Sf59
Tooxin SP 285 Nf40
Topagoruk River USA 15 Cc10
Topaklı TR 131 Mp51
Topar KZ 166 Og21
Topar KZ 166 Oh23
Topaz Lake USA (NV) 20 Ea26
Topčii BG 127 Mg47
Topczewo PL 117 Mc38
Tope de Coroa CV 268 Jh37
Topeka USA (KS) 27 Fc26
Topia RCA 281 Lj43
Topkapı Saray TR 130 Mk49
Toplet RO 124 Mc46
Topley CDN (BC) 18 Dg18
Toplica SCG 126 Mb47
Topli Do SCG 126 Mc47
Toplița RO 125 Mf44
Topoháe MEX (SO) 23 Ee31
Topola SCG 126 Ma46
Topolčani MK 126 Mb49
Topol'čany SK 118 Lt42
Topoli RDC 287 Md44
Topoli RDC 287 Me44
Topolobampo MEX (SL) 38 Ef33
Topolog RO 124 Me45
Topolog RO 125 Mj46
Topolovení RO 125 Mf46
Topolovgrad BG 127 Mg48
Topolovo BG 127 Mf49
Toponica SCG 126 Ma47
Toporu RO 125 Mf46
Toppenish USA (WA) 18 Dk22
Toppur IND (TNU) 193 Ok41
Toprag-Qala UZB 153 Oa25
Topsfield USA (ME) 30 Gg23
Tops, Mount AUS 226 Rg56
Top Springs AUS (NT) 223 Rf54
Topura PNG 244 Sf51
Topusko HR 121 Lr45
Tor ETH 283 Mg42
Torâ E 110 Lb49
Toramarkog VRC (QHI) 171 Pj29
To'raqo'rg'on UZB 159 Of25
Torata PE 72 Ge54
Torbalı TR 129 Mh52
Torbantea AUS (QLD) 235 Sg58
Torbat-e-Heydariyeh IR 155 Nk28
Torbat-e Jam IR 155 Oa28
Torbay CDN (NF) 31 Hd22
Torbay Bay AUS 228 Qj62
Torčyn UA 117 Me40
Tordesillas E 106 Kp51
Töre S 91 Mb13
Töreboda S 93 Lp32
Torekov S 94 Ln34
Torelló E 110 Lc48
Toreno E 106 Ko52
Torfjanovka RUS 96 Mh30
Torgaj KZ 133 Nd21
Torgåsmon S 93 Lo30
Torgau D 113 Ln39
Torgelow D 113 Lp37
Torgun RUS 133 Nd20
Torhout B 103 Ld39
Tori IND (JKD) 191 Pc34
Tori RMM 270 Kj39
Toribio CO 60 Gb44
Tori-Bossito DY 280 Lb42
Torigni-sur-Vire F 102 Kt41
Torija E 109 Kr50
Tori-jima J 185 Re32
Toril E 109 Kt50
Torino I 120 Lh45
Torit SUD 283 Mg43
Torkaman IR 154 Nd27
Tormabum WAL 278 Ke42
Tormac RO 124 Mb45
Torna IND 190 Og36
Tornado Mount CDN 19 Ec20
Tornal'a SK 119 Ma42
Torndirrup N.P. AUS 228 Qj63
Torneälven S 90 Ma12
Torneträsk S 90 Lk11
Torneträsk S 90 Lk11
Tornio FIN 91 Mc13
Tornjoš SCG 124 Lu45
Tornquist RA (BA) 81 Gj65
Toro E 106 Kp51
Toro, Cerro del RA/RCH 76 Gf60
Torö S 93 Ls32
Torobi RI 212 Re46
Torobulu RI 209 Rb48
Torodi RN 271 La39
Toro Doum TCH 273 Lj37
Toro Game Reserve EAU 290 Mf45
Törökbálint H 119 Lt43
Torokina PNG 244 Sh49
Toro Kinkéné CI 279 Kh41
Törökszentmiklós H 119 Ma43
Toroli RMM 271 Kj39
Toro Negro Forest USA 47 Gg36
Toronto CDN (ON) 33 Ga24
Torony H 118 Lr43
Toropec RUS 132 Mf17
Tororo EAU 290 Mh45
Toro Toro, P.N. BOL 72 Gh55
Torpathar IND (CGH) 191 Pb34
Torpo N 92 Lj30
Torpshammar S 93 Lr28
Torqabeh IR 155 Nk27
Torquay AUS (VIC) 237 Sc65
Torquay GB 100 Kr40
Torra Bay NAM 298 Lg56
Torrance USA (CA) 22 Ea29
Torrão P 108 Km48
Torre Annunziata I 122 Lp50
Torrebeleña E 109 Kr50
Torreblanca E 110 La50
Torrecampo E 108 Kq48
Torrecilla en Cameros E 107 Ks52
Torre de Belém P 108 Kl48
Torre de Bujaco E 108 Ko49
Torre de la Higuera E 108 Ko47
Torre del Greco I 122 Lp50
Torre de Moncorvo P 106 Kn51
Torre de'Pásseri I 122 Lo48
Torredonjimeno E 108 Kr47
Torrejón de Ardoz E 109 Kr50
Torrelaguna E 109 Kr50
Torrelavega E 107 Kq53
Torremaggiore I 122 Lq49
Torremolinos E 108 Kq46
Torremormojón E 106 Kq51
Torrens Creek AUS (QLD) 233 Sc56
Torrens River AUS 233 Sc57
Torrent E 109 Ku49
Torreón MEX (COH) 39 Ej33
Torre-Pacheco E 109 Kt47
Torre Péllice I 120 Lh46
Torrequemada E 108 Ko49
Torres BR (RS) 79 Hf60
Torres-de-Alcalá MA 259 Kh28
Torres del Paine, P.N. RCH 82 Gd71
Torres Islands VU 246 Td52
Torres mudéjares de Teruel E 109 Kt50
Torres Novas P 108 Km49
Torres Strait AUS/PNG 230 Sa50
Torres Trench 241 Tb21
Torres Vedras P 108 Kl49
Torrevieja E 109 Ku47
Torrey USA (UT) 21 Ee26
Torricelli Mountains PNG 242 Sb47
Torri del Benaco I 120 Ll45
Torriglia I 120 Lk46
Torrijas E 109 Ku50
Torrijos E 109 Kq49
Torrijos RP 203 Rb39
Tørring DK 94 Lk35
Tørring N 90 Lf13
Torrington GB 100 Kq40
Torrington USA (WY) 21 Eh24
Torrock TCH 273 Lh41
Torroella de Montgrí E 110 Ld48
Torronsuon kansallispuisto FIN 96 Md30
Torsåker S 93 Lr30
Torsås S 95 Lq34
Torsborg S 93 Lo28
Torsby S 93 Ln30
Torshälla S 93 Lr31
Tórshavn DK 88 Kc06
Torsö S 93 Lo32
Tortel RCH 82 Gd69
Történeti Emlékpark H 119 Ma44
Tortiya CI 279 Kh41
Tortkol KZ 158 Oe24
To'rtko'l UZB 153 Oa25
Tortola GB 47 Gh36
Tórtoles de Esgueva E 106 Kq51
Tortoli I 111 Lk51
Tortona I 120 Lj46
Tortorici I 122 Lp52
Tortosa E 110 La50
Tortuguero, P.N. NIC 42 Fj40
Torud IR 154 Nh28
Torue RI 209 Ra46
Torugart KS 159 Oh25
Torul TR 145 Mk25
Toruń PL 116 Lt37
Torup S 95 Lo34
Tõrva EST 96 Mf32
Tory RUS (BUR) 172 Qb20
Tory Island IRL 98 Km35
Tory Sound IRL 98 Km35
Toržkovskaja grjada RUS 132 Mh17
Toržok RUS 132 Mh17
Torzym PL 116 Lq38
Tosagua EC 60 Fk46
Tosanachic MEX (CHH) 23 Eg31
Tosa-shimizu J 185 Rg29
Tosa-wan J 183 Rg29
Tosa-wan J 185 Rg29
Tosbara IND (HYA) 188 Oh31
Tosbotn N 90 Lg13
Tosca SA 299 Mb58
Toshino-Kumano N.P. J 183 Rh29
Toshka Project (Southern Valley Development Project) ET 263 Mf34
Tosi SUD 283 Mf40
Toslak TR 131 Mm54
Tosno RUS 132 Mf16
Tosonchengel MNG 172 Pk21
Toson Hu VRC 169 Pj27
Töss CH 114 Lj43
Tostado RA (SF) 77 Gk60
Tõstamaa EST 96 Md32
Tostedt D 112 Lk37
Tosya TR 144 Mh25
Tószeg H 119 Ma43
Tot EAK 290 Mh45
Totak N 92 Lh31
Totana E 109 Kt47
Totata LB 278 Kf42
Totatiche MEX (JLC) 40 Ej35
Toteng RB 299 Mb56
Totes F 102 Lb41
Totiyas SP 291 Nb44
Tótkomlós H 119 Ma44
Tøtlandsvik N 92 Lg31
Totnes GB 100 Kr40
Totness SME 59 Hb43
Toto ANG 288 Lh49
Toto WAN 280 Ld41
Totok RI 209 Rc45
Totonicapán GCA 41 Fe38
Totontepec MEX (OAX) 40 Fb37
Totora BOL 72 Gh54
Totora BOL 72 Gg54
Totoral RCH 76 Ge59
Totoral RCH 76 Ge59
Totoralejos RA (CD) 76 Gh60
Totora Palca BOL 72 Gh55
Totoras RA (SF) 77 Gk62
Totoya FJI 247 Ua55
Tottenham AUS (NSW) 237 Sd62
Tottori J 183 Rh28
Totumito YV 57 Ge42
Totutla MEX (VC) 40 Fb36

Tou BF 271 Kj39
Touâjil RIM 264 Kd34
Touâret RN 266 Ld35
Touat DZ 259 Kk32
Touba CI 278 Kg41
Touba SN 269 Kc38
Toubakouta SN 269 Kb39
Toubéré Bafal SN 269 Kd38
Toubkal, P.N.du MA 258 Kf30
Touboro CAM 281 Lh42
Toucy F 103 Ld43
Touérât RMM 271 Kj37
Tougan BF 271 Kj39
Tougé RG 278 Ke40
Touggourt DZ 260 Ld29
Tougnifili RG 278 Kc40
Tougouri BF 271 Kk39
Tougoutaou RN 272 Ld38
Touho F 246 Tc56
Touijînet RIM 270 Kf36
Touil RIM 269 Ke38
Toukoroba RMM 270 Kg39
Toukoto RMM 270 Kf39
Toul F 103 Lf42
Touléplеu CI 278 Kf42
Touli RC 179 Ra34
Toulon F 105 Lf47
Toulon-sur-Arroux F 105 Le44
Toulounga TCH 282 Lk40
Toulouse F 104 Lb47
Toumbélaga RN 272 Ld38
Toumkous RN 271 La38
Toumodi CI 279 Kh42
Toumoundjila RG 278 Kf40
Touna RMM 270 Kh39
Tounfafi RN 272 Lc38
Toungo WAN 281 Lg41
Toungoo MYA 196 Pj36
Tougour TCH 274 Lk37
Toura BF 271 Kk39
Toura DY 272 Lb40
Tourassine RIM 264 Ke33
Tourba TCH 273 Lh39
Tourcoing F 103 Ld40
Tour Eiffel F 103 Lc42
Tourine RIM 264 Ke34
Tourlaville F 102 Kt41
Tournai B 103 Ld40
Tournavista PE 66 Gc50
Tourni BF 279 Kh40
Tournon-d'Agenais F 104 Lb46
Tournon-sur-Rhône F 105 Le45
Tournus F 105 Le44
Touros BR (RN) 65 Jc48
Touroua CAM 273 Lg40
Touroua CAM 273 Lg41
Touroug MA 258 Kh30
Tourou kоro BF 279 Kh40
Touroungoumbé RMM 270 Kf38
Tours F 102 La43
Toury F 103 Lb42
Tousséguéla RMM 278 Kg40
Toussiana BF 279 Kh40
Toutes Aides CDN (MB) 24 Fa20
Toutoukro CI 279 Kh42
Toutswemogala Hill RB 299 Md56
Touws SA 302 Ma62
Touws River SA 302 Ma62
Töv MNG 172 Qc22
Tovar YV 56 Ge41
Tovar YV 57 Gg40
Tovarankurichchi IND (TNU) 193 Ok41
Tovarkovskij RUS 133 Mk19
Tovarnik HR 124 Lu45
Tovste UA 125 Mf42
Tovuz AZ 152 Nc25
Tow USA (TX) 28 Fa30
Towada J 183 Sa25
Towada-Hachimantai N.P. J 183 Sa26
Towai LB 278 Kf42
Towakaima GUY 58 Ha42
Towale RI 209 Qk46
Towanda USA (PA) 33 Gb25
Towari RI 211 Ra48
Towcester GB 101 Ku38
Tower = Isla Genovesa EC 60 Ff45
Tower USA (MN) 27 Fd22
Towera AUS (WA) 224 Qh57
Towerhill River AUS 232 Sc56
Tower of London GB 101 Ku39
Tower of Silence IR 154 Nh30
Tower Peak AUS 229 Rb62
Towi RI 209 Ra46
Towla ZW 300 Me56
Towle SA 300 Me57
Towner USA (ND) 24 Ek21
Towner USA (CO) 26 Ej26
Townsend USA (MT) 21 Ee22
Townshend Island AUS 233 Sf57
Townsville AUS (QLD) 233 Sd55
Towot SUD 283 Mh42
Towraghondi AFG 160 Ob28
Towrana AUS (WA) 224 Oh58
Towr Ham AFG 161 Of28
Towson USA (MD) 33 Gb26
Toya-ko J 181 Sb24
Toyama J 183 Rj27
Toyama-wan J 183 Rj27
Toyo J 183 Rh29
Toyohashi J 183 Rj28
Toyokawa J 183 Rj28
Toyooka J 183 Rh28
Toyos HN 42 Fg38
Toyota J 183 Rj28
Toyotomi J 181 Sa23
Toypapkeh RI 211 Qh50
Töysä FIN 96 Md28
To'ytepa UZB 158 Oe25
Tozeur TN 260 Le29
Tozitna River USA 15 Cd13
Tqibuli GE 152 Nb24
Tqvarčeli GE 152 Na24
Trabanca E 106 Ko51
Traben-Trarbach D 114 Lh41
Trablous RL 146 Mh28
Tra Bong VN 197 Qe38
Trabzon TR 145 Mk25
Tracadie CDN (NB) 31 Gh22
Tra Co Beach VN 178 Qd35
Tracy USA (CA) 20 Dk27
Tracy City USA (TN) 34 Fh28
Traditional war-dances RI 206 Pj45
Trælleborg DK 94 Lm35
Trafalgar AUS (VIC) 237 Sd65
Tragacete E 109 Kt50
Tragoncillo E 109 Ks48
Trahiá GR 128 Md53
Traiguén RCH 80 Gd65
Trail CDN (BC) 18 Eb21
Trail USA (OR) 20 Dj24
Train du Désert RIM 264 Kd34
Traipu BR (AL) 71 Jb50
Traírão BR 63 He49
Trairi BR (CE) 65 Ja47
Trairi BR 65 Jc49
Traisen A 115 Lq42
Traiskirchen A 115 Lr42
Trakai LT 97 Me35
Trakan Phut Phon THA 197 Qc38
Tra Kieu Citadel VN 197 Qe38
Traku istorinis n.p. LT 97 Me35
Tralee IRL 100 Kl38
Tralee Bay IRL 100 Kl38
Tramandaí BR (RS) 78 He61
Tramore IRL 100 Kn38
Tra My VN 197 Qe38
Trăn BG 126 Mc48
Tranås S 95 Lp32
Trancas RA (TU) 76 Gh59
Trancoso BR (BA) 75 Ja54
Tranemo S 95 Lo33
Tranent GB 99 Ks35
Trang THA 198 Pk42
Trangan RI 213 Rh49
Trang Bang VN 197 Qd40
Trang Dinh VN 178 Qd34
Trangie AUS (NSW) 237 Sd62
Trani I 123 Lr49
Tranomaro RM 306 Nd58
Tranoroa RM 306 Nc58
Tran Phu VN 197 Qd40
Tranqueras ROU 77 Hc61
Tranšah IR 154 Nd27
Transamazônica BR 63 Hd47
Transantarctic Mountains ANT 312 Jc35
Trans Australian Railway AUS 229 Rg61
Trans-Canada Highway CDN 19 Ee19
Trans-Canada Highway CDN 25 Fh21
Transhimalaya 164 Od12
Transpantaneira BR 69 Hb54
Transsib RUS 133 Na16
Transsib RUS 173 Qh20
Trans-Sumatra-Highway RI 206 Qa45
Transtrand S 93 Lo29
Transua CI 279 Kj42
Transylvania RO 124 Md44
Transylvanian Alps RO 124 Md45
Tra On VN 199 Qc41
Trapalco, Cerro RA 80 Gf65
Trápani I 122 Ln52
Trappstegsforsarna S 90 Lh13
Traralgon AUS (VIC) 237 Sd65
Trarza RIM 269 Kc37
Trasacco I 122 Lo49
Trashigang BHT 194 Pf32
Trás os Montes P 106 Kn51
Trat THA 197 Qb39
Traun A 115 Lp42
Traunreut D 115 Ln43
Traunsee A 115 Lo43
Traunstein D 115 Ln43
Travellers Village AUS (SA) 229 Re61
Travemünde D 113 Ll37
Traverse City USA (MI) 32 Fh23
Traverse Peak USA (AK) 15 Ca13
Travesía de Tunuyán RA 76 Gg62
Travesía Puntana RA 76 Gg63
Tra Vinh VN 199 Qd41
Travnik BIH 121 Ls46
Travo F 111 Lk49
Trawas RI 206 Qb47
Trawniki PL 117 Mc39
Trayning AUS (WA) 228 Qj61
Trbovlje SLO 121 Lq44
Treasure Beach JA 45 Gb37
Treasury Islands SOL 244 Sh49
Trebbia I 120 Lk46
Trebbin D 113 Lo38
Trebel D 113 Ln36
Třebíč CZ 118 Lq41
Trebinje BIH 126 Lt48
Trebisacce I 123 Lr51
Trebisov SK 119 Mb42
Trebinka PL 117 Mb38
Trebnje SLO 121 Lp45
Třeboň CZ 118 Lp41
Trebonne AUS (QLD) 233 Sd55
Trecate I 120 Lj45
Tre Cime I 120 Ln44
Treene D 112 Lk36
Tree of Knowledge AUS 233 Sc57
Treffurt D 112 Ll39
Tregaron GB 100 Kr38
Trégastel-Plage F 102 Kr42
Tregor USA (MT) 18 Ec21
Tregrosse Islets AUS 233 Sf54
Tréguier F 102 Kr42
Treherne CDN (MB) 24 Fa21
Trehgolovyj Gorez RUS 172 Qd19
Treignac F 104 Lb45
Trei Ierarhi RO 125 Mh43
Treinta y Tres ROU 77 Hc62
Treis-Karden D 112 Lh40
Treis-Karden D 114 Lh40
Trejo MEX (OAX) 41 Fc37
Trekkopje NAM 298 Lh57
Trekljano BG 126 Mc48
Trélazé F 102 Ku43
Trelew RA (CB) 80 Gh67
Trelleborg S 95 Lo35
Tremadog Bay GB 100 Kq38
Trembleur Lake CDN 18 Dh18
Trementina USA (NM) 23 Eh28
Tremen, Volcán RA 80 Ge64
Tremezzo I 120 Lk45
Tremonton USA (UT) 21 Ed25
Tremp E 110 La48
Trenary USA (MI) 32 Fg22
Trenčiansky hrad SK 118 Lt42
Trenčín SK 118 Lt42
Trenel RA (LP) 76 Gh63
Trenggalek RI 210 Qf50
Trenino Verde I 111 Lk51
Trenque Lauquen RA (BA) 81 Gj63
Trent GB 101 Ku37
Trentham AUS (VIC) 237 Sc64
Trentham Gardens NZ 238 Th66
Trentino-Alto Adige I 120 Lm44
Trento I 120 Lm44
Trento RP 205 Rd41
Trenton CDN (ON) 33 Gb23
Trenton USA (MO) 27 Fd25
Trenton USA (TN) 29 Ff28
Trenton USA (NJ) 33 Gc25
Trenton USA (FL) 36 Fj31
Trepassey Bay CDN 31 Hd22
Trephina Gorge N.P. AUS 227 Rh57
Tres Altitos, Cerro RA 76 Gf62
Três Arroios BR (RS) 78 Hd59
Tres Arroyos RA (BA) 81 Gk65
Três Barras BR (SC) 79 Hf59
Tres Bocas RA (ER) 77 Ha62
Tres Bocas YV 56 Gd41
Três Casas BR (AM) 62 Gj49
Tres Cerros RA 80 Ge67
Tres Chorros BR (MG) 80 Gf64
Três Corações BR (MG) 75 Hh56
Tres Cruces, Cerro MEX 41 Fd38
Tres Cruces RA (PJ) 72 Gh57
Tres Cruces, Nevado RA/RCH 76 Gf59
Tres Cruces RCH 76 Gf59
Três de Maio BR (RS) 78 Hc59
Tres Esquinas CO 60 Gc45
Tresfjord N 92 Lh28
Tres Isletas RA (CH) 77 Gk59
Três Lagoas BR (MS) 74 He56
Tres Lagos RA (SC) 82 Ge70
Tres Lomas RA (BA) 81 Gj64
Três Mapejos BOL 67 Gh51
Três Marias BR (MG) 75 Hh55
Tres Morros RA (PJ) 72 Gh57
Trespaderne E 107 Kr52
Trespassey CDN (NF) 31 Hd22
Três Passos BR (RS) 78 Hd59
Tres Picos RA (BA) 81 Gj65
Tres Picos, Cerro RA 81 Gj65
Tres Piedras USA (NM) 23 Eh27
Três Pinheiros BR (SC) 78 He59
Três Pontas BR (MG) 75 Hh56
Tres Praias BR (AM) 67 Gg50
Tres Ranchos BR (GO) 74 Hg55
Tres Rios BR (RJ) 75 Hj57
Tressillian AUS (QLD) 233 Sd57
Trestickans n.p. S 92 Lm31
Tres Unidos BR (AM) 67 Gf49
Tres Zapotes MEX 40 Fc36
Tretjakovo RUS 167 Pa20
Tretten N 92 Ll29
Treuchtlingen D 115 Ll42
Treuenbrietzen D 113 Ln38
Trevelín RA (CB) 80 Ge67
Trevi I 121 Ln48
Treviglio I 120 Lk45
Treviso I 120 Ln45
Triabunna AUS (TAS) 236 Sd67
Trianggulasi RI 211 Qh50
Triangle ZW 300 Mf56
Trianon RH 46 Gd36
Tribeč SK 118 Lt42
Tribugá CO 56 Gb43
Tribune USA (KS) 26 Ek26
Tribunj HR 121 Lq47
Trica-Có RA (RN) 80 Gg65
Tricárico I 123 Lr50
Tricase I 123 Lt51
Trichur = Thrissur IND (KER) 192 Oj41
Trichy = Tiruchirapalli IND (TNU) 193 Ok41
Trici BR (CE) 65 Hk48
Tri City USA (OR) 20 Dj24
Trida AUS (NSW) 237 Sc62
Trident Shoal 204 Qh40
Triduba UA 125 Mi42
Triebel D 113 Lo39
Trieben A 115 Lp43
Trier D 114 Lg41
Trieste I 121 Lo45
Trie-sur-Baïse F 104 La47
Trifești RO 125 Mh43
Triglav SLO 121 Lo44
Triglavski narodni park SLO 121 Lo44
Trignac F 102 Ks43
Trigno I 122 Lp49
Trigono GR 126 Mb50
Trikala GR 126 Mb51
Trikéri GR 128 Md51
Trikkandimadu CL 193 Pa43
Trikkavilu IND (KER) 192 Oh41
Trikora Beach RI 207 Qc45
Trilbar AUS (WA) 224 Qj58
Trill RA (LP) 81 Gj63
Trillo E 109 Ks50
Trilsbeck Lake CDN 25 Fj20
Trim IRL 100 Ko37
Trimouille Islands AUS 224 Qh56
Trincheira Bacajá, T.I. BR 63 He48
Trincheira, T.I. BR 62 Ha47
Trincheras MEX (SO) 23 Ee30
Trincomalee CL 193 Pa42
Trindade BR (PE) 71 Hk49
Trindade BR (GO) 74 Hf54
Třinec CZ 118 Lt41
Trinidad AUS (QLD) 234 Sb58
Trinidad BOL 68 Gh53
Trinidad C 44 Fk35
Trinidad CO 56 Ge43
Trinidad PY 77 Hc59
Trinidad ROU 77 Hb62
Trinidad TT 58 Gk40
Trinidad USA (CA) 20 Dh25
Trinidad USA (CO) 23 Eh27
Trinidad and Tobago TT 47 Gk40
Trinidad del Paraná PY 77 Hc59
Trinidade BR (PA) 64 Hf47
Trinitápoli I 123 Lr49
Trinity USA 20 Dj25
Trinity USA (TX) 29 Fc30
Trinity USA 29 Fc30
Trinity Bay AUS (QLD) 233 Sc54
Trinity Bay CDN 31 Hd22
Trinity East CDN (NF) 31 Hd21
Trinity Peninsula 312 Ha31
Trinity Range USA 20 Ea25
Trinity Site USA 23 Eg29
Trinkitat SUD 277 Mj37
Trino I 120 Lj45
Triora I 120 Lh47
Trios BR (PA) 59 Hc44
Tripoli GR 128 Mc53
Tripoli LAR 260 Lg29
Tripoli RL 146 Mh28
Tripolitania LAR 260 Lf30
Tripp USA (SD) 26 Fb24
Tripunithura IND (KER) 192 Oj42
Tripura IND 186 Pc14
Tristan da Cunha GB 253 Ka13
Tristeza, Cerro YV 57 Gj40
Trisul IND 189 Ok30
Trisuli River Rafting NEP 170 Pc32
Tri Ton VN 199 Qc40
Triunvirato RA (BA) 77 Gk63
Trivandrum = Thiruvananthapuram IND (KER) 192 Oj42
Trivento I 122 Lp49
Trjavna BG 127 Mf48
Trnava SK 118 Ls42
Trnovacko jezero SCG 126 Lt47
Trnovo BIH 121 Lt47
Trobriand Islands PNG 244 Sf50
Trocany SK 119 Mb41
Trocará, T.I. BR 64 Hf47
Trocoman RA 80 Ge64
Trödje S 93 Ls30
Troekurovo RUS 133 Mk19
Trofaiach A 115 Lp43
Trofors N 90 Lg13
Trogir HR 121 Lr47
Troglan Bara SCG 126 Mb47
Troglav HR/BIH 121 Lr47
Tróia I 122 Lq49
Tróia P 108 Km48
Troick RUS 140 Oa08
Troickaja RUS 135 Mk23
Troic'ke UA 125 Mi43
Troickoe RUS 180 Rj21
Troisdorf D 112 Lh40
Trois-Pistoles CDN (QC) 30 Gf21
Trois Rivières CDN (QC) 30 Gd22
Trois Sauts F 59 Hd44
Troița Nouă MD 125 Mk44
Troize-Sergieva Lavra RUS 132 Mk17
Troizkij sobor RUS 133 Nc20
Troizki monastyr RUS 133 Na18
Trojaci MK 126 Mb49
Trojan BG 127 Me48
Trojanski manastir BG 127 Me48
Trolla TCH 273 Lh38
Trollhättan S 92 Ln32
Trollhätte kanal S 92 Ln32
Trollstigen N 92 Lh28
Trolltinden N 92 Lh28
Trombetas BR 63 Hb46
Tromelin F 307 Nh53
Tromostovje SLO 121 Lp44
Tromøya N 92 Lj32
Trompsburg SA 303 Mc61
Tromsø N 90 Lk11
Tronador, Cerro RA/RCH 80 Ge66
Tronadora CR 42 Fh40
Troncones MEX (GUR) 40 Ek37
Troncoso MEX (ZCT) 39 Ej34
Trøndelag N 90 Lf14
Trondheim N 90 Lf14
Trondheimsfjorden N 90 Lf14
Tronto I 121 Lo48
Troodos Mountains CY 131 Mn56
Troon GB 99 Kq35
Tropaion Traiani RO 125 Mh46
Tropas BR 63 Hb49
Tropea I 123 Lq52
Tropic of Cancer Beach BS 37 Gc34
Trosa S 93 Ls32
Troškas LV 97 Mg34
Troškūnai LT 97 Me35
Trosna RUS 132 Mh19
Trostan' RUS 132 Mg19
Trostberg D 115 Ln42
Trostjanec' UA 132 Mh20
Trostjanskij RUS 133 Nb20
Trotters USA (ND) 26 Ej22
Trotuș RO 125 Mg44
Trou du Natron TCH 274 Lj35
Troup USA (TX) 29 Fc29
Trourbeck ZW 300 Mg55
Trout Creek CDN (ON) 33 Ga23
Trout Creek USA (MT) 19 Ec22
Trout Lake CDN 24 Fd20
Trout Lake USA (WA) 20 Dk23
Trout Lake USA (MI) 32 Fh22
Trout River CDN 19 Ec17
Trout River CDN (NF) 31 Ha21
Trouville-sur-Mer F 102 La41
Trowbridge GB 101 Ks39
Trowutta AUS (TAS) 236 Sc66
Troy TR 130 Mg51
Troy USA (MT) 19 Ec21
Troy USA (KS) 27 Fc26
Troy USA (OH) 32 Fh25
Troy USA (PA) 33 Gb25
Troy USA (NY) 33 Gd24
Troy USA (AL) 35 Fh30
Troy USA (NC) 35 Ga28
Troya RA 76 Gf59
Troyes F 103 Le42
Troyitsko monastyr UA 132 Mf20
Troy Peak USA 20 Ec26
Troyya G 281 Lg45
Trsa SCG 126 Lt47
Trsat HR 121 Lp45
Tršće HR 121 Lp45
Trstená SK 119 Lu41
Trstenik SCG 126 Ma47
Truant Island AUS 223 Rj51
Truaru, T.I. BR 58 Gk44
Trubčevsk RUS 132 Mg19
Trubetčino RUS 133 Mk19
Truch CDN (BC) 17 Dj17
Truckee USA (CA) 20 Dk26
Trud BG 127 Me48
Truer Range AUS 226 Rf57
Trujillo E 108 Kp49
Trujillo HN 42 Fg38
Trujillo PE 66 Ga50
Trujillo YV 57 Ge41
Trukwel EAK 290 Mh44
Trulli di Alberobello I 123 Ls50
Trumann USA (AR) 29 Fe28
Trumbull, Mount USA 22 Ed27
Trumieje PL 116 Lu37
Trumon RI 198 Pj44
Trun F 102 La42
Trundle AUS (NSW) 237 Sd62
Trunkey AUS (NSW) 237 Se62
Truro CDN (NS) 31 Gj23
Truro GB 100 Kp40
Trusan MAL 204 Qh43
Trușești RO 125 Mh43
Truskavec' UA 119 Md41
Trus Madi, Gunung MAL 204 Qj43
Trussville USA (AL) 34 Fg29
Trustrup DK 94 Ll34
Truth or Consequences USA (NM) 23 Eg29
Trutnov CZ 118 Lq40
Truva TR 130 Mg51
Truyère F 105 Lc45
Tryon USA (NE) 26 Ek25
Tryphena NZ 238 Th64
Trysilelva N 92 Lm29
Trysilfjellet N 92 Lm29
Tryškiai LT 97 Mc34
Tržac BIH 121 Lq46
Trzcianka PL 116 Lr37
Trzcianne PL 117 Mc37
Trzciel PL 116 Lq38
Trzcinna PL 116 Lq38
Trzcińsko-Zdrój PL 116 Lp38
Trzebiatów PL 116 Lq36
Trzebień PL 116 Lq39
Trzebinia PL 117 Lu40
Trzebnica PL 116 Ls39
Trzemeszno PL 116 Ls38
Trzydnik Duży PL 117 Mc40
Tsabit DZ 259 Kk31
Tsadumu IND (KTK) 193 Ok40
Tsagaan Agui Cave MNG 172 Qa23
Tsagaan Chulunta VRC (QHI) 169 Pg26
Tsagaandörvölj MNG 173 Qe23
Tsagaannuur MNG 167 Pe21
Tsagaannuur MNG 173 Qk22
Tsagaan Olom MNG 172 Pj22
Tsagaan-Ovoo MNG 172 Qa23
Tsagaan Shiveet Uul Nature Reserve MNG 167 Pf20
Tsagaan Tsavyn MNG 174 Qe23
Tsagaan Uul MNG 172 Qa20
Tsageri GE 152 Nb24
Tsama RCB 281 Lh46
Tsamia RN 272 Le38
Tsandi NAM 294 Lh54
Tsangano MW 297 Mh53
Tsant MNG 172 Qd22
Tsanyawa WAN 272 Ld39
Tsaobis Leopard Nature Park NAM 298 Lh57
Tsarahonenana RM 305 Ne53
Tsaramandroso RM 306 Nd54
Tsaratanana RM 305 Ne53
Tsaratanana RM 306 Nd54
Tsaravinany RM 306 Ne55
Tsaraxhoogte Pass NAM 298 Lj58
Tsast Uul MNG 167 Pg21
Tsatsu RB 299 Mc58
Tsau RB 299 Mb56
Tsauchab NAM 298 Lh58
Tsavdan MNG 167 Ph21
Tsavo EAK 293 Mk47
Tsavo East N.P. EAK 291 Mk47
Tsavo West N.P. EAK 291 Mk47
Tsawah LAR 267 Lg32
Tseikuru EAK 291 Mk46
Tsembo RCB 288 Lg47
Tsengel MNG 172 Qa21
Tsentralnyye Karakumy TM 153 Nk26
Tsepélovo GR 128 Ma51
Tses NAM 298 Lk58
Tseteng RB 299 Mb57
Tsetserleg MNG 172 Qa22
Tsévié RT 279 La42
Tshabong RB 302 Mb59
Tshako RDC 289 Mb50
Tshala RDC 289 Mb50
Tshane RB 299 Ma57
Tshela RDC 288 Lg48
Tshesebe RB 299 Md56
Tshibala RDC 289 Ma49
Tshibamba RDC 289 Mb50
Tshibambula RDC 289 Mb48
Tshibeke RDC 292 Me47
Tshibuka RDC 289 Ma49
Tshibwika RDC 289 Mb49
Tshidilamolomo SA 299 Mc58
Tshie RDC 289 Mb50
Tshikapa RDC 289 Ma49
Tshikula RDC 289 Mb49
Tshilenge RDC 289 Mb49
Tshimbalanga RDC 289 Mb50
Tshimbok RDC 289 Mc49
Tshimbulu RDC 289 Mb49
Tshimbungu RDC 289 Mb50
Tshinsenda RDC 296 Md52
Tshintshanku RDC 289 Mb49
Tshipise SA 300 Mf57
Tshisenge RDC 289 Ma49
Tshisonge RDC 289 Mb50
Tshitadi RDC 289 Ma49
Tshitanzu RDC 289 Mb50
Tshiturapadsi ZW 300 Mf57
Tshofa RDC 288 Mc48
Tshokwane SA 300 Mf58
Tsholotsho ZW 299 Md55
Tshongwe RDC 289 Mc49
Tshootsha RB 299 Ma57
Tshopo RDC 287 Mc45
Tshuapa RDC 286 Lk46
Tshuapa GUY 58 Gk42
Tshwane = Pretoria SA 299 Me58
Tsiaki RCB 288 Lg47
Tsianaloka RM 306 Nc56
Tsimafana RM 306 Nc55
Tsimanampetsotsa, P.N.de RM 306 Nb58
Tsimazava RM 306 Nc56
Tsimpsean Ind. Res. CDN 17 De18
Tsineng SA 302 Mb59
Tsingtao VRC (SDG) 182 Ra27
Tsingy de Bemaraha, P.N.des RM 306 Nc55
Tsinjoariva RM 306 Nd55
Tsinjomitondraka RM 304 Nd53
Tsintsabis NAM 298 Lj55
Tsiombe RM 306 Nc58
Tsiribihina RM 306 Nc55
Tsiroanomandidy RM 306 Nd55
Tsitondroina RM 306 Nd56
Tsitsikamma N.P. SA 302 Mb63
Tsivory RM 306 Nd58
Tsodilo RB 299 Ma55
Tsodilo Hills RB 299 Ma55
Tsoe RB 299 Mc56
Tsogstsalu MNG 172 Qd22
Tsolo SA 303 Me61
Tsomo SA 303 Md61
Tsomo SA 303 Md62
Tso Morari 161 Ok29
Tsondab NAM 298 Lh57
Tsondabvlei NAM 298 Lh58
Tsonjiyn Chuluu MNG 173 Qf23
Tsqaltubo GE 152 Nb24
Tsu J 183 Rj28
Tsubata J 183 Rj27
Tsuchiura J 183 Sa27
Tsugaru Q.N.P. J 183 Sa25
Tsugaru Strait J 181 Sa25
Tsujima J 182 Re28
Tsuli ZW 299 Md55
Tsumbiri RDC 288 Lj47
Tsumeb NAM 298 Lj55
Tsumis Park NAM 298 Lj57
Tsumkwe NAM 299 Ma55
Tsundupalle IND (APH) 193 Ok40
Tsuruga J 183 Rj28
Tsurugi-san J 183 Rh29
Tsurui J 181 Sc24
Tsuruoka J 183 Rk26
Tsuyama J 183 Rh28
Tswaane RB 299 Mb57
Tswalu Private Desert Reserve SA 302 Mb59
Tswapong Hills RB 299 Md57
T-Tree Bay AUS 235 Sg59
Tual RI 212 Rg48
Tuam IRL 98 Km37
Tua Marine National Park = Bunaken-Manado Tua Marine National Park RI 209 Rc45
Tuamotu Archipelago 317 Cb11
Tuamotu Ridge 317 Cb12
Tuanake Atoll F 249 Ch54
Tuanan RI 208 Qh47
Tuan Giao VN 195 Qb35
Tuangku RI 198 Pj44
Tuao RP 203 Ra37
Tuapse RUS 135 Mk23
Tuaran MAL 204 Qj42
Tua River PNG 243 Sc49
Tuba City USA (AZ) 23 Ee27
Tubaï-Manu F 249 Ce54
Tuban RI 210 Qg49
Tubarão BR (SC) 79 Hf60
Tubaraõ Latunde, T.I. BR 68 Gk52
Tubarjal KSA 146 Mk30
Tubau MAL 208 Qg44
Tubbataha Reef National Marine Park RP 204 Qk41
Tubbergen NL 112 Lg38
Tubeya RDC 289 Mb49
Tubigon RP 205 Rb41
Tübingen D 114 Lk42
Tubisyimita RI 213 Rg46
Tubize B 103 Le40
Tübkaraghan müyis KZ 152 Nf23
Tubo WAN 272 Ld40
Tubod RP 205 Rb41
Tubou FJI 247 Ua55
Tubruq LAR 261 Mb29
Tubruq War Cemeteries LAR 261 Mb29
Tubuai Islands 317 Ca12
Tuburan RP 205 Rb40
Tubutama MEX (SO) 23 Ee30
Tucacas YV 56 Gf40
Tucano BR (BA) 71 Ja51
Tucavaca BOL 73 Ha55
Tuchan F 104 Lc48
Tucheng VRC (GZH) 178 Qc32
Tuchitua CDN (YT) 17 Df15
Tuchola PL 116 Ls37
Tucholski Park Krajobrazowy PL 116 Lt37
Tuchów PL 119 Mb41
Tuckanarra AUS (WA) 224 Qj59
Tucker Glacier 313 Tb33
Tučovo RUS 132 Mj18
Tucson USA (AZ) 23 Ee29
Tucumã BR (AM) 62 Ha49
Tucumã BR (PA) 63 He49
Tucumán RA 55 Gc24
Tucumcari USA (NM) 23 Ej28
Tucunaré PE 66 Ga49
Tucuña CO 61 Ge45
Tucunaré BR (AM) 62 Gh45
Tucupido YV 57 Gh41
Tucupita YV 58 Gj41
Tucuriba BR (AM) 62 Ha48
Tucurui BR (PA) 64 Hf47
Tucu-Tucu RA (SC) 82 Ge70
Tuczna PL 117 Md39
Tuczno PL 116 Lq38
Tuczno PL 116 Lr37
Tudela E 106 Kq51
Tudela de Duero E 106 Kq51
Tudu EST 96 Mg31
Tudulinna EST 96 Mh31
Tudun Wada WAN 272 Le40
Tuejar E 109 Kt49
Tuèkta RUS (ALT) 167 Pc20
Tuena AUS (NSW) 237 Se63
Tu-Endie-Wei S.P. USA 33 Fk26
Tueré BR 63 He47
Tuerjishan Reservoir VRC 182 Rb24
Tufeni RO 125 Me46
Tufi PNG 243 Se50
Tufi Dive Resort PNG 243 Se50
Tug VRC (NMZ) 175 Qe26
Tug Der SP 285 Nd41
Tugela SA 303 Mf60
Tugela SA 303 Mf60
Tugela Ferry SA 303 Mf60
Tughyl KZ 167 Pc22
Tugidak Island USA 16 Cc17
Tugu GH 279 Kk41
Tuguegarao RP 203 Ra37
Tugyi MYA 196 Ph37
Tuhala EST 96 Me31
Tuham, Gunung RI 208 Qg45
Tuherahera F 249 Cf53
Tui E 106 Km52
Tuichi BOL 67 Gf53
Tuilibigeal AUS (NSW) 237 Sd62
Tuin MK 126 Mb49
Tuina RCH 72 Gf57
Tuineje E 264 Kc31
Tuiué BR (AM) 62 Gj48
Tuiyk KZ 159 Ok24
Tūja LV 97 Me33
Tujmazy RUS 133 Ng18
Tujn gol MNG 172 Qa23
Tujun RUS 180 Rg20
Tujuwe RI 211 Ra48
Tukarak Island CDN 25 Ga17
Tukayel ETH 285 Nc41
Tükh ET 263 Mf30
Tuki SOL 244 Sj49
Tukola Tolha VRC (QHI) 171 Ph29
Tukosmera VU 246 Te55
Tukrah LAR 261 Ma29
Tuktoyatuk CDN 10 Db05
Tukuhora F 249 Ch54
Tukums LV 97 Md34
Tukuna Porto Espiritual, T.I. BR 61 Gf48
Tukuna Santo Antonio, T.I. BR 61 Gf48
Tukuna Umariaçu, T.I. BR 61 Gf48
Tukuyu EAT 292 Mg50
Tula EAK 291 Mk46
Tula EAK 291 Mk46
Tula MEX (TM) 39 Fa34
Tula MEX 40 Fa35
Tula RUS 132 Mj18
Tula USA 248 Be53
Tula de Allende MEX (HDG) 40 Fa35
Tulak AFG 160 Ob29
Tulameen CDN (BC) 18 Dk21
Tulancingo MEX (HDG) 40 Fa35
Tulare SCG 126 Mb48
Tulare USA (CA) 22 Ea27
Tulare USA (SD) 26 Fa23
Tularosa USA (NM) 23 Eg29
Tulate GCA 41 Fe38
Tulayhah IRQ 147 Na29
Tula Yiri WAN 273 Lf41
Tulbagh SA 302 Lk62
Tulcán EC 60 Gb45
Tulcea RO 125 Mj45
Tul'čyn UA 134 Me21
Tule RI 205 Rd43
Tulebaevo KZ 166 Ok22
Tüledy araldary KZ 152 Nf23
Tulehu RI 212 Re47
Tulga AUS (QLD) 232 Sb57
Tulghes RO 125 Mf43
Tulia USA (TX) 28 Ek28
Tuli Block RB 299 Md58
Tuligul UA 125 Mj43
Tuligul'nic'kij liman UA 125 Mm44
Tulihe VRC (NMZ) 173 Ra20
Tulijá MEX 41 Fd37
Tuliszków PL 116 Lt38
Tuljupur IND (MHT) 190 Oj37
Tullah AUS (TAS) 236 Sc66
Tullahoma USA (TN) 34 Fg28
Tullamore AUS (NSW) 237 Sd62
Tullamore IRL 100 Kn37
Tulle F 104 Lb45
Tulln A 115 Lr42
Tullos USA (LA) 29 Fd30
Tullow IRL 100 Ko38
Tullus SUD 282 Mc40
Tully AUS (QLD) 233 Sc54
Tulovice PL 116 Ls40
Tulsa USA (OK) 29 Fb27
Tulsipur IND (UPH) 189 Pb32
Tulsipur NEP 170 Pb31
Tulsk IRL 98 Km37
Tulu PNG 243 Sc48
Tuluá CO 56 Gb43
Tulu Bobo ETH 284 Mk41
Tuluca BR (AM) 61 Gf45
Tulu Deemtu ETH 284 Mk42
Tuluksak USA (AK) 14 Bk15
Tulul Al Ashaqif JOR 146 Mj29
Tulum MEX 41 Fg35
Tulum MEX (QTR) 41 Fg35
Tulumayo PE 66 Gc51
Tulumayo RDC 289 Mb49
Tulun RUS 140 Qa08
Tulungagung RI 210 Qf50
Tulungselapan RI 207 Qc47
Tulun Islands PNG 244 Sh48
Tulu Welel ETH 283 Mh41
Tulyčiv UA 117 Me39
Tuma RUS 133 Na18
Tumaco CO 60 Ga45
Tuman PE 66 Ga49
Tumauini RP 203 Ra37
Tumba RDC 289 Mb47
Tumba S 93 Ls31
Tumbangjul RI 208 Qf46
Tumbangkiran RI 208 Qg46
Tumbangmirih RI 208 Qg46
Tumbangsamba RI 208 Qg46
Tumbangtalaken RI 208 Qg46
Tumbanlahung RI 208 Qh46
Tumbarumba AUS (NSW) 237 Sd63
Tumbes PE 60 Fk47
Tumbiscatío de Ruiz MEX (MHC) 40 Ej36
Tumbler Ridge CDN (BC) 18 Dk18
Tumbukut MYA 195 Pj33
Tumbwe RDC 296 Md51
Tumby Bay AUS (SA) 236 Rj63
Tumd Youyi VRC (NMZ) 175 Qf25
Tumd Zuoqi VRC (NMZ) 175 Qf25
Tumen VRC (JLN) 182 Re24
Tumen Gang DVRK/VRC 182 Re24
Tumen Jiang VRC/DVRK 182 Re24
Tumeremo YV 58 Gk42
Tumgaon IND (CGH) 191 Pb35
Tumia, T.I. BR 67 Gg49
Tumindao Island RP 204 Qk43
Tumkur IND (KTK) 193 Oj40
Tumlingtan NEP 170 Pd32
Tumner IND (CGH) 191 Pa36
Tumnin RUS 181 Sa21
Tumpat MAL 199 Qa42
Tumsar IND (MHT) 191 Ok35
Tumu GH 279 Kk40
Tumucumaque, P.N. do BR 63 Hd45
Tumupasa BOL 67 Gg53
Tumut AUS (NSW) 237 Se63
Tuna GH 279 Kj41
Tuna IND (GUJ) 190 Of34
Tunaca YV 57 Gg42
Tunadal S 93 Ls28
Tuna Gain RI 212 Rg47
Tunapa, Cerro BOL 72 Gg55
Tunapuna TT 58 Gk40
Tunari, P.N. BOL 72 Gg54
Tunas de Zaza C 45 Ga35
Tunaydiba SUD 276 Mh40
Tunçbilek TR 130 Mk51
Tunceli TR 145 Mk26
Tunchang VRC (HAN) 178 Qf36
Tuncurry AUS (NSW) 237 Sg62
Tundavala ANG 294 Lg53
Tundi IND (JKD) 194 Pd33
Tundik KZ 166 Oj20
Tundla IND (UPH) 189 Ok32
Tundulu Z 292 Me50
Tunduma EAT 292 Mg50
Tunduru EAT 297 Mj51
Tundža BG 127 Mf48
Tunga WAN 280 Le41
Tungabhadra IND 190 Oj38
Tungabhadra Reservoir IND 192 Oj39
Tungaru SUD 283 Mf40
Tungaztarim VRC (XUZ) 168 Pb27
Tungho RC 179 Ra34
Tungkai RI 207 Qb46
Tungkaranasam RI 208 Qj47
Tungku MAL 204 Qk43
Tungokočen RUS 173 Qh19
Tungsha Islands VRC 179 Qj35
Tungshih RC 179 Ra33
Tungsten CDN (NWT) 17 Df15
Tungting Lake VRC 177 Qg31
Tungurahua, Volcán EC 60 Ga46
Tunguwatu RI 213 Rh48
Tuni IND (APH) 191 Pb37
Tunica USA (MS) 29 Fe28
Tunis TN 260 Lf27
Tunisia TN 253 La06
Tunja CO 56 Gd43
Tunka La IND 194 Pf32
Tunkas MEX (YT) 41 Ff35
Tünkhel MNG 172 Qd21
Tunku Abdul Rahman Park MAL 204 Qj42
Tunnel Creek N.P. AUS 222 Rc54
Tunnel de Tende F/I 105 Lh46
Tunnel du Fréjus F/I 105 Lg45
Tunnel du M Blanc F 105 Lg45
Tunnel las Raices RCH 80 Ge65
Tunnels USA (HI) 16 Ca34
Tunqiu VRC (GZG) 178 Qe33
Tunstall GB 101 Ks36
Tuntum BR (MA) 64 Hh48
Tuntutuliak USA (AK) 14 Bj15
Tununak USA (AK) 14 Bh15
Tununguo EAT 293 Mj49
Tunuyán RA (MD) 76 Gf62
Tunuyán RA 76 Gg62
Tunzam MYA 194 Pg34
Tuolo VRC (GZG) 178 Qd34
Tuol Tel K 197 Qb39
Tuol Totoeng K 197 Qb39
Tuong Duong VN 197 Qc36
Tuotuo He VRC 171 Pf28
Tuotuo Heyan VRC (QHI) 171 Pg28
Tüp KS 159 Ok24
Tupă BR (SP) 74 He56
Tupaceretã BR (MS) 73 Hb55
Tupaciguara BR (MG) 74 Hf55
Tupai Atoll F 249 Ce54
Tupana BR 62 Gk48
Tupanatinga BR (PE) 71 Jb50
Tupanciretã BR (RS) 78 Hd60
Tuparrito CO 57 Gf43
Tuparro CO 57 Gf43
Tupelo USA (OK) 29 Fb28
Tupelo USA (MS) 29 Ff28
Tupi RP 205 Rc42
Tupicino RUS 96 Mj32
Tupilco MEX (TB) 41 Fd36
Tupi Paulista BR (SP) 74 He56
Tupiratins BR (TO) 70 Hf50
Tupiza BOL 72 Gh56
Tüpkaraghan tübegi KZ 152 Nf23
Tupoko YV 58 Gj42
Tupper CDN (BC) 18 Dk18
Tupper Lake USA (NY) 33 Gc23
Tupran IND (APH) 191 Ok37
Tupungato RA (MD) 76 Gf62
Tupungato, Cerro RA/RCH 76 Gf62
Tuquan VRC (NMZ) 173 Ra23
Túquerres CO 60 Gb45
Tuqu Gang VRC 178 Qe36
Tura IND (MGA) 194 Pf33
Tura RUS 140 Qa06
Tura VRC (XUZ) 168 Pd27
Turabah KSA 148 Na35
Turabah KSA 149 Nb31
Turagua, Cerro YV 57 Gh42
Turaida LV 97 Me33
Turaiyur IND (TNU) 193 Ok41
Turama River PNG 243 Sb49
Turan RUS (TUV) 167 Pg19
Turangi NZ 238 Th65
Turan Lowland 142 Oa10
Turar KZ 158 Of24
Turayf KSA 146 Mk30
Turbaco CO 56 Gc40
Turbah YE 150 Nb39
Turbat PK 162 Ob33
Turbeville USA (SC) 35 Ga29
Turbio RA 82 Ge71
Turbjo RCH 76 Ge60
Turbo CO 56 Gb41
Turbo EAK 290 Mh45
Turčianske Teplice SK 119 Lt42
Turco BOL 72 Gf55
Turda RO 124 Md44
Turda SUD 283 Me40
Turee Creek AUS 224 Qj57
Turee Creek AUS (WA) 224 Qk57
Turégano E 106 Kq51
Tureh IR 154 Ne28
Tureia Atoll 317 Da12
Turek PL 116 Lt38
Turen RI 210 Qg50
Tureni RO 124 Md44
Turfan Depression VRC 169 Pe24
Turga RUS 173 Qj20
Turgajskoe plato 138 Oa04
Turgan KZ 159 Oj24
Türgen Uul MNG 167 Pg21
Türgen Uul Nature Reserve MNG 167 Pf21
Turgut TR 131 Mm52
Turgutlu TR 129 Mh52
Turgutreis TR 129 Mh53
Turhal TR 131 Mf50
Turi BR 61 Gf46
Türi EST 96 Mf32
Turiaçu BR (MA) 64 Hh46
Turiaçú BR 64 Hh47
Turicato MEX (MHC) 40 Ek36
Turija UA 117 Me39
Turijs'k UA 117 Me39
Turilari RA (PJ) 72 Gg57
Turin CDN (AB) 19 Ed21
Turin I 120 Lh45
Turis E 109 Ku49
Turiščevo RUS 132 Mh19
Turjak SCG 126 Ma48
Turjak SLO 121 Lp45
Turka RUS (BUR) 172 Qe19
Turka RUS 173 Qe19
Turka UA 119 Md41
Turkana EAK 290 Mh44
Türkeli TR 130 Mh50
Türkeve H 119 Ma43
Turkey TR 142 Mc11
Turkey USA 27 Fe24
Turkey Creek AUS (WA) 222 Re54
Turkistan KZ 158 Oe24
Turkmenabat TM 153 Ob26
Turkmenbashi TM 153 Ng25
Turkmenbashi Bay TM 153 Ng26
Turkmengala TM 155 Ob27
Turkmenistan TM 139 Nb06
Turkmenskiy zaliv TM 153 Ng26
Türkoğlu TR 144 Mj27
Turksad RUS 152 Nc23
Turks and Caicos Islands GB 45 Ge34
Turks Island Passage BS 37 Ge35
Turks Islands GB 45 Ge35
Turku = Åbo FIN 96 Mc30

Turkwel Gorge Reservoir EAK 290 Mh45
Turlock USA (CA) 20 Dk27
Turmalina BR (MG) 75 Hj54
Turmi ETH 284 Mj43
Turnagain Arm USA 15 Ce15
Turnagain River CDN 17 Df16
Turneffe Islands BH 41 Fg37
Turner AUS (WA) 222 Re54
Turner USA (MT) 19 Ef21
Turner Falls Park USA 28 Fb28
Turner Lake CDN 19 Ef17
Turner River AUS 224 Qk56
Turners Peninsula WAL 278 Kd42
Turnhout B 103 Le39
Türnitz A 115 Lq43
Turnor Lake CDN (SK) 19 Ef17
Turnov CZ 118 Lq40
Turnu RO 124 Mb44
Turnu Măgurele RO 127 Me47
Turocak RUS (ALT) 167 Pd19
Turoś PL 117 Mb37
Turpan VRC (XUZ) 169 Pe24
Turrialba CR 42 Fj41
Turriff GB 99 Ks33
Tursaq IRQ 147 Nc29
Tursunzade TJ 158 Oe26
Turt MNG 172 Qa20
Turtel MK 126 Mc49
Turtle Beach USA (FL) 36 Fj32
Turtle Beach YE 151 Ng39
Turtleford CDN (SK) 19 Ef19
Turtle Harbour HN 42 Fg37
Turtle Islands RP 204 Qk42
Turtle Islands Marine Park RP 204 Qk42
Turtle Lake CDN 19 Ef19
Turtle Lake USA (ND) 26 Ek22
Turuépano, P.N. YV 57 Gj40
Turuhansk RUS 140 Pb05
Turu/Mariquita, T.I. BR 64 Hf47
Turuntaevo RUS (BUR) 172 Qd19
Tururu BR (CE) 65 Ja47
Turuvekere IND (KTK) 193 Oj40
Turvânia BR (GO) 74 He54
Turvelândia BR (GO) 74 He54
Turvo BR 69 He54
Turvo BR (PR) 74 He58
Turvo BR 74 Hf56
Turvo BR (SC) 79 Hf60
Turzovka SK 118 Lt41
Tus IR 155 Nk27
Tusaquilla RA (PJ) 72 Gg57
Tuscaloosa USA (AL) 34 Fg29
Tuscánia I 122 Lm48
Tuscany I 120 Ll47
Tuscola USA (TX) 28 Fa29
Tuscumbia USA (MO) 27 Fd26
Tuscumbia USA (AL) 34 Fg28
Tusen-øyane N 91 Ma07
Tushchybas shyghanagh KZ 153 Nk22
Tushkadi BD 194 Pe34
Tuskegee USA (AL) 35 Fh29
Tušnica BIH 121 Ls47
Tustumena Lake USA 15 Ce15
Tutaev RUS 132 Mk17
Tutak TR 145 Nb26
Tuticorin IND (TNU) 193 Ok42
Tutin SCG 126 Ma48
Tutira NZ 238 Tj65
Tutóia BR (MA) 65 Hj47
Tutoko, Mount NZ 239 Te68
Tutova RO 125 Mh44
Tutova RO 125 Mh44
Tutrakan BG 125 Mg46
Tuttlingen D 114 Lj43
Tutuaca MEX 23 Ef31
Tutuala TIM 214 Rd50
Tutubu EAT 292 Mg48
Tutuila Island USA 248 Be53
Tutume RB 299 Md56
Tutupaca, Volcán PE 72 Ge54
Tutut RI 198 Pj43
Tutwiler USA (MS) 29 Fe29
Tutyaka TR 131 Mo52
Tuul Gol MNG 172 Qc22
Tuulos FIN 96 Me29
Tuusniemi FIN 91 Me14
Tuusula FIN 96 Mf30
Tuva RUS 140 Pd08
Tuvalu 219 Tb10
Tuvalu Islands TUV 241 Td20
Tuvana-i-Ra FJI 221 Ua23
Tuvuca FJI 247 Ua54
Tuwayq KSA 149 Nc33
Tuwwal KSA 148 Mk34
Tuxcueca MEX (JLC) 40 Ej35
Tuxedni Bay USA 15 Cd15
Tuxford CDN (SK) 19 Eh20
Tuxpam (Tuxpan) MEX (VC) 40 Fb35
Tuxpan MEX (NYT) 39 Eh35
Tuxpan MEX (JLC) 40 Ej36
Tuxpan MEX 40 Fb35
Tuxpan = Tuxpam MEX (VC) 40 Fb35
Tuxtepec MEX (OAX) 40 Fb36
Tuxtla Gutiérrez MEX (CHP) 41 Fd37
Tuya River CDN 17 De16
Tuy Duc VN 197 Qd39
Tuyen Quang VN 178 Qc35
Tuy Hoa VN 197 Qe39
Tuy Phong VN 197 Qe40
Tuysarkan IR 154 Ne28
Tuža RUS 133 Nd17
Tuzantla MEX (MHC) 40 Ek36
Tuzantlán MEX (GUR) 40 Fa36
Tuz-Ashueue KS 159 Og24
Tuz Gölü TR 131 Mo52
Tuzi SCG 126 Lu48
Tuzigoot Nat. Mon. USA 23 Ee28
Tuz Khurmatu IRQ 147 Nc28
Tuzla BIH 124 Lt46
Tuzla TR 131 Mp52
Tuzla Gölü TR 131 Mq52
Tuzluca TR 145 Nb25
Tuzlukçu TR 131 Mm52
Tuzly UA 125 Ml45
Tuzule RDC 289 Mb49
Tvååker S 94 Ln33
Tvărdica BG 127 Mf48
Tvardita MD 125 Mj44
Tvedestrand N 92 Lj32
Tveitsund N 92 Lj31
Tver' RUS 132 Mh17
Tving S 95 Lq34
Tvrda HR 121 Lt45
Tvrdava SCG 126 Mb47
Tvrdošín SK 119 Lu41
Twardogóra PL 116 Ls39
Tweed GB 99 Ks35
Tweed Heads AUS (NSW) 235 Sg60
Tweedsmuir Prov. Park CDN 18 Dg19
Tweefontein SA 302 Lk62
Tweeling SA 303 Me59
Twee River NAM 298 Lk58
Twee Rivieren SA 302 Ma59
Tweespruit SA 303 Md60
Twello NL 112 Lg38
Twelve Apostles AUS 237 Sb65
Twelve Foot Davis Prov. Hist. Site CDN 19 Eb17
Twentynine Palms USA (CA) 22 Ec28
Twifo-Praso GH 279 Kk43
Twilight Cove AUS 229 Rd62
Twin Bridges USA (MT) 21 Ed23
Twin Falls USA (ID) 21 Ec24
Twingi Z 296 Me51
Twin Lakes CDN (AB) 19 Eb17
Twin Mount USA (AK) 15 Cj13
Twin Peaks AUS (WA) 224 Qh59
Twin Ring Motegi J 183 Sa27
Twin Wells AUS (NSW) 236 Sa62
Twistringen D 112 Lj38
Twitya River CDN 17 Df13
Twizel NZ 239 Tf68
Two Fold Bay AUS 237 Se64
Two Harbors USA (MN) 27 Fe22
Two Hills CDN (AB) 19 Ee19
Two Rivers USA (WI) 32 Fg23
Two Rocks AUS (WA) 228 Qh61
Two Wells AUS (SA) 236 Rk63
Twyfelfontein Rock Engraving NAM 298 Lh56
Tyapukai Aboriginal Cultural Centre AUS (QLD) 233 Sc54
Tychowo PL 116 Lr37
Tychy PL 117 Lu40
Tyczyn PL 119 Mc41
Tyélé RMM 270 Kg39
Tyfors S 93 Lp30
Tygda RUS 180 Rg19
Tygda RUS 180 Rh19
Tyin N 92 Lj29
Tykocin PL 117 Mc37
Tylawa PL 119 Mb41
Tyler USA (TX) 29 Fc29
Tylertown USA (LA) 29 Fe30
Tylisos GR 129 Mf55
Tylkowo PL 117 Ma37
Tylösand S 94 Ln34
Tymkove MD 125 Mk43
Tyndall USA (SD) 26 Fb24
Tyndrum GB 99 Kq34
Tynemouth GB 99 Kt35
Tyner CDN (SK) 19 Ef20
Tyngsjö S 93 Lo30
Tyniec PL 117 Lu40
Týniště nad Orlicí CZ 118 Lr40
Týn nad Vltavou CZ 118 Lp41
Tynset N 92 Ll28
Tyoplye Klyuchi KS 159 Oh24
Tyre RL 146 Mh29
Tyresta n.p. S 93 Ls31
Tyrifjorden N 92 Ll30
Tyringe S 95 Lo34
Tyringham AUS (NSW) 235 Sg61
Tyristrand N 92 Ll30
Tyrma RUS 180 Rg20
Tyrma RUS 180 Rg21
Tyrnyauz RUS (KBA) 152 Nb24
Tyrol Basin Ski Area USA 32 Ff24
Tyrrhenian Sea 86 Lb06
Tysa UA 119 Md42
Tyškivka UA 134 Mf21
Tysnes N 92 Lf30
Tyssebotn N 92 Lf30
Tyssedal N 92 Lg30
Tystberga S 93 Ls32
Tyszowce PL 117 Md40
Tytuvėnai LT 97 Md35
Tywi GB 100 Kr38
Tywyn GB 100 Kq38
Tzaneen SA 300 Mf57
Tzasar 161 Oj29
Tzermiádo GR 129 Mf55
Tzintzuntzan MEX 40 Ek36
Tziscao MEX (CHP) 41 Fe37
Tzucacab MEX (YT) 41 Ff35

U

Uaçá, T.I. BR 59 He44
Uaco Cungo ANG 294 Lh51
Ua Huka F 249 Da50
Uamba ANG 288 Lj49
Uanda AUS (QLD) 233 Sc56
Uangando ANG 294 Lj54
Uanle Uen = Wankawayn SP 291 Nc44
Uape MOC 297 Mk54
Ua Pou F 249 Ck50
Uar Addoi SP 291 Na44
Uarges EAK 290 Mj45
Uar Igarore SP 291 Nb45
Uarini BR (AM) 62 Gh47
Uarini BR 62 Gh47
Uati-Paraná, T.I. BR 61 Gg47
Uatumã BR 62 Ha47
Uauá BR (BA) 71 Ja50
Uauaretê BR (AM) 61 Gf45
Uaupes BR 61 Gf45
Uavala ANG 294 Lj54
Uaxactún GCA 41 Ff37
Ub SCG 124 Ma46
Uba BR (MG) 75 Hj56
Uba KZ 167 Pb20
Uba WAN 273 Lg40
Ubai BR (MG) 75 Hh54
Ubai PNG 244 Sf48
'Ubaid SUD 282 Mc39
Ubaíra BR (BA) 71 Ja52
Ubaitaba BR (BA) 71 Ja53
Ubajara BR (CE) 65 Hk47
Ubajay RA (ER) 77 Ha61
Ubangi RCB/RDC 281 Lj45
Ubar OM 151 Ng36
Ubatã BR (BA) 71 Ja53
Ubate CO 56 Gd43
Ubatuba BR (SP) 75 Hh57
Ubauru PK 163 Oe31
Ubay RP 205 Rc40
Ubaye F 105 Lg46
Ube J 185 Rf29
Úbeda E 109 Kr48
Ubehebe Crater USA 22 Eb27
Uberaba BR 74 Hf55
Uberaba BR (MG) 74 Hg55
Uberlândia BR (MG) 74 Hf55
Überlingen D 114 Lk43
Ubia, Gunung RI 213 Rj48
Ubiaja WAN 280 Ld42
Ubieszyn PL 117 Mc40
Ubir AUS 223 Rg52
Ubiratã BR (PR) 74 Hd58
Ubl'a SK 119 Mc42
Ubli SCG 126 Lt48
Ubol Rat Reservoir THA 197 Qb37
Ubombo SA 303 Mg59
Ubon Ratchathani THA 197 Qc38
Ubovka RUS 180 Rh23
Ubrique E 108 Kp46
Ubudiah Mosque MAL 198 Qa43
Ubundu RDC 287 Mc46
Ucacha RA (CD) 76 Gj62
Ucapinima CO 61 Gf45
Ucar AZ 152 Nd25
Ucayali PE 60 Gc49
Ucero E 107 Kr51
Ucës BY 117 Mf38
Uch PK 163 Of31
Uch-Adzhi TM 153 Ob26
Uchalon IND (WBG) 194 Pd34
Ucharonidge AUS (NT) 223 Rh54
Uchiza PE 66 Gb50
Uchqo'rg'on UZB 159 Og25
Uchquduq UZB 158 Ob24
Uchsoy UZB 153 Nk24
Uchte D 112 Lj38
Uckermark D 113 Lo37
Uckfield GB 101 La40
Ucluelet CDN (BC) 18 Dh21
Üçpınar TR 131 Mn53
Ucross USA (WY) 21 Eg23
Úcua ANG 288 Lh50
Uda RO 125 Me46
Uda RUS 172 Pj19
Uda RUS 172 Qe20
Udačnoe RUS 133 Nd22
Udačnyj RUS 141 Qc05
Udaigiri IND 194 Pd35
Udainagar IND (MPH) 190 Oj34
Udaipur IND (RJT) 190 Og33
Udaipur IND (TRP) 194 Pf34
Udaipura IND (MPH) 191 Ok34
Udakatla IND (APH) 190 Oj37
Udala IND (ORS) 194 Pd35
Udaquiola RA (BA) 81 Ha64
Udayagiri Caves IND 191 Oj34
Udayagiri Caves IND 191 Pc35
Udayd SUD 276 Mh39
Udaypur IND 191 Ok34
Udbina HR 121 Lq46
Uddevalla S 92 Lm32
Uddheden S 93 Ln31
Uddjaure S 90 Lj13
Udegi WAN 280 Ld41
Uden NL 112 Lf39
Udgir IND (MHT) 190 Oj36
Udhampur 161 Oh29
Udi IND (UPH) 189 Ok32
Udi WAN 280 Ld42
Udine I 121 Lo44
Udinsk RUS (BUR) 172 Qe19
Udmurtia 89 Nc07
Udomlja RUS 132 Mh17
Udong K 197 Qc40
Udon Thani THA 197 Qb37
Udumalaippettai IND (TNU) 193 Oj41
Udupi IND (KTK) 192 Oh40
Udu Point FJI 247 Tj54
Udu Point FJI 247 Ua54
Udzungwa Mountains N.P. EAT 293 Mj49
Udzungwa Range EAT 293 Mh50
Ueca ETH 284 Mj41
Uecker D 113 Lo37
Ueckermünde D 113 Lp37
Ueda J 183 Rk27
Uegit = Waajid SP 291 Nb44
Uele RDC 286 Mb44
Uëlen RUS 141 Ub05
Uelzen D 113 Ll38
Uepi Island Resort SOL 245 Sk50
Uere RDC 282 Mc43
Uetersen D 112 Lk37
Uetze D 113 Ll38
Ufa RUS 140 Nd07
Ufa RUS 140 Nd08
Ufeyn SP 285 Ne40
Uffenheim D 114 Ll41
Ugab NAM 298 Lj55
Ugab Rock Finger NAM 298 Lh56
Ugab Vingerklip NAM 298 Lh56
Ugāle LV 97 Mc33
Ugalla EAT 292 Mf48
Ugalla EAT 292 Mf48
Ugalla River Game Reserve EAT 292 Mf48
Ugamas SA 302 Lk60
Uganda 253 Mb09
Uganik Island USA 14 Cd16
Ugao SCG 126 Ma47
Ugărčin BG 127 Me47
Ugarit SYR 146 Mh28
Ugashik Bay USA (AK) 14 Ca17
Ugashik Lake USA (AK) 14 Cb17
Ugba WAN 280 Le42
Ugbala WAN 280 Le42
Ugbenu WAN 280 Lc42
Ugep WAN 280 Le43
Ughelli WAN 280 Ld43
Ugie SA 303 Me61
Ugíjar E 109 Kr46
Ugine F 105 Lg45
Ugjut KS 159 Oh25
Uglegorsk RUS 181 Sb21
Uglekamensk RUS 180 Rg24
Uglič RUS 132 Mk17
Ugljan HR 121 Lq46
Ugljan HR 121 Lq46
Uglovoe RUS 180 Re20
Ugo WAN 280 Ld42
Ugol'nye Kopi RUS 141 Td06
Ugoofaaru MV 192 Og43
Ugra RUS 132 Mh18
Ugtam Nature Reserve MNG 173 Qg21
Ugumji WAN 272 Lf40
Uğurlu TR 144 Mf27
Uğurlu Baraj TR 145 Mj25
Uğurludağ TR 131 Mp50
Uhaymir SUD 276 Mg39
Uhekera EAT 293 Mg48
Uhen WAN 280 Lc42
Uherské Hradiště CZ 118 Ls41
Uherský Brod CZ 118 Ls41
Uhi WAN 280 Ld42
Uhiere WAN 280 Lc42
Uhlenhorst NAM 298 Lj57
Uhly UA 117 Mf39
Uhniv UA 117 Md40
Uhrichsville USA (OH) 33 Fk25
Uhta RUS 140 Nc06
Uibaí BR (BA) 71 Hj51
Uig GB 98 Ko33
Uige ANG 288 Lh49
Uiha Island TO 248 Bc55
Uijongbu ROK 182 Rd27
Uiju DVRK 182 Rc25
Uinta USA 21 Ee25
Uintah and Ouray Ind. Res. USA 21 Ee25
Uinta Mountains USA 21 Ee25
Uirapuru BR (MT) 68 Ha53
Uiraúna BR (PB) 65 Ja49
Uis Myn NAM 298 Lh56
Uisong ROK 182 Re27
Uitenhage SA 303 Mc62
Uithoorn NL 112 Le38
Uithuizen NL 112 Lg37
Uitkyk SA 302 Lk60
Uitsakpan SA 302 Ma59
Uivar RO 124 Ma45
Ujae Atoll MH 241 Tb17
Ujali WAN 280 Ld42
Ujaly KZ 153 Nh23
Ujanmas RI 207 Qb47
Ujar RUS 140 Pc07
Ujdah MA 259 Kk28
Ujelang Atoll MH 240 Ta17
Ujeździec Mały PL 116 Ls39
Újfehértó H 119 Mb43
Ujhani IND (UPH) 189 Ok32
Uji J 183 Rh28
Uji-gunto J 185 Re30
Ujiji EAT 292 Me48
Ujir RI 213 Rh48
Ujjain IND (MPH) 190 Oh34
Ujma PL 116 Lt38
Ujmen' RUS 167 Pd20
Ujohbilang RI 208 Qh45
Ujście PL 116 Lr37
Ujście Warty, P.N. PL 116 Lp38
Ujungbatu RI 206 Qa45
Ujungkulon N.P. RI 210 Qc49
Ujung Pandang RI 209 Qk48
Ujung Pandang RI 211 Ra48
Ukal Sagar IND 190 Og35
Ukata WAN 272 Lc40
Ukdungle 161 Ok29
Ukenyengi EAT 293 Mg47
Ukerewe Island EAT 290 Mg46
uKhahlamba SA 303 Me60
uKhahlamba-Drakensberg N.P. SA 303 Me60
Ukhia BD 194 Pg35
Ukhrul IND (MNP) 194 Ph33
Ukiah USA (CA) 20 Dj26
Ukiah USA (OR) 20 Ea23
Ukiernica PL 116 Lq37
Uki Ni Masi Island SOL 245 Ta51
Ukkamba IND (ORS) 191 Pb36
Ukmergė LT 97 Me35
Ukora Island EAT 290 Mg46
Ukraine 87 Ma05
Ukrainian Cultural Heritage Village CDN 19 Ed19
Ukui RI 206 Qb46
Uku-jima J 185 Re29
Ukwatutu RDC 287 Md43
Ukwi Pan RB 299 Ma57
Ukwipan RB 299 Ma57
Ula TR 130 Mj53
Ulaanbaatar MNG 172 Qd22
Ulaanbulag MNG 172 Qc22
Ulaandel MNG 173 Qg22
Ulaan-Ereg MNG 173 Qe22
Ulaan nuur MNG 174 Qb23
Ulaan Tayga MNG/RUS 172 Pk20
Ulaan-Uul MNG 175 Qf23
Ulaanžirèm MNG 172 Qc23
Ulakmakam RI 206 Qb46
Ulamona PNG 244 Sf48
Ulan VRC (QHI) 174 Pk27
Ulana NIC 42 Fj38
Ulan Bator MNG 172 Qd22
Ulanbel KZ 158 Of23
Ulan Črge RUS (KAL) 135 Nc22
Ulanhot VRC (NMZ) 180 Rb22
Ulanlinggi VRC (XUZ) 169 Pd24
Ulanów PL 117 Mc40
Ulansuhai Nur VRC 175 Qe25
Ulan Tohoi VRC (NMZ) 174 Qa25
Ulan-Ude RUS (BUR) 172 Qd20
Ulan Ul Hu VRC 171 Pf28
Ulapara BD 194 Pe33
Ularbemban RI 207 Qb45
Ulaş TR 144 Mj26
Ulawa Island SOL 245 Ta50
Ulaya EAT 293 Mj49
Ulbanep, Mount PNG 243 Sb47
Ulbi KZ 167 Pb20
Ulbroka LV 97 Me34
Ulcinj SCG 126 Lu49
Ulco SA 303 Mc60
Ul' durga RUS 173 Qh19
Ulefoss N 92 Lk31
Uleila del Campo E 109 Ks47
Ulete EAT 293 Mh50
Ulfborg DK 94 Lj34
Ulft NL 112 Lg39
Ulgai VRC (NMZ) 173 Qk23
Ulianópolis BR (PA) 64 Hg47
Uliastay MNG 172 Pj22
Úlibice CZ 118 Lq40
Ulieș RO 125 Mf44
Ulindi RDC 287 Md46
Ulithi Atoll FSM 240 Rd16
Ul'janovka UA 125 Ml42
Ul'janovka UA 125 Ml43
Uljanovo RUS 97 Mc36
Uljanovsk RUS 133 Ne18
Uljatuj RUS 173 Qj20
Uljin ROK 182 Re27
Ulken KZ 166 Og23
Ülken Borsyk kumy KZ 153 Nk22
Ülken Özen KZ 132 Ne21
Ulken sor KZ 153 Ng23
Ulladulla AUS (NSW) 237 Sf63
Ullal IND (KTK) 192 Oh40
Ullal Beach IND 192 Oh40
Ullapool GB 99 Kp33
Ullared S 94 Ln33
Ullatti S 90 Ma12
Ulla Ulla BOL 67 Gf53
Ullawarra AUS (WA) 224 Qj57
Ulldecona E 110 La50
Ullerslev DK 94 Ll35
Ulloma BOL 72 Gf54
Ullún RA (SJ) 76 Gf61
Ullung ROK 183 Rf27
Ullung Do ROK 183 Rf27
Ulm D 114 Lk42
Ul'ma RUS 180 Rf20
Ulmara AUS (NSW) 235 Sg60
Ulmen D 112 Lg40
Ulmu RO 125 Mh46
Ulongwe MOC 296 Mh53
Ulricehamn S 95 Lo33
Ulrika S 95 Lq32
Ulsan ROK 182 Re28
Ulsta GB 99 Kt30
Ulsteinvik N 92 Lf28
Ulster IRL/GB 98 Kn36
Ulster D 112 Lk40
Ultima AUS (VIC) 237 Sb63
Ulu MYA 198 Pk40
Ulu RI 205 Rc44
Ulu RUS 141 Rb06
Ulu SUD 283 Mg40
Ulubat Gölü TR 130 Mj50
Ulubey TR 130 Mk52
Uluborlu TR 131 Ml52
Ulu Camii (Aksaray) TR 131 Mo52
Ulu Camii (Bolu) TR 131 Mm50
Ulu Camii (Çorum) TR 131 Mp50
Ulu Camii (Divriği) TR 145 Mk26
Ulu Camii (Diyarbakır) TR 145 Na26
Uluçınar TR 144 Mh27
Uludağ Milli Parkı TR 130 Mk50
Uludağ Tepe TR 130 Mk50
Uluderbent TR 130 Mj52
Uludere TR 145 Nb27
Uluggat VRC (XUZ) 168 Oh26
Ulug-Hem = Verhnij Enisej RUS 167 Pg20
Uluguru Mountains EAT 293 Mj49
Ulu Kiran MAL 208 Qf45
Ulukışla TR 131 Mp53
Uluköy TR 130 Mg51
Ulu Layar MAL 208 Qf45
Ulundi SA 303 Mf60
Ulungur He VRC 167 Pe22
Ulungur Hu VRC 167 Pd22
Uluru AUS 226 Rf58
Uluru = Ayers Rock AUS 226 Rf58
Uluru N.P. AUS 226 Rf58
Ulu-Ulu RI 208 Qj44
Ulva AUS (QLD) 233 Sc56
Ulva GB 98 Ko34
Ulvåker S 95 Lo32
Ulveah VU 246 Te54
Ulverston GB 101 Kr36
Ulverstone AUS (TAS) 236 Sd66
Ulvik N 92 Lg30
Ulvila FIN 96 Mb29
Ulvsvåg N 90 Lh11
Ulyanovskii KZ 166 Og20
Ulysses USA (KS) 28 Ek27
Ulz MNG 173 Qg21
Ulz gol MNG 173 Qg21
Uma RDC 287 Md45
Uma VRC (NMZ) 173 Ra19
Uma Daro MAL 208 Qf44
Umag HR 121 Lo45
Umaid-Bahwan-Palace IND 188 Og32
Umaish WAN 280 Ld41
Umán MEX (YT) 41 Ff35
Uman' UA 134 Mf21
Umanak Fjord DK 11 Hb04
Umarga IND (MHT) 190 Oj37
Umari BR 67 Gh50
Umaria IND (MPH) 191 Pa34
Umarkhed IND (MHT) 190 Oj36
Umarkot IND (ORS) 191 Pb36
Umarkot PK 163 Oe33
Umatilla USA (OR) 20 Ea23
Umatilla Ind. Res. USA 20 Ea23
Umba EAT 291 Mk48
Umba Game Reserve EAT 293 Mk48
Umbakumba AUS (NT) 223 Rj52
Umbar Depe TM 155 Od27
Umbarpada IND (GUJ) 190 Og35
Umbe PE 66 Gb50
Umbeara AUS (NT) 226 Rg58
Umbeb Bay VU 246 Td54
Umbelasha SUD 282 Mb41
Umbele RI 209 Rb47
Umbértide I 120 Ln47
Umboi Island PNG 243 Sd48
Umbraj IND (MHT) 190 Oh37
Úmbria I 120 Ln47
Umbukul PNG 243 Se49
Umbulan Balam RI 207 Qb48
Umbulan Gayohpecoh RI 207 Qc47
Umbulan Sumurkucing RI 207 Qc48
Umbumbulu SA 303 Mf61
Umburanas BR (BA) 71 Hk51
Umbuzeiro BR (PB) 65 Jc49
Umčari SCG 124 Ma46
Ume ZW 296 Me54
Umeå S 90 Ma14
Umeälven S 90 Lj13
Umera RI 212 Re46
Umfurudzi Safari Area ZW 296 Mf54
Umiat USA (AK) 15 Cd11
Umiray RP 203 Ra38
U'mista Cult. Centre CDN 18 Dg20
Umka SCG 124 Ma46
Umkomaas SA 303 Mf61
Umlazi SA 303 Mf60
Umling IND (MGA) 194 Pf33
Umm al Aranib LAR 267 Lh32
Umm Al-Ashtan UAE 156 Ng34
Umm al Jamajim KSA 149 Nc32
Umm al Khashab KSA 150 Nb37
Umm al-Qaiwain UAE 156 Nh33
Umm al Qalban KSA 148 Na32
Umm an-Nar UAE 156 Nh33
Ummanz D 113 Lo36
Umm ar Rizam LAR 261 Mb29
Umm Ashar Ash Sharjim KSA 149 Nc32
Umm as-Samim OM 151 Nh35
Umm Az-Zumul UAE 156 Nh34
Umm Badr SUD 275 Md38
Umm Barbit SUD 283 Mg40
Umm Bel SUD 283 Me39
Umm Buru SUD 275 Mb38
Umm Busha SUD 283 Mf39
Umm Dafag SUD 282 Mb40
Umm Dam SUD 283 Mf39
Umm Defeis SUD 283 Mg39
Umm Digulgulaya SUD 282 Mc40
Umm Dubban SUD 276 Me39
Umm Durman SUD 276 Mg39
Umm el-Jimal JOR 146 Mj29
Umm Gamala SUD 283 Me39
Umm Gederri SUD 282 Mc40
Umm Haraz SUD 282 Mb40
Umm Hawsh SUD 283 Mg39
Umm Hisin UAE 156 Ng34
Umm Hitan SUD 283 Mf40
Umm Inderaba SUD 276 Mf39
Umm Kaddada SUD 283 Md39
Umm Lajj KSA 148 Mj33
Umm Marahik SUD 282 Mc39
Umm Qais JOR 146 Mh29
Umm Qasr IRQ 147 Nd30
Umm Qozein SUD 275 Md38
Umm Qurein SUD 276 Me38
Umm Rahaw SUD 276 Mf37
Umm Rumeila SUD 276 Mh38
Umm Rumetla SUD 276 Mf38
Umm Ruwaba SUD 283 Mf39
Umm Sa'ad LAR 262 Mc30
Umm Sagura SUD 283 Me41
Umm Said = Mesaieed Q 156 Nf33
Umm Sayyala SUD 276 Mf39
Umm Segeiti SUD 283 Mf39
Umm Urumah KSA 148 Mj33
Umniati ZW 300 Me55
Umpaqua USA 20 Dh24
Um Phang THA 196 Pk37
Umpire USA (AR) 29 Fc28
Umpuhua MOC 297 Mj53
Ümraniye TR 131 Mm51
Umred IND (MHT) 191 Ok35
Umri IND (MPH) 189 Ok32
Umri IND (MHT) 190 Oj36
Umsini, Gunung RI 213 Rg46
Umsning IND (MGA) 194 Pf33
Umtamvuna Nature Reserve SA 303 Mf61
Umtata SA 303 Me61
Umtata Dam SA 303 Me61
Umtentu SA 303 Mf61
Umuahia WAN 280 Ld43
Umuarama BR (PR) 74 Hd57
Umu-Duru WAN 280 Ld43
Umunede WAN 280 Ld42
Umurbey TR 130 Mg50
Umurga LV 97 Me33
Umurlu TR 129 Mh53
Umutina, T.I. BR (MT) 68 Ha53
Umutombuko Z 292 Me50
Umutu WAN 280 Ld43
Umwukwe Range ZW 296 Mf54
Umzimkulu SA 303 Me61
Umzingwani ZW 300 Me56
Umzinto SA 303 Mf61
Una BIH 121 Lq46
Una BR (BA) 71 Ja53
Una BR 71 Jc50
Una IND (HPH) 189 Oj30
Una IND (GUJ) 190 Of35
Unaðsdalur IS 90 Jj12
Unai BR (MG) 75 Hg54
Unaipass AFG 160 Oe28
Unalakleet USA (AK) 15 Bk14
Unalakleet River USA 15 Bk14
Unalaska USA (AK) 14 Bg19
Unalaska Bay USA (AK) 14 Bg19
Unalaska Island USA 14 Bg19
Unalga Island USA 14 Bh19
Unango MOC 297 Mh52
Unari FIN 91 Mc12
Unauna RI 209 Ra46
Unawari RI 213 Rh47
Unawatuna Beach CL 193 Pa44
Unayzah KSA 149 Nb32
Unbunmaroo, Mount AUS 232 Sa57
Uncastillo E 107 Kt52
Uncompahgre Plateau USA 21 Ef26
Unda RUS 173 Qj20
Undaima SP 285 Nf40
Undara Volcanic N.P. AUS 232 Sc55
Undaunda Z 296 Me53
Unden S 93 Lp32
Undenäs S 93 Lp32
Underberg SA 303 Me60
Undersåker S 90 Lg14
Underwater Caves BS 37 Gb33
Unduma BOL 67 Gg52
Undva neem EST 96 Mb32
Unea Island PNG 243 Se48
Uneča RUS 132 Mg19
Unei BR 61 Gg46
Uneiuxi BR 61 Gg46
Uneiuxi, T.I. BR 61 Gg46
Úněšov CZ 118 Lo41
UNEXSO BS 37 Ga32
Unga Island USA 14 Bk18
Ungalik USA (AK) 15 Bk13
Ungalik River USA 15 Ca13
Ungarra AUS (SA) 236 Rj63
Unga Strait USA 14 Bk18
Ungava Bay CDN 11 Gc07
Ungerem PNG 242 Sa49
Ungheni MD 125 Mh43
Ungheni RO 125 Me44
Ungo RUS 173 Qe20
Unguja EAT 293 Mk48
Unguriņi LV 97 Mf33
Ungwana Bay EAK 291 Na47
Ungwatiri SUD 276 Mh38
Unhe ANG 295 Ma54
Uniab NAM 298 Lg56
União BR (AM) 61 Gf47
União BR (PI) 65 Hj48
União da Vitória BR (PR) 78 He59
União de Minas BR (MG) 74 He55
União dos Palmares BR (AL) 71 Jc50
Uniara IND (RJT) 188 Oj33
Unica BOL 72 Gg55
Unichowo PL 116 Ls36
Uničov CZ 118 Ls41
Uniejów PL 116 Lt39
Unije HR 121 Lp46
Unimak USA (AK) 14 Bh18
Unimak Bay USA (AK) 14 Bh18
Unimak Island USA 14 Bh18
Unimak Pass USA (AK) 14 Bh18
Unini BR 62 Gj46
Unión RA (SL) 76 Gh63
Union USA (OR) 20 Eb23
Union USA (MO) 27 Fe26
Union USA (SC) 35 Fk28
Union WV 47 Gk39
Union Center USA (SD) 26 Ej23
Union City USA (TN) 29 Ff27
Union City USA (PA) 33 Ga25
Union Creek USA (OR) 20 Dj24
Uniondale SA 302 Mb62
Unión de Tula MEX (JLC) 39 Eh36
Unión Hidalgo MEX (OAX) 41 Fc37
Union Juárez MEX (CHP) 41 Fd38
Union Springs USA (AL) 35 Fh29
Uniontown USA (PA) 33 Ga26
Unionville USA (NV) 20 Ea25
Unionville USA (MO) 27 Fd25
Unipouheos Ind. Res. CDN 19 Ee19
Unisław PL 116 Lt37
United Arab Emirates UAE 156 Ng34
United Kingdom 87 Kb04
United States USA 9 Ea06
Unity CDN (SK) 19 Ef19
Unity USA (OR) 20 Ea23
Universal City USA (TX) 28 Fa31
Universal Studios USA 36 Fk31
University Park USA (NM) 23 Eg29
University Place USA (WA) 18 Dj22
Unmet VU 246 Td54
Unna D 112 Lh39
Unnamed Conservation Park AUS 226 Re60
Unnao IND (UPH) 189 Pa32
Unnaryd S 95 Lo34
Uno GNB 269 Kb40
Unpongko VU 246 Te55
Unsan DVRK 182 Rc25
Unst GB 99 Ku30
Unstrut D 113 Ll39
Unteres Odertal, N.P. D 113 Lp38
Unterhaching D 115 Lm42
Unterückersee D 113 Lo37
Unuk River CDN 17 De17
Ünye TR 145 Mj25
Unzen J 185 Rf29
Uoro o Mbini GQ 281 Lf45
Uotsuri Shima J 185 Rb33
Uozo J 183 Rj27
Upa EST 96 Mc32
Upala CR 42 Fh40
Upalco USA (UT) 21 Ee25
Upanema BR (RN) 65 Jb48
Upang RI 207 Qc47
Upata YV 58 Gj41
Upemba, P.N.de l' RDC 292 Md50
Upernavik DK 11 Ha04
Upham USA (ND) 24 Ek21
Upi RP 205 Rc42
Upington SA 302 Ma60
Upinniemi = Obbnäs FIN 96 Me30
Upleta IND (GUJ) 190 Of35
'Upolu Island WS 248 Be52
Upolu Point USA 16 Cc35
Uppalapadu IND (APH) 193 Ok39
Upper Arrow Lake CDN 18 Ea20
Upper Canada Vill. CDN 33 Gc23
Upper Daly A.L. AUS 223 Rf53
Upper Forster Lake CDN 19 Eh17
Upper Guinea 252 Kb09
Upper Karoo SA 302 Ma61
Upper Klamath Lake USA 20 Dj24
Upper Lake USA 20 Ea25
Upper Lough Erne IRL 98 Kn36
Upper Mississippi N.W.R. USA 32 Fe24
Upper-Normandie F 102 La41
Upper Peninsula USA 27 Fh22
Upper Red Lake USA 24 Fc21
Upper Sandusky USA (OH) 32 Fj25
Upper Sioux Ind. Res. USA 27 Fc23
Upper Soda USA (OR) 20 Dj23
Upper Svaneti GE 152 Nb24
Upper Twin Lake CDN 25 Fg20
Uppinangadi IND (KTK) 192 Oh40
Uppland S 93 Ls31
Upplands-Väsby S 93 Ls31
Uppsala S 93 Ls31
Upsala CDN (ON) 25 Fe21
Upsala Glacier RA 82 Gd70
Upshi 161 Oj29
Upton USA (WY) 26 Eh23
Uqban YE 150 Nb38
Uqlat as Suqur KSA 148 Nb33
Ur IRQ 147 Nd30
Uracoa YV 58 Gj41
Urad Houqi VRC (NMZ) 174 Qd25
Urad Qianqi VRC (NMZ) 174 Qe25
Urad Zhongqi VRC (NMZ) 174 Qe25
Urahoro J 181 Sb24
Uraim BR 64 Hg47
Urakawa J 181 Sb24
Ural RUS 140 Nd08
Uralla AUS (NSW) 235 Sf61
Ural Mountains 89 Oa06
Urambo EAT 292 Mg48
Uran IND (MHT) 190 Og36
Urana AUS (NSW) 237 Sd63
Urandangi AUS (QLD) 232 Rk56
Urandi BR (BA) 70 Hj53
Uranga AUS (NSW) 235 Sg61
Uranium City CDN 10 Ec07
Uran-Togoo Tulga Mountain Nature Reserve MNG 172 Qb21
'Uraq SUD 276 Mg39
Uraricuera BR 58 Gk44
Ura-Vajgurore AL 126 Lu50
Uravakonda IND (APH) 193 Oj39
Urayirah KSA 149 Ne33
Urbana USA (IL) 32 Ff25
Urbana USA (OH) 32 Fj25
Urbandale USA (IA) 27 Fd25
Urbânia I 120 Ln47
Urbano Noris C 45 Gb35
Urbano Santos BR (MA) 64 Hj47
Urbi SUD 276 Mf37
Urbinasopon RI 212 Rf46
Urbino I 120 Ln47
Urcos PE 67 Ge52
Urdampilleta RA (BA) 81 Gk64
Urdaneta RP 202 Ra38
Urdgol MNG 167 Pg22
Urdinarrain RA (ER) 77 Ha62
Urd Tamir Gol MNG 172 Qa22
Ure GB 101 Ks36
Ure WAN 280 Ld41
Ureca GQ 280 Le44
Urema RI 213 Rh47
Uren RUS 133 Nc17
Ureña RA 76 Gh59
Ureparapara VU 246 Td52
Ures MEX (SO) 23 Ee31
Urewera N.P. NZ 238 Tj65
Urgal RUS 180 Rg20
Urgal RUS 180 Rg20
Urganch UZB 153 Oa25
Urganlı TR 129 Mh52
Urgench = Urganch UZB 153 Oa25
Urgoma Mountains ETH 284 Mk42
Ürgüp TR 131 Mp52
Urgut UZB 158 Od26
Urho VRC (XUZ) 167 Pc22
Urho Kekkosen kansallispuisto FIN 91 Me11
Uri TCH 275 Lk35
Uria RO 124 Me43
Uriah USA (AL) 34 Fg30
Uribe CO 60 Gb44
Uribia CO 56 Gd40
Uribicha BOL 68 Gj53
Urica YV 57 Gh41
Uri Hauchab Mountains NAM 298 Lh58
Urik RUS 172 Qa19
Uriman YV 58 Gj43
Urique MEX (CHH) 38 Eg32
Urisirima GUY 58 Ha42
Urítiyacu PE 60 Gc48
Uriuk RUS 172 Qd20
Uri Wenz ETH 277 Mk40
Uriž UA 119 Md41
Urjala FIN 96 Md29
Urjumkan RUS 173 Qk20
Urjumkanskij hrebet RUS 173 Qk20
Urjupino RUS 173 Qk19
Urjupinsk RUS 133 Na20
Urk NL 112 Lf38
Urla TR 129 Mg52
Urlati RO 125 Mg46
Urlingford IRL 100 Kn38
Urmary RUS (CHU) 133 Nd18
Urmi RUS 180 Rg21
Urnes N 92 Lh29
Uromi WAN 280 Ld42
Uroševac SCG 126 Mb48
Uroteppa TJ 158 Oe26
Urov RUS 173 Ra20
Urrampinyu Jlijiltjarri A.L. AUS 226 Rg58
Urrao CO 56 Gb42
Ursus Cove USA 15 Cd16
Urszulewo PL 117 Lu38
Urt MNG 174 Qa24
Urt Moron VRC (QHI) 169 Pg27
Uru BR 69 Hf53
Uruachic MEX (CHH) 38 Ef32
Uruaçu BR (GO) 70 Hf53
Uruanã BR (GO) 70 Hf53
Uruapan MEX (BC) 22 Eb30
Uruapan del Progreso MEX (MHC) 40 Ej36
Urucará BR 63 Hd47
Urubamba PE 67 Gd52
Urubamba PE 67 Gd52
Urubaxi BR 62 Gh46
Urubici BR (SC) 79 Hf60
Urubu Branco, T.I. BR 69 He51
Urubu Grande BR 69 Hf51
Urucara BR (AM) 63 Hb47
Urucu BR 62 Gh48
Uruçuca BR (BA) 71 Ja53
Uruçui BR (PI) 64 Hh49
Urucuia BR 70 Hh54
Urucuia BR (MG) 75 Hh54
Uruçui Preto BR 64 Hh50
Urucu Juruá, T.I. BR 64 Hh48
Urucuriana BR 63 Hc45
Uru-Eu-Wau-Wau, T.I. BR 68 Gj51
Urugu EAT 293 Mh48
Uruguai BR 78 Hd59
Uruguaiana BR (RS) 78 Hb60
Uruguay BR/RA 77 Hb60
Uruguay 51 Ha13
Uruguinha BR (AP) 63 He45
Uruk = Erech IRQ 147 Nc30
Urukthapel PAL 203 Rh42
Uruma RI 213 Rh48
Urumaco YV 57 Ge40
Ürümqi VRC (XUZ) 167 Pd24
Uruoca BR (CE) 65 Hk47
Urupadi BR 63 Hb47
Urupês BR (SP) 74 Hf56
Uruq al Awarik KSA 150 Nd36
'Uruq al Mawarid KSA 150 Ne36
'Uruq al Mundafin KSA 150 Nc36
Uruq ar Rumaylah KSA 149 Nd35
Uruq Subay KSA 148 Nb34
Ürür gol MNG 172 Qa20
Urussanga BR (SC) 79 Hf60
Urussu RUS (TAR) 133 Ng18
Uruwira EAT 292 Mf49
Uryzhar KZ 166 Pa22
Urzędów PL 117 Mc39
Urziceni RO 125 Mg46
Us RUS 167 Pg19
Usa J 185 Rf29
Ušačy BY 132 Me18
Usadišče RUS 132 Mg16
Usagari EAT 292 Mg48
Usagre E 108 Ko48
Uşak TR 130 Mk52
Usakos NAM 298 Lh56
Ušakovskoe RUS 141 Ua04
Usambara Mountains EAT 291 Mk48
U.S. Army Aviation Mus. USA 35 Fh30
Usarp Mountains 313 Ta33
'Usaylay KSA 149 Nc33
Uš-Bel'dir RUS (TUV) 172 Pk20
Uschodni BY 132 Md19
Usedom D 113 Lo37
Usedom D 113 Lp36
Useless Loop AUS (WA) 224 Qg59
Usen RUS 133 Nh18
Usengi EAK 290 Mh46
Usfan KSA 148 Mk35
Ushaa Z 295 Mb53
Usharal KZ 158 Of24
Usharal KZ 166 Pa22
'Ushayrah KSA 149 Nc33
Ushetu EAT 292 Mg48
Ushibuka J 185 Rf29
Ushirombo EAT 292 Mf47
Ushtobe KZ 166 Oj23
Ushuaia RA (TF) 82 Gf73
Usib NAM 298 Lh57
Usilampatti IND (TNU) 193 Oj42
Usim RI 212 Rg46
Usina Apiacás BR (MT) 69 Hb51
Usina São Francisco BR (AM) 62 Ha48
Usingen D 114 Lj40
Usino PNG 243 Sc48
Usk CDN (BC) 18 Df18
Usk GB 101 Ks39

Uska IND (UPH) 189 Pb32
Uskoplje BIH 121 Ls47
Uslar D 112 Lk39
Usman RUS 133 Mk19
Usmas ezers LV 97 Mc33
Usmat UZB 158 Od26
Usoke EAT 292 Mg48
Usol'e-Sibirsko RUS 172 Qb19
Uson RP 203 Rb39
Usovo RUS 133 Nb19
Uspallata RA (MD) 76 Gf62
Uspenie manastir BG 126 Mc47
Uspenskij sobor RUS 132 Mf18
Uspenskij sobor Rjazan' RUS 133 Mk18
Uspenskij sobor Tver' RUS 132 Mh17
Usquil PE 66 Ga49
Usran KSA 150 Nb36
Ussel F 104 Lc45
U.S. Space & Rocket Center USA 34 Fg28
Ussuri RUS 180 Rh22
Ussurijsk RUS 180 Rf24
Usta RUS 133 Nd17
Usta USA (SD) 26 Ej23
Usta Muhammad PK 162 Oe31
Ust'-Barguzin RUS (BUR) 172 Qe19
Ust'-Cil'ma RUS 140 Nc05
Ust'-Džeguta RUS (KCH) 152 Na23
Ust'-Džilinda RUS (BUR) 173 Qf19
Ust'-Elegest RUS (TUV) 167 Ph20
Uster CH 114 Lj43
Ustibar BIH 126 Lu47
Ustikolina BIH 126 Lt47
Ust'-Ilimsk RUS 140 Qa07
Ústí nad Labem CZ 118 Lp40
Ústí nad Orlicí CZ 118 Lr41
Ustiprača BIH 126 Lu47
Ustjurt Plateau KZ/UZB 142 Nd10
Ustjužina RUS 132 Mj16
Ustka PL 116 Lr36
Ust'-Kamčatsk RUS 141 Ta07
Ust'-Kan RUS (ALT) 167 Pc20
Ust'Karsk RUS 173 Qk19
Ust'-Koksa RUS (ALT) 167 Pc20
Ust'-Kujga RUS 141 Rd04
Ust'-Kut RUS 140 Qb07
Ust'-Labinsk RUS 135 Mk23
Ust'-Luga RUS 96 Mj31
Ust'-Maja RUS 141 Rc06
Ust'-Nera RUS 141 Sa06
Ust'-Omčug RUS 141 Sb06
Ust'-Ordynsk Buryat Autonomous District RUS 140 Qa08
Ust'-Ordynskij RUS (UOB) 172 Qc19
Ustovo BG 127 Me49
Ustrem BG 127 Mg48
Ustroń PL 119 Lt41
Ustronie Morskie PL 116 Lq36
Ustrzyki Dolne PL 119 Mc41
Ust'Sobolevka RUS 181 Rk22
Ust'-Ulagan RUS (ALT) 167 Pe20
Ust'-Umal'ta RUS 180 Rg20
Ust'-Varga RUS 140 Na06
Ustyluh PL 117 Me40
Ust-Zolotaja RUS 167 Pg19
Usu VRC (XUZ) 167 Pc23
Usuki J 185 Rf29
Usuktuk River USA 15 Cb10
Usulutan ES 41 Ff39
Usumacinta GCA/MEX 41 Fe37
Usur IND (CGH) 191 Pa36
Usutu SA 300 Me57
Usu-zan J 181 Sa24
Usvjaty RUS 132 Mf18
Uta RI 213 Rj48
Utah USA 12 Eb11
Utah Lake USA 21 Ed25
Utajärvi FIN 91 Md13
Utåker N 92 Lf31
Utamballa EAT 292 Mg50
Utangala RI 209 Rb45
Utansjö S 93 Ls28
Utar RI 211 Qj50
Utara Baliem RI 213 Rk48
Utcubamba PE 60 Ga48
Utegi EAT 290 Mh46
Utembo ANG 295 Ma54
Ute Mountain Ind. Res. USA 23 Ee27
Utena LT 97 Mf35
Utete EAT 293 Mk50
U Thai LAO 195 Qa34
Uthai Thani THA 196 Qa38
Uthal PK 162 Od33
Uthomphon LAO 197 Qc37
U Thong THA 196 Pk38
Uthumph on Phisai THA 197 Qc38
Utiariti BR (MT) 68 Ha52
Utiariti, T.I. BR 68 Ha52
Utica CO 56 Gc43
Utica TN 260 Lf27
Utica USA (MS) 29 Fe29
Utica USA (OH) 32 Fj25
Utica USA (NY) 33 Gc24
Utiel E 109 Kt49
Utik Lake CDN 24 Fb18
Utikuma Lake CDN 19 Ec18
Utikuma River CDN 19 Ec17
Utila HN 42 Fg37
Utinga BR (BA) 71 Hk52
Utinga BR 71 Hk52
Utlängan S 95 Lq34
Utne N 92 Lg30
Utnur IND (APH) 191 Ok36
Utö FIN 96 Mb31
Utö S 93 Lt32
Utraula IND (UPH) 189 Pb32
Utrecht NL 112 Lf38
Utrecht SA 303 Mf59
Utrera E 108 Kp47
Utria, P.N. CO 56 Gb43
Utroja RUS 97 Mh34
Utsira N 92 Le31
Utsjoki FIN 91 Md11
Utstein Kloster N 92 Lf31
Utsunomiya J 183 Rk27
Uttampalaiyam IND (TNU) 193 Oj42
Uttangarai IND (TNU) 193 Ok40
Uttaradit THA 196 Qa37
Uttaranchal IND 186 Od12
Uttarkashi IND (UTT) 189 Ok30
Uttar Pradesh IND 186 Pa13
Uttoxeter GB 101 Kt38
Uttukkotta IND (APH) 193 Ok40
Utuado USA (PR) 47 Gg36
Utuana EC 60 Ga48
Utubulak VRC (XUZ) 167 Pd22
Utupua SOL 241 Tb21
Uturoa F 249 Ce54
Uturuncu, Cerro BOL 72 Gg57
Utvin RO 124 Mb45
Uukuniemi FIN 96 Mk29
Uummannaq = Dundas DK 11 Gc03
Uummannarsuaq = Kap Farvel DK 11 Hd07
Uurainen FIN 96 Mf28
Üüreg MNG 167 Pf20
Üüreg nuur MNG 167 Pf20
Uusikaupunki = Nystadt FIN 93 Mb30
Uutapi NAM 294 Lh54
Uvá CO 57 Gf44
Uvalde USA (TX) 28 Fa31
Úvaly CZ 118 Lp40
Uvarovo RUS 133 Nb20
Uvdal N 92 Lj30
Uvdal stavkirke N 92 Lj30
Uvinza EAT 292 Mf48
Uvira RDC 292 Me47
Uvol PNG 244 Sf49
Uvs MNG 167 Pg21
Uvs nuur MNG 167 Pg20
Uvs Nuur Nature Reserve MNG 167 Pg20
Uvungu RDC 289 Mc47
Uwajima J 185 Rg29
Uwa-kai J 185 Rg29
Uwakeka RI 214 Rd49
Uwanda Game Reserve EAT 292 Mg49
Uwanza EAT 293 Mh48
Uwapa RI 213 Rh47
Uwaynat Wannin LAR 260 Lg31
Uwekuli RI 209 Ra47
Uwi RI 199 Qd45
Uwimmerah RI 242 Sa49
Uxal MEX 41 Ff37
Uxin Ju VRC (NMZ) 175 Qe26
Uxin Qi VRC (NMZ) 174 Qe26
Uxmal MEX 41 Ff35
Uyak Bay USA (AK) 14 Cc17
Uyluk Tepe TR 129 Mk54
Uyo WAN 280 Ld43
Uyowa EAT 292 Mf48
Uyuali = Mutúali MOC 297 Mj53
Uyugan RP 203 Ra35
Uyun KSA 149 Ne33
Uyuni BOL 72 Gg56
Üyzen MNG 174 Qd23
Uzbekistan UZB 139 Oa05
Uzdowo PL 117 Ma37
Uzebba WAN 280 Lc42
Uzerche F 104 Lb45
Uzès F 105 Le47
Uzgen KS 159 Og25
Užhorod UA 119 Mc42
Užice SCG 126 Lu47
Uzlovaja RUS 133 Mk19
Užovka RUS 133 Nc18
Üzümlü TR 129 Mk54
Üzümlü TR 131 Mm53
Üzümlü TR 145 Mk26
Uzuncaburç TR 144 Mg27
Uzunköprü TR 130 Mg49
Uzunpınar TR 131 Ml52
Užventis LT 97 Mc35
Uzyn UA 134 Mf21
Uzynaghash KZ 159 Oj24
Uzynaghash KZ 159 Oj24

V

Vaal SA 303 Mc60
Vaalbos N.P. SA 303 Mc60
Vaaldam SA 303 Me59
Vaaldam Nature Reserve SA 303 Me59
Vaalimaa FIN 96 Mh30
Vaalkop Dam SA 299 Md58
Vaalwater SA 299 Me58
Vaasa FIN 91 Ma14
Vaavu Atoll = Felidhoo Atoll MV 192 Og44
Vabalninkas LT 97 Me35
Vabre F 104 Lc47
Vác H 119 Lu43
Váča BG 127 Me48
Vaca Guzmán BOL 73 Gj55
Vacaria BR 70 Hj54
Vacaria BR (RS) 78 He60
Vacaville USA (CA) 20 Dj26
Vacha D 112 Ll40
Vache MOC 297 Mj53
Väckelsång S 95 Lp34
Vada IND (MHT) 190 Og36
Vadakkevila IND (KER) 192 Oj42
Väddö S 93 Lt30
Vadehavet DK 94 Lj35
Vader USA (WA) 18 Dj22
Vadheim N 92 Lf29
Vadodara IND (GUJ) 190 Og34
Vado del Yeso C 45 Gb35
Vadsø N 91 Me10
Vadstena S 93 Lp32
Vaduz FL 114 Lk43
Vadvetjåkka n.p. S 90 Lk11
Værøy N 90 Lg12
Vaga RCB 288 Lh46
Vågåholmen N 90 Lg12
Vågåmo N 92 Lk29
Vaganski vrh HR 121 Lq46
Vagator Beach IND 190 Og38
Vaggeryd S 95 Lp33
Vaghena SOL 245 Sj49
Vagnhärad S 93 Ls32
Vägsele S 90 Lk13
Vågsøy N 92 Lf29
Váh SK 118 Ls42
Váh SK 119 Lu41
Vahš TJ 158 Oe27
Vahto FIN 96 Mc30
Vaiaau F 249 Ce54
Vaiaku TUV 241 Td20
Vaiden USA (MS) 29 Ff29
Vaihingen (Enz) D 114 Lj42
Vai Island PNG 243 Sc47
Vaikam IND (KER) 192 Oj42
Väike-Pakri EST 96 Md31
Vaikuntha Perumal Temple IND 193 Ok40
Vail USA (CO) 21 Eg26
Vailala River PNG 243 Sc49
Vailly-sur-Sauldre F 103 Lc43
Vainikkala FIN 96 Mj30
Vainode LV 97 Mb34
Vaisala WS 248 Bd52
Vaishali IND (BIH) 191 Pc33
Vaishnav Devi Shrine PK 161 Oh29
Vaison-la-Romaine F 105 Lf46
Vaitahu F 249 Da50
Vaitape F 249 Ce54
Vaitupu TUV 241 Td20
Vajszló H 121 Ls45
Vakaga RCA 282 Mb41
Vakfıkebir TR 145 Mk25
Vakhsh TJ 158 Oe26
Vakıf TR 130 Mg50
Vakil Abad IR 157 Nk31
Vaku RDC 288 Lg48
Vakuta PNG 244 Sf50
Vakuta Island PNG 244 Sf50
Valaam monastyr RUS 91 Mf15
Valadim MOC 297 Mj52
Valamon luostari FIN 91 Me14
Valandovo MK 126 Mc49
Valappadi IND (TNU) 193 Ok41
Valaská Belá SK 118 Lt42
Valašská Polanka CZ 118 Ls41
Valašské Meziříčí CZ 118 Ls41
Valavanni IND (PND) 193 Ok41
Valayat IR 156 Nf31
Vålberg S 93 Lo31
Valbo S 93 Lr30
Valbonć AL 126 Lu48
Vălčedrăm BG 126 Md47
Valcheta RA (RN) 80 Gg66
Valcheta RA 80 Gg66
Vălčidol BG 127 Mh47
Valdagno I 120 Lm45
Valdahon F 103 Lg43
Valdaisky N.P. RUS 132 Mg17
Valdaj RUS 132 Mg17
Valdayskaya Vozvyshennost' RUS 132 Mg17
Valdefuentes E 108 Ko49
Valdelagua E 109 Kr49
Valdeltormo E 110 La50
Valdemārpils LV 97 Mc33
Valdemars Slot DK 94 Ll35
Valdemarsvik S 95 Lr32
Valdemeca E 109 Kt50
Valdemoro E 109 Kr50
Valdenoceda E 107 Kr52
Valdepeñas E 109 Kr48
Valdepeñas de Jaén E 109 Kr47
Valderas E 106 Kp52
Val de Reuil F 102 Lb41
Valderrobres E 110 La50
Valdés RA (BA) 77 Gk63
Valdez RP 204 Qj41
Valdez USA (AK) 15 Cg15
Val d'Isère F 105 Lg45
Valdivia RCH 80 Gd65
Valdivia Fracture Zone 54 Fc27
Valdobbiádene I 120 Ln45
Val-d'Or CDN (QC) 30 Gb21
Valdosta USA (GA) 35 Fj30
Valdres N 92 Lj29
Vale USA (OR) 20 Eb24
Valea Argovei RO 125 Mg46
Valea Ierii RO 124 Md44
Valea lui Mihai RO 124 Mc43
Valea Mare-Pravăț RO 125 Mf45
Valea Mărului RO 125 Mh45
Valea Perjei MD 125 Mj44
Valea Sării RO 125 Mg45
Valea Ursului RO 125 Mh44
Valea Uzului RO 125 Mg44
Valea Viilor RO 124 Me44
Vale do Guaporé, T.I. BR 68 Gk52
Valejkiďki BY 97 Mf36
Valemount CDN (BC) 18 Ea19
Valença BR (BA) 71 Ja52
Valença do Minho P 106 Km52
Valença do Piauí BR (PI) 65 Hk49
Valençay F 102 Lb43
Valence F 104 La46
Valence F 105 Le46
Valence-sur-Baïse F 104 La47
València E 109 Kt49
València E 110 Ku51
Valencia RP 205 Rc42
Valencia YV 57 Gg40
Valencia de Alcántara E 108 Kn49
Valencia de Don Juan E 106 Kp52
Valenciennes F 103 Ld40
Vălenii de Munte RO 125 Mg45
Valeni-Stânișoara RO 125 Mf43
Valensole F 105 Lf47
Valentano I 122 Lm48
Valente BR (BA) 71 Ja51
Valentia Island IRL 100 Kk39
Valentim Gentil BR (SP) 74 He56
Valentín ROU 77 Hb61
Valentin RUS 181 Rh24
Valentine USA (NE) 26 Ek24
Valentine N.W.R. USA 26 Ek24
Valenza I 120 Lj45
Våler N 92 Lm30
Valera PE 66 Gb49
Valera YV 57 Ge41
Valeria E 109 Ks49
Valerio MEX (CHH) 38 Eg32
Valesdir VU 246 Te54
Valeuka BY 97 Mf37
Valevåg N 92 Lf31
Vale Verde BR (RS) 78 Hd60
Valga EST 96 Mg33
Val Grande, P.N.della I 120 Lj44
Valguarnera Caropepe I 122 Lp53
Valhalla Prov. Park CDN 18 Eb21
Vali Abad IR 154 Nf27
Valier USA (MT) 19 Ed21
Valira GR 128 Mb53
Vălișoara RO 124 Mc44
Văliug RO 124 Mc45
Val-Jalbert CDN 30 Gd21
Valjevo SCG 126 Lu46
Valka LV 97 Mf33
Valkeakoski FIN 96 Me29
Valkeala FIN 96 Mg30
Valkenswaard NL 112 Lf39
Valkmusan kansallispuisto FIN 96 Mg30
Valko = Valkom FIN 96 Mg30
Valkom = Valko FIN 96 Mg30
Valky UA 133 Mh21
Valkyrjedomen 313 Md33
Valla S 93 Lr31
Valladolid E 106 Kq51
Valladolid EC 60 Ga48
Valladolid MEX (YT) 41 Ff35
Vallargärdet S 93 Lo31
Vall de Boí E 110 La48
Valldemossa E 110 Lc51
Valle N 92 Lh31
Valle Altares RA 80 Gf67
Valle Castor RCH 82 Gf73
Valle d'Aosta I 120 Lh45
Valle de Allende MEX (CHH) 39 Eh32
Valle de Bravo MEX (MEX) 40 Ek36
Valle de Cabuérniga E 107 Kq53
Valle de Calingasta RA 76 Gf61
Valle de Chapalcó RA 80 Gh64
Valle de Guanape YV 57 Gh41
Valle dei Templi I 122 Lo53
Valle de la Luna BOL 72 Gf54
Valle de la Luna = Parque Provincial Ischigualasto RA 76 Gg61
Valle de la Luna RCH 72 Gf57
Valle de la Pascua YV 57 Gh41
Valle del Río Deseado RA 82 Gf69
Valle del Río Elqui RCH 76 Ge60
Valle de Santiago MEX (GJT) 40 Ek35
Valle de Viñales C 44 Fj34
Valle de Zaragoza MEX (CHH) 38 Eh32
Valle do Douro P 106 Kn51
Valledupar CO 56 Gd40
Vallée de la Lufira RDC 296 Md51
Vallée de l'Azaough RMM/RN 271 Lc37
Vallée de l'Azar RMM 271 Lb38
Vallée de l'Ourika MA 258 Kg30
Vallée de Mai N.P. SY 305 Nh48
Valle Edén ROU 77 Hb61
Vallée du Dadès MA 258 Kg30
Vallée du Drâa MA 258 Kg30
Vallée du Ferlo SN 269 Kd38
Vallée du M'Zab DZ 259 Lb29
Valléedu Saloum SN 269 Kc38
Vallée du Serpent RMM 270 Kf38
Vallée du Tîlemsi RMM 271 La36
Vallée du Ziz MA 258 Kh30
Valle Encantado RA 80 Ge66
Valle Fertil RA 76 Gg61
Valle General Racedo RA 80 Gf67
Vallegrande BOL 73 Gh55
Valle Gran Rey E 264 Kb31
Vallehermoso E 264 Kb31
Valle Hermoso MEX (TM) 39 Fb33
Valle Hermoso MEX (QTR) 41 Ff36
Vallei van Verlatheid SA 302 Mb62
Vallejo USA (CA) 20 Dj26
Valle Las Palmas MEX (BC) 22 Eb29
Valle Maracó Grande RA 80 Gh64
Valle-mí PY 73 Hb57
Valle Nacional MEX (OAX) 40 Fb37
Vallenar RCH 76 Ge60
Valle Nerecó RA 80 Gh64
Valle Nevado RCH 76 Ge62
Vallentuna S 93 Lt31
Valletta M 122 Lp55
Valle Ucal RA 81 Gh64
Valley USA (WY) 21 Ef23
Valley USA (AL) 35 Fh29
Valley City USA (ND) 26 Fb22
Valley Falls USA (OR) 20 Dk24
Valley Mills USA (TX) 28 Fb30
Valley of Desolation SA 302 Mb62
Valley of Fire S.P. USA 22 Ec27
Valley of Fires S.P. USA 23 Eg29
Valley of Flowers N.P. IND 189 Ok30
Valley of Lagoons AUS (QLD) 233 Sc55
Valley of the Kings ET 263 Mg33
Valley of wild elephants = Yexianggu VRC 195 Qa34
Valley of Willow USA (AK) 15 Cc11
Valley R. Ind. Res. CDN 24 Ek20
Valley River CDN 24 Ek20
Valley Station USA (KY) 34 Fh26
Valleyview CDN (AB) 19 Eb18
Valli di Comácchio I 120 Ln46
Vallières RH 46 Ge36
Vallon-Pont-d'Arc F 105 Le46
Vallorbe CH 114 Lg44
Valls E 110 Lb49
Vallsta S 93 Lr29
Vallvik S 93 Ls29
Valmanya F 104 Lc48
Val Marie CDN (SK) 19 Eg21
Valmiera LV 97 Mf33
Valognes F 102 Kt41
Valøy N 90 Lf13
Valožyn BY 97 Mg36
Valpaços P 106 Kn51
Val-Paradis CDN (QC) 25 Ga21
Valparai IND (TNU) 193 Oj41
Valparaiso BR (AC) 66 Gd49
Valparaíso BR (SP) 74 He56
Valparaiso CO 60 Gc45
Valparaíso MEX (ZCT) 39 Ej34
Valparaíso RCH 76 Ge62
Valparaiso USA (IN) 32 Fg25
Valpovo HR 121 Lt45
Valréas F 105 Le46
Vals SA 303 Md59
Valsad IND (GUJ) 190 Og35
Valsbaai SA 302 Lk63
Valset N 90 Le14
Valsjöbyn S 90 Lh13
Vals-les-Bains F 105 Le46
Valtellina I 120 Lk44
Valterlândia BR (AM) 67 Gg50
Val-Thorens F 105 Lg45
Valtournenche I 120 Lh45
Valujki RUS 133 Mk20
Valul lui Traian MD 125 Mj44
Valverde E 264 Kb32
Valverde de Júcar E 109 Ks49
Valverde del Camino E 108 Ko47
Valverde de Leganés E 108 Ko48
Valverde del Fresno E 108 Ko50
Vama RO 125 Mf43
Vamberk CZ 118 Lr40
Vamdrup DK 94 Lk35
Våmhus S 93 Lp29
Vamlingbo S 95 Lt33
Vammala FIN 96 Mc29
Vampula FIN 96 Mc29
Van TR 145 Nb26
Vanadzor ARM 152 Nc25
Vanajavesi FIN 96 Me29
Vana-Kuuste EST 96 Mg32
Vanalphensvlei SA 299 Me58
Vanån S 93 Lo29
Vanapa River PNG 243 Sd50
Van Asch van Wijckgebergte SME 59 Hc44
Vânatori RO 124 Mc46
Vânatori RO 125 Me44
Vanavara RUS 140 Qa06
VanBlomme-steinmeer = Brokopondo-stuwmeer SME 59 Hc43
Van Buren USA (AR) 29 Fc28
Van Buren USA (ME) 30 Gg22
Van Canh VN 197 Qe39
Vanceboro USA (ME) 31 Gg23
Vanceburg USA (KY) 35 Fj26
Vancouver CDN (BC) 18 Dj21
Vancouver USA (OR) 20 Dj23
Vancouver Island CDN 18 Df21
Vancouver Island Range CDN 18 Dh21
Vanda = Vantaa FIN 96 Me30
Vanda ANT (NZ) 313 Tb34
Van Daalen RI 213 Rj47
Vandalur IND (TNU) 193 Pa40
Vandavasi IND (TNU) 193 Ok40
Vandekerckhove Lake CDN 24 Ek17
Vanderbijlpark SA 303 Md59
Vandergrift USA (PA) 33 Ga25
Vanderhoof CDN (BC) 18 Dh18
Vanderkloof SA 303 Mc61
Vanderkloof Dam SA 303 Mc61
Vanderlei BR (BA) 70 Hj52
Vanderlin Island AUS 223 Rj53
Van de Wal RI 213 Rk47
Van Diemen Gulf AUS 223 Rf51
Vändra EST 96 Mf32
Vandyksdrif SA 303 Me59
Vandžiogala LT 97 Md35
Vāne LV 97 Mc34
Vanegas MEX (SLP) 39 Ek34
Vänern S 93 Ln32
Vänersborg S 92 Ln32
Vangaindrano RM 306 Nd57
Vangaži LV 97 Me33
Van Gölü TR 145 Nb26
Vangsnes N 92 Lg29
Vangunu SOL 245 Sk50
Vangunu, Mount SOL 245 Sj50
Vang Vieng LAO 197 Qb36
Vanh Ninh VN 197 Qe39
Van Horn USA (TX) 23 Eh30
Vani GE 152 Nb24
Vani IND (MHT) 190 Og35
Vanikolo SOL 241 Tb21
Vanimo PNG 242 Sa47
Vanivilasa Sagara IND 193 Oj40
Vaniyambadi IND (TNU) 193 Ok40
Vânju Mare RO 124 Mc46
Van Lan VN 197 Qe40
Van Mijenfjorden N 91 Lh07
Vanna N 90 Lk10
Vannareid N 90 Lk10
Vännäs S 90 Lk14
Vannes F 102 Ks43
Vannsjø N 92 Ll31
Vanoise, P.N.de la F 105 Lg45
Vanovano SOL 244 Sj50
Van Reenen SA 303 Me60
Vanrhynsdorp SA 302 Lk61
Vanrook AUS (QLD) 232 Sa54
Vansbro S 93 Lp30
Vänsjö S 93 Lq29
Vanstadensrus SA 303 Md60
Vantaa = Vanda FIN 96 Me30
Vantaa FIN 96 Me30
Vantage CDN (SK) 19 Eh21
Vantage USA (WA) 18 Dk22
Van Tassell USA (WY) 21 Eh24
Vanthli IND (GUJ) 190 Of35
Vant's Drift SA 303 Mf60
Vanttauskoski FIN 91 Md12
Vanua Balavu FJI 247 Ua54
Vanua Lava VU 246 Td52
Vanua Levu FJI 247 Tk54
Vanuatu 219 Ta11
Vanuire, T.I. BR 74 He56
Vanvikan N 90 Lf14
Van Wert USA (OH) 32 Fh25
Van Wyksdorp SA 302 Ma62
Van Wyksvlei SA 302 Ma61
Van Zylsrus SA 302 Mb59
Vao F 246 Td57
Vapi LAO 197 Qc38
Vaquería MEX (NL) 39 Fa33
Var F 105 Lg47
Vara S 93 Ln32
Varadero C 44 Fk34
Varades F 102 Kt43
Varakallu IND (APH) 190 Ok38
Varakļāni LV 97 Mg34
Varalé CI 279 Kj41
Varallo I 120 Lj45
Varamin IR 154 Nf28
Varanasi IND (UPH) 191 Pb33
Vărăncău MD 125 Mk43
Varangerbotn N 91 Me10
Varangerfjorden N 91 Mf10
Varangerhaløya N 91 Me10
Varapaeva BY 97 Mh35
Varar IND 190 Oe34
Văratec RO 124 Mc43
Varaždin HR 121 Lr44
Varaždinske Toplice HR 121 Lr44
Varazze I 120 Lj46
Varberg S 94 Ln33
Vărbica BG 127 Mg48
Varbola EST 96 Me31
Várda GR 128 Mb52
Vardannapet IND (APH) 191 Ok37
Vardar MK 126 Mc49
Vardar klisura MK 126 Mc49
Vardarski Rid MK 126 Mc49
Varde DK 94 Lj35
Vardenis ARM 152 Nc25
Vardin IR 154 Nd26
Vardö FIN 93 Ma30
Vårdö FIN 93 Ma30
Vardø N 91 Mf10
Vardzya GE 152 Nb25
Varekil S 94 Lm32
Varel D 112 Lj37
Varela GNB 269 Kb39
Varela RA (SL) 76 Gg63
Varėna LT 97 Me36
Varena I LT 97 Me36
Varengeville-sur-Mer F 102 La41
Varennes-en-Argonne F 103 Lf41
Varennes-sur-Allier F 105 Ld44
Vareš BIH 121 Lt46
Varese I 120 Lj45
Varese Ligure I 120 Lk46
Vârfu Câmpului RO 125 Mg43
Vârfurile RO 124 Mc44
Vårgårda S 95 Ln32
Vargem BR 71 Ja50
Vargem Grande BR (MA) 64 Hj47
Varginha BR (MG) 75 Hh56
Vargön S 92 Ln32
Varhaug N 92 Lf32
Varilhes F 104 Lb47
Varillas PE 72 Ge58
Varirata N.P. PNG 243 Sd50
Váris GR 126 Mb50
Varjota BR (CE) 65 Hk48
Varkala IND (KER) 192 Oj42
Varkan IR 154 Nf29
Varkaus FIN 96 Mh28
Varmahlíð IS 90 Ka13
Värmeln S 93 Ln31
Värmland S 93 Ln30
Värmlandsbro S 93 Lo31
Värmlandsnäs S 93 Lo31
Varna BG 127 Mh47
Värnamo S 95 Lp33
Varniai LT 97 Mc35
Varnja EST 96 Mh32
Varnjany BY 97 Mg36
Varnsdorf CZ 113 Lp40
Varoška Rijeka BIH 121 Lr45
Várpalota H 118 Lt43
Vârșag RO 125 Mf44
Văršec BG 126 Md47
Văršilo BG 127 Mh48
Vartdal N 92 Lg28
Varto TR 145 Na26
Vârtop RO 124 Md46
Vartun IR 154 Ng29
Varva UA 132 Mg20
Varvara BG 127 Me48
Varzaneh IR 154 Ng29
Várzea Alegre BR (CE) 65 Ja49
Várzea da Palma BR (MG) 75 Hh54
Várzea do Poço BR (BA) 71 Hk51
Várzea Grande BR (PI) 64 Hj49
Varzea Grande BR (MT) 69 Hb53
Várzeas BR (BA) 70 Hh52
Varzelândia BR (MG) 70 Hh53
Varzi I 120 Lk46
Varzy F 103 Ld43
Vasa Barris BR 71 Ja50
Vasalemma EST 96 Me31
Vasaloppet S 93 Lp29
Vásárosnamény H 119 Mc42
Vasco da Gama IND (GOA) 190 Og38
Vasconcelos MEX (VC) 41 Fc37
Vasil'evka RUS 180 Rh22
Vasil'evo RUS 96 Mh33
Vasil'evo RUS (TAR) 133 Ne18
Vasilikí GR 128 Ma52
Vasiščeve UA 133 Mj21
Vasjuganskaja ravnina RUS 140 Od07
Vaškai LT 97 Me34
Vaskivesi FIN 96 Md28
Vasknarva EST 96 Mh32
Vas'kovo RUS 91 Na13
Vaslui RO 125 Mh44
Vaslui RO 125 Mh44
Väsman S 93 Lp30
Vassilika GR 126 Md50
Vassílikó GR 128 Md52
Vassilikós GR 128 Ma53
Västansjö S 90 Lh13
Västbacka S 93 Lp29
Västerås S 93 Lr31
Västerbotten S 90 Ma13
Västerdalälven S 93 Lo30
Väster-Götland S 94 Ln32
Västerhaninge S 93 Lt31
Västervik S 95 Lr33
Vasto I 122 Lp48
Våstra S 93 Ls31
Västra Åmtervik S 93 Lo31
Vasvár H 118 Lr43
Vasylivka UA 135 Mh22
Vasyl'kiv UA 134 Mf20
Vasyl'kivka UA 135 Mj21
Vața de Jos RO 124 Mc44
Vatan F 102 Lb43
Vatersay GB 98 Kn34
Váthi GR 126 Mc49
Vathí GR 129 Mg54
Vatican City V 122 Ln49
Vatla EST 96 Md32
Vatnajökull IS 90 Kb13
Vatne N 92 Lg28
Vatoa FJI 221 Ua22
Vatolatsaka RM 306 Nc57
Vatomandry RM 306 Ne55
Vatra MD 125 Mj43
Vatra Dornei RO 125 Mf43
Vatra Moldoviței RO 125 Mf43
Vattaikundu IND (TNU) 193 Oj41
Vattanam IND (TNU) 193 Ok42
Vattaru Channel MV 192 Og44
Vättern S 93 Lp32
Vättlax FIN 96 Mc31
Vatu-i-ra Channel FJI 247 Tk54
Vatulele FJI 247 Tj55
Vatutine UA 134 Mf21
Vaucouleurs F 103 Lf42
Vaudrey F 105 Lf44
Vaughan Springs AUS (NT) 226 Rf57
Vaughn USA (NM) 23 Eh28
Vau i Dejës AL 126 Lu49
Vaukalata BY 97 Mh36
Vaukavysk BY 117 Me37
Vaukavyskae uzvyšša BY 117 Me37
Vaupés CO 61 Ge45
Vauvert F 105 Le47
Vauxhall CDN (AB) 19 Ed20
Vavatenina RM 306 Ne54
Vavau WS 248 Be53
Vava'u Group TO 248 Bd55
Vava'u Island TO 248 Bd55
Väversunda S 93 Lp32
Vavoua CI 278 Kg42
Vavuniya CL 193 Pa42
Vaxholm S 93 Lt31
Växjö S 95 Lp34
Våxtorp S 95 Lo34
Vayittiri = Vythiri IND (KER) 192 Oj41
Vayrac F 104 Lb46
Vazante BR (MG) 75 Hg54
Vazobe RM 306 Nd55
Vazvan IR 154 Nf29
Veal Rinh K 197 Qb40
Vechelde D 113 Ll38
Vechta D 112 Lj38
Vecinos E 106 Kp50
Vecpiebalga LV 97 Mf33
Veclaicene LV 97 Mg33
Vecses H 119 Lu43
Vecumnieki LV 97 Me34
Vedaranyam IND (TNU) 193 Ok41
Veddige S 94 Ln33
Vedea RO 125 Mf46
Vedea RO 127 Mf47
Vedevåg S 93 Lq31
Vedia RA (BA) 77 Gk63
Vedrovo RUS 133 Nb17
Vedshir IND (MHT) 190 Oh36
Veendam NL 112 Lg37
Veenendaal NL 112 Lf39
Veere EST 96 Mc32
Vega N 90 Lf13
Vega USA (TX) 23 Ej28
Vega Baja USA (PR) 47 Gg36
Vega de Alatorre MEX (VC) 40 Fb35
Vegadeo E 106 Kn53
Vegamót IS 90 Jj13
Vegarienza E 106 Ko52
Vegårshei N 92 Lj32
Veghel NL 112 Lf39
Véglie I 123 Ls50
Vegreville CDN (AB) 19 Ed19
Végueta PE 66 Gb51
Vegusdal N 92 Lj32
Vehmaa FIN 96 Mb30
Vehu FIN 96 Me28
Veidelevka RUS 133 Mk20
Veiprty CZ 118 Lo40
Veiru PNG 243 Sc49
Veisiejai LT 97 Md36
Ve Javis AUS (QLD) 234 Sb58
Vejen DK 94 Lk35
Vejer de la Frontera E 108 Kp46
Vejle DK 94 Lk35
Vejle Fjord DK 94 Lk35
Vekilski BG 127 Mh47
Velacruz EC 60 Ga47
Vela Luka HR 121 Lr48
Velanganni IND (TNU) 193 Ok41
Velanídia GR 128 Md54
Velapur IND (MHT) 190 Oh37
Velasco Ibarra EC 60 Ga46
Velasco Ibarra = Empalmé EC 60 Ga46
Vel'aty SK 119 Mb42
Velavadar N.P. IND 190 Og34
Velázquez ROU 77 Hc63
Velbert D 112 Lh39
Velden A 115 Lp44
Veldhoven NL 112 Lf39
Veldrif SA 302 Lk62
Veldurti IND (APH) 193 Oj39
Velebit HR 121 Lq46
Velēna LV 97 Mg33
Velencei-tó H 119 Lt43
Velenje SLO 121 Lq44
Veles MK 126 Mb49
Velestino GR 128 Mc51
Velež BIH 121 Ls47
Vélez CO 56 Gd42
Vélez Blanco E 109 Ks47
Vélez-Málaga E 108 Kq46
Vélez Rubio E 109 Ks47
Vélia I 122 Lq50
Velika GR 128 Mb53
Velika HR 121 Ls45
Velika Gorica HR 121 Lr45
Velikaja RUS 96 Mj33
Velikaja Guba RUS (KAR) 91 Mh14
Velikaja Kema RUS 181 Rj23
Velika Kladuša HR 121 Lq45
Velika Paklenica HR 121 Lq46
Velika Plana SCG 126 Mb47
Velika Planina SCG 126 Mb48
Velika Slatina SCG 126 Ma48
Veliki Dal'nik UA 125 Ml44
Veliki Gradište SCG 124 Mb46
Veliki Grdevac HR 121 Ls45
Veliki kanal SCG 124 Lu45
Veliki Kupci SCG 126 Mb47
Veliki Morava SCG 126 Mb46
Veliki Novosilka UA 135 Mj22
Veliki Plana SCG 124 Mb46
Veliki Preslav BG 127 Mg47
Veliki Radinci SCG 124 Lu45
Veliki Šiljegovac SCG 126 Mb47
Veliki Zdenci HR 121 Ls45
Veliko Tărnovo BG 127 Mf47
Velille PE 67 Ge53
Velimlje SCG 126 Lt48
Velingara SN 269 Kc38
Vélingara SN 269 Kc39
Velingrad BG 127 Me48
Veliž RUS 132 Mf18
Veljun HR 121 Lq45
Velká Biteš CZ 118 Lr41
Veľké Kapušany SK 119 Mc42
Velké Losiny CZ 118 Ls40
Velké Meziříčí CZ 118 Lr41
Velkomstpynten N 91 Lg06
Velký Bor CZ 118 Lo41
Veľký Krtíš SK 119 Lu42
Veľký Šariš SK 119 Mb41
Veľký Tribeč SK 118 Lt42
Vella Lavella SOL 244 Sj49
Vellankulam CL 193 Pa42
Velletri I 122 Ln49
Vellinge S 95 Lo35
Vellmar D 112 Lk39
Vellore IND (TNU) 193 Ok40
Velloso RA (BA) 81 Ha64
Velmerstot D 112 Lj39
Velneshwar Beach IND 190 Og37
Vel'sk RUS 140 Na06
Velugodu IND (APH) 190 Ok38
Veluwezoom, N.P. NL 112 Lg38
Velventós GR 126 Mc50
Velyka Hluša UA 117 Mf39
Velyka Horonycja UA 117 Mf40
Velyka Lepetycha UA 134 Mg22
Velyka Mychajlivka UA 125 Mk43
Velyka Pysarivka UA 132 Mh20
Velyki Dederkaly UA 134 Md21
Velyki Mosty UA 117 Me40
Velykoploske UA 125 Mk43
Velykyj Bereznyj UA 119 Mc42
Velytkyi Burluk UA 133 Mj21
Veman S 93 Lo28
Vemb DK 94 Lj34
Vembanad Lake IND 192 Oj42
Vemdalen S 93 Lo28
Vemork N 92 Lj31
Vempalle IND (APH) 193 Ok39
Vemulavada IND 191 Ok36
Ven S 94 Ln35
Venable Ice Shelf 312 Fc33
Venado MEX (SLP) 39 Ek34
Venado Tuerto RA (SF) 77 Gk62
Venafro I 122 Lp49
Venâncio Aires BR (RS) 78 Hd60
Venarey-les Laumes F 103 Le43
Venčane SCG 124 Ma46
Vence F 105 Lh47
Venda Nova P 106 Kn51
Venda Nova do Imigrante BR (ES) 75 Hk56
Vendas Novas P 108 Km48
Vendée F 102 Kt44
Vendée F 102 Kt44
Vendeuvre-sur-Barse F 103 Le42
Vendôme F 102 Lb43
Venec BG 127 Mg47
Venetie USA (AK) 15 Cg12
Véneto I 120 Lm45
Venev RUS 133 Mk18
Veneza BR (PI) 65 Hj48
Veneza BR (PE) 71 Ja50
Venézia I 120 Ln45
Venezuela 51 Gb09
Venezuela Basin 46 Gf37
Vengurla IND (MHT) 190 Og38
Vengurla Beach IND 190 Og38
Veniaminof Volcano USA 14 Ca17
Venice I 120 Ln45
Venice USA (LA) 29 Ff31
Venice USA (FL) 36 Fj32
Vénissieux F 105 Le45
Venjan S 93 Lo30
Venjanssjön S 93 Lo30
Venkatagiri IND (APH) 193 Ok40
Venkatagirikota IND (APH) 193 Ok40
Venkatapuram IND (APH) 191 Pa36
Venlo NL 112 Lg39
Vennesla N 92 Lh32
Venosa I 123 Lq50
Venray NL 112 Lg39
Venta LT 97 Mc34
Venta LV 97 Mb33
Venta de Ballerías E 107 Ku51
Venta de Baños E 106 Kq51
Ventanas EC 60 Ga46
Ventania BR (PR) 74 He58
Vente LT 97 Mb35
Ventersburg SA 303 Md60
Ventersdorp SA 303 Md59
Venterstad SA 303 Mc61
Ventilla BOL 72 Gg55
Ventimíglia I 120 Lh47
Ventisquero, Cerro RA 80 Ge66
Ventisquero Sur, Cerro RCH 80 Ge67
Ventspils LV 97 Mb33
Ventuari YV 57 Gg43
Ventura USA (CA) 22 Ea28
Venturosa BR (PE) 71 Jb50
Venu IND 190 Oe35
Veppur IND (TNU) 193 Ok41
Vera BR (MT) 69 Hc52
Vera E 109 Kt47
Vera RA (SF) 77 Gk60
Vera Cruz BR (BA) 71 Ja52
Veracruz MEX (VC) 40 Fb36
Veracruz MEX 40 Fb35
Veracruz NIC 42 Fg40
Vera Cruz do Oeste BR (PR) 74 Hd58
Veranópolis BR (RS) 78 He60
Veraval IND (GUJ) 190 Of35
Verbania I 120 Lj45
Verbeek Mountains RI 209 Ra47
Verbier CH 114 Lh44
Vercelli I 120 Lj45
Verchnjadzvimsk BY 132 Md18
Verchnje Syn'ovydne UA 119 Md41
Verchn'odniprovs'k UA 134 Mh21
Verdalsøra N 90 Lf14
Verde MEX 38 Eg32
Verde Island RP 203 Ra39
Verden (Aller) D 112 Lk38
Verdigre USA (NE) 26 Fa24
Verdon F 105 Lg47
Verdun F 103 Lf41
Verdún ROU 77 Hc62
Verdun-sur-le-Doubs F 105 Lf44
Vereeniging SA 303 Md59
Verena SA 299 Me58
Verenal CO 60 Gb44
Vergara ROU 77 Hd62
Vergato I 120 Lm46
Vergeleë SA 299 Mc58
Vergemont AUS (QLD) 232 Sb57
Vergennes USA (VT) 33 Gd23
Vergina GR 126 Mc50
Vergt F 104 La45
Verhneimbatsk RUS 140 Pb06
Verhnetulomskoe Vodohranilišče RUS 91 Mf11
Verhnezejskaja ravnina RUS 141 Rb08
Verhnie Usugh RUS 173 Qh19
Verhnij Baskunčak RUS 133 Nd21
Verhnij Enisej RUS 167 Pg20
Verhnij Mel'gin RUS 180 Rf20
Véria GR 126 Mc50
Verila BG 126 Md48
Verin E 106 Kn51
Verinsko BG 126 Md48
Veriora EST 96 Mh32
Verkehrshaus CH 114 Lj43
Verkhoyanskiy Mountains RUS 141 Rb05
Verkykerskop SA 303 Me59
Verl D 112 Lj39
Verla FIN 96 Mg29
Verlegenhuken N 91 Lj05
Vermandois F 103 Ld41
Vermelho BR 63 Hf49
Vermelho BR 64 Hg50
Vermelho BR 69 He53
Vermenton F 103 Ld43
Vermilion CDN (AB) 19 Ee19
Vermilion Bay CDN (ON) 24 Fd21
Vermilion Bay USA 29 Fe31
Vermilion Lake CDN 24 Fd20
Vermilion River CDN 19 Ed19
Vermillion USA (SD) 27 Fb24
Vermont USA 33 Gd23
Vernadsky ANT (UA) 312 Gc32
Vernal USA (UT) 21 Ef25
Vernazza I 120 Lk46
Vernești RO 125 Mg45
Verneuil-sur-Avre F 102 La42

Verneuk Pan SA 302 Ma60
Vernoe RUS 180 Re20
Vernon CDN (BC) 18 Ea20
Vernon F 103 Lb41
Vernon USA (UT) 21 Ed25
Vernon USA (TX) 28 Fa28
Vernon Islands AUS 223 Rf52
Vero F 111 Lk48
Vero Beach USA (FL) 36 Fk32
Verona I 120 Lm45
Véronica RA (BA) 77 Hb63
Ver-o-Peso (Belém) BR (PA) 64 Hf46
Versailles F 103 Lc42
Versailles USA (MO) 27 Fd26
Versailles USA (IN) 32 Fh26
Versailles USA (KY) 35 Fh26
Versalles CO 56 Gb43
Veršino-Darasunskij RUS 173 Qh19
Versmold D 112 Lj38
Vertelim RUS (MOR) 133 Nc18
Vertentes BR (PE) 71 Jc49
Vertijievka UA 132 Mf20
Vertintes C 45 Ga35
Vertiskos GR 126 Md50
Vértiz RA (LP) 76 Gj63
Vertjačij RUS 133 Nb21
Vertus F 103 Lc42
Verulam SA 303 Mf60
Verviers B 103 Lf40
Vervins F 103 Ld41
Vesanka FIN 96 Mf28
Vesegonsk RUS 132 Mj16
Vesele UA 135 Mh22
Veselij Kut UA 125 Mk44
Veselí nad Lužnicí CZ 118 Lp41
Veselí nad Moravou CZ 118 Ls42
Veselovskoe Vodohranilišče RUS 135 Na22
Vešenskaja RUS 133 Na21
Vesjoloje RUS 117 Lu36
Vesoul F 103 Lg43
Vespaciano BR (MG) 75 Hj55
Vessigebro S 94 Ln34
Vestby N 92 Ll31
Veste Coburg D 115 Ll40
Vesterålen N 90 Lh11
Vesterli N 90 Lh12
Vesterø Havn DK 94 Ll33
Vesterøy N 92 Ll31
Vestfjorden N 90 Lg12
Vestfonna N 91 Lk06
Vestiges préhistoriques et Peintures rupestres RN 266 Le35
Vestmannaeyjar IS 90 Jk14
Vestnes N 92 Lh28
Vestvågøy N 90 Lg11
Vesúvio I 122 Lp50
Veszprém H 118 Ls43
Vetel RO 124 Mc45
Vetlanda S 95 Lq33
Vetluga RUS 133 Nc17
Vetluga RUS 133 Nd17
Vetrişoaia RO 125 Mj44
Větrný Jeníkov CZ 118 Lq41
Veulettes-sur-Mer F 102 La41
Veurne B 103 Lc39
Vevelstad = Forvika N 90 Lg13
Vevey CH 114 Lg44
Vévi GR 126 Mb50
Veymandhoo MV 192 Og44
Veymandhoo Channel MV 192 Og44
Veynes F 105 Lf46
Veys IR 154 Ne30
Vézelay F 103 Ld43
Vézère F 104 Lb45
Vezirköprü TR 144 Mh25
V. Guerrero MEX (BC) 22 Ec29
V. Guerrero MEX (ZCT) 39 Ej34
Vhembe-Dongola N.P. SA 300 Me57
Vi S 93 Ls28
Via Appia I 122 Ln49
Viacha BOL 72 Gf54
Viadana I 120 Ll46
Viaduc-de-Garabit F 105 Ld46
Viaducto la Polvorilla RA 72 Gg58
Viadutos BR (RS) 78 Hd59
Vialadougou CI 278 Kg41
Viale RA (ER) 77 Ha61
Via Lemovicensis F 104 La45
Via Mala CH 114 Lk44
Viamonte RA (CD) 76 Gj62
Viana ANG 288 Lg50
Viana BR (PA) 63 He46
Viana BR (MA) 64 Hh47
Viana BR (ES) 75 Hk56
Viana E 107 Ks52
Viana de Bolo E 106 Kn52
Viana do Alentejo P 108 Kn48
Viana do Castelo P 106 Km51
Vianden L 103 Lg41
Vianen NL 112 Lf39
Viangchan LAO 197 Qb36
Vianópolis BR (GO) 74 Hf54
Via Podiensis F 104 Lb46
Viareggio I 120 Ll47
Vias F 105 Ld47
Viaté G 281 Lf45
Via Tolosana F 104 Lc47
Via Turonensis F 102 La44
Vibble S 95 Lt33
Viborg DK 94 Lk34
Vibo Valéntia I 123 Lr52
Vibraye F 102 La42
Vic E 110 Lc49
Vicam MEX (SO) 38 Ee32
Vicdessos F 104 Lb48
Vic-en-Bigorre F 104 La47
Vicente Guerrero MEX (BC) 22 Ec30
Vicente Guerrero MEX (DGO) 39 Ej34
Vicentinópolis BR (GO) 74 Hf54
Vicenza I 120 Lm45
Vichada CO 57 Gf43
Vichadero ROU 77 Hc61
Viche EC 60 Ga45
Vichina RA 76 Gf60
Vichy F 105 Ld44
Vichy-Bellerive F 105 Ld44
Vici USA (OK) 28 Fa27
Vicksburg USA (MS) 29 Fe29
Vic-le-Comte F 105 Ld45
Vic-le-Fesq F 105 Le47
Vico F 111 Lj48
Viçosa BR (AL) 71 Jb50
Viçosa BR (MG) 75 Hj56
Viçosa do Ceará BR (CE) 65 Hk47
Vicovu de Jos RO 125 Mf43
Vic-sur-Cère F 105 Lc46
Victor USA (ID) 21 Ee24
Victor Harbour AUS (SA) 236 Rk63
Victoria AUS 220 Sa26
Victoria = Limbé CAM 280 Le43
Victoria CDN (BC) 18 Dj21
Victoria CO 56 Gc43
Victoria M 122 Lp54
Victoria RA (ER) 77 Gk62
Victoria RA (LP) 80 Gh64
Victoria RCH 80 Gd65
Victoria RO 125 Me45
Victoria RO 125 Mh43
Victoria RP 203 Ra39
Victoria SY 305 Nh48
Victoria USA (TX) 29 Fb31
Victoria Beach CDN (MB) 24 Fb20
Victoria Bryant S.P. USA 35 Fj28
Victoria Falls ZW 295 Mc54
Victoria Falls ZW/Z 299 Mc54
Victoria Highway AUS 223 Re53
Victoria Island CDN 10 Eb04
Victoria Lake CDN 31 Hb21
Victoria Land ANT 313 Tb33
Victoria Memorial IND 194 Pe34
Victoria, Mount MYA 194 Pg35
Victoria, Mount NZ 239 Tg67
Victoria, Mount PNG 243 Sd50
Victoria Nile EAU 290 Mg45
Victoria Nile EAU 290 Mf44
Victoria Park Racecourse AUS (SA) 236 Rk63
Victoria River AUS (NT) 223 Rf53
Victoria River AUS 223 Rf53
Victoria River CDN 31 Hb21
Victoria River Downs AUS (NT) 223 Rf54
Victorias RP 205 Rb40
Victoria Strait CDN 10 Ed05
Victoriaville CDN (QC) 30 Ge22
Victoria West SA 302 Mb61
Victorino C 45 Gb35
Victor, Mount 313 Mc33
Victor Rosales MEX (ZCT) 39 Ej34
Victorville USA (CA) 22 Eb28
Victory, Mount PNG 243 Se50
Vičuga RUS 133 Na17
Vicuña RCH 76 Ge61
Vicuña Mackenna RA (CD) 76 Gh62
Vicus PE 60 Fk48
Vida USA (OR) 20 Dj23
Vida USA (MT) 21 Eh22
Vidal PE 61 Gd47
Vidal USA (CA) 22 Ec28
Vidalia USA (GA) 35 Fj29
Vidal Junction USA (CA) 22 Ec28
Vidamlja BY 117 Md38
Vidauban F 105 Lg47
Videbæk DK 94 Lj34
Videira BR (SC) 78 He59
Videle RO 125 Mf46
Videsæter N 92 Lh29
Vidice CZ 118 Ln41
Vidigueira P 108 Kn48
Vidin BG 126 Mc47
Vidisha IND (MPH) 191 Oj34
Vidiškiai LT 97 Me35
Vidneva BY 97 Mg36
Vidsel S 90 Ma13
Viduša BIH 121 Lt48
Vidzeme LV 97 Mf33
Vidzy BY 97 Mg35
Viechtach D 115 Ln41
Viedgesville SA 303 Me61
Viedma RA (RN) 81 Gj66
Viedma, Volcán RA 82 Gd70
Vieille Chapelle (Tadoussac) CDN 30 Gf21
Viejo RA 76 Gj60
Viejo, Volcán NIC 42 Fg39
Viekšniai LT 97 Mc34
Vielha E 110 La48
Vielsalm B 103 Lf40
Vienenburg D 113 Ll39
Vieng Kham LAO 195 Qb35
Vieng Phukha LAO 195 Qa35
Vieng Thong LAO 195 Qb35
Vieng Xai LAO 178 Qc35
Vienna A 115 Lr42
Vienna USA (MO) 27 Fe26
Vienna USA (IL) 29 Ff27
Vienna USA (OH) 33 Fk26
Vienne F 102 La44
Vienne F 105 Le45
Vientiane = Viangchan LAO 197 Qb36
Vieques USA 47 Gh36
Vierheim D 114 Lj41
Viersen D 112 Lg39
Vierwaldstätter See CH 114 Lj44
Vierzehnheiligen D 115 Lm40
Vierzon F 103 Lc43
Viesca MEX (COH) 39 Ej33
Viesite LV 97 Mf34
Vieste I 123 Lr49
Vietas S 90 Lk12
Vietnam VN 139 Qa08
Viet Tri VN 178 Qc35
Vieux Bordeaux F 104 Ku46
Vieux Fort WL 47 Gk39
Vif F 105 Lf45
Viga RP 203 Rc39
Vigala EST 96 Me32
Vigan RP 202 Ra37
Vigeland N 92 Lh32
Vigévano I 120 Lj45
Vigia BR (PA) 64 Hf46
Vigia Chico MEX (QTR) 41 Fg36
Vignola I 120 Ll46
Vigo E 106 Km52
Vigra N 92 Lg28
Vigrestad N 92 Lf32
Vihanti FIN 91 Mc13
Vihari PK 161 Og30
Vihiers F 102 Ku43
Vihotraivo RM 306 Ne54
Vihtari FIN 96 Mk28
Vihti FIN 96 Me30
Viiala FIN 96 Md29
Viira EST 96 Md32
Viisarimäki FIN 96 Mg28
Viişoara RO 125 Mg44
Viitasaari FIN 91 Mc14
Viitna EST 96 Mg31
Viivikonna EST 96 Mh31
Vijayapuri North IND (APH) 191 Ok37
Vijayawada IND (APH) 191 Pa37
Vijaydurg IND (MHT) 190 Og37
Vijaydurg Beach IND 190 Og37
Vijosë AL 126 Ma50
Vik IS 90 Ka14
Vik S 95 Lp35
Vika S 93 Lp30
Vikajärvi FIN 91 Md12
Vikanes N 92 Lf30
Vikarabad IND (APH) 190 Oj37
Vikarbyn S 93 Lq30
Vikedal N 92 Lf31
Vikeke TIM 214 Rd50
Viken S 94 Ln34
Vikenara Point SOL 245 Sk50
Vikersund N 92 Lk31
Vikevåg N 92 Lf31
Vikindu EAT 293 Mk49
Viking CDN (AB) 19 Ee19
Vikingskipet N 92 Lm30
Vikna N 90 Lf13
Vikno UA 125 Mf42
Vikos-Aoos N.P. GR 128 Ma51
Vikran N 90 Lk11
Viksjö S 93 Ls28
Viksøyri N 92 Lg29
Vila Aurora BR (PA) 64 Hg47
Vila Bela da São Trinidade BR (MT) 68 Ha53
Vila Capixabas BR (AC) 67 Gg51
Vila Conceição BR (PA) 64 Hg47
Vila de Manica MOC 300 Mg55
Vila de Rei P 108 Km49
Vila de Sena MOC 297 Mh54
Vila do Bispo P (Portugal) 108 Km47
Vila do Maio CV 268 Jj38
Vila dos Remédios BR (RN) 65 Jd47
Vila Flor ANG 294 Lh52
Vila Flor P 106 Kn51
Vilafranca del Maestrat E 109 Ku50
Vilafranca del Penedès E 110 Lb49
Vila Franca de Xira P 108 Km48
Vilagarcia de Arousa E 106 Km52
Vilaine F 102 Ks43
Vilaka LV 97 Mh33
Vilakalaka VU 246 Td53
Vilalba = Villalba E 106 Kn53
Vila Martins BR (AM) 67 Gf49
Vila Meriti BR (AM) 62 Ha48
Vila Mouzinho MOC 296 Mh53
Vila Nazaré BR (AM) 62 Gh47
Viljani LV 97 Mg34
Vilankulo MOC 300 Mh57
Vilano Beach USA (FL) 36 Fk31
Vila Nova ANG 294 Lj52
Vila Nova da Fronteira MOC 297 Mh54
Vila Nova de Famalição P 106 Km51
Vila Nova de Foz Côa P 106 Kn51
Vila Nova de Milfontes P 108 Km47
Vila Nova de Paiva P 106 Kn50
Vila Nova do Piauí BR (PI) 65 Hk49
Vila Nova do Seles ANG 294 Lh51
Vilanova i la Geltrú E 110 Lb49
Vila Nova Sintra CV 268 Jh38
Vila Palestina BR (PA) 64 Hg48
Vila Porto Franco BR (AM) 62 Ha49
Vila Pouca de Aguiar P 106 Kn51
Vilar P 106 Kn50
Vila-real E 109 Ku49
Vila Real P 106 Kn51
Vila Real de Santo Antonio P 108 Kn47
Vilar Formoso P 106 Ko50
Vila Rica BR (MT) 69 He51
Vila Rica BR (MS) 74 Hc57
Vilarinho do Monte BR (PA) 63 Hd46
Vila Sagrado Coração de Jesus BR (AM) 62 Ha48
Vila Tambaqui BR (AM) 62 Gh47
Vila Tepequem BR (RR) 58 Gk44
Vilattikulam IND (TNU) 193 Ok42
Vila Tugendhat CZ 118 Lr41
Vila Valério BR (ES) 75 Hk55
Vila Velha BR (AP) 59 He44
Vila Velha BR 74 He58
Vila Velha BR (ES) 75 Hk56
Vila Velha de Ródão P 108 Kn49
Vila Verde de Ficalho P 108 Kn47
Vila Viçosa P 108 Kn48
Vilcabamba EC 60 Ga48
Vilcabamba Viejo PE 66 Gd52
Vilcashuamán PE 66 Gd52
Vilcas Huaman PE 66 Gd52
Vilches E 109 Kr48
Vilcún RCH 80 Gd65
Vilcún RCH 80 Gd65
Vildbjerg DK 94 Lj34
Vilejka BY 97 Mg36
Vilelas RA (SE) 77 Gj59
Vilhelmina S 90 Lj13
Vilhena BR (RO) 68 Gk52
Viligili MV 192 Og45
Vilija BY 97 Mg36
Viljandi EST 96 Mf32
Viljoenskroon SA 303 Md59
Viljuj RUS 141 Ra06
Viljujsk RUS 141 Ra06
Viljujskoe plato RUS 141 Qc05
Viljujskoe vdhr. RUS 141 Qc06
Vilkaviškis LT 97 Md36
Vilkija LT 97 Md35
Villa Abecia BOL 72 Gh56
Villa Adriana I 122 Ln49
Villa Ahumada MEX (CHH) 23 Eg30
Villa Alegre RCH 80 Ge63
Villa Alemana RCH 76 Ge62
Villa Alhué RCH 76 Ge62
Villa Amengual RCH 80 Gd68
Villa Ana RA (SF) 77 Ha60
Villa Angela RA (CH) 77 Gk59
Villa Atamisqui RA (SE) 76 Gj60
Villa Atuel RA (MD) 76 Gg63
Villa Azueta MEX (VC) 40 Fc36
Villaba RP 205 Rc40
Villa Berthet RA (CH) 77 Gk59
Villablino E 106 Ko52
Villa Bruzual YV 57 Gf41
Villa Bustos RA (LR) 76 Gg60
Villacañas E 109 Kr49
Villa Cañas RA (SF) 77 Gk63
Villacarillo E 109 Kr48
Villa Carlos Paz RA (CD) 76 Gh61
Villacarriedo E 107 Kr53
Villacastin E 106 Kq50
Villach A 115 Lo44
Villacidro I 111 Lj51
Villa Constitución RA (SF) 77 Gk62
Villada E 106 Kq52
Villadama MEX (NL) 39 Ek32
Villa de Arista MEX (SLP) 39 Ek34
Villa de Cura YV 57 Gg40
Villa de Guadelupe MEX (CAM) 41 Fe36
Villa del Carmén ROU 77 Hb62
Villa de Leyva CO 56 Gd43
Villa del Río E 108 Kq47
Villa del Rosario RA (CD) 76 Gj61
Villa del Totoral RA (CD) 76 Gh61
Villa de María RA (CD) 76 Gj60
Villa de Reyes MEX (SLP) 40 Ek35
Villa d'Este I 122 Ln49
Villa de Zaachila MEX (OAX) 40 Fb37
Villadiego E 107 Kq52
Villa Dolores RA (CD) 76 Gh61
Villa Dos Trece RA (FO) 77 Ha59
Villa El Chocón RA (NE) 80 Gf65
Villa Elisa RA (ER) 77 Ha62
Villa Escalante MEX (MHC) 40 Ek36
Villa Figueroa RA (SE) 76 Gj59
Villaflores MEX (CHP) 41 Fd37
Villa Florida PY 77 Hb59
Villa Foscari I 120 Ln45
Villa Franca PY 77 Ha59
Villafranca del Bierzo E 106 Ko52
Villafranca de los Barros E 108 Ko48
Villafranca de los Caballeros E 109 Kr49
Villafranca di Verona I 120 Ll45
Villafranco del Guadalquivir E 108 Ko47
Villa General Belgrano RA (CD) 76 Gh62
Villa General Güemes RA (FO) 73 Ha58
Villa General M.Belgrano RA (FO) 73 Ha58
Villa General Roca RA (SL) 76 Gg62
Villages de Pygmés RDC 287 Me45
Villa Gesell RA (BA) 81 Hb64
Villa Gobernador Gálvez RA (SF) 77 Gk62
Villa González Ortega MEX (ZCT) 39 Ek34
Villa Guadelupe MEX (SO) 22 Ed30
Villaguay RA (ER) 77 Ha61
Villa Guillermina RA (SF) 77 Ha60
Villaharta E 108 Kq48
Villahermosa E 109 Ks48
Villahermosa MEX (SO) 22 Ed30
Villahermosa MEX (TB) 41 Fd36
Villahermosa MEX (CAM) 41 Ff37
Villa Hidalgo MEX (JLC) 40 Ej35
Villahoz E 107 Kr52
Villa Huidobro RA (CD) 76 Gh63
Villa Hvitträsk FIN 96 Me30
Villa Iris RA (BA) 81 Gj65
Villa Jovis I 122 Lp50
Villajoyosa = La Vila Joiosa E 109 Ku48
Villa Juárez MEX (SO) 38 Ef32
Villa Juárez MEX (AGS) 39 Ej34
Villa Junqueiro MOC 297 Mj53
Villa Krause RA (SJ) 76 Gf61
Villa La Angostura RA (NE) 80 Ge66
Villa Larca RA (SL) 76 Gh62
Villalba = Vilalba E 106 Kn53
Villa Lola YV 58 Gj42
Villalón de Campos E 106 Kp52
Villalonga RA (BA) 81 Gj65
Villa López MEX (CHH) 39 Eh32
Villalpando E 106 Kp51
Villa Madero MEX (CAM) 41 Fe36
Villa Mainero MEX (TM) 39 Fa33
Villamalea E 109 Kt49
Villamanrique E 109 Kr48
Villa María RA (CD) 76 Gj62
Villa Martin BOL 72 Gg56
Villamartin E 108 Kp46
Villa Mascardi RA (RN) 80 Ge66
Villa Matamoros MEX (CHH) 39 Eh32
Villamayor E 107 Ku51
Villamayor de Santiago E 109 Ks49
Villa Mazán RA (LR) 76 Gg60
Villa Media Agua RA (SJ) 76 Gf61
Villa Mercedes RA (SL) 76 Gh62
Villa Minetti RA (SF) 77 Gk60
Villa M.Moreno RA (TU) 76 Gh59
Villa Montes BOL 73 Gj56
Villandraut F 104 Ku46
Villandry F 102 La43
Villa Nova de Cerveira P 106 Km51
Villanubla E 106 Kq51
Villanueva BOL 67 Gh51
Villanueva CO 56 Gd40
Villanueva HN 42 Fg38
Villanueva MEX (ZCT) 39 Ej34
Villanueva NIC 42 Fg39
Villa Nueva RA (SJ) 76 Gf61
Villa Nueva RA (MD) 76 Gf62
Villanueva de Alcorón E 109 Ks50
Villanueva de Argaño E 107 Kr52
Villanueva de Córdoba E 108 Kq48
Villanueva de Gállego E 107 Ku51
Villanueva de la Fuente E 109 Ks48
Villanueva de la Jura E 109 Kt49
Villanueva de la Serena E 108 Kp48
Villanueva de la Sierra E 108 Ko50
Villanueva de las Torres E 109 Kr47
Villanueva del Campo E 106 Kp51
Villanueva del Fresno E 108 Kn48
Villanueva del Huerva E 107 Kt51
Villanueva de los Castillejos E 108 Kn47
Villanueva de los Infantes E 109 Kr48
Villanueva del Río y Minas E 108 Kp47
Villány H 121 Lt45
Villa Ocampo RA (SF) 77 Ha60
Villa Ojo de Agua RA (SE) 76 Gj60
Villa Ortega RCH 80 Ge68
Villapalacios E 109 Ks48
Villa Paranacito RA (ER) 77 Ha62
Villapinzon CO 56 Gd43
Villaputzu I 111 Lk51
Villard RH 46 Gd36
Villard-de-Lans F 105 Lf45
Villardeciervos E 106 Ko51
Villar de Domingo García E 109 Ks50
Villardefrades E 106 Kp51
Villar del Arzobispo E 109 Ku49
Villar del Rey E 108 Ko49
Villarreal de los Infantes = Vila-real E 109 Ku49
Villa Reducción RA (CD) 76 Gj62
Villa Regina RA (RN) 80 Gg65
Villarejo de Fuentes E 109 Ks49
Villarejo de Salvanés E 109 Kr50
Villarente E 106 Kp52
Villarica PY 73 Hb58
Villarmayor E 106 Kp51
Villa Romana del Casale I 122 Lp53
Villarpando DOM 46 Ge36
Villarrica RCH 80 Gd65
Villarrica, P.N. RCH 80 Ge65
Villarrica, Volcán RCH 80 Ge65
Villarrin de Campos E 106 Kp51
Villarrobledo E 109 Ks49
Villarroya de la Sierra E 107 Kt51
Villarrubia de los Ojos E 109 Kr49
Villars CH 114 Lh44
Villars-les-Dombes F 105 Lf45
Villarta de los Montes E 108 Kq49
Villarti IND (APH) 191 Pa37
Villasalto I 111 Lk51
Villasana de Mena E 107 Kr53
Villa Sánchez Magallanes MEX (TB) 41 Fd36
Villa San Giovanni I 123 Lq52
Villa San José de Vinchina RA (LR) 76 Gf60
Villa San Martín = Cuidad de Loreto RA (SE) 76 Gh60
Villa Santa María I 122 Lp49
Villa Serano BOL 73 Gh55
Villasimius I 111 Lk51
Villa Trinidad RA (SF) 77 Gk61
Villa Tunari BOL 72 Gh54
Villa Unión MEX (SL) 38 Eg34
Villa Unión MEX (DGO) 39 Eh34
Villa Unión RA (LR) 76 Gf60
Villa Valeria RA (CD) 76 Gh63
Villa Vásquez DOM 46 Ge36
Villavicencio CO 56 Gd43
Villaviciosa E 106 Kp53
Villaviciosa RP 203 Ra37
Villaviciosa de Córdoba E 108 Kp48
Villa Viscarra BOL 72 Gh54
Villa Ygatimí PY 74 Hc58
Villazón BOL 72 Gh57
Villedieu-les-Poêles F 102 Kt42
Villedieu-sur-Indre F 102 Lb44
Villefort F 105 Ld46
Villefranche-de-Conflent F 104 Lc48
Villefranche-de-Lauragais F 104 Lb47
Villefranche-de-Rouergue F 104 Lc46
Villefranche-du-Périgord F 104 Lb46
Villefranche-sur-Cher F 102 Lb43
Villefranche-sur-Mer F 105 Lh47
Villefranche-sur-Saône F 105 Le45
Ville-Marie CDN (QC) 33 Ga22
Villena E 109 Ku48
Villeneuve F 104 Lc46
Villeneuve-lès-Avignon F 105 Le47
Villeneuve-sur-Lot F 104 La46
Villeneuve-sur-Yonne F 103 Ld42
Ville Platte USA (LA) 29 Fd30
Villeréal F 104 La46
Villeroy CDN (QC) 30 Ge22
Villers-Bocage F 102 Ku41
Villers-Bocage F 103 Lc41
Villers- Bretonneux F 103 Lc41
Villers-Cotterêts F 103 Ld41
Villersexel F 103 Lg43
Villerupt F 103 Lf41
Villeurbanne F 105 Le45
Villiers SA 303 Me59
Villiers-Saint-Georges F 103 Ld42
Villingen-Schwenningen D 114 Lj42
Villupuram IND (TNU) 193 Ok41
Vilnius LT 97 Mf36
Vil'njans'k UA 135 Mh22
Vil'nohirs'k UA 134 Mh21
Vilppula FIN 96 Me28
Vils D 115 Lm41
Vils D 115 Ln42
Vilsandi rahvuspark EST 96 Mb32
Vil'šanka UA 125 Mj42
Vil'šany UA 133 Mh20
Vilsbiburg D 115 Ln42
Vilshofen D 115 Lo42
Vimão BR (RS) 78 He61
Vimianzo E 106 Kl53
Vimieiro P 108 Kn48
Vimioso P 106 Ko51
Vimmerby S 95 Lq33
Vimoutiers F 102 La42
Vina CAM 281 Lh42
Vinac BIH 121 Ls46
Viña del Mar RCH 76 Ge62
Vinanivao RM 305 Nf53
Vinarós E 110 La50
Vinay F 105 Lf45
Vincennes USA (IL) 34 Fg26
Vincennes Bay 313 Qb32
Vincent USA (TX) 28 Ek29
Vincente Noble DOM 46 Ge36
Vinces EC 60 Ga46
Vindeln S 90 Lk13
Vinderup DK 94 Lj34
Vindex AUS (QLD) 232 Sb57
Vindhya Range IND 190 Oj34
Vindö S 93 Lt31
Vindrej RUS (MOR) 133 Nb18
Vinegar Hill USA 20 Dk23
Vineland USA (CO) 23 Eh26
Vineland USA (NJ) 33 Gc26
Vinga RO 124 Mb44
Vingåker S 93 Lq31
Vinh VN 197 Qc36
Vinhais P 106 Ko51
Vinh Cam Rah VN 197 Qe40
Vinh Chao VN 197 Qe39
Vinh Da Nang VN 197 Qe37
Vinh Duang Quat VN 197 Qe38
Vinh Hy VN 197 Qe40
Vinh Loc VN 178 Qc35
Vinh Long VN 199 Qc40
Vinh Moc Tunnel VN 197 Qd37
Vinh Padaran VN 197 Qe40
Vinh Phan Ri VN 197 Qe40
Vinh Phan Thiet VN 197 Qe40
Vinh Rach Gia VN 199 Qc41
Vinh Son VN 197 Qe38
Vinh Trang Pagoda VN 197 Qd40
Vinh Van Phong VN 197 Qe39
Vinica MK 126 Mc49
Viniště BG 126 Md47
Vinita USA (OK) 29 Fc27
Vinje N 92 Lg30
Vinkovci HR 124 Lt45
Vinnycja UA 134 Me21
Vinograd BG 127 Mf47
Vinön S 93 Lq31
Vinon-sur-Verdon F 105 Lf47
Vinslöv S 95 Lo34
Vinson Massif 312 Fd34
Vinstra N 92 Lk29
Vintar RP 203 Ra36
Vintermarknad S 90 Lk12
Vinukonda IND (APH) 191 Ok37
Vinza RCB 288 Lh47
Violet Town AUS (VIC) 237 Sc64
Violet Valley A.L. AUS 222 Rd54
Vioolsdrif SA 302 Lj60
Viphya Mountains MW 296 Mg51
Vipiteno = Sterzing I 120 Lm44
Vir HR 121 Lq46
Virac RP 203 Rc39
Virachey K 197 Qd39
Virachey N.P. LAO 197 Qd38
Viralimalai IND (TNU) 193 Ok41
Viramgam IND (GUJ) 190 Og34
Viranşehir TR 145 Mk27
Virar IND (MHT) 190 Og36
Virarajendrapet IND (KTK) 192 Oh40
Virawah PK 163 Of33
Virazon RA 81 Ha65
Virazon RA 81 Ha65
Virbalis LT 97 Mc36
Virden CDN (MB) 24 Ek21
Vire F 102 Ku42
Virei ANG 294 Lg53
Vireši LV 97 Mg33
Virf Cindrel RO 124 Md45
Virf Făncelul RO 125 Mf44
Virf Svinecea RO 124 Mc46
Virgem da Lapa BR (MG) 75 Hj54
Virgin Gorda GB 47 Gh36
Virginia AUS (SA) 236 Rk63
Virginia IRL 98 Kn37
Virginia SA 303 Md60
Virginia USA 13 Ga11
Virginia USA (MN) 27 Fd22
Virginia Beach USA (VA) 35 Gb27
Virginia City USA (NV) 20 Ea26
Virginia City USA (MT) 21 Ee23
Virgin Islands GB 47 Gh36
Virgin Islands GB/USA 47 Gh36
Virgin Is. N.P. USA 47 Gh36
Virginópolis BR (MG) 75 Hj55
Virgin Passage USA 47 Gh36
Virihaure S 90 Lj12
Virkby = Virkkala FIN 96 Md30
Virkkala = Virkby FIN 96 Md30
Virklund DK 94 Lk34
Virojoki FIN 96 Mh30
Virolahden FIN 96 Mh30
Viroqua USA (WI) 27 Fe24
Virovitica HR 121 Ls45
Virpazar SCG 126 Lu48
Virrat FIN 96 Md28
Virsbo S 93 Lq31
Virserum S 95 Lq33
Virsko More HR 121 Lp46
Virtasalmi FIN 96 Mh28
Virton B 103 Lf41
Virtsu EST 96 Md32
Virttaa FIN 96 Mc30
Virú PE 66 Ga50
Viruá, P.N. do BR 62 Gk45
Virudó CO 56 Gb43
Virudunagar IND (TNU) 193 Oj42
Virunga, P.N.des RDC 287 Me46
Vis HR 121 Lr47
Vis HR 121 Lr48
Visaginas LT 97 Mg35
Visalaukė LT 97 Mf36
Visalia USA (CA) 22 Ea27
Visarwari IND (MHT) 190 Oh35
Visayan Sea RP 205 Rb40
Visayas RP 201 Ra16
Visby S 95 Lt33
Vischering D 112 Lh39
Visconde do Rio Branco BR (MG) 75 Hj56
Viscount Melville Sound CDN 11 Ec04
Viscri RO 125 Mf44
Visé B 103 Lf40
Višegrad BIH 126 Lu47
Viseisei FJI 247 Tj54
Viseu BR (PA) 64 Hg46
Viseu P 106 Kn50
Vișeu RO 124 Me43
Vișeu de Sus RO 124 Me43
Vishakhapatnam IND (APH) 191 Pb37
Vishalla Village IND 190 Og34
Vishnupur IND (WBG) 194 Pd34
Vishwa Shanti Stupa IND 191 Pc33
Visina RO 127 Me47
Visingö S 95 Lp32
Visita BR (MT) 62 Ha49
Viskafors S 95 Ln33
Viskån S 94 Ln33
Vislanda S 95 Lp34
Visočica HR 121 Lq46
Viso del Marqués E 109 Kr48
Visoki Dečani SCG 126 Ma48
Visoko BIH 121 Lt47
Visp CH 114 Lh44
Vis Rivier NAM 298 Lj58
Vis Rivier NAM 302 Lj60
Visrivier SA 303 Mc61
Vissannapeta IND (APH) 191 Pa37
Vissefjärda S 95 Lq34
Visselhövede D 112 Lk38
Vista Alegre BR (AM) 61 Gg46
Vista Alegre BR (AM) 62 Gh46
Vistabella del Maestrat E 109 Ku50
Viste Alegre ANG 288 Lh50
Vistula PL 117 Lu38
Vistula Lagoon PL/RUS 117 Lu36
Vištytis LT 97 Mc36
Visuvesi FIN 96 Md28
Visuvisu Point SOL 245 Sj49
Vit BG 127 Me47
Vita IND (MHT) 190 Oh37
Vitaio F 59 Hd44
Vitebsk BY 132 Mf18
Viterbo I 122 Ln48
Vitez BIH 121 Ls46
Vi Thanh VN 199 Qc41
Vithkuq AL 126 Ma50
Vitiaz I Deep 316 Sa08
Vitiaz II Deep 221 Ub23
Vitiaz III Deep 221 Ua25
Vitiaz Strait PNG 243 Sd48
Vitiaz Trench 218 Ta10
Vitichi BOL 72 Gh56
Vitigudino E 106 Ko50
Viti Levu FJI 247 Tj55
Vitim RUS 141 Qc08
Vitim RUS 173 Qg19
Vitimskoe ploskogo RUS 173 Qg19
Vitina SCG 126 Mb48
Vitolište MK 126 Mb49
Vitor PE 72 Ge54
Vitoria BR (PA) 63 Hd47
Vitória BR (ES) 75 Hk56
Vitória da Conquista BR (BA) 71 Hk53
Vitória de Santo Antão BR (PE) 71 Jc50
Vitoria do Mearim BR (MA) 64 Hh47
Vitoria-Gasteiz E 107 Ks52
Vitória Seamount 53 Ja23
Vitorino BR (PR) 78 Hd59
Vitorino Freire BR (MA) 64 Hh48
Vitoša, N.P. BG 126 Md48
Vitré F 102 Kt42
Vitrolles F 105 Lf47
Vitry-le-François F 103 Le42
Vitshumbi RDC 287 Me46
Vitteaux F 103 Le43
Vittel F 103 Lf42
Vittória I 122 Lp54
Vittorio Véneto I 120 Ln45
Vittsjö S 95 Lo34
Viù I 120 Lh45
Viv RUS 140 Pd05
Vivario F 111 Lk48
Viveiro E 106 Kn53
Vivian CDN (MB) 24 Fb21
Vivian USA (SD) 26 Ek24
Viviers F 105 Le46
Vivo SA 300 Me57
Vivonne F 102 La44
Viwa FJI 247 Tj54
Vizcaíno MEX (BCS) 38 Ed32
Vize TR 130 Mh49
Vizianagaram IND (APH) 191 Pb36
Vizille F 105 Lf45
Viziru RO 125 Mh45
Vizovice CZ 118 Ls41
Vizzini I 122 Lp53
Vjalikija Matykaly BY 117 Md38
Vjartsilja RUS (KAR) 91 Mf14
Vjatka RUS 133 Nf17
Vjatskie Poljany RUS 133 Nf17
Vjatskoe RUS 133 Na17
Vjazemskij RUS 180 Rh22
Vjaz'ma RUS 132 Mh18
Vjazniki RUS 133 Nb17
Vlădeni RO 125 Mg43
Vlădeni RO 125 Mh43
Vladikavkaz RUS (SOA) 152 Nc24
Vladimir RUS 133 Na17
Vladimir SCG 126 Lu48
Vladimirovo BG 126 Md47
Vladimirovo RUS 181 Sb21
Vladivostok RUS 182 Rf24
Vlad Țepeș RO 125 Mh46
Vlagtwedde NL 112 Lh37
Vlaháta GR 128 Ma52
Vlaháva GR 126 Mb51
Vlahiá GR 128 Md52
Vlăhița RO 125 Mf44
Vlaming Head Lighthouse AUS 224 Qh56
Vlasenica BIH 126 Lt46
Vlašim CZ 118 Lp41
Vlașin RO 125 Mf46
Vlasotince SCG 126 Mc48
Vlieland NL 112 Lf37
Vlissingen NL 112 Ld39
Vlkolinec SK 119 Lu41
Vlorë AL 126 Lu50
Vlotho D 112 Lj38
Vltava CZ 118 Lp41
Vobkent UZB 158 Oc25
Vöcklabruck A 115 Lo42
Vodice HR 121 Lq47
Vodil UZB 159 Of25
Vodlozersky N.P. RUS 91 Mj14
Vodňany CZ 118 Lp41
vodní nádrž Hracholusky CZ 118 Lq41
vodní nádrž Lipno CZ 118 Lp42
Vodnjan HR 121 Lo46
vodoschovyšče Sjalec BY 117 Me38
Vodskov DK 94 Ll33
Voerde D 112 Lg39
Vogan RT 279 La42
Vogar CDN (MB) 24 Fa20
Vogatsikó GR 126 Mb50
Vogelkop RI 212 Rf46
Vogelkop RI 212 Rf46
Vogelsberg D 112 Lk40
Vogelweide NAM 298 Lk58
Voghera I 120 Lk46
Voh F 246 Tc56
Võhandu EST 96 Mh33
Vohburg D 115 Lm42
Vohemar = Iharana RM 305 Ne52
Vohenstrauß D 115 Ln41
Vohidiala RM 306 Ne54
Vohilava RM 306 Nd56
Vohilengo RM 306 Ne54
Vohimasina RM 306 Ne56
Vohimena RM 306 Ne54
Vohipeno RM 306 Nd56
Vohitrambo RM 306 Nd57
Võhma EST 96 Mc32
Võhma EST 96 Mf32
Voi EAK 293 Mk47
Voi VN 197 Qd36
Voikoski FIN 96 Mg29
Voineasa RO 124 Md45
Voineasa RO 124 Me46
Voineşti RO 125 Mf45
Voinjama LB 278 Kf41
Voiron F 105 Lf45
Võiste EST 96 Me32
Voiteg RO 124 Mb45
Voitsberg A 115 Lq43
Vojens DK 94 Lk35
Vojinka UA 135 Mg23
Vojnić HR 121 Lq45
Vojnica RUS (KAR) 91 Mf13
Vojnika BG 127 Mg48
Vojnovo BG 125 Mh47
Vojutyči UA 119 Md41
Vojvodina SCG 124 Lu45
Vokeo Island PNG 243 Sc47
Volary CZ 118 Lo42
Volborg USA (MT) 21 Eh23
Volcán PA 42 Fj41
Volcán RA (PJ) 72 Gh57
Volcán Alcedo EC 60 Fe46
Volcán Altar EC 60 Ga46
Volcán Antisana EC 60 Ga46
Volcán Antofalla RA 72 Gg58
Volcán Antuco RCH 80 Ge64
Volcán Aracar RA 72 Gg58
Volcán Arenal, P.N. CR 42 Fh40
Volcán Atitlán GCA 41 Fe38
Volcán Barú, P.N. PA 42 Fj41
Volcán Calbuco RCH 80 Gd66
Volcán Callaquí RCH 80 Ge64
Volcán Cayambe EC 60 Ga45
Volcán Chachani PE 72 Ge54
Volcán Chiguana BOL 72 Gg56
Volcán Chillán RCH 80 Ge64
Volcán Chimborazo EC 60 Ga46
Volcán Choshuenco RCH 80 Gd65
Volcán Concepción NIC 42 Fh40
Volcán Copahue RA/RCH 80 Ge64
Volcán Copiapó RCH 76 Gf59
Volcán Corcovado RCH 80 Gd67
Volcán Cotopaxi EC 60 Ga46
Volcán Cumbal CO 60 Gb45
Volcán Darwin EC 60 Fe46
Volcán de Colima MEX 40 Ej36
Volcán de Fuego GCA 41 Fe38
Volcán Domuyo RA 80 Ge64
Volcán Doña Juana CO 60 Gb45
Volcán Fernandina EC 60 Fe46
Volcán Galeras CO 60 Gb45
Volcán G.Pichincha EC 60 Ga46
Volcán Gualłatiri RCH 72 Gf55
Volcán Huequi RCH 80 Gd67
Volcán Illiniza EC 60 Ga46
Volcán Ipala HN 41 Ff38
Volcán Isluga RCH 72 Gf55
Volcán Isluga, P.N. RCH 72 Gf55
Volcán Lanín RCH 80 Ge65
Volcán Lascar RCH 72 Gg57
Volcán Lastarria RCH/RA 72 Gf58
Volcán Las Virgenes MEX 38 Ed32
Volcán Licancábur RCH 72 Gg57
Volcán Llaima RCH 80 Ge65
Volcán Llullaillaco RCH/RA 72 Gf58
Volcán Lonquimay RCH 80 Ge65
Volcán Maipo RCH/RA 76 Gf63
Volcán Masaya, P.N. NIC 42 Fg39
Volcán Michimáhuida RCH 80 Gd67
Volcán Misti PE 72 Ge54
Volcán Momotombo NIC 42 Fg39
Volcano USA (HI) 16 Cc36
Volcán Ollagüe BOL/RCH 72 Gf56
Volcano Mayon RP 203 Rb39
Volcán Osorno RCH 80 Gd66
Volcán Parinacota RCH 72 Gf55
Volcán Peteroa RCH/RA 76 Ge63
Volcán Pico de Orizaba MEX 39 Fb36
Volcan Pico de Orizaba, Volcán MEX 39 Fb36
Volcán Poás, P.N. CR 42 Fh40
Volcán Puracé CO 60 Gb44
Volcán Puyehue RCH 80 Gd66
Volcán Reventador EC 60 Gb46
Volcán Sabancaya PE 67 Ge53
Volcán Sangay EC 60 Ga47
Volcán San José RA/RCH 76 Gf62
Volcán San Pedro RCH 72 Gf56
Volcán Socompa RCH/RA 72 Gf58
Volcán Sotara CO 60 Gb44
Volcans, P.N.des RWA 292 Me46
Volcán Sumaco EC 60 Gb46
Volcán Tacaná GCA/MEX 41 Fd38
Volcán Tacora PE/RCH 72 Gf54
Volcán Tajumulco GCA 41 Fe38

X

Y

Z

Zarqan **IR** 156 Ng31
Zarrentin **D** 113 Ll37
Zarrin **IR** 154 Nh29
Zarrin Abad **IR** 154 Ne28
Zarrine Rud **IR** 154 Nd27
Zarrin Shar **IR** 154 Nf29
Zarskoje Selo **RUS** 132 Mf16
Zaruma **EC** 60 Ga47
Zarumilla **PE** 60 Fk47
Żary **PL** 116 Lq39
Zaryanovsk **KZ** 167 Pc21
Zarza de Granadilla **E** 108 Ko50
Zarzal **CO** 56 Gb43
Zarzis **TN** 260 Lf29
Zasa **LV** 97 Mf34
Zasieki **PL** 116 Lp39
Zaškiv **UA** 134 Mf21
Zasos'e **RUS** 96 Mj31
Zastron **SA** 303 Md61
Žatec **CZ** 118 Lo40
Zatoka Pucka **PL** 116 Lt36
zatoka Syvaš **UA** 135 Mh22
Zätreni **RO** 124 Md46
Zatyššja **UA** 125 Mk43
Zaunguzskiye Karakumy **TM** 153 Nk25
Zavala **BIH** 121 Ls48
Zavalinë **AL** 126 Ma50
Zavalla **RA** (SF) 77 Gk62
Zavalla **USA** (TX) 29 Fc30
Zavareh **IR** 154 Ng29
Zave **ZW** 296 Mf54
Zavet **BG** 127 Mg47
Zavetvoe **RUS** 135 Nb22
Zavety Il'iča **RUS** 181 Sa21
Zavidoviči **BIH** 121 Lt46
Zavitaja **RUS** 180 Re20
Zavitinsk **RUS** 180 Re20
Zavitne **UA** 135 Mj23
Zavizan **HR** 121 Lp46
Zavkhan **MNG** 172 Pj21
Zavkhan Gol **MNG** 167 Ph21
Zavodoukovsk **RUS** 140 Ob07
Zavoj **MK** 126 Ma49
Zavolž'e **RUS** 133 Nb17
Zawady **PL** 117 Ma39
Zawidów **PL** 116 Lq39
Zawiercie **PL** 117 Lu40
Zawilah **LAR** 267 Lh32
Zawita **IRQ** 147 Nb27
Zawiyat al Izziyat **LAR** 261 Mb29
Zawiyat al Murassas **LAR** 261 Mb29
Zawiyat Masus **LAR** 261 Ma30
Zawoja **PL** 119 Lu41
Zayaki Jangal **PK** 162 Oc32
Zayat **MYA** 194 Ph34
Zayat-koun **MYA** 195 Ph35
Zaymah **KSA** 148 Na35
Zaymi **OM** 157 Nj33
Zaza **RUS** 173 Qf19
Zazafotsy **RM** 306 Nd57
Zazhong **VRC** (TIB) 171 Pj31
Zaziatou **RN** 271 Lb39
Zázrivá **SK** 119 Lu41
Zbaraž **UA** 134 Mc21
Zbąszyń **PL** 116 Lq38
Zbečno **CZ** 118 Lo40
Zbiroh **CZ** 118 Lo41
Zblewo **PL** 116 Lt37
Zbójna **PL** 117 Mb37
Zbójno **PL** 117 Lu37
Zboriv **UA** 119 Mf41
Zborov **SK** 119 Mb41
Zborowice **PL** 119 Ma41
Zbruč **UA** 125 Mg42
Zbucznka **PL** 117 Mc38
Žďár **CZ** 118 Lo40
Žďár nad Sázavou **CZ** 118 Lq41
Ždírec nad Doubravou **CZ** 118 Lq41
Zdolbuniv **UA** 134 Md20
Zdunje **MK** 126 Mb49
Zduńska Wola **PL** 116 Lt39
Zduny **PL** 117 Lu38
Zdzieszowice **PL** 116 Lt40
Zebak **AFG** 161 Of27
Zeballos **CDN** (BC) 18 Dg21
Zebediela **SA** 300 Me58
Zé Biel **BR** (TO) 64 Hg49
Zebilla **GH** 279 Kk40
Žebrak **PL** 117 Mc38
Zebreira **P** 108 Kn49
Zedyn Nuruu **MNG** 172 Qb20
Zé Doca **BR** (MA) 64 Hh47
Zéé **DY** 280 Lb42
Zeebrugge **B** 103 Ld39
Zeehan **AUS** (TAS) 236 Sc66
Zeekoegat **SA** 300 Me58
Zeerust **SA** 299 Md58
Zeewyk Channel **AUS** 228 Qg60
Zefat **IL** 146 Mh29
Zefreh **IR** 154 Ng29
Zegbé **CI** 279 Kh43
Zeghamra **DZ** 259 Kj31
Zegon **MYA** 195 Pj34
Zégoua **RMM** 279 Kh40
Zegstey **MNG** 172 Qb22
Zéguédéguen **BF** 271 Kk39
Zehdenick **D** 113 Lo38
Zeil, Mount **AUS** 226 Rg57
Žeimelis **LT** 97 Md34
Žeimena **LT** 97 Mf35
Žeimiai **LT** 97 Md35
Zeist **NL** 112 Lf38
Zeitz **D** 113 Ln39
Zeja **RUS** 180 Rd20
Zejsko-Bureinkaja ravnina **RUS** 180 Re20
Zejskoe vdhr. **RUS** 141 Rb08
Zêkog **VRC** (QHI) 176 Qa28
Želazna **PL** 116 Ls36
Želča **RUS** 96 Mh32
Żelechów **PL** 117 Mb39
Zelená Hora **CZ** 118 Lo41
Zelenaja Rošča **RUS** 96 Mk30
Zelenbreg **MK** 126 Mc49
Zelenčukskaja **RUS** (KCH) 152 Na24
Zelenivka **UA** 135 Mj22
Zelenodol'sk **RUS** (TAR) 133 Ne18
Zelenodol's'k **UA** 134 Mg22
Zelenogirs'ke **UA** 125 Ml43
Zelenograd **RUS** 132 Mj17
Zelenogradsk **RUS** 97 Ma36
Zelenokumsk **RUS** 152 Nb23
Železná Ruda **CZ** 118 Lo41
Železnodorožnyj **RUS** 97 Mb36
Železnogorsk **RUS** 132 Mh19
Zelfana **DZ** 259 Lc29
Želiezovce **SK** 118 Lt42
Želju Vojoda **BG** 127 Mg48
Zella-Mehlis **D** 113 Ll40
Zell am See **A** 115 Ln43
Zell an der Pram **A** 115 Lo42
Zel'tau Ajtau **KZ** 166 Og23
Zelter **MNG** 172 Qc20
Zeltiņi **LV** 97 Mg33
Zeltweg **A** 115 Lp43
Zel'va **BY** 117 Me37
Želva **LT** 97 Mf35
Zelzate **B** 103 Ld39
Žemaičiu Kalvarija **LT** 97 Mc34
Žemaičių Naumiestis **LT** 97 Mb35
Žemaitija **LT** 97 Mc35
Žemaitijos n.p. **LT** 97 Mb34
Žemberovce **SK** 119 Lt42
Zemblak **AL** 126 Ma50
Zembra **TN** 260 Lf27
Zemen **BG** 126 Mc48
Zemenskija prolom **BG** 126 Mc48
Zemgale **LV** 97 Me34
Zemio **RCA** 287 Mc43
Zemite **LV** 97 Mc34
Zemlja Aleksandry **RUS** 140 Nb02
Zemlja Georga **RUS** 140 Nc02
Zemmora **DZ** 259 La28
Zemmour **DARS** 264 Kd33
Zemo Ažara **GE** 152 Na24
Zempléngagárd **H** 119 Mc42
Zempléni-hegység **H** 119 Mb42
Zempoala **MEX** 40 Fb36
Zemurray Gardens Lodge Complex **USA** 29 Fe30
Zendeh Jan **AFG** 160 Oa28
Zenguele **ANG** 288 Lh49
Zenica **BIH** 121 Ls46
Zenkoji **J** 183 Rk27
Zentsuji **J** 183 Rg28
Zenza do Itombe **ANG** 288 Lh50
Žepče **BIH** 121 Lt46
Zephyrhills **USA** (FL) 36 Fj31
Zepita **PE** 72 Gf54
Zepu **VRC** (XUZ) 168 Oj26
Zeralda **DZ** 259 Lb27
Zerauk **AFG** 160 Oe29
Žeravna **BG** 127 Mg48
Zerbst **D** 113 Ln39
Zerdevka **RUS** 133 Na20
Žeredkove **UA** 125 Mk43
Zeribet el Oued **DZ** 260 Ld28
Zerkov Bogojavlenija **RUS** 133 Na17
Zerkov Borisa i Gleba **RUS** 133 Na17
Zerkov pokrova na Nerli **RUS** 133 Na17
Zermatt **CH** 114 Lh44
Zernograd **RUS** 135 Na22
Zerouilet **MA** 259 Kj29
Zerqan **AL** 126 Ma49
Žeskazgan **KZ** 140 Ob09
Zestaponi **GE** 152 Nb24
Zeta **SCG** 126 Lu48
Zêtang **VRC** (TIB) 171 Pf31
Zetel **D** 112 Lh37
Žetikara **KZ** 140 Oa08
Žetikonyr kum **KZ** 166 Oe22
Zeulenroda **D** 113 Lm40
Zeuthen **D** 113 Lo38
Zeven **D** 112 Lk37
Zevenaar **NL** 112 Lf39
Zevenbergen **NL** 112 Le39
Zeyn-od Din **IR** 154 Nh30
Zeytinbağı **TR** 130 Mj50
Zeytındağ **TR** 129 Mh52
Zeytınlı **TR** 130 Mg51
Zgierz **PL** 117 Lu39
Zgniłoche **PL** 117 Ma37
Zgorzelec **PL** 116 Lq39
Zgozhd **AL** 126 Ma49
Zgurița **MD** 125 Mj42
Zhairan **KZ** 166 Of21
Zhaksykylysh **KZ** 153 Ob22
Zhalaghash **KZ** 158 Oc23
Zhalanash **KZ** 159 Ok24
Zhalong Lake Sanctuary **VRC** 180 Rc22
Zhambyl **KZ** 166 Of22
Zhambyl **KZ** 166 Og23
Zhamshi **KZ** 166 Oh22
Zhanaakshiman **KZ** 166 Oj20
Zhanadariya **KZ** 158 Oc23
Zhanakala **KZ** 158 Ob23
Zhanakorghan **KZ** 158 Od24
Zhanang **VRC** (TIB) 171 Pf31
Zhanaozen **KZ** 153 Ng24
Zhanatas **KZ** 158 Oe24
Zhanbay aral **KZ** 152 Ne22
Zhangbei **VRC** (HBI) 175 Qh25
Zhangcunpu **VRC** (AHU) 184 Qh29
Zhang Fei Ci **VRC** 177 Qe30
Zhangguangcai Ling **VRC** 180 Re23
Zhanghe Shuiku **VRC** 177 Qf30
Zhang Hua **VRC** 177 Qg30
Zhanghuang **VRC** (GZG) 178 Qe35
Zhanghyztobe **KZ** 166 Pa21
Zhangjiachuan **VRC** (GSU) 177 Qd28
Zhangjiajie **VRC** (HUN) 177 Qf31
Zhangjiakou **VRC** (HBI) 175 Qh25
Zhangjialing **VRC** (JGX) 184 Qj31
Zhangjiang **VRC** (JGS) 184 Ra30
Zhangla **VRC** (SCH) 176 Qb29
Zhangping **VRC** (FJN) 179 Qj33
Zhangpu **VRC** (FJN) 179 Qj33
Zhangqiu **VRC** (SDG) 175 Qj27
Zhangshu **VRC** (JGX) 184 Qh31
Zhangwu **VRC** (LNG) 182 Rb24
Zhangye **VRC** (GSU) 174 Qa26
Zhangzhou **VRC** (FJN) 179 Qj33
Zhanjiang **VRC** (GDG) 178 Qf35
Zhansugirov **KZ** 166 Ok23
Zhanyi **VRC** (YUN) 195 Qb33
Zhaodong **VRC** (HLG) 180 Rc22
Zhaojue **VRC** (SCH) 176 Qb31
Zhaokua **VRC** (YUN) 195 Qb33
Zhao Ling **VRC** 177 Qe28
Zhaolin Gongyuan **VRC** 180 Rd23
Zhaoping **VRC** (GZG) 178 Qf33
Zhaoqing **VRC** (GDG) 178 Qg34
Zhaosu **VRC** (XUZ) 166 Pa24
Zhaotong **VRC** (YUN) 195 Qb32
Zhao Xian **VRC** (HBI) 175 Qh27
Zhaoxing **VRC** (HLG) 180 Rf22
Zhaoyuan **VRC** (HLG) 180 Rc23
Zhaozhen **VRC** (SCH) 176 Qc30
Zhaozhou **VRC** (HLG) 180 Rc23
Zhaozhou Qiao **VRC** 175 Qh27
Zha po Gang **VRC** 178 Qf35
Zhapu **VRC** (ZJG) 184 Ra30
Zhari Namco **VRC** 170 Pc30
Zharkent **KZ** 166 Ok23
Zharma **KZ** 166 Pa21
Zharyk **KZ** 166 Pa21
Zharykbas **KZ** 158 Of24
Zhaxigang **VRC** (TIB) 170 Ok29
Zhazuo **VRC** (GZH) 178 Qd32
Zhdanovo **KZ** 158 Of24
Zhecheng **VRC** (HNN) 184 Qh28
Zhefang **VRC** (YUN) 195 Pk33
Zhejiang **VRC** 165 Qd13
Zhejue **VRC** (GZH) 195 Qb32
Zhelang **VRC** (GDG) 179 Qh34
Zhen'an **VRC** (SAA) 177 Qe29
Zhenba **VRC** (SAA) 177 Qd29
Zhenbao Ding **VRC** 178 Qf32
Zhenfeng **VRC** (GZH) 178 Qc33
Zhengcheng **VRC** (GDG) 179 Qg34
Zhenghe **VRC** (FJN) 184 Qk32
Zhengxiangbai Qi **VRC** (NMZ) 175 Qh24
Zhengyang **VRC** (HNN) 184 Qh29
Zhengzhou **VRC** (HNN) 177 Qg28
Zhenhai **VRC** (FJN) 179 Qk33
Zhenhai **VRC** (ZJG) 184 Ra31
Zhenjiang **VRC** (JGS) 184 Qk29
Zhenkang **VRC** (YUN) 195 Pk34
Zhenlai **VRC** (JLN) 180 Rb23
Zhenning **VRC** (GZH) 178 Qc32
Zhenping **VRC** (HNN) 177 Qg29
Zhenqian **VRC** (FJN) 184 Qk32
Zhenxiong **VRC** (YUN) 178 Qc32
Zhenyuan **VRC** (GSU) 177 Qd28
Zhenyuan **VRC** (GZH) 178 Qe32
Zhenyuan **VRC** (YUN) 195 Qa33
Zherong **VRC** (FJN) 184 Qk32
Zhesang **VRC** (YUN) 178 Qc34
Zhetibai **KZ** 153 Ng24
Zhetisai **KZ** 158 Oe25
Zhexi Shuiku **VRC** 177 Qf31
Zhicheng **VRC** (HUB) 177 Qf30
Zhidan **VRC** (SAA) 174 Qe27
Zhidoi **VRC** (QHI) 171 Ph29
Zhigan **VRC** (TIB) 170 Pb30
Zhijiang **VRC** (HUB) 177 Qf30
Zhijiang **VRC** (HUN) 178 Qe32
Zhijin **VRC** (GZH) 178 Qc32
Zhi Jin Cave **VRC** 178 Qc32
Zhiqu = Tongtian He **VRC** 171 Ph28
Zhob **PK** 160 Oe30
Zhob **PK** 161 Oe30
Zhombe **ZW** 300 Me55
Zhongba **VRC** (TIB) 170 Pc31
Zhongba **VRC** (GDG) 179 Qh34
Zhongcheng **VRC** (YUN) 176 Qb31
Zhongde **VRC** 184 Qj29
Zhongdian **VRC** (YUN) 195 Pk32
Zhonghe **VRC** (CGQ) 177 Qe31
Zhonghuang **VRC** (GZH) 178 Qe32
Zhongjiang **VRC** (SCH) 176 Qc30
Zhongning **VRC** (NHZ) 174 Qc27
Zhongrankou **VRC** (SCH) 176 Qb29
Zhongshan **VRC** (GZG) 178 Qf33
Zhongshan **VRC** (GDG) 179 Qg34
Zhongwei **VRC** (NHZ) 174 Qc27
Zhongxiang **VRC** (HUB) 177 Qg30
Zhongxin Gang **VRC** 184 Ra29
Zhongxingqiao **VRC** (JGS) 184 Ra29
Zhongzhai **VRC** (ZJG) 184 Rb31
Zhongzhou **VRC** (CGQ) 177 Qe30
Zhorgha **KZ** 166 Oj21
Zhosaly **KZ** 158 Oc23
Zhoukou **VRC** (HNN) 184 Qh29
Zhoukoudian **VRC** 175 Qh26
Zhoulichang **VRC** (SCH) 176 Qc31
Zhouning **VRC** (FJN) 184 Qk32
Zhousahn Qundao **VRC** 184 Ra30
Zhoushan **VRC** (ZJG) 184 Rb30
Zhouxiang **VRC** (ZJG) 184 Ra30
Zhouzhi **VRC** (SAA) 177 Qe28
Zhowagoin **VRC** (TIB) 171 Pj31
Zhuanghe **VRC** (LNG) 182 Rb26
Zhuantobe **KZ** 158 Oe23
Zhucheng **VRC** (SDG) 175 Qk28
Zhud **EC** 60 Ga47
Zhugqu **VRC** (GSU) 176 Qc29
Zhuhai **VRC** (GDG) 179 Qg34
Zhuji **VRC** (ZJG) 184 Ra31
Zhujiang Kou **VRC** 179 Qg34
Zhulin **VRC** (YUN) 178 Qc34
Zhumadian **VRC** (HNN) 177 Qg29
Zhumadian **VRC** (HNN) 184 Qh29
Zhuozhi Z.B. **VRC** 177 Qd28
Zhuo Zhou **VRC** (HBI) 175 Qh26
Zhuozi **VRC** (NMZ) 175 Qg25
Zhuozi Shan **VRC** 174 Qd26
Zhushan **VRC** (HUB) 177 Qf29
Zhuxi **VRC** (HUB) 177 Qe29
Zhuzhou **VRC** (HUN) 179 Qg32
Zia Ind. Res. **USA** 23 Eg28
Ziama **RG** 278 Kf41
Ziama Mansouria **DZ** 260 Lc27
Ziarat **PK** 160 Od30
Žiar nad Hronom **SK** 119 Lt42
Zia-ud-Din **PK** 162 Oe32
Ziban **DZ** 260 Lc28
Zibo **VRC** (SDG) 175 Qk27
Zibo Tombs **VRC** 175 Qk27
Zicavo **F** 111 Lk49
Zichang **VRC** (SAA) 175 Qe27
Zieban **SYR** 147 Na28
Ziębice **PL** 116 Ls40
Zięby **PL** 117 Ma36
Ziehtown **LB** 278 Kf42
Ziēkas **LV** 97 Mb33
Zielona Góra **PL** 116 Lq39
Zielonka **PL** 117 Mb38
Zierikzee **NL** 112 Ld39
Ziesar **D** 113 Ln38
Žiežmariai **LT** 97 Me36
Žigansk **RUS** 141 Ra05
Zigbayo **CI** 278 Kg43
Zighan **LAR** 262 Mb33
Zighout Youcef **DZ** 260 Ld27
Zigon **MYA** 195 Ph34
Zigon **MYA** 196 Ph36
Zigong **VRC** (SCH) 176 Qc31
Ziguéy **TCH** 273 Lh38
Zigui **VRC** (HUB) 177 Qf30
Ziguinchor **SN** 269 Kb39
Zihuaquio **MEX** (GUR) 40 Ek36
Zihuatanejo **MEX** (GUR) 40 Ek37
Zijin **VRC** (GDG) 179 Qh34
Zile **TR** 131 Mq50
Žilina **SK** 118 Lt41
Žilino **RUS** 97 Mb36
Zillah **LAR** 261 Lj31
Ziller **A** 115 Ln43
Zillertaler Alpen **A** 115 Lm43
Zima **RUS** 172 Qa19
Zima **RUS** 172 Qb19
Zimane **MOC** 300 Mg57
Zimapan **MEX** (HDG) 40 Fa35
Zimba **Z** 296 Md54
Zimbabwe 253 Ma11
Zim Bassin Waterfall **RH** 46 Gd36
Zimbor **RO** 124 Md43
Zimmi **WAL** 278 Ke42
Zimna Woda **PL** 117 Ma37
Zimnicea **RO** 127 Mf47
Zimovniki **RUS** 135 Nb22
Zina **CAM** 273 Lh40
Zinapécuaro **MEX** (MHC) 40 Ek36
Zinave, P.N.de **MOC** 300 Mg56
Zincırlı Dağı **TR** 131 Mp51
Zindan Mağarası **TR** 131 Ml52
Zinder **RN** 272 Le39
Zinga **EAT** 293 Mk49
Zinga Mulike **EAT** 293 Mk50
Zingst **D** 113 Ln36
Ziniare **BF** 271 Kk39
Zinjibar **YE** 150 Nc39
Zin'kiv **UA** 132 Mh20
Zinna **WAN** 273 Lf41
Zinnowitz **D** 113 Lo36
Zinzana **RMM** 270 Kh39
Zio **CI** 278 Kg42
Zio **RT** 279 La42
Zion N.P. **USA** 22 Ed27
Ziope **GH** 279 La42
Zipaquira **CO** 56 Gc43
Zi Qu **VRC** 171 Pj29
Ziquite **MOC** 296 Mg54
Zirapur **IND** (MPH) 190 Oj33
Zirc **H** 118 Ls43
Žirje **HR** 121 Lq47
Zirku **UAE** 156 Ng33
Zirndorf **D** 115 Ll41
Zirnovsk **RUS** 133 Nc20
Ziro **IND** (ARP) 194 Pg32
Zi Shui **VRC** 177 Qf31
Zitácuaro **MEX** (MHC) 40 Ek36
Zitava **SK** 118 Lt42
Zitenga **BF** 271 Kk39
Žitište **SCG** 124 Ma45
Žitni Potok **SCG** 126 Mb47
Zitong **VRC** (SCH) 177 Qc30
Žitoradja **SCG** 126 Mb47
Zitouna **DZ** 260 Ld27
Zittau **D** 113 Lp40
Zitundo **MOC** 303 Mg59
Živinice **BIH** 124 Lt46
Ziwani **EAT** 293 Mk48
Ziwa Ruins **ZW** 300 Mg55
Ziway **ETH** 284 Mk41
Ziwu Liang **VRC** 177 Qe28
Zixi **VRC** (JGX) 184 Qj32
Zixing **VRC** (HUN) 179 Qg33
Ziya Abad **IR** 154 Ne27
Ziya He **VRC** 175 Qj26
Ziyang **VRC** (SCH) 176 Qc30
Ziyang **VRC** (SAA) 177 Qe29
Zi Yang Guan Temple **VRC** 182 Rc25
Ziyarat **IR** 157 Nj32
Ziyarat Kalleh **IR** 157 Nj32
Ziyuan **VRC** (GZG) 178 Qf32
Ziyun Miaozu **VRC** (GZH) 178 Qd33
Zizhou **VRC** (SAA) 175 Qf27
Zlaja **RUS** 97 Mb36
Zlarin **HR** 121 Lq47
Zlatarsko jezero **SCG** 126 Lu47
Zlaté Morávce **SK** 118 Lt42
Zlatica **BG** 127 Me48
Zlati Vojvoda **BG** 127 Mg48
Zlatna **RO** 124 Md44
Zlatna Panega **BG** 127 Me47
Zlatni Pjasăci **BG** 127 Mj47
Zlatni Pjasăci, N.P. **BG** 127 Mj47
Zlatoust **RUS** 140 Nd07
Zli **RIM** 269 Kd36
Zlín **CZ** 118 Ls41
Zlitan **LAR** 260 Lh29
Žlobin **BY** 132 Mf19
Złocieniec **PL** 116 Lr37
Złoczew **PL** 116 Lt39
Złotniki Kujawskie **PL** 116 Lt38
Złotoryia **PL** 116 Lq39
Złotów **PL** 116 Ls37
Žlutice **CZ** 118 Lo40
Z'Malet el Emir **DZ** 259 Lb28
Zmeinogorsk **RUS** 167 Pb20
Žmerynka **UA** 134 Me21
Zmievka **RUS** 132 Mj19
Żmigród **PL** 116 Lr39
Zmijiv **UA** 135 Mj21
Zminica **SCG** 126 Lu47
Znamenka **KZ** 166 Ok20
Znamensk **RUS** 97 Mb36
Znamenskoe **RUS** 132 Mh19
Znamienka **BY** 117 Md39
Znamjanka **UA** 134 Mg21
Żnin **PL** 116 Ls38
Znojmo **CZ** 118 Lr42
Zoa **CAM** 281 Lg43
Zoar Village St. Mem. **USA** 33 Fk25
Žodzina **BY** 132 Me18
Zoébefang **CAM** 281 Lf44
Zoétélé **CAM** 281 Lf44
Zoetermeer **NL** 112 Le38
Zofar **IL** 146 Mh30
Zofingen **CH** 114 Lh43
Zogang **VRC** (TIB) 171 Pj31
Zogbodomé **DY** 280 Lb42
Zogora **RB** 299 Mc56
Zogoré **BF** 271 Kj39
Zogqên **VRC** (SCH) 176 Pk29
Zogsool **MNG** 172 Qd22
Zohor **SK** 118 Lr42
Zoigê **VRC** (SCH) 176 Qb29
Zoissa **EAT** 293 Mj48
Zolder **B** 103 Lf40
Zolfo Springs **USA** (FL) 36 Fk32
Zollikofen **CH** 114 Lh44
Zollverein **D** 112 Lh39
Zoločiv **UA** 119 Me41
Zolote **UA** 135 Mk21
Zolotoe-koltso **RUS** 132 Mk17
Zolotonoša **UA** 134 Mg21
Żołynia **PL** 117 Mc40
Zomandao **RM** 306 Nc56
Zomba **MW** 297 Mh53
Zombe **Z** 292 Mf50
Zombitse-Vohibasia, P.N.de **RM** 306 Nc57
Zomin **UZB** 158 Oe26
zone annexe (P.N.des Kundelungu) **RDC** 296 Md51
Zone de Chasse de Djona **DY** 272 Lb40
Zone de Chasse de la Pendjari **DY** 279 La40
Zone de Chasse de l'Atakora **DY** 272 Lb40
Žongar Alatauj **KZ/VRC** 166 Pa23
Zongo **RDC** 286 Lk43
Zongshan **ANT** (VRC) 313 Od32
Zonguldak **TR** 144 Mf25
Zongwe **RDC** 292 Md48
Zongwe **RDC** 292 Mf49
Zongyang **VRC** (AHU) 184 Qj30
Zongza **VRC** (SCH) 176 Pk31
Zoniquera **BOL** 72 Gg56
Zonkwa **WAN** 272 Le41
Zonokoua **CI** 279 Kj42
Zonza **F** 111 Lk49
Zoo Baba **RN** 274 Lg36
Zöölön **MNG** 172 Pk20
Zorats stones **ARM** 152 Nd26
Żórawina **PL** 116 Ls40
Zörbig **D** 113 Ln39
Zorgo **BF** 271 Kk39
Zorita **E** 108 Kp49
Zorleni **RO** 125 Mh44
Zoro **WAN** 273 Lf40
Zoró, T.I. **BR** 68 Gk51
Zorritos **PE** 60 Fk47
Zory **PL** 116 Lt40
Zossen **D** 113 Lo38
Zottegem **B** 103 Ld40
Zou **DY** 279 La42
Zouan-Hounien **CI** 278 Kf42
Zouar **TCH** 267 Lj35
Zouarké **TCH** 274 Lj35
Zouérat **RIM** 264 Kd34
Zoug **DARS** 264 Kc35
Zoûgh **RIM** 270 Kg37
Zougou Pantrossi **DY** 272 Lb40
Zouireg **DZ** 259 La29
Zoukouboué **CI** 278 Kg42
Zoukouzou **RCA** 282 Mb42
Zoulabot I **CAM** 281 Lh44
Zoulabot II **CAM** 281 Lg44
Zoulouma **RCA** 286 Ma43
Zouping **VRC** (SDG) 175 Qj27
Zoupleu **CI** 278 Kf42
Zoushan Dao **VRC** 184 Rb30
Zoushi **VRC** (HUN) 177 Qf31
Zouzoudinga **RN** 267 Lg34
Žovkva **UA** 117 Md40
Žovten' **UA** 125 Ml43
Žovti Vody **UA** 134 Mg21
Žovtneve **UA** 132 Mh20
Žovtyj Jar **UA** 125 Mk45
Zrenjanin **SCG** 124 Ma45
Zruč nad Sázavou **CZ** 118 Lq41
Zsadány **H** 119 Mb44
Zschopau **D** 113 Lo40
Zuata **YV** 57 Gh41
Zuata **YV** 57 Gh41
Zubcov **RUS** 132 Mh17
Zubova Poljana **RUS** (MOR) 133 Nb18
Zubovo **RUS** 91 Mj15
Żubrówka **PL** 117 Md36
Žuč **SCG** 126 Mb47
Zudaire **E** 107 Ks52
Zudañez **BOL** 73 Gh55
Zuénoula **CI** 278 Kg42
Zuera **E** 107 Ku51
Zufaf **KSA** 150 Na37
Zufallspitze = Cevedale **I** 120 Ll44
Zug **CH** 114 Lj43
Zugdidi **GE** 152 Na24
Zugspitze **D/A** 115 Lm43
Zuid-Beveland **NL** 112 Ld39
Zuidhorn **NL** 112 Lg37
Zukovka **RUS** 132 Mg19
Zula **ER** 277 Mk39
Zuli **VRC** 174 Qc27
Zulía **YV** 56 Gd41
Zülpich **D** 112 Lg40
Zulumah **YE** 150 Ne38
Zulumaj **RUS** 172 Qa19
Zülünbulag **MNG** 173 Qh22
Zumarraga **E** 107 Ks53
Zumba **EC** 60 Ga48
Zumbahua **EC** 60 Ga46
Zumbo **MOC** 296 Mf53
Zumbo **ZW** 296 Me54
Zumbrota **USA** (MN) 27 Fd23
Zumpango del Río **MEX** (GUR) 40 Fa37
Zün **MNG** 167 Ph21
Zundert **NL** 112 Le39
Zungeru **WAN** 272 Ld41
Zunheboto **IND** (NGL) 194 Ph33
Zunhua **VRC** (HBI) 175 Qj25
Zuni Ind. Res. **USA** 23 Ef28
Zuni Pueblo **USA** (NM) 23 Ef28
Zunyi **VRC** (GZH) 178 Qd32
Zuoquan **VRC** (SAX) 175 Qg27
Zuoyun **VRC** (SAX) 175 Qg25
Županja **HR** 121 Lt45
Zuqualla Monastery **ETH** 284 Mk41
Zurak **WAN** 273 Lf41
Žuravne **UA** 119 Me41
Żuraw **PL** 116 Lt36
Zurayghit **KSA** 148 Na32
Zuri **BOL** 72 Gg54
Zürich **CH** 114 Lj43
Zürichsee **CH** 114 Lj43
Zurmi **WAN** 272 Ld39
Żuromin **PL** 117 Lu37
Zurong **VRC** (GZG) 178 Qd34
Zurrieq **M** 122 Lp55
Zuru **WAN** 272 Lc40
Zuruahã, T.I. **BR** 67 Gg49
Žut **HR** 121 Lq47
Zutiua **BR** 64 Hh48
Zutphen **NL** 112 Lg38
Züünbayan **MNG** 175 Qf23
Züünbulag **MNG** 173 Qg22
Züünkharaa **MNG** 172 Qd21
Züünkhövöö **MNG** 167 Pg20
Zuunmod **MNG** 172 Qd22
Züün Soyony Nuruu **MNG** 172 Pk20
Zuwa **WAN** 273 Lh40
Zuwarah **LAR** 260 Lg29
Züyl **MNG** 167 Pg22
Zuytdorp Cliffs **AUS** 224 Qg59
Zuytdorp Point **AUS** 224 Qg59
Žužemberk **SLO** 121 Lp45
Zvenigorod **RUS** 132 Mj18
Zvenigovo **RUS** (CHU) 133 Nd18
Zvenyhorodka **UA** 134 Mf21
Zvezdec **BG** 127 Mh48
Zvishavane **ZW** 300 Mf56
Zvolen **SK** 119 Lu42
Zvolensky zámok **SK** 119 Lu42
Zvonce **SCG** 126 Mc48
Zvornik **BIH** 124 Lu46
Zwartkop **SA** 302 Ma61
Zwedru **LB** 278 Kf42
Zweibrücken **D** 114 Lh41
Zweisimmen **CH** 114 Lh44
Zwelitsha **SA** 303 Md62
Zwettl **A** 115 Lq42
Zwickau **D** 113 Ln40
Zwiefalten **D** 114 Lk42
Zwierzyniec **PL** 117 Mc40
Zwiesel **D** 115 Lo41
Zwijndrecht **NL** 112 Le39
Zwinger in Dresden **D** 113 Lo39
Zwinger zu Dresden **D** 113 Lo39
Zwingli **SA** 299 Md58
Zwoleń **PL** 117 Mb39
Zwolle **NL** 112 Lg38
Zwolle **USA** (LA) 29 Fd30
Żychlin **PL** 117 Lu38
Zydačiv **UA** 119 Me41
Zymoetz River **CDN** 18 Dg18
Żyrardów **PL** 117 Ma38
Zyrjanka **RUS** 141 Sc05
Žyrovďčy **BY** 117 Mf37
Žytkavičy **BY** 132 Md19
Žytomyr **UA** 134 Me20
Żywiec **PL** 119 Lu41

Photo Index

Abbreviations:
C = Corbis
DFA = Das Fotoarchiv
G = Getty
H = Huber
M = Mauritius
mcs = Mediacolors
P = Premium

page I–II: Spacecapes, PhotoDisc Vol. 34. page II–III: ©Geospace/EDC 2002. page IV–V: World Landmarks and Travel, PhotoDisc Vol. 60. page VI–VII: P/Stimpson/PI. page VIII–IX: 1, 2, 3 P; 3 H/Damm. page X–XI: 1 Monheim; 2, 3 P; 4 IFA/Jacobs. page XII–XIII: 1 G/Tomlinson; 2 G/Waite; 3 P/Petsch; 4 G/Layda. page XIV: 1 DFA; 2 H/Damm. page XV: P. page XVI–XVII: 1 P/Sekai Bunka; 2 IFA; 3 P/NGS; 4 P/Schwabel. page XVIII: P/Raymer/NGS. page 2: top P; 1 G/TCL; 2, 3, 5, 6 P; 4 M; 7 H/Damm. page 3: 1, 3, 4, 6, 7 P/Marka; 2 zefa/Putz; 5 W + C Kunth. page 4: top C; 1 G; 2 Mau; 3–5 dpa. page 5: 1 H/Bertsch; 2, 3, 6 P; 4 K.U.Müller; 5, 7 G/Cornish. page 6-7 P. page 8: 1, 3, 4, 7 P; 2, 6 G/TCL; 5 M. page 9: 1 P/NGS; 2 DFA/Wheeler; 3 G/Hiser; 4 P/Brandenburg; 5 Gonzalez/Laif. page 10: top – 1 C; 2, 7, 8 P; 3–5 G; 6 H. page 11: 1 G/Walker; 2–4 P; 5, 6 C; 7 H. page 12-13.1 P; 2 M; 3 G/Till; 4 Look/Heeb; 5 C; 6 G/Everts; 7 G/Waugh. page 14: top P; 1, 2 C; 3 M; 4, 5 P; 6 – page 15.3 C; 4 P; 5, 6 C. page 16: top, 1 C; 2–4 P; 5, 6 Pix/Pacific Stock; 7 G/Schafer/Hill. page 17: 1 Panorama Images; 2 Pix/Masterfile; 3 C; 4 Minden/Clifton/P; 5, 6 P; 7 C. page 18: top – 5 P; 6 G/Marshall; 7 P/NGS. page 19: 1 IFA/Hartmann; 2 P/Westlight; 3, 4 Yanagi/P; 5 G/Kennan; 6 DFA/Schmid; 7 – page 20.top P/Sisk; 1 G/Wells; 2 P/Gilchrist; 3 DFA/Schmid; 4, 5 P/Kosuge; 6 G/Coleman; 7 P/Weyers. page 21: 1, 3, 5–7 P/Roda; 2 Pix/Minden/Fitzharris; 4 DFA/Schmid. page 22 – 23.1 P; 2 G/Craddock; 3 P/NGS/Blair; 4 M/AGE; 5 Huber/Laif; 6 G; 7 P. page 24: top, 5 C; 1, 2 P; 4 Essick/Aurora. page 25: 1, 2 First Light/P; 3 Kennedy/C; 4, 5 P; 6 Schermeister/C; 7 M/Canstock. page 26: top IFA/Arnold; 1–4, 6, 7 P; 5 IFA. page 27: 1–3, 5, 6 P; 4 G/Wells. page 28: top P/Sekai Bunka; 1, 2 DFA/Tack; 3 G/PP; 4 DFA/Schumacher; 5 P/Frilet/Stock Image; 6 DFA/Fessel; 7 DFA/Matsumoto. page 29: 1 IFA/Panstock; 2 P; 3, 5 DFA/ Tack; 4 DFA/Moore; 6 G/Bean. page 30: top – 2 C; 3 G/Marcoux; 4 Souders/C; 5 DFA/Müller; 6 Lewis/C. page 31: 1 Wheeler/C; 2 P/ NGS; 3 Souders/C; 4 Probst/C; 5 Steedman/ C; 6 Kaehler/C; 7 Nowitz/C. page 32: top P; 1 C; 2–4 P; 5 G; 6 M; 7 – page 33: 1 P; 2, 3 DFA/Müller; 4, 5, 7 P; 6 C. page 34: top P/Watts/First Light; 1 Zobel/C; 2 Muench/C; 3 Fleming/C; 4 Purcel/C; 5 IFA/ Aberham; 6 DFA/Tack; 7 P. page 35: 1 Huber/Laif; 2 DFA/Wheeler; 3 Olson/Aurora; 4–6 DFA; 7 P. page 36 top – 3, 6, 7 P; 4 R. König; 5 DFA/Tack. page 37: 1 DFA/Schmid; 2–5 P; 6 M/visa image; 7 DFA/Tack. page 38: top – page 39.1 C; 2 P/Siepmann; 3, 6 C; 4, 7 P; 5 G. page 40: top P; 1 G/Frerck; 2 Gonzalez/Laif; 3 P/Brimberg; 4, 6, 7 Pix/Raga; 5 P. page 41: 1, 2 G; 3, 4 P; 5 Gonzalez/Laif; 6, 7 H. page 42: top Schafer/C; 2 Arthus-Bertrand/C; 3 G/Höröld; 4, 5, 7 P; 6 H. page 43: 1 mcs; 2, 3 P; 4, 5 Lehmann/ C; 6 M/AGE; 7 P. page 44: top IFA; 1 Pix; 2 Look/Raach; 3 P; 4 M; 5, 7 C; 6 IFA. page 45: 1 H; 2 Gonzalez/Laif, 3–7 C. page 46: top NN; 1, 2, 6 mcs; 3 C; 4 G; 5 IFA; 7 P. page 47: 1 Eisele; 2 C; 3 H/Giovanni; 4 R. König; 5 M/Pearce; 6 H/Gräfenhain; 7 P. page 48-49. 1 Woodhouse; 2, 3 P; 4 G. page 50: top, 1 G; 2 Woodhouse; 3, 5 Holz; 4, 6 P; 7 Photopress/Köck. page 51: 1 P; 2, 3 G/Pile; 4 Schapowalow/ Hiller; 5 DFA; 6 Focus/Fordrelli. page 52: top G/Prior; 1, 3 P/Pecha; 2 Rowell/C; 4 P/Roda; 5 Woodhouse; 6 Wald/Aurora; 7 mcs. page 53: 1 IFA; 2 Gonzalez/Laif; 4 P/Siering; 5, 6 Jo Holz. page 54: top, 1, 2 P/ Hummel; 3 G; 4 DFA/Schmid; 5 C; 6, 7 P/ Roda. page 55: 1 P; 2, 3 G; 4 Schafer/C; 6 Leask/C; 7 Kaehler/C; 5 P. page 56: top Arthus-Bertrand/C; 1 Horner/C; 2, 3 DFA/Zippel; 4 G/Horner; 5 H/Giovanni; 6 Via/ Gross; 7 M/AGE. page 57: 1 P; 2 Gonzalez/Laif; 3, 7 C; 4–6 Caputo/Aurora. page 58: top, 1 P; 2 G/Armand; 3, 4 C; 5 G/Fisher; 6 Gonzalez/Laif. page 59: 1 C; 2 Randy Olson/Aurora; 3 P; Henseler/ Laif. page 60: top Corral/C; 1–3 P; 4 DFA/Zippel; 5 Horner/C; 7 Rowell/C; 6 IFA. page 61: 1 P/Pecha; 2 Schaefer/C; 3 Creed/C; 4 Corral/C; 5, 6 Kaehler/C. page 62: top Rowell/C; 1 IFA; 2 M; 3 Delevingue/Focus; 4 P/Pecha; 5 R.König; 6 P. page 63: 1 Photobrazil; 2 P; 3 Kaehler/C; 4 G/Prior; 5 M/Wendler; 6 P; 7 Lehmann/C. page 64: top Fordyce/C; 1 Bosshart/C; 2 Laif; 3 Kaehler/C; 4, 5 Bosshart/C; 6 Photobrazil; 7 Azoury/C. page 65: 1 Kaehler/C; 2 Maze/C; 3 Garg/C; 4 Fordyce/C; 5 M/Raga; 6 IFA/Jon Arnold Images. page 66: top Woodhouse; 1 Benn/C; 2 Dagli Orti/C; 3 Gonzalez/Laif; 4 Orti/C; 5, 6 P. page 67: 1 Fogden/C; 2 Braasch/C; 3 C; 4 Laif; 5 Woodhouse; 6 Soumar/C; 7 Archivo iconografico/C. page 68: top P; 1, 2 Branco/Magnum/Focus; 3 Vega; 4, 5 Hodalic; 6 TG/Moody; 7 P. page 69: 1 Feanny; 2 P; 3 Save/Ziesler; 4, 5 Allofs/C; 6 P/Minden; 7 Photobrazil. page 70: top Piepenburg/ Laif; 1, 3 Genevieve Vallee/Alamy; 2 Robert Harding Picture Library/Alamy; 4 Gonzalez/Laif; 5 M/Wendler; 6 World Wide Picture Library/Alamy. page 71: 1 Orezzoli/ C; 2, 3 Piepenburg/Laif; 4 DFA; 5 Yspeert/C; Red/Alamy; 7 P. page 72: top Woodhouse; 1, 2 P; 3–7 DFA/Tack. page 73: 1 M/ AGE; 2 IFA/TPC; 3 DFA/Christoph; 4 mcs; 5, 6 Sparshatt/C; 7 Pitamitz/C. page 74: top, 5, 6 P/Barbudo; 1 Creed/C; 2, 3, 7 mcs; 4 Jo Holz. page 75: 1 mcs; 2 Piepenburg/Laif; 3 IFA/Jon Arnold Images; 4 P/Minden/Lanting; 5 IFA; 6, 7 P. page 76: top –2, 4, 5, 7 Gonzalez/Laif; 3 Harscher/Laif; 6 zefa/Damm. page 77: 1–5 Gonzalez/Laif; 6 P; 7 Kristensen/Laif. page 78: top P; 1 IFA; 2 Laif; 3 G/Parfitt; 4 P/Minden/Lanting; 5 Look/Richter; 6, 7 Gonzalez/Laif. page 79: 1 DFA/ Meyer; 2 P; 3 IFA/Seidenberger; 4, 5, 7 P; 6 mcs. page 80: top P/Hummel; 1, 5, 7 Rowell/C; 2 mcs; 3 Stadler/C; 4 Everton/C; 6 P. page 81: 1 Arthus-Bertrand/C; 2 Shok/C; 3–5 IFA; 6 P; 7 Stadler/C. page 82: top P; 1 Modic/C; 2 Kaehler/C; 3, 4 Stadler/C; 5 Gonzalez/Laif; 6 H; 7 P. page 83: 1 IFA; 2 DFA/Tack; 3 P/Abel/NGS; 4 IFA; 5 mcs; 6 Röchner/TG, 7 C. page 84 – page 85.1, 5 P; page:86 2 Wandmacher; 3 IFA; 6 mcs. page 87: 1 Schapowalow/Holm; 2 DFA/ Morris. page 88: top P; 1 G; 2, 6 P; 3 Bieker; 5 mcs; 7 IFA. page 89: 1 H; 2 Böttcher; 3, 7 mdc; 4, 5 IFA; 6 C. page 90: top, 1 P; 2 Icelandic Images; 3, 7 Laif; 4 P; 5 M/sipa; 6 DFA/ Tack. page 91: 1 IFA; 2 Laif/Modrow; 3 M; 4–6 C; 7 H/Giovanni. page 92: top, 2 G; 1, 3, 6, 7 P; 4, 5 Klammet. page 93: 1, 2 Laif/Meier; 3 C; 4 Laif; 5, 7 P; 6 H. page 94: top C; 1, 5 Klammet; 2, 7 P; 3 Nordis; 4 Pix; 6 DFA. page 95: 1 P; 2 Laif; 3 Klammet; 4–7 – page 96: top Laif; 1 IFA; 2 Laif; 3 Nordis; 4 P/Sekai Bunka; 5 DFA; 6 P; 7 G. page 97: 1, 6 M; 2, 4 H; 3, 5 P. page 98: top, 1, 3–7 P; 2 M/ACE. page 99: 1 DFA/Babowic; 2–4, 6 P; 5 G; 7 M/Nägele. page 100: top, 4 P; 5 M/Kord; 6 Klammet; 7 G/Waite. page 101: 1, 3–5, 7 P; 2 G; 6 Klammet. page 102: top IFA; 1 DFA/Mayer; 2 M; 3 NN; 4 G; 5, 6 P; 7 Herzig. page 103: 1–6 P; 7 DFA. page 104: top, 2, 5, 6 P; 1 IFA; 3 Monheim; 4 G; 7 H. page 105: 1 IFA; 2, 4 P; 3, 5, 7 H; 6 M. page 106: top, 4, 5 P; 1 Laif; 2 Nägele/KM; 3 H; 6 G/Cornish; 7 Pix/ Silberbauer. page 107: 1 G/Thiele; 2, 6, 7 P; 3, 4 H; 5 IFA. page 108: top, 2, 3, 6, 7 P; 1 Gonzalez; 4 Klein/Laif; 5 C/Frerck. page 109: 1 G/Everts; 2 Monheim; 3–5 P; 6 Transglobe/Winter; 7 IFA. page 110: top Gonzalez/Laif; 1, 3, 5–7 P; 2 IFA; 4 GM Schmid. page 111: 1, 3 Bednorz/Monheim; 2, 5 Laif; 4, 7 IFA; 6 M/Raga. page 112: top, 1, 4–7 P; 2 H; 3 M. page 113: 1, 6 H; 2 Dr. Zahn; 4, 5 Böttcher. page 114: top, 1 G; 2 M/Hänel; 3, 5 H; 4 Freyer; 6, 7 P. page 115: 1, 5 Romeis; 2, 3 Freyer; 4 H; 6 Radelt/KM; 7 P. page 116: top Laif; 1 Kalmar; 2 H/Schmid; 3 von Götz; 4, 6 DFA; 5, 7. page 117: 1, 2, 5, 6 P; 3 Laif; 4 Freyer; 7 C/Libra. page 118: top H; 1 IFA; 2, 4, 6 P; 3 Laif; 5 M; 7 Jano/Pix. page 119: 1, 5 P; 2 H; 3, 6 M; 4 Huber/ Laif. page 120: top –2, 5, 7 P; 3, 6 Klammet, Nägele; 4 G. page 121: 1, 2 P; 3 G; 4 Freyer; 5 IFA; 6, 7 H. page 122: top IFA; 2–3, 5, 7 P; 4 G/Layda; 6 M. page 123: 1, 3–5 P; 2 M; 6 H; 7 NN. page 124: top H; 1, 5, 7 DFA/Zippel; 2–4, 6 IFA. page 125: 1 Klammet; 2 G/ Tschanz; 3 IFA; 4 C/Wheeler; 5 G/Jecan; 6 IFA; 7 DFA/Riedmiller. page 126: top, 2 IFA; 1 G; 3 mcs; 4 M/Rossenbach; 5–7 P. page 127: 1, 4–7 Henseler/Laif; 2 Evans; 3 P. page 128 top – page 129.3: P; 4, 7 H/Mehlig; 5 M; 6 DFA. page 130: top –3, 6 P; 4 Laif; 5 C. page 131: 1, 2 P/NGS; 3 M/Hänel; 4, 6 H/Schmid; 5 Krause/Laif; 7 mcs. page 132: top Klasen; 1–5 P; 6 G; 7 Kalmar. page 133: 1, 2, 6 H; 3, 4 P/Buss; 5, 7 C/Schmid. page 134: top C; 1, 2 DFA/Müller; 3 – page 135.2: C; 3 H; 4–7 C. page 136-137 P. page 138: top M/Krinninger; 1, 2 IFA; 3, 4 G; 5 DFA/Morrow; 6 C. page 139: 1 DFA/ Riedmiller; 2 Emmler/Laif. page 140: top Arthus-Bertrand/C; 1 Essik/Arora; 2 B. & C. Alexander Photography/ Alamy; 3 P/ Mikhailov; 4 Klasen; 5 Hilger/Laif; 6 Pölking/TG; 7 P/IC; page 141: 1 Steven Brown/pd; 2–4 Langewin; 5–7 Arthus-Bertrand/C. page 142: top C. page 142: 1 DFA/Cristofori; 2–4 IFA; 5 Wheeler/C; 7 Westermann. page 143: 1, 2, 4, 7 C; 3, 5 IFA; 6 M. page 144: top Pictor/P; 1 Tophoven/ Laif; 2, 3, 5, 6 P. page 144: 4 Antrobus/C; 7 Klammet. page 145: 1 G/Thiele; 2 P; 3–6 IFA; 7 Evans; 8 M/Pigneter. page 146: top P; 1, 2 Laif; 3 H/Schmid; 4 DFA/Künzig; 5 mcs; 6 IFA; 7 H. page 147: 1 G/Mollenhauer; 2, 3 IFA; 4–7 C. page 148: top IFA/Aberham; 1, 3–5 Kaehler; 2 Stier; 6 Shandiz. page 149: 1 O-Rourke; 2 Houser; 3 Thévenart/C. page 150: top IFA/Rölle; 1, 2 C; 3–5 IFA; 6 – page 151: 1, 5 B. Kreißl. page 151: 2–4, 6, 7 IFA. page 152: top C; 1 IFA; 2 Chatelin/Focus; 3 Pix/ Steenmans; 4 G/Weinberg; 5 P; 6 – page 153: 1, 3 G.M.Schmid; 2 Laif; 4 C; 5 G/Wedewarth. page 154: top –2, 5, 7 C; 3, 6 IFA; 4 P. page 155: 1, 2, 5, 7 C; 3 M; 4, 6 P/NGS. page 156: top C; 1 IFA; 2 P; 3 zefa/Maroon; 4, 6 IFA/Tschanz; 5 Westermann; 7 C; page 157: 1 DFA/Sasse; 2 IFA; 3, 4, 7 Westermann; 5 IFA/Aberham; 6 C. page 158: top C; 1 zefa/Anderle; 2 C; 3, 4, 6 M/O–Brien; 5 P/Maiburg. page 159: 1 C; 2–4 P; 5 zefa/Minden/ Lanting; 6, 7 C. page 160: top C; 1, 2, 4 DFA/Maeder; 3 C; 5, 6 IFA; 7 C. page 161: 1 P; 2, 3 C; 4–7 K.U.Müller. page 162: top M; 1 C; 2 IFA; 3 Hub/Laif; 4–6 DFA/Bolesch; 7 – page 163.1 C; 2 Evrad/TG; 3 DFA/Bolesch; 4–7 C. page 164: top –2 P; 3 Sparks/ C; 4 P; 5 K.U.Müller; 6 IFA/Fried; 7 Fiedler. page.164 – page 165.1 P; 2 IFA/Warter; 3 C; 4, 6 P; 5 DFA/Zippel; 7 Moore. page 166: top P/Sekai Bunka; 1 Su/C; 2 Nasa/C; 3 Zhuoming/C; 4 Wier/C; 5 Twight/Aurora; 6 IFA. page 167: 1, 2 IFA/Jung; 3 Wier/C; 4, 5 Arbib/C; 6, 7 K.U.Müller. page 168: top P; 1 Su/C; 2 – page 169.5 K.U.Müller; 6 IFA/ Aberham. page 170: top –2 P; 3 G; 4, 6 DFA/ Gordon, Bolesch; 5 K.U.Müller. page 171: 1, 2, 7 P; 3 H; 4 M; 5, 6 K.U.Müller. page 172: top Pölking/TG; 1 Su/C; 2 Bailey/C; 3 DFA/Cristoph; 4, 7 C; 5, 6 IFA. page 173: 1, 2 DFA/ Cristoph; 3–5 C; 6 IFA; 7 M/Morandi. page 174: top P; 1 IFA; 2–4, 7 K.U.Müller; 5 P; 6 IFA/Schmidt. page 175: 1 IFA/Aberham; 2 K. U.Müller; 3 P; 4 interfoto/TG; 5, 6 P. page 176: top P; 1 Slater/C; 2 Chun Li/C; 3, 4 P/Minden; 5 mcs; 6 C. page 177: 1 K.U.Müller; 2 H; 3 M; 4 DFA/Zippel; 5 C; 6 de Bode/Laif; 7 P. page 178: top IFA/Aberham; 1, 3 P; 4 G/ Su; 5 IFA/Nok; 6 DFA/Wheeler; 7 Raymer. page 179: 1, 3 K.U.Müller; 2 P/Mac Killop; 4 DFA/Sasse; 5 M/Blockhuis; 6, 7 IFA/Arakaki. page 180: top, 3 IFA; 1, 5 mcs; 2, 7 DFA; 4, 6, 7 P. page 181: 1–3, 5, 6 P; 4 IFA. page 182: top G; 1 K.U.Müller; 2, 7 DFA/Stark; 3, 5 M/Gierth; 4 G; 6 P. page 183: 1 Hiroshi Suga/Focus; 2 G/Ehlers; 3 IFA/Aberham; 4, 5 P/Orion; 6 H/Orient; 7 Shintani/MT/ P. page 184: top P; 1 K.U.Müller; 2–6 P. page 185: 1, 3, 5–7 Kumamoto/, Orion/P; 2 DFA/Sasse; 4 K.U.Müller. page 186: top IFA; 1–5 P; 6 DFA/Scheibner; 7 P. page 187: 1, 4, 6, 7 P; 2 M/Krinninger; 3 G; 5 K.U.Müller. page 188: top – 2 P; 3 DFA/Riedm.; 4–6, 8 P, 7 C. + W. Kunth. page 189: 1 Cooke/C; 2 Calder/C; 3 Cassidy/P; 4 Wedewarth/G; 5 P; 6 K.U.Müller. page 190: top Wolinsky/Aurora; 1–5 C; 6 Huber/Laif; 7 H. page 191: 1, 4–7 C; 2 P; 3 DFA. page 192: top Sekai Bunka/P; 1 Fiala/P; 2 Huber/Laif; 3, 4 P; 5, 6 DFA/Scheibner. page 193: 1, 2, 4, 5 H; 3, 6 P. page 194: top P; 1 G/Chesley; 2 Baldev/Sygma/C; 3, 5, 6 P; 4 K.U. Müller; 7 Horner/C. page 195: 1, 7 K.U. Müller; 2, 6 Yamashita/C; 3 Strachan/G; 4, 5 P. page 196: top, 1 P; 2 G/Kavanagh; 3 C; 4, 6 DFA; 5 P; 7 – page 197.1 H; 2, 7 C; 3, 5, 6 P; 4 Pix/Rahn. page 198: top P, 1 DFA; 2 G/Merill; 3, 4 DFA/Müller; 5, 6 DFA/Sasse. page 199: 1–3 C. + W. Kunth; 4, 6 P, 5 DFA/Sasse. page 200: top, 1, 3 P; 2 IFA/ Adams; 4–6 C/Holmes, Lawler. page 201: 1–4, 6 P; 5 G/Austen. page 202: top Pacific Stock/P; 1 Transglobe; 2 H/ Fantuz; 3 C; 4 DFA/Tack; 5 P; 6, 7 C. page 203: 1 P; 2, 4, 7 C; 3, 5 mcs; 6 IFA. page 204: top H; 1 Laif/Riehle, 2 P/Minden; 3, 5 C; 4 P/Lanting; 6, 7 DFA. page 205: 1, 4 P; 2, 5 DFA; 3 H; 6, 7 Laif/Riehle. page 206: top G; 1 IFA; 2 K.U.Müller; 3–5 C; 6 K.U.Müller. page 207: 1, 2, 4–6 C; 5 IFA. page 208: top, 1 C; 2 Eisele; 3 P; 4 Su/G; 5 P/NGS; 6 Fields/C. page 209: 1, 2 Frink/Fogden/C; 3 P; 4 mcs; 5 Fields/C; 6, 7 P. page 210: top IFA; 1 G/Ehlers; 2, 5, 6 C; 3 IFA; 4 P. page 211: 1 P; 2 mcs; 3 G; 4 Emmler/Laif; 5 C; 6 Bilderberg. page 212: top IFA; 1 P/Bavendamm; 2, 3 Wheeler, Lenars/C. page 213: 1 Lawler/C; 2, 3 Schaefer/C; 4 Lenars/C; 5 IFA; 6, 7 B. + C. Alexander/Alamy. page 214: top Stephen Frink Collection/Alamy; 1, 2 Stauder/IPN; 3, 4 Lawler/Fields/C; 5, 7 IFA/ Bail; 6 Wheeler/C. page 215: 1, 2, 4–6 Fields/ C; 3 IFA; 7 Lenars/C. page 216/217 o, 1, 2 P; 3 DFA/Hympendahl. page 218: top IFA; 1 Kaehler/C; 2 Hugh Brown/IPN; 3 Houser/C; 4 IFA; 5 G; 6 P; 7 M. page 219: 1, 2 M; 1 P; 2 Schapowalow/Pratt; 3 TG/Ryman; 4 DFA/Wheeler. page 220: top, 1, 6 C; 2, 5 IFA; 3, 4, 7 P/APL. page 212: 1, 7 IFA; 2, 5 Probst/ C; 3, 6 P; 4 DFA. page 222: top IFA; 1, 2, 5 Arthus-Bertrand/C; 3 Garwood/C; 4 Garvey/C; 6, 7 IFA. page 223: 1 Tweedie/C; 2 IFA; 3, 4 H; 5 TG/Schmitz; 6 IFA/Gottschalk; 7 P. page 224: top Hugh Brown/IPN; 1, 2 C; 3, 7 IFA; 4 M/Nakamura; 5, 6 P. page 225: 1–4 Hugh Brown/IPN; 5 Garvey/C; 6, 7 P. page 226: top P; 1 Pix; 2 M/Drecoli; 3 Nowitz/C, 4 H; 5 Souders/C; 6 IFA. page 227: 1 P; 2 IFA; 3–5 C; 6, 7 P/APL. page 228: top P; 1 C; 2 IFA/Siebig; 3, 4 P/APL; 5, 6 IFA; 7 Gardner/Lane Agency/C. page 229: 1, 2, 7 IFA; 3, 6 P; 4 Gardner/Lane/C; 5 Garwood/C. page 230: top P; 1 Tweedie/Alamy; 2 Lenars/C; 3 Hugh Brown/IPN; 4 Holmes/C; 5, 6 P; 7 Arthus Bertrand/C. page 231: 1 Glover, Ecoscene/C; 2–4 P; 5, 7 IFA; 6 DFA/Tack. page 232: top, 1 P; 2 Orezzoli/ C; 3–6 P. page 233: 1, 2 Arthus-Bertrand, Lehman/C; 3 Matsumoto/DFA; 4, 6, 7 Chesley/G; 5 P/Minden. page 234: top, 1, 3 P/ APL; 2, 4, 5 C. page 235: 1 P. page 235: 2 Emmler/Laif; 3, 4 IFA; 5, 6 C; 7 P. page 236: top P; 1, 2 Houser/C; 3 IFA; 4 Heaton/C; 5 Souder/C; 6 Rowell/C. page 237: 1–4 P; 6 IFA; 5, 7 C. page 238: top G; 1–3, 4 G; 5–7 P. page 239: 1 G; 2–7 P. page 240: top, 1 P; 2, 7 G; 3 Aurora/Ernsting/Bilderberg; 4 IFA; 5 P; 6 zefa/Bell. page 241: 1, 2 Bond/ 4, 5 Sarkis/ 6 Peebles Phot./Alamy; 7 La Roque/ Laif. page 242: top, 2, 3 C, 1 Robert Harding/ Alamy; 4–6 Minden/P. page 243: 1, 3–7 C; 5 mcs. page 244: top, 1, 2 C; 3, 5 Essik/ Aurora; 4 Lenars/C; 6, 7. page 245: 1, 4, 5, 7 C; 2 P; 3 Frink Collection/Alamy; 6 Helms. page 246: top, 1 P; 2 Helms; 3, 4 C; 5 Essik/Aurora; 6 P. page 247: 1, 2, 5, 6 C; 3, 4 P. page 248: top, 1, 2 C; 3–5 Pacific Stock/ P. page 249: 1, 2, 4–6 P; 3 IFA/Jon Arnold Images. page 250-251 P, 4 H. page 252: top Cook/Alamy; 1 P; 2 Pix; 3 G/Parfitt; 4 mcs; 5 M; 6 IFA. page 253: 1 Laif; 2 Cristofori. page 254: top P; 1–3 IFA; 4–6 C. page 255: 1, 3 P; 2 DFA/Riedmiller; 4 Melters/missio/DFA; 6 Scheibner/DFA; 5, 7, 8 C. page 256: top –3 P; 4 Image State/Alamy; 5 IFA; 6, 7 Emmler/Laif. page 257: 1 P; 2 G/Parfitt; 3 P; 4, 7 DFA; 5 Laif; 6 IFA. page 258: top, 7 IFA/ Diaf; 1 Laif; 2 M; 3 G/Grigoriou; 4, 5 H; 6 P. page 259: 1 DFA; 2, 3, 5 IFA; 4 G/Kanus; 6 P; 7 Laif. page 260: top, 7 P; 1 M; 2 G/WPS; 3 IFA; 4 H; 5 M; 6 Laif. page 261: 1–4 IFA; 5 P; 6 H; 7 Laif. page 262: top H; 1, 2, 6 IFA; 3, 7 P; 4 DFA; 5 G/Pigneter. page 263: 1, 3, 7 P; 2, 5 G/Hellier; 4 mcs; 6, 8 IFA. page 264: top P; 1, 4–7 IFA; 2 H; 3 Look/Richter. page 265: 1 P; 2 DFA; 3 IFA; 4, 6, 7 C; 5 Pix. page 266: top G; 1 IFA; 2, 6 Laif; 3 Pix; 2, 4, 5 C; 7 mcs. page 267: 1 Laif; 2 M; 3 IFA; 4, 7 C; 5, 6 IFA. page 268: top, 3, 4 IFA; 1 C; 2, 5 P; 6 – page 269. 1, 2, 4–7 DFA; 3 P. page 270: top P; 1 DFA; 2, 3, 5, 7 C; 4 P; 6 M. page 271: 1 Uluntuncok/Laif; 2 IFA; 3 Arthus-Bertrand/C; 4 P; 5, 7 C; 6 mcs. page 272: top, 1, 3 C; 2, 4 P; 5, 6 DFA. page 273: 1, 3 C; 2 IFAM; 4 Geospace/ EDC; 5, 6 DFA/Christoph. page 274: top, 3, 7 P; 1, 2, 4, 5 IFA; 6 Laif. page 275: 1, 4, 5 IFA; 2, 6, 7 P; 3 Laif. page 276: top IFA; 1, 2, 4–6 C; 3 DFA; 7 Laif. page 277: 1, 2, 5 IFA; 3, 4 P; 6, 7 DFA. page 278: top C; 1, 6 P; 2 IFA; 3–5 C. page 279: 1–4 C; 5 AKG; 6, 7 DFA. page 280: top P; 1 DFA/ Christoph; 2 Buck; 3 Laif/Krause; 4 IFA; 5 Pix/Havi; 6 M; 7 C. page 281: 1, 3 DFA/ Buck; 2 DFA/Christoph; 4 C; 5 P; 6 M/de Foy. page 282: top Oswald Iten; 1, 2 Laif/Riehle; 3, 4 P; 5 Save/ Jecan; 6 Victor Englebert. page 283: 1 Davenport/Aurora; 2–4 O.Iten; 5 Caputo/IPN; 6 M/Ritschel; 7 Campbell/Aurora. page 284: top P; 1 DFA/Scheibner; 2 IFA/Fiedler; 3 Riehle/Laif; 4 H; 5 M; 6 P. page 285: 1, 3, 4 IFA; 2 P; 5 Uluntuncok/Laif; 6 C. page 286: top M; 1 Caputo/Aurora; 2 G/Lange; 3–5 Sygma/C; 6 IFA. page 287: 1, 2 H; 3 C; 4, 6 P; 5 IFA. page 288: top, 2, 3 C; 1 Dr. Janicke; 4 Reporters/Laif; 5–7 Caputo/IPN. page 289: 1, 4 P; 2 M; 3 Gallo/C; 5 Caputo/IPN. page 290: top P; 1, 3 IFA; 2 G/Parfitt; 4 DFA/Stark; 5 G/Petersen; 6 P; 7 C. + W. Kunth. page 291: 1, 5 Riehle/Laif; 2 C. + W. Kunth; 3 P/Sixty-Six; 4 Pölking/P; 6 IFA; 7 Caputo/Aurora. page 292: top IFA/Aberham; 1–3 Ariadne van Zanbergen; 4, 5 C; 6 M/Rosing; 7 P. page 293: 1 P. page 293: 2 Okapia; 3–5 P; 6 DFA/Thomashoff; 7 DFA/Wheeler. page 294: top C; 1 Image State/Alamy; 2 A. Vitale/Alamy; 3 C; 4, 5, 7 P; 6 DFA/Honzera. page 295: 1 Malie Rich-Griffith/Alamy; 2 M/Eichhorn; 3, 4 H; 5 Morgan/Alamy; 6 IFA/BCI. page 296: top Pix; 1, 3 C; 2, 7 P; 4 DFA; 5 M; 6 R. König. page 297: 1 C; 2 Meier/Laif; 3 zefa/Boehnke; 4 DFA/Stark; 5–7 IFA/Pickford. page 298: top, 3 C. + W. Kunth; 1, 2 P; 4–6 IFA; 7 G/ Chard. page 299: 1 C. + W. Kunth; 2 IFA; 3, 4 P; 5 Schapowalow. page 300: top –3, 7 C; 4, 5 IFA/Mielke. page 301: 1, 3, 4 P; 2 G; 5, 6 Emmler/Laif. page 302: top P; 1, 2 IFA; 3–6 Laif; 7 DFA. page 303 1, 2, 5 Emmler/Laif; 3 IFA/Aberham; 4 Riehle/Laif; 6 IFA/ Welsh. page 304: top, 4, 6 P; 5 IFA; 7 C. page 305: 1, 4 P; 2, 5, 6 IFA; 3 C. page 306: top, 2 Arthus-Bertrand/C; 1 DFA; 3, 4 P/Minden; 5 – page 307.1 Hellier/C; 2 DFA; 3–6 IFA; 7, 8 P. page 308–309: P/Sekai Bunka. page 310: top P; 1 Amos/C; 2 Widstrand/C; 3 Pinneo/Aurora; 4 G/TCL; 5 G/ Beatty; 6 G/Heacox; 7 McLain/Aurora. page 311: 1, 3 Rowell/C; 2 Sygma/C; 4 Schafer/ C; 5–7 P. page 312: top, 1, 3 P/Hummel; 2 G/Osborne; 4 G/Rogers; 5 Rowell/C; 6 Hawthorne/C. page 313: 1 Beebe/C; 2 Rainier/C; 3, 4 Rowell/C; 5–7 P/Hummel. page 314: top Randlev/C; 1 P; 2 G/Grigoriou; 3 G/Krechichwost; 4 P; 5 IFA; 6 P. page 315: top, 1, 2, 4 P; 3 M/Bibikow; 5 IFA; 6 Pitamitz/C. page 316–317.1, 3, 7 P; 2, 4, 6 C.

Credits/Contributors

Published in the United States, Canada, and Puerto Rico by
Hammond World Atlas Corporation
Union, New Jersey 07083
www.hammondmap.com

ISBN 0-8437-1982-6

Coordination: Vera Benson
Cover design: Yang Zhao

Innere Wiener Straße 13
81667 Munich
info@geographicmedia.de
www.geographicmedia.de

Concept: Wolfgang Kunth
Cartography: GeoKarta – Ralf van den Berg, Jens Ewers, Bernd Hilberer, Doris Kordisch, Peter Krause, Gabriele Luber, Karen Morlok, Heiner Newe, Beate Reußner, Bernhard Spachmüller, Karin Stemmer
Texts: Manuela Blisse & Uwe Lehmann, Peter Daners, Christian Gehl, Christine Hamel, Bernd Helms, Dr. Siegmar Hohl, Dr. Bernhard Jendricke, Marlis Kappelhoff, Barbara Kreißl, Angelika Kunth-Jakobs, Demetri Lowe, Frank Meinshausen, Michael Schaeffer, Daniela Schetar, Trudie Trox
Text Translation: Demetri Lowe
Picture Research: Max Oberdorfer
Final Checking: Michael Kaiser
Coordination: Heiner Newe, Claus-Peter Waider, Michael Kaiser
Design, Layout: Umlbruch, Munich, Christopher Kunth
Reproduction: Fotolito Varesco, Auer (Italy)

Printed in Spain